The Longman Anthology of British Literature

SECOND COMPACT EDITION

VOLUME B

David Damrosch
COLUMBIA UNIVERSITY

Christopher Baswell
UNIVERSITY OF CALIFORNIA, LOS ANGELES

Clare Carroll
QUEENS COLLEGE, CITY UNIVERSITY OF NEW YORK

Kevin J. H. Dettmar
SOUTHERN ILLINOIS UNIVERSITY

Heather Henderson

Constance Jordan
CLAREMONT GRADUATE UNIVERSITY

Peter J. Manning
STATE UNIVERSITY OF NEW YORK, STONY BROOK

Anne Howland Schotter
WAGNER COLLEGE

William Chapman Sharpe
BARNARD COLLEGE

Stuart Sherman
FORDHAM UNIVERSITY

Jennifer Wicke
UNIVERSITY OF VIRGINIA

Susan J. Wolfson
PRINCETON UNIVERSITY

The Longman Anthology of British Literature
Second Compact Edition

David Damrosch

General Editor

VOLUME B

THE ROMANTICS AND THEIR CONTEMPORARIES
Susan Wolfson *and* Peter Manning

THE VICTORIAN AGE
Heather Henderson *and* William Sharpe

THE TWENTIETH CENTURY
Kevin Dettmar *and* Jennifer Wicke

PEARSON
Longman

New York   San Francisco   Boston
London   Toronto   Sydney   Tokyo   Singapore   Madrid
Mexico City   Munich   Paris   Cape Town   Hong Kong   Montreal

Vice President and Editor-in-Chief: *Joseph Terry*
Development Manager: *Janet Lanphier*
Senior Marketing Manager: *Melanie Craig*
Senior Supplements Editor: *Donna Campion*
Media Supplements Editor: *Nancy Garcia*
Senior Production Manager: *Valerie Zaborski*
Project Coordination and Electronic Page Makeup: *Elm Street Publishing Services, Inc.*
Senior Cover Designer/Manager: *Nancy Danahy*
On the Cover: Detail from *Iron and Coal* (© 1855–60) by William Bell Scott, The National
     Trust, Trevelyan Collection, Wallington Hall, Morpeth, U.K. The complete image appears on
     the back cover.
Photo Researcher: *Photosearch, Inc.*
Manufacturing Buyer: *Lucy Hebard*
Printer and Binder: *Quebecor World/Taunton*
Cover Printer: *Lehigh Press, Inc.*

For permission to use copyrighted material, grateful acknowledgment is made to the copyright
holders on pages 1462–64, which are hereby made part of this copyright page.

Library of Congress Cataloging-in-Publication Data

The Longman anthology of British literature / David Damrosch, general
     editor. — Compact 2nd ed.
          p. cm.
     Includes bibliographical references and index.
     Contents: v. 1. The Middle Ages / Christopher Baswell and Anne Howland
Schotter. The early modern period / Constance Jordan and Clare
Carroll. The Restoration and the 18th century / Stuart Sherman —
v. 2. The Romantics and their contemporaries / Susan Wolfson and Peter
Manning. The Victorian age / Heather Henderson and William Sharpe.
The twentieth century / Kevin Dettmar and Jennifer Wicke.
     ISBN 0-321-19891-3 (v. A) — ISBN 0-321-20239-2 (v. B)
     1. English literature. 2. Great Britain—Literary collections.
I. Damrosch, David.
PR1109.L69 2004
820.8—dc21

                                                                                    2003052707
Copyright © 2004 by Pearson Education, Inc.

Please visit our website at http://www.ablongman.com/damrosch

ISBN 0-321-19891-3 (Volume A)
ISBN 0-321-20239-2 (Volume B)

1 2 3 4 5 6 7 8 9 10—WCT—06 05 04 03

CONTENTS

The Victorian Age

THOMAS CARLYLE

⚒ PERSPECTIVES ⚒
The Industrial Landscape

⇌ PERSPECTIVES ⇌
Victorian Ladies and Gentlemen

❧ PERSPECTIVES ❧
Religion and Science   632

⇒ PERSPECTIVES ⇐
Imagining Childhood   795

▓ OSCAR WILDE AND HIS TIME ▓
Aestheticism, Decadence, and
the *Fin de Siècle*   889

The Twentieth Century

JOSEPH CONRAD

BERNARD SHAW

THOMAS HARDY

⇥ PERSPECTIVES ⇤
The Great War: Confronting the Modern

LIST OF ILLUSTRATIONS

The Romantics and Their Contemporaries

The Victorian Age

Color Plates   *following page 464*

Black-and-White Images

The Twentieth Century

Color Plates

Black-and-White Images

PREFACE

Literature has a double life. Born in one time and place and read in another, literary works are at once products of their age and independent creations, able to live on long after their original world has disappeared. The goal of this anthology is to present a wealth of poetry, prose, and drama from the full sweep of the literary history of the British Isles, and to do so in ways that will bring out both the works' original cultural contexts and their lasting aesthetic power. These aspects are, in fact, closely related: Form and content, verbal music and social meanings, go hand in hand. This double life makes literature, as Aristotle said, "the most philosophical" of all the arts, intimately connected to ideas and to realities that the writer transforms into moving patterns of words. The challenge is to show these works in the contexts in which, and for which, they were written, while at the same time not trapping them within those contexts. The warm response this anthology received from the hundreds of teachers who adopted it in its first edition reflects the growing consensus that we don't have to accept an either/or choice between the literature's aesthetic and cultural dimensions. Our users' responses have now guided us in seeing how we can improve our anthology further, so it can be most pleasurable and stimulating to students, most useful to teachers, and most responsive to ongoing developments in literary studies. This preface can serve as a road map to the new phase in this book's life.

LITERATURE IN ITS TIME—AND IN OURS

When we engage with a rich literary history that extends back over a thousand years, we often encounter writers who assume their readers know all sorts of things that are little known today: historical facts, social issues, literary and cultural references. Beyond specific information, these works will have come out of a very different literary culture than our own. Even the contemporary British Isles present a cultural situation—or a mix of cultures—very different from what North American readers encounter at home, and these differences only increase as we go farther back in time. A major emphasis of this anthology is to bring the works' original cultural moment to life: not because the works simply or naively reflect that moment of origin, but because they do refract it in fascinating ways. British literature is both a major heritage for modern North America and, in many ways, a very distinct culture; reading British literature will regularly give an experience both of connection and of difference. Great writers create imaginative worlds that have their own compelling internal logic, and a prime purpose of this anthology is to help readers to understand the formal means— whether of genre, rhetoric, or style—with which these writers have created works of haunting beauty. At the same time, as Virginia Woolf says in A Room of One's Own, the gossamer threads of the artist's web are joined to reality "with bands of steel." This anthology pursues a range of strategies to bring out both the beauty of these webs of words and their points of contact with reality.

The Longman Anthology brings related authors and works together in several ways:

☞ PERSPECTIVES: **Broad groupings that illuminate underlying issues in a variety of the major works of a period.**

☞ AND ITS TIME: **A focused cluster that illuminates a specific cultural moment or a debate to which an author is responding.**

☞ COMPANION READINGS: **Pairings of works in dialogue with each other.**

These groupings provide a range of means of access to the literary culture of each period. The Perspectives sections do much more than record what major writers thought about an issue: they give a variety of views in a range of voices, to illustrate the wider culture within which the literature was being written. An attack on tobacco by King James the First; theological reflections by the pioneering scientist Isaac Newton; haunting testimony by Victorian child workers concerning their lives; these and many other vivid readings give rhetorical as well as social contexts for the poems, plays, and stories around them. Perspectives sections typically relate to several major authors of the period, as with a section on Government and Self-Government that relates broadly to Spenser's *Faerie Queene* and to Milton's *Paradise Lost*. Most of the writers included in Perspectives sections are important figures of the period who could be neglected if they were listed on their own with just a few pages each; grouping them together has proven to be useful pedagogically as well as intellectually. Perspectives sections may also include work by a major author whose primary listing appears elsewhere in the period; thus, a Perspective section on the abolition of slavery—a hotly debated issue in England from the 1790s through the 1830s—includes poems and other writing on slavery by both Dorothy and William Wordsworth so as to give a rounded presentation of the issue in ways that can inform the reading of those authors in their individual sections.

When we present a major work "And Its Time," we give a cluster of related materials to suggest the context within which the work was written. Thus Sir Philip Sidney's great *Apology for Poetry* is accompanied by readings showing the controversy that was raging at the time concerning the nature and value of poetry. Some of the writers in these groupings and in our Perspectives sections have not traditionally been seen as literary figures, but all have produced lively and intriguing works, from medieval clerics writing about saints and sea monsters, to a polemical seventeenth-century tract giving *The Arraignment of Lewd, Idle, Froward, and Unconstant Women*, to rousing speeches by Winston Churchill as the British faced the Nazis during World War II.

Also, we include "Companion Readings" to present specific prior texts to which a work is responding: when Sir Thomas Wyatt creates a beautiful poem, *Whoso list to hunt*, by making a free translation of a Petrarch sonnet, we include Petrarch's original (with a literal translation) as a companion reading. John Keats's sonnet "On First Looking into Chapman's Homer" is accompanied by excerpts from Chapman's translation of the *Iliad*, as well as by Alexander Pope's rendering (much better known in Keats's time), so readers can directly see why Chapman's vibrant version looked so exciting to Keats in contrast to Pope's polished heroic couplets.

CULTURAL EDITIONS

This edition follows the establishment of an important new series of companion volumes under the general editorship of Susan Wolfson, the Longman Cultural Editions, which carry further the anthology's emphases by presenting major texts along with a generous selection of contextual material. Initial volumes are devoted to *King Lear;* a pairing of *Othello* and Elizabeth Cary's *Tragedie of Mariam; Pride and Prejudice; Frankenstein;* and *Hard Times.* More are currently being developed and are available free, for course use, with the anthology itself. Taken together, our new edition and the Longman Cultural Editions offer an unparalleled set of materials for the enjoyment and study of British literary culture from its first beginnings to the present.

ILLUSTRATING VISUAL CULTURE

Another important context for literary production has been a different kind of culture: the visual. We have newly added in this edition a suite of color plates in each volume, and we also have dozens of black-and-white illustrations throughout the anthology, chosen to show artistic and cultural images that figured importantly for literary creation. Sometimes, a poem refers to a specific painting, or more generally emulates qualities of a school of visual art. At other times, more popular materials like advertisements may underlie scenes in Victorian or Modernist writing. In some cases, visual and literary creation have merged, as in Hogarth's series *A Rake's Progress,* included in Volume A, or Blake's illustrated engravings of his *Songs of Innocence and of Experience,* several of whose plates are reproduced in color in Volume B.

Our cover illustration, *Iron and Coal,* by the Scottish painter William Bell Scott, is an excellent instance of a beautiful image that illustrates both the artistic and the social culture of its times. Scott (1811–1890) was a poet as well as a painter, a lifelong friend of the poet-painter Dante Gabriel Rossetti and a member of the Pre-Raphaelite circle. In 1857 he was asked by Sir Walter and Lady Pauline Trevelyan to create a cycle of paintings for the central hall of Wallington House, their home in Northumberland, in the north of England. Depicting scenes from Northumberland history, the cycle begins with *The Building of the Roman Wall* and culminates with *Iron and Coal,* one of the earliest artistic celebrations of the new commercial world made possible through scientific and industrial progress. The view from the factory—a picture within a picture—portrays a bustling port with a train trellis overhead. Inside, heroically proportioned "strikers" emphasize the immense human labor that underlies industrial work. Caught in mid-swing, they could almost be one striker in a multiple-exposure photograph, a kind of image that would soon be produced in the astonishing photographs of motion by the Victorian photographer Eadweard Muybridge. The pose also suggests that the men themselves are merging with the machinery that underlies England's future prosperity. One of the strikers is in fact a portrait of an heir to Wallington House. The actual owner of the factory is represented in turn by his own children. The boy surveys the world he will literally inherit. The girl is reading a book, but she pauses, looking out from her world into ours.

AIDS TO UNDERSTANDING

We have attempted to contextualize our selections in suggestive rather than exhaustive ways, trying to enhance rather than overwhelm the experience of reading the texts themselves. Thus, when difficult or archaic words need defining in poems, we use glosses in the margins, so as to disrupt the reader's eye as little as possible; footnotes are intended to be concise and informative, rather than massive or interpretive. Important literary and social terms are defined when they are used. At the end of Volume A there are useful summaries of British political and religious organization, and of money, weights, and measures. For further reading, carefully selected, up-to-date bibliographies for each period and for each author can be found at the end of each volume.

LOOKING—AND LISTENING—FURTHER

Beyond the boundaries of the anthology itself, along with this edition we have created a pair of CDs giving a wide range of readings of texts in the anthology and selections of music from each period. It is only in the past century or two that people usually began to read literature silently; most literature has been written in the expectation that it would be read aloud, or even sung in the case of lyric poetry ("lyric" itself means a work meant to be sung to the accompaniment of a lyre or other instruments). The aural power and beauty of these works are a crucial dimension of their experience. For further explorations, we have also expanded our Web site, available to all users at www.awlonline.com/damrosch; this site gives a wealth of information, annotated links to related sites, and an archive of texts for further reading. For instructors, we have revised and expanded our popular companion volume, *Teaching British Literature*, written directly by the anthology's editors, 600 pages in length, available free to everyone who adopts the anthology.

WHAT IS BRITISH LITERATURE?

Turning now to the book itself, let us begin by defining our basic terms: What is "British" literature? What is literature itself? And just what should an anthology of this material look like at the present time? If the term "British" has no ultimate essence, it does have a history. The first British were Celtic people who inhabited the British Isles and the northern coast of France (still called Brittany) before various Germanic tribes of Angles and Saxons moved onto the islands in the fifth and sixth centuries. Gradually the Angles and Saxons amalgamated into the Anglo-Saxon culture that became dominant in the southern and eastern regions of Britain and then spread outward; the old British people were pushed west, toward what became known as Cornwall, Wales, and Ireland, which remained independent kingdoms for centuries, as did Celtic Scotland to the north. By an ironic twist of linguistic fate, the Anglo-Saxons began to appropriate the term British from the Britons they had displaced, and they took as a national hero the early, semi-mythic Welsh King Arthur. By the seventeenth century, English monarchs had extended their sway over Wales, Ireland, and Scotland, and they began to refer to their holdings as "Great Britain." Today, Great Britain includes England, Wales, Scotland, and Northern Ireland, but does not include the Republic of Ireland, which has been independent from England since 1922.

This anthology uses "British" in a broad sense, as a geographical term encompassing the whole of the British Isles. For all its fraught history, it seems a more satisfactory term than to speak simply of "English" literature, for two reasons. First: most speakers of English live in countries that are not the focus of this anthology; second, while the English language and its literature have long been dominant in the British Isles, other cultures in the region have always used other languages and have produced great literature in these languages. Important works by Irish, Welsh, and Scots writers appear regularly in the body of this anthology, some of them written directly in their languages and presented here in translation, and others written in an English inflected by the rhythms, habits of thought, and modes of expression characteristic of these other languages and the people who use them.

We use the term "literature" in a similarly capacious sense. Only in the past hundred years or so has creating "belles lettres" or high literary art been thought of as a sharply separate sphere of activity from other sorts of writing that the same authors would regularly produce. Sometimes, Romantic poets wrote sonnets to explore the deepest mysteries of individual perception and memory; at other times, they wrote sonnets the way a person might now write an Op-Ed piece, and such a sonnet would be published and read along with parliamentary debates and letters to the editor on the most pressing contemporary issues.

WOMEN'S WRITING, AND MEN'S

Literary culture has always involved an interplay between central and marginal regions, groupings, and individuals. A major emphasis in literary study in recent years has been the recovery of writing by women writers, some of them little read until recently, others major figures in their time. This anthology gives an integrated presentation of women's writing in the British Isles from the Middle Ages to the present. The Irish poet Eavan Boland, in fact, appears in both periods—as a translator of medieval Irish verse, and as an important contemporary poet in her own right. Attending to these voices gives us a new variety of compelling works, and helps us rethink the entire periods in which they wrote. The first third of the nineteenth century, for example, can be defined more broadly than as a "Romantic Age" dominated by six male poets; looking closely at women's writing as well as at men's, we can deepen our understanding of the period as a whole, including the specific achievements of Blake, William Wordsworth, Coleridge, Keats, Percy Shelley, and Byron, all of whom continue to have a major presence in these pages as most of them did during the nineteenth century.

VARIETIES OF LITERARY EXPERIENCE

Above all, we have striven to give as full a presentation as possible to the varieties of great literature produced over the centuries in the British Isles, by women as well as by men, in outlying regions as well as in the metropolitan center of London, and in prose, drama, and verse alike. While we have made sure to keep this Compact Edition to a moderate length, judicious pruning has made room for important additions in every period, including Perspectives: Ethnic and Religious Encounters in the Middle Ages; Perspectives: Government and Self-Government in the early modern period; The Beggar's Opera in the eighteenth century; Perspectives: The Sublime, the Beautiful, and the Picturesque in the Romantic era; Perspectives: Imagining Childhood in the Victorian period; and Perspectives: Regendering Modernism in the twentieth century. Finally, lyric poetry appears in profusion throughout the anthology, from early lyrics by anonymous Middle English poets and the trenchantly witty Dafydd ap Gwilym to the powerful contemporary voices of Philip Larkin, Seamus Heaney, Eavan Boland, and Derek Walcott—himself a product of colonial British education, heir of Shakespeare and James Joyce—who closes the anthology with poems about Englishness abroad and foreignness in Britain.

As topical as these contemporary writers are, we hope that this anthology will show that the great works of earlier centuries can also speak to us compellingly today, their value only increased by the resistance they offer to our views of ourselves and our world. To read and reread the full sweep of this literature is to be struck anew by the degree to which the most radically new works are rooted in centuries of prior innovation. Even this preface can close in no better way than by quoting the words written eighteen hundred years ago by Apuleius of Madaura—both a consummate artist and a kind of anthologist of extraordinary tales—when he concluded the prologue to his masterpiece The Golden Ass: Attend, reader, and pleasure is yours.

David Damrosch

ACKNOWLEDGMENTS

In planning and preparing the second compact edition of our anthology, the editors have been fortunate to have the support, advice, and assistance of many people. Our editor, Joe Terry, has been unwavering in his enthusiasm for the book and his commitment to it; he and his associates Roth Wilkofsky, Janet Lanphier, and Melanie Craig have supported us in every possible way throughout the process, ably assisted by Nancy Crochiere, Michele Cronin, and Alison Main. Our developmental editor, Mark Getlein, guided us and our manuscript from start to finish with unfailing acuity and Wildean wit. Daniel Kline and Peter Meyers have devoted enormous energy and creativity to revising our Web site and developing our new audio CDs. Lynn Smith cleared our many text permissions, and Jacqui Sutton of Photosearch, Inc., cleared our many illustration permissions. Finally, Valerie Zaborski oversaw the production with sunny good humor and kept the book successfully on track on a very challenging schedule, working closely with Karin Vonesh at Elm Street Publishing Services.

Our plans for the new edition have been shaped by comments and suggestions from many faculty who have used the book over the past four years. We are specifically grateful for the thoughtful advice of our reviewers for this edition, Alexander M. Bruce (Florida Southern College), Teri Gaston (The University of Texas at Arlington), Stephen J. Harris (University of Massachusetts Amherst), Nancy Knowles (Eastern Oregon University), Ben Kohn (Whatcom Community College), Pat Lonchar (University of the Incarnate Word), Ann Martin (Louisiana State University), Delilah Orr (Fort Lewis College), Mark K. Stevens (Southern Polytechnic State University), Rob Breton (The University of British Columbia), Catherine R. Eskin (Florida Southern College), Carol Hanes (Howard College), Marvin Hunt (North Carolina State University), Helaine Razovsky (Northwestern State University), Gerald Richman (Suffolk University), Maxine Susman (Caldwell College), Marion Hoctor (Nazareth College), Ted Sherman (Middle Tennessee State University), Robert Barrett (University of Pennsylvania), Mary Been (Clovis Community College), Stephen Behrendt (University of Nebraska), James Campbell (University of Central Florida), Linda McFerrin Cook (McLellan Community College), Kevin Gardner (Baylor University), Peter Greenfield (University of Puget Sound), Natalie Grinnell (Wofford College), Wayne Hall (University of Cincinnati), Donna Hamilton (University of Maryland), Carrie Hintz (Queens College), Eric Johnson (Dakota State College), Roxanne Kent-Drury (Northern Kentucky University), Adam Komisaruk (West Virginia University), John Laflin (Dakota State University), Paulino Lim (California State University, Long Beach), Ed Malone (Missouri Western State College), William W. Matter (Richland College), Evan Matthews (Navarro College), Lawrence McCauley (College of New Jersey), Peter E. Medine (University of Arizona), Charlotte Morse (Virginia Commonwealth University), Mary Morse (Rider University), Richard Nordquist (Armstrong Atlantic State University), John Ottenhoff (Alma College), Joyce Cornette Palmer (Texas Women's University), Leslie Palmer (University of North Texas), Rebecca Phillips (West Virginia University), William Rankin (Abilene Christian University), Sherry Rankin (Abilene Christian University), Luke Reinsma (Seattle Pacific University), David Rollison (College of Marin), Kathryn Rummel (California Polytechnic), R. G. Siemens

(Malaspina University-College), Brad Sullivan (Florida Gulf Coast University), Brett Wallen (Cleveland Community College), Daniel Watkins (Duquesne University), and Julia Wright (University of Waterloo).

As if all this help weren't enough, the editors also drew directly on friends and colleagues in many ways, for advice, for information, sometimes for outright contributions to headnotes and footnotes, even (in a pinch) for aid in proofreading. In particular, we wish to thank David Ackiss, Marshall Brown, James Cain, Cathy Corder, Jeffrey Cox, Michael Coyle, Pat Denison, Tom Farrell, Andrew Fleck, Jane Freilich, Laurie Glover, Lisa Gordis, Joy Hayton, Ryan Hibbet, V. Lauryl Hicks, Nelson Hilton, Jean Howard, David Kastan, Stanislas Kemper, Andrew Krull, Ron Levao, Carol Levin, David Lipscomb, Denise MacNeil, Jackie Maslowski, Richard Matlak, Anne Mellor, James McKusick, Melanie Micir, Michael North, David Paroissien, Stephen M. Parrish, Peter Platt, Cary Plotkin, Desma Polydorou, Gina Renee, Alan Richardson, Esther Schor, Catherine Siemann, Lauren Simonetti, Glenn Simshaw, David Tresilian, Shasta Turner, Nicholas Watson, Michael Winckleman, Gillen Wood, and Sarah Zimmerman for all their guidance and assistance.

The pages on the Restoration and the eighteenth century are the work of many collaborators, diligent and generous. Michael F. Suarez, S. J. (Campion Hall, Oxford) edited the Swift and Pope sections; Mary Bly (Fordham University) edited Sheridan's *School for Scandal*. Steven N. Zwicker (Washington University) co-wrote the period introduction, and the headnotes for the Dryden section. Bruce Redford (Boston University) crafted the footnotes for Dryden, Gay, Johnson, and Boswell. Susan Brown, Christine Coch, Tara Czechowski, Paige Reynolds, and Andrew Tumminia helped with texts, footnotes, and other matters throughout; William Pritchard gathered texts, wrote notes, and prepared the bibliography. To all, abiding thanks.

It has been a pleasure to work with all of these colleagues in the ongoing collaborative process that has produced this book and brought it to this new stage of its life and use. This book exists for its readers, whose reactions and suggestions we warmly welcome, as these will in turn reshape this book for later users in the years to come.

Color Plate 1 John Martin, *The Bard*, 1817. "Ruin seize thee, ruthless King!" According to the legend retold in Thomas Gray's 1757 ode *The Bard*, in the thirteenth century Edward I attempted to stamp out Welsh resistance to English power by ordering the court poets, bards, put to death. John Martin's large canvas captures the sublime moment at which the last bard denounced the invading monarch before leaping into the River Conway below. *(Tyne and Wear Museums.)*

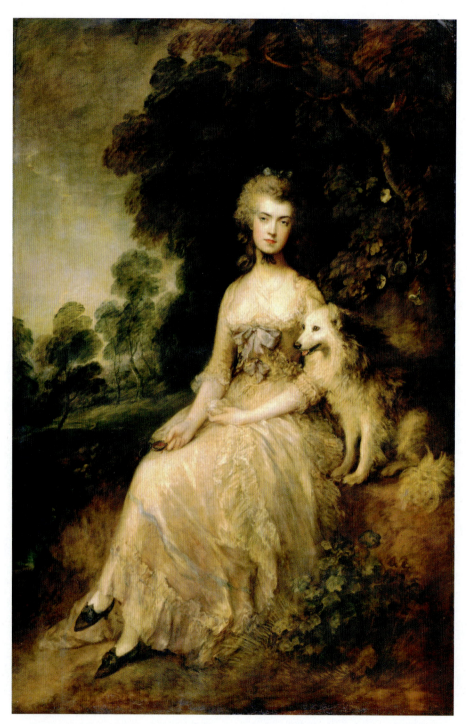

Color Plate 2   Thomas Gainsborough (1727–1788), *Mrs. Mary Robinson ("Perdita")*. Gainsborough was one of the most fashionable portraitists of his day, surpassed only by his rival Sir Joshua Reynolds. His elegant depiction of the actress and poet Mary Robinson is witness to her social triumph. The locket in Robinson's hand reveals a portrait of the Prince of Wales, whose infatuation with her was the cause of her first celebrity. *(By kind permission of the trustees of the Wallace Collection.)*

Color Plate 3 Thomas Phillips (1770–1845), *George Gordon Byron, 6th Baron Byron,* (c. 1835, replicated by Thomas Phillips from an 1813 original). Byron himself was the premier model for the "Byronic hero." He wrote to his mother in 1809, full of admiration for Albanian dress: "the most magnificent in the world, consisting of a long <u>white</u> <u>kilt</u>, old worked cloak, crimson velvet gold laced jacket & waistcoat, silver mounted pistols & daggars." He purchased some outfits for himself: "the only expensive articles in this country they cost 50 guineas each & have so much gold they would cost in England two hundred." *(By courtesy of The National Portrait Gallery, London.)*

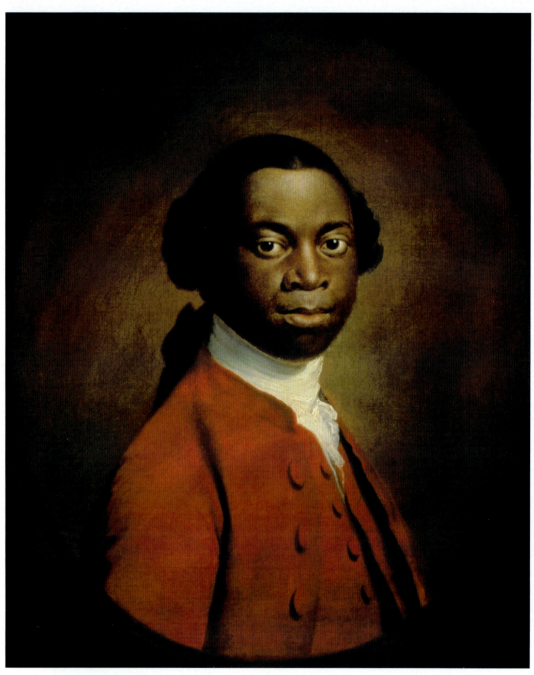

Color Plate 4 *Portrait of Olaudah Equiano*, late-18th century. This handsome portrait vividly attests Equiano's rise from kidnapped slave to British respectability. *(Royal Albert Memorial Museum, Exeter, Devon, UK/Bridgeman Art Library.)*

Color Plate 5 Joseph Mallord William Turner (British 1775–1851), *Slave Ship (Slavers Throwing Overboard the Dead and Dying, Typhoon Coming On)*, 1840. Turner depicts a notorious incident that galvanized the abolition movement. In 1781 the captain of the slave ship *Zong* ordered 133 weak and diseased slaves ejected into shark-infested waters, planning to collect on a policy that held the insurer liable for cargo jettisoned in order to salvage the remainder. In 1783 Olaudah Equiano brought the incident to the attention of the abolition movement; the resulting trial (which debated not the captain's criminal liability but the insurer's financial liability), presided over by Lord Mansfield, sided with the captain. (*Oil on canvas, 90.8 x 122.6 cm [35 3/4 x 48 1/4 in.]. Henry Lillie Pierce Fund. Courtesy, Museum of Fine Arts, Boston.*)

Color Plates 6 and 7 William Blake, two versions of the second plate of *The Little Black Boy*, from *Songs of Innocence*. As can be seen here, Blake sometimes tints the black boy's skin as light as the English boy's (near left); in others, he colors them differently (far left). While the heavenly scene portrays both boys sheltered by the tree and welcomed by Christ, it also puts the black boy outside the inner circle formed by the curve of Christ's body and the praying English boy. The black boy is not part of this configuration of prayer, but rather a witness to it, stroking the hair of the English boy, who has no regard for him. *(Fitzwilliam Museum, University of Cambridge, UK/Bridgeman Art Library.)*

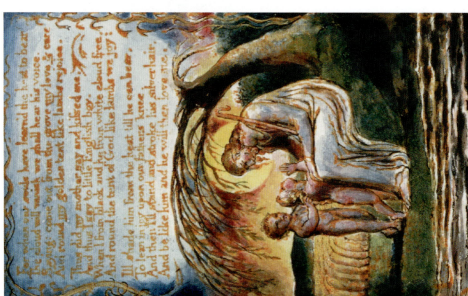

Color Plate 8 (far left) William Blake, *The Tyger*, from *Songs of Experience*. In some copies, Blake colors the tyger in lurid tones; in others, the tyger is colored in pastels. Strangely, the unmenacing, sideways image of the tyger not only fails to display the "fearful symmetry" that alarms the poem's speaker, but also seems no cause for the horrified tone of address. *(Fitzwilliam Museum, University of Cambridge, UK/Bridgeman Art Library.)*

Color Plate 9 (near left) William Blake, *The Sick Rose*, from *Songs of Experience*. The sickness of the rosebush is conveyed not only by its trailing on the ground but also by several particulars: the encircling thorns; the quite visible worm wrapped around the naked body emerging (in joy? in pain?) from the rose; the caterpillars devouring the leaves; a second naked body constricted by a snakelike worm. *(Fitzwilliam Museum, University of Cambridge, UK/Bridgeman Art Library.)*

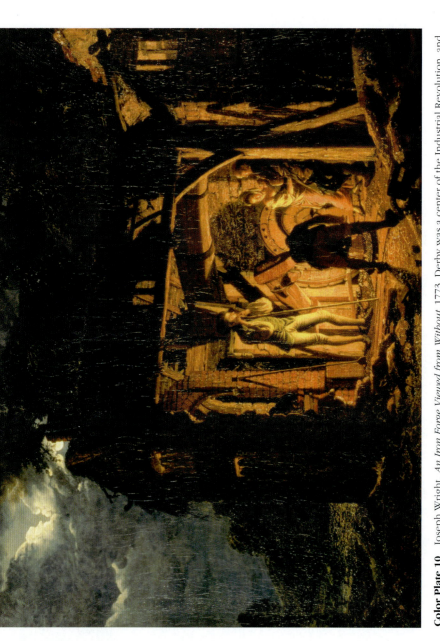

Color Plate 10 Joseph Wright, *An Iron Forge Viewed from Without*, 1773. Derby was a center of the Industrial Revolution, and Wright (1734–1797), a native, gained fame for his treatment of scientific and industrial subjects. He was particularly renowned for his handling of artificial light, and the dramatic contrast of fire and dark in this painting illustrates the romantic effects that could be drawn from technology. The contrast between the lurid forge and the picturesque background also suggests the contemporary spread of manufacture into peaceful landscapes. (*Hermitage, St. Petersburg, Russia/Bridgeman Art Library.*)

The Longman Anthology
of British Literature

SECOND COMPACT EDITION

VOLUME B

Thomas Girtin, *Tintern Abbey,* c. 1793.

The Romantics and Their Contemporaries

LITERATURE AND THE AGE: "NOUGHT WAS LASTING"

Reviewing Mary Shelley's *Frankenstein* in 1818, the *Edinburgh Magazine* remarked that "never was a wilder story imagined." Even so, the reviewer went on, "like most of the fictions of this age, it has an air of reality attached to it, by being connected with the favourite projects and passions of the times. The real events of the world have, in our day, too, been of so wondrous and gigantic a kind,—the shiftings of the scenes in our stupendous drama have been so rapid and various, that Shakespeare himself, in his wildest flights, has been completely distanced by the eccentricities of actual existence." The turbulent world and whirl of real events shaped the years of the "Romantic" period. It was marked on the one end by the revolutions in America and France, and on the other by the reform of Parliament to extend the vote and reconfigure representation, by the emergence of the modern industrial state, and by the abolition of slavery in British colonies. In the early 1820s, Lord Byron protested:

> Talk not of seventy years as age; in seven
>   I have seen more changes, down from monarchs to
> The humblest individual under heaven,
>   Than might suffice a moderate century through.
> I knew that nought was lasting, but now even
>   Change grows too changeable without being new:
> Nought's permanent among the human race ... (*Don Juan* 11.81)

As the nod toward monarchs indicates, the French Revolution of the 1790s cast a long shadow across British consciousness. Its events had announced a radical break in historical continuity—a sudden, cataclysmic overthrow of a monarchy surrounded by high culture, and the eruption of new social order that no one knew how to "read." New, challenging, and often contradictory energies reverberated across Britain and Europe. Enthusiasts heralded the fall of an oppressive aristocracy and the birth of democratic and egalitarian ideals, a new era, shaped by "the rights of man" rather than the entailments of wealth and privilege, while skeptics and reactionaries rued the end of chivalry, lamented the erosion of order, and foresaw the decline of civilization.

Yet whatever side one took, the upheaval bore a stark realization: politically, socially, economically, and philosophically, an irrevocable tide of new ideas had risen against seemingly entrenched structures. "It was now known," as historian E. J. Hobsbawm puts it, "that revolution in a single country could be a European phenomenon, that its doctrines could spread across the frontiers. . . . It was now known that social revolution was possible, that nations existed as something independent of states, peoples as something independent of their rulers, and even that the poor existed as something independent of the ruling classes." Other challenges appeared, framed in the rhetoric of the Revolution debate and animated by appeals to moral law and natural principle. There were arguments for and against the rights of women (not for the vote, but for better principles of education and improved social attitudes); debates over the abolition of Britain's slave trade and of slavery in its colonies (a moral blight but also a source of enormous and widespread commercial profit); movements for social and political remedies for the poor (versus the traditional spiritual consolations); and a newly emergent class consciousness among discontented workers in Britain's fields, mines, factories, and mills.

Polemical essays and pamphlets helped shape the controversies, and so did various forms of literary writing: sonnets and songs, ballads and poetic epistles, tales and plays, the sensationally turned narrative and the didactic novel. Even literature not forged in the social and political turbulence was caught by a sense of revolution. The first generation of writers (those who made their marks in the 1790s and the first decade of the new century) included William Blake, William Wordsworth, Samuel Taylor Coleridge, and Walter Scott, as well as several remarkable women: Anna Barbauld, Charlotte Smith, Hannah More, Mary Wollstonecraft, and Mary Robinson. The second generation (emerging before 1820) adds the younger voices and visions of Percy Shelley, Mary Shelley, John Keats, Lord Byron, and John Clare. It also witnesses the emergence of international literary celebrity, first and foremost in the charismatic figure of Lord Byron, then extending in the 1820s to the adored Felicia Hemans and at last to venerable Wordsworth, who would become a beloved Poet Laureate in 1843. All these writers were invigorated by a sense of participating in the modern world, of defining its values, and of claiming a place for writers as its instructors, prophets, critics, and inspirers. In 1792 Wollstonecraft urged "a REVOLUTION in female manners," and at the end of the decade, Wordsworth's Preface to the second edition of *Lyrical Ballads* announced his break with "known habits of association" in the genre of poetry—a program, as his collaborator Coleridge later said, of "awakening the mind's attention from the lethargy of custom" (*Biographia Literaria*, 1817). The post-Revolutionary poet "strips the veil of familiarity from the world," declared Shelley in *A Defence of Poetry*, a document he concluded by designating poets the "unacknowledged legislators of the world." This enthusiasm inspired innovations in content and literary form. Lyric, epic, and autobiography became radically subjective, spiraling inward to psychological dramas of mind and memory, or projecting outward into prophecies and visions of new worlds formed by new values. Other hybrid forms, such as political ballads and polemical narrative, emerged to address pressing issues of the day, while novelists were producing new kinds of female heroines and new narrative structures to represent family and social life. Still other writers developed forms such as the personal essay, the travelogue, or the journal, to join the personal and the political, the social and the domestic, the world of feeling to the world of thought, and both to the world of action.

ROMANCE, ROMANTICISM, AND THE POWERS OF THE IMAGINATION

In this vibrant culture of new imaginative possibilities, "Imagination" itself became a subject of reflection, and often debate. Eighteenth-century philosophy and science had argued for objective, verifiable truth and the common basis of our experience in a world of concrete, measurable physical realities. Over the century, however, there emerged a competing interest in individual variations, subjective filterings, and the mind's independence of physical realities, or even creative transformation of them: not just a recorder or mirror, the mind was an active, synthetic, dynamic, even visionary power—of particular importance to poets. Poets tended to define "Imagination" against what it was not, even categorically the opposite of: thus, imagination vs. reality; imagination vs. reason; vs. science; vs. the understanding (especially its "fixities" and "certainties"); vs. mere "fancy"; even vs. religious truth. Blake declared its priority: "What is now proved was once, only imagin'd" (*The Marriage of Heaven and Hell*); it is imagination that can "see a World in a Grain of Sand / And a Heaven in a Wild Flower" (*Auguries of Innocence*). Deeming Wordsworth too wedded to observation and description, he scribbled in the margin of Wordsworth's 1815 *Poems*, "One Power alone makes a Poet.—Imagination The Divine Vision." Yet Wordsworth had moods in which he shared Blake's sense of imagination as most potent when severed from ordinary senses and experiences: "Imagination—here the Power so called / Through sad incompetence of human speech— / That awful Power rose from the Mind's abyss / Like an unfathered vapour" (1850 *Prelude* Book 6, 593–96), he writes at a pivotal moment in a work that is the story of imagination, celebrated in his conclusion as the ultimate synthesizing power: "Imagination . . . in truth, / Is but another name for absolute strength / And clearest insight, and amplitude of mind, / And reason in her most exalted mood" (1805 *Prelude* 13.167–70).

Coleridge defined "Primary Imagination" as "the living Power and prime Agent of all human Perception," analogous to but a lesser power than divine creation. Poetry is written by the "secondary Imagination," an "echo" of the Primary "coexisting with conscious will": it dissolves and diffuses the materials of perception "in order to recreate," and thus shows itself "in the balance or reconciliation of opposite or discordant qualities," among these, the general and the individual, the new and the familiar, emotion and order, judgment and enthusiasm, rationality and passion, the artificial and the natural (*Biographia Literaria* chs. 13, 14). Percy Shelley, who also liked binaries, contrasted "Imagination" to "Reason" in the first paragraph of his *Defence of Poetry*, and following Coleridge, coordinated their powers: "Reason is to imagination as the instrument to the agent, as the body to the spirit, as the shadow to the substance." Byron, when he wasn't dramatizing the torments of imagination, was inclined to look wryly: "Imagination droops her pinion, / And the sad truth which hovers o'er my desk / Turns what was once romantic to burlesque" (*Don Juan* 4.3); "And as for other love, the illusion's o'er; / And money, that most pure imagination, / Gleams only through the dawn of its creation" (12.2). Keats proposed the imagination as a link to the ideal world at the dawn of creation: "The Imagination may be compared to Adam's dream—he awoke and found it truth," he suggested, referring to the dream of Eve. But he was ultimately more interested in the way imagination operates on real perception: "probably every mental pursuit takes its reality and worth from the ardour of the pursuer—being in itself a nothing." And like his contemporaries, he was drawn by the involvement of imagination with disease, deviance, delusion, egotism, escapism.

As Keats's analogy of Adam's dream suggests, male imagination often projects an eroticized female or feminized object. How did women writers address the imagination? They were prone to a skeptical bias, accenting dangers, a corruption of rational capacity and moral judgment, an alliance with destructive (rather than creative) passion. This view was not just resistance to male schemes of gender; it was also fueled by a discourse of rational education and intellectual dissent that included both men and women. "The imagination should not be allowed to debauch the understanding before it has gained strength, or vanity will become the forerunner of vice," cautioned Wollstonecraft in *A Vindication of the Rights of Woman;* the best books are those "which exercise the understanding and regulate the imagination." Mary Robinson recognized how, Hamlet-wise, "pall'd imagination, sick'ning, spurns / The sanity of reason!" (*The Sicilian Lover* 15.23–24). When Mary Shelley recalls, "My imagination, unbidden, possessed and guided me, gifting the successive images that arose in my mind with a vividness far beyond the usual bounds of reverie," the gift was *Frankenstein.* Men often wrote about these dangers, but usually in a pattern of alternation with enthusiastic, idealizing, visionary projections. And women were not always or only cautionary. Like Byron, Robinson could wax satiric, especially when her object is a self-styled male poet, his garret "the airy throne / Of bold Imagination, rapture-fraught / Above the herds of mortals" (*The Poet's Garret*). Yet of the women poets, she is probably the most enthusiastic: enchanted by Coleridge's opium-inspired *Kubla Khan*, she addresses him as "Spirit Divine!" and offers to "trace / Imagination's boundless space" with him (*To the Poet Coleridge*); writing a poem for his infant son, she celebrates his fortune in being born among "Romantic mountains! from whose brows sublime / Imagination might to frenzy turn."

Imagination was a heady romance—an inspiring force, a dangerous seduction. Not coincidentally, the issues often took shape in the language of romance. The rapid changes, new demands, and confusions of the age often pressed writers into imagining worlds elsewhere, the impulse of the mode from which the "Romantic" era gets its name: the "Romance." In 1755 Samuel Johnson's great *Dictionary* defined it thus: "A military fable of the middle ages; a tale of wild adventures in war and love." In a variety of genres—ballad, narrative poem, novel—Romance turned to other places and times, or shaped timeless, ahistorical tales of quest and desire, love and adventure. A medieval idiom, which flourished into a "gothic" vogue, supplied vivid language for Byron's *Childe Harold*, Keats's *La Belle Dame* and *The Eve of St. Agnes* (1820), and Hemans's many poems of the age of the Crusades. Romance could inhabit the even more distant pasts of Anglo-Saxon legend or classical mythology. Percy Shelley and Keats turned to the landscapes and myths of ancient Greece as resources of imagination before the age of Christian "truth." As the settings of many of these works indicate, Romance is also fascinated with foreign worlds. *Childe Harold*, Coleridge's *Kubla Khan*, and Hemans's *Tales, and Historic Scenes* testify to the vogue of Eastern materials. Byron intrigued readers with a lexicon of "jelicks" and "baracans," "giaours" and "viziers" (*Don Juan*). "Queen of far-away!" Keats hailed "Romance" itself.

In its various forms and stories, Romances shared a feature that Victorians would take as exemplary of the literary (if not the polemical) imagination of the age: a turn, even an escape, from the tumultuous and confusing here-and-now of England. The appeal lay not only in exotic settings and remote ages themselves but also in the freedom these licensed to explore superstitions and customs that had been dismissed by Enlightenment thinkers who championed faith in "Reason," progress, and universal truths. These historically distant worlds were often sites for prophecy of renewed worlds and alternative values. Defined against "neoclassical" values of proportion, rational order, balanced harmony, and a reverence for the traditions that conveyed these values, the adjective "romantic" had long stood for a recurrent impulse in the history of the arts: a passion for the wild, the unfamiliar, the irregular, the irrational, even anti-rational. Johnson's *Dictionary* offered a suggestive cluster for "romantick": "1) resembling the tales of romances; wild. 2) Improbable; false. 3) Fanciful; full of wild scenery." All these senses infuse one powerful model for the male Romantic poet: the enraptured, entranced "bard." Descended from the Old Testament prophet, Englished by Milton and elaborated in the eighteenth-century ode, the bard emerged in the Romantic era as an electrically visionary poet and prophet for the age. Poets as various and as different from one another as Blake, Wordsworth, Coleridge, Shelley, and Keats assume a bardic stance to credit their dreams, hopes, and visions, even as socially oriented reformists, such as Wollstonecraft advocating "the rights of woman" or Wilberforce arguing for the abolition of slavery, adopt bardic tones to project a better, more moral world.

There was another landscape in the Romantic age that overlapped with these exotic worlds: the psychic terrain of imagination. And here a second definition Johnson supplies for "romance"—"A lie; a fiction"—casts its shadow. Romance is not only the genre of enchanted dreams and inspired visions, but also of superstitions and spells, delusions and nightmares. Coleridge said that the poetry he wrote for *Lyrical Ballads* was devoted to "persons and characters supernatural, or at least romantic." Infused with sensations of supernatural power, or fed by opiated fantasies, the magical mystery tours of supernatural romance may hold the keys to paradise or the passage to hell, or both by turns. The genre of romance fairly bristles with complexities. Acutely aware of the chaos of their historical moment, writers often make the attraction to another world a critical theme: "magic casements," said Keats, "opening on the foam / Of perilous seas, in faery lands forlorn" (*Ode to a Nightingale*). The dubiously magic casements, moreover, may turn into mirrors: Romances often reflect, and reflect on, the world seemingly escaped or effaced from consciousness. The most celebrated romancers were hardly uncritical practitioners of the genre. Byron casts *Childe Harold* as a quest romance, but its path turns repeatedly to modern life, in particular the Napoleonic wars that were ravaging Europe.

At the same time, the prestige of "romance" and "romanticism" posed problems for women writers. Keats suggests one of these when he portrays "Romance" itself as a dangerous seductress (a "Queen of far-away," a "Fair plumed Syren") and opposes her allure to the demands of epic and tragedy (by which male poets claimed their fame). The critique of "Romance" could be tinged with sexism—an irony, since many women writers were inclined to criticize the genre, too. Clara Reeve, Wollstonecraft, Barbauld, and Hannah More—whose opinions divided, often sharply, on a variety of political and social issues—found common ground on the dangers of "Romance." Especially in the popular form of the novel, they felt it encouraged too much "sensibility"—the cultivation of emotional refinement over rational intellect—and fed an appetite for fantasy over sound judgment. Insofar as "Romances" deal in "the wild and extravagant," worried Reeve in *The Progress of Romance* (1785), they are "dangerous" for young readers: "they create and encourage the wildest excursions of imagination." "Novels . . . tend to make women the creatures of sensation," warned Wollstonecraft's *Rights of Woman* (1792); "their character is thus formed in the mould of folly." The genre enfeebled reason and stimulated illusions about "romantic love" that held perilous social consequences. By 1810, Barbauld was willing to argue that good novels could teach good values, but she was still cautious about the power of "romances . . . to impress false ideas on the mind." Urging women to cultivate the Enlightenment values of "Reason" and intellectual strength, these female critics also challenged romance stereotypes proffered as universal truth: the ideals of "feminine" silence, self-sacrifice, passivity, and unquestioning obedience; the ideology of female life contained in the domestic sphere.

There were still more ways that Romance exoticism intersected with the socially immediate world. Encounters with outcasts of all kinds—refugees, the poor, abandoned and fallen women, discharged soldiers, sailors, vagrants, peasants, north-country shepherds and smallholders, abject slaves—supplied the unusual and unexpected, and at the same time provoked social self-reflection. Foreign cultures might be close to home. Scots poet Robert Burns packaged himself as a primitive bard: the son of a tenant-farmer and tenant-farmer himself, a heavy-drinking, illegitimate-child-siring, native genius whose dialect verse and egalitarian sentiments seemed to make him the very voice of the people. William Wordsworth produced incidents from rural life in *Lyrical Ballads*, and his sister Dorothy Wordsworth captured the dialects in her journal. John Clare wrote of rural life in a rural idiom and himself embodied the figure of the peasant poet. Meanwhile, the "wild scenery" of Johnson's definition was caught in new travel books and records of "tours," and "tourists"—a word that emerged around 1800—began to delight in locales ignored by previous generations, or thought unpleasantly rough. Once-isolated Wales became so flooded by tourists that by 1833 a Welsh grammar carried an appendix of useful phrases: "I long to see the monastery"; "Is there a waterfall in this neighbourhood?"

This romance of novelty interplays with a powerful sense of a past that might be renewed. Writers created hybrid forms, building on models anywhere from the middle ages through the eighteenth century. Byron remained loyal to neoclassic poets such as Pope and Dryden, even as he gave their forms new vibrancy and reveled in contemporary political satire. Literary tradition was a cherished, if daunting, national heritage. Many admired Chaucer's tale-telling and descriptive detail; others worked variations on Spenser's allegorical epic, *The Faerie Queene*. Hazlitt honored Spenser as "the poet of our waking dreams," and the Spenserian stanza that conveyed these dreams shaped more than a few new "romances"—among them, Byron's *Childe Harold*, Hemans's *Forest Sanctuary*, Keats's *Eve of St. Agnes*, Shelley's *Revolt of Islam* and his homage to Keats, *Adonais*. Shakespeare and Milton were the great progenitors. Shakespeare was admired for the intensity of his imagery, his spectacular versatility, his unparalleled characterizations, as well as his mastery of "organic" (as opposed to "mechanical") aesthetic form, a concept elaborated in the criticism of Coleridge. He was an early inspiration for Coleridge's lectures and poetry; Wordsworth, Byron, and Hemans could hardly write without alluding to him; Keats named him his "Presider." For this generation of writers, Milton's revolutionary politics provided an example of antimonarchal courage, and *Paradise Lost* was indisputably the most important poem in English literature. Milton's Eve focuses the feminist grievances of Wollstonecraft's *Rights of Woman*, while for poets, as Byron declares in *Don Juan*, "the word 'Miltonic' mean[s] 'sublime,' " stimulating epic ambitions in works as diverse as Blake's *Milton* and *Jerusalem*, Wordsworth's *Prelude*, Percy Shelley's *Prometheus Unbound*, Keats's *Hyperion*, and Byron's *Don Juan*. Milton's Satan, an epitome of the "sublime," is echoed and doubled everywhere, and along with Milton's God and Adam, casts his shadow across the fable of masculine ambition and heroic alienation that Wollstonecraft's daughter Mary Shelley creates for *Frankenstein*.

At the same time (as the protagonist of *Frankenstein* demonstrates), Romantic creativity also defined itself—often defiantly—against tradition, experimenting with new forms and genres. Blake writes visionary epics; Wordsworth spends half a century on his poetic autobiography, "a thing unprecedented in Literary history," he said. Mary Shelley fuses several myths into a complex, interlocking structure of tales and tellers to form *Frankenstein*. Byron interplays stand-up patter with a tale of adventure to shape his burlesque *Don Juan*, "a poem totally of its own species . . . at once the stamp of originality and a defiance of imitation," Percy Shelley exclaimed to him. Individual experience, simultaneously the most exotic and most common region of all, led to excavations of the depths of the single self—which is to say, the unfolding of a self conceived as having depths and mysterious recesses. Reading Wordsworth's *Tintern Abbey*, Keats found "Genius" in its "dark Passages." In the Prospectus to *The Recluse* (1814), Wordsworth himself proclaimed

> Not Chaos, not
> The darkest pit of lowest Erebus,
> Nor aught of blinder vacancy—scooped out
> By help of dreams, can breed such fear and awe
> As fall upon us often when we look
> Into our Minds, into the Mind of Man,
> My haunt, and the main region of my Song.

Byron jibed that Keats's *Sleep and Poetry* was "an ominous title," but when Wordsworth named "the Mind" as his subject, Keats understood completely, and even women poets participated. This post-Enlightenment, bourgeois Protestant individualism moved beyond the rhetorical first-person of eighteenth-century poetry to produce the "I" as an individual authority, for whom the mind, in all its creative powers and passionate testimony of deeply registered sensations, became a compelling focus. The "I" could sponsor extravagant self-display (Robinson and Byron), prophetic self-elevation (Blake and Shelley), poignant song (Hemans), internal debate (Keats), or what Keats, thinking of Wordsworth, called the "egotistical sublime." Many of its forms defined a radical or alienated subjectivity. Wollstonecraft wrote as a nonconformist, Cowper and Hemans were famous for the melancholy autobiography that haunts their poetry, while poets such as Byron, Coleridge, and Shelley cultivated the "I" as antihero: the exile, the damned visionary, the alienated idealist, the outcast, whose affiliates were Cain, Satan, even the paradoxical figure of Napoleon—all joined by the passion of mind and the torments of imagination.

Whether cast as experiment and innovation or allied with liberty and revolution, these new expressive forms were sharpened by a sense of modernity, with their writers often viewing old forms and traditions as tyranny or, at the very least, as the strictures of custom and habit. Revoking the neoclassical argument of Dryden (in the seventeenth century) that the poet is responsible for "putting bounds to a wilde overflowing Fancy," Wordsworth asserted in the Preface to *Lyrical Ballads* (1800) that poetry should be a "spontaneous overflow of powerful feelings," and explained, in a later version, that in his poems "the feeling . . . gives importance to the action and situation, and not the action and situation to the feeling." Framing "incidents of common life," he made the agents of feeling such socially disenfranchised figures as children, bereft mothers, impoverished shepherds, beggars, veterans, and the rural destitute. In a lecture "On the Living Poets" (1818), William Hazlitt sneered at this "mixed rabble of . . . convicts, female vagrants, gipsies, . . . ideot boys and mad mothers . . . peasants, pedlars," but Wordsworth's revolution was to treat them all as vehicles of worthy imagination and passion. Hazlitt had no trouble linking this program to "the sentiments and opinions which produced the French revolution" as well as its "principles and events":

> The change in the belles-lettres was as complete, and . . . as startling, as the change in politics, with which it went hand in hand. . . . According to the prevailing notions, all was to be natural and new. Nothing that was established was to be tolerated. . . . Kings and queens were dethroned from their rank and station in legitimate tragedy or epic poetry, as they were decapitated elsewhere; rhyme was looked upon as a relic of the feudal system, and regular metre was abolished along with regular government.

THE FRENCH REVOLUTION AND ITS REVERBERATIONS

In the 1780s, the American Revolution was a recent memory for the British, at once an inspiration to political progressives, an embarrassment for the prestige of the Empire, and a worry to a conservative ruling class concerned about the arrival of democratic ideas on British shores. When the next Revolution exploded in France only twelve miles across the Channel, rather than a hemisphere away, the press of radical, violent, and inevitable change seemed imminent. With the fall of the Bastille prison, a symbol of royal tyranny, on July 14, 1789, and the *Declaration of the Rights of Man* that soon followed, British consciousness was dominated by French events. Conservatives were alarmed, while liberals welcomed the early phase as a repetition of England's "Glorious Revolution" of 1688, an overdue end to feudal abuse and the inauguration of constitutional government. Radicals hoped for a more thorough-going renovation: "Bliss was it in that dawn to be alive, / But to be young was very heaven!" Wordsworth said in retrospect, in a passage from his poetic autobiography that he published in 1809, and again in 1815 under the title *French Revolution as it Appeared to Enthusiasts at its Commencement.* Everything was infused with "the attraction of a country in Romance!" He was not the only one in rapture. Burns was certain that "man to man the world o'er / Shall brithers be for a' that." In their own idioms, Wollstonecraft, Blake, and Charles Lamb joined the chorus, and in subsequent generations, Byron and Percy Shelley continued to hope that what was started in France could be continued elsewhere with better consequences.

Better consequences, because millenarian dreams were soon undermined by harsh developments: the overthrow of the French monarchy in August 1792 and in the next month, the massacre of more than a thousand prisoners by a Paris mob. When extremist Jacobins prevailed over moderate Girondins, the French Revolution fragmented into the Reign of Terror. Louis XVI was guillotined in January 1793, Queen Marie Antoinette in October. In February 1793, France declared war on Britain and Britain reciprocated, throwing the political ideals of Wordsworth and his generation into sharp conflict with their love of country. Except for the brief interlude of the deceptive Peace of Amiens (1802–1803:

"Peace in a week, war in a month," a British diplomat commented), Britain was at war with France until the final defeat of Napoleon at Waterloo in 1815. The shock of these events lasted for decades and lent retroactive credit to the conservative polemic of Edmund Burke's *Reflections on the Revolution in France*, published in 1790, after the arrest and imprisonment of the royal family. In 1790 Burke seemed a sentimental hysteric to political opponents and was quickly subject to sarcastic challenge in Wollstonecraft's *Vindication of the Rights of Men* (1790) and Tom Paine's *Rights of Man* (1791). In 1793 radical philosopher William Godwin's *Political Justice*, though not directly about the Revolution, offered a vision of a society governed by individual reason, without the oppression of social institutions or private property. But the course of the Revolution confirmed Burke's alarm.

Under the systematic Terror of Robespierre (1793–1794), thousands of aristocrats, their employees, the clergy, and ostensible opponents of the Revolution were guillotined, the violence swallowing up Robespierre himself in 1794. British unease increased when France offered to support all revolutions abroad, and then invaded the Netherlands and the German states in 1794, Italy in 1796, and republican Switzerland in 1798. Now "Oppressors in their turn," Wordsworth wrote, "Frenchmen had changed a war of self-defense / For one of conquest, losing sight of all / Which they had struggled for" (1805 *Prelude* 10.791–94). In 1799 Napoleon, a general who consolidated his power in the Italian and Swiss campaigns, staged a *coup d'état* and was named First Consul for life. The Revolution had evolved into a military dictatorship, its despotism confirmed when Napoleon crowned himself Emperor in 1804. A complex personality—a challenger of entrenched monarchies; a charismatic military genius; a ruthless, egotistical imperialist—he generated nearly two decades of war that ravaged the Continent. Although war barely reached Britain, it was a constant threat, cost thousands of British lives and sent its economy into turmoil.

When Napoleon invaded the Iberian Peninsula in 1807, British support for the spontaneous resistance of the Portuguese and Spanish peoples enabled former radicals to return to the patriotic fold, to see their country as the champion of liberty against French imperialism. Napoleon's actions, claimed Coleridge, produced a "national unanimity unexampled in our history since the reign of Elizabeth . . . and made us all once more Englishmen." English self-definition was energized, the contest with France drawing on historical antagonisms that went back for centuries. Unlike the English, the French rejected their monarchy; if France could thus claim to be the first modern nation in the old world, Britain could feel superior to a country defined by the Terror and then Napoleon. National self-definition had strong literary manifestations. Hemans began her career with patriotic anthems celebrating Britain's support for the "noble" (and highly "romantic") Spanish resistance, and across these decades she published *Welsh Melodies, Greek Songs, Songs of Spain, National Lyrics,* and even the canonical American anthem, "The Landing of the Pilgrim Fathers" (our "Thanksgiving" hymn). Byron wrote *Hebrew Melodies* (1815), got involved with Italian liberation movements, and in his last real-life romance, died in Greece where he had gone to aid the revolution against the Ottoman Empire.

Yet even as this literature tamed class differences into a general culture of songs for the salon, or made nationalism itself a vivid "romance," continuing disturbances pointed to those excluded from Coleridge's idealized whole of "us all . . . Englishmen."

THE CONTRAST
1792

BRITISH LIBERTY.   FRENCH LIBERTY

RELIGION.   MORALITY.   ATHEISM   PERJURY
LOYALTY OBEDIENCE TO THE LAWS   REBELLION.TREASON.ANARCHY MURDER
INDEPENDANCE PERSONAL SECURITY   EQUALITY.MADNESS.CRUELTY. INJUSTICE
JUSTICE INHERITANCE PROTECTION   TREACHERY INGRATITUDE IDLENESS
PROPERTY.INDUSTRY. NATIONAL PROSPERITY   FAMINE NATIONAL & PRIVATE RUIN.
            HAPPINESS   MISERY
                    WHICH IS BEST

Thomas Rowlandson, after a drawing by Lord George Murray, *The Contrast, 1792*.

Its fears heightened by the threat of invasion, the government clamped down on any form of political expression that hinted at French ideas. Efforts to reform Parliament begun in the 1780s were stifled, as was the movement to abolish the slave trade, and even moderates were silenced by accusations of "Jacobinism" (sympathy with Revolutionary extremists). In 1791 authorities in Birmingham connived at three days of riots by a loyal "Church and King" mob against Dissenters who had held a dinner to commemorate the Fall of the Bastille. When his house and laboratory were sacked, the eminent chemist and nonconformist Joseph Priestley fled to London and then emigrated to America. In 1792 Paine fled to France; he was tried and convicted in absentia of sedition for *The Rights of Man*, and his publishers and booksellers were regularly prosecuted. In 1794, twelve London radicals were arrested, including a novelist and playwright, Thomas Holcroft, and Horne Tooke, a philologist whose publications seemed a dangerous attempt to democratize language. Charged with high treason, they were defended by Godwin and acquitted, but the trial was a harbinger.

In 1794 the government suspended the long-established right of habeas corpus, which required the state to show cause for imprisonment and to conduct trials in a timely fashion; now anyone suspected of a crime could be jailed indefinitely. The Gagging Acts of 1795 targeted radical lecturers and societies, defining any criticism of the monarchy as treason and squelching political organization by limiting the size of meetings called to discuss reform. The Combination Act of 1799 forbade workmen, under penalty of conspiracy charges, to unionize or even to associate for purposes of collective bargaining. All these laws were enforced by government spies. Coleridge and Wordsworth, walking and conversing on the coastal hills of the Bristol Channel and plotting nothing more revolutionary than poems for *Lyrical Ballads*, looked suspicious enough to warrant tailing by a government informer. Coleridge was amused that their talk of the philosopher Spinoza was reported as references to "Spy Nozy," but actual radicals suffered severer consequences, for the government was also deploying *agents provocateurs* to incite them into capital offences. These infiltrators played a major role in plotting the Pentridge Rising of 1817 and the Cato Street Conspiracy of 1820, a scheme to murder cabinet ministers (a prime minister had been assassinated in 1812) and stage a coup d'état. "Cato Street" was "exposed" and its radical conspirators hanged or sent to prison in Australia, but the ultimate conspirator had been the government. Policy was still more severe outside England: in Edinburgh, delegates to the first British Convention of reformers were arrested for sedition and doomed to sentences in Australia; in Ireland, where Britain had more troops than on the Continent, a peasants' rebellion was crushed in a bloodbath (1798). Rather than international "fraternity," it was repression at home and wars abroad that defined the legacy of the French Revolution. When Napoleon was finally defeated in 1815 and the Bourbons were restored to the throne of France, the result was to reinforce reactionary measures and despotic monarchies all over Europe.

In the England of 1815, a further affliction was visited on the poor, among whom were many veterans, by Parliament's passage of the Corn Laws. Because importing grain had been impossible during the war years, prices for native grain soared; the Corn Laws now restricted imports in order to sustain the artificially high prices, a boon for landlords and a disaster for the poor, for whom bread was a chief article of diet. Bad harvests further raised costs. For the first time, in the estimate of the *Morning Chronicle*, protests and petitions erupted from "a majority of the adult male population of England," igniting food riots across the country. Under the unreformed electoral system, petitions to Parliament were the only recourse for those without representatives. In 1800 only males, and only five percent of them, were allowed to vote; only Anglicans, members of the state Church, could serve in the House of Lords. Workers did not have a vote, or even a representative in Parliament. The worker-populated cities of Leeds, Manchester, Birmingham, and Sheffield did not have a vote, whereas depopulated "rotten boroughs," consisting of one or two houses owned by a single landlord, enjoyed one or even two representatives in Parliament. As the Prince Regent returned from the opening of Parliament in January 1817, he found his carriage surrounded by a hostile crowd and stoned.

Workers were also being displaced by new machinery; they sometimes retaliated with attacks on the machines themselves, actions punishable by death. (Byron's first speech in the House of Lords was against such a measure, the Frame-breaking Bill provoked by weavers' riots.) Throughout the 1820s, farmworkers, angry at their degraded conditions, erupted into sporadic violence, culminating in a great uprising in 1830, in which barns burned across the countryside, and laborers again attacked machinery. The unemployed starved to death. Men scrambled for employment, while women and children, because they were deemed tractable and obedient, found it at pitiful wages. Prevailing attitudes and institutions were inadequate to ameliorate the misery and consequent disruptions. Since Elizabethan times, England had relied on a network of parishes and justices of the peace: local notables, serving in a largely volunteer capacity that enhanced their status, who kept records, assisted the needy, and administered everyday justice. Indigent newcomers to the cities could not easily be returned to their home parishes for support; they were needed as workers. And the parish system left out many: Irish Catholic immigrants, members of dissenting sects, and those lapsed from an Anglicanism that had failed to build churches for the new populations and at worst seemed remote from their concerns. When Lord John Manners declared that "the only means of Christianizing Manchester" was to revive the monasteries, he made clear the inadequacy of the current state Church to supply moral authority, social structure, and needed assistance.

No wonder that it was in Manchester that the modern vocabulary of class struggle emerged. The eighteenth-century ideal of stable social "orders" and "ranks" was challenged by a growing antagonism between successful capitalist entrepreneurs and their workers. In August 1819, nearly a hundred thousand mill-workers and their families gathered at nearby St. Peter's Field for a peaceful demonstration with banners and parades, capped by an address by the radical "Orator" Hunt calling for parliamentary reform. Alarmed by the spectacle, the local ruling class sent their drunken, sabre-wielding militia to charge the rally and arrest Hunt. Hunt offered no resistance, but the militia struck out at the jeering though unarmed crowd and, backed by mounted Hussars, in ten minutes left an official toll of eleven dead, including one trampled child, and more than four hundred injured, many from sabre wounds. Unreported injuries and later deaths from injury undoubtedly added to the official toll. This pivotal event in nineteenth-century economic and political strife was immediately dubbed "Peterloo" by the left press—a sardonic echo of the celebrated British triumph over Napoleon at Waterloo, four years before. Parliament did not reform, but instead consolidated the repressive measures of previous decades into the notorious Six Acts at the end of 1819. These Acts outlawed demonstrations, empowered magistrates to enter private houses in search of arms, prohibited meetings of more than fifty unless all participants were residents of the parish in which the meeting was held, increased the prosecution of blasphemous or seditious libel (defined as language "tending to bring into hatred or contempt" the monarchy or government), and raised the newspaper tax, thus constricting the circulation of William Cobbett's radical *Political Register* by tripling its price.

THE MONARCHY

Outraged by the situation summed by "Peterloo," Percy Shelley mordantly surveyed *England in 1819*, the title of a sonnet whose language rendered it unpublishable, even in a radical newspaper such as his friend Leigh Hunt's *Examiner*. It began:

> An old, mad, blind, despised, and dying King,
> Princes, the dregs of their dull race, who flow
> Through public scorn,—mud from a muddy spring,—
> Rulers who neither see, nor feel, nor know . . .

The Lear-like king who inspired this contempt was George III, Washington's antagonist in the American Revolution. He had had an episode of mental instability in 1765 and another in 1788: he talked incessantly and rarely slept, and once his eldest son tried to throttle him. The episode at once epitomized their antagonism and reflected the political conflicts of the late Georgian era. The King lived a domestic life and his successive administrations were firmly Tory—that is, socially and politically "conservative," committed to the constitutional power of the monarchy and the

Church, and opposed to concessions of greater religious and political liberties. The Prince lived extravagantly at taxpayers' expense, with a devout Roman Catholic mistress whom he secretly and unconstitutionally married. In 1787, he obtained an extra £10,000 from the King, a relief from Parliament of £100,000 to pay his debts, and an additional £60,000 to build his residence, Carlton House—a total equivalent to almost seven million dollars today. But because his comparative political flexibility held out the hope of some reforms, he was backed by the opposition party, the liberal Whigs. He expected the crown in 1788, but the King unexpectedly recovered, hanging on until November 1810, when he relapsed and became permanently mad. In January 1811 the Prince was appointed "Regent."

In this new position of power, he focused all the contradictions and tensions of the time. In 1812, the *Morning Post* addressed him in the loyalist hyperbole that earned it the nickname of the "Fawning Post": "You are the glory of the People . . . You breathe eloquence, you inspire the Graces—You are an Adonis in loveliness." Leigh and John Hunt replied in *The Examiner*, denouncing "this Adonis in Loveliness" as "a corpulent gentleman of fifty . . . a man who had just closed half a century without one single claim on the gratitude of his country or the respect of posterity." Their scathing rejoinder earned them two-year sentences for libel and fines of £500 each, but Leigh Hunt continued to edit *The Examiner* from his prison cell, which he transformed into a gentleman's parlor, where he was visited as a hero by Byron, Moore, Keats, and Lamb.

Meanwhile, the Prince Regent was transforming the face of London. He and his architects recreated Regent's Park in the north and St. James Park in the south, linking them by extending Regent Street, built Trafalgar Square, elevated Buckingham House into Buckingham Palace, and erected the Hyde Park arch. The "metropolitan improvements" bespoke impressive city planning, but also demarcated the boundaries between rich and poor. The Gothic/Chinese/Indian fantasy of his beloved retreat, the Brighton Pavilion, spoke even more loudly of his distance from the everyday life of his subjects. By 1815, when £150 a year provided a comfortable living for many, he was £339,000 in debt, an extravagance that brought contempt on the monarchy. The pity many still felt for George III did not extend to the son. On his accession to power, he abandoned his Whig friends, separated his estranged Queen Caroline from their daughter Charlotte, and was absent from Charlotte when she died in childbirth in 1817. In 1820, when George III died and he at last became King, he attempted to divorce Caroline by initiating a sordid investigation of her escapades abroad. The scandal rebounded on a man excoriated, in the Hunts' words, as "a libertine over head and heels in debt and disgrace, a despiser of domestic ties," and provided yet another handle for attacks upon him. The personal elegance that had made him "the first gentleman of Europe" had dissipated; already in 1813, Beau Brummell, an aristocratic "dandy" whose impeccable style and social assurance made him a paragon of the era, responded to a slight by the Regent by loudly inquiring of a fellow dandy, "who's your fat friend?" The Prince was too fat to mount his horse by 1816; by 1818 it was reported that "Prinny has let loose his belly which now reaches his knees." Of his official Coronation portrait, Moore acidly noted that it was "disgraceful both to the King & the painter—a lie upon canvas." It was inevitable that satiric sketches would compete for fame.

Thomas Lawrence, *Corona-
tion Portrait of the Prince
Regent* (later, *George IV*), 1820.

INDUSTRIAL ENGLAND AND "NEVER-RESTING LABOUR"

In the decades of this royal extravagance, the general population was rapidly expanding, accompanied by grim social misery. By 1750, the population of England and
Wales was around five-and-a-half million; at the turn of the century, when the first
census was taken, it was about eight million, with most of the increase in the last two
decades. Scotland registered another million and a half, Ireland more than five million. Traditionally viewed as an index to a nation's wealth, population now loomed
as a danger, inspiring the dire prophecy of Thomas Malthus's *On the Principle of Population As It Affects the Future Improvement of Society* (1798): "population, when
unchecked, increases in a geometrical ratio. Subsistence increases only in an arithmetical ratio. A slight acquaintance with numbers will show the immensity of the
first power in comparison of the second." The increase continued: by 1831 the population of Great Britain neared fourteen million.

The numbers tell only part of the story. Ever since the end of the eighteenth century and then with postwar acceleration, the economic base had begun to shift from agriculture, controlled by wealthy aristocrats (the landlords), to manufacture, controlled by new-money industrialists. The war against France fueled a surge: "A race of merchants and manufacturers and bankers and loan jobbers and contractors" was born, remarked Cobbett in 1802. Factories and mills invaded the countryside, pumped small towns into burgeoning cities, and cities into teeming metropolises. In 1800 only London—with about ten percent of the population of England and Wales—had more than a hundred thousand people. By 1837, when Victoria was crowned, there were five such cities, and London was growing by as much as twenty percent a decade. Even more staggering was the growth of the new industrial cities of the north. Manchester's population increased fivefold in fifty years, to 142,000 in 1831. Cobbett denounced these developments as "infernal," and many of his contemporaries, alarmed by the new populations and their demands for wages, food, and housing, feared a repetition at home of the mob violence of France.

This unprecedented concentration was the result of several converging factors. Poor harvests afflicted the countryside in the 1790s, and again in 1815. Scarcities were aggravated by the Corn Laws and an increase of "Enclosure acts"—the consolidation and privatization of old common fields into larger, more efficient farms. The modernizing did improve agricultural yield and animal husbandry, offsetting in some measure Malthus's prediction of an inadequate food supply, but it also produced widespread dislocation and misery. The pattern of country landholding changed. Smallholders, whether independent but modest farmers or proprietors of estates up to a thousand acres, fell away, while the great estates prospered in size and number: "the big bull frog grasps all," Cobbett pungently remarked. Meanwhile, the farmers and herdsmen rendered landless by the enclosure acts had to settle for meager subsistence wages in the country or migrate to the cities. The census of 1811 revealed that for the first time a majority of families were engaged in nonagricultural employment. The yeomen who had represented the mythic heart of sturdy English freedom became day laborers, while others sank into poverty and centuries-old social structures eroded. Sending the Whig leader in Parliament a copy of *Lyrical Ballads* that he hoped might call attention to the plight of the rural poor, Wordsworth lamented that without a "little tract of land" as "a kind of permanent rallying point" in their hardships, "the bonds of domestic feeling . . . have been weakened, and in innumerable instances entirely destroyed."

Uprooted families were pulled by hopes of employment to the new factory towns. Cotton made modern Manchester. By 1802 there were more than fifty spinning mills, and the once-provincial city had become one of the commercial capitals of Europe. Textiles produced in vast quantities by power looms eliminated skilled hand-weavers, and extinguished the traditional supplement to the income of the cottager. The city did not incorporate until 1838, and no regulations controlled manufacture, sanitation, or housing; the unchecked boom enriched the few master manufacturers and immiserated the workers. The factories required a workforce disciplined to the constant output of the machines they tended; families accustomed to the ebb and flow of agricultural rhythms found themselves plunged into a world of industrial clock-time. Twelve- to fifteen-hour shifts, strict discipline, capricious firings, dangerous and unsanitary conditions, injuries, and ruined health were the rule of the day. Children were the preferred staff for the mills, and youngsters of five worked in the mines, their little bodies ideal for hauling coal in the narrow shafts. Workers were often further victimized by debts to their employers for housing and food. There was no philosophy of government restraint and regulation of these practices; all was "laissez-faire," the doctrine associated with Adam Smith's enormously influential *Wealth of Nations* (1777) that national wealth would flourish if businesses were left to operate with unfettered self-interest. By the 1780s there was a measurable gulf between rich and poor, ever more apparent in Manchester in the contrast between the homes of the wealthy in the suburbs and the slums by the polluted city river. "The town is abominably filthy," declared a visitor in 1808, "the Steam Engine is pestiferous, the Dyehouses noisome and offensive, and the water of the river as black as ink or the Stygian lake."

The twin agricultural and industrial revolutions recast both the town and the country and altered the relationship between them. To obtain waterpower, early mills and factories were set by rivers, thereby converting peaceful valleys into sites of production. Gas lighting, first used in such buildings, made possible twenty-four-hour operation, and the resulting spectacle affected contemporaries as a weird and ominous splendor. In regions that were once the "assured domain of calm simplicity / And pensive quiet," wrote Wordsworth in *The Excursion* (1814):

> an unnatural light,
> Prepared for never-resting Labour's eyes,
> Breaks from a many-windowed Fabric huge;
> And at the appointed hour a Bell is heard—
> Of harsher import than the Curfew-knoll
> That spake the Norman Conqueror's stern behest,
> A local summons to unceasing toil!
> Disgorged are now the Ministers of day;
> And, as they issue from the illumined Pile,
> A fresh Band meets them, at the crowded door,—
> And in the Courts—and where the rumbling Stream,
> That turns the multitude of dizzy wheels,
> Glares, like a troubled Spirit, in its bed
> Among the rocks below. Men, Maidens, Youths,
> Mother and little Children, Boys and Girls,
> Enter, and each the wonted task resumes
> Within this Temple—where is offered up
> To Gain—the Master Idol of the Realm,
> Perpetual sacrifice.   (8.169–87)

Industry invaded the most picturesque quarters of the British Isles. A center of tourism, Wales was also home to oppressive slate mines. Richard Pennant of North Wales epitomized the fortunes made in the trade in slaves and new-world commodities. Using the profits from his family's Jamaican sugar plantations, Pennant developed and mechanized the slate quarries on his estates. Elected to Parliament from Liverpool in 1783, he led the planters' defense of the slave trade while boosting the market for slate at home. Slate was an ideal roofing material, and the spread of education created a need for slate blackboards; at Port Penrhyn, the town Pennant established to ship slate, a hundred thousand writing slates were manufactured each year. In the eighteenth century, the quarries employed six hundred and the manufactory thirty more; by 1820 the workforce was a thousand, and it expanded rapidly over the next two decades. The concurrent discovery on the estate of minerals useful to the manufacture of Herculaneum pottery in Liverpool generated still more income. The profits underwrote Penryhn Castle, a lush Norman fantasy constructed (from 1821) by Pennant's heir.

The rhetoric of an 1832 history of Wales obscures the dislocations entailed by the progress it lauds: "About forty years ago, this part of the country bore a most wild, barren, and uncultivated appearance, but it is now covered with handsome villas, well built farm houses, neat cottages, rich meadows, well-cultivated fields, and flourishing plantations; bridges have been built, new roads made, bogs and swampy grounds drained and cultivated, neat fences raised, and barren rocks covered with woods." At Portmadoc, about twelve miles south of the sublime scenery of Mount Snowdon in Wales, William Madocks was performing one of the celebrated technological feats of the day, building a massive embankment (1808–1811), draining the tidal estuary behind it, enlarging the harbor, and founding a model village named after himself, Tremadoc—a project on which Percy Shelley enthusiastically collaborated, until he and his household fled from Wales in 1813 in the wake of a murderous attack. Popular biography ascribed the incident to Shelley's propensity to hallucination, but underlying it were genuine conflicts between idealist radicalism, paternalistic planning, local privilege, and labor unrest.

If Romantic poetry is famous for celebrating "Nature," this affection coincides with the peril to actual nature by modern industry. "Our feeling for nature," wrote Friedrich Schiller in the 1790s, "is like the feeling of an invalid for health." Industry scarred previously rural communities. Visiting Scotland in 1803 with her brother, Dorothy Wordsworth noted of one village: "a pretty place it once has been, but a manufactory is established there; and a townish bustle and ugly stone houses are fast taking the place of the brown-roofed thatched cottages." Of the famous Carron Ironworks, "seen at a distance," she noted, "the sky above them was red with a fiery light." Industry ringed even their beloved Lake District, and on its coast the shafts of the coal mines owned by the employer of Wordsworth's father, Sir James Lowther, ran ever deeper and longer, until they extended under the sea and even caused the collapse of houses in Whitehaven, the planned port city from which the coal was shipped.

The need to bring coal and iron into conjunction spurred improvements in transport. In 1759 the Duke of Bridgewater cut an eleven-mile canal between his colliery at Worsley and Manchester; two years later an extension linked Manchester to the sea. Soon canals transected the country; between 1790 and 1794 alone, eighty-one acts for the construction of canals were passed. The cost of carriage was drastically cut, and the interior of England opened for commerce. By 1811 there were steamboats on the rivers; by 1812 locomotives were hauling coal. Large-scale road-building followed, including arteries between Shrewsbury and Holyhead (the port of departure for Ireland) and another between Carlisle and Glasgow in Scotland. During these years, a Scotsman, John Macadam, developed the road surface that bears his name. Across the country, distant regions were joined by a web of new roads and the Royal Mail coaches that ran along them on regular schedules. Decades later, remembering coach travel as it was in 1812, Thomas De Quincey recalled the new sensation of speed: "we saw it, we felt it as a thrilling; and this speed was not the product of blind insensate agencies, that had no sympathy to give, but was incarnated in the fiery eyeballs of an animal, in his dilated nostril, spasmodic muscles, and echoing hoofs" (*The English Mail-Coach, or the Glory of Motion*, 1849).

In this age of acceleration, the British Empire was expanding, too. Economically and politically, it had become the preeminent world power. The American colonies had been lost, but Canada and the West Indies remained, and Australia, New Zealand, and India marked a global reach. British forces subjugated natives, defeated rival French ambitions, and held the Turks and Russians in check, while the East India Company, originally a trading organization, gradually assumed administrative control of the subcontinent, even to the point of collecting taxes to protect British interests. The Company penetrated every aspect of British life: Warren Hastings, the first governor-general of India, was tried for cruelty and corruption, having amassed a fortune of over £400,000 in India. His trial, lasting from 1788 to 1795, was a *cause célèbre*, establishing the fame of the prosecutors even though he was acquitted. While his profits were exceptional, they marked a trend of great numbers of younger sons seeking fortunes in India. In a pattern common to north-country boys with the right connections, Wordsworth's family destined his younger brother John for service with the East India Company. "I will work for you," he said to William, "and you shall attempt to do something for the world." Although John lost his life in 1805 in the wreck of a tradeship, so widespread was the phenomenon of English fortunes based on Indian gain that "nabob," Hindi for "vicegerent" or "governor," entered the vernacular as a synonym for a wealthy man.

CONSUMERS AND COMMODITIES

Even more remarkable was the role of the East India Company as the prototype for later colonial rule. At a time when Oxford and Cambridge graduates were preparing for clerical orders, the Company college at Haileybury trained its students for their foreign service. Malthus taught there; both James Mill and son John Stuart Mill worked for the Company; Lamb was a clerk in the home office in London. And thousands more indirectly derived livelihoods or pleasures from the Company's activities. Napoleon sneered at Britain as "a nation of shopkeepers," taking this phrase from Smith's *Wealth of Nations*: "To found a great empire for the sole purpose of raising up a people of customers, may at first sight appear a project fit only for a nation of shopkeepers." But Smith's mercantile empire was a perspicacious forecast, confirmed in 1823 by Byron when he named England's pride as its "haughty shopkeepers, who sternly dealt / Their goods and edicts out from pole to pole, / And made the very billows pay them toll" (*Don Juan* 10.65).

Cotton and tea were major goods. So was opium, and behind the dreams of Coleridge's *Kubla Khan*, Keats's *Ode to a Nightingale* (whose poet compares his state of sensation to intoxication by "some dull opiate"), and De Quincey's *Confessions of an English Opium Eater* were grim realities. Laudanum, opium dissolved in alcohol, was widely prescribed for a variety of complaints; it was the chief ingredient in a host of sedatives for children, especially of the poor, whose families had to leave them at home while they worked. It was also a cheap intoxicant. When Marx said that "religion was the opium of the masses," he was not using a random metaphor. Opium virtually defined foreign profiteering. De Quincey's uncle was a colonel in Bengal, in the military service of the East India Company, which reaped enormous profits from producing opium and smuggling it into China against the prohibition of the Chinese government. A Member of Parliament remarked: "If the Chinese are to be poisoned by opium, I would rather they were poisoned for the benefit of our Indian subjects than for the benefit of any other Exchequer." But the profits accrued less to Indian subjects than to the ruling British, even as the Opium Wars served the larger purpose of opening China to Lancashire cotton, as India had been opened earlier: the Wars concluded with the annexation of Hong Kong, and the opening of five treaty ports to British commerce. Meanwhile, the persistence of slave labor in British colonial plantations (not abolished until 1833) continued to raise ethical questions about the traffic in their commodities. International affairs inescapably cast their shadow on national life: "By foreign wealth are British morals chang'd," charged Barbauld in 1791, "And Afric's sons, and India's, smile aveng'd."

As morals adjusted in relation to economic opportunities, the empire also fed a growing appetite for the exotic among those shut up in urban squalor, or merely in an increasingly routinized commercial life. For those who had the wherewithal, the era proffered a new world of objects, which had begun to proliferate in the late eighteenth century. An exemplary instance of the success of marketing joined to new technological advance is Josiah Wedgwood (1730–1795), whose cream-colored earthenware became known as "Queen's ware" because of Queen Charlotte's patronage in 1765, and, aided by that éclat, soon enjoyed a worldwide sale. In the 1770s he discovered how quickly high art could be transformed into status commodity, and began to produce imitation Greek vases, in vogue because of recent excavations at Herculaneum and Pompeii. The Wedgwood fortune enabled Josiah's sons to offer Coleridge an annuity of £150 so that he could devote himself to literature.

Alfred Bird, inventor of "Bird's Custard," pinned up in his Birmingham shop a telling motto mixing morality and the new imperatives of trade: "Early to bed. Early to rise / Stick to your work . . . And Advertise." From the late eighteenth century on, fashion magazines with colored plates advertised to provincial residents the latest styles of the capital. Even as she denounced the enslavement of women by "the perpetual fluctuation of fashion," Mary Hays conceded that "this constant variation of mode is serviceable to commerce, and promotes a brisk circulation of money" (*Letters and Essays*, 1793). This stimulus reached its acme with the arrival of *Forget Me Not, a Christmas and New Year's Present for 1823*. More than sixty annuals emerged to capitalize on this pioneering venture, bearing such titles as *The Book of Beauty*. Partly because they targeted female readers, they were hospitable to female authors, including Shelley and Hemans. And because they paid so well, they also attracted male writers: Wordsworth, Coleridge, and Lamb published in them, even though literary contributions were subordinated to the engravings that were their most compelling feature. The elegantly produced annuals were best-sellers (*The Literary Souvenir* attained a circulation of fifteen thousand); copies were shipped across the empire months in advance.

Not only women and city-dwellers were seduced by the lure of shop windows, magazines, and circulating catalogues. Cobbett hurled jeremiads at the prosperous farmers who aspired to a gentility that set them apart from the workers they had once fed as part of the family:

> Everything about this farm-house was formerly the scene of *plain manners* and *plentiful living*. . . . But all appeared to be in a state of decay and nearly of disuse. There appeared to have been hardly any *family* in that house, where formerly there were, in all probability, from ten to fifteen men, boys, and maids: and, which was the worst of all, there was a *parlour*. Aye, and a *carpet* and a *bell-pull* too! . . . And, there were the decanters, the glasses,

the "dinner-set" of crockery-ware, and all just in the true stock-jobber style. And I dare say it has been 'Squire Charington and the Miss Charingtons; and not plain Master Charington, and his son Hodge, and his daughter Betty Charington, all of whom this accursed system has, in all likelihood, transmuted into a species of mock gentlefolks, while it has ground the labourers down into real slaves. (Rural Rides, 20 October 1825)

This revolution in manners and family structure reduced "family" to its biological nucleus, replacing the economic unit that enfolded laborers, servants, and dependents. This was but one manifestation of the "acceleration" and "agitation" that, in De Quincey's words, characterized the period well before the French Revolution.

AUTHORSHIP, AUTHORITY, AND "ROMANTICISM"

In this fast-moving world, the fortunes of writers, too, began to rise and fall with new speed. Writing in the Edinburgh Review in 1829, the critic Francis Jeffrey meditated on "the perishable nature of modern literary fame":

Since the beginning of our critical career, we have seen a vast deal of beautiful poetry pass into oblivion, in spite of our feeble efforts to recall or retain it in remembrance. The tuneful quartos of Southey are already little better than lumber:—And the rich melodies of Keats and Shelley,—and the fantastical emphasis of Wordsworth,—and the plebeian pathos of Crabbe, are melting fast from the fields of our vision. The novels of Scott have put out his poetry. Even the splendid strains of Moore are fading into distance and dimness, except where they have been married to immortal music; and the blazing star of Byron himself is receding from its place of pride. . . . The two who have the longest withstood this rapid withering of the laurel, and with the least marks of decay on their branches, are Rogers and Campbell; neither of them, it may be remarked, voluminous writers, and both distinguished rather for the fine taste and consummate elegance of their writings, than for the fiery passion, and disdainful vehemence, which seemed for a time to be so much more in favour with the public. . . . If taste and elegance, however, be titles to enduring fame, we might venture securely to promise that rich boon to the author before us.

The author before Jeffrey as he wrote was Felicia Hemans, a poet widely admired on both sides of the Atlantic but by the end of the century forgotten, except for a few anthology favorites. Meanwhile, with nearly three decades of reviewing experience, Jeffrey was unable to predict the durable fame of some of the writers who by the century's end would be deemed quintessential "romantics": Byron, Wordsworth, Keats, and Shelley. And he misguessed about Rogers and Campbell, though it is clear he would have attributed their demise to degraded public taste rather than intrinsic faults. What Jeffrey helps us see is that naming a literary canon is a matter of selection from a wide field, motivated by personal values. Other than Hemans, for instance, he thinks of English literary tradition as defined by men—even though Jane Austen and Mary Shelley proved to have as much durability as anyone in his census (Austen's novels and Shelley's Frankenstein have never been out of print). He also prefers literature of "fine taste" and "elegance" to the fiery passion and disdainful vehemence that other readers would admire in Byron and Shelley.

It was the conservative Jeffrey who first attempted to assess the "new poets," in the inaugural issue of the Edinburgh Review (1802). Here he castigates Southey as a member of a heretical "sect of poets, that has established itself in this country within these ten or twelve years, and is looked upon, we believe, as one of its chief champions and apostles." His polemical intent was to brand with all the excesses of the French Revolution a group he called "the Lakers" (from their residence in the Lake District): Southey, Wordsworth, and Coleridge. Well before Hazlitt, Jeffrey was blaming "the revolution in our literature" on "the agitations of the French revolution, and the discussion as well as the hopes and terrors to which it gave occasion." "A splenetic and idle discontent with the existing institutions of society, seems to be at the bottom of all their serious and peculiar sentiments"; "the ambition of Mr. Southey and some of his associates" is not "of that regulated and manageable sort which usually grows up in old established commonwealths," but "of a more undisciplined and revolutionary character which looks, we think with a jealous and contemptuous eye on the old aristocracy of the literary world."

By the Regency, the revolutionary "Lake School" was joined by the upstart "Cockney School," a term of insult fixed on Londoners Hazlitt, Hunt, and Keats, by the Scotsman John Gibson Lockhart, writing in *Blackwood's* in 1817, partly in response to Hunt's celebration of a vigorous school of "Young Poets" in essays he was writing for *The Examiner*. Hunt was a radical; Lockhart despised his politics. In 1821 ex-Laker and now Poet Laureate Southey identified still a third school. His youthful radicalism well behind him, he denounced the men "of diseased hearts and depraved imaginations" who formed "the Satanic School, . . . characterized by a Satanic spirit of pride and audacious impiety." Provoked by the allusion to himself and Percy Shelley, Byron responded with satiric attacks against both Southey personally and the establishment politics he had come to espouse. All these classifications were politically motivated—in most cases sneers at innovators and nonconformists or class-inflected put-downs. The designation of a "Romantic School" was not a product of the age itself, but was applied much later in the century—by literary historians with their own Victorian motivations and nostalgia.

With no sense of a monolithic movement that could be called "Romanticism," the polemical terms of the age itself mark a field animated by differences of location, class, gender, politics, and audience. The boundaries that appear rigid at one moment re-form when the perspective shifts: to Lockhart, Lakers (whom he respected) and Cockneys were distinct; to Byron, a champion of Pope, Keats was both "a tadpole of the Lakes" and a Cockney brat who "abused Pope and Swift." And except for Hunt and Scott, most of these men bonded across class and political lines in their contempt of "Blue Stockings" (intellectual women) and female writers, even as these women were defining themselves for and against the stigmatized precedent of Wollstonecraft. Liberals, conservatives, and radicals; Byron and Shelley, self-exiled aristocrats in Italy; Wordsworth, Coleridge, and Southey praising domesticity in the Lakes; Keats, Hazlitt, and Hunt, an apprentice surgeon and working journalists, all precariously middle-class Londoners; women novelists, poets, and essayists, Blue Stockings and Wollstonecraftians, moralizers and rebels: the array is diverse and engaged in a contest for attention too keen to call debate or conversation.

The difficulty of specifying the term "Romantic" arises in part because it hovers between chronological and conceptual references. Its literature emerges in the social and literary ferment of the 1780s, a benchmark being the publication of Blake's *Songs of Innocence* in the climactic year of 1789. The period's close is usually seen in the 1830s—the decade in which George IV died, as did several writers who defined the age: Scott, Lamb, Coleridge, Hemans. By this time, too, Keats, Byron, and Percy Shelley, Austen, and most of the first generation were dead. In the same decade, Alfred Lord Tennyson's poetic career began, and Victoria was crowned Queen. Yet the temporal boundaries are fluid: "Romantic" Keats and "Victorian" Thomas Carlyle were born the same year, 1795, and Wordsworth's major poem, *The Prelude*, though he worked on it for a half century beginning in 1797 or so, was not published until the year of his death, 1850, the same year that Tennyson's quintessentially Victorian *In Memoriam* appeared. Much of Keats's poetry appeared for the first time after 1848, reviving interest in him among a new generation of readers.

Yet even with these ambiguous boundaries, the "Romantic" movement, from its first description in the nineteenth century until the mid-1980s, was characterized by men's writing. In the age itself, the powers of literary production—publishers, booksellers, reviews, and the press—were men's domains and not always open to female authors, and the culture as a whole was not receptive to female authority. Wollstonecraft's *Rights of Woman* (1792) was one of the first analyses to define "women" as an oppressed class that cut across national distinctions and historical differences—oppressed by lack of education, by lack of legal rights and access to gainful employment, as well as by a "prevailing opinion" about their character: that women were made to feel and be felt, rather than to think; their duty was to bear children and be domestic drudges, to obey their fathers and their husbands without complaint. Women writers faced more than a few challenges. One was the pervasive cultural attitude that a woman who presumed to authority, published her views, and even aspired to make a living as an author was grossly immodest, decidedly "unfeminine," and probably a truant from her domestic calling. Many women published anonymously, under male pseudonyms, with the proper title "Mrs." or, as in Austen's case, under an anonymous and socially modest signature, "by a Lady" (not one of Austen's novels bore her name). They also maintained propriety by hewing to subjects and genres deemed "feminine"—not political polemic, epic poetry, science or philosophy but children's books, conduct literature, travel writing (if it was clear they had proper escorts), household hints, cookbooks, novels of manners, and poems of sentiment and home, of patriotism and religious piety. Women who transgressed provoked harsh discipline. When Barbauld ventured an anti-imperialist poem, *Eighteen Hundred and Eleven*, the Tory *Quarterly Review* exercised reproof precisely in terms of the gender-genre transgression:

> Mrs. Barbauld turned satirist! . . . We had hoped, indeed, that the empire might have been saved without the intervention of a lady-author. . . . Her former works have been of some utility; her "Lessons for Children," her "Hymns in Prose," her "Selections from the Spectator," . . . but we must take the liberty of warning her to desist from satire . . . writing any more pamphlets in verse. (June 1812)

Barbauld took this advice to heart, and desisted from satire. About fifteen years earlier, Anglican arbiter Richard Polwhele viciously listed a whole set of contemporary female writers in his poem *The Unsex'd Females*, with virulent animosity to Wollstonecraft. They are "unsex'd" by their public stance, parading what "ne'er our fathers saw."

The Tory *British Critic*, on the occasion of praising Hemans's excellence "in painting the strength and the weaknesses of her own lovely sex" and the "womanly nature throughout all her thoughts and her aspirations," kept up the surveillance, taking the opportunity to despise anything that advertised the intellectual and critical authority of women. It opened its review of Hemans (1823) not with a discussion of the work at hand but with an assault on the world that was changing before its eyes, against which it invokes every counterauthority, from divine creation, to modern science, to Shakespeare, to the language of ridicule and disgust:

> We heartily abjure Blue Stockings. We make no compromise with any variation of the colour, from sky-blue to Prussian blue, blue stockings are an outrage upon the eternal fitness of things. It is a principle with us to regard an Academicienne of this Society, with the same charity that a cat regards a vagabond mouse. We are inexorable to special justifications. We would fain make a fire in Charing-Cross, of all the bas bleus in the kingdom, and albums, and commonplace books, as accessaries [sic] before or after the fact, should perish in the conflagration.
>
> Our forefathers never heard of such a thing as a Blue Stocking, except upon their sons' legs; the writers of Natural History make no mention of the name. . . . Shakspeare, who painted all sorts and degrees of persons and things, who compounded or created thousands, which, perhaps, never existed, except in his own prolific mind, even he, in the wildest excursion of his fancy never dreamed of such an extraordinary combination as a Blue Stocking! No!

The extraordinary combination, however, was there to stay, and even with all these constraints, women writers thrived. More, Barbauld, Robinson, Charlotte Smith, and Maria Edgeworth stand out among those who earned both reputation and a living through poetry, novels, and tracts on education and politics, freely crossing the borders between public and private spheres, male and female realms.

POPULAR PROSE

When *The Edinburgh Review* was founded in 1802 as an organ of liberal political opinion, it raised the status of periodical writing. "To be an Edinburgh Reviewer," opined Hazlitt, who freelanced in the journal, "is, I suspect, the highest rank in modern literary society." By the end of the decade, the rival Tory *Quarterly Review* arrived on the scene. The quarterlies favored an authoritative, anonymous voice, while new monthly magazines revived the lighter manner of the eighteenth-century "familiar essay." *Blackwood's* (founded 1817) printed raffish conversations set in a nearby tavern, and the *London* (founded 1820) hosted Lamb's essays and De Quincey's *Confessions of an English Opium Eater*. Whether the topic was imaginative literature, social observation, science, or political commentary, the personality of the essayist and the literary performance—by turns meditative, autobiographical, analytical, whimsical, terse and expansive—were what commanded attention. "All the great geniuses of the day are Periodical," declared John Wilson, writing in *Blackwood's* in 1829—a self-interested judgment, but true insofar as it acknowledges the new importance of the periodical essay. Meanwhile, beneath the realm of the respectable journals, though not out of their anxious sight, thrived Cobbett, who published a weekly newspaper, the *Political Register* (founded 1802), its price low enough to evade the stamp tax (thus becoming known as "The Two-Penny Trash"). It reached a circulation of forty or fifty thousand and helped make him the most widely read writer of his era, and surely the most prolific, with an output estimated at more than twenty million words.

If later decades tended to represent "Romanticism" largely as an age of poetry, in the age itself, poetry, traditionally the genre of prestige, had to compete with prose, and not just the engaging new essay form, but also, and quite emphatically, the once-disreputable novel. The novel had begun to command new attention after the success of Godwin's political romance from the 1790s, *Caleb Williams*, and new respect after the critical and popular success of Scott's *Waverley* (1814). As the occasion indicates, the novel was also a genre in which women achieved considerable success. Hannah More's only novel, *Coelebs in Search of a Wife* (1808), ran through twelve editions in its first year, and before her death in 1833 had sold thirty thousand copies in America alone. Shelley produced a durable masterpiece with *Frankenstein* (1818 and 1831), while Austen's novels caught public interest with their sharp social observation and stories of heroines coming of age in a world of finely calibrated social codes and financial pressures.

Throughout the years, social turmoil and technological change fostered a proliferation of writing. In the Preface to *Lyrical Ballads* (1800) Wordsworth deplored the "multitude of causes unknown to former times . . . now acting with a combined force to blunt the discriminating powers of the mind," and diagnosed the most virulent as "the great national events which are daily taking place, and the encreasing accumulation of men in cities, where the uniformity of their occupations produces a craving for extraordinary incident which the rapid communication of intelligence hourly gratifies." Newspapers, daily and Sunday, multiplied to meet this craving. In 1814 the London *Times* converted to a steam press, and doubled circulation. Newspaper sales reached thirty million, with yet more readers in the coffee-houses and subscription reading-rooms that took papers that taxes rendered too expensive for individual purchase. Parliamentary commissions and boards of review collected information and compiled statistics and summaries as never before on every aspect of the nation's economy and policies, and the press disseminated them. Cobbett ceaselessly lambasted the fundholders who profited from the debts incurred by the war, even as those who had fought suffered from the postwar depression; John Wade investigated sinecures, aristocratic incomes, pluralism in the Church, corruption in Parliament, and the expenditures of the civil list, and published his findings in the sensational *Black Book* (1820), available in sixpenny installments that sold ten thousand copies each.

The explosion of readers at once liberated authors from patronage and exposed them to the turbulent and precarious world of the literary marketplace. In 1812 Jeffrey reckoned that among "the higher classes" there were twenty thousand readers, but at least "two hundred thousand who read for amusement and instruction, among the middling classes of society," defining "middling" as those "who do not aim at distinction or notoriety beyond the circle of their equals in fortune or station." Faced with an audience fissured along class lines, he thought that it was "easy to see" which group an author should please. But others looked to the growing number of literate

THE PRESS, invented much about the same time with the *Reformation,* hath done more mischief to the discipline of our Church, than all the doctrines can make amends for. 'Twas an happy time, when all learning was in manuscript, and some little officer did keep the key of the library! Now, since PRINTING came into the world, such is the mischief, that *a man cannot write a book but presently he is answered!* There have always been ways found out to *fine* not the people, but even the *grounds and fields where they assembled:* but no art yet could prevent these SEDITIOUS MEETINGS OF LETTERS! Two or three brawny fellows in a corner, with meer ink and elbow-grease, do more harm than an *hundred systematic divines.* Their ugly printing *letters,* that look but like so many rotten teeth, how oft have they been pulled out by the public tooth-drawers! And yet these rascally operators of the press have got a trick to fasten them again in a few minutes, that they grow as firm a set, and as biting and talkative as ever! O PRINTING! how thou hast *"disturbed the peace!"* Lead, when moulded into bullets, is not so mortal as when founded into *letters!* There was a mistake sure in the story of Cadmus; and the *serpent's teeth* which he sowed, were nothing else but the *letters* which he invented.

Marvell's Rehearsal transposed, 4to, 1672.

Being marked only with *four and twenty letters,—variously transposed* by the help of a PRINTING PRESS,—PAPER works miracles. The Devil dares no more come near a *Stationer's* heap, or a *Printer's Office,* than *Rats* dare put their noses into a Cheesemonger's Shop.

A Whip for the Devil, 1669, p. 92.

George Cruikshank, *The Press,* from the satirical pamphlet *The Political Showman—at Home!* by William Hone, 1821. We transcribe the text that was originally printed on this pamphlet.

poor who lacked traditional education, vast numbers whose allegiance was fought over by radicals like Cobbett and Paine and conservatives such as More, whose *Cheap Repository Tracts* (1795–1799) were circulated by the millions.

Such journalism diffused and intensified troubled perceptions of the functioning of society and one's place in it. "The beginning of Inquiry is Disease," intoned Carlyle; he inveighed against "the diseased self-conscious state of Literature" but this self-consciousness was its character. Uncertain of the audience(s) by whom they would be read, writers resorted to an ironic wavering that sought to forestall being pinned down to a position and dismissed, or devised various strategies to seduce assent: the development of the authorial "I" whom readers might come to trust as an authentic percipient, personae that insiders would be able to penetrate, and codings that would deepen a sense of solidarity among a constituency. Wordsworth had made his name with the highly personal, but culturally resonant, lyric outpouring of "Lines, written a few miles above Tintern Abbey, On Revisiting the Banks of the Wye during a Tour, July 13, 1798" (*Lyrical Ballads*, 1798); he celebrated his return from France in 1802 with a sonnet "Composed in the Valley, near Dover, On the Day of Landing," rejoicing in familiar sights of rivers and boys at play: "All, all are English." In a neighboring sonnet in the same collection, though, he complained, "The world is too much with us," running our lives with "getting and spending" and alienating our hearts from "Nature."

Wordsworth remained ambivalent about developing a voice and a literature that would gain popular reception, and continued to resent those, such as Scott, who were more successful in these terms. But the new world and the new literatures were finding remarkable sympathy in many quarters. Scott's first romance, *The Lay of the Last Minstrel* (1805), sold well over 2,000 copies within a year of publication, and nearly 10,000 more by 1807. His publisher offered him 1,000 guineas, sight unseen, for his next poetic romance, *Marmion* (1808). Scott said the sum "made men's hair stand on end," but the bargain was a good one on both sides: by 1811 it had sold 28,000 copies. These figures were topped by Byron, who, Scott good-naturedly conceded, drove him from the field of poetry, while his own *Waverley* novels proved still more popular. Over his lifetime, Scott made about £80,000 from his writing. That Byron's *Corsair* (1814) could sell 10,000 copies on the day of publication testifies to the mechanisms of production, publicity, and sales the book trade commanded. Byron was not embarrassed to seek £2600 for *Childe Harold IV* (1818). It must have galled Wordsworth that his publisher gave Thomas Moore 3,000 guineas for *Lalla Rookh*, more than had ever been offered for a single poem. Yet along with these stunning successes, other careers were more modestly compensated, and poets, at least, did not often enjoy the degree of prosperity that the novelists did.

The volatility of the market and of public taste points to salient qualities of the period: a heightened awareness of differences and boundaries, and of the energies generated along their unstable edges, and even more, a heightened awareness of time and history, public and cultural as well as personal. "Romanticism" denotes less a unified concept, or even a congeries of ideas, than an era and a literature of clashing systems, each plausibly claiming allegiance, in a world of rapid change.

Anna Letitia Barbauld
1743–1825

Anna Barbauld's long career exemplifies that of the professional woman of letters: a respected poet (and not only on conventionally feminine themes), a writer on radical causes throughout the 1790s, an early welcomer of Coleridge (who presented her with a prepublication copy of *Lyrical Ballads*), and a friend of Priestley and Hannah More. The daughter of John Aikin, master of Warrington Academy, a celebrated institution of English Dissenting culture where she lived between the ages of fifteen and thirty, Anna Laetitia Aikin is said to have learned to read English by the age of three, Italian and French not long afterward, and Greek and Latin while still a child. Her first volume of *Poems* (1773) went through five editions in four years; in the same year, she published *Miscellaneous Pieces in Prose* with her brother John, later editor of the *Monthly Magazine*, an influential radical journal. In 1774 she married Rochemont Barbauld, a Dissenting clergyman, with whom she ran a school. Samuel Johnson derided the activity as the waste of a fine education, but it led to her often reprinted *Lessons for Children* (1778) and *Hymns in Prose for Children* (1781). After the increasing mental instability of her husband led to the closing of their school, she undertook ambitious editorial projects. In 1794 she produced an edition of Akenside, one of Collins in 1797, and in 1804 a six-volume edition of the *Correspondence of Samuel Richardson*, followed by a fifty-volume set of *The British Novelists* (1810), with biographical introductions and a sophisticated preface arguing for the instructive value of a genre derided as mere entertainment, as well as a popular anthology for young women, *The Female Speaker* (1811). Like Wollstonecraft, she believed that young women should be educated to become wives and mothers. The works included here display her range as a poet. *Washing-Day* (1797) moves from mock-epic to personal recollection to its concluding instance of a recent scientific advance, Montgolfier's balloon ascent, effortlessly crossing the conventional boundaries of private and public, feminine and masculine, realms; *The First Fire* likewise surprisingly joins a celebration of the domestic hearth to a vista of geological process.

The Mouse's Petition to Dr. Priestley[1]

O hear a pensive prisoner's prayer,
   For liberty that sighs;
And never let thine heart be shut
   Against the wretch's cries!

5   For here forlorn and sad I sit,
   Within the wiry grate;
And tremble at the approaching morn,
   Which brings impending fate.

If e'er thy breast with freedom glowed,
10   And spurned a tyrant's chain,
Let not thy strong oppressive force
   A free-born mouse detain!

---

1. The title in early editions is *The Mouse's Petition, Found in the trap where he had been confined all night*, accompanied by a motto from Virgil's *Aeneid* (6.853): "Parcere subjectis & debellare superbos" [To spare the conquered, and subdue the proud]. Joseph Priestley (1733–1804), political radical and eminent chemist who discovered oxygen, had been testing the properties of gases on captured household mice. Tradition has it that Barbauld's petition succeeded, and this mouse was released.

O do not stain with guiltless blood
    Thy hospitable hearth;
15   Nor triumph that thy wiles betrayed
    A prize so little worth.

The scattered gleanings of a feast
    My frugal meals supply;
But if thine unrelenting heart
20   That slender boon deny,—

The cheerful light, the vital air,
    Are blessings widely given;
Let nature's commoners enjoy
    The common gifts of heaven.

25   The well-taught philosophic mind
    To all compassion gives:
Casts round the world an equal eye,
    And feels for all that lives.

If mind,—as ancient sages taught,—
30   A never-dying flame,
Still shifts through matter's varying forms,
    In every form the same;

Beware, lest in the worm you crush
    A brother's soul you find;
35   And tremble lest thy luckless hand
    Dislodge a kindred mind.

Or, if this transient gleam of day
    Be *all* of life we share,
Let pity plead within thy breast
40   That little *all* to spare.

So may thy hospitable board
    With wealth and peace be crowned;
And every charm of heartfelt ease
    Beneath thy roof be found.

45   So when destruction lurks unseen,
    Which men, like mice, may share,
May some kind angel clear thy path,
    And break the hidden snare.

1771   1773

On a Lady's Writing

Her even lines her steady temper show,
Neat as her dress, and polished as her brow;
Strong as her judgment, easy as her air;
Correct though free, and regular though fair:
And the same graces o'er her pen preside,
That form her manners and her footsteps guide.

1773

Remains of quiet: then expect to hear
25 Of sad disasters,—dirt and gravel stains
Hard to efface, and loaded lines at once
Snapped short,—and linen-horse° by dog thrown down,   *drying rack*
And all the petty miseries of life.
Saints have been calm while stretched upon the rack,
30 And Guatimozin[3] smiled on burning coals;
But never yet did housewife notable°   *efficient*
Greet with a smile a rainy washing-day.
But grant the welkin° fair, require not thou   *the heavens*
Who call'st thyself perchance the master there,
35 Or study swept, or nicely dusted coat,
Or usual 'tendance,—ask not, indiscreet,
Thy stockings mended, though the yawning rents
Gape wide as Erebus;[4] nor hope to find
Some snug recess impervious: shouldst thou try
40 The 'customed garden-walks, thine eyes shall rue
The budding fragrance of thy tender shrubs,
Myrtle or rose, all crushed beneath the weight
Of coarse checked apron,—with impatient hand
Twitched off when showers impend: or crossing lines
45 Shall mar thy musings, as the wet, cold sheet
Flaps in thy face abrupt. Woe to the friend
Whose evil stars have urged him forth to claim
On such a day the hospitable rites!
Looks, blank at best, and stinted courtesy,
50 Shall he receive. Vainly he feeds his hopes
With dinner of roast chicken, savory pie,
Or tart, or pudding:—pudding he nor tart
That day shall eat; nor, though the husband try,
Mending what can't be helped, to kindle mirth
55 From cheer deficient, shall his consort's brow
Clear up propitious: the unlucky guest
In silence dines, and early slinks away.
I well remember, when a child, the awe
This day struck into me; for then the maids,
60 I scarce knew why, looked cross, and drove me from them:
Nor soft caress could I obtain; nor hope
Usual indulgences; jelly or creams,
Relic of costly suppers, and set by
For me their petted one, or buttered toast,
65 When butter was forbid; or thrilling tale
Of ghost or witch or murder,—so I went
And sheltered me beside the parlor fire:
There my dear grandmother, eldest of forms,
Tended the little ones, and watched from harm,
70 Anxiously fond, though oft her spectacles
With elfin cunning hid, and oft the pins
Drawn from her ravelled stockings, might have soured
One less indulgent.—

3. Cuauhtemoc, the last Aztec emperor of Mexico, tor-   4. In Greek myth, the dark passage through which souls
tured and executed by Cortés in 1525.   enter Hades.

At intervals my mother's voice was heard,
75   Urging despatch: briskly the work went on,
All hands employed to wash, to rinse, to wring,
To fold, and starch, and clap, and iron, and plait.
Then would I sit me down, and ponder much
Why washings were. Sometimes through hollow bowl
80   Of pipe amused we blew, and sent aloft
The floating bubbles; little dreaming then
To see, Montgolfier,[5] thy silken ball
Ride buoyant through the clouds,—so near approach
The sports of children and the toils of men.
85   Earth, air, and sky, and ocean hath its bubbles,
And verse is one of them,—this most of all.

1797

The First Fire

October 1st, 1815

Ha, old acquaintance! many a month has past
Since last I viewed thy ruddy face; and I,
Shame on me! had mean time well nigh forgot
That such a friend existed. Welcome now!—
5   When summer suns ride high, and tepid airs
Dissolve in pleasing langour; then indeed
We think thee needless, and in wanton pride
Mock at thy grim attire and sooty jaws,
And breath sulphureous, generating spleen,—
10   As Frenchmen say; Frenchmen, who never knew
The sober comforts of a good coal fire.
—Let me imbibe thy warmth, and spread myself
Before thy shrine adoring:—magnet thou
Of strong attraction, daily gathering in
15   Friends, brethren, kinsmen, variously dispersed,
All the dear charities of social life,
To thy close circle. Here a man might stand,
And say, This is my world! Who would not bleed
Rather than see thy violated hearth
20   Prest by a hostile foot? The winds sing shrill;
Heap on the fuel! Not the costly board,
Nor sparkling glass, nor wit, nor music, cheer
Without thy aid. If thrifty thou dispense
Thy gladdening influence, in the chill saloon
25   The silent shrug declares th' unpleased guest.
—How grateful to belated traveller
Homeward returning, to behold the blaze
From cottage window, rendering visible
The cheerful scene within! There sits the sire,
30   Whose wicker chair, in sunniest nook enshrined,
His age's privilege,—a privilege for which
Age gladly yields up all precedence else

5. In 1783, in France, the Montgolfier brothers launched the first hot-air balloon.

In gay and bustling scenes,—supports his limbs.
Cherished by thee, he feels the grateful warmth
35   Creep through his feeble frame and thaw the ice
Of fourscore years, and thoughts of youth arise.
—Nor less the young ones press within, to see
Thy face delighted, and with husk of nuts,
Or crackling holly, or the gummy pine,
40   Feed thy immortal hunger: cheaply pleased
They gaze delighted, while the leaping flames
Dart like an adder's tongue upon their prey;
Or touch with lighted reed thy wreaths of smoke;
Or listen, while the matron sage remarks
45   Thy bright blue scorching flame and aspect clear,
Denoting frosty skies. Thus pass the hours,
While Winter spends without his idle rage.

—Companion of the solitary man,
From gayer scenes withheld! With thee he sits,
50   Converses, moralizes; musing asks
How many eras of uncounted time
Have rolled away since thy black unctuous° food   oily
Was green with vegetative life, and what
This planet then: or marks, in sprightlier mood,
55   Thy flickering smiles play round the illumined room,
And fancies gay discourse, life, motion, mirth,
And half forgets he is a lonely creature.

—Nor less the bashful poet loves to sit
Snug, at the midnight hour, with only thee
60   Of his lone musings conscious. Oft he writes,
And blots, and writes again; and oft, by fits,
Gazes intent with eyes of vacancy
On thy bright face; and still at intervals,
Dreading the critic's scorn, to thee commits,
65   Sole confidant and safe, his fancies crude.

—O wretched he, with bolts and massy bars
In narrow cell immured, whose green, damp walls,
That weep unwholesome dews, have never felt
Thy purifying influence! Sad he sits
70   Day after day till in his youthful limbs
Life stagnates, and the hue of hope is fled
From his wan cheek. And scarce less wretched he,—
When wintry winds blow loud and frosts bite keen,—
The dweller of the clay-built tenement,
75   Poverty-struck, who, heart[h]less, strives to raise
From sullen turf, or stick plucked from the hedge,
The short-lived blaze; while chill around him spreads
The dreary fen, and Ague, sallow-faced,
Stares through the broken pane;—assist him, ye
80   On whose warm roofs the sun of plenty shines,
And feel a glow beyond material fire!

1815   1825

≈⊹ PERSPECTIVES ⊹≈
The Rights of Man and
the Revolution Controversy

"The Revolution in France," wrote Percy Shelley, "overthrew the hierarchy, the aristocracy, and the monarchy, and the whole of that peculiarly insolent and oppressive system on which they were based." Celebrated international center of high culture and progressive philosophy, eighteenth-century France was also a country of profound social inequalities and oppression. Dissatisfaction had been growing against the corrupt and inefficient aristocracy, who relentlessly taxed the lower classes (the "Third Estate": peasants, serfs, yeomen, industrial workers and economically independent bourgeoisie) without granting them political power. Tensions mounted in the 1780s as the government went bankrupt and tried to hold on with more taxation and the imprisonment of dissidents, without trial, in the Bastille prison in Paris. Open rebellion broke out with the storming of the Bastille in 1789 and radiated into a series of cataclysmic events watched from across the English Channel, and witnessed by some English visitors to France, with a mixture of interest, sympathy, and horror.

Support for the Revolution was a coterie enthusiasm in England rather than widespread, but it was still of concern to the government and allied institutions. Following the American Revolution, and close to the centenary of Britain's "Glorious Revolution" of 1688, this latest upheaval underscored to European monarchies the insecurity of long-standing alliances of church, state, and aristocracy, and seemed to herald an inevitable movement of "the spirit of the age" toward liberalism and democracy. Political idealists took fire, enchanted by the bold reformation of French life, including not only a new government but also new street names, a new calendar (Year I beginning 21 September 1792) with new month names, new deities (the goddesses Reason, Liberty), and new national festivals to replace the old religious holidays. "Bliss was it in that dawn to be alive!" exclaimed William Wordsworth in a retrospect published in 1809 (cf. *Prelude* 10.689). But the dream proved short-lived as the French Republic descended into factionalism, extremist purges, internal violence, terrorism, and imperialist war-mongering: the monarchy was overthrown in August 1792, thousands of aristocrats and suspected sympathizers were massacred in September, Louis XVI was guillotined in January 1793, and Queen Marie Antoinette in October. Wordsworth and others fell into disenchantment and despair ("The scenes that I witnessed during the earlier years of the French Revolution when I was resident in France," he wrote in 1835, "come back on me with appalling violence"). Conservatives sounded the alarm and, citing the likelihood of a French invasion, the British government enacted a series of repressive measures in the 1790s—suspending civil rights, spying on and harassing political groups, outlawing and vigorously prosecuting some kinds of assembly and publication. France and Britain declared war, and the countries remained on hostile terms, often at war, through the 1790s and the rise of Napoleon, who was finally defeated by the British at Waterloo in 1815. The Revolution and its sequels had such a profound effect on British political life that in 1823 Samuel Taylor Coleridge could say, "We are not yet aware of the consequences of that event. We are too near it."

⊹→ ≈⊹≈ ←⊹

Helen Maria Williams
1762–1827

When Helen Maria Williams died in Paris in 1827, *Gentleman's Magazine* in England remembered her as "pre-eminent among the violent female devotees of the Revolution." Of Scots and Welsh descent, Williams made her appearance in London literary circles with the publication of *Edwin and Eltruda* (1782). Subsequent works fixed her reputation as a poet of liberal opinions, among them *Peru* (1784), a critique of imperialism, and *A Poem on the Bill lately passed for regulating the Slave Trade* (1788). A poem on the Bastille in her only novel, *Julia* (1790), signaled her enthusiasm for the Revolution. She visited Paris in 1790, returned in 1791, and settled there in 1792. A close friend of the moderate Girondins, she was imprisoned in 1793, but her support for the principles of the Revolution never wavered. The salon she ran until 1816 was a magnet for many expatriates, including Paine and Wollstonecraft. Her *Letters Written in France, in the Summer of 1790* were followed by further volumes of *Letters from France* (1792–1796), and *A Tour in Switzerland* (1798), which recorded the impact of the Revolution on the Swiss Republic. Her admiration for Napoleon dimmed only when he crowned himself Emperor in 1804. Her disillusion can be seen in two later works, published in 1815 and 1819, which carry her account of French life through to the restoration of Louis XVIII, but by then her public identification with radicalism was set. Such sentiments, when joined with her enduring affair with the Unitarian radical John Hurford Stone, tarnished her standing at home, provoking Horace Walpole to call her "a scribbling trollop." But Williams's devotion had produced an unparalleled eyewitness narrative of more than twenty-five turbulent years; perhaps no English subject knew so many of those who shaped the course of the Revolution.

from Letters Written in France, in the Summer of 1790,

to a Friend in England, Containing Various Anecdotes Relative to the French Revolution[1]

[ARRIVAL IN PARIS]

I arrived at Paris, by a very rapid journey, the day before the federation;[2] and when I am disposed to murmur at the evils of my destiny, I shall henceforth put this piece of good fortune into the opposite scale, and reflect how many disappointments it ought to counterbalance. Had the packet which conveyed me from Brighton to Dieppe failed a few hours later; had the wind been contrary; in short, had I not reached Paris at the moment I did reach it, I should have missed the most sublime spectacle which, perhaps, was ever represented on the theatre of this earth.

[A DEPICTION OF A FEDERATION]

I promised to send you a description of the federation: but it is not to be described! One must have been present, to form any judgment of a scene, the sublimity of which depended much less on its external magnificence than on the effect it produced on the minds of the spectators. "The people, sure, the people were the sight!" I may tell you of pavilions, of triumphal arches, of altars on which incense was burnt, of two hundred thousand men walking in procession; but how am I to give you an adequate idea of the behaviour of the spectators? How am I to paint the impetuous feelings of that immense, that exulting multitude? Half a million people assembled at a spectacle, which furnished every image that can elevate the mind of man; which connected the enthusiasm of moral sentiment with the solemn pomp of religious ceremonies; which addressed itself at once to the imagination, the understanding, and the heart!

1. The selections here are drawn from volume 1, letters 1, 2, 4, and 5.
2. The Festival of the Federation was held in Paris on 14 July 1790, to celebrate the first anniversary of the fall of the Bastille and the new constitution.

The Champ de Mars[3] was formed into an immense amphitheatre, round which were erected forty rows of seats, raised one above another with earth, on which wooden forms were placed. Twenty days['] labour, animated by the enthusiasm of the people, accomplished what seemed to require the toil of years. Already in the Champ de Mars the distinctions of rank were forgotten; and, inspired by the same spirit, the highest and lowest orders of citizens gloried in taking up the spade, and assisting the persons employed in a work on which the common welfare of the state depended. Ladies took the instruments of labour in their hands, and removed a little of the earth, that they might be able to boast that they also had assisted in the preparations at the Champ de Mars; and a number of old soldiers were seen voluntarily bestowing on their country the last remains of their strength. A young Abbé of my acquaintance told me, that the people beat a drum at the door of the convent where he lived, and obliged the Superior to let all the Monks come out and work in the Champ de Mars. The Superior with great reluctance acquiesced, "Quant à moi," said the young Abbé, "je ne demandois pas mieux" ["As for me, I desired nothing better"].[4]

At the upper end of the amphitheatre a pavilion was built for the reception of the King, the Queen, their attendants, and the National Assembly,[5] covered with striped tent-cloth of the national colours, and decorated with streamers of the same beloved tints, and fleur de lys. The white flag was displayed above the spot where the King was seated. In the middle of the Champ de Mars L'Autel de la Patrie[6] was placed, on which incense was burnt by priests dressed in long white robes, with sashes of national ribbon. Several inscriptions were written on the altar, but the words visible at the greatest distance were, La Nation, la Loi, et le Roi [The Nation, the Law, and the King].

At the lower end of the amphitheatre, opposite to the pavilion, three triumphal arches were erected, adorned with emblems and allegorical figures.

The procession marched to the Champ de Mars, through the central streets of Paris. At La Place de Louis Quinze, the escorts, who carried the colours, received under their banners, ranged in two lines, the National Assembly, who came from the Tuilleries. When the procession passed the street where Henry the Fourth was assassinated,[7] every man paused as if by general consent: the cries of joy were suspended, and succeeded by a solemn silence. This tribute of regret, paid from the sudden impulse of feeling at such a moment, was perhaps the most honourable testimony to the virtues of that amiable Prince which his memory has yet received.

In the streets, at the windows, and on the roofs of the houses, the people, transported with joy, shouted and wept as the procession passed. Old men were seen kneeling in the streets, blessing God that they had lived to witness that happy moment. The people ran to the doors of their houses loaded with refreshments, which they offered to the troops; and crouds of women surrounded the soldiers, and holding up their infants in their arms, and melting into tears, promised to make their children imbibe, from their earliest age, an inviolable attachment to the principles of the new constitution.

---

3. "The Field of Mars," the former military parade ground on the left bank of the Seine.
4. The translations of French are by Williams, who wanted her work to reach as broad an audience as possible.
5. The legislative assembly made up of the third estate, or commons, that by declaring itself the governing body of the nation had precipitated the revolution in 1789.
6. The Altar of the Fatherland.
7. A king of France known for his love of his people, assassinated in 1610.

[A VISIT TO THE BASTILLE PRISON]

Before I suffered my friends at Paris to conduct me through the usual routine of convents, churches, and palaces, I requested to visit the Bastille; feeling a much stronger desire to contemplate the ruins of that building than the most perfect edifices in Paris. When we got into the carriage, our French servant called to the coachman, with an air of triumph, "A la Bastille—mais nous n'y resterons pas" ["To the Bastille,—but we shall not remain there"]. We drove under that porch which so many wretches have entered never to repass, and alighting from the carriage descended with difficulty into the dungeons, which were too low to admit of our standing upright, and so dark that we were obliged at noon-day to visit them with the light of a candle. We saw the hooks of those chains by which the prisoners were fastened round the neck, to the walls of their cells; many of which being below the level of the water, are in a constant state of humidity; and a noxious vapour issued from them, which more than once extinguished the candle, and was so insufferable that it required a strong spirit of curiosity to tempt one to enter. Good God! and to these regions of horror were human creatures dragged at the caprice of despotic power. What a melancholy consideration, that

————Man! proud man,
Drest in a little brief authority,
Plays such fantastic tricks before high heaven,
As make the angels weep.[8]

There appears to be a greater number of these dungeons than one could have imagined the hard heart of tyranny itself would contrive; for, since the destruction of the building, many subterraneous cells have been discovered underneath a piece of ground which was inclosed within the walls of the Bastille, but which seemed a bank of solid earth before the horrid secrets of this prison-house were disclosed. Some skeletons were found in these recesses, with irons still fastened on their decaying bones.

After having visited the Bastille, we may indeed be surprized, that a nation so enlightened as the French, submitted so long to the oppressions of their government; but we must cease to wonder that their indignant spirits at length shook off the galling yoke.

Those who have contemplated the dungeons of the Bastille, without rejoicing in the French revolution, may, for aught I know, be very respectable persons, and very agreeable companions in the hours of prosperity; but, if my heart were sinking with anguish, I should not fly to those persons for consolation. Sterne[9] says, that a man is incapable of loving one woman as he ought, who has not a sort of an affection for the whole sex; and as little should I look for particular sympathy from those who have no feelings of general philanthropy. If the splendour of a despotic throne can only shine like the radiance of lightning, while all around is involved in gloom and horror, in the name of heaven let its baleful lustre be extinguished for ever. May no such strong contrast of light and shade again exist in the political system of France! but may the beams of liberty, like the beams of day, shed their benign influence on the cottage of

8. Isabella's tirade against the tyranny of Angelo, the agent of the Duke, in Shakespeare's *Measure for Measure* 2.2.117–123.

9. Laurence Sterne, author of *Tristram Shandy* (1759–1767) and *A Sentimental Journey* (1768).

the peasant, as well as on the palace of the monarch! May liberty, which for so many ages past has taken pleasure in softening the evils of the bleak and rugged climates of the north, in fertilizing a barren soil, in clearing the swamp, in lifting mounds against the inundations of the tempest, diffuse her blessings also on the genial land of France, and bid the husbandman rejoice under the shade of the olive and the vine!

[THE ARISTOCRACY]

I am just returned from a visit to Madame Sillery, whose works on education are so well known and so justly esteemed in England[1] * * * Mons. d'Orléans[2] has certainly conferred a most essential obligation upon his children, by placing them under the care of this lady. I never met with young people more amiable in their dispositions, or more charming in their manners, which are equally remote from arrogance, and from those efforts of condescension which I have seen some great people make, with much difficulty to themselves, and much offence to others. The Princess, who is thirteen years of age, has a countenance of the sweetest expression, and appears to me to be Adelaide, the heroine of Madame Sillery's Letters on Education, personified. The three princes, though under Madame Sillery's superintendence, have also preceptors who live in the house, and assist in their education. The eldest prince, Mons. de Chartres, is nearly eighteen years of age, and his attentive politeness formed a striking contrast in my mind, to the manners of those fashionable gentlemen in a certain great metropolis, who consider apathy and negligence as the test of good-breeding. But if I was pleased with the manners of this young Prince, I was still more delighted to find him a confirmed friend to the new constitution of France, and willing, with the enthusiasm of a young and ardent mind, to renounce the splendour of his titles for the general good. When he heard that the sacrifice of fortune also was required, and that the immense property, which he had been taught to consider as his inheritance, was to be divided with his brothers, he embraced them with the utmost affection, declaring that he rejoiced in such a division. To find a democratic Prince, was somewhat singular:[3] I was much less surprized that Madame Sillery had adopted sentiments which are so congenial to an enlarged and comprehensive mind. This lady I have called Sillery, because it is the name by which she is known in England; but, since the decree of the National Assembly, abolishing the nobility, she has renounced with her title the name of Sillery, and has taken that of Brulart.

She talked to me of the distinctions of rank, in the spirit of philosophy, and ridiculed the absurdity of converting the rewards of personal merit into the inheritance of those who had perhaps so little claim to honours, that they were a sort of oblique reproach on their character and conduct. There may be arguments against hereditary rank sufficiently convincing to such an understanding as Madame Brulart's: but I know some French ladies who entertain very different notions on this subject; who see no impropriety in the establishments of nobility; and who have car-

---

1. The Marquise de Sillery, better known as Mme. de Genlis, was the author of *Adele et Theodore, ou Lettres sur l'education* (London ed., 1782); when the Jacobins triumphed in 1793, her husband was guillotined and she and her pupil Mlle. d'Orléans fled to Switzerland.
2. Louis Philippe Joseph, Duke of Orléans (1747–1793), the richest man in France, earned the name Philippe Egalité for his liberal convictions; elected a deputy from Paris to the Convention, he voted for the king's death, but when his eldest son, the Duke of Chartres, deserted to the Austrians, he was arrested and guillotined.
3. Under the old system of primogeniture, the Prince (as eldest son) would have been sole heir. See also Wollstonecraft's critique of primogeniture as a corruption of virtue (page 60, n. 7).

ried their love of aristocratical rights so far as to keep their beds, in a fit of despondency, upon being obliged to relinquish the agreeable epithets of Comtesse or Marquise, to which their ears had been so long accustomed.

But let me do justice to the ladies of France. The number of those who have murmured at the loss of rank, bears a very small proportion to those who have acted with a spirit of distinguished patriotism; who, with those generous affections which belong to the female heart, have gloried in sacrificing titles, fortune, and even the personal ornaments, so dear to female vanity, for the common cause. It was the ladies who gave the example of le don patriotique [the patriotic donation], by offering their jewels at the shrine of liberty; and, if the women of ancient Rome have gained the applause of distant ages for such actions, the women of France will also claim the admiration of posterity.

The women have certainly had a considerable share in the French revolution: for, whatever the imperious lords of the creation may fancy, the most important events which take place in this world depend a little on our influence; and we often act in human affairs like those secret springs in mechanism, by which, though invisible, great movements are regulated.

But let us return to Madame Brulart, who wears at her breast a medallion made of a stone of the Bastille polished. In the middle of the medallion, *Liberté* was written in diamonds; above was marked, in diamonds, the planet that shone on the 14th of July; and below was seen the moon, of the size she appeared that memorable night. The medallion was set in a branch of laurel, composed of emeralds, and tied at the top with the national cockade, formed of brilliant stones of the three national colours.

from Letters from France[1]
[THE EXECUTION OF THE KING]

Paris, Feb. 10, 1793

The faction of the anarchists desired that the French king should be put to death without the tedious forms of a trial. This opinion, however, was confined to the summit of the Mountain,[2] that elevated region, where aloof from all the ordinary feelings of our nature, no one is diverted from his purpose by the weakness of humanity, or the compunction of remorse; where urbanity is considered as an aristocratical infringement of les grands principes, and mercy as a crime de leze-nation [treason].

The trial of the king was decreed by the National Convention, and the eleventh of December was fixed upon for that purpose. Lewis the sixteenth had supported his long imprisonment with fortitude; and, when he heard that the day for his trial was fixed, he said with great calmness, "Eh bien! qu'on me guillotine si on veut; je suis preparé" ["Well! let them *guillotine* me if they will; I am prepared"].

A short time after the taking of the Bastille the king was observed reading the history of Charles the first.[3] "Why, sire," said an attendant, "do you read that history? it will make you melancholy." "Je me mets dans l'esprit," replied the king, "qu'un jour je finirai comme lui" ["I feel an impression on my mind, that one day I shall end like

---

1. The selections here are from the second edition (1796), volume 4, letters 1 and 5.
2. Term for the radical Jacobin deputies, who sat on the high benches in the left of the National Convention.

3. The civil war between Charles I, king of Great Britain from 1625, and the parliamentary forces under Oliver Cromwell, culminated in his execution on 30 January 1649.

him"]. It appears that the French queen has also chosen a model for her behaviour, in the last scene of life, from the English annals; for since her imprisonment she has been employed in reading the history of Mary queen of Scots.[4] Marie Antoinette, however, is in no danger of sharing the same fate: if she were, her haughty indignant spirit, which preferred the chance of losing empire and life to the certainty of retaining any thing less than absolute dominion, would probably meet death with becoming dignity, feeling, that "to be weak is to be miserable, doing or suffering."[5] * * *

History will, indeed, condemn Lewis the sixteenth. The evidence of his guilt is clear; and the historian will fulfil his duty in passing sentence upon his memory; for the historian has not, like the judge, the prerogative to pardon. But Lewis the sixteenth will not stand alone at the bar of posterity. His judges also must appear at that tribunal; on them, also, the historian will pass sentence. He will behold the same men acting at once as accusers, party, and judge; he will behold the unfortunate monarch deprived, not only of his inviolability as a king, but of his rights as a citizen; and perhaps the irrevocable decree of posterity may reverse that of the National Convention.

The detail of the interrogation which the French king underwent at the bar of the National Convention is too well known to need repetition.—He was conducted back to the Temple about six in the evening: the night was dark; but the town was illuminated; and those objects which appeared only half formed, and were seen indistinctly, imagination finished and filled up, as best suited the gloomy impressions of the moment. By the way, since the second of September, when the whole town was lighted up for security, an illumination at Paris appears no gaudy pageant, which beams the symbol of public festivity; but is considered as the harbinger of danger—the signal of alarm—the tocsin of night. A considerable number of horse as well as foot-guards formed the escort of the king; and the trampling of the horses' feet—the hoarse sounds of the collected multitude—the beating of drums—the frequent report of fire-arms—all conspired to excite the most solemn emotions. The long page of human history rushed upon the mind—age after age arose to memory, in sad succession, like the line of Banquo;[6] and each seemed disfigured by crimes or darkened by calamity. The past was clouded with horror—a great experiment was about to be made for the future; but it was impossible to reflect, without trembling anxiety, that the stake was human happiness, and that the issue was doubtful, while all that could be calculated with certainty was, that millions must perish in the trial. It is asserted that the philosophers of France produced the revolution; I believe this to be an error. They, indeed, have disseminated the principles which form the basis of the new fabric of French government; but the ancient system was overthrown, not because it was unphilosophical, but because it could be upheld no longer. The revolution was the effect of imperious necessity; for, whatever permanent good may result from a change of government, the temporary evil is so certain, that every age is disposed to leave that work to a succeeding generation. The instinct of the people teaches them, that in framing a new government they can only hope, like Moses, to see the promised land, but not to enter it. They may plant the seeds of general prosperity, sown with toil and trouble, and bathed in blood; but the blooming vegetation and the golden fruit belong to another race of men.[7]

4. Daughter of James V of Scotland, Mary became queen as an infant; in 1558 she married the Dauphin of France; a romantic figure; for the next three decades, she was the Roman Catholic threat to Elizabeth for the throne of Britain. Imprisoned from 1569 and tried for treason in 1586, she was beheaded in 1587.
5. Paraphrasing Milton's Satan, *Paradise Lost* 1.156–57.

6. See Shakespeare, *Macbeth*, 4.1.112–24. Banquo is murdered by the king's assassins, but his descendants eventually claim the Scottish throne.
7. The witches that inspire Macbeth's ambitions to the throne also chant, in their coven, of "toil and trouble." For the allusion to Moses, see Deuteronomy 34.4.

The defence of Lewis the sixteenth * * * though it failed to prove his innocence, at least interested the humane part of the audience in behalf of his misfortunes: and such of that audience as reflected, that he who now stood an arraigned criminal at the bar of the Convention, had, four years ago, the destiny of twenty-five millions of people at the disposal of his will, felt that, whatever were his sins against the nation, he was already punished enough. * * * The attention of all Europe was fixed in anxious suspense on the issue of this important trial; and the situation of Lewis the sixteenth excited universal sympathy. But at Paris it cast a peculiar horror—a sort of local gloom over the whole city; it seemed as if the National Convention had chosen the very means most proper to re-kindle the dying flame of loyalty. We remembered that the king had betrayed his people, till, by the rigour of their resentment, they made us lose the sense of his guilt in the greatness of his calamities. They wished us to feel indignation at his offence, and they compelled us to weep for his misfortunes. They called on our abhorrence of the ungenerous use he had made of the power with which he was entrusted, and we saw how little magnanimous was the use which they made of theirs. Their decision seemed at once so cruel and so impolitic, that it is not surprising if, instead of appearing to foreign nations in the light of a painful sacrifice made to public security, it bore the aspect of public security sacrificed to inhumanity and vengeance. It were, however, an error to believe, either that Lewis the sixteenth fell the victim of that barbarous thirst for his blood displayed by the chiefs of the Mountain, or that he was devoted to death by the pusillanimity of those who were influenced by considerations of their own personal safety. No; while we admire the heroic courage of such as, in defiance of the popular outcry, pleased with pathetic eloquence the cause of mercy; while we love the humanity of Brissot, the philosophy of Condorcet, we must admit, that amongst those who voted for the death of Lewis the sixteenth are found men equally incapable of being actuated by fear or by vengeance; men, who, considering the king's death as essential to security of the republic, pronounced the fatal sentence in the bitterness of their souls, and as the performance of a cruel duty which their country imperiously required.

The proposition of an appeal to the departments was rejected, because it was apprehended, that such an appeal might lead to civil war. * * * The French king received the intelligence of his approaching fate without dismay. He displayed far more firmness upon the scaffold than he had done upon the throne, and atoned for the weakness and inconsistency of his conduct in life, by the calmness and fortitude of his behaviour in death. The evening before his execution, his family, from whom he had been separated since the commencement of his trial, were conducted to the tower of the Temple, and allowed the sad indulgence of a last interview, unmolested by the presence of his guards. * * * Ah, surely, amidst the agonies of final separation from those to whom we are bound by the strongest ties of nature and affection! surely when we cling to those we love, in the unutterable pang of a last embrace— in such moments the monarch must forget his crown, and the regrets of disappointed ambition must be unfelt amidst the anguish which overwhelms the broken heart. * * *

The king had sufficient firmness to avoid seeing his family on the morning of his execution! He desired the queen might be told that he was unable to bear the sight of her and his children in those last moments! he took a ring off his finger, which contained some of his own hair, of the queen's, and of his two children, and desired it might be given to the queen. He called the municipal officers round him, and told them, it was his dying request, that Clery, his valet-de-chambre, might remain with his son. He then said to Santerre, "Marchons" ["Let us go"]; and after crossing, with a hurried pace, the inner court of the Temple, he got into the mayor's carriage, which was in waiting, and was attended by his confessor.

It is certain that many of those acts of illegal power, which brought the unhappy monarch to the scaffold, were dictated by the fanatical and discontented clergy which swarmed about his palace; by non-juring bishops and archbishops; men who, having lost their wealth and their influence by the revolution, prompted the king to run all risks in order to gratify their own resentment. * * *

The calmness which Lewis the sixteenth displayed on this great trial of human fortitude, is attributed not only to the support his mind received from religious faith, but also to the hope which it is said he cherished, even till his last moment, that the people, whom he meant to address from the scaffold, would demand that his life might be spared. And his confessor, from motives of compassion, had encouraged him in this hope. After ascending the scaffold with a firm step, twice the unhappy monarch attempted to speak, and twice Santerre prevented him from being heard, by ordering the drums to beat immediately. * * * Then it was that despair seized upon the mind of the unfortunate monarch—his countenance assumed a look of horror—twice with agony he repeated, "Je suis perdu! je suis perdu!" ["I am undone! I am undone!"] His confessor mean time called to him from the foot of the scaffold, "Louis, fils de St. Louis, montez au ciel" ["Son of St. Louis, ascend to heaven!"]; and in one moment he was delivered from the evils of mortality.

The executioner held up the bleeding head, and the guards cried "Vive la Republique!" ["Long live the Republic!"] Some dipt their handkerchiefs in the blood—but the greater number, chilled with horror at what had passed, desired the commandant would lead them instantly from the spot. The hair was sold in separate tresses at the foot of the scaffold.

["WHAT THEN IS THE CONCLUSION OF THE WHOLE MATTER?"][8]

Paris, March 1793

* * * The destruction of the monarchy in France on the 10th of August—the horrors of the massacre of the 2d of September,[9] and then the death of the king, finally alienated the minds of Englishmen from the French revolution; rendered popular a war, which otherwise no minister would have dared to undertake; disgusted all wise, and shocked all humane men; and left to us, and all who had espoused the cause, no hope but that Heaven, which knows how to bring good out of evil, would watch over an event so interesting to the welfare of mankind as the French revolution; nor suffer the folly and vice of the agents concerned in it, to spoil the greatest and noblest enterprise ever undertaken by a nation.

A variety of secondary causes operated, in conjunction with these primary ones, to alienate the minds of our countrymen from the French revolution. It is curious, and may be useful to trace a few of them.

Those who have long held the first rank in any society are always reluctant to yield up their place, or suffer others, who were below, to be raised above them. Accustomed to regard their own constitution as the perfection of civil polity, the English found a

---

8. Critic Stephen Blakemore (*Crisis in Representation*, 1997) reports that this letter was written by Williams's friend Thomas Christie.

9. Between 2 and 6 September 1792, more than a thousand prisoners, aristocrats, priests, and purported sympathizers were seized from the Paris jails and summarily executed.

new source of disapprobation of the French institution: they forgot that their dearest privileges, trial by jury, the liberty of the press, and other advantages, had once been regarded by foreign nations as audacious novelties; and had scandalized the despots of Europe and their degraded subjects, as much as the new experiments of the French did at present. It was a common saying in France, under the old system, that "Le roi d'Angleterre / Regne dans l'enfer" ["The king of England reigns in hell"] and the freedom of speech, and of writing on public affairs, the dearest rights of Englishmen, were constantly represented as absurd and noxious privileges, that occasioned eternal commotion in the state, and *disturbed the peace of government*. In spite of these facts, when circumstances arose that hurt their national vanity, by exalting a rival people, many of our countrymen appear to have forgotten the ancient history of England—the nations seemed to have changed sides, and Englishmen talked of France as Frenchmen were wont to talk of England. But truth changes not with the fashions of the times. It was not to be forgotten, that the English had been the first *bold experimenters* in the science of government in modern Europe—the first who carried into practical execution the calumniated principle of EQUALITY—the first people who formally brought a monarch to the scaffold—the first asserters of the neglected *rights of man*. In the common law of England, and the commentaries of the older lawyers on it, I have found all the fundamental principles of the French declaration des droits de l'homme [of the rights of man].

But, said some, we made our revolution without bloodshed, and theirs has been a continued scene of confusion and murder. It is true, the revolution of 1688 was accomplished with little trouble; but it produced the wars of 1715 and 1745, in the last of which the metropolis very nearly fell into the hands of the enemy; a circumstance that would have placed a popish despot on the throne, and annihilated the liberties of England. And it is to be observed, that the revolution of 1688 was but one of many events that formed the English constitution. That system was the fruit of the labours of ages of struggle and confusion. The establishment of our liberties cost us many wars—and amidst the civil dissensions caused by the contest of principles against ancient error, our history records a sad catalogue of crimes and cruelties committed on all sides. Whoever, Madam, will examine these annals, will soon be convinced, that we have not much ground to reproach our neighbours. In France, indeed, a greater number of events have been crowded into a shorter space of time; and the enormities in France have been committed at a period, when, by means of the facility of communication, all public events are more widely and rapidly circulated than in former ages; circumstances that alter the appearance, but not the reality, of the case. We now enjoy the blessings of freedom, and have forgotten the price it cost our ancestors to obtain it. But no people ever travelled to the temple of Liberty by a path strewed with roses; nor has established tyranny ever yielded to reason and justice, till after a severe struggle. I do not pretend to justify the French, but I do not see much right that we at least have to condemn them. We cannot even reproach them with the fate of Louis the sixteenth, without calling up to remembrance that of Charles the first. * * *

If the destruction of the monarchy was absolutely necessary, certainly the death of the king was not; and France might have struck surrounding nations with reverence at her sublime clemency, in place of shocking all Europe by a condemnation, the justice of which was at best doubtful, and which the generality of them at present consider as an atrocious crime. * * * However much indisposed our countrymen were to the French from preceding reasons, it is certain that the death of the king alone prepared their minds for war, and completed the triumph of the enemies of France in England. * * *

Whether France will finally be able to extricate herself from an intestine, as well as external war, which now assail her at once—whether she will be able to support her republic; or, fatigued with anarchy, repose herself in limited monarchy; or finally, overwhelmed by her foes, be forced to accept that constitution which they choose to give her, are points that surpass my powers to decide. Were I to conjecture, I would say, that she will succeed in maintaining her own freedom, but not in communicating it to her neighbours. But should she even be overpowered by her enemies, and should continental despots wish to load her with the most galling chains, I cannot forget, Madam, that Britain is concerned in this transaction! And this recollection cheers my mind; for a free and generous people cannot condemn twenty-five millions of men to be slaves! No: the severest sentence that England can suffer to be pronounced, even on her rival, would be, "Let France be delivered from the dominion of a ferocious mob—let her be delivered from anarchy, and restored to reason and lawful sway!" Thus terminate how it will, I trust the French revolution will promote the good of France, and this prospect consoles me amidst the present evils. * * *

When I said that the French revolution began in wisdom, I admitted that it came afterwards into the hands of fools. But *the foundation was laid in wisdom*. I must intreat you to mark that circumstance; for if even the superstructure should fall, the foundation would remain. The BASTILLE, though honoured by Mr. Burke with the title of the *king's castle* (a shocking satire on every humane and just prince), will never be rebuilt in France; and the declaration of the rights of man will remain eternal, as the truths it contains. In the early ages of the world, the revolutions of the states, and the incursions of barbarians, often overwhelmed knowledge, and occasioned *the loss of principles*: but since the invention of printing has diffused science over Europe, and accumulated the means of extending and preserving truth, PRINCIPLES can no more be lost. Like vigorous seeds committed to the bosom of the fertile earth, accidental circumstances may prevent their vegetation for a time, but they will remain alive, and ready to spring up at the first favourable moment.

What then is the conclusion of the whole matter? This, surely, that PRINCIPLES are never to be abandoned, however unsuccessful may be the attempt to carry them into *practice*. We in England, however, have had practical experience of the good effects of right principles: our maxims of liberty have proved their intrinsic worth, by counteracting even the natural defects of our country. They have made, as Addison happily expresses, "our bleak rocks and barren mountains smile"; and on the careful preservation of these maxims depends the continuance of the blessings they have procured us. But I must conclude:

> O Liberty! expand thy vital ray,
> O'er the dark globe diffuse celestial day;
> Glad distant regions by thy blissful voice,
> Till India's wilds and Afric's sands rejoice;
> Thy spirit breathe, wide as creation's space;
> Exalt, illume, inspire the human race;
> As heaven's own æther thro' expansion whirl'd,
> Attracts, sublimes, and animates the world.[1]

Thus wishes a worthy member of the British Senate, and such are your wishes and mine.

ADIEU

1. Attributed by Williams to John Courtenay (1738–1816), dissenter, abolitionist, supporter of the French Revolution. The prior reference is to Joseph Addison (1672–1719), poet, Whig statesman, and essayist.

Edmund Burke
1729–1797

A political writer and Irish member of Parliament for nearly thirty years, famous for electrifying oratory, Edmund Burke embodied the debates of his century. Although he was allied with the Whigs and not the Tories, and with them often advocated liberal and reform clauses, his politics were never of a piece. The son of a Protestant minister and a Catholic mother, he castigated Britain's handling of Ireland, urging the emancipation of Irish trade, the Irish Parliament, and Irish Catholics. He endorsed William Wilberforce's movement for the abolition of the slave trade, worked for the reform of the East India Company's abuses in India, and argued for better treatment of and greater autonomy for the American colonies. Yet he also supported Britain's right to tax the colonies and was a celebrated opponent of the French Revolution, denouncing it as an unparalleled disaster in modern history.

"Burke never shows his powers, except he is in a passion. The French Revolution was alone a subject fit for him," remarked Samuel Taylor Coleridge. Burke's best known work is *Reflections on the Revolution in France*, published in 1790, after the arrest and imprisonment of Louis XVI and Marie Antoinette but before the Terror and their execution. (Wordsworth, who as a young man saw the Revolution heralding a new golden age in human history, was horrified by the Terror and later praised the "Genius of Burke.") Selling quickly and widely (5,500 copies in seventeen days and 30,000 in the next few years), *Reflections* provoked strong reactions, pro and con. It was championed throughout Europe for a principled conservatism that revered an idealized past and historical continuity, and on this basis defended the moral authority of a nation's institutions: the monarchy, the aristocracy, the church, and the constitution that guaranteed their power. A famous passage dramatized the arrest and imprisonment of the royal family, with a dignified queen as tragic heroine. Sympathizers with the Revolution immediately produced rebuttals, among the first, Mary Wollstonecraft's *Vindication of the Rights of Men,* and the most influential, Tom Paine's *Rights of Man.*

from Reflections on the Revolution in France
["This Strange Chaos"]

All circumstances taken together, the French Revolution is the most astonishing that has hitherto happened in the world. The most wonderful things are brought about in many instances by means the most absurd and ridiculous; in the most ridiculous modes; and, apparently, by the most contemptible instruments. Everything seems out of nature in this strange chaos of levity and ferocity, and of all sorts of crimes jumbled together with all sorts of follies. In viewing this monstrous tragicomic scene, the most opposite passions necessarily succeed, and sometimes mix with each other in the mind; alternate contempt and indignation; alternate laughter and tears; alternate scorn and horror.

It cannot however be denied, that to some this strange scene appeared in quite another point of view. Into them it inspired no other sentiments than those of exultation and rapture. They saw nothing in what has been done in France, but a firm and temperate exertion of freedom; so consistent, on the whole, with morals and with piety as to make it deserving not only of the secular applause of dashing Machiavelian politicians,[1] but to render it a fit theme for all the devout effusions of sacred eloquence.

---

1. Niccolo Machiavelli (1469–1527), Florentine statesman, was famous for *The Prince,* a handbook on power; "Machiavelian" came to refer to a cynical politics of cunning, manipulation, and duplicity.

James Gillray, *Smelling out a Rat;___or The Atheistical Revolutionist disturbed in his Midnight Calculations,* 1790. The picture on the wall depicts *Death of Charles I, or the Glory of Britain;* the King was beheaded in the English Civil Wars of the 1640s. Burke, wielding the symbols of the monarchy and the established Church and bearing his *Reflections* on his brow, detects a "Rat" at his desk writing *The Benefits of Anarchy, Regicide & Atheism;* at his feet are Dr. Richard Price's *Sermon to the Revolution Society* (1789, Burke's incitement to *Reflections*) and *Treatise on the ill effects of order and government on society, and the absurdity of serving GOD and honoring the KING.*

[THE CONSTITUENT PARTS OF A STATE]

The constituent parts of a state are obliged to hold their public faith with each other, and with all those who derive any serious interest under their engagements, as much as the whole state is bound to keep its faith with separate communities. Otherwise competence and power would soon be confounded, and no law be left but the will of a prevailing force. On this principle the succession of the crown has always been what it now is, an hereditary succession by law: in the old line it was a succession by the common law; in the new by the statute law, operating on the principles of the common law, not changing the substance, but regulating the mode, and describing the persons. Both these descriptions of law are of the same force, and are derived from an equal authority, emanating from the common agreement and original compact of the state, *communi sponsione reipublicae,*[2] and as such are equally binding on king and people too, as long as the terms are observed, and they continue the same body politic.

---

2. Burke summons the Latin phrase "common compact of the state" to give classical Roman republican authority to the principle of rule based on mutual agreement.

[LIBERTIES AS AN ENTAILED INHERITANCE]

You will observe, that from Magna Charta to the Declaration of Right,[3] it has been the uniform policy of our constitution to claim and assert our liberties, as an *entailed inheritance* derived to us from our forefathers, and to be transmitted to our posterity; as an estate specially belonging to the people of this kingdom, without any reference whatever to any other more general or prior right. By this means our constitution preserves a unity in so great a diversity of its parts. We have an inheritable crown; an inheritable peerage; and a House of Commons[4] and a people inheriting privileges, franchises, and liberties, from a long line of ancestors.

This policy appears to me to be the result of profound reflection; or rather the happy effect of following nature, which is wisdom without reflection, and above it. A spirit of innovation is generally the result of a selfish temper, and confined views. People will not look forward to posterity, who never look backward to their ancestors. Besides, the people of England well know, that the idea of inheritance furnishes a sure principle of conservation, and a sure principle of transmission; without at all excluding a principle of improvement. It leaves acquisition free; but it secures what it acquires. Whatever advantages are obtained by a state proceeding on these maxims, are locked fast as in a sort of family settlement; grasped as in a kind of mortmain[5] for ever. By a constitutional policy, working after the pattern of nature, we receive, we hold, we transmit our government and our privileges, in the same manner in which we enjoy and transmit our property and our lives. The institutions of policy, the goods of fortune, the gifts of providence, are handed down to us, and from us, in the same course and order. Our political system is placed in a just correspondence and symmetry with the order of the world, and with the mode of existence decreed to a permanent body composed of transitory parts; wherein, by the disposition of a stupendous wisdom, moulding together the great mysterious incorporation of the human race, the whole, at one time, is never old, or middle-aged, or young, but, in a condition of unchangeable constancy, moves on through the varied tenor of perpetual decay, fall, renovation, and progression. Thus, by preserving the method of nature in the conduct of the state, in what we improve, we are never wholly new; in what we retain, we are never wholly obsolete. By adhering in this manner and on those principles to our forefathers, we are guided not by the superstition of antiquarians, but by the spirit of philosophic analogy. In this choice of inheritance we have given to our frame of polity the image of a relation in blood; binding up the constitution of our country with our dearest domestic ties; adopting our fundamental laws into the bosom of our family affections; keeping inseparable, and cherishing with the warmth of all their combined and mutually reflected charities, our state, our hearths, our sepulchres, and our altars.

Through the same plan of a conformity to nature in our artificial institutions, and by calling in the aid of her unerring and powerful instincts, to fortify the fallible and feeble contrivances of our reason, we have derived several other, and those no small benefits, from considering our liberties in the light of an inheritance. Always

---

3. The Magna Carta (Great Charter) of 1215 was forced on King John by the nobles, clergy, and merchants to protect them from taxation without consent and from the seizure of property and persons without due process. The Declaration of Right, a result of the Glorious Revolution of 1688, provided civil liberties for the nobility and subjected the monarchy to the rule of law and the consent of Parliament.

Reflections is framed as a letter to a "gentleman in Paris."
4. Lower house of Parliament, to which those without aristocratic titles could be elected as representatives by their home districts.
5. Literally "dead hand," the term refers to the perpetual possession of property by a corporation independent of the death of any particular person.

acting as if in the presence of canonized forefathers, the spirit of freedom, leading in itself to misrule and excess, is tempered with an awful gravity. This idea of a liberal descent inspires us with a sense of habitual native dignity, which prevents that upstart insolence almost inevitably adhering to and disgracing those who are the first acquirers of any distinction. By this means our liberty becomes a noble freedom. It carries an imposing and majestic aspect. It has a pedigree and illustrating ancestors. It has its bearings and its ensigns armorial. It has its gallery of portraits; its monumental inscriptions; its records, evidences, and titles. We procure reverence to our civil institutions on the principle upon which nature teaches us to revere individual men; on account of their age, and on account of those from whom they are descended. All your sophisters cannot produce anything better adapted to preserve a rational and manly freedom than the course that we have pursued, who have chosen our nature rather than our speculations, our breasts rather than our inventions, for the great conservatories and magazines[6] of our rights and privileges.

[LEVELLERS CAN NEVER EQUALISE]

Your present confusion, like a palsy, has attacked the fountain of life itself. Every person in your country, in a situation to be actuated by a principle of honour, is disgraced and degraded, and can entertain no sensation of life, except in a mortified and humiliated indignation. But this generation will quickly pass away. The next generation of the nobility will resemble the artificers and clowns, and money-jobbers, usurers, and Jews, who will be always their fellows, sometimes their masters. Believe me, Sir, those who attempt to level,[7] never equalise. In all societies, consisting of various descriptions of citizens, some description must be uppermost. The levellers therefore only change and pervert the natural order of things.

[THE REAL RIGHTS OF MEN]

Far am I from denying in theory, full as far is my heart from withholding in practice, (if I were of power to give or to withhold,) the *real* rights of men.[8] In denying their false claims of right, I do not mean to injure those which are real, and are such as their pretended rights would totally destroy. If civil society be made for the advantage of man, all the advantages for which it is made become his right. It is an institution of beneficence; and law itself is only beneficence acting by a rule. Men have a right to live by that rule; they have a right to do justice, as between their fellows, whether their fellows are in public function or in ordinary occupation. They have a right to the fruits of their industry; and to the means of making their industry fruitful. They have a right to the acquisitions of their parents; to the nourishment and improvement of their offspring; to instruction in life, and to consolation in death. Whatever each man can separately do, without trespassing upon others, he has a right to do for himself; and he has a right to a fair portion of all which society, with all its combinations of skill and force, can do in his favour. In this partnership all men have equal rights; but not to equal things. He that has but five shillings in the partnership, has as good a right to it,

6. Storehouses, particularly for arms.
7. An allusion to the Levellers, the radical republicans of the English Civil War period of the 1640s, who advocated principles that were to shape democratic movements in Burke's day: universal suffrage for men, a written constitution, proportional representation in a single governing body, and abolition of the monarchy and class privileges.
8. An allusion to the French Revolutionary Assembly's Declaration of the Rights of Man.

as he that has five hundred pounds has to his larger proportion. But he has not a right to an equal dividend in the product of the joint stock; and as to the share of power, authority, and direction which each individual ought to have in the management of the state, that I must deny to be amongst the direct original rights of man in civil society.

[THE ARREST AND IMPRISONMENT OF THE KING AND QUEEN]

History will record, that on the morning of the 6th of October, 1789, the king and queen of France, after a day of confusion, alarm, dismay, and slaughter, lay down, under the pledged security of public faith, to indulge nature in a few hours of respite, and troubled, melancholy repose. From this sleep the queen was first startled by the voice of the sentinel at her door, who cried out to her to save herself by flight—that this was the last proof of fidelity he could give—that they were upon him, and he was dead. Instantly he was cut down. A band of cruel ruffians and assassins, reeking with his blood, rushed into the chamber of the queen, and pierced with a hundred strokes of bayonets and poniards the bed, from whence this persecuted woman had but just time to fly almost naked, and, through ways unknown to the murderers, had escaped to seek refuge at the feet of a king and husband, not secure of his own life for a moment.

This king, to say no more of him, and this queen, and their infant children, (who once would have been the pride and hope of a great and generous people,) were then forced to abandon the sanctuary of the most splendid palace in the world, which they left swimming in blood, polluted by massacre, and strewed with scattered limbs and mutilated carcases. Thence they were conducted into the capital of their kingdom. Two had been selected from the unprovoked, unresisted, promiscuous slaughter, which was made of the gentlemen of birth and family who composed the king's body guard. These two gentlemen, with all the parade of an execution of justice, were cruelly and publicly dragged to the block, and beheaded in the great court of the palace. Their heads were stuck upon spears, and led the procession; whilst the royal captives who followed in the train were slowly moved along, amidst the horrid yells, and shrilling screams, and frantic dances, and infamous contumelies, and all the unutterable abominations of the furies of hell, in the abused shape of the vilest of women. After they had been made to taste, drop by drop, more than the bitterness of death, in the slow torture of a journey of twelve miles, protracted to six hours, they were, under a guard, composed of those very soldiers who had thus conducted them through this famous triumph, lodged in one of the old palaces of Paris, now converted into a bastile for kings.

Is this a triumph to be consecrated at altars? to be commemorated with grateful thanksgiving? to be offered to the divine humanity with fervent prayer and enthusiastic ejaculation? * * *

Such treatment of any human creatures must be shocking to any but those who are made for accomplishing revolutions. But I cannot stop here. Influenced by the inborn feelings of my nature, and not being illuminated by a single ray of this new sprung modern light, I confess to you, Sir, that the exalted rank of the persons suffering, and particularly the sex, the beauty, and the amiable qualities of the descendant of so many kings and emperors, with the tender age of royal infants, insensible only through infancy and innocence of the cruel outrages to which their parents were exposed, instead of being a subject of exultation, adds not a little to my sensibility on that most melancholy occasion.

I hear that the august person,[9] who was the principal object of our preacher's triumph, though he supported himself, felt much on that shameful occasion. As a man, it became him to feel for his wife and his children, and the faithful guards of his person, that were massacred in cold blood about him; as a prince, it became him to feel for the strange and frightful transformation of his civilized subjects, and to be more grieved for them than solicitous for himself. It derogates little from his fortitude, while it adds infinitely to the honour of his humanity. I am very sorry to say it, very sorry indeed, that such personages are in a situation in which it is not becoming in us to praise the virtues of the great.

I hear, and I rejoice to hear, that the great lady[1] the other object of the triumph, has borne that day, (one is interested that beings made for suffering should suffer well,) and that she bears all the succeeding days, that she bears the imprisonment of her husband, and her own captivity, and the exile of her friends, and the insulting adulation of addresses, and the whole weight of her accumulated wrongs, with a serene patience, in a manner suited to her rank and race, and becoming the offspring of a sovereign distinguished for her piety and her courage: that, like her, she has lofty sentiments; that she feels with the dignity of a Roman matron;[2] that in the last extremity she will save herself from the last disgrace; and that, if she must fall, she will fall by no ignoble hand.[3]

It is now sixteen or seventeen years since I saw the queen of France, then the dauphiness [princess], at Versailles;[4] and surely never lighted on this orb, which she hardly seemed to touch, a more delightful vision. I saw her just above the horizon, decorating and cheering the elevated sphere she just began to move in,—glittering like the morning-star, full of life, and splendour, and joy. Oh! what a revolution! and what a heart must I have to contemplate without emotion that elevation and that fall! Little did I dream when she added titles of veneration to those of enthusiastic, distant, respectful love, that she should ever be obliged to carry the sharp antidote against disgrace concealed in that bosom; little did I dream that I should have lived to see such disasters fallen upon her in a nation of gallant men, in a nation of men of honour, and of cavaliers. I thought ten thousand swords must have leaped from their scabbards to avenge even a look that threatened her with insult. But the age of chivalry is gone. That of sophisters, economists, and calculators, has succeeded; and the glory of Europe is extinguished for ever. Never, never more shall we behold that generous loyalty to rank and sex, that proud submission, that dignified obedience, that subordination of the heart, which kept alive, even in servitude itself, the spirit of an exalted freedom. The unbought grace of life, the cheap defence of nations, the nurse of manly sentiment and heroic enterprise, is gone! It is gone, that sensibility of principle, that chastity of honour, which felt a stain like a wound, which inspired courage whilst it mitigated ferocity, which ennobled whatever it touched, and under which vice itself lost half its evil, by losing all its grossness.

This mixed system of opinion and sentiment had its origin in the ancient chivalry; and the principle, though varied in its appearance by the varying state of human

---

9. King Louis XVI. The preacher is Richard Price (1723–1791), to whose *Discourse on the Love of Our Country* Burke is replying.
1. Queen Marie Antoinette.
2. The women of ancient Rome were famous for dignified self-possession in adversity; Marie Antoinette's mother was the Empress of Austria, Maria Theresa.
3. The ancient Roman action of honor in defeat was to

take one's own life (cf. below: "the sharp antidote to disgrace concealed in that bosom"—a small knife or poison). Such hope was not realized for Marie Antoinette, who was beheaded in a noisy public event in 1793 (three years after the publication of *Reflections*).
4. The royal palace outside Paris from 1682 until the ejection of the royal family here described.

affairs, subsisted and influenced through a long succession of generations, even to the time we live in. If it should ever be totally extinguished, the loss I fear will be great. It is this which has given its character to modern Europe. It is this which has distinguished it under all its forms of government, and distinguished it to its advantage, from the states of Asia, and possibly from those states which flourished in the most brilliant periods of the antique world. It was this, which, without confounding ranks, had produced a noble equality, and handed it down through all the gradations of social life. It was this opinion which mitigated kings into companions, and raised private men to be fellows with kings. Without force or opposition, it subdued the fierceness of pride and power; it obliged sovereigns to submit to the soft collar of social esteem, compelled stern authority to submit to elegance, and gave a dominating vanquisher of laws to be subdued by manners.

But now all is to be changed. All the pleasing illusions, which made power gentle and obedience liberal, which harmonized the different shades of life, and which, by a bland assimilation, incorporated into politics the sentiments which beautify and soften private society, are to be dissolved by this new conquering empire of light and reason.[5] All the decent drapery of life is to be rudely torn off. All the super-added ideas, furnished from the wardrobe of a moral imagination, which the heart owns, and the understanding ratifies, as necessary to cover the defects of our naked, shivering nature, and to raise it to dignity in our own estimation, are to be exploded as a ridiculous, absurd, and antiquated fashion.

On this scheme of things, a king is but a man, a queen is but a woman; a woman is but an animal, and an animal not of the highest order. All homage paid to the sex[6] in general as such, and without distinct views, is to be regarded as romance and folly. Regicide, and parricide, and sacrilege, are but fictions of superstition, corrupting jurisprudence by destroying its simplicity. The murder of a king, or a queen, or a bishop, or a father, are only common homicide; and if the people are by any chance, or in any way, gainers by it, a sort of homicide much the most pardonable, and into which we ought not to make too severe a scrutiny.

On the scheme of this barbarous philosophy, which is the offspring of cold hearts and muddy understandings, and which is as void of solid wisdom as it is destitute of all taste and elegance, laws are to be supported only by their own terrors, and by the concern which each individual may find in them from his own private speculations, or can spare to them from his own private interests. In the groves of *their* academy,[7] at the end of every vista, you see nothing but the gallows. Nothing is left which engages the affections on the part of the commonwealth. On the principles of this mechanic philosophy, our institutions can never be embodied, if I may use the expression, in persons; so as to create in us love, veneration, admiration, or attachment. But that sort of reason which banishes the affections is incapable of filling their place. These public affections, combined with manners, are required sometimes as supplements, sometimes as correctives, always as aids to law. The precept given by a wise man, as well as a great critic, for the construction of poems, is equally true as to states:—*Non satis est pulchra esse poemata, dulcia sunto*.[8] There ought to be a system of manners in every nation, which a well-formed mind would be disposed to relish. To make us love our country, our country ought to be lovely.

---

5. A sarcastic reference to the Enlightenment ideology of Reason championed by political reformers and revolutionaries alike.
6. Women; a common usage.

7. In ancient Greece, philosophers and students met outside under the shade of the trees.
8. "It is not enough that poems be beautiful, they must be sweet [tender, touching]" (Horace, *Ars Poetica*).

But power, of some kind or other, will survive the shock in which manners and opinions perish; and it will find other and worse means for its support. The usurpation which, in order to subvert ancient institutions, has destroyed ancient principles, will hold power by arts similar to those by which it has acquired it. When the old feudal and chivalrous spirit of *fealty*,[9] which, by freeing kings from fear, freed both kings and subjects from the precautions of tyranny, shall be extinct in the minds of men, plots and assassinations will be anticipated by preventive murder and preventive confiscation, and that long roll of grim and bloody maxims, which form the political code of all power, not standing on its own honour, and the honour of those who are to obey it. Kings will be tyrants from policy, when subjects are rebels from principle.

When ancient opinions and rules of life are taken away, the loss cannot possibly be estimated. From that moment we have no compass to govern us; nor can we know distinctly to what port we steer. Europe, undoubtedly, taken in a mass, was in a flourishing condition the day on which your revolution was completed. How much of that prosperous state was owing to the spirit of our old manners and opinions is not easy to say; but as such causes cannot be indifferent in their operation, we must presume, that, on the whole, their operation was beneficial.

We are but too apt to consider things in the state in which we find them, without sufficiently adverting to the causes by which they have been produced, and possibly may be upheld. Nothing is more certain, than that our manners, our civilization, and all the good things which are connected with manners and with civilization, have, in this European world of ours, depended for ages upon two principles; and were indeed the result of both combined; I mean the spirit of a gentleman, and the spirit of religion. The nobility and the clergy, the one by profession, the other by patronage, kept learning in existence, even in the midst of arms and confusions, and whilst governments were rather in their causes, than formed. Learning paid back what it received to nobility and to priesthood; and paid it with usury,[1] by enlarging their ideas, and by furnishing their minds. Happy if they had all continued to know their indissoluble union, and their proper place! Happy if learning, not debauched by ambition, had been satisfied to continue the instructor, and not aspired to be the master! Along with its natural protectors and guardians, learning will be cast into the mire, and trodden down under the hoofs of a swinish multitude.[2]

["THIS GREAT DRAMA"]

[W]hen kings are hurled from their thrones by the Supreme Director[3] of this great drama, and become the objects of insult to the base, and of pity to the good, we behold such disasters in the moral, as we should behold a miracle in the physical, order of things. We are alarmed into reflection; our minds (as it has long since been observed) are purified by terror and pity;[4] our weak, unthinking pride is humbled under the dispensations of a mysterious wisdom. Some tears might be drawn from me, if such a spectacle were exhibited on the stage. I should be truly ashamed of finding in myself that superficial, theatric sense of painted distress, whilst I could exult over

---

9. Medieval ideal of a vassal's obligation of fidelity to his lord; by extension, the faithful allegiance that secures social order both from fear of violent revolt and from preventive lordly tyranny.
1. Interest; here, a positive term.
2. Among the several rebuttals provoked by *Reflections*

was *The Reply of the Swinish Multitude to Mr. Burke.*
3. A metaphor for God.
4. In his extended metaphor of the "great drama," Burke refers to Aristotle's argument in *Poetics* for the salutary effect of drama in its controlled release of sensations of pity and fear.

it in real life. With such a perverted mind, I could never venture to show my face at a tragedy. People would think the tears that Garrick formerly, or that Siddons not long since, have extorted from me, were the tears of hypocrisy;[5] I should know them to be the tears of folly.

Indeed the theatre is a better school of moral sentiments than churches, where the feelings of humanity are thus outraged. Poets who have to deal with an audience not yet graduated in the school of the rights of men, and who must apply themselves to the moral constitution of the heart, would not dare to produce such a triumph as a matter of exultation. There, where men follow their natural impulses, they would not bear the odious maxims of a Machiavelian policy, whether applied to the attainment of monarchical or democratic tyranny. They would reject them on the modern, as they once did on the ancient stage, where they could not bear even the hypothetical proposition of such wickedness in the mouth of a personated tyrant, though suitable to the character he sustained. No theatric audience in Athens would bear what has been borne, in the midst of the real tragedy of this triumphal day; a principal actor weighing, as it were in scales hung in a shop of horrors,—so much actual crime against so much contingent advantage,—and after putting in and out weights, declaring that the balance was on the side of the advantages. They would not bear to see the crimes of new democracy posted as in a ledger against the crimes of old despotism, and the book-keepers of politics finding democracy still in debt, but by no means unable or unwilling to pay the balance. In the theatre, the first intuitive glance, without any elaborate process of reasoning, will show, that this method of political computation would justify every extent of crime. They would see, that on these principles, even where the very worst acts were not perpetrated, it was owing rather to the fortune of the conspirators, than to their parsimony in the expenditure of treachery and blood. They would soon see, that criminal means once tolerated are soon preferred. They present a shorter cut to the object than through the highway of the moral virtues. Justifying perfidy and murder for public benefit, public benefit would soon become the pretext, and perfidy and murder the end; until rapacity, malice, revenge, and fear more dreadful than revenge, could satiate their insatiable appetites. Such must be the consequences of losing, in the splendour of these triumphs of the rights of men, all natural sense of wrong and right.

[THE CONTRACT OF SOCIETY]

To avoid therefore the evils of inconstancy and versatility, ten thousand times worse than those of obstinacy and the blindest prejudice, we have consecrated the state, that no man should approach to look into its defects or corruptions but with due caution; that he should never dream of beginning its reformation by its subversion; that he should approach to the faults of the state as to the wounds of a father, with pious awe and trembling solicitude. By this wise prejudice we are taught to look with horror on those children of their country, who are prompt rashly to hack that aged parent in pieces, and put him into the kettle of magicians, in hopes that

---

5. David Garrick (1717–1779) and Sarah Siddons (1755–1831) were leading actors of the age, both celebrated for their performances in Shakespeare's tragedies; "hypocrisy" is in the same metaphor system, derived from a Greek word for "stage-acting."

by their poisonous weeds, and wild incantations, they may regenerate the paternal constitution, and renovate their father's life.[6]

Society is indeed a contract. Subordinate contracts for objects of mere occasional interest may be dissolved at pleasure—but the state ought not to be considered as nothing better than a partnership agreement in a trade of pepper and coffee, calico or tobacco, or some other such low concern, to be taken up for a little temporary interest, and to be dissolved by the fancy of the parties. It is to be looked on with other reverence; because it is not a partnership in things subservient only to the gross animal existence of a temporary and perishable nature. It is a partnership in all science; a partnership in all art; a partnership in every virtue, and in all perfection. As the ends of such a partnership cannot be obtained in many generations, it becomes a partnership not only between those who are living, but between those who are living, those who are dead, and those who are to be born. Each contract of each particular state is but a clause in the great primaeval contract of eternal society, linking the lower with the higher natures, connecting the visible and invisible world, according to a fixed compact sanctioned by the inviolable oath which holds all physical and all moral natures, each in their appointed place. This law is not subject to the will of those, who by an obligation above them, and infinitely superior, are bound to submit their will to that law. The municipal corporations of that universal kingdom are not morally at liberty at their pleasure, and on their speculations of a contingent improvement, wholly to separate and tear asunder the bands of their subordinate community, and to dissolve it into an unsocial, uncivil, unconnected chaos of elementary principles. It is the first and supreme necessity only, a necessity that is not chosen, but chooses, a necessity paramount to deliberation, that admits no discussion, and demands no evidence, which alone can justify a resort to anarchy. This necessity is no exception to the rule; because this necessity itself is a part too of that moral and physical disposition of things, to which man must be obedient by consent or force: but if that which is only submission to necessity should be made the object of choice, the law is broken, nature is disobeyed, and the rebellious are outlawed, cast forth, and exiled, from this world of reason, and order, and peace, and virtue, and fruitful penitence, into the antagonist world of madness, discord, vice, confusion, and unavailing sorrow.

＋·✦✧✦·＋

Mary Wollstonecraft
1759–1797

Mary Wollstonecraft was living on her own in London on Bastille Day, 14 July 1789, writing for and serving on the staff of the *Analytical Review*, enjoying a lively circle of artists, writers, and intellectuals gathered around Joseph Johnson, its politically radical publisher. *A Vindication of the Rights of Men* (published by Johnson) appeared anonymously, in two printings in rapid succession in late 1790, leading a flood of responses to Burke's *Reflections on the Revolution in France*, which had appeared only weeks earlier. Her title refers to the Declaration of the Rights of Man voted by the French Constituent Assembly in August 1789. Caustic, trenchant, and frequently sarcastic, *Rights of Men* made her reputation when the second edition bore her name in 1790. Concerned chiefly to refute Burke's arguments for the hereditary succession of the crown, the inviolability of a national constitution, and the necessary alliance of church

---

6. Manipulated by the sorceress Medea, the daughters of Pelias, King of Thessaly, took this course of action, not realizing that Medea was in league with Pelias's dispossessed half-nephew, Jason.

and state, Wollstonecraft also drew notice for her collateral arguments about the property of the poor, and for her bitter critiques of naval impressment, antipoaching laws, slavery, and Burke's attitudes about women and gender, which had already irritated her in his widely influential *Inquiry into the Origin of Our Ideas of the Sublime and Beautiful* (1757); see page 302.

For more about Wollstonecraft, see the principal listing, page 149.

from A Vindication of the Rights of Men
in a Letter to the Right Honourable Edmund Burke; Occasioned by his Reflections on the Revolution in France

Mr. Burke's *Reflections on the French Revolution* first engaged my attention as the transient topic of the day. * * * My indignation was roused by the sophistical arguments, that every moment crossed me, in the questionable shape[1] of natural feelings and common sense. * * * I have confined my strictures, in a great measure, to the grand principles at which he has levelled many ingenious arguments in a very specious garb.

[SENSIBILITY]

Sensibility is the *manie* of the day,[2] and compassion the virtue which is to cover a multitude of vices, whilst justice is left to mourn in sullen silence, and balance truth in vain.

In life, an honest man with a confined understanding is frequently the slave of his habits and the dupe of his feelings, whilst the man with a clearer head and colder heart makes the passions of others bend to his interest; but truly sublime is the character that acts from principle. * * * All your pretty flights arise from your pampered sensibility; and that, vain of this fancied pre-eminence of organs, you foster every emotion till the fumes, mounting to your brain, dispel the sober suggestions of reason. It is not in this view surprising, that when you should argue you become impassioned, and that reflection inflames your imagination, instead of enlightening your understanding.

Quitting now the flowers of rhetoric, let us, Sir, reason together.[3] * * *

The birthright of man, to give you, Sir, a short definition of this disputed right, is such a degree of liberty, civil and religious, as is compatible with the liberty of every other individual with whom he is united in a social compact, and the continued existence of that compact.[4]

Liberty, in this simple, unsophisticated sense, I acknowledge, is a fair idea that has never yet received a form in the various governments that have been established on our bounteous globe; the demon of property has ever been at hand to encroach on the sacred rights of men, and to fence round with awful pomp laws that war with

1. A sardonic allusion to Hamlet's first address to his father's ghost: "Angels and ministers of grace defend us! / Be thou a spirit of health or goblin damned, / Bring with thee airs from heaven or blasts from hell, / Be thy intents wicked or charitable, / Thou com'st in such a questionable shape / That I will speak to thee" (*Hamlet* 1.4.39–44).
2. A reference to the "Cult of Sensibility," the elevation of feelings over rationality, particularly by poets and sentimental novelists of both sexes, but with a general sense that such culture is the province of women and men of "feminine" character. *Manie*, a quasi-medical term, combines the senses of emotional hyperactivity and mania, a cultural craze.
3. A parody of Isaiah: "Come now, and let us reason together, saith the Lord: though your sins be as scarlet, they shall be as white as snow" (1.18). Rhetoric, an orna-

mental art, may displace reason; cf. Wollstonecraft's remarks on her style in Introduction to *Rights of Woman*, page 153.
4. John Locke's *Two Treatises on Government* (1690) defines the "*original Compact*," whereby every man "with others incorporates into *one Society*": "by consenting with others to make one Body Politick under one Government, [he] puts himself under an obligation to every one of that Society, to submit to the determination of the *majority*, and to be concluded by it" (2.97). Jean-Jacques Rousseau's *Social Contract* (1762) argues that a free acceptance of this contract involves the surrender of the individual to the State, their reciprocal obligations, and their legal equality. Although Rousseau distrusted democracy and preferred monarchy, this work would be cited by conservatives as the philosophical basis for the "democratic despotism" fostered by the French Revolution.

justice. * * * If there is any thing like argument, or first principles, in your wild declamation, behold the result:—that we are to reverence the rust of antiquity, and term
the unnatural customs, which ignorance and mistaken self-interest have consolidated, the sage fruit of experience: nay, that, if we do discover some errors, our *feelings*
should lead us to excuse, with blind love, or unprincipled filial affection, the venerable vestiges of ancient days. These are gothic notions of beauty[5]—the ivy is beautiful, but, when it insidiously destroys the trunk from which it receives support, who
would not grub it up? * * *

The civilization which has taken place in Europe has been very partial, and, like
every custom that an arbitrary point of honour has established, refines the manners
at the expence of morals, by making sentiments and opinions current in conversation
that have no root in the heart, or weight in the cooler resolves of the mind.—And
what has stopped its progress?—hereditary property—hereditary honours. The man
has been changed into an artificial monster by the station in which he was born, and
the consequent homage that benumbed his faculties like the torpedo's touch;[6]—or a
being, with a capacity of reasoning, would not have failed to discover, as his faculties
unfolded, that true happiness arose from the friendship and intimacy which can only
be enjoyed by equals; and that charity is not a condescending distribution of alms,
but an intercourse of good offices and mutual benefits, founded on respect for justice
and humanity.

[AUTHORITY, SLAVERY, AND NATURAL RIGHTS]

Are we to seek for the rights of men in the ages when a few marks were the only
penalty imposed for the life of a man, and death for death when the property of the
rich was touched? when—I blush to discover the depravity of our nature—when a
deer was killed![7] Are these the laws that it is natural to love, and sacrilegious to
invade?—Were the rights of men understood when the law authorized or tolerated
murder?—or is power and right the same in your creed? * * *

It is necessary emphatically to repeat, that there are rights which men inherit at
their birth, as rational creatures, who were raised above the brute creation by their
improvable faculties; and that, in receiving these, not from their forefathers but, from
God, prescription can never undermine natural rights.

A father may dissipate his property without his child having any right to complain;—but should he attempt to sell him for a slave, or fetter him with laws contrary
to reason; nature, in enabling him to discern good from evil, teaches him to break the
ignoble chain, and not to believe that bread becomes flesh, and wine blood, because
his parents swallowed the Eucharist[8] with this blind persuasion.

There is no end to this implicit submission to authority—some where it must
stop, or we return to barbarism; and the capacity of improvement, which gives us a
natural sceptre on earth, is a cheat, an ignis-fatuus,[9] that leads us from inviting

---

5. A reference to the "gothic" aesthetic of the 18th century, which admired the gloomy, wild, and untamed, and
adored ivy-covered ruins (preferably of medieval Gothic
architecture); ivy is a parasite.
6. The numbing electric discharges of the torpedo, a ray
fish; *torpedo* in Latin means *numbness*.
7. From 1389 to 1831, British law restricted the right to
kill game to wealthy landlords and leaseholders; poach-
ing, a theft of game often motivated by desperate hunger,
was punishable by death.

8. Catholic theology stressed that the communion bread
and wine are inwardly transformed into Christ's body and
blood. Wollstonecraft was religious; her contempt issues
from a general English disdain of Roman Catholicism as
well as from her Enlightenment deism, which distrusted
the authority of an established Church.
9. Latin for false/foolish fire: nighttime lights over marsh-
lands supposedly caused by spontaneous combustion of
gases released by the decay of organic material; by extension, a deceptive guiding light, an illusory ideal.

meadows into bogs and dunghills. And if it be allowed that many of the precautions, with which any alteration was made, in our government, were prudent, it rather proves its weakness that substantiates an opinion of the soundness of the stamina, or the excellence of the constitution.

But on what principle Mr. Burke could defend American independence, I cannot conceive;[1] for the whole tenor of his plausible arguments settles slavery on an everlasting foundation. Allowing his servile reverence for antiquity, and prudent attention to self-interest, to have the force which he insists on, the slave trade ought never to be abolished;[2] and, because our ignorant forefathers, not understanding the native dignity of man, sanctioned a traffic that outrages every suggestion of reason and religion, we are to submit to the inhuman custom, and term an atrocious insult to humanity the love of our country, and a proper submission to the laws by which our property is secured.—Security of property! Behold, in a few words, the definition of English liberty. And to this selfish principle every nobler one is sacrificed.—The Briton takes place of the man, and the image of God is lost in the citizen! But it is not that enthusiastic flame which in Greece and Rome consumed every sordid passion: no, self is the focus; and the disparting rays rise not above our foggy atmosphere. But softly—it is only the property of the rich that is secure; the man who lives by the sweat of his brow has no asylum from oppression. * * * It is a farce to pretend that a man fights *for his country, his hearth, or his altars,* when he has neither liberty nor property.—His property is in his nervous arms—and they are compelled to pull a strange rope at the surly command of a tyrannic boy, who probably obtained his rank on account of his family connections, or the prostituted vote of his father, whose interest in a borough, or voice as a senator, was acceptable to the minister.[3] * * *

Misery, to reach your heart, I perceive, must have its cap and bells;[4] your tears are reserved, very *naturally* considering your character, for the declamation of the theatre, or for the downfall of queens, whose rank alters the nature of folly, and throws a graceful veil over vices that degrade humanity; whilst the distress of many industrious mothers, whose *helpmates* have been torn from them, and the hungry cry of helpless babes, were vulgar sorrows that could not move your commiseration, though they might extort an alms. * * *

A brutal attachment to children has appeared most conspicuous in parents who have treated them like slaves, and demanded due homage for all the property they transferred to them, during their lives. It has led them to force their children to break the most sacred ties; to do violence to a natural impulse, and run into legal prostitution to increase wealth or shun poverty.[5] * * * It appears to be a natural suggestion of reason, that a man should be freed from implicit obedience to parents and private punishments, when he is of an age to be subject to the jurisdiction of the laws of his country; and that the barbarous cruelty of allowing parents to imprison their children, to prevent their contaminating their noble blood by following the dictates of

1. Burke's *Speech on Conciliation with America* (22 March 1775) defended the American Revolution on principles of traditional British liberties (e.g., taxation by consent and representation).
2. The institution of slavery in ancient Greece and Rome poses a contradiction to Burke's support in the 1780s of the parliamentary movement to abolish the slave trade.
3. Naval crews were often supplied by impressment, kidnapping or enforced labor; "nervous" means "well strung, vigorous."
4. A court-jester's bell-tipped hat; hence, any device of foolish entertainment.
5. Marriage for financial reasons rather than mutual love, affection, and esteem—a frequent term in Wollstonecraft's *Rights of Woman,* used earlier by Daniel Defoe in *Conjugal Lewdness: or, Matrimonial Whoredom* (1727).

nature when they chose to marry, or for any misdemeanor that does not come under the cognizance of public justice, is one of the most arbitrary violations of liberty.[6]

Who can recount all the unnatural crimes which the *laudable, interesting* desire of perpetuating a name has produced? The younger children have been sacrificed to the eldest son; sent into exile, or confined in convents, that they might not encroach on what was called, with shameful falsehood, the *family* estate.[7] Will Mr Burke call this parental affection reasonable or virtuous?—No; it is the spurious offspring of over-weening, mistaken pride—and not that first source of civilization, natural parental affection, that makes no difference between child and child, but what reason justifies by pointing out superior merit.

Another pernicious consequence which unavoidably arises from this artificial affection is, the insuperable bar which it puts in the way of early marriages. It would be difficult to determine whether the minds or bodies of our youth are most injured by this impediment. Our young men become selfish coxcombs. * * *

The same system has an equally pernicious effect on female morals.—Girls are sacrificed to family convenience, or else marry to settle themselves in a superior rank, and coquet, without restraint, with the fine gentleman whom I have already described.

[PROPERTY AND VIRTUE]

Property, I do not scruple to aver it, should be fluctuating, which would be the case, if it were more equally divided amongst all the children of a family; else it is an everlasting rampart, in consequence of a barbarous feudal institution, that enables the elder son to overpower talents and depress virtue.[8]

Besides, an unmanly servility, most inimical to true dignity of character is, by this means, fostered in society. Men of some abilities play on the follies of the rich, and mounting to fortune as they degrade themselves, they stand in the way of men of superior talents, who cannot advance in such crooked paths, or wade through the filth which *parasites* never boggle at. Pursuing their way straight forward, their spirit is either bent or broken by the rich man's contumelies[9] or the difficulties they have to encounter.

The only security of property that nature authorizes and reason sanctions is, the right a man has to enjoy the acquisitions which his talents and industry have acquired; and to bequeath them to whom he chooses. * * * Overreaching, adultery, and coquetry, are venial offences, though they reduce virtue to an empty name, and make wisdom consist in saving appearances.

"On this scheme of things[1] a king *is* but a man; a queen *is* but a woman; a woman *is* but an animal, and an animal not of the highest order."—All true, Sir; if she is not more attentive to the duties of humanity than queens and fashionable ladies in general are. I will still further accede to the opinion you have so justly conceived of the spirit which begins to animate this age.—"All homage paid to the sex in general, as such, and without distinct views, is to be regarded as *romance* and folly." Undoubted-

6. In *Letters Written in France in the Summer of 1790*, Helen Maria Williams tells the story of one family that suffered such injustice (chs. 16–22); until 1791, a "lettre de cachet" signed by the king on the petition of an individual permitted imprisonment without trial. Wordsworth tells a story, based on Williams, of French parental tyranny against young lovers at the end of Book 9 of the 1805 *Prelude* (556–935).

7. A reference to primogeniture, a system to preserve the

family estate by restricting inheritance to the first-born son, abolished in the French Revolution. See H. M. Williams, page 40.

8. An argument made in Locke's *Treatises on Government* (2.25–51).

9. Insults and abuses.

1. As you ironically observe [Wollstonecraft's note]. Here and following, she refers to statements in Burke's *Reflections*, page 53, applying her own emphases.

ly; because such homage vitiates them, prevents their endeavouring to obtain solid personal merit; and, in short, makes those beings vain inconsiderate dolls, who ought to be prudent mothers and useful members of society. "Regicide and sacrilege are but fictions of superstition corrupting jurisprudence, by destroying its simplicity. The murder of a king, or a queen, or a bishop, are only common homicide."—Again I agree with you; but you perceive, Sir, that by leaving out the word *father*, I think the whole extent of the comparison invidious.[2]

[ROMANCE AND CHIVALRY]

Whether the glory of Europe is set, I shall not now enquire; but probably the spirit of romance and chivalry is in the wane; and reason will gain by its extinction.

From observing several cold romantic characters I have been led to confine the term romantic to one definition—false, or rather artificial, feelings. Works of genius are read with a prepossession in their favour, and sentiments imitated, because they were fashionable and pretty, and not because they were forcibly felt.

In modern poetry the understanding and memory often fabricate the pretended effusions of the heart, and romance destroys all simplicity; which, in works of taste, is but a synonymous word for truth. This romantic spirit has extended to our prose, and scattered artificial flowers over the most barren heath; or a mixture of verse and prose producing the strangest incongruities. The turgid bombast of some of your periods[3] fully proves these assertions; for when the heart speaks we are seldom shocked by hyperbole, or dry raptures. * * * I am led very often to doubt your sincerity, and to suppose that you have said many things merely for the sake of saying them well. * * * The mock dignity and haughty stalk, only reminds me of the ass in the lion's skin.

A sentiment of this kind glanced across my mind when I read the following exclamation. "Whilst the royal captives, who followed in the train, were slowly moved along, amidst the horrid yells, and shrilling screams, and frantic dances, and infamous contumelies, and all the unutterable abominations of the furies of hell, in the abused shape of the vilest of women."[4] Probably you mean women who gained a livelihood by selling vegetables or fish, who never had any advantages of education; or their vices might have lost part of their abominable deformity, by losing part of their grossness. The queen of France—the great and small vulgar, claim our pity; they have almost insuperable obstacles to surmount in their progress towards true dignity of character; still I have such a plain downright understanding that I do not like to make a distinction without a difference. But it is not very extraordinary that *you* should, for throughout your letter you frequently advert to a sentimental jargon, which has long been current in conversation, and even in books of morals, though it never received the *regal* stamp of reason. A kind of mysterious instinct is *supposed* to reside in the soul, that instantaneously discerns truth, without the tedious labour of ratiocination. This instinct, for I know not what other name to give it, has been termed *common sense*, and more frequently *sensibility*, and, by a kind of *indefeasible* right, it has been *supposed*, for rights of this kind are not easily proved, to reign paramount over the other faculties of the mind, and to be an authority from which there is no appeal. * * * It is to this instinct, without doubt, that you allude, when you talk of the "moral constitution of the heart."

---

2. Burke's sentence says "Regicide, and parricide, and sacrilege"; see page 53.

3. Sentences

4. See Burke's *Reflections*, page 51.

In the name of the people of England, you say, "* * * In England we have not yet been completely emboweled of our natural entrails; we still feel within us, and we cherish and cultivate those inbred sentiments which are the faithful guardians, the active monitors of our duty, the true supporters of all liberal and manly morals."— What do you mean by inbred sentiments? From whence do they come? How were they bred? Are they the brood of folly, which swarms like the insects on the banks of the Nile, when mud and putrefaction have enriched the languid soil? Were these *inbred* sentiments faithful guardians of our duty when the church was an asylum for murderers, and men worshipped bread as a God? when slavery was authorized by law to fasten her fangs on human flesh, and the iron eat into the very soul? If these sentiments are not acquired, if our passive dispositions do not expand into virtuous affections and passions, why are not the Tartars in the first rude horde endued with sentiments white and *elegant* as the driven snow? Why is passion or heroism the child of reflection, the consequence of dwelling with intent contemplation on one object? The appetites are the only perfect inbred powers that I can discern; and they like instincts have a certain aim, they can be satisfied—but improveable reason has not yet discovered the perfection it may arrive at—God forbid!

[THE RICH AND THE POOR]

The rich and weak, a numerous train, will certainly applaud your system, and loudly celebrate your pious reverence for authority and establishments—they find it pleasanter to enjoy than to think; to justify oppression than correct abuses.—*The rights of men* are grating sounds that set their teeth on edge; the impertinent enquiry of philosophic meddling innovation. If the poor are in distress, they will make some *benevolent* exertions to assist them; they will confer obligations, but not do justice. Benevolence is a very amiable specious quality; yet the aversion which men feel to accept a right as a favour, should rather be extolled as a vestige of native dignity, than stigmatized as the odious offspring of ingratitude. The poor consider the rich as their lawful prey; but we ought not too severely to animadvert on[5] their ingratitude. When they receive an alms they are commonly grateful at the moment; but old habits quickly return, and cunning has ever been a substitute for force. * * *

Among all your plausible arguments, and witty illustrations, your contempt for the poor always appears conspicuous, and rouses my indignation. The following paragraph in particular struck me, as breathing the most tyrannic spirit, and displaying the most factitious feelings. "Good order is the foundation of all good things. To be enabled to acquire, the people, without being servile, must be tractable and obedient. The magistrate must have his reverence, the laws their authority. The body of the people must not find the principles of natural subordination by art rooted out of their minds. They *must* respect that property of which they *cannot* partake. *They must labour to obtain what by labour can be obtained; and when they find, as they commonly do, the success disproportioned to the endeavour, they must be taught their consolation in the final proportions of eternal justice.* Of this consolation, whoever deprives them, deadens their industry, and strikes at the root of all acquisition as of all conservation. He that does this, is the cruel oppressor, the merciless enemy, of the poor and wretched; at the same time that, by his wicked speculations, he exposes the fruits of successful industry, and the accumulations of fortune, (ah! there's the rub)[6] to the plunder of the negligent, the disappointed, and the unprosperous."

---

5. Censure.
6. The flaw in the argument; the phrase is from *Hamlet*

3.1.65, referring to the way the attraction of suicide is thwarted by fear of the afterlife.

This is contemptible hard-hearted sophistry, in the specious form of humility, and submission to the will of Heaven.—It is, Sir, *possible* to render the poor happier in this world, without depriving them of the consolation which you gratuitously grant them in the next. They have a right to more comfort than they at present enjoy; and more comfort might be afforded them, without encroaching on the pleasures of the rich: not now waiting to enquire whether the rich have any right to exclusive pleasures. What do I say?—encroaching! No; if an intercourse were established between them, it would impart the only true pleasure that can be snatched in this land of shadows, this hard school of moral discipline.

I know, indeed, that there is often something disgusting in the distresses of poverty, at which the imagination revolts, and starts back to exercise itself in the more attractive Arcadia of fiction.[7] The rich man builds a house, art and taste give it the highest finish. His gardens are planted, and the trees grow to recreate the fancy of the planter, though the temperature of the climate may rather force him to avoid the dangerous damps they exhale, than seek the umbrageous retreat. Every thing on the estate is cherished but man;—yet, to contribute to the happiness of man, is the most sublime of all enjoyments. But if, instead of sweeping pleasure-grounds, obelisks, temples, and elegant cottages, as *objects* for the eye,[8] the heart was allowed to beat true to nature, decent farms would be scattered over the estate, and plenty smile around. Instead of the poor being subject to the griping hand of an avaricious steward, they would be watched over with fatherly solicitude, by the man whose duty and pleasure it was to guard their happiness, and shield from rapacity the beings who, by the sweat of their brow, exalted him above his fellows.

I could almost imagine I see a man thus gathering blessings as he mounted the hill of life; or consolation, in those days when the spirits lag, and the tired heart finds no pleasure in them. It is not by squandering alms that the poor can be relieved, or improved—it is the fostering sun of kindness, the wisdom that finds them employments calculated to give them habits of virtue, that meliorates their condition. * * *

Why cannot large estates be divided into small farms? these dwellings would indeed grace our land. Why are huge forests still allowed to stretch out with idle pomp and all the indolence of Eastern [Asian] grandeur? Why does the brown waste meet the traveller's view, when men want work? But commons cannot be enclosed without *acts of parliament* to increase the property of the rich![9] Why might not the industrious peasant be allowed to steal a farm from the heath? This sight I have seen;—the cow that supported the children grazed near the hut, and the cheerful poultry were fed by the chubby babes, who breathed a bracing air, far from the diseases and the vices of cities. Domination blasts all these prospects; virtue can only flourish amongst equals, and the man who submits to a fellow-creature, because it promotes his worldly interest, and he who relieves only because it is his duty to lay up a treasure in heaven,[1] are much on a par, for both are radically degraded by the habits of their life.

7. In ancient Greece, a region of pastoral simplicity, beauty, and harmony.
8. A reference to the 18th-century vogue of landscaping on aristocratic estates, which frequently involved vast rearrangements of topography and the addition of picturesque enhancements such as pillars, classical temples, instant ruins, quaint cottages.
9. "Brown waste" is arable but untilled land; Wollstonecraft may also be alluding to Lancelot "Capability" Brown, a famous landscaper of aristocratic estates, who devised, among other "improvements," idle, though picturesque, stretches of forests and plains. In the 18th century, Parliament enacted a series of extreme "enclosure" acts, deeding to private ownership formerly public lands (the "commons" being the least arable of these), on which the poor lived, grew crops, and pastured livestock.
1. See Jesus' instruction to "lay up for yourselves treasures in heaven, where neither moth nor rust doth corrupt, and where thieves do not break through nor steal" (Matthew 6.20). Wollstonecraft is referring to charity motivated by self-interest, the belief that such acts will count in one's favor in the judgment of Heaven.

In this great city, that proudly rears its head, and boasts of its population and commerce, how much misery lurks in pestilential corners, whilst idle mendicants assail, on every side, the man who hates to encourage impostors, or repress, with angry frown, the plaints of the poor! How many mechanics, by a flux of trade or fashion, lose their employment; whom misfortunes, not to be warded off, lead to the idleness that vitiates their character and renders them afterwards averse to honest labour! Where is the eye that marks these evils, more gigantic than any of the infringements of property, which you piously deprecate? Are these remediless evils? And is the humane heart satisfied with turning the poor over to *another* world, to receive the blessings this could afford? * * *

What were the outrages of a day[2] to these continual miseries? Let those sorrows hide their diminished head before the tremendous mountain of woe that thus defaces our globe![3] Man preys on man; and you mourn * * * for the empty pageant of a name, when slavery flaps her wing, and the sick heart retires to die in lonely wilds, far from the abodes of men. Did the pangs you felt for insulted nobility, the anguish that rent your heart when the gorgeous robes were torn off the idol human weakness had set up [Queen Marie Antoinette], deserve to be compared with the long-drawn sigh of melancholy reflection, when misery and vice are thus seen to haunt our steps, and swim on the top of every cheering prospect? Why is our fancy to be appalled by terrific perspective of a hell beyond the grave?—Hell stalks abroad;—the lash resounds on the slave's naked sides; and the sick wretch, who can no longer earn the sour bread of unremitting labour, steals to a ditch to bid the world a long good night—or, neglected in some ostentatious hospital, breathes his last amidst the laugh of mercenary attendants.

Such misery demands more than tears—I pause to recollect myself; and smother the contempt I feel rising for your rhetorical flourishes and infantine sensibility.

Second edition, 1790

Thomas Paine
1737–1809

"These are the times that try men's souls," declared Tom Paine in a pamphlet that was read to George Washington's suffering and discouraged troops before the battle of Trenton. Paine was already famous for *Common Sense* (1776), urging the colonies to revolt from Britain; selling briskly, more than 100,000 copies in three months, it was a critical inspiration for the Declaration of Independence and the American Revolution. Born in England, and with only a grammar-school education, Paine endured various unsatisfactory jobs until he met Benjamin Franklin in London. At thirty-seven, with letters of introduction from Franklin, he sailed to America, where he launched his career as a writer, with articles on women's rights and the abolition of slavery. After he returned to England in 1787, he shuttled back and forth to France, and when Burke's *Reflections on the Revolution in France* appeared in 1790, he quickly

2. The 6th of October (1789) [Wollstonecraft's note]; see Burke, *Reflections*, page 51.
3. In *Paradise Lost*, Satan notes how "all the Stars / Hide thir diminisht heads" at the sight of the noonday sun, "that with surpassing Glory crown'd, / Look'st from [its] sole dominion like the God / Of this new World" (4.32–35).

began his rebuttal, *The Rights of Man,* published early the next year. Burke wrote eloquent prose for the educated elite; Paine's simple, electric style was framed for the common reader, and his tract, priced cheaply, was an immediate and widespread success, selling 200,000 copies by 1793—but not without cost. Paine's incitement to revolution over reform and his attack on monarchies sent his bookseller to jail and led to his own indictment for treason. Fleeing to France in 1792 (just after the September Massacres), he was warmly received, elected to the National Assembly and given honorary citizenship. But he soon got into trouble for criticizing the execution of Louis XVI. Imprisoned by the Jacobins, he only narrowly escaped the guillotine himself through the intercession of James Monroe, then American ambassador to France. Convicted in absentia in England, he could not return without imprisonment, so he went back to America. There he completed *The Age of Reason* (1792–1795), a case for Deism begun during his imprisonment in France. Its strident denunciation of institutionalized Christianity and the Bible cost Paine sympathetic readers, however, and his reputation fell further in 1796 when he attacked Washington and federalism. He died in 1809, impoverished, angry, and ostracized. Denounced as an atheist, he was denied a consecrated burial, but in 1819, William Cobbett, a sympathetic English radical, exhumed his remains and took them to England.

from **The Rights of Man**
Being an answer to Mr. Burke's attack on the French Revolution
["Man Has No Property in Man"]

There never did, there never will, and there never can, exist a Parliament, or any description of men, or any generation of men, in any country, possessed of the right or the power of binding and controuling posterity to the *"end of time."* * * * Every age and generation must be as free to act for itself *in all cases* as the ages and generations which preceded it. The vanity and presumption of governing beyond the grave is the most ridiculous and insolent of all tyrannies. Man has no property in man; neither has any generation a property in the generations which are to follow. The Parliament or the people of 1688,[1] or of any other period, had no more right to dispose of the people of the present day, or to bind or to controul them *in any shape whatever,* than the Parliament or the people of the present day have to dispose of, bind or controul those who are to live a hundred or a thousand years hence. Every generation is, and must be, competent to all the purposes which its occasions require. It is the living, and not the dead, that are to be accommodated. When man ceases to be, his power and his wants cease with him; and having no longer any participation in the concerns of this world, he has no longer any authority in directing who shall be its governors, or how its Government shall be organised, or how administered.

I am not contending for nor against any form of Government, nor for nor against any party, here or elsewhere. That which a whole Nation chooses to do, it has a right to do. Mr. Burke says, No. Where, then does the right exist? I am contending for the rights of the *living,* and against their being willed away, and controuled and contracted for, by the manuscript assumed authority of the dead; and Mr. Burke is contending for the authority of the dead over the rights and freedom of the living. There was a time when Kings disposed of their Crowns by will upon their death-beds, and consigned the people, like beasts of the field, to whatever successor they appointed. This is now so exploded as scarcely to be remembered, and so monstrous as hardly to be

---

1. In the Glorious Revolution of 1688 (so named by the Whigs), Parliament deposed Catholic James II and installed Protestant William and Mary, along with a bill of rights that shifted the balance of power from the monarchy to Parliament.

believed; but the Parliamentary clauses upon which Mr. Burke builds his political church are of the same nature.

The laws of every country must be analogous to some common principle. In England no parent or master, nor all the authority of Parliament, omnipotent as it has called itself, can bind or controul the personal freedom even of an individual beyond the age of twenty-one years. On what ground of right, then, could the Parliament of 1688, or any other Parliament, bind all posterity for ever?

Those who have quitted the world, and those who are not yet arrived at it, are as remote from each other as the utmost stretch of mortal imagination can conceive. What possible obligation, then, can exist between them; what rule or principle can be laid down that of two non-entities, the one out of existence and the other not in, and who never can meet in this world, the one should controul the other to the end of time? * * * It is the nature of man to die, and he will continue to die as long as he continues to be born. But Mr. Burke has set up a sort of political Adam, in whom all posterity are bound for ever; he must, therefore, prove that his Adam possessed such a power, or such a right. * * * It requires but a very small glance of thought to perceive that altho' laws made in one generation often continue in force through succeeding generations, yet that they continue to derive their force from the consent of the living. A law not repealed continues in force, not because it *cannot* be repealed, but because it *is not* repealed; and the non-repealing passes for consent.

[PRINCIPLES, NOT PERSONS]

Mr. Burke shows that he is ignorant of the springs and principles of the French Revolution. It was not against Louis XVI, but against the despotic principles of the government, that the Nation revolted. These principles had not their origin in him, but in the original establishment, many centuries back; and they were become too deeply rooted to be removed, and the Augean stable of parasites and plunderers too abominably filthy to be cleansed,[2] by anything short of a complete and universal Revolution. When it becomes necessary to do a thing, the whole heart and soul should go into the measure, or not attempt it. That crisis was then arrived, and there remained no choice but to act with determined vigour, or not to act at all. The King was known to be the friend of the Nation, and this circumstance was favourable to the enterprise.[3] Perhaps no man bred up in the style of an absolute King, ever possessed a heart so little disposed to the exercise of that species of power as the present King of France. But the principles of the Government itself still remained the same. The Monarch and the Monarchy were distinct and separate things; and it was against the established despotism of the latter, and not against the person or principles of the former, that the revolt commenced, and the Revolution has been carried.

Mr. Burke does not attend to the distinction between *men* and *principles;* and, therefore, he does not see that a revolt may take place against the despotism of the latter, while there lies no charge of despotism against the former.

The natural moderation of Louis XVI contributed nothing to alter the hereditary despotism of the Monarchy. All the tyrannies of former reigns, acted under that hereditary despotism, were still liable to be revived in the hands of a successor. It was

2. One of Hercules' labors was to purge the notoriously filthy stables of King Augeas—hence, a place of entrenched corruption.
3. In the 1770s and 1780s, Louis XVI tried unsuccessfully to initiate some reforms, including moderate taxation of the nobility. After the fall of the Bastille in July 1789, he withdrew his troops, reinstated his reform-minded director of the treasury (ousted by reactionary factions), and outwardly accepted the Revolution.

not the respite of a reign that would satisfy France, enlightened as she then was become. A casual discontinuance of the *practice* of despotism, is not a discontinuance of its *principles*; the former depends on the virtue of the individual who is in immediate possession of the power; the latter, on the virtue and fortitude of the nation. In the case of Charles I and James II of England, the revolt was against the personal despotism of the men;[4] whereas in France, it was against the hereditary despotism of the established government. But men who can consign over the rights of posterity for ever on the authority of a mouldy parchment, like Mr. Burke, are not qualified to judge of this Revolution. It takes in a field too vast for their views to explore, and proceeds with a mightiness of reason they cannot keep pace with.

But there are many points of view in which this Revolution may be considered. When despotism has established itself for ages in a country, as in France, it is not in the person of the King only that it resides. It has the appearance of being so in show, and in nominal authority; but it is not so in practice and in fact. It has its standard everywhere. Every office and department has its despotism, founded upon custom and usage. Every place has its Bastille, and every Bastille its despot.[5] The original hereditary despotism resident in the person of the King, divides and subdivides itself into a thousand shapes and forms, till at last the whole of it is acted by deputation. This was the case in France; and against this species of despotism, proceeding on through an endless labyrinth of office till the source of it is scarcely perceptible, there is no mode of redress. It strengthens itself by assuming the appearance of duty, and tyrannises under the pretence of obeying.

When a man reflects on the condition which France was in from the nature of her Government, he will see other causes for revolt than those which immediately connect themselves with the person or character of Louis XVI. There were, if I may so express it, a thousand despotisms to be reformed in France, which had grown up under the hereditary despotism of the monarchy, and became so rooted as to be in great measure independent of it. Between the Monarchy, the Parliament, and the Church, there was a *rivalship* of despotism; besides the feudal despotism operating locally, and the ministerial despotism operating everywhere. But Mr. Burke, by considering the King as the only possible object of a revolt, speaks as if France was a village, in which everything that passed must be known to its commanding officer, and no oppression could be acted but what he could immediately controul. Mr. Burke might have been in the Bastille his whole life, as well under Louis XVI as Louis XIV,[6] and neither the one nor the other have known that such a man as Mr. Burke existed. The despotic principles of the Government were the same in both reigns, though the dispositions of the men were as remote as tyranny and benevolence.

What Mr. Burke considers as a reproach to the French Revolution (that of bringing it forward under a reign more mild than the preceding ones) is one of its highest honours. The Revolutions that have taken place in other European countries, have been excited by personal hatred. The rage was against the man, and he

4. Charles I, son of James I (successor of Elizabeth I), was unpopular for imposing exorbitant taxes, suspending Parliament, and harshly oppressing religious dissent; defeated in the 1640s Civil War with Parliament, he was beheaded for "high treason and other high crimes" in 1649. The monarchy was restored in 1660, and his Roman Catholic son became King James II in 1685, but was soon forced from office for his attempt to restore absolute monarchy and Catholicism as the state religion. Seven powerful nobles, with the consent of Parliament, invited William III of Orange (grandson of Charles I) to "invade" England to protect its liberties and become joint monarch with Charles's Protestant daughter, Mary; William advanced bloodlessly to London with 15,000 troops, and Parliament proclaimed him and Mary monarchs in 1689.

5. The Bastille was France's infamous prison, holding many political prisoners, mostly without trial; it was the icon of the abuse of power that fomented the Revolution, which began with the storming of the Bastille and the liberation of its prisoners on 14 July 1789.

6. Louis XVI's ancestor (1638–1715), known as the Sun King, a notorious spendthrift, advocate of the divine right of kings, and patron of the arts.

became the victim. But, in the instance of France we see a revolution generated in the rational contemplation of the rights of man, and distinguishing from the beginning between persons and principles.

But Mr. Burke appears to have no idea of principles when he is contemplating Governments. "Ten years ago," says he, "I could have felicitated France on her having a Government, without inquiring what the nature of that Government was, or how it was administered." Is this the language of a rational man? Is it the language of a heart feeling as it ought to feel for the rights and happiness of the human race? On this ground, Mr. Burke must compliment all the Governments in the world, while the victims who suffer under them, whether sold into slavery, or tortured out of existence, are wholly forgotten. It is power, and not principles, that Mr. Burke venerates. * * *

As to the tragic paintings by which Mr. Burke has outraged his own imagination, and seeks to work upon that of his readers, they are very well calculated for theatrical representation, where facts are manufactured for the sake of show, and accommodated to produce, through the weakness of sympathy, a weeping effect. But Mr. Burke should recollect that he is writing history, and not *plays*, and that his readers will expect truth, and not the spouting rant of high-toned exclamation.

When we see a man dramatically lamenting in a publication intended to be believed that *"The age of chivalry is gone! that The glory of Europe is extinguished for ever! that the unbought grace of life (if any one knows what it is), the cheap defence of nations, the nurse of manly sentiment and heroic enterprise is gone!"* and all this because the Quixote age of chivalry nonsense is gone, what opinion can we form of his judgment, or what regard can we pay to his facts?[7] In the rhapsody of his imagination he has discovered a world of windmills, and his sorrows are that there are no Quixotes to attack them. But if the age of Aristocracy, like that of Chivalry, should fall (and they had originally some connection), Mr. Burke, the trumpeter of the order, may continue his parody to the end, and finish with exclaiming: *"Othello's occupation's gone!"*[8]

Notwithstanding Mr. Burke's horrid paintings, when the French Revolution is compared with the Revolutions of other countries, the astonishment will be that it is marked with so few sacrifices; but this astonishment will cease when we reflect that *principles*, and not *persons*, were the meditated objects of destruction. The mind of the nation was acted upon by a higher stimulus than what the consideration of persons could inspire, and sought a higher conquest than could be produced by the downfall of an enemy. Among the few who fell there do not appear to be any that were intentionally singled out. They all of them had their fate in the circumstances of the moment. * * * From his violence and his grief, his silence on some points and his excess on others, it is difficult not to believe that Mr. Burke is sorry, extremely sorry, that arbitrary power, the power of the Pope[9] and the Bastille, are pulled down.

Not one glance of compassion, not one commiserating reflection that I can find throughout his book, has he bestowed on those who lingered out the most wretched of lives, a life without hope in the most miserable of prisons. It is painful to behold a man employing his talents to corrupt himself. Nature has been kinder to Mr. Burke than he is to her. He is not affected by the reality of distress touching his heart, but by the showy resemblance of it striking his imagination. He pities the plumage, but forgets

7. Quoting Burke's *Reflections*, pages 52–53, and alluding to Cervantes' Don Quixote, a country gentleman who, fed on chivalric romances, sets out in search of knightly adventure and winds up tilting at windmills in lieu of real opponents.
8. Othello utters this cry, when, falsely convinced of his wife's infidelity, he feels he has nothing more to live for (*Othello* 3.3.354).
9. Pre-Revolutionary France was Catholic (like Burke's Ireland), and so answerable to the Pope, at least in theory.

the dying bird.[1] Accustomed to kiss the aristocratical hand that hath purloined him from himself, he degenerates into a composition of art, and the genuine soul of nature forsakes him. His hero or his heroine must be a tragedy-victim expiring in show, and not the real prisoner of misery, sliding into death in the silence of a dungeon.

[THE DOCTRINE OF EQUAL RIGHTS]

If the mere name of antiquity is to govern in the affairs of life, the people who are to live an hundred or a thousand years hence, may as well take us for a precedent, as we make a precedent of those who lived an hundred or a thousand years ago. The fact is, that portions of antiquity, by proving everything, establish nothing. It is authority against authority all the way, till we come to the divine origin of the rights of man at the creation. Here our inquiries find a resting-place, and our reason finds a home. If a dispute about the rights of man had arisen at the distance of an hundred years from the creation, it is to this source of authority they must have referred, and it is to this same source of authority that we must now refer.

Though I mean not to touch upon any sectarian principle of religion, yet it may be worth observing, that the genealogy of Christ is traced to Adam. Why then not trace the rights of man to the creation of man? I will answer the question. Because there have been upstart Governments, thrusting themselves between and presumptuously working to *un-make* man.

If any generation of men ever possessed the right of dictating the mode by which the world should be governed for ever, it was the first generation that existed; and if that generation did it not, no succeeding generation can show any authority for doing it, nor can set any up. The illuminating and divine principle of the equal rights of man (for it has its origin from the Maker of man) relates, not only to the living individuals, but to generations of men succeeding each other. Every generation is equal in rights to the generations which preceded it, by the same rule that every individual is born equal in rights with his contemporary.

Every history of the creation, and every traditionary account, whether from the lettered or unlettered world, however they may vary in their opinion or belief of certain particulars, all agree in establishing one point, *the unity of man*; by which I mean that men are all of *one degree*, and consequently that all men are born equal, and with equal natural rights, in the same manner as if posterity had been continued by *creation* instead of *generation*, the latter being only the mode by which the former is carried forward; and consequently every child born into the world must be considered as deriving its existence from God. The world is as new to him as it was to the first man that existed, and his natural right in it is of the same kind.

The Mosaic account of the creation,[2] whether taken as divine authority or merely historical, is fully up to this point, *the unity or equality of man*. The expressions admit of no controversy. "And God said, Let us make man in our own image. In the image of God created he him; male and female created he them." The distinction of sexes is pointed out, but no other distinction is even implied. If this be not divine authority, it is at least historical authority, and shows that the equality of man, so far from being a modern doctrine, is the oldest upon record. * * *

1. The most famous sentence in this tract. Royalty frequently ornamented itself with elaborate plumage (feathers); Paine's point is that Burke is so wrapped up in the disgrace of the royal family that he neglects the misery of the state that sustains it, and which itself is dying from poverty and corruption.
2. Moses (adj. Mosaic) was traditionally thought to be the author of Genesis. Paine's ensuing quotation is patched from Genesis 1.26–27; in Genesis 2, which Milton follows in *Paradise Lost*, God creates man first, and woman second.

It is not among the least of the evils of the present existing Governments in all parts of Europe that man, considered as man, is thrown back to a vast distance from his Maker, and the artificial chasm filled up by a succession of barriers, or sort of turnpike gates, through which he has to pass. I will quote Mr. Burke's catalogue of barriers that he has set up between Man and his Maker. Putting himself in the character of a herald, he says: *We fear God—we look with* AWE *to kings—with affection to Parliaments—with duty to magistrates—with reverence to priests, and with respect to nobility.* Mr. Burke has forgotten to put in "*chivalry.*" He has also forgotten to put in Peter.[3]

The duty of man is not a wilderness of turnpike gates, through which he is to pass by tickets from one to the other. It is plain and simple, and consists but of two points. His duty to God, which every man must feel; and with respect to his neighbour, to do as he would be done by. If those to whom power is delegated do well, they will be respected; if not, they will be despised; and with regard to those to whom no power is delegated, but who assume it, the rational world can know nothing of them.

[THE REPUBLICAN SYSTEM]

When we survey the wretched condition of Man, under the monarchical and hereditary systems of Government, dragged from his home by one power, or driven by another, and impoverished by taxes more than by enemies, it becomes evident that those systems are bad, and that a general Revolution in the principle and construction of Governments is necessary.

What is Government more than the management of the affairs of a Nation? It is not, and from its nature cannot be, the property of any particular man or family, but of the whole community, at whose expence it is supported; and though by force and contrivance it has been usurped into an inheritance, the usurpation cannot alter the right of things. Sovereignty, as a matter of right, appertains to the Nation only, and not to any individual; and a Nation has at all times an inherent, indefeasible right to abolish any form of Government it finds inconvenient, and to establish such as accords with its interest, disposition, and happiness. The romantic and barbarous distinction of men into Kings and subjects, though it may suit the conditions of courtiers, cannot that of citizens; and is exploded by the principle upon which Governments are now founded. Every citizen is a member of the sovereignty, and, as such, can acknowledge no personal subjection: and his obedience can be only to the laws.

* * * In this view of Government, the Republican system, as established by America and France, operates to embrace the whole of a Nation. * * * What we formerly called Revolutions, were little more than a change of persons, or an alteration of local circumstances. They rose and fell like things of course, and had nothing in their existence or their fate that could influence beyond the spot that produced them. But what we now see in the world, from the Revolutions of America and France, are a renovation of the natural order of things, a system of principles as universal as truth and the existence of man, and combining moral with political happiness and national prosperity.

──── ✦✦✦ ────

The Anti-Jacobin, or Weekly Examiner

In thirty-six numbers, November 1797 to July 1798, *The Anti-Jacobin*, edited by William Gifford, defended Pitt's government by brilliantly lampooning any and all signs of radical opposition.

---

3. In popular Christian lore, St. Peter keeps the gates to Heaven, deciding whom to admit.

Avowedly devoted to combating the spread of subversive ideas, George Ellis, John Hookham Frere, George Canning, and their fellows deployed a wit as pointed as it was exuberant against political figures and at writers such as Wordsworth and Charles Lamb suspected of dangerous sympathies. Robert Southey's *The Widow* (1796) offered an irresistible target: Frere and Canning derided its classical Sapphic meter as an "absurdity" in true English verse, even as they denounced Southey's "new topics of invective against the pride of property"—a characteristic juxtaposition of abstract republican philanthropy with Jacobin conduct, real or imagined. Their burlesque, *The Friend of Humanity and the Knife-Grinder*, appeared on 27 November 1797, illustrated by the leading caricaturist of the day, James Gillray, with an instantly recognizable portrait of James Tierney, Member of Parliament and of the reformist society, The Friends of the People. The piece caused a sensation. As late as 1890, an editor could say, "perhaps no lines in the English language have been more effective, or oftener quoted." They endure as a vivid index of the charged climate in which the poems of the Romantics emerged.

from The Anti-Jacobin
The Friend of Humanity and the Knife-Grinder

In the specimen of JACOBIN POETRY which we gave in our last number was developed a principle, perhaps one of the most universally recognised in the Jacobin creed; namely, "that the animadversion of *human law* upon *human actions* is for the most part nothing but *gross oppression;* and that, in all cases of the administration of *criminal justice*, the truly benevolent mind will consider only the *severity of the punishment*, without any reference to the *malignity of the crime*." This principle has of late years been laboured with extraordinary industry, and brought forward in a variety of shapes, for the edification of the public. It has been inculcated in bulky quartos, and illustrated in popular novels. It remained only to fit it with a poetical dress, which had been attempted in the INSCRIPTION for CHEPSTOW CASTLE, and which (we flatter ourselves) was accomplished in that for MRS. BROWNRIGG'S CELL.[1]

Another principle, no less devoutly entertained, and no less sedulously disseminated, is the *natural and eternal warfare of the* POOR *and the* RICH. In those orders and gradations of society, which are the natural result of the original difference of talents and of industry among mankind, the Jacobin sees nothing but a graduated scale of violence and cruelty. He considers every rich man as an oppressor, and every person in a lower situation as the victim of avarice, and the slave of aristocratical insolence and contempt. These truths he declares loudly, not to excite compassion, or to soften the consciousness of superiority in the higher, but for the purpose of aggravating discontent in the inferior orders.

A human being, in the lowest state of penury and distress, is a treasure to the reasoner of this cast. He contemplates, he examines, he turns him in every possible light, with a view of extracting from the variety of his wretchedness new topics of invective against the pride of property. He, indeed (if he is a true Jacobin), refrains from *relieving* the object of his compassionate contemplation; as well knowing that every diminution from the general mass of human misery must proportionably diminish the force of his argument.

---

1. The first issue of the *Anti-Jacobin*, 20 November 1797, parodied Robert Southey's sympathetic *Inscription for the Apartment in Chepstow Castle*, where *Henry Marten, the Regicide, was imprisoned thirty years* with an *Inscription for the Door of the Cell in Newgate, where Mrs. Brownrigg, the "Prentice-cide," was confined previous to her Execution.* Henry Marten was a republican who signed the death warrant of Charles I; he was imprisoned at the Restoration in 1660. Mrs. Brownrigg was infamous for her sadistic treatment of young female apprentices. She was executed for her crimes in 1767.

This principle is treated at large by many authors. It is versified in sonnets and elegies without end. We trace it particularly in a poem by the same author from whom we borrowed our former illustration of the Jacobin doctrine of crimes and punishments. In this poem, the pathos of the matter is not a little relieved by the absurdity of the metre. * * * The learned reader will perceive that the metre is SAPPHIC, and affords a fine opportunity for his *scanning* and *proving*, if he has not forgotten them.

The Widow
Sapphics

Cold was the night wind; drifting fast the snows fell;
Wide were the downs, and shelterless and naked;
When a poor wand'rer struggled on her journey,
      Weary and way-sore.

5   Drear were the downs, more dreary her reflections;
Cold was the night wind, colder was her bosom:
She had no home, the world was all before her,[2]
      She had no shelter.

Fast o'er the heath a chariot rattled by her:
10   "Pity me!" feebly cried the poor night wanderer.
"Pity me, strangers! lest with cold and hunger
      Here I should perish.

Once I had friends—but they have all forsook me!
Once I had parents—they are now in heaven!
15   I had a home once—I had once a husband—
      Pity me, strangers!

I had a home once—I had once a husband—
I am a widow, poor and broken-hearted!"
Loud blew the wind, unheard was her complaining;
20   On drove the chariot.

Then on the snow she laid her down to rest her;
She heard a horseman: "Pity me!" she groaned out.
Loud was the wind, unheard was her complaining;
      On went the horseman.

25   Worn out with anguish, toil, and cold and hunger,
Down sunk the wanderer; sleep had seized her senses:
There did the traveller find her in the morning—
      God had released her.

                                        —*Robert Southey* [1796]

We proceed to give our IMITATION, which is of the *Amoeboean* or *Collocutory* kind.[3]

---

2. See Milton, *Paradise Lost* 12.646–47, referring to Adam and Eve's prospects after their expulsion from Eden.

3. A poem composed in strophes with alternating speakers; a dialogue.

Sapphics
The Friend of Humanity and the Knife-Grinder

James Gillray, 1797.

━━┥≡◈≡┝━━

William Blake

1757–1827

It was from William Blake's *Marriage of Heaven and Hell* that a sensationally transgressive rock band of the 1960s, The Doors, took their name:

> If the doors of perception were cleansed
> every thing would appear to man as it is: In-
> -finite.

But unlike The Doors, Blake needed no pharmaceutical assistance in cleansing his vision. His eccentricity and imaginative intensity, which seemed like madness to more than a few contemporaries, emerged from a childhood punctuated by such events as beholding God's face pressed against his window, seeing angels among the haystacks, and being visited by the Old Testament prophet Ezekiel. When his favorite brother died in 1787, Blake claimed that he saw his "released spirit ascend heavenwards, clapping its hand for joy." Soon after, he reports, this spirit visited him with a critical revelation of the method of "Illuminated Printing" that he would use in his major poetical works.

Rebellious, unconventional, fiercely idealistic, Blake became a celebrity in modern counterculture—Allen Ginsberg and many of the Beat poets of the 1950s and 1960s cited him as a major influence. But for a good part of the nineteenth century, he was known only to a coterie. He did not support himself as a poet but got by on patronage and commissions for engraving and painting. His projects included the Book of Job and other scenes from the Bible; Chaucer's Canterbury Pilgrims; characters in Spenser's *Faerie Queene*; Milton's *L'Allegro*, *Il Penseroso*, *Paradise Lost*, and *Paradise Regained*; Gray's *The Bard*; Young's *Night Thoughts*; and Blair's *The Grave*. His obscurity as a poet was due in part to the difficulty of his work after the mid-1790s but chiefly to the very limited issue of his books, a consequence of the painstaking and time-consuming process of "Illuminated Printing." He hoped to reach a wider audience with a private exhibition of his illustrations in 1809, but his adventurous originality, coupled with his cantankerous and combative personality, left him ignored, except by one of the radical journals, *The Examiner*, which called him a lunatic in a vicious review. At the time of his death, he was impoverished and almost entirely unknown except to a small group of younger painters. Only in 1863 did interest begin to grow, thanks to Alexander Gilchrist's biography, *The Life of William Blake: Pictor Ignotus*, its second volume a selection of poems edited by Dante Gabriel Rossetti. The revival was fanned by the enthusiasm of the Pre-Raphaelite circle and subsequent essays by Algernon Charles Swinburne, William Michael Rossetti (Dante Gabriel's brother), and William Butler Yeats.

Although Blake had no formal education, he was an avid reader, immersing himself in English poetry, the Bible, and works of mysticism and philosophy, as well as a study of Greek, Latin, and Hebrew. With precocious talent as a sketcher, he hoped to become a painter, but his father could not afford the tuition, and so apprenticed him at age fourteen as an engraver. During this seven-year term, Blake found time to write the poems gathered into his first publication, *Poetical Sketches* (1783), his only unilluminated volume. The later illuminated books were not products of the letter-press, but of a process of hand-etching designs onto copper plates, using these plates to ink-print pages that were then individually hand-colored and hand-bound into volumes. So labor-intensive a method was not adaptable to any production of quantity: there are, for instance, only twenty-seven known copies of *Songs of Innocence and of Experience* and only nine of *The Marriage of Heaven and Hell*. Yet Blake's commitment to involving his verbal text with pictures and pictorial embellishments created books of extraordinary beauty and an innovative "composite art" of word and image. In this art, the script conveys meaning—flowing versus starkly blocked letters, for instance—and the pictorial elements are significant, sometimes illustrating, sometimes adding another perspective or an ironic comment on the verbal text, sometimes even presenting contradictory information. Our selection of plates shows these dynamics, and our transcriptions of the poetry in all cases follow the linear arrangement on the plates.

Blake's popularity is based chiefly on his earlier and most accessible works from the 1790s. *Songs of Innocence and of Experience* (1789–1794) was much admired in his own day by Samuel Taylor Coleridge, Charles Lamb, and William Wordsworth (even though Blake deemed him too enamored of "Natural Piety"—faith in the natural world as spiritual and poetic resource: "I see in Wordsworth the Natural man rising up against the Spiritual Man Continually, & then he is No Poet but a heathen Philosopher at Enmity against all true Poetry or Inspiration"). *Songs* is notable not only for a concern with the different ways children and adults see and understand their world (a theme that would occupy Wordsworth, too) but also for its acid critiques of social evils, political injustice, and their agents, the triumvirate of "God & his Priest & King" (in the voice of a too-experienced chimney sweeper). Reflecting Blake's familiarity with the range of freethinking contemporary biblical commentary that became the "Higher Criticism," *The Marriage of Heaven and Hell* (1790) brings visionary energy and poetic extravagance to a trenchant argument for imaginative freedom over psychological inhibition, conventional morality, and institutionalized authority. It is also one of the first Romantic-era rethinkings of Milton's *Paradise Lost*, the archetypal story of right and wrong, sin and punishment. Blake takes as an important effect a common reaction (including even Alexander Pope): that Satan and the scenes in Hell provide far more exciting and imaginatively powerful reading than the Angels and God's court in Heaven. "The reason Milton wrote in fetters when / he wrote of Angels & God, and at liberty when of / Devils & Hell," proposes Blake's "Voice of the Devil," is "because he was a true Poet and / of the Devils party without knowing it." Unfettering himself from Milton's moral machinery with this outrageously subversive commentary, Blake presents devils who are a lot more fun than his angels. The *Proverbs of Hell* offer their wisdom with a kind of transgressive glee, sarcastic levity, and diabolical wit that anticipates the sly aphorisms of Oscar Wilde and the exuberance of American Beat poetry.

These works and others of this decade emerge from Blake's involvement with the London circle of bookseller Joseph Johnson, including Mary Wollstonecraft, Tom Paine, and Dr. Joseph Priestley—a radical political group of artists and religious dissenters joined by their sociopolitical criticism and a general support of the French Revolution. Like many of this group, Blake read the revolutions in America and France as heralds of a new millennium, and thus inspired, he produced a sequence of (sometimes abstruse) visionary works celebrating the overthrow of tyranny: *The French Revolution* (1791), *America: A Prophecy* (1793), *Europe: A Prophecy* (1794), and *The Book of Urizen* (1794). His later "prophetic" works—*Milton* (1804) and *Jerusalem* (1804–1820)—develop some of these themes with an increasingly esoteric vocabulary and elaborate personal mythology, and are notoriously difficult to read, although they contain passages of impressive energy and imagination.

An emblematic episode from 1803 suggests the real-life consequences of Blake's uncompromising visions. When a drunken dragoon trespassed onto his cottage garden and refused to leave, Blake vigorously ejected him. In consequence, he was arrested on a spiteful accusation of seditious threats against the crown; with England at war with France, this was a capital offense for which the penalty could have been death. Blake's trial ended in an acquittal loudly applauded by the spectators, but the ordeal exacerbated his memory of having been arrested in 1780 under the suspicion of being a spy for France while on a riverboat sketching excursion, and it crystallized his anger at state authority. Energizing all Blake's works is his commitment to imagination and the potency of visionary idealism, sharpened by resistance to psychological, ideological, institutional, and political tyrannies.

[Plate 1]

The voice of one crying in the
Wilderness[1]

[Plate 2]

All Religions Are One[2]

[Plate 3]

The Argument
As the true meth-
-od of knowledge
is experiment,
the true faculty
of knowing must
be the faculty which
experiences. This
faculty I treat of.

[Plate 4]

PRINCIPLE 1ˢᵗ
That the Poetic Genius is
the true Man, and that
the body or outward form
of Man is derived from the
Poetic Genius. Likewise
that the forms of all things
are derived from their
Genius, which by the
Ancients was calld an
Angel & Spirit & Demon.

[Plate 5]

PRINCIPLE 2ᵈ
As all men are alike in
outward form, So (and
with the same infinite
variety) all are alike in
the Poetic Genius

[Plate 6]

PRINCIPLE 3ᵈ
No man can think
write or speak from his
heart, but he must intend
truth. Thus all sects of
Philosophy are from the
Poetic Genius, adapted
to the weaknesses of
every individual.

1. The prophecy of Isaiah 40.3, which Matthew 3.3 takes to refer to John the Baptist; Blake places himself in this line of visionary authority.
2. Blake asserts that religious sects are only various forms of a central truth, divined by the poet's imagination. He did not subscribe his name to the potentially heretical *All Religions Are One* but presents its argument and principles as if from the voice of a biblical prophet speaking to the modern age.

[Plate 7]

PRINCIPLE 4th

As none by trave
ling over known
lands can find out
the unknown, So,
from already ac
quired knowledge,
Man could not ac
quire more; there
fore an universal
Poetic Genius exists.

[Plate 8]

PRINCIPLE 5th

The Religions of all Nat-
-ions are derived from each
Nations different reception
of the Poetic Genius which
is every where call'd the Spi
rit of Prophecy

[Plate 9]

PRINCIPLE 6th

The Jewish & Chris-
tian Testaments are
An original derivati-
-on from the Poetic Ge-
nius: this is necessary
from the confined natu
re of bodily sensation

[Plate 10]

PRINCIPLE 7th

As all men are alike
(tho' infinitely vari
ous) So all Religions:
& as all similars have
one source,
    The true Man is the
source, he being the
Poetic Genius

SONGS OF INNOCENCE AND OF EXPERIENCE   Blake's most popular work appeared in two phases. In 1789 he published *Songs of Innocence*; five years later he bound these poems with a set of new poems in a volume titled *Songs of Innocence and of Experience Shewing the two contrary States of the Human Soul.* "Innocence" and "Experience" are definitions of consciousness that re-think Milton's existential-mythic states of "Paradise" and the "Fall." Blake's categories are modes of perception that tend to coordinate with a chronological story that would become standard in Romanticism: childhood is a time and a state of protected "innocence," but it is a qualified inno-cence, not immune to the fallen world and its institutions. This world sometimes impinges on childhood itself, and in any event becomes known through "experience," a state of being marked by the loss of childhood vitality, by fear and inhibition, by social and political corruption, and by the manifold oppression of Church, State, and the ruling classes. The volume's "Contrary States" are sometimes signaled by patently repeated or contrasted titles: in *Innocence, Infant Joy,* in *Expe-rience, Infant Sorrow*; in *Innocence, The Lamb*, in *Experience, The Fly* and *The Tyger.*

These contraries are not constructed as simple oppositions, however. Unlike Milton's narrative of the Fall from Paradise, Blake shows either state of soul possible at any moment. Some children, even infants, have already lost their innocence through a soiling contact with the world; some adults, particularly joyously visionary poets, seem able to retain a kind of innocent vitality even as they enter the world of experience. Moreover, the values of "Innocence" and "Experience" are themselves complex. At times, the innocent state of soul reflects a primary, untainted vitality of imagination; but at other times, Blake, like Mary Wollstonecraft, implicates innocence with dangerous ignorance and vulnerability to oppression. Thus, in their rhetorical structure, the poems may present an innocent speaker against dark ironies that a more experienced reader, alert to social and political evil, will grasp. But just as trickily, experience can also define an imagination self-darkened by its own "mind-forg'd manacles." Blake's point is not that children are pure and adults fallen, or that children are naive and adults perspicacious. The contrary possibilities coexist, with different plays and shades of emphasis in different poems. And these values are often further complicated by the ambiguous significance of the illustrations that accompany and often frame the poems' texts. Sometimes these illustrations sustain the speaker's tone and point of view (e.g., *The Lamb*), and sometimes (e.g., *The Little Black Boy*) they offer an ironic counter-commentary.

from SONGS OF INNOCENCE AND OF EXPERIENCE
SHEWING THE TWO CONTRARY STATES OF THE HUMAN SOUL
from Songs of Innocence
Introduction

Piping down the valleys wild
Piping songs of pleasant glee
On a cloud I saw a child
And he laughing said to me.

5   Pipe a song about a Lamb:
So I piped with merry chear,
Piper, pipe that song again—
So I piped, he wept to hear.

Drop thy pipe thy happy pipe
10 Sing thy songs of happy chear,
So I sang the same again
While he wept with joy to hear

Piper sit thee down and write
In a book that all may read—
15 So he vanish'd from my sight
And I pluck'd a hollow reed

And I made a rural pen,
And I stain'd the water clear,
And I wrote my happy songs,
20 Every child may joy to hear

The Ecchoing Green

The Sun does arise,
And make happy the skies.
The merry bells ring

5
      To welcome the Spring.
The sky-lark and thrush,
The birds of the bush,
Sing louder around,
To the bells chearful sound
While our sports shall be seen
10
On the Ecchoing Green.

Old John with white hair
Does laugh away care,
Sitting under the oak,
Among the old folk,
15
They laugh at our play,
And soon they all say,
Such such were the joys
When we all girls & boys,
In our youth time were seen,
20
On the Ecchoing Green.

Till the little ones weary
No more can be merry
The sun does descend,
And our sports have an end:
25
Round the laps of their mothers
Many sisters and brothers,
Like birds in their nest,
Are ready for rest:
And sport no more seen,
30
On the darkening Green.

The Lamb

    Little Lamb who made thee
    Dost thou know who made thee
Gave thee life & bid thee feed,
By the stream & o'er the mead;
5
Gave thee clothing of delight,
Softest clothing wooly bright;
Gave thee such a tender voice,
Making all the vales rejoice:
    Little Lamb who made thee
10
    Dost thou know who made thee

    Little Lamb, I'll tell thee.
    Little Lamb, I'll tell thee;
He is called by thy name
For he calls himself a Lamb:
15
He is meek & he is mild,
He became a little child:
I a child & thou a lamb,
We are called by his name.
    Little Lamb God bless thee
20
    Little Lamb God bless thee

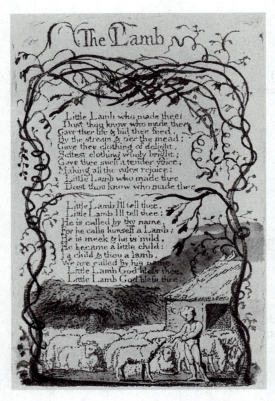

William Blake, *The Lamb*, from *Songs of Innocence*. Blake pictures the boy in a natural state of nakedness among the lambs, all embraced by twining branches.

The Little Black Boy[1]

My mother bore me in the southern wild,
And I am black, but O! my soul is white
White as an angel is the English child:
But I am black as if bereav'd of light.

5   My mother taught me underneath a tree
And sitting down before the heat of day,
She took me on her lap and kissed me,
And, pointing to the east, began to say.

Look on the rising sun: there God does live
10   And gives his light and gives his heat away.
And flowers and trees and beasts and men recieve
Comfort in morning joy in the noon day.

And we are put on earth a little space
That we may learn to bear the beams of love.
15   And these black bodies and this sun-burnt face
Is but a cloud, and like a shady grove.

[handwritten annotations:] representative of all those in servitude

learns about God in nature, not in institution of church

innocence — he believes trusts his mothers words because they are hers

1. See Color Plates 6 and 7. In "Copy B," Blake tints the black boy's skin as light as the English boy's; in others, he colors them differently. While the second plate shows both boys sheltered by the tree and welcomed by Christ, it also puts the black boy outside the inner cirle formed by the curve of Christ's body and the praying English boy. He is not part of this configuration of prayer, but rather a witness to it, stroking the hair of the English boy who has no regard for him.

For when our souls have learn'd the heat to bear
The cloud will vanish we shall hear his voice
Saying: come out from the grove, my love & care,
20   And round my golden tent like lambs rejoice.

Thus did my mother say, and kissed me.
And thus I say to little English boy.
When I from black and he from white cloud free,
And round the tent of God like lambs we joy:

25   Ill shade him from the heat till he can bear,
To lean in joy upon our fathers knee
And then Ill stand and stroke his silver hair,
And be like him and he will then love me.

The Chimney Sweeper[1]

When my mother died I was very young
And my father sold me while yet my tongue
Could scarcely cry weep weep weep weep.[2]
So your chimneys I sweep & in soot I sleep.

5   Theres little Tom Dacre, who cried when his head
That curl'd like a lambs back, was shav'd, so I said:
Hush Tom never mind it, for when your head's bare
You know that the soot cannot spoil your white hair

And so he was quiet, & that very night,
10   As Tom was a sleeping he had such a sight,
That thousands of sweepers Dick, Joe, Ned & Jack
Were all of them lock'd up in coffins of black,

And by came an Angel who had a bright key,
And he open'd the coffins & set them all free.
15   Then down a green plain leaping laughing they run
And wash in a river and shine in the Sun.

Then naked & white, all their bags left behind,
They rise upon clouds, and sport in the wind
And the Angel told Tom if he'd be a good boy,
20   He'd have God for his father & never want joy

And so Tom awoke and we rose in the dark
And got with our bags & our brushes to work.
Tho' the morning was cold, Tom was happy & warm
So if all do their duty they need not fear harm.[3]

1. Chimney-sweeps were mostly young boys, whose impoverished parents sold them into the business, or who were orphans, outcasts, or illegitimate children with no other means of living. It was filthy, health-ruining labor, aggravated by overwork and inadequate clothing, food, and shelter. Among the hazards were burns, permanently blackened skin, deformed legs, black lung disease, and cancer of the scrotum. Protective legislation passed in 1788 was never enforced. Blake's outrage at this exploitation also sounds in "London." Admiring the poem, Charles Lamb sent it to James Montgomery (a topical poet and radical-press editor) for inclusion in *The Chimney-Sweeper's Friend, and Climbing Boy's Album* (1824), which he was assembling for the Society for Ameliorating the Condition of Infant Chimney-Sweepers.
2. With a relevant pun, the child's lisping street cry advertising his trade, "sweep! sweep!"
3. A typical conduct homily.

The Divine Image

To Mercy Pity Peace and Love,
All pray in their distress:
And to these virtues of delight
Return their thankfulness.

5 For Mercy Pity Peace and Love
Is God our father dear:
And Mercy Pity Peace and Love,
Is Man his child and care.

For Mercy has a human heart
10 Pity, a human face:
And Love, the human form divine,
And Peace, the human dress.

Then every man, of every clime
That prays in his distress,
15 Prays to the human form divine
Love Mercy Pity Peace.

And all must love the human form,
In heathen, turk or jew.
Where Mercy, Love & Pity dwell,
20 There God is dwelling too.

HOLY THURSDAY[1]

Twas on a Holy Thursday their innocent faces clean
The children walking two & two in red & blue & green[2]
Grey headed beadles[3] walkd before with wands as white as snow
Till into the high dome of Pauls they like Thames waters flow

5 O what a multitude they seemd these flowers of London town
Seated in companies they sit with radiance all their own
The hum of multitudes was there but multitudes of lambs
Thousands of little boys & girls raising their innocent hands

Now like a mighty wind they raise to heaven the voice of song
10 Or like harmonious thunderings the seats of heaven among
Beneath them sit the aged men wise guardians of the poor
Then cherish pity lest you drive an angel from your door[4]

---

1. One of the poems with a companion in *Experience* (see page 88). Holy Thursday in the calendar of England's official state religion celebrated the Ascension; it was customary to conduct the children in London's charity schools, many of them orphans, to services at St. Paul's, the chief Anglican cathedral.
2. The colors denote different school uniforms.

3. Minor officials charged with ushering and preserving order at services.
4. A conduct homily, perhaps Hebrews 13.1–2: "Let brotherly love continue. Be not forgetful to entertain strangers: for thereby some have entertained angels unawares."

Nurse's Song

When the voices of children are heard on the green
And laughing is heard on the hill,
My heart is at rest within my breast
And everything else is still

5   Then come home my children the sun is gone down
And the dews of night arise
Come come leave off play, and let us away
Till the morning appears in the skies

No no let us play, for it is yet day
10   And we cannot go to sleep
Besides in the sky the little birds fly
And the hills are all coverd with sheep

Well well go & play till the light fades away
And then go home to bed
15   The little ones leaped & shouted & laugh'd
And all the hills ecchoed

Infant Joy

I have no name.
I am but two days old—
What shall I call thee?
I happy am
5   Joy is my name—
Sweet joy befall thee!

Pretty joy!
Sweet joy but two days old.
Sweet joy I call thee:
10   Thou dost smile,
I sing the while,
Sweet joy befall thee

❧

COMPANION READING

Charles Lamb: from *The Praise of Chimney-Sweepers*[1]

I like to meet a sweep; understand me,—not a grown sweeper, (old chimney-sweepers are by no means attractive,) but one of those tender novices, blooming through their first nigritude, the maternal washings not quite effaced from the cheek: such as come forth with the dawn, or somewhat earlier, with their little professional notes sounding like the *peep peep* of a young sparrow; or liker to the matin lark should I pronounce them, in their aërial ascents not seldom anticipating the sun-rise?

    I have a kindly yearning toward these dim specks—poor blots—innocent blacknesses.

---

1. Published in *London Magazine*, May 1822, under the pseudonym "Elia." For more by Lamb, see listing under William Wordsworth (page 231).

I reverence these young Africans of our own growth,—these almost clergy imps, who sport their cloth without assumption; and from their little pulpits, (the tops of chimneys,) in the nipping air of a December morning, preach a lesson of patience to mankind.

When a child, what a mysterious pleasure it was to witness their operation! to see a chit no bigger than one's-self, enter, one knew not by what process, into what seemed the *fauces Averni*,[2]—to pursue him in imagination, as he went sounding on through so many dark stifling caverns, horrid shades!—to shudder with the idea that "now, surely, he must be lost for ever!"—to revive at hearing his feeble shout of discovered day-light—and then (O fulness of delight!) running out of doors, to come just in time to see the sable phenomenon emerge in safety, the brandished weapon of his art victorious like some flag waved over a conquered citadel! I seem to remember having been told that a bad sweep was once left in a stack with his brush, to indicate which way the wind blew. It was an awful spectacle certainly; not much unlike the old stage direction in Macbeth, where the "Apparition of a child crowned, with a tree in his hand, rises."[3]

Reader, if thou meetest one of these small gentry in thy early rambles, it is good to give him a penny. It is better to give him twopence. If it be starving weather, and to the proper troubles of his hard occupation a pair of kibed[4] heels (no unusual accompaniment) be superadded, the demand on thy humanity will surely rise to a tester.[5] * * *

In one of the state-beds at Arundel Castle,[6] a few years since, under a ducal canopy, (that seat of the Howards is an object of curiosity to visitors, chiefly for its beds, in which the late duke was especially a connoisseur,) encircled with curtains of delicatest crimson, with starry coronets inwoven, folded between a pair of sheets whiter and softer than the lap where Venus lulled Ascanius,[7] was discovered by chance, after all methods of search had failed, at noon-day, fast asleep, a lost chimney-sweeper. The little creature, having somehow confounded his passage among the intricacies of those lordly chimneys, by some unknown aperture had alighted upon this magnificent chamber; and, tired with his tedious explorations, was unable to resist the delicious invitement to repose, which he there saw exhibited; so creeping between the sheets very quietly, laid his black head upon the pillow, and slept like a young Howard.

Such is the account given to the visitors at the Castle. But I cannot help seeming to perceive a confirmation of what I had just hinted at in this story. A high instinct was at work in the case, or I am mistaken. Is it probable that a poor child of that description, with whatever weariness he might be visited, would have ventured, under such a penalty as he would be taught to expect, to uncover the sheets of a Duke's bed, and deliberately to lay himself down between them, when the rug, or the carpet, presented an obvious couch still far above his pretensions? Is this probable, I would ask, if the great power of nature, which I contend for, had not been manifested within him, prompting to the adventure? Doubtless this young nobleman (for such my mind misgives me that he must be) was allured by some memory, not amounting to full consciousness, of his condition in infancy, when he was used to be lapped by his mother, or his nurse, in just such sheets as he there found, into which he was now

---

2. The Jaws of Avernus (a phrase from Vergil's *Aeneid*, 6.201); Lake Avernus, near Naples, was thought to lead to the underworld.

3. Cf. *Macbeth* 4.1; the crowned child is a sign that a line other than childless Macbeth's will become Scotland's kings.

4. Ulcerated and inflamed from exposure to the cold.

5. Sixpence.

6. Home of the Howard family, Dukes of Norfolk.

7. Aeneas's young son (*Aeneid* bk. 1) who, protected by Venus, escaped with his father from burning Troy.

but creeping back as into his proper *incunabula* [cradle clothes] and resting-place. By no other theory than by this sentiment of a pre-existent state (as I may call it), can I explain a deed so venturous, and indeed upon any other system, so indecorous, in this tender but unseasonable sleeper.

My pleasant friend Jem White[8] was so impressed with a belief of metamorphoses like this frequently taking place, that in some sort to reverse the wrongs of fortune in these poor changelings, he instituted an annual feast of chimney-sweepers, at which it was his pleasure to officiate as host and waiter. * * * O it was a pleasure to see the sable younkers lick in the unctuous meat, with *his* more unctuous sayings—how he would fit the tit-bits to the puny mouths, reserving the lengthier links for the seniors—how he would intercept a morsel even in the jaws of some young desperado, declaring it "must to the pan again to be browned, for it was not fit for a gentleman's eating"—how he would recommend this slice of white bread, or that piece of kissing-crust,[9] to a tender juvenile, advising them all to have a care of cracking their teeth, which were their best patrimony,—how genteelly he would deal about the small ale, as if it were wine, naming the brewer, and protesting, if it were not good, he should lose their custom; with a special recommendation to wipe the lip before drinking. Then we had our toasts—"The King,"—"the Cloth,"—which, whether they understood or not, was equally diverting and flattering;—and for a crowning sentiment, which never failed, "May the Brush supersede the Laurel!" All these, and fifty other fancies, which were rather felt than comprehended by his guests, would he utter, standing upon tables, and prefacing every sentiment with—"Gentlemen, give me leave to propose so and so," which was a prodigious comfort to those young orphans; every now and then stuffing into his mouth (for it did not do to be squeamish on these occasions) indiscriminate pieces of those reeking sausages, which pleased them mightily, and was the savouriest part, you may believe, of the entertainment.

> Golden lads and lasses must,
> As chimney-sweepers, come to dust.[1]

James White is extinct, and with him these suppers have long ceased. He carried away with him half the fun of the world when he died—of my world at least. His old clients look for him among the pens; and missing him, reproach the altered feast of St. Bartholomew, and the glory of Smithfield departed for ever.

from *Songs of Experience*

Introduction.

> Hear the voice of the Bard!
> Who Present, Past, & Future sees
> Whose ears have heard,
> The Holy Word,[1]
> That walk'd among the ancient trees.

5

---

8. James White, Lamb's schoolmate at Christ's Hospital, a London school for orphans and poor children, also attended by Coleridge and Leigh Hunt.
9. Overhanging crust that touches, or kisses, the crust of another loaf of bread during baking.
1. A couplet from a song in Shakespeare's *Cymbeline* (4.2.262–63); "dust" is both literal for the chimney-sweepers' soot and metaphorical for the return of the body after death to elemental earth.
1. Fallen Adam and Eve (the first lapsed souls) "heard the voice of the Lord God walking in the garden in the cool of the day" and "hid themselves from the presence of the Lord God amongst the trees of the garden" (Genesis 3.8).

Calling the lapsed Soul
And weeping in the evening dew:
That might controll
The starry pole:[2]
10   And fallen fallen light renew!

O Earth O Earth return![3]
Arise from out the dewy grass:
Night is worn.
And the morn
15   Rises from the slumberous mass.

Turn away no more
Why wilt thou turn away
The starry floor
The watry shore
20   Is givn thee till the break of day.

EARTH'S *Answer*[1]

Earth rais'd up her head.
From the darkness dread & drear.
Her light fled:
Stony dread!
5   And her locks cover'd with grey despair.

Prison'd on watry shore
Starry Jealousy does keep my den
Cold and hoar
Weeping o'er
10   I hear the Father of the ancient men.[2]

Selfish father of men
Cruel jealous selfish fear
Can delight
Chain'd in night
15   The virgins of youth and morning bear

Does spring hide its joy
When buds and blossoms grow?
Does the sower?
Sow by night?
20   Or the plowman in darkness plow?

Break this heavy chain.
That does freeze my bones around
Selfish! vain!
Eternal bane!
25   That free Love with bondage bound

---

2. The star above the North Pole (the North Star), its fixed
position making it a symbol of steadfastness and a focus for
navigation; or a term for the entire celestial order.
3. God exhorts his erring people: "O Earth, earth, earth,
hear the word of the Lord" (Jeremiah 22.29). Blake's
placement of "return" at the turn of the verse line is a
poet's pun (*versus* in Latin means *turn*), replayed in *turn*

in lines 16 and 17.
1. Blake's plate design surrounds and penetrates the text
with sinewy plant stems, which along the bottom turn
into a prone serpent, its head slightly raised, with an open
mouth and flickering tongue. One effect is to suggest that
"Earth's answer" comes from this tongue.
2. On some plates "Father" is "father."

William Blake, *The Fly*, from *Songs of Experience*. The activities depicted seem "innocent": a girl bats a shuttlecock; a nurse guides a boy's early steps. But the poem-text provokes a view of the girl as a potential fly-swatter, and, in another frame of reference, of both little ones as analogues to the "little fly." Blake's plate makes the order of the stanzas ambiguous: should we read down or across?

THE FLY

Little Fly
Thy summer's play,
My thoughtless hand
Has brush'd away.[1]

Am not I
A fly like thee?
Or art not thou
A man like me?

For I dance
And drink & sing:
Till some blind hand
Shall brush my wing.

If thought is life
And strength & breath:[2]
And the want
Of thought is death;

Then am I
A happy fly,
If I live,
Or if I die.

---

1. Cf. the blinded Gloucester's bitterly rueful comment in *King Lear*: "As flies to wanton boys, are we to th' gods, / They kill us for their sport" (4.1.36–37).

2. Cf. Descartes' famous statement: "I think, therefore I am."

The CLOD & the PEBBLE

Love seeketh not Itself to please,
Nor for itself hath any care;
But for another gives its ease,
And builds a Heaven in Hells despair.[1]

5   So sung a little Clod of Clay
       Trodden with the cattles feet:
       But a Pebble of the brook,
       Warbled out these metres meet.

Love seeketh only Self to please
10   To bind another to Its delight:
Joys in anothers loss of ease,
And builds a Hell in Heavens despite.[2]

HOLY THURSDAY[1]

Is this a holy thing to see,
In a rich and fruitful land
Babes reducd to misery
Fed with cold and usurous hand?

5   Is that trembling cry a song?
Can it be a song of joy?
And so many children poor?
It is a land of poverty!

And their sun does never shine,
10   And their fields are bleak & bare,
And their ways are fill'd with thorns
It is eternal winter there.

For where-e'er the sun does shine,
And where-e'er the rain does fall:
15   Babe can never hunger there,
Nor poverty the mind appall.

The Tyger[1]

Tyger Tyger, burning bright,
In the forests of the night;[2]
What immortal hand or eye,
Could frame thy fearful symmetry?

---

1. Cf. I Corinthians 13.4: "Charity suffereth long, and is kind; charity envieth not; charity vaunteth not itself, is not puffed up."
2. Cf. Satan's rebellious declaration in *Paradise Lost:* "The mind is its own place, and in itself / Can make a Heaven of Hell, a Hell of Heaven" (1.254–55).

1. See *Holy Thursday* in *Songs of Innocence*, page 82.
1. See Color Plate 8.
2. Not just a time of day but a metaphysical location, characterized by forest mazes—the terrain that conducts to Hell in Dante's *Inferno*. Cf. "midnight streets" in *London*, line 13.

5 In what distant deeps or skies,
Burnt the fire of thine eyes?
On what wings dare he aspire?[3]
What the hand dare sieze the fire?

And what shoulder & what art,
10 Could twist the sinews of thy heart?
And when thy heart began to beat,
What dread hand? & what dread feet?[4]

What the hammer? what the chain,
In what furnace was thy brain?
15 What the anvil? what dread grasp,
Dare its deadly terrors clasp!

When the stars threw down their spears
And water'd heaven with their tears:[5]
Did he smile his work to see?[6]
20 Did he who made the Lamb make thee?[7]

Tyger Tyger burning bright,
In the forests of the night:
What immortal hand or eye,
Dare frame thy fearful symmetry?

The Chimney Sweeper[1]

A little black thing among the snow:
Crying weep, weep, in notes of woe!
Where are thy father & mother? say?
They are both gone up to the church to pray.

5 Because I was happy upon the heath
And smil'd among the winters snow:
They clothed me in the clothes of death,
And taught me to sing the notes of woe.

And because I am happy & dance & sing,
10 They think they have done me no injury:
And are gone to praise God & his Priest & King
Who make up a heaven of our misery.[2]

---

3. Icarus, with his father Dedalus, fashioned wings of feathers and wax to escape from prison. Icarus became enchanted with flight and, ignoring his father's cautions, soared too close to the sun; the wax melted and he fell to his death in the sea.
4. One engraving has, "What dread hand Formd thy dread feet?"
5. In the war in Heaven, *Paradise Lost* (bk. 6), Satan, rebelling against God's authority, is defeated by the Son and driven down to Hell. Blake's verb leaves it undecidable whether the stars "threw down their spears" in des-

perate surrender or in defiance.
6. In a notebook draft, Blake wrote "did he laugh his work to see."
7. An allusion to Jesus, "The Lamb of God" (John 1.29 and 1.36) and, indirectly, to the poem in *Songs of Innocence*, with Blake as the maker.
1. See "The Chimney Sweeper" in *Songs of Innocence*, page 81.
2. In both senses: construct their happiness from the elements of our misery; create an illusion of heavenly will in our misery.

William Blake, *The Chimney Sweeper*, from *Songs of Experience*. The contrasting colors of soot-burdened sweep and snow storm also involve a moral recognition: in the adverse winter world where effective home heating requires clean chimneys, the warm homes are closed to the sweep.

The SICK ROSE[1]

O Rose thou art sick.
The invisible worm,
That flies in the night
In the howling storm:

5 Has found out thy bed
Of crimson joy:
And his dark secret love
Does thy life destroy.

AH! SUN-FLOWER[1]

Ah Sun-flower! weary of time,
Who countest the steps of the Sun:
Seeking after that sweet golden clime
Where the travellers journey is done

5 Where the Youth pined away with desire,
And the pale Virgin shrouded in snow:
Arise from their graves and aspire
Where my Sun-flower wishes to go.

1. See Color Plate 9.
1. In Ovid's *Metamorphoses* (4.192), a nymph spurned by Apollo, the sun god, so pined for him that she turned into a sunflower. Blake personifies the sunflower as a heliotrope—a plant that turns to follow the sun.

The GARDEN of LOVE

I went to the Garden of Love.
And saw what I never had seen:
A Chapel was built in the midst,
Where I used to play on the green.

5   And the gates of this Chapel were shut,
And Thou shalt not, writ over the door;[1]
So I turnd to the Garden of Love,
That so many sweet flowers bore.

And I saw it was filled with graves,
10   And tomb-stones where flowers should be:
And Priests in black gowns, were walking their rounds,
And binding with briars, my joys & desires.[2]

LONDON

lonely / no purpose – whole city too

I wander thro' each charter'd street,[1]
Near where the charter'd Thames does flow
And mark in every face I meet
Marks of weakness, marks of woe.

woe, sadness, suffering is emphasized

5   In every cry of every Man,
In every Infants cry of fear,
In every voice; in every ban,[2]
The mind-forg'd manacles I hear[3]

fetters by created by their minds
repetition – universalizes problem
bound to their misery – no room for imagination
← can't return to innocence
first person P.O.V. – draws attention to suffering but does nothing, no hope

white = pure – he uses black   *irony*
How the Chimney-sweepers cry
10   Every blackning Church appalls.[4]
And the hapless Soldiers sigh
Runs in blood down Palace walls

pun – pale – shocked into inactivity
lack of interaction – solely observation – isolation
images blurred

But most thro' midnight streets I hear
How the youthful Harlots curse[5]
15   Blasts the new-born Infants tear
And blights with plagues the Marriage hearse[6]

ironic – marriage has lost its joy – marriage is dead for Harlots   *death*

The Human Abstract

Pity would be no more,
If we did not make somebody Poor:
And Mercy no more could be,
If all were as happy as we:

1. A parody of the syntax of the Ten Commandments.
2. Alluding to the crown of thorns that tortured Jesus.
1. A charter is a grant of liberty or privilege, as in Magna Carta (1215). Exclusive: granted to some, it forbids others. Whether rights were chartered or natural was contested in the 1790s.
2. Several meanings are involved: political prohibition, public condemnation, curse, announcement of marriage.
3. The forgers of these fetters are the authorities of Church and State (Blake originally wrote "german forged," referring to the German descent of King George III) and the individuals who fetter themselves in fear or compliance. Between this "hear" and its rhyming repeti-

tion at the end of line 13, is an acrostic of the first letters of the third stanza H E A R.
4. The capital C makes it clear that this is the institutional Church of England. Blake's adjective involves the literal blackening of soot with the imagery of moral evil; "appalls" continues the indictment, by drawing into the sense of "dismay" (to which the Church is immune) the literal meaning, "make pale"—that is, clean the soot out of; this color-moral extends into the next stanza's "blasts" and "blights".
5. Many prostitutes were desperately poor girls barely out of childhood, abandoned or disowned by their families.
6. Prenatal blindness caused by sexually transmitted diseases.

5   And mutual fear brings peace:
       Till the selfish loves increase.
       Then Cruelty knits a snare,
       And spreads his baits with care.

       He sits down with holy fears,
10   And waters the ground with tears:
       Then Humility takes its root
       Underneath his foot.

       Soon spreads the dismal shade
       Of Mystery over his head;
15   And the Catterpiller and Fly,
       Feed on the Mystery.

       And it bears the fruit of Deceit,
       Ruddy and sweet to eat:
       And the Raven his nest has made
20   In its thickest shade.

       The Gods of the earth and sea,
       Sought thro' Nature to find this Tree
       But their search was all in vain:
       There grows one in the Human Brain

INFANT SORROW

       My mother groand! my father wept.
       Into the dangerous world I leapt:
       Helpless naked piping loud:
       Like a fiend hid in a cloud.

5   Struggling in my fathers hands:
       Striving against my swadling bands
       Bound and weary I thought best
       To sulk upon my mothers breast.

A POISON TREE

       I was angry with my friend:
       I told my wrath, my wrath did end.
       I was angry with my foe:
       I told it not, my wrath did grow.

5   And I waterd it in fears,
       Night & morning with my tears:
       And I sunned it with smiles.
       And with soft deceitful wiles.

       And it grew both day and night.
10   Till it bore an apple bright.
       And my foe beheld it shine.
       And he knew that it was mine.

William Blake. *A Poison Tree*, from *Songs of Experience*. The poem was originally titled "Christian Forbearance." The tail of the "y" in "My" at the beginning of the last line becomes a clockwise frame of the whole, as a branch of the poison tree. The outstretched body is in the posture of a crucifixion.

And into my garden stole.
When the night had veild the pole.
15   In the morning glad I see.
My foe outstretchd beneath the tree.

A DIVINE IMAGE

Cruelty has a Human Heart
And Jealousy a Human Face
Terror, the Human Form Divine
And Secrecy, the Human Dress

5   The Human Dress, is forged in Iron
The Human Form, a fiery Forge.
The Human Face, a Furnace seal'd
The Human Heart, its hungry Gorge.

The School-Boy[1]

I love to rise in a summer morn,
When the birds sing on every tree;
The distant huntsman winds° his horn,   *blows*
And the sky-lark sings with me.
5   O! what sweet company.

But to go to school in a summer morn
O! it drives all joy away;
Under a cruel eye outworn
The little ones spend the day,
10   In sighing and dismay.

Ah! then at times I drooping sit,
And spend many an anxious hour.
Nor in my book can I take delight,
Nor sit in learnings bower
15   Worn thro' with the dreary shower.

How can the bird that is born for joy,
Sit in a cage and sing,
How can a child when fears annoy,
But droop his tender wing.
20   And forget his youthful spring.

O father & mother, if buds are nip'd,
And blossoms blown away,
And if the tender plants are strip'd
Of their joy in the springing day,
25   By sorrow and cares dismay.

How shall the summer arise in joy.
Or the summer fruits appear   (troy[2]
Or how shall we gather what griefs des
Or bless the mellowing year
30   When the blasts of winter appear.

THE MARRIAGE OF HEAVEN AND HELL   *The Marriage of Heaven and Hell* is Blake's first, though hardly systematic, attempt to present a philosophical vision. His aim is to challenge, even outrage, conventional ideologies of good and evil and the moral rewards of Heaven and Hell. His immediate target is the teachings of Emanuel Swedenborg (1688–1772), a visionary theologian he initially admired but then found fault with: it is Swedenborg's *Memorable Relations*, solemn reports of encounters with angels and devils in his *Treatise Concerning Heaven and Hell* (1778), that are satirized in Blake's *Memorable Fancies*. Most of Blake's targets are still recognizable: scientific materialists like Locke who value reason and the information of the senses over imagination; pious moral philosophies that regard the body and soul as distinct, antithetical entities; conventional strictures, keyed to such philosophies, that shame the body

---

1. This song was originally placed in *Songs of Innocence*, then transferred to *Songs of Experience*.
2. On Blake's plate, the word *destroy* is broken into its two syllables, with the second one placed on the line above, its connection to the first indicated by a left parenthesis. This device is standard printer's practice, when the page space does not allow the whole line to be printed as one, but Blake's plate shows that he might have had plenty of space after "des" had the word not met the tree-trunk of his pictorial design; it is possible that he decided to display a destruction of the very word.

and sexuality. Although Blake assails orthodox Christian pieties, his argument is not with religion per se: he is intensely spiritual, believing in visionary prophecy, presenting the prophets Isaiah and Ezekiel as inspirational allies and fellow poets, and admiring Jesus, not as the enforcer of the Ten Commandments but as a compassionate rebel whose "virtue" is precisely that he "acted from im-/-pulse and not from rules." Blake's poem wields the allied genres of satire, enlightenment treatise, and prophecy (of spiritual revolution, signaled by political revolution). The verse lines in the text below vary from standard editorial transcriptions by following the linear arrangement of Blake's plates. Square brackets to the left give the plate number in Blake's illuminated book.

[Plate 1]

THE
MARRIAGE
of
HEAVEN
and
HELL

[Plate 2]

The Argument.[1]

Rintrah[2] roars & shakes his fires in the burdend air;

Hungry clouds swag° on the deep   *sink; lie heavily*

Once meek, and in a perilous path,
The just man[3] kept his course along
5   The vale of death.
Roses are planted where thorns grow.
And on the barren heath
Sing the honey bees.

Then the perilous path was planted:
10 And a river, and a spring
On every cliff and tomb;
And on the bleached bones[4]
Red clay brought forth.[5]

Till the villain left the paths of ease,
15 To walk in perilous paths, and drive
The just man into barren climes.

---

1. An "Argument" is normally a prose summary of a verse passage to follow; Blake deploys the term both inversely and deceptively: he is using poetry to summarize the prose that follows and not really providing a simplified summary at all.

2. A Blake-name for a wrathful poet-prophet of the Old-Testament type and herald (like John the Baptist) of a new messianic era, this figure is Blake's persona for rebuking the present aridity of society and predicting restorative revolution.

3. An allegorical figure for the spiritual pilgrim and prophet, the original inhabitant of Paradise trying to keep faith after the Fall, helped by Christ (who plants the perilous paths) and thwarted by the villains of the Christian Church.

4. See Ezekiel 37, an account of the resurrection of life from a valley of bones ("can these bones live?").

5. A literal translation of "Adam"; also a reference to the blood of revolutionary violence, and thus its role in redemption (Christ is sometimes called the second Adam). Isaiah 5 prophesies assault by devouring fire and a "roaring" army (30), and chapters 34–35, to which Blake refers on plate 3, prophesy "the day of the Lord's vengeance" on Edom—the destruction of the armies, the dominion of wild beasts, and a land reduced to deserts and thorns and then restored to fertility and the rebirth of faith: "the desert shall . . . blossom as the rose . . . in the wilderness shall waters break out . . . And an highway shall be there . . . called The way of holiness."

Now the sneaking serpent walks
In mild humility.
And the just man rages in the wilds[6]
20   Where lions roam.

Rintrah roars & shakes his fires in the
    burdend air;
Hungry clouds swag on the deep.

[Plate 3]   As a new heaven is begun, and it is now thir-
-ty-three years since its advent:[7] the Eternal Hell[8]
revives. And lo! Swedenborg is the Angel sitting
at the tomb: his writings are the linen clothes folded
up.[9] Now is the dominion of Edom,[1] & the return of
Adam into Paradise; see Isaiah XXXIV & XXXV Chap:[2]

    Without Contraries is no progression. Attraction
and Repulsion, Reason and Energy, Love and
Hate, are necessary to Human existence.

    From these contraries spring what the religious call
Good & Evil. Good is the passive that obeys Reason
Evil is the active springing from Energy.

    Good is Heaven. Evil is Hell.

[Plate 4]   The voice of the
                         Devil[3]

    All   Bibles   or   sacred   codes,   have   been
the causes of the following Errors.

    1. That Man has two real existing princi-
ples Viz: a Body & a Soul.

    2. That Energy, calld Evil, is alone from the
Body, & that Reason, calld Good, is alone from
the Soul.

    3. That God will torment Man in Eternity
for following his Energies.

6. Compare to epigraph for *All Religions Are One*. The voice from the wilderness is prophesied in Isaiah 40.3 and taken by Matthew (3.3) to refer to John the Baptist.

7. In 1757, 33 years before he began this poem in 1790, Blake was born and Swedenborg claimed to have witnessed the Last Judgment and the advent of "New Heaven." At age 33, Christ was crucified and resurrected, hence Blake's sly reference to himself in 1790 in the role of Christ-like prophet.

8. As various sects prophesy new heavens, Hell remains eternal. Blake is also referring to his anti-Swedenborgian writing as the countercreation of his own "Bible of Hell" (see plate 24).

9. See John 20.4–14 for the discovery of Christ's empty sepulchre, the empty burial linens folded and two angels sitting where the body was, and then the appearance of the resurrected body of Christ. Blake puts Swedenborg in the comically ironic situation of announcing his teachings as no longer useful, cast off.

1. See Genesis 27.40: "Edom" is another name for Esau, the honest brother duped out of his inheritance by the trickery of Jacob; their father Isaac assures Esau that "it shall come to pass when thou shalt have the dominion, that thou shalt break [Jacob's] yoke from off thy neck." Isaiah 63 presents the allegory of an Edomite (Esau's descendant) "red in apparel"—bloodspattered from a vengeful trampling down of the rebellious Israelites. "Edom," like "Adam," means "red earth," a literal pun that in the early 1790s would evoke the blood of political revolution that precedes (in Blake's myth) Adam's return to Paradise.

2. In addition to the chapters and verses named (see Argument), Blake is also, defiantly, recalling Isaiah 5.20, which records the warning "Woe unto them that call evil good and good evil."

3. Not necessarily Blake's own voice, but an antidote to conventionally "sacred codes"—"what the religious call Good & Evil." In such codes, "Good" is restraint, obedience, prohibition, and rationality, and "Evil" is its judgment on principles of pleasure, bodily desire, imagination, and rebellion. The diabolic voice argues that Good is only a synonym for sterility unto death and that Evil is energy, freedom, and life.

But the following Contraries to these are True

1. Man has no Body distinct from his Soul for that calld Body is a portion of Soul discernd by the five Senses, the chief inlets of Soul in this age.

2. Energy is the only life and is from the Body and Reason is the bound or outward circumference of Energy.

3. Energy is Eternal Delight

[Plate 5]

Those who restrain desire, do so because theirs is weak enough to be restrained; and the restrainer or reason usurps its place & governs the unwilling.

And being restraind it by degrees becomes passive till it is only the shadow of desire.

The history of this is written in Paradise Lost. & the Governor or Reason is call'd Messiah.[4]

And the original Archangel or possessor of the command of the heavenly host is call'd the Devil or Satan and his children are call'd Sin & Death[5]

But in the Book of Job Miltons Messiah is call'd Satan.[6]

For this history has been adopted by both parties

It indeed appear'd to Reason as if Desire was cast out, but the Devil's account is, that the Messi-

[Plate 6]

ah fell. & formed a heaven of what he stole from the Abyss

This is shewn in the Gospel, where he prays to the Father to send the comforter or Desire that Reason may have Ideas to build on,[7] the Jehovah of the Bible being no other than he   who dwells in flaming fire.

Know that after Christs death, he became Jehovah.

But in Milton; the Father is Destiny, the Son, a Ratio of the five senses.[8] & the Holy-ghost, Vacuum![9]

Note. The reason Milton wrote in fetters when he wrote of Angels & God, and at liberty when of Devils & Hell, is because he was a true Poet and of the Devils party[1] without knowing it

4. In *Paradise Lost*, "Reason" is the highest mental capacity, through which man knows God, and thus the agency by which "lower" faculties such as passion and appetite are disciplined.

5. A reference to Satan's status as Archangel Lucifer before his fall from Heaven along with the rebel faction he commanded in the war against God (*Paradise Lost* 6.824ff.). In 2.746–814, Milton provides a lurid account of the birth of Satan's children: first his daughter Sin, and then their incestuous son, Death.

6. In the Book of Job, God tests Job's faith by allowing Satan to torment him.

7. An ironic twist on Christ's assurance that after his earthly death he will send the Holy Ghost as comforter; see John 14.16–17.

8. Blake puns on the Latin meanings of "sum" and "Reason." Blake argues that philosophical and theological exaltations of reason demote the creative power of imagination.

9. Milton was skeptical of the Trinitarian completion of divinity by the Holy Ghost, but Blake here satirizes what he sees as imaginative emptiness.

1. Both the Devil's point of view and the political faction he led against the authority of God. This "Note" is a famous example of what was later called "Romantic Satanism" and its reading *Paradise Lost* against Milton's "Argument."

A Memorable Fancy

As I was walking among the fires of hell, delighted with the enjoyments of Genius; which to An-
-gels look like torment and insanity. I collected some
of their Proverbs: thinking that as the sayings used
in a nation, mark its character, so the Proverbs of
Hell, shew the nature of Infernal wisdom better
than any description of buildings or garments

When I came home, on the abyss of the five sen-
-ses, where a flat sided steep frowns over the pre-
-sent world. I saw a mighty Devil folded in black
clouds hovering on the sides of the rock, with cor-

[Plate 7] -roding fires[2] he wrote the following sentence now per-
-cieved by the minds of men, & read by them on earth.

How do you know but ev'ry Bird that cuts the airy way,
Is an immense world of delight, clos'd by your senses five?[3]

Proverbs of Hell.[4]

In seed time learn, in harvest teach, in winter enjoy.
Drive your cart and your plow over the bones of the dead.
The road of excess leads to the palace of wisdom.
Prudence is a rich ugly old maid courted by Incapacity.
5 He who desires but acts not, breeds pestilence.
The cut worm forgives the plow.
Dip him in the river who loves water.
A fool sees not the same tree that a wise man sees.
He whose face gives no light, shall never become a star.
10 Eternity is in love with the productions of time.
The busy bee has no time for sorrow.
The hours of folly are measur'd by the clock, but of wis-
-dom: no clock can measure.
All wholsom food is caught without a net or a trap.
15 Bring out number weight & measure in a year of dearth
No bird soars too high. if he soars with his own wings.
A dead body. revenges not injuries.
The most sublime act is to set another before you.
If the fool would persist in his folly he would become
20 Folly is the cloke of knavery.   [wise
Shame is Prides cloke.

---

2. Casting himself and other poets as Devils, Blake refers
to his process of book production, whereby he etched his
designs on copper plates with an acid-resistant fluid, then
washed the plate in acid so that the designs emerged in
relief. Hand-colored, this relief plate was then used to
print the pages. See plate 14 for a reference to the symbolic value of this method.
3. These lines allude to verses by Thomas Chatterton:
"How dydd I know that eve'ry darte, / That cutte the

Airie waie, / Myghte nott find passage toe my harte, /
And close myne eyes for aie?" (*Bristowe Tragedie*). At age
17, Chatterton committed suicide in despair of success
and thereby won celebrity in the Romantic era as a martyred genius.
4. Blake's diabolic version of the Old Testament's Book
of Proverbs as well as his satire on the *Aphorisms* of Kas-
par Lavater (1788), a Swiss moralist and friend of Henry
Fuseli, an artist who was also Blake's friend.

[Plate 8]   Proverbs of Hell

Prisons are built with stones of Law, Brothels with
    bricks of Religion.
The pride of the peacock is the glory of God.
5   The lust of the goat is the bounty of God.
The wrath of the lion is the wisdom of God.
The nakedness of woman is the work of God.
Excess of sorrow laughs. Excess of joy weeps.
The roaring of lions, the howling of wolves the raging
10   of the stormy sea, and the destructive sword, are
    portions of eternity too great for the eye of man.
The fox condemns the trap. not himself.
Joys impregnate. Sorrows bring forth.
Let man wear the fell of the lion. woman the fleece of
15   the sheep.
The bird a nest, the spider a web, man friendship.
The selfish smiling fool. & the sullen frowning fool. shall
    be both thought wise, that they may be a rod.
What is now proved was once, only imagin'd.
20   The rat, the mouse, the fox, the rabbet; watch the roots,
    the lion, the tyger, the horse, the elephant, watch
    the fruits.
The cistern contains: the fountain overflows
One thought. fills immensity.
25   Always be ready to speak your mind, and a base man
    will avoid you.
Every thing possible to be believ'd is an image of truth.
The eagle never lost so much time. as when he submit-
    -ted to learn of the crow.

[Plate 9]   Proverbs of Hell

The fox provides for himself. but God provides for the lion.
Think in the morning. Act in the noon, Eat in the even-
    -ing, Sleep in the night.
5   He who has sufferd you to impose on him knows you.
As the plow follows words, so God rewards prayers.
The tygers of wrath are wiser than the horses of in-
Expect poison from the standing water.   [-struction
You never know what is enough unless you know what is
10   more than enough.
Listen to the fools reproach! it is a kingly title!
The eyes of fire, the nostrils of air, the mouth of water,
    the beard of earth.
The weak in courage is strong in cunning.
15   The apple tree never asks the beech how he shall grow,
    nor the lion, the horse, how he shall take his prey.
The thankful reciever bears a plentiful harvest.
If others had not been foolish. we should be so.
The soul of sweet delight. can never be defil'd,
20   When thou seest an Eagle, thou seest a portion of Ge

-nius. lift up thy head!

As the catterpiller chooses the fairest leaves to lay
    her eggs on, so the priest lays his curse on
    the fairest joys.

25   To create a little flower is the labour of ages.

Damn, braces: Bless relaxes.

The best wine is the oldest. the best water the newest

Prayers plow not! Praises reap not!

Joys laugh not! Sorrows weep not!

[Plate 10]   Proverbs of Hell

The head Sublime, the heart Pathos, the genitals Beauty
    the hands & feet Proportion.

As the air to a bird or the sea to a fish, so is contempt
    to the contemptible.

The crow wish'd every thing was black, the owl, that eve-
-ry thing was white.

Exuberance is Beauty.

If the lion was advised by the fox. he would be cunning.

10   Improvent makes strait roads, but the crooked roads
    without Improvement. are roads of Genius.

Sooner murder an Infant in its cradle than nurse unact
-ed desires

Where man is not nature is barren.

15   Truth can never be told so as to be understood and
    not be believd.

Enough! or Too much

[Plate 11]   The ancient Poets animated all sensible objects
with Gods or Geniuses, calling them by the names and
adorning them with the properties of woods, rivers,
mountains, lakes, cities, nations, and whatever their
enlarged & numerous senses could percieve.

    And particularly they studied the genius of each
city & country. placing it under its mental deity.

    Till a system was formed, which some took ad-
vantage of & enslav'd the vulgar by attempting to
realize or abstract the mental deities from their
objects: thus began Priesthood.

    Choosing forms of worship from poetic tales.

    And at length they pronouncd that the Gods
had orderd such things.

    Thus   men   forgot   that   All   deities   reside
in the human breast.

[Plate 12]   A Memorable Fancy.

    The Prophets Isaiah and Ezekiel dined with
me, and I asked them how they dared so roundly to
assert. that God spake to them; and whether they
did not think at the time, that they would be mis-
-understood, & so be the cause of imposition.

Isaiah answer'd. I saw no God, nor heard any, in a finite organical perception; but my sen--ses discover'd the infinite in every thing, and as I was then perswaded, & remain confirmd; that the voice of honest indignation is the voice of God, I cared not for consequences but wrote.

Then I asked: does a firm perswasion that a thing is so, make it so?

He replied. All poets believe that it does. & in ages of imagination this firm perswasion remo ved mountains; but many are not capable of a firm perswasion of any thing.

Then Ezekiel said. The philosophy of the east taught the first principles of human perception some nations held one principle for the origin & some another; we of Israel taught that the Poetic Genius (as you now call it) was the first principle and all the others merely derivative, which was the cause of our despising the Priests & Philosophers of other countries. and prophecying that all Gods

[Plate 13]

would at last be proved to originate in ours & to be the tributaries of the Poetic Genius, it was this. that our great poet King David desired so fervently & invokes so patheticly, saying by this he conquers enemies & governs kingdoms; and we so loved our God. that we cursed in his name all the deities of surrounding nations, and asserted that they had rebelled; from these opinions the vulgar came to think that all nati--ons would at last be subject to the jews.

This said he, like all firm perswasions, is come to pass, for all nations believe the jews code and wor--ship the jews god, and what greater subjection can be

I heard this with some wonder. & must confess my own conviction. After dinner I ask'd Isaiah to fa-vour the world with his lost works, he said none of equal value was lost. Ezekiel said the same of his.

I also asked Isaiah what made him go naked and barefoot three years?[5] he answerd, the same that made our friend Diogenes the Grecian.

I then asked Ezekiel. why he eat dung, & lay so long on his right & left side?[6] he answerd, the desire of raising other men into a perception of the infinite this the North American tribes practise. & is he hon-est who resists his genius or conscience. only for the sake of present ease or gratification?

5. See Isaiah 20.2; the Lord instructs Isaiah to walk "naked and barefoot."
6. See Ezekiel 4. Ezekiel is instructed to act out with his body the siege of Jerusalem by lying on his left side for 390 days to represent the years of Israel's iniquity and for 40 days on his right side for the years of the iniquity of the house of Judah; he is also ordered to eat barley cakes mixed with dung. Diogenes, famous for searching in daylight with a lantern for one honest man, was a 4th-century Greek Cynic philosopher who led a severely ascetic life. Blake alludes to these extraordinary actions to reflect the eccentricity often associated with visionary prophets.

[Plate 14]   The ancient tradition that the world will be con-
-sumed in fire at the end of six thousand years[7]
is true. as I have heard from Hell.

For the cherub with his flaming sword is
hereby commanded to leave his guard at tree of
life,[8] and when he does, the whole creation will
be consumed and appear infinite. and holy
whereas it now appears finite & corrupt.

This will come to pass by an improvement of
sensual enjoyment.

But first the notion that man has a body
distinct from his soul, is to be expunged; this
I shall do, by printing in the infernal method, by
corrosives, which in Hell are salutary and medicinal, melting apparent surfaces away, and
displaying the infinite which was hid.

If the doors of perception were cleansed
every thing would appear to man as it is: In-
-finite.

For man has closed himself up, till he sees
all things thro' narrow chinks of his cavern.[9]

[Plate 15]   A Memorable Fancy[1]

I was in a Printing house in Hell & saw the
method in which knowledge is transmitted from generation to generation.

In the first chamber was a Dragon-Man, clear-
-ing away the rubbish from a caves mouth; within, a
number of Dragons were hollowing the cave.

In the second chamber was a Viper folding round
the rock & the cave, and others adorning it with gold
silver and precious stones.

In the third chamber was an Eagle, with wings
and feathers of air, he caused the inside of the cave
to be infinite, around were numbers of Eagle like
men, who built palaces in the immense cliffs.

In the fourth chamber were Lions of flaming fire
raging around & melting the metals into living fluids.

7. This prophetic tradition is represented in the Book of
Revelation and based on the translation of the six days of
creation into six millennia (see 2 Peter 3.8); Blake relates
this symbolism to the American and French revolutions.
8. See Genesis 3.24. After evicting Adam and Eve from
Eden, God "placed at the east of the garden of Eden
cherubims, and a flaming sword which turned every way,
to keep the way of the tree of life" (this is one of the last
images in *Paradise Lost* Book 12). Blake in turn imagines
the expulsion of this angelic policeman and the restoration of Adam to the garden, free from sexual shame.
9. Plato's allegory of the Cave (*Republic* 7) compares the
human mind to a cavern where men sit with their backs to
the aperture of daylight, apprehending only shadows cast
by firelight on the wall. Locke's *Essay Concerning Human
Understanding* (1690–1700) describes "external and inter-

nal sensation" as "the only passages . . . of knowledge to
the understanding . . . the windows by which light is let
into [the] dark room" of the mind: "understanding is not
much unlike a closet wholly shut from light, with only
some little openings left, to let in external visible resem-
blances, or ideas of things without" (2.11.17).
1. The caverns continue the imagery of plate 14. The
allegory is cryptic but seems to refer to Blake's creative
process: in the first cavern, a figure of diabolic energy is
clearing away the rubbish of wasted systems; the second
chamber is undergoing artistic restoration; the third is
being made into a place for liberated imagination; in the
fourth and fifth chambers, the metal plates for Blake's
book-making processes are being formed; in the sixth,
men take possession of these books, imaging the decline
from energy to system.

In the fifth chamber were Unnam'd forms, which cast the metals into the expanse.

There they were reciev'd by Men who occupied the sixth chamber, and took the forms of books & were arranged in libraries.

[Plate 16]   The Giants who formed this world into its sensual existence and now seem to live in it in chains; are in truth. the causes of its life & the sources of all activity, but the chains are, the cunning of weak and tame minds which have power to resist energy. according to the pro--verb, the weak in courage is strong in cunning.

Thus one portion of being, is the Prolific. the other, the Devouring: to the devourer it seems as if the producer was in his chains, but it is not so; he only takes portions of existence and fancies that the whole.

But the Prolific would cease to be Prolific unless the Devourer as a sea recieved the excess of his delights.

Some will say, Is not God alone the Prolific? I answer. God only Acts & Is, in existing beings or Men.

These two classes of men are always upon earth. & they should be enemies: whoever tries

[Plate 17]   to reconcile them seeks to destroy existence. Religion is an endeavour to reconcile the two.

Note. Jesus Christ did not wish to unite but to separate them, as in the Parable of sheep and goats! & he says I came not to send Peace but a Sword.[2]

Messiah or Satan or Tempter was formerly thought to be one of the Antediluvians[3] who are our Energies.

A Memorable Fancy[4]

An Angel came to me and said. O pitiable foolish young man! O horrible! O dreadful state! consider the hot burning dungeon thou art preparing for thyself to all eternity, to which thou art going in such career.

I said. perhaps you will be willing to shew me my eternal lot & we will contemplate together upon it and see whether your lot or mine is most desirable.

2. The Prolific (diabolical creators) and the Devourers (sterile pious reasoners) accord with the parable of the sheep and goats (Matthew 25.32–33): Jesus, the Shepherd, separates the sheep on his right hand, admitting them to his kingdom, and the goats on his left, condemning them to the punishment of everlasting fire—having cautioned, "think not that I am come to send peace on earth: I came not to send peace, but a sword" (10.34).
3. Inhabitants of the earth "before the flood" survived by Noah.

4. In this Memorable Fancy, a kind of dream allegory, Blake wages an elaborately comic argument with a pious Swedenborgian Angel, the voice of conventional morality and religion. The geography of their fantastic tour images the decline of Christianity, beginning in the stable of Christ's birth and the church founded in His name, and descending into the vault, the cave, the mill, and the abyss—into the rigidity of institutional religion.

So he took me thro' a stable & thro' a church
& down into the church vault at the end of which
was a mill: thro' the mill we went, and came to a
cave. down the winding cavern we groped our tedi-
-ous way till a void boundless as a nether sky ap-
-peard beneath us & we held by the roots of trees
and hung over this immensity: but I said, if you
please we will commit ourselves to this void, and
see whether providence is here also, if you will not
I will? but he answerd, do not presume O young-
man but as we here remain behold thy lot which
will soon appear when the darkness passes away
    So I remaind with him sitting in the twisted

[Plate 18] root of an oak; he was suspended in a fungus
which hung with the head downward into the deep:
    By degrees we beheld the infinite Abyss, fiery
as the smoke of a burning city; beneath us at an
immense distance was the sun, black but shining
round it were fiery tracks on which revolv'd vast
spiders, crawling after their prey; which flew or
rather swum in the infinite deep, in the most ter-
-rific shapes of animals sprung from corruption.
& the air was full of them, & seemd composed
of them; these are Devils. and are called Powers
of the air. I now asked my companion which was my
eternal lot? he said, between the black & white spiders
    But now, from between the black & white spiders
a cloud and fire burst and rolled thro the deep
blackning all beneath, so that the nether deep grew
black as a sea & rolled with a terrible noise: be-
-neath us was nothing now to be seen but a black
tempest, till looking east between the clouds & the
waves, we saw a cataract of blood mixed with fire
and not many stones throw from us appeard and
sunk again the scaly fold of a monstrous serpent.
at last to the east, distant about three degrees[5] ap-
-peard a fiery crest above the waves slowly it rear-
-ed like a ridge of golden rocks till we discoverd
two globes of crimson fire, from which the sea
fled away in clouds of smoke, and now we saw, it
was the head of Leviathan.[6] his forehead was divided into streaks of green & purple like those on
a tygers forehead: soon we saw his mouth & red
gills hang just above the raging foam, tinging the
black deep with beams of blood, advancing toward

5. The longitudinal position of Paris, heart of the French Revolution, relative to London.
6. A beast described in the Bible (Job 41.1, Isaiah 27.1, Psalms 104.26), and alluded to by Thomas Hobbes (1588–1679) in his famous treatise on government, *Leviathan, or the Matter, Form, and Power of a Common-* *wealth, Ecclesiastical and Civil* (1651), written during the commonwealth and defending a secular monarchy; Hobbes argues that appetitive self-interest must be controlled only by the laws and institutions of government, whose authority is agreed upon by common contract. In Blake's view, this vision of the state is monstrous.

[Plate 19]   us with all the fury of a spiritual exsitence.

My friend the Angel climb'd up from his station into the mill; I remain'd alone, & then this
appearance was no more, but I found myself sitting on a pleasant bank beside a river by moon
light hearing a harper who sung to the harp. &
his theme was, The man who never alters his
opinion is like standing water, & breeds reptiles
of the mind.

But I arose, and sought for the mill &
there I found my Angel, who surprised asked
me, how I escaped?

I answerd. All that we saw was owing to your
metaphysics: for when you ran away, I found myself
on a bank by moonlight hearing a harper, But
now we have seen my eternal lot, shall I shew you
yours? he laughd at my proposal; but I by force
suddenly caught him in my arms, & flew westerly
thro' the night, till we were elevated above the
earths shadow: then I flung myself with him directly into the body of the sun, here I clothed myself in
white,[7] & taking in my hand Swedenborgs volumes
sunk from the glorious clime, and passed all the
planets till we came to saturn, here I staid to rest
& then leap'd into the void, between saturn & the
fixed stars.

Here said I! is your lot, in this space, if space
it may be calld. Soon we saw the stable and the
church, & I took him to the altar and open'd the
Bible, and lo! it was a deep pit, into which I de-
-scended driving the Angel before me, soon we saw
seven houses of brick,[8] one we enterd; in it were a

[Plate 20]   number of monkeys, baboons, & all of that species
chaind by the middle, grinning and snatching at
one another, but witheld by the shortness of their
chains:[9] however I saw that they sometimes grew nu
merous, and then the weak were caught by the strong
and with a grinning aspect first coupled with & then
devourd, by plucking off first one limb & then ano-
-ther till the body was left a helpless trunk. this after
grinning & kissing it with seeming fondness they de-
-vourd too; and here & there I saw one savourily pic-
-king the flesh off of his own tail; as the stench ter-
-ribly annoyd us both we went into the mill, & I in
my hand brought the skeleton of a body, which in
the mill was Aristotles Analytics.[1]

---

7. In Revelation 7.9, those who have been redeemed
appear before the throne of Christ in white robes.
8. The seven churches to whom John addresses the Book
of Revelation (1.4).
9. Blake's satire of theological dispute.

1. A "skeleton" both in the sense of an abstract summary
and as a symbolic comment on the lifeless form of knowledge represented by Aristotle's treatise on logic as the
highest kind of mental discipline. Compare the reference
to "bleached bones" in the Argument.

So the Angel said: thy phantasy has imposed
upon me & thou oughtest to be ashamed.

I answer: we impose upon one another. & it is
but lost time to converse with you whose works
are only Analytics

Opposition is true Friendship[2]

[Plate 21]

I have always found that Angels have the vani-
-ty to speak of themselves as the only wise; this they
do with a confident insolence sprouting from systema-
-tic reasoning:

Thus Swedenborg boasts that what he writes is
new: tho' it is only the Contents or Index of already
publish'd books

A man carried a monkey about for a shew, & be-
-cause he was a little wiser than the monkey, grew
vain, and conciev'd himself as much wiser than se-
-ven men. It is so with Swedenborg: he shews the
folly of churches & exposes hypocrites, till he im-
-agines that all are religious, & himself the single

[Plate 22]

one on earth that ever broke a net.

Now hear a plain fact: Swedenborg has not writ-
-ten one new truth: Now hear another: he has written
all the old falshoods.

And now hear the reason. He conversed with Angels
who are all religious. & conversed not with Devils who
all hate religion for he was incapable thro' his conceited
notions.

Thus Swedenborgs writings are a recapitulation of
all superficial opinions, and an analysis of the more
sublime. but no further.

Have now another plain fact: Any man of mechani-
-cal talents may from the writings of Paracelsus or Ja-
-cob Behmen,[3] produce ten thousand volumes of equal
value with Swedenborg's, and from those of Dante or
Shakespear, an infinite number.

But when he has done this, let him not say that he
knows better than his master, for he only holds a can-
-dle in sunshine.

A Memorable Fancy

Once I saw a Devil in a flame of fire, who arose be
fore an Angel that sat on a cloud, and the Devil ut-
-terd these words.

The worship of God is. Honouring his gifts in other
men each according to his genius. and loving the

---

2. This motto appears in only three of the nine known
copies of the poem.
3. Paracelsus (1493–1541) was a Swiss physician,
occultist, and alchemist; Behmen is Jakob Boehme
(1575–1624), a German mystic, who believed that God
was knowable from the unity of the natural world.

[Plate 23]

greatest men best, those who envy or calumniate great men hate God, for there is no other God.

The Angel hearing this became almost blue but mastering himself he grew yellow, & at last white pink & smiling. and then replied,

Thou Idolater, is not God One? & is not he visible in Jesus Christ? and has not Jesus Christ given his sanction to the law of ten commandments and are not all other men fools sinners & nothings?

The Devil answer'd; bray a fool in a morter with wheat yet shall not his folly be beaten out of him[4] if Jesus Christ is the greatest man, you ought to love him in the greatest degree; now hear how he has given his sanction to the law of ten command -ments: did he not mock at the sabbath, and so mock the sabbaths God? murder those who were murderd because of him? turn away the law from the woman taken in adultery? steal the labor of others to support him? bear false witness when he omitted making a defence before Pilate? covet when he pray'd for his disciples, and when he bid them shake off the dust of their feet against such as refused to lodge them? I tell you, no virtue can exist without breaking these ten command-ments: Jesus was all virtue, and acted from im-

[Plate 24]

-pulse: not from rules.[5]

When he had so spoken, I beheld the Angel who stretched out his arms embracing the flame of fire & he was consumed and arose as Elijah.[6]

Note. This Angel, who is now become a Devil, is my particular friend: we often read the Bible to--gether in its infernal or diabolical sense which the world shall have if they behave well.

I have also: **The Bible of Hell**:[7] which the world shall have whether they will or no.

One Law for the Lion & Ox is Oppression

1790–1793   1793–1825

---

4. See Proverbs 27.22: "Though thou shouldest bray [crush] a fool in a mortar among wheat with a pestle, yet will not his foolishness depart from him."
5. For Jesus' breaking of Jewish law, see John 8.2–11, and Matthew 9.14–17, 12.1–8, and 27.11–14.

6. See 2 Kings 2.11: "there appeared a chariot of fire, and horses of fire, and . . . Elijah went up by a whirlwind into heaven."
7. Blake's own scripture—that is, his illuminated poems.

⇒⧻ PERSPECTIVES ⧻⇐
The Abolition of Slavery and the Slave Trade

Slavery and the slave trade provoked sharp controversy in the age of Romanticism, and literary writing played a major role in shaping public opinion. From 1783 to 1793 more than 300,000 slaves were sold in the British colonies, at a value of over £15,000,000. A "triangular trade" flourished, whereby British merchants financed expeditions to the African Gold Coast to buy or kidnap human cargo, to be shipped (the "Middle Passage") under brutal conditions to markets in the West Indies and South America. About 13 percent of this cargo died, while the survivors suffered heat, cramped quarters, fettering, physical abuse, poor sanitation, and disease. With the profits, which usually exceeded a hundred percent of the initial investment, traders filled their ships with exotic colonial goods—tobacco, sugar, molasses, rum, spices, cotton—which they sold in Europe, also at tremendous profits. Moral opposition to this trade, spearheaded by the Quakers and Evangelical Christian sects, was invigorated by Lord Mansfield's ruling in 1772 declaring the absence of any legal basis for slavery in England. Over the 1770s, several abolitionist tracts appeared, and by the end of the decade, bills were being introduced in Parliament to regulate the trade. National attention was galvanized by the scandal of the slave ship *Zong* (1781) whose captain ordered 133 weak and diseased slaves ejected into shark-infested waters in order to collect on a policy that held the insurer liable for cargo jettisoned in order to salvage the remainder. Color Plate 5 shows J. M. W. Turner's famous painting of this event.

In the 1780s the Quakers continued to petition Parliament and distribute pamphlets, while other abolitionists wrote tracts challenging the scriptural as well as economic justifications for slavery, and reformed slave-traders published memoirs detailing the horrors of the trade. By the end of the decade, William Wilberforce was heading a Parliamentary investigation and the former slave Olaudah Equiano's *Interesting Narrative* quickly became a best-seller. But the advent of the French Revolution in 1789 increased fear of slave revolts, and Wilberforce's first bill for abolition was defeated in 1791.

Yet the abolition movement persisted. In 1792 Edmund Burke's *Sketch of a Negro Code* gave a plan for orderly abolition and emancipation, and in 1793 Wilberforce's second bill for abolition at least won in the House of Commons. By the decade's end, the British treasury was reeling under the cost of regulating the trade and defending the plantation owners. The abolition movement achieved its first major success in 1807, when Parliament abolished British slave-trading. Wilberforce's stirring *Letter on the Abolition of the Slave Trade* (1807), praising the moral importance of the event, helped sustain the movement for abolishing slavery itself (still legal in the colonies)—as did Thomas Clarkson's gripping *History of the Abolition of the African Slave-Trade by the British Parliament* (1808), which detailed the horrors of the trade both for the slaves and the seamen. By the 1820s, the movement was benefiting from the increasing involvement of women, who were horrified by the often violent and sexually abusive treatment of female slaves. In 1823 Clarkson and Wilberforce founded the influential *Anti-Slavery Monthly Reporter*, which relentlessly publicized all the horrors, and Parliament seriously addressed the issue, with Foreign Secretary George Canning arguing that "the spirit of the Christian religion is hostile to slavery." The year 1831 was a critical one, marked not only by a massive slave rebellion in Jamaica, with severe reprisals against slaves and sympathetic missionaries, but also by the publication of former slave Mary Prince's autobiography, with searing reports of atrocities, especially to female slaves. The Reform Parliament of 1832 proved hospitable to emancipation, and in 1833 it passed the Emancipation Bill, liberating 800,000 slaves in British colonies and compensating the owners with more than £20,000,000.

It was the planters and the merchants in Bristol and Liverpool, enjoying immense profits, who opposed abolition. Supported by their Standing Committee in Parliament, they justified slavery by arguing that Africans had already enslaved each other; that they were mental and moral primitives, animals and heathens, to whom plantation life brought a work ethic, civilized behavior, and the grace of Christian religion; and finally, that British abolition would not end the trade, only leave the profits to other nations. Their literary propaganda tended toward the genre of "romance," pastoral stories with happy endings in which slaves are grateful and planters benevolent. Their appeals to social stability were amplified by alarm at the French Revolution, and in 1791 a massive slave revolt in Santo Domingo made it possible to link abolitionism to Jacobinism and to embarrass at least the Evangelical abolitionists, who tended to be critical of the Revolution.

Abolitionists came from differing, often opposed political groups: Tory, Evangelical, Quaker, Unitarian, Dissenter, Nonconformist, radical. Some, such as Anna Barbauld, Mary Wollstonecraft, and Tom Paine, energized abolitionism with related commitments to social reform and the new philosophies of "the rights of man" and "the rights of woman." Wordsworth's excoriation of slavery in *The Prelude* powerfully sounds this note. But others, including the Parliamentarians Burke and Wilberforce and most Evangelical Christians, were politically conservative, often wealthy; wanting to avoid political arguments, the Evangelicals condemned slavery as a moral blight on a Christian nation and advocated Parliamentary reform. They refuted the planters' claims of kind treatment on slave-ships and plantations, and vividly purveyed what amounts to a pornography of atrocities, even as the moral stress was on common humanity and Christian values. With their own version of African primitivism, their fables evoked sympathy for the slaves' childlike simplicity and the pathos of their destroyed families, their physical tortures and suffering. In these narratives, redemption for the slaves appears not through rebellion, but through the salvational processes of Christian conversion, forbearance, and an appeal to enlightened authority.

Many well-known writers entered the debate, rallying support by using vivid stories to exemplify the broad social and ethical issues involved. The texts that follow show the range of literary resources, and the range of viewpoints, employed by writers who composed poems, essays, and stories as part of the protracted struggle over abolition.

Olaudah Equiano
c. 1745–1797

In the parliamentary inquiry into the condition of the slave trade between 1788 and 1789, evidence came almost exclusively from the traders. Olaudah Equiano's *Interesting Narrative* was crucial for presenting dramatic evidence from the slaves' harrowing experiences. Born to a high-ranking, prosperous, slave-owning family of the Ebo tribe, in the region of modern Nigeria, Equiano was kidnapped by freelance slavers at age ten, shipped first to Barbados, then North America. The disorienting effects of this brutal experience are reflected in the series of names he was given by successive owners: on the slave-ship he was "Michael," then named "Jacob" by a Virginia plantation owner, and then dubbed "Gustavus Vassa," after a sixteenth-century Swedish hero, when he was purchased by Lieutenant Michael Pascal of the British navy. Pascal took him to England in 1757, and then to Canada where he fought in the Seven Years' War in 1758; he was baptized in 1759, and worked for the British navy in the Mediterranean as a servant and gunner's mate. Pascal then sold him to Captain James Doran. In the West Indies, he was sold, again, to an American Quaker merchant, Robert King, on whose trading ships he worked. With profits from private trade conducted by his own initiative and entrepreneurial skill, he earned enough from the system he abhorred to purchase his freedom, for £70, in 1766. Subsequent adventures took him on a Grand Tour of the Mediterranean, to the Caribbean, and even on an expedition to the Arctic in 1773 (seeking a polar route to India), where a shipmate was young Horatio Nelson (later, one of England's celebrated naval heroes). At various times, Equiano managed a plantation in Central America, earned a living as a hairdresser in London, and worked for the Sierra Leone project (a planned colony for freed slaves in Africa), until he protested against financial mismanagement and was dismissed.

Once settled in England, he renewed his commitment to Christianity and worked with the Evangelicals, campaigned tirelessly for abolition, and became an acquaintance of the founder of the radical working-class London Corresponding Society. In 1792 Equiano married an English woman with whom he had two daughters, and was well enough off at his death in 1797 to leave his one surviving daughter an inheritance of £950 on her twenty-first birthday in 1816. Equiano's *Interesting Narrative* witnesses the cruelty of the Middle Passage, the violence of slavery, and the uncertain status of even the free black; at the same time, it is a vivid picaresque adventure, a religious conversion narrative, and a document of surprising social mobility. A story of triumph as well as oppression, the *Narrative* has a complexity the more compelling for its seeming artlessness. It was an immediate sensation, selling 5,000 copies the first year, and going through thirty-six editions over the next half century. Published as far afield as Germany and Russia, it was influential in promoting abolition, a cause that Equiano continued to serve as a devoted public speaker until the end of his life. For his portrait, see Color Plate 4.

From **The Interesting Narrative of the Life of Olaudah Equiano**
or Gustavus Vassa, the African
[THE SLAVE SHIP AND ITS CARGO]

The first object that saluted my eyes when I arrived on the coast was the sea, and a slave ship, which was then riding at anchor, and waiting for its cargo.[1] These filled me with astonishment, that was soon converted into terror, which I am yet at a loss to describe, and much more the then feelings of my mind when I was carried on board. I was immediately handled and tossed up to see if I was sound, by some of the crew; and I was now persuaded that I had got into a world of bad spirits, and that they were going to kill me. Their complexions too, differing so much from ours, their long hair, and the language they spoke, which was very different from any I had ever heard, united to confirm me in this belief. Indeed such were the horrors of my views and fears at the moment, that if ten thousand worlds had been my own, I would have freely parted with them all to have exchanged my condition with the meanest slave in my own country. When I looked round the ship too, and saw a large furnace or copper boiling and a multitude of black people, of every description, chained to-gether, every one of their countenances expressing dejection and sorrow, I no longer doubted of my fate; and, quite overpowered with horror and anguish, I fell motionless on the deck, and fainted. When I recovered a little, I found some black people about me, who I believed were some of those who brought me on board, and had been receiving their pay: they talked to me in order to cheer me, but all in vain. I asked them if we were not to be eaten by those white men with horrible looks, red faces, and long hair. They told me I was not: and one of the crew brought me a small por-tion of spirituous liquor in a wine glass; but, being afraid of him, I would not take it

1. Captured by slavers along with his sister, Equiano was soon separated from her and sold to different masters over a peri-od of several months before reaching the African coast for shipment to Barbados.

out of his hand. One of the blacks therefore took it from him and gave it to me, and I took a little down my palate, which, instead of reviving me, as they thought it would, threw me into the greatest consternation at the strange feeling it produced, having never tasted any such liquor before.

Soon after this the blacks who brought me on board went off, and left me abandoned to despair. I now saw myself deprived of all chance of returning to my native country, or even the least glimpse of gaining the shore, which I now considered as friendly; and I even wished for my former slavery, in preference to my present situation, which was filled with horrors of every kind, still heightened by my ignorance of what I was to undergo. I was not long suffered to indulge my grief. I was soon put down under the decks, and there I received such a salutation in my nostrils as I had never experienced in my life: so that, with the loathsomeness of the stench, and with my crying together, I became so sick and low that I was not able to eat, nor had I the least desire to taste any thing. I now wished for the last friend, death, to relieve me; but soon, to my grief, two of the white men offered me eatables; and, on my refusing to eat, one of them held me fast by the hands, and laid me across, I think, the windlass, and tied my feet, while the other flogged me severely. I had never experienced any thing of this kind before, and although, not being used to the water, I naturally feared that element the first time I saw it, yet nevertheless, could I have got over the nettings, I would have jumped over the side, but I could not; and besides the crew used to watch us very closely, who were not chained down to the decks, lest we should leap into the water. I have seen some of these poor African prisoners most severely cut for attempting to do so, and hourly whipped for not eating. This indeed was often the case with myself. In a little time after, amongst the poor chained men, I found some of my own nation, which in a small degree gave ease to my mind. I inquired of these what was to be done with us. They gave me to understand we were to be carried to these white people's country to work for them. I was then a little revived, and thought if it were no worse than working, my situation was not so desperate. But still I feared I should be put to death, the white people looked and acted, as I thought, in so savage a manner; for I had never seen among any people such instances of brutal cruelty: and this is not only shewn towards us blacks, but also to some of the whites themselves. One white man in particular I saw, when we were permitted to be on deck, flogged so unmercifully with a large rope near the foremast, that he died in consequence of it; and they tossed him over the side as they would have done a brute. This made me fear these people the more; and I expected nothing less than to be treated in the same manner. I could not help expressing my fearful apprehensions to some of my countrymen; I asked them if these people had no country, but lived in this hollow place, the ship. They told me they did not, but came from a distant one. "Then," said I, "how comes it, that in all our country we never heard of them?" They told me, because they lived so very far off. I then asked, where their women were: had they any like themselves. I was told they had. "And why," said I, "do we not see them?" They answered, because they were left behind. I asked how the vessel could go. They told me they could not tell; but that there was cloth put upon the masts by the help of the ropes I saw, and then the vessel went on; and the white men had some spell or magic they put in the water, when they liked, in order to stop the vessel. I was exceedingly amazed at this account, and really thought they were spirits. I therefore wished much to be from amongst them, for I expected they would sacrifice me; but my wishes were in vain, for we were so quartered that it was impossible for any of us to make our escape.

[EQUIANO, AGE 12, REACHES ENGLAND]

One morning, when I got upon deck, I perceived it covered over with the snow that fell overnight. As I had never seen any thing of the kind before, I thought it was salt; so I immediately ran down to the mate and desired him, as well as I could, to come and see how somebody in the night had thrown salt all over the deck. He, knowing what it was, desired me to bring some of it down to him; accordingly I took up a handful of it, which I found very cold indeed; and when I brought it to him he desired me to taste it. I did so, and was surprised above measure. I then asked him what it was; he told me it was snow; but I could not by any means understand him. He asked me if we had no such thing in our country; and I told him "No." I then asked him the use of it, and who made it; he told me a great man in the heavens, called God: but here again I was to all intents and purposes at a loss to understand him; and the more so, when a little after I saw the air filled with it, in a heavy shower, which fell down on the same day.

After this I went to church; and having never been at such a place before, I was again amazed at seeing and hearing the service. I asked all I could about it; and they gave me to understand it was "worshiping God, who made us and all things." I was still at a loss, and soon got into an endless field of inquiries, as well as I was able to speak and ask about things. However, my dear little friend Dick[2] used to be my best interpreter; for I could make free with him and he always instructed me with pleasure. And from what I could understand by him of this God, and in seeing that these white people did not sell one another as we did, I was much pleased: and in this I thought they were much happier than we Africans. I was astonished at the wisdom of the white people in all things which I beheld; but I was greatly amazed at their not sacrificing, not making any offerings, and at their eating with unwashen hands, and touching of the dead. I also could not help remarking the particular slenderness of their women, which I did not at first like, and I thought them not so modest and shamefaced as the African women.

I had often seen my master Dick employed in reading; and I had a great curiosity to talk to the books, as I thought they did; and so to learn how all things had a beginning. For that purpose I have often taken up a book and talked to it, and then put my ears to it, when alone, in hopes it would answer me; and I have been very much concerned when I found it remaining silent.

[READING THE BIBLE; FINDING A "FATHER"; SOLD AGAIN INTO SLAVERY]

There was also one Daniel Queen, about forty years of age, a man very well educated, who messed with me on board this ship,[3] and he likewise dressed and attended the captain. Fortunately this man soon became very much attached to me, and took great pains to instruct me in many things. He taught me to shave, and dress hair a little, and also to read in the Bible, explaining many passages to me, which I did not comprehend. I was wonderfully surprised to see the laws and rules of my own country written almost exactly here; a circumstance which, I believe, tended to impress our manners and customs more deeply on my memory. I used to tell him of this resemblance, and many a time we have sat up the whole night together at this employment. In short, he was like a father to me; and some used even to call me after his name: they also styled me "the black Christian." Indeed I almost loved him with the affection of

---

2. Richard Baker, an American boy four or five years older than Equiano.

3. The *Etna*, of which Pascal had been given command in 1759; messed: ate.

a son. Many things I have denied myself, that he might have them; and when I used to play at marbles or any other game, and won a few halfpence, or got some money for shaving any one, I used to buy him a little sugar or tobacco, as far as my stock of money would go. He used to say that he and I never should part, and that when our ship was paid off, as I was free as himself or any other man on board, he would instruct me in his business, by which I might gain a good livelihood. This gave me new life and spirits; and my heart burned within me, while I thought the time long till I obtained my freedom. For though my master had not promised it to me, yet, besides the assurances I had often received that he had no right to detain me,[4] he always treated me with the greatest kindness, and reposed in me an unbounded confidence. He even paid attention to my morals, and would never suffer me to deceive him, or tell lies, of which he used to tell me the consequences; and that if I did so, God would not love me. So that from all this tenderness I had never once supposed, in all my dreams of freedom, that he would think of detaining me any longer than I wished.

In pursuance of our orders we sailed from Portsmouth for the Thames, and arrived at Deptford the 10th of December, where we cast anchor just as it was high water. The ship was up about half an hour, when my master ordered the barge to be manned; and, all in an instant, without having before given me the least reason to suspect any thing of the matter, he forced me into the barge, saying, I was going to leave him, but he would take care that I did not. I was so struck with the unexpectedness of this proceeding, that for some time I did not make a reply, only I made an offer to go for my books and chest of clothes, but he swore I should not move out of his sight; and if I did, he would cut my throat, at the same time taking out his hanger.[5] I told him that I was free, and he could not by law serve me so. But this only enraged him the more; and he continued to swear, and said he would soon let me know whether he would or not, and at that instant sprung himself into the barge, from the ship, to the astonishment and sorrow of all on board.

The tide, rather unluckily for me, had just turned downward, so that we quickly fell down the river along with it, till we came among some outwardbound West Indiamen; for he was resolved to put me on board the first vessel he could get to receive me. The boat's crew, who pulled against their will, became quite faint at different times, and would have gone ashore, but he would not let them. Some of them strove then to cheer me, and told me he could not sell me, and that they would stand by me, which revived me a little, and I still entertained hopes; for as they pulled me along he asked some vessels to receive me, and they refused.

But, just as we had got a little below Gravesend, we came alongside of a ship going away the next tide for the West-Indies; her name was the Charming Sally, Captain James Doran. My master went on board and agreed with him for me; and in little time I was sent for into the cabin. When I came there Captain Doran asked me if I knew him; I answered I did not: "Then," said he, "you are now my slave." I told him my master could not sell me to him nor to any one else. "Why," said he, "did not your master buy you?" I confessed he did. "But I have served him," said I, "many years, and he has taken all my wages and prize-money,[6] for I only got one sixpence during the war. Besides this I have been baptized; and, by the laws of the land, no man has a right to sell me." And I added, that I had heard a lawyer, and others, at

---

4. Even before the Mansfield Decision of 1772, contemporary opinion held that Royal Navy ships were British territory, on which slavery was inappropriate.

5. Short sword.

6. Profits from an enemy ship and its cargo seized during war, traditionally shared among the victorious crew.

different times tell my master so. They both then said, that those people who told me so, were not my friends: but I replied—it was very extraordinary that other people did not know the law as well as they. Upon this, Captain Doran said I talked too much English, and if I did not behave myself well and be quiet, he had a method on board to make me. I was too well convinced of his power over me to doubt what he said; and my former sufferings in the slave-ship presenting themselves to my mind, the recollection of them made me shudder. However, before I retired I told them, that as I could not get any right among men here, I hoped I should hereafter in Heaven, and I immediately left the cabin, filled with resentment and sorrow.

The only coat I had with me my master took away with him, and said, "if your prize-money had been £10,000, I had a right to it all, and would have taken it." I had about nine guineas, which, during my long sea-faring life, I had scraped together from trifling perquisites and little ventures; and I hid it that instant, lest my master should take that from me likewise, still hoping that, by some means or other, I should make my escape to the shore. Indeed some of my old shipmates told me not to despair, for they would get me back again; and that, as soon as they could get their pay, they would immediately come to Portsmouth to me, where this ship was going. But, alas, all my hopes were baffled, and the hour of my deliverance was, as yet, far off. My master, having soon concluded his bargain with the captain, came out of the cabin, and he and his people got into the boat and put off. I followed them with aching eyes as long as I could, and when they were out of sight I threw myself on the deck, with a heart ready to burst with sorrow and anguish.

[EMPLOYMENT IN THE WEST INDIES]

I had the good fortune to please my master[7] in every department in which he employed me; and there was scarcely any part of his business, or household affairs, in which I was not occasionally engaged. I often supplied the place of a clerk, in receiving and delivering cargoes to the ships, in tending stores, and delivering goods; and, besides this, I used to shave and dress my master, when convenient, and take care of his horse; and when it was necessary, which was very often, I worked likewise on board of his different vessels. By these means I became very useful to my master, and saved him, as he used to acknowledge, above a hundred pounds a year. Nor did he scruple to say I was of more advantage to him than any of his clerks; tho' their usual wages in the West-Indies are from sixty to a hundred pounds current a year.

I have sometimes heard it asserted that a negro cannot earn his master the first cost; but nothing can be further from the truth. I suppose nine tenths of the mechanics throughout the West-Indies are negro slaves; and I well know the coopers[8] among them earn two dollars a-day; the carpenters the same, and oftentimes more; also the masons, smiths, and fishermen, &c. and I have known many slaves whose masters would not take a thousand pounds current for them. But surely this assertion refutes itself: for, if it be true, why do the planters and merchants pay such a price for slaves? And, above all, why do those, who make this assertion, exclaim the most loudly against the abolition of the slave trade? So much are men blinded, and to such inconsistent arguments are they driven by mistaken interest! I grant, indeed, that slaves are sometimes, by half-feeding, half-clothing, over-working, and stripes,[9] reduced so low, that they are turned out as unfit for service, and left to perish in the woods, or to expire on a dunghill.

---

7. Robert King, an American merchant.
8. Barrel-makers.

9. Lashings and the welts they leave.

My master was several times offered by different gentlemen one hundred guineas[1] for me; but he always told them he would not sell me, to my great joy: and I used to double my diligence and care for fear of getting into the hands of these men, who did not allow a valuable slave the common support of life. Many of them used to find fault with my master for feeding his slaves so well as he did; although I often went hungry, and an Englishman might think my fare very indifferent: but he used to tell them he always would do it, because the slaves thereby looked better and did more work.

While I was thus employed by my master, I was often a witness to cruelties of every kind, which were exercised on my unhappy fellowslaves. I used frequently to have different cargoes of new negroes in my care for sale; and it was almost a constant practice with our clerks, and other whites, to commit violent depredations on the chastity of the female slaves; and to these atrocities I was, though with reluctance, obliged to submit at all times, being unable to help them. When we have had some of these slaves on board my master's vessels to carry them to other islands, or to America, I have known our mates commit these acts most shamefully, to the disgrace not of christians only, but of men. I have even known them gratify their brutal passion with females not ten years old; and these abominations some of them practised to such a scandalous excess, that one of our captains discharged the mate and others on that account. And yet in Montserrat[2] I have seen a negro-man staked to the ground, and cut most shockingly, and then his ears cut off, bit by bit, because he had been connected with a white woman, who was a common prostitute! As if it were no crime in the whites to rob an innocent African girl of her virtue; but most heinous in a black man only to gratify a passion of nature, where the temptation was offered by one of a different colour, though the most abandoned woman of her species.

[THE PERILS OF BEING A FREEMAN]

I have since often seen in Jamaica and other islands, free men, whom I have known in America, thus villainously trepanned[3] and kept in bondage. I have heard of two similar practices even in Philadelphia: and were it not for the benevolence of the Quakers in that city, many of the sable race, who now breathe the air of liberty, would, I believe, be groaning under some planter's chains. These things opened my mind to a new scene of horror, to which I had been before a stranger. Hitherto I had thought only slavery dreadful; but the state of a free negro appeared to me now equally so at least, and in some respects even worse; for they live in constant alarm for their liberty, which is but nominal; and they are universally insulted and plundered without the possibility of redress; such being the equity of the West-Indian laws, that no free negro's evidence will be admitted in their courts of justice. * * *

I determined to make every exertion to obtain my freedom, and to return to Old England. For this purpose I thought a knowledge of Navigation might be of use to me; for, though I did not intend to run away unless I should be ill used, yet, in such a case, if I understood navigation, I might attempt my escape in our sloop, which was one of the swiftest sailing vessels in the West-Indies, and I could be at no loss for hands to join me. Had I made this attempt, I had intended to go in her to England; but this, as I said, was only to be in the event of my meeting with any ill usage. I

1. The guinea coin, first struck in 1663 by a company of merchants chartered by the British crown to obtain slaves from the Guinea coast of Africa (hence the name), was worth 21 shillings; made of gold, it often traded for more than its face value and connoted a certain prestige.
2. Island in the British West Indies.
3. Betrayed.

therefore employed the mate of our vessel to teach me Navigation, for which I agreed to give him twenty-four dollars, and actually paid him part of the money down; though when the captain, some time after, came to know that the mate was to have such a sum for teaching me, he rebuked him, and said it was a shame for him to take any money from me. However, my progress in this useful art was much retarded by the constancy of our work.

Had I wished to run away I did not want opportunities, which frequently presented themselves; and particularly at one time, soon after this. When we were at the island of Guadaloupe there was a large fleet of merchantmen bound for Old France; and seamen then being very scarce, they gave from fifteen to twenty pounds a man for the run. Our mate and all the white sailors left our vessel on this account, and went aboard of the French ships. They would have had me also to go with them, for they regarded me, and swore to protect me, if I would go: and, as the fleet was to sail the next day, I really believe I could have got safe to Europe at that time. However, as my master was kind, I would not attempt to leave him; still remembering the old maxim, that *honesty is the best policy*, I suffered them to go without me. Indeed my captain was much afraid of my leaving him and the vessel at that time, as I had so fair an opportunity: but, I thank God, this fidelity of mine turned out much to my advantage hereafter, when I did not in the least think of it; and made me so much in favour with the captain, that he used now and then to teach me some parts of Navigation himself. But some of our passengers, and others, seeing this, found much fault with him for it, saying it was a very dangerous thing to let a negro know Navigation; and thus I was hindered again in my pursuits.

[MANUMISSION]

When we had unladen the vessel, and I had sold my venture,[4] finding myself master of about forty-seven pounds, I consulted my true friend, the Captain, how I should proceed in offering my master the money for my freedom.[5] He told me to come on a certain morning, when he and my master would be at breakfast together. Accordingly, on that morning I went, and met the Captain there, as he had appointed. When I went in I made my obeisance to my master, and with my money in my hand, and many fears in my heart, I prayed him to be as good as his offer to me, when he was pleased to promise me my freedom as soon as I could purchase it. This speech seemed to confound him; he began to recoil; and my heart that instant sunk within me. "What," said he, "give you your freedom? Why, where did you get the money? Have you got forty pounds sterling?" "Yes, sir," I answered. "How did you get it?" replied he. I told him, "very honestly." The Captain then said he knew I got the money very honestly and with much industry, and that I was particularly careful. On which my master replied, I got money much faster than he did; and said he would not have made me the promise which he did, had he thought I should have got the money so soon. "Come, come," said my worthy Captain, clapping my master on the back, "Come, Robert, (which was his name) I think you must let him have his freedom. You have laid your money out very well; you have received good interest for it all this time, and here is now the principal at last. I know GUSTAVUS has earned you more than a hundred a year, and he will still save you money, as he will not leave you. Come, Robert, take the money." My master then said, he would not be worse than his promise; and, taking the money, told me to go to the Secretary at the Register Office, and get my manumission[6] drawn up.

4. The stock he was permitted to trade for himself.
5. In 1763 Equiano was sold to Robert King, a Quaker merchant, and thereafter served in the West Indies in one of his ships under Captain Thomas Farmer.
6. The formal liberation of a slave.

These words of my master were like a voice from heaven to me: in an instant all my trepidation was turned into unutterable bliss, and I most reverently bowed myself with gratitude, unable to express my feelings, but by the overflowing of my eyes, and a heart replete with thanks to God; while my true and worthy friend, the Captain, congratulated us both with a peculiar degree of heartfelt pleasure. As soon as the first transports of my joy were over, and that I had expressed my thanks to these my worthy friends in the best manner I was able, I rose with a heart full of affection and reverence, and left the room, in order to obey my master's joyful mandate of going to the Register Office. As I was leaving the house I called to mind the words of the Psalmist, in the 126th Psalm, and like him, "I glorified God in my heart, in whom I trusted."[7] These words had been impressed on my mind from the very day I was forced from Deptford[8] to the present hour, and I now saw them, as I thought, fulfilled and verified.

My imagination was all rapture as I flew to the Register Office; and in this respect, like the apostle Peter (whose deliverance from prison was so sudden and extraordinary, that he thought he was in a vision)[9] I could scarcely believe I was awake. Heavens! who could do justice to my feelings at this moment? Not conquering heroes themselves, in the midst of a triumph—Not the tender mother who has just regained her long-lost infant, and presses it to her heart—Not the weary, hungry mariner, at the sight of the desired friendly port—Not the lover, when he once more embraces his beloved mistress, after she has been ravished from his arms!—All within my breast was tumult, wildness, and delirium! My feet scarcely touched the ground; for they were winged with joy, and, like Elijah, as he rose to Heaven, they "were with lightning sped as I went on."[1] Every one I met I told of my happiness, and blazed about the virtue of my amiable master and Captain. * * *

In short, the fair as well as black people immediately styled me by a new appellation,—to me the most desirable in the world,—which was "Freeman," and, at the dances I gave, my Georgia superfine blue clothes made no indifferent appearance, as I thought. Some of the sable females, who formerly stood aloof, now began to relax and appear less coy; but my heart was still fixed on London, where I hoped to be ere long. So that my worthy Captain, and his owner, my late master, finding that the bent of my mind was towards London, said to me, "We hope you won't leave us, but that you will still be with the vessels." Here gratitude bowed me down; and none but the generous mind can judge of my feelings, struggling between inclination and duty. However, notwithstanding my wish to be in London, I obediently answered my benefactors that I would go in the vessel, and not leave them; and from that day I was entered on board as an able-bodied seaman, at thirty-six shillings per month, besides what perquisites I could make.[2] My intention was to make a voyage or two, entirely to please these my honoured patrons; but I determined that the year following, if it pleased God, I would see Old England once more, and surprise my old master, Captain Pascal, who was hourly in my mind: for I still loved him, notwithstanding his usage to me, and I pleased myself with thinking of what he would say when he saw what the Lord had done for me in so short a time, instead of being, as he might perhaps suppose, under the cruel yoke of some planter.

---

7. Psalm 126 celebrates release from captivity; the phrase Equiano quotes does not appear there, though it echoes several other psalms (28, 33, 86, 125).
8. A borough southeast of London, where in 1762 Captain Michael Henry Pascal sold Equiano back into slavery, after several years' service. See excerpt above.

9. Acts 12.9 [Equiano's note].
1. In 2 Kings (2.11), Elijah has a vision of a chariot of fire and is carried to Heaven in a whirlwind.
2. Equiano has the right to trade for himself and to receive tips.

Mary Prince
c. 1788–after 1833

The History of Mary Prince, a West Indian Slave, Related by Herself is the earliest known slave narrative by a woman. Sponsored by the Anti-Slavery Society to galvanize support for abolition, especially from Britain's women, its saga of overwork, abuse, and sexual violence was chronicled in unprecedented depth and detail. Mary Prince's *History* was a sensation, reaching a third edition the year it was published, 1831.

Prince was born a slave on a farm in Bermuda, a British colony whose major industries were shipbuilding and salting, and whose population was half slave. In her childhood, she was treated with relative kindness, but things changed dramatically when she was twelve. She was sold to sadistic, sexually abusive new owners. After several years of brutality, she was sold to an even more ghastly situation in the "cruel, horrible" salt ponds of Turks Island, about 200 miles northeast of Bermuda, where her labor left her legs covered with boils and eventually crippled her with rheumatism. Perpetually beaten, and sexually assaulted by an "indecent master," she requested to be sold to a merchant from Antigua, who was impressed by her reputation as a good worker. Overworked and exhausted, she began to rebel at her status there, and suffered imprisonment and repeated beatings and floggings. In 1827, with the help of abolitionist sympathizers, she escaped from these owners, when they took her to London. There Thomas Pringle, a Methodist and secretary of the Anti-Slavery Society, employed her as a domestic servant. He also edited her *History* as publicity for the movement; it sparked a national controversy when attacked in *Blackwood's Edinburgh Magazine* and *The Glasgow Courier* as fraudulent propaganda by a loose-moraled liar. Libel suits erupted, Prince's owner suing Pringle, and Pringle suing *Blackwood's*. *Blackwood's* declined to cross-examine her, letting her statement stand, but Pringle lost the other case because he couldn't produce witnesses from the West Indies to substantiate the allegations of *The History*. Even so, *The History* commanded wide readership, influencing the cause not only in its representation of general atrocities, but also in its image of Prince's individual resilience and determination. "All slaves want to be free," she declared in the final paragraph; "to be free is very sweet. . . . I can tell by myself what other slaves feel, and by what they have told me. The man that says slaves be quite happy in slavery—that they don't want to be free—that man is either ignorant or a lying person. I never heard a slave say so."

from The History of Mary Prince, a West Indian Slave
Related by Herself

It was night when I reached my new home. The house was large, and built at the bottom of a very high hill; but I could not see much of it that night. I saw too much of it afterwards. The stones and the timber were the best things in it; they were not so hard as the hearts of the owners.[1]

Before I entered the house, two slave women, hired from another owner, who were at work in the yard, spoke to me, and asked who I belonged to? I replied, "I am come to live here." "Poor child, poor child!" they both said; "you must keep a good heart, if you are to live here."—When I went in, I stood up crying in a corner. Mrs. I—— came and took off my hat, a little black silk hat Miss Pruden[2] made for me, and said in a rough voice, "You are not come here to stand up in corners and cry, you are come here to work." She then put a child into my arms, and, tired as I was, I was

---

1. These strong expressions, and all of a similar character in this little narrative, are given verbatim as uttered by Mary Prince [Thomas Pringle's note].

2. Prince's first owner, Mrs. Williams, had fallen on hard times and hired her out at age 12 to Mrs. Pruden; with Mrs. Williams's death, she was sold to "Captain I—."

forced instantly to take up my old occupation of a nurse.—I could not bear to look at my mistress, her countenance was so stern. She was a stout tall woman with a very dark complexion, and her brows were always drawn together into a frown. I thought of the words of the two slave women when I saw Mrs. I——, and heard the harsh sound of her voice.

The person I took the most notice of that night was a French Black called Hetty, whom my master took in privateering[3] from another vessel, and made his slave. She was the most active woman I ever saw, and she was tasked to her utmost. A few minutes after my arrival she came in from milking the cows, and put the sweet-potatoes on for supper. She then fetched home the sheep, and penned them in the fold; drove home the cattle, and staked them about the pond side;[4] fed and rubbed down my master's horse, and gave the hog and the fed cow[5] their suppers; prepared the beds, and undressed the children, and laid them to sleep. I liked to look at her and watch all her doings, for hers was the only friendly face I had as yet seen, and I felt glad that she was there. She gave me my supper of potatoes and milk, and a blanket to sleep upon, which she spread for me in the passage before the door of Mrs. I——'s chamber.

I got a sad fright, that night. I was just going to sleep, when I heard a noise in my mistress's room; and she presently called out to inquire if some work was finished that she had ordered Hetty to do. "No, Ma'am, not yet," was Hetty's answer from below. On hearing this, my master started up from his bed, and just as he was, in his shirt, ran down stairs with a long cow-skin in his hand.[6] I heard immediately after, the cracking of the thong, and the house rang to the shrieks of poor Hetty, who kept crying out, "Oh, Massa! Massa! me dead. Massa! have mercy upon me—don't kill me outright."—This was a sad beginning for me. I sat up upon my blanket, trembling with terror, like a frightened hound, and thinking that my turn would come next. At length the house became still, and I forgot for a little while all my sorrows by falling fast asleep.

The next morning my mistress set about instructing me in my tasks. She taught me to do all sorts of household work; to wash and bake, pick cotton and wool, and wash floors, and cook. And she taught me (how can I ever forget it!) more things than these; she caused me to know the exact difference between the smart of the rope, the cart-whip, and the cow-skin, when applied to my naked body by her own cruel hand. And there was scarcely any punishment more dreadful than the blows I received on my face and head from her hard heavy fist. She was a fearful woman, and a savage mistress to her slaves.

There were two little slave boys in the house, on whom she vented her bad temper in a special manner. One of these children was a mulatto,[7] called Cyrus, who had been bought while an infant in his mother's arms; the other, Jack, was an African from the coast of Guinea, whom a sailor had given or sold to my master. Seldom a day passed without these boys receiving the most severe treatment, and often for no fault at all. Both my master and mistress seemed to think that they had a right to ill-use them at their pleasure; and very often accompanied their commands with blows, whether the children were behaving well or ill. I have seen their flesh ragged and raw with licks.—Lick—lick—they were never secure one moment from a blow, and their lives were passed in continual fear. My mistress was not contented with using the

3. Sanctioned raiding of enemy ships by armed private vessels.
4. The cattle on a small plantation in Bermuda are, it seems, often thus staked or tethered, both night and day, in situations where grass abounds. [Pringle's note].
5. A cow fed for slaughter. [Pringle's note].
6. A thong of hard twisted hide, known by this name in the West Indies [Pringle's note].
7. A person of mixed African and Caucasian descent.

whip, but often pinched their cheeks and arms in the most cruel manner. My pity for these poor boys was soon transferred to myself; for I was licked, and flogged, and pinched by her pitiless fingers in the neck and arms, exactly as they were. To strip me naked—to hang me up by the wrists and lay my flesh open with the cow-skin, was an ordinary punishment for even a slight offence. My mistress often robbed me too of the hours that belong to sleep. She used to sit up very late, frequently even until morning; and I had then to stand at a bench and wash during the greater part of the night, or pick wool and cotton; and often I have dropped down overcome by sleep and fatigue, till roused from a state of stupor by the whip, and forced to start up to my tasks.

Poor Hetty, my fellow slave, was very kind to me, and I used to call her my Aunt; but she led a most miserable life, and her death was hastened (at least the slaves all believed and said so), by the dreadful chastisement she received from my master during her pregnancy. It happened as follows. One of the cows had dragged the rope away from the stake to which Hetty had fastened it, and got loose. My master flew into a terrible passion, and ordered the poor creature to be stripped quite naked, notwithstanding her pregnancy, and to be tied up to a tree in the yard. He then flogged her as hard as he could lick, both with the whip and cow-skin, till she was all over streaming with blood. He rested, and then beat her again and again. Her shrieks were terrible. The consequence was that poor Hetty was brought to bed before her time, and was delivered after severe labour of a dead child. She appeared to recover after her confinement, so far that she was repeatedly flogged by both master and mistress afterwards; but her former strength never returned to her. Ere long her body and limbs swelled to a great size; and she lay on a mat in the kitchen, till the water burst out of her body and she died. All the slaves said that death was a good thing for poor Hetty; but I cried very much for her death. The manner of it filled me with horror. I could not bear to think about it; yet it was always present to my mind for many a day.

After Hetty died all her labours fell upon me, in addition to my own. I had now to milk eleven cows every morning before sunrise, sitting among the damp weeds; to take care of the cattle as well as the children; and to do the work of the house. There was no end to my toils—no end to my blows. I lay down at night and rose up in the morning in fear and sorrow; and often wished that like poor Hetty I could escape from this cruel bondage and be at rest in the grave. But the hand of God whom then I knew not, was stretched over me; and I was mercifully preserved for better things. It was then, however, my heavy lot to weep, weep, weep, and that for years; to pass from one misery to another, and from one cruel master to a worse. But I must go on with the thread of my story.

One day a heavy squall of wind and rain came on suddenly, and my mistress sent me round the corner of the house to empty a large earthen jar. The jar was already cracked with an old deep crack that divided it in the middle, and in turning it upside down to empty it, it parted in my hand. I could not help the accident, but I was dreadfully frightened, looking forward to a severe punishment. I ran crying to my mistress, "O mistress, the jar has come in two." "You have broken it, have you?" she replied; "come directly here to me." I came trembling; she stripped and flogged me long and severely with the cow-skin; as long as she had strength to use the lash, for she did not give over till she was quite tired.—When my master came home at night, she told him of my fault; and oh, frightful! how he fell a swearing. After abusing me with every ill name he could think of, (too, too bad to speak in England,) and giving me several heavy blows with his hand, he said, "I shall come home to-morrow morning at twelve, on purpose to give you a round hundred." He kept his word—Oh sad for me! I cannot easily forget it. He tied me up upon a ladder, and gave me a hundred lashes with his own hand, and master Benjy[8] stood by to count them for him. When he had licked me for some time he sat down to take breath; then after resting, he beat me again and again, until he was quite wearied, and so hot (for the weather was very sultry), that he sank back in his chair, almost like to faint. While my mistress went to bring him drink, there was a dreadful earthquake.[9] Part of the roof fell down, and every thing in the house went—clatter, clatter, clatter. Oh I thought the end of all things near at hand; and I was so sore with the flogging, that I scarcely cared whether I lived or died. The earth was groaning and shaking; every thing tumbling about; and my mistress and the slaves were shrieking and crying out, "The earthquake! the earthquake!" It was an awful day for us all. * * *

Some little time after this, one of the cows got loose from the stake, and eat one of the sweet-potatoe slips.[1] I was milking when my master found it out. He came to me, and without any more ado, stooped down, and taking off his heavy boot, he struck me such a severe blow in the small of my back, that I shrieked with agony, and thought I was killed; and I feel a weakness in that part to this day. The cow was frightened at his violence, and kicked down the pail and spilt the milk all about. My master knew that this accident was his own fault, but he was so enraged that he seemed glad of an excuse to go on with his ill usage. I cannot remember how many licks he gave me then, but he beat me till I was unable to stand, and till he himself was weary.

After this I ran away and went to my mother, who was living with Mr. Richard Darrel.[2] My poor mother was both grieved and glad to see me; grieved because I had been so ill used, and glad because she had not seen me for a long, long while. She dared not receive me into the house, but she hid me up in a hole in the rocks near, and brought me food at night, after every body was asleep. My father, who lived at Crow-Lane, over the salt-water channel, at last heard of my being hid up in the cavern, and he came and took me back to my master. Oh I was loth, loth to go back; but as there was no remedy, I was obliged to submit.

When we got home, my poor father said to Cap. I——, "Sir, I am sorry that my child should be forced to run away from her owner; but the treatment she has received is enough to break her heart. The sight of her wounds has nearly broke mine.—I entreat you, for the love of God, to forgive her for running away, and that you will be a kind master to her in future." Capt. I—— said I was used as well as I deserved, and that I ought to be punished for running away. I then took courage and said that I could stand the floggings no longer; that I was weary of my life, and therefore I had run away to my mother; but mothers could only weep and mourn over their children, they could not save them from cruel masters—from the whip, the rope, and the cow-skin. He told me to hold my tongue and go about my work, or he would find a way to settle me. He did not, however, flog me that day. * * *

For five years after this I remained in his house, and almost daily received the same harsh treatment. At length he put me on a sloop, and to my great joy sent me away to Turk's Island. I was not permitted to see my mother or father, or poor sisters and brothers, to say good bye, though going away to a strange land, and might never see them again. Oh the Buckra [white] people who keep slaves think that black people are like cattle, without natural affection. But my heart tells me it is far otherwise. * * *

8. Captain I——'s son, about Prince's age.
9. An earthquake shook Bermuda on 19 February 1801.
1. A cutting, rooted and planted.

2. Captain Darrell had purchased Prince and her mother, and then gave Prince to his daughter-in-law, Mrs. Williams.

My new master was one of the owners or holders of the salt ponds, and he received a certain sum for every slave that worked upon his premises, whether they were young or old. This sum was allowed him out of the profits arising from the salt works. I was immediately sent to work in the salt water with the rest of the slaves. The work was perfectly new to me. I was given a half barrel and a shovel, and had to stand up to my knees in the water from four o'clock in the morning till nine, when we were given some Indian corn boiled in water, which we were obliged to swallow as fast as we could for fear the rain should come on and melt the salt. We were then called again to our tasks, and worked through the heat of the day; the sun flaming upon our heads like fire, and raising salt blisters in those parts which were not completely covered. Our feet and legs, from standing in the salt water for so many hours, soon became full of dreadful boils, which eat down in some cases to the very bone, afflicting the sufferers with great torment. We came home at twelve; ate our corn soup, called *blawly*, as fast as we could, and went back to our employment till dark at night. We then shovelled up the salt in large heaps, and went down to the sea, where we washed the pickle from our limbs, and cleaned the barrows and shovels from the salt. When we returned to the house, our master gave us each our allowance of raw Indian corn, which we pounded in a mortar and boiled in water for our suppers.

We slept in a long shed, divided into narrow slips, like the stalls used for cattle. Boards fixed upon stakes driven into the ground, without mat or covering, were our only beds. On Sundays, after we had washed the salt bags, and done other work required of us, we went into the bush and cut the long soft grass, of which we made trusses for our legs and feet to rest upon, for they were so full of the salt boils that we could get no rest lying upon the bare boards.

Though we worked from morning till night, there was no satisfying Mr. D———. I hoped, when I left Capt. I———, that I should have been better off, but I found it was but going from one butcher to another. There was this difference between them: my former master used to beat me while raging and foaming with passion;   Mr. D——— was usually quite calm. He would stand by and give orders for a slave to be cruelly whipped, and assist in the punishment, without moving a muscle of his face, walking about and taking snuff with the greatest composure. Nothing could touch his hard heart—neither sighs, nor tears, nor prayers, nor streaming blood: he was deaf to our cries, and careless of our sufferings.—Mr. D——— has often stripped me naked, hung me up by the wrists, and beat me with the cow-skin with his own hand, till my body was raw with gashes. Yet there was nothing very remarkable in this; for it might serve as a sample of the common usage of slaves on that horrible island.

≡◆≡

Thomas Bellamy
1745–1800

Thomas Bellamy had various careers, as a hosier, a bookseller's clerk, magazine publisher, writer, and proprietor of a circulating library. In 1789 he wrote *The Benevolent Planters* in support of the anti-emancipation West Indian lobby. Staged at the Theatre Royal, Haymarket, with some of the leading actors of the day, his playlet presents a world of kindly paternal masters whose slaves proclaim their happiness and gratitude.

The Benevolent Planters
A Dramatic Piece

Scene, Jamaica

Characters

Planters: GOODWIN, STEADY, HEARTFREE
Slaves: ORAN, SELIMA
Archers, &c. &c.

Prologue (By a Friend)[1]

AN AFRICAN SAILOR:

> To Afric's torrid clime, where every day
> The sun oppresses with his scorching ray,
> My birth I owe; and here for many a year,
> I tasted pleasure free from every care.
> 5   There 'twas my happy fortune long to prove
> The fond endearments of parental love.
> 'Twas there my Adela, my favourite maid,
> Return'd my passion, love with love repaid.
> Oft on the banks where golden rivers flow,
> 10   And aromatic woods enchanting grow,
> With my lov'd Adela I pass'd the day,
> While suns on suns roll'd unperceiv'd away.
> But ah! this happiness was not to last,
> Clouds now the brightness of my fate o'ercast;
> 15   For the white savage fierce upon me sprung,
> Wrath in his eye, and fury on his tongue,
> And dragg'd me to a loathsome vessel near,
> Dragg'd me from every thing I held most dear,
> And plung'd me in the horrors of despair.
> 20   Insensible to all that pass'd around,
> Till, in a foreign clime, myself I found,
> And sold to slavery!—There with constant toil,
> Condemn'd in burning suns to turn the soil.
> Oh! if I told you what I suffer'd there,
> 25   From cruel masters, and the lash severe,
> Eyes most unus'd to melt, would drop the tear.
> But fortune soon a kinder master gave,
> Who made me soon forget I was a slave,
> And brought me to this land, this generous land,°   *Jamaica*
> 30   Where, they inform me, that an hallow'd band,
> Impelled by soft humanity's kind laws,
> Take up with fervent zeal the Negroe's cause,
> And at this very moment, anxious try,
> To stop the widespread woes of slavery.

---

1. Spoken by Stephen George Kemble, a leading tragic actor, as "An African Sailor." In the play Kemble performed Olah, whose beloved, Selima, was performed by his wife. The anti-slavetrade, pro-liberty prologue is not disputed by the playlet, which instead presents a humane, anti-emancipation image of plantation life.

35   But of this hallow'd band a part appears,
        Exult my heart, and flow my grateful tears.
        Oh sons of mercy! whose extensive mind
        Takes in at once the whole of human kind,
        Who know the various nations of the earth,
40   To whatsoever clime they owe their birth,
        Or of whatever colour they appear,
        All children of one gracious Parent are.
        And thus united by paternal love,
        To all mankind, of all the friend you prove.
45   With fervent zeal pursue your godlike plan,
        And man deliver from the tyrant man!
        What tho' at first you miss the wish'd-for end,
        Success at last your labours will attend.
        Then shall your worth, extoll'd in grateful strains,
50   Resound through Gambia's and Angola's plains.[2]
        Nations unborn your righteous zeal shall bless,
        To them the source of peace and happiness.
        Oh mighty Kannoah, thou most holy power,
        Whom humbly we thy sable race adore!
55   Prosper the great design—thy children free
        From the oppressor's hand, and give them liberty!

Scene 1

A Room in Goodwin's House; Enter Goodwin, meeting Steady and Heartfree.

GOODWIN: Good morrow, neighbours, friend Steady,[3] is your jetty tribe ready for the diversions?

STEADY: My tribe is prepared and ready to meet thine, and my heart exults on beholding so many happy countenances. But an added joy is come home to my bosom. This English friend, who, some time since, came to settle among us, in order that he might exhibit to his brother Planters, the happy effects of humanity, in the treatment of those who, in the course of human chance, are destined to the bonds of slavery, has honoured my dwelling with his presence, and gladdened my heart with his friendship.

HEARTFREE: A cause like the present, makes brothers of us all, and may heaven increase the brothers of humanity—Friend Steady informs me, that we are to preside as directors of the different diversions.

GOODWIN: It is our wish to prevent a repetition of disorders, that last year disturbed the general happiness. They were occasioned by the admission of one of those games, which, but too often, begin in sport, and end in passion. The offenders, however, were soon made sensible of the folly of attacking each other without provocation, and with no other view than to shew their superior skill, in an art, which white men have introduced among them.[4]

HEARTFREE: If that art was only made use of as a defence against the attacks of an unprincipled and vulgar violence, no man could with propriety form a wish of checking its progress. But while it opens another field where the gambler fills his

2. Gambia: northwest African country, with a strong British colonial presence. Angola: Portuguese colony on the southwest coast.
3. "Friend" evokes the Quaker term of address; Bellamy

may be trying to suggest that not all Quakers were adamant abolitionists.
4. Perhaps boxing or duelling.

pocket at the expence of the credulous and unsuspecting, whose families too often mourn in poverty and distress the effects of their folly; every member of society will hold up his hand against it, if his heart feels as it ought. I am sorry likewise to add, that too many recent instances of its fatal effects among my own countrymen, have convinced me of the guilt and folly of venturing *a life* to display *a skill*.

GOODWIN: We are happy to find our union strengthened by corresponding sentiments.

HEARTFREE: The sports, I find, are to continue six days; repeat your design, respecting the successful archers.

STEADY: The archers, friend, to the number of twelve, consist of selected slaves, whose honest industry and attachment have rendered them deserving of reward. They are to advance in pairs, and the youth who speeds the arrow surest, is to be proclaimed victor.

HEARTFREE: And what is his reward?

STEADY: A portion of land for himself, and his posterity—freedom for his life, and the maiden of his heart.

HEARTFREE: Generous men! humanity confers dignity upon authority. The grateful Africans have hearts as large as ours, and shame on the degrading lash, when it can be spared—Reasonable obedience is what we expect, and let those who look for more, feel and severely feel the sting of disappointment.

STEADY: Will your poor fellow attend the festival?

HEARTFREE: He will. I respect your feelings for the sorrows of the worthy Oran.

GOODWIN: Oran, did you say? What know you of him; pardon my abruptness, but relate his story, it may prove a task of pleasure.

HEARTFREE: By the fate of war,[5] Oran had been torn from his beloved Selima. The conquerors were on the point of setting fire to the consuming pile to which he was bound, while the partner of his heart, who was devoted[6] to the arms of the chief of the adverse party, was rending the air with her cries; at this instant a troop of Europeans broke in upon them, and bore away a considerable party to their ships; among the rest was the rescued Oran, who was happily brought to our mart, where I had the good fortune to become his master—he has since served me well and affectionately. But sorrow for his Selima is so deeply rooted in his feeling bosom, that I fear I shall soon lose an excellent domestic and as valuable a friend, whose only consolation springs from a sense of dying in the possession of Christian principles, from whence he acknowledges to have drawn comforts inexpressible.

GOODWIN: And comfort he shall still draw from a worldly as well as a heavenly source. For know, I can produce the Selima he mourns. She has told me her story, which is indeed a tale of woe. Inward grief has preyed upon her mind, and like her faithful Oran, she is bending to her grave. But happiness, love, and liberty shall again restore them.

HEARTFREE: When the mind has made itself up to misery—discoveries admitting of more than hope, ought ever to be made with caution. But you have a heart to feel for the distress of another, and conduct to guide you in giving relief to sorrow; leave me to my poor fellow, and do you prepare his disconsolate partner.

GOODWIN: I'll see her immediately, and when we take our seats on the plain of sports, we will communicate to each other the result of our considerations.

STEADY: Till then, my worthy associates, farewell. [*Exeunt*]

5. Tribal warfare in Africa.   6. Destined.

Scene II

Another Apartment in Goodwin's house. Enter Goodwin and Selima.

GOODWIN: Come, my poor disconsolate, be composed, and prepare to meet your friends on those plains, where you never shall experience sorrow; but on the contrary, enjoy every happiness within the power of thy grateful master to bestow; you once told me, Selima, that my participation of your griefs abated their force; will you then indulge me with that pleasing tho' mournful Song you have made, on the loss of him, who, perhaps, may one day be restored?

SELIMA: Good and generous Master! ever consoling me with hope, can I deny you who have given me mind, taught me your language, comforted me with the knowledge of books, and made me every thing I am? Prepared too, my soul for joys, which you say are to succeed the patient bearing of human misery. Oh, Sir, with what inward satisfaction do I answer a request in every way grateful to my feelings!

SONG. SET TO MUSIC BY MR. REEVE[7]

How vain to me the hours of ease,
  When every daily toil is o'er;
In my sad heart no hope I find,
  For Oran is, alas! no more.

Not sunny Africa could please,
  Nor friends upon my native shore,
To me the dreary world's a cave,
  For Oran is, alas! no more.

In bowers of bliss beyond the moon,
  The white man says, his sorrow's o'er,
And comforts me with soothing hope,
  Tho' Oran is, alas, no more.

O come then, messenger of death,
  Convey me to yon starry shore,
Where I may meet with my true love,
  And never part with Oran more.

GOODWIN: There's my kind Selima! and now attend to a discovery, on which depends your future happiness; not only liberty, but love awaits you.

SELIMA: The first I want not—the last can never be! for where shall I find another Oran?

GOODWIN: O my good girl, your song of sorrow shall be changed into that of gladness. For know—the hours of anguish are gone by, your Oran lives, and lives but to bless his faithful Selima.

SELIMA [*after a pause*]: To that invisible Being who has sustained my suffering heart, I kneel, overwhelmed with an awful[8] sense of his protecting power. But how?

GOODWIN: As we walk on, I will explain every thing. You soon will embrace your faithful Oran, and his beloved Selima shall mourn no more. [*Exeunt.*]

7. William Reeve (1757–1815), actor and composer.   8. Awe-filled.

Scene III

An open Plain.

[*On one side a range of men-slaves; on the other a range of women-slaves—at some distance, seated on decorated chairs, Heartfree, Goodwin, and Steady—twelve archers close the line on the men-side, meeting the audience with Oran at their head, distinguished from the rest by a rich dress—Oran, advancing to the front of the stage, stands in a dejected posture.*]

HEARTFREE: Now let the air echo to the sound of the enlivening instruments, and beat the ground to their tuneful melody; while myself and my two worthy friends, who since our last festival have reaped the benefit of your honest labours, in full goblets drink to your happiness.

[*Flourish of music, and a dance.*]

HEARTFREE: Now let the archers advance in pairs, and again, in replenished cups, health and domestic peace to those who surest speed the arrow.

[*Flourish. Here the archers advance in pairs to the middle of the Stage, and discharge their arrows through the side wings—the victor is saluted by two female slaves, who present to him the maiden of his choice—then a flourish of music, and the parties fall back to the side. After the ceremony has been repeated five times to as many pair of archers, and Oran and Almaboe only remain to advance as the sixth pair, Oran appears absorbed in grief, which is observed with evident concern by Heartfree.*]

HEARTFREE: Why Oran, with looks divided between earth and heaven, dost thou appear an alien among those who are encompassed with joy and gladness? Though your beloved Selima is torn from your widowed arms, yet it is a duty you owe yourself, as a man, an obligation due to me, as your friend, to take to your bosom one whom I have provided for you. A contest with Almaboe is needless; he has fixed on his partner, to whom, according to your request, he is now presented. [*A flourish of music—two female slaves advance with a third, who is presented to Almaboe—the parties embrace.*] It remains, therefore, for you to comply with the wishes of those who honour your virtues, and have respected your sorrows.

ORAN: Kind and benevolent masters; I indeed came hither unwillingly, to draw the bow, with a heart already pierced with the arrow of hopeless anguish. You have done generously by my friend, to whom I meant to have relinquished the victor's right, had the chance been mine. For alas, Sirs! Selima was my first and only love; and when I lost her, joy fled from a bosom it will never again revisit. The short date of my existence is therefore devoted alone to that Power whom you have taught me to revere. Sacred to gratitude, and sacred to her whose beckoning spirit seems at this moment to call on me from yonder sky—

GOODWIN: What say you, Oran, if I should produce a maiden whose virtues will bring you comfort, and whose affection you will find as strong as hers, whose loss you so feelingly deplore?

ORAN: O Sirs! had you but known my Selima, you would not attempt to produce her equal! Poor lost excellence! Yes, thy spirit, released from all its sufferings, is now looking down upon its Oran! But let not imagination too far transport me: perhaps she yet lives, a prey to brutal lust. [*Turns to Almaboe.*] Brother of my choice, and friend of my adverse hour, long may your Coanzi be happy in the endearments of her faithful Almaboe. And O my friend! when thy poor Oran is no more, if [it] chance that Selima yet lives, if blessed Providence *should* lead her to these happy shores, if she should escape the cruel enemy, and be brought hither with honour unsullied;[9] tell her how much she owes to these generous men; comfort her afflicted spirit, and teach her to adore the God of truth and mercy.

ALMABOE: Oran must himself endeavour to live for that day, and not by encouraging despair, sink self-devoted to the grave.[1] The same Providence, my friend, which has turned the terrors of slavery into willing bondage, may yet restore thy Selima.

ORAN: The words of Almaboe come charged with the force of truth, and erring Oran bends to offended Heaven! Yet erring Oran must still feel his loss, and erring Oran must for ever lament it.

GOODWIN: It is true, Oran, our arguments to urge thee to be happy, have hitherto proved fruitless. But know, thou man of sorrow, we are possessed of the means which will restore thee to thyself and to thy friends. Hear, then, the important secret, and know, that thy Selima yet lives!

ORAN [after a pause]: Yet lives! Selima yet lives! what my Selima! my own dear angel! O speak again, your words have visited my heart, and it is lost in rapture.

HEARTFREE: Nay, Oran, but be calm.

ORAN: I am calm—Heaven will permit me to support my joy, but do you relieve me from suspence.

GOODWIN: Let the instruments breathe forth the most pleasing strains—Advance, my happy virgins, with your charge, and restore to Oran his long-lost Selima. You receive her pure as when you parted, with a mind released from the errors of darkness, and refined by its afflictions.

[Soft music—Selima comes down the stage, attended by six virgins in fancied dresses, who present her to Oran—the lovers embrace—flourish of music, and a shout.]

ORAN: Lost in admiration, gratitude, and love, Oran has no words, but can only in silence own the hand of Heaven; while to his beating heart he clasps his restored treasure. And O my masters! for such, though free, suffer me still to call you; let my restored partner and myself bend to such exalted worth; while for ourselves, and for our surrounding brethren, we declare, that you have proved yourselves *The Benevolent Planters*, and that under subjection like yours,

SLAVERY IS BUT A NAME

SONG. TO THE TUNE OF *RULE BRITANNIA*.[2]

In honour of this happy day,
  Let Afric's sable sons rejoice;
To mercy we devote the lay,
  To heaven-born mercy raise the voice.
Long may she reign, and call each heart her own,
And nations guard her sacred throne.

Fair child of heaven, our rites approve,
  With smiles attend the votive song,
Inspire with universal love,
  For joy and peace to thee belong.
Long may'st thou reign, and call each heart thy own,
While nations guard thy sacred throne.

9. Not sexually compromised either by rape or forced consent.
1. By suicide; "devoted" means "doomed."

2. A famous song, written by James Thomson in 1740, with music by Thomas Arne.

William Cowper
1731–1800

The son of a rector and a mother who traced her descent to Henry III and John Donne, William Cowper was beset through his life with manic, sometimes suicidal, depressions, aggravated by his attraction to sects emphasizing man's original sin. He studied law but found poetry more congenial, and with the Evangelical minister and abolitionist John Newton published a volume of hymns in 1779, including Newton's great hymn *Amazing Grace*. He followed with a series of moral satires in the early 1780s, and his most famous poem, *The Task* (1785), whose second book opens with a strong critique of slavery. Feeling deeply the moral blight of slavery as an institution sustained only by greed, Cowper responded to Wilberforce's call for popular abolitionist literature with four ballads in 1788 that were widely reprinted. The poet of *The Morning Dream* envisions the goddess Britannia sailing west to a "slave-cultured island" to confront the cruel "Demon" of slave-ownership, who sickens and dies at her sight; the balladeer of *Pity for Poor Africans*, insisting that he is "shock'd at the purchase of slaves," justifies his participation by arguing that foreigners will not give up the trade: "He shar'd in the plunder, but he pitied the man." *Sweet Meat Has Sour Sauce: or, The Slave-Trader in the Dumps*, printed here, is the ditty of a trader lamenting the inevitable abolition of his business and trying to unload his gear. Cowper grew so depressed with his involvement in the slavery issue that eventually he had to stop writing about it.

Sweet Meat Has Sour Sauce
or, The Slave-Trader in the Dumps

A trader I am to the African shore,
But since that my trading is like to be o'er,
I'll sing you a song that you ne'er heard before,
    Which nobody can deny, deny,
5   Which nobody can deny.

When I first heard the news it gave me a shock,
Much like what they call an electrical knock,
And now I am going to sell off my stock,
    Which nobody can deny.

10 'Tis a curious assortment of dainty regales,°   *choice pieces*
To tickle the Negroes with when the ship sails—
Fine chains for the neck, and a cat with nine tails,[1]
    Which nobody can deny.

Here's supple-jack plenty, and store of rat-tan,[2]
15 That will wind itself round the sides of a man,
As close as a hoop round a bucket or can,
    Which nobody can deny.

Here's padlocks and bolts, and screws for the thumbs,
That squeeze them so lovingly till the blood comes;

---

1. Cat-o'-nine-tails: a whip of nine knotted lashes.
2. Both supple-jack (a woody vine) and rattan (a climbing palm) were used to make whips, canes, and ropes.

20   They sweeten the temper like comfits or plums,
                Which nobody can deny.

        When a Negro his head from his victuals withdraws,
        And clenches his teeth and thrusts out his paws,
        Here's a notable engine to open his jaws,[3]
25   Which nobody can deny.

        Thus going to market, we kindly prepare
        A pretty black cargo of African ware,
        For what they must meet with when they get there,
                Which nobody can deny.

30   'Twould do your heart good to see 'em below
        Lie flat on their backs all the way as we go,[4]
        Like sprats on a gridiron, scores in a row,[5]
                Which nobody can deny.

        But ah! if in vain I have studied an art
35   So gainful to me, all boasting apart,
        I think it will break my compassionate heart,
                Which nobody can deny.

        For oh! how it enters my soul like an awl!
        This pity, which some people self-pity call,
40   Is sure the most heart-piercing pity of all,
                Which nobody can deny.

        So this is my song, as I told you before;
        Come, buy off my stock, for I must no more
        Carry Caesars and Pompeys to Sugar-cane shore,[6]
45   Which nobody can deny, deny,
                Which nobody can deny.

Dorothy Wordsworth
1771–1855

Dorothy Wordsworth was an ardent advocate of abolition, and closely followed Parliamentary events, writing to a friend in May 1792, "I hope you were an *immediate* abolitionist and are angry with the House of Commons for continuing the traffic in human flesh so long as till 96 but you will also rejoice that so much has been done. I hate Mr. Dundas" (the member of Parliament who created the plan to delay abolition until 1796). Her Grasmere journal records the story of a slave-ship sailor, whom she views as a collateral victim of the trade; her brother William touches obliquely on this issue in Book 4 of *The Prelude*, in his recollection of his encounter with a gaunt veteran of service in "the Tropic isles."

For more on Dorothy Wordsworth, see her principal listing, page 290.

---

3. Force-feeding of a slave meaning to starve to death.
4. A reference to the tortuous tight-packing of slave cargo.
5. Sprats are herrings (metaphorically, insignificant people); a gridiron is a griddle—an image of slaves cooking

in hot cargo-holds.
6. Caesar and Pompey were famous ancient Romans (many slaves were royalty in their African cultures); "Sugar-cane shore" is the West Indies.

from **The Grasmere Journals**

Monday Morning [March 15, 1802]. . . . a sailor who was travelling from Liverpool[1] to Whitehaven called he was faint & pale when he knocked at the door, a young Man very well dressed. We sate by the kitchen fire talking with him for 2 hours—he told us most interesting stories of his life. His name was Isaac Chapel—he had been at sea since he was 15 years old. He was by trade a sail-maker. His last voyage was to the Coast of Guinea.[2] He had been on board a slave ship the Captain's name Maxwell where one man had been killed a Boy put to lodge with the pigs & was half eaten, one Boy set to watch in the hot sun till he dropped down dead. He had been cast away in North America & had travelled 30 days among the Indians where he had been well treated—He had twice swum from a King's ship in the Night & escaped, he said he would rather be in hell than be pressed.[3] He was now going to wait in England to appear against Captain Maxwell. "O he's a Rascal, Sir, he ought to be put in the papers!" The poor man had not been in bed since Friday Night—he left Liverpool at 2 o'clock on Saturday morning, he had called at a farm house to beg victuals & had been refused. The woman said she would give him nothing. "Won't you? Then I can't help it." He was excessively like my Brother John.[4]

━━ ≡✦≡ ━━

William Wordsworth
1770–1850

William Wordsworth's sonnet *To Toussaint L'Ouverture* honors François Dominique Toussaint (1743?–1803), a self-educated slave freed shortly before the 1791 revolt in San Domingo, who became a leader of the revolutionaries (dubbed "L'Ouverture" for his skill in "opening" gaps in enemy ranks, he adopted this as a surname). In 1801, he conquered San Domingo and became governor of the whole island. When, in 1802, he resisted Napoleon's attempt to re-establish French rule and slavery, he was arrested and dungeoned in the French Alps, where he died in April 1803, after ten months of cold and hunger. Wordsworth published his sonnet in *The Morning Post* in February 1803, and then in *Poems* of 1807 under "Sonnets Dedicated to Liberty." In some writing he demonstrates his unwavering moral revulsion at slavery and contempt for the economic justifications for it. But in a letter of 1833, he joined the now Tory Poet Laureate Southey in declining to contribute to a volume of antislavery poetry, expressing qualified sympathy for the planters, who, he suggests, have been too one-sidedly villainized.

For more about Wordsworth, see the principal listing on page 194.

To Toussaint L'Ouverture

Toussaint, the most unhappy man of men!
Whether the whistling Rustic tend his plough
Within thy hearing, or thy head be now
Pillowed in some deep dungeon's earless den;—
5   O miserable Chieftain! where and when
Wilt thou find patience? Yet die not; do thou
Wear rather in thy bonds a cheerful brow:
Though fallen thyself, never to rise again,

---

1. Along with Bristol, a chief center for the slave trade.
2. West coast of Africa.
3. Kidnapped and forced into service, a kind of white
male slavery.
4. John Wordsworth was captain of a merchant vessel; he would drown in a shipwreck in 1805.

Live, and take comfort. Thou hast left behind
10   Powers that will work for thee; air, earth, and skies;
There's not a breathing of the common wind
That will forget thee; thou hast great allies;
Thy friends are exultations, agonies,
And love, and man's unconquerable mind.

1802   1807

from **The Prelude**[1]

When to my native Land,
(After a whole year's absence) I return'd
I found the air yet busy with the stir
Of a contention which had been rais'd up
205   Against the Traffickers in Negro blood,
An effort, which though baffled, nevertheless
Had call'd back old forgotten principles
Dismiss'd from service, had diffus'd some truths
And more of virtuous feeling through the heart
210   Of the English People.[2] And no few of those
So numerous (little less in verity
Than a whole Nation crying with one voice)
Who had been cross'd in this their just intent
And righteous hope, thereby were well prepared
215   To let that journey sleep a while and join
Whatever other Caravan appear'd
To travel forward towards Liberty
With more success. For me that strife had ne'er
Fasten'd on my affections, nor did now
220   Its unsuccessful issue much excite
My sorrow, having laid this faith to heart,
That if France prosper'd good Men would not long
Pay fruitless worship to humanity,
And this most rotten branch of human shame,
225   Object, as seem'd, of a superfluous pains,
Would fall together with its parent tree.

1805   1926

Letter to Mary Ann Rawson[1]

[ca. May 1833]

Dear Madam,

Your letter which I lose no time in replying to, has placed me under some embarrassment, as I happen to possess some Mss verses of my own[2] upon the subject to
which you solicit my attention. But I frankly own to you, that neither with respect to

---

1. This passage, from Book 10, was written during the
abolition controversy (c. 1805); a revised text appears in
the version of *The Prelude* published in 1850, a moment
when it could address the abolition movement in the
United States, where *The Prelude* was also published.
2. Wordsworth returned from revolutionary France late
in 1792; the "effort" to which he refers is Wilberforce's

unsuccessful 1793 bill for abolition.
1. An original member of the Sheffield Female Anti-
Slavery Society (founded in 1825), Rawson began in 1826
to collect pieces for an anthology of antislavery prose and
poetry, *The Bow in the Cloud,* which she published in 1834,
after colonial Emancipation, in a small edition of 500.
2. *Humanity,* written in 1829 and published in 1835.

this subject nor to the kindred one, the Slavery of the children in the Factories,[3] which is adverted to in the same Poem, am I prepared to add to the excitement already existing in the public mind upon these, and so many other points of legislation and government. Poetry, if good for any thing, must appeal forcibly to the Imagination and the feelings; but what at this period we want above every thing, is patient examination and sober judgement. It can scarcely be necessary to add that my mind revolts as strongly as any one's can, from the law that permits one human being to sell another. It is in principle monstrous, but it is not the worst thing in human nature. Let precipitate advocates for its destruction bear this in mind. But I will not enter farther into the question than to say, that there are three parties—the Slave—the Slave owner—and the imperial Parliament, or rather the people of the British Islands, acting through that Organ. Surely the course at present pursued is hasty, intemperate, and likely to lead to gross injustice. Who in fact are most to blame? the people—who, by their legislation, have sanctioned not to say encouraged, slavery. But now we are turning round at once upon the planters, and heaping upon them indignation without measure, as if we wished that the Slaves should believe that their Masters alone were culpable—and they alone fit objects of complaint and resentment.

> Excuse haste and believe me Dear Madam
> respectfully yours,
> Wᵐ Wordsworth

+ ⟨◆⟩ +

The Edinburgh Review

One of the most influential quarterly journals of the day, the *Edinburgh Review* was edited by its cofounder Francis Jeffrey (1773–1850) from its inception in 1802 until 1829. Although Jeffrey tended to conservative standards as a literary critic (famously attacking the Lake School for presenting peasants sympathetically), the *Edinburgh* was an important organ for liberal political opinion and was committed to supporting the Whigs in their parliamentary campaign for reform. Among its other cofounders, Henry Brougham (1778–1868) was a leader in the abolitionist movement, and Sydney Smith (1771–1845) excoriated the slave trade as an "enormous wickedness." Although England had abolished the trade in 1807, other countries, including France and the United States, remained involved, and slavery was still legal in England's colonies. Reports such as the one below (October 1821) kept public attention focused on the atrocities.

from Abstract of the Information laid on the Table of the House of Commons, on the Subject of the Slave Trade

The French ship Le Rodeur, of two hundred tons burden, sailed from the port of Havre for the river Calabar on the coast of Africa, where she arrived after a prosperous voyage, and anchored at Bonny on the fourteenth of March. Her crew, of twenty-two men, had enjoyed perfect health; and this continued during her stay of three weeks, while she received on board one hundred and sixty negroes, with whom she set sail for Guadaloupe[1] on the sixth of April. No traces of any epidemy had been perceived among the natives; the cargo (as it is called), no more than the crew, exhibited any

---

3. A Parliamentary commission issued a shocking report in 1832 about child labor in factories that led to the "Act of 1833," preventing those under 9 from such labor and limited those under 13 to 48 hours a week, with no more than 9 hours in any one day; it also required these children to receive at least two hours of schooling a day. It failed in its goal to secure a 10-hour day for teenagers.
1. In the Caribbean.

symptoms of disease; and the first fortnight of the voyage to the West Indies promised a continuance of all the success which had seemed to attend the earlier stages of the expedition. The vessel had now approached the line,[2] when a frightful malady broke out. At first the symptoms were slight, little more than a redness of the eyes; and this being confined to the negroes, was ascribed to the want of air in the hold, and the narrow space between the decks, into which so large a number of those unhappy beings were crowded; something, too, was imagined to arise from the scarcity of water, which had thus early begun to be felt, and pressed chiefly upon the slaves; for they were allowed only eight ounces, which was soon reduced to half a wine glass per day. By the surgeon's advice, therefore, they were suffered, for the first time, to breathe the purer air upon the deck, where they were brought in succession; but many of these poor creatures being affected with that mighty desire of returning to their native country, which is so strong as to form a disease, termed *Nostalgia* by the physicians, no sooner found they were at liberty, than they threw themselves into the sea, locked in each other's arms, in the vain hope, known to prevail among them, of thus being swiftly transported again to their homes. With the view of counteracting this propensity, the Captain ordered several who were stopt in the attempt, to be shot or hanged in the sight of their companions; but this terrible example was unavailing to deter them; and it became necessary, once more, to confine them entirely to the hold.

The disease proved to be a virulent ophthalmia, and it now spread with irresistible rapidity among the Africans, all of whom were seized; but it soon attacked the crew; and its ravages were attended, perhaps its violence exasperated, by a dysentery, which the use of rain-water was found to have produced. A sailor who slept near the hatch communicating with the hold, was the first who caught it; next day a landsman was taken ill; and in three days more, the Captain and almost all the rest of the crew were infected. The resources of medicine were tried in vain; the sufferings of the people, and the number of the blind, were daily increasing; and they were in constant expectation that the negroes, taking advantage of their numbers, would rise and destroy them. From this danger they were only saved by the mutual hatred of the tribes to which these unfortunate beings belonged, and which was so fierce and inextinguishable, that, even under the load of chains and sickness, they were ready every instant, in their fury, to tear one another in pieces. * * *

The consternation now became general and horrid; but it did not preclude calculation; for, thirty-six of the negroes having become quite blind, were *thrown into the sea and drowned*, in order to save the expense of supporting slaves rendered unsaleable, and to obtain grounds for a claim against the under-writers.[3] * * *

The reader may think that we have been going back to the times when the slave-trade flourished under the protection of the law in England and France; and that we have been citing from the writings of some political author, some advocate for the abolition. Not so. All these horrors darken the history of the year 1819; and the tale is almost all told incidentally by the scientific compilers of a Medical Journal. Yes—in 1819 * * * twelve years after England had forbidden the traffic—eight years after she had declared it a crime—and four years after France, first by law, and then by solemn treaty, had become a party to its positive, unqualified, immediate abolition.

2. Equator.
3. The notorious precedent was the case of the slave ship Zong (1781), whose captain ordered 133 weak and diseased slaves ejected into shark-infested waters in order to collect on a policy that held the insurer liable for cargo jettisoned in order to salvage the remainder. The insurance trial (not about the captain's criminal liability but the underwriter's financial liability) was presided over by Mansfield, who ruled in favor of the captain.

Dreadful as are the scenes disclosed in the case of the Rodeur, there are even worse horrors in the Parliamentary Papers of which the abstract lies before us. In March 1820, the Tartar, commanded by Sir George Collier, boarded a French vessel, called La Jeune Estelle of Martinique, after a long chase. The captain admitted that he had been engaged in the slave-trade, but denied that he had any slaves on board, declaring that he had been plundered of his cargo. The English officers, however, observed that all the French seamen appeared agitated and alarmed; and this led to an examination of the hold. Nothing, however, was found; and they would have departed with the belief that the captain's story was a true one, had not a sailor happened to strike a cask, and hear, or fancy he heard, a faint voice issue from within. The cask was opened, and two negro girls were found crammed into it, and in the last stage of suffocation. Being brought upon the deck of the Tartar, they were recognised by a person who had before seen them in the possession of an American who had died on the coast. An investigation now took place; and it was ascertained that they formed part of a cargo of fourteen slaves, whom the French captain had carried off by an attack which he and his crew made on the American's property after his decease. This led to a new search of the slave-ship for the other twelve, whom he was thus proved to have obtained by the robbery; when a platform was discovered, on which the negroes must have been laid in a space twenty-three inches in height, and beneath it a negro was found, not, however, one of the twelve, jammed into the crevice between two water casks. Still there were no traces of those twelve slaves; and the French captain persisted in his story, that he had been plundered by a Spanish pirate. But suddenly a most horrible idea darted across the minds of the English officers and men; they recollected that, when the chase began, they had seen several casks floating past them, which, at the time, they could not account for; but now, after the examination of the one which remained on board the Jeune Estelle, little doubt could be entertained that those casks contained the wretched slaves, whom the infernal monster had thus thrown overboard, to prevent the detection that would have ensued, either upon their being found in his ship, or by their bodies floating exposed on the sea. * * *

May we not then appeal to the body of our most enlightened European neighbours, and call upon them to stimulate their rulers not only to follow the example set by England and America in classing the slave-trade among heinous crimes, but to join them in that measure which, if those three great maritime powers adopt it, must speedily become the law of all nations? That the French people at large are prepared for such a step, there can be little reason to doubt. All their ablest statesmen have the most sound views upon this important question; and the remains of prejudice with respect to the means, when so generous an anxiety is entertained for the attainment of the object, must soon give way to the enlightened genius of the age; and certainly, what has passed in America, is calculated to assist in dispelling those prejudices beyond any thing we can conceive.

Our attention has, in this article, been confined to the portion of the Parliamentary Papers which treats of the French slave-trade, as out of all comparison the most important in every point of view. Much to lament and to amend is, however, contained in the correspondence with Spain, Portugal, and the Netherlands; and it is to be hoped that our Government, acting under the control of the almost unanimous opinion upon this subject entertained both by Parliament and the country, will be enabled, before long, to obtain some more satisfactory arrangements with those three powers. The late Revolutions, and the establishment of a popular constitution in Portugal and Spain, afford additional grounds for such expectations.

END OF PERSPECTIVES: THE ABOLITION OF SLAVERY AND THE SLAVE TRADE

+·+ ≡◆≡ +·+

Mary Robinson
1758–1800

As a child, Mary Darby attended a school run by Hannah More's sisters in Bristol. In her teens she married Thomas Robinson, a clerk who landed them and their daughter in debtor's prison. Her beauty and talent rescued her: under the patronage of Richard Brinsley Sheridan and David Garrick, she made her debut in 1776 as Juliet at Drury Lane Theatre, where she appeared with great success for four seasons. Her performance in Shakespeare's *The Winter's Tale* captivated the young Prince of Wales (afterward George IV), who in his letters assumed the role of Florizel to her Perdita, the name by which she was ever afterward known. She became his mistress, but the liaison ended within a year, and the Prince reneged on a promised financial settlement of £20,000. With the aid of the prominent Whig Charles James Fox, also a lover, she obtained an annuity of £500. A series of affairs with such fashionable figures as Colonel Banastre Tarleton, who had fought under Cornwallis in America and later became a Member of Parliament, kept her in the public eye even after her retirement from the stage. Witness this paragraph, under the head "Ship News," from the *Morning Post:*

> Yesterday, a messenger arrived in town, with the very interesting and pleasing intelligence of the Tarleton, armed ship, having, after a chace of some months, captured the Perdita frigate, and brought her safe into Egham port. The Perdita is a prodigious fine clean bottomed vessel, and had taken many prizes during her cruize, particularly the Florizel, a most valuable ship belonging to the Crown, but which was immediately released, after taking out the cargo. The Perdita was captured some time ago by the Fox, but was, afterwards, retaken by the Malden, and had a sumptuous suit of new rigging, when she fell in with the Tarleton. Her manoeuvering to escape was admirable; but the Tarleton, fully determined to take her, or perish, would not give up the chace; and at length, coming alongside the Perdita, fully determined to board her, sword in hand, she instantly surrendered at discretion.

At the height of her fame, Robinson was painted by Cosway, Reynolds, Gainsborough, and Romney. (See the Gainsborough portrait, Plate Ref.) A miscarriage in 1783 paralyzed her legs, but the affair with Tarleton did not end until he married an heiress in 1798. Though Robinson's literary career was inseparable from her notoriety, it both predated and outlasted her life on the stage. Her first volume of poems appeared in 1775, and the two-volume *Poems* of 1791–1793 attracted 600 subscribers. Working in a variety of genres from the sentimental verse with which she began through ballads, tales, light occasional verse, and odes, producing plays and seven successful novels, Robinson confirmed her twofold status as celebrity and writer, and supported herself, her mother, and her daughter. *Sappho and Phaon* (1796) brought her the title of "the English Sappho" that to some degree overlaid her identity as "Perdita"; arguing in the preface for the "legitimate" Petrarchan sonnet, Robinson combined a poetry of passion (for which Sappho was an honorific female precursor) with formal control, and made a notable contribution to the revival of the sonnet upon which Wordsworth was to capitalize. Succeeding Southey as poetry editor of the *Morning Post,* she became an established figure on the London literary scene. Coleridge thought her "a woman of undoubted Genius . . . she overloads everything; but I never knew a human being with so full a mind—bad, good, and indifferent, I grant you—but full and overflowing." Her collection *Lyrical Tales* (1800), published in the last year of her life, acknowledges *Lyrical Ballads;* Coleridge thought the meter of *The Haunted Beach* "fascinating," and sent her *Kubla Khan* in manuscript, inspiring one of her last works, *To the Poet Coleridge,* a record of response to the poem sixteen years before it was printed. Her career exemplifies the opportunities for self-fashioning the burgeoning literary marketplace offered a resourceful woman.

Ode to Beauty

EXULTING BEAUTY:—phantom of an hour,
    Whose magic spells enchain the heart,
Ah! what avails thy fascinating pow'r,
    Thy thrilling smile, thy witching art?
5   Thy lip, where balmy nectar glows;
        Thy cheek, where round the damask rose
    A thousand nameless Graces move,
        Thy mildly speaking azure eyes,
    Thy golden hair, where cunning Love
10   In many a mazy ringlet lies?
    Soon as thy radiant form is seen,
    Thy native blush, thy timid mien,°   *appearance*
Thy hour is past! thy charms are vain!
ILL-NATURE haunts thee with her sallow train,
15 Mean JEALOUSY deceives thy list'ning ear,
And SLANDER stains thy cheek with many a bitter tear.

In calm retirement form'd to dwell,
    NATURE, thy handmaid fair and kind,
    For thee a beauteous garland twin'd;
20 The vale-nurs'd Lily's downcast bell
        Thy modest mien display'd,
    The snow-drop, April's meekest child,
    With myrtle blossoms undefil'd.
        Thy mild and spotless mind pourtray'd;
25   Dear blushing maid, of cottage birth,
    'Twas thine, o'er dewy meads to stray,
    While sparkling health, and frolic mirth,
        Led on thy laughing Day.

Lur'd by the babbling tongue of FAME,
30 Too soon, insidious FLATT'RY came;
    Flush'd VANITY her footsteps led,
        To charm thee from thy blest repose,
    While Fashion twin'd about thy head
        A wreath of wounding woes;
35 See Dissipation smoothly glide,
    Cold Apathy, and puny Pride,
    Capricious Fortune, dull, and blind,
        O'er splendid Folly throws her veil,
        While Envy's meagre tribe assail
40 Thy gentle form, and spotless mind.

Their spells prevail! no more those eyes
    Shoot undulating fires;
On thy wan cheek, the young rose dies,
    Thy lip's deep tint expires;
45 Dark Melancholy chills thy mind;
    Thy silent tear reveals thy woe;
TIME strews with thorns thy mazy way;
Where'er thy giddy footsteps stray,

Thy thoughtless heart is doom'd to find
50   An unrelenting foe.

'Tis thus, the infant Forest flow'r,
Bespangled o'er with glitt'ring dew,
At breezy morn's refreshing hour,
Glows with pure tints of varying hue,
55 Beneath an aged oak's wide spreading shade,
Where no rude winds, or beating storms invade.
Transplanted from its lonely bed,
No more it scatters perfumes round,
No more it rears its gentle head,
60   Or brightly paints the mossy ground;
For ah! the beauteous bud, too soon,
Scorch'd by the burning eye of day,
Shrinks from the sultry glare of noon,
Droops its enamell'd brow, and blushing, dies away.

1791

January, 1795

Pavement slippery, people sneezing
Lords in ermine, beggars freezing;
Titled gluttons dainties carving,
Genius in a garret starving.

5 Lofty mansions, warm and spacious;
Courtiers cringing and voracious;
Misers scarce the wretched heeding;
Gallant soldiers fighting, bleeding.

Wives who laugh at passive spouses;
10 Theatres, and meeting houses;
Balls, where simpering misses languish;
Hospitals, and groans of anguish.

Arts and sciences bewailing;
Commerce drooping, credit failing;
15 Placemen° mocking subjects loyal;   *political appointees*
Separations, weddings royal.

Authors who can't earn a dinner;
Many a subtle rogue a winner;
Fugitives for shelter seeking;
20 Misers hoarding, tradesmen breaking.°   *going bankrupt*

Taste and talents quite deserted;
All the laws of truth perverted;
Arrogance o'er merit soaring;
Merit silently deploring.

25 Ladies gambling night and morning;
Fools the works of genius scorning;
Ancient dames for girls mistaken;
Youthful damsels quite forsaken.

Some in luxury delighting;
30   More in talking than in fighting;
Lovers old, and beaux decrepid;
Lordlings empty and insipid.

Poets, painters, and musicians;
Lawyers, doctors, politicians;
35   Pamphlets, newspapers, and odes,
Seeking fame by different roads.

Gallant souls with empty purses;
Generals only fit for nurses;
School-boys, smit with martial spirit,
40   Taking places of veteran merit.

Honest men who can't get places,
Knaves who show unblushing faces;
Ruin hastened, peace retarded;
Candour spurn'd, and art° rewarded.   *hypocrisy*

1795   1795

from **Sappho and Phaon, in a Series of Legitimate Sonnets**[1]

Flendus amor meus est; elegeia flebile carmen;
Non facit ad lacrymas barbitos ulla meas.   OVID

Love taught my tears in sadder notes to flow,
And tuned my heart to elegies of woe.   POPE

4

Why, when I gaze on Phaon's beauteous eyes,
    Why does each thought in wild disorder stray?
    Why does each fainting faculty decay,
And my chill'd breast in throbbing tumults rise?
5   Mute on the ground my lyre neglected lies,
    The Muse forgot, and lost the melting lay;
    My down-cast looks, my faltering lips betray,
That stung by hopeless passion;—Sappho dies!
    Now on a bank of cypress° let me rest;   *emblem of death*
10   Come, tuneful maids, ye pupils of my care,
    Come, with your dulcet° numbers soothe my breast;   *sweet, melodious*
And, as the soft vibrations float on air,
    Let pity waft my spirit to the blest,
To mock the barbarous triumphs of despair!

1. The Greek lyric poet Sappho of Lesbos (c. 600 B.C.) was particularly famous for love poems addressed to other women. Little is known of her life; she is said to have been banished from Lesbos, and gone to Sicily. According to legend, she fell in love with Phaon, a Lesbian boatman granted youth and beauty by Aphrodite, and when her love was not returned, perished by throwing herself from the Leucadian rock into the sea. Robinson narrates these events in a series of 44 sonnets, taking her epigraph from Epistle XV of the *Heroides*, by Ovid (43 B.C.–A.D. 18), which popularized the story; the translation is from *Sappho to Phaon* (1712), a free rendering by Alexander Pope (1688–1744) (7–8).

7

Come. Reason, come! each nerve rebellious bind,²
   Lull the fierce tempest of my fev'rish soul;
   Come, with the magic of thy meek controul,
And check the wayward wand'rings of my mind:
5   Estrang'd from thee, no solace can I find;
   O'er my rapt brain, where pensive visions stole,
   Now passion reigns and stormy tumults roll—
So the smooth Sea obeys the furious wind!
   In vain Philosophy unfolds his³ store,
10 O'erwhelm'd is every source of pure delight;
   Dim is the golden page of wisdom's lore;
All nature fades before my sick'ning sight;
   For what bright scene can fancy's eye explore,
'Midst dreary labyrinths of mental night?

11

O Reason! vaunted Sov'reign of the mind!
   Thou pompous vision with a sounding name!
   Can'st thou the soul's rebellious passions tame?
Can'st thou in spells the vagrant fancy bind?
5   Ah, no! capricious as the wav'ring wind
   Are sighs of Love that dim thy boasted flame,
   While Folly's torch consumes the wreath of fame,
And Pleasure's hands the sheaves of Truth unbind.
   Press'd by the storms of fate, hope shrinks and dies,
10 Frenzy darts forth in mightiest ills array'd;
   Around thy throne destructive tumults rise,
And hell-fraught jealousies, thy rights invade!
   Then, what art thou? O Idol of the wise!
A visionary theme!—a gorgeous shade!°   *shadow; ghost*

12

Now, o'er the tesselated° pavement strew   *mosaic*
   Fresh saffron, steep'd in essence of the rose,
   While down yon agate column gently flows
A glittering streamlet of ambrosial⁴ dew!
5   My Phaon smiles! the rich carnation's hue,
   On his flush'd cheek in conscious lustre glows,
   While o'er his breast enamour'd Venus throws
Her starry mantle of celestial blue!
   Breathe soft, ye dulcet flutes, among the trees
10 Where clustering boughs with golden citron° twine;   *citrus fruit*
   While slow vibrations, dying on the breeze
Shall soothe his soul with harmony divine!

---

2. Robinson implicitly disputes the force of such arguments as Wollstonecraft's, in *Rights of Woman*, for the rational control of erotic passion.

3. Later revised to "her."

4. In Greek mythology, ambrosia is the nectar of the gods; hence, divinely sweet.

Then let my form his yielding fancy seize,
And all his fondest wishes blend with mine.

18

Why art thou changed? O Phaon! tell me why?
  Love flies reproach, when passion feels decay;
  Or, I would paint the raptures of that day,
When, in sweet converse, mingling sigh with sigh,
5 I mark'd the graceful languor of thine eye
  As on a shady bank entranced we lay:
  O! eyes! whose beamy radiance stole away,
As stars fade trembling from the burning sky!
  Why art thou changed, dear source of all my woes?
10 Though dark my bosom's tint, through every vein
  A ruby tide of purest lustre flows,
Warm'd by thy love, or chill'd by thy disdain;
  And yet no bliss this sensate being knows;
Ah! why is rapture so allied to pain?

30

O'er the tall cliff that bounds the billowy main,
  Shadowing the surge that sweeps the lonely strand,
  While the thin vapours break along the sand,
Day's harbinger unfolds the liquid plain.
5 The rude sea murmurs, mournful as the strain
  That love-lorn minstrels strike with trembling hand,
  While from their green beds rise the Syren[5] band
With tongues aerial to repeat my pain!
  The vessel rocks beside the pebbly shore,
10 The foamy curls its gaudy trappings lave;
  Oh! bark propitious! bear me gently o'er;
Breathe soft, ye winds! rise slow, O swelling wave!
  Lesbos, these eyes shall meet thy sands no more:
I fly, to seek my lover, or my grave!

37

When, in the gloomy mansion of the dead,
  This withering heart, this faded form shall sleep:
  When these fond eyes at length shall cease to weep,
And earth's cold lap receive this feverish head;
5 Envy shall turn away, a tear to shed,
  And time's obliterating pinions sweep
  The spot, where poets shall their vigils keep,
To mourn and wander near my freezing bed!
  Then, my pale ghost, upon th' Elysian shore,
10 Shall smile, released from every mortal care;
  While, doom'd love's victim to repine no more,

---

5. The Sirens were mythical sea nymphs who lured men to destruction by their singing.

My breast shall bathe in endless rapture there!
    Ah! no! my restless shade would still deplore,
Nor taste that bliss, which Phaon did not share.

1796

The Camp

      Tents, <i>marquees</i>,° and baggage-waggons;   <i>military tents</i>
      Suttling-houses,° beer in flagons;   <i>provision shops</i>
      Drums and trumpets, singing, firing;
      Girls seducing, beaux admiring;
   5 Country lasses gay and smiling,
      City lads their hearts beguiling;
      Dusty roads, and horses frisky,
      Many an <i>Eton Boy</i> in whisky;¹
      Tax'd carts full of farmers' daughters;
  10 Brutes condemn'd, and man who slaughters!
      Public-houses,° booths, and castles,   <i>pubs</i>
      Belles of fashion, serving vassals;
      Lordly gen'rals fiercely staring,
      Weary soldiers, sighing, swearing!
  15 <i>Petit-maitres</i>° always dressing,   <i>dandies</i>
      In the glass themselves caressing;
      Perfum'd, painted, patch'd, and blooming
      Ladies—manly airs assuming!
      Dowagers of fifty, simp'ring,
  20 Misses for their lovers whimp'ring;
      Husbands drill'd to household tameness;
      Dames heart sick of wedded sameness.
      Princes setting girls a-madding,
      Wives for ever fond of gadding;
  25 Princesses with lovely faces,
      Beauteous children of the Graces!
      Britain's pride and virtue's treasure,
      Fair and gracious beyond measure!
      Aid-de-camps° and youthful pages,   officers' assistants
  30 Prudes and vestals° of all ages!   <i>virgins</i>
      Old coquets and matrons surly,
      Sounds of distant hurly-burly!
      Mingled voices, uncouth singing,
      Carts full laden, forage bringing;
  35 Sociables° and horses weary,   <i>carriages</i>
      Houses warm, and dresses airy;
      Loads of fatten'd poultry; pleasure
      Serv'd (to nobles) without measure;
      Doxies,° who the waggons follow;   <i>prostitutes</i>
  40 Beer, for thirsty hinds° to swallow;   <i>peasants</i>
      Washerwomen, fruit-girls cheerful,

---

1. Eton is an elite public (in American usage, private) school. Whisky is a light carriage, and perhaps also the liquor.

Ancient ladies—*chaste* and *fearful!!*
Tradesmen, leaving shops, and seeming
More of *war* than profit dreaming;
45 Martial sounds and braying asses,
Noise, that ev'ry noise surpasses!
All confusion, din, and riot,
Nothing clean—and nothing quiet.

1799   1802

The Haunted Beach[1]

Upon a lonely desart Beach
   Where the white foam was scatter'd,
A little shed uprear'd its head
   Though lofty Barks° were shatter'd.   *sailing ships*
5 The Sea-weeds gath'ring near the door,
   A sombre path display'd;
And, all around, the deaf'ning roar,
Re-echo'd on the chalky shore,
   By the green billows made.

10 Above, a jutting cliff was seen
   Where Sea Birds hover'd, craving;
And all around, the craggs were bound
   With weeds—for ever waving.
And here and there, a cavern wide
15   Its shad'wy jaws display'd;
And near the sands, at ebb of tide,
A shiver'd mast was seen to ride
   Where the green billows stray'd.

And often, while the moaning wind
20   Stole o'er the Summer Ocean;
The moonlight scene, was all serene,
   The waters scarce in motion:
Then, while the smoothly slanting sand
   The tall cliff wrapp'd in shade,
25 The Fisherman beheld a band
Of Spectres, gliding hand in hand—
   Where the green billows play'd.

And pale their faces were, as snow,
   And sullenly they wander'd:
30 And to the skies with hollow eyes
   They look'd as though they ponder'd.
And sometimes, from their hammock shroud,
   They dismal howlings made,
And while the blast blew strong and loud
35 The clear moon mark'd the ghastly croud,
   Where the green billows play'd!

---

1. One of the poems in *Lyrical Tales*, a volume published in 1800.

And then, above the haunted hut
   The Curlews° screaming hover'd;   *snipes; small birds*
And the low door with furious roar
40   The frothy breakers cover'd.
For, in the Fisherman's lone shed
   A MURDER'D MAN was laid,
With ten wide gashes in his head
And deep was made his sandy bed
45   Where the green billows play'd.

A Shipwreck'd Mariner was he,
   Doom'd from his home to sever;
Who swore to be thro' wind and sea
   Firm and undaunted ever!
50 And when the wave resistless roll'd,
     About his arm he made
A packet rich of Spanish gold,
And, like a British sailor, bold,
   Plung'd, where the billows play'd!

55 The Spectre band, his messmates brave
   Sunk in the yawning ocean,
While to the mast he lash'd him fast
   And brav'd the storm's commotion.
The winter moon, upon the sand
60   A silv'ry carpet made,
And mark'd the Sailor reach the land,
And mark'd his murd'rer wash his hand
   Where the green billows play'd.

And since that hour the Fisherman
65   Has toil'd and toil'd in vain!
For all the night, the moony light
   Gleams on the specter'd main!
And when the skies are veil'd in gloom,
   The Murd'rer's liquid way
70 Bounds o'er the deeply yawning tomb,
And flashing fires the sands illume,
   Where the green billows play!

Full thirty years his task has been,
   Day after day more weary;
75 For Heav'n design'd, his guilty mind
   Should dwell on prospects dreary.
Bound by a strong and mystic chain,
   He has not pow'r to stray;
But, destin'd mis'ry to sustain,
80 He wastes, in Solitude and Pain—
   A loathsome life away.

                                    1800

London's Summer Morning

Who has not wak'd to list° the busy sounds   *listen to; tally*
Of summer's morning, in the sultry smoke

Of noisy London? On the pavement hot
The sooty chimney-boy, with dingy face
5 And tatter'd covering, shrilly bawls his trade,
Rousing the sleepy housemaid. At the door
The milk-pail rattles, and the tinkling bell
Proclaims the dustman's office; while the street
Is lost in clouds impervious. Now begins
10 The din of hackney-coaches, waggons, carts;
While tinmen's shops, and noisy trunk-makers,
Knife-grinders, coopers, squeaking cork-cutters,
Fruit-barrows, and the hunger-giving cries
Of vegetable venders, fill the air.
15 Now ev'ry shop displays its varied trade,
And the fresh-sprinkled pavement cools the feet
Of early walkers. At the private door
The ruddy housemaid twirls the busy mop,[1]
Annoying the smart 'prentice,° or neat girl,   *apprentice*
20 Tripping with band-box° lightly. Now the sun   *hat box*
Darts burning splendour on the glitt'ring pane,
Save where the canvas awning throws a shade
On the gay merchandize. Now, spruce and trim,
In shops (where beauty smiles with industry,)
25 Sits the smart damsel; while the passenger
Peeps thro' the window, watching ev'ry charm.
Now pastry dainties catch the eye minute
Of humming insects, while the limy snare
Waits to enthral them. Now the lamp-lighter
30 Mounts the tall ladder, nimbly vent'rous,
To trim the half-fill'd lamp; while at his feet
The pot-boy° yells discordant! All along   *server of drinks*
The sultry pavement, the old-clothes-man cries
In tone monotonous, and side-long views
35 The area for his traffic: now the bag
Is slily open'd, and the half-worn suit
(Sometimes the pilfer'd treasure of the base
Domestic spoiler), for one half its worth,
Sinks in the green abyss. The porter now
40 Bears his huge load along the burning way;
And the poor poet wakes from busy dreams,
To paint the summer morning.

1800   1806

The Old Beggar

Do you see the OLD BEGGAR who sits at yon gate,
 With his beard silver'd over like snow?
Tho' he smiles as he meets the keen arrows of fate,
 Still his bosom is wearied with woe.

---

1. The detail recalls Jonathan Swift, "A Description of the Morning" (1709): "Now Moll had whirl'd her mop with dex'trous Airs" (7).

Many years has he sat at the foot of the hill,
    Many days seen the summer sun rise;
And at evening the traveller passes him still,
    While the shadows steal over the skies.

In the bleak blast of winter he hobbles along
    O'er the heath, at the dawning of day;
And the *dew-drops* that freeze the rude thistles among,
    Are the *stars* that illumine his way.

How mild is his aspect, how modest his eye,
    How meekly his soul bears each wrong!
How much does he speak by his eloquent sigh,
    Tho' no accent is heard from his tongue.

Time was, when this beggar, in martial trim dight,°   *dressed*
    Was as bold as the chief of his throng;
When he march'd thro' the storms of the day or the night,
    And still smil'd as he journey'd along.

Then his form was athletic, his eyes' vivid glance
    Spoke the lustre of youth's glowing day!
And the village all mark'd, in the combat and dance,
    The brave younker° still valiant as gay.   *youth*

When the prize was propos'd, how his footsteps wou'd bound,
    While the MAID *of his heart* led the throng,
While the ribands that circled the May-pole around,
    Wav'd the trophies of garlands among!

But love o'er his bosom triumphantly reign'd,
    Love taught him in secret to pine;
Love wasted his youth, yet he never complain'd,
    For the silence of love—is divine!

The dulcet° ton'd word, and the plaint° of despair,   *sweet / lament*
    Are no signs of the soul-wasting smart;
'Tis the pride of affection to cherish its care,
    And to count the quick throbs of the heart.

Amidst the loud din of the battle he stood,
    Like a lion, undaunted and strong;
But the tear of compassion was mingled with blood,
    When his sword was the first in the throng.

When the bullet whizz'd by, and his arm bore away,
    Still he shrunk not, with anguish oppress'd;
And when victory shouted the fate of the day,
    Not a groan check'd the joy of his breast.

To his dear native shore the poor wand'rer hied;
    But he came to complete his despair:
For the maid of his soul was that morning *a bride!*
    And a gay *lordly rival* was there!

From that hour, o'er the world he has wander'd forlorn;
    But still LOVE his companion would go;

5

10

15

20

25

30

35

40

45

50

And tho' deeply fond memory planted its thorn,
    Still he silently cherish'd his woe.

See him now, while with age and with sorrow oppress'd,
    He the gate opens slowly, and sighs!
55   See him drop the big tears on his woe-wither'd breast,
    The big tears that fall fast from his eyes!

See his habit all tatter'd, his shrivell'd cheek pale;
    See his locks, waving thin in the air;
See his lip is half froze with the sharp cutting gale,
60   And his head, o'er the temples, all bare!

His eye-beam no longer in lustre displays
    The warm sunshine that visits his breast;
For deep sunk is its orbit, and darken'd its rays,
    And he sighs for the grave's silent rest.

65   And his voice is grown feeble, his accent is slow,
    And he sees not the distant hill's side;
And he hears not the breezes of morn as they blow,
    Nor the streams that soft murmuring glide.

To him all is silent, and mournful, and dim,
70   E'en the seasons pass dreary and slow;
For affliction has plac'd its cold fetters on him,
    And his soul is enamour'd of woe.

See the TEAR, which, imploring, is fearful to roll,
    Tho' in silence he bows as you stray;
75   'Tis the eloquent silence which speaks to the soul,
    'Tis the *star* of his *slow-setting day*!

Perchance, ere the *May-blossoms* cheerfully wave,
    Ere the *zephyrs* of SUMMER soft sigh;
The sun-beams shall dance on the grass o'er his GRAVE,
80   And his *journey* be mark'd—TO THE SKY.
1799   1806

To the Poet Coleridge[1]

Rapt in the visionary theme!
    Spirit Divine! with thee I'll wander!
Where the blue, wavy, lucid stream
    Mid forest glooms shall slow meander!
5   With thee I'll trace the circling bounds
    Of thy new paradise, extended;
And listen to the varying sounds
    Of winds, and foamy torrents blended!

Now by the source, which lab'ring heaves
10   The mystic fountain, bubbling, panting,[2]

1. A response to Samuel Taylor Coleridge's *Kubla Khan*, written between 1797 and 1798, and recited to friends for many years prior to its publication in 1816.
2. Cf. *Kubla Khan*, 18–19.

While gossamer° its network weaves   *fine cobwebs*
   Adown the blue lawn, slanting—
I'll mark thy "sunny dome," and view
Thy "caves of ice," thy fields of dew,[3]
15 Thy ever-blooming mead, whose flow'r
Waves to the cold breath of the moonlight hour!
Or when the day-star,° peering bright   *sun*
On the grey wing of parting night;
While more than vegetating pow'r
20 Throbs, grateful to the burning hour,
As summer's whispered sighs unfold
Her million million buds of gold!—

Then will I climb the breezy bounds
   Of thy new paradise, extended,
25 And listen to the distant sounds
   Of winds, and foamy torrents blended!

   Spirit Divine! with thee I'll trace
   Imagination's boundless space!
With thee, beneath thy "sunny dome,"
30   I'll listen to the minstrel's lay
   Hymning the gradual close of day;
In "caves of ice" enchanted roam,
Where on the glitt'ring entrance plays
The moon's beam with its silv'ry rays;
35 Or, when the glassy stream
That through the deep dell flows,
Flashes the noon's hot beam
   The noon's hot beam, that midway shows
Thy flaming temple, studded o'er
40 With all Peruvia's lustrous store![4]
There will I trace the circling bounds
   Of thy new paradise, extended!
And listen to the awful° sounds   *awe-inspiring*
   Of winds, and foamy torrents blended!

45 And now I'll pause to catch the moan
   Of distant breezes, cavern-pent;
Now, ere the twilight tints are flown,
   Purpling the landscape far and wide,
   On the dark promontory's side
50 I'll gather wild flowers, dew besprent,°   *sprinkled over*
And weave a crown for thee,
Genius of heav'n-taught poesy!
While, opening to my wond'ring eyes,
Thou bid'st a new creation rise,
55 I'll raptured trace the circling bounds
   Of thy rich paradise, extended,
And listen to the varying sounds
   Of winds, and foamy torrents blended.

3. Cf. *Kubla Khan*, 35–36.   4. Peru was famed for mineral and gem mines.

And now, with lofty tones inviting,
60   Thy nymph, her dulcimer swift-smiting,
Shall wake me in ecstatic measures
Far, far removed from mortal pleasures;[5]
In cadence rich, in cadence strong,
Proving the wondrous witcheries of song!
65   I hear her voice—thy "sunny dome,"
Thy "caves of ice," aloud repeat—
Vibrations, madd'ning sweet,
Calling the visionary wand'rer home.
She sings of thee, oh favoured child
70   Of minstrelsy, sublimely wild!—
Of thee whose soul can feel the tone
Which gives to airy dreams a magic all thy own!

                                                    SAPPHO

1800   1801

❈❈❈

Mary Wollstonecraft
1759–1797

It is hard to imagine how anyone advocating the education of young women, the virtues of sense over sensibility, chastity for men as well as women, school uniforms, and regular physical exercise, could be reviled as a radical revolutionary, an atheist, a slut, and a pathologically castrating threat to masculine authority. But Mary Wollstonecraft suffered all these abuses. The attacks were provoked, in part, by her principled, frequently caustic refutation in A *Vindication of the Rights of Men* of Edmund Burke's *Reflections on the Revolution in France*. She went further in her *Vindication of the Rights of Woman*, a trenchant critique of the ideologies of gender in such culturally revered works as Milton's *Paradise Lost* and the admired "conduct" literature of the day—advice to young women on how to be attractive to men and cultivate the Christian virtues of submission, obedience, and service. It was not only Wollstonecraft's publications that provoked censure; it was also her private life, taken to be the basis of her ideas. The litany included helping a sister run away from an abusive husband (an assault on the social institution and religious sacrament of marriage); her financial independence and career as a professional writer (very unfeminine); her enamored pursuit of Swiss artist Henry Fuseli in the early 1790s (most immodest) and the outright sinfulness of her tempestuous affair with American adventurer Gilbert Imlay a few years later; her out-of-wedlock daughter by Imlay; the two attempts at suicide provoked by Imlay's infidelities; her affair with William Godwin and a premarital pregnancy. When she died from complications in childbirth, her detractors intuited divine judgment.

   A brilliant thinker and conversationalist, a prolific polemical writer, a commanding social presence, Wollstonecraft led a life of passionate commitments, and was one of the most impressive figures of the radical circle in England in the 1790s. Born in 1759, she spent a childhood suffering the consequences of her father's failures at various enterprises, as he squandered a large inheritance and sought refuge in drink; more than once she defended her mother from his drunken rages. To escape, she became a lady's companion in Bath but returned after two years to nurse her mother. After her mother's death, she left home for good, supporting herself with

---

5. Cf. *Kubla Khan*, 37.

eye-straining work as a seamstress and then as a schoolmistress in North London with a friend and another sister. When the school failed, Wollstonecraft wrote to pay off her debts, publishing *Thoughts on the Education of Daughters* in 1786; she worked for a year as a governess in an Irish aristocratic family, during which time she wrote her first novel, *Mary, A Fiction*.

Determined to make a living as a writer, she returned to London where she met Joseph Johnson, a radical bookseller, who in 1788, published *Mary* and her book for children, *Original Stories from Real Life*, and in 1789, her anthology, *The Female Reader* (under a male pen name). He also hired her to work for and write articles for *The Analytical Review* and to produce translations of German and French moral philosophers. In London Wollstonecraft became part of Johnson's lively circle of artists, writers, liberal political thinkers, progressive philosophers, and religious Dissenters—among them, Anna Laetitia Barbauld, Tom Paine, William Blake, Joel Barlow, Joseph Priestley, Fuseli, and her future husband, Godwin. Blake and Robert Southey were completely enamored of her, though Godwin was at first put off by her forwardness in conversation. In 1790 Johnson published *A Vindication of the Rights of Men*, a rapid response to Edmund Burke's *Reflections on the Revolution in France*; it was anonymous, and when Wollstonecraft signed her name to the second edition in 1791, her fame was established.

She began *Rights of Woman* the same year and early in 1792 spent time with Talleyrand, the French minister of education, on his visit to London; she dedicated *Rights of Woman* to him when its second edition was published later that year. Her reasonable, modest proposals for the improved education and social development of young women were etched with acid comparisons of the state of women to that of plantation and harem slaves, equally oppressed, tyrannized, and brutalized by morally illegitimate masters. Wollstonecraft called for a "revolution in female manners," arguing that no agenda for "the rights of man" could claim moral authority if it entailed the unchanged degradation of women. At the end of 1792, she left on her own for Paris, partly to wean herself from her crush on Fuseli and partly to witness Revolutionary France. Here she met Helen Maria Williams, and within a few months, Imlay, dashing veteran of the American Revolution. Paris in 1793 was a dangerous world, still reeling from the September massacres of 1792 and the arrest and trial of Louis XVI, who was beheaded in January 1793. Over the course of this year, the Reign of Terror beheaded thousands more, including Wollstonecraft's friend Madame Roland and Queen Marie Antoinette in October. Wollstonecraft left Paris to seek safety in the suburbs, but returned to register as Imlay's wife at the American embassy in order to gain protection as an American citizen, France being at war with England. Early in 1794, she and Imlay went to Le Havre, where their daughter Fanny was born. They all returned to Paris; then Imlay went to London, leaving wife and daughter behind.

Wollstonecraft's *Historical and Moral View of the Origin and Progress of the French Revolution* was published later that year. On returning to London, she was devastated to discover Imlay living with an actress. He prevented her attempted suicide, and to distance himself from her, sent her (with Fanny and a French nurse) on a business trip to Scandinavia during the summer of 1795. She returned in October to find him living with yet another actress and again attempted suicide, jumping off a bridge into the Thames. Imlay left for Paris with his new amour in November, and Wollstonecraft, ever resourceful, decided to publish her letters to him recording her experiences in Scandinavia. When *Letters Written during a Short Residence in Sweden, Norway, and Denmark* appeared the following year, Godwin exclaimed, "If ever there was a book calculated to make a man in love with its author, this appears to me to be the book." They renewed their friendship in January 1796 and by the summer, "friendship melting into love," and they became lovers. When she became pregnant at the end of the year, they set aside principle and decided to marry. They were wed in March, but insisted on keeping separate residences. Mary Wollstonecraft Godwin— the future Mary Shelley—was born in August; in ten days, her mother, having suffered agonizing pain from poisoning by an incompletely expelled placenta, was dead, at age thirty-seven.

When Godwin published a *Memoir* of her and her unfinished novel, *The Wrongs of Woman, or Maria* in 1798, both works fed anti-Jacobin attacks on her ideas and moral character. His grief clouded his judgment about what he could recount without offending propriety, and the *Memoir* proved a scandal, embarrassing even those who had welcomed *Rights of Woman*. An anonymous *Defence of the Character and Conduct of the Late Mary Wollstonecraft Godwin* (often credited to Mary Hays, her friend and fellow feminist) appeared in 1803, but the defense could hardly rest. Hays did not feel safe including her in her *Female Biography, or Memoirs of Illustrious and Celebrated Women of all Ages and Countries* (also 1803), even though she found space for the Lesbian Sappho and Marat's assassin Charlotte Corday. Decades later, in 1869, John Stuart Mill forgot to mention *Rights of Woman* in his *Subjection of Women*. Attacks on Wollstonecraft's character and conduct persisted well into the 1970s, not only stigmatizing the arguments of her writing but providing antifeminists with fuel to impugn any advocacy of women's rights. Yet there always persisted a community of admiration for her courage and intelligence, including (for better or worse) Percy Shelley, and over ensuing decades, such women of intellect as George Eliot, Emma Goldman, and Virginia Woolf.

Selections from *A Vindication of the Rights of Men* are included in Perspectives: The Rights of Man and the Revolution Controversy, page 57.

A VINDICATION OF THE RIGHTS OF WOMAN   With the French Revolutionary Assembly's Declaration of the Rights of Man granting participatory citizenship only to men, Wollstonecraft's "second *Vindication*" responds to a concern of many progressive women, namely, that the vibrant declarations of the "Rights of Man" were all too serious about the *fraternity* of "liberty, fraternity, equality." Bluntly comparing marriage to slavery and tyrannical oppression, Wollstonecraft boldly challenges the ideology that sustains and frequently idealizes this subjection: the view of women's subordination as a universal fact of nature, human history, rational philosophy, and divine ordination. She proceeds first to identify this view as a sociocultural text, a "prevailing opinion," and then to subject it to a sharp critical reading. This textual critique is embedded in the overt literary criticism that fills her pages, incisive and often sarcastic examinations of the attitudes about gender in long-standing misogynist myths (Pandora) and in the most influential works of her day: John Milton's *Paradise Lost* (and its informing biblical stories); Alexander Pope's second *Moral Essay*, "Of the Characters of Women" (1735); Samuel Richardson's *Clarissa* (1747–1748); Jean-Jacques Rousseau's influential education novel *Émile* (1762) and his *Julie, ou la Nouvelle Héloïse* (1791); Dr. John Gregory's *A Father's Legacy to His Daughters* (1774); Dr. James Fordyce's *Sermons to Young Women* (1765). Her literary criticism extends to an unforgiving focus on a set of interlocked key terms used to flatter women into subjection—"innocent," "delicate," "feminine," "beautiful"—embellished with praise for their "fair defects" of character (an oxymoron she despises) and reverence for them as "angels" or "girls," rather than rationally capable, intelligent, mature adults.

Wollstonecraft's argument for a gender-neutral capacity of "reason" simultaneously draws on eighteenth-century rationalist philosophy and democratizes the Miltonic value of "Reason" as the highest mental capacity. For Milton, this capacity is located in men only; Wollstonecraft argues that this hierarchical arrangement is not a divine but a social formation. She counters that if God is Reason, He surely would not have created women without this capacity, the source of both virtuous conduct and spiritual salvation—a religious argument Wollstonecraft uses not only to refute appeals to divine ordination, but also to invest her social polemic with what she hopes will be an unimpeachable moral foundation. Alongside this moral argument, her *Vindication* wields the discourse of tyranny and revolution that already had currency with her male colleagues, allowing her to point out the reactionary attitudes about women that may be tolerated, even supported, by progressive political thinkers.

from A Vindication of the Rights of Woman

Introduction

After considering the historic page, and viewing the living world with anxious solicitude, the most melancholy emotions of sorrowful indignation have depressed my spirits, and I have sighed when obliged to confess, that either nature has made a great difference between man and man, or that the civilization which has hitherto taken place in the world has been very partial. I have turned over various books written on the subject of education, and patiently observed the conduct of parents and the management of schools; but what has been the result?—a profound conviction that the neglected education of my fellow-creatures is the grand source of the misery I deplore; and that women, in particular, are rendered weak and wretched by a variety of concurring causes, originating from one hasty conclusion. The conduct and manners of women, in fact, evidently prove that their minds are not in a healthy state; for, like the flowers which are planted in too rich a soil, strength and usefulness are sacrificed to beauty; and the flaunting leaves, after having pleased a fastidious eye, fade, disregarded on the stalk, long before the season when they ought to have arrived at maturity.—One cause of this barren blooming I attribute to a false system of education, gathered from the books written on this subject by men who, considering females rather as women than human creatures, have been more anxious to make them alluring mistresses than affectionate wives and rational mothers; and the understanding of the sex has been so bubbled[1] by this specious homage, that the civilized women of the present century, with a few exceptions, are only anxious to inspire love, when they ought to cherish a nobler ambition, and by their abilities and virtues exact respect.

In a treatise, therefore, on female rights and manners, the works which have been particularly written for their improvement must not be overlooked; especially when it is asserted, in direct terms, that the minds of women are enfeebled by false refinement; that the books of instruction, written by men of genius, have had the same tendency as more frivolous productions; and that, in the true style of Mahometanism, they are treated as a kind of subordinate beings, and not as a part of the human species,[2] when improveable reason is allowed to be the dignified distinction which raises men above the brute creation, and puts a natural sceptre in a feeble hand.

Yet, because I am a woman, I would not lead my readers to suppose that I mean violently to agitate the contested question respecting the equality or inferiority of the sex; but as the subject lies in my way, and I cannot pass it over without subjecting the main tendency of my reasoning to misconstruction, I shall stop a moment to deliver, in a few words, my opinion.—In the government of the physical world it is observable that the female in point of strength is, in general, inferior to the male. This is the law of nature; and it does not appear to be suspended or abrogated in favour of woman. A degree of physical superiority cannot, therefore, be denied—and it is a noble prerogative! But not content with this natural pre-eminence, men endeavour to sink us still lower, merely to render us alluring objects for a moment; and women, intoxicated by the adoration which men, under the influence of their senses, pay them, do not seek to obtain a durable interest in their hearts, or to become the friends of the fellow creatures who find amusement in their society.

1. Gas-filled; deluded.
2. A European misconception that the sacred texts of Islam stated that women lack souls and therefore have no afterlife in Heaven.

I am aware of an obvious inference:—from every quarter have I heard exclamations against masculine women; but where are they to be found? If by this appellation men mean to inveigh against their ardour in hunting, shooting, and gaming, I shall most cordially join in the cry; but if it be against the imitation of manly virtues, or, more properly speaking, the attainment of those talents and virtues, the exercise of which ennobles the human character, and which raise females in the scale of animal being, when they are comprehensively termed mankind;—all those who view them with a philosophic eye must, I should think, wish with me, that they may every day grow more and more masculine.

This discussion naturally divides the subject. I shall first consider women in the grand light of human creatures, who, in common with men, are placed on this earth to unfold their faculties; and afterwards I shall more particularly point out their peculiar designation.

I wish also to steer clear of an error which many respectable writers have fallen into; for the instruction which has hitherto been addressed to women, has rather been applicable to *ladies*, if the little indirect advice, that is scattered through Sandford and Merton, be excepted;[3] but, addressing my sex in a firmer tone, I pay particular attention to those in the middle class, because they appear to be in the most natural state.[4] Perhaps the seeds of false-refinement, immorality, and vanity, have ever been shed by the great. Weak, artificial beings, raised above the common wants and affections of their race, in a premature unnatural manner, undermine the very foundation of virtue, and spread corruption through the whole mass of society! As a class of mankind they have the strongest claim to pity; the education of the rich tends to render them vain and helpless, and the unfolding mind is not strengthened by the practice of those duties which dignify the human character.—They only live to amuse themselves, and by the same law which in nature invariably produces certain effects, they soon only afford barren amusement.

But as I purpose taking a separate view of the different ranks of society, and of the moral character of women, in each, this hint is, for the present, sufficient; and I have only alluded to the subject, because it appears to me to be the very essence of an introduction to give a cursory account of the contents of the work it introduces.

My own sex, I hope, will excuse me, if I treat them like rational creatures, instead of flattering their *fascinating* graces, and viewing them as if they were in a state of perpetual childhood, unable to stand alone. I earnestly wish to point out in what true dignity and human happiness consists—I wish to persuade women to endeavour to acquire strength, both of mind and body, and to convince them that the soft phrases, susceptibility of heart, delicacy of sentiment, and refinement of taste, are almost synonymous with epithets of weakness, and that those beings who are only the objects of pity and that kind of love, which has been termed its sister, will soon become objects of contempt.

Dismissing then those pretty feminine phrases, which the men condescendingly use to soften our slavish dependence, and despising that weak elegancy of mind, exquisite sensibility, and sweet docility of manners, supposed to be the sexual characteristics of the weaker vessel, I wish to shew that elegance is inferior to virtue, that the first object of laudable ambition is to obtain a character as a human being,

3. The tutor in Thomas Day's popular children's story, *The History of Sandford and Merton* (1786–1789, influenced by Rousseau's *Émile*), tells several moral tales.

4. "Ladies" are upper-class; Wollstonecraft suggests that the middle class is the most "natural" state because it has not been corrupted by extremes of wealth or poverty.

regardless of the distinction of sex; and that secondary views should be brought to this simple touchstone.

This is a rough sketch of my plan; and should I express my conviction with the energetic emotions that I feel whenever I think of the subject, the dictates of experience and reflection will be felt by some of my readers. Animated by this important object, I shall disdain to cull my phrases or polish my style;—I aim at being useful, and sincerity will render me unaffected; for, wishing rather to persuade by the force of my arguments, than dazzle by the elegance of my language, I shall not waste my time in rounding periods,[5] or in fabricating the turgid bombast of artificial feelings, which, coming from the head, never reach the heart.—I shall be employed about things, not words!—and, anxious to render my sex more respectable members of society, I shall try to avoid that flowery diction which has slided from essays into novels, and from novels into familiar letters and conversation.

These pretty superlatives, dropping glibly from the tongue, vitiate the taste, and create a kind of sickly delicacy that turns away from simple unadorned truth; and a deluge of false sentiments and over-stretched feelings, stifling the natural emotions of the heart, render the domestic pleasures insipid, that ought to sweeten the exercise of those severe duties, which educate a rational and immortal being for a nobler field of action.

The education of women has, of late, been more attended to than formerly; yet they are still reckoned a frivolous sex, and ridiculed or pitied by the writers who endeavour by satire or instruction to improve them. It is acknowledged that they spend many of the first years of their lives in acquiring a smattering of accomplishments; meanwhile strength of body and mind are sacrificed to libertine notions of beauty, to the desire of establishing themselves,—the only way women can rise in the world,—by marriage. And this desire making mere animals of them, when they marry they act as such children may be expected to act:—they dress; they paint, and nickname God's creatures.[6]—Surely these weak beings are only fit for a seraglio![7]—Can they be expected to govern a family with judgment, or take care of the poor babes whom they bring into the world?

If then it can be fairly deduced from the present conduct of the sex,[8] from the prevalent fondness for pleasure which takes place of ambition and those nobler passions that open and enlarge the soul; that the instruction which women have hitherto received has only tended, with the constitution of civil society, to render them insignificant objects of desire—mere propagators of fools!—if it can be proved that in aiming to accomplish them, without cultivating their understandings, they are taken out of their sphere of duties, and made ridiculous and useless when the short-lived bloom of beauty is over,[9] I presume that *rational* men will excuse me for endeavouring to persuade them to become more masculine and respectable.

Indeed the word masculine is only a bugbear: there is little reason to fear that women will acquire too much courage or fortitude; for their apparent inferiority with respect to bodily strength, must render them, in some degree, dependent on men in

5. Crafting elaborate sentences—the oratorical style for which Burke was famous.

6. A reference to Hamlet's misogynist diatribe at Ophelia, whom he suspects of treachery: "God hath given you one face, and you make yourselves another. You jig and amble, and you lisp; you nickname God's creatures and make your wantonness [seem] your ignorance" (*Hamlet* 3.1.145–48).

7. Harem.

8. The female sex, a common usage.

9. A lively writer . . . asks what business women turned of forty have to do in the world? [Wollstonecraft's note.]

the various relations of life; but why should it be increased by prejudices that give a sex to virtue,[1] and confound simple truths with sensual reveries?

Women are, in fact, so much degraded by mistaken notions of female excellence, that I do not mean to add a paradox when I assert, that this artificial weakness produces a propensity to tyrannize, and gives birth to cunning, the natural opponent of strength, which leads them to play off those contemptible infantine airs that undermine esteem even whilst they excite desire. Let men become more chaste and modest, and if women do not grow wiser in the same ratio, it will be clear that they have weaker understandings. It seems scarcely necessary to say, that I now speak of the sex in general. Many individuals have more sense than their male relatives; and, as nothing preponderates where there is a constant struggle for an equilibrium, without it has naturally more gravity, some women govern their husbands without degrading themselves, because intellect will always govern.

from *Chapter 1. The Rights and Involved Duties of Mankind Considered*

In the present state of society it appears necessary to go back to first principles in search of the most simple truths, and to dispute with some prevailing prejudice every inch of ground. To clear my way, I must be allowed to ask some plain questions, and the answers will probably appear as unequivocal as the axioms on which reasoning is built; though, when entangled with various motives of action, they are formally contradicted, either by the words or conduct of men.

In what does man's pre-eminence over the brute creation consist? The answer is as clear as that a half is less than the whole; in Reason.

What acquirement exalts one being above another? Virtue; we spontaneously reply.

For what purpose were the passions implanted? That man by struggling with them might attain a degree of knowledge denied to the brutes; whispers Experience.

Consequently the perfection of our nature and capability of happiness, must be estimated by the degree of reason, virtue, and knowledge, that distinguish the individual, and direct the laws which bind society: and that from the exercise of reason, knowledge and virtue naturally flow, is equally undeniable, if mankind be viewed collectively.

The rights and duties of man thus simplified, it seems almost impertinent to attempt to illustrate truths that appear so incontrovertible; yet such deeply rooted prejudices have clouded reason, and such spurious qualities have assumed the name of virtues, that it is necessary to pursue the course of reason as it has been perplexed and involved in error, by various adventitious circumstances, comparing the simple axiom with casual deviations.

Men, in general, seem to employ their reason to justify prejudices, which they have imbibed, they can scarcely trace how, rather than to root them out. The mind must be strong that resolutely forms its own principles; for a kind of intellectual cowardice prevails which makes many men shrink from the task, or only do it by halves. Yet the imperfect conclusions thus drawn, are frequently very plausible, because they are built on partial experience, on just, though narrow, views. * * *

The civilization of the bulk of the people of Europe is very partial; nay, it may be made a question, whether they have acquired any virtues in exchange for innocence, equivalent to the misery produced by the vices that have been plastered over unsightly

1. The prevailing opinion that only men have the rational and hence moral capacity for virtuous behavior.

ignorance, and the freedom which has been bartered for splendid slavery. The desire of dazzling by riches, the most certain pre-eminence that man can obtain, the pleasure of commanding flattering sycophants, and many other complicated low calculations of doting self-love, have all contributed to overwhelm the mass of mankind, and make liberty a convenient handle for mock patriotism. For whilst rank and titles are held of the utmost importance, before which Genius "must hide its diminished head,"[1] it is, with a few exceptions, very unfortunate for a nation when a man of abilities, without rank or property, pushes himself forward to notice.—Alas! what unheard of misery have thousands suffered to purchase a cardinal's hat for an intriguing obscure adventurer, who longed to be ranked with princes, or lord it over them by seizing the triple crown![2] * * *

Nothing can set the regal character in a more contemptible point of view, than the various crimes that have elevated men to the supreme dignity.—Vile intrigues, unnatural crimes, and every vice that degrades our nature, have been the steps to this distinguished eminence; yet millions of men have supinely allowed the nerveless limbs of the posterity of such rapacious prowlers to rest quietly on their ensanguined thrones.[3]

What but a pestilential vapour can hover over society when its chief director is only instructed in the invention of crimes, or the stupid routine of childish ceremonies? Will men never be wise?—will they never cease to expect corn from tares, and figs from thistles?[4]

It is impossible for any man, when the most favourable circumstances concur, to acquire sufficient knowledge and strength of mind to discharge the duties of a king, entrusted with uncontrouled power; how then must they be violated when his very elevation is an insuperable bar to the attainment of either wisdom or virtue; when all the feelings of a man are stifled by flattery, and reflection shut out by pleasure! Surely it is madness to make the fate of thousands depend on the caprice of a weak fellow creature, whose very station sinks him *necessarily* below the meanest of his subjects! But one power should not be thrown down to exalt another—for all power inebriates weak man; and its abuse proves that the more equality there is established among men, the more virtue and happiness will reign in society. But this and any similar maxim deduced from simple reason, raises an outcry—the church or the state is in danger, if faith in the wisdom of antiquity is not implicit; and they who, roused by the sight of human calamity, dare to attack human authority, are reviled as despisers of God, and enemies of man. These are bitter calumnies, yet they reached one of the best of men,[5] whose ashes still preach peace, and whose memory demands a respectful pause, when subjects are discussed that lay so near his heart.—

After attacking the sacred majesty of Kings, I shall scarcely excite surprise by adding my firm persuasion that every profession, in which great subordination of rank constitutes its power, is highly injurious to morality.

1. A sardonic reference to Satan's noting how "all the Stars / Hide thir diminisht heads" at the sight of the noonday sun "that with surpassing Glory crown'd, / Look'st from [its] sole dominion like the God / Of this new World" (*Paradise Lost* 4.32–35). Wollstonecraft also quotes this phrase in *Rights of Men*; see page 64.

2. Papal crown.

3. "Could there be a greater insult offered to the rights of man than the beds of justice in France, when an infant was made the organ of the detestable Dubois!" [Wollstonecraft's note.] Guillaume Dubois (1656–1723) was foreign affairs advisor to Philippe II, Duc d'Orleans, the appointed regent (acting ruler) of France during the minority of Louis XV (1710–1774), who became king at age five

(Louis XVI, king in 1792, was his grandson and successor).

4. See Jesus' Sermon on the Mount: "Beware of false prophets. . . . Ye shall know them by their fruits. Do men gather . . . figs of thistles? (Matthew 7.15–16); tares: weeds; see also Shakespeare, *Hamlet* (2.2.310).

5. Dr. Price [Wollstonecraft's note]. "Calumnies" are maliciously false charges. Wollstonecraft's friend Richard Price, dissenting minister and radical political writer, championed the American and French Revolutions. His lecture to the Revolution Society in 1789, *A Discourse on the Love of our Country*, provoked sharp criticism in Burke's *Reflections on the Revolution in France* (see James Gillray's cartoon, *Smelling Out a Rat*, page 48) and spirited defense in Wollstonecraft's *Vindication of the Rights of Men*.

A standing army, for instance, is incompatible with freedom; because subordination and rigour are the very sinews of military discipline; and despotism is necessary to give vigour to enterprizes that one will directs. A spirit inspired by romantic notions of honour, a kind of morality founded on the fashion of the age, can only be felt by a few officers, whilst the main body must be moved by command, like the waves of the sea; for the strong wind of authority pushes the crowd of subalterns forward, they scarcely know or care why, with headlong fury.

Besides, nothing can be so prejudicial to the morals of the inhabitants of country towns as the occasional residence of a set of idle superficial young men, whose only occupation is gallantry, and whose polished manners render vice more dangerous, by concealing its deformity under gay ornamental drapery. An air of fashion, which is but a badge of slavery, and proves that the soul has not a strong individual character, awes simple country people into an imitation of the vices, when they cannot catch the slippery graces, of politeness. Every corps is a chain of despots, who, submitting and tyrannizing without exercising their reason, become dead weights of vice and folly on the community. A man of rank or fortune, sure of rising by interest, has nothing to do but to pursue some extravagant freak; whilst the needy *gentleman*, who is to rise, as the phrase turns, by his merit, becomes a servile parasite or vile pander.

Sailors, the naval gentlemen, come under the same description, only their vices assume a different and a grosser cast. They are more positively indolent, when not discharging the ceremonials of their station; whilst the insignificant fluttering of soldiers may be termed active idleness. More confined to the society of men, the former acquire a fondness for humour and mischievous tricks; whilst the latter, mixing frequently with well-bred women, catch a sentimental cant.—But mind is equally out of the question, whether they indulge the horse-laugh, or polite simper.

May I be allowed to extend the comparison to a profession where more mind is certainly to be found; for the clergy have superior opportunities of improvement, though subordination almost equally cramps their faculties? The blind submission imposed at college to forms of belief serves as a novitiate to the curate, who must obsequiously respect the opinion of his rector or patron, if he mean to rise in his profession. Perhaps there cannot be a more forcible contrast than between the servile dependent gait of a poor curate and the courtly mien of a bishop. And the respect and contempt they inspire render the discharge of their separate functions equally useless.

It is of great importance to observe that the character of every man is, in some degree, formed by his profession. A man of sense may only have a cast of countenance that wears off as you trace his individuality, whilst the weak, common man has scarcely ever any character, but what belongs to the body; at least, all his opinions have been so steeped in the vat consecrated by authority, that the faint spirit which the grape of his own vine yields cannot be distinguished.

Society, therefore, as it becomes more enlightened, should be very careful not to establish bodies of men who must necessarily be made foolish or vicious by the very constitution of their profession.

from *Chapter 2. The Prevailing Opinion of a Sexual Character Discussed*

To account for, and excuse the tyranny of man, many ingenious arguments have been brought forward to prove, that the two sexes, in the acquirement of virtue, ought to aim at attaining a very different character: or, to speak explicitly, women are not allowed to have sufficient strength of mind to acquire what really deserves the name of virtue. Yet it should seem, allowing them to have souls, that there is but one way appointed by Providence to lead *mankind* to either virtue or happiness.

If then women are not a swarm of ephemeron[1] triflers, why should they be kept in ignorance under the specious name of innocence? Men complain, and with reason, of the follies and caprices of our sex, when they do not keenly satirize our headstrong passions and groveling vices.—Behold, I should answer, the natural effect of ignorance! The mind will ever be unstable that has only prejudices to rest on, and the current will run with destructive fury when there are no barriers to break its force. Women are told from their infancy, and taught by the example of their mothers, that a little knowledge of human weakness, justly termed cunning, softness of temper, *outward* obedience, and a scrupulous attention to a puerile kind of propriety, will obtain for them the protection of man; and should they be beautiful, every thing else is needless, for, at least, twenty years of their lives.

Thus Milton describes our first frail mother; though when he tells us that women are formed for softness and sweet attractive grace,[2] I cannot comprehend his meaning, unless, in the true Mahometan strain, he meant to deprive us of souls, and insinuate that we were beings only designed by sweet attractive grace, and docile blind obedience, to gratify the senses of man when he can no longer soar on the wing of contemplation.

How grossly do they insult us who thus advise us only to render ourselves gentle, domestic brutes! For instance, the winning softness so warmly, and frequently, recommended, that governs by obeying. What childish expressions, and how insignificant is the being—can it be an immortal one? who will condescend to govern by such sinister methods! "Certainly," says Lord Bacon, "man is of kin to the beasts by his body; and if he be not of kin to God by his spirit, he is a base and ignoble creature!"[3] Men, indeed, appear to me to act in a very unphilosophical manner when they try to secure the good conduct of women by attempting to keep them always in a state of childhood. Rousseau was more consistent when he wished to stop the progress of reason in both sexes, for if men eat of the tree of knowledge, women will come in for a taste; but, from the imperfect cultivation which their understandings now receive, they only attain a knowledge of evil.[4]

Children, I grant, should be innocent; but when the epithet is applied to men, or women, it is but a civil term for weakness. For if it be allowed that women were destined by Providence to acquire human virtues, and by the exercise of their understandings, that stability of character which is the firmest ground to rest our future hopes upon, they must be permitted to turn to the fountain of light, and not forced to shape their course by the twinkling of a mere satellite. Milton, I grant, was of a very different opinion; for he only bends to the indefeasible right of beauty, though it would be difficult to render two passages which I now mean to contrast, consistent. But into similar inconsistencies are great men often led by their senses.

To whom thus Eve with *perfect beauty* adorn'd.

"My Author and Disposer, what thou bidst

---

1. Flying insect that lives for only a day.
2. See Satan's first view of Adam and Eve in *Paradise Lost*: "Not equal, as thir sex not equal seem'd; / For contemplation hee and valor form'd, / For softness shee and sweet attractive Grace, / He for God only, shee for God in him" (4.296–99). Fordyce quotes these lines in *Sermons to Young Women*, ch. 13.
3. Francis Bacon, *Essay 16*, "Of Atheism" (1606).
4. See Rousseau's *Émile* (1.1): "Only reason teaches us good from evil."

> *Unargued* I obey; So God ordains;
> God is *thy law, thou* mine: to know no more
> Is Woman's *happiest* knowledge and her *praise*."[5]

These are exactly the arguments that I have used to children; but I have added, your reason is now gaining strength, and, till it arrives at some degree of maturity, you must look up to me for advice—then you ought to *think*, and only rely on God.

Yet in the following lines Milton seems to coincide with me; when he makes Adam thus expostulate with his Maker.

> Hast thou not made me here thy substitute,
> And these inferior far beneath me set?
> Among *unequals* what society
> Can sort, what harmony or true delight?
> Which must be mutual, in proportion due
> Giv'n and receiv'd; but in *disparity*
> The one intense, the other still remiss
> Cannot well suit with either, but soon prove
> Tedious alike: of *fellowship* I speak
> Such as I seek, fit to participate
> All rational delight[6]—

In treating, therefore, of the manners of women, let us, disregarding sensual arguments, trace what we should endeavour to make them in order to co-operate, if the expression be not too bold, with the supreme Being.

By individual education, I mean, for the sense of the word is not precisely defined, such an attention to a child as will slowly sharpen the senses, form the temper, regulate the passions as they begin to ferment, and set the understanding to work before the body arrives at maturity; so that the man may only have to proceed, not to begin, the important task of learning to think and reason. * * *

In fact, it is a farce to call any being virtuous whose virtues do not result from the exercise of its own reason. This was Rousseau's opinion respecting men: I extend it to women, and confidently assert that they have been drawn out of their sphere by false refinement, and not by an endeavour to acquire masculine qualities. Still the regal homage which they receive is so intoxicating, that till the manners of the times are changed, and formed on more reasonable principles, it may be impossible to convince them that the illegitimate power, which they obtain, by degrading themselves, is a curse, and that they must return to nature and equality, if they wish to secure the placid satisfaction that unsophisticated affections impart. But for this epoch we must wait—wait, perhaps, till kings and nobles, enlightened by reason, and, preferring the real dignity of man to childish state, throw off their gaudy hereditary trappings: and if then women do not resign the arbitrary power of beauty—they will prove that they have *less* mind than man.

I may be accused of arrogance; still I must declare what I firmly believe, that all the writers who have written on the subject of female education and manners from Rousseau to Dr. Gregory, have contributed to render women more artificial, weak characters, than they would otherwise have been; and, consequently, more useless

---

5. *Paradise Lost* 4.634–38; Wollstonecraft's emphases.   6. *Paradise Lost* 8.381–91; Wollstonecraft's emphases.

members of society.[7] * * * My objection extends to the whole purport of those books, which tend, in my opinion, to degrade one half of the human species, and render women pleasing at the expense of every solid virtue.

Though, to reason on Rousseau's ground, if man did attain a degree of perfection of mind when his body arrived at maturity, it might be proper, in order to make a man and his wife *one*, that she should rely entirely on his understanding; and the graceful ivy, clasping the oak that supported it, would form a whole in which strength and beauty would be equally conspicuous. But, alas! husbands, as well as their help-mates, are often only overgrown children; nay, thanks to early debauchery, scarcely men in their outward form—and if the blind lead the blind, one need not come from heaven to tell us the consequence.[8] * * *

Probably the prevailing opinion, that woman was created for man, may have taken its rise from Moses's poetical story;[9] yet, as very few, it is presumed, who have bestowed any serious thought on the subject, ever supposed that Eve was, literally speaking, one of Adam's ribs, the deduction must be allowed to fall to the ground; or, only be so far admitted as it proves that man, from the remotest antiquity, found it convenient to exert his strength to subjugate his companion, and his invention to shew that she ought to have her neck bent under the yoke, because the whole creation was only created for his convenience or pleasure.

Let it not be concluded that I wish to invert the order of things; I have already granted, that, from the constitution of their bodies, men seem to be designed by Providence to attain a greater degree of virtue. I speak collectively of the whole sex; but I see not the shadow of a reason to conclude that their virtues should differ in respect to their nature. In fact, how can they, if virtue has only one eternal standard? I must therefore, if I reason consequentially, as strenuously maintain that they have the same simple direction, as that there is a God.

It follows then that cunning should not be opposed to wisdom, little cares to great exertions, or insipid softness, varnished over with the name of gentleness, to that fortitude which grand views alone can inspire.

I shall be told that woman would then lose many of her peculiar graces, and the opinion of a well known poet might be quoted to refute my unqualified assertion. For Pope has said, in the name of the whole male sex,

> Yet ne'er so sure our passion to create,
> As when she touch'd the brink of all we hate.

In what light this sally[1] places men and women, I shall leave to the judicious to determine; meanwhile I shall content myself with observing, that I cannot discover why, unless they are mortal, females should always be degraded by being made sub-servient to love or lust.

To speak disrespectfully of love is, I know, high treason against sentiment and fine feelings; but I wish to speak the simple language of truth, and rather to address

7. In *Émile*, ch. 5, "Sophy or Woman," Rousseau advises that a "woman's education must . . . be planned in rela-tion to man. To be pleasing in his sight, to win his respect and love, to train him in childhood, to tend him in manhood, to counsel and console, to make his life pleasant and happy"; at any state of life, she "will always be in subjection to a man, or to man's judgment, and she will never be free to set her own opinion above his." Dr. John Gregory (1724–1773) wrote a popular English con-duct book, *A Father's Legacy to His Daughters* (1774).
8. See Jesus' admonition, "if the blind lead the blind,

both shall fall into the ditch" (Matthew 15.14). "Rousseau's ground" is given in *Émile*, ch. 5.
9. The first five books of the Old Testament are tradi-tionally attributed to Moses; Genesis gives two versions of the creation of woman: in 1.27, God creates man and woman simultaneously; in 2.21–23, the one followed by Milton, God creates Eve out of Adam's rib.
1. The "sally" (an attack by besieged troops; an outburst of wit) is from Pope's *Epistle II, to a Lady*, "Of the Charac-ters of Women" (1735), 51–52.

the head than the heart. To endeavour to reason love out of the world, would be to out Quixote Cervantes, and equally offend against common sense;[2] but an endeavour to restrain this tumultuous passion, and to prove that it should not be allowed to dethrone superior powers, or to usurp the sceptre which the understanding should ever coolly wield, appears less wild.

Youth is the season for love in both sexes; but in those days of thoughtless enjoyment provision should be made for the more important years of life, when reflection takes place of sensation. But Rousseau, and most of the male writers who have followed his steps, have warmly inculcated that the whole tendency of female education ought to be directed to one point:—to render them pleasing.[3]

Let me reason with the supporters of this opinion who have any knowledge of human nature, do they imagine that marriage can eradicate the habitude of life? The woman who has only been taught to please will soon find that her charms are oblique sunbeams, and that they cannot have much effect on her husband's heart when they are seen every day, when the summer is passed and gone. Will she then have sufficient native energy to look into herself for comfort, and cultivate her dormant faculties? or, is it not more rational to expect that she will try to please other men; and, in the emotions raised by the expectation of new conquests, endeavour to forget the mortification her love or pride has received? When the husband ceases to be a lover—and the time will inevitably come, her desire of pleasing will then grow languid, or become a spring of bitterness; and love, perhaps, the most evanescent of all passions, gives place to jealousy or vanity.

I now speak of women who are restrained by principle or prejudice; such women, though they would shrink from an intrigue with real abhorrence, yet, nevertheless, wish to be convinced by the homage of gallantry that they are cruelly neglected by their husbands; or, days and weeks are spent in dreaming of the happiness enjoyed by congenial souls till their health is undermined and their spirits broken by discontent. How then can the great art of pleasing be such a necessary study? it is only useful to a mistress; the chaste wife, and serious mother, should only consider her power to please as the polish of her virtues, and the affection of her husband as one of the comforts that render her task less difficult and her life happier.— But, whether she be loved or neglected, her first wish should be to make herself respectable, and not to rely for all her happiness on a being subject to like infirmities with herself. * * *

Women ought to endeavour to purify their heart;[4] but can they do so when their uncultivated understandings make them entirely dependent on their senses for employment and amusement, when no noble pursuit sets them above the little vanities of the day, or enables them to curb the wild emotions that agitate a reed over which every passing breeze has power? To gain the affections of a virtuous man is affectation necessary? Nature has given woman a weaker frame than man; but, to ensure her husband's affections, must a wife, who by the exercise of her mind and body whilst she was discharging the duties of a daughter, wife, and mother, has allowed her constitution to retain its natural strength, and her nerves a healthy tone, is she, I say, to condescend to use art and feign a sickly delicacy in order to secure her husband's affection? Weakness may excite tenderness, and gratify the arrogant pride

2. To outdo Cervantes' comic hero Don Quixote in ineffectual idealism, including the ideals of courtly love.
3. See *Émile*, ch. 5.

4. Jesus teaches, "Blessed are the pure of heart: for they shall see God" (Matthew 5.8).

of man; but the lordly caresses of a protector will not gratify a noble mind that pants for, and deserves to be respected. Fondness is a poor substitute for friendship!

In a seraglio, I grant, that all these arts are necessary; the epicure must have his palate tickled, or he will sink into apathy; but have women so little ambition as to be satisfied with such a condition? Can they supinely dream life away in the lap of pleasure, or the languor of weariness, rather than assert their claim to pursue reasonable pleasures and render themselves conspicuous by practising the virtues which dignify mankind? Surely she has not an immortal soul who can loiter life away merely employed to adorn her person, that she may amuse the languid hours, and soften the cares of a fellow-creature who is willing to be enlivened by her smiles and tricks, when the serious business of life is over.

Besides, the woman who strengthens her body and exercises her mind will, by managing her family and practising various virtues, become the friend, and not the humble dependent of her husband; and if she, by possessing such substantial qualities, merit his regard, she will not find it necessary to conceal her affection, nor to pretend to an unnatural coldness of constitution to excite her husband's passions. In fact, if we revert to history, we shall find that the women who have distinguished themselves have neither been the most beautiful nor the most gentle of their sex. * * *

I own it frequently happens that women who have fostered a romantic unnatural delicacy of feeling,[5] waste their lives in *imagining* how happy they should have been with a husband who could love them with a fervid increasing affection every day, and all day. But they might as well pine married as single—and would not be a jot more unhappy with a bad husband than longing for a good one. That a proper education; or, to speak with more precision, a well stored mind, would enable a woman to support a single life with dignity, I grant; but that she should avoid cultivating her taste, lest her husband should occasionally shock it, is quitting a substance for a shadow. To say the truth, I do not know of what use is an improved taste, if the individual be not rendered more independent of the casualties of life; if new sources of enjoyment, only dependent on the solitary operations of the mind, are not opened. People of taste, married or single, without distinction, will ever be disgusted by various things that touch not less observing minds. On this conclusion the argument must not be allowed to hinge; but in the whole sum of enjoyment is taste to be denominated a blessing? * * *

But to view the subject in another point of view. Do passive indolent women make the best wives? Confining our discussion to the present moment of existence, let us see how such weak creatures perform their part? Do the women who, by the attainment of a few superficial accomplishments, have strengthened the prevailing prejudice, merely contribute to the happiness of their husbands? Do they display their charms merely to amuse them? And have women, who have early imbibed notions of passive obedience, sufficient character to manage a family or educate children? So far from it, that, after surveying the history of woman, I cannot help, agreeing with the severest satirist, considering the sex as the weakest as well as the most oppressed half of the species. What does history disclose but marks of inferiority, and how few women have emancipated themselves from the galling yoke of sovereign man?—So few, that the exceptions remind me of an ingenious conjecture respecting Newton: that he was probably a being of a superior order, accidentally caged in a

---

5. For example, the herd of novelists [Wollstonecraft's note, attacking the influence of popular sentimental fiction].

human body.[6] Following the same train of thinking, I have been led to imagine that the few extraordinary women who have rushed in eccentrical directions out of the orbit prescribed to their sex, were *male* spirits, confined by mistake in female frames. But if it be not philosophical to think of sex when the soul is mentioned, the inferiority must depend on the organs; or the heavenly fire, which is to ferment the clay, is not given in equal portions.[7] * * *

from *Chapter 3. The Same Subject Continued*

If it be granted that woman was not created merely to gratify the appetite of man, or to be the upper servant, who provides his meals and takes care of his linen, it must follow, that the first care of those mothers or fathers, who really attend to the education of females, should be, if not to strengthen the body, at least, not to destroy the constitution by mistaken notions of beauty and female excellence; nor should girls ever be allowed to imbibe the pernicious notion that a defect can, by any chemical process of reasoning, become an excellence. In this respect, I am happy to find, that the author of one of the most instructive books, that our country has produced for children, coincides with me in opinion; I shall quote his pertinent remarks to give the force of his respectable authority to reason.[1]

But should it be proved that woman is naturally weaker than man, whence does it follow that it is natural for her to labour to become still weaker than nature intended her to be? Arguments of this cast are an insult to common sense, and savour of passion. The *divine right* of husbands, like the divine right of kings, may, it is to be hoped, in this enlightened age, be contested without danger, and, though conviction may not silence many boisterous disputants, yet, when any prevailing prejudice is attacked, the wise will consider, and leave the narrow-minded to rail with thoughtless vehemence at innovation.

The mother, who wishes to give true dignity of character to her daughter, must, regardless of the sneers of ignorance, proceed on a plan diametrically opposite to that which Rousseau has recommended with all the deluding charms of eloquence and philosophical sophistry: for his eloquence renders absurdities plausible, and his dogmatic conclusions puzzle, without convincing, those who have not ability to refute them.

Throughout the whole animal kingdom every young creature requires almost continual exercise, and the infancy of children, conformable to this intimation, should be passed in harmless gambols, that exercise the feet and hands, without requiring very minute direction from the head, or the constant attention of a nurse. In fact, the care necessary for self-preservation is the first natural exercise of the

---

6. Isaac Newton (1642–1727), brilliant physicist and mathematician.
7. In the 18th century, the question whether the soul was marked by a sexual character, like the body, was widely debated. "Clay" is a familiar term for the body.
1. "If women are in general feeble both in body and mind, it arises less from nature than from education. We encourage a vicious indolence and inactivity, which we falsely call delicacy; instead of hardening their minds by the severer principles of reason and philosophy, we breed them to useless arts, which terminate in vanity and sensuality. In most of the countries which I had visited, they are taught nothing of an higher nature than a few modulations of the voice, or useless postures of the body; their time is consumed in sloth or trifles, and trifles become the only pursuits capable of interesting them. We seem to forget, that it is upon the qualities of the female sex that our own domestic comforts and the education of our children must depend. And what are the comforts or the education which a race of beings, corrupted from their infancy, and unacquainted with all the duties of life, are fitted to bestow? To touch a musical instrument with useless skill, to exhibit their natural or affected graces to the eyes of indolent and debauched young men, to dissipate their husband's patrimony [his inheritance as well as his children's] in riotous and unneccessary [sic] expences, these are the only arts cultivated by women in most of the polished nations I had seen. And the consequences are uniformly such as may be expected to proceed from such polluted sources, private misery and public servitude . . . ." Mr. [Thomas] Day's *Sandford and Merton*, Vol III [Wollstonecraft's note].

understanding, as little inventions to amuse the present moment unfold the imagination. But these wise designs of nature are counteracted by mistaken fondness or blind zeal. The child is not left a moment to its own direction, particularly a girl, and thus rendered dependent—dependence is called natural.

To preserve personal beauty, woman's glory! the limbs and faculties are cramped with worse than Chinese bands,[2] and the sedentary life which they are condemned to live, whilst boys frolic in the open air, weakens the muscles and relaxes the nerves.— As for Rousseau's remarks, which have since been echoed by several writers, that they have naturally, that is from their birth, independent of education, a fondness for dolls, dressing, and talking[3]—they are so puerile as not to merit a serious refutation. That a girl, condemned to sit for hours together listening to the idle chat of weak nurses, or to attend at her mother's toilet,[4] will endeavour to join the conversation, is, indeed, very natural; and that she will imitate her mother or aunts, and amuse herself by adorning her lifeless doll, as they do in dressing her, poor innocent babe! is undoubtedly a most natural consequence. For men of the greatest abilities have seldom had sufficient strength to rise above the surrounding atmosphere; and, if the page of genius have always been blurred by the prejudices of the age, some allowance should be made for a sex, who, like kings, always see things through a false medium.

Pursuing these reflections, the fondness for dress, conspicuous in women, may be easily accounted for, without supposing it the result of a desire to please the sex on which they are dependent. The absurdity, in short, of supposing that a girl is naturally a coquette, and that a desire connected with the impulse of nature to propagate the species, should appear even before an improper education has, by heating the imagination, called it forth prematurely, is so unphilosophical, that such a sagacious observer as Rousseau would not have adopted it, if he had not been accustomed to make reason give way to his desire of singularity, and truth to a favorite paradox.[5] * * *

I have, probably, had an opportunity of observing more girls in their infancy than J. J. Rousseau[6]—I can recollect my own feelings, and I have looked steadily around me; yet, so far from coinciding with him in opinion respecting the first dawn of the female character, I will venture to affirm, that a girl, whose spirits have not been damped by inactivity, or innocence tainted by false shame, will always be a romp, and the doll will never excite attention unless confinement allows her no alternative. Girls and boys, in short, would play harmlessly together, if the distinction of sex was not inculcated long before nature makes any difference.—I will go further, and affirm, as an indisputable fact, that most of the women, in the circle of my observation, who have acted like rational creatures, or shewn any vigour of intellect, have accidentally been allowed to run wild—as some of the elegant formers of the fair sex would insinuate. * * *

I once knew a weak woman of fashion, who was more than commonly proud of her delicacy and sensibility. She thought a distinguishing taste and puny appetite the height of all human perfection, and acted accordingly.—I have seen this weak sophisticated being neglect all the duties of life, yet recline with self-complacency on a sofa, and boast of her want of appetite as a proof of delicacy that extended to, or, perhaps, arose from, her exquisite sensibility: for it is difficult to render intelligible such ridiculous jargon.—Yet, at the moment, I have seen her insult a worthy old

2. The Chinese practice of binding girls' feet to keep them delicately small often left them crippled for life, reinforcing dependency.
3. See *Émile*, ch. 5.

4. Grooming and dressing.
5. See *Émile*, ch. 5.
6. Wollstonecraft was the eldest sister in a family with three girls and had also worked as a governess.

gentlewoman, whom unexpected misfortunes had made dependent on her ostentatious bounty, and who, in better days, had claims on her gratitude. Is it possible that a human creature could have become such a weak and depraved being, if, like the Sybarites,[7] dissolved in luxury, every thing like virtue had not been worn away, or never impressed by precept, a poor substitute, it is true, for cultivation of mind, though it serves as a fence against vice?

Such a woman is not a more irrational monster than some of the Roman emperors, who were depraved by lawless power. Yet, since kings have been more under the restraint of law, and the curb, however weak, of honour, the records of history are not filled with such unnatural instances of folly and cruelty, nor does the despotism that kills virtue and genius in the bud, hover over Europe with that destructive blast which desolates Turkey, and renders the men, as well as the soil, unfruitful.[8] * * *

It is time to effect a revolution in female manners—time to restore to them their lost dignity—and make them, as a part of the human species, labour by reforming themselves to reform the world. It is time to separate unchangeable morals from local manners.—If men be demi-gods—why let us serve them! And if the dignity of the female soul be as disputable as that of animals—if their reason does not afford sufficient light to direct their conduct whilst unerring instinct is denied—they are surely of all creatures the most miserable! and, bent beneath the iron hand of destiny, must submit to be a *fair defect* in creation. But to justify the ways of Providence respecting them, by pointing out some irrefragable reason for thus making such a large portion of mankind accountable and not accountable, would puzzle the subtilest casuist.[9] * * *

I must relieve myself by drawing a different picture.

Let fancy now present a woman with a tolerable understanding, for I do not wish to leave the line of mediocrity, whose constitution, strengthened by exercise, has allowed her body to acquire its full vigour; her mind, at the same time, gradually expanding itself to comprehend the moral duties of life, and in what human virtue and dignity consist.

Formed thus by the discharge of the relative duties of her station, she marries from affection, without losing sight of prudence, and looking beyond matrimonial felicity, she secures her husband's respect before it is necessary to exert mean arts to please him and feed a dying flame, which nature doomed to expire when the object became familiar, when friendship and forbearance take place of a more ardent affection.—This is the natural death of love, and domestic peace is not destroyed by struggles to prevent its extinction. I also suppose the husband to be virtuous; or she is still more in want of independent principles.

Fate, however, breaks this tie.—She is left a widow, perhaps, without a sufficient provision; but she is not desolate! The pang of nature is felt; but after time has softened sorrow into melancholy resignation, her heart turns to her children with redoubled fondness, and anxious to provide for them, affection gives a sacred heroic cast to her maternal duties. She thinks that not only the eye sees her virtuous efforts from whom all her comfort now must flow, and whose approbation is life; but her imagination, a little abstracted and exalted by grief, dwells on the fond hope that the eyes which her trembling hand closed, may still see how she subdues every wayward passion to fulfil the double duty of being the father as well as the mother of her children.

---

7. The inhabitants of a 5th-century Greek colony in Italy famed for luxurious decadence.
8. Both the hot, dusty winds from the deserts to the south and the infamously despotic Ottoman Empire.

9. For "fair defect," see *Paradise Lost* 8.891–92; Milton begins his epic invoking divine inspiration to "justify the ways of God to men" (1.26); a casuist is one who debates ethical questions with overtones of dishonesty.

Raised to heroism by misfortunes, she represses the first faint dawning of a natural inclination, before it ripens into love, and in the bloom of life forgets her sex—forgets the pleasure of an awakening passion, which might again have been inspired and returned. She no longer thinks of pleasing, and conscious dignity prevents her from priding herself on account of the praise which her conduct demands. Her children have her love, and her brightest hopes are beyond the grave, where her imagination often strays.

I think I see her surrounded by her children, reaping the reward of her care. The intelligent eye meets hers, whilst health and innocence smile on their chubby cheeks, and as they grow up the cares of life are lessened by their grateful attention. She lives to see the virtues which she endeavoured to plant on principles, fixed into habits, to see her children attain a strength of character sufficient to enable them to endure adversity without forgetting their mother's example.

The task of life thus fulfilled, she calmly waits for the sleep of death, and rising from the grave, may say—Behold, thou gavest me a talent—and here are five talents.[1]

I wish to sum up what I have said in a few words, for I here throw down my gauntlet, and deny the existence of sexual virtues, not excepting modesty.[2] For man and woman, truth, if I understand the meaning of the word, must be the same; yet the fanciful female character, so prettily drawn by poets and novelists, demanding the sacrifice of truth and sincerity, virtue becomes a relative idea, having no other foundation than utility, and of that utility men pretend arbitrarily to judge, shaping it to their own convenience.

Women, I allow, may have different duties to fulfil; but they are *human* duties, and the principles that should regulate the discharge of them, I sturdily maintain, must be the same. * * *

from *Chapter 13. Some Instances of the Folly Which the Ignorance of Women Generates; with Concluding Reflections on the Moral Improvement That a Revolution in Female Manners Might Naturally Be Expected to Produce*
[CONCLUDING REFLECTIONS]

That women at present are by ignorance rendered foolish or vicious, is, I think, not to be disputed; and, that the most salutary effects tending to improve mankind might be expected from a REVOLUTION in female manners, appears, at least, with a face of probability, to rise out of the observation. For as marriage has been termed the parent of those endearing charities which draw man from the brutal herd, the corrupting intercourse that wealth, idleness, and folly, produce between the sexes, is more universally injurious to morality than all the other vices of mankind collectively considered. To adulterous lust the most sacred duties are sacrificed, because before marriage, men, by a promiscuous intimacy with women, learned to consider love as a

1. An extravagant rewriting of Jesus' parable of the talents (Matthew 25.15–28), on the duty to make good use of God's gifts. A master, having given one servant five talents (a talent is a silver coin worth about $1,000 today), another two, and another only one, is pleased to learn that first two have doubled their money; but he is so enraged at the timidity of the third servant, who has only buried his talent, that he takes the money away from him and gives it to the first servant.

2. To throw down one's gauntlet, the glove of armor, is a challenge to combat. By "sexual virtues," she means sex-specific; "modesty" (usually regarded as a "feminine" characteristic) refers to the general moral discipline of self-restraint and respect for others desirable in both sexes.

selfish gratification—learned to separate it not only from esteem, but from the affection merely built on habit, which mixes a little humanity with it. Justice and friendship are also set at defiance, and that purity of taste is vitiated which would naturally lead a man to relish an artless display of affection rather than affected airs. But that noble simplicity of affection, which dares to appear unadorned, has few attractions for the libertine, though it be the charm, which by cementing the matrimonial tie, secures to the pledges of a warmer passion the necessary parental attention; for children will never be properly educated till friendship subsists between parents. Virtue flies from a house divided against itself—and a whole legion of devils take up their residence there.[1]

The affection of husbands and wives cannot be pure when they have so few sentiments in common, and when so little confidence is established at home, as must be the case when their pursuits are so different. That intimacy from which tenderness should flow, will not, cannot subsist between the vicious.

Contending, therefore, that the sexual distinction which men have so warmly insisted upon, is arbitrary, I have dwelt on an observation, that several sensible men, with whom I have conversed on the subject, allowed to be well founded; and it is simply this, that the little chastity to be found amongst men, and consequent disregard of modesty, tend to degrade both sexes; and further, that the modesty of women, characterized as such, will often be only the artful veil of wantonness instead of being the natural reflection of purity, till modesty be universally respected.[2]

From the tyranny of man, I firmly believe, the greater number of female follies proceed; and the cunning, which I allow makes at present a part of their character, I likewise have repeatedly endeavoured to prove, is produced by oppression.

Were not dissenters,[3] for instance, a class of people, with strict truth, characterized as cunning? And may I not lay some stress on this fact to prove, that when any power but reason curbs the free spirit of man, dissimulation is practised, and the various shifts of art are naturally called forth? Great attention to decorum, which was carried to a degree of scrupulosity, and all that puerile bustle about trifles and consequential solemnity, which Butler's caricature of a dissenter, brings before the imagination, shaped their persons as well as their minds in the mould of prim littleness.[4] I speak collectively, for I know how many ornaments to human nature have been enrolled amongst sectaries; yet, I assert, that the same narrow prejudice for their sect, which women have for their families, prevailed in the dissenting part of the community, however worthy in other respects; and also that the same timid prudence, or headstrong efforts, often disgraced the exertions of both. Oppression thus formed many of the features of their character perfectly to coincide with that of the oppressed half of mankind; or is it not notorious that dissenters were, like women, fond of deliberating together, and asking advice of each other, till by a complication of little contrivances, some little end was brought about? A similar attention to preserve their reputation was conspicuous in the dissenting and female world, and was produced by a similar cause.

1. An allusion to Jesus' lesson that "if a house be divided against itself, that house cannot stand" (Mark 3.25).
2. By chastity and modesty, Wollstonecraft means sexual self-control and self-discipline; male chastity entails fidelity, not sexual self-denial, in marriage.
3. Those who dissented from the established Church of England to form independent religious sects; many of Wollstonecraft's friends were dissenters.
4. Samuel Butler's mock-heroic, satirical poem *Hudibras* (1663–1678) takes aim at Puritans (dissenters who formed the commonwealth government after the execution of Charles I); Sir Hudibras, pedant and hypocrite, is a country justice who sets out to reform England of various popular entertainments.

Asserting the rights which women in common with men ought to contend for, I have not attempted to extenuate their faults; but to prove them to be the natural consequence of their education and station in society. If so, it is reasonable to suppose that they will change their character, and correct their vices and follies, when they are allowed to be free in a physical, moral, and civil sense.[5]

Let woman share the rights and she will emulate the virtues of man; for she must grow more perfect when emancipated, or justify the authority that chains such a weak being to her duty.—If the latter, it will be expedient to open a fresh trade with Russia for whips; a present which a father should always make to his son-in-law on his wedding day, that a husband may keep his whole family in order by the same means; and without any violation of justice reign, wielding this sceptre, sole master of his house, because he is the only being in it who has reason:—the divine, indefeasible earthly sovereignty breathed into man by the Master of the universe. Allowing this position, women have not any inherent rights to claim; and, by the same rule, their duties vanish, for rights and duties are inseparable.

Be just then, O ye men of understanding! and mark not more severely what women do amiss, than the vicious tricks of the horse or the ass for whom ye provide provender—and allow her the privileges of ignorance, to whom ye deny the rights of reason, or ye will be worse than Egyptian task-masters, expecting virtue where nature has not given understanding!

❧ "A VINDICATION" AND ITS TIME ❧

The Wollstonecraft Controversy and the Rights of Women

Wollstonecraft's *Vindication of the Rights of Woman* challenged an age when women had no legal standing as daughters or wives, being under the coverture (legal identity) of their fathers and husbands. They could not own property, form contracts, or conduct business. "Obedience" was expected behavior, sanctioned by religion, law, and custom; a rebellious daughter (one, for instance, refusing her father's choice of her husband) could be disowned; divorce was granted only by husbands, who retained custody of all property (including dowry) as well as the children (a prime reason many women remained in abusive marriages). Female suffrage was so outrageous a notion that it could not be debated for another century or so. Far from having any power to change the law by vote, women did not even have legal status, or any representatives for their concerns in Parliament. It was not until 1870 that the Married Woman's Property Act was passed, allowing such women to keep their earnings, and not until 1882 that it was amended to allow them to keep the property, including personal property, that they brought to the marriage (dowry) or acquired during it; this act also gave a woman the right to enter legal contracts and to sue in courts, as well as a legally distinct identity from her husband.

---

5. I had further enlarged on the advantages which might reasonably be expected to result from an improvement in female manners, towards the general reformation of society; but it appeared to me that such reflections would more properly close the last volume. [Wollstonecraft's note; no further volumes were published].

England was not alone in the 1790s in resisting change: even in France the case for women's rights fared so poorly with the Revolutionary government that its champions were sent to the guillotine. French women did not secure the vote until 1944, nearly a century after American feminists presented the Declaration of Sentiments and Resolutions at Seneca Falls. The way was paved for these changes by the constant debate from the 1790s onward over systems of female education, women's rights, and social policy—a debate that even among women involved ideologically disparate, even opposed, commitments. When Maria Edgeworth proposed to Anna Barbauld that they coedit a periodical featuring "the literary ladies of the present day," Barbauld declined on the question of common cause: "There is no bond of union among literary women, any more than among literary men; different sentiments and different connections separate them much more than the joint interest of their sex would unite them. Mrs. Hannah More would not write along with you or me, and we should probably hesitate at joining Miss Hays, or if she were living, Mrs. Godwin" [Wollstonecraft]. Our selections from this tremendous body of literature show the wide range of concerns in this debate and the wide range of responses it involved, in particular to Wollstonecraft—a lightning rod in this charged atmosphere.

Catherine Macaulay
from *Letters on Education*[1]
from *Letter 22: No Characteristic Difference in Sex*

The great difference that is observable in the characters of the sexes, Hortensia,[2] as they display themselves in the scenes of social life, has given rise to much false speculation on the natural qualities of the female mind.—For though the doctrine of innate ideas, and innate affections, are in a great measure exploded by the learned, yet few persons reason so closely and so accurately on abstract subjects as, through a long chain of deductions, to bring forth a conclusion which in no respect militates with their premises.

It is a long time before the crowd give up opinions they have been taught to look upon with respect. * * * It is from such causes that the notion of a sexual difference in the human character has, with very few exceptions, universally prevailed from the earliest times, and the pride of one sex, and the ignorance and vanity of the other, have helped to support an opinion which a close observation of Nature, and a more accurate way of reasoning, would disprove.

It must be confessed, that the virtues of the males among the human species, though mixed and blended with a variety of vices and errors, have displayed a bolder and a more consistent picture of excellence than female nature has hitherto done. It is on these reasons that, when we compliment the appearance of a more than ordinary energy in the female mind, we call it masculine; and hence it is, that Pope has elegantly said *a perfect woman's but a softer man.*[3] And if we take in the consideration, that there can be but one rule of moral excellence for beings made of the same materials, organized after the same manner, and subjected to similar laws of

1. *Letters on Education*, published in 1790, deeply influenced Wollstonecraft, who called Macaulay "the woman of the greatest abilities, undoubtedly, that this country has ever produced." Wollstonecraft also admired Macaulay's eight-volume, anti-monarchial *History of England*. Macaulay did not live to see the publication of *Rights of Woman*, in which Wollstonecraft praises her "strong and clear" intellect and echoes many of her polemics: the attack on the gender ideologies proffered by Rousseau and Pope and on the cultural systems that educate women into

"a state of slavery"; a disdain of "coquetry" (the female art of manipulating men through their passions); a scathing critique of the language of female compliments; and advocacy of coeducation and a gender-neutral standard of "rational" conduct.

2. The fictitious recipient of the letter.

3. A slight misquotation of *Epistle II*, "Of the Characters of Women": "Heaven, when it strives to polish all it can / Its last best work, but forms a softer man" (271–72).

Nature, we must either agree with Mr. Pope, or we must reverse the proposition, and say, that *a perfect man is a woman formed after a coarser mold*. The difference that actually does subsist between the sexes, is too flattering for men to be willingly imputed to accident; for what accident occasions, wisdom might correct; and it is better, says Pride, to give up the advantages we might derive from the perfection of our fellow associates, than to own that Nature has been just in the equal distribution of her favours. These are the sentiments of the men: but mark how readily they are yielded to by the women; not from humility I assure you, but merely to preserve with character those fond vanities on which they set their hearts. No; suffer them to idolize their persons, to throw away their life in the pursuit of trifles, and to indulge in the gratification of the meaner passions, and they will heartily join in the sentence of their degradation.

Among the most strenuous asserters of a sexual difference in character, Rousseau is the most conspicuous, both on account of that warmth of sentiment which distinguishes all his writings, and the eloquence of his compositions: but never did enthusiasm and the love of paradox, those enemies to philosophical disquisition, appear in more strong opposition to plain sense than in Rousseau's definition of this difference.[4] He sets out with a supposition, that Nature intended the subjection of the one sex to the other; that consequently there must be an inferiority of intellect in the subjected party; but as man is a very imperfect being, and apt to play the capricious tyrant, Nature, to bring things nearer to an equality, bestowed on the woman such attractive graces, and such an insinuating address, as to turn the balance on the other scale. Thus Nature, in a giddy mood, recedes from her purposes, and subjects prerogative to an influence which must produce confusion and disorder in the system of human affairs. Rousseau saw this objection; and in order to obviate it, he has made up a moral person of the union of the two sexes, which, for contradiction and absurdity, outdoes every metaphysical riddle that was ever formed in the schools. In short, it is not reason, it is not wit; it is pride and sensuality that speak in Rousseau, and, in this instance, has lowered the man of genius to the licentious pedant. * * * for so little did a wise and just Providence intend to make the condition of slavery an unalterable law of female nature, that in the same proportion as the male sex have consulted the interest of their own happiness, they have relaxed in their tyranny over women; and such is their use in the system of mundane creation, and such their natural influence over the male mind, that were these advantages properly exerted, they might carry every point of any importance to their honour and happiness. However, till that period arrives in which women will act wisely, we will amuse ourselves in talking of their follies.

The situation and education of women, Hortensia, is precisely that which must necessarily tend to corrupt and debilitate both the powers of mind and body. From a false notion of beauty and delicacy, their system of nerves is depraved before they come out of their nursery; and this kind of depravity has more influence over the mind, and consequently over morals, than is commonly apprehended. But it would be well if such causes only acted towards the debasement of the sex; their moral education is, if possible, more absurd than their physical. The principles and nature of virtue, which is never properly explained to boys, is kept quite a mystery to girls. They are told indeed, that they must abstain from those vices which are contrary to their personal happiness, or they will be regarded as criminals, both by God and man;

4. Rousseau's arguments throughout *Émile*, especially ch. 5 ("Sophy").

but all the higher parts of rectitude, every thing that ennobles our being, and that renders us both innoxious and useful, is either not taught, or is taught in such a manner as to leave no proper impression on the mind. This is so obvious a truth, that the defects of female education have ever been a fruitful topic of declamation for the moralist; but not one of this class of writers have laid down any judicious rules for amendment. Whilst we still retain the absurd notion of a sexual excellence, it will mitigate against the perfecting a plan of education for either sex. The judicious Addison animadverts on the absurdity of bringing a young lady up with no higher idea of the end of education than to make her agreeable to a husband, and confining the necessary excellence for this happy acquisition to the mere graces of person.[5]

Every parent and tutor may not express himself in the same manner as is marked out by Addison; yet certain it is, that the admiration of the other sex is held out to women as the highest honour they can attain; and whilst this is considered as their *summum bonum* [highest good] and the beauty of their persons the chief *desideratum* [thing wanted] of men, Vanity, and its companion Envy, must taint, in their characters, every native and every acquired excellence. Nor can you, Hortensia, deny, that these qualities, when united to ignorance, are fully equal to the engendering and rivetting all those vices and foibles which are peculiar to the female sex; vices and foibles which have caused them to be considered, in ancient times, as beneath cultivation, and in modern days have subjected them to the censure and ridicule of writers of all descriptions, from the deep thinking philosopher to the man of ton[6] and gallantry, who, by the bye, sometimes distinguishes himself by qualities which are not greatly superior to those he despises in women. Nor can I better illustrate the truth of this observation than by the following picture, to be found in the polite and gallant Chesterfield. "Women," says his Lordship, "are only children of a larger growth. They have an entertaining tattle, sometimes wit; but for solid reasoning, and good sense, I never in my life knew one that had it, or who acted or reasoned in consequence of it for four and twenty hours together. A man of sense only trifles with them, plays with them, humours and flatters them, as he does an engaging child; but he neither consults them, nor trusts them in serious matters."[7]

Richard Polwhele
from *The Unsex'd Females* [1]

Thou, who with all the poet's genuine rage,
Thy "fine eye rolling" o'er "this aweful age,"[2]

5. Joseph Addison (1672–1719), essayist and poet. Macaulay wrongly attributes to Addison an unsigned essay on this subject in *The Spectator* by his collaborator, Richard Steele. Animadverts: criticizes.
6. Fashion.
7. *Letters to His Son* no. 294 (16 November 1752), also cited in *Rights of Woman*, ch. 4. Philip Chesterfield (1694–1773), statesman, author, and wit, wrote letters of advice to his illegitimate son from age five until his own death; published in 1774, these became famous (or infamous) for their comments on sexual behavior and rituals.
1. *The Unsex'd Females* appeared in 1798, at the end of a decade of vigorous debate about women's rights inaugurated by Macaulay's *Letters on Education* (1790) and Wollstonecraft's *Rights of Woman* (1792). Polwhele (1760–1838) wrote poetry, histories, theological tracts, and essays for conservative journals. Polwhele lumps together a wide range of women writers as "unsex'd" radicals, further developing his poem's polemics in his massive footnotes, which form a key part of his work.
2. The addressee is another Tory conservative scourge, Thomas James Mathias, whose long satirical poem *The Pursuits of Literature* (1794–1797), also encased in footnotes, inspired Polwhele's. In his Preface to the 4th dialogue of this popular poem (16 editions), Mathias lamented that "our *unsexed* female writers now instruct, or confuse, us and themselves, in the labyrinth of politics, or turn us wild with Gallic frenzy"—French-inspired ideas and fashions. He begins representing himself "not unconscious of this awful age" (1.7), echoing Milton's representation of himself and other visionary poets as chastisers of their own age, "fall'n on evil days" (*Paradise Lost* 7.25). Theseus in *A Midsummer Night's Dream* describes "the poet's eye, in a fine frenzy rolling" (5.1.12).

Where polish'd life unfolds its various views,
Hast mark'd the magic influence of the muse;
5 Sever'd, with nice precision, from her beam
Of genial power, her false and feeble gleam;
Expos'd the Sciolist's[3] vain-glorious claim,
And boldly thwarted Innovation's aim,
Where witlings wildly think, or madly dare,[4]
10 With Honor, Virtue, Truth, announcing war;
Survey with me, what ne'er our fathers saw,
A female band despising NATURE's law,[5]
As "proud defiance"[6] flashes from their arms,
And vengeance smothers all their softer charms.
15   I shudder at the new unpictur'd scene,
Where unsex'd woman vaunts the imperious mien;
Where girls, affecting to dismiss the heart,
Invoke the Proteus of petrific art;[7]
With equal ease, in body or in mind,
20 To Gallic freaks or Gallic faith[8] resign'd,
The crane-like neck, as Fashion bids, lay bare,
Or frizzle, bold in front, their borrow'd hair;°   *wigs*
Scarce by a gossamery film carest,
Sport, in full view, the meretricious breast;[9]
25 Loose the chaste cincture,[1] where the graces shone,
And languish'd all the Loves, the ambrosial zone;
As lordly domes inspire dramatic rage,
Court prurient Fancy to the private stage;
With bliss botanic[2] as their bosoms heave,

---

3. Displayer of superficial learning.
4. "Greatly think, or nobly die." Pope [Polwhele's note, slightly misquoting l.10 of *Elegy to the Memory of an Unfortunate Lady*, about a woman who seems to have committed suicide in despair of love].
5. Nature is the grand basis of all laws human and divine: and the woman, who has no regard to nature, either in the decoration of her person, or the culture of her mind, will soon "walk after the flesh, in the lust of uncleanness, and despise government" [Polwhele's note, quoting 2 Peter 2.10; Rousseau and other defenders of sexual inequality routinely invoke "Natural" or "Nature's" law].
6. "A troop came next, who crowns and armour wore, / And proud defiance in their looks they bore." Pope. The Amazonian band—the female Quixotes of the new philosophy, are, here, too justly characterised [Polwhele's note. The quotation is from *The Temple of Fame* (1711, ll.342–343), the troop answering "the direful trump of Slander." The Amazons, legendary race of warrior women from Scythia, near the Black Sea, frequently assailed the Greeks; they were fabled to have burnt off the right breast (*a*, without; *mazos*, breast) to facilitate use of bow or javelin; the term is used, not always disparagingly, for any "masculine" woman, or, disparagingly, as a synonym for virago. Quixotes (from Cervantes' hero) are impractical idealists.
7. Proteus: god able to change shapes at will; petrific: able to turn to stone, as if a Medusa, an unfeeling woman.

8. French fashions and the new French (Godless) religion.
9. To "sport a face," is a cant phrase in one of our Universities, by which is meant an impudent obtrusion of a man's person in company. It is not inapplicable, perhaps, to the open bosom—a fashion which we have never invited or sanctioned. The fashions of France, which have been always imitated by the English, were, heretofore, unexceptionable in a moral point of view; since, however ridiculous or absurd, they were innocent. But they have now their source among prostitutes—among women of the most abandoned character. [Polwhele's note]. Meretricious: whorish. An 18th-century French aristocratic fashion was a fancy-gown neckline plunged below the bosom, displaying it bare.
1. A wide belt around the waist and sometimes the bosom, as a girdle; it is "chaste" for concealing breasts and hips.
2. Botany has lately become a fashionable amusement with the ladies. But how the study of the sexual system of plants can accord with female modesty, I am not able to comprehend. I had first written: "More eager for illicit knowlege [sic] pant, / With lustful boys anatomize a plant; / The virtues of its dust prolific speak, / Or point its pistill with unblushing cheek." I have, several times, seen boys and girls botanizing together [Polwhele's note]. Such judgment of the immodesty of botanizing was probably fueled by Erasmus Darwin, whose popular poem, *The Botanic Garden*, especially Part II, *The Loves of the Plants* (1789; 1791), is explicit about sexual organs and activity.

30   Still pluck forbidden fruit, with mother Eve,
        For puberty in sighing florets pant,
        Or point the prostitution of a plant;
        Dissect[3] its organ of unhallow'd lust,
        And fondly gaze the titillating[4] dust;
35   With liberty's sublimer views expand,
        And o'er the wreck of kingdoms[5] sternly stand;
        And, frantic, midst the democratic storm,
        Pursue, Philosophy! thy phantom-form.
            Far other is the female shape and mind,
40   By modest luxury heighten'd and refin'd;
        Those limbs, that figure, tho' by Fashion grac'd,
        By Beauty polish'd, and adorn'd by Taste;
        That soul, whose harmony perennial flows,
        In Music trembles, and in Color glows;
45   Which bids sweet Poesy reclaim the praise
        With faery light to gild fastidious days,
        From sullen clouds relieve domestic care,
        And melt in smiles the withering frown of war.
        Ah! once the female Muse, to NATURE true,
50   The unvalued store from FANCY, FEELING drew;
        Won, from the grasp of woe, the roseate hours,
        Cheer'd life's dim vale, and strew'd the grave with flowers.
        But lo! where, pale amidst the wild,[6] she draws
        Each precept cold from sceptic Reason's[7] vase;
55   Pours with rash arm the turbid stream along,
        And in the foaming torrent whelms the throng.[8]
        Alas! her pride sophistic° flings a gloom,   *specious*

3. Miss Wollstonecraft does not blush to say, in an introduction to a book designed for the use of young ladies, that, "in order to lay the axe at the root of corruption, it would be proper to familiarize the sexes to an unreserved discussion of those topics, which are generally avoided in conversation from a principle of false delicacy; and that it would be right to speak of the organs of generation as freely as we mention our eyes or our hands." To such language our botanizing girls are doubtless familiarized: and, they are in a fair way of becoming worthy disciples of Miss W. If they do not take heed to their ways, they will soon exchange the blush of modesty for the bronze of impudence [Polwhele's note, alluding to Luke 3.9]. He misrepresents Wollstonecraft's statement in "Introductory Address to Parents," *Elements of Morality, For the Use of Children* (1792): concerned with masturbation and other "impure" practices, she contends that "the most efficacious method to root out this dreadful evil, which poisons the source of human happiness, would be to speak to children of the organs of generation as freely as we speak of the other parts of the body, and explain to them the noble use which they were designed for, and how they may be injured." In *Rights of Woman* (ch. 7: "Modesty") she refutes as "absurd" the "gross idea" that botany is inconsistent with female modesty, and lists it among the subjects that boys and girls might study together (ch. 12: "On National Education").
4. "Each pungent grain of titillating dust." Pope; "The

prolific dust"—of the botanist [Polwhele's note, alluding to the "Charge of *Snuff*"—"The pungent Grains of titillating Dust"—Belinda hurls at her adversary in *The Rape of the Lock* (5.84)].
5. The female advocates of Democracy in this country, though they have had no opportunity of imitating the French ladies, in their atrocious acts of cruelty; have yet assumed a stern serenity in the contemplation of those savage excesses. "To express their abhorrence of royalty, they (the French ladies) threw away the character of their sex, and bit the amputated limbs of their murdered countrymen.—I say this on the authority of a young gentleman who saw it.—I am sorry to add, that the relation, accompanied with looks of horror and disgust, only provoked a contemptuous smile from an illuminated British fair-one." See Robinson [Polwhele's note, quoting *Proofs of a Conspiracy*].
6. "A wild, where flowers and weeds promiscuous shoot; / A garden tempting with forbidden fruit." Pope [Polwhele's note, quoting *Essay on Man* (1733): Epistle I, 7–8].
7. A troubled stream only, can proceed from the vase of scepticism [Polwhele's note, alluding to the Revolutionaries' (Godless) ideology of "Reason"].
8. "Raging waves, foaming out their own shame"—St. Jude. Such were those infamous publications of Paine and others, which, like the torrents of December, threatened to sweep all before them—to overwhelm the multitude [Polwhele's note].

To chase, sweet Innocence! thy vernal bloom,
Of each light joy to damp the genial glow,
60   And with new terrors clothe the groupe of woe,
Quench the pure daystar° in oblivion deep,   *sun*
And, Death! restore thy "long, unbroken sleep."[9]
    See Wollstonecraft, whom no decorum checks,
Arise, the intrepid champion of her sex;
65   O'er humbled man assert the sovereign claim,
And slight the timid blush[1] of virgin fame.
    "Go, go (she cries) ye tribes of melting maids,
Go, screen your softness in sequester'd shades;
With plaintive whispers woo the unconscious grove,
70   And feebly perish, as depis'd ye love.
What tho' the fine Romances of Rousseau
Bid the frame flutter, and the bosom glow;
Tho' the rapt Bard, your empire fond to own,
Fall prostrate and adore your living throne,
75   The living throne his hands presum'd to rear,
Its seat a simper, and its base a tear;[2]
Soon shall the sex disdain the illusive sway,
And wield the sceptre in yon blaze of day;
Ere long, each little artifice discard,
80   No more by weakness[3] winning fond regard;
Nor eyes, that sparkle from their blushes, roll,
Nor catch the languors of the sick'ning soul,
Nor the quick flutter, nor the coy reserve,
But nobly boast the firm gymnastic nerve;[4]
85   Nor more affect with Delicacy's fan
To hide the emotion from congenial man;
To the bold heights where glory beams, aspire,
Blend mental energy with Passion's fire,
Surpass their rivals in the powers of mind
90   And vindicate *the Rights of womankind.*"

9. "We, the great, the valiant and the wise, / When once the seal of death hath clos'd our eyes, / Shut in the hollow tomb obscure and deep, / Slumber, to wake no more, one long unbroken sleep." Moschus [Polwhele's note; Moschus: 2nd-century B.C. Greek pastoral poet, whom he translated in a well-received publication of 1786].
1. That Miss Wollstonecraft was a sworn enemy to blushes, I need not remark. But many of my readers, perhaps, will be astonished to hear, that at several of our boarding-schools for young ladies, a blush incurs a penalty [Polwhele's note].
2. According to Rousseau, the empire of women is the empire of softness—of address: their commands, are caresses; their menaces, are tears. [Polwhele's note, referring to Rousseau's views on women in *La Nouvelle*

Heloise (1760) and *Émile* (1762), both criticized in *Rights of Woman.*]
3. "Like monarchs, we have been flattered into imbecillity, by those who wish to take advantage of our weakness," says Mary Hays (*Essays and Letters*, p. 92). But, whether flattered or not, women were always weak: and female weakness hath accomplished, what the force of arms could not effect [Polwhele's note, quoting her passionate endorsement of Wollstonecraft's *Rights of Woman.* Hays's feminist *Appeal to the Men of Great Britain on Behalf of Women* appeared anonymously in 1798.]
4. Miss Wollstonecraft seriously laments the neglect of all muscular exercises, at our female Boarding-schools [Polwhele's note].

She spoke: and veteran BARBAULD[5] caught the strain,
And deem'd her songs of Love, her Lyrics vain;
And ROBINSON[6] to Gaul her Fancy gave,
And trac'd the picture of a Deist's grave!
95   And charming SMITH[7] resign'd her power to please,
Poetic feeling and poetic ease;
And HELEN,[8] fir'd by Freedom, bade adieu
To all the broken visions of Peru.
And YEARSELEY,[9] who had warbled, Nature's child,
100 Midst twilight dews, her minstrel ditties wild,
(Tho' soon a wanderer from her meads and milk,
She long'd to rustle, like her sex, in silk)

5. Here . . . I have formed a groupe of female Writers; whose productions have been appreciated by the public as works of learning or genius—though not praised with that extravagance of panegyric, which was once a customary tribute to the literary compositions of women. In this country, a female author was formerly esteemed a Phenomenon in Literature: and she was sure of a favourable reception among the critics, in consideration of her sex. This species of gallantry, however, conveyed no compliment to her understanding. It implied such an inferiority of woman in the scale of intellect as was justly humiliating: and critical forbearance was mortifying to female vanity. At the present day, indeed, our literary women are so numerous, that their judges, wa[i]ving all complimentary civilities, decide upon their merits with the same rigid impartiality as it seems right to exercise towards the men. The tribunal of criticism is no longer charmed into complacence by the blushes of modest apprehension. It no longer imagines the pleading eye of feminine diffidence that speaks a consciousness of comparative imbecillity, or a fearfulness of having offended by intrusion. Experience hath drawn aside the flimsy veil of affected timidity, that only served to hide the smile of complacency; the glow of self-gratulation. Yet, alas! the crimsoning blush of modesty, will be always more attractive, than the sparkle of confident intelligence.—Mrs. Barbauld stands the most conspicuous figure in the groupe. She is a veteran in Literature . . . Her poetry . . . is certainly, chaste and elegant. . . . I was sorry to find Mrs. B. . . . classed with such females as a Wollstonecraft. . . . But though Mrs. B. has lately published several political tracts, which if not discreditable to her talents and virtues, can by no means add to her reputation, yet, I am sure, she must reprobate, with me, the alarming eccentricities of Miss Wollstonecraft [Polwhele's note].
6. In Mrs. Robinson's Poetry, there is a peculiar delicacy: but her Novels, as literary compositions, have no great claim to approbation—As containing the doctrines of Philosophism, they merit the severest censure. Would that, for the sake of herself and her beautiful daughter (whose personal charms are only equalled by the elegance of her mind) would, that, for the sake of the public morality, Mrs. Robinson were persuaded to dismiss the gloomy phantom of annihilation; to think seriously of a future retribution; and to communicate to the world, a recantation of errors that originated in levity, and have been nursed by pleasure! I have seen her, "glittering like the morning-star, full of life, and splendor and joy!" Such, and more glorious, may I meet her again, when the just "shall shine forth as the brightness of the firmament, and as the stars for ever and ever!" [Polwhele, quoting Burke's famous description of his first sight of princess Marie Antoinette; see Reflections, page 52.] "Philosophism" refers to the Enlightenment ideology of progress and human perfectibility through reason.
7. The Sonnets of Charlotte Smith, have a pensiveness peculiarly their own. It is not the monotonous plaintiveness of Shenstone, the gloomy melancholy of Gray, or the meek subdued spirit of Collins. It is a strain of wild, yet softened sorrow, that breathes a romantic air, without losing, for a moment, its mellowness. Her images, often original, are drawn from nature: the most familiar, have a new and charming aspect. Sweetly picturesque, she creates with the pencil of a Gilpin, and infuses her own soul into the landscape. There is so uncommon a variety in her expression, that I could read a thousand of such sonnets without lassitude. In general, a very few Sonnets fatigue attention, partly owing to the sameness of their construction. Petrarch, indeed, I can relish for a considerable time: but Spenser and Milton soon produce somnolence. . . . But why does she suffer her mind to be infected with the Gallic mania? [Polwhele's note. Other references are to the 18th-century poets William Shenstone, Thomas Gray, and William Collins, and to William Gilpin (1724–1804), author of illustrated picturesque tours of Britain.]
8. Miss Helen Williams is, doubtless, a true poet. But is it not extraordinary, that such a genius, a female and so young, should have become a politician—that the fair Helen, whose notes of love have charmed the moonlight vallies, should stand forward, an intemperate advocate for Gallic licentiousness—that such a woman should import with her, a blast more pestilential than that of Avernus, though she has so often delighted us with melodies, soft as the sighs of the Zephyr, delicious as the airs of Paradise? [Polwhele's note. See Williams's Letters from France (1792–1796), pages 37–46; her long political poem condemning imperial conquest, Peru, was published in 1784. Avernus is a lake in Italy thought to be the gate to the underworld; zephyr is the spring breeze.]
9. Mrs. Yearseley's [sic] Poems, as the product of an untutored milk-woman, certainly entitled her to patronage: and patronage she received, from Miss H. More, liberal beyond example. Yet, such is the depravity of the human heart, that this milk-woman had no sooner her hut cheered by the warmth of benevolence, than she spurned her benefactor from her door. . . . My business, however, with Mrs. Y. is to recall her, if possible, from her Gallic wanderings—if an appeal to native ingenuousness be not too late; if the fatal example of the Arch-priestess of female Libertinism, have any influence on a mind once stored with the finest moral sentiment [Polwhele's note].

Now stole that modish grin, the sapient sneer,
And flippant HAYS[1] assum'd a cynic leer ＊＊＊

1798

Hannah More

from *Strictures on the Modern System of Female Education;*[1]
*with a View of the Principles and Conduct Prevalent
among Women of Rank and Fortune*
from *Introduction*

It is a singular injustice which is often exercised towards women, first to give them a very defective education, and then to expect from them the most undeviating purity of conduct;—to train them in such a manner as shall lay them open to the most dangerous faults, and then to censure them for not proving faultless. Is it not unreasonable and unjust, to express disappointment if our daughters should, in their subsequent lives, turn out precisely that very kind of character for which it would be evident to an unprejudiced by-stander that the whole scope and tenour of their instruction had been systematically preparing them?

Some reflections on the present erroneous system are here with great deference submitted to public consideration. The author is apprehensive that she shall be accused of betraying the interests of her sex by laying open their defects; but surely an earnest wish to turn their attention to objects calculated to promote their true dignity, is not the office of an enemy. So to expose the weakness of the land, as to suggest the necessity of internal improvement, and to point out the means of effectual defence, is not treachery, but patriotism. ＊＊＊

Let it not be suspected that the author arrogantly conceives *herself* to be exempt from that natural corruption of the heart which it is one chief object of this slight work to exhibit; that she superciliously erects herself into the impeccable censor of her sex and of the world; as if from the critic's chair she were coldly pointing out the faults and errors of another order of beings, in whose welfare she had not that lively interest which can only flow from the tender and intimate participation of fellow-feeling.

Bath, March 14, 1799

1. Mary Hays from her "Letters and Essays" . . . is evidently a Wollstonecraftian. "I cannot mention (says she) the admirable advocate for the rights of women, without pausing to pay a tribute of grateful respect, in the name of my sex, to the virtue and talents of a writer, who with equal courage and ability, hath endeavoured to rescue the female mind from those prejudices which have been the canker of genuine virtue. . . . The rights of woman and the name of Wollstonecraft, will go down to posterity with reverence." Mary Hays ridicules "the good lady who studied her Bible, and obliged her children to say their prayers, and go stately to church." Her expressions respecting the European Governments are, in a high degree, inflammatory [Polwhele's note]. The attacks on Wollstonecraft continue in subsequent notes, recounting her infatuation with the married Fuseli, her affair with Imlay, her suicide attempts despite a young daughter, her premarital affair with Godwin, and her lack of church attendance or death-bed conversion. "I cannot but think, that the Hand of Providence is visible, in her life, her death and in [Godwin's] Memoirs. . . . As she was given up to her 'heart's lusts,' and let 'to follow her own imaginations,' that the fallacy of and the effects of an irreligious conduct, might be manifested to the world; and as she died a death that strongly marked the distinction of the sexes, by pointing out the destiny of women and the diseases to which they are liable."

1. First published in 1799, *Strictures on Female Education* went through thirteen editions and was in demand for decades, selling 19,000 copies. Raised in a High Church–Tory family, More criticized both the French Revolution and Wollstonecraft's arguments for the rights of women. ("We shall be hearing of the rights of Children next!" she scoffed.) Yet she shared Wollstonecraft's emphasis on rationality, chastity, and "practiced education," and herself learned several languages, joined London literary circles, and wrote several bestselling works.

from *Chapter 8. On Female Study*

Will it not be ascribed to a captious singularity, if I venture to remark that real knowledge and real piety, though they may have gained in many instances, have suffered in others from that profusion of little, amusing, sentimental books with which the youthful library overflows? Abundance has its dangers as well as scarcity. In the first place, may not the multiplicity of these alluring little works increase the natural reluctance to those more dry and uninteresting studies, of which, after all, the rudiments of every part of learning *must* consist? And, secondly, is there not some danger (though there are many honourable exceptions) that some of those engaging narratives may serve to infuse into the youthful heart a sort of spurious goodness, a confidence of virtue, a parade of charity? And that the benevolent actions with the recital of which they abound, when they are not made to flow from any source but *feeling*, may tend to inspire a self-complacency, a self-gratulation, a "stand by, for I am holier than thou?" May not the success with which the good deeds of the little heroes are uniformly crowned; the invariable reward which is made the instant concomitant of well-doing, furnish the young reader with false views of the condition of life, and the nature of the divine dealings with men? May they not help to suggest a false standard of morals, to infuse a love of popularity and an anxiety for praise, in the place of that simple and unostentatious rule of doing whatever good we do, *because it is the will of God?* The universal substitution of this principle would tend to purify the worldly morality of many a popular little story. And there are few dangers which good parents will more carefully guard against than that of giving their children a mere political piety; that sort of religion which just goes to make people more respectable, and to stand well with the world; a religion which is to save appearances without inculcating realities; a religion which affects to "preach peace and good will to men," but which forgets to give "glory to God in the highest."[1]

There is a certain precocity of mind which is much helped on by these superficial modes of instruction; for frivolous reading will produce its correspondent effect, in much less time than books of solid instruction; the imagination being liable to be worked upon, and the feelings to be set a going, much faster than the understanding can be opened and the judgment enlightened. A talent for conversation should be the result of instruction, not its precursor: it is a golden fruit when suffered to ripen gradually on the tree of knowledge; but if forced in the hot-bed of a circulating library,[2] it will turn out worthless and vapid in proportion as it was artificial and premature. Girls who have been accustomed to devour a multitude of frivolous books, will converse and write with a far greater appearance of skill, as to style and sentiment, at twelve or fourteen years old, than those of a more advanced age, who are under the discipline of severer studies; but the former having early attained to that low standard which had been held out to them, become stationary; while the latter, quietly progressive, are passing through just gradations to a higher strain of mind; and those who early begin with talking and writing like women, commonly end with thinking and acting like children.

I would not, however, prohibit such works of imagination as suit this early period. When moderately used, they serve to stretch the faculties and expand the mind;

1. An ingenious (and in many respects useful) French Treatise on Education has too much encouraged this political piety [More's note; her quotations are from Luke 2.14].

2. Lending libraries that flourished from the 1790s carried stores of popular fiction, much of it written by and for women.

but I should prefer works of vigorous genius and pure unmixed fable to many of those tame and more affected moral stories, which are not grounded on Christian principle. I should suggest the use, on the one hand, of original and acknowledged fictions; and, on the other, of accurate and simple facts; so that truth and fable may ever be kept separate and distinct in the mind. * * *

This suggestion is, however, by no means intended to exclude works of taste and imagination, which must always make the ornamental part, and of course a very considerable part of female studies. It is only intimated, that they should not form them entirely and exclusively. For what is called dry tough reading, independent of the knowledge it conveys, is useful as a habit, and wholesome as an exercise. Serious study serves to harden the mind for more trying conflicts; it lifts the reader from sensation to intellect; it abstracts her from the world and its vanities; it fixes a wandering spirit and fortifies a weak one; it divorces her from matter; it corrects that spirit of trifling which she naturally contracts from the frivolous turn of female conversation and the petty nature of female employments. * * *

Far be it from me to desire to make scholastic ladies or female dialecticians; but there is little fear that the kind of books here recommended, if thoroughly studied, and not superficially skimmed, will make them pedants, or induce conceit; for by showing them the possible powers of the human mind, you will bring them to see the littleness of their own: and surely to get acquainted with the mind, to regulate, to inform it; to show it its own ignorance and its own weakness, does not seem the way to puff it up. But let her who is disposed to be elated with her literary acquisitions check the rising vanity by calling to mind the just remark of Swift, "that after all her boasted acquirements, a woman will, generally speaking, be found to possess less of what is called learning than a common school-boy."[3]

Neither is there any fear that this sort of reading will convert ladies into authors. The direct contrary effect will be likely to be produced by the perusal of writers who throw the generality of readers at such an unapproachable distance as to check presumption, instead of exciting it. Who are those ever-multiplying authors, that with unparalleled fecundity are overstocking the world with their quick-succeeding progeny? They are NOVEL-WRITERS: the easiness of whose productions is at once the cause of their own fruitfulness, and of the almost infinitely numerous race of imitators to whom they give birth. Such is the frightful facility of this species of composition, that every raw girl, while she reads, is tempted to fancy that she can also write. And as Alexander, on perusing the Iliad, found by congenial sympathy the image of Achilles stamped on his own ardent soul, and felt himself the hero he was studying; and as Corregio, on first beholding a picture which exhibited the perfection of the graphic art, prophetically felt all his own future greatness, and cried out in rapture, "And I, too, am a painter!" so a thorough-paced novel-reading Miss, at the close of every tissue of hackneyed adventures, feels within herself the stirring impulse of corresponding genius, and triumphantly exclaims, "And I, too, am an author!" The glutted imagination soon overflows with the redundance of cheap sentiment and plentiful incident, and by a sort of arithmetical proportion, is enabled by the perusal of any three novels, to produce a fourth; till every fresh production, like the prolific progeny

3. From *Letter to a Young Lady* (1727) by Jonathan Swift: "Those who are commonly called Learned Women have lost all manner of Credit by their impertinent Talkativeness and Conceit of themselves; but there is an easy remedy for this, if you once consider, that after all the pains you may be at, you can never arrive in point of learning to the perfection of a School-boy."

of Banquo, is followed by "Another, and another, and another!"[4] Is a lady, however destitute of talents, education, or knowledge of the world, whose studies have been completed by a circulating library, in any distress of mind? the writing a novel suggests itself as the best soother of her sorrows! Does she labour under any depression of circumstances? writing a novel occurs as the readiest receipt for mending them! and she solaces her imagination with the conviction that the subscription which has been extorted by her importunity, or given to her necessities, has been offered as a homage to her genius; and this confidence instantly levies a fresh contribution for a succeeding work. Capacity and cultivation are so little taken into the account, that writing a book seems to be now considered as the only sure resource which the idle and the illiterate have always in their power.

May the Author be indulged in a short digression, while she remarks, though rather out of its place, that the corruption occasioned by these books has spread so wide, and descended so low, as to have become one of the most universal, as well as most pernicious, sources of corruption among us. Not only among milliners, mantua-makers, and other trades where numbers work together, the labour of one girl is frequently sacrificed that she may be spared to read those mischievous books to the others; but she has been assured by clergymen who have witnessed the fact, that they are procured and greedily read in the wards of our hospitals! an awful hint, that those who teach the poor to read, should not only take care to furnish them with principles which will lead them to abhor corrupt books, but that they should also furnish them with such books as shall strengthen and confirm their principles.[5]

from *Chapter 14. The Practical Use of Female Knowledge, with a Sketch of the Female Character, and a Comparative View of the Sexes*

The chief end to be proposed, in cultivating the understandings of women is to qualify them for the practical purposes of life. Their knowledge is not often, like the learning of men, to be reproduced in some literary composition, and never in any learned profession; but it is to come out in conduct: it is to be exhibited in life and manners. A lady studies, not that she may qualify herself to become an orator or a pleader; not that she may learn to debate, but to act. She is to read the best books, not so much to enable her to talk to them, as to bring the improvement which they furnish to the rectification of her principles and the formation of her habits. The great uses of study to a woman are to enable her to regulate her own mind, and to be instrumental to the good of others. * * *

But there is one *human* consideration which would perhaps more effectually tend to damp in an aspiring woman the ardours of literary vanity—I speak not of real genius, though there the remark often applies—than any which she will derive from motives of humility, or propriety, or religion; which is, that in the judgment passed on her performances, she will have to encounter the mortifying circumstance of having her sex always taken into account, and her highest exertions will probably be

---

4. References are to the famous anecdote of Alexander the Great's sympathy with the Greek hero Achilles in Homer's epic of the Trojan War; the Italian Renaissance painter; and to the vision of Banquo's royal heirs that frustrates Macbeth (4.1).
5. The above facts furnish no argument on the side of those who would keep the poor in ignorance. Those who cannot *read* can *hear*, and are likely to hear to worse purpose than those who have been better taught. And that ignorance furnishes no security for integrity either in morals or politics, the late revolts in more than one country, remarkable for the ignorance of the poor, fully illustrate. It is earnestly hoped that the above facts may tend to impress ladies with the importance of superintending the instruction of the poor, and of making it an indispensable part of their charity to give them moral and religious books [More's note].

received with the qualified approbation *that it is really extraordinary for a woman*. Men of learning, who are naturally disposed to estimate works in proportion as they appear to be the result of art, study, and institution, are inclined to consider even the happier performances of the other sex as the spontaneous productions of a fruitful but shallow soil, and to give them the same kind of praise which we bestow on certain salads, which often draw from us a sort of wondering commendation, not, indeed, as being worth much in themselves, but because, by the lightness of the earth, and a happy knack of the gardener, these indifferent cresses spring up in a night, and therefore we are ready to wonder they are no worse.

As to men of sense, however, they need be the less hostile to the improvement of the other sex, as they themselves will be sure to be gainers by it; the enlargement of the female understanding being the most likely means to put an end to those petty and absurd contentions for equality which female smatterers so anxiously maintain. I say smatterers, for between the first class of both sexes the question is much more rarely and always more temperately agitated. Cooperation, and not competition, is, indeed, the clear principle we wish to see reciprocally adopted by those higher minds in each sex which really approximate the nearest to each other. The more a woman's understanding is improved, the more obviously she will discern that there can be no happiness in any society where there is a perpetual struggle for power; and the more her judgment is rectified, the more accurate views will she take of the station she was born to fill, and the more readily will she accommodate herself to it. * * *

There is this singular difference between a woman vain of her wit, and a woman vain of her beauty; * * * she who is vain of her genius, more liberal at least in her vanity, is jealous for the honour of her whole sex, and contends for the equality of their pretensions as a body, in which she feels that her own are involved as an individual. The beauty vindicates her own rights, the wit the rights of women; * * * and while the more selfish though more moderate beauty "would but be Queen for life," the public-spirited wit struggles to abrogate the Salique law of intellect, and to enthrone "a whole sex of Queens."[1]

At the revival of letters in the sixteenth and the following century, the controversy about this equality was agitated with more warmth than wisdom; and the process was instituted and carried on, on the part of the female complainant, with that sort of acrimony which always raises a suspicion of the justice of any cause; for violence commonly implies doubt, and invective indicates weakness rather than strength. * * * Among the innovations of this innovating period, the imposing term of *rights* has been produced to sanctify the claim of our female pretenders,[2] with a view not only to rekindle in the minds of women a presumptuous vanity, dishonourable to their sex, but produced with a view to excite in their hearts an impious discontent with the post which God has assigned them in this world.[3]

But *they* little understand the true interests of woman who would lift her from the important duties of her allotted station, to fill, with fantastic dignity, a loftier

---

1. Pope's *Epistle II*, "of the Characters of Women," assumes that "ev'ry Lady would be Queen for life" and shudders at the thought of "a whole Sex of Queens! / Pow'r all their end" (218–20). Salique (Salic) law, deriving from old French law, excludes females from the line of succession to a throne.

2. False claimants, especially to a throne; More is also suggesting "fantasizers" and dissemblers.
3. This was written soon after the publication of a work intitled "The Rights of Woman" [More's note, referring to Wollstonecraft's *Vindication of the Rights of Woman*].

but less appropriate niche. Nor do they understand her true happiness, who seek to annihilate distinctions from which she derives advantages, and to attempt innovations which would depreciate her real value. Each sex has its proper excellences, which would be lost were they melted down into the common character by the fusion of the new philosophy. Why should we do away distinctions which increase the mutual benefits and enhance the satisfactions of life? Whence, but by carefully preserving the original marks of difference, stamped by the hand of the Creator, would be derived the superior advantage of mixed society? Is either sex so abounding in perfection, as to be independent on the other for improvement? Have men no need to have their rough angles filed off, and their harshnesses and asperities smoothed and polished by assimilating with beings of more softness and refinement? Are the ideas of women naturally so *very* judicious, are their principles so *invincibly* firm, are their views so *perfectly* correct, are their judgments so *completely* exact, that there is occasion for no additional weight, no superadded strength, no increased clearness, none of that enlargement of mind, none of that additional invigoration, which may be derived from the aids of the stronger sex? What identity could advantageously supersede such an enlivening opposition, such an interesting variety of character? * * *

Natural propensities best mark the designations of Providence as to their application. The fin was not more clearly bestowed on the fish that he should swim, nor the wing given to the bird that he should fly, than superior strength of body and a firmer texture of mind were given to man, that he might preside in the deep and daring scenes of action and of council; in the complicated arts of government, in the contention of arms, in the intricacies and depths of science, in the bustle of commerce, and in those professions which demand a higher reach and a wider range of powers. The true value of woman is not diminished by the imputation of inferiority in those talents which do not belong to her, of those qualities in which her claim to excellence does not consist. She has other requisites, better adapted to answer the end and purposes of her being, from "Him who does all things well;" who suits the agent to the action; who accommodates the instrument to the work.

Let not, then, aspiring, because ill-judging, woman view with pining envy the keen satirist, hunting vice through all the doublings and windings of the heart; the sagacious politician, leading senates, and directing the fate of empires; the acute lawyer, detecting the obliquities of fraud; and the skilful dramatist, exposing the pretensions of folly; but let her ambition be consoled by reflecting, that those who thus excel, to all that Nature bestows and books can teach, must add besides that consummate knowledge of the world to which a delicate woman has no fair avenues, and which, even if she could attain, she would never be supposed to have come honestly by.

In almost all that comes under the description of polite letters, in all that captivates by vivid imagery or warms by just and affecting sentiment, women are excellent. They possess in a high degree that delicacy and quickness of perception, and that nice discernment between the beautiful and defective which comes under the denomination of taste. Both in composition and in action they excel in details; but they do not so much generalise their ideas as men, nor do their minds seize a great subject with so large a grasp. They are acute observers, and accurate judges of life and manners, as far as their own sphere of observation extends, but they describe a smaller circle. A woman sees the world, as it were, from a little elevation in her own garden, whence she makes an exact survey of home scenes, but takes not in that wider range of distant prospects which he who stands on a loftier eminence commands.

William Thompson and Anna Wheeler

*Appeal of One Half the Human Race, Women, Against the
Pretensions of the Other Half, Men, To Retain Them in Political, and Thence in Civil
and Domestic Slavery* [1]

"'Tis all stern duty on the female side;
On man's, mere sensual gust and surly pride."[2]

from *Introductory Letter to Mrs. Wheeler*

The days of dedication and patronage are gone by. It is *not* with the view of obtaining the support of your name or your influence to the cause of truth and humanity that these lines are addressed to you. * * * I address you then simply to perform towards you a debt of justice. * * * Anxious that you should take up the cause of your proscribed sex, and state to the world in writing, in your own name, what you have so often and so well stated in conversation, and under feigned names in such of the periodical publications of the day as would tolerate such a theme, I long hesitated to arrange our common ideas, even upon a branch of the subject like the present. Anxious that the hand of a woman should have the honor of raising from the dust that neglected banner which a woman's hand nearly thirty years ago unfolded boldly, in face of the prejudices of thousands of years, and for which a woman's heart bled, and her life was all but the sacrifice—I hesitated to write. Were courage the quality wanting, you would have shown, what every day's experience proves, that women have more fortitude in endurance than men. Were comprehensiveness of mind, above the narrow views which too often marred Mary Wolstonecroft's [sic] pages and narrowed their usefulness, the quality wanting,—above the timidity and impotence of conclusion accompanying the gentle eloquence of Mary Hays, addressed, about the same time that Mary Wolstonecroft wrote, in the shape of an "Appeal" to the then closed ears of unreasoning men;[3] yours was the eye which no prejudice obscured, open to the rays of truth from whatever quarter they might emanate. But leisure and resolution to undertake the drudgery of the task were wanting. A few only therefore of the following pages are the exclusive produce of your mind and pen, and written with your own hand. The remainder are our joint property, I being your interpreter and the scribe of your sentiments. * * *

You look forward, as I do, to a state of society very different from that which now exists, in which the effort of all is to out wit, supplant, and snatch from each other; where interest is systematically opposed to duty; where the so-called system of morals is little more than a mass of hypocrisy preached by knaves, unpractised by them, to keep their slaves, male as well as female, in blind uninquiring obedience; and where the whole motley fabric is kept together by fear and blood. You look forward to a better

---

1. The work of two leading Irish socialists of the 1820s, *Appeal* is the most important English feminist document between Wollstonecraft's *Rights of Woman* (1792) and John Stuart Mill's *Subjection of Women* (1869). Building on Wollstonecraft's arguments, Thompson and Wheeler extend them into a critique of the underlying social system and ally the cure for women's rights with those of workers and slaves.
2. A slight misquotation of Dryden's *Palamon and Arcite* in *Fables Ancient and Modern* (1700); the virgin Emily begs the goddess Cynthia to accept her as a votress, pleading, "Like Death, thou know'st, I loath the Nuptial state, / And

Man, the Tyrant of our Sex, I hate, / A lowly Servant, but a lofty Mate. / Where Love is Duty, on the Female side; / On theirs meer sensual Gust, and sought with surly Pride" (227–32); "Gust" is appetite. In *Rights of Woman*, ch. 6, Wollstonecraft uses these lines to gloss the lack of "satisfaction" that any woman of delicate affections would confront "in a union with such a man."
3. Mary Hays, disciple and friend of Wollstonecraft, published her feminist polemic, *Appeal to the Men of Great Britain in Behalf of Women* anonymously in 1798, by which time Wollstonecraft was a scandal and the English political climate increasingly conservative.

aspect of society, where the principle of benevolence shall supersede that of fear; where restless and anxious individual competition shall give place to mutual co-operation and joint possession; where individuals in large numbers, male and female, forming voluntary associations, shall become a mutual guarantee to each other for the supply of all useful wants, and form an unsalaried and uninsolvent insurance company against all insurable casualties; where perfect freedom of opinion and perfect equality will reign amongst the co-operators; and where the children of all will be equally educated and provided for by the whole, even these children longer the slaves of individual caprice.

In truth, under the present arrangements of society, the principle of individual competition remaining, as it is, the master-key and moving principle of the whole social organization, *individual* wealth the great object sought after by all, and the quantum of happiness of each individual (other things being equal) depending on the quantum of wealth, the means of happiness, possessed by each; it seems impossible—even were all unequal legal and unequal moral restraints removed, and were no secret current of force or influence exerted to baffle new regulations of equal justice—that women should attain to equal happiness with men. Two circumstances—permanent inferiority of strength, and occasional loss of time in gestation and rearing infants—must eternally render the average exertions of women in the race of the competition for wealth less successful than those of men. The pleasant compensation that men now affect to give for these two natural sources of inferior accumulation of wealth on the part of women (aggravated a thousand degrees by their exclusions from knowledge and almost all means of useful exertions, (the very lowest only excepted)), is the existing system of marriage; under which, for the mere faculty of eating, breathing and living, in whatever degree of comfort husbands may think fit, women are reduced to domestic slavery, without will of their own, or power of locomotion, otherwise than as permitted by their respective masters. * * *

With you I would equally elevate both sexes. Really enlightened women, disdaining equally the submissive tricks of the slave and the caprices of the despot, breathing freely only in the air of the esteem of equals, and of mutual, *unbought, uncommanded,* affection, would find it difficult to meet with associates worthy of them in men as now formed, full of ignorance and vanity, priding themselves on a *sexual* superiority, entirely independent of any merit, any superior qualities, or pretensions to them, claiming respect from the strength of their arm and the lordly faculty of producing beards attached by nature to their chins! No: unworthy of, as incapable of appreciating, the delight of the society of such women, are the great majority of the existing race of men. The pleasures of mere animal appetite, the pleasures of commanding (the prettier and more helpless the slave, the greater these pleasures of the brute), are the only pleasures which the majority of men seek for from women, are the only pleasures which their education and the hypocritical system of morals with which they have been necessarily imbued, permit them to expect. * * *

Even under the present arrangements of society, founded as they all are on the basis of individual competition, nothing could be more easy than to put the *rights* of women, political and civil, on a perfect equality with those of men. It is only to abolish all prohibitory and exclusive laws,—statute or what are called "common,"—the remnants of the barbarous customs of our ignorant ancestors; particularly the horrible and odious inequality and indissolubility of that disgrace of civilization, the present marriage code. Women then might exert in a free career with men their faculties of mind and body, to whatever degree developed, in pursuit of happiness by means of exertion, as men do. But this would not raise women to an equality of happiness with men: their rights might be equal, but not their happiness, because unequal powers under free competition must produce unequal effects.

In truth, the system of the most enlightened of the school of those reformers called political economists, is still founded on exclusions. Its basis is too narrow for human happiness. A more comprehensive system, founded on equal benevolence, on the true development of the principle of Utility, is wanting.[4] Let the *competitive* political economists be satisfied with the praise of causing the removal of some of the rubbish of ignorant restrictions, under the name of laws, impeding the development of human exertion in the production of wealth. To build up a new fabric of social happiness, comprehending equally the interests of all existing human beings, has never been contemplated by them, and is altogether beyond the scope of their little theories; aiming at the utmost at increasing the number of what they style the happy middling orders, but leaving the great bulk of human beings to eternal ignorance and toil, requited by the mere means of prolonging from day to day an unhealthy and precarious existence. To a new science, the *social science*, or the science of promoting human happiness, that of political economy, or the mere science of producing wealth by individual competition, must give way.

from *Part 2*

[ON DAUGHTERS]

Business, professions, political concerns, local affairs, the whole field of sciences and arts, are open to the united and mutually sympathizing efforts of the males. To their mutual judgments and speculations, the disposal of the family income and capital are intrusted. From all these commanding sources of intellectual and muscular activity, the daughters, like the little children, are excluded, previous care having been taken, by shutting them out from all means of intellectual culture, and from the view of and participation in the real incidents of active life, to render them as unfit for, as unambitious of, such high occupations. Confined, like other domestic animals, to the house and its little details, their "sober wishes" are never permitted "to stray" into the enlarged plains of general speculation and action. The dull routine of domestic incidents is the world to them. * * *

So much more completely is the interest of the sons involved than that of the daughters in the interest of fathers, that as soon as the daughters become adult, they, necessarily operated upon by the system under which they live, look out of their artificial cages of restraint and imbecility, to catch glances at the world with the hope of freedom from parental control, by leaving behind them the very name of their fathers, and vainly hoping for happiness without independence, in the gratification of one passion, love, round which their absurd training for blind male sensuality, has caused all their little anxieties to centre. The adult sons go in and out of the father's house when they choose: they are frequently treated with liberality as visitors or equals. But the adult daughters are, for the most part, under as much restraint as little children: they must ask leave to open the door or take a walk: not one of their actions that does not depend on the will of another: they are never permitted, like the sons, to regulate their conduct by their own notions of propriety and prudence and to restrain them where necessary, like rational beings, from a regard to their consequences: every thing is prescribed to them: their reason and foresight are not cultivated like those of the

---

4. The philosophy of utilitarianism, formulated by contemporaries Jeremy Bentham and James Mill, that there is no inherent right and wrong; the only issue is consequence, whether an action contributes to "the happiness of man."

sons; and the despotism which creates their imbecility, adduces its own work as a justification of its unrelenting pressure and of its eternal duration. To marriage therefore, as the only means allowed them of emerging from paternal control; as the only means of gratifying one passion, to which all their thoughts have been exclusively directed, but which they are at the same time told it is highly improper they should wish to enjoy; as the only means of obtaining, through cunning and blandishment, that direction of their own voluntary actions, which all rational beings ought to possess, and which is the sure and only basis of intelligence and morals; to marriage, as the fancied haven of pleasure and freedom—the freedom of the slave to-be-sure, to be acquired not by right but by coaxing, by the influence of passions inapplicable to the cold despotism of the fathers—daughters look forward. No sooner adult, than their home and their name are daughters anxious to get rid of, because the retaining of them is made incompatible with the only views of happiness presented to them.

[ON WIVES]

By way of distinguishing and honoring this class of the proscribed half of the human race, man condescends to enter into what he calls a *contract* with certain women, for certain purposes, the most important of which is, the producing and rearing of children to maturity. Each man yokes a woman to his establishment, and calls it a *contract*. Audacious falsehood! A contract! where are any of the attributes of contracts, of equal and just contracts, to be found in this transaction? A contract implies the voluntary assent of both the contracting parties. Can even both the parties, man and woman, by agreement alter the terms, as to *indissolubility* and *inequality*, of this pretended contract? No. Can any individual man divest himself, were he even so inclined, of his power of despotic control? He cannot. Have women been consulted as to the terms of this pretended contract? A contract, all of whose enjoyments—wherever nature has not imposed a physical bar on the depravity of selfishness—are on one side, while all of its pains and privations are on the other! A contract, giving all power, arbitrary will and unbridled enjoyment to the one side; to the other, unqualified obedience, and enjoyments meted out or withheld at the caprice of the ruling and enjoying party. Such a contract, as the owners of *slaves* in the West Indies and every other slave-polluted soil, enter into with their slaves—the law of the stronger imposed on the weaker, *in contempt* of the interests and wishes of the weaker. * * *

As soon as adult daughters become wives, their civil rights disappear; they fall back again, and remain all their lives—should their owners and directors live so long—into the state of children or idiots, the passive property of their owners; protected by the law in some few respects only, like other slaves, from the excessive abuse of despotic power.

Woman is then compelled, in marriage, by the possession of superior strength on the part of men, by the want of knowledge, skill and wealth, by the positive, cruel, partial, and cowardly enactments of law, by the terrors of superstition, by the mockery of a pretended vow of obedience, and to crown all, and as the result of all, by the force of an unrelenting, unreasoning, unfeeling, public opinion, to be the literal unequivocal *slave* of the man who may be styled her husband. I say emphatically the slave; for a slave is a person whose actions and earnings, instead of being, under his own control, liable only to equal laws, to public opinion, and to his own calculations, under these, of his own interest, are under the arbitrary control of any other human being, by whatever name called. This is the essence of slavery, and what distinguishes it from freedom. A domestic, a civil, a political slave, in the plain unsophisticated sense of the word—in no metaphorical sense—is every married woman. No matter with what wealth she may be surrounded, with what dainties she may be fed, with what splendor of trappings adorned, with what voluptuousness her corporeal, mental, or moral sweets may be gathered; that high prerogative of human nature, the faculty of self-government, the basis of intellectual development, without which no moral conduct can exist, is to her wanting. * * * Till laws afford married women the same protection against the restraints and violence of the men to whom they are married, that they affect to afford them against all other individuals; till they afford them the same protection against the restraints and violence of their husbands, that their husbands enjoy against their caprices and violence, the social condition of the civilized wife will remain more completely slavish than that of the female slave of the West Indies.

[EXHORTATION TO MEN]

Be consistent, men! Ye stronger half of the race, be at length rational! Three or four thousand years have worn threadbare your vile cloak of hypocrisy. Even women, your poor, weak, contented slaves, at whose impotence of penetration, the result of your vile exclusions, you have been accustomed to laugh, begin to see through it and to shudder at the loathsomeness beneath. Cast aside this tattered cloak before it leaves you naked and exposed. Clothe yourselves with the new garments of sincerity. Be rational human beings, not mere male sexual creatures. Cast aside the ferocious brute of your nature: give up the pleasures of the brute, those of mere lust and command, for the pleasures of the rational being. So shall you enjoy the love of your *equals,* enlightened, benevolent, graceful, like yourselves, founded on an appreciation of your real merits: so shall you be happy. For the intercourse of the *bought* prostitute, or of the *commanded* household slave, you shall have full and equal participation in the compounded and associated pleasures of sense, intellect and benevolence. To the highest enjoyments of which your nature is susceptible, there is no shorter road than the simple road of equal justice.

[WHAT DO WOMEN WANT?]

The simple and modest request is, that they may be permitted equal enjoyments with men, *provided they can by the free and equal development and exercise of their faculties procure for themselves such enjoyments.* They ask the same means that men possess of acquiring every species of knowledge, of unfolding every one of their faculties of mind and body that can be made tributary to their happiness. They ask every facility of access to every art, occupation, profession, from the highest to the lowest, without one exception, to which their inclination and talents may direct and may fit them to occupy. They ask the removal of *all* restraints and exclusions not applicable to men of equal capacities. They ask for perfectly equal political, civil and domestic rights. They ask for equal obligations and equal punishments from the law with men in case of infraction of the same law by either party. They ask for an equal system of morals, founded on utility instead of caprice and unreasoning despotism, in which the same action attended with the same consequences, whether done by man or woman, should be attended with the same portion of approbation or disapprobation; in which every pleasure, accompanied or followed by no preponderant evil, should be equally permitted to women and to men; in which every pleasure accompanied or followed by preponderant evil should be equally censured in women and in men.

* * *

Women of England! women, in whatever country ye breathe—wherever ye breathe, degraded—awake! Awake to the contemplation of the happiness that awaits you when all your faculties of mind and body shall be fully cultivated and developed;

when every path in which ye can exercise those improved faculties shall be laid open and rendered delightful to you, even as to them who now ignorantly enslave and degrade you. If degradation from long habitude have lost its sting, if the iron have penetrated so deeply into your frame that it has been gradually taken up into the system and mingles unperceived amidst the fluids of your life; if the prostration of reason and the eradication of feeling have kept pace within you, so that you are insensible alike to what you suffer and to what you might enjoy,—your case were all but hopeless. Nothing less, then, than the sight presented before your eyes, of the superior happiness enjoyed by other women, under arrangements of perfect equality with men, could arouse you. Such a sight, even under such circumstances, would excite your envy and kindle up all your extinct desires. But you are not so degraded. The unvaried despotism of so many thousand years, has not so entirely degraded you, has not been able to extinguish within you the feelings of nature, the love of happiness and of equal justice. The united exertions of law, superstition, and pretended morals of past ages of ignorance, have not entirely succeeded. * * *

Nor will your fellow-creatures, men, long resist the change. They are too deeply concerned to continue long to oppose what palpably tends to their happiness: they are too deeply concerned not to be compelled to re-consider the barbarous systems of law and morals under which they have been brought up. In justice, in pity to them, submit no longer; no longer *willingly* submit to their caprices. Though your bodies may be a little longer kept in servitude, degrade not yourselves by the repetition of superfluous vows of obedience: cease to kiss the rod: let your *minds* be henceforth free. The morn of loosening your physical chains will not be far distant.

O woman, from your auspicious hands may the new destiny of your species proceed! The collective voices of your sex raised against oppression will ultimately make men themselves your advocates and debtors. Reflect then seriously on your miserable and degraded position—your youth, your beauty, your feelings, your opinions, your actions, your time, your few years' fever of meritricious life—all made tributary to the appetites and passions of men. Whatever pleasures you enjoy, are permitted you for man's sake. Nothing is your own; protection of person and of property are alike withheld from you. Nothing is yours, but secret pangs, the bitter burning tears of regret, the stifled sobs of outraged nature thrown back upon your own hearts, where the vital principle itself stands checked, or is agitated with malignant passions, until body and mind become the frequent prey to overwhelming disease; now finding vent in sudden phrensy, now plunged in pining melancholy, or bursting the weak tenement of reason, seeking relief in self-destruction.

How many thousand of your sex *daily* perish thus unpitied and unknown; often victims of pressing want, always of privation and the arbitrary laws of heartless custom; condemned to cheerless solitude, or an idiot round of idle fashionable pursuits; your morning of life perhaps passed by, and with it the lingering darling hope of sympathy expired—puppets once of doting ignorant parents, whose tenderness for you outlived not your first youth; who, careless of your future fate, "launched you into life without an oar," indigent and ignorant, to eat the tear-steeped bread of dependence as wives, sisters, hired mistresses or unpitied prostitutes! This is the fate of the many, nay, of all your sex, subject only to those shades of difference arising from very peculiar circumstances or the accident of independent fortune; though even here the general want of knowledge, withheld from your sex, keeps even those individuals who are favored by fortune bowed to the relentless yoke which man's laws, his superstitions, and hypocritical morality, have prepared for you.

For once then instruct man in what is good, wash out the foul stain, equally disgraceful to both sexes—that your sex has unbounded influence in making men to do evil, but cannot induce them to do good.

How many Thaises are there, who, vain of the empire they hold over the passions of men, exercise at all risks this contemptible and pernicious influence—the only influence permitted them—in stimulating these masters of the world to destroy cities; and, regardless of the whispers of conscience and humanity, often shake men's tardy resolutions to repair the evils they have caused![1]—Shall none be found with sufficient knowledge and elevation of mind to persuade men to do good, to make the most certain step towards the regeneration of degraded humanity, by opening a free course for justice and benevolence, for intellectual and social enjoyments, by no colour, by no sex to be restrained? As your bondage has chained down man to the ignorance and vices of despotism, so will your liberation reward him with knowledge, with freedom and with happiness.[2]

END OF "A VINDICATION" AND THE WOLLSTONECRAFT CONTROVERSY
AND THE RIGHTS OF WOMEN

Robert Burns
1759–1796

A "striking example of native genius bursting through the obscurity of poverty and the obstructions of laborious life" exclaimed the *Edinburgh Magazine* when Burns's *Poems, Chiefly in the Scottish Dialect* appeared from provincial Kilmarnock in 1786. Yet the reality of the "heaven-taught plowman" was more complex. A tenant farmer like his father, Burns planned to accept a position on a Jamaican plantation until the success of his poetry provided another means of escape from a hard existence. Though poor, Burns was well read; his poems, if "chiefly" in dialect, were never exclusively so: the accents and forms of folk culture play against a range of polite English genres. Fame brought Burns to Edinburgh, where he enlarged and reprinted his book. On the profits, Burns returned to farming and married Jean Armour, who had borne him children in 1786 and 1788.

The farm failed, as had its three predecessors, and Burns moved his family to Dumfries, where he obtained the post of exciseman, or tax-inspector. Government employment might seem anomalous for one who championed the American and French Revolutions, who believed in the goodness of man against the tenets of the Scots church, which he repeatedly satirized, and flamboyantly defied in his many erotic escapades, but Burns fulfilled his duties responsibly. An invitation in 1787 to contribute to *The Scots Musical Museum* intensified his sense of his Scots identity: for the next six years Burns became "absolutely crazed," as he put it, with collecting and editing traditional songs for the successive volumes, and wrote more than two hundred himself, new or adapted. When the fourth volume was finished in 1792, Burns agreed to participate in a *Select Collection of Scottish Airs*, a far more genteelly refining version of Scottish poetry. The more earthy energies of Burns's poetry appear in the posthumously

1. Probably the 4th-century B.C. Athenian courtesan, patronized by Alexander the Great and then by the King of Egypt; she was said to have accompanied Alexander on his conquests. Another Thais was a 1st-century Alexan- / drian, famous for her beauty, wealth, and sexual indulgences, who repented and converted to Christianity and a life of piety.
2. The last paragraph of *Appeal*.

published *Merry Muses of Caledonia* (1799–1800), a collection printed at least partly from Burns's papers following his early death from heart disease at the age of thirty-seven. The second version of *Comin' Thro' the Rye* and *The Fornicator* appeared in this work.

To a Mouse

On Turning Her Up in Her Nest with the Plough, November, 1785

	Wee, sleekit,° cowrin, tim'rous beastie,	*sleek*
	O, what a panic's in thy breastie!	
	Thou need na start awa sae° hasty	*so*
	Wi' bickering brattle!°	*scurry*
5	I wad be laith° to rin an' chase thee,	*loath*
	Wi' murdering pattle!°	*plough-scraper*
	I'm truly sorry man's dominion	
	Has broken Nature's social union,	
	An' justifies that ill opinion	
10	Which makes thee startle	
	At me, thy poor, earth-born companion	
	An' fellow mortal!	
	I doubt na, whyles,° but thou may thieve;	*sometimes*
	What then? poor beastie, thou maun° live!	*must*
15	A daimen icker in a thrave°	*odd ear in 24 sheaves*
	'S a sma' request;	
	I'll get a blessin wi' the lave,°	*rest*
	An' never miss 't!	
	Thy wee-bit housie, too, in ruin!	
20	Its silly wa's° the win's are strewin!	*feeble walls*
	An' naething, now, to big° a new ane,	*build*
	O' foggage° green!	*coarse grass*
	An' bleak December's win's ensuin,	
	Baith snell° an' keen!	*bitter*
25	Thou saw the fields laid bare an' waste,	
	An' weary winter comin fast,	
	An' cozie here, beneath the blast,	
	Thou thought to dwell,	
	Till crash! the cruel coulter° past	*plow-blade*
30	Out thro' thy cell.	
	That wee bit heap o' leaves an' stibble,°	*stubble*
	Has cost thee monie a weary nibble!	
	Now thou's turned out, for a' thy trouble,	
	But° house or hald,°	*without / goods*
35	To thole° the winter's sleety dribble,	*endure*
	An' cranreuch° cauld!	*hoarfrost*
	But Mousie, thou art no thy lane,°	*not alone*
	In proving foresight may be vain:	
	The best-laid schemes o' mice an' men	
40	Gang aft agley,°	*go oft awry*

An' lea'e us nought but grief an' pain,
    For promis'd joy!

Still thou art blest, compared wi' me!
The present only toucheth thee:
45 But och! I backward cast my e'e,
    On prospects drear!
An' forward, tho' I canna see,
    I guess an' fear!

1785   1786

Comin' Thro' the Rye (1)[1]

CHORUS
O, Jenny's a' weet, poor body,
    Jenny's seldom dry:
She draigl't° a' her petticoatie,   *bedraggled*
    Comin thro' the rye!

5 Comin thro' the rye, poor body,
    Comin thro' the rye,
She draigl't a' her petticoatie,
    Comin thro' the rye!

Gin° a body meet a body   *if*
10   Comin thro' the rye,
Gin a body kiss a body,
    Need a body cry?

Gin a body meet a body
    Comin thro' the glen,
15 Gin a body kiss a body,
    Need the warld ken?°   *know*

CHORUS
1796

Comin' Thro' the Rye (2)

CHORUS
O gin a body meet a body,
    Comin throu the rye;
Gin a body f—k a body,
    Need a body cry.

5 Comin' thro' the rye, my jo,°   *sweetheart*
    An' comin' thro' the rye;
She fand a staun° o' staunin' graith,°   *stand / tools*
    Comin' thro' the rye.

1. A revision and expansion of an old song, also popular in various bawdy versions, as in the second version which follows, with obscenities tactfully hyphenated by the 1800 publisher.

10
Gin a body meet a body,
    Comin' thro' the glen;
Gin a body f—k a body,
    Need the warld ken.

Gin a body meet a body,
    Comin' thro' the grain;
15
Gin a body f—k a body,
    C—t's a body's ain.°   *own*

Gin a body meet a body,
    By a body's sel,
What na body f—s a body,
20
    Wad a body tell.

Mony a body meets a body,
    They dare na weel avow;
Mony a body f—s a body,
    Ye wadna think it true.

                                               1799–1800

Scots, wha hae wi' Wallace bled[1]

Scots, wha hae° wi' Wallace bled,[2]   *who have*
Scots, wham° Bruce has aften led,   *whom*
Welcome to your gory bed
    Or to victorie!

5
Now's the day, and now's the hour:
See the front o' battle lour,°   *glare*
See approach proud Edward's° power—   *Edward II*
    Chains and slaverie!

Wha will be a traitor knave?
10
Wha can fill a coward's grave?
Wha sae base as be a slave?—
    Let him turn, and flee!

Wha for Scotland's King and Law
Freedom's sword will strongly draw,
15
Freeman stand or freeman fa',°   *fall*
    Let him follow me!

By Oppression's woes and pains,
By your sons in servile chains,

1. On 26 August 1787, Burns visited the field of Bannockburn, where Robert the Bruce vanquished the far larger English army in 1314. The victory gave Bruce the Scottish throne. Begged to make "soft verses" for the tune popularly believed to be Bruce's march at the battle, Burns said he "had no idea of giving myself any trouble on the subject, till the accidental recollection of that glorious struggle for Freedom . . . roused my rhyming mania." First published in *The Morning Chronicle*, May 1794, the poem spoke to current events—the French Revolution and the Edinburgh sedition trials—as much as to medieval history.
2. Sir William Wallace, famous Scots patriot, executed by the English King Edward I in 1305.

We will drain our dearest veins
20   But they shall be free!

Lay the proud usurpers low!
Tyrants fall in every foe!
Liberty's in every blow!
      Let us do, or die!

1793   1794

A Red, Red Rose[1]

O, my luve is like a red, red rose,
    That's newly sprung in June.
O, my luve is like the melodie,
    That's sweetly play'd in tune.

5   As fair art thou, my bonie lass,
    So deep in luve am I,
And I will luve thee still, my dear,
    Till a' the seas gang° dry.   *go*

Till a' the seas gang dry, my dear,
10   And the rocks melt wi' the sun!
And I will luve thee still, my dear,
    While the sands o' life shall run.

And fare thee weel, my only luve,
    And fare thee weel a while!
15   And I will come again, my luve,
    Tho' it were ten thousand mile!

1794   1796

Auld Lang Syne

Should auld acquaintance be forgot,
    And never brought to mind?
Should auld acquaintance be forgot,
    And auld lang syne!°   *long ago times*

CHORUS
5   For auld lang syne, my dear,
          For auld lang syne,
      We'll tak a cup o' kindness yet
          For auld lang syne!

And surely ye'll be° your pint-stowp,°   *buy / pint-cup*
10   And surely I'll be mine,
And we'll tak a cup o' kindness yet
    For auld lang syne!

1. This poem incorporates elements of several old ballads and folk songs, a common practice of amalgamation at which Burns had great success.

CHORUS

We twa hae run about the braes,°   *slopes*
        And pou'd° the gowans° fine,   *pulled / daisies*
15 But we've wander'd monie a weary fit°   *foot*
        Sin'° auld lang syne.   *since*

CHORUS

We twa hae paidl'd in the burn[1]
        Frae morning sun till dine,°   *dinner (noon)*
But seas between us braid° hae roar'd   *broad*
20   Sin' auld lang syne.

CHORUS

And there's a hand, my trusty fiere,°   *friend*
        And gie's a hand o' thine,
And we'll tak a right guid-willie waught°   *good-will swig*
        For auld lang syne!

CHORUS

25   For auld lang syne, my dear,
                    For auld lang syne,
                We'll tak a cup o' kindness yet
                    For auld lang syne!

1788   1796

The Fornicator. A New Song
Tune, Clout the Caldron

Ye jovial boys who love the joys
        The blissful joys of lovers;
Yet dare avow with dauntless brow,
        When the bony lass discovers:[1]
5 I pray draw near and lend an ear,
        And welcome in a Frater,°   *brother*
For I've lately been on quarantine,
        A proven Fornicator.

Before the Congregation wide
10   I pass'd the muster fairly,[2]
My handsome Betsey by my side,[3]
        We gat° our ditty° rarely;   *received / reproof*
But my downcast eye by chance did spy
        What made my lips to water,
15 Those limbs so clean where I, between
        Commenc'd a Fornicator.

---

1. Stream; waters used for brewing. "Burns" would especially appreciate the double sense.
1. Reveals her pregnancy.
2. In the Scottish Church those found guilty of fornication were required to sit, clothed in black, for three successive Sundays on a raised "stool of repentance."
3. Usually taken as Elizabeth Paton, with whom Burns had an illegitimate child.

With rueful face and signs of grace
    I pay'd the buttock-hire,[4]
The night was dark and thro the park
20   I could not but convoy her;
A parting kiss, what could I less,
    My vows began to scatter,
My Betsey fell—lal de dal lal lal,
    I am a Fornicator.

25   But for her sake this vow I make,
    And solemnly I swear it,
That while I own a single crown,
    She's welcome for to share it;
And my roguish boy his Mother's joy,
30   And the darling of his Pater,°   *father*
For him I boast my pains and cost,
    Although a Fornicator.

Ye wenching blades whose hireling jades[5]
Have tipt you off blue-boram,[6]
35   I tell you plain, I do disdain
    To rank you in the Quorum;
But a bony lass upon the grass
    To teache her esse Mater,°   *to be a mother*
And no reward but for regard,
40   O that's a Fornicator.

Your warlike kings and heroes bold,
    Great Captains and Commanders;
Your mighty Cèsars fam'd of old,
    And Conquering Alexanders;
45   In fields they fought and laurels bought
    And bulwarks strong did batter,
But still they grac'd our noble list
    And ranked Fornicator!!!

1784–1785   1799

⊷ ⊨✦⊨ ⊶

William Wordsworth
1770–1850

Meeting Wordsworth in 1815, Byron told his wife that he had "but one feeling . . . reverence!" The exemplar of "plain living and high thinking," Wordsworth provided an image of poetry and "the Poet" as at once humble and exalted, domestic and severely moral. By the end of his life he had become a cultural institution, respected even by those who opposed his politics. Admirers made pilgrimages to his home at Rydal Mount in the Lake District. His beginnings

---

4. There was a six-pound fine for fornication.
5. Worn-out horses, a contemptuous term for women.

6. Infected you with syphilis. The term probably derives from the notorious Blue Boar Tavern in London.

were less auspicious. Born in the Lake District, Wordsworth was the son of the steward of Lord Lonsdale (James Lowther), the dominant landowner of the beautiful but isolated region. The death of Wordsworth's mother when he was eight years old broke a stable middle-class family life; William and his three brothers were sent to Hawkshead to school, and his sister Dorothy sent to live with various distant relatives. His father died five years later, at which point Lord Lonsdale resisted paying the monies owed to him; the children did not receive their inheritance until 1802, when a new Lord Lonsdale, who became Wordsworth's patron, succeeded to the title. "The props of my affection were removed, / And yet the building stood," Wordsworth exclaimed in a passage of the *Prelude* that readers have taken to refer obliquely to these early losses and separations; "taught to feel, perhaps too much, / The self-sufficing power of Solitude," Wordsworth developed a potent myth of himself as a "favoured being" shaped by the severe but mysteriously benevolent ministry of Nature.

In 1787 Wordsworth entered St. John's College, Cambridge, taking his degree in 1791 without distinction. As his autobiographical poem *The Prelude* testifies, his travels left deeper impressions than his studies: a summer walking tour in 1790 that brought him to France a year after the fall of the Bastille, then a trip through North Wales in 1791, and a year-long stay in France (1791–1792). There he became an active partisan in the heady early phase of the Revolution. "Bliss was it in that dawn to be alive, / But to be young was very Heaven!" as he wrote in *The Prelude*. The millenarian hopes of a new era were suffused with personal attachments: he had a love affair with Annette Vallon, who bore their daughter in December 1792. By then, lack of funds had forced him back to England, and the English declaration of war against France precluded his return until 1802. In him as in many of his generation, the war produced a crisis of loyalties, aggravated by the increasing violence of revolutionary France. "Sick, wearied out with contrarieties," Wordsworth recovered "a saving intercourse with [his] true self" only through the struggles that his poetry records.

A turning point came in 1795, when a small legacy of £900 from a friend enabled Wordsworth to devote himself to poetry. He reunited with Dorothy, and met Coleridge; in 1797 brother and sister moved to Alfoxden, to be near Coleridge at Nether Stowey. "[B]uoyant spirits / . . . were our daily portion when we first / Together wantoned in wild poesy," Wordsworth later wrote; comfortably housed, free to wander the countryside, Wordsworth and Coleridge collaborated on the poems that became *Lyrical Ballads*, published anonymously in 1798 to mixed reviews. The strangeness of *The Rime of the Ancyent Marinere* disconcerted some readers, and the audacious simplicity of Wordsworth's subjects and style offended more. But others felt the "power and pathos" of the poetry, even (in Hazlitt's words) "the sense of a new style and a new spirit." In 1800 Wordsworth published a second edition under his own name, adding a volume containing *Michael* and the "Lucy" poems and others written during the cold and lonely winter that he and Dorothy had passed in Germany between 1798 and 1799. A new Preface, defending his principles and repudiating the expectations of his readers, set the terms of his reception and continued to govern the charges against him by critics such as Francis Jeffrey for decades afterwards.

In late 1799 William and Dorothy returned to the Lakes and settled in the beautiful Grasmere valley, where they remained together for the rest of their lives: first at Dove Cottage, then, after 1813, at the more spacious Rydal Mount. In 1802 their household had expanded when Wordsworth married a childhood friend, and the tenor of their life was steady thereafter, though the years were marred by grave losses—his brother John drowned in 1805, when the ship he captained went down in a storm, two of William's five children died in 1812, and a rift with Coleridge was not patched up until the 1820s. Harsh reviews of *Poems, in Two Volumes* (1807) and *The Excursion* (1814) paradoxically attested to Wordsworth's emerging centrality, and the publication of his revised and reordered *Poems* in 1815 asserted his claim to enter the canon of English poetry. Wordsworth continued to write and publish almost to the end of his long life. Though his increasingly conservative politics led some of the next generation to regard him as having betrayed his republican youth, and put him in opposition to the democratic and commercializing spirit of post-Reform Bill England, his reputation grew steadily, and in 1843 he was appointed Poet Laureate.

The Prelude, the poem that has most compelled modern readers, was published posthumously. Wordsworth had held back the work ("Title not yet fixed upon") that he had referred to variously as "the poem to Coleridge," "the poem on the growth of my own mind," and "the poem on my own poetical education," in part because he thought it "unprecedented" that an author should talk so much about himself, in part so as to bequeath its copyright as a legacy to his family. Reserving his most intimate and ambitious poem while revising it across four decades must have affected his often touchy attitude to his critics; by the time *The Prelude* appeared in 1850, the same year as Tennyson's *In Memoriam*, not even the "jacobinical" strain that Thomas Macaulay detected could much alter the image of him. For the Victorians, Wordsworth was the poet of nature, whose writings made the Lake District a tourist spot (much to his disgruntlement) and provided a moral philosophy of life, of childhood and "joy in widest commonalty spread," and above all, of memory and consolation. It was chiefly Wordsworth's "healing power" that led Matthew Arnold to declare in 1879 that Wordsworth stood third only to Milton and Shakespeare in English poetry since the Renaissance. Twentieth-century readers have been captivated by the visionary power of his language, those transient moments when "forms and substances . . . through the turnings intricate of verse, / Present themselves as objects recognized, / In flashes, and with a glory scarce their own." In Wordsworth's sustained effort in *The Prelude* to trace the growth of his mind while attending to experiences lying beyond and beneath the rational mind's grasp—"Points have we all of us within our souls / Where all stand single; this I feel, and make / Breathings for incommunicable powers"—some critics have discerned the beginnings of modern subjectivity. For Geoffrey Hartman, Wordsworth is "the most isolated figure among the great English poets." Other readers, though, have found in the tensions and ambivalences of Wordsworth's project a particularly rich embodiment of the strains of the pivotal decades in which he wrote, and he remains a crucial focus for understanding the vivid and contradictory currents of his age.

Other writing by Wordsworth appears in Perspectives: The Abolition of Slavery and the Slave Trade, page 131.

LYRICAL BALLADS In spring 1798 the young Wordsworth and Coleridge had been near neighbors in Somerset for almost a year. In the fall of 1797, they had decided to pay for a brief walking tour by collaborating on a poem to be sold to the *Monthly Magazine*. Uncompleted at the time, *The Rime of the Ancyent Marinere* became the opening poem of a more substantial enterprise: *Lyrical Ballads, with a few other poems*, the joint collection they published anonymously in October 1798. The exchange that nourished the project had been so close that Coleridge said that the two poets regarded the volume as "one work, in kind, though not in degree, as an ode is one work; and that our different poems are stanzas, good, relatively rather than absolutely," though of the twenty-three poems he wrote only four. A friend, Bristol bookseller Joseph Cottle, agreed to pay the poets £30 for the copyright; before the book appeared they had departed for Germany, Coleridge to study philosophy at Göttingen and Wordsworth to learn German at Goslar, in hopes of later earning money as a translator. Priced at five shillings, the volume sold steadily and earned favorable reviews, but the simplicity of style, the focus on rural life and language, and the obscurity of the *Ancyent Marinere* provoked memorably sharp criticism. The volume had been prefixed by an Advertisement describing the majority of the poems as "experiments" to "ascertain how far the language of conversation in the middle and lower classes of society is adapted to the purposes of poetic pleasure." Attacking "the gaudiness and inane phraseology of many modern writers," and anticipating that "readers of superior judgment" would find that many of the poems would not "suit their taste," the Advertisement deliberately positioned the volume as an affront to "pre-established codes of decision," and thereby claimed for its authors the status of innovators.

Returned from Germany in 1800 and living in the Lake District, Wordsworth planned a second edition, which he sold to Longman, an established London publisher. He now dominated the project: the whole collection was published under his name alone, and Wordsworth replaced the Advertisement with an extended Preface vindicating his principles. A new second volume was made up entirely of his poems; the archaisms of the *Ancyent Marinere* were trimmed, and the poem, retitled *The Ancient Mariner: A Poet's Reverie*, was moved from the head of the first volume to the twenty-third position, accompanied by a condescending note ("The Poem of my Friend has indeed great defects"). The expanded collection sold quickly, and by 1802 a revised third edition appeared, with a significant addition to the Preface, "What is a poet?" The harsh critique by Francis Jeffrey in the newly founded *Edinburgh Review* (page 228) may be seen as sealing the notoriety that Wordsworth had been courting; it surely helped propel the final edition of *Lyrical Ballads* in 1805, after which the contents were dispersed among the author's separate publications. Years later, in 1843, Wordsworth dictated notes on the circumstances of the poems' composition; these notes, recorded by Isabella Fenwick, are indicated as "[I.F.]."

from LYRICAL BALLADS (1798)
Simon Lee[1]
The Old Huntsman, with an incident in which he was concerned.

In the sweet shire of Cardigan,
Not far from pleasant Ivor-hall,
An old man dwells, a little man,
I've heard he once was tall.
5   Of years he has upon his back,
No doubt, a burthen weighty;
He says he is three score and ten,°   *seventy years old*
But others say he's eighty.

A long blue livery-coat° has he,   *servant's uniform*
10   That's fair behind, and fair before;
Yet, meet him where you will, you see
At once that he is poor.
Full five and twenty years he lived
A running huntsman merry;
15   And, though he has but one eye left,
His cheek is like a cherry.

---

1. "This old man had been huntsman to the squires of Alfoxden. . . . The old man's cottage stood upon the common, a little way from the entrance to Alfoxden Park. . . . I have, after an interval of 45 years, the image of the old man as fresh before my eyes as if I had seen him yesterday" [I.F.]. Wordsworth has relocated the poem from Somersetshire, where he and his sister Dorothy lived from 1797 to 1798, to Cardiganshire, a former county of southwest Wales. A huntsman manages the hunt and has charge of the hounds. In the Preface of 1800, Wordsworth said he wrote the poem to provoke his readers' feelings "from ordinary moral sensations."

No man like him the horn could sound,
And no man was so full of glee;
To say the least, four counties round
20 Had heard of Simon Lee;
His master's dead, and no one now
Dwells in the hall of Ivor;
Men, dogs, and horses, all are dead;
He is the sole survivor.

25 His hunting feats have him bereft
Of his right eye, as you may see:
And then, what limbs those feats have left
To poor old Simon Lee!
He has no son, he has no child,
30 His wife, an aged woman,
Lives with him, near the waterfall,
Upon the village common.²

And he is lean and he is sick,
His little body's half awry
35 His ancles they are swoln and thick;
His legs are thin and dry.
When he was young he little knew
Of husbandry or tillage;
And now he's forced to work, though weak,
40 —The weakest in the village.

He all the country could outrun,
Could leave both man and horse behind;
And often, ere the race was done,
He reeled and was stone-blind.
45 And still there's something in the world
At which his heart rejoices;
For when the chiming hounds are out,
He dearly loves their voices!³

Old Ruth works out of doors with him,
50 And does what Simon cannot do;
For she, not over stout° of limb,   *hardy*
Is stouter of the two.
And though you with your utmost skill
From labour could not wean them,
55 Alas! 'tis very little, all
Which they can do between them.

Beside their moss-grown hut of clay,
Not twenty paces from the door,
A scrap of land they have, but they

---

2. Common lands were progressively being enclosed as private property. Wordsworth successfully fought the enclosure of Grasmere's commons.

3. "The expression when the hounds were out, 'I dearly love their voices,' was word for word from his own lips" [I.F.].

60 Are poorest of the poor.
This scrap of land he from the heath
Enclosed when he was stronger;
But what avails the land to them,
Which they can till no longer?

65 Few months of life has he in store,
As he to you will tell,
For still, the more he works, the more
His poor old ancles swell.
My gentle reader, I perceive
70 How patiently you've waited,
And I'm afraid that you expect
Some tale will be related.

O reader! had you in your mind
Such stores as silent thought can bring,
75 O gentle° reader! you would find   *kind, well-born*
A tale in every thing.
What more I have to say is short,
I hope you'll kindly take it;
It is no tale; but should you think,
80 Perhaps a tale you'll make it.

One summer-day I chanced to see
This old man doing all he could
About the root of an old tree,
A stump of rotten wood.
85 The mattock° totter'd in his hand;   *pick-ax*
So vain was his endeavour
That at the root of the old tree
He might have worked for ever.

"You're overtasked, good Simon Lee,
90 Give me your tool" to him I said;
And at the word right gladly he
Received my proffer'd aid.
I struck, and with a single blow
The tangled root I sever'd,
95 At which the poor old man so long
And vainly had endeavour'd.

The tears into his eyes were brought,
And thanks and praises seemed to run
So fast out of his heart, I thought
100 They never would have done.
—I've heard of hearts unkind, kind deeds
With coldness still returning.
Alas! the gratitude of men
Has oftner left me mourning.

1798   1798

We Are Seven[1]

A simple child, dear brother Jim,
That lightly draws its breath,
And feels its life in every limb,
What should it know of death?

5   I met a little cottage girl,
She was eight years old, she said;
Her hair was thick with many a curl
That cluster'd round her head.

She had a rustic, woodland air,
10   And she was wildly clad;
Her eyes were fair, and very fair,
—Her beauty made me glad.

"Sisters and brothers, little maid,
How many may you be?"
15   "How many? seven in all," she said,
And wondering looked at me.

"And where are they, I pray you tell?"
She answered, "Seven are we,
And two of us at Conway° dwell,   *Welsh seaport*
20   And two are gone to sea.

"Two of us in the church-yard lie,
My sister and my brother,
And in the church-yard cottage, I
Dwell near them with my mother."

25   "You say that two at Conway dwell,
And two are gone to sea,
Yet you are seven; I pray you tell
Sweet Maid, how this may be?"

Then did the little Maid reply,
30   "Seven boys and girls are we;
Two of us in the church-yard lie,
Beneath the church-yard tree."

"You run about, my little Maid,
Your limbs they are alive;
35   If two are in the church-yard laid,
Then ye are only five."

"Their graves are green, they may be seen,"
The little Maid replied,
"Twelve steps or more from my mother's door,
40   And they are side by side.

---

1. "The little girl who is the heroine I met within the area of Goodrich Castle in the year 1793. . . . I composed it while walking in the grove at Alfoxden. My friends will not deem it too trifling to relate that while walking to and fro I composed the last stanza first having begun with the last line" [I.F.]. Coleridge wrote the first stanza. Wordsworth's own mother died when he was turning eight, the age of the girl in the poem.

"My stockings there I often knit,
My 'kerchief there I hem;
And there upon the ground I sit—
I sit and sing to them.

45   "And often after sunset, Sir,
When it is light and fair,
I take my little porringer,°   *porridge-bowl*
And eat my supper there.

"The first that died was little Jane;
50   In bed she moaning lay,
Till God released her of her pain,
And then she went away.

"So in the church-yard was she laid;
And all the summer dry,
55   Together round her grave we played,
My brother John and I.

"And when the ground was white with snow,
And I could run and slide,
My brother John was forced to go,
60   And he lies by her side."

"How many are you then," said I,
"If they two are in Heaven?"
The little Maiden did reply,
"O Master! we are seven."

65   "But they are dead; those two are dead!
Their spirits are in heaven!"
'Twas throwing words away; for still
The little Maid would have her will,
And said, "Nay, we are seven!"

1798   1798

Lines Written in Early Spring

I heard a thousand blended notes,
While in a grove I sate reclined,
In that sweet mood when pleasant thoughts
Bring sad thoughts to the mind.

5   To her fair works did nature link
The human soul that through me ran;
And much it griev'd my heart to think
What man has made of man.

Through primrose-tufts, in that sweet bower,
10   The periwinkle trail'd its wreathes;
And 'tis my faith that every flower
Enjoys the air it breathes.

The birds around me hopp'd and play'd:
Their thoughts I cannot measure,°   *assess, put in meters*

15 But the least motion which they made,
   It seem'd a thrill of pleasure.

   The budding twigs spread out their fan,
   To catch the breezy air;
   And I must think, do all I can,
20 That there was pleasure there.

   If I these thoughts may not prevent,
   If such be of my creed the plan,
   Have I not reason to lament
   What man has made of man?

1798   1798

TINTERN ABBEY   "No poem of mine was composed under circumstances more pleasant for me to remember than this. I began it upon leaving Tintern, after crossing the Wye, and concluded it just as I was entering Bristol in the evening, after a ramble of 4 or 5 days, with my sister. Not a line of it was altered, and not any part of it written down till I reached Bristol." So Wordsworth recalled in 1843, but he had been practicing the gestures of the poem for some time: a manuscript fragment of 1796–1797 underlies the seemingly spontaneous opening and one of its central formulations: "Yet once again do I behold the forms / Of these huge mountains, and yet once again, / Standing beneath these elms, I hear thy voice, / Beloved Derwent, that peculiar voice / Heard in the stillness of the evening air, / Half-heard and half-created." Wordsworth first visited the Wye valley in August 1793, on a solo walking tour; the return with his sister in July 1798 prompted this spacious meditation on time and memory, in which the ruined Abbey (see Girtin's illustration, page 2), a famous picturesque destination, does not appear. Instead, it is replaced by the inward "fluxes and refluxes of the mind" that shape the poem, which concludes the 1798 *Lyrical Ballads*. In 1800 Wordsworth added a note on the elevated manner: "I have not ventured to call this Poem an Ode; but it was written with a hope that in the transitions, and the impassioned music of the versification, would be found the principal requisites of that species of composition."

Lines Written a Few Miles above Tintern Abbey
On Revisiting the Banks of the Wye during a Tour, July 13, 1798

   Five years have passed; five summers, with the length
   Of five long winters! and again I hear
   These waters, rolling from their mountain-springs
   With a sweet inland murmur.[1]—Once again
5 Do I behold these steep and lofty cliffs,
   Which on a wild secluded scene impress
   Thoughts of more deep seclusion; and connect
   The landscape with the quiet of the sky.
   The day is come when I again repose
10 Here, under this dark sycamore, and view
   These plots of cottage-ground, these orchard-tufts,
   Which, at this season, with their unripe fruits,
   Among the woods and copses lose themselves,
   Nor, with their green and simple hue, disturb
15 The wild green landscape. Once again I see
   These hedge-rows, hardly hedge-rows, little lines

1. The river is not affected by the tides a few miles above Tintern [Wordsworth's note, 1798].

Of sportive wood run wild; these pastoral farms
Green to the very door; and wreathes of smoke
Sent up, in silence, from among the trees,
20   With some uncertain notice, as might seem,
Of vagrant dwellers in the houseless woods,
Or of some hermit's cave, where by his fire
The hermit° sits alone.   *religious recluse*

                    Though absent long,
These forms of beauty have not been to me,
25   As is a landscape to a blind man's eye:
But oft, in lonely rooms, and mid the din
Of towns and cities, I have owed to them,
In hours of weariness, sensations sweet,
Felt in the blood, and felt along the heart,
30   And passing even into my purer mind
With tranquil restoration:—feelings too
Of unremembered pleasure; such, perhaps,
As may have had no trivial influence
On that best portion of a good man's life;
35   His little, nameless, unremembered acts
Of kindness and of love. Nor less, I trust,
To them I may have owed another gift,
Of aspect more sublime; that blessed mood,
In which the burthen° of the mystery,[2]   *burden*
40   In which the heavy and the weary weight
Of all this unintelligible world
Is lighten'd:—that serene and blessed mood,
In which the affections gently lead us on,
Until, the breath of this corporeal frame,
45   And even the motion of our human blood
Almost suspended, we are laid asleep
In body, and become a living soul:
While with an eye made quiet by the power
Of harmony, and the deep power of joy,
50   We see into the life of things.

                    If this
Be but a vain belief, yet, oh! how oft,
In darkness, and amid the many shapes
Of joyless day-light; when the fretful stir
Unprofitable, and the fever of the world,
55   Have hung upon the beatings of my heart,[3]
How oft, in spirit, have I turned to thee
O sylvan Wye! Thou wanderer through the wood
How often has my spirit turned to thee!

And now, with gleams of half-extinguish'd thought,
60   With many recognitions dim and faint,

2. Keats thought this phrase the core of Wordsworth's "genius."
3. Echoing Macbeth's sense of life's fitful fever (3.2.23)

and Hamlet's view of life as "weary, stale, flat, and unprofitable" (1.2.133).

And somewhat of a sad perplexity,
The picture of the mind revives again:
While here I stand, not only with the sense
Of present pleasure, but with pleasing thoughts
65 That in this moment there is life and food
For future years. And so I dare to hope
Though changed, no doubt, from what I was, when first
I came among these hills; when like a roe
I bounded o'er the mountains, by the sides
70 Of the deep rivers, and the lonely streams,
Wherever nature led; more like a man
Flying from something that he dreads, than one
Who sought the thing he loved. For nature then
(The coarser pleasures of my boyish days,
75 And their glad animal movements all gone by,)
To me was all in all.—I cannot paint
What then I was. The sounding cataract
Haunted me like a passion: the tall rock,
The mountain, and the deep and gloomy wood,
80 Their colours and their forms, were then to me
An appetite: a feeling and a love,
That had no need of a remoter charm,
By thought supplied, or any interest
Unborrowed from the eye.—That time is past,
85 And all its aching joys are now no more,
And all its dizzy raptures. Not for this
Faint° I, nor mourn nor murmur: other gifts   *lose heart*
Have followed, for such loss, I would believe,
Abundant recompence. For I have learned
90 To look on nature, not as in the hour
Of thoughtless youth, but hearing oftentimes
The still, sad music of humanity,
Not harsh nor grating, though of ample power
To chasten and subdue. And I have felt
95 A presence that disturbs me with the joy
Of elevated thoughts; a sense sublime
Of something far more deeply interfused,
Whose dwelling is the light of setting suns,
And the round ocean, and the living air,
100 And the blue sky, and in the mind of man,
A motion and a spirit, that impels
All thinking things, all objects of all thought,
And rolls through all things. Therefore am I still
A lover of the meadows and the woods,
105 And mountains; and of all that we behold
From this green earth; of all the mighty world
Of eye and ear, both what they half-create,[4]

4. This line has a close resemblance to an admirable line of Young, the exact expression of which I cannot recollect [Wordsworth's note]. He is thinking of Edward Young's "half create the wondrous world they see" (*The Complaint or Night Thoughts* [1744], 6.427).

And what perceive; well pleased to recognize
In nature and the language of the sense,
110   The anchor of my purest thoughts, the nurse,
The guide, the guardian of my heart, and soul
Of all my moral being.

                    Nor, perchance,
If I were not thus taught, should I the more
Suffer my genial° spirits to decay: *she is outlet for spontaneous emotion*   creative
115   For thou art with me, here, upon the banks
Of this fair river; thou, my dearest Friend,[5]
My dear, dear Friend, and in thy voice I catch°   sense, arrest
The language of my former heart, and read
My former pleasures in the shooting lights   *- he sees*
120   Of thy wild eyes. Oh! yet a little while   *himself in her*
May I behold in thee what I was once,   *↳she repeats his*
My dear, dear Sister! And this prayer I make,   *experience*
Knowing that Nature never did betray   *↳ it is open for*
The heart that loved her; 'tis her privilege,   *all*
125   Through all the years of this our life, to lead   *↳ emotion*
From joy to joy: for she can so inform   *recollected in*
The mind that is within us, so impress   *tranquility*
With quietness and beauty, and so feed
With lofty thoughts, that neither evil tongues,[6]
130   Rash judgments, nor the sneers of selfish men,
Nor greetings where no kindness is, nor all
The dreary intercourse of daily life,   *- he turns away*
Shall e'er prevail against us, or disturb   *from nature*
Our chearful faith that all which we behold   *towards another*
135   Is full of blessings. Therefore let the moon   *human being*
Shine on thee in thy solitary walk;
And let the misty mountain winds be free
To blow against thee: and in after years,
When these wild ecstasies shall be matured
140   Into a sober pleasure, when thy mind
Shall be a mansion for all lovely forms,
Thy memory be as a dwelling-place
For all sweet sounds and harmonies; Oh! then,
If solitude, or fear, or pain, or grief,
145   Should be thy portion,° with what healing thoughts   dowry, bequest
Of tender joy wilt thou remember me,
And these my exhortations! Nor, perchance,
If I should be, where I no more can hear   *future*
Thy voice, nor catch from thy wild eyes these gleams   *message*
150   Of past existence, wilt thou then forget   *(coping life)*
That on the banks of this delightful stream
We stood together; and that I, so long
A worshipper of Nature, hither came,

5. His sister Dorothy. The language echoes Psalm 23: "Yea, through I walk through the valley of the shadow of death, I will fear no evil: for thou art with me."

6. An echo of Milton's claim to "Sing with mortal voice, unchang'd / To hoarse or mute, though fall'n on evil days, / . . . and evil tongues" (*Paradise Lost* 7.24–26).

155   Unwearied in that service: rather say
       With warmer love, oh! with far deeper zeal
       Of holier love. Nor wilt thou then forget,
       That after many wanderings, many years
       Of absence, these steep woods and lofty cliffs,
       And this green pastoral landscape, were to me
160   More dear, both for themselves, and for thy sake.
1798   1798

from LYRICAL BALLADS (1800, 1802)

from **Preface**[1]

The first Volume of these Poems has already been submitted to general perusal.[2] It was published, as an experiment, which, I hoped, might be of some use to ascertain, how far, by fitting to metrical arrangement a selection of the real language of men in a state of vivid sensation, that sort of pleasure and that quantity of pleasure may be imparted, which a Poet may rationally endeavour to impart. * * *

It is supposed, that by the act of writing in verse an Author makes a formal engagement that he will gratify certain known habits of association; that he not only thus apprizes the Reader that certain classes of ideas and expressions will be found in his book, but that others will be carefully excluded. This exponent or symbol held forth by metrical language must in different eras of literature have excited very different expectations * * * I will not take upon me to determine the exact import of the promise which by the act of writing in verse an Author in the present day makes to his reader: but it will undoubtedly appear to many persons that I have not fulfilled the terms of an engagement thus voluntarily contracted. They who have been accustomed to the gaudiness and inane phraseology of many modern writers, if they persist in reading this book to its conclusion, will, no doubt, frequently have to struggle with feelings of strangeness and aukwardness: they will look round for poetry, and will be induced to inquire by what species of courtesy these attempts can be permitted to assume that title. * * * I hope therefore the Reader will not censure me, if I attempt to state what I have proposed to myself to perform.

[THE PRINCIPAL OBJECT OF THE POEMS. HUMBLE AND RUSTIC LIFE]

The principal object, then, which I proposed to myself in these Poems was to chuse incidents and situations from common life, and to relate or describe them, throughout, as far as was possible, in a selection of language really used by men; and, at the same time, to throw over them a certain colouring of imagination, whereby ordinary things should be presented to the mind in an unusual way; and, further, and above all, to make these incidents and situations interesting by tracing in them, truly though not ostentatiously, the primary laws of our nature: chiefly, as far as regards the manner in which we associate ideas in a state of excitement. Low and rustic life was generally chosen, because in that condition, the essential passions of the heart find a better soil in which they can attain their maturity, are less under restraint, and speak a plainer and more emphatic language; because in that condition of life our elementary feelings co-exist in a state of greater simplicity, and, consequently, may be more accurately contemplated, and more forcibly communicated because the manners of

---

1. First published in 1800, the text here is the revised Preface of 1802.

2. *Lyrical Ballads*, 1798 was (for the most part) the first volume of the two-volume edition of 1800.

rural life germinate from those elementary feelings; and, from the necessary character of rural occupations, are more easily comprehended; and are more durable; and lastly, because in that condition the passions of men are incorporated with the beautiful and permanent forms of nature. The language, too, of these men is adopted (purified indeed from what appear to be its real defects, from all lasting and rational causes of dislike or disgust) because such men hourly communicate with the best objects from which the best part of language is originally derived; and because, from their rank in society and the sameness and narrow circle of their intercourse, being less under the influence of social vanity they convey their feelings and notions in simple and unelaborated expressions. Accordingly, such a language, arising out of repeated experience and regular feelings, is a more permanent, and a far more philosophical language, than that which is frequently substituted for it by Poets, who think that they are conferring honour upon themselves and their art, in proportion as they separate themselves from the sympathies of men, and indulge in arbitrary and capricious habits of expression, in order to furnish food for fickle tastes, and fickle appetites of their own creation.³

["THE SPONTANEOUS OVERFLOW OF POWERFUL FEELINGS"]

[A]ll good poetry is the spontaneous overflow of powerful feelings: but though this be true, Poems to which any value can be attached, were never produced on any variety of subjects but by a man who, being possessed of more than usual organic sensibility, had also thought long and deeply. For our continued influxes of feeling are modified and directed by our thoughts, which are indeed the representatives of all our past feelings; and, as by contemplating the relation of these general representatives to each other we discover what is really important to men, so, by the repetition and continuance of this act, our feelings will be connected with important subjects, till at length, if we be originally possessed of much sensibility, such habits of mind will be produced, that, by obeying blindly and mechanically the impulses of those habits, we shall describe objects, and utter sentiments, of such a nature, and in such connection with each other, that the understanding of the being to whom we address ourselves must necessarily be in some degree enlightened, and his affections ameliorated.

I have said that each of these poems has a purpose. I have also informed my Reader what this purpose will be found principally to be: namely to illustrate the manner in which our feelings and ideas are associated in a state of excitement. But, speaking in language somewhat more appropriate, it is to follow the fluxes and refluxes of the mind when agitated by the great and simple affections of our nature. * * * I should mention one other circumstance which distinguishes these Poems from the popular Poetry of the day; it is this, that the feeling therein developed gives importance to the action and situation and not the action and situation to the feeling. * * * I will not suffer a sense of false modesty to prevent me from asserting, that I point my Reader's attention to this mark of distinction, far less for the sake of these particular Poems than from the general importance of the subject. The subject is indeed important! For the human mind is capable of being excited without the application of gross and violent stimulants; and he must have a very faint perception

3. It is worth while here to observe that the affecting parts of Chaucer are almost always expressed in language pure and universally intelligible even to this day [Wordsworth's note].

of its beauty and dignity who does not know this, and who does not further know, that one being is elevated above another, in proportion as he possesses this capability. It has therefore appeared to me, that to endeavour to produce or enlarge this capability is one of the best services in which, at any period, a Writer can be engaged; but this service, excellent at all times, is especially so at the present day. For a multitude of causes, unknown to former times, are now acting with a combined force to blunt the discriminating powers of the mind, and unfitting it for all voluntary exertion to reduce it to a state of almost savage torpor. The most effective of these causes are the great national events which are daily taking place, and the encreasing accumulation of men in cities, where the uniformity of their occupations produces a craving for extraordinary incident, which the rapid communication of intelligence hourly gratifies.[4] To this tendency of life and manners the literature and theatrical exhibitions of the country have conformed themselves. The invaluable works of our elder writers, I had almost said the works of Shakespear and Milton, are driven into neglect by frantic novels, sickly and stupid German Tragedies, and deluges of idle and extravagant stories in verse.[5]—When I think upon this degrading thirst after outrageous stimulation, I am almost ashamed to have spoken of the feeble effort with which I have endeavoured to counteract it; and, reflecting upon the magnitude of the general evil, I should be oppressed with no dishonorable melancholy, had I not a deep impression of certain inherent and indestructible qualities of the human mind, and likewise of certain powers in the great and permanent objects that act upon it which are equally inherent and indestructible; and did I not further add to this impression a belief, that the time is approaching when the evil will be systematically opposed, by men of greater powers, and with far more distinguished success.

[THE LANGUAGE OF POETRY]

Having dwelt thus long on the subjects and aim of these Poems, I shall request the Reader's permission to apprize him of a few circumstances relating to their *style*, in order, among other reasons, that I may not be censured for not having performed what I never attempted. The Reader will find that personifications of abstract ideas rarely occur in these volumes; and, I hope, are utterly rejected as an ordinary device to elevate the style, and raise it above prose. I have proposed to myself to imitate, and, as far as is possible, to adopt the very language of men; and assuredly such personifications do not make any natural or regular part of that language. They are, indeed, a figure of speech occasionally prompted by passion, and I have made use of them as such; but I have endeavoured utterly to reject them as a mechanical device of style, or as a family language which Writers in metre seem to lay claim to by prescription. I have wished to keep my Reader in the company of flesh and blood, persuaded that by so doing I shall interest him. I am, however, well aware that others who pursue a different track may interest him likewise; I do not interfere with their claim, I only wish to prefer a different claim of my own. There will also be found in these volumes little of what is usually called poetic diction; I have taken much pains to avoid it as others ordinarily take to produce it; this I have done for the reason already alleged, to bring my language near to the language of men, and further, because the pleasure which I have proposed to myself to

---

4. That is, the rapid increase in daily newspaper production at this time. The "events" include the war with France, the Irish rebellion, and the sedition trials at home.

5. For example, sentimental melodramas and the popular Gothic novels of Ann Radcliffe and "Monk" Lewis.

impart is of a kind very different from that which is supposed by many persons to be the proper object of poetry. I do not know how without being culpably particular I can give my Reader a more exact notion of the style in which I wished these poems to be written, than by informing him that I have at all times endeavoured to look steadily at my subject, consequently, I hope that there is in these Poems little false-hood of description, and that my ideas are expressed in language fitted to their respective importance. Something I must have gained by this practice, as it is friendly to one property of all good poetry, namely, good sense; but it has necessar-ily cut me off from a large portion of phrases and figures of speech which from father to son have long been regarded as the common inheritance of Poets. I have also thought it expedient to restrict myself still further, having abstained from the use of many expressions, in themselves proper and beautiful, but which have been foolishly repeated by bad Poets, till such feelings of disgust are connected with them as it is scarcely possible by any art of association to overpower.

If in a poem there should be found a series of lines, or even a single line, in which the language, though naturally arranged and according to the strict laws of metre, does not differ from that of prose, there is a numerous class of critics, who, when they stumble upon these prosaisms as they call them, imagine that they have made a notable discovery, and exult over the Poet as over a man ignorant of his own profession. Now these men would establish a canon of criticism which the Reader will conclude he must utterly reject, if he wishes to be pleased with these volumes. And it would be a most easy task to prove to him, that not only the language of a large portion of every good poem, even of the most elevated character, must neces-sarily, except with reference to the metre, in no respect differ from that of good prose, but likewise that some of the most interesting parts of the best poems will be found to be strictly the language of prose, when prose is well written. The truth of this asser-tion might be demonstrated by innumerable passages from almost all the poetical writings, even of Milton himself. * * * [T]o illustrate the subject in a general manner, I will here adduce a short composition of Gray,[6] who was at the head of those who by their reasonings have attempted to widen the space of separation betwixt Prose and Metrical composition, and was more than any other man curiously elaborate in the structure of his own poetic diction.

> In vain to me the smiling mornings shine,
> And reddening Phœbus° lifts his golden fire: [sun god]
> The birds in vain their amorous descant° join,   [song]
> Or chearful fields resume their green attire:
> These ears alas! for other notes repine;°   [languish]
> *A different object do these eyes require;*
> *My lonely anguish melts no heart but mine;*
> *And in my breast the imperfect joys expire;*
> Yet Morning smiles the busy race to cheer,
> And new-born pleasure brings to happier men;
> The fields to all their wonted tribute bear;
> To warm their little loves the birds complain.

---

6. Thomas Gray (1716–1771) is best known for *Elegy Written in a Country Churchyard* (1751). The poem Wordsworth quotes (adding italics) is *Sonnet On the Death of Richard West* (1775). Gray had said to West that "the language of the age is never the language of poetry."

> *I fruitless mourn to him that cannot hear*
> *And weep the more because I weep in vain.*

It will easily be perceived that the only part of this Sonnet which is of any value is the lines printed in Italics: it is equally obvious, that, except in the rhyme, and in the use of the single word "fruitless" for fruitlessly, which is so far a defect, the language of these lines does in no respect differ from that of prose.

By the foregoing quotation I have shewn that the language of Prose may yet be well adapted to Poetry; and I have previously asserted that a large portion of the language of every good poem can in no respect differ from that of good Prose. I will go further. I do not doubt that it may be safely affirmed, that there neither is, nor can be, any essential difference between the language of prose and metrical composition. * * * They both speak by and to the same organs; the bodies in which both of them are clothed may be said to be of the same substance, their affections are kindred, and almost identical, not necessarily differing even in degree; Poetry[7] sheds no tears "such as Angels weep," but natural and human tears; she can boast of no celestial ichor that distinguishes her vital juices from those of prose; the same human blood circulates through the veins of them both. * * *

[WHAT IS A POET?]

What is a Poet? To whom does he address himself? And what language is to be expected from him? He is a man speaking to men: a man, it is true, endued with more lively sensibility, more enthusiasm and tenderness, who has a greater knowledge of human nature, and a more comprehensive soul, than are supposed to be common among mankind; a man pleased with his own passions and volitions, and who rejoices more than other men in the spirit of life that is in him; delighting to contemplate similar volitions and passions as manifested in the goings-on of the Universe, and habitually impelled to create them where he does not find them. To these qualities he has added a disposition to be affected more than other men by absent things as if they were present; an ability of conjuring up in himself passions, which are indeed far from being the same as those produced by real events, yet (especially in those parts of the general sympathy which are pleasing and delightful) do more nearly resemble the passions produced by real events, than any thing which, from the motions of their own minds merely, other men are accustomed to feel in themselves; whence, and from practice, he has acquired a greater readiness and power in expressing what he thinks and feels, and especially those thoughts and feelings which, by his own choice, or from the structure of his own mind, arise in him without immediate external excitement.

But, whatever portion of this faculty we may suppose even the greatest Poet to possess, there cannot be a doubt but that the language which it will suggest to him, must, in liveliness and truth, fall far short of that which is uttered by men in real life, under the actual pressure of those passions, certain shadows of which the Poet thus produces, or feels to be produced, in himself. However exalted a notion we would wish to cherish of the character of a Poet, it is obvious, that, while he describes and imitates passions, his situation is altogether slavish and mechanical, compared with

---

7. In a footnote, Wordsworth says that he means "Poetry" as opposed to "Prose, and synonymous with metrical composition"; he concedes that "much confusion has been introduced into criticism by this contradistinction of Poetry and Prose, instead of the more philosophical one of Poetry and Matter of fact, or Science. The only strict antithesis to Prose is Metre; nor is this, in truth, a *strict* antithesis; because lines and passages of metre so naturally occur in writing prose, that it would be scarcely possible to avoid them, even were it desirable." The quotation is from *Paradise Lost*, 1.620.

the freedom and power of real and substantial action and suffering. So that it will be the wish of the Poet to bring his feelings near to those of the persons whose feelings he describes, nay, for short spaces of time perhaps, to let himself slip into an entire delusion, and even confound and identify his own feelings with theirs; modifying only the language which is thus suggested to him, by a consideration that he describes for a particular purpose, that of giving pleasure. Here, then, he will apply the principle on which I have so much insisted, namely, that of selection; on this he will depend for removing what would otherwise be painful or disgusting in the passion; he will feel that there is no necessity to trick out or to elevate nature: and, the more industriously he applies this principle, the deeper will be his faith that no words, which his fancy or imagination can suggest, will be to be compared with those which are the emanations of reality and truth. * * *

Aristotle, I have been told, hath said, that Poetry is the most philosophic of all writing: it is so: its object is truth, not individual and local, but general, and operative; not standing upon external testimony, but carried alive into the heart by passion; truth which is its own testimony, which gives strength and divinity to the tribunal to which it appeals, and receives them from the same tribunal. Poetry is the image of man and nature. The obstacles which stand in the way of the fidelity of the Biographer and Historian, and of their consequent utility, are incalculably greater than those which are to be encountered by the Poet who has an adequate notion of the dignity of his art. The Poet writes under one restriction only, namely, the necessity of giving immediate pleasure to a human Being possessed of that information which may be expected from him, not as a lawyer, a physician, a mariner, an astronomer or a natural philosopher, but as a Man. * * *

Nor let this necessity of producing immediate pleasure be considered as a degradation of the Poet's art. It is far otherwise. It is * * * a homage paid to the native and naked dignity of man, to the grand elementary principle of pleasure, by which he knows, and feels, and lives, and moves. We have no sympathy but what is propagated by pleasure. * * * We have no knowledge, that is, no general principles drawn from the contemplation of particular facts, but what has been built up by pleasure, and exists in us by pleasure alone. The Man of Science, the Chemist and Mathematician, whatever difficulties and disgusts they may have had to struggle with, know and feel this. However painful may be the objects with which the Anatomist's knowledge is connected, he feels that his knowledge is pleasure; and where he has no pleasure he has no knowledge. What then does the Poet? He considers man and the objects that surround him as acting and re-acting upon each other, so as to produce an infinite complexity of pain and pleasure. * * *

The knowledge both of the Poet and the Man of science is pleasure; but the knowledge of the one cleaves to us as a necessary part of our existence, our natural and unalienable inheritance; the other is a personal and individual acquisition, slow to come to us, and by no habitual and direct sympathy connecting us with our fellow-beings. The Man of Science seeks truth as a remote and unknown benefactor; he cherishes and loves it in his solitude: the Poet, singing a song in which all human beings join with him, rejoices in the presence of truth as our visible friend and hourly companion. Poetry is the breath and finer spirit of all knowledge; it is the impassioned expression which is in the countenance of all Science. Emphatically may it be said of the Poet, as Shakspeare hath said of man, "that he looks before and after."[8] He is the

---

8. Hamlet's comment (4.4.34). Shelley alludes to this same phrase in *To a Sky-Lark* (86).

rock of defence for human nature; an upholder and preserver, carrying every where with him relationship and love. In spite of difference of soil and climate, of language and manners, of laws and customs, in spite of things silently gone out of mind, and things violently destroyed, the Poet binds together by passion and knowledge the vast empire of human society, as it is spread over the whole earth, and over all time.

["EMOTION RECOLLECTED IN TRANQUILLITY"]

I have said that Poetry is the spontaneous overflow of powerful feelings: it takes its origin from emotion recollected in tranquillity: the emotion is contemplated till by a species of reaction the tranquillity gradually disappears, and an emotion, kindred to that which was before the subject of contemplation, is gradually produced, and does itself actually exist in the mind. In this mood successful composition generally begins, and in a mood similar to this it is carried on; but the emotion, of whatever kind and in whatever degree, from various causes is qualified by various pleasures, so that in describing any passions whatsoever, which are voluntarily described, the mind will upon the whole be in a state of enjoyment. Now, if Nature be thus cautious in preserving in a state of enjoyment a being thus employed, the Poet ought to profit by the lesson thus held forth to him, and ought especially to take care, that whatever passions he communicates to his Reader, those passions, if his Reader's mind be sound and vigorous, should always be accompanied with an overbalance of pleasure. Now the music of harmonious metrical language, the sense of difficulty overcome, and the blind association of pleasure which has been previously received from works of rhyme or metre of the same or similar construction, an indistinct perception perpetually renewed of language closely resembling that of real life, and yet, in the circumstance of metre, differing from it so widely[,] all these imperceptibly make up a complex feeling of delight, which is of the most important use in tempering the painful feeling which will always be found intermingled with powerful descriptions of the deeper passions.

There was a Boy[1]

There was a Boy; ye knew him well, ye Cliffs
And Islands of Winander![2] many a time,
At evening, when the earliest stars had just begun
To move along the edges of the hills,
5   Rising or setting, would he stand alone,
Beneath the trees, or by the glimmering lake,
And there, with fingers interwoven, both hands
Press'd closely palm to palm and to his mouth
Uplifted, he, as through an instrument,
10 Blew mimic hootings to the silent owls
That they might answer him. And they would shout
Across the wat'ry vale and shout again
Responsive to his call, with quivering peals,
And long halloos, and screams, and echoes loud

1. First drafted in Germany in 1798 in the first person, these lines were later assimilated to *The Prelude* Book 5 as an example of education by "Nature." In his collection of 1815, Wordsworth had this poem lead off the subsection "Poems of the Imagination," commenting in his Preface that it displayed "one of the earliest processes of Nature in the development of this faculty. Guided by one of my own primary consciousnesses, I have presented a commutation and transfer of internal feelings, co-operating with external accidents, to plant, for immortality, images of sound and sight, in the celestial soil of the Imagination."
2. Windermere, in the Lake District.

15   Redoubled and redoubled, a wild scene
       Of mirth and jocund din! And, when it chanced
       That pauses of deep silence mock'd his skill,
       Then, sometimes, in that silence, while he hung
       Listening, a gentle shock of mild surprize
20   Has carried far into his heart the voice
       Of mountain-torrents; or the visible scene
       Would enter unawares into his mind
       With all its solemn imagery, its rocks,
       Its woods, and that uncertain heaven receiv'd
25   Into the bosom of the steady lake.
          Fair are the woods, and beauteous is the spot,
       The vale where he was born: the Church-yard hangs
       Upon a slope above the village school;[3]
       And there along that bank where I have pass'd
30   At evening, I believe, that near his grave
       A full half-hour together I have stood,
       Mute—for he died when he was ten years old.

1797–1798   1800

Strange fits of passion have I known[1]

       Strange fits of passion have I known,
       And I will dare to tell,
       But in the lover's ear alone,
       What once to me befel.

5   When she I lov'd, was strong and gay
       And like a rose in June,
       I to her cottage bent my way,
       Beneath the evening moon.

       Upon the moon I fix'd my eye,
10   All over the wide lea;
       My horse trudg'd on, and we drew nigh
       Those paths so dear to me.

       And now we reach'd the orchard plot,
       And, as we climb'd the hill,
15   Towards the roof of Lucy's cot°   *cottage*
       The moon descended still.

       In one of those sweet dreams I slept,
       Kind Nature's gentlest boon!
       And, all the while, my eyes I kept
20   On the descending moon.

       My horse mov'd on; hoof after hoof
       He rais'd, and never stopp'd:

3. Hawkshead Grammar School, which Wordsworth attended in the Lake District village of Esthwaite.
1. This and the three following lyrics, all written during a lonely winter that William and Dorothy spent in Germany, compose four of five lyrics traditionally called the "Lucy Poems." Lucy has not been conclusively identified. The name "Lucy" comes from the Latin "lux" (light); "Lucina" is an old name for the goddess of the moon.

When down behind the cottage roof
At once the planet dropp'd.

25   What fond and wayward thoughts will slide
Into a Lover's head—
"O mercy!" to myself I cried,
"If Lucy should be dead!"[2]

1798–1799   1800

Song ("She dwelt among th' untrodden ways")

She dwelt among th' untrodden ways
   Beside the springs of Dove,[1]
A Maid whom there were none to praise
   And very few to love:

5   A Violet by a mossy stone
   Half-hidden from the Eye![2]
—Fair, as a star when only one
   Is shining in the sky!

She *liv'd* unknown, and few could know
10   When Lucy ceas'd to be;
But she is in her Grave, and Oh!
   The difference to me!

1798   1800

Three years she grew in sun and shower

Three years she grew in sun and shower,
Then Nature said, "A lovelier flower
On earth was never sown;
This Child I to myself will take
5   She shall be mine, and I will make
A Lady of my own.

"Myself will to my darling be
Both law and impulse, and with me
The Girl in rock and plain,
10   In earth and heaven, in glade and bower,
Shall feel an overseeing power
To kindle or restrain.

"She shall be sportive as the fawn
That wild with glee across the lawn
15   Or up the mountain springs,
And hers shall be the breathing balm,
And hers the silence and the calm
Of mute insensate things.

---

2. A manuscript from 1799 shows a final stanza later deleted: "I told her this: her laughter light / Is ringing in my ears: / And when I think upon that night / My eyes are dim with tears."

1. A river in England.
2. See Gray's *Elegy Written in a Country Churchyard*: "Full many a flower is born to blush unseen" (55).

20   "The floating clouds their state shall lend
      To her; for her the willow bend,
      Nor shall she fail to see
      Even in the motions of the storm
      Grace that shall mould the Maiden's form
      By silent sympathy.

25   "The stars of midnight shall be dear
      To her, and she shall lean her ear
      In many a secret place
      Where rivulets dance their wayward round,
      And beauty born of murmuring sound
30   Shall pass into her face.

      "And vital feelings of delight
      Shall rear her form to stately height,
      Her virgin bosom swell,
      Such thoughts to Lucy I will give
35   While she and I together live
      Here in this happy dell."

      Thus Nature spake—The work was done—
      How soon my Lucy's race was run!
      She died, and left to me
40   This heath, this calm and quiet scene,
      The memory of what has been,
      And never more will be.
1798–1799   1800

Song ("A slumber did my spirit seal")[1]

      A slumber did my spirit seal;
         I had no human fears:
      She seem'd a thing that could not feel
         The touch of earthly years.

5   No motion has she now, no force
         She neither hears nor sees
      Roll'd round in earth's diurnal° course,   *daily*
         With rocks, and stones, and trees.
1798–1799   1800

Nutting[1]

                    It seems a day
         (I speak of one from many singled out)
         One of those heavenly days that cannot die;

---

1. Coleridge wrote to a friend, "Some months ago Wordsworth transmitted to me a most sublime Epitaph. Whether it had any reality, I cannot say. Most probably, in some gloomier moment he had fancied the moment in which his Sister might die."
1. "Intended as part of a poem on my own life, but struck out as not being wanted there. Like most of my schoolfellows I was an impassioned nutter. For this pleasure, the vale of Esthwaite, abounding in coppice-wood, furnished a very wide range. The verses arose out of the remembrance of feelings I had when a boy" [I.F.].

When forth I walked from our cottage-door,[2]
5   And with a wallet o'er my shoulder slung,
    A nutting-crook in hand; and turn'd my steps
    Towards the distant wood, a Figure quaint,
    Trick'd out in proud disguise of Beggar's weeds°   *clothing*
    Put on for the occasion, by advice
10 And exhortation of my frugal Dame.
    Motley accoutrement! of power to smile
    At thorns, and brakes, and brambles, and, in truth,
    More ragged than need was. Among the woods,
    And o'er the pathless rocks, I forc'd my way
15 Until, at length, I came to one dear nook
    Unvisited, where not a broken bough
    Droop'd with its wither'd leaves, ungracious sign
    Of devastation, but the hazels rose
    Tall and erect, with milk-white clusters hung,
20 A virgin scene![3]—A little while I stood,
    Breathing with such suppression of the heart
    As joy delights in; and with wise restraint
    Voluptuous, fearless of a rival, eyed
    The banquet; or beneath the trees I sate
25 Among the flowers, and with the flowers I play'd;
    A temper known to those, who, after long
    And weary expectation, have been bless'd
    With sudden happiness beyond all hope.—
    —Perhaps it was a bower beneath whose leaves
30 The violets of five seasons re-appear
    And fade, unseen by any human eye,
    Where fairy water-breaks[4] do murmur on
    For ever, and I saw the sparkling foam,
    And with my cheek on one of those green stones
35 That, fleec'd with moss, beneath the shady trees,
    Lay round me, scatter'd like a flock of sheep,
    I heard the murmur and the murmuring sound,
    In that sweet mood when pleasure loves to pay
    Tribute to ease, and, of its joy secure
40 The heart luxuriates with indifferent things,
    Wasting its kindliness on stocks° and stones,   *tree stumps*
    And on the vacant air. Then up I rose,
    And dragg'd to earth both branch and bough, with crash
    And merciless ravage: and the shady nook
45 Of hazels, and the green and mossy bower
    Deform'd and sullied, patiently gave up
    Their quiet being: and unless I now
    Confound my present feelings with the past,

2. The house at which I boarded during the time I was at School [Wordsworth's note]; supervised by Ann Tyson, the Dame of line 10.
3. The moral terrain of the bower entails two precedents:

Spenser's "Bower of Blisse" in *The Faerie Queene*, a dangerously seductive pleasure garden, and the Garden of Eden in Milton's *Paradise Lost*, which Satan invades to ravage Eve.
4. Wordsworth's coinage for "little rapids."

Even then, when from[5] the bower I turn'd away,
50   Exulting, rich beyond the wealth of kings
I felt a sense of pain when I beheld
The silent trees, and saw the intruding sky.—

Then, dearest Maiden![6] move along these shades°   shadows, spirits
In gentleness of heart; with gentle hand
55   Touch,—for there is a Spirit in the woods.
1798–1799   1800

MICHAEL Sending a copy of the 1800 *Lyrical Ballads* to Charles James Fox, leader of the Whig opposition in Parliament, Wordsworth drew attention to *Michael*: "I have attempted to draw a picture of the domestic affections . . . amongst a class of men who are now almost confined to the North of England. They are small independent *proprietors* of land here called statesmen, men of respectable education who daily labour on their own little properties. The domestic affections will always be strong amongst men who live in a country not crowded with population, if these men are placed above poverty. But if they are proprietors of small estates, which have descended to them from their ancestors, the power which these affections will acquire . . . is inconceivable by those who have only had an opportunity of observing hired labourers, farmers, and the manufacturing Poor. Their little tract of land serves as a kind of permanent rallying point for their domestic feelings, as a tablet upon which they are written which makes them objects of memory in a thousand instances when they would otherwise be forgotten"; *Michael* shows "that men who do not wear fine cloaths can feel deeply." Later that year Wordsworth wrote to a friend, "I have attempted to give a picture of a man, of strong mind and lively sensibility, agitated by two of the most powerful affections of the human heart; the parental affection, and the love of property, *landed* property, including the feelings of inheritance, home, and personal and family independence." Wordsworth drew on two local tales, one of "the son of an old couple having become dissolute and run away from his parents" (who once owned Dove Cottage, Wordsworth's home at the time); and one of "an old shepherd having been seven years in building up a sheepfold in a solitary valley." The austere biblical aura of the "covenant" between Michael and his son evokes Old Testament prototypes, and Luke is the Gospel that contains the parable of the Prodigal Son (15.11–32). In focusing on contemporary conditions and refusing to provide any relief except in Michael's "comfort in the strength of love," Wordsworth significantly revises the genre of pastoral.

Michael
A Pastoral Poem

If from the public way you turn your steps
Up the tumultuous brook of Green-head Gill,[1]
You will suppose that with an upright path
Your feet must struggle; in such bold ascent
5   The pastoral Mountains front you, face to face.
But, courage! for around that boisterous Brook
The mountains have all open'd out themselves,
And made a hidden valley of their own.

---

5. Later revised to "ere from," making the "sense of pain" precede rather than coincide with "exulting."
6. In a much longer manuscript draft, Wordsworth preceded this poem with the story of a "Lucy" who had been ravaging a bower—her ungentle, unmaidenly action pro-

voking her companion to recount this episode from his past, seemingly to admonish her with his remorse.
1. Green-head Gill (valley) and the poem's other settings are near Wordsworth's cottage at Grasmere.

No habitation can be seen; but such
10   As journey thither find themselves alone
With a few sheep, with rocks and stones, and kites°   *hawks*
That overhead are sailing in the sky.

It is in truth an utter solitude;
Nor should I have made mention of this Dell
15   But for one object which you might pass by,
Might see and notice not. Beside the brook
There is a straggling heap of unhewn stones!
And to that place a story appertains,
Which, though it be ungarnish'd with events,
20   Is not unfit, I deem, for the fire-side,
Or for the summer shade. It was the first,
The earliest of those tales that spake to me
Of Shepherds, dwellers in the valleys, men
Whom I already lov'd; not verily
25   For their own sakes, but for the fields and hills
Where was their occupation and abode.
And hence this Tale, while I was yet a boy
Careless of books, yet having felt the power
Of Nature, by the gentle agency
30   Of natural objects, led me on to feel
For passions that were not my own, and think
At random and imperfectly indeed
On man; the heart of man, and human life.
Therefore, although it be a history
35   Homely and rude, I will relate the same
For the delight of a few natural hearts,
And with yet fonder feeling, for the sake
Of youthful Poets, who among these Hills
Will be my second self when I am gone.

40   Upon the Forest-side in Grasmere Vale
There dwelt a Shepherd, Michael was his name,
An old man, stout of heart, and strong of limb.
His bodily frame had been from youth to age
Of an unusual strength; his mind was keen
45   Intense and frugal, apt for all affairs,
And in his Shepherd's calling he was prompt
And watchful more than ordinary men.
Hence had he learn'd the meaning of all winds,
Of blasts of every tone, and often-times,
50   When others heeded not, He heard the South°   *south wind*
Make subterraneous music, like the noise
Of Bagpipers on distant Highland hills;
The Shepherd, at such warning, of his flock
Bethought him, and he to himself would say
55   The winds are now devising work for me!
And truly at all times the storm, that drives
The Traveller to a shelter, summon'd him
Up to the mountains: he had been alone

Amid the heart of many thousand mists
60   That came to him, and left him, on the heights.
So liv'd he till his eightieth year was pass'd.

And grossly that man errs, who should suppose
That the green Valleys, and the Streams and Rocks
Were things indifferent to the Shepherd's thoughts.
65   Fields, where with chearful spirits he had breath'd
The common air; the hills, which he so oft
Had climb'd, with vigorous steps; which had impress'd
So many incidents upon his mind
Of hardship, skill or courage, joy or fear;
70   Which, like a book, preserv'd the memory
Of the dumb animals, whom he had sav'd,
Had fed or shelter'd, linking to such acts,
So grateful in themselves, the certainty
Of honourable gains; these fields, these hills
75   Which were his living Being, even more
Than his own Blood—what could they less? had laid
Strong hold on his affections, were to him
A pleasurable feeling of blind love,
The pleasure which there is in life itself.

80   He had not passed his days in singleness.
He had a Wife, a comely Matron, old
Though younger than himself full twenty years.
She was a woman of a stirring life
Whose heart was in her house: two wheels she had
85   Of antique form; this large, for spinning wool,
That small for flax; and if one wheel had rest,
It was because the other was at work.
The Pair had but one Inmate° in their house,   *resident*
An only Child, who had been born to them
90   When Michael telling° o'er his years began   *counting*
To deem that he was old, in Shepherd's phrase,
With one foot in the grave. This only son,
With two brave sheep dogs tried° in many a storm,   *tested*
The one of an inestimable worth,
95   Made all their Household. I may truly say,
That they were as a proverb in the vale
For endless industry. When day was gone,
And from their occupations out of doors
The Son and Father were come home, even then
100   Their labour did not cease, unless when all
Turn'd to the cleanly supper-board, and there
Each with a mess of pottage° and skimm'd milk,   *stew*
Sate round the basket pil'd with oaten cakes,
And their plain home-made cheese. Yet when their meal
105   Was ended, LUKE (for so the Son was nam'd)
And his old Father, both betook themselves
To such convenient work as might employ
Their hands by the fire-side; perhaps to card°   *comb out*

Wool for the House-wife's spindle, or repair
110   Some injury done to sickle, flail, or scythe,
Or other implement of house or field.

Down from the ceiling, by the chimney's edge,
That in our ancient uncouth country style
Did with a huge projection overbrow
115   Large space beneath, as duly as the light
Of day grew dim, the House-wife hung a lamp;
An aged utensil, which had perform'd
Service beyond all others of its kind.
Early at evening did it burn and late,
120   Surviving Comrade of uncounted Hours
Which going by from year to year had found
And left the Couple neither gay perhaps
Nor chearful, yet with objects and with hopes
Living a life of eager industry.
125   And now, when LUKE was in his eighteenth year,
There by the light of this old lamp they sate,
Father and Son, while late into the night
The House-wife plied her own peculiar work,
Making the cottage thro' the silent hours
130   Murmur as with the sound of summer flies.
Not with a waste of words, but for the sake
Of pleasure, which I know that I shall give
To many living now, I of this Lamp
Speak thus minutely: for there are no few
135   Whose memories will bear witness to my tale.
This Light was famous in its neighbourhood,
And was a public Symbol of the life,
That thrifty Pair had liv'd. For, as it chanc'd,
Their Cottage on a plot of rising ground
140   Stood single, with large prospect North and South,
High into Easedale, up to Dunmal-Raise,
And Westward to the village near the Lake;
And from this constant light so regular
And so far seen, the House itself by all
145   Who dwelt within the limits of the vale,
Both old and young, was nam'd The Evening Star.

Thus living on through such a length of years,
The Shepherd, if he lov'd himself, must needs
Have lov'd his Help-mate; but to Michael's heart
150   This Son of his old age was yet more dear—
Effect which might perhaps have been produc'd
By that instinctive tenderness, the same
Blind Spirit, which is in the blood of all,
Or that a child, more than all other gifts,
155   Brings hope with it, and forward-looking thoughts,
And stirrings of inquietude, when they
By tendency of nature needs must fail.
From such, and other causes, to the thoughts

160   Of the old Man his only Son was now
The dearest object that he knew on earth.
Exceeding was the love he bare to him,
His Heart and his Heart's joy! For oftentimes
Old Michael, while he was a babe in arms,
165   Had done him female service, not alone
For dalliance and delight, as is the use
Of Fathers, but with patient mind enforc'd
To acts of tenderness; and he had rock'd
His cradle, as with a woman's gentle hand.

And in a later time, ere yet the Boy
170   Had put on Boy's attire, did Michael love,
Albeit of a stern unbending mind,
To have the young one in his sight, when he
Had work by his own door, or when he sate
With sheep before him on his Shepherd's stool,
175   Beneath that large old Oak, which near their door
Stood, and from its enormous breadth of shade
Chosen for the Shearer's covert from the sun,
Thence in our rustic dialect was call'd
The CLIPPING TREE,[2] a name which yet it bears.
180   There, while they two were sitting in the shade,
With others round them, earnest all and blithe,
Would Michael exercise his heart with looks
Of fond correction and reproof bestow'd
Upon the child, if he disturb'd the sheep
185   By catching at their legs, or with his shouts
Scar'd them, while they lay still beneath the shears.

And when by Heaven's good grace the Boy grew up
A healthy Lad, and carried in his cheek
Two steady roses that were five years old,
190   Then Michael from a winter coppice° cut   *grove of small trees*
With his own hand a sapling, which he hoop'd
With iron, making it throughout in all
Due requisites a perfect Shepherd's Staff,
And gave it to the Boy; wherewith equipp'd
195   He as a Watchman oftentimes was plac'd
At gate or gap, to stem or turn the flock,
And to his office prematurely call'd
There stood the urchin, as you will divine,
Something between a hindrance and a help,
200   And for this cause not always, I believe,
Receiving from his Father hire of praise.
Though nought was left undone which staff or voice,
Or looks, or threatening gestures, could perform.
But soon as Luke, full ten years old, could stand
205   Against the mountain blasts, and to the heights,
Not fearing toil, nor length of weary ways,

---

2. Clipping is the word used in the North of England for shearing [Wordsworth's note].

He with his Father daily went, and they
Were as companions, why should I relate
That objects which the Shepherd loved before
210 Were dearer now? that from the Boy there came
Feelings and emanations, things which were
Light to the sun and music to the wind;
And that the Old Man's heart seemed born again.
Thus in his Father's sight the Boy grew up:
215 And now, when he had reached his eighteenth year,
He was his comfort and his daily hope.

While this good household thus were living on
From day to day, to Michael's ear there came
Distressful tidings. Long before the time
220 Of which I speak, the Shepherd had been bound
In surety° for his Brother's Son, a man   *guaranteed a loan*
Of an industrious life, and ample means;
But unforeseen misfortunes suddenly
Had press'd upon him, and old Michael now
225 Was summon'd to discharge the forfeiture,°   *collateral*
A grievous penalty, but little less
Than half his substance. This un-look'd for claim,
At the first hearing, for a moment took
More hope out of his life than he supposed
230 That any old man ever could have lost.
As soon as he had gather'd so much strength
That he could look his trouble in the face,
It seem'd that his sole refuge was to sell
A portion of his patrimonial fields.
235 Such was his first resolve; he thought again,
And his heart fail'd him. "Isabel," said he,
Two evenings after he had heard the news,
"I have been toiling more than seventy years,
And in the open sun-shine of God's love
240 Have we all liv'd; yet if these fields of ours
Should pass into a Stranger's hand, I think
That I could not lie quiet in my grave.
Our lot is a hard lot; the Sun itself
Has scarcely been more diligent than I,
245 And I have liv'd to be a fool at last
To my own family. An evil Man
That was, and made an evil choice, if he
Were false to us; and if he were not false,
There are ten thousand to whom loss like this
250 Had been no sorrow. I forgive him—but
'Twere better to be dumb than to talk thus.
When I began, my purpose was to speak
Of remedies and of a chearful hope.
Our Luke shall leave us, Isabel; the land
255 Shall not go from us, and it shall be free;°   *not mortgaged*
He° shall possess it, free as is the wind   *Luke*

That passes over it. We have, thou knowest,
Another Kinsman, he will be our friend
In this distress. He is a prosperous man,
260 Thriving in trade, and Luke to him shall go,
And with his Kinsman's help and his own thrift,
He quickly will repair this loss, and then
May come again to us. If here he stay,
What can be done? Where every one is poor
265 What can be gained?" At this the old Man paus'd,
And Isabel sate silent, for her mind
Was busy, looking back into past times.
There's Richard Bateman, thought she to herself,[3]
He was a parish-boy° at the church-door   *on welfare*
270 They made a gathering for him, shillings, pence,
And halfpennies, wherewith the Neighbours bought
A Basket, which they fill'd with Pedlar's wares,
And with this Basket on his arm, the Lad
Went up to London, found a Master° there,   *employer*
275 Who out of many chose the trusty Boy
To go and overlook his merchandise
Beyond the seas, where he grew wond'rous rich,
And left estates and monies to the poor,
And at his birth-place, built a Chapel, floor'd
280 With Marble, which he sent from foreign lands.
These thoughts, and many others of like sort,
Pass'd quickly thro' the mind of Isabel,
And her face brighten'd. The old Man was glad,
And thus resum'd. "Well! Isabel, this scheme
285 These two days, has been meat and drink to me.
Far more than we have lost is left us yet.
—We have enough—I wish indeed that I
Were younger, but this hope is a good hope.
—Make ready Luke's best garments, of the best
290 Buy for him more, and let us send him forth
To-morrow, or the next day, or to-night:
—If he could go, the Boy should go to-night."

Here Michael ceas'd, and to the fields went forth
With a light heart. The House-wife for five days
295 Was restless° morn and night, and all day long   *without rest*
Wrought on with her best fingers to prepare
Things needful for the journey of her Son.
But Isabel was glad when Sunday came
To stop her in her work; for, when she lay
300 By Michael's side, she through the last two nights
Heard him, how he was troubled in his sleep:
And when they rose at morning she could see
That all his hopes were gone. That day at noon
She said to Luke, while they two by themselves

3. The story alluded to here is well known in the country [Wordsworth's note, 1802].

305   Were sitting at the door, "Thou must not go,
   We have no other Child but thee to lose,
   None to remember—do not go away,
   For if thou leave thy Father he will die."[4]
   The Lad made answer with a jocund voice,
310   And Isabel, when she had told her fears,
   Recover'd heart. That evening her best fare
   Did she bring forth, and all together sate
   Like happy people round a Christmas fire.

   Next morning Isabel resum'd her work,
315   And all the ensuing week the house appear'd
   As chearful as a grove in Spring: at length
   The expected letter from their Kinsman came,
   With kind assurances that he would do
   His utmost for the welfare of the Boy,
320   To which requests were added, that forthwith
   He might be sent to him. Ten times or more
   The letter was read over; Isabel
   Went forth to shew it to the neighbours round:
   Nor was there at that time on English Land
325   A prouder heart than Luke's. When Isabel
   Had to her house return'd, the Old Man said,
   "He shall depart to-morrow." To this word
   The House-wife answered, talking much of things
   Which, if at such short notice he should go,
330   Would surely be forgotten. But at length
   She gave consent, and Michael was at ease.

   Near the tumultuous brook of Green-head Gill,
   In that deep Valley, Michael had design'd
   To build a Sheep-fold;[5] and, before he heard
335   The tidings of his melancholy loss,
   For this same purpose he had gathered up
   A heap of stones, which close to the brook side
   Lay thrown together, ready for the work.
   With Luke that evening thitherward he walk'd;
340   And soon as they had reach'd the place he stopp'd,
   And thus the Old Man spake to him. "My Son,
   To-morrow thou wilt leave me; with full heart
   I look upon thee, for thou art the same
   That wert a promise to me ere thy birth,
345   And all thy life hast been my daily joy.
   I will relate to thee some little part
   Of our two histories; 'twill do thee good
   When thou art from me, even if I should speak
   On things thou canst not know of.—After thou

4. Echoing the story of Joseph in Genesis 44.22: "The lad cannot leave his father: for if he should leave his father, his father would die."
5. A sheepfold in these mountains is an unroofed build-ing of stone walls, with different divisions. It is generally placed by the side of a brook [Wordsworth's note, 1802]. "The Sheepfold . . . remains, or rather ruins of it," Wordsworth remarked in 1843.

350 First cam'st into the world—as oft befalls
To new-born infants, thou didst sleep away
Two days, and blessings from thy Father's tongue
Then fell upon thee. Day by day pass'd on,
And still I lov'd thee with encreasing love.
355 Never to living ear came sweeter sounds
Than when I heard thee by our own fire-side
First uttering without words a natural tune,
While thou, a feeding babe, didst in thy joy
Sing at thy Mother's breast. Month followed month,
360 And in the open fields my life was pass'd
And on the mountains, else I think that thou
Hadst been brought up upon thy father's knees.
—But we were playmates, Luke; among these hills,
As well thou know'st, in us the old and young
365 Have play'd together, nor with me didst thou
Lack any pleasure which a boy can know."

Luke had a manly heart; but at these words
He sobb'd aloud. The Old Man grasp'd his hand,
And said, "Nay do not take it so—I see
370 That these are things of which I need not speak.
—Even to the utmost I have been to thee
A kind and a good Father: and herein
I but repay a gift which I myself
Receiv'd at others' hands, for, though now old
375 Beyond the common life of man, I still
Remember them who lov'd me in my youth.
Both of them sleep together: here they liv'd,
As all their Forefathers had done, and when
At length their time was come, they were not loth
380 To give their bodies to the family mold.
I wish'd that thou should'st live the life they liv'd.
But 'tis a long time to look back, my Son,
And see so little gain from sixty years.
These fields were burthen'd° when they came to me;   *mortgaged*
385 'Till I was forty years of age, not more
Than half of my inheritance was mine.
I toil'd and toil'd; God bless'd me in my work,
And 'till these three weeks past the land was free.
—It looks as if it never could endure
390 Another Master. Heaven forgive me, Luke,
If I judge ill for thee, but it seems good
That thou should'st go." At this the Old Man paus'd;
Then, pointing to the Stones near which they stood,
Thus, after a short silence, he resum'd:
395 "This was a work for us, and now, my Son,
It is a work for me. But, lay one Stone—
Here, lay it for me, Luke, with thine own hands.
I for the purpose brought thee to this place.
Nay, Boy, be of good hope:—we both may live

400 To see a better day. At eighty-four
     I still am strong and stout;°—do thou thy part;   *hardy*
     I will do mine[6]—I will begin again
     With many tasks that were resign'd to thee;
     Up to the heights, and in among the storms,
405 Will I without thee go again, and do
     All works which I was wont to do alone,
     Before I knew thy face.—Heaven bless thee, Boy!
     Thy heart these two weeks has been beating fast
     With many hopes—it should be so—yes—yes—
410 I knew that thou could'st never have a wish
     To leave me, Luke, thou hast been bound to me
     Only by links of love, when thou art gone
     What will be left to us!—But, I forget
     My purposes. Lay now the corner-stone,
415 As I requested, and hereafter, Luke,
     When thou art gone away, should evil men
     Be thy companions, let this sheep-fold be
     Thy anchor and thy shield; amid all fear
     And all temptation, let it be to thee
420 An emblem of the life thy Fathers liv'd,
     Who, being innocent, did for that cause
     Bestir them in good deeds. Now, fare thee well—
     When thou return'st, thou in this place wilt see
     A work which is not here, a covenant
425 'Twill be between us—but, whatever fate
     Befall thee, I shall love thee to the last,
     And bear thy memory with me to the grave."

     The Shepherd ended here; and Luke stoop'd down,
     And as his Father had requested, laid
430 The first stone of the Sheep-fold; at the sight
     The Old Man's grief broke from him, to his heart
     He press'd his Son, he kissed him and wept;
     And to the House together they return'd.

     Next morning, as had been resolv'd, the Boy
435 Began his journey, and when he had reach'd
     The public Way, he put on a bold face;
     And all the Neighbours, as he pass'd their doors
     Came forth with wishes and with farewell pray'rs,
     That follow'd him 'till he was out of sight.

440 A good report did from their Kinsman come,
     Of Luke and his well-doing; and the Boy
     Wrote loving letters, full of wond'rous news,
     Which, as the House-wife phrased it, were throughout
     The prettiest letters that were ever seen.
445 Both parents read them with rejoicing hearts.
     So, many months pass'd on: and once again

---

6. "Nature . . . hath done her part; / Do thou but thine," Raphael instructs Adam about his responsibility for Eve (*Paradise Lost* 8.561–62); "God toward thee hath done his part, do thine," Adam cautions Eve, before she goes off alone in Eden, the prelude to her Fall (9.375).

The Shepherd went about his daily work
With confident and chearful thoughts; and now
Sometimes when he could find a leisure hour
450 He to that valley took his way, and there
Wrought at the Sheep-fold. Meantime Luke began
To slacken in his duty; and, at length
He in the dissolute city gave himself
To evil courses: ignominy and shame
455 Fell on him, so that he was driven at last
To seek a hiding-place beyond the seas.

There is a comfort in the strength of love;
'Twill make a thing endurable, which else
Would break the heart:—Old Michael found it so.
460 I have convers'd with more than one who well
Remember the Old Man, and what he was
Years after he had heard this heavy news.
His bodily frame had been from youth to age
Of an unusual strength. Among the rocks
465 He went, and still look'd up upon the sun,
And listen'd to the wind; and as before
Perform'd all kinds of labour for his Sheep,
And for the land, his small inheritance.
And to that hollow Dell from time to time
470 Did he repair, to build the Fold of which
His flock had need. 'Tis not forgotten yet
The pity which was then in every heart
For the Old Man—and 'tis believed by all
That many and many a day he thither went,
475 And never lifted up a single stone.

There, by the Sheep-fold, sometimes was he seen
Sitting alone, with that his faithful Dog,
Then old, beside him, lying at his feet.
The length of full seven years from time to time
480 He at the building of this Sheep-fold wrought,
And left the work unfinished when he died.

Three years, or little more, did Isabel,
Survive her Husband: at her death the estate
Was sold, and went into a Stranger's hand.
485 The Cottage which was nam'd The Evening Star
Is gone, the ploughshare has been through the ground
On which it stood;[7] great changes have been wrought
In all the neighbourhood, yet the Oak is left
That grew beside their Door; and the remains

7. The grazing fields have been enclosed for agriculture; also evoking the strife between the herdsman Abel and his farming brother Cain.

490   Of the unfinished Sheep-fold may be seen
           Beside the boisterous brook of Green-head Gill.
1800   1800

༚‿༚

COMPANION READINGS
Francis Jeffrey: [On "the new poetry"][1]

Poetry has this much, at least, in common with religion, that its standards were fixed
long ago, by certain inspired writers, whose authority it is no longer lawful to call in
question; and that many profess to be entirely devoted to it, who have no *good works*
to produce in support of their pretensions. * * * The author who is now before us,
belongs to a *sect* of poets, that has established itself in this country within these ten or
twelve years, and is looked upon, we believe, as one of its chief champions and apostles. The peculiar doctrines of this sect, it would not, perhaps, be very easy to explain;
but, that they are *dissenters* from the established systems in poetry and criticism, is
admitted, and proved indeed, by the whole tenor of their compositions. Though they
lay claim, we believe, to a creed and a revelation of their own, there can be little
doubt, that their doctrines are of *German* origin, and have been derived from some of
the great modern reformers in that country. Some of their leading principles, indeed,
are probably of an earlier date, and seem to have been borrowed from the great apostle
of Geneva.[2] * * *

    The disciples of this school boast much of its originality, and seem to value
themselves very highly, for having broken loose from the bondage of ancient authority, and re-asserted the independence of genius. Originality, however, we are persuaded, is rarer than mere alteration; and a man may change a good master for a bad
one, without finding himself at all nearer to independence. * * * The productions of
this school, we conceive, are so far from being entitled to the praise of originality, that
they cannot be better characterised, than by an enumeration of the sources from which
their materials have been derived. The greater part of them, we apprehend, will be
found to be composed of the following elements: 1. The antisocial principles, and dis-
tempered sensibility of Rousseau—his discontent with the present constitution of society—his paradoxical morality, and his perpetual hankerings after some unattainable
state of voluptuous virtue and perfection. 2. The simplicity and energy (*horresco refer-
ens* [I dread to say it]) of Kotzebue and Schiller. 3. The homeliness and harshness of
some of Cowper's language and versification, interchanged occasionally with the *innocence* of Ambrose Philips, or the quaintness of Quarles and Dr Donne.[3] * * *

    The authors, of whom we are now speaking [Southey, Wordsworth, and
Coleridge], have, among them, unquestionably, a very considerable portion of poeti-

---

1. By 1802, when this essay appeared in *The Edinburgh
Review* (its occasion was Robert Southey's exotic verse
romance, *Thalaba, the Destroyer*), the second edition of
Lyrical Ballads, with the Preface, had appeared. Southey,
like fellow "Lake Poet" Wordsworth, advocated political
reform in the 1790s. Francis Jeffrey (1773–1850) was the
editor and chief literary critic for the *Edinburgh*, soon to
be one of the most influential reviews of the age. His
tastes were more neoclassical than modern, and his
attacks on Wordsworth's poetic principles persisted for
decades. For another of his *Edinburgh* essays, see the

Companion Readings for Felicia Hemans (page 415).
2. Referring chiefly to Goethe and to German poets of
sensational verse narrative. The apostle of Geneva is
Rousseau.
3. August von Kotzebue was famed for his sentimental
plays. Ambrose Phillips (1675–1749) was admired and
ridiculed for his sweet verses; Francie Quarles was best
known for *Emblems* (1635), a book of devotional poems
with quaint illustrations. John Donne (1572–1631) wrote
boldly experimental poetry famed for its passion, its
rough meters, and its extravagant wit.

cal talent, and have, consequently, been enabled to seduce many into an admiration of the false taste (as it appears to us) in which most of their productions are composed. They constitute, at present, the most formidable conspiracy that has lately been formed against sound judgment in matters poetical; and are entitled to a larger share of our censorial notice, than could be spared for an individual delinquent. * * *

Their most distinguishing symbol, is undoubtedly an affection of great simplicity and familiarity of language. They disdain to make use of the common poetical phraseology, or to ennoble their diction by a selection of fine or dignified expressions. There would be too much *art* in this, for that great love of nature with which they are all of them inspired; and their sentiments, they are determined shall be indebted, for their effect, to nothing but their intrinsic tenderness or elevation. There is something very noble and conscientious, we will confess, in this plan of composition; but the misfortune is, that there are passages in all poems, that can neither be pathetic nor sublime; and that, on these occasions, a neglect of the embellishments of language is very apt to produce absolute meanness and insipidity. * * * It is in such passages, accordingly, that we are most frequently offended with low and inelegant expressions; and that the language, which was intended to be simple and natural, is found oftenest to degenerate into mere slovenliness and vulgarity. * * *

One of their own authors, indeed, has very ingeniously set forth, (in a kind of manifesto that preceded one of their most flagrant acts of hostility), that it was their capital object "to adapt to the uses of poetry, the ordinary language of conversation among the middling and lower orders of the people." What advantages are to be gained by the success of this project, we confess ourselves unable to conjecture. The language of the higher and more cultivated orders may fairly be presumed to be better than that of their inferiors: at any rate, it has all those associations in its favour, by means of which, a style can ever appear beautiful or exalted, and is adapted to the purposes of poetry, by having been long consecrated to its use. The language of the vulgar, on the other hand, has all the opposite associations to contend with; and must seem unfit for poetry, (if there were no other reason), merely because it has scarcely ever been employed in it. A great genius may indeed overcome these disadvantages; but we can scarcely conceive that he should court them. We may excuse a certain homeliness of language in the productions of a ploughman or a milkwoman;[4] but we cannot bring ourselves to admire it in an author, who has had occasion to indite odes to his college bell, and inscribe hymns to the Penates.[5]

But the mischief of this new system is not confined to the depravation of language only; it extends to the sentiments and emotions, and leads to the debasement of all those feelings which poetry is designed to communicate. It is absurd to suppose, that an author should make use of the language of the vulgar, to express the sentiments of the refined. His professed object, in employing that language, is to bring his compositions nearer to the true standard of nature; and his intention to copy the sentiments of the lower orders, is implied in his resolution to make use of their style. Now, the different classes of society have each of them a distinct character, as well as a separate idiom; and the names of the various passions to which they are subject respectively, have a signification that varies essentially, according to the condition of the persons to whom they are applied. The love, or grief, or indignation of an

---

4. Alluding to the popularity of Robert Burns (Scots farmer poet) and Anne Yearsley, "the poetical milkwoman."

5. A sarcastic reference to Southey's mock ode *The Chapel-Bell* (1793) and his long *Hymn to the Penates* (1796); penates were Roman household deities.

enlightened and refined character, is not only expressed in a different language, but is in itself a different emotion from the love, or grief, or anger, of a clown,[6] a tradesman, or a market-wench. The things themselves are radically and obviously distinct; and the representation of them is calculated to convey a very different train of sympathies and sensations to the mind. The question, therefore, comes simply to be—which of them is the most proper object for poetical imitation? It is needless for us to answer a question, which the practice of all the world has long ago decided irrevocably. The poor and vulgar may interest us, in poetry, by their *situation;* but never, we apprehend, by any sentiments that are peculiar to their condition, and still less by any language that is characteristic of it. The truth is, that is impossible to copy their diction or their sentiments correctly, in a serious composition; and this, not merely because poverty makes men ridiculous, but because just taste and refined sentiment are rarely to be met with among the uncultivated part of mankind; and a language, fitted for their expression, can still more rarely form any part of their "ordinary conversation."

* * * It has been argued, indeed, (for men will argue in support of what they do not venture to practice), that as the middling and lower orders of society constitute by far the greater part of mankind, so, their feelings and expressions should interest more extensively, and may be taken, more fairly than any other, for the standards of what is natural and true. To this, it seems obvious to answer, that the arts that aim at exciting admiration and delight, do not take their models from what is ordinary, but from what is excellent; and that our interest in the representation of any event, does not depend upon our familiarity with the original, but on its intrinsic importance, and the celebrity of the parties it concerns. The sculptor employs his art in delineating the graces of Antinous or Apollo, and not in the representation of those ordinary forms that belong to the crowd of his admirers. When a chieftain perishes in battle, his followers mourn more for him, than for thousands of their equals that may have fallen around him. * * *

The qualities of style and imagery, however, form but a small part of the characteristics by which a literary faction is to be distinguished. The subject and object of their compositions, and the principles and opinions they are calculated to support, constitute a far more important criterion, and one to which it is usually altogether easy to refer. Some poets are sufficiently described as the flatterers of greatness and power, and others as the champions of independence. One set of writers is known by its antipathy to decency and religion; another, by its methodistical cant and intolerance. Our new school of poetry has a moral character also; though it may not be possible, perhaps, to delineate it quite so concisely.

A splenetic and idle discontent with the existing institutions of society, seems to be at the bottom of all their serious and peculiar sentiments. Instead of contemplating the wonders and the pleasures which civilization has created for mankind, they are perpetually brooding over the disorders by which its progress has been attended. They are filled with horror and compassion at the sight of poor men spending their blood in the quarrels of princes, and brutifying their sublime capabilities in the drudgery of unremitting labour. For all sorts of vice and profligacy in the lower orders of society, they have the same virtuous horror, and the same tender compassion. While the existence of these offences overpowers them with grief and confusion, they never permit themselves to feel the smallest indignation or dislike towards the offenders. The present vicious constitution of society alone is responsible for all these enormities: the poor sinners are but the helpless victims or

6. A peasant.

instruments of its disorders, and could not possibly have avoided the errors into which they have been betrayed. Though they can bear with crimes, therefore, they cannot reconcile themselves to punishments; and have an unconquerable antipathy to prisons, gibbets, and houses of correction, as engines of oppression, and instruments of atrocious injustice. While the plea of moral necessity is thus artfully brought forward to convert all the excesses of the poor into innocent misfortunes, no sort of indulgence is shown to the offences of the powerful and rich. Their oppressions, and seductions, and debauch-eries, are the theme of many an angry verse; and the indignation and abhorrence of the reader is relentlessly conjured up against those perturbators of society, and scourges of mankind.

It is not easy to say, whether the fundamental absurdity of this doctrine, or the partiality of its application, be entitled to the severest reprehension.

1802

Charles Lamb: from *Letter to William Wordsworth* [1]

[Jan. 30, 1801]

Thanks for your Letter and Present. I had already borrowed your second volume.[2] What most please me are, the Song of Lucy. * * * *Simon's sickly daughter* in the Sexton made me cry.[3] * * * I will mention one more: the delicate and curious feeling in the wish for the Cumberland Beggar, that he may have about him the melody of Birds, altho' he hear them not. Here the mind knowingly passes a fiction upon herself, first substituting her own feelings for the Beggar's, and, in the same breath detecting the fallacy, will not part with the wish.— * * * I will just add that it appears to me a fault in the Beggar, that the instructions conveyed in it are too direct and like a lecture:[4] they don't slide into the mind of the reader, while he is imagining no such matter. An intelligent reader finds a sort of insult in being told, I will teach you how to think upon this subject. * * * There is implied an unwritten compact between Author and reader; I will tell you a story, and I suppose you will understand it. * * *—I am sorry that Coleridge has christened his Ancient Marinere "a poet's Reverie"—it is as bad as Bottom the Weaver's declaration that he is not a Lion but only the scenical representation of a Lion.[5] What new idea is gained by this Title, but one subversive of all credit, which the tale should force upon us, of its truth? For me, I was never so affected with any human Tale. After first reading it, I was totally possessed with it for many days.—I dislike all the miraculous part of it, but the feelings of the man under the operation of such scenery dragged me along like Tom Piper's magic whistle. I totally differ from your idea that the Marinere should have had a character and profession. This is a Beauty in Gulliver's Travels, where the mind is kept in a placid state of little wonderments; but the Ancient Marinere undergoes such Trials, as overwhelm and bury all individuality or memory of what he was, like the state of a man in a Bad dream, one terrible peculiarity of which is: that all consciousness of

1. At the time of these letters, Lamb was an old friend of Coleridge and a newer acquaintance of the Wordsworths; he had published a novel and some verses, but his major career as an essayist was still to come.
2. Wordsworth had sent the two-volume *Lyrical Ballads* (1800) to Lamb, who knew the poems in the first volume from the 1798 edition. The poems he discusses are newly published in volume 2.
3. Referring to *Song* (*She dwelt among th'untrodden ways*) and *To a Sexton*, where the charnel house worker is chas-

tised for disturbing the bones of the dead, including Simon's daughter.
4. The poem includes a polemic by Wordsworth against forcing beggars into miserable workhouses (lines 177–78).
5. In 1800, the poem was subtitled "A Poet's Reverie." In Shakespeare's *Midsummer Night's Dream* (5.1), Snug the Joiner says this, on Bottom's fervent recommendation, fearing that the ladies in the audience will take him for a real lion (5.1.220 ff; cf. Bottom, 3.1.35–45).

personality is gone. Your other observation is I think as well a little unfounded: the Marinere from being conversant in supernatural events *has* acquired a supernatural and strange cast of *phrase*, eye, appearance, &c. which frighten the wedding guest. You will excuse my remarks, because I am hurt and vexed that you should think it necessary, with a prose apology,[6] to open the eyes of dead men that cannot see. To sum up a general opinion of the second vol.—I do not feel any one poem in it so forcibly as the Ancient Marinere, the Mad Mother, and the Lines at Tintern Abbey in the first.—I could, too, have wished the Critical preface had appeared in a separate treatise. All its dogmas are true and just, and most of them new, *as* criticism. But they associate a *diminishing* idea with the Poems which follow, as having been written for *Experiment* on the public taste, more than having sprung (as they must have done) from living and daily circumstances.—I am prolix, because I am gratifyed in the opportunity of writing to you, and I don't well know when to leave off. I ought before this to have reply'd to your very kind invitation into Cumberland.[7] With you and your Sister I could gang any where. But I am afraid whether I shall ever be able to afford so desperate a Journey. Separate from the pleasure of your company, I don't much care if I never see a mountain in my life. I have passed all my days in London, until I have formed as many and intense local attachments, as any of you mountaineers can have done with dead nature. The Lighted shops of the Strand and Fleet Street, the innumerable trades, tradesmen and customers, coaches, waggons, playhouses, all the bustle and wickedness round about Covent Garden, the very women of the Town, the Watchmen, drunken scenes, rattles,[8]—life awake, if you awake, at all hours of the night, the impossibility of being dull in Fleet Street, the crowds, the very dirt & mud, the Sun shining upon houses and pavements, the print shops, the old book stalls, parsons cheap'ning books, coffee houses, steams of soups from kitchens, the pantomimes, London itself a pantomime and a masquerade,—all these things work themselves into my mind and feed me, without a power of satiating me. The wonder of these sights impells me into night-walks about her crowded streets, and I often shed tears in the motley Strand from fulness of joy at so much Life.—All these emotions must be strange to you. So are your rural emotions to me. But consider, what must I have been doing all my life, not to have lent great portions of my heart with usury to such scenes?——

Charles Lamb: from *Letter to Thomas Manning*[1]

[Feb. 15, 1801]

I had need be cautious henceforward what opinion I give of the "Lyrical Ballads." All the North of England are in a turmoil. Cumberland and Westmoreland have already declared a state of war.[2] I lately received from Wordsworth a copy of the second volume, accompanied by an acknowledgement of having received from me many months since a copy of a certain Tragedy,[3] with excuses for not having made any acknowledgement sooner, it being owing to an "almost insurmountable aversion from Letter-writing." This letter I answered in due form and time, and enumerated several of the passages which had most affected me, adding, unfortunately, that no single piece had moved me so

6. The Preface of 1800.
7. In the Lake District.
8. Watchmen's alarms.
1. One of Lamb's closest friends, Manning (1772–1840), mathematician and traveler, was considered the first scholar of Chinese literature in Europe; he was the first

and, for many years, only Englishman to enter the holy city of Lhasa, Tibet.
2. Coleridge was living in Cumberland county, the Wordsworths in Westmoreland.
3. By Lamb.

forcibly as the "Ancient Mariner," "The Mad Mother," or the "Lines at Tintern Abbey." The Post did not sleep a moment. I received almost instantaneously a long letter of four sweating pages from my Reluctant Letter-Writer, the purport of which was, that he was sorry his 2d vol. had not given me more pleasure (Devil a hint did I give that it had *not pleased me*), and "was compelled to wish that my range of sensibility was more extended, being obliged to believe that I should receive large influxes of happiness and happy Thoughts" (I suppose from the L. B.)—With a deal of stuff about a certain Union of Tenderness and Imagination, which in the sense he used Imagination was not the characteristic of Shakspeare, but which Milton possessed in a degree far exceeding other Poets: which Union, as the highest species of Poetry, and chiefly deserving that name, "He was most proud to aspire to;" then illustrating the said Union by two quotations from his own 2d vol. (which I had been so unfortunate as to miss) [quotes *Michael* 349–53]. These lines [352–53] were thus undermarked, and then followed "This Passage, as combining in an extraordinary degree that Union of Imagination and Tenderness which I am speaking of, I consider as one of the Best I ever wrote!" * * * good Poetry: but after one has been reading Shakspeare twenty of the best years of one's life, to have a fellow start up, and prate about some unknown quality, which Shakspeare possessed in a degree inferior to Milton and *somebody else!!* This was not to be *all* my castigation. Coleridge, who had not written to me some months before, starts up from his bed of sickness to reprove me for my hardy presumption: four long pages, equally sweaty and more tedious, came from him; assuring me that, when the works of a man of true genius such as W. undoubtedly was, do not please me at first sight, I should suspect the fault to lie "in me and not in them," etc. etc. etc. etc. etc. What am I to do with such people? I certainly shall write them a very merry Letter. Writing to *you*, I may say that the 2d vol. has no such pieces. * * * It is full of original thinking and an observing mind, but it does not often make you laugh or cry.—It too artfully aims at simplicity of expression. And you sometimes doubt if Simplicity be not a cover for Poverty. The best Piece in it I will send you, being *short*. I have grievously offended my friends in the North by declaring my undue preference; but I need not fear you:—[quotes *Song* (*She dwelt among th'untrodden ways*)]. This is choice and genuine, and so are many, many more. But one does not like to have 'em rammed down one's throat. "Pray, take it—it's very good—let me help you—eat faster."

SONNETS, 1802–1807[1]
Prefatory Sonnet

> Nuns fret not at their Convent's narrow room;[2]
> And Hermits are contented with their Cells;
> And Students with their pensive Citadels;
> Maids at the Wheel, the Weaver at his Loom,
> 5   Sit blithe and happy; Bees that soar for bloom,

---

1. Wordsworth's first publication was his sonnet *On seeing Miss Helen Maria Williams Weep at a Tale of Distress* (1787) and he was encouraged by the revival of sonnet-writing at the end of the 18th century as well as by Milton's political sonnets. He composed many of the sonnets in this section in 1802, when he briefly visited France during the Peace of Amiens to settle affairs with Annette Vallon, prior to his marriage.

2. In 1802 Wordsworth praised Milton's sonnets for their "energetic and varied flow of sound crowding into narrow room more of the combined effect of rhyme and blank verse than can be done by any other kind of verse that I know of." He particularly liked Milton's stanzaic and linear enjambments (see his own wit about this device in line 10 where *bound* is thus unbound).

High as the highest Peak of Furness-fells,°   *mountains*
Will murmur by the hour in Foxglove bells:
In truth, the prison, into which we doom
Ourselves, no prison is: and hence for me,
10   In sundry moods, 'twas pastime to be bound
Within the Sonnet's scanty plot of ground:
Pleas'd if some Souls (for such there needs must be)
Who have felt the weight of too much liberty,
Should find brief solace there, as I have found.

The world is too much with us

The world is too much with us; late and soon,
Getting and spending, we lay waste our powers:
Little we see in nature that is ours;
We have given our hearts away, a sordid boon!
5   The Sea that bares her bosom to the moon;
The Winds that will be howling at all hours
And are up-gathered now like sleeping flowers;
For this, for everything, we are out of tune;
It moves us not. Great God! I'd rather be
10   A Pagan° suckled in a creed outworn;   *pre-Christian*
So might I, standing on this pleasant lea,
Have glimpses that would make me less forlorn;
Have sight of Proteus rising from the sea;
Or hear old Triton blow his wreathed horn.[1]

Composed upon Westminster Bridge, Sept. 3, 1802[1]

Earth has not anything to shew more fair:
Dull would he be of soul who could pass by
A sight so touching in its majesty:
This City now doth like a garment wear
5   The beauty of the morning; silent, bare,
Ships, towers, domes, theatres, and temples lie
Open unto the fields, and to the sky;
All bright and glittering in the smokeless air.
Never did sun more beautifully steep
10   In his first splendour, valley, rock, or hill;
Ne'er saw I, never felt, a calm so deep!
The river glideth at his own sweet will:
Dear God! the very houses seem asleep;
And all that mighty heart is lying still!

1. Proteus is the shape-changing herdsman of the sea; Triton, usually depicted blowing a conch shell, is a sea deity. Cf. the personified "Sea" in line 5.
1. "Composed on the roof of a coach, on my way to France" [I.F., 1843]. For a description of the circumstances, see Dorothy Wordsworth's *Grasmere Journals*, July 1802, page 297. Wordsworth misremembered the date as September (the time of his return, not his departure), and gave the year as 1803 (corrected to 1802 in the edition of 1838). His confusion about the date may have had to do with his anxiety about his reunion with—and final departure from—Annette Vallon and their daughter Caroline.

It is a beauteous Evening[1]

It is a beauteous Evening, calm and free;
The holy time is quiet as a Nun
Breathless with adoration; the broad sun
Is sinking down in its tranquillity;
5   The gentleness of heaven is on the Sea:[2]
Listen! the mighty Being is awake
And doth with his eternal motion make
A sound like thunder—everlastingly.
Dear Child! dear Girl! that walkest with me here,[3]
10   If thou appear'st untouch'd by solemn thought,
Thy nature is not therefore less divine:
Thou liest in Abraham's bosom[4] all the year;
And worshipp'st at the Temple's inner shrine,
God being with thee when we know it not.

I griev'd for Buonaparte[1]

I griev'd for Buonaparte, with a vain
And an unthinking grief! the vital blood
Of that Man's mind what can it be? What food
Fed his first hopes? What knowledge could *He* gain?
5   'Tis not in battles that from youth we train
The Governor who must be wise and good,
And temper with the sternness of the brain
Thoughts motherly, and meek as womanhood.
Wisdom doth live with children round her knees:
10   Books, leisure, perfect freedom, and the talk
Man holds with week-day man in the hourly walk
Of the mind's business: these are the degrees
By which true Sway° doth mount; this is the stalk   *authority*
True Power doth grow on; and her rights are these.

London, 1802[1]

Milton! thou should'st be living at this hour:
England hath need of thee: she is a fen

---

1. This was composed on the beach near Calais, in the autumn of 1802 [Wordsworth's note, 1843].
2. In 1836 Wordsworth changed "is on" to "broods o'er."
3. Wordsworth's daughter Caroline.
4. Christ's description of the resting place for heaven-bound souls (Luke 16.22).
1. One afternoon in 1801, my sister read to me the Sonnets of Milton. I had long been well acquainted with them, but I was particularly struck on that occasion with the dignified simplicity and majestic harmony that runs through most of them,—in character so totally different from the Italian, and still more so from Shakespeare's fine sonnets. I took fire, if I may be allowed to say so, and produced three Sonnets the same afternoon, the first I ever wrote except an irregular one at school. Of these three, the only one I distinctly remember is, "I grieved for

Buonaparté" [I.F., 1843]. He misremembers the date, which Dorothy Wordsworth records as 21 May 1802. Buonaparte named himself First Consul of France for life in 1802, taking the name Napoleon. His forces invaded Switzerland in October. Wordsworth's sonnet was first published in *The Morning Post* in September 1802.
1. One of the sonnets "written immediately after my return from France to London, when I could not but be struck . . . with the vanity and parade of our own country, especially in great towns and cities as contrasted with the quiet, and I may say desolation, that the revolution had produced in France. This must be borne in mind, or else the reader may think . . . I have exaggerated the mischief engendered and fostered among us by undisturbed wealth" [Wordsworth's note, 1843].

Of stagnant waters: altar, sword, and pen,
Fireside, the heroic wealth of hall and bower,
5   Have forfeited their ancient English dower
Of inward happiness. We are selfish men;
Oh! raise us up, return to us again;
And give us manners, virtue, freedom, power.
Thy soul was like a Star and dwelt apart:
10   Thou hadst a voice whose sound was like the sea;
Pure as the naked heavens, majestic, free,
So didst thou travel on life's common way,
In chearful godliness; and yet thy heart
The lowliest duties on itself did lay.

COMPANION READINGS

Charlotte Smith: from *Elegiac Sonnets*[1]

To Melancholy. Written on the Banks of the Arun, October, 1785

When latest Autumn spreads her evening veil
          And the grey mists from these dim waves arise,
          I love to listen to the hollow sighs,
Thro' the half leafless wood that breathes the gale.
5   For at such hours the shadowy phantom pale,
          Oft seems to fleet before the poet's eyes;
          Strange sounds are heard, and mournful melodies,
As of night wanderers, who their woes bewail!
Here, by his native stream, at such an hour,
10   Pity's own Otway,[2] I methinks could meet,
               And hear his deep sighs swell the sadden'd wind!
Oh Melancholy!—such thy magic power,
          That to the soul these dreams are often sweet,
               And soothe the pensive visionary mind!

1789

Far on the Sands

Far on the sands, the low, retiring tide,
          In distant murmurs hardly seems to flow,
And o'er the world of waters, blue and wide,
          The sighing summer-wind, forgets to blow.
5   As sinks the day star in the rosy West,
          The silent wave, with rich reflection glows;
Alas! can tranquil nature give *me* rest,

1. Charlotte Smith was born in 1749; a disastrous marriage when she was sixteen culminated in her spendthrift husband's imprisonment for debt in 1783. Pregnant with her twelfth child, Smith was left to support herself and her family by her pen. The successful first edition of *Elegiac Sonnets* (1784) led to eight more, ever-expanding editions by 1800. Though the ten novels she produced in those years were far more lucrative, poetry was the more exalted genre, and she was admired for the sonnets, her substantial blank-verse poem *The Emigrants* (1793), and her final work, *Beachy-Head*, published in 1807, the year of her death. Coleridge acknowledged Bowles and Smith as "they who first made the Sonnet popular in English," and Wordsworth was reading her sonnets in 1802 as he worked on his own sonnet sequence.

2. Thomas Otway (1652–1685), author of the dramas *The Orphan* and *Venice Preserved*, was known for the pathos of his work.

Or scenes of beauty, soothe me to repose?
Can the soft lustre of the sleeping main,
10   Yon radiant heaven, or all creation's charms,
"Erase the written troubles of the brain,"[1]
        Which Memory tortures, and which Guilt alarms?
Or bid a bosom transient quiet prove,
That bleeds with vain remorse, and unextinguish'd love!

1800

To Tranquillity

In this tumultuous sphere, for thee unfit,
        How seldom art thou found—Tranquillity!
        Unless 'tis when with mild and downcast eye
By the low cradles, thou delight'st to sit,
5   Of sleeping infants—watching the soft breath,
        And bidding the sweet slumberers easy lie;
Or sometimes hanging o'er the bed of death,
        Where the poor languid sufferer—hopes to die.
Oh! beauteous sister of the halcyon peace![1]
10   I sure shall find thee in that heavenly scene
        Where care and anguish shall their power resign;
Where hope alike, and vain regret shall cease;
        And Memory—lost in happiness serene,
Repeat no more—that misery has been mine!

1789

∽

THE PRELUDE   Now regarded as Wordsworth's major work, *The Prelude* was unknown in his lifetime except to a small circle of family and friends. Though the poem was largely complete by 1805, Wordsworth continued to rework and polish it for the remaining forty-five years of his life, in an ongoing and intense self-inquiry into his childhood and youth. Published posthumously in 1850, *The Prelude* incorporates passages first written in the late 1790s. On first reading, *The Prelude* appears to be a paean to the recovery of the past; on closer acquaintance it emerges as a great, self-conscious testimony to the construction of the past out of the urgent needs of the present. To compose the poem was also to compose the poet, to create Wordsworth as The Poet, a meditative and resolute figure who had struggled through years of family disruption and revolutionary turmoil to a position of authority.

   The Prelude evolved in three principal versions. Isolated in Germany in the coldest winter of the century, 1798–1799, Wordsworth wrote several passages drawing on his childhood experiences in nature, sketches for *The Recluse*, a philosophic poem that Coleridge had urged him to write. By the time he and his sister Dorothy had settled in Grasmere in 1799, he had completed a two-part poem of almost a thousand lines of blank verse, narrating his life from schooldays through the age of seventeen.

   In 1801 Wordsworth began to revise his poem, though it was not until 1804 that he set to work in earnest. An initial plan to write it in five books quickly gave way to a greater

---

1. Macbeth asks his wife's doctor, "Canst thou not minister to a mind diseased, / Pluck from the memory of a rooted sorrow, / Race out the written troubles of the brain?" He replies, "Therein the patient / Must minister to himself" (5.3.39–46).

1. When her husband perished in a shipwreck, Halcyone threw herself into the sea; in pity the gods changed the pair into kingfishers and calmed the sea for a brief interval each year so they could mate. A halcyon peace is a blessed interval of calm amid adversity.

expansion into thirteen books, including an account of experiences in France and the crisis that followed the failure of his hopes for the French Revolution. The full version finished in 1805 combines earlier and later material, not always in chronological order, suggesting that the sequence of Wordsworth's life is less important than the imperatives shaping its argument. Further revised over the years, the poem was finally published by Wordsworth's widow in 1850. This was the only known text until 1926, when Ernest de Selincourt published that of 1805, the version printed here.

Part confession, a crisis-autobiography descended from Saint Augustine's exemplary *Confessions*, *The Prelude* is also a consciously English document. Exceptionally personal, it is also a representative story of one seduced by youthful radicalism from his native heritage and returning from his errors to become a national poet. To this degree, *The Prelude* stands as a rejoinder to Rousseau's notorious *Confessions*, but its chief parallel is Milton's *Paradise Lost*, with which it regularly challenges comparison. *The Prelude* turns epic inward even as it claims the growth of the poet's mind as an exalted subject. But *The Prelude* is not everywhere epic and prophetic: it is also an epistle to Coleridge, intimate and domestic, a record of friendship. The result is a shifting interplay between high genre and familiar conversation, between the adult poet looking back and trying to explain and the boy from whose sense of the mysterious the poem derives its originating power. Writing his story, Wordsworth sometimes felt possessed by "Two consciousnesses, conscious of myself / And of some other Being" (2.32–33). As he tries to close the gap in the act of writing, the ungraspable, elusive vacancies generate a structure that circles back in its large patterns, animated throughout by countermovements that uncannily create the effect of authenticity:

> As oftentimes a River, it might seem,
> Yielding in part to old remembrances,
> Part sway'd by fear to tread an onward road
> That leads direct to the devouring sea,
> Turns and will measure back his course, far back
> Towards the very regions which he cross'd
> In his first outset; so have we long time
> Made motions retrograde, in like pursuit
> Detain'd.   (9.1–9)

The simile, in suggesting the "fear" of concluding as well as the pull of "old remembrances," lays open to view the conflicting dynamics of Wordsworth's autobiographical enterprise.

from THE PRELUDE, OR GROWTH OF A POET'S MIND

Book First. Introduction, Childhood, and School time

> Oh there is blessing in this gentle breeze[1]
> That blows from the green fields and from the clouds
> And from the sky: it beats against my cheek
> And seems half conscious of the joy it gives.
5 > O welcome Messenger! O welcome Friend!
> A Captive greets thee, coming from a house
> Of bondage,[2] from yon City's walls set free,
> A prison where he hath been long immured.
> Now I am free, enfranchis'd and at large,

---

1. Lines 1–54, which Wordsworth later called his "glad preamble" (7.4), were composed in late 1799 or 1800. Nature itself is his inspiring Muse or spirit ("spiritus" in

Latin means both "spirit" and "breeze").
2. Cf. Exodus 13.14: "the Lord brought us out from Egypt, from the house of bondage."

10   May fix my habitation where I will.
        What dwelling shall receive me? In what Vale
        Shall be my harbour? Underneath what grove
        Shall I take up my home, and what sweet stream
        Shall with its murmurs lull me to my rest?
15   The earth is all before me:[3] with a heart
        Joyous, nor scar'd at its own liberty
        I look about, and should the guide I chuse
        Be nothing better than a wandering cloud
        I cannot miss my way. I breathe again;
20   Trances of thought and mountings of the mind
        Come fast upon me: it is shaken off,
        As by miraculous gift 'tis shaken off,
        That burthen of my own unnatural self,
        The heavy weight of many a weary day
25   Not mine, and such as were not made for me.
        Long months of peace (if such bold word accord
        With any promises of human life)
        Long months of ease and undisturb'd delight
        Are mine in prospect: whither shall I turn
30   By road or pathway or through open field,
        Or shall a twig or any floating thing
        Upon the river, point me out my course?
            Enough that I am free; for months to come
        May dedicate myself to chosen tasks;
35   May quit the tiresome sea, and dwell on shore,
        If not a settler on the soil, at least
        To drink wild water, and to pluck green herbs,
        And gather fruits fresh from their native bough.
        Nay more, if I may trust myself, this hour
40   Hath brought a gift that consecrates my joy;
        For I, methought, while the sweet breath of Heaven
        Was blowing on my body, felt within
        A corresponding mild creative breeze,
        A vital breeze which travell'd gently on
45   O'er things which it had made, and is become
        A tempest, a redundant° energy   *abounding*
        Vexing its own creation. 'Tis a power
        That does not come unrecognis'd, a storm,
        Which, breaking up a long continued frost
50   Brings with it vernal° promises, the hope   *springtime*
        Of active days, of dignity and thought,
        Of prowess in an honorable field,
        Pure passions, virtue, knowledge, and delight,
        The holy life of music and of verse.
55   Thus far, O Friend! did I, not used to make
        A present joy the matter of my Song,[4]

3. Compare the ending of *Paradise Lost*, when Adam and Eve leave Eden: "the world was all before them" (12.646ff.).
4. The poem is addressed to Coleridge; in the Preface to *Lyrical Ballads*, Wordsworth describes poetic creation as "emotion recollected in tranquillity."

Pour out, that day, my soul in measur'd strains,
Even in the very words which I have here
Recorded: to the open fields I told
60 A prophecy: poetic numbers° came   *verses*
Spontaneously, and cloth'd in priestly robe
My spirit, thus singled out, as it might seem,
For holy services: great hopes were mine;
My own voice chear'd me, and, far more, the mind's
65 Internal echo of the imperfect sound:
To both I listen'd, drawing from them both
A chearful confidence in things to come.
    Whereat, being not unwilling now to give
A respite to this passion, I paced on
70 Gently, with careless steps, and came erelong
To a green shady place where down I sate
Beneath a tree, slackening my thoughts by choice
And settling into gentler happiness.
'Twas Autumn, and a calm and placid day,
75 With warmth as much as needed from a sun
Two hours declin'd towards the west, a day
With silver clouds, and sunshine on the grass
And, in the shelter'd grove where I was couch'd,
A perfect stillness. On the ground I lay
80 Passing through many thoughts, yet mainly such
As to myself pertain'd. I made a choice
Of one sweet Vale° whither my steps should turn   *Grasmere*
And saw, methought, the very house and fields
Present before my eyes: nor did I fail
85 To add, meanwhile, assurance of some work
Of glory, there forthwith to be begun,[5]
Perhaps, too, there perform'd. Thus, long I lay
Chear'd by the genial pillow of the earth
Beneath my head, sooth'd by a sense of touch
90 From the warm ground, that balanced me, though lost
Entirely, seeing nought, nought hearing, save
When here and there, about the grove of Oaks
Where was my bed, an acorn from the trees
Fell audibly, and with a startling sound.
95   Thus occupied in mind, I linger'd here
Contented, nor rose up until the sun
Had almost touch'd the horizon; bidding then
A farewell to the City left behind,
Even on the strong temptation of that hour
100 And with its chance equipment, I resolved
To journey towards the Vale which I had chosen.
It was a splendid evening: and my soul
Did once again make trial of her strength
Restored to her afresh; nor did she want
105 Eolian visitations; but the harp[6]

5. *The Recluse* (never finished).
6. The Aeolian harp, named for Aeolus, mythic god of   the winds, resounds at the wind's touch.

Was soon defrauded, and the banded host
Of harmony dispers'd in straggling sounds
And, lastly, utter silence. "Be it so,
It is an injury," said I, "to this day
110 To think of any thing but present joy."
So like a Peasant I pursued my road
Beneath the evening sun; nor had one wish
Again to bend the sabbath of that time
To a servile yoke. What need of many words?
115 A pleasant loitering journey, through two days
Continued, brought me to my hermitage.°   *secluded dwelling*
      I spare to speak, my Friend, of what ensued,
The admiration and the love, the life
In common things; the endless store of things
120 Rare, or at least so seeming, every day
Found all about me in one neighbourhood,
The self-congratulation,° the complete   *rejoicing*
Composure, and the happiness entire.
But speedily a longing in me rose
125 To brace myself to some determin'd aim,
Reading or thinking, either to lay up
New stores, or rescue from decay the old
By timely interference, I had hopes
Still higher, that with a frame of outward life,
130 I might endue,° might fix in a visible home   *endow*
Some portion of those phantoms of conceit°   *mental images*
That had been floating loose about so long,
And to such Beings temperately deal forth
The many feelings that oppress'd my heart.
135 But I have been discouraged: gleams of light
Flash often from the East, then disappear
And mock me with a sky that ripens not
Into a steady morning: if my mind,
Remembering the sweet promise of the past,
140 Would gladly grapple with some noble theme,
Vain is her wish; where'er she turns she finds
Impediments from day to day renew'd.
      And now it would content me to yield up
Those lofty hopes a while for present gifts
145 Of humbler industry. But, O dear Friend!
The Poet, gentle creature as he is,
Hath, like the Lover, his unruly times;
His fits when he is neither sick nor well,
Though no distress be near him but his own
150 Unmanageable thoughts. The mind itself,
The meditative mind, best pleased, perhaps,
While she, as duteous as the Mother Dove,
Sits brooding,[7] lives not always to that end
But hath less quiet instincts, goadings-on

7. In *Paradise Lost*, the epic narrator asks for inspiration from the Holy Spirit who, at Creation, "Dove-like satst brooding on the vast Abyss / And mad'st it pregnant" (1.21–2).

155   That drive her, as in trouble, through the groves.
        With me is now such passion, which I blame
        No otherwise than as it lasts too long.
           When, as becomes a man who would prepare
        For such a glorious work, I through myself
160   Make rigorous inquisition, the report
        Is often chearing; for I neither seem
        To lack, that first great gift! the vital soul,
        Nor general truths which are themselves a sort
        Of Elements and Agents, Under-Powers,
165   Subordinate helpers of the living mind.
        Nor am I naked in external things,
        Forms, images; nor numerous other aids
        Of less regard, though won perhaps with toil,
        And needful to build up a Poet's praise.
170   Time, place, and manners;° these I seek, and these   *customs*
        I find in plenteous store; but nowhere such
        As may be singled out with steady choice;
        No little Band of yet remember'd names
        Whom I, in perfect confidence, might hope
175   To summon back from lonesome banishment
        And make them inmates in the hearts of men
        Now living, or to live in times to come.
        Sometimes, mistaking vainly, as I fear,
        Proud spring-tide swellings for a regular sea
180   I settle on some British theme, some old
        Romantic tale, by Milton left unsung:[8]
        More often, resting at some gentle place
        Within the groves of Chivalry, I pipe
        Among the Shepherds, with reposing Knights
185   Sit by a Fountain-side, and hear their tales.
        Sometimes, more sternly mov'd, I would relate
        How vanquish'd Mithridates northward pass'd,
        And, hidden in the cloud of years, became
        That Odin, Father of a Race by whom
190   Perish'd the Roman Empire:[9] how the Friends
        And Followers of Sertorius, out of Spain
        Flying, found shelter in the Fortunate Isles;[1]
        And left their usages, their arts, and laws
        To disappear by a slow gradual death;
195   To dwindle and to perish one by one
        Starved in those narrow bounds: but not the Soul
        Of Liberty, which fifteen hundred years
        Surviv'd, and when the European° came   *Spanish conquerors*
        With skill and power that could not be withstood,

8. Milton considered writing tales of "Heroic Martyrdom" or an epic about Arthurian knights before settling on his biblical theme; a "Romantic" tale is a story of knightly adventure.

9. In his *Decline and Fall of the Roman Empire* (1776–1788), Edward Gibbon had proposed that the

Norse god Odin was originally a tribal chieftain who had attacked Rome, his story taking on elements from the historical King Mithridates of Asia Minor, defeated by the Romans in the 1st century B.C.

1. The Canary Islands. Sertorius was a Roman general and ally of Mithridates, assassinated in 72 B.C.

200   Did like a pestilence maintain its hold,
       And wasted down by glorious death that Race
       Of natural Heroes: or I would record
       How in tyrannic times some unknown Man,
       Unheard of in the Chronicles of Kings,
205   Suffer'd in silence for the love of truth:
       How that one Frenchman,[2] through continued force
       Of meditation on the inhuman deeds
       Of the first Conquerors of the Indian Isles,
       Went single in his ministry across
210   The Ocean, not to comfort the Oppress'd,
       But, like a thirsty wind, to roam about,
       Withering the Oppressor: how Gustavus found
       Help at his need in Dalecarlia's Mines;[3]
       How Wallace fought for Scotland,[4] left the name
215   Of Wallace to be found like a wild flower,
       All over his dear Country, left the deeds
       Of Wallace, like a Family of Ghosts,
       To people the steep rocks and river banks,
       Her natural sanctuaries, with a local soul
220   Of independence and stern liberty.
       Sometimes it suits me better to shape out
       Some Tale from my own heart, more near akin
       To my own passions and habitual thoughts,
       Some variegated story, in the main
225   Lofty, with interchange of gentler things;
       But deadening admonitions will succeed,
       And the whole beauteous Fabric seems to lack
       Foundation, and, withal, appears throughout
       Shadowy and unsubstantial. Then, last wish,
230   My last and favorite aspiration! then
       I yearn towards some philosophic Song
       Of Truth that cherishes° our daily life;   *holds dear*
       With meditations passionate from deep
       Recesses in man's heart, immortal verse
235   Thoughtfully fitted to the Orphean lyre;[5]
       But from this awful° burthen I full soon   *solemn*
       Take refuge, and beguile myself with trust
       That mellower years will bring a riper mind
       And clearer insight. Thus from day to day
240   I live, a mockery of the brotherhood
       Of vice and virtue, with no skill to part
       Vague longing that is bred by want of power
       From paramount impulse not to be withstood,

2. In 1568 Dominique de Gourges "went to Florida to avenge the massacre of the French by the Spaniards there" [Wordsworth's note, 1850].
3. Gustavus I of Sweden (1496–1530) planned his country's liberation from Danish rule, while hiding in the Dalecarlia mines of Sweden.
4. William Wallace was a Scottish hero who fought for the liberty of his country; he was executed by the British in 1305. See Robert Burns, *Scots wha' hae*, page 191.
5. In Greek myth, Orpheus singing and playing on his lyre could enthrall the natural world as well as people. Coleridge later praised *The Prelude* as "an Orphic Tale indeed."

A timorous capacity from prudence;
From circumspection infinite delay.
Humility and modest awe themselves
Betray me, serving often for a cloak
To a more subtle selfishness, that now
Doth lock my functions up in blank reserve,°   *inertia*
Now dupes me by an over anxious eye
That with a false activity beats off
Simplicity and self-presented truth.
—Ah! better far than this, to stray about
Voluptuously° through fields and rural walks,   *luxuriantly*
And ask no record of the hours, given up
To vacant musing, unreprov'd neglect
Of all things, and deliberate holiday:
Far better never to have heard the name
Of zeal and just ambition, than to live
Thus baffled by a mind that every hour
Turns recreant to her task, takes heart again
Then feels immediately some hollow thought
Hang like an interdict° upon her hopes.   *prohibition*
This is my lot; for either still I find
Some imperfection in the chosen theme;
Or see of absolute accomplishment
Much wanting, so much wanting in myself,
That I recoil and droop, and seek repose
In indolence from vain perplexity,
Unprofitably travelling towards the grave,
Like a false Steward who hath much receiv'd
And renders nothing back.⁶—Was it for this
That one, the fairest of all Rivers,⁷ lov'd
To blend his murmurs with my Nurse's song
And from his alder shades and rocky falls,
And from his fords and shallows sent a voice
That flow'd along my dreams? For this didst Thou,
O Derwent! travelling over the green Plains
Near my sweet birth-place,⁸ didst thou, beauteous Stream,
Make ceaseless music through the night and day
Which with its steady cadence tempering
Our human waywardness, composed my thoughts
To more than infant softness, giving me,
Among the fretful dwellings of mankind,
A knowledge, a dim earnest of the calm
Which Nature breathes among the hills and groves.
    When, having left his Mountains, to the Towers
Of Cockermouth that beauteous River came,
Behind my Father's House he pass'd, close by,

245
250
255
260
265
270
275
280
285

6. An allusion to the parable of the steward who fails to use his talents (literally a coin, metaphorically, God-given abilities), Matthew 25.14–30. Milton refers to this same parable in his famous sonnet, *On His Blindness*.

7. The Derwent flows behind Wordsworth's childhood residence in Cockermouth, Cumberland.
8. Quoting Coleridge's *Frost at Midnight* (28).

290 Along the margin of our Terrace Walk.
He was a Playmate whom we dearly lov'd.
Oh! many a time have I, a five years' Child,
A naked Boy, in one delightful Rill,
A little Mill-race sever'd from his stream,
295 Made one long bathing of a summer's day,
Bask'd in the sun, and plunged, and bask'd again,
Alternate all a summer's day, or cours'd
Over the sandy fields, leaping through groves
Of yellow grunsel,° or when crag and hill,   *ragweed*
300 The woods, and distant Skiddaw's⁹ lofty height,
Were bronz'd with a deep radiance, stood alone
Beneath the sky, as if I had been born
On Indian Plains,° and from my Mother's hut   *in America*
Had run abroad in wantonness, to sport,
305 A naked Savage, in the thunder shower.
    Fair seed-time had my soul, and I grew up
Foster'd alike by beauty and by fear;
Much favor'd in my birth-place, and no less
In that beloved Vale¹ to which, erelong,
310 I was transplanted. Well I call to mind,
('Twas at an early age, ere I had seen
Nine summers) when upon the mountain slope
The frost, and breath of frosty wind had snapp'd
The last autumnal crocus, 'twas my joy
315 To wander half the night among the Cliffs
And the smooth Hollows, where the woodcocks ran
Along the open turf. In thought and wish,
That time, my shoulder all with springes° hung,   *bird-traps*
I was a fell destroyer. On the heights
320 Scudding away from snare to snare, I plied
My anxious visitation, hurrying on,
Still hurrying, hurrying onward: moon and stars
Were shining o'er my head; I was alone
And seem'd to be a trouble to the peace
325 That was among them. Sometimes it befel
In these night-wanderings, that a strong desire
O'erpower'd my better reason, and the bird
Which was the captive of another's toils°   *labors, snares*
Became my prey; and, when the deed was done,
330 I heard among the solitary hills
Low breathings coming after me, and sounds
Of undistinguishable motion, steps
Almost as silent as the turf they trod.
    Nor less in spring-time when on southern banks
335 The shining sun had from her knot of leaves
Decoy'd the primrose flower, and when the Vales
And woods were warm, was I a plunderer then

---

9. At 3,053 feet, one of the highest peaks of the Lake District, nine miles east of Cockermouth.

1. Esthwaite, where Wordsworth went to school, 35 miles from Cockermouth.

In the high places, on the lonesome peaks
Where'er, among the mountains and the winds,
340 The Mother Bird had built her lodge. Though mean
My object, and inglorious, yet the end
Was not ignoble. Oh! when I have hung
Above the raven's nest, by knots of grass,
And half-inch fissures in the slippery rock
345 But ill sustain'd, and almost, as it seem'd,
Suspended by the blast which blew amain,
Shouldering the naked crag; Oh! at that time,
While on the perilous ridge I hung alone,
With what strange utterance did the loud dry wind
350 Blow through my ears! the sky seem'd not a sky
Of earth, and with what motion mov'd the clouds!
      The mind of man is framed even like the breath
And harmony of music. There is a dark
Invisible workmanship that reconciles
355 Discordant elements, and makes them move
In one society. Ah me! that all
The terrors, all the early miseries,
Regrets, vexations, lassitudes, that all
The thoughts and feelings which have been infus'd
360 Into my mind should ever have made up
The calm existence that is mine when I
Am worthy of myself. Praise to the end!
Thanks likewise for the means! But I believe
That Nature, oftentimes, when she would frame
365 A favor'd Being, from his earliest dawn
Of infancy doth open out the clouds,
As at the touch of lightning, seeking him
With gentlest visitation: not the less,
Though haply° aiming at the self-same end,   *perhaps*
370 Does it delight her sometimes to employ
Severer interventions, ministry
More palpable, and so she dealt with me.
      One evening (surely I was led by her)
I went alone into a Shepherd's Boat,
375 A Skiff that to a Willow tree was tied
Within a rocky Cave, its usual home.
'Twas by the Shores of Patterdale, a Vale
Wherein I was a Stranger, thither come,
A School-boy Traveller, at the Holidays.
380 Forth rambled from the Village Inn alone
No sooner had I sight of this small Skiff,
Discover'd thus by unexpected chance,
Than I unloos'd her tether and embark'd.
The moon was up, the Lake was shining clear
385 Among the hoary mountains: from the Shore
I push'd, and struck the oars and struck again
In cadence, and my little Boat mov'd on
Even like a Man who walks with stately step

Though bent on speed. It was an act of stealth
390   And troubled pleasure: nor without the voice
Of mountain echoes did my Boat move on,
Leaving behind her still on either side
Small circles glittering idly in the moon
Until they melted all into one track
395   Of sparkling light. A rocky steep uprose
Above the Cavern of the Willow tree
And now, as suited one who proudly row'd
With his best skill, I fix'd a steady view
Upon the top of that same craggy ridge,[2]
400   The bound of the horizon, for behind
Was nothing but the stars and the grey sky.
She was an elfin Pinnace;° lustily   *a small boat*
I dipp'd my oars into the silent Lake,
And, as I rose upon the stroke, my Boat
405   Went heaving through the water, like a Swan,
When from behind that craggy Steep, till then
The bound of the horizon, a huge Cliff,
As if with voluntary power instinct,°   *endowed*
Uprear'd its head: I struck, and struck again,
410   And, growing still in stature, the huge Cliff
Rose up between me and the stars, and still,
With measur'd motion, like a living thing,
Strode after me. With trembling hands I turn'd,
And through the silent water stole my way
415   Back to the Cavern of the Willow tree.
There, in her mooring-place, I left my Bark
And, through the meadows homeward went with grave
And serious thoughts: and after I had seen
That spectacle, for many days my brain
420   Work'd with a dim and undetermin'd sense
Of unknown modes of being: in my thoughts
There was a darkness, call it solitude,
Or blank desertion, no familiar shapes
Of hourly objects, images of trees,
425   Of sea, or sky, no colours of green fields;
But huge and mighty Forms that do not live
Like living men mov'd slowly through my mind
By day and were the trouble of my dreams.
      Wisdom and Spirit of the Universe![3]
430   Thou Soul that art the Eternity of Thought!
And giv'st to forms and images a breath
And everlasting motion! not in vain,
By day or starlight thus from my first dawn
Of Childhood didst Thou intertwine for me
435   The passions that build up our human Soul,

2. The rower faces the stern and fixes his sight on a shore-point, in order to move the boat in a straight line.
3. Coleridge published 429–90 in *The Friend* (December 1809), under the title "Growth of Genius from the Influence of Natural Objects, on the Imagination in Boyhood, and Early Youth."

Not with the mean and vulgar° works of Man,   *lowly and ordinary*
But with high objects, with enduring things,
With life and nature, purifying thus
The elements of feeling and of thought,
440   And sanctifying by such discipline
Both pain and fear until we recognise
A grandeur in the beatings of the heart.
    Nor was this fellowship vouchsaf'd to me
With stinted kindness. In November days
445   When vapours, rolling down the valleys, made
A lonely scene more lonesome; among woods
At noon, and 'mid the calm of summer nights,
When by the margin of the trembling Lake
Beneath the gloomy hills I homeward went
450   In solitude, such intercourse was mine;
'Twas mine among the fields both day and night,
And by the waters all the summer long.
—And in the frosty season, when the sun
Was set, and, visible for many a mile,
455   The cottage windows through the twilight blaz'd,
I heeded not the summons:—happy time
It was indeed for all of us; to me
It was a time of rapture: clear and loud
The village clock toll'd six; I wheel'd about,
460   Proud and exulting, like an untired horse,
That cares not for its home.—All shod with steel
We hiss'd along the polish'd ice, in games
Confederate, imitative of the chace,
And woodland pleasures, the resounding horn,
465   The Pack, loud bellowing, and the hunted hare.
So through the darkness and the cold we flew,
And not a voice was idle: with the din,
Meanwhile, the precipices rang aloud,
The leafless trees, and every icy crag
470   Tinkled like iron, while the distant hills
Into the tumult sent an alien sound
Of melancholy, not unnoticed, while the stars,
Eastward, were sparkling clear, and in the west,
The orange sky of evening died away.
475   Not seldom from the uproar I retired
Into a silent bay, or sportively
Glanced sideway, leaving the tumultuous throng,
To cut across the image of a star
That gleam'd upon the ice: and oftentimes,
480   When we had given our bodies to the wind,
And all the shadowy banks, on either side,
Came sweeping through the darkness, spinning still
The rapid line of motion; then at once
Have I, reclining back upon my heels,
485   Stopp'd short, yet still the solitary Cliffs
Wheel'd by me, even as if the earth had roll'd

With visible motion her diurnal° round;   *daily*
Behind me did they stretch in solemn train
Feebler and feebler, and I stood and watch'd
490   Till all was tranquil as [   ]⁴
          Ye Presences of Nature, in the sky
Or on the earth! Ye Visions of the hills!
And Souls of lonely places! can I think
A vulgar hope was yours when Ye employ'd
495   Such ministry, when Ye through many a year
Haunting me thus among my boyish sports,
On caves and trees, upon the woods and hills,
Impress'd upon all forms the characters°   *marks, signs*
Of danger or desire, and thus did make
500   The surface of the universal earth
With triumph, and delight, and hope, and fear
Work° like a sea.   *seethe*
                    Not uselessly employ'd,
I might pursue this theme through every change
Of exercise and play, to which the year
505   Did summon us in its delightful round.
—We were a noisy crew; the sun in heaven
Beheld not vales more beautiful than ours
Nor saw a race, in happiness and joy
More worthy of the fields where they were sown.
510   I would record with no reluctant voice
The woods of autumn and their hazel bowers⁵
With milk-white clusters hung; the rod and line,
True symbol of the foolishness of hope,
Which with its strong enchantment led us on
515   By rocks and pools, shut out from every star
All the green summer, to forlorn cascades
Among the windings of the mountain-brooks.
—Unfading recollections! at this hour
The heart is almost mine with which I felt
520   From some hill-top, on sunny afternoons,
The Kite high up among the fleecy clouds
Pull at its rein, like an impatient Courser,°   *race-horse*
Or, from the meadows sent on gusty days
Beheld her breast the wind, then suddenly
525   Dash'd headlong; and rejected by the storm.
          Ye lowly Cottages in which we dwelt,
A ministration of your own was yours,
A sanctity, a safeguard, and a love!
Can I forget you, being as ye were
530   So beautiful among the pleasant fields
In which ye stood? Or can I here forget
The plain and seemly countenance with which
Ye dealt out your plain comforts? Yet had ye

---

4. Wordsworth left the end of this line blank in 1805. In   5. *Nutting* (page 215) was originally part of this poem.
1809, it was completed as "a dreamless sleep."

Delights and exultations of your own.
535 Eager and never weary we pursued
Our home amusements by the warm peat fire
At evening; when with pencil and with slate,
In square divisions parcell'd out, and all
With crosses and with cyphers scribbled o'er,°   *tic-tac-toe*
540 We schemed and puzzled, head opposed to head,
In strife too humble to be named in Verse;
Or round the naked Table, snow-white deal,°   *pine*
Cherry, or maple, sate in close array,
And to the combat, Lu or Whist,° led on   *card games*
545 A thick-ribb'd Army, not as in the world
Neglected and ungratefully thrown by
Even for the very service they had wrought,
But husbanded through many a long campaign.
Uncouth assemblage was it, where no few
550 Had changed their functions, some, plebean cards,
Which Fate beyond the promise of their birth
Had glorified, and call'd to represent
The persons of departed Potentates.
Oh! with what echoes on the Board they fell!
555 Ironic Diamonds; Clubs, Hearts, Diamonds, Spades,
A congregation piteously akin;
Cheap matter did they give to boyish wit,
Those sooty Knaves, precipitated down
With scoffs and taunts, like Vulcan out of Heaven,
560 The paramount Ace, a moon in her eclipse,
Queens, gleaming through their splendour's last decay,
And Monarchs, surly at the wrongs sustain'd
By royal visages. Meanwhile, abroad
The heavy rain was falling, or the frost
565 Raged bitterly, with keen and silent tooth,
And, interrupting the impassion'd game,
From Esthwaite's neighbouring Lake the splitting ice,
While it sank down towards the water, sent,
Among the meadows and the hills, its long
570 And dismal yellings, like the noise of wolves
When they are howling round the Bothnic Main.°   *Baltic Sea*
     Nor, sedulous[6] as I have been to trace
How Nature by extrinsic passion first
Peopled my mind with beauteous forms or grand,
575 And made me love them, may I well forget
How other pleasures have been mine, and joys
Of subtler origin; how I have felt
Not seldom, even in that tempestuous time,
Those hallow'd and pure motions of the sense
580 Which seem, in their simplicity, to own
An intellectual charm, that calm delight
Which, if I err not, surely must belong

---

6. Diligent; revising Milton's claim that he is "Not sedulous by Nature" to treat epic themes (*Paradise Lost* 9.27).

To those first-born affinities that fit
Our new existence to existing things
585 And, in our dawn of being, constitute
The bond of union betwixt life and joy.
Yes, I remember, when the changeful earth,
And twice five seasons on my mind had stamp'd
The faces of the moving year, even then,
590 A Child, I held unconscious intercourse
With the eternal Beauty, drinking in
A pure organic pleasure from the lines
Of curling mist, or from the level plain
Of waters colour'd by the steady clouds.
595 The Sands of Westmoreland, the Creeks and Bays
Of Cumbria's rocky limits, they can tell
How when the Sea threw off his evening shade
And to the Shepherd's hut beneath the crags
Did send sweet notice of the rising moon,
600 How I have stood to fancies such as these,
Engrafted in the tenderness of thought,
A stranger, linking with the spectacle
No conscious memory of a kindred sight,
And bringing with me no peculiar sense
605 Of quietness or peace, yet have I stood,
Even while mine eye has mov'd o'er three long leagues°   *about 9 miles*
Of shining water, gathering, as it seem'd,
Through every hair-breadth of that field of light,
New pleasure, like a bee among the flowers.
610 Thus, often in those fits of vulgar° joy   *ordinary*
Which through all seasons, on a child's pursuits
Are prompt attendants, 'mid that giddy bliss
Which, like a tempest, works along the blood
And is forgotten; even then I felt
615 Gleams like the flashing of a shield: the earth
And common face of Nature spake to me
Rememberable things: sometimes, 'tis true,
By chance collisions, and quaint accidents
Like those ill-sorted unions, work suppos'd
620 Of evil-minded fairies, yet not vain,
Nor profitless, if haply they impress'd
Collateral° objects and appearances,   *secondary*
Albeit lifeless then, and doom'd to sleep
Until maturer seasons call'd them forth
625 To impregnate and to elevate the mind.
And if the vulgar joy by its own weight
Wearied itself out of the memory
The scenes which were a witness of that joy
Remained, in their substantial lineaments
630 Depicted on the brain, and to the eye
Were visible, a daily sight: and thus,
By the impressive discipline of fear,
By pleasure, and repeated happiness,

Are quicken'd, are more vigorous, his mind spreads,
Tenacious of the forms which it receives.
255 In one beloved presence, nay and more,
In that most apprehensive habitude°   *capacity to assimilate*
And those sensations which have been deriv'd
From this beloved Presence, there exists
A virtue which irradiates and exalts
260 All objects through all intercourse of sense.
No outcast he, bewilder'd and depress'd:
Along his infant veins are interfus'd
The gravitation and the filial bond
Of nature, that connect him with the world.
265 Emphatically such a Being lives,
An inmate of this *active* universe;
From nature largely he receives; nor so
Is satisfied, but largely gives again,
For feeling has to him imparted strength,
270 And powerful in all sentiments of grief,
Of exultation, fear, and joy, his mind,
Even as an agent of the one great mind,
Creates, creator and receiver both,
Working but in alliance with the works
275 Which it beholds.——Such, verily, is the first
Poetic spirit of our human life;
By uniform controul of after years
In most abated and suppress'd, in some,
Through every change of growth or of decay,
280 Pre-eminent till death.
                              From early days,
Beginning not long after that first time
In which, a Babe, by intercourse of touch,
I held mute dialogues with my Mother's heart,
I have endeavour'd to display the means
285 Whereby the infant sensibility,
Great birth-right of our Being, was in me
Augmented and sustain'd. Yet is a path
More difficult before me, and I fear
That in its broken windings we shall need
290 The chamois'° sinews, and the eagle's wing: *mountain antelope*
For now a trouble came into my mind
From unknown causes. I was left alone,
Seeking the visible world, nor knowing why.
The props of my affections were remov'd,
295 And yet the building stood, as if sustain'd
By its own spirit!⁴ All that I beheld
Was dear to me, and from this cause it came,
That now to Nature's finer influxes°   *influences, impressions*
My mind lay open, to that more exact
300 And intimate communion which our hearts

---

4. Perhaps an oblique reference to the death of Wordsworth's mother when he was almost eight years old.

Maintain with the minuter properties
Of objects which already are belov'd,
And of those only.

from Book Sixth. Cambridge, and the Alps

[TRAVELLING IN THE ALPS. SIMPLON PASS]

Yet still in me, mingling with these delights°   *of travel*
Was something of stern mood, an under thirst
490   Of vigour, never utterly asleep.
Far different dejection once was mine,
A deep and genuine sadness then I felt:
The circumstances I will here relate
Even as they were. Upturning with a Band
495   Of Travellers, from the Valais we had clomb
Along the road that leads to Italy;°   *Simplon Pass*
A length of hours, making of these our guides
Did we advance, and having reach'd an Inn
Among the mountains, we together ate
500   Our noon's repast, from which the Travellers rose,
Leaving us at the Board. Erelong we follow'd,
Descending by the beaten road that led
Right to a rivulet's edge, and there broke off.
The only track now visible was one
505   Upon the further side, right opposite,
And up a lofty Mountain. This we took
After a little scruple,° and short pause,   *hesitation*
And climb'd with eagerness, though not, at length,
Without surprize and some anxiety
510   On finding that we did not overtake
Our Comrades gone before. By fortunate chance,
While every moment now encreas'd our doubts,
A Peasant met us and from him we learn'd
That to the place which had perplex'd us first
515   We must descend, and there should find the road
Which in the stony channel of the Stream
Lay a few steps, and then along its Banks,
And, further, that thenceforward all our course
Was downwards, with the current of that Stream.
520   Hard of belief we questioned him again,
And all the answers which the Man return'd
To our inquiries, in their sense and substance,
Translated by the feelings which we had,
Ended in this, that we had cross'd the Alps.
525   Imagination! lifting up itself
Before the eye and progress of my Song°   *this poem*
Like an unfather'd vapour; here that Power,
In all the might of its endowments, came
Athwart me; I was lost as in a cloud,
530   Halted without a struggle to break through,

And now[1] recovering to my Soul I say
I recognize thy glory; in such strength
Of usurpation, in such visitings
Of awful° promise, when the light of sense   *awe-filled*
535 Goes out in flashes that have shewn to us
The invisible world, doth Greatness make abode,
There harbours whether we be young or old.
Our destiny, our nature, and our home
Is with infinitude, and only there;
540 With hope it is, hope that can never die,
Effort, and expectation, and desire,
And something evermore about to be.
The mind beneath such banners militant
Thinks not of spoils, trophies nor of aught
545 That may attest its prowess, blest in thoughts
That are their own perfection and reward,
Strong in itself, and in the access of joy
Which hides it like the overflowing Nile.
        The dull and heavy slackening which ensu'd
550 Upon those tidings by the Peasant given
Was soon dislodg'd; downwards we hurried fast,
And enter'd with the road which we had miss'd
Into a narrow chasm: the brook and road[2]
Were fellow-travellers in this gloomy Pass,
555 And with them did we journey several hours
At a slow step. The immeasurable height
Of woods decaying, never to be decay'd,
The stationary blasts of waterfalls,
And every where along the hollow rent
560 Winds thwarting winds, bewilder'd and forlorn,[3]
The torrents shooting from the clear blue sky,
The rocks that mutter'd close upon our ears,
Black drizzling crags that spake by the way-side
As if a voice were in them, the sick sight
565 And giddy prospect of the raving stream,
The unfetter'd clouds, and region of the heavens,
Tumult and peace, the darkness and the light
Were all like workings of one mind, the features
Of the same face, blossoms upon one tree,
570 Characters° of the great Apocalyps,   *signs, letters*
The types and symbols of Eternity,
Of first and last, and midst, and without end.[4]
        That night our lodging was an Alpine House,
An Inn or Hospital, as they are named,
575 Standing in that same valley by itself
And close upon the confluence of two streams,

1. This apostrophe was written in 1804, 14 years after the
disappointment of the missed climax.
2. Lines 553 (from "the") through 572 were published as
The Simplon Pass in Wordsworth's 1845 *Poems,* under
"Poems of the Imagination."
3. A contrasting echo of 2.261.

4. Milton's terms for God (*Paradise Lost* 5.165), echoing
God's description of himself in the book of Revelation
(the Apocalypse) as "Alpha and Omega, the beginning
and the ending"—the first and last letters of the Greek
alphabet. "Types" are people or events that foreshadow
God's future works.

A dreary Mansion, large beyond all need,
With high and spacious rooms, deafen'd and stunn'd
By noise of waters, making innocent Sleep
580   Lie melancholy among weary bones.[5]
      Uprisen betimes, our journey we renew'd
Led by the Stream, ere noon-day magnified
Into a lordly River, broad and deep,
Dimpling along in silent majesty,
585   With mountains for its neighbours, and in view
Of distant mountains and their snowy tops,
And thus proceeding to Locarno's Lake,
Fit resting-place for such a Visitant.
    ——Locarno, spreading out in width like Heaven,
590   And Como, thou a treasure by the earth
Kept to itself, a darling bosom'd up
In Abyssinian[6] privacy, I spake
Of thee, thy chesnut woods, and garden plots
Of Indian corn tended by dark-eyed Maids,
595   Thy lofty steeps, and path-ways roof'd with vines
Winding from house to house, from town to town,
Sole link that binds them to each other, walks
League after league, and cloistral avenues
Where silence is, if music be not there:
600   While yet a Youth, undisciplined in Verse,
Through fond ambition of my heart, I told
Your praises; nor can I approach you now,
Ungreeted by a more melodious Song,
Where tones of learned Art and Nature mix'd
605   May frame enduring language. Like a breeze
Or sunbeam over your domain I pass'd
In motion without pause; but Ye have left
Your beauty with me, an impassion'd sight
Of colours and of forms, whose power is sweet
610   And gracious, almost might I dare to say,
As virtue is, or goodness, sweet as love
Or the remembrance of a noble deed,
Or gentlest visitations of pure thought
When God, the Giver of all joy, is thank'd
615   Religiously, in silent blessedness,
Sweet as this last itself, for such it is.
      Through those delightful pathways we advanced
Two days, and still in presence of the Lake,
Which, winding up among the Alps, now changed
620   Slowly its lovely countenance, and put on
A sterner character. The second night,
In eagerness, and by report misled
Of those Italian Clocks that speak the time
In fashion different from ours, we rose
625   By moonshine, doubting not that day was near,

---

5. King-killer Macbeth laments the loss of "innocent sleep" (2.2.35).

6. Abyssinia was a legendary location of Paradise.

And that, meanwhile, coasting the Water's edge,
As hitherto, and with as plain a track
To be our guide, we might behold the scene
In its most deep repose.—We left the Town
630 Of Gravedona with this hope; but soon
Were lost, bewilder'd among woods immense,
Where, having wander'd for a while, we stopp'd
And on a rock sate down, to wait for day.
An open place it was, and overlook'd
635 From high the sullen water underneath,
On which a dull red image of the moon
Lay bedded, changing oftentimes its form
Like an uneasy snake: long time we sate,
For scarcely more than one hour of the night,
640 Such was our error, had been gone, when we
Renew'd our journey. On the rock we lay,
And wish'd to sleep but could not for the stings
Of insects, which with noise like that of noon
Fill'd all the woods: the cry of unknown birds,
645 The mountains, more by darkness visible[7]
And their own size than any outward light,
The breathless wilderness of clouds, the clock
That told with unintelligible voice
The widely-parted hours, the noise of streams
650 And sometimes rustling motions nigh at hand
Which did not leave us free from personal fear,
And lastly the withdrawing Moon, that set
Before us while she yet was high in heaven,
These were our food; and such a summer night
655 Did to that pair of golden days succeed,
With now and then a doze and snatch of sleep,
On Como's Banks, the same delicious Lake.

from Book Tenth. Residence in France and French Revolution

[THE REIGN OF TERROR. CONFUSION. RETURN TO ENGLAND]

It was a beautiful and silent day
That overspread the countenance of earth,
Then fading, with unusual quietness
When from the Loire I parted, and through scenes
5   Of vineyard, orchard, meadow-ground and tilth,°   *tilled land*
Calm waters, gleams of sun, and breathless trees
Towards the fierce Metropolis turn'd my steps
Their homeward way to England. From his Throne
The King had fallen;[1] the congregated Host,
10   Dire cloud upon the front of which was written
The tender mercies of the dismal wind

---

7. Recalling Milton's description of Hell (*Paradise Lost* 1.61ff.), which resonates throughout this passage.
1. Louis XVI was imprisoned in August 1792, and the invading armies of Austria and Prussia were defeated by the French at Valmy on 20 September 1792, a month before Wordsworth returned from Orleans to Paris.

That bore it, on the Plains of Liberty
Had burst innocuously:—say more, the swarm
That came elate and jocund, like a Band
15 Of Eastern Hunters, to enfold in ring
Narrowing itself by moments and reduce
To the last punctual° spot of their despair   *precise*
A race of victims, so they deem'd, themselves
Had shrunk from sight of their own task, and fled
20 In terror; desolation and dismay
Remain'd for them whose fancies had grown rank
With evil expectations, confidence
And perfect triumph to the better cause.
The State, as if to stamp the final seal
25 On her security, and to the world
Shew what she was, a high and fearless soul,
Or rather in a spirit of thanks to those
Who had stirr'd up her slackening faculties
To new transition, had assumed with joy
30 The body and the venerable name
Of a Republic:[2] lamentable crimes
'Tis true had gone before this hour, the work
Of massacre in which the senseless sword
Was pray'd to as a judge; but these were past,
35 Earth free from them for ever, as was thought,
Ephemeral monsters, to be seen but once,
Things that could only shew themselves and die.
    This was the time in which enflam'd with hope,
To Paris I return'd. Again I rang'd,
40 More eagerly than I had done before,
Through the wide City and in progress pass'd
The Prison where the unhappy Monarch lay
Associate with his Children and his Wife
In bondage; and the Palace lately storm'd
45 With roar of canon, and a numerous Host.
I cross'd, (a blank and empty area then)
The Square of the Carousel, few weeks back
Heap'd up with dead and dying,[3] upon these
And other sights looking as doth a man
50 Upon a volume whose contents he knows
Are memorable, but from him lock'd up,
Being written in a tongue he cannot read;
So that he questions the mute leaves with pain
And half upbraids their silence. But that night
55 When on my bed I lay I was most mov'd
And felt most deeply in what world I was;
My room was high and lonely, near the roof
Of a large Mansion° or Hotel, a spot   *townhouse*
That would have pleas'd me in more quiet times

2. On 22 September 1792.
3. The royal palace had been stormed by a mob in

August, with over a thousand lives lost; their bodies were
cremated in the square in front of the palace.

60   Nor was it wholly without pleasure then.
    With unextinguish'd taper I kept watch,
    Reading at intervals; the fear gone by
    Press'd on me almost like a fear to come;
    I thought of those September Massacres,
65   Divided from me by a little month,[4]
    And felt and touch'd them, a substantial dread;
    The rest was conjured up from tragic fictions
    And mournful Calendars° of true history,   *records*
    Remembrances and dim admonishments.
70   "The horse is taught his manage° and the wind   *paces*
    Of heaven wheels round and treads in his own steps,[5]
    Year follows year, the tide returns again,
    Day follows day, all things have second birth;
    The earthquake is not satisfied at once."
75   And in such way I wrought upon myself
    Until I seem'd to hear a voice that cried
    To the whole City, "Sleep no more."[6] To this
    Add comments of a calmer mind, from which
    I could not gather full security,
80   But at the best it seemed a place of fear,
    Unfit for the repose of night,
    Defenceless as a wood where tigers roam.
       Betimes next morning to the Palace Walk
    Of Orleans I repair'd and entering there
85   Was greeted, among divers° other notes,   *various*
    By voices of the Hawkers in the crowd
    Bawling, *Denunciation of the crimes*
    Of Maximilian Robespierre: the speech
    Which in their hands they carried was the same
90   Which had been recently pronounced the day
    When Robespierre, well-knowing for what mark
    Some words of indirect reproof had been
    Intended, rose in hardihood and dared
    The Man who had an ill surmise of him
95   To bring his charge in openness: whereat
    When a dead pause ensued and no one stirr'd,
    In silence of all present, from his seat
    Louvet walked singly through the avenue
    And took his station in the Tribune,° saying   *rostrum*
100   "I, Robespierre, accuse thee"! 'Tis well known
    What was the issue of that charge, and how
    Louvet was left alone without support
    Of his irresolute Friends:[7] but these are things

4. Between 2 and 7 September, Robespierre's newly powerful radical faction of the Republican government organized massacres in which 3,000 prisoners were executed. Wordsworth echoes Hamlet's anger at his mother's betrayal of his recently deceased father (1.2.147).
5. The National Convention of France now met at a former riding school near the Tuileries. The quotation is from Shakespeare's *As You Like It* (1.1.11–12).
6. Macbeth's guilty fantasy after he has murdered his

king: "Methought I heard a voice cry 'Sleep no more!'" (*Macbeth* 2.2.35).
7. In the National Convention, on 29 October 1792, the moderate Girondist J. B. Louvet de Couvray accused Robespierre of dictatorial behavior and aspirations. The phrase "walked singly" in line 98 evokes the solitary resistance of archangel Abdiel to Satan's revolt against God (*Paradise Lost* 5.877ff.).

Of which I speak only as they were storm
105 Or sunshine to my individual mind,
No further. Let me then relate that now
In some sort seeing with my proper° eyes   *own*
That Liberty, and Life and Death would soon
To the remotest corners of the Land
110 Lie in the arbitriment° of those who ruled   *government*
The capital City, what was struggled for,
And by what combatants victory must be won,
The indecision on their° part whose aim   *Girondin moderates*
Seem'd best, and the straight-forward path of those
115 Who in attack or in defense alike
Were strong through their impiety,° greatly I   *the Jacobin radicals*
Was agitated; yea I could almost
Have pray'd that throughout earth upon all souls
Worthy of liberty, upon every soul
120 Matured to live in plainness and in truth
The gift of tongues might fall,[8] and men arrive
From the four quarters of the winds to do
For France what without help she could not do,
A work of honour: think not that to this
125 I added work of safety; from such thought
And the least fear about the end of things
I was as far as Angels are from guilt.
    Yet did I grieve, nor only grieved, but thought
Of opposition and of remedies,
130 An insignificant Stranger, and obscure,
Mean° as I was, and little graced with powers   *humble*
Of eloquence even in my native speech,
And all unfit for tumult and intrigue,
Yet would I willingly have taken up
135 A service at this time for cause so great,
However dangerous. Inly I revolved
How much the destiny of man had still°   *always*
Hung upon single persons, that there was,
Transcendant to all local patrimony,
140 One Nature, as there is one Sun in heaven,
That objects, even as they are great, thereby
Do come within the reach of humblest eyes,
That Man was only weak through his mistrust
And want of hope, where evidence divine
145 Proclaim'd to him that hope should be most sure,
That, with desires heroic and firm sense,
A Spirit thoroughly faithful to itself,
Unquenchable, unsleeping, undismay'd,[9]
Was as an instinct among men, a stream
150 That gather'd up each petty straggling rill
And vein of water, glad to be roll'd on

8. Apostles began to speak in tongues at Pentecost, miraculously understood by foreigners of many languages (Acts 2).

9. Again evoking Abdiel's faithful heroism (*Paradise Lost* 5.897-99).

In safe obedience, that a mind whose rest
Was where it ought to be, in self-restraint,
In circumspection and simplicity,
155 Fell rarely in entire discomfiture
Below its aim, or met with from without
A treachery that defeated it, or foil'd.
—On the other side I call'd to mind those truths
Which are the common-places of the Schools,
160 A theme° for Boys, too trite even to be felt,   *essay subject*
Yet with a revelation's liveliness
In all their comprehensive bearings known
And visible to Philosophers of old,
Men who, to business of the world untrain'd,
165 Liv'd in the Shade, and to Harmodius known
And his Compeer Aristogiton, known
To Brutus,[1] that tyrannic Power is weak,
Hath neither gratitude, nor faith, nor love,
Nor the support of good or evil men
170 To trust in, that the Godhead which is ours
Can never utterly be charm'd° or still'd,   *expelled*
That nothing hath a natural right to last
But equity and reason, that all else
Meets foes irreconcilable, and at best
175 Doth live but by variety of disease.

    Well might my wishes be intense, my thoughts
Strong and perturb'd, not doubting at that time,
Creed which ten shameful years[2] have not annull'd,
But that the virtue of one paramount mind
180 Would have abash'd those impious crests, have quell'd
Outrage and bloody power, and in despite
Of what the People were through ignorance
And immaturity, and, in the teeth
Of desperate opposition from without,
185 Have clear'd a passage for just government,
And left a solid birth-right to the State,
Redeem'd according to example given
By ancient Lawgivers.
                    In this frame of mind
Reluctantly to England I return'd,[3]
190 Compell'd by nothing less than absolute want
Of funds for my support, else, well assured
That I both was and must be of small worth,
No better than an alien in the Land,
I doubtless should have made a common cause
195 With some who perish'd, haply° perish'd too,[4]   *perhaps*

1. Harmodius and Aristogiton were killed when they tried to overthrow the tyrant Hippias in 514 B.C. in Athens. Brutus was the idealistic assassin of Julius Caesar, who seemed ready in 44 B.C. to name himself emperor.
2. Since 1793.

3. Late in 1792.
4. Wordsworth's sympathies were with the moderate Girondins, almost all of whom were executed or committed suicide following Robespierre's rise to power.

A poor mistaken and bewilder'd offering,
Should to the breast of Nature have gone back
With all my resolutions, all my hopes,
A Poet only to myself, to Men

200   Useless, and even, beloved Friend, a soul
To thee unknown.[5]

[FURTHER EVENTS IN FRANCE]

In France, the Men who for their desperate ends
Had pluck'd up mercy by the roots were glad
Of this new enemy. Tyrants, strong before

310   In devilish pleas were ten times stronger now,[6]
And thus beset with Foes on every side
The goaded Land wax'd mad; the crimes of few
Spread into madness of the many, blasts
From hell came sanctified like airs from heaven;[7]

315   The sternness of the Just,[8] the faith of those
Who doubted not that Providence had times
Of anger and vengeance, theirs who throned
The human understanding paramount
And made of that their God,[9] the hopes of those

320   Who were content to barter short-lived pangs
For a paradise of ages,[1] the blind rage
Of insolent tempers, the light vanity
Of intermeddlers, steady purposes
Of the suspicious, slips of the indiscreet,

325   And all the accidents of life were press'd
Into one service, busy with one work;
The Senate was heart-stricken, not a voice
Uplifted, none to oppose or mitigate:
Domestic carnage now fill'd all the year

330   With Feast-days; the Old Man from the chimney-nook,
The Maiden from the bosom of her Love,
The Mother from the Cradle of her Babe,
The Warrior from the Field, all perish'd,
Friends, enemies, of all parties, ages, ranks,

335   Head after head, and never heads enough
For those who bade them fall: they found their joy,
They made it, ever thirsty.[2]—As a Child,
(If light desires of innocent little Ones
May with such heinous appetites be match'd)

340   Having a toy, a windmill, though the air

5. Wordsworth met Coleridge in 1795.
6. After France declared war on England in February 1793, England joined the coalition against France led by Austria and Prussia. Except for a brief peace in 1802, England would be at war with France until 1815.
7. Echoing Hamlet's doubt whether his murdered father's ghost brings "airs from heaven or blasts from hell" (Hamlet 1.4.41).
8. Referring obliquely to Robespierre's associate Louis St.

Just, a leader of the Terror.
9. "La Raison" (Reason) was a goddess of the Republic, and churches were turned into Temples of Reason.
1. Radicals regarded the terror as a necessary purge to secure the safety of the Republic.
2. At the height of the Terror in 1793, 1,376 people were guillotined in Paris in 49 days, and in the city of Nantes 15,000 by the end of the year.

Do of itself blow fresh, and makes the vane
Spin in his eyesight, he is not content,
But with the play-thing at arm's length, he sets
His front against the blast, and runs amain°   *full force*
345   To make it whirl the faster.
                              In the depth
Of these enormities, even thinking minds
Forgot at seasons whence they had their being,
Forgot that such a sound was ever heard
As Liberty, upon earth; yet all beneath
350   Her innocent authority was wrought,
Nor could have been without her blessed name.
The illustrious Wife of Roland, in the hour
Of her composure, felt that agony
And gave it vent in her last words.³ O Friend!
355   It was a lamentable time for man
Whether a hope had e'er been his or not,
A woful time for them whose hopes did still
Outlast the shock, most woful for those few—
They had the deepest feeling of the grief—
360   Who still were flatter'd,° and had trust in man.   *deluded*
Meanwhile, the Invaders fared as they deserv'd;
The Herculean Commonwealth had put forth her arms
And throttled with an infant Godhead's might
The snakes about her cradle:⁴ that was well
365   And as it should be, yet no cure for those
Whose souls were sick with pain of what would be
Hereafter brought in charge against mankind;
Most melancholy at that time, O Friend!
Were my day thoughts, my dreams were miserable;
370   Through months, through years, long after the last beat
Of those atrocities (I speak bare truth,
As if to thee alone in private talk)
I scarcely had one night of quiet sleep,
Such ghastly visions had I of despair
375   And tyranny and implements of death,
And long orations which in dreams I pleaded
Before unjust Tribunals, with a voice
Labouring, a brain confounded, and a sense
Of treachery and desertion in the place
380   The holiest that I knew of, my own soul.

[THE DEATH OF ROBESPIERRE AND RENEWED OPTIMISM]⁵

when a Traveller
Chancing to pass, I carelessly inquired

---

3. Madame Roland, Wollstonecraft's friend and an important supporter of the Girondins, was guillotined in November 1793. Her famous last words were: "O Liberté, que des crimes l'on commet en ton nom!" ("O Liberty, what crimes one commits in thy name!").
4. As an infant in his cradle, Hercules strangled the two serpents sent by Hera to destroy him, just as the infant Republic had repelled foreign invasions.
5. Wordsworth is back in England, spending the summer on the coast near Peele Castle. On 28 July 1794, Robespierre and 21 associates were guillotined. Wordsworth was walking near the shore when he heard the news.

If any news were stirring: he replied
In the familiar language of the day
535 That "*Robespierre was dead.*" Nor was a doubt,
On further question, left within my mind
But that the tidings were substantial truth,
That he and his supporters all were fallen.
    Great was my glee of spirit, great my joy
540 In vengeance, and eternal justice, thus
Made manifest. "Come now ye golden times,"
Said I, forth-breathing on those open Sands
A Hymn of triumph, "as the morning comes
Out of the bosom of the night, come Ye:
545 Thus far our trust is verified; behold!
They who with clumsy desperation brought
A river of blood, and preach'd that nothing else
Could cleanse the Augean Stable,[6] by the might
Of their own helper have been swept away;
550 Their madness is declared and visible,
Elsewhere will safety now be sought,[7] and Earth
March firmly towards righteousness and peace."
Then schemes I framed more calmly, when and how
The madding Factions might be tranquillised,
555 And though through hardships manifold and long,
The mighty renovation would proceed:
Thus, interrupted by uneasy bursts
Of exultation, I pursued my way
Along that very Shore which I had skimm'd
560 In former times, when, spurring from the Vale
Of Nightshade and St Mary's mouldering Fane°   *shrine*
And the Stone Abbot, after circuit made
In wantonness of heart, a joyous Crew
Of School-boys, hastening to their distant home,
565 Along the margin of the moonlight Sea,
We beat with thundering hoofs the level Sand.

               * * *

    O pleasant exercise of hope and joy![8]
690 For great were the auxiliars° which then stood   *allies*
Upon our side, we who were strong in love;
Bliss was it in that dawn to be alive,
But to be young was very heaven: O times,
In which the meagre, stale, forbidding ways
695 Of custom, law and statute took at once
The attraction of a Country in Romance;
When Reason seem'd the most to assert her rights
When most intent on making of herself
A prime Enchanter to assist the work

---

6. In one of his 12 labors, Hercules cleaned the filthy stables of King Augeus, by diverting two rivers through them.
7. Instead of with Robespierre's Committee of Public Safety, which had instigated the Terror.
8. Wordsworth's renewed faith in the French Republic extended to hope for peaceful reforms in England. He published this passage in Coleridge's journal *The Friend* in 1809 and in his *Poems* of 1815, as "French Revolution as It Appeared to Enthusiasts at Its Commencement," classing it with "Poems of the Imagination."

700   Which then was going forwards in her name:
       Not favor'd spots alone, but the whole earth
       The beauty wore of promise, that which sets,
       To take an image which was felt, no doubt,
       Among the bowers of paradise itself,
705   The budding rose above the rose full blown.
       What temper° at the prospect did not wake   *temperament*
       To happiness unthought-of? The inert
       Were rouz'd, and lively natures rapt° away.   *carried, enraptured*
       They who had fed their childhood upon dreams,
710   The Play-fellows of Fancy, who had made
       All powers of swiftness, subtlety, and strength
       Their ministers, used to stir in lordly wise
       Among the grandest objects of the sense
       And deal with whatsoever they found there
715   As if they had within some lurking right
       To wield it:—they too, who, of gentle mood,
       Had watch'd all gentle motions, and to these
       Had fitted their own thoughts, schemers more mild,
       And in the region of their peaceful selves—
720   Did now find helpers to their heart's desire,
       And stuff at hand, plastic° as they could wish,   *malleable*
       Were call'd upon to exercise their skill,
       Not in Utopia, subterraneous fields,
       Or some secreted Island Heaven knows where;
725   But in the very world which is the world
       Of all of us, the place on which in the end
       We find our happiness, or not at all.

[BRITAIN DECLARES WAR ON FRANCE.
THE RISE OF NAPOLEON AND IMPERIALIST FRANCE]

           In the main outline, such, it might be said
       Was my condition, till with open war
       Britain opposed the Liberties of France:[9]
760   This threw me first out of the pale° of love,   *boundary*
       Sour'd, and corrupted upwards to the source
       My sentiments, was° not, as hitherto,   *this was*
       A swallowing up of lesser things in great;
       But change of them into their opposites,
765   And thus a way was open'd for mistakes
       And false conclusions of the intellect
       As gross in their degree and in their kind
       Far, far more dangerous. What had been a pride
       Was now a shame; my likings and my loves
770   Ran in new channels, leaving old ones dry,
       And thus a blow which in maturer age
       Would but have touch'd the judgement struck more deep
       Into sensations near the heart: meantime,
       As from the first, wild theories were afloat

9. France declared war on 1 February 1793. Ten days later, England reciprocated.

775 Unto the subtleties of which at least
 I had but lent a careless ear, assured
 Of this, that time would soon set all things right,
 Prove that the multitude had been oppress'd,
 And would be so no more.
         But when events
780 Brought less encouragement, and unto these
 The immediate proof of principles no more
 Could be entrusted, while the events themselves,
 Worn out in greatness and in novelty,
 Less occupied the mind and sentiments,
785 Could through my understanding's natural growth
 No longer justify themselves through faith
 Of inward consciousness, and hope that laid
 Its hand upon its object; evidence
 Safer, of universal application, such
790 As could not be impeach'd was sought elsewhere.

  And now, become Oppressors in their turn,
 Frenchmen had changed a war of self-defense
 For one of conquest, losing sight of all
 Which they had struggled for; and mounted up
795 Openly in the view of earth and heaven
 The scale of Liberty.[1] I read her doom,
 Vex'd inly somewhat, it is true, and sore,
 But not dismay'd, nor taking to the shame
 Of a false Prophet; but, rouz'd up, I stuck
800 More firmly to old tenets, and to prove
 Their temper,° strain'd them more, and thus in heat   *test their strength*
 Of contest did opinions every day
 Grow into consequence till round my mind
 They clung, as if they were the life of it.
805 This was the time when all things tended fast
 To depravation; the Philosophy
 That promised to abstract the hopes of man
 Out of his feelings, to be fix'd thenceforth
 For ever in a purer element.
810 Found ready welcome.[2] Tempting region that
 For Zeal to enter and refresh herself
 Where passions had the privilege to work,
 And never hear the sound of their own names:
 But, speaking more in charity, the dream
815 Was flattering° to the young ingenuous mind,   *seductive*
 Pleas'd with extremes, and not the least with that
 Which makes the human Reason's naked self
 The object of its fervour: what delight!
 How glorious! in self-knowledge and self-rule
820 To look through all the frailties of the world

1. Initially fighting only in self-defense, by late 1794 France extended the war to several foreign fronts.
2. A reference to William Godwin's *Political Justice* (1793), which argued for the power of individual rational judgment to bring about reform.

920   My office upon earth, and nowhere else,
           And lastly, Nature's self, by human love
           Assisted, through the weary labyrinth
           Conducted me again to open day,
           Revived the feelings of my earlier life,
925   Gave me that strength, and knowledge full of peace,
           Enlarged, and never more to be disturb'd,
           Which through the steps of our degeneracy,
           All degradation of this age, hath still
           Upheld me, and upholds me at this day°   1804
930   In the catastrophe (for so they dream,
           And nothing less) when finally, to close
           And rivet up the gains of France, a Pope
           Is summon'd in, to crown an Emperor;
           This last opprobrium° when we see the dog   disgrace
935   Returning to his vomit,[4] when the sun
           That rose in splendour, was alive, and moved
           In exultation among living clouds
           Hath put his function and his glory off,
           And, turn'd into a gewgaw, a machine,°   stage machine
940   Sets like an opera phantom. * * *

─────────⚬─────────

COMPANION READING
William Wordsworth: from *The Prelude* (1850)

[APOSTROPHE TO EDMUND BURKE][1]

           Genius of Burke! forgive the pen seduced
           By specious wonders, and too slow to tell
           Of what the ingenuous, what bewildered men,
515   Beginning to mistrust their boastful guides,
           And wise men, willing to grow wiser, caught,
           Rapt auditors! from thy most eloquent tongue—
           Now mute, for ever mute in the cold grave.
           I see him,—old, but vigorous in age,—
520   Stand like an oak whose stag-horn branches start
           Out of its leafy brow, the more to awe
           The younger brethren of the grove. But some—
           While he forewarns, denounces, launches forth,
           Against all systems built on abstract rights,
525   Keen ridicule; the majesty proclaims
           Of Institutes and Laws, hallowed by time;
           Declares the vital power of social ties
           Endeared by Custom; and with high disdain,
           Exploding upstart Theory, insists

───

4. In November 1804 Pope Pius VII attended Napoleon's
coronation as Emperor; as Pius was about to crown him,
Napoleon snatched the crown and put it on himself.
Wordsworth alludes to 2 Peter 2.22: the persistently evil
man is like a dog "turned to his own vomit again."

1. This passage, composed in 1832, appears in Book 7 of
the 1850 *Prelude*, as Wordsworth pauses before Parliament and remembers Burke's parliamentary career and
his antirevolutionary *Reflections on the Revolution in
France* (see page 47).

530 Upon the allegiance to which men are born—
 Some—say at once a froward° multitude—   *willful*
 Murmur (for truth is hated, where not loved)
 As the winds fret within the Aeolian cave,
 Gall'd by their monarch's chain.[2] The times were big
535 With ominous change, which, night by night, provoked
 Keen struggles, and black clouds of passion raised;
 But memorable moments intervened,
 When Wisdom, like the Goddess° from Jove's brain,   *Athena*
 Broke forth in armour of resplendent words,
540 Startling the Synod.° Could a youth, and one   *Parliament*
 In ancient story versed, whose breast had heaved
 Under the weight of classic eloquence,
 Sit, see, and hear, unthankful, uninspired?

from Book Eleventh. Imagination, How Impaired and Restored

[IMAGINATION RESTORED BY NATURE]

 Long time hath Man's unhappiness and guilt
 Detain'd us; with what dismal sights beset
 For the outward view, and inwardly oppress'd
 With sorrow, disappointment, vexing thoughts,
5 Confusion of the judgement, zeal decay'd
 And lastly, utter loss of hope itself,
 And things to hope for. Not with these began
 Our Song; and not with these our Song must end:
 Ye motions of delight that through the fields
10 Stir gently, breezes and soft airs that breathe
 The breath of paradise, and find your way
 To the recesses of the soul! Ye Brooks
 Muttering along the stones, a busy noise
 By day, a quiet one in silent night,
15 And you, Ye Groves, whose ministry it is
 To interpose the covert of your shades,
 Even as a sleep, betwixt the heart of man
 And the uneasy world, 'twixt man himself,
 Not seldom, and his own unquiet heart,
20 Oh! that I had a music and a voice,
 Harmonious as your own, that I might tell
 What ye have done for me. The morning shines,
 Nor heedeth Man's perverseness; Spring returns,
 I saw the Spring return when I was dead
25 To deeper hope, yet had I joy for her,
 And welcomed her benevolence, rejoiced
 In common with the Children of her Love,
 Plants, insects, beast in field, and bird in bower.
 So neither were complacency° nor peace   *satisfaction*
30 Nor tender yearnings wanting° for my good   *lacking*

2. The god Aeolus kept the winds chained in a cave.

Through those distracted times; in Nature still
Glorying, I found a counterpoise in her,
Which, when the spirit of evil was at height
Maintain'd for me a secret happiness;
35   Her I resorted to, and lov'd so much
I seem'd to love as much as heretofore;
And yet this passion, fervent as it was,
Had suffer'd change; how could there fail to be
Some change, if merely hence, that years of life
40   Were going on, and with them loss or gain
Inevitable, sure alternative.
    This History, my Friend, hath chiefly told
Of intellectual° power, from stage to stage   *mental and spiritual*
Advancing, hand in hand with love and joy,
45   And of imagination teaching truth
Until that natural graciousness of mind
Gave way to over-pressure of the times
And their disastrous issues. What avail'd,
When Spells forbade the Voyager to land,
50   The fragrance which did ever and anon
Give notice° of the Shore, from arbours breathed   *reports*
Of blessed sentiment and fearless love?
What did such sweet remembrances avail,
Perfidious then, as seem'd, what serv'd they then?
55   My business was upon the barren seas,
My errand was to sail to other coasts:
Shall I avow that I had hope to see,
I mean that future times would surely see
The man to come parted as by a gulph
60   From him who had been, that I could no more
Trust the elevation which had made me one
With the great Family that here and there
Is scatter'd through the abyss of ages past,
Sage, Patriot, Lover, Hero; for it seem'd
65   That their best virtues were not free from taint
Of something false and weak which could not stand
The open eye of Reason. Then I said,
Go to the Poets; they will speak to thee
More perfectly of purer creatures, yet
70   If Reason be nobility in man
Can aught be more ignoble than the man
Whom they describe, would fasten if they may
Upon our love by sympathies of truth.
    Thus strangely did I war against myself.

["SPOTS OF TIME." TWO MEMORIES FROM CHILDHOOD AND LATER REFLECTIONS][1]

In truth, this degradation, howsoe'er
Induced, effect in whatsoe'er degree

---

1. This sequence, which concludes Book 11, was drafted in 1799. Originally placed early in Book 1 of the *Two-Part Prelude* with other boyhood memories (boat-stealing, ice-skating, the drowned man), the discussion of "spots of time" explores the way memories can have a restorative power on the imagination. By transferring these early memories to this late point in his autobiography, Wordsworth empowers them to enact what they describe—the revivification of poetic powers through recollection.

245 Of custom, that prepares such wantonness
 As makes the greatest things give way to least,
 Of any other cause which hath been named,
 Or, lastly, aggravated by the times,
 Which with their passionate sounds might often make
250 The milder minstrelsies of rural scenes
 Inaudible, was transient; I had felt
 Too forcibly, too early in my life
 Visitings of imaginative power,
 For this to last: I shook the habit off
255 Entirely and for ever, and again
 In Nature's presence stood, as I stand now,
 A sensitive and a creative Soul.
  There are in our existence spots of time,
 Which with distinct preeminence retain
260 A renovating Virtue,° whence, depress'd   *power*
 By false opinion and contentious thought,
 Or aught of heavier or more deadly weight
 In trivial occupations, and the round
 Of ordinary intercourse, our minds
265 Are nourish'd, and invisibly repair'd,
 A virtue by which pleasure is enhanced
 That penetrates, enables us to mount
 When high, more high, and lifts us up when fallen.
 This efficacious spirit chiefly lurks
270 Among those passages of life in which
 We have had deepest feeling that the mind
 Is lord and master, and that outward sense
 Is but the obedient servant of her will.
 Such moments, worthy of all gratitude,
275 Are scatter'd every where, taking their date
 From our first childhood; in our childhood even
 Perhaps are most conspicuous. Life with me
 As far as memory can look back, is full
 Of this beneficent influence. At a time
280 When scarcely (I was then not six years old)
 My hand could hold a bridle, with proud hopes
 I mounted, and we rode towards the hills:
 We were a pair of Horsemen; honest James[2]
 Was with me, my encourager and guide.
285 We had not travell'd long ere some mischance
 Disjoin'd me from my Comrade, and through fear
 Dismounting, down the rough and stony Moor
 I led my Horse, and, stumbling on, at length
 Came to a bottom,° where in former times   *dell*
290 A Murderer had been hung in iron chains.
 The Gibbet mast was moulder'd down, the bones
 And iron case were gone; but on the turf
 Hard by, soon after that fell deed was wrought
 Some unknown hand had carved the Murderer's name.

2. Later identified as "an ancient servant of my father's house."

295   The monumental writing was engraven
       In times long past, and still, from year to year,
       By superstition of the neighbourhood
       The grass is clear'd away; and to this hour
       The letters are all fresh and visible.
300   Faltering, and ignorant where I was, at length
       I chanced to espy those characters inscribed
       On the green sod: forthwith I left the spot
       And, reascending the bare Common,° saw   *field*
       A naked Pool that lay beneath the hills,
305   The Beacon on the summit, and more near
       A Girl who bore a Pitcher on her head
       And seem'd with difficult steps to force her way
       Against the blowing wind. It was, in truth,
       An ordinary sight; but I should need
310   Colours and words that are unknown to man
       To paint the visionary dreariness
       Which, while I look'd all round for my lost Guide,
       Did at that time invest the naked Pool,
       The Beacon on the lonely Eminence,
315   The Woman, and her garments vex'd and toss'd
       By the strong wind. When in a blessed season[3]
       With those two dear Ones,[4] to my heart so dear,
       When in the blessed time of early love,
       Long afterwards, I roam'd about
320   In daily presence of this very scene;
       Upon the naked pool and dreary crags,
       And on the melancholy Beacon, fell
       The spirit of pleasure, and youth's golden gleam;
       And think ye not with radiance more divine
325   From these remembrances, and from the power
       They left behind? So feeling comes in aid
       Of feeling, and diversity of strength
       Attends us, if but once we have been strong.
       Oh! mystery of Man, from what a depth
330   Proceed thy honours! I am lost, but see
       In simple childhood something of the base
       On which thy greatness stands, but this I feel,
       That from thyself it is that thou must give,
       Else never canst receive. The days gone by
335   Come back upon me from the dawn almost
       Of life: the hiding-places of my power
       Seem open; I approach, and then they close;[5]
       I see by glimpses now; when age comes on
       May scarcely see at all, and I would give,
340   While yet we may, as far as words can give,
       A substance and a life to what I feel:

3. Wordsworth wrote this verse, to the end of the paragraph, in 1804, just after completing the "Intimations" ode. The season recalled was before his departure to France.
4. His sister and Mary Hutchinson, whom he would marry in 1802.
5. In the 1850 text, this line became "I would approach them, but they close" (12.280).

I would enshrine the spirit of the past
For future restoration. Yet another
Of these to me affecting incidents
With which we will conclude.

345   One Christmas-time,
The day before the Holidays began,
Feverish, and tired, and restless, I went forth
Into the fields, impatient for the sight
Of those two Horses which should bear us home,
350 My Brothers and myself.[6] There was a Crag,
An Eminence, which from the meeting point
Of two high-ways ascending, overlook'd
At least a long half-mile of those two roads,
By each of which the expected Steeds might come,
355 The choice uncertain. Thither I repair'd,
Up to the highest summit: 'twas a day
Stormy, and rough and wild, and on the grass
I sate, half shelter'd by a naked wall:
Upon my right hand was a single sheep,
360 A whistling hawthorn on my left, and there
With those Companions at my side, I watch'd,
Straining my eyes intensely, as the mist
Gave intermitting prospect of the wood
And plain beneath. Ere I to School return'd
365 That dreary time, ere I had been ten days
A Dweller in my Father's House, he died
And I and my two Brothers, Orphans then,
Followed his Body to the Grave.[7] The event
With all the sorrow which it brought appear'd
370 A chastisement; and when I call'd to mind
That day so lately pass'd, when from the crag
I look'd in such anxiety of hope,
With trite reflections of morality,
Yet in the deepest passion, I bow'd low
375 To God, who thus corrected my desires;
And afterwards, the wind and sleety rain
And all the business of the elements,
The single sheep, and the one blasted tree,
And the bleak music of that old stone wall,
380 The noise of wood and water, and the mist
Which on the line of each of those two Roads
Advanced in such indisputable shapes,[8]
All these were spectacles and sounds to which
I often would repair, and thence would drink
385 As at a fountain: and I do not doubt
That in this later time, when storm and rain

---

6. December 1783; they were away from home at Hawkshead Grammar School.
7. Wordsworth's father died on 30 December 1783; his
mother had died five years earlier.

8. An echo of Hamlet's cry to his father's ghost: "Thou
com'st in such a questionable shape / That I will speak to
thee" (*Hamlet* 1.4.43–44).

So molds them and endues, abstracts, combines
80   Or by abrupt and unhabitual influence
     Doth make one object so impress itself
     Upon all others, and pervade them so
     That even the grossest minds must see and hear
     And cannot chuse but feel. The Power which these
85   Acknowledge when thus moved, which Nature thus
     Thrusts forth upon the senses, is the express
     Resemblance, in the fullness of its strength
     Made visible, a genuine Counterpart
     And Brother of the glorious faculty
90   Which higher minds bear with them as their own;
     This is the very spirit in which they deal
     With all the objects of the universe.
     They from their native selves can send abroad
     Like transformation, for themselves create
95   A like existence, and whene'er it is
     Created for them catch it by an instinct;
     Them the enduring and the transient both
     Serve to exalt; they build up greatest things
     From least suggestions; ever on the watch,
100 Willing to work and to be wrought upon,
     They need not extraordinary calls
     To rouze them, in a world of life they live
     By sensible impressions not enthrall'd,
     But quicken'd, rouz'd, and made thereby more fit
105 To hold communion with the invisible world.
     Such minds are truly from the Deity;
     For they are Powers; and hence the highest bliss
     That can be known is theirs, the consciousness
     Of whom they are habitually infused
110 Through every image, and through every thought,
     And all impressions: hence religion, faith,
     And endless occupation for the soul
     Whether discursive or intuitive,[5]
     Hence sovereignty within and peace at will,
115 Emotion which best foresight need not fear,
     Most worthy then of trust when most intense:
     Hence chearfulness in every act of life,
     Hence truth in moral judgements and delight
     That fails not in the external universe.
120   Oh! who is he that hath his whole life long
     Preserved, enlarged this freedom in himself!
     For this alone is genuine Liberty.
     Witness, ye Solitudes! where I received
     My earliest visitations, careless then
125 Of what was given me, and which now I roam
     A meditative, oft a suffering Man,
     And yet, I trust, with undiminish'd powers,

5. Archangel Raphael tells Adam that the soul has powers of Reason "Discursive or Intuitive" (*Paradise Lost* 5. 485–88); discursive: learned.

Witness, whatever falls my better mind,
Revolving with the accidents of life,
130 May have sustain'd, that, howsoe'er misled,
I never, in the quest of right and wrong,
Did tamper with myself° from private aims;   *my conscience*
Nor was in any of my hopes the dupe
Of selfish passions; nor did wilfully
135 Yield ever to mean cares and low pursuits;
But rather did with jealousy° shrink back   *vigilance*
From every combination that might aid
The tendency, too potent in itself,
Of habit to enslave the mind, I mean
140 Oppress it by the laws of vulgar° sense,   *mere*
And substitute a universe of death,[6]
The falsest of all worlds, in place of that
Which is divine and true. To fear and love,
To love, as first and chief, for there fear ends,
145 Be this ascribed; to early intercourse,
In presence of sublime and lovely Forms,
With the adverse principles of pain and joy,
Evil, as one° is rashly named by those   *i.e., pain*
Who know not what they say.[7] From love, for here
150 Do we begin and end, all grandeur comes,
All truth and beauty, from pervading love,
That gone, we are as dust. Behold the fields
In balmy spring-time, full of rising flowers
And blissful Creatures: see that Pair, the Lamb
155 And the Lamb's Mother, and their tender ways
Shall touch thee to the heart: in some green bower
Rest, and be not alone, but have thou there
The One who is thy choice of all the world;
There linger, lull'd, and lost, and rapt away,
160 Be happy to thy fill: thou call'st this love,
And so it is; but there is higher love
Than this, a love that comes into the heart
With awe and a diffusive° sentiment;   *bountiful*
Thy love is human merely; this proceeds
165 More from the brooding Soul, and is divine.
      This love more intellectual° cannot be   *spiritual*
Without Imagination, which in truth
Is but another name for absolute strength
And clearest insight, amplitude of mind,
170 And reason in her most exalted mood.
This faculty hath been the moving soul
Of our long labour: we have traced the stream
From darkness, and the very place of birth
In its blind cavern, whence is faintly heard
175 The sound of waters, follow'd it to light
And open day, accompanied its course

6. Milton's description of Hell (*Paradise Lost* 2.622).   7. Echoing Jesus' description of his executioners (Luke 23.34).

Among the ways of Nature; afterwards
Lost sight of it, bewilder'd and engulph'd,
Then given it greeting, as it rose once more
180   With strength, reflecting in its solemn breast
The works of man and face of human life,
And lastly, from its progress have we drawn
The feeling of life endless, the one thought
By which we live, Infinity and God.
185   Imagination having been our theme,
So also hath that intellectual love,
For they are each in each, and cannot stand
Dividually.°—Here must thou be, O Man!   *separately*
Strength to thyself; no Helper hast thou here;
190   Here keepest thou thy individual state:
No other can divide with thee this work,
No secondary hand can intervene
To fashion this ability; 'tis thine,
The prime and vital principle is thine
195   In the recesses of thy nature, far
From any reach of outward fellowship,
Else 'tis not thine at all.—But joy to him,
O joy to him who here hath sown, hath laid
Here the foundations of his future years!
200   For all that friendship, all that love can do,
All that a darling countenance can look
Or dear voice utter to complete the man,
Perfect him, made imperfect in himself,
All shall be his: and he whose soul hath risen
205   Up to the height of feeling intellect
Shall want no humbler tenderness, his heart
Be tender as a nursing Mother's heart,
Of female softness shall his life be full,
Of little loves and delicate desires,
210   Mild interests and gentlest sympathies.

[Concluding Retrospect and Prophecy]

Having now
Told what best merits mention, further pains
Our present labour seems not to require
370   And I have other tasks. Call back to mind
The mood in which this Poem was begun,
O Friend! the termination of my course
Is nearer now, much nearer; yet even then
In that distraction and intense desire
375   I said unto the life which I had lived,
Where art thou? Hear I not a voice from thee
Which 'tis reproach to hear?[8] Anon I rose
As if on wings, and saw beneath me stretch'd

---

8. Recalling Coleridge's urging that he should undertake a major philosophical epic, Book 1.625–72.

380	Vast prospect of the world which I had been	
	And was;[9] and hence this Song which like a lark	
	I have protracted, in the unwearied Heavens	
	Singing,[1] and often with more plaintive voice	
	Attemper'd to the sorrows of the earth;	
	Yet centring all in love, and in the end	
385	All gratulant° if rightly understood.	*expressing joy*
	Whether to me shall be allotted life,	
	And with life power to accomplish aught of worth	
	Sufficient to excuse me in men's sight	
	For having given this Record of myself	
390	Is all uncertain: but, beloved Friend,	
	When, looking back, thou seest in clearer view	
	Than any sweetest sight of yesterday	
	That summer when on Quantock's grassy Hills[2]	
	Far ranging, and among the sylvan Coombs°	*small valleys*
395	Thou in delicious words with happy heart	
	Didst speak the Vision of that Ancient Man,	
	The bright-eyed Mariner, and rueful woes	
	Didst utter of the Lady Christabel	
	And I, associate in such labour, walk'd	
400	Murmuring of him who, joyous hap! was found,	
	After the perils of his moonlight ride	
	Near the loud Waterfall; or her who sate	
	In misery near the miserable Thorn;[3]	
	When thou dost to that summer turn thy thoughts,	
405	And hast before thee all which then we were,	
	To thee, in memory of that happiness	
	It will be known, by thee at least, my Friend,	
	Felt, that the history of a Poet's mind	
	Is labour not unworthy of regard.	
410	To thee the work shall justify itself.	
	The last, and later portions of this Gift	
	Which I for Thee design have been prepared	
	In times which have from those wherein we first	
	Together wanton'd in wild Poesy,	
415	Differ'd thus far, that they have been, O Friend,	
	Times of much sorrow, of a private grief	
	Keen and enduring,[4] which the frame of mind	
	That in this meditative History	
	Hath been described, more deeply makes me feel;	
420	Yet likewise hath enabled me to bear	
	More firmly; and a comfort now, a hope,	
	One of the dearest which this life can give,	
	Is mine; that Thou art near and wilt be soon	

9. Echoing Eve's dream (*Paradise Lost* 5.86–88).
1. Echoing Shakespeare, Sonnet 29 (9–12).
2. Above Alfoxden, in Somerset, where the Wordsworths lived, near Coleridge, from 1797 to 1798.
3. Referring to the lyrical ballads Wordsworth wrote then (*The Idiot Boy* and *The Thorn*), and to Coleridge's *Rime of the Ancyent Marinere* and *Christabel*.
4. Wordsworth's younger brother John drowned in a shipwreck, 5 February 1805.

Restored to us in renovated health:[5]
425   When, after the first mingling of our tears,
'Mong other consolations we may find
Some pleasure from this Offering of my love.
    Oh! yet a few short years of useful life,
And all will be complete, thy race be run,
430   Thy monument of glory will be raised;
Then, though, too weak to tread the ways of truth,
This Age fall back to old idolatry,
Though men return to servitude as fast
As the tide ebbs, to ignominy and shame
435   By Nations° sink together, we shall still   *nation by nation*
Find solace in the knowledge which we have,
Bless'd with true happiness if we may be
United helpers forward of a day
Of firmer trust, joint-labourers in the work,
440   (Should Providence such grace to us vouchsafe)
Of their redemption, surely yet to come.
Prophets of Nature, we to them will speak
A lasting inspiration, sanctified
By reason and by truth: what we have loved
445   Others will love; and we may teach them how,
Instruct them how the mind of man becomes
A thousand times more beautiful than the earth
On which he dwells, above this Frame of things
(Which 'mid all revolutions in the hopes
450   And fears of men doth still remain unchanged)
In beauty exalted, as it is itself
Of substance and of fabric more divine.

1798–1805   1850, 1926

I wandered lonely as a cloud[1]

I wandered lonely as a cloud
That floats on high o'er vales and hills,
When all at once I saw a crowd,
A host, of golden daffodils;
5   Beside the lake, beneath the trees,
Fluttering and dancing in the breeze.

Continuous as the stars that shine
And twinkle on the milky way,
They stretched in never-ending line
10   Along the margin of a bay:
Ten thousand saw I at a glance,
Tossing their heads in sprightly dance.

The waves beside them danced; but they
Outdid the sparkling waves in glee:—
15   A Poet could not but be gay,

5. Coleridge had gone to the Mediterranean island of
Malta for his health.

1. Compare Dorothy Wordsworth's *Grasmere Journal*, 15
April 1802, page 296.

In such a jocund company:
I gazed—and gazed—but little thought
What wealth the show to me had brought:

20 For oft when on my couch I lie
In vacant or in pensive mood,
They flash upon that inward eye
Which is the bliss of solitude;[2]
And then my heart with pleasure fills,
And dances with the daffodils.

1804/1815   1807/1815

My heart leaps up

My heart leaps up when I behold
    A Rainbow in the sky:
So was it when my life began;
So is it now I am a Man;
5 So be it when I shall grow old,
    Or let me die!
The Child is Father of the Man;
And I could wish my days to be
Bound each to each by natural piety.

1802   1807

Ode: Intimations of Immortality from Recollections of Early Childhood
In a letter from 1814, Wordsworth remarks, "The poem rests entirely on two recollections
of childhood, one that of a splendour in the objects of sense which is passed away, and the
other an indisposition to bend to the law of death as applying to our particular case. A
Reader who has not a vivid recollection of these feelings having existed in his mind cannot
understand that Poem." In 1843 he recalled, "Two years at least passed between the writing
of the four first stanzas and the remaining part. To the attentive and competent reader the
whole sufficiently explains itself; but there may be no harm in adverting here to particular
feelings or *experiences* of my own mind on which the structure of the poem partly rests.
Nothing was more difficult for me in childhood than to admit the notion of death as a state
applicable to my own being. I have said elsewhere—

A simple child,
That lightly draws its breath,
And feels its life in every limb,
What should it know of death!—[*We Are Seven*, 1–4]

But it was not so much from feelings of animal vivacity that my difficulty came as from a sense
of the indomitableness of the Spirit within me. I used to brood over the stories of Enoch and
Elijah, and almost to persuade myself that, whatever might become of others, I should be translated, in something of the same way, to heaven.[1] With a feeling congenial to this, I was often
unable to think of external things as having external existence, and I communed with all that
I saw as something not apart from, but inherent in, my own immaterial nature. Many times

2. Lines 21–22 were composed by Wordsworth's wife. He
thought them the "two best lines," though Coleridge called
them "mental bombast" (*Biographia Literaria*, ch. 22).

1. Old Testament prophets: Enoch did not die, but was tak-
en directly to heaven (Genesis 5.24) and Elijah was carried
to heaven in a chariot of fire (2 Kings 2.11).

5

Our birth is but a sleep and a forgetting:
The Soul that rises with us, our life's Star,°   *the sun*
60   Hath had elsewhere its setting,
        And cometh from afar:
     Not in entire forgetfulness,
     And not in utter nakedness,
But trailing clouds of glory do we come⁵
65   From God, who is our home:
Heaven lies about us in our infancy!
Shades of the prison-house begin to close
     Upon the growing Boy,
But He beholds the light, and whence it flows,
70   He sees it in his joy;
The Youth, who daily farther from the east
     Must travel, still is Nature's Priest,
     And by the vision splendid
     Is on his way attended;
75 At length the Man perceives it die away,
And fade into the light of common day.

6

Earth fills her lap with pleasures of her own;
Yearnings she hath in her own natural kind,
And, even with something of a Mother's mind,
80   And no unworthy aim,
     The homely° Nurse doth all she can   *simple*
To make her Foster-child, her Inmate° Man,   *resident*
     Forget the glories he hath known,
And that imperial palace whence he came.

7

85 Behold the Child among his new-born blisses,
A six years' Darling of a pigmy size!
See, where 'mid work of his own hand he lies,
Fretted by sallies of his mother's kisses,
With light upon him from his father's eyes!
90 See, at his feet, some little plan or chart,
Some fragment from his dream of human life,
Shaped by himself with newly-learned art;
     A wedding or a festival,
     A mourning or a funeral;
95   And this hath now his heart,
And unto this he frames his song:
     Then will he fit his tongue
To dialogues of business, love, or strife;
     But it will not be long
100   Ere this be thrown aside,
     And with new joy and pride

5. Revising a famous line in Thomas Gray's *Elegy Written in a Country Churchyard* (1751): "The paths of glory lead but to the grave."

The little Actor cons another part;
Filling from time to time his "humorous stage"[6]
With all the Persons, down to palsied Age,
105   That Life brings with her in her equipage;
      As if his whole vocation
      Were endless imitation.

8

Thou, whose exterior semblance doth belie
    Thy Soul's immensity;
110   Thou best Philosopher, who yet dost keep
Thy heritage, thou Eye among the blind,
That, deaf and silent, read'st the eternal deep,
Haunted for ever by the eternal mind,—
      Mighty Prophet! Seer blest!
115   On whom those truths do rest,
Which we are toiling all our lives to find,
In darkness lost, the darkness of the grave;
Thou, over whom thy Immortality
Broods like the Day, a Master o'er a Slave,
120   A Presence which is not to be put by;
Thou little Child, yet glorious in the might
Of heaven-born freedom on thy being's height,
Why with such earnest pains dost thou provoke
The years to bring the inevitable yoke,
125   Thus blindly with thy blessedness at strife?
Full soon thy Soul shall have her earthly freight,
And custom lie upon thee with a weight,
Heavy as frost, and deep almost as life!

9

      O joy! that in our embers
130   Is something that doth live,
      That nature yet remembers
      What was so fugitive!
The thought of our past years in me doth breed
Perpetual benediction: not indeed
135   For that which is most worthy to be blest;
Delight and liberty, the simple creed
Of Childhood, whether busy or at rest,
With new-fledged hope still fluttering in his breast:—
      Not for these I raise
140   The song of thanks and praise;
      But for those obstinate questionings
      Of sense and outward things,
      Fallings from us, vanishings;
      Blank misgivings of a Creature
145   Moving about in worlds not realised,°   *seeming unreal*
High instincts before which our mortal Nature

---

6. A phrase from the dedicatory sonnet for Samuel Daniel's *Musophilus* (1599), referring to the different character types of Renaissance drama, defined by their "humors" (natural temperaments).

Did tremble like a guilty Thing surprised:[7]
  But for those first affections,
  Those shadowy recollections,
150   Which, be they what they may,
Are yet the fountain light of all our day,
Are yet a master light of all our seeing;
  Uphold us, cherish, and have power to make
Our noisy years seem moments in the being
155 Of the eternal Silence: truths that wake,
   To perish never;
Which neither listlessness, nor mad endeavour,
   Nor Man nor Boy,
Nor all that is at enmity with joy,
160 Can utterly abolish or destroy!
   Hence in a season of calm weather
   Though inland far we be,
Our Souls have sight of that immortal sea
   Which brought us hither,
165   Can in a moment travel thither,
And see the Children sport upon the shore,
And hear the mighty waters rolling evermore.

10

Then sing, ye Birds, sing, sing a joyous song!
  And let the young Lambs bound
170   As to the tabor's sound!
We in thought will join your throng,
  Ye that pipe and ye that play,
  Ye that through your hearts to-day
  Feel the gladness of the May!
175 What though the radiance which was once so bright
Be now for ever taken from my sight,
  Though nothing can bring back the hour
Of splendour in the grass, of glory in the flower;
  We will grieve not, rather find
180   Strength in what remains behind;
  In the primal sympathy
  Which having been must ever be;
  In the soothing thoughts that spring
  Out of human suffering;
185   In the faith that looks through death,
In years that bring the philosophic mind.

11

And O, ye Fountains, Meadows, Hills, and Groves,
Forebode not any severing of our loves!
Yet in my heart of hearts I feel your might;
190 I only have relinquished one delight
To live beneath your more habitual sway.

---

7. At dawn, the ghost of Hamlet's father "started, like a guilty thing / Upon a fearful summons" and mysteriously vanished (*Hamlet* 1.1.148–49).

I love the Brooks which down their channels fret,
Even more than when I tripped lightly as they;
The innocent brightness of a new-born Day
    Is lovely yet;
195
The Clouds that gather round the setting sun
Do take a sober colouring from an eye
That hath kept watch o'er man's mortality;
Another race hath been, and other palms° are won.   *prizes*
200
Thanks to the human heart by which we live,
Thanks to its tenderness, its joys, and fears,
To me the meanest° flower that blows can give   *humblest*
Thoughts that do often lie too deep for tears.

1802–1804/1815   1807/1815

The Solitary Reaper[1]

Behold her, single in the field,
Yon solitary Highland Lass!
Reaping and singing by herself;
Stop here, or gently pass!
5
Alone she cuts, and binds the grain,
And sings a melancholy strain;
O listen! for the Vale profound
Is overflowing with the sound.

No Nightingale did ever chaunt
10
More welcome notes to weary bands
Of Travellers in some shady haunt,
Among Arabian Sands:
No sweeter voice was ever heard[2]
In spring-time from the Cuckoo-bird,
15
Breaking the silence of the seas
Among the farthest Hebrides.°   *Scottish islands*

Will no one tell me what she sings?—
Perhaps the plaintive numbers flow
For old, unhappy, far-off things,
20
And battles long ago:
Or is it some more humble lay,
Familiar matter of today?
Some natural sorrow, loss, or pain,
That has been, and may be again!

25
Whate'er the theme, the Maiden sang
As if her song could have no ending;
I saw her singing at her work,
And o'er the sickle bending;—
I listen'd till I had my fill.[3]

---

1. Suggested by Wordsworth's reading in manuscript of "a beautiful sentence" in Thomas Wilkinson's *Tours to the British Mountains* (1824): "Passed a female who was reaping alone: she sung in Erse [Scottish Gaelic] as she bended over her sickle; the sweetest human voice I ever heard: her strains were tenderly melancholy, and felt delicious, long after they were heard no more."
2. "A voice so thrilling ne'er was heard" (1836).
3. "I listened, motionless and still" (1820).

30   And, as I mounted up the hill,
      The music in my heart I bore,
      Long after it was heard no more.
1805   1807

Surprized by joy

      Surprized by joy—impatient as the Wind
      I turned to share the transport—Oh! with whom
      But thee, long buried in the silent Tomb,
      That spot which no vicissitude can find?[1]
5   Love, faithful love, recalled thee to my mind—
      But how could I forget thee? Through what power,
      Even for the least division of an hour,
      Have I been so beguiled as to be blind
      To my most grievous loss!—That thought's return
10   Was the worst pang that sorrow ever bore,
      Save one, one only, when I stood forlorn,
      Knowing my heart's best treasure was no more;
      That neither present time, nor years unborn
      Could to my sight that heavenly face restore.
1812–1815   1815

Dorothy Wordsworth
1771–1855

Dorothy Wordsworth would probably be surprised to see herself in our pages, for unlike just about everyone else here, she did not think of herself primarily as a writer, and she did not aspire to publication. Her brother William did put a few of her poems in his volumes (including *Address to a Child* and *Floating Island*), specifying them as "By my Sister"—an apt credit, for this was Dorothy's own chief self-identification. When friends urged her to publish her remarkable account of her community's response to a local tragedy (*George and Sarah Green*, 1808), she protested that she had written it only at her brother's urging and only as a local record; "I should detest the idea of setting myself as an Author," she said. Similar encouragement for her journals of her tours of Scotland and Europe was similarly rebuffed, Dorothy insisting that she had written only for family and friends. When she began her Grasmere journal, she told herself that she was writing to give William "pleasure."

Born in the Lake District of England in 1771, Dorothy Wordsworth lived happily there with her four brothers until 1778, when their mother died. Their father, who was often absent on business, felt unable to sustain the household and sent the boys away to school and Dorothy to live with a series of distant relatives, in situations ranging from happy to bleak. She saw her brothers rarely and especially missed William, with whom she was closest, less than two years his junior. As soon as they were reunited in 1787, they longed to have a home together, and in 1795, with the advantage of William's legacy from a college friend, they were able to realize this dream. They first lived in southwest England, in Dorset, as a quasi-family with a friend's young son as their ward. Moving to Alfoxden in 1797 to be near Samuel Taylor Coleridge, they became acquainted with Charles and Mary Lamb and Robert Southey. During

---

1. The Wordsworths' daughter Catherine, who died in 1812 at age 3.

their summer tour of the Wye valley in 1798, William wrote *Tintern Abbey* with its homage to Dorothy's companionship and her continuing inspiration to him. They spent the next winter miserably in Goslar, Germany (following Coleridge there on a scheme to learn the language); after they returned to England, they settled at the end of 1799 in Grasmere, in their beloved native Lake District, where they remained together for the rest of their lives.

Dorothy began her Grasmere journal in May 1800, just as William was beginning to court their childhood friend, Mary Hutchinson, and she left off at the beginning of 1803, a few months after Mary and William returned from their honeymoon. There was never any question about her remaining in the household: Mary married *them*. A beloved aunt to their children, Dorothy was really more a third parent. She not only shared the domestic labors but functioned for William as companion, encourager, sounding board, secretary, and (along with Mary) perpetual transcriber of his drafts into fair-copy. In 1829 she was stricken by the first in a series of devastating illnesses, with relapses and new afflictions occurring over the next six years, each event wracking her with pain and leaving her further debilitated. By 1835 it was clear that her temperament and mental acuity were also afflicted, a pre-senile dementia akin to Alzheimer's disease. Cared for with affection by her family, she lived a kind of invalid half-life, with lucid intervals, for the next twenty years, surviving her brother by five.

This demise is especially poignant, given the intelligence, sensitivity, and physical vitality with which she had impressed everyone. It was not until the end of the nineteenth century that her poems and journals were collected and published, and for a long time the journals were read chiefly for information about Coleridge, William, and the circumstances of the poems he wrote between 1798 and 1802. Placed alongside these poems, however, some of Dorothy's passages suggest that William may have been inspired as much by her language as by events and appearances in the external world; and recently, Dorothy Wordsworth has been taken seriously as a writer in her own right. Her Grasmere journal is a fascinating chronicle of early nineteenth-century life in the Lake District—full of brilliantly detailed descriptions of nature (admired by Virginia Woolf), accounts of domestic life and household labors, precise observations of the people, the social textures and economic distresses of rural England. In the cast of characters that cross her pages— children, neighbors, local laborers, tinkers and itinerants, beggars and vagrants, abandoned wives and mothers, a leech-gatherer, discharged and often injured soldiers, sailors, and veterans— Dorothy Wordsworth captures, as much as her brother hoped his poetry would, the "language really used by men" (and women). In addition to journals, records of tours, numerous letters, and ceaseless secretarial work and manuscript transcription for William, Dorothy wrote about thirty poems. Composed sporadically from 1805 to 1840, these often allude to or converse with her brother's poetry, sometimes marking different investments of imagination, alternative views of the world they share, or a different sensibility—one less solitary and more social in orientation, less visionary than domestic in idiom, and more self-effacing and self-discrediting in character, especially about the vocation and practice of writing poetry.

A selection from Dorothy Wordsworth's journal appears in Perspectives: The Abolition of Slavery and the Slave Trade, page 131.

Address to a Child
During a boisterous Winter Evening in a high wind[1]

What way does the wind come? what way does he go?
He rides over the water and over the snow,
Through wood, and through vale; and o'er rocky height

---

1. Written in 1806 for nephew Johnny; see her comment in late 1805: "what a fearful thing a windy night is now at our house! I am too often haunted with dreadful images of Shipwrecks and the Sea when I am in bed and hear a stormy wind"—evoking the loss of her beloved brother John in a shipwreck in 1805. Published unsigned in William's *Poems*, 1815; our text follows this version, with significant variants from the ms. ("An address to a Child in a high wind") indicated.

Which the goat cannot climb takes his sounding flight.[2]
5   He tosses about in every bare tree,
As, if you look up you plainly may see
But how he will come, and whither he goes
There's never a Scholar in England knows.

He will suddenly stop in a cunning nook
10   And rings a sharp larum:°—but if you should look   *call to arms*
There's nothing to see but a cushion of snow,
Round as a pillow and whiter than milk
And softer than if it were cover'd with silk.

Sometimes he'll hide in the cave of a rock;
15   Then whistle as shrill as the buzzard cock;
—Yet seek him and what shall you find in his place
Nothing but silence and empty space
Save in a corner a heap of dry leaves
That he's left for a bed for beggars or thieves.

20   As soon as 'tis daylight tomorrow with me
You shall go to the orchard & then you will see
That he has been there, & made a great rout,°   *debacle*
And cracked the branches, & strew'd them about:
Heaven grant that he spare but that one upright twig
25   That look'd up at the sky so proud & so big
All last summer, as well you know
Studded with apples, a beautiful shew!

Hark! over the roof he makes a pause
And growls as if he would fix his claws
30   Right in the slates, and with a huge rattle
Drive them down like men in a battle.
—But let him range round; he does us no harm
We build up the fire; we're snug and warm,
Untouch'd by his breath see the candle shines bright,
35   And burns with a clear and steady light;
Books have we to read,—hush! that half-stifled knell,
Methinks 'tis the sound of the eight o'clock bell.[3]

Come, now we'll to bed, and when we are there
He may work his own will, & what shall we care.
40   He may knock at the door—we'll not let him in
May drive at the windows—we'll laugh at his din
Let him seek his own home wherever it be
Here's a cozy warm house for Edward and me.[4]

1806   1815

---

2. Manuscript: "Through the valley, and over the hill / And roars as loud as a thundering Mill" (waterfall where a mill is located).
3. Manuscript lines: "Old Madam has brought us plenty of coals / And the Glazier has closed up all the holes / In

every window that Johnny broke / And the walls are tighter than Molly's new cloak."
4. In the manuscript, the synonym *canny* is used instead of *cozy*; Edward is a pseudonym to protect Johnny's privacy.

Thoughts on My Sick-bed[1]

And has the remnant of my life
Been pilfered of this sunny Spring?
And have its own prelusive sounds
Touched in my heart no echoing string?

5   Ah! say not so—the hidden life
Couchant° within this feeble frame   *lying down*
Hath been enriched by kindred gifts,
That, undesired, unsought-for, came

With joyful heart in youthful days
10   When fresh each season in its Round
I welcomed the earliest Celandine[2]
Glittering upon the mossy ground;

With busy eyes I pierced the lane
In quest of known and *un*known things,
15   —The primrose a lamp on its fortress rock,
The silent butterfly spreading its wings,

The violet betrayed by its noiseless breath,
The daffodil dancing in the breeze,
The carolling thrush, on his naked perch,
20   Towering above the budding trees.[3]

Our cottage-hearth no longer our home,
Companions of Nature were we,
The Stirring, the Still, the Loquacious, the Mute—
To all we gave our sympathy.

25   Yet never in those careless days
When spring-time in rock, field, or bower
Was but a fountain of earthly hope
A promise of fruits & the *splendid* flower.[4]

No! then I never felt a bliss
30   That might with *that* compare
Which, piercing to my couch of rest,
Came on the vernal air.

When loving Friends an offering brought,
The first flowers of the year,
35   Culled from the precincts of our home,
From nooks to Memory dear.[5]

---

1. Written in spring 1832, by which time Dorothy was stricken with a series of debilitating illnesses.
2. A resilient flower, addressed by William in *The Small Celandine* (1804; 1807) as an emblem of inevitable old age.
3. A bouquet of loaded references to William's poems: *The Primrose of the Rock* (c. 1831, about a flower on the Grasmere-Rydal road); *To a Butterfly* ("Stay near me") and *To a Butterfly* ("I've watched you") (both 1802; 1807); *Song* ("*She dwelt among th'untrodden ways*") ("a violet by a mossy stone, half hidden from the eye"); *I wandered lonely as a cloud* ("golden daffodils . . . dancing in the breeze").
4. W. Wordsworth's "Intimations" *Ode*: "Though nothing can bring back the hour / Of splendour in the grass, of glory in the flower; / We will grieve not, rather find / Strength in what remains behind" (177–80).
5. "Intimations" *Ode*: "The fulness of your bliss, I feel—I feel it all. / O evil day! if I were sullen / While Earth herself is adorning, / This sweet May-morning, / And the Children are culling / On every side, / In a thousand valleys far and wide, / Fresh flowers" (41–48).

With some sad thoughts the work was done,[6]
Unprompted and unbidden,
But joy it brought to my *hidden* life,
40   To consciousness no longer hidden.

I felt a Power unfelt before,
Controlling weakness, languor, pain;
It bore me to the Terrace walk
I trod the Hills again;—

45   No prisoner in this lonely room,
I *saw* the green Banks of the Wye,
Recalling thy prophetic words,
Bard, Brother, Friend from infancy![7]

No need of motion, or of strength,[8]
50   Or even the breathing air:
—I thought of Nature's loveliest scenes;
And with Memory I was there.

1832

When Shall I Tread Your Garden Path?[1]

When shall I tread your garden path?
Or climb your sheltering hill?
When shall I wander, free as air,
And track the foaming rill?

5   A prisoner on my pillowed couch
Five years in feebleness I've lain,
Oh! shall I e'er with vigorous step
Travel the hills again?

To Mr Carter DW
Novr 11—1835

from The Grasmere Journals

[HOME ALONE]

May 14 1800 [*Wednesday*]. Wm and John set off into Yorkshire[1] after dinner at 1/2 past 2 o'clock—cold pork in their pockets. I left them at the turning of the Low-wood bay under the trees. My heart was so full that I could hardly speak to W when I gave him a farewell kiss. I sate a long time upon a stone at the margin of the lake, & after a flood of tears my heart was easier. The lake looked to me I knew not why dull and melancholy, the weltering on the shores seemed a heavy sound. I walked as long as I could amongst the stones of the shore. The wood rich in flowers. A beautiful yellow, palish yellow flower, that looked thick round & double, and smelt very sweet—I

---

6. W. Wordsworth's *Lines Written in Early Spring* ("I sate reclined, / In that sweet mood when pleasant thoughts / Bring sad thoughts to the mind") and *Three Years She Grew* ("Thus nature spake—The work was done— / How soon my Lucy's race was run! / She died").
7. See *Tintern Abbey*, especially 111ff.
8. W. Wordsworth's *A slumber did my spirit seal* ("No

motion has she now, no force").
1. Addressed to John Carter, William's assistant in the stamp office and their handyman for more than 40 years.
1. William and younger brother John, who lived with them at Dove Cottage in 1800; the trip through Yorkshire was to visit childhood friend Mary Hutchinson, whom William would marry in October 1802.

supposed it was a ranunculus—Crowfoot, the grassy-leaved Rabbit-toothed white flower, strawberries, Geranium—scentless violet, anemones two kinds, orchises, primroses. The heckberry very beautiful. * * * Met a blind man, driving a very large beautiful Bull & a cow—he walked with two sticks. Came home by Clappersgate. The valley very green, many sweet views up to Rydale head when I could juggle away the fine houses, but they disturbed me even more than when I have been happier—one beautiful view of the Bridge, without Sir Michaels.[2] Sate down very often, tho' it was cold. I resolved to write a journal of the time till W & J return, and I set about keeping my resolve because I will not quarrel with myself, & because I shall give Wm Pleasure by it when he comes home again. At Rydale a woman of the village, stout & well dressed, begged a halfpenny—she had never she said done it before, but these hard times—Arrived at home with a bad head-ach, set some slips of privett. The evening cold had a fire—my face now flame-coloured. It is nine o'clock. I shall soon go to bed. A young woman begged at the door—she had come from Manchester on Sunday morn with two shillings & a slip of paper which she supposed a Bank note—it was a cheat. She had buried her husband & three children within a year & a half—all in one grave—burying very dear—paupers all put in one place—20 shillings paid for as much ground as will bury a man—a stone to be put over it or the right will be lost—11/6 each time the ground is opened.[3] Oh! that I had a letter from William!

Sunday [*18th.*] Went to church, slight showers, a cold air. The mountains from this window look much greener & I think the valley is more green than ever. The corn begins to shew itself. The ashes are still bare. * * * A little girl from Coniston came to beg. She had lain out all night—her step-mother had turned her out of doors.

[THE GRASMERE MAILMAN]

Monday Morning 8th February 1802. It was very windy & rained very hard all the morning. William worked at his poem & I read a little in Lessing and the Grammar.[4] A chaise came past to fetch Ellis the Carrier who had hurt his head. After dinner (i.e. we set off at about 1/2 past 4) we went towards Rydale[5] for letters. It was a cold "*Cauld Clash*"—the Rain had been so cold that it hardly melted the snow. We stopped at Park's to get some straw in William's shoes. The young mother was sitting by a bright wood fire with her youngest child upon her lap & the other two sate on each side of the chimney. The light of the fire made them a beautiful sight, with their innocent countenances, their rosy cheeks & glossy curling hair. We sate & talked about poor Ellis, and our journey over the Hawes. It had been reported that we came over in the night. Willy told us of 3 men who were once lost in crossing that way in the night, they had carried a lantern with them—the lantern went out at the Tarn[6] & they all perished. Willy had seen their cloaks drying at the public house in Patterdale[7] the day before their funeral. We walked on very wet through the clashy cold roads in bad spirits at the idea of having to go as far as Rydale, but

2. Rydal Hall, the home of Sir Michael le Fleming; in 1813, the Wordsworth household would move to Rydal Mount, the substantial residence next door, where they lived the rest of their lives.
3. Eleven shillings, 6 pence; dear: expensive. William and Dorothy lived modestly but comfortably on £130–40 a year.
4. William's poem is *The Pedlar*, abandoned as an independent piece and later incorporated into the first part of Book 1 of his long poem, *The Excursion* (1814). Lessing (1729–1781) is a German dramatist, art theorist, and critic; "the Grammar" is most likely a German grammar (Dorothy had learned German in Germany).
5. About a mile away.
6. Mountain lake.
7. An inn in the village several miles away, reached by treacherous pass over the high mountains.

before we had come again to the shore of the Lake, we met our patient, bow-bent Friend with his little wooden box at his Back. "Where are you going?" said he. "To Rydale for letters.—I have two for you in my Box." We lifted up the lid & there they lay. Poor Fellow, he straddled & pushed on with all his might but we soon outstripped him far away when we had turned back with our letters. We were very thankful that we had not to go on, for we should have been sadly tired. In thinking of this I could not help comparing lots with him! He goes at that slow pace every morning, & after having wrought a hard days work returns at night, however weary he may be, takes it all quietly, & though perhaps he neither feels thankfulness, nor pleasure when he eats his supper, & has no luxury to look forward to but falling asleep in bed, yet I daresay he neither murmurs nor thinks it hard. He seems mechanized to labour.

[A Vision of the Moon]

[18 March 1802] * * * As we came along Ambleside vale in the twilight—it was a grave evening—there was something in the air that compelled me to serious thought—the hills were large, closed in by the sky. It was nearly dark * * * night was come on & the moon was overcast. But as I climbed Moss the moon came out from behind a Mountain Mass of Black clouds—O the unutterable darkness of the sky & the Earth below the Moon! & the glorious brightness of the moon itself! There was a vivid sparkling streak of light at this end of Rydale water but the rest was very dark & Loughrigg fell and Silver How were white & bright as if they were covered with hoar frost.[8] The moon retired again & appeared & disappeared several times before I reached home. Once there was no moonlight to be seen but upon the Island house & the promontory of the Island where it stands, "That needs must be a holy place" &c—&c.[9] I had many many exquisite feelings and when I saw this lowly Building in the waters among the dark & lofty hills, with that bright soft light upon it—it made me more than half a poet. I was tired when I reached home. I could not sit down to reading & tried to write verses but alas! I gave up expecting William & went soon to bed. Fletcher's carts came home late.[1]

[A Field of Daffodils]

Thursday 15th. [April 1802] * * * When we were in the woods beyond Gowbarrow[2] park we saw a few daffodils close to the water side, we fancied that the lake had floated the seeds ashore & that the little colony had so sprung up—But as we went along there were more & yet more & at last under the boughs of the trees, we saw that there was a long belt of them along the shore, about the breadth of a country turnpike road.[3] I never saw daffodils so beautiful they grew among the mossy stones about & about them, some rested their heads upon these stones as on a pillow for weariness & the rest tossed & reeled & danced & seemed as if they verily laughed with the wind that blew upon them over the Lake, they looked so gay ever glancing ever changing. This wind blew directly over the lake to them. There was here & there a little knot & a few stragglers

---

8. The places mentioned are White Moss Common, Rydale water (a lake nearby Grasmere Lake and the Common), and two peaks to the south of these lakes, Loughrigg and Silver How.
9. Perhaps recalling an early draft of Coleridge's *Kubla Khan*, line 14, or William's feeling in *Home at Grasmere* that "dwellers in this holy place / Must need themselves

be hallow'd" (366–67).
1. William's ride, via the mail carrier.
2. Several miles away in another part of the Lake district, near Patterdale on Ullswater.
3. Dorothy erased the next words, "the end we did not see." Cf. W. Wordsworth's poem, *I wandered lonely as a cloud*: "They stretched in never-ending line."

a few yards higher up but they were so few as not to disturb the simplicity & unity & life of that one busy highway. We rested again & again. The Bays were stormy, & we heard the waves at different distances and in the middle of the water like the Sea.

[A BEGGAR WOMAN FROM COCKERMOUTH[4]]

Tuesday 4th May [1802]. William had slept pretty well & though he went to bed nervous & jaded in the extreme he rose refreshed. I wrote the Leech Gatherer[5] for him which he had begun the night before & of which he wrote several stanzas in bed this Monday morning. It was very hot, we called at Mr Simpson's door as we passed but did not go in. We rested several times by the way, read & repeated the Leech Gatherer. We were almost melted before we were at the top of the hill. * * * William & I ate a Luncheon, then went on towards the Waterfall. It is a glorious wild solitude under that lofty purple crag. It stood upright by itself. Its own self and its shadow below, one mass—all else was sunshine. We went on further. A Bird at the top of the crags was flying round & round & looked in thinness & transparency, shape & motion, like a moth. We climbed the hill but looked in vain for a shade except at the foot of the great waterfall, & there we did not like to stay on account of the loose stones above our heads. We came down & rested upon a moss covered Rock, rising out of the bed of the River. There we lay ate our dinner & stayed there till about 4 o clock or later. Wm & C[6] repeated & read verses. I drank a little Brandy & water & was in Heaven. The Stags horn is very beautiful & fresh springing upon the fells. Mountain ashes, green. * * * On the Rays we met a woman with 2 little girls one in her arms the other about 4 years old walking by her side, a pretty little thing, but half starved. She had on a pair of slippers that had belonged to some gentlemans child, down at the heels it was not easy to keep them on but, poor thing! young as she was, she walked carefully with them. Alas too young for such cares & such travels. The Mother when we accosted her told us that her husband had left her & gone off with another woman & how she "*pursued*" them. Then her fury kindled & her eyes rolled about. She changed again to tears. She was a Cockermouth woman 30 years of age—a child at Cockermouth when I was. I was moved & gave her a shilling—I believe 6[d] more than I ought to have given.[7] We had the crescent moon with the "auld moon in her arms."[8] We rested often—always upon the Bridges. Reached home at about 10 o clock.

[THE CIRCUMSTANCES OF "COMPOSED UPON WESTMINISTER BRIDGE"[9]]

[*27 July 1802*] * * * After various troubles & disasters we left London on Saturday morning at 1/2 past 5 or 6. * * * we mounted the Dover Coach at Charing Cross. It was a beautiful morning. The City, St Pauls, with the River & a multitude of little Boats, made a most beautiful sight as we crossed Westminster Bridge. The houses were not overhung by their cloud of smoke & they were spread out endlessly, yet the sun shone

4. The town where Dorothy and her brothers were born and spent their childhood before the break-up of the household.
5. The early title for *Resolution and Independence*.
6. Coleridge, whom they met up with on their excursion.
7. Six pence; Dorothy inserted "30 years of age—a child at Cockermouth when I was" to explain the generosity.
8. A line from *Sir Patrick Spence*, also quoted by Coleridge in his epigraph for *Dejection: An Ode*.

9. See page 234; William and Dorothy are on their way to Calais, France, sailing from Dover, to settle affairs with Annette Vallon and her daughter by William, Caroline, prior to William's marriage to Mary Hutchinson in October. The City is Westminster, a district of London where Parliament, Westminster Abbey, and Buckingham Palace are located; St. Paul's is the chief Anglican church. Westminster Bridge crosses the Thames river.

so brightly with such a pure light that there was even something like the purity of one of nature's own grand Spectacles.

[The Circumstances of "It is a beauteous Evening"[1]]

[1 August 1802] * * * We walked by the sea-shore almost every Evening with Annette & Caroline or Wm & I alone.[2] * * * there was always light, & life, & joy upon the Sea.—One night, though, I shall never forget. The day had been very hot, & William & I walked alone together upon the pier—the sea was gloomy for there was a blackness over all the sky except when it was overspread with lightning which often revealed to us a distant vessel. Near us the waves roared & broke against the pier, & as they broke & as they travelled towards us, they were interfused with greenish fiery light. The more distant sea always black & gloomy. It was also beautiful on the calm hot night to see the little Boats row out of harbour with wings of fire & the sail boats with the fiery track which they cut as they went along & which closed up after them with a hundred thousand sparkles balls shootings, & streams of glowworm light. Caroline was delighted.

[The Household in Winter, with William's New Wife. Gingerbread]

[25 December 1802] * * * It is today Christmas-day Saturday 25th December 1802. I am 31 years of age.—It is a dull frosty day. * * *

Tuesday January 11th [1803] A very cold day. Wm promised me he would rise as soon as I had carried him his Breakfast but he lay in bed till between 12 & one. We talked of walking, but the blackness of the Cold made us slow to put forward & we did not walk at all. Mary read the Prologue to Chaucer's tales to me, in the morning William was working at his poem to C.[3] Letter from Keswick & from Taylor on Wm's marriage. C poorly, in bad spirits. Canaries.[4] Before tea I sate 2 hours in the parlour—read part of The Knight's Tale with exquisite delight. Since Tea Mary has been down stairs copying out Italian poems for Stuart. Wm has been working beside me, & here ends this imperfect summary. I will take a nice Calais Book[5] & will for the future write regularly &, if I can legibly, so much for this my resolution on Tuesday night, January 11th 1803. Now I am going to take Tapioca for my supper, & Mary an Egg. William some cold mutton—his poor chest is tired.

Wednesday 12th. Very cold, & cold all the week.

Sunday the 16th. Intensely cold. Wm had a fancy for some ginger-bread I put on Molly's Cloak & my Spenser,[6] and we walked towards Matthew Newtons.[7] I went into the house. The blind Man & his Wife & Sister were sitting by the fire, all dressed very clean in their Sunday's Clothes, the sister reading. They took their little stock of gingerbread out of the cubboard & I bought 6 pennyworth. They were so grateful when I paid them for it that I could not find it in my heart to tell them we were going to make Gingerbread ourselves. I had asked them if they had no thick "No" answered Matthew "there was none on Friday but we'll endeavour to get some." The next Day the woman came just when we were baking & we bought 2 pennyworth.

---

1. See William's sonnet, page 235.
2. Without Annette, that is.
3. The Prelude, known during William's lifetime as Poem to Coleridge, his addressee; The Knight's Tale is one of Chaucer's Canterbury Tales.
4. Canary Islands, where Coleridge hoped to go for his

health.
5. A blank notebook purchased in Calais; Dorothy did not continue her journal.
6. Heavy overcoat.
7. A gingerbread shop in Grasmere.

==+ PERSPECTIVES +==
The Sublime, the Beautiful, and the Picturesque

Touring Scotland with William and Coleridge in 1803, Dorothy Wordsworth recorded in her journal an encounter at the famous destination of Cora Linn, the Falls of the River Clyde:

> We sat upon a bench, placed for the sake of one of these views, whence we looked down upon the waterfall, and over the open country, and saw a ruined tower (called Wallace's Tower), which stands at a very little distance from the fall, and is an interesting object. A lady and gentleman, more expeditious tourists than we, came to the spot; they left us at the seat, and we found them again at another station above the Falls. C., who is always good-natured enough to enter into conversation with anybody whom he meets in his way, began to talk with the gentleman, who observed that it was a *"majestic* waterfall." Coleridge was delighted with the accuracy of the epithet, particularly as he had been settling in his own mind the precise meaning of the words grand, majestic, sublime, etc., and had discussed the subject with Wm. at some length the day before. "Yes sir," says Coleridge, "it *is* a majestic waterfall." "Sublime and beautiful," replied his friend. Poor C. could make no answer, and, not very desirous to continue the conversation, came to us and related the story, laughing heartily.

More than a decade later Coleridge inserted the episode in one of his own essays, *On the Principles of Genial Criticism:* "Many years ago, the writer, in company with an accidental party of travelers, was gazing on a cataract of great height, breadth, and impetuosity, the summit of which appeared to blend with the sky and clouds, while the lower part was hidden by rocks and trees, and, on his observing, that it was, in the strictest sense of the word, a sublime object, a lady present assented with warmth to the remark, adding—"Yes! and it is not only sublime, but beautiful and absolutely pretty." The joke in both versions is the indifference of his tourist interlocutor to distinctions that the philosopher wishes to make "precise." The published text, by dispensing with "majestic," focuses it more finely on the couple of "sublime" and "beautiful." By transposing the respondent from male to female Coleridge invidiously genders the contrast between philosophic rigor and casual conversation: "pretty," a condescending term, made still more ludicrously inappropriate by conjunction with the force of "absolutely," marks the distance of this "warm" woman from intellectual pursuits.

And yet, as his laughter in the first version suggests, the joke tells against Coleridge too, for trying to demarcate terms that inevitably implicated one another and gained currency through the easy looseness of their application. The concept of the *beautiful* had a long pedigree, whether reaching back to the Platonic identification of the beautiful with the true and the good or merely characterizing that which is pleasing to the senses. The concept of the *sublime* derived from the first-century rhetorician Longinus, whose treatise *Peri Hupsous,* rediscovered in the Renaissance, was variously translated into English in the seventeenth century as *Of the Height of Eloquence* and *Of the Loftiness or Elegancy of Speech* and into French by Boileau as *Du Sublime* (1674). As the English titles suggest, the term initially characterized literary style, where the sublime was understood as "the echo of a great soul," but its use rapidly spread to cover those features of landscape that inspired profound sensations. The third key term, the *picturesque,* was the most recent and problematic; absent from both versions of Coleridge's encounter, it saturates Dorothy's journal entry and motivates the whole.

In its most general signification meaning "that which is suitable for painting," the picturesque carried more specific qualities. As early as 1748, in his Spenserian *Castle of Indolence,* James Thomson identified the painters whose works were to influence British representations of landscape for decades to come: "Whate'er *Lorrain* light-touched with softening Hue, / Or

Thomas Rowlandson, *Dr. Syntax Sketching by the Lake,* from *The Tour of Dr. Syntax in Search of the Picturesque,* 1812. The first issue of Rudolf Ackermann's *Poetical Magazine* contained *The Schoolmaster's Tour,* a couplet satire written by William Combe (1749–1823) and illustrated by Thomas Rowlandson (1756–1827). The pedantic Dr. Syntax and the caricatures proved so popular that in 1812 Ackermann published *Doctor Syntax in Search of the Picturesque,* which was followed by *Doctor Syntax in Search of Consolation* (1820) and yet a further sequel, *Doctor Syntax in Search of a Wife* (1821). Dr. Syntax, shown here sketching near Keswick in this plate, is shortly to be thrown into the lake by his carelessly grazing horse.

savage *Rosa* dash'd, or learned *Poussin* drew" (I.38). Connoisseurs with tastes formed on the seventeenth-century artists Claude Lorrain, Salvator Rosa, Nicolas Poussin and his brother Gaspard Dughet sought in nature the compositions and colors they knew from art, generating an endlessly oscillating loop between the two realms. If picturesque nature served as a counter-aesthetic to neoclassical correctness and regularity, to the proprieties of social man, it was always in danger of revealing itself as just another form of artifice.

Before that self-defeating moment was manifest, however, the concept of the picturesque animated several fields. As a quality said to inhere in the world, it fueled the search for it, substantially contributing to the contemporary transformation of travel into touring and tourism. The picturesque traveler became a recognized type, equipped with his Claude glass—a folding pocket mirror tinted brown, the preeminent color of the picturesque, that enabled the viewer to frame the scene by turning his back on it, to look at its composed reflection rather than directly. Tinted glasses were also popular, making it possible to alter the color balance of the viewed scene into cool morning or warm evening hues. Remote spots such as Wales and Scotland drew travelers such as the Wordsworths and Coleridge in expeditions codified and publicized in guidebooks, spawning an industry of roads, lodgings, transportation, and local agents. Each particular spot, moreover, soon developed a favored observation point, the place from which the attraction, be it mountain, gorge, valley, or castle, could be best appreciated.

Dorothy's journal entry is replete with the material trappings that accompanied the nexus of the sublime, the beautiful, and the picturesque. The visit to Cora Linn is only the first testimony to the social power of this discourse. The "bench, placed for the sake of one of these views," marks the careful management of the scene—the analogy between landscape viewing and stage sets is recurrent in the period—and the "ruined tower (called Wallace's Tower) . . . an interesting

Joseph Mallord William Turner, *The Passage of the St. Gothard,* 1804. This large watercolor, over 3 feet high by 2 feet wide, stems from the sketchbooks Turner (1775–1851) made on his first trip to the Continent in 1802 during the Peace of Amiens. The craggy Alpine scene, dwarfing the pack animals, their path disappearing into the chasm obscured by the rising cloud, exemplifies the romantic sublime. John Constable (1776–1837), his fellow artist, observed years later of Turner's developed style: Turner "seems to paint with tinted steam, so evanescent, and so airy."

object" furnishes the virtually indispensable prompt to ruminations on personal and historical mutability. To undertake the tour in which Cora Linn prominently figures signaled participation in contemporary aesthetic discourse and the possession of the leisure (and usually the means) to realize it for oneself. Access to the experience depended on the relations of property: in this public space, one needed to follow the paths provided by the landlord, who required remuneration for the privilege; when the famous spot stood on a nobleman's estate, access required the appearance of gentility, and the senior servant who showed one round expected a tip for the favor, such gratuities being among the cherished perquisites of his position. Major theorists of the picturesque, such as Uvedale Price (*Essays on the Picturesque,* 1794) and his friend and neighboring squire Richard Payne Knight (*Analytical Inquiry into the Principles of Taste,* 1805), were substantial landowners who transformed their estates according to their aesthetic principles.

Inexact as the relations between the sublime, the beautiful, and the picturesque might be in common parlance, and infinitely repetitive as their combinations and permutations might become—for example, the composer Charles Avison's characterization of the rugged landscape of the Lake District, cited by Gilpin, "Here is beauty indeed—Beauty lying in the lap of Horrour!"—the very buzzing confusion of this discourse attests to the energy of a phenomenon at once pictorial, literary, cultural, economic, and psychological. The selections that follow illustrate its features and its staying power.

→← ⊨⊹⊒ →←

Edmund Burke
1729–1797

Edmund Burke was not yet thirty when A *Philosophical Enquiry into the Origin of Our Ideas of the Sublime and Beautiful* appeared in 1757. Educated at Trinity College, Dublin, he entered the Middle Temple in 1750 to study law. Publication was a means to attract attention and the patronage he needed; he wrote for the *Annual Register*, became a founding member of the Club surrounding Dr. Johnson, and by 1765 attained the post of secretary to the Whig prime minister, the Marquis of Rockingham, and entered Parliament. The *Enquiry* set the terms of subsequent discussion, less by subtlety than by the rhetorical brilliance that distinguished Burke's political career. From the outset Burke's bold formulations provoked resistance from more cautious thinkers; Payne Knight noticed that Burke's derivation of sublimity from "whatever is fitted in any sort to excite the ideas of pain, and danger" required the vague qualification of "at certain distances, and with certain modifications," left unspecified. He was equally skeptical of Burke's linkage of astonishment and the sublime:

> If during this period [of Burke's celebrated indictment of Warren Hastings and the abuses of the East India Company] he had walked up St. James's Street without his breeches, it would have occasioned great and universal *astonishment*; and if he had, at the same time, carried a loaded blunderbuss in his hands, the astonishment would have been mixed with no small portion of terror; but I do not believe that the unified effects of these two power-ful passions would have produced any sensation approaching to sublime, even in the breast of those who had the strongest sense of self-preservation.

Funny as this riposte is, and exemplary of the exuberant *ad hominem* character of eighteenth-century debate, it misses the point. If Burke can be dismayingly positivist in connecting physi-cal objects to mental states, he is far subtler than Knight is here about the mind's capacity to respond to its own fantasies, figures, and fictions.

For more on Burke, see the entry in Perspectives: The Rights of Man and the Revolution Controversy (page 47).

from A Philosophical Enquiry into the Origin of Our Ideas of the Sublime and Beautiful
Of the Sublime

Whatever is fitted in any sort to excite the ideas of pain and danger, that is to say, whatever is in any sort terrible, or is conversant about terrible objects, or operates in a manner analogous to terror, is a source of the *sublime;* that is, it is productive of the strongest emotion which the mind is capable of feeling. I say the strongest emotion, because I am satisfied the ideas of pain are much more powerful than those which enter on the part of pleasure. Without all doubt, the torments which we may be made to suffer, are much greater in their effect on the body and mind, than any pleasures which the most learned voluptuary could suggest, or than the liveliest imagination, and the most sound and exquisitely sensible body, could enjoy. Nay I am in great doubt whether any man could be found who would earn a life of the most perfect sat-isfaction, at the price of ending it in the torments, which justice inflicted in a few hours on the late unfortunate regicide in France.[1] But as pain is stronger in its opera-tion than pleasure, so death is in general a much more affecting idea than pain; because there are very few pains, however exquisite, which are not preferred to

---

1. Robert-François Damiens was publicly tortured and executed by quartering in March 1757 for having attempted to take the life of Louis XV.

Benjamin Robert Haydon, *Study after the Elgin Marbles,* from *Annals of the Fine Arts,* 1819. The painter Benjamin Haydon (1786–1846), Keats's friend, tirelessly promoted the Elgin Marbles (see note to Keats's *On Seeing the Elgin Marbles,* page 425), here in the periodical he dominated, the *Annals of the Fine Arts,* and elsewhere. In this "comparison between the Venetian Horse's Head, said to be by Lysippus, and the Horse's Head from the Parthenon, in the Elgin Collection," the realism and vigor of the Parthenon horse, with his prominent eye and flaring nostril, recall the passage from Job that Burke had cited as an instance of the sublime (see page 305). Haydon proclaimed that "in as much as the Elgin Horse's head differs in form and is superior to the head of Lysippus so do the rest of the Elgin marbles differ from and are superior to all other statues of this, and every subsequent age."

death; nay, what generally makes pain itself, if I may say so, more painful, is, that it is considered as an emissary of this king of terrors. When danger or pain press too nearly, they are incapable of giving any delight, and are simply terrible; but at certain distances, and with certain modifications, they may be, and they are delightful, as we every day experience. The cause of this I shall endeavour to investigate hereafter.

Of the passion caused by the Sublime

The passion caused by the great and sublime in *nature,* when those causes operate most powerfully, is astonishment; and astonishment is that state of the soul, in which all its motions are suspended, with some degree of horror. In this case the mind is so entirely filled with its object, that it cannot entertain any other, nor by consequence reason on that object which employs it. Hence arises the great power of the sublime, that, far from being produced by them, it anticipates our reasonings, and hurries us on by an irresistible force. Astonishment, as I have said, is the effect of the sublime in its highest degree; the inferior effects are admiration, reverence, and respect.

from *Terror*

No passion so effectually robs the mind of all its powers of acting and reasoning as fear. For fear being an apprehension of pain or death, it operates in a manner that resembles actual pain. Whatever therefore is terrible, with regard to sight, is sublime too, whether this cause of terror be endued with greatness of dimensions or not; for it is impossible to look on any thing as trifling, or contemptible, that may be dangerous.

from *Obscurity*

To make any thing very terrible, obscurity seems in general to be necessary. When we know the full extent of any danger, when we can accustom our eyes to it, a great deal of the apprehension vanishes. Every one will be sensible of this, who considers how greatly night adds to our dread, in all cases of danger, and how much the notions of ghosts and goblins, of which none can form clear ideas, affect minds which give credit to the popular tales concerning such sorts of beings. * * * No person seems better to have understood the secret of heightening, or of setting terrible things, if I may use the expression, in their strongest light by the force of a judicious obscurity, than Milton. His description of Death in the second book is admirably studied; it is astonishing with what a gloomy pomp, with what a significant and expressive uncertainty of strokes and colouring, he has finished the portrait of the king of terrors:

> The other shape,
> If shape it might be call'd that shape had none
> Distinguishable, in member, joint, or limb;
> Or substance might be call'd that shadow seemed;
> For such seemed either; black he stood as night;
> Fierce as ten furies; terrible as hell;
> And shook a deadly dart. What seem'd his head
> The likeness of a kingly crown had on.[2]

In this description all is dark, uncertain, confused, terrible, and sublime to the last degree.

* * *

In nature, dark, confused, uncertain images have a greater power on the fancy to form the grander passions, than those have which are more clear and determinate. * * * I am sensible that this idea has met with opposition, and is likely still to be rejected by several. But let it be considered that hardly any thing can strike the mind with its greatness, which does not make some sort of approach towards infinity; which nothing can do whilst we are able to perceive its bounds; but to see an object distinctly, and to perceive its bounds, is one and the same thing. A clear idea is therefore another name for a little idea.

from *Power*

Besides those things which *directly* suggest the idea of danger, and those which produce a similar effect from a mechanical cause, I know of nothing sublime, which is not some modification of power. And this branch rises as naturally as the other two branches, from terror, the common stock of every thing that is sublime. * * * Look at a man, or any other animal of prodigious strength, and what is your idea before reflection? Is it that this strength will be subservient to you, to your ease, to your pleasure, to your interest in any sense? No; the emotion you feel is, lest this enormous strength

---

2. Satan encounters Sin and Death, in an infernal parody of the Trinity (*Paradise Lost*, 2.666–73).

should be employed to the purposes of rapine and destruction. That power derives all its sublimity from the terror with which it is generally accompanied, will appear evidently from its effect in the very few cases, in which it may be possible to strip a considerable degree of strength of its ability to hurt. When you do this, you spoil it of every thing sublime, and it immediately becomes contemptible. An ox is a creature of vast strength; but he is an innocent creature, extremely serviceable, and not at all dangerous; for which reason the idea of an ox is by no means grand. A bull is strong too; but his strength is of another kind; often very destructive, seldom (at least amongst us) of any use in our business; the idea of a bull is therefore great, and it has frequently a place in sublime descriptions, and elevating comparisons. Let us look at another strong animal in the two distinct lights in which we may consider him. The horse in the light of an useful beast, fit for the plough, the road, the draught; in every social useful light, the horse has nothing of the sublime; but it is thus that we are affected with him, *whose neck is cloathed with thunder, the glory of whose nostrils is terrible, who swalloweth the ground with fierceness and rage, neither believeth that it is the sound of the trumpet?*[3] In this description the useful character of the horse entirely disappears, and the terrible and the sublime blaze out together. * * * In short, wheresoever we find strength, and in what light soever we look upon power, we shall all along observe the sublime the concomitant of terror, and contempt the attendant on a strength that is subservient and innoxious. The race of dogs in many of their kinds, have generally a competent degree of strength and swiftness; and they exert these, and other valuable qualities which they possess, greatly to our convenience and pleasure. Dogs are indeed the most social, affectionate, and amiable animals of the whole brute creation; but love approaches much nearer to contempt than is commonly imagined; and accordingly, though we caress dogs, we borrow from them an appellation of the most despicable kind, when we employ terms of reproach; and this appellation is the common mark of the last vileness and contempt in every language.

from *Privation*

All *general* privations are great, because they are all terrible; *Vacuity, Darkness, Solitude,* and *Silence.*

from *Vastness*

Greatness of dimension is a powerful cause of the sublime. This is too evident, and the observation too common, to need any illustration; it is not so common, to consider in what ways greatness of dimension, vastness of extent, or quantity, has the most striking effect. Extension is either in length, height, or depth. Of these the length strikes least; an hundred yards of even ground will never work such an effect as a tower an hundred yards high, or a rock or mountain of that altitude. I am apt to imagine likewise, that height is less grand than depth; and that we are more struck at looking down from a precipice, than at looking up at an object of equal height: but of that I am not very positive. A perpendicular has more force in forming the sublime, than an inclined plane; and the effects of a rugged and broken surface seem stronger than where it is smooth and polished.

from *Infinity*

Another source of the sublime, is *Infinity;* if it does not rather belong to the last. Infinity has a tendency to fill the mind with that sort of delightful horror, which is the most genuine effect, and truest test of the sublime.

3. Job 39.19–24.

from *Difficulty*

Another source of greatness is *Difficulty*. When any work seems to have required immense force and labour to effect it, the idea is grand. Stonehenge,[4] neither for disposition nor ornament, has any thing admirable; but those huge rude masses of stone, set on end, and piled on each other, turn the mind on the immense force necessary for such a work. Nay, the rudeness of the work increases this cause of grandeur, as it excludes the idea of art and contrivance; for dexterity produces another sort of effect, which is different enough from this.

from *Perfection not the cause of Beauty*

There is another notion current, pretty closely allied to the former; that *Perfection* is the constituent cause of beauty. This opinion has been made to extend much farther than to sensible objects. But in these, so far is perfection, considered as such, from being the cause of beauty; that this quality, where it is highest, in the female sex, almost always carries with it an idea of weakness and imperfection. Women are very sensible of this; for which reason, they learn to lisp, to totter in their walk, to counterfeit weakness, and even sickness.[5] In all this they are guided by nature. Beauty in distress is much the most affecting beauty. Blushing has little less power; and modesty in general, which is a tacit allowance of imperfection, is itself considered as an amiable quality, and certainly heightens every other that is so.

from *Beautiful objects small*

The most obvious point that presents itself to us in examining any object, is its extent or quantity. And what degree of extent prevails in bodies that are held beautiful, may be gathered from the usual manner of expression concerning it. I am told that, in most languages, the objects of love are spoken of under diminutive epithets. It is so in all the languages of which I have any knowledge.

from *Smoothness*

The next property constantly observable in such objects is *Smoothness:* A quality so essential to beauty, I do not now recollect any thing beautiful that is not smooth. In trees and flowers, smooth leaves are beautiful; smooth slopes of earth in gardens; smooth streams in the landscape; smooth coats of birds and beasts in animal beauties; in fine women, smooth skins; and in several sorts of ornamental furniture, smooth and polished surfaces.

from *Gradual Variation*

But as perfectly beautiful bodies are not composed of angular parts, so their parts never continue long in the same right line. They vary their direction every moment, and they change under the eye by a deviation continually carrying on, but for whose beginning or end you will find it difficult to ascertain a point. * * * Observe that part of a beautiful woman where she is perhaps the most beautiful, about the neck and breasts; the smoothness; the softness; the easy and insensible swell; the variety of the surface, which is never for the smallest space the same; the deceitful maze, through

4. The monumental Druid stone circle.
5. Burke echoes Hamlet's denunciation of women to Ophelia: "You jig and amble, and you lisp; you nickname God's creatures and make your wantonness your ignorance" (3.1.146–48).

which the unsteady eye slides giddily, without knowing where to fix, or whither it is carried. Is not this a demonstration of that change of surface, continual, and yet hardly perceptible at any point, which forms one of the great constituents of beauty?

from *The physical cause of Love*

When we have before us such objects as excite love and competency, the body is affected, so far as I could observe, much in the following manner. The head reclines something on one side; the eyelids are more closed than usual, and the eyes roll gently with an inclination to the object, the mouth is a little opened, and the breath drawn slowly, with now and then a low sigh: the whole body is composed, and the hands fall idly to the sides. All this is accompanied with an inward sense of melting and languor. These appearances are always proportioned to the degree of beauty in the object, and of sensibility in the observer. And this gradation from the highest pitch of beauty and sensibility, even to the lowest of mediocrity and indifference, and their correspondent effects, ought to be kept in view, else this description will seem exaggerated, which it certainly is not. But from this description it is almost impossible not to conclude, that beauty acts by relaxing the solids of the whole system. There are all the appearances of such a relaxation; and a relaxation somewhat below the natural tone seems to me the cause of all positive pleasure.

from *How Words influence the passions*

In painting we may represent any fine figure we please; but we never can give it those enlivening touches which it may receive from words. To represent an angel in a picture, you can only draw a beautiful young man winged: but what painting can furnish any thing so grand as the addition of one word, "the angel of the *Lord?*" It is true, I have here no clear idea; but these words affect the mind more than the sensible image did; which is all I contend for. A picture of Priam dragged to the altar's foot, and there murdered, if it were well executed, would undoubtedly be very moving; but there are very aggravating circumstances which it could never represent:

> *Sanguine faedantem quos ipse sacraverat ignes.*[6]

As a further instance, let us consider those lines of Milton, where he describes the travels of the fallen angels through their dismal habitation,

> —O'er many a dark and dreary vale
> They pass'd, and many a region dolorous;
> O'er many a frozen, many a fiery Alp;
> Rocks, caves, lakes, fens, bogs, dens, and shades of death,
> A universe of death.[7]

Here is displayed the force of union in

> Rocks, caves, lakes, dens, bogs, fens, and shades—;

which yet would lose the greatest part of the effect, if they were not the

> *Rocks, caves, lakes, dens, bogs, fens, and shades——*
> *——of Death.*

---

6. Aeneas recounts the sight of Priam "polluting with his blood the fires he / himself had hallowed" (Virgil, *Aeneid*   2.502, trans. Mandelbaum).
7. *Paradise Lost*, 2.618–22.

This idea or this affection caused by a word, which nothing but a word could annex to the others, raises a very great degree of the sublime; and this sublime is raised yet higher by what follows, a *"universe of Death."* Here are again two ideas not presentable but by language; and an union of them great and amazing beyond conception; if they may properly be called ideas which present no distinct image to the mind:—but still it will be difficult to conceive how words can move the passions which belong to real objects, without representing those objects clearly. This is difficult to us, because we do not sufficiently distinguish, in our observations upon language, between a clear expression, and a strong expression. These are frequently confounded with each other, though they are in reality extremely different. The former regards the understanding; the latter belongs to the passions. The one describes a thing as it is; the other describes it as it is felt. * * * The truth is, all verbal description, merely as naked description, though never so exact, conveys so poor and insufficient an idea of the thing described, that it could scarcely have the smallest effect, if the speaker did not call in to his aid those modes of speech that mark a strong and lively feeling in himself. Then by the contagion of our passions, we catch a fire already kindled in another, which probably might never have been struck out by the object described. Words, by strongly conveying the passions, by those means which we have already mentioned, fully compensate for their weakness in other respects.

1747–1754   1757, 1759

+ ✦ +

William Gilpin
1724–1804

No name is more associated with the fashion of the picturesque than that of William Gilpin, from 1777 the vicar of Boldre. He traveled throughout the British Isles, and the records of his tours, illustrated with pen and wash drawings, circulated widely in manuscript before publication made them the handbooks of picturesque travel and picturesque sketching. Such works as his *Observations on the River Wye, and Several Parts of South Wales, relative chiefly to Picturesque Beauty; made in the Summer of 1770* (1782), read by Thomas Gray, who left a journal of his tour in the Lake District, before his death in 1771, *Observations relative chiefly to Picturesque Beauty, Made in the Year 1772, on several Parts of England; particularly the Mountains, and Lakes of Cumberland, and Westmoreland* (1786), and *Observations, relative chiefly to Picturesque Beauty, Made in the Year 1776, on Several Parts of Great Britain; particularly the High-Lands of Scotland* (1789) promoted travel to hitherto neglected regions and fixed the discourse of appreciation. The *Three Essays*, excerpted below, contained aquatints precisely illustrating how the addition of detail and management of lighting could convert a smoothly regular landscape into an appealingly varied picturesque prospect. How closely Gilpin's taste accorded with and in turn shaped artistic practice may be gauged by comparing his description of Tintern Abbey with the images of Thomas Girtin and Edward Dayes:

> No part of the ruins of Tintern is seen from the river, except the abbey-church. It has been an elegant Gothic pile; but it does not make that appearance as a *distant* object, which we expected. . . . No ruins of the tower are left, which might give form, and contrast to the walls, and buttresses, and other inferior parts. Instead of this, a number of gabel-ends hurt the eye with their regularity; and disgust it by the vulgarity of their shape. A mallet judiciously used (but who durst use it?) might be of service in fracturing some of them. . . . But if *Tintern-abbey* be less striking as a distant object, it exhibits, on a *nearer* view (when the whole together cannot be seen, but the eye settles on some of its nobler parts,) a

Edward Dayes, *Tintern Abbey from across the Wye,* 1794. The draftsman Edward Dayes (1763–1804), to whom Thomas Girtin was apprenticed (see page 2), made this drawing of Tintern Abbey in 1794. William Gilpin had commented in his Observations on the River Wye (1782): "were the building ever so beautiful, incompassed as it is with shabby houses, it could make no appearance from the river." The presentation of the building amid the surrounding scenery was nonetheless attractive enough for the drawing to be reproduced.

very inchanting piece of ruin. Nature has now made it her own. Time has worn off all traces of the rule: it has blunted the sharp edges of the chissel, and broken the regularity of opposing parts. The figured ornaments of the east window are gone; those of the west-window are left. Most of the other windows, with their principal ornaments, remain. To these are superadded the ornaments of time. Ivy, in masses uncommonly large, has taken possession of many parts of the wall; and gives a happy contrast to the grey-coloured stone, of which the building is composed. Nor is this undecorated. Mosses of various hues, with lychens, maiden-hair, penny-leaf, and other humble plants, overspread the surface, or hang from every joint, and crevice. . . . Such is the beautiful appearance, which Tintern-abbey exhibits on the *outside.* . . . But when we *enter it,* we see it in most perfection. . . . The roof is gone, but the walls, pillars, and abutments, which supported it, are intire. A few of the pillars indeed have given way; and here, and there, a piece of the facing of the wall: but in correspondent parts, one always remains to tell the story. . . . When we stood at one end of this awful piece of ruin; and surveyed the whole in one view—the elements of air, and earth, its only covering, and pavement, and the grand, and venerable remains, which terminated both—perfect enough to form the perspective, yet broken enough to destroy the regularity; the eye was above measure delighted with the beauty, the greatness, and the novelty of the scene.

from Three Essays on Picturesque Beauty, on Picturesque Travel, and on Sketching Landscape
from *Essay 1, on Picturesque Beauty*

Disputes about beauty might perhaps be involved in less confusion, if a distinction were established, which certainly exists, between such objects as are *beautiful,* and such as are *picturesque*—between those, which please the eye in their *natural state*; and those, which please from some quality, capable of being *illustrated by painting*.

Ideas of beauty vary with the objects, and with the eye of the spectator. The stone-mason sees beauties in a well-jointed wall, which escape the architect, who surveys the building under a different idea. And thus the painter, who compares his object with the rules of his art, sees it in a different light from the man of general taste, who surveys it only as simply beautiful.

As the difference therefore between the *beautiful*, and the *picturesque* appears really to exist, and must depend upon some peculiar construction of the object; it may be worth while to examine, what that peculiar construction is. We inquire not into the *general sources of beauty*, either in nature, or in representation. This would lead into a nice, and scientific discussion, in which it is not our purpose to engage. The question simply is, *What is that quality in objects, which particularly marks them as picturesque?*

In examining the *real object*, we shall find one source of beauty arise from that species of elegance, which we call *smoothness*, or *neatness*; for the terms are nearly synonymous. The higher the marble is polished, the brighter the silver is rubbed, and the more the mahogany shines, the more each is considered as an object of beauty: as if the eye delighted in gliding smoothly over a surface. * * *

But in *picturesque representation* it seems somewhat odd, yet perhaps we shall find it equally true, that the reverse of this is the case; and that the ideas of *neat* and *smooth*, instead of being picturesque, in reality strip the object, in which they reside, of all pretensions to *picturesque beauty*.—Nay, farther, we do not scruple to assert, that *roughness* forms the most essential point of difference between the *beautiful* and the *picturesque*; as it seems to be that particular quality which makes objects chiefly pleasing in painting.—I use the general term *roughness*; but properly speaking roughness relates only to the surfaces of bodies: when we speak of their delineation, we use the word *ruggedness*. * * *

A piece of Palladian[1] architecture may be elegant in the last degree. The proportion of its parts—the propriety of its ornaments—and the symmetry of the whole may be highly pleasing. But if we introduce it in a picture, it immediately becomes a formal object, and ceases to please. Should we wish to give it picturesque beauty, we must use the mallet, instead of the chisel: we must beat down one half of it, deface the other, and throw the mutilated members around in heaps. In short, from a *smooth* building we must turn it into a *rough* ruin. No painter, who had the choice of the two objects, would hesitate which to choose.

Again, why does an elegant piece of garden-ground make no figure on canvas? The shape is pleasing; the combination of the objects, harmonious; and the widening of the walk in the very line of beauty. All this is true, but the *smoothness* of the whole, tho right, and as it should be in nature, offends in picture. Turn the lawn into a piece of broken ground: plant rugged oaks instead of flowering shrubs: break the edges of the walk give it the rudeness of a road; mark it with wheel-tracks; and scatter around a few stones, and brushwood; in a word, instead of making the whole *smooth*, make it rough; and you make it also *picturesque*. * * *

That lovely face of youth smiling with all its sweet, dimpling charms, how attractive is it in life! How beautiful in representation! It is one of those objects, that please, as many do, both in nature, and on canvas. But would you see the human face

---

1. In the manner of the Italian neoclassical architect Andrea Palladio (1518–1580), whose designs influenced building in England.

in its brightest form of *picturesque beauty*, examine that patriarchal head. What is it, which gives that dignity of character; that force of expression; those lines of wisdom, and experience; that energetic meaning, so far beyond the rosy hue, or even the bewitching smile of youth? What is it, but the forehead furrowed with wrinkles? The prominent cheek-bone, catching the light? The muscles of the cheek strongly marked, and losing themselves in the shaggy beard? And, above all, the austere brow, projecting over the eye—the feature which particularly struck Homer in his idea of Jupiter, and which he had probably seen finely represented in some statue; in a word, what is it, but the *rough* touches of age? * * *

Animal life, as well as human, is, in general, beautiful both in nature, and on canvas. We admire the horse, as a *real object*; the elegance of his form; the stateliness of his tread, the spirit of all his motions; and the glossiness of his coat. We admire him also in *representation*. But as an object of picturesque beauty, we admire more the worn-out cart-horse, the cow, the goat, or the ass; whose harder lines, and rougher coats, exhibit more the graces of the pencil. * * * Smooth-coated animals could not produce so picturesque an effect. * * *

It is not however merely for the sake of his *execution*, that the artist values a rough object. He finds it in many other respects accommodated to his art. In the first place, his *composition* requires it. If the history-painter threw all his draperies smooth over his figures; his groups, and combinations would be very awkward. And in *landscape-painting* smooth objects would produce no composition at all. In a mountain-scene what composition could arise from the corner of a smooth knoll coming forward on one side, intersected by a smooth knoll on the other; with a smooth plain perhaps in the middle, and a smooth mountain in the distance. The very idea is disgusting. Picturesque composition consists in uniting in one whole a variety of parts; and these parts can only be obtained from rough objects. If the smooth mountains, and plains were broken by different objects, the composition might be good, on a supposition the great lines of it were so before. * * *

Some quibbling opponent may throw out, that wherever there is smoothness, there must also be roughness. The smoothest plain consists of many rougher parts; and the roughest rock of many smoother; and there is such a variety of degrees in both, that it is hard to say, where you have the precise ideas of *rough* and *smooth*.

To this it is enough, that the province of the picturesque eye is to *survey nature*; not to *anatomize matter*. It throws its glances around in the broad-cast style. It comprehends an extensive tract at each sweep. It examines *parts*, but never *particles*.

from *Essay 2, on Picturesque Travel*

Enough has been said to shew the difficulty of *assigning causes*: let us then take another course, and amuse ourselves with *searching after effects*. This is the general intention of picturesque travel. We mean not to bring it into competition with any of the more useful ends of traveling. But as many travel without any end at all, amusing themselves without being able to give a reason why they are amused, we offer an end, which may possibly engage some vacant minds; and may indeed afford a rational amusement to such as travel for more important purposes.

In treating of picturesque travel, we may consider first its *object*; and secondly its sources of *amusement*.

Its *object* is beauty of every kind, which either art or nature can produce; but it is chiefly that species of *beauty*, which we have endeavoured to characterize in the preceding essay as *picturesque*. This great object we pursue through the scenery of nature. We seek it among all the ingredients of landscape—trees—rocks—broken-grounds—woods—rivers—lakes—plains—vallies—mountains—and   distances. These objects *in themselves* produce infinite variety. * * *

That we may examine picturesque objects with more ease, it may be useful to class them into the *sublime*, and the *beautiful*; tho, in fact this distinction is rather inaccurate. *Sublimity alone* cannot make an object *picturesque*. However grand the mountain, or the rock may be, it has no claim to this epithet, unless its form, its colour, or its accompaniments have *some degree of beauty*. Nothing can be more sublime, than the ocean: but wholly unaccompanied, it has little of the picturesque. When we talk therefore of a sublime object, we always understand, that it is also beautiful: and we call it sublime, or beautiful, only as the idea of sublimity, or of simple beauty prevail. * * *

The first source of amusement to the picturesque traveler, is the *pursuit* of his object—the expectation of new scenes continually opening, and arising to his view. We suppose the country to have been unexplored. Under this circumstance the mind is kept constantly in an agreeable suspense. The love of novelty is the foundation of this pleasure. Every distant horizon promises something new; and with this pleasing expectation we follow her through all her walks. We pursue her from hill to dale; and hunt after those various beauties, with which she everywhere abounds. * * *

After the pursuit we are gratified with the *attainment* of the object. Our amusement, on this head, arises from the employment of the mind in examining the beautiful scenes we have found. Sometimes we examine them under the idea of a *whole*: we admire the composition, the colouring, and the light, in one *comprehensive view*. When we are fortunate enough to fall in with scenes of this kind, we are highly delighted. But as we have less frequent opportunities of being thus gratified, we are more commonly employed in analyzing the *parts of scenes*; which may be exquisitely beautiful, tho unable to produce a whole. We examine what would amend the composition; how little is wanting to reduce it to the rules of our art; how trifling a circumstance sometimes forms the limit between beauty, and deformity. Or we compare the objects before us with other objects of the same kind: or perhaps we compare them with the imitations of art. From all these operations of the mind results great amusement.

But it is not from this *scientifical* employment, that we derive our chief pleasure. We are most delighted, when some grand scene, tho perhaps of an incorrect composition, rising before the eye, strikes us beyond the power of thought—when the *vox faucibus haeret*;[2] and every mental operation is suspended. In this pause of intellect; this deliquium of the soul, an enthusiastic sensation of pleasure overspreads it, previous to any examination by the rules of art. The general idea of the scene makes an impression, before any appeal is made to the judgment. We rather *feel*, than *survey* it. * * *

Having gained by a minute examination of incidents a complete idea of an object, our next amusement arises from inlarging, and correcting our general stock of ideas. * * *

From this correct knowledge of objects arises another amusement; that of representing, by a few strokes in a sketch, those ideas, which have made the most impression upon us. * * * There may be more pleasure in recollecting, and recording, from a few transient lines, the scenes we have admired, than in the present enjoyment of them. If the scenes indeed have *peculiar greatness*, this secondary pleasure cannot be

2. Stunned by the image of his lost wife Creusa Aeneas finds his "voice held fast within / [his] jaws" (Virgil, *Aeneid*, 2.774); see also Turnus's horror (12.868).

attended with those enthusiastic feelings, which accompanied the real exhibition. But, in general, tho it may be a calmer species of pleasure, it is more uniform, and uninterrupted. It flatters us too with the idea of a sort of creation of our own; and it is unallayed with that fatigue, which is often a considerable abatement to the pleasures of traversing the wild, and savage parts of nature. * * *

We are in some degree, also amused by the very visions of fancy itself. Often, when slumber has half-closed the eye, and shut out all the objects of sense, especially after the enjoyment of some splendid scene; the imagination, active, and alert, collects its scattered ideas, transposes, combines, and shifts them into a thousand forms, producing such exquisite scenes, such sublime arrangements, such glow, and harmony of colouring, such brilliant lights, such depth, and clearness of shadow, as equally foil description, and every attempt of artificial colouring. * * *

The more refined our taste grows from the *study of nature*, the more insipid are the *works of art*. Few of its efforts please. The idea of the great original is so strong, that the copy must be pure, if it do not disgust. But the varieties of nature's charts are such, that, study them as we can, new varieties will always arise: and let our taste be ever so refined, her works, on which it is formed (at least when we consider them as *objects*), must always go beyond it; and furnish fresh sources both of pleasure and amusement.

from *Essay 3, on The Art of Sketching Landscape*

Your intention in taking *views from nature*, may either be to *fix them in your own memory*—or to *convey, in some degree, your ideas to others*.

With regard to the former, when you meet a scene you wish to sketch, your first consideration is to get it in the best point of view. A few paces to the right, or left, make a great difference. The ground, which folds awkwardly here, appears to fold more easily there: and that long black curtain of the castle, which is so unpleasing a circumstance, as you stand on one side, is agreeably broken by a buttress on another. * * *

But when a sketch is intended *to convey in some degree, our ideas to others*, it is necessary, that it should be somewhat more adorned. To *us* the scene, familiar to our recollection, may be suggested by a few rough strokes: but if you wish to raise the idea, *where none existed before*, and to do it *agreeably*, there should be some *composition* in your sketch—a degree of *correctness, and expression* in the out-line—and some *effect of light*. A little *ornament* also from figures, and other circumstances may be introduced. In short, it should be so far dressed, as to give some idea of a picture. I call this an *adorned sketch*; and should sketch nothing that was not capable of being thus dressed. * * *

But the *composition*, you say, is already fixed by the *original sketch*.

It is true, but still it may admit many little alterations, by which the forms of objects may be assisted; and yet the remembrance not disfigured: as the same piece of music, performed by different masters, and graced variously by each, may yet continue still the same. We must ever recollect that nature is most defective in composition; and *must* be a little assisted. Her ideas are too vast for picturesque use, without the restraint of rules. * * *

In a hasty transcript *from nature*, it is sufficient to take the lines of the country just as you find them: but in your *adorned sketch* you must grace them a little, where they run false. You must contrive to hide offensive parts with wood; to cover such as are too bald, with bushes; and to remove little objects, which in nature push themselves too much in sight, and serve only to introduce too many parts into your *composition*.

1794

→ ‡◆‡ ←

Jane Austen
1775–1817

All of Jane Austen's novels were published between 1811 and 1818, and their general subject is a young woman's finding her way in and place in the world, usually through the trials of her relationships with her family, her close friends, and above all, men whom she might, or might not, marry. Her second novel, *Pride and Prejudice* (1813), is her most famous. Leading up to the passage excerpted here, the novel's heroine, Elizabeth Bennet, had angrily refused a proposal of marriage from Mr. Darcy, believing him to be an arrogant snob and the cause of misery to her sister. Darcy sent her a letter of apology, with new information that has altered her view of him. Not having seen him since, she is now on a tour of Derbyshire with her aunt and uncle and, believing Darcy to be absent, she agrees to a tour of his estate.

from **Pride and Prejudice**
from **Chapter 43**

[A VISIT TO FITZWILLIAM DARCY'S ESTATE IN DERBYSHIRE]

Elizabeth, as they drove along, watched for the first appearance of Pemberley Woods with some perturbation; and when at length they turned in at the lodge,[1] her spirits were in a high flutter.

The park[2] was very large, and contained great variety of ground. They entered it in one of its lowest points, and drove some time through a beautiful wood, stretching over a wide extent.

Elizabeth's mind was too full for conversation, but she saw and admired every remarkable spot and point of view. They gradually ascended for half a mile, and then found themselves at the top of a considerable eminence, where the wood ceased, and the eye was instantly caught by Pemberley House, situated on the opposite side of a valley, into which the road with some abruptness wound. It was a large, handsome, stone building, standing well on rising ground, and backed by a ridge of high woody hills;—and in front, a stream of some natural importance was swelled into greater, but without any artificial appearance. Its banks were neither formal, nor falsely adorned. Elizabeth was delighted. She had never seen a place for which nature had done more, or where natural beauty had been so little counteracted by an awkward taste.[3] They were all of them warm in their admiration; and at that moment she felt, that to be mistress of Pemberley might be something!

1813

→ ‡◆‡ ←

Mary Wollstonecraft
1759–1797

Mary Wollstonecraft's *A Vindication of the Rights of Men*, published anonymously in 1790, was one of the first replies to Edmund Burke's *Reflections on the Revolution in France*. In joining with

---

1. An out-building for use by recreational hunters.
2. A vast estate of land, of hundreds of acres. (Darcy is one of the richest men in England.)
3. The late critic Donald Greene persuasively revived the speculation that the original of Austen's Pemberley is the great estate of the Dukes of Devonshire, Chatsworth. If so, what Elizabeth sees as nature was the result of an

extensive, expensive reshaping of the estate by the landscape architect Lancelot "Capability" Brown. The point does not depend on reference. Austen's language exquisitely hints at the paradoxes of the picturesque project: the stream is naturally important, but has been swelled; natural beauty has not been "counteracted" by bad taste, but may have been improved by a sophisticated one.

her attack on Burke's reaction a severe critique of the invidious gendering that operates in his *Philosophical Enquiry into the Origin of Our Ideas of the Sublime and Beautiful*, first published more than thirty years before, Wollstonecraft not only discloses the continuities between Burke's aesthetics and his politics, but also tacitly acknowledges the continuing currency of the earlier work. Despite her political differences from Burke, Wollstonecraft's treatment of nature in her fiction and in *Letters Written During a Short Residence in Sweden, Norway, and Denmark* (1796) remained imbued with Burkean categories.

For more on Wollstonecraft, see the entry in Perspectives: The Rights of Man and the Revolution Controversy (page 36) and the main entry under her name (page 56).

from A Vindication of the Rights of Men
[WOLLSTONECRAFT'S CRITIQUE OF BURKE]

Where is the dignity, the infallibility of sensibility, in the fair ladies, whom, if the voice of rumour is to be credited, the captive negroes curse in all the agony of bodily pain, for the unheard of tortures they invent? It is probable that some of them, after the sight of a flagellation, compose their ruffled spirits and exercise their tender feelings by the perusal of the last imported novel.—How true these tears are to nature, I leave you to determine. But these ladies may have read your Enquiry concerning the origin of our ideas of the Sublime and Beautiful, and, convinced by your arguments, may have laboured to be pretty, by counterfeiting weakness.[1]

You may have convinced them that *littleness* and *weakness* are the very essence of beauty; and that the Supreme Being, in giving women beauty in the most supereminent degree, seemed to command them, by the powerful voice of Nature, not to cultivate the moral virtues that might chance to excite respect, and interfere with the pleasing sensations they were created to inspire. Thus confining truth, fortitude, and humanity, within the rigid pale of manly morals, they might justly argue, that to be loved, woman's high end and great distinction! They should "learn to lisp, to totter in their walk, and nick-name God's creatures." Never, they might repeat after you, was any man, much less a woman, rendered amiable by the force of those exalted qualities, fortitude, justice, wisdom, and truth; and thus forewarned of the sacrifice they must make to those austere, unnatural virtues, they would be authorized to turn all their attention to their persons, systematically neglecting morals to secure beauty.—Some rational old woman indeed might chance to stumble at this doctrine, and hint, that in avoiding atheism you had not steered clear of the mussulman's [Muslim's] creed; but you could readily exculpate yourself by turning the charge on Nature, who made our idea of beauty independent of reason. Nor would it be necessary for you to collect, that if virtue has any other foundation than worldly utility, you have clearly proved that one half of the human species, at least, have not souls; and that Nature, by making women *little, smooth, delicate, fair* creatures, never designed that they should exercise their reason to acquire the virtues that produce opposite, if not contradictory, feelings. The affection they excite, to be uniform and perfect, should not be tinctured with the respect which moral virtues inspire, lest pain should be blended with pleasure, and admiration disturb the soft intimacy of love. This laxity of morals in the female world is certainly more captivating to a libertine imagination than the cold arguments of reason, that give no sex to virtue. If beautiful weakness be interwoven in a woman's frame, if the chief business of her life

1. See the excerpt from the section "Perfection not the cause of Beauty," in Burke's *Enquiry*, above (page 306).

be (as you insinuate) to inspire love, and Nature has made an eternal distinction between the qualities that dignify a rational being and this animal perfection, her duty and happiness in this life must clash with any preparation for a more exalted state. So that Plato and Milton were grossly mistaken in asserting that human love led to heavenly, and was only an exaltation of the same affection; for the love of the Deity, which is mixed with the most profound reverence, must be love of perfection, and not compassion for weakness.

To say the truth, I not only tremble for the souls of women, but for the good natured man, whom every one loves. The *amiable* weakness of his mind is a strong argument against its immateriality, and seems to prove that beauty relaxes the *solids* of the soul as well as the body.[2]

It follows then immediately, from your own reasoning, that respect and love are antagonist principles; and that, if we really wish to render men more virtuous, we must endeavour to banish all enervating modifications of beauty from civil society. We must, to carry your argument a little further, return to Spartan regulations, and settle the virtues of men on the stern foundation of mortification and self-denial; for any attempt to civilize the heart, to make it humane by implanting reasonable principles, is a mere philosophic dream. If refinement invariably lessens respect for virtue, by rendering beauty, the grand tempter, more seductive; if these relaxing feelings are incompatible with the nervous exertions of morality, the sun of Europe is not set; it begins to dawn, when cold metaphysicians try to make the head give laws to the heart.[3]

But should experience prove that there is a beauty in virtue, a charm in order which necessarily implies exertion, a depraved sensual taste may give way to a more manly one—and *melting* feelings to rational satisfactions. Both may be equally natural to man; the test is their moral difference, and that point reason alone can decide.

Such a glorious change can only be produced by liberty.

1790   1790

Immanuel Kant
1724–1804

The Critique of Pure Reason, published at Riga in 1781, quickly established the stature of the German philosopher Immanuel Kant. By the 1790s his name had begun to appear in British journals; reviews and essays on his system multiplied, including a significant piece by Coleridge's friend the physician Thomas Beddoes in *The Monthly Magazine* (1796), followed by books, translations, and courses of lectures. Coleridge declared in Chapter 9 of the *Biographia Literaria* (1817) that

> the writings of the illustrious sage of Köningsberg, the founder of the Critical Philosophy, at once invigorated and disciplined my understanding. The originality, the depth, and the compression of the thoughts, the novelty and subtlety, yet solidity and importance, of the distinctions; the adamantine chain of the logic; and I will venture to add (paradox as it will appear to those who have taken their notion of IMMANUEL KANT, from Reviewers and Frenchmen) the *clearness* and *evidence*. . . . took possession of me as with a giant's hand.

---

2. See the excerpt from the section "The physical cause of Love," in Burke's *Enquiry*, above (page 307).
3. See Burke's paean to Marie Antoinette and chivalry in the excerpt from *Reflections on the Revolution in France* (page 52).

Declaring that after fifteen years' familiarity he "still read" Kant "with undiminished delight and increasing admiration," Coleridge became the chief propagator of Kant's reputation in England. As the sneer at "Frenchmen" suggests, the increasing importance of German culture (for example, Carlyle's devotion to Goethe) flagged a shift away from what had come to seem for many the shallow and dangerous rationalism of the French enlightenment. The "*all-to-nothing-crushing* KANT*,*" as Coleridge translated the epithet coined by Moses Mendelssohn, became the foundation of a new conception of ethics and polity.

In the *Critique of Judgement,* published at Leipzig in 1790, Kant acknowledges that Burke "deserves to be called the foremost" of those who have developed "a merely empirical exposition of the sublime and beautiful," but rejects the sensationist approach to ground the experience of the sublime in the operations of the mind itself. His account of the unease that the sublime arouses and the resurgent sense of the superiority of the mind it provokes should be compared to Wordsworth's staging of the "spots of time" in *The Prelude.*

from The Critique of Judgement
from Book 2, Analytic of the Sublime
A. The Mathematically sublime

from SECTION 25, DEFINITION OF THE TERM "SUBLIME"

Sublime is the name given to what is *absolutely great.* But to be great and to be a magnitude are entirely different concepts (*magnitudo* and *quantitas*). In the same way to *Assert without qualification (simpliciter)* that something is great, is quite a different thing from saying that it is *absolutely great (absolute, non comparative magnum).* The latter is *what is beyond all comparison great.* * * * If, however, we call anything not alone great, but, without qualification, absolutely, and in every respect (beyond all comparison) great, that is to say, sublime, we soon perceive that it is not permissible to seek an appropriate standard outside itself, but merely in itself. It is a greatness comparable to itself alone. Hence it comes that the sublime is not to be looked for in things of nature, but only in our own ideas. * * * But precisely because there is a striving in our imagination towards progress *ad infinitum,* while reason demands absolute totality, as a real idea, that same inability on the part of our faculty for the estimation of the magnitude of things of the world of sense to attain to this idea, is the awakening of a feeling of a supersensible faculty[1] within us, and it is the use to which judgment naturally puts particular objects on behalf of this latter feeling, and not the object of sense, that is absolutely great, and every other contrasted employment small. Consequently it is the disposition of soul evoked by a particular representation engaging the attention of the reflective judgement, and not the Object, that is to be called sublime.

The forgoing formulae defining the sublime may, therefore, be supplemented by yet another: *The sublime is that, the mere capacity of thinking which evidences a faculty of mind transcending every standard of sense.*

from SECTION 27, QUALITY OF THE DELIGHT IN OUR ESTIMATE OF THE SUBLIME

The feeling of the sublime is, therefore, at once a feeling of displeasure, arising from the inadequacy of the imagination in the aesthetic estimation of magnitude to attain to its estimation by reason, and a simultaneously awakened pleasure, arising from this very judgement of inadequacy of the greatest faculty of sense being in accord with ideas of reason, so far as the effort to attain to these is for us a law. * * *

---

1. Above and beyond the senses; not sensual; intellectual.

Therefore the inner perception of the inadequacy of every standard of sense to serve for the rational estimation of magnitude is a coming into accord with reason's laws, and a displeasure that makes us alive to the feeling of the supersensible side of our being, according to which it is final, and consequently a pleasure, to find every standard of sensibility falling short of the ideas of reason.

The mind feels itself *set in motion* in the representation of the sublime in nature; whereas in the aesthetic judgment upon what is beautiful therein it is in *restful* contemplation. This movement, especially in its inception, may be compared with a vibration, i.e. with a rapidly alternating repulsion and attraction to the same Object. The point of excess for the imagination (towards which it is driven in the apprehension of the intuition) is like an abyss in which it fears to lose itself; yet again for the rational idea of the supersensible it is not excessive, but conformable to law, and directed to drawing out such an effort on the part of the imagination: and so in turn as much a source of attraction as it was repellent to mere sensibility.

B. *The Dynamically Sublime in Nature*

from SECTION 28, NATURE AS MIGHT

Might is a power which is superior to great hindrances. It is termed *dominion* if it is also superior to the resistance of that which itself possesses might. Nature considered in an aesthetic judgement as might that has no dominion over us, is *dynamically sublime.*

If we are to estimate nature as dynamically sublime, it must be represented as a source of fear (though the converse, that every object that is a source of fear is, in our aesthetic judgement, sublime, does not hold). For in forming an aesthetic estimate (no concept being present) the superiority to hindrances can only be estimated according to the greatness of the resistance. Now that which we strive to resist is an evil, and, if we do not find our powers commensurate to the task, an object of fear. * * *

Bold, overhanging, and as it were, threatening rocks, thunderclouds piled up the vault of heaven, borne along with flashes and peals, volcanoes in all their violence of destruction, hurricanes leaving desolation in their track, the boundless ocean rising with rebellious force, the high waterfall of some mighty river, and the like, make our power of resistance of trifling moment in comparison with their might. But, provided our own position is secure, their aspect is all the more attractive for its fearfulness; and we readily call these objects sublime, because they raise the forces of the soul above the height of vulgar commonplace, and discover within us a power of resistance of quite another kind, which gives us courage to be able to measure ourselves against the seeming omnipotence of nature.

In the immeasurableness of nature and the incompetence of our faculty for adopting a standard proportionate to the aesthetic estimation of the magnitude of its *realm*, we found our own limitation. But with this we also found in our rational faculty another non-sensuous standard, one which has that infinity itself under it as a unit, and in comparison with which everything in nature is small, and so found in our minds a preeminence over nature even in its immeasurability. Now in just the same way the irresistibility of the might of nature forces upon us the recognition of our physical helplessness as beings of nature, but at the same time reveals a faculty of estimating ourselves as independent of nature, and discovers a pre-eminence above nature that is the foundation of a self-preservation of quite another kind from that which may be assailed and brought into danger by external nature. This saves humanity in our own person from humiliation, even though as mortal men we have to submit to external violence. In this way external nature is not estimated in our aesthetic judgement as sublime so far as exciting fear, but rather because it challenges our power (one not of nature) to regard as small those things of which we are wont to be solicitous (worldly goods, health, and life), and hence to regard its might (to which in these matters we are no doubt subject) as exercising over us and our personality no such rude dominion that we should bow down before it, once the question becomes one of our highest principles and of our asserting or forsaking them. Therefore nature is here called sublime merely because it raises the imagination to a presentation of those cases in which the mind can make itself sensible of the appropriate sublimity of the sphere of its own being, even above nature. * * *

Sublimity, therefore, does not reside in any of the things of nature, but only in our own mind, in so far as we may become conscious of our superiority over nature within, and thus also over nature without us (as exerting influence upon us). Everything that provokes this feeling in us, including the *might* of nature which challenges our strength, is then, though improperly, called sublime, and it is only under presupposition of the idea within us, and in relation to it, that we are capable of attaining to the sublimity of that Being which inspires deep respect in us, not by the mere display of its might in nature, but more by the faculty which is planted in us of estimating the might without fear, and of regarding our estate as exalted above it.

1790

﹅

John Ruskin
1819–1900

John Ruskin's first book, Modern Painters, if one can call a book a project published over more than a decade and a half (1843–1860) and running in the end to five volumes, was an impassioned defense of the greatness of the art of J. M. W. Turner. In the excerpt below one sees the continuing uses of the term "picturesque," and the metamorphoses it could take in the hands of a brilliant critic and fierce moralist. The Reverend Gilpin acknowledged the paradox that "moral and picturesque ideas do not always coincide," but shied away from exploring its implications: "In a moral view, the industrious mechanic is a more pleasing object than the loitering peasant. But in a picturesque light, it is otherwise. The arts of industry are rejected; and even idleness, if I may so speak, adds dignity to a character" (The *Tour* to the Lakes, 1786). Ruskin turns and turns the paradox, first criticizing the callousness of the hunter after ruin and misery, then conceding the possibility of increased sympathy. More: if the endurance that Ruskin attributes to Calais Church and the innate dignity of the unconsciously suffering laborer (think of Wordsworth's Michael) that he finds in the noble picturesque cannot be neatly cordoned off from the condescension of the "low school of the surface-picturesque," Ruskin's wielding of his distinction is urgent. The picturesque had begun as a counter to eighteenth-century ideals of symmetry, harmony, and regularity; in Ruskin's mid-nineteenth century deepening it is a weapon against a rootless, industrializing, utilitarian modernity.

For more on Ruskin, see the principal listing on page 737.

from Modern Painters
from *Of the Turnerian Picturesque*[1]

And the most interesting of these subjects of inquiry, with which, therefore, it may be best to begin, is the precise form under which he has admitted into his work the

1. From vol. 4, part 5, "Of Mountain Beauty."

modern feeling of the picturesque, which, so far as it consists in a delight in ruin, is perhaps the most suspicious and questionable of all the characters distinctively belonging to our temper, and art. * * *

The essence of picturesque character has already been defined to be a sublimity not inherent in the nature of the thing, but caused by something external to it; as the ruggedness of a cottage roof possesses something of a mountain aspect, not belonging to the cottage as such. And this sublimity may be either in mere external ruggedness, and other visible character, or it may lie deeper, in an expression of sorrow and old age, attributes which are both sublime; not a dominant expression, but one mingled with such familiar and common characters as prevent the object from becoming perfectly pathetic in its sorrow, or perfectly venerable in its age.

For instance, I cannot find words to express the intense pleasure I have always in first finding myself, after some prolonged stay in England, at the foot of the old tower of Calais church. The large neglect, the noble unsightliness of it; the record of its years written so visibly, yet without sign of weakness or decay; its stern wasteness and gloom, eaten away by the Channel winds, and overgrown with the bitter sea grasses; its slates and tiles all shaken and rent, and yet not falling, its desert of brickwork full of bolts, and holes, and ugly fissures, and yet strong, like a bare brown rock; its carelessness of what any one thinks or feels about it, putting forth no claim, having no beauty nor desirableness, pride, nor grace; yet neither asking for pity; not, as ruins are, useless and piteous, feebly or fondly garrulous of better days; but useful still, going through its own daily work,—as some old fisherman beaten gray by storm, yet drawing his daily nets: so it stands, with no complaint about its past youth, in blanched and meagre massiveness and serviceableness, gathering human souls together underneath it; the sound of its bells for prayer still rolling through its rents; and the grey peak of it seen far across the sea, principal of the three that rise above the waste of surfy sand and hillocked shore,—the lighthouse for life, and the belfry for labour, and this for patience and praise.

I cannot tell the half of the strange pleasures and thoughts that come about me at the sight of that old tower, for, in some sort, it is the epitome of all that makes the Continent of Europe interesting, as opposed to new countries; and, above all, it completely expresses that agedness in the midst of active life which binds the old and the new into harmony. We, in England, have our new street, our new inn, our green shaven lawn, and our piece of ruin emergent from it,—a mere *specimen* of the middle ages put on a bit of velvet carpet to be shown, which, but for its size, might as well be on a museum shelf at once, under cover. But, on the Continent, the links are unbroken between the past and present, and in such use as they can serve for, the grey-headed wrecks are suffered to stay with men; while, in unbroken line, the generations of spared buildings are seen succeeding each in its place. And thus in its largeness, in its permitted evidence of slow decline, in its poverty, in its absence of all pretence, of all show and care for outside aspect, that Calais tower has an infinite of symbolism in it, all the more striking because usually seen in contrast with English scenes expressive of feelings the exact reverse of these. * * *

Now, I have insisted long on this English character, because I want the reader to understand thoroughly the opposite element of the noble picturesque; its expression, namely, of *suffering* of *poverty*, or *decay*, nobly endured by unpretending strength of heart. Nor only unpretending, but unconscious. If there be visible pensiveness in the building, as in a ruined abbey, it becomes, or claims to become, beautiful; but the picturesqueness is in the unconscious suffering,—the look that an old labourer has, not knowing that there is anything pathetic in his grey hair, and withered arms, and sun-burnt breast; and thus there are the two extremes, the consciousness of pathos in the confessed ruin, which may or may not be beautiful, according to the kind of it; and the entire denial of all human calamity and care, in the swept proprieties and neat-nesses of English modernism: and, between these, there is the unconscious confession of the facts of distress and decay, in the by-words; the world's hard-work being gone through all this while, and no pity asked for, nor contempt feared. And this is the expression of that Calais spire, and of all picturesque things, in so far as they have mental or human expression at all.

I say, in so far as they have mental expression, because their merely outward delightfulness—that which makes them pleasant in painting, or, in the literal sense, pic-turesque—is their actual variety of colour and form. A broken stone has necessarily more various forms in it than a whole one; a bent roof has more various curves in it than a straight one; every excrescence or cleft indicates some additional complexity of light and shade, and every stain of moss on eaves or wall adds to the delightfulness of colour. Hence, in a completely picturesque object, as of an old cottage or mill, there are intro-duced, by various circumstances not essential to it, but, on the whole, generally some-what detrimental to it as cottage or mill, such elements of sublimity—complex light and shade, varied colour, undulatory form, and so on—as can generally be found only in noble natural objects, woods, rocks, and mountains. This sublimity, belonging in a para-sitical manner, to the building, renders it, in the usual sense of the word, "picturesque."

Now, if this outward sublimity be sought for by the painter, without any regard for the real nature of the thing, and without any comprehension of the pathos of character hidden beneath it, it forms the low school of the surface-picturesque; that which fills ordinary drawing-books and scrap-books, and the most popular living landscape painters of France, England, and Germany. But if these same outward characters be sought for in subordination to the inner character of the object, every source of pleasurableness being refused which is incompatible with that, while per-fect sympathy is felt at the same time with the object as to all that it tells of itself in those sorrowful by-words, we have the school of true or noble picturesque; still distin-guished from the school of pure beauty or sublimity, because, in its subjects, the pathos and sublimity are all *by the way,* as in Calais old spire,—not inherent, as in a lovely tree or mountain; while it is distinguished still more from the schools of the lower picturesque by its tender sympathy, and its refusal of all sources of pleasure inconsistent with the perfect nature of the thing to be studied. ✳ ✳ ✳

It is mainly because the one painter has communion of heart with his subject, and the other only casts his eyes upon it feelinglessly, that the work of the one is greater than that of the other.[2] And, as we think farther over the matter, we shall see that this is indeed the eminent cause of the difference between the lower pic-turesque and the higher. For, in a certain sense, the lower picturesque ideal is emi-nently a *heartless* one; the lover of it seems to go forth in the world in a temper as merciless as its rocks. All other men feel some regret at the sight of disorder and ruin. He alone delights in both; it matters not of what. Fallen cottage—desolate vil-la—deserted village—blasted heath—mouldering castle—to him, so that they do but show jagged angles of stone and timber, all are sights equally joyful. Poverty, and darkness, and guilt, bring in their several contributions to his treasury of pleasant

2. Before this point Ruskin has paired and contrasted studies of windmills by Turner and Clarkson Stanfield, "the first master of the lower picturesque, among our living artists."

thoughts. The shattered window, opening into black and ghastly rents of wall, the foul rag or straw wisp stopping them, the dangerous roof, decrepit floor and stair, ragged misery or wasting age of the inhabitants,—all these conduce, each in due measure, to the fulness of his satisfaction. What is it to him that the old man has passed his seventy years in helpless darkness and untaught waste of soul? The old man has at last accomplished his destiny, and filled the corner of a sketch, where something of an unshapely nature was wanting. What is it to him that the people fester in that feverish misery in the low quarter of the town, by the river? Nay, it is much to him. What else were they made for? what could they have done better? The black timbers, and the green water, and the soaking wrecks of boats, and the torn remnants of clothes hung out to dry in the sun;—truly the fever-struck creatures, whose lives have been given for the production of these materials of effect, have not died in vain.

Yet, for all this, I do not say the lover of the lower picturesque is a monster in human form. He is by no means this, though truly we might at first think so, if we came across him unawares, and had not met with any such sort of person before. Generally speaking, he is kind-hearted, innocent of evil, but not broad in thought; somewhat selfish, and incapable of acute sympathy with others; gifted at the same time with strong artistic instincts and capacities for the enjoyment of varied form, and light, and shade, in pursuit of which enjoyment his life is passed, as the lives of other men are, for the most part, in the pursuit of what *they* also like,—be it honour, or money, or indolent pleasure,—very irrespective of the poor people living by the stagnant canal. And, in some sort, the hunter of the picturesque is better than many of these; inasmuch as he is simple-minded and capable of unostentatious and economical delights, which, if not very helpful to other people, are at all events utterly uninjurious, even to the victims or subjects of his picturesque fancies; while to many others his work is entertaining and useful. And, more than all this, even that delight which he *seems* to take in misery is not altogether unvirtuous. Through all his enjoyment there runs a certain undercurrent of tragical passion,— a real vein of human sympathy;—it lies at the root of all those strange morbid hauntings of his; a sad excitement, such as other people feel at a tragedy, only less in degree, just enough, indeed, to give a deeper tone to his pleasure, and to make him choose for his subject the broken stones of a cottage wall rather than a road-side bank, the picturesque beauty of form in each being supposed precisely the same: and, together with this slight tragical feeling, there is also a humble and romantic sympathy; a vague desire, in his own mind, to live in cottages rather than palaces; a joy in humble things, a contentment and delight in makeshifts, a secret persuasion (in many respects a true one) that there is in these ruined cottages a happiness often quite as great as in kings' palaces, and a virtue and nearness to God infinitely greater and holier than can commonly be found in any other kind of place; so that the misery in which he exults is not, as he sees it, misery, but noble-ness, "poor, and sick in body, and beloved by the Gods." And thus, being nowise sure that these things can be mended at all, and very sure that he knows not how to mend them, and also that the strange pleasure he feels in them *must* have some good reason in the nature of things, he yields to his destiny, enjoys his dark canal without scruple, and mourns over every improvement in the town, and every movement made by its sanitary commissioners, as a miser would over a planned robbery of his chest; in this being not only innocent, but even respectable and admirable, compared with the kind of person who has *no* pleasure in sights of this kind, but only in fair façades, trim gardens, and park palings, and who would thrust all poverty and misery out of his way, collecting it into back alleys, or sweeping it finally out of the world, so that the street might give wider play for his chariot wheels, and the breeze less offence to his nobility.

Therefore, even the love for the lower picturesque ought to be cultivated with care, wherever it exists; not with any special view to artistic, but to merely humane, education. It will never really or seriously interfere with practical benevolence; on the contrary, it will constantly lead, if associated with other benevolent principles, to a truer sympathy with the poor, and better understanding of the right ways of helping them; and, in the present stage of civilization, it is the most important element of character, not directly moral, which can be cultivated in youth; since it is mainly for the want of this feeling that we destroy so many ancient monuments, in order to erect "handsome" streets and shops instead, which might just as well have been erected elsewhere, and whose effect on our minds, so far as they have any, is to increase every disposition to frivolity, expense, and display.

1868

⇥ END OF PERSPECTIVES: THE SUBLIME, THE BEAUTIFUL, AND THE PICTURESQUE ⇤

Samuel Taylor Coleridge
1772–1834

"Come back into memory, like as thou wert in the dayspring of thy fancies, with hope like a fiery column before thee—the dark pillar not yet turned—Samuel Taylor Coleridge—Logician, Metaphysician, Bard!—How have I seen the casual passer through the cloisters stand still, entranced with admiration . . . while the walls of the old Grey Friars re-echoed to the accents of the *inspired charity-boy!*" When Charles Lamb thus memorialized his former schoolfellow, Coleridge had more than a decade yet to live, but he had already made himself into the mythic Romantic figure of promise and failure whom Lamb salutes.

Born in 1772, the last child of the vicar of Ottery St. Mary's in Devon, Coleridge developed a reputation for precocity even before the death of his father led to his enrollment at Christ's Hospital, a London boarding school for the sons of distressed families, where Lamb met him. A brilliant career at Jesus College, Cambridge, ended in an unhappy attempt to enlist in the army under an assumed name, and he left without a degree in 1794. With Robert Southey, a fellow Oxford enthusiast for poetry and radical politics, he planned an ideal democratic community on the banks of the Susquehanna in Pennsylvania, to be named "Pantisocracy," or equal rule by all. The project collapsed in a dispute over whether they would have servants, but not before Coleridge had cemented the social bonds by becoming engaged to Sara Fricker, the sister of Southey's fiancée; the marriage proved unhappy. Coleridge later minimized his youthful "squeaking baby-trumpet of sedition," but he founded a short-lived antigovernment periodical. *The Watchman* (1796); to earn a living, he was pointing in the unorthodox direction of the Unitarian ministry until he was relieved by a moderate annuity of £150 from the Wedgwoods, of the famous pottery firm. In 1796 he published *Poems on Various Subjects*, containing the poem later titled *The Eolian Harp*, and in 1797 he began the collaboration with Wordsworth that produced *Lyrical Ballads* (1798), headed by *The Rime of the Ancyent Marinere*, as the poem was called in its archaizing first version. Before the volume was published, Coleridge and the Wordsworths departed for Germany, where Coleridge studied philosophy at Göttingen. Charges of plagiarism have swirled ever since around the readings of Kant, Schiller, Schelling, and Fichte that animated his lifelong effort to combat what he regarded as the spiritless mechanical world of eighteenth-century British empiricism.

In 1800 Coleridge followed the Wordsworths to the Lake District, where his love for Sara Hutchinson, sister of Wordsworth's future wife, sharpened his estrangement from his own wife. He became addicted to laudanum (opium dissolved in alcohol), a standard medical remedy for the rheumatic pains he suffered, but the stomach disorders it produced increased his dependency. The physiology of addiction was not understood in his day, and what was a widespread social phenomenon Coleridge regarded as an individual moral flaw. His inability to break the habit produced a spiral of depression: guilt, a paralytic doubt of his strength of will, the fear that he was unworthy of love. By 1802, in *Dejection: An Ode*, he declared the failure of his "genial spirits" and "shaping spirit of Imagination," but he carried on an active public career. An important political commentator in the newspapers, he also undertook another periodical, *The Friend* (1809–1810), saw his play *Remorse* succeed at Drury Lane (1813), and gave a series of brilliant lectures on Shakespeare, Milton, poetry, drama, and philosophy (1808–1818). That these enterprises often fell short of the triumphant fullness he forecast for them fixed the myth of promise unfulfilled, even as his accomplishments won increasing influence. From 1816 on, he lived in a London suburb under the care of a young doctor, James Gillman, and he flourished in this stable environment. The fabled talk of the "Sage of Highgate," as Carlyle called him, "had a charm much more than literary, a charm almost religious and prophetic." If the "practical intellects of the world did not much heed him," Carlyle continued, "to the rising spirits of the young generation he had this dusky sublime character; and sat there as a kind of *Magus*." Coleridge became, in the judgment of John Stuart Mill, one of the two seminal minds of the nineteenth century, the idealist, Christian, philosopher of organic unity around whose work the opposition to Benthamite utilitarianism crystalized.

In his final decades, Coleridge joined new work and old into a substantial body of publication. *Christabel*, long known by reputation, appeared with Byron's enthusiastic sponsorship, in 1816, together with *Kubla Khan*. 1817 brought *Sibylline Leaves* (Coleridge's collected poems, including the marginal-gloss version of the lyrical ballad now titled *The Rime of the Ancient Mariner*) and *Biographia Literaria*, the account of his "literary life and opinions" that has provided the starting-point for much twentieth-century literary criticism. In a series of works, Coleridge explicated conservative principles continuous with but far evolved from the Jacobin associations that had led him to urge anonymous publication of the *Lyrical Ballads* because "Wordsworth's name is nothing, and mine stinks": two *Lay Sermons* (1816–1817), articulating his views in the debate over reform; *The Friend*, expanded in 1818 into a three-volume collection of essays on "politics, morals, and religion"; *Aids to Reflection* (1825), emphasizing Christianity as "personal revelation"; and *On the Constitution of Church and State* (1830), outlining conceptions of national culture (and the "clerisy" responsible for preserving it) that resonate throughout the Victorian period. *Table Talk* (1836) posthumously captured the echoes of his voice, and Coleridge has enjoyed a resurrection in our own day. As new scholarly editions bring more writings to light, they deepen the fascination of a man who was the author of some of the most suggestive poems in the language and an erudite philosopher, a poet who in the *Biographia Literaria* transformed the role of the critic, a theorist of the unifying imagination whose works and life are marked by fragments and discontinuities, a believer in the unity of all whose own method has been aptly described as marginal glosses on the works of others, and an idealist engaged with the daily politics of a turbulent era.

The Eolian Harp[1]

Composed at Clevedon, Somersetshire

My pensive Sara![2] thy soft cheek reclined
Thus on mine arm, most soothing sweet it is
To sit beside our cot,° our cot o'ergrown   *cottage*
With white-flowered jasmin, and the broad-leaved myrtle,
5   (Meet emblems they of Innocence and Love!)
And watch the clouds, that late were rich with light,
Slow saddening round, and mark the star of eve
Serenely brilliant (such should wisdom be)
Shine opposite! How exquisite the scents
10   Snatched from yon bean-field! and the world so hushed!
The stilly murmur of the distant sea
Tells us of silence.

           And that simplest lute,
Placed length-ways in the clasping casement, hark!
How by the desultory breeze caressed,
15   Like some coy maid half yielding to her lover,
It pours such sweet upbraiding,° as must needs   *reproach*
Tempt to repeat the wrong! And now, its strings
Boldlier swept, the long sequacious° notes   *rhythmic, flowing*
Over delicious surges sink and rise,
20   Such a soft floating witchery of sound
As twilight Elfins make, when they at eve
Voyage on gentle gales from Fairy-Land,
Where Melodies round honey-dropping flowers,
Footless and wild, like birds of Paradise,[3]
25   Nor pause, nor perch, hovering on untamed wing!
O the one life within us and abroad,
Which meets all motion and becomes its soul,
A light in sound, a sound-like power in light
Rhythm in all thought, and joyance everywhere—
30   Methinks, it should have been impossible
Not to love all things in a world so filled;
Where the breeze warbles, and the mute still air
Is Music slumbering on her instrument.[4]

          And thus, my love! as on the midway slope
35   Of yonder hill I stretch my limbs at noon,
Whilst through my half-closed eyelids I behold
The sunbeams dance, like diamonds, on the main,
And tranquil muse upon tranquillity;
Full many a thought uncalled and undetained,
40   And many idle flitting phantasies,

1. Named after Aeolus, the Greek god of winds, the harp consisted of a guitarlike box, set in an open window where the breeze would cause its strings to sound. Originally titled *Effusion* XXXV *Composed August 20th, at Clevedon, Somersetshire.* The poem was first published in 1796; we print the text of 1834.

2. Sara Fricker, Coleridge's new bride. This poem was written on the honeymoon.
3. Tropical birds famed for colorful plumage.
4. Lines 26–34 were first printed in 1817, not in the poem, but on a corrections page at the front of the volume, marked for insertion here.

Traverse my indolent and passive brain,
As wild and various as the random gales
That swell and flutter on this subject lute!

    And what if all of animated nature
45   Be but organic harps diversely framed,
That tremble into thought, as o'er them sweeps
Plastic and vast, one intellectual breeze,
At once the Soul of each, and God of All?
    But thy more serious eye a mild reproof
50   Darts, O beloved woman! nor such thoughts
Dim and unhallowed dost thou not reject,
And biddest me walk humbly with my God.
Meek daughter in the family of Christ!
Well hast thou said and holily dispraised
55   These shapings of the unregenerate mind;
Bubbles that glitter as they rise and break
On vain Philosophy's aye-babbling spring.
For never guiltless may I speak of him,
The Incomprehensible! save when with awe
60   I praise him, and with Faith that inly feels;
Who with his saving mercies healed me,
A sinful and most miserable man,
Wildered and dark, and gave me to possess
Peace, and this cot, and thee, heart-honoured Maid!

1796/1817/1834   1796, 1817

The Rime of the Ancient Mariner,[1]

IN SEVEN PARTS

Facile credo, plures esse Naturas invisibiles quam visibiles in
rerum universitate. Sed horum omnium familiam quis nobis
enarrabit, et gradus et cognationes et discrimina et singulo-
rum munera? Quid agunt? quae loca habitant? Harum rerum
notitiam semper ambivit ingenium humanum, nunquam
attigit. Juvat, interea, non diffiteor, quandoque in animo,
tanquam in tabulâ, majoris et melioris mundi imaginem con-
templari: ne mens assuefacta hodiernae vitae minutiis se
contrahat nimis, et tota subsidat in pusillas cogitationes. Sed
veritati interea invigilandum est, modusque servandus, ut
certa ab incertis, diem a nocte, distinguamus.[2]

T. Burnet. *Archaeol. Phil.* p. 68.

1. A somewhat revised *Rime* appeared in the 1800 *Lyrical Ballads*, and each publication thereafter reflected further revisions. In his own signed collection of 1817 (*Sibylline Leaves*) Coleridge replaced the "Argument" with the Latin epigraph and added the marginal glosses.
2. From English theologian Thomas Burnet's *Archaeologiae Philosophicae* (1692): "I can easily believe that there are more invisible creatures in the universe than visible ones. But who will tell us to what family each belongs, their ranks and relationships, and what their distinguishing characteristics may be? What do they do? Where do they live? The human mind has always circled around these matters without finding satisfaction. But I do not doubt that it is beneficial sometimes to contemplate in the mind, as in a picture, the image of a grander and better world; for if the mind becomes used to the trival things of everyday life, it may limit itself too much and decline completely into worthless thinking. Meanwhile, however, we must be on the lookout for the truth, keeping a sense of proportion so that we can distinguish what is sure from what is uncertain, and day from night."

An ancient Mariner
meeteth three Gallants
bidden to a wedding-
feast, and detaineth
one.

IT is an ancient Mariner,
And he stoppeth one of three.
"By thy long gray beard and glittering eye,
Now wherefore stopp'st thou me?

"The Bridegroom's doors are opened wide,   5
And I am next of kin;
The guests are met, the feast is set:
May'st hear the merry din."

He holds him with his skinny hand,
"There was a ship," quoth he.   10
"Hold off! unhand me, grey-beard loon!"
Eftsoons° his hand dropt he.   *immediately*

The wedding-guest is
spellbound by the eye
of the old sea-faring
man, and constrained
to hear his tale.

He holds him with his glittering eye—
The wedding-guest stood still,
And listens like a three years' child: 15
The Mariner hath his will.

The wedding-guest sat on a stone:
He can not choose but hear;
And thus spake on that ancient man,
The bright-eyed Mariner.   20

The ship was cheer'd, the harbour clear'd,
Merrily did we drop
Below the kirk,° below the hill,   *church*
Below the light-house top.

The Mariner tells how
the ship sailed
southward with a good
wind and fair weather,
till it reached the line.

The Sun came up upon the left,   25
Out of the sea came he;
And he shone bright, and on the right
Went down into the sea.

Higher and higher every day,
Till over the mast at noon—   30
The Wedding-Guest here beat his breast,
For he heard the loud bassoon.

The wedding-guest
heareth the bridal
music; but the Mariner
continueth his tale.

The bride hath paced into the hall,
Red as a rose is she;
Nodding their heads before her goes   35
The merry minstrelsy.

The Wedding-Guest he beat his breast,
Yet he can not choose but hear;
And thus spake on that ancient man,
The bright-eyed Mariner.   40

The ship drawn by a
storm toward the south
pole.

And now the STORM-BLAST came, and he
Was tyrannous and strong:
He struck with his o'ertaking wings,
And chased us south along.

With sloping masts and dipping prow,   45
As who pursued with yell and blow

Still treads the shadow of his foe
And forward bends his head,
The ship drove fast, loud roared the blast,
And southward aye° we fled.   *continuously*

And now there came both mist and snow,
And it grew wondrous cold:
And ice, mast-high, came floating by,
As green as emerald.

The land of ice, and of
fearful sounds, where
no living thing was to
be seen.

And through the drifts the snowy clifts   55
Did send a dismal sheen:
Nor shapes of men nor beast we ken°—   *knew*
The ice was all between.

The ice was here, the ice was there,
The ice was all around: 60
It cracked and growled, and roared and howled,
Like noises in a swound!

Till a great sea-bird
called the Albatross,
came through the
snow-fog, and was
received with great joy
and hospitality.

At length did cross an Albatross,
Thorough the fog it came;
As if it had been a Christian soul,   65
We hailed it in God's name.

It ate the food it ne'er had eat,
And round and round it flew.
The ice did split with a thunder-fit;
The helmsman steered us through!   70

And lo! the Albatross
proveth a bird of good
omen, and followeth
the ship as it returned
northward through fog
and floating ice.

And a good south wind sprung up behind;
The Albatross did follow,
And every day, for food or play,
Came to the mariner's hollo!

In mist or cloud, on mast or shroud,   75
It perched for vespers nine;
Whiles all the night, through fog-smoke white,
Glimmered the white moon-shine.

The ancient Mariner
inhospitably killeth
the pious bird of good
omen

"God save thee, ancient Mariner!
From the fiends, that plague thee thus!—   80
Why look'st thou so?"—With my cross-bow
I shot the ALBATROSS.

Part the Second

THE Sun now rose upon the right:
Out of the sea came he,
Still hid in mist, and on the left   85
Went down into the sea.

And the good south wind still blew behind,
But no sweet bird did follow,
Nor any day for food or play
Came to the mariners' hollo!   90

His shipmates cry out against the ancient Mariner, for killing the bird of good luck.

And I had done a hellish thing,
And it would work 'em woe:
For all averred, I had killed the bird
That made the breeze to blow.
Ah wretch! said they, the bird to slay,   95
That made the breeze to blow!

But when the fog cleared off, they justify the same, and thus make themselves accomplices in the crime.

Nor dim nor red, like God's own head,
The glorious Sun uprist:
Then all averred, I had killed the bird
That brought the fog and mist.   100
'Twas right, said they, such birds to slay,
That bring the fog and mist.

The fair breeze continues; the ship enters the Pacific Ocean, and sails northward, even till it reaches the Line.

The fair breeze blew, the white foam flew,
The furrow followed free;
We were the first that ever burst   105
Into that silent sea.

The ship hath been suddenly becalmed.

Down dropt the breeze, the sails dropt down,
'Twas sad as sad could be;
And we did speak only to break
The silence of the sea!   110

All in a hot and copper sky,
The bloody Sun, at noon,
Right up above the mast did stand,
No bigger than the Moon.

Day after day, day after day,   115
We stuck, nor breath nor motion;
As idle as a painted ship
Upon a painted ocean.

And the Albatross begins to be avenged.

Water, water, every where,
And all the boards did shrink;   120
Water, water, every where,
Nor any drop to drink.

A spirit had followed them; one of the invisible inhabitants of this planet, neither departed souls nor angels; concerning whom the learned Jew, Josephus, and the Platonic Constantinopolitan, Michael Psellus, may be consulted. They are very numerous, and there is no climate or element without one or more.

The very deep did rot: O Christ!
That ever this should be!
Yea, slimy things did crawl with legs   125
Upon the slimy sea.

About, about, in reel and rout
The death-fires° danced at night;   *phosphorescent plankton*
The water, like a witch's oils,
Burnt green, and blue and white.   130

And some in dreams assured were
Of the Spirit that plagued us so;
Nine fathom deep he had followed us
From the land of mist and snow.

And every tongue, through utter drought,   135
Was withered at the root;
We could not speak, no more than if
We had been choak'd with soot.

The shipmates, in
their sore distress,
would fain throw the
whole guilt on the
ancient Mariner; in
sign whereof they hang
the dead sea-bird
round his neck.

Ah! well a-day! what evil looks
Had I from old and young!   140
Instead of the cross, the Albatross
About my neck was hung.

Part the Third

THERE passed a weary time. Each throat
Was parched, and glazed each eye.
A weary time! a weary time!   145
How glazed each weary eye,
The ancient Mariner
beholdeth a sign in the
element afar off.
When looking westward, I beheld
A something in the sky.

At first it seemed a little speck,
And then it seemed a mist;   150
It moved and moved, and took at last
A certain shape, I wist.°   *knew*

A speck, a mist, a shape, I wist!
And still it neared and neared:
As if it dodged a water-sprite,   155
It plunged and tacked and veered.

At its nearer approach,
it seemeth him to be a
ship; and at a dear
ransom he freeth his
speech from the bonds
of thirst.
With throats unslaked, with black lips baked,
We could nor laugh nor wail;
Through utter drought all dumb we stood!
I bit my arm, I sucked the blood,   160
And cried, A sail! a sail!

With throats unslaked, with black lips baked,
Agape they heard me call:
A flash of joy.
Gramercy! they for joy did grin,
And all at once their breath drew in,   165
As they were drinking all.

And horror follows.
For can it be a *ship*
that comes onward
without wind or tide?
See! see! (I cried) she tacks no more!
Hither to work us weal;°   *benefit*
Without a breeze, without a tide,
She steadies with upright keel!   170

The western wave was all a-flame.
The day was well nigh done!
Almost upon the western wave
Rested the broad bright Sun;
When that strange shape drove suddenly   175
Betwixt us and the Sun.

It seemeth him but the
skeleton of a ship.
And straight the Sun was flecked with bars,
(Heaven's Mother send us grace!)
As if through a dungeon-grate he peer'd
With broad and burning face.   180

And its ribs are seen as bars on the face of the setting Sun.

Alas! (thought I, and my heart beat loud)
How fast she nears and nears!
Are those *her* sails that glance in the Sun,
Like restless gossameres?°   cobwebs

The spectre-woman and her death-mate, and no other on board the skeleton-ship.

Are those *her* ribs through which the Sun   185
Did peer, as through a grate?
And is that Woman all her crew?
Is that a DEATH? and are there two?
Is DEATH that woman's mate?

Like vessel, like crew!

Her lips were red, *her* looks were free,   190
Her locks were yellow as gold:
Her skin was as white as leprosy,
The Night-Mair LIFE-IN-DEATH was she,
Who thicks man's blood with cold.

DEATH, and LIFE-IN-DEATH have diced for the ship's crew, and she (the latter) winneth the ancient Mariner.

The naked hulk alongside came,   195
And the twain were casting dice;
"The game is done! I've, I've won!"
Quoth she, and whistles thrice.[3]

No twilight within the courts of the Sun.

The Sun's rim dips; the stars rush out:
At one stride comes the dark;   200
With far-heard whisper, o'er the sea,
Off shot the spectre-bark.

At the rising of the Moon,

We listened and looked sideways up!
Fear at my heart, as at a cup,
My life-blood seemed to sip!   205
The stars were dim, and thick the night,
The steersman's face by his lamp gleamed white;

From the sails the dew did drip—
Till clomb above the eastern bar
The horned Moon, with one bright star   210
Within the nether tip.

One after another,

One after one, by the star-dogged Moon,
Too quick for groan or sigh,
Each turned his face with a ghastly pang,
And cursed me with his eye.   215

His ship-mates drop down dead;

Four times fifty living men
(And I heard nor sigh nor groan),
With heavy thump, a lifeless lump,
They dropped down one by one.

But LIFE-IN-DEATH begins her work on the ancient Mariner.

The souls did from their bodies fly,—   220
They fled to bliss or woe!
And every soul, it passed me by,
Like the whizz of my CROSS-BOW!

3. In 1817 only, this stanza followed: "A gust of wind sterte up behind / And whistled through the bones; / Through the holes of his eyes and the hole of his mouth, / Half whistles and half groans." Coleridge wanted to erase this stanza.

Part the Fourth

The wedding-guest feareth that a spirit is talking to him;

"I FEAR thee, ancient Mariner!
I fear thy skinny hand!
And thou art long, and lank, and brown,
As is the ribbed sea-sand.   225

But the ancient Mariner assureth him of his bodily life, and proceedeth to relate his horrible penance.

I fear thee and thy glittering eye,
And thy skinny hand, so brown."—
Fear not, fear not, thou Wedding-Guest!   230
This body dropt not down.

Alone, alone, all, all alone,
Alone on a wide wide sea!
And never a saint took pity on
My soul in agony.   235

He despiseth the creatures of the calm,

The many men, so beautiful!
And they all dead did lie:
And a thousand thousand slimy things
Lived on; and so did I.

And envieth that *they* should live, and so many lie dead.

I looked upon the rotting sea,   240
And drew my eyes away;
I looked upon the rotting deck,
And there the dead men lay.

I looked to Heaven, and tried to pray;
But or ever a prayer had gusht,   245
A wicked whisper came, and made
My heart as dry as dust.

I closed my lids, and kept them close,
And the balls like pulses beat;
For the sky and the sea, and the sea and the sky   250
Lay, like a load, on my weary eye,
And the dead were at my feet.

But the curse liveth for him in the eye of the dead men.

The cold sweat melted from their limbs,
Not rot nor reek did they:
The look with which they looked on me   255
Had never passed away.

In his loneliness and fixedness he yearneth towards the journeying Moon, and the stars that still sojourn, yet still move onward; and every where the blue sky belongs to them, and is their appointed rest, and their native country, and their own natural homes, which they enter unannounced, as

An orphan's curse would drag to Hell
A spirit from on high;
But oh! more horrible than that
Is the curse in a dead man's eye!   260
Seven days, seven nights, I saw that curse,
And yet I could not die.

The moving Moon went up the sky,
And nowhere did abide:
Softly she was going up,   265
And a star or two beside—

lords that are certainly
expected, and yet there
is a silent joy at their
arrival.

Her beams bemocked the sultry main,
Like April hoar-frost spread;
But where the ship's huge shadow lay,
The charmed water burnt alway   270
A still and awful red.

By the light of the
Moon he beholdeth
God's creatures of the
great calm.

Beyond the shadow of the ship,
I watched the water-snakes:
They moved in tracks of shining white,
And when they reared, the elfish light   275
Fell off in hoary flakes.

Within the shadow of the ship
I watched their rich attire:
Blue, glossy green, and velvet black,
They coiled and swam; and every track   280
Was a flash of golden fire.

Their beauty and their
happiness.

O happy living things! no tongue
Their beauty might declare:
A spring of love gushed from my heart,

He blesseth them in
his heart.

And I blessed them unaware!   285
Sure my kind saint took pity on me,
And I blessed them unaware.

The spell begins to
break.

The self same moment I could pray;
And from my neck so free
The Albatross fell off, and sank   290
Like lead into the sea.

Part the Fifth

By grace of the holy
Mother, the ancient
Mariner is refreshed
with rain.

O SLEEP! it is a gentle thing,
Belov'd from pole to pole!
To Mary Queen the praise be given!
She sent the gentle sleep from Heaven,   295
That slid into my soul.

The silly° buckets on the deck,   *helpless*
That had so long remained,
I dreamt that they were filled with dew;
And when I awoke, it rained.   300

My lips were wet, my throat was cold,
My garments all were dank;
Sure I had drunken in my dreams,
And still my body drank.

He heareth sounds and
seeth strange sights
and commotions in the
sky and the element.

I moved, and could not feel my limbs: 305
I was so light—almost
I thought that I had died in sleep,
And was a blessed ghost.

And soon I heard a roaring wind:
It did not come anear;   310

But with its sound it shook the sails,
That were so thin and sere.

The upper air burst into life!
And a hundred fire-flags° sheen,   *meteors*
To and fro they were hurried about!   315
And to and fro, and in and out,
The wan stars danced between.

And the coming wind did roar more loud,
And the sails did sigh like sedge;°   *marsh grass*
And the rain poured down from one black cloud;   320
The Moon was at its edge.

The thick black cloud was cleft, and still
The Moon was at its side:
Like waters shot from some high crag,
The lightning fell with never a jag,   325
A river steep and wide.

The bodies of the ship's crew are inspirited, and the ship moves on.

The loud wind never reached the ship,
Yet now the ship moved on!
Beneath the lightning and the Moon
The dead men gave a groan.   330

They groaned, they stirred, they all uprose,
Nor spake, nor moved their eyes;
It had been strange, even in a dream,
To have seen those dead men rise.

The helmsman steered, the ship moved on;   335
Yet never a breeze up blew;
The mariners all 'gan work the ropes,
Where they were wont to do;
They raised their limbs like lifeless tools—
We were a ghastly crew.   340

The body of my brother's son
Stood by me, knee to knee:
The body and I pulled at one rope,
But he said naught to me.

But not by the souls of the men, nor by daemons of earth or middle air, but by a blessed troop of angelic spirits, sent down by the invocation of the guardian saint.

"I fear thee, ancient Mariner!"   345
Be calm, thou Wedding-Guest!
'Twas not those souls that fled in pain,
Which to their corses came again,
But a troop of spirits blest:

For when it dawned—they dropped their arms,   350
And clustered round the mast;
Sweet sounds rose slowly through their mouths,
And from their bodies passed.

Around, around, flew each sweet sound,
Then darted to the Sun;   355

Slowly the sounds came back again,
Now mixed, now one by one.

Sometimes a-dropping from the sky
I heard the sky-lark sing;
Sometimes all little birds that are,   360
How they seemed to fill the sea and air
With their sweet jargoning!°   *warbling*

And now 'twas like all instruments,
Now like a lonely flute;
And now it is an angel's song,   365
That makes the heavens be mute.

It ceased; yet still the sails made on
A pleasant noise till noon,
A noise like of a hidden brook
In the leafy mouth of June,   370
That to the sleeping woods all night
Singeth a quiet tune.

Till noon we quietly sailed on,
Yet never a breeze did breathe:
Slowly and smoothly went the ship,   375
Moved onward from beneath.

The lonesome spirit from the south-pole carries on the ship as far as the line, in obedience to the angelic troop, but still requireth vengeance.

Under the keel nine fathom deep,
From the land of mist and snow,
The spirit slid: and it was he
That made the ship to go.   380
The sails at noon left off their tune,
And the ship stood still also.

The Sun, right up above the mast,
Had fixt her to the ocean;
But in a minute she 'gan stir,   385
With a short uneasy motion—
Backwards and forwards half her length,
With a short uneasy motion.

Then like a pawing horse let go,
She made a sudden bound: 390
It flung the blood into my head,
And I fell down in a swound.

The Polar Spirit's fellow-daemons, the invisible inhabitants of the element, take part in his wrong; and two of them relate, one to the other, that penance long and heavy for the ancient Mariner hath been accorded to the Polar Spirit, who returneth southward.

How long in that same fit I lay,
I have not to declare;
But ere my living life returned,   395
I heard and in my soul discerned
Two VOICES in the air.

"Is it he?" quoth one, "Is this the man?
By him who died on cross,
With his cruel bow he laid full low,   400
The harmless Albatross.

The spirit who bideth by himself
In the land of mist and snow,
He loved the bird that loved the man
Who shot him with his bow."   405

The other was a softer voice,
As soft as honey-dew.
Quoth he, "The man hath penance done,
And penance more will do."

Part the Sixth

FIRST VOICE.
"But tell me, tell me! speak again,   410
Thy soft response renewing—
What makes that ship drive on so fast?
What is the OCEAN doing?"

SECOND VOICE.
"Still as a slave before his lord,
The OCEAN hath no blast;   415
His great bright eye most silently
Up to the Moon is cast—

If he may know which way to go;
For she guides him smooth or grim.
See, brother, see! how graciously   420
She looketh down on him."

FIRST VOICE.
"But why drives on that ship so fast,
Without or wave or wind?"

SECOND VOICE.
"The air is cut away before,
And closes from behind.   425

Fly, brother, fly! more high, more high!
Or we shall be belated:
For slow and slow that ship will go,
When the Mariner's trance is abated."

I woke, and we were sailing on   430
As in a gentle weather:
'Twas night, calm night, the moon was high;
The dead men stood together.

All stood together on the deck,
For a charnel-dungeon fitter: 435
All fixed on me their stony eyes,
That in the Moon did glitter.

The pang, the curse, with which they died,
Had never passed away:
I could not draw my eyes from theirs,   440
Nor turn them up to pray.

The Mariner hath been cast into a trance; for the angelic power causeth the vessel to drive northward, faster than human life could endure.

The supernatural motion is retarded; the Mariner awakes, and his penance begins anew.

The curse is finally
expiated.

And now this spell was snapt: once more
I viewed the ocean green,
And looked far forth, yet little saw
Of what had else been seen—   445

Like one, that on a lonesome road
Doth walk in fear and dread,
And having once turn'd round, walks on,
And turns no more his head;
Because he knows, a frightful fiend   450
Doth close behind him tread.

But soon there breathed a wind on me,
Nor sound nor motion made:
Its path was not upon the sea,
In ripple or in shade.   455

It raised my hair, it fanned my cheek
Like a meadow-gale of spring—
It mingled strangely with my fears,
Yet it felt like a welcoming.

Swiftly, swiftly flew the ship,   460
Yet she sailed softly too:
Sweetly, sweetly blew the breeze—
On me alone it blew.

And the ancient
Mariner beholdeth his
native country.

Oh! dream of joy! is this indeed
The light-house top I see?   465
Is this the hill? is this the kirk?
Is this mine own countree?

We drifted o'er the harbour-bar,
And I with sobs did pray—
O let me be awake, my God!   470
Or let me sleep alway.

The harbour-bay was clear as glass,
So smoothly it was strewn!
And on the bay the moonlight lay,
And the shadow of the moon.   475

The rock shone bright, the kirk no less,
That stands above the rock:
The moonlight steeped in silentness
The steady weathercock.

And the bay was white with silent light,   480
Till rising from the same,

The angelic spirits
leave the dead bodies,

Full many shapes, that shadows were,
In crimson colours came.

And appear in their
own forms of light.

A little distance from the prow
Those crimson shadows were: 485

I turned my eyes upon the deck—
Oh, Christ! what saw I there!

Each corse lay flat, lifeless and flat,
And, by the holy rood!°   *cross*
A man all light, a seraph-man,   490
On every corse there stood.

This seraph-band, each waved his hand:
It was a heavenly sight!
They stood as signals to the land,
Each one a lovely light;   495

This sera ph-band, each waved his hand,
No voice did they impart—
No voice; but oh! the silence sank
Like music on my heart.

But soon I heard the dash of oars,   500
I heard the Pilot's cheer;
My head was turned perforce away
And I saw a boat appear.

The Pilot, and the Pilot's boy,
I heard them coming fast: 505
Dear Lord in Heaven! it was a joy
The dead men could not blast.

I saw a third—I heard his voice:
It is the Hermit good!
He singeth loud his godly hymns   510
That he makes in the wood.
He'll shrieve° my soul, he'll wash away   *absolve*
The Albatross's blood.

Part the Seventh

The Hermit of the
Wood,

This Hermit good lives in that wood
Which slopes down to the sea.   515
How loudly his sweet voice he rears!
He loves to talk with marineres
That come from a far countree.

He kneels at morn, and noon, and eve—
He hath a cushion plump: 520
It is the moss that wholly hides
The rotted old oak-stump.

The Skiff-boat neared: I heard them talk,
"Why, this is strange, I trow!
Where are those lights so many and fair,   525
That signal made but now?"

Approacheth the ship
with wonder.

"Strange, by my faith!" the Hermit said—
"And they answered not our cheer!

The planks looked warped! and see those sails,
How thin they are and sere!   530
I never saw aught like to them,
Unless perchance it were

"Brown skeletons of leaves that lag
My forest-brook along;
When the ivy-tod° is heavy with snow,   clump   535
And the owlet whoops to the wolf below,
That eats the she-wolf's young."

"Dear Lord! it hath a fiendish look—
(The Pilot made reply)
I am a-feared"—"Push on, push on!"   540
Said the Hermit cheerily.

The boat came closer to the ship,
But I nor spake nor stirred;
The boat came close beneath the ship,
And straight a sound was heard.   545

The boat came closer to the ship,

Under the water it rumbled on,
Still louder and more dread:
It reachd the ship, it split the bay;
The ship went down like lead.

Stunned by that loud and dreadful sound,   550
Which sky and ocean smote,
Like one that hath been seven days drowned,
My body lay afloat;
But swift as dreams, myself I found
Within the Pilot's boat.   555

Upon the whirl, where sank the ship,
The boat spun round and round;
And all was still, save that the hill
Was telling of the sound.

I moved my lips—the Pilot shrieked   560
And fell down in a fit;
The holy Hermit raised his eyes,
And prayed where he did sit.

I took the oars: the Pilot's boy,
Who now doth crazy go,   565
Laughed loud and long, and all the while
His eyes went to and fro.
"Ha! ha!" quoth he, "full plain I see,
The Devil knows how to row."

And now, all in my own countree,   570
I stood on the firm land!
The Hermit stepped forth from the boat,
And scarcely he could stand.

The ancient Mariner
earnestly entreateth
the Hermit to shrieve
him; and the penance
of life falls on him.
"O shrieve me, shrieve me, holy man!"
The Hermit crossed his brow.   575
"Say quick," quoth he, "I bid thee say—
What manner of man art thou?"

Forthwith this frame of mine was wrenched
With a woeful agony,
Which forced me to begin my tale;   580
And then it left me free.

And ever and anon
throughout his future
life an agony
constraineth him to
travel from land to
land,
Since then, at an uncertain hour,
That agony returns:
And till my ghastly tale is told,
This heart within me burns.   585

I pass, like night, from land to land;
I have strange power of speech;
That moment that his face I see,
I know the man that must hear me:
To him my tale I teach.   590

What loud uproar bursts from that door!
The wedding-guests are there:
But in the garden-bower the bride
And bride-maids singing are;
And hark the little vesper bell,   595
Which biddeth me to prayer!

O Wedding-Guest! this soul hath been
Alone on a wide wide sea:
So lonely 'twas, that God himself
Scarce seemed there to be.   600

O sweeter than the marriage-feast,
'Tis sweeter far to me,
To walk together to the kirk
With a goodly company!—

To walk together to the kirk,   605
And all together pray,
While each to his great Father bends,
Old men, and babes, and loving friends,
And youths and maidens gay!

And to teach by his
own example, love and
reverence to all things
that God made and
loveth.
Farewell, farewell! but this I tell   610
To thee, thou Wedding-Guest!
He prayeth well, who loveth well
Both man and bird and beast.

He prayeth best, who loveth best
All things both great and small;   615

For the dear God who loveth us,
He made and loveth all."

The Mariner, whose eye is bright,
Whose beard with age is hoar,
Is gone: and now the Wedding-Guest   620
Turned from the bridegroom's door.

He went like one that hath been stunned,
And is of sense forlorn:
A sadder and a wiser man,
He rose the morrow morn.   625
1817–1834   1817

COMPANION READING

Samuel Taylor Coleridge: from *Table Talk*

May 31, 1830. Mrs. Barbauld[1] once told me that she admired the Ancient Mariner very much, but that there were two faults in it, it was improbable, and had no moral. As for the probability, I owned that that might admit some question; but as to the want of a moral, I told her that in my own judgment the poem had too much; and that the only, or chief fault, if I might say so, was the obtrusion of the moral senti-ment so openly on the reader as a principle or cause of action in a work of such pure imagination. It ought to have had no more moral than the Arabian Nights' tale of the merchant's sitting down to eat dates by the side of a well, and throwing the shells aside, and lo! a genie starts up, and says he *must* kill the aforesaid merchant, *because* one of the date shells had, it seems, put out the eye of the genie's son.

Kubla Khan *or, A Vision in a Dream.*[1]
A Fragment

Of the Fragment of Kubla Khan

The following fragment is here published at the request of a poet of great and deserv-ing celebrity,[2] and, as far as the Author's own opinions are concerned, rather as a psy-chological curiosity, than on the ground of any supposed *poetic* merits.

In the summer of the year 1797, the Author, then in ill health, had retired to a lonely farmhouse between Porlock and Linton, on the Exmoor confines of Somerset and Devonshire. In consequence of a slight indisposition, an anodyne[3] had been pre-scribed, from the effects of which he fell asleep in his chair at the moment that he was reading the following sentence, or words of the same substance, in "Purchas's Pilgrim-age":[4] "Here the Khan Kubla commanded a palace to be built, and a stately garden thereunto. And thus ten miles of fertile ground were inclosed with a wall." The

1. Anna Letitia Barbauld; see page 29.
1. Kubla Khan was the grandson of Genghis Khan and Emperor of China in the 13th century.
2. Byron, who convinced his own publisher to issue the poem, together with *Christabel* and *The Pains of Sleep*.

3. A painkiller, probably laudanum.
4. A collection of often fantastical accounts of foreign lands compiled by Samuel Purchas (1613). As a boy, Coleridge was an avid reader of such literature.

Author continued for about three hours in a profound sleep, at least of the external senses, during which time he has the most vivid confidence, that he could not have composed less than from two to three hundred lines; if that indeed can be called composition in which all the images rose up before him as *things*, with a parallel production of the correspondent expressions, without any sensation or consciousness of effort. On awaking he appeared to himself to have a distinct recollection of the whole, and taking his pen, ink, and paper, instantly and eagerly wrote down the lines that are here preserved. At this moment he was unfortunately called out by a person on business from Porlock, and detained by him above an hour, and on his return to his room, found to his no small surprise and mortification, that though he still retained some vague and dim recollection of the general purpose of the vision, yet, with the exception of some eight or ten scattered lines and images, all the rest had passed away like the images on the surface of a stream into which a stone has been cast, but, alas! without the after restoration of the latter:

> Then all the charm
> Is broken—all that phantom-world so fair
> Vanishes, and a thousand circlets spread,
> And each mis-shape the other. Stay awhile,
> Poor youth! who scarcely dar'st lift up thine eyes—
> The stream will soon renew its smoothness, soon
> The visions will return! And lo, he stays,
> And soon the fragments dim of lovely forms
> Come trembling back, unite, and now once more
> The pool becomes a mirror.[5]

Yet from the still surviving recollections in his mind, the Author has frequently purposed to finish for himself what had been originally, as it were, given to him. Σαμερον αδιον ασω:[6] but the to-morrow is yet to come.

As a contrast to this vision, I have annexed a fragment of a very different character, describing with equal fidelity the dream of pain and disease.[7]

(1816)

Kubla Khan

> In Xanadu did KUBLA KHAN
> A stately pleasure-dome decree:
> Where ALPH, the sacred river, ran
> Through caverns measureless to man
> 5   Down to a sunless sea.
> So twice five miles of fertile ground
> With walls and towers were girdled round;
> And here were gardens bright with sinuous rills,
> Where blossom'd many an incense-bearing tree;
> 10   And here were forests ancient as the hills,
> And folding sunny spots of greenery.
>
> But oh that deep romantic chasm which slanted
> Down the green hill athwart a cedarn cover!

5. From Coleridge's *The Picture* (lines 91–100).
6. Misquoting Theocritus, *Idyls*, line 1.145: "I'll sing a sweeter song tomorrow."
7. *The Pains of Sleep*.

A savage place! as holy and inchanted
15 As e'er beneath a waning moon was haunted
By woman wailing for her demon-lover!
And from this chasm, with ceaseless turmoil seething,
As if this earth in fast thick pants were breathing,
A mighty fountain momently was forced:
20 Amid whose swift half-intermitted Burst
Huge fragments vaulted like rebounding hail,
Or chaffy grain beneath the thresher's flail:
And mid these dancing rocks at once and ever
It flung up momently the sacred river.
25 Five miles meandering with a mazy motion
Through wood and dale the sacred river ran,
Then reached the caverns measureless to man,
And sank in tumult to a lifeless ocean:
And 'mid this tumult Kubla heard from far
30 Ancestral voices prophesying war!

    The shadow of the dome of pleasure
    Floated midway on the waves;
    Where was heard the mingled measure
    From the fountain and the caves.
35 It was a miracle of rare device,
A sunny pleasure-dome with caves of ice!

    A damsel with a dulcimer
    In a vision once I saw:
    It was an Abyssinian maid
40   And on her dulcimer she play'd,
    Singing of Mount Abora.
    Could I revive within me
    Her symphony and song,
    To such a deep delight 'twould win me,
45 That with music loud and long,
I would build that dome in air,
That sunny dome! those caves of ice!
And all who heard should see them there,
And all should cry, Beware! Beware!
50 His flashing eyes, his floating hair!
Weave a circle round him thrice,
And close your eyes with holy dread:
For he on honey-dew hath fed,
And drank[8] the milk of Paradise.

1797–1798   1816

Frost at Midnight

The Frost performs its secret ministry,
Unhelped by any wind. The owlet's cry
Came loud—and hark, again! loud as before.

8. Changed to "drunk" in 1832.

The inmates of my cottage, all at rest,
5   Have left me to that solitude, which suits
Abstruser musings: save that at my side
My cradled infant slumbers peacefully.
'Tis calm indeed! so calm, that it disturbs
And vexes meditation with its strange
10 And extreme silentness. Sea, hill, and wood
This populous village! Sea, and hill, and wood,
With all the numberless goings on of life,
Inaudible as dreams! the thin blue flame
Lies on my low burnt fire, and quivers not;
15 Only that film,[1] which fluttered on the grate,
Still flutters there, the sole unquiet thing.
Methinks, its motion in this hush of nature
Gives it dim sympathies with me who live,
Making it a companionable form,
20 Whose puny flaps and freaks the idling Spirit
By its own moods interprets, everywhere
Echo or mirror seeking of itself,
And makes a toy of Thought.

But O! how oft,
How oft, at school, with most believing mind,
25 Presageful, have I gazed upon the bars,
To watch that fluttering stranger! and as oft
With unclosed lids, already had I dreamt
Of my sweet birth-place, and the old church-tower,
Whose bells, the poor man's only music, rang
30 From morn to evening, all the hot fair-day,
So sweetly, that they stirred and haunted me
With a wild pleasure, falling on mine ear
Most like articulate sounds of things to come!
So gazed I, till the soothing things I dreamt
35 Lulled me to sleep, and sleep prolonged my dreams!
And so I brooded all the following morn,
Awed by the stern preceptor's° face, mine eye   *teacher's*
Fixed with mock study on my swimming book:
Save if the door half opened, and I snatched
40 A hasty glance, and still my heart leaped up,
For still I hoped to see the stranger's face,
Townsman, or aunt, or sister more beloved,
My playmate when we both were clothed alike![2]

Dear Babe, that sleepest cradled by my side,
45 Whose gentle breathings, heard in this deep calm,
Fill up the interspersed vacancies
And momentary pauses of the thought!
My babe so beautiful! it thrills my heart
With tender gladness, thus to look at thee,

1. A piece of soot. "In all parts of the kingdom these films   some absent friend" (Coleridge's note in 1798).
are called *strangers* and supposed to portend the arrival of   2. Boys and girls wore the same clothes until age 5.

50 And think that thou shalt learn far other lore
And in far other scenes! For I was reared
In the great city, pent 'mid cloisters dim,
And saw naught lovely but the sky and stars.
But *thou*, my babe! shalt wander like a breeze
55 By lakes and sandy shores, beneath the crags
Of ancient mountain, and beneath the clouds,
Which image in their bulk both lakes and shores
And mountain crags: so shalt thou see and hear
The lovely shapes and sounds intelligible
60 Of that eternal language, which thy God
Utters, who from eternity doth teach
Himself in all, and all things in himself.
Great universal Teacher! he shall mould
Thy spirit, and by giving make it ask.

65   Therefore all seasons shall be sweet to thee,
Whether the summer clothe the general earth
With greenness, or the redbreast sit and sing
Betwixt the tufts of snow on the bare branch
Of mossy apple-tree, while the nigh thatch
70 Smokes in the sun-thaw; whether the eave-drops fall
Heard only in the trances of the blast,
Or if the secret ministry of frost
Shall hang them up in silent icicles,
Quietly shining to the quiet Moon.

February 1798   1798/1817

Dejection: An Ode[1]

Late, late yestreen I saw the new Moon,
With the old Moon in her arms;
And I fear, I fear, my Master dear!
We shall have a deadly storm.

BALLAD OF SIR PATRICK SPENCE

I

Well! If the Bard was weather-wise, who made
    The grand old ballad of Sir Patrick Spence,
        This night, so tranquil now, will not go hence
Unroused by winds, that ply a busier trade
5 Than those which mould yon cloud in lazy flakes,
Or the dull sobbing draft, that moans and rakes
        Upon the strings of this Eolian lute,[2]
        Which better far were mute.
    For lo! the New-moon winter-bright!

1. *Dejection* evolved from a long verse-letter that Coleridge wrote to Sara Hutchinson in April 1802, after hearing the opening stanzas of Wordsworth's *Ode: Intimations of Immortality* (see page 284). Cutting the verse letter by half, Coleridge published it on 4 October 1802, Wordsworth's wedding day and the seventh anniversary of his own unhappy marriage. We print the text of 1834. 2. An instrument named after Aeolus, the Greek god of winds; see *The Eolian Harp*, page 325.

10   And overspread with phantom light,
        (With swimming phantom light o'erspread
        But rimmed and circled by a silver thread)
      I see the old Moon in her lap, foretelling
        The coming on of rain and squally blast.
15   And oh! that even now the gust were swelling,
        And the slant night-shower driving loud and fast!
      Those sounds which oft have raised me, whilst they awed,
          And sent my soul abroad,
      Might now, perhaps, their wonted impulse give,
20   Might startle this dull pain, and make it move and live!

                          II
      A grief without a pang, void, dark, and drear,
        A stifled, drowsy, unimpassioned grief,
        Which finds no natural outlet, no relief,
          In word, or sigh, or tear—
25   O Lady! in this wan and heartless mood,
      To other thoughts by yonder throstle° woo'd,   *thrush*
          All this long eve, so balmy and serene,
      Have I been gazing on the western sky,
          And its peculiar tint of yellow green:
30   And still I gaze—and with how blank an eye!
      And those thin clouds above, in flakes and bars,
      That give away their motion to the stars;
      Those stars, that glide behind them or between,
      Now sparkling, now bedimmed, but always seen:
35   Yon crescent Moon, as fixed as if it grew
      In its own cloudless, starless lake of blue;
      I see them all so excellently fair,
      I see, not feel how beautiful they are!

                          III
          My genial° spirits fail;[3]   *creative*
40   And what can these avail
      To lift the smothering weight from off my breast?
            It were a vain endeavor,
            Though I should gaze forever
      On that green light that lingers in the west:
45   I may not hope from outward forms to win
      The passion and the life, whose fountains are within.

                          IV
      O Lady! we receive but what we give,
      And in our life alone does Nature live:
      Ours is her wedding-garment, ours her shroud!
50   And would we aught behold, of higher worth,
      Than that inanimate° cold world allowed   *soulless*
      To the poor loveless ever-anxious crowd,
          Ah! from the soul itself must issue forth,

3. Compare *Tintern Abbey*, lines 114 ff.

A light, a glory, a fair luminous cloud
55   Enveloping the Earth—
And from the soul itself must there be sent
     A sweet and potent voice, of its own birth,
Of all sweet sounds the life and element!

V

O pure of heart; thou need'st not ask of me
60 What this strong music in the soul may be!
What, and wherein it doth exist,
This light, this glory, this fair luminous mist,
This beautiful and beauty-making power.
     Joy, virtuous Lady! Joy that ne'er was given,
65 Save to the pure, and in their purest hour,
Life, and Life's effluence, cloud at once and shower
Joy, Lady! is the spirit and the power
Which wedding Nature to us gives in dower,
     A new Earth and new Heaven,
70 Undreamt of by the sensual and the proud—
Joy is the sweet voice, Joy the luminous cloud—
     We in ourselves rejoice!
And thence flows all that charms or ear or sight,
     All melodies the echoes of that voice,
75 All colors a suffusion from that light.

VI

There was a time when, though my path was rough,
     This joy within me dallied with distress,
And all misfortunes were but as the stuff
     Whence Fancy made me dreams of happiness:
80 For hope grew round me, like the twining vine,
And fruits, and foliage, not my own, seemed mine.
But now afflictions bow me down to earth:
Nor care I that they rob me of my mirth,
     But oh! each visitation
85 Suspends what nature gave me at my birth,
     My shaping spirit of Imagination.
For not to think of what I needs must feel,
     But to be still and patient, all I can;
And haply by abstruse research to steal
90   From my own nature all the natural man—
     This was my sole resource, my only plan:
Till that which suits a part infects the whole,
And now is almost grown the habit of my soul.

VII

Hence, viper thoughts, that coil around my mind,
95   Reality's dark dream!
I turn from you, and listen to the wind,
     Which long has raved unnoticed. What a scream
Of agony by torture lengthened out
That lute sent forth! Thou Wind, that ravest without,
100 Bare craig, or mountain-tairn,° or blasted tree,   *pond*

Or pine-grove whither woodman never clomb,
Or lonely house, long held the witches' home,
   Methinks were fitter instruments for thee,
Mad Lutanist! who in this month of showers,
105 Of dark-brown gardens, and of peeping flowers,
Mak'st Devils' yule,° with worse than wintry song,   *Christmas*
The blossoms, buds, and timorous leaves among.
   Thou Actor, perfect in all tragic sounds!
Thou mighty Poet, e'en to frenzy bold!
110   What tell'st thou now about?
     'Tis of the rushing of a host in rout,
   With groans of trampled men, with smarting wounds—
At once they groan with pain, and shudder with the cold!
But hush! there is a pause of deepest silence!
115   And all that noise, as of a rushing crowd,
With groans and tremulous shudderings—all is over—
   It tells another tale, with sounds less deep and loud!
     A tale of less affright,
     And tempered with delight,
120 As Otway's self had framed the tender lay[4]
     'Tis of a little child,
     Upon a lonesome wild,
Not far from home, but she hath lost her way:
And now moans low in bitter grief and fear,
125 And now screams loud, and hopes to make her mother hear.

VIII

'Tis midnight, but small thoughts have I of sleep;
Full seldom may my friend such vigils keep!
Visit her, gentle Sleep! with wings of healing,
   And may this storm be but a mountain-birth,°   *short-lived*
130 May all the stars hang bright above her dwelling,
   Silent as though they watched the sleeping Earth!
     With light heart may she rise,
     Gay fancy, cheerful eyes,
   Joy lift her spirit, joy attune her voice;
135 To her may all things live, from pole to pole,
Their life the eddying of her living soul!
   O simple spirit, guided from above,
Dear Lady! friend devoutest of my choice,
Thus mayest thou ever, evermore rejoice.

1802   1802

Work Without Hope[1]
Lines Composed 21st February, 1825

All Nature seems at work. Slugs leave their lair—
The bees are stirring—birds are on the wing—

---

4. Thomas Otway, author of *The Orphan* (1680) and other tragedies noted for their pathos. In earlier versions the reference is to "William," probably alluding to Wordsworth's *Lucy Gray*.

1. First published in *The Bijou*, a gift-book annual.

And Winter slumbering in the open air,
Wears on his smiling face a dream of Spring!
5 And I, the while, the sole unbusy thing,
Nor honey make, nor pair, nor build, nor sing.

Yet well I ken° the banks where amaranths° blow,   *know / unfading flowers*
Have traced the fount whence streams of nectar flow.
Bloom, O ye amaranths! bloom for whom ye may,
10 For me ye bloom not! Glide, rich streams, away!
With lips unbrightened, wreathless brow, I stroll:
And would you learn the spells that drowse my soul?
Work without Hope draws nectar in a sieve,
And Hope without an object cannot live.

1825   1828

Constancy to an Ideal Object

Since all that beat about in Nature's range,
Or° veer or vanish; why shouldst thou remain   *either*
The only constant in a world of change,
O yearning Thought! that liv'st but in the brain?
5 Call to the Hours, that in the distance play,
The faery people of the future day—
Fond Thought! not one of all that shining swarm
Will breathe on thee with life-enkindling breath,
Till when, like strangers shelt'ring from a storm,
10 Hope and Despair meet in the porch of Death!
Yet still thou haunt'st me; and though well I see,
She is not thou, and only thou art she,
Still, still as though some dear embodied Good,
Some living Love before my eyes there stood
15 With answering look a ready ear to lend,
I mourn to thee and say—"Ah! loveliest friend!
That this the meed of all my toils might be,
To have a home, an English home, and thee!"
Vain repetition! Home and Thou are one.
20 The peacefull'st cot,° the moon shall shine upon,   *cottage*
Lulled by the thrush, and wakened by the lark,
Without thee were but a becalmed bark,°   *boat*
Whose Helmsman on an ocean waste and wide
Sits mute and pale his mouldering helm beside.

25 And art thou nothing? Such thou art, as when
The woodman winding westward up the glen
At wintry dawn, where o'er the sheep-track's maze
The viewless° snow-mist weaves a glist'ning haze,   *invisible*
Sees full before him, gliding without tread,
30 An image with a glory round its head;[1]

---

1. Coleridge refers to the phenomenon in which a walker in the mountains, the sun behind him, casts a magnified vertical self-image on the crystalized mists before him. See *Dejection: An Ode*, line 54.

The enamored rustic worships its fair hues,
Nor knows he makes the shadow, he pursues!

(1804–1826?)   1834

Epitaph

Stop, Christian Passer-by—Stop, child of God,
And read with gentle breast. Beneath this sod
A poet lies, or that which once seem'd he—
O lift one thought in prayer for S. T. C.;[1]
5   That he who many a year with toil of breath
Found death in life, may here find life in death!
Mercy for° praise—to be forgiven for° fame   *instead of*
He ask'd, and hoped, through Christ. Do thou the same!
9 November 1833   1834

BIOGRAPHIA LITERARIA   In 1803 Coleridge contemplated writing "my metaphysical works *as my life, & in* my life—intermixed with all the other events of history of the mind and fortunes of S.T. Coleridge." Nothing came of this characteristically Romantic interfusion of personal experience and philosophical generalization until 1815, when Coleridge decided to prefix a collected edition of his poems with "a general preface . . . on the principles" of criticism. Wordsworth's *Poems* (1815), with an extensive essay supplementary to the *Lyrical Ballads* Preface (1800–1802), further prompted Coleridge to clarify his theoretical divergences from his former collaborator. The resulting *Biographia Literaria*, grown from preface to two independent volumes, is an extraordinary work: a revisionary autobiography, in which Coleridge minimizes his youthful radicalism; a philosophical argument to establish the freedom of the will, yet so enmeshed in the material exigencies of book production that publication was delayed for two years; a meditation on original genius heavily indebted to recent German thought; and, in Chapter 13, a comic masquerade that has proved one of the seminal passages for subsequent literary studies. In his sustained, probing commentary on Wordsworth, unprecedented in discussions of modern literature, Coleridge confirmed Wordsworth's stature and, at the same time, by claiming to understand Wordsworth better than he did himself, institutionalized the role of the critic as the reader who completes the poet's task. *Lyrical Ballads* (1798) had been a joint project of Wordsworth and Coleridge; Coleridge said in 1800 that the Preface added in that year "contains our joint opinions on Poetry," but by 1802 he had begun "to suspect, that there is, somewhere or other, a *radical* difference in our opinions."

from Biographia Literaria
or Biographical Sketches of My Literary Life and Opinions

from Chapter 13

[IMAGINATION AND FANCY]

Thus far had the work been transcribed for the press, when I received the following letter from a friend,[1] whose practical judgement I have had ample reason to estimate and revere, and whose taste and sensibility preclude all the excuses which my self-love might possibly have prompted me to set up in plea against the decision of advisers of equal good sense, but with less tact and feeling.

---

1. Coleridge commented that he was "better known by the Initials of his name than by the Name Itself." He   died July 25, 1834.
1. Coleridge wrote the letter himself.

Dear C.

You ask my opinion concerning your Chapter on the Imagination, both as to the impressions it made on myself, and as to those which I think it will make on the PUBLIC, i.e. that part of the public, who from the title of the work and from its forming a sort of introduction to a volume of poems, are likely to constitute the great majority of your readers.

As to myself, and stating in the first place the effect on my understanding, your opinions and method of argument were not only so new to me, but so directly the reverse of all I had ever been accustomed to consider as truth, that even if I had comprehended your premises sufficiently to have admitted them, and had seen the necessity of your conclusions, I should still have been in that state of mind, which in your note, p. 75, 76, you have so ingeniously evolved, as the antithesis to that in which a man is, when he makes a bull.[2] In your own words, I should have felt as if I had been standing on my head.

The effect on my feelings, on the other hand, I cannot better represent, than by supposing myself to have known only our light airy modern chapels of ease, and then for the first time to have been placed, and left alone, in one of our largest Gothic cathedrals in a gusty moonlight night of autumn. "Now in glimmer, and now in gloom;"[3] often in palpable darkness not without a chilly sensation of terror; then suddenly emerging into broad yet visionary lights with coloured shadows, of fantastic shapes yet all decked with holy insignia and mystic symbols; and ever and anon coming out full upon pictures and stone-work images of great men, with whose names I was familiar, but which looked upon me with countenances and an expression, the most dissimilar to all I had been in the habit of connecting with those names. Those whom I had been taught to venerate as almost super-human in magnitude of intellect, I found perched in little fret-work niches, as grotesque dwarfs; while the grotesques, in my hitherto belief, stood guarding the high altar with all the characters of Apotheosis.[4] In short, what I had supposed substances were thinned away into shadows, while every where shadows were deepened into substances:

> If substance may be call'd what shadow seem'd,
> For each seem'd either!
>
> Milton[5]

Yet after all, I could not but repeat the lines which you had quoted from a MS. poem of your own in the FRIEND,[6] and applied to a work of Mr. Wordsworth's though with a few of the words altered:

> ————————An orphic tale indeed,
> A tale obscure of high and passionate thoughts
> To a strange music chaunted![7]

Be assured, however, that I look forward anxiously to your great book on the CONSTRUCTIVE PHILOSOPHY,[8] which you have promised and announced: and that I will do my best to understand it. Only I will not promise to descend into the dark cave of Trophonius[9] with you, there to rub my own eyes, in order to make the sparks and figured flashes, which I am required to see.

---

2. When he unwittingly contradicts himself, inviting ridicule.

3. *Christabel*, line 169.

4. Divinity.

5. A famous description of Death; *Paradise Lost*, 2.669–70. Cf. Burke, page 304.

6. The journal produced by Coleridge in 1809–1810.

7. To *William Wordsworth*, lines 45–47 (variant), referring to the 1805 *Prelude*.

8. Perhaps the *Logic* or *Opus Maximum*, or a general reference to Coleridge's Kantian model of systematic philosophy.

9. Legendary architect of the temple of Apollo at Delphi. After his death an oracle was consecrated to him; visitors were dragged into a cave filled with strange sounds and glaring lights, where they received the oracle's messages.

So much for myself. But as for the PUBLIC, *I do not hesitate a moment in advising and urging you to withdraw the Chapter from the present work, and to reserve it for your announced treatises on the Logos or communicative intellect in Man and Deity.[1] First, because imperfectly as I understand the present Chapter, I see clearly that you have done too much, and yet not enough. You have been obliged to omit so many links, from the necessity of compression, that what remains, looks (if I may recur to my former illustration) like the fragments of the winding steps of an old ruined tower. Secondly, a still stronger argument (at least one that I am sure will be more forcible with you) is, that your readers will have both right and reason to complain of you. This Chapter, which cannot, when it is printed, amount to so little as an hundred pages, will of necessity greatly increase the expense of the work; and every reader who, like myself, is neither prepared or perhaps calculated for the study of so abstruse a subject so abstrusely treated, will, as I have before hinted, be almost entitled to accuse you of a sort of imposition on him. For who, he might truly observe, could from your title-page, viz. "𝔐𝔶 𝔏𝔦𝔱𝔢𝔯𝔞𝔯𝔶 𝔏𝔦𝔣𝔢 𝔞𝔫𝔡 𝔒𝔭𝔦𝔫𝔦𝔬𝔫𝔰," published too as introductory to a volume of miscellaneous poems, have anticipated, or even conjectured, a long treatise on ideal Realism, which holds the same relation in abstruseness to Plotinus, as Plotinus does to Plato.[2] It will be well, if already you have not too much of metaphysical disquisition in your work, though as the larger part of the disquisition is historical, it will doubtless be both interesting and instructive to many to whose unprepared minds your speculations on the esemplastic[3] power would be utterly unintelligible. Be assured, if you do publish this Chapter in the present work, you will be reminded of Bishop Berkley's Siris,[4] announced as an Essay on Tar-water, which beginning with Tar ends with the Trinity, the omne scibile [everything knowable] forming the interspace. I say in the* present *work. In that greater work to which you have devoted so many years, and study so intense and various, it will be in its proper place. Your prospectus will have described and announced both its contents and their nature; and if any persons purchase it, who feel no interest in the subjects of which it treats, they will have themselves only to blame.*

I could add to these arguments one derived from pecuniary[5] motives, and particularly from the probable effects on the sale of your present publication; but they would weigh little with you compared with the preceding. Besides, I have long observed, that arguments drawn from your own personal interests more often act on you as narcotics than as stimulants, and that in money concerns you have some small portion of pig nature in your moral idiosyncracy, and like these amiable creatures, must occasionally be pulled backward from the boat in order to make you enter it. All success attend you, for if hard thinking and hard reading are merits, you have deserved it.

Your affectionate, & c.

In consequence of this very judicious letter, which produced complete conviction on my mind, I shall content myself for the present with stating the main result of the Chapter, which I have reserved for that future publication, a detailed prospectus of which the reader will find at the close of the second volume.

---

1. The Word of God, incarnated in Jesus Christ. Coleridge announced a study of the Gospel of John as part of a work that never appeared, the *Logosophia*.
2. Coleridge saw himself as an "ideal realist," rejecting the Platonic distinction between the essence and appearance of things for an idea of the world intuited whole by the indwelling human spirit, a position derived from Plato's inheritor Plotinus.

3. Coleridge's invented word, meaning unifying or synthesizing.
4. George Berkeley (1685–1753), Irish bishop and philosopher. *Siris* (1744) begins with a chemical description of the medicinal advantages of tar and proceeds to reflections on theology. Coleridge admired philosophy tied to the empirical truths of the natural sciences.
5. Financial.

The IMAGINATION then I consider either as primary, or secondary. The primary IMAGINATION I hold to be the living Power and prime Agent of all human Perception, and as a repetition in the finite mind of the eternal act of creation in the infinite I AM. The secondary I consider as an echo of the former, co-existing with the conscious will, yet still as identical with the primary in the *kind* of its agency, and differing only in *degree*, and in the *mode* of its operation. It dissolves, diffuses, dissipates, in order to re-create; or where this process is rendered impossible, yet still at all events it struggles to idealize and to unify. It is essentially *vital*, even as all objects (*as* objects) are essentially fixed and dead.

FANCY, on the contrary, has no other counters to play with, but fixities and definites. The Fancy is indeed no other than a mode of Memory emancipated from the order of time and space; and blended with, and modified by that empirical phenomenon of the will, which we express by the word CHOICE. But equally with the ordinary memory it must receive all its materials ready made from the law of association.

Whatever more than this, I shall think it fit to declare concerning the powers and privileges of the imagination in the present work, will be found in the critical essay on the uses of the Supernatural in poetry and the principles that regulate its introduction: which the reader will find prefixed to the poem of 𝕿𝖍𝖊 𝕬𝖓𝖈𝖎𝖊𝖓𝖙 𝕸𝖆𝖗𝖎𝖓𝖊𝖗.[6]

from *Chapter 14*

[OCCASION OF THE *LYRICAL BALLADS*—PREFACE TO THE SECOND EDITION— THE ENSUING CONTROVERSY]

During the first year that Mr. Wordsworth and I were neighbours, our conversations turned frequently on the two cardinal points of poetry, the power of exciting the sympathy of the reader by a faithful adherence to the truth of nature, and the power of giving the interest of novelty by the modifying colours of imagination. The sudden charm, which accidents of light and shade, which moon-light or sun-set diffused over a known and familiar landscape, appeared to represent the practicability of combining both. These are the poetry of nature. The thought suggested itself (to which of us I do not recollect) that a series of poems might be composed of two sorts. In the one, the incidents and agents were to be, in part at least, supernatural; and the excellence aimed at was to consist in the interesting of the affections by the dramatic truth of such emotions, as would naturally accompany such situations, supposing them real. And real in *this* sense they have been to every human being who, from whatever source of delusion, has at any time believed himself under supernatural agency. For the second class, subjects were to be chosen from ordinary life; the characters and incidents were to be such, as will be found in every village and its vicinity, where there is a meditative and feeling mind to seek after them, or to notice them, when they present themselves.

In this idea originated the plan of the *Lyrical Ballads;* in which it was agreed, that my endeavours should be directed to persons and characters supernatural, or at least romantic; yet so as to transfer from our inward nature a human interest and a semblance of truth sufficient to procure for these shadows of imagination that willing suspension of disbelief for the moment, which constitutes poetic faith. Mr. Wordsworth,

6. The essay did not appear.

on the other hand, was to propose to himself as his object, to give the charm of novelty to things of every day, and to excite a feeling analogous to the supernatural, by
awakening the mind's attention from the lethargy of custom, and directing it to the
loveliness and the wonders of the world before us; an inexhaustible treasure, but for
which in consequence of the film of familiarity and selfish solicitude we have eyes,
yet see not, ears that hear not, and hearts that neither feel nor understand.[1]

With this view I wrote the "Ancient Mariner," and was preparing among other
poems, the "Dark Ladie," and the "Christabel," in which I should have more nearly
realized my ideal, than I had done in my first attempt. But Mr. Wordsworth's industry had proved so much more successful, and the number of his poems so much
greater, that my compositions, instead of forming a balance, appeared rather an
interpolation of heterogeneous matter. Mr. Wordsworth added two or three poems
written in his own character, in the impassioned, lofty, and sustained diction, which
is characteristic of his genius. In this form the *Lyrical Ballads* were published; and
were presented by him, as an *experiment*,[2] whether subjects, which from their nature
rejected the usual ornaments and extra-colloquial style of poems in general, might
not be so managed in the language of ordinary life as to produce the pleasurable
interest, which it is the peculiar business of poetry to impart. To the second edition
he added a preface of considerable length; in which notwithstanding some passages
of apparently a contrary import, he was understood to contend for the extension of
this style to poetry of all kinds, and to reject as vicious and indefensible all phrases
and forms of style that were not included in what he (unfortunately, I think, adopting an equivocal expression) called the language of *real life*. From this preface, prefixed to poems in which it was impossible to deny the presence of original genius,
however mistaken its direction might be deemed, arose the whole long continued
controversy. For from the conjunction of perceived power with supposed heresy I
explain the inveteracy[3] and in some instances, I grieve to say, the acrimonious passions, with which the controversy has been conducted by the assailants.

Had Mr. Wordsworth's poems been the silly, the childish things, which they
were for a long time described as being; had they been really distinguished from the
compositions of other poets merely by meanness of language and inanity of thought;
had they indeed contained nothing more than what is found in the parodies and pretended imitations of them; they must have sunk at once, a dead weight, into the
slough of oblivion, and have dragged the preface along with them. But year after year
increased the number of Mr. Wordworth's admirers. They were found too not in the
lower classes of the reading public, but chiefly among young men of strong sensibility
and meditative minds; and their admiration (inflamed perhaps in some degree by
opposition) was distinguished by its intensity, I might almost say, by its *religious* fervour. These facts, and the intellectual energy of the author, which was more or less
consciously felt, where it was outwardly and even boisterously denied, meeting with
sentiments of aversion to his opinions, and of alarm at their consequences, produced
an eddy of criticism, which would of itself have borne up the poems by the violence,
with which it whirled them round and round. With many parts of this preface in the
sense attributed to them and which the words undoubtedly seem to authorise, I never
concurred; but on the contrary objected to them as erroneous in principle, and as
contradictory (in appearance at least) both to other parts of the same preface, and to
the author's own practice in the greater number of the poems themselves. Mr.

---

1. Echoing Jeremiah 5.21 and Isaiah 6.10.
2. "Experiments" is Wordsworth's term in the Advertisement to the 1798 *Lyrical Ballads*.
3. Deep-seated prejudice.

Wordsworth in his recent collection[4] has, I find, degraded this prefatory disquisition to the end of his second volume, to be read or not at the reader's choice. But he has not, as far as I can discover, announced any change in his poetic creed. [At] all events, considering it as the source of a controversy, in which I have been honored more, than I deserve, by the frequent conjunction of my name with his, I think it expedient to declare once for all, in what points I coincide with his opinions, and in what points I altogether differ. But in order to render myself intelligible I must previously, in as few words as possible, explain my ideas, first, of a POEM; and secondly, of POETRY itself, in *kind*, and in *essence*.

[PHILOSOPHIC DEFINITIONS OF A POEM AND POETRY]

A poem is that species of composition, which is opposed to works of science, by proposing for its *immediate* object pleasure, not truth; and from all other species (having *this* object in common with it) it is discriminated by proposing to itself such delight from the *whole*, as is compatible with a distinct gratification from each component *part*. * * *

But if this should be admitted as a satisfactory character of a poem, we have still to seek for a definition of poetry. The writings of PLATO, and Bishop TAYLOR, and the *Theoria Sacra* of BURNET,[5] furnish undeniable proofs that poetry of the highest kind may exist without metre, and even without the contra-distinguishing objects of a poem. The first chapter of Isaiah (indeed a very large proportion of the whole book) is poetry in the most emphatic sense; yet it would be not less irrational than strange to assert, that pleasure, and not truth, was the immediate object of the prophet. In short, whatever *specific* import we attach to the word, poetry, there will be found involved in it, as a necessary consequence, that a poem of any length neither can be, or ought to be, all poetry. * * *

What is poetry? is so nearly the same question with, what is a poet? that the answer to the one is involved in the solution of the other. For it is a distinction resulting from the poetic genius itself, which sustains and modifies the images, thoughts, and emotions of the poet's own mind. The poet, described in ideal perfection, brings the whole soul of man into activity, with the subordination of its faculties to each other, according to their relative worth and dignity. He diffuses a tone, and spirit of unity, that blends, and (as it were) *fuses*, each into each, by that synthetic and magical power, to which we have exclusively appropriated the name of imagination. This power, first put in action by the will and understanding, and retained under their irremissive, though gentle and unnoticed, controul (*laxis effertur habenis* [guided by loose reins]) reveals itself in the balance or reconciliation of opposite or discordant qualities: of sameness, with difference; of the general, with the concrete; the idea, with the image; the individual, with the representative; the sense of novelty and freshness, with old and familiar objects; a more than usual state of emotion, with more than usual order; judgement ever awake and steady self-possession, with enthusiasm and feeling profound or vehement; and while it blends and harmonizes the natural and the artificial, still subordinates art to nature; the manner to the matter; and our admiration of the poet to our sympathy with the poetry. * * *

Finally, GOOD SENSE is the BODY of poetic genius, FANCY its DRAPERY, MOTION its LIFE, and IMAGINATION the SOUL that is every where, and in each; and forms all into one graceful and intelligent whole.

4. *Poems* (1815).
5. Greek philosopher Plato; Jeremy Taylor, author of *Holy Living* and *Holy Dying* (1650–1651); and the 17th-century theologian Thomas Burnet (whose work supplies the epigraph for the 1817 *Ancient Mariner*).

‹‹ ►◄◊►◄ ››

George Gordon, Lord Byron
1788–1824

"Mad—bad—and dangerous to know," pronounced Lady Caroline Lamb, before becoming his lover; a "splendid and imperishable excellence of sincerity and strength," declared Matthew Arnold: the fascination that made Byron the archetypal Romantic, in Europe even more than in Britain, grew from both judgments. He was born in London in 1788, the son of Captain John "Mad Jack" Byron and his second wife, Catherine Gordon, a Scots heiress. The Captain quickly ran through her fortune and departed; Byron and his mother withdrew to Aberdeen in 1789. He passed the next ten years in straitened circumstances, sensitive to the clubfoot with which he had been born, left with a mother who displaced resentment against her absconded husband onto him, and tended by a Calvinist nurse whom he later said had early awakened his sexuality. In 1798 his great-uncle the fifth Baron Byron, "the wicked Lord," died childless, and just after his tenth birthday Byron unexpectedly inherited his title. He asked his mother "whether she perceived any difference in him since he had been made a lord, as he perceived none himself," but the difference shaped the poet.

Byron and his mother returned to England and moved into Newstead Abbey, near Nottingham, the now debt-ridden estate presented to the Byrons by Henry VIII; to the lonely boy, the Gothic hall embodied his tempestuous family heritage. In 1801 Byron was sent to school at Harrow; in the same year he probably met his half-sister Augusta. He entered Trinity College, Cambridge, in 1805, living extravagantly and entangling himself with moneylenders, but also making enduring friendships.

Byron's first published volume, *Hours of Idleness*, appeared in 1807, when he was nineteen; the lofty pose he struck as "Lord Byron: A Minor" provoked a savage notice from the *Edinburgh Review*, to which he retaliated in 1809 with a satire in Popean couplets, *English Bards and Scotch Reviewers*. "Written when I was very young and very angry," Byron later confessed to Coleridge, the poem "has been a thorn in my side ever since; more particularly as almost all the Persons animadverted upon became subsequently my acquaintances, and some of them my friends." He suppressed the fifth edition, but so memorable were its attacks on Coleridge, Southey, Wordsworth, and others that pirated editions continued to appear. Byron took his seat in the House of Lords that same year, and then departed on a grand tour shaped by the Napoleonic wars, which barred much of Europe. He sailed to Lisbon, crossed Spain, and proceeded to Greece and Albania, through country little known to Western Europeans. There he began *Childe Harold's Pilgrimage*. In March 1810 he sailed for Constantinople, visited the site of Troy and swam the Hellespont in imitation of the mythical Greek lover Leander. In the East, Byron found a world in which the love of an older aristocrat for a beautiful boy was accepted, and he also developed a political identity as the Western hero who would liberate Greece from the Turks.

Byron returned to London in July 1811, but too late to see his mother before she died. In February 1812 he made his first speech in the House of Lords, denouncing the death penalty proposed for weavers who had smashed the machines they blamed for their loss of work. Byron's parliamentary activity was superseded the next month when the first two cantos of *Childe Harold's Pilgrimage* appeared and he "woke to find himself famous." The poem joined the immediacy of a travelogue to the disillusionment of a speaker who voiced the melancholy of a generation wearied by prolonged war. Despite Byron's claim that Harold was a fiction designed merely to connect a picaresque narrative, readers heard his author speaking passionately of his own concerns. The magnetism of this personality offset the cynicism the poem displayed: the handsome, aristocratic poet, returned from exotic travels, himself became a figure of force. Byron followed this success with a series of "Eastern" tales that added to his aura:

one, *The Corsair* (1814), written in ten days, sold ten thousand copies on the day of publication. *Hebrew Melodies* (1815) contains some of Byron's most famous lyrics (*She walks in beauty*) and accorded with the vogue for nationalist themes. Byron was both a sensational commercial success and a noble who gave away his copyrights because aristocrats do not write for money. Like all myths, "Byron" embodied contradictions more than he resolved them.

This literary celebrity was enhanced by Byron's lionizing in Whig society. Liaisons with Lady Caroline Lamb and the "autumnal" Lady Oxford magnified his notoriety, but it was his relationship with his half-sister Augusta, now married, that gave rise to most scandal; her daughter Medora, born in 1814 and given the name of the heroine of *The Corsair*, was widely thought to be Byron's, and probably was. Seeking to escape these agitating affairs, and also to repair his debts, Byron proposed to Annabella Milbanke. They married in January 1815; their daughter Augusta Ada was born at the end of the year, but a few weeks later Annabella left Byron to live with her parents, amid rumors of insanity, incest, and sodomy. Pirated editions of Byron's poems on the separation made marital discord into public scandal.

In April 1816 Byron quit England, bearing the pageant of his bleeding heart, in Matthew Arnold's famous phrase, across Europe. He settled in Geneva, near Percy Bysshe Shelley and Mary Godwin, who had eloped two years before. They were joined by Mary's stepsister, Claire Clairmont, with whom Byron resumed an affair he had begun in England. Poetry was as much in the air as romance: Byron reported that Shelley "dosed him with Wordsworth physic even to nausea"; the influence and resistance the phrase shows are both evident in the third canto of *Childe Harold* (1816). He wrote *The Prisoner of Chillon* at this time and began the closet-drama *Manfred* (1817). At the end of the summer the Shelley party left for England, where Claire gave birth to Byron's illegitimate daughter Allegra; in October Byron departed for Venice, where he rented a palazzo on the Grand Canal.

Byron described his Venetian life in brilliant letters, some of which were meant for circulation in the circle of his publisher John Murray. To a ceaseless round of sexual activity, he joined substantial literary productivity. He studied Armenian, completed *Manfred,* and visited Rome, gathering materials for a fourth canto of *Childe Harold* (1818). The canto was his longest and most sublime, and its invocation of Freedom's torn banner streaming "*against* the wind" fixed his revolutionary reputation. Yet Byron began to feel trapped by the modes that had won him popularity; determining to "repel charges of monotony and mannerism," he wrote *Beppo*, a comic verse tale of a Venetian *ménage-à-trois* (1818). In its colloquial, digressive ease, Byron was testing the form of his greatest poem, *Don Juan*, at once fictional autobiography, picaresque narrative, literary burlesque, and exposure of social, sexual, and religious hypocrisies. The first two cantos were published in 1819 in an expensive edition meant to forestall charges of blasphemy and bearing neither the author's nor the publisher's name. The authorship was nonetheless known: *Blackwood's Magazine* criticized Byron for "a filthy and impious" attack on his wife, and the second canto, which turns to shipwreck and cannibalism, redoubled charges of nihilism. Shocking the proprieties of one audience, Byron moved toward another; the poem sold well in increasingly cheap editions.

In April 1819 Byron met his "last attachment," Countess Teresa Gamba Guiccioli, nineteen years old and married to a man nearly three times her age. Through her family, Byron was initiated into the Carbonari, a clandestine revolutionary organization devoted to achieving Italian independence from Austria. While continuing *Don Juan*, he wrote *Marino Faliero, Sardanapalus,* and *The Two Foscari* (all 1821), historical dramas exploring the relationship between the powerful individual and the post-revolutionary state. To the same year belongs *Cain*, a "mystery" drama refused copyright for its unorthodoxy and immediately pirated by radicals.

When Teresa's father and brother were exiled for their part in an abortive uprising, she followed them, and Byron reluctantly went with her to Pisa. There he reunited with Percy Shelley, with whom he planned a radical journal, *The Liberal*. The first number contained *The*

Vision of Judgment, a devastating rebuttal to a eulogy of George III by Robert Southey, in the preface to which the poet laureate had alluded to Byron as the head of a "Satanic School."

Restive in the domesticity of life with Teresa, Byron agreed to act as agent of a London committee aiding the Greeks in their struggle for independence. In July 1823 he left for Cephalonia, an island in western Greece. Clear of debt and now attentive to his literary income, Byron devoted his fortune to the cause. Philhellenic idealism was soon confronted by motley reality, but Byron founded, paid, and trained a brigade of soldiers. A serious illness in February 1824, followed by the usual remedy of bleeding, weakened him; in April he contracted a fever, treated by further bleeding, from which he died on 19 April at the age of thirty-six. Deeply mourned, he became a Greek national hero, and throughout Europe his name became synonymous with Romanticism. In England, the stunned reaction of the young Tennyson spoke for many: on hearing the news, he sadly wrote on a rock "Byron is dead." As Arnold later recalled, in placing Byron with Wordsworth as the great English poets of the century, he had "subjugated" his readers, and his influence was immense and lasting.

She walks in beauty[1]

1

She walks in beauty, like the night
　　Of cloudless climes and starry skies;
And all that's best of dark and bright
　　Meet in her aspect and her eyes:
5　Thus mellow'd to that tender light
　　Which heaven to gaudy day denies.

2

One shade the more, one ray the less,
　　Had half impair'd the nameless grace
Which waves in every raven tress,
10　Or softly lightens o'er her face;
Where thoughts serenely sweet express
　　How pure, how dear their dwelling-place.

3

And on that cheek, and o'er that brow,
　　So soft, so calm, yet eloquent,
15　The smiles that win, the tints that glow,
　　But tell of days in goodness spent,
A mind at peace with all below,
　　A heart whose love is innocent!

1814   1815

So, we'll go no more a-roving[1]

1

So, we'll go no more a-roving
　　So late into the night,

---

1. The first poem in *Hebrew Melodies*, a collection initiated by Jewish composer Isaac Nathan, and published with his music. The subject is Anne Wilmot, the wife of Byron's cousin, whom he had seen at a party wearing "mourning, with dark spangles on her dress."

1. The poem first appeared in a letter Byron wrote from Venice to Thomas Moore: "The Carnival—that is, the latter part of it—and sitting up late o'nights, had knocked me up a little. But it is over—and it is now Lent . . . though I did not dissipate much upon the whole, yet I find 'the sword wearing out the scabbard,' though I have but just turned the corner of twenty-nine." "Carnival," literally farewell to flesh, is the period of festival before Lent.

Though the heart be still as loving,
And the moon be still as bright.

2

5 For the sword outwears its sheath,
And the soul wears out the breast,
And the heart must pause to breathe,
And love itself have rest.

3

Though the night was made for loving,
10 And the day returns too soon,
Yet we'll go no more a roving
By the light of the moon.

1817   1830

from CHILDE HAROLD'S PILGRIMAGE, CANTO THE THIRD[1]

[THUNDERSTORM IN THE ALPS][2]

92

860 Thy sky is changed!—and such a change! Oh night,
And storm, and darkness, ye are wondrous strong,
Yet lovely in your strength, as is the light
Of a dark eye in woman! Far along,
From peak to peak, the rattling crags among
865 Leaps the live thunder! Not from one lone cloud,
But every mountain now hath found a tongue,
And Jura answers, through her misty shroud,
Back to the joyous Alps, who call to her aloud![3]

93

And this is in the night:—Most glorious night!
870 Thou wert not sent for slumber! let me be
A sharer in thy fierce and far delight,—
A portion of the tempest and of thee!
How the lit lake shines, a phosphoric sea,
And the big rain comes dancing to the earth!
875 And now again 'tis black,—and now, the glee
Of the loud hills shakes with its mountain-mirth,
As if they did rejoice o'er a young earthquake's birth.

1. The first two cantos of *Childe Harold's Pilgrimage* appeared in 1812. As their subtitle "A Romaunt" indicated, Byron had adopted the form of romance for his unnervingly contemporary poem. The Spenserian stanzas and mock-archaisms—a "childe" is a youth of noble birth—played discordantly against the account of his travels in 1809–1811 through Spain (and his acerbic commentary on the Peninsular War; see Introduction, pages 356–58) and then on into parts of Greece unfrequented by Westerners. The overwhelming success of the poem ensured that Byron would be identified with Childe Harold. Byron protested, but the connection is reinforced by the manuscripts themselves, which disclose that Childe Harold was once Childe Burun, an ancient form of his family name. Canto 3, published in 1816, is

independent, though the continuity reflects the degree to which protagonist and poet had come to figure each other. Byron left England on 25 April 1816, and wrote the opening stanzas while crossing the Channel.
2. "The thunder-storms to which these lines refer occurred on the thirteenth of June, 1816, at midnight. I have seen among the Acroceraunian mountains of Chimari several more terrible, but none more beautiful" [Byron's note]. Byron had settled in the Villa Diodati on 10 June, near the Shelley party; a few days after these storms Mary Shelley began *Frankenstein* in Byron's new residence.
3. The Jura Mountains, north and west of Geneva, form the boundary between Switzerland and France; the Alps run to the east and south.

94

Now, where the swift Rhone cleaves his way between
Heights which appear as lovers who have parted
In hate, whose mining depths so intervene,
That they can meet no more, though broken-hearted!
Though in their souls, which thus each other thwarted,
Love was the very root of the fond rage
Which blighted their life's bloom, and then departed:
Itself expired, but leaving them an age
Of years all winters,—war within themselves to wage.[4]

95

Now, where the quick Rhone thus hath cleft his way,
The mightiest of the storms hath ta'en his stand:
For here, not one, but many, make their play,
And fling their thunder-bolts from hand to hand,
Flashing and cast around: of all the band,
The brightest through these parted hills hath fork'd
His lightnings, as if he did understand,
That in such gaps as desolation work'd,
There the hot shaft should blast whatever therein lurk'd.

96

Sky, mountains, river, winds, lake, lightnings! ye!
With night, and clouds, and thunder, and a soul
To make these felt and feeling, well may be
Things that have made me watchful; the far roll
Of your departing voices, is the knoll
Of what in me is sleepless,—if I rest.
But where of ye, oh tempests! is the goal?
Are ye like those within the human breast?
Or do ye find, at length, like eagles, some high nest?

97

Could I embody and unbosom now
That which is most within me,—could I wreak
My thoughts upon expression, and thus throw
Soul, heart, mind, passions, feelings, strong or weak,
All that I would have sought, and all I seek,
Bear, know, feel, and yet breathe—into *one* word,
And that one word were Lightning, I would speak;
But as it is, I live and die unheard,
With a most voiceless thought, sheathing it as a sword.

[BYRON'S STRAINED IDEALISM. APOSTROPHE TO HIS DAUGHTER]

111

Thus far have I proceeded in a theme
Renew'd with no kind auspices°:—to feel   *hopeful signs*

4. The simile of lovers parted in hate obliquely recalls Byron's separation from his wife and illustrates his tendency to turn nature into sublime self-projection.

We are not what we have been, and to deem
We are not what we should be,—and to steel
1035   The heart against itself; and to conceal,
With a proud caution, love, or hate, or aught,—
Passion or feeling, purpose, grief, or zeal,—
Which is the tyrant spirit of our thought,
Is a stern task of soul:—No matter,—it is taught.

112

1040   And for these words, thus woven into song,
It may be that they are a harmless wile,—
The colouring of the scenes which fleet along,
Which I would seize, in passing, to beguile
My breast, or that of others, for a while.
1045   Fame is the thirst of youth,—but I am not
So young as to regard men's frown or smile,
As loss or guerdon° of a glorious lot;   prize
I stood and stand alone,—remember'd or forgot.

113

I have not loved the world, nor the world me;
1050   I have not flatter'd its rank breath,[5] nor bow'd
To its idolatries a patient knee,—
Nor coin'd my cheek to smiles,—nor cried aloud
In worship of an echo; in the crowd
They could not deem me one of such; I stood
1055   Among them, but not of them; in a shroud
Of thoughts which were not their thoughts, and still could,
Had I not filed[6] my mind, which thus itself subdued.

114

I have not loved the world, not the world me,—
But let us part fair foes; I do believe,
1060   Though I have found them not, that there may be
Words which are things,—hopes which will not deceive,
And virtues which are merciful, nor weave
Snares for the failing: I would also deem
O'er others' griefs that some sincerely grieve;
1065   That two, or one, are almost what they seem,—
That goodness is no name, and happiness no dream.

115

My daughter! with thy name this song begun—
My daughter! with thy name thus much shall end—
I see thee not,—I hear thee not,—but none
1070   Can be so wrapt in thee; thou art the friend
To whom the shadows of far years extend:
Albeit my brow thou never should'st behold,
My voice shall with thy future visions blend

5. See Shakespeare, *Coriolanus*, 3.1.66–67. Byron frequently voices himself through allusions to Shakespeare's
willful Roman general, who retorts to the plebeians who
banish him: "I banish you" (3.3.124).

6. Defiled. Byron adds a note citing Shakespeare's *Macbeth*, 3.1.65

And reach into thy heart,—when mine is cold,—
1075 A token and a tone, even from thy father's mould.

116

To aid thy mind's developement,—to watch
Thy dawn of little joys,—to sit and see
Almost thy very growth,—to view thee catch
Knowledge of objects,—wonders yet to thee!
1080 To hold thee lightly on a gentle knee,
And print on thy soft cheek a parent's kiss,—
This, it should seem, was not reserved for me;
Yet this was in my nature:—as it is,
I know not what is there, yet something like to this.

117

1085 Yet, though dull Hate as duty should be taught,
I know that thou wilt love me; though my name
Should be shut from thee, as a spell still fraught
With desolation,—and a broken claim:
Though the grave closed between us,—'twere the same,
1090 I know that thou wilt love me; though to drain
My blood from out thy being were an aim,
And an attainment,—all would be in vain,—
Still thou would'st love me, still that more than life retain.

118

The child of love,—though born in bitterness
1095 And nurtured in convulsion. Of thy sire
These were the elements,—and thine no less.
As yet such are around thee,—but thy fire
Shall be more temper'd, and thy hope far higher.
Sweet be thy cradled slumbers! O'er the sea,
1100 And from the mountains where I now respire,
Fain would I waft such blessing upon thee,
As, with a sigh, I deem thou might'st have been to me!

from Canto the Fourth[1]

[THE COLISEUM. THE DYING GLADIATOR]

139

And here the buzz of eager nations ran,
In murmur'd pity, or loud-roar'd applause,
1245 As man was slaughter'd by his fellow man.[2]
And wherefore slaughter'd? wherefore, but because
Such were the bloody Circus' genial laws,
And the imperial pleasure. Wherefore not?

1. Byron began Canto 4 in June 1817, and published it in April 1818. In the dedication he announced that the reader would find "less of the pilgrim" than in the preceding cantos: "I had become weary," he declared in ending the division between the narrator and Harold, "of drawing a line which every one seemed determined not to perceive." Canto 4 is spoken in his own person and carries

the account of his travels into Italy.
2. The partly ruined Coliseum, a vast amphitheater completed about A.D. 80, was the site of gladiatorial combats in which prisoners of war or slaves fought to the death. Spectators could signal mercy to the defeated by waving handkerchiefs; turning thumbs down doomed the combatant.

What matters where we fall to fill the maws°   *stomachs*
1250   Of worms—on battle-plains or listed spot?
Both are but theatres where the chief actors rot.

140

I see before me the Gladiator lie:
He leans upon his hand—his manly brow
Consents to death, but conquers agony,
1255   And his droop'd head sinks gradually low—
And through his side the last drops, ebbing slow
From the red gash, fall heavy, one by one,
Like the first of a thunder-shower; and now
The arena swims around him—he is gone,
1260   Ere ceased the inhuman shout which hail'd the wretch who won.

141

He heard it, but he heeded not—his eyes
Were with his heart, and that was far away:
He reck'd not of the life he lost nor prize,
But where his rude hut by the Danube lay,
1265   *There* were his young barbarians all at play,
There was their Dacian mother[3]—he, their sire,
Butcher'd to make a Roman holiday—
All this rush'd with his blood—Shall he expire
And unavenged?—Arise! ye Goths, and glut your ire![4]

142

1270   But here, where Murder breathed her bloody steam;
And here, where buzzing nations choked the ways,
And roar'd or murmur'd like a mountain stream
Dashing or winding as its torrent strays;
Here, where the Roman millions' blame or praise
1275   Was death or life, the playthings of a crowd,
My voice sounds much—and fall the stars' faint rays
On the arena void—seats crush'd—walls bow'd—
And galleries, where my steps seem echoes strangely loud.

143

A ruin—yet what ruin! from its mass
1280   Walls, palaces, half-cities, have been rear'd;
Yet oft the enormous skeleton ye pass,
And marvel where the spoil could have appear'd.
Hath it indeed been plunder'd, or but clear'd?
Alas! developed,° opens the decay,   *disclosed*
1285   When the colossal fabric's form is near'd:
It will not bear the brightness of the day,
Which streams too much on all years, man, have reft° away.   *ravaged*

---

3. The Dacians, a people north of the Danube River in what is now Romania, harried the Romans until their defeat by the Emperor Trajan (A.D. 101–107).
4. The Goths were Germanic tribes who overran the Roman Empire in the 5th century A.D. The stanza was inspired by the statue of a dying Gaul in the Capitoline Museum, in Byron's day thought to be a gladiator.

144

But when the rising moon begins to climb
Its topmost arch, and gently pauses there;
1290   When the stars twinkle through the loops of time,
And the low night-breeze waves along the air
The garland forest, which the gray walls wear,
Like laurels on the bald first Caesar's head;[5]
When the light shines serene but doth not glare,
1295   Then in this magic circle raise the dead:
Heroes have trod this spot—'tis on their dust ye tread.

145

"While stands the Coliseum, Rome shall stand;
When falls the Coliseum, Rome shall fall;
And when Rome falls—the World."[6] From our own land
1300   Thus spake the pilgrims o'er this mighty wall
In Saxon times, which we are wont to call
Ancient;[7] and these three mortal things are still
On their foundations, and unalter'd all;
Rome and her Ruin past Redemption's skill,
1305   The World, the same wide den—of thieves, or what ye will.

[APOSTROPHE TO THE OCEAN. CONCLUSION]

178

There is a pleasure in the pathless woods,
1595   There is a rapture on the lonely shore,
There is society, where none intrudes,
By the deep Sea, and music in its roar:
I love not Man the less, but Nature more,
From these our interviews, in which I steal
1600   From all I may be, or have been before,
To mingle with the Universe, and feel
What I can ne'er express, yet can not all conceal.

179

Roll on, thou deep and dark blue Ocean—roll!
Ten thousand fleets sweep over thee in vain;
1605   Man marks the earth with ruin—his control
Stops with the shore;—upon the watery plain
The wrecks are all thy deed, nor doth remain
A shadow of man's ravage, save his own,
When, for a moment, like a drop of rain,
1610   He sinks into thy depths with bubbling groan,
Without a grave, unknell'd, uncoffin'd, and unknown.

5. Roman historian Suetonius records that Julius Caesar (102–44 B.C.) was particularly gratified by a decree of the Roman Senate that permitted him to wear a laurel wreath (an emblem of victory) at all times, because it hid his baldness.
6. A note by Byron directs the reader to chapter 71 of The Decline and Fall of the Roman Empire, by Edward Gibbon (1737–1794), a work he had known since adolescence: "Reduced to its naked majesty, the Flavian amphitheatre was contemplated with awe and admiration by the pilgrims of the North: and their rude enthusiasm broke forth in a sublime proverbial expression, which is recorded in the eighth century in the fragments of the venerable Bede."
7. The Anglo-Saxon kingdoms in Britain, established following the withdrawal of the Romans in the 4th century A.D., consolidated into one Saxon kingdom that lasted until the Norman Conquest of 1066.

180

His steps are not upon thy paths,—thy fields
Are not a spoil for him,—thou dost arise
And shake him from thee; the vile strength he wields
1615 For earth's destruction thou dost all despise,
Spurning him from thy bosom to the skies,
And send'st him, shivering in thy playful spray
And howling, to his Gods, where haply lies
His petty hope in some near port or bay,
1620 And dashest him again to earth:—there let him lay.[8]

181

The armaments which thunderstrike the walls
Of rock-built cities, bidding nations quake,
And monarchs tremble in their capitals,
The oak leviathans, whose huge ribs make
1625 Their clay creator the vain title take
Of lord of thee, and arbiter of war;[9]
These are thy toys, and, as the snowy flake,
They melt into thy yeast of waves, which mar
Alike the Armada's pride, or spoils of Trafalgar.[1]

182

1630 Thy shores are empires, changed in all save thee—
Assyria, Greece, Rome, Carthage, what are they?
Thy waters washed them power while they were free,
And many a tyrant since; their shores obey
The stranger, slave, or savage; their decay
1635 Has dried up realms to deserts:—not so thou,
Unchangeable save to thy wild waves' play—
Time writes no wrinkle on thine azure brow—
Such as creation's dawn beheld, thou rollest now.

183

Thou glorious mirror, where the Almighty's form
1640 Glasses itself in tempests; in all time,
Calm or convulsed—in breeze, or gale, or storm,
Icing the pole, or in the torrid clime
Dark-heaving;—boundless, endless, and sublime—
The image of Eternity—the throne
1645 Of the Invisible; even from out thy slime
The monsters of the deep are made; each zone
Obeys thee; thou goest forth, dread, fathomless, alone.

8. When his publisher's reader queried, "I have a doubt about *lay*" (instead of *lie*, perhaps the most famous solecism in English poetry), Byron replied: "So have I—but the *post* and *indolence* and *illness!*" He "manages his pen with the careless and negligent ease of a man of quality," Scott wrote of Byron; the nonchalant manner marked his aristocratic status.
9. The imagery is from the Book of Job: bemoaning his condition, Job acknowledges that God has made him "as the clay" (Job 10.9); God, showing his power, asks: "Canst thou draw out leviathan with a hook?" (41.1). The comparison of ships to this sea beast was familiar.
1. Storms severely damaged the Spanish fleet sent against England in 1588; a subsequent storm destroyed many of the ships taken as prizes in Admiral Nelson's victory over the French fleet at Trafalgar (1805).

184

And I have loved thee, Ocean! and my joy
Of youthful sports was on thy breast to be
1650   Borne, like thy bubbles, onward: from a boy
I wanton'd with thy breakers—they to me
Were a delight; and if the freshening sea
Made them a terror—'twas a pleasing fear,
For I was as it were a child of thee,
1655   And trusted to thy billows far and near,
And laid my hand upon thy mane—as I do here.

185

My task is done—my song hath ceased—my theme
Has died into an echo; it is fit
The spell should break of this protracted dream.
1660   The torch shall be extinguish'd which hath lit
My midnight lamp—and what is writ, is writ,—
Would it were worthier! but I am not now
That which I have been—and my visions flit
Less palpably before me—and the glow
1665   Which in my spirit dwelt is fluttering, faint, and low.

186

Farewell! a word that must be, and hath been—
A sound which makes us linger;—yet—farewell!
Ye! who have traced the Pilgrim to the scene
Which is his last, if in your memories dwell
1670   A thought which once was his, if on ye swell
A single recollection, not in vain
He wore his sandal-shoon, and scallop-shell;[2]
Farewell! with *him* alone may rest the pain,
If such there were—with you, the moral of his strain!

∞

COMPANION READINGS

John Wilson: from A Review of *Childe Harold's Pilgrimage*[1]

It might, on a hasty consideration, seem to us, that such undisguised revelation of feelings and passions, which the becoming pride of human nature, jealous of its own dignity, would, in general, desire to hold in unviolated silence, could produce in the public mind only pity, sorrow, or repugnance. But, in the case of men of real genius, like

2. The shell of a scallop found on the Mediterranean coast was formerly worn by pilgrims returned from the Holy Land.
1. Scotsman John Wilson (1785–1844), a staunch Tory, was elected Professor of Moral Philosophy at Edinburgh University in 1820, a position for which he had been recommended by Wordsworth, whose reputation Wilson had helped to establish. Though he wrote popular poems, his fame rests on his irreverent contributions to Black-

wood's *Magazine*, which he joined in 1817, under the pseudonym "Christopher North." "He is a perverse mortal—not to say worse of him," Wordsworth later declared. This unsigned review of *Childe Harold's Pilgrimage* appeared in the *Edinburgh Review* in 1818. Of it Byron remarked, "Wilson's [is] the review of a poet, too, on another—his *idol;* for he likes me better than he chooses to avow to the public, with all his eulogy. I speak, judging only from the article, for I don't know him personally."

Rousseau or Byron, it is otherwise. Each of us must have been aware in himself of a singular illusion, by which these disclosures, when read with that tender or high interest which attaches to poetry, seem to have something of the nature of private and confidential communications. They are not felt, while we read, as declarations published to the world,—but almost as secrets whispered to chosen ears. Who is there that feels, for a moment, that the voice which reaches the inmost recesses of his heart is speaking to the careless multitudes around him? Or, if we do so remember, the words seem to pass by others like air, and to find their way to the hearts for whom they were intended,—kindred and sympathizing spirits, who discern and own that secret language, of which the privacy is not violated, though spoken in hearing of the uninitiated,—because it is not understood. There is an unobserved beauty that smiles on us alone; and the more beautiful to us, because we feel as if chosen out from a crowd of lovers. * * *

But there are other reasons why we read with complacency writings which, by the most public declaration of most secret feelings, ought, it might seem, to shock and revolt our sympathy. A great poet may address the whole world in the language of intensest passion, concerning objects of which, rather than speak, face to face, with any one human being on earth, he would perish in his misery. For it is in solitude that he utters what is to be wafted by all the winds of heaven. There are, during his inspiration, present with him only the shadows of men. He is not daunted, or perplexed, or disturbed, or repelled by real living breathing features. He can updraw just as much as he chuses of the curtain that hangs between his own solitude and the world of life. He thus pours his soul out, partly to himself alone,—partly to the ideal abstractions, and impersonated images that float round him at his own conjuration,—and partly to human beings like himself, moving in the dark distance of the every-day world. He confesses himself, not before men, but before the Spirit of Humanity. And he thus fearlessly lays open his heart,—assured that nature never prompted unto genius that which will not triumphantly force its wide way into the human heart. We can thus easily imagine the poet whom, in real life, the countenances and voices of his fellow men might silence into shame, or fastidiousness, or timidity, or aversion or disdain,—yet kindling in his solitude into irrepressible passion and enthusiasm towards human nature and all its transitory concerns,—anxiously moulding himself into the object of men's most engrossing and vehement love or aversion,—identifying his own existence with all their strongest and profoundest passions,—claiming kindred with them, not in their virtues alone, but in their darkest vices and most fatal errors; yet, in the midst of all this, proudly guarding his own prevailing character, so that it shall not merge in the waves of a common nature, but stand "in shape and gesture proudly eminent,"[2] contemplated with still-increasing interest by the millions that, in spite of themselves, feel and acknowledge its strange and unaccountable ascendency.

John Scott: [Lord Byron's Creations][1]

Lord Byron's creations * * * are addressed to the poetical sympathies of his readers while their main interest is derived from awakening a recollection of some fact of the author's life, or a conviction of an analogy to the author's own character. A confusion

2. Milton's description of Satan (*Paradise Lost* 1.590).
1. John Scott, author of the lively travelogues *A Visit to Paris* (1814) and *Paris Revisited* (1815), edited *The London Magazine* in its most brilliant days. His attack on the irresponsibilities of the rival *Blackwood's* led J. G. Lockhart, Walter Scott's son-in-law, to challenge him to a duel; the clumsy resolution of the quarrel prompted a counter-challenge from John Scott, who was then killed by a friend of Lockhart. This critique of Byron appeared in *The London Magazine* in 1821.

is thus occasioned, in the breast of him whose attention is captivated by the productions in question, unfavourable altogether to right and pure feeling. The impression left on the mind, is neither strictly that of a work of art, to be pronounced upon according to the rules applicable to art,—nor of a matter-of-fact, appealing to the principles of sound judgment in such cases;—but what is striking in poetry is made a set-off against what is objectionable in morals,—while that which would be condemned as false, theatrical, or inconsistent, according to laws of poetical criticism, is often rendered the most taking part of the whole composition by its evident connection with real and private circumstances, that are of a nature to tickle the idle, impertinent, and most unpoetical curiosity of the public.

DON JUAN   "Give me a poem," Byron's publisher John Murray wrote him in January 1817, "a good Venetian tale describing manners formerly from the story itself, and now from your own observations." The response was Beppo, which Byron based on an anecdote that he had heard from the husband of his mistress, turning it into a seemingly effortless comparison of Italian and British manners. Its success led Murray to ask in July 1818: "Have you not another lively tale like Beppo? Or will you not give me some prose in three volumes?—all the adventures that you have undergone, seen, heard of, or imagined, with your reflections on life and manners." In the same week Byron had begun Don Juan; his own inclination consorted with the publisher's sketch of a suitable "work to open [his] campaign" for fall sales.

For a work of which he remarked "I have no plan—I had no plan—but I had or have materials," Byron found an ideal model in the seriocomic Italian romances of the fifteenth and sixteenth centuries by Pulci, Berni, and Ariosto. Their episodic, digressive mode, flexible enough to incorporate a wide range of moods and stylistic levels, enabled Byron to stage aspects of himself that had not appeared in the titanism of his Eastern tales and the loftiness of Childe Harold's Pilgrimage. He sought to treat public issues with the conversational fluency of a skeptical intelligence engaged with the ordinary materiality of the world: brand names and ship's pumps, indigestion and thinning hair, literary rivalries and reviewers. Byron regarded the story as a "hinge" on which to mount his reflections, and as the poem proceeds its title character retreats before the ceaseless inventions of the narrator, who both is and is not Byron. "If people contradict themselves," he wrote, "can I / Help contradicting them, and everybody, / Even my veracious self?" Truth's streams, he continued, "cut through such canals of contradiction, / That she must often navigate o'er fiction" (15.88). Such teasing of the borders between fiction and fact intrigued readers, and enhanced the allure of the figure of "Byron" the words create. Don Juan is a seemingly inexhaustible improvisatory monologue—sixteen cantos were published between 1819 and 1823, with a fragmentary seventeenth left uncompleted at Byron's death. Through a range of voices, by allusion and quotation, and in the number of perspectives entertained or denounced by the narrator, the poem generates a sense of dialogue and exchange. As the critic Jerome McGann has argued, the poem superimposes three historical levels: Juan's own story is set in the late eighteenth century and was planned to end in the French Revolution; the narrator's reminiscences arise from Byron's years of fame in Regency London (1812–1816); lastly, the narrator's commentary engages the post-Napoleonic moment of the actual writing (1818–1823). As it proceeds, Don Juan depicts Greek pirates and Turkish harems, Russian armies and Spanish families, British highwaymen and British aristocrats, story and commentary together building a critical portrait of the Europe of Byron's era, torn by revolution and now subsiding into the conservative restoration the poet condemns. Though he might have begun the poem intending only "to giggle and make giggle," Byron's purposes deepened as he advanced against the opposition of his friends and publisher.

Byron intensifies the sense that he is speaking in *Don Juan*—forms of the first-person pronoun occur almost two thousand times—and he repeatedly reminds the reader of his capricious playing with form, but the poem is personal in a more specific way as well. Readers familiar with Byron's life—and his celebrity had assured that many were—could perceive in Juan's mother, Donna Inez, a caricature of Byron's estranged wife Annabella, Lady Byron. The account of Juan's youth with Inez also draws on Byron's childhood, "an only son left with an only mother" (1.37). Like Wordsworth's *Prelude*, *Don Juan* is autobiography—but in the form of oblique and theatricalized fiction. It is also picaresque adventure, satire, and mock-Homeric epic, whose hero belies the legacy of his name, seduced more often than seducing, kindhearted rather than ruthless and conniving. As Byron's rhymes make clear (*Juan* rhymes with *new one*), this half-Englished modern hero is not the legendary Don Juan. Byron's genre-crossing revision of literary tradition made "something wholly new & relative to the age," as Shelley recognized.

Much of the poem's power arises from Byron's fluent handling of the ottava rima stanza, rhyming *ababab cc*. He credited *The Monks and the Giants* (1817) by his friend John Hookham Frere for the inspiration, but Frere's work shows little of Byron's deftness. Byron employed a fantastic wealth of rhymes ("Plato" with "potato," "intellectual" with "hen-peck'd you all"), often emphasizing the snap of the concluding couplet for comic surprise; he could also downplay the rhymes and enjamb lines to yield a rhythm like blank verse. "The most readable poem of its length ever written," Virginia Woolf marveled, because its "method is a discovery by itself . . . an elastic shape which will hold whatever you choose to put in it." "Like all free and easy things," she added, "only the skilled and mature really bring them off successfully. But Byron was full of ideas—a quality that gives his verse a toughness." The rare combination of ease and power to which both Shelley and Woolf point keeps *Don Juan* subversively fresh today.

from DON JUAN
Dedication[1]

1

Bob Southey! You're a poet, Poet-laureate,[2]
   And representative of all the race,
Although 'tis true that you turn'd out a Tory at
   Last,—yours has lately been a common case,—
5   And now, my Epic Renegade! what are ye at?
      With all the Lakers,[3] in and out of place?
A nest of tuneful persons, to my eye
Like "four and twenty Blackbirds in a pye;[4]

2

"Which pye being open'd they began to sing"
10   (This old song and new simile holds good),
"A dainty dish to set before the King,"
   Or Regent, who admires such kind of food;—

And Coleridge, too, has lately taken wing,
    But like a hawk encumber'd with his hood,—
15 Explaining metaphysics to the nation—
    I wish he would explain his Explanation.[5]

3

You, Bob! are rather insolent, you know,
    At being disappointed in your wish
To supersede all warblers here below,
20   And be the only Blackbird in the dish;
And then you overstrain yourself, or so,
    And tumble downward like the flying fish
Gasping on deck, because you soar too high, Bob,
And fall, for lack of moisture quite a-dry, Bob![6]

4

25 And Wordsworth, in a rather long "Excursion"[7]
    (I think the quarto holds five hundred pages),
Has given a sample from the vasty version
    Of his new system to perplex the sages;
'Tis poetry—at least by his assertion,
30   And may appear so when the dog-star rages—
And he who understands it would be able
To add a story to the Tower of Babel.[8]

5

You—Gentlemen! by dint of long seclusion
    From better company, have kept your own
35 At Keswick,[9] and, through still continued fusion
    Of one another's minds, at last have grown
To deem as a most logical conclusion,
    That Poesy has wreaths for you alone:
There is a narrowness in such a notion,
40 Which makes me wish you'd change your lakes for ocean.

6

I would not imitate the petty thought,
    Nor coin my self-love to so base a vice,
For all the glory your conversion brought,
    Since gold alone should not have been its price.
45 You have your salary; was't for that you wrought?
    And Wordsworth has his place in the Excise.[1]
You're shabby fellows—true—but poets still,
And duly seated on the immortal hill.°   Parnassus

5. Referring to *The Statesman's Manual* (1816) and
Biographia Literaria (1817).
6. A "dry bob" was slang for sex without ejaculation.
7. This nine-book poem appeared in 1814.
8. To punish human presumption, God destroys the Tower of Babel and institutes the multiplicity of languages (Genesis 11.1–9); note the pun on "story."

9. Southey's home, where the Coleridges moved in 1800; Wordsworth lived nearby in Grasmere.
1. In March 1813 Wordsworth obtained a sinecure as distributor of tax stamps for Westmoreland through the aid of his patron, the Earl of Lonsdale, to whom he dedicated *The Excursion*.

7

Your bays° may hide the baldness of your brows²—   *laurel wreaths*
50   Perhaps some virtuous blushes;—let them go—
To you I envy neither fruit nor boughs—
   And for the fame you would engross below,
The field is universal, and allows
   Scope to all such as feel the inherent glow:
55   Scott, Rogers, Campbell, Moore, and Crabbe,³ will try
'Gainst you the question with posterity.

8

For me, who, wandering with pedestrian Muses,
   Contend not with you on the winged steed,⁴
I wish your fate may yield ye, when she chooses,
60   The fame you envy, and the skill you need;
And recollect a poet nothing loses
   In giving to his brethren their full meed°   *reward*
Of merit, and complaint of present days
Is not the certain path to future praise.

9

65   He that reserves his laurels for posterity
   (Who does not often claim the bright reversion)
Has generally no great crop to spare it, he
   Being only injured by his own assertion;
And although here and there some glorious rarity
70   Arise like Titan from the sea's immersion,
The major part of such appellants go
To—God knows where—for no one else can know.

10

If, fallen in evil days on evil tongues,
   Milton appeal'd to the Avenger, Time,⁵
75   If Time, the Avenger, execrates his wrongs,
   And makes the word "Miltonic" mean "*sublime*,"
He deign'd not to belie his soul in songs,
   Nor turn his very talent to a crime;
He did not loathe the Sire to laud the Son,
80   But closed the tyrant-hater he begun.⁶

11

Think'st thou, could he—the blind Old Man—arise
   Like Samuel from the grave, to freeze once more

2. See *Childe Harold* 4.1293 (page 364).
3. In ranking the living poets in an 1813 journal, Byron declared Walter Scott the "Monarch of Parnassus," Samuel Rogers (1763–1855) next, Thomas Moore (1779–1852) and Thomas Campbell (1777–1844) third, "Southey-Wordsworth-Coleridge" below these. George Crabbe (1754–1832) he elsewhere praised for being "free" of the "wrong revolutionary poetical system" that he and his contemporaries exemplified: "and if I had to begin again—I would model myself accordingly—

Crabbe's the man."
4. The "musa pedestris" of Latin poet Horace (65–8 B.C.) signals a humble, as opposed to exalted or epic, style (*Satires* 2.6.17). The winged horse Pegasus is an old symbol of poetic imagination.
5. Milton's self-description in Book 7 of *Paradise Lost*: "On evil days though fall'n, and evil tongues" (26).
6. A supporter of the Commonwealth party that overthrew Charles I in 1649, Milton held to principle and did not praise Charles II after the Restoration in 1660.

The blood of monarchs with his prophecies,[7]
Or be alive again—again all hoar
85   With time and trials, and those helpless eyes,
And heartless daughters[8]—worn—and pale—and poor;
Would *he* adore a sultan? *he* obey
The intellectual eunuch Castlereagh?[9]

12

Cold-blooded, smooth-faced, placid miscreant!
90   Dabbling its sleek young hands in Erin's° gore,   *Ireland's*
And thus for wider carnage taught to pant,
Transferr'd to gorge upon a sister shore,
The vulgarest tool that Tyranny could want,
With just enough of talent, and no more,
95   To lengthen fetters by another fix'd,
And offer poison long already mix'd.[1]

13

An orator of such set trash of phrase
Ineffably—legitimately vile,[2]
That even its grossest flatterers dare not praise,
100   Nor foes—all nations—condescend to smile,—
Not even a sprightly blunder's spark can blaze
From that Ixion grindstone's ceaseless toil,[3]
That turns and turns to give the world a notion
Of endless torments and perpetual motion.

14

105   A bungler even in its disgusting trade,
And botching, patching, leaving still behind
Something of which its masters are afraid,
States to be curb'd, and thoughts to be confined,
Conspiracy or Congress to be made—[4]
110   Cobbling at manacles for all mankind—
A tinkering slave-maker, who mends old chains,
With God and man's abhorrence for its gains.

---

7. King Saul, attacked by the Philistines, raises the ghost of the prophet Samuel to ask advice, only to learn that he has disobeyed the Lord and will be delivered to the enemy (1 Samuel 28).
8. "Milton's two elder daughters are said to have robbed him of his books, besides cheating and plaguing him in the economy of his house" [Byron's note].
9. Irish nobleman Robert Stewart, Viscount Castlereagh, as chief secretary for Ireland (1799–1801), suppressed the Irish rebellion and secured the Act of Union with England that ended the Irish Parliament. As British Foreign Secretary (1812–1822), he was instrumental in arranging the balance of power in post-Napoleonic Europe, for which he was detested by Byron and the liberals.
1. His opponents regarded Castlereagh as the pawn of the Austrian foreign minister, Prince Metternich.

2. Castlereagh's poor speaking was notorious: "It is the first time indeed since the Normans," Byron wrote in the preface to Cantos 6–8, "that England has been insulted by a *Minister* (at least) who could not speak English, and that Parliament permitted itself to be dictated to in the language of Mrs. Malaprop" [the character from R. B. Sheridan's *The Rivals* (1773) who has given her name to verbal slips].
3. In Greek mythology Ixion is punished in Hades by being chained to a perpetually rolling wheel.
4. In 1814 Austria, Russia, Prussia, and England formed the Quadruple Alliance; after the fall of Napoleon, Castlereagh and Metternich reestablished the "legitimate" governments of Europe at the Congress of Vienna (1815), restoring the Bourbons in France and acknowledging Ferdinand VII in Spain.

15

If we may judge of matter by the mind,
   Emasculated to the marrow *It*
Hath but two objects, how to serve, and bind,
   Deeming the chain it wears even men may fit,
Eutropius[5] of its many masters,—blind
   To worth as freedom, wisdom as to wit,
Fearless—because *no* feeling dwells in ice,
Its very courage stagnates to a vice.

115

120

16

Where shall I turn me not to *view* its bonds,
   For I will never *feel* them;—Italy!
Thy late reviving Roman soul desponds
   Beneath the lie this State-thing breathed o'er thee—
Thy clanking chain, and Erin's yet green wounds,
   Have voices—tongues to cry aloud for me.
Europe has slaves—allies—kings—armies still,
And Southey lives to sing them very ill.

125

17

Meantime—Sir Laureate—I proceed to dedicate,
   In honest simple verse, this song to you.
And, if in flattering strains I do not predicate,
   'Tis that I still retain my "buff and blue";[6]
My politics as yet are all to educate:
   Apostasy's so fashionable, too,
To keep *one* creed's a task grown quite Herculean;
Is it not so, my Tory, ultra-Julian?[7]

130

135

from Canto 1

1

I want a hero: an uncommon want,
   When every year and month sends forth a new one,
Till, after cloying the gazettes with cant,
   The age discovers he is not the true one;
Of such as these I should not care to vaunt,
   I'll therefore take our ancient friend Don Juan—
We all have seen him, in the pantomime,
Sent to the devil somewhat ere his time.[1]

5

5. The career of Eutropius, a eunuch who became a magistrate and general in the Eastern Roman Empire (395–408), is narrated by Gibbon, *Decline and Fall* (ch. 32). Byron's denunciation of Castlereagh as a "eunuch" and an "It" may hint at private knowledge. Castlereagh's suicide in 1822, officially attributed to overwork, was preceded by an attempt to blackmail him on the grounds of homosexuality: sodomy was a capital crime.
6. Colors adopted by the Whigs and by the *Edinburgh Review*.
7. Julian was raised as a Christian, but on becoming Roman emperor in 361 he revived the worship of the pagan gods. He was killed in battle in 363. See Gibbon, *Decline and Fall*, ch. 23.
1. Popular melodrama portrayed Don Juan as a seducer who ends in hell; Byron plays against his own reputation as notorious lover by presenting Juan as an innocent boy overwhelmed by women. His attention may have been drawn to the figure by Coleridge's discussion in *Biographia Literaria* (ch. 23). "Juan" is Anglicized into two syllables, as the rhymes with "true one" and "new one" indicate. "Inez" rhymes with "fine as" and "Jóse" with "nosey."

2

Vernon, the butcher Cumberland, Wolfe, Hawke,
10   Prince Ferdinand, Granby, Burgoyne, Keppel, Howe,[2]
Evil and good, have had their tithe of talk,
      And fill'd their sign-posts then, like Wellesley now;[3]
Each in their turn like Banquo's monarchs stalk,
      Followers of fame, "nine farrow" of that sow:[4]
15   France, too, had Buonaparté and Dumourier
Recorded in the Moniteur and Courier.[5]

3

Barnave, Brissot, Condorcet, Mirabeau,
      Petion, Clootz, Danton, Marat, La Fayette,[6]
Were French, and famous people, as we know;
20   And there were others, scarce forgotten yet,
Joubert, Hoche, Marceau, Lannes, Desaix, Moreau,
      With many of the military set,
Exceedingly remarkable at times,
But not at all adapted to my rhymes.

4

25   Nelson was once Britannia's god of war,
      And still should be so, but the tide is turn'd;
There's no more to be said of Trafalgar
      'Tis with our hero quietly inurn'd;[7]
Because the army's grown more popular,
30   At which the naval people are concern'd;
Besides, the prince is all for the land-service,
Forgetting Duncan, Nelson, Howe, and Jervis.[8]

5

Brave men were living before Agamemnon[9]
      And since, exceeding valorous and sage,
35   A good deal like him too, though quite the same none;
      But then they shone not on the poet's page,
And so have been forgotten:—I condemn none,
      But can't find any in the present age
Fit for my poem (that is, for my new one);
40   So, as I said, I'll take my friend Don Juan.

---

2. Recent military heroes. The Duke of Cumberland defeated the Stuart army in 1745; he earned the title "Butcher" for his subsequent suppression of Jacobitism in Scotland.
3. Arthur Wellesley, Duke of Wellington, born in Ireland, the most celebrated British general of his time. Granted a peerage for his victory over the French at Talavera (1808), he led the British forces at Waterloo.
4. In Shakespeare's Macbeth (4.1), the witches show Macbeth a vision of future Scots kings descended from the murdered Banquo, establishing the triumph of his line and the frustration of Macbeth's ambitions.
5. Charles Dumouriez was a French general and Girondist (moderate); suspected by the Jacobins in 1793, he fled to the Austrians whom he had defeated the year before. He settled in England in 1804, and advised the British in their war against Buonaparte. The Moniteur and Courier were French newspapers.
6. All figures of the French Revolution. Jean Baptiste, Baron von Cloots, a zealot, dropped his title and took the pseudonym Anacharsis; elected to the Convention in 1792, he voted for the King's death and was himself executed in 1794. Byron wrote that he meant Juan "to finish as Anacharsis Cloots—in the French Revolution."
7. Admiral Horatio Nelson died in the Battle of Trafalgar (1805) at which he defeated the French fleet.
8. Byron plays the four distinguished British admirals against the Regent's support of the army.
9. An adaptation of Horace (Odes 4.9.25–28): "Many heroes lived before Agamemnon; but all are overwhelmed in unending night, unwept, unknown, because they lacked a sacred bard" (trans. by C. E. Bennett).

6

Most epic poets plunge "in medias res"
  (Horace makes this the heroic turnpike road),[1]
And then your hero tells, whene'er you please,
  What went before—by way of episode,
45   While seated after dinner at his ease,
  Beside his mistress in some soft abode,
Palace, or garden, paradise, or cavern,
Which serves the happy couple for a tavern.

7

That is the usual method, but not mine—
50   —My way is to begin with the beginning;
The regularity of my design
  Forbids all wandering as the worst of sinning,[2]
And therefore I shall open with a line
  (Although it cost me half an hour in spinning)
55   Narrating somewhat of Don Juan's father,
And also of his mother, if you'd rather.

8

In Seville was he born, a pleasant city,
  Famous for oranges and women—he
Who has not seen it will be much to pity,
60   So says the proverb—and I quite agree;
Of all the Spanish towns is none more pretty,
  Cadiz perhaps—but that you soon may see:—
Don Juan's parents lived beside the river,
A noble stream, and call'd the Guadalquivir.

9

65 His father's name was Jóse—Don, of course,
  A true Hidalgo,° free from every stain   *nobleman*
Of Moor or Hebrew blood, he traced his source
  Through the most Gothic gentlemen of Spain;
A better cavalier ne'er mounted horse,
70   Or, being mounted, e'er got down again,
Than Jóse, who begot our hero, who
Begot—but that's to come———Well, to renew:

10

His mother was a learned lady, famed
  For every branch of every science known—
75 In every Christian language ever named,
  With virtues equall'd by her wit alone,
She made the cleverest people quite ashamed,
  And even the good with inward envy groan,
Finding themselves so very much exceeded
80 In their own way by all the things that she did.

---

1. In *Ars Poetica* Horace recommends that the epic poet begin dramatically, like Homer, by taking the audience directly "into the midst of things."

2. That is, digression, literally "off the path." The Latin word for "wandering," *erratus*, also means "sinning."

11

Her memory was a mine: she knew by heart
    All Calderon and greater part of Lopé,[3]
So that if any actor miss'd his part
    She could have served him for the prompter's copy;
85   For her Feinagle's were an useless art,[4]
    And he himself obliged to shut up shop—he
Could never make a memory so fine as
That which adorn'd the brain of Donna Inez.

12

Her favourite science was the mathematical,
90   Her noblest virtue was her magnanimity,
Her wit (she sometimes tried at wit) was Attic° all,   *refined*
    Her serious sayings darken'd to sublimity;
In short, in all things she was fairly what I call
    A prodigy—her morning dress was dimity,°   *plain cotton*
95   Her evening silk, or, in the summer, muslin,
And other stuffs, with which I won't stay puzzling.

13

She knew the Latin—that is, "the Lord's prayer,"
    And Greek—the alphabet—I'm nearly sure;
She read some French romances here and there,
100   Although her mode of speaking was not pure;
For native Spanish she had no great care,
    At least her conversation was obscure;
Her thoughts were theorems, her words a problem,
As if she deem'd that mystery would ennoble 'em.

14

105   She liked the English and the Hebrew tongue,
    And said there was analogy between 'em;
She proved it somehow out of sacred song,
    But I must leave the proofs to those who've seen 'em,
But this I heard her say, and can't be wrong,
110   And all may think which way their judgments lean 'em,
"'Tis strange—the Hebrew noun which means 'I am,'[5]
The English always use to govern d—n."

15

Some women use their tongues—she *look'd* a lecture,
    Each eye a sermon, and her brow a homily,
115   An all-in-all-sufficient self-director,
    Like the lamented late Sir Samuel Romilly,
The Law's expounder, and the State's corrector,
    Whose suicide was almost an anomaly—

3. Pedro Calderón de la Barca (1600–1681) and Lopé de Vega (1562–1635), Spanish dramatists.
4. In 1812 Gregor von Feinagle lectured on mnemonics, under bluestocking patronage.
5. "God," *Yahweh* in Hebrew, which God renders to Moses as "I AM THAT I AM" (Exodus 3.14).

One sad example more, that "All is vanity,"—
120 (The jury brought their verdict in "Insanity.")[6]

16

In short, she was a walking calculation,
   Miss Edgeworth's novels stepping from their covers,
Or Mrs. Trimmer's books on education,
   Or "Cœlebs' Wife" set out in quest of lovers,[7]
125 Morality's prim personification,
   In which not Envy's self a flaw discovers;
To others' share let "female errors fall,"[8]
For she had not even one—the worst of all.

17

Oh! she was perfect past all parallel—
130   Of any modern female saint's comparison;
So far above the cunning powers of hell,
   Her guardian angel had given up his garrison;
Even her minutest motions went as well
   As those of the best time-piece made by Harrison:[9]
135 In virtues nothing earthly could surpass her,
Save thine "incomparable oil," Macassar![1]

18

Perfect she was, but as perfection is
   Insipid in this naughty world of ours,
Where our first parents never learn'd to kiss
140   Till they were exiled from their earlier bowers,
Where all was peace, and innocence, and bliss
   (I wonder how they got through the twelve hours)
Don Jóse, like a lineal son of Eve,
Went plucking various fruit without her leave.

19

145 He was a mortal of the careless kind,
   With no great love for learning, or the learn'd,
Who chose to go where'er he had a mind,
   And never dream'd his lady was concern'd;
The world, as usual, wickedly inclined
150   To see a kingdom or a house o'erturn'd,
Whisper'd he had a mistress, some said *two*,
But for domestic quarrels *one* will do.

---

6. Romilly (1757–1818), a liberal member of Parliament, accepted a retainer to represent Byron in the separation proceedings but then switched to Lady Byron. Even his suicide did not soften Byron's resentment; Murray refused to print this stanza in the first edition. "All is vanity" (emptiness) is the Preacher's refrain in Ecclesiastes.
7. Maria Edgeworth was a popular Irish novelist and educational writer; Sarah Trimmer (1741–1810) was a popular writer on education and of children's books. *Cœlebs in*

Search of a Wife (1809)—its title deliberately misquoted by Byron—was the only, but quite successful, novel of Hannah More.
8. Alexander Pope, *The Rape of the Lock* (1714), 2.17.
9. In 1762 English clockmaker John Harrison claimed the government prize of £20,000 for a chronometer able to determine longitude. Byron called Lady Byron "the Princess of Parellelograms."
1. Byron cites the advertisements of the firm A. Rowland and Son for their widely used hair oil.

20

Now Donna Inez had, with all her merit,
   A great opinion of her own good qualities;
155 Neglect, indeed, requires a saint to bear it,
   And such, indeed, she was in her moralities;
But then she had a devil of a spirit,
   And sometimes mix'd up fancies with realities,
And let few opportunities escape
160 Of getting her liege lord into a scrape.

21

This was an easy matter with a man
   Oft in the wrong, and never on his guard;
And even the wisest, do the best they can,
   Have moments, hours, and days, so unprepared,
165 That you might "brain them with their lady's fan";[2]
   And sometimes ladies hit exceeding hard,
And fans turn into falchions° in fair hands,   *swords*
And why and wherefore no one understands.

22

'Tis pity learned virgins ever wed
170   With persons of no sort of education,
Or gentlemen, who, though well born and bred,
   Grow tired of scientific conversation:
I don't choose to say much upon this head,
   I'm a plain man, and in a single station,
175 But—Oh! ye lords of ladies intellectual,
Inform us truly, have they not hen-peck'd you all?

23

Don Jóse and his lady quarrell'd—*why*,
   Not any of the many could divine,
Though several thousand people chose to try,
180   'Twas surely no concern of theirs nor mine;
I loathe that low vice—curiosity;
   But if there's any thing in which I shine,
'Tis in arranging all my friends' affairs,
Not having, of my own, domestic cares.

24

185 And so I interfered, and with the best
   Intentions, but their treatment was not kind;
I think the foolish people were possess'd,
   For neither of them could I ever find,
Although their porter afterwards confess'd—
190   But that's no matter, and the worst's behind,
For little Juan o'er me threw, down stairs,
A pail of housemaid's water unawares.

2. Shakespeare, *1 Henry IV*, 2.3.23.

25

A little curly-headed, good-for-nothing,
  And mischief-making monkey from his birth;
His parents ne'er agreed except in doting
  Upon the most unquiet imp on earth;
Instead of quarrelling, had they been but both in
  Their senses, they'd have sent young master forth
To school, or had him soundly whipp'd at home,
To teach him manners for the time to come.

26

Don Jóse and the Donna Inez led
  For some time an unhappy sort of life,
Wishing each other, not divorced, but dead;
  They lived respectably as man and wife,
Their conduct was exceedingly well-bred,
  And gave no outward signs of inward strife,
Until at length the smother'd fire broke out,
And put the business past all kind of doubt.

27

For Inez call'd some druggists, and physicians,
  And tried to prove her loving lord was *mad*,[3]
But as he had some lucid intermissions,
  She next decided he was only *bad*;
Yet when they ask'd her for her depositions,
  No sort of explanation could be had,
Save that her duty both to man and God
Required this conduct—which seem'd very odd.

28

She kept a journal, where his faults were noted,
  And open'd certain trunks of books and letters,
All which might, if occasion served, be quoted;
  And then she had all Seville for abettors,
Besides her good old grandmother (who doted);
  The hearers of her case became repeaters,
Then advocates, inquisitors, and judges,
Some for amusement, others for old grudges.

29

And then this best and meekest woman bore
  With such serenity her husband's woes,
Just as the Spartan ladies did of yore,
  Who saw their spouses kill'd, and nobly chose
Never to say a word about them more—
  Calmly she heard each calumny that rose,

195

200

205

210

215

220

225

230

---

3. As Byron believed Lady Byron had tried to do; stanzas 27 and 28 replay details of their separation.

And saw *his* agonies with such sublimity,
That all the world exclaim'd, "What magnanimity!"

30

No doubt this patience, when the world is damning us,
 Is philosophic in our former friends;
235 'Tis also pleasant to be deem'd magnanimous,
 The more so in obtaining our own ends;
And what the lawyers call a *"malus animus"*°   *ill will*
 Conduct like this by no means comprehends:
Revenge in person's certainly no virtue,
240 But then 'tis not *my* fault, if *others* hurt you.

31

And if our quarrels should rip up old stories,
 And help them with a lie or two additional,
I'm not to blame, as you well know—no more is
 Any one else—they were become traditional;
245 Besides, their resurrection aids our glories
 By contrast, which is what we just were wishing all:
And science profits by this resurrection—
Dead scandals form good subjects for dissection.

32

Their friends had tried at reconciliation,
250 Then their relations, who made matters worse.
('Twere hard to tell upon a like occasion
 To whom it may be best to have recourse—
I can't say much for friend or yet relation):
 The lawyers did their utmost for divorce,
255 But scarce a fee was paid on either side
Before, unluckily, Don Jóse died.

33

He died: and most unluckily, because,
 According to all hints I could collect
From counsel learned in those kinds of laws,
260 (Although their talk's obscure and circumspect)
His death contrived to spoil a charming cause;
 A thousand pities also with respect
To public feeling, which on this occasion
Was manifested in a great sensation.

34

265 But ah! he died; and buried with him lay
 The public feeling and the lawyers' fees:
His house was sold, his servants sent away,
 A Jew took one of his two mistresses,
A priest the other—at least so they say:
270 I ask'd the doctors after his disease—
He died of the slow fever call'd the tertian,°   *malaria*
And left his widow to her own aversion.

35

Yet Jóse was an honourable man,[4]
　　That I must say, who knew him very well;
275 Therefore his frailties I'll no further scan,
　　Indeed there were not many more to tell:
And if his passions now and then outran
　　Discretion, and were not so peaceable
As Numa's (who was also named Pompilius),[5]
280 He had been ill brought up, and was born bilious.

36

Whate'er might be his worthlessness or worth,
　　Poor fellow! he had many things to wound him.
Let's own—since it can do no good on earth—
　　It was a trying moment that which found him
285 Standing alone beside his desolate hearth,
　　Where all his household gods lay shiver'd round him
No choice was left his feelings or his pride,
Save death or Doctors' Commons[6]—so he died.

37

Dying intestate,° Juan was sole heir   *without a will*
290 　　To a chancery suit, and messuages,° and lands,   *houses*
Which, with a long minority and care,
　　Promised to turn out well in proper hands:
Inez became sole guardian, which was fair,
　　And answer'd but to nature's just demands;
295 An only son left with an only mother
Is brought up much more wisely than another.

38

Sagest of women, even of widows, she
　　Resolved that Juan should be quite a paragon,
And worthy of the noblest pedigree:
300 　　(His sire was of Castile, his dam from Aragon.)
Then for accomplishments of chivalry,
　　In case our lord the king should go to war again,
He learn'd the arts of riding, fencing, gunnery,
And how to scale a fortress—or a nunnery.

39

305 But that which Donna Inez most desired,
　　And saw into herself each day before all
The learned tutors whom for him she hired,
　　Was, that his breeding should be strictly moral:
Much into all his studies she enquired,
310 　　And so they were submitted first to her, all,
Arts, sciences, no branch was made a mystery
To Juan's eyes, excepting natural history.

---

4. Parodying Marc Antony's ironic praise of assassin Brutus
at Caesar's funeral (*Julius Caesar* 3.2.84).
5. The second king of Rome, renowned for his piety.

6. The court that presided over divorces; Chancery
presided over inheritance.

40

The languages, especially the dead,
  The sciences, and most of all the abstruse,
315 The arts, at least all such as could be said
  To be the most remote from common use,
In all these he was much and deeply read;
  But not a page of any thing that's loose,
Or hints continuation of the species,
320 Was ever suffer'd, lest he should grow vicious.

41

His classic studies made a little puzzle,
  Because of filthy loves of gods and goddesses,
Who in the earlier ages raised a bustle,
  But never put on pantaloons or bodices;
325 His reverend tutors had at times a tussle,
  And for their Aeneids, Iliads, and Odysseys,
Were forced to make an odd sort of apology,
For Donna Inez dreaded the Mythology.

42

Ovid's a rake, as half his verses show him,
330 Anacreon's morals are a still worse sample,
Catullus scarcely has a decent poem,
  I don't think Sappho's Ode a good example,
Although Longinus tells us there is no hymn
  Where the sublime soars forth on wings more ample;
335 But Virgil's songs are pure, except that horrid one
Beginning with "Formosum Pastor Corydon."[7]

43

Lucretius' irreligion is too strong
  For early stomachs, to prove wholesome food;
I can't help thinking Juvenal was wrong,
340 Although no doubt his real intent was good,
For speaking out so plainly in his song,
  So much indeed as to be downright rude;
And then what proper person can be partial
To all those nauseous epigrams of Martial?[8]

44

345 Juan was taught from out the best edition,
  Expurgated by learned men, who place,
Judiciously, from out the schoolboy's vision,
  The grosser parts; but fearful to deface
Too much their modest bard by this omission,

---

7. Classical erotic poets: the Roman Ovid (43 B.C.–A.D. 18), author of the *Amores* and *The Art of Love*; Anacreon, 6th-century B.C.; Catullus (c. 84–54 B.C.); Sappho, 7th-century B.C. Greek poet; her ode beginning "To me he seems like a god / as he sits facing you" (trans. by Willis Barnstone) was praised by Longinus in his essay *On the Sublime* (1st century B.C.). The second Eclogue of Virgil (70–19 B.C.), is a homoerotic text beginning: "Corydon the shepherd burned for lovely Alexis, / His master's beloved."
8. *De Rerum Natura* ("On the Nature of Things"), by 1st-century B.C. Roman poet Lucretius, argues a materialistic view of the world; the 16 satires of Juvenal (c. A.D. 60–130) sternly denounce Roman society; the epigrams of Martial (A.D. 40–104) are witty but often blunt.

350   And pitying sore his mutilated case,
    They only add them all in an appendix,
    Which saves, in fact, the trouble of an index;[9]

45

    For there we have them all "at one fell swoop,"
      Instead of being scatter'd through the pages;
355   They stand forth marshall'd in a handsome troop,
      To meet the ingenuous youth of future ages,
    Till some less rigid editor shall stoop
      To call them back into their separate cages,
    Instead of standing staring altogether,
360   Like garden gods—and not so decent either.

46

    The Missal too (it was the family Missal)
      Was ornamented in a sort of way
    Which ancient mass-books often are, and this all
      Kinds of grotesques illumined; and how they,
365   Who saw those figures on the margin kiss all,
      Could turn their optics to the text and pray,
    Is more than I know—but Don Juan's mother
    Kept this herself, and gave her son another.

47

    Sermons he read, and lectures he endured,
370   And homilies, and lives of all the saints;
    To Jerome and to Chrysostom inured,[1]
      He did not take such studies for restraints;
    But how faith is acquired, and then ensured,
      So well not one of the aforesaid paints
375   As Saint Augustine in his fine Confessions,
    Which make the reader envy his transgressions.[2]

48

    This, too, was a seal'd book to little Juan—
      I can't but say that his mamma was right,
    If such an education was the true one.
380   She scarcely trusted him from out her sight;
    Her maids were old, and if she took a new one,
      You might be sure she was a perfect fright,
    She did this during even her husband's life—
    I recommend as much to every wife.

49

385   Young Juan wax'd in goodliness and grace;
      At six a charming child, and at eleven
    With all the promise of as fine a face

---

9. "Fact. There is, or was, such an edition, with all the obnoxious epigrams of Martial placed by themselves at the end" [Byron's note].
1. St. Jerome (340–420), translator of the Vulgate, and St. John Chrysostom (c. 345–407) were known for asceticism.
2. In his *Confessions* (397–398) Augustine describes his life in Carthage, "a hissing cauldron of lust," before his conversion to Christianity.

As e'er to man's maturer growth was given:
He studied steadily, and grew apace,
390   And seem'd, at least, in the right road to heaven,
For half his days were pass'd at church, the other
Between his tutors, confessor, and mother.

50

At six, I said, he was a charming child,
At twelve he was a fine, but quiet boy;
395   Although in infancy a little wild,
They tamed him down amongst them: to destroy
His natural spirit not in vain they toil'd.
At least it seem'd so; and his mother's joy
Was to declare how sage, and still, and steady,
400   Her young philosopher was grown already.

51

I had my doubts, perhaps I have them still,
But what I say is neither here nor there:
I knew his father well, and have some skill
In character—but it would not be fair
405   From sire to son to augur good or ill:
He and his wife were an ill-sorted pair—
But scandal's my aversion—I protest
Against all evil speaking, even in jest.

52

For my part I say nothing—nothing—but
410   *This* I will say—my reasons are my own—
That if I had an only son to put
To school (as God be praised that I have none),
'Tis not with Donna Inez I would shut
Him up to learn his catechism alone,
415   No—no—I'd send him out betimes to college,
For there it was I pick'd up my own knowledge.

53

For there one learns—'tis not for me to boast,
Though I acquired—but I pass over *that,*
As well as all the Greek I since have lost:
420   I say that there's the place—but "*Verbum sat,*"[3]
I think I pick'd up too, as well as most,
Knowledge of matters—but no matter *what*—
I never married—but, I think, I know
That sons should not be educated so.

54

425   Young Juan now was sixteen years of age,
Tall, handsome, slender, but well knit: he seem'd
Active, though not so sprightly, as a page;
And every body but his mother deem'd

3. Proverbial: "A word to the wise suffices."

Him almost man; but she flew in a rage
430   And bit her lips (for else she might have scream'd)
If any said so, for to be precocious
Was in her eyes a thing the most atrocious.

55

Amongst her numerous acquaintance, all
     Selected for discretion and devotion,
435 There was the Donna Julia, whom to call
     Pretty were but to give a feeble notion
Of many charms in her as natural
     As sweetness to the flower, or salt to ocean,
Her zone to Venus,[4] or his bow to Cupid,
440 (But this last simile is trite and stupid.)

56

The darkness of her Oriental eye
     Accorded with her Moorish origin;
(Her blood was not all Spanish, by the by;
     In Spain, you know, this is a sort of sin.)
445 When proud Granada fell, and, forced to fly,
     Boabdil[5] wept, of Donna Julia's kin
Some went to Africa, some stay'd in Spain,
Her great great grandmamma chose to remain.

57

She married (I forget the pedigree)
450   With an Hidalgo, who transmitted down
His blood less noble than such blood should be;
     At such alliances his sires would frown,
In that point so precise in each degree
     That they bred in and in, as might be shown,
455 Marrying their cousins—nay, their aunts, and nieces,
Which always spoils the breed, if it increases.

58

This heathenish cross restored the breed again,
     Ruin'd its blood, but much improved its flesh;
For from a root the ugliest in Old Spain
460   Sprung up a branch as beautiful as fresh;
The sons no more were short, the daughters plain:
     But there's a rumour which I fain would hush,
'Tis said that Donna Julia's grandmamma
Produced her Don more heirs at love than law.

59

465 However this might be, the race went on
     Improving still through every generation,
Until it centred in an only son,
     Who left an only daughter; my narration

---

4. The belt ("zone") of Venus made its wearer sexually attractive.

5. Mohammed XI, the last Moorish king of Granada, expelled by Ferdinand and Isabella in 1492.

May have suggested that this single one
470   Could be but Julia (whom on this occasion
I shall have much to speak about), and she
Was married, charming, chaste, and twenty-three.

60

Her eye (I'm very fond of handsome eyes)
    Was large and dark, suppressing half its fire
475 Until she spoke, then through its soft disguise
    Flash'd an expression more of pride than ire,
And love than either; and there would arise
    A something in them which was not desire,
But would have been, perhaps, but for the soul
480 Which struggled through and chasten'd down the whole.

61

Her glossy hair was cluster'd o'er a brow
    Bright with intelligence, and fair, and smooth;
Her eyebrow's shape was like th' aërial bow,
    Her cheek all purple with the beam of youth,
485 Mounting, at times, to a transparent glow,
    As if her veins ran lightning; she, in sooth,
Possess'd an air and grace by no means common:
Her stature tall—I hate a dumpy woman.

62

Wedded she was some years, and to a man
490   Of fifty, and such husbands are in plenty;
And yet, I think, instead of such a ONE
    'Twere better to have TWO of five-and-twenty,
Especially in countries near the sun:
    And now I think on't, "mi vien in mente,"°   *it comes to mind*
495 Ladies even of the most uneasy virtue
Prefer a spouse whose age is short of thirty.

63

'Tis a sad thing, I cannot choose but say,
    And all the fault of that indecent sun,
Who cannot leave alone our helpless clay,
500   But will keep baking, broiling, burning on,
That howsoever people fast and pray,
    The flesh is frail, and so the soul undone:
What men call gallantry, and gods adultery,
Is much more common where the climate's sultry.

64

505 Happy the nations of the moral North!
    Where all is virtue, and the winter season
Sends sin, without a rag on, shivering forth
    ('Twas snow that brought St. Anthony to reason);[6]

---

6. As Byron later realized, it was St. Francis of Assisi (1181?–1226) who cast himself into ditches full of snow to quell his desires.

Where juries cast up what a wife is worth,
510   By laying whate'er sum, in mulct,° they please on   *penalty*
The lover, who must pay a handsome price,
Because it is a marketable vice.

from Canto 11[1]

[JUAN IN ENGLAND][2]

21

Through Groves, so call'd as being void of trees,
    (Like *lucus* from *no* light);[3] through prospects named
Mount Pleasant, as containing nought to please,
    Nor much to climb; through little boxes framed
165   Of bricks, to let the dust in at your ease,
    With "To be let,"° upon their doors proclaim'd;   *rented*
Through "Rows" most modestly call'd "Paradise,"
Which Eve might quit without much sacrifice;—

22

Through coaches, drays, choked turnpikes, and a whirl
170   Of wheels, and roar of voices, and confusion;
Here taverns wooing to a pint of "purl,"°   *gin and beer*
    There mails° fast flying off like a delusion;   *mail-coaches*
There barbers' blocks with periwigs in curl
    In windows; here the lamplighter's infusion
175   Slowly distill'd into the glimmering glass
(For in those days we had not got to gas—);[4]

23

Through this, and much, and more, is the approach
    Of travellers to mighty Babylon:
Whether they come by horse, or chaise, or coach,
180   With slight exceptions, all the ways seem one.
I could say more, but do not choose to encroach
    Upon the Guide-book's privilege. The sun
Had set some time, and night was on the ridge
Of twilight, as the party cross'd the bridge.

24

185   That's rather fine, the gentle sound of Thamis°—   *River Thames*
    Who vindicates a moment, too, his stream—
Though hardly heard through multifarious "damme's."
    The lamps of Westminster's more regular gleam,

1. Composed October 1822. John Hunt published Cantos 9–11 together in August 1823, again anonymously.
2. Having distinguished himself at Ismail, Juan is sent to St. Petersburg, where he becomes the favorite of Empress Catherine the Great, whose sexual appetite was notorious. Amply rewarded but exhausted, Juan is sent on a diplomatic mission to England to restore his declining health. Juan's journey across Europe enabled Byron lightly to revisit the materials of *Childe Harold's Pilgrimage*, and his arrival in England returns the poem, in a vivid act of memory, to the Regency England in which Byron had shined. Here Juan is approaching London.
3. In a famous ancient false etymology, it was speculated that the Latin word for "grove," *lucus*, derived from the lack of light (*lux*) under the trees.
4. Gas came into use in London in 1812.

The breadth of pavement, and yon shrine[5] where fame is
190   A spectral resident—whose pallid beam
In shape of moonshine hovers o'er the pile—
Make this a sacred part of Albion's isle.

25

The Druids' groves are gone—so much the better:
      Stone-Henge[6] is not—but what the devil is it?—
195 But Bedlam still exists with its sage fetter,
      That madmen may not bite you on a visit;
The Bench too seats or suits full many a debtor;
      The Mansion House too (though some people quiz it)
To me appears a stiff yet grand erection;
200 But then the Abbey's worth the whole collection.[7]

26

The line of lights too up to Charing Cross,
      Pall Mall,[8] and so forth, have a coruscation°   sparkle
Like gold as in comparison to dross,
      Match'd with the Continent's illumination,
205 Whose cities Night by no means deigns to gloss.
      The French were not yet a lamp-lighting nation,
And when they grew so—on their new-found lantern,
Instead of wicks, they made a wicked man turn.[9]

27

A row of gentlemen along the streets
210   Suspended, may illuminate mankind,
As also bonfires made of country seats;
      But the old way is best for the purblind:
The other looks like phosphorus on sheets,
      A sort of ignis fatuus° to the mind,   will o' the wisp
215 Which, though 'tis certain to perplex and frighten,
Must burn more mildly ere it can enlighten.

28

But London's so well lit, that if Diogenes
      Could recommence to hunt his *honest man*,[1]
And found him not amidst the various progenies
220   Of this enormous city's spreading spawn,
'Twere not for want of lamps to aid his dodging his
      Yet undiscover'd treasure. What *I* can,
I've done to find the same throughout life's journey,
But see the world is only one attorney.

* * *

5. Westminster Abbey, filled with monuments to the famous.
6. Interest in the ancient Celtic Druids, to whom the oak was sacred, and Stonehenge, the Druid stone circle on Salisbury Plain, had grown in the 18th century.
7. London sites: Bedlam, a corruption of Bethlehem Hospital for the insane; the Bench, the Court of Common Pleas; the Mansion House, the residence of the Lord Mayor.

8. Juan is proceeding to the fashionable West End.
9. A punning capsule history, from the rationalism of the Enlightenment to the hanging of offending persons from lampposts during the French Revolution.
1. Greek philosopher Diogenes the Cynic (c. 423–323 B.C.) took a lantern in broad daylight to search for an honest man.

65[2]

His morns he pass'd in business—which dissected,
    Was like all business, a laborious nothing,
515 That leads to lassitude, the most infected
    And Centaur Nessus garb of mortal clothing,[3]
And on our sofas makes us lie dejected,
    And talk in tender horrors of our loathing
All kinds of toil, save for our country's good—.
520 Which grows no better, though 'tis time it should.

66

His afternoons he pass'd in visits, luncheons,
    Lounging, and boxing; and the twilight hour
In riding round those vegetable puncheons
    Call'd "Parks," where there is neither fruit nor flower
525 Enough to gratify a bee's slight munchings;
    But after all it is the only "bower,"
(In Moore's phrase) where the fashionable fair
Can form a slight acquaintance with fresh air.

67

Then dress, then dinner, then awakes the world!
    Then glare the lamps, then whirl the wheels, then roar
530 Through street and square fast flashing chariots hurl'd
    Like harness'd meteors; then along the floor
Chalk mimics painting; then festoons are twirl'd;
    Then roll the brazen thunders of the door,
535 Which opens to the thousand happy few
An earthly Paradise of "Or Molu."[4]

* * *

74

585 Our hero, as a hero, young and handsome,
    Noble, rich, celebrated, and a stranger,
Like other slaves of course must pay his ransom
    Before he can escape from so much danger
As will environ a conspicuous man.[5] Some
590   Talk about poetry, and "rack and manger,"°   *rack and ruin*
And ugliness, disease, as toil and trouble;—
I wish they knew the life of a young noble.

75

They are young, but know not youth—it is anticipated;
    Handsome but wasted, rich without a sou;
595 Their vigour in a thousand arms is dissipated;

2. The intervening stanzas record Juan's enthusiastic reception by high society.
3. When her husband Hercules was unfaithful, Deianira sent him the tunic of the Centaur Nessus, whom he had killed, believing it to be a love charm. Instead Hercules died in agony.
4. Gilded bronze, an ornamental material popular in the Regency.
5. Echoing Samuel Butler's satiric poem, *Hudibras* (1663–1678), "Ah me! what perils do environ / The man who meddles with cold iron" (pt. 1, ch. 3).

Their cash comes *from*, their wealth goes to a Jew;
Both senates see their nightly votes participated
  Between the tyrant's and the tribunes' crew;[6]
And having voted, dined, drank, gamed, and whored,
600 The family vault receives another lord.
1822   1823

Stanzas[1]

When a man hath no freedom to fight for at home,
  Let him combat for that of his neighbours;
Let him think of the glories of Greece and of Rome,
  And get knock'd on the head for his labours.

5   To do good to mankind is the chivalrous plan,
  And is always as nobly requited;
Then battle for freedom wherever you can,
  And, if not shot or hang'd, you'll get knighted.
1820   1830

On This Day I Complete My Thirty-Sixth Year
Missolonghi, Jan. 22. 1824[1]

'Tis time this heart should be unmoved,
  Since others it hath ceased to move:
Yet, though I cannot be beloved,
  Still let me love!

5   My days are in the yellow leaf;[2]
  The flowers and fruits of love are gone;
The worm, the canker, and the grief
  Are mine alone!

The fire that on my bosom preys
10   Is lone as some volcanic isle;
No torch is kindled at its blaze—
  A funeral pile!

The hope, the fear, the jealous care,
  The exalted portion of the pain
15 And power of love, I cannot share,
  But wear the chain.

But 'tis not *thus*—and 'tis not *here*—
  Such thoughts should shake my soul, nor *now*,
Where glory decks the hero's bier,
20   Or binds his brow.

---

6. The tyrants are the Tories, in power; the tribunes, representatives of the people, are the opposition Whigs and radicals. The Jews are moneylenders.
1. Sent to Thomas Moore in a letter of 5 November 1820, the poem reflects—with his usual irony—Byron's involvement with the Carbonari, rebels against Austrian domination of Italy.
1. Two weeks earlier, Byron had arrived in Missolonghi, a marshy town in western Greece, to support the Greeks in their war against Turkish rule. The poem is the final entry in his Missolonghi journal; he died from a fever and the ignorant medical practice of the day on 19 April. The poem reflects Byron's feelings for his 15-year-old page, Loukas Chalandritsanos.
2. Echoing Shakespeare, *Macbeth*, 5.3.22.

The sword, the banner, and the field,
  Glory and Greece, around me see!
The Spartan, borne upon his shield,[3]
  Was not more free.

25 Awake! (not Greece—she *is* awake!)
  Awake, my spirit! Think through *whom*
Thy life-blood tracks its parent lake,
  And then strike home!

Tread those reviving passions down,
30 Unworthy manhood!—unto thee
Indifferent should the smile or frown
  Of beauty be.

If thou regret'st thy youth, *why* live?
  The land of honourable death
35 Is here:—up to the field, and give
  Away thy breath!

Seek out—less often sought than found—
  A soldier's grave, for thee the best;
Then look around, and choose thy ground,
40 And take thy rest.

1824   1824

Percy Bysshe Shelley
1792–1822

One of the most radically visionary of the Romantics, Percy Bysshe Shelley has always had countercultural prestige. In the nineteenth century, Karl Marx and Friedrich Engels praised his "prophetic genius," and in the twentieth century, Paul Foot, head of England's Socialist Workers Party, edited an inexpensive volume of his political writing both to answer "the enthusiasm of the members of the SWP for Shelley's revolutionary writings" and to give socialists a means to disseminate their views not "with dogmatic propaganda but with the poetry which carries revolutionary ideas through the centuries."

Shelley's esteem in these countercultures emerges from a selective reading of his work and life, the full range of which complicates and challenges partisan evaluation. Variously described as a selflessly devoted, often misunderstood idealist and as appallingly selfish, Shelley was always a risk-taker, and could be careless of the consequences. As an Oxford undergraduate, he collaborated with a friend on *The Necessity of Atheism*, a pamphlet that got them promptly expelled after they sent it to every university professor and administrative official, as well as every bishop in the United Kingdom. His first long poem *Queen Mab* included a vitriolic attack on "Priestcraft" and "Kingcraft" that earned him celebrity in the radical press and infamy in the conservative press; well into the nineteenth century, these atheist and revolutionary passages were expurgated. This censorship was part of the refashioning of Shelley in the Victorian period. In a well-orchestrated campaign by his grieving widow and devoted disciples of his poetry, he was made safe for parlors, refurbished from a dangerous thinker into an impossibly delicate visionary given to chanting at skylarks, "Hail to thee, blithe Spirit!"

3. Spartan warriors were exhorted not to drop their shields and flee battle but to return either with their shields or carried, dead, upon them.

Shelley's life is marked by idealism, scandal, and passionate but shifting emotional commitments, especially to women. Grandson of a wealthy landowner and son of a member of Parliament, he was born into conservative aristocracy. Expected to continue in this world, he was sent to the best schools. But he began to rebel early. At Eton (1804–1810), he challenged the tyrannical system of "fagging," whereby upperclassmen had the privilege of abusing their juniors. He no sooner enrolled in Oxford, in 1810, than he got himself expelled for that pamphlet on atheism, an event that at once surprised him and enraged his father. He took off for London, where he met Harriet Westbrook and, believing her oppressed by her father, convinced her to elope with him in August 1811 (he was eighteen, she sixteen). The next year, he was in Ireland irritating its Protestant aristocracy by distributing pamphlets urging Catholic emancipation and improved conditions for its large population of the poor. Eager to meet William Godwin, author of *Political Justice*, he returned to London, and began *Queen Mab*, a Godwinian dream vision. In 1813 Harriet bore a daughter, and he published *Mab* at his own expense. At once celebrated (and pirated) by the radical press and denounced by the Tory press, this poem would be linked to Shelley for the rest of his life, its infamy persisting even into his obituaries.

In the heat of his Godwinian enthusiasms and mindful of Godwin's disdain of the institution of marriage, Shelley allowed himself to tire of Harriet and become enamored of Godwin and Wollstonecraft's beautiful, intelligent daughter Mary. In July 1814, he and Mary eloped to France, accompanied by her stepsister Claire Clairmont. After a six-week tour of Europe, marveling at the Alps and dismayed by the ravages of the Napoleonic wars, they returned to England and the scandal of their elopement. In December Harriet bore her second child by Percy but declined his invitation to join their menage as a platonic sister. When Shelley's grandfather died at the beginning of 1815, he gained a modest fortune of £1000 per year, one-fifth of which was paid directly to Harriet and a good portion of which he would always spend on philanthropy and loans to friends. Mary's first child, a daughter, was born prematurely in February, and died within a few weeks, an event that devastated her. During this year, they experimented with an "open" relationship, in which Percy had a romance with Claire and she with his college friend T. J. Hogg (collaborator on the pamphlet on atheism). Still at odds with their fathers, Mary and Percy were further strained by debts and a constant shift of residences to avoid their creditors and the bailiffs. Percy wrote *Alastor*, a somewhat equivocally framed story of a young visionary poet alienated by life in the world who seeks visionary fulfillment, finding this ultimately in death. Their second child, William, was born early in 1816.

They left for Switzerland in May 1816 with Claire, to meet Lord Byron, now Claire's lover. During this summer, Mary wrote *Frankenstein*, and Percy wrote *Hymn to Intellectual Beauty* and *Mont Blanc*, and toured the lakes with Byron. At the summer's end, the Shelley party returned to England and several catastrophes. Mary's half-sister Fanny Imlay committed suicide in October on discovering that Godwin was not her father, and in November, Harriet, pregnant by a new lover and in despair over rejection by him, drowned herself. Percy and Mary were now able to marry, but the scandal of his life and political writings cost him custody of his children by Harriet—an extraordinary ruling in an age when fathers automatically had custody. He was shocked by this judgment, which deepened his self-mythology as an idealist persecuted by social and political injustice and despised by a world unable to appreciate his "beautiful idealisms of moral excellence" (as he would phrase it in the Preface to *Prometheus Unbound*).

Over the course of 1817, Shelley consoled himself with new political writing and his friendship with Leigh Hunt, minor poet and editor of the radical newspaper *The Examiner*; through Hunt he met John Keats. Mary was pregnant again, and Clara was born in September. In 1818 they moved to Europe. Eager to spend as much time as possible with Byron, now in Italy, Percy subjected his family to much arduous travel during an oppressively hot summer. Clara did not fare well and died in September. The year 1819 was a productive one for Shelley's writing. He finished *Prometheus Unbound*, an epic "closet-drama" begun the year before about the Titan's war with his oppressor; he wrote *The Cenci*, a Jacobean political tragedy of incestuous rape, parricide, and persecution; several other political poems, including *The Mask of Anarchy*, in reaction to the infamous "Peterloo Massacre" of a peaceful workers' rally; a long proto-Marxist political pamphlet, *A Philosophical View of Reform;* and a witty satire of Wordsworth (*Peter Bell the Third*), energized by dismay at the middle-aged poet's didacticism and swing to the political right. He also composed one of his most famous poems, *Ode to the West Wind*, an impassioned cry for spiritual transformation rendered in the astonishingly intricate, overflowing verse of terza-rima sonnet-stanzas. The death of William in June, at age three and a half, wrenched the Shelleys with a grief only partly allayed by the birth, five months later, of a second son, Percy Florence—the only of their children to survive into adulthood.

Shelley continued to write poetry over the next two years, including *To a Sky-Lark*, and *Adonais*, an elegy for Keats, representing him as a martyr to vicious, politically motivated reviews. Increasingly identifying with this myth himself, and despairing of his bid for poetic fame, in 1821 he began his *Defence of Poetry* (published posthumously by Mary in 1840), in which he set forth his views on the relation of poets both to their immediate social and historical circumstances and to the "Eternity" that authorized their visions and would vindicate their merits. He was also becoming infatuated with Jane Williams, who with her common-law husband Edward had joined their circle in Pisa, Italy. The Williamses and the Shelleys decided to live together on the Bay of Spezia in the summer of 1822. More and more alienated from Mary, who was understandably moody (pregnant for the fifth time in six years and still grieving for her first three children), Percy frequently left her behind to enjoy excursions with the Williamses or Jane alone. He was charmed by their company, jealous of their relationship, and in love with Jane, to whom he addressed a set of beautiful lyrics interwoven with his affection for her, his resentment of Edward, and his withdrawal from Mary. Mary suffered a nearly fatal miscarriage in June. In July, Percy and Edward sailed to Leghorn to greet Leigh Hunt, who was joining Shelley and Byron in Italy to establish *The Liberal*, a journal of opinion and the arts. On the sail back, Percy and Edward were caught in a sudden storm, and both drowned. Byron wrote to his publisher, sponsor of the most influential Tory periodical of the day, *The Quarterly Review* (which had savaged Shelley): "You are all brutally mistaken about Shelley who was without exception—the *best* and least selfish man I ever knew.—I never knew one who was not a beast in comparison." Whether or not one shares this judgment of the man, Shelley's accomplishment as an artist has always compelled admiration. Wordsworth, who thought him too fantastic by half and who was famously sparing in praise of other poets, judged Shelley "one of the best *artists* of us all . . . in workmanship of style."

Mont Blanc
Lines Written in the Vale of Chamouni[1]

1

The everlasting universe of things
Flows through the mind, and rolls its rapid waves,
Now dark—now glittering—now reflecting gloom—

---

1. At nearly 16,000 feet Mont Blanc, in the French Alps, is the highest peak in Europe, a must-see on everyone's Grand Tour as the epitome of "the sublime" (see pages 299–323) its summit had been attained only a few times by 1816. In Mary's *History of a Six Weeks' Tour*, Percy said the poem "was composed under the immediate impression of the deep and powerful feelings excited by the objects which it attempts to describe; and, as an undisciplined overflowing of the soul, rests its claim to approbation on an attempt to imitate the untamable wildness and inaccessible solemnity from which those feelings sprang." The "imitation" involves a dizzying play of imagery and language: wildly dilated and piled-up syntaxes, dazzling verbal transformations and a welter of sublime negatives (e.g. *unknown, infinite, unearthly, unfathomable, viewless*). Amid this drama, Shelley poses questions of the mind's ability to comprehend transcendent power, and ultimately its existence. He portrays the perceiving "mind" with metaphors drawn from the scene before him, as he stands on a bridge over the River Arve, a deep ravine, and the valley below, the mountain and glacier above. Echoing with a difference Wordsworth's love for "all the mighty world / Of eye, and ear,—both what they half create, / And what perceive; well pleased to recognise / In nature and the language of the sense / The anchor of my purest thoughts" (*Tintern Abbey* 105–109, pages 204–205), Shelley's poetry alludes to and contests this philosophy of "Nature."

Now lending splendour, where from secret springs
5   The source of human thought its tribute brings
Of waters,—with a sound but half its own,
Such as a feeble brook will oft assume
In the wild woods, among the mountains lone,
Where waterfalls around it leap for ever,
10   Where woods and winds contend, and a vast river
Over its rocks ceaselessly bursts and raves.[2]

2

Thus thou, Ravine of Arve—dark, deep Ravine—
Thou many-coloured, many-voiced vale,
Over whose pines and crags and caverns sail
15   Fast cloud-shadows and sunbeams: awful° scene,   *awesome*
Where Power in likeness of the Arve comes down
From the ice gulphs that gird his secret throne,
Bursting thro' these dark mountains like the flame
Of lightning through the tempest;—thou dost lie,—
20   Thy giant brood of pines around thee clinging,
Children of elder° time, in whose devotion   *older and earlier*
The chainless winds still come and ever came
To drink their odours, and their mighty swinging
To hear, an old and solemn harmony;
25   Thine earthly rainbows stretched across the sweep
Of the ethereal waterfall, whose veil
Robes some unsculptured image;[3] the strange sleep
Which, when the voices of the desart fail,
Wraps all in its own deep eternity;—
30   Thy caverns echoing to the Arve's commotion,
A loud, lone sound no other sound can tame;
Thou art pervaded with that ceaseless motion
Thou art the path of that unresting sound—
Dizzy Ravine! and when I gaze on thee
35   I seem as in a trance sublime and strange
To muse on my own separate phantasy,°   *fantasy, delusion*
My own, my human mind, which passively
Now renders and receives fast influencings,
Holding an unremitting interchange
40   With the clear universe of things around;
One legion of wild thoughts, whose wandering wings
Now float above thy darkness, and now rest
Where that° or thou° art no unbidden guest,   *thy darkness / ravine*
In the still cave of the witch Poesy,
45   Seeking among the shadows that pass by,
Ghosts of all things that are, some shade of thee,
Some phantom, some faint image; till the breast
From which they fled recalls them, thou art there![4]

---

2. Coleridge's *Kubla Khan* (pub. 1816) 17–21, page 343;
the landscape of this poem also appears at 122.
3. Rocks behind the waterfall in shapes not sculpted by
human artistry.
4. Plato's allegory in *Republic* 7 compares the mind to a
cave in which our sense of reality consists of the shadows
cast by firelight on its walls, ignorant of the light of
"Reality" outside. Shelley's difficult syntax blurs the distinction of inner and outer, human mind and Ravine.

3

Some say that gleams of a remoter world
50 Visit the soul in sleep,[5]—that death is slumber,
And that its shapes the busy thoughts outnumber
Of those who wake and live.—I look on high;
Has some unknown omnipotence unfurled
The veil of life and death?[6] or do I lie
55 In dream, and does the mightier world of sleep
Spread far around and inaccessibly
Its circles? For the very spirit fails,
Driven like a homeless cloud from steep to steep
That vanishes among the viewless° gales!   *unseeing, invisible*
60 Far, far above, piercing the infinite sky,
Mont Blanc appears,—still, snowy, and serene—
Its subject mountains their unearthly forms
Pile around it, ice and rock; broad vales between
Of frozen floods, unfathomable deeps,
65 Blue as the overhanging heaven, that spread
And wind among the accumulated steeps;
A desart peopled by the storms alone,
Save° when the eagle brings some hunter's bone,   *except*
And the wolf tracts° her there—how hideously   *tracks, traces*
70 Its shapes are heaped around! rude, bare, and high,
Ghastly, and scarred, and riven.°—Is this the scene   *split*
Where the old Earthquake-dæmon[7] taught her young
Ruin? Were these their toys? or did a sea
Of fire, envelope once this silent snow?
75 None can reply—all seems eternal now.
The wilderness has a mysterious tongue
Which teaches awful doubt,° or faith so mild,   *awe-filled questioning*
So solemn, so serene, that man may be
But for such faith, with nature reconciled.[8]
80 Thou hast a voice, great Mountain, to repeal
Large codes of fraud and woe; not understood
By all, but which the wise and great and good
Interpret, or make felt, or deeply feel.

4

The fields, the lakes, the forests, and the streams,
85 Ocean, and all the living things that dwell
Within the daedal[9] earth, lightning, and rain,
Earthquake, and fiery flood, and hurricane,
The torpor of the year when feeble dreams

5. Inverting Wordsworth's philosophy of Platonic amnesia in stanza 5 of the "Intimations" *Ode* (see page 286), Shelley entertains the idea that this spiritual reality is not forgotten but visits the soul in sleep.
6. The screen of phenomena separating physical from spiritual reality (lifted in sleep, in daydreams and visions).
7. In Greek mythology daemons are (often playful) spirits, usually personifications of natural forces.
8. Shelley first wrote "In such wise faith with Nature reconciled," then revised to "But for such faith" and lowercased

"nature." The sense is ambiguous: "But for" may indicate "Only by means of" faith in Nature over the "Large codes of fraud and woe" promulgated by institutional religions (81). Or it may mean "Except for": man might be reconciled to the mysteries of nature's violent power, did this not require a bland faith in a nature that is unknowable and perhaps indifferent to human needs and values.
9. From Daedalus, architect of the famous labyrinth in Crete, and of wings for flight crafted with feathers and wax; hence, a wonderfully wrought, inspired creation.

Visit the hidden buds, or dreamless sleep
90   Holds every future leaf and flower;—the bound
With which from that detested trance they leap;
The works and ways of man, their death and birth,
And that of him, and all that his may be;
All things that move and breathe with toil and sound
95   Are born and die; revolve, subside, and swell.
Power dwells apart in its tranquillity
Remote, serene, and inaccessible:
And *this,* the naked countenance of earth,
On which I gaze, even these primaeval mountains
100   Teach the adverting mind. The glaciers creep
Like snakes that watch their prey, from their far fountains,
Slow rolling on; there, many a precipice,
Frost and the Sun in scorn of mortal power
Have piled: dome, pyramid, and pinnacle,
105   A city of death, distinct with many a tower
And wall impregnable of beaming ice.
Yet not a city, but a flood of ruin
Is there, that from the boundary of the sky
Rolls its perpetual stream; vast pines are strewing
110   Its destined path, or in the mangled soil
Branchless and shattered stand: the rocks, drawn down
From yon remotest waste, have overthrown
The limits of the dead and living world,
Never to be reclaimed. The dwelling-place
115   Of insects, beasts, and birds, becomes its spoil;
Their food and their retreat for ever gone,
So much of life and joy is lost. The race
Of man, flies far in dread; his work and dwelling
Vanish, like smoke before the tempest's stream,
120   And their place is not known.[1] Below, vast caves
Shine in the rushing torrent's restless gleam,
Which from those secret chasms in tumult welling
Meet in the vale, and one majestic River,
The breath and blood of distant lands, for ever
125   Rolls its loud waters to the ocean waves,
Breathes its swift vapours to the circling air.

5

Mont Blanc yet gleams on high:—the power is there,
The still and solemn power, of many sights,
And many sounds, and much of life and death.
130   In the calm darkness of the moonless nights,
In the lone glare of day, the snows descend
Upon that Mountain; none beholds them there,
Nor when the flakes burn in the sinking sun,
Or the star-beams dart through them:—Winds contend
135   Silently there, and heap the snow with breath

1. Echoing Psalm 103: "As for man, his days are as grass . . . For the wind passeth over it, and it is gone; and the place thereof shall know it no more" (15–16).

Rapid and strong, but silently! Its home
The voiceless lightning in these solitudes
Keeps innocently, and like vapour broods
Over the snow. The secret strength of things
140 Which governs thought, and to the infinite dome
Of heaven is as a law, inhabits thee!
And what were thou,° and earth, and stars, and sea,   *Mont Blanc*
If to the human mind's imaginings
Silence and solitude were vacancy?

23 July 1816   1817

Hymn to Intellectual Beauty[1]

1

The awful shadow of some unseen Power
   Floats, though unseen, amongst us, visiting
   This various world with as inconstant wing
As summer winds that creep from flower to flower.—
5 Like moonbeams that behind some piny mountain shower,°   *(verb)*
     It visits with inconstant glance
     Each human heart and countenance;
Like hues and harmonies of evening,—
   Like clouds in starlight widely spread,—
10   Like memory of music fled,—
   Like aught that for its grace may be
Dear, and yet dearer for its mystery.

2

Spirit of BEAUTY, that dost consecrate
   With thine own hues all thou dost shine upon
15   Of human thought or form,—where art thou gone?
Why dost thou pass away, and leave our state,
This dim vast vale of tears, vacant and desolate?—
     Ask why the sunlight not for ever
     Weaves rainbows o'er yon mountain river;
20 Why aught should fail and fade that once is shown;
     Why fear and dream and death and birth
     Cast on the daylight of this earth
     Such gloom,—why man has such a scope
For love and hate, despondency and hope?

3

25 No voice from some sublimer world hath ever
   To sage or poet these responses given—
   Therefore the names of God and ghost and Heaven,
Remain the records of their° vain endeavour,   *sages and poets*
Frail spells—whose uttered charm might not avail to sever
30   From all we hear and all we see,

---

1. Composed the same summer as *Mont Blanc* (1816), *Hymn* shares its metaphysics. "Intellectual" refers to the ideal Platonic spirit apprehended by the mind, over the faint and fleeting information of the senses; Shelley may have taken this term from Wollstonecraft's lament in *Rights of Woman* over the low cultural esteem of women's "intellectual beauty" (ch. 3). As in *Mont Blanc*, "unseen Power" is evoked by a language of negation, unanswered questions, and merely proximate similes.

Doubt, chance, and mutability.[2]
Thy light alone like mist o'er mountains driven,
    Or music by the night wind sent
    Through strings of some still instrument,[3]
35   Or moonlight on a midnight stream,
Gives grace and truth to life's unquiet dream.

4

Love, Hope, and Self-esteem, like clouds depart
    And come, for some uncertain moments lent.
    Man were° immortal, and omnipotent,   *would be*
40   Didst thou,° unknown and awful as thou art,   *if thou didst*
Keep with thy glorious train firm state within his heart.
    Thou messenger of sympathies
    That wax and wane in lovers' eyes—
Thou, that to human thought art nourishment,
45   Like darkness to a dying flame![4]
    Depart not—as thy shadow came:
    Depart not, lest the grave should be,
Like life and fear, a dark reality!

5

While yet a boy, I sought for ghosts, and sped
50   Through many a listening chamber, cave and ruin,
    And starlight wood, with fearful steps pursuing
Hopes of high talk with the departed dead.[5]
I called on poisonous names with which our youth is fed.[6]
    I was not heard—I saw them not—
55   When musing deeply on the lot
Of life at that sweet time when winds are wooing
    All vital things that wake to bring
    News of birds and blossoming,—
    Sudden, thy shadow fell on me;
60 I shrieked, and clasped my hands in extasy!

6

I vowed that I would dedicate my powers
    To thee and thine—have I not kept the vow?
    With beating heart and streaming eyes, even now
I call the phantoms of a thousand hours
65 Each from his voiceless grave: they have in visioned bowers
    Of studious zeal or love's delight
    Outwatched with me the envious night—
They know that never joy illumed my brow
    Unlinked with hope that thou wouldst free
70   This world from its dark slavery,
    That thou, O awful LOVELINESS,
Wouldst give whate'er these words cannot express.

2. Although some "responses" have been given to the questions in stanza 2, even the potent vocabulary of institutional religion has been unable to allay all doubts and fears.
3. An aeolian or "wind" harp; see Coleridge's *The Eolian Harp*, page 325.
4. Darkness aesthetically nourishes a flame by offsetting its glow, even as the flame ultimately dies into darkness;

thus Intellectual Beauty nourishes frail human intellect.
5. An alignment of his childhood with Wordsworth's shadowy recollection in the "Intimations" *Ode* of a boyhood sense of a spiritual reality behind the veil of phenomena; see especially lines 141–147 (pages 287–88).
6. The vocabulary for divinity in institutional religions; see line 27. Shelley is referring to boyhood experiments in conjuration.

7

The day becomes more solemn and serene
    When noon is past—there is a harmony
75   In autumn, and a lustre in its sky,
Which through the summer is not heard or seen,
As if it could not be, as if it had not been!
    Thus let thy power, which like the truth
    Of Nature on my passive youth
80   Descended, to my onward life supply
    Its calm—to one who worships thee,
    And every form containing thee,
Whom, SPIRIT fair, thy spells did bind
To fear° himself, and love all humankind.   *revere, fear for*

1816   1817

Ozymandias[1]

I met a traveller from an antique land
Who said: "Two vast and trunkless° legs of stone   *lacking a torso*
Stand in the desert. . . . Near them on the sand,
Half sunk, a shattered visage° lies, whose frown,   *face*
5   And wrinkled lip, and sneer of cold command,
Tell that its sculptor well those passions read
Which yet survive, stamped on these lifeless things,
The hand that mocked them, and the heart that fed.[2]
And on the pedestal, these words appear:
10   "My name is Ozymandias, King of Kings:
Look on my works, ye Mighty, and despair!"[3]
Nothing beside remains. Round the decay
Of that colossal[4] Wreck, boundless and bare,
The lone and level sands stretch far away."

1817   1818

Ode to the West Wind[1]

1

O wild West Wind, thou breath of Autumn's being,
Thou from whose unseen presence the leaves dead
Are driven like ghosts from an enchanter fleeing,

1. Ozymandias (the Greek name for Ramses II) reigned 1292–1225 B.C.; he is thought to be the pharaoh of Exodus whom Moses challenged. The story of the statue and its inscription is taken from the Greek historian Diodorus Siculus, 1st century B.C.
2. The sculptor read well those passions that survive his hand (that mocked them) and the tyrant's heart (that fed them); "mocked": "imitated," with a sense of caricature or derision. The passions survive both on the images of the stone fragments and in the hearts of modern tyrants; Shelley published this sonnet in 1818 in Leigh Hunt's radical paper, *The Examiner*.
3. According to Diodorus, this is the actual boast; by Shelley's time, its language echoes ironically against the subsequent application of this title to Christ.

4. An adjective derived from "colossus," the term in antiquity for any large statue; there were several such of 50–60 feet in height in ancient Egypt. Shelley is also recalling the depiction of Julius Caesar by one of the conspirators in his assassination: "he doth bestride the narrow world / Like a Colossus" (*Julius Caesar* 1.2.135–36).
1. There is a long tradition, as old as the Bible, of wind as metaphor of life and inspiration—particularly the West Wind, as bearer of new weather, the harbinger of future seasons, events, and transformations, not only in the natural weather, but by symbolic extension, in emotional, spiritual, and political life. The Latin word for "wind," *spiritus*, also means "breath" (1) and soul or spirit (13, 61–62), as well as being the root-word for "inspiration" (a taking-in of energy).

Yellow, and black, and pale, and hectic° red,   *feverish*
5   Pestilence-stricken multitudes!² O Thou
Who chariotest to their dark wintry bed

The winged seeds, where they lie cold and low,
Each like a corpse within its grave, until
Thine azure sister of the Spring° shall blow   *spring wind*

10 Her clarion° o'er the dreaming earth, and fill   *shrill trumpet*
(Driving sweet buds like flocks to feed in air)
With living hues and odours plain and hill:

Wild Spirit, which art moving everywhere;
Destroyer and Preserver;³ hear, O hear!

2

15 Thou on whose stream, mid the steep sky's commotion,
Loose clouds like earth's decaying leaves are shed,
Shook from the tangled boughs of heaven and ocean,

Angels° of rain and lightning! there are spread   *messengers*
On the blue surface of thine airy surge,
20 Like the bright hair uplifted from the head

Of some fierce Maenad, even from the dim verge
Of the horizon to the zenith's height,
The locks of the approaching storm.⁴ Thou dirge°   *funeral chant*

Of the dying year, to which this closing night
25 Will be the dome of a vast sepulchre,
Vaulted with all thy congregated might

Of vapours, from whose solid atmosphere
Black rain, and fire, and hail, will burst: Oh hear!

3

Thou who didst waken from his summer dreams
30 The blue Mediterranean, where he lay,
Lulled by the coil of his crystalline streams,

Beside a pumice° isle in Baiae's bay,   *volcanic*
And saw in sleep old palaces and towers
Quivering within the wave's intenser day,

35 All overgrown with azure moss, and flowers
So sweet, the sense faints picturing them!⁵ Thou
For whose path the Atlantic's level powers

---

2. An allusion to a traditional epic simile (Milton, Dante, Virgil) comparing the dead to wind-driven fallen leaves.
3. Titles for major Hindu gods, Siva the Destroyer and Vishnu the Preserver.
4. The Greek god of wine Bacchus was attended by Maenads, female votaries who danced in wild worship. Viewing a sculpture of them in Florence, Shelley commented: "The tremendous spirit of superstition aided by drunkenness . . . seems to have caught them in its whirlwinds, and

to bear them over the earth as the rapid volutions of a tempest have the ever-changing trunk of a water-spout. . . . Their hair, loose and floating, seems caught in tempest of their own tumultuous motion." Associated in general with vegetation, Bacchus was fabled to die in the autumn and be reborn in the spring.
5. Ruins of imperial Roman villas in the Bay of Baiae, west of Naples.

Cleave themselves into chasms, while far below
The sea-blooms and the oozy woods which wear
40 The sapless foliage of the ocean, know

Thy voice, and suddenly grow grey with fear,
And tremble and despoil themselves:[6] O hear!

4

If I were a dead leaf thou mightest bear;
If I were a swift cloud to fly with thee;
45 A wave to pant beneath thy power, and share

The impulse of thy strength, only less free
Than thou, O uncontrollable! if even
I were as in my boyhood, and could be

The comrade of thy wanderings over heaven,
50 As then, when to outstrip thy skiey speed
Scarce seemed a vision,—I would ne'er have striven

As thus with thee in prayer in my sore need.
Oh lift me as a wave, a leaf, a cloud!
I fall upon the thorns of life![7] I bleed!

55 A heavy weight of hours has chained and bowed
One too like thee—tameless, and swift, and proud.

5

Make me thy lyre,[8] even as the forest is:
What if my leaves are falling like its own?
The tumult of thy mighty harmonies

60 Will take from both a deep autumnal tone,
Sweet though in sadness. Be thou, Spirit fierce,
My spirit! Be thou me, impetuous one![9]

Drive my dead thoughts over the universe,
Like withered leaves, to quicken a new birth;
65 And, by the incantation of this verse,

Scatter, as from an unextinguished hearth
Ashes and sparks, my words among mankind!
Be through my lips to unawakened earth

The trumpet of a prophecy! O Wind,
70 If Winter comes, can Spring be far behind?

1819   1820

---

6. In a note, Shelley says he is alluding to the seasonal change (despoiling) of seaweed, a process he imagines as instigated by the autumn wind.
7. A risky self-comparison to Jesus' torture by a crown of thorns.

8. A wind-harp, an image used in Coleridge's *The Eolian Harp.*
9. Shelley hazards the ungrammatical objective case ("me" instead of "I") not only to chime with "Be" but also to represent himself as an object.

To a Sky-Lark

Hail to thee, blithe Spirit!
    Bird thou never wert—
That from Heaven or near it
    Pourest thy full heart
5   In profuse strains of unpremeditated art.[1]

    Higher still and higher
        From the earth thou springest,
    Like a cloud of fire;
        The blue deep thou wingest,
10   And singing still dost soar, and soaring ever singest.

    In the golden lightning
        Of the sunken sun,
    O'er which clouds are bright'ning,
        Thou dost float and run,
15   Like an unbodied joy whose race is just begun.

    The pale purple even°   *evening*
        Melts around thy flight;
    Like a star of Heaven,
        In the broad daylight
20   Thou art unseen, but yet I hear thy shrill delight—

    Keen as are the arrows
        Of that silver sphere°   *morning star*
    Whose intense lamp narrows
        In the white dawn clear
25   Until we hardly see—we feel, that it is there.

    All the earth and air
        With thy voice is loud,
    As, when night is bare,
        From one lonely cloud
30   The moon rains out her beams, and Heaven is overflowed.

    What thou art we know not;
        What is most like thee?
    From rainbow clouds there flow not
        Drops so bright to see
35   As from thy presence showers a rain of melody:—

    Like a Poet hidden
        In the light of thought,
    Singing hymns unbidden,
        Till the world is wrought
40   To sympathy with hopes and fears it heeded not:

---

1. The skylark sings only in flight; Shelley evokes Milton's thanks to his "Celestial patroness," who "inspires / Easy [his] unpremeditated Verse" (*Paradise Lost* 9.21–24).

Like a high-born maiden
  In a palace tower,
Soothing her love-laden
  Soul in secret hour

45   With music sweet as love which overflows her bower:

Like a glow-worm golden
  In a dell of dew,
Scattering unbeholden
  Its aerial hue

50   Among the flowers and grass which screen it from the view:

Like a rose embowered
  In its own green leaves,
By warm winds deflowered,
  Till the scent it gives

55   Makes faint with too much sweet these heavy-winged thieves:

Sound of vernal° showers   *springtime*
  On the twinkling grass,
Rain-awakened flowers,
  All that ever was,

60   Joyous and clear and fresh,—thy music doth surpass.

Teach us, Sprite° or Bird,   *spirit, fairy*
  What sweet thoughts are thine:
I have never heard
  Praise of love or wine

65   That panted forth a flood of rapture so divine.

Chorus Hymeneal°   *wedding song*
  Or triumphal° chaunt,   *military*
Matched with thine, would be all
  But an empty vaunt—

70   A thing wherein we feel there is some hidden want.

What objects are the fountains
  Of thy happy strain?
What fields, or waves, or mountains?
  What shapes of sky or plain?

75   What love of thine own kind? what ignorance of pain?

With thy clear keen joyance
  Languor cannot be:
Shadow of annoyance
  Never came near thee:

80   Thou lovest—but ne'er knew love's sad satiety.°   *(over)fullness*

Waking or asleep,
  Thou of death must deem
Things more true and deep
  Than we mortals dream,

85   Or how could thy notes flow in such a crystal stream?

We look before and after,[2]
   And pine for what is not:
Our sincerest laughter
   With some pain is fraught;
90   Our sweetest songs are those that tell of saddest thought.

Yet if we could scorn
   Hate and pride and fear,
If we were things born
   Not to shed a tear,
95   I know not how thy joy we ever should come near.

Better than all measures
   Of delightful sound,
Better than all treasures
   That in books are found,
100   Thy skill to poet were, thou scorner of the ground!

Teach me half the gladness
   That thy brain must know,
Such harmonious madness[3]
   From my lips would flow
105   The world should listen then—as I am listening now.

1820   1820

----- ≡◆≡ -----

Felicia Hemans
1793–1835

A best-selling poet in England and America through most of the nineteenth century, Felicia Hemans (née Browne) was a prolific writer. In addition to numerous publications in magazines and gift-books, she produced nineteen volumes of poems and plays between 1808 and 1834. Lord Byron, with whom she shared the publisher John Murray, was sensitive to the competition. In letters to Murray, he tags her "your feminine *He-Man*" or "Mrs. Hewoman's," his punning turning her commercial prowess into a monstrous mockery of sexual identity. Byron preferred women in their place, not his. "I do not despise Mrs. Heman—but if [she] knit blue stockings instead of wearing them it would be better," he declared to Murray, referring to the "bluestockings," a derisive term for learned women.

     Born in Liverpool in 1793, the year of the Terror in France and the execution of its king and queen, Felicia Browne was raised in the distant calms of North Wales. Under the devoted tutelage of her mother, she became a child prodigy, learning Latin, German, French, and Italian, devouring Shakespeare, and quickly developing a talent for writing; when she was fourteen, her

2. Echoing Hamlet's comment on the human capability of "looking before and after" (4.4.36), as well as alluding to Wordsworth's use of this phrase in Preface to *Lyrical Ballads* (see page 206).

3. Echoing Wordsworth's rhyme in *Resolution and Independence*: "We Poets in our youth begin in gladness; / But thereof come in the end despondency and madness" (48–49).

Edward Smith, after a painting by Edward Robertson, *Portrait of Felicia Hemans,* 1831. Robertson's portrait captures the melancholy beauty that was the poet's hallmark.

parents underwrote the publication of her first volume. Learning of her talents and beauty, Percy Shelley ventured a correspondence, but (fortunately for the young poet) her mother intervened and nothing came of his overture. The romance that did blossom was with Captain Alfred Hemans, a veteran of the Peninsular Campaign in Spain in which her brothers also served. They married in 1812, the year of her nineteenth birthday and third volume, *The Domestic Affections.* By 1818, she had produced three more volumes to favorable reviews, as well as five sons. Just before the birth of the last, the Captain left for Italy; the "story" was ill health. They never saw each other again, the breach mirroring her father's desertion of his wife and children in 1810, for a fresh start in Canada. The collapse of her own and her mother's marriages haunts the idealism of home for which "Mrs. Hemans" was becoming famous, shadowing it with repeated stories of men's unreliability or treachery and the necessity of maternal responsibility.

Determined to support herself and her sons with her writing, Hemans returned to her mother's home in Wales. With no wifely obligations or husband to "obey," and with sisters, mother, and brothers to help care for her boys and run the home, Hemans had considerable time to read, study, write, and publish. There was a related cultural advantage. As a daughter under "the maternal wing" and an "affectionate, tender, and vigilant mother" herself (as prefaces to her works later in the century put it), the professional writer was immunized against the stigma of "unfeminine" independence. The death of her mother in 1827 was a deep and devastating grief, aggravated by the disintegration of her home as sons grew up and brothers and sisters married or moved away. Her health suffered, and after a long decline, she died in Dublin in 1835, a few months before her forty-second birthday. William Wordsworth warmly honored her in the memorial verses of his *Extempore Effusion,* even as he indicated his discomfort with her ignorance of household skills and her affectation of being a "literary lady."

Among Hemans's most successful volumes, both critically and commercially, were *Tales, and Historic Scenes in Verse* (1819), *The Forest Sanctuary* (1825), *Records of Woman* (1828), which she dedicated to Joanna Baillie, and *Songs of the Affections* (1830). She was popular well into the Victorian age, especially among women. By the middle of the twentieth century, she was remembered only by a few favorite poems, including *The Homes of England*, *The Landing of the Pilgrim Fathers* ("The breaking waves dashed high, / On a stern and rockbound coast") and *Casabianca* ("The boy stood on the burning deck")—this last a parlor-recitation and school-assembly favorite, as well as the subject of multiple parodies. By the 1980s, she was virtually forgotten. In the subsequent recovery of the "lost" women writers of the Romantic era, her work has received fresh attention, especially for its reflection of many of the key social, psychological, and emotional concerns for women in her day. These involve not only woman's celebrated roles as a patient, devoted, and often long-suffering lover, wife, and mother, but also persistent tensions within these definitions. Some readers still read her poetry as texts of traditional gender values: women's place at home and her value in upholding "domestic affections," religious faith, and patriotic sentiment. But to others this same poetry seems only tenuously conservative and far from replete—haunted by sensations of the futility and vulnerability of the very ideals it celebrates, invaded by sadness, melancholy, betrayal, suffering, and violence, and repeatedly staging women's heroism in scenes of defeat and death. Hemans's imagination was particularly tuned to conflicts besetting women who achieve fame in nontraditional roles, especially as artists, typically at great cost in personal happiness.

from TALES, AND HISTORIC SCENES, IN VERSE

The Wife of Asdrubal

"This governor, who had braved death when it was at a distance, and protested that the sun should never see him survive Carthage,[1] this fierce Asdrubal, was so mean-spirited, as to come alone, and privately throw himself at the conqueror's feet. The general, pleased to see his proud rival humbled, granted his life, and kept him to grace his triumph. The Carthaginians in the citadel no sooner understood that their commander had abandoned the place, than they threw open the gates, and put the proconsul in possession of Byrsa. The Romans had now no enemy to contend with but the nine hundred deserters, who, being reduced to despair, retired into the temple of Esculapius, which was a second citadel within the first: there the proconsul attacked them; and these unhappy wretches, finding there was no way to escape, set fire to the temple. As the flames spread, they retreated from one part to another, till they got to the roof of the building: there Asdrubal's wife appeared in her best apparel, as if the day of her death had been a day of triumph; and after having uttered the most bitter imprecations against her husband, whom she saw standing below with Emilianus,[2]—'Base coward!' said she, 'the mean things thou hast done to save thy life shall not avail thee; thou shalt die this instant, at least in thy two children.' Having thus spoken, she drew out a dagger, stabbed them both, and while they were yet struggling for life, threw them from the top of the temple, and leaped down after them into the flames."

Ancient Universal History [London, 1736–1744]

---

1. A powerful city-state on Africa's northern coast; its control of the western Mediterranean was challenged by the Roman empire, which finally destroyed it in the Third Punic War (149–146 B.C.).

2. Scipio Africanus Minor, the Roman general (son of Aemilius Paullus). The surviving Carthaginians were sold into slavery, and Asdrubal lived comfortably as a state prisoner in Italy.

The sun sets brightly—but a ruddier glow
O'er Afric's heaven the flames of Carthage throw;
Her walls have sunk, and pyramids of fire
In lurid splendor from her domes aspire;
5   Sway'd by the wind, they wave—while glares the sky
As when the desert's red Simoom° is nigh;   *desert wind*
The sculptured altar, and the pillar'd hall,
Shine out in dreadful brightness ere they fall;
Far o'er the seas the light of ruin streams,
10   Rock, wave, and isle, are crimson'd by its beams;
While captive thousands, bound in Roman chains,
Gaze in mute horror on their burning fanes;°   *temples*
And shouts of triumph, echoing far around,
Swell from the victor's tents with ivy crown'd.[3]

15   But mark! from yon fair temple's loftiest height
What towering form bursts wildly on the sight,
All regal in magnificent attire,
And sternly beauteous in terrific ire?
She might be deem'd a Pythia[4] in the hour
20   Of dread communion and delirious power;
A being more than earthly, in whose eye
There dwells a strange and fierce ascendancy.
The flames are gathering round—intensely bright,
Full on her features glares their meteor-light,
25   But a wild courage sits triumphant there,
The stormy grandeur of a proud despair;
A daring spirit, in its woes elate,
Mightier than death, untameable by fate.
The dark profusion of her locks unbound,
30   Waves like a warrior's floating plumage round;
Flush'd is her cheek, inspired her haughty mien,
She seems th' avenging goddess of the scene.

Are those *her* infants, that with suppliant-cry
Cling round her, shrinking as the flame draws nigh,
35   Clasp with their feeble hands her gorgeous vest,
And fain would rush for shelter to her breast?
Is that a mother's glance, where stern disdain,
And passion awfully vindictive, reign?

Fix'd is her eye on Asdrubal, who stands,
40   Ignobly safe, amidst the conquering bands;
On him, who left her to that burning tomb,
Alone to share her children's martyrdom;
Who when his country perish'd, fled the strife,

3. It was a Roman custom to adorn the tents of victors with ivy [Hemans's note].
4. Priestess and medium of Apollo at the oracle of Delphi, whose entranced, frenzied communications required interpretation by male priests.

And knelt to win the worthless boon of life.
45 "Live, traitor, live!" she cries, "since dear to thee,
E'en in thy fetters, can existence be!
Scorn'd and dishonour'd, live!—with blasted name,
The Roman's triumph° not to grace, but shame.   *victory parade*
O slave in spirit! bitter be thy chain
50 With tenfold anguish to avenge my pain!
Still may the manès° of thy children rise   *avenging spirits*
To chase calm slumber from thy wearied eyes;
Still may their voices on the haunted air
In fearful whispers tell thee to despair,
55 Till vain remorse thy wither'd heart consume,
Scourged by relentless shadows of the tomb!
E'en now my sons shall die—and thou, their sire,
In bondage safe, shalt yet in them expire.
Think'st thou I love them not?—'Twas thine to fly—
60 'Tis mine with these to suffer and to die.
Behold their fate!—the arms that cannot save
Have been their cradle, and shall be their grave."

Bright in her hand the lifted dagger gleams,
Swift from her children's hearts the life-blood streams;
65 With frantic laugh she clasps them to the breast
Whose woes and passions soon shall be at rest;
Lifts one appealing, frenzied glance on high,
Then deep midst rolling flames is lost to mortal eye.

1819

from RECORDS OF WOMAN[1]

Properzia Rossi

Properzia Rossi, a celebrated female sculptor of Bologna, possessed also of talents for poetry and music, died in consequence of an unrequited attachment.—A painting by Ducis, represents her showing her last work, a basso-relievo of Ariadne, to a Roman Knight, the object of her affection, who regards it with indifference.[2]

———Tell me no more, no more
Of my soul's lofty gifts! Are they not vain
To quench its haunting thirst for happiness?
Have I not lov'd, and striven, and fail'd to bind
One true heart unto me, whereon my own
Might find a resting-place, a home for all

1. Hemans's most popular volume was published in 1828, with a dedication to Joanna Baillie; as in Wollstonecraft, "Woman" identifies a universal category. There was a sub-section of *Miscellaneous Poems* that included *The Homes of England*.
2. Hemans's headnote refers to Properzia de'Rossi (c. 1491–1530) and Louis Ducis, a French painter (1775–1847). The subject of Rossi's sculpture, Ariadne,

was the daughter of King Minos of Crete, who imprisoned the Greek prince Theseus in his labyrinth, there to be killed by the Minotaur. In love with Theseus, Ariadne told him how to slay the monster and escape the labyrinth. He married her, but after they left Crete, he abandoned her on the Greek isle of Naxos, where she pined away for him.

Its burden of affections? I depart,
Unknown, tho' Fame goes with me; I must leave
The earth unknown. Yet it may be that death
Shall give my name a power to win such tears
As would have made life precious.[3]

1

One dream of passion and of beauty more!
And in its bright fulfilment let me pour
My soul away! Let earth retain a trace
Of that which lit my being, tho' its race
5   Might have been loftier far.—Yet one more dream!
From my deep spirit one victorious gleam
Ere I depart! For thee alone, for thee!
May this last work, this farewell triumph be,
Thou, lov'd so vainly! I would leave enshrined
10   Something immortal of my heart and mind,
That yet may speak to thee when I am gone,
Shaking thine inmost bosom with a tone
Of lost affection;—something that may prove
What she hath been, whose melancholy love
15   On thee was lavish'd; silent pang and tear,
And fervent song, that gush'd when none were near,
And dream by night, and weary thought by day,
Stealing the brightness from her life away,—
While thou———Awake! not yet within me die,
20   Under the burden and the agony
Of this vain tenderness,—my spirit, wake!
Ev'n for thy sorrowful affection's sake,
Live! in thy work breathe out!—that he may yet,
Feeling sad mastery there, perchance regret
25   Thine unrequited gift.

2

It comes,—the power
Within me born, flows back; my fruitless dower
That could not win me love. Yet once again
I greet it proudly, with its rushing train
Of glorious images:—they throng—they press—
30   A sudden joy lights up my loneliness,—
I shall not perish all!
                  The bright work grows
Beneath my hand, unfolding, as a rose,
Leaf after leaf, to beauty; line by line,
I fix my thought, heart, soul, to burn, to shine,
35   Thro' the pale marble's veins. It grows—and now

3. The epigraph is also by Hemans.

I give my own life's history to thy brow,
Forsaken Ariadne! thou shalt wear
My form, my lineaments; but oh! more fair,
Touch'd into lovelier being by the glow
40   Which in me dwells, as by the summer-light
All things are glorified. From thee my wo
    Shall yet look beautiful to meet his sight,
When I am pass'd away. Thou art the mould
Wherein I pour the fervent thoughts, th' untold,
45 The self-consuming! Speak to him of me,
Thou, the deserted by the lonely sea,
With the soft sadness of thine earnest eye,
Speak to him, lorn one! deeply, mournfully,
Of all my love and grief! Oh! could I throw
50 Into thy frame a voice, a sweet, and low,
And thrilling voice of song! when he came nigh,
To send the passion of its melody
Thro' his pierc'd bosom—on its tones to bear
My life's deep feeling, as the southern air
55 Wafts the faint myrtle's breath,—to rise, to swell,
To sink away in accents of farewell,
Winning but one, *one* gush of tears, whose flow
Surely my parted spirit yet might know,
If love be strong as death!

                  3
                Now fair thou art,
60 Thou form, whose life is of my burning heart!
Yet all the vision that within me wrought,
    I cannot make thee! Oh! I might have given
Birth to creations of far nobler thought,
    I might have kindled, with the fire of heaven,
65 Things not of such as die! But I have been
Too much alone; a heart whereon to lean,
With all these deep affections, that o'erflow[4]
My aching soul, and find no shore below;
An eye to be my star, a voice to bring
70 Hope o'er my path, like sounds that breathe of spring,
These are denied me—dreamt of still in vain,—
Therefore my brief aspirings from the chain,
Are ever but as some wild fitful song,
Rising triumphantly, to die ere long
75 In dirge-like echoes.

                  4
                Yet the world will see
Little of this, my parting work, in thee,
    Thou shalt have fame! Oh, mockery! give the reed
From storms a shelter,—give the drooping vine

4. The verb, reflected in Hemans's enjambment, evokes both "flow over from" and "overwhelm."

Something round which its tendrils may entwine,—
80   Give the parch'd flower a rain-drop, and the meed
Of love's kind words to woman! Worthless fame!
That in *his* bosom wins not for my name
Th' abiding-place it ask'd! Yet how my heart,
In its own fairy world of song and art,
85   Once beat for praise!—Are those high longings o'er?
That which I have been can I be no more?—
Never, oh! never more; tho' still thy sky
Be blue as then, my glorious Italy!
And tho' the music, whose rich breathings fill
90   Thine air with soul, be wandering past me still,
And tho' the mantle of thy sunlight streams,
Unchang'd on forms, instinct° with poet-dreams;   *inspired*
Never, oh! never more! Where'er I move,
The shadow of this broken-hearted love
95   Is on me and around! Too well *they* know,
      Whose life is all within, too soon and well,
When there the blight hath settled;—but I go
      Under the silent wings of peace to dwell;
From the slow wasting, from the lonely pain,
100 The inward burning of those words—*"in vain,"*
      Sear'd on the heart—I go. 'Twill soon be past.
Sunshine, and song, and bright Italian heaven,
      And thou, oh! thou, on whom my spirit cast
Unvalued wealth,—who know'st not what was given
105 In that devotedness,—the sad, and deep,
And unrepaid—farewell! If I could weep
Once, only once, belov'd one! on thy breast,
Pouring my heart forth ere I sink to rest!
But that were happiness, and unto me
110 Earth's gift is *fame*. Yet I was form'd to be
So richly blest! With thee to watch the sky,
Speaking not, feeling but that thou wert nigh;
With thee to listen, while the tones of song
Swept ev'n as part of our sweet air along,
115 To listen silently;—with thee to gaze
On forms, the deified of olden days,
This had been joy enough;—and hour by hour,
From its glad well-springs drinking life and power,
How had my spirit soar'd, and made its fame
120   A glory for thy brow!—Dreams, dreams!—the fire
Burns faint within me. Yet I leave my name—
      As a deep thrill may linger on the lyre
When its full chords are hush'd—awhile to live,
And one day haply in thy heart revive
125 Sad thoughts of me:—I leave it, with a sound,
A spell o'er memory, mournfully profound,
I leave it, on my country's air to dwell,—
Say proudly yet—*"Twas her's who lov'd me well!"*

The Homes of England

"Where's the coward that would not dare
To fight for such a land?"   —*Marmion*[1]

The stately Homes of England,
    How beautiful they stand!
Amidst their tall ancestral trees,
    O'er all the pleasant land.
5   The deer across their greensward bound
    Through shade and sunny gleam,
And the swan glides past them with the sound
    Of some rejoicing stream.

The merry Homes of England!
10   Around their hearths by night,
What gladsome looks of household love
    Meet, in the ruddy light!
There woman's voice flows forth in song,
    Or childhood's tale is told,
15   Or lips move tunefully along
    Some glorious page of old.

The blessed Homes of England!
    How softly on their bowers
Is laid the holy quietness
20   That breathes from Sabbath-hours!
Solemn, yet sweet, the church-bell's chime
    Floats through their woods at morn;
All other sounds, in that still time,
    Of breeze and leaf are born.

25   The Cottage Homes of England!
    By thousands on her plains,
They are smiling o'er the silvery brooks,
    And round the hamlet-fanes.
Thro' glowing orchards forth they peep,
30   Each from its nook of leaves,
And fearless there the lowly° sleep,   *the poor*
    As the bird beneath their eaves.

The free, fair Homes of England!
    Long, long, in hut and hall,
35   May hearts of native proof be rear'd
    To guard each hallowed wall!
And green for ever be the groves,
    And bright the flowery sod,
Where first the child's glad spirit loves
40   Its country and its God!

                                      1828

1827

1. A poetic romance (1808) by Walter Scott.

Corinne at the Capitol[1]

"Les femmes doivent penser [. . .] qu'il est dans cette carrière bien peu de sorts qui puissent valoir la plus obscure vie d'une femme aimée et d'une mère heureuse." —*Madame de Staël* [2]

Daughter of th' Italian heaven!
Thou, to whom its fires are given,
Joyously thy car hath roll'd
Where the conqueror's pass'd of old;
5   And the festal sun that shone,
O'er three hundred triumphs gone,[3]
Makes thy day of glory bright,
With a shower of golden light.

Now thou tread'st th' ascending road,
10   Freedom's foot so proudly trode;
While, from tombs of heroes borne,
From the dust of empire shorn,
Flowers upon thy graceful head,
Chaplets° of all hues, are shed,   head-wreaths
15   In a soft and rosy rain,
Touch'd with many a gemlike stain.

Thou hast gain'd the summit now!
Music hails thee from below;—
Music, whose rich notes might stir
20   Ashes of the sepulchre;
Shaking with victorious notes
All the bright air as it floats.
Well may woman's heart beat high
Unto that proud harmony!

25   Now afar it rolls—it dies—
And thy voice is heard to rise
With a low and lovely tone
In its thrilling power alone;
And thy lyre's deep silvery string,

1. Hemans's title is that of Book 2 of Germaine de Staël's *Corinne, ou l'Italie* (1807). Quickly translated into English, this novel was immensely popular, especially with women, not only Hemans, but also Jane Austen, Mary Godwin (Shelley), Elizabeth Barrett (Browning), George Eliot, and Harriet Beecher (Stowe). It was read as the definitive story of female "genius"—an inspirational and cautionary tale about artistic celebrity at the cost of domestic happiness. De Staël was famous for her intellect, her social charm, her essays, her forthright conversation (including blunt criticism of Napoleon), and her salons, attended by political and literary celebrities. Her heroine, Corinne, half English and half Italian, is a famous performing poet living in Italy, where she meets the English Lord Nelvil. With him, we see her for the first time, at the Roman Capitol, celebrated in all her glorious genius. De Staël elaborates her triumph, transcribing "Corinne's Improvisation at the Capitol," and concluding in apotheosis: "No longer a fearful woman, she was an inspired priestess, joyously devoting herself to the cult of genius." Corinne and Nelvil fall in love, but she declines his proposal of marriage, fearing a too-constrained life as an English wife. He returns to England and marries her half sister, a fully proper English maid. When Corinne learns of this, she dies of grief.

2. *De L'influence des Passions* (1796): "Women should consider that in this career there are very few destinies equal in worth to the most obscure life of a beloved wife and a happy mother." *Femme* means both *wife* and *woman*.

3. The trebly hundred triumphs.—Byron [Hemans's note, referring to *Childe Harold's Pilgrimage*, 4.731, a comment on the number of triumphs (victory parades), in ancient Rome.]

30   Touch'd as by a breeze's wing,
       Murmurs tremblingly at first,
       Ere the tide of rapture burst.

       All the spirit of thy sky
       Now hath lit thy large dark eye,
35   And thy cheek a flush hath caught
       From the joy of kindled thought;
       And the burning words of song
       From thy lip flow fast and strong,
       With a rushing stream's delight
40   In the freedom of its might.

       Radiant daughter of the sun!
       Now thy living wreath is won.
       Crown'd of Rome!—Oh! art thou not
       Happy in that glorious lot?—
45   Happier, happier far than thou,
       With the laurel on thy brow,[4]
       She that makes the humblest hearth
       Lovely but to one on earth!

1827   1830

Woman and Fame[1]

       Happy—happier far than thou,
       With the laurel on thy brow;
       She that makes the humblest hearth,
       Lovely but to one on earth.

       Thou hast a charmed cup, O Fame!
         A draught° that mantles° high,   *drink / blushes*
       And seems to lift this earthly frame
         Above mortality.
5   Away! to me—a woman—bring
       Sweet waters from affection's spring.

       Thou hast green laurel-leaves that twine
         Into so proud a wreath;[2]
       For that resplendent gift of thine,
10   Heroes have smiled in death.
       Give *me* from some kind hand a flower,
       The record of one happy hour!

       Thou hast a voice, whose thrilling tone
         Can bid each life-pulse beat,
15   As when a trumpet's note hath blown,
         Calling the brave to meet:
       But mine, let mine—a woman's breast,
       By words of home-born love be bless'd.

4. The laurel wreath is a public honor for glorious accomplishment; laurel is the badge of Apollo, classical god of poetry (whence "Poet Laureate").

1. Published in *The Amulet*, an annual. The epigraph is a self-quotation from the end of *Corinne at the Capitol*.
2. See n. 4 to *Corinne at the Capitol*.

A hollow sound is in thy song,
20   A mockery in thine eye,
To the sick heart that doth but long
        For aid, for sympathy;
For kindly looks to cheer it on,
For tender accents that are gone.

25   Fame, Fame! thou canst not be the stay
        Unto the drooping reed,
The cool fresh fountain, in the day
        Of the soul's feverish need;
Where must the lone one turn or flee?—
30   Not unto thee, oh! not to thee!

1827–1829   1829

§

COMPANION READING
Francis Jeffrey: from *A Review of Felicia Hemans's Poetry*[1]

Women we fear, cannot do every thing; nor even every thing they attempt. But what they can do, they do, for the most part, excellently—and much more frequently with an absolute and perfect success, than the aspirants of our rougher and more ambitious sex. They cannot, we think, represent naturally the fierce and sullen passions of men—nor their coarser vices—nor even scenes of actual business or contention—and the mixed motives, and strong and faulty characters, by which affairs of moment are usually conducted on the great theatre of the world. For much of this they are disqualified by the delicacy of their training and habits, and the still more disabling delicacy which pervades their conceptions and feelings; and from much they are excluded by their actual inexperience of the realities they might wish to describe—by their substantial and incurable ignorance of business—of the way in which serious affairs are actually managed—and the true nature of the agents and impulses that give movement and direction to the stronger currents of ordinary life. Perhaps they are also incapable of long moral or political investigations, where many complex and indeterminate elements are to be taken into account, and a variety of opposite probabilities to be weighed before coming to a conclusion. They are generally too impatient to get at the ultimate results, to go well through with such discussions; and either stop short at some imperfect view of the truth, or turn aside to repose in the shadow of some plausible error. This, however, we are persuaded, arises entirely from their being seldom set on such tedious tasks. Their proper and natural business is the practical regulation of private life, in all its bearings, affections, and concerns; and the questions with which they have to deal in that most important department, though often of the utmost difficulty and nicety, involve, for the most part, but few elements; and may generally be better described as delicate than intricate;—requiring for their solution rather a quick tact and fine perception than a patient or laborious examination. For the same reason, they rarely succeed in long works, even on subjects the best suited to their genius; their natural training rendering them equally averse to long doubt and long labour.

1. Francis Jeffrey cofounded the quarterly *Edinburgh Review* in 1802 and was its editor and chief literary reviewer until 1829. Appearing in one of the most influential periodicals of these decades, his essay on Hemans is relevant not just to her popularity (it was generously excerpted by publishers of her collected works), but also for its comments about women writers and its sense of which contemporary male writers seemed destined for posterity.

For all other intellectual efforts, however, either of the understanding or the fancy, and requiring a thorough knowledge either of man's strength or his weakness, we apprehend them to be, in all respects, as well qualified as their brethren of the stronger sex; while, in their perceptions of grace, propriety, ridicule—their power of detecting artifice, hypocrisy, and affectation—the force and promptitude of their sympathy, and their capacity of noble and devoted attachment, and of the efforts and sacrifices it may require, they are, beyond all doubt, our superiors.

Their business being, as we have said, with actual or social life, and the colours it receives from the conduct and dispositions of individuals, they unconsciously acquire, at a very early age, the finest perception of character and manners, and are almost as soon instinctively schooled in the deep and dangerous learning of feeling and emotion; while the very minuteness with which they make and meditate on these interesting observations, and the finer shades and variations of sentiment which are thus treasured and recorded, trains their whole faculties to a nicety and precision of operation, which often discloses itself to advantage in their application to studies of a very different character. When women, accordingly, have turned their minds—as they have done but too seldom—to the exposition or arrangement of any branch of knowledge, they have commonly exhibited, we think, a more beautiful accuracy, and a more uniform and complete justness of thinking, than their less discriminating brethren. There is a finish and completeness about every thing they put out of their hands, which indicates not only an inherent taste for elegance and neatness, but a habit of nice observation, and singular exactness of judgment.

It has been so little the fashion, at any time, to encourage women to write for publication, that it is more difficult than it should be, to prove these truths by examples. Yet there are enough, within the reach of a very careless and superficial glance over the open field of literature, to enable us to explain, at least, and illustrate, if not entirely to verify, our assertions. No *man*, we will venture to say, could have written the Letters of Madame de Sevigné, or the Novels of Miss Austin, or the Hymns and Early Lessons of Mrs Barbauld, or the Conversations of Mrs Marcet.[2] These performances, too, are not only essentially and intensely feminine, but they are, in our judgment, decidedly more perfect than any masculine productions with which they can be brought into comparison. They accomplish more completely all the ends at which they aim, and are worked out with a gracefulness and felicity of execution which excludes all idea of failure, and entirely satisfies the expectations they may have raised. We might easily have added to these instances. There are many parts of Miss Edgeworth's earlier stories, and of Miss Mitford's sketches and descriptions, and not a little of Mrs Opie's, that exhibit the same fine and penetrating spirit of observation, the same softness and delicacy of hand, and unerring truth of delineation, to which we have alluded as characterising the purer specimens of female art.[3] * * *

We think the poetry of Mrs Hemans a fine exemplification of Female Poetry—and we think it has much of the perfection which we have ventured to ascribe to the happier productions of female genius.

2. Marie de Rabutin-Chantal, Marquise de Sévigné (1626–1696), French lady of fashion, famous for her lively letters to her daughter and friends describing life in the court, the city, the country, and at home. "Austin" is Jane Austen. For Barbauld, see the principal listing; her *Hymns in Prose for Children* (1781) was translated into several European languages. Jane Marcet (1769–1858) was famous for her educational series *Conversations on Chemistry, intended especially for the Female Sex* (1806; 15 later editions), *Conversations on Natural Philosophy* (1815), science for children; and her especially admired *Conversations on Political Economy* (1816; much reprinted).

3. Maria Edgeworth (1767–1829), best-selling Irish novelist; Mary Russell Mitford (1787–1859), woman of letters, whose sketches, *Our Village*, began to appear in 1824; Amelia Opie (1769–1853), fiction writer, poet, and abolitionist.

It may not be the best imaginable poetry, and may not indicate the very highest or most commanding genius; but it embraces a great deal of that which gives the very best poetry its chief power of pleasing; and would strike us, perhaps, as more impassioned and exalted, if it were not regulated and harmonized by the most beautiful taste. It is infinitely sweet, elegant, and tender—touching, perhaps, and contemplative, rather than vehement and overpowering; and not only finished throughout with an exquisite delicacy, and even serenity of execution, but informed with a purity and loftiness of feeling, and a certain sober and humble tone of indulgence and piety, which must satisfy all judgments, and allay the apprehensions of those who are most afraid of the passionate exaggerations of poetry. The diction is always beautiful, harmonious, and free—and the themes, though of infinite variety, uniformly treated with a grace, originality and judgment, which mark the same master hand. These themes she has borrowed, with the peculiar interest and imagery that belong to them, from the legends of different nations, and the most opposite states of society; and has contrived to retain much of what is interesting and peculiar in each of them, without adopting, along with it, any of the revolting or extravagant excesses which may characterise the taste or manners of the people or the age from which it has been derived. She has thus transfused into her German or Scandinavian legends the imaginative and daring tone of the originals, without the mystical exaggerations of the one, or the painful fierceness and coarseness of the other—she has preserved the clearness and elegance of the French, without their coldness or affectation—and the tenderness and simplicity of the early Italians, without their diffuseness or languor. Though occasionally expatiating, somewhat fondly and at large, amongst the sweets of her own planting, there is, on the whole, a great condensation and brevity in most of her pieces, and, almost without exception, a most judicious and vigorous conclusion. The great merit, however, of her poetry, is undoubtedly in its tenderness and its beautiful imagery. * * *

We have seen too much of the perishable nature of modern literary fame, to venture to predict to Mrs Hemans that hers will be immortal, or even of very long duration. Since the beginning of our critical career, we have seen a vast deal of beautiful poetry pass into oblivion, in spite of our feeble efforts to recall or retain it in remembrance. The tuneful quartos of Southey are already little better than lumber:—And the rich melodies of Keats and Shelley,—and the fantastical emphasis of Wordsworth,—and the plebeian pathos of Crabbe, are melting fast from the fields of our vision. The novels of Scott have put out his poetry. Even the splendid strains of Moore are fading into distance and dimness, except where they have been married to immortal music; and the blazing star of Byron himself is receding from its place of pride. We need say nothing of Milman, and Croly, and Atherstone, and Hood, and a legion of others, who, with no ordinary gifts of taste and fancy, have not so properly survived their fame, as been excluded by some hard fatality from what seemed their just inheritance. The two who have the longest withstood this rapid withering of the laurel, and with the least marks of decay on their branches, are Rogers and Campbell; neither of them, it may be remarked, voluminous writers, and both distinguished rather for the fine taste and consummate elegance of their writings, than for that fiery passion, and disdainful vehemence, which seemed for a time to be so much more in favour with the public.[4]

---

4. For Keats, Shelley, Byron (all dead by this time), and Wordsworth, see their listings. Other writers mentioned are Robert Southey (1774–1843), Sir Walter Scott (1771–1832), Thomas Moore (1779–1852), George Crabbe (1754–1832), Thomas Campbell (1777–1844), Thomas Hood (1799–1845)—all read through the 19th century and beyond—and Samuel Rogers (1763–1855), George Croly (1780–1860), Edwin Atherstone (1788–1872), and Henry Hart Milman (1791–1868).

If taste and elegance, however, be titles to enduring fame, we might venture securely to promise that rich boon to the author before us; who adds to those great merits a tenderness and loftiness of feeling, and an ethereal purity of sentiment, which could only emanate from the soul of a woman. She must beware of becoming too voluminous; and must not venture again on any thing so long as the "Forest Sanctuary."[5] But, if the next generation inherits our taste for short poems, we are persuaded it will not readily allow her to be forgotten. For we do not hesitate to say, that she is, beyond all comparison, the most touching and accomplished writer of occasional verses that our literature has yet to boast of.

⊶ ⊱

John Clare
1793–1864

The horizon of John Clare's world was defined by the village of Helpston, Northamptonshire, in which he was born, to a barely literate farmhand and an illiterate mother. His formal education was sparse, though his poetry shows his knowledge of Milton and Thomson and he read Wordsworth, Coleridge, Keats, and Byron (two late long poems are entitled *Childe Harold* and *Don Juan*). By the "indefatigable savings of a penny and a half-penny," the young Clare purchased fairy tales from hawkers, recalling that "I firmly believed every page I read and considerd I possessd in these the chief learning and literature of the country." His own writing was produced swiftly and with few revisions in time seized from agricultural labor, then hid "with all secresy possible" in "an old unused cubbard" or hole in the wall.

Clare's condition placed him in the line of those "natural geniuses" eagerly sought by eighteenth-century primitivism: Stephen Duck "The Thresher Poet" (1705–1756), Robert Bloomfield (*The Farmer's Boy*, 1800), Ann Yearsley "The Milkmaid Poet" (1752–1806), and Robert Burns (1759–1796) had all been fit into the stereotype of the peasant poet. In 1817 Keats's publisher John Taylor saw Clare's proposal to publish a volume of poetry by subscription; in 1820 his firm brought out *Poems Descriptive of Rural Life and Scenery*, marketing it as the work of a young "Northamptonshire Peasant," a description that fixed Clare's regional and class identity. The book enjoyed critical and popular success, with four editions in a year. The vogue that brought Clare attention quickly came to constrain him: his Evangelical patron disapproved of his social criticism and "vulgar" manner, while Taylor sought to broaden his appeal by standardizing his language and cutting his poems. Clare's pungent dialect usages—which illustrate by contrast how thoroughly Wordsworth "purified" the "language really used by men" in *Lyrical Ballads*—and belief "that what ever is intellig[i]ble to others is grammer and what ever is commonsense is not far from correctness" offended the norms of polite literature. "Grammer in learning," Clare adamantly insisted to Taylor in a phrase that by linking style and politics makes clear the twin offenses he posed to the urban book-buying public, "is like Tyranny in government—confound the bitch Ill never be her slave." Taylor found himself in the awkward position of intermediary between an audience for poetry increasingly represented by genteel women and a prickly lower-class male writer: "*false delicasy* damn it I hate it beyond every thing those primpt up misses brought up in those seminaries of mysterious wickedness (Boarding Schools) what will please 'em? why we well know—but while their heart & soul loves to extravagance (what we dare not mention) false delicasy's seriousness muscles [muzzles] up the mouth & condemns it." If that explosion reminds one of the "rhodomontade" with which Keats defended his sexually more explicit revisions to *The Eve of St. Agnes*, the distance

5. Jeffrey's article takes as occasion the second editions of *Records of Woman* and *The Forest Sanctuary*, an epic romance that Hemans regarded as "almost, if not altogether, the best" of her works.

between the literariness of Keats, whom Clare admired, and Clare's plainness is manifest in his objection that Keats "keeps up a constant alusion or illusion to the grecian mythology & there I cannot follow . . . the frequency of such classical accompaniment makes it wearisome to the reader where behind every rose bush he looks for a Venus & under every laurel a thrumming Appollo."

Before long, readers lost interest in Clare's rough independence from their expectations of verse. *The Village Minstrel* (1821) sold badly and *The Shepherd's Calendar* (1827) even more disappointingly; *The Rural Muse* (1835) got good reviews but not a readership. By then Clare had left Helpston for Northborough, where he moved to a cottage provided by another patron, hoping to set himself up as a farmer. Though the move measured only a few miles, it broke his firm sense of place. In 1837 Clare was admitted to an asylum for the mentally ill in southeast England, from which he escaped in 1841, walking back the eighty miles to Northborough. He was recommitted to an asylum in Northampton, where he spent the remaining years of his life. Yet Clare never ceased to write. His early poetry depicts with marked individuality a rural existence threatened by enclosure and by widening difference between classes; long and close observation of the landscape, of animals and birds, produced sharply detailed images in "a language that is ever green" (*Pastoral Poesy*) and far removed from the "egotistical sublime" to which Wordsworth's experience of nature gives rise. Clare once proclaimed of *Composed Upon Westminster Bridge* "I think it (& woud say it to the teeth of the critic in spite of his rule & compass) that it owns no equal in the English language," but he mocked Wordsworth's "affectations of simplicity." The delusions and instabilities of Clare's identity in the asylum period led to a poetry of fantasized memory and loss that possesses a strange and often visionary power.

New editions of Clare's writings have freed his texts from the emendations of their first publication and have brought unpublished materials to view, winning him the audience he missed in his own time. As illustration, we print two versions of *Written in November*, the first from the manuscripts edited by Eric Robinson and David Powell, the source of our texts, the second as the poem appeared in *The Village Minstrel* (1821).

Written in November (1)

Autumn I love thy latter end to view
In cold novembers day so bleak & bare
When like lifes dwindled thread worn nearly thro
Wi lingering pottering° pace & head bleached bare   dawdling, uncertain
5   Thou like an old man bids the world adieu
I love thee well & often when a child
Have roamd the bare brown heath a flower to find
& in the moss clad vale & wood bank wild
Have cropt the little bell flowers paley blue
10   That trembling peept the sheltering bush behind
When winnowing north winds cold & blealy° blew   coldly, bleakly
How have I joyd wi dithering° hands to find   shivering
Each fading flower & still how sweet the blast
Would bleak novembers hour Restore the joy thats past

Written in November (2)

Autumn, I love thy parting look to view
    In cold November's day, so bleak and bare,
When, thy life's dwindled thread worn nearly thro',
    With ling'ring pott'ring pace, and head bleach'd bare,
5   Thou, like an old man, bidd'st the world adieu.

I love thee well: and often, when a child,
Have roam'd the bare brown heath a flower to find;
    And in the moss-clad vale, and wood-bank wild
Have cropt the little bell-flowers, pearly blue,
10   That trembling peep the shelt'ring bush behind.
When winnowing north-winds cold and bleaky blew,
    How have I joy'd, with dithering hands, to find
Each fading flower; and still how sweet the blast,
Would bleak November's hour restore the joy that's past.

c. 1812   1821

Clock a Clay°   *lady-bug*

In the cowslips peeps° I lye[1]   *primrose blossoms*
Hidden from the buzzing fly
While green grass beneath me lies
Pearled wi' dew like fishes eyes
5   Here I lye a Clock a clay
Waiting for the time o' day[2]

While grassy forests quake surprise
And the wild wind sobs and sighs
My gold home rocks as like to fall
10 On its pillars green and tall
When the pattering rain drives bye
Clock a Clay keeps warm and dry

Day by day and night by night
All the week I hide from sight
15 In the cowslips peeps I lye
In rain and dew still warm and dry
Day and night and night and day
Red black spotted clock a clay

My home it shakes in wind and showers
20 Pale green pillar top't wi' flowers
Bending at the wild winds breath
Till I touch the grass beneath
Here still I live lone clock a clay
Watching for the time of day

c. 1848   1873

"I Am"

I am—yet what I am, none cares or knows;
    My friends forsake me like a memory lost:—
I am the self-consumer of my woes;—
    They rise and vanish in oblivion's host,
5   Like shadows in love's frenzied stifled throes:—
    And yet I am, and live—like vapours tost

---

1. Echoing Ariel's song in Shakespeare, *The Tempest*, 5.1.89: "In a cowslip's bell I lie."

2. Refers to the children's game of counting the taps needed to make the lady-bug fly away home.

Into the nothingness of scorn and noise,—
　　Into the living sea of waking dreams,
Where there is neither sense of life or joys,
10　　But the vast shipwreck of my lifes esteems;
Even the dearest, that I love the best
Are strange—nay, rather stranger than the rest.

I long for scenes, where man hath never trod
　　A place where woman never smiled or wept
15　There to abide with my Creator, God;
And sleep as I in childhood, sweetly slept,
Untroubling, and untroubled where I lie,
The grass below—above the vaulted sky.

c. 1842　　　　　　　　　　　　　　　　　　　　　　1848

◆━━◆

John Keats
1795–1821

"A thing of beauty is a joy for ever"; "tender is the night"; "Beauty is truth; truth Beauty"—these phrases are so well known that we may forget that they were unheard before John Keats. Keats's brief career ran only from 1814, when he wrote his first poem, to 1820, when he revised his sonnet *Bright Star* on board a ship to Italy. "Oh, for ten years, that I may overwhelm / Myself in poesy," he said in 1816. Not even getting this decade, his active life as a writer stopped around his twenty-fourth birthday. At age twenty-four, Chaucer had yet to write anything, and if Shakespeare had died at twenty-four, he would be known only (if at all) by a few early works. What if Keats had lived until 1881, like that Victorian sage Thomas Carlyle, also born in 1795?

The drama of Keats is not just the poignancy of genius cut off in youth but also his humble origins—a focus of ridicule during and after his lifetime by class-conscious reviewers and aristocratic poets. Son of a livery-stable keeper who had married the owner's daughter and inherited the suburban London business, Keats attended the progressive Enfield School. Here he was tutored and befriended by Charles Cowden Clarke, the headmaster's son, who introduced him to literature, music, the theater. When Keats was nine years old, his father died in a riding accident and his mother remarried immediately; her commitment to her children was as erratic as it was doting, and her presence at home was inconstant. Keats was deeply attached to her and devastated when she disappeared for four years, leaving them all with his grandmother. When she returned sick and consumptive, he nursed her, and she died when he was fourteen; the welter of emotions she left in him is reflected in the series of adored, inconstant women around which so much of his poetry revolves. The children were remanded to the guardianship of a practical businessman whose chief concern was to apprentice the boys to some viable trade. Unimaginative himself and unsympathetic to any passion for learning and poetry, he apprenticed Keats to a London hospital surgeon in the grim days before anesthesia. Keats stayed with this training long enough to be licensed as an apothecary (more a general practitioner than a druggist), but he frequently took time off to read and to write poetry. When he came of age in 1817, he gave up medicine and set out to make a living as a poet.

Keats was already enjoying the society of Clarke and his circle of politically progressive thinkers, artists, poets, journalists, and publishers, many of whom became close friends—among them Leigh Hunt, also a poet as well as a radical journalist. Hunt launched Keats's career, publishing him in his weekly paper, *The Examiner*, and advertising him as one of the rising "Young

Poets." It was through Hunt that Keats met some of the chief nonestablishment writers of the day—William Wordsworth, William Hazlitt, Charles Lamb, Percy Shelley—and the controversial painter Benjamin Robert Haydon. His inaugural volume, published in 1817, included twenty sonnets, a favorite form for him, as well as Spenserian stanzas, odes, verse epistles, romance fragments, and meditative long poems on the subject of poetry itself. The writers that mattered most to him were Spenser (his first poem, written in 1814, was a deft "Imitation of Spenser" in Spenserian stanzas), Shakespeare, and ambivalently, Milton, and among his contemporaries, Wordsworth and Byron, though again with intelligent ambivalence. Keats warmly dedicated the 1817 *Poems* to Hunt and in a long concluding piece (*Sleep and Poetry*) voiced sharp criticism of what he saw as the arid formalism of eighteenth-century neoclassical poetry, which still had prestige with conservative or aristocratic writers, including Byron. He never forgave Keats for this tirade, and it immediately provoked the Tory journalists, who were only too eager to jab at their political enemy Hunt through his protégé. Published in a year when civil rights were weakened and the radical publisher William Hone brought to trial, *Poems* was viciously ridiculed in reviews marked by social snobbery and political prejudice and Keats was indelibly tagged "the Cockney Poet"—one of Hunt's suburban radicals. He was stung, but determined to prove himself with his next effort, *Endymion*, initiated as part of a contest with Hunt and Shelley to see who could write a 4,000-line poem by the end of 1817. The only one to complete the challenge, Keats set off with a sense that it would be "a test" or "trial" of his talents. "A thing of beauty is a joy for ever" begins this tale of a shepherd-prince who dreams of a goddess, and on waking is profoundly alienated from ordinary life in the world. Book I narrates this episode; over the course of the next three books, Endymion dreams of her again, loses her, searches high (more dreams) and low (underground to the Bower of Venus and Adonis and several other labyrinthine terrains), and finally gives up, falling for a maid he finds abandoned in the woods. She turns out to be his goddess in disguise, and his dream comes true. This is the last time in Keats's poetry that dreams are so happily realized.

The same reviewers who had hooted at Keats's debut were waiting to savage *Endymion*, which they did with glee in the summer of 1818. But Keats himself had already grown weary of this poem, calling it "slipshod," and coming to feel that the most powerful poets did not write escapist, "golden-tongued Romance" but embraced the "fierce dispute" of life in the world. In 1818 he was attending Hazlitt's London lectures on English poetry, rereading *Paradise Lost*, *Hamlet*, *King Lear*, and Henry Cary's recent translation of Dante's *Divine Comedy*. He was also acknowledging that Wordsworth, whose didacticism and egotism he disliked, had a profoundly modern sense of the "dark passages" of life—the misfortunes, miseries, and griefs that could not be dispelled by simple romance or explained away by simplistic moral philosophies. It was in this temper that Keats began a revisionary Miltonic epic, *Hyperion*, whose hero was intended to be Apollo, the god of knowledge, poetry, and medicine—a linkage dear to Keats. Its most deeply felt poetry, however—in the two books that Keats completed—involved the sorrows and anxieties of gods suffering their ejection from heaven, and the plight of the sun-god Hyperion, not yet fallen but sensing his fate. When Keats turned to Apollo in Book 3, he lost inspiration, in part because he was feeling acutely the very mortal pain of nursing his beloved brother Tom, dying of tuberculosis, the disease that had killed their mother and that would kill Keats himself three years later (already he was suffering from a chronically sore throat).

Tom died at the end of 1818, and Keats sought relief in his poetry. In a burst of inspiration that lasted well into the fall of 1819 (when he revised *Hyperion*), he produced the work that established his fame: *The Eve of St. Agnes* (a part serious, part ironic romance), *La Belle Dame sans Mercy* (a romance with a vengeance), *Lamia* (a wickedly satirical, bitter romance), all the Great Odes, and a clutch of brilliant sonnets, including *Bright Star*. Although (unlike most of his contemporaries) he wrote no prefaces, defenses, self-promoting polemics, or theoretical essays, his letters display a critical intelligence as brilliant as the poetic talent. A number of their off-the-cuff formulations—the "finer tone" of repetition, "negative capability," "the camelion Poet," "the egotistical sublime," truth "proved upon our pulses"—have become standard terms in literary criticism and

Charles Brown, *Portrait of John Keats,* 1819.

theory, and his letters from their first publication, after his death, have been admired for their generosity and playfulness, their insight, their candor, and their critical penetration.

His health worsening over the course of 1819, Keats suffered a major lung hemorrhage early in 1820; with the accuracy of his medical training, he read his "death warrant" and was devastated. For despite the shaky reception of *Poems* and *Endymion*, he was hopeful about his forthcoming volume and full of plans for new writing (journalism or plays); he was also deeply in love with the girl next door, Fanny Brawne, whom he secretly betrothed and hoped to marry once he was financially capable. He sailed to Italy in September, seeking health in a warmer climate, but died at the end of the next February, four months after his twenty-fifth birthday—far from Fanny and his friends and in such despair of fame that he asked his tombstone to be inscribed "Here lies one whose name was writ in water." Yet he did live long enough to see some favorable reviews of his 1820 volume. Shelley's fable in *Adonais* of Keats killed by hostile reviewers, though often credited, could not have been more out of tune with Keats's own resilience. "This is a mere matter of the moment," he assured his brother George, adding, "I think I shall be among the English Poets after my death."

On First Looking into Chapman's Homer[1]

> Much have I travell'd in the realms of gold,
>   And many goodly states and kingdoms seen;

---

1. Written the morning after Keats had stayed up all night with Clarke reading George Chapman's vibrant, early 17th-century translation of Homer at a time when Pope's rendering in polished heroic couplets was the standard. Keats describes his reading as a Homeric voyage through the Greek isles where classical literature had its golden age. In *A Defence of Poesie* (1595), Sidney wrote that poets "deliver a golden" world from the "brazen" world of nature. Keats extends the language of traveling in "realms of gold" to Renaissance-era voyages of discovery to the New World in quest of gold by adventurers such as the conquistador of Mexico, Cortez.

Round many western islands have I been
Which bards in fealty to Apollo° hold.   *god of poetry*
5   Oft of one wide expanse had I been told
That deep-brow'd Homer ruled as his demesne;°   *realm*
Yet did I never breathe its pure serene°   *clear sky*
Till I heard Chapman speak out loud and bold:
Then felt I like some watcher of the skies
10   When a new planet swims into his ken;[2]
Or like stout Cortez when with eagle eyes
He star'd at the Pacific—and all his men
Look'd at each other with a wild surmise—
Silent, upon a peak in Darien.[3]

1816   1816, 1817

COMPANION READINGS
Alexander Pope: Homer's Iliad [1]
from *Book 5*

[THE ARMOR OF DIOMEDES, A GREEK WARRIOR]

High on his helm celestial lightnings play,
His beamy shield emits a living ray;
Th' unwearied blaze incessant streams supplies,
Like the red star that fires th' autumnal skies,
5   When fresh he rears his radiant orb to sight,
And bath'd in Ocean, shoots a keener light.
Such glories Pallas[2] on the chief bestow'd,
Such, from his arms, the fierce effulgence flow'd:
Onward she drives him, furious to engage,
10 Where the fight burns, and where the thickest rage.

George Chapman: Homer's Iliad [3]
from *Book 5*

From his bright helme and shield did burne a most unwearied fire,
Like rich Autumnus' golden lampe, whose brightnesse men admire
Past all the other host of starres, when, with his cheaerfull face
Fresh washt in loftir ocean waves he doth the skies enchase.
5   To let whose glory lose no sight, still Pallas made him turne
Where tumult most expresst his powre, and where the fight did burne.

---

2. Uranus was discovered in 1781; ken: range of apprehension.
3. Mountain range in eastern Panama.
1. When Books 1–4 of Pope's *Iliad* were published in 1715 (Book 5 in 1716), he was acclaimed the greatest poet of the age; the successful sale inaugurated the first poetic career in England able to sustain itself independent of political or aristocratic patronage.

2. Pallas Athene, an epithet of Athena, Greek goddess of war (and later, wisdom).
3. Chapman uses the fourteener, an iambic seven-beat line, most common in ballad verse (as two lines of four and three beats). Although both Pope and Chapman turn Homer's unrhymed lines into couplets, Keats preferred Chapman's rougher lines and direct language.

On Seeing the Elgin Marbles[1]

My spirit is too weak—mortality
   Weighs heavily on me like unwilling sleep,
   And each imagined pinnacle and steep
Of godlike hardship, tells me I must die
5   Like a sick eagle looking at the sky.
   Yet 'tis a gentle luxury to weep
   That I have not the cloudy winds to keep
Fresh for the opening of the morning's eye.
Such dim-conceived glories of the brain
10   Bring round the heart an undescribable feud;
So do these wonders a most dizzy pain
   That mingles Grecian grandeur with the rude
Wasting of old time—with a billowy main°   *sea*
   A sun—a shadow of a magnitude.

1817   1817, 1818

Sonnet: When I have fears

When I have fears that I may cease to be[1]
   Before my pen has glean'd my teeming brain,
Before high piled books in charact'ry°   *written symbols*
   Hold like rich garners the full-ripened grain;
5   When I behold upon the night's starred face,
   Huge cloudy symbols of a high romance,
And think that I may never live to trace
   Their shadows with the magic hand of chance;
And when I feel, fair creature of an hour,
10   That I shall never look upon thee more,
Never have relish in the fairy power
   Of unreflecting love—then on the shore
Of the wide world I stand alone and think,
Till love and fame to nothingness do sink.

January 1818   1848

THE EVE OF ST. AGNES   Keats began this poem in the winter months of early 1819, setting it on St. Agnes' Eve, when, according to legend, a young virgin who has performed certain rituals may dream of her future husband. Agnes is the patron saint of virgins, and her story is quite violent. A thirteen-year-old Christian martyr in early fourth-century Rome, she was condemned to

1. Keats viewed these sculptural fragments from the Athenian Parthenon with Haydon, a champion of Lord Elgin's purchase of them in 1806 from the Turks, then occupying Greece. Elgin (hard *g*) was motivated both by admiration for their powerful beauty and a desire to preserve them from erosion and the further peril of being turned into mortar or used for target practice by Turkish soldiers. Their aesthetic value was debated (some found them crude and even inauthentic), and their purchase by the British government in 1816 for deposit in the British Museum (they are still there) was (and still is) controversial. Keats's sonnet appeared in *The Examiner* in 1817 (our text) and in Haydon's *Annals of the Fine Arts* in 1818. For Haydon's enthusiasm, see page 303.

1. Keats's sonnet plays several allusive echoes: Shakespeare's "When I do count the clock that tells the time"; Wordsworth's "few could know / When Lucy ceased to be" (*She dwelt among th'untrodden ways;* see page 214); Shelley's lament that by 1816 the radical Wordsworth should "cease to be" (*To Wordsworth*); Milton's sonnet, "When I consider how my light is spent / Ere half my days, in this dark world and wide . . ."

a night of rape in the brothels before her execution. This preliminary torture was prevented by a miraculous storm of thunder and lightning, a climate that Keats writes into the end of his poem. Working in the intricate form of Spenserian stanzas, repopularized by Byron's *Childe Harold's Pilgrimage* (1812–1818), Keats spins an ironic romance—at once indulging the traditional pleasures of the genre (love, imagination, gorgeous sensuality with a spiritual aura) and bringing a playful, sometimes satiric, sometimes darkly shaded perspective to its illusions. With *Romeo and Juliet* in mind, Keats at first portrayed the sexual desire of his hero and heroine, but his publishers, worried about indecency, forced him to revise. Though he complied with angry reluctance, the imagery of stars and flowers in stanza 36 shows his skill in retaining some of the original pulsation. We give some of his original draft in our footnotes.

The Eve of St. Agnes

1

St. Agnes' Eve—Ah, bitter chill it was!
The owl, for all his feathers, was a-cold;
The hare limp'd trembling through the frozen grass,
And silent was the flock in woolly fold:
5 Numb were the Beadsman's fingers, while he told
His rosary,[1] and while his frosted breath,
Like pious incense from a censer old,
Seem'd taking flight for heaven, without a death,
Past the sweet Virgin's picture, while his prayer he saith.

2

10 His prayer he saith, this patient, holy man;
Then takes his lamp, and riseth from his knees,
And back returneth, meagre, barefoot, wan,
Along the chapel aisle by slow degrees:
The sculptur'd dead, on each side, seem to freeze,
15 Emprison'd in black, purgatorial rails:
Knights, ladies, praying in dumb orat'ries,°   *chapels*
He passeth by; and his weak spirit fails
To think how they may ache in icy hoods and mails.

3

Northward he turneth through a little door,
20 And scarce three steps, ere Music's golden tongue
Flatter'd to tears this aged man and poor;
But no—already had his deathbell rung;
The joys of all his life were said and sung:
His was harsh penance on St. Agnes' Eve:
25 Another way he went, and soon among
Rough ashes sat he for his soul's reprieve,
And all night kept awake, for sinners' sake to grieve.

4

That ancient Beadsman heard the prelude soft;
And so it chanc'd, for many a door was wide,
30 From hurry to and fro. Soon, up aloft,
The silver, snarling trumpets 'gan to chide:

1. A pensioner paid to say prayers, this beadsman is saying a rosary in the estate's cold chapel for the salvation of the ancestors.

The level chambers, ready with their pride,
Were glowing to receive a thousand guests:
The carved angels, ever eager-eyed,
35   Star'd, where upon their heads the cornice rests,
With hair blown back, and wings put cross-wise on their breasts.

5

At length burst in the argent° revelry,   *silvery*
With plume, tiara, and all rich array,
Numerous as shadows haunting fairily
40   The brain, new stuff'd, in youth with triumphs gay
Of old romance.[2] These let us wish away,
And turn, sole-thoughted, to one Lady there,
Whose heart had brooded, all that wintry day,
On love, and wing'd St. Agnes' saintly care,
45   As she had heard old dames full many times declare.

6

They told her how, upon St. Agnes' Eve,
Young virgins might have visions of delight,
And soft adorings from their loves receive
Upon the honey'd middle of the night,
50   If ceremonies due they did aright;
As, supperless to bed they must retire,
And couch supine their beauties, lily white;
Nor look behind, nor sideways, but require°   *beseech*
Of Heaven with upward eyes for all that they desire.[3]

7

55   Full of this whim was thoughtful Madeline:[4]
The music, yearning like a God in pain
She scarcely heard: her maiden eyes divine,
Fix'd on the floor, saw many a sweeping train°   *long skirt*
Pass by—she heeded not at all: in vain
60   Came many a tiptoe, amorous cavalier,
And back retir'd; not cool'd by high disdain,
But she saw not: her heart was otherwhere:
She sigh'd for Agnes' dreams, the sweetest of the year.

8

She danc'd along with vague, regardless eyes,
65   Anxious her lips, her breathing quick and short:[5]
The hallow'd hour was near at hand: she sighs
Amid the timbrels,° and the throng'd resort   *tambourines*
Of whisperers in anger, or in sport;
'Mid looks of love, defiance, hate, and scorn,
70   Hoodwink'd° with faery fancy; all amort,°   *blinded / dead*

---

2. The literary genre.
3. Keats's publishers forced him to cancel as too explicitly erotic a stanza that followed this one, recounting the fable of a maid's "future lord" appearing in her dreams, bringing "delicious food even to her lips": "Viands, and wine, and fruit, and sugared cream, / To touch her palate with the fine extreme / Of relish; the soft music heard; and then / More pleasures followed in a dizzy stream, /

Palpable almost; then to wake again / Warm in the virgin morn, no weeping Magdalen"—i.e., Mary Magdalen, the prostitute befriended by Jesus; in Keats's day hospitals for unwed mothers were called Magdalens.
4. A name derived from Magdalen.
5. Originally: "Her anxious lips mouth full pulp'd with rosy thoughts."

Save to St. Agnes and her lambs unshorn,
And all the bliss to be before to-morrow morn.[6]

9

So, purposing each moment to retire,
She linger'd still. Meantime, across the moors,
75   Had come young Porphyro,[7] with heart on fire
For Madeline. Beside the portal doors,
Buttress'd from moonlight,[8] stands he, and implores
All saints to give him sight of Madeline,
But for one moment in the tedious hours,
80   That he might gaze and worship all unseen:
Perchance speak, kneel, touch, kiss—in sooth such things have been.

10

He ventures in: let no buzz'd whisper tell:
All eyes be muffled, or a hundred swords
Will storm his heart,[9] Love's fev'rous citadel:
85   For him, those chambers held barbarian hordes,
Hyena foemen, and hot-blooded lords,
Whose very dogs would execrations howl
Against his lineage: not one breast affords
Him any mercy, in that mansion foul,
90   Save one old beldame,[1] weak in body and in soul.

11

Ah, happy chance! the aged creature came,
Shuffling along with ivory-headed wand,°   *staff*
To where he stood, hid from the torch's flame,
Behind a broad hall-pillar, far beyond
95   The sound of merriment and chorus bland:°   *soft*
He startled her; but soon she knew his face,
And grasp'd his fingers in her palsied hand,
Saying, "Mercy, Porphyro! hie thee from this place;
They are all here to-night, the whole blood-thirsty race!

12

100   "Get hence! get hence! there's dwarfish Hildebrand;
He had a fever late, and in the fit
He cursed thee and thine, both house and land:
Then there's that old Lord Maurice, not a whit
More tame for his grey hairs—Alas me! flit!
105   Flit like a ghost away."—"Ah, Gossip° dear,   *confidant*
We're safe enough; here in this arm-chair sit,
And tell me how"—"Good Saints! not here, not here;
Follow me, child, or else these stones will be thy bier."°   *coffin-platform*

6. It was a custom at St. Agnes' Day mass, during the singing of Agnus Dei (Lamb of God), to bless two white unshorn lambs, whose wool nuns then spun and wove.
7. From porphyra, "purple," a precious dye for garments of the nobility; "purple blood" signifies royalty and nobility; a porphyre is a purple-colored serpent. Moreover, Porphyry (3rd c. A.D.), famous antagonist of Christianity, instituted Neoplatonism throughout the Roman Empire a few decades before the martyrdom of St. Agnes.
8. Hidden in the shadow of a buttress (the external archi-

tecture that supports the castle walls).
9. Keats echoes Burke's famous account of the arrest of Marie Antoinette: "A band of cruel ruffians and assassins . . . rushed into the chamber of the queen, and pierced with a hundred strokes of bayonets and poniards the bed, from whence this persecuted woman had but just time to fly almost naked" (see *Reflections*, page 51).
1. Grandmother or old nurse; Angela evokes Juliet's nurse Angelica in *Romeo and Juliet*, also a go-between for the lovers.

13

He follow'd through a lowly arched way,
110 Brushing the cobwebs with his lofty plume,
And as she mutter'd "Well-a—well-a-day!"
He found him in a little moonlight room,
Pale, lattic'd, chill, and silent as a tomb.
"Now tell me where is Madeline," said he,
115 "O tell me, Angela, by the holy loom
Which none but secret sisterhood may see,
When they St. Agnes' wool are weaving piously."

14

"St. Agnes! Ah! it is St. Agnes' Eve—
Yet men will murder upon holy days:
120 Thou must hold water in a witch's sieve,
And be liege-lord of all the Elves and Fays,°   *fairies*
To venture so: it fills me with amaze
To see thee, Porphyro!—St. Agnes' Eve!
God's help! my lady fair the conjuror plays
125 This very night: good angels her deceive!
But let me laugh awhile, I've mickle° time to grieve."   *much*

15

Feebly she laugheth in the languid moon,
While Porphyro upon her face doth look,
Like puzzled urchin on an aged crone
130 Who keepeth clos'd a wond'rous riddle-book,
As spectacled she sits in chimney nook.
But soon his eyes grew brilliant, when she told
His lady's purpose; and he scarce could brook°   *hold back*
Tears, at the thought of those enchantments cold,
135 And Madeline asleep in lap of legends old.

16

Sudden a thought came like a full-blown rose,
Flushing his brow, and in his pained heart
Made purple riot:[2] then doth he propose
A stratagem, that makes the beldame start:
140 "A cruel man and impious thou art:
Sweet lady, let her pray, and sleep, and dream
Alone with her good angels, far apart
From wicked men like thee. Go, go!—I deem
Thou canst not surely be the same that thou didst seem."

17

145 "I will not harm her, by all saints I swear,"
Quoth Porphyro: "O may I ne'er find grace
When my weak voice shall whisper its last prayer,
If one of her soft ringlets I displace.
Or look with ruffian passion in her face:
150 Good Angela, believe me by these tears;
Or I will, even in a moment's space,
Awake, with horrid shout, my foemen's ears,
And beard° them, though they be more fang'd than wolves and bears."   *defy*

2. Originally: Heated his Brow / Made riot fierce.

18

"Ah! why wilt thou affright a feeble soul?

155   A poor, weak, palsy-stricken, churchyard thing,
Whose passing-bell° may ere the midnight toll;   *death knell*
Whose prayers for thee, each morn and evening,
Were never miss'd."—Thus plaining,° doth she bring   *lamenting*
A gentler speech from burning Porphyro;

160   So woeful, and of such deep sorrowing,
That Angela gives promise she will do
Whatever he shall wish, betide her weal or woe.

19

Which was, to lead him, in close secrecy,
Even to Madeline's chamber, and there hide

165   Him in a closet,° of such privacy   *private room*
That he might see her beauty unespied,
And win perhaps that night a peerless bride,
While legion'd fairies pac'd the coverlet,
And pale enchantment held her sleepy-eyed.

170   Never on such a night have lovers met,
Since Merlin paid his Demon all the monstrous debt.[3]

20

"It shall be as thou wishest," said the Dame:
"All cates° and dainties shall be stored there   *delicacies*
Quickly on this feast-night: by the tambour frame[4]

175   Her own lute thou wilt see: no time to spare,
For I am slow and feeble, and scarce dare
On such a catering trust my dizzy head.
Wait here, my child, with patience; kneel in prayer
The while: Ah! thou must needs the lady wed,

180   Or may I never leave my grave among the dead."

21

So saying, she hobbled off with busy fear.
The lover's endless minutes slowly pass'd;
The dame return'd, and whisper'd in his ear
To follow her; with aged eyes aghast

185   From fright of dim espial.[5] Safe at last,
Through many a dusky gallery, they gain
The maiden's chamber, silken, hush'd, and chaste;
Where Porphyro took covert,[6] pleas'd amain.°   *fully*
His poor guide hurried back with agues° in her brain.   *trembling*

22

190   Her falt'ring hand upon the balustrade,°   *bannister*
Old Angela was feeling for the stair,
When Madeline, St. Agnes' charmed maid,
Rose, like a mission'd spirit,[7] unaware:
With silver taper's° light, and pious care,   *candle's*

195   She turn'd, and down the aged gossip led

---

3. In Arthurian legend, the magician Merlin had his powers
turned against him by the enchantress Vivien, who repaid
his love by imprisoning him in a cave, where he died.
4. Frame for embroidering, shaped like a tambourine.

5. Being espied, even in dim light.
6. Originally: where he in panting covert.
7. Commissioned, as if an angel-messenger.

To a safe level matting. Now prepare,
Young Porphyro, for gazing on that bed;
She comes, she comes again, like ring-dove fray'd° and fled.   *frightened*

23

Out went the taper° as she hurried in;   *candle*
200   Its little smoke, in pallid moonshine, died:
She clos'd the door, she panted, all akin
To spirits of the air, and visions wide:
No utter'd syllable, or, woe betide!
But to her heart, her heart was voluble,
205   Paining with eloquence her balmy side;
As though a tongueless nightingale should swell
Her throat in vain, and die, heart-stifled, in her dell.[8]

24

A casement° high and triple-arch'd there was,   *window*
All garlanded with carven imag'ries
210   Of fruits, and flowers, and bunches of knot-grass,
And diamonded with panes of quaint device,
Innumerable of stains and splendid dyes,
As are the tiger-moth's deep-damask'd wings;
And in the midst, 'mong thousand heraldries,°   *genealogical emblems*
215   And twilight saints, and dim emblazonings,
A shielded scutcheon blush'd with blood of queens and kings.[9]

25

Full on this casement shone the wintry moon,
And threw warm gules° on Madeline's fair breast,   *red*
As down she knelt for heaven's grace and boon;°   *favor*
220   Rose-bloom fell on her hands, together prest,
And on her silver cross soft amethyst,
And on her hair a glory,° like a saint: *halo*
She seem'd a splendid angel, newly drest,
Save wings, for heaven:—Porphyro grew faint:
225   She knelt, so pure a thing, so free from mortal taint.

26

Anon his heart revives: her vespers done,
Of all its wreathed pearls her hair she frees;
Unclasps her warmed jewels one by one;
Loosens her fragrant bodice;[1] by degrees
230   Her rich attire creeps rustling to her knees:
Half-hidden, like a mermaid in sea-weed,
Pensive awhile she dreams awake, and sees,
In fancy, fair St. Agnes in her bed,
But dares not look behind, or all the charm is fled.[2]

---

8. In a story in Ovid's *Metamorphoses*, Tereus, after raping his wife's sister Philomela, cut out her tongue to prevent her report; but she wove its imagery, which her sister understood, and was so enraged that she butchered her and Tereus's son and fed him a dinner made from the flesh. With Tereus on the verge of violent revenge, all three were turned into birds, Philomela into a nightingale; her name means "lover of honey, sweetness, song."
9. Scutcheon: shield; although "blood" aptly evokes bloodshed, here it refers to Madeline's royal bloodline.

1. Keats's drafts: her bosom jewels / loosens her bursting boddice / her Boddice lace string / her Boddice and her bosom bar[e] / Loosens her fragrant boddice and does bare her.
2. Evoking the myth of Orpheus and Eurydice, with Madeline in the male role of the lover who wins the opportunity to lead his dead beloved back to life from Hades, on the condition that he not look back at her until they reach the upper world. Orpheus violated this injunction and lost Eurydice forever.

27

235 Soon, trembling in her soft and chilly nest,
In sort of wakeful swoon, perplex'd she lay,
Until the poppied° warmth of sleep oppress'd   *fragrant, narcotic*
Her soothed limbs, and soul fatigued away;
Flown, like a thought, until the morrow-day;
240 Blissfully haven'd both from joy and pain;
Clasp'd like a missal where swart Paynims pray;[3]
Blinded alike from sunshine and from rain,
As though a rose should shut, and be a bud again.

28

Stol'n to this paradise,[4] and so entranced,
245 Porphyro gazed upon her empty dress,
And listen'd to her breathing, if it chanced
To wake into a slumberous tenderness;
Which when he heard, that minute did he bless,
And breath'd himself: then from the closet crept,
250 Noiseless as fear in a wide wilderness,
And over the hush'd carpet, silent, stept,
And 'tween the curtains peep'd, where, lo!—how fast she slept.

29

Then by the bed-side, where the faded moon
Made a dim, silver twilight, soft he set
255 A table, and, half anguish'd, threw thereon
A cloth of woven crimson, gold, and jet:—
O for some drowsy Morphean amulet![5]
The boisterous, midnight, festive clarion,
The kettle-drum, and far-heard clarionet,
260 Affray° his ears, though but in dying tone:—   *frighten*
The hall door shuts again, and all the noise is gone.

30

And still she slept an azure-lidded sleep,
In blanched linen, smooth, and lavender'd,
While he from forth the closet brought a heap
265 Of candied apple, quince, and plum, and gourd;°   *melon*
With jellies soother[6] than the creamy curd,
And lucent syrops, tinct° with cinnamon;   *clear syrups, tinged*
Manna° and dates, in argosy° transferr'd   *rare food / merchant fleet*
From Fez; and spiced dainties, every one,
270 From silken Samarcand to cedar'd Lebanon.[7]

31

These delicates he heap'd with glowing hand
On golden dishes and in baskets bright
Of wreathed silver: sumptuous they stand

---

3. Clasped shut and held like a prayer-book concealed from the sight of hostile, dark-skinned pagans (Muslims); "clasped" also suggests "arrested," with "pray" punning as "prey" (on), or persecute.
4. Alluding to Satan's entry into the Garden of Eden to corrupt Eve (*Paradise Lost*, bk. 9).
5. Sleep-inducing charm; Morpheus is the divine agent of sleep.
6. A Keats-coinage: smoother and more soothing.
7. All major places in the British trade in exotic goods, the luxuries of the feudal aristocracy: Fez in northern Morocco was a source of sugar; the ancient Persian city of Samarkand was famous for its silk markets, and Lebanon for its fine cedar timber.

In the retired quiet of the night,
275 Filling the chilly room with perfume light.—
     "And now, my love, my seraph° fair, awake!   *angel*
     Thou art my heaven, and I thine eremite:°   *hermit*
     Open thine eyes, for meek St. Agnes' sake,
Or I shall drowse beside thee, so my soul doth ache."

32

280 Thus whispering, his warm, unnerved° arm   *weak, unmanned*
     Sank in her pillow. Shaded was her dream
     By the dusk curtains:—'twas a midnight charm
     Impossible to melt as iced stream:
     The lustrous salvers° in the moonlight gleam: *trays*
285 Broad golden fringe upon the carpet lies:
     It seem'd he never, never could redeem
     From such a steadfast spell his lady's eyes;
So mus'd awhile, entoil'd in woofed° phantasies.   *woven*

33

     Awakening up, he took her hollow lute,—
290 Tumultuous,—and, in chords that tenderest be,
     He play'd an ancient ditty, long since mute,
     In Provence call'd, "La belle dame sans mercy":[8]
     Close to her ear touching the melody;—
     Wherewith disturb'd, she utter'd a soft moan:
295 He ceased—she panted quick—and suddenly
     Her blue affrayed° eyes wide open shone: *frightened*
Upon his knees he sank, pale as smooth-sculptured stone.

34

     Her eyes were open, but she still beheld,
     Now wide awake, the vision of her sleep:
300 There was a painful change, that nigh expell'd
     The blisses of her dream so pure and deep
     At which fair Madeline began to weep,
     And moan forth witless° words with many a sigh;   *uncomprehending*
     While still her gaze on Porphyro would keep;
305 Who knelt, with joined hands and piteous eye,
Fearing to move or speak, she look'd so dreamingly.

35

     "Ah, Porphyro!" said she, "but even now
     Thy voice was at sweet tremble in mine ear,
     Made tuneable with every sweetest vow;
310 And those sad eyes were spiritual and clear:
     How chang'd thou art! how pallid, chill, and drear!
     Give me that voice again, my Porphyro,
     Those looks immortal, those complainings° dear!   *laments*
     Oh leave me not in this eternal woe,
315 For if thou diest, my Love, I know not where to go."

---

8. Provence is a region of southern France famed for troubadours; in the poem by Alain Chartier (1424; translated by Chaucer), a lady earns this title for her determined refusal of a suitor. In a few months, Keats would write his own ballad of a lady "sans mercy"/"sans merci": see n. 1 to *La Belle Dame sans Mercy* (page 435).

36

Beyond a mortal man impassion'd far
At these voluptuous accents, he arose,
Ethereal, flush'd, and like a throbbing star
Seen mid the sapphire heaven's deep repose;
320 Into her dream he melted, as the rose
Blendeth its odour with the violet,[9]—
Solution° sweet: meantime the frost-wind blows   *fusion*
Like Love's alarum,° pattering the sharp sleet   *Cupid's warning*
Against the window-panes; St. Agnes' moon hath set.

37

325 'Tis dark: quick pattereth the flaw-blown° sleet: *storm-driven*
"This is no dream, my bride, my Madeline!"
'Tis dark: the iced gusts still rave and beat:
"No dream, alas! alas! and woe is mine!
Porphyro will leave me here to fade and pine.—
330 Cruel! what traitor could thee hither bring?
I curse not, for my heart is lost in thine,
Though thou forsakest a deceived thing;—
A dove forlorn and lost with sick unpruned° wing."   *bedraggled*

38

"My Madeline! sweet dreamer! lovely bride!
335 Say, may I be for aye° thy vassal blest?[1]   *ever*
Thy beauty's shield, heart-shaped and vermeil° dyed?   *vermillion*
Ah, silver shrine, here will I take my rest
After so many hours of toil and quest,
A famish'd pilgrim,—saved by miracle.
340 Though I have found, I will not rob thy nest
Saving of thy sweet self; if thou think'st well
To trust, fair Madeline, to no rude infidel.°   *unbeliever*

39

"Hark! 'tis an elfin-storm from faery land,
Of haggard° seeming, but a boon indeed: *wild, bewitched*
345 Arise—arise! the morning is at hand;—
The bloated wassaillers will never heed:—
Let us away, my love, with happy speed;
There are no ears to hear, or eyes to see,—
Drown'd all in Rhenish and the sleepy mead:°   *sweet wine*
350 Awake! arise! my love, and fearless be,
For o'er the southern moors I have a home for thee."

40

She hurried at his words, beset with fears,
For there were sleeping dragons all around,
At glaring watch, perhaps, with ready spears—
355 Down the wide stairs a darkling° way they found.—   *dark, in the dark*
In all the house was heard no human sound.
A chain-droop'd lamp was flickering by each door;

---

9. Keats's publishers refused his revision of 314–22, in which Porphyro's "arms encroaching slow . . . zon'd her, heart to heart" as he spoke into "her burning ear," and then "with her wild dream . . . mingled as a rose / Mar-

ryeth its odour to a violet."
1. Keats would tell Fanny Brawne (25 July 1819): "the very first week I knew you I wrote myself your vassal" (page 447). Vassal: devoted servant.

The arras,° rich with horseman, hawk, and hound,   *tapestry*
Flutter'd in the besieging wind's uproar;
360   And the long carpets rose along the gusty floor.

41

They glide, like phantoms, into the wide hall;
Like phantoms to the iron porch they glide;
Where lay the Porter,° in uneasy sprawl,   *gate-keeper*
With a huge empty flagon by his side:
365   The wakeful bloodhound rose, and shook his hide,
But his sagacious eye an inmate owns:[2]
By one, and one, the bolts full easy slide:—
The chains lie silent on the footworn stones;—
The key turns, and the door upon its hinges groans.

42

370   And they are gone: ay, ages long ago
These lovers fled away into the storm.
That night the Baron dreamt of many a woe,
And all his warrior-guests, with shade and form
Of witch, and demon, and large coffin-worm,
375   Were long be-nightmar'd. Angela the old
Died palsy-twitch'd, with meagre face deform;
The Beadsman, after thousand aves told,[3]
For aye unsought for slept among his ashes cold.

1819   1820

La Belle Dame sans Mercy[1]

Ah, what can ail thee, wretched wight,°   *fellow*
Alone and palely loitering;
The sedge° is wither'd from the lake,   *marsh grass*
And no birds sing.

5   Ah, what can ail thee wretched wight,
So haggard and so woe-begone?
The squirrel's granary is full,
And the harvest's done.

I see a lily on thy brow,
10   With anguish moist and fever dew;
And on thy cheeks a fading rose
Fast withereth too.[2]

---

2. Recognizes a resident (i.e., Madeline).
3. "Ave Maria" ("Hail Mary") prayers, part of the rosary ritual.
1. Published in Hunt's aesthetic (as opposed to political) journal, *The Indicator*; a version in a letter of April 1819, with slight differences in title ("La Belle Dame sans Merci") some words and stanza ordering, became, after it was first published in 1848, the preferred version, in part because it was shorn of association with Hunt. Our text is the version published in the Romantic era. The letter version, its French title taken from a medieval poem (see

Eve of St. Agnes 292), gives the lady both more agency and more remorse. "La Belle Dame" means "the beautiful lady"; "Merci" suggests "Mercy" but carries a sense of gracious obligation. Both words derive from the medieval French *merces*, price paid or wages, suggesting the economy of exchange (the granting of sexual favor in exchange for gifts and service) that courted women are expected to honor. Keats situates the "Belle Dame" of his literary ballad in a long literary tradition of "femmes fatales," temptresses whose seduction proves fatal.
2. Traditional emblems: the lily, death; the rose, love.

I met a Lady in the meads°³   *meadows*
     Full beautiful, a fairy's child;
15   Her hair was long, her foot was light,
     And her eyes were wild.

I set her on my pacing steed,⁴
     And nothing else saw all day long;
For sideways would she lean, and sing
20   A fairy's song.

I made a garland for her head,
     And bracelets too, and fragrant zone;°   *belt*
She look'd at me as° she did love,   *while, as if*
     And made sweet moan.

25   She found me roots of relish sweet,
     And honey wild, and manna dew;⁵
And sure in language strange she said,
     I love thee true.

She took me to her elfin grot,°   *grotto*
30   And there she gaz'd and sighèd deep,
And there I shut her wild sad eyes—
     So kiss'd to sleep.

And there she slumber'd on the moss,
     And there I dream'd, ah woe betide,
35   The latest° dream I ever dream'd   *last, most recent*
     On the cold hill side

I saw pale kings, and princes too,
     Pale warriors, death-pale were they all;
Who cry'd—"La belle Dame sans mercy
40   Hath thee in thrall!"°   *enslaved, enthralled*

I saw their starv'd lips in the gloom
     With horrid warning gapèd wide,
And I awoke, and found me here
     On the cold hill side.

45   And this is why I sojourn here
     Alone and palely loitering,
Though the sedge is wither'd from the lake,
     And no birds sing.

1819   1820

---

3. This stanza seems to begin the wretched wight's reply to his questioner, but the initial questioner may be continuing with his own story.
4. In the letter, this stanza was transposed with the next.
5. In Exodus 16, God feeds the Israelites in the wilderness with a miraculous dew that hardens into food called manna; the context here may recall lines Keats marked in *Paradise Lost* describing fallen angel Belial's sophistry: "all was false and hollow, though his Tongue / Dropt Manna" (2.112–13). See also *The Eve of St. Agnes*, line 268 (page 432).

Incipit Altera Sonneta[1]

I have been endeavouring to discover a better sonnet stanza than we have. The legitimate does not suit the language over-well from the pouncing rhymes—the other kind appears too elegaiac[2]—and the couplet at the end of it has seldom a pleasing effect—I do not pretend to have succeeded—it will explain itself—

    If by dull rhymes our English° must be chain'd,   *English language*
    And, like Andromeda,[3] the Sonnet sweet
    Fetter'd in spite of pained loveliness;
    Let us find out, if we must be constrain'd,
5   Sandals more interwoven & complete
    To fit the naked foot of Poesy;[4]
    Let us inspect the Lyre,[5] & weigh the stress
    Of every chord & see what may be gain'd
    By ear industrious & attention meet;°   *appropriate*
10 Misers of sound & syllable, no less
    Than Midas of his coinage,[6] let us be
    Jealous of dead leaves in the bay wreath Crown;[7]
    So if we may not let the Muse be free,
    She will be bound with Garlands of her own.

1819   1836; 1848

THE ODES OF 1819   In Keats's career of ode-writing (from *Ode to Apollo*, 1814, to *Ode to Fanny*, 1820), the remarkable group composed in a burst of inspiration between April and September 1819 is regarded as his highest achievement. The odes reflect personal, cultural, and political contexts of 1819, having to do with everything from the Elgin Marbles controversy, to the widespread use of opium as a painkiller, to social misery and political unrest, to Keats's grief over one brother's death and the other's emigration to America, to his nagging sensation that he was doomed to die young. Their language is enriched by literary allusion, as dense as it is casual, ranging through the Bible, Keats's earlier poetry and the hostile reviews of it, and favorite writers: Spenser, Shakespeare, Milton, Thomson, Collins, Chatterton, Coleridge, and Wordsworth. Even so, the odes also have an independent appeal that has made them, like Shakespeare's sonnets, general primers of the pleasure of reading poetry—of how verbal nuance and reverberation, and complex interplays of imagery, shape a dynamic process of thought. Nineteenth-century readers admired the beautiful phrases and sensuous language—the tactile, auditory, visual qualities, even sensations of smell and taste. Later readers have added an enthusiasm for the intellectual complexity and mental drama, variously described as a poetry of "internal debate," a structure of "paradox" and "contradiction," a "rhetoric of irony" or a poetics of "indeterminacy."

1. Latin: "Here begins another Sonnet"; Keats's heading for this poem in a letter, to his brothers (30 April 1819), containing this sonnet. Although every sonnet implicitly comments on sonnet tradition, Keats's *Incipit*, like Wordsworth's *Nuns fret not* and *Scorn not the sonnet* , is an explicit reading of the tradition and his relation to it. Keats had written more than 60 sonnets by this point (not counting ones embedded in longer poems), but he would write only a few more after. Several allusions to Ovid's *Metamorphoses* reflect his concern with formal transformation.
2. The Petrarchan ("legitimate") sonnet opens with "pouncing rhymes": *abbaabba*; the "other" kind, the Shakespearean sonnet, deploys three "elegaic" stanzas

(quatrains rhymed *abab; cdcd; efef*).
3. In Ovid's fable, beautiful Andromeda was fettered to a rock to be ravaged by a sea serpent; she was rescued by Perseus on his winged horse, Pegasus, an emblem of poetic inspiration.
4. Alluding to "poetic feet"—that is, meter.
5. The instrument of Apollo, god of poetry.
6. When Ovid's miserly king got his wish that everything he touched would turn to gold, he found he was unable to eat.
7. A head-wreath of bay laurel signifying poetic fame (hence, "poet laureate"); in *Metamorphoses*, when the nymph Daphne escapes Apollo's amorous pursuit by turning into a laurel, he takes the laurel as his emblem.

Keats once suggested that "a question is the best beacon toward a little speculation," and that knowledge was less a matter of "seeming sure points of Reasoning" than of "question and answer—a little pro and con." The key questions in his odes—"Was it a vision, or a waking dream?"; "What leaf-fringed legend haunts about thy shape . . . ?"; "Where are the songs of spring?"—are met less with answers than with pro and con: a poet's mind as a "rosy sanctuary" and a place of mere "shadowy thought"; a bird-song that evokes "full-throated ease" and "easeful death"; a world of art in which human figures are both "for ever young" and a "cold pastoral"; an intensity of "Beauty" that is always a "Beauty that must die"; a sensuous "indolence" that cannot stay "sheltered from annoy" of busy thoughts; an autumn that is inextricably a season of ripe fruition and of death.

Ode to a Nightingale[1]

1

My heart aches, and a drowsy numbness pains
    My sense, as though of hemlock I had drunk,
Or emptied some dull opiate to the drains
    One minute past, and Lethe-wards had sunk:[2]
5 'Tis not through envy of thy happy lot,
    But being too happy in thine happiness,—
      That thou, light-winged Dryad° of the trees,   *wood-nymph*
        In some melodious plot
    Of beechen green, and shadows numberless,
10   Singest of summer in full-throated ease.

2

O, for a draught of vintage!° that hath been   *wine*
    Cool'd a long age in the deep-delved earth,
Tasting of Flora and the country green,
    Dance, and Provençal song, and sunburnt mirth![3]
15 O for a beaker full of the warm South,
    Full of the true, the blushful Hippocrene,[4]
      With beaded bubbles winking at the brim,
        And purple-stained mouth;
    That I might drink, and leave the world unseen,[5]
20   And with thee fade away into the forest dim:

3

Fade far away, dissolve, and quite forget
    What thou among the leaves hast never known,
The weariness, the fever, and the fret
    Here, where men sit and hear each other groan;
25 Where palsy shakes a few, sad, last gray hairs,

---

1. First published in *Annals of the Fine Arts*, 1819. Keats's stanza incorporates sonnet elements: a Shakespearean quatrain (*abab*) followed by a Petrarchan sestet (*cdecde*), also the form of the ode on "Melancholy." The nightingale in literary tradition (including Milton, Wordsworth, Coleridge) often evokes Ovid's story of Philomela; see page 431, n. 8. Keats was also inspired by an actual nightingale's song at the house where he was living.

2. In small doses hemlock is a sedative; in large doses, such as Socrates', it is fatal; an opiate is any sense-duller, particularly opium, widely used as a painkiller; Lethe is the mythic river of the underworld whose waters produce forgetfulness of previous life.

3. Magician Merlin dwells "in a deep delve, farre from the view of day, / That of no living wight he mote be found" (*Faerie Queene* 3.3.7). Flora: Roman goddess of flowers; see *Sleep and Poetry* 102. Provence: region in southern France famed for troubadours.

4. The fountain of the muses on Mount Helicon.

5. "Unseen" can modify both "I" and "world."

Where youth grows pale, and spectre-thin, and dies;[6]
    Where but to think is to be full of sorrow
    And leaden-eyed despairs,
Where Beauty cannot keep her lustrous eyes,
30   Or new Love pine at them beyond to-morrow.

4

Away! away! for I will fly to thee,
    Not charioted by Bacchus and his pards,[7]
But on the viewless wings of Poesy,
    Though the dull brain perplexes and retards:
35 Already with thee! tender is the night,
    And haply° the Queen-Moon is on her throne,   *happily, perhaps*
      Cluster'd around by all her starry Fays;°   *fairies*
      But here there is no light,
    Save what from heaven is with the breezes blown
40   Through verdurous glooms and winding mossy ways.

5

I cannot see what flowers are at my feet,
    Nor what soft incense hangs upon the boughs,
But, in embalmed darkness, guess each sweet
    Wherewith the seasonable month endows
45 The grass, the thicket, and the fruit-tree wild;
    White hawthorn, and the pastoral eglantine;
      Fast fading violets cover'd up in leaves;
      And mid-May's eldest child,
    The coming musk-rose, full of dewy wine,
50   The murmurous haunt of flies on summer eves.[8]

6

Darkling° I listen; and, for many a time   *in the dark*
    I have been half in love with easeful Death,
Call'd him soft names in many a mused rhyme,
    To take into the air my quiet breath;
55 Now more than ever seems it rich to die,
    To cease upon the midnight with no pain,
      While thou art pouring forth thy soul abroad
      In such an ecstasy!
    Still wouldst thou sing, and I have ears in vain—
60   To thy high requiem° become a sod.   *funeral mass*

7

Thou wast not born for death, immortal Bird!
    No hungry generations tread thee down;
The voice I hear this passing night was heard

6. An echo of Wordsworth's memory in *Tintern Abbey* of himself in "darkness, and amid the many shapes / Of joyless day-light; when the fretful stir / Unprofitable, and the fever of the world, / Have hung upon the beatings of my heart" (52–55). Both Wordsworth and Keats recall Macbeth's envy of Duncan "in his grave; / After life's fitful fever he sleeps well" (*Macbeth* 3.322–323). Also echoed is Wordsworth's image of an ideal life "from diminution safe

and weakening age; / While man grows old, and dwindles, and decays" (*Excursion* 4.759–60).
7. Bacchus, god of wine and revelry, whose chariot is drawn by leopards.
8. This guessing of flowers echoes Oberon's description in *A Midsummer Night's Dream* of a verdant bank where one may find a snake-skin whose juices make a sleeper fall in love with whatever is first seen on waking (2.1.249–58).

rustic, peasant

In ancient days by emperor and clown:°
65   Perhaps the self-same song that found a path
  Through the sad heart of Ruth, when, sick for home,
    She stood in tears amid the alien corn;[9]
      The same that oft-times hath
  Charm'd magic casements, opening on the foam
70   Of perilous seas, in faery lands forlorn.

8

Forlorn! the very word is like a bell
  To toll me back from thee to my sole self!
Adieu! the fancy cannot cheat so well[1]
  As she is fam'd to do, deceiving elf.
75   Adieu! adieu! thy plaintive anthem fades
  Past the near meadows, over the still stream,
    Up the hill-side; and now 'tis buried deep
      In the next valley-glades:
  Was it a vision, or a waking dream?
  Fled is that music:—Do I wake or sleep?

Ode on a Grecian Urn[1]

1

Thou still unravish'd bride of quietness,
  Thou foster-child of silence and slow time,
Sylvan° historian, who canst thus express   woodland
  A flowery tale more sweetly than our rhyme:
5   What leaf-fring'd legend haunts about thy shape
  Of deities or mortals, or of both,
    In Tempe or the dales of Arcady?[2]
  What men or gods are these? What maidens loth?
What mad pursuit? What struggle to escape?
10   What pipes and timbrels?° What wild ecstasy?   tambourines

2

Heard melodies are sweet, but those unheard
  Are sweeter; therefore, ye soft pipes, play on;
Not to the sensual° ear, but, more endear'd,   physical

---

9. See Ruth 1–2: compelled by famine to leave her home, Ruth eked out a living as a gleaner in faraway fields.
1. The adieu echoes the opening line of Charlotte Smith's *On the Departure of the Nightingale* (1784), "Sweet poet of the woods!—a long adieu!" The closing question bears several echoes: *Psyche* 5–6; the opening of Spenser's *Amoretti* 77: "Was it a dreame, or did I see it playne?"; Hazlitt's remark that "Spenser was the poet of our waking dreams," his "music . . . lulling the senses into a deep oblivion of the jarring noises of the world from which we have no wish ever to be recalled" (*On Chaucer and Spenser*, 1818); a spellbound lover's confusion in *Midsummer Night's Dream*: "Are you sure / That we are awake? It seems to me / That yet we sleep, we dream" (4.1.194–96); Wordsworth's lament in the "Intimations" *Ode*, "Whith-

er is fled the visionary gleam? / Where is it now, the glory and the dream?" (56–57), and his phrase "waking dream" in *Yarrow Visited* (pub. 1815).
1. First published in *Annals of the Fine Arts*. Keats describes three scenes on an imaginary urn. The first is an image of revelry and sexual pursuit; the second (stanzas 2–3) is either a detail of this or another: a piper, and a lover in pursuit of a fair maid; in both, the story of Pan is implied. The third (stanza 4) is a sacrificial ritual, perhaps inspired by one of the Elgin Marble friezes.
2. A design of leaves frames a "legend" or caption on some vases; Tempe and Arcadia are districts of ancient Greece famed for beauty and serenity, where the gods often frolicked.

15   Pipe to the spirit ditties of no tone:
      Fair youth, beneath the trees, thou canst not leave
      Thy song, nor ever can those trees be bare;
      Bold Lover, never, never canst thou kiss,
      Though winning near the goal—yet, do not grieve;
      She cannot fade, though thou hast not thy bliss,
20   For ever wilt thou love, and she be fair!

                              3
      Ah, happy, happy° boughs! that cannot shed   *joyous, fortunate*
      Your leaves, nor ever bid the Spring adieu;
      And, happy melodist, unwearied,
      For ever piping songs for ever new;
25   More happy love! more happy, happy love!
      For ever warm and still to be enjoy'd,
          For ever panting, and for ever young;
      All breathing human passion far above,
      That leaves a heart high-sorrowful and cloy'd,
30   A burning forehead, and a parching tongue.

                              4
      Who are these coming to the sacrifice?
      To what green altar, O mysterious[3] priest,
      Lead'st thou that heifer lowing at the skies,
      And all her silken flanks with garlands drest?
35   What little town by river or sea shore,
          Or mountain-built with peaceful citadel,°   *fortress*
          Is emptied of this folk, this pious morn?
      And, little town, thy streets for evermore
          Will silent be; and not a soul to tell
40   Why thou art desolate, can e'er return.

                              5
      O Attic shape! Fair attitude!° with brede°   *pose / intricate design*
      Of marble men and maidens overwrought,[4]
      With forest branches and the trodden weed;
          Thou, silent form, dost tease us out of thought
45   As doth eternity: Cold Pastoral!
          When old age shall this generation waste,
          Thou shalt remain, in midst of other woe
      Than ours, a friend to man, to whom thou say'st,
          Beauty is truth, truth beauty,—that is all
50   Ye know on earth, and all ye need to know.[5]

---

3. "Unknown"; also denoting religious "mysteries" or rites.
4. The urn, made in Attica (where Athens is located), is "overwrought" (overlaid) with its design; Keats may be implying "over-elaborated," with a hint of psychological or emotional anguish in the frozen figures; thus "brede" puns on what cannot happen, "breed."
5. In the 1820 volume, but in no other draft, quotation marks are placed around "Beauty is truth, truth beauty." Keats ponders the relation between "beauty" and "truth" throughout his career.

Ode on Melancholy[1]

1

No, no, go not to Lethe,° neither twist   *river of forgetfulness*
  Wolf's-bane, tight-rooted, for its poisonous wine;
Nor suffer thy pale forehead to be kiss'd
  By nightshade, ruby grape of Proserpine;[2]
5 Make not your rosary of yew-berries,[3]
    Nor let the beetle, nor the death-moth be
      Your mournful Psyche,[4] nor the downy owl
A partner in your sorrow's mysteries;°   *secret rites*
  For shade to shade will come too drowsily,
10   And drown the wakeful anguish of the soul.

2

But when the melancholy fit shall fall
  Sudden from heaven like a weeping cloud,
That fosters the droop-headed flowers all,
  And hides the green hill in an April shroud;
15 Then glut thy sorrow on a morning rose,
    Or on the rainbow of the salt sand-wave,
      Or on the wealth of globed peonies;
Or if thy mistress some rich anger shows,
  Emprison her soft hand, and let her rave,
20   And feed deep, deep upon her peerless eyes.

3

She[5] dwells with Beauty—Beauty that must die;
  And Joy, whose hand is ever at his lips
Bidding adieu; and aching Pleasure nigh,
  Turning to poison while the bee-mouth sips:
25 Ay, in the very temple of Delight
    Veil'd Melancholy has her sovran shrine,
      Though seen of none save him whose strenuous tongue
Can burst Joy's grape against his palate fine;°   *sensitive, refined*
  His soul shall taste the sadness of her might,
30   And be among her cloudy trophies hung.

1. In May 1819, Keats paraphrased a couplet from Wordsworth's "Intimations" *Ode:* "Nothing can bring back the hour / Of splendour in the grass and glory in the flower" (cf. 177–78; page 288), commenting, "I once thought this a Melancholist's dream." "Melancholy" is a traditional term for "the blues," or even "black" moods; Hamlet is famously "The Melancholy Dane." Robert Burton's treatise, *Anatomy of Melancholy* (1621), which Keats studied, offers an elaborate medical analysis as well as an anthology of notable remarks. Taking a stock subject for poets in the 18th century, Keats prizes melancholy as a sensibility that accepts, even relishes, evanescence. He originally began the ode with a macabre, mock-heroic stanza about the quest for the goddess Melancholy: "Though you should build a bark of dead men's bones, / And rear a phantom gibbet for a mast, / Stitch creeds together for a sail, with groans / To fill it out, blood-stained and aghast; / Although your rudder be a Dragon's tail, / Long sever'd, yet still hard with agony, / Your cordage large uprootings from the skull / Of bald Medusa: certes you would fail / To find the Melancholy, whether she / Dreameth in any isle of Lethe dull . . ."
2. Wolfsbane and nightshade are poisons; Proserpine was abducted to the underworld by its ruler, Hades, but an appeal by her mother Ceres (goddess of grain) allowed her an annual sojourn in the upper world from spring to fall—a fable of seasonal flux relevant to the aesthetic of Melancholy.
3. Yew is an emblem of death; rosary: prayer beads.
4. In Greek, "psyche" means both "soul" and "butterfly" (its emblem); the markings on the death's-head moth resemble a human skull; the beetle may be the scarab, a jewel-bug placed in tombs by the ancient Egyptians as a portent of resurrection.
5. A double reference, to the mistress and to the goddess Melancholy.

To Autumn[1]

1

Season of mists and mellow fruitfulness,
    Close bosom-friend of the maturing sun;
Conspiring with him how to load and bless
    With fruit the vines that round the thatch-eaves[2] run;
5   To bend with apples the moss'd cottage-trees,
    And fill all fruit with ripeness to the core;
        To swell the gourd, and plump the hazel shells
With a sweet kernel; to set budding more,
    And still more, later flowers for the bees,
10   Until they think warm days will never cease,
        For Summer has o'er-brimm'd their clammy cells.

2

Who hath not seen thee oft amid thy store?
    Sometimes whoever seeks abroad may find
Thee sitting careless on a granary floor,
15   Thy hair soft-lifted by the winnowing wind;
Or on a half-reap'd furrow sound asleep,
    Drows'd with the fume of poppies, while thy hook°   *scythe*
        Spares the next swath and all its twined flowers:
And sometimes like a gleaner thou dost keep
20   Steady thy laden head across a brook;
    Or by a cyder-press, with patient look,
        Thou watchest the last oozings hours by hours.

3

Where are the songs of Spring? Ay, where are they?[3]
    Think not of them, thou hast thy music too,—
25   While barred clouds bloom the soft-dying day,
    And touch the stubble-plains with rosy hue;
Then in a wailful choir the small gnats mourn
    Among the river sallows,[4] borne aloft
        Or sinking as the light wind lives or dies;
30   And full-grown lambs loud bleat from hilly bourn;°   *boundary, region*
    Hedge-crickets sing; and now with treble soft°   *faint high pitch*
    The red-breast whistles from a garden-croft;°   *enclosure*
        And gathering swallows twitter in the skies.

1. Composed 19–21 September 1819 in Winchester, a tranquil town in southern England, from which Keats wrote to a friend: "How beautiful the season is now— How fine the air. A temperate sharpness about it. . . . I never lik'd stubble fields so much as now—Aye better than the chilly green of the spring. Somehow a stubble plain looks warm—in the same way that some pictures look warm—this struck me so much in my sunday's walk that I composed upon it." The ode evokes two competing but related senses of autumn: the social context of harvest bounty; and the symbolic association with death— the reaper as grim reaper, autumn as the presage of winter (see Shakespeare's Sonnet 73, "That time of year thou may'st in me behold"). Among other poems echoed are Thomson's *Autumn* in *The Seasons* (1740) and the last stanza of Coleridge's *Frost at Midnight*.
2. The eaves of thatched cottage roofs.
3. A sounding of the "Ubi sunt" trope ("where are they now?"), which traditionally prefaces a nostalgic lament for lost worlds, the implied answer being "gone"; cf. Wordsworth's version at the end of stanza 4 of the "Intimations" *Ode* (page 285).
4. Willows (an emblem of death).

This living hand[1]

This living hand, now warm and capable
Of earnest grasping, would, if it were cold
and in the icy silence of the tomb,
So haunt thy days and chill thy dreaming nights
5 That thou would wish thine own hea[r]t[2] dry of blood
So in my veins red life might stream again,
and thou be conscience-calm'd—see here it is—
I hold it towards you—

c. 1819   1898

Bright Star[1]

Bright Star, would I were stedfast as thou art—
   Not in lone splendor hung aloft the night,
And watching, with eternal lids apart,
   Like nature's patient, sleepless Eremite,°   *hermit*
5 The moving waters at their priestlike task
   Of pure ablution° round earth's human shores,   *ritual washing*
Or gazing on the new soft-fallen masque[2]
   Of snow upon the mountains and the moors—
No—yet still stedfast, still unchangeable
10   Pillow'd upon my fair love's ripening breast,
To feel for ever its soft swell and fall.
   Awake for ever in a sweet unrest,
Still, still to hear her tender-taken breath,
And so live ever—or else swoon to death—

1820   1838

<hr>

LETTERS[1]
To George and Thomas Keats[2]
["INTENSITY" AND "NEGATIVE CAPABILITY"]

My dear Brothers   December 181[7]

[21 Dec.] * * * I saw Kean return to the public in Richard III,[3] & finely he did it. * * *
Hone the publisher's trial, you must find very amusing; & as Englishmen very encouraging—his <u>Not Guilty</u> is a thing, which not to have been, would have dulled still more

<hr>

1. A mysterious fragment, context unknown; "hand" is also a term for "handwriting": for the relation of these two senses, see *Fall of Hyperion* 1.16–18.
2. Keats inserted "heat" as superscript between "thine" and "own"; his characteristic dropping of "r" in handwriting makes it possible that he meant "heart," which best fits the context (although "heat" is relevant).
1. In summer 1818, Keats remarked that the scenery of the lake country "refine[s] one's sensual vision into a sort of north star which can never cease to be open lidded and stedfast over the wonders of the great Power"; sometime before summer 1819, he drafted this sonnet, then wrote this revised version in early autumn 1820 into the volume of Shakespeare's poems he took to Italy; perhaps the last poetry he wrote, its title in 19th-century editions was "Keats's last sonnet." The opening recalls the heroic self-description of Julius Caesar: "I could be well moved . . .

but I am constant as the Northern Star, / Of whose true-fixed and resting quality / There is no fellow in the firmament" (*Julius Caesar* 3.1.58–62).
2. Punning on "mask," the word used in the 1819 draft.
1. In order to convey the character of Keats's letter-writing, idiosyncrasies of spelling, punctuation, and capitalization are for the most part preserved. Our insertions for clarity appear in square brackets [ ].
2. The brothers had lived together since 1816; George (1797–1841) had taken Tom to Teignmouth, Devonshire, for his health.
3. Edmund Kean (1787–1833), charismatic and scandal-ridden actor who revolutionized the Shakespearean stage with his passionate performances. Richard III was one of his celebrated roles; Keats had just published an article on him in *The Champion*.

Liberty's Emblazoning—Lord Ellenborough has been paid in his own coin—Wooler & Hone have done us an essential service[4]—I spent Friday evening with Wells & went the next morning to see <u>Death on the Pale horse.</u>[5] It is a wonderful picture, when West's age is considered; But there is nothing to be intense upon; no women one feels mad to kiss; no face swelling into reality. the excellence of every Art is its intensity, capable of making all disagreeables evaporate, from their being in close relationship with Beauty & Truth—Examine King Lear[6] & you will find this examplified throughout; but in this picture we have unpleasantness without any momentous depth of speculation excited, in which to bury its repulsiveness. * * * [?27 Dec.] * * * I had not a dispute but a disquisition with Dilke, on various subjects;[7] several things dovetailed in my mind, & at once it struck me, what quality went to form a Man of Achievement especially in Literature & which Shakespeare posessed so enormously—I mean <u>Negative Capability</u>, that is when man is capable of being in uncertainties, Mysteries, doubts, without any irritable reaching after fact & reason[8]—Coleridge, for instance, would let go by a fine isolated verisimilitude caught from the Penetralium of mystery, from being incapable of remaining content with half knowledge.[9] This pursued through Volumes would perhaps take us no further than this, that with a great poet the sense of Beauty overcomes every other consideration, or rather obliterates all consideration.

Shelley's poem is out & there are words about its being objected too, as much as Queen Mab was. Poor Shelley I think he has his Quota of good qualities, in sooth la!![1] Write soon to your most sincere friend & affectionate Brother

John

To Richard Woodhouse[2]

[THE "CAMELION POET" VS. THE "EGOTISTICAL SUBLIME"]

My dear Woodhouse,   27 October 1818

Your Letter gave me a great satisfaction; more on account of its friendliness, than any relish of that matter in it which is accounted so acceptable in the 'genus irritabile'[3] The best answer I can give you is in a clerklike manner to make some observations on

---

4. Two notorious prosecutions. William Hone had just been found not guilty on three counts of blasphemous libel for his parodies of the liturgy, of which nearly 100,000 copies had sold. A conservative Lord Chief Justice Ellenborough, who had earlier sentenced John and Leigh Hunt for libel, presided at two of his trials and was humiliated by the loudly applauded verdict. Thomas Wooler, politician, journalist, and editor of the radical weekly *The Black Dwarf*, was acquitted on similar charges the previous June. The trials were well attended and extremely amusing because the "offenses" had to be read into the record, thus gaining audience not only in the courtroom but also in reports in the "legitimate" press.
5. Wells was a schoolmate of Tom; *Death on a Pale Horse*, by American painter Benjamin West, is based on the image in Revelation of the fourth horseman of the apocalypse.
6. West's painting of the storm scene in the play, not the play itself.
7. Disquisition: legalese for formal inquiry. Charles Dilke (1789–1864), government worker and amateur scholar, was a new friend.
8. "Negative Capability," Keats's most famous formulation, is a self-conscious oxymoron, wittily defined by its refrain from positing certainties of "fact & reason"; compare

Keats's antipathy to egotistical assertions of "certain philosophy," "resting places and seeming sure points of Reasoning" (letters to Reynolds, 3 February and 3 May 1818).
9. In 1817, Coleridge published *Biographia Literaria* and *The Rime of the Ancient Mariner* with an explanatory marginal gloss. "Penetralium" is Keats's faux-Latin singular of "penetralia," the inmost chamber of a temple.
1. Shelley was forced to withdraw *Laon and Cythna* (1817), an epic featuring the incestuous love of its sibling hero and heroine; the outcry was as heated as that against *Queen Mab* (1813), a visionary political epic attacking "Kingcraft, Priestcraft, and Statecraft." Keats's "sooth la!" ("the truth!") echoes Cleopatra as she tries, ineptly, to help Antony put on his armor after their night of debauchery (*Antony and Cleopatra* 4.4.8).
2. Legal and literary adviser to Keats's second publishers, Woodhouse adored Keats and assiduously preserved or transcribed his letters, manuscripts, and proof-sheets, as well as collected anecdotes. This is one of Keats's most famous letters, written after a summer of negative reviews in highly visible journals.
3. Horace's term for poets, "the irritable tribe" (*Epistles* 2.2.102).

two principle points, which seem to point like indices into the midst of the whole pro and con, about genius, and views and achievements and ambition and cœtera. 1ˢᵗ As to the poetical Character itself, (I mean that sort of which, if I am any thing, I am a Member; that sort distinguished from the wordsworthian or egotistical sublime;[4] which is a thing per se and stands alone[5]) it is not itself—it has no self—it is every thing and nothing—It has no character—it enjoys light and shade; it lives in gusto, be it foul or fair, high or low, rich or poor, mean or elevated—It has as much delight in conceiving an Iago as an Imogen.[6] What shocks the virtuous philosop[h]er, delights the camelion[7] Poet. It does no harm from its relish of the dark side of things any more than from its taste for the bright one; because they both end in speculation. A Poet is the most unpoetical of any thing in existence; because he has no Identity—he is continually in for[ming?]—and filling some other Body—The Sun, the Moon, the Sea and Men and Women who are creatures of impulse are poetical and have about them an unchangeable attribute—the poet has none; no identity—he is certainly the most unpoetical of all God's Creatures. If then he has no self, and if I am a Poet, where is the Wonder that I should say I would ~~right~~ write no more? Might I not at that very instant [have] been cogitating on the Characters of saturn and Ops?[8] It is a wretched thing to confess; but is a very fact that not one word I ever utter can be taken for granted as an opinion growing out of my identical nature—how can it, when I have no nature? When I am in a room with People if I ever am free from speculating on creations of my own brain, then not myself goes home to myself: but the identity of every one in the room begins to press upon me that, I am in a very little time an[ni]hilated—not only among Men; it would be the same in a Nursery of children: I know not whether I make myself wholly understood: I hope enough so to let you see that no dependence is to be placed on what I said that day.

In the second place I will speak of my views, and of the life I purpose to myself—I am ambitious of doing the world some good: if I should be spared that may be the work of maturer years—in the interval I will assay to reach to as high a summit in Poetry as the nerve bestowed upon me will suffer. The faint conceptions I have of Poems to come brings the blood frequently into my forehead—All I hope is that I may not lose all interest in human affairs—that the solitary indifference I feel for applause even from the finest Spirits, will not blunt any acuteness of vision I may have. I do not think it will—I feel assured I should write from the mere yearning and fondness I have for the Beautiful even if my night's labours should be burnt every morning and no eye ever shine upon them. But even now I am perhaps not speaking from myself; but from some character in whose soul I now live. I am sure however that this next sentence is from myself. I feel your anxiety, good opinion and friendliness in the highest degree, and am

Your's most sincerely

John Keats

4. "Character" means not only a poet's personality but also the degree to which his identity, biases, philosophy, etc. are visible in his work. In Keats's day, Shakespeare was admired, by Coleridge and others, for the invisibility of this "character"; in an influential lecture of 1818 (attended by Keats), Hazlitt called Shakespeare "the least of an egotist that it was possible to be. He was nothing in himself; but . . . all that others were." Milton and Wordsworth were typically summoned for contrast, as poets of egotism.
5. A foolish soldier in Shakespeare's Troilus and Cressida is described as "a very man per se" who "stands alone"

(1.2.15–16).
6. Iago is the scheming villain of Othello; Imogen is the virtuous heroine of Cymbeline.
7. Chameleon, a creature able to change color according to circumstance.
8. Keats had remarked to Woodhouse that he felt preempted by the great poets of the past. In Greek mythology, Saturn is the king of the Titan gods and Ops a harvest goddess; cast out of heaven by the revolt of their children, the fallen Titans focus the major part of the poem Keats was working on during these months, Hyperion.

To Fanny Brawne[9]
["YOU TAKE POSSESSION OF ME"]

My sweet Girl,   25 July 1819 Sunday Night.

    I hope you did not blame me much for not obeying your request of a Letter on Saturday: we have had four in our small room playing at cards night and morning leaving me no undisturb'd opportunity to write. [. . .] Brown to my sorrow confirms the account you give of your ill health. You cannot conceive how I ache to be with you: how I would die for one hour—for what is in the world? I say you cannot conceive; it is impossible you should look with such eyes upon me as I have upon you: it cannot be. Forgive me if I wander a little this evening, for I have been all day employ'd in a very abstr[a]ct Poem[1] and I am in deep love with you—two things which must excuse me. I have, believe me, not been an age in letting you take possession of me; the very first week I knew you I wrote myself your vassal; but burnt the Letter as the very next time I saw you I thought you manifested some dislike to me. If you should ever feel for Man at the first sight what I did for you, I am lost. Yet I should not quarrel with you, but hate myself if such a thing were to happen—only I should burst if the thing were not as fine as a Man as you are as a Woman. Perhaps I am too vehement, then fancy me on my knees, especially when I mention a part of you Letter which hurt me; you say speaking of Mr Severn[2] "but you must be satisfied in knowing that I admired you much more than your friend." My dear love, I cannot believe there ever was or ever could be any thing to admire in me especially as far as sight goes—I cannot be admired, I am not a thing to be admired. You are, I love you; all I can bring you is a swooning admiration of your Beauty. I hold that place among Men which snub-nos'd brunettes with meeting eyebrows do among women—they are trash to me—unless I should find one among them with a fire in her heart like the one that burns in mine. You absorb me in spite of myself—you alone: for I look not forward with any pleasure to what is call'd being settled in the world; I tremble at domestic cares—yet for you I would meet them, though if it would leave you the happier I would rather die than do so. I have two luxuries to brood over in my walks, your Loveliness and the hour of my death. O that I could have possession of them both in the same minute.[3] I hate the world: it batters too much the wings of my self-will, and would I could take a sweet poison from your lips to send me out of it. From no others would I take it. I am indeed astonish'd to find myself so careless of all cha[r]ms but yours—rememb[e]ring as I do the time when even a bit of ribband was a matter of interest with me. What softer words can I find for you after this—what it is I will not read. Nor will I say more here, but in a Postscript answer any thing else you may have mentioned in your Letter in so many words—for I am distracted with a thousand thoughts. I will imagine you Venus tonight and pray, pray, pray to your star like a Hethen.

Your's ever, fair Star,

John Keats.

To Percy Bysshe Shelley

["An Artist Must Serve Mammon"]

My dear Shelley,   16 August 1820

I am very much gratified that you, in a foreign country, and with a mind almost over occupied, should write to me in the strain of the Letter beside me. If I do not take advantage of your invitation it will be prevented by a circumstance I have very much at heart to prophesy.[4] There is no doubt that an english winter would put an end to me, and do so in a lingering hateful manner, therefore I must either voyage or journey to Italy as a soldier marches up to a battery. My nerves at present are the worst part of me, yet they feel soothed when I think that come what extreme may, I shall not be destined to remain in one spot long enough to take a hatred of any four particular bed-posts. I am glad you take any pleasure in my poor Poem;[5]—which I would willingly take the trouble to unwrite, if possible, did I care so much as I have done about Reputation. I received a copy of the Cenci, as from yourself from Hunt. There is only one part of it I am judge of; the Poetry, and dramatic effect, which by many spirits now a days is considered the mammon.[6] A modern work it is said must have a purpose, which may be the God—an artist must serve Mammon—he must have "self concentration" selfishness perhaps. You I am sure will forgive me for sincerely remarking that you might curb your magnanimity and be more of an artist, and "load every rift" of your subject with ore.[7] The thought of such discipline must fall like cold chains upon you, who perhaps never sat with your wings furl'd for six Months together. And is not this extraordina[r]ly talk for the writer of Endymion? whose mind was like a pack of scattered cards—I am pick'd up and sorted to a pip.[8] My Imagination is a Monastry and I am its Monk—you must explain my [metaphysics] to yourself. I am in expectation of Prometheus[9] every day. Could I have my own wish for its interest effected you would have it still in manuscript—or be but now putting an end to the second act. I remember you advising me not to publish my first-blights, on Hampstead heath[1]—I am returning advice upon your hands. Most of the Poems in the volume I send you have been written above two years, and would never have been publish'd but from a hope of gain;[2] so you see I am inclined enough to take your advice now. I must exp[r]ess once more my deep sense of your kindness, adding my sincere thanks and respects for Mrs Shelley. In the hope of soon seeing you I remain

most sincerely yours,

John Keats—

---

4. Learning of Keats's grave ill health from Hunt, Shelley offered him hospitality in the warmer climate of Italy; Keats accepted the invitation, first going to Rome, where he died.
5. Sympathetic to the sting of negative reviews, Shelley had written some encouraging remarks about Endymion.
6. The false idol of money and worldly goods, against whom Jesus cautions, "Ye cannot serve God and mammon" (Matthew 6.24). In the Preface of The Cenci (1820), a tragedy of incestuous rape, tyranny, and parricide, Shelley proffered a moral judgment of its heroine Beatrice Cenci.

7. From the ceiling of the Palace of Mammon in Spenser's Faerie Queene hang stalactites "Embost with massy gold of glorious gift, / And with rich metall loaded every rift, / That heavy ruine they did seeme to threat" (2.7.28).
8. Arranged in order; pips are marks on playing cards.
9. Shelley's drama, Prometheus Unbound, just published.
1. Many of the pieces in Keats's 1817 Poems took inspiration from the landscape of Hampstead Heath; Keats met Shelley through Hunt, who lived there.
2. The 1820 volume; Keats was eager for financial "gain" as a requisite for marriage to Fanny Brawne.

To Charles Brown[3]
[KEATS'S LAST LETTER]

My dear Brown,   Rome. 30 November 1820.

'Tis the most difficult thing in the world to me to write a letter. My stomach continues so bad, that I feel it worse on opening any book,—yet I am much better than I
was in Quarantine.[4] Then I am afraid to encounter the proing and conning of any
thing interesting to me in England. I have an habitual feeling of my real life having
past, and that I am leading a posthumous existence. God knows how it would have
been—but it appears to me—however, I will not speak of that subject. I must have
been at Bedhampton nearly at the time you were writing to me from Chichester—
how unfortunate—and to pass on the river too![5] There was my star predominant! I
cannot answer any thing in your letter, which followed me from Naples to Rome,
because I am afraid to look it over again. I am so weak (in mind) that I cannot bear
the sight of any hand writing of a friend I love so much as I do you. Yet I ride the little horse,[6]—and, at my worst, even in Quarantine, summoned up more puns, in a sort
of desperation, in one week than in any year of my life. There is one thought enough
to kill me—I have been well, healthy, alert &c, walking with her[7]—and now—the
knowledge of contrast, feeling for light and shade, all that information (primitive
sense) necessary for a poem are great enemies to the recovery of the stomach. There,
you rogue, I put you to the torture,—but you must bring your philosophy to bear—as
I do mine, really—or how should I be able to live? Dr Clarke is very attentive to me;
he says, there is very little the matter with my lungs, but my stomach, he says, is very
bad. I am well disappointed in hearing good news from George,—for it runs in my
head we shall all die young.[8] I have not written to x x x x x yet, which he must think
very neglectful; being anxious to send him a good account of my health, I have
delayed it from week to week. If I recover, I will do all in my power to correct the
mistakes made during sickness; and if I should not, all my faults will be forgiven. I
shall write to x x x to-morrow, or next day. I will write to x x x x x in the middle of
next week. Severn is very well, though he leads so dull a life with me. Remember me
to all friends, and tell x x x x I should not have left London without taking leave of
him, but from being so low in body and mind. Write to George as soon as you receive
this, and tell him how I am, as far as you can guess;—and also a note to my sister—
who walks about my imagination like a ghost—she is so like Tom. I can scarcely bid
you good bye even in a letter. I always made an awkward bow.

God bless you!
John Keats.

---

3. Charles Brown (1787–1842), a man of various literary
and amorous pursuits, was a close friend, traveling companion, and housemate. He cared assiduously for Keats
after his first major hemorrhage in February 1820, but left
for his usual summer vacation in May. Keats's earnest
wish was for Brown to accompany him to Italy, but he
could not be located.
4. The ship on which Keats sailed was held for quarantine
outside Naples, in oppressive summer weather.

5. The towns are near Portsmouth harbor, from which
Keats would sail.
6. Recommended by Keats's doctor in Rome as exercise.
7. Fanny Brawne; Brown deleted her name, as well as
those of Keats's friends, when he included the letter in a
biography of Keats.
8. Tom died at 19, George lived to his mid-forties, and
the youngest, Fanny, lived into her eighties.

Gustave Doré, *Ludgate Hill*, from *London: A Pilgrimage,* 1872.

The Victorian Age

✦ᘰ◈ᘰ✦

1832–1901

> Never since the beginning of Time was there, that we hear or read
> of, so intensely self-conscious a Society. Our whole relations to the
> Universe and to our fellow-man have become an Inquiry, a Doubt.
>
> —*Thomas Carlyle, 1831*

Nothing characterizes Victorian society so much as its quest for self-definition. The
sixty-three years of Victoria's reign were marked by momentous and intimidating
social changes, startling inventions, prodigious energies; the rapid succession of
events produced wild prosperity and unthinkable poverty, humane reforms and flagrant exploitation, immense ambitions and devastating doubts. Between 1800 and
1850 the population doubled from nine to eighteen million, and Britain became the
richest country on earth, the first urban industrial society in history. For some, it
was a period of great achievement, deep faith, indisputable progress. For others, it
was "an age of destruction," religious collapse, vicious profiteering. To almost everyone it was apparent that, as Sir Henry Holland put it in 1858, "we are living in *an
age of transition.*"

But what Matthew Arnold called the "multitudinousness" of British culture
overwhelmed all efforts to give the era a collective identity or a clear sense of purpose. Dazzled and dazed by their steam-powered printing presses, their railways and
telegraphs, journalism and junk mail, Victorians suffered from both future shock and
the information explosion. For the first time a nation had become self-consciously
modern: people were sure only of their differences from previous generations, certain
only that traditional ways of life were fast being transformed into something perilous-
ly unstable and astonishingly new. As the novelist William Makepeace Thackeray
noted, "We are of the time of chivalry. . . . We are of the age of steam."

VICTORIA AND THE VICTORIANS

In an unpredictable, tumultuous era, the stern, staid figure of Queen Victoria came to
represent stability and continuity. The adjective "Victorian" was first used in 1851 to
celebrate the nation's mounting pride in its institutions and commercial success.
That year, the global predominance of British industry had emerged incontestably at
the original "world's fair" in London, the "Great Exhibition of the Works of Industry
of All Nations," which Prince Albert helped organize. Arrayed for the world to see in
a vast "Crystal Palace" of iron and glass, the marvels of British manufacture achieved
a regal stature of their own and cast their allure upon the monarchy in turn. In the
congratulatory rhetoric that surrounded the event, the conservative, retiring queen
emerged as the durable symbol of her dynamic, aggressively businesslike realm.

Sunlight Soap advertisement commemorating the 1897 Jubilee of Victoria's reign.

In succeeding decades, the official portraits of Queen Victoria, gradually aging, reflected her country's sense of its own maturation as a society and world power. Etched by conflict with her prime ministers, the birth of nine children, and the early death of her beloved Prince Albert, Victoria's once pretty face became deeply lined and heavily jowled. Represented as a fairy-tale teenaged queen at her coronation in 1837, she radiated a youthful enthusiasm that corresponded to the optimism of the earlier 1830s. It seemed a decade of new beginnings. Settling into the role of fertile matron-monarch, she offered a domestic image to match the booming productivity of the 1850s. Reclusive after Albert died in 1861, she eventually took on the austere role of the black-satined Empress of India, projecting a world-weary glumness that lent gravity to the imperial heyday of the 1870s. Finally, as the aged, venerated Widow of Windsor, she became a universal icon, prompting the nostalgic worldwide spectacles of the Golden and Diamond Jubilees in 1887 and 1897. When Victoria died in 1901, after the longest reign in English history, a newspaper wrote: "Few of us, perhaps, have realized till now how large a part she had in the life of everyone of us; how the thread of her life [bound] the warp of the nation's progress."

During the seven decades of her rule, Victoria's calm profile, stamped on currency and displayed in offices and outposts from London to Bombay, presided over the expansion of Britain into the world's greatest empire. Economically and politically, Britannia ruled not only the waves but more than a quarter of the globe's landmass. Among its domains were Canada, Australia, New Zealand, South Africa, the Indian subcontinent and Ceylon, Malaya, Hong Kong, Singapore, Burma, Jamaica, Trinidad,

British Guiana, Bermuda, the Bahamas, Rhodesia, Kenya, Uganda, and Nigeria. By the 1890s one out of every four people on earth was a "subject" of Queen Victoria.

Victoria stood not only for England and Empire, but also for Duty, Family, and, especially, Propriety. "We have come to regard the Crown as the head of our morality" wrote the historian Walter Bagehot. As a description of behavior, "Victorian" signifies social conduct governed by strict rules, formal manners, and rigidly defined gender roles. Relations between the sexes were hedged about with sexual prudery and an intense concern for maintaining the appearance of propriety in public, whatever the private facts. But although she was presented as the ultimate role model, Victoria herself could not escape the contradictions of her era. The most powerful woman on earth, she denounced "this mad, wicked folly of Women's Rights." Her quiet reserve restored the dignity of the monarchy after the rakish ways of George IV, but she allowed advertisers to trade shamelessly on her image and product endorsements. Her face was universally known, featured on everything from postage stamps to tea trays, yet after Albert's death she lived in seclusion, rarely seeing either her ministers or the public. An icon of motherhood, she detested pregnancy, childbirth, and babies. As an emblem of Britain's greatness, Queen Victoria gave her subjects the public identity and purpose that privately they—and she, in her diaries—recognized as an unfulfilled ideal.

The Victorians have left us a contradictory picture of themselves. On the one hand, they were phenomenally energetic, dedicated to the Gospel of Work and driven by a solemn sense of duty to the Public Good. Popular authors like Dickens and Trollope churned out three-volume novels, engaged in numerous philanthropic projects, devoured twelve-course dinners, took twenty-mile walks, and produced a voluminous correspondence. Explorers and missionaries such as Burton, Speke, Stanley, and Livingston took enormous risks to map uncharted territory or spread Christianity "in darkest Africa." Although an invalid, Florence Nightingale revamped the entire British military medical and supply system from her bedroom office. All this activity was sustained by belief in its implicit moral benefit. In matters of character Victorians prized respectability, earnestness, a sense of duty and public service; most would have regarded an industrious, pious conventionality as the best road not only to material recompense but to heavenly rewards as well.

Yet the fabled self-confidence of this overachieving society often rings hollow. Their literature conveys an uneasy sense that their obsession with work was in part a deliberate distraction, as if Victorians were discharging public responsibilities in order to ease nagging doubts about their religious faith, about changing gender roles, about the moral quandaries of class privilege and imperial rule. Much of the era's social conservatism, such as its resistance to women's rights and to class mobility, may be traced to the fear of change. They struggled to dominate the present moment in order to keep an uncertain future at bay. Few questioned that tremendous advances were taking place in science, public health, transportation, and the general standard of living, but each new idea or discovery seemed to have unexpected, distressing repercussions.

The critic J. A. Froude remarked in 1841 that "the very truths which have come forth have produced doubts . . . this dazzle has too often ended in darkness." Discoveries in geology, biology, and textual scholarship shattered belief in the literal truth of the Bible. The Industrial Revolution shifted power from the landed aristocracy toward an insecure, expanding middle class of businessmen and professionals, impoverishing millions of once rural laborers along the way. Strident, riotous campaigns to extend voting rights to males of the middle and working classes produced fears of armed insurrection. Coupled with the agitations for and against trade unions, women's equality, socialism, and the separation of church and state, the fitful transformation of Britain's political and economic structure often teetered on the brink of open class warfare. In the national clamor for reform, every sector of the population fought for its privileges and feared for its rights. The following pages introduce the Victorian period by looking at several key issues: the era's energy and invention, its doubts about religion and industrialism, its far-reaching social reforms, its conflicted fascination with Empire, the commercialization and expansion of the reading public, and the period's vigorous self-scrutiny in the mirror of literature.

THE AGE OF ENERGY AND INVENTION

The most salient characteristic of life in this latter portion of the 19th century is its SPEED.

—W. R. Greg, Life at High Pressure, 1875

The "newness" of Victorian society—its speed, progress, and triumphant ingenuity— was epitomized by the coming of the railway. Until the 1830s, the fastest ways to travel or transport goods were still the most ancient ones, by sail or horse. But on seeing the first train pass through the Rugby countryside in 1839, Thomas Arnold astutely remarked: "Feudality is gone forever." The earliest passenger railway line opened in 1830 between Liverpool and Manchester; by 1855, eight thousand miles of track had been laid. Speeds of fifty miles per hour were soon routine; the journey from London to Edinburgh that had taken two weeks in 1800 now took less than a day.

Carrying passengers, freight, newspapers, and mail, the railways helped create a national consciousness by linking once remote parts of the country into a single economy and culture. Networks of information, distribution, and services moved news, goods, and people from one end of Britain to the other to the rhythm of the railway timetable. The accelerating pace of life that railways introduced became one of the defining features of the age.

Moreover, the railway irrevocably altered the face of the landscape. Its bridges, tunnels, cuttings, crossings, viaducts, and embankments permanently scarred a rural landscape whose fields, hedgerows, and highways were rooted deep in history. In the cities, engineers and entrepreneurs carved room for vast railyards and stations by demolishing populous districts. Discharging commodities and crowds, the railways transformed town centers everywhere, bolstering local economies and stimulating construction as they arrived, but depriving once thriving coaching inns and former mail routes of traffic and trade. Underground trains restructured the experience of travel within the city as well: the world's first subway line opened in 1863 in London; a complete inner London system was operating by 1884. Finally, railway-sponsored mass tourism eroded the regional distinctiveness and insularity of individual places. The inventor of the organized excursion, Thomas Cook, saw his advertising slogan, "RAILWAYS FOR THE MILLIONS," turned into a simple statement of fact.

Optimistic social prophets envisioned all classes reaping the fruits of the Industrial Revolution. The widespread Victorian belief in Progress was sustained by many factors, including rising incomes, the greater availability of goods, the perception of surplus production, and the leading role of Britain in world affairs. Many people were

Robert Howlett, *Portrait of Isambard Kingdom Brunel and Launching Chains of the Great Eastern,* 1857. Howlett's interest in contemporary subjects, ranging from steamships and Crimean War heroes to telescopic views of the moon, exemplified the belief that as a new medium itself, photography was supremely suited to capture "progress" in all its manifestations. In his portrait of Brunel, the audacious engineer who designed the Great Western Railway and the world's largest steamship, *The Great Eastern,* Howlett evoked both industrial might and Victorian self-confidence; the man of genius dominates the chains that dwarf him.

awed by the sheer size of industrial achievement: the heaviest ships, the longest tunnels, the biggest warehouses, the most massive factory outputs ever known, all contributed to a sublimity of scale that staggered the public's imagination.

Every decade brought impressive innovations that transformed the rhythms of everyday life. The first regular Atlantic steamship crossings began in 1838, flouting the age-old dependence on wind and tide, importing tea from China, cotton from India or Alabama, beef from Australia, and exporting to world markets finished goods ranging from Sheffield cutlery and Manchester textiles to Pear's Soap and the latest Dickens novel.

Equally momentous in its own way was Henry Fox Talbot's discovery between 1839 and 1841 of how to produce and print a photographic negative. The technology of his "sun-pictures" revolutionized the entire visual culture and changed the human relationship to the past. A moment in time could now be "fixed" forever. Thus, more than a century later, we have photographic records of many subsequent innovations: the construction of the London sewer system; the laying of the transatlantic cable in 1865, putting London and New York in almost instantaneous contact via telegraph; the popularity in the 1890s of bicycles, gramophones, electric trams, and the first regular motion picture shows; and in the year of Victoria's death, 1901, Marconi's first transatlantic wireless radio message.

Capturing the public mood, Disraeli wrote in 1862: "It is a privilege to live in this age of rapid and brilliant events. What an error to consider it a utilitarian age. It is one of infinite romance." For the growing middle class there was an Aladdin-like sense of wonderment at the astounding abundance of *things*: an incredible hodge-podge of inventions, gimmicks, and gadgets began to make up the familiar parapher-nalia of modern life, including chain stores, washing and sewing machines, postage stamps, canned foods, toothpaste, sidewalk newsstands, illustrated magazines and newspapers, typewriters, breakfast cereal, slide projectors, skin creams, diet pills, shampoo, ready-to-wear clothes, sneakers (called "plimsolls"), and even a cumber-some prototype computer, designed by Charles Babbage.

Victorian architecture, interior design, and clothing embodied the obsession with plenitude, presenting a bewildering variety of prefabricated, highly ornamented styles. A house might feature Gothic revival, neoclassical, Egyptian, Moorish, baronial, or Arts-and-Crafts motifs, every inch of its interior covered with wallpapers, etchings, draperies, carvings, lacework, and knickknacks. Though fashions varied, men and women were usually as well upholstered as their furniture, tightly buttoned from top to toe in sturdy fabrics, their clothes complexly layered on the outside (men's waistcoats, jackets, cravats, and watches) and inside (women's crinolines, petticoats, bustles, corsets, and drawers).

In a Protestant culture that linked industriousness with godliness, both capitalism and consumerism were fueled by prevailing religious attitudes. For Thomas Carlyle, work itself had a divine sanction: "Produce! Produce!" he wrote in *Sartor Resartus*: "Were it but the pitifullest infinitesimal fraction of a Product, produce it in God's name!" His compatriots obliged: by 1848 Britain's output of cotton cloth and iron was more than half of the world total, and the coal output two-thirds of world production. At the Great Exhibition of 1851, when Britain was dubbed "the workshop of the world," the display struck the Reverend Charles Kingsley as triumphant evidence of God's will: "If these forefathers of ours could rise from their graves this day they would be inclined to see in our hospitals, in our railroads, in the achievements of our physical science . . . proofs of the kingdom of God . . . vaster than any of which they had dreamed."

But for Karl Marx, laboring to write *Das Kapital* (1867) at a desk in the British Museum Reading Room, it was not enough to find God in the material world. He saw that through the hoopla of the marketplace, products had acquired a "mystical char-acter" and "theological niceties" of their own. Yet Marx did not regard commodities as proof of God's existence; instead, he argued that they functioned as deities in their own right. An ignored subversive stationed at the heart of the empire, Marx per-ceived how status-filled objects seemed to take on lives that defined human social relations, even as they degraded the workers that produced them. Looking around at the wonders of British industry, Marx decided that people had become, finally, less important than things. For him, it was the Age of Commodity Fetishism.

THE AGE OF DOUBT

> It was the age of science, new knowledge, searching criticism, fol-lowed by multiplied doubts and shaken beliefs.
>
> —*John Morley*

Despite their reverence for material accomplishment and the tenets of organized reli-gion, the Victorians were deeply conflicted in their beliefs and intentions. In retro-spect, the forces that shook the foundations of Victorian society might be summed up in two names, Marx and Darwin: though he was virtually unknown at the time, Marx's radical critique of unbridled free enterprise brought to the most acute level contemporary analyses of economic injustice and the class system. Darwin's staggering evolutionary theories implied that biblical accounts of creation could not be literally true. But well before either had published a word, British thought was in crisis: "The Old has passed away," wrote Carlyle in 1831, "but, alas, the New appears not in its stead." In his 1851 novel *Yeast*, Charles Kingsley described how deluged the Victorians felt by challenges to their faith and social order: "The various stereotyped systems . . . received by tradition [are] breaking up under them like ice in a thaw," he wrote; "a thousand facts and notions, which they know not how to classify, [are] pouring in on them like a flood."

The Crisis of Faith

In the midst of this tumult, the Victorians were troubled by Time. On the one hand, there was not enough of it: the accelerated pace of change kept people too busy to assimilate the torrent of new ideas and technologies. In the 1880s the essayist F. R. Harrison contended that Victorians were experiencing "a life lived so full . . . that we have no time to reflect where we have been and whither we intend to go." On the other hand, there was too much time: well before Darwin, scientists were showing that vast eons of geological and cosmic development had preceded human history, itself suddenly lengthening due to such discoveries as the Neanderthal skeletons found in 1856.

Their sense of worth diminished by both time clocks and time lines, Victorians felt they had little opportunity for reflection and often took scant comfort in it. Matthew Arnold complained of "this strange disease of modern life with its sick hurry, its divided aims." Yet this climate of anxious uncertainty provoked intense religious fervor, and debates about church doctrine and the proper forms of Christian worship occupied the national consciousness throughout the century. "This is the age of experiment," wrote the historian E. P. Hood in 1850, regarding the constant testing of belief, "but the cheerful fact is, that almost all men are yearning after a faith."

The most influential group were the "Evangelicals," a term which covers not only "dissenting" or "nonconformist" Protestant sects outside the Church of England (such as Methodists, Presbyterians, Congregationalists, and Baptists), but also the Evangelical party or "Low Church" faction within the Church of England. Anti-Catholic, Bible-oriented, concerned with humanitarian issues, and focused on the salvation of individual souls within a rigid framework of Christian conduct, Evangelicalism dominated the religious and often the social life of working- and middle-class Britons. Evangelicals practiced self-denial and frugality; they rejected most forms of entertainment as sinful or frivolous, and regarded any but the simplest church service as a "popish" throwback to Catholicism, which they abhorred on nationalistic as well as religious grounds. It was Evangelicalism that was largely responsible for the freeing of slaves in the British colonies in 1833, for the strictness of Victorian morality at home, and for British missionary zeal abroad.

At the other end of the spectrum were the Anglo-Catholics of the Tractarian or Oxford Movement, which flourished in the 1830s and 1840s. Through an appeal to early church history, they sought to revitalize the power and spiritual intensity of the Church of England, insisting on the authority of the Church hierarchy, and reaffirming the Church's traditional position as a grace-granting intermediary between

Christians and their God. The movement collapsed when its leader, John Henry Newman, converted to Roman Catholicism in 1845. But the antirational, romantic spirit of this small group left a substantial legacy in the renewed ritualism of "High Church" practices. Gothic revival architecture, the burning of altar candles and incense, the resplendent vestments of the clergy—all these were aspects of a religious apprehension of sensuous beauty and mysticism that had not been seen in England since before the Reformation. This "High Church" aestheticism came into direct and ongoing conflict with "Low Church" sobriety.

The crisis of religious doubt occasioned by biblical scholarship and scientific discoveries hit Christian belief hard. But it prompted an array of coping strategies and new ideas about the position of human beings in the universe that remain significant to this day. Most Victorian authors and intellectuals found a way to reassert religious ideas. Thus George Eliot, for instance, maintained that an Evangelical sense of duty and ethics was essential as a social "glue" to prevent the disintegration of society in the absence of religious authority. That it was still an era which *wanted* to believe is evident from the huge success of Tennyson's *In Memoriam* (1850), in which the poet's hard-won religious faith finally triumphs over science-induced despair. Extending evolutionary theory to spiritual advantage, Tennyson hoped man might transcend animality by encouraging his divine soul to "Move upward, working out the beast, / And let the ape and tiger die." Even Darwin's defender Thomas Huxley, who coined the word "agnostic," also celebrated Auguste Comte's positivism and "the Religion of Humanity." Huxley spoke for many who had renounced organized religion but not spiritual impulses when he said that Carlyle's *Sartor Resartus* "led me to know that a deep sense of religion was compatible with the entire absence of theology." Finally, some artists and writers used Christian icons as an avant-garde protest against the secular direction of modern life. "The more materialistic science becomes," said the artist Edward Burne-Jones, "the more angels shall I paint."

The Industrial Catastrophe

In principle, the Victorian crisis of faith should at least have pleased the Utilitarians. The creed of these atheistic, rationalist followers of Jeremy Bentham was strictly practical: measure all human endeavor by its ability to produce "the greatest happiness for the greatest number." Sharing a committed, "can do" philosophy of social reform, Utilitarianism and Evangelicalism were the two dominant ideologies shaping early and mid-Victorian life. But despite the significant changes they effected in government and education during the 1820s and 1830s, even the Utilitarians ran out of self-assurance and moral steam in the morass of mid-Victorian cultural ferment.

A few energetic idealists dreamed of leveling age-old inequalities. "Glory to Man in the highest!" wrote Swinburne in 1869, "for Man is the master of things." But here too a form of evolutionary theory was undercutting the conventional pieties of social discourse. "Love thy neighbor" had no more moral authority for the "Social Darwinist" than it had historical accuracy for the textual scholar. Summed up in the phrase "survival of the fittest"—coined by the philosopher Herbert Spencer in 1852, seven years before *The Origin of Species* appeared—Social Darwinism viewed as dangerous any attempt to regulate the supposedly immutable laws of society. Evolutionary forces decreed that only the fittest should survive in capitalist competition as well as in nature. Applied to nations and races as well as individuals, this theory supported the apparent destiny of England to prosper and rule the world.

Social Darwinism was a brutal offshoot of the influential economic theory of laissez-faire capitalism. Drawing on Adam Smith's *The Wealth of Nations* (1776), businessmen argued that the unfettered pursuit of self-interest, in the form of unrestricted competition in a free market, would be best for society. This was an idea that Utilitarians and many Evangelicals rejected in favor of legislative regulation, since their view of the imperfections of humanity indicated that one person's self-interest was likely to mean another's exploitation. The desperate need to protect the poor and disadvantaged, and the difficulty of doing so, was cause for much soul-searching, particularly among those who had made a religion of social reform.

Concern about the fairness and efficacy of the social structure was exacerbated by the unprecedented rate of urbanization. "Our age is preeminently the age of great cities" declared historian Robert Vaughan in 1843. At the beginning of the nineteenth century only one-fifth of the British population lived in cities; by the end of the century, more than three-quarters did. Such vast numbers of people crowding into the cities created hideous problems of housing, sanitation, and disease. For the poor, living and working conditions were appalling, particularly in the 1830s and 1840s, when neither housing nor factories were regulated. Industrial workers labored six days a week, for as many as fourteen or sixteen hours a day, in stifling, deafening, dangerous workshops, then went home to unheated rooms they often shared with other families, six or seven people to a bed of rags. Drinking water often came from rivers filled with industrial pollution and human waste. Without job security, health-care, or pensions, the injured, the sick, and the aged fell by the wayside. In manufacturing cities the competition for survival was indeed intense: the life expectancy among working people in Manchester in 1841 was about twenty years.

The Crystal Palace, site of the Great Exhibition of 1851, after its re-erection at Sydenham, c. 1855.

Foreign visitors in particular were struck with wonder and horror at the conjunction of so much misery and so much wealth. "From this filthy sewer pure gold flows," marveled the French historian Alexis de Tocqueville: "From this foul drain the greatest stream of human industry flows out to fertilize the whole world." Friedrich Engels spent a year in Manchester, producing the most detailed and shocking firsthand account of Victorian industrial life, *The Condition of the Working Class in England in 1844*. Karl Marx, who lived in England for thirty-four years, worked his observations into his famous theory of "surplus labor value." Under the current system, he said, wretched factory hands would never receive adequate payment for the wealth they created by transforming raw materials into precious commodities. Like many people at the time, both liberal and conservative, Marx expected that violent class warfare was imminent.

On average real wages went up and prices went down in Victoria's reign, with per capita income doubling between 1800 and 1860. But the boom-and-bust cycles of free trade made for unsteady wages, seesaw prices, sudden layoffs, and volatile labor relations, as Britain made a lurching transition to an industrial and commercial economy. There were serious depressions or slowdowns almost every decade, but the worst took place during "the Hungry Forties." Scarce food, widespread unemployment, and general despair provoked riots and fears of revolution. The statesman Charles Greville noted in his diary in 1842, "There is an immense and continually increasing population, no adequate demand for labor . . . no confidence, but a universal alarm, disquietude, and discontent." An American observer of the industrial scene named Henry Coleman remarked, "Every day that I live I thank Heaven that I am not a poor man with a family in England." When the economy recovered, many fled. Between the years 1850 and 1880, three million emigrants left Britain, two-thirds for the United States.

THE AGE OF REFORM

> The whole meaning of Victorian England is lost if it is thought of as a country of stuffy complacency and black top-hatted moral priggery. Its frowsty crinolines and dingy hansom cabs, its gas-lit houses and over-ornate draperies, concealed a people engaged in a tremendously exciting adventure—the daring experiment of fitting industrial man into a democratic society.
>
> —*Historian David Thompson, 1950*

Despite crushing problems and the threat of social breakdown, the Victorian period can justly be called an age of reform. Each of the issues that threatened to bring the country into open conflict or destroy the social fabric was in the course of the century addressed peacefully through legislation: voting rights were extended, working conditions improved, and women's rights began to gain ground, without the bloody revolutions or insurrections that struck France in 1838, 1848, and 1870, and Germany in 1848. As fears of revolution receded, the subtler worries of Mill and Arnold, based on their observation of American democracy, seemed more to the point. How could liberty of thought be preserved in a mass culture dedicated to majority rule? How could the best ideas elevate, rather than succumb to, the lowest common denominator?

Politics and Class

The key to the century's relatively peaceful progress was the passage of legislation for political and social reform. The start of the Victorian era is often dated 1832, five years before Victoria's coronation, because in that year the First Reform Bill was enacted. It gave representation to the new industrial towns, such as Manchester, Birmingham, and Leeds, all cities of over 100,000 inhabitants that had lacked a single seat in Parliament. It also enlarged the electorate by about 50 percent, granting the vote to some propertied portions of the middle class. Still, only one in six adult males could vote, and the aristocracy retained parliamentary control. Agitation for reform continued, especially in the Chartist movement of 1838–1848. Taking its name from the People's Charter of 1838, it was a loose alliance of artisans and factory workers that called for sweeping reforms, including universal male suffrage, the secret ballot, equal electoral districts, and annual elections. Chartism was the world's first independent working-class movement, its membership swelling into the millions during the depressions of the 1840s. The Chartists presented giant petitions, signed by one to five million people, to Parliament in 1839, 1842, and 1848. But each time they were rejected, and the movement collapsed after a government show of force effectively defused the demonstrations accompanying the petition of 1848.

The lot of workers was to improve piecemeal, not through the grand political reorganization envisioned by Chartism, as Parliament grudgingly passed acts regulating food, factories, and the right to unionize. An important breakthrough came with the repeal of the Corn Laws in 1846. The laws levied tariffs on the importation of foreign grain; they were sponsored by the landed aristocracy to protect the high price of their home-grown grains (called "corn" in Britain). Therefore, as the poet Thomas Hood wrote in 1842, "bread was dear and flesh and blood were cheap." The new urban business interests fought the protectionist tariffs in the name of "Free Trade." They preferred a stable, better-fed workforce to one that rioted or starved in times of scarcity, but they also wanted cheap bread to keep their workers' wages down. Later, the Public Health acts of 1848 and 1869 improved the availability of tea, sugar, and beer. In the 1870s the importation of wheat from the United States and refrigerated meat and fruit from Australia and New Zealand meant a more varied diet for the working classes, who could by now also afford the new custom of having large bacon-and-egg breakfasts.

Beginning in 1833, a crucial series of Factory Acts slowly curtailed the horrors of industrial labor. The 1833 Act provided for safety inspections of machinery, prohibited the employment of children under nine, and limited the workweek to forty-eight hours for children under twelve. Though the law was poorly enforced, a trend had begun. The Ten Hours Act of 1847 limited the time women and children could work daily in textile factories, and ensuing acts gradually regulated safety and working conditions in other industries. Workers' political power increased when the Second Reform Bill (1867) doubled the electorate, including all male urban householders. During this period employers also felt increasing pressure from extralegal trade union movements, including miners, textile workers, and women garment workers. An uncomprehending middle class (including Dickens and Gaskell) often regarded unionists as anarchists and murderers. But trade unions were finally legalized in 1871, and the first working-class Members of Parliament were unionist miners elected in 1874. By the 1890s there were 1.5 million trade union members, many of them part of the growing Socialist movement, and the foundations of the modern Labour Party had been laid.

Thus the high hopes of Chartism had in a sense succeeded, many of its supposedly dangerous demands eventually met. As Engels noted, these changes also benefited the middle class who resisted them, as people realized the value—social as well as economic—of reduced hostilities and improved cooperation between classes. Everyone also gained from related reforms that reflected weakening class barriers and increasing social mobility. In 1870 the Education Act initiated nationally funded public education in England and Wales. In the 1880s, middle-class investigators and social workers spearheaded the "discovery of poverty" in London's East End, one of a range of efforts that brought better housing, nutrition, and education to the poor. Finally, the nation as a whole benefited from what historian Asa Briggs has called "the one great political invention in Victorian England"—a civil service staffed through open examinations rather than patronage.

By the last decades of the century, Britain had become a more democratic and pluralistic society; it enjoyed greater freedom in matters of religion, political views, and intellectual life than any other country. Overall, the middle class were the chief generators and beneficiaries of social change. Outsiders before 1832, they became key players in the Victorian period. Though they never dominated politics, which remained largely an aristocratic preserve, they set the tone and agenda for the era's socioeconomic evolution.

"The Woman Question"

Still, one group found almost all doors closed against it. Throughout much of Victoria's reign, women had few opportunities for higher education or satisfying employment: from scullery maids to governesses, female workers of all ranks were severely exploited, and prior to the 1870s married women had no legal rights. What contemporaries called "the Woman Question" was hotly debated in every decade, but only at the end of the century were the first women allowed to vote in local elections. Full female suffrage came only after World War I. Despite articulate champions such as Harriet Martineau and John Stuart Mill, and the examples of successful women such as George Eliot, the Brontës, Florence Nightingale, and the Queen herself, proponents of women's rights made slow headway against prevailing norms. Though Victorians acknowledged the undeniable literary achievements of numerous women writers, many regarded this "brain-work" as a serious aberration that unfitted women for motherhood. The medical establishment backed the conventional view that women were physically and intellectually inferior, a "weaker sex" that would buckle under the weight of strong passion, serious thought, or vigorous exercise. Only in their much vaunted "femininity" did women have an edge, as nurturers of children and men's better instincts.

The ideal Victorian woman was supposed to be domestic and pure, selflessly motivated by the desire to serve others rather than fulfill her own needs. In particular, her duty was to soothe the savage beast her husband might become as he fought in the jungle of free trade. Her role prescribed by Coventry Patmore's wildly popular poem, *The Angel in the House* (1854–1862), the model woman would provide her family with an uplifting refuge from the moral squalor of the working world. Only a small portion of the nation's women could afford to remain at home, but the constant celebration of home and hearth by politicians, the press, and respected authors made conspicuous domesticity the expected role for well-born and well-married women. Many upper- and middle-class women spent their days paying social calls or acquiring "female accomplishments" such as needlework, sketching, or flower arranging. Though this leisure played an important part in generating new literary markets targeted at women, it provoked devastating satires of time-wasting females by Elizabeth Barrett Browning, Charles Dickens, and Florence Nightingale, among others. By the 1860s, with the birth of the department store and modern advertising, leisured women were also for the first time wooed as consumers and portrayed as smart shoppers.

Though their contribution was minimized, women were in fact heavily involved in the labor force, making up one-third of all workers, and 90 percent of the nation's largest labor category, household servants. For so-called "redundant" women who could not find husbands or work, the situation was especially grim. Low wages and unemployment drove tens of thousands of girls and women into prostitution, which, due to the growth of the military and repressive Victorian sexual mores, became one more "boom industry" whose workers reaped few rewards.

If a woman's life was economically precarious outside marriage, her existence was legally terminated within that bond. A woman lost the few civil rights she had as she became "one body" with her husband. Married women had, at the start of the era, no legal right to custody of their own children or to own property. The Divorce and Matrimonial Causes Act of 1857 established a civil divorce court in London, and subsequent acts created protection against assault, desertion, and cruelty, but only a wealthy few could afford legal proceedings. The Married Women's Property Acts of 1870 and 1882, however, gave women the right to possess wages they earned after marriage, as well as any property they owned before it.

Gradually, with the aid of male allies, women created educational opportunities for themselves. The first women's college opened in London in 1848, and the first women's colleges opened at Cambridge in 1869 and at Oxford in 1879—though women were not allowed to take Oxbridge degrees. Elizabeth Blackwell, the first woman M.D., became an accredited physician both in Britain and the United States in 1859; by 1895 there were 264 women doctors. In the 1890s, the much parodied image of the liberated "New Woman" began circulating in the press. By then many young women were braving a conservative backlash to take new positions in office work, the civil service, nursing, and teaching. They also enjoyed the social freedom that accompanied their expanding role in the economy. The novelist Walter Besant wrote admiringly in 1897 of the "personal independence that is the keynote of the situation. . . . The girls go off by themselves on their bicycles; they go about as they please. . . . For the first time in man's history it is regarded as a right and proper thing to trust a girl as a boy insists on being trusted."

The uphill battle that feminists faced is conveyed in the cautious motto of a national-market periodical for women. Published from 1890 to 1912, *Woman* magazine declared its mission: "Forward, but not too fast." Antisuffragists of both sexes found willing allies among those who regarded women as weak and unworldly, better equipped for housekeeping than speechmaking. As the nineteenth century waned, many women and most men would still have endorsed Dickens's parodic view of the public woman, Mrs Jellyby in *Bleak House*: she is so focused on missionary work in Africa that she cannot see the lamentable state of her family in the very next room.

The Age of Empire

I contend that we are the first race in the world, and the more of
the world we inhabit, the better it is for the human race.

—*Cecil Rhodes*

With the prime meridian conveniently located at Greenwich, just southeast of London, Victorians could measure all the world in relation to a British focal point, culturally as well as geographically. Abroad, as at home, it was an Englishman's duty to rule whatever childlike or womanly peoples he came across, for their own good. For Queen Victoria, the mission of empire was obvious: "to protect the poor natives and advance civilization." The conviction of innate superiority was reinforced by the implacable desire of British business to dominate world markets. The vast size of Britain's naval and commercial fleets and its head start in industrial production helped the cause, and Britain's military and commercial might was unsurpassed. Victorian advertising reveals the global realities and hopes of the emerging merchant empires. Tetley's tea ads depicted their plantations in Ceylon, as well as the ships, trains, and turbanned laborers that secured "the largest sale in the world." Pear's Soap advertising campaigns kept up with British expeditionary forces worldwide, finding potential customers in temporary adversaries such as the "Fuzzy-Wuzzies" of the Sudanese wars or the Boers of South Africa. One advertiser even challenged convention by speaking of "Brightest Africa"—because of the continent's vast market potential.

Yet the empire was hard to assemble and expensive—monetarily and morally—to maintain. Slavery was abolished in British dominions in 1833, but many fortunes still depended on the cheap production of sugar at West Indian plantations, as well as slave-produced cotton from the United States. Thus British implication in the slave trade remained a volatile issue. All Britain took sides in the Governor Eyre scandal of 1865, when the acting governor of Jamaica imposed severe martial law to put down a rebellion by plantation workers. Carlyle, Dickens, and Ruskin supported the executions and floggings, while John Stuart Mill sought to have Eyre tried for murder.

Closer to home, the perennial "Irish Question" resurfaced urgently during the potato famine of 1845–1847. Through the British government's callousness and ineptitude, a million and a half Irish died of starvation and disease and an equal number emigrated. In the wake of this disaster, the Irish engaged in rebellions, uprisings, and massive political efforts to gain parliamentary "Home Rule" for Ireland. But concern about the unity of the Empire, the safety of Protestants in the north of Ireland, and the supposed inability of the Irish to govern themselves led Parliament to defeat all efforts at Irish autonomy during Victoria's reign.

The Asian empire captured the popular imagination for the first time through the so-called "Indian Mutiny" of 1857–1859, a broad-based rebellion against the East India Company, the commercial entity that ruled most of India. The gory details of Indian atrocities, followed by equally bloody and more extensive British reprisals, filled the press and inflamed the public. The crown now took possession, and henceforth British policy was much more guarded, attempting to respect local institutions and practices. Later, as Rudyard Kipling recorded in his novel *Kim* (1901), India became an important setting for the "Great Game" of espionage to prevent foreign destabilization of British interests worldwide.

Color Plate 11   Sir John Everett Millais, *Mariana*, 1851. Millais based this painting on Tennyson's poem *Mariana* (page 586). When first exhibited, the painting was accompanied by these lines: "She only said, 'My life is dreary, / He cometh not,' she said; / She said, 'I am aweary, aweary, / I would that I were dead!'" Millais's painting is typically Pre-Raphaelite in its use of bright colors, narrative details, and medieval trappings. The stained glass windows depict the Annunciation, suggesting an ironic contrast between the Virgin's fulfillment and Mariana's frustration. Not everyone was moved by this vision of anguished longing; the art critic John Ruskin snorted derisively that had Millais "depicted Mariana working in a meadowed grange, instead of idle in a moated one, it had been to better purpose." *(Tate Gallery, London/Art Resource, NY.)*

Color Plate 12 William Holman Hunt, *The Awakening Conscience*, 1853. A "kept" woman (she wears no wedding ring) and her lover have been blithely singing at the piano when suddenly she has a spiritual revelation: she sees the light and realizes it is not too late to reform. The painting is full of symbolic details: the cat toying with the bird suggests the true nature of the gentleman's relationship with his mistress; the glove carelessly tossed aside hints at her probable future as a prostitute. Ruskin wrote, "the very hem of the poor girl's dress, at which the painter has laboured so closely, thread by thread, has a story in it, if we think how soon its pure whiteness may be soiled with dust and rain, her outcast feet failing in the street." The sunny garden reflected in the mirror symbolizes the possibility of redemption if she can escape the importuning arms that encircle her. *(Tate Gallery, London/Art Resource, NY.)*

Color Plate 13 Ford Madox Brown, *Work*, 1852–1865. Inspired by the sight of men laying sewers in London, this Dickensian novel of a painting portrays work across the entire social spectrum. Brown called the young British excavator in the center "The outward and visible type of Work"—he is the hero, "the strong fully developed navvy who does his work and loves his beer." On horseback is a very rich gentleman, "probably a Colonel in the army, with a seat in Parliament, and fifteen thousand a year" and his daughter. Standing on the right are two influential intellectuals, Thomas Carlyle and the Reverend F. D. Maurice (who founded the Working Man's College where Brown taught art); they are "the brain workers, who seeming to be idle, work, and are the cause of well-ordained work and happiness, in others." The beer seller, who grew up in the slums of Birmingham, is "humpbacked, dwarfish, and . . . vulgar," yet has prospered through energy and hard work; "in his way he also is a sort of hero." The flower seller is a "ragged wretch who has never been taught to work." The neglected children are motherless, as "the baby's black ribbons and their extreme dilapidation indicate," and "the care of the two little ones is an anxious charge for the elder girl." *(© Manchester Art Gallery.)*

Color Plates 14 and 15 Augustus Egg, *Past and Present, No. 1* (above) and *Past and Present, No. 3* (below), 1858. *Past and Present* tells the story of an adulterous woman's downfall in three scenes. In the first, the distraught husband holds the letter that has just revealed his wife's infidelity; she lies prostrate with grief and shame, while the house of cards their children are building collapses (on the wall one picture depicts the expulsion of Adam and Eve from Eden; the other shows a shipwreck). The third scene takes place five years later; the mother is now a homeless outcast, huddled under a bridge with her illegitimate child (behind her a poster advertises two plays, *Victims* and *The Cure for Love*, while another describes "Pleasure Excursions to Paris"). Meanwhile, in the second scene (not illustrated here) her two orphaned daughters gaze forlornly at the same moon as their mother, from whom they are forever separated. Egg's use of symbolic detail recalls Holman Hunt's *The Awakening Conscience* (Color Plate 12), another version of the theme of the "fallen woman." (*Tate Gallery, London/Art Resource, NY.*)

Color Plate 16 William Morris, *Guenevere*, or *La Belle Iseult*, 1858. Morris published his first book of poems, *The Defence of Guenevere*, in March 1858, and this painting was long believed to depict Guenevere, King Arthur's adulterous queen, standing beside her rumpled bed. Arthurian themes were enormously popular among the Victorians (Tennyson published his first *Idylls of the King* in 1858). But the picture is now thought to portray Queen Iseult grieving over the absence of her exiled lover, Sir Tristram. Either way, the brooding posture of the "fallen woman" is accentuated by the sensuous richness of her dress and surroundings: the illuminated missal, Turkish carpet, and elaborately patterned hangings and tapestries. The model was Jane Burden, whom Morris married the following year. (*Tate Gallery, London/Art Resource, NY.*)

Color Plate 17 Dante Gabriel Rossetti, *The Blessed Damozel*, 1871–1879. Rossetti based this painting on his poem *The Blessed Damozel*, written before he was 20 years old. The Damozel, surrounded by angels, leans over the golden bar of Heaven and gazes wistfully down toward her lover below on earth. The painting is split into two parts—rather like a Renaissance altarpiece—emphasizing the separation of the lovers. *(Courtesy, National Museums Liverpool [The Walker].)*

Color Plate 18   James Abbott McNeill Whistler, *Nocturne in Black and Gold: The Falling Rocket,* c. 1875. Working at the limit of representation, Whistler aggressively opposed the literary, anecdotal qualities of Pre-Raphaelite and mainstream Victorian art. This painting of fireworks exploding at the Cremorne Gardens amusement park so riled the critic John Ruskin that he wrote, "I have seen, and heard, much of Cockney impudence before now; but never expected to hear a coxcomb ask two hundred guineas for flinging a pot of paint in the public's face." Whistler sued Ruskin for libel, and Whistler's brilliant defense of his work at the ensuing trial paved the way for the impressionist and abstract styles of the modern era. (For Whistler's manifesto of art for art's sake, see his "Ten O'Clock" lecture, page 895.) *(Gift of Dexter M. Ferry, Jr. Photograph© 1988 The Detroit Institute of Arts.)*

Color Plate 19 John William Waterhouse, *The Lady of Shalott*, 1888. Tennyson's poem *The Lady of Shalott* (page 588) inspired many Victorian paintings, including one by Holman Hunt (page 589). Hunt shows the lady imprisoned in her tower; Waterhouse depicts her floating "down the river's dim expanse / Like some bold seer in a trance" toward Camelot. The painting shows her loosening the boat's chain and "singing her last song," as in the poem, but Waterhouse has added the crucifix and candles. *(Tate Gallery, London/Art Resource, NY.)*

Color Plate 20 Sir Edward Burne-Jones, *Love Among the Ruins*, 1894. The painting's title is taken from Robert Browning's poem (page 668), but it is not so much an illustration of the poem as a romantic evocation of its subject. The languid poses and pale faces, sumptuous colors and flowing drapery, show how the Pre-Raphaelite influence continued late in the century. Unlike narrative paintings (such as *Mariana, The Awakening Conscience,* and *Past and Present,* Color Plates 11, 12, 14, and 15), there is no story to be "read" in the details. As Burne-Jones wrote, "I mean by a picture, a beautiful romantic dream of something that never was, never will be—in a better light than any light that ever shone—in a land that no-one can define or remember, only desire—and the forms divinely beautiful." *(Wightwick Manor, The Mander Collection [The National Trust] NTPL. Photo by Derrick E. Witty.)*

PEARS' SOAP IN THE SOUDAN.
"Even if our invasion of the Soudan has done nothing else it has at any rate left the Arab something to puzzle his fuzzy head over, for the legend   at
             PEARS' SOAP IS THE BEST,
inscribed in huge white characters on the rock which marks the forthest point of our advance towards Berber,
will tax all the wits of the Dervishes of the Desert to translate."—Phil Robinson, War Correspondent
(in the Soudan) of the Daily Telegraph in London, 1884.

"The Formula of British Conquest," Pears' Soap advertisement from *Illustrated London
News,* 27 August 1887.

In the second half of the century, frequent and often bungled conflicts riveted public attention. The Crimean War of 1854–1856, in which Britain fought on the side of Turkey to prevent Russian expansion in the Middle East, cost 21,000 British lives but made little change in the European balance of power. "Some one had blunder'd," as Tennyson wrote in *The Charge of the Light Brigade.* The newspapers' exposure of the gross mismanagement of the war effort, however, led to improved supply systems, medical care, and weapons, and the rebuilding of the armed forces, all of which served Britain in ensuing colonial wars. A veteran of the Crimea, General George Gordon, rose to fame in 1860, capturing Peking and protecting far-flung Britons in the Second Opium War. But in 1884 he and several thousand others were massacred at Khartoum in the Sudan after a year's siege by religiously inspired rebels. Governmental dithering caused the British relief force to arrive two days too late. On another front, the Boer War of 1899–1902 stimulated war mania at home but tarnished Britain's image throughout the world. In pursuit of freer access to South African gold and diamond mines, the world's greatest military power bogged down in a guerilla war that ended only when British forces herded Afrikaner civilians into concentration camps, where 20,000 died.

Many viewed these conflicts as part of "the White Man's burden," as Kipling phrased it: the duty to spread British order and culture throughout the world. Yet imperialism had many opponents. In 1877 the Liberal leader William Gladstone argued that the Empire was a drain on the economy and population, serving only "to compromise British character in the judgment of the impartial world." Even Queen Victoria complained of the "overbearing and offensive behavior" of the Indian Civil Service for "trying to trample on the people and continually reminding them and making them feel that they are a conquered people." Like the growth of Victorian cities, the unplanned agglomeration of British colonies involved such a haphazard mixture of economic expansion, high-minded sentiment, crass exploitation, political expediency, and blatant racism that it apparently had no clear rationale. "We seem," said Cambridge historian J. R. Seeley in 1883, "to have conquered and peopled half the world in a fit of absence of mind."

Victorians did not only go to the ends of the earth; they saw the world's abundance come home to them. Britain and especially London became a magnet for all manner of people and things, a world within a world. There were many distinguished foreign sojourners at the center of empire. Among the artists, exiles, and expatriates who visited or stayed were the deposed French emperor Louis Napoleon, the painters Vincent Van Gogh and James McNeill Whistler, and the writers Arthur Rimbaud, Paul Verlaine, and Stephen Crane. Many of the era's great images and cultural moments came from outsiders: London was memorably painted by Claude Monet, anatomized by Henry James, serenaded by Frédéric Chopin and Franz Liszt, and entertained by Buffalo Bill. It received possibly its most searching critique from Karl Marx and Friedrich Engels, who drafted the *Communist Manifesto* there in 1847. Not only the country's prosperity and cultural prestige attracted people, but also its tolerance and democracy. Despite the wage slavery and imperialist ideology that he saw only too clearly, Engels was forced to admit: "England is unquestionably the freest—that is, the least unfree—country in the world, North America not excepted."

THE AGE OF READING

Even idleness is eager now,—eager for amusement; prone to excursion-trains, art-museums, periodical literature, and exciting novels.

—*George Eliot*

Publishing was a major industry in the Victorian period. Magazines, newspapers, novels, poetry, histories, travel narratives, sporting news, scandal sheets, and penny cyclopedias kept people entertained and informed as never before. A thriving commercial literary culture was built on rising literacy rates, with as many as 97 percent of both sexes able to read by 1900. The expansion of the reading public went hand-in-hand with new print technologies, including steam-powered presses, the introduction of cheaper wood-pulp (instead of rag-based) paper, and, eventually, mechanized typesetting. Illustrations were widely used, notably in serialized fiction, where they helped unpracticed readers to follow the story. After 1875 wood engravings gave way to photogravure, and in the 1880s halftone printing enabled photographs to replace hand-drawn works as the primary means of visual communication. Colored illustrations were handtinted at first, often by poor women and children working at home; later chromolithography made colored reproductions of artwork possible. British publishing gradually transformed itself into a modern industry with worldwide distribution and influence. Copies of *The Times* circulated in uncharted Africa; illustrations torn from magazines adorned bushmen's huts in the Great Karoo.

Readers' tastes varied according to class, income, and education. The well-educated but unintellectual upper class formed only a small portion of the Victorian reading public. As the historian Walter Bagehot noted at the time, "A great part of the 'best' English people keep their minds in a state of decorous dullness." At the other end of the social scale, working-class literacy rates were far below the general standard but increased as working hours diminished, housing improved, and public libraries spread. The appetite for cheap literature steadily grew, feeding on a diet of religious tracts, self-help manuals, reprints of classics, penny newspapers, and the expanding range of sensational entertainment: "penny dreadfuls and shilling shockers," serials, bawdy ballads, and police reports of lurid crimes.

It was the burgeoning middle class, however, that formed the largest audience for new prose and poetry and produced the authors to meet an increasing demand for books that would edify, instruct, and entertain. This was the golden age of the English novel, but poetry and serious nonfiction also did a brisk trade, as did "improving" works on religion, science, philosophy, and economics. But new books, especially fiction, were still a luxury in the earlier Victorian period. Publishers inflated prices so that readers would rent novels and narrative poems—just as people rent videos today—from commercial circulating libraries, which provided a larger and steadier income than individual sales. The collaboration between publishers and libraries required authors to produce "three deckers," long novels packaged in three separate volumes that thereby tripled rental fees and allowed three readers to peruse a single novel at one time. An economical alternative was to buy the successive "numbers" of a book as they appeared in individual, illustrated monthly installments. This form of publication became common with the tremendous success of Dickens's first novel, *Pickwick Papers*, which came out in parts in 1836 and 1837. By the 1860s most novels were serialized in weekly or monthly magazines, giving the reader a wealth of additional material for about the same price.

The serialization of novels had a significant impact on literary form. Most of the major novelists, including Dickens, Thackeray, Collins, Gaskell, Trollope, and Eliot, had to organize their work into enticing, coherent morsels that kept characters and story lines clear from month to month, and left readers eager to buy the next installment. Authors felt pressure to keep ahead of deadlines, often not knowing which turn a story might take. But they also enjoyed the opportunity to stay in the public eye, to weave in references to current events, or to make adjustments based on sales and reviews. For their part, readers experienced literature as an ongoing part of their lives. They had time to absorb and interpret their reading, and even to influence the outcome of literary events: throughout his career, Dickens was badgered by readers who wanted to see more of one character, less of another, or prevent the demise of a third.

The close relationship authors shared with their public had its drawbacks: writers had to censor their content to meet the prim standards of "circulating library morality." In keeping with the Evangelical temper of the times, middle-class Victorian recreation centered on the home, where one of the most sacred institutions was

A NOVEL FACT.

Old-fashioned Party (with old-fashioned prejudices). "AH! VERY CLEVER, I DARE SAY. BUT I SEE IT'S WRITTEN BY A LADY, AND
I WANT A BOOK THAT MY DAUGHTERS MAY READ. GIVE ME SOMETHING ELSE!"

Cartoon from *Punch* magazine, 1867.

the family reading circle. Usually wives or daughters read aloud to the rest of the
household. Any hint of impropriety, anything that might bring "a blush to the cheek
of the Young Person"—as Dickens warily satirized the trend—was aggressively ferreted out by publishers and libraries. Even revered poets such as Tennyson and Barrett
Browning found themselves edited by squeamish publishers.

A better testimony to the intelligence and perceptiveness of the Victorian reading
public is the fact that so many of today's classics were best-sellers then, including the
novels of the Brontës, Dickens, and George Eliot; the poetry of Tennyson, Elizabeth and
Robert Browning, and Christina Rossetti; and the essays of Carlyle, Ruskin, and Arnold.
These works were addressed to readers who had an impressive level of literary and general culture, kept up to snuff by the same magazines and reviews in which the best fiction,
poetry, and prose appeared. Educated Victorians had an insatiable appetite for "serious"
literature on religious issues, socioeconomic theory, scientific developments, and general information of all sorts. It was an era of outstanding, influential periodicals that combined entertaining writing with intellectual substance: politically oriented quarterlies
such as the Whig *Edinburgh Review* and the Benthamite *Westminster Review*; more varied
monthlies such as *Fraser's Magazine,* where Carlyle's *Sartor Resartus* first appeared, and
Cornhill, which published works by Ruskin, Thackeray, Eliot, Trollope, and Hardy; the
satirical weekly *Punch,* still published today; and Dickens's low-priced weeklies *Household Words* and *All the Year Round* for a more general readership. As a rule, the public had
faith in the press, regarding it as a forum essential to the progress and management of
democracy. At the same time, as political and cultural power broadened, the press took
seriously its new role as creator, shaper, and transmitter of public opinion.

Celebrated authors were hailed as heroes, regarded as public property, and respected as sages; they inspired a passionate adulation. Robert Browning first approached Elizabeth Barrett by writing her a fan letter. The public sought instruction and guidance from authors, who were alternately flattered and dismayed by the responsibilities thrust upon them. The critic Walter Houghton points out that "every writer had his congregation of devoted or would-be devoted disciples who read his work in much the spirit they had once read the Bible." Robert Browning lived to see an international proliferation of Browning Societies, dedicated to expounding his supposed moral teachings. Hero worship was yet another Victorian invention.

THE AGE OF SELF-SCRUTINY

The energy of Victorian literature is its most striking trait, and self-exploration is its favorite theme. Victorians produced a staggeringly large body of literature, renowned for its variety and plenitude. Their writing is distinguished by its particularity, eccentricity, long-windedness, earnestness, ornateness, fantasy, humor, experimentation, and self-consciousness. As befits a scientific age, most authors exhibited a willingness to experiment with new forms of representation, coupled with a penchant for realism, a love of closely observed detail: Tennyson was famous for his myopic descriptions of flowers; Browning transcribed tics of speech like a clinical psychologist; Eliot compared her scenes to Dutch genre paintings; and Dickens indignantly defended the accuracy of his characterization and the plausibility of his plots. Sustained labor was as important as keen observation: "lyric" poems ran to hundreds of lines, novels spanned a thousand pages, essayists constructed lengthy paragraphs with three or four generous sentences. One single book, alternately discredited and revered, underpinned the whole literary enterprise. The King James Version of the Bible shaped the cadences, supplied the imagery, and proposed the structures through which Victorians apprehended the universe; knowledge of it immensely deepens one's appreciation of the time.

Like the photographic close-ups invented by Julia Margaret Cameron, much Victorian literature tries to get at what Matthew Arnold called "the buried life" of individuals struggling for identity in a commercial, technocratic society. In the 1830s Carlyle was already alluding to "these autobiographical times of ours." Autobiography rapidly assumed new importance as a literary form, driven by the apparent necessity of each person working out a personal approach to the universe and a position within the culture. As Matthew Arnold announced in 1853, "the dialogue of the mind with itself has commenced."

Often written under intense emotional pressure, nonfiction prose on social or aesthetic issues turned into an art form as personal as lyric poetry, expressing the writers' interior lives as well as their ideas. Yet the very variety of disguised or semiautobiographical forms (such as the dramatic monologue) suggests that introspection produced its own moral perplexities. In a culture that stressed action, production, civic duty, and family responsibility, such apparently self-indulgent self-scrutiny might well seem unworthy: "I sometimes hold it half a sin / To put in words the grief I feel," said Tennyson about the loss of his best friend. Thus the guilty confessional impulse was forced underground to reemerge almost everywhere: in first-person narratives, devotional poems, travelogues, novels of religious or emotional crisis, intimate essays, dramatic lyrics, fictionalized memoirs, and recollections of famous people and places.

The Major Genres

Victorian literature is remarkable in that there were three great literary genres: non-fiction prose emerged as the artistic equal of poetry and fiction. Topical and influential in their day, the criticism and essays of such writers as Carlyle, Mill, Newman, Ruskin, Darwin, Arnold, Nightingale, and Wilde achieved classic status by virtue of their distinctive styles and force of intellect. In richly varied rhythms they record the process of original minds seeking to understand the relation of individuals to nature and culture in the new industrial world. Though their works might be categorized as religion, politics, aesthetics, or science, all these authors wrote revealingly of their intellectual development, and all explored the literary resources of the language, from simile and metaphor to fable and fantasy. Oscar Wilde argued for the supreme creativity of the autobiographical critic-as-artist: "That is what the highest criticism really is, the record of one's own soul." His teacher Walter Pater remarked simply that prose is "the special and opportune art of the modern world."

Poets struggled to refute this sentiment. Poetry commanded more respect than prose as a literary genre, but despite the immense success of Tennyson, it gradually lost ground in popularity. Whether this occurred because of, or in spite of, poetry's deliberate cultivation of a mass audience is difficult to say. But whereas Victorians regarded the Romantic poets as visionaries who opened dazzling new vistas onto the self and nature, they encouraged contemporary poets to keep their ideas down to earth, to offer practical advice about managing the vicissitudes of heart and soul in a workaday world. What was viewed, with some suspicion, as the Romantic emphasis on self-expression gave way to more qualified soul-searching with an eye toward moral content that the public could grasp and apply. Carlyle's famous admonition in *Sartor Resartus* set the tone for the period: "Close thy *Byron;* open thy *Goethe.*" In other words, forget the tormented introspection and alienation associated with Byronic heroes; strive instead to improve society and practice greater artistic control; know your work and do it.

Whether they felt guilty, inspired, infuriated, or amused over their audience's thirst for instruction, Victorian poets took advantage of it to expand the resources of poetry in English. Though there are obvious lines of influence from the Romantics—Tennyson acknowledged Keats, Shelley was an early influence on Browning, and Arnold steeped himself in Wordsworth—the innovations are perhaps even more striking. Eclectic poets introduced their readers to a bewildering variety of rhythms, stanzas, topics, words, and ideas. Contemporary social concerns vied with—and sometimes merged into—Greek mythology and Arthurian legend as subject matter. Hopkins engaged in verbal pyrotechnics that produced new meters amid an ecstasy of sound; Elizabeth Barrett Browning unleashed stormy feminist lyrics marked by a dazzling intellect; Arnold captured readers with his startling emotional honesty; Christina Rossetti whittled her lines down to a thought-teasing purity; Arthur Symons and William Ernest Henley adapted French *vers libre* to create modern "free verse."

Perhaps the most important development was the rise of the dramatic monologue. Almost every poet found occasion to speak through characters apparently quite foreign in time, place, or social situation. Tennyson's liquid vowel sounds and Browning's clotted consonant clusters are trademarks of very different styles, but both poets use their distinctive music to probe the psychology of the speakers in their dramatic poems.

Adapting the sound of their lines to fit the rhythms of their speakers' thoughts, poets acquired a more conversational tone and expanded the psychological range of their craft. While Browning was preoccupied with extreme psychological states, many poets shared his desire to represent a person or event from multiple perspectives, through shifting voices and unreliable narrators. These relativistic approaches also encouraged poets to experiment with new angles of vision suggested by the initially disorienting array of developments in visual culture. Photography, panoramas, stereopticons, impressionist painting, illustrated newspapers, and the mass reproduction of art images all left their mark on poetic practice. The ultimate effect was to engender poems whose ability to please or even communicate depended on the active participation of the reader.

Though nonfiction prose and poetry flourished, the Victorian era is still considered the great age of British fiction. Novelists strove to embody the character and genius of the time. The novel's triumphant adaptation of practically any material into "realistic" narrative and detail fueled an obsession with storytelling that spilled over into anecdotal painting, program music, and fictive or autobiographical frames for essays and histories. The novels themselves generally explored the relation between individuals and their society through the mechanism of a central love plot, around which almost any subject could be investigated, including the quest for self-knowledge, religious crises, industrialism, education, women's roles, crime and punishment, or the definition of gentlemanliness.

Convoluted by later standards, Victorian novels received their most famous assessment from Henry James, who regarded them as "loose baggy monsters." The English novel, he said, is "a treasure house of detail, but an indifferent whole." Shrewd as the observation was, it overlooks the thematic density that unifies Dickens's sprawling three-deckers; the moral consciousness that registers every nuance of thought in George Eliot's rural panoramas; the intricate narrative structures and ardent self-questioning that propel the tormented romances of the Brontës. Their novels work within an established social frame, focusing on the characters' freedom to act within fairly narrow moral codes in an unpredictable universe; they deal with questions of social responsibility and personal choice, the impulses of passion and the dictates of conscience. Yet even as they portrayed familiar details of contemporary social life, novelists challenged the confines of "realist" fiction, experimenting with multiple perspectives, unreliable narrators, stories within stories, direct appeals to the reader, and strange extremes of behavior.

The Role of Art in Society

"The past for poets, the present for pigs." This polemical statement by the painter Samuel Palmer sums up much of the period's literary debate. Because Victorian times seemed so thoroughly to break from the past, "modern" became a common but often prejudicial word. Was there anything of lasting artistic value to be found in ordinary everyday life? Many writers felt there was not; they preferred to indulge instead in what Tennyson called the "passion of the past." Most poetry shunned the details of contemporary urban existence, and even the great novelists like Dickens, Eliot, and Thackeray situated much of their work in the pre-Victorian world of their parents. Some of this writing was escapist, but many authors saw in earlier times a more ethically and aesthetically coherent world that could serve as a model for Victorian social reform. The Pre-Raphaelite painters and their literary allies sought out medieval models, while Matthew Arnold returned to the Greco-Roman classics: "They, at any rate, knew what they wanted in art, and we do not."

But another group vigorously disagreed; they stressed the importance of creating an up-to-date art that would validate or at least grapple with the uniqueness of Victorian life. In *Aurora Leigh* Elizabeth Barrett Browning contended that "this live throbbing age" should take precedence over all other topics: "if there's room for poets in this world," she said, "Their sole work is to represent the age / Their age, not Charlemagne's." In 1850 the critic F. G. Stephens argued that poets should emphasize "the poetry of the things about us; our railways, factories, mines, roaring cities, steam vessels, and the endless novelties and wonders produced every day." As the century wore on, there was a broadening in social scope: the life of the working classes became a serious literary topic, and in the 1870s and 1880s "naturalist" writers probed the structures of everyday life at near-subsistence level. Thomas Hardy wrote searching studies of rural life; George Gissing, whose first wife was a prostitute, documented in harsh detail "the nether world" of back-street London.

Whether they favored the past or present as a literary landscape, whether they criticized or lauded the times they lived in, most Victorian writers felt at home in their era. Though they had their own interests, they did not act as alienated outcasts but addressed social needs and responded to the public desire for instruction and reassurance. They recognized the force of John Stuart Mill's remark: "Whatever we may think or affect to think of the present age, we cannot get out of it; we must suffer with its sufferings, and enjoy with its enjoyments; we must share in its lot."

Amid all this energetic literary production, a substantial portion of readers demanded to know if literature had any value at all. Utilitarians regarded art as a waste of time and energy, while Evangelicals were suspicious of art's appeal to the senses and emotions rather than the soul and the conscience. "All poetry is misrepresentation," said the founder of Utilitarianism, Jeremy Bentham, who could not see how fanciful words might be of service to humanity. Such was the temper of the time that writers strove mightily to prove that audiences could derive moral and religious benefit from impractical things like circuses or watercolors. Even secular critics sought to legitimize art's role in society by contending that if religion failed, literature would take its place as a guiding light. "Literature is but a branch of Religion," said Carlyle; "in our time, it is the only branch that still shows any greenness." "More and more," said Arnold, "mankind will discover that we have to turn to poetry to interpret life for us, to console us, to sustain us."

The great expectations most Victorians had for their literature inevitably produced reactions against such moral earnestness. In the theater, a huge variety of comedies, melodramas, pantomimes, and music-hall skits amused all classes; 150,000 people a day went to theaters in London during the 1860s. Yet in comparison to other literary forms, little of lasting value remains. Though leading authors such as Browning, Tennyson, and Henry James tried their hand at writing for the stage, it was not until the 1890s, with the sophisticated wit of Oscar Wilde, the subtle social inquiry of Arthur Wing Pinero, and the provocative "problem plays" of Bernard Shaw, that British theater offered more than light entertainment for the masses. The way for serious drama had been prepared by the wonderfully clever musicals of W. S. Gilbert and Arthur Sullivan, which satirized such topics as Aestheticism (*Patience*, 1881), the House of Lords (*Iolanthe*, 1882), and the struggle for sexual equality (*Princess Ida*, 1884). Victorian social drama came into its own late in the era, when it began directly to explore its own relevance, dissecting social and theatrical conventions even as it questioned whether art could—or should—teach anything at all.

Doubts about the mission of art to improve society culminated in the Aesthetic movement of the 1880s and 1890s, whose writers sought to show, in Oscar Wilde's words, that "there is no such thing as a moral or an immoral book. Books are well written or badly written. That is all." In an era of practicality, art declared its freedom by positing its sheer uselessness. Wilde argued that it is "through Art, and through Art only, that we can shield ourselves from the sordid perils of actual existence." Thus many authors at the end of the Victorian period renounced the values that characterize the age as a whole.

And yet the Aesthetes were still quintessentially Victorian in feeling that, as writers, they had to expose their inner being, whether uplifting or shocking, to the public gaze. In their thoughts and deeds, but especially in their words, writers were expected to harness their autobiographical impulses to society's need for guidance and amusement—or even outrage. "I never travel without my diary," one of Wilde's characters remarks: "One should always have something sensational to read in the train."

Every generalization about the Victorians comes with a ready-made contradiction: they were materialist but religious, self-confident but insecure, monstrous exploiters who devoted themselves to humane reforms; they were given to blanket pronouncements about the essential nature of sexes and races, the social order, and the Christian universe, but they relentlessly probed the foundations of their thought; they demanded a moral literature and thrilled to mindless page-turners. Yet in all these matters they were constantly concerned with rules, codes of duty and behavior, their places in a complex and often frustrating social order. Even the alienated rebels of the 1890s cared intensely (a favorite word) what people thought and how shocking their calculated transgressions might make them.

For a few decades after World War I, the Victorians' obsession with the tightly buttoned structures of everyday life seemed their only legacy, offering an easy target for Modernists who sought to declare their own free-thinking independence. "Queen Victoria was like a great paper-weight," wrote H. G. Wells, "that for half a century sat upon men's minds, and when she was removed their ideas began to blow about all over the place haphazardly." But the end of the Victorian period is now a century past, and the winds of change have blown many Victorian ideas back into favor. More and more readers delight to discover beneath the stiff manners and elaborate conventions of a bygone era an anxious, humorous, dynamic people very much like ourselves.

Thomas Carlyle
1795–1881

Thomas Carlyle was a difficult and cranky character whose imaginative, eccentric works of history and social criticism had an immense influence on his fellow Victorians. Mill, Tennyson, Browning, Dickens, Ruskin, and many others idolized him. George Eliot believed that even if all Carlyle's books were burnt, "it would be only like cutting down an oak after its acorns have sown a forest. For there is hardly a superior or active mind of this generation that has not been modified by Carlyle's writings; there has hardly been an English book written for the last ten or twelve years that would not have been different if Carlyle had not lived."

Carlyle was born in the small village of Ecclefechan in Scotland, the eldest son of a stonemason and his wife who gave their numerous children a strict Calvinist upbringing. From his devout and self-disciplined parents, Carlyle learned early the value of hard work, and he later preached the Gospel of Work to his generation. His parents recognized his exceptional abilities and sent him to the University of Edinburgh to study for the ministry.

Religious doubts, however, prevented him from seeking ordination; at nineteen he wrote, "I am growing daily and hourly more lukewarm about this preaching business." He tried school-teaching instead, but hated it, and feared that his youth was "hurrying darkly and uselessly away." Tormented by ill health and his lack of a vocation, Carlyle gradually turned to a literary career. Inspired by German literature and philosophy, he began reviewing and translating.

In 1821 Carlyle met Jane Welsh. Middle-class, well-educated, and with literary aspirations of her own, Jane did not at first take Carlyle seriously as a suitor, but he was determined to marry her. Prophetically, he wrote to a friend that he expected their marriage to be "the most turbulent, incongruous thing on earth—a mixture of honey and wormwood" with "thunder and lightning and furious storms—all mingled together into the same season—and the sunshine always in the *smallest* quantity!" Despite this gloomy forecast, they married in 1826, embarking on one of the century's most famous, and most speculated about, marriages. Jane was sharp-tongued and high-strung, Thomas was perpetually irritable, depressed, and complaining, yet they stayed together for nearly forty years. Samuel Butler rather nastily remarked that "it was very good of God to let Carlyle and Mrs. Carlyle marry one another and so make only two people miserable instead of four, besides being very amusing."

In 1828 they left the social and intellectual pleasures of Edinburgh for six years of self-imposed exile in Craigenputtoch, a bleak, remote sheep farm. Here Carlyle wrote the essays that would begin to make his name, *Signs of the Times*, *On History*, and *Characteristics*, as well as his first book, *Sartor Resartus* (1833–1834). A symbolic autobiography, *Sartor* records Carlyle's struggle to find meaning in life after his loss of faith. A decade earlier, during a period of despair and spiritual crisis which he terms "The Everlasting No," Carlyle had experienced a kind of epiphany, a profound and lifelong conviction of the existence of a transcendent reality. *Sartor*, however, is a strange book, mixing metaphorical philosophy and narrative hijinks in the reconstruction of the odd life of its comic hero, Diogenes Teufelsdröckh. Carlyle had a long and discouraging struggle to find a publisher for it.

In 1834 the Carlyles moved to London, to a house in Chelsea where they spent the rest of their lives. The bustling city was a great contrast to the lonely farm, providing more access to stimulating books and friendships, but Carlyle continued to struggle with poverty, poor health, and insomnia. He set to work on his chronicle of *The French Revolution* (1837), the most dramatic and apocalyptic event in recent European history. In impassioned and impressionistic prose, he traced the downfall of an aristocracy of corrupt impostors, who had to be swept away to allow for the rebirth of a healthy society. In their destruction he read a warning for England, whose leaders seemed to be abandoning the country to democracy and laissez-faire capitalism.

Julia Margaret Cameron, *Thomas Carlyle*, 1867. The greatest of Victorian portrait photographers, Cameron lived near Tennyson on the Isle of Wight, and by virtue of her irrepressible personality managed to get his many distinguished visitors to sit through grueling photo sessions in her drafty greenhouse. Tennyson once brought the American poet Longfellow to her, saying "You will have to do whatever she tells you. I will come back soon and see what is left of you." Cameron's portrait of Carlyle conveys not only his stern prophetic power but also her own sense of photography's ability to discover a transcendent energy in simple human features: "My mortal but yet divine! Art of photography."

After completing the first of three volumes, Carlyle suffered a catastrophic setback: he lent the manuscript to his friend John Stuart Mill, whose housemaid accidentally burned it in the fireplace. Carlyle was devastated, but he forced himself to begin again. Rewriting was torture: Carlyle called *The French Revolution* "a wild savage Book" that "has come out of my own soul; born in blackness, whirl-wind and sorrow."

Yet, to his own surprise, this was the book that finally brought him widespread public recognition and some relief from financial strain. He enjoyed the admiration, and savored his new role as Sage and Prophet—though he complained that nobody listened when he addressed his contemporaries on a variety of social issues. Invited to give a series of lectures, later published as *On Heroes and Hero-Worship* (1841), Carlyle offered historical examples of what he considered true leadership. Then, in *Past and Present* (1843), he contrasted the coherent social and religious fabric of life in the Middle Ages with the chaos of the modern world. Democracy, to Carlyle, meant the breakdown of political order, the "despair of finding any heroes to govern you." He urged the "Captains of Industry" to become modern heroes, as feudal lords had been in an idealized medieval past, and to reestablish a sense of human community in mechanized England.

Carlyle believed that strong leaders were the only hope for social reform. Turning to history once again for examples, he wrote about *Oliver Cromwell* (1845) and *Frederick the Great* (1858–1865). Six volumes long, *Frederick* was hailed as Carlyle's masterpiece, and Carlyle was elected Rector of Edinburgh University. While he was in Scotland delivering his inaugural speech in 1866, Jane Welsh Carlyle died. In his grief, Carlyle wrote a moving memoir of his wife, to which he added others, including portraits of his friend Edward Irving, and Wordsworth; these were published after his death as *Reminiscences* (1881).

Although Carlyle continued to have public honors heaped upon him in old age, a reaction against his authoritarianism had begun as early as 1850, when he published the *Latter-Day Pamphlets*, a jeremiad against democracy, and *Shooting Niagara, and After?* (1867), an attack on the Second Reform Bill. While he remained an important figure, admired and respected, he was frustrated at feeling, as the critic G. B. Tennyson has put it, "everywhere honored and nowhere heeded." Carlyle's lifelong insistence on divine purpose at work in the universe was deeply attractive to a society in the grip of social unrest and religious malaise—but few were willing to accept the tasks that Carlyle claimed God had set for them. Carlyle's reputation rests on his vigorous denunciation of a materialist society and his rousing calls for social reform. Like a biblical prophet, Carlyle exhorts his followers to mend their ways. In powerfully idiosyncratic language, he condemns laziness and greed, alienation and mechanization, and urges the necessity for spiritual rebirth.

from Past and Present[1]
Midas[2]
[THE CONDITION OF ENGLAND]

The condition of England, on which many pamphlets are now in the course of publication, and many thoughts unpublished are going on in every reflective head, is justly regarded as one of the most ominous, and withal one of the strangest, ever seen in this world. England is full of wealth, of multifarious produce, supply for human want in every kind; yet England is dying of inanition. With unabated bounty the land of England blooms and grows; waving with yellow harvests; thick-studded with workshops, industrial implements, with fifteen millions of workers, understood to be the strongest, the cunningest and the willingest our Earth ever had; these men are here; the work they have done, the fruit they have realised is here, abundant, exuberant on every hand of us: and behold, some baleful fiat as of Enchantment has gone forth, saying, "Touch it not, ye workers, ye master-workers, ye master-idlers; none of you can touch it, no man of you shall be the better for it; this is enchanted fruit!" On the poor workers such fiat falls first, in its rudest shape; but on the rich master-workers too it falls; neither can the rich master-idlers, nor any richest or highest man escape, but all are like to be brought low with it, and made "poor" enough, in the money sense or a far fataler one.

Of these successful skilful workers some two millions, it is now counted, sit in Workhouses, Poor-law Prisons;[3] or have "out-door relief"[4] flung over the wall to them,—the workhouse Bastille[5] being filled to bursting, and the strong Poor-law broken asunder by a stronger. They sit there, these many months now; their hope of

---

1. *Past and Present* (1843) was Carlyle's response to the crisis of poverty and class estrangement during the Hungry Forties. Unemployment among industrial workers, combined with appalling conditions for the relief of the poor, had led to violent rioting. Even the Chartist movement's more peaceful attempts to address social and economic injustices through political reform aroused fears of revolution. Carlyle called for strong leaders to take charge. He contrasted the selfish indifference of laissez-faire industrialists and privileged aristocrats to the responsible paternalism of feudal lords and medieval monks. Medieval inequality and lack of personal freedom, he argued, were preferable to the modern "liberty to starve."
2. From Book 1, ch. 1. Midas was a legendary king who was granted his wish that everything he touched might

turn to gold; belatedly he realized he could not eat, for food became gold in his mouth.
3. Under the Poor Law Amendment Act of 1834, workhouses were established to provide relief to the poor. To deter loafers, the workhouses were made as unpleasant as possible: the standard of living was deliberately rendered worse than that of the lowest paid worker, and the inmates were expected to perform prison labor, such as picking oakum or breaking stones. Men and women were housed separately so that families were broken up.
4. Under the system of "outdoor relief," which existed prior to the Poor Law Amendment Act of 1834, each parish provided for its own poor through minimum allowances.
5. The Bastille was a Parisian prison and a symbol of oppression; the storming of the Bastille in 1789 marked the opening of the French Revolution.

deliverance as yet small. In workhouses, pleasantly so-named, because work cannot be done in them. Twelve-hundred-thousand workers in England alone; their cunning right-hand lamed, lying idle in their sorrowful bosom; their hopes, outlooks, share of this fair world, shut-in by narrow walls. They sit there, pent up, as in a kind of horrid enchantment; glad to be imprisoned and enchanted, that they may not perish starved. The picturesque Tourist, in a sunny autumn day, through this bounteous realm of England, descries the Union Workhouse on his path. "Passing by the Work-house of St. Ives in Huntingdonshire, on a bright day last autumn," says the pic-turesque Tourist, "I saw sitting on wooden benches, in front of their Bastille and within their ring-wall and its railings, some half-hundred or more of these men. Tall robust figures, young mostly or of middle age; of honest countenance, many of them thoughtful and even intelligent-looking men. They sat there, near by one another; but in a kind of torpor, especially in a silence, which was very striking. In silence: for, alas, what word was to be said? An Earth all lying round, crying, Come and till me, come and reap me;—yet we here sit enchanted! In the eyes and brows of these men hung the gloomiest expression, not of anger, but of grief and shame and manifold inarticulate distress and weariness; they returned my glance with a glance that seemed to say, "Do not look at us. We sit enchanted here, we know not why. The Sun shines and the Earth calls; and, by the governing Powers and Impotences of this Eng-land, we are forbidden to obey. It is impossible, they tell us!" There was something that reminded me of Dante's Hell in the look of all this; and I rode swiftly away."

So many hundred thousands sit in workhouses: and other hundred thousands have not yet got even workhouses; and in thrifty Scotland itself, in Glasgow or Edin-burgh City, in their dark lanes, hidden from all but the eye of God, and of rare Benevolence the minister of God, there are scenes of woe and destitution and desola-tion, such as, one may hope, the Sun never saw before in the most barbarous regions where men dwelt. Competent witnesses, the brave and humane Dr. Alison,[6] who speaks what he knows, whose noble Healing Art in his charitable hands becomes once more a truly sacred one, report these things for us: these things are not of this year, or of last year, have no reference to our present state of commercial stagnation, but only to the common state. Not in sharp fever-fits, but in chronic gangrene of this kind is Scotland suffering. A Poor-law, any and every Poor-law, it may be observed, is but a temporary measure; an anodyne, not a remedy: Rich and Poor, when once the naked facts of their condition have come into collision, cannot long subsist together on a mere Poor-law. True enough:—and yet, human beings cannot be left to die! Scotland too, till something better come, must have a Poor-law, if Scotland is not to be a byword among the nations. O, what a waste is there; of noble and thrice-noble national virtues; peasant Stoicisms, Heroisms; valiant manful habits, soul of a Nation's worth,—which all the metal of Potosi[7] cannot purchase back; to which the metal of Potosi, and all you can buy with it, is dross and dust!

Why dwell on this aspect of the matter? It is too indisputable, not doubtful now to any one. Descend where you will into the lower class, in Town or Country, by what avenue you will, by Factory Inquiries, Agricultural Inquiries, by Revenue Returns, by Mining-Labourer Committees, by opening your own eyes and looking, the same sorrowful result discloses itself: you have to admit that the working body of

---

6. William Pulteney Alison, Scottish physician and author of *Observations on the Management of the Poor in Scotland* (1840).

7. Bolivian city noted for its silver, tin, lead, and copper mines.

this rich English Nation has sunk or is fast sinking into a state, to which, all sides of it considered, there was literally never any parallel. At Stockport Assizes,—and this too has no reference to the present state of trade, being of date prior to that,—a Mother and a Father are arraigned and found guilty of poisoning three of their children, to defraud a "burial-society" of some 3l.8s. due on the death of each child: they are arraigned, found guilty; and the official authorities, it is whispered, hint that perhaps the case is not solitary, that perhaps you had better not probe farther into that department of things. This is in the autumn of 1841; the crime itself is of the previous year or season. "Brutal savages, degraded Irish," mutters the idle reader of Newspapers; hardly lingering on this incident. Yet it is an incident worth lingering on; the depravity, savagery and degraded Irishism being never so well admitted. In the British land, a human Mother and Father, of white skin and professing the Christian religion, had done this thing; they, with their Irishism and necessity and savagery, had been driven to do it. Such instances are like the highest mountain apex emerged into view; under which lies a whole mountain region and land, not yet emerged. A human Mother and Father had said to themselves, What shall we do to escape starvation? We are deep sunk here, in our dark cellar; and help is far.—Yes, in the Ugolino Hunger-tower stern things happen; best-loved little Gaddo fallen dead on his Father's knees![8]—The Stockport Mother and Father think and hint: Our poor little starveling Tom, who cries all day for victuals, who will see only evil and not good in this world: if he were out of misery at once; he well dead, and the rest of us perhaps kept alive? It is thought, and hinted; at last it is done. And now Tom being killed, and all spent and eaten, Is it poor little starveling Jack that must go, or poor little starveling Will?—What a committee of ways and means!

In starved sieged cities, in the uttermost doomed ruin of old Jerusalem fallen under the wrath of God, it was prophesied and said, "The hands of the pitiful women have sodden their own children."[9] The stern Hebrew imagination could conceive no blacker gulf of wretchedness; that was the ultimatum of degraded god-punished man. And we here, in modern England, exuberant with supply of all kinds, besieged by nothing if it be not by invisible Enchantments, are we reaching that?—How come these things? Wherefore are they, wherefore should they be?

Nor are they of the St. Ives workhouses, of the Glasgow lanes, and Stockport cellars, the only unblessed among us. This successful industry of England, with its plethoric wealth, has as yet made nobody rich; it is an enchanted wealth, and belongs yet to nobody. We might ask, Which of us has it enriched? We can spend thousands where we once spent hundreds; but can purchase nothing good with them. In Poor and Rich, instead of noble thrift and plenty, there is idle luxury alternating with mean scarcity and inability. We have sumptuous garnitures for our Life, but have forgotten to *live* in the middle of them. It is an enchanted wealth; no man of us can yet touch it. The class of men who feel that they are truly better off by means of it, let them give us their name!

Many men eat finer cookery, drink dearer liquors,—with what advantage they can report, and their Doctors can: but in the heart of them, if we go out of the dyspeptic stomach, what increase of blessedness is there? Are they better, beautifuler, stronger, braver? Are they even what they call "happier"? Do they look with satisfaction on more

8. Count Ugolino and his sons and grandsons were starved to death in a tower by his political opponents; in Canto 33 of the *Inferno* Dante implies that Ugolino, out of starvation and desperation, cannibalized his children's corpses.
9. Cf. Lamentations 4.10.

things and human faces in this God's-Earth; do more things and human faces look with satisfaction on them? Not so. Human faces gloom discordantly, disloyally on one another. Things, if it be not mere cotton and iron things, are growing disobedient to man. The Master Worker is enchanted, for the present, like his Workhouse Workman; clamours, in vain hitherto, for a very simple sort of "Liberty": the liberty "to buy where he finds it cheapest, to sell where he finds it dearest." With guineas jingling in every pocket, he was no whit richer; but now, the very guineas threatening to vanish, he feels that he is poor indeed. Poor Master Worker! And the Master Unworker, is not he in a still fataler situation? Pausing amid his game-preserves, with awful eye,—as he well may! Coercing fifty-pound tenants;[1] coercing, bribing, cajoling; "doing what he likes with his own." His mouth full of loud futilities, and arguments to prove the excellence of his Corn-law;[2] and in his heart the blackest misgiving, a desperate half-consciousness that his excellent Corn-law is indefensible, that his loud arguments for it are of a kind to strike men too literally *dumb*.

To whom, then, is this wealth of England wealth? Who is it that it blesses; makes happier, wiser, beautifuler, in any way better? Who has got hold of it, to make it fetch and carry for him, like a true servant, not like a false mock-servant; to do him any real service whatsoever? As yet no one. We have more riches than any Nation ever had before; we have less good of them than any Nation ever had before. Our successful industry is hitherto unsuccessful; a strange success, if we stop here! In the midst of plethoric plenty, the people perish; with gold walls, and full barns, no man feels himself safe or satisfied. Workers, Master Workers, Unworkers, all men, come to a pause; stand fixed, and cannot farther. Fatal paralysis spreading inwards, from the extremities, in St. Ives workhouses, in Stockport cellars, through all limbs, as if towards the heart itself. Have we actually got enchanted, then; accursed by some god?—

Midas longed for gold, and insulted the Olympians. He got gold, so that whatsoever he touched became gold,—and he, with his long ears, was little the better for it. Midas had misjudged the celestial music-tones; Midas had insulted Apollo and the gods: the gods gave him his wish, and a pair of long ears, which also were a good appendage to it. What a truth in these old Fables!

from *Gospel of Mammonism*[1]
[THE IRISH WIDOW]

One of Dr. Alison's Scotch facts struck us much. A poor Irish Widow, her husband having died in one of the Lanes of Edinburgh, went forth with her three children, bare of all resource, to solicit help from the Charitable Establishments of that City. At this Charitable Establishment and then at that she was refused; referred from one to the other, helped by none;—till she had exhausted them all; till her strength and heart failed her: she sank down in typhus-fever; died, and infected her Lane with fever, so that "seventeen other persons" died of fever there in consequence. The humane Physician asks thereupon, as with a heart too full for speaking, Would it not have been *economy* to help this poor Widow? She took typhus-fever, and killed seventeen of you!—Very curious. The forlorn Irish Widow applies to her fellow-creatures, as if saying, "Behold I am sinking, bare of help: ye must help me! I am your

---

1. The Reform Bill of 1832 enfranchised tenants who paid 50 pounds or more in annual rent.
2. The Corn Laws regulated the import of grain into Eng-

land. Intended to protect domestic agriculture, they also limited food supplies and raised food prices.
1. From Book 3, ch. 2.

sister, bone of your bone; one God made us: ye must help me!" They answer, "No, impossible; thou art no sister of ours." But she proves her sisterhood; her typhus-fever kills *them:* they actually were her brothers, though denying it! Had human creature ever to go lower for a proof?

For, as indeed was very natural in such case, all government of the Poor by the Rich has long ago been given over to Supply-and-demand, Laissez-faire and such-like,[2] and universally declared to be "impossible." "You are no sister of ours; what shadow of proof is there? Here are our parchments, our padlocks, proving indisputably our money-safes to be *ours*, and you to have no business with them. Depart! It is impossible!"—Nay, what wouldst thou thyself have us do? cry indignant readers. Nothing, my friends,—till you have got a soul for yourselves again. Till then all things are "impossible." Till then I cannot even bid you buy, as the old Spartans would have done, two-pence worth of powder and lead, and compendiously shoot to death this poor Irish Widow: even that is "impossible" for you. Nothing is left but that she prove her sisterhood by dying, and infecting you with typhus. Seventeen of you lying dead will not deny such proof that she *was* flesh of your flesh; and perhaps some of the living may lay it to heart.

from *Labour*[1]
[KNOW THY WORK]

For there is a perennial nobleness, and even sacredness, in Work. Were he never so benighted, forgetful of his high calling, there is always hope in a man that actually and earnestly works: in Idleness alone is there perpetual despair. Work, never so Mammonish,[2] mean, *is* in communication with Nature; the real desire to get Work done will itself lead one more and more to truth, to Nature's appointments and regulations, which are truth.

The latest Gospel in this world is, Know thy work and do it. "Know thyself": long enough has that poor "self" of thine tormented thee; thou wilt never get to "know" it, I believe! Think it not thy business, this of knowing thyself; thou art an unknowable individual: know what thou canst work at; and work at it, like a Hercules![3] That will be thy better plan.

It has been written, "an endless significance lies in Work"; a man perfects himself by working. Foul jungles are cleared away, fair seedfields rise instead, and stately cities; and withal the man himself first ceases to be a jungle and foul unwholesome desert thereby. Consider how, even in the meanest sorts of Labour, the whole soul of a man is composed into a kind of real harmony, the instant he sets himself to work! Doubt, Desire, Sorrow, Remorse, Indignation, Despair itself, all these like helldogs lie beleaguering the soul of the poor dayworker, as of every man: but he bends himself with free valour against his task, and all these are stilled, all these shrink murmuring far off into their caves. The man is now a man. The blessed glow of Labour in him, is it not as purifying fire, wherein all poison is burnt up, and of sour smoke itself there is made bright blessed flame!

2. The free trade philosophy of British industrialists who believed in the market's ability to regulate itself and in the right to do business unhampered by government regulation.

1. From Book 3, ch. 9.
2. Mammon is the personification of material wealth. "Ye cannot serve God and mammon" (Matthew 7.24).
3. Hercules had to perform twelve labors.

Destiny, on the whole, has no other way of cultivating us. A formless Chaos, once set it *revolving*, grows round and ever rounder; ranges itself, by mere force of gravity, into strata, spherical courses; is no longer a Chaos, but a round compacted World. What would become of the Earth, did she cease to revolve? In the poor old Earth, so long as she revolves, all inequalities, irregularities disperse themselves; all irregularities are incessantly becoming regular. Hast thou looked on the Potter's wheel,—one of the venerablest objects; old as the Prophet Ezechiel and far older? Rude lumps of clay, how they spin themselves up, by mere quick whirling, into beautiful circular dishes. And fancy the most assiduous Potter, but without his wheel; reduced to make dishes, or rather amorphous botches, by mere kneading and baking! Even such a Potter were Destiny, with a human soul that would rest and lie at ease, that would not work and spin! Of an idle unrevolving man the kindest Destiny, like the most assiduous Potter without wheel, can bake and knead nothing other than a botch; let her spend on him what expensive colouring, what gilding and enamelling she will, he is but a botch. Not a dish; no, a bulging, kneaded, crooked, shambling, squint-cornered, amorphous botch,—a mere enamelled vessel of dishonour! Let the idle think of this.

Blessed is he who has found his work; let him ask no other blessedness. He has a work, a life-purpose; he has found it, and will follow it! How, as a free-flowing channel, dug and torn by noble force through the sour mud-swamp of one's existence, like an ever-deepening river there, it runs and flows;—draining-off the sour festering water, gradually from the root of the remotest grass-blade; making, instead of pestilential swamp, a green fruitful meadow with its clear-flowing stream. How blessed for the meadow itself, let the stream and *its* value be great or small! Labour is Life: from the inmost heart of the Worker rises his god-given Force, the sacred celestial Life-essence breathed into him by Almighty God; from his inmost heart awakens him to all nobleness,—to all knowledge, "self-knowledge" and much else, so soon as Work fitly begins. Knowledge? The knowledge that will hold good in working, cleave thou to that; for Nature herself accredits that, says Yea to that. Properly thou hast no other knowledge but what thou hast got by working: the rest is yet all a hypothesis of knowledge; a thing to be argued of in schools, a thing floating in the clouds, in endless logic-vortices, till we try it and fix it. "Doubt, of whatever kind, can be ended by Action alone."

Captains of Industry[1]

If I believed that Mammonism with its adjuncts was to continue henceforth the one serious principle of our existence, I should reckon it idle to solicit remedial measures from any Government, the disease being insusceptible of remedy. Government can do much, but it can in nowise do all. Government, as the most conspicuous object in Society, is called upon to give signal of what shall be done; and, in many ways, to preside over, further, and command the doing of it. But the Government cannot do, by all its signaling and commanding, what the Society is radically indisposed to do. In the long-run every Government is the exact symbol of its People, with their wisdom and unwisdom; we have to say, Like People like Government.—The main substance of this immense Problem of Organising Labour, and first of all of Managing the Working Classes, will, it is very clear, have to be solved by those who stand prac-

1. From Book 4, ch. 4.

tically in the middle of it; by those who themselves work and preside over work. Of all that can be enacted by any Parliament in regard to it, the germs must already lie potentially extant in those two Classes, who are to obey such enactment. A Human Chaos *in* which there is no light, you vainly attempt to irradiate by light shed *on* it: order never can arise there.

But it is my firm conviction that the "Hell of England" will *cease* to be that of "not making money"; that we shall get a nobler Hell and a nobler Heaven! I antici-pate light *in* the Human Chaos, glimmering, shining more and more; under manifold true signals from without That light shall shine. Our deity no longer being Mam-mon,—O Heavens, each man will then say to himself: "Why such deadly haste to make money? I shall not go to Hell, even if I do not make money! There is another Hell, I am told!" Competition, at railway-speed, in all branches of commerce and work will then abate:—good felt-hats for the head, in every sense, instead of seven-feet lath-and-plaster hats on wheels, will then be discoverable! Bubble-periods,[2] with their panics and commercial crises, will again become infrequent; steady modest industry will take the place of gambling speculation. To be a noble Master, among noble Workers, will again be the first ambition with some few; to be a rich Master only the second. How the Inventive Genius of England, with the whirr of its bobbins and billy-rollers[3] shoved somewhat into the backgrounds of the brain, will contrive and devise, not cheaper produce exclusively, but fairer distribution of the produce at its present cheapness! By degrees, we shall again have a Society with something of Heroism in it, something of Heaven's Blessing on it; we shall again have, as my Ger-man friend[4] asserts, "instead of Mammon-Feudalism with unsold cotton-shirts and Preservation of the Game, noble just Industrialism and Government by the Wisest!"

It is with the hope of awakening here and there a British man to know himself for a man and divine soul, that a few words of parting admonition, to all persons to whom the Heavenly Powers have lent power of any kind in this land, may now be addressed. And first to those same Master-Workers, Leaders of Industry; who stand nearest and in fact powerfulest, though not most prominent, being as yet in too many senses a Virtuality rather than an Actuality.

The Leaders of Industry, if Industry is ever to be led, are virtually the Captains of the World! if there be no nobleness in them, there will never be an Aristocracy more. But let the Captains of Industry consider: once again, are they born of other clay than the old Captains of Slaughter; doomed forever to be no Chivalry, but a mere gold-plated *Doggery*,—what the French well name *Canaille*, "Doggery" with more or less gold carrion at its disposal? Captains of Industry are the true Fighters, henceforth recognisable as the only true ones: Fighters against Chaos, Necessity and the Devils and Jötuns;[5] and lead on Mankind in that great, and alone true, and uni-versal warfare; the stars in their courses fighting for them, and all Heaven and all Earth saying audibly, Well done! Let the Captains of Industry retire into their own hearts, and ask solemnly, If there is nothing but vulturous hunger, for fine wines, valet reputation and gilt carriages, discoverable there? Of hearts made by the Almighty God I will not believe such a thing. Deep-hidden under wretchedest god-forgetting Cants, Epicurisms, Dead-Sea Apisms;[6] forgotten as under foulest fat Lethe mud and weeds, there is yet, in all hearts born into this God's-World, a spark of the

2. Ups and downs in the stock market.
3. Machines that prepare cotton or wool for spinning.
4. Teufelsdröckh, the central character in *Sartor Resartus*.
5. Giants in Norse mythology.

6. An Islamic myth held that a tribe living near the Dead Sea were turned into apes because they refused to heed the prophecies of Moses.

Godlike slumbering. Awake, O nightmare sleepers; awake, arise, or be forever fallen! This is not playhouse poetry; it is sober fact. Our England, our world cannot live as it is. It will connect itself with a God again, or go down with nameless throes and fire-consummation to the Devils. Thou who feelest aught of such a Godlike stirring in thee, any faintest intimation of it as through heavy-laden dreams, follow *it*, I conjure thee. Arise, save thyself, be one of those that save thy country.

Bucaniers, Chactaw Indians, whose supreme aim in fighting is that they may get the scalps, the money, that they may amass scalps and money: out of such came no Chivalry, and never will! Out of such came only gore and wreck, infernal rage and misery; desperation quenched in annihilation. Behold it, I bid thee, behold there, and consider! What is it that thou have a hundred thousand-pound bills laid-up in thy strong-room, a hundred scalps hung-up in thy wigwam? I value not them or thee. Thy scalps and thy thousand-pound bills are as yet nothing, if no nobleness from within irradiate them; if no Chivalry, in action, or in embryo ever struggling towards birth and action, be there.

Love of men cannot be bought by cash-payment; and without love men cannot endure to be together. You cannot lead a Fighting World without having it regiment-ed, chivalried: the thing, in a day, becomes impossible; all men in it, the highest at first, the very lowest at last, discern consciously, or by a noble instinct, this necessity. And can you any more continue to lead a Working World unregimented, anarchic? I answer, and the Heavens and Earth are now answering, No! The thing becomes not "in a day" impossible; but in some two generations it does. Yes, when fathers and mothers, in Stockport hunger-cellars, begin to eat their children, and Irish widows have to prove their relationship by dying of typhus-fever; and amid Governing "Cor-porations of the Best and Bravest," busy to preserve their game by "bushing," dark millions of God's human creatures start up in mad Chartisms, impracticable Sacred-Months, and Manchester Insurrections;[7]—and there is a virtual Industrial Aristocra-cy as yet only half-alive, spell-bound amid money-bags and ledgers; and an actual Idle Aristocracy seemingly near dead in somnolent delusions, in trespasses and double-barrels; "sliding," as on inclined-planes, which every new year they *soap* with new Hansard's-jargon[8] under God's sky, and so are "sliding," ever faster, towards a "scale" and balance-scale whereon is written *Thou art found Wanting*:—in such days, after a generation or two, I say, it does become, even to the low and simple, very palpably impossible! No Working World, any more than a Fighting World, can be led on without a noble Chivalry of Work, and laws and fixed rules which follow out of that,—far nobler than any Chivalry of Fighting was. As an anarchic multitude on mere Supply-and-demand, it is becoming inevitable that we dwindle in horrid suici-dal convulsion and self-abrasion, frightful to the imagination, into *Chactaw* Workers. With wigwams and scalps,—with palaces and thousand-pound bills; with savagery, depopulation, chaotic desolation! Good Heavens, will not one French Revolution and Reign of Terror suffice us, but must there be two? There will be two if needed; there will be twenty if needed; there will be precisely as many as are needed. The Laws of Nature will have themselves fulfilled. That is a thing certain to me.

Your gallant battle-hosts and work-hosts, as the others did, will need to be made loyally yours; they must and will be regulated, methodically secured in their just share

7. Manchester was the site of Chartist agitation in 1838–1839. In 1819, the infamous "Peterloo Massacre" occurred there when charging cavalry killed a dozen peo-ple at an outdoor workers' meeting.
8. *Hansard* is the official record of Parliamentary debate.

of conquest under you;—joined with you in veritable brotherhood, sonhood, by quite other and deeper ties than those of temporary day's wages! How would mere red-coated regiments, to say nothing of chivalries, fight for you, if you could discharge them on the evening of the battle, on payment of the stipulated shillings,—and they discharge you on the morning of it! Chelsea Hospitals,[9] Pensions, promotions, rigorous lasting covenant on the one side and on the other, are indispensable even for a hired fighter. The Feudal Baron, much more,—how could he subsist with mere temporary mercenaries round him, at sixpence a day; ready to go over to the other side, if sevenpence were offered? He could not have subsisted;—and his noble instinct saved him from the necessity of even trying! The Feudal Baron had a Man's Soul in him; to which anarchy, mutiny, and the other fruits of temporary mercenaries, were intolerable: he had never been a Baron otherwise, but had continued a Chactaw and Bucanier. He felt it precious, and at last it became habitual, and his fruitful enlarged existence included it as a necessity, to have men round him who in heart loved him; whose life he watched over with rigour yet with love; who were prepared to give their life for him, if need came. It was beautiful; it was human! Man lives not otherwise, nor can live contented, anywhere or anywhen. Isolation is the sum-total of wretchedness to man. To be cut off, to be left solitary: to have a world alien, not your world; all a hostile camp for you; not a home at all, of hearts and faces who are yours, whose you are! It is the frightfulest enchantment; too truly a work of the Evil One. To have neither superior, nor inferior, nor equal, united manlike to you. Without father, without child, without brother. Man knows no sadder destiny. "How is each of us," exclaims Jean Paul,[1] "so lonely in the wide bosom of the All!" Encased each as in his transparent "ice-palace"; our brother visible in his, making signals and gesticulations to us;—visible, but forever unattainable: on his bosom we shall never rest, nor he on ours. It was not a God that did this; no!

Awake, ye noble Workers, warriors in the one true war: all this must be remedied. It is you who are already half-alive, whom I will welcome into life; whom I will conjure, in God's name, to shake off your enchanted sleep, and live wholly! Cease to count scalps, gold-purses; not in these lies your or our salvation. Even these, if you count only these, will not long be left. Let bucaniering be put far from you; alter, speedily abrogate all laws of the bucaniers, if you would gain any victory that shall endure. Let God's justice, let pity, nobleness and manly valour, with more gold-purses or with fewer, testify themselves in this your brief Life-transit to all the Eternities, the Gods and Silences. It is to you I call; for ye are not dead, ye are already half-alive: there is in you a sleepless dauntless energy, the prime-matter of all nobleness in man. Honour to you in your kind. It is to you I call: ye know at least this, That the mandate of God to His creature man is: Work! The future Epic of the World rests not with those that are near dead, but with those that are alive, and those that are coming into life.

Look around you. Your world-hosts are all in mutiny, in confusion, destitution; on the eve of fiery wreck and madness! They will not march farther for you, on the sixpence a day and supply-and-demand principle: they will not; nor ought they, nor can they. Ye shall reduce them to order, begin reducing them. To order, to just subordination; noble loyalty in return for noble guidance. Their souls are driven nigh mad; let yours be sane and ever saner. Not as a bewildered bewildering mob; but as a firm regimented mass, with real captains over them, will these men march any more. All

---

9. A home and hospital for disabled soldiers.   1. Jean Paul Richter (1763–1825), German writer.

human interests, combined human endeavours, and social growths in this world, have, at a certain stage of their development, required organising: and Work, the grandest of human interests, does now require it.

God knows, the task will be hard: but no noble task was ever easy. This task will wear away your lives, and the lives of your sons and grandsons: but for what purpose, if not for tasks like this, were lives given to men? Ye shall cease to count your thousand-pound scalps, the noble of you shall cease! Nay the very scalps, as I say, will not long be left if you count only these. Ye shall cease wholly to be barbarous vulturous Chactaws, and become noble European Nineteenth-Century Men. Ye shall know that Mammon, in never such gigs[2] and flunky "respectabilities," is not the alone God; that of himself he is but a Devil, and even a Brute-god.

Difficult? Yes, it will be difficult. The short-fibre cotton; that too was difficult. The waste cotton-shrub, long useless, disobedient, as the thistle by the wayside,— have ye not conquered it: made it into beautiful bandana webs; white woven shirts for men; bright-tinted air-garments wherein flit goddesses? Ye have shivered mountains asunder, made the hard iron pliant to you as soft putty: the Forest-giants, Marsh-jötuns bear sheaves of golden-grain; Aegir the Sea-demon himself stretches his back for a sleek highway to you, and on Firehorses and Windhorses ye career. Ye are most strong. Thor red-bearded, with his blue sun-eyes, with his cheery heart and strong thunder-hammer, he and you have prevailed. Ye are most strong, ye Sons of the icy North, of the far East,—far marching from your rugged Eastern Wildernesses, hitherward from the gray Dawn of Time! Ye are Sons of the Jötun-land; the land of Difficulties Conquered. Difficult? You must try this thing. Once try it with the understanding that it will and shall have to be done. Try it as ye try the paltrier thing, making of money! I will bet on you once more, against all Jötuns, Tailor-gods, Double-barrelled Law-wards, and Denizens of Chaos whatsoever!

1843   1843

2. A two-wheeled, one-horse carriage.

⇒ PERSPECTIVES ⇐
The Industrial Landscape

"The most fundamental transformation of human life in the history of the world"—this is how the historian Eric Hobsbawm describes the Industrial Revolution. In economic terms, the arrival of the "Machine Age" was a huge success: thanks to its technological preeminence, Britain's wealth and prosperity increased enormously. This increase, coupled with pride in the improvements themselves, created a sense of excitement, of living in stirring times, and bolstered the optimistic conviction that further progress was certain. But the rapidity with which industrialization took place was also profoundly disorienting. Overnight, it seemed, the world had been transformed.

The first wave of the Industrial Revolution took place in the cotton industry. During the eighteenth century, new inventions had changed the technique of spinning and speeded up production of thread. This in turn had created a demand for more weavers. But with the development of steam-powered looms in the 1820s, weaving began to be done in factories rather than at home, and handloom weavers became obsolete. Large numbers of people found themselves without a job. Rural workers flocked to the cities to find work, and the population burgeoned in northern cities such as Manchester, Liverpool, Leeds, Birmingham, Sheffield, and Glasgow.

Britain grew richer, but it was not the poor who benefited from this revolution. In the early decades of the century, before legislation was passed to address some of the worst evils of the factory system, workers—including children—toiled for up to sixteen hours a day, six days a week, under inhuman conditions: deafening noise, poor ventilation, dangerous machinery, demanding overseers, and no insurance or benefits to protect them in the event of an accident or illness. Periodic economic depressions resulted in massive unemployment: being "in work" was bad enough, but being out of work could mean actual starvation.

The factory system disrupted not only traditional patterns of work but also family life. As more and more women and children were employed in factories, mills, and mines, there was an inevitable loss of paternal authority. Women had always worked, but never before had their labor been so visible. The "factory girl" became a focus for fears about promiscuity and the undermining of the family structure.

John Leech, *Horseman pursued by a train engine named "Time."*

The overcrowded conditions in the cities created urban slums of unimaginable wretchedness. Whole families—sometimes several families—might live in a single room. Tens of thousands of people lived in damp cellars. Because of the lack of sanitation, raw sewage overflowed everywhere, and fresh water was often impossible to obtain. When typhoid and cholera broke out, epidemics spread rampantly among the inhabitants of these foul dens; contagion was impossible to avoid.

Industrial pollution was another byproduct of the machine age. Factories spewed smoke into the air, and cities dumped sewage directly into the rivers. The outlying areas of Birmingham came to be known as "The Black Country." In *Contrasts* (1836) A. W. N. Pugin vividly depicted the sheer ugliness of a landscape dominated by smokestacks. In *The Storm-Cloud of the Nineteenth Century* (1884) John Ruskin denounced the devastation wrought by industrialism: "Blanched Sun,—blighted grass,—blinded man."

The second phase of the Industrial Revolution was brought about by the railway boom of the 1840s. The spreading network of rails linked the cities and allowed the iron and coal industries to flourish. The railroad transfigured the landscape in ways that were terribly disruptive but also immensely thrilling. More than any other technological innovation, it symbolized the dizzying speed with which Britain was changing.

Psychologically, it was hard to assimilate such a rapidly altering environment. Many people felt that the world of their childhood had been obliterated. In 1860 the novelist William Makepeace Thackeray voiced this sense of bewilderment:

> It was only yesterday; but what a gulf between now and then! *Then* was the old world. Stage-coaches, more or less swift, riding-horses, pack-horses, highwaymen, knights in armour, Norman invaders, Roman legions, Druids, Ancient Britons painted blue, and so forth—all these belong to the old period. . . . But your railroad starts the new era. . . . We who lived before railways, and survive out of the ancient world, are like Father Noah and his family out of the Ark.

Writers throughout the nineteenth century shared Thackeray's wistful longing for a romanticized past. Pugin, Carlyle, Tennyson, Morris, and many others used their vision of an idealized medieval England, aesthetically pleasing and socially harmonious, as a device to castigate the evils of industrialization.

This harking back to the past was not mere nostalgia: it reflected the trauma of the experience of industrialization. The transformation from a rural agrarian economy to a machine-dominated system of factories, mines, and railroads meant a very real shift in ancient patterns of life. The clock rather than the natural rhythms of the seasons now dictated working-class existence, and the laissez-faire pursuit of profit changed the relations between masters and men. Despite the huge accumulation of national wealth, the gulf between rich and poor had never been wider. In 1844 Friedrich Engels observed that "class warfare is so open and shameless that it has to be seen to be believed." Hunger, misery, and hopelessness found expression in strikes and trade union activity. The Chartist movement, in which the workers hoped for some relief from their distress by presenting a list of demands to Parliament, fizzled. Far from gaining middle-class compassion, it aroused hostility, and even fears of a revolution in Britain.

Among the key literary responses to the "condition of England" question were Carlyle's *Past and Present* (1843), Elizabeth Gaskell's *Mary Barton* (1848) and *North and South* (1855), and Dickens's *Hard Times* (1854). Their writing helped to focus attention on the human costs of the Industrial Revolution. In an effort to prick the consciences of their readers, they dramatized the sufferings of factory workers, and tried to put a human face on the inflammatory figure of the Chartist; they warned of the dangers of selfish individualism, and urged sympathy, communication, and benevolent leadership as remedies for class alienation.

The Steam Loom Weaver

In traditional bawdy ballads, the lovers meet under a hedge or by a stream, and their agrarian pursuits—herding sheep, milking cows, grinding corn, weaving cotton by hand—provide the pastoral setting and imagery for a sexual encounter. But the Industrial Revolution sent tens of thousands of rural people to live and work in cities. This humorous working-class ballad takes its imagery from the new industrial occupations of the factories, where steam engines powered the weavers' looms in cotton mills. Broadside ballads like this one were printed on flimsy paper and sold in the street for a penny or less; in the early nineteenth century, they were the most common form of reading matter for the urban poor.

The Steam Loom Weaver

One morning in summer I did ramble,
In the pleasant month of June,
The birds did sing the lambkins play,
Two lovers walking in their bloom,
5   The lassie was a steam loom weaver,
The lad an engine driver keen,
All their discourse was about weaving.
And the getting up of steam.

She said my loom is out of fettle,
10   Can you right it yes or no,
You say you are an engine driver,
Which makes the steam so rapid flow;
My lambs and jacks[1] are out of order,
My laith in motion has not been,
15   So work away without delay,
And quickly muster up the steam.

I said fair maid you seem determined,
No longer for to idle be,
Your healds and laith[2] I'll put in motion,
20   Then work you can without delay,
She said young man a pair of pickers,[3]
A shuttle too I want you ween,
Without these three I cannot weave,
So useless would be the steam.

25   Dear lass these things I will provide,
But when to labour will you begin
As soon my lad as things are ready
My loom shop you can enter in.
A shuttle true and pickers too,
30   This young man did provide amain.

---

1. Jacks are levers that raise the harness supporting the warp threads; lambs are foot pedals that operate the jacks.
2. Healds are loops through which the warp threads pass; the laith is the supporting stand of the loom.
3. Pickers are attachments to the picking stick which propels the shuttle through the warp threads.

And soon her loom was put in tune
So well it was supplied with steam.

Her loom worked well the shuttle flew,
His nickers play'd the tune nick-nack,
35   Her laith did move with rapid motion,
Her temples, healds, long-lambs and jacks,
Her cloth beam rolled the cloth up tight,
The yarn beam emptied soon its seam,
The young man cried your loom works, light
40   And quickly then off shot the steam.

She said young man another web,
Upon the beam let's get don't strike,
But work away while yet it's day,
This steam loom weaving well I like.
45   He said good lass I cannot stay,
But if a fresh warp you will beam
If ready when I come this way,
I'd strive for to get up the steam.

                                          c. 1830

Fanny Kemble
1809–1893

The Liverpool and Manchester Railway, opened in 1830, was Britain's first passenger railway, built despite powerful opposition. During the debates in Parliament it had been argued that cows would cease to give milk, hens would be prevented from laying, and horses would become extinct if this monstrosity were allowed to deface the countryside. Fanny Kemble, a popular young actress, was the first woman to ride on the steam locomotive. She was accompanied by George Stephenson himself, the engineer who had designed the railroad. Her vivid description captures the startling newness of the experience, and the sense of traveling at astonishing speeds.

from Record of a Girlhood
[FIRST RIDE ON A STEAM ENGINE]

Liverpool, August 26th

My dear H————,

A common sheet of paper is enough for love, but a foolscap extra[1] can alone contain a railroad and my ecstasies. * * * We were introduced to the little engine which was to drag us along the rails. She (for they make these curious little fire-horses all mares) consisted of a boiler, a stove, a small platform, a bench, and behind the bench a barrel containing enough water to prevent her being thirsty for fifteen miles,—the whole machine not bigger than a common fire-engine. She goes upon two wheels, which are her feet, and are moved by bright steel legs called pistons; these are propelled by steam, and in proportion as more steam is applied to the upper extremities (the hip-joints, I suppose) of these pistons, the faster they move the wheels; and when

---

1. An extra-long sheet of writing paper.

it is desirable to diminish the speed, the steam, which unless suffered to escape would burst the boiler, evaporates through a safety-valve into the air. The reins, bit, and bridle of this wonderful beast—a small steel handle, which applies or withdraws the steam from its legs or pistons, so that a child might manage it. The coals, which are its oats, were under the bench, and there was a small glass tube affixed to the boiler, with water in it, which indicates by its fulness or emptiness when the creature wants water, which is immediately conveyed to it from its reservoirs. There is a chimney to the stove, but as they burn coke there is none of the dreadful black smoke which accompanies the progress of a steam-vessel. This snorting little animal, which I felt rather inclined to pat, was then harnessed to our carriage, and, Mr. Stephenson having taken me on the bench of the engine with him, we started at about ten miles an hour. * * * You can't imagine how strange it seemed to be journeying on thus, without any visible cause of progress other than the magical machine, with its flying white breath and rhythmical, unvarying pace, between these rocky walls, which are already clothed with moss and ferns and grasses; and when I reflected that these great masses of stone had been cut asunder to allow our passage thus far below the surface of the earth, I felt as if no fairy tale was ever half so wonderful as what I saw. * * *

* * * He explained to me the whole construction of the steam-engine, and said he could soon make a famous engineer of me, which, considering the wonderful things he *has* achieved, I dare not say is impossible. * * * The engine having received its supply of water * * * set off at its utmost speed, thirty-five miles an hour, swifter than a bird flies (for they tried the experiment with a snipe). You cannot conceive what that sensation of cutting the air was; the motion is as smooth as possible, too. I could either have read or written. * * * When I closed my eyes this sensation of flying was quite delightful, and strange beyond description; yet, strange as it was, I had a perfect sense of security, and not the slightest fear * * * [as] this brave little she-dragon of ours flew on.

1830   1878

+—⚐—+

Thomas Babington Macaulay
1800–1859

Not everyone deplored the high human cost of rapid industrialization: the historian Thomas Babington Macaulay saw it as evidence of social progress. He was a firm believer in "the natural tendency of society to improvement," and he took great pride in the material achievements of his age. He expressed his views forcefully in reviewing Robert Southey, whose *Colloquies on the Progress and Prospects of Society* (1829) had criticized industrialism and urged a return to a romanticized rural past. In reply, Macaulay argued that in the nineteenth century "people live longer because they are better fed, better lodged, better clothed, and better attended in sickness, and that these improvements are owing to that increase of national wealth which the manufacturing system has produced."

For more about Macaulay, see Perspectives: Religion and Science, page 633.

from A Review of Southey's Colloquies
[THE NATURAL PROGRESS OF SOCIETY]

History is full of the signs of this natural progress of society. We see in almost every part of the annals of mankind how the industry of individuals, struggling up against wars, taxes, famines, conflagrations, mischievous prohibitions, and more mischievous protections, creates faster than governments can squander, and repairs whatever invaders can destroy. We see the wealth of nations increasing, and all the arts of life approaching nearer and nearer to perfection, in spite of the grossest corruption and the wildest profusion on the part of rulers.

The present moment is one of great distress. But how small will that distress appear when we think over the history of the last forty years; a war, compared with which all other wars sink into insignificance;[1] taxation, such as the most heavily taxed people of former times could not have conceived; a debt larger than all the public debts that ever existed in the world added together; the food of the people studiously rendered dear; the currency imprudently debased, and imprudently restored. Yet is the country poorer than in 1790? We firmly believe that, in spite of all the misgovernment of her rulers, she has been almost constantly becoming richer and richer. Now and then there has been a stoppage, now and then a short retrogression; but as to the general tendency there can be no doubt. A single breaker may recede; but the tide is evidently coming in.

If we were to prophesy that in the year 1930 a population of fifty millions, better fed, clad, and lodged than the English of our time, will cover these islands, that Sussex and Huntingdonshire will be wealthier than the wealthiest parts of the West Riding of Yorkshire now are, that cultivation, rich as that of a flower garden, will be carried up to the very tops of Ben Nevis and Helvelyn,[2] that machines constructed on principles yet undiscovered will be in every house, that there will be no highways but railroads, no traveling but by steam, that our debt, vast as it seems to us, will appear to our great-grandchildren a trifling encumbrance, which might easily be paid off in a year or two, many people would think us insane. We prophesy nothing; but this we say: If any person had told the Parliament which met in perplexity and terror after the crash in 1720 that in 1830 the wealth of England would surpass all their wildest dreams, that the annual revenue would equal the principal of that debt which they considered as an intolerable burden, that for one man of ten thousand pounds then living there would be five men of fifty thousand pounds, that London would be twice as large and twice as populous, and that nevertheless the rate of mortality would have diminished to one-half of what it then was, that the post office would bring more into the exchequer than the excise and customs had brought in together under Charles the Second,[3] that stage coaches would run from London to York in twenty-four hours, that men would be in the habit of sailing without wind, and would be beginning to ride without horses, our ancestors would have given as much credit to the prediction as they gave to *Gulliver's Travels*. Yet the prediction would have been true; and they would have perceived that it was not altogether absurd, if they had considered that the country was then raising every year a sum which would have purchased the fee-simple[4] of the revenue of the Plantagenets, ten times what supported the Government of Elizabeth, three times what, in the time of Cromwell,[5] had been thought intolerably oppressive. To almost all men the state of things under which they have been used to live seems to be the necessary state of things. We have heard it said that five per cent is the natural interest of money, that twelve is the natural

---

1. The Napoleonic Wars, which took place from 1792 until 1815.
2. Mountains in Scotland and the Lake District of England.
3. Reigned 1660–1685.

4. Complete ownership of their estates. The Plantagenets ruled England from 1154 to 1399.
5. Elizabeth reigned from 1558 to 1603. Oliver Cromwell was Lord Protector from 1653 to 1658.

number of a jury, that forty shillings is the natural qualification of a county voter. Hence it is that, though in every age everybody knows that up to his own time progressive improvement has been taking place, nobody seems to reckon on any improvement during the next generation. We cannot absolutely prove that those are in error who tell us that society has reached a turning point, that we have seen our best days. But so said all who came before us, and with just as much apparent reason. "A million a year will beggar us," said the patriots of 1640. "Two millions a year will grind the country to powder," was the cry in 1660. "Six millions a year, and a debt of fifty millions!" exclaimed Swift, "the high allies have been the ruin of us." "A hundred and forty millions of debt!" said Junius;[6] "well may we say that we owe Lord Chatham more than we shall ever pay, if we owe him such a load as this." "Two hundred and forty millions of debt!" cried all the statesmen of 1783 in chorus; "what abilities, or what economy on the part of a minister, can save a country so burdened?" We know that if, since 1783, no fresh debt had been incurred, the increased resources of the country would have enabled us to defray that debt at which Pitt, Fox, and Burke[7] stood aghast, nay, to defray it over and over again, and that with much lighter taxation than what we have actually borne. On what principle is it that, when we see nothing but improvement behind us, we are to expect nothing but deterioration before us?

It is not by the intermeddling of Mr Southey's idol, the omniscient and omnipotent State, but by the prudence and energy of the people, that England has hitherto been carried forward in civilization; and it is to the same prudence and the same energy that we now look with comfort and good hope. Our rulers will best promote the improvement of the nation by strictly confining themselves to their own legitimate duties, by leaving capital to find its most lucrative course, commodities their fair price, industry and intelligence their natural reward, idleness and folly their natural punishment, by maintaining peace, by defending property, by diminishing the price of law, and by observing strict economy in every department of the State. Let the Government do this: the People will assuredly do the rest.

1830

Parliamentary Papers ("Blue Books")

Factories, mills, and mines all employed women and children as cheap labor. They often worked grueling hours under appalling conditions, for wages that barely enabled them to subsist. Their misery attracted the attention of various official fact-finding commissions, whose horrifying reports, known as the "Blue Books," revealed that five-year-old children slaved in pitch-dark mines for twelve hours a day, and that pregnant and half-naked women crawled through mine shafts hauling heavy loads of coal. Such investigations helped bring about the 1833 and 1842 Factory Acts that prohibited the employment of children under nine and limited those under twelve to forty-eight hours of work per week. In the following passages young girls testify before Parliamentary commissions about the circumstances of their lives.

---

6. Pseudonym of a political commentator (active from 1769 to 1772) who supported William Pitt, Earl of Chatham. Pitt led the costly war against France.

7. William Pitt, Charles James Fox, and Edmund Burke were 18th-century statesmen.

Testimony of Hannah Goode, a Child Textile Worker

I work at Mr. Wilson's mill. I attend the drawing-head.[1] I get 5s. 9d. It is four or five years since we worked double hours. We only worked an hour over then. We got a penny for that. We went in the morning at six o'clock by the mill clock. It is about half past five by our clock at home when we go in, and we are about a quarter too fast by Nottingham. We come out at seven by the mill. The clock is in the engine-house. It goes like other clocks. I think the youngest child is about seven. There are only two males in the mill. I dare say there are twenty under nine years. They go in when we do and come out when we do. The smallest children work at the cards,[2] and doffing the spinning bobbins.[3] I work in that room. We never stop to take our meals, except at dinner. It has gone on so this six years and more. It is called an hour for dinner from coming out to going in. We have a full hour. Some stop in, if they have a mind. The men stop half an hour at dinner-time to clean the wheels. The children stop to clean their own work; that may take them five or ten minutes or so. That is taken out of the dinner-time. William Crookes is overlooker in our room; he is cross-tempered sometimes. He does not beat me; he beats the little children if they do not do their work right. They want beating now and then. He has a strap; he never beats them with any thing else, except his hand. The children are in a middling way as to goodness. I have sometimes seen the little children drop asleep or so, but not lately. If they are catched asleep they get the strap. They are always very tired at night. I have weakened[4] them sometimes to prevent Crookes seeing them; not very often, because they don't often go to sleep. Sometimes they play about the street when they come out; sometimes they go home. The girls often go home and sew. I sit up often till nine or ten o'clock at home, picking the spinners waste. I get 2½d. a pound for that. I can pick about half a pound a night, working very hard. I have known the people complain of their children getting beat. There is no rule about not beating the children. When the engine stops, all stops except the reeling. The reelers are all grown up. I can read a little; I can't write. I used to go to school before I went to the mill; I have [not] since. I am sixteen. We have heard nothing in our mill about not working so long.

1833

Testimony of Ann and Elizabeth Eggley, Child Mineworkers

Ann Eggley, eighteen years old.————I'm sure I don't know how to spell my name. We go at four in the morning, and sometimes at half-past four. We begin to work as soon as we get down. We get out after four, sometimes at five, in the evening. We work the whole time except an hour for dinner, and sometimes we haven't time to eat. I hurry[1] by myself, and have done so for long. I know the corves are very heavy they are the biggest corves anywhere about. The work is far too hard for me; the sweat runs off me all over sometimes. I am very tired at night. Sometimes when we get home at night we have not power to wash us, and then we go to bed. Sometimes we fall asleep in the chair. Father said last night it was both a shame and a disgrace for

---

1. The drawing frame, a machine which drew out, or lengthened, the wool after it had been carded.
2. Work at the carding machine, which consisted of rollers studded with wires to comb the wool and remove debris.
3. Removing the full bobbins or spindles of wool, and tak-ing them to other machines to be made into thread.
4. Wakened.
1. A hurrier pushed carriages loaded with ore through the mine shafts. These handtrucks, called corves, weighed as much as 800 pounds.

girls to work as we do, but there was nought else for us to do. I have tried to get wind-ing[2] to do, but could not. I begun to hurry when I was seven and I have been hurrying ever since. I have been 11 years in the pit. The girls are always tired. I was poorly twice this winter; it was with headache. I hurry for Robert Wiggins; he is not akin to me. I riddle[3] for him. We all riddle for them except the littlest when there is two. We don't always get enough to eat and drink, but we get a good supper. I have known my father go at two in the morning to work when we worked at Twibell's, where there is a day-hole to the pit, and he didn't come out till four. I am quite sure that we work constantly 12 hours except on Saturdays. We wear trousers and our shifts[4] in the pit, and great big shoes clinkered and nailed. The girls never work naked to the waist in our pit. The men don't insult us in the pit. The conduct of the girls in the pit is good enough sometimes, and sometimes bad enough. I never went to a day-school. I went a little to a Sunday-school, but I soon gave it over. I thought it too bad to be con-fined both Sundays and week-days. I walk about and get the fresh air on Sundays. I have not learnt to read. I don't know my letters. I never learnt nought. I never go to church or chapel; there is no church or chapel at Gawber, there is none nearer than a mile. If I was married I would not go to the pits, but I know some married women that do. The men do not insult the girls with us, but I think they do in some. I have never heard that a good man came into the world who was God's Son to save sinners. I never heard of Christ at all. Nobody has ever told me about him, nor have my father and mother ever taught me to pray. I know no prayer: I never pray. I have been taught nothing about such things.

Elizabeth Eggley, sixteen years old.————I am sister to the last witness. I hurry in the same pit, and work for my father. I find my work very much too hard for me. I hurry alone. It tires me in my arms and back most. We go to work between four and five in the morning. If we are not there by half past five we are not allowed to go down at all. We come out at four, five, or six at night as it happens. We stop in gen-erally 12 hours, and sometimes longer. We have to hurry only from the bank-face down to the horse-gate and back. I am sure it is very hard work and tires us very much; it is too hard for girls to do. We sometimes go to sleep before we get to bed. We haven't a very good house; we have but two rooms for all the family. I have never been to school except four times, and then I gave over because I could not get things to go in.[5] I cannot read: I do not know my letters. I don't know who Jesus Christ was. I never heard of Adam either. I never heard about them at all. I have often been obliged to stop in bed all Sunday to rest myself. I never go to church or chapel.

1842

Charles Dickens
1812–1870

During the "railway mania" of the 1840s, nearly nine thousand miles of new track were laid across Britain. In 1842 the young Queen Victoria took her first railway journey, and was "quite charmed by it"—though she was also criticized for having risked her life. The railroads were a visible symbol of progress, but as Dickens dramatizes in his novel *Dombey and Son*, their con-struction brought about a vast demolition of neighborhoods and upheaval of the landscape. In

---

2. Helping to hoist the coal up the shaft to the surface.
3. Sift the coal through a sieve.

4. Loose-fitting undergarments.
5. I.e., proper clothing.

the later novel *Hard Times*, Dickens portrays industrial Manchester as "Coketown" because of the coal residue that blackened the city. He emphasizes the dreary regimentation and the loss of personal identity produced by the mechanization of labor. The workers who tended the machines were called "hands," a term that aptly symbolized their dehumanization. But, as Dickens insists throughout *Hard Times*, oppressive working conditions were only part of the problem; the factory system also fostered alienation and hostility between classes, and the masters were apparently content for their workers to be deprived of education, religion, and even entertainment.

from Dombey and Son
[THE COMING OF THE RAILWAY]

The first shock of a great earthquake had, just at that period, rent the whole neighbourhood to its centre.[1] Traces of its course were visible on every side. Houses were knocked down; streets broken through and stopped; deep pits and trenches dug in the ground; enormous heaps of earth and clay thrown up; buildings that were undermined and shaking, propped by great beams of wood. Here, a chaos of carts, overthrown and jumbled together, lay topsy-turvy at the bottom of a steep unnatural hill; there, confused treasures of iron soaked and rusted in something that had accidentally become a pond. Everywhere were bridges that led nowhere; thoroughfares that were wholly impassable; Babel towers[2] of chimneys, wanting half their height; temporary wooden houses and enclosures, in the most unlikely situations; carcases of ragged tenements, and fragments of unfinished walls and arches, and piles of scaffolding, and wildernesses of bricks, and giant forms of cranes, and tripods straddling above nothing. There were a hundred thousand shapes and substances of incompleteness, wildly mingled out of their places, upside down, burrowing in the earth, aspiring in the air, mouldering in the water, and unintelligible as any dream. Hot springs and fiery eruptions, the usual attendants upon earthquakes, lent their contributions of confusion to the scene. Boiling water hissed and heaved within dilapidated walls; whence, also, the glare and roar of flames came issuing forth; and mounds of ashes blocked up rights of way, and wholly changed the law and custom of the neighbourhood.

In short, the yet unfinished and unopened Railroad was in progress; and, from the very core of all this dire disorder, trailed smoothly away, upon its mighty course of civilisation and improvement.

But as yet, the neighbourhood was shy to own the Railroad. One or two bold speculators had projected streets; and one had built a little, but had stopped among the mud and ashes to consider farther of it. A bran-new Tavern, redolent of fresh mortar and size, and fronting nothing at all, had taken for its sign The Railway Arms; but that might be rash enterprise—and then it hoped to sell drink to the workmen. So, the Excavators' House of Call had sprung up from a beer-shop; and the old-established Ham and Beef Shop had become the Railway Eating House, with a roast leg of pork daily, through interested motives of a similar immediate and popular description. Lodging-house keepers were favourable in like manner; and for the like

---

1. Dickens is describing the construction of the London-Birmingham railway, which demolished many buildings in Camden Town, an area in London he knew as a boy. The line opened in 1838.
2. The tower of Babel was supposed to have been built high enough to reach heaven (Genesis 11).

reasons were not to be trusted. The general belief was very slow. There were frowzy fields, and cow-houses, and dunghills, and dustheaps, and ditches, and gardens, and summer-houses, and carpet-beating grounds, at the very door of the Railway. Little tumuli[3] of oyster shells in the oyster season, and of lobster shells in the lobster season, and of broken crockery and faded cabbage leaves in all seasons, encroached upon its high places. Posts, and rails, and old cautions to trespassers, and backs of mean houses, and patches of wretched vegetation, stared it out of countenance. Nothing was the better for it, or thought of being so. If the miserable waste ground lying near it could have laughed, it would have laughed it to scorn, like many of the miserable neighbours.

1846

from Hard Times

[COKETOWN]

Coketown, to which Messrs Bounderby and Gradgrind[1] now walked, was a triumph of fact; it had no greater taint of fancy in it than Mrs Gradgrind herself. Let us strike the key-note, Coketown, before pursuing our tune.

It was a town of red brick, or of brick that would have been red if the smoke and ashes had allowed it; but, as matters stood it was a town of unnatural red and black like the painted face of a savage. It was a town of machinery and tall chimneys, out of which interminable serpents of smoke trailed themselves for ever and ever, and never got uncoiled. It had a black canal in it, and a river that ran purple with ill-smelling dye, and vast piles of building full of windows where there was a rattling and a trembling all day long, and where the piston of the steam-engine worked monotonously up and down, like the head of an elephant in a state of melancholy madness. It contained several large streets all very like one another, and many small streets still more like one another, inhabited by people equally like one another, who all went in and out at the same hours, with the same sound upon the same pavements, to do the same work, and to whom every day was the same as yesterday and tomorrow, and every year the counterpart of the last and the next.

These attributes of Coketown were in the main inseparable from the work by which it was sustained; against them were to be set off, comforts of life which found their way all over the world, and elegancies of life which made, we will not ask how much of the fine lady, who could scarcely bear to hear the place mentioned. The rest of its features were voluntary, and they were these.

You saw nothing in Coketown but what was severely workful. If the members of a religious persuasion built a chapel there—as the members of eighteen religious persuasions had done—they made it a pious warehouse of red brick, with sometimes (but this only in highly ornamented examples) a bell in a bird-cage on the top of it. The solitary exception was the New Church; a stuccoed edifice with a square steeple over the door, terminating in four short pinnacles like florid wooden legs. All the public inscriptions in the town were painted alike, in severe characters of black and white. The jail might have been the infirmary, the infirmary

---

3. Artificial mounds. Oysters, a luxury today, were popular with poor people in Dickens's day; in *Pickwick Papers* Sam Weller says: "Poverty and oysters always seem to go together."

1. Bounderby is a mill owner; Gradgrind runs a school on Utilitarian principles.

might have been the jail, the town-hall might have been either, or both, or anything else, for anything that appeared to the contrary in the graces of their construction. Fact, fact, fact, everywhere in the material aspect of the town; fact, fact,
fact, everywhere in the immaterial. The M'Choakumchild school was all fact, and
the school of design was all fact, and the relations between master and man were
all fact, and everything was fact between the lying-in hospital and the cemetery,
and what you couldn't state in figures, or show to be purchaseable in the cheapest
market and saleable in the dearest, was not, and never should be, world without
end, Amen.[2]

A town so sacred to fact, and so triumphant in its assertion, of course got on
well? Why no, not quite well. No? Dear me!

No. Coketown did not come out of its own furnaces, in all respects like gold
that had stood the fire. First, the perplexing mystery of the place was, Who
belonged to the eighteen denominations? Because, whoever did, the labouring people did not. It was very strange to walk through the streets on a Sunday morning,
and note how few of *them* the barbarous jangling of bells that was driving the sick
and nervous mad, called away from their own quarter, from their own close rooms,
from the corners of their own streets, where they lounged listlessly, gazing at all the
church and chapel going, as at a thing with which they had no manner of concern.
Nor was it merely the stranger who noticed this, because there was a native organization in Coketown itself, whose members were to be heard of in the House of
Commons every session, indignantly petitioning for acts of parliament that should
make these people religious by main force. Then, came the Teetotal Society, who
complained that these same people *would* get drunk, and showed in tabular statements that they did get drunk, and proved at tea parties that no inducement,
human or Divine (except a medal), would induce them to forego their custom of
getting drunk. Then, came the chemist and druggist, with other tabular statements,
showing that when they didn't get drunk, they took opium. Then, came the experienced chaplain of the jail, with more tabular statements, outdoing all the previous
tabular statements, and showing that the same people *would* resort to low haunts,
hidden from the public eye, where they heard low singing and saw low dancing,
and mayhap joined in it; and where A. B., aged twenty-four next birthday, and
committed for eighteen months' solitary, had himself said (not that he had ever
shown himself particularly worthy of belief) his ruin began, as he was perfectly sure
and confident that otherwise he would have been a tip-top moral specimen. Then,
came Mr Gradgrind and Mr Bounderby, the two gentlemen at this present moment
walking through Coketown, and both eminently practical, who could, on occasion,
furnish more tabular statements derived from their own personal experience, and
illustrated by cases they had known and seen, from which it clearly appeared—in
short it was the only clear thing in the case—that these same people were a bad lot
altogether, gentlemen; that do what you would for them they were never thankful
for it, gentlemen; that they were restless, gentlemen; that they never knew what
they wanted; that they lived upon the best, and bought fresh butter, and insisted
on Mocha coffee, and rejected all but prime parts of meat, and yet were eternally
dissatisfied and unmanageable.

1854

2. The conclusion of the Anglican form of the Lord's Prayer.

Benjamin Disraeli
1804–1881

The subtitle of Benjamin Disraeli's novel *Sybil*, "The Two Nations," encapsulates the Victorians' uneasy sense of being a divided society. The Hungry Forties were a time of unprecedented economic distress: Britain was the world's wealthiest nation, yet people were starving in the streets, and many feared that a revolution was in the offing. Thomas Carlyle had argued in *Past and Present* that "isolation is the sum-total of wretchedness to man." Here, Disraeli echoes his call for cooperation and benevolent paternalism to forge new relations between classes. Disraeli went on to become a Conservative Prime Minister, noted both for his nostalgic vision of aristocratic leadership, and for the domestic social reforms that took place during his administration.

from Sybil
[THE TWO NATIONS]

"It is a community of purpose that constitutes society," continued the younger stranger; "without that, men may be drawn into contiguity, but they still continue virtually isolated."

"And is that their condition in cities?"

"It is their condition everywhere; but in cities that condition is aggravated. A density of population implies a severer struggle for existence, and a consequent repulsion of elements brought into too close contact. In great cities men are brought together by the desire of gain. They are not in a state of co-operation, but of isolation, as to the making of fortunes; and for all the rest they are careless of neighbours. Christianity teaches us to love our neighbour as ourself; modern society acknowledges no neighbour."

"Well, we live in strange times," said Egremont, struck by the observation of his companion, and relieving a perplexed spirit by an ordinary exclamation, which often denotes that the mind is more stirred than it cares to acknowledge, or at the moment is able to express.

"When the infant begins to walk, it also thinks that it lives in strange times," said his companion.

"Your inference?" asked Egremont.

"That society, still in its infancy, is beginning to feel its way."

"This is a new reign," said Egremont, "perhaps it is a new era."

"I think so," said the younger stranger.

"I hope so," said the elder one.

"Well, society may be in its infancy," said Egremont, slightly smiling; "but, say what you like, our Queen reigns over the greatest nation that ever existed."

"Which nation?" asked the younger stranger, "for she reigns over two."

The stranger paused; Egremont was silent, but looked inquiringly.

"Yes," resumed the younger stranger after a moment's interval. "Two nations; between whom there is no intercourse and no sympathy; who are as ignorant of each other's habits, thoughts, and feelings, as if they were dwellers in different zones, or inhabitants of different planets; who are formed by a different breeding, are fed by a different food, are ordered by different manners, and are not governed by the same laws."

"You speak of—" said Egremont, hesitatingly.

"The Rich and the Poor."

1845

➤ ⇥✦⇤ ↠

Friedrich Engels
1820–1895

In the manufacturing city of Manchester, whose size had increased more than tenfold between 1760 and 1830, the average life expectancy of working people in 1841 was only twenty years. Friedrich Engels, a German who had come to Manchester to study the cotton trade, was so appalled by his observations of the urban poor that he wrote an exposé of their degradation, stressing the "hypocritical town planning" that insulated the middle class from the sight of squalor and suffering. Engels's book was published in German in 1845; it became a socialist classic, and laid the groundwork for Engels's collaboration with Karl Marx. Lenin called the book "a terrible indictment of capitalism and of the middle classes." It was finally translated into English in 1892.

from The Condition of the Working Class in England in 1844
from *The Great Towns*

London is unique, because it is a city in which one can roam for hours without leaving the built-up area and without seeing the slightest sign of the approach of open country. This enormous agglomeration of population on a single spot has multiplied a hundred-fold the economic strength of the two and a half million inhabitants concentrated there. This great population has made London the commercial capital of the world and has created the gigantic docks in which are assembled the thousands of ships which always cover the River Thames. I know nothing more imposing than the view one obtains of the river when sailing from the sea up to London Bridge. Especially above Woolwich the houses and docks are packed tightly together on both banks of the river. The further one goes up the river the thicker becomes the concentration of ships lying at anchor, so that eventually only a narrow shipping lane is left free in mid-stream. Here hundreds of steamships dart rapidly to and fro. All this is so magnificent and impressive that one is lost in admiration. The traveller has good reason to marvel at England's greatness even before he steps on English soil.

It is only later that the traveller appreciates the human suffering which has made all this possible. He can only realise the price that has been paid for all this magnificence after he has tramped the pavements of the main streets of London for some days and has tired himself out by jostling his way through the crowds and by dodging the endless stream of coaches and carts which fills the streets. It is only when he has visited the slums of this great city that it dawns upon him that the inhabitants of modern London have had to sacrifice so much that is best in human nature in order to create those wonders of civilisation with which their city teems. The vast majority of Londoners have had to let so many of their potential creative faculties lie dormant, stunted and unused in order that a small, closely-knit group of their fellow citizens could develop to the full the qualities with which nature has endowed them. The restless and noisy activity of the crowded streets is highly distasteful, and it is surely abhorrent to human nature itself. Hundreds of thousands of men and women drawn from all classes and ranks of society pack the streets of London. Are they not all human beings with the same innate characteristics and potentialities? Are they not all equally interested in the pursuit of happiness? And do they not all aim at happiness by following similar methods? Yet they rush past each other as if they had

Augustus Welby Northmore Pugin, *Catholic Town in 1440 / Same Town in 1840*, from *Contrasts*, 1836. Pugin, an architect, anticipated Ruskin's belief that art is an index of spiritual values. He argued for a revival of Gothic architecture as a means of regenerating Victorian morality. In *Contrasts* he juxtaposed medieval and Victorian scenes to display the superiority of Gothic styles, institutions, and attitudes. Here, church spires have given way to smokestacks; trees and open fields have been replaced by looming factories, a lunatic asylum, and an enormous panoptic jail; the social and spiritual harmony of a preindustrial age has fragmented into a hodgepodge of competing religious sects.

nothing in common. They are tacitly agreed on one thing only—that everyone should keep to the right of the pavement so as not to collide with the stream of people moving in the opposite direction. No one even thinks of sparing a glance for his neighbour in the streets. The more that Londoners are packed into a tiny space, the more repulsive and disgraceful becomes the brutal indifference with which they ignore their neighbours and selfishly concentrate upon their private affairs. We know well enough that this isolation of the individual—this narrow-minded egotism—is everywhere the fundamental principle of modern society. But nowhere is this selfish egotism so blatantly evident as in the frantic bustle of the great city. The disintegration of society into individuals, each guided by his private principles and each pursuing his own aims has been pushed to its furthest limits in London. Here indeed human society has been split into its component atoms.

From this it follows that the social conflict—the war of all against all—is fought in the open. * * * Here men regard their fellows not as human beings, but as pawns in the struggle for existence. Everyone exploits his neighbour with the result that the stronger tramples the weaker under foot. The strongest of all, a tiny group of capitalists, monopolise everything, while the weakest, who are in the vast majority, succumb to the most abject poverty.

What is true of London, is true also of all the great towns, such as Manchester, Birmingham and Leeds. Everywhere one finds on the one hand the most barbarous indifference and selfish egotism and on the other the most distressing scenes of misery and poverty. Signs of social conflict are to be found everywhere. Everyone turns his house into a fortress to defend himself—under the protection of the law—from the depredations of his neighbours. Class warfare is so open and shameless that it has to be seen to be believed. The observer of such an appalling state of affairs must shudder at the consequences of such feverish activity and can only marvel that so crazy a social and economic structure should survive at all.

Capital is the all-important weapon in the class war. Power lies in the hands of those who own, directly or indirectly, foodstuffs and the means of production. The poor, having no capital, inevitably bear the consequences of defeat in the struggle. Nobody troubles about the poor as they struggle helplessly in the whirlpool of modern industrial life. The working man may be lucky enough to find employment, if by his labour he can enrich some member of the middle classes. But his wages are so low that they hardly keep body and soul together. If he cannot find work, he can steal, unless he is afraid of the police; or he can go hungry and then the police will see to it that he will die of hunger in such a way as not to disturb the equanimity of the middle classes. While I was in England at least twenty or thirty people died of hunger under the most scandalous circumstances, and yet when an inquest was held the jury seldom had the courage to bring in a verdict in accordance with the facts. However clear and unequivocal the evidence, the middle classes, from whom the juries were drawn, always found a loophole which enabled them to avoid a verdict of "death from starvation." In such circumstances the middle classes dare not tell the truth, because if they did so, they would be condemning themselves out of their own mouths. * * *

Every great town has one or more slum areas into which the working classes are packed. Sometimes, of course, poverty is to be found hidden away in alleys close to the stately homes of the wealthy. Generally, however, the workers are segregated in separate districts where they struggle through life as best they can out of sight of the more fortunate classes of society. The slums of the English towns have much in common—the worst houses in a town being found in the worst districts. They are generally unplanned wildernesses of one- or two-storied terrace houses built of brick. Wherever possible these have cellars which are also used as dwellings. These little houses of three or four rooms and a kitchen are called cottages, and throughout England, except for some parts of London, are where the working classes normally live. The streets themselves are usually unpaved and full of holes. They are filthy and strewn with animal and vegetable refuse. Since they have neither gutters nor drains the refuse accumulates in stagnant, stinking puddles. Ventilation in the slums is inadequate owing to the hopelessly unplanned nature of these areas. A great many people live huddled together in a very small area, and so it is easy to imagine the nature of the air in these workers' quarters. However, in fine weather the streets are used for the drying of washing and clothes lines are stretched across the streets from house to house and wet garments are hung out on them.

We propose to describe some of these slums in detail. In London there is the well-known "rookery"[1] of St. Giles. * * * St. Giles is situated in the most densely-populated part of London and is surrounded by splendid wide streets which are used by the fashionable world. It is close to Oxford Street, Trafalgar Square and the Strand. It is a confused conglomeration of tall houses of three or four stories. The narrow, dirty streets are just as crowded as the main thoroughfares, but in St. Giles one sees only members of the working classes. The narrowness of the roads is accentuated by the presence of streetmarkets in which baskets of rotting and virtually uneatable vegetables and fruit are exposed for sale. The smell from these and from the butchers' stalls is appalling. The houses are packed from cellar to attic and they are as dirty inside as outside. No human being would willingly inhabit such dens. Yet even worse conditions are to be found in the houses which lie off the main road down narrow alleys leading to the courts. These dwellings are approached by covered passages between the houses. The extent to which these filthy passages are falling into decay beggars all description. There is hardly an unbroken windowpane to be seen, the walls are crumbling, the door posts and window frames are loose and rotten. The doors, where they exist, are made of old boards nailed together. Indeed in this nest of thieves doors are superfluous, because there is nothing worth stealing. Piles of refuse and ashes lie all over the place and the slops thrown out into the street collect in pools which emit a foul stench. Here live the poorest of the poor. Here the worst-paid workers rub shoulders with thieves, rogues and prostitutes. Most of them have come from Ireland or are of Irish extraction. Those who have not yet been entirely engulfed in the morass of iniquity by which they are surrounded are daily losing the power to resist the demoralising influences of poverty, dirt and low environment. * * *

However wretched may be the dwellings of some of the workers—who do at least have a roof over their heads—the situation of the homeless is even more tragic. Every morning fifty thousand Londoners wake up not knowing where they are going to sleep at night. The most fortunate are those who have a few pence in their pocket in the evening and can afford to go to one of the many lodging houses which exist in all the big cities. But these establishments only provide the most miserable accommodation. They are crammed full of beds from top to bottom—four, five and even six beds in a room—until there is no room for more. Each bed is filled to capacity and

---

1. An overcrowded and deteriorating district of tenement dwellings.

may contain as many as four, five or even six lodgers. The lodging house keeper allocates his accommodation to all his customers in rotation as they arrive. No attempt is made to segregate the sick and the healthy, the old and the young, the men and the women, the drunk and the sober. If these ill-assorted bed-fellows do not agree there are quarrels and fights which often lead to injuries. But if they do agree among themselves, it is even worse, for they are either planning burglaries or are engaged in practices of so bestial a nature that no words exist in a modern civilised tongue to describe them. Those who cannot afford a bed in a lodging house sleep where they can, in passages, arcades or any corner where the police and the owners are unlikely to disturb their slumbers. * * *

If we cross Blackstone Edge on foot or take the train we reach Manchester, the regional capital of South Lancashire, and enter the classic home of English industry. This is the masterpiece of the Industrial Revolution and at the same time the mainspring of all the workers' movements. Once more we are in a beautiful hilly countryside. The land slopes gently down towards the Irish Sea, intersected by the charming green valleys of the Ribble, the Irwell, the Mersey and their tributaries. A hundred years ago this region was to a great extent thinly populated marsh-land. Now it is covered with towns and villages and is the most densely-populated part of England. In Lancashire—particularly in Manchester—is to be found not only the origin but the heart of the industry of the United Kingdom. Manchester Exchange is the thermometer which records all the fluctuations of industrial and commercial activity. The evolution of the modern system of manufacture has reached its climax in Manchester. It was in the South Lancashire cotton industry that water and steam power first replaced hand machines. It was here that such machines as the power-loom and the self-acting mule replaced the old hand-loom and spinning wheel. It is here that the division of labour has been pushed to its furthest limits. These three factors are the essence of modern industry. In all three of them the cotton industry was the pioneer and remains ahead in all branches of industry. In the circumstances it is to be expected that it is in this region that the inevitable consequences of industrialisation in so far as they affect the working classes are most strikingly evident. Nowhere else can the life and conditions of the industrial proletariat be studied in all their aspects as in South Lancashire. Here can be seen most clearly the degradation into which the worker sinks owing to the introduction of steam power, machinery and the division of labour. Here, too, can be seen most the strenuous efforts of the proletariat to raise themselves from their degraded situation. I propose to examine conditions in Manchester in greater detail for two reasons. In the first place, Manchester is the classic type of modern industrial town. Secondly, I know Manchester as well as I know my native town and I know more about it than most of its inhabitants. * * *

* * * Owing to the curious lay-out of the town it is quite possible for someone to live for years in Manchester and to travel daily to and from his work without ever seeing a working-class quarter or coming into contact with an artisan. He who visits Manchester simply on business or for pleasure need never see the slums, mainly because the working-class districts and the middle-class districts are quite distinct. This division is due partly to deliberate policy and partly to instinctive and tacit agreement between the two social groups. In those areas where the two social groups happen to come into contact with each other the middle classes sanctimoniously ignore the existence of their less fortunate neighbours. In the centre of Manchester there is a fairly large commercial district, which is about half a mile long and half a mile broad. This district is almost entirely given over to offices and warehouses. Nearly the whole of this district

has no permanent residents and is deserted at night, when only policemen patrol its dark, narrow thoroughfares with their bull's eye lanterns. This district is intersected by certain main streets which carry an enormous volume of traffic. The lower floors of the buildings are occupied by shops of dazzling splendour. A few of the upper stories on these premises are used as dwellings and the streets present a relatively busy appearance until late in the evening. Around this commercial quarter there is a belt of built up areas on the average one and a half miles in width, which is occupied entirely by working-class dwellings. This area of workers' houses includes all Manchester proper, except the centre. * * * The upper classes enjoy healthy country air and live in luxurious and comfortable dwellings which are linked to the centre of Manchester by omnibuses which run every fifteen or thirty minutes. To such an extent has the convenience of the rich been considered in the planning of Manchester that these plutocrats can travel from their houses to their places of business in the centre of the town by the shortest routes, which run entirely through working-class districts, without even realising how close they are to the misery and filth which lie on both sides of the road. This is because the main streets which run from the Exchange in all directions out of the town are occupied almost uninterruptedly on both sides by shops, which are kept by members of the lower middle classes. In their own interests these shopkeepers should keep the outsides of their shops in a clean and respectable condition, and in fact they do so. These shops have naturally been greatly influenced by the character of the population in the area which lies behind them. Those shops which are situated in the vicinity of commercial or middle class residential districts are more elegant than those which serve as a facade for the workers' grimy cottages. Nevertheless, even the less pretentious shops adequately serve their purpose of hiding from the eyes of wealthy ladies and gentlemen with strong stomachs and weak nerves the misery and squalor which are part and parcel of their own riches and luxury. * * *

I am quite aware of the fact that this hypocritical town-planning device is more or less common to all big cities. * * * But in my opinion Manchester is unique in the systematic way in which the working classes have been barred from the main streets. Nowhere else has such care been taken to avoid offending the tender susceptibilities of the eyes and the nerves of the middle classes. Yet Manchester is the very town in which building has taken place in a haphazard manner with little or no planning or interference from the authorities. When the middle classes zealously proclaim that all is well with the working classes, I cannot help feeling that the politically "progressive" industrialists, the Manchester "bigwigs," are not quite so innocent of this shameful piece of town planning as they pretend.

* * * I will now give a description of the working-class districts of Manchester. The first of them is the Old Town, which lies between the northern limit of the commercial quarter and the River Irk. * * * Here one is really and truly in a district which is quite obviously given over entirely to the working classes, because even the shopkeepers and the publicans[2] of Long Millgate make no effort to give their establishments a semblance of cleanliness. The condition of this street may be deplorable, but it is by no means as bad as the alleys and courts which lie behind it, and which can be approached only by covered passages so narrow that two people cannot pass. Anyone who has never visited these courts and alleys can have no idea of the fantastic way in which the houses have been packed together in disorderly confusion in impudent defiance of all reasonable principles of town planning. And the fault lies not merely in the

---

2. Pub-keepers.

survival of old property from earlier periods in Manchester's history. Only in quite modern times has the policy of cramming as many houses as possible on to such space as was not utilised in earlier periods reached its climax. The result is that today not an inch of space remains between the houses and any further building is now physically impossible. * * *

* * * To the right and left a number of covered passages from Long Millgate give access to several courts. On reaching them one meets with a degree of dirt and revolting filth, the like of which is not to be found elsewhere. The worst courts are those leading down to the Irk, which contain unquestionably the most dreadful dwellings I have ever seen. In one of these courts, just at the entrance where the covered passage ends there is a privy without a door. This privy is so dirty that the inhabitants of the court can only enter or leave the court if they are prepared to wade through puddles of stale urine and excrement. Anyone who wishes to confirm this description should go to the first court on the bank of the Irk above Ducie Bridge. Several tanneries are situated on the bank of the river and they fill the neighbourhood with the stench of animal putrefaction. The only way of getting to the courts below Ducie Bridge is by going down flights of narrow dirty steps and one can only reach the houses by treading over heaps of dirt and filth. * * * The view from this bridge, which is mercifully concealed by a high parapet from all but the tallest mortals, is quite characteristic of the whole district. At the bottom the Irk flows, or rather, stagnates. It is a narrow, coal-black, stinking river full of filth and rubbish which it deposits on the more low-lying right bank. In dry weather this bank presents the spectacle of a series of the most revolting blackish-green puddles of slime from the depths of which bubbles of miasmatic[3] gases constantly rise and create a stench which is unbearable even to those standing on the bridge forty or fifty feet above the level of the water. Moreover, the flow of the river is continually interrupted by numerous high weirs, behind which large quantities of slime and refuse collect and putrefy. Above Ducie Bridge there are some tall tannery buildings, and further up there are dye-works, bone mills and gasworks. All the filth, both liquid and solid, discharged by these works finds its way into the River Irk, which also receives the contents of the adjacent sewers and privies. The nature of the filth deposited by this river may well be imagined. If one looks at the heaps of garbage below Ducie Bridge one can gauge the extent to which accumulated dirt, filth and decay permeates the courts on the steep left bank of the river. The houses are packed very closely together and since the bank of the river is very steep it is possible to see a part of every house. All of them have been blackened by soot, all of them are crumbling with age and all have broken window panes and window frames. * * * In the background one sees the paupers' cemetery, and the stations of the railways to Liverpool and Leeds. Behind these buildings is situated the workhouse, Manchester's "Poor Law Bastille."[4] The workhouse is built on a hill and from behind its high walls and battlements seems to threaten the whole adjacent working-class quarter like a fortress.

* * * The recently constructed extension of the Leeds railway which crosses the Irk at this point has swept away some of these courts and alleys, but it has thrown open to public gaze some of the others. So it comes about that there is to be found immediately under the railway bridge a court which is even filthier and more revolting than all the others. This is simply because it was formerly so hidden and secluded that it could only

3. Heavy, vaporous, and possibly disease ridden.
4. The Poor Laws of the 1830s established workhouses for the poor, where conditions were so appalling that they were likened to prisons such as the Bastille in Paris.

be reached with considerable difficulty, [but is now exposed to the human eye]. I thought I knew this district well, but even I would never have found it had not the railway viaduct made a breach in the slums at this point. One walks along a very rough path on the river bank, in between clothes-posts and washing lines to reach a chaotic group of little, one-storied, one-roomed cabins. Most of them have earth floors, and working, living and sleeping all take place in the one room. In such a hole, barely six feet long and five feet wide, I saw two beds—and what beds and bedding!—which filled the room, except for the fireplace and the doorstep. Several of these huts, as far as I could see, were completely empty, although the door was open and the inhabitants were leaning against the door posts. In front of the doors filth and garbage abounded. I could not see the pavement, but from time to time, I felt it was there because my feet scraped it. This whole collection of cattle sheds for human beings was surrounded on two sides by houses and a factory and on a third side by the river. * * *

Enough of this! All along the Irk slums of this type abound. There is an unplanned and chaotic conglomeration of houses, most of which are more or less unhabitable. The dirtiness of the interiors of these premises is fully in keeping with the filth that surrounds them. How can people dwelling in such places keep clean! There are not even adequate facilities for satisfying the most natural daily needs. There are so few privies that they are either filled up every day or are too far away for those who need to use them. How can these people wash when all that is available is the dirty water of the Irk? Pumps and piped water are to be found only in the better-class districts of the town. Indeed no one can blame these helots[5] of modern civilisation if their homes are no cleaner than the occasional pigsties which are a feature of these slums. * * *

This, then, is the Old Town of Manchester. On re-reading my description of the Old Town I must admit that, far from having exaggerated anything, I have not written vividly enough to impress the reader with the filth and dilapidation of a district which is quite unfit for human habitation. The shameful lay-out of the Old Town has made it impossible for the wretched inhabitants to enjoy cleanliness, fresh air, and good health. And such a district of at least twenty to thirty thousand inhabitants lies in the very centre of the second city in England, the most important factory town in the world. It is here that one can see how little space human beings need to move about in, how little air—and what air!—they need to breathe in order to exist, and how few of the decencies of civilisation are really necessary in order to survive. It is true that this is the *Old Town* and Manchester people stress this when their attention is drawn to the revolting character of this hell upon earth. But that is no defence. Everything in this district that arouses our disgust and just indignation is of relatively recent origin and belongs to the industrial age. The two or three hundred houses which survive from the earlier period of Manchester's history have long ago been deserted by their original inhabitants. It is only industry which has crammed them full of the hordes of workers who now live there. It is only the modern industrial age which has built over every scrap of ground between these old houses to provide accommodation for the masses who have migrated from the country districts and from Ireland. It is only the industrial age that has made it possible for the owners of these shacks, fit only for the accommodation of cattle, to let them at high rents for human habitations. It is only modern industry which permits these owners to take

5. Serfs or slaves.

advantage of the poverty of the workers, to undermine the health of thousands to enrich themselves. Only industry has made it possible for workers who have barely emerged from a state of serfdom to be again treated as chattels and not as human beings. The workers have been caged in dwellings which are so wretched that no one else will live in them, and they actually pay good money for the privilege of seeing these dilapidated hovels fall to pieces about their ears. Industry alone has been responsible for all this and yet this same industry could not flourish except by degrading and exploiting the workers.

1845

✦ ✠ ✦

Henry Mayhew
1812–1887

In London, the most visible occupations of children were in the streets. They earned a precarious living hawking goods, begging, performing, and providing various services, from running errands to prostitution. Mayhew interviewed hundreds of street people, gathering four volumes of testimony about the lives of this exploited and neglected underclass. With an extraordinary ear for slang and oddities of speech, he shaped each narrative into a kind of dramatic monologue. By publishing "the history of a people, from the lips of the people themselves . . . in their own 'unvarnished' language," Mayhew gave voice to a multitude of forgotten workers. The critic John D. Rosenberg has described Mayhew's image of London as "a vast, ingeniously balanced mechanism in which each class subsists on the drippings and droppings of the stratum above, all the way from the rich, whom we scarcely glimpse, down to the deformed and starving, whom we see groping for bits of salvageable bone or decaying vegetables in the markets."

from London Labour and the London Poor
Watercress Girl

The little watercress girl who gave me the following statement, although only eight years of age, had entirely lost all childish ways, and was, indeed, in thoughts and manner, a woman. There was something cruelly pathetic in hearing this infant, so young that her features had scarcely formed themselves, talking of the bitterest struggles of life, with the calm earnestness of one who had endured them all. I did not know how to talk with her. At first I treated her as a child, speaking on childish subjects; so that I might, by being familiar with her, remove all shyness, and get her to narrate her life freely. I asked her about her toys and her games with her companions; but the look of amazement that answered me soon put an end to any attempt at fun on my part. I then talked to her about the parks, and whether she ever went to them. "The parks!" she replied in wonder, "where are they?" I explained to her, telling her that they were large open places with green grass and tall trees, where beautiful carriages drove about, and people walked for pleasure, and children played. Her eyes brightened up a little as I spoke; and she asked, half doubtingly, "Would they let such as me go there—just to look?" All her knowledge seemed to begin and end with water-cresses,[1] and what they fetched. She knew no more of London than that part

---

1. An herb whose leaves are used in salads and as garnishes.

she had seen on her rounds, and believed that no quarter of the town was handsomer or pleasanter than it was at Farringdon-market or at Clerkenwell, where she lived. Her little face, pale and thin with privation, was wrinkled where the dimples ought to have been, and she would sigh frequently. When some hot dinner was offered to her, she would not touch it, because, if she eat too much, "it made her sick," she said; "and she wasn't used to meat, only on a Sunday."

The poor child, although the weather was severe, was dressed in a thin cotton gown, with a threadbare shawl wrapped round her shoulders. She wore no covering to her head, and the long rusty hair stood out in all directions. When she walked she shuffled along, for fear that the large carpet slippers that served her for shoes should slip off her feet.

"I go about the streets with water-creases, crying, 'Four bunches a penny, water-creases.' I am just eight years old—that's all, and I've a big sister, and a brother and a sister younger than I am. On and off, I've been very near a twelve-month in the streets. Before that, I had to take care of a baby for my aunt. No, it wasn't heavy—it was only two months old; but I minded it for ever such a time—till it could walk. It was a very nice little baby, not a very pretty one; but, if I touched it under the chin, it would laugh. Before I had the baby, I used to help mother, who was in the fur trade; and, if there was any slits in the fur, I'd sew them up. My mother learned me to needle-work and to knit when I was about five. I used to go to school, too; but I wasn't there long. I've forgot all about it now, it's such a time ago; and mother took me away because the master whacked me, though the missus use'n't to never touch me. I didn't like him at all. What do you think? he hit me three times, ever so hard, across the face with his cane, and made me go dancing down stairs; and when mother saw the marks on my cheek, she went to blow him up,[2] but she couldn't see him— he was afraid. That's why I left school.

"The creases is so bad now, that I haven't been out with 'em for three days. They're so cold, people won't buy 'em; for when I goes up to them, they say, 'They'll freeze our bellies.' Besides, in the market, they won't sell a ha'penny handful now— they're ris to[3] a penny and tuppence. In summer there's lots, and 'most as cheap as dirt; but I have to be down at Farringdon-market between four and five, or else I can't get any creases, because everyone almost—especially the Irish—is selling them, and they're picked up so quick. Some of the saleswomen—we never calls 'em ladies—is very kind to us children, and some of them altogether spiteful. The good one will give you a bunch for nothing, when they're cheap; but the others, cruel ones, if you try to bate them a farden less[4] than they ask you, will say, 'Go along with you, you're no good.' I used to go down to market along with another girl, as must be about fourteen, 'cos she does her back hair up. When we've bought a lot, we sits down on a door-step, and ties up the bunches. We never goes home to breakfast till we've sold out; but, if it's very late, then I buys a penn'orth of pudden, which is very nice with gravy. I don't know hardly one of the people, as goes to Farringdon, to talk to; they never speaks to me, so I don't speak to them. We children never play down there, 'cos we're thinking of our living. No; people never pities me in the street—excepting one gentleman, and he says, says he, 'What do you do out so soon in the morning?' but he gave me nothink—he only walked away.

---

2. Scold him.

3. Their price has risen to.

4. Give them a farthing (a quarter of a penny) less.

"It's very cold before winter comes on reg'lar—specially getting up of a morning. I gets up in the dark by the light of the lamp in the court. When the snow is on the ground, there's no creases. I bears the cold—you must; so I puts my hands under my shawl, though it hurts 'em to take hold of the creases, especially when we takes 'em to the pump to wash 'em. No; I never see any children crying—it's no use.

"Sometimes I make a great deal of money. One day I took 1s. 6d., and the creases cost 6d.; but it isn't often I get such luck as that. I oftener makes 3d. or 4d. than 1s.; and then I'm at work, crying, 'Creases, four bunches a penny, creases!' from six in the morning to about ten. What do you mean by mechanics?—I don't know what they are. The shops buys most of me. Some of 'em says, 'Oh! I ain't a-goin' to give a penny for these;' and they want 'em at the same price as I buys 'em at.

"I always give mother my money, she's so very good to me. She don't often beat me; but, when she do, she don't play with me. She's very poor, and goes out cleaning rooms sometimes, now she don't work at the fur. I ain't got no father, he's a father-in-law. No; mother ain't married again—he's a father-in-law. He grinds scissors, and he's very good to me. No; I dont mean by that that he says kind things to me, for he never hardly speaks. When I gets home, after selling creases, I stops at home. I puts the room to rights: mother don't make me do it, I does it myself. I cleans the chairs, though there's only two to clean. I takes a tub and scrubbing-brush and flannel, and scrubs the floor—that's what I do three or four times a week.

"I don't have no dinner. Mother gives me two slices of bread-and-butter and a cup of tea for breakfast, and then I go till tea, and has the same. We has meat of a Sunday, and, of course, I should like to have it every day. Mother has just the same to eat as we has, but she takes more tea—three cups, sometimes. No; I never has no sweet-stuff; I never buy none—I don't like it. Sometimes we has a game of 'honey-pots' with the girls in the court, but not often. Me and Carry H— carries the little 'uns. We plays, too, at 'kiss-in-the-ring.' I knows a good many games, but I don't play at 'em, 'cos going out with creases tires me. On a Friday night, too, I goes to a Jew's house till eleven o'clock on Saturday night. All I has to do is to snuff the candles and poke the fire. You see they keep their Sabbath then, and they won't touch anything; so they gives me my wittals[5] and 1½d., and I does it for 'em. I have a reg'lar good lot to eat. Supper of Friday night, and tea after that, and fried fish of a Saturday morning, and meat for dinner, and tea, and supper, and I like it very well.

"Oh, yes; I've got some toys at home. I've a fire-place, and a box of toys, and a knife and fork, and two little chairs. The Jews gave 'em to me where I go to on a Friday, and that's why I said they was very kind to me. I never had no doll; but I misses little sister—she's only two years old. We don't sleep in the same room; for father and mother sleeps with little sister in the one pair, and me and brother and other sister sleeps in the top room. I always goes to bed at seven, 'cos I has to be up so early.

"I am a capital hand at bargaining—but only at buying watercreases. They can't take me in. If the woman tries to give me a small handful of creases, I says, 'I ain't a goin' to have that for a ha'porth,' and I go to the next basket, and so on, all round. I know the quantities very well. For a penny I ought to have a full market hand, or as much as I could carry in my arms at one time, without spilling. For 3d. I has a lap full, enough to earn about a shilling; and for 6d. I gets as many as crams my basket. I can't read or write, but I knows how many pennies goes to a shilling, why, twelve, of

5. Victuals, food.

The Boy Crossing-Sweepers. After a daguerreotype by Richard Beard, from Henry Mayhew's *London Labour and the London Poor,* 1851.

course, but I don't know how many ha'pence there is, though there's two to a penny. When I've bought 3*d.* of creases, I ties 'em up into as many little bundles as I can. They must look biggish, or the people won't buy them, some puffs them out as much as they'll go. All my money I earns I puts in a club and draws it out to buy clothes with. It's better than spending it in sweet-stuff, for them as has a living to earn. Besides it's like a child to care for sugar-sticks, and not like one who's got a living and vittals to earn. I ain't a child, and I shan't be a woman till I'm twenty, but I'm past eight, I am. I don't know nothing about what I earns during the year, I only know how many pennies goes to a shilling, and two ha'pence goes to a penny, and four fardens goes to a penny. I knows, too, how many fardens goes to tuppence—eight. That's as much as I wants to know for the markets."

[A Boy Crossing-Sweeper]

I found the lad who first gave me an insight into the proceedings of the associated crossing-sweepers crouched on the stone steps of a door in Adelaide-street, Strand; and when I spoke to him he was preparing to settle down in a corner and go to sleep—his legs and body being curled round almost as closely as those of a cat on a hearth.

The moment he heard my voice he was upon his feet, asking me to "give a halfpenny to poor little Jack."

He was a good-looking lad, with a pair of large mild eyes, which he took good care to turn up with an expression of supplication as he moaned for his halfpenny.

A cap, or more properly a stuff bag, covered a crop of hair which had matted itself into the form of so many paint-brushes, while his face, from its roundness of feature and the complexion of dirt, had an almost Indian look about it; the colour of his hands, too, was such that you could imagine he had been shelling walnuts.

He ran before me, treading cautiously with his naked feet, until I reached a convenient spot to take down his statement, which was as follows:—

"I've got no mother or father; mother has been dead for two years, and father's been gone more than that—more nigh five years—he died at Ipswich, in Suffolk.

* * *

* * * "I used, when I was with mother, to go to school in the morning, and go at nine and come home at twelve to dinner, then go again at two and leave off at half-past four,—that is, if I behaved myself and did all my lessons right; for if I did not I was kept back till I *did* them so. Mother used to pay one shilling a-week, and extra for the copy-books and things. I can read and write— oh, yes, I mean read and write well— read anything, even old English; and I write pretty fair,—though I don't get much reading now, unless it's a penny paper—I've got one in my pocket now—it's the *London Journal*—there's a tale in it now about two brothers, and one of them steals the child away and puts another in his place, and then he gets found out, and all that, and he's just been falling off a bridge now. * * *

"After mother died, sister still kept on making nets,[1] and I lived with her for some time, until she told me she couldn't afford to keep me no longer, though she seemed to have a pretty good lot to do; but she would never let me go with her to the shops, though I could crochet, which she'd learned me, and used to run and get her all her silks and things what she wanted. But she was keeping company with a young man, and one day they went out, and came back and said they'd been and got married. It was him as got rid of me.

"He was kind to me for the first two or three months, while he was keeping her company; but before he was married he got a little cross, and after he was married he begun to get more cross, and used to send me to play in the streets, and tell me not to come home again till night. One day he hit me, and I said I wouldn't be hit about by him, and then at tea that night sister gave me three shillings, and told me I must go and get my own living. So I bought a box and brushes (they cost me just the money) and went cleaning boots, and I done pretty well with them, till my box was stole from me by a boy where I was lodging. He's in prison now—got six calendar for picking pockets.

"Sister kept all my clothes. When I asked her for 'em, she said they was disposed of along with all mother's goods; but she gave me some shirts and stockings, and such-like, and I had very good clothes, only they was all worn out. I saw sister after I left her, many times. I asked her many times to take me back, but she used to say, 'It was not her likes, but her husband's, or she'd have had me back;' and I think it was true, for until he came she was a kind-hearted girl; but he said he'd enough to do to look after his own living; he was a fancy-baker by trade.

"I was fifteen the 24th of last May, sir, and I've been sweeping crossings now near upon two years. There's a party of six of us, and we have the crossings from St. Martin's Church as far as Pall Mall. I always go along with them as lodges in the same place as I do. In the daytime, if it's dry, we do anythink we can—open cabs, or

---

1. Hair nets, which she sold to hairdressers.

anythink; but if it's wet, we separate, and I and another gets a crossing—those who gets on it first, keeps it,—and we stand on each side and take our chance.

"We do it in this way:—if I was to see two gentlemen coming, I should cry out, 'Two toffs!' and then they are mine; and whether they give me anythink or not they are mine, and my mate is bound not to follow them; for if he did he would get a hiding from the whole lot of us. If we both cry out together, then we share. If it's a lady and gentleman, then we cries, 'A toff and a doll!' Sometimes we are caught out in this way. Perhaps it is a lady and gentleman and a child; and if I was to see them, and only say, 'A toff and a doll,' and leave out the child, then my mate can add the child; and as he is right and I wrong, then it's his party.

"If there's a policeman close at hand we mustn't ask for money; but we are always on the look-out for the policemen, and if we see one, then we calls out 'Phillup!' for that's our signal. One of the policemen at St. Martin's Church—Bandy, we calls him—knows what Phillup means, for he's up to us; so we had to change the word. (At the request of the young crossing-sweeper the present signal is omitted.)

"Yesterday on the crossing I got threepence halfpenny, but when it's dry like to-day I do nothink, for I haven't got a penny yet. We never carries no pockets, for if the policemen find us we generally pass the money to our mates, for if money's found on us we have fourteen days in prison. * * *

"When we see the rain we say together, 'Oh! there's a jolly good rain! we'll have a good day to-morrow.' If a shower comes on, and we are at our room, which we general are about three o'clock, to get somethink to eat—besides, we general go there to see how much each other's taken in the day—why, out we run with our brooms. * * *

"When we gets home at half-past three in the morning, whoever cries out 'first wash' has it. First of all we washes our feet, and we all uses the same water. Then we washes our faces and hands, and necks, and whoever fetches the fresh water up has first wash; and if the second don't like to go and get fresh, why he uses the dirty. Whenever we come in the landlady makes us wash our feet. Very often the stones cuts our feet and makes them bleed; then we bind a bit of rag round them. * * *

"When there's snow on the ground we puts our money together, and goes and buys an old shovel, and then, about seven o'clock in the morning, we goes to the shops and asks them if we shall scrape the snow away. We general gets twopence every house, but some gives sixpence, for it's very hard to clean the snow away, particular when it's been on the ground some time. It's awful cold, and gives us chilblains on our feet; but we don't mind it when we're working, for we soon gets hot then.

1849–1850   1861–1862

END OF PERSPECTIVES: THE INDUSTRIAL LANDSCAPE

John Stuart Mill
1806–1873

The name John Stuart Mill has become synonymous with genius. But for the Victorians it was also associated with outrageously radical views: Mill advocated sexual equality, the right to divorce, universal suffrage, free speech, and proportional representation. He first gained public attention as a social reformer, promoting the rationalist ideas of his godfather, Jeremy

Bentham, founder of Utilitarianism. Mill went on to become the era's leading philosopher and political theorist, an outspoken member of Parliament, and Britain's most prestigious proponent of women's rights.

Mill's education is legendary: the Victorians were fond of social experiments, but few were stranger or more disturbing than James Mill's efforts to prove that a child could learn so much so early in life. He began teaching his son Greek at the age of three, making him memorize long lists of Greek words and their English translations. He also "home-schooled" his son in history, languages, calculus, logic, political economy, geography, psychology, and rhetoric. The boy's responsibilities included tutoring his younger siblings—eventually, eight of them— in these subjects. All this went on while his father, busy writing his multivolume *History of British India,* surveyed his children from the other end of the dining-room table.

As Mill's *Autobiography* shows, the human cost of the experiment was high. In an early draft he wrote that "I . . . grew up in the absence of love & in the presence of fear." His stern father denied Mill both pleasures and playmates, and so dominated the boy's mother that he interpreted her submissiveness as indifference to his existence. At fourteen, when his father declared his education finished, Mill had, by his own account, the knowledge of a man of forty—but he still could not brush his own hair.

Undaunted by such trivia, Mill decided he wanted to be "a reformer of the world." When he was seventeen, he founded the Utilitarian Society, which vigorously debated how to achieve the Utilitarian goal of bringing the greatest happiness to the greatest number of people. But at twenty he was plunged into depression when he realized that achieving all his goals would not satisfy him: "I seemed to have nothing left to live for." Overwork and the utter neglect of human emotion in his otherwise comprehensive education led Mill to a nervous breakdown in 1826.

Discovering that "the habit of analysis has a tendency to wear away the feelings," Mill gradually recovered by reading poetry, especially that of Wordsworth. The poet aroused his interest in "the common feelings and common destiny of human beings." Despite his assessment of himself as an "unpoetical nature," Mill became one of the most astute critics of his generation, recognizing before anyone else the unusual strengths and psychological motivations of both Tennyson and Browning. His essay *What is Poetry?* (1833) argues that true poetry expresses the passionate, solitary meditations of the author; it is not so much heard as "*over*heard."

In 1823 Mill followed in his father's footsteps by taking a clerkship in the Examiner's Office of the East India Company, the commercial enterprise that, in effect, governed British India. He eventually headed the department, as his father had before him. The center of his professional life, however, was his own writing and political activism. His position allowed him time to become an energetic propagandist for radical causes and legal reform—he was even arrested at age seventeen, a few weeks after the job began, for distributing information on birth control. He also edited the *London and Westminster Review* (1836–1840), while writing important essays on Coleridge and Jeremy Bentham. His *System of Logic* (1843) and *Principles of Political Economy* (1848) immediately became standard works in the field; he followed these with influential books on philosophy, politics, and economics, including *Thoughts on Parliamentary Reform* (1859), *Utilitarianism* (1861), *Representative Government* (1861), and *Auguste Comte and Positivism* (1865).

The most significant event of Mill's adult life was meeting the brilliant and beautiful Harriet Taylor in 1830. She shared his radical views on women's rights, and they soon formed an intimate friendship. But she was married and the mother of three children, a fact which lent piquancy to their efforts to establish the legal right of divorce. They finally married in 1851, after the death of her husband. Mill claimed that she deserved equal credit for his works, calling them "joint productions" of their intellectual life together. "When two persons have their thoughts and speculations completely in common," he wrote in his *Autobiography*, "it is of little consequence . . . which of them holds the pen." After Harriet Taylor died in 1858, her daughter Helen became Mill's companion; she carried on their work in woman's rights into the twentieth century.

Mill retired from the East India Company in 1858 when the British government took over the company's affairs. Although he refused to seek votes or curry favor with any constituency, Mill was elected Member of Parliament for Westminster from 1865 to 1868, making memorable speeches on behalf of political reform, Irish freedom, and women's voting rights. A century ahead of mainstream Anglo-American lawmakers, he demanded nonsexist language for legislation, including a proposal that the Second Reform Bill (1867) be rewritten to replace the word "man" with the word "person." After his defeat in the election of 1868, Mill spent most of his remaining years in Avignon, France, where he died in 1873.

In the twentieth century, Mill's reputation has been sustained by the continuing relevance of his work. *On Liberty* (1859) has become the classic defense of the individual's right, in a modern society dominated by bureaucracy and mass culture, to resist the constraints of both government and public opinion. *The Subjection of Women* (1869) insists that men should grant "perfect equality" to women, demonstrating that "what is now called the nature of women is an eminently artificial thing—the result of forced repression in some directions, unnatural stimulation in others." Finally, the *Autobiography* (1873) poignantly applies these insights to the construction of the author's own identity, revealing how Mill's life was shaped by the forced repressions and stimulations of his unusual family environment.

These three works also embody Mill's distinctive qualities as a writer and thinker: he advances his arguments with exceptional clarity, anticipating objections and providing interesting examples to prove his points; he makes his appeals to the reader on the basis of reason, no matter how emotionally charged the topic may be; and he displays an underlying concern for what is good for the public at large. Never content merely to assert human rights or display moral outrage, Mill dedicated himself to convincing others that freedom of thought and action—for women as well as for men—is not simply right but beneficial to society as a whole.

from **On Liberty**
from Chapter 2. Of the Liberty of Thought and Discussion

The time, it is to be hoped, is gone by, when any defence would be necessary of the "liberty of the press" as one of the securities against corrupt or tyrannical government. * * * If all mankind minus one, were of one opinion, and only one person were of the contrary opinion, mankind would be no more justified in silencing that one person, than he, if he had the power, would be justified in silencing mankind. Were an opinion a personal possession of no value except to the owner; if to be obstructed in the enjoyment of it were simply a private injury, it would make some difference whether the injury was inflicted only on a few persons or on many. But the peculiar evil of silencing the expression of an opinion is, that it is robbing the human race; posterity as well as the existing generation; those who dissent from the opinion, still more than those who hold it. If the opinion is right, they are deprived of the opportunity of exchanging error for truth: if wrong, they lose, what is almost as great a benefit, the clearer perception and livelier impression of truth, produced by its collision with error.

* * * The majority of the eminent men of every past generation held many opinions now known to be erroneous, and did or approved numerous things which no one will now justify. Why is it, then, that there is on the whole a preponderance among mankind of rational opinions and rational conduct? If there really is this preponderance—which there must be unless human affairs are, and have always been, in an almost desperate state—it is owing to a quality of the human mind, the source of

everything respectable in man either as an intellectual or as a moral being, namely, that his errors are corrigible. He is capable of rectifying his mistakes, by discussion and experience. Not by experience alone. There must be discussion, to show how experience is to be interpreted. Wrong opinions and practices gradually yield to fact and argument: but facts and arguments, to produce any effect on the mind, must be brought before it. Very few facts are able to tell their own story, without comments to bring out their meaning. The whole strength and value, then, of human judgment, depending on the one property, that it can be set right when it is wrong, reliance can be placed on it only when the means of setting it right are kept constantly at hand. In the case of any person whose judgment is really deserving of confidence, how has it become so? Because he has kept his mind open to criticism of his opinions and conduct. Because it has been his practice to listen to all that could be said against him; to profit by as much of it as was just, and expound to himself, and upon occasion to others, the fallacy of what was fallacious. Because he has felt, that the only way in which a human being can make some approach to knowing the whole of a subject, is by hearing what can be said about it by persons of every variety of opinion, and studying all modes in which it can be looked at by every character of mind. No wise man ever acquired his wisdom in any mode but this. * * *

In the present age—which has been described as "destitute of faith, but terrified at scepticism"[1]—in which people feel sure, not so much that their opinions are true, as that they should not know what to do without them—the claims of an opinion to be protected from public attack are rested not so much on its truth, as on its importance to society. There are, it is alleged, certain beliefs, so useful, not to say indispensable to well-being, that it is as much the duty of governments to uphold those beliefs, as to protect any other of the interests of society. In a case of such necessity, and so directly in the line of their duty, something less than infallibility may, it is maintained, warrant, and even bind, governments, to act on their own opinion, confirmed by the general opinion of mankind. It is also often argued, and still oftener thought, that none but bad men would desire to weaken these salutary beliefs; and there can be nothing wrong, it is thought, in restraining bad men, and prohibiting what only such men would wish to practise. This mode of thinking makes the justification of restraints on discussion not a question of the truth of doctrines, but of their usefulness; and flatters itself by that means to escape the responsibility of claiming to be an infallible judge of opinions. But those who thus satisfy themselves, do not perceive that the assumption of infallibility is merely shifted from one point to another. The usefulness of an opinion is itself matter of opinion: as disputable, as open to discussion, and requiring discussion as much, as the opinion itself. There is the same need of an infallible judge of opinions to decide an opinion to be noxious, as to decide it to be false, unless the opinion condemned has full opportunity of defending itself. And it will not do to say that the heretic may be allowed to maintain the utility or harmlessness of his opinion, though forbidden to maintain its truth. The truth of an opinion is part of its utility. If we would know whether or not it is desirable that a proposition should be believed, is it possible to exclude the consideration of whether or not it is true? * * *

1. By Thomas Carlyle in *Memoirs of the Life of Scott* (1838).

We have now recognised the necessity to the mental well-being of mankind (on which all their other well-being depends) of freedom of opinion, and freedom of the expression of opinion, on four distinct grounds; which we will now briefly recapitulate.

First, if any opinion is compelled to silence, that opinion may, for aught we can certainly know, be true. To deny this is to assume our own infallibility.

Secondly, though the silenced opinion be an error, it may, and very commonly does, contain a portion of truth; and since the general or prevailing opinion on any subject is rarely or never the whole truth, it is only by the collision of adverse opinions that the remainder of the truth has any chance of being supplied.

Thirdly, even if the received opinion be not only true, but the whole truth; unless it is suffered to be, and actually is, vigorously and earnestly contested, it will, by most of those who receive it, be held in the manner of a prejudice, with little comprehension or feeling of its rational grounds. And not only this, but, fourthly, the meaning of the doctrine itself will be in danger of being lost, or enfeebled, and deprived of its vital effect on the character and conduct: the dogma becoming a mere formal profession, inefficacious for good, but cumbering the ground, and preventing the growth of any real and heartfelt conviction, from reason or personal experience.

from *Chapter 3. Of Individuality, as One of the Elements of Well-Being*

* * * The majority, being satisfied with the ways of mankind as they now are (for it is they who make them what they are), cannot comprehend why those ways should not be good enough for everybody; and what is more, spontaneity forms no part of the ideal of the majority of moral and social reformers, but is rather looked on with jealousy, as a troublesome and perhaps rebellious obstruction to the general acceptance of what these reformers, in their own judgment, think would be best for mankind. Few persons, out of Germany, even comprehend the meaning of the doctrine which Wilhelm Von Humboldt, so eminent both as a *savant* and as a politician, made the text of a treatise—that "the end of man, or that which is prescribed by the eternal or immutable dictates of reason, and not suggested by vague and transient desires, is the highest and most harmonious development of his powers to a complete and consistent whole;" that, therefore, the object "towards which every human being must ceaselessly direct his efforts, and on which especially those who design to influence their fellowmen must ever keep their eyes, is the individuality of power and development;" that for this there are two requisites, "freedom, and variety of situations;" and that from the union of these arise "individual vigour and manifold diversity," which combine themselves in "originality."[1]

Little, however, as people are accustomed to a doctrine like that of Von Humboldt, and surprising as it may be to them to find so high a value attached to individuality, the question, one must nevertheless think, can only be one of degree. No one's idea of excellence in conduct is that people should do absolutely nothing but copy one another. No one would assert that people ought not to put into their mode of life, and into the conduct of their concerns, any impress whatever of their own judgment, or of their own individual character. On the other hand, it would be absurd to pretend that people ought to live as if nothing whatever had been known in the world before they came into it; as if experience had as yet done nothing

---

1. From *The Sphere and Duties of Government* by Baron Wilhelm von Humboldt. Although written in 1791, this treatise was not published until 1852; it was translated into English in 1854.

towards showing that one mode of existence, or of conduct, is preferable to another. Nobody denies that people should be so taught and trained in youth, as to know and benefit by the ascertained results of human experience. But it is the privilege and proper condition of a human being, arrived at the maturity of his faculties, to use and interpret experience in his own way. It is for him to find out what part of recorded experience is properly applicable to his own circumstances and character. * * *

He who lets the world, or his own portion of it, choose his plan of life for him, has no need of any other faculty than the ape-like one of imitation. He who chooses his plan for himself, employs all his faculties. * * * A person whose desires and impulses are his own—are the expression of his own nature, as it has been developed and modified by his own culture—is said to have a character. One whose desires and impulses are not his own, has no character, no more than a steam-engine has a character. If, in addition to being his own, his impulses are strong, and are under the government of a strong will, he has an energetic character. Whoever thinks that individuality of desires and impulses should not be encouraged to unfold itself, must maintain that society has no need of strong natures—is not the better for containing many persons who have much character—and that a high general average of energy is not desirable.

In some early states of society, these forces might be, and were, too much ahead of the power which society then possessed of disciplining and controlling them. There has been a time when the element of spontaneity and individuality was in excess, and the social principle had a hard struggle with it. The difficulty then was, to induce men of strong bodies or minds to pay obedience to any rules which required them to control their impulses. To overcome this difficulty, law and discipline, like the Popes struggling against the Emperors, asserted a power over the whole man, claiming to control all his life in order to control his character—which society had not found any other sufficient means of binding. But society has now fairly got the better of individuality; and the danger which threatens human nature is not the excess, but the deficiency, of personal impulses and preferences. Things are vastly changed, since the passions of those who were strong by station or by personal endowment were in a state of habitual rebellion against laws and ordinances, and required to be rigorously chained up to enable the persons within their reach to enjoy any particle of security. In our times, from the highest class of society down to the lowest, every one lives as under the eye of a hostile and dreaded censorship. Not only in what concerns others, but in what concerns only themselves, the individual or the family do not ask themselves—what do I prefer? or, what would suit my character and disposition? or, what would allow the best and highest in me to have fair play, and enable it to grow and thrive? They ask themselves, what is suitable to my position? what is usually done by persons of my station and pecuniary circumstances? or (worse still) what is usually done by persons of a station and circumstances superior to mine? I do not mean that they choose what is customary, in preference to what suits their own inclination. It does not occur to them to have any inclination, except for what is customary. Thus the mind itself is bowed to the yoke: even in what people do for pleasure, conformity is the first thing thought of; they like in crowds; they exercise choice only among things commonly done: peculiarity of taste, eccentricity of conduct, are shunned equally with crimes: until by dint of not following their own nature, they have no nature to follow: their human capacities are withered and starved: they become incapable of any strong wishes or native pleasures, and are generally without either opinions or feelings of home growth, or properly their own. Now is this, or is it not, the desirable condition of human nature?* * *

Having said that Individuality is the same thing with development, and that it is only the cultivation of individuality which produces, or can produce, well-developed human beings, I might here close the argument: for what more or better can be said of any condition of human affairs, than that it brings human beings themselves nearer to the best thing they can be? or what worse can be said of any obstruction to good, than that it prevents this? Doubtless, however, these considerations will not suffice to convince those who most need convincing; and it is necessary further to show, that these developed human beings are of some use to the undeveloped—to point out to those who do not desire liberty, and would not avail themselves of it, that they may be in some intelligible manner rewarded for allowing other people to make use of it without hindrance.

In the first place, then, I would suggest that they might possibly learn something from them. It will not be denied by anybody, that originality is a valuable element in human affairs. There is always need of persons not only to discover new truths, and point out when what were once truths are true no longer, but also to commence new practices, and set the example of more enlightened conduct, and better taste and sense in human life. * * * Persons of genius, it is true, are, and are always likely to be, a small minority; but in order to have them, it is necessary to preserve the soil in which they grow. Genius can only breathe freely in an *atmosphere* of freedom. Persons of genius are, *ex vi termini* [by definition], *more* individual than any other people—less capable, consequently, of fitting themselves, without hurtful compression, into any of the small number of moulds which society provides in order to save its members the trouble of forming their own character. If from timidity they consent to be forced into one of these moulds, and to let all that part of themselves which cannot expand under the pressure remain unexpanded, society will be little the better for their genius. If they are of a strong character, and break their fetters, they become a mark for the society which has not succeeded in reducing them to commonplace, to point at with solemn warning as "wild," "erratic," and the like; much as if one should complain of the Niagara river for not flowing smoothly between its banks like a Dutch canal.* * *

In sober truth, whatever homage may be professed, or even paid, to real or supposed mental superiority, the general tendency of things throughout the world is to render mediocrity the ascendant power among mankind. In ancient history, in the middle ages, and in a diminishing degree through the long transition from feudality to the present time, the individual was a power in himself; and if he had either great talents or a high social position, he was a considerable power. At present individuals are lost in the crowd. In politics it is almost a triviality to say that public opinion now rules the world. The only power deserving the name is that of masses, and of governments while they make themselves the organ of the tendencies and instincts of masses. This is as true in the moral and social relations of private life as in public transactions. Those whose opinions go by the name of public opinion, are not always the same sort of public: in America they are the whole white population; in England, chiefly the middle class. But they are always a mass, that is to say, collective mediocrity. And what is a still greater novelty, the mass do not now take their opinions from dignitaries in Church or State, from ostensible leaders, or from books. Their thinking is done for them by men much like themselves, addressing them or speaking in their name, on the spur of the moment, through the newspapers. I am not complaining of all this. I do not assert that anything better is compatible, as a general rule, with the present low state of the human mind. But that does not hinder the government of mediocrity from being mediocre government. No government by a democracy or a numerous aristocracy, either in its political acts or in the opinions, qualities, and tone of mind which it fosters, ever did or could rise above mediocrity, except in so far as the sovereign Many have let themselves be guided (which in their best times they always have done) by the counsels and influence of a more highly gifted and instructed One or Few. The initiation of all wise or noble things, comes and must come from individuals; generally at first from some one individual. The honour and glory of the average man is that he is capable of following that initiative; that he can respond internally to wise and noble things, and be led to them with his eyes open. I am not countenancing the sort of "hero-worship" which applauds the strong man of genius for forcibly seizing on the government of the world and making it do his bidding in spite of itself.[2] All he can claim is, freedom to point out the way. The power of compelling others into it, is not only inconsistent with the freedom and development of all the rest, but corrupting to the strong man himself. It does seem, however, that when the opinions of masses of merely average men are everywhere become or becoming the dominant power, the counterpoise and corrective to that tendency would be, the more and more pronounced individuality of those who stand on the higher eminences of thought. It is in these circumstances most especially, that exceptional individuals, instead of being deterred, should be encouraged in acting differently from the mass. In other times there was no advantage in their doing so, unless they acted not only differently, but better. In this age, the mere example of nonconformity, the mere refusal to bend the knee to custom, is itself a service. Precisely because the tyranny of opinion is such as to make eccentricity a reproach, it is desirable, in order to break through that tyranny, that people should be eccentric. Eccentricity has always abounded when and where strength of character has abounded; and the amount of eccentricity in a society has generally been proportional to the amount of genius, mental vigour, and moral courage which it contained. That so few now dare to be eccentric, marks the chief danger of the time. * * *

* * * We have discarded the fixed costumes of our forefathers; every one must still dress like other people, but the fashion may change once or twice a year. We thus take care that when there is change it shall be for change's sake, and not from any idea of beauty or convenience; for the same idea of beauty or convenience would not strike all the world at the same moment, and be simultaneously thrown aside by all at another moment. But we are progressive as well as changeable: we continually make new inventions in mechanical things, and keep them until they are again superseded by better; we are eager for improvement in politics, in education, even in morals, though in this last our idea of improvement chiefly consists in persuading or forcing other people to be as good as ourselves. It is not progress that we object to; on the contrary, we flatter ourselves that we are the most progressive people who ever lived. It is individuality that we war against: we should think we had done wonders if we had made ourselves all alike; forgetting that the unlikeness of one person to another is generally the first thing which draws the attention of either to the imperfection of his own type, and the superiority of another, or the possibility, by combining the advantages of both, of producing something better than either. We have a warning example in China—a nation of much talent, and, in some respects, even wisdom, owing to the rare good fortune of having been provided at an early period with a particularly good set of customs, the work, in some measure, of men to whom

2. Cf. Thomas Carlyle, *On Heroes and Hero-Worship* (1841).

even the most enlightened European must accord, under certain limitations, the title of sages and philosophers. They are remarkable, too, in the excellence of their appa-ratus for impressing, as far as possible, the best wisdom they possess upon every mind in the community, and securing that those who have appropriated most of it shall occupy the posts of honour and power. Surely the people who did this have discov-ered the secret of human progressiveness, and must have kept themselves steadily at the head of the movement of the world. On the contrary, they have become station-ary—have remained so for thousands of years; and if they are ever to be farther improved, it must be by foreigners. They have succeeded beyond all hope in what English philanthropists are so industriously working at—in making a people all alike, all governing their thoughts and conduct by the same maxims and rules; and these are the fruits. The modern *régime* of public opinion is, in an unorganized form, what the Chinese educational and political systems are in an organized; and unless indi-viduality shall be able successfully to assert itself against this yoke, Europe, notwith-standing its noble antecedents and its professed Christianity, will tend to become another China.

1859

from The Subjection of Women[1]
from Chapter 1

The object of this essay is to explain as clearly as I am able, the grounds of an opinion which I have held from the very earliest period when I had formed any opinions at all on social or political matters, and which, instead of being weakened or modified, has been constantly growing stronger by the progress of reflection and the experience of life: That the principle which regulates the existing social relations between the two sexes—the legal subordination of one sex to the other—is wrong in itself, and now one of the chief hindrances to human improvement; and that it ought to be replaced by a principle of perfect equality, admitting no power or privilege on the one side, nor disability on the other. * * *

* * * If the authority of men over women, when first established, had been the result of a conscientious comparison between different modes of constituting the gov-ernment of society; if, after trying various other modes of social organization—the gov-ernment of women over men, equality between the two, and such mixed and divided modes of government as might be invented—it had been decided, on the testimony of experience, that the mode in which women are wholly under the rule of men, having no share at all in public concerns, and each in private being under the legal obligation of obedience to the man with whom she has associated her destiny, was the arrange-ment most conducive to the happiness and well being of both; its general adoption might then be fairly thought to be some evidence that, at the time when it was adopt-ed, it was the best: though even then the considerations which recommended it may, like so many other primeval social facts of the greatest importance, have subsequently, in the course of ages, ceased to exist. But the state of the case is in every respect the reverse of this. In the first place, the opinion in favour of the present system, which entirely subordinates the weaker sex to the stronger, rests upon theory only; for there never has been trial made of any other: so that experience, in the sense in which it is

1. See Mary Wollstonecraft's A Vindication of the Rights of   Its Time, page 168.
Woman (1792), page 152, and also "A Vindication" and

vulgarly opposed to theory, cannot be pretended to have pronounced any verdict. And in the second place, the adoption of this system of inequality never was the result of deliberation, or forethought, or any social ideas, or any notion whatever of what conduced to the benefit of humanity or the good order of society. It arose simply from the fact that from the very earliest twilight of human society, every woman (owing to the value attached to her by men, combined with her inferiority in muscular strength) was found in a state of bondage to some man. * * *

Some will object, that a comparison cannot fairly be made between the government of the male sex and the forms of unjust power which I have adduced in illustration of it,[2] since these are arbitrary, and the effect of mere usurpation, while it on the contrary is natural. But was there ever any domination which did not appear natural to those who possessed it? There was a time when the division of mankind into two classes, a small one of masters and a numerous one of slaves, appeared, even to the most cultivated minds, to be a natural, and the only natural, condition of the human race. No less an intellect, and one which contributed no less to the progress of human thought, than Aristotle, held this opinion without doubt or misgiving; and rested it on the same premises on which the same assertion in regard to the dominion of men over women is usually based, namely that there are different natures among mankind, free natures, and slave natures; that the Greeks were of a free nature, the barbarian races of Thracians and Asiatics of a slave nature.[3] But why need I go back to Aristotle? Did not the slaveowners of the Southern United States maintain the same doctrine, with all the fanaticism with which men cling to the theories that justify their passions and legitimate their personal interests? Did they not call heaven and earth to witness that the dominion of the white man over the black is natural, that the black race is by nature incapable of freedom, and marked out for slavery? —some even going so far as to say that the freedom of manual labourers is an unnatural order of things anywhere. * * * The subjection of women to men being a universal custom, any departure from it quite naturally appears unnatural. But how entirely, even in this case, the feeling is dependent on custom, appears by ample experience. Nothing so much astonishes the people of distant parts of the world, when they first learn anything about England, as to be told that it is under a queen: the thing seems to them so unnatural as to be almost incredible. To Englishmen this does not seem in the least degree unnatural, because they are used to it; but they do feel it unnatural that women should be soldiers or members of Parliament. In the feudal ages, on the contrary, war and politics were not thought unnatural to women, because not unusual; it seemed natural that women of the privileged classes should be of manly character, inferior in nothing but bodily strength to their husbands and fathers. The independence of women seemed rather less unnatural to the Greeks than to other ancients, on account of the fabulous Amazons (whom they believed to be historical), and the partial example afforded by the Spartan women; who, though no less subordinate by law than in other Greek states, were more free in fact, and being trained to bodily exercises in the same manner with men, gave ample proof that they were not naturally disqualified for them. There

2. Mill has been describing slave owners' power over slaves, or tyrants' power over their subjects.
3. In *Politics* Aristotle asserts that it is as natural for free men to rule over slaves as for men to rule over women (sec. 1260a2–14).

can be little doubt that Spartan experience suggested to Plato, among many other of his doctrines, that of the social and political equality of the two sexes.[4]

But, it will be said, the rule of men over women differs from all these others in not being a rule of force: it is accepted voluntarily; women make no complaint, and are consenting parties to it. In the first place, a great number of women do not accept it. Ever since there have been women able to make their sentiments known by their writings (the only mode of publicity which society permits to them), an increasing number of them have recorded protests against their present social condition: and recently many thousands of them, headed by the most eminent women known to the public, have petitioned Parliament for their admission to the Parliamentary Suffrage.[5] The claim of women to be educated as solidly, and in the same branches of knowledge, as men, is urged with growing intensity, and with a great prospect of success; while the demand for their admission into professions and occupations hitherto closed against them, becomes every year more urgent. Though there are not in this country, as there are in the United States, periodical Conventions and an organized party to agitate for the Rights of Women, there is a numerous and active Society organized and managed by women, for the more limited object of obtaining the political franchise. * * *

All causes, social and natural, combine to make it unlikely that women should be collectively rebellious to the power of men. They are so far in a position different from all other subject classes, that their masters require something more from them than actual service. Men do not want solely the obedience of women, they want their sentiments. All men, except the most brutish, desire to have, in the woman most nearly connected with them, not a forced slave but a willing one, not a slave merely, but a favourite. They have therefore put everything in practice to enslave their minds. The masters of all other slaves rely, for maintaining obedience, on fear; either fear of themselves, or religious fears. The masters of women wanted more than simple obedience, and they turned the whole force of education to effect their purpose. All women are brought up from the very earliest years in the belief that their ideal of character is the very opposite to that of men; not self-will, and government by self-control, but submission, and yielding to the control of others. All the moralities tell them that it is the duty of women, and all the current sentimentalities that it is their nature, to live for others; to make complete abnegation of themselves, and to have no life but in their affections. And by their affections are meant the only ones they are allowed to have—those to the men with whom they are connected, or to the children who constitute an additional and indefeasible tie between them and a man. When we put together three things—first, the natural attraction between opposite sexes; secondly, the wife's entire dependence on the husband, every privilege or pleasure she has being either his gift, or depending entirely on his will; and lastly, that the principal object of human pursuit, consideration, and all objects of social ambition, can in general be sought or obtained by her only through him—it would be a miracle if the object of being attractive to men had not become the polar star of feminine education and formation of character. * * *

* * * But I may go farther, and maintain that the course of history, and the tendencies of progressive human society, afford not only no presumption in favour of

---

4. See *The Republic*, 5: "Then, if we are to set women to the same tasks as men, we must teach them the same things. They must have the same two branches of training for mind and body and also be taught the art of war, and they must receive the same treatment" (trans. by F. M. Cornford).

5. This petition was presented in the House of Commons in 1866 by Mill himself; he was the first member of Parliament to advocate women's suffrage.

this system of inequality of rights, but a strong one against it; and that, so far as the whole course of human improvement up to this time, the whole stream of modern tendencies, warrants any inference on the subject, it is, that this relic of the past is discordant with the future, and must necessarily disappear.

For, what is the peculiar character of the modern world—the difference which chiefly distinguishes modern institutions, modern social ideas, modern life itself, from those of times long past? It is, that human beings are no longer born to their place in life, and chained down by an inexorable bond to the place they are born to, but are free to employ their faculties, and such favourable chances as offer, to achieve the lot which may appear to them most desirable. * * *

The social subordination of women thus stands out an isolated fact in modern social institutions; a solitary breach of what has become their fundamental law; a single relic of an old world of thought and practice exploded in everything else, but retained in the one thing of most universal interest; as if a gigantic dolmen,[6] or a vast temple of Jupiter Olympius, occupied the site of St. Paul's and received daily worship, while the surrounding Christian churches were only resorted to on fasts and festivals. * * *

Neither does it avail anything to say that the *nature* of the two sexes adapts them to their present functions and position, and renders these appropriate to them. Standing on the ground of common sense and the constitution of the human mind, I deny that any one knows, or can know, the nature of the two sexes, as long as they have only been seen in their present relation to one another. If men had ever been found in society without women, or women without men, or if there had been a society of men and women in which the women were not under the control of the men, something might have been positively known about the mental and moral differences which may be inherent in the nature of each. What is now called the nature of women is an eminently artificial thing—the result of forced repression in some directions, unnatural stimulation in others. It may be asserted without scruple, that no other class of dependents have had their character so entirely distorted from its natural proportions by their relation with their masters; for, if conquered and slave races have been, in some respects, more forcibly repressed, whatever in them has not been crushed down by an iron heel has generally been let alone, and if left with any liberty of development, it has developed itself according to its own laws; but in the case of women, a hot-house and stove cultivation has always been carried on of some of the capabilities of their nature, for the benefit and pleasure of their masters. * * *

Even the preliminary knowledge, what the differences between the sexes now are, apart from all question as to how they are made what they are, is still in the crudest and most incomplete state. Medical practitioners and physiologists have ascertained, to some extent, the differences in bodily constitution; and this is an important element to the psychologist: but hardly any medical practitioner is a psychologist. Respecting the mental characteristics of women; their observations are of no more worth than those of common men. It is a subject on which nothing final can be known, so long as those who alone can really know it, women themselves, have given but little testimony, and that little, mostly suborned. It is easy to know stupid women. Stupidity is much the same all the world over. A stupid person's notions and feelings may confidently be inferred from those which prevail in the circle by which the person is surrounded. Not

6. Tablelike prehistoric monument of standing stones, associated with pagan religious rites.

so with those whose opinions and feelings are an emanation from their own nature and faculties. It is only a man here and there who has any tolerable knowledge of the character even of the women of his own family. I do not mean, of their capabilities; these nobody knows, not even themselves, because most of them have never been called out. I mean their actually existing thoughts and feelings. Many a man thinks he perfectly understands women, because he has had amatory relations with several, perhaps with many of them. If he is a good observer, and his experience extends to quality as well as quantity, he may have learnt something of one narrow department of their nature—an important department, no doubt. But of all the rest of it, few persons are generally more ignorant, because there are few from whom it is so carefully hidden. The most favourable case which a man can generally have for studying the character of a woman, is that of his own wife: for the opportunities are greater, and the cases of complete sympathy not so unspeakably rare. And in fact, this is the source from which any knowledge worth having on the subject has, I believe, generally come. But most men have not had the opportunity of studying in this way more than a single case: accordingly one can, to an almost laughable degree, infer what a man's wife is like, from his opinions about women in general. To make even this one case yield any result, the woman must be worth knowing, and the man not only a competent judge, but of a character so sympathetic in itself, and so well adapted to hers, that he can either read her mind by sympathetic intuition, or has nothing in himself which makes her shy of disclosing it. Hardly anything, I believe, can be more rare than this conjunction. It often happens that there is the most complete unity of feeling and community of interests as to all external things, yet the one has as little admission into the internal life of the other as if they were common acquaintance. Even with true affection, authority on the one side and subordination on the other prevent perfect confidence. Though nothing may be intentionally withheld, much is not shown. * * * When we further consider that to understand one woman is not necessarily to understand any other woman; that even if he could study many women of one rank, or of one country, he would not thereby understand women of other ranks or countries; and even if he did, they are still only the women of a single period of history; we may safely assert that the knowledge which men can acquire of women, even as they have been and are, without reference to what they might be, is wretchedly imperfect and superficial, and always will be so, until women themselves have told all that they have to tell.

And this time has not come; nor will it come otherwise than gradually. It is but of yesterday that women have either been qualified by literary accomplishments, or permitted by society, to tell anything to the general public. As yet very few of them dare tell anything, which men, on whom their literary success depends, are unwilling to hear. Let us remember in what manner, up to a very recent time, the expression, even by a male author, of uncustomary opinions, or what are deemed eccentric feelings, usually was, and in some degree still is, received; and we may form some faint conception under what impediments a woman, who is brought up to think custom and opinion her sovereign rule, attempts to express in books anything drawn from the depths of her own nature. * * * Literary women are becoming more freespoken, and more willing to express their real sentiments. Unfortunately, in this country especially, they are themselves such artificial products, that their sentiments are compounded of a small element of individual observation and consciousness, and a very large one of acquired associations. This will be less and less the case, but it will remain true to a great extent, as long as social institutions do not admit the same free development of originality in women which is possible to men. When that time comes, and not before, we shall see, and not merely hear, as much as it is necessary to know of the nature of women, and the adaptation of other things to it. * * *

One thing we may be certain of—that what is contrary to women's nature to do, they never will be made to do by simply giving their nature free play. The anxiety of mankind to interfere in behalf of nature, for fear lest nature should not succeed in effecting its purpose, is an altogether unnecessary solicitude. What women by nature cannot do, it is quite superfluous to forbid them from doing. What they can do, but not so well as the men who are their competitors, competition suffices to exclude them from; since nobody asks for protective duties and bounties in favour of women; it is only asked that the present bounties and protective duties in favour of men should be recalled. If women have a greater natural inclination for some things than for others, there is no need of laws or social inculcation to make the majority of them do the former in preference to the latter. Whatever women's services are most wanted for, the free play of competition will hold out the strongest inducements to them to undertake. And, as the words imply, they are most wanted for the things for which they are most fit; by the apportionment of which to them, the collective faculties of the two sexes can be applied on the whole with the greatest sum of valuable result.

The general opinion of men is supposed to be, that the natural vocation of a woman is that of a wife and mother. I say, is supposed to be, because, judging from acts—from the whole of the present constitution of society—one might infer that their opinion was the direct contrary. They might be supposed to think that the alleged natural vocation of women was of all things the most repugnant to their nature; insomuch that if they are free to do anything else—if any other means of living, or occupation of their time and faculties, is open, which has any chance of appearing desirable to them— there will not be enough of them who will be willing to accept the condition said to be natural to them. If this is the real opinion of men in general, it would be well that it should be spoken out. I should like to hear somebody openly enunciating the doctrine (it is already implied in much that is written on the subject)—"It is necessary to society that women should marry and produce children. They will not do so unless they are compelled. Therefore it is necessary to compel them." The merits of the case would then be clearly defined. It would be exactly that of the slaveholders of South Carolina and Louisiana. "It is necessary that cotton and sugar should be grown. White men cannot produce them. Negroes will not, for any wages which we choose to give. *Ergo* they must be compelled." An illustration still closer to the point is that of impressment.[7] Sailors must absolutely be had to defend the country. It often happens that they will not voluntarily enlist. Therefore there must be the power of forcing them. How often has this logic been used! and, but for one flaw in it, without doubt it would have been successful up to this day. But it is open to the retort—First pay the sailors the honest value of their labour. When you have made it as well worth their while to serve you, as to work for other employers, you will have no more difficulty than others have in obtaining their services. To this there is no logical answer except "I will not": and as people are now not only ashamed, but are not desirous, to rob the labourer of his hire,[8] impressment is no longer advocated. Those who attempt to force women into marriage by closing all other doors against them, lay themselves open to a similar retort. If they mean what they say, their opinion must evidently be, that men do not render the married

---

7. The practice of seizing men and forcing them to serve as sailors in the navy.   8. Luke 10.7.

condition so desirable to women, as to induce them to accept it for its own recommendations. It is not a sign of one's thinking the boon one offers very attractive, when one allows only Hobson's choice, "that or none." And here, I believe, is the clue to the feelings of those men, who have a real antipathy to the equal freedom of women. I believe they are afraid, not lest women should be unwilling to marry, for I do not think that any one in reality has that apprehension; but lest they should insist that marriage should be on equal conditions; lest all women of spirit and capacity should prefer doing almost anything else, not in their own eyes degrading, rather than marry, when marrying is giving themselves a master, and a master too of all their earthly possessions. And truly, if this consequence were necessarily incident to marriage, I think that the apprehension would be very well founded. I agree in thinking it probable that few women, capable of anything else, would, unless under an irresistible *entrainement* [enchantment], rendering them for the time insensible to anything but itself, choose such a lot, when any other means were open to them of filling a conventionally honourable place in life: and if men are determined that the law of marriage shall be a law of despotism, they are quite right, in point of mere policy, in leaving to women only Hobson's choice. But, in that case, all that has been done in the modern world to relax the chain on the minds of women, has been a mistake. They never should have been allowed to receive a literary education. Women who read, much more women who write, are, in the existing constitution of things, a contradiction and a disturbing element: and it was wrong to bring women up with any acquirements but those of an odalisque,[9] or of a domestic servant.

1860   1869

Statement Repudiating the Rights of Husbands[1]

6th March 1851

Being about, if I am so happy as to obtain her consent, to enter into the marriage relation with the only woman I have ever known, with whom I would have entered into that state; and the whole character of the marriage relation as constituted by law being such as both she and I entirely and conscientiously disapprove, for this among other reasons, that it confers upon one of the parties to the contract, legal power and control over the person, property, and freedom of action of the other party, independent of her own wishes and will; I, having no means of legally divesting myself of these odious powers (as I most assuredly would do if an engagement to that effect could be made legally binding on me), feel it my duty to put on record a formal protest against the existing law of marriage, in so far as conferring such powers; and a solemn promise never in any case or under any circumstances to use them. And in the event of marriage between Mrs. Taylor and me I declare it to be my will and intention, and the condition of the engagement between us, that she retains in all respects whatever the same absolute freedom of action, and freedom of disposal of herself and of all that does or may at any time belong to her, as if no such marriage had taken place; and I absolutely disclaim and repudiate all pretence to have acquired any *rights* whatever by virtue of such marriage.

J. S. Mill

9. Concubine in a harem.
1. At the time Mill wrote this, shortly before his marriage to Harriet Taylor, married women occupied a peculiar position under British law. A woman, upon her marriage, entered into a state called coverture. This meant she was subsumed into the legal personhood of her husband, and could neither sign legal contracts nor own property. Cf. Caroline Norton's *Letter to the Queen* (1855) in Perspectives: Victorian Ladies and Gentlemen, page 565.

Elizabeth Barrett Browning

1806–1861

Elizabeth Barrett Browning was the most celebrated woman poet of the Victorian era. She was admired by contemporaries as varied as William Wordsworth, Queen Victoria, Edgar Allan Poe (who introduced an American edition of her work), Christina Rossetti, and John Ruskin (who proclaimed *Aurora Leigh* the greatest poem in English). Her popularity was especially remarkable because she interspersed her ardent love lyrics with hard-hitting poems on radical political causes and feminist themes. In the United States, she influenced not only sequestered writers like Emily Dickinson but also political activists like Susan B. Anthony.

The eldest of eleven children, Elizabeth Barrett grew up in a country manor house called Hope End in Hertfordshire. The Barretts were a wealthy family whose fortune derived from a slave plantation in Jamaica. While her submissive mother, Mary Clark, encouraged her to write, it was her protective but authoritarian father, Edward Moulton-Barrett, who dominated her affections and received laudatory poems on his birthdays. From an early age Barrett envisioned herself combining male and female attributes to become "the feminine of Homer." As the critic Dorothy Mermin has pointed out, the ambitious child-poet was already imaginatively inhabiting two gender roles, the imprisoned female muse and the active male quester: "At five I supposed myself a heroine and in my day dreams of bliss I constantly imaged to myself a forlorn damsel in distress rescued by some noble knight."

Barrett took advantage of her family's resources to give herself an exceptional education, unusual for a woman of her day. Her passion for Greek poetry led her to translate Aeschylus's *Prometheus Bound* (1833). Two earlier works also reflected her wide reading: at twelve she wrote a four-book epic, *The Battle of Marathon*, which her father had privately printed, and at twenty she anonymously published a long philosophical poem, *An Essay on Mind, with Other Poems* (1826). But her intellectual development was offset by an illness that broke her health at the age of fifteen. Thereafter, her bold aspirations and mental energy were at odds with her semi-invalid state. Her sense of isolation increased in 1828 when her mother died, and again when declining family fortunes led her father to move the family from the home she loved, first to Sidmouth, Devon, in 1832 and then to London in 1835, where they eventually settled at 50 Wimpole Street.

It was here that Barrett became almost a recluse. Disliking the dirty, foggy city, she hardly left the house, but she corresponded avidly with a circle of literary and public figures. In 1838 chronic lung disease weakened her further; she already had developed what would be a lifelong dependence on morphine as a painkiller. Her doctors insisted that she go to Mediterranean climes, but the farthest her father would allow was Torquay, on the south coast of England. She lived there for three years, returning prostrate with grief after her brother Edward died in a boating accident. For the next several years, her spirits sustained only by her poetry, she worked, slept, and received visitors on a couch in a room sealed against the London air. Often exhausted, she was unable to see the aged Wordsworth when he came to pay his respects.

As she and her small circle of friends were quick to realize, Elizabeth Barrett had become like Tennyson's Lady of Shalott, having no other life but to weave her poetic web in solitude. *The Seraphim and Other Poems* (1838) established her reputation, and the two volumes of *Poems* (1844) consolidated her position as the era's finest "poetess." The latter book included *A Drama of Exile*, a sequel to Milton's *Paradise Lost* in which Eve emerges as a heroine, and also *The Cry of the Children*, condemning child labor in factories. Despite her oppositional politics, the suppleness of her thought and her passionate voice were so highly regarded by critics and public alike that she was mentioned as a candidate for Poet Laureate when Wordsworth died in 1850.

But by then she had utterly transformed her life. In 1845 she began corresponding with Robert Browning—she was nearly forty, and famous; he was thirty-three and his only reputation was for obscurity. Their literary friendship rapidly blossomed into romance, which they had to hide from her father, who had tacitly forbidden his children to marry. After a secret marriage in London in 1846, the couple eloped to Italy, where they settled in Florence at Casa Guidi. There, the fairy tale continued: happily married and living in a warm climate, she recovered much of her health, wrote her best work, gained the love of the Italians with her nationalistic verse, and gave birth to a son, Robert Weidemann Browning ("Pen"), in 1849. She had prophetically written to Browning, in the last letter before their elopement: "I begin to think that none are so bold as the timid, when they are fairly roused."

Her union with Robert Browning was responsible for two works that have since formed the cornerstone of her reputation. The first is their justly famous correspondence. The story of their courtship was widely known, but its intimate details were not revealed until the publication of their letters in 1899. Second, as their relationship developed she wrote a series of love poems to Browning. She finished the last poem two days before their wedding, and the collection was published in 1850, under the deliberately misleading title *Sonnets from the Portuguese*. Among the most significant sonnet sequences since those of Shakespeare and Sidney, these poems revived the form in Victorian England and revised in brilliant new ways what had hitherto been a primarily masculine poetic tradition. Casting the male recipient of her sonnets in the role of sexual object, yet also allowing for his reciprocal passion and poetic drive, Barrett Browning records the interplay of gifted lovers whose desire is inseparable from their quest for verbal mastery.

In her final years Barrett Browning's career continued to flourish. She and her husband enjoyed a wide circle of friends, including Tennyson, Ruskin, Carlyle, Rossetti, and Margaret Fuller. They traveled a great deal, to Rome, Paris, and several times back to London where they were warmly received by both their families—with the exception of her father, who refused to forgive or even see her again. In 1851 she published *Casa Guidi Windows*, which promoted the cause of Italian independence from Austria. *Poems Before Congress* (1860) stirred controversy in England over its volatile and "unwomanly" political views, particularly its scathing attack on American slavery. But her health was failing, and after recurrent illnesses, she died in Florence in her husband's arms. *Last Poems* appeared posthumously in 1862.

Her greatest achievement, however, lies in her verse novel, *Aurora Leigh* (1856), a daring combination of epic, romance, and *bildungsroman*. The first major poem in English in which the heroine, like the author, is a woman writer, *Aurora Leigh* rewrites Wordsworth's *The Prelude* from a female point of view. With its Miltonic echoes, the blank-verse format claims epic importance not only for the growth of the woman poet, but also for a woman's struggle to achieve artistic and economic independence in modern society. The poem blends these themes, moreover, with a witty, Byronic treatment of Victorian manners and social issues, and an emotionally charged love plot that recalls Charlotte Brontë's *Jane Eyre*. The story of how the aspiring poet Aurora Leigh overcomes the prejudices of both a masculine audience and the man she loves, in order to find fame and happiness in Italy, closely mirrors Barrett Browning's own. The poem was an overwhelming success, even though many contemporary readers were scandalized by its radical revision of Victorian ideals of femininity and its picture of how the two sexes might work together so that each could achieve its fullest human potential. Scorning to measure herself against any but the greatest male authors, Elizabeth Barrett Browning was the first to show English readers the enormous possibilities of a poetic tradition in which women participated on equal terms.

from **Sonnets from the Portuguese**[1]

1

I thought once how Theocritus had sung
Of the sweet years, the dear and wished-for years,
Who each one in a gracious hand appears
To bear a gift for mortals, old or young:[2]
5 And, as I mused it in his antique tongue,[3]
I saw, in gradual vision through my tears,
The sweet, sad years, the melancholy years,
Those of my own life, who by turns had flung
A shadow across me. Straightway I was 'ware,
10 So weeping, how a mystic Shape did move
Behind me, and drew me backward by the hair;
And a voice said in mastery, while I strove,—
"Guess now who holds thee?"—"Death," I said. But, there,
The silver answer rang,—"Not Death, but Love."

13

And wilt thou have me fashion into speech
The love I bear thee, finding words enough,
And hold the torch out, while the winds are rough,
Between our faces, to cast light on each?—
5 I drop it at thy feet. I cannot teach
My hand to hold my spirit so far off
From myself—me—that I should bring thee proof
In words, of love hid in me out of reach.
Nay, let the silence of my womanhood
10 Commend my woman-love to thy belief,—
Seeing that I stand unwon, however wooed,
And rend the garment of my life, in brief,
By a most dauntless, voiceless fortitude,
Lest one touch of this heart convey its grief.

21

Say over again, and yet once over again,
That thou dost love me. Though the word repeated
Should seem "a cuckoo-song,"[4] as thou dost treat it,
Remember, never to the hill or plain,
5 Valley and wood, without her cuckoo-strain
Comes the fresh Spring in all her green completed.
Belovèd, I, amid the darkness greeted
By a doubtful spirit-voice, in that doubt's pain

---

1. These very personal poems chronicle Elizabeth Barrett's courtship with Robert Browning. She did not show them to him until after they were married, when he pronounced them "the finest sonnets written in any language since Shakespeare's." He overcame her reluctance to publish them by proposing the somewhat cryptic title implying that they are merely translations.

2. In *Idylls* 15, Theocritus, a Greek pastoral poet of the 3rd century B.C., tells how "the dainty-footed Hours" brought Adonis to Aphrodite. The song celebrates the return of spring, the season when Elizabeth Barrett first met Robert Browning.
3. I.e., Greek.
4. Repetitious, like the cuckoo's song.

Cry, "Speak once more—thou lovest!" Who can fear
10 Too many stars, though each in heaven shall roll,
Too many flowers, though each shall crown the year?
Say thou dost love me, love me, love me—toll
The silver iterance!° —only minding, Dear,   *repetition*
To love me also in silence with thy soul.

22

When our two souls stand up erect and strong,
Face to face, silent, drawing nigh and nigher,
Until the lengthening wings break into fire
At either curvèd point,—what bitter wrong
5   Can the earth do to us, that we should not long
Be here contented? Think. In mounting higher,
The angels would press on us and aspire
To drop some golden orb of perfect song
Into our deep, dear silence. Let us stay
10 Rather on earth, Belovèd,—where the unfit
Contrarious moods of men recoil away
And isolate pure spirits, and permit
A place to stand and love in for a day,
With darkness and the death-hour rounding it.

28

My letters! all dead paper, mute and white!
And yet they seem alive and quivering
Against my tremulous hands which loose the string
And let them drop down on my knee to-night.
5   This said,—he wished to have me in his sight
Once, as a friend: this fixed a day in spring⁵
To come and touch my hand . . . a simple thing,
Yet I wept for it!—this, . . . the paper's light . . .
Said, *Dear, I love thee*; and I sank and quailed
10 As if God's future thundered on my past.
This said, *I am thine*—and so its ink has paled
With lying at my heart that beat too fast.
And this . . . O Love, thy words have ill availed
If, what this said, I dared repeat at last!

[handwritten annotation: moon = symbol of change (traditional) change fulness]

32

The first time that the sun rose on thine oath
To love me, I looked forward to the moon
To slacken all those bonds which seemed too soon
And quickly tied to make a lasting troth.
5   Quick-loving hearts, I thought, may quickly loathe;
And, looking on myself, I seemed not one
For such man's love!—more like an out-of-tune

[handwritten annotations: love as my environment; quick, uncertain, unexpected, overwhelming, sudden, changeful; feels herself unworthy]

5. On 17 May 1845, Robert Browning wrote to arrange their first meeting: "I will call at two on Tuesday."

Worn viol, a good singer would be wroth
To spoil his song with, and which, snatched in haste,
10   Is laid down at the first ill-sounding note.
I did not wrong myself so, but I placed
A wrong on *thee*. For perfect strains may float
'Neath master-hands, from instruments defaced,—
And great souls, at one stroke, may do and doat.

38

First time he kissed me, he but only kissed
The fingers of this hand wherewith I write;
And ever since, it grew more clean and white,
Slow to world-greetings, quick with its "Oh, list,"°   listen
5   When the angels speak. A ring of amethyst
I could not wear here, plainer to my sight,
Than that first kiss. The second passed in height
The first, and sought the forehead, and half missed,
Half falling on the hair. O beyond meed!°   deserving
10   That was the chrism[6] of love, which love's own crown,
With sanctifying sweetness, did precede.
The third upon my lips was folded down
In perfect, purple state; since when, indeed,
I have been proud and said, "My love, my own."

43

How do I love thee? Let me count the ways.
I love thee to the depth and breadth and height
My soul can reach, when feeling out of sight
For the ends of Being and ideal Grace.
5   I love thee to the level of everyday's
Most quiet need, by sun and candle-light.
I love thee freely, as men strive for Right;
I love thee purely, as they turn from Praise.
I love thee with the passion put to use
10   In my old griefs, and with my childhood's faith.
I love thee with a love I seemed to lose
With my lost saints,—I love with the breath,
Smiles, tears, of all my life!—and, if God choose,
I shall but love thee better after death.

1845–1847   1850

from Aurora Leigh[1]

from Book 1

[SELF-PORTRAIT]

Of writing many books there is no end;
And I who have written much in prose and verse

---

6. Consecrated oil used to anoint during a coronation.
1. Barrett Browning called *Aurora Leigh*, a poem in nine books, a "verse novel." It portrays the struggles of a young poet to find her artistic voice and pursue her vocation despite the obstacles confronting a woman writer.

For others' uses, will write now for mine,—
Will write my story for my better self,
As when you paint your portrait for a friend,
Who keeps it in a drawer and looks at it
Long after he has ceased to love you, just
To hold together what he was and is.
I, writing thus, am still what men call young;
I have not so far left the coasts of life
To travel inward, that I cannot hear
That murmur of the outer Infinite
Which unweaned babies smile at in their sleep
When wondered at for smiling; not so far,
But still I catch my mother at her post
Beside the nursery door, with finger up,
"Hush, hush—here's too much noise!" while her sweet eyes
Leap forward, taking part against her word
In the child's riot. Still I sit and feel
My father's slow hand, when she had left us both,
Stroke out my childish curls across his knee,
And hear Assunta's daily jest (she knew
He liked it better than a better jest)
Inquire how many golden scudi[2] went
To make such ringlets. O my father's hand,
Stroke heavily, heavily the poor hair down,
Draw, press the child's head closer to thy knee!
I'm still too young, too young, to sit alone.
I write. My mother was a Florentine,
Whose rare blue eyes were shut from seeing me
When scarcely I was four years old, my life
A poor spark snatched up from a failing lamp
Which went out therefore. She was weak and frail;
She could not bear the joy of giving life,
The mother's rapture slew her. If her kiss
Had left a longer weight upon my lips
It might have steadied the uneasy breath,
And reconciled and fraternised my soul
With the new order. As it was, indeed,
I felt a mother-want about the world,
And still went seeking, like a bleating lamb
Left out at night in shutting up the fold,—
As restless as a nest-deserted bird
Grown chill through something being away, though what
It knows not. I, Aurora Leigh, was born
To make my father sadder, and myself
Not overjoyous, truly. Women know
The way to rear up children (to be just),
They know a simple, merry, tender knack
Of tying sashes, fitting baby-shoes,

2. Italian coins; Assunta was Aurora's nurse.

And stringing pretty words that make no sense,
And kissing full sense into empty words,
Which things are corals to cut life upon,
Although such trifles: children learn by such,
55   Love's holy earnest in a pretty play
And get not over-early solemnised,
But seeing, as in a rose-bush, Love's Divine
Which burns and hurts not,—not a single bloom,—
Become aware and unafraid of Love.
60   Such good do mothers. Fathers love as well
—Mine did, I know,—but still with heavier brains,
And wills more consciously responsible,
And not as wisely, since less foolishly;
So mothers have God's license to be missed.

65   My father was an austere Englishman,
Who, after a dry lifetime spent at home
In college-learning, law, and parish talk,
Was flooded with a passion unaware,
His whole provisioned and complacent past
70   Drowned out from him that moment. As he stood
In Florence, where he had come to spend a month
And note the secret of Da Vinci's drains,[3]
He musing somewhat absently perhaps
Some English question . . . whether men should pay
75   The unpopular but necessary tax
With left or right hand—in the alien sun
In that great square of the Santissima[4]
There drifted past him (scarcely marked enough
To move his comfortable island scorn)
80   A train of priestly banners, cross and psalm,
The white-veiled rose-crowned maidens holding up
Tall tapers, weighty for such wrists, aslant
To the blue luminous tremor of the air,
And letting drop the white wax as they went
85   To eat the bishop's wafer[5] at the church;
From which long trail of chanting priests and girls,
A face flashed like a cymbal on his face
And shook with silent clangour brain and heart,
Transfiguring him to music. Thus, even thus,
90   He too received his sacramental gift
With eucharistic meanings; for he loved.

[HER MOTHER'S PORTRAIT]

And as I grew
In years, I mixed, confused, unconsciously,
Whatever I last read or heard or dreamed,

---

3. Leonardo da Vinci (1452–1519) was an architect and engineer, as well as an artist; he designed the aqueduct that supplied Milan's water.

4. The Florentine church of the Santissima Annunziata, or Holy Annunciation.
5. To take Holy Communion.

Abhorrent, admirable, beautiful,
150   Pathetical, or ghastly, or grotesque,
With still that face . . . which did not therefore change,
But kept the mystic level of all forms,
Hates, fears, and admirations, was by turns
Ghost, fiend, and angel, fairy, witch, and sprite,
155   A dauntless Muse who eyes a dreadful Fate,
A loving Psyche who loses sight of Love,[6]
A still Medusa[7] with mild milky brows
All curdled and all clothed upon with snakes
Whose slime falls fast as sweat will; or anon
160   Our Lady of the Passion, stabbed with swords
Where the Babe sucked; or Lamia[8] in her first
Moonlighted pallor, ere she shrunk and blinked
And shuddering wriggled down to the unclean;
Or my own mother, leaving her last smile
165   In her last kiss upon the baby-mouth
My father pushed down on the bed for that,—
Or my dead mother, without smile or kiss,
Buried at Florence. All which images,
Concentred on the picture, glassed themselves
170   Before my meditative childhood, as
The incoherencies of change and death
Are represented fully, mixed and merged,
In the smooth fair mystery of perpetual Life.

[AURORA'S EDUCATION]

Then, land!—then, England! oh, the frosty cliffs[9]
Looked cold upon me. Could I find a home
Among those mean red houses through the fog?
And when I heard my father's language first
255   From alien lips which had no kiss for mine
I wept aloud, then laughed, then wept, then wept,
And some one near me said the child was mad
Through much sea-sickness. The train swept us on:
Was this my father's England? the great isle?
260   The ground seemed cut up from the fellowship
Of verdure, field from field,[1] as man from man;
The skies themselves looked low and positive,
As almost you could touch them with a hand,
And dared to do it they were so far off
265   From God's celestial crystals;[2] all things blurred
And dull and vague. Did Shakespeare and his mates
Absorb the light here?—not a hill or stone

---

6. Psyche was beloved of Cupid (or Eros), whom she had never seen because he always came to her after dark; one night she lit her lamp to look at him as he slept, whereupon he left her.

7. A gorgon, a female monster with serpents for hair, the sight of whom turned people to stone.

8. A monster with the head and upper body of a maiden, and lower body of a serpent.

9. The white chalk cliffs of Dover.

1. English fields are divided by hedgerows.

2. The stars, or perhaps the crystalline sphere the ancients believed lay beyond them.

With heart to strike a radiant colour up
Or active outline on the indifferent air.

270 I think I see my father's sister stand
Upon the hall-step of her country-house
To give me welcome. She stood straight and calm,
Her somewhat narrow forehead braided tight
As if for taming accidental thoughts
275 From possible pulses;[3] brown hair pricked with gray
By frigid use of life (she was not old,
Although my father's elder by a year),
A nose drawn sharply, yet in delicate lines;
A close mild mouth, a little soured about
280 The ends, through speaking unrequited loves
Or peradventure niggardly half-truths;
Eyes of no colour,—once they might have smiled,
But never, never have forgot themselves
In smiling; cheeks, in which was yet a rose
285 Of perished summers, like a rose in a book,
Kept more for ruth° than pleasure,—if past bloom,   *remorse*
Past fading also.

                    She had lived, we'll say,
A harmless life, she called a virtuous life,
A quiet life, which was not life at all
290 (But that, she had not lived enough to know),
Between the vicar and the country squires,
The lord-lieutenant looking down sometimes
From the empyrean to assure their souls
Against chance vulgarisms, and, in the abyss,
295 The apothecary, looked on once a year
To prove their soundness of humility.
The poor-club exercised her Christian gifts
Of knitting stockings, stitching petticoats,
Because we are of one flesh, after all,
300 And need one flannel° (with a proper sense   *petticoat*
Of difference in the quality)—and still
The book-club, guarded from your modern trick
Of shaking dangerous questions from the crease,[4]
Preserved her intellectual. She had lived
305 A sort of cage-bird life, born in a cage,
Accounting that to leap from perch to perch
Was act and joy enough for any bird.
Dear heaven, how silly are the things that live
In thickets, and eat berries!

                    I, alas,
310 A wild bird scarcely fledged, was brought to her cage,
And she was there to meet me. Very kind.

---

3. Pulsations of strong emotion.   the folds, or creases, to open the pages and read the book.
4. Books were sold with their pages uncut; one had to cut

Bring the clean water, give out the fresh seed.

* * *

So it was.

385 I broke the copious curls upon my head
In braids, because she liked smooth-ordered hair.
I left off saying my sweet Tuscan words
Which still at any stirring of the heart
Came up to float across the English phrase

390 As lilies (*Bene* or *Che che*[5]), because
She liked my father's child to speak his tongue.
I learnt the collects and the catechism,
The creeds, from Athanasius back to Nice,
The Articles,[6] the Tracts *against* the times[7]

395 (By no means Buonaventure's "Prick of Love"[8]),
And various popular synopses of
Inhuman doctrines never taught by John,[9]
Because she liked instructed piety.
I learnt my complement of classic French

400 (Kept pure of Balzac and neologism[1])
And German also, since she liked a range
Of liberal education,—tongues, not books.
I learnt a little algebra, a little
Of the mathematics,—brushed with extreme flounce

405 The circle of the sciences, because
She misliked women who are frivolous.
I learnt the royal genealogies
Of Oviedo, the internal laws
Of the Burmese empire,—by how many feet

410 Mount Chimborazo outsoars Teneriffe.
What navigable river joins itself
To Lara, and what census of the year five
Was taken at Klagenfurt,—because she liked
A general insight into useful facts.

415 I learnt much music,—such as would have been
As quite impossible in Johnson's day[2]
As still it might be wished—fine sleights of hand
And unimagined fingering, shuffling off
The hearer's soul through hurricanes of notes

420 To a noisy Tophet;° and I drew . . . costumes   *Hell*
From French engravings, nereids neatly draped
(With smirks of simmering godship): I washed in°   *water-colored*
Landscapes from nature (rather say, washed out).

5. "Good" and "no, indeed" (Italian).
6. The Thirty-nine Articles are the principles of Anglican faith; collects are Anglican prayers.
7. An ironic reference to the High Church movement's *Tracts for the Times*, written by Newman, Keble, and Pusey; thus, the aunt is Low Church.
8. Saint Buonaventure (1221–1274) wrote of ecstatic, mystical Christian experiences; he believed in the power of love over the power of reason.

9. The author of the gospel.
1. Honoré de Balzac (1799–1850), French realist novelist who described things considered unpleasant or immoral, hence unsuitable reading for young ladies. A neologism is a newly coined word.
2. When informed that a piece of music being played by a young lady was extremely difficult, Samuel Johnson responded, "Would that it had been impossible."

I danced the polka and Cellarius,
425   Spun glass, stuffed birds, and modelled flowers in wax,
Because she liked accomplishments in girls.
I read a score of books on womanhood
To prove, if women do not think at all,
They may teach thinking (to a maiden aunt
430   Or else the author),—books that boldly assert
Their right of comprehending husband's talk
When not too deep, and even of answering
With pretty "may it please you," or "so it is,"—
Their rapid insight and fine aptitude,
435   Particular worth and general missionariness,
As long as they keep quiet by the fire
And never say "no" when the world says "ay,"
For that is fatal,—their angelic reach
Of virtue, chiefly used to sit and darn,
440   And fatten household sinners,—their, in brief,
Potential faculty in everything
Of abdicating power in it: she owned
She liked a woman to be womanly,
And English women, she thanked God and sighed
445   (Some people always sigh in thanking God)
Were models to the universe. And last
I learnt cross-stitch, because she did not like
To see me wear the night with empty hands
A-doing nothing. So, my shepherdess
450   Was something after all (the pastoral saints
Be praised for't), leaning lovelorn with pink eyes
To match her shoes, when I mistook the silks;
Her head uncrushed by that round weight of hat
So strangely similar to the tortoise-shell
455   Which slew the tragic poet.[3]

                              By the way,
The works of women are symbolical.
We sew, sew, prick our fingers, dull our sight,
Producing what? A pair of slippers, sir,
To put on when you're weary—or a stool
460   To stumble over and vex you . . . "curse that stool!"
Or else at best, a cushion, where you lean
And sleep, and dream of something we are not
But would be for your sake. Alas, alas!
This hurts most, this—that, after all, we are paid
465   The worth of our work, perhaps.

                              In looking down
Those years of education (to return)
I wonder if Brinvilliers suffered more

---

3. The Greek playwright Aeschylus was supposed to have been killed when an eagle, mistaking his bald head for a stone, dropped a tortoise on it to break the shell.

In the water-torture[4] . . . flood succeeding flood
To drench the incapable throat and split the veins . . .
470   Than I did. Certain of your feebler souls
Go out in such a process; many pine
To a sick, inodorous light; my own endured:
I had relations in the Unseen, and drew
The elemental nutriment and heat
475   From nature, as earth feels the sun at nights,
Or as a babe sucks surely in the dark.
I kept the life thrust on me, on the outside
Of the inner life with all its ample room
For heart and lungs, for will and intellect,
480   Inviolable by conventions. God,
I thank thee for that grace of thine!

[DISCOVERY OF POETRY]

815   The cygnet finds the water, but the man
Is born in ignorance of his element
And feels out blind at first, disorganised
By sin i' the blood,—his spirit-insight dulled
And crossed by his sensations. Presently
820   He feels it quicken in the dark sometimes,
When, mark, be reverent, be obedient,
For such dumb motions of imperfect life
Are oracles of vital Deity
Attesting the Hereafter. Let who says
825   "The soul's a clean white paper," rather say,
A palimpsest,[5] a prophet's holograph
Defiled, erased and covered by a monk's,—
The apocalypse, by a Longus![6] poring on
Which obscene text, we may discern perhaps
830   Some fair, fine trace of what was written once,
Some upstroke of an alpha and omega
Expressing the old scripture.
             Books, books, books!
I had found the secret of a garret-room
Piled high with cases in my father's name,
835   Piled high, packed large,—where, creeping in and out
Among the giant fossils of my past,
Like some small nimble mouse between the ribs
Of a mastodon, I nibbled here and there
At this or that box, pulling through the gap,
840   In heats of terror, haste, victorious joy,
The first book first. And how I felt it beat
Under my pillow, in the morning's dark,

---

4. In 1676 Marie Marguerite, Marquise de Brinvilliers, was tortured by having water forced down her throat, then executed.
5. Parchment where the original writing has been scraped off so it can be reused.
6. I.e., imagine that the words of the apocalypse have been erased and written over by Longus, a Greek writer of romances.

An hour before the sun would let me read!
My books! At last because the time was ripe,
845   I chanced upon the poets.

                              As the earth
Plunges in fury, when the internal fires
Have reached and pricked her heart, and, throwing flat
The marts and temples, the triumphal gates
And towers of observation, clears herself
850   To elemental freedom—thus, my soul,
At poetry's divine first finger-touch,
Let go conventions and sprang up surprised,
Convicted of the great eternities
Before two worlds.

                              What's this, Aurora Leigh,
855   You write so of the poets, and not laugh?
Those virtuous liars, dreamers after dark,
Exaggerators of the sun and moon,
And soothsayers in a tea-cup?

                              I write so
Of the only truth-tellers now left to God,
860   The only speakers of essential truth,
Opposed to relative, comparative,
And temporal truths; the only holders by
His sun-skirts, through conventional gray glooms;
The only teachers who instruct mankind
865   From just a shadow on a charnel-wall[7]
To find man's veritable stature out
Erect, sublime,—the measure of a man,
And that's the measure of an angel, says
The apostle. Ay, and while your common men
870   Lay telegraphs, gauge railroads, reign, reap, dine,
And dust the flaunty carpets of the world
For kings to walk on, or our president,
The poet suddenly will catch them up
With his voice like a thunder,—"This is soul,
875   This is life, this word is being said in heaven,
Here's God down on us! what are you about?"
How all those workers start amid their work,
Look round, look up, and feel, a moment's space,
That carpet-dusting, though a pretty trade,
880   Is not the imperative labour after all.

from *Book 2*
[WOMAN AND ARTIST]

Times followed one another. Came a morn
I stood upon the brink of twenty years,

---

7. Wall of a building where bodies or bones are deposited.

And looked before and after, as I stood
Woman and artist,—either incomplete,
5   Both credulous of completion. There I held
The whole creation in my little cup,
And smiled with thirsty lips before I drank
"Good health to you and me, sweet neighbor mine,
And all these peoples."

                    I was glad, that day;
10   The June was in me, with its multitudes
Of nightingales all singing in the dark,
And rosebuds reddening where the calyx[1] split.
I felt so young, so strong, so sure of God!
So glad, I could not choose be very wise!
15   And, old at twenty, was inclined to pull
My childhood backward in a childish jest
To see the face of't once more, and farewell!
In which fantastic mood I bounded forth
At early morning,—would not wait so long
20   As even to snatch my bonnet by the strings,
But, brushing a green trail across the lawn
With my gown in the dew, took will and away
Among the acacias of the shrubberies,
To fly my fancies in the open air
25   And keep my birthday, till my aunt awoke
To stop good dreams. Meanwhile I murmured on
As honeyed bees keep humming to themselves,
"The worthiest poets have remained uncrowned
Till death has bleached their foreheads to the bone;
30   And so with me it must be unless I prove
Unworthy of the grand adversity,
And certainly I would not fail so much.
What, therefore, if I crown myself to-day
In sport, not pride, to learn the feel of it,
35   Before my brows be numbed as Dante's own
To all the tender pricking of such leaves?
Such leaves! what leaves?"

                    I pulled the branches down
To choose from.

              "Not the bay![2] I choose no bay
(The fates deny us if we are overbold),
40   Nor myrtle—which means chiefly love; and love
Is something awful which one dares not touch
So early o' mornings. This verbena strains
The point of passionate fragrance; and hard by,
This guelder-rose, at far too slight a beck
45   Of the wind, will toss about her flower-apples.
Ah—there's my choice,—that ivy on the wall,

1. The green outer leaves which protect a flowerbud.   laurel leaves.
2. Laurel; Apollo, the god of poetry, wore a wreath of

That headlong ivy! not a leaf will grow
But thinking of a wreath. Large leaves, smooth leaves,
Serrated like my vines, and half as green.
50   I like such ivy, bold to leap a height
'Twas strong to climb; as good to grow on graves
As twist about a thyrsus;[3] pretty too
(And that's not ill) when twisted round a comb."
Thus speaking to myself, half singing it,
55   Because some thoughts are fashioned like a bell
To ring with once being touched, I drew a wreath
Drenched, blinding me with dew, across my brow,
And fastening it behind so, turning faced
. . . My public!—cousin Romney—with a mouth
60   Twice graver than his eyes.

                    I stood there fixed,—
My arms up, like the caryatid,[4] sole
Of some abolished temple, helplessly
Persistent in a gesture which derides
A former purpose. Yet my blush was flame,
65   As if from flax, not stone.

                    "Aurora Leigh,
The earliest of Auroras!"[5]

                    Hand stretched out
I clasped, as shipwrecked men will clasp a hand,
Indifferent to the sort of palm. The tide
Had caught me at my pastime, writing down
70   My foolish name too near upon the sea
Which drowned me with a blush as foolish. "You,
My cousin!"

                    The smile died out in his eyes
And dropped upon his lips, a cold dead weight,
For just a moment, "Here's a book I found!
75   No name writ on it—poems, by the form;
Some Greek upon the margin,—lady's Greek
Without the accents. Read it? Not a word.
I saw at once the thing had witchcraft in't,
Whereof the reading calls up dangerous spirits:
80   I rather bring it to the witch."

                    "My book.
You found it" . . .

                    "In the hollow by the stream
That beech leans down into—of which you said
The Oread in it has a Naiad's heart
And pines for waters."[6]

---

3. Ivy-covered staff carried by the Greek god Dionysus.
4. Female figure with upraised arms, used as a supporting
architectural column.

5. Aurora, the goddess of the dawn.
6. An Oread is a tree nymph; a Naiad is a water nymph.

         "Thank you."

                     "Thanks to *you*

85   My cousin! that I have seen you not too much
        Witch, scholar, poet, dreamer, and the rest,
        To be a woman also."

                  With a glance
        The smile rose in his eyes again and touched
        The ivy on my forehead, light as air.
90   I answered gravely "Poets needs must be
        Or men or women—more's the pity."

                        "Ah,
        But men, and still less women, happily,
        Scarce need be poets. Keep to the green wreath,
        Since even dreaming of the stone and bronze
95   Brings headaches, pretty cousin, and defiles
        The clean white morning dresses."

                    "So you judge!
        Because I love the beautiful I must
        Love pleasure chiefly, and be overcharged
        For ease and whiteness! well, you know the world,
100   And only miss your cousin, 'tis not much.
        But learn this; I would rather take my part
        With God's Dead, who afford to walk in white
        Yet spread His glory, than keep quiet here
        And gather up my feet from even a step
105   For fear to soil my gown in so much dust.
        I choose to walk at all risks.—Here, if heads
        That hold a rhythmic thought, much ache perforce,
        For my part I choose headaches,—and to-day's
        My birthday."

            "Dear Aurora, choose instead
110   To cure them. You have balsams."

                     "I perceive.
        The headache is too noble for my sex.
        You think the heartache would sound decenter,
        Since that's the woman's special, proper ache,
        And altogether tolerable, except
115   To a woman."

                [NO FEMALE CHRIST]

               "There it is!—
180   You play beside a death-bed like a child,
        Yet measure to yourself a prophet's place
        To teach the living. None of all these things
        Can women understand. You generalise
        Oh, nothing,—not even grief! Your quick-breathed hearts,
185   So sympathetic to the personal pang,

Close on each separate knife-stroke, yielding up
A whole life at each wound, incapable
Of deepening, widening a large lap of life
To hold the world-full woe. The human race
190   To you means, such a child, or such a man,
You saw one morning waiting in the cold,
Beside that gate, perhaps. You gather up
A few such cases, and when strong sometimes
Will write of factories and of slaves, as if
195   Your father were a negro, and your son
A spinner in the mills. All's yours and you,
All, coloured with your blood, or otherwise
Just nothing to you. Why, I call you hard
To general suffering. Here's the world half-blind
200   With intellectual light, half-brutalised
With civilisation, having caught the plague
In silks from Tarsus,[7] shrieking east and west
Along a thousand railroads, mad with pain
And sin too! . . . does one woman of you all
205   (You who weep easily) grow pale to see
This tiger shake his cage?—does one of you
Stand still from dancing, stop from stringing pearls,
And pine and die because of the great sum
Of universal anguish?—Show me a tear
210   Wet as Cordelia's,[8] in eyes bright as yours,
Because the world is mad. You cannot count,
That you should weep for this account, not you!
You weep for what you know. A red-haired child
Sick in a fever, if you touch him once,
215   Though but so little as with a finger-tip,
Will set you weeping; but a million sick . . .
You could as soon weep for the rule of three
Or compound fractions. Therefore, this same world,
Uncomprehended by you, must remain
220   Uninfluenced by you.—Women as you are,
Mere women, personal and passionate,
You give us doating mothers, and perfect wives,
Sublime Madonnas, and enduring saints!
We get no Christ from you,—and verily
225   We shall not get a poet, in my mind."

[AURORA'S REJECTION OF ROMNEY]

There he glowed on me
With all his face and eyes. "No other help?"

---

7. I.e., with civilized luxuries come evils, just as the trading ships bringing silks from Tarsus—a wealthy center of
trade in the ancient Middle East—might also have
brought rats that spread the plague.
8. Cordelia weeps when she is reunited with her father

(*King Lear*, 4.7.71); her feelings are entirely personal.
Romney mentions Cordelia to bolster his argument that
women cannot play any role in world affairs because
they are incapable of taking a broad view of human
suffering.

345   Said he—"no more than so?"9

                         "What help?" I asked.
     "You'd scorn my help,—as Nature's self, you say,
     Has scorned to put her music in my mouth
     Because a woman's. Do you now turn round
     And ask for what a woman cannot give?"

350   "For what she only can, I turn and ask,"
     He answered, catching up my hands in his,
     And dropping on me from his high-eaved brow
     The full weight of his soul,—"I ask for love,
     And that, she can; for life in fellowship
355   Through bitter duties—that, I know she can;
     For wifehood—will she?"

                "Now," I said, "may God
     Be witness 'twixt us two!" and with the word,
     Meseemed I floated into a sudden light
     Above his stature,—"am I proved too weak
360   To stand alone, yet strong enough to bear
     Such leaners on my shoulder? poor to think,
     Yet rich enough to sympathise with thought?
     Incompetent to sing, as blackbirds can,
     Yet competent to love, like HIM?"

                   I paused;
365   Perhaps I darkened, as the lighthouse will
     That turns upon the sea. "It's always so.
     Anything does for a wife."

                "Aurora, dear,
     And dearly honoured,"—he pressed in at once
     With eager utterance,—"you translate me ill.
370   I do not contradict my thought of you
     Which is most reverent, with another thought
     Found less so. If your sex is weak for art
     (And I, who said so, did but honour you
     By using truth in courtship), it is strong
375   For life and duty. Place your fecund heart
     In mine, and let us blossom for the world
     That wants love's colour in the grey of time.
     My talk, meanwhile, is arid to you, ay,
     Since all my talk can only set you where
380   You look down coldly on the arena-heaps
     Of headless bodies, shapeless, indistinct!
     The Judgment-Angel scarce would find his way
     Through such a heap of generalised distress
     To the individual man with lips and eyes,
385   Much less Aurora. Ah, my sweet, come down,

9. Romney wants to alleviate the misery of the poor through social reform. Aurora has offered her approval of his plans, but he asks if she can offer him another kind of help—i.e., to be his wife or "helpmate" (line 402 below).

And hand in hand we'll go where yours shall touch
These victims, one by one! till, one by one,
The formless, nameless trunk of every man
Shall seem to wear a head with hair you know,
390   And every woman catch your mother's face
To melt you into passion."

                "I am a girl,"
I answered slowly; "you do well to name
My mother's face. Though far too early, alas,
God's hand did interpose 'twixt it and me,
395   I know so much of love as used to shine
In that face and another. Just so much;
No more indeed at all. I have not seen
So much love since, I pray you pardon me,
As answers even to make a marriage with
400   In this cold land of England. What you love
Is not a woman, Romney, but a cause:
You want a helpmate, not a mistress, sir,
A wife to help your ends,—in her no end.
Your cause is noble, your ends excellent,
405   But I, being most unworthy of these and that,
Do otherwise conceive of love. Farewell."

"Farewell, Aurora? you reject me thus?"
He said.

         "Sir, you were married long ago.
You have a wife already whom you love,
410   Your social theory. Bless you both, I say.
For my part, I am scarcely meek enough
To be the handmaid of a lawful spouse.
Do I look a Hagar,[1] think you?"
                "So you jest."

"Nay, so, I speak in earnest," I replied.
415   "You treat of marriage too much like, at least,
A chief apostle: you would bear with you
A wife . . . a sister . . . shall we speak it out?
A sister of charity."

            "Then, must it be
Indeed farewell? And was I so far wrong
420   In hope and in illusion, when I took
The woman to be nobler than the man,
Yourself the noblest woman, in the use
And comprehension of what love is,—love,
That generates the likeness of itself
425   Through all heroic duties? so far wrong,

---

1. In Genesis 16, Hagar was the handmaiden of Abraham's lawful wife, Sarah; Hagar bore Abraham a son, Ishmael, when it appeared that Sarah was barren.

In saying bluntly, venturing truth on love,
'Come, human creature, love and work with me,'—
Instead of 'Lady, thou art wondrous fair,
And, where the Graces walk before, the Muse
430 Will follow at the lightning of their eyes,
And where the Muse walks, lovers need to creep:
Turn round and love me, or I die of love.'"

With quiet indignation I broke in.
"You misconceive the question like a man,
435 Who sees a woman as the complement
Of his sex merely. You forget too much
That every creature, female as the male,
Stands single in responsible act and thought
As also in birth and death. Whoever says
440 To a loyal woman, 'Love and work with me,'
Will get fair answers if the work and love,
Being good themselves, are good for her—the best
She was born for. Women of a softer mood,
Surprised by men when scarcely awake to life,
445 Will sometimes only hear the first word, love,
And catch up with it any kind of work,
Indifferent, so that dear love go with it.
I do not blame such women, though, for love,
They pick much oakum;[2] earth's fanatics make
450 Too frequently heaven's saints. But *me* your work
Is not the best for,—nor your love the best,
Nor able to commend the kind of work
For love's sake merely. Ah, you force me, sir,
To be overbold in speaking of myself:
455 I too have my vocation,—work to do,
The heavens and earth have set me since I changed
My father's face for theirs, and, though your world
Were twice as wretched as you represent,
Most serious work, most necessary work
460 As any of the economists'. Reform,
Make trade a Christian possibility,
And individual right no general wrong;
Wipe out earth's furrows of the Thine and Mine,
And leave one green for men to play at bowls,[3]
465 With innings for them all! . . . What then, indeed,
If mortals are not greater by the head
Than any of their prosperities? what then,
Unless the artist keep up open roads
Betwixt the seen and unseen,—bursting through
470 The best of your conventions with his best,
The speakable, imaginable best
God bids him speak, to prove what lies beyond

2. Prisoners and paupers in workhouses were forced to pick oakum (untwist strands of old rope); it was tedious and humble labor.
3. Lawn bowling.

Both speech and imagination? A starved man
Exceeds a fat beast: we'll not barter, sir,
475 The beautiful for barley.—And, even so,
I hold you will not compass your poor ends
Of barley-feeding and material ease,
Without a poet's individualism
To work your universal. It takes a soul,
480 To move a body: it takes a high-souled man,
To move the masses, even to a cleaner stye:
It takes the ideal, to blow a hair's-breadth off
The dust of the actual.—Ah, your Fouriers[4] failed,
Because not poets enough to understand
485 That life develops from within.—For me,
Perhaps I am not worthy, as you say,
Of work like this: perhaps a woman's soul
Aspires, and not creates: yet we aspire,
And yet I'll try out your perhapses, sir,
490 And if I fail . . . why, burn me up my straw[5]
Like other false works—I'll not ask for grace;
Your scorn is better, cousin Romney. I
Who love my art, would never wish it lower
To suit my stature. I may love my art.
495 You'll grant that even a woman may love art,
Seeing that to waste true love on anything
Is womanly, past question."

                              I retain
The very last word which I said that day,
As you the creaking of the door, years past,
500 Which let upon you such disabling news
You ever after have been graver. He,
His eyes, the motions in his silent mouth,
Were fiery points on which my words were caught,
Transfixed for ever in my memory
505 For his sake, not their own. And yet I know
I did not love him . . . nor he me . . . that's sure . . .
And what I said is unrepented of,
As truth is always. Yet . . . a princely man!—
If hard to me, heroic for himself!
510 He bears down on me through the slanting years,
The stronger for the distance. If he had loved,
Ay, loved me, with that retributive face, . . .
I might have been a common woman now
And happier, less known and less left alone,
515 Perhaps a better woman after all,
With chubby children hanging on my neck
To keep me low and wise. Ah me, the vines
That bear such fruit are proud to stoop with it.

---

4. François Marie Charles Fourier (1772–1837), a French
social theorist who advocated communal property.

5. I.e., destroy my poetry.

The palm stands upright in a realm of sand.
520 And I, who spoke the truth then, stand upright,
Still worthy of having spoken out the truth,
By being content I spoke it though it set
Him there, me here.—O woman's vile remorse,
To hanker after a mere name, a show,
525 A supposition, a potential love!
Does every man who names love in our lives
Become a power for that?

from *Book 3*

[THE WOMAN WRITER IN LONDON]

Why what a pettish, petty thing I grow,—
A mere mere woman, a mere flaccid nerve,
A kerchief left out all night in the rain,
Turned soft so,—overtasked and overstrained
40 And overlived in this close London life!
And yet I should be stronger.

                              Never burn
Your letters, poor Aurora! for they stare
With red seals from the table, saying each,
"Here's something that you know not." Out, alas,
45 'Tis scarcely that the world's more good and wise
Or even straighter and more consequent
Since yesterday at this time—yet, again,
If but one angel spoke from Ararat[1]
I should be very sorry not to hear:
50 So open all the letters! let me read.
Blanche Ord, the writer in the "Lady's Fan,"
Requests my judgment on . . . that, afterwards.
Kate Ward desires the model of my cloak,
And signs "Elisha to you."[2] Pringle Sharpe
55 Presents his work on "Social Conduct," craves
A little money for his pressing debts . . .
From me, who scarce have money for my needs;
Art's fiery chariot which we journey in
Being apt to singe our singing-robes to holes,
60 Although you ask me for my cloak, Kate Ward!
Here's Rudgely knows it,—editor and scribe;
He's "forced to marry where his heart is not,
Because the purse lacks where he lost his heart."
Ah,——lost it because no one picked it up;
65 That's really loss,—(and passable impudence).
My critic Hammond flatters prettily,
And wants another volume like the last.
My critic Belfair wants another book

---

1. The mountain where Noah's ark rested after the Flood and where God spoke to Noah (Genesis 8).
2. When the prophet Elijah was carried to heaven in a chariot of fire, his cloak fell to earth and was taken up by his successor Elisha (2 Kings 2.1–15); Kate Ward means that she wants to copy Aurora's cloak.

Entirely different, which will sell (and live?),
70   A striking book, yet not a startling book,
The public blames originalities
(You must not pump spring-water unawares
Upon a gracious public full of nerves):
Good things, not subtle, new yet orthodox,
75   As easy reading as the dog-eared page
That's fingered by said public fifty years,
Since first taught spelling by its grandmother,
And yet a revelation in some sort:
That's hard, my critic Belfair. So—what next?
80   My critic Stokes objects to abstract thoughts;
"Call a man John, a woman Joan," says he,
"And do not prate so of *humanities:*"
Whereat I call my critic simply, Stokes.
My critic Jobson recommends more mirth
85   Because a cheerful genius suits the times,
And all true poets laugh unquenchably
Like Shakespeare and the gods. That's very hard.
The gods may laugh, and Shakespeare; Dante smiled
With such a needy heart on two pale lips,
90   We cry "Weep rather, Dante." Poems are
Men, if true poems: and who dares exclaim
At any man's door, "Here, 'tis understood
The thunder fell last week and killed a wife
And scared a sickly husband—what of that?
95   Get up, be merry, shout and clap your hands,
Because a cheerful genius suits the times—"?
None says so to the man, and why indeed
Should any to the poem? A ninth seal;[3]
The apocalypse is drawing to a close.
100   Ha,—this from Vincent Carrington,—"Dear friend,
I want good counsel. Will you lend me wings
To raise me to the subject, in a sketch
I'll bring to-morrow—may I? at eleven?
A poet's only born to turn to use:
105   So save you! for the world . . . and Carrington."
"(Writ after.) Have you heard of Romney Leigh,
Beyond what's said of him in newspapers,
His phalansteries[4] there, his speeches here,
His pamphlets, pleas, and statements, everywhere?
110   He dropped *me* long ago, but no one drops
A golden apple—though indeed one day
You hinted that, but jested. Well, at least
You know Lord Howe who sees him . . . whom he sees
And *you* see and I hate to see,—for Howe
115   Stands high upon the brink of theories,

---

3. In Revelation 5.1 there is a book closed with seven seals, the opening of which will herald the Apocalypse. The reference to a ninth seal satirically suggests some-thing more extreme than the Apocalypse itself.
4. The communes advocated by the socialist Fourier.

Observes the swimmers and cries 'Very fine,'
But keeps dry linen equally,—unlike
That gallant breaster, Romney. Strange it is,
Such sudden madness seizing a young man
120 To make earth over again,—while I'm content
To make the pictures. Let me bring the sketch.
A tiptoe Danae,[5] overbold and hot,
Both arms a-flame to meet her wishing Jove
Halfway, and burn him faster down; the face
125 And breasts upturned and straining, the loose locks
All glowing with the anticipated gold.
Or here's another on the self-same theme.[6]
She lies here—flat upon her prison-floor,
The long hair swathed about her to the heel
130 Like wet seaweed. You dimly see her through
The glittering haze of that prodigious rain,
Half blotted out of nature by a love
As heavy as fate. I'll bring you either sketch.
I think, myself, the second indicates
More passion."

135   Surely. Self is put away,
And calm with abdication. She is Jove,
And no more Danae—greater thus. Perhaps
The painter symbolises unaware
Two states of the recipient artist-soul,
140 One, forward, personal, wanting reverence,
Because aspiring only. We'll be calm,
And know that, when indeed our Joves come down,
We all turn stiller than we have ever been.

* * *

Serene and unafraid of solitude,
170 I worked the short days out,—and watched the sun
On lurid morns or monstrous afternoons
(Like some Druidic idol's fiery brass
With fixed unflickering outline of dead heat,
From which the blood of wretches pent inside
175 Seems oozing forth to incarnadine the air[7])
Push out through fog with his dilated disk,
And startle the slant roofs and chimney-pots
With splashes of fierce colour. Or I saw
Fog only, the great tawny weltering fog,
180 Involve the passive city, strangle it
Alive, and draw it off into the void,
Spires, bridges, streets, and squares, as if a sponge
Had wiped out London,—or as noon and night
Had clapped together and utterly struck out

---

5. Carrington has sketched Danae, the beloved of Zeus, whom Zeus visited in a shower of gold.
6. I.e., the second picture is also of Danae and the golden

shower ("prodigious rain") that is Zeus.
7. It was believed that ancient Celtic druids performed human sacrifices.

185   The intermediate time, undoing themselves
       In the act. Your city poets see such things
       Not despicable. Mountains of the south,
       When drunk and mad with elemental wines
       They rend the seamless mist and stand up bare,
190   Make fewer singers, haply. No one sings,
       Descending Sinai: on Parnassus mount[8]
       You take a mule to climb and not a muse
       Except in fable and figure: forests chant
       Their anthems to themselves, and leave you dumb.
170   But sit in London at the day's decline,
       And view the city perish in the mist
       Like Pharaoh's armaments in the deep Red Sea,[9]
       The chariots, horsemen, footmen, all the host,
       Sucked down and choked to silence—then, surprised
       By a sudden sense of vision and of tune,
       You feel as conquerors though you did not fight,
       And you and Israel's other singing girls,
       Ay, Miriam[1] with them, sing the song you choose.

from *Book 5*
[EPIC ART AND MODERN LIFE]

       The critics say that epics have died out
140   With Agamemnon and the goat-nursed gods;[1]
       I'll not believe it. I could never deem,
       As Payne Knight[2] did (the mythic mountaineer
       Who travelled higher than he was born to live,
       And showed sometimes the goitre in his throat[3]
145   Discoursing of an image seen through fog),
       That Homer's heroes measured twelve feet high.
       They were but men:—his Helen's hair turned grey
       Like any plain Miss Smith's who wears a front;[4]
       And Hector's infant whimpered at a plume[5]
150   As yours last Friday at a turkey-cock.
       All actual heroes are essential men,
       And all men possible heroes: every age,
       Heroic in proportions, double-faced,
       Looks backward and before, expects a morn

8. Sinai is the mountain where God gave the Commandments to Moses; Parnassus is the mountain where the Muses, the Greek goddesses of the arts and of knowledge, dwelled. The idea is that neither biblical nor classical sources can provide poetic inspiration for the modern poet; only the city can do so.
9. In Exodus 14.21–30, God parts the Red Sea so the Israelites can escape from Egypt but drowns Pharaoh's pursuing armies.
1. Miriam, the sister of Moses and Aaron, led the women of Israel in singing to celebrate the drowning of the Egyptian army (Exodus 15.19–21).

1. Agamemnon led the Greeks in the Trojan War, as chronicled in Homer's epic, the *Iliad*; Zeus was nursed by a goat.
2. Richard Payne Knight (1750–1824), a classical scholar who speculated about Homer and the Elgin marbles.
3. A swelling of the throat (caused by lack of iodine in the water at high altitudes), symbolizing the foolishness of Payne Knight's utterances.
4. Hairpiece worn over the forehead; artificial bangs.
5. When the Trojan warrior Hector tried to embrace his infant son before going into battle, the baby was terrified of his father's plumed helmet.

155   And claims an epos.°   *epic poem*
                        Ay, but every age
        Appears to souls who live in't (ask Carlyle[6])
        Most unheroic. Ours, for instance, ours:
        The thinkers scout it, and the poets abound
        Who scorn to touch it with a finger-tip:
160   A pewter age,[7]—mixed metal, silver-washed;
        An age of scum, spooned off the richer past,
        An age of patches for old gaberdines,°   *overcoats*
        An age of mere transition,[8] meaning nought
        Except that what succeeds must shame it quite
165   If God please. That's wrong thinking, to my mind,
        And wrong thoughts make poor poems.

                                        Every age,
        Through being beheld too close, is ill-discerned
        By those who have not lived past it. We'll suppose
        Mount Athos carved, as Alexander schemed,
170   To some colossal statue of a man.[9]
        The peasants, gathering brushwood in his ear,
        Had guessed as little as the browsing goats
        Of form or feature of humanity
        Up there,—in fact, had travelled five miles off
175   Or ere the giant image broke on them,
        Full human profile, nose and chin distinct,
        Mouth, muttering rhythms of silence up the sky
        And fed at evening with the blood of suns;
        Grand torso,—hand, that flung perpetually
180   The largesse of a silver river down
        To all the country pastures. 'Tis even thus
        With times we live in,—evermore too great
        To be apprehended near.

                                But poets should
        Exert a double vision; should have eyes
185   To see near things as comprehensively
        As if afar they took their point of sight,
        And distant things as intimately deep
        As if they touched them. Let us strive for this.
        I do distrust the poet who discerns
190   No character or glory in his times,
        And trundles back his soul five hundred years,
        Past moat and drawbridge, into a castle-court,

6. In *On Heroes and Hero Worship* (1841) Thomas Carlyle urges a renewal of the idea of the heroic.
7. Inferior to the Golden, the Silver, or even the Bronze Age; Hesiod proposed that history is a constant process of decline.
8. In *The Spirit of the Age* (1831) John Stuart Mill says the present era is "an age of transition."
9. Alexander the Great thought of having Mount Athos carved in the form of a gigantic statue of a conqueror, with a basin in one hand to collect water for the pastures below.

To sing—oh, not of lizard or of toad
Alive i' the ditch there,—'twere excusable,
195   But of some black chief, half knight, half sheep-lifter,
Some beauteous dame, half chattel and half queen,
As dead as must be, for the greater part,
The poems made on their chivalric bones;
And that's no wonder: death inherits death.

200   Nay, if there's room for poets in this world
A little overgrown (I think there is),
Their sole work is to represent the age,
Their age, not Charlemagne's,[1]—this live, throbbing age,
That brawls, cheats, maddens, calculates, aspires,
205   And spends more passion, more heroic heat,
Betwixt the mirrors of its drawing-rooms,
Than Roland with his knights at Roncesvalles.[2]
To flinch from modern varnish, coat or flounce,
Cry out for togas and the picturesque,
210   Is fatal,—foolish too. King Arthur's self
Was commonplace to Lady Guenever;
And Camelot to minstrels seemed as flat
As Fleet Street to our poets.[3]

                      Never flinch,
But still, unscrupulously epic, catch
215   Upon the burning lava of a song
The full-veined, heaving, double-breasted Age:
That, when the next shall come, the men of that
May touch the impress with reverent hand, and say
"Behold,—behold the paps we all have sucked!
220   This bosom seems to beat still, or at least
It sets ours beating: this is living art,
Which thus presents and thus records true life."

1853–1856   1856

1. Charlemagne was king of the Franks (768–814) and emperor of the West, laying the foundation for the Holy Roman Empire.
2. Legendary hero whose defeat at Roncesvalles (in the Spanish Pyrenees) was disastrous for Charlemagne's forces; his exploits are the subject of a medieval epic poem, Le Chanson de Roland.
3. I.e., to his wife Guinevere, even the glorious King Arthur was ordinary, and his kingdom was no more a subject for the poets of his own time than Fleet Street—location of London publishers and newspaper offices—is for the poets of the 19th century.

� PERSPECTIVES ⟷
Victorian Ladies and Gentlemen

As Victorian society prospered, social divisions became more fluid, but at the same time class consciousness became more intense. The terms "lady" and "gentleman" had enormous significance, particularly for those aspiring to these ranks, or for those in danger of slipping out of them. Some social distinctions were obvious: regardless of conduct, people born into the aristocracy and landed gentry were indisputably ladies and gentlemen; people who worked with their hands in home, field, or factory were not. The upper and lower boundaries of the middle class were blurred, however, and everyone was alert to fine gradations. Manners, money, birth, occupation, and leisure time were crucial indicators of social standing, determining not only one's place in society but one's freedom to act, speak, learn, and earn.

Ladies and gentlemen endeavored to conform to the ideology of separate spheres that dominated Victorian thinking about gender. Middle-class women were to preside over the domestic sphere, the home and family, while men entered the fray of the world. Woman's "mission" was to provide a sanctified haven from the rough-and-tumble world of business and politics. Her virtuous passivity, selflessness, and spiritual purity gave her moral authority in the social and domestic realm. The first mass-circulation women's periodical, launched in 1852, was called, significantly, *Englishwoman's Domestic Magazine*.

Meanwhile, the world of action and aggression belonged to men: as Ruskin put it in *Sesame and Lilies* (1865): "The man, in his rough work in the open world, must encounter all peril and trial . . . often he must be wounded, or subdued, often misled; and *always* hardened. But he guards the woman from all this; within his house, as ruled by her . . . need enter no danger, no temptation, no cause of error or offense." Tennyson's *The Princess* (1847) gave the polarization of gender roles the aura of timeless law:

> Man for the field and woman for the hearth:
> Man for the sword and for the needle she:
> Man with the head and woman with the heart:
> Man to command and woman to obey:
> All else confusion.

Among middle-class men, the clearest social division was between those who had attended a public school (an elite boarding school) and those who had not. The ideal of gentlemanliness inculcated by these schools became a way for society to remake the upstart middle classes in the image of the aristocracy. Emphasizing character over intellect, the public schools taught boys how to assimilate the manners and customs of those above them socially, and gave them a familiarity with Greek, Latin, and school games such as cricket and rugby—hallmarks of an upper-class education. Instilling the values of duty, loyalty, and public service, these schools helped to create a new administrative elite, based more on merit and training than birth, who ran both the Civil Service and the Empire. Sustained by the "old boy" network, in which former schoolmates assisted each other's careers, graduates of places such as Eton, Harrow, Winchester, and Rugby could look forward to positions of influence and affluence.

Although the daughters of some well-to-do families might attend a fashionable boarding school, education was not primarily what determined a woman's claim to be considered a lady. Her position derived from her parents or her husband, and her unproductive leisure was a visible signal of rank. Since aspirations to "refinement" effectively precluded middle-class women from employment, ladies had, as the novelist Dinah Maria Mulock put it in 1858, "literally nothing whatever to do." She complained that "their whole energies are devoted to the massacre of old Time. They prick him to death with crochet and embroidery needles; strum him

The Parliamentary Female, from *Punch* magazine, 1853. A caption offered this dialogue:

FATHER OF THE FAMILY: Come, dear; we so seldom go out together now—Can't you take us all
   to the Play to-night?

MISTRESS OF THE HOUSE, AND M.P.: How you talk, Charles! Don't you see that I am too Busy. I
   have a Committee to-morrow morning, and I have my Speech on the Great Crochet Question
   to prepare for the evening.

deaf with piano and harp playing—*not* music; cut him up with morning visitors, or leave his
carcass in ten-minute parcels at every 'friend's' house they can think of." In her autobiography
Harriet Martineau described the expectations in her day: "It was not thought proper for young
ladies to study very conspicuously. . . . If ever I shut myself into my own room for an hour of
solitude, I knew it was at the risk of being sent for to join the sewing-circle, or to read aloud."

It was a way of life that at once exalted women and paralyzed them. They could not
work outside the home; they could not vote; they had no legal rights, even over their own
children; they could not attend university or enter the professions. Legally, they were classed
with criminals, idiots, and minors. Rejecting women's education, the painter Edward Burne-
Jones argued, "The great point is, not that they should understand us, but that they should
worship and obey us." Ironically, only economic necessity or illness could liberate a lady
from the burden of enforced idleness. When Harriet Martineau's family went bankrupt she
was enabled to pursue her dream of authorship, for "we had lost our gentility." Similarly, the
death of both parents freed Mary Kingsley to travel, and her own recurrent ill health allowed
Isabella Bird to go off in search of a "cure." Florence Nightingale made time for a career by
taking to her bed, where only her persistent indisposition released her from the demands of
family and social life. Definitions of masculinity and femininity were earnestly contested
throughout the period—with increasingly sharp assaults on traditional roles coming from
aesthetes and decadents at the end of the century. The following selections illustrate the
kinds of arguments and experiences that figured prominently in debates on gender roles in
the early and mid-Victorian periods.

Sarah Stickney Ellis
1799–1872

Author of numerous popular guides to female conduct, including *The Women of England* (1839), *The Daughters of England* (1842), *The Wives of England* (1843), and *The Mothers of England* (1845), Sarah Stickney Ellis advised women to accept their inferiority to men and devote themselves to the happiness and moral elevation of their brothers, husbands, and sons. Idealizing the family home as the center of middle-class English life, Ellis fostered the notion of women's separate domestic sphere. Although she ran a school for girls, Ellis discouraged intellectual ambitions, demanding precisely the sort of self-sacrificing domesticity that Florence Nightingale, and many other talented and capable women, found so intolerably confining.

from The Women of England:
Their Social Duties and Domestic Habits
[THE INFLUENCE OF WOMEN]

It is not to be presumed that women *possess* more power than men; but happily for them, such are their early impressions, associations, and general position in the world, that their moral feelings are less liable to be impaired by the pecuniary objects which too often constitute the chief end of man, and which, even under the limitations of better principle, necessarily engage a large portion of his thoughts. There are many humble-minded women, not remarkable for any particular intellectual endowments, who yet possess so clear a sense of the right and wrong of individual actions, as to be of essential service in aiding the judgments of their husbands, brothers, or sons, in those intricate affairs in which it is sometimes difficult to dissever worldly wisdom from religious duty.

* * * And surely they now need more than ever all the assistance which Providence has kindly provided, to win them away from this warfare, to remind them that they are hastening on towards a world into which none of the treasures they are amassing can be admitted; and, next to those holier influences which operate through the medium of revelation, or through the mysterious instrumentality of Divine love, I have little hesitation in saying, that the society of woman in her highest moral capacity, is best calculated to effect this purpose.

How often has man returned to his home with a mind confused by the many voices, which in the mart, the exchange, or the public assembly, have addressed themselves to his inborn selfishness, or his worldly pride; and while his integrity was shaken, and his resolution gave way beneath the pressure of apparent necessity, or the insidious pretences of expediency, he has stood corrected before the clear eye of woman, as it looked directly to the naked truth, and detected the lurking evil of the specious act he was about to commit. Nay, so potent may have become this secret influence, that he may have borne it about with him like a kind of second conscience, for mental reference, and spiritual counsel, in moments of trial; and when the snares of the world were around him, and temptations from within and without have bribed over the witness in his own bosom, he has thought of the humble monitress who sat alone, guarding the fireside comforts of his distant home; and the remembrance of her character, clothed in moral beauty, has scattered the clouds before his mental vision, and sent him back to that beloved home, a wiser and a better man.

The women of England, possessing the grand privilege of being better instruct-ed than those of any other country, in the minutiae of domestic comfort, have obtained a degree of importance in society far beyond what their unobtrusive virtues would appear to claim. The long-established customs of their country have placed in their hands the high and holy duty of cherishing and protecting the minor morals of life, from whence springs all that is elevated in purpose, and glori-ous in action. The sphere of their direct personal influence is central, and conse-quently small; but its extreme operations are as widely extended as the range of human feeling. They may be less striking in society than some of the women of other countries, and may feel themselves, on brilliant and stirring occasions, as simple, rude, and unsophisticated in the popular science of excitement; but as far as the noble daring of Britain has sent forth her adventurous sons, and that is to every point of danger on the habitable globe, they have borne along with them a gen-erosity, a disinterestedness, and a moral courage, derived in no small measure from the female influence of their native country.

It is a fact well worthy of our most serious attention, and one which bears imme-diately upon the subject under consideration, that the present state of our national affairs is such as to indicate that the influence of woman in counteracting the grow-ing evils of society is about to be more needed than ever. ✳ ✳ ✳

Will an increase of intellectual attainments, or a higher style of accomplish-ments, effect this purpose? Will the common-place frivolities of morning calls, or an interminable range of superficial reading, enable them to assist their brothers, their husbands, or their sons in becoming happier and better men?—No: let the aspect of society be what it may, man is a social being, and beneath the hard sur-face he puts on, to fit him for the wear and tear of every day, he has a heart as true to the kindly affections of our nature, as that of woman—as true, though not as suddenly awakened to every pressing call. He has therefore need of all her sisterly services—and under the pressure of the present times, he needs them more than ever—to foster in his nature, and establish in his character that higher tone of feel-ing, without which he can enjoy nothing beyond a kind of animal existence. ✳ ✳ ✳

In order to ascertain what kind of education is most effective in making woman what she ought to be, the best method is to inquire into the character, station, and peculiar duties of woman throughout the largest portion of her earthly career; and then ask, for what she is most valued, admired, and beloved?

In answer to this, I have little hesitation in saying,—For her disinterested kindness. Look at all the heroines, whether of romance or reality—at all the female characters that are held up to universal admiration—at all who have gone down to honoured graves, amongst the tears and the lamentations of their sur-vivors. Have these been the learned, the accomplished women; the women who could speak many languages, who could solve problems, and elucidate systems of philosophy? No: or if they have, they have also been women who were dignified with the majesty of moral greatness—women who regarded not themselves, their own feebleness, or their own susceptibility of pain, but who, endued with an almost super-human energy, could trample under foot every impediment that intervened between them and the accomplishment of some great object upon which their hopes were fixed, while that object was wholly unconnected with their own personal exaltation or enjoyment, and related only to some beloved object, whose suffering was their sorrow, whose good their gain. * * *

Never yet, however, was woman great, because she had great acquirements; nor can she ever be great in herself—personally, and without instrumentality—as an object, not an agent. * * *

Let us single out from any particular seminary a child who has been there from the years of ten to fifteen, and reckon, if it can be reckoned, the pains that have been spent in making that child a proficient in Latin. Have the same pains been spent in making her disinterestedly kind? And yet what man is there in existence who would not rather his wife should be free from selfishness, than be able to read Virgil without the use of a dictionary. * * *

Taking into consideration the various excellencies and peculiarities of woman, I am inclined to think that the sphere which of all others admits of the highest development of her character, is the chamber of sickness; and how frequently and mournfully familiar are the scenes in which she is thus called to act and feel, let the private history of every family declare.

There is but a very small proportion of the daughters of farmers, manufacturers, and tradespeople, in England, who are ever called upon for their Latin, their Italian, or even for their French; but all women in this sphere of life are liable to be called upon to visit and care for the sick; and if in the hour of weakness and of suffering, they prove to be unacquainted with any probable means of alleviation, and wholly ignorant of the most judicious and suitable mode of offering relief and consolation, they are indeed deficient in one of the highest attainments in the way of usefulness, to which a woman can aspire. * * *

Women have the choice of many means of bringing their principles into exercise, and of obtaining influence, both in their own domestic sphere, and in society at large. Amongst the most important of these is *conversation*, an engine so powerful upon the minds and characters of mankind in general, that beauty fades before it, and wealth in comparison is but as leaden coin. If match-making were indeed the great object of human life, I should scarcely dare to make this assertion, since few men choose women for their conversation, where wealth or beauty are to be had. * * *

* * * But if she has no intellectual hold upon her husband's heart, she must inevitably become that most helpless and pitiable of earthly objects—a slighted wife.

Conversation, understood in its proper character, as distinct from mere talk, might rescue her from this. Not conversation upon books, if her husband happens to be a fox-hunter; nor upon fox-hunting, if he is a book-worm; but exactly that kind of conversation which is best adapted to his tastes and habits, yet at the same time capable of leading him a little out of both into a wider field of observation, and subjects he may never have derived amusement from before, simply from the fact of their never having been presented to his notice.—How pleasantly the evening hours may be made to pass, when a woman who really can converse, will thus beguile the time. But, on the other hand, how wretched is the portion of that man who dreads the dulness of his own fireside! who sees the clog of his existence ever seated there— the same, in the deadening influence she has upon his spirits to-day, as yesterday, to-morrow, and the next day, and the next!

1839

Charlotte Brontë
1816–1855

To be a governess or schoolteacher was one of the very few professions open to a middle-class woman, but it was not an enviable life. Rarely was the governess treated as an equal by her employers, even though she was expected to be a "lady." Poorly paid and often rudely treated, she could be fired at a moment's notice, for there was an abundance of needy single women eager to take her place. Charlotte Brontë's novel *Jane Eyre* (1847) portrayed the social isolation of a governess, who is ridiculed to her face by visiting ladies. Brontë's own experiences were unhappy, as this letter to her sister reveals. In another letter, Brontë wrote that it was better to be "a housemaid or kitchen girl, rather than a baited, trampled, desolate, distracted governess."

from Letter to Emily Brontë[1]
[*The Horrors of Governessing*]

STONEGAPPE, June 8th, 1839

∗ ∗ ∗ I have striven hard to be pleased with my new situation. The country, the house, and the grounds are, as I have said, divine. But, alack-a-day! there is such a thing as seeing all beautiful around you—pleasant woods, winding white paths, green lawns, and blue sunshiny sky—and not having a free moment or a free thought left to enjoy them in. The children are constantly with me, and more riotous, perverse, unmanageable cubs never grew. As for correcting them, I soon quickly found that was entirely out of the question: they are to do as they like. A complaint to Mrs Sidgwick brings only black looks upon oneself, and unjust, partial excuses to screen the children. I have tried that plan once. It succeeded so notably that I shall try it no more. I said in my last letter that Mrs Sidgwick did not know me. I now begin to find that she does not intend to know me, that she cares nothing in the world about me except to contrive how the greatest possible quantity of labour may be squeezed out of me, and to that end she overwhelms me with oceans of needlework, yards of cambric to hem, muslin nightcaps to make, and, above all things, dolls to dress. I do not think she likes me at all, because I can't help being shy in such an entirely novel scene, surrounded as I have hitherto been by strange and constantly changing faces. I used to think I should like to be in the stir of grand folks' society but I have had enough of it—it is dreary work to look on and listen. I see now more clearly than I have ever done before that a private governess has no existence, is not considered as a living and rational being except as connected with the wearisome duties she has to fulfil. While she is teaching the children, working for them, amusing them, it is all right. If she steals a moment for herself she is a nuisance. Nevertheless, Mrs Sidgwick is universally considered an amiable woman. Her manners are fussily affable. She talks a great deal, but as it seems to me not much to the purpose. Perhaps I may like her better after a while.

---

1. Text taken from *The Brontës: Their Lives, Friendships and Correspondence*, vol. 1 (1933, rpt. 1980).

Richard Redgrave, *The Poor Teacher,* 1844. Narrative painting was enormously popular with the Victorians, who delighted in "reading" the story in symbolic visual details and drawing a moral from it. Here Redgrave, whose sisters were governesses, draws attention to his subject's social and emotional isolation. Dressed in mourning, the solitary governess sits indoors while her gaily-clad pupils skip rope in the sunlight, apparently indifferent to the bad news contained in her black-bordered letter. She has been playing "Home Sweet Home" on the piano. With copy books still to correct, she is about to consume her supper, a meager slice of bread and a tiny cup of tea. Contemporary observers speculated that she was an orphan, whose pallor revealed that she was already wasting away from illness and overwork.

At present I have no call to her. Mr Sidgwick is in my opinion a hundred times better—less profession, less bustling condescension, but a far kinder heart. It is very seldom that he speaks to me, but when he does I always feel happier and more settled for some minutes after. He never asks me to wipe the children's smutty noses or tie their shoes or fetch their pinafores or set them a chair. * * *

Anne Brontë
1820–1849

Like her older sisters, Charlotte and Emily, Anne Brontë tried to earn her living as a governess. All of them were made miserable by the constant drudgery and humiliations, and by being cut off, as governesses usually were, from family and friends. Her autobiographical novel *Agnes Grey* (1847) dramatizes Anne Brontë's own experience of working as a governess.

Initially, she had looked forward to the job: "How delightful it would be to be a governess!" says Agnes: "To go out into the world; to enter into a new life; to act for myself; to exercise my unused faculties." But Agnes had not yet realized the drawbacks of a governess's anomalous social status: caught between disrespectful children and contemptuous parents, she was made grimly conscious of her dependent position.

from Agnes Grey
[THE GOVERNESS TORMENTED BY HER CHARGES]

I returned, however, with unabated vigour to my work—a more arduous task than any one can imagine, who has not felt something like the misery of being charged with the care and direction of a set of mischievous turbulent rebels, whom his utmost exertions cannot bind to their duty; while, at the same time, he is responsible for their conduct to a higher power, who exacts from him what cannot be achieved without the aid of the superior's more potent authority: which, either from indolence, or the fear of becoming unpopular with the said rebellious gang, the latter refuses to give. I can conceive few situations more harassing than that wherein, however you may long for success, however you may labour to fulfil your duty, your efforts are baffled and set at nought by those beneath you, and unjustly censured and misjudged by those above. * * *

I particularly remember one wild, snowy afternoon, soon after my return in January; the children had all come up from dinner, loudly declaring that they meant "to be naughty"; and they had well kept their resolution, though I had talked myself hoarse, and wearied every muscle in my throat, in the vain attempt to reason them out of it. I had got Tom pinned up in a corner, whence, I told him, he should not escape till he had done his appointed task. Meantime, Fanny had possessed herself of my work-bag, and was rifling its contents—and spitting into it besides. I told her to let it alone, but to no purpose, of course.

"Burn it, Fanny!" cried Tom; and *this* command she hastened to obey. I sprang to snatch it from the fire, and Tom darted to the door.

"Mary Ann, throw her desk[1] out of the window!" cried he: and my precious desk, containing my letters and papers, my small amount of cash, and all my valuables, was about to be precipitated from the three-story window. I flew to rescue it. Meanwhile Tom had left the room, and was rushing down the stairs, followed by Fanny. Having secured my desk, I ran to catch them, and Mary Ann came scampering after. All three escaped me, and ran out of the house into the garden, where they plunged about in the snow, shouting and screaming in exultant glee.

What must I do? If I followed them, I should probably be unable to capture one, and only drive them farther away; if I did not, how was I to get them in? and what would their parents think of me, if they saw or heard the children rioting, hatless, bonnetless, gloveless, and bootless, in the deep, soft snow?

While I stood in this perplexity, just without the door, trying by grim looks and angry words, to awe them into subjection, I heard a voice behind me, in harshly piercing tones, exclaiming,—

"Miss Grey! Is it possible? What, in the devil's name, can you be thinking about?"

"I can't get them in, sir," said I, turning round, and beholding Mr Bloomfield, with his hair on end, and his pale blue eyes bolting from their sockets.

"But I INSIST upon their being got in!" cried he, approaching nearer, and looking perfectly ferocious.

---

1. Portable box for writing materials and letters, sometimes with a sloping surface for writing on.

"Then, sir, you must call them yourself, if you please, for they won't listen to me," I replied, stepping back.

"Come in with you, you filthy brats! or I'll horsewhip you, every one!" roared he; and the children instantly obeyed. "There, you see! they come at the first word!"

"Yes, when *you* speak."

"And it's very strange, that when you've the care of 'em, you've no better control over 'em than that!—Now, there they are, gone upstairs with their nasty snowy feet! Do go after 'em and see them made decent, for Heaven's sake!"

That gentleman's mother was then staying in the house; and, as I ascended the stairs and passed the drawing-room door, I had the satisfaction of hearing the old lady declaiming aloud to her daughter-in-law to this effect (for I could only distinguish the most emphatic words)—

"Gracious Heavens!—never in all my life!—!—get their death as sure as—! Do you think, my dear, she's a *proper person*? Take my word for it—"

I heard no more, but that sufficed.

1847

John Henry Cardinal Newman
1801–1890

The ideal of gentlemanliness was central to the Victorians' notion of themselves, yet for a society in flux it was a concept increasingly difficult to pin down. What exactly *was* a gentleman? In most people's minds, property, birth, courage, and athleticism were essential ingredients. And, of course, a gentleman was assumed to be a Christian. But John Henry Cardinal Newman distinguishes between the two: in a series of lectures about the purposes of a liberal education he said that while the gentleman has "a cultivated intellect, a delicate taste, a candid, equitable, dispassionate mind, a noble and courteous bearing in the conduct of life . . . they are no guarantee for sanctity or even for conscientiousness; they may attach to the man of the world, to the profligate, to the heartless." Thus for Newman, who was both, a gentleman is not necessarily a Christian: one may have character and education but not faith. He subtly suggests the vanity behind the gentleman's courtesy; gentility and virtue are not necessarily the same thing.

For more about Newman, see Perspectives: Religion and Science, page 646.

from The Idea of a University
[A DEFINITION OF A GENTLEMAN]

Hence it is that it is almost a definition of a gentleman to say he is one who never inflicts pain. This description is both refined and, as far as it goes, accurate. He is mainly occupied in merely removing the obstacles which hinder the free and unembarrassed action of those about him; and he concurs with their movements rather than takes the initiative himself. His benefits may be considered as parallel to what are called comforts or conveniences in arrangements of a personal nature: like an easy chair or a good fire, which do their part in dispelling cold and fatigue, though nature provides both means of rest and animal heat without them. The true gentleman in like manner carefully avoids whatever may cause a jar or a jolt in the minds of those with whom he is cast;—all clashing of opinion, or collision of feeling, all restraint, or suspicion, or gloom, or resentment; his great concern being to make every one at their ease and at home. He has his eyes on all his company; he is tender towards the bashful, gentle towards the distant, and merciful towards the absurd; he can recollect to whom he is speaking; he guards against unseasonable allusions, or topics which may irritate; he is seldom prominent in conversation, and never wearisome. He makes light of favours while he does them, and seems to be receiving when he is conferring. He never speaks of himself except when compelled, never defends himself by a mere retort, he has no ears for slander or gossip, is scrupulous in imputing motives to those who interfere with him, and interprets every thing for the best. He is never mean or little in his disputes, never takes unfair advantage, never mistakes personalities or sharp sayings for arguments, or insinuates evil which he dare not say out. From a longsighted prudence, he observes the maxim of the ancient sage, that we should ever conduct ourselves towards our enemy as if he were one day to be our friend. He has too much good sense to be affronted at insults, he is too well employed to remember injuries, and too indolent to bear malice. He is patient, forbearing, and resigned, on philosophical principles; he submits to pain, because it is inevitable, to bereavement, because it is irreparable, and to death, because it is his destiny. If he engages in controversy of any kind, his disciplined intellect preserves him from the blundering discourtesy of better, perhaps, but less educated minds; who, like blunt weapons, tear and hack instead of cutting clean, who mistake the point in argument, waste their strength on trifles, misconceive their adversary, and leave the question more involved than they find it. He may be right or wrong in his opinion, but he is too clear-headed to be unjust; he is as simple as he is forcible, and as brief as he is decisive. Nowhere shall we find greater candour, consideration, indulgence: he throws himself into the minds of his opponents, he accounts for their mistakes. He knows the weakness of human reason as well as its strength, its province and its limits. If he be an unbeliever, he will be too profound and large-minded to ridicule religion or to act against it; he is too wise to be a dogmatist or fanatic in his infidelity. He respects piety and devotion; he even supports institutions as venerable, beautiful, or useful, to which he does not assent; he honours the ministers of religion, and it contents him to decline its mysteries without assailing or denouncing them. He is a friend of religious toleration, and that, not only because his philosophy has taught him to look on all forms of faith with an impartial eye, but also from the gentleness and effeminacy of feeling, which is the attendant on civilization.

1852

┼─ ╪◆╪ ─┼

Caroline Norton
1808–1877

In the nineteenth century, a woman's person and property were at her husband's disposal, not merely by custom but by law. The thinking was that "husband and wife are one person, and the husband is that person." The celebrated case of Caroline Norton, trapped in a disastrous marriage to a brutal man, helped bring this injustice into the public eye. Her husband denied her access to their three sons (a father had sole custody of his children) and tried to seize her earnings as a writer. Norton's passionate and articulate agitation aided passage of the Infant Custody Act (1839) and the Divorce and Matrimonial Causes Act (1857). But not until after her death, with the Married Women's Property Act of 1882, did married women finally gain the right to hold property.

from A Letter to the Queen

A married woman in England has *no legal existence:* her being is absorbed in that of her husband. Years of separation or desertion can not alter this position. Unless divorced by special enactment in the House of Lords, the legal fiction holds her to be *"one"* with her husband, even though she may never see or hear of him.

She has no possessions, unless by special settlement; her property is *his* property. Lord Ellenborough mentions a case in which a sailor bequeathed "all he was worth" to a woman he cohabited with; and afterwards married, in the West Indies, a woman of considerable fortune. At this man's death it was held,—notwithstanding the hardship of the case,—that the will swept away from his widow, in favour of his mistress, every shilling of the property. It is now provided that a will shall be revoked by marriage: but the claim of *the husband* to all that is his wife's exists in full force. An English wife has no legal right even to her clothes or ornaments; her husband may take them and sell them if he pleases, even though they be the gifts of relatives or friends, or bought before marriage.

An English wife cannot make a will. She may have children or kindred whom she may earnestly desire to benefit;—she may be separated from her husband, who may be living with a mistress; no matter: the law gives what she has to him, and no will she could make would be valid.

An English wife cannot legally claim her own earnings. Whether wages for manual labour, or payment for intellectual exertion, whether she weed potatoes, or keep a school, her salary is *the husband's;* and he could compel a second payment, and treat the first as void, if paid to the wife without his sanction.

An English wife may not leave her husband's house. Not only can he sue her for "restitution of conjugal rights," but he has a right to enter the house of any friend or relation with whom she may take refuge, and who may "harbour her,"—as it is termed,—and carry her away by force, with or without the aid of the police.

If the wife sue for separation for cruelty, it must be "cruelty that endangers life or limb," and if she has once forgiven, or, in legal phrase, "*condoned*" his offences, she cannot plead them; though her past forgiveness only proves that she endured as long as endurance was possible.

If her husband take proceedings for a divorce, she is not, in the first instance, allowed to defend herself. She has no means of proving the falsehood of his allegation. She is not represented by attorney, nor permitted to be considered a party to the suit between him and her supposed lover, for "damages." Lord Brougham affirmed in the House of Lords: "*in the action the character of the woman was at immediate issue, although she was not prosecuted. The consequence not unfrequently was, that the character of a woman was sworn away; instances were known in which, by collusion between the husband and a pretended paramour, the character of the wife has been destroyed. All this could take place, and yet the wife had no defence; she was excluded from Westminster-hall, and behind her back, by the principles of our jurisprudence, her character was tried between her husband and the man called her paramour.*"

If an English wife be guilty of infidelity, her husband can divorce *her* so as to marry again; but she cannot divorce the husband *a vinculo,*[1] however profligate he may be. No law court can divorce in England. A special Act of Parliament annulling

---

1. A nullification of the marriage, granted only for reasons of mental incompetence, sexual impotence, or fraud.

the marriage, is passed for each case. The House of Lords grants this almost as a matter of course to the husband, but not to the wife. In only four instances (two of which
were cases of incest), has the wife obtained a divorce to marry again.

She cannot prosecute for a libel. Her husband must prosecute; and in cases of
enmity and separation, of course she is without a remedy.

She cannot sign a lease, or transact responsible business.

She cannot claim support, as a matter of personal right, from her husband. The
general belief and nominal rule is, that her husband is "bound to maintain her." That
is not the law. He is not bound to *her*. He is bound to his country; bound to see that
she does not cumber the parish in which she resides. If it be proved that means sufficient are at her disposal, from relatives or friends, her husband is quit of his obligation, and need not contribute a farthing:[2] even if he have deserted her; or be in
receipt of money which is hers by inheritance. ***

Separation from her husband by consent, or for his ill usage, does not alter their
mutual relation. He retains the right to divorce her *after* separation,—as before,—
though he himself be unfaithful.

Her being, on the other hand, of spotless character, and without reproach, gives
her no advantage in law. She may have withdrawn from his roof knowing that he
lives with "his faithful housekeeper": having suffered personal violence at his hands;
having "condoned" much, and being able to prove it by unimpeachable testimony: or
he may have shut the doors of her house against her: all this is quite immaterial: the
law takes no cognisance of which is to blame. As *her husband*, he has a right to all
that is hers: as *his wife*, she has no right to anything that is his. As her husband, he
may divorce her (if truth or false swearing can do it): as his wife, the utmost "divorce"
she could obtain, is permission to reside alone,—married to his name. The marriage
ceremony is a civil bond for him,—and an indissoluble sacrament for her; and the
rights of mutual property which that ceremony is ignorantly supposed to confer, are
made absolute for him, and null for her.

Of course, an opposite picture may be drawn. There are bad, wanton,
irreclaimable women, as there are vicious, profligate, tyrannical men: but the difference is *this*: that to punish and restrain bad wives, there are laws, and very severe laws
(to say nothing of social condemnation); while to punish or restrain bad husbands,
there is, in England, no adequate law whatever. Indeed, the English law holds out a
sort of premium on infidelity; for there is no doubt that the woman, who is divorced
for a lover and marries him, suffers less (except in conscience) than the woman who
does not deserve to suffer at all—the wife of a bad husband, who can inflict what he
pleases, whether she remain in her home, or attempt to leave it.

Such, however, is "the law": and if anything could add to the ridicule, confusion, and injustice of its provision, it would be the fact, that though it is law for the
rich, it is not law for the poor; and though it is the law in England, it is not the law
in Scotland!

It is not law for the poor.

Since the days of Henry VIII, for whose passions it was contrived, our method of
divorce has remained an indulgence sacred to the aristocracy of England. The poorer
classes have no form of divorce amongst them. The rich man makes a new marriage,
having divorced his wife in the House of Lords: his new marriage is legal; his children

2. A quarter of a penny.

are legitimate; his bride occupies, in all respects, the same social position as if he had never previously been wedded. The poor man makes a new marriage, *not* having divorced his wife in the House of Lords; his new marriage is null; his children are bastards; and he himself is liable to be put on his trial for bigamy: the allotted punishment for which crime, at one time was hanging, and is now imprisonment. Not always offending knowingly,—for nothing can exceed the ignorance of the poor on this subject; they believe a Magistrate can divorce them, that an absence of seven years constitutes a nullity of the marriage tie, or that they can give each other reciprocal permission to divorce: and among some of our rural populations, the grosser belief prevails, that a man may legally *sell* his wife, and so break the bond of union! They believe anything,—rather than what is the fact,—viz., that *they* cannot do legally, that which they know is done legally in the classes above them; that the comfort of the rich man's home, or the indulgence of the rich man's passions, receives a consideration in England which the poor need not expect to obtain.

It is not the law of Scotland. In your Majesty's kingdom, nothing but "The rapid running of the silver Tweed" divides that portion of the realm where women are protected by law,—from that portion where they are *unprotected*, though living under the same Sovereign and the same government!

1855

George Eliot
1819–1880

George Eliot was the pen name of Mary Ann Evans, who scandalized Victorian society by her decision in 1854 to live openly with a married man. Her family refused to have anything more to do with the "fallen woman," but the socially outcast Eliot went on to become one of the most revered novelists of the age. Writing under a male pseudonym, she discovered her creative genius in midlife and published a series of highly successful novels, including *Adam Bede* (1859), *The Mill on the Floss* (1860), *Silas Marner* (1861), *Romola* (1863), *Felix Holt* (1866), *Middlemarch* (1871–1872), and *Daniel Deronda* (1876). Although her formal education had ended at sixteen, George Eliot read widely on her own, teaching herself foreign languages and studying philosophy and theology; in her thirties, she became an editor of the influential *Westminster Review*. In this essay, she argues eloquently against the popular notion that an ignorant woman makes the best wife: "Men pay a heavy price for their reluctance to encourage self-help and independent resources in women."

Margaret Fuller and Mary Wollstonecraft[1]

The dearth of new books just now gives us time to recur to less recent ones which we have hitherto noticed but slightly; and among these we choose the late edition of Margaret Fuller's *Woman in the Nineteenth Century*, because we think it has been unduly thrust into the background by less comprehensive and candid productions on the same subject. Notwithstanding certain defects of taste and a sort of vague spiritualism and grandiloquence which belong to all but the very best American writers, the

---

1. This essay, originally published in *The Leader* (1855), reviews two influential feminist works. Margaret Fuller (1810–1850), an American associated with the New England transcendentalist movement, was the author of *Woman in the Nineteenth Century* (1843; 1855). Mary Wollstonecraft (1759–1797), the wife of William Godwin and mother of Mary Shelley, was best-known for writing *A Vindication of the Rights of Woman* (1792), page 152.

book is a valuable one: it has the enthusiasm of a noble and sympathetic nature, with the moderation and breadth and large allowance of a vigorous and cultivated understanding. There is no exaggeration of woman's moral excellence or intellectual capabilities; no injudicious insistence on her fitness for this or that function hitherto engrossed by men; but a calm plea for the removal of unjust laws and artificial restrictions, so that the possibilities of her nature may have room for full development, a wisely stated demand to disencumber her of the

> parasitic forms
> That seem to keep her up, but drag her down—
> And leave her field to burgeon and to bloom
> From all within her, make herself her own
> To give or keep, to live and learn and be
> All that not harms distinctive womanhood.[2]

It is interesting to compare this essay of Margaret Fuller's, published in its earliest form in 1843, with a work on the position of woman, written between sixty and seventy years ago—we mean Mary Wollstonecraft's *Rights of Woman*. The latter work was not continued beyond the first volume; but so far as this carries the subject, the comparison, at least in relation to strong sense and loftiness of moral tone, is not at all disadvantageous to the woman of the last century. There is in some quarters a vague prejudice against the *Rights of Woman* as in some way or other a reprehensible book, but readers who go to it with this impression will be surprised to find it eminently serious, severely moral, and withal rather heavy—the true reason, perhaps, that no edition has been published since 1796, and that it is now rather scarce. There are several points of resemblance, as well as of striking difference, between the two books. A strong understanding is present in both; but Margaret Fuller's mind was like some regions of her own American continent, where you are constantly stepping from the sunny "clearings" into the mysterious twilight of the tangled forest—she often passes in one breath from forcible reasoning to dreamy vagueness; moreover, her unusually varied culture gives her great command of illustration. Mary Wollstonecraft, on the other hand, is nothing if not rational; she has no erudition, and her grave pages are lit up by no ray of fancy. In both writers we discern, under the brave bearing of a strong and truthful nature, the beating of a loving woman's heart, which teaches them not to undervalue the smallest offices of domestic care or kindliness. But Margaret Fuller, with all her passionate sensibility, is more of the literary woman, who would not have been satisfied without intellectual production; Mary Wollstonecraft, we imagine, wrote not at all for writing's sake, but from the pressure of other motives. So far as the difference of date allows, there is a striking coincidence in their trains of thought; indeed, every important idea in the *Rights of Woman*, except the combination of home education with a common day-school for boys and girls, reappears in Margaret Fuller's essay.

One point on which they both write forcibly is the fact that, while men have a horror of such faculty or culture in the other sex as tends to place it on a level with their own, they are really in a state of subjection to ignorant and feeble-minded women. Margaret Fuller says:—

2. Tennyson, *The Princess* 7.253–58. See page 598.

Wherever man is sufficiently raised above extreme poverty or brutal stupidity, to care for the comforts of the fireside, or the bloom and ornament of life, woman has always power enough, if she choose to exert it, and is usually disposed to do so, in proportion to her ignorance and childish vanity. Unacquainted with the importance of life and its purposes, trained to a selfish coquetry and love of petty power, she does not look beyond the pleasure of making herself felt at the moment, and governments are shaken and commerce broken up to gratify the pique of a female favourite. The English shopkeeper's wife does not vote, but it is for her interest that the politician canvasses by the coarsest flattery.

Again:—

All wives, bad or good, loved or unloved, inevitably influence their husbands from the power their position not merely gives, but necessitates of colouring evidence and infusing feelings in hours when the—patient, shall I call him?—is off his guard.

Hear now what Mary Wollstonecraft says on the same subject:—

Women have been allowed to remain in ignorance and slavish dependence many, very many years, and still we hear of nothing but their fondness of pleasure and sway, their preference of rakes and soldiers, their childish attachment to toys, and the vanity that makes them value accomplishments more than virtues. History brings forward a fearful catalogue of the crimes which their cunning has produced, when the weak slaves have had sufficient address to overreach their masters. . . . When, therefore, I call women slaves, I mean in a political and civil sense; for indirectly they obtain too much power, and are debased by their exertions to obtain illicit sway. . . . The libertinism,[3] and even the virtues of superior men, will always give women of some description great power over them; and these weak women, under the influence of childish passions and selfish vanity, *will throw a false light over the objects which the very men view with their eyes who ought to enlighten their judgment.* Men of fancy, and those sanguine[4] characters who mostly hold the helm of human affairs in general, relax in the society of women; and surely I need not cite to the most superficial reader of history the numerous examples of vice and oppression which the private intrigues of female favourites have produced; not to dwell on the mischief that naturally arises from the blundering interposition of well-meaning folly. *For in the transactions of business it is much better to have to deal with a knave than a fool, because a knave adheres to some plan, and any plan of reason may be seen through sooner than a sudden flight of folly.* The power which vile and foolish women have had over wise men who possessed sensibility is notorious.

There is a notion commonly entertained among men that an instructed woman, capable of having opinions, is likely to prove an impracticable yoke-fellow, always pulling one way when her husband wants to go the other, oracular in tone, and prone to give curtain lectures[5] on metaphysics. But surely, so far as obstinacy is concerned, your unreasoning animal is the most unmanageable of creatures, where you are not allowed to settle the question by a cudgel, a whip and bridle, or even a string to the leg. For our own parts, we see no consistent or commodious medium between the old plan of corporal discipline and that thorough education of women which will make them rational beings in the highest sense of the word. Wherever weakness is not harshly controlled it must *govern*, as you may see when a strong man holds a little child by the hand, how he is pulled hither and thither, and wearied in his walk by his submission to the whims and feeble movements of his companion. A really cultured

3. Licentiousness.
4. Confident.

5. I.e., she would lecture him privately, behind the bed curtains.

woman, like a really cultured man, will be ready to yield in trifles. So far as we see, there is no indissoluble connexion between infirmity of logic and infirmity of will, and a woman quite innocent of an opinion in philosophy, is as likely as not to have an indomitable opinion about the kitchen. As to airs of superiority, no woman ever had them in consequence of true culture, but only because her culture was shallow or unreal, only as a result of what Mrs Malaprop[6] well calls "the ineffectual qualities in a woman"—mere acquisitions carried about, and not knowledge thoroughly assimilated so as to enter into the growth of the character.

To return to Margaret Fuller, some of the best things she says are on the folly of absolute definitions of woman's nature and absolute demarcations of woman's mission. "Nature," she says, "seems to delight in varying the arrangements, as if to show that she will be fettered by no rule; and we must admit the same varieties that she admits." Again: "If nature is never bound down, nor the voice of inspiration stifled, that is enough. We are pleased that women should write and speak, if they feel need of it, from having something to tell; but silence for ages would be no misfortune, if that silence be from divine command, and not from man's tradition." And here is a passage, the beginning of which has been often quoted:—

> If you ask me what offices they (women) may fill, I reply—any. I do not care what case you put; let them be sea-captains if you will. I do not doubt there are women well fitted for such an office, and, if so, I should be as glad as to welcome the Maid of Saragossa, or the Maid of Missolonghi, or the Suliote heroine, or Emily Plater.[7] I think women need, especially at this juncture, a much greater range of occupation than they have, to rouse their latent powers. . . . In families that I know, some little girls like to saw wood, others to use carpenter's tools. Where these tastes are indulged, cheerfulness and good-humour are promoted. Where they are forbidden, because "such things are not proper for girls," they grow sullen and mischievous. Fouriet[8] had observed these wants of women, as no one can fail to do who watches the desires of little girls, or knows the *ennui* that haunts grown women, except where they make to themselves a serene little world by art of some kind. He, therefore, in proposing a great variety of employments, in manufactures or the care of plants and animals, allows for one third of women as likely to have a taste for masculine pursuits, one third of men for feminine. . . . I have no doubt, however, that a large proportion of women would give themselves to the same employments as now, because there are circumstances that must lead them. Mothers will delight to make the nest soft and warm. Nature would take care of that; no need to clip the wings of any bird that wants to soar and sing, or finds in itself the strength of pinion[9] for a migratory flight unusual to its kind. The difference would be that *all* need not be constrained to employments for which *some* are unfit.

A propos of the same subject, we find Mary Wollstonecraft offering a suggestion which the women of the United States have already begun to carry out. She says:—

> Women, in particular, all want to be ladies. Which is simply to have nothing to do, but listlessly to go they scarcely care where, for they cannot tell what. But what have women to do in society? I may be asked, but to loiter with easy grace; surely you would not condemn them all to suckle fools and chronicle small beer.[1] No. *Women might certainly study the art of healing, and be physicians as well as nurses.* . . . Business of various kinds they

---

6. In Richard Sheridan's play *The Rivals* (1775), Mrs. Malaprop misuses words in hilarious ways: when complimented on her "intellectual accomplishments," she replies: "Ah! few gentlemen, nowadays, know how to value the ineffectual qualities in a woman!"

7. Women who fought heroically for their countries.
8. Charles Fourier, French social reformer and author of *The New Industrial World* (1829–1830).
9. Wing.
1. Iago's view of women in *Othello* 2.1.159.

might likewise pursue, if they were educated in a more orderly manner. . . . Women would not then marry for a support, as men accept of places under government, and neglect the implied duties.

Men pay a heavy price for their reluctance to encourage self-help and independent resources in women. The precious meridian years of many a man of genius have to be spent in the toil of routine, that an "establishment" may be kept up for a woman who can understand none of his secret yearnings, who is fit for nothing but to sit in her drawing-room like a doll-Madonna in her shrine. No matter. Anything is more endurable than to change our established formulae about women, or to run the risk of looking up to our wives instead of looking down on them. *Sit divus, dummodo non sit vivus* (let him be a god, provided he be not living), said the Roman magnates of Romulus;[2] and so men say of women, let them be idols, useless absorbents of precious things, provided we are not obliged to admit them to be strictly fellow-beings, to be treated, one and all, with justice and sober reverence.

On one side we hear that woman's position can never be improved until women themselves are better; and, on the other, that women can never become better until their position is improved—until the laws are made more just, and a wider field opened to feminine activity. But we constantly hear the same difficulty stated about the human race in general. There is a perpetual action and reaction between individuals and institutions; we must try and mend both by little and little—the only way in which human things can be mended. Unfortunately, many over-zealous champions of women assert their actual equality with men—nay, even their moral superiority to men—as a ground for their release from oppressive laws and restrictions. They lose strength immensely by this false position. If it were true, then there would be a case in which slavery and ignorance nourished virtue, and so far we should have an argument for the continuance of bondage. But we want freedom and culture for woman, because subjection and ignorance have debased her, and with her, Man; for—

> If she be small, slight-natured, miserable,
> How shall men grow?[3]

Both Margaret Fuller and Mary Wollstonecraft have too much sagacity to fall into this sentimental exaggeration. Their ardent hopes of what women may become do not prevent them from seeing and painting women as they are. On the relative moral excellence of men and women Mary Wollstonecraft speaks with the most decision:—

> Women are supposed to possess more sensibility,[4] and even humanity, than men, and their strong attachments and instantaneous emotions of compassion are given as proofs; but the clinging affection of ignorance has seldom anything noble in it, and may mostly be resolved into selfishness, as well as the affection of children and brutes. I have known many weak women whose sensibility was entirely engrossed by their husbands; and as for their humanity, it was very faint indeed, or rather it was only a transient emotion of compassion. Humanity does not consist "in a squeamish ear," says an eminent orator. "It belongs to the mind as well as to the nerves." But this kind of exclusive affection, though it degrades the individual, should not be brought forward as a proof of the inferiority of the sex, because it is the natural consequence of confined views; for even women of superior sense, having their attention turned to little employments and private plans, rarely rise to

---

2. Romulus and Remus were the legendary founders of Rome. After Romulus vanished in a thunderstorm, he was worshipped as the god Quirinus; in *Lives* Plutarch says the patricians were suspected of murdering Romulus and start-

ing the rumor of his translation to godhood to keep people from inquiring too closely into his disappearance.
3. Tennyson, *The Princess* 7.249–50; see page 598.
4. Awareness of and responsiveness to emotions.

heroism, unless when spurred on by love! and love, as an heroic passion, like genius, appears but once in an age. I therefore agree with the moralist who asserts "that women have seldom so much generosity as men"; and that their narrow affections, to which justice and humanity are often sacrificed, render the sex apparently inferior, especially as they are commonly inspired by men; but I contend that the heart would expand as the understanding gained strength, if women were not depressed[5] from their cradles.

We had marked several other passages of Margaret Fuller's for extract, but as we do not aim at an exhaustive treatment of our subject, and are only touching a few of its points, we have, perhaps, already claimed as much of the reader's attention as he will be willing to give to such desultory material.

1855

✦ ⟡ ✦

Thomas Hughes
1822–1896

Thomas Hughes's famous portrait of Victorian public school life was based on his own experiences at Rugby under the headmastership of Thomas Arnold, the renowned educator and father of Matthew Arnold. Appointed in 1828, Arnold brought an evangelical fervor to the task of reforming the English public schools so as to instill moral character and Christian virtue in the future leaders of society. He made team sports a big part of school life; the playing fields would foster physical prowess, courage, and manliness. The curriculum was dominated by Latin and Greek—the hallmarks of a gentleman's education—but scholarship wasn't really the point: musing about his reasons for sending his son to Rugby, Tom Brown's father declares, "I don't care a straw for Greek particles. . . . If he'll only turn out a brave, helpful, truth-telling Englishman, and a gentleman, and a Christian, that's all I want."

from Tom Brown's School Days
[THE HEAD BOY ADDRESSES THE SCHOOL]

Then Warner, the head of the house,[1] gets up and wants to speak, but he can't, for every boy knows what's coming; and the big boys who sit at the tables pound them and cheer; and the small boys who stand behind pound one another, and cheer, and rush about the hall cheering. Then silence being made, Warner reminds them of the old School-house custom of drinking the healths, on the first night of singing, of those who are going to leave at the end of the half. "He sees that they know what he is going to say already—(loud cheers)—and so won't keep them, but only ask them to treat the toast as it deserves. It is the head of the eleven, the head of big-side football, their leader on this glorious day—Pater[2] Brooke!"

And away goes the pounding and cheering again, becoming deafening when old Brooke gets on his legs: till, a table having broken down, and a gallon or so of beer been upset, and all throats getting dry, silence ensues, and the hero speaks, leaning his hands on the table, and bending a little forwards. No action, no tricks or oratory; plain, strong, and straight, like his play.

"Gentlemen of the School-house! I am very proud of the way in which you have received my name, and I wish I could say all I should like in return. But I know I shan't.

---

5. Repressed, kept down.
1. A public school such as Rugby would be divided into houses; Tom Brown belongs to the School-house, which

has just beaten the whole of the School in a rugby match.
2. Father (Latin). Brooke is "head of the eleven," i.e., captain of the School-house rugby team.

However, I'll do the best I can to say what seems to me ought to be said by a fellow who's just going to leave, and who has spent a good slice of his life here. Eight years it is, and eight such years as I can never hope to have again. So now I hope you'll all listen to me—(loud cheers of 'that we will')—for I'm going to talk seriously. You're bound to listen to me, for what's the use of calling me 'pater,' and all that, if you don't mind what I say? And I'm going to talk seriously, because I feel so. It's a jolly time, too, getting to the end of the half, and a goal kicked by us first day—(tremendous applause)—after one of the hardest and fiercest day's play I can remember in eight years—(frantic shoutings). The School played splendidly, too, I will say, and kept it up to the last. That last charge of theirs would have carried away a house. I never thought to see anything again of old Crab there, except little pieces, when I saw him tumbled over by it—(laughter and shouting, and great slapping on the back of Jones by the boys nearest him). Well, but we beat 'em—(cheers). Ay, but why did we beat 'em? answer me that—(shouts of 'your play'). Nonsense! 'Twasn't the wind and kick-off either—that wouldn't do it. 'Twasn't because we've half-a-dozen of the best players in the school, as we have. I wouldn't change Warner, and Hedge, and Crab, and the young un, for any six on their side—(violent cheers). But half-a-dozen fellows can't keep it up for two hours against two hundred. Why is it, then? I'll tell you what I think. It's because we've more reliance on one another, more of a house feeling, more fellowship than the School can have. Each of us knows and can depend on his next hand man better—that's why we beat 'em to-day. We've union, they've division—there's the secret—(cheers). But how's this to be kept up? How's it to be improved? That's the question. For I take it, we're all in earnest about beating the School, whatever else we care about. I know I'd sooner win two School-house matches running than get the Balliol scholarship[3] any day—(frantic cheers).

"Now, I'm as proud of the house as any one. I believe it's the best house in the school, out-and-out—(cheers). But it's a long way from what I want to see it. First, there's a deal of bullying going on. I know it well. I don't pry about and interfere; that only makes it more underhand, and encourages the small boys to come to us with their fingers in their eyes telling tales, and so we should be worse off than ever. It's very little kindness for the sixth[4] to meddle generally—you youngsters, mind that. You'll be all the better football players for learning to stand it, and to take your own parts, and fight it through. But depend on it, there's nothing breaks up a house like bullying. Bullies are cowards, and one coward makes many; so good-bye to the School-house match if bullying gets ahead here. (Loud applause from the small boys, who look meaningly at Flashman and other boys at the tables.) Then there's fuddling about in the public-house, and drinking bad spirits, and punch, and such rot-gut stuff. That won't make good drop-kicks or charges of you, take my word for it. You get plenty of good beer here, and that's enough for you; and drinking isn't fine or manly, whatever some of you may think of it. ✳ ✳ ✳

✳ ✳ ✳ But before I sit down I must give you a toast to be drunk with three-times-three and all the honours. It's a toast which I hope every one of us, wherever he may go hereafter, will never fail to drink when he thinks of the brave bright days of his boy-hood. It's a toast which should bind us all together, and to those who've gone before, and who'll come after us here. It is the dear old School-house—the best house of the best school in England!"

1857

3. Prize scholarship to attend Balliol College at Oxford.
4. The sixth form—i.e., the oldest boys, who were in   charge of the younger ones.

Isabella Beeton
1836–1865

The home was a near-sacred institution in Victorian England, and when Isabella Beeton published her book of advice on household management it became a best-seller second only to the
Bible. In over a thousand pages of small print, she instructed women on matters ranging from the
supervision of servants to the care of the sick, from meal planning to proper conduct during a
social call. Mrs. Beeton's portrait of the mistress of the house reflects a complex, somewhat contradictory sense of a woman's role: she is at once "the commander of an army"—with the housekeeper as her "second in command"—and a lady of leisure, enjoying "the pleasures of literature"
and "the innocent delights of the garden." Yet, like a child, she needs to be scolded to rise early
and be punctual. Although Mrs. Beeton was just twenty-four, she was respected as an oracle in
the domestic sphere; her cookbook is still used today. She died in childbirth at twenty-eight.

from The Book of Household Management

I must frankly own, that if I had known, beforehand, that this book would have
cost me the labour which it has, I should never have been courageous enough to
commence it. What moved me, in the first instance, to attempt a work like this,
was the discomfort and suffering which I had seen brought upon men and women
by household mismanagement. I have always thought that there is no more fruitful
source of family discontent than a housewife's badly-cooked dinners and untidy
ways. Men are now so well served out of doors,—at their clubs, well-ordered taverns, and dining-houses, that in order to compete with the attractions of these
places, a mistress must be thoroughly acquainted with the theory and practice of
cookery, as well as be perfectly conversant with all the other arts of making and
keeping a comfortable home. * * *

As with the Commander of an Army, or the leader of any enterprise, so is it with
the mistress of a house. Her spirit will be seen through the whole establishment; and
just in proportion as she performs her duties intelligently and thoroughly, so will her
domestics follow in her path. Of all those acquirements, which more particularly
belong to the feminine character, there are none which take a higher rank, in our
estimation, than such as enter into a knowledge of household duties; for on these are
perpetually dependent the happiness, comfort, and well-being of a family. * * *

Early Rising is one of the most Essential Qualities which enter into good Household Management, as it is not only the parent of health, but of innumerable other
advantages. Indeed, when a mistress is an early riser, it is almost certain that her
house will be orderly and well-managed. On the contrary, if she remain in bed till a
late hour, then the domestics, who, as we have before observed, invariably partake
somewhat of their mistress's character, will surely become sluggards. * * *

Friendships should not be hastily formed, nor the heart given, at once, to every
new-comer. There are ladies who uniformly smile at, and approve everything and
everybody, and who possess neither the courage to reprehend vice, nor the generous
warmth to defend virtue. The friendship of such persons is without attachment, and
their love without affection or even preference. * * *

Hospitality is a most Excellent Virtue; but care must be taken that the love of
company, for its own sake, does not become a prevailing passion; for then the habit is
no longer hospitality, but dissipation. * * * With respect to the continuance of friendships * * * it may be found necessary, in some cases, for a mistress to relinquish, on

assuming the responsibility of a house-hold, many of those commenced in the earlier part of her life. * * *

In Conversation, Trifling Occurrences, such as small disappointments, petty annoyances, and other every-day incidents, should never be mentioned to your friends. The extreme injudiciousness of repeating these will be at once apparent, when we reflect on the unsatisfactory discussions which they too frequently occasion, and on the load of advice which they are the cause of being tendered, and which is, too often, of a kind neither to be useful nor agreeable. * * * If the mistress be a wife, never let an account of her husband's failings pass her lips. * * *

After Breakfast is over, it will be well for the mistress to make a round of the kitchen and other offices, to see that all are in order, and that the morning's work has been properly performed by the various domestics. The orders for the day should then be given, and any questions which the domestics desire to ask, respecting their several departments, should be answered, and any special articles they may require, handed to them from the store-closet. * * *

After this General Superintendence of her servants, the mistress, if a mother of a young family, may devote herself to the instruction of some of its younger members, or to the examination of the state of their wardrobe, leaving the later portion of the morning for reading, or for some amusing recreation. * * *

Unless the means of the mistress be very circumscribed, and she be obliged to devote a great deal of her time to the making of her children's clothes, and other economical pursuits, it is right that she should give some time to the pleasures of literature, the innocent delights of the garden, and to the improvement of any special abilities for music, painting, and other elegant arts, which she may, happily, possess. * * *

After Luncheon, Morning Calls and Visits may be made and received. These may be divided under three heads: those of ceremony, friendship, and congratulation or condolence. Visits of ceremony, or courtesy, which occasionally merge into those of friendship, are to be paid under various circumstances. Thus, they are uniformly required after dining at a friend's house, or after a ball, picnic, or any other party. These visits should be short, a stay of from fifteen to twenty minutes being quite sufficient. A lady paying a visit may remove her boa or neckerchief; but neither her shawl nor bonnet.

When other visitors are announced, it is well to retire as soon as possible, taking care to let it appear that their arrival is not the cause. When they are quietly seated, and the bustle of their entrance is over, rise from your chair, taking a kind leave of the hostess, and bowing politely to the guests. Should you call at an inconvenient time, not having ascertained the luncheon hour, or from any other inadvertence, retire as soon as possible, without, however, showing that you feel yourself an intruder. It is not difficult for any well-bred or even good-tempered person, to know what to say on such an occasion, and, on politely withdrawing, a promise can be made to call again, if the lady you have called on, appear really disappointed.

In Paying Visits of Friendship, it will not be so necessary to be guided by etiquette as in paying visits of ceremony; and if a lady be pressed by her friend to remove her shawl and bonnet, it can be done if it will not interfere with her subsequent arrangements. * * * During these visits, the manners should be easy and cheerful, and the subjects of conversation such as may be readily terminated. Serious discussions or arguments are to be altogether avoided.

1861

Queen Victoria
1819–1901

Queen Victoria, who ruled from 1837 to 1901, was the most prominent woman of the age, and during her reign the monarchy came to symbolize the far-flung power of the British Empire. Although she was a capable woman who wielded genuine political influence, she felt uncomfortably thrust into greatness and often deplored the contradictions of her position. A firm believer in the notion that men and women should occupy separate spheres, the queen regarded campaigns for women's rights as "dangerous and unchristian and unnatural." The mother of nine children, Victoria was revered as the embodiment of domestic propriety, but her views on maternity were decidedly unsentimental. Her letters to her eldest daughter lament the sufferings of pregnancy, and in the 1850s Queen Victoria pioneered the use of chloroform in childbirth, thus making anesthesia acceptable for other women.

Letters and Journal Entries on the Position of Women
Journal[1]

20 June 1837

I was awoke at 6 o'clock by Mamma,[2] who told me that the Archbishop of Canterbury and Lord Conyngham were here, and wished to see me. I got out of bed and went into my sitting-room (only in my dressing-gown), and alone, and saw them. Lord Conyngham then acquainted me that my poor Uncle, the King, was no more, and had expired at 12 minutes p. 2 this morning, and consequently that I am Queen. Lord Conyngham knelt down and kissed my hand, at the same time delivering to me the official announcement of the poor King's demise. The Archbishop then told me that the Queen[3] was desirous that he should come and tell me the details of the last moments of my poor, good Uncle; he said that he had directed his mind to religion and had died in a perfectly happy, quiet state of mind, and was quite prepared for his death. He added that the King's sufferings at the last were not very great but that there was a good deal of uneasiness. Lord Conyngham, who I charged to express my feelings of condolence and sorrow to the poor Queen, returned directly to Windsor. I then went to my room and dressed.

Since it has pleased Providence to place me in this station, I shall do my utmost to fulfil my duty towards my country; I am very young and perhaps in many, though not in all things, inexperienced, but I am sure, that very few have more real good will and more real desire to do what is fit and right than I have. * * *

To Princess Frederick William[4]

24 March 1858

That you should feel shy sometimes I can easily understand. I do so very often to this hour. But being married gives one one's position which nothing else can. Think

---

1. From *Queen Victoria in Her Letters and Journals*, ed. Christopher Hibbert (1985).
2. Victoria's mother was the widow of Edward, Duke of Kent, the fourth son of George III. Since Edward died when Victoria was an infant, she was brought up by her mother. She had just turned 18 when she became queen on the death of her uncle, King William IV.
3. Adelaide, the widow of William IV.

4. This and the following letters on marriage and childbirth are from *Dearest Child: Letters between Queen Victoria and the Princess Royal, 1858–1861*, ed. Roger Fulford (1964). On 25 January 1858, at the age of 17, Victoria's eldest daughter had married Prince Frederick ("Fritz"), later Crown Prince of Prussia. Her mother wrote her frequent letters full of maternal advice.

Edwin Landseer, *Windsor Castle in Modern Times*, 1841–1845, showing Queen Victoria and Prince Albert at home with their eldest child Princess Victoria.

however what it was for me, a girl of 18 all alone, not brought up at court as you were—but very humbly at Kensington Palace—with trials and difficulties, to receive and be everywhere the first! No, no one knows what a life of difficulties mine was—and is! How thankful I am that none of you, please God! ever will have that anomalous and trying position. Now do enter into this in your letters, you so seldom do that, except to answer a question.

Now to reply to your observation that you find a married woman has much more liberty than an unmarried one; in one sense of the word she has,—but what I meant was—in a physical point of view—and if you have hereafter (as I had constantly for the first 2 years of my marriage)—aches—and sufferings and miseries and plagues—which you must struggle against—and enjoyments etc. to give up—constant precautions to take, you will feel the yoke of a married woman! Without that—certainly it is unbounded happiness—if one has a husband one worships! It is a foretaste of heaven. And you have a husband who adores you, and is, I perceive, ready to meet every wish and desire of your's. I had 9 times for 8 months[5] to bear with those above-named enemies and real misery (besides many duties) and I own it tried me sorely; one feels so pinned down—one's wings clipped—in fact, at the best (and few were or are better than I was) only half oneself—particularly the first and second time. This I call the "shadow side" as much as being torn away from one's loved home, parents and brothers and sisters. And therefore—I think our sex a most unenviable one.

5. Victoria alludes to her nine pregnancies.

26 May 1858

The horrid news contained in Fritz's letter to Papa [that the Princess was preg-nant] upset us dreadfully. The more so as I feel certain almost it will all end in nothing.

15 June 1858

What you say of the pride of giving life to an immortal soul is very fine, dear, but I own I cannot enter into that; I think much more of our being like a cow or a dog at such moments; when our poor nature becomes so very animal and unecstatic—but for you, dear, if you are sensible and reasonable not in ecstasy nor spending your day with nurses and wet nurses, which is the ruin of many a refined and intellectual young lady, without adding to her real maternal duties, a child will be a great resource. Above all, dear, do remember never to lose the modesty of a young girl towards others (without being prude); though you are married don't become a matron at once to whom every-thing can be said, and who minds saying nothing herself—I remained particular to a degree (indeed feel so now) and often feel shocked at the confidences of other married ladies. I fear abroad they are very indelicate about these things.

29 January 1859

God be praised for all his mercies, and for bringing you safely through this awful time![6] Our joy, our gratitude knows no bounds.

My precious darling, you suffered much more that I ever did—and how I wish I could have lightened them for you! Poor dear Fritz—how he will have suffered for you! I think and feel much for him; the dear little boy if I could but see him for one minute, give you one kiss. It is hard, very hard. But we are so happy, so grateful! And people here are all in ecstasies—such pleasure, such delight—as if it was their own prince and so it is too! All the children so delighted! You will and must feel so thank-ful all is over! But don't be alarmed for the future, it never can be so bad again!

20 April 1859

I really think I shall never let your sisters marry—certainly not to be so constant-ly away and see so little of their parents—as till now, you have done, contrary to all that I was originally promised and told. I am so glad to see that you so entirely enter into all my feelings as a mother. Yes, dearest, it is an awful moment to have to give one's innocent child up to a man, be he ever so kind and good—and to think of all that she must go through! I can't say what I suffered, what I felt—what struggles I had to go through—(indeed I have not quite got over it yet) and that last night when we took you to your room, and you cried so much, I said to Papa as we came back "after all, it is like taking a poor lamb to be sacrificed." You now know—what I meant, dear. I know that God has willed it so and that these are the trials which we poor women must go through; no father, no man can feel this! Papa never would enter into it all! As in fact he seldom can in my very violent feelings. It really makes me shudder when I look around at all your sweet, happy, unconscious sisters—and think that I must give them up too—one by one!! Our dear Alice,[7] has seen and

---

6. After a difficult and dangerous labor, Victoria's daugh-ter had given birth on 27 January 1859; her son was the future Kaiser Wilhelm II, who led Germany against

England in the First World War.
7. Princess Alice, Victoria's second daughter, was 15.

heard more (of course not what no one ever can know before they marry and before they have had children) than you did, from your marriage—and quite enough to give her a horror rather of marrying.

4 May 1859

Abstractedly, I have no *tendre* for them [babies] till they have become a little human; an ugly baby is a very nasty object—and the prettiest is frightful when undressed—till about four months; in short as long as they have their big body and little limbs and that terrible frog-like action. But from four months, they become prettier and prettier. And I repeat it—your child would delight me at any age.

15 June 1859

Now I must scold you a wee bit for an observation which really seems at variance with your own expressions. You say "how glad" Ada[8] "must be" at being again in that most charming situation, which you yourself very frequently told me last year was so wretched. How can anyone, who has not been married above two years and three quarters, (like Ada) rejoice at being a third time in that condition? I positively think those ladies who are always *enceinte* quite disgusting; it is more like a rabbit or guinea-pig than anything else and really it is not very nice.

16 May 1860

All marriage is such a lottery—the happiness is always an exchange—though it may be a very happy one—still the poor woman is bodily and morally the husband's slave. That always sticks in my throat. When I think of a merry, happy, free young girl—and look at the ailing, aching state a young wife generally is doomed to—which you can't deny is the penalty of marriage.

17 November 1860

My beloved child, these lines are to wish you heartily and warmly joy of your 20th birthday—an important age—though married nearly three years and with two children it seems but of little consequence. Still to bid adieu to one's "teens" is a serious thing!

18 December 1861

What is to become of us all?[9] Of the unhappy country, of Europe, of all? For you all, the loss of such a father is totally irreparable! I will do all I can to follow out all his wishes—to live for you all and for my duties. But how I, who leant on him for all and everything—without whom I did nothing, moved not a finger, arranged not a print or photograph, didn't put on a gown or bonnet if he didn't approve it shall be able to go on, to live, to move, to help myself in difficult moments? How I shall long to ask

8. The Queen's niece, married to Prince Frederick of Schleswig-Holstein.
9. Victoria was grief stricken at the death her husband, Prince Albert, on 14 December 1861; after his death she mourned him obsessively, going into virtual seclusion for many years. Beatrice was her ninth child, born in 1857. This letter is from *Queen Victoria in Her Letters and Journals*, ed. Christopher Hibbert (1985).

his advice! Oh! it is too, too weary! The day—the night (above all the night) is too sad and weary. The days never pass! I try to feel and think that I am living on with him, and that his pure and perfect spirit is guiding and leading me and inspiring me!

Sweet little Beatrice comes to lie in my bed every morning which is a comfort. I long so to cling to and clasp a loving being. Oh! how I admired Papa! How in love I was with him! How everything about him was beautiful and precious in my eyes! Oh! how, how I miss all, all! Oh! Oh! the bitterness of this—of this woe!

To William Gladstone[1]

6 May 1870

The circumstances respecting the Bill to give women the same position as men with respect to Parliamentary franchise gives her an opportunity to observe that she had for some time past wished to call Mr Gladstone's attention to the mad & utterly demoralizing movement of the present day to place women in the same position as to professions—as *men*;—& amongst others, in the *Medical Line*.

* * * And she is *most* anxious that it should be known how she not only disapproves but *abhors* the attempts to destroy all propriety & womanly feeling which will inevitably be the result of what has been proposed. The Queen is a woman herself—& knows what an anomaly her *own* position is:—but that can be reconciled with reason & propriety tho' it is a terribly difficult & trying one. But to tear away all the barriers which surround a woman, & to propose that they should study with *men*—things which could not be named before them—certainly not *in a mixed* audience—would be to introduce a total disregard of what must be considered as belonging to the rules & principles of morality.

The Queen feels so strongly upon this dangerous & unchristian & unnatural *cry* & movement of "woman's rights,"—in which she knows Mr Gladstone *agrees*, (as he sent her that excellent Pamphlet by Lady) that she is most anxious that Mr Gladstone & others should take some steps to check this alarming danger & to make whatever use they can of her name. * * *

Let woman be what God intended; a helpmate for a man—but with totally different duties & vocations.

To Sir Theodore Martin[2]

29 May 1870

The Queen is most anxious to enlist every one who can speak or write to join in checking this mad, wicked folly of "Woman's Rights," with all its attendant horrors, on which her poor feeble sex is bent, forgetting every sense of womanly feeling and propriety. Lady—ought to get a *good whipping*.

It is a subject which makes the Queen so furious that she cannot contain herself. God created men and women different—then let them remain each in their own position. Tennyson has some beautiful lines on the difference of men and women in

1. Gladstone (1809–1898) was the prime minister in four Liberal governments (1868–1874, 1880–1885, 1886, 1892–1894). This letter is from *The Queen and Mr. Gladstone* (1933) edited by Philip Guedalla. The Queen refers to the recurrence of the proposal to give women the vote, first presented to the House of Commons in 1866 by J. S. Mill.

2. This letter is from *Queen Victoria As I Knew Her* (1908) by Sir Theodore Martin, a lawyer and man of letters.

The Princess.[3] Woman would become the most hateful, heartless, and disgusting of human beings were she allowed to unsex herself; and where would be the protection which man was intended to give the weaker sex? The Queen is sure that Mrs Martin agrees with her.

+—+ ≳◆≲ +—+

Charles Kingsley
1819–1875

Charles Kingsley was a hearty country clergyman and prolific writer whose sermons praised physical prowess and manly pursuits such as riding, hunting, and fishing. He was a vigorous Protestant, suspicious of celibacy and of what he considered the feminine monasticism of Catholicism: an injudicious remark of his about the dishonesty of the Catholic clergy prompted Newman's *Apologia Pro Vita Sua*. Kingsley is so often paired with Thomas Hughes, author of *Tom Brown's School Days*, that he has been called "the most famous Brown in the Victorian period;" although he didn't go to Rugby, he embodied the spirit of its headmaster Dr. Arnold. "Muscular Christianity" was originally a term of mocking disparagement for boisterous assertions of bodily strength and energy as the foundation of a pure moral life. But the blending of Christianity with manliness was part of an emerging middle-class identity that strove toward an ideal of public service: both Hughes and Kingsley embraced Christian socialism, a movement to respond to the injustices of industrialism.

from Letters and Memories
[MUSCULAR CHRISTIANITY]

[From a letter to his fiancée, Frances Grenfell:]

There has always seemed to me something impious in the neglect of personal health, strength, and beauty, which the religious, and sometimes clergymen of this day affect. It is very often a mere form of laziness. . . . I could not do half the little good I do do here, if it were not for that strength and activity which some consider coarse and degrading. Do not be afraid of my overworking myself. If I stop, I go down. I must work. . . . How merciful God has been in turning all the strength and hardihood I gained in snipe shooting and hunting, and rowing, and jack-fishing in those magnificent fens[1] to His work! While I was following my own fancies, He was preparing me for His work. . . . Is it not an awful proof that matter is not necessarily evil, that we shall be clothed in bodies even in our perfect state? Think of that! . . . It seems all so harmonious to me. It is all so full of God, that I see no inconsistency in making my sermons while I am cutting wood; and no "bizarrerie" in talking one moment to one man about the points of a horse, and the next moment to another about the mercy of God to sinners. I try to catch men by their leading ideas, and so draw them off insensibly to my leading idea. And so I find—shall I tell you? that God is really permitting me to do His work—I find that dissent is decreasing; people are coming to church who never went anywhere before; that I am loved and respected—or rather that God's ministry, which has been here deservedly despised, alas! is beginning to be respected; and above all, that the young wild fellows who are considered as hopeless by most

3. See *The Princess* (page 597): "For woman is not undevelopt man, / But diverse: could we make her as the man, / Sweet Love were slain: his dearest bond is this, / Not like to like, but like in difference."
1. Low marshy areas.

men, because most men are what they call "spoony Methodists," *i.e.*, effeminate ascetics—dare not gainsay, but rather look up to a man who they see is their superior, if he chose to exert his power, in physical as well as intellectual skill. * * *
1842   1877

[From a letter to the Reverend F. D. Maurice:]

I do feel very deeply the truth which John Mill has set forth in a one-sided way in his new book on Liberty[2] * * * about the past morality of Christendom having taken a somewhat abject tone, and requiring, as a complement, the old Pagan virtues, which our forefathers learnt from Plutarch's Lives, and of which the memory still lingers in our classical education. I do not believe, of course, that the want really exists: but that it was created, principally by the celibate misanthropy of the patristic and mediaeval church. But I have to preach the divineness of the whole manhood, and am content to be called a Muscular Christian, or any other impertinent name, by men who little dream of the weakness of character, sickness of body, and misery of mind, by which I have bought what little I know of the human heart.
1857   1877

Sir Henry Newbolt
1862–1938

Sir Henry Newbolt's rousing patriotic poems make explicit the link between public school games and the romantic ideology of empire. Schoolboy sports were not merely about keeping fit; with their emphasis on manliness, mettle, and pluck, they were preparing the upper classes to regard imperialism as a grand adventure. School loyalty merged with national patriotism. Games fostered the notion that wars were won by team spirit, holding up the side, and never quitting. Young English officers carried this schoolboy code into combat: they saw war itself as a "great game," and battlefields as playing fields. Their letters from the front during World War I described the action in the language of sports. One officer actually dribbled a soccer ball as he led his men to their deaths in the battle of the Somme.

Vitaï Lampada[1]

There's a breathless hush in the Close[2] to-night—
    Ten to make and the match to win—
    A bumping pitch and a blinding light,
    An hour to play and the last man in.
5   And it's not for the sake of a ribboned coat,
      Or the selfish hope of a season's fame,
    But his Captain's hand on his shoulder smote—
    "Play up! play up! and play the game!"

    The sand of the desert is sodden red,—
10   Red with the wreck of a square that broke;—

---

2. On *Liberty* (1859); see page 515.
1. The Torch of Life; a reference to a relay race, described in Lucretius's *De Rerum Natura*, where runners hand off a

flaming torch.
2. The playing fields at a public school.

The Gatling's[3] jammed and the Colonel dead,
   And the regiment blind with dust and smoke.
The river of death has brimmed his banks,
   And England's far, and Honour a name,
15   But the voice of a schoolboy rallies the ranks:
   "Play up! play up! and play the game!"

This is the word that year by year,
   While in her place the School is set,
Every one of her sons must hear,
20   And none that hears it dare forget.
This they all with a joyful mind
   Bear through life like a torch in flame,
And falling fling to the host behind—
25   "Play up! play up! and play the game!"

                                       1897

➤➤ END OF PERSPECTIVES: VICTORIAN LADIES AND GENTLEMEN ➤➤

Alfred, Lord Tennyson
1809–1892

"There, that is the first money you have ever earned by your poetry, and, take my word for it, it will be the last." These were the words of Tennyson's crusty grandfather, as he doled out ten shillings for the teenager's ode on the death of his grandmother. The pen proved mightier than the prediction, however, as Tennyson went on to become the most celebrated poet of the age. His books sold tens of thousands of copies; the Queen and Parliament named him Poet Laureate, then Lord, and finally Baron Tennyson; his annual income surpassed ten thousand pounds a year; and he was widely regarded as something more than a poet—a prophet, a sage, and an infallible moneymaker. A New York publisher once offered him a thousand pounds for any three-stanza poem he cared to write.

It is often said that Tennyson's greatness lay in eloquently presenting the anxieties and aspirations of his era. In poems such as *Ulysses, In Memoriam,* and *Idylls of the King,* he expressed the energy, resolve, faith, and idealism of an industrious society that was nonetheless racked by deep doubts about its materialism, the truth of the Bible, and the possibility of achieving a truly Christian society. But Tennyson was not just a mouthpiece for his age: in the early and mid-Victorian period Tennyson was one of its most progressive voices, espousing views that were all the more daring for a shy and sensitive man struggling to realize his dream of becoming "a *popular* poet." His assertion in *The Princess* (1847) that "the woman's cause is man's" anticipates Mill's *The Subjection of Women* by more than twenty years; in the course of writing *In Memoriam* (1850) he lucidly formulated some of the main principles of evolutionary theory well before Darwin's *Origin of Species* (1859); he called public attention to the industrialized misery and revolutionary anger of the poor during the 1840s while the contemporaneous works of Marx and Engels were virtually unknown; and in *Locksley Hall* (1842) he evoked the technological promise of the future as compellingly as any science fiction writer.

3. An early form of machine gun.

One key to Tennyson's poetic success was his prosaic devotion to the Victorian gospel of hard work. He labored patiently, in poverty and without recognition, to overcome his troubled background. Born in Somersby, Lincolnshire, Tennyson was the third surviving son in a close-knit but emotionally unstable family of eleven children, two of whom suffered lifelong mental illness, while two more were addicted to drugs and alcohol. The poet's father, George, was an awkward, tormented man whose ill temper was aggravated into alcoholism and violence when he was disinherited in favor of his younger brother and then forced to accept a position as village rector. It seems that the entire family was prone to epilepsy. Well into maturity, Alfred was haunted by fear of "the black blood of the Tennysons."

Tennyson's grim childhood was brightened by his mother's warmth and affection, his father's extensive library, and both parents' love of poetry. The rectory was surrounded by large gardens and open countryside, and as a child Tennyson composed nature poetry in the manner of James Thomson's *Seasons*. Early years at a brutally strict grammar school, followed by intensive tutoring from his erudite father, gave Tennyson a solid grounding in Greek, Latin, English, and modern languages by the time he went to Cambridge University in 1827. He had already mastered the styles of poets ranging from Horace and Virgil to Shakespeare, Milton, Scott, and Byron, and earlier that year he published his first book, *Poems by Two Brothers*. It was written with his brother Charles, with whom he used to exchange lines on their country walks, shouting them out across the hedges. The habit of building poems around a series of sonorous individual lines would remain with Tennyson all his life.

At Cambridge the timid country boy began gradually to assume the artistic persona that would be revered throughout the empire. Tall, ruggedly handsome, and with a faraway look in his eyes that was actually due to myopia, Tennyson fit everyone's idea of how a poet should look. He distinguished himself by the quality of his talk, his humorous storytelling, and his acting ability. In 1829 he received the Chancellor's Medal for *Timbuctoo*, the first poem in blank verse ever to win. The same year he and his best friend Arthur Henry Hallam joined "The Apostles," a select group of undergraduates who met to discuss social, philosophical, and literary issues. Members became lifelong friends, and their admiration of his early work helped convince the reticent Tennyson to publish *Poems, Chiefly Lyrical* in 1830. The book received mixed reviews.

In 1831 his father died, and Tennyson had to return home without a degree. Yet Tennyson persevered, issuing in 1832 a new volume, *Poems*. This time, the reviews were actively hostile. Tennyson's morale was sustained only by the visits to Somersby of Hallam, who by now was engaged to Tennyson's sister Emily. Then in 1833 Hallam died suddenly of a cerebral hemorrhage while on a trip to Vienna, and Tennyson's life changed forever.

Within a week of hearing the news, Tennyson began work on his greatest poem, though he did not know then that the brief lyric passages of love, loss, and doubt that he composed to assuage his grief would eventually become *In Memoriam*, an epic meditation on mortality, evolution, and the hard-won consolations of inner faith. He was already proficient, like his early hero Byron, in turning his own private misery into virtuoso evocations of emotionally charged landscapes. As John Stuart Mill wrote in 1835, Tennyson excelled in "the power of *creating* scenery, in keeping with some state of human feeling, so fitted to it as to be the embodied symbol of it, and to summon up the state of feeling itself, with a force not to be surpassed by anything but reality." Quoting *Mariana* as an example, Mill concluded that "words surely never created a more vivid feeling of physical and spiritual dreariness."

Outwardly Tennyson was calm, actively reading, writing, and socializing, but in his poetry he pictured himself as a weeping widower who mourned "a loss forever new." In 1842 he reluctantly published a two-volume edition of *Poems*, improving earlier works and introducing new ones, most notably *Ulysses* and *Morte d'Arthur*. Although his reputation was now rising, the poet was at a low ebb. He was so poor and hampered by responsibilities to his unraveling family that he was forced to postpone indefinitely his marriage to Emily Sellwood, to whom he had become engaged in 1838.

At this point Tennyson lost all his money in a scheme for carving wood by machinery. His friends feared he was on the verge of suicide. Here, as at other dark times in his life, he relied on sheer willpower to follow the advice he once offered to a depressed friend: "Just go grimly on." Eventually travel, hydropathic cures, new acquaintances, and improving finances assuaged his melancholia. Publication of *The Princess* in 1847 finally gave him the popular notice he had long sought.

But it was not until 1850 that Tennyson triumphed in life and art. In May, after seventeen years' brooding, he published *In Memoriam* to great acclaim; on 13 June he married Emily; and by the end of June one reviewer was calling him "the greatest living poet." The sentiment was timely, since Wordsworth had died in April, and by November Tennyson was named Poet Laureate. In 1852 his first son, Hallam, was born, and in 1853 the Tennysons moved to a neo-Gothic country estate called Farringford on the Isle of Wight.

His experimental "monodrama" *Maud* (1855) sold well though it baffled the critics, one of whom remarked that there was one vowel too many, no matter which, in the title. But the combined sales of his works enabled him to buy Farringford, where he could work in peace amid wreaths of tobacco smoke, adored by Emily and protected from his fans by a large staff. There he entertained great personages of the day, from Prince Albert and Garibaldi to his neighbor Julia Margaret Cameron, who badgered him into photographic immortality. Henceforth, whenever he visited London, he was sought after in society and mobbed by admirers.

The stability of his new life enabled Tennyson to pursue many longer projects, including the best-selling narrative poem *Enoch Arden* (1864) and several successful plays. Most of his energies were taken up, however, with the great work of his later life, *Idylls of the King*. A trip to Wales helped fuel his interest in Arthurian legends, and he published groups of *Idylls* in 1859 and 1869. As with *In Memoriam* and *Maud,* the poet gradually felt his way, as he composed the parts, toward a larger design for the whole. All the while he held before him the image of "my lost Arthur," until recollections of his actual friend Arthur Hallam blended with the two literary Arthurs of *In Memoriam* and *Idylls of the King*. He rounded out his tale to an epic twelve books, not producing a final version until 1888, just a few years before his death.

Max Beerbohm, *Tennyson Reading "In Memoriam" to his Sovereign,* 1904.

In the *Idylls* as in much of his earlier poetry, Tennyson is a poet of deferment. His most memorable characters—Mariana, the Lotos Eaters, Ulysses, Tithonus, and the speakers of *In Memoriam* and *Maud*, among them—long for reunions and releases that are ever yet to come, as distant as the return of King Arthur from Avalon. In old age Tennyson remembered of his youth that even before he could read, "the words 'far, far away' always had a strange charm for me."

After Tennyson's death in 1892 and his burial with great pomp in Westminster Abbey, his reputation suffered a decline that lasted till the end of the Modernist period around 1945. But Tennyson's lyric genius was admired by poets as various as the Pre-Raphaelites and Whitman, Poe, and Hopkins. Auden and Eliot were in rare agreement that he had "the finest ear of any English poet since Milton." Critics continue to dispute whether the sense of Tennyson's poetry is equal to its magnificent sound, but any close reading of his work will reveal Tennyson's deep ambivalence about the world of which he gradually became both oracle and icon. Often beneath his harmonies we hear echoes of his favorite childhood sound, "voices crying in the wind." As Eliot observed, Tennyson was "the most instinctive rebel against the society in which he was the most perfect conformist."

The Kraken[1]

Below the thunders of the upper deep;
Far, far beneath in the abysmal sea,
His ancient, dreamless, uninvaded sleep
The Kraken sleepeth: faintest sunlights flee
5   About his shadowy sides: above him swell
Huge sponges of millennial growth and height;
And far away into the sickly light,
From many a wondrous grot° and secret cell   grotto, cave
Unnumber'd and enormous polypi°   octopuses
10   Winnow with giant arms the slumbering green.
There hath he lain for ages and will lie
Battening upon huge seaworms in his sleep,
Until the latter fire[2] shall heat the deep;
Then once by man and angels to be seen,
15   In roaring he shall rise and on the surface die.

                                                            1830

Mariana

"Mariana in the moated grange."[1]

Measure for Measure

With blackest moss the flower-plots
    Were thickly crusted, one and all:
The rusted nails fell from the knots
    That held the pear to the gable-wall.
5   The broken sheds look'd sad and strange:
    Unlifted was the clinking latch;
    Weeded and worn the ancient thatch

---

1. Giant mythical sea monster.
2. The fire of Judgment Day, which will consume the world.
1. The *moated grange* was no particular grange, but one which rose to the music of Shakespeare's words: "There,

at the moated grange, resides this dejected Mariana" (*Measure for Measure* Act 3. Sc. 1) [Tennyson's note]. In Shakespeare's play, Angelo refuses to marry Mariana after her brother and her dowry are lost in a shipwreck. See John Everett Millais's painting *Mariana* (Color Plate 11).

Upon the lonely moated grange.
   She only said, "My life is dreary,
10   He cometh not," she said;
   She said, "I am aweary, aweary,
     I would that I were dead!"

Her tears fell with the dews at even;
   Her tears fell ere the dews were dried;
15 She could not look on the sweet heaven.
   Either at morn or eventide.
After the flitting of the bats,
   When thickest dark did trance° the sky,   *traverse*
   She drew her casement-curtain by,
20 And glanced athwart the glooming flats.
   She only said, "The night is dreary,
      He cometh not," she said;
   She said, "I am aweary, aweary,
     I would that I were dead!"

25 Upon the middle of the night,
   Waking she heard the night-fowl crow:
The cock sung out an hour ere light:
   From the dark fen the oxen's low
Came to her: without hope of change,
30   In sleep she seem'd to walk forlorn,
Till cold winds woke the gray-eyed morn
About the lonely moated grange.
   She only said, "The day is dreary,
      He cometh not," she said;
35 She said, "I am aweary, aweary,
     I would that I were dead!"

About a stone-cast from the wall
   A sluice with blacken'd waters slept,
And o'er it many, round and small,
40   The cluster'd marish-mosses² crept.
Hard by a poplar shook alway,
   All silver-green with gnarled bark:
For leagues no other tree did mark
The level waste, the rounding gray.
45   She only said, "My life is dreary,
      He cometh not," she said;
   She said, "I am aweary, aweary,
     I would that I were dead!"

And ever when the moon was low,
50   And the shrill winds were up and away,
In the white curtain, to and fro,
   She saw the gusty shadow sway.
But when the moon was very low,

2. The little marsh-moss lumps that float on the surface of water [Tennyson's note].

And wild winds bound within their cell,[3]
55 The shadow of the poplar fell
Upon her bed, across her brow.
    She only said, "The night is dreary,
        He cometh not," she said;
    She said, "I am aweary, aweary,
60   I would that I were dead!"

All day within the dreamy house,
    The doors upon their hinges creak'd;
The blue fly sung in the pane; the mouse
    Behind the mouldering wainscot shriek'd,
65 Or from the crevice peer'd about.
    Old faces glimmer'd thro' the doors,
    Old footsteps trod the upper floors,
Old voices called her from without.
    She only said, "My life is dreary,
70   He cometh not," she said;
    She said, "I am aweary, aweary,
        I would that I were dead!"

The sparrow's chirrup on the roof,
    The slow clock ticking, and the sound
75 Which to the wooing wind aloof
    The poplar made, did all confound
Her sense; but most she loathed the hour
    When the thick-moted sunbeam lay
    Athwart the chambers, and the day
80 Was sloping toward his western bower.
    Then, said she, "I am very dreary,
        He will not come," she said;
    She wept, "I am aweary, aweary,
        Oh God, that I were dead!"

                                    1830

The Lady of Shalott[1]

Part 1

On either side the river lie
Long fields of barley and of rye,
That clothe the wold° and meet the sky;   *rolling uplands*
And thro' the field the road runs by
5   To many-tower'd Camelot;
And up and down the people go,
Gazing where the lilies blow°   *bloom*

---

3. The cave of Aeolus, god of the winds.
1. The Lady of Shalott is evidently the Elaine of the *Morte
d'Arthur,* but I do not think that I had ever heard of the

latter when I wrote the former [Tennyson's note]. In Malory, Elaine dies of grief for love of Lancelot, but the curse,
the weaving, and the mirror are all Tennyson's inventions.

William Holman Hunt, *The Lady of Shalott*, from the Moxon edition of Tennyson's poems, 1857. This edition was a high point in Victorian book illustration, including drawings by Rossetti and Millais as well as Hunt. Tennyson, however, complained about this illustration because it depicts the lady entangled in the threads of her tapestry, making her unable to leave the loom, as she does in his poem. Hunt responded: "I had only half a page on which to convey the impression of weird fate, whereas you use about fifteen pages to give expression to the complete idea." See also *The Lady of Shalott* by John William Waterhouse (Color Plate 19).

      Round an island there below,
           The island of Shalott.
10   Willows whiten, aspens quiver,
      Little breezes dusk and shiver
      Thro' the wave that runs for ever
      By the island in the river
           Flowing down to Camelot.
15   Four gray walls, and four gray towers,
      Overlook a space of flowers,
      And the silent isle imbowers
           The Lady of Shalott.

      By the margin, willow-veil'd,
20   Slide the heavy barges trail'd
      By slow horses; and unhail'd
      The shallop° flitteth silken-sail'd   *small boat*
           Skimming down to Camelot:
      But who hath seen her wave her hand?
25   Or at the casement seen her stand?
      Or is she known in all the land,
           The Lady of Shalott?

      Only reapers, reaping early
      In among the bearded barley,

30   Hear a song that echoes cheerly
From the river winding clearly,
        Down to tower'd Camelot:
And by the moon the reaper weary,
Piling sheaves in uplands airy,
35   Listening, whispers "'Tis the fairy
        Lady of Shalott.'"

Part 2

There she weaves by night and day
A magic web with colours gay.
She has heard a whisper say,
40   A curse is on her if she stay
        To look down to Camelot.
She knows not what the curse may be,
And so she weaveth steadily,
And little other care hath she,
45   The Lady of Shalott.

And moving thro' a mirror clear[2]
That hangs before her all the year,
Shadows of the world appear.
There she sees the highway near
50   Winding down to Camelot:
There the river eddy whirls,
And there the surly village-churls,°   *peasants*
And the red cloaks of market girls,
        Pass onward from Shalott.

55   Sometimes a troop of damsels glad,
An abbot on an ambling pad,°   *horse*
Sometimes a curly shepherd-lad,
Or long-hair'd page in crimson clad,
        Goes by to tower'd Camelot;
60   And sometimes thro' the mirror blue
The knights come riding two and two:
She hath no loyal knight and true,
        The Lady of Shalott.

But in her web she still delights
65   To weave the mirror's magic sights,
For often thro' the silent nights
A funeral, with plumes and lights
        And music, went to Camelot:
Or when the moon was overhead,
70   Came two young lovers lately wed;
"I am half sick of shadows," said
        The Lady of Shalott.

2. Working from the back of their tapestries, weavers placed mirrors on the other side to see the effect of their work.

Part 3

A bow-shot from her bower-eaves,
He rode between the barley-sheaves,
75   The sun came dazzling thro' the leaves,
And flamed upon the brazen greaves°   leg armor
    Of bold Sir Lancelot.[3]
A red-cross knight for ever kneel'd
To a lady in his shield,[4]
80   That sparkled on the yellow field,
        Beside remote Shalott.

The gemmy bridle glitter'd free,
Like to some branch of stars we see
Hung in the golden Galaxy.
85   The bridle bells rang merrily
        As he rode down to Camelot:
And from his blazon'd baldric° slung   ornamented belt
A mighty silver bugle hung,
And as he rode his armour rung,
90   Beside remote Shalott.

All in the blue unclouded weather
Thick-jewell'd shone the saddle-leather,
The helmet and the helmet-feather
Burn'd like one burning flame together,
95   As he rode down to Camelot.
As often thro' the purple night,
Below the starry clusters bright,
Some bearded meteor, trailing light,
        Moves over still Shalott.

100   His broad clear brow in sunlight glow'd;
On burnish'd hooves his war-horse trode;
From underneath his helmet flow'd
His coal-black curls as on he rode,
        As he rode down to Camelot.
105   From the bank and from the river
He flash'd into the crystal mirror,
"Tirra lirra," by the river
        Sang Sir Lancelot.

She left the web, she left the loom,
110   She made three paces thro' the room,
She saw the water-lily bloom,
She saw the helmet and the plume,
        She look'd down to Camelot.
Out flew the web and floated wide;
115   The mirror crack'd from side to side;
"The curse is come upon me," cried
        The Lady of Shalott.

---

3. The greatest of King Arthur's knights, Lancelot was in love with Queen Guinevere.
4. Lancelot's shield depicts the Redcrosse Knight—a character in Spenser's *Faerie Queene* who champions holiness—kneeling in homage to his lady.

Part 4

In the stormy east-wind straining,
The pale yellow woods were waning,
120   The broad stream in his banks complaining,
Heavily the low sky raining
      Over tower'd Camelot;
Down she came and found a boat
Beneath a willow left afloat,
125   And round about the prow she wrote
      The Lady of Shalott.

And down the river's dim expanse
Like some bold seër in a trance,
Seeing all his own mischance—
130   With a glassy countenance
      Did she look to Camelot.
And at the closing of the day
She loosed the chain, and down she lay;
The broad stream bore her far away,
135   The Lady of Shalott.

Lying, robed in snowy white
That loosely flew to left and right—
The leaves upon her falling light—
Thro' the noises of the night
140   She floated down to Camelot:
And as the boat-head wound along
The willowy hills and fields among,
They heard her singing her last song,
      The Lady of Shalott.

145   Heard a carol, mournful, holy,
Chanted loudly, chanted lowly,
Till her blood was frozen slowly,
And her eyes were darken'd wholly,
      Turn'd to tower'd Camelot.
150   For ere she reach'd upon the tide
The first house by the water-side,
Singing in her song she died,
      The Lady of Shalott.

Under tower and balcony,
155   By garden-wall and gallery,
A gleaming shape she floated by,
Dead-pale between the houses high,
      Silent into Camelot.
Out upon the wharfs they came;
160   Knight and burgher, lord and dame,
And round the prow they read her name,
      The Lady of Shalott.

Who is this? and what is here?
And in the lighted palace near

165   Died the sound of royal cheer;
    And they cross'd themselves for fear,
        All the knights at Camelot:
    But Lancelot mused a little space;
    He said, "She has a lovely face;
170   God in his mercy lend her grace,
        The Lady of Shalott."

                                    1832, 1842

Ulysses[1]

    It little profits that an idle king,
    By this still hearth, among these barren crags,
    Match'd with an aged wife, I mete and dole
    Unequal laws unto a savage race,
5   That hoard, and sleep, and feed, and know not me.

    I cannot rest from travel: I will drink
    Life to the lees: all times I have enjoy'd
    Greatly, have suffer'd greatly, both with those
    That loved me, and alone; on shore, and when
10   Thro' scudding drifts the rainy Hyades[2]
    Vext the dim sea: I am become a name;
    For always roaming with a hungry heart
    Much have I seen and known; cities of men
    And manners, climates, councils, governments,
15   Myself not least, but honour'd of them all;
    And drunk delight of battle with my peers,
    Far on the ringing plains of windy Troy.
    I am a part of all that I have met;
    Yet all experience is an arch wherethro'
20   Gleams that untravell'd world, whose margin fades
    For ever and for ever when I move.
    How dull it is to pause, to make an end,
    To rust unburnish'd, not to shine in use!
    As tho' to breathe were life. Life piled on life
25   Were all too little, and of one to me
    Little remains: but every hour is saved
    From that eternal silence, something more,
    A bringer of new things; and vile it were
    For some three suns to store and hoard myself,
30   And this gray spirit yearning in desire
    To follow knowledge like a sinking star,
    Beyond the utmost bound of human thought.

1. The poem was written soon after Arthur Hallam's death, and it gives the feeling about the need of going further and braving the struggle of life perhaps more simply than anything in In Memoriam [Tennyson's note]. In Homer's Odyssey, Ulysses returns home to Ithaca, after ten years of wandering following the fall of Troy, and slays the suitors who have been harassing his wife Penelope. "My father," wrote Tennyson's son, "takes up the story of further wanderings at the end of the Odyssey. Ulysses has lived in Ithaca for a long while before the craving for fresh travel seizes him. The comrades he addresses are of the same heroic mould as his old comrades." Dante also has Ulysses set off on another voyage, this time westward through the Strait of Gibraltar (Inferno 26).

2. The Hyades were a constellation of seven stars whose rising was believed to bring rain.

This is my son, mine own Telemachus,
To whom I leave the sceptre and the isle—
35 Well-loved of me, discerning to fulfil
This labour, by slow prudence to make mild
A rugged people, and thro' soft degrees
Subdue them to the useful and the good.
Most blameless is he, centred in the sphere
40 Of common duties, decent not to fail
In offices of tenderness, and pay
Meet adoration to my household gods,
When I am gone. He works his work, I mine.

There lies the port; the vessel puffs her sail:
45 There gloom the dark broad seas. My mariners,
Souls that have toil'd, and wrought, and thought with me—
That ever with a frolic welcome took
The thunder and the sunshine, and opposed
Free hearts, free foreheads—you and I are old;
50 Old age hath yet his honour and his toil;
Death closes all: but something ere the end,
Some work of noble note, may yet be done,
Not unbecoming men that strove with Gods.
The lights begin to twinkle from the rocks:
55 The long day wanes: the slow moon climbs: the deep
Moans round with many voices. Come, my friends,
'Tis not too late to seek a newer world.
Push off, and sitting well in order smite
The sounding furrows; for my purpose holds
60 To sail beyond the sunset, and the baths
Of all the western stars,[3] until I die.
It may be that the gulfs will wash us down:
It may be we shall touch the Happy Isles,[4]
And see the great Achilles, whom we knew.
65 Tho' much is taken, much abides; and tho'
We are not now that strength which in old days
Moved earth and heaven; that which we are, we are;
One equal temper of heroic hearts,
Made weak by time and fate, but strong in will
70 To strive, to seek, to find, and not to yield.

1833   1842

Break, Break, Break[1]

Break, break, break,
    On thy cold gray stones, O Sea!
And I would that my tongue could utter
    The thoughts that arise in me.

3. The Greeks believed that the flat earth was encircled by an ocean into which the stars dipped at times.
4. The Islands of the Blessed were a land of perpetual summer thought to lie in the western ocean beyond the Pillars of Hercules (the Straits of Gibraltar). Great heroes—such as Achilles, the Greek warrior who killed the Trojan prince, Hector—were sent by the gods to live there as immortals.
1. Inspired by the death of the poet's friend, Arthur Hallam. Cf. In Memoriam, page 600.

5   O well for the fisherman's boy,
       That he shouts with his sister at play!
    O well for the sailor lad,
       That he sings in his boat on the bay!

    And the stately ships go on
10   To their haven under the hill;
    But O for the touch of a vanish'd hand,
       And the sound of a voice that is still!

    Break, break, break
       At the foot of thy crags, O Sea!
15   But the tender grace of a day that is dead
       Will never come back to me.

1834   1842

The Epic [Morte d'Arthur][1]

At Francis Allen's on the Christmas-eve,—
The game of forfeits[2] done—the girls all kiss'd
Beneath the sacred bush° and past away—   *mistletoe*
The parson Holmes, the poet Everard Hall,
5   The host, and I sat round the wassail-bowl,°   *punch bowl*
Then half-way ebb'd: and there we held a talk,
How all the old honour had from Christmas gone,
Or gone, or dwindled down to some odd games
In some odd nooks like this; till I, tired out
10   With cutting eights that day upon the pond,
Where, three times slipping from the outer edge,
I bump'd the ice into three several stars,
Fell in a doze; and half-awake I heard
The parson taking wide and wider sweeps,
15   Now harping on the church-commissioners,[3]
Now hawking at Geology and schism;[4]
Until I woke, and found him settled down
Upon the general decay of faith
Right thro' the world, "at home was little left,
20   And none abroad: there was no anchor, none,
To hold by." Francis, laughing, clapt his hand
On Everard's shoulder, with "I hold by him."
"And I," quoth Everard, "by the wassail-bowl."
"Why yes," I said, "we knew your gift that way
25   At college: but another which you had,
I mean of verse (for so we held it then),

---

1. One of Tennyson's lifelong projects was an epic poem about King Arthur, which ultimately became the *Idylls of the King*. The last poem in the sequence, describing the death of Arthur, was actually written first: it was begun in 1833, when Arthur Hallam died, and was called *Morte d'Arthur*. Tennyson framed the poem with *The Epic*, a description of contemporary (i.e., 19th century) Christmas Eve festivities, during which the poet—here called

Everard Hall—was encouraged to read *Morte d'Arthur* aloud.
2. A party game where players have to forfeit an item, then redeem it by performing a silly task.
3. In 1835 the government set up a system of commissioners to oversee the finances of the Anglican Church.
4. A reference to current scientific and religious controversies.

What came of that?" "You know," said Frank, "he burnt
His epic, his King Arthur, some twelve books"—
And then to me demanding why? "Oh, sir,
30   He thought that nothing new was said, or else
Something so said 'twas nothing—that a truth
Looks freshest in the fashion of the day;
God knows: he has a mint of reasons: ask.
It pleased _me_ well enough." "Nay, nay," said Hall,
35   "Why take the style of those heroic times?
For nature brings not back the Mastodon,
Nor we those times; and why should any man
Remodel models? these twelve books of mine
Were faint Homeric echoes,[5] nothing-worth,
40   Mere chaff and draff, much better burnt." "But I,"
Said Francis, "pick'd the eleventh from this hearth
And have it: keep a thing, its use will come.
I hoard it as a sugar-plum for Holmes."
He laugh'd, and I, tho' sleepy, like a horse
45   That hears the corn-bin open, prick'd my ears;
For I remember'd Everard's college fame
When we were Freshmen: then at my request
He brought it; and the poet little urged,
But with some prelude of disparagement,
50   Read, mouthing out his hollow oes and aes,
Deep-chested music, and to this result.[6]

                    * * *

Here ended Hall, and our last light, that long
325   Had wink'd and threaten'd darkness, flared and fell:
At which the Parson, sent to sleep with sound,
And waked with silence, grunted "Good!" but we
Sat rapt: it was the tone with which he read—
Perhaps some modern touches here and there
330   Redeem'd it from the charge of nothingness—
Or else we loved the man, and prized his work;
I know not: but we sitting, as I said,
The cock crew loud; as at that time of year
The lusty bird takes every hour for dawn:
335   Then Francis, muttering, like a man ill-used,
"There now—that's nothing!" drew a little back,
And drove his heel into the smoulder'd log,
That sent a blast of sparkles up the flue:
And so to bed; where yet in sleep I seem'd
340   To sail with Arthur under looming shores,
Point after point; till on to dawn, when dreams
Begin to feel the truth and stir of day,

5. I.e., Hall claims his poems merely echoed the great epics of Homer. He may have been fishing for a compliment: when the poet Walter Savage Landor read Tennyson's _Morte d'Arthur_ in manuscript, he declared, "it is more Homeric than any poem of our time, and rivals some of the noblest parts of the Odyssey."
6. At this point Hall reads aloud _Morte d'Arthur_.

To me, methought, who waited with a crowd,
There came a bark that, blowing forward, bore
345 King Arthur, like a modern gentleman
Of stateliest port;° and all the people cried,   *bearing*
"Arthur is come again: he cannot die."[7]
Then those that stood upon the hills behind
Repeated—"Come again, and thrice as fair;"
350 And, further inland, voices echo'd—"Come
With all good things, and war shall be no more."
At this a hundred bells began to peal,
That with the sound I woke, and heard indeed
The clear church-bells ring in the Christmas-morn.

1833–1838   1842

from THE PRINCESS[1]

Tears, Idle Tears[1]

Tears, idle tears, I know not what they mean,
Tears from the depth of some divine despair
Rise in the heart, and gather to the eyes,
In looking on the happy Autumn-fields,
5 And thinking of the days that are no more.

Fresh as the first beam glittering on a sail,
That brings our friends up from the underworld,
Sad as the last which reddens over one
That sinks with all we love below the verge;
10 So sad, so fresh, the days that are no more.

Ah, sad and strange as in dark summer dawns
The earliest pipe of half-awaken'd birds
To dying ears, when unto dying eyes
The casement° slowly grows a glimmering square;   *window*
15 So sad, so strange, the days that are no more.

Dear as remember'd kisses after death,
And sweet as those by hopeless fancy feign'd
On lips that are for others; deep as love,
Deep as first love, and wild with all regret;
20 O Death in Life, the days that are no more.

---

7. There is a legend that King Arthur will return once more to lead his people.
1. *The Princess* (1847) is a long narrative poem, set in a fairy-tale realm, about the effort to found a women's college. (The first British institution for the higher education of women, Queen's College, London, opened the next year.) The story is interspersed with brief "songs" or lyrics—some of them added later—whose musicality and depth of emotion soon won them admiration as independent works of art.
1. This song came to me on the yellowing autumn-tide at Tintern Abbey, full for me of its bygone memories [Tennyson's note]. The poet would remember not only Wordsworth's poem *Lines Written a Few Miles above Tintern Abbey*, but also his dead friend Hallam, buried not far away.

["The Woman's Cause Is Man's"][1]

"Blame not thyself too much," I said, "nor blame
240   Too much the sons of men and barbarous laws;
These were the rough ways of the world till now.
Henceforth thou hast a helper, me, that know
The woman's cause is man's: they rise or sink
Together, dwarf'd or godlike, bond or free:
245   For she that out of Lethe[2] scales with man
The shining steps of Nature, shares with man
His nights, his days, moves with him to one goal,
Stays all the fair young planet in her hands[3]—
If she be small, slight-natured, miserable,
250   How shall men grow? but work no more alone!
Our place is much: as far as in us lies
We two will serve them both in aiding her—
Will clear away the parasitic forms
That seem to keep her up but drag her down—
255   Will leave her space to burgeon out of all
Within her—let her make herself her own
To give or keep, to live and learn and be
All that not harms distinctive womanhood.
For woman is not undevelopt man,
260   But diverse: could we make her as the man,
Sweet Love were slain: his dearest bond is this,
Not like to like, but like in difference.
Yet in the long years liker must they grow;
The man be more of woman, she of man;
265   He gain in sweetness and in moral height,
Nor lose the wrestling thews° that throw the world;   *muscles*
She mental breadth, nor fail in childward care,
Nor lose the childlike in the larger mind;
Till at the last she set herself to man,
270   Like perfect music unto noble words;
And so these twain, upon the skirts of Time,
Sit side by side, full-summ'd in all their powers,
Dispensing harvest, sowing the To-be,
Self-reverent each and reverencing each,
275   Distinct in individualities,
But like each other ev'n as those who love.
Then comes the statelier Eden back to men:

1. Princess Ida, the heroine of *The Princess*, founds a women's college, and swears she will never marry. But through various exploits—including masquerading as a woman to attend her college—Prince Florian convinces her that her feminist experiment is futile. She turns her college into a hospital and agrees to marry him. In this, his concluding speech (from Book 7), Florian envisions a future in which men and women will be more alike, and the relations between them will be improved.
2. The waters of forgetfulness, here implying a new beginning.
3. Hallam Tennyson notes: "Cf. Ross Wallace's lines:

'The hand that rocks the cradle is the hand that rules the world.' My father felt that woman must train herself more earnestly than heretofore to do the large work that lies before her, even though she may not be destined to be wife or mother, cultivating her understanding not her memory only, her imagination in its highest phases, her inborn spirituality and her sympathy with all that is pure, noble and beautiful, rather than mere social accomplishments; and that then and then only will she further the progress of humanity, then and then only men will continue to hold her in reverence."

Then reign the world's great bridals, chaste and calm:
Then springs the crowning race of humankind.
280   May these things be!"
                        Sighing she spoke "I fear
They will not."
             "Dear, but let us type them now
In our own lives, and this proud watchword rest
Of equal; seeing either sex alone
Is half itself, and in true marriage lies
285   Nor equal, nor unequal: each fulfils
Defect in each, and always thought in thought,
Purpose in purpose, will in will, they grow,
The single pure and perfect animal,
The two-cell'd heart beating, with one full stroke,
290   Life."
          And again sighing she spoke: "A dream
That once was mine! what woman taught you this?"
1839–1847   1847

IN MEMORIAM A. H. H.   When Tennyson was twenty-four, his closest friend Arthur Henry Hallam died suddenly in Vienna. Regarded by all who knew him as the most promising intellect of his generation, Hallam had been Tennyson's confidante, best critic, and strongest supporter. It was Hallam who encouraged Tennyson to publish, helped him get his work through the press, and sustained him amidst criticism, self-doubt, and family crises. His perceptive review of the early poems remains among the best essays ever written on Tennyson. The poet learned of Hallam's death on 1 October 1833, and soon began composing short lyrics exploring the dark questions raised by so devastating an event. "I did not write them with any view of weaving them into a whole," Tennyson later said, "or for publication, until I found I had written so many."

The 131 sections of *In Memoriam*, produced over sixteen years, constitute a new type of elegy, what T. S. Eliot called "the concentrated diary" of a man confessing his love, sorrow, and doubts about the immortality of the soul. Tennyson drew on many sources, ranging from Greek pastoral elegy and Horace's *Odes*, to the sonnet sequences of Petrarch and Shakespeare. As in traditional elegy, the death of a friend blights joy in all living things, until the poet asserts his omnipresence in nature. But Tennyson expands his personal loss into the potential death of the human species, questioning the direction of evolution, science's challenges to Christian belief, and the ultimate destiny of the human spirit. The result is an intensely private autobiography of grief that nonetheless registers the troubled spiritual condition of Victorian England.

Presented as a broken narrative of the poet's fitful progress from despair to solace, *In Memoriam* covers a three-year period, from the death of Hallam in the autumn of 1833 to the spring of 1836. Sections 9–15 describe the return of Hallam's body to England by sea; section 19, its burial. The structural heart of the poem is the succession of three Christmases (sections 28–30, 78, 104–106), whose celebration of Christian rebirth gradually rings less hollow, more convincing. The poet's acceptance of his loss also deepens over the three springs that follow (sections 39, 86, and 115); the timeless renewal of nature eventually reawakens the poet to life. Yet for many readers, the bleak evidence of blindly predatory Nature at the poem's emotional nadir (sections 54, 55, and 56) nearly overshadows the brighter hopes of later sections. As Eliot remarked, *In Memoriam* triumphs not "because of the quality of its faith, but because of the quality of its doubt."

The form of the poem is justly famous. At the time he was writing Tennyson mistakenly thought he had created a new stanza—iambic tetrameter quatrains, rhyming *abba*—unaware that Sidney and Jonson had preceded him. But Tennyson's brilliant, sustained use of the quatrains was so well adapted to his material that the form has come to be called "the In Memoriam stanza." The first line-ending lingers in the memory while the central couplet pushes other sounds to the fore, then the rhyme is completed across that divide just as the stanza ends. This aural pattern of separation and completion parallels the intellectual and emotional progress of the poem: sound and substance combine in a verbal embrace of Tennyson's loss.

from **In Memoriam A. H. H.**

Obiit MDCCCXXXIII[1]

1

I held it truth, with him who sings
　　To one clear harp in divers tones,[2]
　　That men may rise on stepping-stones
Of their dead selves to higher things.

5　　But who shall so forecast the years
　　And find in loss a gain to match?
　　Or reach a hand thro' time to catch
The far-off interest of tears?[3]

Let Love clasp Grief lest both be drown'd,
10　　Let darkness keep her raven gloss:
　　Ah, sweeter to be drunk with loss,
To dance with death, to beat the ground,

Than that the victor Hours should scorn
　　The long result of love, and boast,
15　　"Behold the man that loved and lost,
But all he was is overworn."

2

Old Yew, which graspest at the stones
　　That name the under-lying dead,
　　Thy fibres net the dreamless head,
Thy roots are wrapt about the bones.

5　　The seasons bring the flower again,
　　And bring the firstling to the flock;
　　And in the dusk of thee, the clock
Beats out the little lives of men.

O not for thee the glow, the bloom,
10　　Who changest not in any gale,
　　Nor branding summer suns avail
To touch thy thousand years of gloom:[4]

And gazing on thee, sullen tree,
　　Sick° for thy stubborn hardihood,　　　　　　　　　　　　　*envious*
15　　I seem to fail from out my blood
And grow incorporate into thee.

* * *

1. Died 1833.
2. Goethe, according to Tennyson.
3. The good that grows for us out of grief [Tennyson's note].
4. Hallam Tennyson says: "No autumn tints ever change the green gloom of the yew."

5

I sometimes hold it half a sin
   To put in words the grief I feel;
   For words, like Nature, half reveal
And half conceal the Soul within.

5   But, for the unquiet heart and brain,
   A use in measured language lies;
   The sad mechanic exercise,
Like dull narcotics, numbing pain.

In words, like weeds,° I'll wrap me o'er,   *mourning clothes*
10   Like coarsest clothes against the cold:
   But that large grief which these enfold
Is given in outline and no more.

* * *

7

Dark house, by which once more I stand
   Here in the long unlovely street,[5]
   Doors, where my heart was used to beat
So quickly, waiting for a hand,

5   A hand that can be clasp'd no more—
   Behold me, for I cannot sleep,
   And like a guilty thing I creep
At earliest morning to the door.

He is not here;[6] but far away
10   The noise of life begins again,
   And ghastly thro' the drizzling rain
On the bald street breaks the blank day.

* * *

9

Fair ship, that from the Italian shore
   Sailest the placid ocean-plains
   With my lost Arthur's loved remains,
Spread thy full wings, and waft him o'er.

5   So draw him home to those that mourn
   In vain; a favourable speed
   Ruffle thy mirror'd mast, and lead
Thro' prosperous floods his holy urn.

All night no ruder air perplex
10   Thy sliding keel, till Phosphor,[7] bright
   As our pure love, thro' early light
Shall glimmer on the dewy decks.

Sphere all your lights around, above;
   Sleep, gentle heavens, before the prow;

---

5. Hallam's house at 67 Wimpole Street in London.
6. "He is not here, but is risen," said the angel at Jesus'
tomb (Luke 24.6).
7. The morning star.

15   Sleep, gentle winds, as he sleeps now,
        My friend, the brother of my love;

        My Arthur, whom I shall not see
            Till all my widow'd race be run;
            Dear as the mother to the son,
20   More than my brothers are to me.

                    * * *
                    14

        If one should bring me this report,
            That thou° hadst touch'd the land to-day,   *the ship*
            And I went down unto the quay,
            And found thee lying in the port;

5   And standing, muffled round with woe,
            Should see thy passengers in rank
            Come stepping lightly down the plank,
            And beckoning unto those they know;

        And if along with these should come
10   The man I held as half-divine;
            Should strike a sudden hand in mine,
            And ask a thousand things of home;

        And I should tell him all my pain,
            And how my life had droop'd of late,
15   And he should sorrow o'er my state
            And marvel what possess'd my brain;

        And I perceived no touch of change,
            No hint of death in all his frame,
            But found him all in all the same,
20   I should not feel it to be strange.

                    * * *
                    19

        The Danube to the Severn[8] gave
            The darken'd heart that beat no more;
            They laid him by the pleasant shore,
            And in the hearing of the wave.

5   There twice a day the Severn fills;
            The salt sea-water passes by,
            And hushes half the babbling Wye,[9]
            And makes a silence in the hills.

        The Wye is hush'd nor moved along,
10   And hush'd my deepest grief of all,
            When fill'd with tears that cannot fall,
            I brim with sorrow drowning song.

---

8. Arthur Hallam died in Vienna, which is on the Danube, and was buried at Clevedon, near the Severn River in southwest England.

9. Taken from my own observation—the rapids of the Wye are stilled by the incoming sea [Tennyson's note]. The Wye is a tributary of the Severn, a tidal river.

The tide flows down, the wave again
   Is vocal in its wooded walls;
15   My deeper anguish also falls,
And I can speak a little then.

* * *

27

I envy not in any moods
   The captive void of noble rage,
   The linnet° born within the cage,   *finch*
That never knew the summer woods:

5 I envy not the beast that takes
   His license in the field of time,
   Unfetter'd by the sense of crime,
To whom a conscience never wakes;

Nor, what may count itself as blest,
10   The heart that never plighted troth
   But stagnates in the weeds of sloth;
Nor any want-begotten rest.[1]

I hold it true, whate'er befall;
   I feel it, when I sorrow most;
15   'Tis better to have loved and lost
Than never to have loved at all.

28

The time draws near the birth of Christ:[2]
   The moon is hid; the night is still;
   The Christmas bells from hill to hill
Answer each other in the mist.

5 Four voices of four hamlets round,
   From far and near, on mead and moor,
   Swell out and fail, as if a door
Were shut between me and the sound:

Each voice four changes[3] on the wind,
10   That now dilate, and now decrease,
   Peace and goodwill, goodwill and peace,
Peace and goodwill, to all mankind.

This year I slept and woke with pain,
   I almost wish'd no more to wake,
15   And that my hold on life would break
Before I heard those bells again:

But they my troubled spirit rule,
   For they controll'd me when a boy;
   They bring me sorrow touch'd with joy,
20 The merry merry bells of Yule.

* * *

1. Peace of mind owing to lack or "want" of having made commitments.

2. The first Christmas after Hallam's death.
3. Arrangements of church bell ringing.

30

With trembling fingers did we weave
    The holly round the Christmas hearth;
    A rainy cloud possess'd the earth,
And sadly fell our Christmas-eve.

5   At our old pastimes in the hall
    We gambol'd, making vain pretence
    Of gladness, with an awful sense
Of one mute Shadow watching all.

We paused: the winds were in the beech:
10   We heard them sweep the winter land;
    And in a circle hand-in-hand
Sat silent, looking each at each.

Then echo-like our voices rang;
    We sung, tho' every eye was dim,
15   A merry song we sang with him
Last year: impetuously we sang:

We ceased: a gentler feeling crept
    Upon us: surely rest is meet:°   *fitting*
    "They rest," we said, "their sleep is sweet,"
20   And silence follow'd, and we wept.

Our voices took a higher range;
    Once more we sang: "They do not die
    Nor lose their mortal sympathy,
Nor change to us, although they change;

25   "Rapt° from the fickle and the frail   *carried away*
    With gather'd power, yet the same,
    Pierces the keen seraphic flame
From orb° to orb, from veil to veil."   *star*

Rise, happy morn, rise, holy morn,
30   Draw forth the cheerful day from night:
    O Father, touch the east, and light
The light that shone when Hope was born.

* * *

39

Old warder[4] of these buried bones,
    And answering now my random stroke
    With fruitful cloud and living smoke,[5]
Dark yew, that graspest at the stones

5   And dippest toward the dreamless head,
    To thee too comes the golden hour
    When flower is feeling after flower;
But Sorrow—fixt upon the dead,

---

4. The yew tree that stands by Hallam's grave; cf. Section 2. This section was written and added in 1868.

5. The yew, when flowering, in a wind or if struck sends up its pollen like smoke [Tennyson's note].

And darkening the dark graves of men,—
  What whisper'd from her lying lips?
  Thy gloom is kindled at the tips,[6]
And passes into gloom again.

* * *

50

Be near me when my light is low,
  When the blood creeps, and the nerves prick
  And tingle; and the heart is sick,
And all the wheels of Being slow.

Be near me when the sensuous frame
  Is rack'd with pangs that conquer trust;
  And Time, a maniac scattering dust,
And Life, a Fury slinging flame.[7]

Be near me when my faith is dry,
  And men the flies of latter spring,
  That lay their eggs, and sting and sing
And weave their petty cells and die.

Be near me when I fade away,
  To point the term of human strife,
  And on the low dark verge of life
The twilight of eternal day.

* * *

54

Oh yet we trust that somehow good
  Will be the final goal of ill,
  To pangs of nature, sins of will,
Defects of doubt, and taints of blood;

That nothing walks with aimless feet;
  That not one life shall be destroy'd,
  Or cast as rubbish to the void,
When God hath made the pile complete;

That not a worm is cloven in vain;
  That not a moth with vain desire
  Is shrivell'd in a fruitless fire,
Or but subserves another's gain.

Behold, we know not anything;
  I can but trust that good shall fall
  At last—far off—at last, to all,
And every winter change to spring.

So runs my dream: but what am I?
  An infant crying in the night:
  An infant crying for the light:
And with no language but a cry.

6. The tips of the yew branches are in flower.   7. The Furies—avengers of crime—carry torches.

55

The wish, that of the living whole
    No life may fail beyond the grave,
    Derives it not from what we have
The likest God within the soul?[8]

Are God and Nature then at strife,
    That Nature lends such evil dreams?
    So careful of the type[9] she seems,
So careless of the single life;

That I, considering everywhere
    Her secret meaning in her deeds,
    And finding that of fifty seeds
She often brings but one to bear,

I falter where I firmly trod,
    And falling with my weight of cares
    Upon the great world's altar-stairs
That slope thro' darkness up to God,

I stretch lame hands of faith, and grope,
    And gather dust and chaff, and call
    To what I feel is Lord of all,
And faintly trust the larger hope.[1]

56

"So careful of the type?" but no.
    From scarpèd[2] cliff and quarried stone
    She° cries, "A thousand types are gone: *Nature*
I care for nothing, all shall go.

"Thou makest thine appeal to me:
    I bring to life, I bring to death:
    The spirit does but mean the breath:
I know no more." And he, shall he,

Man, her last work, who seem'd so fair,
    Such splendid purpose in his eyes,
    Who roll'd the psalm to wintry skies,
Who built him fanes° of fruitless prayer,   *temples*

Who trusted God was love indeed
    And love Creation's final law—
    Tho' Nature, red in tooth and claw
With ravine, shriek'd against his creed—

Who loved, who suffer'd countless ills,
    Who battled for the True, the Just,

8. The inner consciousness—the divine in man [Tennyson's note].
9. Species; i.e., Nature ensures the preservation of the species but is indifferent to the fate of the individual.

1. Hallam Tennyson notes: "My father means by 'the larger hope' that the whole human race would through, perhaps, ages of suffering, be at length purified and saved."
2. Steep cut-away cliffs with the strata exposed.

Be blown about the desert dust,
20 Or seal'd° within the iron hills?   *fossilized*

No more? A monster then, a dream,
    A discord. Dragons of the prime,
    That tare° each other in their slime,[3]   *tore*
Were mellow music match'd° with him.   *compared*

25 O life as futile, then, as frail!
    O for thy voice to soothe and bless!
    What hope of answer, or redress?
Behind the veil, behind the veil.

* * *

67

When on my bed the moonlight falls,
    I know that in thy place of rest
    By that broad water of the west,[4]
There comes a glory on the walls;

5   Thy marble bright in dark appears,
    As slowly steals a silver flame
    Along the letters of thy name,
And o'er the number of thy years.

The mystic glory swims away;
10   From off my bed the moonlight dies;
    And closing eaves of wearied eyes
I sleep till dusk is dipt in gray:

And then I know the mist is drawn
    A lucid veil from coast to coast,
15   And in the dark church like a ghost
Thy tablet glimmers to the dawn.

* * *

78

Again at Christmas[5] did we weave
    The holly round the Christmas hearth;
    The silent snow possess'd the earth,
And calmly fell our Christmas-eve:

5   The yule-clog° sparkled keen with frost,   *log*
    No wing of wind the region swept,
    But over all things brooding slept
The quiet sense of something lost.

As in the winters left behind,
10   Again our ancient games had place,
    The mimic picture's breathing grace,[6]
And dance and song and hoodman-blind.°   *blindman's bluff*

---

3. The geologic monsters of the early ages [Tennyson's note].
4. The Severn, near which Hallam was buried at Clevedon.

5. The second Christmas after Hallam's death.
6. Tableaux-vivants, an entertainment in which performers reenact a well-known work of art or historical event.

Who show'd a token of distress?
   No single tear, no mark of pain:
15   O sorrow, then can sorrow wane?
O grief, can grief be changed to less?

O last regret, regret can die!
   No—mixt with all this mystic frame,
   Her° deep relations are the same,   *sorrow's*
20 But with long use her tears are dry.

         * * *
         86
Sweet after showers, ambrosial air,
   That rollest from the gorgeous gloom
   Of evening over brake and bloom
And meadow, slowly breathing bare

5 The round of space, and rapt below
   Thro' all the dewy-tassell'd wood,
   And shadowing down the hornèd flood[7]
In ripples, fan my brows and blow

The fever from my cheek, and sigh
10   The full new life that feeds thy breath
   Throughout my frame, till Doubt and Death,
Ill brethren, let the fancy fly

From belt to belt of crimson seas
   On leagues of odour streaming far,
15   To where in yonder orient star
A hundred spirits whisper "Peace."

         * * *
         95
By night we linger'd on the lawn,
   For underfoot the herb was dry;
   And genial warmth; and o'er the sky
The silvery haze of summer drawn;

5 And calm that let the tapers burn
   Unwavering: not a cricket chirr'd:
   The brook alone far-off was heard,
And on the board the fluttering urn:[8]

And bats went round in fragrant skies,
10   And wheel'd or lit the filmy shapes°   *moths*
   That haunt the dusk, with ermine capes
And woolly breasts and beaded eyes;

While now we sang old songs that peal'd
   From knoll to knoll, where, couch'd at ease,
15   The white kine° glimmer'd, and the trees   *cows*
Laid their dark arms about the field.

---

7. Between two promontories [Tennyson's note].
8. Hot-water urn for making tea or coffee, heated by a   fluttering flame.

But when those others, one by one,
    Withdrew themselves from me and night,
    And in the house light after light
20   Went out, and I was all alone,

A hunger seized my heart; I read
    Of that glad year which once had been,
    In those fall'n leaves which kept their green,
The noble letters of the dead:

25   And strangely on the silence broke
    The silent-speaking words, and strange
    Was love's dumb cry defying change
To test his worth; and strangely spoke

The faith, the vigour, bold to dwell
30   On doubts that drive the coward back,
    And keen thro' wordy snares to track
Suggestion to her inmost cell.

So word by word, and line by line,
    The dead man touch'd me from the past.
35   And all at once it seem'd at last
The living soul[9] was flash'd on mine,

And mine in this was wound, and whirl'd
    About empyreal heights of thought,
    And came on that which is, and caught
40   The deep pulsations of the world,

Aeonian music[1] measuring out
    The steps of Time—the shocks of Chance—
    The blows of Death. At length my trance
Was cancell'd, stricken thro' with doubt.[2]

45   Vague words! but ah, how hard to frame
    In matter-moulded forms of speech,
    Or ev'n for intellect to reach
Thro' memory that which I became:

Till now the doubtful dusk reveal'd
50   The knolls once more where, couch'd at ease,
    The white kine glimmer'd, and the trees
Laid their dark arms about the field:

And suck'd from out the distant gloom
    A breeze began to tremble o'er
55   The large leaves of the sycamore,
And fluctuate all the still perfume,

And gathering freshlier overhead,
    Rock'd the full-foliaged elms, and swung

9. "His living soul" in the first edition; the next line originally read "And mine in his was wound." Tennyson said
that the first version "troubled me, as perhaps giving a
wrong impression."

1. The music of the aeons.
2. The trance came to an end in a moment of critical
doubt, but the doubt was dispelled by the glory of the
dawn of the "boundless day" [Tennyson's note].

The heavy-folded rose, and flung
60   The lilies to and fro, and said

"The dawn, the dawn," and died away;
    And East and West, without a breath,
    Mixt their dim lights, like life and death,
To broaden into boundless day.

* * *

104

The time draws near the birth of Christ;[3]
    The moon is hid, the night is still;
    A single church below the hill
Is pealing, folded in the mist.

5   A single peal of bells below,
    That wakens at this hour of rest
    A single murmur in the breast,
That these are not the bells I know.

Like strangers' voices here they sound,
10   In lands where not a memory strays,
    Nor landmark breathes of other days,
But all is new unhallow'd ground.

* * *

106

Ring out, wild bells, to the wild sky,
    The flying cloud, the frosty light:
    The year is dying in the night;
Ring out, wild bells, and let him die.

5   Ring out the old, ring in the new,
    Ring, happy bells, across the snow:
    The year is going, let him go;
Ring out the false, ring in the true.

Ring out the grief that saps the mind,
10   For those that here we see no more;
    Ring out the feud of rich and poor,
Ring in redress to all mankind.

Ring out a slowly dying cause,
    And ancient forms of party strife;
15   Ring in the nobler modes of life,
With sweeter manners, purer laws.

Ring out the want, the care, the sin,
    The faithless coldness of the times;
    Ring out, ring out my mournful rhymes,
20   But ring the fuller minstrel in.

---

3. It is now the third Christmas since Hallam's death.

Ring out false pride in place and blood,
   The civic slander and the spite;
   Ring in the love of truth and right,
Ring in the common love of good.

25   Ring out old shapes of foul disease;
   Ring out the narrowing lust of gold;
   Ring out the thousand wars of old,
Ring in the thousand years of peace.

Ring in the valiant man and free,
30   The larger heart, the kindlier hand;
   Ring out the darkness of the land,
Ring in the Christ that is to be.

* * *

115

Now fades the last long streak of snow,
   Now burgeons every maze of quick[4]
   About the flowering squares, and thick
By ashen roots the violets blow.

5   Now rings the woodland loud and long,
   The distance takes a lovelier hue,
   And drown'd in yonder living blue
The lark becomes a sightless song.

Now dance the lights on lawn and lea,
10   The flocks are whiter down the vale,
   And milkier every milky sail
On winding stream or distant sea;

Where now the seamew pipes, or dives
   In yonder greening gleam, and fly
15   The happy birds, that change their sky
To build and brood; that live their lives

From land to land; and in my breast
   Spring wakens too; and my regret
   Becomes an April violet,
20 And buds and blossoms like the rest.

* * *

118

Contemplate all this work of Time,
   The giant labouring in his youth;
   Nor dream of human love and truth,
As dying Nature's earth and lime;

5   But trust that those we call the dead
   Are breathers of an ampler day
   For ever nobler ends. They° say,   *scientists*
The solid earth whereon we tread

4. Hawthorn hedges are budding; the "flowering squares" in the next line are fields.

In tracts of fluent heat began,
10   And grew to seeming-random forms,
    The seeming prey of cyclic storms,
Till at the last arose the man;

Who throve and branch'd from clime to clime,
    The herald of a higher race,
15   And of himself in higher place,
If so he type[5] this work of time

Within himself, from more to more;
    Or, crown'd with attributes of woe
    Like glories, move his course, and show
20 That life is not as idle ore,

But iron dug from central gloom,
    And heated hot with burning fears,
    And dipt in baths of hissing tears,
And batter'd with the shocks of doom

25 To shape and use. Arise and fly
    The reeling Faun, the sensual feast;
    Move upward, working out the beast,
And let the ape and tiger die.

119

Doors, where my heart was used to beat
    So quickly, not as one that weeps
    I come once more;[6] the city sleeps;
I smell the meadow in the street;

5 I hear a chirp of birds; I see
    Betwixt the black fronts long-withdrawn
    A light-blue lane of early dawn,
And think of early days and thee,

And bless thee, for thy lips are bland,
10   And bright the friendship of thine eye;
    And in my thoughts with scarce a sigh
I take the pressure of thine hand.

120

I trust I have not wasted breath:
    I think we are not wholly brain,
    Magnetic mockeries;° not in vain,   *automatons*
Like Paul with beasts,[7] I fought with Death;

5 Not only cunning casts in clay:
    Let Science prove we are, and then

---

5. Typifies or prefigures.
6. Tennyson has returned to Hallam's house in London; see Section 7, page 601.

7. Saint Paul said: "If after the manner of men I have fought with beasts at Ephesus, what advantageth it me, if the dead rise not" (1 Corinthians 15.32).

What matters Science unto men,
  At least to me? I would not stay.

  Let him, the wiser man who springs
10   Hereafter, up from childhood shape
    His action like the greater ape,[8]
But I was *born* to other things.

* * *

123

There rolls the deep where grew the tree.
  O earth, what changes hast thou seen!
  There where the long street roars, hath been
The stillness of the central sea.

5 The hills are shadows, and they flow
    From form to form, and nothing stands;
    They melt like mist, the solid lands,
Like clouds they shape themselves and go.

  But in my spirit will I dwell,
10   And dream my dream, and hold it true;
    For tho' my lips may breathe adieu,
I cannot think the thing farewell.

124

That which we dare invoke to bless;
  Our dearest faith; our ghastliest doubt;
  He, They, One, All; within, without;
The Power in darkness whom we guess;

5 I found Him not in world or sun,
    Or eagle's wing, or insect's eye;[9]
    Nor thro' the questions men may try,
The petty cobwebs we have spun:

  If e'er when faith had fall'n asleep,
10   I heard a voice "believe no more"
    And heard an ever-breaking shore
That tumbled in the Godless deep;

  A warmth within the breast would melt
    The freezing reason's colder part,
15   And like a man in wrath the heart
Stood up and answer'd "I have felt."

  No, like a child in doubt and fear:
    But that blind clamour made me wise;
    Then was I as a child that cries,
20 But, crying, knows his father near;

---

8. Spoken ironically against mere materialism, not against evolution [Tennyson's note].
9. Tennyson rejects the argument that God's existence can be inferred from Nature—i.e., that the design of the universe is so orderly and complex that there must have been a designer.

And what I am beheld again
    What is, and no man understands;
    And out of darkness came the hands
That reach thro' nature, moulding men.

* * *

130

Thy voice is on the rolling air;
    I hear thee where the waters run;
    Thou standest in the rising sun,
And in the setting thou art fair.

5   What art thou then? I cannot guess;
    But tho' I seem in star and flower
    To feel thee some diffusive power,
I do not therefore love thee less:

My love involves the love before;
10   My love is vaster passion now;
    Tho' mix'd with God and Nature thou,
I seem to love thee more and more.

Far off thou art, but ever nigh;
    I have thee still, and I rejoice;
15   I prosper, circled with thy voice;
I shall not lose thee tho' I die.

131

O living will[1] that shalt endure
    When all that seems shall suffer shock,
    Rise in the spiritual rock,[2]
Flow thro' our deeds and make them pure,

5   That we may lift from out of dust
    A voice as unto him that hears,
    A cry above the conquer'd years
To one that with us works, and trust,

With faith that comes of self-control,
10   The truths that never can be proved
    Until we close with all we loved,
And all we flow from, soul in soul.

* * *

---

1. That which we know as Free-will in man [Tennyson's note].

2. "And did all drink the same spiritual drink: for they drank of that spiritual Rock that followed them: and that Rock was Christ" (1 Corinthians 10.4).

The Charge of the Light Brigade[1]

1

Half a league, half a league,
Half a league onward,
All in the valley of Death
   Rode the six hundred.
5 "Forward, the Light Brigade!
Charge for the guns!" he said:
Into the valley of Death
   Rode the six hundred.[2]

2

"Forward, the Light Brigade!"
10 Was there a man dismay'd?
Not tho' the soldier knew
   Some one had blunder'd:
Their's not to make reply,
Their's not to reason why,
15 Their's but to do and die:
Into the valley of Death
   Rode the six hundred.

3

Cannon to right of them,
Cannon to left of them,
20 Cannon in front of them
   Volley'd and thunder'd;
Storm'd at with shot and shell,
Boldly they rode and well,
Into the jaws of Death,
25 Into the mouth of Hell
   Rode the six hundred.

4

Flash'd all their sabres bare,
Flash'd as they turn'd in air
Sabring the gunners there,
30 Charging an army, while
   All the world wonder'd:
Plunged in the battery-smoke
Right thro' the line they broke;
Cossack and Russian
35 Reel'd from the sabre-stroke
   Shatter'd and sunder'd.
Then they rode back, but not
   Not the six hundred.

---

1. In 1854, during the Crimean War, a misunderstood order caused a brigade of 600 British cavalry to make a foolhardy charge upon the batteries of Russian artillery at Balaclava, near Sebastopol. More than 400 soldiers were killed.

2. In his Lincolnshire accent, Tennyson apparently pronounced "hundred" as "hunderd"—thus making it an exact rhyme with "blundered" and "thundered."

5

Cannon to right of them,
40   Cannon to left of them,
Cannon behind them
    Volley'd and thunder'd;
Storm'd at with shot and shell,
While horse and hero fell,
45   They that had fought so well
Came thro' the jaws of Death,
Back from the mouth of Hell,
All that was left of them,
    Left of six hundred.

6

50   When can their glory fade?
O the wild charge they made!
    All the world wonder'd.
Honour the charge they made!
Honour the Light Brigade,
55   Noble six hundred!
1854   1854

Crossing the Bar[1]

Sunset and evening star,
    And one clear call for me!
And may there be no moaning of the bar,[2]
    When I put out to sea,

5   But such a tide as moving seems asleep,
    Too full for sound and foam,
When that which drew from out the boundless deep
    Turns again home.

Twilight and evening bell,
10   And after that the dark!
And may there be no sadness of farewell,
    When I embark;

For tho' from out our bourne° of Time and Place   boundary
    The flood may bear me far,
15   I hope to see my Pilot face to face[3]
    When I have crost the bar.
1889   1889

---

1. Tennyson instructed that this poem should appear at the end of every collection of his work, though it was not in fact the last poem he wrote. The poem, he said, "came in a moment" while he was crossing the Solent to return home to Farringford on the Isle of Wight.
2. The sandbank that forms at the mouth of a harbor. The "moaning" may be the sound of the river and the sea meeting.
3. The pilot has been on board all the while, but in the dark I have not seen him [Tennyson's note]. Cf. 1 Corinthians 13.12: "For now we see through a glass, darkly; but then face to face: now I know in part; but then shall I know even as also I am known."

Charles Darwin
1809–1882

Charles Darwin's five-year excursion on the *Beagle* has become the stuff of legend. No voyage since that of Columbus has had such a profound impact on the world. Darwin's ideas concerning evolution and natural selection brought about a revolution in human thought; they radically transformed our sense of our place in the universe. Yet *The Voyage of the Beagle* is a modestly written account of the meticulous observations of a young naturalist, as interested in ordinary beetles and coral formations as in the weirdly monstrous creatures he saw on the Galapagos Islands.

Nothing in Darwin's youth suggested a great man in the making. His father once warned him, "You care for nothing but shooting, dogs, and rat-catching, and you will be a disgrace to yourself and all your family." Darwin's father was a prosperous doctor, and he sent his son to Edinburgh University for two years to study medicine, but Darwin detested the subject and neglected his studies. Casting about for an occupation for this unpromising son, his father proposed the undemanding career of a country clergyman. Darwin agreed and spent the next three years at Cambridge where, according to his autobiography, he did little except collect beetles.

Although he considered his formal education a complete waste, Darwin was busy educating himself in natural history. The turning point in his life was an invitation to become the ship's naturalist on the H.M.S. *Beagle*'s surveying expedition. Knowing the ship would be away for years, Darwin's father initially refused permission to accept. At a time when the word "scientist" did not even exist, he could not see how such an undertaking could lead to any respectable profession. But he left a loophole, telling his son, "If you can find any man of common sense, who advises you to go, I will give my consent." Fortunately, Darwin's uncle supported the idea, and in 1831 the *Beagle* sailed for South America with the twenty-two-year-old Darwin aboard.

Darwin had to put up with cramped quarters, seasickness, and the captain's volatile temper, but he accomplished an extraordinary amount of work. He collected specimens, filled eighteen notebooks with scientific observations, and spent long periods ashore studying plants and animals, fossils, and indigenous cultures. He also kept a diary that eventually became the basis of *The Voyage of the Beagle* (1839, rev. 1845), one of the great classics of travel literature. Out of these investigations, particularly in the volcanic Galapagos Islands off the coast of South America, grew the theory of evolution.

Yet it is a myth that Darwin had a sudden insight concerning the origin of species while examining the strange tortoises, lizards, and finches in the Galapagos. Though he had read with interest the evolutionary speculations of his grandfather, Erasmus Darwin, he had remained a creationist: during the voyage he continued to believe that species were fixed forever at the moment of their creation, as described in the Bible. Only back in England, working through his huge volume of notes, did he become convinced of the mutability of species.

Within a few months of his return home in 1836, Darwin had accepted evolution as the explanation for the natural phenomena he had observed. But he was in no hurry to publish his findings. In fact, twenty years went by before he learned in 1858 that a young naturalist, Alfred Russel Wallace, had arrived independently at the theory of natural selection. A joint paper of their findings was presented to the Linnaean Society, and Darwin at long last rushed to compile and publish *On the Origin of Species by Means of Natural Selection* (1859). Darwin realized that most living organisms produce far more offspring than can survive: not every acorn becomes an oak. Certain genetically favored individuals have a competitive edge in the struggle for life. Nature thus ensures the "survival of the fittest," and eventually their descendants evolve into new and better-adapted species.

The book created an immediate sensation. The original edition sold out the day it was published. Darwin was not the first to propose a theory of evolution, but he was the first to

Thomas Landseer, after a drawing by C. Martens, *A Fuegian at Portrait Cove*, 1839. This illustration appeared in the *Narrative of the Surveying Voyages of His Majesty's Ships Adventure and Beagle, between the Years 1826 and 1836* (1839); Darwin's part of this report became *The Voyage of the Beagle.*

offer a persuasive account of the means by which evolution works. Geologists such as Charles Lyell had already shown that the earth was immensely older than six thousand years, the traditional estimate based on biblical chronology. In further undermining the biblical account of creation, Darwin shook the faith of his contemporaries.

Darwin was not eager to offend people, nor did he enjoy controversy. Thus in *The Origin of Species* he tactfully avoided any discussion of human origins, although he was already confident that evolution applied to human beings as well. In *The Descent of Man* (1871) he finally made his position clear: man is an animal. Darwin's ideas were profoundly unsettling. No longer sure of belonging to an ordered world overseen by a beneficent Creator, many people felt they had been set adrift in an indifferent cosmos. Tennyson's memorable phrase, "Nature, red in tooth and claw," expressed the Victorians' collective horror at Darwin's vision of nature as a cruel and violent battlefield.

Darwin's theories were earthshaking, but his private life was not. When the *Beagle* voyage ended, he debated the pros and cons of marriage, telling himself that a wife would provide "an object to be beloved and played with—better than a dog anyhow." Despite these unromantic musings, his marriage to his cousin Emma Wedgwood was long and happy. They settled down in a country house and had many children. For the rest of his life Darwin suffered from mysterious illnesses; they prevented his going into society, but they did not stop him working and writing. He never traveled again.

from **The Voyage of the Beagle**

from Chapter 10. Tierra Del Fuego[1]

December 17th, 1832.—Having now finished with Patagonia[2] and the Falkland Islands, I will describe our first arrival in Tierra del Fuego. A little after noon we doubled Cape St. Diego, and entered the famous strait of Le Maire. We kept close to the Fuegian shore, but the outline of the rugged, inhospitable Staten-land was visible amidst the clouds. In the afternoon we anchored in the Bay of Good Success. While entering we were saluted in a manner becoming the inhabitants of this savage land. A group of Fuegians partly concealed by the entangled forest, were perched on a wild point overhanging the sea; and as we passed by, they sprang up and waving their tattered cloaks sent forth a loud and sonorous shout. The savages followed the ship, and just before dark we saw their fire, and again heard their wild cry. The harbour consists of a fine piece of water half surrounded by low rounded mountains of clay-slate, which are covered to the water's edge by one dense gloomy forest. A single glance at the landscape was sufficient to show me how widely different it was from any thing I had ever beheld. At night it blew a gale of wind, and heavy squalls from the mountains swept past us. It would have been a bad time out at sea, and we, as well as others, may call this Good Success Bay.

In the morning the Captain sent a party to communicate with the Fuegians. When we came within hail, one of the four natives who were present advanced to receive us, and began to shout most vehemently, wishing to direct us where to land. When we were on shore the party looked rather alarmed, but continued talking and making gestures with great rapidity. It was without exception the most curious and interesting spectacle I ever beheld: I could not have believed how wide was the difference between savage and civilized man: it is greater than between a wild and domesticated animal, inasmuch as in man there is a greater power of improvement. The chief spokesman was old, and appeared to be the head of the family; the three others were powerful young men, about six feet high. The women and children had been sent away. These Fuegians are a very different race from the stunted, miserable wretches farther westward; and they seem closely allied to the famous Patagonians of the Strait of Magellan. Their only garment consists of a mantle made of guanaco[3] skin, with the wool outside; this they wear just thrown over their shoulders, leaving their persons as often exposed as covered. Their skin is of a dirty copper red colour.

The old man had a fillet[4] of white feathers tied round his head, which partly confined his black, coarse, and entangled hair. His face was crossed by two broad transverse bars; one, painted bright red, reached from ear to ear and included the upper lip; the other, white like chalk, extended above and parallel to the first, so that even his eyelids were thus coloured. The other two men were ornamented by streaks of black powder, made of charcoal. The party altogether closely resembled the devils which come on the stage in plays like Der Freischutz.[5]

Their very attitudes were abject, and the expression of their countenances distrustful, surprised, and startled. After we had presented them with some scarlet cloth, which they immediately tied round their necks, they became good friends. This was shown by the old man patting our breasts, and making a chuckling kind of noise, as people do when feeding chickens. I walked with the old man, and this demonstration of friendship was repeated several times; it was concluded by three hard slaps, which

---

1. A group of islands off the southern tip of South America.
2. The southernmost region of South America.
3. A South American mammal with fawn-colored fur.
4. A headband.

5. An 1817 opera by Carl Maria von Weber (1786–1826), first performed in London in 1824. The story concerns Max, a forester who nearly sells his soul to the devil.

were given me on the breast and back at the same time. He then bared his bosom for me to return the compliment, which being done, he seemed highly pleased. The language of these people, according to our notions, scarcely deserves to be called articulate. Captain Cook has compared it to a man clearing his throat, but certainly no European ever cleared his throat with so many hoarse, guttural, and clicking sounds.

They are excellent mimics: as often as we coughed or yawned, or made any odd motion, they immediately imitated us. Some of our party began to squint and look awry; but one of the young Fuegians (whose whole face was painted black, excepting a white band across his eyes) succeeded in making far more hideous grimaces. They could repeat with perfect correctness each word in any sentence we addressed them, and they remembered such words for some time. Yet we Europeans all know how difficult it is to distinguish apart the sounds in a foreign language. Which of us, for instance, could follow an American Indian through a sentence of more than three words? All savages appear to possess, to an uncommon degree, this power of mimicry. I was told, almost in the same words, of the same ludicrous habit among the Caffres:[6] the Australians, likewise, have long been notorious for being able to imitate and describe the gait of any man, so that he may be recognized. How can this faculty be explained? is it a consequence of the more practised habits of perception and keener senses, common to all men in a savage state, as compared with those long civilized?

When a song was struck up by our party, I thought the Fuegians would have fallen down with astonishment. With equal surprise they viewed our dancing; but one of the young men, when asked, had no objection to a little waltzing. Little accustomed to Europeans as they appeared to be, yet they knew and dreaded our fire-arms; nothing would tempt them to take a gun in their hands. They begged for knives, calling them by the Spanish word "cuchilla." They explained also what they wanted, by acting as if they had a piece of blubber in their mouth, and then pretending to cut instead of tear it.

I have not as yet noticed the Fuegians whom we had on board. During the former voyage of the Adventure and Beagle in 1826 to 1830, Captain Fitz Roy[7] seized on a party of natives, as hostages for the loss of a boat, which had been stolen, to the great jeopardy of a party employed on the survey; and some of these natives, as well as a child whom he bought for a pearl-button, he took with him to England, determining to educate them and instruct them in religion at his own expense. To settle these natives in their own country, was one chief inducement to Captain Fitz Roy to undertake our present voyage; and before the Admiralty had resolved to send out this expedition, Captain Fitz Roy had generously chartered a vessel, and would himself have taken them back. The natives were accompanied by a missionary, R. Matthews; of whom and of the natives, Captain Fitz Roy has published a full and excellent account. Two men, one of whom died in England of the smallpox, a boy and a little girl, were originally taken; and we had now on board, York Minster, Jemmy Button (whose name expresses his purchase-money), and Fuegia Basket. York Minster was a full-grown, short, thick, powerful man: his disposition was reserved, taciturn, morose, and when excited violently passionate; his affections were very strong towards a few friends on board; his intellect good. Jemmy Button was a universal favourite, but likewise passionate; the expression of his face at once showed his nice disposition. He was merry and often laughed, and was remarkably sympathetic with any one in pain: when the water was rough, I was often a little seasick, and he used to come to me and say in a plaintive voice, "Poor, poor fellow!" but the notion, after his aquatic life, of a man being sea-sick, was too ludicrous, and he was gen-

6. Kaffirs are a Bantu-speaking African people.
7. Robert Fitz Roy (1805–1865) was the captain of the

Beagle; he and Darwin had a sometimes difficult relationship.

erally obliged to turn on one side to hide a smile or laugh, and then he would repeat his "Poor, poor fellow!" He was of a patriotic disposition; and he liked to praise his own tribe and country, in which he truly said there were "plenty of trees," and he abused all the other tribes: he stoutly declared that there was no Devil in his land. Jemmy was short, thick, and fat, but vain of his personal appearance; he used to wear gloves, his hair was neatly cut, and he was distressed if his well-polished shoes were dirtied. He was fond of admiring himself in a looking-glass; and a merry-faced little Indian boy from the Rio Negro, whom we had for some months on board, soon perceived this, and used to mock him: Jemmy, who was always rather jealous of the attention paid to this little boy, did not at all like this, and used to say, with rather a contemptuous twist of his head, "Too much skylark." It seems yet wonderful to me, when I think over all his many good qualities, that he should have been of the same race, and doubtless partaken of the same character, with the miserable, degraded savages whom we first met here. Lastly, Fuegia Basket was a nice, modest, reserved young girl, with a rather pleasing but sometimes sullen expression, and very quick in learning anything, especially languages. This she showed in picking up some Portuguese and Spanish, when left on shore for only a short time at Rio de Janeiro and Monte Video, and in her knowledge of English. York Minster was very jealous of any attention paid to her; for it was clear he determined to marry her as soon as they were settled on shore. * * *

It was interesting to watch the conduct of the savages, when we landed, towards Jemmy Button: they immediately perceived the difference between him and ourselves, and held much conversation one with another on the subject. The old man addressed a long harangue to Jemmy, which it seems was to invite him to stay with them. But Jemmy understood very little of their language, and was, moreover, thoroughly ashamed of his countrymen. When York Minster afterwards came on shore, they noticed him in the same way, and told him he ought to shave; yet he had not twenty dwarf hairs on his face, whilst we all wore our untrimmed beards. They examined the colour of his skin, and compared it with ours. One of our arms being bared, they expressed the liveliest surprise and admiration at its whiteness, just in the same way in which I have seen the ourang-outang do at the Zoological Gardens. We thought that they mistook two or three of the officers, who were rather shorter and fairer, though adorned with large beards, for the ladies of our party. The tallest among the Fuegians was evidently much pleased at his height being noticed. When placed back to back with the tallest of the boat's crew, he tried his best to edge on higher ground, and to stand on tiptoe. He opened his mouth to show his teeth, and turned his face for a side view; and all this was done with such alacrity, that I dare say he thought himself the handsomest man in Tierra del Fuego. After our first feeling of grave astonishment was over, nothing could be more ludicrous than the odd mixture of surprise and imitation which these savages every moment exhibited. * * *

December 25th, 1832.— * * * While going one day on shore near Wollaston Island, we pulled alongside a canoe with six Fuegians. These were the most abject and miserable creatures I anywhere beheld. On the east coast the natives, as we have seen, have guanaco cloaks, and on the west, they possess seal-skins. Amongst these central tribes the men generally have an otter-skin, or some small scrap about as large as a pocket-handkerchief, which is barely sufficient to cover their backs as low down as their loins. It is laced across the breast by strings, and according as the wind blows, it is shifted from side to side. But these Fuegians in the canoe were quite naked, and even one full-grown woman was absolutely so. It was raining heavily, and the fresh water, together with the spray, trickled down her body. In another harbour not far distant, a woman, who was suckling a recently-born child, came one day alongside the vessel, and remained there out of mere curiosity, whilst the sleet fell and thawed on her naked bosom, and on the skin of her naked baby! These poor wretches were stunted in their growth, their hideous faces bedaubed with white paint, their skins filthy and greasy, their hair entangled, their voices discordant, and their gestures violent. Viewing such men, one can hardly make oneself believe that they are fellow-creatures, and inhabitants of the same world. It is a common subject of conjecture what pleasure in life some of the lower animals can enjoy: how much more reasonably the same question may be asked with respect to these barbarians! At night, five or six human beings, naked and scarcely protected from the wind and rain of this tempestuous climate, sleep on the wet ground coiled up like animals. Whenever it is low water, winter or summer, night or day, they must rise to pick shellfish from the rocks; and the women either dive to collect sea-eggs, or sit patiently in their canoes, and with a baited hairline without any hook, jerk out little fish. If a seal is killed, or the floating carcass of a putrid whale discovered, it is a feast; and such miserable food is assisted by a few tasteless berries and fungi. * * *

The different tribes have no government or chief; yet each is surrounded by other hostile tribes, speaking different dialects, and separated from each other only by a deserted border or neutral territory: the cause of their warfare appears to be the means of subsistence. Their country is a broken mass of wild rocks, lofty hills, and useless forests: and these are viewed through mists and endless storms. The habitable land is reduced to the stones on the beach; in search of food they are compelled unceasingly to wander from spot to spot, and so steep is the coast, that they can only move about in their wretched canoes. They cannot know the feeling of having a home, and still less that of domestic affection; for the husband is to the wife a brutal master to a laborious slave. Was a more horrid deed ever perpetrated, than that witnessed on the west coast by Byron, who saw a wretched mother pick up her bleeding dying infant-boy, whom her husband had mercilessly dashed on the stones for dropping a basket of sea-eggs! How little can the higher powers of the mind be brought into play: what is there for imagination to picture, for reason to compare, for judgment to decide upon? to knock a limpet from the rock does not require even cunning, that lowest power of the mind. Their skill in some respects may be compared to the instinct of animals; for it is not improved by experience: the canoe, their most ingenious work, poor as it is, has remained the same, as we know from Drake, for the last two hundred and fifty years.

Whilst beholding these savages, one asks, whence have they come? What could have tempted, or what change compelled a tribe of men, to leave the fine regions of the north, to travel down the Cordillera[8] or backbone of America, to invent and build canoes, which are not used by the tribes of Chile, Peru, and Brazil, and then to enter on one of the most inhospitable countries within the limits of the globe? Although such reflections must at first seize on the mind, yet we may feel sure that they are partly erroneous. There is no reason to believe that the Fuegians decrease in number; therefore we must suppose that they enjoy a sufficient share of happiness, of whatever kind it may be, to render life worth having. Nature by making habit omnipotent, and its effects hereditary, has fitted the Fuegian to the climate and the productions of his miserable country. * * *

January 15th, 1833.—The *Beagle* anchored in Goeree Roads. Captain Fitz Roy having resolved to settle the Fuegians, according to their wishes, in Ponsonby Sound, four boats were equipped to carry them there through the Beagle Channel. * * *

19th.—Three whale-boats and the yawl, with a party of twenty-eight, started under the command of Captain Fitz Roy. In the afternoon we entered the eastern

8. Andean mountain range.

mouth of the channel, and shortly afterwards found a snug little cove concealed by some surrounding islets. Here we pitched our tents and lighted our fires. * * *

Few if any of these natives could ever have seen a white man; certainly nothing could exceed their astonishment at the apparition of the four boats. Fires were lighted on every point (hence the name of Tierra del Fuego, or the land of fire), both to attract our attention and to spread far and wide the news. Some of the men ran for miles along the shore. I shall never forget how wild and savage one group appeared: suddenly four or five men came to the edge of an overhanging cliff; they were absolutely naked, and their long hair streamed about their faces; they held rugged staffs in their hands, and, springing from the ground, they waved their arms round their heads, and sent forth the most hideous yells. * * *

22nd.— * * * At night we slept close to the junction of Ponsonby Sound with the Beagle Channel. A small family of Fuegians, who were living in the cove, were quiet and inoffensive, and soon joined our party round a blazing fire. We were well clothed, and though sitting close to the fire were far from too warm; yet these naked savages, though further off, were observed, to our great surprise, to be streaming with perspiration at undergoing such a roasting. They seemed, however, very well pleased, and all joined in the chorus of the seamen's songs: but the manner in which they were invariably a little behindhand was quite ludicrous. * * *

The next morning after our arrival (the 24th) the Fuegians began to pour in, and Jemmy's mother and brothers arrived. Jemmy recognized the stentorian voice of one of his brothers at a prodigious distance. The meeting was less interesting than that between a horse, turned out into a field, when he joins an old companion. There was no demonstration of affection; they simply stared for a short time at each other; and the mother immediately went to look after her canoe. We heard, however, through York, that the mother had been inconsolable for the loss of Jemmy, and had searched everywhere for him, thinking that he might have been left after having been taken in the boat. The women took much notice of and were very kind to Fuegia. We had already perceived that Jemmy had almost forgotten his own language. I should think there was scarcely another human being with so small a stock of language, for his English was very imperfect. It was laughable, but almost pitiable, to hear him speak to his wild brother in English, and then ask him in Spanish ("no sabe?") whether he did not understand him. * * *

February 6th.— * * * It was quite melancholy leaving the three Fuegians with their savage countrymen; but it was a great comfort that they had no personal fears. York, being a powerful resolute man, was pretty sure to get on well, together with his wife Fuegia. Poor Jemmy looked rather disconsolate, and would then, I have little doubt, have been glad to have returned with us. His own brother had stolen many things from him; and as he remarked, "what fashion call that?" He abused his countrymen, "all bad men, no sabe (know) nothing," and, though I never heard him swear before, "damned fools." Our three Fuegians, though they had been only three years with civilized men, would, I am sure, have been glad to have retained their new habits; but this was obviously impossible. I fear it is more than doubtful, whether their visit will have been of any use to them. * * *

On the 5th of March, we anchored in the cove at Woollya, but we saw not a soul there. We were alarmed at this, for the natives in Ponsonby Sound showed by gestures, that there had been fighting; and we afterwards heard that the dreaded Oens men had made a descent. Soon a canoe, with a little flag flying, was seen approaching, with one of the men in it washing the paint off his face. This man was poor Jemmy,—now a thin haggard savage, with long disordered hair, and naked, except a bit of a blanket round his waist. We did not recognize him till he was close to us; for he was ashamed of himself, and turned his back to the ship. We had left him plump, fat, clean, and well dressed;—I never saw so complete and grievous a change. As soon however as he was clothed, and the first flurry was over, things wore a good appearance. He dined with Captain Fitz Roy, and ate his dinner as tidily as formerly. He told us he had "too much" (meaning enough) to eat, that he was not cold, that his relations were very good people, and that he did not wish to go back to England: in the evening we found out the cause of this great change in Jemmy's feelings, in the arrival of his young and nice-looking wife. With his usual good feeling, he brought two beautiful otter-skins for two of his best friends, and some spear-heads and arrows made with his own hands for the Captain. He said he had built a canoe for himself, and he boasted that he could talk a little of his own language! But it is a most singular fact, that he appears to have taught all his tribe some English: an old man spontaneously announced "Jemmy Button's wife." Jemmy had lost all his property. He told us that York Minster had built a large canoe, and with his wife Fuegia, had several months since gone to his own country, and had taken farewell by an act of consummate villainy; he persuaded Jemmy and his mother to come with him, and then on the way deserted them by night, stealing every article of their property.

Jemmy went to sleep on shore, and in the morning returned, and remained on board till the ship got under weigh, which frightened his wife, who continued crying violently till he got into his canoe. He returned loaded with valuable property. Every soul on board was heartily sorry to shake hands with him for the last time. I do not now doubt that he will be as happy as, perhaps happier than, if he had never left his own country. Every one must sincerely hope that Captain Fitz Roy's noble hope may be fulfilled, of being rewarded for the many generous sacrifices which he made for these Fuegians, by some shipwrecked sailor being protected by the descendants of Jemmy Button and his tribe! When Jemmy reached the shore, he lighted a signal fire, and the smoke curled up, bidding us a last and long farewell, as the ship stood on her course into the open sea.

from *Chapter 17. Galapagos Archipelago*[1]

In the morning (17th)[2] we landed on Chatham Island, which, like the others, rises with a tame and rounded outline, broken here and there by scattered hillocks, the remains of former craters. Nothing could be less inviting than the first appearance. A broken field of black basaltic lava, thrown into the most rugged waves, and crossed by great fissures, is every where covered by stunted, sunburnt brushwood, which shows little signs of life. The dry and parched surface, being heated by the noonday sun, gave to the air a close and sultry feeling, like that from a stove: we fancied even that the bushes smelt unpleasantly. Although I diligently tried to collect as many plants as possible, I succeeded in getting very few; and such wretched-looking little weeds would have better become an arctic than an equatorial Flora. The brushwood appears, from a short distance, as leafless as our trees during winter; and it was some time before I discovered that not only almost every plant was now in full leaf, but that the greater number were in flower. * * *

The *Beagle* sailed round Chatham Island, and anchored in several bays. One night I slept on shore on a part of the island, where black truncated cones were extraordinarily numerous: from one small eminence I counted sixty of them, all surmounted by craters

---

1. A group of islands located 400 miles off the coast of Ecuador.   2. Of September 1835.

more or less perfect. The greater number consisted merely of a ring of red scoriae[3] or slags, cemented together: and their height above the plain of lava was not more than from fifty to a hundred feet: none had been very lately active. The entire surface of this part of the island seems to have been permeated, like a sieve, by the subterranean vapours: here and there the lava, whilst soft, has been blown into great bubbles; and in other parts, the tops of caverns similarly formed have fallen in, leaving circular pits with steep sides. From the regular form of the many craters, they gave to the country an artificial appearance, which vividly reminded me of those parts of Staffordshire, where the great iron-foundries are most numerous. The day was glowing hot, and the scrambling over the rough surface and through the intricate thickets, was very fatiguing; but I was well repaid by the strange Cyclopean[4] scene. As I was walking along I met two large tortoises, each of which must have weighed at least two hundred pounds: one was eating a piece of cactus, and as I approached, it stared at me and slowly stalked away; the other gave a deep hiss, and drew in its head. These huge reptiles, surrounded by the black lava, the leafless shrubs, and large cacti, seemed to my fancy like some antediluvian[5] animals. The few dull-coloured birds cared no more for me, than they did for the great tortoises. * * *

The natural history of these islands is eminently curious, and well deserves attention. Most of the organic productions are aboriginal creations, found nowhere else; there is even a difference between the inhabitants of the different islands; yet all show a marked relationship with those of America, though separated from that continent by an open space of ocean, between 500 and 600 miles in width. The archipelago is a little world within itself, or rather a satellite attached to America, whence it has derived a few stray colonists, and has received the general character of its indigenous productions. Considering the small size of these islands, we feel the more astonished at the number of their aboriginal beings, and at their confined range. Seeing every height crowned with its crater, and the boundaries of most of the lava-streams still distinct, we are led to believe that within a period, geologically recent, the unbroken ocean was here spread out. Hence, both in space and time, we seem to be brought somewhat near to that great fact—that mystery of mysteries—the first appearance of new beings on this earth. * * *

The tortoises, when purposely moving towards any point, travel by night and day, and arrive at their journey's end much sooner than would be expected. The inhabitants, from observing marked individuals, consider that they travel a distance of about eight miles in two or three days. One large tortoise, which I watched, walked at the rate of sixty yards in ten minutes, that is 360 yards in the hour, or four miles a day,—allowing a little time for it to eat on the road. During the breeding season, when the male and female are together, the male utters a hoarse roar or bellowing, which, it is said, can be heard at the distance of more than a hundred yards. The female never uses her voice, and the male only at these times; so that when the people hear this noise, they know that the two are together. They were at this time (October) laying their eggs. The female, where the soil is sandy, deposits them together, and covers them up with sand; but where the ground is rocky she drops them indiscriminately in any hole: Mr. Bynoe[6] found seven placed in a fissure. The egg is white and spherical; one which I measured was seven inches and three-eighths in circumference, and therefore larger than a hen's egg. The young tortoises, as soon as they are hatched, fall a prey in great numbers to the carrion-feeding buzzard. The old ones seem generally to die from accidents, as from falling down

3. Lava.

4. Darwin may mean that the landscape is savage and wild, like that inhabited by the Cyclopes in Homer's

Odyssey.

5. Ancient; literally, before the Flood.

6. Naval surgeon aboard the *Beagle*.

precipices: at least, several of the inhabitants told me, that they had never found one dead without some evident cause.

The inhabitants believe that these animals are absolutely deaf; certainly they do not overhear a person walking close behind them. I was always amused when overtaking one of these great monsters, as it was quietly pacing along, to see how suddenly, the instant I passed, it would draw in its head and legs, and uttering a deep hiss fall to the ground with a heavy sound, as if struck dead. I frequently got on their backs, and then giving a few raps on the hinder part of their shells, they would rise up and walk away;— but I found it very difficult to keep my balance. The flesh of this animal is largely employed, both fresh and salted; and a beautifully clear oil is prepared from the fat. * * *

There can be little doubt that this tortoise is an aboriginal inhabitant of the Galapagos; for it is found on all, or nearly all, the islands, even on some of the smaller ones where there is no water; had it been an imported species, this would hardly have been the case in a group which has been so little frequented. * * *

I have not as yet noticed by far the most remarkable feature in the natural history of this archipelago; it is, that the different islands to a considerable extent are inhabited by a different set of beings. My attention was first called to this fact by the Vice-Governor, Mr. Lawson, declaring that the tortoises differed from the different islands, and that he could with certainty tell from which island any one was brought. I did not for some time pay sufficient attention to this statement, and I had already partially mingled together the collections from two of the islands. I never dreamed that islands, about fifty or sixty miles apart, and most of them in sight of each other, formed of precisely the same rocks, placed under a quite similar climate, rising to a nearly equal height, would have been differently tenanted; but we shall soon see that this is the case. It is the fate of most voyagers, no sooner to discover what is most interesting in any locality, than they are hurried from it; but I ought, perhaps, to be thankful that I obtained sufficient material to establish this most remarkable fact in the distribution of organic beings. * * *

If we now turn to the Flora, we shall find the aboriginal plants of the different islands wonderfully different. * * *

Hence we have the truly wonderful fact, that in James Island, of the thirty-eight Galapageian plants, or those found in no other part of the world, thirty are exclusively confined to this one island; and in Albemarle Island, of the twenty-six aboriginal Galapageian plants, twenty-two are confined to this one island, that is, only four are at present known to grow in the other islands of the archipelago; and so on. * * *

The distribution of the tenants of this archipelago would not be nearly so wonderful, if, for instance, one island had a mocking-thrush, and a second island some other quite distinct genus;—if one island had its genus of lizard, and a second island another distinct genus, or none whatever; * * * But it is the circumstance, that several of the islands possess their own species of the tortoise, mocking-thrush, finches, and numerous plants, these species having the same general habits, occupying analogous situations, and obviously filling the same place in the natural economy of this archipelago, that strikes me with wonder. * * * I must repeat, that neither the nature of the soil, nor height of the land, nor the climate, nor the general character of the associated beings, and therefore their action one on another, can differ much in the different islands. * * *

The only light which I can throw on this remarkable difference in the inhabitants of the different islands, is, that very strong currents of the sea running in a westerly and W.N.W. direction must separate, as far as transportal by the sea is concerned, the southern islands from the northern ones; and between these northern islands a strong N.W. current was observed, which must effectually separate James and Albemarle Islands. As the archipelago is free to a most remarkable degree from gales of wind, neither the birds, insects, nor lighter seeds, would be blown from island to island. And lastly, the profound depth of the ocean between the islands, and their apparently recent (in a geological sense) volcanic origin, render it highly unlikely that they were ever united; and this, probably, is a far more important consideration than any other, with respect to the geographical distribution of their inhabitants. Reviewing the facts here given, one is astonished at the amount of creative force, if such an expression may be used, displayed on these small, barren, and rocky islands; and still more so, at its diverse yet analogous action on points so near each other. I have said that the Galapagos Archipelago might be called a satellite attached to America, but it should rather be called a group of satellites, physically similar, organically distinct, yet intimately related to each other, and all related in a marked, though much lesser degree, to the great American continent.

I will conclude my description of the natural history of these islands, by giving an account of the extreme tameness of the birds.

This disposition is common to all the terrestrial species; namely, to the mocking-thrushes, the finches, wrens, tyrant-fly-catchers, the dove, and carrion-buzzard. All of them often approached sufficiently near to be killed with a switch, and sometimes, as I myself tried, with a cap or hat. A gun is here almost superfluous; for with the muzzle I pushed a hawk off the branch of a tree. One day, whilst lying down, a mocking-thrush alighted on the edge of a pitcher, made of the shell of a tortoise, which I held in my hand, and began very quietly to sip the water; it allowed me to lift it from the ground whilst seated on the vessel: I often tried, and very nearly succeeded, in catching these birds by their legs. * * *

From these several facts we may, I think, conclude, first, that the wildness of birds with regard to man, is a particular instinct directed against *him*, and not dependent on any general degree of caution arising from other sources of danger; secondly, that it is not acquired by individual birds in a short time, even when much persecuted; but that in the course of successive generations it becomes hereditary. With domesticated animals we are accustomed to see new mental habits or instincts acquired and rendered hereditary; but with animals in a state of nature, it must always be most difficult to discover instances of acquired hereditary knowledge. In regard to the wildness of birds towards man, there is no way of accounting for it, except as an inherited habit: comparatively few young birds, in any one year, have been injured by man in England, yet almost all, even nestlings, are afraid of him; many individuals, on the other hand, both at the Galapagos and at the Falklands, have been pursued and injured by man, but yet have not learned a salutary dread of him. We may infer from these facts, what havoc the introduction of any new beast of prey must cause in a country, before the instincts of the indigenous inhabitants have become adapted to the stranger's craft or power.

1839, 1845

from On the Origin of Species by Means of Natural Selection

or

The Preservation of Favoured Races in the Struggle for Life
from Chapter 3. Struggle for Existence

Before entering on the subject of this chapter, I must make a few preliminary remarks, to show how the struggle for existence bears on Natural Selection. * * * The mere existence of individual variability and of some few well-marked varieties, though necessary as the foundation for the work, helps us but little in understanding how species arise in nature. How have all those exquisite adaptations of one part of the organisation to another part, and to the conditions of life, and of one distinct organic being to another being, been perfected? We see these beautiful co-adaptations most plainly in the wood-pecker and missletoe; and only a little less plainly in the humblest parasite which clings to the hairs of a quadruped or feathers of a bird; in the structure of the beetle which dives through the water; in the plumed seed which is wafted by the gentlest breeze; in short, we see beautiful adaptations everywhere and in every part of the organic world.

Again, it may be asked, how is it that varieties which I have called incipient species, become ultimately converted into good and distinct species, which in most cas-es obviously differ from each other far more than do the varieties of the same species? How do those groups of species, which constitute what are called distinct genera,[1] and which differ from each other more than do the species of the same genus, arise? All these results, as we shall more fully see in the next chapter, follow inevitably from the struggle for life. Owing to this struggle for life, any variation, however slight and from whatever cause proceeding, if it be in any degree profitable to an individual of any species, in its infinitely complex relations to other organic beings and to external nature, will tend to the preservation of that individual, and will generally be inherited by its offspring. The offspring, also, will thus have a better chance of surviving, for, of the many individuals of any species which are periodically born, but a small number can survive. I have called this principle, by which each slight variation, if useful, is pre-served, by the term of Natural Selection, in order to mark its relation to man's power of selection. We have seen that man by selection can certainly produce great results, and can adapt organic beings to his own uses, through the accumulation of slight but useful variations, given to him by the hand of Nature. But Natural Selection, as we shall here-after see, is a power incessantly ready for action, and is as immeasurably superior to man's feeble efforts, as the works of Nature are to those of Art.

We will now discuss in a little more detail the struggle for existence. * * * Nothing is easier than to admit in words the truth of the universal struggle for life, or more diffi-cult—at least I have found it so—than constantly to bear this conclusion in mind. Yet unless it be thoroughly engrained in the mind, I am convinced that the whole economy of nature, with every fact on distribution, rarity, abundance, extinction, and variation, will be dimly seen or quite misunderstood. We behold the face of nature bright with gladness, we often see superabundance of food; we do not see, or we forget, that the birds which are idly singing round us mostly live on insects or seeds, and are thus constantly destroying life; or we forget how largely these songsters, or their eggs, or their nestlings, are destroyed by birds and beasts of prey; we do not always bear in mind, that though food may be now superabundant, it is not so at all seasons of each recurring year.

I should premise that I use the term Struggle for Existence in a large and metaphorical sense, including dependence of one being on another, and including (which is more important) not only the life of the individual, but success in leaving progeny. Two canine animals in a time of dearth, may be truly said to struggle with each other which shall get food and live. But a plant on the edge of a desert is said to struggle for life against the drought, though more properly it should be said to be dependent on the moisture. A plant which annually produces a thousand seeds, of which on an average only one comes to maturity, may be more truly said to struggle with the plants of the same and other kinds which already clothe the ground. The missletoe is dependent on the apple and a few other trees, but can only in a far-fetched sense be said to struggle with these trees, for if too many of these parasites grow on the same tree, it will languish and die. But several seedling missletoes, growing close

---

1. Plural of genus, a class of species with common characteristics.

together on the same branch, may more truly be said to struggle with each other. As the missletoe is disseminated by birds, its existence depends on birds; and it may metaphorically be said to struggle with other fruit-bearing plants, in order to tempt birds to devour and thus disseminate its seeds rather than those of other plants. In these several senses, which pass into each other, I use for convenience sake the general term of struggle for existence.

A struggle for existence inevitably follows from the high rate at which all organic beings tend to increase. Every being, which during its natural lifetime produces several eggs or seeds, must suffer destruction during some period of its life, and during some season or occasional year, otherwise, on the principle of geometrical increase, its numbers would quickly become so inordinately great that no country could support the product. Hence, as more individuals are produced than can possibly survive, there must in every case be a struggle for existence, either one individual with another of the same species, or with the individuals of distinct species or with the physical conditions of life. It is the doctrine of Malthus[2] applied with manifold force to the whole animal and vegetable kingdoms; for in this case there can be no artificial increase of food, and no prudential restraint from marriage. Although some species may be now increasing, more or less rapidly, in numbers, all cannot do so, for the world would not hold them.

There is no exception to the rule that every organic being naturally increases at so high a rate, that if not destroyed, the earth would soon be covered by the progeny of a single pair. Even slow-breeding man has doubled in twenty-five years, and at this rate, in a few thousand years, there would literally not be standing room for his progeny. Linnaeus[3] has calculated that if an annual plant produced only two seeds—and there is no plant so unproductive as this—and their seedlings next year produced two, and so on, then in twenty years there would be a million plants. The elephant is reckoned to be the slowest breeder of all known animals, and I have taken some pains to estimate its probable minimum rate of natural increase: it will be under the mark to assume that it breeds when thirty years old, and goes on breeding till ninety years old, bringing forth three pairs of young in this interval; if this be so, at the end of the fifth century there would be alive fifteen million elephants, descended from the first pair.

But we have better evidence on this subject than mere theoretical calculations, namely, the numerous recorded cases of the astonishingly rapid increase of various animals in a state of nature, when circumstances have been favourable to them during two or three following seasons. Still more striking is the evidence from our domestic animals of many kinds which have run wild in several parts of the world: if the statements of the rate of increase of slow-breeding cattle and horses in South America, and latterly in Australia, had not been well authenticated, they would have been quite incredible. So it is with plants: cases could be given of introduced plants which have become common throughout whole islands in a period of less than ten years. * * *

In looking at Nature, it is most necessary to keep the foregoing considerations always in mind—never to forget that every single organic being around us may be said to be striving to the utmost to increase in numbers; that each lives by a struggle at some period of its life; that heavy destruction inevitably falls either on the young or old, during each generation or at recurrent intervals. Lighten any check, mitigate the destruction ever so little, and the number of the species will almost instantaneously increase to any amount. The face of Nature may be compared to a yielding surface,

2. In his *Essay on the Principle of Population* (1803), English economist Thomas Malthus argued that unchecked population growth would threaten the food supply; he proposed "moral restraint" as a partial solution.
3. Carl von Linné (1707–1778), Swedish botanist and founder of scientific classification systems.

with ten thousand sharp wedges packed close together and driven inwards by incessant blows, sometimes one wedge being struck, and then another with greater force. * * *

The amount of food for each species of course gives the extreme limit to which each can increase; but very frequently it is not the obtaining food, but the serving as prey to other animals, which determines the average numbers of a species. Thus, there seems to be little doubt that the stock of partridges, grouse, and hares on any large estate depends chiefly on the destruction of vermin. If not one head of game were shot during the next twenty years in England, and, at the same time, if no vermin were destroyed, there would, in all probability, be less game than at present, although hundreds of thousands of game animals are now annually killed. On the other hand, in some cases, as with the elephant and rhinoceros, none are destroyed by beasts of prey: even the tiger in India most rarely dares to attack a young elephant protected by its dam.

Climate plays an important part in determining the average numbers of a species, and periodical seasons of extreme cold or drought, I believe to be the most effective of all checks. I estimated that the winter of 1854–55 destroyed four-fifths of the birds in my own grounds; and this is a tremendous destruction, when we remember that ten per cent. is an extraordinarily severe mortality from epidemics with man. The action of climate seems at first sight to be quite independent of the struggle for existence; but in so far as climate chiefly acts in reducing food, it brings on the most severe struggle between the individuals, whether of the same or of distinct species, which subsist on the same kind of food. Even when climate, for instance extreme cold, acts directly, it will be the least vigorous, or those which have got least food through the advancing winter, which will suffer most. When we travel from south to north, or from a damp region to a dry, we invariably see some species gradually getting rarer and rarer, and finally disappearing; and the change of climate being conspicuous, we are tempted to attribute the whole effect to its direct action. But this is a very false view: we forget that each species, even where it most abounds, is constantly suffering enormous destruction at some period of its life, from enemies or from competitors for the same place and food; and if these enemies or competitors be in the least degree favoured by any slight change of climate, they will increase in numbers, and, as each area is already fully stocked with inhabitants, the other species will decrease. * * *

That climate acts in main part indirectly by favouring other species, we may clearly see in the prodigious number of plants in our gardens which can perfectly well endure our climate, but which never become naturalised, for they cannot compete with our native plants, nor resist destruction by our native animals. * * *

Many cases are on record showing how complex and unexpected are the checks and relations between organic beings, which have to struggle together in the same country. I will give only a single instance, which, though a simple one, has interested me. In Staffordshire, on the estate of a relation where I had ample means of investigation, there was a large and extremely barren heath, which had never been touched by the hand of man; but several hundred acres of exactly the same nature had been enclosed twenty-five years previously and planted with Scotch fir. The change in the native vegetation of the planted part of the heath was most remarkable, more than is generally seen in passing from one quite different soil to another: not only the proportional numbers of the heath-plants were wholly changed, but twelve species of plants (not counting grasses and carices) flourished in the plantations, which could not be found on the heath. The effect on the insects must have been still greater, for six insectivorous birds were very common in the plantations, which were not to be seen on the heath; and the heath was frequented by two or three distinct insectivorous birds. Here we see how potent has been the effect of the introduction of a single tree, nothing whatever else having been done, with the exception that the land had been enclosed, so that cattle could not enter. * * *

A corollary of the highest importance may be deduced from the foregoing remarks, namely, that the structure of every organic being is related, in the most essential yet often hidden manner, to that of all other organic beings, with which it comes into competition for food or residence, or from which it has to escape, or on which it preys. This is obvious in the structure of the teeth and talons of the tiger; and in that of the legs and claws of the parasite which clings to the hair on the tiger's body. But in the beautifully plumed seed of the dandelion, and in the flattened and fringed legs of the water-beetle, the relation seems at first confined to the elements of air and water. Yet the advantage of plumed seeds no doubt stands in the closest relation to the land being already thickly clothed by other plants; so that the seeds may be widely distributed and fall on unoccupied ground. In the water-beetle, the structure of its legs, so well adapted for diving, allows it to compete with other aquatic insects, to hunt for its own prey, and to escape serving as prey to other animals.

The store of nutriment laid up within the seeds of many plants seems at first sight to have no sort of relation to other plants. But from the strong growth of young plants produced from such seeds (as peas and beans), when sown in the midst of long grass, I suspect that the chief use of the nutriment in the seed is to favour the growth of the young seedling, whilst struggling with other plants growing vigorously all around.

Look at a plant in the midst of its range, why does it not double or quadruple its numbers? We know that it can perfectly well withstand a little more heat or cold, dampness or dryness, for elsewhere it ranges into slightly hotter or colder, damper or drier districts. In this case we can clearly see that if we wished in imagination to give the plant the power of increasing in number, we should have to give it some advantage over its competitors, or over the animals which preyed on it. On the confines of its geographical range, a change of constitution with respect to climate would clearly be an advantage to our plant; but we have reason to believe that only a few plants or animals range so far, that they are destroyed by the rigour of the climate alone. Not until we reach the extreme confines of life, in the arctic regions or on the borders of an utter desert, will competition cease. The land may be extremely cold or dry, yet there will be competition between some few species, or between the individuals of the same species, for the warmest or dampest spots.

Hence, also, we can see that when a plant or animal is placed in a new country amongst new competitors, though the climate may be exactly the same as in its former home, yet the conditions of its life will generally be changed in an essential manner. If we wished to increase its average numbers in its new home, we should have to modify it in a different way to what we should have done in its native country; for we should have to give it some advantage over a different set of competitors or enemies.

It is good thus to try in our imagination to give any form some advantage over another. Probably in no single instance should we know what to do, so as to succeed. It will convince us of our ignorance on the mutual relations of all organic beings; a conviction as necessary, as it seems to be difficult to acquire. All that we can do, is to keep steadily in mind that each organic being is striving to increase at a geometrical ratio; that each at some period of its life, during some season of the year, during each generation or at intervals, has to struggle for life, and to suffer great destruction. When we reflect on this struggle, we may console ourselves with the full belief, that the war of nature is not incessant, that no fear is felt, that death is generally prompt, and that the vigorous, the healthy, and the happy survive and multiply.

≈+ PERSPECTIVES +≈
Religion and Science

"If only the Geologists would let me alone, I could do very well, but those dreadful Hammers! I hear the clink of them at the end of every cadence of the Bible verses." John Ruskin's anxious words reflect the widespread fear that science was chipping away at the foundations of faith. The fossil record showed that the earth was vastly older than anyone had thought, thus casting doubt on the biblical account of Creation, conventionally dated around four thousand years before the birth of Christ. Suddenly a scale of millions and even billions of years was being employed. "The riddle of the rocks" having been deciphered, the physicist John Tyndall said in 1874, "the leaves of that stone book . . . carry the mind back into abysses of past time."

Yet, far from being opposed to science, many early Victorian clergymen were amateur geologists and naturalists. The word "scientist" did not even exist until 1840, and science was scarcely imagined as an independent profession: for all his love of natural history, Charles Darwin studied to be a clergyman. In his day, it was common to take a university degree with no scientific education at all. Until the mid-nineteenth century, science and religion had often been seen as being in harmony. In *Natural Theology* (1802) the philosopher and Anglican priest William Paley had proposed a famous analogy: when we see a complex mechanism such as a watch, we infer that the watch must have had a maker; similarly, when we see the order and beauty of the universe, we must infer the existence of a Creator. Paley's "Argument from Design" was enormously influential. As the geologist Hugh Miller put it, "I am confident that there is not half the ingenuity, or half the mathematical knowledge, displayed in the dome of St Paul's at London, that we find exhibited in the construction of this simple shell."

Increasingly, though, scientists began to question the evidence of God's artistry. In *Principles of Geology* (1830–1833), Charles Lyell argued that geological phenomena resulted from the gradual actions of nature over immense stretches of time. And in 1859, Darwin's *The Origin of Species* extended this perspective to the formation of living creatures, including human beings. Years of scientific observations had convinced him that the animate world is not the product of divine creation but of natural selection: "We can no longer argue that, for instance, the beautiful hinge of a bivalve shell must have been made by an intelligent being. . . . There seems to be no more design in the variability of organic beings and in the action of natural selection, than in the course which the wind blows."

Scientific methods, moreover, were being applied to the study of the Bible itself. Even as scientists undermined "natural" theology, a new wave of biblical criticism from Germany undermined the "revealed" theology given in the Bible. These scholars treated Scripture like any other text, probing into questions of dates and sources, authorship and authenticity. They concluded that Moses could not have written the Pentateuch, and that many episodes in the Bible could not be regarded as historically accurate; some even denied that Jesus was the son of God.

The claims of both science and the "Higher Criticism" provoked storms of controversy. They shattered certainties about the nature of truth, the meaning of life, and man's place in the universe. The historian J. A. Froude recalled the 1840s as a period when "All round us, the intellectual lightships had broken from their moorings. . . . The present generation . . . will never know what it was to find the lights all drifting, the compasses all awry, and nothing left to steer by except the stars." This was not only a personal problem; many assumed that a collapse of Christian faith would lead to the disintegration of society as a whole. The critic Walter Houghton points out the connection to the fear of revolution: in the reviews of *The Descent of Man* (1871) Darwin was severely censured for "revealing his zoological conclusions to the general public at a moment when the sky of Paris was red with the incendiary flames of the Commune."

Some—particularly the literal-minded Evangelicals—reacted to these upheavals by denying any validity to the new scientific theories; others struggled to repress their concerns. The educator Thomas Arnold suggested that doubts "should be kept, I think, to ourselves, and not talked of even to our nearest friends." If we put a searching question to our neighbor, wrote Ruskin, we risk discovering "that he doubts of many things which we ourselves do not believe strongly enough to hear doubted without danger." To some Victorians, on the other hand, the new theories offered an opportunity for a fresh assessment of long-unquestioned beliefs. George Eliot wrote with exhilaration that her soul had been "liberated from the wretched giant's bed of dogmas on which it has been racked and stretched." The philosopher Leslie Stephen welcomed agnosticism: "I did not feel that the solid ground was giving way beneath my feet, but rather that I was being relieved of a cumbrous burden."

Stopping short of agnosticism, the liberal "Broad Church" centrists of the Church of England sought a clarified, "demythologized" faith, finding moral rather than historical truths in the old stories of creation. At times they treated even Jesus' miracles as more on a par with his parables than as crucial historical events. Bishop William Colenso's careful weighing of historical probabilities, excerpted below, struck many of his first readers as scandalous, but over time mainstream Church of England thought came to accept a comparable coexistence of myth and history in the biblical stories. The book of nature and the book of the acts of God alike now required active and engaged readers, in a world less of facts and certainties than of hypotheses and interpretations.

◆━━ ▅◈▅ ━━◆

Thomas Babington Macaulay
1800–1859

Always a staunch believer in material progress, Macaulay extolled scientific achievements as entirely beneficial for society. In 1837 his lavish and unqualified praise of applied science did not jar any sensibilities, for religion and science had not yet clashed as violently as they were to do later in the century. Railroads and steamships, feats of engineering and astronomy, military and industrial technology—it was still possible to admire them all unreservedly. Macaulay's enthusiasm for science was untempered by any sense of the possible dangers of science, or of the threat science would soon pose to the very foundations of religious belief.

An additional work by Macaulay is included in Perspectives: The Industrial Landscape, page 491.

from **Lord Bacon**
[SCIENCE AS PROGRESS]

It has lengthened life; it has mitigated pain; it has extinguished diseases; it has increased the fertility of the soil; it has given new securities to the mariner; it has furnished new arms to the warrior; it has spanned great rivers and estuaries with bridges of form unknown to our fathers; it has guided the thunderbolt innocuously from heaven to earth; it has lighted up the night with the splendour of the day; it has extended the range of the human vision; it has multiplied the power of the human muscles; it has accelerated motion; it has annihilated distance; it has facilitated intercourse, correspondence, all friendly offices, all despatch of business; it has enabled man to descend to the depths of the sea, to soar into the air, to penetrate securely into the noxious recesses of the earth, to traverse the land in cars which whirl along without horses, and the ocean in ships which run ten knots an hour against the wind. These are but a part of its fruits, and of its first fruits. For it is a philosophy which never rests, which has never attained, which is never perfect. Its law is progress. A point which yesterday was invisible is its goal today, and will be its starting-post to-morrow.

1837

Charles Dickens
1812–1870

Victorian morality permeated British life in the mid-nineteenth century—but there was sharp disagreement as to how that morality should be fostered and expressed. In this selection, Dickens argues passionately for a relaxed standard of Sunday observance, against the strict rules that the Evangelicals were attempting to legislate. A broadly based group that included Methodists, Congregationalists, Baptists, and "Low Church" Anglicans, Evangelicals were concerned not only with individual salvation (through rigorous conduct, prayer, and Bible reading) but also with the moral reform of society. In the mid-1830s, Sir Andrew Agnew repeatedly proposed a Sunday Observance Bill in Parliament. As Dickens points out in his scathing attack, the effects of the Bill would have been felt disproportionately by the lower classes, for whom Sunday was the only day of relaxation; he argues that the cause of religion itself, as well as working people's well-being, would be harmed by overly strict observance.

from Sunday Under Three Heads

The provisions of the bill introduced into the House of Commons by Sir Andrew Agnew, and thrown out by that House on the motion for the second reading, on the 18th of May in the present year, by a majority of 32, may very fairly be taken as a test of the length to which the fanatics, of which the honourable Baronet is the distinguished leader, are prepared to go. * * *

The proposed enactments of the bill are briefly these:—All work is prohibited on the Lord's day, under heavy penalties, increasing with every repetition of the offence. There are penalties for keeping shops open—penalties for drunkenness—penalties for keeping open houses of entertainment—penalties for being present at any public meeting or assembly—penalties for letting carriages, and penalties for hiring them—penalties for travelling in steam-boats, and penalties for taking passengers—penalties on vessels commencing their voyage on Sundays—penalties on the owners of cattle who suffer them to be driven on the Lord's day—penalties on constables who refuse to act, and penalties for resisting them when they do. In addition to these trifles, the constables are invested with arbitrary, vexatious, and most extensive powers; and all this in a bill which sets out with the hypocritical and canting declaration that "nothing is more acceptable to God than the *true and sincere* worship of Him according to His holy will, and that it is the bounden duty of Parliament to promote the observance of the Lord's day, by protecting every class of society against being required to sacrifice their comfort, health, religious privileges, and conscience, for the convenience, enjoyment, or supposed advantage of any other class on the Lord's day"! The idea of making a man truly moral through the ministry of constables, and sincerely religious under the influence of penalties, is worthy of the mind which could form such a mass of monstrous absurdity as this bill is composed of. * * *

In the first place, it is by no means the worst characteristic of this bill, that it is a bill of blunders: it is, from beginning to end, a piece of deliberate cruelty, and crafty injustice. If the rich composed the whole population of this country, not a single comfort of one single man would be affected by it. It is directed exclusively, and without the exception of a solitary instance, against the amusements and recreations of the poor. * * *

Take the very first clause, the provision that no man shall be allowed to work on Sunday—"That no person, upon the Lord's day, shall do, or hire, or employ any person to do any manner of labour, or any work of his or her ordinary calling." What class of persons does this affect? The rich man? No. Menial servants, both male and female, are specially exempted from the operation of the bill. "Menial servants" are among the poor people. The bill has no regard for them. The Baronet's dinner must be cooked on Sunday, the Bishop's horses must be groomed, and the Peer's carriage must be driven. So the menial servants are put utterly beyond the pale of grace;— unless indeed, they are to go to heaven through the sanctity of their masters, and possibly they might think even that, rather an uncertain passport. * * *

With one exception, there are perhaps no clauses in the whole bill, so strongly illustrative of its partial operation, and the intention of its framer, as those which relate to travelling on Sunday. Penalties of ten, twenty, and thirty pounds, are mercilessly imposed upon coach proprietors who shall run their coaches on the Sabbath; one, two, and ten pounds upon those who hire, or let to hire, horses and carriages upon the Lord's day, but not one syllable about those who have no necessity to hire, because they have carriages and horses of their own; not one word of a penalty on liveried coachmen and footmen. The whole of the saintly venom is directed against the hired cabriolet, the humble fly, or the rumbling hackney coach, which enables a man of the poorer class to escape for a few hours from the smoke and dirt, in the midst of which he has been confined throughout the week: while the escutcheoned[1] carriage and the dashing cab, may whirl their wealthy owners to Sunday feasts and private oratorios, setting constables, informers, and penalties, at defiance. Again, in the description of the places of public resort which it is rendered criminal to attend on Sunday, there are no words comprising a very fashionable promenade. Public discussions, public debates, public lectures and speeches, are cautiously guarded against; for it is by their means that the people become enlightened enough, to deride the last efforts of bigotry and superstition. There is a stringent provision for punishing the poor man who spends an hour in a news-room, but there is nothing to prevent the rich one, from lounging away the day in the Zoological Gardens.

There is, in four words, a mock proviso, which affects to forbid travelling "with any animal" on the Lord's day. This, however, is revoked, as relates to the rich man, by a subsequent provision. We have then a penalty of not less than fifty, nor more than one hundred pounds, upon any person participating in the controul, or having the command of any vessel which shall commence her voyage on the Lord's day, should the wind prove favourable. The next time this bill is brought forward (which will no doubt be at an early period of the next session of Parliament) perhaps it will be better to amend this clause by declaring, that from and after the passing of the act, it shall be deemed unlawful for the wind to blow at all upon the Sabbath. It would remove a great deal of temptation from the owners and captains of vessels. * * *

---

1. Bearing a coat of arms.

Let us suppose such a bill as this, to have actually passed both branches of the legislature; to have received the royal assent; and to have come into operation. Imagine its effect in a great city like London.

Sunday comes, and brings with it a day of general gloom and austerity. The man who has been toiling hard all the week, has been looking towards the Sabbath, not as to a day of rest from labour, and healthy recreation, but as one of grievous tyranny and grinding oppression. The day which his Maker intended as a blessing, man has converted into a curse. Instead of being hailed by him as his period of relaxation, he finds it remarkable only as depriving him of every comfort and enjoyment. He has many children about him, all sent into the world at an early age, to struggle for a livelihood; one is kept in a warehouse all day, with an interval of rest too short to enable him to reach home, another walks four or five miles to his employment at the docks, a third earns a few shillings weekly, as an errand boy, or office messenger; and the employment of the man himself, detains him at some distance from his home from morning till night. Sunday is the only day on which they could all meet together, and enjoy a homely meal in social comfort; and now they sit down to a cold and cheerless dinner: the pious guardians of the man's salvation, having, in their regard for the welfare of his precious soul, shut up the bakers' shops.[2] The fire blazes high in the kitchen chimney of these well-fed hypocrites, and the rich steams of the savoury dinner scent the air. What care they to be told that this class of men have neither a place to cook in—nor means to bear the expense, if they had?

Look into your churches—diminished congregations, and scanty attendance. People have grown sullen and obstinate, and are becoming disgusted with the faith which condemns them to such a day as this, once in every seven. And as you cannot make people religious by Act of Parliament, or force them to church by constables, they display their feeling by staying away.

Turn into the streets, and mark the rigid gloom that reigns over everything around. The roads are empty, the fields are deserted, the houses of entertainment are closed. Groups of filthy and discontented-looking men, are idling about at the street corners, or sleeping in the sun; but there are no decently-dressed people of the poorer class, passing to and fro. Where should they walk to? It would take them an hour, at least, to get into the fields, and when they reached them, they could procure neither bit nor sup, without the informer and the penalty. Now and then, a carriage rolls smoothly on, or a well-mounted horseman followed by a liveried attendant, canters by; but with these exceptions, all is as melancholy and quiet, as if a pestilence had fallen on the city.

Bend your steps through the narrow and thickly-inhabited streets, and observe the sallow faces of the men and women, who are lounging at the doors, or lolling from the windows. Regard well, the closeness of these crowded rooms, and the noisome exhalations that rise from the drains and kennels; and then laud the triumph of religion and morality, which condemns people to drag their lives out in such stews[3] as these, and makes it criminal for them to eat or drink in the fresh air, or under the clear sky. * * *

It may be asked, what motives can actuate a man who has so little regard for the comfort of his fellow-beings, so little respect for their wants and necessities, and so distorted a notion of the beneficence of his Creator. I reply, an envious, heartless,

---

2. Lacking ovens at home, working people brought their dinners to cook at bakers' shops on Sundays. Dickens returned to the subject in *A Christmas Carol*, where the reformed Scrooge is indignant about Sunday closings, particularly of bakeries.

3. Overheated, congested areas.

ill-conditioned dislike, to seeing those whom fortune has placed below him, cheerful and happy—an intolerant confidence in his own high worthiness before God, and a lofty impression of the demerits of others—pride, selfish pride, as inconsistent with the spirit of Christianity itself, as opposed to the example of its Founder upon earth.

1836

David Friedrich Strauss
1808–1874

Evolution and geology were not the only threats to traditional Christian faith: German scholars who applied methods of historical and literary analysis to the Bible demonstrated that it was, as the historian J. A. Froude put it, "a human composition—parts of it of doubtful authenticity." Such scholarship, known as the "higher criticism," undermined the Bible's stature as divine revelation. Biblical criticism made Charles Kingsley, the Anglican clergyman associated with "Muscular Christianity," feel as though he were standing "on a cliff which is crumbling beneath one, and falling piecemeal into the dark sea." But it liberated George Eliot from her evangelical beliefs. In 1846 she helped bring German scholarship to the attention of the British public with her translation, excerpted here, of *Das Leben Jesu*, David Friedrich Strauss's controversial treatment of Jesus as an historical figure, not the son of God.

from The Life of Jesus Critically Examined
Translated by George Eliot

Having shown the possible existence of the mythical and the legendary in the gospels, both on extrinsic and intrinsic grounds, and defined their distinctive characteristics, it remains in conclusion to inquire how their actual presence may be recognized in individual cases?

The mythus[1] presents two phases; in the first place it is not history; in the second it is fiction, the product of the particular mental tendency of a certain community. These two phases afford the one a negative, the other a positive criterion, by which the mythus is to be recognized.

I. *Negative*. That an account is not historical—that the matter related could not have taken place in the manner described is evident.

First. When the narration is irreconcileable with the known and universal laws which govern the course of events. * * *

Secondly. An account which shall be regarded as historically valid must neither be inconsistent with itself, nor in contradiction with other accounts. * * *

It may here be asked: is it to be regarded as a contradiction if one account is wholly silent respecting a circumstance mentioned by another? In itself, apart from all other considerations, the argumentum ex silentio is of no weight; but it is certainly to be accounted of moment when, at the same time, it may be shown that had the author known the circumstance he could not have failed to mention it, and also that he must have known it had it actually occurred.

II. *Positive*. The positive characters of legend and fiction are to be recognized sometimes in the form, sometimes in the substance of a narrative.

---

1. Myth; this was a contentious word to use in connection with Scripture.

If the form be poetical, if the actors converse in hymns, and in a more diffuse and elevated strain than might be expected from their training and situations, such discourses, at all events, are not to be regarded as historical. The absence of these marks of the unhistorical do not however prove the historical validity of the narration, since the mythus often wears the most simple and apparently historical form: in which case the proof lies in the substance.

If the contents of a narrative strikingly accords with certain ideas existing and prevailing within the circle from which the narrative proceeded, which ideas themselves seem to be the product of preconceived opinions rather than of practical experience, it is more or less probable, according to circumstances, that such a narrative is of mythical origin. The knowledge of the fact, that the Jews were fond of representing their great men as the children of parents who had long been childless, cannot but make us doubtful of the historical truth of the statement that this was the case with John the Baptist;[2] knowing also that the Jews saw predictions every where in the writings of their prophets and poets, and discovered types[3] of the Messiah in all the lives of holy men recorded in their Scriptures; when we find details in the life of Jesus evidently sketched after the pattern of these prophecies and prototypes, we cannot but suspect that they are rather mythical than historical. * * *

Yet each of these tests, on the one hand, and each narrative on the other, considered apart, will rarely prove more than the possible or probable unhistorical character of the record. The concurrence of several such indications, is necessary to bring about a more definite result. The accounts of the visit of the Magi, and of the murder of the innocents at Bethlehem, harmonize remarkably with the Jewish Messianic notion, built upon the prophecy of Balaam, respecting the star which should come out of Jacob; and with the history of the sanguinary command of Pharaoh.[4] Still this would not alone suffice to stamp the narratives as mythical. But we have also the corroborative facts that the described appearance of the star is contrary to the physical, the alleged conduct of Herod to the psychological laws; that Josephus,[5] who gives in other respects so circumstantial an account of Herod, agrees with all other historical authorities in being silent concerning the Bethlehem massacre; and that the visit of the Magi together with the flight into Egypt related in the one Gospel, and the presentation in the temple related in another Gospel, mutually exclude one another.[6] Wherever, as in this instance, the several criteria of the mythical character concur, the result is certain, and certain in proportion to the accumulation of such grounds of evidence. * * *

In these last remarks we are, to a certain extent, anticipating the question which is, in conclusion, to be considered: viz., whether the mythical character is restricted to those features of the narrative, upon which such character is actually stamped; and whether a contradiction between two accounts invalidates one account only, or both? That is to say, what is the precise boundary line between the historical and the unhistorical?—the most difficult question in the whole province of criticism.

2. Elizabeth, the mother of John the Baptist, was well past childbearing years when he was born. See Luke 1.5–25.
3. Antecedents who foreshadowed the coming of the Messiah.
4. The Magi were the three kings or wise men who visited the infant Jesus (Matthew 2.1); the "murder of the innocents" refers to King Herod's slaughter of all the male infants in Bethlehem (Matthew 2.16); Balaam's words in Numbers 24.17 have been interpreted as a prophecy concerning Jesus; the Pharaoh of Egypt, fearing the people of Israel, plotted to kill all the male infants born to them (Exodus 1.8, 22).
5. Flavius Josephus (37–c.100), Jewish historian.
6. Joseph and Mary fled into Egypt with their child, Jesus, after a dream warning of the wrath of Herod (Matthew 2.13–15); when Jesus was 12, his parents took him to the Temple in Jerusalem, where he amazed the rabbis with his wisdom (Luke 2.41–52).

In the first place, when two narratives mutually exclude one another, one only is thereby proved to be unhistorical. If one be true the other must be false, but though the one be false the other may be true. Thus, in reference to the original residence of the parents of Jesus, we are justified in adopting the account of Luke which places it at Nazareth, to the exclusion of that of Matthew, which plainly supposes it to have been at Bethlehem; and, generally speaking, when we have to choose between two irreconcileable accounts, in selecting as historical that which is the least opposed to the laws of nature, and has the least correspondence with certain national or party opinions. But upon a more particular consideration it will appear that, since one account is false, it is possible that the other may be so likewise: the existence of a mythus respecting some certain point, shows that the imagination has been active in reference to that particular subject; (we need only refer to the genealogies); and the historical accuracy of either of two such accounts cannot be relied upon, unless substantiated by its agreement with some other well-authenticated testimony.

Concerning the different parts of one and the same narrative: it might be thought for example, that though the appearance of an angel, and his announcement to Mary that she should be the Mother of the Messiah,[7] must certainly be regarded as unhistorical, still, that Mary should have indulged this hope before the birth of the child, is not in itself incredible. But what should have excited this hope in Mary's mind? It is at once apparent that that which is credible in itself is nevertheless unhistorical when it is so intimately connected with what is incredible that, if you discard the latter, you at the same time remove the basis on which the former rests. * * *

The following examples will serve to illustrate the mode of deciding in such cases. According to the narrative, as Mary entered the house and saluted her cousin Elizabeth, who was then pregnant, the babe leaped in her womb, she was filled with the Holy Ghost, and she immediately addressed Mary as the mother of the Messiah. This account bears indubitable marks of an unhistorical character. Yet, it is not, in itself, impossible that Mary should have paid a visit to her cousin, during which every thing went on quite naturally. The fact is, however, that there are psychological difficulties connected with this journey of the betrothed; and that the visit, and even the relationship of the two women, seem to have originated entirely in the wish to exhibit a connexion between the mother of John the Baptist, and the mother of the Messiah. Or when in the history of the transfiguration[8] it is stated, that the men who appeared with Jesus on the Mount were Moses and Elias; and that the brilliancy which illuminated Jesus was supernatural; it might seem here also that, after deducting the marvellous, the presence of two men and a bright morning beam might be retained as the historical facts. But the legend was predisposed, by virtue of the current idea concerning the relation of the Messiah to these two prophets, not merely to make any two men (whose persons, object, and conduct, if they were not what the narrative represents them, remain in the highest degree mysterious) into Moses and Elias, but to create the whole occurrence; and in like manner not merely to conceive of some certain illumination as a supernatural effulgence (which, if a natural one, is much exaggerated and misrepresented), but to create it at once after the pattern of the brightness which illuminated the face of Moses on Mount Sinai.

---

7. See Luke 1.26.
8. Jesus took several disciples up a mountain, "And was transfigured before them: and his face did shine as the sun, and his raiment was white as the light. And, behold, there appeared unto them Moses and Elias talking with him" (Matthew 17.1–3).

Hence is derived the following rule. Where not merely the particular nature and manner of an occurrence is critically suspicious, its external circumstances represented as miraculous and the like; but where likewise the essential substance and groundwork is either inconceivable in itself, or is in striking harmony with some Messianic idea of the Jews of that age, then not the particular alleged course and mode of the transaction only, but the entire occurrence must be regarded as unhistorical. Where on the contrary, the form only, and not the general contents of the narration, exhibits the characteristics of the unhistorical, it is at least possible to suppose a kernel of historical fact; although we can never confidently decide whether this kernel of fact actually exists, or in what it consists; unless, indeed, it be discoverable from other sources. In legendary narratives, or narratives embellished by the writer, it is less difficult,—by divesting them of all that betrays itself as fictitious imagery, exaggeration, &c.—by endeavouring to abstract from them every extraneous adjunct and to fill up every hiatus—to succeed, proximately at least, in separating the historical groundwork.

The boundary line, however, between the historical and the unhistorical, in records, in which as in our Gospels this latter element is incorporated, will ever remain fluctuating and unsusceptible of precise attainment. Least of all can it be expected that the first comprehensive attempt to treat these records from a critical point of view should be successful in drawing a sharply defined line of demarcation. In the obscurity which criticism has produced, by the extinction of all lights hitherto held historical, the eye must accustom itself by degrees to discriminate objects with precision; and at all events the author of this work, wishes especially to guard himself, in those places where he declares he knows not what happened, from the imputation of asserting that he knows that nothing happened.

1835; 1846

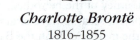

Charlotte Brontë
1816–1855

Charlotte Brontë's savage portrait in her novel *Jane Eyre* of an evangelical clergyman as a sadistic and hypocritical bully is based on a real-life figure, the founder of the school where her two elder sisters died. The Reverend Mr. Brocklehurst, who hectors a small child about death and hell-fire, represents the worst excesses of the Evangelical movement. Convinced of mankind's essentially sinful nature, Evangelicals stressed Bible reading, prayer, and regular examinations of conscience as the means to salvation. Brontë satirizes the self-serving piety which urges humility and self-denial on others—particularly dependents—while complacently exempting itself.

from Jane Eyre

I feared to return to the nursery, and feared to go forward to the parlour; ten minutes I stood in agitated hesitation; the vehement ringing of the breakfast-room bell decided me; I *must* enter.

"Who could want me?" I asked inwardly, as with both hands I turned the stiff door-handle which, for a second or two, resisted my efforts. "What should I see besides Aunt Reed in the apartment?—a man or a woman?" The handle turned, the door unclosed, and passing through and curtseying low, I looked up at—a black pillar!—such, at least, appeared to me, at first sight, the straight, narrow, sable-clad shape standing erect on the rug; the grim face at the top was like a carved mask, placed above the shaft by way of capital.

Mrs Reed occupied her usual seat by the fireside; she made a signal to me to approach; I did so, and she introduced me to the stony stranger with the words—

"This is the little girl respecting whom I applied to you."

He—for it was a man—turned his head slowly towards where I stood, and having examined me with the two inquisitive looking gray eyes which twinkled under a pair of bushy brows, said solemnly, and in a bass voice—

"Her size is small; what is her age?"

"Ten years."

"So much?" was the doubtful answer; and he prolonged his scrutiny for some minutes. Presently he addressed me—

"Your name, little girl?"

"Jane Eyre, sir."

In uttering these words I looked up: he seemed to me a tall gentleman, but then I was very little; his features were large, and they and all the lines of his frame were equally harsh and prim.

"Well, Jane Eyre, and are you a good child?"

Impossible to reply to this in the affirmative: my little world held a contrary opinion: I was silent. Mrs Reed answered for me by an expressive shake of the head, adding soon, "Perhaps the less said on that subject the better, Mr Brocklehurst."

"Sorry indeed to hear it! She and I must have some talk"; and bending from the perpendicular, he installed his person in the arm-chair, opposite Mrs Reed's. "Come here," he said.

I stepped across the rug: he placed me square and straight before him. What a face he had, now that it was almost on a level with mine! what a great nose! and what a mouth! and what large, prominent teeth!

"No sight so sad as that of a naughty child," he began, "especially a naughty little girl. Do you know where the wicked go after death?"

"They go to hell," was my ready and orthodox answer.

"And what is hell? Can you tell me that?"

"A pit full of fire."

"And should you like to fall into that pit, and to be burning there for ever?"

"No, sir."

"What must you do to avoid it?"

I deliberated a moment: my answer, when it did come, was objectionable: "I must keep in good health, and not die."

"How can you keep in good health? Children younger than you die daily. I buried a little child of five years old only a day or two since—a good little child, whose soul is now in heaven. It is to be feared the same could not be said of you, were you to be called thence."

Not being in a condition to remove his doubt, I only cast my eyes down on the two large feet planted on the rug, and sighed, wishing myself far enough away.

"I hope that sigh is from the heart, and that you repent of ever having been the occasion of discomfort to your excellent benefactress."

"Benefactress! benefactress!" said I inwardly: "they all call Mrs Reed my benefactress; if so, a benefactress is a disagreeable thing."

"Do you say your prayers night and morning?" continued my interrogator.

"Yes, sir."

"Do you read your Bible?"

"Sometimes."

"With pleasure? Are you fond of it?"

"I like Revelations, and the Book of Daniel, and Genesis, and Samuel, and a little bit of Exodus, and some parts of Kings and Chronicles, and Job and Jonah."

"And the Psalms? I hope you like them?"

"No, sir."

"No? Oh, shocking! I have a little boy, younger than you, who knows six Psalms by heart: and when you ask him which he would rather have, a ginger-bread-nut to eat, or a verse of a Psalm to learn, he says: 'Oh! the verse of a Psalm! angels sing Psalms,' says he; 'I wish to be a little angel here below.' He then gets two nuts in recompense for his infant piety."

"Psalms are not interesting," I remarked.

"That proves you to have a wicked heart; and you must pray to God to change it: to give you a new and clean one: to take away your heart of stone and give you a heart of flesh."

I was about to propound a question, touching the manner in which that operation of changing my heart was to be performed, when Mrs Reed interposed, telling me to sit down; she then proceeded to carry on the conversation herself.

1847

—— ≡✦≡ ——

Arthur Hugh Clough
1819–1861

Clever, witty, and ironic, Arthur Hugh Clough satirized religious hypocrisy and bankrupt values. But his humor only thinly veiled his genuine concern at the erosion of Christianity's spiritual authority. Clough took religion seriously enough to resign his Oxford fellowship rather than subscribe to the Thirty-Nine Articles of Anglican doctrine. He used his poetry to probe the ways Victorians had adjusted their religion to suit an increasingly secular age. The title *Epi-strauss-ium* refers to David Friedrich Strauss, whose *Life of Jesus* denied the divinity of Christ: the poem concludes that the Sun/Son of God can still illuminate, despite skepticism about the authenticity of the gospels. *The Latest Decalogue* casts a cynical eye on a materialist version of the Ten Commandments. *"There is no God," the Wicked Saith*, a lyric interlude from his long poem *Dipsychus*, contrasts the self-absorption of doubters to those whose love, innocence, or suffering make them believers.

Epi-strauss-ium[1]

Matthew and Mark and Luke and holy John
Evanished all and gone!
Yea, he° that erst, his dusky curtains quitting,   *the sun*
Through Eastern pictured panes his level beams transmitting,
5   With gorgeous portraits blent,
On them his glories intercepted spent,

1. "On-Strauss-ism."

Southwestering now, through windows plainly glassed,
On the inside face his radiance keen hath cast,
And in the lustre lost, invisible and gone,
10 Are, say you, Matthew, Mark and Luke and holy John?
Lost, is it? lost, to be recovered never?
However,
The place of worship the meantime with light
Is, if less richly, more sincerely bright,
15 And in blue skies the Orb is manifest to sight.

1847   1869

The Latest Decalogue[1]

Thou shalt have one God only; who
Would be at the expense of two?
No graven images may be
Worshipped, except the currency:
5 Swear not at all; for for thy curse
Thine enemy is none the worse:
At church on Sunday to attend
Will serve to keep the world thy friend:
Honour thy parents; that is, all
10 From whom advancement may befall:

Thou shalt not kill; but needst not strive
Officiously to keep alive:
Do not adultery commit;
Advantage rarely comes of it:
15 Thou shalt not steal; an empty feat,
When it's so lucrative to cheat:
Bear not false witness; let the lie
Have time on its own wings to fly:
Thou shalt not covet; but tradition
20 Approves all forms of competition.

The sum of all is, thou shalt love,
If any body, God above:
At any rate shall never labour
More than thyself to love thy neighbour.

1862; 1951

from **Dipsychus**[1]
"There Is No God," the Wicked Saith

"There is no God," the wicked saith,
    "And truly it's a blessing,
For what he might have done with us
    It's better only guessing."

---

1. The Ten Commandments. The last four lines were not published until 1951; they were added from Clough's manuscript.

1. Dipsychus ("two-souled" or "of two minds") is the hero of a long poem by Clough, published in 1865; this excerpt from scene 5 was published separately in 1862.

5   "There is no God," a youngster thinks,
           "Or really, if there may be,
       He surely didn't mean a man
           Always to be a baby."

       "There is no God, or if there is,"
10   The tradesman thinks, "'twere funny
       If he should take it ill in me
           To make a little money."

       "Whether there be," the rich man says,
           "It matters very little,
15   For I and mine, thank somebody,
           Are not in want of victual."

       Some others, also, to themselves
           Who scarce so much as doubt it,
       Think there is none, when they are well,
20   And do not think about it.

       But country folks who live beneath
           The shadow of the steeple;
       The parson and the parson's wife,
           And mostly married people;

25   Youths green and happy in first love,
           So thankful for illusion;
       And men caught out in what the world
           Calls guilt, in first confusion;

       And almost every one when age,
30   Disease, or sorrows strike him,
       Inclines to think there is a God,
           Or something very like Him.

1850   1862

━━◆━━

John William Colenso
1814–1883

Shortly after *The Origin of Species* appeared in 1859, an even greater furor erupted, this time
with the publication of a work of biblical criticism written by an Anglican bishop. A mathematician who had become the Bishop of Natal in South Africa, Colenso was translating the
Scriptures into Zulu when he began to have doubts about their historical veracity. His knowledge of geology made him realize that the Flood "could not possibly have taken place." Further
research convinced him that Moses had not written the first five books of the Bible. Colenso
was angrily attacked for challenging the divine authenticity of the Bible—he was even accused
of insanity. He was deposed as bishop and excommunicated, though later reinstated. Colenso
argued, however, that a vital religious belief could not ultimately conflict with the findings of
historical scholarship, and that modern Christianity would be strengthened by being freed
from outdated mythological beliefs.

from The Pentateuch and Book of Joshua Critically Examined

You will, of course, expect that, since I have had the charge of this Diocese, I have been closely occupied in the study of the Zulu tongue, and in translating the Scriptures into it. Through the blessing of God, I have now translated the New Testament completely, and several parts of the Old, among the rest the books of Genesis and Exodus. In this work I have been aided by intelligent natives; and, having also published a Zulu Grammar and Dictionary, I have acquired sufficient knowledge of the language, to be able to have intimate communion with the native mind. * * *

Here, however, as I have said, amidst my work in this land, I have been brought face to face with the very questions which I then put by. While translating the story of the Flood, I have had a simple-minded, but intelligent, native,—one with the docility of a child, but the reasoning powers of mature age,—look up, and ask, "Is all that true? Do you really believe that all this happened thus,—that all the beasts, and birds, and creeping things, upon the earth, large and small, from hot countries and cold, came thus by pairs, and entered into the ark with Noah? And did Noah gather food for them *all*, for the beasts and birds of prey, as well as the rest?" My heart answered in the words of the Prophet, "Shall a man speak lies in the Name of the Lord?" Zech.xiii.3. I dared not do so. My own knowledge of some branches of science, of Geology in particular, had been much increased since I left England; and I now knew for certain, on geological grounds, a fact, of which I had only had misgivings before, viz. that a *Universal* Deluge, such as the Bible manifestly speaks of, could not possibly have taken place in the way described in the Book of Genesis, not to mention other difficulties which the story contains. * * * Of course, I am well aware that some have attempted to show that Noah's Deluge was only a *partial* one. But such attempts have ever seemed to me to be made in the very teeth of the Scripture statements, which are as plain and explicit as words can possibly be. Nor is anything really gained by supposing the Deluge to have been partial. For, as waters must find their own level on the Earth's surface, without a special miracle, of which the Bible says nothing, a Flood, which should begin by covering the top of Ararat,[1] (if that were conceivable), or a much lower mountain, must necessarily become universal, and in due time sweep over the hills of Auvergne.[2] Knowing this, I felt that I dared not, as a servant of the God of Truth, urge my brother man to believe that, which I did not myself believe, which I knew to be untrue, as a matter-of-fact, historical, narrative. I gave him, however, such a reply as satisfied him for the time, without throwing any discredit upon the general veracity of the Bible history.

But I was thus driven,—against my will at first, I may truly say,—to search more deeply into these questions; and I have since done so, to the best of my power, with the means at my disposal in this colony. And now I tremble at the result of my enquiries, rather, I should do so, were it not that I believe firmly in a God of Righteousness and Truth and Love, who both "IS, and is a rewarder of them that diligently seek him." * * *

The first five books of the Bible,—commonly called the Pentateuch (ἡ πεντα τευχος βιβλος, Pentateuchus, sc. liber), or Book of Five Volumes,—are supposed by most English readers of the Bible to have been written by Moses, except the last

---

1. A mountain in Turkey on which Noah's ark was supposed to have landed at the end of the Flood (Genesis 8.4).   2. Part of the Massif Central in France.

chapter of Deuteronomy, which records the death of Moses, and which, of course, it is generally allowed, must have been added by another hand, perhaps that of Joshua. It is believed that Moses wrote under such special guidance and teaching of the Holy Spirit, that he was preserved from making any error in recording those matters, which came within his own cognisance, and was instructed also in respect of events, which took place before he was born,—before, indeed, there was a human being on the earth to take note of what was passing. He was in this way, it is supposed, enabled to write a true account of the Creation. And, though the accounts of the Fall and of the Flood, as well as of later events, which happened in the time of Abraham, Isaac, and Jacob, may have been handed down by tradition from one generation to another, and even, some of them, perhaps, written down in words, or represented in hieroglyphics, and Moses may, probably, have derived assistance from these sources also in the composition of his narrative, yet in all his statements, it is believed, he was under such constant control and superintendence of the Spirit of God, that he was kept from making any serious error, and certainly from writing anything altogether untrue. We may rely with undoubting confidence—such is the statement usually made—on the historical veracity, and infallible accuracy, of the Mosaic narrative in all its main particulars. * * *

But, among the many results of that remarkable activity in scientific enquiry of every kind, which, by God's own gift, distinguishes the present age, this also must be reckoned, that attention and labour are now being bestowed, more closely and earnestly than ever before, to search into the real foundations for such a belief as this. * * * The time is come, as I believe, in the Providence of God, when this question can no longer be put by,—when it must be resolutely faced, and the whole matter fully and freely examined, if we would be faithful servants of the God of Truth. * * *

The result of my enquiry is this, that I have arrived at the conviction,—as painful to myself at first, as it may be to my reader, though painful now no longer under the clear shining of the Light of Truth,—that the Pentateuch, as a whole, cannot possibly have been written by Moses, or by any one acquainted personally with the facts which it professes to describe, and, further, that the (so-called) Mosaic narrative, by whomsoever written, and though imparting to us, as I fully believe it does, revelations of the Divine Will and Character, cannot be regarded as *historically true*.

1862

—≡◆≡—

John Henry Cardinal Newman
1801–1890

Newman's conversion to Catholicism in 1845 sent shock waves throughout England. Newman, an Anglican clergyman and a leading figure in the Oxford Movement, was well known for his efforts to construct a *via media*, or middle way, between Protestantism and Catholicism. But his struggle to locate the authority of the Anglican church in early church history gradually convinced him that Rome was right. Anti-Catholic feeling was strong, and Newman's "going over" was regarded as a terrible betrayal of his friends and colleagues. But when Charles Kingsley incautiously accused him of lying, Newman finally got a chance to explain his conversion to the public; the *Apologia Pro Vita Sua* became a classic of spiritual autobiography.

Unlike some of his contemporaries, whose religious beliefs were shaken by scientific discoveries and biblical criticism, Newman's faith never wavered: "Ten thousand difficulties do not make one doubt."

For more about Newman, see Perspectives: Victorian Ladies and Gentlemen, page 563.

from Apologia Pro Vita Sua

from Chapter 1. History of My Religious Opinions to the Year 1833

I was brought up from a child to take great delight in reading the Bible; but I had no formed religious convictions till I was fifteen. Of course I had a perfect knowledge of my Catechism.[1]

After I was grown up, I put on paper my recollections of the thoughts and feelings on religious subjects, which I had at the time that I was a child and a boy,—such as had remained on my mind with sufficient prominence to make me then consider them worth recording. Out of these, written in the Long Vacation of 1820, and transcribed with additions in 1823, I select two, which are at once the most definite among them, and also have a bearing on my later convictions.

1. "I used to wish the Arabian Tales were true: my imagination ran on unknown influences, on magical powers, and talismans. . . . I thought life might be a dream, or I an Angel, and all this world a deception, my fellow-angels by a playful device concealing themselves from me, and deceiving me with the semblance of a material world."

Again: "Reading in the Spring of 1816 a sentence from [Dr. Watts's] 'Remnants of Time,'[2] entitled 'the Saints unknown to the world,' to the effect, that 'there is nothing in their figure or countenance to distinguish them,' &c, &c, I supposed he spoke of Angels who lived in the world, as it were disguised."

2. The other remark is this: "I was very superstitious, and for some time previous to my conversion [when I was fifteen] used constantly to cross myself on going into the dark."

Of course I must have got this practice from some external source or other; but I can make no sort of conjecture whence; and certainly no one had ever spoken to me on the subject of the Catholic religion, which I only knew by name. The French master was an émigré Priest, but he was simply made a butt, as French masters too commonly were in that day, and spoke English very imperfectly. There was a Catholic family in the village, old maiden ladies we used to think; but I knew nothing about them. I have of late years heard that there were one or two Catholic boys in the school; but either we were carefully kept from knowing this, or the knowledge of it made simply no impression on our minds. My brother[3] will bear witness how free the school was from Catholic ideas. * * *

When I was fifteen, (in the autumn of 1816), a great change of thought took place in me. I fell under the influences of a definite Creed, and received into my intellect impressions of dogma, which, through God's mercy, have never been effaced or obscured. * * * [I] believed that the inward conversion of which I was conscious, (and of which I still am more certain than that I have hands and feet,) would last into the next life, and that I was elected to eternal glory. I have no consciousness

---

1. A summary of religious doctrine (in Newman's case, the Church of England's) set forth in a series of questions and answers.
2. Isaac Watts (1674–1748), Nonconformist cleric; the full title is The Improvement of the Mind, with a discourse

on Education, and the Remnants of Time, employed in prose and verse.
3. Francis William Newman (1805–1897), professor of Latin at University College, London, and a prominent freethinker.

that this belief had any tendency whatever to lead me to be careless about pleasing God. I retained it till the age of twenty-one, when it gradually faded away; but I believe that it had some influence on my opinions, in the direction of those childish imaginations which I have already mentioned, viz. in isolating me from the objects which surrounded me, in confirming me in my mistrust of the reality of material phenomena, and making me rest in the thought of two and two only absolute and luminously self-evident beings, myself and my Creator;—for while I considered myself predestined to salvation, my mind did not dwell upon others, as fancying them simply passed over, not predestined to eternal death. I only thought of the mercy to myself. * * *

Calvinists[4] make a sharp separation between the elect and the world; there is much in this that is cognate or parallel to the Catholic doctrine; but they go on to say, as I understand them, very differently from Catholicism,—that the converted and the unconverted can be discriminated by man, that the justified are conscious of their state of justification, and that the regenerate cannot fall away. Catholics on the other hand shade and soften the awful antagonism between good and evil, which is one of their dogmas, by holding that there are different degrees of justification, that there is a great difference in point of gravity between sin and sin, that there is the possibility and the danger of falling away, and that there is no certain knowledge given to any one that he is simply in a state of grace, and much less that he is to persevere to the end:—of the Calvinistic tenets the only one which took root in my mind was the fact of heaven and hell, divine favour and divine wrath, of the justified and the unjustified. The notion that the regenerate and the justified were one and the same, and that the regenerate, as such, had the gift of perseverance, remained with me not many years, as I have said already. * * *

I am obliged to mention, though I do it with great reluctance, another deep imagination, which at this time, the autumn of 1816, took possession of me,—there can be no mistake about the fact; viz. that it would be the will of God that I should lead a single life. This anticipation, which has held its ground almost continuously ever since,—with the break of a month now and a month then, up to 1829, and, after that date, without any break at all,—was more or less connected in my mind with the notion, that my calling in life would require such a sacrifice as celibacy involved; as, for instance, missionary work among the heathen, to which I had a great drawing for some years. It also strengthened my feeling of separation from the visible world, of which I have spoken above.

from *Chapter 5. The Position of My Mind Since 1845*

From the time that I became a Catholic, of course I have no further history of my religious opinions to narrate. In saying this, I do not mean to say that my mind has been idle, or that I have given up thinking on theological subjects; but that I have had no variations to record, and have had no anxiety of heart whatever. I have been in perfect peace and contentment; I never have had one doubt. I was not conscious to myself, on my conversion, of any change, intellectual or moral, wrought in my mind. I was not conscious of firmer faith in the fundamental truths of Revelation, or of more self-command; I had not more fervour; but it was like coming into port after a rough sea; and my happiness on that score remains to this day without interruption.

---

4. Followers of John Calvin (1509–1564), French theologian whose doctrines included predestination, the natural depravity of human beings, and salvation through God's grace.

Nor had I any trouble about receiving those additional articles, which are not found in the Anglican Creed. Some of them I believed already, but not any one of them was a trial to me. I made a profession of them upon my reception with the greatest ease, and I have the same ease in believing them now. I am far of course from denying that every article of the Christian Creed, whether as held by Catholics or by Protestants, is beset with intellectual difficulties; and it is simple fact, that, for myself, I cannot answer those difficulties. Many persons are very sensitive of the difficulties of Religion; I am as sensitive of them as any one; but I have never been able to see a connexion between apprehending those difficulties, however keenly, and multiplying them to any extent, and on the other hand doubting the doctrines to which they are attached. Ten thousand difficulties do not make one doubt, as I understand the subject; difficulty and doubt are incommensurate. There of course may be difficulties in the evidence; but I am speaking of difficulties intrinsic to the doctrines themselves, or to their relations with each other. A man may be annoyed that he cannot work out a mathematical problem, of which the answer is or is not given to him, without doubting that it admits of an answer, or that a certain particular answer is the true one. Of all points of faith, the being of a God is, to my own apprehension, encompassed with most difficulty, and yet borne in upon our minds with most power.

People say that the doctrine of Transubstantiation[1] is difficult to believe; I did not believe the doctrine till I was a Catholic. I had no difficulty in believing it, as soon as I believed that the Catholic Roman Church was the oracle of God, and that she had declared this doctrine to be part of the original revelation. It is difficult, impossible, to imagine, I grant;—but how is it difficult to believe? Yet Macaulay thought it so difficult to believe, that he had need of a believer in it of talents as eminent as Sir Thomas More,[2] before he could bring himself to conceive that the Catholics of an enlightened age could resist "the overwhelming force of the argument against it." "Sir Thomas More," he says, "is one of the choice specimens of wisdom and virtue; and the doctrine of transubstantiation is a kind of proof charge. A faith which stands that test, will stand any test." But for myself, I cannot indeed prove it, I cannot tell *how* it is; but I say, "Why should it not be? What's to hinder it? What do I know of substance or matter? just as much as the greatest philosophers, and that is nothing at all;"—so much is this the case, that there is a rising school of philosophy now, which considers phenomena to constitute the whole of our knowledge in physics. The Catholic doctrine leaves phenomena alone. It does not say that the phenomena go; on the contrary, it says that they remain; nor does it say that the same phenomena are in several places at once. It deals with what no one on earth knows any thing about, the material substances themselves. And, in like manner, of that majestic Article of the Anglican as well as of the Catholic Creed,—the doctrine of the Trinity in Unity.[3] What do I know of the Essence of the Divine Being? I know that my abstract idea of three is simply incompatible with my idea of one; but when I come to the question of concrete fact, I have no means of proving that there is not a sense in which one and three can equally be predicated of the Incommunicable God.

But I am going to take upon myself the responsibility of more than the mere Creed of the Church; as the parties accusing me are determined I shall do. They say, that now, in that I am a Catholic, though I may not have offences of my own against

1. Doctrine that the elements of bread and wine in the rite of Holy Communion are actually converted into the Body and Blood of Christ in all but external appearance.
2. Sir Thomas More (1478–1535) was an English statesman beheaded for his opposition to the church policy of Henry VIII. Macaulay invokes More in his 1840 review of Ranke's *History of the Popes*.
3. The belief that God is three (Father, Son, and Holy Spirit) and yet only one.

honesty to answer for, yet, at least, I am answerable for the offences of others, of my co-religionists, of my brother priests, of the Church herself. I am quite willing to accept the responsibility; and, as I have been able, as I trust, by means of a few words, to dissipate, in the minds of all those who do not begin with disbelieving me, the suspicion with which so many Protestants start, in forming their judgment of Catholics, viz. that our Creed is actually set up in inevitable superstition and hypocrisy, as the original sin of Catholicism; so now I will proceed, as before, identifying myself with the Church and vindicating it,—not of course denying the enormous mass of sin and error which exists of necessity in that world-wide multiform Communion,—but going to the proof of this one point, that its system is in no sense dishonest, and that therefore the upholders and teachers of that system, as such, have a claim to be acquitted in their own persons of that odious imputation.

Starting then with the being of a God, (which, as I have said, is as certain to me as the certainty of my own existence, though when I try to put the grounds of that certainty into logical shape I find a difficulty in doing so in mood and figure to my satisfaction,) I look out of myself into the world of men, and there I see a sight which fills me with unspeakable distress. The world seems simply to give the lie to that great truth, of which my whole being is so full; and the effect upon me is, in consequence, as a matter of necessity, as confusing as if it denied that I am in existence myself. If I looked into a mirror, and did not see my face, I should have the sort of feeling which actually comes upon me, when I look into this living busy world, and see no reflexion of its Creator. This is, to me, one of those great difficulties of this absolute primary truth, to which I referred just now. Were it not for this voice, speaking so clearly in my conscience and my heart, I should be an atheist, or a pantheist, or a polytheist when I looked into the world. I am speaking for myself only; and I am far from denying the real force of the arguments in proof of a God, drawn from the general facts of human society and the course of history, but these do not warm me or enlighten me; they do not take away the winter of my desolation, or make the buds unfold and the leaves grow within me, and my moral being rejoice. The sight of the world is nothing else than the prophet's scroll, full of "lamentations, and mourning, and woe."[4]

To consider the world in its length and breadth, its various history, the many races of man, their starts, their fortunes, their mutual alienation, their conflicts; and then their ways, habits, governments, forms of worship; their enterprises, their aimless courses, their random achievements and acquirements, the impotent conclusion of long-standing facts, the tokens so faint and broken of a superintending design, the blind evolution of what turn out to be great powers or truths, the progress of things, as if from unreasoning elements, not towards final causes, the greatness and littleness of man, his far-reaching aims, his short duration, the curtain hung over his futurity, the disappointments of life, the defeat of good, the success of evil, physical pain, mental anguish, the prevalence and intensity of sin, the pervading idolatries, the corruptions, the dreary hopeless irreligion, that condition of the whole race, so fearfully yet exactly described in the Apostle's words, "having no hope and without God in the world,"[5]—all this is a vision to dizzy and appal; and inflicts upon the mind the sense of a profound mystery, which is absolutely beyond human solution.

What shall be said to this heart-piercing, reason-bewildering fact? I can only answer, that either there is no Creator, or this living society of men is in a true sense discarded from His presence. Did I see a boy of good make and mind, with the tokens

4. Ezekiel 2.9–10.   5. Ephesians 2.12.

on him of a refined nature, cast upon the world without provision, unable to say whence he came, his birth-place or his family connexions, I should conclude that there was some mystery connected with his history, and that he was one, of whom, from one cause or other, his parents were ashamed. Thus only should I be able to account for the contrast between the promise and the condition of his being. And so I argue about the world;—*if* there be a God, *since* there is a God, the human race is implicated in some terrible aboriginal calamity. It is out of joint with the purposes of its Creator. This is a fact, a fact as true as the fact of its existence; and thus the doctrine of what is theologically called original sin becomes to me almost as certain as that the world exists, and as the existence of God.

And now, supposing it were the blessed and loving will of the Creator to interfere in this anarchical condition of things, what are we to suppose would be the methods which might be necessarily or naturally involved in His purpose of mercy? Since the world is in so abnormal a state, surely it would be no surprise to me, if the interposition were of necessity equally extraordinary—or what is called miraculous. But that subject does not directly come into the scope of my present remarks. Miracles as evidence, involve a process of reason, or an argument; and of course I am thinking of some mode of interference which does not immediately run into argument. I am rather asking what must be the face-to-face antagonist, by which to withstand and baffle the fierce energy of passion and the all-corroding, all-dissolving scepticism of the intellect in religious inquiries? I have no intention at all of denying, that truth is the real object of our reason, and that, if it does not attain to truth, either the premiss or the process is in fault; but I am not speaking here of right reason, but of reason as it acts in fact and concretely in fallen man. I know that even the unaided reason, when correctly exercised, leads to a belief in God, in the immortality of the soul, and in a future retribution; but I am considering the faculty of reason actually and historically; and in this point of view, I do not think I am wrong in saying that its tendency is towards a simple unbelief in matters of religion. No truth, however sacred, can stand against it, in the long run; and hence it is that in the pagan world, when our Lord came, the last traces of the religious knowledge of former times were all but disappearing from those portions of the world in which the intellect had been active and had had a career.

And in these latter days, in like manner, outside the Catholic Church things are tending,—with far greater rapidity than in that old time from the circumstance of the age,—to atheism in one shape or other. What a scene, what a prospect, does the whole of Europe present at this day! and not only Europe, but every government and every civilization through the world, which is under the influence of the European mind! Especially, for it most concerns us, how sorrowful, in the view of religion, even taken in its most elementary, most attenuated form, is the spectacle presented to us by the educated intellect of England, France, and Germany! Lovers of their country and of their race, religious men, external to the Catholic Church, have attempted various expedients to arrest fierce wilful human nature in its onward course, and to bring it into subjection. The necessity of some form of religion for the interests of humanity, has been generally acknowledged: but where was the concrete representative of things invisible, which would have the force and the toughness necessary to be a breakwater against the deluge? Three centuries ago the establishment of religion, material, legal, and social, was generally adopted as the best expedient for the purpose, in those countries which separated from the Catholic Church; and for a long time it was successful; but now the crevices of those establishments are admitting the enemy. Thirty years ago, education was relied upon: ten years ago there was a hope that wars would cease for ever, under the influence of commercial enterprise and the reign of the useful and fine arts; but will any one venture to say that there is any thing any where on this earth, which will afford a fulcrum for us, whereby to keep the earth from moving onwards? * * *

Supposing then it to be the Will of the Creator to interfere in human affairs, and to make provisions for retaining in the world a knowledge of Himself, so definite and distinct as to be proof against the energy of human scepticism, in such a case,—I am far from saying that there was no other way,—but there is nothing to surprise the mind, if He should think fit to introduce a power into the world, invested with the prerogative of infallibility in religious matters. Such a provision would be a direct, immediate, active, and prompt means of withstanding the difficulty; it would be an instrument suited to the need; and, when I find that this is the very claim of the Catholic Church, not only do I feel no difficulty in admitting the idea, but there is a fitness in it, which recommends it to my mind. And thus I am brought to speak of the Church's infallibility, as a provision, adapted by the mercy of the Creator, to preserve religion in the world, and to restrain that freedom of thought, which of course in itself is one of the greatest of our natural gifts, and to rescue it from its own suicidal excesses. And let it be observed that, neither here nor in what follows, shall I have occasion to speak directly of Revelation in its subject-matter, but in reference to the sanction which it gives to truths which may be known independently of it,—as it bears upon the defence of natural religion. I say, that a power, possessed of infallibility in religious teaching, is happily adapted to be a working instrument, in the course of human affairs, for smiting hard and throwing back the immense energy of the aggressive, capricious, untrustworthy intellect:—and in saying this, as in the other things that I have to say, it must still be recollected that I am all along bearing in mind my main purpose, which is a defence of myself.

I am defending myself here from a plausible charge brought against Catholics, as will be seen better as I proceed. The charge is this:—that I, as a Catholic, not only make profession to hold doctrines which I cannot possibly believe in my heart, but that I also believe in the existence of a power on earth, which at its own will imposes upon men any new set of *credenda* [beliefs], when it pleases, by a claim to infallibility; in consequence, that my own thoughts are not my own property; that I cannot tell that to-morrow I may not have to give up what I hold to-day, and that the necessary effect of such a condition of mind must be a degrading bondage, or a bitter inward rebellion relieving itself in secret infidelity, or the necessity of ignoring the whole subject of religion in a sort of disgust, and of mechanically saying every thing that the Church says, and leaving to others the defence of it. As then I have above spoken of the relation of my mind towards the Catholic Creed, so now I shall speak of the attitude which it takes up in the view of the Church's infallibility.

And first, the initial doctrine of the infallible teacher must be an emphatic protest against the existing state of mankind. Man had rebelled against his Maker. It was this that caused the divine interposition: and to proclaim it must be the first act of the divinely-accredited messenger. The Church must denounce rebellion as of all possible evils the greatest. She must have no terms with it; if she would be true to her Master, she must ban and anathematize it. This is the meaning of a statement of mine which has furnished matter for one of those special accusations to which I am at present replying: I have, however, no fault at all to confess in regard to it; I have nothing to withdraw, and in consequence I here deliberately repeat it. I said, "The

Catholic Church holds it better for the sun and moon to drop from heaven, for the earth to fail, and for all the many millions on it to die of starvation in extremest agony, as far as temporal affliction goes, than that one soul, I will not say, should be lost, but should commit one single venial sin, should tell one wilful untruth, or should steal one poor farthing without excuse." I think the principle here enunciated to be the mere preamble in the formal credentials of the Catholic Church, as an Act of Parliament might begin with a "Whereas." It is because of the intensity of the evil which has possession of mankind, that a suitable antagonist has been provided against it; and the initial act of that divinely-commissioned power is of course to deliver her challenge and to defy the enemy. Such a preamble then gives a meaning to her position in the world, and an interpretation to her whole course of teaching and action. * * *

* * * We live in a wonderful age; the enlargement of the circle of secular knowledge just now is simply a bewilderment, and the more so, because it has the promise of continuing, and that with greater rapidity, and more signal results. Now these discoveries, certain or probable, have in matter of fact an indirect bearing upon religious opinions, and the question arises how are the respective claims of revelation and of natural science to be adjusted. Few minds in earnest can remain at ease without some sort of rational grounds for their religious belief; to reconcile theory and fact is almost an instinct of the mind. When then a flood of facts, ascertained or suspected, comes pouring in upon us, with a multitude of others in prospect, all believers in Revelation, be they Catholic or not, are roused to consider their bearing upon themselves, both for the honour of God, and from tenderness for those many souls who, in consequence of the confident tone of the schools of secular knowledge, are in danger of being led away into a bottomless liberalism of thought.

I am not going to criticize here that vast body of men, in the mass, who at this time would profess to be liberals in religion; and who look towards the discoveries of the age, certain or in progress, as their informants, direct or indirect, as to what they shall think about the unseen and the future. The Liberalism which gives a colour to society now, is very different from that character of thought which bore the name thirty or forty years ago. Now it is scarcely a party; it is the educated lay world.

1864

━━◄◆►━━

Thomas Henry Huxley
1825–1895

Huxley was known as "Darwin's bulldog" for the vigorous way he defended Darwin in the controversies over *The Origin of Species*. In 1860 he took on Bishop Wilberforce in a famous debate at Oxford: when the bishop asked sarcastically whether "it was through his grandfather or his grandmother that he claimed his descent from a monkey?" Huxley carried the day by replying that "he was not ashamed to have a monkey for his ancestor; but he would be ashamed to be connected with a man who used great gifts to obscure the truth." In *Evolution and Ethics* he built on Darwinian ideas, arguing that although humankind is the natural product of evolutionary forces, we are inescapably at war with nature. Huxley rejected any direct "social Darwinist" view of society as a struggle for the survival of the fittest, and sought instead to envision a humanist ethics free from natural and from supernatural control alike.

from **Evolution and Ethics**
from *Prolegomena*
[MAN'S WAR WITH NATURE]

It may be safely assumed that, two thousand years ago, before Caesar set foot in southern Britain,[1] the whole country-side visible from the windows of the room in which I write, was in what is called "the state of nature." Except, it may be, by raising a few sepulchral mounds, such as those which still, here and there, break the flowing contours of the downs, man's hands had made no mark upon it; and the thin veil of vegetation which overspread the broad-backed heights and the shelving sides of the coombs[2] was unaffected by his industry. The native grasses and weeds, the scattered patches of gorse, contended with one another for the possession of the scanty surface soil; they fought against the droughts of summer, the frosts of winter, and the furious gales which swept, with unbroken force, now from the Atlantic, and now from the North Sea, at all times of the year; they filled up, as they best might, the gaps made in their ranks by all sorts of underground and overground animal ravagers. One year with another, an average population, the floating balance of the unceasing struggle for existence among the indigenous plants, maintained itself. It is as little to be doubted, that an essentially similar state of nature prevailed, in this region, for many thousand years before the coming of Caesar; and there is no assignable reason for denying that it might continue to exist through an equally prolonged futurity, except for the intervention of man.

Reckoned by our customary standards of duration, the native vegetation, like the "everlasting hills" which it clothes, seems a type of permanence. The little Amarella Gentians, which abound in some places to-day, are the descendants of those that were trodden underfoot by the prehistoric savages who have left their flint tools about, here and there; and they followed ancestors which, in the climate of the glacial epoch, probably flourished better than they do now. Compared with the long past of this humble plant, all the history of civilized men is but an episode.

Yet nothing is more certain than that, measured by the liberal scale of time-keeping of the universe, this present state of nature, however it may seem to have gone and to go on for ever, is but a fleeting phase of her infinite variety; merely the last of the series of changes which the earth's surface has undergone in the course of the millions of years of its existence. Turn back a square foot of the thin turf, and the solid foundation of the land, exposed in cliffs of chalk five hundred feet high on the adjacent shore, yields full assurance of a time when the sea covered the site of the "everlasting hills"; and when the vegetation of what land lay nearest, was as different from the present Flora of the Sussex downs, as that of Central Africa now is. No less certain is it that between the time during which the chalk was formed and that at which the original turf came into existence, thousands of centuries elapsed, in the course of which, the state of nature of the ages during which the chalk was deposited, passed into that which now is, by changes so slow that, in the coming and going of the generations of men, had such witnessed them, the contemporary conditions would have seemed to be unchanging and unchangeable.

But it is also certain that, before the deposition of the chalk, a vastly longer period had elapsed, throughout which it is easy to follow the traces of the same process of ceaseless modification and of the internecine struggle for existence of living things;

---

1. Julius Caesar conquered Britain for the Roman Empire   2. Deep valleys.
in the last century B.C.

and that even when we can get no further back, it is not because there is any reason to think we have reached the beginning, but because the trail of the most ancient life remains hidden, or has become obliterated.

Thus that state of nature of the world of plants, which we began by considering, is far from possessing the attribute of permanence. Rather its very essence is impermanence. It may have lasted twenty or thirty thousand years, it may last for twenty or thirty thousand years more, without obvious change; but, as surely as it has followed upon a very different state, so it will be followed by an equally different condition. That which endures is not one or another association of living forms, but the process of which the cosmos is the product, and of which these are among the transitory expressions. And in the living world, one of the most characteristic features of this cosmic process is the struggle for existence, the competition of each with all, the result of which is the selection, that is to say, the survival of those forms which, on the whole, are best adapted to the conditions which at any period obtain; and which are, therefore, in that respect, and only in that respect, the fittest. The acme reached by the cosmic process in the vegetation of the downs is seen in the turf, with its weeds and gorse. Under the conditions, they have come out of the struggle victorious; and, by surviving, have proved that they are the fittest to survive. * * *

As a natural process, of the same character as the development of a tree from its seed, or of a fowl from its egg, evolution excludes creation and all other kinds of supernatural intervention. As the expression of a fixed order, every stage of which is the effect of causes operating according to definite rules, the conception of evolution no less excludes that of chance. It is very desirable to remember that evolution is not an explanation of the cosmic process, but merely a generalized statement of the method and results of that process. And, further, that, if there is proof that the cosmic process was set going by any agent, then that agent will be the creator of it and of all its products, although supernatural intervention may remain strictly excluded from its further course.

So far as that limited revelation of the nature of things, which we call scientific knowledge, has yet gone, it tends, with constantly increasing emphasis, to the belief that, not merely the world of plants, but that of animals; not merely living things, but the whole fabric of the earth; not merely our planet, but the whole solar system; not merely our star and its satellites, but the millions of similar bodies which bear witness to the order which pervades boundless space, and has endured through boundless time; are all working out their predestined courses of evolution.

* * * Three or four years have elapsed since the state of nature, to which I have referred, was brought to an end, so far as a small patch of the soil is concerned, by the intervention of man. The patch was cut off from the rest by a wall; within the area thus protected, the native vegetation was, as far as possible, extirpated; while a colony of strange plants was imported and set down in its place. In short, it was made into a garden. At the present time, this artificially treated area presents an aspect extraordinarily different from that of so much of the land as remains in the state of nature, outside the wall. Trees, shrubs, and herbs, many of them appertaining to the state of nature of remote parts of the globe, abound and flourish. Moreover, considerable quantities of vegetables, fruits, and flowers are produced, of kinds which neither now exist, nor have ever existed, except under conditions such as obtain in the garden; and which, therefore, are as much works of the art of man as the frames and glass-houses in which some of them are raised. That the "state of Art," thus created in the state of nature by man, is sustained by and dependent on him, would at once become apparent, if the watchful

supervision of the gardener were withdrawn, and the antagonistic influences of the general cosmic process were no longer sedulously warded off, or counteracted. The walls and gates would decay; quadrupedal and bipedal intruders would devour and tread down the useful and beautiful plants; birds, insects, blight, and mildew would work their will; the seeds of the native plants, carried by winds or other agencies, would immigrate, and in virtue of their long-earned special adaptation to the local conditions, these despised native weeds would soon choke their choice exotic rivals. A century or two hence, little beyond the foundations of the wall and of the houses and frames would be left, in evidence of the victory of the cosmic powers at work in the state of nature, over the temporary obstacles to their supremacy, set up by the art of the horticulturist.

It will be admitted that the garden is as much a work of art,[3] or artifice, as anything that can be mentioned. The energy localised in certain human bodies, directed by similarly localised intellects, has produced a collocation[4] of other material bodies which could not be brought about in the state of nature. The same proposition is true of all the works of man's hands, from a flint implement to a cathedral or a chronometer; and it is because it is true, that we call these things artificial, term them works of art, or artifice, by way of distinguishing them from the products of the cosmic process, working outside man, which we call natural, or works of nature. The distinction thus drawn between the works of nature and those of man, is universally recognised; and it is, as I conceive, both useful and justifiable. * * *

The process of colonization presents analogies to the formation of a garden which are highly instructive. Suppose a shipload of English colonists sent to form a settlement, in such a country as Tasmania was in the middle of the last century. On landing, they find themselves in the midst of a state of nature, widely different from that left behind them in everything but the most general physical conditions. The common plants, the common birds and quadrupeds, are as totally distinct as the men from anything to be seen on the side of the globe from which they come. The colonists proceed to put an end to this state of things over as large an area as they desire to occupy. They clear away the native vegetation, extirpate or drive out the animal population, so far as may be necessary, and take measures to defend themselves from the re-immigration of either. In their place, they introduce English grain and fruit trees; English dogs, sheep, cattle, horses; and English men; in fact, they set up a new Flora and Fauna and a new variety of mankind, within the old state of nature. Their farms and pastures represent a garden on a great scale, and themselves the gardeners who have to keep it up, in watchful antagonism to the old *régime*. Considered as a whole, the colony is a composite unit introduced into the old state of nature; and, thenceforward, a competitor in the struggle for existence, to conquer or be vanquished.

Under the conditions supposed, there is no doubt of the result, if the work of the colonists be carried out energetically and with intelligent combination of all their forces. On the other hand, if they are slothful, stupid, and careless; or if they waste their energies in contests with one another, the chances are that the old state of nature will have the best of it. The native savage will destroy the immigrant civilized man; of the English animals and plants some will be extirpated by their

---

3. The sense of the term "Art" is becoming narrowed; "work of Art" to most people means a picture, a statue, or a piece of *bijouterie*; by way of compensation "artist" has included in its wide embrace cooks and ballet girls, no less than painters and sculptors [Huxley's note].
4. Bringing together.

indigenous rivals, others will pass into the feral state and themselves become components of the state of nature. In a few decades, all other traces of the settlement will have vanished. ✳ ✳ ✳

Moralists of all ages and of all faiths, attending only to the relations of men towards one another in an ideal society, have agreed upon the "golden rule," "Do as you would be done by." In other words, let sympathy be your guide; put yourself in the place of the man towards whom your action is directed; and do to him what you would like to have done to yourself under the circumstances. However much one may admire the generosity of such a rule of conduct; however confident one may be that average men may be thoroughly depended upon not to carry it out to its full logical consequences; it is nevertheless desirable to recognise the fact that these consequences are incompatible with the existence of a civil state, under any circumstances of this world which have obtained, or, so far as one can see, are, likely to come to pass.

For I imagine there can be no doubt that the great desire of every wrongdoer is to escape from the painful consequences of his actions. If I put myself in the place of the man who has robbed me, I find that I am possessed by an exceeding desire not to be fined or imprisoned; if in that of the man who has smitten me on one cheek, I contemplate with satisfaction the absence of any worse result than the turning of the other cheek for like treatment. Strictly observed, the "golden rule" involves the negation of law by the refusal to put it in motion against law-breakers; and, as regards the external relations of a polity,[5] it is the refusal to continue the struggle for existence. It can be obeyed, even partially, only under the protection of a society which repudiates it. Without such shelter, the followers of the "golden rule" may indulge in hopes of heaven, but they must reckon with the certainty that other people will be masters of the earth.

What would become of the garden if the gardener treated all the weeds and slugs and birds and trespassers as he would like to be treated, if he were in their place? ✳ ✳ ✳

That progressive modification of civilization which passes by the name of the "evolution of society," is, in fact, a process of an essentially different character, both from that which brings about the evolution of species, in the state of nature, and from that which gives rise to the evolution of varieties, in the state of art.

There can be no doubt that vast changes have taken place in English civilization since the reign of the Tudors.[6] But I am not aware of a particle of evidence in favour of the conclusion that this evolutionary process has been accompanied by any modification of the physical, or the mental, characters of the men who have been the subjects of it. I have not met with any grounds for suspecting that the average Englishmen of to-day are sensibly different from those that Shakspere knew and drew. We look into his magic mirror of the Elizabethan age, and behold, nowise darkly, the presentment of ourselves.

During these three centuries, from the reign of Elizabeth to that of Victoria, the struggle for existence between man and man has been so largely restrained among the great mass of the population (except for one or two short intervals of civil war), that it can have had little, or no, selective operation. As to anything comparable to direct selection, it has been practised on so small a scale that it may also be neglected. The criminal law, in so far as by putting to death, or by subjecting to long periods of imprisonment, those who infringe its provisions, it prevents the propagation of hereditary criminal tendencies; and the poor-law, in so far as it separates married

---

5. Government.   6. Reigned 1485–1603.

couples, whose destitution arises from hereditary defects of character, are doubtless selective agents operating in favour of the non-criminal and the more effective members of society. But the proportion of the population which they influence is very small; and, generally, the hereditary criminal and the hereditary pauper have propagated their kind before the law affects them. In a large proportion of cases, crime and pauperism have nothing to do with heredity; but are the consequence, partly, of circumstances and, partly, of the possession of qualities, which, under different conditions of life, might have excited esteem and even admiration. It was a shrewd man of the world who, in discussing sewage problems, remarked that dirt is riches in the wrong place; and that sound aphorism has moral applications. The benevolence and open-handed generosity which adorn a rich man, may make a pauper of a poor one; the energy and courage to which the successful soldier owes his rise, the cool and daring subtlety to which the great financier owes his fortune, may very easily, under unfavourable conditions, lead their possessors to the gallows, or to the hulks. Moreover, it is fairly probable that the children of a "failure" will receive from their other parent just that little modification of character which makes all the difference. I sometimes wonder whether people, who talk so freely about extirpating the unfit, ever dispassionately consider their own history. Surely, one must be very "fit," indeed, not to know of an occasion, or perhaps two, in one's life, when it would have been only too easy to qualify for a place among the "unfit."

In my belief the innate qualities, physical, intellectual, and moral, of our nation have remained substantially the same for the last four or five centuries. If the struggle for existence has affected us to any serious extent (and I doubt it) it has been, indirectly, through our military and industrial wars with other nations. * * *

To return, once more, to the parallel of horticulture. In the modern world, the gardening of men by themselves is practically restricted to the performance, not of selection, but of that other function of the gardener, the creation of conditions more favourable than those of the state of nature; to the end of facilitating the free expansion of the innate faculties of the citizen, so far as it is consistent with the general good. And the business of the moral and political philosopher appears to me to be the ascertainment, by the same method of observation, experiment, and ratiocination, as is practised in other kinds of scientific work, of the course of conduct which will best conduce to that end.

But, supposing this course of conduct to be scientifically determined and carefully followed out, it cannot put an end to the struggle for existence in the state of nature; and it will not so much as tend, in any way, to the adaptation of man to that state. Even should the whole human race be absorbed in one vast polity, within which "absolute political justice" reigns, the struggle for existence with the state of nature outside it, and the tendency to the return of the struggle within, in consequence of over-multiplication, will remain; and, unless men's inheritance from the ancestors who fought a good fight in the state of nature, their dose of original sin, is rooted out by some method at present unrevealed, at any rate to disbelievers in supernaturalism, every child born into the world will still bring with him the instinct of unlimited self-assertion. He will have to learn the lesson of self-restraint and renunciation. But the practice of self-restraint and renunciation is not happiness, though it may be something much better.

That man, as a "political animal," is susceptible of a vast amount of improvement, by education, by instruction, and by the application of his intelligence to the adaptation of the conditions of life to his higher needs, I entertain not the slightest doubt. But, so long as he remains liable to error, intellectual or moral; so long as he is compelled to be perpetually on guard against the cosmic forces, whose ends are not his ends, without and within himself; so long as he is haunted by inexpugnable memories and hopeless aspirations; so long as the recognition of his intellectual limitations forces him to acknowledge his incapacity to penetrate the mystery of existence; the prospect of attaining untroubled happiness, or of a state which can, even remotely, deserve the title of perfection, appears to me to be as misleading an illusion as ever was dangled before the eyes of poor humanity. And there have been many of them.

That which lies before the human race is a constant struggle to maintain and improve, in opposition to the State of Nature, the State of Art of an organized polity; in which, and by which, man may develop a worthy civilization, capable of maintaining and constantly improving itself, until the evolution of our globe shall have entered so far upon its downward course that the cosmic process resumes its sway; and, once more, the State of Nature prevails over the surface of our planet.

1893

━━ END OF PERSPECTIVES: RELIGION AND SCIENCE ━━

━━ ✦ ━━

Robert Browning
1812–1889

Throughout his life Robert Browning was something of an enigma, a Byronic dandy sporting lemon-yellow gloves and gorgeous waistcoats, who loved dining out and yet kept both his private life and poetic practice out of the conversation. He longed for public recognition but would not make his work more accessible by stepping from behind his elaborate artistic masks. Unable to reconcile the hearty dinner guest with the experimental poet, Henry James concluded that Browning lived equally on both sides of an inner wall which "contained an invisible door through which, working the lock at will, he could swiftly pass." Although Browning sometimes suggested that he was a mere ventriloquist or puppeteer, the genius with which he impersonated other voices extended the range and complexity of English poetry in bold new directions. More than any other nineteenth-century figure, Browning shaped the poetry of the twentieth, influencing British and American poets from Hardy and Yeats to Eliot, Pound, Frost, Lowell, and Stevens.

Browning's early years were quiet, even sheltered. He was born in Camberwell, a rural suburb south of London, and with the exception of a year spent at London University, he lived at home with his parents and sister until the age of thirty-four. His father was an official in the Bank of England, and his mother a pious Nonconformist, both of whom encouraged their son in his passion for poetry, painting, and music. The chief source of his education was extensive, haphazard reading in his father's vast private library. Brought up to be a gentleman, Browning received lessons in dancing, fencing, boxing, drawing, and music, as well as Greek and Latin. His doting parents denied him nothing: when, at fourteen, he expressed an interest in the poetry of Shelley—whose works were unavailable because of his atheism—Browning's devout mother took him to London to find an out-of-print copy.

Uncertain what his genuine calling was, Browning considered and rejected careers in art, music, law, and business. A turning point came in October 1832, when he saw the aging Edmund Kean play Richard III. Stunned by the power of a performance in which the brilliant but weary actor alternately electrified and embarrassed the audience as he struggled to dominate his role, Browning found dramatic confirmation of his evolving theory that all personality was staged and variable. Taking Shakespeare as a model, he envisioned himself as performer, playwright, and stage manager of his own artistic world. That night he conceived a grand plan to "assume I know not how many different characters" in order to write poems, operas, novels, and speeches under different names so that "the world was never to guess" that Robert Browning had been the author.

It is a fascinating literary mystery why Browning should have wanted simultaneously to conceal his own identity and yet dazzle the world by impersonating other people—especially since the authors he most admired (Byron, Keats, and particularly Shelley) seemed to him to speak too personally. In 1833, Browning began his career anonymously with a long romantic poem, *Pauline*, in which he took an indirect approach, speaking through a narrator who confided: "I will tell / My state, as though 'twere none of mine." *Pauline* failed to sell a single copy, but the book found its way to John Stuart Mill, who commented that the poet possessed "a more intense and morbid self-consciousness than I ever knew in any sane being."

In the next decade Browning produced a string of introspective plays and experimental dramatic poems, including *Paracelsus* (1835), *Strafford* (1837), *Sordello* (1840), and *Pippa Passes* (1841). The notorious difficulty of these unpopular works gave Browning a reputation for obscurity that he labored for the rest of his life to overcome. But by the early 1840s he had discovered where his talent lay: applying to lyric poetry his theatrical instincts and his aversion to self-revelation, he found he could produce startling new effects. Henceforth he would present his audience with a cast of aberrant personalities, each starring in his or her own miniplay. In language adapted to their insecurities and obsessions, Browning's characters unwittingly reveal their own, often shocking secrets—but only if readers make the effort to follow the uncanny logic of their contorted confessions.

In the advertisement for his breakthrough book, *Dramatic Lyrics* (1842), Browning offered the disclaimer that, though the poems are "lyric in expression," they are the "utterances of so many imaginary persons, not mine." These imaginary persons range from the Greek goddess Artemis to lovers in a Venetian gondola, from a medieval damsel in distress to a Spanish monk so consumed by hatred that his soliloquy begins with a growl: "Gr-r-r." The sheer physicality of Browning's words, the thick-textured lines, the aggressive consonant clusters that seem to mock Tennyson's liquid vowels, the staccato lines and convoluted syntax that convey the twistings of tongue and mind struggling to express themselves—all are trademarks of Browning's style. As Gerard Manley Hopkins said, Browning talks like "a man bouncing up from table with his mouth full of bread and cheese and saying that he meant to stand no blasted nonsense."

Browning did not invent the poetic form known as the dramatic monologue—it is used in such classics as Marvell's *To His Coy Mistress* and Tennyson's *Ulysses*—but he brought the form to new levels of complexity. He usually situates his speakers in specific historical places and periods. Sometimes they are well-known figures from the past, such as the Italian painters Andrea del Sarto and Fra Lippo Lippi, or literary characters, such as Caliban and Childe Roland. Browning catches them at a moment of great emotional intensity as they attempt to explain why they think and act as they do. In these passionate outbursts, they reveal their characters as much by idiomatic language, patterns of imagery, speech rhythms, and unintended ironies as by what they actually say.

Browning induces his readers to sympathize—even identify—with speakers of dubious morality and intentions. His gallery of rogues includes a duke who may have murdered his wife, a painter who savors his own cuckoldry, and a dying bishop who recalls with gusto the fleshly delights he has enjoyed. As the critic Robert Langbaum has pointed out, "the utter outrageousness" of such behavior "makes condemnation the least interesting response." Just as Satan becomes the most intriguing figure in *Paradise Lost,* so Browning's narrators elicit a reluctant fascination. Alternating between admiration and revulsion, and compelled by the intricacies of human motivation to suspend judgment, the reader struggles to come to terms with these disclosures.

This theatrical world of passionate utterance spilled over into reality in 1845, when Browning became the coauthor and hero of his own romantic drama. On 10 January, he wrote a fan letter to the famous poet Elizabeth Barrett, whom he had never seen. He was thirty-three, she nearly forty, and her poetry was far better known than his. "I love your verses with all my heart," he wrote boldly, "—and I love you too." Her reply was encouraging, and thus began the century's most celebrated literary correspondence. She was an invalid suffering from tuberculosis, and they did not meet until May. But when Browning entered her darkened room, he fell instantly in love with the frail, fiery woman lying on her couch swathed in shawls and blankets. For more than a year and half they kept the nature of their relationship secret, to circumvent the wrath of her tyrannical father, who had permitted none of his children to marry. Finally, Browning decided they must break free: they were married secretly during a morning walk, in September 1846, and eloped to Italy, where they eventually settled in Florence.

Though their marriage was rhapsodic, Browning was frustrated with his art. Preoccupied with his wife, her work, their son "Pen" (born in 1849), and the charms of Florence, the usually prolific Browning wrote only one poem in the first three years of marriage and published just two books in the fifteen years they lived together. Though she acknowledged his genius, Elizabeth joined with her husband's friends in urging him to write "in the most directest and most impressive way, the mask thrown off." Unable or unwilling to do so, Browning gloomily found that he had acquired a further mask that he had not sought: that of "Mrs. Browning's husband."

Hoping finally to make his name with a wider public, Browning channeled his energies into a new project, fifty monologues published in 1855 as *Men and Women.* These animated self-portraits by artists, lovers, questors, skeptics, and impostors form a dazzling picture gallery containing many of Browning's greatest poems, including *Love Among the Ruins, Fra Lippo Lippi,* and *Childe Roland.* The plural title of *Men and Women* insists on the variability of human experience and the centrality of sexual difference to every individual's self-definition. But the book was poorly received at the time, except by the Pre-Raphaelites, and was soon overshadowed by the tumultuous acclaim bestowed on Elizabeth Barrett Browning's *Aurora Leigh* in 1856. Dejected by his readers' failure to make the effort to comprehend his art, Browning complained to his friend John Ruskin: "I cannot begin writing poetry till my imaginary reader has conceded licenses to me. . . . You would have me paint it all plain out, which can't be; but by various artifices I try to make shift with touches and bits of outlines which *succeed* if they bear the conception from me to you. You ought, I think, to keep pace with the thought."

Elizabeth Barrett Browning died suddenly in 1861 in Florence. "My life is fixed and sure now," the devastated widower wrote to his sister, "I shall live out the remainder in her direct influence." Browning returned to England with his son and settled down to a steady rhythm of writing and dining out. But with renewed vigor he resumed his demanding experiments with dramatic lyrics, more determined than ever to pursue the indirect forms of expression that the reading public had resisted.

The result was his second masterpiece, *The Ring and the Book,* a novel in verse published in four monthly installments, between 1868 and 1869. The poem reimagines a sensational seventeenth-century Roman murder trial. In extended monologues the various participants tell their versions of the story. We hear the pleas of the dying young bride Pompilia, her cruel husband Guido, her priest and would-be rescuer Caponsacchi, and then the rationale of the Pope, who decides the case. In this sordid tale of marital abuse and dubious justice, Browning explores the relativity of human understanding, the rights of women, and the role of religious belief in determining earthly action.

"Art remains the one way possible," the poet says, "Of speaking truth. . . . " But then, typically, he hedges his assertion: "—to mouths like mine, at least." In a world of becoming, no single perspective is ever sufficient, but Browning shows how, seen from the inside, each self, no matter how bizarre, finds words to justify its actions. Browning's truth is always contingent, evolving, and dependent on the flawed language we have to express it: "For how else know we save by worth of word?"

The success of *The Ring and the Book*, together with the increasing popularity of his earlier work, meant that in the 1870s and 1880s Browning was finally recognized as sharing with Tennyson the title of the era's leading poet. He was especially amused and gratified by the adulation of the Browning Societies that sprang up in England and around the world during his later years. When asked if he objected to the amateurish enthusiasm of the clubs that met to discuss his philosophy of life, he replied: "Object to it? No, I like it! . . . I have waited forty years for it, and now—I like it!" In the United States, where Browning mania hit hardest, brown clothing, curtains, and tableware became the rage, and his works were excerpted on railroad timetables. Mark Twain even gave a series of readings of which he boasted: "I can read Browning so Browning himself can understand it."

Browning's last book, *Asolando*, was published to wide acclaim the day he died at his son's home in Venice. Shortly before his death, Browning read aloud from the book's *Epilogue* the stanza that described his dogged determination to keep on striving in a world of limitation and imperfection: "One who never turned his back but marched breast forward, / Never doubted clouds would break." Ultimately, this confidence underlies the bold relativity and deep skepticism that animate Browning's work. Like Hopkins, Browning insists that all of nature, even human nature, bespeaks some part of an unknowable absolute. Thus everything becomes material for poetry, the dirty, deformed, and despicable no less than the beautiful, pure, and radiantly good. As Browning says in *Fra Lippo Lippi*, "This world's no blot for us, / Nor blank; it means intensely, and means good: / To find its meaning is my meat and drink."

Porphyria's Lover[1]

The rain set early in to-night,
    The sullen wind was soon awake,
It tore the elm-tops down for spite,
    And did its worst to vex the lake:
5   I listened with heart fit to break.
When glided in Porphyria; straight
    She shut the cold out and the storm,
And kneeled and made the cheerless grate
    Blaze up, and all the cottage warm;
10   Which done, she rose, and from her form
Withdrew the dripping cloak and shawl,
    And laid her soiled gloves by, untied
Her hat and let the damp hair fall,
    And, last, she sat down by my side
15   And called me. When no voice replied,
She put my arm about her waist,
    And made her smooth white shoulder bare,
And all her yellow hair displaced,
    And, stooping, made my cheek lie there,

1. The poem was originally published with another of Browning's dramatic monologues, *Johannes Agricola in Meditation*, under the general title of *Madhouse Cells*.

20 And spread, o'er all, her yellow hair,
Murmuring how she loved me—she
Too weak, for all her heart's endeavour,
To set its struggling passion free
From pride, and vainer ties dissever,
25 And give herself to me for ever.
But passion sometimes would prevail,
Nor could to-night's gay feast restrain
A sudden thought of one so pale
For love of her, and all in vain:
30 So, she was come through wind and rain.
Be sure I looked up at her eyes
Happy and proud; at last I knew
Porphyria worshipped me; surprise
Made my heart swell, and still it grew
35 While I debated what to do.
That moment she was mine, mine, fair,
Perfectly pure and good: I found
A thing to do, and all her hair
In one long yellow string I wound
40 Three times her little throat around,
And strangled her. No pain felt she;
I am quite sure she felt no pain.
As a shut bud that holds a bee,
I warily oped her lids: again
45 Laughed the blue eyes without a stain.
And I untightened next the tress
About her neck; her cheek once more
Blushed bright beneath my burning kiss:
I propped her head up as before,
50 Only, this time my shoulder bore
Her head, which droops upon it still:
The smiling rosy little head,
So glad it has its utmost will,
That all it scorned at once is fled,
55 And I, its love, am gained instead!
Porphyria's love: she guessed not how
Her darling one wish would be heard.
And thus we sit together now,
And all night long we have not stirred,
60 And yet God has not said a word!

c. 1835   1836, 1842

My Last Duchess[1]
Ferrara

That's my last Duchess painted on the wall,
Looking as if she were alive. I call

That piece a wonder, now: Fràà Pandolf's[2] hands
Worked busily a day, and there she stands.
5   Will't please you sit and look at her? I said
"Fràà Pandolf" by design, for never read
Strangers like you that pictured countenance,
The depth and passion of its earnest glance,
But to myself they turned (since none puts by
10 The curtain I have drawn for you, but I)
And seemed as they would ask me, if they durst,
How such a glance came there; so, not the first
Are you to turn and ask thus. Sir, 'twas not
Her husband's presence only, called that spot
15 Of joy into the Duchess' cheek: perhaps
Fràà Pandolf chanced to say "Her mantle laps
Over my lady's wrist too much," or "Paint
Must never hope to reproduce the faint
Half-flush that dies along her throat:" such stuff
20 Was courtesy, she thought, and cause enough
For calling up that spot of joy. She had
A heart—how shall I say?—too soon made glad,
Too easily impressed; she liked whate'er
She looked on, and her looks went everywhere.
25 Sir, 'twas all one! My favour at her breast,
The dropping of the daylight in the West,
The bough of cherries some officious fool
Broke in the orchard for her, the white mule
She rode with round the terrace—all and each
30 Would draw from her alike the approving speech,
Or blush, at least. She thanked men,—good! but thanked
Somehow—I know not how—as if she ranked
My gift of a nine-hundred-years-old name
With anybody's gift. Who'd stoop to blame
35 This sort of trifling? Even had you skill
In speech—(which I have not)—to make your will
Quite clear to such an one, and say, "Just this
Or that in you disgusts me; here you miss,
Or there exceed the mark"—and if she let
40 Herself be lessoned so, nor plainly set
Her wits to yours, forsooth, and made excuse,
—E'en then would be some stooping; and I choose
Never to stoop. Oh sir, she smiled, no doubt,
Whene'er I passed her, but who passed without
45 Much the same smile? This grew; I gave commands;
Then all smiles stopped together. There she stands
As if alive. Will't please you rise? We'll meet
The company below, then. I repeat,
The Count your master's known munificence
50 Is ample warrant that no just pretence
Of mine for dowry will be disallowed;

---

2. Brother Pandolf, the imaginary painter of the duchess's portrait.

Though his fair daughter's self, as I avowed
At starting, is my object.[3] Nay, we'll go
Together down, sir. Notice Neptune, though,
55   Taming a sea-horse, thought a rarity,
Which Claus of Innsbruck cast in bronze for me!

1842   1842

The Bishop Orders His Tomb at Saint Praxed's Church[1]
Rome, 15——

Vanity, saith the preacher, vanity![2]
Draw round my bed: is Anselm keeping back?
Nephews—sons mine[3] . . . ah God, I know not! Well—
She, men would have to be your mother once,
5   Old Gandolf envied me, so fair she was!
What's done is done, and she is dead beside,
Dead long ago, and I am Bishop since,
And as she died so must we die ourselves,
And thence ye may perceive the world's a dream.
10   Life, how and what is it? As here I lie
In this state-chamber, dying by degrees,
Hours and long hours in the dead night, I ask
"Do I live, am I dead?" Peace, peace seems all.
Saint Praxed's ever was the church for peace;
15   And so, about this tomb of mine. I fought
With tooth and nail to save my niche, ye know:
—Old Gandolf cozened me,° despite my care;   cheated
Shrewd was that snatch from out the corner South
He graced his carrion with, God curse the same!
20   Yet still my niche is not so cramped but thence
One sees the pulpit o' the epistle-side,[4]
And somewhat of the choir, those silent seats,
And up into the aery dome where live
The angels, and a sunbeam's sure to lurk:
25   And I shall fill my slab of basalt there,
And 'neath my tabernacle[5] take my rest,
With those nine columns round me, two and two,
The odd one at my feet where Anselm stands:
Peach-blossom marble all, the rare, the ripe
30   As fresh-poured red wine of a mighty pulse.[6]

---

3. Only now does the reader learn that the duke is con-
ducting negotiations for his second marriage and has
been addressing the envoy of his bride-to-be's father.
1. John Ruskin admired Browning's portrait of a dying
bishop's obsession with ordering a sumptuous tomb: "I
know of no other piece of modern English, prose or poetry, in which there is so much told, as in these lines, of the
Renaissance spirit—its worldliness, inconsistency, pride,
hypocrisy, ignorance of itself, love of art, of luxury, and of
good Latin. It is nearly all that I have said of the central
Renaissance in thirty pages of the *Stones of Venice*, put
into as many lines, Browning's also being the antecedent

work" (*Modern Painters*, vol. 4, ch. 20, sec. 34).
2. "Vanity of vanities, saith the Preacher, vanity of vanities; all is vanity" (Ecclesiastes 1.2).
3. The supposedly celibate clergy could not marry but
sometimes took mistresses; the Bishop euphemistically
calls his illegitimate sons "nephews."
4. The right side, as one faces the altar, from which the
Epistles of the New Testament are read.
5. Stone canopy beneath which the sculpted effigy of the
bishop will repose on his tomb.
6. The pulpy mash of grapes from which strong wine
could be made.

—Old Gandolf with his paltry onion-stone,°   *cheap marble*
Put me where I may look at him! True peach,
Rosy and flawless: how I earned the prize!
Draw close: that conflagration of my church
35   —What then? So much was saved if aught were missed!
My sons, ye would not be my death? Go dig
The white-grape vineyard where the oil-press stood,
Drop water gently till the surface sink,
And if ye find . . . Ah God, I know not, I! . . .
40   Bedded in store of rotten fig-leaves soft,
And corded up in a tight olive-frail,°   *basket*
Some lump, ah God, of *lapis lazuli*,[7]
Big as a Jew's head cut off at the nape,
Blue as a vein o'er the Madonna's breast . . .
45   Sons, all have I bequeathed you, villas, all,
That brave Frascati[8] villa with its bath,
So, let the blue lump poise between my knees,
Like God the Father's globe on both his hands
Ye worship in the Jesu Church so gay,
50   For Gandolf shall not choose but see and burst!
Swift as a weaver's shuttle fleet our years:[9]
Man goeth to the grave, and where is he?
Did I say basalt for my slab, sons? Black—
'Twas ever antique-black I meant! How else
55   Shall ye contrast my frieze° to come beneath?   *sculpted band*
The bas-relief in bronze ye promised me,
Those Pans and Nymphs ye wot of, and perchance
Some tripod, thyrsus, with a vase or so,
The Saviour at his sermon on the mount,
60   Saint Praxed in a glory, and one Pan
Ready to twitch the Nymph's last garment off,
And Moses with the tables[1] . . . but I know
Ye mark me not! What do they whisper thee,
Child of my bowels, Anselm? Ah, ye hope
65   To revel down my villas while I gasp
Bricked o'er with beggar's mouldy travertine°   *limestone*
Which Gandolf from his tomb-top chuckles at!
Nay, boys, ye love me—all of jasper, then!
'Tis jasper ye stand pledged to, lest I grieve.
70   My bath must needs be left behind, alas!
One block, pure green as a pistachio-nut,
There's plenty jasper somewhere in the world—
And have I not Saint Praxed's ear to pray
Horses for ye, and brown Greek manuscripts,
75   And mistresses with great smooth marbly limbs?
—That's if ye carve my epitaph aright,

7. A semiprecious bright blue stone.
8. A resort near Rome.
9. Job 7.6: "My days are swifter than a weaver's shuttle
and are spent without hope." The next line alludes to Job
7.9 and 14.10.

1. The bronze bas-relief sculptures will mingle pagan and
Christian scenes, the goatlike lecherous Pan next to
Moses receiving the Ten Commandments. In *Contrasts*
(1841) A. W. Pugin criticized such juxtapositions, which
were typical of the Renaissance.

Choice Latin, picked phrase, Tully's every word,
No gaudy ware like Gandolf's second line—
Tully, my masters? Ulpian serves his need![2]
80 And then how I shall lie through centuries,
And hear the blessed mutter of the mass,
And see God made and eaten all day long,[3]
And feel the steady candle-flame, and taste
Good strong thick stupefying incense-smoke!
85 For as I lie here, hours of the dead night,
Dying in state and by such slow degrees,
I fold my arms as if they clasped a crook,
And stretch my feet forth straight as stone can point,
And let the bedclothes, for a mortcloth, drop
90 Into great laps and folds of sculptor's-work:[4]
And as yon tapers dwindle, and strange thoughts
Grow, with a certain humming in my ears,
About the life before I lived this life,
And this life too, popes, cardinals and priests,
95 Saint Praxed at his sermon on the mount,[5]
Your tall pale mother with her talking eyes,
And new-found agate urns as fresh as day,
And marble's language, Latin pure, discreet,
—Aha, ELUCESCEBAT[6] quoth our friend?
100 No Tully, said I, Ulpian at the best!
Evil and brief hath been my pilgrimage.[7]
All *lapis*, all, sons! Else I give the Pope
My villas! Will ye ever eat my heart?
Ever your eyes were as a lizard's quick,
105 They glitter like your mother's for my soul,
Or ye would heighten my impoverished frieze,
Piece out its starved design, and fill my vase
With grapes, and add a vizor and a Term,[8]
And to the tripod ye would tie a lynx
110 That in his struggle throws the thyrsus down,
To comfort me on my entablature°   platform
Whereon I am to lie till I must ask
"Do I live, am I dead?" There, leave me, there!
For ye have stabbed me with ingratitude
115 To death—ye wish it—God, ye wish it! Stone—
Gritstone, a-crumble![9] Clammy squares which sweat

---

2. Domitius Ulpianus (A.D. 170–228) was considered inferior to Marcus Tullius Cicero (106–43 B.C.), regarded during the Renaissance as the greatest Latin prose stylist.
3. According to the doctrine of transubstantiation, the bread and wine of Holy Communion become the body and blood of Christ.
4. As he lies in bed, the bishop positions himself like a carved effigy lying on a tomb, holding his ceremonial staff and draping his bedsheets like a "mortcloth" over a corpse.
5. Jesus gave the sermon on the mount, not St. Praxed

(who was a woman); the bishop's mind is getting confused.
6. Gandolf's epitaph: "He was illustrious." The bishop disapproves of the verb form; Cicero would have written *elucebat*.
7. Cf. Genesis 47.9, where Jacob says: "The days of the years of my pilgrimage are an hundred and thirty years: few and evil have the days of the years of my life been."
8. The vizor of a helmet is sometimes represented in sculpture; the bishop suggests that his sons might also add a statue of Terminus, the Roman god of boundaries.
9. He fears they might use crumbly sandstone after all.

As if the corpse they keep were oozing through—
And no more *lapis* to delight the world!
Well go! I bless ye. Fewer tapers there,
120   But in a row: and, going, turn your backs
—Ay, like departing altar-ministrants,
And leave me in my church, the church for peace,
That I may watch at leisure if he leers—
Old Gandolf, at me, from his onion-stone,
125   As still he envied me, so fair she was!
1844   1845

Love Among the Ruins[1]

1

Where the quiet-coloured end of evening smiles,
        Miles and miles
On the solitary pastures where our sheep
        Half-asleep
5   Tinkle homeward thro' the twilight, stray or stop
        As they crop—
Was the site once of a city great and gay,
        (So they say)
Of our country's very capital, its prince
10   Ages since
Held his court in, gathered councils, wielding far
        Peace or war.

2

Now,—the country does not even boast a tree
        As you see,
15   To distinguish slopes of verdure, certain rills
        From the hills
Intersect and give a name to, (else they run
        Into one)
Where the domed and daring palace shot its spires
20   Up like fires
O'er the hundred-gated circuit of a wall
        Bounding all,
Made of marble, men might march on nor be pressed
        Twelve abreast.

3

25   And such plenty and perfection, see, of grass
        Never was!
Such a carpet as, this summer-time, o'erspreads
        And embeds
Every vestige of the city, guessed alone,
30   Stock or stone—

1. The poem's scenery suggests the Roman Campagna but may also allude to archaeological excavations at Babylon, Nineveh, and Egyptian Thebes. Browning invented this stanza form. See Edward Burne-Jones's painting of the same name (Color Plate 20).

Where a multitude of men breathed joy and woe
    Long ago;
Lust of glory pricked their hearts up, dread of shame
    Struck them tame;
35 And that glory and that shame alike, the gold
    Bought and sold.

4

Now,—the single little turret that remains
    On the plains,
By the caper° overrooted, by the gourd   *shrub*
40   Overscored,
While the patching houseleek's head of blossom winks
    Through the chinks—
Marks the basement whence a tower in ancient time
    Sprang sublime,
45 And a burning ring, all round, the chariots traced
    As they raced,
And the monarch and his minions and his dames
    Viewed the games.

5

And I know, while thus the quiet-coloured eve
50   Smiles to leave
To their folding, all our many-tinkling fleece
    In such peace,
And the slopes and rills in undistinguished grey
    Melt away—
55 That a girl with eager eyes and yellow hair
    Waits me there
In the turret whence the charioteers caught soul
    For the goal,
When the king looked, where she looks now, breathless, dumb
60   Till I come.

6

But he looked upon the city, every side,
    Far and wide,
All the mountains topped with temples, all the glades'
    Colonnades,
65 All the causeys,° bridges, aqueducts,—and then,   *causeways*
    All the men!
When I do come, she will speak not, she will stand,
    Either hand
On my shoulder, give her eyes the first embrace
70   Of my face,
Ere we rush, ere we extinguish sight and speech
    Each on each.

7

In one year they sent a million fighters forth
    South and North,

75   And they built their gods a brazen pillar high
        As the sky,
     Yet reserved a thousand chariots in full force—
        Gold, of course.
     Oh heart! oh blood that freezes, blood that burns!
80   Earth's returns
     For whole centuries of folly, noise and sin!
        Shut them in,
     With their triumphs and their glories and the rest!
        Love is best.

c. 1852   1855

"Childe Roland to the Dark Tower Came"[1]

(See Edgar's Song in "Lear")[2]

1

My first thought was, he lied in every word,
    That hoary cripple, with malicious eye
    Askance to watch the working of his lie
On mine, and mouth scarce able to afford
5   Suppression of the glee, that pursed and scored
    Its edge, at one more victim gained thereby.

2

What else should he be set for, with his staff?
    What, save to waylay with his lies, ensnare
    All travellers who might find him posted there,
10   And ask the road? I guessed what skull-like laugh
Would break, what crutch 'gin write my epitaph
    For pastime in the dusty thoroughfare,

3

If at his counsel I should turn aside
    Into that ominous tract which, all agree,
15   Hides the Dark Tower. Yet acquiescingly
I did turn as he pointed: neither pride
Nor hope rekindling at the end descried,
    So much as gladness that some end might be.

4

For, what with my whole world-wide wandering,
20   What with my search drawn out thro' years, my hope
    Dwindled into a ghost not fit to cope
With that obstreperous joy success would bring,—
I hardly tried now to rebuke the spring
    My heart made, finding failure in its scope.

1. Roland was a hero of Charlemagne legends, and a "childe" was a young candidate for knighthood. Although critics have proposed many different interpretations of Roland's strange, nightmarish quest, Browning himself said only that the poem "came upon me as a kind of dream. I had to write it, then and there, and I finished it the same day, I believe. But it was simply that I had to do it. I did not know then what I meant beyond that, and I'm sure I don't know now. But I am very fond of it."
2. In Shakespeare's *King Lear*, Edgar, disguised as the mad beggar Poor Tom, sings: "Child Rowland to the dark tower came; / His word was still, 'Fie, foh and fum, / I smell the blood of a British man'" (3.4.181–83).

5

25　As when a sick man very near to death
　　　Seems dead indeed, and feels begin and end
　　　The tears and takes the farewell of each friend,
　　And hears one bid the other go, draw breath
　　Freelier outside, ("since all is o'er," he saith,
30　　　"And the blow fallen no grieving can amend;")

6

　　While some discuss if near the other graves
　　　Be room enough for this, and when a day
　　　Suits best for carrying the corpse away,
　　With care about the banners, scarves and staves:
35　And still the man hears all, and only craves
　　　He may not shame such tender love and stay.

7

　　Thus, I had so long suffered in this quest,
　　　Heard failure prophesied so oft, been writ
　　　So many times among "The Band"—to wit,
40　The knights who to the Dark Tower's search addressed
　　Their steps—that just to fail as they, seemed best,
　　　And all the doubt was now—should I be fit?

8

　　So, quiet as despair, I turned from him,
　　　That hateful cripple, out of his highway
45　　　Into the path he pointed. All the day
　　Had been a dreary one at best, and dim
　　Was settling to its close, yet shot one grim
　　　Red leer to see the plain catch its estray.°   *stray animal*

9

　　For mark! no sooner was I fairly found
50　　　Pledged to the plain, after a pace or two,
　　　Than, pausing to throw backward a last view
　　O'er the safe road, 'twas gone; grey plain all round:
　　Nothing but plain to the horizon's bound.
　　　I might go on; nought else remained to do.

10

55　So, on I went. I think I never saw
　　　Such starved ignoble nature; nothing throve:
　　　For flowers—as well expect a cedar grove!
　　But cockle, spurge,° according to their law   *weeds*
　　Might propagate their kind, with none to awe,
60　　　You'd think; a burr had been a treasure-trove.

11

　　No! penury, inertness and grimace,
　　　In some strange sort, were the land's portion. "See
　　　Or shut your eyes," said Nature peevishly,
　　"It nothing skills: I cannot help my case:
65　'Tis the Last Judgment's fire must cure this place,
　　　Calcine° its clods and set my prisoners free."   *burn to ashes*

12

If there pushed any ragged thistle-stalk
   Above its mates, the head was chopped; the bents°   *coarse grasses*
   Were jealous else. What made those holes and rents
70 In the dock's° harsh swarth leaves, bruised as to baulk   *weed*
All hope of greenness? 'tis a brute must walk
   Pashing° their life out, with a brute's intents.   *crushing*

13

As for the grass, it grew as scant as hair
   In leprosy; thin dry blades pricked the mud
75   Which underneath looked kneaded up with blood.
One stiff blind horse, his every bone a-stare,
Stood stupefied, however he came there:
   Thrust out past service from the devil's stud!

14

Alive? he might be dead for aught I know,
80   With that red gaunt and colloped neck a-strain,
   And shut eyes underneath the rusty mane;
Seldom went such grotesqueness with such woe;
I never saw a brute I hated so;
   He must be wicked to deserve such pain.

15

85 I shut my eyes and turned them on my heart.
   As a man calls for wine before he fights,
   I asked one draught of earlier, happier sights,
Ere fitly I could hope to play my part.
Think first, fight afterwards—the soldier's art:
90   One taste of the old time sets all to rights.

16

Not it! I fancied Cuthbert's reddening face
   Beneath its garniture of curly gold,
   Dear fellow, till I almost felt him fold
An arm in mine to fix me to the place,
95 That way he used. Alas, one night's disgrace!
   Out went my heart's new fire and left it cold.

17

Giles then, the soul of honour—there he stands
   Frank as ten years ago when knighted first.
   What honest man should dare (he said) he durst.
100 Good—but the scene shifts—faugh! what hangman-hands
Pin to his breast a parchment? His own bands
   Read it. Poor traitor, spit upon and curst!

18

Better this present than a past like that;
   Back therefore to my darkening path again!
105   No sound, no sight as far as eye could strain.
Will the night send a howlet° or a bat?   *owl*
I asked: when something on the dismal flat
   Came to arrest my thoughts and change their train.

19

110   A sudden little river crossed my path
         As unexpected as a serpent comes.
         No sluggish tide congenial to the glooms;
     This, as it frothed by, might have been a bath
     For the fiend's glowing hoof—to see the wrath
         Of its black eddy bespate with flakes and spumes.

20

115   So petty yet so spiteful! All along,
         Low scrubby alders kneeled down over it;
         Drenched willows flung them headlong in a fit
     Of mute despair, a suicidal throng:
     The river which had done them all the wrong,
120   Whate'er that was, rolled by, deterred no whit.

21

     Which, while I forded,—good saints, how I feared
         To set my foot upon a dead man's cheek,
         Each step, or feel the spear I thrust to seek
     For hollows, tangled in his hair or beard!
125   —It may have been a water-rat I speared,
         But, ugh! it sounded like a baby's shriek.

22

     Glad was I when I reached the other bank.
         Now for a better country. Vain presage!
         Who were the strugglers, what war did they wage,
130   Whose savage trample thus could pad° the dank   *tread*
     Soil to a plash? Toads in a poisoned tank,
         Or wild cats in a red-hot iron cage—

23

     The fight must so have seemed in that fell cirque.°   *terrible arena*
         What penned them there, with all the plain to choose?
135   No foot-print leading to that horrid mews,
     None out of it. Mad brewage set to work
     Their brains, no doubt, like galley-slaves the Turk
         Pits for his pastime, Christians against Jews.

24

     And more than that—a furlong on—why, there!
140   What bad use was that engine for, that wheel,
         Or brake, not wheel—that harrow fit to reel
     Men's bodies out like silk? with all the air
     Of Tophet's° tool, on earth left unaware,   *hell's*
         Or brought to sharpen its rusty teeth of steel.

25

145   Then came a bit of stubbed ground, once a wood,
         Next a marsh, it would seem, and now mere earth
         Desperate and done with; (so a fool finds mirth,
     Makes a thing and then mars it, till his mood
     Changes and off he goes!) within a rood°—   *quarter of an acre*
150   Bog, clay and rubble, sand and stark black dearth.

26

Now blotches rankling, coloured gay and grim,
  Now patches where some leanness of the soil's
  Broke into moss or substances like boils;
Then came some palsied oak, a cleft in him
155 Like a distorted mouth that splits its rim
  Gaping at death, and dies while it recoils.

27

And just as far as ever from the end!
  Nought in the distance but the evening, nought
  To point my footstep further! At the thought,
160 A great black bird, Apollyon's[3] bosom-friend,
  Sailed past, nor beat his wide wing dragon-penned°   pinioned
  That brushed my cap—perchance the guide I sought.

28

For, looking up, aware I somehow grew,
  'Spite of the dusk, the plain had given place
165 All round to mountains—with such name to grace
Mere ugly heights and heaps now stolen in view.
  How thus they had surprised me,—solve it, you!
  How to get from them was no clearer case.

29

Yet half I seemed to recognize some trick
170 Of mischief happened to me, God knows when—
  In a bad dream perhaps. Here ended, then,
Progress this way. When, in the very nick
Of giving up, one time more, came a click
  As when a trap shuts—you're inside the den!

30

175 Burningly it came on me all at once,
  This was the place! those two hills on the right,
  Crouched like two bulls locked horn in horn in fight;
While to the left, a tall scalped mountain . . . Dunce,
Dotard, a-dozing at the very nonce,°   moment
180 After a life spent training for the sight!

31

What in the midst lay but the Tower itself?
  The round squat turret, blind as the fool's heart,[4]
  Built of brown stone, without a counterpart
In the whole world. The tempest's mocking elf
185 Points to the shipman thus the unseen shelf
  He strikes on, only when the timbers start.

32

Not see? because of night perhaps?—why, day
  Came back again for that! before it left,

3. Devil mentioned in Revelation 9.11 and in Bunyan's   4. "The fool hath said in his heart, There is no God"
Pilgrim's Progress.   (Psalm 14.1).

The dying sunset kindled through a cleft:
190   The hills, like giants at a hunting, lay,
Chin upon hand, to see the game at bay,—
"Now stab and end the creature—to the heft!"°   hilt

33

Not hear? when noise was everywhere! it tolled
Increasing like a bell. Names in my ears
195   Of all the lost adventurers my peers,—
How such a one was strong, and such was bold,
And such was fortunate, yet each of old
Lost, lost! one moment knelled the woe of years.

34

There they stood, ranged along the hill-sides, met
200   To view the last of me, a living frame
For one more picture! in a sheet of flame
I saw them and I knew them all. And yet
Dauntless the slug-horn⁵ to my lips I set,
And blew. *"Childe Roland to the Dark Tower came."*

c. 1852   1855

Fra Lippo Lippi¹

I am poor brother Lippo, by your leave!
You need not clap your torches to my face.
Zooks, what's to blame? you think you see a monk!
What, 'tis past midnight, and you go the rounds,
5   And here you catch me at an alley's end
Where sportive ladies leave their doors ajar?
The Carmine's my cloister:² hunt it up,
Do,—harry out, if you must show your zeal,
Whatever rat, there, haps on his wrong hole,
10   And nip each softling of a wee white mouse,
Weke, weke, that's crept to keep him company!
Aha, you know your betters! Then, you'll take
Your hand away that's fiddling on my throat,
And please to know me likewise. Who am I?
15   Why, one, sir, who is lodging with a friend
Three streets off—he's a certain . . . how d'ye call?
Master—a . . . Cosimo of the Medici,³
I' the house that caps the corner. Boh! you were best!
Remember and tell me, the day you're hanged,
20   How you affected such a gullet's-gripe!⁴

5. Scottish word for slogan, or battle cry, though Browning seems to mean "trumpet."
1. Filippo Lippi (1406–1469) was an early Renaissance painter and monk whose life is described in Giorgio Vasari's *The Lives of the Painters* (1550, 1568); "Fra" means brother.

2. Santa Maria del Carmine, a Carmelite monastery in Florence.
3. Cosimo de' Medici (1389–1464), a banker and ruler of Florence, was Lippi's patron.
4. How you choked me by the throat.

But you, sir,[5] it concerns you that your knaves
Pick up a manner nor discredit you:
Zooks, are we pilchards,° that they sweep the streets   *sardines*
And count fair prize what comes into their net?

25   He's Judas to a tittle, that man is![6]
Just such a face! Why, sir, you make amends:
Lord, I'm not angry! Bid your hangdogs go
Drink out this quarter-florin to the health
Of the munificent House that harbours me

30   (And many more beside, lads! more beside!)
And all's come square again. I'd like his face—
His, elbowing on his comrade in the door
With the pike and lantern,—for the slave that holds
John Baptist's head a-dangle by the hair

35   With one hand ("Look you, now," as who should say)
And his weapon in the other, yet unwiped!
It's not your chance to have a bit of chalk,
A wood-coal or the like? or you should see!
Yes, I'm the painter, since you style me so.

40   What, brother Lippo's doings, up and down,
You know them and they take you? like enough!
I saw the proper twinkle in your eye—
'Tell you, I liked your looks at very first.
Let's sit and set things straight now, hip to haunch.

45   Here's spring come, and the nights one makes up bands
To roam the town and sing out carnival,[7]
And I've been three weeks shut within my mew,
A-painting for the great man, saints and saints
And saints again. I could not paint all night—

50   Ouf! I leaned out of window for fresh air.
There came a hurry of feet and little feet,
A sweep of lute-strings, laughs, and whifts of song,—
Flower o' the broom,
Take away love, and our earth is a tomb!

55   *Flower o' the quince,*
I let Lisa go, and what good in life since?
Flower o' the thyme[8]—and so on. Round they went.
Scarce had they turned the corner when a titter
Like the skipping of rabbits by moonlight,—three slim shapes,

60   And a face that looked up .... zooks, sir, flesh and blood,
That's all I'm made of! Into shreds it went,
Curtain and counterpane and coverlet,
All the bed-furniture—a dozen knots,
There was a ladder! Down I let myself,

65   Hands and feet, scrambling somehow, and so dropped,
And after them. I came up with the fun

---

5. Lippi now addresses the leader of the watchmen.
6. One of the watchmen is the spitting image of Judas.
7. A season of festivities before Lent.

8. The "flower songs" Lippi sings are called *stornelli*,
three-line Tuscan folk songs.

Hard by Saint Laurence,[9] hail fellow, well met,—
Flower o' the rose,
If I've been merry, what matter who knows?
70   And so as I was stealing back again
To get to bed and have a bit of sleep
Ere I rise up to-morrow and go work
On Jerome[1] knocking at his poor old breast
With his great round stone to subdue the flesh,
75   You snap me of the sudden. Ah, I see!
Though your eye twinkles still, you shake your head—
Mine's shaved[2]—a monk, you say—the sting's in that!
If Master Cosimo announced himself,
Mum's the word naturally; but a monk!
80   Come, what am I a beast for? tell us, now!
I was a baby when my mother died
And father died and left me in the street.
I starved there, God knows how, a year or two
On fig-skins, melon-parings, rinds and shucks,
85   Refuse and rubbish. One fine frosty day,
My stomach being empty as your hat,
The wind doubled me up and down I went.
Old Aunt Lapaccia trussed me with one hand,
(Its fellow was a stinger as I knew)
90   And so along the wall, over the bridge,
By the straight cut to the convent. Six words there,
While I stood munching my first bread that month:
"So, boy, you're minded," quoth the good fat father
Wiping his own mouth, 'twas refection-time,°—   *mealtime*
95   "To quit this very miserable world?
Will you renounce" . . . "the mouthful of bread?" thought I;
By no means! Brief, they made a monk of me;
I did renounce the world, its pride and greed,
Palace, farm, villa, shop and banking-house,
100 Trash, such as these poor devils of Medici
Have given their hearts to—all at eight years old.
Well, sir, I found in time, you may be sure,
'Twas not for nothing—the good bellyful,
The warm serge and the rope that goes all round,
105 And day-long blessed idleness beside!
"Let's see what the urchin's fit for"—that came next.
Not overmuch their way, I must confess.
Such a to-do! They tried me with their books:
Lord, they'd have taught me Latin in pure waste!
110 *Flower o' the clove,*
All the Latin I construe is, "amo," I love!
But, mind you, when a boy starves in the streets
Eight years together, as my fortune was,
Watching folk's faces to know who will fling

9. The Church of San Lorenzo.
1. The pleasure-loving Lippi is painting the chaste and
ascetic St. Jerome.

2. The tonsure, or partially shaved head, was the emblem
of the monk.

115   The bit of half-stripped grape-bunch he desires,
       And who will curse or kick him for his pains,—
       Which gentleman processional and fine,
       Holding a candle to the Sacrament,
       Will wink and let him lift a plate and catch
120   The droppings of the wax to sell again,
       Or holla for the Eight[3] and have him whipped,—
       How say I?—nay, which dog bites, which lets drop
       His bone from the heap of offal in the street,—
       Why, soul and sense of him grow sharp alike,
125   He learns the look of things, and none the less
       For admonition from the hunger-pinch.
       I had a store of such remarks, be sure,
       Which, after I found leisure, turned to use.
       I drew men's faces on my copy-books,
130   Scrawled them within the antiphonary's marge,[4]
       Joined legs and arms to the long music-notes,
       Found eyes and nose and chin for A's and B's,
       And made a string of pictures of the world
       Betwixt the ins and outs of verb and noun,
135   On the wall, the bench, the door. The monks looked black.
       "Nay," quoth the Prior, "turn him out, d' ye say?
       In no wise. Lose a crow and catch a lark.
       What if at last we get our man of parts,
       We Carmelites, like those Camaldolese
140   And Preaching Friars, to do our church up fine
       And put the front on it that ought to be!"[5]
       And hereupon he bade me daub away.
       Thank you! my head being crammed, the walls a blank,
       Never was such prompt disemburdening.
145   First, every sort of monk, the black and white,
       I drew them, fat and lean: then, folk at church,
       From good old gossips waiting to confess
       Their cribs° of barrel-droppings, candle-ends,—   *small thefts*
       To the breathless fellow at the altar-foot,
150   Fresh from his murder,[6] safe and sitting there
       With the little children round him in a row
       Of admiration, half for his beard and half
       For that white anger of his victim's son
       Shaking a fist at him with one fierce arm,
155   Signing himself[7] with the other because of Christ
       (Whose sad face on the cross sees only this
       After the passion° of a thousand years)   *suffering*
       Till some poor girl, her apron o'er her head,
       (Which the intense eyes looked through) came at eve
160   On tiptoe, said a word, dropped in a loaf,

3. Send for the magistrates of Florence.
4. The margin of his hymn book.
5. The Prior, or head of the monastery, wants to outdo
rival orders of monks by having Lippi paint the church
splendidly.
6. Criminals could take refuge in the church because it
was a sanctuary where civil law had no power.
7. Making the sign of the cross.

Her pair of earrings and a bunch of flowers
(The brute took growling), prayed, and so was gone.
I painted all, then cried " 'Tis ask and have;
Choose, for more's ready!"—laid the ladder flat,
165 And showed my covered bit of cloister-wall
The monks closed in a circle and praised loud
Till checked, taught what to see and not to see,
Being simple bodies,—"That's the very man!
Look at the boy who stoops to pat the dog!
170 That woman's like the Prior's niece[8] who comes
To care about his asthma: it's the life!"
But there my triumph's straw-fire flared and funked;°   smoked
Their betters took their turn to see and say:
The Prior and the learned pulled a face
175 And stopped all that in no time. "How? what's here?
Quite from the mark of painting, bless us all!
Faces, arms, legs and bodies like the true
As much as pea and pea! it's devil's-game!
Your business is not to catch men with show,
180 With homage to the perishable clay,
But lift them over it, ignore it all,
Make them forget there's such a thing as flesh.
Your business is to paint the souls of men—
Man's soul, and it's a fire, smoke . . . no, it's not . . .
185 It's vapour done up like a new-born babe—
(In that shape when you die it leaves your mouth)
It's . . . well, what matters talking, it's the soul!
Give us no more of body than shows soul!
Here's Giotto,[9] with his Saint a-praising God,
190 That sets us praising,—why not stop with him?
Why put all thoughts of praise out of our head
With wonder at lines, colours, and what not?
Paint the soul, never mind the legs and arms!
Rub all out, try at it a second time.
195 Oh, that white smallish female with the breasts,
She's just my niece . . . Herodias, I would say,—
Who went and danced and got men's heads cut off![1]
Have it all out!" Now, is this sense, I ask?
A fine way to paint soul, by painting body
200 So ill, the eye can't stop there, must go further
And can't fare worse! Thus, yellow does for white
When what you put for yellow's simply black,
And any sort of meaning looks intense
When all beside itself means and looks nought.
205 Why can't a painter lift each foot in turn,
Left foot and right foot, go a double step,
Make his flesh liker and his soul more like,

8. Probably a euphemism for the Prior's mistress.
9. Giotto di Bondone (c. 1266–1337), late-medieval Florentine artist and architect.
1. The gospel of Matthew tells how Herod's niece Salomé

danced before him and requested as a reward the head of
John the Baptist (14.6–8). According to Vasari, however,
it was Salomé's mother, Herodias, who danced.

Both in their order? Take the prettiest face,
The Prior's niece . . . patron-saint—is it so pretty
210 You can't discover if it means hope, fear,
Sorrow or joy? won't beauty go with these?
Suppose I've made her eyes all right and blue,
Can't I take breath and try to add life's flash,
And then add soul and heighten them threefold?
215 Or say there's beauty with no soul at all—
(I never saw it—put the case the same—)
If you get simple beauty and nought else,
You get about the best thing God invents:
That's somewhat: and you'll find the soul you have missed,
220 Within yourself, when you return him thanks.
"Rub all out!" Well, well, there's my life, in short,
And so the thing has gone on ever since.
I'm grown a man no doubt, I've broken bounds:
You should not take a fellow eight years old
225 And make him swear to never kiss the girls.
I'm my own master, paint now as I please—
Having a friend, you see, in the Corner-house!°   *Medici palace*
Lord, it's fast holding by the rings in front—
Those great rings serve more purposes than just
230 To plant a flag in, or tie up a horse!
And yet the old schooling sticks, the old grave eyes
Are peeping o'er my shoulder as I work,
The heads shake still—"It's art's decline, my son!
You're not of the true painters, great and old;
235 Brother Angelico's the man, you'll find;
Brother Lorenzo stands his single peer:[2]
Fag° on at flesh, you'll never make the third!"   *struggle*
Flower o' the pine,
You keep your mistr . . . manners, and I'll stick to mine!
240 I'm not the third, then: bless us, they must know!
Don't you think they're the likeliest to know,
They with their Latin? So, I swallow my rage,
Clench my teeth, suck my lips in tight, and paint
To please them—sometimes do and sometimes don't;
245 For, doing most, there's pretty sure to come
A turn, some warm eve finds me at my saints—
A laugh, a cry, the business of the world—
(*Flower o' the peach,*
Death for us all, and his own life for each!)
250 And my whole soul revolves, the cup runs over,
The world and life's too big to pass for a dream,
And I do these wild things in sheer despite,
And play the fooleries you catch me at,
In pure rage! The old mill-horse, out at grass
255 After hard years, throws up his stiff heels so,

---

2. Fra Angelico (1387–1455) and Lorenzo Monaco (1370–1425) were important painters in the traditional formalist style.

Although the miller does not preach to him
The only good of grass is to make chaff.°   *straw*
What would men have? Do they like grass or no—
May they or mayn't they? all I want's the thing
260   Settled for ever one way. As it is,
You tell too many lies and hurt yourself:
You don't like what you only like too much,
You do like what, if given you at your word,
You find abundantly detestable.
265   For me, I think I speak as I was taught;
I always see the garden and God there
A-making man's wife: and, my lesson learned,
The value and significance of flesh,
I can't unlearn ten minutes afterwards.

270   You understand me: I'm a beast, I know.
But see, now—why, I see as certainly
As that the morning-star's about to shine,
What will hap some day. We've a youngster here
Comes to our convent, studies what I do,
275   Slouches and stares and lets no atom drop:
His name is Guidi—he'll not mind the monks—
They call him Hulking Tom,[3] he lets them talk—
He picks my practice up—he'll paint apace,
I hope so—though I never live so long,
280   I know what's sure to follow. You be judge!
You speak no Latin more than I, belike,
However, you're my man, you've seen the world
—The beauty and the wonder and the power,
The shapes of things, their colours, lights and shades,
285   Changes, surprises,—and God made it all!
—For what? Do you feel thankful, ay or no,
For this fair town's face, yonder river's line,
The mountain round it and the sky above,
Much more the figures of man, woman, child,
290   These are the frame to? What's it all about?
To be passed over, despised? or dwelt upon,
Wondered at? oh, this last of course!—you say.
But why not do as well as say,—paint these
Just as they are, careless what comes of it?
295   God's works—paint anyone, and count it crime
To let a truth slip. Don't object, "His works
Are here already; nature is complete:
Suppose you reproduce her—(which you can't)
There's no advantage! you must beat her, then."
300   For, don't you mark? we're made so that we love
First when we see them painted, things we have passed
Perhaps a hundred times nor cared to see;

---

3. Tommaso Guidi (1401–1428), called Masaccio ("Sloppy Tom"), was probably Lippi's teacher, but Browning casts him as his pupil. Both painters revolted against the highly stylized conventions of medieval art in favor of increased realism.

And so they are better, painted—better to us,
Which is the same thing. Art was given for that;
305   God uses us to help each other so,
Lending our minds out. Have you noticed, now,
Your cullion's hanging face?[4] A bit of chalk,
And trust me but you should, though! How much more,
If I drew higher things with the same truth!
310   That were to take the Prior's pulpit-place,
Interpret God to all of you! Oh, oh,
It makes me mad to see what men shall do
And we in our graves! This world's no blot for us,
Nor blank; it means intensely, and means good:
315   To find its meaning is my meat and drink.
"Ay, but you don't so instigate to prayer!"
Strikes in the Prior: "when your meaning's plain
It does not say to folk—remember matins,°   *morning prayers*
Or, mind you fast next Friday!" Why, for this
320   What need of art at all? A skull and bones,
Two bits of stick nailed crosswise, or, what's best,
A bell to chime the hour with, does as well.
I painted a Saint Laurence six months since
At Prato, splashed the fresco in fine style:
325   "How looks my painting, now the scaffold's down?"
I ask a brother: "Hugely," he returns—
Already not one phiz° of your three slaves   *face*
Who turn the Deacon off his toasted side,[5]
But's scratched and prodded to our heart's content,
330   The pious people have so eased their own
With coming to say prayers there in a rage:
We get on fast to see the bricks beneath.
Expect another job this time next year,
For pity and religion grow i' the crowd—
335   Your painting serves its purpose!" Hang the fools!

      —That is—you'll not mistake an idle word
Spoke in a huff by a poor monk, God wot,
Tasting the air this spicy night which turns
The unaccustomed head like Chianti wine!
340   Oh, the church knows! don't misreport me, now!
It's natural a poor monk out of bounds
Should have his apt word to excuse himself:
And hearken how I plot to make amends.
I have bethought me: I shall paint a piece
345   . . . There's for you! Give me six months, then go, see
Something in Sant' Ambrogio's![6] Bless the nuns!
They want a cast o' my office. I shall paint
God in the midst, Madonna and her babe,

4. That rascal's drooping face (or perhaps "born to be hanged"—cf. line 19).
5. St. Laurence, a deacon who was martyred by being roasted, is reputed to have asked to be turned over, as he was done on one side.
6. Lippi's *Coronation of the Virgin* was painted for the church of Sant' Ambrogio's convent in Florence.

Ringed by a bowery flowery angel-brood,
350 Lilies and vestments and white faces, sweet
As puff on puff of grated orris-root
When ladies crowd to Church at midsummer.
And then i' the front, of course a saint or two—
355 Saint John, because he saves the Florentines,
Saint Ambrose, who puts down in black and white
The convent's friends and gives them a long day,
And Job, I must have him there past mistake,
The man of Uz (and Us without the z,
Painters who need his patience). Well, all these
360 Secured at their devotion, up shall come
Out of a corner when you least expect,
As one by a dark stair into a great light,
Music and talking, who but Lippo! I!—
Mazed, motionless and moonstruck—I'm the man!
365 Back I shrink—what is this I see and hear?
I, caught up with my monk's-things by mistake,
My old serge gown and rope that goes all round,
I, in this presence, this pure company!
Where's a hole, where's a corner for escape?
370 Then steps a sweet angelic slip of a thing
Forward, puts out a soft palm—"Not so fast!"
—Addresses the celestial presence, "nay—
He made you and devised you, after all,
Though he's none of you! Could Saint John there draw—
375 His camel-hair[7] make up a painting-brush?
We come to brother Lippo for all that,
Iste perfecit opus!"[8] So, all smile—
I shuffle sideways with my blushing face
Under the cover of a hundred wings
380 Thrown like a spread of kirtles° when you're gay   _skirts_
And play hot cockles,[9] all the doors being shut,
Till, wholly unexpected, in there pops
The hothead husband! Thus I scuttle off
To some safe bench behind, not letting go
385 The palm of her, the little lily thing
That spoke the good word for me in the nick,
Like the Prior's niece . . . Saint Lucy, I would say.[1]
And so all's saved for me, and for the church
A pretty picture gained. Go, six months hence!
390 Your hand, sir, and good-bye: no lights, no lights!
The street's hushed, and I know my own way back,
Don't fear me! There's the grey beginning. Zooks!

1853   1855

---

7. "And John was clothed with camel's hair, and with a girdle of a skin about his loins; and he did eat locusts and wild honey" (Mark 1.6). John the Baptist is the patron saint of Florence.
8. "This man made the work." These words appear beside a figure in the painting, which was assumed to be a self-portrait of Lippi. (It actually depicts the patron who ordered the painting.)
9. A blindfolded game, here a euphemism for sex.
1. Lippi will paint the Prior's "niece" as the virgin martyr Lucy, whom he has imagined interceding on his behalf with "the celestial presence" (lines 370–377).

Andrea del Sarto[1]
(called "The Faultless Painter")

But do not let us quarrel any more,
No, my Lucrezia; bear with me for once:
Sit down and all shall happen as you wish.
You turn your face, but does it bring your heart?
5   I'll work then for your friend's friend, never fear,
Treat his own subject after his own way,
Fix his own time, accept too his own price,
And shut the money into this small hand
When next it takes mine. Will it? tenderly?
10 Oh, I'll content him,—but to-morrow, Love!
I often am much wearier than you think,
This evening more than usual, and it seems
As if—forgive now—should you let me sit
Here by the window with your hand in mine
15 And look a half-hour forth on Fiesole,[2]
Both of one mind, as married people use,
Quietly, quietly the evening through,
I might get up to-morrow to my work
Cheerful and fresh as ever. Let us try.
20 To-morrow, how you shall be glad for this!
Your soft hand is a woman of itself,
And mine the man's bared breast she curls inside.
Don't count the time lost, neither; you must serve
For each of the five pictures we require:
25 It saves a model. So! keep looking so—
My serpentining beauty, rounds on rounds!
—How could you ever prick those perfect ears,
Even to put the pearl there! oh, so sweet—
My face, my moon, my everybody's moon,
30 Which everybody looks on and calls his,
And, I suppose, is looked on by in turn,
While she looks—no one's: very dear, no less.
You smile? why, there's my picture ready made,
There's what we painters call our harmony!
35 A common greyness silvers everything,[3]—
All in a twilight, you and I alike
—You, at the point of your first pride in me
(That's gone you know),—but I, at every point;
My youth, my hope, my art, being all toned down
40 To yonder sober pleasant Fiesole.

1. Browning's depiction of Andrea del Sarto (1486–1531), a technically gifted Florentine Renaissance painter who never quite lived up to his early promise, is based in part on Giorgio Vasari's *The Lives of the Painters* (1550, 1568). Vasari, who had been Andrea's pupil, considered that "had his spirit been as bold as his judgment was profound, he would doubtless have been unequaled. But a timidity of spirit and a yielding simple nature prevented him from exhibiting a burning ardour and dash that, joined to his other qualities, would have made him divine."
2. A suburb of Florence.
3. The grey tones of Andrea del Sarto's paintings were regarded in Browning's day as characteristic of his art (rather than the effect of fading and aging); the unusually muted rhythms of this poem attempt to convey the same qualities of restraint and understatement.

There's the bell clinking from the chapel-top;
That length of convent-wall across the way
Holds the trees safer, huddled more inside;
The last monk leaves the garden; days decrease,
45   And autumn grows, autumn in everything.
Eh? the whole seems to fall into a shape
As if I saw alike my work and self
And all that I was born to be and do,
A twilight-piece. Love, we are in God's hand.
50   How strange now, looks the life he makes us lead;
So free we seem, so fettered fast we are!
I feel he laid the fetter: let it lie!
This chamber for example—turn your head—
All that's behind us! You don't understand
55   Nor care to understand about my art,
But you can hear at least when people speak:
And that cartoon,° the second from the door   *drawing*
—It is the thing, Love! so such things should be—
Behold Madonna!—I am bold to say.
60   I can do with my pencil what I know,
What I see, what at bottom of my heart
I wish for, if I ever wish so deep—
Do easily, too—what I say, perfectly,
I do not boast, perhaps: yourself are judge,
65   Who listened to the Legate's[4] talk last week,
And just as much they used to say in France.
At any rate 'tis easy, all of it!
No sketches first, no studies, that's long past:
I do what many dream of, all their lives,
70   —Dream? strive to do, and agonize to do,
And fail in doing. I could count twenty such
On twice your fingers, and not leave this town,
Who strive—you don't know how the others strive
To paint a little thing like that you smeared
75   Carelessly passing with your robes afloat,—
Yet do much less, so much less, Someone[5] says,
(I know his name, no matter)—so much less!
Well, less is more, Lucrezia: I am judged.
There burns a truer light of God in them,
80   In their vexed beating stuffed and stopped-up brain,
Heart, or whate'er else, than goes on to prompt
This low-pulsed forthright craftsman's hand of mine.
Their works drop groundward, but themselves, I know,
Reach many a time a heaven that's shut to me,
85   Enter and take their place there sure enough,
Though they come back and cannot tell the world.
My works are nearer heaven, but I sit here.
The sudden blood of these men! at a word—
Praise them, it boils, or blame them, it boils too.

---

4. A representative of the Pope.   5. Probably Michelangelo.

90   I, painting from myself and to myself,
      Know what I do, am unmoved by men's blame
      Or their praise either. Somebody remarks
      Morello's[6] outline there is wrongly traced,
      His hue mistaken; what of that? or else,
95   Rightly traced and well ordered; what of that?
      Speak as they please, what does the mountain care?
      Ah, but a man's reach should exceed his grasp,
      Or what's a heaven for? All is silver-grey
      Placid and perfect with my art: the worse!
100   I know both what I want and what might gain,
      And yet how profitless to know, to sigh
      "Had I been two, another and myself,
      Our head would have o'erlooked the world!" No doubt.
      Yonder's a work now, of that famous youth
105   The Urbinate who died five years ago.[7]
      ('Tis copied, George Vasari sent it me.)
      Well, I can fancy how he did it all,
      Pouring his soul, with kings and popes to see,
      Reaching, that heaven might so replenish him,
110   Above and through his art—for it gives way;
      That arm is wrongly put—and there again—
      A fault to pardon in the drawing's lines,
      Its body, so to speak: its soul is right,
      He means right—that, a child may understand.
115   Still, what an arm! and I could alter it:
      But all the play, the insight and the stretch—
      Out of me, out of me! And wherefore out?
      Had you enjoined them on me, given me soul,
      We might have risen to Rafael, I and you!
120   Nay, Love, you did give all I asked, I think—
      More than I merit, yes, by many times.
      But had you—oh, with the same perfect brow,
      And perfect eyes, and more than perfect mouth,
      And the low voice my soul hears, as a bird
125   The fowler's pipe, and follows to the snare—
      Had you, with these the same, but brought a mind!
      Some women do so. Had the mouth there urged
      "God and the glory! never care for gain.
      The present by the future, what is that?
130   Live for fame, side by side with Agnolo![8]
      Rafael is waiting: up to God, all three!"
      I might have done it for you. So it seems:
      Perhaps not. All is as God over-rules.
      Beside, incentives come from the soul's self;
135   The rest avail not. Why do I need you?

6. A mountain near Florence.
7. Raphael (1483–1520) was born in Urbino. Thus the poem is set in 1525 (when, far from being in autumnal decline, Andrea was at the height of his powers).
8. Michelangelo (Michel Agnolo Buonarroti), Italian painter (1475–1564).

What wife had Rafael, or has Agnolo?
In this world, who can do a thing, will not;
And who would do it, cannot, I perceive:
Yet the will's somewhat—somewhat, too, the power—
140 And thus we half-men struggle. At the end,
God, I conclude, compensates, punishes.
'Tis safer for me, if the award be strict,
That I am something underrated here,
Poor this long while, despised, to speak the truth.
145 I dared not, do you know, leave home all day,
For fear of chancing on the Paris lords.[9]
The best is when they pass and look aside;
But they speak sometimes; I must bear it all.
Well may they speak! That Francis, that first time,
150 And that long festal year at Fontainebleau!
I surely then could sometimes leave the ground,
Put on the glory, Rafael's daily wear,
In that humane great monarch's golden look,—
One finger in his beard or twisted curl
155 Over his mouth's good mark that made the smile,
One arm about my shoulder, round my neck,
The jingle of his gold chain in my ear,
I painting proudly with his breath on me,
All his court round him, seeing with his eyes,
160 Such frank French eyes, and such a fire of souls
Profuse, my hand kept plying by those hearts,—
And, best of all, this, this, this face beyond,
This in the background, waiting on my work,
To crown the issue with a last reward!
165 A good time, was it not, my kingly days?
And had you not grown restless . . . but I know—
'Tis done and past; 'twas right, my instinct said;
Too live the life grew, golden and not grey,
And I'm the weak-eyed bat no sun should tempt
170 Out of the grange whose four walls make his world.
How could it end in any other way?
You called me, and I came home to your heart.
The triumph was—to reach and stay there; since
I reached it ere the triumph, what is lost?
175 Let my hands frame your face in your hair's gold,
You beautiful Lucrezia that are mine!
"Rafael did this, Andrea painted that;
The Roman's[1] is the better when you pray,
But still the other's Virgin was his wife—"
180 Men will excuse me. I am glad to judge
Both pictures in your presence; clearer grows

9. In 1518 Andrea was invited to Fontainebleau by the French king, Francis I, who became his patron. Rumor had it that when he left the court to return to Italy, the king entrusted him with funds, which he spent on a house for Lucrezia. Now he is ashamed to face the scorn of visiting French nobles.
1. Raphael worked in Rome after 1509.

My better fortune, I resolve to think.
For, do you know, Lucrezia, as God lives,
Said one day Agnolo, his very self,
185   To Rafael . . . I have known it all these years . . .
(When the young man was flaming out his thoughts
Upon a palace-wall for Rome to see,
Too lifted up in heart because of it)
"Friend, there's a certain sorry little scrub[2]
190   Goes up and down our Florence, none cares how,
Who, were he set to plan and execute
As you are, pricked on by your popes and kings,
Would bring the sweat into that brow of yours!"
To Rafael's!—And indeed the arm is wrong.
195   I hardly dare . . . yet, only you to see,
Give the chalk here—quick, thus the line should go!
Ay, but the soul! he's Rafael! rub it out!
Still, all I care for, if he spoke the truth,
(What he? why, who but Michel Agnolo?
200   Do you forget already words like those?)[3]
If really there was such a chance, so lost,—
Is, whether you're—not grateful—but more pleased.
Well, let me think so. And you smile indeed!
This hour has been an hour! Another smile?
205   If you would sit thus by me every night
I should work better, do you comprehend?
I mean that I should earn more, give you more.
See, it is settled dusk now; there's a star;
Morello's gone, the watch-lights show the wall,
210   The cue-owls[4] speak the name we call them by.
Come from the window, love,—come in, at last,
Inside the melancholy little house
We built to be so gay with. God is just.
King Francis may forgive me: oft at nights
215   When I look up from painting, eyes tired out,
The walls become illumined, brick from brick
Distinct, instead of mortar, fierce bright gold,
That gold of his I did cement them with!
Let us but love each other. Must you go?
220   That Cousin here again?[5] he waits outside?
Must see you—you, and not with me? Those loans?
More gaming debts to pay? you smiled for that?
Well, let smiles buy me! have you more to spend?
While hand and eye and something of a heart
225   Are left me, work's my ware, and what's it worth?
I'll pay my fancy. Only let me sit

2. I.e., Andrea, who is boasting to Lucrezia that Michelangelo once praised his abilities to Raphael.
3. Lucrezia, bored, has lost the thread of Andrea's story.

4. Owls whose cry sounds like the Italian word *ciù*.
5. Lucrezia's lover, whose gambling debts Andrea has already agreed to pay (lines 5–10).

The grey remainder of the evening out,
Idle, you call it, and muse perfectly
How I could paint, were I but back in France,
230   One picture, just one more—the Virgin's face,
Not yours this time! I want you at my side
To hear them—that is, Michel Agnolo—
Judge all I do and tell you of its worth.
Will you? To-morrow, satisfy your friend.
235   I take the subjects for his corridor,
Finish the portrait out of hand—there, there,
And throw him in another thing or two
If he demurs; the whole should prove enough
To pay for this same Cousin's freak. Beside,
240   What's better and what's all I care about,
Get you the thirteen scudi° for the ruff!   *coins*
Love, does that please you? Ah, but what does he,
The Cousin! what does he to please you more?

I am grown peaceful as old age to-night.
245   I regret little, I would change still less.
Since there my past life lies, why alter it?
The very wrong to Francis!—it is true
I took his coin, was tempted and complied,
And built this house and sinned, and all is said.
250   My father and my mother died of want.[6]
Well, had I riches of my own? you see
How one gets rich! Let each one bear his lot.
They were born poor, lived poor, and poor they died:
And I have laboured somewhat in my time
255   And not been paid profusely. Some good son
Paint my two hundred pictures—let him try!
No doubt, there's something strikes a balance. Yes,
You loved me quite enough, it seems to-night.
This must suffice me here. What would one have?
260   In heaven, perhaps, new chances, one more chance—
Four great walls in the New Jerusalem,[7]
Meted° on each side by the angel's reed,   *measured*
For Leonard,[8] Rafael, Agnolo and me
To cover—the three first without a wife,
265   While I have mine! So—still they overcome
Because there's still Lucrezia,—as I choose.

Again the Cousin's whistle! Go, my Love.

c. 1853   1855

---

6. Vasari claimed that Andrea abandoned his aged parents and spent his money on Lucrezia and her family.
7. Cf. Revelation 21.10–21.

8. Leonardo da Vinci (1452–1519), third in the trio of great Italian Renaissance artists whom del Sarto has failed to equal.

POPULAR SHORT FICTION

During the 1880s and 1890s, short stories enjoyed a golden age in Britain. H. G. Wells said that "People talked about them tremendously, compared them, and ranked them. That was the thing that mattered." Yet short stories had been popular in America and Europe for decades before they caught on in Britain. Previously, the public's appetite for fiction had been sated by novels, which often appeared serially in the leading periodicals. Although many novelists, including Charles Dickens, George Eliot, Anthony Trollope, and Wilkie Collins, occasionally tried their hand at short fiction, three-decker novels were far more profitable—and far more prestigious. Where the novel might be regarded as "serious," stories smacked of the sensational. Henry James observed that "the little story is but scantily relished in England, where readers take their fiction rather by the volume than by the page." Not until late in the century did writers such as Stevenson, Kipling, and Doyle build their careers on short stories, and only then did the genre gain the status of a distinct artistic form.

The growing visibility of short stories was fueled by innovations in the printing process that allowed low-cost mass-circulation periodicals to flourish; Somerset Maugham later argued that "the rich abundance of short stories during the nineteenth century was directly occasioned by the opportunity which the periodicals afforded." Thanks in part to the rage for Sherlock Holmes, *The Strand* sold half-a-million copies a month during the 1890s. Literary magazines were often shaped by the taste and vision of the founding editor; *Household Words*, for example—where Elizabeth Gaskell first published *Cranford*—bore the characteristic stamp of its creator, Charles Dickens.

The market for cheap reading matter was strengthened by the excitement of new-found and nearly universal literacy. The demands of an expanding readership spurred the development of the short story as an emerging literary form, one that ran the gamut from mystery stories, detective stories, and ghost stories to fairy tales, fables, and fantasies. The best story writers have always made every detail count; they achieve powerful effects through poetic compression of meaning into a narrow space. But they must do more than convey a unified mood or atmosphere; Hardy believed that their subject matter should be exceptional, too: "We tale-tellers are all Ancient Mariners, and none of us is warranted in stopping Wedding Guests (in other words, the hurrying public) unless he has something more unusual to relate than the ordinary experience of every average man and woman."

The examples that follow suggest the range of technique and experience the short story form could accommodate.

Elizabeth Gaskell
1810–1865

The narrator of *Cranford* speaks of having "vibrated all my life" between the rural setting of Cranford and a nearby commercial city. The same was true of Elizabeth Gaskell, who grew up in the small town of Knutsford, but went to live in the industrial city of Manchester after her marriage to a Unitarian minister in 1832. She grappled with the changes wrought by industrialism in novels of social protest, including *Mary Barton* (1848), *Ruth* (1853), and *North and South* (1855). Even in the idyllic village of Cranford, the "obnoxious" new railroad impinges dramatically. The middle-aged spinsters with their out-of-date clothes and manners are only dimly aware of the bustling modern world; they linger on as representatives of a bygone era. The story is set in the 1830s, when Dickens's lively comic novel *Pickwick Papers* was hot off the presses, the epitome of modern literature; the Cranford ladies' preference for the stately prose of the eighteenth-century Dr. Johnson humorously dramatizes a society in transition. The young narrator records their eccentricities fondly, but with a subtle sense of the absurd. Yet despite their faintly ridiculous obsession with gentility and "elegant economy," the women of Cranford retain the humanity, compassion, and moral integrity conspicuously lacking in the industrial world.

Our Society at Cranford[1]

In the first place, Cranford is in possession of the Amazons;[2] all the holders of houses above a certain rent are women. If a married couple come to settle in the town, somehow the gentleman disappears; he is either fairly frightened to death by being the only man in the Cranford evening parties, or he is accounted for by being with his regiment, his ship, or closely engaged in business all the week in the great neighbouring commercial town of Drumble,[3] distant only twenty miles on a railroad. In short, whatever does become of the gentlemen, they are not at Cranford. What could they do if they were there? The surgeon has his round of thirty miles, and sleeps at Cranford; but every man cannot be a surgeon. For keeping the trim gardens full of choice flowers without a weed to speck them; for frightening away little boys who look wistfully at the said flowers through the railings; for rushing out at the geese that occasionally venture into the gardens if the gates are left open; for deciding all questions of literature and politics without troubling themselves with unnecessary reasons or arguments; for obtaining clear and correct knowledge of everybody's affairs in the parish; for keeping their neat maid-servants in admirable order; for kindness (somewhat dictatorial) to the poor, and real tender good offices to each other whenever they are in distress, the ladies of Cranford are quite sufficient. "A man," as one of them observed to me once, "is *so* in the way in the house!" Although the ladies of Cranford know all each other's proceedings, they are exceedingly indifferent to each other's opinions. Indeed, as each has her own individuality, not to say eccentricity, pretty strongly developed, nothing is so easy as verbal retaliation; but, somehow, good-will reigns among them to a considerable degree.

The Cranford ladies have only an occasional little quarrel, spirited out in a few peppery words and angry jerks of the head; just enough to prevent the even tenor of their lives from becoming too flat. Their dress is very independent of fashion; as they observe, "What does it signify how we dress here at Cranford, where everybody knows us?" And if they go from home, their reason is equally cogent, "What does it signify how we dress here, where nobody knows us?" The materials of their clothes are, in general, good and plain, and most of them are nearly as scrupulous as Miss Tyler, of cleanly memory;[4] but I will answer for it, the last gigot, the last tight and scanty petticoat in wear in England, was seen in Cranford—and seen without a smile.[5]

I can testify to a magnificent family red silk umbrella, under which a gentle little spinster, left alone of many brothers and sisters, used to patter to church on rainy

1. First published as a self-contained story in December 1851 in *Household Words*, a periodical edited by Charles Dickens. Although Gaskell later said that "I never meant to write more," Dickens persuaded her to continue the story in subsequent issues. In 1853 the collected sketches appeared in book form as *Cranford*.
2. In Greek legend, the Amazons were fierce warriors who formed an all-female state.

3. Manchester.
4. The aunt of Robert Southey (1774–1843)—Poet Laureate at the time when *Cranford* takes place—was famous for her passion for cleanliness.
5. By the mid-1830s, the old-fashioned leg-of-mutton sleeve and straight skirt had given way to the hooped skirt.

days. Have you any red silk umbrellas in London? We had a tradition of the first that had ever been seen in Cranford; and the little boys mobbed it, and called it "a stick in petticoats." It might have been the very red silk one I have described, held by a strong father over a troop of little ones; the poor little lady—the survivor of all—could scarcely carry it.

Then there were rules and regulations for visiting and calls; and they were announced to any young people who might be staying in the town, with all the solemnity with which the old Manx laws were read once a year on the Tinwald Mount.[6]

"Our friends have sent to inquire how you are after your journey to-night, my dear" (fifteen miles in a gentleman's carriage); "they will give you some rest to-morrow, but the next day, I have no doubt, they will call; so be at liberty after twelve—from twelve to three are our calling hours."

Then, after they had called—

"It is the third day; I dare say your mamma has told you, my dear, never to let more than three days elapse between receiving a call and returning it; and also, that you are never to stay longer than a quarter of an hour."

"But am I to look at my watch? How am I to find out when a quarter of an hour has passed?"

"You must keep thinking about the time, my dear, and not allow yourself to forget it in conversation."

As everybody had this rule in their minds, whether they received or paid a call, of course no absorbing subject was ever spoken about. We kept ourselves to short sentences of small talk, and were punctual to our time.

I imagine that a few of the gentlefolks of Cranford were poor, and had some difficulty in making both ends meet; but they were like the Spartans,[7] and concealed their smart under a smiling face. We none of us spoke of money, because that subject savoured of commerce and trade, and though some might be poor, we were all aristocratic. The Cranfordians had that kindly *esprit de corps* which made them overlook all deficiencies in success when some among them tried to conceal their poverty. When Mrs Forrester, for instance, gave a party in her baby-house of a dwelling, and the little maiden disturbed the ladies on the sofa by a request that she might get the tea-tray out from underneath, every one took this novel proceeding as the most natural thing in the world, and talked on about household forms and ceremonies as if we all believed that our hostess had a regular servants' hall, second table, with housekeeper and steward, instead of the one little charity-school maiden,[8] whose short ruddy arms could never have been strong enough to carry the tray upstairs, if she had not been assisted in private by her mistress, who now sat in state, pretending not to know what cakes were sent up, though she knew, and we knew, and she knew that we knew, and we knew that she knew that we knew, she had been busy all the morning making tea-bread and sponge-cakes.

There were one or two consequences arising from this general but unacknowledged poverty, and this very much acknowledged gentility, which were not amiss, and which might be introduced into many circles of society to their great improvement. For instance, the inhabitants of Cranford kept early hours, and clattered

---

6. The population of the Isle of Man customarily assembled once a year on Tynwald Hill to hear the new laws read aloud.
7. The Spartans of ancient Greece were known for their courage and self-control in the face of hardship.
8. Charity schools trained poor children for domestic work; that one such pupil formed Mrs. Forrester's entire domestic staff indicates her meager standard of living.

home in their pattens,[9] under the guidance of a lantern-bearer, about nine o'clock at night; and the whole town was abed and asleep by half-past ten. Moreover, it was considered "vulgar" (a tremendous word in Cranford) to give anything expensive, in the way of eatable or drinkable, at the evening entertainments. Wafer bread-and-butter and sponge-biscuits were all that the Honourable Mrs Jamieson gave; and she was sister-in-law to the late Earl of Glenmire, although she did practise such "elegant economy."

"Elegant economy!" How naturally one falls back into the phraseology of Cranford! There, economy was always "elegant," and money-spending always "vulgar and ostentatious;" a sort of sour-grapeism which made us very peaceful and satisfied. I never shall forget the dismay felt when a certain Captain Brown came to live at Cranford, and openly spoke about his being poor—not in a whisper to an intimate friend, the doors and windows being previously closed, but in the public street! in a loud military voice! alleging his poverty as a reason for not taking a particular house. The ladies of Cranford were already rather moaning over the invasion of their territories by a man and a gentleman. He was a half-pay captain,[1] and had obtained some situation on a neighbouring railroad, which had been vehemently petitioned against by the little town;[2] and if, in addition to his masculine gender, and his connection with the obnoxious railroad, he was so brazen as to talk of being poor—why, then, indeed, he must be sent to Coventry.[3] Death was as true and as common as poverty; yet people never spoke about that, loud out in the streets. It was a word not to be mentioned to ears polite. We had tacitly agreed to ignore that any with whom we associated on terms of visiting equality could ever be prevented by poverty from doing anything that they wished. If we walked to or from a party, it was because the night was so fine, or the air so refreshing, not because sedan-chairs were expensive.[4] If we wore prints, instead of summer silks, it was because we preferred a washing material; and so on, till we blinded ourselves to the vulgar fact that we were, all of us, people of very moderate means. Of course, then, we did not know what to make of a man who could speak of poverty as if it was not a disgrace. Yet, somehow, Captain Brown made himself respected in Cranford, and was called upon, in spite of all resolutions to the contrary. I was surprised to hear his opinions quoted as authority at a visit which I paid to Cranford about a year after he had settled in the town. My own friends had been among the bitterest opponents of any proposal to visit the Captain and his daughters, only twelve months before; and now he was even admitted in the tabooed hours before twelve. True, it was to discover the cause of a smoking chimney, before the fire was lighted; but still Captain Brown walked upstairs, nothing daunted, spoke in a voice too large for the room, and joked quite in the way of a tame man about the house. He had been blind to all the small slights, and omissions of trivial ceremonies, with which he had been received. He had been friendly, though the Cranford ladies had been cool; he had answered small sarcastic compliments in good faith; and with his manly frankness had overpowered all the shrinking which met him as a man who was not ashamed to be poor. And, at last, his excellent masculine common sense, and his facility in devising expedients to overcome domestic dilemmas, had gained him an extraordinary place as authority among the Cranford ladies. He himself went on

9. Wooden platform shoes to protect one's shoes from mud.
1. A retired officer who stayed on reserve at half pay.
2. The railroads were new, and still looked on with suspicion by many country-dwellers.

3. Ostracized.
4. Enclosed chairs carried by servants; more common in the 18th century.

in his course, as unaware of his popularity as he had been of the reverse; and I am sure he was startled one day when he found his advice so highly esteemed as to make some counsel which he had given in jest to be taken in sober, serious earnest.

It was on this subject: An old lady had an Alderney cow, which she looked upon as a daughter. You could not pay the short quarter of an hour call without being told of the wonderful milk or wonderful intelligence of this animal. The whole town knew and kindly regarded Miss Betsy Barker's Alderney; therefore great was the sympathy and regret when, in an unguarded moment, the poor cow tumbled into a lime-pit.[5] She moaned so loudly that she was soon heard and rescued; but meanwhile the poor beast had lost most of her hair, and came out looking naked, cold, and miserable, in a bare skin. Everybody pitied the animal, though a few could not restrain their smiles at her droll appearance. Miss Betsy Barker absolutely cried with sorrow and dismay; and it was said she thought of trying a bath of oil. This remedy, perhaps, was recommended by some one of the number whose advice she asked; but the proposal, if ever it was made, was knocked on the head by Captain Brown's decided "Get her a flannel waistcoat and flannel drawers, ma'am, if you wish to keep her alive. But my advice is, kill the poor creature at once."

Miss Betsy Barker dried her eyes, and thanked the Captain heartily; she set to work, and by-and-by all the town turned out to see the Alderney meekly going to her pasture, clad in dark grey flannel. I have watched her myself many a time. Do you ever see cows dressed in grey flannel in London?

Captain Brown had taken a small house on the outskirts of the town, where he lived with his two daughters. He must have been upwards of sixty at the time of the first visit I paid to Cranford after I had left it as a residence. But he had a wiry, well-trained, elastic figure, a stiff military throw-back of his head, and a springing step, which made him appear much younger than he was. His eldest daughter looked almost as old as himself, and betrayed the fact that his real was more than his apparent age. Miss Brown must have been forty; she had a sickly, pained, careworn expression on her face, and looked as if the gaiety of youth had long faded out of sight. Even when young she must have been plain and hard featured. Miss Jessie Brown was ten years younger than her sister, and twenty shades prettier. Her face was round and dimpled. Miss Jenkyns once said, in a passion against Captain Brown (the cause of which I will tell you presently), "that she thought it was time for Miss Jessie to leave off her dimples, and not always to be trying to look like a child." It was true there was something childlike in her face; and there will be, I think, till she dies, though she should live to a hundred. Her eyes were large blue wondering eyes, looking straight at you; her nose was unformed and snub, and her lips were red and dewy; she wore her hair, too, in little rows of curls, which heightened this appearance. I do not know whether she was pretty or not; but I liked her face, and so did everybody, and I do not think she could help her dimples. She had something of her father's jauntiness of gait and manner; and any female observer might detect a slight difference in the attire of the two sisters—that of Miss Jessie being about two pounds per annum more expensive than Miss Brown's. Two pounds was a large sum in Captain Brown's annual disbursements.

Such was the impression made upon me by the Brown family when I first saw them all together in Cranford Church. The Captain I had met before—on the occasion of the smoky chimney, which he had cured by some simple alteration in the

---

5. A pit in which tanners dress skins with lime to remove the hair.

flue. In church, he held his double eye-glass to his eyes during the Morning Hymn, and then lifted up his head erect and sang out loud and joyfully. He made the responses louder than the clerk—an old man with a piping feeble voice, who, I think, felt aggrieved at the Captain's sonorous bass, and quavered higher and higher in consequence.

On coming out of church, the brisk Captain paid the most gallant attention to his two daughters. He nodded and smiled to his acquaintances; but he shook hands with none until he had helped Miss Brown to unfurl her umbrella, had relieved her of her prayer-book, and had waited patiently till she, with trembling nervous hands, had taken up her gown to walk through the wet roads.

I wondered what the Cranford ladies did with Captain Brown at their parties. We had often rejoiced, in former days, that there was no gentleman to be attended to, and to find conversation for, at the card-parties. We had congratulated ourselves upon the snugness of the evenings; and, in our love for gentility, and distaste of mankind, we had almost persuaded ourselves that to be a man was to be "vulgar"; so that when I found my friend and hostess, Miss Jenkyns, was going to have a party in my honour, and that Captain and the Miss Browns were invited, I wondered much what would be the course of the evening. Card-tables, with green baize tops, were set out by daylight, just as usual; it was the third week in November, so the evenings closed in about four. Candles, and clean packs of cards were arranged on each table. The fire was made up; the neat maid-servant had received her last directions; and there we stood, dressed in our best, each with a candle-lighter in our hands, ready to dart at the candles as soon as the first knock came. Parties in Cranford were solemn festivities, making the ladies feel gravely elated as they sat together in their best dresses. As soon as three had arrived, we sat down to "Preference," I being the unlucky fourth.[6] The next four comers were put down immediately to another table; and presently the tea-trays, which I had seen set out in the store-room as I passed in the morning, were placed each on the middle of a card-table. The china was delicate egg-shell; the old-fashioned silver glittered with polishing; but the eatables were of the slightest description. While the trays were yet on the tables, Captain and the Miss Browns came in; and I could see that, somehow or other, the Captain was a favourite with all the ladies present. Ruffled brows were smoothed, sharp voices lowered at his approach. Miss Brown looked ill, and depressed almost to gloom. Miss Jessie smiled as usual, and seemed nearly as popular as her father. He immediately and quietly assumed the man's place in the room; attended to every one's wants, lessened the pretty maid-servant's labour by waiting on empty cups and bread-and-butterless ladies; and yet did it all in so easy and dignified a manner, and so much as if it were a matter of course for the strong to attend to the weak, that he was a true man throughout. He played for threepenny points with as grave an interest as if they had been pounds; and yet, in all his attention to strangers, he had an eye on his suffering daughter—for suffering I was sure she was, though to many eyes she might only appear to be irritable. Miss Jessie could not play cards: but she talked to the sitters-out, who, before her coming, had been rather inclined to be cross. She sang, too, to an old cracked piano, which I think had been a spinet[7] in its youth. Miss Jessie sang "Jock of Hazeldean"[8] a little out of tune; but we were none of us musical, though Miss Jenkyns beat time, out of time, by way of appearing to be so.

6. "Unlucky" because only three people can play this card game at once; the dealer has to sit out.
7. An earlier keyboard instrument, popular before the invention of the piano.
8. A ballad written in 1816 by Sir Walter Scott.

It was very good of Miss Jenkyns to do this; for I had seen that, a little before, she had been a good deal annoyed by Miss Jessie Brown's unguarded admission (à propos of Shetland wool) that she had an uncle, her mother's brother, who was a shopkeeper in Edinburgh. Miss Jenkyns tried to drown this confession by a terrible cough—for the Honourable Mrs Jamieson was sitting at the card-table nearest Miss Jessie, and what would she say or think if she found out she was in the same room with a shopkeeper's niece! But Miss Jessie Brown (who had no tact, as we all agreed the next morning) would repeat the information, and assure Miss Pole she could easily get her the identical Shetland wool required, "through my uncle, who has the best assortment of Shetland goods of any one in Edinbro'." It was to take the taste of this out of our mouths, and the sound of this out of our ears, that Miss Jenkyns proposed music; so I say again, it was very good of her to beat time to the song.

When the trays re-appeared with biscuits and wine, punctually at a quarter to nine, there was conversation, comparing of cards, and talking over tricks; but by-and-by Captain Brown sported a bit of literature.

"Have you seen any numbers of 'The Pickwick Papers'?" said he. (They were then publishing in parts.)[9] "Capital thing!"

Now Miss Jenkyns was daughter of a deceased rector of Cranford; and, on the strength of a number of manuscript sermons, and a pretty good library of divinity, considered herself literary, and looked upon any conversation about books as a challenge to her. So she answered and said, "Yes, she had seen them; indeed, she might say she had read them."

"And what do you think of them?" exclaimed Captain Brown. "Aren't they famously good?"

So urged, Miss Jenkyns could not but speak.

"I must say, I don't think they are by any means equal to Dr Johnson.[1] Still, perhaps, the author is young. Let him persevere, and who knows what he may become if he will take the great Doctor for his model?" This was evidently too much for Captain Brown to take placidly; and I saw the words on the tip of his tongue before Miss Jenkyns had finished her sentence.

"It is quite a different sort of thing, my dear madam," he began.

"I am quite aware of that," returned she. "And I make allowances, Captain Brown."

"Just allow me to read you a scene out of this month's number," pleaded he. "I had it only this morning, and I don't think the company can have read it yet."

"As you please," said she, settling herself with an air of resignation. He read the account of the "swarry" which Sam Weller gave at Bath.[2] Some of us laughed heartily. I did not dare, because I was staying in the house. Miss Jenkyns sat in patient gravity. When it was ended, she turned to me, and said with mild dignity—

"Fetch me 'Rasselas,'[3] my dear, out of the bookroom."

When I brought it to her, she turned to Captain Brown—

"Now allow me to read you a scene, and then the present company can judge between your favourite, Mr Boz, and Dr Johnson."

9. Dickens published The Pickwick Papers serially in 1836 and 1837 under the pseudonym "Boz." Although this form of publication was considered "vulgar," the humorous escapades of Mr. Pickwick were phenomenally successful. When Cranford first appeared in Dickens's Household Words, he substituted Thomas Hood for himself, to Gaskell's annoyance.
1. Samuel Johnson (1708–1784) wrote more than a hundred years before Dickens; he was noted for his stately, balanced prose.

2. A reference to an episode in Pickwick Papers where Mr. Pickwick's servant Sam Weller attends a "soirée" for the footmen at Bath. The quick-witted Sam mocks the pompous servants, but they don't realize it.
3. Rasselas is a series of dialogues on moral themes between the prince of Abyssinia and his spiritual mentor, Imlac. Unlike the lively Pickwick, it is a serious and slow-paced philosophical work.

She read one of the conversations between Rasselas and Imlac, in a high-pitched majestic voice: and when she had ended, she said, "I imagine I am now justified in my preference of Dr Johnson as a writer of fiction." The Captain screwed his lips up, and drummed on the table, but he did not speak. She thought she would give a finishing blow or two.

"I consider it vulgar, and below the dignity of literature, to publish in numbers."

"How was the *Rambler*[4] published, ma'am?" asked Captain Brown in a low voice, which I think Miss Jenkyns could not have heard.

"Dr Johnson's style is a model for young beginners. My father recommended it to me when I began to write letters—I have formed my own style upon it; I recommend it to your favourite."

"I should be very sorry for him to exchange his style for any such pompous writing," said Captain Brown.

Miss Jenkyns felt this as a personal affront, in a way of which the Captain had not dreamed. Epistolary writing she and her friends considered as her *forte*. Many a copy of many a letter have I seen written and corrected on the slate, before she "seized the half-hour just previous to post-time to assure" her friends of this or of that; and Dr Johnson was, as she said, her model in these compositions. She drew herself up with dignity, and only replied to Captain Brown's last remark by saying, with marked emphasis on every syllable, "I prefer Dr Johnson to Mr Boz."

It is said—I won't vouch for the fact—that Captain Brown was heard to say, *sotto voce*, "D—n Dr Johnson!" If he did, he was penitent afterwards, as he showed by going to stand near Miss Jenkyns's arm-chair, and endeavouring to beguile her into conversation on some more pleasing subject. But she was inexorable. The next day she made the remark I have mentioned about Miss Jessie's dimples.

2

It was impossible to live a month at Cranford and not know the daily habits of each resident; and long before my visit was ended I knew much concerning the whole Brown trio. There was nothing new to be discovered respecting their poverty; for they had spoken simply and openly about that from the very first. They made no mystery of the necessity for their being economical. All that remained to be discovered was the Captain's infinite kindness of heart, and the various modes in which, unconsciously to himself, he manifested it. Some little anecdotes were talked about for some time after they occurred. As we did not read much, and as all the ladies were pretty well suited with servants, there was a dearth of subjects for conversation. We therefore discussed the circumstance of the Captain taking a poor old woman's dinner out of her hands one very slippery Sunday. He had met her returning from the bakehouse as he came from church, and noticed her precarious footing; and, with the grave dignity with which he did everything, he relieved her of her burden, and steered along the street by her side, carrying her baked mutton and potatoes safely home.[5] This was thought very eccentric; and it was rather expected that he would pay a round of calls, on the Monday morning, to explain and apologise to the Cranford sense of propriety: but he did no such thing: and then it was decided that he was ashamed, and was keeping out of sight. In a kindly pity for him, we began to say,

---

4. A periodical started in 1750 by Dr. Johnson and written almost entirely by himself.

5. Poor people often brought their meals to cook in the ovens of baker's shops on Sundays and holidays.

"After all, the Sunday morning's occurrence showed great goodness of heart," and it was resolved that he should be comforted on his next appearance amongst us; but, lo! he came down upon us, untouched by any sense of shame, speaking loud and bass as ever, his head thrown back, his wig as jaunty and well-curled as usual, and we were obliged to conclude he had forgotten all about Sunday.

Miss Pole and Miss Jessie Brown had set up a kind of intimacy on the strength of the Shetland wool and the new knitting stitches; so it happened that when I went to visit Miss Pole I saw more of the Browns than I had done while staying with Miss Jenkyns, who had never got over what she called Captain Brown's disparaging remarks upon Dr Johnson as a writer of light and agreeable fiction. I found that Miss Brown was seriously ill of some lingering, incurable complaint, the pain occasioned by which gave the uneasy expression to her face that I had taken for unmitigated crossness. Cross, too, she was at times, when the nervous irritability occasioned by her disease became past endurance. Miss Jessie bore with her at these times, even more patiently than she did with the bitter self-upbraidings by which they were invariably succeeded. Miss Brown used to accuse herself, not merely of hasty and irritable temper, but also of being the cause why her father and sister were obliged to pinch, in order to allow her the small luxuries which were necessaries in her condition. She would so fain have made sacrifices for them, and have lightened their cares, that the original generosity of her disposition added acerbity to her temper. All this was borne by Miss Jessie and her father with more than placidity—with absolute tenderness. I forgave Miss Jessie her singing out of tune, and her juvenility of dress, when I saw her at home. I came to perceive that Captain Brown's dark Brutus wig and padded coat[6] (alas! too often threadbare) were remnants of the military smartness of his youth, which he now wore unconsciously. He was a man of infinite resources, gained in his barrack experience. As he confessed, no one could black his boots to please him except himself; but, indeed, he was not above saving the little maid-servant's labours in every way—knowing, most likely, that his daughter's illness made the place a hard one.

He endeavoured to make peace with Miss Jenkyns soon after the memorable dispute I have named, by a present of a wooden fire-shovel (his own making), having heard her say how much the grating of an iron one annoyed her. She received the present with cool gratitude, and thanked him formally. When he was gone, she bade me put it away in the lumber-room; feeling, probably, that no present from a man who preferred Mr Boz to Dr Johnson could be less jarring than an iron fire-shovel.

Such was the state of things when I left Cranford and went to Drumble. I had, however, several correspondents, who kept me *au fait* as to the proceedings of the dear little town. There was Miss Pole, who was becoming as much absorbed in crochet as she had been once in knitting, and the burden of whose letter was something like, "But don't you forget the white worsted at Flint's" of the old song; for at the end of every sentence of news came a fresh direction as to some crochet commission which I was to execute for her. Miss Matilda Jenkyns (who did not mind being called Miss Matty, when Miss Jenkyns was not by) wrote nice, kind, rambling letters, now and then venturing into an opinion of her own; but suddenly pulling herself up, and either begging me not to name what she had said, as Deborah thought differently, and *she* knew, or else putting in a postscript to the effect that, since writing the

6. A short, curly hairstyle popular during the French Revolution; padded coats were fashionable in the early 19th century.

above, she had been talking over the subject with Deborah, and was quite convinced that, &c.—(here probably followed a recantation of every opinion she had given in the letter). Then came Miss Jenkyns—Debōrah, as she liked Miss Matty to call her, her father having once said that the Hebrew name ought to be so pronounced. I secretly think she took the Hebrew prophetess for a model in character; and, indeed, she was not unlike the stern prophetess[7] in some ways, making allowance, of course, for modern customs and difference in dress. Miss Jenkyns wore a cravat, and a little bonnet like a jockey-cap, and altogether had the appearance of a strong-minded woman; although she would have despised the modern idea of women being equal to men. Equal, indeed! she knew they were superior. But to return to her letters. Everything in them was stately and grand like herself. I have been looking them over (dear Miss Jenkyns, how I honoured her!), and I will give an extract, more especially because it relates to our friend Captain Brown:—

"The Honourable Mrs Jamieson has only just quitted me; and, in the course of conversation, she communicated to me the intelligence that she had yesterday received a call from her revered husband's quondam[8] friend, Lord Mauleverer. You will not easily conjecture what brought his lordship within the precincts of our little town. It was to see Captain Brown, with whom, it appears, his lordship was acquainted in the 'plumed wars,' and who had the privilege of averting destruction from his lordship's head when some great peril was impending over it, off the misnomered Cape of Good Hope. You know our friend the Honourable Mrs Jamieson's deficiency in the spirit of innocent curiosity; and you will therefore not be so much surprised when I tell you she was quite unable to disclose to me the exact nature of the peril in question. I was anxious, I confess, to ascertain in what manner Captain Brown, with his limited establishment, could receive so distinguished a guest; and I discovered that his lordship retired to rest, and, let us hope, to refreshing slumbers, at the Angel Hotel; but shared the Brunonian[9] meals during the two days that he honoured Cranford with his august presence. Mrs Johnson, our civil butcher's wife, informs me that Miss Jessie purchased a leg of lamb; but, besides this, I can hear of no preparation whatever to give a suitable reception to so distinguished a visitor. Perhaps they entertained him with 'the feast of reason and the flow of soul;'[1] and to us, who are acquainted with Captain Brown's sad want of relish for 'the pure wells of English undefiled,'[2] it may be matter for congratulation that he has had the opportunity of improving his taste by holding converse with an elegant and refined member of the British aristocracy. But from some mundane failings who is altogether free?"

Miss Pole and Miss Matty wrote to me by the same post. Such a piece of news as Lord Mauleverer's visit was not to be lost on the Cranford letter-writers: they made the most of it. Miss Matty humbly apologised for writing at the same time as her sister, who was so much more capable than she to describe the honour done to Cranford; but in spite of a little bad spelling, Miss Matty's account gave me the best idea of the commotion occasioned by his lordship's visit, after it had occurred; for, except the people at the Angel, the Browns, Mrs Jamieson, and a little lad his lordship had sworn at for driving a dirty hoop against the aristocratic legs, I could not hear of any one with whom his lordship had held conversation.

7. Deborah was one of the leaders of Israel (Judges 4–5).
8. Former.
9. A pretentious, Latinized version of Brown, part of Miss Jenkyns's unintentionally comic imitation of the style of Dr. Johnson.

1. Alexander Pope, *Imitations of Horace*, Satire 1, Book 2.128 (1733).
2. Edmund Spenser, *The Faerie Queene*, 4.2.32 (1596); the reference is to Chaucer.

My next visit to Cranford was in the summer. There had been neither births, deaths, nor marriages since I was there last. Everybody lived in the same house, and wore pretty nearly the same well-preserved, old-fashioned clothes. The greatest event was, that Miss Jenkynses had purchased a new carpet for the drawing-room. Oh, the busy work Miss Matty and I had in chasing the sunbeams, as they fell in an afternoon right down on this carpet through the blindless window! We spread newspapers over the places, and sat down to our book or our work; and, lo! in a quarter of an hour the sun had moved, and was blazing away on a fresh spot; and down again we went on our knees to alter the position of the newspapers. We were very busy, too, one whole morning, before Miss Jenkyns gave her party, in following her directions, and in cutting out and stitching together pieces of newspaper so as to form little paths to every chair set for the expected visitors, lest their shoes might dirty or defile the purity of the carpet. Do you make paper paths for every guest to walk upon in London?

Captain Brown and Miss Jenkyns were not very cordial to each other. The literary dispute, of which I had seen the beginning, was a "raw," the slightest touch on which made them wince. It was the only difference of opinion they had ever had; but that difference was enough. Miss Jenkyns could not refrain from talking *at* Captain Brown; and, though he did not reply, he drummed with his fingers, which action she felt and resented as very disparaging to Dr Johnson. He was rather ostentatious in his preference of the writings of Mr Boz; would walk through the streets so absorbed in them that he all but ran against Miss Jenkyns; and though his apologies were earnest and sincere, and though he did not, in fact, do more than startle her and himself, she owned to me she had rather he had knocked her down, if he had only been reading a higher style of literature. The poor, brave Captain! he looked older, and more worn, and his clothes were very threadbare. But he seemed as bright and cheerful as ever, unless he was asked about his daughter's health.

"She suffers a great deal, and she must suffer more: we do what we can to alleviate her pain;—God's will be done!" He took off his hat at these last words. I found, from Miss Matty, that everything had been done, in fact. A medical man, of high repute in that country neighbourhood, had been sent for, and every injunction he had given was attended to, regardless of expense. Miss Matty was sure they denied themselves many things in order to make the invalid comfortable; but they never spoke about it; and as for Miss Jessie!—"I really think she's an angel," said poor Miss Matty, quite overcome. "To see her way of bearing with Miss Brown's crossness, and the bright face she puts on after she's been sitting up a whole night and scolded above half of it, is quite beautiful. Yet she looks as neat and as ready to welcome the Captain at breakfast-time as if she had been asleep in the Queen's bed all night. My dear! you could never laugh at her prim little curls or her pink bows again if you saw her as I have done." I could only feel very penitent, and greet Miss Jessie with double respect when I met her next. She looked faded and pinched; and her lips began to quiver, as if she was very weak, when she spoke of her sister. But she brightened, and sent back the tears that were glittering in her pretty eyes, as she said—

"But, to be sure, what a town Cranford is for kindness! I don't suppose any one has a better dinner than usual cooked but the best part of all comes in a little covered basin for my sister. The poor people will leave their earliest vegetables at our door for her. They speak short and gruff, as if they were ashamed of it; but I am sure it often goes to my heart to see their thoughtfulness." The tears now came back and overflowed; but after a minute or two she began to scold herself, and ended by going away the same cheerful Miss Jessie as ever.

"But why does not this Lord Mauleverer do something for the man who saved his life?" said I.

"Why, you see, unless Captain Brown has some reason for it, he never speaks about being poor; and he walked along by his lordship looking as happy and cheerful as a prince; and as they never called attention to their dinner by apologies, and as Miss Brown was better that day, and all seemed bright, I dare say his lordship never knew how much care there was in the background. He did send game in the winter pretty often, but now he is gone abroad."

I had often occasion to notice the use that was made of fragments and small opportunities in Cranford; the rose-leaves that were gathered ere they fell to make into a potpourri for some one who had no garden; the little bundles of lavender flowers sent to strew the drawers of some town-dweller, or to burn in the chamber of some invalid. Things that many would despise, and actions which it seemed scarcely worth while to perform, were all attended to in Cranford. Miss Jenkyns stuck an apple full of cloves, to be heated and smell pleasantly in Miss Brown's room; and as she put in each clove she uttered a Johnsonian sentence. Indeed, she never could think of the Browns without talking Johnson; and, as they were seldom absent from her thoughts just then, I heard many a rolling, three-piled sentence.

Captain Brown called one day to thank Miss Jenkyns for many little kindnesses, which I did not know until then that she had rendered. He had suddenly become like an old man; his deep bass voice had a quavering in it, his eyes looked dim, and the lines on his face were deep. He did not—could not—speak cheerfully of his daughter's state, but he talked with manly, pious resignation, and not much. Twice over he said, "What Jessie has been to us, God only knows!" and after the second time, he got up hastily, shook hands all round without speaking, and left the room.

That afternoon we perceived little groups in the street, all listening with faces aghast to some tale or other. Miss Jenkyns wondered what could be the matter for some time before she took the undignified step of sending Jenny out to inquire.

Jenny came back with a white face of terror. "Oh, ma'am! oh, Miss Jenkyns, ma'am! Captain Brown is killed by them nasty cruel railroads!" and she burst into tears. She, along with many others, had experienced the poor Captain's kindness.

"How?—where—where? Good God! Jenny, don't waste time in crying, but tell us something." Miss Matty rushed out into the street at once, and collared the man who was telling the tale.

"Come in—come to my sister at once, Miss Jenkyns, the rector's daughter. Oh, man, man! say it is not true," she cried, as she brought the affrighted carter, sleeking down his hair, into the drawing-room, where he stood with his wet boots on the new carpet, and no one regarded it.

"Please, mum, it is true. I seed it myself," and he shuddered at the recollection. "The Captain was a-reading some new book as he was deep in, a-waiting for the down train; and there was a little lass as wanted to come to its mammy, and gave its sister the slip, and came toddling across the line. And he looked up sudden, at the sound of the train coming, and seed the child, and he darted on the line and cotched it up, and his foot slipped, and the train came over him in no time. O Lord, Lord! Mum, it's quite true—and they've come over to tell his daughters. The child's safe, though, with only a bang on its shoulder as he threw it to its mammy. Poor Captain would be glad of that, mum, wouldn't he? God bless him!" The great rough carter puckered up his manly face, and turned away to hide his tears. I turned to Miss Jenkyns. She looked very ill, as if she were going to faint, and signed to me to open the window.

"Matilda, bring me my bonnet. I must go to those girls. God pardon me, if ever I have spoken contemptuously to the Captain!"

Miss Jenkyns arrayed herself to go out, telling Miss Matilda to give the man a glass of wine. While she was away, Miss Matty and I huddled over the fire, talking in a low and awestruck voice. I know we cried quietly all the time.

Miss Jenkyns came home in a silent mood, and we durst not ask her many questions. She told us that Miss Jessie had fainted, and that she and Miss Pole had had some difficulty in bringing her round; but that, as soon as she recovered, she begged one of them to go and sit with her sister.

"Mr Hoggins says she cannot live many days, and she shall be spared this shock," said Miss Jessie, shivering with feelings to which she dared not give way.

"But how can you manage, my dear?" asked Miss Jenkyns; "you cannot bear up, she must see your tears."

"God will help me—I will not give way—she was asleep when the news came; she may be asleep yet. She would be so utterly miserable, not merely at my father's death, but to think of what would become of me; she is so good to me." She looked up earnestly in their faces with her soft true eyes, and Miss Pole told Miss Jenkyns afterwards she could hardly bear it, knowing, as she did, how Miss Brown treated her sister.

However, it was settled according to Miss Jessie's wish. Miss Brown was to be told her father had been summoned to take a short journey on railway business. They had managed it in some way—Miss Jenkyns could not exactly say how. Miss Pole was to stop with Miss Jessie. Mrs Jamieson had sent to inquire. And this was all we heard that night; and a sorrowful night it was. The next day a full account of the fatal accident was in the county paper which Miss Jenkyns took in. Her eyes were very weak, she said, and she asked me to read it. When I came to the "gallant gentleman was deeply engaged in the perusal of a number of 'Pickwick,' which he had just received," Miss Jenkyns shook her head long and solemnly, and then sighed out, "Poor, dear, infatuated man!"

The corpse was to be taken from the station to the parish church, there to be interred. Miss Jessie had set her heart on following it to the grave; and no dissuasives could alter her resolve. Her restraint upon herself made her almost obstinate; she resisted all Miss Pole's entreaties and Miss Jenkyns's advice. At last Miss Jenkyns gave up the point; and after a silence, which I feared portended some deep displeasure against Miss Jessie, Miss Jenkyns said she should accompany the latter to the funeral.

"It is not fit for you to go alone. It would be against both propriety and humanity were I to allow it."

Miss Jessie seemed as if she did not half like this arrangement; but her obstinacy, if she had any, had been exhausted in her determination to go to the interment. She longed, poor thing, I have no doubt, to cry alone over the grave of the dear father to whom she had been all in all, and to give way, for one little half-hour, uninterrupted by sympathy and unobserved by friendship. But it was not to be. That afternoon Miss Jenkyns sent out for a yard of black crape, and employed herself busily in trimming the little black silk bonnet I have spoken about. When it was finished she put it on, and looked at us for approbation—admiration she despised. I was full of sorrow, but, by one of those whimsical thoughts which come unbidden into our heads, in times of deepest grief, I no sooner saw the bonnet than I was reminded of a helmet; and in that hybrid bonnet, half helmet, half jockey-cap, did Miss Jenkyns attend Captain Brown's funeral, and, I believe, supported Miss Jessie with a tender, indulgent firmness which was invaluable, allowing her to weep her passionate fill before they left.

Miss Pole, Miss Matty, and I, meanwhile attended to Miss Brown: and hard work we found it to relieve her querulous and never-ending complaints. But if we were so weary and dispirited, what must Miss Jessie have been! Yet she came back almost calm, as if she had gained a new strength. She put off her mourning dress, and came in, looking pale and gentle, thanking us each with a soft long pressure of the hand. She could even smile—a faint, sweet, wintry smile—as if to reassure us of her power to endure; but her look made our eyes fill suddenly with tears, more than if she had cried outright.

It was settled that Miss Pole was to remain with her all the watching livelong night; and that Miss Matty and I were to return in the morning to relieve them, and give Miss Jessie the opportunity for a few hours of sleep. But when the morning came, Miss Jenkyns appeared at the breakfast-table, equipped in her helmet-bonnet, and ordered Miss Matty to stay at home, as she meant to go and help to nurse. She was evidently in a state of great friendly excitement, which she showed by eating her breakfast standing, and scolding the household all round.

No nursing—no energetic strong-minded woman could help Miss Brown now. There was that in the room as we entered which was stronger than us all, and made us shrink into solemn awestruck helplessness. Miss Brown was dying. We hardly knew her voice, it was so devoid of the complaining tone we had always associated with it. Miss Jessie told me afterwards that it, and her face too, were just what they had been formerly, when her mother's death left her the young anxious head of the family, of whom only Miss Jessie survived.

She was conscious of her sister's presence, though not, I think, of ours. We stood a little behind the curtain: Miss Jessie knelt with her face near her sister's, in order to catch the last soft awful whispers.

"Oh, Jessie! Jessie! How selfish I have been! God forgive me for letting you sacrifice yourself for me as you did! I have so loved you—and yet I have thought only of myself. God forgive me!"

"Hush, love! hush!" said Miss Jessie, sobbing.

"And my father! my dear, dear father! I will not complain now, if God will give me strength to be patient. But, oh, Jessie! tell my father how I longed and yearned to see him at last, and to ask his forgiveness. He can never know now how I loved him—oh! if I might but tell him, before I die! What a life of sorrow his has been, and I have done so little to cheer him!"

A light came into Miss Jessie's face. "Would it comfort you, dearest, to think that he does know?—would it comfort you, love, to know that his cares, his sorrows"— Her voice quivered, but she steadied it into calmness—"Mary! he has gone before you to the place where the weary are at rest.[3] He knows now how you loved him."

A strange look, which was not distress, came over Miss Brown's face. She did not speak for some time, but then we saw her lips form the words, rather than heard the sound—"Father, mother, Harry, Archy;"—then, as if it were a new idea throwing a filmy shadow over her darkened mind—"But you will be alone, Jessie!"

Miss Jessie had been feeling this all during the silence, I think; for the tears rolled down her cheeks like rain, at these words, and she could not answer at first. Then she put her hands together tight, and lifted them up, and said—but not to us—

"Though He slay me, yet will I trust in Him."[4]

3. Job 3.17.   4. Job 13.15.

In a few moments more Miss Brown lay calm and still—never to sorrow or murmur more.

After this second funeral, Miss Jenkyns insisted that Miss Jessie should come to stay with her rather than go back to the desolate house, which, in fact, we learned from Miss Jessie, must now be given up, as she had not wherewithal to maintain it. She had something above twenty pounds a year, besides the interest of the money for which the furniture would sell; but she could not live upon that: and so we talked over her qualifications for earning money.

"I can sew neatly," said she, "and I like nursing. I think, too, I could manage a house, if any one would try me as housekeeper; or I would go into a shop, as saleswoman, if they would have patience with me at first."

Miss Jenkyns declared, in an angry voice, that she should do no such thing; and talked to herself about "some people having no idea of their rank as a captain's daughter," nearly an hour afterwards, when she brought Miss Jessie up a basin of delicately-made arrowroot, and stood over her like a dragoon until the last spoonful was finished; then she disappeared. Miss Jessie began to tell me some more of the plans which had suggested themselves to her, and insensibly fell into talking of the days that were past and gone, and interested me so much I neither knew nor heeded how time passed. We were both startled when Miss Jenkyns reappeared, and caught us crying. I was afraid lest she would be displeased, as she often said that crying hindered digestion, and I knew she wanted Miss Jessie to get strong; but, instead, she looked queer and excited, and fidgeted round us without saying anything. At last she spoke.

"I have been so much startled—no, I've not been at all startled—don't mind me, my dear Miss Jessie—I've been very much surprised—in fact, I've had a caller, whom you knew once, my dear Miss Jessie"—

Miss Jessie went very white, then flushed scarlet, and looked eagerly at Miss Jenkyns.

"A gentleman, my dear, who wants to know if you would see him."

"Is it?—it is not"—stammered out Miss Jessie—and got no farther.

"This is his card," said Miss Jenkyns, giving it to Miss Jessie; and while her head was bent over it, Miss Jenkyns went through a series of winks and odd faces to me, and formed her lips into a long sentence, of which, of course, I could not understand a word.

"May he come up?" asked Miss Jenkyns, at last.

"Oh, yes! certainly!" said Miss Jessie, as much as to say, this is your house, you may show any visitor where you like. She took up some knitting of Miss Matty's and began to be very busy, though I could see how she trembled all over.

Miss Jenkyns rang the bell, and told the servant who answered it to show Major Gordon upstairs; and, presently, in walked a tall, fine, frank-looking man of forty or upwards. He shook hands with Miss Jessie; but he could not see her eyes, she kept them so fixed on the ground. Miss Jenkyns asked me if I would come and help her to tie up the preserves in the store-room; and, though Miss Jessie plucked at my gown, and even looked up at me with begging eye, I durst not refuse to go where Miss Jenkyns asked. Instead of tying up preserves in the store-room, however, we went to talk in the dining-room; and there Miss Jenkyns told me what Major Gordon had told her; how he had served in the same regiment with Captain Brown, and had become acquainted with Miss Jessie, then a sweet-looking, blooming girl of eighteen; how the acquaintance had grown into love on his part, though it had been some years before he had spoken; how, on becoming possessed, through the will of an uncle, of a good estate in Scotland, he had offered and been refused, though with so much agitation and evident distress that he was sure she was not indifferent to him; and how he had discovered that the obstacle was the fell disease which was, even then, too surely threatening her sister. She had mentioned that the surgeons foretold intense suffering; and there was no one but herself to nurse her poor Mary, or cheer and comfort her father during the time of illness. They had had long discussions; and on her refusal to pledge herself to him as his wife when all should be over, he had grown angry, and broken off entirely, and gone abroad, believing that she was a cold-hearted person whom he would do well to forget. He had been travelling in the East, and was on his return home when, at Rome, he saw the account of Captain Brown's death in *Galignani*.[5]

Just then Miss Matty, who had been out all the morning, and had only lately returned to the house, burst in with a face of dismay and outraged propriety.

"Oh, goodness me!" she said. "Deborah, there's a gentleman sitting in the drawing-room with his arm round Miss Jessie's waist!" Miss Matty's eyes looked large with terror.

Miss Jenkyns snubbed her down in an instant.

"The most proper place in the world for his arm to be in. Go away, Matilda, and mind your own business." This from her sister, who had hitherto been a model of feminine decorum, was a blow for poor Miss Matty, and with a double shock she left the room.

The last time I ever saw poor Miss Jenkyns was many years after this. Mrs Gordon had kept up a warm and affectionate intercourse with all at Cranford. Miss Jenkyns, Miss Matty, and Miss Pole had all been to visit her, and returned with wonderful accounts of her house, her husband, her dress, and her looks. For, with happiness, something of her early bloom returned; she had been a year or two younger than we had taken her for. Her eyes were always lovely, and, as Mrs Gordon, her dimples were not out of place. At the time to which I have referred, when I last saw Miss Jenkyns, that lady was old and feeble, and had lost something of her strong mind. Little Flora Gordon was staying with the Misses Jenkyns, and when I came in she was reading aloud to Miss Jenkyns, who lay feeble and changed on the sofa. Flora put down the *Rambler* when I came in.

"Ah!" said Miss Jenkyns, "you find me changed, my dear. I can't see as I used to do. If Flora were not here to read to me, I hardly know how I should get through the day. Did you ever read the *Rambler*? It's a wonderful book—wonderful! and the most improving reading for Flora" (which I dare say it would have been, if she could have read half the words without spelling, and could have understood the meaning of a third), "better than that strange old book, with the queer name, poor Captain Brown was killed for reading—that book by Mr Boz, you know—'Old Poz'; when I was a girl—but that's a long time ago—I acted Lucy in 'Old Poz.' "[6] She babbled on long enough for Flora to get a good long spell at the "Christmas Carol,"[7] which Miss Matty had left on the table.

1851, 1853

5. An English newspaper published in Paris and read by tourists and expatriates.
6. A children's play by Maria Edgeworth (1795); Lucy is the young heroine.
7. Published by Dickens in 1843. The topicality of Dickens's works helps date the events of *Cranford*.

Sir Arthur Conan Doyle
1859–1930

Sherlock Holmes may not have been the first detective in English fiction, but he quickly became *the* detective, a near-mythic character whose cloak and deerstalker cap, pipe and magnifying glass have defined our image of the "private eye" for over a century. Edgar Allan Poe, Charles Dickens, and Wilkie Collins had preceded Doyle in creating detectives of their own, but Doyle's genius was to construct a rational aesthete: Holmes's languid manner and bohemian tastes suggest *fin de siècle* decadence, but his suave imperturbability stems from his extraordinary powers of reasoning and observation. A quintessentially urban figure, Sherlock Holmes penetrates the foggy chaos of London with his mastery of disguise and his uncanny ability to guess occupations through telltale signs. In an urban world of anonymous strangers, Holmes can "place" people instantly, deciphering the clues to identity that elude and perplex the ordinary observer. Like his plodding sidekick Watson, readers trail along in the wake of Holmes's deft ratiocinations, awed and reassured by his effortless omniscience. His successful detections keep at bay threats to middle-class values and social harmony; he offers a comforting promise of legibility, order, and justice.

Holmes's adventures appeared monthly in *The Strand Magazine,* and they were the making of Arthur Conan Doyle, a doctor-turned-writer who capitalized on the Victorian fascination with crime. So wildly popular was his brilliant investigator that when Doyle grew bored and decided to slay his hero, the public wore mourning-bands, and Doyle was forced to revive him. Indeed, Sherlock Holmes has always seemed oddly more real than his creator: T. S. Eliot wrote that when we talk of Holmes, "we invariably fall into the fancy of his existence." To this day, thousands of letters are addressed to him at 221B Baker Street.

A Scandal in Bohemia[1]

To Sherlock Holmes she is always *the* woman. I have seldom heard him mention her under any other name. In his eyes she eclipses and predominates the whole of her sex. It was not that he felt any emotion akin to love for Irene Adler. All emotions, and that one particularly, were abhorrent to his cold, precise, but admirably balanced mind. He was, I take it, the most perfect reasoning and observing machine that the world has seen; but, as a lover, he would have placed himself in a false position. He never spoke of the softer passions, save with a gibe and a sneer. They were admirable things for the observer—excellent for drawing the veil from men's motives and actions. But for the trained reasoner to admit such intrusions into his own delicate and finely adjusted temperament was to introduce a distracting factor which might throw a doubt upon all his mental results. Grit in a sensitive instrument, or a crack in one of his own high-power lenses, would not be more disturbing than a strong emotion in a nature such as his. And yet there was but one woman to him, and that woman was the late Irene Adler, of dubious and questionable memory.

I had seen little of Holmes lately. My marriage had drifted us away from each other. My own complete happiness, and the home-centred interests which rise up around the man who first finds himself master of his own establishment, were sufficient to absorb all my attention; while Holmes, who loathed every form of society with his whole Bohemian soul,[2] remained in our lodgings in Baker-street, buried

---

1. First published in *The Strand Magazine* in July 1891.
2. Like the artists in Henri Murger's *Scènes de la vie de Bohème* (1848), Holmes's tastes are aesthetic and eccen-

tric. His bohemianism contrasts with the conventional soul of the King of Bohemia later in the story.

among his old books, and alternating from week to week between cocaine and ambition, the drowsiness of the drug, and the fierce energy of his own keen nature. He was still, as ever, deeply attracted by the study of crime, and occupied his immense faculties and extraordinary powers of observation in following out those clues, and clearing up those mysteries, which had been abandoned as hopeless by the official police. From time to time I heard some vague account of his doings: of his summons to Odessa in the case of the Trepoff murder, of his clearing up of the singular tragedy of the Atkinson brothers at Trincomalee, and finally of the mission which he had accomplished so delicately and successfully for the reigning family of Holland. Beyond these signs of his activity, however, which I merely shared with all the readers of the daily press, I knew little of my former friend and companion.

One night—it was on the 20th of March, 1888—I was returning from a journey to a patient (for I had now returned to civil practice),[3] when my way led me through Baker-street. As I passed the well-remembered door, which must always be associated in my mind with my wooing, and with the dark incidents of the Study in Scarlet,[4] I was seized with a keen desire to see Holmes again, and to know how he was employing his extraordinary powers. His rooms were brilliantly lit, and, even as I looked up, I saw his tall spare figure pass twice in a dark silhouette against the blind. He was pacing the room swiftly, eagerly, with his head sunk upon his chest, and his hands clasped behind him. To me, who knew his every mood and habit, his attitude and manner told their own story. He was at work again. He had arisen out of his drug-created dreams, and was hot upon the scent of some new problem. I rang the bell, and was shown up to the chamber which had formerly been in part my own.

His manner was not effusive. It seldom was; but he was glad, I think, to see me. With hardly a word spoken, but with a kindly eye, he waved me to an armchair, threw across his case of cigars, and indicated a spirit case and a gasogene in the corner.[5] Then he stood before the fire, and looked me over in his singular introspective fashion.

"Wedlock suits you," he remarked. "I think, Watson, that you have put on seven and a half pounds since I saw you."

"Seven," I answered.

"Indeed, I should have thought a little more. Just a trifle more, I fancy, Watson. And in practice again, I observe. You did not tell me that you intended to go into harness."

"Then, how do you know?"

"I see it, I deduce it. How do I know that you have been getting yourself very wet lately, and that you have a most clumsy and careless servant girl?"

"My dear Holmes," said I, "this is too much. You would certainly have been burned, had you lived a few centuries ago.[6] It is true that I had a country walk on Thursday and came home in a dreadful mess; but, as I have changed my clothes, I can't imagine how you deduce it. As to Mary Jane, she is incorrigible, and my wife has given her notice; but there again I fail to see how you work it out."

He chuckled to himself and rubbed his long nervous hands together.

"It is simplicity itself," said he; "my eyes tell me that on the inside of your left shoe, just where the fire-light strikes it, the leather is scored by six almost parallel cuts. Obviously they have been caused by someone who has very carelessly scraped

3. Watson, who had been invalided out of the Army medical corps, had resumed private practice upon his marriage.
4. Doyle's first Sherlock Holmes novel (1887).

5. I.e., he invited Watson to make himself a drink (a gasogene makes carbonated water).
6. I.e., his uncanny powers would have led to his being burned at the stake as a warlock.

round the edges of the sole in order to remove crusted mud from it. Hence, you see, my double deduction that you had been out in vile weather, and that you had a particularly malignant boot-slitting specimen of the London slavey.[7] As to your practice, if a gentleman walks into my rooms smelling of iodoform, with a black mark of nitrate of silver upon his right fore-finger, and a bulge on the side of his top-hat to show where he has secreted his stethoscope, I must be dull indeed, if I do not pronounce him to be an active member of the medical profession."

I could not help laughing at the ease with which he explained his process of deduction. "When I hear you give your reasons," I remarked, "the thing always appears to me to be so ridiculously simple that I could easily do it myself, though at each successive instance of your reasoning I am baffled, until you explain your process. And yet I believe that my eyes are as good as yours."

"Quite so," he answered, lighting a cigarette, and throwing himself down into an armchair. "You see, but you do not observe. The distinction is clear. For example, you have frequently seen the steps which lead up from the hall to this room."

"Frequently."

"How often?"

"Well, some hundreds of times."

"Then how many are there?"

"How many! I don't know."

"Quite so! You have not observed. And yet you have seen. That is just my point. Now, I know that there are seventeen steps, because I have both seen and observed. By the way, since you are interested in these little problems, and since you are good enough to chronicle one or two of my trifling experiences, you may be interested in this." He threw over a sheet of thick pink-tinted notepaper which had been lying open upon the table. "It came by the last post," said he. "Read it aloud."

The note was undated, and without either signature or address.

"There will call upon you to-night, at a quarter to eight o'clock," it said, "a gentleman who desires to consult you upon a matter of the very deepest moment. Your recent services to one of the Royal Houses of Europe have shown that you are one who may safely be trusted with matters which are of an importance which can hardly be exaggerated. This account of you we have from all quarters received. Be in your chamber then at that hour, and do not take it amiss if your visitor wear a mask."

"This is indeed a mystery," I remarked. "What do you imagine that it means?"

"I have no data yet. It is a capital mistake to theorise before one has data. Insensibly one begins to twist facts to suit theories, instead of theories to suit facts. But the note itself. What do you deduce from it?"

I carefully examined the writing, and the paper upon which it was written.

"The man who wrote it was presumably well to do," I remarked, endeavouring to imitate my companion's processes. "Such paper could not be bought under half a crown a packet. It is peculiarly strong and stiff."

"Peculiar—that is the very word," said Holmes. "It is not an English paper at all. Hold it up to the light."

I did so, and saw a large E with a small g, a P, and a large G with a small t woven into the texture of the paper.

"What do you make of that?" asked Holmes.

"The name of the maker, no doubt; or his monogram, rather."

"Not at all. The G with the small *t* stands for 'Gesellschaft,' which is the German for 'Company.' It is a customary contraction like our 'Co.' *P*, of course, stands for 'Papier.' Now for the *Eg*. Let us glance at our Continental Gazetteer." He took down a heavy brown volume from his shelves. "Eglow, Eglonitz—here we are, Egria. It is in a German-speaking country—in Bohemia,[8] not far from Carlsbad. 'Remarkable as being the scene of the death of Wallenstein, and for its numerous glass factories and paper mills.' Ha, ha, my boy, what do you make of that?" His eyes sparkled, and he sent up a great blue triumphant cloud from his cigarette.

"The paper was made in Bohemia," I said.

"Precisely. And the man who wrote the note is a German. Do you note the peculiar construction of the sentence—'This account of you we have from all quarters received.' A Frenchman or Russian could not have written that. It is the German who is so uncourteous to his verbs. It only remains, therefore, to discover what is wanted by this German who writes upon Bohemian paper, and prefers wearing a mask to showing his face. And here he comes, if I am not mistaken, to resolve all our doubts."

As he spoke there was the sharp sound of horses' hoofs and grating wheels against the curb, followed by a sharp pull at the bell. Holmes whistled.

"A pair, by the sound," said he. "Yes," he continued, glancing out of the window. "A nice little brougham and a pair of beauties.[9] A hundred and fifty guineas apiece. There's money in this case, Watson, if there is nothing else."

"I think that I had better go, Holmes."

"Not a bit, Doctor. Stay where you are. I am lost without my Boswell.[1] And this promises to be interesting. It would be a pity to miss it."

"But your client—"

"Never mind him. I may want your help, and so may he. Here he comes. Sit down in that armchair, Doctor, and give us your best attention."

A slow and heavy step, which had been heard upon the stairs and in the passage, paused immediately outside the door. Then there was a loud and authoritative tap.

"Come in!" said Holmes.

A man entered who could hardly have been less than six feet six inches in height, with the chest and limbs of a Hercules. His dress was rich with a richness which would, in England, be looked upon as akin to bad taste. Heavy bands of Astrakhan[2] were slashed across the sleeves and fronts of his double-breasted coat, while the deep blue cloak which was thrown over his shoulders was lined with flame-coloured silk, and secured at the neck with a brooch which consisted of a single flaming beryl. Boots which extended half way up his calves, and which were trimmed at the tops with rich brown fur, completed the impression of barbaric opulence which was suggested by his whole appearance. He carried a broad-brimmed hat in his hand, while he wore across the upper part of his face, extending down past the cheekbones, a black vizard mask,[3] which he had apparently adjusted that very moment, for his hand was still raised to it as he entered. From the lower part of the face he appeared to be a man of strong character, with a thick, hanging lip, and a long straight chin, suggestive of resolution pushed to the length of obstinacy.

---

8. Country in Eastern Central Europe, then part of the Austrian Empire, now part of the Czech Republic. Prague was the capital.
9. A closed four-wheeled carriage drawn by two horses.
1. James Boswell (1740–1795), biographer of Samuel

Johnson.
2. A luxurious wool, made from lambs who are killed in their mother's womb.
3. A mask that conceals the eyes.

"You had my note?" he asked, with a deep harsh voice and a strongly marked German accent. "I told you that I would call." He looked from one to the other of us, as if uncertain which to address.

"Pray take a seat," said Holmes. "This is my friend and colleague, Dr Watson, who is occasionally good enough to help me in my cases. Whom have I the honour to address?"

"You may address me as the Count Von Kramm, a Bohemian nobleman. I understand that this gentleman, your friend, is a man of honour and discretion, whom I may trust with a matter of the most extreme importance. If not, I should much prefer to communicate with you alone."

I rose to go, but Holmes caught me by the wrist and pushed me back into my chair. "It is both, or none," said he. "You may say before this gentleman anything which you may say to me."

The Count shrugged his broad shoulders. "Then I must begin," said he, "by binding you both to absolute secrecy for two years, at the end of that time the matter will be of no importance. At present it is not too much to say that it is of such weight that it may have an influence upon European history."

"I promise," said Holmes.

"And I."

"You will excuse this mask," continued our strange visitor. "The august person who employs me wishes his agent to be unknown to you, and I may confess at once that the title by which I have just called myself is not exactly my own."

"I was aware of it," said Holmes dryly.

"The circumstances are of great delicacy, and every precaution has to be taken to quench what might grow to be an immense scandal and seriously compromise one of the reigning families of Europe. To speak plainly, the matter implicates the great House of Ormstein, hereditary kings of Bohemia."

"I was also aware of that," murmured Holmes, settling himself down in his armchair, and closing his eyes.

Our visitor glanced with some apparent surprise at the languid, lounging figure of the man who had been no doubt depicted to him as the most incisive reasoner, and most energetic agent in Europe. Holmes slowly reopened his eyes, and looked impatiently at his gigantic client.

"If your Majesty would condescend to state your case," he remarked, "I should be better able to advise you."

The man sprang from his chair, and paced up and down the room in uncontrollable agitation. Then, with a gesture of desperation, he tore the mask from his face and hurled it upon the ground. "You are right," he cried, "I am the King. Why should I attempt to conceal it?"

"Why, indeed?" murmured Holmes. "Your Majesty had not spoken before I was aware that I was addressing Wilhelm Gottsreich Sigismond von Ormstein, Grand Duke of Cassel-Felstein, and hereditary King of Bohemia."

"But you can understand," said our strange visitor, sitting down once more and passing his hand over his high, white forehead, "you can understand that I am not accustomed to doing such business in my own person. Yet the matter was so delicate that I could not confide it to an agent without putting myself in his power. I have come incognito from Prague for the purpose of consulting you."

"Then, pray consult," said Holmes, shutting his eyes once more.

"The facts are briefly these: Some five years ago, during a lengthy visit to Warsaw, I made the acquaintance of the well-known adventuress Irene Adler. The name is no doubt familiar to you."

"Kindly look her up in my index, Doctor," murmured Holmes, without opening his eyes. For many years he had adopted a system of docketing all paragraphs concerning men and things, so that it was difficult to name a subject or a person on which he could not at once furnish information. In this case I found her biography sandwiched in between that of a Hebrew Rabbi and that of a staff-commander who had written a monograph upon the deep sea fishes.

"Let me see," said Holmes. "Hum! Born in New Jersey in the year 1858. Contralto—hum! La Scala,[4] hum! Prima donna Imperial Opera of Warsaw—Yes! Retired from operatic stage—ha! Living in London—quite so! Your Majesty, as I understand, became entangled with this young person, wrote her some compromising letters, and is now desirous of getting those letters back."

"Precisely so. But how—"

"Was there a secret marriage?"

"None."

"No legal papers or certificates?"

"None."

"Then I fail to follow your Majesty. If this young person should produce her letters for blackmailing or other purposes, how is she to prove their authenticity?"

"There is the writing."

"Pooh, pooh! Forgery."

"My private notepaper."

"Stolen."

"My own seal."

"Imitated."

"My photograph."

"Bought."

"We were both in the photograph."

"Oh dear! That is very bad! Your Majesty has indeed committed an indiscretion."

"I was mad—insane."

"You have compromised yourself seriously."

"I was only Crown Prince then. I was young. I am but thirty now."

"It must be recovered."

"We have tried and failed."

"Your Majesty must pay. It must be bought."

"She will not sell."

"Stolen, then."

"Five attempts have been made. Twice burglars in my pay ransacked her house. Once we diverted her luggage when she travelled. Twice she has been waylaid. There has been no result."

"No sign of it?"

"Absolutely none."

Holmes laughed. "It is quite a pretty little problem," said he.

---

4. A famous opera house in Milan.

"But a very serious one to me," returned the King, reproachfully.

"Very, indeed. And what does she propose to do with the photograph?"

"To ruin me."

"But how?"

"I am about to be married."

"So I have heard."

"To Clotilde Lothman von Saxe-Meningen, second daughter of the King of Scandinavia. You may know the strict principles of her family. She is herself the very soul of delicacy. A shadow of a doubt as to my conduct would bring the matter to an end."

"And Irene Adler?"

"Threatens to send them the photograph. And she will do it. I know that she will do it. You do not know her, but she has a soul of steel. She has the face of the most beautiful of women, and the mind of the most resolute of men. Rather than I should marry another woman, there are no lengths to which she would not go—none."

"You are sure that she has not sent it yet?"

"I am sure."

"And why?"

"Because she has said that she would send it on the day when the betrothal was publicly proclaimed. That will be next Monday."

"Oh, then, we have three days yet," said Holmes, with a yawn. "That is very fortunate, as I have one or two matters of importance to look into just at present. Your Majesty will, of course, stay in London for the present?"

"Certainly. You will find me at the Langham, under the name of the Count Von Kramm."

"Then I shall drop you a line to let you know how we progress."

"Pray do so. I shall be all anxiety."

"Then, as to money?"

"You have *carte blanche*."[5]

"Absolutely?"

"I tell you that I would give one of the provinces of my kingdom to have that photograph."

"And for present expenses?"

The king took a heavy chamois leather bag from under his cloak, and laid it on the table.

"There are three hundred pounds in gold, and seven hundred in notes," he said.

Holmes scribbled a receipt upon a sheet of his note-book, and handed it to him.

"And mademoiselle's address?" he asked.

"Is Briony Lodge, Serpentine-avenue, St. John's Wood."[6]

Holmes took a note of it. "One other question," said he. "Was the photograph a cabinet?"[7]

"It was."

"Then, good night, your Majesty, and I trust that we shall soon have some good news for you. And good night, Watson," he added, as the wheels of the Royal brougham rolled down the street. "If you will be good enough to call tomorrow afternoon, at three o'clock, I should like to chat this little matter over with you."

---

5. I.e., complete freedom of action and unlimited funds.
6. A London area favored by authors, artists, and well-

known courtesans.
7. A cabinet photo was $5\frac{1}{2}$ by 4 inches.

2

At three o'clock precisely I was at Baker-street, but Holmes had not yet returned. The landlady informed me that he had left the house shortly after eight o'clock in the morning. I sat down beside the fire, however, with the intention of awaiting him, however long he might be. I was already deeply interested in his inquiry, for, though it was surrounded by none of the grim and strange features which were associated with the two crimes which I have already recorded,[8] still, the nature of the case and the exalted station of his client gave it a character of its own. Indeed, apart from the nature of the investigation which my friend had on hand, there was something in his masterly grasp of a situation, and his keen, incisive reasoning, which made it a pleasure to me to study his system of work, and to follow the quick, subtle methods by which he disentangled the most inextricable mysteries. So accustomed was I to his invariable success that the very possibility of his failing had ceased to enter into my head.

It was close upon four before the door opened, and a drunken-looking groom, ill-kempt and side-whiskered, with an inflamed face and disreputable clothes, walked into the room. Accustomed as I was to my friend's amazing powers in the use of disguises, I had to look three times before I was certain that it was indeed he. With a nod he vanished into the bedroom, whence he emerged in five minutes tweed-suited and respectable, as of old. Putting his hands into his pockets, he stretched out his legs in front of the fire, and laughed heartily for some minutes.

"Well, really!" he cried, and then he choked; and laughed again until he was obliged to lie back, limp and helpless, in the chair.

"What is it?"

"It's quite too funny. I am sure you could never guess how I employed my morning, or what I ended by doing."

"I can't imagine. I suppose that you have been watching the habits, and perhaps the house, of Miss Irene Adler."

"Quite so, but the sequel was rather unusual. I will tell you, however. I left the house a little after eight o'clock this morning, in the character of a groom out of work. There is a wonderful sympathy and freemasonry among horsey men. Be one of them, and you will know all that there is to know. I soon found Briony Lodge. It is a *bijou* villa,[9] with a garden at the back, but built out in front right up to the road, two stories. Chubb lock to the door. Large sitting-room on the right side, well furnished, with long windows almost to the floor, and those preposterous English window fasteners which a child could open. Behind there was nothing remarkable, save that the passage window could be reached from the top of the coach-house. I walked round it and examined it closely from every point of view, but without noting anything else of interest.

"I then lounged down the street, and found, as I expected, that there was a mews[1] in a lane which runs down by one wall of the garden. I lent the ostlers a hand in rubbing down their horses, and I received in exchange twopence, a glass of half-and-half, two fills of shag tobacco, and as much information as I could desire about Miss Adler, to say nothing of half a dozen other people in the neighbourhood in whom I was not in the least interested, but whose biographies I was compelled to listen to."

"And what of Irene Adler?" I asked.

---

8. In *A Study in Scarlet* (1887) and *The Sign of the Four* (1890).

9. A small, charming house.

1. A back lane, used for stables and deliveries.

"Oh, she has turned all the men's heads down in that part. She is the daintiest thing under a bonnet on this planet. So say the Serpentine-mews, to a man. She lives quietly, sings at concerts, drives out at five every day, and returns at seven sharp for dinner. Seldom goes out at other times, except when she sings. Has only one male visitor, but a good deal of him. He is dark, handsome, and dashing; never calls less than once a day, and often twice. He is a Mr Godfrey Norton, of the Inner Temple.[2] See the advantages of a cabman as a confidant. They had driven him home a dozen times from Serpentine-mews, and knew all about him. When I had listened to all that they had to tell, I began to walk up and down near Briony Lodge once more, and to think over my plan of campaign.

"This Godfrey Norton was evidently an important factor in the matter. He was a lawyer. That sounded ominous. What was the relation between them, and what the object of his repeated visits? Was she his client, his friend, or his mistress? If the former, she had probably transferred the photograph to his keeping. If the latter, it was less likely. On the issue of this question depended whether I should continue my work at Briony Lodge, or turn my attention to the gentleman's chambers in the Temple. It was a delicate point, and it widened the field of my inquiry. I fear that I bore you with these details, but I have to let you see my little difficulties, if you are to understand the situation."

"I am following you closely," I answered.

"I was still balancing the matter in my mind, when a hansom cab drove up to Briony Lodge, and a gentleman sprang out. He was a remarkably handsome man, dark, aquiline, and moustached—evidently the man of whom I had heard. He appeared to be in a great hurry, shouted to the cabman to wait, and brushed past the maid who opened the door with the air of a man who was thoroughly at home.

"He was in the house about half an hour, and I could catch glimpses of him, in the windows of the sitting-room, pacing up and down, talking excitedly and waving his arms. Of her I could see nothing. Presently he emerged, looking even more flurried than before. As he stepped up to the cab, he pulled a gold watch from his pocket and looked at it earnestly. 'Drive like the devil,' he shouted, 'first to Gross & Hankey's in Regent-street, and then to the church of St. Monica in the Edgware-road. Half a guinea if you do it in twenty minutes!'

"Away they went, and I was just wondering whether I should not do well to follow them, when up the lane came a neat little landau, the coachman with his coat only half buttoned, and his tie under his ear, while all the tags of his harness were sticking out of the buckles. It hadn't pulled up before she shot out of the hall door and into it. I only caught a glimpse of her at the moment, but she was a lovely woman, with a face that a man might die for.

" 'The Church of St. Monica, John,' she cried, 'and half a sovereign if you reach it in twenty minutes.'

"This was quite too good to lose, Watson. I was just balancing whether I should run for it, or whether I should perch behind her landau, when a cab came through the street. The driver looked twice at such a shabby fare; but I jumped in before he could object. 'The Church of St. Monica,' said I, 'and half a sovereign if you reach it in twenty minutes.' It was twenty-five minutes to twelve, and of course it was clear enough what was in the wind.[3]

---

2. One of the four Inns of Court, where the offices and residences of barristers are located.

3. Until 1886, marriages could only be legally performed before noon.

"My cabby drove fast. I don't think I ever drove faster, but the others were there before us. The cab and the landau with their steaming horses were in front of the door when I arrived. I paid the man, and hurried into the church. There was not a soul there save the two whom I had followed and a surpliced clergyman, who seemed to be expostulating with them. They were all three standing in a knot in front of the altar. I lounged up the side aisle like any other idler who has dropped into a church. Suddenly, to my surprise, the three at the altar faced round to me, and Godfrey Norton came running as hard as he could towards me.

" 'Thank God!' he cried. 'You'll do. Come! Come!'

" 'What then?' I asked.

" 'Come man, come, only three minutes, or it won't be legal.'

"I was half dragged up to the altar, and, before I knew where I was, I found myself mumbling responses which were whispered in my ear, and vouching for things of which I knew nothing, and generally assisting in the secure tying up of Irene Adler, spinster, to Godfrey Norton, bachelor. It was all done in an instant, and there was the gentleman thanking me on the one side and the lady on the other, while the clergyman beamed on me in front. It was the most preposterous position in which I ever found myself in my life, and it was the thought of it that started me laughing just now. It seems that there had been some informality about their licence, that the clergyman absolutely refused to marry them without a witness of some sort, and that my lucky appearance saved the bridegroom from having to sally out into the streets in search of a best man. The bride gave me a sovereign, and I mean to wear it on my watch chain in memory of the occasion."

"This is a very unexpected turn of affairs," said I; "and what then?"

"Well, I found my plans very seriously menaced. It looked as if the pair might take an immediate departure, and so necessitate very prompt and energetic measures on my part. At the church door, however, they separated, he driving back to the Temple, and she to her own house. 'I shall drive out in the Park at five as usual,' she said as she left him. I heard no more. They drove away in different directions, and I went off to make my own arrangements."

"Which are?"

"Some cold beef and a glass of beer," he answered, ringing the bell. "I have been too busy to think of food, and I am likely to be busier still this evening. By the way, Doctor, I shall want your co-operation."

"I shall be delighted."

"You don't mind breaking the law?"

"Not in the least."

"Nor running a chance of arrest?"

"Not in a good cause."

"Oh, the cause is excellent!"

"Then I am your man."

"I was sure that I might rely on you."

"But what is it you wish?"

"When Mrs Turner has brought in the tray I will make it clear to you. Now," he said, as he turned hungrily on the simple fare that our landlady had provided, "I must discuss it while I eat, for I have not much time. It is nearly five now. In two hours we must be on the scene of action. Miss Irene, or Madame, rather, returns from her drive at seven. We must be at Briony Lodge to meet her."

"And what then?"

"You must leave that to me. I have already arranged what is to occur. There is only one point on which I must insist. You must not interfere, come what may. You understand?"

"I am to be neutral?"

"To do nothing whatever. There will probably be some small unpleasantness. Do not join in it. It will end in my being conveyed into the house. Four or five minutes afterwards the sitting-room window will open. You are to station yourself close to that open window."

"Yes."

"You are to watch me, for I will be visible to you."

"Yes."

"And when I raise my hand—so—you will throw into the room what I give you to throw, and will, at the same time, raise the cry of fire. You quite follow me?"

"Entirely."

"It is nothing very formidable," he said, taking a long cigar-shaped roll from his pocket. "It is an ordinary plumber's smoke rocket,[4] fitted with a cap at either end to make it self-lighting. Your task is confined to that. When you raise your cry of fire, it will be taken up by quite a number of people. You may then walk to the end of the street, and I will rejoin you in ten minutes. I hope that I have made myself clear?"

"I am to remain neutral, to get near the window, to watch you, and, at the signal, to throw in this object, then to raise the cry of fire, and to await you at the corner of the street."

"Precisely."

"Then you may entirely rely on me."

"That is excellent. I think perhaps it is almost time that I prepared for the new rôle I have to play."

He disappeared into his bedroom, and returned in a few minutes in the character of an amiable and simple-minded Nonconformist clergyman. His broad black hat, his baggy trousers, his white tie, his sympathetic smile, and general look of peering and benevolent curiosity were such as Mr John Hare[5] alone could have equalled. It was not merely that Holmes changed his costume. His expression, his manner, his very soul seemed to vary with every fresh part that he assumed. The stage lost a fine actor, even as science lost an acute reasoner, when he became a specialist in crime.

It was a quarter past six when we left Baker-street, and it still wanted ten minutes to the hour when we found ourselves in Serpentine-avenue. It was already dusk, and the lamps were just being lighted as we paced up and down in front of Briony Lodge, waiting for the coming of its occupant. The house was just such as I had pictured it from Sherlock Holmes's succinct description, but the locality appeared to be less private than I expected. On the contrary, for a small street in a quiet neighbourhood, it was remarkably animated. There was a group of shabbily-dressed men smoking and laughing in a corner, a scissors grinder with his wheel,[6] two guardsmen who were flirting with a nurse-girl, and several well-dressed young men who were lounging up and down with cigars in their mouths.

"You see," remarked Holmes, as we paced to and fro in front of the house, "this marriage rather simplifies matters. The photograph becomes a double-edged weapon now. The chances are that she would be as averse to its being seen by Mr Godfrey

---

4. A device to test pipes for leaks.
5. A popular character actor of the era.

6. A door-to-door knife sharpener.

Norton, as our client is to its coming to the eyes of his Princess. Now the question is—Where are we to find the photograph?"

"Where, indeed?"

"It is most unlikely that she carries it about with her. It is cabinet size. Too large for easy concealment about a woman's dress. She knows that the King is capable of having her waylaid and searched. Two attempts of the sort have already been made. We may take it then that she does not carry it about with her."

"Where, then?"

"Her banker or her lawyer. There is that double possibility. But I am inclined to think neither. Women are naturally secretive, and they like to do their own secreting. Why should she hand it over to anyone else? She could trust her own guardianship, but she could not tell what indirect or political influence might be brought to bear upon a business man. Besides, remember that she had resolved to use it within a few days. It must be where she can lay her hands upon it. It must be in her own house."

"But it has twice been burgled."

"Pshaw! They did not know how to look."

"But how will you look?"

"I will not look."

"What then?"

"I will get her to show me."

"But she will refuse."

"She will not be able to. But I hear the rumble of wheels. It is her carriage. Now carry out my orders to the letter."

As he spoke the gleam of the sidelights of a carriage came round the curve of the avenue. It was a smart little landau which rattled up to the door of Briony Lodge. As it pulled up one of the loafing men at the corner dashed forward to open the door in the hope of earning a copper, but was elbowed away by another loafer who had rushed up with the same intention. A fierce quarrel broke out, which was increased by the two guardsmen, who took sides with one of the loungers, and by the scissors grinder, who was equally hot upon the other side. A blow was struck, and in an instant the lady, who had stepped from her carriage, was the centre of a little knot of flushed and struggling men who struck savagely at each other with their fists and sticks. Holmes dashed into the crowd to protect the lady; but, just as he reached her, he gave a cry and dropped to the ground, with the blood running freely down his face. At his fall the guardsmen took to their heels in one direction and the loungers in the other, while a number of better dressed people who had watched the scuffle without taking part in it, crowded in to help the lady and to attend to the injured man. Irene Adler, as I will still call her, had hurried up the steps; but she stood at the top with her superb figure outlined against the lights of the hall, looking back into the street.

"Is the poor gentleman much hurt?" she asked.

"He is dead," cried several voices.

"No, no, there's life in him," shouted another. "But he'll be gone before you can get him to hospital."

"He's a brave fellow," said a woman. "They would have had the lady's purse and watch if it hadn't been for him. They were a gang, and a rough one too. Ah, he's breathing now."

"He can't lie in the street. May we bring him in, marm?"

"Surely. Bring him into the sitting-room. There is a comfortable sofa. This way, please!"

Slowly and solemnly he was borne into Briony Lodge, and laid out in the principal room, while I still observed the proceedings from my post by the window. The lamps had been lit, but the blinds had not been drawn, so that I could see Holmes as he lay upon the couch. I do not know whether he was seized with compunction at that moment for the part he was playing, but I know that I never felt more heartily ashamed of myself in my life than when I saw the beautiful creature against whom I was conspiring, or the grace and kindliness with which she waited upon the injured man. And yet it would be the blackest treachery to Holmes to draw back now from the part which he had entrusted to me. I hardened my heart, and took the smoke-rocket from under my ulster.[7] After all, I thought, we are not injuring her. We are but preventing her from injuring another.

Holmes had sat up upon the couch, and I saw him motion like a man who is in need of air. A maid rushed across and threw open the window. At the same instant I saw him raise his hand, and at the signal I tossed my rocket into the room with a cry of "Fire." The word was no sooner out of my mouth than the whole crowd of spectators, well dressed and ill—gentlemen, ostlers, and servant maids—joined in a general shriek of "Fire." Thick clouds of smoke curled through the room, and out at the open window. I caught a glimpse of rushing figures, and a moment later the voice of Holmes from within, assuring them that it was a false alarm. Slipping through the shouting crowd I made my way to the corner of the street, and in ten minutes was rejoiced to find my friend's arm in mine, and to get away from the scene of uproar. He walked swiftly and in silence for some few minutes, until we had turned down one of the quiet streets which lead towards the Edgware-road.

"You did it very nicely, Doctor," he remarked. "Nothing could have been better. It is all right."

"You have the photograph!"

"I know where it is."

"And how did you find out?"

"She showed me, as I told you that she would."

"I am still in the dark."

"I do not wish to make a mystery," said he laughing. "The matter was perfectly simple. You, of course, saw that everyone in the street was an accomplice. They were all engaged for the evening."

"I guessed as much."

"Then, when the row broke out, I had a little moist red paint in the palm of my hand. I rushed forward, fell down, clapped my hand to my face, and became a piteous spectacle. It is an old trick."

"That also I could fathom."

"Then they carried me in. She was bound to have me in. What else could she do? And into her sitting-room, which was the very room which I suspected. It lay between that and her bedroom, and I was determined to see which. They laid me on a couch, I motioned for air, they were compelled to open the window, and you had your chance."

"How did that help you?"

"It was all-important. When a woman thinks that her house is on fire, her instinct is at once to rush to the thing which she values most. It is a perfectly overpowering impulse, and I have more than once taken advantage of it. In the case of the Darling-

7. A long, loose overcoat.

ton Substitution Scandal it was of use to me, and also in the Arnsworth Castle business. A married woman grabs at her baby—an unmarried one reaches for her jewel box. Now it was clear to me that our lady of to-day had nothing in the house more precious to her than what we are in quest of. She would rush to secure it. The alarm of fire was admirably done. The smoke and shouting were enough to shake nerves of steel. She responded beautifully. The photograph is in a recess behind a sliding panel just above the right bell pull. She was there in an instant, and I caught a glimpse of it as she half drew it out. When I cried out that it was a false alarm, she replaced it, glanced at the rocket, rushed from the room, and I have not seen her since. I rose, and, making my excuses, escaped from the house. I hesitated whether to attempt to secure the photograph at once; but the coachman had come in, and, as he was watching me narrowly, it seemed safer to wait. A little over-precipitance may ruin all."

"And now?" I asked.

"Our quest is practically finished. I shall call with the King to-morrow, and with you, if you care to come with us. We will be shown into the sitting-room to wait for the lady, but it is probable that when she comes she may find neither us nor the photograph. It might be a satisfaction to His Majesty to regain it with his own hands."

"And when will you call?"

"At eight in the morning. She will not be up, so that we shall have a clear field. Besides, we must be prompt, for this marriage may mean a complete change in her life and habits. I must wire to the King without delay."

We had reached Baker-street, and had stopped at the door. He was searching his pockets for the key, when someone passing said:—

"Good-night, Mister Sherlock Holmes."

There were several people on the pavement at the time, but the greeting appeared to come from a slim youth in an ulster who had hurried by.

"I've heard that voice before," said Holmes, staring down the dimly lit street. "Now, I wonder who the deuce that could have been."

3

I slept at Baker-street that night, and we were engaged upon our toast and coffee in the morning when the King of Bohemia rushed into the room.

"You have really got it!" he cried, grasping Sherlock Holmes by either shoulder, and looking eagerly into his face.

"Not yet."

"But you have hopes?"

"I have hopes."

"Then, come. I am all impatience to be gone."

"We must have a cab."

"No, my brougham is waiting."

"Then that will simplify matters." We descended, and started off once more for Briony Lodge.

"Irene Adler is married," remarked Holmes.

"Married! When?"

"Yesterday."

"But to whom?"

"To an English lawyer named Norton."

"But she could not love him?"

"I am in hopes that she does."

"And why in hopes?"

"Because it would spare your Majesty all fear of future annoyance. If the lady loves her husband, she does not love your Majesty. If she does not love your Majesty, there is no reason why she should interfere with your Majesty's plan."

"It is true. And yet—! Well! I wish she had been of my own station! What a queen she would have made!" He relapsed into a moody silence which was not broken, until we drew up in Serpentine-avenue.

The door of Briony Lodge was open, and an elderly woman stood upon the steps. She watched us with a sardonic eye as we stepped from the brougham.

"Mr Sherlock Holmes, I believe?" said she.

"I am Mr Holmes," answered my companion, looking at her with a questioning and rather startled gaze.

"Indeed! My mistress told me that you were likely to call. She left this morning with her husband, by the 5.15 train from Charing-cross, for the Continent."

"What!" Sherlock Holmes staggered back, white with chagrin and surprise. "Do you mean that she has left England?"

"Never to return."

"And the papers?" asked the King, hoarsely. "All is lost."

"We shall see." He pushed past the servant, and rushed into the drawing-room, followed by the King and myself. The furniture was scattered about in every direction, with dismantled shelves, and open drawers, as if the lady had hurriedly ransacked them before her flight. Holmes rushed at the bell-pull, tore back a small sliding shutter, and, plunging in his hand, pulled out a photograph and a letter. The photograph was of Irene Adler herself in evening dress, the letter was superscribed to "Sherlock Holmes, Esq. To be left till called for." My friend tore it open, and we all three read it together. It was dated at midnight of the preceding night, and ran in this way:—

"My Dear Mr Sherlock Holmes,—You really did it very well. You took me in completely. Until after the alarm of fire, I had not a suspicion. But then, when I found how I had betrayed myself, I began to think. I had been warned against you months ago. I had been told that, if the King employed an agent, it would certainly be you. And your address had been given me. Yet, with all this, you made me reveal what you wanted to know. Even after I became suspicious, I found it hard to think evil of such a dear, kind old clergyman. But, you know, I have been trained as an actress myself. Male costume is nothing new to me. I often take advantage of the freedom which it gives. I sent John, the coachman, to watch you, ran upstairs, got into my walking clothes, as I call them, and came down just as you departed.

"Well, I followed you to your door, and so made sure that I was really an object of interest to the celebrated Mr Sherlock Holmes. Then I, rather imprudently, wished you good night, and started for the Temple to see my husband.

"We both thought the best resource was flight, when pursued by so formidable an antagonist; so you will find the nest empty when you call to-morrow. As to the photograph, your client may rest in peace. I love and am loved by a better man than he. The King may do what he will without hindrance from one whom he has cruelly wronged. I keep it only to safeguard myself, and to preserve a weapon which will always secure me from any steps which he might take in the future. I leave a photograph which he might care to possess; and I remain, dear Mr Sherlock Holmes, very truly yours,

"Irene Norton, née Adler."

"What a woman—oh, what a woman!" cried the King of Bohemia, when we had all three read this epistle. "Did I not tell you how quick and resolute she was? Would she not have made an admirable queen? Is it not a pity that she was not on my level?"

"From what I have seen of the lady, she seems, indeed, to be on a very different level to your Majesty," said Holmes, coldly. "I am sorry that I have not been able to bring your Majesty's business to a more successful conclusion."

"On the contrary, my dear sir," cried the King. "Nothing could be more successful. I know that her word is inviolate. The photograph is now as safe as if it were in the fire."

"I am glad to hear your Majesty say so."

"I am immensely indebted to you. Pray tell me in what way I can reward you. This ring—." He slipped an emerald snake ring from his finger, and held it out upon the palm of his hand.

"Your Majesty has something which I should value even more highly," said Holmes.

"You have but to name it."

"This photograph!"

The King stared at him in amazement.

"Irene's photograph!" he cried. "Certainly, if you wish it."

"I thank your Majesty. Then there is no more to be done in the matter. I have the honour to wish you a very good morning." He bowed, and, turning away without observing the hand which the King had stretched out to him, he set off in my company for his chambers.

And that was how a great scandal threatened to affect the kingdom of Bohemia, and how the best plans of Mr Sherlock Holmes were beaten by a woman's wit. He used to make merry over the cleverness of women, but I have not heard him do it of late. And when he speaks of Irene Adler, or when he refers to her photograph, it is always under the honourable title of *the* woman.

1891

Rudyard Kipling
1865–1936

"The infant monster," Henry James called him. In his early twenties the "shockingly precocious" Rudyard Kipling was already a literary celebrity, acclaimed for his vivid stories of life in India. Like Dickens, to whom he was inevitably compared, Kipling was both popular and prolific. In addition to hundreds of short stories, he wrote poetry, essays, and children's books, including the *Jungle Books* (1894, 1895) and *Just So Stories* (1902). He also wrote several novels, of which the best-known are *The Light That Failed* (1890), *Captains Courageous* (1896–1897), and *Kim* (1901). In 1907 he became the first English writer to win the Nobel Prize for literature.

Rudyard Kipling was born in Bombay, and his idyllic early years gave him a lifelong attachment to India. He and his younger sister were cared for by indulgent servants with whom they spoke Hindustani; English was almost a second language, "haltingly translated out of the vernacular idiom that one thought and dreamed in." But when he was five years old Kipling's parents sent the children "home" to England, where they were badly treated by the English family who were paid to look after them. They did not see their parents for five years. After this period of bitter unhappiness, boarding school came as a relief; Kipling later recorded his experiences of schoolboy life in the stories of *Stalky & Co.* (1899).

In 1882, not yet seventeen, Kipling returned to India to work as a journalist. Once again the people and landscape got under his skin: "I would wander till dawn in all manner of odd places—liquor-shops, gambling- and opium-dens . . . wayside entertainments such as puppet-shows, native dances; or in and about the narrow gullies under the Mosque of Wazir Khan for the sheer sake of looking." After seven years in India, he returned to England with a growing literary reputation, for his first collection of stories, *Plain Tales from the Hills* (1888), had caught the public's imagination. His exotic settings and vigorous prose struck readers as fresh and original—particularly in contrast to the writing of his jaded *fin-de-siècle* contemporaries. Somerset Maugham described the magic of Kipling's Indian stories: "They give you the tang of the East, the smell of the bazaars, the torpor of the rains, the heat of the sun-scorched earth, the rough life of the barracks."

Many critics consider Kipling the greatest short story writer in English. Describing his own economy of style, Kipling wrote that tightening up his stories had taught him "that a tale from which pieces have been raked out is like a fire that has been poked." His intense and enigmatic stories reveal a meticulous attention to detail. In addition, Kipling captured the cadences of everyday speech in many dialects and accents—Indian, Cockney, Yorkshire, Irish, Sussex—and he was adept with an astonishing range of narrative voices. He particularly excelled at reproducing the slang and shoptalk of the rough-and-ready men doing the work of empire: soldiers, sailors, engineers. Kipling's genius for capturing the "language of common men,"—to use Wordsworth's phrase from his preface to *Lyrical Ballads* (1800)—is even more pronounced in his poetry than in his prose. *Barrack-Room Ballads* (1892), for instance, pursues the Wordsworthian fascination with the imaginative side of ordinary life, but life as it is lived at the ends of a far-flung Empire, to the tempo of a military band. His first book of poems, *Departmental Ditties* (1886), revealed that he had learned his swinging rhythms and ballad meters from Swinburne and Scott, while he also admired the American dialect styles of Bret Harte, Mark Twain, and Joel Chandler Harris's Uncle Remus stories.

Fusing these varied influences with subject matter that was completely new to English verse, he deliberately rejected the introspective poetry of private life that the Aesthetes were making fashionable. Instead Kipling produced a public-oriented poetry that dealt with the wider world of Empire, using poetry as a vehicle to express the social and political views of his down-to-earth narrators. Though his exceptional skill with rhyme and meter has been widely praised, people often quote Kipling without realizing it, when they use such phrases as "a good cigar is a Smoke," "the female of the species," "but that is another story," or "the White Man's burden."

At times Kipling has been better known for his political views than for his literary works. But attention to the more reactionary moments of his later life (his opposition to Home Rule in India, for instance) has obscured the complexity of his attitudes. His opinions of imperialism, the colonies, and people of other cultures can be extremely hard to pin down. Like Robert Browning or Joseph Conrad, he adopts a range of narrative devices and speaking voices, presenting himself in a variety of roles, from the common British soldier to the Islamic sage. Though he is often accused of supporting British imperialism, Kipling persistently probes the human toll that empire building takes on those who bear the brunt of it: British soldiers and administrators on the one hand and native soldiers and servants on the other.

A reading of Kipling's work on its own terms reveals a complicated art in which human qualities such as love, fidelity, and devotion to duty can bridge national and racial boundaries. What comes through strongly in Kipling's writing is his respect for hard work and his admiration for courage in the face of death. He satirizes and condemns vanity and bullying among all peoples. Above all else, perhaps, he is fascinated with both subtle and crude manifestations of English power: its uses, abuses, and—especially—its painful responsibilities. Kipling's sympathy for both colonized and colonizer, as well as his evident pleasure in the myriad inflections and accents of speech, makes his work, as the critic Craig Raine has said, "the expression of a profoundly democratic artistry."

Without Benefit of Clergy[1]

"But if it be a girl?"

"Lord of my life, it cannot be. I have prayed for so many nights, and sent gifts to Sheikh Badl's shrine so often, that I know God will give us a son—a man-child that shall grow into a man. Think of this and be glad. My mother shall be his mother till I can take him again, and the mullah[2] of the Pattan mosque shall cast his nativity—God send he be born in an auspicious hour!—and then, and then thou wilt never weary of me, thy slave."

"Since when hast thou been a slave, my queen?"

"Since the beginning—till this mercy[3] came to me. How could I be sure of thy love when I knew that I had been bought with silver?"

"Nay, that was the dowry. I paid it to thy mother."

"And she has buried it, and sits upon it all day long like a hen. What talk is yours of dower! I was bought as though I had been a Lucknow dancing-girl[4] instead of a child."

"Art thou sorry for the sale?"

"I have sorrowed; but to-day I am glad. Thou wilt never cease to love me now?— answer, my king."

"Never—never. No."

"Not even though the *mem-log*—the white women of thy own blood—love thee? And remember, I have watched them driving in the evening; they are very fair."

"I have seen fire-balloons[5] by the hundred. I have seen the moon, and—then I saw no more fire-balloons."

Ameera clapped her hands and laughed. "Very good talk," she said. Then with an assumption of great stateliness: "It is enough. Thou hast my permission to depart,—if thou wilt."

The man did not move. He was sitting on a low red-lacquered couch in a room furnished only with a blue and white floor-cloth, some rugs, and a very complete collection of native cushions. At his feet sat a woman of sixteen, and she was all but all the world in his eyes. By every rule and law she should have been otherwise, for he was an Englishman, and she a Mussulman's daughter bought two years before from her mother, who, being left without money, would have sold Ameera shrieking to the Prince of Darkness if the price had been sufficient.

It was a contract entered into with a light heart; but even before the girl had reached her bloom she came to fill the greater portion of John Holden's life. For her, and the withered hag her mother, he had taken a little house overlooking the great red-walled city, and found,—when the marigolds had sprung up by the well in the courtyard, and Ameera had established herself according to her own ideas of comfort, and her mother had ceased grumbling at the inadequacy of the cooking-places, the distance from the daily market, and at matters of house-keeping in general,—that the

---

1. First published in *Macmillan's Magazine* (1890). "Benefit of clergy" means the traditional right of clergymen to be tried by a church court; Kipling, however, means that the union of the two protagonists has not been blessed by the clergy—i.e., they are unmarried.

2. Muslim religious leader.
3. I.e., her pregnancy.
4. Dancing girls were considered prostitutes; Ameera's mother has sold her as if she were a prostitute.
5. Hot-air balloons.

house was to him his home. Any one could enter his bachelor's bungalow by day or night, and the life that he led there was an unlovely one. In the house in the city his feet only could pass beyond the outer courtyard to the women's rooms; and when the big wooden gate was bolted behind him he was king in his own territory, with Ameera for queen. And there was going to be added to this kingdom a third person whose arrival Holden felt inclined to resent. It interfered with his perfect happiness. It disarranged the orderly peace of the house that was his own. But Ameera was wild with delight at the thought of it, and her mother not less so. The love of a man, and particularly a white man, was at the best an inconstant affair, but it might, both women argued, be held fast by a baby's hands. "And then," Ameera would always say, "then he will never care for the white *mem-log*. I hate them all—I hate them all."

"He will go back to his own people in time," said the mother; "but by the blessing of God that time is yet afar off."

Holden sat silent on the couch thinking of the future, and his thoughts were not pleasant. The drawbacks of a double life are manifold. The Government, with singular care, had ordered him out of the station for a fortnight on special duty in the place of a man who was watching by the bedside of a sick wife. The verbal notification of the transfer had been edged by a cheerful remark that Holden ought to think himself lucky in being a bachelor and a free man. He came to break the news to Ameera.

"It is not good," she said slowly, "but it is not all bad. There is my mother here, and no harm will come to me—unless indeed I die of pure joy. Go thou to thy work and think no troublesome thoughts. When the days are done I believe . . . nay, I am sure. And—and then I shall lay *him* in thy arms, and thou wilt love me for ever. The train goes tonight, at midnight is it not? Go now, and do not let thy heart be heavy by cause of me. But thou wilt not delay in returning? Thou wilt not stay on the road to talk to the bold white *mem-log*. Come back to me swiftly, my life."

As he left the courtyard to reach his horse that was tethered to the gatepost, Holden spoke to the white-haired old watchman who guarded the house, and bade him under certain contingencies despatch the filled-up telegraph-form that Holden gave him. It was all that could be done, and with the sensations of a man who has attended his own funeral Holden went away by the night-mail to his exile. Every hour of the day he dreaded the arrival of the telegram, and every hour of the night he pictured to himself the death of Ameera. In consequence his work for the State was not of first-rate quality, nor was his temper towards his colleagues of the most amiable. The fortnight ended without a sign from his home, and, torn to pieces by his anxieties, Holden returned to be swallowed up for two precious hours by a dinner at the club, wherein he heard, as a man hears in a swoon, voices telling him how execrably he had performed the other man's duties, and how he had endeared himself to all his associates. Then he fled on horseback through the night with his heart in his mouth. There was no answer at first to his blows on the gate, and he had just wheeled his horse round to kick it in when Pir Khan appeared with a lantern and held his stirrup.

"Has aught occurred?" said Holden.

"The news does not come from my mouth, Protector of the Poor, but—" He held out his shaking hand as befitted the bearer of good news who is entitled to a reward.

Holden hurried through the courtyard. A light burned in the upper room. His horse neighed in the gateway and he heard a shrill little wail that sent all the blood into the apple of his throat. It was a new voice, but it did not prove that Ameera was alive.

"Who is there?" he called up the narrow brick staircase.

There was a cry of delight from Ameera, and then the voice of the mother, tremulous with old age and pride—"We be two women and—the—man—thy—son."

On the threshold of the room Holden stepped on a naked dagger, that was laid there to avert ill-luck, and it broke at the hilt under his impatient heel.

"God is great!" cooed Ameera in the half-light. "Thou hast taken his misfortunes on thy head."

"Ay, but how is it with thee, life of my life? Old woman, how is it with her?"

"She has forgotten her sufferings for joy that the child is born. There is no harm; but speak softly," said the mother.

"It only needed thy presence to make me all well," said Ameera. "My king, thou hast been very long away. What gifts hast thou for me? Ah, ah! It is I that bring gifts this time. Look, my life, look. Was there ever such a babe? Nay, I am too weak even to clear my arm from him."

"Rest then, and do not talk. I am here, bachari (little woman)."

"Well said, for there is a bond and a heel-rope (peecharee) between us now that nothing can break. Look—canst thou see in this light? He is without spot or blemish. Never was such a man-child. Ya illah! [My God] he shall be a pundit[6]—no, a trooper of the Queen. And, my life, dost thou love me as well as ever, though I am faint and sick and worn? Answer truly."

"Yea. I love as I have loved, with all my soul. Lie still, pearl, and rest."

"Then do not go. Sit by my side here—so. Mother, the lord of this house needs a cushion. Bring it." There was an almost imperceptible movement on the part of the new life that lay in the hollow of Ameera's arm. "Aho!" she said, her voice breaking with love. "The babe is a champion from his birth. He is kicking me in the side with mighty kicks. Was there ever such a babe! And he is ours to us—thine and mine. Put thy hand on his head, but carefully, for he is very young, and men are unskilled in such matters."

Very cautiously Holden touched with the tips of his fingers the downy head.

"He is of the Faith," said Ameera; "for lying here in the night-watches I whispered the call to prayer and the profession of faith into his ears. And it is most marvellous that he was born upon a Friday,[7] as I was born. Be careful of him, my life; but he can almost grip with his hands."

Holden found one helpless little hand that closed feebly on his finger. And the clutch ran through his limbs till it settled about his heart. Till then his sole thought had been for Ameera. He began to realize that there was some one else in the world, but he could not feel that it was a veritable son with a soul. He sat down to think, and Ameera dozed lightly.

"Get hence, sahib,"[8] said her mother under her breath. "It is not good that she should find you here on waking. She must be still."

"I go," said Holden submissively. "Here be rupees. See that my baba gets fat and finds all that he needs."

The chink of the silver roused Ameera. "I am his mother, and no hireling," she said weakly. "Shall I look to him more or less for the sake of money? Mother, give it back. I have born my lord a son."

The deep sleep of weakness came upon her almost before the sentence was completed. Holden went down to the courtyard very softly with his heart at ease. Pir Khan, the old watchman, was chuckling with delight. "This house is now complete,"

6. Teacher.
7. The Islamic holy day.

8. A deferential term meaning lord or master.

he said, and without further comment thrust into Holden's hands the hilt of a sabre worn many years ago when he, Pir Khan, served the Queen in the police. The bleat of a tethered goat came from the well-kerb.

"There be two," said Pir Khan, "two goats of the best. I bought them, and they cost much money; and since there is no birth-party assembled their flesh will be all mine. Strike craftily, *sahib!* 'Tis an ill-balanced sabre at the best. Wait till they raise their heads from cropping the marigolds."

"And why?" said Holden, bewildered.

"For the birth-sacrifice. What else? Otherwise the child being unguarded from fate may die. The Protector of the Poor knows the fitting words to be said."

Holden had learned them once with little thought that he would ever speak them in earnest. The touch of the cold sabre-hilt in his palm turned suddenly to the clinging grip of the child up stairs—the child that was his own son—and a dread of loss filled him.

"Strike!" said Pir Khan. "Never life came into the world but life was paid for it. See, the goats have raised their heads. Now! With a drawing cut!"

Hardly knowing what he did Holden cut twice as he muttered the Mohammedan prayer that runs:—"Almighty! In place of this my son I offer life for life, blood for blood, head for head, bone for bone, hair for hair, skin for skin." The waiting horse snorted and bounded in his pickets at the smell of the raw blood that spirted over Holden's riding-boots.

"Well smitten!" said Pir Khan wiping the sabre. "A swordsman was lost in thee. Go with a light heart, Heaven-born. I am thy servant, and the servant of thy son. May the Presence live a thousand years and. . . . the flesh of the goats is all mine?" Pir Khan drew back richer by a month's pay. Holden swung himself into the saddle and rode off through the low-hanging wood-smoke of the evening. He was full of riotous exultation, alternating with a vast vague tenderness directed towards no particular object, that made him choke as he bent over the neck of his uneasy horse. "I never felt like this in my life," he thought. "I'll go to the club and pull myself together."

A game of pool was beginning, and the room was full of men. Holden entered, eager to get to the light and the company of his fellows, singing at the top of his voice:

> In Baltimore a-walking, a lady I did meet!

"Did you?" said the club-secretary from his corner. "Did she happen to tell you that your boots were wringing wet? Great goodness, man, it's blood!"

"Bosh!" said Holden, picking his cue from the rack. "May I cut in? It's dew. I've been riding through high crops. My faith! my boots are in a mess though!

> And if it be a girl she shall wear a wedding ring,
> And if it be a boy he shall fight for his king,
> With his dirk, and his cap, and his little jacket blue,
> He shall walk the quarter-deck—"

"Yellow on blue—green next player," said the marker monotonously.

"He *shall walk the quarter-deck*,—am I green, marker? He *shall walk the quarter-deck*,—eh! that's a bad shot,—*as his daddy used to do!*"

"I don't see that you have anything to crow about," said a zealous junior civilian acidly. "The Government is not exactly pleased with your work when you relieved Sanders."

"Does that mean a wigging[9] from head-quarters?" said Holden with an abstracted smile. "I think I can stand it."

The talk beat up round the ever-fresh subject of each man's work, and steadied Holden till it was time to go to his dark empty bungalow, where his butler received him as one who knew all his affairs. Holden remained awake for the greater part of the night, and his dreams were pleasant ones.

2

"How old is he now?"

"*Ya illah!* What a man's question! He is all but six weeks old; and on this night I go up to the house-top with thee, my life, to count the stars. For that is auspicious. And he was born on a Friday under the sign of the sun, and it has been told to me that he will outlive us both and get wealth. Can we wish for aught better, beloved?"

"There is nothing better. Let us go up to the roof, and thou shalt count the stars—but a few only, for the sky is heavy with cloud."

"The winter rains are late, and maybe they come out of season. Come, before all the stars are hid. I have put on my richest jewels."

"Thou hast forgotten the best of all."

"*Ai!* Ours. He comes also. He has never yet seen the skies."

Ameera climbed the narrow staircase that led to the flat roof. The child, placid and unwinking, lay in the hollow of her right arm, gorgeous in silver-fringed muslin with a small skull-cap on his head. Ameera wore all that she valued most. The diamond nose-stud that takes the place of the Western patch[1] in drawing attention to the curve of the nostril, the gold ornament in the centre of the forehead studded with tallow-drop emeralds and flawed rubies, the heavy circlet of beaten gold that was fastened round her neck by the softness of the pure metal, and the chinking curb-patterned silver anklets hanging low over the rosy ankle-bone. She was dressed in jade-green muslin as befitted a daughter of the Faith, and from shoulder to elbow and elbow to wrist ran bracelets of silver tied with floss silk, frail glass bangles slipped over the wrist in proof of the slenderness of the hand, and certain heavy gold bracelets that had no part in her country's ornaments but, since they were Holden's gift and fastened with a cunning European snap, delighted her immensely.

They sat down by the low white parapet of the roof, overlooking the city and its lights.

"They are happy down there," said Ameera. "But I do not think that they are as happy as we. Nor do I think the white *mem-log* are as happy. And thou?"

"I know they are not."

"How dost thou know?"

"They give their children over to the nurses."

"I have never seen that," said Ameera with a sigh, "nor do I wish to see. *Ahi!*"— she dropped her head on Holden's shoulder,—"I have counted forty stars, and I am tired. Look at the child, love of my life, he is counting too."

The baby was staring with round eyes at the dark of the heavens. Ameera placed him in Holden's arms, and he lay there without a cry.

---

9. Reprimand.   in the 18th century.
1. Reference to the "beauty patches" popular in England

"What shall we call him among ourselves?" she said. "Look! Art thou ever tired of looking? He carries thy very eyes. But the mouth—"

"Is thine, most dear. Who should know better than I?"

" 'Tis such a feeble mouth. Oh, so small! And yet it holds my heart between its lips. Give him to me now. He has been too long away."

"Nay, let him lie; he has not yet begun to cry."

"When he cries thou wilt give him back—eh! What a man of mankind thou art! If he cried he were only the dearer to me. But, my life, what little name shall we give him?"

The small body lay close to Holden's heart. It was utterly helpless and very soft. He scarcely dared to breathe for fear of crushing it. The caged green parrot that is regarded as a sort of guardian spirit in most native households moved on its perch and fluttered a drowsy wing.

"There is the answer," said Holden. "Mian Mittu has spoken. He shall be the parrot. When he is ready he will talk mightily and run about. Mian Mittu is the parrot in thy—in the Mussulman tongue, is it not?"

"Why put me so far off?" said Ameera fretfully. "Let it be like unto some English name—but not wholly. For he is mine."

"Then call him Tota, for that is likest English."

"Ay, Tota, and that is still the parrot. Forgive me, my lord, for a minute ago, but in truth he is too little to wear all the weight of Mian Mittu for name. He shall be Tota—our Tota to us. Hearest thou, oh, small one? Littlest, thou art Tota." She touched the child's cheek, and he waking wailed, and it was necessary to return him to his mother, who soothed him with the wonderful rhyme of *Aré koko, Ja ré koko!* which says:

Oh, crow! Go crow! Baby's sleeping sound,
And the wild plums grow in the jungle, only a penny a pound.
Only a penny a pound, *baba*, only a penny a pound.

Reassured many times as to the price of those plums, Tota cuddled himself down to sleep. The two sleek, white well-bullocks in the courtyard were steadily chewing the cud of their evening meal; old Pir Khan squatted at the head of Holden's horse, his police sabre across his knees, pulling drowsily at a big water-pipe that croaked like a bull-frog in a pond. Ameera's mother sat spinning in the lower verandah, and the wooden gate was shut and barred. The music of a marriage procession came to the roof above the gentle hum of the city, and a string of flying-foxes crossed the face of the low moon.

"I have prayed," said Ameera after a long pause, "I have prayed for two things. First, that I may die in thy stead if thy death is demanded, and in the second that I may die in the place of the child. I have prayed to the Prophet and to Beebee Miriam [the Virgin Mary]. Thinkest thou either will hear?"

"From thy lips who would not hear the lightest word?"

"I asked for straight talk, and thou hast given me sweet talk. Will my prayers be heard?"

"How can I say? God is very good."

"Of that I am not sure. Listen now. When I die, or the child dies, what is thy fate? Living, thou wilt return to the bold white *mem-log*, for kind calls to kind."

"Not always."

"With a woman, no; with a man it is otherwise. Thou wilt in this life, later on, go back to thine own folk. That I could almost endure, for I should be dead. But in thy very death thou wilt be taken away to a strange place and a paradise that I do not know."

"Will it be paradise?"

"Surely, for who would harm thee? But we two—I and the child—shall be elsewhere, and we cannot come to thee, nor canst thou come to us. In the old days, before the child was born, I did not think of these things; but now I think of them always. It is very hard talk."

"It will fall as it will fall. Tomorrow we do not know, but to-day and love we know well. Surely we are happy now."

"So happy that it were well to make our happiness assured. And thy Beebee Miriam should listen to me; for she is also a woman. But then she would envy me! It is not seemly for men to worship a woman."

Holden laughed aloud at Ameera's little spasm of jealousy.

"Is it not seemly? Why didst thou not turn me from worship of thee, then?"

"Thou a worshipper! And of me! My king, for all thy sweet words, well I know that I am thy servant and thy slave, and the dust under thy feet. And I would not have it otherwise. See!"

Before Holden could prevent her she stooped forward and touched his feet; recovering herself with a little laugh she hugged Tota closer to her bosom. Then, almost savagely—

"Is it true that the bold white *mem-log* live for three times the length of my life? Is it true that they make their marriages not before they are old women?"

"They marry as do others—when they are women."

"That I know, but they wed when they are twenty-five. Is that true?"

"That is true."

"*Ya illah!* At twenty-five! Who would of his own will take a wife even of eighteen? She is a woman—ageing every hour. Twenty-five! I shall be an old woman at that age, and—Those *mem-log* remain young for ever. How I hate them!"

"What have they to do with us?"

"I cannot tell. I know only that there may now be alive on this earth a woman ten years older than I who may come to thee and take thy love ten years after I am an old woman, grey headed, and the nurse of Tota's son. That is unjust and evil. They should die too."

"Now, for all thy years thou art a child, and shalt be picked up and carried down the staircase."

"Tota! Have a care for Tota, my lord! Thou at least art as foolish as any babe!" Ameera tucked Tota out of harm's way in the hollow of her neck, and was carried down stairs laughing in Holden's arms, while Tota opened his eyes and smiled after the manner of the lesser angels.

He was a silent infant, and, almost before Holden could realize that he was in the world, developed into a small gold-coloured little god and unquestioned despot of the house overlooking the city. Those were months of absolute happiness to Holden and Ameera—happiness withdrawn from the world, shut in behind the wooden gate that Pir Khan guarded. By day Holden did his work with an immense pity for such as were not so fortunate as himself, and a sympathy for small children that amazed and amused many mothers at the little station-gatherings. At nightfall he returned to Ameera,—Ameera full of the wondrous doings of Tota, how he had been seen to clap his hands together and move his fingers with intention and purpose—which was manifestly a miracle—how later, he had of his own initiative crawled out of his low bedstead on to the floor and swayed on both feet for the space of three breaths.

"And they were long breaths, for my heart stood still with delight," said Ameera. Then he took the beasts into his councils—the well-bullocks, the little grey squirrels, the mongoose that lived in a hole near the well, and especially Mian Mittu, the parrot, whose tail he grievously pulled, and Mian Mittu screamed till Ameera and Holden arrived.

"Oh, villain! Child of strength! This to thy brother on the house-top! *Tobah, tobah!* Fie! Fie! But I know a charm to make him wise as Suleiman and Aflatoun [Solomon and Plato]. Now look," said Ameera. She drew from an embroidered bag a handful of almonds. "See! we count seven. In the name of God!"

She placed Mian Mittu, very angry and rumpled, on the top of his cage, and seating herself between the babe and the bird she cracked and peeled an almond less white than her teeth. "This is a true charm, my life, and do not laugh. See! I give the parrot one half and Tota the other." Mian Mittu with careful beak took his share from between Ameera's lips, and she kissed the other half into the mouth of the child, who ate it slowly with wondering eyes. "This I will do each day of seven, and without doubt he who is ours will be a bold speaker and wise. Eh, Tota, what wilt thou be when thou art a man and I am grey-headed?" Tota tucked his fat legs into adorable creases. He could crawl, but he was not going to waste the spring of his youth in idle speech. He wanted Mian Mittu's tail to tweak.

When he was advanced to the dignity of a silver belt—which, with a magic-square engraved on silver and hung round his neck, made up the greater part of his clothing— he staggered on a perilous journey down the garden to Pir Khan and proffered him all his jewels in exchange for one little ride on Holden's horse, having seen his mother's mother chaffering with pedlars in the verandah. Pir Khan wept and set the untried feet on his own grey head in sign of fealty, and brought the bold adventurer to his mother's arms, vowing that Tota would be a leader of men ere his beard was grown.

One hot evening while he sat on the roof between his father and mother watching the never-ending warfare of the kites, that the city boys flew, he demanded a kite of his own with Pir Khan to fly it, because he had a fear of dealing with anything larger than himself, and when Holden called him a "spark," he rose to his feet and answered slowly in defence of his newfound individuality: "*Hum 'park nahin hai. Hom admi hai.* (I am no spark, but a man.)"

The protest made Holden choke and devote himself very seriously to a consideration of Tota's future. He need hardly have taken the trouble. The delight of that life was too perfect to endure. Therefore it was taken away as many things are taken away in India—suddenly and without warning. The little lord of the house, as Pir Khan called him, grew sorrowful and complained of pains who had never known the meaning of pain. Ameera, wild with terror, watched him through the night, and in the dawning of the second day the life was shaken out of him by fever—the seasonal autumn fever. It seemed altogether impossible that he could die, and neither Ameera nor Holden at first believed the evidence of the little body on the bedstead. Then Ameera beat her head against the wall and would have flung herself down the well in the garden had Holden not restrained her by main force.

One mercy only was granted to Holden. He rode to his office in broad daylight and found waiting him an unusually heavy mail that demanded concentrated attention and hard work. He was not, however, alive to this kindness of the gods.

3

The first shock of a bullet is no more than a brisk pinch. The wrecked body does not send in its protest to the soul till ten or fifteen seconds later. Holden realized his pain slowly, exactly as he had realized his happiness, and with the same imperious necessity for hiding all trace of it. In the beginning he only felt that there had been a loss, and that Ameera needed comforting, where she sat with her head on her knees shivering as Mian Mittu from the house-top called, *Tota! Tota! Tota!* Later all his world and the daily life of it rose up to hurt him. It was an outrage that any one of the children at the band-stand in the evening should be alive and clamorous, when his own child lay dead. It was more than mere pain when one of them touched him, and stories told by over-fond fathers of their children's latest performances cut him to the quick. He could not declare his pain. He had neither help, comfort, nor sympathy; and Ameera at the end of each weary day would lead him through the hell of self-questioning reproach which is reserved for those who have lost a child, and believe that with a little—just a little more care—it might have been saved.

"Perhaps," Ameera would say, "I did not take sufficient heed. Did I, or did I not? The sun on the roof that day when he played so long alone and I was—*ahi!* braiding my hair—it may be that the sun then bred the fever. If I had warned him from the sun he might have lived. But, oh my life, say that I am guiltless! Thou knowest that I loved him as I love thee. Say that there is no blame on me, or I shall die—I shall die!"

"There is no blame,—before God, none. It was written and how could we do aught to save? What has been, has been. Let it go, beloved."

"He was all my heart to me. How can I let the thought go when my arm tells me every night that he is not here? *Ahi! Ahi!* Oh Tota come back to me—come back again, and let us be all together as it was before!"

"Peace, peace! For thine own sake, and for mine also, if thou lovest me—rest."

"By this I know thou dost not care; and how shouldst thou? The white men have hearts of stone and souls of iron. Oh that I had married a man of mine own people—though he beat me, and had never eaten the bread of an alien!"

"Am I an alien—mother of my son?"

"What else—*sahib?* . . . Oh forgive me—forgive! The death has driven me mad. Thou art the life of my heart, and the light of my eyes, and the breath of my life, and—and I have put thee from me though it was but for a moment. If thou goest away to whom shall I look for help? Do not be angry. Indeed, it was the pain that spoke and not thy slave."

"I know, I know. We be two who were three. The greater need therefore that we should be one."

They were sitting on the roof as of custom. The night was a warm one in early spring, and sheet-lightning was dancing on the horizon to a broken tune played by far-off thunder. Ameera settled herself in Holden's arms.

"The dry earth is lowing like a cow for the rain, and I—I am afraid. It was not like this when we counted the stars. But thou lovest me as much as before, though a bond is taken away? Answer!"

"I love more because a new bond has come out of the sorrow that we have eaten together, and that thou knowest."

"Yea, I knew," said Ameera in a very small whisper. "But it is good to hear thee say so, my life, who art so strong to help. I will be a child no more, but a woman and an aid to thee. Listen! Give me my *sitar*[2] and I will sing bravely."

She took the light silver-studded *sitar* and began a song of the great hero Rajah Rasalu. The hand failed on the strings, the tune halted, checked, and at a low note turned off to the poor little nursery-rhyme about the wicked crow:

And the wild plums grow in the jungle, only a penny a pound.
Only a penny a pound, *baba*—only . . .

Then came the tears, and the piteous rebellion against fate till she slept, moaning a little in her sleep, with the right arm thrown clear of the body as though it protected something that was not there. It was after this night that life became a little easier for Holden. The ever-present pain of loss drove him into his work, and the work repaid him by filling up his mind for eight or nine hours a day. Ameera sat alone in the house and brooded, but grew happier when she understood that Holden was more at ease, according to the custom of women. They touched happiness again, but this time with caution.

"It was because we loved Tota that he died. The jealousy of God was upon us," said Ameera. "I have hung up a large black jar before our window to turn the evil eye from us, and we must make no protestations of delight but go softly underneath the stars, lest God find us out. Is that not good talk, worthless one?"

She had shifted the accent on the word that means "beloved," in proof of the sincerity of her purpose. But the kiss that followed the new christening was a thing that any deity might have envied. They went about henceforward saying, "It is naught, it is naught;" and hoping that all the Powers heard.

The Powers were busy on other things. They had allowed thirty million people four years of plenty wherein men fed well and the crops were certain and the birth-rate rose year by year: the districts reported a purely agricultural population varying from nine hundred to two thousand to the square mile of the overburdened earth; and the Member for Lower Tooting,[3] wandering about India in top-hat and frock-coat talked largely of the benefits of British rule, and suggested as the one thing needful the establishment of a duly qualified electoral system and a general bestowal of the franchise. His long-suffering hosts smiled and made him welcome, and when he paused to admire, with pretty picked words, the blossom of the blood-red *dhak* tree that had flowered untimely for a sign of what was coming, they smiled more than ever.

It was the Deputy Commissioner of Kot-Kumharsen, staying at the club for a day, who lightly told a tale that made Holden's blood run cold as he overheard the end.

"He won't bother any one any more. Never saw a man so astonished in my life. By Jove, I thought he meant to ask a question in the House about it. Fellow-passenger in his ship—dined next him—bowled over by cholera and died in eighteen hours. You needn't laugh, you fellows. The Member for Lower Tooting is awfully angry about it; but he's more scared. I think he's going to take his enlightened self out of India."

"I'd give a good deal if he were knocked over. It might keep a few vestrymen[4] of his kidney to their own parish. But what's this about cholera? It's full early for anything of that kind," said a warden of an unprofitable salt-lick.

2. Indian stringed instrument.
3. A Member of Parliament who has come to India to give advice on matters about which, Kipling suggests, he knows nothing.
4. Members of a Church of England parish council; Kipling uses the term satirically to refer to Members of Parliament.

"Don't know," said the Deputy Commissioner reflectively. "We've got locusts with us. There's sporadic cholera all along the north—at least we're calling it sporadic for decency's sake. The spring crops are short in five districts, and nobody seems to know where the rains are. It's nearly March now. I don't want to scare anybody, but it seems to me that Nature's going to audit her accounts with a big red pencil this summer."

"Just when I wanted to take leave, too!" said a voice across the room.

"There won't be much leave this year, but there ought to be a great deal of promotion. I've come in to persuade the Government to put my pet canal on the list of famine relief-works. It's an ill-wind that blows no good. I shall get that canal finished at last."

"Is it the old programme then," said Holden; "famine, fever, and cholera?"

"Oh no. Only local scarcity and an unusual prevalence of seasonal sickness. You'll find it all in the reports if you live till next year. You're a lucky chap. You haven't got a wife to put out of harm's way. The hill-stations ought to be full of women this year."

"I think you're inclined to exaggerate the talk in the *bazars*," said a young civilian in the Secretariat. "Now I have observed——"

"I dare say you have," said the Deputy Commissioner, "but you've a great deal more to observe, my son. In the meantime, I wish to observe to you—" and he drew him aside to discuss the construction of the canal that was so dear to his heart. Holden went to his bungalow and began to understand that he was not alone in the world, and also that he was afraid for the sake of another,—which is the most soul-satisfying fear known to man.

Two months later, as the Deputy had foretold, Nature began to audit her accounts with a red pencil. On the heels of the spring-reapings came a cry for bread, and the Government, which had decreed that no man should die of want, sent wheat. Then came the cholera from all four quarters of the compass. It struck a pilgrim-gathering of half a million at a sacred shrine. Many died at the feet of their god; the others broke and ran over the face of the land carrying the pestilence with them. It smote a walled city and killed two hundred a day. The people crowded the trains, hanging on to the foot-boards and squatting on the roofs of the carriages, and the cholera followed them, for at each station they dragged out the dead and the dying. They died by the roadside, and the horses of the Englishmen shied at the corpses in the grass. The rains did not come, and the earth turned to iron lest man should escape death by hiding in her. The English sent their wives away to the hills and went about their work, coming forward as they were bidden to fill the gaps in the fighting-line. Holden, sick with fear of losing his chiefest treasure on earth, had done his best to persuade Ameera to go away with her mother to the Himalayas.

"Why should I go?" said she one evening on the roof.

"There is sickness, and people are dying, and all the white *mem-log* have gone."

"All of them?"

"All—unless perhaps there remain some old scald-head who vexes her husband's heart by running risk of death."

"Nay; who stays is my sister, and thou must not abuse her, for I will be a scald-head too. I am glad all the bold *mem-log* are gone."

"Do I speak to a woman or a babe? Go to the hills and I will see to it that thou goest like a queen's daughter. Think, child. In a red-lacquered bullock cart, veiled and curtained, with brass peacocks upon the pole and red cloth hangings. I will send two orderlies for guard and—"

"Peace! Thou art the babe in speaking thus. What use are those toys to me? *He* would have patted the bullocks and played with the housings. For his sake, perhaps,—thou hast made me very English—I might have gone. Now, I will not. Let the *mem-log* run."

"Their husbands are sending them, beloved."

"Very good talk. Since when hast thou been my husband to tell me what to do? I have but born thee a son. Thou art only all the desire of my soul to me. How shall I depart when I know that if evil befall thee by the breadth of so much as my littlest fingernail—is that not small?—I should be aware of it though I were in paradise. And here, this summer thou mayst die—*ai, janee,* die! and in dying they might call to tend thee a white woman, and she would rob me in the last of thy love!"

"But love is not born in a moment or on a death-bed!"

"What dost thou know of love, stone-heart? She would take thy thanks at least and, by God and the Prophet and Beebee Miriam the mother of thy Prophet, that I will never endure. My lord and my love, let there be no more foolish talk of going away. Where thou art, I am. It is enough." She put an arm round his neck and a hand on his mouth.

There are not many happinesses so complete as those that are snatched under the shadow of the sword. They sat together and laughed, calling each other openly by every pet name that could move the wrath of the gods. The city below them was locked up in its own torments. Sulphur fires blazed in the streets; the conches in the Hindu temples screamed and bellowed, for the gods were inattentive in those days. There was a service in the great Mahomedan shrine, and the call to prayer from the minarets was almost unceasing. They heard the wailing in the houses of the dead, and once the shriek of a mother who had lost a child and was calling for its return. In the grey dawn they saw the dead borne out through the city gates, each litter with its own little knot of mourners. Wherefore they kissed each other and shivered.

It was a red and heavy audit, for the land was very sick and needed a little breathing-space ere the torrent of cheap life should flood it anew. The children of immature fathers and undeveloped mothers made no resistance. They were cowed and sat still, waiting till the sword should be sheathed in November if it were so willed. There were gaps among the English, but the gaps were filled. The work of superintending famine-relief, cholera-sheds, medicine-distribution, and what little sanitation was possible, went forward because it was so ordered.

Holden had been told to keep himself in readiness to move to replace the next man who should fall. There were twelve hours in each day when he could not see Ameera, and she might die in three. He was considering what his pain would be if he could not see her for three months, or if she died out of his sight. He was absolutely certain that her death would be demanded—so certain that when he looked up from the telegram and saw Pir Khan breathless in the doorway, he laughed aloud, "And?" said he,——

"When there is a cry in the night and the spirit flutters into the throat, who has a charm that will restore? Come swiftly, Heaven-born! It is the black cholera."

Holden galloped to his home. The sky was heavy with clouds, for the long deferred rains were near and the heat was stifling. Ameera's mother met him in the courtyard, whimpering, "She is dying. She is nursing herself into death. She is all but dead. What shall I do, *sahib*?"

Ameera was lying in the room in which Tota had been born. She made no sign when Holden entered because the human soul is a very lonely thing and, when it is getting ready to go away, hides itself in a misty borderland where the living may not follow. The black cholera does its work quietly and without explanation. Ameera was being thrust out of life as though the Angel of Death had himself put his hand upon her. The quick breathing seemed to show that she was neither afraid nor in pain, but neither eyes nor mouth gave any answer to Holden's kisses. There was nothing to be said or done. Holden could only wait and suffer. The first drops of the rain began to fall on the roof and he could hear shouts of joy in the parched city.

The soul came back a little and the lips moved. Holden bent down to listen. "Keep nothing of mine," said Ameera. "Take no hair from my head. *She* would make thee burn it later on. That flame I should feel. Lower! Stoop lower! Remember only that I was thine and bore thee a son. Though thou wed a white woman to-morrow, the pleasure of receiving in thy arms thy first son is taken from thee for ever. Remember me when thy son is born—the one that shall carry thy name before all men. His misfortunes be on my head. I bear witness—I bear witness"—the lips were forming the words on his ear—"that there is no God but—thee, beloved!"

Then she died. Holden sat still, and all thought was taken from him,—till he heard Ameera's mother lift the curtain.

"Is she dead, *sahib?*"

"She is dead."

"Then I will mourn, and afterwards take an inventory of the furniture in this house. For that will be mine. The *sahib* does not mean to resume it? It is so little, so very little, *sahib*, and I am an old woman. I would like to lie softly."

"For the mercy of God be silent, a while. Go out and mourn where I cannot hear."

"*Sahib*, she will be buried in four hours."

"I know the custom. I shall go ere she is taken away. That matter is in thy hands. Look to it, that the bed on which—on which she lies—"

"Aha! That beautiful red-lacquered bed. I have long desired——"

"That the bed is left here untouched for my disposal. All else in the house is thine. Hire a cart, take everything, go hence, and before sunrise let there be nothing in this house but that which I have ordered thee to respect."

"I am an old woman. I would stay at least for the days of mourning, and the rains have just broken. Whither shall I go?"

"What is that to me? My order is that there is a going. The house-gear is worth a thousand rupees and my orderly shall bring thee a hundred rupees to-night."

"That is very little. Think of the cart-hire."

"It shall be nothing unless thou goest, and with speed. O woman, get hence and leave me to my dead!"

The mother shuffled down the staircase, and in her anxiety to take stock of the house-fittings forgot to mourn. Holden stayed by Ameera's side and the rain roared on the roof. He could not think connectedly by reason of the noise, though he made many attempts to do so. Then four sheeted ghosts glided dripping into the room and stared at him through their veils. They were the washers of the dead. Holden left the room and went out to his horse. He had come in a dead, stifling calm through ankle-deep dust. He found the court-yard a rain-lashed pond alive with frogs; a torrent of yellow water ran under the gate, and a roaring wind drove the bolts of the rain like buck-shot against the mud walls. Pir Khan was shivering in his little hut by the gate, and the horse was stamping uneasily in the water.

"I have been told the *sahib*'s order," said Pir Khan. "It is well. This house is now desolate. I go also, for my monkey-face would be a reminder of that which has been.

Concerning the bed, I will bring that to thy house yonder in the morning; but remember, *sahib*, it will be to thee a knife turned in a green wound. I go upon a pilgrimage, and I will take no money. I have grown fat in the protection of the Presence whose sorrow is my sorrow. For the last time I hold his stirrup."

He touched Holden's foot with both hands and the horse sprang out into the road, where the creaking bamboos were whipping the sky and all the frogs were chuckling. Holden could not see for the rain in his face. He put his hands before his eyes and muttered,

"Oh you brute! You utter brute!"

The news of his trouble was already in his bungalow. He read the knowledge in his butler's eyes when Ahmed Khan brought in food, and for the first and last time in his life laid a hand upon his master's shoulder, saying: "Eat, *sahib*, eat. Meat is good against sorrow. I also have known. Moreover the shadows come and go, *sahib*; the shadows come and go. These be curried eggs."

Holden could neither eat nor sleep. The heavens sent down eight inches of rain in that night and washed the earth clean. The waters tore down walls, broke roads, and scoured open the shallow graves on the Mahomedan burying-ground. All next day it rained, and Holden sat still in his house considering his sorrow. On the morning of the third day he received a telegram which said only: "Rickells, Myndonie. Dying. Holden relieve. Immediate." Then he thought that before he departed he would look at the house wherein he had been master and lord. There was a break in the weather, and the rank earth steamed with vapour.

He found that the rains had torn down the mud pillars of the gateway, and the heavy wooden gate that had guarded his life hung lazily from one hinge. There was grass three inches high in the courtyard; Pir Khan's lodge was empty, and the sodden thatch sagged between the beams. A gray squirrel was in possession of the verandah, as if the house had been untenanted for thirty years instead of three days. Ameera's mother had removed everything except some mildewed matting. The *tick-tick* of the little scorpions as they hurried across the floor was the only sound in the house. Ameera's room and the other one where Tota had lived were heavy with mildew; and the narrow staircase leading to the roof was streaked and stained with rain-borne mud. Holden saw all these things, and came out again to meet in the road Durga Dass, his landlord,—portly, affable, clothed in white muslin, and driving a C-spring buggy. He was overlooking his property to see how the roofs stood the stress of the first rains.

"I have heard," said he, "you will not take this place any more, *sahib*?"

"What are you going to do with it?"

"Perhaps I shall let it again."

"Then I will keep it on while I am away."

Durga Dass was silent for some time. "You shall not take it on, *sahib*," he said. "When I was a young man I also——, but to-day I am a member of the Municipality. Ho! Ho! No. When the birds have gone what need to keep the nest? I will have it pulled down—the timber will sell for something always. It shall be pulled down, and the Municipality shall make a road across, as they desire, from the burning-*ghaut*[5] to the city wall, so that no man may say where this house stood."

1890

[END OF POPULAR SHORT FICTION]

5. Place where bodies are cremated.

John Ruskin

1819–1900

John Ruskin began his career as the most perceptive English art critic of the nineteenth century. But for Ruskin, art was inextricably linked to the moral temper of the age in which it was produced. Thus he was drawn inevitably from art criticism to social criticism, denouncing ugliness and injustice as aspects of the same spiritual decline. His prodigious output of books on painting, literature, architecture, politics, and society culminated with a beautiful and moving autobiography, *Praeterita*, which means "of things past."

For all the magnificence of his prose and the brilliance of his vision, John Ruskin was a rather peculiar man. He was the only child of middle-class parents who lived in the suburbs near London and whose dearest wish, he wrote, was "to make an evangelical clergyman of me." Forbidden toys, he passed his time studying the patterns in the nursery carpet and garden leaves, delighting already in the visual pleasures that would engross him all his life. His upbringing was strict, secluded, and overprotected: he was educated at home until his mother accompanied him to Oxford, where she remained for the duration of his studies.

Perhaps because he was so sheltered, Ruskin's love life was a series of disastrous ordeals. As a teenager he suffered a hopeless passion for Adèle Domecq, who was rich, French, and Catholic—unsuitable on every count. Later, a miserable six-year marriage to his cousin Effie Gray was annulled on the grounds of nonconsummation (she then married the Pre-Raphaelite painter John Everett Millais, with whom she had many children). The annulment created a scandal, and the whole episode was so painful that Ruskin omitted any reference to his marriage in *Praeterita*. Finally, he became morbidly obsessed with Rose La Touche, thirty years his junior, and only nine years old when he met her. His tragic relationship with her became a secret thread running through his later work.

Ruskin's intensity of vision was already evident in his first book, *Modern Painters*, in which he declared that "to see clearly is poetry, prophecy, and religion—all in one." Ruskin insisted that the impressionistic canvasses of J. M. W. Turner were actually more faithful to nature than the carefully rendered detail of Dutch realists. Reading *Modern Painters*, Charlotte Brontë wrote: "I feel . . . as if I had been walking blindfold—this book seems to give me eyes." Published over seventeen years (1843–1860), the five volumes of *Modern Painters* reflect their author's changing preoccupations: from art and nature in the early volumes to humanism and society in the last one, following an experience of religious "unconversion" in 1858.

From boyhood Ruskin loved to travel on the Continent, and his autobiography relates with deep pleasure the many journeys he took, usually with his parents. Venice aroused him to write what the critic John Rosenberg has called "the most elaborate and eloquent monument to a city in our literature," *The Stones of Venice* (1851–1853). Ruskin's Venice is "a ghost upon the sands of the sea, so weak—so quiet,—so bereft of all but her loveliness." The decline and fall of the Venetian empire serves as a warning to the British, which, "if it forget their example, may be led through prouder eminence to less pitied destruction."

The book's central chapter, *The Nature of Gothic*, became the touchstone for Ruskin's subsequent radical social critique of England. He argues that Gothic workmanship, though rude and imperfect, reflected a culture that respected the individual soul of the workman. Societies which demand machinelike perfection dehumanize the craftsman, turning him into a soulless operative. Ruskin thus mingled his hymn to the beauty of Venice with a scathing indictment of the Industrial Revolution.

In *Modern Manufacture and Design* (1859) and *Unto This Last* (1862), Ruskin turned from architecture to economics, raging like a biblical prophet against the savagery of laissez-faire capitalism and exhorting employers to take responsibility for the well-being of their workers.

Contemporary response was hostile, but Ruskin's reforms have had a lasting influence on radical political thinkers from the founders of the British Labour Party to Gandhi, who felt himself transformed by reading *Unto This Last:* "All Ruskin's words captivated me . . . I lay awake all night and there and then I decided to change my whole life."

Ruskin's later writings became increasingly fragmented as he suffered a long, slow decline into madness. "The doctors said I went mad . . . from overwork," he wrote, but "I went mad because nothing came of my work." Yet from 1871 to 1884 he was able to lecture about art at Oxford and to produce an impassioned series of open letters to English workmen, entitled *Fors Clavigera.* Many of the letters describe the Guild of St. George, a utopian society Ruskin had founded. Tormented by the brutality and folly he saw everywhere around him, Ruskin chose in his final work to record only "what it gives me joy to remember."

from Modern Painters
from Definition of Greatness in Art[1]

Painting, or art generally, as such, with all its technicalities, difficulties, and particular ends, is nothing but a noble and expressive language, invaluable as the vehicle of thought, but by itself nothing. He who has learned what is commonly considered the whole art of painting, that is, the art of representing any natural object faithfully, has as yet only learned the language by which his thoughts are to be expressed. He has done just as much towards being that which we ought to respect as a great painter, as a man who has learnt how to express himself grammatically and melodiously has towards being a great poet. The language is, indeed, more difficult of acquirement in the one case than in the other, and possesses more power of delighting the sense, while it speaks to the intellect; but it is, nevertheless, nothing more than language, and all those excellences which are peculiar to the painter as such, are merely what rhythm, melody, precision, and force are in the words of the orator and the poet, necessary to their greatness, but not the tests of their greatness. It is not by the mode of representing and saying, but by what is represented and said, that the respective greatness either of the painter or the writer is to be finally determined. * * *

If I say that the greatest picture is that which conveys to the mind of the spectator the greatest number of the greatest ideas, I have a definition which will include as subjects of comparison every pleasure which art is capable of conveying. If I were to say, on the contrary, that the best picture was that which most closely imitated nature, I should assume that art could only please by imitating nature; and I should cast out of the pale of criticism those parts of works of art which are not imitative, that is to say, intrinsic beauties of colour and form, and those works of art wholly, which, like the Arabesques of Raffaelle in the Loggias,[2] are not imitative at all. Now, I want a definition of art wide enough to include all its varieties of aim. I do not say, therefore, that the art is greatest which gives most pleasure, because perhaps there is some art whose end is to teach, and not to please. I do not say that the art is greatest which teaches us most, because perhaps there is some art whose end is to please, and not to teach. I do not say that the art is greatest which imitates best, because perhaps there is some art whose end is to create and not to imitate. But I say that the art is greatest which conveys to the mind of the spectator, by any means whatsoever, the greatest number of the greatest ideas; and I call an idea great in proportion as it is

1. From vol. 1, part 1, sec. 1, ch. 2.
2. The Italian Renaissance painter Raphael (1483–1520) decorated the Loggia of the Vatican with arabesques,
wall paintings of interwoven foliage, animals, and human figures.

received by a higher faculty of the mind, and as it more fully occupies, and in occupying, exercises and exalts, the faculty by which it is received.

If this, then, be the definition of great art, that of a great artist naturally follows. He is the greatest artist who has embodied, in the sum of his works, the greatest number of the greatest ideas.

1843

from **The Stones of Venice**
from *The Nature of Gothic*[1]

I shall endeavour therefore to give the reader in this chapter an idea, at once broad and definite, of the true nature of *Gothic* architecture, properly so called; not of that of Venice only, but of universal Gothic: for it will be one of the most interesting parts of our subsequent inquiry to find out how far Venetian architecture reached the universal or perfect type of Gothic, and how far it either fell short of it, or assumed foreign and independent forms.

The principal difficulty in doing this arises from the fact that every building of the Gothic period differs in some important respect from every other; and many include features which, if they occurred in other buildings, would not be considered Gothic at all; so that all we have to reason upon is merely, if I may be allowed so to express it, a greater or less degree of *Gothicness* in each building we examine. And it is this Gothicness,—the character which, according as it is found more or less in a building, makes it more or less Gothic,—of which I want to define the nature. * * * That is to say, pointed arches do not constitute Gothic, nor vaulted roofs, nor flying buttresses, nor grotesque sculptures; but all or some of these things, and many other things with them, when they come together so as to have life. * * *

* * * We shall find that Gothic architecture has external forms and internal elements. Its elements are certain mental tendencies of the builders, legibly expressed in it; as fancifulness, love of variety, love of richness, and such others. Its external forms are pointed arches, vaulted roofs, etc. And unless both the elements and the forms are there, we have no right to call the style Gothic. It is not enough that it has the Form, if it have not also the power and life. It is not enough that it has the Power, if it have not the form. * * *

I believe, then, that the characteristic or moral elements of Gothic are the following, placed in the order of their importance:

1. Savageness.
2. Changefulness.
3. Naturalism.
4. Grotesqueness.
5. Rigidity.
6. Redundance.

These characters are here expressed as belonging to the building; as belonging to the builder, they would be expressed thus:—1. Savageness or Rudeness. 2. Love of Change. 3. Love of Nature. 4. Disturbed Imagination. 5. Obstinacy. 6. Generosity. And I repeat, that the withdrawal of any one, or any two, will not at once destroy the

---

1. From vol. 2, ch. 6.

Gothic character of a building, but the removal of a majority of them will. I shall proceed to examine them in their order.

(1.) SAVAGENESS. I am not sure when the word "Gothic" was first generically applied to the architecture of the North; but I presume that, whatever the date of its original usage, it was intended to imply reproach, and express the barbaric character of the nations among whom that architecture arose. It never implied that they were literally of Gothic lineage, far less that their architecture had been originally invented by the Goths themselves;[2] but it did imply that they and their buildings together exhibited a degree of sternness and rudeness, which, in contradistinction to the character of Southern and Eastern nations, appeared like a perpetual reflection of the contrast between the Goth and the Roman in their first encounter. And when that fallen Roman, in the utmost impotence of his luxury, and insolence of his guilt, became the model for the imitation of civilized Europe,[3] at the close of the so-called Dark ages, the word Gothic became a term of unmitigated contempt, not unmixed with aversion. From that contempt, by the exertion of the antiquaries and architects of this century, Gothic architecture has been sufficiently vindicated; and perhaps some among us, in our admiration of the magnificent science of its structure, and sacredness of its expression, might desire that the term of ancient reproach should be withdrawn, and some other, of more apparent honourableness, adopted in its place. There is no chance, as there is no need, of such a substitution. As far as the epithet was used scornfully, it was used falsely; but there is no reproach in the word, rightly understood; on the contrary, there is a profound truth, which the instinct of mankind almost unconsciously recognizes. It is true, greatly and deeply true, that the architecture of the North is rude and wild; but it is not true, that, for this reason, we are to condemn it, or despise. Far otherwise: I believe it is in this very character that it deserves our profoundest reverence.

The charts of the world which have been drawn up by modern science have thrown into a narrow space the expression of a vast amount of knowledge, but I have never yet seen any one pictorial enough to enable the spectator to imagine the kind of contrast in physical character which exists between Northern and Southern countries. We know the differences in detail, but we have not that broad glance and grasp which would enable us to feel them in their fulness. We know that gentians grow on the Alps, and olives on the Apennines; but we do not enough conceive for ourselves that variegated mosaic of the world's surface which a bird sees in its migration, that difference between the district of the gentian and of the olive which the stork and the swallow see far off, as they lean upon the sirocco wind.[4] Let us, for a moment, try to raise ourselves even above the level of their flight, and imagine the Mediterranean lying beneath us like an irregular lake, and all its ancient promontories sleeping in the sun: here and there an angry spot of thunder, a grey stain of storm, moving upon the burning field; and here and there a fixed wreath of white volcano smoke, surrounded by its circle of ashes; but for the most part a great peacefulness of light, Syria and Greece, Italy and Spain, laid like pieces of a golden pavement into the sea-blue, chased, as we stoop nearer to them, with bossy beaten work of mountain chains, and glowing softly with terraced gardens, and flowers heavy with frankincense, mixed among masses of laurel, and orange, and plumy palm, that abate with their grey-green

2. The Goths, a Germanic people who overran the Roman Empire, were regarded as barbarians.
3. A reference to the Renaissance rediscovery of the clas-

sical world. Ruskin despised Renaissance architecture, which he found excessively ornate and morally suspect.
4. Hot Mediterranean wind.

shadows the burning of the marble rocks, and of the ledges of porphyry[5] sloping under lucent sand. Then let us pass farther towards the north, until we see the orient colours change gradually into a vast belt of rainy green, where the pastures of Switzerland, and poplar valleys of France, and dark forests of the Danube and Carpathians stretch from the mouths of the Loire to those of the Volga, seen through clefts in grey swirls of rain-cloud and flaky veils of the mist of the brooks, spreading low along the pasture lands: and then, farther north still, to see the earth heave into mighty masses of leaden rock and heathy moor, bordering with a broad waste of gloomy purple that belt of field and wood, and splintering into irregular and grisly islands amidst the northern seas, beaten by storm, and chilled by ice-drift, and tormented by furious pulses of contending tide, until the roots of the last forests fail from among the hill ravines, and the hunger of the north wind bites their peaks into barrenness; and, at last, the wall of ice, durable like iron, sets, deathlike, its white teeth against us out of the polar twilight. And, having once traversed in thought this gradation of the zoned iris of the earth in all its material vastness, let us go down nearer to it, and watch the parallel change in the belt of animal life; the multitudes of swift and brilliant creatures that glance in the air and sea, or tread the sands of the southern zone; striped zebras and spotted leopards, glistening serpents, and birds arrayed in purple and scarlet. Let us contrast their delicacy and brilliancy of colour, and swiftness of motion, with the frost-cramped strength, and shaggy covering, and dusky plumage of the northern tribes; contrast the Arabian horse with the Shetland, the tiger and leopard with the wolf and bear, the antelope with the elk, the bird of paradise with the osprey; and then, submissively acknowledging the great laws by which the earth and all that it bears are ruled throughout their being, let us not condemn, but rejoice in the expression by man of his own rest in the statutes of the lands that gave him birth. Let us watch him with reverence as he sets side by side the burning gems, and smooths with soft sculpture the jasper pillars, that are to reflect a ceaseless sunshine, and rise into a cloudless sky: but not with less reverence let us stand by him, when, with rough strength and hurried stroke, he smites an uncouth animation out of the rocks which he has torn from among the moss of the moorland, and heaves into the darkened air the pile of iron buttress and rugged wall, instinct with work of an imagination as wild and wayward as the northern sea; creatures of ungainly shape and rigid limb, but full of wolfish life; fierce as the winds that beat, and changeful as the clouds that shade them.

There is, I repeat, no degradation, no reproach in this, but all dignity and honourableness: and we should err grievously in refusing either to recognize as an essential character of the existing architecture of the North, or to admit as a desirable character in that which it yet may be, this wildness of thought, and roughness of work; this look of mountain brotherhood between the cathedral and the Alp; this magnificence of sturdy power, put forth only the more energetically because the fine finger-touch was chilled away by the frosty wind, and the eye dimmed by the moor-mist, or blinded by the hail; this out-speaking of the strong spirit of men who may not gather redundant fruitage from the earth, nor bask in dreamy benignity of sunshine, but must break the rock for bread, and cleave the forest for fire, and show, even in what they did for their delight, some of the hard habits of the arm and heart that grew on them as they swung the axe or pressed the plough.

5. Dark red or purple rock.

If, however, the savageness of Gothic architecture, merely as an expression of its origin among Northern nations, may be considered, in some sort, a noble character, it possesses a higher nobility still, when considered as an index, not of climate, but of religious principle.

In the 13th and 14th paragraphs of Chapter XXI of the first volume of this work, it was noticed that the systems of architectural ornament, properly so called, might be divided into three:—1. Servile ornament, in which the execution or power of the inferior workman is entirely subjected to the intellect of the higher;—2. Constitutional ornament, in which the executive inferior power is, to a certain point, emancipated and independent, having a will of its own, yet confessing its inferiority and rendering obedience to higher powers;—and 3. Revolutionary ornament, in which no executive inferiority is admitted at all. I must here explain the nature of these divisions at somewhat greater length.

Of Servile ornament, the principal schools are the Greek, Ninevite,[6] and Egyptian; but their servility is of different kinds. The Greek master-workman was far advanced in knowledge and power above the Assyrian or Egyptian. Neither he nor those for whom he worked could endure the appearance of imperfection in anything; and, therefore, what ornament he appointed to be done by those beneath him was composed of mere geometrical forms,—balls, ridges, and perfectly symmetrical foliage,—which could be executed with absolute precision by line and rule, and were as perfect in their way, when completed, as his own figure sculpture. The Assyrian and Egyptian, on the contrary, less cognisant of accurate form in anything, were content to allow their figure sculpture to be executed by inferior workmen, but lowered the method of its treatment to a standard which every workman could reach, and then trained him by discipline so rigid, that there was no chance of his falling beneath the standard appointed. The Greek gave to the lower workman no subject which he could not perfectly execute. The Assyrian gave him subjects which he could only execute imperfectly, but fixed a legal standard for his imperfection. The workman was, in both systems, a slave.

But in the mediaeval, or especially Christian, system of ornament, this slavery is done away with altogether; Christianity having recognized, in small things as well as great, the individual value of every soul. But it not only recognizes its value; it confesses its imperfection, in only bestowing dignity upon the acknowledgment of unworthiness. That admission of lost power and fallen nature, which the Greek or Ninevite felt to be intensely painful, and, as far as might be, altogether refused, the Christian makes daily and hourly, contemplating the fact of it without fear, as tending, in the end, to God's greater glory. Therefore, to every spirit which Christianity summons to her service, her exhortation is: Do what you can, and confess frankly what you are unable to do; neither let your effort be shortened for fear of failure, nor your confession silenced for fear of shame. And it is, perhaps, the principal admirableness of the Gothic schools of architecture, that they thus receive the results of the labour of inferior minds; and out of fragments full of imperfection, and betraying that imperfection in every touch, indulgently raise up a stately and unaccusable whole.

But the modern English mind has this much in common with that of the Greek, that it intensely desires, in all things, the utmost completion or perfection

6. Nineveh was an ancient Assyrian city.

compatible with their nature. This is a noble character in the abstract, but becomes ignoble when it causes us to forget the relative dignities of that nature itself, and to prefer the perfectness of the lower nature to the imperfection of the higher; not considering that as, judged by such a rule, all the brute animals would be preferable to man, because more perfect in their functions and kind. * * * And therefore, while in all things that we see or do, we are to desire perfection, and strive for it, we are nevertheless not to set the meaner thing, in its narrow accomplishment, above the nobler thing, in its mighty progress; not to esteem smooth minuteness above shattered majesty; not to prefer mean victory to honourable defeat; not to lower the level of our aim, that we may the more surely enjoy the complacency of success. But, above all, in our dealings with the souls of other men, we are to take care how we check, by severe requirement or narrow caution, efforts which might otherwise lead to a noble issue; and, still more, how we withhold our admiration from great excellencies, because they are mingled with rough faults. Now, in the make and nature of every man, however rude or simple, whom we employ in manual labour, there are some powers for better things; some tardy imagination, torpid capacity of emotion, tottering steps of thought, there are, even at the worst; and in most cases it is all our own fault that they *are* tardy or torpid. But they cannot be strengthened, unless we are content to take them in their feebleness, and unless we prize and honour them in their imperfection above the best and most perfect manual skill. And this is what we have to do with all our labourers; to look for the *thoughtful* part of them, and get that out of them, whatever we lose for it, whatever faults and errors we are obliged to take with it. For the best that is in them cannot manifest itself, but in company with much error. Understand this clearly: You can teach a man to draw a straight line, and to cut one; to strike a curved line, and to carve it; and to copy and carve any number of given lines or forms, with admirable speed and perfect precision; and you find his work perfect of its kind: but if you ask him to think about any of those forms, to consider if he cannot find any better in his own head, he stops; his execution becomes hesitating; he thinks, and ten to one he thinks wrong; ten to one he makes a mistake in the first touch he gives to his work as a thinking being. But you have made a man of him for all that. He was only a machine before, an animated tool.

And observe, you are put to stern choice in this matter. You must either make a tool of the creature, or a man of him. You cannot make both. Men were not intended to work with the accuracy of tools, to be precise and perfect in all their actions. If you will have that precision out of them, and make their fingers measure degrees like cogwheels, and their arms strike curves like compasses, you must unhumanize them. All the energy of their spirits must be given to make cogs and compasses of themselves. All their attention and strength must go to the accomplishment of the mean act. The eye of the soul must be bent upon the finger-point, and the soul's force must fill all the invisible nerves that guide it, ten hours a day, that it may not err from its steely precision, and so soul and sight be worn away, and the whole human being be lost at last—a heap of sawdust, so far as its intellectual work in this world is concerned: saved only by its Heart, which cannot go into the form of cogs and compasses, but expands, after the ten hours are over, into fireside humanity. On the other hand, if you will make a man of the working creature, you cannot make a tool. Let him but begin to imagine, to think, to try to do anything worth doing; and the engine-turned precision is lost at once. Out come all his roughness, all his dulness, all his incapability; shame upon shame, failure upon failure, pause after pause: but out comes the whole majesty of him also; and we know the height of it only when we see the clouds settling upon him. And, whether the clouds be bright or dark, there will be transfiguration behind and within them.

And now, reader, look round this English room of yours, about which you have been proud so often, because the work of it was so good and strong, and the ornaments of it so finished. Examine again all those accurate mouldings, and perfect polishings, and unerring adjustments of the seasoned wood and tempered steel. Many a time you have exulted over them, and thought how great England was, because her slightest work was done so thoroughly. Alas! if read rightly, these perfectnesses are signs of a slavery in our England a thousand times more bitter and more degrading than that of the scourged African, or helot[7] Greek. Men may be beaten, chained, tormented, yoked like cattle, slaughtered like summer flies, and yet remain in one sense, and the best sense, free. But to smother their souls within them, to blight and hew into rotting pollards[8] the suckling branches of their human intelligence, to make the flesh and skin which, after the worm's work on it, is to see God,[9] into leathern thongs to yoke machinery with,—this is to be slave-masters indeed; and there might be more freedom in England, though her feudal lords' lightest words were worth men's lives, and though the blood of the vexed husbandman dropped in the furrows of her fields, than there is while the animation of her multitudes is sent like fuel to feed the factory smoke, and the strength of them is given daily to be wasted into the fineness of a web, or racked into the exactness of a line.

And, on the other hand, go forth again to gaze upon the old cathedral front, where you have smiled so often at the fantastic ignorance of the old sculptors: examine once more those ugly goblins, and formless monsters, and stern statues, anatomiless and rigid; but do not mock at them, for they are signs of the life and liberty of every workman who struck the stone; a freedom of thought, and rank in scale of being, such as no laws, no charters, no charities can secure; but which it must be the first aim of all Europe at this day to regain for her children.

Let me not be thought to speak wildly or extravagantly. It is verily this degradation of the operative into a machine, which, more than any other evil of the times, is leading the mass of the nations everywhere into vain, incoherent, destructive struggling for a freedom of which they cannot explain the nature to themselves. Their universal outcry against wealth, and against nobility, is not forced from them either by the pressure of famine, or the sting of mortified pride. These do much, and have done much in all ages; but the foundations of society were never yet shaken as they are at this day. It is not that men are ill fed, but that they have no pleasure in the work by which they make their bread, and therefore look to wealth as the only means of pleasure. It is not that men are pained by the scorn of the upper classes, but they cannot endure their own; for they feel that the kind of labour to which they are condemned is verily a degrading one, and makes them less than men. Never had the upper classes so much sympathy with the lower, or charity for them, as they have at this day, and yet never were they so much hated by them: for, of old, the separation between the noble and the poor was merely a wall built by law; now it is a veritable difference in level of standing, a precipice between upper and lower grounds in the field of humanity, and there is pestilential air at the bottom of it. * * *

---

7. Serf or slave.
8. Trees that are artificially shaped by pruning.

9. "And though after my skin worms destroy this body, yet in my flesh shall I see God" (Job 19.26).

We have much studied and much perfected, of late, the great civilized invention of the division of labour; only we give it a false name. It is not, truly speaking, the labour that is divided; but the men:—Divided into mere segments of men—broken into small fragments and crumbs of life; so that all the little piece of intelligence that is left in a man is not enough to make a pin, or a nail, but exhausts itself in making the point of a pin or the head of a nail. Now it is a good and desirable thing, truly, to make many pins in a day; but if we could only see with what crystal sand their points were polished,—sand of human soul, much to be magnified before it can be discerned for what it is—we should think there might be some loss in it also. And the great cry that rises from all our manufacturing cities, louder than their furnace blast, is all in very deed for this,—that we manufacture everything there except men; we blanch cotton, and strengthen steel, and refine sugar, and shape pottery; but to brighten, to strengthen, to refine, or to form a single living spirit, never enters into our estimate of advantages. And all the evil to which that cry is urging our myriads can be met only in one way: not by teaching nor preaching, for to teach them is but to show them their misery, and to preach to them, if we do nothing more than preach, is to mock at it. It can be met only by a right understanding, on the part of all classes, of what kinds of labour are good for men, raising them, and making them happy; by a determined sacrifice of such convenience, or beauty, or cheapness as is to be got only by the degradation of the workman; and by equally determined demand for the products and results of healthy and ennobling labour.

And how, it will be asked, are these products to be recognized, and this demand to be regulated? Easily: by the observance of three broad and simple rules:

1. Never encourage the manufacture of any article not absolutely necessary, in the production of which *Invention* has no share.

2. Never demand an exact finish for its own sake, but only for some practical or noble end.

3. Never encourage imitation or copying of any kind, except for the sake of preserving records of great works.

The second of these principles is the only one which directly rises out of the consideration of our immediate subject; but I shall briefly explain the meaning and extent of the first also, reserving the enforcement of the third for another place.

1. Never encourage the manufacture of anything not necessary, in the production of which invention has no share.

For instance. Glass beads are utterly unnecessary, and there is no design or thought employed in their manufacture. They are formed by first drawing out the glass into rods; these rods are chopped up into fragments of the size of beads by the human hand, and the fragments are then rounded in the furnace. The men who chop up the rods sit at their work all day, their hands vibrating with a perpetual and exquisitely timed palsy, and the beads dropping beneath their vibration like hail. Neither they, nor the men who draw out the rods or fuse the fragments, have the smallest occasion for the use of any single human faculty; and every young lady, therefore, who buys glass beads is engaged in the slave-trade, and in a much more cruel one than that which we have so long been endeavouring to put down.

But glass cups and vessels may become the subjects of exquisite invention; and if in buying these we pay for the invention, that is to say, for the beautiful form, or colour, or engraving, and not for mere finish of execution, we are doing good to humanity.

So, again, the cutting of precious stones, in all ordinary cases, requires little exertion of any mental faculty; some tact and judgment in avoiding flaws, and so on, but nothing to bring out the whole mind. Every person who wears cut jewels merely for the sake of their value is, therefore, a slave-driver.

But the working of the goldsmith, and the various designing of grouped jewellery and enamel-work, may become the subject of the most noble human intelligence. Therefore, money spent in the purchase of well-designed plate, of precious engraved vases, cameos, or enamels, does good to humanity; and, in work of this kind, jewels may be employed to heighten its splendour; and their cutting is then a price paid for the attainment of a noble end, and thus perfectly allowable.

I shall perhaps press this law farther elsewhere, but our immediate concern is chiefly with the second, namely, never to demand an exact finish, when it does not lead to a noble end. For observe, I have only dwelt upon the rudeness of Gothic, or any other kind of imperfectness, as admirable, where it was impossible to get design or thought without it. If you are to have the thought of a rough and untaught man, you must have it in a rough and untaught way; but from an educated man, who can without effort express his thoughts in an educated way, take the graceful expression, and be thankful. Only *get* the thought, and do not silence the peasant because he cannot speak good grammar, or until you have taught him his grammar. Grammar and refinement are good things, both, only be sure of the better thing first. And thus in art, delicate finish is desirable from the greatest masters, and is always given by them. In some places Michael Angelo, Leonardo, Phidias, Perugino, Turner,[1] all finished with the most exquisite care; and the finish they give always leads to the fuller accomplishment of their noble purposes. But lower men than these cannot finish, for it requires consummate knowledge to finish consummately, and then we must take their thoughts as they are able to give them. So the rule is simple: Always look for invention first, and after that, for such execution as will help the invention, and as the inventor is capable of without painful effort, and *no more*. Above all, demand no refinement of execution where there is no thought, for that is slaves' work, unredeemed. Rather choose rough work than smooth work, so only that the practical purpose be answered, and never imagine there is reason to be proud of anything that may be accomplished by patience and sand-paper.

I shall only give one example, which however will show the reader what I mean, from the manufacture already alluded to, that of glass. Our modern glass is exquisitely clear in its substance, true in its form, accurate in its cutting. We are proud of this. We ought to be ashamed of it. The old Venice glass was muddy, inaccurate in all its forms, and clumsily cut, if at all. And the old Venetian was justly proud of it. For there is this difference between the English and Venetian workman, that the former thinks only of accurately matching his patterns, and getting his curves perfectly true and his edges perfectly sharp, and becomes a mere machine for rounding curves and sharpening edges; while the old Venetian cared not a whit whether his edges were sharp or not, but he invented a new design for every glass that he made, and never moulded a handle or a lip without a new fancy in it. And therefore, though some Venetian glass is ugly and clumsy enough when made by clumsy and uninventive workmen, other Venetian glass is so lovely in its forms

1. Michelangelo Buonarroti (1475–1564), Italian painter, sculptor, architect, and poet; Leonardo da Vinci (1452–1519), Italian painter, sculptor, architect, and engineer; Phidias (5th century B.C.), ancient Greek sculptor; Pietro Vannucci Perugino (1446–1523), Italian painter; J. M. W. Turner (1775–1851), English painter.

that no price is too great for it; and we never see the same form in it twice. Now you cannot have the finish and the varied form too. If the workman is thinking about his edges, he cannot be thinking of his design; if of his design, he cannot think of his edges. Choose whether you will pay for the lovely form or the perfect finish, and choose at the same moment whether you will make the worker a man or a grindstone.

Nay, but the reader interrupts me,—"If the workman can design beautifully, I would not have him kept at the furnace. Let him be taken away and made a gentleman, and have a studio, and design his glass there, and I will have it blown and cut for him by common workmen, and so I will have my design and my finish too."

All ideas of this kind are founded upon two mistaken suppositions: the first, that one man's thoughts can be, or ought to be, executed by another man's hands; the second, that manual labour is a degradation, when it is governed by intellect.

On a large scale, and in work determinable by line and rule, it is indeed both possible and necessary that the thoughts of one man should be carried out by the labour of others; in this sense I have already defined the best architecture to be the expression of the mind of manhood by the hands of childhood. But on a smaller scale, and in a design which cannot be mathematically defined, one man's thoughts can never be expressed by another: and the difference between the spirit of touch of the man who is inventing, and of the man who is obeying directions, is often all the difference between a great and a common work of art. How wide the separation is between original and second-hand execution, I shall endeavour to show elsewhere; it is not so much to our purpose here as to mark the other and more fatal error of despising manual labour when governed by intellect; for it is no less fatal an error to despise it when thus regulated by intellect, than to value it for its own sake. We are always in these days endeavouring to separate the two; we want one man to be always thinking, and another to be always working, and we call one a gentleman, and the other an operative; whereas the workman ought often to be thinking, and the thinker often to be working, and both should be gentlemen, in the best sense. As it is, we make both ungentle, the one envying, the other despising, his brother; and the mass of society is made up of morbid thinkers, and miserable workers. Now it is only by labour that thought can be made healthy, and only by thought that labour can be made happy, and the two cannot be separated with impunity. ✳ ✳ ✳

I should be led far from the matter in hand, if I were to pursue this interesting subject. Enough, I trust, has been said to show the reader that the rudeness or imperfection which at first rendered the term "Gothic" one of reproach is indeed, when rightly understood, one of the most noble characters of Christian architecture, and not only a noble but an *essential* one. It seems a fantastic paradox, but it is nevertheless a most important truth, that no architecture can be truly noble which is *not* imperfect. And this is easily demonstrable. For since the architect, whom we will suppose capable of doing all in perfection, cannot execute the whole with his own hands, he must either make slaves of his workmen in the old Greek, and present English fashion, and level his work to a slave's capacities, which is to degrade it; or else he must take his workmen as he finds them, and let them show their weaknesses together with their strength, which will involve the Gothic imperfection, but render the whole work as noble as the intellect of the age can make it.

But the principle may be stated more broadly still. I have confined the illustration of it to architecture, but I must not leave it as if true of architecture only. Hitherto I have used the words imperfect and perfect merely to distinguish between work grossly unskilful, and work executed with average precision and science; and I have been pleading that any degree of unskilfulness should be admitted, so only that the labourer's mind had room for expression. But, accurately speaking, no good work whatever can be perfect, and *the demand for perfection is always a sign of a misunderstanding of the ends of art.*

This for two reasons, both based on everlasting laws. The first, that no great man ever stops working till he has reached his point of failure: that is to say, his mind is always far in advance of his powers of execution, and the latter will now and then give way in trying to follow it; besides that he will always give to the inferior portions of his work only such inferior attention as they require; and according to his greatness he becomes so accustomed to the feeling of dissatisfaction with the best he can do, that in moments of lassitude or anger with himself he will not care though the beholder be dissatisfied also. I believe there has only been one man who would not acknowledge this necessity, and strove always to reach perfection, Leonardo; the end of his vain effort being merely that he would take ten years to a picture and leave it unfinished. And therefore, if we are to have great men working at all, or less men doing their best, the work will be imperfect, however beautiful. Of human work none but what is bad can be perfect, in its own bad way.[2]

The second reason is, that imperfection is in some sort essential to all that we know of life. It is the sign of life in a mortal body, that is to say, of a state of progress and change. Nothing that lives is, or can be, rigidly perfect; part of it is decaying, part nascent. The foxglove blossom,—a third part bud, a third part past, a third part in full bloom,—is a type of the life of this world. And in all things that live there are certain irregularities and deficiencies which are not only signs of life, but sources of beauty. No human face is exactly the same in its lines on each side, no leaf perfect in its lobes, no branch in its symmetry. All admit irregularity as they imply change; and to banish imperfection is to destroy expression, to check exertion, to paralyze vitality. All things are literally better, lovelier, and more beloved for the imperfections which have been divinely appointed, that the law of human life may be Effort, and the law of human judgment, Mercy.

Accept this then for a universal law, that neither architecture nor any other noble work of man can be good unless it be imperfect; and let us be prepared for the otherwise strange fact, which we shall discern clearly as we approach the period of the Renaissance, that the first cause of the fall of the arts of Europe was a relentless requirement of perfection, incapable alike either of being silenced by veneration for greatness, or softened into forgiveness of simplicity.

Thus far then of the Rudeness or Savageness, which is the first mental element of Gothic architecture. It is an element in many other healthy architectures also, as the Byzantine and Romanesque; but true Gothic cannot exist without it.

1851–1853

---

2. The Elgin marbles are supposed by many persons to be "perfect." In the most important portions they indeed approach perfection, but only there. The draperies are unfinished, the hair and wool of the animals are unfinished, and the entire bas-reliefs of the frieze are roughly cut [Ruskin's note]. The Elgin marbles are sculptures (including the Parthenon frieze) that were taken from Athens to England by Lord Elgin at the beginning of the 19th century.

Matthew Arnold

1822–1888

"I am glad you like the Gipsy Scholar," Matthew Arnold wrote to a friend in 1853, "—but what does it *do* for you?" No Victorian gave more attention than Arnold to the momentous question of how art should affect an audience, and no writer was ever more tortured by it. For much as he delighted in creating the "pleasing melancholy" of *The Scholar-Gipsy*, one of his greatest poems, Arnold felt that literature must directly address the moral needs of readers, "to *animate* and *ennoble* them." This concern with the practical emotional effects of art, Arnold said simply, is "the basis of my nature—and of my poetics."

But in trying to realize his goal, Arnold became a deeply divided man. Author of the era's most distinctive poems of alienation and doubt, he gave up poetry to work for the public good, passionately defending classic literature as a means of remaking the materialist society he abhorred. As a social critic, he aspired to embody his ideal of a balanced mind, to be a man "who saw life steadily and saw it whole." But as a private individual he viewed himself as a forlorn romantic quester, disenchanted with modernity. Unable to believe in the religion of the past and unwilling to accept the secular values of the present, he described himself as "wandering between two worlds, one dead, / The other powerless to be born." Arnold is unique among the eminent Victorian writers, admired equally for his heartfelt poetry of disillusionment and for his sophisticated prose aimed at pragmatic social reform.

Matthew Arnold was the oldest son of Dr. Thomas Arnold, headmaster of Rugby School, who had become famous for reshaping the curriculum to instill a healthy respect for Christian values, classical languages, and competitive games. Matthew's mother, Mary Penrose Arnold, encouraged her son to be creative, self-conscious, and alert to the comic or dramatic side of daily events. Nicknamed "Crabby" by his father when he wore leg braces for two years, Arnold adopted a sidelong, crab-like approach to his goal of becoming a poet. A lazy, dilettantish, facetious student, Arnold managed through last-minute heroics to win the top prizes: a scholarship in 1840 to Balliol College, Oxford; the renowned Newdigate Prize for poetry in 1843; and in 1845 a Fellowship at Oriel College.

Throughout his life, Arnold seemed most comfortable outdoors and free of the classroom, whether blasting away at game on the English moors (he was a terrible shot) or hiking in the Alps. He spent his early childhood at Laleham, a village on the Thames, perhaps the source of his frequent river imagery. When he should have been studying at Oxford, he roamed the idyllic countryside surrounding it, hunting, fishing, and composing verses. He once pranced naked on a riverbank after swimming, prompting a rebuke from a passing clergyman. Waving his towel, Arnold replied: "Is it possible that you see anything indelicate in the human form divine?"

In 1847 Arnold became private secretary to the liberal politician Lord Lansdowne, spending most of his time in London, working on his poetry, and arguing about poetry and religion with his best friend, the poet Arthur Hugh Clough. They both agreed on the spiritual bankruptcy of modern life: "These are damned times," Arnold wrote to Clough in 1849; "everything is against one . . . the absence of great *natures*, the unavoidable contact with millions of small ones . . . our own selves, and the sickening consciousness of our difficulties."

Arnold dealt with these difficulties by casting them in poetic form. His first book of poems, *The Strayed Reveller, and Other Poems*, by "A," appeared in 1849, followed by *Empedocles on Etna, and Other Poems* (1852) and *Poems* (1853). Many other important poems, including *Dover Beach*, also date from this fertile period, though not published until later, in *Poems, Second Series* (1855) and *New Poems* (1867).

Arnold's finest poetry is imbued with a love of the countryside. He spent family vacations in the Lake District, whose beauty and poetic associations made a deep impression on him. His parents were friendly with Wordsworth, who was to become the chief influence on Arnold's poetry; when Wordsworth died he mourned, "who will teach us how to feel?" Like Wordsworth, Arnold evokes memorable landscapes in many of his key works in order to ponder the relation between hidden emotions and external objects, and to explore the themes of lost childhood, nostalgia for the past, and the quest for identity. But Arnold rarely found in nature a means of contact with other people or with a deeper self: "The disease of the present age," he wrote in his journal, "is divorce from oneself."

Arnold felt a growing dissatisfaction with his society and with his own poetry. In a controversial preface to his *Poems* of 1853, he justified not reprinting his major earlier work, *Empedocles on Etna*, because he felt that it failed to "inspirit and rejoice" readers and teach them how to live. He went on to condemn poetry that merely presents "a continuous state of mental distress . . . unrelieved by incident, hope, or resistance; in which there is everything to be endured, nothing to be done." In these words he accurately summed up—and dismissed—what was most powerful and moving in his own work.

Provoking a heated debate about the poet's relation to contemporary life, Arnold urged that modern poets should turn from their own troubles to build upon timeless, universal "great actions," such as those found in Sophocles and Aeschylus. The Victorian age, he concluded, was an unlikely source of poetic material, because it was "an age wanting in moral grandeur . . . an age of spiritual discomfort."

Too much a man of his time to be able to follow his own advice, Arnold largely abandoned poetry after the mid-1850s. In 1851, two important events occurred that contributed to this abdication: his marriage to Frances Lucy Wightman and his taking a job as a school inspector to support his family. This turned out to be a grueling position assessing the quality of instruction in government-funded schools for the poor. Initially surmising that the job would do well enough "for the next three or four years," Arnold doggedly kept at it for thirty-five years, traveling constantly throughout Britain and later in Europe. He soon realized the importance of expanding and reforming public education, arguing for the schools' crucial role "in civilizing the next generation of the lower classes, who, as things are going, will have most of the political power of the country in their hands."

Thus the anguished poet transformed himself into an energetic public servant, strenuously trying to remedy with his progressive criticism a society that he privately despaired of as hopelessly materialist. In 1857 Arnold was elected Professor of Poetry at Oxford University. He was the first to lecture in English rather than Latin, and for the next ten years he used the occasion of his public lectures to reach the broadest possible audience, promoting his belief that a careful reading of classic literature produces civilizing and morally sustaining effects. He reworked many of his lectures into books and essays, including *On Translating Homer* (1861) and *On the Modern Element in Literature* (1869). The work begun at Oxford eventually helped establish literature as a cornerstone of university programs in the liberal arts.

In his most important work of social criticism, *Culture and Anarchy* (1869), Arnold called for "disinterested" analysis free of partisan politics. He deplored English pride in "doing as one likes" and found in the self-serving behavior of all classes an anarchic lack of concern for the public good. Only education, he contended, could unite the antagonistic factions of British society, by teaching respect for beauty and intellect—what Arnold termed the virtues of "sweetness and light."

The mocking irony, Olympian assurance, and lucid, cascading style of his works make them exhilarating—or exasperating—reading. Arnold's high-minded attitudes enraged many of his opponents, and his loftiness of tone led even his friends and family to nickname him "the Emperor." For Arnold, education was a lifelong task, and few measured up to the cosmopolitan,

European standards he set. He was particularly savage with anyone he considered guilty of self-interest or fuzzy thinking, and he attacked politicians and bishops by name. Leslie Stephen, Virginia Woolf's father, remarked satirically that "I often wished . . . that I too had a little sweetness and light that I might be able to say such nasty things of my enemies."

In the 1870s, Arnold scandalized many people with his attacks on orthodox religion in *St. Paul and Protestantism* (1870), *Literature and Dogma* (1873), and *God and the Bible* (1875). In *The Study of Poetry* (1880), he went so far as to argue that "most of what now passes for religion and philosophy will be replaced by poetry."

In 1883, weary, in debt, and desperate to retire, Arnold tried to raise money by selecting, with his daughter Nelly, 365 mottoes to create a *Matthew Arnold Birthday Book*. In the same year he went on a money-making lecture tour of the United States, meeting with mixed success. The chief intellectual product of his travel was *Discourses in America* (1885), which contained his essay *Literature and Science*. There, Arnold defended the idea of a liberal arts education founded on ancient and modern literatures against Thomas Huxley's contention in *Science and Culture* (1881) that an education based on the natural sciences would do just as well. Arnold felt that the debate had particular relevance for Americans, whose respect for "the average man" was fraught with "danger to the ideal of a high and rare excellence," best conveyed by a humanistic education. Arnold died suddenly of a heart attack in 1888.

Arnold was not a prophetic critic like Carlyle, nor a visionary poet of social reform like Elizabeth Barrett Browning, nor a moral crusader like Dickens. Instead, Arnold offered thoughtful prescriptions for guiding a changing and increasingly democratic society to a fuller understanding of its problems, and a more effective realization of its goals. As a school inspector he developed a deeper understanding of ineffective institutions and the ignorance of the British public than any other important Victorian author. While few have agreed fully with his pronouncements on literature and society, he has influenced almost every significant English-speaking critic since his time, including T. S. Eliot, F. R. Leavis, Lionel Trilling, and Raymond Williams.

Arnold has remained a literary force to be reckoned with as well. In its honest, introspective, sometimes awkward way, Arnold's poetry speaks unforgettably of the anxieties of his era. Though he saw himself as having "less poetical sentiment than Tennyson, and less intellectual vigor and abundance than Browning," he felt that his more balanced "fusion" of these qualities would continue to assure him an audience. His open approach to his innermost feelings is echoed almost everywhere in modern poetry.

Dover Beach

The sea is calm to-night.
The tide is full, the moon lies fair
Upon the straits; on the French coast the light
Gleams and is gone; the cliffs of England stand,
5   Glimmering and vast, out in the tranquil bay.
Come to the window, sweet is the night-air!
Only, from the long line of spray
Where the sea meets the moon-blanched land,
Listen! you hear the grating roar
10   Of pebbles which the waves draw back, and fling,
At their return, up the high strand,
Begin, and cease, and then again begin,
With tremulous cadence slow, and bring
The eternal note of sadness in.

15   Sophocles long ago
        Heard it on the Aegean,[1] and it brought
        Into his mind the turbid ebb and flow
        Of human misery; we
        Find also in the sound a thought,
20   Hearing it by this distant northern sea.

        The Sea of Faith
        Was once, too, at the full, and round earth's shore
        Lay like the folds of a bright girdle° furled.   *sash*
        But now I only hear
25   Its melancholy, long, withdrawing roar,
        Retreating, to the breath
        Of the night-wind, down the vast edges drear
        And naked shingles° of the world.   *pebble beaches*

        Ah, love, let us be true
30   To one another! for the world, which seems
        To lie before us like a land of dreams,
        So various, so beautiful, so new,
        Hath really neither joy, nor love, nor light,
        Nor certitude, nor peace, nor help for pain;
35   And we are here as on a darkling plain
        Swept with confused alarms of struggle and flight,
        Where ignorant armies clash by night.

c. 1851   1867

from Culture and Anarchy[1]
from Sweetness and Light

The disparagers of culture make its motive curiosity; sometimes, indeed, they make its motive mere exclusiveness and vanity. The culture which is supposed to plume itself on a smattering of Greek and Latin is a culture which is begotten by nothing so intellectual as curiosity; it is valued either out of sheer vanity and ignorance or else as an engine of social and class distinction, separating its holder, like a badge or title, from other people who have not got it. No serious man would call this *culture*, or attach any value to it, as culture, at all. To find the real ground for the very different estimate which serious people will set upon culture, we must find some motive for culture in the terms of which may lie a real ambiguity; and such a motive the word *curiosity* gives us.

I have before now pointed out that we English do not, like the foreigners, use this word in a good sense as well as in a bad sense. With us the word is always used in

1. Sophocles was a 5th century B.C. Greek dramatist; the Aegean Sea lies between Greece and Turkey.
1. Arnold's most important work of social criticism, *Culture and Anarchy* (1869) grew out of his final Oxford lecture in 1867. Deploring English pride in "doing as one likes," Arnold connected the self-serving behavior of all classes to the worst effects of laissez-faire capitalism. He felt that Britain was heading toward anarchy; no one seemed to have any concern for the public good. The best of Western culture, Arnold contended, depends on a balance between the Judeo-Christian emphasis on moral conduct (Hebraism) and the Greek ideal of intellectual and artistic cultivation (Hellenism). But in his view a Puritan "strictness of conscience" was now impeding a classical "spontaneity of consciousness." There was only one way to bridge the gap between privileged "Barbarians" (the aristocracy), intolerant "Philistines" (the middle classes), and the uneducated "Populace" (the working classes): by spreading to all parts of society a Hellenistic respect for beauty and intellect—what Arnold termed "sweetness and light."

a somewhat disapproving sense. A liberal and intelligent eagerness about the things of the mind may be meant by a foreigner when he speaks of curiosity, but with us the word always conveys a certain notion of frivolous and unedifying activity. In the *Quarterly Review*, some little time ago, was an estimate of the celebrated French critic, M. Sainte-Beuve,[2] and a very inadequate estimate it in my judgment was. And its inadequacy consisted chiefly in this: that in our English way it left out of sight the double sense really involved in the word *curiosity*, thinking enough was said to stamp M. Sainte-Beuve with blame if it was said that he was impelled in his operations as a critic by curiosity, and omitting either to perceive that M. Sainte-Beuve himself, and many other people with him, would consider that this was praiseworthy and not blameworthy, or to point out why it ought really to be accounted worthy of blame and not of praise. For as there is a curiosity about intellectual matters which is futile, and merely a disease, so there is certainly a curiosity,—a desire after the things of the mind simply for their own sakes and for the pleasure of seeing them as they are,— which is, in an intelligent being, natural and laudable. Nay, and the very desire to see things as they are implies a balance and regulation of mind which is not often attained without fruitful effort, and which is the very opposite of the blind and diseased impulse of mind which is what we mean to blame when we blame curiosity. Montesquieu[3] says: "The first motive which ought to impel us to study is the desire to augment the excellence of our nature, and to render an intelligent being yet more intelligent." This is the true ground to assign for the genuine scientific passion, however manifested, and for culture, viewed simply as a fruit of this passion; and it is a worthy ground, even though we let the term *curiosity* stand to describe it.

But there is of culture another view, in which not solely the scientific passion, the sheer desire to see things as they are, natural and proper in an intelligent being, appears as the ground of it. There is a view in which all the love of our neighbour, the impulses towards action, help, and beneficence, the desire for removing human error, clearing human confusion, and diminishing human misery, the noble aspiration to leave the world better and happier than we found it,—motives eminently such as are called social,—come in as part of the grounds of culture, and the main and pre-eminent part. Culture is then properly described not as having its origin in curiosity, but as having its origin in the love of perfection; it is *a study of perfection*. It moves by the force, not merely or primarily of the scientific passion for pure knowledge, but also of the moral and social passion for doing good. As, in the first view of it, we took for its worthy motto Montesquieu's words: "To render an intelligent being yet more intelligent!" so, in the second view of it, there is no better motto which it can have than these words of Bishop Wilson: "To make reason and the will of God prevail!"[4] * * *

The pursuit of perfection, then, is the pursuit of sweetness and light.[5] He who works for sweetness and light, works to make reason and the will of God prevail. He who works for machinery, he who works for hatred, works only for confusion. Culture looks beyond machinery, culture hates hatred; culture has one great passion,

---

2. Charles Augustine Sainte-Beuve (1804–1869), French critic whom Arnold admired.
3. Baron de la Brède et de Montesquieu (1689–1755), French political and legal philosopher.
4. Thomas Wilson (1663–1755), Bishop of Sodor and Man. His *Maxims*, though little known, were a favorite of Arnold's.

5. The phrase comes from a fable in Swift's *The Battle of the Books* (1704): the Bee (representing ancient culture) ventures forth to fill its hive with honey and wax for light-giving candles, but the home-bound Spider (representing modern culture) produces from itself only cobwebs and poison. The Bee thus provides "the two noblest of things, which are sweetness and light."

the passion for sweetness and light. It has one even yet greater!—the passion for making them *prevail*. It is not satisfied till we *all* come to a perfect man; it knows that the sweetness and light of the few must be imperfect until the raw and unkindled masses of humanity are touched with sweetness and light. If I have not shrunk from saying that we must work for sweetness and light, so neither have I shrunk from saying that we must have a broad basis, must have sweetness and light for as many as possible. Again and again I have insisted how those are the happy moments of humanity, how those are the marking epochs of a people's life, how those are the flowering times for literature and art and all the creative power of genius, when there is a *national* glow of life and thought, when the whole of society is in the fullest measure permeated by thought, sensible to beauty, intelligent and alive. Only it must be *real* thought and *real* beauty; *real* sweetness and *real* light. Plenty of people will try to give the masses, as they call them, an intellectual food prepared and adapted in the way they think proper for the actual condition of the masses. The ordinary popular literature is an example of this way of working on the masses. Plenty of people will try to indoctrinate the masses with the set of ideas and judgments constituting the creed of their own profession or party. Our religious and political organisations give an example of this way of working on the masses. I condemn neither way; but culture works differently. It does not try to teach down to the level of inferior classes; it does not try to win them for this or that sect of its own, with ready-made judgments and watchwords. It seeks to do away with classes; to make the best that has been thought and known in the world current everywhere; to make all men live in an atmosphere of sweetness and light, where they may use ideas, as it uses them itself, freely,—nourished, and not bound by them.

* * *

from *Hebraism and Hellenism*

This fundamental ground is our preference of doing to thinking. Now this preference is a main element in our nature, and as we study it we find ourselves opening up a number of large questions on every side.

Let me go back for a moment to Bishop Wilson, who says: "First, never go against the best light you have; secondly, take care that your light be not darkness."[6] We show, as a nation, laudable energy and persistence in walking according to the best light we have, but are not quite careful enough, perhaps, to see that our light be not darkness. This is only another version of the old story that energy is our strong point and favourable characteristic, rather than intelligence. But we may give to this idea a more general form still, in which it will have a yet larger range of application. We may regard this energy driving at practice, this paramount sense of the obligation of duty, self-control, and work, this earnestness in going manfully with the best light we have, as one force. And we may regard the intelligence driving at those ideas which are, after all, the basis of right practice, the ardent sense for all the new and changing combinations of them which man's development brings with it, the indomitable impulse to know and adjust them perfectly, as another force. And these two forces we may regard as in some sense rivals,—rivals not by the necessity of their own nature, but as exhibited in man and his history,—and rivals dividing the empire of the world between them. And to give these forces names from the two races of

6. Quoting Thomas Wilson, *Maxims* (see page 753, n. 4).

men who have supplied the most signal and splendid manifestations of them, we may call them respectively the forces of Hebraism and Hellenism.[7] Hebraism and Hellenism,—between these two points of influence moves our world. At one time it feels more powerfully the attraction of one of them, at another time of the other; and it ought to be, though it never is, evenly and happily balanced between them.

The final aim of both Hellenism and Hebraism, as of all great spiritual disciplines, is no doubt the same: man's perfection or salvation. The very language which they both of them use in schooling us to reach this aim is often identical. * * *

Still, they pursue this aim by very different courses. The uppermost idea with Hellenism is to see things as they really are; the uppermost idea with Hebraism is conduct and obedience. Nothing can do away with this ineffaceable difference. The Greek quarrel with the body and its desires is, that they hinder right thinking; the Hebrew quarrel with them is, that they hinder right acting. * * *

* * * Eighteen hundred years ago it was altogether the hour of Hebraism. Primitive Christianity was legitimately and truly the ascendant force in the world at that time, and the way of mankind's progress lay through its full development. Another hour in man's development began in the fifteenth century, and the main road of his progress then lay for a time through Hellenism. Puritanism was no longer the central current of the world's progress, it was a side stream crossing the central current and checking it. The cross and the check may have been necessary and salutary, but that does not do away with the essential difference between the main stream of man's advance and a cross or side stream. For more than two hundred years the main stream of man's advance has moved towards knowing himself and the world, seeing things as they are, spontaneity of consciousness; the main impulse of a great part, and that the strongest part, of our nation has been towards strictness of conscience. They have made the secondary the principal at the wrong moment, and the principal they have at the wrong moment treated as secondary. This contravention of the natural order has produced, as such contravention always must produce, a certain confusion and false movement, of which we are now beginning to feel, in almost every direction, the inconvenience. In all directions our habitual courses of action seem to be losing efficaciousness, credit, and control, both with others and even with ourselves. Everywhere we see the beginnings of confusion, and we want a clue to some sound order and authority. This we can only get by going back upon the actual instincts and forces which rule our life, seeing them as they really are, connecting them with other instincts and forces, and enlarging our whole view and rule of life.

from *Conclusion*

And so we bring to an end what we had to say in praise of culture, and in evidence of its special utility for the circumstances in which we find ourselves, and the confusion which environs us. Through culture seems to lie our way, not only to perfection, but even to safety. Resolutely refusing to lend a hand to the imperfect operations of our Liberal friends, disregarding their impatience, taunts, and reproaches, firmly bent on trying to find in the intelligible laws of things a firmer and sounder basis for future practice than any which we have at present, and believing this search and discovery to be, for our generation and circumstances, of yet more vital and pressing importance

---

7. In Arnold's view Hebraism (the Judeo-Christian tradition) emphasizes duty, industriousness, and a sense of sin. In contrast, Hellenism (the Greek tradition) values rationality, "clearness of mind," and the quest for perfection. While Arnold emphasizes the importance of both traditions, it is Hellenism that he associates with sweetness and light.

than practice itself, we nevertheless may do more, perhaps, we poor disparaged follow-ers of culture, to make the actual present, and the frame of society in which we live, solid and seaworthy, than all which our bustling politicians can do.

For we have seen how much of our disorders and perplexities is due to the disbelief, among the classes and combinations of men, Barbarian or Philistine, which have hither-to governed our society, in right reason, in a paramount best self; to the inevitable decay and break-up of the organisations by which, asserting and expressing in these organisa-tions their ordinary self only, they have so long ruled us; and to their irresolution, when the society, which their conscience tells them they have made and still manage not with right reason but with their ordinary self, is rudely shaken, in offering resistance to its sub-verters. But for us,—who believe in right reason, in the duty and possibility of extricat-ing and elevating our best self, in the progress of humanity towards perfection,—for us the framework of society, that theatre on which this august drama has to unroll itself, is sacred; and whoever administers it, and however we may seek to remove them from their tenure of administration, yet, while they administer, we steadily and with undivid-ed heart support them in repressing anarchy and disorder; because without order there can be no society, and without society there can be no human perfection.

And this opinion of the intolerableness of anarchy we can never forsake, however our Liberal friends may think a little rioting, and what they call popular demonstra-tions, useful sometimes to their own interests and to the interests of the valuable prac-tical operations they have in hand, and however they may preach the right of an Eng-lishman to be left to do as far as possible what he likes, and the duty of his government to indulge him and connive as much as possible and abstain from all harshness of repression. And even when they artfully show us operations which are undoubtedly precious, such as the abolition of the slave-trade, and ask us if, for their sake, foolish and obstinate governments may not wholesomely be frightened by a little disturbance, the good design in view and the difficulty of overcoming opposition to it being consid-ered,—still we say no, and that monster-processions in the streets and forcible irrup-tions into the parks, even in professed support of this good design, ought to be unflinch-ingly forbidden and repressed; and that far more is lost than is gained by permitting them. Because a State in which law is authoritative and sovereign, a firm and settled course of public order, is requisite if man is to bring to maturity anything precious and lasting now, or to found anything precious and lasting for the future. * * *

                                                                                    1867–1868; 1869

⊶ ⊷

Christina Rossetti
1830–1894

"Here is a great discovery," Christina Rossetti wrote to her brother Dante Gabriel in 1870, as he tried to advise her about her poetic career: " 'Women are not Men,' and you must not expect me to possess a tithe of your capacities, though I humbly—or proudly—lay claim to family-likeness." The remark hints at many sides of Rossetti's complex nature: her modest yet firm manner; the touch of irony in her deference; and the "family-likeness" not only of poetic genius but personal temperament—their parents called them the "two storms" in childhood because they were both difficult, irritable, volatile, and creative. Her declaration signals Rossetti's recognition that as a woman and artist she had had to take a very different path from her more famous brother. She renounced from an early age any pleasures or relationships that did not conform to her strict Anglo-Catholic principles—even to the point of giving up chess because it made her too eager to win. Instead she found poetic fulfillment in haunting lyrics about goblin men and love beyond the grave.

Rossetti was born in London in 1830, the youngest of four precocious children of Gabriele Rossetti, an Italian poet-in-exile, and his English-Italian wife, Frances Polidori, whose brother John was Byron's physician and traveling companion. Amid a stream of foreign visitors the bilingual Rossetti children listened to animated discussions of art, music, and revolutionary politics. This atmosphere "made us . . . not a little different from British children," her brother William recalled, "and, when Dante and Christina Rossetti proved, as poetic writers, somewhat devious from the British tradition and the insular mind, we may say, if not 'so much the better,' at any rate, 'no wonder.'"

Like many Victorian women of letters, Christina Rossetti suffered from mysterious maladies that served to protect her time and talent. "I am rejoiced to feel that my health does really unfit me for miscellaneous governessing *en permanence*," she confided to William in 1855. Freed from "the necessity of teaching the small daughters of the neighbouring hairdresser or the neighbouring pork-butcher their p's and q's," she was "anxious to secure any literary pickings which might offer."

Shy, devout, and self-sacrificing, Rossetti nevertheless found time for a literary and social life that included as acquaintances Browning, Ruskin, Swinburne, Lewis Carroll, Edmund Gosse, and the Pre-Raphaelites. She modeled as the Virgin Mary in two of Dante Gabriel's finest paintings, *The Girlhood of Mary Virgin* (1848–1849) and *Ecce Ancilla Domini* (1849–1850). Because of her sex, Christina was denied membership in the Pre-Raphaelite Brotherhood, but she did publish her first poems in their journal, *The Germ*, in 1850. With the appearance of *Goblin Market and Other Poems* in 1862, she acquired a growing critical and popular following. Hailed by Gosse as the "High Priestess of Pre-Raphaelitism" because of her superb technique and keenness of observation, she won even wider fame as an author of religious poetry, inspiring, among others, Gerard Manley Hopkins.

Admirers of Rossetti's passionate, frustrated love poetry have long puzzled over the scanty details of her romantic life. She rejected two suitors because she found their faith wanting. Early biographers assumed that these broken relationships blighted Rossetti's life, but recently critics have regarded her choice of a single life as an act of artistic self-preservation. For Christina not only witnessed Dante's tormented affairs but also had the opportunity to view passion's consequences in a clinical light during the decade she worked as a volunteer at the Highgate House of Charity for "fallen women."

Though brightened by many touches of humor, Rossetti's writing focuses mostly on religious topics or some combination of themes arising from troubled love, grave illness, and anticipations of death—themes she must have pondered during the extended periods she spent taking care of dying family members at home, beginning with her father and continuing with her sister, her brother Dante, her mother (who was always her closest companion), and two maiden aunts. Despite severe illness in later life, she maintained a strict professionalism toward her career, publishing new work during the 1870s and 1880s, then issuing revised editions until her death in 1894.

A spontaneous writer whose lucidity of phrasing has sometimes caused readers to overlook her emotional and symbolic depths, Rossetti mastered a variety of forms, ranging from hymns and a sonnet-sequence to nursery rhymes and a well-known Christmas carol, *In the Bleak Mid-Winter*. Like Emily Dickinson, whose poems she admired when the first selection was published in 1890, Rossetti displays a quirky independence of vision, mingling the morbid, the whimsical, the cooly ironic. What is today her most famous poem, *Goblin Market*, features the enticements of sensual knowledge. Regarded chiefly as a children's tale in the nineteenth century, the poem has subsequently attracted much critical attention, including analyses of it as a struggle between self and soul, a comment on sex as a capitalist commodity, a parable of feminist solidarity, a lesson about poetry's subversive power, and a lesbian love story. This fable about the danger of desire provides insight into the dualistic world of Victorian fantasy. Magical events permitted writers and readers to enter forbidden realms of violence, temptation, and transformation, yet moralized endings sought to tame even the wildest tales for social and ethical instruction. Something similar may be said of Christina Rossetti's life and art: a stormy nature finds release in the tight formal control of the polished artist.

Song

When I am dead, my dearest,
  Sing no sad songs for me;
Plant thou no roses at my head,
  Nor shady cypress tree:
5 Be the green grass above me
  With showers and dewdrops wet;
And if thou wilt, remember,
  And if thou wilt, forget.

I shall not see the shadows,
10 I shall not feel the rain;
I shall not hear the nightingale
  Sing on, as if in pain:
And dreaming through the twilight
  That doth not rise nor set,
15 Haply° I may remember,   *perhaps*
  And haply may forget.

1848   1862

In an Artist's Studio

One face looks out from all his canvasses,[1]
One selfsame figure sits or walks or leans;
We found her hidden just behind those screens,
That mirror gave back all her loveliness.

---

1. Christina's brother, William Michael Rossetti, wrote: "The reference is apparently to our brother's studio, and to his constantly repeated heads of the lady whom he afterwards married, Miss Siddal."

5   A queen in opal or in ruby dress,
           A nameless girl in freshest summer greens,
           A saint, an angel;—every canvass means
       The same one meaning, neither more nor less.
       He feeds upon her face by day and night,
10   And she with true kind eyes looks back on him
       Fair as the moon and joyful as the light:
           Not wan with waiting, not with sorrow dim;
       Not as she is, but was when hope shone bright;
           Not as she is, but as she fills his dream.

1856   1896

Goblin Market

       Morning and evening
       Maids heard the goblins cry:
       "Come buy our orchard fruits,
       Come buy, come buy:
5   Apples and quinces,
       Lemons and oranges,
       Plump unpecked cherries,
       Melons and raspberries,
       Bloom-down-cheeked peaches,
10   Swart°-headed mulberries,   *dark*
       Wild free-born cranberries,
       Crab-apples, dewberries,
       Pine-apples, blackberries,
       Apricots, strawberries;—
15   All ripe together
       In summer weather,—
       Morns that pass by,
       Fair eves that fly;
       Come buy, come buy:
20   Our grapes fresh from the vine,
       Pomegranates full and fine,
       Dates and sharp bullaces,
       Rare pears and greengages,
       Damsons[1] and bilberries,
25   Taste them and try:
       Currants and gooseberries,
       Bright-fire-like barberries,
       Figs to fill your mouth,
       Citrons from the South,
30   Sweet to tongue and sound to eye;
       Come buy, come buy."

       Evening by evening
       Among the brookside rushes,
       Laura bowed her head to hear,
35   Lizzie veiled her blushes:

1. Bullaces, greengages, and damsons are types of plums.

Dante Gabriel Rossetti,
frontispiece to the first
edition of Christina
Rossetti's *Goblin Market*,
1862.

> Crouching close together
> In the cooling weather,
> With clasping arms and cautioning lips,
> With tingling cheeks and finger tips.
> 40   "Lie close," Laura said,
> Pricking up her golden head:
> "We must not look at goblin men,
> We must not buy their fruits:
> Who knows upon what soil they fed
> 45   Their hungry thirsty roots?"
> "Come buy," call the goblins
> Hobbling down the glen.
> "Oh," cried Lizzie, "Laura, Laura,
> You should not peep at goblin men."
> 50   Lizzie covered up her eyes,
> Covered close lest they should look;
> Laura reared her glossy head,
> And whispered like the restless brook:
> "Look, Lizzie, look, Lizzie,
> 55   Down the glen tramp little men.
> One hauls a basket,
> One bears a plate,

One lugs a golden dish
Of many pounds weight.
60 How fair the vine must grow
Whose grapes are so luscious;
How warm the wind must blow
Thro' those fruit bushes."
"No," said Lizzie: "No, no, no;
65 Their offers should not charm us,
Their evil gifts would harm us."
She thrust a dimpled finger
In each ear, shut eyes and ran:
Curious Laura chose to linger
70 Wondering at each merchant man.
One had a cat's face,
One whisked a tail,
One tramped at a rat's pace,
One crawled like a snail,
75 One like a wombat prowled obtuse and furry,
One like a ratel[2] tumbled hurry skurry.
She heard a voice like voice of doves
Cooing all together:
They sounded kind and full of loves
80 In the pleasant weather.

Laura stretched her gleaming neck
Like a rush-imbedded swan,
Like a lily from the beck,°   brook
Like a moonlit poplar branch,
85 Like a vessel at the launch
When its last restraint is gone.

Backwards up the mossy glen
Turned and trooped the goblin men,
With their shrill repeated cry,
90 "Come buy, come buy."
When they reached where Laura was
They stood stock still upon the moss,
Leering at each other,
Brother with queer brother;
95 Signalling each other,
Brother with sly brother.
One set his basket down,
One reared his plate;
One began to weave a crown
100 Of tendrils, leaves and rough nuts brown
(Men sell not such in any town);
One heaved the golden weight
Of dish and fruit to offer her:
"Come buy, come buy," was still their cry.

2. A tropical badgerlike nocturnal animal (pronounced "ray-tell").

105   Laura stared but did not stir,
        Longed but had no money:
        The whisk-tailed merchant bade her taste
        In tones as smooth as honey,
        The cat-faced purr'd,
110   The rat-paced spoke a word
        Of welcome, and the snail-paced even was heard;
        One parrot-voiced and jolly
        Cried "Pretty Goblin" still for "Pretty Polly;"—
        One whistled like a bird.

115   But sweet-tooth Laura spoke in haste:
        "Good folk, I have no coin;
        To take were to purloin:
        I have no copper in my purse,
        I have no silver either,
120   And all my gold is on the furze[3]
        That shakes in windy weather
        Above the rusty heather."
        "You have much gold upon your head,"
        They answered all together:
125   "Buy from us with a golden curl."
        She clipped a precious golden lock,
        She dropped a tear more rare than pearl,
        Then sucked their fruit globes fair or red:
        Sweeter than honey from the rock.
130   Stronger than man-rejoicing wine,
        Clearer than water flowed that juice;
        She never tasted such before,
        How should it cloy with length of use?
        She sucked and sucked and sucked the more
135   Fruits which that unknown orchard bore;
        She sucked until her lips were sore;
        Then flung the emptied rinds away
        But gathered up one kernel-stone,
        And knew not was it night or day
140   As she turned home alone.

        Lizzie met her at the gate
        Full of wise upbraidings:
        "Dear, you should not stay so late,
        Twilight is not good for maidens;
145   Should not loiter in the glen
        In the haunts of goblin men.
        Do you not remember Jeanie,
        How she met them in the moonlight,
        Took their gifts both choice and many,
150   Ate their fruits and wore their flowers
        Plucked from bowers

---

3. An evergreen shrub that grows on the heath.

Where summer ripens at all hours?
But ever in the noonlight
She pined and pined away;
155 Sought them by night and day,
Found them no more but dwindled and grew grey;
Then fell with the first snow,
While to this day no grass will grow
Where she lies low:
160 I planted daisies there a year ago
That never blow.
You should not loiter so."
"Nay, hush," said Laura:
"Nay, hush, my sister:
165 I ate and ate my fill,
Yet my mouth waters still;
Tomorrow night I will
Buy more:" and kissed her:
"Have done with sorrow;
170 I'll bring you plums tomorrow
Fresh on their mother twigs,
Cherries worth getting;
You cannot think what figs
My teeth have met in,
175 What melons icy-cold
Piled on a dish of gold
Too huge for me to hold,
What peaches with a velvet nap,
Pellucid° grapes without one seed: *translucent*
180 Odorous indeed must be the mead
Whereon they grow, and pure the wave they drink
With lilies at the brink,
And sugar-sweet their sap."

Golden head by golden head,
185 Like two pigeons in one nest
Folded in each other's wings,
They lay down in their curtained bed:
Like two blossoms on one stem,
Like two flakes of new-fall'n snow,
190 Like two wands of ivory
Tipped with gold for awful° kings.   *awe-inspiring*
Moon and stars gazed in at them,
Wind sang to them lullaby,
Lumbering owls forbore to fly,
195 Not a bat flapped to and fro
Round their rest:
Cheek to cheek and breast to breast
Locked together in one nest.

Early in the morning
200 When the first cock crowed his warning,
Neat like bees, as sweet and busy,

Laura rose with Lizzie:
Fetched in honey, milked the cows,
Aired and set to rights the house,
205   Kneaded cakes of whitest wheat,
Cakes for dainty mouths to eat,
Next churned butter, whipped up cream,
Fed their poultry, sat and sewed;
Talked as modest maidens should:
210   Lizzie with an open heart,
Laura in an absent dream,
One content, one sick in part;
One warbling for the mere bright day's delight,
One longing for the night.

215   At length slow evening came:
They went with pitchers to the reedy brook;
Lizzie most placid in her look,
Laura most like a leaping flame.
They drew the gurgling water from its deep;
220   Lizzie plucked purple and rich golden flags,
Then turning homewards said: "The sunset flushes
Those furthest loftiest crags;
Come, Laura, not another maiden lags,
No wilful squirrel wags,
225   The beasts and birds are fast asleep."
But Laura loitered still among the rushes
And said the bank was steep.

And said the hour was early still,
The dew not fall'n, the wind not chill:
230   Listening ever, but not catching
The customary cry,
"Come buy, come buy,"
With its iterated jingle
Of sugar-baited words:
235   Not for all her watching
Once discerning even one goblin
Racing, whisking, tumbling, hobbling;
Let alone the herds
That used to tramp along the glen,
240   In groups or single,
Of brisk fruit-merchant men.
Till Lizzie urged, "O Laura, come;
I hear the fruit-call but I dare not look:
You should not loiter longer at this brook:
245   Come with me home.
The stars rise, the moon bends her arc,
Each glowworm winks her spark,
Let us get home before the night grows dark:
For clouds may gather
250   Tho' this is summer weather,

Put out the lights and drench us thro';
Then if we lost our way what should we do?"

Laura turned cold as stone
To find her sister heard that cry alone,
255   That goblin cry,
"Come buy our fruits, come buy."
Must she then buy no more such dainty fruit?
Must she no more such succous° pasture find,   *juicy*
Gone deaf and blind?
260   Her tree of life drooped from the root:
She said not one word in her heart's sore ache;
But peering thro' the dimness, nought discerning,
Trudged home, her pitcher dripping all the way;
So crept to bed, and lay
265   Silent till Lizzie slept;
Then sat up in a passionate yearning,
And gnashed her teeth for baulked desire, and wept
As if her heart would break.

Day after day, night after night,
270   Laura kept watch in vain
In sullen silence of exceeding pain.
She never caught again the goblin cry:
"Come buy, come buy;"—
She never spied the goblin men
275   Hawking their fruits along the glen:
But when the noon waxed bright
Her hair grew thin and gray;
She dwindled, as the fair full moon doth turn
To swift decay and burn
280   Her fire away.

One day remembering her kernel-stone
She set it by a wall that faced the south;
Dewed it with tears, hoped for a root,
Watched for a waxing shoot,
285   But there came none;
It never saw the sun,
It never felt the trickling moisture run:
While with sunk eyes and faded mouth
She dreamed of melons, as a traveller sees
290   False waves in desert drouth
With shade of leaf-crowned trees,
And burns the thirstier in the sandful breeze.

She no more swept the house,
Tended the fowls or cows,
295   Fetched honey, kneaded cakes of wheat,
Brought water from the brook:
But sat down listless in the chimney-nook
And would not eat.

Tender Lizzie could not bear
300   To watch her sister's cankerous° care   *festering*
Yet not to share.
She night and morning
Caught the goblins' cry:
"Come buy our orchard fruits,
305   Come buy, come buy:"—
Beside the brook, along the glen,
She heard the tramp of goblin men,
The voice and stir
Poor Laura could not hear;
310   Longed to buy fruit to comfort her,
But feared to pay too dear.
She thought of Jeanie in her grave,
Who should have been a bride;
But who for joys brides hope to have
315   Fell sick and died
In her gay prime,
In earliest Winter time,
With the first glazing rime,
With the first snow-fall of crisp Winter time.

320   Till Laura dwindling
Seemed knocking at Death's door:
Then Lizzie weighed no more
Better and worse;
But put a silver penny in her purse,
325   Kissed Laura, crossed the heath with clumps of furze
At twilight, halted by the brook:
And for the first time in her life
Began to listen and look.

Laughed every goblin
330   When they spied her peeping:
Came towards her hobbling,
Flying, running, leaping,
Puffing and blowing,
Chuckling, clapping, crowing,
335   Clucking and gobbling,
Mopping and mowing,
Full of airs and graces,
Pulling wry faces,
Demure grimaces,
340   Cat-like and rat-like,
Ratel- and wombat-like,
Snail-paced in a hurry,
Parrot-voiced and whistler,
Helter skelter, hurry skurry,
345   Chattering like magpies,
Fluttering like pigeons,
Gliding like fishes,—
Hugged her and kissed her,

Squeezed and caressed her:
350   Stretched up their dishes,
Panniers, and plates:
"Look at our apples
Russet and dun,
Bob at our cherries,
355   Bite at our peaches,
Citrons and dates,
Grapes for the asking,
Pears red with basking
Out in the sun,
360   Plums on their twigs;
Pluck them and suck them,
Pomegranates, figs."—

"Good folk," said Lizzie,
Mindful of Jeanie:
365   "Give me much and many:"—
Held out her apron,
Tossed them her penny.
"Nay, take a seat with us,
Honour and eat with us,"
370   They answered grinning:
"Our feast is but beginning.
Night yet is early,
Warm and dew-pearly,
Wakeful and starry:
375   Such fruits as these
No man can carry;
Half their bloom would fly,
Half their dew would dry,
Half their flavour would pass by.
380   Sit down and feast with us,
Be welcome guest with us,
Cheer you and rest with us."—
"Thank you," said Lizzie: "But one waits
At home alone for me:
385   So without further parleying,
If you will not sell me any
Of your fruits tho' much and many,
Give me back my silver penny
I tossed you for a fee."—
390   They began to scratch their pates,
No longer wagging, purring,
But visibly demurring,
Grunting and snarling.
One called her proud,
395   Cross-grained, uncivil;
Their tones waxed loud,
Their looks were evil.
Lashing their tails

They trod and hustled her,
400   Elbowed and jostled her,
Clawed with their nails,
Barking, mewing, hissing, mocking,
Tore her gown and soiled her stocking,
Twitched her hair out by the roots,
405   Stamped upon her tender feet,
Held her hands and squeezed their fruits
Against her mouth to make her eat.
White and golden Lizzie stood,
Like a lily in a flood,—
410   Like a rock of blue-veined stone
Lashed by tides obstreperously,—
Like a beacon left alone
In a hoary roaring sea,
Sending up a golden fire,—
415   Like a fruit-crowned orange-tree
White with blossoms honey-sweet
Sore beset by wasp and bee,—
Like a royal virgin town
Topped with gilded dome and spire
420   Close beleaguered by a fleet
Mad to tug her standard down.

One may lead a horse to water,
Twenty cannot make him drink.
Tho' the goblins cuffed and caught her,
425   Coaxed and fought her,
Bullied and besought her,
Scratched her, pinched her black as ink,
Kicked and knocked her,
Mauled and mocked her,
430   Lizzie uttered not a word;
Would not open lip from lip
Lest they should cram a mouthful in:
But laughed in heart to feel the drip
Of juice that syrupped all her face,
435   And lodged in dimples of her chin,
And streaked her neck which quaked like curd.
At last the evil people
Worn out by her resistance
Flung back her penny, kicked their fruit
440   Along whichever road they took,
Not leaving root or stone or shoot;
Some writhed into the ground,
Some dived into the brook
With ring and ripple,
445   Some scudded on the gale without a sound,
Some vanished in the distance.
In a smart, ache, tingle,
Lizzie went her way;
Knew not was it night or day;

450 Sprang up the bank, tore thro' the furze,
    Threaded copse and dingle,
    And heard her penny jingle
    Bouncing in her purse,
    Its bounce was music to her ear.
455 She ran and ran
    As if she feared some goblin man
    Dogged her with gibe or curse
    Or something worse:
    But not one goblin skurried after,
460 Nor was she pricked by fear;
    The kind heart made her windy-paced
    That urged her home quite out of breath with haste
    And inward laughter.

    She cried "Laura," up the garden,
465   "Did you miss me?
    Come and kiss me.
    Never mind my bruises,
    Hug me, kiss me, suck my juices
    Squeezed from goblin fruits for you,
470 Goblin pulp and goblin dew.
    Eat me, drink me, love me;
    Laura, make much of me:
    For your sake I have braved the glen
    And had to do with goblin merchant men."

475 Laura started from her chair,
    Flung her arms up in the air,
    Clutched her hair:
    "Lizzie, Lizzie, have you tasted
    For my sake the fruit forbidden?
480 Must your light like mine be hidden,
    Your young life like mine be wasted,
    Undone in mine undoing
    And ruined in my ruin,
    Thirsty, cankered, goblin-ridden?"—
485 She clung about her sister,
    Kissed and kissed and kissed her:
    Tears once again
    Refreshed her shrunken eyes,
    Dropping like rain
490 After long sultry drouth;
    Shaking with aguish fear, and pain,
    She kissed and kissed her with a hungry mouth.

    Her lips began to scorch,
    That juice was wormwood to her tongue,
495 She loathed the feast:
    Writhing as one possessed she leaped and sung,
    Rent all her robe, and wrung
    Her hands in lamentable haste,
    And beat her breast.

500 Her locks streamed like the torch
    Borne by a racer at full speed,
    Or like the mane of horses in their flight,
    Or like an eagle when she stems° the light   *makes headway against*
    Straight toward the sun,
505 Or like a caged thing freed,
    Or like a flying flag when armies run.

    Swift fire spread thro' her veins, knocked at her heart,
    Met the fire smouldering there
    And overbore its lesser flame;
510 She gorged on bitterness without a name:
    Ah! fool, to choose such part
    Of soul-consuming care!
    Sense failed in the mortal strife:
    Like the watch-tower of a town
515 Which an earthquake shatters down,
    Like a lightning-stricken mast,
    Like a wind-uprooted tree
    Spun about,
    Like a foam-topped waterspout
520 Cast down headlong in the sea,
    She fell at last;
    Pleasure past and anguish past,
    Is it death or is it life?

    Life out of death.
525 That night long Lizzie watched by her,
    Counted her pulse's flagging stir,
    Felt for her breath,
    Held water to her lips, and cooled her face
    With tears and fanning leaves:
530 But when the first birds chirped about their eaves,
    And early reapers plodded to the place
    Of golden sheaves,
    And dew-wet grass
    Bowed in the morning winds so brisk to pass,
535 And new buds with new day
    Opened of cup-like lilies on the stream,
    Laura awoke as from a dream,
    Laughed in the innocent old way,
    Hugged Lizzie but not twice or thrice;
540 Her gleaming locks showed not one thread of grey,
    Her breath was sweet as May
    And light danced in her eyes.

    Days, weeks, months, years
    Afterwards, when both were wives
545 With children of their own;
    Their mother-hearts beset with fears,
    Their lives bound up in tender lives;
    Laura would call the little ones

And tell them of her early prime,
550   Those pleasant days long gone
Of not-returning time:
Would talk about the haunted glen,
The wicked, quaint fruit-merchant men,
Their fruits like honey to the throat
555   But poison in the blood;
(Men sell not such in any town:)
Would tell them how her sister stood
In deadly peril to do her good,
And win the fiery antidote:
560   Then joining hands to little hands
Would bid them cling together,
"For there is no friend like a sister
In calm or stormy weather;
To cheer one on the tedious way,
565   To fetch one if one goes astray,
To lift one if one totters down,
To strengthen whilst one stands."

1859   1862

"No, Thank You, John"

I never said I loved you, John:
    Why will you teaze me day by day,
And wax a weariness to think upon
    With always "do" and "pray"?

5   You know I never loved you, John;
    No fault of mine made me your toast:
Why will you haunt me with a face as wan
    As shows an hour-old ghost?

I dare say Meg or Moll would take
10   Pity upon you, if you'd ask:
And pray don't remain single for my sake
    Who can't perform that task.

I have no heart?—Perhaps I have not;
    But then you're mad to take offence
15   That I don't give you what I have not got:
    Use your own common sense.

Let bygones be bygones:
    Don't call me false, who owed not to be true:
I'd rather answer "No" to fifty Johns
20   Than answer "Yes" to you.

Let's mar our pleasant days no more,
    Song-birds of passage, days of youth:
Catch at today, forget the days before:
    I'll wink at your untruth.

25   Let us strike hands as hearty friends;
       No more, no less; and friendship's good:
     Only don't keep in view ulterior ends,
       And points not understood

     In open treaty. Rise above
30   Quibbles and shuffling off and on:
     Here's friendship for you if you like; but love,—
       No, thank you, John.

1860   1862

Promises Like Pie-Crust[1]

Promise me no promises,
    So will I not promise you;
Keep we both our liberties,
    Never false and never true:
5   Let us hold the die uncast,
     Free to come as free to go;
For I cannot know your past,
    And of mine what can you know?

You, so warm, may once have been
10   Warmer towards another one;
I, so cold, may once have seen
    Sunlight, once have felt the sun:
Who shall show us if it was
    Thus indeed in time of old?
15 Fades the image from the glass
    And the fortune is not told.

If you promised, you might grieve
    For lost liberty again;
If I promised, I believe
20   I should fret to break the chain:
Let us be the friends we were,
    Nothing more but nothing less;
Many thrive on frugal fare
    Who would perish of excess.

1861   1896

Sleeping at Last

Sleeping at last, the trouble & tumult over,
Sleeping at last, the struggle & horror past,
Cold & white out of sight of friend & of lover
Sleeping at last.

5   No more a tired heart downcast or overcast,
No more pangs that wring or shifting fears that hover,
Sleeping at last in a dreamless sleep locked fast.

1. English proverb: "Promises are like pie-crust, made to be broken."

Fast asleep. Singing birds in their leafy cover
Cannot wake her, nor shake her the gusty blast.
10   Under the purple thyme & the purple clover
Sleeping at last.

c. 1893   1896

+ ·+· ☲◊☲ ·+· +

Gerard Manley Hopkins
1844–1889

Gerard Manley Hopkins is the most modern of Victorian poets, and the most Victorian of modern poets. His stunningly original poems were, with a few exceptions, not published until 1918, placing him at first glance in the company of Eliot and Pound. But his struggle to maintain religious faith, his respect for conventional verse forms, and his quest to find proof of God's work in nature all mark him as quintessentially Victorian. Hopkins combines a microscopic keenness of vision with a Joycean genius for compound words, new coinages, unexpected rhymes, and startling distortions of syntax. The result is a poetry of modernist intensity and compression, fraught with bold ellipses and daring line breaks, but nonetheless dedicated to describing a world "charged with the grandeur of God." Orthodox and self-denying in matters of religion, Hopkins was also the era's most radical literary rebel.

Hopkins was born into a prosperous, pious Anglican family. After attending school in London, he went in 1863 to study classics at Balliol College, Oxford, where the agnostic aesthete Walter Pater was one of his tutors. At the same time, Hopkins came under the influence of the "Oxford Movement." He read John Henry Newman's account of his gravitation toward Roman Catholicism in *Apologia Pro Vita Sua*; subsequent talks with Newman led to Hopkins's own agonizing conversion to Catholicism in 1866. In 1868 he entered the novitiate of the Society of Jesus and burned almost all his early, Keatsian poems. He called his action the "slaughter of the innocents," and resolved "to write no more, as not belonging to my profession, unless it were by the wish of my superiors."

Seven years of poetic silence ensued, as Hopkins studied for the priesthood. But he was also meditating on his idiosyncratic theories of poetic composition. When five nuns were drowned in a shipwreck in 1875, he was suddenly moved to compose the first poem in his new style, *The Wreck of the Deutschland*. But there was no audience prepared to fathom his highly wrought style. Hopkins offered the work to a Jesuit magazine but, he said, "they dared not print it." He never again tried to publish.

Hopkins was ordained a Jesuit priest in 1877. Joyous, he produced a series of radiant sonnets celebrating the presence of God in nature. But his remaining years tested his faith sorely. Often in ill-health, he labored as a parish priest and teacher throughout Britain, including missionary work in the slums of Liverpool. He suffered physically and spiritually from the "vice and horrors" he found in his dreary urban duties: "It made even life a burden to me," he confessed. Then in 1884 he was appointed Professor of Greek and Latin at the Catholic, newly formed University College in Dublin. Already estranged from his family and the English church, he felt separated from his country, too. "I am in Ireland now," he wrote in a sonnet, "now I am at a third / Remove." Yet even as he despaired of accomplishing work of lasting value, he produced many of his best poems, including the famed "terrible sonnets" that describe his sense of spiritual and poetic sterility. Exhausted by his strenuous duties, Hopkins died in Dublin of typhoid at the age of forty-five.

Although Hopkins read the important nineteenth-century poets with care, he deliberately carved his own way. "The effect of studying masterpieces," he said, "is to make me admire and do otherwise." In his journals Hopkins often sounds like an English Thoreau, finely attuned to every nuance of the natural world. His entries are always searching to grasp the essential particularity of a thing, its inner landscape—what he called "inscape." Elaborating his theory in a letter to Robert Bridges, an Oxford friend who later became Poet Laureate, Hopkins admitted that "no doubt my poetry errs on the side of oddness. . . . it is the vice of distinctiveness to become queer." But he asserted the absolute importance of such "distinctiveness"—this "design, pattern or what I am in the habit of calling *inscape* is what I above all aim at in poetry." Hopkins needed another term to express the dynamic energy that not only makes the inscape cohere but also projects it outward toward the observer. This force that both unifies an object and arouses the senses of its beholder Hopkins called "instress." Taken together, the terms "inscape" and "instress" convey the organic beauty that for Hopkins speaks of God's presence in nature.

To apply these concepts poetically, Hopkins developed a new verse line based on "sprung rhythm." As in Old English poetry or nursery rhymes, each line in sprung rhythm has a fixed number of stresses, but the number and placement of unstressed syllables can vary widely. Many poets had employed individual lines of this type, but Hopkins took the idea of flexible metrics to new heights. He loaded his lines with internal rhyme, alliteration, assonance, and strong Anglo-Saxon words, and drove them forward with crashing consonants and wrenching enjambments. Responding to Bridges's confusion, he explained: "Why do I employ sprung rhythm at all? Because it is the nearest to the rhythm of prose, that is the native and natural rhythm of speech, the least forced, the most rhetorical and emphatic of all possible rhythms." Since Hopkins connected the sight and sound of individual words to the religious intensity with which he viewed objects in nature, the effect is akin to impassioned prayer. "My verse is less to be read than heard," he concluded; "it is oratorical."

In his later poetry a tangle of religious and sexual imagery expresses his sense of thwarted love and meager poetic production. He portrays himself as a sapless tree, or as barren sand: "I am soft sift / In an hourglass." In 1885 he wrote to Bridges in frustration, "if I could but produce work I should not mind its being buried, silenced, and going no further; but it kills me to be time's eunuch and never to beget." Such passages, with their images of sexual impotency, poetic infertility, and self-abnegation, suggest what Bridges called "the naked encounter of sensualism and asceticism" in Hopkins's work.

Despite his disclaimers, Hopkins was preoccupied with his lack of an audience. He once informed Bridges: "You are my public and I hope to convert you." Missionary-like, Hopkins's poetry seeks to "convert" the reader with its ecstatic particularity, its intensity of perception. But he speaks of his efforts as a one-way correspondence to God and his public; his poems are "cries like dead letters sent / To dearest him that lives alas! away." Hopkins could not have known that Bridges, despite his difficulty grasping these "dead letters," would finally publish the poems to great acclaim at the close of World War I. Then, like the works of Emily Dickinson and Vincent Van Gogh, they would suddenly seize a central artistic place in a past that had been unaware of their existence. And yet, Hopkins did recognize that his mingling of sensuality and spirituality allied him with another great proto-modernist. "I always knew in my heart Walt Whitman's mind to be more like my own than any other man's living," he told Bridges. "As he is a great scoundrel this is not a pleasant confession."

God's Grandeur

The world is charged with the grandeur of God.
    It will flame out, like shining from shook foil;[1]
    It gathers to a greatness, like the ooze of oil
Crushed.[2] Why do men then now not reck° his rod?   *heed*

---

1. I mean foil in its sense of leaf or tinsel. . . . Shaken goldfoil gives off broad glares like sheet lightning and also, and this is true of nothing else, owing to its zigzag dints and creasings and network of small many cornered facets, a sort of fork lightning too [Hopkins's note].
2. Oil made by crushing seeds or olives.

5   Generations have trod, have trod, have trod;
       And all is seared with trade; bleared, smeared with toil;
       And wears man's smudge and shares man's smell: the soil
    Is bare now, nor can foot feel, being shod.

    And for° all this, nature is never spent;   *despite*
10   There lives the dearest freshness deep down things;
    And though the last lights off the black West went
       Oh, morning, at the brown brink eastward, springs—
    Because the Holy Ghost over the bent
       World broods with warm breast and with ah! bright wings.

1877   1895

The Windhover:[1]

To Christ Our Lord

I caught this morning morning's minion,[2] king-
    dom of daylight's dauphin,[3] dapple-dawn-drawn Falcon, in his riding
    Of the rolling level underneath him steady air, and striding
High there, how he rung upon the rein[4] of a wimpling wing
5   In his ecstasy! then off, off forth on swing,
    As a skate's heel sweeps smooth on a bow-bend: the hurl and gliding
    Rebuffed the big wind. My heart in hiding
Stirred for a bird,—the achieve of, the mastery of the thing!

Brute beauty and valour and act, oh, air, pride, plume, here
10   Buckle! AND the fire that breaks from thee then, a billion
Times told lovelier, more dangerous, O my chevalier!

No wonder of it: shéer plód makes plough down sillion[5]
Shine, and blue-bleak embers, ah my dear,
    Fall, gall[6] themselves, and gash gold-vermilion.

1877   1918

Pied[1] Beauty

Glory be to God for dappled things—
    For skies of couple-colour as a brinded[2] cow;
       For rose-moles all in stipple[3] upon trout that swim;
Fresh-firecoal chestnut-falls;[4] finches' wings;
5   Landscape plotted and pieced—fold, fallow, and plough;[5]
       And áll trádes, their gear and tackle and trim.°   *equipment*

All things counter,[6] original, spare, strange;
    Whatever is fickle, freckled (who knows how?)

---

1. Kestrel falcon—a small hawk—that appears to hover in the air.
2. Darling, from the French *mignon.*
3. The dauphin was the heir to the French throne.
4. In falconry, a bird rings when it rises in spirals (like a horse circling at the end of a tether or rein). Wimpling means rippling.
5. The furrows of a plowed field.

6. Break their surfaces.
1. Blotched with different colors.
2. Brindled, having dark patches on a tawny ground.
3. Stippled, painted or drawn with dots instead of lines.
4. Chestnuts as bright as coals [Hopkins's journal].
5. Landscape of differently colored fields, some used as pasture ("fold"), some lying fallow, some plowed.
6. Contrary; "spare" means rare.

With swift, slow; sweet, sour; adazzle, dim;
10   He fathers-forth whose beauty is past change:
                    Praise him.

1877   1918

Felix Randal

Felix Randal the farrier,[1] O he is dead then? my duty all ended,
Who have watched his mould of man, big-boned and hardy-handsome
Pining, pining, till time when reason rambled in it and some
Fatal four disorders, fleshed there, all contended?

5   Sickness broke him. Impatient he cursed at first, but mended
Being anointed[2] and all; though a heavenlier heart began some
Months earlier, since I had our sweet reprieve and ransom[3]
Tendered to him. Ah well, God rest him all road ever° he offended!   *however*

This seeing the sick endears them to us, us too it endears.
10   My tongue had taught thee comfort, touch had quenched thy tears,
Thy tears that touched my heart, child, Felix, poor Felix Randal;

How far from then forethought of, all thy more boisterous years,
When thou at the random[4] grim forge, powerful amidst peers,
Didst fettle° for the great grey drayhorse his bright and battering sandal!   *prepare*

1880   1918

Spring and Fall:
to a young child

Márgarét, are you gríeving
Over Goldengrove unleaving?
Leáves, líke the things of man, you
With your fresh thoughts care for, can you?
5   Áh! ás the heart grows older
It will come to such sights colder
By and by, nor spare a sigh
Though worlds of wanwood leafmeal lie;[1]
And yet you wíll weep and know why.
10   Now no matter, child, the name:
Sórrow's spríngs áre the same.
Nor mouth had, no nor mind, expressed
What heart heard of, ghost° guessed: *spirit*
It ís the blight man was born for,
15   It is Margaret you mourn for.
1880   1918

1. Blacksmith.
2. Having received Extreme Unction, the sacrament for the dying.
3. Confession, absolution, and Holy Communion.

4. Built of rough irregular stones.
1. The leaves of pale trees lie scattered; "leafmeal" is derived from "piecemeal."

As Kingfishers Catch Fire

As kingfishers catch fire, dragonflies dráw fláme;
As tumbled over rim in roundy wells
Stones ring; like each tucked° string tells, each hung bell's   plucked
Bow swung finds tongue to fling out broad its name;
5   Each mortal thing does one thing and the same:
Deals out that being indoors each one dwells;
Selves—goes itself; *myself* it speaks and spells;
Crying *Whát I dó is me: for that I came.*

Í say móre: the just man justices;
10 Kéeps gráce; thát keeps all his goings graces;
Acts in God's eye what in God's eye he is—
Chríst—for Christ plays in ten thousand places,
Lovely in limbs, and lovely in eyes not his
To the Father through the features of men's faces.

1881–1882?   1918

[Carrion Comfort][1]

Not, I'll not, carrion comfort, Despair, not feast on thee;
Not untwist—slack they may be—these last strands of man
In me ór, most weary, cry *I can no more.* I can;
Can something, hope, wish day come, not choose not to be.
5   But ah, but O thou terrible, why wouldst thou rude on me
Thy wring-world right foot rock? lay a lionlimb against me? scan
With darksome devouring eyes my bruisèd bones? and fan,
O in turns of tempest, me heaped there; me frantic to avoid thee and flee?

Why? That my chaff might fly; my grain lie, sheer and clear.
10 Nay in all that toil, that coil,[2] since (seems) I kissed the rod,
Hand rather,[3] my heart lo! lapped strength, stole joy, would laugh, chéer.
Cheer whom though? the hero whose heaven-handling flung me, fóot tród
Me? or me that fought him? O which one? is it each one? That night, that year
Of now done darkness I wretch lay wrestling with (my God!) my God.

1885   1918

No Worst, There Is None

No worst, there is none. Pitched past pitch of grief,
More pangs will, schooled at forepangs, wilder wring.
Comforter, where, where is your comforting?
Mary, mother of us, where is your relief?
5   My cries heave, herds-long;[1] huddle in a main, a chief
Woe, world-sorrow; on an age-old anvil wince and sing—

---

1. The title was added by Robert Bridges. This poem is one of the "terrible sonnets" of 1885, as are the next two.
2. Turmoil.

3. I.e., the hand that holds the rod the speaker has kissed.
1. Like a cry of sheep or cattle repeated successively the length of the herd.

Then lull, then leave off. Fury had shrieked "No ling-
ering! Let me be fell:° force° I must be brief."   *fierce / perforce*

    O the mind, mind has mountains; cliffs of fall
10   Frightful, sheer, no-man-fathomed. Hold them cheap
May who ne'er hung there. Nor does long our small
Durance° deal with that steep or deep. Here! creep,   *endurance*
Wretch, under a comfort serves in a whirlwind: all
Life death does end and each day dies with sleep.
1885   1918

I Wake and Feel the Fell of Dark, Not Day

I wake and feel the fell[1] of dark, not day.
What hours, O what black hoürs we have spent
This night! what sights you, heart, saw; ways you went!
And more must, in yet longer light's delay.
5   With witness I speak this. But where I say
Hours I mean years, mean life. And my lament
Is cries countless, cries like dead letters sent
To dearest him that lives alas! away.

    I am gall, I am heartburn. God's most deep decree
10   Bitter would have me taste: my taste was me;
Bones built in me, flesh filled, blood brimmed the curse.
    Selfyeast of spirit a dull dough sours. I see
The lost° are like this, and their scourge to be   *souls in Hell*
As I am mine, their sweating selves; but worse.
1885   1918

Thou Art Indeed Just, Lord

    Justus quidem tu es, Domine, si disputem tecum: verumtamen
        justa loquar ad te: Quare via impiorum prosperatur? &c.[1]

Thou art indeed just, Lord, if I contend
With thee; but, sir, so what I plead is just.
Why do sinners' ways prosper? and why must
Disappointment all I endeavour end?
5   Wert thou my enemy, O thou my friend,
How wouldst thou worse, I wonder, than thou dost
Defeat, thwart me? Oh, the sots and thralls of lust
Do in spare hours more thrive than I that spend,
Sir, life upon thy cause. See, banks and brakes°   *thickets*
10   Now, leavèd how thick! lacèd they are again
With fretty chervil,° look, and fresh wind shakes   *cow-parsley*
Them; birds build—but not I build; no, but strain,
Time's eunuch, and not breed one work that wakes.
Mine, O thou lord of life, send my roots rain.
1889   1893

---

1. Gall, bitterness; but also a hide or covering; a wasteland; as an adjective, "fell" means fierce or cruel.

1. The first lines of the poem translate these words from
Jeremiah 12.1.

Lewis Carroll
1832–1898

With their disconcerting mix of fantasy and parody, wordplay and violent, outrageous nonsense, *Alice in Wonderland* (1865) and its sequel, *Through the Looking-Glass* (1871), enchanted the Victorian public. The Alice stories make fun of manners, school lessons, politics, royalty, and the values of the middle class. Lewis Carroll's rare ability to enter the imaginative world of childhood, coupled with his surrealistic, tumultuous vision of what would entertain a ten-year-old, transformed children's literature. His extravagant, eccentric characters—the White Rabbit, the Mad Hatter, the Cheshire Cat, Tweedledee and Tweedledum—badger Alice with absurd advice, but ultimately the books themselves offer no moral whatsoever.

The creator of Wonderland was a shy but playful professor of mathematics named Charles Lutwidge Dodgson. He had settled early on the chief activities of his life: puzzling over logical problems and entertaining children. The oldest son of an Anglican clergyman, Dodgson delighted his seven sisters and three brothers with his puppet shows, invented games, and comic writing. A prize-winning student at Rugby School, he went on to Oxford, where he became a fellow of Christ Church in 1855. Some readers find it peculiar that the greatest nonsense writer in English should also be the author of *Curiosa Mathematica: A New Theory of Parallels* (1888) and *Symbolic Logic* (1896), but others have enjoyed the mathematical and logical brainteasers embedded in his stories. His sense of fun emerged in his serious work, too, as in a passage in a textbook he wrote where Euclid's ghost tries to prevent a professor from altering his classical geometry manual.

Dodgson was the epitome of the Oxford don—set in his ways, devoted to his work and his spinster sisters, a confirmed bachelor who kept the same cluttered rooms in college for thirty years. To separate the retiring scholar from the irreverent author of fiction and poetry, Dodgson invented a pseudonym: he reversed his first two names, translated them into Latin, and then back again, with schoolboy mistakes, into English. "Lewis Carroll" became in some sense an uninhibited alter ego. Like all instructors at Oxford, Dodgson was an ordained clergyman. The insecure Reverend Dodgson could not bear to hear a religious joke, yet Lewis Carroll gleefully parodied hymns and moralizing poems. While the identity of the Reverend Dodgson and Mr. Carroll was an open secret, Dodgson refused to acknowledge publicly the authorship of the Alice books. When Queen Victoria, who was a fan of *Alice*, asked him to send her a copy of his next book, he duly obliged with an inscribed copy of *An Elementary Treatise on Determinants* (1867), by C. L. Dodgson. And when a dinner guest unwittingly raised the forbidden topic, Dodgson fled the house. Like Alice, he seems to have been "very fond of pretending to be two people."

The story of how *Alice in Wonderland* came to be written is famous. On 4 July 1862 Dodgson and another don, Robinson Duckworth, invited Alice Liddell, daughter of the Dean of Christ Church, and her sisters on a boating trip. The children clamored for a story, and Dodgson obliged, inventing tales about a fictional child also named Alice. "In a desperate attempt to strike out some new line of fairy lore," Dodgson recalled, he precipitated his heroine "straight down a rabbit hole . . . without the least idea what was to happen afterwards." Later on, at Alice Liddell's request, he began drafting a fuller version which he illustrated himself. Revised, the book was published with superb illustrations by John Tenniel. When it was finally presented to Alice on the third anniversary of the boat trip in 1865, the actual Alice was already thirteen, though her fictional counterpart was only seven.

Even in a pre-Freudian era, Dodgson's friends were struck by his unusual interest in little girls. He invited them to tea and escorted them on outings. He struck up conversations with girls on trains and at the seaside, and afterward wrote them letters. He also took their pictures. Dodgson took up photography in 1856, the same year he created "Lewis Carroll." Though he produced fine portraits of Tennyson, Thackeray, Ruskin, and the Rossettis, his passion was photographing children. He preferred his sitters to be solitary and, if possible, nude. He wrote to one mother, "what I like best of all is to have *two* hours of leisure time before me, *one* child to photograph, and *no* restrictions as to costume! (It is a descending Arithmetical Series—2, 1, 0)." While the *Dictionary of Literary Biography* concludes that his attentions were "pronounced though proper," it is hard nowadays not to find his behavior rather odd. In any case, it is clear that the story of Alice would never have been told without Dodgson's extraordinary desire to please one particular little girl.

The fractured narrative structure of *Alice's Adventures* combines the abrupt, topsy-turvy transitions of nursery rhymes with some of the classic motifs of Western literature. It is part quest-romance toward a miniature Edenic garden, part Dantean descent into a fearful underworld. Mocking didactic literature and rejecting the sentimental view of childhood, Dodgson sends a bold but nervous Alice into a menacing, anarchic landscape replete with birth trauma (the fall down the hole), identity crisis ("Who in the world am I?"), and exaggerated growth pangs ("sending presents to one's own feet!"). In Wonderland, sudden change is the keynote—Alice's body, the rules of society, and even animal species suffer unexpected transformations—as Dodgson invokes Victorian anxiety about the instability of a world racked by speed, industry, and evolutionary theory.

One of Dodgson's innovations was the seamless way his narrative incorporates the poetic "lessons" that Alice hears or recites. Shredding conventional pieties, the poems crazily spoof the dignity of old age ("You are old, Father William"), the instructive events of animal fables ("The Lobster Quadrille," "The Walrus and the Carpenter"), and the purported wisdom of rural folk ("The White Knight's Song"). Even Dodgson's dedicatory verse, "Child of the Pure Unclouded Brow," refuses to honor its genre: instead of celebrating innocence, its ominous view of "bedtime" reveals an underlying fear of growth, sex, and death that lurks at the heart of the Alice stories. Dodgson's scenes frequently take on a nightmarish quality based on estrangement from the body, whether by physical constriction, painful alteration, or some form of extinction, such as "shutting up like a telescope."

Cumulatively, the "lessons" given to Alice and her readers bespeak a universe of randomness and chance, where rules are ridiculous, animals loquacious, everybody illogical, and words arbitrary and out of control. "Lewis Carroll" reveled in what Charles Dodgson repressed, and this subversive, exhilarating flirting with excesses of language and behavior has led not only to the popularity of the Alice stories but to innumerable interpretations. Are they allegories about the Church of England, studies in pyschological and social regression, devastating attacks on English education? For some critics, Lewis Carroll expresses Dodgson's deepest religious doubts—in a world of nonsense, there is no divine guidance shaping human life or guaranteeing the meaning of sacred texts. Others see his irrepressible wordplay as a joyful liberation from the Victorian prison house of stuffy etiquette and stifling morality. The variety of responses even in his own day did not surprise Dodgson/Carroll. As he explained to perplexed readers, "words mean more than we mean to express whenever we use them, so a whole book ought to mean a great deal more than the writer meant."

from Alice's Adventures in Wonderland
Chapter 1. Down the Rabbit-Hole

Alice was beginning to get very tired of sitting by her sister on the bank and of having nothing to do: once or twice she had peeped into the book her sister was reading, but it had no pictures or conversations in it, "and what is the use of a book," thought Alice, "without pictures or conversations?"

So she was considering, in her own mind (as well as she could, for the hot day made her feel very sleepy and stupid), whether the pleasure of making a daisy-chain would be worth the trouble of getting up and picking the daisies, when suddenly a White Rabbit with pink eyes ran close by her.

There was nothing so *very* remarkable in that; nor did Alice think it so *very* much out of the way to hear the Rabbit say to itself "Oh dear! Oh dear! I shall be too late!" (when she thought it over afterwards it occurred to her that she ought to have wondered at this, but at the time it all seemed quite natural); but, when the Rabbit actually *took a watch out of its waistcoat-pocket,* and looked at it, and then hurried on, Alice started to her feet, for it flashed across her mind that she had never before seen a rabbit with either a waistcoat-pocket, or a watch to take out of it, and burning with curiosity, she ran across the field after it, and was just in time to see it pop down a large rabbit-hole under the hedge.

In another moment down went Alice after it, never once considering how in the world she was to get out again.

The rabbit-hole went straight on like a tunnel for some way, and then dipped suddenly down, so suddenly that Alice had not a moment to think about stopping herself before she found herself falling down what seemed to be a very deep well.

Either the well was very deep, or she fell very slowly, for she had plenty of time as she went down to look about her, and to wonder what was going to happen next. First, she tried to look down and make out what she was coming to, but it was too dark to see anything: then she looked at the sides of the well, and noticed that they were filled with cupboards and book-shelves: here and there she saw maps and pictures hung upon pegs. She took down a jar from one of the shelves as she passed: it was labeled "ORANGE MARMALADE," but to her great disappointment it was empty: she did not like to drop the jar, for fear of killing somebody underneath, so managed to put it into one of the cupboards as she fell past it.

"Well!" thought Alice to herself. "After such a fall as this, I shall think nothing of tumbling down-stairs! How brave they'll all think me at home! Why, I wouldn't say anything about it, even if I fell off the top of the house!" (Which was very likely true.)

Down, down, down. Would the fall *never* come to an end? "I wonder how many miles I've fallen by this time?" she said aloud. "I must be getting somewhere near the centre of the earth. Let me see: that would be four thousand miles down, I think—" (for, you see, Alice had learnt several things of this sort in her lessons in the schoolroom, and though this was not a *very* good opportunity for showing off her knowledge, as there was no one to listen to her, still it was good practice to say it over) "—yes, that's about the right distance, but then I wonder what Latitude or Longitude I've got to?" (Alice had not the slightest idea what Latitude was, or Longitude either, but she thought they were nice grand words to say.)

Presently she began again. "I wonder if I shall fall right *through* the earth! How funny it'll seem to come out among the people that walk with their heads downwards! The antipathies,[1] I think—" (she was rather glad there *was* no one listening, this time, as it didn't sound at all the right word) "—but I shall have to ask them what the name of the country is, you know. Please, Ma'am, is this New Zealand? Or Australia?" (and she tried to curtsey as she spoke—fancy, *curtseying* as you're falling through the air! Do you think you could manage it?) "And what an ignorant little girl she'll think me for asking! No, it'll never do to ask: perhaps I shall see it written up somewhere."

Down, down, down. There was nothing else to do, so Alice soon began talking again. "Dinah'll miss me very much to-night, I should think!" (Dinah was the cat.) "I hope they'll remember her saucer of milk at tea-time. Dinah, my dear! I wish you

---

1. Alice means "Antipodes," or places on opposite sides of the globe; for England, that would be Australia.

were down here with me! There are no mice in the air, I'm afraid, but you might catch a bat, and that's very like a mouse, you know. But do cats eat bats, I wonder?" And here Alice began to get rather sleepy, and went on saying to herself, in a dreamy sort of way, "Do cats eat bats? Do cats eat bats?" and sometimes "Do bats eat cats?" for, you see, as she couldn't answer either question, it didn't much matter which way she put it. She felt that she was dozing off, and had just begun to dream that she was walking hand in hand with Dinah, and was saying to her, very earnestly, "Now, Dinah, tell me the truth: did you ever eat a bat?" when suddenly, thump! thump! down she came upon a heap of sticks and dry leaves, and the fall was over.

Alice was not a bit hurt, and she jumped up on to her feet in a moment: she looked up, but it was all dark overhead: before her was another long passage, and the White Rabbit was still in sight, hurrying down it. There was not a moment to be lost: away went Alice like the wind, and was just in time to hear it say, as it turned a corner, "Oh my ears and whiskers, how late it's getting!" She was close behind it when she turned the corner, but the Rabbit was no longer to be seen: she found herself in a long, low hall, which was lit up by a row of lamps hanging from the roof.

There were doors all round the hall, but they were all locked; and when Alice had been all the way down one side and up the other, trying every door, she walked sadly down the middle, wondering how she was ever to get out again.

Suddenly she came upon a little three-legged table, all made of solid glass: there was nothing on it but a tiny golden key, and Alice's first idea was that this might belong to one of the doors of the hall; but, alas! either the locks were too large, or the key was too small, but at any rate it would not open any of them. However, on the second time round, she came upon a low curtain she had not noticed before, and behind it was a little door about fifteen inches high: she tried the little golden key in the lock, and to her great delight it fitted!

Alice opened the door and found that it led into a small passage, not much larger than a rat-hole: she knelt down and looked along the passage into the loveliest garden you ever saw. How she longed to get out of that dark hall, and wander about among those beds of bright flowers and those cool fountains, but she could not even get her head through the doorway: "and even if my head *would* go through," thought poor Alice, "it would be of very little use without my shoulders. Oh, how I wish I could shut up like a telescope! I think I could, if I only knew how to begin." For, you see, so many out-of-the-way things had happened lately, that Alice had begun to think that very few things indeed were really impossible.

There seemed to be no use in waiting by the little door, so she went back to the table, half hoping she might find another key on it, or at any rate a book of rules for shutting people up like telescopes: this time she found a little bottle on it ("which certainly was not here before," said Alice), and tied around the neck of the bottle was a paper label, with the words "DRINK ME" beautifully printed on it in large letters.

It was all very well to say "Drink me," but the wise little Alice was not going to do *that* in a hurry. "No, I'll look first," she said, "and see whether it's marked '*poison*' or not"; for she had read several nice little stories about children who had got burnt, and eaten up by wild beasts, and other unpleasant things, all because they *would* not remember the simple rules their friends had taught them: such as, that a red-hot poker will burn you if you hold it too long; and that, if you cut your finger *very* deeply with a knife, it usually bleeds; and she had never forgotten that, if you drink much from a bottle marked "poison," it is almost certain to disagree with you, sooner or later.

However, this bottle was *not* marked "poison," so Alice ventured to taste it, and, finding it very nice (it had, in fact, a sort of mixed flavour of cherry-tart, custard, pine-apple, roast turkey, toffy, and hot buttered toast), she very soon finished it off.

* * * *

* * *

* * * *

"What a curious feeling!" said Alice. "I must be shutting up like a telescope!"

And so it was indeed: she was now only ten inches high, and her face brightened up at the thought that she was now the right size for going through the little door into that lovely garden. First, however, she waited for a few minutes to see if she was going to shrink any further: she felt a little nervous about this; "for it might end, you know," said Alice to herself, "in my going out altogether, like a candle. I wonder what I should be like then?" And she tried to fancy what the flame of a candle looks like after the candle is blown out, for she could not remember ever having seen such a thing.

After a while, finding that nothing more happened, she decided on going into the garden at once; but, alas for poor Alice! when she got to the door, she found she had forgotten the little golden key, and when she went back to the table for it, she found she could not possibly reach it: she could see it quite plainly through the glass, and she tried her best to climb up one of the legs of the table, but it was too slippery; and when she had tired herself out with trying, the poor little thing sat down and cried.

"Come, there's no use in crying like that!" said Alice to herself rather sharply. "I advise you to leave off this minute!" She generally gave herself very good advice (though she very seldom followed it), and sometimes she scolded herself so severely as to bring tears into her eyes; and once she remembered trying to box her own ears for having cheated herself in a game of croquet she was playing against herself, for this curious child was very fond of pretending to be two people. "But it's no use now," thought poor Alice, "to pretend to be two people! Why, there's hardly enough of me left to make *one* respectable person!"

Soon her eye fell on a little glass box that was lying under the table: she opened it, and found in it a very small cake, on which the words "EAT ME" were beautifully marked in currants. "Well, I'll eat it," said Alice, "and if it makes me grow larger, I can reach the key; and if it makes me grow smaller, I can creep under the door: so either way I'll get into the garden, and I don't care which happens!"

She ate a little bit, and said anxiously to herself "Which way? Which way?", holding her hand on the top of her head to feel which way it was growing; and she was quite surprised to find that she remained the same size. To be sure, this is what generally happens when one eats cake; but Alice had got so much into the way of expecting nothing but out-of-the-way things to happen, that it seemed quite dull and stupid for life to go on in the common way.

So she set to work, and very soon finished off the cake.

* * * *

* * *

* * *

from *Chapter 2. The Pool of Tears*

"Curiouser and curiouser!" cried Alice (she was so much surprised, that for the moment she quite forgot how to speak good English). "Now I'm opening out like the largest telescope that ever was! Good-bye, feet!" (for when she looked down at her feet, they seemed to be almost out of sight, they were getting so far off). "Oh, my

John Tenniel, illustration to
Alice in Wonderland, 1865.

poor little feet, I wonder who will put on your shoes and stockings for you now, dears? I'm sure *I* sha'n't be able! I shall be a great deal too far off to trouble myself about you: you must manage the best way you can—but I must be kind to them," thought Alice, "or perhaps they wo'n't walk the way I want to go! Let me see. I'll give them a new pair of boots every Christmas."

And she went on planning to herself how she would manage it. "They must go by the carrier," she thought; "and how funny it'll seem, sending presents to one's own feet! And how odd the directions will look!

> *Alice's Right Foot, Esq.*
> *Hearthrug,*
> *near the Fender,*[1]
> *(with Alice's love).*

Oh dear, what nonsense I'm talking!"

Just at this moment her head struck against the roof of the hall: in fact she was now rather more than nine feet high, and she at once took up the little golden key and hurried off to the garden door.

Poor Alice! It was as much as she could do, lying down on one side, to look through into the garden with one eye; but to get through was more hopeless than ever: she sat down and began to cry again.

"You ought to be ashamed of yourself," said Alice, "a great girl like you," (she might well say this), "to go on crying in this way! Stop this moment, I tell you!" But she went on all the same, shedding gallons of tears, until there was a large pool around her, about four inches deep, and reaching half down the hall.

1. A low fence in front of a fireplace to keep coals from falling out.

After a time she heard a little pattering of feet in the distance, and she hastily dried her eyes to see what was coming. It was the White Rabbit returning, splendidly dressed, with a pair of white kid-gloves in one hand and a large fan in the other: he came trotting along in a great hurry, muttering to himself, as he came, "Oh! The Duchess, the Duchess! Oh! Wo'n't she be savage if I've kept her waiting!" Alice felt so desperate that she was ready to ask help of any one: so, when the Rabbit came near her, she began, in a low, timid voice, "If you please, Sir—" The Rabbit started violently, dropped the white kid-gloves and the fan, and scurried away into the darkness as hard as he could go.

Alice took up the fan and gloves, and, as the hall was very hot, she kept fanning herself all the time she went on talking. "Dear, dear! How queer everything is to-day! And yesterday things went on just as usual. I wonder if I've changed in the night? Let me think: was I the same when I got up this morning? I almost think I can remember feeling a little different. But if I'm not the same, the next question is 'Who in the world am I?' Ah, *that's* the great puzzle!" And she began thinking over all the children she knew that were of the same age as herself, to see if she could have been changed for any of them.

"I'm sure I'm not Ada," she said, "for her hair goes in such long ringlets, and mine doesn't go in ringlets at all; and I'm sure I ca'n't be Mabel, for I know all sorts of things, and she, oh, she knows such a very little! Besides, *she's* she, and *I'm* I, and—oh dear, how puzzling it all is! I'll try if I know all the things I used to know. Let me see: four times five is twelve, and four times six is thirteen, and four times seven is—oh dear! I shall never get to twenty at that rate! However, the Multiplication-Table doesn't signify: let's try Geography. London is the capital of Paris, and Paris is the capital of Rome, and Rome—no, *that's* all wrong, I'm certain! I must have been changed for Mabel! I'll try and say 'How doth the little—'," and she crossed her hands on her lap as if she were saying lessons, and began to repeat it, but her voice sounded hoarse and strange, and the words did not come the same as they used to do:—

> "How doth the little crocodile
>   Improve his shining tail,
> And pour the waters of the Nile
>   On every golden scale!
>
> "How cheerfully he seems to grin.
>   How neatly spreads his claws,
> And welcomes little fishes in,
>   With gently smiling jaws![2]

"I'm sure those are not the right words," said poor Alice, and her eyes filled with tears again as she went on, "I must be Mabel after all, and I shall have to go and live in that poky little house, and have next to no toys to play with, and oh, ever so many lessons to learn! No, I've made up my mind about it: if I'm Mabel, I'll stay down here. It'll be no use their putting their heads down and saying 'Come up again, dear!' I shall only look up and say 'Who am I, then? Tell me that first, and then, if I like being that person, I'll come up: if not, I'll stay down here till I'm somebody else'— but, oh dear!" cried Alice, with a sudden burst of tears, "I do wish they *would* put their heads down! I am so *very* tired of being all alone here!"

2. The poem Alice is trying to recite is Isaac Watts's *Against Idleness and Mischief* (1715): "How doth the little busy bee / Improve each shining hour, / And gather honey all the day / from every opening flower! / How skillfully she builds her cell! / How neatly she spreads the wax! / And labours hard to store it well / With the sweet food she makes."

You are old, Father William[1]

"You are old, Father William," the young man said,
    "And your hair has become very white;
And yet you incessantly stand on your head—
    Do you think, at your age, it is right?"

5 "In my youth," Father William replied to his son,
    "I feared it might injure the brain;
But, now that I'm perfectly sure I have none,
    Why, I do it again and again."

"You are old," said the youth, "as I mentioned before,
10   And have grown most uncommonly fat;
Yet you turned a back-somersault in at the door—
    Pray, what is the reason of that?"

"In my youth," said the sage, as he shook his grey locks,
    "I kept all my limbs very supple
15 By the use of this ointment—one shilling the box—
    Allow me to sell you a couple?"

"You are old," said the youth, "and your jaws are too weak
    For anything tougher than suet;
Yet you finished the goose, with the bones and the beak—
20   Pray, how did you manage to do it?"

"In my youth," said his father, "I took to the law,
    And argued each case with my wife;
And the muscular strength, which it gave to my jaw
    Has lasted the rest of my life."

25 "You are old," said the youth, "one would hardly suppose
    That your eye was as steady as ever;
Yet you balanced an eel on the end of your nose—
    What made you so awfully clever?"

"I have answered three questions, and that is enough,"
30   Said his father. "Don't give yourself airs!
Do you think I can listen all day to such stuff?
    Be off, or I'll kick you down-stairs!"

The Lobster-Quadrille[1]

"Will you walk a little faster?" said a whiting to a snail,
"There's a porpoise close behind us, and he's treading on my tail.
See how eagerly the lobsters and the turtles all advance!

---

1. From *Alice's Adventures in Wonderland* (ch. 5). The
Caterpillar orders Alice to recite a pious poem, Robert
Southey's *The Old Man's Comforts, and How He Gained
Them* (1799); to her own dismay, what comes out of her
mouth is this parody.
1. From *Alice's Adventures in Wonderland* (ch. 10); the

Mock-Turtle sings this, "very slowly and sadly." It is a
parody of Mary Howitt's moralistic poem, *The Spider and
the Fly* (1834), which begins, "'Will you walk into my
parlor?' said the Spider to the Fly, / 'Tis the prettiest little
parlor that ever you did spy.'"

They are waiting on the shingle[2]—will you come and join the dance?
5   Will you, wo'n't you, will you, wo'n't you, will you join the dance?
    Will you, wo'n't you, will you, wo'n't you, wo'n't you join the dance?

"You can really have no notion how delightful it will be
When they take us up and throw us, with the lobsters, out to sea!"
But the snail replied "Too far, too far!", and gave a look askance—
10 Said he thanked the whiting kindly, but he would not join the dance.
    Would not, could not, would not, could not, could not join the dance.
    Would not, could not, would not, could not, could not join the dance.

"What matters it how far we go?" his scaly friend replied.
"There is another shore, you know, upon the other side.
15 The further off from England the nearer is to France—
Then turn not pale, beloved snail, but come and join the dance.
    Will you, wo'n't you, will you, wo'n't you, will you join the dance?
    Will you, wo'n't you, will you, wo'n't you, wo'n't you join the dance?"

from Through the Looking-Glass
Child of the pure unclouded brow[1]

Child of the pure unclouded brow
    And dreaming eyes of wonder!
Though time be fleet, and I and thou
    Are half a life asunder,
5 Thy loving smile will surely hail
    The love-gift of a fairy-tale.

I have not seen thy sunny face,
    Nor heard thy silver laughter:
No thought of me shall find a place
10   In thy young life's hereafter—
Enough that now thou wilt not fail
To listen to my fairy-tale.

A tale begun in other days,
    When summer suns were glowing—
15 A simple chime, that served to time
    The rhythm of our rowing—
Whose echoes live in memory yet,
Though envious years would say "forget."

Come, hearken then, ere voice of dread,
20   With bitter tidings laden,
Shall summon to unwelcome bed
    A melancholy maiden!
We are but older children, dear,
Who fret to find our bedtime near.

2. Pebble beach.
1. Introductory poem to *Through the Looking-Glass* (1871),
    the sequel to *Alice*.

25 Without, the frost, the blinding snow,
        The storm-wind's moody madness—
    Within, the firelight's ruddy glow,
        And childhood's nest of gladness.
    The magic words shall hold thee fast:
30 Thou shalt not heed the raving blast.

    And, though the shadow of a sigh
        May tremble through the story,
    For "happy summer days" gone by,
        And vanish'd summer glory—
35 It shall not touch, with breath of bale,
        The pleasance[2] of our fairy-tale.

Jabberwocky[1]

    'Twas brillig, and the slithy toves
        Did gyre and gimble in the wabe:
    All mimsy were the borogoves,
        And the mome raths outgrabe.

5   "Beware the Jabberwock, my son!
        The jaws that bite, the claws that catch!
    Beware the Jubjub bird, and shun
        The frumious Bandersnatch!"

    He took his vorpal sword in hand:
10   Long time the manxome foe he sought—
    So rested he by the Tumtum tree,
        And stood awhile in thought.

    And, as in uffish thought he stood,
        The Jabberwock, with eyes of flame,
15 Came whiffling through the tulgey wood,
        And burbled as it came!

    One, two! One, two! And through and through
        The vorpal blade went snicker-snack!
    He left it dead, and with its head
20   He went galumphing back.

    "And, hast thou slain the Jabberwock?
        Come to my arms, my beamish boy!
    O frabjous day! Callooh! Callay!"
        He chortled in his joy.

25 'Twas brillig, and the slithy toves
        Did gyre and gimble in the wabe:

---

2. Pleasance was Alice Liddell's middle name. By 1871, when *Through the Looking-Glass* was published, Alice Liddel was 16; in the book she is seven.
1. From *Through the Looking-Glass* (ch. 1). Alice finds a book in which all the words are printed backwards; when she realizes it's a Looking-glass book, she holds it up to the mirror and reads this poem. Afterwards she remarks that "it's *rather* hard to understand!" Later in *Through the Looking-Glass* Humpty Dumpty explicates the poem (see below).

> All mimsy were the borogoves,
>   And the mome raths outgrabe.

[HUMPTY DUMPTY ON JABBERWOCKY][1]

"You seem very clever at explaining words, Sir," said Alice. "Would you kindly tell me the meaning of the poem called 'Jabberwocky'?"

"Let's hear it," said Humpty Dumpty. "I can explain all the poems that ever were invented—and a good many that haven't been invented just yet."

This sounded very hopeful, so Alice repeated the first verse:—

> *"'Twas brillig, and the slithy toves*
> *Did gyre and gimble in the wabe:*
> *All mimsy were the borogoves,*
> *And the mome raths outgrabe."*

"That's enough to begin with," Humpty Dumpty interrupted: "there are plenty of hard words there. '*Brillig*' means four o'clock in the afternoon—the time when you begin *broiling* things for dinner."

"That'll do very well," said Alice: "and '*slithy*'?"

"Well, '*slithy*' means 'lithe and slimy.' 'Lithe' is the same as 'active.' You see it's like a pormanteau[2]—there are two meanings packed up into one word."

"I see it now," Alice remarked thoughtfully: "and what are '*toves*'?"

"Well '*toves*' are something like badgers—they're something like lizards—and they're something like corkscrews."

"They must be very curious-looking creatures."

"They are that," said Humpty Dumpty; "also they make their nests under sundials—also they live on cheese."

"And what's to '*gyre*' and to '*gimble*'?"

"To '*gyre*' is to go round and round like a gyroscope. To '*gimble*' is to make holes like a gimlet."

"And '*the wabe*' is the grass-plot round a sun-dial, I suppose?" said Alice, surprised at her own ingenuity.

"Of course it is. It's called '*wabe*' you know, because it goes a long way before it, and a long way behind it—"

"And a long way beyond it on each side," Alice added.

"Exactly so. Well then, '*mimsy*' is 'flimsy and miserable' (there's another portmanteau for you). And a '*borogove*' is a thin shabby-looking bird with its feathers sticking out all round—something like a live mop."

"And then '*mome raths*'?" said Alice. "I'm afraid I'm giving you a great deal of trouble."

"Well, a '*rath*' is a sort of green pig: but '*mome*' I'm not certain about. I think it's short for 'from home'—meaning that they'd lost their way, you know."

---

1. From *Through the Looking-Glass* (ch. 6).
2. A word formed by combining two other words (e.g., *brunch, motel*). In the preface to *The Hunting of the Snark* (1876), Carroll wrote about the "hard words" in *Jabberwocky*: "Humpty Dumpty's theory, of two meanings packed into one word like a portmanteau, seems to me the right explanation for all. For instance, take the two words 'fuming' and 'furious.' Make up your mind that you will say both words, but leave it unsettled which you will say first. Now open your mouth and speak. If your thoughts incline ever so little towards 'fuming,' you will say 'fuming-furious,' if they turn, by even a hair's breadth, towards 'furious,' you will say 'furious-fuming,' but if you have the rarest of gifts, a perfectly balanced mind, you will say 'frumious.'"

"And what does 'outgrabe' mean?"

"Well, 'outgribing' is something between bellowing and whistling, with a kind of sneeze in the middle: however, you'll hear it done, maybe—down in the wood yonder—and, when you've once heard it, you'll be *quite* content. Who's been repeating all that hard stuff to you?"

"I read it in a book," said Alice.

The Walrus and the Carpenter[1]

The sun was shining on the sea,
    Shining with all his might:
He did his very best to make
    The billows smooth and bright—
5   And this was odd, because it was
    The middle of the night.

The moon was shining sulkily,
    Because she thought the sun
Had got no business to be there
10   After the day was done—
"It's very rude of him," she said,
    "To come and spoil the fun!"

The sea was wet as wet could be,
    The sands were dry as dry.
15   You could not see a cloud, because
    No cloud was in the sky:
No birds were flying overhead—
    There were no birds to fly.

The Walrus and the Carpenter
20   Were walking close at hand:
They wept like anything to see
    Such quantities of sand:
"If this were only cleared away,"
    They said, "it would be grand!"

25   "If seven maids with seven mops
    Swept it for half a year,
Do you suppose," the Walrus said,
    "That they could get it clear?"
"I doubt it," said the Carpenter,
30   And shed a bitter tear.

"O Oysters, come and walk with us!"
    The Walrus did beseech.
"A pleasant walk, a pleasant talk,
    Along the briny beach:
35   We cannot do with more than four,
    To give a hand to each."

1. From *Through the Looking-Glass* (ch. 4); Tweedledee recites this poem to Alice, choosing it because it "is the longest."

The eldest Oyster looked at him,
 But never a word he said:
The eldest Oyster winked his eye,
40 And shook his heavy head—
Meaning to say he did not choose
 To leave the oyster-bed.

But four young Oysters hurried up,
 All eager for the treat:
45 Their coats were brushed, their faces washed,
  Their shoes were clean and neat—
And this was odd, because, you know,
 They hadn't any feet.

Four other Oysters followed them,
50 And yet another four;
And thick and fast they came at last,
 And more, and more, and more—
All hopping through the frothy waves,
 And scrambling to the shore.

55 The Walrus and the Carpenter
  Walked on a mile or so,
And then they rested on a rock
 Conveniently low:
And all the little Oysters stood
60 And waited in a row.

"The time has come," the Walrus said,
 "To talk of many things:
Of shoes—and ships—and sealing wax—
 Of cabbages—and kings—
65 And why the sea is boiling hot—
 And whether pigs have wings."

"But wait a bit," the Oysters cried,
 "Before we have our chat;
For some of us are out of breath,
70 And all of us are fat!"
"No hurry!" said the Carpenter.
 They thanked him much for that.

"A loaf of bread," the Walrus said,
 "Is what we chiefly need:
75 Pepper and vinegar besides
 Are very good indeed—
Now, if you're ready, Oysters dear,
 We can begin to feed."

"But not on us!" the Oysters cried,
80 Turning a little blue.
"After such kindness, that would be
 A dismal thing to do!"
"The night is fine," the Walrus said.
 "Do you admire the view?"

85 "It was so kind of you to come!
      And you are very nice!"
   The Carpenter said nothing but
      "Cut us another slice.
   I wish you were not quite so deaf—
90   I've had to ask you twice!"

   "It seems a shame," the Walrus said,
      "To play them such a trick.
   After we've brought them out so far,
      And made them trot so quick!"
95 The Carpenter said nothing but
      "The butter's spread too thick!"

   "I weep for you," the Walrus said:
      "I deeply sympathize."
   With sobs and tears he sorted out
100   Those of the largest size,
   Holding his pocket-handkerchief
      Before his streaming eyes.

   "O Oysters," said the Carpenter,
      "You've had a pleasant run!
105 Shall we be trotting home again?"
      But answer came there none—
   And this was scarcely odd, because
      They'd eaten every one.

The White Knight's Song[1]

   I'll tell thee everything I can:
      There's little to relate.
   I saw an aged aged man,
      A-sitting on a gate.
5 "Who are you, aged man?" I said.
      "And how is it you live?"
   And his answer trickled through my head,
      Like water through a sieve.

   He said "I look for butterflies
10   That sleep among the wheat:
   I make them into mutton-pies,
      And sell them in the street.
   I sell them unto men," he said,
      "Who sail on stormy seas;
15 And that's the way I get my bread—
      A trifle, if you please."

   But I was thinking of a plan
      To dye one's whiskers green,

---

1. From *Through the Looking-Glass* (ch. 8); the White Knight sings it to Alice. It is a parody of Wordsworth's *Resolution and Independence*.

And always use so large a fan
    That they could not be seen.
20   So, having no reply to give
    To what the old man said,
I cried "Come, tell me how you live!"
    And thumped him on the head.

25   His accents mild took up the tale:
    He said "I go my ways,
And when I find a mountain-rill,
    I set it in a blaze;
And thence they make a stuff they call
30   Rowland's Macassar-Oil—
Yet twopence-halfpenny is all
    They give me for my toil."

But I was thinking of a way
    To feed oneself on batter,
35   And so go on from day to day
    Getting a little fatter.
I shook him well from side to side,
    Until his face was blue:
"Come, tell me how you live," I cried,
40   "And what it is you do!"

He said "I hunt for haddocks' eyes
    Among the heather bright,
And work them into waistcoat-buttons
    In the silent night.
45   And these I do not sell for gold
    Or coin of silvery shine,
But for a copper halfpenny,
    And that will purchase nine.

"I sometimes dig for buttered rolls,
50   Or set limed twigs for crabs:
I sometimes search for grassy knolls
    For wheels of Hansom-cabs.
And that's the way" (he gave a wink)
    "By which I get my wealth—
55   And very gladly will I drink
    Your Honour's noble health."

I heard him then, for I had just
    Completed my design
To keep the Menai bridge from rust
60   By boiling it in wine.
I thanked him much for telling me
    The way he got his wealth,
But chiefly for his wish that he
    Might drink my noble health.

65   And now, if e'er by chance I put
    My fingers into glue,

Or madly squeeze a right-hand foot
   Into a left-hand shoe,
Or if I drop upon my toe
70   A very heavy weight,
I weep, for it reminds me so
   Of that old man I used to know—

Whose look was mild, whose speech was slow,
Whose hair was whiter than the snow,
75 Whose face was very like a crow,
With eyes, like cinders, all aglow,
Who seemed distracted with his woe,
Who rocked his body to and fro,
And muttered mumblingly and low,
80 As if his mouth were full of dough,
Who snorted like a buffalo—
That summer evening long ago,
   A-sitting on a gate.

≈✦ PERSPECTIVES ✦≈

Imagining Childhood

The nineteenth century has been called the Golden Age of children's literature, for the period saw a remarkable flourishing of writing for and about children. Much of this writing aimed not merely to instruct or admonish children but to delight them. Lewis Carroll's *Alice* books may be the best-known examples, but they are hardly alone: Edward Lear produced several enormously popular volumes of nonsense, writers from John Ruskin to Oscar Wilde tried their hand at the modern fairy tale, Christina Rossetti and Robert Louis Stevenson produced deceptively simple nursery rhymes, and fantasy writing by Charles Kingsley, George MacDonald, and Edith Nesbit paved the way for early-twentieth-century classics such as *Peter Pan*, *The Wind in the Willows*, and *Winnie-the-Pooh*. In addition, the era saw an explosion of adventure stories by novelists such as Rudyard Kipling and Robert Louis Stevenson; of detective fiction, most famously by Sir Arthur Conan Doyle (see *A Scandal in Bohemia*, page 706); and of tales of ghosts and the supernatural. Thomas Hughes's *Tom Brown's School Days* (see page 572) gave rise to another popular genre known as the "school story."

Although the distinction between writing for adults and writing for children was less marked than it is today, much of this literature was produced with a juvenile audience in mind. But it wasn't just the audience who was young: child protagonists featured in countless Victorian novels. The first child hero, Dickens's Oliver Twist (1837), was soon followed by Charlotte Brontë's Jane Eyre, Emily Brontë's Cathy Earnshaw and Heathcliff, William Makepeace Thackeray's Amelia Sedley and Becky Sharp, George Eliot's Tom and Maggie Tulliver—and, of course, a host of subsequent child protagonists in Dickens's own novels, from David Copperfield to Pip. The youthful characters who filled the pages of nineteenth-century fiction served, in part, as vehicles for the authors to come to terms with their own early years. Many of the best-known writers for children, including Dickens, Carroll, and Lear, had memories of difficult childhoods; hence, they frequently idealized and sentimentalized childhood or fantasized about escape to secret gardens and wonderlands. Simultaneously, the century saw a flood of autobiographical writing.

Although childhood was often part of the plot in eighteenth-century novels, it was Blake and Wordsworth who made children into central characters. The Victorians built on the Romantic vision of the child as source of both innocence and imagination, a vision expressed by Wordsworth in his ode *Intimations of Immortality*: "And not in utter nakedness, / But trailing clouds of glory do we come / From God, who is our home." Such ideas about the natural goodness of children owed much to the French philosopher Jean-Jacques Rousseau (1712–1778), who saw children's instinctive innocence as a spiritual touchstone for adults.

The Victorians were engaged in an ongoing debate about the meaning and nature of childhood. What was special about that period of life? Were children born in original sin and thus in need of perpetual training and vigilance in order to ensure the salvation of their souls? Or were they born in a state of innocence, only gradually to be sullied through initiation into adult cares? Did children possess heightened perceptions that would gradually fade with time? Did they have a clearer vision or a purer moral nature? Were their minds really blank slates— John Locke's *tabula rasa*—upon which teaching and experience would later be imprinted? Or did they have inborn instincts, innate predispositions? (Darwin, for example, observed in his baby that ideas arose "independently of any instruction.")

The answers to such questions determined, among other things, how children were brought up. Evangelical households subordinated every other aim and pleasure to the goal of saving the souls of their offspring: strict Sabbath observance meant putting away all the toys except Noah's ark and reading only sermons or perhaps *Pilgrim's Progress*. Darwin, ever the

Advertisement for Pears' soap. Children in earlier eras were often depicted as miniature adults, standing stiffly beside their parents in dignified family portraits. Victorian painters, aided by photographs, tried to convey their liveliness and playfulness. The painting here was created in 1886 by Sir John Everett Millais, one of the original Pre-Raphaelites, and depicts his grandson wearing a Little Lord Fauntleroy suit and blowing bubbles—symbol of the ephemeral beauty of childhood. Millais called it *A Child's World*. But this sort of idealization of childhood readily leant itself to commercialization, and without Millais's knowledge, the owner of his picture sold it to the Pears Soap Company, along with the rights to reproduction. Retitled *Bubbles* and shown with a bar of soap added at the lower right and the word "Pears" in the upper left, the art-advertisement went on to become one of the most widely diffused images in the British Empire.

scientist, regarded his children as part and parcel of the natural world and thus as objects of study every bit as fascinating as finches or coral reefs; he preferred, therefore, to work on his children's "good feelings" rather than exert authoritarian control.

The Victorians were the first generation of parents to be bombarded with books on child rearing; the 1830s alone saw the publication of *Advice to Young Men . . . on How to Be a Father* (1829), *The Mother at Home, or the Principles of Maternal Duty* (1830), *Nursery Government* (1836), *Thoughts of a Parent on Education* (1837), *Hints to Mothers* (1837), *Physical Education, or the Nurture and Management of Children* (1838), and *Advice to Mothers* (1839). Such books were full of information about bathing, dressing, feeding, and disciplining children; some even offered suggestions for decorating the nursery. All of this sometimes conflicting advice could confuse well-meaning and well-read parents: as Elizabeth Gaskell exclaimed anxiously in the diary she kept from 1835 to 1838 to record her feelings as a first-time mother, "Books do so differ." Gaskell herself was most influenced by *L'Education progressive* (1828–1832), written by a French mother who took issue with Rousseau on the question of parental authority: "Perhaps Rousseau has made you uneasy as to the lawfulness of your authority. But if your child be exposed to a real danger . . . your theories are all forgotten." Such books put a great deal of pressure on conscientious women to live up to the high responsibilities of maternity; child rearing was no longer considered merely a matter of affection and common sense.

The novelist Anthony Trollope—whose own, notoriously miserable childhood he later recorded in his autobiography—disapproved of permissive American methods of upbringing:

> I must protest that American babies are an unhappy race. They eat and drink just as they please; they are never punished; they are never banished, snubbed, and kept in the back ground as children are kept with us; and yet they are wretched and uncomfortable. My heart has bled for them as I have heard them squalling by the hour together in agonies of discontent and dyspepsia. Can it be, I wonder, that the children are happier when they are made to obey orders and are sent to bed at six o'clock, than when allowed to regulate their own conduct; that bread and milk is more favourable to laughter and soft childish ways than beefsteak and pickles three times a day; that an occasional whipping, even, will conduce to rosy cheeks? It is an idea which I should never dare to broach to an American mother; but I must confess that after my travels on the western continent my opinions have a tendency in that direction. Beefsteak and pickles certainly produce smart[1] little men and women. Let that be taken for granted. But rosy laughter and winning childish ways are, I fancy, the produce of bread and milk.

Trollope's observations give a glimpse of contemporary British nursery life, with its strict discipline, bland diet, and early bedtimes. Middle- and upper-class children spent most of their day under the care of nurses and governesses, seeing their parents only at scheduled times. Trollope subscribes to a prevalent ideal of childhood—rosy cheeks and soft childish ways—that he feels should be protected; the American system of a rich diet and early independence encourages children to grow up too soon, to become "smart little men and women."

For some, there were nurseries and nannies; for others, factories and mines—American children weren't the only ones growing up too soon. The comfortable childhoods depicted in *Alice's Adventures in Wonderland* or *A Child's Garden of Verses*—full of toys and storybooks, nice clothes and good manners—existed alongside appalling child labor and poverty. Children as young as five or six put in twelve-hour days as chimney sweeps or mill workers. Large numbers of children were employed in domestic service or agricultural labor. Others worked in coal

1. Trollope probably means "shrewd." Other English travelers to America, including Trollope's mother, Frances Trollope, and Isabella Bird, also deplored the "smartness" of American children and their passion for making money.

mines or as street hawkers or prostitutes. Thus, while popular ideology regarded children as innocents to be cherished, admired, and safeguarded, they were very often allowed to endure unspeakable wretchedness.

Of course, these were not the *same* children; as the following remarks on pregnancy illustrate, class distinctions were taken for granted: "We know that it is utterly impossible for the wife of the labouring man to give up work, and, what is called 'take care of herself,' as others can. Nor is it necessary. 'The back is made for its burthen.' It would be just as injurious for the labourer's wife to give up her daily work, as for the lady to take to sweeping her own carpets or cooking the dinner" (from *Cassell's Household Guide*). As with the mother-to-be, so with the child: the privileges of one class and the sufferings of the other were divinely appointed, or at least inevitable. As a Nottingham master sweep explained, many customers *insisted* on having their chimneys swept by children rather than machines, even "ladies who professed to pity the boys." For further reading about the lives of working children, see Blake's "The Chimney Sweeper" (page 89), as well as the testimony of child workers excerpted from the Parliamentary Papers (page 493) and Henry Mayhew's accounts of his interviews with street children (page 508).

The nineteenth century saw gradual improvement in the lot of such children, beginning with the Factory Act of 1833, which limited those under thirteen to an eight-hour work day. It was the first time that childhood had been legally defined by age. The findings of the Children's Employment Commission of 1842–1843 shocked the public conscience, but not until 1901 was a Factory Act passed to prohibit children under twelve from employment in any factory or workshop. In other areas, too, humanitarian efforts slowly brought about protective legislation: the Education Act of 1870 made the first move toward compulsory education, and the 1889 Prevention of Cruelty to Children Act enabled authorities to remove abused children from the custody of their parents. The imprisonment of children under sixteen was not abolished until 1908.

Any discussion of Victorian childhood must also consider the reality of infant mortality. Throughout much of the century, the death rate in England remained fairly constant at over 15 percent of live births (the lowest in Europe). But in industrialized cities, the figure was far higher. Even at midcentury, as many as half of all children did not survive to see their fifth birthday. In addition to malnutrition and poor hygiene, the lack of antibiotics made many deaths from childhood diseases unavoidable. Yet it is a mistake to think that people in earlier times were resigned to losing their children. Darwin wrote a heartbreaking account of the death of his ten-year-old daughter Annie; when her infant son succumbed to scarlet fever, Elizabeth Gaskell wrote, "I don't believe Heaven itself can obliterate the memory of that agony." Then, as now, the loss of a child was one of life's worst blows. It is hardly surprising, then, that pathetic deathbed scenes figure largely in Victorian literature: the most notorious is the death of Little Nell in Dickens's *The Old Curiosity Shop* (1841), which made grown men sob. In contrast, Christina Rossetti's nursery lyrics *"Why did baby die"* and *"Baby lies so fast asleep"* treat the topic with a poignant matter-of-factness.

Child mortality was only one of many complex factors that led the Victorians to make a cult of childhood. They fetishized eternal youth, from Little Nell to Dorian Gray, and on to Peter Pan. Some men, including Ruskin and Carroll and Lear, sought out young children for intense friendships. The notion that the spiritual purity of a young child could bring about the moral redemption of an adult became a frequent theme, from *A Christmas Carol* to Frances Hodgson Burnett's *Little Lord Fauntleroy* (1886). In the same year that Burnett's novel sparked a craze for dressing boys in velvet suits, lace collars, and long curls, John Everett Millais painted his grandson blowing bubbles in just such an outfit. The portrait of this golden-headed child became one of the most popular images of the century. It evokes a vision of childhood as a golden, fragile realm of innocence, a paradisiacal time that many idealized and longed to recapture. The great children's writers, themselves often in revolt against the strictures of adult society, created imaginary worlds for the amusement of their younger readers and the solace of their older ones. Fairy tales and fantasies, anarchic nonsense verse and thrilling tales of adventure, all were part of the period's ongoing discovery and recovery of childhood. As Charles

Dickens wrote, in an essay called *Frauds on Fairies* (1853), "everyone who has considered the subject knows full well that a nation without fancy, without some romance, never did, never can, never will, hold a great place under the sun."

⊷—⊷ ☰◇☰ ⊷—⊷

Charles Darwin
1809–1882

"My first child was born on December 27th, 1839, and I at once commenced to make notes on the first dawn of the various expressions which he exhibited, for I felt convinced, even at this early period, that the most complex and fine shades of expression must all have had a gradual and natural origin." Darwin thus explains in his *Autobiography* how he carefully observed the behavior of his baby, recording his findings with the same objectivity and detachment he brought to any other subject of scientific inquiry. His speculations are free of any sentimentality about children or any religious concerns about their innate guilt or innocence; rather, his approach is typically and sometimes amusingly "Darwinian." He wonders whether throwing things in anger is an inherited male trait and whether a child's fear of large animals derives from a primal memory of "ancient savage times." He matter-of-factly notes similarities between the human infant and various animals: his baby's instinctive anger reminds him of the snapping jaws of a young crocodile, and he contrasts his son's pleasure in looking at himself in the mirror to the puzzlement of apes (and his younger sister). In a final surprise, Darwin hints at a permissive system of child rearing more associated with contemporary America than Victorian England. Although written in 1839–1841, this path-breaking study in child development was not published until 1877.

For more about Charles Darwin, see his principal listing on page 617.

from A Biographical Sketch of an Infant

During the first seven days various reflex actions, namely sneezing, hickuping, yawning, stretching, and of course sucking and screaming, were well performed by my infant. On the seventh day, I touched the naked sole of his foot with a bit of paper, and he jerked it away, curling at the same time his toes, like a much older child when tickled. The perfection of these reflex movements shows that the extreme imperfection of the voluntary ones is not due to the state of the muscles or of the coordinating centres, but to that of the seat of the will. * * *

* * *

Anger.—It was difficult to decide at how early an age anger was felt; on his eighth day he frowned and wrinkled the skin round his eyes before a crying fit, but this may have been due to pain or distress, and not to anger. When about ten weeks old, he was given some rather cold milk and he kept a slight frown on his forehead all the time that he was sucking, so that he looked like a grown-up person made cross from being compelled to do something which he did not like. When nearly four months old, and perhaps much earlier, there could be no doubt, from the manner in which the blood gushed into his whole face and scalp, that he easily got into a violent passion. A small cause sufficed; thus, when a little over seven months old, he screamed with rage because a lemon slipped away and he could not seize it with his hands. When eleven months old, if a wrong plaything was given him, he would push it away and beat it; I presume that the beating was an instinctive sign of anger, like the snapping of the jaws by a young crocodile just out of the egg, and not that he imagined he could hurt the plaything. When two years and three months old, he became a great adept at throwing books or sticks, &c., at anyone who offended him; and so it was with some of my other sons. On the other hand, I could never see a trace of such aptitude in my infant daughters; and this makes me think that a tendency to throw objects is inherited by boys.

Fear.—This feeling probably is one of the earliest which is experienced by infants, as shown by their starting at any sudden sound when only a few weeks old, followed by crying. Before the present one was $4\frac{1}{2}$ months old I had been accustomed to make close to him many strange and loud noises, which were all taken as excellent jokes, but at this period I one day made a loud snoring noise which I had never done before; he instantly looked grave and then burst out crying. Two or three days afterwards, I made through forgetfulness the same noise with the same result. About the same time (*viz.* on the 137th day) I approached with my back towards him and then stood motionless: he looked very grave and much surprised, and would soon have cried, had I not turned round; then his face instantly relaxed into a smile. It is well known how intensely older children suffer from vague and undefined fears, as from the dark, or in passing an obscure corner in a large hall, &c. I may give as an instance that I took the child in question, when $2\frac{1}{4}$ years old, to the Zoological Gardens, and he enjoyed looking at all the animals which were like those that he knew, such as deer, antelopes &c., and all the birds, even the ostriches, but was much alarmed at the various larger animals in cages. He often said afterwards that he wished to go again, but not to see "beasts in houses"; and we could in no manner account for his fear. May we not suspect that the vague but very real fears of children, which are quite independent of experience, are the inherited effects of real dangers and abject superstitions during ancient savage times? It is quite conformable with what we know of the transmission of formerly well-developed characters, that they should appear at an early period of life, and afterwards disappear.

* * *

Affection.—This probably arose very early in life, if we may judge by his smiling at those who had charge of him when under two months old; though I had no distinct evidence of his distinguishing and recognizing anyone, until he was nearly four months old. When nearly five months old, he plainly showed his wish to go to his nurse. But he did not spontaneously exhibit affection by overt acts until a little above a year old, namely, by kissing several times his nurse who had been absent for a short time. With respect to the allied feeling of sympathy, this was clearly shown at 6 months and 11 days by his melancholy face, with the corners of his mouth well depressed, when his nurse pretended to cry. Jealousy was plainly exhibited when I fondled a large doll, and when I weighed his infant sister, he being $15\frac{1}{2}$ months old. Seeing how strong a feeling jealousy is in dogs, it would probably be exhibited by infants at an earlier age than that just specified, if they were tried in a fitting manner.

Association of Ideas, Reason, &c.—The first action which exhibited, as far as I observed, a kind of practical reasoning, has already been noticed, namely, the slipping his hand down my finger so as to get the end of it into his mouth; and this happened on the 114th day. When four and a half months old, he repeatedly smiled at my image and his own in a mirror, and no doubt mistook them for real objects; but he showed sense in being evidently surprised at my voice coming from behind him. Like all infants he much enjoyed thus looking at himself, and in less than two months per-fectly understood that it was an image; for if I made quite silently any odd grimace, he would suddenly turn round to look at me. He was, however, puzzled at the age of sev-en months, when being out of doors he saw me on the inside of a large plate-glass window, and seemed in doubt whether or not it was an image. Another of my infants, a little girl, when exactly a year old, was not nearly so acute, and seemed quite per-plexed at the image of a person in a mirror approaching her from behind. The higher apes which I tried with a small looking-glass behaved differently; they placed their hands behind the glass, and in doing so showed their sense, but far from taking plea-sure in looking at themselves they got angry and would look no more.

When five months old, associated ideas arising independently of any instruction became fixed in his mind; thus as soon as his hat and cloak were put on, he was very cross if he was not immediately taken out of doors. When exactly seven months old, he made the great step of associating his nurse with her name, so that if I called it out he would look round for her. Another infant used to amuse himself by shaking his head laterally: we praised and imitated him, saying "Shake your head"; and when he was seven months old, he would sometimes do so on being told without any other guide. * * * The facility with which associated ideas due to instruction and others spon-taneously arising were acquired, seemed to me by far the most strongly marked of all the distinctions between the mind of an infant and that of the cleverest full-grown dog that I have ever known. What a contrast does the mind of an infant present to that of the pike, described by Professor Möbius,[1] who during three whole months dashed and stunned himself against a glass partition which separated him from some minnows; and when, after at least learning that he could not attack them with impunity, he was placed in the aquarium with these same minnows, then in a persistent and senseless manner he would not attack them!

* * *

Moral Sense.—The first sign of moral sense was noticed at the age of nearly 13 months. I said "Doddy (his nickname) won't give poor papa a kiss,—naughty Doddy". These words, without doubt, made him feel slightly uncomfortable; and at last when I had returned to my chair, he protruded his lips as a sign that he was ready to kiss me; and he then shook his hand in an angry manner until I came and received his kiss. Nearly the same little scene recurred in a few days, and the reconciliation seemed to give him so much satisfaction, that several times afterwards he pretended to be angry and slapped me, and then insisted on giving me a kiss. So that here we have a touch of the dramatic art, which is so strongly pronounced in most young children. About this time it became easy to work on his feelings and make him do whatever was wanted. When 2 years and 3 months old, he gave his last bit of gingerbread to his little sister, and then cried out with high self-approbation "Oh kind Doddy, kind Doddy." Two months later, he became extremely sensitive to ridicule, and was so suspicious that he often thought people who were laughing and talking together were laughing at him. A little later (2 years and 7½ months old) I met him coming out of the dining room with his eyes unnaturally bright, and an odd unnatural or affected manner, so that I went into the room to see who was there, and found that he had been taking pounded sug-ar, which he had been told not to do. As he had never been in any way punished, his odd manner certainly was not due to fear, and I suppose it was pleasurable excitement struggling with conscience. A fortnight afterwards, I met him coming out of the same

---

1. Karl August Möbius (1825–1908), German zoologist and marine biologist.

room, and he was eyeing his pinafore which he had carefully rolled up; and again his manner was so odd that I determined to see what was within his pinafore, notwithstanding that he said that there was nothing and repeatedly commanded me to "go away," and I found it stained with pickle-juice; so that here was carefully planned deceit. As this child was educated solely by working on his good feelings, he soon became as truthful, open, and tender, as anyone could desire.

1839–1841   1877

◂—◂═◆═▸—▸

Moral Verses

Much of what was written for children in the nineteenth century had a strong flavor of the didactic and morally improving, as illustrated by the anonymous *Table Rules for Little Folks*. The lessons could be hard-hitting: the popular but unsentimental Eliza Cook's little mouse actually *dies* as a punishment for not sharing his cake with his brothers! Translated into English in 1848, Heinrich Hoffmann's *Struwwelpeter* was the first sustained parody of the "awful warnings" of earlier moral verse; he inspired many imitators, most notably Hilaire Belloc's *Cautionary Tales for Children* (1907). Yet it's never quite clear whether Hoffmann is truly mocking the awful warnings or comically reinventing them—for the "sin" of defying his parents by refusing his soup, Augustus ends up dead. In a different vein Thomas Miller, a popular working-class poet, sought to arouse the moral sympathies of his young readers with the plight of the freezing and half-starved watercress seller; the implied contrast with their own comfort would presumably teach them to be grateful for their blessings. In contrast, the Scots poem *Willie Winkie*—the title character is the personification of Sleep—takes a cheerful view of mischievous "weans" who won't go to bed.

Table Rules for Little Folks

In silence I must take my seat,
And give God thanks before I eat;
Must for my food in patience wait,
Till I am asked to hand my plate;
5   I must not scold, nor whine, nor pout,
Nor move my chair nor plate about;
With knife, or fork, or napkin ring,
I must not play, nor must I sing.
I must not speak a useless word,
10   For children should be seen, not heard;
I must not talk about my food,
Nor fret if I don't think it good;
I must not say, "The bread is old,"
"The tea is hot," "The coffee's cold";
15   My mouth with food I must not crowd,
Nor while I'm eating speak aloud;
Must turn my head to cough or sneeze,
And when I ask, say "If you please";
The tablecloth I must not spoil,
20   Nor with my food my fingers soil;
Must keep my seat when I have done,
Nor round the table sport or run;
When told to rise, then I must put

25 My chair away with noiseless foot;
And lift my heart to God above,
In praise for all his wondrous love.

c. 1858

Eliza Cook: The Mouse and the Cake

A mouse found a beautiful piece of plum cake,
The richest and sweetest that mortal could make;
'Twas heavy with citron and fragrant with spice,
And covered with sugar all sparkling as ice.

5 "My stars!" cried the mouse, while his eye beamed with glee,
"Here's a treasure I've found: what a feast it will be;
But, hark! there's a noise, 'tis my brothers at play;
So I'll hide with the cake, lest they wander this way.

"Not a bit shall they have, for I know I can eat
10 Every morsel myself, and I'll have such a treat."
So off went the mouse as he held the cake fast;
While his hungry young brothers went scampering past.

He nibbled, and nibbled, and panted, but still
He kept gulping it down till he made himself ill;
15 Yet he swallowed it all, and 'tis easy to guess,
He was soon so unwell that he groaned with distress.

His family heard him, and as he grew worse,
They sent for the doctor, who made him rehearse
How he'd eaten the cake to the very last crumb,
20 Without giving his playmates and relatives some.

"Ah me!" cried the doctor, "advice is too late;
You must die before long, so prepare for your fate.
If you had but divided the cake with your brothers,
'Twould have done you no harm, and been good for the others.

25 "Had you shared it, the treat had been wholesome enough;
But eaten by *one*, it was dangerous stuff;
So prepare for the worst—" and the word had scarce fled,
When the doctor turned round, and the patient was dead.

Now all little people the lesson may take,
30 And *some* large ones may learn from the mouse and the cake;
Not to be over-selfish with what we may gain,
Or the best of our pleasures may turn into pain.

1849

Heinrich Hoffmann: The Story of Augustus who would Not have any Soup

Augustus was a chubby lad;
Fat ruddy cheeks Augustus had:
And everybody saw with joy

The plump and hearty, healthy boy.
5   He ate and drank as he was told,
And never let his soup get cold.
But one day, one cold winter's day,
He screamed out "Take the soup away!
O take the nasty soup away!
10   I won't have any soup today."

Next day, now look, the picture shows
How lank and lean Augustus grows!
Yet, though he feels so weak and ill,
The naughty fellow cries out still
15   "Not any soup for me, I say:
O take the nasty soup away!
I *won't* have any soup today."

The third day comes: Oh what a sin!
To make himself so pale and thin.
20   Yet, when the soup is put on table,
He screams, as loud as he is able,
"Not any soup for me, I say:
O take the nasty soup away!
I WON'T have any soup today."

25   Look at him, now the fourth day's come!
He scarcely weighs a sugar-plum;
He's like a little bit of thread,
And, on the fifth day, he was—dead!

1844   1848

Thomas Miller: The Watercress Seller[1]

Now all aloud the wind and rain
Beat sharp upon the window pane,
   And though 'tis hardly light,
I hear that little girl go by,
5   Who does "Fine watercresses" cry,
   Morning, and noon, and night.

I saw her pass by yesterday,
The snow upon the pavement lay,
   Her hair was white with sleet;
10 She shook with cold, as she did cry,
"Fine watercresses, come and buy,"
   And naked were her feet.

And with one hand, so red and cold,
She did her tattered bonnet hold,
15   The other held her shawl,
Which was too thin to keep her warm,

1. See also Henry Mayhew, the *Watercress Girl*, page 508.

But naked left each little arm,
    It was so very small.

20   Her watercresses froze together,
    Yet she, through the cold, bitter weather,
        Went on from street to street:
    And thus she goes out every day,
    For she can earn no other way
        The bread which she doth eat.

1850

William Miller: Willie Winkie

Wee Willie Winkie rins through the town,
Up stairs and doon stairs in his nicht-gown,
Tirling° at the window, crying at the lock,   *rapping*
"Are the weans° in their bed, for it's now ten o'clock?"   *children*

5   "Hey, Willie Winkie, are ye coming ben°?   *in*
The cat's singing grey thrums° to the sleeping hen,   *purring*
The dog's spelder'd° on the floor, and disna gie a cheep, *sprawled*
But here's a waukrife° laddie, that winna fa' asleep."   *wakeful*

Onything but sleep, you rogue! glow'ring like the moon,
10   Rattling in an airn° jug wi' an airn spoon,   *iron*
Rumbling, tumbling round about, crawing like a cock,
Skirling like a kenna-what,° wauk'ning sleeping fock.   *shrieking like anything*

"Hey, Willie Winkie—the wean's in a creel,°   *in a state*
Wambling° aff a bodie's knee like a very eel,   *squirming*
15   Rugging° at the cat's lug,° and ravelling a'her thrums— *tugging / ear*
Hey, Willie Winkie—see, there he comes!"

Wearied is the mither° that has a stoorie° wean,   *mother / restless*
A wee stumpie stoussie,° that canna rin his lane,°   *munchkin / run alone*
That has a battle aye wi' sleep before he'll close an e'e—
20   But a kiss frae aff his rosy lips gies strength anew to me.

1841

·—· ⛬ ·—·

Edward Lear
1812–1888

"I see life as basically tragic and futile and the only thing that matters is making little jokes," wrote the landscape painter Edward Lear in his diary. The twentieth child of a bankrupt stockbroker, he suffered from depression and poor health. Yet this unhappy, enigmatic figure produced some of the most amusing writing of the era, accompanied by his own surreal sketches. Like Lewis Carroll, whose *Alice* (1865) appeared nearly twenty years after Lear's *A Book of Nonsense* (1846), Lear created an absurdist nonsense world in reaction to the stuffy conventions of Victorian social life. His sense of himself as a misfit is reflected not only in the autobiographical "How Pleasant to Know Mr. Lear," but also in the gallery of eccentrics who people his limericks. Many of his peculiar Old Men and whimsical Young Ladies come to a violent end at the hands of a mocking and intolerant "they"; others do away with themselves for no apparent reason, suggesting nihilism at the heart of nonsense. In later verses, such as "The Owl and the Pussy-Cat," alienation is transformed as preposterously mismatched couples enact a fantasy of joyful romantic escape. The bouncing energy of Lear's verses and the chaotic anarchy of his nonsense vision culminate in the Jumblies' fantastical and nutty adventures at sea.

[SELECTED LIMERICKS]

There was an Old Man with a beard,
Who said, "It is just as I feared!—
Two Owls and a Hen, four Larks and a Wren,
Have all built their nests in my beard!"

There was an Old Man with a nose,
Who said, "If you choose to suppose,
That my nose is too long, you are certainly wrong!"
That remarkable Man with a nose.

There was a Young Lady of Norway,
Who casually sat in a doorway;
When the door squeezed her flat, she exclaimed "What of that?"
This courageous Young Lady of Norway.

There was an Old Man of the Dee,
Who was sadly annoyed by a flea;
When he said, "I will scratch it"—they gave him a hatchet,
Which grieved that Old Man of the Dee.

There was an Old Man of Whitehaven,
Who danced a quadrille with a Raven;
But they said—"It's absurd, to encourage this bird!"
So they smashed that Old Man of Whitehaven.

There was a young lady, whose nose,
Continually prospers and grows;
When it grew out of sight, she exclaimed in a fright,
"Oh! Farewell to the end of my nose!"

The Owl and the Pussy-Cat

1

The Owl and the Pussy-cat went to sea
   In a beautiful pea-green boat,
They took some honey, and plenty of money,
   Wrapped up in a five-pound note.
5 The Owl looked up to the stars above,
   And sang to a small guitar,
"O lovely Pussy! O Pussy, my love,
   What a beautiful Pussy you are,
     You are,
10   You are!
   What a beautiful Pussy you are!"

2

Pussy said to the Owl, "You elegant fowl!
   How charmingly sweet you sing!
O let us be married! too long we have tarried:
15   But what shall we do for a ring?"

They sailed away, for a year and a day,
  To the land where the Bong-tree grows
And there in a wood a Piggy-wig stood
  With a ring at the end of his nose,
20   His nose,
      His nose,
With a ring at the end of his nose.

3

"Dear Pig, are you willing to sell for one shilling
  Your ring?" Said the Piggy, "I will."
25 So they took it away, and were married next day
  By the Turkey who lives on the hill.
They dined on mince, and slices of quince,
  Which they ate with a runcible spoon;
And hand in hand, on the edge of the sand,
30   They danced by the light of the moon,
      The moon,
      The moon,
    They danced by the light of the moon.

1871

How pleasant to know Mr. Lear!

How pleasant to know Mr. Lear!
  Who has written such volumes of stuff!
Some think him ill-tempered and queer,
  But a few think him pleasant enough.

5 His mind is concrete and fastidious,
  His nose is remarkably big;
His visage is more or less hideous,
  His beard it resembles a wig.

He has ears, and two eyes, and ten fingers,
10 Leastways if you reckon two thumbs:
Long ago he was one of the singers,
  But now he is one of the dumbs.

He sits in a beautiful parlour,
  With hundreds of books on the wall;
15 He drinks a great deal of Marsala,
  But never gets tipsy at all.

He has many friends, laymen and clerical;
  Old Foss is the name of his cat;
His body is perfectly spherical,
20 He weareth a runcible hat.

When he walks in a waterproof white,
  The children run after him so!
Calling out, "He's come out in his night-
  Gown, that crazy old Englishman, oh!"

25 He weeps by the side of the ocean,
  He weeps on the top of the hill;

He purchases pancakes and lotion,
    And chocolate shrimps from the mill.

He reads but he cannot speak Spanish,
30   He cannot abide ginger-beer;
Ere the days of his pilgrimage vanish,
    How pleasant to know Mr. Lear!

1879   1912

Robert Louis Stevenson
1850–1894

The Scottish author of adventure novels such as *Treasure Island* (1883) and *Kidnapped* (1886), Robert Louis Stevenson also produced the century's most important collection of poems for children, the immensely popular *A Child's Garden of Verses* (1885). The poems are written from a child's perspective yet tinged with adult nostalgia for lost innocence and simplicity. Like Stevenson himself, who suffered from poor health, the protagonist is a sickly child with a vivid imaginative life. The poems recreate the child's world: his delight in make-believe, his wonder at the moon and stars and wind, his curiosity about dreams and shadows. They also evoke the more everyday experiences of having to worry about good manners and to go to bed while it's still light out. Yet along with the pleasures of teatime and toys, cozy counterpanes and dreamy reverie, runs a thread of anxiety, as though middle-class comforts are bulwarks against nighttime fears. The precariousness of this world is suggested, too, in the child's awareness of how poor children and foreign children do not have the security of regular meals and a rich papa. The wider world entices the child, who longs to visit foreign lands or venture out at night like the lamplighter, yet his desire to explore mingles with a fearful sense of the dangers that lurk abroad.

from A Child's Garden of Verses
Whole Duty of Children

A child should always say what's true
And speak when he is spoken to,
And behave mannerly at table;
At least as far as he is able.

The Land of Counterpane°   *bedspread*

When I was sick and lay a-bed,
I had two pillows at my head,
And all my toys beside me lay
To keep me happy all the day.

5   And sometimes for an hour or so
I watched my leaden soldiers go,
With different uniforms and drills,
Among the bed-clothes, through the hills;

And sometimes sent my ships in fleets
10   All up and down among the sheets;
Or brought my trees and houses out,

And planted cities all about.

I was the giant great and still
That sits upon the pillow-hill,
15   And sees before him, dale and plain,
The pleasant land of counterpane.

System

Every night my prayers I say,
And get my dinner every day;
And every day that I've been good,
I get an orange after food.

5   The child that is not clean and neat,
With lots of toys and things to eat,
He is a naughty child, I'm sure—
Or else his dear papa is poor.

Escape at Bedtime

The lights from the parlour and kitchen shone out
   Through the blinds and the windows and bars;
And high overhead and all moving about,
   There were thousands of millions of stars.
5   There ne'er were such thousands of leaves on a tree,
   Nor of people in church or the Park,
As the crowds of the stars that looked down upon me,
   And that glittered and winked in the dark.

The Dog, and the Plough, and the Hunter, and all,
10   And the star of the sailor, and Mars,
These shone in the sky, and the pail by the wall
   Would be half full of water and stars.
They saw me at last, and they chased me with cries,
   And they soon had me packed into bed;
15   But the glory kept shining and bright in my eyes,
   And the stars going round in my head.

Happy Thought

The world is so full of a number of things,
I'm sure we should all be as happy as kings.

Shadow March

All round the house is the jet-black night;
   It stares through the window-pane;
It crawls in the corners, hiding from the light,
   And it moves with the moving flame.

5   Now my little heart goes a-beating like a drum,
   With the breath of the Bogie in my hair;
And all round the candle the crooked shadows come,
   And go marching along up the stair.

The shadow of the balusters, the shadow of the lamp,
10   The shadow of the child that goes to bed—
All the wicked shadows coming tramp, tramp, tramp,
With the black night overhead.

                                                                1885

* ⛭ *

Hilaire Belloc
1870–1953

Born in France, Hilaire Belloc grew up in England, where he became a novelist, biographer, journalist, essayist, critic, and travel writer. His book of whimsical verse, *The Bad Child's Book of Beasts* (1896), was a runaway best-seller, soon followed by *More Beasts for Worse Children* (1897). These lively comic verses parody the heavy-handed moral lessons for children so prevalent earlier in the century. Their wry sophistication and subversive energy make them as entertaining for adults as for children—though it is the adults who usually appear pompous and slightly absurd. The illustrations by Belloc's friend Basil Blackwood interact cleverly with the texts, as in "The Tiger," where the image of the tiger's bulging stomach elucidates why the overworked mother might find such a creature a handy pet.

from The Bad Child's Book of Beasts
Introduction

I call you bad, my little child,
    Upon the title page,
Because a manner rude and wild
    Is common at your age.

5   The Moral of this priceless work
        (If rightly understood)
    Will make you—from a little Turk—
        Unnaturally good.

    Do not as evil children do,
10   Who on the slightest grounds
    Will imitate the Kangaroo,
        With wild unmeaning bounds.

    Do not as children badly bred,
        Who eat like little Hogs,
15 And when they have to go to bed
        Will whine like Puppy Dogs:

    Who take their manners from the Ape,
        Their habits from the Bear,
    Indulge the loud unseemly jape,°   *joke*
20   And never brush their hair.

    But so control your actions that
        Your friends may all repeat,
    "This child is dainty as the cat
        And as the Owl discreet."

                                                                1896

The Yak

As a friend to the children commend me the Yak.
    You will find it exactly the thing:
It will carry and fetch, you can ride on its back,
    Or lead it about with a string.

5 The Tartar who dwells on the plains of Thibet
    (A desolate region of snow)
Has for centuries made it a nursery pet,
    And surely the Tartar should know!

Then tell your papa where the Yak can be got,
10   And if he is awfully rich
He will buy you the creature—or else he will *not*.
    (I cannot be positive which.)

1896

The Tiger

The Tiger, on the other hand,

                                is kittenish and mild,
He makes a pretty playfellow for any little child;
And mothers of large families (who claim to common sense)

Will find a Tiger well repay the trouble and expense.

1896

Beatrix Potter
1866–1943

Anticipating Kenneth Grahame's *The Wind in the Willows* (1908) and A. A. Milne's *Winnie-the-Pooh* (1926), Beatrix Potter's books take place in a magical pastoral landscape inhabited by talking animals who lead remarkably domestic middle-class English lives. *The Tale of Peter Rabbit* began as a letter to comfort a sick child; but its popularity encouraged Potter to write many more little books for children, twenty-three in all, populated by a gallery of rabbits and squirrels and mice, illustrated with her own exquisite watercolors and told with an elegant economy of style. Although it may initially seem to be a moral fable—the naughty Peter disobeys his mother and goes to bed without supper—there is more than a hint of subversiveness in this tale. To the mischievous hero, "Don't go into Mr McGregor's garden" sounds like an implicit invitation rather than a warning. Peter ventures into a forbidden paradise, braves an assortment of dangers, and returns safely home to domestic warmth and maternal comfort. This archetypal story of transgression and redemption is told with humorous understatement; a comic providence watches over Peter, who pays for his temporary escape with scarcely a moment's repentance.

The Tale of Peter Rabbit

Once upon a time there were four little Rabbits, and their names were—Flopsy, Mopsy, Cotton-tail, and Peter.

They lived with their Mother in a sand-bank, underneath the root of a very big fir-tree.

"Now, my dears," said old Mrs Rabbit one morning, "you may go into the fields or down the lane, but don't go into Mr McGregor's garden: your Father had an accident there; he was put in a pie by Mrs McGregor."

"Now run along, and don't get into mischief. I am going out."

Then old Mrs Rabbit took a basket and her umbrella, and went through the wood to the baker's. She bought a loaf of brown bread and five currant buns.

Flopsy, Mopsy, and Cotton-tail, who were good little bunnies, went down the lane to gather blackberries: but Peter, who was very naughty, ran straight away to Mr McGregor's garden, and squeezed under the gate!

First he ate some lettuces and some French beans; and then he ate some radishes; and then, feeling rather sick, he went to look for some parsley.

But round the end of a cucumber frame, whom should he meet but Mr McGregor!

Mr McGregor was on his hands and knees planting out young cabbages, but he jumped up and ran after Peter, waving a rake and calling out, "Stop thief!"

Peter was most dreadfully frightened; he rushed all over the garden, for he had forgotten the way back to the gate.

He lost one of his shoes among the cabbages, and the other shoe amongst the potatoes.

After losing them, he ran on four legs and went faster, so that I think he might have got away altogether if he had not unfortunately run into a gooseberry net, and got caught by the large buttons on his jacket. It was a blue jacket with brass buttons, quite new.

Peter gave himself up for lost, and shed big tears; but his sobs were overheard by some friendly sparrows, who flew to him in great excitement, and implored him to exert himself.

Mr McGregor came up with a sieve, which he intended to pop upon the top of Peter; but Peter wriggled out just in time, leaving his jacket behind him. And rushed into the toolshed, and jumped into a can. It would have been a beautiful thing to hide in, if it had not had so much water in it.

Mr McGregor was quite sure that Peter was somewhere in the tool-shed, perhaps hidden underneath a flower-pot. He began to turn them over carefully, looking under each.

Presently Peter sneezed—"Kertyschoo!" Mr McGregor was after him in no time.

And tried to put his foot upon Peter, who jumped out of a window, upsetting three plants. The window was too small for Mr McGregor, and he was tired of running after Peter. He went back to his work.

Peter sat down to rest; he was out of breath and trembling with fright, and he had not the least idea which way to go. Also he was very damp with sitting in that can.

After a time he began to wander about, going lippity—lippity—not very fast, and looking all round.

He found a door in a wall; but it was locked, and there was no room for a fat little rabbit to squeeze underneath.

An old mouse was running in and out over the stone doorstep, carrying peas and beans to her family in the wood. Peter asked her the way to the gate, but she had such a large pea in her mouth that she could not answer. She only shook her head at him. Peter began to cry.

Then he tried to find his way straight across the garden, but he became more and more puzzled. Presently, he came to a pond where Mr McGregor filled his water-cans. A white cat was staring at some gold-fish, she sat very, very still, but now and then the tip of her tail twitched as if it were alive. Peter thought it best to go away without speaking to her; he had heard about cats from his cousin, little Benjamin Bunny.

He went back towards the tool-shed, but suddenly, quite close to him, he heard the noise of a hoe—scr-r-ritch, scratch, scratch, scritch. Peter scuttered underneath the bushes. But presently, as nothing happened, he came out, and climbed upon a wheelbarrow and peeped over. The first thing he saw was Mr McGregor hoeing onions. His back was turned towards Peter, and beyond him was the gate!

Peter got down very quietly off the wheelbarrow, and started running as fast as he could go, along a straight walk behind some black-currant bushes.

Mr McGregor caught sight of him at the corner, but Peter did not care. He slipped underneath the gate, and was safe at last in the wood outside the garden.

Mr McGregor hung up the little jacket and the shoes for a scare-crow to frighten the blackbirds.

Peter never stopped running or looked behind him till he got home to the big fir-tree.

He was so tired that he flopped down upon the nice soft sand on the floor of the rabbit-hole and shut his eyes. His mother was busy cooking; she wondered what he had done with his clothes. It was the second little jacket and pair of shoes that Peter had lost in a fortnight!

I am sorry to say that Peter was not very well during the evening.

His mother put him to bed, and made some camomile tea; and she gave a dose of it to Peter!

"One table-spoonful to be taken at bed-time."

But Flopsy, Mopsy, and Cotton-tail had bread and milk and blackberries for supper.

THE END

Daisy Ashford
1881–1972

The Young Visiters has been called "the greatest novel ever written by a nine-year-old." Margaret Mary ("Daisy") Ashford wrote the book in 1890, but it was not published for nearly thirty years, when the manuscript was rediscovered. Thanks in part to a preface by J. M. Barrie (the author of Peter Pan), it became an instant best-seller in 1919. By then in her late thirties, Ashford was able to marry on the proceeds; she lived a modest uneventful life until her death at ninety. She had written nothing since the age of thirteen, when she renounced her earlier ambition to become "an authoress." No one could quite believe that The Young Visiters had been produced by a child of nine: Winston Churchill, for one, was convinced that Barrie had written it himself, and a journalist is said to have chased the publisher down a London street shouting, "Did he or did she?" The novel is a comic masterpiece, an unintentionally hilarious portrait of late Victorian high life as seen from the nursery. The peregrinations of Mr. Salteena and Ethel are recounted with a mixture of exuberance, innocence, and misspelling. Ashford's readings of adult social codes are remarkably astute; she intuitively grasps the relationships between class and money, sex and social ambition.

from The Young Visiters; or, Mr Salteena's Plan
Quite a Young Girl

Mr Salteena was an elderly man of 42 and was fond of asking peaple to stay with him. He had quite a young girl staying with him of 17 named Ethel Monticue. Mr Salteena had dark short hair and mustache and wiskers which were very black and twisty. He was middle sized and he had very pale blue eyes. He had a pale brown suit but on Sundays he had a black one and he had a topper[1] every day as he thorght it more becoming. Ethel Monticue had fair hair done on the top and blue eyes. She had a blue velvit frock which had grown rarther short in the sleeves. She had a black straw hat and kid gloves.

One morning Mr Salteena came down to brekfast and found Ethel had come down first which was strange. Is the tea made Ethel he said rubbing his hands. Yes said Ethel and such a quear shaped parcel has come for you Yes indeed it was a quear shape parcel it was a hat box tied down very tight and a letter stuffed between the string. Well well said Mr Salteena parcels do turn quear I will read the letter first and so saying he tore open the letter and this is what it said

MY DEAR ALFRED.

I want you to come for a stop with me so I have sent you a top hat wraped up in tishu paper inside the box. Will you wear it staying with me because it is very uncommon. Please bring one of your young ladies whichever is the prettiest in the face.

I remain Yours truely
BERNARD CLARK

Well said Mr Salteena I shall take you to stay Ethel and fancy him sending me a top hat. Then Mr S. opened the box and there lay the most splendid top hat of a lovly rich tone rarther like grapes with a ribbon round compleat.

---

1. Top hat.

Well said Mr Salteena peevishly I dont know if I shall like it the bow of the ribbon is too flighty for my age. Then he sat down and eat the egg which Ethel had so kindly laid for him. After he had finished his meal he got down and began to write to Bernard Clark he ran up stairs on his fat legs and took out his blotter with a loud sniff and this is what he wrote

MY DEAR BERNARD

Certinly I shall come and stay with you next Monday I will bring Ethel Monticue commonly called Miss M. She is very active and pretty. I do hope I shall enjoy myself with you. I am fond of digging in the garden and I am parshial to ladies if they are nice I suppose it is my nature. I am not quite a gentleman but you would hardly notice it but cant be helped anyhow. We will come by the 3–15.

Your old and valud friend
ALFRED SALTEENA

Perhaps my readers will be wondering why Bernard Clark had asked Mr Salteena to stay with him. He was a lonely man in a remote spot and he liked peaple and partys but he did not know many. What rot muttered Bernard Clark as he read Mr Salteenas letter. He was rarther a presumshious man.

from *Starting Gaily*

When the great morning came Mr Salteena did not have an egg for his brekfast in case he should be sick on the jorney.

What top hat will you wear asked Ethel.

I shall wear my best black and my white alpacka coat to keep off the dust and flies replied Mr Salteena.

I shall put some red ruge on my face said Ethel because I am very pale owing to the drains in this house.

You will look very silly said Mr Salteena with a dry laugh.

Well so will you said Ethel in a snappy tone and she ran out of the room with a very superier run throwing out her legs behind and her arms swinging in rithum.

Well said the owner of the house she has a most idiotick run.

Presently Ethel came back in her best hat and a lovly velvit coat of royal blue. Do I look nice in my get up she asked.

Mr Salteena survayed her. You look rarther rash my dear your colors dont quite match your face but never mind I am just going up to say goodbye to Rosalind the housemaid.

Well dont be long said Ethel. Mr S. skipped upstairs to Rosalinds room. Goodbye Rosalind he said I shall be back soon and I hope I shall enjoy myself.

I make no doubt of that sir said Rosalind with a blush as Mr Salteena silently put 2/6 on the dirty toilet cover.

Take care of your bronkitis said Mr S. rarther bashfully and he hastilly left the room waving his hand carelessly to the housemaid.

Come along cried Ethel powdering her nose in the hall let us get into the cab. Mr Salteena did not care for powder but he was an unselfish man so he dashed into the cab. Sit down said Ethel as the cabman waved his whip you are standing on my luggage. Well I am paying for the cab said Mr S. so I might be allowed to put my feet were I like.

They traveled 2nd class in the train and Ethel was longing to go first but thought perhaps least said soonest mended. Mr Salteena got very excited in the train about his visit. Ethel was calm but she felt excited inside. Bernard has a big house said Mr S. gazing at Ethel he is inclined to be rich.

Oh indeed said Ethel looking at some cows flashing past the window. Mr S. felt rarther disheartened so he read the paper till the train stopped and the porters shouted Rickamere station. We had better collect our traps said Mr Salteena and just then a very exalted footman in a cocked hat and olive green uniform put his head in at the window. Are you for Rickamere Hall he said in impressive tones.

Well yes I am said Mr Salteena and so is this lady.

Very good sir said the noble footman if you will alight I will see to your luggage there is a convayance awaiting you.

Oh thankyou thankyou said Mr S. and he and Ethel stepped along the platform. Outside they found a lovely cariage lined with olive green cushons to match the footman and the horses had green bridles and bows on their manes and tails. They got gingerly in. Will he bring our luggage asked Ethel nervously.

I expect so said Mr Salteena lighting a very long cigar.

Do we tip him asked Ethel quietly.

Well no I dont think so not yet we had better just thank him perlitely.

Just then the footman staggered out with the bagage. Ethel bowed gracefully over the door of the cariage and Mr S. waved his hand as each bit of luggage was hoisted up to make sure it was all there. Then he said thankyou my good fellow very politely. Not at all sir said the footman and touching his cocked hat he jumped actively to the box.

I was right not to tip him whispered Mr Salteena the thing to do is to leave 2/6 on your dressing table when your stay is over.

Does he find it asked Ethel who did not really know at all how to go on at a visit. I beleeve so replied Mr Salteena anyhow it is quite the custom and we cant help it if he does not. Now my dear what do you think of the sceenery

Very nice said Ethel gazing at the rich fur rug on her knees. Just then the cariage rolled into a beautifull drive with tall trees and big red flowers growing amid shiny dark leaves. Presently the haughty coachman pulled up with a great clatter at a huge front door with tall pillers each side a big iron bell and two very clean scrapers. The doors flung open as if by majic causing Ethel to jump and a portly butler appeared on the scene with a very shiny shirt front and a huge pale face. Welcome sir he exclaimed good naturedly as Mr Salteena alighted rarther quickly from the viacle and please to step inside.

Mr Salteena stepped in as bid followed by Ethel. The footman again struggled with the luggage and the butler Francis Minnit by name kindly lent a hand. The hall was very big and hung round with guns and mats and ancesters giving it a gloomy but a grand air. The butler then showed them down a winding corridor till he came to a door which he flung open shouting Mr Salteena and a lady sir.

A tall man of 29 rose from the sofa. He was rarther bent in the middle with very nice long legs fairish hair and blue eyes. Hullo Alf old boy he cried so you have got here all safe and no limbs broken.

None thankyou Bernard replied Mr Salteena shaking hands and let me introduce Miss Monticue she is very pleased to come for this visit. Oh yes gasped Ethel blushing through her red ruge. Bernard looked at her keenly and turned a dark red. I am glad to see you he said I hope you will enjoy it but I have not arranged any partys yet as I dont know anybody.

Dont worry murmered Ethel I dont mix much in Socierty and she gave him a dainty smile.

* * *

I have given the best spare room to Miss Monticue said Bernard with a gallant bow and yours turning to Mr Salteena opens out of it so you will be nice and friendly both the rooms have big windows and a handsome view.

How charming said Ethel. Yes well let us go up replied Bernard and he led the way up many a winding stairway till they came to an oak door with some lovly swans and bull rushes painted on it. Here we are he cried gaily. Ethels room was indeed a handsome compartment with purple silk curtains and a 4 post bed draped with the same shade. The toilit set was white and mouve and there were some violets in a costly varse. Oh I say cried Ethel in supprise. I am glad you like it said Bernard and here we have yours Alf. He opened the dividing doors and portrayed a smaller but dainty room all in pale yellow and wild primroses. My own room is next the bath room said Bernard it is decerated dark red as I have somber tastes. The bath room has got a tip up bason and a hose thing for washing your head.

A good notion said Mr Salteena who was secretly getting jellus.

Here we will leave our friends to unpack and end this Chapter.

from *Mr Salteenas Plan*

Mr Salteena woke up rarther early next day and was supprised and delighted to find Horace the footman entering with a cup of tea.

Oh thankyou my man said Mr Salteena rolling over in the costly bed. Mr Clark is nearly out of the bath sir anounced Horace I will have great plesure in turning it on for you if such is your desire. Well yes you might said Mr Salteena seeing it was the idear and Horace gave a profound bow.

Ethel are you getting up shouted Mr Salteena.

Very nearly replied Ethel faintly from the next room.

I say said Mr Salteena excitedly I have had some tea in bed.

So have I replied Ethel.

Then Mr Salteena got into a mouve dressing goun with yellaw tassles and siezing his soap he wandered off to the bath room which was most sumpshous. It had a lovly white shiny bath and sparkling taps and several towels arrayed in readiness by thourghtful Horace. It also had a step for climbing up the bath and other good dodges of a rich nature. Mr Salteena washed himself well and felt very much better. After brekfast Mr Salteena asked Bernard if he could have some privite conversation with him. Well yes replied Bernard if you will come into my study we can have a few words.

Cant I come too muttered Ethel sulkily.

No my dear said Mr Salteena this is privite.

Perhaps later I might have a privite chat with you Miss Monticue said Bernard kindly.

Oh do lets said Ethel.

Then Bernard and Mr S. strolled to the study and sat upon two arm chairs. Fire away said Bernard lighting his pipe. Well I cant exactly do that said Mr Salteena in slow tones it is a searious matter and you can advise me as you are a thorugh gentleman I am sure.

Well yes said Bernard what can I do for you eh Alf?

You can help me perhaps to be more like a gentleman said Mr Salteena getting rarther hot I am quite alright as they say but I would like to be the real thing can it be done he added slapping his knees.

I dont quite know said Bernard it might take a good time.

Might it said Mr S. but I would slave for years if need be. Bernard scratched his head. Why dont you try the Crystal Pallace he asked several peaple Earls and even dukes have privite compartments there.[2]

But I am not an Earl said Mr Salteena in a purplexed tone.

True replied Bernard but I understand there are sort of students there who want to get into the War Office and notable banks.

Would that be a help asked Mr Salteena egerly.

Well it might said Bernard I can give you a letter to my old pal the Earl of Clincham who lives there he might rub you up and by mixing with him you would probably grow more seemly.

Oh ten thousand thanks said Mr Salteena I will go there as soon as it can be arranged if you would be so kind as to keep an eye on Ethel while I am away.

Oh yes said Bernard I may be running up to town for a few days and she could come too.

You are too kind said Mr Salteena and I dont think you will find her any trouble.

No I dont think I shall said Bernard she is a pretty girl cheerful and active. And he blushed rarther red.

[MR SALTEENA GOES TO THE CRYSTAL PALACE IN LONDON TO MEET THE EARL OF CLINCHAM]

The Earl gave a slight cough and gazed at Mr Salteena thourghtfully.

Have you much money he asked and are you prepared to spend a good deal.

Oh yes quite gasped Mr Salteena I have plenty in the bank and £10 in ready gold in my purse.

You see these compartments are the haunts of the Aristockracy said the earl and they are kept going by peaple who have got something funny in their family and who want to be less mere if you can comprehend.

Indeed I can said Mr Salteena.

Personally I am a bit parshial to mere people said his Lordship but the point is that we charge a goodly sum for our training here but however if you cant pay you need not join.

I can and will proclaimed Mr Salteena and he placed a £10 note on the desk. His Lordship slipped it in his trouser pocket. It will be £42 before I have done with you he said but you can pay me here and there as convenient.

Oh thankyou cried Mr Salteena.

Not at all said the Earl and now to bissness. While here you will live in compartments in the basement known as Lower Range. You will get many hints from the Groom of the Chambers as to clothes and ettiquett to menials. You will mix with me for grammer and I might take you out hunting or shooting sometimes to give you a few tips. Also I have lots of ladies partys which you will attend occasionally.

Mr Salteenas eyes flashed with excitement. I shall enjoy that he cried.

2. The Crystal Palace was a huge glass and iron structure in London designed to house the Great Exhibition of 1851 (see photo, page 459); it was not a palace where aristocrats had apartments.

from *A Gay Call*

[ETHEL GOES TO LONDON WITH BERNARD CLARK, THEN CALLS ON THE EARL]

What pleasant compartments you have cried Ethel in rarther a socierty tone.

Fairly so so responded the Earl do you live in London he added in a loud tone as someone was playing a very difficult peice on the piano.

Well no I dont said Ethel my home is really in Northumberland but I am at present stopping with Mr Clark at the Gaierty Hotel she continued in a somewhat showing off tone.

Oh I see said the earl well shall I introduce you to a few of my friends.

Oh please do said Ethel with a dainty blow at her nose.

The earl disserppeard into the madding crowd and presently came back with a middle aged gentleman. This is Lord Hyssops he said my friend Miss Monticue he added genially.

Ethel turned a dull yellow. Lord Hyssops she said in a faint voice why it is Mr Salteena I know him well.

Hush cried the Earl it is a title bestowd recently by my friend the Prince of Wales. Yes indeed murmered Mr Salteena deeply flabber-gasted by the ready wit of the earl.

Oh indeed said Ethel in a peevish tone well how do you come to be here.

I am stopping with his Lordship said Mr Salteena and have a set of compartments in the basement so there.

I dont care said huffy Ethel I am in handsome rooms at the Gaierty.

Nothing could be nicer I am sure struck in the earl what do you say Hyssops eh.

Doubtless it is charming said Mr Salteena who was wanting peace tell me Ethel how did you leave Bernard.

I have not left him said Ethel in an annoying voice I am stopping with him at the gaierty and we have been to lots of theaters and dances.

Well I am glad you are enjoying yourself said Mr Salteena kindly you had been looking pale of late.

No wonder in your stuffy domain cried Ethel well have you got any more friends she added turning to the earl.

Well I will see said the obliging earl and he once more disapeared.

I dont know why you should turn against me Ethel said Mr Salteena in a low tone.

Ethel patted her hair and looked very sneery. Well I call it very mysterious you going off and getting a title said Ethel and I think our friendship had better stop as no doubt you will soon be marrying a duchess or something.

Not at all said Mr Salteena you must know Ethel he said blushing a deep red I always wished to marry you some fine day.

This is news to me cried Ethel still peevish.

But not to me murmered Mr Salteena and his voice trembled in his chest. I may add that I have always loved you and now I seem to do so madly he added passionately.

But I dont love you responded Ethel.

But if you married me you might get to said Mr Salteena.

I think not replied Ethel and all the same it is very kind of you to ask me and she smiled more nicely at him.

This is agony cried Mr Salteena clutching hold of a table my life will be sour grapes and ashes without you.

Be a man said Ethel in a gentle whisper and I shall always think of you in a warm manner.

from *A Proposale*

Let us now bask under the spreading trees said Bernard in a passiunate tone.

Oh yes lets said Ethel and she opened her dainty parasole and sank down upon the long green grass. She closed her eyes but she was far from asleep. Bernard sat beside her in profound silence gazing at her pink face and long wavy eye lashes. He puffed at his pipe for some moments while the larks gaily caroled in the blue sky. Then he edged a trifle closer to Ethels form.

Ethel he murmured in a trembly voice.

Oh what is it said Ethel hastily sitting up.

Words fail me ejaculated Bernard horsly my passion for you is intense he added fervently. It has grown day and night since I first beheld you.

Oh said Ethel in supprise I am not prepared for this and she lent back against the trunk of the tree.

Bernard placed one arm tightly round her. When will you marry me Ethel he uttered you must be my wife it has come to that I love you so intensely that if you say no I shall perforce dash my body to the brink of yon muddy river he panted wildly.

Oh dont do that implored Ethel breathing rarther hard.

Then say you love me he cried.

Oh Bernard she sighed fervently I certinly love you madly you are to me like a Heathen god she cried looking at his manly form and handsome flashing face I will indeed marry you.

How soon gasped Bernard gazing at her intensly.

As soon as possible said Ethel gently closing her eyes.

My Darling whispered Bernard and he seiezed her in his arms we will be marrid next week.

Oh Bernard muttered Ethel this is so sudden.

No no cried Bernard and taking the bull by both horns he kissed her violently on her dainty face. My bride to be he murmered several times.

Ethel trembled with joy as she heard the mistick words.

Oh Bernard she said little did I ever dream of such as this and she suddenly fainted into his out stretched arms.

Oh I say gasped Bernard and laying the dainty burden on the grass he dashed to the waters edge and got a cup full of the fragrant river to pour on his true loves pallid brow.

She soon came to and looked up with a sickly smile Take me back to the Gaierty hotel she whispered faintly.

With plesure my darling said Bernard I will just pack up our viands ere I unloose the boat.

Ethel felt better after a few drops of champagne and began to tidy her hair while Bernard packed the remains of the food. Then arm in arm they tottered to the boat.

I trust you have not got an illness my darling murmured Bernard as he helped her in.

Oh no I am very strong said Ethel I fainted from joy she added to explain matters.

Oh I see said Bernard handing her a cushon well some people do he added kindly and so saying they rowed down the dark stream now flowing silently beneath a golden moon. All was silent as the lovers glided home with joy in their hearts and radiance on their faces only the sound of the mysterious water lapping against the frail vessel broke the monotony of the night.

So I will end my chapter.

How It Ended

Mr Salteena by the aid of the earl and the kindness of the Prince of Wales managed to get the job his soul craved and any day might be seen in Hyde park or Pickadilly galloping madly after the Royal Carrage in a smart suit of green velvit with knicker-bockers compleat. At first he was rarther terrified as he was not used to riding and he found his horse bumped him a good deal and he had to cling on desperately to its flowing main. At other times the horse would stop dead and Mr Salteena would use his spurs and bad languige with no avail. But he soon got more used to his fresh and sultry steed and His Royal Highness seemed satisfide.

The Earl continued his merry life at the Compartments till finally he fell in love with one of the noble ladies who haunted them. She was not so pretty as Ethel as she had rarther a bulgy figure and brown eyes but she had lovely raven tresses a pointed nose and a rose like complexion of a dainty hue. She had very nice feet and plenty of money. Her name was called Lady Helena Herring and her age was 25 and she mated well with the earl.

Mr Salteena grew very lonely after the earl was marrid and he could not bear a single life any more so failing Ethel he marrid one of the maids in waiting at Buck-ingham palace by name Bessie Topp a plesant girl of 18 with a round red face and rarther stary eyes.

So now that all our friends are marrid I will add a few words about their familys. Ethel and Bernard returned from their Honymoon with a son and hair a nice fat baby called Ignatius Bernard. They soon had six more children four boys and three girls and some of them were twins which was very exciting.

The Earl only got two rarther sickly girls called Helen and Marie because the last one looked slightly french.

Mr Salteena had a large family of 10 five of each but he grew very morose as the years rolled by and his little cottage was very noisy and his wife was a bit annoying at times especially when he took to dreaming of Ethel and wishing he could have mar-rid her. Still he was a pius man in his way and found relief in prayer.

Bernard Clark was the happiest of our friends as he loved Ethel to the bitter end and so did she him and they had a nice house too.

The Earl soon got tired of his sickly daughters and his wife had a savage temper so he thourght he would divorce her and try again but he gave up the idear after sev-eral attempts and decided to offer it up as a Mortification.[3]

So now my readers we will say farewell to the characters in this book.

1890   1919

Henry James
1845–1916

The expatriate American novelist Henry James spent most of his adult life in England and based many of his novels there. In *What Maisie Knew* (1897) he explores the consciousness

---

3. As a penance (for one's sins).

of a young girl confronted by the amorous entanglements of her divorced upper-middle-class parents, a self-absorbed and promiscuous pair who do not hesitate to use their daughter as a weapon against one another. Their behavior is "the tomb of Maisie's childhood." Maisie is vividly but unprotestingly aware of their neglect: the adult society observed by this fictive child is a far bleaker and more sordid place than the jolly world of grown-up romance imagined by the actual child Daisy Ashford. Yet Maisie transcends the abuse to which she is subjected, keeping—as James later wrote in his Preface—"the torch of virtue alive in an air tending infinitely to smother it" and sowing "on barren strands" "the seed of the moral life." In using a child's perspective, limited by its own innocence, to portray the perplexities and complexities of life, James had many Victorian predecessors, notably Charlotte Brontë in *Jane Eyre* (1847), Charles Dickens in *David Copperfield* (1849–1850), and George Eliot in *The Mill on the Floss* (1860). If the nineteenth century could lay claim to the Invention of Childhood, this fin-de-siècle satire, with its portrayal of the death of childhood, pronounces its ironic epitaph.

from What Maisie Knew
[PROLOGUE]

The litigation had seemed interminable and had in fact been complicated; but by the decision on the appeal the judgement of the divorce-court was confirmed as to the assignment of the child. The father, who, though bespattered from head to foot, had made good his case, was, in pursuance of this triumph, appointed to keep her: it was not so much that the mother's character had been more absolutely damaged as that the brilliancy of a lady's complexion (and this lady's, in court, was immensely remarked) might be more regarded as showing the spots. Attached, however, to the second pronouncement was a condition that detracted, for Beale Farange, from its sweetness—an order that he should refund to his late wife the twenty-six hundred pounds put down by her, as it was called, some three years before, in the interest of the child's maintenance and precisely on a proved understanding that he would take no proceedings: a sum of which he had had the administration and of which he could render not the least account. The obligation thus attributed to her adversary was no small balm to Ida's resentment; it drew a part of the sting from her defeat and compelled Mr Farange perceptibly to lower his crest. He was unable to produce the money or to raise it in any way; so that after a squabble scarcely less public and scarcely more decent than the original shock of battle his only issue from his predicament was a compromise proposed by his legal advisers and finally accepted by hers.

His debt was by this arrangement remitted to him and the little girl disposed of in a manner worthy of the judgement-seat of Solomon.[1] She was divided in two and the portions tossed impartially to the disputants. They would take her, in rotation, for six months at a time; she would spend half the year with each. This was odd justice in the eyes of those who still blinked in the fierce light projected from the tribunal—a light in which neither parent figured in the least as a happy

---

1. King Solomon of Israel proposed to solve a dispute over a baby claimed by two women by cutting the child in half (I Kings 3.16–28).

example to youth and innocence. What was to have been expected on the evidence was the nomination, *in loco parentis*,[2] of some proper third person, some respectable or at least some presentable friend. Apparently, however, the circle of the Faranges had been scanned in vain for any such ornament; so that the only solution finally meeting all the difficulties was, save that of sending Maisie to a Home, the partition of the tutelary office in the manner I have mentioned. There were more reasons for her parents to agree to it than there had ever been for them to agree to anything; and they now prepared with her help to enjoy the distinction that waits upon vulgarity sufficiently attested. Their rupture had resounded, and after being perfectly insignificant together they would be decidedly striking apart. Had they not produced an impression that warranted people in looking for appeals in the newspapers for the rescue of the little one—reverberation, amid a vociferous public, of the idea that some movement should be started or some benevolent person should come forward? A good lady came indeed a step or two: she was distantly related to Mrs Farange, to whom she proposed that, having children and nurseries wound up and going, she should be allowed to take home the bone of contention and, by working it into her system, relieve at least one of the parents. This would make every time, for Maisie, after her inevitable six months with Beale, much more of a change.

"More of a change?" Ida cried. "Won't it be enough of a change for her to come from that low brute to the person in the world who detests him most?"

"No, because you detest him so much that you'll always talk to her about him. You'll keep him before her by perpetually abusing him."

Mrs Farange stared. "Pray, then, am I to do nothing to counteract his villainous abuse of *me*?"

The good lady, for a moment, made no reply: her silence was a grim judgement of the whole point of view. "Poor little monkey!" she at last exclaimed; and the words were an epitaph for the tomb of Maisie's childhood. She was abandoned to her fate. What was clear to any spectator was that the only link binding her to either parent was this lamentable fact of her being a ready vessel for bitterness, a deep little porcelain cup in which biting acids could be mixed. They had wanted her not for any good they could do her, but for the harm they could, with her unconscious aid, do each other. She should serve their anger and seal their revenge, for husband and wife had been alike crippled by the heavy hand of justice, which in the last resort met on neither side their indignant claim to get, as they called it, everything. If each was only to get half this seemed to concede that neither was so base as the other pretended, or, to put it differently, offered them both as bad indeed, since they were only as good as each other. The mother had wished to prevent the father from, as she said, "so much as looking" at the child; the father's plea was that the mother's lightest touch was "simply contamination." These were the opposed principles in which Maisie was to be educated—she was to fit them together as she might. Nothing could have been more touching at first than her failure to suspect the ordeal that awaited her little unspotted soul. There were persons horrified to think what those in charge of it would combine to try to

2. In the place of a parent (Latin); to be responsible for a child.

make of it: no one could conceive in advance that they would be able to make nothing ill.

from Chapter 1

The child was provided for, but the new arrangement was inevitably confounding to a young intelligence intensely aware that something had happened which must matter a good deal and looking anxiously out for the effects of so great a cause. It was to be the fate of this patient little girl to see much more than she at first understood, but also even at first to understand much more than any little girl, however patient, had perhaps ever understood before. Only a drummer-boy in a ballad or a story could have been so in the thick of the fight. She was taken into the confidence of passions on which she fixed just the stare she might have had for images bounding across the wall in the slide of a magic lantern.[3] Her little world was phantasmagoric—strange shadows dancing on a sheet. It was as if the whole performance had been given for her—a mite of a half-scared infant in a great dim theatre. She was in short introduced to life with a liberality in which the selfishness of others found its account, and there was nothing to avert the sacrifice but the modesty of her youth.

Her first term was with her father, who spared her only in not letting her have the wild letters addressed to her by her mother: he confined himself to holding them up at her and shaking them, while he showed his teeth, and then amusing her by the way he chucked them, across the room, bang into the fire. Even at that moment, however, she had a scared anticipation of fatigue, a guilty sense of not rising to the occasion, feeling the charm of the violence with which the stiff unopened envelopes, whose big monograms—Ida bristled with monograms—she would have liked to see, were made to whizz, like dangerous missiles, through the air. The greatest effect of the great cause was her own greater importance, chiefly revealed to her in the larger freedom with which she was handled, pulled hither and thither and kissed, and the proportionately greater niceness she was obliged to show. Her features had somehow become prominent; they were so perpetually nipped by the gentlemen who came to see her father and the smoke of whose cigarettes went into her face. Some of these gentlemen made her strike matches and light their cigarettes; others, holding her on knees violently jolted, pinched the calves of her legs till she shrieked—her shriek was much admired—and reproached them with being toothpicks. The word stuck in her mind and contributed to her feeling from this time that she was deficient in something that would meet the general desire. She found out what it was; it was a congenital tendency to the production of a substance to which Moddle, her nurse, gave a short ugly name, a name painfully associated at dinner with the part of the joint that she didn't like. She had left behind her the time when she had no desires to meet, none at least save Moddle's, who, in Kensington Gardens, was always on the bench when she came back to see if she had been playing too far. Moddle's desire was merely that she shouldn't do that, and she met it so easily that the only spots

---

3. An early form of slide projector.

in that long brightness were the moments of her wondering what would become of her if, on her rushing back, there should be no Moddle on the bench. They still went to the Gardens, but there was a difference even there; she was impelled perpetually to look at the legs of other children and ask her nurse if *they* were toothpicks. Moddle was terribly truthful; she always said: "Oh my dear, you'll not find such another pair as your own." It seemed to have to do with something else that Moddle often said: "You feel the strain—that's where it is; and you'll feel it still worse, you know."

Thus from the first Maisie not only felt it, but knew she felt it. A part of it was the consequence of her father's telling her he felt it too, and telling Moddle, in her presence, that she must make a point of driving that home. She was familiar, at the age of six, with the fact that everything had been changed on her account, everything ordered to enable him to give himself up to her. She was to remember always the words in which Moddle impressed upon her that he did so give himself: "Your papa wishes you never to forget, you know, that he has been dreadfully put about." * * *

She had the knowledge that on a certain occasion which every day brought nearer her mother would be at the door to take her away, and this would have darkened all the days if the ingenious Moddle hadn't written on a paper in very big easy words ever so many pleasures that she would enjoy at the other house. These promises ranged from "a mother's fond love" to "a nice poached egg for your tea," and took by the way the prospect of sitting up ever so late to see the lady in question dressed, in silks and velvets and diamonds and pearls, to go out: so that it was a real support to Maisie, at the supreme hour, to feel how, by Moddle's direction, the paper was thrust away in her pocket and there clenched in her fist. The supreme hour was to furnish her with a vivid reminiscence, that of a strange outbreak in the drawing-room on the part of Moddle, who, in reply to something her father had just said, cried aloud: "You ought to be perfectly ashamed of yourself—you ought to blush, sir, for the way you go on!" The carriage, with her mother in it, was at the door; a gentleman who was there, who was always there, laughed out very loud; her father, who had her in his arms, said to Moddle: "My dear woman, I'll settle *you* presently!"—after which he repeated, showing his teeth more than ever at Maisie while he hugged her, the words for which her nurse had taken him up. Maisie was not at the moment so fully conscious of them as of the wonder of Moddle's sudden disrespect and crimson face; but she was able to produce them in the course of five minutes when, in the carriage, her mother, all kisses, ribbons, eyes, arms, strange sounds and sweet smells, said to her: "And did your beastly papa, my precious angel, send any message to your own loving mamma?" Then it was that she found the words spoken by her beastly papa to be, after all, in her little bewildered ears, from which, at her mother's appeal, they passed, in her clear shrill voice, straight to her little innocent lips. "He said I was to tell you, from him," she faithfully reported, "that you're a nasty horrid pig!"

1897

≈+ END OF PERSPECTIVES: IMAGINING CHILDHOOD +≈

Oscar Wilde

1854–1900

"He hasn't a single redeeming vice." Oscar Wilde's witticism hardly applied to himself: his character was a quixotic mixture of brilliance and folly. Flamboyant, extravagant, outrageous, the most splendid playwright of the century lived his own life on center stage. Though his flagrant self-promotion irritated many, he was generous and good-natured, unable to imagine that the Victorian morality he satirized would finally bring about his own fall.

Wilde was born in Dublin, and although he spent much of his adult life in England, he never lost the sense of himself as a foreigner. His parents—Irish Protestants, ardent nationalists, and prolific writers—were notable figures in their own right: Sir William Robert Wilde was a famous surgeon, fathered three illegitimate children, and was sued by a former patient who claimed he had drugged and raped her. Lady Wilde, who changed her name from Jane Frances to Speranza Francesca, was a self-dramatizing and unconventional woman whom her son adored.

Wilde was educated in Ireland until 1874 when he won a scholarship to Oxford. Here he began to establish a reputation as an Aesthete and an admirer of Pre-Raphaelite poets such as Swinburne, Rossetti, and William Morris. He was also attracted to the contradictory artistic creeds of both John Ruskin and Walter Pater, Ruskin proclaiming that all good art is moral art, Pater preferring "poetic passion, the desire of beauty, the love of art for art's sake." Wilde dressed ostentatiously, wore his hair long, and decorated his rooms with lilies, a favorite symbol of the Aesthetes. His literary abilities won him both the Newdigate Prize for poetry and a double first (highest honors). But along with these academic awards he was celebrated for a remark which seemed to epitomize aestheticism: "I find it harder and harder every day to live up to my blue china."

Following his triumphs at Oxford, Wilde cast about for a career. His father had died leaving only a small inheritance, and Wilde's attempts to win a university fellowship failed. In London he set about making himself conspicuous, and soon he was the center of the social scene. Few could help being dazzled by his witty conversation. Yet some were skeptical, including an actress who said: "What has he done, this young man, that one meets him everywhere? Oh yes he talks well, but what has he done? He has written nothing, he does not sing or paint or act—he does nothing but talk."

Wilde's talk, however, was glorious and eventually would find lasting expression in his plays. Meanwhile, he played the dandy, and was satirized by Gilbert and Sullivan in *Patience* (1881) as the most illustrious Aesthete of the day, who had walked "down Piccadilly with a poppy or a lily in his medieval hand." Wilde reacted with good humor, observing that "To have done it was nothing, but to make people think one had done it was a triumph."

In the early 1880s Wilde began to refute the charge that he did nothing but talk. He wrote his first play, called *Vera; or, The Nihilists* (1880), about Russian czars and revolutionaries; the play's portrayal of an assassination attempt made it politically unacceptable, and the production was canceled. He privately published a book of poems in 1881, opening with the sonnet *Hélas!* They were praised by Matthew Arnold and by Swinburne, but elsewhere denounced as immoral.

Wilde's finances received an unexpected boost when the New York production of *Patience* led to an invitation to lecture in the United States. His arrival in New York in 1882 was a media event: he was mobbed by reporters, and his every utterance was quoted or misquoted in both the American and British press. He was reported to have been disappointed in the Atlantic—"It is not so majestic as I expected"—and to have told the customs officers, "I have nothing to declare except my genius." He stayed a full year, earned quite a lot of money, and returned home internationally famous.

Wilde followed up his conquest of America with a few months in Paris, where he met many leading painters and writers. Back in London, and short of money once again, his

Oscar Wilde and Lord Alfred Douglas, 1893.

thoughts turned to marriage, and in 1884 he wed Constance Lloyd. She was well-educated and well-off, and at first Wilde enjoyed the new roles of husband and then father to two sons, Cyril and Vyvyan. But he soon found married life a bore. Even during his honeymoon in Paris his thoughts were elsewhere: he became enamored of a book known as the Bible of decadence, *A Rebours* (1884) by Joris-Karl Huysmans. As his biographer Richard Ellmann has put it, this book "summoned him towards an underground life."

Wilde was a celebrity. He spent several years lecturing and reviewing, then entered the most inventive period of his life. Although he would later remark, "I have put only my talent into my works. I have put my genius into my life," the creative work of the early 1890s belies him. He articulated his theories on Art and Nature in two dialogues full of provocative paradoxes, *The Decay of Lying* (1888) and *The Critic as Artist* (1890). Then in his essay *The Soul of Man Under Socialism* (1891) he argued that the final goal of social evolution was joyous individualism. He continued his exploration of the relation of art to life in his only novel, *The Picture of Dorian Gray* (1890), which tells of a promising golden boy fascinated by the seductively amoral ideas of a jaded cynic. Dorian makes a Faustian bargain: his corrupted soul will be mirrored, not in his own face—he remains eternally youthful—but in his portrait. Much influenced by *A Rebours*, *Dorian Gray* achieved instantaneous notoriety, not so much for its aestheticism as for its thinly veiled suggestions of homosexuality.

Lady Windermere's Fan (1891) met with the opposite reception: this sparkling comedy depicting a mother's secret sacrifice for her daughter was an immediate success. Inspired in part by the French symbolist poet, Stéphane Mallarmé, Wilde was also writing—in French—a very different play, *Salomé*, about the fatal perversity of love and desire. To Wilde's indignation, *Salomé* was banned in England. However, in 1894 he published an English translation, with dramatic and daring illustrations by Aubrey Beardsley.

Wilde wrote two more comedies, *A Woman of No Importance* and *An Ideal Husband*, followed by his masterpiece, *The Importance of Being Earnest* (1895). Its philosophy, Wilde said, is "That we should treat all trivial things very seriously, and all the serious things of life with sincere and studied triviality." The triumphant opening night of this delightfully sophisticated farce marked the culmination of Wilde's career.

Then, at the very crest of success, Wilde was brought down by catastrophe. Although homosexuality was a criminal offense in Britain, Wilde had made little effort to conceal his relations with younger men, particularly Lord Alfred Douglas. But if society turned a blind eye, Douglas's father, the Marquess of Queensberry, did not. He hounded his son's lover relentlessly, finally sending Wilde a ludicrously misspelled note calling him a "Somdomite." Egged on by Douglas, Wilde sued for libel. It was a fatal mistake. His private affairs were mercilessly exposed in court, and he lost the case. Wilde himself was then prosecuted for committing indecent acts, convicted, and sentenced to two years at hard labor.

His obsession with the young aristocrat—beautiful, vicious, and volatile—had been ruinous in every sense. Wilde was disgraced and bankrupted. So great was the collective repugnance for him that both of his currently running plays, *An Ideal Husband* and *The Importance of Being Earnest*, were obliged to close. But the nightmare was only beginning: following the public humiliation of the trials was the horror of prison. Confined in a small cell with a bare plank bed, revolting food, and no latrine, he suffered constantly from diarrhea. He was allowed only one twenty-minute visit every three months. No talking was permitted. Dreading that he might lose his sanity, Wilde pleaded in vain for early release.

He gave vent to his sufferings in a long letter to Douglas entitled *De Profundis*. It is a terrible indictment of Douglas's selfish behavior, but more than that it is an autobiography, the anguished confession of a soul coming face to face with itself. Painfully he reviews the events that led to his downfall, finding at last his own salvation in forgiveness: "I don't write this letter to put bitterness into your heart, but to pluck it out of mine. For my own sake I must forgive you." Wilde was allowed to take the letter with him when he left prison, but chose not to have it published until after his death.

Wilde emerged from the degradation of prison a broken and penniless man. He spent the remainder of his life in exile outside Britain. He was never again allowed to see his young sons, and their surname was changed to protect them from scandal. All but a few loyal friends shunned him. The man who had lavished champagne on his friends was reduced to scrounging drinks from strangers who pitied him. He was unable to resume his writing, except for *The Ballad of Reading Gaol* (1898), a long poem based upon his prison experience. He converted to Catholicism on his deathbed, in a Paris hotel, but continued bravely inventing witticisms to the end: "I am dying beyond my means."

Impression du Matin[1]

The Thames nocturne of blue and gold
   Changed to a harmony in gray:[2]
   A barge with ochre-coloured hay
Dropt° from the wharf: and chill and cold   *went downstream*

5   The yellow fog came creeping down
   The bridges, till the houses' walls

---

1. Impression of the morning (French). The title evokes the paintings of the French Impressionists and their attempts to show how light transforms the landscape. The group received its name in 1874 when a critic singled out Monet's *Impression: Sunrise* as representative.
2. The American James McNeill Whistler painted a series of Thames night scenes, called "nocturnes" (including the famous *Nocturne in Blue and Gold: Old Battersea Bridge*, c. 1875). He entitled some of his daytime scenes "harmonies." His close friendship with Wilde turned into a bitter rivalry by the mid-1880s; Whistler accused Wilde of plagiarizing his ideas.

Seemed changed to shadows and St. Paul's
Loomed like a bubble o'er the town.

10   Then suddenly arose the clang
        Of waking life; the streets were stirred
        With country wagons: and a bird
Flew to the glistening roofs and sang.

    But one pale woman all alone,
        The daylight kissing her wan hair,
15   Loitered beneath the gas lamps' flare,
With lips of flame and heart of stone.

1877   1881

Symphony in Yellow[1]

An omnibus across the bridge
    Crawls like a yellow butterfly,
And, here and there, a passer-by
    Shows like a little restless midge.

5 Big barges full of yellow hay
    Are moored against the shadowy wharf,
And, like a yellow silken scarf,
    The thick fog hangs along the quay.

    The yellow leaves begin to fade
10   And flutter from the Temple elms,[2]
And at my feet the pale green Thames
    Lies like a rod of rippled jade.

                                               1889

from The Decay of Lying[1]
An Observation

A dialogue. Persons: Cyril and Vivian.[2]

SCENE: *The library of a country house in Nottinghamshire.*

CYRIL (*coming in through the open window from the terrace*): My dear Vivian, don't coop yourself up all day in the library. It is a perfectly lovely afternoon. The air is exquisite. There is a mist upon the woods, like the purple bloom upon a plum. Let us go and lie on the grass, and smoke cigarettes, and enjoy Nature.

1. The title suggests Whistler's series of paintings that he called "symphonies" in various colors. The Aesthetic vogue for titles that mingle the arts originated with the French poet Théophile Gautier, who in 1852 named a poem *Symphony in White Major.* In the 1880s yellow—the color of sunflowers and paperback French novels—became associated with the Aesthetic movement.
2. The Middle Temple and Inner Temple form part of the Inns of Court; their garden runs down to the River Thames.
1. Published in January 1889 in *The Nineteenth Century,* then revised and reprinted in Wilde's *Intentions* (1891). This essay adopts the form of a Platonic dialogue in order

to reconsider Plato's famous assertion in *The Republic* that art is falsehood. Wilde agrees with Plato that the artist tells lies, but instead of finding this morally repugnant, he praises the artist's imaginative victory over nature and mere fact. Questioning Plato's claim that art is a shadowy reflection of real life, Wilde claims that art comes first: "life is the mirror, and art the reality." As he explores the paradoxes of his theory that life imitates art, Wilde seeks to shock his audience into revising its aesthetic values; he wittily subverts the Victorian reverence for nature, sincerity, moral teaching, and artistic verisimilitude.
2. Wilde's two sons, aged three and two at the time Wilde wrote this, were named Cyril and Vyvyan.

VIVIAN: Enjoy Nature! I am glad to say that I have entirely lost that faculty. People tell us that Art makes us love Nature more than we loved her before; that it reveals her secrets to us; and that after a careful study of Corot and Constable we see things in her that had escaped our observation. My own experience is that the more we study Art, the less we care for Nature. What Art really reveals to us is Nature's lack of design, her curious crudities, her extraordinary monotony, her absolutely unfinished condition. Nature has good intentions, of course, but, as Aristotle once said, she cannot carry them out.[3] When I look at a landscape I cannot help seeing all its defects. It is fortunate for us, however, that Nature is so imperfect, as otherwise we should have had no art at all. Art is our spirited protest, our gallant attempt to teach Nature her proper place. As for the infinite variety of Nature, that is a pure myth. It is not to be found in Nature herself. It resides in the imagination, or fancy, or cultivated blindness of the man who looks at her.

CYRIL: Well, you need not look at the landscape. You can lie on the grass and smoke and talk.

VIVIAN: But Nature is so uncomfortable. Grass is hard and lumpy and damp, and full of dreadful black insects. Why, even Morris' poorest workman[4] could make you a more comfortable seat than the whole of Nature can. Nature pales before the furniture of "the street which from Oxford has borrowed its name," as the poet you love so much once vilely phrased it.[5] I don't complain. If Nature had been comfortable, mankind would never have invented architecture, and I prefer houses to the open air. In a house we all feel of the proper proportions. Everything is subordinated to us, fashioned for our use and our pleasure. Egotism itself, which is so necessary to a proper sense of human dignity, is entirely the result of indoor life. Out of doors one becomes abstract and impersonal. One's individuality absolutely leaves one. And then Nature is so indifferent, so unappreciative. Whenever I am walking in the park here, I always feel that I am no more to her than the cattle that browse on the slope, or the burdock that blooms in the ditch. Nothing is more evident than that Nature hates Mind. Thinking is the most unhealthy thing in the world, and people die of it just as they die of any other disease. Fortunately, in England at any rate, thought is not catching. Our splendid physique as a people is entirely due to our national stupidity. I only hope we shall be able to keep this great historic bulwark of our happiness for many years to come; but I am afraid that we are beginning to be over-educated; at least everybody who is incapable of learning has taken to teaching—that is really what our enthusiasm for education has come to. In the meantime, you had better go back to your wearisome uncomfortable Nature, and leave me to correct my proofs.

CYRIL: Writing an article! That is not very consistent after what you have just said.

VIVIAN: Who wants to be consistent? The dullard and the doctrinaire, the tedious people who carry out their principles to the bitter end of action, to the *reductio ad absurdum* of practice. Not I. Like Emerson, I write over the door of my library the word "Whim."[6] Besides, my article is really a most salutary and valuable warning. If it is attended to, there may be a new Renaissance of Art.

---

3. In the *Poetics*, Aristotle suggests that, through mimesis or imitation of life, the artist completes nature's work.
4. William Morris employed skilled craftsmen to produce handmade furniture and textiles.
5. The goods sold on Oxford Street in London outshine the products of Wordsworth's beloved Nature. The line in Wordsworth's *The Power of Music* actually reads: "In the street that from Oxford hath borrowed its name."
6. Ralph Waldo Emerson, the American essayist, wrote in *Self-Reliance* (1841): "I shun father and mother and wife and brother when my genius calls me. I would write on the lintels of the doorpost, *Whim*."

CYRIL: What is the subject?

VIVIAN: I intend to call it "The Decay of Lying: A Protest."

CYRIL: Lying! I should have thought that our politicians kept up that habit.

VIVIAN: I assure you that they do not. They never rise beyond the level of misrepresentation, and actually condescend to prove, to discuss, to argue. How different from the temper of the true liar, with his frank, fearless statements, his superb irresponsibility, his healthy, natural disdain of proof of any kind! After all, what is a fine lie? Simply that which is its own evidence. If a man is sufficiently unimaginative to produce evidence in support of a lie, he might just as well speak the truth at once. No, the politicians won't do. Something may, perhaps, be urged on behalf of the Bar. The mantle of the Sophist[7] has fallen on its members. Their feigned ardours and unreal rhetoric are delightful. They can make the worse appear the better cause, as though they were fresh from Leontine schools,[8] and have been known to wrest from reluctant juries triumphant verdicts of acquittal for their clients, even when those clients, as often happens, were clearly and unmistakeably innocent. But they are briefed by the prosaic, and are not ashamed to appeal to precedent. In spite of their endeavours, the truth will out. Newspapers, even, have degenerated. They may now be absolutely relied upon. One feels it as one wades through their columns. It is always the unreadable that occurs. I am afraid that there is not much to be said in favour of either the lawyer or the journalist. Besides, what I am pleading for is Lying in art. Shall I read you what I have written? It might do you a great deal of good.

CYRIL: Certainly, if you give me a cigarette. Thanks. By the way, what magazine do you intend it for?

VIVIAN: For the *Retrospective Review*.[9] I think I told you that the elect had revived it.

CYRIL: Whom do you mean by "the elect"?

VIVIAN: Oh, The Tired Hedonists of course.[1] It is a club to which I belong. We are supposed to wear faded roses in our button-holes when we meet, and to have a sort of cult for Domitian.[2] I am afraid you are not eligible. You are too fond of simple pleasures.

CYRIL: I should be black-balled on the ground of animal spirits, I suppose?

VIVIAN: Probably. Besides, you are a little too old. We don't admit anybody who is of the usual age.

CYRIL: Well, I should fancy you are all a good deal bored with each other.

VIVIAN: We are. That is one of the objects of the club. Now, if you promise not to interrupt too often, I will read you my article.

CYRIL: You will find me all attention.

VIVIAN (*reading in a very clear, musical voice*): "THE DECAY OF LYING: A PROTEST.— One of the chief causes that can be assigned for the curiously commonplace character of most of the literature of our age is undoubtedly the decay of Lying as an art, a science, and a social pleasure. The ancient historians gave us delightful fiction in the form of fact; the modern novelist presents us with dull facts under the

---

7. The Sophists were Greek philosophers who taught the art of rhetoric; the word now refers to a deceptive reasoner.

8. Leontini was a Greek colony in Sicily where the sophist and rhetorician Gorgias (c. 483–375 B.C.) was educated.

9. A periodical, published in the 1820s and again in the

1850s, that promoted interest in earlier literature. It was not, in fact, revived in the 1890s.

1. Hedonists believe that pleasure is the greatest good in life; a tired hedonist would be one exhausted by pleasure (a parody of Wilde's own image).

2. Emperor of Rome (A.D. 81–96), Domitian was famous for his cruelty.

guise of fiction. The Blue-Book[3] is rapidly becoming his ideal both for method and manner. He has his tedious '*document humain,*'[4] his miserable little '*coin de la création,*' into which he peers with his microscope. He is to be found at the Librairie Nationale, or at the British Museum, shamelessly reading up his subject. He has not even the courage of other people's ideas, but insists on going directly to life for everything, and ultimately, between encyclopaedias and personal experience, he comes to the ground, having drawn his types from the family circle or from the weekly washerwoman, and having acquired an amount of useful information from which never, even in his most meditative moments, can he thoroughly free himself.

"The loss that results to literature in general from this false ideal of our time can hardly be overestimated. People have a careless way of talking about a 'born liar,' just as they talk about a 'born poet.' But in both cases they are wrong. Lying and poetry are arts—arts, as Plato saw, not unconnected with each other—and they require the most careful study, the most disinterested devotion. Indeed, they have their technique, just as the more material arts of painting and sculpture have, their subtle secrets of form and colour, their craft-mysteries, their deliberate artistic methods. As one knows the poet by his fine music, so one can recognize the liar by his rich rhythmic utterance, and in neither case will the casual inspiration of the moment suffice. Here, as elsewhere, practice must precede perfection. But in modern days while the fashion of writing poetry has become far too common, and should, if possible, be discouraged, the fashion of lying has almost fallen into disrepute. Many a young man starts in life with a natural gift for exaggeration which, if nurtured in congenial and sympathetic surroundings, or by the imitation of the best models, might grow into something really great and wonderful. But, as a rule, he comes to nothing. He either falls into careless habits of accuracy—"

CYRIL: My dear fellow!

VIVIAN: Please don't interrupt in the middle of a sentence. "He either falls into careless habits of accuracy, or takes to frequenting the society of the aged and the well-informed. Both things are equally fatal to his imagination, as indeed they would be fatal to the imagination of anybody, and in a short time he develops a morbid and unhealthy faculty of truth-telling, begins to verify all statements made in his presence, has no hesitation in contradicting people who are much younger than himself, and often ends by writing novels which are so like life that no one can possibly believe in their probability. This is no isolated instance that we are giving. It is simply one example out of many; and if something cannot be done to check, or at least to modify, our monstrous worship of facts, Art will become sterile, and Beauty will pass away from the land." * * *

* * * Believe me, my dear Cyril, modernity of form and modernity of subject-matter are entirely and absolutely wrong. We have mistaken the common livery of the age for the vesture of the Muses, and spend our days in the sordid streets and hideous suburbs of our vile cities when we should be out on the hillside with Apollo. Certainly we are a degraded race, and have sold our birthright for a mess of facts.[5]

---

3. Parliamentary reports. The whole passage is aimed at contemporary Realist and Naturalist novelists, such as George Gissing and Émile Zola, who sought to document everyday life, especially among the poor.
4. Human document, from the title of an essay by Zola,

who wrote in *What I Hate:* "A work of art is a nook of creation ("un coin de la création") seen from the perspective of a temperament."
5. When he was hungry, Esau sold his birthright to his brother Jacob for "a mess of pottage" (Genesis 25.30–34).

CYRIL: There is something in what you say, and there is no doubt that whatever amusement we may find in reading a purely modern novel, we have rarely any artistic pleasure in re-reading it. And this is perhaps the best rough test of what is literature and what is not. If one cannot enjoy reading a book over and over again, there is no use reading it at all. But what do you say about the return to Life and Nature? This is the panacea that is always being recommended to us.

VIVIAN: I will read you what I say on that subject. The passage comes later on in the article, but I may as well give it to you now:—

"The popular cry of our time is 'Let us return to Life and Nature; they will recreate Art for us, and send the red blood coursing through her veins; they will shoe her feet with swiftness and make her hand strong.' But, alas! we are mistaken in our amiable and well-meaning efforts. Nature is always behind the age. And as for Life, she is the solvent that breaks up Art, the enemy that lays waste her house."

CYRIL: What do you mean by saying that Nature is always behind the age?

VIVIAN: Well, perhaps that is rather cryptic. What I mean is this. If we take Nature to mean natural simple instinct as opposed to self-conscious culture, the work produced under this influence is always old-fashioned, antiquated, and out of date. One touch of Nature may make the whole world kin, but two touches of Nature will destroy any work of Art. If, on the other hand, we regard Nature as the collection of phenomena external to man, people only discover in her what they bring to her. She has no suggestions of her own. Wordsworth went to the lakes, but he was never a lake poet. He found in stones the sermons he had already hidden there.[6] He went moralizing about the district, but his good work was produced when he returned, not to Nature but to poetry. Poetry gave him "Laodamia," and the fine sonnets, and the great Ode,[7] such as it is. Nature gave him "Martha Ray" and "Peter Bell," and the address to Mr Wilkinson's spade.

CYRIL: I think that view might be questioned. I am rather inclined to believe in the "impulse from a vernal wood,"[8] though of course the artistic value of such an impulse depends entirely on the kind of temperament that receives it, so that the return to Nature would come to mean simply the advance to a great personality. You would agree with that, I fancy. However, proceed with your article.

VIVIAN (reading): "Art begins with abstract decoration, with purely imaginative and pleasurable work dealing with what is unreal and nonexistent. This is the first stage. Then Life becomes fascinated with this new wonder, and asks to be admitted into the charmed circle. Art takes life as part of her rough material, recreates it, and refashions it in fresh forms, is absolutely indifferent to fact, invents, imagines, dreams, and keeps between herself and reality the impenetrable barrier of beautiful style, of decorative or ideal treatment. The third stage is when Life gets the upper hand, and drives Art out into the wilderness. This is the true decadence, and it is from this that we are now suffering.

"Take the case of the English drama. At first in the hands of the monks Dramatic Art was abstract, decorative, and mythological. Then she enlisted Life in her service, and using some of life's external forms, she created an entirely new race of beings, whose sorrows were more terrible than any sorrow man has ever

---

6. "And this our life, exempt from public haunt, / Finds tongues in trees, books in the running brooks, / Sermons in stones, and good in every thing" (*As You Like It* 2.1.15–17).

7. Presumably Wordsworth's *Ode: Intimations of Immortal-*

ity. Vivian next mentions several distinctly lesser poems.

8. "One impulse from a vernal wood / May teach you more of man / Of moral evil and of good / Than all the sages can." From Wordsworth's *The Tables Turned.*

felt, whose joys were keener than lover's joys, who had the rage of the Titans[9] and the calm of the gods, who had monstrous and marvellous sins, monstrous and marvellous virtues. To them she gave a language different from that of actual use, a language full of resonant music and sweet rhythm, made stately by solemn cadence, or made delicate by fanciful rhyme, jewelled with wonderful words, and enriched with lofty diction. She clothed her children in strange raiment and gave them masks, and at her bidding the antique world rose from its marble tomb. A new Caesar stalked through the streets of risen Rome, and with purple sail and flute-led oars another Cleopatra passed up the river to Antioch.[1] Old myth and legend and dream took shape and substance. History was entirely re-written, and there was hardly one of the dramatists who did not recognize that the object of Art is not simple truth but complex beauty. In this they were perfectly right. Art itself is really a form of exaggeration; and selection, which is the very spirit of art, is nothing more than an intensified mode of over-emphasis.

"But Life soon shattered the perfection of the form. Even in Shakespeare we can see the beginning of the end. It shows itself by the gradual breaking up of the blank-verse in the later plays, by the predominance given to prose, and by the over-importance assigned to characterization. The passages in Shakespeare—and they are many—where the language is uncouth, vulgar, exaggerated, fantastic, obscene even, are entirely due to Life calling for an echo of her own voice, and rejecting the intervention of beautiful style, through which alone should Life be suffered to find expression. Shakespeare is not by any means a flawless artist. He is too fond of going directly to life, and borrowing life's natural utterance. He forgets that when Art surrenders her imaginative medium she surrenders everything. Goethe says, somewhere—

In der Beschränkung zeigt sich erst der Meister,[2]

"'It is in working within limits that the master reveals himself,' and the limitation, the very condition of any art is style. However, we need not linger any longer over Shakespeare's realism. The Tempest is the most perfect of palinodes.[3] All that we desired to point out was, that the magnificent work of the Elizabethan and Jacobean artists contained within itself the seeds of its own dissolution, and that, if it drew some of its strength from using life as rough material, it drew all its weakness from using life as an artistic method. As the inevitable result of this substitution of an imitative for a creative medium, this surrender of an imaginative form, we have the modern English melodrama. The characters in these plays talk on the stage exactly as they would talk off it; they have neither aspirations nor aspirates; they are taken directly from life and reproduce its vulgarity down to the smallest detail; they present the gait, manner, costume, and accent of real people; they would pass unnoticed in a third-class railway carriage. And yet how wearisome the plays are! They do not succeed in producing even that impression of reality at which they aim, and which is their only reason for existing. As a method, realism is a complete failure.

"What is true about the drama and the novel is no less true about those arts that we call the decorative arts. The whole history of these arts in Europe is the record of the struggle between Orientalism, with its frank rejection of imitation,

9. Mythological giants who were overthrown by the gods.
1. References to Shakespeare's Julius Caesar and Antony and Cleopatra.

2. From Nature and Art by Johann Wolfgang von Goethe (1749–1832).
3. A retraction or recantation.

its love of artistic convention, its dislike to the actual representation of any object in Nature, and our own imitative spirit. Wherever the former has been paramount, as in Byzantium, Sicily, and Spain, by actual contact, or in the rest of Europe by the influence of the Crusades, we have had beautiful and imaginative work in which the visible things of life are transmuted into artistic conventions, and the things that Life has not are invented and fashioned for her delight. But wherever we have returned to Life and Nature, our work has always become vulgar, common, and uninteresting. Modern tapestry, with its aërial effects, its elaborate perspective, its broad expanses of waste sky, its faithful and laborious realism, has no beauty whatsoever. The pictorial glass of Germany is absolutely detestable. We are beginning to weave possible carpets in England, but only because we have returned to the method and spirit of the East. Our rugs and carpets of twenty years ago, with their solemn depressing truths, their inane worship of Nature, their sordid reproductions of visible objects, have become, even to the Philistine,[4] a source of laughter. A cultured Mahomedan once remarked to us, "You Christians are so occupied in misinterpreting the fourth commandment that you have never thought of making an artistic application of the second."[5] He was perfectly right, and the whole truth of the matter is this: The proper school to learn art in is not Life but Art."

And now let me read you a passage which seems to me to settle the question very completely.

"It was not always thus. We need not say anything about the poets, for they, with the unfortunate exception of Mr Wordsworth, have been really faithful to their high mission, and are universally recognized as being absolutely unreliable. But in the works of Herodotus, who, in spite of the shallow and ungenerous attempts of modern sciolists[6] to verify his history, may justly be called the 'Father of Lies'; in the published speeches of Cicero and the biographies of Suetonius; in Tacitus at his best; in Pliny's *Natural History;* in Hanno's *Periplus;* in all the early chronicles; in the Lives of the Saints; in Froissart and Sir Thomas Mallory; in the travels of Marco Polo; in Olaus Magnus, and Aldrovandus, and Conrad Lycosthenes, with his magnificent *Prodigiorum et Ostentorum Chronicon;* in the autobiography of Benvenuto Cellini; in the memoirs of Casanuova; in Defoe's *History of the Plague;* in Boswell's *Life of Johnson;* in Napoleon's despatches, and in the works of our own Carlyle, whose *French Revolution* is one of the most fascinating historical novels ever written, facts are either kept in their proper subordinate position, or else entirely excluded on the general ground of dullness. Now, everything is changed. Facts are not merely finding a footing-place in history, but they are usurping the domain of Fancy, and have invaded the kingdom of Romance. Their chilling touch is over everything. They are vulgarizing mankind. The crude commercialism of America, its materializing spirit, its indifference to the poetical side of things, and its lack of imagination and of high unattainable ideals, are entirely due to that country having adopted for its national hero a man, who according to

4. In *Culture and Anarchy* (1869), Matthew Arnold used this term to refer to the materialistic and uncultured middle classes.
5. The Fourth Commandment is "Remember the Sabbath day, to keep it holy"; the Second is "Thou shalt not make unto thee any graven image, or any likeness of any thing that is in heaven above, or that is in the earth beneath, or that is in the water underneath the earth" (Exodus 20.4–5). Islamic art is traditionally decorative rather than imitative, in observance of the second commandment.
6. Know-it-alls.

his own confession, was incapable of telling a lie, and it is not too much to say that the story of George Washington and the cherry-tree has done more harm, and in a shorter space of time, than any other moral tale in the whole of literature."

CYRIL: My dear boy!

VIVIAN: I assure you it is the case, and the amusing part of the whole thing is that the story of the cherry-tree is an absolute myth. However, you must not think that I am too despondent about the artistic future either of America or of our own country. Listen to this:—

"That some change will take place before this century has drawn to its close we have no doubt whatsoever. Bored by the tedious and improving conversation of those who have neither the wit to exaggerate nor the genius to romance, tired of the intelligent person whose reminiscences are always based upon memory, whose statements are invariably limited by probability, and who is at any time liable to be corroborated by the merest Philistine who happens to be present, Society sooner or later must return to its lost leader, the cultured and fascinating liar. Who he was who first, without ever having gone out to the rude chase, told the wondering cavemen at sunset how he had dragged the Megatherium[7] from the purple darkness of its jasper cave, or slain the Mammoth in single combat and brought back its gilded tusks, we cannot tell, and not one of our modern anthropologists, for all their much-boasted science, has had the ordinary courage to tell us. Whatever was his name or race, he certainly was the true founder of social intercourse. For the aim of the liar is simply to charm, to delight, to give pleasure. He is the very basis of civilized society, and without him a dinner party, even at the mansions of the great, is as dull as a lecture at the Royal Society, or a debate at the Incorporated Authors, or one of Mr Burnand's farcical comedies.[8]

"Nor will he be welcomed by society alone. Art, breaking from the prison-house of realism, will run to greet him, and will kiss his false, beautiful lips, knowing that he alone is in possession of the great secret of all her manifestations, the secret that Truth is entirely and absolutely a matter of style; while Life—poor, probable, uninteresting human life—tired of repeating herself for the benefit of Mr Herbert Spencer,[9] scientific historians, and the compilers of statistics in general, will follow meekly after him, and try to reproduce, in her own simple and untutored way, some of the marvels of which he talks.

"No doubt there will always be critics who, like a certain writer in the *Saturday Review*, will gravely censure the teller of fairy tales for his defective knowledge of natural history,[1] who will measure imaginative work by their own lack of any imaginative faculty, and will hold up their inkstained hands in horror if some honest gentleman, who has never been farther than the yew-trees of his own garden, pens a fascinating book of travels like Sir John Mandeville, or, like great Raleigh, writes a whole history of the world, without knowing anything whatsoever about the past.[2] To excuse themselves they will try and shelter under the shield of him[3] who made Prospero the magician, and gave him Caliban and Ariel as his servants, who heard the Tritons blowing their horns round the coral reefs of the Enchanted Isle, and the fairies singing to each other in a wood near Athens, who led the

---

7. Large extinct animal.

8. Frances Cowley Burnand (1836–1917), editor of *Punch* and popular dramatist.

9. English philosopher and theorist of evolution (1820–1903).

1. Wilde alludes to an anonymous review of his fairy tale,

The Happy Prince.

2. Mandeville was the purported author of a highly fanciful medieval book of travels in the East; Sir Walter Raleigh published his *History of the World* in 1614.

3. I.e., Shakespeare. The sentence alludes to *The Tempest*, *A Midsummer Night's Dream*, and *Macbeth*.

phantom kings in dim procession across the misty Scottish heath, and hid Hecate in a cave with the weird sisters. They will call upon Shakespeare—they always do—and will quote that hackneyed passage about Art holding the mirror up to Nature, forgetting that this unfortunate aphorism is deliberately said by Hamlet in order to convince the bystanders of his absolute insanity in all art-matters."[4]

CYRIL: Ahem! Another cigarette, please.

VIVIAN: My dear fellow, whatever you may say, it is merely a dramatic utterance, and no more represents Shakespeare's real views upon art than the speeches of Iago represent his real views upon morals.[5] But let me get to the end of the passage: "Art finds her own perfection within, and not outside of, herself. She is not to be judged by any external standard of resemblance. She is a veil, rather than a mirror. She has flowers that no forests know of, birds that no woodland possesses. She makes and unmakes many worlds, and can draw the moon from heaven with a scarlet thread. Hers are the "forms more real than living man,"[6] and hers the great archetypes of which things that have existence are but unfinished copies. Nature has, in her eyes, no laws, no uniformity. She can work miracles at her will, and when she calls monsters from the deep they come. She can bid the almond tree blossom in winter, and send the snow upon the ripe cornfield. At her word the frost lays its silver finger on the burning mouth of June, and the winged lions creep out from the hollows of the Lydian hills. The dryads peer from the thicket as she passes by, and the brown fauns smile strangely at her when she comes near them. She has hawk-faced gods that worship her, and the centaurs gallop at her side."

CYRIL: I like that. I can see it. Is that the end?

VIVIAN: No. There is one more passage, but it is purely practical. It simply suggests some methods by which we could revive this lost art of Lying.

CYRIL: Well, before you read it to me, I should like to ask you a question. What do you mean by saying that life, "poor, probable, uninteresting human life," will try to reproduce the marvels of art? I can quite understand your objection to art being treated as a mirror. You think it would reduce genius to the position of a cracked looking-glass. But you don't mean to say that you seriously believe that Life imitates Art, that Life in fact is the mirror, and Art the reality?

VIVIAN: Certainly I do. Paradox though it may seem—and paradoxes are always dangerous things—it is none the less true that Life imitates art far more than Art imitates life. We have all seen in our own day in England how a certain curious and fascinating type of beauty, invented and emphasized by two imaginative painters,[7] has so influenced Life that whenever one goes to a private view or to an artistic salon one sees, here the mystic eyes of Rossetti's dream, the long ivory throat, the strange square-cut jaw, the loosened shadowy hair that he so ardently loved, there the sweet maidenhood of "The Golden Stair," the blossom-like mouth and weary loveliness of the "Laus Amoris," the passion-pale face of Andromeda, the thin hands and lithe beauty of the Vivien in "Merlin's Dream." And it has always been so. A great artist invents a type, and Life tries to copy it, to reproduce it in a popular form, like an enterprising publisher. Neither Holbein nor

---

4. Explaining why performers should not overact, Hamlet says: "For anything so o'erdone is [apart] from the purpose of playing, whose end, both at the first and now, was and is, to hold, as 't were, the mirror up to nature" (*Hamlet* 3.2.19–22).

5. Iago is the villain in Shakespeare's *Othello*.

6. Shelley, *Prometheus Unbound*, line 748.

7. The Pre-Raphaelites Dante Gabriel Rossetti and Edward Burne-Jones; Wilde lists typical features of Rossetti's works, followed by the titles of three of Burne-Jones's paintings.

Vandyck[8] found in England what they have given us. They brought their types with them, and Life with her keen imitative faculty set herself to supply the master with models. The Greeks, with their quick artistic instinct, understood this, and set in the bride's chamber the statue of Hermes or of Apollo, that she might bear children as lovely as the works of art that she looked at in her rapture or her pain. They knew that Life gains from Art not merely spirituality, depth of thought and feeling, soul-turmoil or soul-peace, but that she can form herself on the very lines and colours of art, and can reproduce the dignity of Pheidias as well as the grace of Praxiteles.[9] Hence came their objection to realism. They disliked it on purely social grounds. They felt that it inevitably makes people ugly, and they were perfectly right. We try to improve the conditions of the race by means of good air, free sunlight, wholesome water, and hideous bare buildings for the better housing of the lower orders. But these things merely produce health, they do not produce beauty. For this, Art is required, and the true disciples of the great artist are not his studio-imitators, but those who become like his works of art, be they plastic as in Greek days, or pictorial as in modern times; in a word, Life is Art's best, Art's only pupil. * * *

* * * All that I desire to point out is the general principle that Life imitates Art far more than Art imitates Life, and I feel sure that if you think seriously about it you will find that it is true. Life holds the mirror up to Art, and either reproduces some strange type imagined by painter or sculptor, or realizes in fact what has been dreamed in fiction. Scientifically speaking, the basis of life—the energy of life, as Aristotle would call it[1]—is simply the desire for expression, and Art is always presenting various forms through which this expression can be attained. Life seizes on them and uses them, even if they be to her own hurt. Young men have committed suicide because Rolla did so, have died by their own hand because by his own hand Werther died.[2] Think of what we owe to the imitation of Christ, of what we owe to the imitation of Caesar.

CYRIL: The theory is certainly a very curious one, but to make it complete you must show that Nature, no less than Life, is an imitation of Art. Are you prepared to prove that?

VIVIAN: My dear fellow, I am prepared to prove anything.

CYRIL: Nature follows the landscape painter then, and takes her effects from him?

VIVIAN: Certainly. Where, if not from the Impressionists,[3] do we get those wonderful brown fogs that come creeping down our streets, blurring the gas-lamps and changing the houses into monstrous shadows? To whom, if not to them and their master, do we owe the lovely silver mists that brood over our river, and turn to faint forms of fading grace curved bridge and swaying barge? The extraordinary change that has taken place in the climate of London during the last ten years is entirely due to this particular school of Art. You smile. Consider the matter from a scientific or a metaphysical point of view, and you will find that I am right. For what is Nature? Nature is no great mother who has borne us. She is our creation. It is in our brain that she quickens to life. Things are because we see them, and what we see, and how we see it, depends on the Arts that have influenced us. To

8. Hans Holbein the younger (c. 1497–1543) and Sir Anthony Van Dyke (1599–1641), Dutch portrait painters who greatly influenced English painters. Holbein became the court painter to Henry VIII, and Van Dyke became court painter under James I.
9. Ancient Greek sculptors.
1. In his *Physics*, Aristotle equates nature with energy.
2. Rolla is the Byronic hero of *Rolla* (1833), by the French poet Alfred de Musset; Werther is the romantic hero of Goethe's *The Sorrows of Young Werther* (1774).
3. French Impressionist painters such as Monet, Renoir, and Pissarro sought to capture the interplay of light, atmosphere, and the elements, but it was Whistler (probably the "master" alluded to in the next sentence) who discovered London fogs, barges, and misty bridges as artistic subjects.

look at a thing is very different from seeing a thing. One does not see anything until one sees its beauty. Then, and then only, does it come into existence. At present, people see fogs, not because there are fogs, but because poets and painters have taught them the mysterious loveliness of such effects. There may have been fogs for centuries in London. I dare say there were. But no one saw them, and so we do not know anything about them. They did not exist till Art had invented them. Now, it must be admitted, fogs are carried to excess. They have become the mere mannerism of a clique, and the exaggerated realism of their method gives dull people bronchitis. Where the cultured catch an effect, the uncultured catch cold. And so, let us be humane, and invite Art to turn her wonderful eyes elsewhere. She has done so already, indeed. That white quivering sunlight that one sees now in France, with its strange blotches of mauve, and its restless violet shadows, is her latest fancy, and, on the whole, Nature reproduces it quite admirably. Where she used to give us Corots and Daubignys, she gives us now exquisite Monets and entrancing Pisaros.[4] Indeed there are moments, rare, it is true, but still to be observed from time to ime, when Nature becomes absolutely modern. Of course she is not always to be relied upon. The fact is that she is in this unfortunate position. Art creates an incomparable and unique effect, and, having done so, passes on to other things. Nature, upon the other hand, forgetting that imitation can be made the sincerest form of insult, keeps on repeating this effect until we all become absolutely wearied of it. Nobody of any real culture, for instance, ever talks nowadays about the beauty of a sunset. Sunsets are quite old-fashioned. They belong to the time when Turner was the last note in art.[5] To admire them is a distinct sign of provincialism of temperament. Upon the other hand they go on. Yesterday evening Mrs Arundel insisted on my going to the window, and looking at the glorious sky, as she called it. Of course I had to look at it. She is one of those absurdly pretty Philistines, to whom one can deny nothing. And what was it? It was simply a very second-rate Turner, a Turner of a bad period, with all the painter's worst faults exaggerated and over-emphasized. Of course, I am quite ready to admit that Life very often commits the same error. She produces her false Renés and her sham Vautrins, just as Nature gives us, on one day a doubtful Cuyp, and on another a more than questionable Rousseau.[6] Still, Nature irritates one more when she does things of that kind. It seems so stupid, so obvious, so unnecessary. A false Vautrin might be delightful. A doubtful Cuyp is unbearable. However, I don't want to be too hard on Nature. I wish the Channel, especially at Hastings, did not look quite so often like a Henry Moore,[7] grey pearl with yellow lights, but then, when Art is more varied, Nature will, no doubt, be more varied also. That she imitates Art, I don't think even her worst enemy would deny now. It is the one thing that keeps her in touch with civilized man. But have I proved my theory to your satisfaction?

CYRIL: You have proved it to my dissatisfaction, which is better. But even admitting this strange imitative instinct in Life and Nature, surely you would acknowledge that Art expresses the temper of its age, the spirit of its time, the

4. Earlier in the century, Corot and Daubigny had painted muted landscapes; Wilde's contemporaries Claude Monet and Camille Pissarro produced bright, Impressionist canvasses.
5. The atmospheric landscape paintings of J. M. W. Turner (1775–1851) were much admired by Ruskin in *Modern Painters* (1843–1860).
6. François-René de Chateaubriand's *René* (1802) told

the story of a superior but sorrowful young man who flees to the wilderness of America to seek solitude; Vautrin, villain of a series of novels by Honoré de Balzac (1799–1850); Albert Cuyp (1620–1691), Dutch painter of wintry pastoral landscapes; Théodore Rousseau (1812–1867), French painter of the Barbizon school.
7. English painter (1831–1895) who specialized in seascapes.

moral and social conditions that surround it, and under whose influence it is produced.

VIVIAN: Certainly not! Art never expresses anything but itself. This is the principle of my new aesthetics; and it is this, more than that vital connection between form and substance, on which Mr Pater dwells,[8] that makes music the type of all the arts. Of course, nations and individuals, with that healthy natural vanity which is the secret of existence, are always under the impression that it is of them that the Muses are talking, always trying to find in the calm dignity of imaginative art some mirror of their own turbid passions, always forgetting that the singer of life is not Apollo, but Marsyas.[9] Remote from reality, and with her eyes turned away from the shadows of the cave,[1] Art reveals her own perfection, and the wondering crowd that watches the opening of the marvellous, many-petalled rose fancies that it is its own history that is being told to it, its own spirit that is finding expression in a new form. But it is not so. The highest art rejects the burden of the human spirit, and gains more from a new medium or a fresh material than she does from any enthusiasm for art, or from any lofty passion, or from any great awakening of the human consciousness. She develops purely on her own lines. She is not symbolic of any age. It is the ages that are her symbols.

Even those who hold that Art is representative of time and place and people, cannot help admitting that the more imitative an art is, the less it represents to us the spirit of its age. The evil faces of the Roman emperors look out at us from the foul porphyry and spotted jasper in which the realistic artists of the day delighted to work, and we fancy that in those cruel lips and heavy sensual jaws we can find the secret of the ruin of the Empire. But it was not so. The vices of Tiberius could not destroy that supreme civilization, any more than the virtues of the Antonines could save it.[2] It fell for other, for less interesting reasons. The sibyls and prophets of the Sistine may indeed serve to interpret for some that new birth of the emancipated spirit that we call the Renaissance; but what do the drunken boors and brawling peasants of Dutch art tell us about the great soul of Holland? The more abstract, the more ideal an art is, the more it reveals to us the temper of its age. If we wish to understand a nation by means of its art, let us look at its architecture or its music.

CYRIL: I quite agree with you there. The spirit of an age may be best expressed in the abstract ideal arts, for the spirit itself is abstract and ideal. Upon the other hand, for the visible aspect of an age, for its look, as the phrase goes, we must of course go to the arts of imitation.

VIVIAN: I don't think so. After all, what the imitative arts really give us are merely the various styles of particular artists, or of certain schools of artists. Surely you don't imagine that the people of the Middle Ages bore any resemblance at all to the figures on mediaeval stained glass, or in mediaeval stone and wood carving, or on mediaeval metal-work, or tapestries, or illuminated MSS.[3] They were probably very ordinary-looking people, with nothing grotesque, or remarkable, or fantastic in their appearance. The Middle Ages, as we know them in art, are simply a defi-

8. Walter Pater's views of art influenced Wilde; Vivian refers to Pater's *The School of Giorgione*, an essay added to *The Renaissance* in 1888, where Pater says, "All art constantly aspires towards the condition of music."
9. A flute player who challenged Apollo, the god of music, to a contest; he was defeated and flayed alive for his presumption.
1. In the *Republic*, Plato suggests that reality is to the

absolute what shadows in a cave are to the objects which cast the shadows—i.e., dim and imperfect indications.
2. Tiberius (44 B.C.–A.D. 37) was a cruel and lustful Roman emperor; Antoninus Pius and his son-in-law, the philosopher Marcus Aurelius, were later emperors noted for their wisdom and good character.
3. Manuscripts.

nite form of style, and there is no reason at all why an artist with this style should not be produced in the nineteenth century. No great artist ever sees things as they really are. If he did, he would cease to be an artist. Take an example from our own day. I know that you are fond of Japanese things. Now, do you really imagine that the Japanese people, as they are presented to us in art, have any existence? If you do, you have never understood Japanese art at all. The Japanese people are the deliberate self-conscious creation of certain individual artists. If you set a picture by Hokusai, or Hokkei,[4] or any of the great native painters, beside a real Japanese gentleman or lady, you will see that there is not the slightest resemblance between them. The actual people who live in Japan are not unlike the general run of English people; that is to say, they are extremely commonplace, and have nothing curious or extraordinary about them. In fact the whole of Japan is a pure invention. There is no such country, there are no such people. One of our most charming painters[5] went recently to the Land of the Chrysanthemum in the foolish hope of seeing the Japanese. All he saw, all he had the chance of painting, were a few lanterns and some fans. He was quite unable to discover the inhabitants, as his delightful exhibition at Messrs Dowdeswell's Gallery showed only too well. He did not know that the Japanese people are, as I have said, simply a mode of style, an exquisite fancy of art. And so, if you desire to see a Japanese effect, you will not behave like a tourist and go to Tokio. On the contrary, you will stay at home, and steep yourself in the work of certain Japanese artists, and then, when you have absorbed the spirit of their style, and caught their imaginative manner of vision, you will go some afternoon and sit in the Park or stroll down Piccadilly, and if you cannot see an absolutely Japanese effect there, you will not see it anywhere. Or, to return again to the past, take as another instance the ancient Greeks. Do you think that Greek art ever tells us what the Greek people were like? Do you believe that the Athenian women were like the stately dignified figures of the Parthenon frieze, or like those marvellous goddesses who sat in the triangular pediments of the same building? If you judge from the art, they certainly were so. But read an authority, like Aristophanes[6] for instance. You will find that the Athenian ladies laced tightly, wore high-heeled shoes, dyed their hair yellow, painted and rouged their faces, and were exactly like any silly fashionable or fallen creature of our own day. The fact is that we look back on the ages entirely through the medium of Art, and Art, very fortunately, has never once told us the truth.

CYRIL: But modern portraits by English painters, what of them? Surely they are like the people they pretend to represent?

VIVIAN: Quite so. They are so like them that a hundred years from now no one will believe in them. The only portraits in which one believes are portraits where there is very little of the sitter, and a very great deal of the artist. Holbein's drawings of the men and women of his time impress us with a sense of their absolute reality. But this is simply because Holbein compelled life to accept his conditions, to restrain itself within his limitations, to reproduce his type, and to appear as he wished it to appear. It is style that makes us believe in a thing—nothing but style. Most of our

4. Katsushika Hokusai (1760–1849) and Hokkei (1780–1850), Japanese artists.
5. Mortimer Menpes, Australian artist and disciple of

Whistler who gave a Japanese exhibition at Dowdeswell's Gallery in 1888.
6. Athenian satiric dramatist (c. 448–c. 380 B.C.).

modern portrait painters are doomed to absolute oblivion. They never paint what they see. They paint what the public sees, and the public never sees anything.

CYRIL: Well, after that I think I should like to hear the end of your article.

VIVIAN: With pleasure. Whether it will do any good I really cannot say. Ours is certainly the dullest and most prosaic century possible. * * * However, I must read the end of my article:—

"What we have to do, what at any rate it is our duty to do, is to revive this old art of Lying. Much of course may be done, in the way of educating the public, by amateurs in the domestic circle, at literary lunches, and at afternoon teas. But this is merely the light and graceful side of lying, such as was probably heard at Cretan dinner parties. There are many other forms. Lying for the sake of gaining some immediate personal advantage, for instance—lying with a moral purpose, as it is usually called—though of late it has been rather looked down upon, was extremely popular with the antique world. Athena laughs when Odysseus tells her 'his words of sly devising,' as Mr William Morris phrases it,[7] and the glory of mendacity illumines the pale brow of the stainless hero of Euripidean tragedy,[8] and sets among the noble women of the past the young bride of one of Horace's most exquisite odes.[9] Later on, what at first had been merely a natural instinct was elevated into a self-conscious science. Elaborate rules were laid down for the guidance of mankind, and an important school of literature grew up round the subject. Indeed, when one remembers the excellent philosophical treatise of Sanchez[1] on the whole question, one cannot help regretting that no one has ever thought of publishing a cheap and condensed edition of the works of that great casuist. A short primer, 'When to Lie and How,' if brought out in an attractive and not too expensive a form, would no doubt command a large sale, and would prove of real practical service to many earnest and deep-thinking people. Lying for the sake of the improvement of the young, which is the basis of home education, still lingers amongst us, and its advantages are so admirably set forth in the early books of Plato's Republic[2] that it is unnecessary to dwell upon them here. It is a mode of lying for which all good mothers have peculiar capabilities, but it is capable of still further development, and has been sadly overlooked by the School Board. Lying for the sake of a monthly salary is of course well known in Fleet Street, and the profession of a political leader-writer is not without its advantages. But it is said to be a somewhat dull occupation, and it certainly does not lead to much beyond a kind of ostentatious obscurity. The only form of lying that is absolutely beyond reproach is Lying for its own sake, and the highest development of this is, as we have already pointed out, Lying in Art. Just as those who do not love Plato more than Truth cannot pass beyond the threshold of the Academe,[3] so those who do not love Beauty more than Truth never know the inmost shrine of Art. The solid stolid British intellect lies in the desert sands like the Sphinx in Flaubert's marvel-

---

7. Wilde quotes Morris's translation of the Odyssey (bk. 13), where Odysseus lies to Athena, his patron goddess, when she appears to him in disguise.

8. In Euripides' Ion the hero lies about his parentage.

9. Horace tells how Hypermnestra saved her husband's life by warning him that her father, Danaus, was conspiring to kill him; thus she was "splendidly false / to her treacherous father" (Horace, Odes, 3.11.34–35; trans. by David Mulroy, 1994).

1. Fernando Sanchez, author of A Treatise on the Noble

and High Science of Nescience [Ignorance] (1581).

2. In Books 2 and 3, which discuss the education of the future Guardians of the ideal republic, Plato advocates suppressing stories that evoke the terror of death or that portray the gods as undignified or immoral.

3. A gibe at Plato's coercive method of teaching. Wilde reverses Aristotle's remark, "Plato is dear to me, but dearer still is truth." Plato's school in Athens was called the Academy because he taught his students in an olive grove dedicated to the hero Academus.

lous tale,[4] and fantasy, *La Chimère*, dances round it, and calls to it with her false, flute-toned voice. It may not hear her now, but surely some day, when we are all bored to death with the commonplace character of modern fiction, it will hearken to her and try to borrow her wings.

"And when that day dawns, or sunset reddens, how joyous we shall all be! Facts will be regarded as discreditable, Truth will be found mourning over her fetters, and Romance, with her temper of wonder, will return to the land. The very aspect of the world will change to our startled eyes. Out of the sea will rise Behemoth and Leviathan,[5] and sail round the high-pooped galleys, as they do on the delightful maps of those ages when books on geography were actually readable. Dragons will wander about the waste places, and the phoenix will soar from her nest of fire into the air. We shall lay our hands upon the basilisk, and see the jewel in the toad's head. Champing his gilded oats, the Hippogriff will stand in our stalls, and over our heads will float the Blue Bird singing of beautiful and impossible things, of things that are lovely and that never happen, of things that are not and that should be. But before this comes to pass we must cultivate the lost art of Lying."

CYRIL: Then we must certainly cultivate it at once. But in order to avoid making any error I want you to tell me briefly the doctrines of the new aesthetics.

VIVIAN: Briefly, then, they are these. Art never expresses anything but itself. It has an independent life, just as Thought has, and develops purely on its own lines. It is not necessarily realistic in an age of realism, nor spiritual in an age of faith. So far from being the creation of its time, it is usually in direct opposition to it, and the only history that it preserves for us is the history of its own progress. Sometimes it returns upon its footsteps, and revives some antique form, as happened in the archaistic movement of late Greek Art, and in the pre-Raphaelite movement of our own day. At other times it entirely anticipates its age, and produces in one century work that it takes another century to understand, to appreciate, and to enjoy. In no case does it reproduce its age. To pass from the art of a time to the time itself is the great mistake that all historians commit.

The second doctrine is this. All bad art comes from returning to Life and Nature, and elevating them into ideals. Life and Nature may sometimes be used as part of Art's rough material, but before they are of any real service to art they must be translated into artistic conventions. The moment Art surrenders its imaginative medium it surrenders everything. As a method Realism is a complete failure, and the two things that every artist should avoid are modernity of form and modernity of subject-matter. To us, who live in the nineteenth century, any century is a suitable subject for art except our own. The only beautiful things are the things that do not concern us. It is, to have the pleasure of quoting myself, exactly because Hecuba is nothing to us that her sorrows are so suitable a motive for a tragedy.[6] Besides, it is only the modern that ever becomes old-fashioned. M. Zola sits down to give us a picture of the Second Empire.[7] Who cares for the Second

---

4. *The Temptation of Saint Anthony* (1874) by French novelist Gustave Flaubert.

5. The hippopotamus and the whale in the Book of Job. The rest of the paragraph refers to fabulous mythical animals: the phoenix was a legendary bird that immolated itself on a pyre, then rose regenerated from the ashes; the basilisk was a reptile whose breath and glance were fatal; the hippogriff was part gryphon and part horse.

6. Hecuba, queen of Troy, lost her sons and her husband when the Greeks defeated Troy. Wilde alludes to a scene in *Hamlet* where an actor recites a speech about her suffering and Hamlet asks himself, "What's Hecuba to him, or he to Hecuba, / That he should weep for her?" (2.2.559–60).

7. In France, the period from 1852 to 1870.

Empire now? It is out of date. Life goes faster than Realism, but Romanticism is always in front of Life.

The third doctrine is that Life imitates Art far more than Art imitates Life. This results not merely from Life's imitative instinct, but from the fact that the self-conscious aim of Life is to find expression, and that Art offers it certain beautiful forms through which it may realize that energy. It is a theory that has never been put forward before, but it is extremely fruitful, and throws an entirely new light upon the history of Art.

It follows, as a corollary from this, that external Nature also imitates Art. The only effects that she can show us are effects that we have already seen through poetry, or in paintings. This is the secret of Nature's charm, as well as the explanation of Nature's weakness.

The final revelation is that Lying, the telling of beautiful untrue things, is the proper aim of Art. But of this I think I have spoken at sufficient length. And now let us go out on the terrace, where "droops the milk-white peacock like a ghost,"[8] while the evening star "washes the dusk with silver."[9] At twilight nature becomes a wonderfully suggestive effect, and is not without loveliness, though perhaps its chief use is to illustrate quotations from the poets. Come! We have talked long enough.

1889, 1891

Preface to *The Picture of Dorian Gray*[1]

The artist is the creator of beautiful things.

To reveal art and conceal the artist is art's aim.

The critic is he who can translate into another manner or a new material his impression of beautiful things.

The highest as the lowest form of criticism is a mode of autobiography.

Those who find ugly meanings in beautiful things are corrupt without being charming. This is a fault.

Those who find beautiful meanings in beautiful things are the cultivated. For these there is hope.

They are the elect to whom beautiful things mean only Beauty.

There is no such thing as a moral or an immoral book.

Books are well written, or badly written. That is all.

The nineteenth century dislike of Realism is the rage of Caliban[2] seeing his own face in a glass.

The nineteenth century dislike of Romanticism is the rage of Caliban not seeing his own face in a glass.

The moral life of man forms part of the subject-matter of the artist, but the morality of art consists in the perfect use of an imperfect medium.

No artist desires to prove anything. Even things that are true can be proved.

---

8. From Tennyson's *The Princess* (1847).

9. From Blake's *To the Evening Star* (1783).

1. When Wilde's novel *Dorian Gray* first appeared in *Lippincott's Monthly Magazine* in July 1890, it scandalized readers with its portrayal of a cruelly hedonistic young man who remains unblemished by his crimes while his portrait ages hideously. Responding to his critics' charges that the novel fostered immoral ideas, Wilde published the preface separately in *The Fortnightly Review* in March 1891. He then added it to the revised novel when it came out in book form a month later. In its defiant tone and "art for art's sake" insistence that literature has no moral content, Wilde's preface echoes Théophile Gautier's preface to *Mademoiselle de Maupin* (1835), a founding text of the Aesthetic movement.

2. In Shakespeare's *The Tempest*, the "monster" Caliban is the offspring of the witch Sycorax and is a native of Prospero's island.

No artist has ethical sympathies. An ethical sympathy in an artist is an unpardonable mannerism of style.

No artist is ever morbid. The artist can express everything.

Thought and language are to the artist instruments of an art.

Vice and virtue are to the artist materials for an art.

From the point of view of form, the type of all the arts is the art of the musician. From the point of view of feeling, the actor's craft is the type.

All art is at once surface and symbol.

Those who go beneath the surface do so at their peril.

Those who read the symbol do so at their peril.

It is the spectator, and not life, that art really mirrors.

Diversity of opinion about a work of art shows that the work is new, complex, and vital.

When critics disagree the artist is in accord with himself.

We can forgive a man for making a useful thing as long as he does not admire it. The only excuse for making a useless thing is that one admires it intensely.

All art is quite useless.

Oscar Wilde

THE IMPORTANCE OF BEING EARNEST   Wilde's last play, *The Importance of Being Earnest,* is one of the great comedies in the English language. Fast-paced and sparkling, the play opened on 14 February 1895, to widespread acclaim. But it was forced to close less than three months later, amidst the scandal surrounding Wilde's trials for sodomy in April 1895. Eventually, however, the play's reputation was firmly established, and Wilde's witty masterpiece took its place in an Anglo-Irish tradition of classic comedies that includes Goldsmith's *She Stoops to Conquer,* Sheridan's *The Rivals,* and Synge's *Playboy of the Western World.* The title alludes to the Victorian obsession with earnestness as both character trait and moral ideal. The play's philosophy, Wilde claimed, was that "We should treat all the trivial things of life seriously, and all the serious things of life with sincere and studied triviality." In the dandified world of this drama, paying scrupulous attention to surfaces is an act of the deepest sincerity.

Wilde drafted the play in four acts, then at the request of the producer revised it to a tauter three-act version that has become the standard text for performance and reading. Formally, *The Importance of Being Earnest* shows the clever construction and neat resolution popular in nineteenth-century British and French drama. But it also fulfills the classical definition of comedy as beginning in error and confusion, and ending in knowledge, recognition, and self-discovery. Questioning social hierarchies based on birth, the plot turns on the mysteries of social and personal identity: "Would you kindly inform me who I am?" asks Jack Worthing at the play's climactic moment.

To explore the fictions of personality, Wilde meticulously sketches the trivialities that constitute social ritual and class distinction. From cucumber sandwiches at the start of the play to champagne and muffins in Act 3, the way Wilde's well-bred sophisticates consume food and drink becomes evidence of their character, emotional state, and social status. While the rigid conventions of this world apparently force young men like Jack and Algy to live double lives, they freely exploit their fictive selves as events dictate. Yet they are easily stage-managed by the women they love. Gwendolen and Cecily, who are more preoccupied with writing in their diaries than with the events they record in them, deploy their self-conscious sexual innocence to make life and love conform to the conventions of literature. *The Importance of Being Earnest* presents life as an aesthetic spectacle, in which the careful observation of outward form is the truest path toward an ironic authenticity and self-fulfillment.

"If I were asked of myself as a dramatist," Wilde mused, "I would say that my unique position was that I had taken the Drama, the most objective form known to art, and made it as personal a mode of expression as the Lyric or the Sonnet, while enlarging the characterization of the stage." Wilde refashioned the late-Victorian theater in his own image through the self-conscious brilliance of his language and the outrageousness of his comic invention. He delighted in artifice and exaggeration for their own sake. As he argued in *The Decay of Lying*, art is not an imitation of life but a more aesthetically satisfying restructuring of it. With droll wordplay, paradox, and ridiculous coincidence casting existential dilemmas into comic relief, *The Importance of Being Earnest* anticipates the modern Theater of the Absurd; it heralds the profound slapstick of Pirandello, Ionesco, Beckett, and Stoppard.

The Importance of Being Earnest
A Trivial Comedy for Serious People

FIRST ACT

SCENE: *Morning-room in Algernon's flat in Half Moon Street.*[1] *The room is luxuriously and artistically furnished. The sound of a piano is heard in the adjoining room.*

[*Lane is arranging afternoon tea on the table, and after the music has ceased, Algernon enters.*]

ALGERNON: Did you hear what I was playing, Lane?

LANE: I didn't think it polite to listen, sir.

ALGERNON: I'm sorry for that, for your sake. I don't play accurately—anyone can play accurately—but I play with wonderful expression. As far as the piano is concerned, sentiment is my forte. I keep science for Life.

LANE: Yes, sir.

ALGERNON: And, speaking of the science of Life, have you got the cucumber sandwiches cut for Lady Bracknell?

LANE: Yes, sir. [*Hands them on a salver.*]

ALGERNON [*inspects them, takes two, and sits down on the sofa*]: Oh! . . . by the way, Lane, I see from your book that on Thursday night, when Lord Shoreham and Mr Worthing were dining with me, eight bottles of champagne are entered as having been consumed.

LANE: Yes, sir; eight bottles and a pint.

ALGERNON: Why is it that at a bachelor's establishment the servants invariably drink the champagne? I ask merely for information.

LANE: I attribute it to the superior quality of the wine, sir. I have often observed that in married households the champagne is rarely of a first-rate brand.

ALGERNON: Good Heavens! Is marriage so demoralizing as that?

LANE: I believe it *is* a very pleasant state, sir. I have had very little experience of it myself up to the present. I have only been married once. That was in consequence of a misunderstanding between myself and a young person.

ALGERNON [*languidly*]: I don't know that I am much interested in your family life, Lane.

LANE: No, sir; it is not a very interesting subject. I never think of it myself.

ALGERNON: Very natural, I am sure. That will do, Lane, thank you.

---

1. A fashionable address in the West End of London.

LANE: Thank you, sir. [*Lane goes out.*]

ALGERNON: Lane's views on marriage seem somewhat lax. Really, if the lower orders don't set us a good example, what on earth is the use of them? They seem, as a class, to have absolutely no sense of moral responsibility.

[*Enter Lane.*]

LANE: Mr Ernest Worthing.

[*Enter Jack. Lane goes out.*]

ALGERNON: How are you, my dear Ernest? What brings you up to town?

JACK: Oh, pleasure, pleasure! What else should bring one anywhere? Eating as usual, I see, Algy!

ALGERNON [*stiffly*]: I believe it is customary in good society to take some slight refreshment at five o'clock. Where have you been since last Thursday?

JACK [*sitting down on the sofa*]: In the country.

ALGERNON: What on earth do you do there?

JACK [*pulling off his gloves*]: When one is in town one amuses oneself. When one is in the country one amuses other people. It is excessively boring.

ALGERNON: And who are the people you amuse?

JACK [*airily*]: Oh, neighbours, neighbours.

ALGERNON: Got nice neighbours in your part of Shropshire?[2]

JACK: Perfectly horrid! Never speak to one of them.

ALGERNON: How immensely you must amuse them! [*Goes over and takes sandwich.*] By the way, Shropshire is your county, is it not?

JACK: Eh? Shropshire? Yes, of course. Hallo! Why all these cups? Why cucumber sandwiches? Why such reckless extravagance in one so young? Who is coming to tea?

ALGERNON: Oh! merely Aunt Augusta and Gwendolen.

JACK: How perfectly delightful!

ALGERNON: Yes, that is all very well; but I am afraid Aunt Augusta won't quite approve of your being here.

JACK: May I ask why?

ALGERNON: My dear fellow, the way you flirt with Gwendolen is perfectly disgraceful. It is almost as bad as the way Gwendolen flirts with you.

JACK: I am in love with Gwendolen. I have come up to town expressly to propose to her.

ALGERNON: I thought you had come up for pleasure? . . . I call that business.

JACK: How utterly unromantic you are!

ALGERNON: I really don't see anything romantic in proposing. It is very romantic to be in love. But there is nothing romantic about a definite proposal. Why, one may be accepted. One usually is, I believe. Then the excitement is all over. The very essence of romance is uncertainty. If I ever get married, I'll certainly try to forget the fact.

JACK: I have no doubt about that, dear Algy. The Divorce Court was specially invented for people whose memories are so curiously constituted.

ALGERNON: Oh! there is no use speculating on that subject. Divorces are made in Heaven—[*Jack puts out his hand to take a sandwich. Algernon at once interferes.*] Please don't touch the cucumber sandwiches. They are ordered specially for Aunt Augusta. [*Takes one and eats it.*]

JACK: Well, you have been eating them all the time.

---

2. Worthing's estate is actually in Hertfordshire, which is a long way from Shropshire.

ALGERNON: That is quite a different matter. She is my aunt. [*Takes plate from below.*] Have some bread and butter. The bread and butter is for Gwendolen. Gwendolen is devoted to bread and butter.

JACK [*advancing to table and helping himself*]: And very good bread and butter it is too.

ALGERNON: Well, my dear fellow, you need not eat as if you were going to eat it all. You behave as if you were married to her already. You are not married to her already, and I don't think you ever will be.

JACK: Why on earth do you say that?

ALGERNON: Well, in the first place girls never marry the men they flirt with. Girls don't think it right.

JACK: Oh, that is nonsense!

ALGERNON: It isn't. It is a great truth. It accounts for the extraordinary number of bachelors that one sees all over the place. In the second place, I don't give my consent.

JACK: Your consent!

ALGERNON: My dear fellow, Gwendolen is my first cousin. And before I allow you to marry her, you will have to clear up the whole question of Cecily. [*Rings bell.*]

JACK: Cecily! What on earth do you mean? What do you mean, Algy, by Cecily? I don't know anyone of the name of Cecily.

[*Enter Lane.*]

ALGERNON: Bring me that cigarette case Mr Worthing left in the smoking-room the last time he dined here.

LANE: Yes, sir. [*Lane goes out.*]

JACK: Do you mean to say you have had my cigarette case all this time? I wish to goodness you had let me know. I have been writing frantic letters to Scotland Yard[3] about it. I was very nearly offering a large reward.

ALGERNON: Well, I wish you would offer one. I happen to be more than usually hard up.

JACK: There is no good offering a large reward now that the thing is found.

[*Enter Lane with the cigarette case on a salver. Algernon takes it at once. Lane goes out.*]

ALGERNON: I think that is rather mean of you, Ernest, I must say. [*Opens case and examines it.*] However, it makes no matter, for, now that I look at the inscription inside, I find that the thing isn't yours after all.

JACK: Of course it's mine. [*Moving to him.*] You have seen me with it a hundred times, and you have no right whatsoever to read what is written inside. It is a very ungentlemanly thing to read a private cigarette case.

ALGERNON: Oh! it is absurd to have a hard-and-fast rule about what one should read and what one shouldn't. More than half of modern culture depends on what one shouldn't read.

JACK: I am quite aware of the fact, and I don't propose to discuss modern culture. It isn't the sort of thing one should talk of in private. I simply want my cigarette case back.

ALGERNON: Yes; but this isn't your cigarette case. This cigarette case is a present from someone of the name of Cecily, and you said you didn't know anyone of that name.

JACK: Well, if you want to know, Cecily happens to be my aunt.

ALGERNON: Your aunt!

---

3. London police headquarters.

JACK: Yes. Charming old lady she is, too. Lives at Tunbridge Wells.[4] Just give it back to me, Algy.

ALGERNON [*retreating to back of sofa*]: But why does she call herself little Cecily if she is your aunt and lives at Tunbridge Wells? [*Reading.*] "From little Cecily with her fondest love."

JACK [*moving to sofa and kneeling upon it*]: My dear fellow, what on earth is there in that? Some aunts are tall, some aunts are not tall. That is a matter that surely an aunt may be allowed to decide for herself. You seem to think that every aunt should be exactly like your aunt! That is absurd! For Heaven's sake give me back my cigarette case. [*Follows Algernon round the room.*]

ALGERNON: Yes. But why does your aunt call you her uncle? "From little Cecily, with her fondest love to her dear Uncle Jack." There is no objection, I admit, to an aunt being a small aunt, but why an aunt, no matter what her size may be, should call her own nephew her uncle, I can't quite make out. Besides, your name isn't Jack at all; it is Ernest.

JACK: It isn't Ernest; it's Jack.

ALGERNON: You have always told me it was Ernest. I have introduced you to everyone as Ernest. You answer to the name of Ernest. You look as if your name was Ernest. You are the most earnest looking person I ever saw in my life. It is perfectly absurd your saying that your name isn't Ernest. It's on your cards. Here is one of them. [*Taking it from case.*] "Mr Ernest Worthing, B. 4, The Albany." I'll keep this as a proof that your name is Ernest if ever you attempt to deny it to me, or to Gwendolen, or to anyone else. [*Puts the card in his pocket.*]

JACK: Well, my name is Ernest in town and Jack in the country, and the cigarette case was given to me in the country.

ALGERNON: Yes, but that does not account for the fact that your small Aunt Cecily, who lives at Tunbridge Wells, calls you her dear uncle. Come, old boy, you had much better have the thing out at once.

JACK: My dear Algy, you talk exactly as if you were a dentist. It is very vulgar to talk like a dentist when one isn't a dentist. It produces a false impression.

ALGERNON: Well, that is exactly what dentists always do. Now, go on! Tell me the whole thing. I may mention that I have always suspected you of being a confirmed and secret Bunburyist, and I am quite sure of it now.

JACK: Bunburyist? What on earth do you mean by a Bunburyist?

ALGERNON: I'll reveal to you the meaning of that incomparable expression as soon as you are kind enough to inform me why you are Ernest in town and Jack in the country.

JACK: Well, produce my cigarette case first.

ALGERNON: Here it is. [*Hands cigarette case.*] Now produce your explanation, and pray make it improbable. [*Sits on sofa.*]

JACK: My dear fellow, there is nothing improbable about my explanation at all. In fact it's perfectly ordinary. Old Mr Thomas Cardew, who adopted me when I was a little boy, made me in his will guardian to his granddaughter, Miss Cecily Cardew. Cecily who addresses me as her uncle from motives of respect that you could not possibly appreciate, lives at my place in the country under the charge of her admirable governess, Miss Prism.

ALGERNON: Where is that place in the country, by the way?

4. A fashionable resort.

JACK: That is nothing to you, dear boy. You are not going to be invited. . . . I may tell you candidly that the place is not in Shropshire.

ALGERNON: I suspected that, my dear fellow! I have Bunburyed all over Shropshire on two separate occasions. Now, go on. Why are you Ernest in town and Jack in the country?

JACK: My dear Algy, I don't know whether you will be able to understand my real motives. You are hardly serious enough. When one is placed in the position of guardian, one has to adopt a very high moral tone on all subjects. It's one's duty to do so. And as a high moral tone can hardly be said to conduce very much to either one's health or one's happiness, in order to get up to town I have always pretended to have a younger brother of the name of Ernest, who lives in the Albany, and gets into the most dreadful scrapes. That, my dear Algy, is the whole truth pure and simple.

ALGERNON: The truth is rarely pure and never simple. Modern life would be very tedious if it were either, and modern literature a complete impossibility!

JACK: That wouldn't be at all a bad thing.

ALGERNON: Literary criticism is not your forte, my dear fellow. Don't try it. You should leave that to people who haven't been at a University. They do it so well in the daily papers. What you really are is a Bunburyist. I was quite right in saying you were a Bunburyist. You are one of the most advanced Bunburyists I know.

JACK: What on earth do you mean?

ALGERNON: You have invented a very useful younger brother called Ernest, in order that you may be able to come up to town as often as you like. I have invented an invaluable permanent invalid called Bunbury, in order that I may be able to go down into the country whenever I choose. Bunbury is perfectly invaluable. If it wasn't for Bunbury's extraordinary bad health, for instance, I wouldn't be able to dine with you at Willis's[5] tonight, for I have been really engaged[6] to Aunt Augusta for more than a week.

JACK: I haven't asked you to dine with me anywhere tonight.

ALGERNON: I know. You are absurdly careless about sending out invitations. It is very foolish of you. Nothing annoys people so much as not receiving invitations.

JACK: You had much better dine with your Aunt Augusta.

ALGERNON: I haven't the smallest intention of doing anything of the kind. To begin with, I dined there on Monday, and once a week is quite enough to dine with one's own relations. In the second place, whenever I do dine there I am always treated as a member of the family, and sent down[7] with either no woman at all, or two. In the third place, I know perfectly well whom she will place me next to, tonight. She will place me next Mary Farquhar, who always flirts with her own husband across the dinner-table. That is not very pleasant. Indeed, it is not even decent . . . and that sort of thing is enormously on the increase. The amount of women in London who flirt with their own husbands is perfectly scandalous. It looks so bad. It is simply washing one's clean linen in public. Besides, now that I know you to be a confirmed Bunburyist I naturally want to talk to you about Bunburying. I want to tell you the rules.

JACK: I'm not a Bunburyist at all. If Gwendolen accepts me, I am going to kill my brother, indeed I think I'll kill him in any case. Cecily is a little too much interested in him. It is rather a bore. So I am going to get rid of Ernest. And I strongly advise you to do the same with Mr . . . with your invalid friend who has the absurd name.

---

5. An expensive London restaurant.
6. I.e., pledged to attend her dinner party.

7. Sent in to the dining room as someone's escort.

ALGERNON: Nothing will induce me to part with Bunbury, and if you ever get married, which seems to me extremely problematic, you will be very glad to know Bunbury. A man who marries without knowing Bunbury has a very tedious time of it.

JACK: That is nonsense. If I marry a charming girl like Gwendolen, and she is the only girl I ever saw in my life that I would marry, I certainly won't want to know Bunbury.

ALGERNON: Then your wife will. You don't seem to realize, that in married life three is company and two is none.

JACK [sententiously]: That, my dear young friend, is the theory that the corrupt French Drama[8] has been propounding for the last fifty years.

ALGERNON: Yes; and that the happy English home has proved in half the time.

JACK: For heaven's sake, don't try to be cynical. It's perfectly easy to be cynical.

ALGERNON: My dear fellow, it isn't easy to be anything nowadays. There's such a lot of beastly competition about. [The sound of an electric bell is heard.] Ah! that must be Aunt Augusta. Only relatives, or creditors, ever ring in that Wagnerian manner.[9] Now, if I get her out of the way for ten minutes, so that you can have an opportunity for proposing to Gwendolen, may I dine with you tonight at Willis's?

JACK: I suppose so, if you want to.

ALGERNON: Yes, but you must be serious about it. I hate people who are not serious about meals. It is so shallow of them.

[Enter Lane.]

LANE: Lady Bracknell and Miss Fairfax.

[Algernon goes forward to meet them. Enter Lady Bracknell and Gwendolen.]

LADY BRACKNELL: Good afternoon, dear Algernon, I hope you are behaving very well.

ALGERNON: I'm feeling very well, Aunt Augusta.

LADY BRACKNELL: That's not quite the same thing. In fact the two things rarely go together. [Sees Jack and bows to him with icy coldness.]

ALGERNON [to Gwendolen]: Dear me, you are smart![1]

GWENDOLEN: I am always smart! Aren't I, Mr Worthing?

JACK: You're quite perfect, Miss Fairfax.

GWENDOLEN: Oh! I hope I am not that. It would leave no room for developments, and I intend to develop in many directions. [Gwendolen and Jack sit down together in the corner.]

LADY BRACKNELL: I'm sorry if we are a little late, Algernon, but I was obliged to call on dear Lady Harbury. I hadn't been there since her poor husband's death. I never saw a woman so altered; she looks quite twenty years younger. And now I'll have a cup of tea, and one of those nice cucumber sandwiches you promised me.

ALGERNON: Certainly, Aunt Augusta. [Goes over to tea-table.]

LADY BRACKNELL: Won't you come and sit here, Gwendolen?

GWENDOLEN: Thanks, mamma, I'm quite comfortable where I am.

ALGERNON [picking up empty plate in horror]: Good heavens! Lane! Why are there no cucumber sandwiches? I ordered them specially.

LANE [gravely]: There were no cucumbers in the market this morning, sir. I went down twice.

---

8. Late 19th-century French plays frequently focused on marital infidelity.

9. I.e., loud and dramatic, like the grand operas of

Richard Wagner (1813–1883).

1. Chic.

ALGERNON: No cucumbers!

LANE: No, sir. Not even for ready money.

ALGERNON: That will do, Lane, thank you.

LANE: Thank you, sir. [*Goes out.*]

ALGERNON: I am greatly distressed, Aunt Augusta, about there being no cucumbers, not even for ready money.

LADY BRACKNELL: It really makes no matter, Algernon. I had some crumpets with Lady Harbury, who seems to me to be living entirely for pleasure now.

ALGERNON: I hear her hair has turned quite gold from grief.

LADY BRACKNELL: It certainly has changed its colour. From what cause I, of course, cannot say. [*Algernon crosses and hands tea.*] Thank you. I've quite a treat for you tonight, Algernon. I am going to send you down with Mary Farquhar. She is such a nice woman, and so attentive to her husband. It's delightful to watch them.

ALGERNON: I am afraid, Aunt Augusta, I shall have to give up the pleasure of dining with you tonight after all.

LADY BRACKNELL [*frowning*]: I hope not, Algernon. It would put my table completely out. Your uncle would have to dine upstairs. Fortunately he is accustomed to that.

ALGERNON: It is a great bore, and, I need hardly say, a terrible disappointment to me, but the fact is I have just had a telegram to say that my poor friend Bunbury is very ill again. [*Exchanges glances with Jack.*] They seem to think I should be with him.

LADY BRACKNELL: It is very strange. This Mr Bunbury seems to suffer from curiously bad health.

ALGERNON: Yes; poor Bunbury is a dreadful invalid.

LADY BRACKNELL: Well, I must say, Algernon, that I think it is high time that Mr Bunbury made up his mind whether he was going to live or to die. This shilly-shallying with the question is absurd. Nor do I in any way approve of the modern sympathy with invalids. I consider it morbid. Illness of any kind is hardly a thing to be encouraged in others. Health is the primary duty of life. I am always telling that to your poor uncle, but he never seems to take much notice . . . as far as any improvement in his ailments goes. I should be much obliged if you would ask Mr Bunbury, from me, to be kind enough not to have a relapse on Saturday, for I rely on you to arrange my music for me. It is my last reception, and one wants something that will encourage conversation, particularly at the end of the season[2] when everyone has practically said whatever they had to say, which, in most cases, was probably not much.

ALGERNON: I'll speak to Bunbury, Aunt Augusta, if he is still conscious, and I think I can promise you he'll be all right by Saturday. Of course the music is a great difficulty. You see, if one plays good music, people don't listen, and if one plays bad music people don't talk. But I'll run over the programme I've drawn out, if you will kindly come into the next room for a moment.

LADY BRACKNELL: Thank you, Algernon. It is very thoughtful of you. [*Rising, and following Algernon.*] I'm sure the programme will be delightful, after a few expurgations. French songs I cannot possibly allow. People always seem to think that they are improper, and either look shocked, which is vulgar, or laugh, which is worse. But German sounds a thoroughly respectable language, and indeed, I believe is so. Gwendolen, you will accompany me.

---

2. Fashionable people left their country estates to spend the social season in London; it began in late spring and lasted through July.

GWENDOLEN: Certainly, mamma.

[*Lady Bracknell and Algernon go into the music-room, Gwendolen remains behind.*]

JACK: Charming day it has been, Miss Fairfax.

GWENDOLEN: Pray don't talk to me about the weather, Mr Worthing. Whenever people talk to me about the weather, I always feel quite certain that they mean something else. And that makes me so nervous.

JACK: I do mean something else.

GWENDOLEN: I thought so. In fact, I am never wrong.

JACK: And I would like to be allowed to take advantage of Lady Bracknell's temporary absence . . .

GWENDOLEN: I would certainly advise you to do so. Mamma has a way of coming back suddenly into a room that I have often had to speak to her about.

JACK [*nervously*]: Miss Fairfax, ever since I met you I have admired you more than any girl . . . I have ever met since . . . I met you.

GWENDOLEN: Yes, I am quite aware of the fact. And I often wish that in public, at any rate, you had been more demonstrative. For me you have always had an irresistible fascination. Even before I met you I was far from indifferent to you. [*Jack looks at her in amazement.*] We live, as I hope you know, Mr Worthing, in an age of ideals. The fact is constantly mentioned in the more expensive monthly magazines, and has reached the provincial pulpits I am told: and my ideal has always been to love some one of the name of Ernest. There is something in that name that inspires absolute confidence. The moment Algernon first mentioned to me that he had a friend called Ernest, I knew I was destined to love you.

JACK: You really love me, Gwendolen?

GWENDOLEN: Passionately!

JACK: Darling! You don't know how happy you've made me.

GWENDOLEN: My own Ernest!

JACK: But you don't really mean to say that you couldn't love me if my name wasn't Ernest?

GWENDOLEN: But your name is Ernest.

JACK: Yes, I know it is. But supposing it was something else? Do you mean to say you couldn't love me then?

GWENDOLEN [*glibly*]: Ah! that is clearly a metaphysical speculation, and like most metaphysical speculations has very little reference at all to the actual facts of real life, as we know them.

JACK: Personally, darling, to speak quite candidly, I don't much care about the name of Ernest . . . I don't think the name suits me at all.

GWENDOLEN: It suits you perfectly. It is a divine name. It has a music of its own. It produces vibrations.

JACK: Well, really, Gwendolen, I must say that I think there are lots of other much nicer names. I think Jack, for instance, a charming name.

GWENDOLEN: Jack? . . . No, there is very little music in the name Jack, if any at all, indeed. It does not thrill. It produces absolutely no vibrations . . . I have known several Jacks, and they all, without exception, were more than usually plain. Besides, Jack is a notorious domesticity for John! And I pity any woman who is married to a man called John. She would probably never be allowed to know the entrancing pleasure of a single moment's solitude. The only really safe name is Ernest.

JACK: Gwendolen, I must get christened at once—I mean we must get married at once. There is no time to be lost.

GWENDOLEN: Married, Mr Worthing?[3]

JACK [*astounded*]: Well . . . surely. You know that I love you, and you led me to believe, Miss Fairfax, that you were not absolutely indifferent to me.

GWENDOLEN: I adore you. But you haven't proposed to me yet. Nothing has been said at all about marriage. The subject has not even been touched on.

JACK: Well . . . may I propose to you now?

GWENDOLEN: I think it would be an admirable opportunity. And to spare you any possible disappointment, Mr Worthing, I think it only fair to tell you quite frankly beforehand that I am fully determined to accept you.

JACK: Gwendolen!

GWENDOLEN: Yes, Mr Worthing, what have you got to say to me?

JACK: You know what I have got to say to you.

GWENDOLEN: Yes, but you don't say it.

JACK: Gwendolen, will you marry me? [*Goes on his knees.*]

GWENDOLEN: Of course I will, darling. How long you have been about it! I am afraid you have had very little experience in how to propose.

JACK: My own one, I have never loved anyone in the world but you.

GWENDOLEN: Yes, but men often propose for practice. I know my brother Gerald does. All my girl-friends tell me so. What wonderfully blue eyes you have, Ernest! They are quite, quite, blue. I hope you will always look at me just like that, especially when there are other people present.

[*Enter Lady Bracknell.*]

LADY BRACKNELL: Mr Worthing! Rise, sir, from this semi-recumbent posture. It is most indecorous.

GWENDOLEN: Mamma! [*He tries to rise; she restrains him.*] I must beg you to retire. This is no place for you. Besides, Mr Worthing has not quite finished yet.

LADY BRACKNELL: Finished what, may I ask?

GWENDOLEN: I am engaged to Mr Worthing, mamma. [*They rise together.*]

LADY BRACKNELL: Pardon me, you are not engaged to anyone. When you do become engaged to some one, I, or your father, should his health permit him, will inform you of the fact. An engagement should come on a young girl as a surprise, pleasant or unpleasant, as the case may be. It is hardly a matter that she could be allowed to arrange for herself. . . . And now I have a few questions to put to you, Mr Worthing. While I am making these inquiries, you, Gwendolen, will wait for me below in the carriage.

GWENDOLEN [*reproachfully*]: Mamma!

LADY BRACKNELL: In the carriage, Gwendolen! [*Gwendolen goes to the door. She and Jack blow kisses to each other behind Lady Bracknell's back. Lady Bracknell looks vaguely about as if she could not understand what the noise was. Finally turns round.*] Gwendolen, the carriage!

GWENDOLEN: Yes, mamma. [*Goes out, looking back at Jack.*]

LADY BRACKNELL [*sitting down*]: You can take a seat, Mr Worthing.

[*Looking in her pocket for note-book and pencil.*]

JACK: Thank you, Lady Bracknell, I prefer standing.

LADY BRACKNELL [*pencil and note-book in hand*]: I feel bound to tell you that you are not down on my list of eligible young men, although I have the same list as the dear Duchess of Bolton has. We work together, in fact. However, I am quite ready

3. Gwendolen reverts to using Jack's last name when she is reminded that he has not yet formally proposed.

to enter your name, should your answers be what a really affectionate mother requires. Do you smoke?

JACK: Well, yes, I must admit I smoke.

LADY BRACKNELL: I am glad to hear it. A man should always have an occupation of some kind. There are far too many idle men in London as it is. How old are you?

JACK: Twenty-nine.

LADY BRACKNELL: A very good age to be married at. I have always been of opinion that a man who desires to get married should know either everything or nothing. Which do you know?

JACK [after some hesitation]: I know nothing, Lady Bracknell.

LADY BRACKNELL: I am pleased to hear it. I do not approve of anything that tampers with natural ignorance. Ignorance is like a delicate exotic fruit; touch it and the bloom is gone. The whole theory of modern education is radically unsound. Fortunately in England, at any rate, education produces no effect whatsoever. If it did, it would prove a serious danger to the upper classes, and probably lead to acts of violence in Grosvenor Square.[4] What is your income? *Riots in Trafalgar Sqr. when Wilde was writing*

JACK: Between seven and eight thousand a year.

LADY BRACKNELL [makes a note in her book]: In land, or in investments?

JACK: In investments, chiefly.

LADY BRACKNELL: That is satisfactory. What between the duties expected of one during one's lifetime, and the duties exacted from one after one's death,[5] land has ceased to be either a profit or a pleasure. It gives one position, and prevents one from keeping it up. That's all that can be said about land.

JACK: I have a country house with some land, of course, attached to it, about fifteen hundred acres, I believe; but I don't depend on that for my real income. In fact, as far as I can make out, the poachers are the only people who make anything out of it.

LADY BRACKNELL: A country house! How many bedrooms? Well, that point can be cleared up afterwards. You have a town house, I hope? A girl with a simple, unspoiled nature, like Gwendolen, could hardly be expected to reside in the country.

JACK: Well, I own a house in Belgrave Square,[6] but it is let by the year to Lady Bloxham. Of course, I can get it back whenever I like, at six months' notice.

LADY BRACKNELL: Lady Bloxham? I don't know her.

JACK: Oh, she goes about very little. She is a lady considerably advanced in years.

LADY BRACKNELL: Ah, nowadays that is no guarantee of respectability of character. What number in Belgrave Square?

JACK: 149.

LADY BRACKNELL [shaking her head]: The unfashionable side. I thought there was something. However, that could easily be altered.

JACK: Do you mean the fashion, or the side?

LADY BRACKNELL [sternly]: Both, if necessary, I presume. What are your politics?

JACK: Well, I am afraid I really have none. I am a Liberal Unionist.[7]

LADY BRACKNELL: Oh, they count as Tories. They dine with us. Or come in the evening, at any rate. Now to minor matters. Are your parents living?

JACK: I have lost both my parents.

4. A fashionable area in the West End of London.
5. "Death duties" are inheritance taxes.
6. A fashionable West End address in Belgravia.

7. In 1886 Liberal Unionists joined the Conservatives (the "Tories") in voting against the Liberal Prime Minister Gladstone's bill supporting Home Rule for Ireland.

LADY BRACKNELL: Both? To lose one parent may be regarded as a misfortune—to lose *both* seems like carelessness. Who was your father? He was evidently a man of some wealth. Was he born in what the Radical papers call the purple of commerce, or did he rise from the ranks of the aristocracy?

JACK: I am afraid I really don't know. The fact is, Lady Bracknell, I said I had lost my parents. It would be nearer the truth to say that my parents seem to have lost me . . . I don't actually know who I am by birth. I was . . . well, I was found.

LADY BRACKNELL: Found!

JACK: The late Mr Thomas Cardew, an old gentleman of a very charitable and kindly disposition, found me, and gave me the name of Worthing, because he happened to have a first-class ticket for Worthing in his pocket at the time. Worthing is a place in Sussex. It is a seaside resort.

LADY BRACKNELL: Where did the charitable gentleman who had a first-class ticket for this seaside resort find you?

JACK [*gravely*]: In a hand-bag.

LADY BRACKNELL: A hand-bag?

JACK [*very seriously*]: Yes, Lady Bracknell. I was in a hand-bag—a somewhat large, black leather hand-bag, with handles to it—an ordinary hand-bag in fact.

LADY BRACKNELL: In what locality did this Mr James, or Thomas, Cardew come across this ordinary hand-bag?

JACK: In the cloak-room at Victoria Station. It was given to him in mistake for his own.

LADY BRACKNELL: The cloak-room at Victoria Station?

JACK: Yes. The Brighton line.

LADY BRACKNELL: The line is immaterial. Mr Worthing, I confess I feel somewhat bewildered by what you have just told me. To be born, or at any rate bred, in a hand-bag, whether it had handles or not, seems to me to display a contempt for the ordinary decencies of family life that reminds one of the worst excesses of the French Revolution. And I presume you know what that unfortunate movement led to? As for the particular locality in which the hand-bag was found, a cloak-room at a railway station might serve to conceal a social indiscretion—has probably, indeed, been used for that purpose before now—but it could hardly be regarded as an assured basis for a recognized position in good society.

JACK: May I ask you then what you would advise me to do? I need hardly say I would do anything in the world to ensure Gwendolen's happiness.

LADY BRACKNELL: I would strongly advise you, Mr Worthing, to try and acquire some relations as soon as possible, and to make a definite effort to produce at any rate one parent, of either sex, before the season is quite over.

JACK: Well, I don't see how I could possibly manage to do that. I can produce the hand-bag at any moment. It is in my dressing-room at home. I really think that should satisfy you, Lady Bracknell.

LADY BRACKNELL: Me, sir! What has it to do with me? You can hardly imagine that I and Lord Bracknell would dream of allowing our only daughter—a girl brought up with the utmost care—to marry into a cloak-room, and form an alliance with a parcel? Good morning, Mr Worthing!

[*Lady Bracknell sweeps out in majestic indignation.*]

JACK: Good morning! [*Algernon, from the other room, strikes up the Wedding March. Jack looks perfectly furious, and goes to the door.*] For goodness' sake don't play that ghastly tune, Algy! How idiotic you are!

[*The music stops, and Algernon enters cheerily.*]

ALGERNON: Didn't it go off all right, old boy? You don't mean to say Gwendolen refused you? I know it is a way she has. She is always refusing people. I think it is most ill-natured of her.

JACK: Oh, Gwendolen is as right as a trivet.[8] As far as she is concerned, we are engaged. Her mother is perfectly unbearable. Never met such a Gorgon[9] . . . I don't really know what a Gorgon is like, but I am quite sure Lady Bracknell is one. In any case, she is a monster, without being a myth, which is rather unfair . . . I beg your pardon, Algy, I suppose I shouldn't talk about your own aunt in that way before you.

ALGERNON: My dear boy, I love hearing my relations abused. It is the only thing that makes me put up with them at all. Relations are simply a tedious pack of people, who haven't got the remotest knowledge of how to live, nor the smallest instinct about when to die.

JACK: Oh, that is nonsense!

ALGERNON: It isn't!

JACK: Well, I won't argue about the matter. You always want to argue about things.

ALGERNON: That is exactly what things were originally made for.

JACK: Upon my word, if I thought that, I'd shoot myself . . . [A pause.] You don't think there is any chance of Gwendolen becoming like her mother in about a hundred and fifty years, do you Algy?

ALGERNON: All women become like their mothers. That is their tragedy. No man does. That's his.

JACK: Is that clever?

ALGERNON: It is perfectly phrased! and quite as true as any observation in civilized life should be.

JACK: I am sick to death of cleverness. Everybody is clever nowadays. You can't go anywhere without meeting clever people. The thing has become an absolute public nuisance. I wish to goodness we had a few fools left.

ALGERNON: We have.

JACK: I should extremely like to meet them. What do they talk about?

ALGERNON: The fools? Oh! about the clever people, of course.

JACK: What fools!

ALGERNON: By the way, did you tell Gwendolen the truth about your being Ernest in town, and Jack in the country?

JACK [in a very patronizing manner]: My dear fellow, the truth isn't quite the sort of thing one tells to a nice sweet refined girl. What extraordinary ideas you have about the way to behave to a woman!

ALGERNON: The only way to behave to a woman is to make love to her,[1] if she is pretty, and to someone else if she is plain.

JACK: Oh, that is nonsense.

ALGERNON: What about your brother? What about the profligate Ernest?

JACK: Oh, before the end of the week I shall have got rid of him. I'll say he died in Paris of apoplexy. Lots of people die of apoplexy, quite suddenly, don't they?

ALGERNON: Yes, but it's hereditary, my dear fellow. It's a sort of thing that runs in families. You had much better say a severe chill.

JACK: You are sure a severe chill isn't hereditary, or anything of that kind?

---

8. Reliable and steady, like a stand used to hold a pot over the fire.

9. A mythical female monster with snakes for hair.

1. I.e., to flirt with or court her.

ALGERNON: Of course it isn't!

JACK: Very well, then. My poor brother Ernest is carried off suddenly in Paris, by a severe chill. That gets rid of him.

ALGERNON: But I thought you said that . . . Miss Cardew was a little too much interested in your poor brother Ernest? Won't she feel his loss a good deal?

JACK: Oh, that is all right. Cecily is not a silly romantic girl, I am glad to say. She has got a capital appetite, goes long walks, and pays no attention at all to her lessons.

ALGERNON: I would rather like to see Cecily.

JACK: I will take very good care you never do. She is excessively pretty, and she is only just eighteen.

ALGERNON: Have you told Gwendolen yet that you have an excessively pretty ward who is only just eighteen?

JACK: Oh! one doesn't blurt these things out to people. Cecily and Gwendolen are perfectly certain to be extremely great friends. I'll bet you anything you like that half an hour after they have met, they will be calling each other sister.

ALGERNON: Women only do that when they have called each other a lot of other things first. Now, my dear boy, if we want to get a good table at Willis's, we really must go and dress. Do you know it is nearly seven?

JACK [irritably]: Oh! it always is nearly seven.

ALGERNON: Well, I'm hungry.

JACK: I never knew you when you weren't. . . .

ALGERNON: What shall we do after dinner? Go to a theatre?

JACK: Oh no! I loathe listening.

ALGERNON: Well, let us go to the Club?

JACK: Oh, no! I hate talking.

ALGERNON: Well, we might trot round to the Empire[2] at ten?

JACK: Oh, no! I can't bear looking at things. It is so silly.

ALGERNON: Well, what shall we do?

JACK: Nothing!

ALGERNON: It is awfully hard work doing nothing. However, I don't mind hard work where there is no definite object of any kind.

[Enter Lane.]

LANE: Miss Fairfax.

[Enter Gwendolen. Lane goes out.]

ALGERNON: Gwendolen, upon my word!

GWENDOLEN: Algy, kindly turn your back. I have something very particular to say to Mr Worthing.

ALGERNON: Really, Gwendolen, I don't think I can allow this at all.

GWENDOLEN: Algy, you always adopt a strictly immoral attitude towards life. You are not quite old enough to do that.

[Algernon retires to the fireplace.]

JACK: My own darling!

GWENDOLEN: Ernest, we may never be married. From the expression on mamma's face I fear we never shall. Few parents nowadays pay any regard to what their children say to them. The old-fashioned respect for the young is fast dying out. Whatever influence I ever had over mamma, I lost at the age of three. But although

2. A popular music hall.

she may prevent us from becoming man and wife, and I may marry someone else, and marry often, nothing that she can possibly do can alter my eternal devotion to you.

JACK: Dear Gwendolen!

GWENDOLEN: The story of your romantic origin, as related to me by mamma, with unpleasing comments, has naturally stirred the deeper fibres of my nature. Your Christian name has an irresistible fascination. The simplicity of your character makes you exquisitely incomprehensible to me. Your town address at the Albany I have. What is your address in the country?

JACK: The Manor House, Woolton, Hertfordshire.

[Algernon, who has been carefully listening, smiles to himself, and writes the address on his shirt-cuff. Then picks up the Railway Guide.]

GWENDOLEN: There is a good postal service, I suppose? It may be necessary to do something desperate. That of course will require serious consideration. I will communicate with you daily.

JACK: My own one!

GWENDOLEN: How long do you remain in town?

JACK: Till Monday.

GWENDOLEN: Good! Algy, you may turn round now.

ALGERNON: Thanks, I've turned round already.

GWENDOLEN: You may also ring the bell.

JACK: You will let me see you to your carriage, my own darling?

GWENDOLEN: Certainly.

JACK [to Lane, who now enters]: I will see Miss Fairfax out.

LANE: Yes, sir. [Jack and Gwendolen go off.]

[Lane presents several letters on a salver to Algernon. It is to be surmised that they are bills, as Algernon, after looking at the envelopes, tears them up.]

ALGERNON: A glass of sherry, Lane.

LANE: Yes, sir.

ALGERNON: Tomorrow, Lane, I'm going Bunburying.

LANE: Yes, sir.

ALGERNON: I shall probably not be back till Monday. You can put up my dress clothes, my smoking jacket, and all the Bunbury suits . . .

LANE: Yes, sir. [Handing sherry.]

ALGERNON: I hope tomorrow will be a fine day, Lane.

LANE: It never is, sir.

ALGERNON: Lane, you're a perfect pessimist.

LANE: I do my best to give satisfaction, sir.

[Enter Jack. Lane goes off.]

JACK: There's a sensible, intellectual girl! the only girl I ever cared for in my life. [Algernon is laughing immoderately.] What on earth are you so amused at?

ALGERNON: Oh, I'm a little anxious about poor Bunbury, that is all.

JACK: If you don't take care, your friend Bunbury will get you into a serious scrape some day.

ALGERNON: I love scrapes. They are the only things that are never serious.

JACK: Oh, that's nonsense, Algy. You never talk anything but nonsense.

ALGERNON: Nobody ever does.

[Jack looks indignantly at him, and leaves the room. Algernon lights a cigarette, reads his shirt-cuff, and smiles.]   ACT DROP

SECOND ACT

SCENE: *Garden at the Manor House. A flight of gray stone steps leads up to the house. The garden, an old-fashioned one, full of roses. Time of year, July. Basket chairs, and a table covered with books, are set under a large yew tree.*

[*Miss Prism discovered seated at the table. Cecily is at the back watering flowers.*]

MISS PRISM [*calling*]: Cecily, Cecily! Surely such a utilitarian occupation as the watering of flowers is rather Moulton's duty than yours? Especially at a moment when intellectual pleasures await you. Your German grammar is on the table. Pray open it at page fifteen. We will repeat yesterday's lesson.

CECILY [*coming over very slowly*]: But I don't like German. It isn't at all a becoming language. I know perfectly well that I look quite plain after my German lesson.

MISS PRISM: Child, you know how anxious your guardian is that you should improve yourself in every way. He laid particular stress on your German, as he was leaving for town yesterday. Indeed, he always lays stress on your German when he is leaving for town.

CECILY: Dear Uncle Jack is so very serious! Sometimes he is so serious that I think he cannot be quite well.

MISS PRISM [*drawing herself up*]: Your guardian enjoys the best of health, and his gravity of demeanour is especially to be commended in one so comparatively young as he is. I know no one who has a higher sense of duty and responsibility.

CECILY: I suppose that is why he often looks a little bored when we three are together.

MISS PRISM: Cecily! I am surprised at you. Mr Worthing has many troubles in his life. Idle merriment and triviality would be out of place in his conversation. You must remember his constant anxiety about that unfortunate young man his brother.

CECILY: I wish Uncle Jack would allow that unfortunate young man, his brother, to come down here sometimes. We might have a good influence over him, Miss Prism. I am sure you certainly would. You know German, and geology, and things of that kind influence a man very much. [*Cecily begins to write in her diary.*]

MISS PRISM [*shaking her head*]: I do not think that even I could produce any effect on a character that according to his own brother's admission is irretrievably weak and vacillating. Indeed I am not sure that I would desire to reclaim him. I am not in favour of this modern mania for turning bad people into good people at a moment's notice. As a man sows so let him reap.[3] You must put away your diary, Cecily. I really don't see why you should keep a diary at all.

CECILY: I keep a diary in order to enter the wonderful secrets of my life. If I didn't write them down I should probably forget all about them.

MISS PRISM: Memory, my dear Cecily, is the diary that we all carry about with us.

CECILY: Yes, but it usually chronicles the things that have never happened, and couldn't possibly have happened. I believe that Memory is responsible for nearly all the three-volume novels that Mudie sends us.[4]

MISS PRISM: Do not speak slightly of the three-volume novel, Cecily. I wrote one myself in earlier days.

CECILY: Did you really, Miss Prism? How wonderfully clever you are! I hope it did not end happily? I don't like novels that end happily. They depress me so much.

3. "Be not deceived; God is not mocked: for whatsoever a man soweth, that shall he also reap" (Galatians 6.7).
4. Mudie's Select Library lent novels to subscribers for a fee; at the time of this play, both Mudie's and the three-volume novel were becoming outmoded.

MISS PRISM: The good ended happily, and the bad unhappily. That is what Fiction means.

CECILY: I suppose so. But it seems very unfair. And was your novel ever published?

MISS PRISM: Alas! no. The manuscript unfortunately was abandoned. I use the word in the sense of lost or mislaid. To your work, child, these speculations are profitless.

CECILY [smiling]: But I see dear Dr Chasuble coming up through the garden.

MISS PRISM [rising and advancing]: Dr Chasuble! This is indeed a pleasure.
    [Enter Canon Chasuble.][5]

CHASUBLE: And how are we this morning? Miss Prism, you are, I trust, well?

CECILY: Miss Prism has just been complaining of a slight headache. I think it would do her so much good to have a short stroll with you in the Park, Dr Chasuble.

MISS PRISM: Cecily, I have not mentioned anything about a headache.

CECILY: No, dear Miss Prism, I know that, but I felt instinctively that you had a headache. Indeed I was thinking about that, and not about my German lesson, when the Rector came in.

CHASUBLE: I hope Cecily, you are not inattentive.

CECILY: Oh, I am afraid I am.

CHASUBLE: That is strange. Were I fortunate enough to be Miss Prism's pupil, I would hang upon her lips. [Miss Prism glares.] I spoke metaphorically.—My metaphor was drawn from bees. Ahem! Mr Worthing I suppose, has not returned from town yet?

MISS PRISM: We do not expect him till Monday afternoon.

CHASUBLE: Ah yes, he usually likes to spend his Sunday in London. He is not one of those whose sole aim is enjoyment, as, by all accounts, that unfortunate young man his brother seems to be. But I must not disturb Egeria[6] and her pupil any longer.

MISS PRISM: Egeria? My name is Laetitia, Doctor.

CHASUBLE [bowing]: A classical allusion merely, drawn from the Pagan authors. I shall see you both no doubt at Evensong?[7]

MISS PRISM: I think, dear Doctor, I will have a stroll with you. I find I have a headache after all, and a walk might do it good.

CHASUBLE: With pleasure, Miss Prism, with pleasure. We might go as far as the schools and back.

MISS PRISM: That would be delightful. Cecily, you will read your Political Economy in my absence. The chapter on the Fall of the Rupee you may omit.[8] It is somewhat too sensational. Even these metallic problems have their melodramatic side. [Goes down the garden with Dr Chasuble.]

CECILY [picks up books and throws them back on table]: Horrid Political Economy! Horrid Geography! Horrid, horrid German!
    [Enter Merriman with a card on a salver.]

MERRIMAN: Mr Ernest Worthing has just driven over from the station. He has brought his luggage with him.

CECILY [takes the card and reads it]: "Mr Ernest Worthing, B.4 The Albany, W." Uncle Jack's brother! Did you tell him Mr Worthing was in town?

MERRIMAN: Yes, Miss. He seemed very much disappointed. I mentioned that you and Miss Prism were in the garden. He said he was anxious to speak to you privately for a moment.

---

5. A canon is a cathedral clergyman; a chasuble is a vestment.
6. Roman goddess of fountains; her name was used for a woman who instructed other women.

7. Evening church services.
8. The declining value of the Indian rupee would hurt British civil servants in India, who were paid in rupees.

CECILY: Ask Mr Ernest Worthing to come here. I suppose you had better talk to the housekeeper about a room for him.

MERRIMAN: Yes, Miss. [*Merriman goes off.*]

CECILY: I have never met any really wicked person before. I feel rather frightened. I am so afraid he will look just like everyone else.

[*Enter Algernon, very gay and debonair.*]

He does!

ALGERNON [*raising his hat*]: You are my little cousin Cecily, I'm sure.

CECILY: You are under some strange mistake. I am not little. In fact, I believe I am more than usually tall for my age. [*Algernon is rather taken aback.*] But I am your cousin Cecily. You, I see from your card, are Uncle Jack's brother, my cousin Ernest, my wicked cousin Ernest.

ALGERNON: Oh! I am not really wicked at all, cousin Cecily. You mustn't think that I am wicked.

CECILY: If you are not, then you have certainly been deceiving us all in a very inexcusable manner. I hope you have not been leading a double life, pretending to be wicked and being really good all the time. That would be hypocrisy.

ALGERNON [*looks at her in amazement*]: Oh! Of course I have been rather reckless.

CECILY: I am glad to hear it.

ALGERNON: In fact, now you mention the subject, I have been very bad in my own small way.

CECILY: I don't think you should be so proud of that, although I am sure it must have been very pleasant.

ALGERNON: It is much pleasanter being here with you.

CECILY: I can't understand how you are here at all. Uncle Jack won't be back till Monday afternoon.

ALGERNON: That is a great disappointment. I am obliged to go up by the first train on Monday morning. I have a business appointment that I am anxious . . . to miss.

CECILY: Couldn't you miss it anywhere but in London?

ALGERNON: No: the appointment is in London.

CECILY: Well, I know, of course, how important it is not to keep a business engagement, if one wants to retain any sense of the beauty of life, but still I think you had better wait till Uncle Jack arrives. I know he wants to speak to you about your emigrating.

ALGERNON: About my what?

CECILY: Your emigrating. He has gone up to buy your outfit.

ALGERNON: I certainly wouldn't let Jack buy my outfit. He has no taste in neckties at all.

CECILY: I don't think you will require neckties. Uncle Jack is sending you to Australia.[9]

ALGERNON: Australia! I'd sooner die.

CECILY: Well, he said at dinner on Wednesday night, that you would have to choose between this world, the next world, and Australia.

ALGERNON: Oh, well! The accounts I have received of Australia and the next world are not particularly encouraging. This world is good enough for me, cousin Cecily.

CECILY: Yes, but are you good enough for it?

ALGERNON: I'm afraid I'm not that. That is why I want you to reform me. You might make that your mission, if you don't mind, cousin Cecily.

CECILY: I'm afraid I've no time, this afternoon.

ALGERNON: Well, would you mind my reforming myself this afternoon?

9. Australia was no longer a penal colony, but it was still a place where families sent their ne'er-do-well sons.

CECILY: It is rather Quixotic[1] of you. But I think you should try.

ALGERNON: I will. I feel better already.

CECILY: You are looking a little worse.

ALGERNON: That is because I am hungry.

CECILY: How thoughtless of me. I should have remembered that when one is going to lead an entirely new life, one requires regular and wholesome meals. Won't you come in?

ALGERNON: Thank you. Might I have a buttonhole[2] first? I never have any appetite unless I have a buttonhole first.

CECILY: A Maréchal Niel?[3] [*Picks up scissors.*]

ALGERNON: No, I'd sooner have a pink rose.

CECILY: Why? [*Cuts a flower.*]

ALGERNON: Because you are like a pink rose, Cousin Cecily.

CECILY: I don't think it can be right for you to talk to me like that. Miss Prism never says such things to me.

ALGERNON: Then Miss Prism is a short-sighted old lady. [*Cecily puts the rose in his buttonhole.*] You are the prettiest girl I ever saw.

CECILY: Miss Prism says that all good looks are a snare.

ALGERNON: They are a snare that every sensible man would like to be caught in.

CECILY: Oh! I don't think I would care to catch a sensible man. I shouldn't know what to talk to him about.

[*They pass into the house. Miss Prism and Dr Chasuble return.*]

MISS PRISM: You are too much alone, dear Dr Chasuble. You should get married. A misanthrope I can understand—a womanthrope, never!

CHASUBLE [*with a scholar's shudder*][4]: Believe me, I do not deserve so neologistic a phrase. The precept as well as the practice of the Primitive Church was distinctly against matrimony.[5]

MISS PRISM [*sententiously*]: That is obviously the reason why the Primitive Church has not lasted up to the present day. And you do not seem to realize, dear Doctor, that by persistently remaining single, a man converts himself into a permanent public temptation. Men should be more careful; this very celibacy leads weaker vessels astray.

CHASUBLE: But is a man not equally attractive when married?

MISS PRISM: No married man is ever attractive except to his wife.

CHASUBLE: And often, I've been told, not even to her.

MISS PRISM: That depends on the intellectual sympathies of the woman. Maturity can always be depended on. Ripeness can be trusted. Young women are green. [*Dr Chasuble starts.*] I spoke horticulturally. My metaphor was drawn from fruits. But where is Cecily?

CHASUBLE: Perhaps she followed us to the schools.

[*Enter Jack slowly from the back of the garden. He is dressed in the deepest mourning, with crape hat-band and black gloves.*]

MISS PRISM: Mr Worthing!

CHASUBLE: Mr Worthing?

---

1. Hopelessly idealistic, like Don Quixote.
2. A flower to wear in his lapel.
3. A yellow rose.
4. He shudders because Miss Prism has mangled the language by coining a word, "womanthrope," to describe someone who dislikes women, instead of using the correct term, "misogynist." A neologism is a newly invented word.
5. Protestant clergy are allowed to marry, but as a High Church Anglican, Chasuble is interested in preserving the rituals and practices of the early Catholic church.

MISS PRISM: This is indeed a surprise. We did not look for you till Monday afternoon.

JACK [*shakes Miss Prism's hand in a tragic manner*]: I have returned sooner than I expected. Dr Chasuble, I hope you are well?

CHASUBLE: Dear Mr Worthing, I trust this garb of woe does not betoken some terrible calamity?

JACK: My brother.

MISS PRISM: More shameful debts and extravagance?

CHASUBLE: Still leading his life of pleasure?

JACK [*shaking his head*]: Dead!

CHASUBLE: Your brother Ernest dead?

JACK: Quite dead.

MISS PRISM: What a lesson for him! I trust he will profit by it.

CHASUBLE: Mr Worthing, I offer you my sincere condolence. You have at least the consolation of knowing that you were always the most generous and forgiving of brothers.

JACK: Poor Ernest! He had many faults, but it is a sad, sad blow.

CHASUBLE: Very sad indeed. Were you with him at the end?

JACK: No. He died abroad; in Paris, in fact. I had a telegram last night from the manager of the Grand Hotel.

CHASUBLE: Was the cause of death mentioned?

JACK: A severe chill, it seems.

MISS PRISM: As a man sows, so shall he reap.

CHASUBLE [*raising his hand*]: Charity, dear Miss Prism, charity! None of us are perfect. I myself am peculiarly susceptible to draughts. Will the interment take place here?

JACK: No. He seemed to have expressed a desire to be buried in Paris.

CHASUBLE: In Paris! [*Shakes his head.*] I fear that hardly points to any very serious state of mind at the last. You would no doubt wish me to make some slight allusion to this tragic domestic affliction next Sunday. [*Jack presses his hand convulsively.*] My sermon on the meaning of the manna in the wilderness[6] can be adapted to almost any occasion, joyful, or, as in the present case, distressing. [*All sigh.*] I have preached it at harvest celebrations, christenings, confirmations, on days of humiliation and festal days. The last time I delivered it was in the Cathedral, as a charity sermon on behalf of the Society for the Prevention of Discontent among the Upper Orders. The Bishop, who was present, was much struck by some of the analogies I drew.

JACK: Ah! that reminds me, you mentioned christenings I think, Dr Chasuble? I suppose you know how to christen all right? [*Dr Chasuble looks astounded.*] I mean, of course, you are continually christening, aren't you?

MISS PRISM: It is, I regret to say, one of the Rector's most constant duties in this parish. I have often spoken to the poorer classes on the subject. But they don't seem to know what thrift is.

CHASUBLE: But is there any particular infant in whom you are interested, Mr Worthing? Your brother was, I believe, unmarried, was he not?

JACK: Oh, yes.

MISS PRISM [*bitterly*]: People who live entirely for pleasure usually are.

JACK: But it is not for any child, dear Doctor. I am very fond of children. No! the fact is, I would like to be christened myself, this afternoon, if you have nothing better to do.

CHASUBLE: But surely, Mr Worthing, you have been christened already?

JACK: I don't remember anything about it.

6. An episode in Exodus 16.

CHASUBLE: But have you any grave doubts on the subject?

JACK: I certainly intend to have. Of course I don't know if the thing would bother you in any way, or if you think I am a little too old now.

CHASUBLE: Not at all. The sprinkling, and, indeed, the immersion of adults is a perfectly canonical practice.

JACK: Immersion!

CHASUBLE: You need have no apprehensions. Sprinkling is all that is necessary, or indeed I think advisable. Our weather is so changeable. At what hour would you wish the ceremony performed?

JACK: Oh, I might trot round about five if that would suit you.

CHASUBLE: Perfectly, perfectly! In fact I have two similar ceremonies to perform at that time. A case of twins that occurred recently in one of the outlying cottages on your own estate. Poor Jenkins the carter, a most hard-working man.

JACK: Oh! I don't see much fun in being christened along with other babies. It would be childish. Would half-past five do?

CHASUBLE: Admirably! Admirably! [Takes out watch.] And now, dear Mr Worthing, I will not intrude any longer into a house of sorrow. I would merely beg you not to be too much bowed down by grief. What seem to us bitter trials are often blessings in disguise.

MISS PRISM: This seems to me a blessing of an extremely obvious kind.

[Enter Cecily from the house.]

CECILY: Uncle Jack! Oh, I am pleased to see you back. But what horrid clothes you have got on! Do go and change them.

MISS PRISM: Cecily!

CHASUBLE: My child! my child!

[Cecily goes towards Jack; he kisses her brow in a melancholy manner.]

CECILY: What is the matter, Uncle Jack? Do look happy! You look as if you had toothache, and I have got such a surprise for you. Who do you think is in the dining-room? Your brother!

JACK: Who?

CECILY: Your brother Ernest. He arrived about half an hour ago.

JACK: What nonsense! I haven't got a brother.

CECILY: Oh, don't say that. However badly he may have behaved to you in the past he is still your brother. You couldn't be so heartless as to disown him. I'll tell him to come out. And you will shake hands with him, won't you, Uncle Jack? [Runs back into the house.]

CHASUBLE: These are very joyful tidings.

MISS PRISM: After we had all been resigned to his loss, his sudden return seems to me peculiarly distressing.

JACK: My brother is in the dining-room? I don't know what it all means. I think it is perfectly absurd.

[Enter Algernon and Cecily hand in hand. They come slowly up to Jack.]

JACK: Good heavens! [Motions Algernon away.]

ALGERNON: Brother John, I have come down from town to tell you that I am very sorry for all the trouble I have given you, and that I intend to lead a better life in the future.

[Jack glares at him and does not take his hand.]

CECILY: Uncle Jack, you are not going to refuse your own brother's hand?

JACK: Nothing will induce me to take his hand. I think his coming down here disgraceful. He knows perfectly well why.

CECILY: Uncle Jack, do be nice. There is some good in everyone. Ernest has just been telling me about his poor invalid friend Mr Bunbury whom he goes to visit so often. And surely there must be much good in one who is kind to an invalid, and leaves the pleasures of London to sit by a bed of pain.

JACK: Oh! he has been talking about Bunbury has he?

CECILY: Yes, he has told me all about poor Mr Bunbury, and his terrible state of health.

JACK: Bunbury! Well, I won't have him talk to you about Bunbury or about anything else. It is enough to drive one perfectly frantic.

ALGERNON: Of course I admit that the faults were all on my side. But I must say that I think that Brother John's coldness to me is peculiarly painful. I expected a more enthusiastic welcome, especially considering it is the first time I have come here.

CECILY: Uncle Jack, if you don't shake hands with Ernest I will never forgive you.

JACK: Never forgive me?

CECILY: Never, never, never!

JACK: Well, this is the last time I shall ever do it. [Shakes hands with Algernon and glares.]

CHASUBLE: It's pleasant, is it not, to see so perfect a reconciliation? I think we might leave the two brothers together.

MISS PRISM: Cecily, you will come with us.

CECILY: Certainly, Miss Prism. My little task of reconciliation is over.

CHASUBLE: You have done a beautiful action today, dear child.

MISS PRISM: We must not be premature in our judgements.

CECILY: I feel very happy. [They all go off.]

JACK: You young scoundrel, Algy, you must get out of this place as soon as possible. I don't allow any Bunburying here.

[Enter Merriman.]

MERRIMAN: I have put Mr Ernest's things in the room next to yours, sir. I suppose that is all right?

JACK: What?

MERRIMAN: Mr Ernest's luggage, sir. I have unpacked it and put it in the room next to your own.

JACK: His luggage?

MERRIMAN: Yes, sir. Three portmanteaus, a dressing-case, two hat-boxes, and a large luncheon-basket.

ALGERNON: I am afraid I can't stay more than a week this time.

JACK: Merriman, order the dog-cart[7] at once. Mr Ernest has been suddenly called back to town.

MERRIMAN: Yes, sir. [Goes back into the house.]

ALGERNON: What a fearful liar you are, Jack. I have not been called back to town at all.

JACK: Yes, you have.

ALGERNON: I haven't heard anyone call me.

JACK: Your duty as a gentleman calls you back.

ALGERNON: My duty as a gentleman has never interfered with my pleasures in the smallest degree.

JACK: I can quite understand that.

ALGERNON: Well, Cecily is a darling.

JACK: You are not to talk of Miss Cardew like that. I don't like it.

---

7. A horse-drawn cart with seats, and a box for hunting dogs.

ALGERNON: Well, I don't like your clothes. You look perfectly ridiculous in them. Why on earth don't you go up and change? It is perfectly childish to be in deep mourning for a man who is actually staying for a whole week with you in your house as a guest. I call it grotesque.

JACK: You are certainly not staying with me for a whole week as a guest or anything else. You have got to leave . . . by the four-five train.

ALGERNON: I certainly won't leave you so long as you are in mourning. It would be most unfriendly. If I were in mourning you would stay with me, I suppose. I should think it very unkind if you didn't.

JACK: Well, will you go if I change my clothes?

ALGERNON: Yes, if you are not too long. I never saw anybody take so long to dress, and with such little result.

JACK: Well, at any rate, that is better than being always over-dressed as you are.

ALGERNON: If I am occasionally a little over-dressed, I make up for it by being always immensely over-educated.

JACK: Your vanity is ridiculous, your conduct an outrage, and your presence in my garden utterly absurd. However, you have got to catch the four-five, and I hope you will have a pleasant journey back to town. This Bunburying, as you call it, has not been a great success for you. [Goes into the house.]

ALGERNON: I think it has been a great success. I'm in love with Cecily, and that is everything.

[Enter Cecily at the back of the garden. She picks up the can and begins to water the flowers.]

But I must see her before I go, and make arrangements for another Bunbury. Ah, there she is.

CECILY: Oh, I merely came back to water the roses. I thought you were with Uncle Jack.

ALGERNON: He's gone to order the dog-cart for me.

CECILY: Oh, is he going to take you for a nice drive?

ALGERNON: He's going to send me away.

CECILY: Then have we got to part?

ALGERNON: I am afraid so. It's a painful parting.

CECILY: It is always painful to part from people whom one has known for a very brief space of time. The absence of old friends one can endure with equanimity. But even a momentary separation from anyone to whom one has just been introduced is almost unbearable.

ALGERNON: Thank you.

[Enter Merriman.]

MERRIMAN: The dog-cart is at the door, sir.

[Algernon looks appealingly at Cecily.]

CECILY: It can wait, Merriman . . . for . . . five minutes.

MERRIMAN: Yes, Miss. [Exit Merriman.]

ALGERNON: I hope, Cecily, I shall not offend you if I state quite frankly and openly that you seem to me to be in every way the visible personification of absolute perfection.

CECILY: I think your frankness does you great credit, Ernest. If you will allow me I will copy your remarks into my diary. [Goes over to table and begins writing in diary.]

ALGERNON: Do you really keep a diary? I'd give anything to look at it. May I?

CECILY: Oh no. [Puts her hand over it.] You see, it is simply a very young girl's record of her own thoughts and impressions, and consequently meant for publication. When it appears in volume form I hope you will order a copy. But pray, Ernest,

don't stop. I delight in taking down from dictation. I have reached "absolute perfection." You can go on. I am quite ready for more.

ALGERNON [*somewhat taken aback*]: Ahem! Ahem!

CECILY: Oh, don't cough, Ernest. When one is dictating one should speak fluently and
not cough. Besides, I don't know how to spell a cough. [*Writes as Algernon speaks.*]

ALGERNON [*speaking very rapidly*]: Cecily, ever since I first looked upon your wonderful and incomparable beauty, I have dared to love you wildly, passionately,
devotedly, hopelessly.

CECILY: I don't think that you should tell me that you love me wildly, passionately,
devotedly, hopelessly. Hopelessly doesn't seem to make much sense, does it?

ALGERNON: Cecily!

[*Enter Merriman.*]

MERRIMAN: The dog-cart is waiting, sir.

ALGERNON: Tell it to come round next week, at the same hour.

MERRIMAN [*looks at Cecily, who makes no sign*]: Yes, sir. [*Merriman retires.*]

CECILY: Uncle Jack would be very much annoyed if he knew you were staying on
till next week, at the same hour.

ALGERNON: Oh, I don't care about Jack. I don't care for anybody in the whole
world but you. I love you, Cecily. You will marry me, won't you?

CECILY: You silly boy! Of course. Why, we have been engaged for the last three
months.

ALGERNON: For the last three months?

CECILY: Yes, it will be exactly three months on Thursday.

ALGERNON: But how did we become engaged?

CECILY: Well, ever since dear Uncle Jack first confessed to us that he had a younger
brother who was very wicked and bad, you of course have formed the chief topic of
conversation between myself and Miss Prism. And of course a man who is much
talked about is always very attractive. One feels there must be something in him
after all. I daresay it was foolish of me, but I fell in love with you, Ernest.

ALGERNON: Darling! And when was the engagement actually settled?

CECILY: On the 14th of February last. Worn out by your entire ignorance of my
existence, I determined to end the matter one way or the other, and after a long
struggle with myself I accepted you under this dear old tree here. The next day I
bought this little ring in your name, and this is the little bangle with the true
lovers' knot I promised you always to wear.

ALGERNON: Did I give you this? It's very pretty, isn't it?

CECILY: Yes, you've wonderfully good taste, Ernest. It's the excuse I've always giv-
en for your leading such a bad life. And this is the box in which I keep all your
dear letters. [*Kneels at table, opens box, and produces letters tied up with blue ribbon.*]

ALGERNON: My letters! But my own sweet Cecily, I have never written you any letters.

CECILY: You need hardly remind me of that, Ernest. I remember only too well that
I was forced to write your letters for you. I wrote always three times a week, and
sometimes oftener.

ALGERNON: Oh, do let me read them, Cecily?

CECILY: Oh, I couldn't possibly. They would make you far too conceited. [*Replaces
box.*] The three you wrote me after I had broken off the engagement are so beautiful,
and so badly spelled, that even now I can hardly read them without crying a little.

ALGERNON: But was our engagement ever broken off?

CECILY: Of course it was. On the 22nd of last March. You can see the entry if you like. [*Shows diary.*] "Today I broke off my engagement with Ernest. I feel it is better to do so. The weather still continues charming."

ALGERNON: But why on earth did you break it off? What had I done? I had done nothing at all. Cecily, I am very much hurt indeed to hear you broke it off. Particularly when the weather was so charming.

CECILY: It would hardly have been a really serious engagement if it hadn't been broken off at least once. But I forgave you before the week was out.

ALGERNON [*crossing to her, and kneeling*]: What a perfect angel you are, Cecily.

CECILY: You dear romantic boy. [*He kisses her, she puts her fingers through his hair.*] I hope your hair curls naturally, does it?

ALGERNON: Yes, darling, with a little help from others.

CECILY: I am so glad.

ALGERNON: You'll never break off our engagement again, Cecily?

CECILY: I don't think I could break it off now that I have actually met you. Besides, of course, there is the question of your name.

ALGERNON: Yes, of course. [*Nervously.*]

CECILY: You must not laugh at me, darling, but it had always been a girlish dream of mine to love some one whose name was Ernest. [*Algernon rises, Cecily also.*] There is something in that name that seems to inspire absolute confidence. I pity any poor married woman whose husband is not called Ernest.

ALGERNON: But, my dear child, do you mean to say you could not love me if I had some other name?

CECILY: But what name?

ALGERNON: Oh, any name you like—Algernon—for instance . . .

CECILY: But I don't like the name of Algernon.

ALGERNON: Well, my own dear, sweet, loving little darling, I really can't see why you should object to the name of Algernon. It is not at all a bad name. In fact, it is rather an aristocratic name. Half of the chaps who get into the Bankruptcy Court are called Algernon. But seriously, Cecily . . . [*moving to her*] . . . if my name was Algy, couldn't you love me?

CECILY [*rising*]: I might respect you, Ernest, I might admire your character, but I fear that I should not be able to give you my undivided attention.

ALGERNON: Ahem! Cecily! [*Picking up hat.*] Your Rector here is, I suppose, thoroughly experienced in the practice of all the rites and ceremonials of the Church?

CECILY: Oh yes. Dr Chasuble is a most learned man. He has never written a single book, so you can imagine how much he knows.

ALGERNON: I must see him at once on a most important christening—I mean on most important business.

CECILY: Oh!

ALGERNON: I shan't be away more than half an hour.

CECILY: Considering that we have been engaged since February the 14th, and that I only met you today for the first time, I think it is rather hard that you should leave me for so long a period as half an hour. Couldn't you make it twenty minutes?

ALGERNON: I'll be back in no time. [*Kisses her and rushes down the garden.*]

CECILY: What an impetuous boy he is! I like his hair so much. I must enter his proposal in my diary.

  [*Enter Merriman.*]

MERRIMAN: A Miss Fairfax has just called to see Mr Worthing. On very important business Miss Fairfax states.

CECILY: Isn't Mr Worthing in his library?

MERRIMAN: Mr Worthing went over in the direction of the Rectory some time ago.

CECILY: Pray ask the lady to come out here; Mr Worthing is sure to be back soon. And you can bring tea.

MERRIMAN: Yes, Miss. [Goes out.]

CECILY: Miss Fairfax! I suppose one of the many good elderly women who are associated with Uncle Jack in some of his philanthropic work in London. I don't quite like women who are interested in philanthropic work. I think it is so forward of them.
[Enter Merriman.]

MERRIMAN: Miss Fairfax.
[Enter Gwendolen. Exit Merriman.]

CECILY [advancing to meet her]: Pray let me introduce myself to you. My name is Cecily Cardew.

GWENDOLEN: Cecily Cardew? [Moving to her and shaking hands.] What a very sweet name! Something tells me that we are going to be great friends. I like you already more than I can say. My first impressions of people are never wrong.

CECILY: How nice of you to like me so much after we have known each other such a comparatively short time. Pray sit down.

GWENDOLEN [still standing up]: I may call you Cecily, may I not?

CECILY: With pleasure!

GWENDOLEN: And you will always call me Gwendolen, won't you.

CECILY: If you wish.

GWENDOLEN: Then that is all quite settled, is it not?

CECILY: I hope so.
[A pause. They both sit down together.]

GWENDOLEN: Perhaps this might be a favourable opportunity for my mentioning who I am. My father is Lord Bracknell. You have never heard of papa, I suppose?

CECILY: I don't think so.

GWENDOLEN: Outside the family circle, papa, I am glad to say, is entirely unknown. I think that is quite as it should be. The home seems to me to be the proper sphere for the man. And certainly once a man begins to neglect his domestic duties he becomes painfully effeminate, does he not? And I don't like that. It makes men so very attractive. Cecily, mamma, whose views on education are remarkably strict, has brought me up to be extremely short-sighted; it is part of her system; so do you mind my looking at you through my glasses?

CECILY: Oh! not at all, Gwendolen. I am very fond of being looked at.

GWENDOLEN [after examining Cecily carefully through a lorgnette]: You are here on a short visit I suppose.

CECILY: Oh no! I live here.

GWENDOLEN [severely]: Really? Your mother, no doubt, or some female relative of advanced years, resides here also?

CECILY: Oh no! I have no mother, nor, in fact, any relations.

GWENDOLEN: Indeed?

CECILY: My dear guardian, with the assistance of Miss Prism, has the arduous task of looking after me.

GWENDOLEN: Your guardian?

CECILY: Yes, I am Mr Worthing's ward.

GWENDOLEN: Oh! It is strange he never mentioned to me that he had a ward. How secretive of him! He grows more interesting hourly. I am not sure, however, that the news inspires me with feelings of unmixed delight. [*Rising and going to her.*] I am very fond of you, Cecily; I have liked you ever since I met you! But I am bound to state that now that I know that you are Mr Worthing's ward, I cannot help expressing a wish you were—well just a little older than you seem to be— and not quite so very alluring in appearance. In fact, if I may speak candidly—

CECILY: Pray do! I think that whenever one has anything unpleasant to say, one should always be quite candid.

GWENDOLEN: Well, to speak with perfect candour, Cecily, I wish that you were fully forty-two, and more than usually plain for your age. Ernest has a strong upright nature. He is the very soul of truth and honour. Disloyalty would be as impossible to him as deception. But even men of the noblest possible moral character are extremely susceptible to the influence of the physical charms of others. Modern, no less than Ancient History, supplies us with many most painful examples of what I refer to. If it were not so, indeed, History would be quite unreadable.

CECILY: I beg your pardon, Gwendolen, did you say Ernest?

GWENDOLEN: Yes.

CECILY: Oh, but it is not Mr Ernest Worthing who is my guardian. It is his brother— his elder brother.

GWENDOLEN [*sitting down again*]: Ernest never mentioned to me that he had a brother.

CECILY: I am sorry to say they have not been on good terms for a long time.

GWENDOLEN: Ah! that accounts for it. And now that I think of it I have never heard any man mention his brother. The subject seems distasteful to most men. Cecily, you have lifted a load from my mind. I was growing almost anxious. It would have been terrible if any cloud had come across a friendship like ours, would it not? Of course you are quite, quite sure that it is not Mr Ernest Worthing who is your guardian?

CECILY: Quite sure. [*A pause.*] In fact, I am going to be his.

GWENDOLEN [*enquiringly*]: I beg your pardon?

CECILY [*rather shy and confidingly*]: Dearest Gwendolen, there is no reason why I should make a secret of it to you. Our little county newspaper is sure to chronicle the fact next week. Mr Ernest Worthing and I are engaged to be married.

GWENDOLEN [*quite politely, rising*]: My darling Cecily, I think there must be some slight error. Mr Ernest Worthing is engaged to me. The announcement will appear in the "Morning Post" on Saturday at the latest.

CECILY [*very politely, rising*]: I am afraid you must be under some misconception. Ernest proposed to me exactly ten minutes ago. [*Shows diary.*]

GWENDOLEN [*examines diary through her lorgnette carefully*]: It is certainly very curious, for he asked me to be his wife yesterday afternoon at 5.30. If you would care to verify the incident, pray do so. [*Produces diary of her own.*] I never travel without my diary. One should always have something sensational to read in the train. I am so sorry, dear Cecily, if it is any disappointment to you, but I am afraid I have the prior claim.

CECILY: It would distress me more than I can tell you, dear Gwendolen, if it caused you any mental or physical anguish, but I feel bound to point out that since Ernest proposed to you he clearly has changed his mind.

GWENDOLEN [*meditatively*]: If the poor fellow has been entrapped into any foolish promise I shall consider it my duty to rescue him at once, and with a firm hand.

CECILY [*thoughtfully and sadly*]: Whatever unfortunate entanglement my dear boy may have got into, I will never reproach him with it after we are married.

GWENDOLEN: Do you allude to me, Miss Cardew, as an entanglement? You are presumptuous. On an occasion of this kind it becomes more than a moral duty to speak one's mind. It becomes a pleasure.

CECILY: Do you suggest, Miss Fairfax, that I entrapped Ernest into an engagement? How dare you? This is no time for wearing the shallow mask of manners. When I see a spade I call it a spade.

GWENDOLEN [satirically]: I am glad to say that I have never seen a spade. It is obvious that our social spheres have been widely different.

[Enter Merriman, followed by the footman. He carries a salver, table cloth, and plate stand. Cecily is about to retort. The presence of the servants exercises a restraining influence, under which both girls chafe.]

MERRIMAN: Shall I lay tea here as usual, Miss?

CECILY [sternly, in a calm voice]: Yes, as usual.

[Merriman begins to clear table and lay cloth. A long pause. Cecily and Gwendolen glare at each other.]

GWENDOLEN: Are there many interesting walks in the vicinity, Miss Cardew?

CECILY: Oh! yes! a great many. From the top of one of the hills quite close one can see five counties.

GWENDOLEN: Five counties! I don't think I should like that. I hate crowds.

CECILY [sweetly]: I suppose that is why you live in town?

[Gwendolen bites her lip, and beats her foot nervously with her parasol.]

GWENDOLEN [looking round]: Quite a well-kept garden this is, Miss Cardew.

CECILY: So glad you like it, Miss Fairfax.

GWENDOLEN: I had no idea there were any flowers in the country.

CECILY: Oh, flowers are as common here, Miss Fairfax, as people are in London.

GWENDOLEN: Personally, I cannot understand how anybody manages to exist in the country, if anybody who is anybody does. The country always bores me to death.

CECILY: Ah! This is what the newspapers call agricultural depression,[8] is it not? I believe the aristocracy are suffering very much from it just at present. It is almost an epidemic amongst them, I have been told. May I offer you some tea, Miss Fairfax?

GWENDOLEN [with elaborate politeness]: Thank you. [Aside.] Detestable girl! But I require tea!

CECILY [sweetly]: Sugar?

GWENDOLEN [superciliously]: No, thank you. Sugar is not fashionable any more.

[Cecily looks angrily at her, takes up the tongs and puts four lumps of sugar into the cup.]

CECILY [severely]: Cake or bread and butter?

GWENDOLEN [in a bored manner]: Bread and butter, please. Cake is rarely seen at the best houses nowadays.

CECILY [cuts a very large slice of cake, and puts it on the tray]: Hand that to Miss Fairfax.

[Merriman does so, and goes out with footman. Gwendolen drinks the tea and makes a grimace. Puts down cup at once, reaches out her hand to the bread and butter, looks at it, and finds it is cake. Rises in indignation.]

GWENDOLEN: You have filled my tea with lumps of sugar, and though I asked most distinctly for bread and butter, you have given me cake. I am known for the gentleness of my disposition, and the extraordinary sweetness of my nature, but I warn you, Miss Cardew, you may go too far.

---

8. A pun on the word "depression"; beginning in the 1870s, British agriculture had been in a slump, causing losses and hardship among landowners.

CECILY [*rising*]: To save my poor, innocent, trusting boy from the machinations of any other girl there are no lengths to which I would not go.

GWENDOLEN: From the moment I saw you I distrusted you. I felt that you were false and deceitful. I am never deceived in such matters. My first impressions of people are invariably right.

CECILY: It seems to me, Miss Fairfax, that I am trespassing on your valuable time. No doubt you have many other calls of a similar character to make in the neighbourhood.

[*Enter Jack.*]

GWENDOLEN [*catching sight of him*]: Ernest! My own Ernest!

JACK: Gwendolen! Darling! [*Offers to kiss her.*]

GWENDOLEN [*drawing back*]: A moment! May I ask if you are engaged to be married to this young lady? [*Points to Cecily.*]

JACK [*laughing*]: To dear little Cecily! Of course not! What could have put such an idea into your pretty little head?

GWENDOLEN: Thank you. You may! [*Offers her cheek.*]

CECILY [*very sweetly*]: I knew there must be some misunderstanding, Miss Fairfax. The gentleman whose arm is at present round your waist is my dear guardian, Mr John Worthing.

GWENDOLEN: I beg your pardon?

CECILY: This is Uncle Jack.

GWENDOLEN [*receding*]: Jack! Oh!

[*Enter Algernon.*]

CECILY: Here is Ernest.

ALGERNON [*goes straight over to Cecily without noticing anyone else*]: My own love! [*Offers to kiss her.*]

CECILY [*drawing back*]: A moment, Ernest! May I ask you—are you engaged to be married to this young lady?

ALGERNON [*looking round*]: To what young lady? Good heavens! Gwendolen!

CECILY: Yes, to good heavens, Gwendolen, I mean to Gwendolen.

ALGERNON [*laughing*]: Of course not! What could have put such an idea into your pretty little head?

CECILY: Thank you. [*Presenting her cheek to be kissed.*] You may.

[*Algernon kisses her.*]

GWENDOLEN: I felt there was some slight error, Miss Cardew. The gentleman who is now embracing you is my cousin, Mr Algernon Moncrieff.

CECILY [*breaking away from Algernon*]: Algernon Moncrieff! Oh!

[*The two girls move towards each other and put their arms round each other's waists as if for protection.*]

CECILY: Are you called Algernon?

ALGERNON: I cannot deny it.

CECILY: Oh!

GWENDOLEN: Is your name really John?

JACK [*standing rather proudly*]: I could deny it if I liked. I could deny anything if I liked. But my name certainly is John. It has been John for years.

CECILY [*to Gwendolen*]: A gross deception has been practised on both of us.

GWENDOLEN: My poor wounded Cecily!

CECILY: My sweet wronged Gwendolen!

GWENDOLEN [*slowly and seriously*]: You will call me sister, will you not?

[*They embrace. Jack and Algernon groan and walk up and down.*]

CECILY [*rather brightly*]: There is just one question I would like to be allowed to ask my guardian.

GWENDOLEN: An admirable idea! Mr Worthing, there is just one question I would like to be permitted to put to you. Where is your brother Ernest? We are both engaged to be married to your brother Ernest, so it is a matter of some importance to us to know where your brother Ernest is at present.

JACK [*slowly and hesitatingly*]: Gwendolen—Cecily—It is very painful for me to be forced to speak the truth. It is the first time in my life that I have ever been reduced to such a painful position, and I am really quite inexperienced in doing anything of the kind. However I will tell you quite frankly that I have no brother Ernest. I have no brother at all. I never had a brother in my life, and I certainly have not the smallest intention of ever having one in the future.

CECILY [*surprised*]: No brother at all?

JACK [*cheerily*]: None!

GWENDOLEN [*severely*]: Had you never a brother of any kind?

JACK [*pleasantly*]: Never. Not even of any kind.

GWENDOLEN: I am afraid it is quite clear, Cecily, that neither of us is engaged to be married to anyone.

CECILY: It is not a very pleasant position for a young girl suddenly to find herself in. Is it?

GWENDOLEN: Let us go into the house. They will hardly venture to come after us there.

CECILY: No, men are so cowardly, aren't they?

[*They retire into the house with scornful looks.*]

JACK: This ghastly state of things is what you call Bunburying, I suppose?

ALGERNON: Yes, and a perfectly wonderful Bunbury it is. The most wonderful Bunbury I have ever had in my life.

JACK: Well, you've no right whatsoever to Bunbury here.

ALGERNON: That is absurd. One has a right to Bunbury anywhere one chooses. Every serious Bunburyist knows that.

JACK: Serious Bunburyist! Good heavens!

ALGERNON: Well, one must be serious about something, if one wants to have any amusement in life. I happen to be serious about Bunburying. What on earth you are serious about I haven't got the remotest idea. About everything, I should fancy. You have such an absolutely trivial nature.

JACK: Well, the only small satisfaction I have in the whole of this wretched business is that your friend Bunbury is quite exploded. You won't be able to run down to the country quite so often as you used to do, dear Algy. And a very good thing too.

ALGERNON: Your brother is a little off colour, isn't he, dear Jack? You won't be able to disappear to London quite so frequently as your wicked custom was. And not a bad thing either.

JACK: As for your conduct towards Miss Cardew, I must say that your taking in a sweet, simple, innocent girl like that is quite inexcusable. To say nothing of the fact that she is my ward.

ALGERNON: I can see no possible defence at all for your deceiving a brilliant, clever, thoroughly experienced young lady like Miss Fairfax. To say nothing of the fact that she is my cousin.

JACK: I wanted to be engaged to Gwendolen, that is all. I love her.

ALGERNON: Well, I simply wanted to be engaged to Cecily. I adore her.

JACK: There is certainly no chance of your marrying Miss Cardew.

ALGERNON: I don't think there is much likelihood, Jack, of you and Miss Fairfax being united.

JACK: Well, that is no business of yours.

ALGERNON: If it was my business, I wouldn't talk about it. [*Begins to eat muffins.*] It is very vulgar to talk about one's business. Only people like stockbrokers do that, and then merely at dinner parties.

JACK: How you can sit there, calmly eating muffins when we are in this horrible trouble, I can't make out. You seem to me to be perfectly heartless.

ALGERNON: Well, I can't eat muffins in an agitated manner. The butter would probably get on my cuffs. One should always eat muffins quite calmly. It is the only way to eat them.

JACK: I say it's perfectly heartless your eating muffins at all, under the circumstances.

ALGERNON: When I am in trouble, eating is the only thing that consoles me. Indeed, when I am in really great trouble, as anyone who knows me intimately will tell you, I refuse everything except food and drink. At the present moment I am eating muffins because I am unhappy. Besides, I am particularly fond of muffins. [*Rising.*]

JACK [*rising*]: Well, that is no reason why you should eat them all in that greedy way.

[*Takes muffins from Algernon.*]

ALGERNON [*offering tea-cake*]: I wish you would have tea-cake instead. I don't like tea-cake.

JACK: Good heavens! I suppose a man may eat his own muffins in his own garden.

ALGERNON: But you have just said it was perfectly heartless to eat muffins.

JACK: I said it was perfectly heartless of you, under the circumstances. That is a very different thing.

ALGERNON: That may be. But the muffins are the same. [*He seizes the muffin-dish from Jack.*]

JACK: Algy, I wish to goodness you would go.

ALGERNON: You can't possibly ask me to go without having some dinner. It's absurd. I never go without my dinner. No one ever does, except vegetarians and people like that. Besides I have just made arrangements with Dr Chasuble to be christened at a quarter to six under the name of Ernest.

JACK: My dear fellow, the sooner you give up that nonsense the better. I made arrangements this morning with Dr Chasuble to be christened myself at 5.30, and I naturally will take the name of Ernest. Gwendolen would wish it. We can't both be christened Ernest. It's absurd. Besides, I have a perfect right to be christened if I like. There is no evidence at all that I ever have been christened by anybody. I should think it extremely probable I never was, and so does Dr Chasuble. It is entirely different in your case. You have been christened already.

ALGERNON: Yes, but I have not been christened for years.

JACK: Yes, but you have been christened. That is the important thing.

ALGERNON: Quite so. So I know my constitution can stand it. If you are not quite sure about your ever having been christened, I must say I think it rather dangerous your venturing on it now. It might make you very unwell. You can hardly have forgotten that someone very closely connected with you was very nearly carried off this week in Paris by a severe chill.

JACK: Yes, but you said yourself that a severe chill was not hereditary.

ALGERNON: It usen't to be, I know—but I daresay it is now. Science is always making wonderful improvements in things.

JACK [picking up the muffin-dish]: Oh, that is nonsense; you are always talking nonsense.

ALGERNON: Jack, you are at the muffins again! I wish you wouldn't. There are only two left. [Takes them.] I told you I was particularly fond of muffins.

JACK: But I hate tea-cake.

ALGERNON: Why on earth then do you allow tea-cake to be served up for your guests? What ideas you have of hospitality!

JACK: Algernon! I have already told you to go. I don't want you here. Why don't you go!

ALGERNON: I haven't quite finished my tea yet! and there is still one muffin left.

[Jack groans, and sinks into a chair. Algernon still continues eating.]   ACT DROP

THIRD ACT

SCENE: Morning-room[9] at the Manor House.

[Gwendolen and Cecily are at the window, looking out into the garden.]

GWENDOLEN: The fact that they did not follow us at once into the house, as anyone else would have done, seems to me to show that they have some sense of shame left.

CECILY: They have been eating muffins. That looks like repentance.

GWENDOLEN [after a pause]: They don't seem to notice us at all. Couldn't you cough?

CECILY: But I haven't got a cough.

GWENDOLEN: They're looking at us. What effrontery!

CECILY: They're approaching. That's very forward of them.

GWENDOLEN: Let us preserve a dignified silence.

CECILY: Certainly. It's the only thing to do now.

[Enter Jack followed by Algernon. They whistle some dreadful popular air from a British Opera.][1]

GWENDOLEN: This dignified silence seems to produce an unpleasant effect.

CECILY: A most distasteful one.

GWENDOLEN: But we will not be the first to speak.

CECILY: Certainly not.

GWENDOLEN: Mr Worthing, I have something very particular to ask you. Much depends on your reply.

CECILY: Gwendolen, your common sense is invaluable. Mr Moncrieff, kindly answer me the following question. Why did you pretend to be my guardian's brother?

ALGERNON: In order that I might have an opportunity of meeting you.

CECILY [to Gwendolen]: That certainly seems a satisfactory explanation, does it not?

GWENDOLEN: Yes, dear, if you can believe him.

CECILY: I don't. But that does not affect the wonderful beauty of his answer.

GWENDOLEN: True. In matters of grave importance, style, not sincerity is the vital thing. Mr Worthing, what explanation can you offer to me for pretending to have a brother? Was it in order that you might have an opportunity of coming up to town to see me as often as possible?

JACK: Can you doubt it, Miss Fairfax?

GWENDOLEN: I have the gravest doubts upon the subject. But I intend to crush them. This is not the moment for German scepticism.[2] [Moving to Cecily.] Their

9. An informal room for receiving morning calls from friends (afternoon visitors were received in the formal drawing room).
1. Probably a reference to Gilbert and Sullivan, who had made fun of Wilde and the Aesthetic movement in Patience (1881); see page 893.
2. Many 19th-century German scholars were skeptical in their treatment of religious texts.

explanations appear to be quite satisfactory, especially Mr Worthing's. That seems to me to have the stamp of truth upon it.

CECILY: I am more than content with what Mr Moncrieff said. His voice alone inspires one with absolute credulity.

GWENDOLEN: Then you think we should forgive them?

CECILY: Yes. I mean no.

GWENDOLEN: True! I had forgotten. There are principles at stake that one cannot surrender. Which of us should tell them? The task is not a pleasant one.

CECILY: Could we not both speak at the same time?

GWENDOLEN: An excellent idea! I nearly always speak at the same time as other people. Will you take the time from me?

CECILY: Certainly.

[Gwendolen beats time with uplifted finger.]

GWENDOLEN AND CECILY [speaking together]: Your Christian names are still an insuperable barrier. That is all!

JACK AND ALGERNON [speaking together]: Our Christian names! Is that all? But we are going to be christened this afternoon.

GWENDOLEN [to Jack]: For my sake you are prepared to do this terrible thing?

JACK: I am.

CECILY [to Algernon]: To please me you are ready to face this fearful ordeal?

ALGERNON: I am!

GWENDOLEN: How absurd to talk of the equality of the sexes! Where questions of self-sacrifice are concerned, men are infinitely beyond us.

JACK: We are. [Clasps hands with Algernon.]

CECILY: They have moments of physical courage of which we women know absolutely nothing.

GWENDOLEN [to Jack]: Darling!

ALGERNON [to Cecily]: Darling! [They fall into each other's arms.]

[Enter Merriman. When he enters he coughs loudly, seeing the situation.]

MERRIMAN: Ahem! Ahem! Lady Bracknell!

JACK: Good heavens!

[Enter Lady Bracknell. The couples separate in alarm.] [Exit Merriman.]

LADY BRACKNELL: Gwendolen! What does this mean?

GWENDOLEN: Merely that I am engaged to be married to Mr Worthing, mamma.

LADY BRACKNELL: Come here. Sit down. Sit down immediately. Hesitation of any kind is a sign of mental decay in the young, of physical weakness in the old. [Turns to Jack.] Apprised, sir, of my daughter's sudden flight by her trusty maid, whose confidence I purchased by means of a small coin, I followed her at once by a luggage train. Her unhappy father is, I am glad to say, under the impression that she is attending a more than usually lengthy lecture by the University Extension Scheme on the Influence of a permanent income on Thought. I do not propose to undeceive him. Indeed I have never undeceived him on any question. I would consider it wrong. But of course, you will clearly understand that all communication between yourself and my daughter must cease immediately from this moment. On this point, as indeed on all points, I am firm.

JACK: I am engaged to be married to Gwendolen, Lady Bracknell!

LADY BRACKNELL: You are nothing of the kind, sir. And now, as regards Algernon! . . . Algernon!

ALGERNON: Yes, Aunt Augusta.

LADY BRACKNELL: May I ask if it is in this house that your invalid friend Mr Bunbury resides?

ALGERNON [*stammering*]: Oh! No! Bunbury doesn't live here. Bunbury is somewhere else at present. In fact, Bunbury is dead.

LADY BRACKNELL: Dead! When did Mr Bunbury die? His death must have been
extremely sudden.

ALGERNON [*airily*]: Oh! I killed Bunbury this afternoon. I mean poor Bunbury
died this afternoon.

LADY BRACKNELL: What did he die of?

ALGERNON: Bunbury? Oh, he was quite exploded.

LADY BRACKNELL: Exploded! Was he the victim of a revolutionary outrage?[3] I
was not aware that Mr Bunbury was interested in social legislation. If so, he is well
punished for his morbidity.

ALGERNON: My dear Aunt Augusta, I mean he was found out! The doctors found
out that Bunbury could not live, that is what I mean—so Bunbury died.

LADY BRACKNELL: He seems to have had great confidence in the opinion of his
physicians. I am glad, however, that he made up his mind at the last to some definite course of action, and acted under proper medical advice. And now that we
have finally got rid of this Mr Bunbury, may I ask, Mr Worthing, who is that
young person whose hand my nephew Algernon is now holding in what seems to
me a peculiarly unnecessary manner?

JACK: That lady is Miss Cecily Cardew, my ward.

[*Lady Bracknell bows coldly to Cecily.*]

ALGERNON: I am engaged to be married to Cecily, Aunt Augusta.

LADY BRACKNELL: I beg your pardon?

CECILY: Mr Moncrieff and I are engaged to be married, Lady Bracknell.

LADY BRACKNELL [*with a shiver, crossing to the sofa and sitting down*]: I do not
know whether there is anything peculiarly exciting in the air of this particular
part of Hertfordshire, but the number of engagements that go on seems to me considerably above the proper average that statistics have laid down for our guidance.
I think some preliminary enquiry on my part would not be out of place. Mr Worthing, is Miss Cardew at all connected with any of the larger railway stations in
London? I merely desire information. Until yesterday I had no idea that there
were any families or persons whose origins was a Terminus.[4]

[*Jack looks perfectly furious, but restrains himself.*]

JACK [*in a clear, cold voice*]: Miss Cardew is the granddaughter of the late Mr
Thomas Cardew of 149, Belgrave Square, S.W.; Gervase Park, Dorking, Surrey;
and the Sporran, Fifeshire, N.B.[5]

LADY BRACKNELL: That sounds not unsatisfactory. Three addresses always
inspire confidence, even in tradesmen. But what proof have I of their authenticity?

JACK: I have carefully preserved the Court Guides[6] of the period. They are open to
your inspection, Lady Bracknell.

LADY BRACKNELL [*grimly*]: I have known strange errors in that publication.

JACK: Miss Cardew's family solicitors are Messrs Markby, Markby, and Markby.

LADY BRACKNELL: Markby, Markby, and Markby? A firm of the very highest
position in their profession. Indeed I am told that one of the Mr Markbys is occasionally to be seen at dinner parties. So far I am satisfied.

---

3. Anarchy and political assassination were much in the
news; Wilde's earliest drama, *Vera, or the Nihilists* (1881),
dealt with the subject.
4. A railway station at the end of the line.

5. North Britain, i.e., Scotland.
6. Annual publications listing the names and London
addresses of the upper classes.

JACK [*very irritably*]: How extremely kind of you, Lady Bracknell! I have also in my possession, you will be pleased to hear, certificates of Miss Cardew's birth, baptism, whooping cough, registration, vaccination, confirmation, and the measles; both the German and the English variety.

LADY BRACKNELL: Ah! A life crowded with incident, I see; though perhaps somewhat too exciting for a young girl. I am not myself in favour of premature experiences. [*Rises, looks at her watch.*] Gwendolen! the time approaches for our departure. We have not a moment to lose. As a matter of form, Mr Worthing, I had better ask you if Miss Cardew has any little fortune?

JACK: Oh! about a hundred and thirty thousand pounds in the Funds.[7] That is all. Goodbye, Lady Bracknell. So pleased to have seen you.

LADY BRACKNELL [*sitting down again*]: A moment, Mr Worthing. A hundred and thirty thousand pounds! And in the Funds! Miss Cardew seems to me a most attractive young lady, now that I look at her. Few girls of the present day have any really solid qualities, any of the qualities that last, and improve with time. We live, I regret to say, in an age of surfaces. [*To Cecily.*] Come over here, dear. [*Cecily goes across.*] Pretty child! your dress is sadly simple, and your hair seems almost as Nature might have left it. But we can soon alter all that. A thoroughly experienced French maid produces a really marvellous result in a very brief space of time. I remember recommending one to young Lady Lancing, and after three months her own husband did not know her.

JACK [*aside*]: And after six months nobody knew her.

LADY BRACKNELL [*glares at Jack for a few moments. Then bends, with a practised smile, to Cecily.*]: Kindly turn round, sweet child. [*Cecily turns completely round.*] No, the side view is what I want. [*Cecily presents her profile.*] Yes, quite as I expected. There are distinct social possibilities in your profile. The two weak points in our age are its want of principle and its want of profile. The chin a little higher, dear. Style largely depends on the way the chin is worn. They are worn very high, just at present. Algernon!

ALGERNON: Yes, Aunt Augusta!

LADY BRACKNELL: There are distinct social possibilities in Miss Cardew's profile.

ALGERNON: Cecily is the sweetest, dearest, prettiest girl in the whole world. And I don't care twopence about social possibilities.

LADY BRACKNELL: Never speak disrespectfully of Society, Algernon. Only people who can't get into it do that. [*To Cecily.*] Dear child, of course you know that Algernon has nothing but his debts to depend upon. But I do not approve of mercenary marriages. When I married Lord Bracknell I had no fortune of any kind. But I never dreamed for a moment of allowing that to stand in my way. Well, I suppose I must give my consent.

ALGERNON: Thank you, Aunt Augusta.

LADY BRACKNELL: Cecily, you may kiss me!

CECILY [*kisses her*]: Thank you, Lady Bracknell.

LADY BRACKNELL: You may also address me as Aunt Augusta for the future.

CECILY: Thank you, Aunt Augusta.

LADY BRACKNELL: The marriage, I think, had better take place quite soon.

ALGERNON: Thank you, Aunt Augusta.

CECILY: Thank you, Aunt Augusta.

---

7. The Consolidated Funds, reliable interest-bearing government bonds.

LADY BRACKNELL: To speak frankly, I am not in favour of long engagements. They give people the opportunity of finding out each other's character before marriage, which I think is never advisable.

JACK: I beg your pardon for interrupting you, Lady Bracknell, but this engagement is quite out of the question. I am Miss Cardew's guardian, and she cannot marry without my consent until she comes of age. That consent I absolutely decline to give.

LADY BRACKNELL: Upon what grounds may I ask? Algernon is an extremely, I may almost say an ostentatiously, eligible young man. He has nothing, but he looks everything. What more can one desire?

JACK: It pains me very much to have to speak frankly to you, Lady Bracknell, about your nephew, but the fact is that I do not approve at all of his moral character. I suspect him of being untruthful.

[Algernon and Cecily look at him in indignant amazement.]

LADY BRACKNELL: Untruthful! My nephew Algernon? Impossible! He is an Oxonian.[8]

JACK: I fear there can be no possible doubt about the matter. This afternoon, during my temporary absence in London on an important question of romance, he obtained admission to my house by means of the false pretence of being my brother. Under an assumed name he drank, I've just been informed by my butler, an entire pint bottle of my Perrier-Jouet, Brut, '89; a wine I was specially reserving for myself. Continuing his disgraceful deception, he succeeded in the course of the afternoon in alienating the affections of my only ward. He subsequently stayed to tea, and devoured every single muffin. And what makes his conduct all the more heartless is, that he was perfectly well aware from the first that I have no brother, that I never had a brother, and that I don't intend to have a brother, not even of any kind. I distinctly told him so myself yesterday afternoon.

LADY BRACKNELL: Ahem! Mr Worthing, after careful consideration I have decided entirely to overlook my nephew's conduct to you.

JACK: That is very generous of you, Lady Bracknell. My own decision, however, is unalterable. I decline to give my consent.

LADY BRACKNELL [to Cecily]: Come here, sweet child. [Cecily goes over.] How old are you, dear?

CECILY: Well, I am really only eighteen, but I always admit to twenty when I go to evening parties.

LADY BRACKNELL: You are perfectly right in making some slight alteration. Indeed, no woman should ever be quite accurate about her age. It looks so calculating. . . . [In a meditative manner.] Eighteen, but admitting to twenty at evening parties. Well, it will not be very long before you are of age and free from the restraints of tutelage. So I don't think your guardian's consent is, after all, a matter of any importance.

JACK: Pray excuse me, Lady Bracknell, for interrupting you again, but it is only fair to tell you that according to the terms of her grandfather's will Miss Cardew does not come legally of age till she is thirty-five.

LADY BRACKNELL: That does not seem to me to be a grave objection. Thirty-five is a very attractive age. London society is full of women of the very highest birth who have, of their own free choice, remained thirty-five for years. Lady Dumbleton is an instance in point. To my own knowledge she has been thirty-five ever since she arrived at the age of forty, which was many years ago now. I see no reason why

---

8. I.e., he attended Oxford University.

our dear Cecily should not be even still more attractive at the age you mention than she is at present. There will be a large accumulation of property.

CECILY: Algy, could you wait for me till I was thirty-five?

ALGERNON: Of course I could, Cecily. You know I could.

CECILY: Yes, I felt it instinctively, but I couldn't wait all that time. I hate waiting even five minutes for anybody. It always makes me rather cross. I am not punctual myself, I know, but I do like punctuality in others, and waiting, even to be married, is quite out of the question.

ALGERNON: Then what is to be done, Cecily?

CECILY: I don't know, Mr Moncrieff.

LADY BRACKNELL: My dear Mr Worthing, as Miss Cardew states positively that she cannot wait till she is thirty-five—a remark which I am bound to say seems to me to show a somewhat impatient nature—I would beg of you to reconsider your decision.

JACK: But my dear Lady Bracknell, the matter is entirely in your own hands. The moment you consent to my marriage with Gwendolen, I will most gladly allow your nephew to form an alliance with my ward.

LADY BRACKNELL [rising and drawing herself up]: You must be quite aware that what you propose is out of the question.

JACK: Then a passionate celibacy is all that any of us can look forward to.

LADY BRACKNELL: That is not the destiny I propose for Gwendolen. Algernon, of course, can choose for himself. [Pulls out her watch.] Come, dear; [Gwendolen rises.] we have already missed five, if not six, trains. To miss any more might expose us to comment on the platform.

[Enter Dr Chasuble.]

CHASUBLE: Everything is quite ready for the christenings.

LADY BRACKNELL: The christenings, sir! Is not that somewhat premature?

CHASUBLE [looking rather puzzled, and pointing to Jack and Algernon]: Both these gentlemen have expressed a desire for immediate baptism.

LADY BRACKNELL: At their age? The idea is grotesque and irreligious! Algernon, I forbid you to be baptized. I will not hear of such excesses. Lord Bracknell would be highly displeased if he learned that that was the way in which you wasted your time and money.

CHASUBLE: Am I to understand then that there are to be no christenings at all this afternoon?

JACK: I don't think that, as things are now, it would be of much practical value to either of us, Dr Chasuble.

CHASUBLE: I am grieved to hear such sentiments from you, Mr Worthing. They savour of the heretical views of the Anabaptists,[9] views that I have completely refuted in four of my unpublished sermons. However, as your present mood seems to be one peculiarly secular, I will return to the church at once. Indeed, I have just been informed by the pew-opener[1] that for the last hour and a half Miss Prism has been waiting for me in the vestry.

LADY BRACKNELL [starting]: Miss Prism! Did I hear you mention a Miss Prism?

CHASUBLE: Yes, Lady Bracknell. I am on my way to join her.

LADY BRACKNELL: Pray allow me to detain you for a moment. This matter may prove to be one of vital importance to Lord Bracknell and myself. Is this Miss Prism a female of repellent aspect, remotely connected with education?

9. A 16th-century Protestant sect that believed in adult   1. Usher.
baptism.

CHASUBLE [*somewhat indignantly*]: She is the most cultivated of ladies, and the very picture of respectability.

LADY BRACKNELL: It is obviously the same person. May I ask what position she holds in your household?

CHASUBLE [*severely*]: I am a celibate, madam.

JACK [*interposing*]: Miss Prism, Lady Bracknell, has been for the last three years Miss Cardew's esteemed governess and valued companion.

LADY BRACKNELL: In spite of what I hear of her, I must see her at once. Let her be sent for.

CHASUBLE [*looking off*]: She approaches; she is nigh.

[*Enter Miss Prism hurriedly.*]

MISS PRISM: I was told you expected me in the vestry, dear Canon. I have been waiting for you there for an hour and three quarters. [*Catches sight of Lady Bracknell who has fixed her with a stony glare. Miss Prism grows pale and quails. She looks anxiously round as if desirous to escape.*]

LADY BRACKNELL [*in a severe, judicial voice*]: Prism! [*Miss Prism bows her head in shame.*] Come here, Prism! [*Miss Prism approaches in a humble manner.*] Prism! Where is that baby? [*General consternation. The Canon starts back in horror. Algernon and Jack pretend to be anxious to shield Cecily and Gwendolen from hearing the details of a terrible public scandal.*] Twenty-eight years ago, Prism, you left Lord Bracknell's house, Number 104, Upper Grosvenor Street, in charge of a perambulator that contained a baby, of the male sex. You never returned. A few weeks later, through the elaborate investigations of the Metropolitan police, the perambulator was discovered at midnight, standing by itself in a remote corner of Bayswater.[2] It contained the manuscript of a three-volume novel of more than usually revolting sentimentality. [*Miss Prism starts in involuntary indignation.*] But the baby was not there! [*Everyone looks at Miss Prism.*] Prism! Where is that baby? [*A pause.*]

MISS PRISM: Lady Bracknell, I admit with shame that I do not know. I only wish I did. The plain facts of the case are these. On the morning of the day you mention, a day that is for ever branded on my memory, I prepared as usual to take the baby out in its perambulator. I had also with me a somewhat old, but capacious handbag in which I had intended to place the manuscript of a work of fiction that I had written during my few unoccupied hours. In a moment of mental abstraction, for which I never can forgive myself, I deposited the manuscript in the bassinette, and placed the baby in the hand-bag.

JACK [*who has been listening attentively*]: But where did you deposit the hand-bag?

MISS PRISM: Do not ask me, Mr Worthing.

JACK: Miss Prism, this is a matter of no small importance to me. I insist on knowing where you deposited the hand-bag that contained that infant.

MISS PRISM: I left it in the cloak-room of one of the larger railway stations in London.

JACK: What railway station?

MISS PRISM [*quite crushed*]: Victoria. The Brighton line. [*Sinks into a chair.*]

JACK: I must retire to my room for a moment. Gwendolen, wait here for me.

GWENDOLEN: If you are not too long, I will wait here for you all my life.

[*Exit Jack in great excitement.*]

CHASUBLE: What do you think this means, Lady Bracknell?

---

2. An area in the West End of London, near Kensington Gardens.

LADY BRACKNELL: I dare not even suspect, Dr Chasuble. I need hardly tell you that in families of high position strange coincidences are not supposed to occur. They are hardly considered the thing.

[*Noises heard overhead as if someone was throwing trunks about. Everyone looks up.*]

CECILY: Uncle Jack seems strangely agitated.

CHASUBLE: Your guardian has a very emotional nature.

LADY BRACKNELL: This noise is extremely unpleasant. It sounds as if he was having an argument. I dislike arguments of any kind. They are always vulgar, and often convincing.

CHASUBLE [*looking up*]: It has stopped now. [*The noise is redoubled.*]

LADY BRACKNELL: I wish he would arrive at some conclusion.

GWENDOLEN: This suspense is terrible. I hope it will last.

[*Enter Jack with a hand-bag of black leather in his hand.*]

JACK [*rushing over to Miss Prism*]: Is this the hand-bag, Miss Prism? Examine it carefully before you speak. The happiness of more than one life depends on your answer.

MISS PRISM [*calmly*]: It seems to be mine. Yes, here is the injury it received through the upsetting of a Gower Street omnibus in younger and happier days. Here is the stain on the lining caused by the explosion of a temperance beverage, an incident that occurred at Leamington. And here, on the lock, are my initials. I had forgotten that in an extravagant mood I had had them placed there. The bag is undoubtedly mine. I am delighted to have it so unexpectedly restored to me. It has been a great inconvenience being without it all these years.

JACK [*in a pathetic voice*]: Miss Prism, more is restored to you than this hand-bag. I was the baby you placed in it.

MISS PRISM [*amazed*]: You?

JACK [*embracing her*]: Yes . . . mother!

MISS PRISM [*recoiling in indignant astonishment*]: Mr Worthing! I am unmarried!

JACK: Unmarried! I do not deny that is a serious blow. But after all, who has the right to cast a stone against one who has suffered?[3] Cannot repentance wipe out an act of folly? Why should there be one law for men, and another for women? Mother, I forgive you. [*Tries to embrace her again.*]

MISS PRISM [*still more indignant*]: Mr Worthing, there is some error. [*Pointing to Lady Bracknell.*] There is the lady who can tell you who you really are.

JACK [*after a pause*]: Lady Bracknell, I hate to seem inquisitive, but would you kindly inform me who I am?

LADY BRACKNELL: I am afraid that the news I have to give you will not altogether please you. You are the son of my poor sister, Mrs Moncrieff, and consequently Algernon's elder brother.

JACK: Algy's elder brother! Then I have a brother after all. I knew I had a brother! I always said I had a brother! Cecily—how could you have ever doubted that I had a brother. [*Seizes hold of Algernon.*] Dr Chasuble, my unfortunate brother. Miss Prism, my unfortunate brother. Gwendolen, my unfortunate brother. Algy, you young scoundrel, you will have to treat me with more respect in the future. You have never behaved to me like a brother in all your life.

ALGERNON: Well, not till today, old boy, I admit. I did my best, however, though I was out of practice. [*Shakes hands.*]

GWENDOLEN [*to Jack*]: My own! But what own are you? What is your Christian name, now that you have become someone else?

---

3. Jesus saves a woman who is about to be stoned for committing adultery, saying, "He that is without sin among you, let him first cast a stone at her" (John 8.7).

JACK: Good heavens! . . . I had quite forgotten that point. Your decision on the subject of my name is irrevocable, I suppose?

GWENDOLEN: I never change, except in my affections.

CECILY: What a noble nature you have, Gwendolen!

JACK: Then the question had better be cleared up at once. Aunt Augusta, a moment. At the time when Miss Prism left me in the hand-bag, had I been christened already?

LADY BRACKNELL: Every luxury that money could buy, including christening, had been lavished on you by your fond and doting parents.

JACK: Then I was christened! That is settled. Now, what name was I given? Let me know the worst.

LADY BRACKNELL: Being the eldest son you were naturally christened after your father.

JACK [irritably]: Yes, but what was my father's Christian name?

LADY BRACKNELL [meditatively]: I cannot at the present moment recall what the General's Christian name was. But I have no doubt he had one. He was eccentric, I admit. But only in later years. And that was the result of the Indian climate, and marriage, and indigestion, and other things of that kind.

JACK: Algy! Can't you recollect what our father's Christian name was?

ALGERNON: My dear boy, we were never even on speaking terms. He died before I was a year old.

JACK: His name would appear in the Army Lists of the period, I suppose, Aunt Augusta?

LADY BRACKNELL: The General was essentially a man of peace, except in his domestic life. But I have no doubt his name would appear in any military directory.

JACK: The Army Lists of the last forty years are here. These delightful records should have been my constant study. [Rushes to bookcase and tears the books out.] M. Generals . . . Mallam, Maxbohm,[4] Magley, what ghastly names they have— Markby, Migsby, Mobbs, Moncrieff! Lieutenant 1840, Captain, Lieutenant-Colonel, Colonel, General 1869, Christian names, Ernest John. [Puts book very quietly down and speaks quite calmly.] I always told you, Gwendolen, my name was Ernest, didn't I? Well, it is Ernest after all. I mean it naturally is Ernest.

LADY BRACKNELL: Yes, I remember now that the General was called Ernest. I knew I had some particular reason for disliking the name.

GWENDOLEN: Ernest! My own Ernest! I felt from the first that you could have no other name!

JACK: Gwendolen, it is a terrible thing for a man to find out suddenly that all his life he has been speaking nothing but the truth. Can you forgive me?

GWENDOLEN: I can. For I feel that you are sure to change.

JACK: My own one!

CHASUBLE [to Miss Prism]: Laetitia! [Embraces her.]

MISS PRISM [enthusiastically]: Frederick! At last!

ALGERNON: Cecily! [Embraces her.] At last!

JACK: Gwendolen! [Embraces her.] At last!

LADY BRACKNELL: My nephew, you seem to be displaying signs of triviality.

JACK: On the contrary, Aunt Augusta, I've now realized for the first time in my life the vital Importance of Being Earnest.

TABLEAU   CURTAIN

1894, performed 1895   1899

---

4. A pun on the name of Wilde's friend Max Beerbohm.

Aphorisms[1]

On arriving in America: I have nothing to declare except my genius.

F. Harris, Oscar Wilde

We have really everything in common with America nowadays, except, of course, language.

The Canterville Ghost

A poet can survive everything but a misprint.

The Children of the Poets

Meredith is a prose Browning, and so is Browning. He used poetry as a medium for writing in prose.

The Critic as Artist

Anybody can make history. Only a great man can write it.

Ibid.

The one duty we owe to history is to rewrite it.

Ibid.

A little sincerity is a dangerous thing, and a great deal of it is absolutely fatal.

Ibid.

There is only one thing in the world worse than being talked about, and that is not being talked about.

The Picture of Dorian Gray

Being natural is simply a pose, and the most irritating pose I know.

Ibid.

A man cannot be too careful in the choice of his enemies.

Ibid.

American girls are as clever at concealing their parents, as English women are at concealing their past.

Ibid.

Perhaps, after all, America never has been discovered. I myself would say that it had merely been detected.

Ibid.

Women give to men the very gold of their lives. But they invariably want it back in such very small change.

Ibid.

I hate vulgar realism in literature. The man who could call a spade a spade should be compelled to use one. It is the only thing he is fit for.

Ibid.

1. Wilde's aphorisms often cleverly invert a cliché in order to produce a seeming paradox; they are perhaps his most characteristic form of expression in his conversation and writing alike. Wilde kept track of his favorite maxims, sometimes revising them in later works. In addition to the epigrammatic preface to *Dorian Gray*, he published two selections: *A Few Maxims for the Instruction of the Over-Educated* appeared anonymously in the *Saturday Review* in November 1894; *Phrases and Philosophies for the Use of the Young* was published in *The Chameleon* in December 1894.

It is better to be beautiful than to be good. But . . . it is better to be good than to be ugly.

Ibid.

I can resist everything except temptation.

Lady Windermere's Fan

It's most dangerous nowadays for a husband to pay any attention to his wife in public. It always makes people think that he beats her when they're alone.

Ibid.

We are all in the gutter, but some of us are looking at the stars.

Ibid.

In this world there are only two tragedies. One is not getting what one wants, and the other is getting it.

Ibid.

What is a cynic? A man who knows the price of everything and the value of nothing.

Ibid.

Experience is the name everyone gives to their mistakes.

Ibid.

Repentance is quite out of date. And besides, if a woman really repents, she has to go to a bad dressmaker, otherwise no one believes in her.

Ibid.

It is perfectly monstrous the way people go about, nowadays, saying things against one behind one's back that are absolutely and entirely true.

A Woman of No Importance

The youth of America is their oldest tradition. It has been going on now for three hundred years.

Ibid.

The English country gentleman galloping after a fox—the unspeakable in full pursuit of the uneatable.

Ibid.

Twenty years of romance make a woman look like a ruin; but twenty years of marriage make her look like a public building.

Ibid.

One should never trust a woman who tells one her real age. A woman who would tell one that, would tell one anything.

Ibid.

The first duty in life is to be as artificial as possible. What the second duty is no one has as yet discovered.

Phrases and Philosophies for the Use of the Young

To love oneself is the beginning of a lifelong romance.

Ibid.

My wallpaper and I are fighting a duel to the death. One or the other of us has to go.

Richard Ellmann, *Oscar Wilde*

❂ OSCAR WILDE AND HIS TIME ❂

Aestheticism, Decadence, and the Fin de Siècle

"I belong to the Beardsley period," Max Beerbohm remarked audaciously in 1894, when he and Aubrey Beardsley were both just twenty-two. Time has proved him correct. The late-Victorian period, the age of Beardsley and Wilde, Kipling and Conan Doyle, has indeed come to be seen as a distinctive era in which the aesthetic and moral values of the nineteenth century were twisted or transmuted into the revolutionary forces of modernism, in a blaze of daring new styles, attitudes, and modes of behavior.

By the early 1880s most of the major mid-Victorian writers had died or were well past their prime. As the Empire reached its peak, Britain's self-confidence eroded under the strain of maintaining its military might and economic supremacy against competition from the United States and Germany. About 1890, the general sense of fatigue and anxiety found expression in the French phrase *fin de siècle*—the "end of the age." The term suggested that Victorian values and energies had become exhausted and that an unsettling, amoral, post-Darwinian world was emerging in which contradictory impulses vied for attention: exquisite delicacy in poetry and brutal realism in fiction, effete dandyism among some men and hearty imperialism among others, socialism and Catholicism. The proliferation of women in the workforce ran headlong into the diagnosis of inherent female debility by medical authorities. Meanwhile, discussion clubs formed where both sexes openly debated the merits of marriage and free love. It was the era of the Manly Woman and the Womanly Man, the moment when sexology was invented and words like "homosexual," "lesbian," and—belatedly—"heterosexual" were coined to regulate the mysteries of sexual identity.

Partly in flight from the devastated industrial landscape, partly in rebellion against middle-class mores and artistic norms, Aesthetes like Pater, Wilde, Whistler, Beardsley, and Symons sought to create a pure art of flawless formal design, divorced from moral concerns but open to hitherto unexplored subject matter—the often artificial beauties of cosmetics, music halls, gaslit faces, or city streets seen through mist and rain. By the 1870s, critics were giving the labels "impressionist" and "aesthetic" to paintings by Whistler and Dante Gabriel Rossetti, and to poems by Rossetti, Swinburne, and Morris. With the help of flamboyant personalities such as Whistler and Wilde, Aestheticism became known in the 1880s as an entire way of life, involving flowing dress for both men and women, medieval- or Japanese-style home furnishings, and ostentatious worship of the beautiful in all the arts. There was even a distinctive Aesthetic vocabulary: "Constantly yearning for the intense," said one observer, "the language of the Aesthetes is tinged with somewhat exaggerated metaphor, and their adjectives are usually superlative—as supreme, consummate, utter, quite too preciously sublime."

Though its excesses were easy to mock, Aestheticism took hold so forcefully because its various strands had been developing, abroad and at home, for several generations. In 1873 Tennyson complained with some reason that Aesthetes lived on "poisonous honey stolen from France." Swinburne was clearly influenced by the French poets Théophile Gautier and Charles Baudelaire when he declared in 1866: "Art for art's sake first of all," explaining that "her business is not to do good on other grounds, but to be good on her own." Yet Tennyson himself was a pivotal figure for the Aesthetes and their immediate predecessors, the Pre-Raphaelites; both groups were inspired by his medievalism and sonorous morbidity.

Aestheticism often shaded over into Decadence, a term that was confusingly applied not only to the deliberately mannered works of the late Victorians, but also to the scandalous or effeminate conduct of their creators. By the 1890s the word had become a vague and fashionable label of both moral censure and avant-garde respect. The naturalist fiction of George Gissing and Émile Zola was called decadent because of its tawdry subject matter and amoral

J'AI BAISÉ TA BOVCHE
IOKANAAN
J'AI BAISÉ TA BOVCHE

Aubrey Beardsley, *"J'ai baisé ta bouche, Iokanaan."* Illustration for Oscar Wilde's *Salomé,* 1893.
Wilde wrote his play *Salomé* in French, but its production on the English stage (starring Sarah
Bernhardt) was banned because of its depiction of biblical characters. Beardsley's outrageous illustrations for the English translation (1894) instantly made the book a decadent *cause célèbre* and a
classic of Art Nouveau design. Beardsley depicts the play's climatic scene, in which Salomé, who
has demanded John the Baptist's head as a reward for her dancing, kisses the dead lips of the
prophet who had scorned her love.

THE SIX-MARK TEA-POT.

Æsthetic Bridegroom. "IT IS QUITE CONSUMMATE, IS IT NOT?"
Intense Bride. "IT IS, INDEED! OH, ALGERNON, LET US LIVE UP TO IT!"

George Du Maurier, *The Six-Mark Tea-Pot,* from *Punch* magazine, 1880. Born in Paris, Du Maurier shuttled between London and Paris, and studies in art and science, until he settled on a career as a magazine illustrator, joining the staff of *Punch* in 1864. His wittily captioned cartoons of Aesthetes fixed the movement in the public imagination. Having established his reputation as a keen satirist of cultural trends, he achieved international fame with his novel *Trilby* (1894), which was based on his days with Whistler as an art student in Paris.

attitudes; Wilde on the other hand claimed that decadent pleasures alone made life worth living. Depending on one's point of view, "decadent" could describe, with praise or blame, a dissipated young man like Wilde's Dorian Gray, or a vigorous freethinking feminist like the heroine of Grant Allen's *The Woman Who Did* (1895). In most cases the word suggested an ultra-refined sophistication of taste allied with moral perversity; and many feared that decadent ideas and behavior heralded social collapse and apocalyptic change for Western culture. Max Nordau's 1895 best-seller *Degeneration* portrayed decadence as evidence of "a twilight mood" in Europe; "degeneration and hysteria," he felt, were "the convulsions and spasms of exhaustion" in Western civilization. Delighting in this anxiety, Wilde told Yeats that Pater's *Renaissance* "is the very flower of decadence; the last trumpet should have sounded the moment it was written."

Together, the *fin de siècle* writers helped free English literature of moral inhibition, producing a richly descriptive poetry and prose marked by deep learning, love of London, bold sensuality, spiritual intensity, and a new focus on images rather than events. The concept of Decadence depended on a Christian mentality haunted by notions of sin, forgiveness, and damnation. Dissatisfied with life and art, and tempted by drugs and drinking, opium and absinthe, some writers met early deaths from dissipation or suicide. The quest for absolution led many, including Beardsley and Wilde, to convert to Catholicism.

While they strove for a refined art purified of morality and narrative content, Aesthetes and Decadents made it clear that art had a definitely sexual if often elusive essence. Though "consummate" was a favorite word, much of their work expressed a frustrated longing for a fleeting taste of forbidden fruits. Often both male and female writers envisioned women as dangerous idols, worshipped at first as chaste images of noble art but finally revealed as seductive vampires who sap masculine energy with insatiable desire.

As the critic Elaine Showalter points out, "The decadent or aesthete was the masculine counterpart to the New Woman" lauded by feminist fiction writers of the 1890s. More prevalent in art than life, these two literary figures spurred fears of a sexual revolution and cast doubt on Britain's ability to procreate future generations of Empire rulers. The anxiety over the blurring of gender boundaries helps explain the strange conflux of misogynist, homoerotic, androgynous, utopianly healthy, and luridly diseased discourses of sexuality that surfaced at this time—culminating in Bram Stoker's *Dracula* (1897), which portrayed the New Woman as an insatiable sexual vampire poised to destroy British manhood. Even a radical advocate of socialist free love, Karl Marx's daughter Eleanor, denounced "the effeminate man and the masculine woman" as horrifyingly unnatural. With slight exaggeration, Max Beerbohm alluded to "that amalgamation of the sexes which is one of the chief planks in the decadent platform."

The heyday of Aestheticism and Decadence came to an end with the trials of Oscar Wilde. When Wilde was arrested for sodomy in 1895, newspapers reported that he carried the notorious decadent magazine, *The Yellow Book*, with him to jail (it was actually a yellow-backed French novel). Mobs stoned the publisher's office; Beardsley, its editor, was fired; the magazine failed. A savage conservative backlash suddenly ended the vogue of the bold New Woman and the languid Aesthete. But it was in the "degenerate" turmoil of the *fin de siècle* that modernism got its start: James, Gissing, Dowson, Yeats, Bennett, Wells, Shaw, Ford, and Conrad all published in *The Yellow Book* or its short-lived successor, *The Savoy*. Though the Aesthetic creed seemed like an underground current to many during the Victorian period, by the turn of the century belief in the autonomy of the artist was on the brink of becoming modernism's main stream.

W. S. Gilbert
1836–1911

William Schwenk Gilbert is best known for his lengthy partnership with the composer Arthur Sullivan. Together they wrote fourteen light operas from 1871 to 1896, immensely popular entertainments that continue to be performed throughout the world today. Known as the "Savoy Operas" because they debuted at the Savoy Theatre built by Richard D'Oyly Carte expressly for their production, Gilbert and Sullivan's works include H.M.S. *Pinafore* (1878), *The Pirates of Penzance* (1879), and *The Mikado* (1885). Typically, these comic operettas poke gentle fun at British institutions such as the law, Parliament, and the navy, while also mocking Victorian obsessions with topics such as social hierarchy or orphanhood. Although Gilbert's satirical librettos perfectly complement Sullivan's sprightly scores, they can be read on their own as nimble evocations of Victorian foibles and follies. *Patience* spoofed Aestheticism just as it reached the public consciousness in the early 1880s; in the process the opera helped to articulate and spread the ideas it mocked. A composite caricature of Whistler and Wilde, the "ultra-poetical, super-aesthetical" Bunthorne is made to confess that his exquisite refinement is just a pose meant to attract the ladies.

If You're Anxious for to Shine in the High Aesthetic Line

Am I alone,
   And unobserved? I am!
Then let me own
   I'm an aesthetic sham!
5 This air severe
   Is but a mere
      Veneer!
This cynic smile
   Is but a wile
10   Of guile!
This costume chaste
   Is but good taste
      Misplaced!
Let me confess!
15   A languid love for lilies does *not* blight me!
   Lank limbs and haggard cheeks do *not* delight me!
I do *not* care for dirty greens
   By any means.
I do *not* long for all one sees
20 That's Japanese.
I am *not* fond of uttering platitudes
   In stained-glass attitudes.
In short, my mediaevalism's affectation,
Born of a morbid love of admiration![1]

Song

25 If you're anxious for to shine in the high aesthetic line as a man of culture rare,
You must get up all the germs of the transcendental terms,[2] and plant them
  everywhere.
You must lie upon the daisies and discourse in novel phrases of your com-
  plicated state of mind,
The meaning doesn't matter if it's only idle chatter of a transcendental kind.
      And every one will say,
30   As you walk your mystic way,
"If this young man expresses himself in terms too deep for *me,*
Why, what a very singularly deep young man this deep young man must be!"

Be eloquent in praise of the very dull old days which have long since
  passed away,
And convince 'em, if you can, that the reign of good Queen Anne[3] was
  Culture's palmiest day.

---

1. Stereotypical Aesthetic behavior, combining traits of Rossetti, Whistler, and Wilde, particularly as they were spoofed by the cartoonist George Du Maurier. Lilies and languid yet soul-tormented lovers figure in the work of Rossetti, as do medieval subjects and stained glass; Whistler's paintings featuring Japanese props and perspective helped create a vogue for Japanese art, dress, and decoration; Wilde's elaborate clothing and ostentatious worship of beauty were said to be merely attention-getting poses.

2. Transcendental philosophy values individual visionary understanding over objective, materialist apprehension of the world. *The Germ* (1850) was a short-lived Pre-Raphaelite journal that sought to promote a more spiritual art and poetry in Britain.
3. Queen of Great Britain from 1702–1714; the simplicity of the era's neoclassical architecture and design found favor with Aesthetes tired of Victorian ornateness.

35   Of course you will pooh-pooh whatever's fresh and new, and declare it's
        crude and mean,
     For Art stopped short in the cultivated court of the Empress Josephine.[4]
            And every one will say,
            As you walk your mystic way,
     "If that's not good enough for him which is good enough for *me*,
40   Why, what a very cultivated kind of youth this kind of youth must be!"

     Then a sentimental passion of a vegetable fashion must excite your languid
        spleen,[5]
     An attachment *à la* Plato for a bashful young potato, or a not-too-French
        French bean!
     Though the Philistines may jostle, you will rank as an apostle in the high
        aesthetic band,
     If you walk down Piccadilly[6] with a poppy or a lily in your mediaeval hand.
45   And every one will say,
            As you walk your flowery way,
     "If he's content with a vegetable love which would certainly not suit *me*,
     Why, what a most particularly pure young man this pure young man must be!"

1881

James Abbott McNeill Whistler
1834–1903

An American artist who settled in London in the early 1860s, Whistler provided much of the intellectual energy that inspired the Aesthetic Movement in the 1880s. He studied art in Paris, where he became friends with Gustav Courbet and Henri Fantin-Latour, absorbed the aesthetic doctrine of Théophile Gautier and Charles Baudelaire, and later came to know and influence Claude Monet and the poet Stéphane Mallarmé. Although Whistler never fully abandoned a representational style, he insisted that viewers accept a painting as an arrangement of lines and colors on a flat canvas. "I care nothing for the past, present, or future of the black figure," he said about a shadowy human outline in one of his paintings; "it was placed there because black was wanted at that spot."

Whistler's *Nocturne in Black and Gold: The Falling Rocket* (1875) (see Color Plate 18) earned the ire of Ruskin, who declared that he was an impudent coxcomb who was "flinging a pot of paint in the public's face." Whistler sued Ruskin for libel, and the ensuing trial of 1878 marked a turning point in English art and taste. Whistler won, and the Ruskinian notion of art as a social and moral force yielded ground to Whistler's concept of art as an expression of the artist's subjective vision, something beyond common comprehension.

Whistler delivered the following lecture in London on 20 February 1885, to an invitation-only audience that included journalists, artists, writers, and society figures. He chose to deliver his "Ten O'Clock" lecture at 10 P.M. so that his fashionable audience would not have to rush dinner. It is the era's clearest manifesto of art for art's sake, setting the artist above and beyond his moment in history. The lecture and its fastidious presentation brought to a larger audience

---

4. Wife of Napoleon Bonaparte and empress of France 1804–1809.
5. I. e., shake you out of your melancholy. The Aesthetes supposedly cherished an idealized, platonic love of such

flowering "vegetable" entities as poppies and lilies; here Gilbert applies the concept literally.
6. A fashionable thoroughfare in London. Wilde, whose passion for lilies was well known, is said to have done this.

the essentials of Whistler's artistic platform: the attention-getting declaration of artistic independence, the sarcastic dismissals of other theories, and the aggressively elitist public posture
that made him "The Master" for other Aesthetes. Mallarmé translated the essay into French in
1888; Whistler himself published it in English in 1890, in *The Gentle Art of Making Enemies*.
Struck by one of Whistler's witticisms, Oscar Wilde once confessed that he wished *he* had
uttered it himself. Whistler replied dryly, "You will, Oscar, you will."

from Mr. Whistler's "Ten O'Clock"

LADIES AND GENTLEMEN:

∗ ∗ ∗ Art is upon the Town!—to be chucked under the chin by the passing gallant—to
be enticed within the gates of the householder—to be coaxed into company, as a proof
of culture and refinement.

If familiarity can breed contempt, certainly Art—or what is currently taken for
it—has been brought to its lowest stage of intimacy.

The people have been harassed with Art in every guise, and vexed with many
methods as to its endurance. They have been told how they shall love Art, and live
with it. Their homes have been invaded, their walls covered with paper, their very
dress taken to task—until, roused at last, bewildered and filled with the doubts and
discomforts of senseless suggestion, they resent such intrusion, and cast forth the false
prophets, who have brought the very name of the beautiful into disrepute, and derision upon themselves.

Alas! ladies and gentlemen, Art has been maligned. She has naught in common
with such practices. She is a goddess of dainty thought—reticent of habit, abjuring
all obtrusiveness, purposing in no way to better others.

She is, withal, selfishly occupied with her own perfection only—having no
desire to teach—seeking and finding the beautiful in all conditions and in all times,
as did her high priest Rembrandt, when he saw picturesque grandeur and noble dignity in the Jews' quarter of Amsterdam, and lamented not that its inhabitants were
not Greeks.[1]

As did Tintoret and Paul Veronese,[2] among the Venetians, while not halting to
change the brocaded silks for the classic draperies of Athens.

As did, at the Court of Philip, Velasquez, whose Infantas, clad in inaesthetic
hoops, are, as works of Art, of the same quality as the Elgin marbles.[3]

No reformers were these great men—no improvers of the way of others! Their
productions alone were their occupation, and, filled with the poetry of their science,
they required not to alter their surroundings—for, as the laws of their Art were
revealed to them they saw, in the development of their work, that real beauty which,
to them, was as much a matter of certainty and triumph as is to the astronomer the
verification of the result, foreseen with the light given to him alone. In all this, their
world was completely severed from that of their fellow-creatures with whom sentiment is mistaken for poetry; and for whom there is no perfect work that shall not be
explained by the benefit conferred upon themselves.

---

1. Rembrandt (1606–1669) was an important influence
on Whistler. The Dutch artist painted many contemporary subjects and even used the costume of his day when
portraying classical subjects, as in *Aristotle Contemplating
the Bust of Homer*.
2. Tintoretto and Paolo Veronese, Italian Renaissance
painters.
3. Diego Rodrigo de Silva y Velasquez (1599–1660), painter
at the court of Philip IV of Spain. The Infantas were daughters of the monarch; in their hooped skirts they seemed no
less artistic to Whistler than classical Greek statuary.

Humanity takes the place of Art, and God's creations are excused by their usefulness. Beauty is confounded with virtue, and, before a work of Art, it is asked: "What good shall it do?"

Hence it is that nobility of action, in this life, is hopelessly linked with the merit of the work that portrays it; and thus the people have acquired the habit of looking, as who should say, not *at* a picture, but *through* it, at some human fact, that shall, or shall not, from a social point of view, better their mental or moral state. So we have come to hear of the painting that elevates, and of the duty of the painter—of the picture that is full of thought, and of the panel that merely decorates.

A favourite faith, dear to those who teach, is that certain periods were especially artistic, and that nations, readily named, were notably lovers of Art.

So we are told that the Greeks were, as a people, worshippers of the beautiful, and that in the fifteenth century Art was engrained in the multitude.

That the great masters lived in common understanding with their patrons—that the early Italians were artists—all—and that the demand for the lovely thing produced it.

That we, of to-day, in gross contrast to this Arcadian[4] purity, call for the ungainly, and obtain the ugly. * * *

Listen! There never was an artistic period.

There never was an Art-loving nation.

In the beginning, man went forth each day—some to do battle, some to the chase; others, again, to dig and to delve in the field—all that they might gain and live, or lose and die. Until there was found among them one, differing from the rest, whose pursuits attracted him not, and so he stayed by the tents with the women, and traced strange devices with a burnt stick upon a gourd.

This man, who took no joy in the ways of his brethren—who cared not for conquest, and fretted in the field—this designer of quaint patterns—this deviser of the beautiful—who perceived in Nature about him curious curvings, as faces are seen in the fire—this dreamer apart, was the first artist.

And when, from the field and from afar, there came back the people, they took the gourd—and drank from out of it.

And presently there came to this man another—and, in time, others—of like nature, chosen by the Gods—and so they worked together; and soon they fashioned, from the moistened earth, forms resembling the gourd. And with the power of creation, the heirloom of the artist, presently they went beyond the slovenly suggestion of Nature, and the first vase was born, in beautiful proportion. * * *

And centuries passed in this using, and the world was flooded with all that was beautiful, until there arose a new class, who discovered the cheap, and foresaw fortune in the facture of the sham.

Then sprang into existence the tawdry, the common, the gewgaw.

The taste of the tradesman supplanted the science of the artist, and what was born of the million went back to them, and charmed them, for it was after their own heart; and the great and the small, the statesman and the slave, took to themselves the abomination that was tendered, and preferred it—and have lived with it ever since!

And the artist's occupation was gone, and the manufacturer and the huckster took his place.

4. Simple, rustic.

And now the heroes filled from the jugs and drank from the bowls—with understanding—noting the glare of their new bravery, and taking pride in its worth.

And the people—this time—had much to say in the matter—and all were satisfied. And Birmingham and Manchester[5] arose in their might—and Art was relegated to the curiosity shop.

Nature contains the elements, in colour and form, of all pictures, as the keyboard contains the notes of all music.

But the artist is born to pick, and choose, and group with science, these elements, that the result may be beautiful—as the musician gathers his notes, and forms his chords, until he bring forth from chaos glorious harmony.

To say to the painter, that Nature is to be taken as she is, is to say to the player, that he may sit on the piano.

That Nature is always right, is an assertion, artistically, as untrue, as it is one whose truth is universally taken for granted. Nature is very rarely right, to such an extent even, that it might almost be said that Nature is usually wrong: that is to say, the condition of things that shall bring about the perfection of harmony worthy a picture is rare, and not common at all.

This would seem, to even the most intelligent, a doctrine almost blasphemous. So incorporated with our education has the supposed aphorism become, that its belief is held to be part of our moral being, and the words themselves have, in our ear, the ring of religion. Still, seldom does Nature succeed in producing a picture.

The sun blares, the wind blows from the east, the sky is bereft of cloud, and without, all is of iron. The windows of the Crystal Palace[6] are seen from all points of London. The holiday-maker rejoices in the glorious day, and the painter turns aside to shut his eyes.

How little this is understood, and how dutifully the casual in Nature is accepted as sublime, may be gathered from the unlimited admiration daily produced by a very foolish sunset.

The dignity of the snow-capped mountain is lost in distinctness, but the joy of the tourist is to recognise the traveller on the top. The desire to see, for the sake of seeing, is, with the mass, alone the one to be gratified, hence the delight in detail.

And when the evening mist clothes the riverside with poetry, as with a veil, and the poor buildings lose themselves in the dim sky, and the tall chimneys become campanili,[7] and the warehouses are palaces in the night, and the whole city hangs in the heavens, and fairy-land is before us—then the wayfarer hastens home; the working man and the cultured one, the wise man and the one of pleasure, cease to understand, as they have ceased to see, and Nature, who, for once, has sung in tune, sings her exquisite song to the artist alone, her son and her master—her son in that he loves her, her master in that he knows her.

To him her secrets are unfolded, to him her lessons have become gradually clear. He looks at her flower, not with the enlarging lens, that he may gather facts for the botanist, but with the light of the one who sees in her choice selection of brilliant tones and delicate tints, suggestions of future harmonies.

5. Large manufacturing towns.
6. Built in Hyde Park, London, to house the Great Exhibition of 1851, the Crystal Palace was three times the size of St. Paul's Cathedral. Resembling a gigantic greenhouse, it was the world's first building of this size to be constructed of metal and glass, and was considered one of the wonders of the age. In 1855 it was re-erected in Sydenham, Southeast London.
7. Italian bell towers.

He does not confine himself to purposeless copying, without thought, each blade of grass, as commended by the inconsequent, but, in the long curve of the narrow leaf, corrected by the straight tall stem, he learns how grace is wedded to dignity, how strength enhances sweetness, that elegance shall be the result. * * *

Why this lifting of the brow in deprecation of the present—this pathos in reference to the past?

If Art be rare to-day, it was seldom heretofore.

It is false, this teaching of decay.

The master stands in no relation to the moment at which he occurs—a monument of isolation—hinting at sadness—having no part in the progress of his fellow men.

He is also no more the product of civilisation than is the scientific truth asserted dependent upon the wisdom of a period. The assertion itself requires the *man* to make it. The truth was from the beginning.

So Art is limited to the infinite, and beginning there cannot progress. * * *

False again, the fabled link between the grandeur of Art and the glories and virtues of the State, for Art feeds not upon nations, and peoples may be wiped from the face of the earth, but Art *is*.

It is indeed high time that we cast aside the weary weight of responsibility and co-partnership, and know that, in no way, do our virtues minister to its worth, in no way do our vices impede its triumph!

How irksome! how hopeless! how superhuman the self-imposed task of the nation! How sublimely vain the belief that it shall live nobly or art perish.

Let us reassure ourselves, at our own option is our virtue. Art we in no way affect.

A whimsical goddess, and a capricious, her strong sense of joy tolerates no dulness, and, live we never so spotlessly, still may she turn her back upon us.

As, from time immemorial, she has done upon the Swiss in their mountains.

What more worthy people! Whose every Alpine gap yawns with tradition, and is stocked with noble story; yet, the perverse and scornful one will none of it, and the sons of patriots are left with the clock that turns the mill, and the sudden cuckoo, with difficulty restrained in its box!

For this was Tell a hero! For this did Gessler die![8]

Art, the cruel jade,[9] cares not, and hardens her heart, and hies her off to the East, to find, among the opium-eaters of Nankin,[1] a favourite with whom she lingers fondly—caressing his blue porcelain, and painting his coy maidens, and marking his plates with her six marks of choice—indifferent in her companionship with him, to all save the virtue of his refinement!

He it is who calls her—he who holds her!

And again to the West, that her next lover may bring together the Gallery at Madrid, and show to the world how the Master towers above all;[2] and in their intimacy they revel, he and she, in this knowledge; and he knows the happiness untasted by other mortal.

---

8. William Tell was a legendary 14th-century Swiss hero whose defiance of Gessler, an Austrian bailiff, led to his well-known punishment: shooting an apple off his son's head. In revenge, Tell killed Gessler and led a revolt to liberate his country from Austrian control.
9. Disreputable woman.

1. The Chinese city of Nanjing.
2. Philip II of Spain created the Prado Gallery in Madrid; its collection was substantially enlarged by Philip IV. The Prado contains many works by "the Master" Velasquez, whose art greatly influenced Whistler.

She is proud of her comrade, and promises that in after-years, others shall pass that way, and understand.

So in all time does this superb one cast about for the man worthy her love—and Art seeks the Artist alone. * * *

Therefore have we cause to be merry!—and to cast away all care—resolved that all is well—as it ever was—and that it is not meet that we should be cried at, and urged to take measures!

Enough have we endured of dulness! Surely are we weary of weeping, and our tears have been cozened from us falsely, for they have called out woe! when there was no grief—and, alas! where all is fair!

We have then but to wait—until, with the mark of the Gods upon him—there come among us again the chosen—who shall continue what has gone before. Satisfied that, even were he never to appear, the story of the beautiful is already complete—hewn in the marbles of the Parthenon—and broidered, with the birds, upon the fan of Hokusai—at the foot of Fusiyama.[3]

1885   1890

H. Montgomery Hyde
from *The Trials of Oscar Wilde*[1]

[THE FIRST TRIAL]

Queensberry's leading counsel[2] rose from his place in the front row of barristers' seats in the Old Bailey courtroom to begin his cross-examination of the prosecutor. As he faced his old college classmate in the witness box, the two figures on whom every eye in court was now fixed presented a striking contrast. There was Wilde, dressed in the height of fashion, a flower in the buttonhole of his frock coat, and exuding an air of easy confidence; opposite him stood Carson, tall, saturnine, and with the most determined expression on his lantern-jawed countenance. * * *

The opening question immediately revealed the cross-examiner's skill. * * *

"You stated that your age was thirty-nine. I think you are over forty. You were born on the 16th of October 1854?" Carson emphasized the point by holding up a copy of the witness's birth certificate.

Wilde appeared momentarily disconcerted, but he quickly recovered his composure. "I have no wish to pose as being young," he replied sweetly. "You have my certificate and that settles the matter."

"But," Carson persisted, "being born in 1854 makes you more than forty?"

"Ah! Very well," Wilde agreed with a sigh, as if to congratulate his opponent on a remarkable feat of mathematics.

3. Katsushika Hokusai (1760–1849), Japanese artist; Fujiyama or Mount Fuji, the highest mountain in Japan and a frequent subject in Hokusai's works.
1. After Lord Alfred Douglas's father, the Marquess of Queensberry, accused Wilde of sodomy, Wilde brought suit for libel. Wilde lost his case, and was in turn prosecuted, in two subsequent criminal trials, for committing indecent acts. He was found guilty and sentenced to two years in prison with hard labor. The three trials took place in 1895, in the Old Bailey in London, and were the focus of immense public curiosity; the sensational story was followed daily in almost every London newspaper. The following excerpts are from H. Montgomery Hyde's *The Trials of Oscar Wilde* (1948); it should be noted that since no authoritative transcripts of the court proceedings exist, his book is a reconstruction of events based on contemporary press reports and personal reminiscences.
2. Edward Carson, a renowned barrister, had been a classmate of Wilde's at Trinity College, Dublin. He successfully defended Queensberry against Wilde's charge of libel in the first trial.

It was a small point that Carson had scored in this duel of wits, but not without considerable importance. At the very outset Wilde had been detected in a stupid lie, the effect of which was not lost upon the jury, particularly when Carson followed it up by contrasting Wilde's true age with that of Lord Alfred Douglas,[3] with whom Wilde admitted to having stayed at many places, including hotels, both in England and on the Continent. Furthermore, it appeared that Douglas had also contributed to *The Chameleon*,[4] namely two poems. Wilde was asked about these poems, which he admitted that he had seen. "I thought them exceedingly beautiful poems," he added. "One was 'In Praise of Shame' and the other 'Two Loves.'"[5]

"These loves," Carson asked, with a note of distaste in his voice. "They were two boys?"

"Yes."

"One boy calls his love 'true love,' and the other boy calls his love 'shame'?"

"Yes."

"Did you think they made any improper suggestion?"

"No, none whatever."

Carson passed on to "The Priest and the Acolyte," which Wilde admitted that he had read.

"You have no doubt whatever that that was an improper story?"

"From the literary point of view it was highly improper. It is impossible for a man of literature to judge it otherwise; by literature, meaning treatment, selection of subject, and the like. I thought the treatment rotten and the subject rotten."

"You are of opinion, I believe, that there is no such thing as an immoral book?"

"Yes."

"May I take it that you think 'The Priest and the Acolyte' was not immoral?"

"It was worse. It was badly written."[6]

"Was not the story that of a priest who fell in love with a boy who served him at the altar, and was discovered by the rector in the priest's room, and a scandal arose?"

"I have read it only once, last November, and nothing will induce me to read it again. I don't care for it. It doesn't interest me."

"Do you think the story blasphemous?"

"I think it violated every artistic canon of beauty."

"That is not an answer."

"It is the only one I can give."

"I want to see the position you pose in."

"I do not think you should say that."

"I have said nothing out of the way. I wish to know whether you thought the story blasphemous."

"The story filled me with disgust. The end was wrong."

"Answer the question, sir," Carson rapped out sharply. "Did you or did you not consider the story blasphemous?"

"I thought it disgusting."

3. Douglas was 24 years old; Wilde was 40.
4. Edited by Jack Bloxam, an Oxford undergraduate, *The Chameleon* was a literary magazine with a homoerotic tone; it appeared only once, in 1894. Bloxam was the author of *The Priest and the Acolyte*. At Douglas's request, Wilde had submitted some of his aphorisms to the magazine, and his legal opponents sought to make Wilde appear guilty by association with the allegedly immoral contributions of Douglas and Bloxam.
5. These poems appear on pages 915–17.
6. Wilde is paraphrasing his preface to *The Picture of Dorian Gray* (see page 846).

Professing himself satisfied with this reply, Carson turned to a particular incident in the story. "You know that when the priest in the story administers poison to the boy, he uses the words of the sacrament of the Church of England?"

"That I entirely forgot."

"Do you consider that blasphemous?"

"I think it is horrible. 'Blasphemous' is not a word of mine." When Carson put the passage in question to him and asked whether he approved of the words used by the author, Wilde repeated his previous opinion: "I think them disgusting, perfect twaddle."

"I think you will admit that anyone who would approve of such a story would pose as guilty of improper practices?"

"I do not think so in the person of another contributor to the magazine. It would show very bad literary taste. Anyhow I strongly objected to the whole story. * * * Of course, I am aware that *The Chameleon* may have circulated among the undergraduates of Oxford. But I do not believe that any book or work of art ever had any effect whatever on morality."

"Am I right in saying that you do not consider the effect in creating morality or immorality?"

"Certainly, I do not."

"So far as your works are concerned, you pose as not being concerned about morality or immorality?"

"I do not know whether you use the word 'pose' in any particular sense."

"Is it a favourite word of your own?"

"Is it? I have no pose in this matter. In writing a play or a book, I am concerned entirely with literature—that is, with art. I aim not at doing good or evil, but in trying to make a thing that will have some quality of beauty." * * *

Carson now turned to *The Picture of Dorian Gray*[7] * * *

" 'There is no such thing as a moral or an immoral book. Books are well written or badly written.' That expresses your view?"

"My view on art, yes."

"Then I take it, no matter how immoral a book may be, if it is well written, it is, in your opinion, a good book?"

"Yes, if it were well written so as to produce a sense of beauty, which is the highest sense of which a human being can be capable. If it were badly written, it would produce a sense of disgust."

"Then a well-written book putting forward perverted moral views may be a good book?"

"No work of art ever puts forward views. Views belong to people who are not artists."

"A perverted novel might be a good book?" Carson persisted.

"I don't know what you mean by a 'perverted' novel," Wilde answered crisply.

This gave Carson the opening he sought. "Then I will suggest *Dorian Gray* is open to the interpretation of being such a novel?"

Wilde brushed aside the suggestion with contempt. "That could only be to brutes and illiterates," he said. "The views of Philistines on art are unaccountable."

"An illiterate person reading *Dorian Gray* might consider it such a novel?"

"The views of illiterates on art are unaccountable. I am concerned only with my own view of art. I don't care twopence what other people think of it."

---

7. Wilde's novel describes the passion felt by an artist, Basil Hallward, for a beautiful young man, Dorian Gray, whose portrait he paints.

"The majority of persons come under your definition of Philistines and illiterates?"

"I have found wonderful exceptions."

"Do you think that the majority of people live up to the position you are giving us?"

"I am afraid they are not cultivated enough."

"Not cultivated enough to draw the distinction between a good book and a bad book?" The note of sarcasm in Carson's voice was unmistakable.

"Certainly not," Wilde replied blandly.

"The affection and love of the artist of *Dorian Gray* might lead an ordinary individual to believe that it might have a certain tendency?"

"I have no knowledge of the views of ordinary individuals."

"You did not prevent the ordinary individual from buying your book?"

"I have never discouraged him!" * * *

Having covered Wilde's published writings, Carson passed on to the allegedly compromising letters Wilde had written to Lord Alfred Douglas. * * *

"Why should a man of your age address a boy nearly twenty years younger as 'My own Boy'?"[8]

"I was fond of him. I have always been fond of him."

"Do you adore him?"

"No, but I have always liked him." Wilde then went on to elaborate upon the letter. "I think it is a beautiful letter. It is a poem. I was not writing an ordinary letter. You might as well cross-examine me as to whether *King Lear* or a sonnet of Shakespeare was proper."

"Apart from art, Mr Wilde?"

"I cannot answer apart from art."

"Suppose a man who was not an artist had written this letter, would you say it was a proper letter?"

"A man who was not an artist could not have written that letter."

"Why?"

"Because nobody but an artist could write it. He certainly could not write the language unless he were a man of letters."

"I can suggest, for the sake of your reputation, that there is nothing very wonderful in this 'red rose-leaf lips of yours'?"

"A great deal depends on the way it is read."

" 'Your slim gilt soul walks between passion and poetry,' " Carson continued. "Is that a beautiful phrase?"

"Not as you read it, Mr Carson. You read it very badly."

It was now Carson's turn to be nettled. "I do not profess to be an artist," he exclaimed, "and when I hear you give evidence, I am glad I am not."

These words immediately brought Sir Edward Clarke[9] to his feet. "I don't think my learned friend should talk like that," he observed. Then, turning towards his client in the witness box, he added: "Pray do not criticize my learned friend's reading again."

This clash caused a buzz of excitement in the courtroom. When it had died down, Carson went on with his cross-examination, indicating the document he was holding in his hand. "Is not that an exceptional letter?"

"It is unique, I should say." Wilde's answer produced loud laughter in court, which was still largely on the side of the witness.

"Was that the ordinary way in which you carried on your correspondence?"

---

8. For the text of this letter, a response to Douglas's poem *In Praise of Shame*, see page 906, n. 3.   9. Clarke was Wilde's attorney in all three trials.

"No. But I have often written to Lord Alfred Douglas, though I never wrote to another young man in the same way."

"Have you often written letters in the same style as this?"

"I don't repeat myself in style."

Carson held out another sheet of paper. "Here is another letter which I believe you also wrote to Lord Alfred Douglas. Will you read it?"

Wilde refused this invitation. "I don't see why I should," he said.

"Then I will," retorted Carson.

> Savoy Hotel
> Victoria Embankment
> London
>
> Dearest of all Boys,
>
> Your letter was delightful, red and yellow wine to me; but I am sad and out of sorts. Bosie, you must not make scenes with me. They kill me, they wreck the loveliness of life. I cannot see you, so Greek and gracious, distorted with passion. I cannot listen to your curved lips saying hideous things to me. I would sooner—than have you bitter unjust, hating. . . .
>
> I must see you soon. You are the divine thing I want, the thing of grace and beauty; but I don't know how to do it. Shall I come to Salisbury? My bill here is £49 for a week. I have also got a new sitting-room. . . .
>
> Why are you not here, my dear, my wonderful boy? I fear I must leave—no money, no credit, and a heart of lead.
>
> Your own
> OSCAR

"Is that an ordinary letter?" Carson asked, when he had finished reading it.

"Everything I wrote is extraordinary," Wilde answered with a show of impatience. "I do not pose as being ordinary, great heavens! Ask me any question you like about it."

Carson had only one question to ask about this letter, but its effect was deadly. "Is it the kind of letter a man writes to another?"

[THE SECOND TRIAL]

"During 1893 and 1894 you were a great deal in the company of Lord Alfred Douglas?"

"Oh, yes."

"Did he read that poem to you?"[1]

"Yes."

"You can perhaps understand that such verses as these would not be acceptable to the reader with an ordinary balanced mind?"

"I am not prepared to say," Wilde answered. "It appears to me to be a question of taste, temperament, and individuality. I should say that one man's poetry is another man's poison!"

"I daresay!" commented Gill[2] dryly, when the laughter had subsided. "The next poem is one described as 'Two Loves.' * * * Was that poem explained to you?"

---

1. Douglas's sonnet *In Praise of Shame* appears on page 915.

2. Charles Gill was counsel for the prosecution during the second and third trial.

"I think that is clear."

"There is no question as to what it means?"

"Most certainly not."

"Is it not clear that the love described relates to natural love and unnatural love?"

"No."

"What is the 'Love that dare not speak its name'?"[3] Gill now asked.

" 'The love that dare not speak its name' in this century is such a great affection of an elder for a younger man as there was between David and Jonathan, such as Plato made the very basis of his philosophy, and such as you find in the sonnets of Michelangelo and Shakespeare.[4] It is that deep, spiritual affection that is as pure as it is perfect. It dictates and pervades great works of art like those of Shakespeare and Michelangelo, and those two letters of mine, such as they are. It is in this century misunderstood, so much misunderstood that it may be described as the 'Love that dare not speak its name,' and on account of it I am placed where I am now. It is beautiful, it is fine, it is the noblest form of affection. There is nothing unnatural about it. It is intellectual, and it repeatedly exists between an elder and a younger man, when the elder has intellect, and the younger man has all the joy, hope, and glamour of life before him. That it should be so, the world does not understand. The world mocks at it and sometimes puts one in the pillory for it."

Wilde's words produced a spontaneous outburst of applause from the public gallery, mingled with some hisses, which moved the judge to say he would have the Court cleared if there were any further manifestation of feeling.

Oscar Wilde

"Out of the depths" [have I cried unto thee, O Lord] (Latin), the first words of Psalm 130. While imprisoned in Reading Gaol, Wilde was allowed pen and paper only to write letters. He thus composed a meditation on his life in the form of a long letter to Lord Alfred Douglas (nicknamed Bosie), written from January to March 1897. Wilde referred to the text as "Epistola: In Carcere et Vinculis" (Letter: In Prison and in Chains). When he was released, he gave the manuscript to his friend, Robert Ross ("Robbie"), who entitled it *De Profundis* and published an abridged version—omitting all mention of Douglas—in 1905, after Wilde's death. In 1949, when Douglas had died, Wilde's son Vyvyan published a fuller text, based on an unreliable typescript supplied by Ross. Only in 1962, when scholars were allowed to consult the original manuscript—given by Ross to the British Museum—did a complete version finally appear.

from *De Profundis*

[January–March 1897]   H.M. Prison, Reading

Dear Bosie, After long and fruitless waiting I have determined to write to you myself, as much for your sake as for mine, as I would not like to think that I had passed through two long years of imprisonment without ever having received a single line from you, or any news or message even, except such as gave me pain.

Our ill-fated and most lamentable friendship has ended in ruin and public infamy for me, yet the memory of our ancient affection is often with me, and the

---

3. Cf. *Two Loves*, line 74, page 917.
4. King David of Israel, and Jonathan, the son of King Saul, were inseparable friends. On Jonathan's death, David declared that "your love to me was wonderful, passing the love of women" (2 Samuel 1.26). Plato argued that the passion of an older man for a younger one could be translated into a contemplation of the ideal and the universal. Both Shakespeare and Michelangelo wrote sonnets that can be read as describing platonic and/or erotic love between men.

thought that loathing, bitterness and contempt should for ever take that place in my heart once held by love is very sad to me: and you yourself will, I think, feel in your heart that to write to me as I lie in the loneliness of prison-life is better than to publish my letters without my permission or to dedicate poems to me unasked, though the world will know nothing of whatever words of grief or passion, of remorse or indifference you may choose to send as your answer or your appeal.

I have no doubt that in this letter in which I have to write of your life and of mine, of the past and of the future, of sweet things changed to bitterness and of bitter things that may be turned into joy, there will be much that will wound your vanity to the quick. If it prove so, read the letter over and over again till it kills your vanity. If you find in it something of which you feel that you are unjustly accused, remember that one should be thankful that there is any fault of which one can be unjustly accused. If there be in it one single passage that brings tears to your eyes, weep as we weep in prison where the day no less than the night is set apart for tears. It is the only thing that can save you. If you go complaining to your mother, as you did with reference to the scorn of you I displayed in my letter to Robbie, so that she may flatter and soothe you back into self-complacency or conceit, you will be completely lost. If you find one false excuse for yourself, you will soon find a hundred, and be just what you were before. Do you still say, as you said to Robbie in your answer, that I "*attribute unworthy motives*" to you? Ah! you had no motives in life. You had appetites merely. A motive is an intellectual aim. That you were "*very young*" when our friendship began? Your defect was not that you knew so little about life, but that you knew so much. The morning dawn of boyhood with its delicate bloom, its clear pure light, its joy of innocence and expectation you had left far behind. With very swift and running feet you had passed from Romance to Realism. The gutter and the things that live in it had begun to fascinate you. That was the origin of the trouble in which you sought my aid, and I, so unwisely according to the wisdom of this world, out of pity and kindness gave it to you. You must read this letter right through, though each word may become to you as the fire or knife of the surgeon that makes the delicate flesh burn or bleed. Remember that the fool in the eyes of the gods and the fool in the eyes of man are very different. One who is entirely ignorant of the modes of Art in its revolution or the moods of thought in its progress, of the pomp of the Latin line or the richer music of the vowelled Greek, of Tuscan sculpture or Elizabethan song may yet be full of the very sweetest wisdom. The real fool, such as the gods mock or mar, is he who does not know himself. I was such a one too long. You have been such a one too long. Be so no more. Do not be afraid. The supreme vice is shallowness. Everything that is realised is right. Remember also that whatever is misery to you to read, is still greater misery to me to set down. To you the Unseen Powers have been very good. They have permitted you to see the strange and tragic shapes of Life as one sees shadows in a crystal. The head of Medusa that turns living men to stone,[1] you have been allowed to look at in a mirror merely. You yourself have walked free among the flowers. From me the beautiful world of colour and motion has been taken away.

I will begin by telling you that I blame myself terribly. As I sit here in this dark cell in convict clothes, a disgraced and ruined man, I blame myself. In the perturbed and fitful nights of anguish, in the long monotonous days of pain, it is myself I blame. I blame myself for allowing an unintellectual friendship, a friendship whose primary

---

1. Medusa was a snake-haired monster, so horrifying that anyone who looked at her turned to stone.

aim was not the creation and contemplation of beautiful things, to entirely dominate my life. From the very first there was too wide a gap between us. You had been idle at your school, worse than idle at your university. You did not realise that an artist, and especially such an artist as I am, one, that is to say, the quality of whose work depends on the intensification of personality, requires for the development of his art the companionship of ideas, and intellectual atmosphere, quiet, peace, and solitude. You admired my work when it was finished: you enjoyed the brilliant successes of my first nights, and the brilliant banquets that followed them: you were proud, and quite naturally so, of being the intimate friend of an artist so distinguished: but you could not understand the conditions requisite for the production of artistic work. I am not speaking in phrases of rhetorical exaggeration but in terms of absolute truth to actual fact when I remind you that during the whole time we were together I never wrote one single line. Whether at Torquay, Goring, London, Florence or elsewhere, my life, as long as you were by my side, was entirely sterile and uncreative. And with but few intervals you were, I regret to say, by my side always. * * *

You send me a very nice poem, of the undergraduate school of verse, for my approval: I reply by a letter of fantastic literary conceits:[2] I compare you to Hylas, or Hyacinth, Jonquil or Narcisse,[3] or someone whom the great god of Poetry favoured, and honoured with his love. The letter is like a passage from one of Shakespeare's sonnets, transposed to a minor key. It can only be understood by those who have read the *Symposium* of Plato, or caught the spirit of a certain grave mood made beautiful for us in Greek marbles. It was, let me say frankly, the sort of letter I would, in a happy if wilful moment, have written to any graceful young man of either University who had sent me a poem of his own making, certain that he would have sufficient wit or culture to interpret rightly its fantastic phrases. Look at the history of that letter! It passes from you into the hands of a loathsome companion: from him to a gang of blackmailers: copies of it are sent about London to my friends, and to the manager of the theatre where my work is being performed: every construction but the right one is put on it: Society is thrilled with the absurd rumours that I have had to pay a huge sum of money for having written an infamous letter to you: this forms the basis of your father's worst attack: I produce the original letter myself in Court to show what it really is: it is denounced by your father's Counsel as a revolting and insidious attempt to corrupt Innocence: ultimately it forms part of a criminal charge: the Crown takes it up: the Judge sums up on it with little learning and much morality: I go to prison for it at last. That is the result of writing you a charming letter. * * *

Other miserable men, when they are thrown into prison, if they are robbed of the beauty of the world, are at least safe, in some measure, from the world's most deadly slings, most awful arrows. They can hide in the darkness of their cells, and of their very disgrace make a mode of sanctuary. The world, having had its will, goes its way, and they are left to suffer undisturbed. With me it has been different. Sorrow after sorrow has come beating at the prison doors in search of me. They have opened the

2. Douglas's poem, *In Praise of Shame*, appears on page 915. Wilde's letter, written in January 1893, was eventually read aloud at his trial:
My own Boy,
  Your sonnet is quite lovely, and it is a marvel that those red rose-leaf lips of yours should have been made no less for the music of song than for madness of kisses. Your slim gilt soul walks between passion and poetry. I know Hyacinthus, whom Apollo loved so madly, was

you in Greek days.
  Why are you alone in London, and when do you go to Salisbury? Do go there to cool your hands in the grey twilight of Gothic things, and come here whenever you like. It is a lovely place—it only lacks you; but go to Salisbury first.
  Always, with undying love,
                                            Yours, Oscar
3. Beautiful young men whom Apollo loved.

gates wide and let them in. Hardly, if at all, have my friends been suffered to see me. But my enemies have had full access to me always. Twice in my public appearances at the Bankruptcy Court, twice again in my public transferences from one prison to another, have I been shown under conditions of unspeakable humiliation to the gaze and mockery of men. The messenger of Death has brought me his tidings and gone his way,[4] and in entire solitude, and isolated from all that could give me comfort, or suggest relief, I have had to bear the intolerable burden of misery and remorse that the memory of my mother placed upon me, and places on me still. Hardly has that wound been dulled, not healed, by time, when violent and bitter and harsh letters come to me from my wife through her solicitor. I am, at once, taunted and threatened with poverty. That I can bear. I can school myself to worse than that. But my two children are taken from me by legal procedure.[5] That is and always will remain to me a source of infinite distress, of infinite pain, of grief without end or limit. That the law should decide, and take upon itself to decide, that I am one unfit to be with my own children is something quite horrible to me. The disgrace of prison is as nothing compared to it. I envy the other men who tread the yard along with me. I am sure that their children wait for them, look for their coming, will be sweet to them.

The poor are wiser, more charitable, more kind, more sensitive than we are. In their eyes prison is a tragedy in a man's life, a misfortune, a casualty, something that calls for sympathy in others. They speak of one who is in prison as of one who is *"in trouble"* simply. It is the phrase they always use, and the expression has the perfect wisdom of Love in it. With people of our rank it is different. With us prison makes a man a pariah. I, and such as I am, have hardly any right to air and sun. Our presence taints the pleasures of others. We are unwelcome when we reappear. To revisit the glimpses of the moon is not for us.[6] Our very children are taken away. Those lovely links with humanity are broken. We are doomed to be solitary, while our sons still live. We are denied the one thing that might heal us and help us, that might bring balm to the bruised heart, and peace to the soul in pain.

And to all this has been added the hard, small fact that by your actions and by your silence, by what you have done and by what you have left undone,[7] you have made every day of my long imprisonment still more difficult for me to live through. The very bread and water of prison fare you have by your conduct changed. You have rendered the one bitter and the other brackish to me. The sorrow you should have shared you have doubled, the pain you should have sought to lighten you have quickened to anguish. I have no doubt that you did not mean to do so. I know that you did not mean to do so. It was simply that "one really fatal defect of your character, your entire lack of imagination."

And the end of it all is that I have got to forgive you. I must do so. I don't write this letter to put bitterness into your heart, but to pluck it out of mine. For my own sake I must forgive you. One cannot always keep an adder in one's breast to feed on one, nor rise up every night to sow thorns in the garden of one's soul. It will not be difficult at all for me to do so, if you help me a little. Whatever you did to me in old days I always readily forgave. It did you no good then. Only one whose life is without stain of any kind can forgive sins. But now when I sit in humiliation and disgrace it is

4. Wilde's mother died while he was in prison.
5. In February 1897 Constance Wilde petitioned for custody of their children, Cyril and Vyvyan, whom Wilde never saw again. Their surname was changed to Holland.

6. Cf. *Hamlet* 1.4.51–53.
7. The Anglican rite of confession asks forgiveness "for what we have done and for what we have left undone."

different. My forgiveness should mean a great deal to you now. Some day you will realise it. Whether you do so early or late, soon or not at all, my way is clear before me. I cannot allow you to go through life bearing in your heart the burden of having ruined a man like me. The thought might make you callously indifferent, or morbidly sad. I must take the burden from you and put it on my own shoulders.

I must say to myself that neither you nor your father, multiplied a thousand times over, could possibly have ruined a man like me: that I ruined myself: and that nobody, great or small, can be ruined except by his own hand. I am quite ready to do so. I am trying to do so, though you may not think it at the present moment. If I have brought this pitiless indictment against you, think what an indictment I bring without pity against myself. Terrible as what you did to me was, what I did to myself was far more terrible still.

I was a man who stood in symbolic relations to the art and culture of my age. I had realised this for myself at the very dawn of my manhood, and had forced my age to realise it afterwards. Few men hold such a position in their own lifetime and have it so acknowledged. It is usually discerned, if discerned at all, by the historian, or the critic, long after both the man and his age have passed away. With me it was different. I felt it myself, and made others feel it. Byron was a symbolic figure, but his relations were to the passion of his age and its weariness of passion. Mine were to something more noble, more permanent, of more vital issue, of larger scope.

The gods had given me almost everything. I had genius, a distinguished name, high social position, brilliancy, intellectual daring: I made art a philosophy, and philosophy an art: I altered the minds of men and the colours of things: there was nothing I said or did that did not make people wonder: I took the drama, the most objective form known to art, and made it as personal a mode of expression as the lyric or the sonnet, at the same time that I widened its range and enriched its characterisation: drama, novel, poem in rhyme, poem in prose, subtle or fantastic dialogue, whatever I touched I made beautiful in a new mode of beauty: to truth itself I gave what is false no less than what is true as its rightful province, and showed that the false and the true are merely forms of intellectual existence. I treated Art as the supreme reality, and life as a mere mode of fiction: I awoke the imagination of my century so that it created myth and legend around me: I summed up all systems in a phrase, and all existence in an epigram.

Along with these things, I had things that were different. I let myself be lured into long spells of senseless and sensual ease. I amused myself with being a *flâneur* [idle stroller], a dandy, a man of fashion. I surrounded myself with the smaller natures and the meaner minds. I became the spendthrift of my own genius, and to waste an eternal youth gave me a curious joy. Tired of being on the heights I deliberately went to the depths in the search for new sensations. What the paradox was to me in the sphere of thought, perversity became to me in the sphere of passion. Desire, at the end, was a malady, or a madness, or both. I grew careless of the lives of others. I took pleasure where it pleased me and passed on. I forgot that every little action of the common day makes or unmakes character, and that therefore what one has done in the secret chamber one has some day to cry aloud on the housetops. I ceased to be Lord over myself. I was no longer the Captain of my Soul, and did not know it. I allowed you to dominate me, and your father to frighten me. I ended in horrible disgrace. There is only one thing for me now, absolute Humility: just as there is only one thing for you, absolute Humility also. You had better come down into the dust and learn it beside me.

I have lain in prison for nearly two years. Out of my nature has come wild despair; an abandonment to grief that was piteous even to look at: terrible and impotent rage:

bitterness and scorn: anguish that wept aloud: misery that could find no voice: sorrow that was dumb. I have passed through every possible mood of suffering. Better than Wordsworth himself I know what Wordsworth meant when he said:

> Suffering is permanent, obscure, and dark
> And has the nature of Infinity.[8]

But while there were times when I rejoiced in the idea that my sufferings were to be endless, I could not bear them to be without meaning. Now I find hidden away in my nature something that tells me that nothing in the whole world is meaningless, and suffering least of all. That something hidden away in my nature, like a treasure in a field, is Humility.

It is the last thing left in me, and the best: the ultimate discovery at which I have arrived: the starting-point for a fresh development. It has come to me right out of myself, so I know that it has come at the proper time. It could not have come before, nor later. Had anyone told me of it, I would have rejected it. Had it been brought to me, I would have refused it. As I found it, I want to keep it. I must do so. It is the one thing that has in it the elements of life, of a new life, a *Vita Nuova*[9] for me. Of all things it is the strangest. One cannot give it away, and another may not give it to one. One cannot acquire it, except by surrendering everything that one has. It is only when one has lost all things, that one knows that one possesses it.

Now that I realise that it is in me, I see quite clearly what I have got to do, what, in fact, I must do. And when I use such a phrase as that, I need not tell you that I am not alluding to any external sanction or command. I admit none. I am far more of an individualist than I ever was. Nothing seems to me of the smallest value except what one gets out of oneself. My nature is seeking a fresh mode of self-realisation. That is all I am concerned with. And the first thing that I have got to do is to free myself from any possible bitterness of feeling against you.

I am completely penniless, and absolutely homeless. Yet there are worse things in the world than that. I am quite candid when I tell you that rather than go out from this prison with bitterness in my heart against you or against the world I would gladly and readily beg my bread from door to door. If I got nothing at the house of the rich, I would get something at the house of the poor. Those who have much are often greedy. Those who have little always share. I would not a bit mind sleeping in the cool grass in summer, and when winter came on sheltering myself by the warm close-thatched rick, or under the penthouse of a great barn, provided I had love in my heart. The external things of life seem to me now of no importance at all. You can see to what intensity of individualism I have arrived, or am arriving rather, for the journey is long, and "where I walk there are thorns."[1]

Of course I know that to ask for alms on the highway is not to be my lot, and that if ever I lie in the cool grass at night-time it will be to write sonnets to the Moon. When I go out of prison, Robbie will be waiting for me on the other side of the big iron-studded gate, and he is the symbol not merely of his own affection, but of the affection of many others besides. I believe I am to have enough to live on for about eighteen months at any rate, so that, if I may not write beautiful books, I may at least read beautiful books, and what joy can be greater? After that, I hope to be able to recreate my creative faculty. But were things different: had I not a friend left

---

8. From *The Borderers*, (act 3).
9. New life (Italian); Dante's book of this name was one of the few books Wilde was able to have sent to him in prison.
1. From Wilde's play, *A Woman of No Importance* (act 4).

in the world: were there not a single house open to me even in pity: had I to accept the wallet and ragged cloak of sheer penury: still as long as I remained free from all resentment, hardness, and scorn, I would be able to face life with much more calm and confidence than I would were my body in purple and fine linen, and the soul within it sick with hate. And I shall really have no difficulty in forgiving you. But to make it a pleasure for me you must feel that you want it. When you really want it you will find it waiting for you.

I need not say that my task does not end there. It would be comparatively easy if it did. There is much more before me. I have hills far steeper to climb, valleys much darker to pass through. And I have to get it all out of myself. Neither Religion, Morality, nor Reason can help me at all.

Morality does not help me. I am a born antinomian.[2] I am one of those who are made for exceptions, not for laws. But while I see that there is nothing wrong in what one does, I see that there is something wrong in what one becomes. It is well to have learned that.

Religion does not help me. The faith that others give to what is unseen, I give to what one can touch, and look at. My Gods dwell in temples made with hands, and within the circle of actual experience is my creed made perfect and complete: too complete it may be, for like many or all of those who have placed their Heaven in this earth, I have found in it not merely the beauty of Heaven, but the horror of Hell also. When I think about Religion at all, I feel as if I would like to found an order for those who cannot believe: the Confraternity of the Fatherless one might call it, where on an altar, on which no taper burned, a priest, in whose heart peace had no dwelling, might celebrate with unblessed bread and a chalice empty of wine. Everything to be true must become a religion. And agnosticism should have its ritual no less than faith. It has sown its martyrs, it should reap its saints, and praise God daily for having hidden Himself from man. But whether it be faith or agnosticism, it must be nothing external to me. Its symbols must be of my own creating. Only that is spiritual which makes its own form. If I may not find its secret within myself, I shall never find it. If I have not got it already, it will never come to me.

Reason does not help me. It tells me that the laws under which I am convicted are wrong and unjust laws, and the system under which I have suffered a wrong and unjust system. But, somehow, I have got to make both of these things just and right to me. And exactly as in Art one is only concerned with what a particular thing is at a particular moment to oneself, so it is also in the ethical evolution of one's character. I have got to make everything that has happened to me good for me. The plankbed, the loathsome food, the hard ropes shredded into oakum[3] till one's fingertips grow dull with pain, the menial offices with which each day begins and finishes, the harsh orders that routine seems to necessitate, the dreadful dress that makes sorrow grotesque to look at, the silence, the solitude, the shame—each and all of these things I have to transform into a spiritual experience. There is not a single degradation of the body which I must not try and make into a spiritualising of the soul.

I want to get to the point when I shall be able to say, quite simply and without affectation, that the two great turning-points of my life were when my father sent me to Oxford, and when society sent me to prison. I will not say that it is the best thing that could have happened to me, for that phrase would savour of too great

---

bitterness towards myself. I would sooner say, or hear it said of me, that I was so typical a child of my age that in my perversity, and for that perversity's sake, I turned the good things of my life to evil, and the evil things of my life to good. What is said, however, by myself or by others matters little. The important thing, the thing that lies before me, the thing that I have to do, or be for the brief remainder of my days one maimed, marred, and incomplete, is to absorb into my nature all that has been done to me, to make it part of me, to accept it without complaint, fear, or reluctance. The supreme vice is shallowness. Whatever is realised is right.

When first I was put into prison some people advised me to try and forget who I was. It was ruinous advice. It is only by realising what I am that I have found comfort of any kind. Now I am advised by others to try on my release to forget that I have ever been in a prison at all. I know that would be equally fatal. It would mean that I would be always haunted by an intolerable sense of disgrace, and that those things that are meant as much for me as for anyone else—the beauty of the sun and the moon, the pageant of the seasons, the music of daybreak and the silence of great nights, the rain falling through the leaves, or the dew creeping over the grass and making it silver—would all be tainted for me, and lose their healing power and their power of communicating joy. To reject one's own experiences is to arrest one's own development. To deny one's own experiences is to put a lie into the lips of one's own life. It is no less than a denial of the Soul.

"Michael Field"

Katharine Bradley	and	Edith Cooper
1846–1914		1862–1913

"I have found a new poet," announced Robert Browning to a hushed dinner party in 1885. He had actually found two poets, both women. "Michael Field" was the pseudonym of Katharine Bradley and her niece Edith Cooper; they were hailed as "the double-headed nightingale" by admirers. Their long collaboration produced twenty-seven poetic dramas on historical themes, and eight volumes of lyric poetry. Their work was praised by Meredith, Swinburne, and Wilde; but the general public was unaware that in lauding "Mr. Field," they were speaking of an aunt who esteemed William Michael Rossetti (Dante and Christina's brother) and a niece nicknamed "Field." Bradley had helped rear Cooper, the child of her invalid sister. In 1878 they moved to Bristol, where they both attended University College, living together from then on in a close emotional and sexual relationship. Commenting on the fabled intimacy of Robert and Elizabeth Barrett Browning, Bradley noted in her diary "*we are closer married.*" Having independent means, they spent their time reading, writing, and visiting galleries; they dressed and decorated their rooms in Aesthetic style, and their journals record their acute impressions of the many artists and writers they met. In 1907 both converted to Catholicism, apparently because of the death of their dog Whym Chow, a Dionysian presence who not only inspired a volume of love poems but also killed Kipling's pet rabbit during a visit.

"We have many things to say," they wrote to Browning, "that the world will not tolerate from a woman's lips. . . . We cannot be stifled in drawing-room conventionalities." Their first joint volume of poems, *Long Ago* (1889), dared to complete Sappho's fragments in modern lyrics that highlighted the lesbian nature of the Greek poems. In a poem they proclaimed they would remain "Poets and lovers evermore . . . Indifferent to heaven and hell." Despite the passionate paganism of their early career, they condemned what they saw as the depravity of Zola and Beardsley, and withdrew one of their poems from *The Yellow Book*. "From decadence, Good Lord deliver us!" they exclaimed in a diary entry in 1891. Their poetry is notable for its subtle music and technical improvisation, as well as their sympathetic rendering of the femme-fatale imagery common at the time. Exploring the nature of womanhood was both a personal mission and an artistic ideal: "We hold ourselves bound in life and in literature," Bradley wrote in her diary, "to reveal . . . the beauty of the high feminine standard of *the ought to be*."

La Gioconda[1]

Leonardo Da Vinci

THE LOUVRE

Historic, side-long, implicating eyes;
A smile of velvet's lustre on the cheek;
Calm lips the smile leads upward; hand that lies
Glowing and soft, the patience in its rest
5   Of cruelty that waits and doth not seek
For prey; a dusky forehead and a breast
Where twilight touches ripeness amorously:
Behind her, crystal rocks, a sea and skies
Of evanescent blue on cloud and creek;
10   Landscape that shines suppressive of its zest
For those vicissitudes by which men die.

1892

A Pen-Drawing of Leda[1]

Sodoma[2]

THE GRAND DUKE'S PALACE AT WEIMAR

'Tis Leda lovely, wild and free,
Drawing her gracious Swan down through the grass to see
    Certain round eggs without a speck:
One hand plunged in the reeds and one dinting the downy neck,
5   Although his hectoring bill
    Gapes toward her tresses,
She draws the fondled creature to her will.

    She joys to bend in the live light
Her glistening body toward her love, how much more bright!
10   Though on her breast the sunshine lies
And spreads its affluence on the wide curves of her waist and thighs,
        To her meek, smitten gaze

---

1. Leonardo's painting (c. 1503), also known as the *Mona Lisa*, hangs in the Louvre in Paris. The authors would have known Pater's famous description of it in *The Renaissance*. This and the following poem appeared in their collection *Sight and Song* (1892), which sought "to translate into verse what the lines and colours of certain chosen pictures sing in themselves."

1. In Greek myth Zeus took the form of a swan to have sex with Leda, a mortal; she subsequently gave birth to Helen of Troy. Compare this view of Leda to Yeats's poem *Leda and the Swan*, page 1125.
2. Nickname of the Sienese artist Giovanni Antonio Bazzi (1477–1549).

Where her hand presses
The Swan's white neck sink Heaven's concentred rays.

1892

"A Girl"

A girl,
    Her soul a deep-wave pearl
Dim, lucent of all lovely mysteries;
    A face flowered for heart's ease,
5   A brow's grace soft as seas
Seen through faint forest-trees:
    A mouth, the lips apart,
Like aspen-leaflets trembling in the breeze
From her tempestuous heart.
10   Such: and our souls so knit,
I leave a page half-writ—
    The work begun
Will be to heaven's conception done,
    If she come to it.

1893

Lionel Johnson
1867–1902

"Life is ritual," Lionel Johnson was fond of telling his close friend William Butler Yeats, and in his poetry he sought to achieve the elegant simplicity and graceful, lasting form he associated with religious practice. Born in Kent, Johnson was educated in classics at Oxford, where Pater was his tutor, then moved to London in 1890 to work as a literary journalist. He converted to Roman Catholicism in 1891 and considered becoming a priest. In that year he also joined the Rhymers' Club, which met frequently to read and discuss poetry at a London pub, the Cheshire Cheese. Other members included Yeats, Arthur Symons, and his constant drinking companion, Ernest Dowson. Seeking a pure poetry, Johnson lived a celibate, bookish life, brightened by whiskey and conversation, during which he repeated verbatim imaginary conversations he had had with Cardinal Newman and Prime Minister Gladstone. Yeats, who greatly admired his work, remembered Johnson as representative of "The Tragic Generation" of the 1890s, whose unhappy lives and dissipation prevented them from realizing their talent. A sufferer from insomnia and alcoholism, Johnson died at thirty-five as a result of falling off a barstool.

Johnson was ambivalent about the idea of decadence as a literary style and deeply distressed about it as a code of behavior. Since the 1890s were "an age of afterthought," Johnson argued, the era encouraged poets to "careful meditation on life." But it also weakened them, he said, with "the vice of over-subtilty and of affectation, when thought thinks upon itself, and when emotions become entangled with the consciousness of them." His own poetry hovers between these virtues and vices: distinguished by learning, polish, and musicality, his lines pit an intensity of religious and sensual passion against the classical restraint of their form. A *Decadent's Lyric*, probably meant as a parody of Symons, shamelessly indulges in sexual synaesthesia. *The Destroyer of a Soul* bristles with hatred, guilt, remorse, and despair: it is addressed to Oscar Wilde, who he thought had seduced his friend Lord Alfred Douglas.

The Destroyer of a Soul

To—.[1]

I hate you with a necessary hate.
First, I sought patience: passionate was she:
My patience turned in very scorn of me,
That I should dare forgive a sin so great,
5   As this, through which I sit disconsolate;
Mourning for that live soul, I used to see;
Soul of a saint, whose friend I used to be:
Till you came by! a cold, corrupting, fate.

Why come you now? You, whom I cannot cease
10   With pure and perfect hate to hate? Go, ring
The death-bell with a deep, triumphant toll!
Say you, my friend sits by me still? Ah, peace!
Call you this thing my friend? this nameless thing?
This living body, hiding its dead soul?

                                                    1892

A Decadent's Lyric

Sometimes, in very joy of shame,
Our flesh becomes one living flame:
And she and I
Are no more separate, but the same.

5   Ardour and agony unite;
Desire, delirium, delight:
And I and she
Faint in the fierce and fevered night.

Her body music is: and ah,
10   The accords of lute and viola!
When she and I
Play on live limbs love's opera!

                                                    1897

Lord Alfred Douglas
1870–1945

Lord Alfred Douglas embodied the new sexual freedom of the early 1890s, both in his life and in his polished verses on erotic themes. He was the son of the pugnacious Marquess of Queensberry, who had established the rules of boxing but who violated almost every social

---

1. Almost certainly Oscar Wilde; Johnson met Wilde at Oxford when the latter paid a visit to Johnson's tutor, Walter Pater. Johnson in turn introduced Wilde to his friend and fellow undergraduate Lord Alfred Douglas in June 1891, after having lent Douglas his copy of *The Picture of Dorian Gray*. Johnson's letters reveal he was successively enamored of all three men.

code in his public antagonism toward his son. In 1891, while Douglas was still an undergraduate at Oxford, Lionel Johnson introduced him to Oscar Wilde, who encouraged both his affections and his writing. Their tempestuous relationship lasted until Wilde's death in 1900, despite Queensberry's constant efforts to disgrace them both. During Wilde's trials, provoked largely by the desire of father and son to injure each other, Douglas stayed safely in France, at Wilde's request. Their reunion after Wilde's imprisonment was marked by mutual recrimination; Wilde addressed to Douglas the bitter accusations detailed in *De Profundis*, and Douglas contended that he alone among Wilde's friends had remained true. In 1902 Douglas surprised everyone by secretly marrying the poet Olive Custance, whom he had met the year before. The marriage ended in 1913, by which time Douglas had converted to Catholicism and renounced his earlier homosexual activity. In his later life Douglas wrote much about his relationship with Wilde, including *Oscar Wilde and Myself* (1914) and *Oscar Wilde: A Summing Up* (1940). Like his father, he took pleasure in attacking the integrity of other people, and in 1923–1924 spent six months in prison for criminally libeling Winston Churchill.

Douglas's early career coincided with the period of sexual openness and homosexual activism that occurred between 1885 and 1895. The term "homosexuality" was invented in 1869, and entered English just as Parliament criminalized all homosexual activity in 1885; medical theories of homosexual "degeneration" soon followed. Yet this climate also inspired resistance among authors who lauded the spiritual and emotional rewards of same-sex relationships. Douglas, by contrast, explored the dangerous pleasures of all kinds of sexuality: he translated Wilde's *Salomé* (1894) from French to English, and his own *Impression de Nuit: London* combines the aesthetic preference for urban artifice with the decadent penchant for monstrously appetitive female bodies. *Two Loves* was a contribution to *The Chameleon* (1894), an Oxford magazine with a distinctly homoerotic slant. The prosecution read the poem at Wilde's second trial in an effort to make Wilde appear guilty by association. Already outraged by the exposure of male prostitution in the Cleveland Street Scandal of 1889, the jury and the public found confirmation in Douglas's poetry that a new threat to the nation had arisen, the "deviant" or "invert."

In Praise of Shame

Last night unto my bed methought there came
Our lady of strange dreams, and from an urn
She poured live fire, so that mine eyes did burn
At sight of it. Anon the floating flame
5 Took many shapes, and one cried: "I am Shame
That walks with Love, I am most wise to turn
Cold lips and limbs to fire; therefore discern
And see my loveliness, and praise my name."

And afterwards, in radiant garments dressed
10 With sound of flutes and laughing of glad lips,
A pomp of all the passions passed along
All the night through; till the white phantom ships
Of dawn sailed in. Whereat I said this song,
"Of all sweet passions Shame is loveliest."

1894

Two Loves

I dreamed I stood upon a little hill,
And at my feet there lay a ground that seemed
Like a waste garden, flowering at its will
With buds and blossoms. There were pools that dreamed
5   Black and unruffled; there were white lilies
A few, and crocuses, and violets,
Purple or pale, snake-like fritillaries¹
Scarce seen for the rank grass, and through green nets
Blue eyes of shy pervenche² winked in the sun.
10   And there were curious flowers, before unknown,
Flowers that were stained with moonlight, or with shades
Of Nature's wilful moods; and here a one
That had drunk in the transitory tone
Of one brief moment in a sunset; blades
15   Of grass that in an hundred springs had been
Slowly but exquisitely nurtured by the stars,
And watered with the scented dew long cupped
In lilies, that for rays of sun had seen
Only God's glory, for never a sunrise mars
20   The luminous air of Heaven. Beyond, abrupt,
A grey stone wall, o'ergrown with velvet moss,
Uprose; and gazing I stood long, all mazed
To see a place so strange, so sweet, so fair.
And as I stood and marvelled, lo! across
25   The garden came a youth; one hand he raised
To shield him from the sun, his wind-tossed hair
Was twined with flowers, and in his hand he bore
A purple bunch of bursting grapes, his eyes
Were clear as crystal, naked all was he,
30   White as the snow on pathless mountains frore,°   *frozen*
Red were his lips as red wine-spilth that dyes
A marble floor, his brow chalcedony.°   *quartz*
And he came near me, with his lips uncurled
And kind, and caught my hand and kissed my mouth,
35   And gave me grapes to eat, and said, "Sweet friend,
Come, I will show thee shadows of the world
And images of life. See from the South
Comes the pale pageant that hath never an end."
And lo! within the garden of my dream
40   I saw two walking on a shining plain
Of golden light. The one did joyous seem
And fair and blooming, and a sweet refrain
Came from his lips; he sang of pretty maids
And joyous love of comely girl and boy;
45   His eyes were bright, and 'mid the dancing blades
Of golden grass his feet did trip for joy;

---

1. A flower similar to the lily.   2. Periwinkle, a small blue flower.

And in his hands he held an ivory lute
With strings of gold that were as maidens' hair,
And sang with voice as tuneful as a flute,
50   And round his neck three chains of roses were.
      But he that was his comrade walked aside;
He was full sad and sweet, and his large eyes
      Were strange with wondrous brightness, staring wide
With gazing; and he sighed with many sighs
55   That moved me, and his cheeks were wan and white
Like pallid lilies, and his lips were red
      Like poppies, and his hands he clenchèd tight
And yet again unclenchèd, and his head
      Was wreathed with moon-flowers[3] pale as lips of death.
60   A purple robe he wore, o'erwrought in gold
      With the device of a great snake, whose breath
Was like curved flame: which when I did behold
      I fell a-weeping, and I cried, "Sweet youth,
Tell me why, sad and sighing, thou dost rove
65   These pleasant realms? I pray thee, speak me sooth,
What is thy name?" He said, "My name is Love."
      Then straight the first did turn himself to me
And cried: "He lieth, for his name is Shame,
      But I am Love, and I was wont to be
70   Alone in this fair garden, till he came
      Unasked by night; I am true Love, I fill
The hearts of boy and girl with mutual flame."
      Then sighing, said the other: "Have thy will,
I am the love that dare not speak its name."

                                          1894

Olive Custance
(Lady Alfred Douglas)
1874–1944

In April 1895, *Punch* published a satiric poem by an "Angry Old Buffer" concerned about the masculine New Woman and the effeminate Decadent:

> . . . a new fear my bosom vexes;
> To-morrow there may be *no* sexes!
> Unless, as end to all pother,
> Each one in fact becomes the other.

Olive Custance contributed notably to the era's uncertainty about gender roles and the nature of romantic love. Coming from a well-to-do upper-class background, she fell in love at sixteen with the decadent poet John Gray, who was Oscar Wilde's lover at the time. Nothing came of this infatuation but poetry; by the age of twenty she was known in fashionable society as a beautiful young poet, friend to Aubrey Beardsley and contributor to the daring *Yellow Book* magazine. She called her first book *Opals* (1897), after the semiprecious stones that are said to bring the wearer

---

3. A fragrant morning glory.

bad luck; she liked to be called "Opal" herself, and sometimes "Wild Olive." Her poetry, like the long letters she wrote to friends, is remarkable for its intensity and emotional candor.

In 1901 she received a passionate fan letter from Natalie Clifford Barney, an American poet and heiress living in Paris. Custance replied with a daring poem:

> For I would dance to make you smile, and sing
> Of those who with some sweet mad sin have played,
> And how Love walks with delicate feet afraid
> 'Twixt maid and maid.

During their brief, stormy relationship, evoked in the poem *The White Witch*, Barney introduced Custance to the lesbian literary scene in Paris. By the time they traveled to Venice together in 1902, however, Custance was already in love with Wilde's friend Lord Alfred Douglas, to whom *she* had sent a fan letter in 1901. His imagined resemblance to a Roman statue inspired several poems, including the decadent classic, *Statues*, which revises the gender terms of the Pygmalion myth. Jilting an earl to whom she had just become engaged, Custance secretly married Douglas in March 1902. By the time the marriage ended in 1913, partially due to Douglas's conversion to Catholicism, Custance had stopped writing. After a reconciliation in 1932, they lived apart but saw each other almost every day until her death. Douglas wrote in his autobiography that "the very thing she loved in me was that which I was always trying to suppress and keep under: I mean the feminine part."

The Masquerade

> Masked dancers in the Dance of life
> We move sedately . . . wearily together,
> Afraid to show a sign of inward strife,
> We hold our souls in tether.
>
> 5   We dance with proud and smiling lips,
> With frank appealing eyes, with shy hands clinging.
> We sing, and few will question if there slips
> A sob into our singing.
>
> Each has a certain step to learn;
> 10   Our prisoned feet move staidly in set paces,
> And to and fro we pass, since life is stern,
> Patiently, with masked faces.
>
> Yet some there are who will not dance,
> They sit apart most sorrowful and splendid,
> 15   But all the rest trip on as in a trance,
> Until the Dance is ended.

1902

Statues

> I have loved statues . . . spangled dawns have seen
> Me bowed before their beauty . . . when the green
> And silver world of Spring wears radiantly
> The morning rainbows of an opal sky . . .

5   And I have chanted curious madrigals[1]
To charm their coldness, twined for coronals[2]
Blossoming branches, thinking thus to change
Their still contempt for mortal love, their bright
Proud scorn to something delicate and strange,
10   More sweet, more marvellous, than mere delight!

I have loved statues—passionately prone
My body worshipped the white form of stone!
And like a flower that lifts its chalice up
Towards the light—my soul became a cup
15   That over-brimming with enchanted wine
Of ecstasy—was raised to the divine
Indifferent lips of some young silent God
Standing aloof from all our tears and strife,
Tranced in the paradise of dreams, he trod
20   In the untroubled summer of his life!

I have loved statues . . . at night the cold
Mysterious moon behind a mask of gold—
Or veiled in silver veils—has seen my pride
Utterly broken—seen the dream denied
25   For which I pleaded—heedless that for me
The miracle of joy could never be . . .
As in old legends beautiful and strange,
When bright gods loved fair mortals born to die,
And the frail daughters of despair and change
30   Become the brides of immortality?

c. 1902   1905

The White Witch

Her body is a dancing joy, a delicate delight,
Her hair a silver glamour in a net of golden light.

Her face is like the faces that a dreamer sometimes meets,
A face that Leonardo would have followed through the streets.

5   Her eyelids are like clouds that spread white wings across blue skies,
Like shadows in still water are the sorrows in her eyes.

How flower-like are the smiling lips so many have desired,
Curled lips that love's long kisses have left a little tired.

c. 1901   1902

END OF OSCAR WILDE AND AESTHETICISM, DECADENCE, AND THE *FIN DE SIÈCLE*

---

1. Love poems, often sung by several unaccompanied voices.   2. Wreathlike crowns.

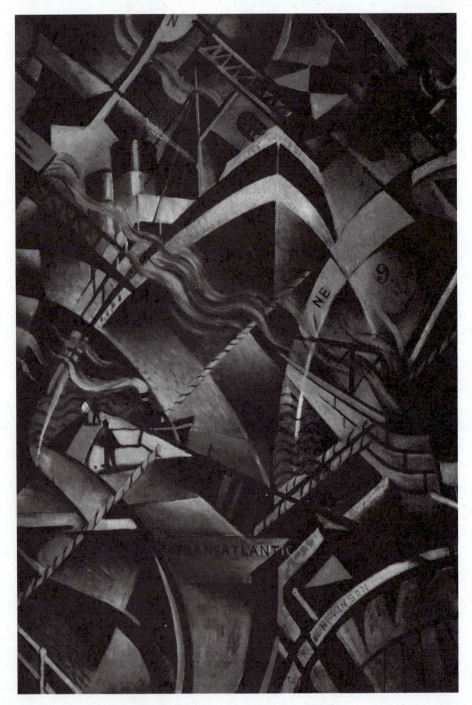

Richard Nevinson, *The Arrival*, 1913–1914.

The Twentieth Century

BEYOND THE PALE

Modern British literature has consistently been distinguished by its movement "beyond the pale." The Pale was originally the fenced-in territory established around Dublin by the invading English in the medieval period, a border between English civilization and Celtic foreignness. In later usage, the phrase "beyond the pale" came to have a purely metaphoric meaning: to stand outside the conventional boundaries of law, behavior, or social class. To snobbish members of the British elite, a poor flower-seller like Eliza Doolittle in Shaw's *Pygmalion* would be beyond the pale in a social sense; at its most serious, the phrase can designate actions violating universal standards of human decency, such as the colonists' appalling treatment of Africans that Conrad chillingly describes in *Heart of Darkness*. Throughout the twentieth century, writers active in the British Isles increasingly probed actions and locations beyond the pale of proper middle-class Englishness. Many of the century's greatest writers, such as the Pole Joseph Conrad, the Irishmen William Butler Yeats and James Joyce, and the Americans Ezra Pound and T. S. Eliot, themselves came from beyond the boundaries of England; others came from social strata within England less often visible before: provincial working-class writers like D. H. Lawrence and the Scots writer James Kelman; women like Rebecca West and Katherine Mansfield; men and women whose sexuality transcended conventional boundaries, such as E. M. Forster and Virginia Woolf.

As the century went on, more and more writers active in the British Isles and its former colonies have been "beyond the pale" in a very literal sense, as people of color: Salman Rushdie, who grew up in India and Pakistan before establishing himself as a writer in England; Ngugi wa-Thiongo, educated by British missionaries in Kenya; Derek Walcott, whose poetry moves between the Caribbean, England, North America, and Africa. With the ending of England's role as a colonial power, a new and dynamic relation of former colonies and colonizers has arisen, a pervasive interfusion of people and of roles. British literature has become a world literature, overflowing what were once its borders.

Earlier centuries had periodically seen the eruption of writers, and of issues, from beyond the pale of accepted norms and educated social groups, but these writers had often faced severe struggles against dominant values of upper-middle-class propriety and the strictures of established literary conventions. The fate of Oscar Wilde was a case in point: his arrest on sodomy charges in 1895 at the peak of his career as a playwright, his sentencing to hard labor and then his exile and death in France in 1900, all pointed up the ways in which late Victorian society could retaliate against the challenges posed by a brilliant, flamboyant, homosexual Irishman. A new generation of writers at the turn of the century set themselves to change this situation, seeking variously to infiltrate the Pale of established British literary expression, to expand its dimensions, or to abolish it altogether. For many of these young writers, a prime strategy for achieving these goals was to attack their predecessors, and they set about this task with gusto.

BURYING VICTORIA

Writing in 1928, Virginia Woolf described the cultural atmosphere of the Victorian era in the following way:

> Damp now began to make its way into every house. . . . The damp struck within. Men felt the chill in their hearts; the damp in their minds. . . . The life of the average woman was a succession of childbirths. She married at nineteen and had fifteen or eighteen children by the time she was thirty; for twins abounded. Thus the British Empire came into existence; and thus—for there is no stopping damp; it gets into inkpots as it gets into the wood-work—sentences swelled, adjectives multiplied, lyrics became epics, and little trifles that had been essays a column long were now encyclopedias in ten or twenty volumes.

Woolf of course exaggerates here for her own effect; yet this passage does capture nicely the stereotypical view of the Victorians that flourished during the modern period—and helped make it possible. Ezra Pound, for instance, called the later nine-teenth century "a rather blurry, messy sort of period, a rather sentimentalistic, man-nerish sort of period." Polemical descriptions like these served the rhetorical purposes of writers at the start of the new century as they attempted to stake out their terrain and to forge a literature and a perspective of their own.

The opening decade of the new century was a time of transition. Woolf later sug-gested, her tongue perhaps in her cheek, that as a result of a Post-Impressionist exhibi-tion of paintings in London, "on or about December, 1910, human character changed." Almost no one, however, seems to have maintained that anything changed very deci-sively on the morning of 1 January 1900. Queen Victoria, at that time on the throne for nearly sixty-five years and in mourning for Prince Albert for almost forty, lived and ruled on into the following year; the subsequent reign of Edward VII (1901–1910) dif-fered only slightly from that of his mother in many respects, the entire nation mourn-ing the loss of their queen as she had the loss of her husband. But Woolf, in a 1924 essay, saw a gulf between herself and the Edwardians: Edwardian novelists, she writes, "established conventions which do their business; and that business is not our busi-ness." Edward VII himself, in fact, was clearly not a Victorian. He had a reputation as a playboy and implicitly rebelled against the conventions that his mother had upheld. During his reign, the mannered decadence of the 1890s modulated into a revived social realism seen in ambitious novels like Joseph Conrad's *Nostromo* and H. G. Wells's darkly comic masterpiece *Tono-Bungay*, while poets like Yeats and Hardy produced major poems probing the relations of self, society, and history. Writers in general con-sidered themselves to be voices of a nation taking stock of its place in the world in a new century. They saw their times as marked by accelerating social and technological change and by the burden of a worldwide empire, which achieved its greatest extent in the years between 1900 and 1914—encompassing as much as a quarter of the world's population and dominating world trade through a global network of ports.

This period of consolidation and reflection abruptly came to an end four years into the reign of George V, with the start of World War I in August 1914; the relatively tranquil prewar years of George's early reign were quickly memorialized, and nostal-gized, in the wake of the war's disruption to the traditionally English way of life. This first Georgian period was abruptly elevated into a cultural "golden age" by the British public and British publishers, a process that was typified by the pastoral poetry gathered by Edward Marsh in his hugely popular series of five anthologies called *Georgian Poetry*, the first of which was published in 1912. As a consequence of Marsh's skill as a tastemaker, this brief period before the war is frequently known as the Georgian period in British literature, though George V himself remained on the throne until 1936, when the distant rumble of World War II was to be heard by those with ears to hear.

The quarter century from 1914 until the start of the war in 1939 is now conventionally known as the modernist period. To be modern was, in one respect, to rebel openly and loudly against one's philosophical and artistic inheritance, in much the same way that the Romantic writers of the late eighteenth and early nineteenth centuries had sought to distinguish themselves from their Augustan forebears. This gesture—the way in which a new artistic movement seeks to define itself through caricature of the movement(s) that gave it birth—is a recurrent feature in literary history, but it took on a particular urgency and energy among the modernists, who advanced the view summarized in Pound's bold slogan, "Make It New." A great modernist monument to this anti-Victorian sentiment was Lytton Strachey's elegantly ironic *Eminent Victorians* (1918), whose probing biographical portraits punctured a series of Victorian pieties. Much of Bernard Shaw's writing (including *Pygmalion*) is animated by anti-Victorian animus as well, taking the theatrical wit of Oscar Wilde and turning it against specific targets. Exaggerated though it was, the ritualized slaughter performed by modernists like Woolf, Strachey, and Shaw seems to have achieved a clearing of the literary and artistic terrain that formed a necessary prelude to further innovation. The modernists' "Victorians" were oversimplified, sometimes straw figures, but the battle that was waged against them was real indeed, and the principles of modernism were forged and refined in the process.

THE FOUNDATIONS OF MODERN SKEPTICISM

The best Victorian writers had not been afraid to ask difficult, unsettling questions. Tennyson's restless skepticism in *In Memoriam,* for example, exemplifies the spirit of Victorian inquiry. But the conclusion of that poem foresees an ongoing progress toward future perfection, guided by "One God, one law, one element, / And one far-off divine event, / To which the whole creation moves." Tennyson himself doubted that such unities could be embodied in the present; twentieth-century writers found increasing fragmentation around them and became more and more suspicious of narratives of historical progress and of social unity.

Modern explorations are undertaken with absolutely no confidence as to the results that will be discovered, still less that a public exists who could understand the writers' discoveries. For that reason Thomas Hardy's ruthless skepticism now seems quintessentially modern. This new attitude is quite clear in Ford Madox Ford's *The Good Soldier* (1915), the first installment of which was published in the inaugural issue of Wyndham Lewis's violently modern magazine *Blast*. John Dowell, the narrator/protagonist of Ford's novel, worries for 250 pages about his sense that the "givens" of civil society seem to have been knocked out from under him, and that he has been left to create values and meaning on his own. Struggling to extract the moral of the story he tells us—the story of his wife's long-standing affair with his best friend, and their consequent deaths—Dowell can only conclude:

> I don't know. And there is nothing to guide us. And if everything is so nebulous about a
> matter so elementary as the morals of sex, what is there to guide us in the more subtle

morality of all other personal contacts, associations, and activities? Or are we meant to act on impulse alone? It is all a darkness.

In Conrad's *Heart of Darkness*, the narrator Charlie Marlow suffers from a similar moral vertigo. When, at the novella's close, he resolves to perform an action he finds deeply repugnant—to tell a lie—he worries that his willful violation of the moral order will provoke an immediate act of divine retribution. None, however, is forthcoming: "It seemed to me that the house would collapse before I could escape, that the heavens would fall upon my head. But nothing happened. The heavens do not fall for such a trifle." In works like these, a voyage is undertaken into a vast, unknown, dark expanse. Those few who come out alive have seen too much ever to be the same.

Similar perceptions underlie modern humor. The Theater of the Absurd that flourished in the 1950s and 1960s, in the work of playwrights like Samuel Beckett and Harold Pinter, had roots in Wilde and Shaw and their comic explorations of the arbitrary conventionality of long-held social values. Throughout the twentieth century, writers devoted themselves to unfolding many varieties of irony—from the severe ironies of Conrad and Yeats to the more tender ironies of Woolf and Auden, to the farcical absurdities of Tom Stoppard and Joe Orton. Joyce described his mixture of high and low comedy as "jocoserious"; asked the meaning of his dense book *Finnegans Wake*, he replied, "It's meant to make you laugh."

Whether seen in comic or tragic light, the sense of a loss of moorings was pervasive. Following the rapid social and intellectual changes of the previous century, the early twentieth century suffered its share of further concussions tending to heighten modern uncertainty. It was even becoming harder to understand the grounds of uncertainty itself. The critiques of Marx and Darwin had derived new messages from bodies of evidence available in principle to all literate citizens; the most important paradigm shifts of the early twentieth century, on the other hand, occurred in the fields of philosophy, psychology, and physics, and often rested on evidence invisible to the average citizen. The German philosopher Friedrich Nietzsche (1844–1900) was, as his dates suggest, wholly a nineteenth-century man, yet his ideas had their most profound impact in the twentieth century. Nietzsche described his lifelong philosophical project as "the revaluation of all values"; in his 1882 treatise *The Joyful Science*, he went so far as to assert that "God is dead." This deliberately provocative statement came as the culmination of a long and complicated argument, and did not mean simply that Nietzsche was an atheist (though he was). Nietzsche was suggesting that traditional religion had been discredited by advances in the natural and physical sciences, and as transcendent standards of truth disappeared, so logically must all moral and ethical systems depending on some faith for their force. It was from this base that Nietzsche created the idea of the *Übermensch*, the "superman" who because of his intellectual and moral superiority to others must not be bound by social conventions. Conrad's tragic figure Kurtz and Shaw's comic Professor Henry Higgins represent two very different takes on this idea, building on Nietzsche's interest in showing how all values are "constructed" rather than given—at some level arbitrary, all truths being merely opinions, all social identities merely roles.

The new psychology, whose earliest stirrings are to be found in the last decades of the nineteenth century, came of age at the turn of the twentieth. Sigmund Freud's *The Interpretation of Dreams* (1900) and *Psychopathology of Everyday Life* (1901) together illustrate in an especially vivid way his evolving theories about the influence of the unconscious mind, and past (especially childhood) experience, on our daily lives. The whole of Freud's work was translated into English by James Strachey (Lytton's brother), and was published in conjunction with the Hogarth Press, owned and run by Leonard and Virginia Woolf; for this reason, among others, the Freudian revolution was felt early, and strongly, among the London intelligentsia. The new psychology was frequently distorted and misunderstood by the larger public; among the artistic community Freud provoked a wide range of response, from the enthusiastic adoption of his theories by some to nervous rejection by writers like Joyce. This response is complicated, in part, by the fact that Freud himself took an interest in artistic and creative processes, and presumed to explain to writers the psychopathology at the heart of their own genius; as the Freudian literary critic Lionel Trilling succinctly put it, "the poet is a poet by reason of his sickness as well as by reason of his power." As Freud's supporter W. H. Auden wrote in his elegy, *In Memory of Sigmund Freud* (1939):

> If often he was wrong and at times absurd,
> To us he is no more a person
> Now but a whole climate of opinion
> Under whom we conduct our different lives.

A further intellectual shock wave was the revolution in physics that was spearheaded by Albert Einstein's *Special Theory of Relativity* (1905). In both this theory (dealing with motion) and later in the General Theory of Relativity (dealing with gravity), Einstein shook the traditional understanding of the universe and our relationship to it; the certainty and predictability of the Newtonian description of the universe had been undone. The "uncertainty" of Einstein's universe was seemingly reinforced by developments in quantum physics, such as the work of Niels Bohr (who won the Nobel Prize in physics in 1922) and Werner Heisenberg, author of the famous "Uncertainty Principle" and the principle of complementarity, which together assert that the movement of subatomic particles can only be predicted by probability and not measured, as the very act of measurement alters their behavior. Ironically enough, the true import of these ideas is not, as the truism has it, that "everything is relative"—in fact, Einstein says almost the exact opposite. In Einstein's vision of the world, *nothing* is relative: everything is absolute, and absolutely fixed—except for us, fallible and limited observers, who have no secure standpoint from which "to see the thing as in itself it really is," to quote Matthew Arnold's 1867 formulation of the critic's goal. The only way to experience the truth, it would seem, would be to find what T. S. Eliot called "the still point of the turning world," an "unmoved mover" outside the flux and change of our day-to-day world. Einstein himself never really rejected the idea of transcendent truth; he once said to an interviewer that to him, the idea of our universe without a Creator was inconceivable. In this case, however, the popular fiction has been more influential than the facts, and the work of Einstein, Heisenberg, and Bohr has been used to support the widespread sense that, as Sean O'Casey's character Captain Jack Boyle puts it in *Juno and the Paycock* (1924), "the whole worl's in a state o' chassis!"

The philosophical and moral upheavals of these years were given added force by the profound shock of World War I—"The Great War," as it came to be known. The British entered the conflict against Germany partly in order to preserve their influence in Europe and their dominance around the globe, and partly out of altruistic notions of gallantry and fair play—to aid their weaker allies against German aggression. The conflict was supposed to take a few weeks; it lasted four grueling years and cost hundreds of thousands of British lives. Notions of British invincibility, of honor, even of the viability of civilization all weakened over the years of vicious trench warfare in France. The progress of technology, which had raised Victorian standards of living, now led to a mechanization of warfare that produced horrific numbers of deaths—as many as a million soldiers died in the single protracted battle of the Somme in 1916. As poets discovered as they served in the trenches, and as the people back home came to learn, modernity had arrived with a vengeance.

REVOLUTIONS OF STYLE

The end of the war was accompanied by a sense of physical and moral exhaustion. To be modern has been defined as a persistent sense of having arrived on the stage of history after history has finished. The critic Perry Meisel, for instance, describes modernism as "a structure of compensation, a way of adjusting to the paradox of belatedness." Behind Ezra Pound's struggle to reinvent poetry lay a nagging suspicion that there was nothing new left to make or say, and Pound claimed that the very slogan "Make It New" was taken off the bathtub of an ancient Chinese emperor. As T. S. Eliot explains in his essay *Tradition and the Practice of Poetry,* "The perpetual task of poetry is to *make all things new.* Not necessarily to make new things. . . . It is always partly a revolution, or a reaction, from the work of the previous generation."

That revolution was carried out both on the level of subject matter and often on the level of style as well. Some important early twentieth-century fiction writers, like John Galsworthy, and H. G. Wells, felt no real need to depart from inherited narrative models, and hewed more or less to a realist or naturalist line, carrying on from the French naturalists like Emile Zola and the Norwegian dramatist Henrik Ibsen. But for those writers we now call modernist, these conventions came to seem too limiting and lifeless. The modern writer was faced with an enormous, Nietzschean task: to create new and appropriate values for modern culture, and a style appropriate to those values. As a consequence, there is often a probing, nervous quality in the modernist explorations of ultimate questions. This quality can be seen at the very start of the century in Conrad's *Heart of Darkness,* a novel about psychological depth and social disintegration that simultaneously implicates its readers in the moral ambiguities of its events. These ambiguities, moreover, are reflected in the very presentation of the narrative itself. In the modern novel, we are no longer allowed to watch from a safe distance while our protagonists mature and change through their trials; instead, we are made to undergo those trials ourselves, through the machinations of the narrative. This technique had already been employed in the nineteenth century, as for instance in the dramatic monologues of Robert Browning; but this narrative of process becomes pervasive in modernist texts, where the uncertainties of the form, the waverings and unpredictability of the narrative, mirror similar qualities in the mind of the narrator or protagonist. Often the reader is drawn into the story's crisis by a heightened use of the technique of plunging the narrative suddenly *in medias res:* "There was no hope for him this time: it was the third stroke" (Joyce, *The Sisters*); "A sudden blow:" (Yeats, *Leda and the Swan*); " 'Yes, of course, if it's fine tomorrow,' said Mrs. Ramsay" (Woolf, *To the Lighthouse*). The customary preliminary information—the sort of dossier about the characters that we expect—isn't given; the reader is put in the position of a detective who has to sort all this information out unaided. This narrative decontextualization reaches its culmination in the theater of Beckett and Pinter, who typically

Soldiers of the 9th Cameronians division prepare to go "over the top" during a daylight raid near Arras, France, 24 March 1917. During such an offensive, troops would make their way quickly across the contested territory between the opposing armies' trenches—the area known as No Man's Land—and attempt to take control of an enemy trench in order to conduct bombing raids and gain whatever intelligence might be found in the abandoned foxholes. The pace of this warfare—where a week's progress might be measured in yards, rather than miles—was, according to troops on both sides, the most salient feature of trench warfare. The human costs included diseases caused by standing water (like infamous "trench foot") and emotional disorders caused by the stress of waiting and constant shelling ("shell shock").

withhold any and all background information about characters. "Confusion," Samuel Beckett told an interviewer in 1956, "is all around us and our only chance now is to let it in. The only chance of renovation is to open our eyes and see the mess. It is not a mess you can make sense of."

Early in the century, a number of poets began to dispense with the frames of reference provided by conventional poetic forms. The first real Anglo-American poetic movement of the century was Imagism, a reaction against the expansive wordiness of Victorian poetry like Tennyson's *Idylls of the King* or Browning's *The Ring and the Book*. Imagists like Pound and H. D. wrote short, spare poems embodying a revelatory image or moment. The most memorable Imagist poems have the concentrated impact of a haiku. But the form leaves little scope for narrative development; that path seems to have been opened by a rediscovery of the seventeenth-century metaphysical poets, notably by T. S. Eliot. The techniques of metaphysical poets like John Donne suggested to Eliot a means for expanding the repertory of Imagist poetry, which he used to good effect in poems like *The Love Song of J. Alfred Prufrock*, which opens with a thoroughly modernized metaphysical conceit:

> Let us go then, you and I,
> when the evening is spread out against the sky
> Like a patient etherized upon a table.

One strategy for making literature new was to make it difficult; this notion was, in part, a response to the proliferation of popular entertainments during the early twentieth century, a development that both disturbed and intrigued many artists, writers, and cultural critics. In such a context, "difficult" literature (such as the densely allusive poetry of Eliot, or the multilayered prose of Joyce) was seen to be of greater artistic merit than the products of an easily consumable mass culture—even as both Eliot and Joyce drew on popular culture and diction as they reshaped the norms of their literary art. Thus, while one of the primary targets of modernist renovation was Victorian literary manners, another was the complacent taste and sensibility of a large, and growing, middle class. Artists had been declaring the need to shock the bourgeoisie since time immemorial; Matthew Arnold worried publicly, and at length, about the dilution of a natural aristocracy of taste by the pseudoculture of newly educated British philistines, at the same time that he campaigned for greatly expanded public education. The Education Act of 1870 resulted in the explosive growth of elementary education, which meant that the reading class grew exponentially. Within the art world, the most obvious result of this anxiety was the "art for art's sake" movement associated with Walter Pater that began in the 1870s. Art was becoming its own material—as, for instance, in French artist Marcel Duchamp's mustache on the Mona Lisa.

In some ways modernist art and literature turned inward, becoming cannibalistic and self-referential. This is demonstrated well in Joyce's novel A Portrait of the Artist as a Young Man, whose protagonist is autobiographical in genesis yet critical in intent; the way Joyce accomplishes this is by moving Stephen Dedalus, his artist-protagonist, through various prose poses—writing now like Gustave Flaubert, now like Cardinal Newman, now like Pater. Stephen can only mimic—not create—a style; such is the situation of the modern writer, Joyce suggests, and his novel Ulysses dramatizes this by adopting a kaleidoscopic array of styles in its eighteen chapters. It thus becomes increasingly difficult to think of "style" as the achievement of an individual, and more and more it becomes the culmination of a cultural, national, or ethnic project or history. As the French critic Roland Barthes has written, the text in the modern period becomes a "multidimensional space in which a variety of writings, none of them original, blend and clash," "a tissue of quotations drawn from innumerable centres of culture"—an apt and dramatic description of modernist texts like Eliot's The Waste Land, Joyce's Ulysses, and Pound's Cantos. To be textual is, during this period, to be intertextual and interdisciplinary as well.

The stylistic experimentation of modernist writers was fueled by the era's technological advances. From the mid-nineteenth century on, Britain had prided itself on its industrial strength and leadership; with the electrification of Britain at the turn of the century, however, the Industrial Revolution was gradually overtaken by a technological revolution. If the sinking of the Titanic on her maiden voyage in 1912 stands as a symbol of the vulnerability of progress—a sort of watery funeral for traditional British industry—the first transatlantic flight in 1919 pointed toward the future. Advances in photographic technology made documentary photographs a part of daily life and brought a heightened visual dimension to political campaigns and to

Color Plate 21 Paul Nash, *We Are Making a New World*, 1918. An Irish painter especially noted for his extraordinary depictions of World War I, Nash is perhaps best known for this stark landscape of the no-man's-land nightmare of trench warfare, a scene empty of human beings, an apocalyptic vision of the horrors created by the modern technology of war, the nightmare "new world" of his painting's ironic title. *(The Imperial War Museum, London.)*

Color Plate 22 Charles Ginner (1878–1952), *Piccadilly Circus*, 1912. A depiction of London shortly before World War I, the scene features a seemingly quaint flower seller in the midst of urban change. Like Eliza Doolittle in Bernard Shaw's *Pygmalion* (page 1005), she is surrounded by evidence of the energies and transformations of the modern city: automobiles, advertising, and even a woman boldly strolling alone down the sidewalk. The word "new" on the poster sums up the social scene. (*© Charles Ginner. Tate Gallery, London/Art Resource, NY.*)

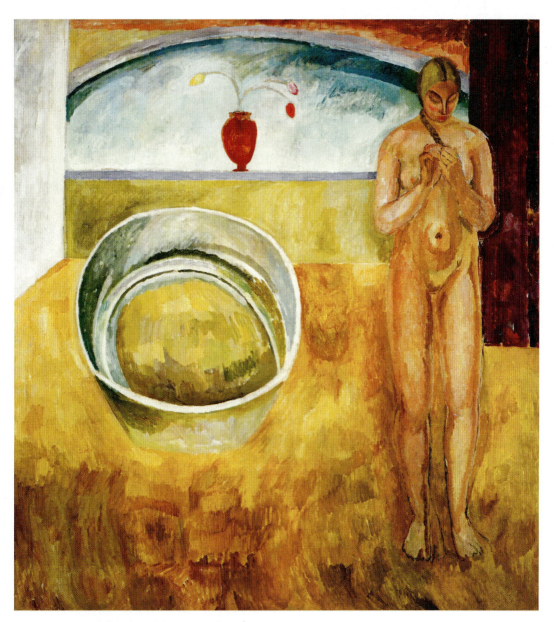

Color Plate 23 Vanessa Bell (1879–1961), *The Tub*, 1917. Bell was Virginia Woolf's sister and, like her, a member of the Bloomsbury Group—a casual association of friends, family, and lovers who were at the forefront of Britain's literary, artistic, and cultural scene for three decades. Bell was a gifted painter with an astonishing color sense; her innovative abstract and figural paintings make her England's strongest female artist of the period. She was known as well for decorative and crafts work such as the furniture, painting and china she created for Omega Workshops, led by Roger Fry. Together with Duncan Grant and Clive Bell, she decorated Charleston, the legendary Bloomsbury country house now on England's register of cultural landmarks. (*© Vanessa Bell. Tate Gallery, London/Art Resource, NY.*)

Color Plate 24 Vera Willoughby, *General Joy*, 1928. As the 20th century opened, public transportation systems in and around London—including the city's impressive subway system, known as the Underground or the Tube—were consolidated under the direction of a single company, soon known as the Underground Group. A commitment to innovative and effective maps, signs, and advertising quickly earned the Underground Group a place in the forefront of graphic design, and together with its successor organizations it remained a strong patron of the arts for much of the century. Posters commissioned by the Authority from new and established artists often advertised underground or ground transportation in novel and artistic ways. *General Joy* reflects the exuberance of London in the 1920s, but just as often the posters offered public art, political messages, and cultural rallying points. Clarissa Dalloway's daughter Elizabeth rides just such an open-air bus through a sparkling London day in June in Virginia Woolf's *Mrs Dalloway*. *(London's Transport Museum.)*

Color Plate 25 L. D. Luard, *The Spirit of 1943*, 1943. By the 1940s the Underground Group had been absorbed into the still larger London Transport company, but the emphasis on strong graphic design and the tradition of commissioning posters from artists continued. This striking graphic image conveys Britain's determination in the midst of World War II. It was meant to bolster the fighting spirit of a country still two years and hundreds of thousands of deaths away from victory over the Axis forces. *(London's Transport Museum.)*

Color Plate 26 Stanley Spencer, *Shipbuilding on the Clyde: Furnaces*, 1946. Twentieth-century British painting is unusual in modern art, for the best of it is not abstract but rather portrays the human figure. Spencer's work was resolutely figural, yet it manages to be modern nonetheless because of the almost transcendent, mystical effects his human figures create. Spencer spent most of his eccentric life in a small English village, whose citizens he depicted swept up in great religious mysteries, such as the Annunciation or the Resurrection. Even his portraits of everyday activities such as shipbuilding or baking are gilded with radiant transfiguration. *(Imperial War Museum, London.)*

Color Plate 27   Francis Bacon, *Study After Velasquez*, 1950. Irish painter Francis Bacon lived for most of his life in London, where his squalid studio, now reconstructed at the Hugh Lane Gallery in Dublin, was famous as a hub of creativity. Bacon was surely one of the great artists of the modern period; his innovations in portraiture are unforgettable icons of modernity. Perhaps his most iconic works are the series of screaming popes. Based on classical portraits of a pope by Velasquez, Bacon's nameless pope has a face haunted with knowledge of the holocausts of the twentieth century. He seems to scream at us from behind a wasteland of totalitarian bars. Bacon was a highly literary painter, and he was inspired to create some of his most tragic and innovative painting by the poetry of Eliot and Yeats. *(© 2004 The Estate of Francis Bacon/ARS, New York/DACS, London.)*

Color Plate 28 Gilbert and George (b. 1943, b. 1942), *Death Hope Life Fear*, 1984. Performance artists and photographers, the gay couple Gilbert and George have offered provocative art for decades, beginning with their first performance piece, for which they gilded themselves with metallic paint and stood motionless for a long, long time. Other pieces have included simply declaring their everyday life to be performance art. Since the 1980s they have also produced huge photographic canvases with religious, political, and homoerotic imagery. Cultural agents-provocateurs, Gilbert and George try to create witty yet highly charged confrontations between spectators and their own cultural beliefs, wishes, and secrets. (*© Gilbert and George. Tate Gallery, London/Art Resource, NY.*)

Color Plate 29 David Hockney, *Great Pyramid at Giza with Broken Head from Thebes*, 1963. Hockney has become a premier artist of our time by reinventing portraiture. Unlike Francis Bacon, who basically deconstructed the human body in his work, Hockney's paintings are filled with sunlight and color. Long stints in Los Angeles have made Hockney the visual poet of the California swimming pool, its aqua waters set shimmering by the beautiful young men Hockney places there. Branching out into many media, Hockney's recent work includes photographic collages and theater stage design. The Egyptian scene depicted here is less typical, but it shows his fascination both with other cultures and countries and with the "deadpan vistas of postmodern and postimperial tourism." *(Earl of Pembroke, Wilton House, Wilton, Salisbury, UK.)*

Color Plate 30 Chris Ofili, *No Woman, No Cry*, 1998. In the 1990s London took the crown from New York as the world's hottest art scene. Young British visual artists have caused a veritable Sensation—the name of one of their group shows—and even prompted the Tate Gallery to build an entirely new wing to house contemporary work. Chris Ofili is one of the most exciting painters in the group. Nigerian by birth, Ofili represents the multicultural Britain that is remaking British art, literature, and popular culture. Ofili integrates African cultural symbols into a painting style drawn from American pop art and British figural painting. Titled after a Bob Marley song, the painting here makes a vivid icon of a black British woman, her clothes a landscape of hot color studded with dried elephant dung, a sacred substance in African rites. "Mr. Ofili generously supports the six London Zoo elephants whose dung is dried for his paintings." *(Acrylic, oil, and mixed media on canvas. © Chris Ofili. Courtesy, Victoria Miro Gallery, London. Photo: Tate Gallery, London/Art Resource, NY.)*

advertising; the advent of quick and inexpensive newspaper photographs put vivid images of the carnage of World War I on Britain's breakfast tables. The texture and pace of daily life changed in the early years of the century to such a degree that average men and women were comfortable referring to themselves by that hopelessly awkward designation, "modern" (from the Latin *modo*, "just now"). And clearly, the London inhabited by the denizens of Eliot's *Waste Land* is a profoundly different place from the London of Dickens. Eliot portrays a woman who works in an office, composes letters on a typewriter, talks to clients on the telephone, plays records on the phonograph at her flat after having casual sex with a co-worker, and eats her evening meal from tins.

The advent of technology had far-reaching effects on the writing of the period. Beckett, famously, imagined a tape recorder before he had ever seen one in order to make possible the memory play of his *Krapp's Last Tape* (1959); more generally, the technology of the transistor radio, and government sponsorship of radio and television by the British Broadcasting Corporation, made possible wholly new literary genres. Beckett and Dylan Thomas were among the first to take advantage of the new media, writing plays for radio and then for television. A generation earlier, Joyce made use of early art film strategies in his "Circe" episode of *Ulysses*. In the most advanced writing of the modernist period we find an increasing sense that the technologies of print affect the text itself. Pound's *Cantos* were composed, not just transcribed, on a typewriter, and cannot be imagined in their current form composed with pen and ink; Joyce plays with the typographic conventions of newspaper headlines in the "Aeolus" chapter of *Ulysses* to create an ironic running commentary on the action. A crucial scene in Joyce's *Finnegans Wake* features a television broadcast (which was not available commercially when the novel was published), blending with a nuclear explosion (also several years before the fact). The scene culminates in "the abnihilisation of the etym"—both a destruction of atom/Adam/etym and its recovery *from* ("ab") nothingness.

MODERNISM AND THE MODERN CITY

Paralleling the new social and artistic opportunities of the twentieth century was a kind of anomie or alienation created by the rush toward industrialization. Vast numbers of human figures remained undifferentiated and the mass-manufactured hats and clothing worn by British industrial workers served only to heighten the monotony of their daily routines. Newspapers eagerly published photographs of thousands of sooty-faced miners. The members of the workforce, which Marx had called "alienated labor," were seen to be estranged not just from their work but from one another as well, as they themselves became mass products. This situation is dramatized especially vividly in the silent films of the period—from the dystopian vision of Fritz Lang's *Metropolis* (1926) to the more comic vision presented by the British-American Charlie Chaplin in *Modern Times* (1936). The sense of major cities being overrun by crowds of nameless human locusts recurs in the poetry of the period:

> A crowd flowed over London Bridge, so many,
> I had not thought death had undone so many.
> Sighs, short and infrequent, were exhaled,
> And each man fixed his eyes before his feet.
>
> (Eliot, *The Waste Land*)

I have met them at close of day
Coming with vivid faces
From counter or desk among grey
Eighteenth-century houses.

(Yeats, *Easter 1916*)

The Victorian concern over huge numbers of urban poor was seconded by a fear of large numbers of restive urban lower-middle class workers and their families.

The city also appeared in far more positive guises, as the modernists were urban sophisticates above all else. Joyce famously remarked that if Dublin were one day destroyed, it could be recreated whole from the pages of his *Ulysses*. Virginia Woolf's great novel *Mrs Dalloway* is among other things a glowing tribute to London as the center of incongruous juxtapositions and unexpected connections, the quintessence of life itself: "Heaven only knows why one loves it so," Clarissa Dalloway thinks,

> how one sees it so, making it up, building it round one, tumbling it, creating it every moment afresh. . . . In people's eyes, in the swing, tramp, and trudge; in the bellow and the uproar; the carriages, motor cars, omnibuses, vans, sandwich men shuffling and swinging; brass bands; barrel organs; in the triumph and the jingle and the strange high singing of some aeroplane overhead was what she loved; life; London; this moment of June.

London had a magnetic attraction for many American writers as well, as a transatlantic literary culture blossomed. Henry James based novels like *The American* and *Portrait of a Lady* on the adventures of Americans living abroad; James himself was an American who lived most of the last thirty-five years of his life in London, and was naturalized as a British citizen three months before his death. T. S. Eliot moved to London in 1915 and lived there until his death in 1965, becoming a British subject, a communicant of the Church of England, and being knighted along the way. The great comic writer P. G. Wodehouse commuted back and forth across the Atlantic in the 1920s and 1930s as his plays and musical comedies were staged in New York and London. In many ways, New York and London had never been so close. This artistic diaspora resulted in a richer, more complex and urbane literature.

PLOTTING THE SELF

The Freudian revolution grew from and reinforced an intense interest in the workings of the individual psyche, and modernists like Woolf and Joyce devoted themselves to capturing the mind's modulations. Both Woolf and Joyce employed versions of what came to be known as the "stream-of-consciousness" technique, in which fragmentary thoughts gradually build up a portrayal of characters' perceptions and of their unstated concerns. Consider this passage from the "interior monologue" of Joyce's protagonist Leopold Bloom, as he prepares a saucer of milk for his cat:

> They call them stupid. They understand what we say better than we understand them. She understands all she wants to. Vindictive too. Wonder what I look like to her. Height of a tower? No, she can jump me. . . . Cruel. Her nature. Curious mice never squeal. Seem to like it.

On the surface, Bloom's staccato thoughts reflect on the cat; at the same time, he identifies the cat with his unfaithful wife Molly, and—without admitting it to himself—he reflects on the cat's foreign psyche as a way of coming to terms with Molly's needs and desires. The development of stream-of-consciousness narrative grows out of a sense that the self is not "natural" or "given" but a construction—specifically a social construction—and that, consequently, traditional methods for depicting character no longer suffice. We are all the products of our own past and we are also, powerfully, products of larger social forces that shape the stories we tell about ourselves, and which others tell about us.

In the Victorian novel, plot crises were typically resolved in some definitive way, such as by a marriage or a change in the financial status of the protagonist. In the modern novel, lasting resolutions growing out of a common vision are few and far between. Walter Pater had counseled his readers, at the conclusion of *The Renaissance*, that "to burn always with a hard, gemlike flame, to maintain this ecstasy" was "success in life"; in the modern period, everyone wants that ecstasy, but no one is sure quite what it looks like amid the ruthless individualism of modern life. "We live as we dream, alone," Conrad's narrator Marlow mutters despondently; "Only connect," the epigraph to E. M. Forster's *Howards End* (1910) implores. On the eve of the London Blitz, however, the characters in Woolf's *Between the Acts* (still the most powerful British novel of World War II) are united only as they sing the refrain, "Dispersed are we." The texts of the modern period, bookended as they are by two world wars, represent a real, agonized meditation on how modern individuals can become united as community again. Woolf herself was skeptical of the possibility and her last novel remains unfinished—or finished only by her husband Leonard—because she took her own life before she could complete it. In the novels of Woolf and Joyce, and in the poetry of Yeats and Auden, community is the glimpsed prospect, the promised land: seen as a possibility but never realized, or embodied precariously in a gesture, a moment, a metaphor, and above all in art itself.

After the modernist high-water mark of the 1920s, the atmosphere darkened amid the international financial depression of the 1930s triggered by the U.S. stock market crash of 1929. The decade saw the growth of British Marxism and widespread labor agitation. The decade also witnessed the international growth of fascism and totalitarianism; writers like Shaw, Wyndham Lewis, Eliot, Yeats, Pound, and Lawrence for a time saw the order and stability promised by authoritarian governments as the only antidote to the "mere anarchy" Yeats decries in his poem *The Second Coming*. In the late thirties, however, intellectual sentiment turned increasingly against the fascist movements being led in Germany by Hitler, in Italy by Mussolini and in Spain by Franco. During Spain's brutal civil war (1936–1939), many writers supported the democratic Republicans against the ultimately victorious fascist General Franco. Meanwhile a series of weak British governments did little to oppose Hitler's increasing belligerence and extremism; the failure to stand up for democratic principles, coupled with worldwide economic depression, led many young intellectuals and artists to became Leftists.

Compared to the stylistic experiments of the previous two decades, British writing of the 1930s sometimes looks rather flat, neutral. This can be attributed in part to the disillusionment that followed World War I, and the very real sense throughout the thirties that things were building up to another war, that art had become something of an irrelevancy. The German cultural critic Theodor Adorno was to write after the war, "no poetry after Auschwitz"; writers of the thirties seem to have had this sense well in advance of Auschwitz. Yeats admired the character in Auguste de Villiers de L'Isle-Adam's drama *Axël* who said, "As for living, we let the servants do that for us"; the young writers of the thirties, however, were concerned that (in Auden's phrase) "poetry makes nothing happen," and were committed to the idea that it must. "Late modernism," as the critic Tyrus Miller has described this writing, was newly engaged with popular culture and political events alike.

THE RETURN OF THE REPRESSED

Modern British literature is characterized by the increasing presence of women's voices, working-class voices, and voices expressing varied ethnic, religious, and sexual perspectives which, whether methodically or inadvertently, had often been excluded from the British literary tradition. The writings of an author like Woolf made England think hard about who she really was, as did, in another sense, the writings of the former colonial administrator George Orwell. In the modern period, Britain begins to deal in a fully conscious way with its human rights problems—most significantly, its treatment of women and the diverse ethnic groups of its colonial possessions.

The gradual enfranchisement and political and economic liberation of British women in the early years of the twentieth century comprised a fundamental social change; the novelist D. H. Lawrence, a rather equivocal friend of the women's movement, called it "perhaps the greatest revolution of modern times." The Women's Property Act—passed in 1882, the year of Woolf's birth—for the first time allowed married women to own property. Decades of sometimes violent suffragist agitation led finally to full voting rights for women in 1928 and to the gradual opening up of opportunities in higher education and the professions.

The quick pace of these changes naturally made many men uneasy. In their monumental three-volume study *No Man's Land: The Place of the Woman Writer in the Twentieth Century*, critics Sandra Gilbert and Susan Gubar suggest that this "war between the sexes" was one of the primary driving forces behind the modernist literary movement. Having emphasized the revolutionary force of the women's movement, Lawrence goes on to warn that the movement, "is even going beyond, and becoming a tyranny of woman, of the individual woman in the house, and of the feminine ideas and ideals in the world." In a half-serious essay titled *Cocksure Women and Hensure Men*, Lawrence complained of women

> more cocky, in their assurance, than the cock himself. . . . It is really out of scheme, it is not in relation to the rest of things. . . . They find, so often, that instead of having laid an egg, they have laid a vote, or an empty ink-bottle, or some other absolutely unhatchable object, which means nothing to them.

On the level of literary principles, a masculinist emphasis can be seen in Ezra Pound's insistence that modern poetry should "move against poppy-cock," "be harder and saner . . . 'nearer the bone' . . . as much like granite as it can be."

Other writers, male and female, supported women's rights; almost all writers sought to rebel against Victorian sexual norms and gender roles. Joyce battled with censors beginning in 1906, and his *Ulysses* was put on trial in New York on obscenity charges in 1933 (and cleared of those charges in the same week that the United States repealed Prohibition). Defending his sexual and scatological scenes, Joyce put the modernists' case for frankness this way:

The modern writer has other problems facing him, problems which are more intimate and unusual. We prefer to search in the corners for what has been hidden, and moods, atmospheres and intimate relationships are the modern writers' theme. . . . The modern theme is the subterranean forces, those hidden tides which govern everything and run humanity counter to the apparent flood: those poisonous subtleties which envelop the soul, the ascending fumes of sex.

In defense of his "dirty" book *Lady Chatterley's Lover* (1928), whose full text was banned as obscene until 1960, Lawrence wrote: "In spite of all antagonism, I put forth this novel as an honest, healthy book, necessary for us today. . . . We are today, as human beings, evolved and cultured far beyond the taboos which are inherent in our culture. . . . The mind has an old groveling fear of the body and the body's potencies. It is the mind we have to liberate, to civilize on these points." In a rich irony, Joyce and Lawrence hated one another's writing: Joyce insisted on calling Lawrence's best-known novel "Lady Chatterbox's Lover." He dismissed the novel as "a piece of propaganda in favour of something which, outside of D. H. L.'s country at any rate, makes all the propaganda for itself." Lawrence, for his part, thought the last chapter of *Ulysses* (Molly Bloom's famous soliloquy) "the dirtiest, most indecent, obscene thing ever written."

Sexuality of all stripes was on trial. The lesbian writer Radclyffe Hall was tried for obscenity in 1928 for her novel *The Well of Loneliness*—whose most obscene sentence is, "That night they were not divided." The trial became a public spectacle, and was a rallying point for writers like Woolf and E. M. Forster, who spoke valiantly in favor of Hall's right to explore her subject, which was primarily the loneliness, rather than the fleshly joys, of same-sex love. Forster's overtly homosexual writings, including his novel *Maurice*, were not published until after his death in 1970. Woolf was somewhat more open in her novel *Orlando* (1928), whose protagonist changes sex from male to female. In Joyce's *Ulysses*, Leopold Bloom fantasizes about becoming a "new womanly man" and dreams of being chastised by a dominatrix who appears first as Bella and then as Bello Cohen. It was not only sexual taboos that were challenged in the writing of the period; in practice there began to be a loosening of the strict gender and sexual roles, which had been reinforced by the homophobia resulting from Oscar Wilde's trial. Gay, lesbian, and bisexual writers like Forster, Woolf, Hall, Stein, Natalie Barney, Djuna Barnes, H. D., Ronald Firbank, and Carl Van Vechten pushed the comfort level of the British reading public; even the "healthy" version of sexuality celebrated by D. H. Lawrence in his greatest novel *Women in Love* begins to suggest that heterosexuality and homosexuality are shifting boundaries, not immutable categories.

The growing independence of the individual subject began to be matched by drives for independence among imperial subjects as well. In "John Bull's other island," as Bernard Shaw called Ireland in his play of that title, agitations for independence grew widespread from the late nineteenth century onward, culminating in the Easter Rising of 1916 and the 1922 partitioning of Ireland, when the Irish Republic became an independent nation while Northern Ireland remained part of Great Britain. No match for England militarily, the Irish used words as their chief weapon in the struggle for independence.

The liberation of Britain's overseas colonial holdings began in the early decades of the century and gathered momentum thereafter. The history of Great Britain in the twentieth century is, in some ways, the story of the centrifugal forces that have largely stripped Britain of its colonial possessions. Britain suffered humiliating losses in the Boer War (1899–1902), fought by the British to take possession of the Boer Republic of South Africa. Half a million British troops were unable to win outright victory over eighty thousand Boers; finally the British adopted a scorched-earth policy that entailed massive arrests and the deaths of thousands of captives in unsanitary camps. This debilitating and unsavory conquest marked the low point of British imperialism, and public disgust led to a reaction against empire itself. Independence movements sprang up in colonies around the world, most notably in India, Britain's largest colony, "the jewel in the crown" of Queen Victoria, where Mohandas Gandhi's Congress Party struggled through nonviolent resistance to force Britain to grant its independence.

WORLD WAR II AND ITS AFTERMATH

The year 1939 and the start of World War II closed the modernist era. It was the year that saw the publication of Joyce's *Finnegans Wake,* which the critic Ihab Hassan calls a "monstrous prophecy" of postmodernity. The seminal modernist careers of Joyce, Woolf, Yeats, Ford, and Freud all came to an end—as did the social and political order of the previous decades. Throughout the late thirties, the government had engaged in futile efforts at diplomacy as Hitler expanded German control in central Europe. Prime Minister Neville Chamberlain finally denounced Hitler when the Germans invaded Czechoslovakia early in 1939; on September 1, Germany invaded Poland, and within days Britain declared war. In contrast to the "Great War," this conflict began with few illusions—but with the knowledge that Britain was facing an implacable and better-armed enemy. Unlike the Great War, fought on foreign soil, the new war hit home directly; during "the Blitz" from July 1940 through 1941, the German Luftwaffe carried out massive bombing raids on London and many other targets around Britain.

During these years, Winston Churchill emerged as a pivotal figure both strategically and morally. First as commander in chief of the navy, and starting in May 1940 as prime minister, he directed British military operations while rallying popular support through stirring speeches and radio addresses. The war had profound effects throughout British society, as almost every man—and many women—between the ages of 14 and 64 came to be involved in the war effort, in conditions that weakened old divisions of region and class and that provided the impetus for new levels of government involvement in social planning. At the war's end in September of 1945, Britain emerged victorious, in concert with its allies. In contrast with the United States, though, Britain had suffered enormous civilian casualties and crushing economic losses, both within Great Britain and throughout its far-flung colonies. As much as a quarter of Britain's national wealth had been consumed by the war. The great city of London had undergone horrific bombing during the the Blitz, whose attacks left the face of this world capital as scarred as had the Great Fire three centuries before. Although morally and socially triumphant in its defeat of Nazism and fascism, Britain was left shattered economically and exhausted spiritually. Its people had come through the war gallantly, only to face grim conditions at home and political unrest throughout the empire.

London during the Blitz, seen from the north transept of St. Paul's Cathedral.

The global effort of that war, whose battles were fought not only in Europe but in Africa, Asia, Latin America, the Middle East, and the Pacific, had forced Britain to draw massively on its colonies for raw materials, money, and soldiers. Since the resistance to the British empire had begun long before World War II, the drafting of millions of already restive colonial subjects into the armed forces intensified the tensions and the conflicts running beneath the surface of the empire. One of the most important political phenomena of the twentieth century was about to hit a depleted Britain with a vengeance: the decolonization of most of the conquered globe in the great wave of independence movements that swept the world after 1945. One by one, with greater and lesser degrees of violence and agony, colonies slipped out of Britain's imperial net. From the independence of India (1947) to the independence struggles of Kenya, Nigeria, Zaire, Palestine, Egypt, and many others, Britain experienced the accelerated loss of the largest empire in Western history. Retaining only a handful of Caribbean, Latin American, and Pacific Rim possessions, the empire had radically shrunk. India, Pakistan, Canada, Australia, and a few other countries adopted commonwealth status, remaining commercially linked but becoming essentially independent politically. The empire on which the sun never set was fast becoming largely confined to England, Scotland, Wales, and Northern Ireland—an ongoing area of tension and conflict to the present day.

The dizzying pace of decolonization after the war put Britain in a paradoxically modern position ahead of many other Western countries: the unquestioned ability, and the rarely questioned right, of Western societies to dominate the globe had finally encountered decisive opposition. Within fifty years Britain found itself transformed from the dominant global power into a relatively small and, for a time, impoverished island nation, no longer a dictator of the world's history, but merely part of it. This dislocation was profoundly registered in British culture, and British writers strove to assess these losses—and to define the new possibilities for a freer and more open society that might emerge from the wreckage of empire.

One of the exciting aspects of British literature after World War II, then, is its very incoherence. New players not only joined the game, but in some instances began to call the shots, as the struggles for independence from British colonial control provided vivid and critical literary subjects—"subjects" in the sense of topics as well as those newly empowered writers whose subjectivity emerged on the page. At the same time, the shrinking of empire was turning Great Britain back into a small nation. Vita Sackville-West's story *Seducers in Ecuador* serves as a beautiful pre-war parable of Britain's precarious global significance; its main character travels around the Mediterranean by yacht with a group of fellow English citizens, with many if not most of their exotic ports of call under British imperial control. When the man buys a pair of blue spectacles in Egypt, he finds that he cannot bear to take them off: the story subtly suggests that they are imperial sunglasses, affording him a way of looking at the world—a gaze of control and domination—that ironically destroys his life when he tries to wear them back in England. The British literature that comes after the loss of Suez, of Egypt and Palestine and Arabia, reverses Sackville-West's prescient parable. The inhabitants of colonized zones don spectacles themselves, and use them to look unsparingly at their colonizers.

A new generation of writers also took on the task of evaluating English culture from inside. John of Gaunt's beautiful paean to "this sceptered isle, this England," in Shakespeare's *Richard II* had to be rewritten now: what was "this England" to be? In the absence of its colonial possessions, and in the general misery of shortages and rationing after the war, there was suddenly a sharp new scrutiny of British society. Its class-bound hierarchies appeared in an even harsher light, and its failures at home became the source of profound self-examination. Rage and anger accompanied this process of self-awareness, and a generation of literary artists dubbed the "angry young men" arose to meet the failures head-on, often in realist drama so faithful to its shabby subjects it was called "kitchen sink" drama, after the cold-water flat settings where the characters played out their rage. Playwrights such as John Osborne (as in the aptly titled *Look Back in Anger*) and novelists such as Anthony Burgess (*A Clockwork Orange*) angrily or satirically probed the discrepancy between England's glorious past and its seemingly squalid present.

A sense of diminishment in the world's eyes led to a passionate critique of British institutions, particularly its class structure, even where the literature produced was conservative in its looking backward. The extraordinary poet Philip Larkin might be seen as a key figure in this generation of writers. Larkin was a librarian in a rural town for most of his adult life. His poetry takes on the sardonic voice of the disenfranchised and the dispossessed—speaking not for the poor or the downtrodden but instead articulating the sense of loss and fury of middle- and upper-class England, bereft of its historical prestige, impoverished by modern culture. He sings of nature, home, and country in a voice that is lacerating and self-mocking, using jazzy and colloquial poetic diction and Anglo-Saxon expletives. As one of his poems memorably declares:

> They fuck you up, your mum and dad.
>   They may not mean to, but they do.
> They fill you with the faults they had
>   And add some extra, just for you.

Larkin also wrote several notable novels at this time, among them *A Girl in Winter*, which explores from a surprisingly feminine and even feminist point of view the struggles of an emigré to Britain who must conceal the traumas her family experienced during the war, in order to "fit in" with a blithe and cavalier aristocratic British family. Larkin's artistry joins that of a host of other postwar writers, mostly male, who write from the center of an England now put off-kilter by the wrenching changes after the war.

Profound historical changes were to continue after the war with the commencement of the Cold War, in which the new world superpowers, the United States and the former Soviet Union, became locked in an intense battle for ideological, political, and economic dominance. Human beings now possessed the technological means to destroy the planet and its inhabitants, and these weapons of destruction were amassed by two societies with sharply conflicting goals. Britain along with Western Europe unequivocally aligned itself on the side of the United States, joining in the long fight against communism and Soviet socialism. While not itself a superpower, Britain had to shape its own social goals in light of the Cold War raging around it. A supremely eloquent voice in the articulation of what was at stake was that of the British writer George Orwell, known for his lucid essays on politics and language, including *Politics and the English Language*, to cite one of his classic works. Immediately after the war Orwell crafted *1984*, an enduring parable of Cold War culture. This book envisions a future society in the year 1984 when the infamous "Big Brother" is watching everyone. That tale of a society of totalitarian surveillance was a thinly veiled allegory of the possibilities inherent not only in a Soviet takeover but even in Western societies and their implicit tendencies toward control and bureaucracy. It may be that Orwell was able to be prophetic about the cultural touchstones of the next several decades because as a British writer he wrote from an oblique angle: the colonial relationship of Britain to the United States had become reversed, with Britain almost becoming an outpost of the United States in terms of its Cold War dominance, reminiscent of Britain's dominance of the fate of the American colonies in the centuries leading up to the American Revolution. It is sometimes possible to see more clearly from a position outside the exact center— and Britain was, in this sense, no longer the center of English-speaking Western civilization. Strangely enough, that ex-centricity granted its literary writers a certain kind of insight.

The British novel after World War II made a retreat from modernist experimentalism. One explanation for a return to the realism that Woolf had so passionately argued against comes, paradoxically, from feminism of the very sort Woolf espouses in *A Room of One's Own* and *Three Guineas*. For as women began to write in large numbers, the novel with characters and a plot became a kind of room these writers needed to make their own. A host of important women writers emerged who revived the novel—which had been declared dead by the French, at least, around 1950—by using its traditions to incorporate their experiences as women, "making it new" not by formal experiments, but by opening that familiar, even a little shabby, room to new voices and new stories. Among the practitioners of this "feminist realism"—although some of them would vehemently deny the label "feminist"—are Jean Rhys, Doris Lessing, Margaret Drabble, A. S. Byatt, Muriel Spark, Iris Murdoch, Nadine Gordimer, and Buchi Emecheta. In every case these are writers who ring changes on ostensibly traditional forms.

A particularly vibrant arena of British literary innovation after the postwar period was British drama; the dramatic form seemed to lend itself to the staging of new social and aesthetic experiments which, with the exception of women's writing as noted above, largely bypassed the British novel of this period. The most innovative of all British dramatists of the twentieth century after World War I was indubitably the Irishman Samuel Beckett. Living in a form of self-imposed exile in France, and a further self-imposed exile within the French language, Beckett moved from being the writer of mordant novels (*Molloy; Malone Dies*) to becoming an extraordinary dramatist. He often wrote his plays first in French, later translating them into English, so that English was their "secondary" language, leading to multiple puns in both English and French. Beckett's contribution to dramatic form, for which he received the Nobel Prize, is nonetheless a creation within British literature. Beckett sculpted his plays out of silence, paring down lines of dialogue until their short sentences and sometimes single words reverberate with the unspoken. More than any other dramatist in English, Samuel Beckett found the pockets of silence in English speech, and made those silences speak. His characters do not inhabit a real place, like England, but instead occupy an abstract space of human existence, where the human predicaments of longing and desire for redemption, the failures of understanding, and the bafflement of death are experienced in their purest form.

Within England a host of dramatic luminaries gave vital energy to the British stage after 1945. While John Osborne created realist dramas of rage and dispossession, Harold Pinter emphasized the careful chiseling of language, bringing out the full ambiguity hidden in seemingly innocuous social conversation. Tom Stoppard joins Harold Pinter in his postwar longevity as a master of the British drama, despite or perhaps because of being an immigrant—"a bounced Czech," as he has called himself. Stoppard employs a brilliant rhetorical surface in his plays, which are often modernist puzzle boxes in their annihilation of the rules of time and space. In his meteoric but short dramatic career the playwright Joe Orton took a reverse tack to that of Beckettian silence and economy, or Pinterian ordinary language, and returned to the example of Oscar Wilde. Using a wildly baroque vocabulary and an epigrammatic wit, Orton brought an explicit gay drama and gay sensibility to the postwar theater, in works like *Loot*, which revolves around a seductive lower-class character who wreaks sexual havoc with all the inhabitants of a country estate, male and female, young and old. In *What the Butler Saw*, Orton imagines a monumental statue, bearing the national "phallus," which is hilariously blown to bits.

The impoverishment of the fifties abated in the sixties, at least for the middle class, as British banking and finance reinvigorated the economy. "Swinging London" became a household phrase, as British urban culture set the pace in music, fashion, and style. The Carnaby Street mode of dress and fashion mavens like Mary Quant, Jean Muir, and Zandra Rhodes were copied all over the world, worn by Jean

Shrimpton and Twiggy, who were among the first supermodels. British film came out of a postwar slump and movies like *Morgan* and *Georgy Girl* had huge audiences at home and in the United States. A delirious excitement invested British popular culture, and London became a hub of the new once more. The critique of British society mounted by Joe Orton's work found its double in the youth culture of "Mods" and "Rockers." Asked which he was, the Beatles' drummer Ringo Starr claimed to synthesize both: "I'm a mocker."

Amid the cultural ferment of the sixties and seventies, successive British governments struggled with intractable problems of inflation and unemployment, punctuated by frequent strikes by Britain's powerful unions, and rising violence in Northern Ireland. The generally pro-union government of Harold Wilson (1964–1970) was followed by the Conservative government of Edward Heath, who put new stress on private enterprise. A major shift away from the "welfare state," however, came only at the end of the decade, when Heath was succeeded by the formidable Margaret Thatcher, the prime minister of Britain for a record twelve years. The daughter of a lower middle-class family, Thatcher vaulted into politics when that was an exceptionally rare opportunity not only for a woman, but for a person whose father was a shop-keeper. Trained as a chemist, Thatcher worked long and hard for the (Tory) Conservative Party, even as Britain was ruled by a succession of Labour and Socialist governments. When her chance came to lead England as its Tory prime minister, Thatcher and her political and ideological colleagues began a governmental revolution by adopting free-market policies similar to those identified with the Ronald Reagan school of U.S. Republicanism. Thatcher set about dismantling as much of the welfare state of postwar modern Britain as she could—and that was a considerable amount.

Margaret Thatcher had an enormous impact on British identity, as well as on British society. Among the very small number of women worldwide who have ever wielded such substantial political power—Golda Meir and Indira Gandhi come to mind as others—Thatcher's polished good looks, her extreme toughness, and her uncompromising political dictates combined to produce a caricature of her as the domineering English governess, laying down the rules of what would be good for Britain's unruly citizens. Thatcher's economic policies emphasized productivity as never before; under her rule, an entrepreneurial culture began to flourish at the expense of once-sacred British social entitlements in education, health care, and civic subsidy of the arts and culture. Margaret Thatcher's most breathtaking quotation, and the one summing up her philosophy of government, was uttered in response to complaints about what was happening to the fabric of British society and, especially, to its poor, elderly, immigrants, and the mass numbers of the unemployed. "There is no such thing as society," she declared. What she meant was that government had no role to play in creating a unitary, egalitarian society. The forces of the unleashed free market, and the will of private individuals, would replace any notion of a social contract or social compact between and among British citizens. There was irony, of course, in Thatcher's seeming to turn her back on members of her own class and those below it, and despite the power and immense reputation she acquired worldwide, there was always scathing and vocal opposition to her within Britain, as she privatized the universities and abolished tenure, made inroads on the National Health Service, dissolved city councils and established poll taxes. Prime Minister Thatcher declared and fought Britain's last imperial war of modern times, against Argentina over the control of the Falkland Islands,

The Beatles preparing for a television broadcast, c. 1963.

and she was fierce opponent of nationalist sentiment among the Scottish and the Welsh, a firm upholder of Britain's right to control Northern Ireland in perpetuity, and strongly against the move toward joining the European Community. Thatcher became an icon in Britain, as well as its longest-governing Prime Minister: an icon for her certainty, confidence, and her personification of the huge changes she brought about. Though she provoked sharp opposition, her brilliance and energy were never in question, nor was her international influence.

Major changes have occurred in the last several years of the twentieth century, changes sweeping enough to have diminished Margaret Thatcher's iconic stature, and to have partially reversed the social revolution she began. At the turn of the century, the Labour Party reclaimed countrol of the country, changing course economically and emphasizing the very social contract Thatcher had set aside. Britain is an increasingly pivotal member of the European Community alliance, and its own internal divisions have come productively to the fore. Surprisingly, the twentieth century ended in much the same way as did the nineteenth century for Britain, with a nationwide debate on home rule. In 1886 and again in 1893 the eminent British prime minister William Gladstone fought for the establishment of a separate Irish parliament—thus the term "home rule"—to allow the Irish colony, with its differing religion of Roman Catholicism and its unique Gaelic culture, to have control over its own internal affairs. Gladstone and his Liberal Party formed an alliance with the Irish National Party's members of Parliament, who were led by the great Charles Steward Parnell, a Protestant Irishman known as "the uncrowned king of Ireland." Parnell's political fall due to an extramarital scandal removed a key player in Gladstone's strategy, and his final attempt in 1893 at voting in home rule failed. This failure led to the Irish revolution, the Irish

Civil War, and the continuing violence within Northern Ireland, the six counties still belonging to Britain and occupied by their army.

Britain's new prime minister, Anthony Blair, was elected in 1997 from the Labour Party, breaking the Conservative Party's eighteen-year hold on the position under Thatcher and her chosen successor, the rather low-key John Major. One of Blair's main campaign promises was bringing home rule to both Scotland and Wales, regions of Britain with their own language and dialect, their own cultural mores, and a long history of armed conflict with England. The referendum on the Scottish parliament, with the power to raise and lower income taxes within Scotland, and a considerable budget to operate as Scotland chooses, for its schools, health, housing and transport, overwhelmingly passed the popular vote; Wales has voted as well for the creation of a Welsh assembly with many of the same powers and responsibilities. While the Republic of Ireland is now a nation in its own right, Tony Blair's commitment to the peace talks in Northern Ireland, and to the inclusion of Sinn Fein in those talks, has also provided the first stirrings of political momentum in resolving the century-old conflict between Northern Irish Protestants who largely wish to remain attached to Britain, and the Northern Irish Catholics who have fought for the autonomy of this part of Ireland.

LANGUAGE AND IDENTITY

Complicated questions of language and identity have increasingly come to dominate the most recent phase of British literature. A great paradox of the British postwar period, in its time of imperial shrinkage, involves the fate of the English language. Britain may have been "kicked out" of many of its former colonies as a governing presence, but English was rarely shown the door at the same time. For economic and cultural reasons English as a global language became even more widely dispersed and dominant after World War II. Of course, the spread of U.S. interests has played a role in the hegemony of English. However, the old contours of the British empire continue to shape much of the production of English literature today. In this way, the former British empire has become part of the fabric of British literature.

Salman Rushdie, who is of Pakistani parentage, is an intriguing example of this process of crossing the increasingly porous boundaries of Britishness, as well as a cautionary tale of how powerful literature can be. Rushdie's novels are part of British literature at its modernist best, drawing on the entire English literary tradition, yet informed by a cosmopolitan and a non-Western literary tradition as well. Eight years after he achieved great acclaim for his novel *Midnight's Children* (1980), a book that adapted the "magic realism" of Latin American fiction to the history of Indian independence, Rushdie published *The Satanic Verses*. This novel recounts a magical mystery tour of sorts, the arrival of two South Asian refugees to modern London: one a film star from Bombay, the other a kind of trickster figure. Embedded in this complex tale of migration and identity is a brief dream sequence satirizing the prophet Mohammed. In response to this dream-within-a-dream passage, the Iranian theocratic government delivered a *fatwa*—an edict sentencing Rushdie to death for treachery to the religion of Islam. Rushdie did not write the book in Arabic, nor did he write it for a Muslim audience, but that was irrelevant to the clerics who pronounced sentence on him before millions of devout adherents. From that time until a few years ago, Rushdie was forced to live in a form of self-imposed house arrest, guarded by the

British government. In an ironic twist, British literature itself had become his prison house of language, his internal exile. It is this tradition that "protects" him as a great writer, and, because of its porous literary borders, is responsible for his predicament.

In recent years British literature has been infused with new life both from foreign-born writers and from new voices bubbling up from within the British Isles, in the shape of Welsh, Scottish, and Irish literary prose and poetry. The Nobel Prize-winning Irish poet Seamus Heaney is a kind of internal outsider, since, as he has written, he does not consider himself to be part of "British" literature as ordinarily defined, while he nonetheless writes English poetry deeply influenced by English poets from Milton to Wordsworth to Eliot. Some writers have deliberately taken themselves out of British literature for political and literary reasons, using the strongest means possible: they have decided to write in a language other than English. For example, the Kenyan writer Ngugi wa-Thiongo, educated by British missionaries and then at a British university, whose first memorized poem was Wordsworth's *Daffodils*, now writes in the Kikuyu language, and translates his work into English. The Irish poet Nuala Ní Dhomhnaill has made a similar decision: she writes and publishes her poetry first in Irish, and only later translates it into English as a "second" language.

In recent years British writing has been invigorated from "below," as well as from "outside": there has been a profusion of working-class or lower-middle-class novelists, poets, and screenwriters, many of whom adopt the dialect or argot of lower-class Welsh, Scottish, and Irish English. The Scottish writer Irvine Welsh is one example of this cross-fertilization today; his novel *Trainspotting* received ample literary accolades and was made into a widely seen film that, like the book, circulated throughout Europe, the Americas, and much of the globe. Its picaresque tale of down-and-out yet lively and smart urban twenty-somethings trying to find fulfillment in drugs, travel, and petty crime made Glaswegian knockabouts and their dialect emblematic of the modern condition. When James Kelman won the Booker Prize for the best novel published in England in 1994, there was widespread outrage: the working-class, expletive-laced speech of his Scottish protagonist was deemed unliterary by many, or at least unreadable and not in conformity with what was revered as the Queen's English. Poetry too has become a vehicle for a range of literary experiments, linking music and film to rhymed and unrhymed, and often performed, verse, connecting the popular and the literary. This upsurge of vivacious and often provocative writing is primarily the work of younger writers, and in many instances the novels are almost immediately being turned into films with international audiences.

In the past hundred years British literature has seen upheavals of aesthetic form, of geographic location, and of linguistic content. What is no longer in question, oddly enough, despite the current age of cyberspace and interactive media, is whether literature itself will survive. As Mark Twain once commented dryly after reading his own obituary in the newspaper: "The reports of my death are greatly exaggerated." The reports of literature's inevitable eclipse at the hands of media and mass culture have, it seems, been greatly exaggerated too. At this moment, British literary creativity is fed from many streams, welling up unpredictably, located in unexpected places. British literature has not merely survived; it remains a vital index of contemporary social and cultural life, and a crucial indication of the shape of things to come.

Joseph Conrad
1857–1924

One of the ironies of twentieth-century British literature is that many of its greatest writers were not conventionally "British." In the case of Joseph Conrad, arguably the first modern British writer, the irony is even more extreme, because Conrad was born a Pole, and learned English only when he was in his twenties. The transformation of Josef Konrad Nalecz Korzeniowski into "Joseph Conrad" is as fascinating and mysterious a story as the transforming journeys at the heart of his fiction.

Joseph Conrad was a lifelong exile from a country that no longer existed on the map of Europe as a separate country. At the time of Conrad's birth in 1857, Poland was divided between Russia and the Austro-Hungarian empire. His parents, Apollo and Eva, were Polish patriots, and after an uprising against Russia in 1863, the family was exiled to a village in the far north of Russia. Eva died when Josef was seven years old; Apollo when he was twelve. Apollo had been both a political activist and a man of letters, a poet and a translator of French and English literature into Polish. In a sense, by becoming a British novelist writing in English, Conrad was carrying on a project of translation begun by his father, a translation across cultures and literatures as well as languages. Hidden within Conrad's poetic and impressionistic literary language is a secret language—Polish—and a secret history of exile from his homeland.

After Conrad's parents died, he was raised by a cosmopolitan uncle, Tadeusz Bobrowski, who was also imbued with patriotic political leanings and a deep love of literature. Josef was sent to school in Cracow, Poland, where he was bored and restless. His uncle then sent him to Switzerland with a private tutor; they argued constantly for a year, and the tutor resigned. Not quite seventeen years old, Conrad proceeded to Marseilles and joined the French merchant navy. He spent twenty years as a sailor and as a ship's captain, spending four years sailing under the French flag, and then sixteen years with British trading ships. In 1894 Josef Korzeniowski completed his transformation into the writer Joseph Conrad by changing his name and settling in England to become a full-time writer.

By the end of the nineteenth century, the nationalistic wars that had led to a divided Poland had been followed by another historical phenomenon: the dividing-up of the globe by the nations of Europe as these powers consolidated empires. The oceans were crucial pathways in these struggles, not simply vast, watery landscapes outside of history. The seafaring Conrad, who had wanted to leave the frustrations of school behind him and see the world, became intimately involved in the everyday business of the making of empires, playing a minor role behind the scenes of the major political forces of the age. Merchant ships of the kind he served on traced the routes of trade and commerce, which now had become the routes of colonization and political conquest as well. As he came to realize he was an eyewitness to modern history in the making, Joseph Conrad discovered his abiding subject as a writer.

Conrad's voyages during this twenty-year odyssey took him East and West, to Indonesia and the Philippines, to Venezuela, the West Indies, and Africa. Working all the while, he watched as bit by bit the patchwork quilt of empire was put together. Wishing to avoid conscription in the French navy when he came of age, in 1878 Conrad joined the British merchant navy. The British empire had become the most extensive and mighty of any imperial power, and in his capacity as seaman Conrad worked in the main ports of call of the empire upon which the sun supposedly never set. He adopted British citizenship in 1886; after his uncle Tadeusz's death in 1894, Conrad made the final decision to become a writer, and to write in English rather than in French. At the age of thirty-seven, Joseph Conrad was newly born.

As a British writer, Conrad was a sort of ventriloquist. On the surface, he was as English as any other writer in his circle: he married an Englishwoman, Jessie George, and became a recognized part of British literary life, forming friendships with other major writers like Henry James and Ford Madox Ford, and achieving great popularity with the British reading public. A stranger from an exotically foreign place, by British standards, a newcomer to the English language, he nonetheless spoke through an English "voice" he created. From his distanced perspective, he was able to make English do things it had not done in the past for native writers of English. Language in Conrad's writing is always a bit off kilter, reading as if it had been translated instead of being, as it was, originally written in English. His prose has a hallucinatory effect, and a poetic intensity linked to his approaching the words of the English language afresh. The most famous of Conrad's narrators is the character Marlow, who appears in several of his major works as an elusive commentator on the action. His Englishness is as real as it can be, for an imitation. Marlow is perhaps even more British than the British, lapsing often into British slang like "By Jove!" as if to authenticate the reality of Conrad's vision of the British world. Through narrative voices like that of Marlow, Conrad can tell stories that may appear to be familiar and ordinary but are in fact anything but that. If modernist writers succeed in making us doubt that we can truly be at home in the world, Conrad can be said to have been the first writer to convey this homelessness in English.

There is another paradox at the heart of Joseph Conrad's work. His writing straddles the nineteenth and the twentieth centuries, with the five major works he wrote in the years before 1900— *Almayer's Folly*, *The Nigger of the "Narcissus," Heart of Darkness, Lord Jim*, and *Typhoon*—thought of by many critics as more modernist and experimental than later novels he wrote in the twentieth century—*Nostromo, The Secret Agent, Under Western Eyes, Chance*, and *Victory*. The critic Ian Watt claims that the "intense experimentation which began in 1896 and ended in 1900" resulted from Conrad's concentration in those five earlier works on his own personal experience, a personal experience of travel, exile, and solitude that was a radical premonition of the conditions of modernity. Works like *Heart of Darkness*, written during Queen Victoria's reign, for Watt present "the obdurate incompatibility of the self and the world in which it exists." In book after book, he sets a lone individual into confrontation with the complexities of the modern world, whether the world be that of European imperialism, or political anarchism, or the secret world of spies, or the world of political revolution. His heroes and (much less often) heroines have to find their bearings as society crumbles around them, and Conrad usually depicts them at a moment of choice, when they have to act on their lonely knowledge without any guarantee that they have chosen rightly.

A reliance on personal experience might seem to be a recipe for a straightforward, realist style, but Conrad's prose throughout his work is complex and symbolic, relying on images that are spun into complicated and ambiguous webs of symbolism. What stands out prominently in Conrad's style is its visual nature, the emphasis on making the reader "see." Critics of Conrad's writing early on seized on the strikingly visual aspect of his effects, and his friend and fellow modernist writer Ford Madox Ford wrote an essay in 1913, *On Impressionism*, which put Conrad in a newly invented camp of impressionist writers. Conrad never fully agreed with this description of his style, nor did he have any special fondness for impressionist painting or the works of its greatest practitioners, Monet and Cézanne. Nonetheless, his own preface to *The Nigger of the "Narcissus"* describes all successful art as based on "an impression conveyed through the senses," and in each of his first five books narrators recount what they have *seen*. The narrator goes back over an experience in retelling it to an audience, an experience whose significance is not necessarily clear even to the narrator but whose meaning is revealed through the accumulation of imagistic details. The powers of sight are directly related to the powers of insight, or self-knowledge. A famous passage from *Heart of Darkness* explains the storytelling technique of the narrator Marlow, but also explains a philosophical conviction at the core of Conrad's writing: "The yarns of seamen have a direct simplicity, the whole meaning of which lies within the shell of a cracked nut. But Marlow was not typical (if his propensity to spin yarns be excepted), and to him the meaning of an episode was not inside like a kernel but outside, enveloping the tale which brought it out only as a glow brings out a haze, in the likeness of one of these misty halos that are sometimes made visible by the spectral illumination of moonshine." Events cast a visual glow and haze where meaning can be found only in the most subtle shades and ambiguous highlights of language. The reader must participate in the gradual, and partial, process of accumulating meaning.

Heart of Darkness is a work at the heart of modern British literature. First published serially in Blackwood's Magazine in 1899, it was reprinted as a complete work along with a companion novella, Youth, in 1902, and writers have returned to it again and again, in the form of quotations and allusions and imitations of its style; its story has been rewritten by each successive generation, in novels, films like Apocalypse Now, and even rock lyrics. Almost mythic in resonance, Heart of Darkness itself is structured around a mythical core—that is, the hero's quest. The journey or quest motif pervades world literature and English literature alike, from the Odyssey and the Epic of Gilgamesh to Dante's Divine Comedy, Bunyan's Pilgrim's Progress, and Byron's Childe Harold. Heart of Darkness condenses in its pages an epic range of theme and experience, both the social themes of empire and cultural clash, and the personal theme of the hero's quest for self-discovery.

As with all his early work, Conrad based Heart of Darkness on his own experience, in this case a trip he took up the Congo River in 1890 in order to become captain of a small steamship. The trip was an unusual one even by Conrad's standards, as he had been sailing the major oceans of the world on large ships. Conrad had reasons for choosing the assignment, however; he had been fascinated by maps since boyhood, and the blank space on the continent of Africa represented by the then-unexplored interior impelled him on. He was curious to see for himself the scandalous imperial practices of the Belgian King Leopold II in the Congo, who possessed what he called the Congo Free State (now Zaire) as his own private property, draining it of raw materials like ivory, while claiming to be suppressing savagery and spreading European civilization. After traveling two hundred miles upriver to Kinshasa to join his ship, however, he found it was undergoing repairs. He traveled as a passenger on a trip to Stanley Falls, to bring back an ailing company agent, Georges Klein, who died on the return trip to Kinshasa. These events provided the germ of Conrad's novella, which transformed Klein ("Little," in German) into the uncanny figure of Kurtz.

A diary Conrad kept during his journey (excerpted as a Companion Reading following Heart of Darkness) records his dawning awareness that King Leopold's policy in the Congo was nothing other than slave labor, ultimately causing the deaths of more than a million Africans. Initially an observer, Conrad became a passionately informed partisan, and made known his findings in the form of journalism and essays in the attempt to halt the King's genocidal policies. Heart of Darkness records these evils, and the ravages of Belgian colonialism on the African tribal societies it encountered and uprooted. Scholars of African history have shown how accurate his descriptions are, from the bit of white thread worn around the neck of a certain tribal group, to the construction of the railroad to Kinshasa and its devastating human impact. Conrad never names the Congo, nor the places and landmarks his character Marlow visits, yet he himself later called the book a "Kodak," or a snapshot, of the Congo.

The location is left unnamed in part because Conrad wishes to show that the heart of this darkness can shift on its axis. Marlow is telling the tale to several anonymous Englishmen as they sail the Thames on their yacht. Under the Roman empire, Britain had itself been thought of as a savage wilderness, a dark continent. The journey upriver, as Marlow points out, has been a reverse journey as well, a journey back from Africa to the darkness that lies at the heart of an England that claims to be civilizing those whom it is merely conquering. The seemingly clear-cut boundaries of light and dark, black and white, have blurred and even reversed themselves, and the nested narrative of the story itself challenges our understanding and even our sense of self. In this narrative, as in Conrad's other works, we are confronted with the tragic irony that human knowledge always comes too late.

Preface to *The Nigger of the "Narcissus"*[1]

A work that aspires, however humbly, to the condition of art should carry its justification in every line. And art itself may be defined as a single-minded attempt to render the highest kind of justice to the visible universe, by bringing to light the truth, manifold and one, underlying its every aspect. It is an attempt to find in its forms, in its colours, in its light, in its shadows, in the aspects of matter, and in the facts of life what of each is fundamental, what is enduring and essential—their one illuminating and convincing quality—the very truth of their existence. The artist, then, like the thinker or the scientist, seeks the truth and makes his appeal. Impressed by the aspect of the world the thinker plunges into ideas, the scientist into facts—whence, presently, emerging they make their appeal to those qualities of our being that fit us best for the hazardous enterprise of living. They speak authoritatively to our common sense, to our intelligence, to our desire of peace, or to our desire of unrest; not seldom to our prejudices, sometimes to our fears, often to our egoism—but always to our credulity. And their words are heard with reverence, for their concern is with weighty matters: with the cultivation of our minds and the proper care of our bodies, with the attainment of our ambitions, with the perfection of the means and the glorification of our precious aims.

It is otherwise with the artist.

Confronted by the same enigmatical spectacle the artist descends within himself, and in that lonely region of stress and strife, if he be deserving and fortunate, he finds the terms of his appeal. His appeal is made to our less obvious capacities: to that part of our nature which, because of the warlike conditions of existence, is necessarily kept out of sight within the more resisting and hard qualities—like the vulnerable body within a steel armour. His appeal is less loud, more profound, less distinct, more stirring—and sooner forgotten. Yet its effect endures for ever. The changing wisdom of successive generations discards ideas, questions facts, demolishes theories. But the artist appeals to that part of our being which is not dependent on wisdom; to that in us which is a gift and not an acquisition—and, therefore, more permanently enduring. He speaks to our capacity for delight and wonder, to the sense of mystery surrounding our lives; to our sense of pity, and beauty, and pain; to the latent feeling of fellowship with all creation—and to the subtle but invincible conviction of solidarity that knits together the loneliness of innumerable hearts, to the solidarity in dreams, in joy, in sorrow, in aspirations, in illusions, in hope, in fear, which binds men to each other, which binds together all humanity—the dead to the living and the living to the unborn.

It is only some such train of thought, or rather of feeling, that can in a measure explain the aim of the attempt, made in the tale which follows, to present an unrestful episode in the obscure lives of a few individuals out of all the disregarded multitude of the bewildered, the simple, and the voiceless. For, if any part of truth dwells in the belief confessed above, it becomes evident that there is not a place of splendour or a dark corner of the earth that does not deserve, if only a passing glance of wonder and pity. The motive, then, may be held to justify the matter of the work; but this preface, which is simply an avowal of endeavour, cannot end here—for the avowal is not yet complete.

---

1. Conrad's novella *The Nigger of the "Narcissus"* deals with the tragic death of a black seaman aboard a merchant ship named the *Narcissus*; Conrad had served as first mate on a ship of that name in the Indian Ocean in 1883. He published the novella in *The New Review* in 1897, then added this preface when it came out in book form in 1898.

Fiction—if it at all aspires to be art—appeals to temperament. And in truth it must be, like painting, like music, like all art, the appeal of one temperament to all the other innumerable temperaments whose subtle and resistless power endows passing events with their true meaning, and creates the moral, the emotional atmosphere of the place and time. Such an appeal to be effective must be an impression conveyed through the senses; and, in fact, it cannot be made in any other way, because temperament, whether individual or collective, is not amenable to persuasion. All art, therefore, appeals primarily to the senses, and the artistic aim when expressing itself in written words must also make its appeal through the senses, if its high desire is to reach the secret spring of responsive emotions. It must strenuously aspire to the plasticity of sculpture, to the colour of painting, and to the magic suggestiveness of music—which is the art of arts. And it is only through complete, unswerving devotion to the perfect blending of form and substance; it is only through an unremitting never-discouraged care for the shape and ring of sentences that an approach can be made to plasticity, to colour, and that the light of magic suggestiveness may be brought to play for an evanescent instant over the commonplace surface of words: of the old, old words, worn thin, defaced by ages of careless usage.

The sincere endeavour to accomplish that creative task, to go as far on that road as his strength will carry him, to go undeterred by faltering, weariness, or reproach, is the only valid justification for the worker in prose. And if his conscience is clear, his answer to those who, in the fullness of a wisdom which looks for immediate profit, demand specifically to be edified, consoled, amused; who demand to be promptly improved, or encouraged, or frightened, or shocked, or charmed, must run thus: My task which I am trying to achieve is, by the power of the written word to make you hear, to make you feel—it is, before all, to make you see. That—and no more, and it is everything. If I succeed, you shall find there according to your deserts: encouragement, consolation, fear, charm—all you demand—and, perhaps, also that glimpse of truth for which you have forgotten to ask.

To snatch in a moment of courage, from the remorseless rush of time, a passing phase of life, is only the beginning of the task. The task approached in tenderness and faith is to hold up unquestioningly, without choice and without fear, the rescued fragment before all eyes in the light of a sincere mood. It is to show its vibration, its colour, its form; and through its movement, its form, and its colour, reveal the substance of its truth—disclose its inspiring secret: the stress and passion within the core of each convincing moment. In a single-minded attempt of that kind, if one be deserving and fortunate, one may perchance attain to such clearness of sincerity that at last the presented vision of regret or pity, of terror or mirth, shall awaken in the hearts of the beholders that feeling of unavoidable solidarity; of the solidarity in mysterious origin, in toil, in joy, in hope, in uncertain fate, which binds men to each other and all mankind to the visible world.

It is evident that he who, rightly or wrongly, holds by the convictions expressed above cannot be faithful to any one of the temporary formulas of his craft. The enduring part of them—the truth which each only imperfectly veils—should abide with him as the most precious of his possessions, but they all: Realism, Romanticism, Naturalism, even the unofficial sentimentalism (which, like the poor, is exceedingly difficult to get rid of), all these gods must, after a short period of fellowship, abandon him—even on the very threshold of the temple—to the stammerings of his conscience and to the outspoken consciousness of the difficulties of his work. In that uneasy solitude the supreme cry of Art for Art itself, loses the exciting ring of its apparent immorality. It sounds far off. It has ceased to be a cry, and is heard only as a whisper, often incomprehensible, but at times and faintly encouraging.

Sometimes, stretched at ease in the shade of a roadside tree, we watch the motions of a labourer in a distant field, and after a time, begin to wonder languidly as to what the fellow may be at. We watch the movements of his body, the waving of his arms, we see him bend down, stand up, hesitate, begin again. It may add to the charm of an idle hour to be told the purpose of his exertions. If we know he is trying to lift a stone, to dig a ditch, to uproot a stump, we look with a more real interest at his efforts; we are disposed to condone the jar of his agitation upon the restfulness of the landscape; and even, if in a brotherly frame of mind, we may bring ourselves to forgive his failure. We understood his object, and, after all, the fellow has tried, and perhaps he had not the strength—and perhaps he had not the knowledge. We forgive, go on our way—and forget.

And so it is with the workman of art. Art is long and life is short, and success is very far off. And thus, doubtful of strength to travel so far, we talk a little about the aim—the aim of art, which, like life itself, is inspiring, difficult—obscured by mists. It is not in the clear logic of a triumphant conclusion; it is not in the unveiling of one of those heartless secrets which are called the Laws of Nature. It is not less great, but only more difficult.

To arrest, for the space of a breath, the hands busy about the work of the earth, and compel men entranced by the sight of distant goals to glance for a moment at the surrounding vision of form and colour, of sunshine and shadows; to make them pause for a look, for a sigh, for a smile—such is the aim, difficult and evanescent, and reserved only for a very few to achieve. But sometimes, by the deserving and the fortunate, even that task is accomplished. And when it is accomplished—behold!—all the truth of life is there: a moment of vision, a sigh, a smile—and the return to an eternal rest.

Heart of Darkness

1

The *Nellie*, a cruising yawl,[1] swung to her anchor without a flutter of the sails, and was at rest. The flood had made, the wind was nearly calm, and being bound down the river, the only thing for it was to come to and wait for the turn of the tide.

The sea-reach of the Thames stretched before us like the beginning of an interminable waterway. In the offing the sea and the sky were welded together without a joint, and in the luminous space the tanned sails of the barges drifting up with the tide seemed to stand still in red clusters of canvas sharply peaked, with gleams of varnished sprits. A haze rested on the low shores that ran out to sea in vanishing flatness. The air was dark above Gravesend, and farther back still seemed condensed into a mournful gloom, brooding motionless over the biggest, and the greatest, town on earth.[2]

The Director of Companies was our captain and our host. We four affectionately watched his back as he stood in the bows looking to seaward. On the whole river there was nothing that looked half so nautical. He resembled a pilot, which to a seaman is trustworthiness personified. It was difficult to realise his work was not out there in the luminous estuary, but behind him, within the brooding gloom.

Between us there was, as I have already said somewhere, the bond of the sea. Besides holding our hearts together through long periods of separation, it had the effect of making us tolerant of each other's yarns—and even convictions. The

1. A two-masted ship.
2. London. Gravesend is the last major town on the   Thames estuary, from which the river joins the North Sea.

Lawyer—the best of old fellows—had, because of his many years and many virtues, the only cushion on deck, and was lying on the only rug. The Accountant had brought out already a box of dominoes, and was toying architecturally with the bones. Marlow sat cross-legged right aft, leaning against the mizzen-mast.[3] He had sunken cheeks, a yellow complexion, a straight back, an ascetic aspect, and, with his arms dropped, the palms of hands outwards, resembled an idol. The Director, satisfied the anchor had good hold, made his way aft and sat down amongst us. We exchanged a few words lazily. Afterwards there was silence on board the yacht. For some reason or other we did not begin that game of dominoes. We felt meditative, and fit for nothing but placid staring. The day was ending in a serenity of still and exquisite brilliance. The water shone pacifically; the sky, without a speck, was a benign immensity of unstained light; the very mist on the Essex marshes was like a gauzy and radiant fabric, hung from the wooded rises inland, and draping the low shores in diaphanous folds. Only the gloom to the west, brooding over the upper reaches, became more sombre every minute, as if angered by the approach of the sun.

And at last, in its curved and imperceptible fall, the sun sank low, and from glowing white changed to a dull red without rays and without heat, as if about to go out suddenly, stricken to death by the touch of that gloom brooding over a crowd of men.

Forthwith a change came over the waters, and the serenity became less brilliant but more profound. The old river in its broad reach rested unruffled at the decline of day, after ages of good service done to the race that peopled its banks, spread out in the tranquil dignity of a waterway leading to the uttermost ends of the earth. We looked at the venerable stream not in the vivid flush of a short day that comes and departs for ever, but in the august light of abiding memories. And indeed nothing is easier for a man who has, as the phrase goes, "followed the sea" with reverence and affection, than to evoke the great spirit of the past upon the lower reaches of the Thames. The tidal current runs to and fro in its unceasing service, crowded with memories of men and ships it has borne to the rest of home or to the battles of the sea. It had known and served all the men of whom the nation is proud, from Sir Francis Drake to Sir John Franklin, knights all, titled and untitled—the great knights-errant of the sea.[4] It had borne all the ships whose names are like jewels flashing in the night of time, from the *Golden Hind* returning with her round flanks full of treasure, to be visited by the Queen's Highness and thus pass out of the gigantic tale, to the *Erebus* and *Terror*, bound on other conquests—and that never returned. It had known the ships and the men. They had sailed from Deptford, from Greenwich, from Erith—the adventurers and the settlers; kings' ships and the ships of men on 'Change; captains, admirals, the dark "interlopers" of the Eastern trade, and the commissioned "generals" of East India fleets.[5] Hunters for gold or pursuers of fame, they all had gone out on that stream, bearing the sword, and often the torch, messengers of the might within the land, bearers of a spark from the sacred fire. What greatness had not floated on the ebb of that river into the mystery of an unknown earth! . . . The dreams of men, the seed of commonwealths, the germs of empires.

---

3. A secondary mast at the stern of the ship.
4. Sir Francis Drake (1540–1596) was captain of *The Golden Hind* in the service of Queen Elizabeth I; his reputation came from the successful raids he mounted against Spanish ships returning laden with gold from the New World (South America). In 1845 Sir John Franklin led an expedition in the *Erebus* and *Terror* in search of the Northwest Passage (to the Pacific); all perished.
5. Deptford, Greenwich, and Erith lie on the Thames between London and Gravesend; "men on 'Change" are brokers on the Stock Exchange; the East India Company, a commercial and trading concern, became *de facto* ruler of large tracts of India in the 18th and 19th centuries.

The sun set; the dusk fell on the stream, and lights began to appear along the shore. The Chapman lighthouse, a three-legged thing erect on a mudflat, shone strongly. Lights of ships moved in the fairway—a great stir of lights going up and going down. And farther west on the upper reaches the place of the monstrous town was still marked ominously on the sky, a brooding gloom in sunshine, a lurid glare under the stars.

"And this also," said Marlow suddenly, "has been one of the dark places of the earth."

He was the only man of us who still "followed the sea." The worst that could be said of him was that he did not represent his class. He was a seaman, but he was a wanderer too, while most seamen lead, if one may so express it, a sedentary life. Their minds are of the stay-at-home order, and their home is always with them—the ship; and so is their country—the sea. One ship is very much like another, and the sea is always the same. In the immutability of their surroundings the foreign shores, the foreign faces, the changing immensity of life, glide past, veiled not by a sense of mystery but by a slightly disdainful ignorance; for there is nothing mysterious to a seaman unless it be the sea itself, which is the mistress of his existence and as inscrutable as Destiny. For the rest, after his hours of work, a casual stroll or a casual spree on shore suffices to unfold for him the secret of a whole continent, and generally he finds the secret not worth knowing. The yarns of seamen have a direct simplicity, the whole meaning of which lies within the shell of a cracked nut. But Marlow was not typical (if his propensity to spin yarns be excepted), and to him the meaning of an episode was not inside like a kernel but outside, enveloping the tale which brought it out only as a glow brings out a haze, in the likeness of one of these misty halos that sometimes are made visible by the spectral illumination of moonshine.

His remark did not seem at all surprising. It was just like Marlow. It was accepted in silence. No one took the trouble to grunt even; and presently he said, very slow,—

"I was thinking of very old times, when the Romans first came here, nineteen hundred years ago[6]—the other day. . . . Light came out of this river since—you say Knights? Yes; but it is like a running blaze on a plain, like a flash of lightning in the clouds. We live in the flicker—may it last as long as the old earth keeps rolling! But darkness was here yesterday. Imagine the feelings of a commander of a fine—what d'ye call 'em?—trireme in the Mediterranean, ordered suddenly to the north; run overland across the Gauls in a hurry;[7] put in charge of one of these craft the legionaries,—a wonderful lot of handy men they must have been too—used to build, apparently by the hundred, in a month or two, if we may believe what we read. Imagine him here—the very end of the world, a sea the colour of lead, a sky the colour of smoke, a kind of ship about as rigid as a concertina—and going up this river with stores, or orders, or what you like. Sandbanks, marshes, forests, savages,—precious little to eat fit for a civilised man, nothing but Thames water to drink. No Falernian wine here, no going ashore. Here and there a military camp lost in a wilderness, like a needle in a bundle of hay—cold, fog, tempests, disease, exile, and death,—death skulking in the air, in the water, in the bush. They must have been dying like flies here. Oh yes—he did it. Did it very well, too, no doubt, and without thinking much about it either, except afterwards to brag of what he had gone through in his time, perhaps. They were men enough to face the darkness. And perhaps he was cheered

6. A Roman force under Julius Caesar landed in Britain in 55 B.C., but it was not until A.D. 43 that the Emperor Claudius decided to conquer the island.
7. A *trireme* is an ancient warship, propelled by oarsmen;

the Gauls were the pre-Roman tribes who occupied present-day France; they were subdued by Julius Caesar between 58–50 B.C.

by keeping his eye on a chance of promotion to the fleet at Ravenna by-and-by, if he had good friends in Rome and survived the awful climate. Or think of a decent young citizen in a toga—perhaps too much dice, you know—coming out here in the train of some prefect, or tax-gatherer, or trader even, to mend his fortunes. Land in a swamp, march through the woods, and in some inland post feel the savagery, the utter savagery, had closed round him,—all that mysterious life of the wilderness that stirs in the forest, in the jungles, in the hearts of wild men. There's no initiation either into such mysteries. He has to live in the midst of the incomprehensible, which is also detestable. And it has a fascination, too, that goes to work upon him. The fascination of the abomination—you know. Imagine the growing regrets, the longing to escape, the powerless disgust, the surrender, the hate."

He paused.

"Mind," he began again, lifting one arm from the elbow, the palm of the hand outwards, so that, with his legs folded before him, he had the pose of a Buddha preaching in European clothes and without a lotus-flower—"Mind, none of us would feel exactly like this. What saves us is efficiency—the devotion to efficiency. But these chaps were not much account, really. They were no colonists; their administration was merely a squeeze, and nothing more, I suspect. They were conquerors, and for that you want only brute force—nothing to boast of, when you have it, since your strength is just an accident arising from the weakness of others. They grabbed what they could get for the sake of what was to be got. It was just robbery with violence, aggravated murder on a great scale, and men going at it blind—as is very proper for those who tackle a darkness. The conquest of the earth, which mostly means the taking it away from those who have a different complexion or slightly flatter noses than ourselves, is not a pretty thing when you look into it too much. What redeems it is the idea only. An idea at the back of it; not a sentimental pretence but an idea; and an unselfish belief in the idea—something you can set up, and bow down before, and offer a sacrifice to. . . ."

He broke off. Flames glided in the river, small green flames, red flames, white flames, pursuing, overtaking, joining, crossing each other—then separating slowly or hastily. The traffic of the great city went on in the deepening night upon the sleepless river. We looked on, waiting patiently—there was nothing else to do till the end of the flood; but it was only after a long silence, when he said, in a hesitating voice, "I suppose you fellows remember I did once turn fresh-water sailor for a bit," that we knew we were fated, before the ebb began to run, to hear about one of Marlow's inconclusive experiences.

"I don't want to bother you much with what happened to me personally," he began, showing in this remark the weakness of many tellers of tales who seem so often unaware of what their audience would best like to hear; "yet to understand the effect of it on me you ought to know how I got out there, what I saw, how I went up that river to the place where I first met the poor chap. It was the farthest point of navigation and the culminating point of my experience. It seemed somehow to throw a kind of light on everything about me—and into my thoughts. It was sombre enough too—and pitiful—not extraordinary in any way—not very clear either. No, not very clear. And yet it seemed to throw a kind of light.

"I had then, as you remember, just returned to London after a lot of Indian Ocean, Pacific, China Seas—a regular dose of the East—six years or so, and I was loafing about, hindering you fellows in your work and invading your homes, just as though I had got a heavenly mission to civilise you. It was very fine for a time, but after a bit I did get tired of resting. Then I began to look for a ship—I should think the hardest work on earth. But the ships wouldn't even look at me. And I got tired of that game too.

"Now when I was a little chap I had a passion for maps. I would look for hours at South America, or Africa, or Australia, and lose myself in all the glories of exploration. At that time there were many blank spaces on the earth, and when I saw one that looked particularly inviting on a map (but they all look that) I would put my finger on it and say, When I grow up I will go there. The North Pole was one of these places, I remember. Well, I haven't been there yet, and shall not try now. The glamour's off. Other places were scattered about the Equator, and in every sort of latitude all over the two hemispheres. I have been in some of them, and . . . well, we won't talk about that. But there was one yet—the biggest, the most blank, so to speak— that I had a hankering after.

"True, by this time it was not a blank space any more. It had got filled since my boyhood with rivers and lakes and names. It had ceased to be a blank space of delightful mystery—a white patch for a boy to dream gloriously over. It had become a place of darkness. But there was in it one river especially, a mighty big river, that you could see on the map, resembling an immense snake uncoiled, with its head in the sea, its body at rest curving afar over a vast country, and its tail lost in the depths of the land. And as I looked at the map of it in a shop-window, it fascinated me as a snake would a bird—a silly little bird. Then I remembered there was a big concern, a Company for trade on that river. Dash it all! I thought to myself, they can't trade without using some kind of craft on that lot of fresh water—steamboats! Why shouldn't I try to get charge of one. I went on along Fleet Street, but could not shake off the idea. The snake had charmed me.

"You understand it was a Continental concern, that Trading Society; but I have a lot of relations living on the Continent, because it's cheap and not so nasty as it looks, they say.

"I am sorry to own I began to worry them. This was already a fresh departure for me. I was not used to get things that way, you know. I always went my own road and on my own legs where I had a mind to go. I wouldn't have believed it of myself; but, then—you see—I felt somehow I must get there by hook or by crook. So I worried them. The men said 'My dear fellow,' and did nothing. Then—would you believe it?—I tried the women. I, Charlie Marlow, set the women to work—to get a job. Heavens! Well, you see, the notion drove me. I had an aunt, a dear enthusiastic soul. She wrote: 'It will be delightful. I am ready to do anything, anything for you. It is a glorious idea. I know the wife of a very high personage in the Administration, and also a man who has lots of influence with,' &c., &c. She was determined to make no end of fuss to get me appointed skipper of a river steamboat, if such was my fancy.

"I got my appointment—of course; and I got it very quick. It appears the Company had received news that one of their captains had been killed in a scuffle with the natives. This was my chance, and it made me the more anxious to go. It was only months and months afterwards, when I made the attempt to recover what was left of the body, that I heard the original quarrel arose from a misunderstanding about some hens. Yes, two black hens. Fresleven—that was the fellow's name, a Dane—thought himself wronged somehow in the bargain, so he went ashore and started to hammer the chief of the village with a stick. Oh, it didn't surprise me in the least to hear this, and at the same time to be told that Fresleven was the gentlest, quietest creature that ever walked on two legs. No doubt he was; but he had been a couple of years already out there engaged in the noble cause, you know, and he probably felt the need at last of asserting his self-respect in some way. Therefore he whacked the old nigger mercilessly, while a big crowd of his people watched him, thunderstruck, till some man,—I was told the chief's son,—in desperation at hearing the old chap yell, made a tentative jab with a spear at the white man—and of course it went quite easy between the shoulder-blades. Then the whole population cleared into the forest, expecting all kinds of calamities to happen, while, on the other hand, the steamer Fresleven commanded left also in a bad panic, in charge of the engineer, I believe. Afterwards nobody seemed to trouble much about Fresleven's remains, till I got out and stepped into his shoes. I couldn't let it rest, though; but when an opportunity offered at last to meet my predecessor, the grass growing through his ribs was tall enough to hide his bones. They were all there. The supernatural being had not been touched after he fell. And the village was deserted, the huts gaped black, rotting, all askew within the fallen enclosures. A calamity had come to it, sure enough. The people had vanished. Mad terror had scattered them, men, women, and children, through the bush, and they had never returned. What became of the hens I don't know either. I should think the cause of progress got them, anyhow. However, through this glorious affair I got my appointment, before I had fairly begun to hope for it.

"I flew around like mad to get ready, and before forty-eight hours I was crossing the Channel to show myself to my employers, and sign the contract. In a very few hours I arrived in a city that always makes me think of a whited sepulchre.[8] Prejudice no doubt. I had no difficulty in finding the Company's offices. It was the biggest thing in the town, and everybody I met was full of it. They were going to run an oversea empire, and make no end of coin by trade.

"A narrow and deserted street in deep shadow, high houses, innumerable windows with venetian blinds, a dead silence, grass sprouting between the stones, imposing carriage archways right and left, immense double doors standing ponderously ajar. I slipped through one of these cracks, went up a swept and ungarnished staircase, as arid as a desert, and opened the first door I came to. Two women, one fat and the other slim, sat on straw-bottomed chairs, knitting black wool. The slim one got up and walked straight at me—still knitting with downcast eyes—and only just as I began to think of getting out of her way, as you would for a somnambulist, stood still, and looked up. Her dress was as plain as an umbrella-cover, and she turned round without a word and preceded me into a waiting-room. I gave my name, and looked about. Deal table in the middle, plain chairs all round the walls, on one end a large shining map, marked with all the colours of a rainbow. There was a vast amount of red—good to see at any time, because one knows that some real work is done in there, a deuce of a lot of blue, a little green, smears of orange, and, on the East Coast, a purple patch, to show where the jolly pioneers of progress drink the jolly lagerbeer.[9] However, I wasn't going into any of these. I was going into the yellow. Dead in the centre. And the river was there—fascinating—deadly—like a snake. Ough! A door opened, a white-haired secretarial head, but wearing a compassionate expression, appeared, and a skinny forefinger beckoned me into the sanctuary. Its light was dim, and a heavy writing-desk squatted in the middle. From behind that structure came out an impression of pale plumpness in a frock-coat. The great man himself. He was five feet six, I should judge, and had his grip on the handle-end of ever so many millions. He shook hands, I fancy, murmured vaguely, was satisfied with my French. *Bon voyage*.

8. Brussels was the headquarters of the Société Anonyme Belge pour le Commerce du Haut-Congo (Belgian Corporation for Trade in the Upper Congo), with which Conrad obtained his post through the influence of his aunt, Marguerite Poradowska.
9. British territories were traditionally marked in red on colonial maps; lager was originally a continental beer, not much drunk in England.

"In about forty-five seconds I found myself again in the waiting-room with the compassionate secretary, who, full of desolation and sympathy, made me sign some document. I believe I undertook amongst other things not to disclose any trade secrets. Well, I am not going to.

"I began to feel slightly uneasy. You know I am not used to such ceremonies, and there was something ominous in the atmosphere. It was just as though I had been let into some conspiracy—I don't know—something not quite right; and I was glad to get out. In the outer room the two women knitted black wool feverishly. People were arriving, and the younger one was walking back and forth introducing them. The old one sat on her chair. Her flat cloth slippers were propped up on a foot-warmer, and a cat reposed on her lap. She wore a starched white affair on her head, had a wart on one cheek, and silver-rimmed spectacles hung on the tip of her nose. She glanced at me above the glasses. The swift and indifferent placidity of that look troubled me. Two youths with foolish and cheery countenances were being piloted over, and she threw at them the same quick glance of unconcerned wisdom. She seemed to know all about them and about me too. An eerie feeling came over me. She seemed uncanny and fateful. Often far away there I thought of these two, guarding the door of Darkness, knitting black wool as for a warm pall, one introducing, introducing continuously to the unknown, the other scrutinising the cheery and foolish faces with unconcerned old eyes. *Ave!* Old knitter of black wool. *Morituri te salutant.*[1] Not many of those she looked at ever saw her again—not half, by a long way.

"There was yet a visit to the doctor. 'A simple formality,' assured me the secretary, with an air of taking an immense part in all my sorrows. Accordingly a young chap wearing his hat over the left eyebrow, some clerk I suppose,—there must have been clerks in the business, though the house was as still as a house in a city of the dead,—came from somewhere upstairs, and led me forth. He was shabby and careless, with ink-stains on the sleeves of his jacket, and his cravat was large and billowy, under a chin shaped like the toe of an old boot. It was a little too early for the doctor, so I proposed a drink, and thereupon he developed a vein of joviality. As we sat over our vermouths he glorified the Company's business, and by-and-by I expressed casually my surprise at him not going out there. He became very cool and collected all at once. 'I am not such a fool as I look, quoth Plato to his disciples,' he said sententiously, emptied his glass with great resolution, and we rose.

"The old doctor felt my pulse, evidently thinking of something else the while. 'Good, good for there,' he mumbled, and then with a certain eagerness asked me whether I would let him measure my head. Rather surprised, I said Yes, when he produced a thing like calipers and got the dimensions back and front and every way, taking notes carefully. He was an unshaven little man in a threadbare coat like a gaberdine, with his feet in slippers, and I thought him a harmless fool. 'I always ask leave, in the interests of science, to measure the crania of those going out there,' he said. 'And when they come back too?' I asked. 'Oh, I never see them,' he remarked; 'and moreover, the changes take place inside, you know.' He smiled, as if at some quiet joke. 'So you are going out there. Famous. Interesting too.' He gave me a searching glance, and made another note. 'Ever any madness in your family?' he asked, in a matter-of-fact tone. I felt very annoyed. 'Is that question in the interests of science too?' 'It would be,' he said, without taking notice of my irritation, 'interesting for science to watch the mental changes of individuals, on the spot, but . . .' 'Are you an

---

1. Hail! . . . Those who are about to die salute you!—traditional cry of Roman gladiators.

alienist?'[2] I interrupted. 'Every doctor should be—a little,' answered that original, imperturbably. 'I have a little theory which you Messieurs who go out there must help me to prove. This is my share in the advantages my country shall reap from the possession of such a magnificent dependency. The mere wealth I leave to others. Pardon my questions, but you are the first Englishman coming under my observation . . .' I hastened to assure him I was not in the least typical. 'If I were,' said I, 'I wouldn't be talking like this with you.' 'What you say is rather profound, and probably erroneous,' he said, with a laugh. 'Avoid irritation more than exposure to the sun. Adieu. How do you English say, eh? Good-bye. Ah! Good-bye. Adieu. In the tropics one must before everything keep calm.' . . . He lifted a warning forefinger. . . . 'Du calme, du calme. Adieu.'

"One thing more remained to do—say good-bye to my excellent aunt. I found her triumphant. I had a cup of tea—the last decent cup of tea for many days—and in a room that most soothingly looked just as you would expect a lady's drawing-room to look, we had a long quiet chat by the fireside. In the course of these confidences it became quite plain to me I had been represented to the wife of the high dignitary, and goodness knows to how many more people besides, as an exceptional and gifted creature—a piece of good fortune for the Company—a man you don't get hold of every day. Good heavens! and I was going to take charge of a twopenny-half-penny river-steamboat with a penny whistle attached! It appeared, however, I was also one of the Workers, with a capital—you know. Something like an emissary of light, something like a lower sort of apostle. There had been a lot of such rot let loose in print and talk just about that time, and the excellent woman, living right in the rush of all that humbug, got carried off her feet. She talked about 'weaning those ignorant millions from their horrid ways,' till, upon my word, she made me quite uncomfortable. I ventured to hint that the Company was run for profit.

" 'You forget, dear Charlie, that the labourer is worthy of his hire,' she said, brightly.[3] It's queer how out of touch with truth women are. They live in a world of their own, and there had never been anything like it, and never can be. It is too beautiful altogether, and if they were to set it up it would go to pieces before the first sunset. Some confounded fact we men have been living contentedly with ever since the day of creation would start up and knock the whole thing over.

"After this I got embraced, told to wear flannel, be sure to write often, and so on—and I left. In the street—I don't know why—a queer feeling came to me that I was an impostor. Odd thing that I, who used to clear out for any part of the world at twenty-four hours' notice, with less thought than most men give to the crossing of a street, had a moment—I won't say of hesitation, but of startled pause, before this commonplace affair. The best way I can explain it to you is by saying that, for a second or two, I felt as though, instead of going to the centre of a continent, I were about to set off for the centre of the earth.

"I left in a French steamer, and she called in every blamed port they have out there, for, as far as I could see, the sole purpose of landing soldiers and custom-house officers. I watched the coast. Watching a coast as it slips by the ship is like thinking about an enigma. There it is before you—smiling, frowning, inviting, grand, mean, insipid, or savage, and always mute with an air of whispering, Come and find out. This one was almost featureless, as if still in the making, with an aspect of monotonous grimness. The edge of a colossal jungle, so dark-green as to be almost black, fringed with white surf, ran straight, like a ruled line, far, far away along a blue sea whose glitter was blurred by a creeping mist. The sun was fierce, the land seemed to glisten and drip with steam. Here and there greyish-whitish specks showed up, clustered inside the white surf, with a flag flying above them perhaps—settlements some centuries old, and still no bigger than pin-heads on the untouched expanse of their background. We pounded along, stopped, landed soldiers; went on, landed custom-house clerks to levy toll in what looked like a Godforsaken wilderness, with a tin shed and a flag-pole lost in it; landed more soldiers—to take care of the custom-house clerks, presumably. Some, I heard, got drowned in the surf; but whether they did or not, nobody seemed particularly to care. They were just flung out there, and on we went. Every day the coast looked the same, as though we had not moved; but we passed various places—trading places—with names like Gran' Bassam, Little Popo,[4] names that seemed to belong to some sordid farce acted in front of a sinister back-cloth. The idleness of a passenger, my isolation amongst all these men with whom I had no point of contact, the oily and languid sea, the uniform sombreness of the coast, seemed to keep me away from the truth of things, within the toil of a mournful and senseless delusion. The voice of the surf heard now and then was a positive pleasure, like the speech of a brother. It was something natural, that had its reason, that had a meaning. Now and then a boat from the shore gave one a momentary contact with reality. It was paddled by black fellows. You could see from afar the white of their eyeballs glistening. They shouted, sang; their bodies streamed with perspiration; they had faces like grotesque masks—these chaps; but they had bone, muscle, a wild vitality, an intense energy of movement, that was as natural and true as the surf along their coast. They wanted no excuse for being there. They were a great comfort to look at. For a time I would feel I belonged still to a world of straightforward facts; but the feeling would not last long. Something would turn up to scare it away. Once, I remember, we came upon a man-of-war anchored off the coast. There wasn't even a shed there, and she was shelling the bush. It appears the French had one of their wars going on thereabouts. Her ensign dropped limp like a rag; the muzzles of the long eight-inch guns stuck out all over the low hull; the greasy, slimy swell swung her up lazily and let her down, swaying her thin masts. In the empty immensity of earth, sky, and water, there she was, incomprehensible, firing into a continent. Pop, would go one of the eight-inch guns; a small flame would dart and vanish, a little white smoke would disappear, a tiny projectile would give a feeble screech—and nothing happened. Nothing could happen. There was a touch of insanity in the proceeding, a sense of lugubrious drollery in the sight; and it was not dissipated by somebody on board assuring me earnestly there was a camp of natives—he called them enemies!—hidden out of sight somewhere.

"We gave her letters (I heard the men in that lonely ship were dying of fever at the rate of three a day) and went on. We called at some more places with farcical names, where the merry dance of death and trade goes on in a still and earthy atmosphere as of an overheated catacomb;[5] all along the formless coast bordered by dangerous surf, as if Nature herself had tried to ward off intruders; in and out of rivers, streams of death in life, whose banks were rotting into mud, whose waters, thickened into slime, invaded the contorted mangroves, that seemed to writhe at us in the extremity of an impotent despair. Nowhere did we stop long enough to get a particularised impression, but the general sense of vague and oppressive wonder grew upon me. It was like a weary pilgrimage amongst hints for nightmares.

"It was upward of thirty days before I saw the mouth of the big river. We anchored off the seat of the government. But my work would not begin till some two hundred miles farther on. So as soon as I could I made a start for a place thirty miles higher up.

"I had my passage on a little sea-going steamer. Her captain was a Swede, and knowing me for a seaman, invited me on the bridge. He was a young man, lean, fair, and morose, with lanky hair and a shuffling gait. As we left the miserable little wharf, he tossed his head contemptuously at the shore. 'Been living there?' he asked. I said, 'Yes.' 'Fine lot these government chaps—are they not?' he went on, speaking English with great precision and considerable bitterness. 'It is funny what some people will do for a few francs a month. I wonder what becomes of that kind when it goes up country?' I said to him I expected to see that soon. 'So-o-o!' he exclaimed. He shuffled athwart, keeping one eye ahead vigilantly. 'Don't be too sure,' he continued. 'The other day I took up a man who hanged himself on the road. He was a Swede, too.' 'Hanged himself! Why, in God's name?' I cried. He kept on looking out watchfully. 'Who knows? The sun too much for him, or the country perhaps.'

"At last we opened a reach. A rocky cliff appeared, mounds of turned-up earth by the shore, houses on a hill, others, with iron roofs, amongst a waste of excavations, or hanging to the declivity. A continuous noise of the rapids above hovered over this scene of inhabited devastation. A lot of people, mostly black and naked, moved about like ants. A jetty projected into the river. A blinding sunlight drowned all this at times in a sudden recrudescence of glare. 'There's your Company's station,' said the Swede, pointing to three wooden barrack-like structures on the rocky slope. 'I will send your things up. Four boxes did you say? So. Farewell.'

"I came upon a boiler wallowing in the grass, then found a path leading up the hill. It turned aside for the boulders, and also for an undersized railway-truck lying there on its back with its wheels in the air. One was off. The thing looked as dead as the carcass of some animal. I came upon more pieces of decaying machinery, a stack of rusty rails. To the left a clump of trees made a shady spot, where dark things seemed to stir feebly. I blinked, the path was steep. A horn tooted to the right, and I saw the black people run. A heavy and dull detonation shook the ground, a puff of smoke came out of the cliff, and that was all. No change appeared on the face of the rock. They were building a railway. The cliff was not in the way or anything; but this objectless blasting was all the work going on.

"A slight clinking behind me made me turn my head. Six black men advanced in a file, toiling up the path. They walked erect and slow, balancing small baskets full of earth on their heads, and the clink kept time with their footsteps. Black rags were wound round their loins, and the short ends behind wagged to and fro like tails. I could see every rib, the joints of their limbs were like knots in a rope; each had an iron collar on his neck, and all were connected together with a chain whose bights swung between them, rhythmically clinking. Another report from the cliff made me think suddenly of that ship of war I had seen firing into a continent. It was the same kind of ominous voice; but these men could by no stretch of imagination be called enemies. They were called criminals, and the outraged law, like the bursting shells, had come to them, an insoluble mystery from over the sea. All their meagre breasts panted together, the violently dilated nostrils quivered, the eyes stared stonily up-hill. They passed me within six inches, without a glance, with that complete, deathlike indifference of unhappy savages. Behind this raw matter one of the reclaimed, the product of the new forces at work, strolled despondently, carrying a rifle by its middle. He had a uniform jacket with one button off, and seeing a white man on the path, hoisted his weapon to his shoulder with alacrity. This was simple prudence, white men being so much alike at a distance that he could not tell who I might be. He was speedily reassured, and with a large, white, rascally grin, and a glance at his charge, seemed to take me into partnership in his exalted trust. After all, I also was a part of the great cause of these high and just proceedings.

"Instead of going up, I turned and descended to the left. My idea was to let that chain-gang get out of sight before I climbed the hill. You know I am not particularly tender; I've had to strike and to fend off. I've had to resist and to attack sometimes—that's only one way of resisting—without counting the exact cost, according to the demands of such sort of life as I had blundered into. I've seen the devil of violence, and the devil of greed, and the devil of hot desire; but, by all the stars! these were strong, lusty, red-eyed devils, that swayed and drove men—men, I tell you. But as I stood on this hillside, I foresaw that in the blinding sunshine of that land I would become acquainted with a flabby, pretending, weak-eyed devil of a rapacious and pitiless folly. How insidious he could be, too, I was only to find out several months later and a thousand miles farther. For a moment I stood appalled, as though by a warning. Finally I descended the hill, obliquely, towards the trees I had seen.

"I avoided a vast artificial hole somebody had been digging on the slope, the purpose of which I found it impossible to divine. It wasn't a quarry or a sandpit, anyhow. It was just a hole. It might have been connected with the philanthropic desire of giving the criminals something to do. I don't know. Then I nearly fell into a very narrow ravine, almost no more than a scar in the hillside. I discovered that a lot of imported drainage-pipes for the settlement had been tumbled in there. There wasn't one that was not broken. It was a wanton smash-up. At last I got under the trees. My purpose was to stroll into the shade for a moment; but no sooner within than it seemed to me I had stepped into the gloomy circle of some Inferno. The rapids were near, and an uninterrupted, uniform, headlong, rushing noise filled the mournful stillness of the grove, where not a breath stirred, not a leaf moved, with a mysterious sound—as though the tearing pace of the launched earth had suddenly become audible.

"Black shapes crouched, lay, sat between the trees, leaning against the trunks, clinging to the earth, half coming out, half effaced within the dim light, in all the attitudes of pain, abandonment, and despair. Another mine on the cliff went off, followed by a slight shudder of the soil under my feet. The work was going on. The work! And this was the place where some of the helpers had withdrawn to die.

"They were dying slowly—it was very clear. They were not enemies, they were not criminals, they were nothing earthly now,—nothing but black shadows of disease and starvation, lying confusedly in the greenish gloom. Brought from all the recesses of the coast in all the legality of time contracts, lost in uncongenial surroundings, fed on unfamiliar food, they sickened, became inefficient, and were then allowed to crawl away and rest. These moribund shapes were free as air—and nearly as thin. I began to distinguish the gleam of eyes under the trees. Then, glancing down, I saw a face near my hand. The black bones reclined at full length with one shoulder against the tree, and slowly the eyelids rose and the sunken eyes looked up at me, enormous and vacant, a kind of blind, white flicker in the depths of the orbs, which died out slowly. The man seemed young—almost a boy—but you know with them it's hard to tell. I found nothing else to do but to offer him one of my good Swede's ship's biscuits I had in my pocket. The fingers closed slowly on it and held—there was no other movement and no other glance. He had tied a bit of white worsted round his neck—Why? Where did he get it? Was it a badge—an ornament—a charm—a propitiatory act? Was there any idea at all connected with it? It looked startling round his black neck, this bit of white thread from beyond the seas.

"Near the same tree two more bundles of acute angles sat with their legs drawn up. One, with his chin propped on his knees, stared at nothing, in an intolerable and appalling manner: his brother phantom rested its forehead, as if overcome with a great weariness; and all about others were scattered in every pose of contorted collapse, as in some picture of a massacre or a pestilence. While I stood horror-struck, one of these creatures rose to his hands and knees, and went off on all-fours towards the river to drink. He lapped out of his hand, then sat up in the sunlight, crossing his shins in front of him, and after a time let his woolly head fall on his breastbone.

"I didn't want any more loitering in the shade, and I made haste towards the station. When near the buildings I met a white man, in such an unexpected elegance of get-up that in the first moment I took him for a sort of vision. I saw a high starched collar, white cuffs, a light alpaca jacket, snowy trousers, a clear silk necktie, and varnished boots. No hat. Hair parted, brushed, oiled, under a green-lined parasol held in a big white hand. He was amazing, and had a penholder behind his ear.

"I shook hands with this miracle, and I learned he was the Company's chief accountant, and that all the book-keeping was done at this station. He had come out for a moment, he said, 'to get a breath of fresh air.' The expression sounded wonderfully odd, with its suggestion of sedentary desk-life. I wouldn't have mentioned the fellow to you at all, only it was from his lips that I first heard the name of the man who is so indissolubly connected with the memories of that time. Moreover, I respected the fellow. Yes; I respected his collars, his vast cuffs, his brushed hair. His appearance was certainly that of a hairdresser's dummy; but in the great demoralisation of the land he kept up his appearance. That's backbone. His starched collars and got-up shirt-fronts were achievements of character. He had been out nearly three years; and, later on, I could not help asking him how he managed to sport such linen. He had just the faintest blush, and said modestly, 'I've been teaching one of the native women about the station. It was difficult. She had a distaste for the work.' Thus this man had verily accomplished something. And he was devoted to his books, which were in apple-pie order.

"Everything else in the station was in a muddle,—heads, things, buildings. Strings of dusty niggers with splay feet arrived and departed; a stream of manufactured goods, rubbishy cottons, beads, and brass-wire sent into the depths of darkness, and in return came a precious trickle of ivory.

"I had to wait in the station for ten days—an eternity. I lived in a hut in the yard, but to be out of the chaos I would sometimes get into the accountant's office. It was built of horizontal planks, and so badly put together that, as he bent over his high desk, he was barred from neck to heels with narrow strips of sunlight. There was no need to open the big shutter to see. It was hot there too; big flies buzzed fiendishly, and did not sting, but stabbed. I sat generally on the floor, while, of faultless appearance (and even slightly scented), perching on a high stool, he wrote, he wrote. Sometimes he stood up for exercise. When a truckle-bed with a sick man (some invalided agent from up-country) was put in there, he exhibited a gentle annoyance. 'The groans of this sick person,' he said, 'distract my attention. And without that it is extremely difficult to guard against clerical errors in this climate.'

"One day he remarked, without lifting his head, 'In the interior you will no doubt meet Mr Kurtz.' On my asking who Mr Kurtz was, he said he was a first-class agent; and seeing my disappointment at this information, he added slowly, laying down his pen, 'He is a very remarkable person.' Further questions elicited from him that Mr Kurtz was at present in charge of a trading-post, a very important one, in the true ivory-country, at 'the very bottom of there. Sends in as much ivory as all the others put together . . .' He began to write again. The sick man was too ill to groan. The flies buzzed in a great peace.

"Suddenly there was a growing murmur of voices and a great tramping of feet. A caravan had come in. A violent babble of uncouth sounds burst out on the other side of the planks. All the carriers were speaking together, and in the midst of the uproar the lamentable voice of the chief agent was heard 'giving it up' tearfully for the twentieth time that day. . . . He rose slowly. 'What a frightful row,' he said. He crossed the room gently to look at the sick man, and returning, said to me, 'He does not hear.' 'What! Dead?' I asked, startled. 'No, not yet,' he answered, with great composure. Then, alluding with a toss of the head to the tumult in the station-yard, 'When one has got to make correct entries, one comes to hate those savages—hate them to the death.' He remained thoughtful for a moment. 'When you see Mr Kurtz,' he went on, 'tell him from me that everything here'—he glanced at the desk—'is very satisfactory. I don't like to write to him—with those messengers of ours you never know who may get hold of your letter—at that Central Station.' He stared at me for a moment with his mild, bulging eyes. 'Oh, he will go far, very far,' he began again. 'He will be a somebody in the Administration before long. They, above—the Council in Europe, you know—mean him to be.'

"He turned to his work. The noise outside had ceased, and presently in going out I stopped at the door. In the steady buzz of flies the homeward-bound agent was lying flushed and insensible; the other, bent over his books, was making correct entries of perfectly correct transactions; and fifty feet below the doorstep I could see the still tree-tops of the grove of death.

"Next day I left that station at last, with a caravan of sixty men, for a two-hundred-mile tramp.

"No use telling you much about that. Paths, paths, everywhere; a stamped-in network of paths spreading over the empty land, through long grass, through burnt grass, through thickets, down and up chilly ravines, up and down stony hills ablaze with heat; and a solitude, a solitude, nobody, not a hut. The population had cleared out a long time ago. Well, if a lot of mysterious niggers armed with all kinds of fearful weapons suddenly took to travelling on the road between Deal[6] and Gravesend, catching the yokels right and left to carry heavy loads for them, I fancy every farm and cottage thereabouts would get empty very soon. Only here the dwellings were gone too. Still, I passed through several abandoned villages. There's something pathetically childish in the ruins of grass walls. Day after day, with the stamp and shuffle of sixty pair of bare feet behind me, each pair under a 60-lb. load. Camp, cook, sleep, strike camp, march. Now and then a carrier dead in harness, at rest in the long grass near the path, with an empty water-gourd and his long staff lying by his side. A great silence around and above. Perhaps on some quiet night the tremor of far-off drums, sinking, swelling, a tremor vast, faint; a sound weird, appealing, suggestive, and wild—and perhaps with as profound a meaning as the sound of bells in a Christian country. Once a white man in an unbuttoned uniform, camping on the

6. An English port.

path with an armed escort of lank Zanzibaris,[7] very hospitable and festive—not to say drunk. Was looking after the upkeep of the road, he declared. Can't say I saw any road or any upkeep, unless the body of a middle-aged negro, with a bullet-hole in the forehead, upon which I absolutely stumbled three miles farther on, may be considered as a permanent improvement. I had a white companion too, not a bad chap, but rather too fleshy and with the exasperating habit of fainting on the hot hillsides, miles away from the least bit of shade and water. Annoying, you know, to hold your own coat like a parasol over a man's head while he is coming-to. I couldn't help asking him once what he meant by coming there at all. 'To make money, of course. What do you think?' he said, scornfully. Then he got fever, and had to be carried in a hammock slung under a pole. As he weighed sixteen stone I had no end of rows with the carriers. They jibbed, ran away, sneaked off with their loads in the night—quite a mutiny. So, one evening, I made a speech in English with gestures, not one of which was lost to the sixty pairs of eyes before me, and the next morning I started the hammock off in front all right. An hour afterwards I came upon the whole concern wrecked in a bush—man, hammock, groans, blankets, horrors. The heavy pole had skinned his poor nose. He was very anxious for me to kill somebody, but there wasn't the shadow of a carrier near. I remembered the old doctor,—'It would be interesting for science to watch the mental changes of individuals, on the spot.' I felt I was becoming scientifically interesting. However, all that is to no purpose. On the fifteenth day I came in sight of the big river again, and hobbled into the Central Station. It was on a back water surrounded by scrub and forest, with a pretty border of smelly mud on one side, and on the three others enclosed by a crazy fence of rushes. A neglected gap was all the gate it had, and the first glance at the place was enough to let you see the flabby devil was running that show. White men with long staves in their hands appeared languidly from amongst the buildings, strolling up to take a look at me, and then retired out of sight somewhere. One of them, a stout, excitable chap with black moustaches, informed me with great volubility and many digressions, as soon as I told him who I was, that my steamer was at the bottom of the river. I was thunderstruck. What, how, why? Oh, it was 'all right.' The 'manager himself' was there. All quite correct. 'Everybody had behaved splendidly! splendidly!'—'You must,' he said in agitation, 'go and see the general manager at once. He is waiting!'

"I did not see the real significance of that wreck at once. I fancy I see it now, but I am not sure—not at all. Certainly the affair was too stupid—when I think of it—to be altogether natural. Still. . . . But at the moment it presented itself simply as a confounded nuisance. The steamer was sunk. They had started two days before in a sudden hurry up the river with the manager on board, in charge of some volunteer skipper, and before they had been out three hours they tore the bottom out of her on stones, and she sank near the south bank. I asked myself what I was to do there, now my boat was lost. As a matter of fact, I had plenty to do in fishing my command out of the river. I had to set about it the very next day. That, and the repairs when I brought the pieces to the station, took some months.

"My first interview with the manager was curious. He did not ask me to sit down after my twenty-mile walk that morning. He was commonplace in complexion, in feature, in manners, and in voice. He was of middle size and of ordinary build. His eyes, of the usual blue, were perhaps remarkably cold, and he certainly could make his glance fall on one as trenchant and heavy as an axe. But even at these times the rest of his person seemed to disclaim the intention. Otherwise there was only an indefinable, faint

---

7. Africans from Zanzibar, in East Africa; they were widely used as mercenaries.

expression of his lips, something stealthy—a smile—not a smile—I remember it, but I can't explain. It was unconscious, this smile was, though just after he had said something it got intensified for an instant. It came at the end of his speeches like a seal applied on the words to make the meaning of the commonest phrase appear absolutely inscrutable. He was a common trader, from his youth up employed in these parts—nothing more. He was obeyed, yet he inspired neither love nor fear, nor even respect. He inspired uneasiness. That was it! Uneasiness. Not a definite mistrust—just uneasiness—nothing more. You have no idea how effective such a . . . a . . . faculty can be. He had no genius for organising, for initiative, or for order even. That was evident in such things as the deplorable state of the station. He had no learning, and no intelligence. His position had come to him—why? Perhaps because he was never ill . . . He had served three terms of three years out there . . . Because triumphant health in the general rout of constitutions is a kind of power in itself. When he went home on leave he rioted on a large scale—pompously. Jack ashore—with a difference—in externals only. This one could gather from his casual talk. He originated nothing, he could keep the routine going—that's all. But he was great. He was great by this little thing that it was impossible to tell what could control such a man. He never gave that secret away. Perhaps there was nothing within him. Such a suspicion made one pause—for out there there were no external checks. Once when various tropical diseases had laid low almost every 'agent' in the station, he was heard to say, 'Men who come out here should have no entrails.' He sealed the utterance with that smile of his, as though it had been a door opening into a darkness he had in his keeping. You fancied you had seen things—but the seal was on. When annoyed at meal-times by the constant quarrels of the white men about precedence, he ordered an immense round table to be made, for which a special house had to be built. This was the station's mess-room. Where he sat was the first place—the rest were nowhere. One felt this to be his unalterable conviction. He was neither civil nor uncivil. He was quiet. He allowed his 'boy'—an overfed young negro from the coast—to treat the white men, under his very eyes, with provoking insolence.

"He began to speak as soon as he saw me. I had been very long on the road. He could not wait. Had to start without me. The up-river stations had to be relieved. There had been so many delays already that he did not know who was dead and who was alive, and how they got on—and so on, and so on. He paid no attention to my explanations, and, playing with a stick of sealing-wax, repeated several times that the situation was 'very grave, very grave.' There were rumours that a very important station was in jeopardy, and its chief, Mr Kurtz, was ill. Hoped it was not true. Mr Kurtz was . . . I felt weary and irritable. Hang Kurtz, I thought. I interrupted him by saying I had heard of Mr Kurtz on the coast. 'Ah! So they talk of him down there,' he murmured to himself. Then he began again, assuring me Mr Kurtz was the best agent he had, an exceptional man, of the greatest importance to the Company; therefore I could understand his anxiety. He was, he said, 'very, very uneasy.' Certainly he fidgeted on his chair a good deal, exclaimed, 'Ah, Mr Kurtz!' broke the stick of sealing-wax and seemed dumbfounded by the accident. Next thing he wanted to know 'how long it would take to' . . . I interrupted him again. Being hungry, you know, and kept on my feet too, I was getting savage. 'How can I tell?' I said. 'I haven't even seen the wreck yet—some months, no doubt.' All this talk seemed to me so futile. 'Some months,' he said. 'Well, let us say three months before we can make a start. Yes. That ought to do the affair.' I flung out of his hut (he lived all alone in a clay hut with a sort of verandah) muttering to myself my opinion of him. He was a chattering idiot. Afterwards I took it back when it was borne in upon me startlingly with what extreme nicety he had estimated the time requisite for the 'affair.'

"I went to work the next day, turning, so to speak, my back on that station. In that way only it seemed to me I could keep my hold on the redeeming facts of life. Still, one must look about sometimes; and then I saw this station, these men strolling aimlessly about in the sunshine of the yard. I asked myself sometimes what it all meant. They wandered here and there with their absurd long staves in their hands, like a lot of faithless pilgrims bewitched inside a rotten fence. The word 'ivory' rang in the air, was whispered, was sighed. You would think they were praying to it. A taint of imbecile rapacity blew through it all, like a whiff from some corpse. By Jove! I've never seen anything so unreal in my life. And outside, the silent wilderness surrounding this cleared speck on the earth struck me as something great and invincible, like evil or truth, waiting patiently for the passing away of this fantastic invasion.

"Oh, those months! Well, never mind. Various things happened. One evening a grass shed full of calico, cotton prints, beads, and I don't know what else, burst into a blaze so suddenly that you would have thought the earth had opened to let an avenging fire consume all that trash. I was smoking my pipe quietly by my dismantled steamer, and saw them all cutting capers in the light, with their arms lifted high, when the stout man with moustaches came tearing down to the river, a tin pail in his hand, assured me that everybody was 'behaving splendidly, splendidly,' dipped about a quart of water and tore back again. I noticed there was a hole in the bottom of his pail.

"I strolled up. There was no hurry. You see the thing had gone off like a box of matches. It had been hopeless from the very first. The flame had leaped high, driven everybody back, lighted up everything—and collapsed. The shed was already a heap of embers glowing fiercely. A nigger was being beaten near by. They said he had caused the fire in some way; be that as it may, he was screeching most horribly. I saw him, later on, for several days, sitting in a bit of shade looking very sick and trying to recover himself: afterwards he arose and went out—and the wilderness without a sound took him into its bosom again. As I approached the glow from the dark I found myself at the back of two men, talking. I heard the name of Kurtz pronounced, then the words, 'take advantage of this unfortunate accident.' One of the men was the manager. I wished him a good evening. 'Did you ever see anything like it—eh? it is incredible,' he said, and walked off. The other man remained. He was a first-class agent, young, gentlemanly, a bit reserved, with a forked little beard and a hooked nose. He was stand-offish with the other agents, and they on their side said he was the manager's spy upon them. As to me, I had hardly ever spoken to him before. We got into talk, and by-and-by we strolled away from the hissing ruins. Then he asked me to his room, which was in the main building of the station. He struck a match, and I perceived that this young aristocrat had not only a silver-mounted dressing-case but also a whole candle all to himself. Just at that time the manager was the only man supposed to have any right to candles. Native mats covered the clay walls; a collection of spears, assegais,[8] shields, knives was hung up in trophies. The business intrusted to this fellow was the making of bricks—so I had been informed; but there wasn't a fragment of a brick anywhere in the station, and he had been there more than a year—waiting. It seems he could not make bricks without something, I don't know what—straw maybe. Anyway, it could not be found there, and as it was not likely to be sent from Europe, it did not appear clear to me what he was waiting for. An act of special creation perhaps. However, they were all waiting—all the sixteen or twenty pilgrims of them—for something; and upon my word it did not seem an uncongenial occupation, from the way they took it, though the only thing that ever came to them

8. Slender African spears.

was disease—as far as I could see. They beguiled the time by backbiting and intriguing against each other in a foolish kind of way. There was an air of plotting about that station, but nothing came of it, of course. It was as unreal as everything else—as the philanthropic pretence of the whole concern, as their talk, as their government, as their show of work. The only real feeling was a desire to get appointed to a trading-post where ivory was to be had, so that they could earn percentages. They intrigued and slandered and hated each other only on that account,—but as to effectually lifting a little finger—oh, no. By heavens! there is something after all in the world allowing one man to steal a horse while another must not look at a halter. Steal a horse straight out. Very well. He has done it. Perhaps he can ride. But there is a way of looking at a halter that would provoke the most charitable of saints into a kick.

"I had no idea why he wanted to be sociable, but as we chatted in there it suddenly occurred to me the fellow was trying to get at something—in fact, pumping me. He alluded constantly to Europe, to the people I was supposed to know there—putting leading questions as to my acquaintances in the sepulchral city, and so on. His little eyes glittered like mica discs—with curiosity,—though he tried to keep up a bit of superciliousness. At first I was astonished, but very soon I became awfully curious to see what he would find out from me. I couldn't possibly imagine what I had in me to make it worth his while. It was very pretty to see how he baffled himself, for in truth my body was full of chills, and my head had nothing in it but that wretched steamboat business. It was evident he took me for a perfectly shameless prevaricator. At last he got angry, and, to conceal a movement of furious annoyance, he yawned. I rose. Then I noticed a small sketch in oils, on a panel, representing a woman, draped and blind-folded, carrying a lighted torch. The background was sombre—almost black. The movement of the woman was stately, and the effect of the torchlight on the face was sinister.

"It arrested me, and he stood by civilly, holding a half-pint champagne bottle (medical comforts) with the candle stuck in it. To my question he said Mr Kurtz had painted this—in this very station more than a year ago—while waiting for means to go to his trading-post. 'Tell me, pray,' said I, 'who is this Mr Kurtz?'

" 'The chief of the Inner Station,' he answered in a short tone, looking away. 'Much obliged,' I said, laughing. 'And you are the brickmaker of the Central Station. Every one knows that.' He was silent for a while. 'He is a prodigy,' he said at last. 'He is an emissary of pity, and science, and progress, and devil knows what else. We want,' he began to declaim suddenly, 'for the guidance of the cause intrusted to us by Europe, so to speak, higher intelligence, wide sympathies, a singleness of purpose.' 'Who says that?' I asked. 'Lots of them,' he replied. 'Some even write that; and so he comes here, a special being, as you ought to know.' 'Why ought I to know?' I interrupted, really surprised. He paid no attention. 'Yes. To-day he is chief of the best station, next year he will be assistant-manager, two years more and . . . but I daresay you know what he will be in two years' time. You are of the new gang—the gang of virtue. The same people who sent him specially also recommended you. Oh, don't say no. I've my own eyes to trust.' Light dawned upon me. My dear aunt's influential acquaintances were producing an unexpected effect upon that young man. I nearly burst into a laugh. 'Do you read the Company's confidential correspondence?' I asked. He hadn't a word to say. It was great fun. 'When Mr Kurtz,' I continued severely, 'is General Manager, you won't have the opportunity.'

"He blew the candle out suddenly, and we went outside. The moon had risen. Black figures strolled about listlessly, pouring water on the glow, whence proceeded a sound of hissing; steam ascended in the moonlight; the beaten nigger groaned somewhere. 'What a row the brute makes!' said the indefatigable man with the moustaches, appearing near us. 'Serve him right. Transgression—punishment—bang! Pitiless, pitiless. That's the only way. This will prevent all conflagrations for the future. I was just telling the manager . . .' He noticed my companion, and became crestfallen all at once. 'Not in bed yet,' he said, with a kind of servile heartiness; 'it's so natural. Ha! Danger—agitation.' He vanished. I went on to the river-side, and the other followed me. I heard a scathing murmur at my ear, 'Heap of muffs—go to.' The pilgrims could be seen in knots gesticulating, discussing. Several had still their staves in their hands. I verily believe they took these sticks to bed with them. Beyond the fence the forest stood up spectrally in the moonlight, and through the dim stir, through the faint sounds of that lamentable courtyard, the silence of the land went home to one's very heart,—its mystery, its greatness, the amazing reality of its concealed life. The hurt nigger moaned feebly somewhere near by, and then fetched a deep sigh that made me mend my pace away from there. I felt a hand introducing itself under my arm. 'My dear sir,' said the fellow, 'I don't want to be misunderstood, and especially by you, who will see Mr Kurtz long before I can have that pleasure. I wouldn't like him to get a false idea of my disposition. . . .'

"I let him run on, this papier-mâché Mephistopheles,[9] and it seemed to me that if I tried I could poke my forefinger through him, and would find nothing inside but a little loose dirt, maybe. He, don't you see, had been planning to be assistant-manager by-and-by under the present man, and I could see that the coming of that Kurtz had upset them both not a little. He talked precipitately, and I did not try to stop him. I had my shoulders against the wreck of my steamer, hauled up on the slope like a carcass of some big river animal. The smell of mud, of primeval mud, by Jove! was in my nostrils, the high stillness of primeval forest was before my eyes; there were shiny patches on the black creek. The moon had spread over everything a thin layer of silver—over the rank grass, over the mud, upon the wall of matted vegetation standing higher than the wall of a temple, over the great river I could see through a sombre gap glittering, glittering, as it flowed broadly by without a murmur. All this was great, expectant, mute, while the man jabbered about himself. I wondered whether the stillness on the face of the immensity looking at us two were meant as an appeal or as a menace. What were we who had strayed in here? Could we handle that dumb thing, or would it handle us? I felt how big, how confoundedly big, was that thing that couldn't talk, and perhaps was deaf as well. What was in there? I could see a little ivory coming out from there, and I had heard Mr Kurtz was in there. I had heard enough about it too—God knows! Yet somehow it didn't bring any image with it— no more than if I had been told an angel or a fiend was in there. I believed it in the same way one of you might believe there are inhabitants in the planet Mars. I knew once a Scotch sailmaker who was certain, dead sure, there were people in Mars. If you asked him for some idea how they looked and behaved, he would get shy and mutter something about 'walking on all-fours.' If you as much as smiled, he would— though a man of sixty—offer to fight you. I would not have gone so far as to fight for Kurtz, but I went for him near enough to a lie. You know I hate, detest, and can't bear a lie, not because I am straighter than the rest of us, but simply because it appals me. There is a taint of death, a flavour of mortality in lies,—which is exactly what I hate and detest in the world—what I want to forget. It makes me miserable and sick, like biting something rotten would do. Temperament, I suppose. Well, I went near enough to it by letting the young fool there believe anything he liked to imagine as to my influence in Europe. I became in an instant as much of a pretence as the rest of

9. One of the devils who tempts Faust.

the bewitched pilgrims. This simply because I had a notion it somehow would be of help to that Kurtz whom at the time I did not see—you understand. He was just a word for me. I did not see the man in the name any more than you do. Do you see him? Do you see the story? Do you see anything? It seems to me I am trying to tell you a dream—making a vain attempt, because no relation of a dream can convey the dream-sensation, that commingling of absurdity, surprise, and bewilderment in a tremor of struggling revolt, that notion of being captured by the incredible which is of the very essence of dreams. . . ."

He was silent for a while.

". . . No, it is impossible; it is impossible to convey the life-sensation of any given epoch of one's existence,—that which makes its truth, its meaning—its subtle and penetrating essence. It is impossible. We live, as we dream—alone. . . ."

He paused again as if reflecting, then added—

"Of course in this you fellows see more than I could then. You see me, whom you know. . . ."

It had become so pitch dark that we listeners could hardly see one another. For a long time already he, sitting apart, had been no more to us than a voice. There was not a word from anybody. The others might have been asleep, but I was awake. I listened, I listened on the watch for the sentence, for the word, that would give me the clue to the faint uneasiness inspired by this narrative that seemed to shape itself without human lips in the heavy night-air of the river.

". . . Yes—I let him run on," Marlow began again, "and think what he pleased about the powers that were behind me. I did! And there was nothing behind me! There was nothing but that wretched, old, mangled steamboat I was leaning against, while he talked fluently about 'the necessity for every man to get on.' 'And when one comes out here, you conceive, it is not to gaze at the moon.' Mr Kurtz was a 'universal genius,' but even a genius would find it easier to work with 'adequate tools—intelligent men.' He did not make bricks—why, there was a physical impossibility in the way—as I was well aware; and if he did secretarial work for the manager, it was because 'no sensible man rejects wantonly the confidence of his superiors.' Did I see it? I saw it. What more did I want? What I really wanted was rivets, by heaven! Rivets. To get on with the work—to stop the hole. Rivets I wanted. There were cases of them down at the coast—cases—piled up—burst—split! You kicked a loose rivet at every second step in that station yard on the hillside. Rivets had rolled into the grove of death. You could fill your pockets with rivets for the trouble of stooping down—and there wasn't one rivet to be found where it was wanted. We had plates that would do, but nothing to fasten them with. And every week the messenger, a lone negro, letter-bag on shoulder and staff in hand, left our station for the coast. And several times a week a coast caravan came in with trade goods,—ghastly glazed calico that made you shudder only to look at it, glass beads value about a penny a quart, confounded spotted cotton handkerchiefs. And no rivets. Three carriers could have brought all that was wanted to set that steamboat afloat.

"He was becoming confidential now, but I fancy my unresponsive attitude must have exasperated him at last, for he judged it necessary to inform me he feared neither God nor devil, let alone any mere man. I said I could see that very well, but what I wanted was a certain quantity of rivets—and rivets were what really Mr Kurtz wanted, if he had only known it. Now letters went to the coast every week. . . . 'My dear sir,' he cried, 'I write from dictation.' I demanded rivets. There was a way—for an intelligent man. He changed his manner; became very cold, and suddenly began to talk about a hippopotamus; wondered whether sleeping on board the steamer (I stuck to my salvage night and day) I wasn't disturbed. There was an old hippo that had the bad habit of getting out on the bank and roaming at night over the station grounds. The pilgrims used to turn out in a body and empty every rifle they could lay hands on at him. Some even had sat up o' nights for him. All this energy was wasted, though. 'That animal has a charmed life,' he said; 'but you can say this only of brutes in this country. No man—you apprehend me?—no man here bears a charmed life.' He stood there for a moment in the moonlight with his delicate hooked nose set a little askew, and his mica eyes glittering without a wink, then, with a curt Good night, he strode off. I could see he was disturbed and considerably puzzled, which made me feel more hopeful than I had been for days. It was a great comfort to turn from that chap to my influential friend, the battered, twisted, ruined, tin-pot steamboat. I clambered on board. She rang under my feet like an empty Huntley & Palmer[1] biscuit-tin kicked along a gutter; she was nothing so solid in make, and rather less pretty in shape, but I had expended enough hard work on her to make me love her. No influential friend would have served me better. She had given me a chance to come out a bit—to find out what I could do. No, I don't like work. I had rather laze about and think of all the fine things that can be done. I don't like work—no man does—but I like what is in the work,—the chance to find yourself. Your own reality—for yourself, not for others—what no other man can ever know. They can only see the mere show, and never can tell what it really means.

"I was not surprised to see somebody sitting aft, on the deck, with his legs dangling over the mud. You see I rather chummed with the few mechanics there were in that station, whom the other pilgrims naturally despised—on account of their imperfect manners, I suppose. This was the foreman—a boiler-maker by trade—a good worker. He was a lank, bony, yellow-faced man, with big intense eyes. His aspect was worried, and his head was as bald as the palm of my hand; but his hair in falling seemed to have stuck to his chin, and had prospered in the new locality, for his beard hung down to his waist. He was a widower with six young children (he had left them in charge of a sister of his to come out there), and the passion of his life was pigeon-flying. He was an enthusiast and a connoisseur. He would rave about pigeons. After work hours he used sometimes to come over from his hut for a talk about his children and his pigeons; at work, when he had to crawl in the mud under the bottom of the steamboat, he would tie up that beard of his in a kind of white serviette[2] he brought for the purpose. It had loops to go over his ears. In the evening he could be seen squatted on the bank rinsing that wrapper in the creek with great care, then spreading it solemnly on a bush to dry.

"I slapped him on the back and shouted 'We shall have rivets!' He scrambled to his feet exclaiming 'No! Rivets!' as though he couldn't believe his ears. Then in a low voice, 'You . . . eh?' I don't know why we behaved like lunatics. I put my finger to the side of my nose and nodded mysteriously. 'Good for you!' he cried, snapped his fingers above his head, lifting one foot. I tried a jig. We capered on the iron deck. A frightful clatter came out of that hulk, and the virgin forest on the other bank of the creek sent it back in a thundering roll upon the sleeping station. It must have made some of the pilgrims sit up in their hovels. A dark figure obscured the lighted doorway of the manager's hut, vanished, then, a second or so after, the doorway itself vanished too. We stopped, and the silence driven away by the stamping of our feet flowed back again from the recesses of the land. The great wall of vegetation, an exuberant and entangled mass of trunks, branches, leaves, boughs, festoons, motionless

---

1. A brand of English cookies.   2. Napkin.

in the moonlight, was like a rioting invasion of soundless life, a rolling wave of plants, piled up, crested, ready to topple over the creek, to sweep every little man of us out of his little existence. And it moved not. A deadened burst of mighty splashes and snorts reached us from afar, as though an ichthyosaurus had been taking a bath of glitter in the great river. 'After all,' said the boiler-maker in a reasonable tone, 'why shouldn't we get the rivets?' Why not, indeed! I did not know of any reason why we shouldn't. 'They'll come in three weeks,' I said, confidently.

"But they didn't. Instead of rivets there came an invasion, an infliction, a visitation. It came in sections during the next three weeks, each section headed by a donkey carrying a white man in new clothes and tan shoes, bowing from that elevation right and left to the impressed pilgrims. A quarrelsome band of footsore sulky niggers trod on the heels of the donkey; a lot of tents, camp-stools, tin boxes, white cases, brown bales would be shot down in the courtyard, and the air of mystery would deepen a little over the muddle of the station. Five such instalments came, with their absurd air of disorderly flight with the loot of innumerable outfit shops and provision stores, that, one would think, they were lugging, after a raid, into the wilderness for equitable division. It was an inextricable mess of things decent in themselves but that human folly made look like the spoils of thieving.

"This devoted band called itself the Eldorado Exploring Expedition,[3] and I believe they were sworn to secrecy. Their talk, however, was the talk of sordid buccaneers: it was reckless without hardihood, greedy without audacity, and cruel without courage; there was not an atom of foresight or of serious intention in the whole batch of them, and they did not seem aware these things are wanted for the work of the world. To tear treasure out of the bowels of the land was their desire, with no more moral purpose at the back of it than there is in burglars breaking into a safe. Who paid the expenses of the noble enterprise I don't know; but the uncle of our manager was leader of that lot.

"In exterior he resembled a butcher in a poor neighbourhood, and his eyes had a look of sleepy cunning. He carried his fat paunch with ostentation on his short legs, and during the time his gang infested the station spoke to no one but his nephew. You could see these two roaming about all day long with their heads close together in an everlasting confab.

"I had given up worrying myself about the rivets. One's capacity for that kind of folly is more limited than you would suppose. I said Hang!—and let things slide. I had plenty of time for meditation, and now and then I would give some thought to Kurtz. I wasn't very interested in him. No. Still, I was curious to see whether this man, who had come out equipped with moral ideas of some sort, would climb to the top after all, and how he would set about his work when there."

2

"One evening as I was lying flat on the deck of my steamboat, I heard voices approaching—and there were the nephew and the uncle strolling along the bank. I laid my head on my arm again, and had nearly lost myself in a doze, when somebody said in my ear, as it were: 'I am as harmless as a little child, but I don't like to be dictated to. Am I the manager—or am I not? I was ordered to send him there. It's incredible.' . . . I became aware that the two were standing on the shore alongside the forepart of the steamboat, just below my head. I did not move; it did not occur to me

3. Eldorado, legendary land of gold in South America and the object of many fruitless 16th-century Spanish expeditions.

to move: I was sleepy. 'It is unpleasant,' grunted the uncle. 'He has asked the Administration to be sent there,' said the other, 'with the idea of showing what he could do; and I was instructed accordingly. Look at the influence that man must have. Is it not frightful?' They both agreed it was frightful, then made several bizarre remarks: 'Make rain and fine weather—one man—the Council—by the nose'—bits of absurd sentences that got the better of my drowsiness, so that I had pretty near the whole of my wits about me when the uncle said, 'The climate may do away with this difficulty for you. Is he alone there?' 'Yes,' answered the manager; 'he sent his assistant down the river with a note to me in these terms: "Clear this poor devil out of the country, and don't bother sending more of that sort. I had rather be alone than have the kind of men you can dispose of with me." It was more than a year ago. Can you imagine such impudence?' 'Anything since then?' asked the other, hoarsely. 'Ivory,' jerked the nephew; 'lots of it—prime sort—lots—most annoying, from him.' 'And with that?' questioned the heavy rumble. 'Invoice,' was the reply fired out, so to speak. Then silence. They had been talking about Kurtz.

"I was broad awake by this time, but, lying perfectly at ease, remained still, having no inducement to change my position. 'How did that ivory come all this way?' growled the elder man, who seemed very vexed. The other explained that it had come with a fleet of canoes in charge of an English half-caste clerk Kurtz had with him; that Kurtz had apparently intended to return himself, the station being by that time bare of goods and stores, but after coming three hundred miles, had suddenly decided to go back, which he started to do alone in a small dug-out with four paddlers, leaving the half-caste to continue down the river with the ivory. The two fellows there seemed astounded at anybody attempting such a thing. They were at a loss for an adequate motive. As to me, I seemed to see Kurtz for the first time. It was a distinct glimpse: the dug-out, four paddling savages, and the lone white man turning his back suddenly on the headquarters, on relief, on thoughts of home—perhaps; setting his face towards the depths of the wilderness, towards his empty and desolate station. I did not know the motive. Perhaps he was just simply a fine fellow who stuck to his work for its own sake. His name, you understand, had not been pronounced once. He was 'that man.' The half-caste, who, as far as I could see, had conducted a difficult trip with great prudence and pluck, was invariably alluded to as 'that scoundrel.' The 'scoundrel' had reported that the 'man' had been very ill—had recovered imperfectly. . . . The two below me moved away then a few paces, and strolled back and forth at some little distance. I heard: 'Military post—doctor—two hundred miles—quite alone now—unavoidable delays—nine months—no news—strange rumours.' They approached again, just as the manager was saying, 'No one, as far as I know, unless a species of wandering trader—a pestilential fellow, snapping ivory from the natives.' Who was it they were talking about now? I gathered in snatches that this was some man supposed to be in Kurtz's district, and of whom the manager did not approve. 'We will not be free from unfair competition till one of these fellows is hanged for an example,' he said. 'Certainly,' grunted the other; 'get him hanged! Why not? Anything—anything can be done in this country. That's what I say; nobody here, you understand, *here*, can endanger your position. And why? You stand the climate—you outlast them all. The danger is in Europe; but there before I left I took care to—' They moved off and whispered, then their voices rose again. 'The extraordinary series of delays is not my fault. I did my possible.' The fat man sighed, 'Very sad.' 'And the pestiferous absurdity of his talk,' continued the other; 'he bothered me enough when he was here. "Each station should be like a beacon on the road towards better things, a centre for trade of course, but also for humanising, improving, instructing." Conceive you—that ass! And he wants to be manager! No, it's—' Here he got choked by excessive indignation, and I lifted my head the least bit. I was surprised to see how near they were—right under me. I could have spat upon their hats. They were looking on the ground, absorbed in thought. The manager was switching his leg with a slender twig: his sagacious relative lifted his head. 'You have been well since you came out this time?' he asked. The other gave a start. 'Who? I? Oh! Like a charm—like a charm. But the rest—oh, my goodness! All sick. They die so quick, too, that I haven't the time to send them out of the country—it's incredible!' 'H'm. Just so,' grunted the uncle. 'Ah! my boy, trust to this—I say, trust to this.' I saw him extend his short flipper of an arm for a gesture that took in the forest, the creek, the mud, the river,—seemed to beckon with a dishonouring flourish before the sunlit face of the land a treacherous appeal to the lurking death, to the hidden evil, to the profound darkness of its heart. It was so startling that I leaped to my feet and looked back at the edge of the forest, as though I had expected an answer of some sort to that black display of confidence. You know the foolish notions that come to one sometimes. The high stillness confronted these two figures with its ominous patience, waiting for the passing away of a fantastic invasion.

"They swore aloud together—out of sheer fright, I believe—then, pretending not to know anything of my existence, turned back to the station. The sun was low; and leaning forward side by side, they seemed to be tugging painfully uphill their two ridiculous shadows of unequal length, that trailed behind them slowly over the tall grass without bending a single blade.

"In a few days the Eldorado Expedition went into the patient wilderness, that closed upon it as the sea closes over a diver. Long afterwards the news came that all the donkeys were dead. I know nothing as to the fate of the less valuable animals. They, no doubt, like the rest of us, found what they deserved. I did not inquire. I was then rather excited at the prospect of meeting Kurtz very soon. When I say very soon I mean it comparatively. It was just two months from the day we left the creek when we came to the bank below Kurtz's station.

"Going up that river was like travelling back to the earliest beginnings of the world, when vegetation rioted on the earth and the big trees were kings. An empty stream, a great silence, an impenetrable forest. The air was warm, thick, heavy, sluggish. There was no joy in the brilliance of sunshine. The long stretches of the waterway ran on, deserted, into the gloom of overshadowed distances. On silvery sandbanks hippos and alligators sunned themselves side by side. The broadening waters flowed through a mob of wooded islands; you lost your way on that river as you would in a desert, and butted all day long against shoals, trying to find the channel, till you thought yourself bewitched and cut off for ever from everything you had known once—somewhere—far away—in another existence perhaps. There were moments when one's past came back to one, as it will sometimes when you have not a moment to spare to yourself; but it came in the shape of an unrestful and noisy dream, remembered with wonder amongst the overwhelming realities of this strange world of plants, and water, and silence. And this stillness of life did not in the least resemble a peace. It was the stillness of an implacable force brooding over an inscrutable intention. It looked at you with a vengeful aspect. I got used to it afterwards; I did not see it any more; I had no time. I had to keep guessing at the channel; I had to discern, mostly by inspiration, the signs of hidden banks; I watched for sunken stones; I was learning to clap my teeth smartly before my heart flew out, when I shaved by a fluke some infernal sly old snag that would have ripped the life out of the tin-pot steamboat and drowned all the pilgrims; I had to keep a look-out for the signs of dead wood we could cut up in the night for next day's steaming.

When you have to attend to things of that sort, to the mere incidents of the surface, the reality—the reality, I tell you—fades. The inner truth is hidden—luckily, luckily. But I felt it all the same; I felt often its mysterious stillness watching me at my monkey tricks, just as it watches you fellows performing on your respective tight-ropes for—what is it? half-a-crown a tumble—"

"Try to be civil, Marlow," growled a voice, and I knew there was at least one listener awake besides myself.

"I beg your pardon. I forgot the heartache which makes up the rest of the price. And indeed what does the price matter, if the trick be well done? You do your tricks very well. And I didn't do badly either, since I managed not to sink that steamboat on my first trip. It's a wonder to me yet. Imagine a blindfolded man set to drive a van over a bad road. I sweated and shivered over that business considerably, I can tell you. After all, for a seaman, to scrape the bottom of the thing that's supposed to float all the time under his care is the unpardonable sin. No one may know of it, but you never forget the thump—eh? A blow on the very heart. You remember it, you dream of it, you wake up at night and think of it—years after—and go hot and cold all over. I don't pretend to say that steamboat floated all the time. More than once she had to wade for a bit, with twenty cannibals splashing around and pushing. We had enlisted some of these chaps on the way for a crew. Fine fellows—cannibals—in their place. They were men one could work with, and I am grateful to them. And, after all, they did not eat each other before my face: they had brought along a provision of hippo-meat which went rotten, and made the mystery of the wilderness stink in my nostrils. Phoo! I can sniff it now. I had the manager on board and three or four pilgrims with their staves—all complete. Sometimes we came upon a station close by the bank, clinging to the skirts of the unknown, and the white men rushing out of a tumble-down hovel, with great gestures of joy and surprise and welcome, seemed very strange,—had the appearance of being held there captive by a spell. The word 'ivory' would ring in the air for a while—and on we went again into the silence, along empty reaches, round the still bends, between the high walls of our winding way, reverberating in hollow claps the ponderous beat of the stern-wheel. Trees, trees, millions of trees, massive, immense, running up high; and at their foot, hugging the bank against the stream, crept the little begrimed steamboat, like a sluggish beetle crawling on the floor of a lofty portico. It made you feel very small, very lost, and yet it was not altogether depressing that feeling. After all, if you were small, the grimy beetle crawled on—which was just what you wanted it to do. Where the pilgrims imagined it crawled to I don't know. To some place where they expected to get something, I bet! For me it crawled towards Kurtz—exclusively; but when the steam-pipes started leaking we crawled very slow. The reaches opened before us and closed behind, as if the forest had stepped leisurely across the water to bar the way for our return. We penetrated deeper and deeper into the heart of darkness. It was very quiet there. At night sometimes the roll of drums behind the curtain of trees would run up the river and remain sustained faintly, as if hovering in the air high over our heads, till the first break of day. Whether it meant war, peace, or prayer we could not tell. The dawns were heralded by the descent of a chill stillness; the woodcutters slept, their fires burned low; the snapping of a twig would make you start. We were wanderers on a pre-historic earth, on an earth that wore the aspect of an unknown planet. We could have fancied ourselves the first of men taking possession of an accursed inheritance, to be subdued at the cost of profound anguish and of excessive toil. But suddenly, as we struggled round a bend, there would be a glimpse of rush walls, of peaked grass-roofs, a burst of yells, a whirl of black limbs, a mass of hands clapping, of feet stamping, of bodies swaying, of eyes rolling, under the droop of heavy and motionless foliage. The steamer toiled along slowly on the edge of a black and incomprehensible frenzy. The prehistoric man was cursing us, praying to us, welcoming us—who could tell? We were cut off from the comprehension of our surroundings; we glided past like phantoms, wondering and secretly appalled, as sane men would be before an enthusiastic outbreak in a madhouse. We could not understand, because we were too far and could not remember, because we were travelling in the night of first ages, of those ages that are gone, leaving hardly a sign—and no memories.

"The earth seemed unearthly. We are accustomed to look upon the shackled form of a conquered monster, but there—there you could look at a thing monstrous and free. It was unearthly, and the men were—No, they were not inhuman. Well, you know, that was the worst of it—this suspicion of their not being inhuman. It would come slowly to one. They howled, and leaped, and spun, and made horrid faces; but what thrilled you was just the thought of their humanity—like yours—the thought of your remote kinship with this wild and passionate uproar. Ugly. Yes, it was ugly enough; but if you were man enough you would admit to yourself that there was in you just the faintest trace of a response to the terrible frankness of that noise, a dim suspicion of there being a meaning in it which you—you so remote from the night of first ages—could comprehend. And why not? The mind of man is capable of anything—because everything is in it, all the past as well as all the future. What was there after all? Joy, fear, sorrow, devotion, valour, rage—who can tell?—but truth—truth stripped of its cloak of time. Let the fool gape and shudder—the man knows, and can look on without a wink. But he must at least be as much of a man as these on the shore. He must meet that truth with his own true stuff—with his own inborn strength. Principles? Principles won't do. Acquisitions, clothes, pretty rags—rags that would fly off at the first good shake. No; you want a deliberate belief. An appeal to me in this fiendish row—is there? Very well; I hear; I admit, but I have a voice too, and for good or evil mine is the speech that cannot be silenced. Of course, a fool, what with sheer fright and fine sentiments, is always safe. Who's that grunting? You wonder I didn't go ashore for a howl and a dance? Well, no—I didn't. Fine sentiments, you say? Fine sentiments be hanged! I had no time. I had to mess about with white-lead and strips of woollen blanket helping to put bandages on those leaky steam-pipes—I tell you. I had to watch the steering, and circumvent those snags, and get the tin-pot along by hook or by crook. There was surface-truth enough in these things to save a wiser man. And between whiles I had to look after the savage who was fireman. He was an improved specimen; he could fire up a vertical boiler. He was there below me, and, upon my word, to look at him was as edifying as seeing a dog in a parody of breeches and a feather hat, walking on his hind-legs. A few months of training had done for that really fine chap. He squinted at the steam-gauge and at the water-gauge with an evident effort of intrepidity—and he had filed teeth too, the poor devil, and the wool of his pate shaved into queer patterns, and three ornamental scars on each of his cheeks. He ought to have been clapping his hands and stamping his feet on the bank, instead of which he was hard at work, a thrall to strange witchcraft, full of improving knowledge. He was useful because he had been instructed; and what he knew was this—that should the water in that transparent thing disappear, the evil spirit inside the boiler would get angry through the greatness of his thirst, and take a terrible vengeance. So he sweated and fired up and watched the glass fearfully (with an impromptu charm, made of rags, tied to his arm, and a piece of polished bone, as big as a watch, stuck flatways through his lower lip), while the wooded banks slipped past us slowly, the short noise was left behind, the interminable miles of silence—and we crept on, towards

Kurtz. But the snags were thick, the water was treacherous and shallow, the boiler seemed indeed to have a sulky devil in it, and thus neither that fireman nor I had any time to peer into our creepy thoughts.

"Some fifty miles below the Inner Station we came upon a hut of reeds, an inclined and melancholy pole, with the unrecognisable tatters of what had been a flag of some sort flying from it, and a neatly stacked wood-pile. This was unexpected. We came to the bank, and on the stack of firewood found a flat piece of board with some faded pencil-writing on it. When deciphered it said: 'Wood for you. Hurry up. Approach cautiously.' There was a signature, but it was illegible—not Kurtz—a much longer word. Hurry up. Where? Up the river? 'Approach cautiously.' We had not done so. But the warning could not have been meant for the place where it could be only found after approach. Something was wrong above. But what—and how much? That was the question. We commented adversely upon the imbecility of that telegraphic style. The bush around said nothing, and would not let us look very far, either. A torn curtain of red twill hung in the doorway of the hut, and flapped sadly in our faces. The dwelling was dismantled; but we could see a white man had lived there not very long ago. There remained a rude table—a plank on two posts; a heap of rubbish reposed in a dark corner, and by the door I picked up a book. It had lost its covers, and the pages had been thumbed into a state of extremely dirty softness; but the back had been lovingly stitched afresh with white cotton thread, which looked clean yet. It was an extraordinary find. Its title was, 'An Inquiry into some Points of Seamanship,' by a man Tower, Towson—some such name—Master in his Majesty's Navy. The matter looked dreary reading enough, with illustrative diagrams and repulsive tables of figures, and the copy was sixty years old. I handled this amazing antiquity with the greatest possible tenderness, lest it should dissolve in my hands. Within, Towson or Towser was inquiring earnestly into the breaking strain of ships' chains and tackle, and other such matters. Not a very enthralling book; but at the first glance you could see there a singleness of intention, an honest concern for the right way of going to work, which made these humble pages, thought out so many years ago, luminous with another than a professional light. The simple old sailor, with his talk of chains and purchases, made me forget the jungle and the pilgrims in a delicious sensation of having come upon something unmistakably real. Such a book being there was wonderful enough; but still more astounding were the notes pencilled in the margin, and plainly referring to the text. I couldn't believe my eyes! They were in cipher! Yes, it looked like cipher. Fancy a man lugging with him a book of that description into this nowhere and studying it—and making notes—in cipher at that! It was an extravagant mystery.

"I had been dimly aware for some time of a worrying noise, and when I lifted my eyes I saw the wood-pile was gone, and the manager, aided by all the pilgrims, was shouting at me from the river-side. I slipped the book into my pocket. I assure you to leave off reading was like tearing myself away from the shelter of an old and solid friendship.

"I started the lame engine ahead. 'It must be this miserable trader—this intruder,' exclaimed the manager, looking back malevolently at the place we had left. 'He must be English,' I said. 'It will not save him from getting into trouble if he is not careful,' muttered the manager darkly. I observed with assumed innocence that no man was safe from trouble in this world.

"The current was more rapid now, the steamer seemed at her last gasp, the stern-wheel flopped languidly, and I caught myself listening on tiptoe for the next beat of the float, for in sober truth I expected the wretched thing to give up every moment. It was like watching the last flickers of a life. But still we crawled. Sometimes I would pick out a tree a little way ahead to measure our progress towards Kurtz by, but I lost it invariably before we got abreast. To keep the eyes so long on one thing was too much for human patience. The manager displayed a beautiful resignation. I fretted and fumed and took to arguing with myself whether or no I would talk openly with Kurtz; but before I could come to any conclusion it occurred to me that my speech or my silence, indeed any action of mine, would be a mere futility. What did it matter what any one knew or ignored? What did it matter who was manager? One gets sometimes such a flash of insight. The essentials of this affair lay deep under the surface, beyond my reach, and beyond my power of meddling.

"Towards the evening of the second day we judged ourselves about eight miles from Kurtz's station. I wanted to push on; but the manager looked grave, and told me the navigation up there was so dangerous that it would be advisable, the sun being very low already, to wait where we were till next morning. Moreover, he pointed out that if the warning to approach cautiously were to be followed, we must approach in daylight—not at dusk, or in the dark. This was sensible enough. Eight miles meant nearly three hours' steaming for us, and I could also see suspicious ripples at the upper end of the reach. Nevertheless, I was annoyed beyond expression at the delay, and most unreasonably too, since one night more could not matter much after so many months. As we had plenty of wood, and caution was the word, I brought up in the middle of the stream. The reach was narrow, straight, with high sides like a railway cutting. The dusk came gliding into it long before the sun had set. The current ran smooth and swift, but a dumb immobility sat on the banks. The living trees, lashed together by the creepers and every living bush of the undergrowth, might have been changed into stone, even to the slenderest twig, to the lightest leaf. It was not sleep—it seemed unnatural, like a state of trance. Not the faintest sound of any kind could be heard. You looked on amazed, and began to suspect yourself of being deaf—then the night came suddenly, and struck you blind as well. About three in the morning some large fish leaped, and the loud splash made me jump as though a gun had been fired. When the sun rose there was a white fog, very warm and clammy, and more blinding than the night. It did not shift or drive; it was just there, standing all round you like something solid. At eight or nine, perhaps, it lifted as a shutter lifts. We had a glimpse of the towering multitude of trees, of the immense matted jungle, with the blazing little ball of the sun hanging over it—all perfectly still—and then the white shutter came down again, smoothly, as if sliding in greased grooves. I ordered the chain, which we had begun to heave in, to be paid out again. Before it stopped running with a muffled rattle, a cry, a very loud cry, as of infinite desolation, soared slowly in the opaque air. It ceased. A complaining clamour, modulated in savage discords, filled our ears. The sheer unexpectedness of it made my hair stir under my cap. I don't know how it struck the others: to me it seemed as though the mist itself had screamed, so suddenly, and apparently from all sides at once, did this tumultuous and mournful uproar arise. It culminated in a hurried outbreak of almost intolerably excessive shrieking, which stopped short, leaving us stiffened in a variety of silly attitudes, and obstinately listening to the nearly as appalling and excessive silence. 'Good God! What is the meaning—?' stammered at my elbow one of the pilgrims,—a little fat man, with sandy hair and red whiskers, who wore side-spring boots, and pink pyjamas tucked into his socks. Two others remained open-mouthed a whole minute, then dashed into the little cabin, to rush out incontinently and stand darting scared glances, with Winchesters at 'ready' in their hands. What we could see was just the steamer we were on, her outlines blurred as though she had been on the point of dissolving, and a misty strip of water, perhaps two feet broad, around her—and that was all. The rest of the world was nowhere, as far as our eyes and ears were concerned. Just nowhere. Gone, disappeared; swept off without leaving a whisper or a shadow behind.

"I went forward, and ordered the chain to be hauled in short, so as to be ready to trip the anchor and move the steamboat at once if necessary. 'Will they attack?' whispered an awed voice. 'We will all be butchered in this fog,' murmured another. The faces twitched with the strain, the hands trembled slightly, the eyes forgot to wink. It was very curious to see the contrast of expressions of the white men and of the black fellows of our crew, who were as much strangers to that part of the river as we, though their homes were only eight hundred miles away. The whites, of course greatly discomposed, had besides a curious look of being painfully shocked by such an outrageous row. The others had an alert, naturally interested expression; but their faces were essentially quiet, even those of the one or two who grinned as they hauled at the chain. Several exchanged short, grunting phrases, which seemed to settle the matter to their satisfaction. Their headman, a young, broad-chested black, severely draped in dark-blue fringed cloths, with fierce nostrils and his hair all done up artfully in oily ringlets, stood near me. 'Aha!' I said, just for good fellowship's sake. 'Catch 'im,' he snapped, with a bloodshot widening of his eyes and a flash of sharp teeth— 'catch 'im. Give 'im to us.' 'To you, eh?' I asked; 'what would you do with them?' 'Eat 'im!' he said, curtly, and, leaning his elbow on the rail, looked out into the fog in a dignified and profoundly pensive attitude. I would no doubt have been properly horrified, had it not occurred to me that he and his chaps must be very hungry: that they must have been growing increasingly hungry for at least this month past. They had been engaged for six months (I don't think a single one of them had any clear idea of time, as we at the end of countless ages have. They still belonged to the beginnings of time—had no inherited experience to teach them, as it were), and of course, as long as there was a piece of paper written over in accordance with some farcical law or other made down the river, it didn't enter anybody's head to trouble how they would live. Certainly they had brought with them some rotten hippo-meat, which couldn't have lasted very long, anyway, even if the pilgrims hadn't, in the midst of a shocking hullabaloo, thrown a considerable quantity of it overboard. It looked like a high-handed proceeding; but it was really a case of legitimate self-defence. You can't breathe dead hippo waking, sleeping, and eating, and at the same time keep your precarious grip on existence. Besides that, they had given them every week three pieces of brass wire, each about nine inches long; and the theory was they were to buy their provisions with that currency in river-side villages. You can see how *that* worked. There were either no villages, or the people were hostile, or the director, who like the rest of us fed out of tins, with an occasional old he-goat thrown in, didn't want to stop the steamer for some more or less recondite reason. So, unless they swallowed the wire itself, or made loops of it to snare the fishes with, I don't see what good their extravagant salary could be to them. I must say it was paid with a regularity worthy of a large and honourable trading company. For the rest, the only thing to eat—though it didn't look eatable in the least—I saw in their possession was a few lumps of some stuff like half-cooked dough, of a dirty lavender colour, they kept wrapped in leaves, and now and then swallowed a piece of, but so small that it seemed done more for the looks of the thing than for any serious purpose of sustenance. Why in the name of all the gnawing devils of hunger they didn't go for us—they were thirty to five—and have a good tuck-in for once, amazes me now when I think of it. They were big powerful men, with not much capacity to weigh the consequences, with courage, with strength, even yet, though their skins were no longer glossy and their muscles no longer hard. And I saw that something restraining, one of those human secrets that baffle probability, had come into play there. I looked at them with a swift quickening of interest—not because it occurred to me I might be eaten by them before very long, though I own to you that just then I perceived—in a new light, as it were—how unwholesome the pilgrims looked, and I hoped, yes, I positively hoped, that my aspect was not so—what shall I say?—so—unappetising: a touch of fantastic vanity which fitted well with the dream-sensation that pervaded all my days at that time. Perhaps I had a little fever too. One can't live with one's finger everlastingly on one's pulse. I had often 'a little fever,' or a little touch of other things—the playful paw-strokes of the wilderness, the preliminary trifling before the more serious onslaught which came in due course. Yes; I looked at them as you would on any human being, with a curiosity of their impulses, motives, capacities, weaknesses, when brought to the test of an inexorable physical necessity. Restraint! What possible restraint? Was it superstition, disgust, patience, fear—or some kind of primitive honour? No fear can stand up to hunger, no patience can wear it out, disgust simply does not exist where hunger is; and as to superstition, beliefs, and what you may call principles, they are less than chaff in a breeze. Don't you know the devilry of lingering starvation, its exasperating torment, its black thoughts, its sombre and brooding ferocity? Well, I do. It takes a man all his inborn strength to fight hunger properly. It's really easier to face bereavement, dishonour, and the perdition of one's soul—than this kind of prolonged hunger. Sad, but true. And these chaps too had no earthly reason for any kind of scruple. Restraint! I would just as soon have expected restraint from a hyena prowling amongst the corpses of a battlefield. But there was the fact facing me—the fact dazzling, to be seen, like the foam on the depths of the sea, like a ripple on an unfathomable enigma, a mystery greater—when I thought of it—than the curious, inexplicable note of desperate grief in this savage clamour that had swept by us on the river-bank, behind the blind whiteness of the fog.

"Two pilgrims were quarrelling in hurried whispers as to which bank. 'Left.' 'No, no; how can you? Right, right, of course.' 'It is very serious,' said the manager's voice behind me; 'I would be desolated if anything should happen to Mr Kurtz before we came up.' I looked at him, and had not the slightest doubt he was sincere. He was just the kind of man who would wish to preserve appearances. That was his restraint. But when he muttered something about going on at once, I did not even take the trouble to answer him. I knew, and he knew, that it was impossible. Were we to let go our hold of the bottom, we would be absolutely in the air—in space. We wouldn't be able to tell where we were going to—whether up or down stream, or across—till we fetched against one bank or the other,—and then we wouldn't know at first which it was. Of course I made no move. I had no mind for a smash-up. You couldn't imagine a more deadly place for a shipwreck. Whether drowned at once or not, we were sure to perish speedily in one way or another. 'I authorise you to take all the risks,' he said, after a short silence. 'I refuse to take any,' I said shortly; which was just the answer he expected, though its tone might have surprised him. 'Well, I must defer to your judgment. You are captain,' he said, with marked civility. I turned my shoulder to him in sign of my appreciation, and looked into the fog. How long would it last? It was the most hopeless look-out. The approach to this Kurtz grubbing for ivory in the wretched bush was beset by as many dangers as though he had been an enchanted princess sleeping in a fabulous castle. 'Will they attack, do you think?' asked the manager, in a confidential tone.

"I did not think they would attack, for several obvious reasons. The thick fog was one. If they left the bank in their canoes they would get lost in it, as we would be if we attempted to move. Still, I had also judged the jungle of both banks quite impenetrable—and yet eyes were in it, eyes that had seen us. The river-side bushes were certainly very thick; but the undergrowth behind was evidently penetrable. However, during the short lift I had seen no canoes anywhere in the reach—certainly not abreast of the steamer. But what made the idea of attack inconceivable to me was the nature of the noise—of the cries we had heard. They had not the fierce character boding of immediate hostile intention. Unexpected, wild, and violent as they had been, they had given me an irresistible impression of sorrow. The glimpse of the steamboat had for some reason filled those savages with unrestrained grief. The danger, if any, I expounded, was from our proximity to a great human passion let loose. Even extreme grief may ultimately vent itself in violence—but more generally takes the form of apathy. . . .

"You should have seen the pilgrims stare! They had no heart to grin, or even to revile me; but I believe they thought me gone mad—with fright, maybe. I delivered a regular lecture. My dear boys, it was no good bothering. Keep a look-out? Well, you may guess I watched the fog for the signs of lifting as a cat watches a mouse; but for anything else our eyes were of no more use to us than if we had been buried miles deep in a heap of cotton-wool. It felt like it too—choking, warm, stifling. Besides, all I said, though it sounded extravagant, was absolutely true to fact. What we afterwards alluded to as an attack was really an attempt at repulse. The action was very far from being aggressive—it was not even defensive, in the usual sense: it was undertaken under the stress of desperation, and in its essence was purely protective.

"It developed itself, I should say, two hours after the fog lifted, and its commencement was at a spot, roughly speaking, about a mile and a half below Kurtz's station. We had just floundered and flopped round a bend, when I saw an islet, a mere grassy hummock of bright green, in the middle of the stream. It was the only thing of the kind; but as we opened the reach more, I perceived it was the head of a long sandbank, or rather of a chain of shallow patches stretching down the middle of the river. They were discoloured, just awash, and the whole lot was seen just under the water, exactly as a man's backbone is seen running down the middle of his back under the skin. Now, as far as I did see, I could go to the right or to the left of this. I didn't know either channel, of course. The banks looked pretty well alike, the depth appeared the same; but as I had been informed the station was on the west side, I naturally headed for the western passage.

"No sooner had we fairly entered it than I became aware it was much narrower than I had supposed. To the left of us there was the long uninterrupted shoal, and to the right a high, steep bank heavily overgrown with bushes. Above the bush the trees stood in serried ranks. The twigs overhung the current thickly, and from distance to distance a large limb of some tree projected rigidly over the stream. It was then well on in the afternoon, the face of the forest was gloomy, and a broad strip of shadow had already fallen on the water. In this shadow we steamed up—very slowly, as you may imagine. I sheered her well inshore—the water being deepest near the bank, as the sounding-pole informed me.

"One of my hungry and forbearing friends was sounding in the bows just below me. This steamboat was exactly like a decked scow.[4] On the deck there were two little teak-wood houses, with doors and windows. The boiler was in the fore-end, and the machinery right astern. Over the whole there was a light roof, supported on stanchions. The funnel projected through that roof, and in front of the funnel a small cabin built of light planks served for a pilot-house. It contained a couch, two camp-stools, a loaded Martini-Henry[5] leaning in one corner, a tiny table, and the steering-wheel. It had a wide door in front and a broad shutter at each side. All these were always thrown open, of course. I spent my days perched up there on the extreme fore-end of

4. A flat-bottomed boat.   5. A rifle.

that roof, before the door. At night I slept, or tried to, on the couch. An athletic black belonging to some coast tribe, and educated by my poor predecessor, was the helmsman. He sported a pair of brass earrings, wore a blue cloth wrapper from the waist to the ankles, and thought all the world of himself. He was the most unstable kind of fool I had ever seen. He steered with no end of a swagger while you were by; but if he lost sight of you, he became instantly the prey of an abject funk, and would let that cripple of a steamboat get the upper hand of him in a minute.

"I was looking down at the sounding-pole, and feeling much annoyed to see at each try a little more of it stick out of that river, when I saw my poleman give up the business suddenly, and stretch himself flat on the deck, without even taking the trouble to haul his pole in. He kept hold on it though, and it trailed in the water. At the same time the fireman, whom I could also see below me, sat down abruptly before his furnace and ducked his head. I was amazed. Then I had to look at the river mighty quick, because there was a snag in the fairway. Sticks, little sticks, were flying about— thick: they were whizzing before my nose, dropping below me, striking behind me against my pilot-house. All this time the river, the shore, the woods, were very quiet—perfectly quiet. I could only hear the heavy splashing thump of the stern-wheel and the patter of these things. We cleared the snag clumsily. Arrows, by Jove! We were being shot at! I stepped in quickly to close the shutter on the landside. That fool-helmsman, his hands on the spokes, was lifting his knees high, stamping his feet, champing his mouth, like a reined-in horse. Confound him! And we were staggering within ten feet of the bank. I had to lean right out to swing the heavy shutter, and I saw a face amongst the leaves on the level with my own, looking at me very fierce and steady; and then suddenly, as though a veil had been removed from my eyes, I made out, deep in the tangled gloom, naked breasts, arms, legs, glaring eyes,—the bush was swarming with human limbs in movement, glistening, of bronze colour. The twigs shook, swayed, and rustled, the arrows flew out of them, and then the shutter came to. 'Steer her straight,' I said to the helmsman. He held his head rigid, face forward; but his eyes rolled, he kept on lifting and setting down his feet gently, his mouth foamed a little. 'Keep quiet!' I said in a fury. I might just as well have ordered a tree not to sway in the wind. I darted out. Below me there was a great scuffle of feet on the iron deck; confused exclamations; a voice screamed, 'Can you turn back?' I caught sight of a V-shaped ripple on the water ahead. What? Another snag! A fusillade burst out under my feet. The pilgrims had opened with their Winchesters, and were simply squirting lead into that bush. A deuce of a lot of smoke came up and drove slowly forward. I swore at it. Now I couldn't see the ripple or the snag either. I stood in the doorway, peering, and the arrows came in swarms. They might have been poisoned, but they looked as though they wouldn't kill a cat. The bush began to howl. Our wood-cutters raised a warlike whoop; the report of a rifle just at my back deafened me. I glanced over my shoulder, and the pilot-house was yet full of noise and smoke when I made a dash at the wheel. The fool-nigger had dropped everything, to throw the shutter open and let off that Martini-Henry. He stood before the wide opening, glaring, and I yelled at him to come back, while I straightened the sudden twist out of that steamboat. There was no room to turn even if I had wanted to, the snag was somewhere very near ahead in that confounded smoke, there was no time to lose, so I just crowded her into the bank—right into the bank, where I knew the water was deep.

"We tore slowly along the overhanging bushes in a whirl of broken twigs and flying leaves. The fusillade below stopped short, as I had foreseen it would when the squirts got empty. I threw my head back to a glinting whizz that traversed the pilot-house, in at one shutter-hole and out at the other. Looking past that mad helmsman, who was shaking the empty rifle and yelling at the shore, I saw vague forms of men running bent double, leaping, gliding, distinct, incomplete, evanescent. Something big appeared in the air before the shutter, the rifle went overboard, and the man stepped back swiftly, looked at me over his shoulder in an extraordinary, profound, familiar manner, and fell upon my feet. The side of his head hit the wheel twice, and the end of what appeared a long cane clattered round and knocked over a little camp-stool. It looked as though after wrenching that thing from somebody ashore he had lost his balance in the effort. The thin smoke had blown away, we were clear of the snag, and looking ahead I could see that in another hundred yards or so I would be free to sheer off, away from the bank; but my feet felt so very warm and wet that I had to look down. The man had rolled on his back and stared straight up at me; both his hands clutched that cane. It was the shaft of a spear that, either thrown or lunged through the opening, had caught him in the side just below the ribs; the blade had gone in out of sight, after making a frightful gash; my shoes were full; a pool of blood lay very still, gleaming dark-red under the wheel; his eyes shone with an amazing lustre. The fusillade burst out again. He looked at me anxiously, gripping the spear like something precious, with an air of being afraid I would try to take it away from him. I had to make an effort to free my eyes from his gaze and attend to the steering. With one hand I felt above my head for the line of the steam-whistle, and jerked out screech after screech hurriedly. The tumult of angry and warlike yells was checked instantly, and then from the depths of the woods went out such a tremulous and prolonged wail of mournful fear and utter despair as may be imagined to follow the flight of the last hope from the earth. There was a great commotion in the bush; the shower of arrows stopped, a few dropping shots rang out sharply—then silence, in which the languid beat of the stern-wheel came plainly to my ears. I put the helm hard astarboard at the moment when the pilgrim in pink pyjamas, very hot and agitated, appeared in the doorway. 'The manager sends me—' he began in an official tone, and stopped short. 'Good God!' he said, glaring at the wounded man.

"We two whites stood over him, and his lustrous and inquiring glance enveloped us both. I declare it looked as though he would presently put to us some question in an understandable language; but he died without uttering a sound, without moving a limb, without twitching a muscle. Only in the very last moment, as though in response to some sign we could not see, to some whisper we could not hear, he frowned heavily, and that frown gave to his black death-mask an inconceivably sombre, brooding, and menacing expression. The lustre of inquiring glance faded swiftly into vacant glassiness. 'Can you steer?' I asked the agent eagerly. He looked very dubious; but I made a grab at his arm, and he understood at once I meant him to steer whether or no. To tell you the truth, I was morbidly anxious to change my shoes and socks. 'He is dead,' murmured the fellow, immensely impressed. 'No doubt about it,' said I, tugging like mad at the shoelaces. 'And, by the way, I suppose Mr Kurtz is dead as well by this time.'

"For the moment that was the dominant thought. There was a sense of extreme disappointment, as though I had found out I had been striving after something altogether without a substance. I couldn't have been more disgusted if I had travelled all this way for the sole purpose of talking with Mr Kurtz. Talking with . . . I flung one shoe overboard, and became aware that that was exactly what I had been looking forward to—a talk with Kurtz. I made the strange discovery that I had never imagined him as doing, you know, but as discoursing. I didn't say to myself, 'Now I will never see him,' or 'Now I will never shake him by the hand,' but, 'Now I will never hear him.' The man presented himself as a voice. Not of course that I did not connect him with some sort of action. Hadn't I been told in all the tones of jealousy and admiration that he had collected, bartered, swindled, or stolen more ivory than all the other agents together. That was not the point. The point was in his being a gifted creature, and that of all his gifts the one that stood out pre-eminently, that carried with it a sense of real presence, was his ability to talk, his words—the gift of expression, the bewildering, the illuminating, the most exalted and the most contemptible, the pulsating stream of light, or the deceitful flow from the heart of an impenetrable darkness.

"The other shoe went flying unto the devil-god of that river. I thought, By Jove! it's all over. We are too late; he has vanished—the gift has vanished, by means of some spear, arrow, or club. I will never hear that chap speak after all,—and my sorrow had a startling extravagance of emotion, even such as I had noticed in the howling sorrow of these savages in the bush. I couldn't have felt more of lonely desolation somehow, had I been robbed of a belief or had missed my destiny in life. . . . Why do you sigh in this beastly way, somebody? Absurd? Well, absurd. Good Lord! mustn't a man ever—Here, give me some tobacco." . . .

There was a pause of profound stillness, then a match flared, and Marlow's lean face appeared, worn, hollow, with downward folds and dropped eyelids, with an aspect of concentrated attention; and as he took vigorous draws at his pipe, it seemed to retreat and advance out of the night in the regular flicker of the tiny flame. The match went out.

"Absurd!" he cried. "This is the worst of trying to tell . . . Here you all are, each moored with two good addresses, like a hulk with two anchors, a butcher round one corner, a policeman round another, excellent appetites, and temperature normal—you hear—normal from year's end to year's end. And you say, Absurd! Absurd be—exploded! Absurd! My dear boys, what can you expect from a man who out of sheer nervousness had just flung overboard a pair of new shoes? Now I think of it, it is amazing I did not shed tears. I am, upon the whole, proud of my fortitude. I was cut to the quick at the idea of having lost the inestimable privilege of listening to the gifted Kurtz. Of course I was wrong. The privilege was waiting for me. Oh yes, I heard more than enough. And I was right, too. A voice. He was very little more than a voice. And I heard—him—it—this voice—other voices—all of them were so little more than voices—and the memory of that time itself lingers around me, impalpable, like a dying vibration of one immense jabber, silly, atrocious, sordid, savage, or simply mean, without any kind of sense. Voices, voices—even the girl herself—now—"

He was silent for a long time.

"I laid the ghost of his gifts at last with a lie," he began suddenly. "Girl! What? Did I mention a girl? Oh, she is out of it—completely. They—the women I mean—are out of it—should be out of it. We must help them to stay in that beautiful world of their own, lest ours gets worse. Oh, she had to be out of it. You should have heard the disinterred body of Mr Kurtz saying, "My Intended." You would have perceived directly then how completely she was out of it. And the lofty frontal bone of Mr Kurtz! They say the hair goes on growing sometimes, but this—ah—specimen was impressively bald. The wilderness had patted him on the head, and, behold, it was like a ball—an ivory ball; it had caressed him, and—lo!—he had withered; it had taken him, loved him, embraced him, got into his veins, consumed his flesh, and sealed his soul to its own by the inconceivable ceremonies of some devilish initiation. He was its spoiled and pampered favourite. Ivory? I should think so. Heaps of it, stacks of it. The old mud shanty was bursting with it. You would think there was not a single tusk left either above or below the ground in the whole country. 'Mostly fossil,' the manager had remarked disparagingly. It was no more fossil than I am; but they call it fossil when it is dug up. It appears these niggers do bury the tusks sometimes—but evidently they couldn't bury this parcel deep enough to save the gifted Mr Kurtz from his fate. We filled the steamboat with it, and had to pile a lot on the deck. Thus he could see and enjoy as long as he could see, because the appreciation of this favour had remained with him to the last. You should have heard him say, 'My ivory.' Oh yes, I heard him. 'My Intended, my ivory, my station, my river, my—' everything belonged to him. It made me hold my breath in expectation of hearing the wilderness burst into a prodigious peal of laughter that would shake the fixed stars in their places. Everything belonged to him—but that was a trifle. The thing was to know what he belonged to, how many powers of darkness claimed him for their own. That was the reflection that made you creepy all over. It was impossible—it was not good for one either—trying to imagine. He had taken a high seat amongst the devils of the land—I mean literally. You can't understand. How could you?—with solid pavement under your feet, surrounded by kind neighbours ready to cheer you or to fall on you, stepping delicately between the butcher and the policeman, in the holy terror of scandal and gallows and lunatic asylums—how can you imagine what particular region of the first ages a man's untrammelled feet may take him into by the way of solitude—utter solitude without a policeman—by the way of silence—utter silence, where no warning voice of a kind neighbour can be heard whispering of public opinion? These little things make all the great difference. When they are gone you must fall back upon your own innate strength, upon your own capacity for faithfulness. Of course you may be too much of a fool to go wrong—too dull even to know you are being assaulted by the powers of darkness. I take it, no fool ever made a bargain for his soul with the devil: the fool is too much of a fool, or the devil too much of a devil—I don't know which. Or you may be such a thunderingly exalted creature as to be altogether deaf and blind to anything but heavenly sights and sounds. Then the earth for you is only a standing place—and whether to be like this is your loss or your gain I won't pretend to say. But most of us are neither one nor the other. The earth for us is a place to live in, where we must put up with sights, with sounds, with smells too, by Jove!—breathe dead hippo, so to speak, and not be contaminated. And there, don't you see? your strength comes in, the faith in your ability for the digging of unostentatious holes to bury the stuff in—your power of devotion, not to yourself, but to an obscure, back-breaking business. And that's difficult enough. Mind, I am not trying to excuse or even explain—I am trying to account to myself for—for—Mr Kurtz—for the shade of Mr Kurtz. This initiated wraith from the back of Nowhere honoured me with its amazing confidence before it vanished altogether. This was because it could speak English to me. The original Kurtz had been educated partly in England, and—as he was good enough to say himself—his sympathies were in the right place. His mother was half-English, his father was half-French. All Europe contributed to the making of Kurtz; and by-and-by I learned that, most appropriately, the International Society for the Suppression of Savage Customs had intrusted him with the making of a report, for its future guidance. And he had written it too. I've seen it. I've read it. It was eloquent, vibrating with eloquence, but too high-strung, I think. Seventeen pages of close writing he had found time for! But this must have been before his—let us say—nerves went wrong, and caused him to preside at certain midnight dances ending with unspeakable rites, which—as far as I reluctantly gathered from what I heard at various times—were offered up to him—do you understand?—to Mr Kurtz himself. But it was a beautiful piece of writing. The opening paragraph, however, in the light of later information, strikes me now as ominous. He began with the argument that we whites, from the point of development we had arrived at, 'must necessarily appear to them [savages] in the nature of supernatural beings—we approach them with the might as of a deity,' and so on, and so on. 'By the simple exercise of our will we can exert a power for good practically unbounded,' &c., &c. From that point he soared and took me with him. The peroration was magnificent, though difficult to remember, you know. It gave me the notion of an exotic Immensity ruled by an august Benevolence. It made me tingle with enthusiasm. This was the unbounded power of eloquence—of words—of burning noble words. There were no practical hints to interrupt the magic current of phrases, unless a kind of note at the foot of the last page, scrawled evidently much later, in an unsteady hand, may be regarded as the exposition of a method. It was very simple, and at the end of that moving appeal to every altruistic sentiment it blazed at you, luminous and terrifying, like a flash of lightning in a serene sky: 'Exterminate all the brutes!' The curious part was that he had apparently forgotten all about that valuable postscriptum, because, later on, when he in a sense came to himself, he repeatedly entreated me to take good care of 'my pamphlet' (he called it), as it was sure to have in the future a good influence upon his career. I had full information about all these things, and, besides, as it turned out, I was to have the care of his memory. I've done enough for it to give me the indisputable right to lay it, if I choose, for an everlasting rest in the dust-bin of progress, amongst all the sweepings and, figuratively speaking, all the dead cats of civilisation. But then, you see, I can't choose. He won't be forgotten. Whatever he was, he was not common. He had the power to charm or frighten rudimentary souls into an aggravated witch-dance in his honour; he could also fill the small souls of the pilgrims with bitter misgivings: he had one devoted friend at least, and he had conquered one soul in the world that was neither rudimentary nor tainted with self-seeking. No; I can't forget him, though I am not prepared to affirm the fellow was exactly worth the life we lost in getting to him. I missed my late helmsman awfully,—I missed him even while his body was still lying in the pilot-house. Perhaps you will think it passing strange this regret for a savage who was no more account than a grain of sand in a black Sahara. Well, don't you see, he had done something, he had steered; for months I had him at my back—a help—an instrument. It was a kind of partnership. He steered for me—I had to look after him, I worried about his deficiencies, and thus a subtle bond had been created, of which I only became aware when it was suddenly broken. And the intimate profundity of that look he gave me when he received his hurt remains to this day in my memory—like a claim of distant kinship affirmed in a supreme moment.

"Poor fool! If he had only left that shutter alone. He had no restraint, no restraint—just like Kurtz—a tree swayed by the wind. As soon as I had put on a dry pair of slippers, I dragged him out, after first jerking the spear out of his side, which operation I confess I performed with my eyes shut tight. His heels leaped together over the little doorstep; his shoulders were pressed to my breast; I hugged him from behind desperately. Oh! he was heavy, heavy; heavier than any man on earth, I should imagine. Then without more ado I tipped him overboard. The current snatched him as though he had been a wisp of grass, and I saw the body roll over twice before I lost sight of it for ever. All the pilgrims and the manager were then congregated on the awning-deck about the pilot-house, chattering at each other like a flock of excited magpies, and there was a scandalised murmur at my heartless promptitude. What they wanted to keep that body hanging about for I can't guess. Embalm it, maybe. But I had also heard another, and a very ominous, murmur on the deck below. My friends the woodcutters were likewise scandalised, and with a better show of reason—though I admit that the reason itself was quite inadmissible. Oh, quite! I had made up my mind that if my late helmsman was to be eaten, the fishes alone should have him. He had been a very second-rate helmsman while alive, but now he was dead he might have become a first-class temptation, and possibly cause some startling trouble. Besides, I was anxious to take the wheel, the man in pink pyjamas showing himself a hopeless duffer at the business.

"This I did directly the simple funeral was over. We were going half-speed, keeping right in the middle of the stream, and I listened to the talk about me. They had given up Kurtz, they had given up the station; Kurtz was dead, and the station had been burnt—and so on—and so on. The red-haired pilgrim was beside himself with the thought that at least this poor Kurtz had been properly revenged. 'Say! We must have made a glorious slaughter of them in the bush. Eh? What do you think? Say?' He positively danced, the bloodthirsty little gingery beggar. And he had nearly fainted when he saw the wounded man! I could not help saying, 'You made a glorious lot of smoke, anyhow.' I had seen, from the way the tops of the bushes rustled and flew, that almost all the shots had gone too high. You can't hit anything unless you take aim and fire from the shoulder; but these chaps fired from the hip with their eyes shut. The retreat, I maintained—and I was right—was caused by the screeching of the steam-whistle. Upon this they forgot Kurtz, and began to howl at me with indignant protests.

"The manager stood by the wheel murmuring confidentially about the necessity of getting well away down the river before dark at all events, when I saw in the distance a clearing on the river-side and the outlines of some sort of building. 'What's this?' I asked. He clapped his hands in wonder. 'The station!' he cried. I edged in at once, still going half-speed.

"Through my glasses I saw the slope of a hill interspersed with rare trees and perfectly free from undergrowth. A long decaying building on the summit was half buried in the high grass; the large holes in the peaked roof gaped black from afar; the jungle and the woods made a background. There was no enclosure or fence of any kind; but there had been one apparently, for near the house half-a-dozen slim posts remained in a row, roughly trimmed, and with their upper ends ornamented with round carved balls. The rails, or whatever there had been between, had disappeared. Of course the forest surrounded all that. The river-bank was clear, and on the waterside I saw a white man under a hat like a cart-wheel beckoning persistently with his whole arm. Examining the edge of the forest above and below, I was almost certain I could see movements—human forms gliding here and there. I steamed past prudently, then stopped the engines and let her drift down. The man on the shore began to shout, urging us to land. 'We have been attacked,' screamed the manager. 'I know—I know. It's all right,' yelled back the other, as cheerful as you please. 'Come along. It's all right. I am glad.'

"His aspect reminded me of something I had seen—something funny I had seen somewhere. As I manoeuvred to get alongside, I was asking myself, 'What does this fellow look like?' Suddenly I got it. He looked like a harlequin. His clothes had been made of some stuff that was brown holland[6] probably, but it was covered with patch-es all over, with bright patches, blue, red, and yellow,—patches on the back, patches on front, patches on elbows, on knees; coloured binding round his jacket, scarlet edg-ing at the bottom of his trousers; and the sunshine made him look extremely gay and wonderfully neat withal, because you could see how beautifully all this patching had been done. A beardless, boyish face, very fair, no features to speak of, nose peeling, little blue eyes, smiles and frowns chasing each other over that open countenance like sunshine and shadow on a wind-swept plain. 'Look out, captain!' he cried; 'there's a snag lodged in here last night.' What! Another snag? I confess I swore shamefully. I had nearly holed my cripple, to finish off that charming trip. The harle-quin on the bank turned his little pug nose up to me. 'You English?' he asked, all smiles. 'Are you?' I shouted from the wheel. The smiles vanished, and he shook his head as if sorry for my disappointment. Then he brightened up. 'Never mind!' he cried encouragingly. 'Are we in time?' I asked. 'He is up there,' he replied, with a toss of the head up the hill, and becoming gloomy all of a sudden. His face was like the autumn sky, overcast one moment and bright the next.

"When the manager, escorted by the pilgrims, all of them armed to the teeth, had gone to the house, this chap came on board. 'I say, I don't like this. These natives are in the bush,' I said. He assured me earnestly it was all right. 'They are simple peo-ple,' he added; 'well, I am glad you came. It took me all my time to keep them off.' 'But you said it was all right,' I cried. 'Oh, they meant no harm,' he said; and as I stared he corrected himself, 'Not exactly.' Then vivaciously, 'My faith, your pilot-house wants a clean-up!' In the next breath he advised me to keep enough steam on the boiler to blow the whistle in case of any trouble. 'One good screech will do more for you than all your rifles. They are simple people,' he repeated. He rattled away at such a rate he quite overwhelmed me. He seemed to be trying to make up for lots of silence, and actually hinted, laughing, that such was the case. 'Don't you talk with Mr Kurtz?' I said. 'You don't talk with that man—you listen to him,' he exclaimed with severe exaltation. 'But now—' He waved his arm, and in the twinkling of an eye was in the uttermost depths of despondency. In a moment he came up again with a jump, possessed himself of both my hands, shook them continuously, while he gab-bled: 'Brother sailor . . . honour . . . pleasure . . . delight . . . introduce myself . . . Russian . . . son of an arch-priest . . . Government of Tambov[7] . . . What? Tobacco! English tobacco; the excellent English tobacco! Now, that's brotherly. Smoke? Where's a sailor that does not smoke?'

"The pipe soothed him, and gradually I made out he had run away from school, had gone to sea in a Russian ship; ran away again; served some time in English ships; was now reconciled with the arch-priest. He made a point of that. 'But when one is young one must see things, gather experience, ideas; enlarge the mind.' 'Here!' I interrupted. 'You can never tell! Here I have met Mr Kurtz,' he said, youthfully solemn and reproachful. I held my tongue after that. It appears he had persuaded a Dutch trading-house on the coast to fit him out with stores and goods, and had start-ed for the interior with a light heart, and no more idea of what would happen to him than a baby. He had been wandering about that river for nearly two years alone, cut off from everybody and everything. 'I am not so young as I look. I am twenty-five,' he said. 'At first old Van Shuyten would tell me to go to the devil,' he narrated with

---

6. A smooth linen fabric.   7. A province of Western Russia.

keen enjoyment; 'but I stuck to him, and talked and talked, till at last he got afraid I would talk the hind-leg off his favorite dog, so he gave me some cheap things and a few guns, and told me he hoped he would never see my face again. Good old Dutchman, Van Shuyten. I sent him one small lot of ivory a year ago, so that he can't call me a little thief when I get back. I hope he got it. And for the rest, I don't care. I had some wood stacked for you. That was my old house. Did you see?'

"I gave him Towson's book. He made as though he would kiss me, but restrained himself. 'The only book I had left, and I thought I had lost it,' he said, looking at it ecstatically. 'So many accidents happen to a man going about alone, you know. Canoes get upset sometimes—and sometimes you've got to clear out so quick when the people get angry.' He thumbed the pages. 'You made notes in Russian?' I asked. He nodded. 'I thought they were written in cipher,' I said. He laughed, then became serious. 'I had lots of trouble to keep these people off,' he said. 'Did they want to kill you?' I asked. 'Oh no!' he cried, and checked himself. 'Why did they attack us?' I pursued. He hesitated, then said shamefacedly, 'They don't want him to go.' 'Don't they?' I said, curiously. He nodded a nod full of mystery and wisdom. 'I tell you,' he cried, 'this man has enlarged my mind.' He opened his arms wide, staring at me with his little blue eyes that were perfectly round."

3

"I looked at him, lost in astonishment. There he was before me, in motley, as though he had absconded from a troupe of mimes, enthusiastic, fabulous. His very existence was improbable, inexplicable, and altogether bewildering. He was an insoluble problem. It was inconceivable how he had existed, how he had succeeded in getting so far, how he had managed to remain—why he did not instantly disappear. 'I went a little farther,' he said, 'then still a little farther—till I had gone so far that I don't know how I'll ever get back. Never mind. Plenty time. I can manage. You take Kurtz away quick—quick—I tell you.' The glamour of youth enveloped his particoloured rags, his destitution, his loneliness, the essential desolation of his futile wanderings. For months—for years—his life hadn't been worth a day's purchase; and there he was gallantly, thoughtlessly alive, to all appearance indestructible solely by the virtue of his few years and of his unreflecting audacity. I was seduced into something like admiration—like envy. Glamour urged him on, glamour kept him unscathed. He surely wanted nothing from the wilderness but space to breathe in and to push on through. His need was to exist, and to move onwards at the greatest possible risk, and with a maximum of privation. If the absolutely pure, uncalculating, unpractical spirit of adventure had ever ruled a human being, it ruled this be-patched youth. I almost envied him the possession of this modest and clear flame. It seemed to have consumed all thought of self so completely, that, even while he was talking to you, you forgot that it was he—the man before your eyes—who had gone through these things. I did not envy him his devotion to Kurtz, though. He had not meditated over it. It came to him, and he accepted it with a sort of eager fatalism. I must say that to me it appeared about the most dangerous thing in every way he had come upon so far.

"They had come together unavoidably, like two ships becalmed near each other, and lay rubbing sides at last. I suppose Kurtz wanted an audience, because on a certain occasion, when encamped in the forest, they had talked all night, or more probably Kurtz had talked. 'We talked of everything,' he said, quite transported at the recollection. 'I forgot there was such a thing as sleep. The night did not seem to last an hour. Everything! Everything! . . . Of love too.' 'Ah, he talked to you of love!' I said, much amused. 'It isn't what you think,' he cried, almost passionately. 'It was in general. He made me see things—things.'

"He threw his arms up. We were on deck at the time, and the headman of my wood-cutters, lounging near by, turned upon him his heavy and glittering eyes. I looked around, and I don't know why, but I assure you that never, never before, did this land, this river, this jungle, the very arch of this blazing sky, appear to me so hopeless and so dark, so impenetrable to human thought, so pitiless to human weakness. 'And, ever since, you have been with him, of course?' I said.

"On the contrary. It appears their intercourse had been very much broken by various causes. He had, as he informed me proudly, managed to nurse Kurtz through two illnesses (he alluded to it as you would to some risky feat), but as a rule Kurtz wandered alone, far in the depths of the forest. 'Very often coming to this station, I had to wait days and days before he would turn up,' he said. 'Ah, it was worth waiting for!—sometimes.' 'What was he doing? exploring or what?' I asked. 'Oh yes, of course'; he had discovered lots of villages, a lake too—he did not know exactly in what direction; it was dangerous to inquire too much—but mostly his expeditions had been for ivory. 'But he had no goods to trade with by that time,' I objected. 'There's a good lot of cartridges left even yet,' he answered, looking away. 'To speak plainly, he raided the country,' I said. He nodded. 'Not alone, surely!' He muttered something about the villages round that lake. 'Kurtz got the tribe to follow him, did he?' I suggested. He fidgeted a little. 'They adored him,' he said. The tone of these words was so extraordinary that I looked at him searchingly. It was curious to see his mingled eagerness and reluctance to speak of Kurtz. The man filled his life, occupied his thoughts, swayed his emotions. 'What can you expect?' he burst out; 'he came to them with thunder and lightning, you know—and they had never seen anything like it—and very terrible. He could be very terrible. You can't judge Mr Kurtz as you would an ordinary man. No, no, no! Now—just to give you an idea—I don't mind telling you, he wanted to shoot me too one day—but I don't judge him.' 'Shoot you!' I cried. 'What for?' 'Well, I had a small lot of ivory the chief of that village near my house gave me. You see I used to shoot game for them. Well, he wanted it, and wouldn't hear reason. He declared he would shoot me unless I gave him the ivory and then cleared out of the country, because he could do so, and had a fancy for it, and there was nothing on earth to prevent him killing whom he jolly well pleased. And it was true too. I gave him the ivory. What did I care! But I didn't clear out. No, no. I couldn't leave him. I had to be careful, of course, till we got friendly again for a time. He had his second illness then. Afterwards I had to keep out of the way; but I didn't mind. He was living for the most part in those villages on the lake. When he came down to the river, sometimes he would take to me, and sometimes it was better for me to be careful. This man suffered too much. He hated all this, and somehow he couldn't get away. When I had a chance I begged him to try and leave while there was time; I offered to go back with him. And he would say yes, and then he would remain; go off on another ivory hunt; disappear for weeks; forget himself amongst these people—forget himself—you know.' 'Why! he's mad,' I said. He protested indignantly. Mr Kurtz couldn't be mad. If I had heard him talk, only two days ago, I wouldn't dare hint at such a thing. . . . I had taken up my binoculars while we talked, and was looking at the shore, sweeping the limit of the forest at each side and at the back of the house. The consciousness of there being people in that bush, so silent, so quiet—as silent and quiet as the ruined house on the hill—made me uneasy. There was no sign on the face of nature of this amazing tale that was not so much told as suggested to me in desolate exclamations, completed by shrugs, in interrupted phrases, in hints ending in deep sighs. The woods were unmoved, like a mask—heavy, like the closed door of a prison—they looked with their air of hidden knowledge, of patient expectation, of unapproachable silence. The Russian was explaining to me that it was only lately that Mr Kurtz had come down to the river, bringing along with him all the fighting men of that lake tribe. He had been absent for several months—getting himself adored, I suppose—and had come down unexpectedly, with the intention to all appearance of making a raid either across the river or down stream. Evidently the appetite for more ivory had got the better of the—what shall I say?—less material aspirations. However, he had got much worse suddenly. 'I heard he was lying helpless, and so I came up—took my chance,' said the Russian. 'Oh, he is bad, very bad.' I directed my glass to the house. There were no signs of life, but there was the ruined roof, the long mud wall peeping above the grass, with three little square window-holes, no two of the same size; all this brought within reach of my hand, as it were. And then I made a brusque movement, and one of the remaining posts of that vanished fence leaped up in the field of my glass. You remember I told you I had been struck at the distance by certain attempts at ornamentation, rather remarkable in the ruinous aspect of the place. Now I had suddenly a nearer view, and its first result was to make me throw my head back as if before a blow. Then I went carefully from post to post with my glass, and I saw my mistake. These round knobs were not ornamental but symbolic; they were expressive and puzzling, striking and disturbing—food for thought and also for the vultures if there had been any looking down from the sky; but at all events for such ants as were industrious enough to ascend the pole. They would have been even more impressive, those heads on the stakes, if their faces had not been turned to the house. Only one, the first I had made out, was facing my way. I was not so shocked as you may think. The start back I had given was really nothing but a movement of surprise. I had expected to see a knob of wood there, you know. I returned deliberately to the first I had seen—and there it was, black, dried, sunken, with closed eyelids,—a head that seemed to sleep at the top of that pole, and, with the shrunken dry lips showing a narrow white line of the teeth, was smiling too, smiling continuously at some endless and jocose dream of that eternal slumber.

"I am not disclosing any trade secrets. In fact the manager said afterwards that Mr Kurtz's methods had ruined the district. I have no opinion on that point, but I want you clearly to understand that there was nothing exactly profitable in these heads being there. They only showed that Mr Kurtz lacked restraint in the gratification of his various lusts, that there was something wanting in him—some small matter which, when the pressing need arose, could not be found under his magnificent eloquence. Whether he knew of this deficiency himself I can't say. I think the knowledge came to him at last—only at the very last. But the wilderness had found him out early, and had taken on him a terrible vengeance for the fantastic invasion. I think it had whispered to him things about himself which he did not know, things of which he had no conception till he took counsel with this great solitude—and the whisper had proved irresistibly fascinating. It echoed loudly within him because he was hollow at the core. . . . I put down the glass, and the head that had appeared near enough to be spoken to seemed at once to have leaped away from me into inaccessible distance.

"The admirer of Mr Kurtz was a bit crestfallen. In a hurried, indistinct voice he began to assure me he had not dared to take these—say, symbols—down. He was not afraid of the natives; they would not stir till Mr Kurtz gave the word. His ascendancy was extraordinary. The camps of these people surrounded the place, and the chiefs came every day to see him. They would crawl . . . 'I don't want to know anything of the ceremonies used when approaching Mr Kurtz,' I shouted. Curious, this feeling that came over me that such details would be more intolerable than those heads drying on the stakes under Mr Kurtz's windows. After all, that was only a savage sight, while I seemed at one bound to have been transported into some lightless region of subtle horrors, where pure, uncomplicated savagery was a positive relief, being something that had a right to exist—obviously—in the sunshine. The young man looked at me with surprise. I suppose it did not occur to him Mr Kurtz was no idol of mine. He forgot I hadn't heard any of these splendid monologues on, what was it? on love, justice, conduct of life—or what not. If it had come to crawling before Mr Kurtz, he crawled as much as the veriest savage of them all. I had no idea of the conditions, he said: these heads were the heads of rebels. I shocked him excessively by laughing. Rebels! What would be the next definition I was to hear? There had been enemies, criminals, workers—and these were rebels. Those rebellious heads looked very subdued to me on their sticks. 'You don't know how such a life tries a man like Kurtz,' cried Kurtz's last disciple. 'Well, and you?' I said. 'I! I! I am a simple man. I have no great thoughts. I want nothing from anybody. How can you compare me to . . . ?' His feelings were too much for speech, and suddenly he broke down. 'I don't understand,' he groaned. 'I've been doing my best to keep him alive, and that's enough. I had no hand in all this. I have no abilities. There hasn't been a drop of medicine or a mouthful of invalid food for months here. He was shamefully abandoned. A man like this, with such ideas. Shamefully! Shamefully! I—I—haven't slept for the last ten nights. . . .'

"His voice lost itself in the calm of the evening. The long shadows of the forest had slipped down-hill while we talked, had gone far beyond the ruined hovel, beyond the symbolic row of stakes. All this was in the gloom, while we down there were yet in the sunshine, and the stretch of the river abreast of the clearing glittered in a still and dazzling splendour, with a murky and overshadowed bend above and below. Not a living soul was seen on the shore. The bushes did not rustle.

"Suddenly round the corner of the house a group of men appeared, as though they had come up from the ground. They waded waist-deep in the grass, in a compact body, bearing an improvised stretcher in their midst. Instantly, in the emptiness of the landscape, a cry arose whose shrillness pierced the still air like a sharp arrow flying straight to the very heart of the land; and, as if by enchantment, streams of human beings—of naked human beings—with spears in their hands, with bows, with shields, with wild glances and savage movements, were poured into the clearing by the dark-faced and pensive forest. The bushes shook, the grass swayed for a time, and then everything stood still in attentive immobility.

" 'Now, if he does not say the right thing to them we are all done for,' said the Russian at my elbow. The knot of men with the stretcher had stopped too, half-way to the steamer, as if petrified. I saw the man on the stretcher sit up, lank and with an uplifted arm, above the shoulders of the bearers. 'Let us hope that the man who can talk so well of love in general will find some particular reason to spare us this time,' I said. I resented bitterly the absurd danger of our situation, as if to be at the mercy of that atrocious phantom had been a dishonouring necessity. I could not hear a sound, but through my glasses I saw the thin arm extended commandingly, the lower jaw moving, the eyes of that apparition shining darkly far in its bony head that nodded with grotesque jerks. Kurtz—Kurtz—that means 'short' in German—don't it? Well, the name was as true as everything else in his life—and death. He looked at least seven feet long. His covering had fallen off, and his body emerged from it pitiful and appalling as from a winding-sheet. I could see the cage of his ribs all astir, the bones of his arm waving. It was as though an animated image of death carved out of old ivory had been shaking its hand with menaces at a motionless crowd of men made of dark and glittering bronze. I saw him open his mouth wide—it gave him a weirdly voracious aspect, as though he had wanted to swallow all the air, all the earth, all the men before him. A deep voice reached me faintly. He must have been shouting. He fell back suddenly. The stretcher shook as the bearers staggered forward again, and almost at the same time I noticed that the crowd of savages was vanishing without any perceptible movement of retreat, as if the forest that had ejected these beings so suddenly had drawn them in again as the breath is drawn in a long aspiration.

"Some of the pilgrims behind the stretcher carried his arms—two shot-guns, a heavy rifle, and a light revolver-carbine—the thunderbolts of that pitiful Jupiter. The manager bent over him murmuring as he walked beside his head. They laid him down in one of the little cabins—just a room for a bed-place and a camp-stool or two, you know. We had brought his belated correspondence, and a lot of torn envelopes and open letters littered his bed. His hand roamed feebly amongst these papers. I was struck by the fire of his eyes and the composed languor of his expression. It was not so much the exhaustion of disease. He did not seem in pain. This shadow looked satiated and calm, as though for the moment it had had its fill of all the emotions.

"He rustled one of the letters, and looking straight in my face said, 'I am glad.' Somebody had been writing to him about me. These special recommendations were turning up again. The volume of tone he emitted without effort, almost without the trouble of moving his lips, amazed me. A voice! a voice! It was grave, profound, vibrating, while the man did not seem capable of a whisper. However, he had enough strength in him—factitious no doubt—to very nearly make an end of us, as you shall hear directly.

"The manager appeared silently in the doorway; I stepped out at once and he drew the curtain after me. The Russian, eyed curiously by the pilgrims, was staring at the shore. I followed the direction of his glance.

"Dark human shapes could be made out in the distance, flitting indistinctly against the gloomy border of the forest, and near the river two bronze figures, leaning on tall spears, stood in the sunlight under fantastic head-dresses of spotted skins, warlike and still in statuesque repose. And from right to left along the lighted shore moved a wild and gorgeous apparition of a woman.

"She walked with measured steps, draped in striped and fringed cloths, treading the earth proudly, with a slight jingle and flash of barbarous ornaments. She carried her head high; her hair was done in the shape of a helmet; she had brass leggings to the knee, brass wire gauntlets to the elbow, a crimson spot on her tawny cheek, innumerable necklaces of glass beads on her neck; bizarre things, charms, gifts of witchmen, that hung about her, glittered and trembled at every step. She must have had the value of several elephant tusks upon her. She was savage and superb, wild-eyed and magnificent; there was something ominous and stately in her deliberate progress. And in the hush that had fallen suddenly upon the whole sorrowful land, the immense wilderness, the colossal body of the fecund and mysterious life seemed to look at her, pensive, as though it had been looking at the image of its own tenebrous and passionate soul.

"She came abreast of the steamer, stood still, and faced us. Her long shadow fell to the water's edge. Her face had a tragic and fierce aspect of wild sorrow and of dumb pain mingled with the fear of some struggling, half-shaped resolve. She stood looking at us without a stir, and like the wilderness itself, with an air of brooding over an inscrutable purpose. A whole minute passed, and then she made a step forward. There was a low jingle, a glint of yellow metal, a sway of fringed draperies, and she stopped as if her heart had failed her. The young fellow by my side growled. The pilgrims murmured at my back. She looked at us all as if her life had depended upon the unswerving steadiness of her glance. Suddenly she opened her bared arms and threw them up rigid above her head, as though in an uncontrollable desire to touch the sky, and at the same time the swift shadows darted out on the earth, swept around on the river, gathering the steamer in a shadowy embrace. A formidable silence hung over the scene.

"She turned away slowly, walked on, following the bank, and passed into the bushes to the left. Once only her eyes gleamed back at us in the dusk of the thickets before she disappeared.

"'If she had offered to come aboard I really think I would have tried to shoot her,' said the man of patches, nervously. 'I had been risking my life every day for the last fortnight to keep her out of the house. She got in one day and kicked up a row about those miserable rags I picked up in the storeroom to mend my clothes with. I wasn't decent. At least it must have been that, for she talked like a fury to Kurtz for an hour, pointing at me now and then. I don't understand the dialect of this tribe. Luckily for me, I fancy Kurtz felt too ill that day to care, or there would have been mischief. I don't understand. . . . No—it's too much for me. Ah, well, it's all over now.'

"At this moment I heard Kurtz's deep voice behind the curtain, 'Save me!—save the ivory, you mean. Don't tell me. Save *me!* Why, I've had to save you. You are interrupting my plans now. Sick! Sick! Not so sick as you would like to believe. Never mind. I'll carry my ideas out yet—I will return. I'll show you what can be done. You with your little peddling notions—you are interfering with me. I will return. I . . .'

"The manager came out. He did me the honour to take me under the arm and lead me aside. 'He is very low, very low,' he said. He considered it necessary to sigh, but neglected to be consistently sorrowful. 'We have done all we could for him—haven't we? But there is no disguising the fact, Mr Kurtz has done more harm than good to the Company. He did not see the time was not ripe for vigorous action. Cautiously, cautiously—that's my principle. We must be cautious yet. The district is closed to us for a time. Deplorable! Upon the whole, the trade will suffer. I don't deny there is a remarkable quantity of ivory—mostly fossil. We must save it, at all events—but look how precarious the position is—and why? Because the method is unsound.' 'Do you,' said I, looking at the shore, 'call it "unsound method"?' 'Without doubt,' he exclaimed, hotly. 'Don't you?' . . . 'No method at all,' I murmured after a while. 'Exactly,' he exulted. 'I anticipated this. Shows a complete want of judgment. It is my duty to point it out in the proper quarter.' 'Oh,' said I, 'that fellow—what's his name?—the brickmaker, will make a readable report for you.' He appeared confounded for a moment. It seemed to me I had never breathed an atmosphere so vile, and I turned mentally to Kurtz for relief—positively for relief. 'Nevertheless, I think Mr Kurtz is a remarkable man,' I said with emphasis. He started, dropped on me a cold heavy glance, said very quietly, 'He was,' and turned his back on me. My hour of favour was over; I found myself lumped along with Kurtz as a partisan of methods for which the time was not ripe: I was unsound! Ah! but it was something to have at least a choice of nightmares.

"I had turned to the wilderness really, not to Mr Kurtz, who, I was ready to admit, was as good as buried. And for a moment it seemed to me as if I also were buried in a vast grave full of unspeakable secrets. I felt an intolerable weight

oppressing my breast, the smell of the damp earth, the unseen presence of victorious corruption, the darkness of an impenetrable night. . . . The Russian tapped me
on the shoulder. I heard him mumbling and stammering something about 'brother
seaman—couldn't conceal—knowledge of matters that would affect Mr Kurtz's
reputation.' I waited. For him evidently Mr Kurtz was not in his grave; I suspect
that for him Mr Kurtz was one of the immortals. 'Well!' said I at last, 'speak out. As
it happens, I am Mr Kurtz's friend—in a way.'

   "He stated with a good deal of formality that had we not been 'of the same profession,' he would have kept the matter to himself without regard to consequences.
He suspected 'there was an active ill-will towards him on the part of these white men
that—' 'You are right,' I said, remembering a certain conversation I had overheard.
'The manager thinks you ought to be hanged.' He showed a concern at this intelligence which amused me at first. 'I had better get out of the way quietly,' he said,
earnestly. 'I can do no more for Kurtz now, and they would soon find some excuse.
What's to stop them? There's a military post three hundred miles from here.' 'Well,
upon my word,' said I, 'perhaps you had better go if you have any friends amongst the
savages near by.' 'Plenty,' he said. 'They are simple people—and I want nothing, you
know.' He stood biting his lip, then: 'I don't want any harm to happen to these
whites here, but of course I was thinking of Mr Kurtz's reputation—but you are a
brother seaman and—' 'All right,' said I, after a time. 'Mr Kurtz's reputation is safe
with me.' I did not know how truly I spoke.

   "He informed me, lowering his voice, that it was Kurtz who had ordered the attack
to be made on the steamer. 'He hated sometimes the idea of being taken away—and
then again . . . But I don't understand these matters. I am a simple man. He thought it
would scare you away—that you would give it up, thinking him dead. I could not stop
him. Oh, I had an awful time of it this last month.' 'Very well,' I said. 'He is all right
now.' 'Ye-e-es,' he muttered, not very convinced apparently. 'Thanks,' said I; 'I shall
keep my eyes open.' 'But quiet—eh?' he urged, anxiously. 'It would be awful for his reputation if anybody here—' I promised a complete discretion with great gravity. 'I have a
canoe and three black fellows waiting not very far. I am off. Could you give me a few
Martini-Henry cartridges?' I could, and did, with proper secrecy. He helped himself,
with a wink at me, to a handful of my tobacco. 'Between sailors—you know—good
English tobacco.' At the door of the pilot-house he turned round—'I say, haven't you a
pair of shoes you could spare?' He raised one leg. 'Look.' The soles were tied with knotted strings sandal-wise under his bare feet. I rooted out an old pair, at which he looked
with admiration before tucking it under his left arm. One of his pockets (bright red)
was bulging with cartridges, from the other (dark blue) peeped 'Towson's Inquiry,' &c.,
&c. He seemed to think himself excellently well equipped for a renewed encounter
with the wilderness. 'Ah! I'll never, never meet such a man again. You ought to have
heard him recite poetry—his own too it was, he told me. Poetry!' He rolled his eyes at
the recollection of these delights. 'Oh, he enlarged my mind!' 'Good-bye,' said I. He
shook hands and vanished in the night. Sometimes I ask myself whether I had ever
really seen him—whether it was possible to meet such a phenomenon! . . .

   "When I woke up shortly after midnight his warning came to my mind with its
hint of danger that seemed, in the starred darkness, real enough to make me get up
for the purpose of having a look round. On the hill a big fire burned, illuminating fit-
fully a crooked corner of the station-house. One of the agents with a picket of a few
of our blacks, armed for the purpose, was keeping guard over the ivory; but deep within the forest, red gleams that wavered, that seemed to sink and rise from the ground
amongst confused columnar shapes of intense blackness, showed the exact position

of the camp where Mr Kurtz's adorers were keeping their uneasy vigil. The monotonous beating of a big drum filled the air with muffled shocks and a lingering vibration. A steady droning sound of many men chanting each to himself some weird incantation came out from the black, flat wall of the woods as the humming of bees comes out of a hive, and had a strange narcotic effect upon my half-awake senses. I believe I dozed off leaning over the rail, till an abrupt burst of yells, an overwhelming outbreak of a pent-up and mysterious frenzy, woke me up in a bewildered wonder. It was cut short all at once, and the low droning went on with an effect of audible and soothing silence. I glanced casually into the little cabin. A light was burning within, but Mr Kurtz was not there.

"I think I would have raised an outcry if I had believed my eyes. But I didn't believe them at first—the thing seemed so impossible. The fact is, I was completely unnerved by a sheer blank fright, pure abstract terror, unconnected with any distinct shape of physical danger. What made this emotion so overpowering was—how shall I define it?—the moral shock I received, as if something altogether monstrous, intolerable to thought and odious to the soul, had been thrust upon me unexpectedly. This lasted of course the merest fraction of a second, and then the usual sense of commonplace, deadly danger, the possibility of a sudden onslaught and massacre, or something of the kind, which I saw impending, was positively welcome and composing. It pacified me, in fact, so much, that I did not raise an alarm.

"There was an agent buttoned up inside an ulster[8] and sleeping on a chair on deck within three feet of me. The yells had not awakened him; he snored very slightly; I left him to his slumbers and leaped ashore. I did not betray Mr Kurtz—it was ordered I should never betray him—it was written I should be loyal to the nightmare of my choice. I was anxious to deal with this shadow by myself alone,—and to this day I don't know why I was so jealous of sharing with any one the peculiar blackness of that experience.

"As soon as I got on the bank I saw a trail—a broad trail through the grass. I remember the exultation with which I said to myself, 'He can't walk—he is crawling on all-fours—I've got him.' The grass was wet with dew. I strode rapidly with clenched fists. I fancy I had some vague notion of falling upon him and giving him a drubbing. I don't know. I had some imbecile thoughts. The knitting old woman with the cat obtruded herself upon my memory as a most improper person to be sitting at the other end of such an affair. I saw a row of pilgrims squirting lead in the air out of Winchesters held to the hip. I thought I would never get back to the steamer, and imagined myself living alone and unarmed in the woods to an advanced age. Such silly things—you know. And I remember I confounded the beat of the drum with the beating of my heart, and was pleased at its calm regularity.

"I kept to the track though—then stopped to listen. The night was very clear: a dark blue space, sparkling with dew and starlight, in which black things stood very still. I thought I could see a kind of motion ahead of me. I was strangely cocksure of everything that night. I actually left the track and ran in a wide semicircle (I verily believe chuckling to myself) so as to get in front of that stir, of that motion I had seen—if indeed I had seen anything. I was circumventing Kurtz as though it had been a boyish game.

"I came upon him, and, if he had not heard me coming, I would have fallen over him too, but he got up in time. He rose, unsteady, long, pale, indistinct, like a vapour

8. Long overcoat.

exhaled by the earth, and swayed slightly, misty and silent before me; while at my back the fires loomed between the trees, and the murmur of many voices issued from the forest. I had cut him off cleverly; but when actually confronting him I seemed to come to my senses, I saw the danger in its right proportion. It was by no means over yet. Suppose he began to shout? Though he could hardly stand, there was still plenty of vigour in his voice. 'Go away—hide yourself,' he said, in that profound tone. It was very awful. I glanced back. We were within thirty yards from the nearest fire. A black figure stood up, strode on long black legs, waving long black arms, across the glow. It had horns—antelope horns, I think—on its head. Some sorcerer, some witch-man, no doubt: it looked fiend-like enough. 'Do you know what you are doing?' I whispered. 'Perfectly,' he answered, raising his voice for that single word: it sounded to me far off and yet loud, like a hail through a speaking-trumpet. If he makes a row we are lost, I thought to myself. This clearly was not a case for fisticuffs, even apart from the very natural aversion I had to beat that Shadow—this wandering and tormented thing. 'You will be lost,' I said—'utterly lost.' One gets sometimes such a flash of inspiration, you know. I did say the right thing, though indeed he could not have been more irretrievably lost than he was at this very moment, when the foundations of our intimacy were being laid—to endure—to endure—even to the end—even beyond.

"'I had immense plans,' he muttered irresolutely. 'Yes,' said I; 'but if you try to shout I'll smash your head with—' there was not a stick or a stone near. 'I will throttle you for good,' I corrected myself. 'I was on the threshold of great things,' he pleaded, in a voice of longing, with a wistfulness of tone that made my blood run cold. 'And now for this stupid scoundrel—' 'Your success in Europe is assured in any case,' I affirmed, steadily. I did not want to have the throttling of him, you understand—and indeed it would have been very little use for any practical purpose. I tried to break the spell—the heavy, mute spell of the wilderness—that seemed to draw him to its pitiless breast by the awakening of forgotten and brutal instincts, by the memory of gratified and monstrous passions. This alone, I was convinced, had driven him out to the edge of the forest, to the bush, towards the gleam of fires, the throb of drums, the drone of weird incantations; this alone had beguiled his unlawful soul beyond the bounds of permitted aspirations. And, don't you see, the terror of the position was not in being knocked on the head—though I had a very lively sense of that danger too—but in this, that I had to deal with a being to whom I could not appeal in the name of anything high or low. I had, even like the niggers, to invoke him—himself—his own exalted and incredible degradation. There was nothing either above or below him, and I knew it. He had kicked himself loose of the earth. Confound the man! he had kicked the very earth to pieces. He was alone, and I before him did not know whether I stood on the ground or floated in the air. I've been telling you what we said—repeating the phrases we pronounced,—but what's the good? They were common everyday words,—the familiar, vague sounds exchanged on every waking day of life. But what of that? They had behind them, to my mind, the terrific suggestiveness of words heard in dreams, of phrases spoken in nightmares. Soul! If anybody had ever struggled with a soul, I am the man. And I wasn't arguing with a lunatic either. Believe me or not, his intelligence was perfectly clear—concentrated, it is true, upon himself with horrible intensity, yet clear; and therein was my only chance—barring, of course, the killing him there and then, which wasn't so good, on account of unavoidable noise. But his soul was mad. Being alone in the wilderness, it had looked within itself, and, by heavens! I tell you, it had gone mad. I had—for my sins, I suppose—to go through the ordeal of looking into it myself. No eloquence could have been so withering to one's belief in mankind as his final burst of sincerity. He struggled with himself, too. I saw it,—I heard it. I saw the inconceivable mystery of a soul that knew no restraint, no faith, and no fear, yet struggling blindly with itself. I kept my head pretty well; but when I had him at last stretched on the couch, I wiped my forehead, while my legs shook under me as though I had carried half a ton on my back down that hill. And yet I had only supported him, his bony arm clasped round my neck—and he was not much heavier than a child.

"When next day we left at noon, the crowd, of whose presence behind the curtain of trees I had been acutely conscious all the time, flowed out of the woods again, filled the clearing, covered the slope with a mass of naked, breathing, quivering, bronze bodies. I steamed up a bit, then swung down-stream, and two thousand eyes followed the evolutions of the splashing, thumping, fierce river-demon beating the water with its terrible tail and breathing black smoke into the air. In front of the first rank, along the river, three men, plastered with bright red earth from head to foot, strutted to and fro restlessly. When we came abreast again, they faced the river, stamped their feet, nodded their horned heads, swayed their scarlet bodies; they shook towards the fierce river-demon a bunch of black feathers, a mangy skin with a pendent tail—something that looked like a dried gourd; they shouted periodically together strings of amazing words that resembled no sounds of human language; and the deep murmurs of the crowd, interrupted suddenly, were like the responses of some satanic litany.

"We had carried Kurtz into the pilot-house: there was more air there. Lying on the couch, he stared through the open shutter. There was an eddy in the mass of human bodies, and the woman with helmeted head and tawny cheeks rushed out to the very brink of the stream. She put out her hands, shouted something, and all that wild mob took up the shout in a roaring chorus of articulated, rapid, breathless utterance.

" 'Do you understand this?' I asked.

"He kept on looking out past me with fiery, longing eyes, with a mingled expression of wistfulness and hate. He made no answer, but I saw a smile, a smile of indefinable meaning, appear on his colourless lips that a moment after twitched convulsively. 'Do I not?' he said slowly, gasping, as if the words had been torn out of him by a supernatural power.

"I pulled the string of the whistle, and I did this because I saw the pilgrims on deck getting out their rifles with an air of anticipating a jolly lark. At the sudden screech there was a movement of abject terror through that wedged mass of bodies. 'Don't! don't! you frighten them away,' cried some one on deck disconsolately. I pulled the string time after time. They broke and ran, they leaped, they crouched, they swerved, they dodged the flying terror of the sound. The three red chaps had fallen flat, face down on the shore, as though they had been shot dead. Only the barbarous and superb woman did not so much as flinch, and stretched tragically her bare arms after us over the sombre and glittering river.

"And then that imbecile crowd down on the deck started their little fun, and I could see nothing more for smoke.

"The brown current ran swiftly out of the heart of darkness, bearing us down towards the sea with twice the speed of our upward progress; and Kurtz's life was running swiftly too, ebbing, ebbing out of his heart into the sea of inexorable time. The manager was very placid, he had no vital anxieties now, he took us both in with a comprehensive and satisfied glance: the 'affair' had come off as well as could be wished. I saw the time approaching when I would be left alone of the party of 'unsound method.' The pilgrims looked upon me with disfavour. I was, so to speak, numbered with the dead. It is strange how I accepted this unforeseen partnership, this choice of nightmares forced upon me in the tenebrous land invaded by these mean and greedy phantoms.

"Kurtz discoursed. A voice! a voice! It rang deep to the very last. It survived his strength to hide in the magnificent folds of eloquence the barren darkness of his heart. Oh, he struggled! he struggled! The wastes of his weary brain were haunted by shadowy images now—images of wealth and fame revolving obsequiously round his unextinguishable gift of noble and lofty expression. My Intended, my station, my career, my ideas—these were the subjects for the occasional utterances of elevated sentiments. The shade of the original Kurtz frequented the bedside of the hollow sham, whose fate it was to be buried presently in the mould of primeval earth. But both the diabolic love and the unearthly hate of the mysteries it had penetrated fought for the possession of that soul satiated with primitive emotions, avid of lying fame, of sham distinction, of all the appearances of success and power.

"Sometimes he was contemptibly childish. He desired to have kings meet him at railway-stations on his return from some ghastly Nowhere, where he intended to accomplish great things. 'You show them you have in you something that is really profitable, and then there will be no limits to the recognition of your ability,' he would say. 'Of course you must take care of the motives—right motives—always.' The long reaches that were like one and the same reach, monotonous bends that were exactly alike, slipped past the steamer with their multitude of secular[9] trees looking patiently after this grimy fragment of another world, the forerunner of change, of conquest, of trade, of massacres, of blessings. I looked ahead—piloting. 'Close the shutter,' said Kurtz suddenly one day; 'I can't bear to look at this.' I did so. There was a silence. 'Oh, but I will wring your heart yet!' he cried at the invisible wilderness.

"We broke down—as I had expected—and had to lie up for repairs at the head of an island. This delay was the first thing that shook Kurtz's confidence. One morning he gave me a packet of papers and a photograph,—the lot tied together with a shoestring. 'Keep this for me,' he said. 'This noxious fool' (meaning the manager) 'is capable of prying into my boxes when I am not looking.' In the afternoon I saw him. He was lying on his back with closed eyes, and I withdrew quietly, but I heard him mutter, 'Live rightly, die, die . . .' I listened. There was nothing more. Was he rehearsing some speech in his sleep, or was it a fragment of a phrase from some newspaper article? He had been writing for the papers and meant to do so again, 'for the furthering of my ideas. It's a duty.'

"His was an impenetrable darkness. I looked at him as you peer down at a man who is lying at the bottom of a precipice where the sun never shines. But I had not much time to give him, because I was helping the engine-driver to take to pieces the leaky cylinders, to straighten a bent connecting-rod, and in other such matters. I lived in an infernal mess of rust, filings, nuts, bolts, spanners, hammers, ratchet-drills—things I abominate, because I don't get on with them. I tended the little forge we fortunately had aboard; I toiled wearily in a wretched scrap-heap—unless I had the shakes too bad to stand.

"One evening coming in with a candle I was startled to hear him say a little tremulously, 'I am lying here in the dark waiting for death.' The light was within a

9. Ancient.

foot of his eyes. I forced myself to murmur, 'Oh, nonsense!' and stood over him as if transfixed.

"Anything approaching the change that came over his features I have never seen before, and hope never to see again. Oh, I wasn't touched. I was fascinated. It was as though a veil had been rent. I saw on that ivory face the expression of sombre pride, of ruthless power, of craven terror—of an intense and hopeless despair. Did he live his life again in every detail of desire, temptation, and surrender during that supreme moment of complete knowledge? He cried in a whisper at some image, at some vision,—he cried out twice, a cry that was no more than a breath—

"'The horror! The horror!'

"I blew the candle out and left the cabin. The pilgrims were dining in the mess-room, and I took my place opposite the manager, who lifted his eyes to give me a questioning glance, which I successfully ignored. He leaned back, serene, with that peculiar smile of his sealing the unexpressed depths of his meanness. A continuous shower of small flies streamed upon the lamp, upon the cloth, upon our hands and faces. Suddenly the manager's boy put his insolent black head in the doorway, and said in a tone of scathing contempt—

"'Mistah Kurtz—he dead.'

"All the pilgrims rushed out to see. I remained, and went on with my dinner. I believe I was considered brutally callous. However, I did not eat much. There was a lamp in there—light, don't you know—and outside it was so beastly, beastly dark. I went no more near the remarkable man who had pronounced a judgment upon the adventures of his soul on this earth. The voice was gone. What else had been there? But I am of course aware that next day the pilgrims buried something in a muddy hole.

"And then they very nearly buried me.

"However, as you see, I did not go to join Kurtz there and then. I did not. I remained to dream the nightmare out to the end, and to show my loyalty to Kurtz once more. Destiny. My destiny! Droll thing life is—that mysterious arrangement of merciless logic for a futile purpose. The most you can hope from it is some knowledge of yourself—that comes too late—a crop of unextinguishable regrets. I have wrestled with death. It is the most unexciting contest you can imagine. It takes place in an impalpable greyness, with nothing underfoot, with nothing around, without spectators, without clamour, without glory, without the great desire of victory, without the great fear of defeat, in a sickly atmosphere of tepid scepticism, without much belief in your own right, and still less in that of your adversary. If such is the form of ultimate wisdom, then life is a greater riddle than some of us think it to be. I was within a hair's-breadth of the last opportunity for pronouncement, and I found with humiliation that probably I would have nothing to say. This is the reason why I affirm that Kurtz was a remarkable man. He had something to say. He said it. Since I had peeped over the edge myself, I understand better the meaning of his stare, that could not see the flame of the candle, but was wide enough to embrace the whole universe, piercing enough to penetrate all the hearts that beat in the darkness. He had summed up—he had judged. 'The horror!' He was a remarkable man. After all, this was the expression of some sort of belief; it had candour, it had conviction, it had a vibrating note of revolt in its whisper, it had the appalling face of a glimpsed truth—the strange commingling of desire and hate. And it is not my own extremity I remember best—a vision of greyness without form filled with physical pain, and a careless contempt for the evanescence of all things—even of this pain itself. No! It is his extremity that I seem to have lived through. True, he had made that last stride, he had stepped over the edge, while I had been permitted to draw back my hesitating foot. And perhaps in this is the whole difference; perhaps all the wisdom, and all truth, and all sincerity, are just compressed into that inappreciable moment of time in which we step over the threshold of the invisible. Perhaps! I like to think my summing-up would not have been a word of careless contempt. Better his cry—much better. It was an affirmation, a moral victory paid for by innumerable defeats, by abominable terrors, by abominable satisfactions. But it was a victory! That is why I have remained loyal to Kurtz to the last, and even beyond, when a long time after I heard once more, not his own voice, but the echo of his magnificent eloquence thrown to me from a soul as translucently pure as a cliff of crystal.

"No, they did not bury me, though there is a period of time which I remember mistily, with a shuddering wonder, like a passage through some inconceivable world that had no hope in it and no desire. I found myself back in the sepulchral city resenting the sight of people hurrying through the streets to filch a little money from each other, to devour their infamous cookery, to gulp their unwholesome beer, to dream their insignificant and silly dreams. They trespassed upon my thoughts. They were intruders whose knowledge of life was to me an irritating pretence, because I felt so sure they could not possibly know the things I knew. Their bearing, which was simply the bearing of commonplace individuals going about their business in the assurance of perfect safety, was offensive to me like the outrageous flauntings of folly in the face of a danger it is unable to comprehend. I had no particular desire to enlighten them, but I had some difficulty in restraining myself from laughing in their faces, so full of stupid importance. I daresay I was not very well at that time. I tottered about the streets—there were various affairs to settle—grinning bitterly at perfectly respectable persons. I admit my behaviour was inexcusable, but then my temperature was seldom normal in these days. My dear aunt's endeavours to 'nurse up my strength' seemed altogether beside the mark. It was not my strength that wanted nursing, it was my imagination that wanted soothing. I kept the bundle of papers given me by Kurtz, not knowing exactly what to do with it. His mother had died lately, watched over, as I was told, by his Intended. A clean-shaved man, with an official manner and wearing gold-rimmed spectacles, called on me one day and made inquiries, at first circuitous, afterwards suavely pressing, about what he was pleased to denominate certain 'documents.' I was not surprised, because I had had two rows with the manager on the subject out there. I had refused to give up the smallest scrap out of that package, and I took the same attitude with the spectacled man. He became darkly menacing at last, and with much heat argued that the Company had the right to every bit of information about its 'territories.' And, said he, 'Mr Kurtz's knowledge of unexplored regions must have been necessarily extensive and peculiar—owing to his great abilities and to the deplorable circumstances in which he had been placed: therefore—' I assured him Mr Kurtz's knowledge, however extensive, did not bear upon the problems of commerce or administration. He invoked then the name of science. 'It would be an incalculable loss if,' &c., &c. I offered him the report on the 'Suppression of Savage Customs,' with the postscriptum torn off. He took it up eagerly, but ended by sniffing at it with an air of contempt. 'This is not what we had a right to expect,' he remarked. 'Expect nothing else,' I said. 'There are only private letters.' He withdrew upon some threat of legal proceedings, and I saw him no more; but another fellow, calling himself Kurtz's cousin, appeared two days later, and was anxious to hear all the details about his dear relative's last moments. Incidentally he gave me to understand that Kurtz had been essentially a great musician. 'There was the making of an immense success,' said the man, who was an organist, I believe, with lank grey hair flowing over a greasy coat-collar. I had no reason to doubt his statement; and to this day I am unable to say what was Kurtz's profession, whether he ever had any—which was the greatest of his talents. I had taken him for a painter who wrote for the papers, or else for a journalist who could paint—but even the cousin (who took snuff during the interview) could not tell me what he had been—exactly. He was a universal genius—on that point I agreed with the old chap, who thereupon blew his nose noisily into a large cotton handkerchief and withdrew in senile agitation, bearing off some family letters and memoranda without importance. Ultimately a journalist anxious to know something of the fate of his 'dear colleague' turned up. This visitor informed me Kurtz's proper sphere ought to have been politics 'on the popular side.' He had furry straight eyebrows, bristly hair cropped short, an eye-glass on a broad ribbon, and, becoming expansive, confessed his opinion that Kurtz really couldn't write a bit—'but heavens! how that man could talk! He electrified large meetings. He had faith—don't you see?—he had the faith. He could get himself to believe anything—anything. He would have been a splendid leader of an extreme party.' 'What party?' I asked. 'Any party,' answered the other. 'He was an—an—extremist.' Did I not think so? I assented. Did I know, he asked, with a sudden flash of curiosity, 'what it was that had induced him to go out there?' 'Yes,' said I, and forthwith handed him the famous Report for publication, if he thought fit. He glanced through it hurriedly, mumbling all the time, judged 'it would do,' and took himself off with this plunder.

"Thus I was left at last with a slim packet of letters and the girl's portrait. She struck me as beautiful—I mean she had a beautiful expression. I know that the sunlight can be made to lie too, yet one felt that no manipulation of light and pose could have conveyed the delicate shade of truthfulness upon those features. She seemed ready to listen without mental reservation, without suspicion, without a thought for herself. I concluded I would go and give her back her portrait and those letters myself. Curiosity? Yes; and also some other feeling perhaps. All that had been Kurtz's had passed out of my hands: his soul, his body, his station, his plans, his ivory, his career. There remained only his memory and his Intended—and I wanted to give that up too to the past, in a way,—to surrender personally all that remained of him with me to that oblivion which is the last word of our common fate. I don't defend myself. I had no clear perception of what it was I really wanted. Perhaps it was an impulse of unconscious loyalty, or the fulfilment of one of those ironic necessities that lurk in the facts of human existence. I don't know. I can't tell. But I went.

"I thought his memory was like the other memories of the dead that accumulate in every man's life,—a vague impress on the brain of shadows that had fallen on it in their swift and final passage; but before the high and ponderous door, between the tall houses of a street as still and decorous as a well-kept alley in a cemetery, I had a vision of him on the stretcher, opening his mouth voraciously, as if to devour all the earth with all its mankind. He lived then before me; he lived as much as he had ever lived—a shadow insatiable of splendid appearances, of frightful realities; a shadow darker than the shadow of the night, and draped nobly in the folds of a gorgeous eloquence. The vision seemed to enter the house with me—the stretcher, the phantom-bearers, the wild crowd of obedient worshippers, the gloom of the forests, the glitter of the reach between the murky bends, the beat of the drum, regular and muffled like the beating of a heart—the heart of a conquering darkness. It was a moment of triumph for the wilderness, an invading and vengeful rush which, it seemed to me, I would have to keep back alone for the salvation of another soul. And the memory of what I had heard him say afar there, with the horned shapes stirring at my back, in the glow of fires, within the patient woods, those broken phrases came back to me, were heard again in their ominous and terrifying simplicity. I remembered his abject pleading, his abject threats, the colossal scale of his vile desires, the meanness, the torment, the tempestuous anguish of his soul. And later on I seemed to see his collected languid manner, when he said one day, 'This lot of ivory now is really mine. The Company did not pay for it. I collected it myself at a very great personal risk. I am afraid they will try to claim it as theirs though. H'm. It is a difficult case. What do you think I ought to do—resist? Eh? I want no more than justice.' . . . He wanted no more than justice—no more than justice. I rang the bell before a mahogany door on the first floor, and while I waited he seemed to stare at me out of the glassy panel—stare with that wide and immense stare embracing, condemning, loathing all the universe. I seemed to hear the whispered cry, 'The horror! The horror!'

"The dusk was falling. I had to wait in a lofty drawing-room with three long windows from floor to ceiling that were like three luminous and bedraped columns. The bent gilt legs and backs of the furniture shone in indistinct curves. The tall marble fireplace had a cold and monumental whiteness. A grand piano stood massively in a corner, with dark gleams on the flat surfaces like a sombre and polished sarcophagus. A high door opened—closed. I rose.

"She came forward, all in black, with a pale head, floating towards me in the dusk. She was in mourning. It was more than a year since his death, more than a year since the news came; she seemed as though she would remember and mourn for ever. She took both my hands in hers and murmured, 'I had heard you were coming.' I noticed she was not very young—I mean not girlish. She had a mature capacity for fidelity, for belief, for suffering. The room seemed to have grown darker, as if all the sad light of the cloudy evening had taken refuge on her forehead. This fair hair, this pale visage, this pure brow, seemed surrounded by an ashy halo from which the dark eyes looked out at me. Their glance was guileless, profound, confident, and trustful. She carried her sorrowful head as though she were proud of that sorrow, as though she would say, I—I alone know how to mourn for him as he deserves. But while we were still shaking hands, such a look of awful desolation came upon her face that I perceived she was one of those creatures that are not the playthings of Time. For her he had died only yesterday. And, by Jove! the impression was so powerful that for me too he seemed to have died only yesterday—nay, this very minute. I saw her and him in the same instant of time—his death and her sorrow—I saw her sorrow in the very moment of his death. Do you understand? I saw them together—I heard them together. She had said, with a deep catch of the breath, 'I have survived'; while my strained ears seemed to hear distinctly, mingled with her tone of despairing regret, the summing-up whisper of his eternal condemnation. I asked myself what I was doing there, with a sensation of panic in my heart as though I had blundered into a place of cruel and absurd mysteries not fit for a human being to behold. She motioned me to a chair. We sat down. I laid the packet gently on the little table, and she put her hand over it. . . . 'You knew him well,' she murmured, after a moment of mourning silence.

" 'Intimacy grows quickly out there,' I said. 'I knew him as well as it is possible for one man to know another.'

" 'And you admired him,' she said. 'It was impossible to know him and not to admire him. Was it?'

"'He was a remarkable man,' I said, unsteadily. Then before the appealing fixity of her gaze, that seemed to watch for more words on my lips, I went on, 'It was impossible not to—'

"'Love him,' she finished eagerly, silencing me into an appalled dumbness. 'How true! how true! But when you think that no one knew him so well as I! I had all his noble confidence. I knew him best.'

"'You knew him best,' I repeated. And perhaps she did. But with every word spoken the room was growing darker, and only her forehead, smooth and white, remained illumined by the unextinguishable light of belief and love.

"'You were his friend,' she went on. 'His friend,' she repeated, a little louder. 'You must have been, if he had given you this, and sent you to me. I feel I can speak to you—and oh! I must speak. I want you—you who have heard his last words—to know I have been worthy of him. . . . It is not pride. . . . Yes! I am proud to know I understood him better than any one on earth—he told me so himself. And since his mother died I have had no one—no one—to—to—'

"I listened. The darkness deepened. I was not even sure whether he had given me the right bundle. I rather suspect he wanted me to take care of another batch of his papers which, after his death, I saw the manager examining under the lamp. And the girl talked, easing her pain in the certitude of my sympathy; she talked as thirsty men drink. I had heard that her engagement with Kurtz had been disapproved by her people. He wasn't rich enough or something. And indeed I don't know whether he had not been a pauper all his life. He had given me some reason to infer that it was his impatience of comparative poverty that drove him out there.

"'. . . Who was not his friend who had heard him speak once?' she was saying. 'He drew men towards him by what was best in them.' She looked at me with intensity. 'It is the gift of the great,' she went on, and the sound of her low voice seemed to have the accompaniment of all the other sounds, full of mystery, desolation, and sorrow, I had ever heard—the ripple of the river, the soughing of the trees swayed by the wind, the murmurs of wild crowds, the faint ring of incomprehensible words cried from afar, the whisper of a voice speaking from beyond the threshold of an eternal darkness. 'But you have heard him! You know!' she cried.

"'Yes, I know,' I said with something like despair in my heart, but bowing my head before the faith that was in her, before that great and saving illusion that shone with an unearthly glow in the darkness, in the triumphant darkness from which I could not have defended her—from which I could not even defend myself.

"'What a loss to me—to us!'—she corrected herself with beautiful generosity; then added in a murmur, 'To the world.' By the last gleams of twilight I could see the glitter of her eyes, full of tears—of tears that would not fall.

"'I have been very happy—very fortunate—very proud,' she went on. 'Too fortunate. Too happy for a little while. And now I am unhappy for—for life.'

"She stood up; her fair hair seemed to catch all the remaining light in a glimmer of gold. I rose too.

"'And of all this,' she went on, mournfully, 'of all his promise, and of all his greatness, of his generous mind, of his noble heart, nothing remains—nothing but a memory. You and I—'

"'We shall always remember him,' I said, hastily.

"'No!' she cried. 'It is impossible that all this should be lost—that such a life should be sacrificed to leave nothing—but sorrow. You know what vast plans he had. I knew of them too—I could not perhaps understand,—but others knew of them. Something must remain. His words, at least, have not died.'

" 'His words will remain,' I said.

" 'And his example,' she whispered to herself. 'Men looked up to him,—his goodness shone in every act. His example—'

" 'True,' I said; 'his example too. Yes, his example. I forgot that.'

" 'But I do not. I cannot—I cannot believe—not yet. I cannot believe that I shall never see him again, that nobody will see him again, never, never, never.'

"She put out her arms as if after a retreating figure, stretching them black and with clasped pale hands across the fading and narrow sheen of the window. Never see him! I saw him clearly enough then. I shall see this eloquent phantom as long as I live, and I shall see her too, a tragic and familiar Shade, resembling in this gesture another one, tragic also, and bedecked with powerless charms, stretching bare brown arms over the glitter of the infernal stream, the stream of darkness. She said suddenly very low, 'He died as he lived.'

" 'His end,' said I, with dull anger stirring in me, 'was in every way worthy of his life.'

" 'And I was not with him,' she murmured. My anger subsided before a feeling of infinite pity.

" 'Everything that could be done—' I mumbled.

" 'Ah, but I believed in him more than any one on earth—more than his own mother, more than—himself. He needed me! Me! I would have treasured every sigh, every word, every sign, every glance.'

"I felt like a chill grip on my chest. 'Don't,' I said, in a muffled voice.

" 'Forgive me. I—I—have mourned so long in silence—in silence. . . . You were with him—to the last? I think of his loneliness. Nobody near to understand him as I would have understood. Perhaps no one to hear. . . .'

" 'To the very end,' I said, shakily. 'I heard his very last words. . . .' I stopped in a fright.

" 'Repeat them,' she said in a heart-broken tone. 'I want—I want—something—something—to—to live with.'

"I was on the point of crying at her, 'Don't you hear them?' The dusk was repeating them in a persistent whisper all around us, in a whisper that seemed to swell menacingly like the first whisper of a rising wind. 'The horror! the horror!'

" 'His last word—to live with,' she murmured. 'Don't you understand I loved him—I loved him—I loved him!'

"I pulled myself together and spoke slowly.

" 'The last word he pronounced was—your name.'

"I heard a light sigh, and then my heart stood still, stopped dead short by an exulting and terrible cry, by the cry of inconceivable triumph and of unspeakable pain. 'I knew it—I was sure!' . . . She knew. She was sure. I heard her weeping; she had hidden her face in her hands. It seemed to me that the house would collapse before I could escape, that the heavens would fall upon my head. But nothing happened. The heavens do not fall for such a trifle. Would they have fallen, I wonder, if I had rendered Kurtz that justice which was his due? Hadn't he said he wanted only justice? But I couldn't. I could not tell her. It would have been too dark—too dark altogether. . . ."

Marlow ceased, and sat apart, indistinct and silent, in the pose of a meditating Buddha. Nobody moved for a time. "We have lost the first of the ebb," said the Director, suddenly. I raised my head. The offing was barred by a black bank of clouds, and the tranquil waterway leading to the uttermost ends of the earth flowed sombre under an overcast sky—seemed to lead into the heart of an immense darkness.

Bernard Shaw

1856–1950

Few writers so dominate their times that their names become household words, let alone, as with (George) Bernard Shaw, their initials: three letters as identifiable during his lifetime as a brand name or a logo is today. G.B.S. was the shorthand code for one of the most celebrated and controversial writers of the twentieth century—a novelist, music critic, playwright, pamphleteer, political theorist, educator, and essayist. Shaw's life arc stretched a venerable ninety-four years from the midpoint of the nineteenth century to the midpoint of the twentieth. In his very long and almost unbelievably prolific career Shaw articulated most of the new ideas associated with modernity, whether in the dramatic form of the plays he is best remembered for today, or in the philosophical and political essays for which he was equally famed during his lifetime. He was awarded the Nobel Prize for literature in 1925, although in characteristically defiant fashion, he refused to accept the money, saying that the honor "is greater than is good for my spiritual health." By the same token, when the British government tried to award him the Order of Merit, he riposted, "I have already conferred it upon myself." So well known was he, and so influential as an iconoclast, that the adjective "Shavian" sprang from his last name, denoting a worldview of exuberant and profound contradictions, where opposing ideas are brought into comic, and ultimately serious, artistic and social synthesis.

A major force on the London stage and in British cultural life, Shaw was not conventionally British. He was Irish, born in Dublin in 1856, the third child of George Carr Shaw and Bessie Gurly. Brought up in "an awful little kennel with primitive sanitary arrangements" on Synge Street in Dublin, Shaw had a startlingly unusual childhood: his father, an alchoholic clerk on his way down the social scale, had permitted Shaw's mother Bessie to bring her vocal coach and lover, Vandeleur Lee, to live in the family house. As Shaw once remarked, Bessie "was simply not a wife or mother at all." Bessie's brother Walter Gurly, a ship's surgeon, was another part of the menage; an ebullient man who electrifyingly proclaimed his idiosyncratic views of the Bible, Gurly became Shaw's "third father." The eccentricities of his upbringing, with three fathers and an absentee mother, led to Shaw's firm belief that parents and children were inevitably mismatched, and to his strong activism for equal rights for all members of the family constellation.

Shaw's experiments with schooling were abysmal failures, largely because only vocational training was available to a family of his means, and by the age of fifteen he had seen his last of school, which he likened to a jail designed "to keep the little devils locked up where they cannot drive their mothers mad." What took the place of formal schooling was Shaw's self-education as a voracious reader of Homer, Shakespeare, Shelley, Dickens, and much popular literature—"all normal people require both classics and trash," he wrote—and his constant immersion in the rich musical life of Dublin. In 1873 his "father" Vandeleur Lee left for London to become a musical impresario, followed soon after by Bessie Shaw and young Bernard's two sisters, leaving Shaw essentially abandoned in Dublin. Thrown back on his own resources, he worked miserably as a clerk and lived in a rooming house, teaching himself to play the piano and organizing musicales with other clerks in their off hours. So acute did his misery grow that in 1876 he decided to go to London himself, and moved in with his mother, Lee, and his sister Lucy.

The move to London altered everything for Shaw. London was the cornucopia that the deprived and impoverished colonial city of Dublin was not, and Shaw was simultaneously intoxicated with its grandeur and disillusioned by its poverty and inequalities. He recognized London as "the literary center of the English language," and he quickly established himself as a budding essayist and critic, and a would-be playwright, while also writing four novels that received rejection notices labeling them "sordid" and "perverse." The hub of Shaw's endeavors was the British Museum's famous reading room and library. Sitting at his assigned carrel (unbeknownst to him, Lenin sat nearby), Shaw read large numbers of books, among them Karl Marx's *Das Kapital*, a book that ironically had been written in that very same reading room. "It was the only book that ever turned me upside down," Shaw confessed, and he began attending meetings of every radical society he could find, until the Fabian Society claimed his loyalty. He delivered a paper before the group in 1884, beginning a long career as a political theorist and polemicist, writing essays such as *The Intelligent Woman's Guide to Socialism and Capitalism*.

Shaw became a charismatic public lecturer on social and political topics, and he began to write art and music criticism. In vivid essays he argued that the innovations of such radical composers as Wagner were parallel to the radical changes in politics and social arrangements Shaw also championed. Like James Joyce, he fervently admired Henrik Ibsen, the Norwegian playwright whose plays seemed to sound the death knell for Victorian social certainties. Ibsen's *The Doll House*, for example, dramatized the growing movement for the emancipation of women, a cause Shaw adamantly supported. Ibsen's drama pointed the way for Shaw's own development into a great playwright: he realized through Ibsen's example that he need not adopt an "art for art's sake" philosophy, as the reigning vision of the *fin de siècle* described its ideal; instead, art could be fully engaged in ideas, and could have as its mission nothing less than changing the world.

Shaw struggled for seven years to break free of Victorian dramatic constraints and the rigid structures of nineteenth-century drama, until in 1895 he had created his first play, *Widower's Houses*. While the play is not particularly memorable, its subtitle does give a sense of the special goals of Shavian drama at this early stage: "An Original Didactic Realist Play in Three Acts, Designed to Induce People to Vote on the Progressive Side at the Next County Council in London." Art for art's sake, indeed. "Why would art if it was just for art's sake interest me at all?" Shaw asked.

The political play of ideas was the form Shaw crafted and perfected over the next thirty years, drawing on a rich history of political thought and philosophical inquiry. He borrowed from British thinkers like Carlyle and from the German philosopher Friedrich Nietzsche, whose controversial writings argued that human beings make their own truth and thus create their own values. In plays like *Man and Superman*, *Androcles and the Lion*, *Arms and the Man*, and *The Doctor's Dilemma*, Shaw staged debates over values that only seem to be universal or eternal, likening the contemporary values of Edwardian Britain to outmoded garments that his society should change. Shaw was a political iconoclast whose democratic ideals were meshed with an unsentimental acknowledgment of human nature. He wanted the best cultural goods—education, art, freedom from drudgery—to be distributed equally to all without regard to sex, class, or race. However, he never romanticized the working class nor any other political group, and, never a utopian, Shaw always argued that lasting change should gradually be pressed with pragmatism, common sense, and energetic wit.

The "Shavian" element of all the plays, and of Shaw's essays and reviews, resides in an unwillingness to propose a simple answer to social problems, or to establish a clear-cut "right" and "wrong." Shaw's thinking is dialectical in style: ideas bounce and ricochet off one another, and things happen in his plays by means of a quicksilver collision of ideas that yields a new and unexpected synthesis. Shaw's characters are not simply ideas dressed up to look like people; instead, the characters embody the ever-changing and often arbitrary flow of ideas as these come to life in real, quirky, individual human beings, embroiled in verbal duels. One of his characters puts it this way: "I want to be an active verb." There are no outright villains, and no pure heroes or heroines, in a Shaw play: for example, while ruthless capitalism is a social evil in Shaw's universe, his plays are full of capitalist *characters* who are wise and winning.

It is helpful—if somewhat dizzying—to remember that Bernard Shaw and Sigmund Freud were born in the same year, and that each man was a powerful voice in transforming modern ideas of sex, gender, and "the woman question." Shaw in fact commented on this unexpected affinity when he first stumbled on Freud's writings in 1911, and pronounced "I have said it all before him." For Freud, the Rosetta Stone of understanding was sex, and his great discovery was that women are also sexual beings. For Shaw, too, sex is everywhere, but it is never the problem—sex is liberating for men and women alike. Shaw was an ardent proponent of free love, and had many romances and affairs, although most of them appear to have been limited to the pages of his torrid correspondence. In 1898, at the age of forty-two, he married Charlotte Payne-Townshend, a wealthy supporter of Fabian socialist causes, but he remained attached, at least on paper, to several other women.

In his famous essay *The Quintessence of Ibsenism*, Shaw used his commentary on Ibsen's plays as a way of proclaiming his own discoveries about the New Woman: "There is no such species in creation as 'Woman, lovely Woman,' the woman being simply the female of the human species, and to have one conception of humanity for the woman and another for the man, or one law for the woman and another for the man, or one artistic convention for the woman and another for the man, or, for that matter, a skirt for the woman and a pair of breeches for the man . . . is unnatural and unworkable." Shaw was dedicated to tearing down what he saw as the oppressive veil of Victorian ideals of womanhood—that women are self-sacrificing, pure, noble, and passive. Women are usually the social visionaries in his plays, not because he thought of women as "better," or even as fundamentally different, but because their struggles with orthodoxy were basic. The modern woman can change into "modern dress"—the radical costumes of the mind—with much more ease and enthusiasm, indeed, more lightheartedly and playfully, than can men. By allying women with the newest of the new ideas, in plays including *Major Barbara, Mrs. Warren's Profession, Pygmalion, Misalliance*, and *Saint Joan*, Shaw indicates the excitement, the vitality, and the innovation behind women who have burst out of the confines of domestic duty.

Shaw's plays employ classic comic situations, with elements drawn from Roman comedy and from Shakespeare. Yet for all their classical economy, Shaw's plays feel experimental, perhaps because they are constructed musically rather than dramatically. Shaw, who is still considered to be the most distinguished music critic of modern times, loves to draw on the musical style of a harmony of voices rather than singling out one or two main protagonists, often creating a kind of chamber play that is reliant on its ensemble. *Pygmalion* has this ensemble structure—we don't get a "full" portrait of any single character in the play, since the characters, like the colored glass bits of a kaleidoscope, change in relation to one another and form new patterns from scene to scene.

Pygmalion—first performed in London and New York in 1914, and published in 1916—is Shaw's most enduringly popular play, due in no small part to the big-budget 1964 Warner Brothers film adaptation *My Fair Lady*, starring Rex Harrison as Professor Henry Higgins and Audrey Hepburn as Eliza Doolittle and featuring songs by the gifted team of Lerner and Loewe. *Pygmalion* foregrounds most of Shaw's characteristic themes: his distaste for and distrust of the British class system, his impatience with the second-class status afforded women in the early decades of the twentieth century, and the hollowness of what Eliza's father refers to as "middle class morality." *Pygmalion* is also characteristic in the way that Shaw uses comic means—as well as a long brow-beating postscript—to put his ideas for social reform across. In the end, aristocratic status is made to look like something of a parlor trick—and that while elegant costume and genteel pronunciation might get one accepted into polite society there is, as W. B. Yeats wrote in his poem "A Coat," "more enterprise / In walking naked."

Bernard Shaw is at once a brilliant comic dramatist—in his essays and his letters as in his plays—and one of the great political playwrights of modern British literature, infusing all his work with the conviction that our social, economic, and sexual lives need transformation. For Shaw, it is comedy and laughter that draw an audience into a generous, collective ensemble—one rather like the ensemble of characters in his plays, none of whom could exist as a full-fledged human being without the others. Shaw disarms us with laughter, dismantling our expectations about what is natural, necessary, or inevitable. In his comedy, words are deeds and gestures speak, always pointedly.

Pygmalion

Preface: A Professor of Phonetics

As will be seen later on, Pygmalion needs, not a preface, but a sequel, which I have supplied in its due place.

The English have no respect for their language, and will not teach their children to speak it. They cannot spell it because they have nothing to spell it with but an old foreign alphabet of which only the consonants—and not all of them—have any agreed speech value. Consequently no man can teach himself what it should sound like from reading it; and it is impossible for an Englishman to open his mouth without making some other Englishman despise him. Most European languages are now accessible in black and white to foreigners: English and French are not thus accessible even to Englishmen and Frenchmen. The reformer we need most today is an energetic phonetic enthusiast: that is why I have made such a one the hero of a popular play.

There have been heroes of that kind crying in the wilderness for many years past. When I became interested in the subject towards the end of the eighteen-seventies, the illustrious Alexander Melville Bell, the inventor of Visible Speech, had emigrated to Canada, where his son invented the telephone; but Alexander J. Ellis was still a London patriarch, with an impressive head always covered by a velvet skull cap, for which he would apologize to public meetings in a very courtly manner. He and Tito Pagliardini, another phonetic veteran, were men whom it was impossible to dislike. Henry Sweet, then a young man, lacked their sweetness of character: he was about as conciliatory to conventional mortals as Ibsen[1] or Samuel Butler.[2] His great ability as a phonetician (he was, I think, the best of them all at his job) would have entitled him to high official recognition, and perhaps enabled him to popularize his subject, but for his Satanic contempt for all academic dignitaries and persons in general who thought more of Greek than of phonetics. Once, in the days when the Imperial Institute rose in South Kensington, and Joseph Chamberlain[3] was booming the Empire, I induced the editor of a leading monthly review to commission an article from Sweet on the imperial importance of his subject. When it arrived, it contained nothing but a savagely derisive attack on a professor of language and literature whose chair Sweet regarded as proper to a phonetic expert only. The article, being libellous, had to be returned as impossible; and I had to renounce my dream of dragging its author into the limelight. When I met him afterwards, for the first time for many years, I found to my astonishment that he, who had been a quite tolerably presentable young man, had actually managed by sheer scorn to alter his personal appearance until he had become a sort of walking repudiation of Oxford and all its traditions. It must have been largely in his own despite that he was squeezed into something called a Readership of phonetics there. The future of phonetics rests probably with his pupils, who all swore by him; but nothing could bring the man himself into any sort of compliance with the university to which he nevertheless clung by divine right in an intensely Oxonian way. I daresay his papers, if he has left any, include some satires that may be published without too destructive results fifty years hence. He was, I believe, not in the least an ill-natured man: very much the opposite, I should say; but he would not suffer fools gladly; and to him all scholars who were not rabid phoneticians were fools.

1. Henrik Ibsen (1828–1906), Norwegian playwright whose realist plays dealing with contemporary social problems were a large influence on Shaw.

2. Samuel Butler (1835–1902), whose satirical novels were admired by Shaw.

3. Joseph Chamberlain (1836–1914), British statesman.

Those who knew him will recognize in my third act the allusion to the Current Shorthand in which he used to write postcards. It may be acquired from a four and sixpenny manual published by the Clarendon Press. The postcards which Mrs Higgins describes are such as I have received from Sweet. I would decipher a sound which a cockney would represent by *zerr*, and a Frenchman by *seu*, and then write demanding with some heat what on earth it meant. Sweet, with boundless contempt for my stupidity, would reply that it not only meant but obviously was the word Result, as no other word containing that sound, and capable of making sense with the context, existed in any language spoken on earth. That less expert mortals should require fuller indications was beyond Sweet's patience. Therefore, though the whole point of his Current Shorthand is that it can express every sound in the language perfectly, vowels as well as consonants, and that your hand has to make no stroke except the easy and current ones with which you write m, n, and u, l, p, and q, scribbling them at whatever angle comes easiest to you, his unfortunate determination to make this remarkable and quite legible script serve also as a shorthand reduced it in his own practice to the most inscrutable of cryptograms. His true objective was the provision of a full, accurate, legible script for our language; but he was led past that by his contempt for the popular Pitman system of shorthand, which he called the Pitfall system. The triumph of Pitman was a triumph of business organization: there was a weekly paper to persuade you to learn Pitman: there were cheap textbooks and exercise books and transcripts of speeches for you to copy, and schools where experienced teachers coached you up to the necessary proficiency. Sweet could not organize his market in that fashion. He might as well have been the Sybil who tore up the leaves of prophecy that nobody would attend to. The four and sixpenny manual, mostly in his lithographed hand-writing, that was never vulgarly advertized, may perhaps some day be taken up by a syndicate and pushed upon the public as The Times pushed the Encyclopaedia Britannica; but until then it will certainly not prevail against Pitman. I have bought three copies of it during my lifetime; and I am informed by the publishers that its cloistered existence is still a steady and healthy one. I actually learned the system two several[4] times; and yet the shorthand in which I am writing these lines is Pitman's. And the reason is, that my secretary cannot transcribe Sweet, having been perforce taught in the schools of Pitman. In America I could use the commercially organized Gregg shorthand, which has taken a hint from Sweet by making its letters writable (current, Sweet would have called them) instead of having to be geometrically drawn like Pitman's; but all these systems, including Sweet's, are spoilt by making them available for verbatim reporting, in which complete and exact spelling and word division are impossible. A complete and exact phonetic script is neither practicable nor necessary for ordinary use; but if we enlarge our alphabet to the Russian size, and make our spelling as phonetic as Spanish, the advance will be prodigious.

Pygmalion[5] Higgins is not a portrait of Sweet, to whom the adventure of Eliza Doolittle would have been impossible; still, as will be seen, there are touches of Sweet in the play. With Higgins's physique and temperament Sweet might have set the Thames on fire. As it was, he impressed himself professionally on Europe to an extent that made his comparative personal obscurity, and the failure of Oxford to do justice to his eminence, a puzzle to foreign specialists in his subject. I do not blame Oxford, because I think Oxford is quite right in demanding a certain social amenity

---

4. Different.
5. In Greek myth, Pygmalion was king of Cyprus and a sculptor; he fell in love with his own creation, and Aphrodite brought the statue, Galatea, to life.

from its nurslings (heaven knows it is not exorbitant in its requirements!); for although I well know how hard it is for a man of genius with a seriously underrated subject to maintain serene and kindly relations with the men who underrate it, and who keep all the best places for less important subjects which they profess without originality and sometimes without much capacity for them, still, if he overwhelms them with wrath and disdain, he cannot expect them to heap honors on him.

Of the later generations of phoneticians I know little. Among them towered Robert Bridges, to whom perhaps Higgins may owe his Miltonic sympathies, though here again I must disclaim all portraiture. But if the play makes the public aware that there are such people as phoneticians, and that they are among the most important people in England at present, it will serve its turn.

I wish to boast that Pygmalion has been an extremely successful play, both on stage and screen, all over Europe and North America as well as at home. It is so intensely and deliberately didactic, and its subject is esteemed so dry, that I delight in throwing it at the heads of the wiseacres who repeat the parrot cry that art should never be didactic. It goes to prove my contention that great art can never be anything else.

Finally, and for the encouragement of people troubled with accents that cut them off from all high employment, I may add that the change wrought by Professor Higgins in the flower-girl is neither impossible nor uncommon. The modern concierge's daughter who fulfils her ambition by playing the Queen of Spain in Ruy Blas at the Théâtre Français is only one of many thousands of men and women who have sloughed off their native dialects and acquired a new tongue. Our West End shop assistants and domestic servants are bi-lingual. But the thing has to be done scientifically, or the last state of the aspirant may be worse than the first. An honest slum dialect is more tolerable than the attempts of phonetically untaught persons to imitate the plutocracy. Ambitious flower-girls who read this play must not imagine that they can pass themselves off as fine ladies by untutored imitation. They must learn their alphabet over again, and different, from a phonetic expert. Imitation will only make them ridiculous.

NOTE FOR TECHNICIANS. A complete representation of the play as printed for the first time in this edition is technically possible only on the cinema screen or on stages furnished with exceptionally elaborate machinery. For ordinary theatrical use the scenes separated by rows of asterisks are to be omitted.

In the dialogue an e upside down indicates the indefinite vowel, sometimes called obscure or neutral, for which, though it is one of the commonest sounds in English speech, our wretched alphabet has no letter.

ACT 1

London at 11.15 p.m. Torrents of heavy summer rain. Cab whistles blowing frantically in all directions. Pedestrians running for shelter into the portico of St Paul's church (not Wren's[1] cathedral but Inigo Jones's[2] church in Covent Garden vegetable market), among them a lady and her daughter in evening dress. All are peering out gloomily at the rain, except one man with his back turned to the rest, wholly preoccupied with a notebook in which he is writing.

The church clock strikes the first quarter.

1. Sir Christopher Wren (1632–1723), English architect.   2. Inigo Jones (1573–1652), English architect.

THE DAUGHTER [*in the space between the central pillars, close to the one on her left*]: I'm getting chilled to the bone. What can Freddy be doing all this time? He's been gone twenty minutes.

THE MOTHER [*on her daughter's right*]: Not so long. But he ought to have got us a cab by this.

A BYSTANDER [*on the lady's right*]: He wont get no cab not until half-past eleven, missus, when they come back after dropping their theatre fares.

THE MOTHER: But we must have a cab. We cant stand here until half-past eleven. It's too bad.

THE BYSTANDER: Well it aint my fault, missus.

THE DAUGHTER: If Freddy had a bit of gumption, he would have got one at the theatre door.

THE MOTHER: What could he have done, poor boy?

THE DAUGHTER: Other people get cabs. Why couldnt he?

[*Freddy rushes in out of the rain from the Southampton Street side, and comes between them closing a dripping umbrella. He is a young man of twenty, in evening dress, very wet round the ankles.*]

THE DAUGHTER: Well, havnt you got a cab?

FREDDY: Theres not one to be had for love or money.

THE MOTHER: Oh, Freddy, there must be one. You cant have tried.

THE DAUGHTER: It's too tiresome. Do you expect us to go and get one ourselves?

FREDDY: I tell you theyre all engaged. The rain was so sudden: nobody was prepared; and everybody had to take a cab. Ive been to Charing Cross one way and nearly to Ludgate Circus the other; and they were all engaged.

THE MOTHER: Did you try Trafalgar Square?

FREDDY: There wasnt one at Trafalgar Square.

THE DAUGHTER: Did you try?

FREDDY: I tried as far as Charing Cross Station. Did you expect me to walk to Hammersmith?

THE DAUGHTER: You havnt tried at all.

THE MOTHER: You really are very helpless, Freddy. Go again; and dont come back until you have found a cab.

FREDDY: I shall simply get soaked for nothing.

THE DAUGHTER: And what about us? Are we to stay here all night in this draught, with next to nothing on? You selfish pig—

FREDDY: Oh, very well: I'll go. I'll go. [*He opens his umbrella and dashes off Strand-wards, but comes into collision with a flower girl who is hurrying in for shelter, knocking her basket out of her hands. A blinding flash of lightning, followed instantly by a rattling peal of thunder, orchestrates the incident.*]

THE FLOWER GIRL: Nah then, Freddy: look wh'y' gowin, deah.

FREDDY: Sorry. [*He rushes off.*]

THE FLOWER GIRL [*picking up her scattered flowers and replacing them in the basket*]: Theres menners f'yer! Tə-oo banches o voylets trod into the mad.

[*She sits down on the plinth of the column, sorting her flowers, on the lady's right. She is not at all a romantic figure. She is perhaps eighteen, perhaps twenty, hardly older. She wears a little sailor hat of black straw that has long been exposed to the dust and soot of London and has seldom if ever been brushed. Her hair needs washing rather badly: its mousy color can hardly be natural. She wears a shoddy black coat that reaches*] nearly to her knees and is shaped to her waist. She has a brown skirt with a coarse apron. Her boots are much the worse for wear. She is no doubt as clean as she can afford to be; but compared to the ladies she is very dirty. Her features are no worse than theirs; but their condition leaves something to be desired; and she needs the services of a dentist.]

THE MOTHER: How do you know that my son's name is Freddy, pray?

THE FLOWER GIRL: Ow, eez, yə -ooa san, is e? Wal, fewd dan y' d-ooty bawmz a mather should, eed now bettern to spawl a pore gel's flahrzn than ran awy athaht pyin. Will ye-oo py me f'them? [Here, with apologies, this desperate attempt to represent her dialect without a phonetic alphabet must be abandoned as unintelligible outside London.]

THE DAUGHTER: Do nothing of the sort, mother. The idea!

THE MOTHER: Please allow me, Clara. Have you any pennies?

THE DAUGHTER: No. Ive nothing smaller than sixpence.

THE FLOWER GIRL [hopefully]: I can give you change for a tanner, kind lady.

THE MOTHER [to Clara]: Give it to me. [Clara parts reluctantly.] Now [to the girl] This is for your flowers.

THE FLOWER GIRL: Thank you kindly, lady.

THE DAUGHTER: Make her give you the change. These things are only a penny a bunch.

THE MOTHER: Do hold your tongue, Clara. [To the girl] You can keep the change.

THE FLOWER GIRL: Oh, thank you, lady.

THE MOTHER: Now tell me how you know that young gentleman's name.

THE FLOWER GIRL: I didnt.

THE MOTHER: I heard you call him by it. Dont try to deceive me.

THE FLOWER GIRL [protesting]: Who's trying to deceive you? I called him Freddy or Charlie same as you might yourself if you was talking to a stranger and wished to be pleasant.

THE DAUGHTER: Sixpence thrown away! Really, mamma, you might have spared Freddy that. [She retreats in disgust behind the pillar.]

[An elderly gentleman of the amiable military type rushes into the shelter, and closes a dripping umbrella. He is in the same plight as Freddy, very wet about the ankles. He is in evening dress, with a light overcoat. He takes the place left vacant by the daughter.]

THE GENTLEMAN: Phew!

THE MOTHER [to the gentleman]: Oh, sir, is there any sign of its stopping?

THE GENTLEMAN: I'm afraid not. It started worse than ever about two minutes ago. [He goes to the plinth beside the flower girl; puts up his foot on it; and stoops to turn down his trouser ends.]

THE MOTHER: Oh dear! [She retires sadly and joins her daughter.]

THE FLOWER GIRL [taking advantage of the military gentleman's proximity to establish friendly relations with him]: If it's worse, it's a sign it's nearly over. So cheer up, Captain; and buy a flower off a poor girl.

THE GENTLEMAN: I'm sorry. I havnt any change.

THE FLOWER GIRL: I can give you change, Captain.

THE GENTLEMAN: For a sovereign? Ive nothing less.

THE FLOWER GIRL: Garn! Oh do buy a flower off me, Captain. I can change half-a-crown. Take this for tuppence.

THE GENTLEMAN: Now dont be troublesome: theres a good girl. [*Trying his pock-ets.*] I really havnt any change—Stop: heres three hapence, if thats any use to you [*he retreats to the other pillar*].

THE FLOWER GIRL [*disappointed, but thinking three halfpence better than nothing*]: Thank you, sir.

THE BYSTANDER [*to the girl*]: You be careful: give him a flower for it. Theres a bloke here behind taking down every blessed word youre saying. [*All turn to the man who is taking notes.*]

THE FLOWER GIRL [*springing up terrified*]: I aint done nothing wrong by speaking to the gentleman. Ive a right to sell flowers if I keep off the kerb. [*Hysterically.*] I'm a respectable girl: so help me. I never spoke to him except to ask him to buy a flower off me.

[*General hubbub, mostly sympathetic to the flower girl, but deprecating her excessive sensibility. Cries of* Dont start hollerin. Who's hurting you? Nobody's going to touch you. Whats the good of fussing? Steady on. Easy easy, etc., *come from the elderly staid spectators, who pat her comfortingly. Less patient ones bid her shut her head, or ask her roughly what is wrong with her. A remoter group, not knowing what the matter is, crowd in and increase the noise with question and answer:* Whats the row? What-she-do? Where is he? A tec[3] taking her down. What! him? Yes: him over there: Took money off the gentleman, etc.]

THE FLOWER GIRL [*breaking through them to the gentleman, crying wildly*]: Oh, sir, dont let him charge me. You dunno what it means to me. Theyll take away my character and drive me on the streets for speaking to gentlemen. They—

THE NOTE TAKER [*coming forward on her right, the rest crowding after him*]: There! there! there! there! Who's hurting you, you silly girl? What do you take me for?

THE BYSTANDER: It's aw rawt: e's a genleman: look at his bə -oots. [*Explaining to the note taker.*] She thought you was a copper's nark, sir.

THE NOTE TAKER [*with quick interest*]: Whats a copper's nark?

THE BYSTANDER [*inapt at definition*]: It's a—well, it's a copper's nark, as you might say. What else would you call it? A sort of informer.

THE FLOWER GIRL [*still hysterical*]: I take my Bible oath I never said a word—

THE NOTE TAKER [*overbearing but good-humored*]: Oh, shut up, shut up. Do I look like a policeman?

THE FLOWER GIRL [*far from reassured*]: Then what did you take down my words for? How do I know whether you took me down right? You just shew[4] me what youve wrote about me. [*The note taker opens his book and holds it steadily under her nose, though the pressure of the mob trying to read it over his shoulders would upset a weaker man.*] Whats that? That aint proper writing. I cant read that.

THE NOTE TAKER: I can. [*Reads, reproducing her pronunciation exactly.*] "Cheer ap, Keptin; n' baw ya flahr orf a pore gel."

THE FLOWER GIRL [*much distressed*]: It's because I called him Captain. I meant no harm. [*To the gentleman.*] Oh, sir, dont let him lay a charge agen me for a word like that. You—

THE GENTLEMAN: Charge! I make no charge. [*To the note taker.*] Really, sir, if you are a detective, you need not begin protecting me against molestation by young women until I ask you. Anybody could see that the girl meant no harm.

3. Detective.   4. Show.

THE BYSTANDERS GENERALLY [*demonstrating against police espionage*]: Course they could. What business is it of yours? You mind your own affairs. He wants promotion, he does. Taking down people's words! Girl never said a word to him. What harm if she did? Nice thing a girl cant shelter from the rain without being insulted, etc., etc., etc. [*She is conducted by the more sympathetic demonstrators back to her plinth, where she resumes her seat and struggles with her emotion.*]

THE BYSTANDER: He aint a tec. He's a blooming busy-body: thats what he is. I tell you, look at his bə -oots.

THE NOTE TAKER [*turning on him genially*]: And how are all your people down at Selsey?

THE BYSTANDER [*suspiciously*]: Who told you my people come from Selsey?

THE NOTE TAKER: Never you mind. They did. [*To the girl.*] How do you come to be up so far east? You were born in Lisson Grove.

THE FLOWER GIRL [*appalled*]: Oh, what harm is there in my leaving Lisson Grove? It wasnt fit for a pig to live in; and I had to pay four-and-six a week. [*In tears.*] Oh, boo—hoo—oo—

THE NOTE TAKER: Live where you like; but stop that noise.

THE GENTLEMAN [*to the girl*]: Come, come! he cant touch you: you have a right to live where you please.

A SARCASTIC BYSTANDER [*thrusting himself between the note taker and the gentleman*]: Park Lane, for instance. I'd like to go into the Housing Question with you, I would.

THE FLOWER GIRL [*subsiding into a brooding melancholy over her basket, and talking very low-spiritedly to herself*]: I'm a good girl, I am.

THE SARCASTIC BYSTANDER [*not attending to her*]: Do you know where I come from?

THE NOTE TAKER [*promptly*]: Hoxton.

[*Titterings. Popular interest in the note taker's performance increases.*]

THE SARCASTIC ONE [*amazed*]: Well, who said I didnt? Bly me! you know everything, you do.

THE FLOWER GIRL [*still nursing her sense of injury*]: Aint no call to meddle with me, he aint.

THE BYSTANDER [*to her*]: Of course he aint. Dont you stand it from him. [*To the note taker.*] See here: what call have you to know about people what never offered to meddle with you?

THE FLOWER GIRL: Let him say what he likes. I dont want to have no truck with him.

THE BYSTANDER: You take us for dirt under your feet, dont you? Catch you taking liberties with a gentleman!

THE SARCASTIC BYSTANDER: Yes: tell him where he come from if you want to go fortune-telling.

THE NOTE TAKER: Cheltenham, Harrow, Cambridge, and India.

THE GENTLEMAN: Quite right.

[*Great laughter. Reaction in the note taker's favor. Exclamations of* He knows all about it. Told him proper. Hear him tell the toff where he come from? *etc.*]

THE GENTLEMAN: May I ask, sir, do you do this for your living at a music hall?

THE NOTE TAKER: I've thought of that. Perhaps I shall some day.

[*The rain has stopped; and the persons on the outside of the crowd begin to drop off.*]

THE FLOWER GIRL [*resenting the reaction*]: He's no gentleman, he aint, to interfere with a poor girl.

THE DAUGHTER [*out of patience, pushing her way rudely to the front and displacing the gentleman, who politely retires to the other side of the pillar*]: What on earth is Freddy doing? I shall get pneumownia if I stay in this draught any longer.

THE NOTE TAKER [*to himself, hastily making a note of her pronunciation of "monia"*]: Earlscourt.

THE DAUGHTER [*violently*]: Will you please keep your impertinent remarks to yourself.

THE NOTE TAKER: Did I say that out loud? I didnt mean to. I beg your pardon. Your mother's Epsom, unmistakeably.

THE MOTHER [*advancing between the daughter and the note taker*]: How very curious! I was brought up in Largelady Park, near Epsom.

THE NOTE TAKER [*uproariously amused*]: Ha! ha! what a devil of a name! Excuse me. [*To the daughter.*] You want a cab, do you?

THE DAUGHTER: Dont dare speak to me.

THE MOTHER: Oh, please, please, Clara. [*Her daughter repudiates her with an angry shrug and retires haughtily.*] We should be so grateful to you, sir, if you found us a cab. [*The note taker produces a whistle.*] Oh, thank you. [*She joins her daughter. The note taker blows a piercing blast.*]

THE SARCASTIC BYSTANDER: There! I knowed he was a plain-clothes copper.

THE BYSTANDER: That aint a police whistle: thats a sporting whistle.

THE FLOWER GIRL [*still preoccupied with her wounded feelings*]: He's no right to take away my character. My character is the same to me as any lady's.

THE NOTE TAKER: I dont know whether youve noticed it; but the rain stopped about two minutes ago.

THE BYSTANDER: So it has. Why didnt you say so before? And us losing our time listening to your silliness! [*He walks off towards the Strand.*]

THE SARCASTIC BYSTANDER: I can tell where you come from. You come from Anwell. Go back there.

THE NOTE TAKER [*helpfully*]: Hanwell.

THE SARCASTIC BYSTANDER [*affecting great distinction of speech*]: Thenk you, teacher. Haw haw! So long. [*He touches his hat with mock respect and strolls off.*]

THE FLOWER GIRL: Frightening people like that! How would he like it himself?

THE MOTHER: It's quite fine now, Clara. We can walk to a motor bus. Come. [*She gathers her skirts above her ankles and hurries off towards the Strand.*]

THE DAUGHTER: But the cab—[*her mother is out of hearing*]. Oh, how tiresome! [*She follows angrily.*]

[*All the rest have gone except the note taker, the gentleman, and the flower girl, who sits arranging her basket, and still pitying herself in murmurs.*]

THE FLOWER GIRL: Poor girl! Hard enough for her to live without being worried and chivied.

THE GENTLEMAN [*returning to his former place on the note taker's left*]: How do you do it, if I may ask?

THE NOTE TAKER: Simply phonetics. The science of speech. Thats my profession: also my hobby. Happy is the man who can make a living by his hobby! You can spot an Irishman or a Yorkshireman by his brogue. *I* can place any man within six miles. I can place him within two miles in London. Sometimes within two streets.

THE FLOWER GIRL: Ought to be ashamed of himself, unmanly coward!

THE GENTLEMAN: But is there a living in that?

THE NOTE TAKER: Oh, yes. Quite a fat one. This is an age of upstarts. Men begin in Kentish Town with £80 a year, and end in Park Lane with a hundred thousand. They want to drop Kentish Town; but they give themselves away every time they open their mouths. Now I can teach them—

THE FLOWER GIRL: Let him mind his own business and leave a poor girl—

THE NOTE TAKER [*explosively*]: Woman: cease this detestable boohooing instantly: or else seek the shelter of some other place of worship.

THE FLOWER GIRL [*with feeble defiance*]: Ive a right to be here if I like, same as you.

THE NOTE TAKER: A woman who utters such depressing and disgusting sounds has no right to be anywhere—no right to live. Remember that you are a human being with a soul and the divine gift of articulate speech: that your native language is the language of Shakespear and Milton and The Bible; and dont sit there crooning like a bilious pigeon.

THE FLOWER GIRL [*quite overwhelmed, looking up at him in mingled wonder and deprecation without daring to raise her head*]: Ah-ah-ah-ow-ow-ow-oo!

THE NOTE TAKER [*whipping out his book*]: Heavens! what a sound! [*He writes; then holds out the book and reads, reproducing her vowels exactly.*] Ah-ah-ah-ow-ow-ow-oo!

THE FLOWER GIRL [*tickled by the performance, and laughing in spite of herself*]: Garn!

THE NOTE TAKER: You see this creature with her kerbstone English: the English that will keep her in the gutter to the end of her days. Well, sir, in three months I could pass that girl off as a duchess at an ambassador's garden party. I could even get her a place as lady's maid or shop assistant, which requires better English.

THE FLOWER GIRL: What's that you say?

THE NOTE TAKER: Yes, you squashed cabbage leaf, you disgrace to the noble architecture of these columns, you incarnate insult to the English language: I could pass you off as the Queen of Sheba. [*To the Gentleman.*] Can you believe that?

THE GENTLEMAN: Of course I can. I am myself a student of Indian dialects; and—

THE NOTE TAKER [*eagerly*]: Are you? Do you know Colonel Pickering, the author of Spoken Sanscrit?

THE GENTLEMAN: I am Colonel Pickering. Who are you?

THE NOTE TAKER: Henry Higgins, author of Higgins's Universal Alphabet.

PICKERING [*with enthusiasm*]: I came from India to meet you.

HIGGINS: I was going to India to meet you.

PICKERING: Where do you live?

HIGGINS: 27A Wimpole Street. Come and see me tomorrow.

PICKERING: I'm at the Carlton. Come with me now and lets have a jaw over some supper.

HIGGINS: Right you are.

THE FLOWER GIRL [*to Pickering, as he passes her*]: Buy a flower, kind gentleman. I'm short for my lodging.

PICKERING: I really havnt any change. I'm sorry. [*He goes away.*]

HIGGINS [*shocked at the girl's mendacity*]: Liar. You said you could change half-a-crown.

THE FLOWER GIRL [*rising in desperation*]: You ought to be stuffed with nails, you ought. [*Flinging the basket at his feet.*] Take the whole blooming basket for sixpence. [*The church clock strikes the second quarter.*]

HIGGINS [*hearing in it the voice of God, rebuking him for his Pharisaic want of charity to the poor girl*]: A reminder. [*He raises his hat solemnly; then throws a handful of money into the basket and follows Pickering.*]

THE FLOWER GIRL [*picking up a half-crown*]: Ah-ow-ooh! [*picking up a couple of florins*] Aaah-ow-ooh! [*picking up several coins*] Aaaaaaah-ow-ooh! [*picking up a half-sovereign*] Aaaaaaaaaaaah-ow-ooh!!!

FREDDY [*springing out of a taxicab*]: Got one at last. Hallo! [*To the girl.*] Where are the two ladies that were here?

THE FLOWER GIRL: They walked to the bus when the rain stopped.

FREDDY: And left me with a cab on my hands! Damnation!

THE FLOWER GIRL [*with grandeur*]: Never mind, young man. I'm going home in a taxi. [*She sails off to the cab. The driver puts his hand behind him and holds the door firmly shut against her. Quite understanding his mistrust, she shews him her handful of money.*] A taxi fare aint no object to me, Charlie. [*He grins and opens the door.*] Here. What about the basket?

THE TAXIMAN: Give it here. Tuppence extra.

LIZA: No: I dont want nobody to see it. [*She crushes it into the cab and gets in, continuing the conversation through the window.*] Goodbye, Freddy.

FREDDY [*dazedly raising his hat*]: Goodbye.

TAXIMAN: Where to?

LIZA: Bucknam Pellis [Buckingham Palace].

TAXIMAN: What d'ye mean—Bucknam Pellis?

LIZA: Dont you know where it is? In the Green Park, where the King lives. Goodbye, Freddy. Dont let me keep you standing there. Goodbye.

FREDDY: Goodbye. [*He goes.*]

TAXIMAN: Here? Whats this about Bucknam Pellis? What business have you at Bucknam Pellis?

LIZA: Of course I havnt none. But I wasnt going to let him know that. You drive me home.

TAXIMAN: And wheres home?

LIZA: Angel Court, Drury Lane, next Meiklejohn's oil shop.

TAXIMAN: That sounds more like it, Judy. [*He drives off.*]

*   *   *

Let us follow the taxi to the entrance to Angel Court, a narrow little archway between two shops, one of them Meiklejohn's oil shop. When it stops there, Eliza gets out, dragging her basket with her.

LIZA: How much?

TAXIMAN [*indicating the taximeter*]: Cant you read? A shilling.

LIZA: A shilling for two minutes!!

TAXIMAN: Two minutes or ten: it's all the same.

LIZA: Well. I dont call it right.

TAXIMAN: Ever been in a taxi before?

LIZA [*with dignity*]: Hundreds and thousands of times, young man.

TAXIMAN [*laughing at her*]: Good for you. Judy, Keep the shilling, darling, with best love from all at home. Good luck! [*He drives off.*]

LIZA [*humiliated*]: Impidence!

[*She picks up the basket and trudges up the alley with it to her lodging: a small room with very old wall paper hanging loose in the damp places. A broken pane in the window is mended with paper. A portrait of a popular actor and a fashion plate of ladies' dresses, all wildly beyond poor Eliza's means, both torn from newspapers, are pinned up on the wall. A birdcage hangs in the window; but its tenant died long ago: it remains as a memorial only.*

These are the only visible luxuries: the rest is the irreducible minimum of poverty's needs: a wretched bed heaped with all sorts of coverings that have any warmth in them, a draped packing case with a basin and jug on it and a little looking glass over it, a chair and table, the refuse of some suburban kitchen, and an American alarum clock on the shelf above the unused fireplace: the whole lighted with a gas lamp with a penny in the slot meter. Rent: four shillings a week.

Here Eliza, chronically weary, but too excited to go to bed, sits, counting her new riches and dreaming and planning what to do with them, until the gas goes out, when she enjoys for the first time the sensation of being able to put in another penny without grudging it. This prodigal mood does not extinguish her gnawing sense of the need for economy sufficiently to prevent her from calculating that she can dream and plan in bed more cheaply and warmly than sitting up without a fire. So she takes off her shawl and skirt and adds them to the miscellaneous bedclothes. Then she kicks off her shoes and gets into bed without any further change.]

ACT 2

Next day at 11 a.m. Higgins's laboratory in Wimpole Street. *It is a room on the first floor, looking on the street, and was meant for the drawing room. The double doors are in the middle of the back wall; and persons entering find in the corner to their right two tall file cabinets at right angles to one another against the wall. In this corner stands a flat writing-table, on which are a phonograph, a laryngoscope, a row of tiny organ pipes with a bellows, a set of lamp chimneys for singing flames with burners attached to a gas plug in the wall by an indiarubber tube, several tuning-forks of different sizes, a life-size image of half a human head, shewing in section the vocal organs, and a box containing a supply of wax cylinders for the phonograph.*

Further down the room, on the same side, is a fireplace, with a comfortable leather-covered easy-chair at the side of the hearth nearest the door, and a coal-scuttle. There is a clock on the mantel-piece. Between the fireplace and the phonograph table is a stand for newspapers.

On the other side of the central door, to the left of the visitor, is a cabinet of shallow drawers. On it is a telephone and the telephone directory. The corner beyond, and most of the side wall, is occupied by a grand piano, with the keyboard at the end furthest from the door, and a bench for the player extending the full length of the keyboard. On the piano is a dessert dish heaped with fruit and sweets, mostly chocolates.

The middle of the room is clear. Besides the easy-chair, the piano bench, and two chairs at the phonograph table, there is one stray chair. It stands near the fireplace. On the walls, engravings: mostly Piranesi[1] and mezzotint[2] portraits. No paintings.

Pickering is seated at the table, putting down some cards and a tuning-fork which he has been using. Higgins is standing up near him, closing two or three file drawers which are hanging out. He appears in the morning light as a robust, vital, appetizing sort of man of forty or thereabouts, dressed in a professional-looking black frock-coat with a white linen collar and black silk tie. He is of the energetic scientific type, heartily, even violently interested in everything that can be studied as a scientific subject, and careless about himself and other people, including their feelings. He is,

1. Giovanni Piranesi (1720–1778), Italian architect and engraver.   2. Prints produced with copper or steel engraved plates.

in fact, but for his years and size, rather like a very impetuous baby 'taking notice' eagerly and loudly, and requiring almost as much watching to keep him out of unintended mischief. His manner varies from genial bullying when he is in a good humor to stormy petulance when anything goes wrong: but he is so entirely frank and void of malice that he remains likeable even in his least reasonable moments.

HIGGINS [*as he shuts the last drawer*]: Well, I think thats the whole show.

PICKERING: It's really amazing. I havnt taken half of it in, you know.

HIGGINS: Would you like to go over any of it again?

PICKERING [*rising and coming to the fireplace, where he plants himself with his back to the fire*]: No, thank you: not now. I'm quite done up for this morning.

HIGGINS [*following him, and standing beside him on his left*]: Tired of listening to sounds?

PICKERING: Yes. It's a fearful strain. I rather fancied myself because I can pronounce twenty-four distinct vowel sounds; but your hundred and thirty beat me. I cant hear a bit of difference between most of them.

HIGGINS [*chuckling, and going over to the piano to eat sweets*]: Oh, that comes with practice. You hear no difference at first; but you keep on listening, and presently you find theyre all as different as A from B. [*Mrs Pearce looks in: she is Higgins's housekeeper.*] Whats the matter?

MRS PEARCE [*hesitating, evidently perplexed*]: A young woman asks to see you, sir.

HIGGINS: A young woman! What does she want?

MRS PEARCE: Well, sir, she says youll be glad to see her when you know what she's come about. She's quite a common girl, sir. Very common indeed. I should have sent her away, only I thought perhaps you wanted her to talk into your machines. I hope Ive not done wrong; but really you see such queer people sometimes—youll excuse me, I'm sure, sir—

HIGGINS: Oh, thats all right, Mrs Pearce. Has she an interesting accent?

MRS PEARCE: Oh, something dreadful, sir, really. I dont know how you can take an interest in it.

HIGGINS [*to Pickering*]: Lets have her up. Shew her up, Mrs Pearce. [*He rushes across to his working table and picks out a cylinder to use on the phonograph.*]

MRS PEARCE [*only half resigned to it*]: Very well, sir. It's for you to say. [*She goes downstairs.*]

HIGGINS: This is rather a bit of luck. I'll shew you how I make records. We'll set her talking; and I'll take it down first in Bell's Visible Speech; then in broad Romic; and then we'll get her on the phonograph so that you can turn her on as often as you like with the written transcript before you.

MRS PEARCE [*returning*]: This is the young woman, sir.

[*The flower girl enters in state. She has a hat with three ostrich feathers, orange, sky-blue, and red. She has a nearly clean apron and the shoddy coat has been tidied a little. The pathos of this deplorable figure, with its innocent vanity and consequential air, touches Pickering, who has already straightened himself in the presence of Mrs Pearce. But as to Higgins, the only distinction he makes between men and women is that when he is neither bullying nor exclaiming to the heavens against some featherweight cross, he coaxes women as a child coaxes its nurse when it wants to get anything out of her.*]

HIGGINS [*brusquely, recognizing her with unconcealed disappointment, and at once, baby-like, making an intolerable grievance of it*]: Why, this is the girl I jotted down last night. She's no use: Ive got all the records I want of the Lisson Grove lingo; and I'm not going to waste another cylinder on it. [*To the girl.*] Be off with you: I dont want you.

THE FLOWER GIRL: Dont you be so saucy. You aint heard what I come for yet. [*To Mrs Pearce, who is waiting at the door for further instructions.*] Did you tell him I come in a taxi?

MRS PEARCE: Nonsense, girl! what do you think a gentleman like Mr Higgins cares what you came in?

THE FLOWER GIRL: Oh, we are proud! He aint above giving lessons, not him: I heard him say so. Well, I aint come here to ask for any compliment; and if my money's not good enough I can go elsewhere.

HIGGINS: Good enough for what?

THE FLOWER GIRL: Good enough for yə -oo. Now you know, dont you? I'm coming to have lessons, I am. And to pay for em tə -oo: make no mistake.

HIGGINS [*stupent*][3]: Well!!! [*Recovering his breath with a gasp.*] What do you expect me to say to you?

THE FLOWER GIRL: Well, if you was a gentleman, you might ask me to sit down, I think. Dont I tell you I'm bringing you business?

HIGGINS: Pickering: shall we ask this baggage to sit down, or shall we throw her out of the window?

THE FLOWER GIRL [*running away in terror to the piano, where she turns at bay*]: Ah-ah-oh-ow-ow-ow-oo! [*Wounded and whimpering.*] I wont be called a baggage when Ive offered to pay like any lady.

[*Motionless, the two men stare at her from the other side of the room, amazed.*]

PICKERING [*gently*]: But what is it you want?

THE FLOWER GIRL: I want to be a lady in a flower shop stead of sellin at the corner of Tottenham Court Road. But they wont take me unless I can talk more genteel. He said he could teach me. Well, here I am ready to pay him—not asking any favor—and he treats me zif I was dirt.

MRS PEARCE: How can you be such a foolish ignorant girl as to think you could afford to pay Mr Higgins?

THE FLOWER GIRL: Why shouldnt I? I know what lessons cost as well as you do; and I'm ready to pay.

HIGGINS: How much?

THE FLOWER GIRL [*coming back to him triumphant*]: Now youre talking! I thought youd come off it when you saw a chance of getting back a bit of what you chucked at me last night. [*Confidentially.*] Youd had a drop in, hadnt you?

HIGGINS [*peremptorily*]: Sit down.

THE FLOWER GIRL: Oh, if youre going to make a compliment of it—

HIGGINS [*thundering at her*]: Sit down.

MRS PEARCE [*severely*]: Sit down, girl. Do as youre told.

THE FLOWER GIRL: Ah-ah-ah-ow-ow-oo! [*She stands, half rebellious, half-bewildered.*]

PICKERING [*very courteous*]: Wont you sit down? [*He places the stray chair near the hearthrug between himself and Higgins.*]

LIZA [*coyly*]: Dont mind if I do. [*She sits down. Pickering returns to the hearthrug.*]

HIGGINS: Whats your name?

THE FLOWER GIRL: Liza Doolittle.

HIGGINS [*declaiming gravely*]: Eliza, Elizabeth, Betsy and Bess,
    They went to the woods to get a bird's nes':

3. Astonished.

PICKERING: They found a nest with four eggs in it:

HIGGINS: They took one apiece, and left three in it.

[*They laugh heartily at their own fun.*]

LIZA: Oh, dont be silly.

MRS PEARCE [*placing herself behind Eliza's chair*]: You mustnt speak to the gentleman like that.

LIZA: Well, why wont he speak sensible to me?

HIGGINS: Come back to business. How much do you propose to pay me for the lessons?

LIZA: Oh, I know whats right. A lady friend of mine gets French lessons for eighteenpence an hour from a real French gentleman. Well, you wouldnt have the face to ask me the same for teaching me my own language as you would for French; so I wont give more than a shilling. Take it or leave it.

HIGGINS [*walking up and down the room, ratting his keys and his cash in his pockets*]: You know, Pickering, if you consider a shilling, not as a simple shilling, but as a percentage of this girl's income, it works out as fully equivalent to sixty or seventy guineas from a millionaire.

PICKERING: How so?

HIGGINS: Figure it out. A millionaire has about £150 a day. She earns about half-a-crown.

LIZA [*haughtily*]: Who told you I only—

HIGGINS [*continuing*]: She offers me two-fifths of her day's income for a lesson. Two-fifths of a millionaire's income for a day would be somewhere about £60. It's handsome. By George, it's enormous! it's the biggest offer I ever had.

LIZA [*rising, terrified*]: Sixty pounds! What are you talking about? I never offered you sixty pounds. Where would I get—

HIGGINS: Hold your tongue.

LIZA [*weeping*]: But I aint got sixty pounds. Oh—

MRS PEARCE: Dont cry, you silly girl. Sit down. Nobody is going to touch your money.

HIGGINS: Somebody is going to touch you, with a broom-stick, if you dont stop snivelling. Sit down.

LIZA [*obeying slowly*]: Ah-ah-ah-ow-oo-o! One would think you was my father.

HIGGINS: If I decide to teach you, I'll be worse than two fathers to you. Here [*he offers her his silk handkerchief*]!

LIZA: Whats this for?

HIGGINS: To wipe your eyes. To wipe any part of your face that feels moist. Remember: thats your handkerchief; and thats your sleeve. Dont mistake the one for the other if you wish to become a lady in a shop.

[*Liza, utterly bewildered, stares helplessly at him.*]

MRS PEARCE: It's no use talking to her like that, Mr Higgins: she doesnt understand you. Besides, youre quite wrong: she doesnt do it that way at all. [*She takes the handkerchief.*]

LIZA [*snatching it*]: Here! You give me that handkerchief. He gev it to me, not to you.

PICKERING [*laughing*]: He did. I think it must be regarded as her property, Mrs Pearce.

MRS PEARCE [*resigning herself*]: Serve you right, Mr Higgins.

PICKERING: Higgins: I'm interested. What about the ambassador's garden party? I'll say youre the greatest teacher alive if you make that good. I'll bet you all the expenses of the experiment you cant do it. And I'll pay for the lessons.

LIZA: Oh, you are real good. Thank you, Captain.

HIGGINS [*tempted, looking at her*]: It's almost irresistible. She's so deliciously low— so horribly dirty—

LIZA [*protesting extremely*]: Ah-ah-ah-ah-ow-oo-oo!!! I aint dirty: I washed my face and hands afore I come, I did.

PICKERING: Youre certainly not going to turn her head with flattery, Higgins.

MRS PEARCE [*uneasy*]: Oh, dont say that, sir: theres more ways than one of turning a girl's head; and nobody can do it better than Mr Higgins, though he may not always mean it. I do hope, sir, you wont encourage him to do anything foolish.

HIGGINS [*becoming excited as the idea grows on him*]: What is life but a series of inspired follies? The difficulty is to find them to do. Never lose a chance: it doesnt come every day. I shall make a duchess of this draggletailed guttersnipe.

LIZA [*strongly deprecating this view of her*]: Ah-ah-ah-ow-ow-oo!

HIGGINS: [*carried away*]: Yes: in six months—in three if she has a good ear and a quick tongue—I'll take her anywhere and pass her off as anything. We'll start today: now! this moment! Take her away and clean her, Mrs Pearce. Monkey Brand,[4] if it wont come off any other way. Is there a good fire in the kitchen?

MRS PEARCE [*protesting*]: Yes; but—

HIGGINS [*storming on*]: Take all her clothes off and burn them. Ring up Whiteley or somebody for new ones. Wrap her up in brown paper til they come.

LIZA: Youre no gentleman, youre not, to talk of such things. I'm a good girl, I am; and I know what the like of you are, I do.

HIGGINS: We want none of your Lisson Grove prudery here, young woman. Youve got to learn to behave like a duchess. Take her away, Mrs Pearce. If she gives you any trouble, wallop her.

LIZA [*springing up and running between Pickering and Mrs Pearce for protection*]: No! I'll call the police, I will.

MRS PEARCE: But Ive no place to put her.

HIGGINS: Put her in the dustbin.

LIZA: Ah-ah-ah-ow-ow-oo!

PICKERING: Oh come, Higgins! Be reasonable.

MRS PEARCE [*resolutely*]: You must be reasonable, Mr Higgins: really you must. You cant walk over everybody like this.

[*Higgins, thus scolded, subsides. The hurricane is succeeded by a zephyr of amiable surprise.*]

HIGGINS [*with professional exquisiteness of modulation*]: I walk over everybody! My dear Mrs Pearce, my dear Pickering, I never had the slightest intention of walking over anyone. All I propose is that we should be kind to this poor girl. We must help her to prepare and fit herself for her new station in life. If I did not express myself clearly it was because I did not wish to hurt her delicacy, or yours.

[*Liza, reassured, steals back to her chair.*]

MRS PEARCE [*to Pickering*]: Well, did you ever hear anything like that, sir?

PICKERING [*laughing heartily*]: Never, Mrs Pearce: never.

4. Widely advertised brand of household cleanser—"won't wash clothes!"

HIGGINS [*patiently*]: Whats the matter?

MRS PEARCE: Well, the matter is, sir, that you cant take a girl up like that as if you were picking up a pebble on the beach.

HIGGINS: Why not?

MRS PEARCE: Why not! But you dont know anything about her. What about her parents? She may be married.

LIZA: Garn!

HIGGINS: There! As the girl very properly says, Garn! Married indeed! Dont you know that a woman of that class looks a worn out drudge of fifty a year after she's married?

LIZA: Whood marry me?

HIGGINS [*suddenly resorting to the most thrillingly beautiful low tones in his best elocutionary style*]: By George, Eliza, the streets will be strewn with the bodies of men shooting themselves for your sake before Ive done with you.

MRS PEARCE: Nonsense, sir. You mustnt talk like that to her.

LIZA [*rising and squaring herself determinedly*]: I'm going away. He's off his chump, he is. I dont want no balmies teaching me.

HIGGINS [*wounded in his tenderest point by her insensibility to his elocution*]: Oh, indeed! I'm mad, am I? Very well, Mrs Pearce: you neednt order the new clothes for her. Throw her out.

LIZA [*whimpering*]: Nah-ow. You got no right to touch me.

MRS PEARCE: You see now what comes of being saucy. [*Indicating the door.*] This way, please.

LIZA [*almost in tears*]: I didnt want no clothes. I wouldnt have taken them. [*She throws away the handkerchief.*] I can buy my own clothes.

HIGGINS [*deftly retrieving the handkerchief and intercepting her on her reluctant way to the door*]: Youre an ungrateful wicked girl. This is my return for offering to take you out of the gutter and dress you beautifully and make a lady of you.

MRS PEARCE: Stop, Mr Higgins. I wont allow it. It's you that are wicked. Go home to your parents, girl; and tell them to take better care of you.

LIZA: I aint got no parents. They told me I was big enough to earn my own living and turned me out.

MRS PEARCE: Wheres your mother?

LIZA: I aint got no mother. Her that turned me out was my sixth stepmother. But I done without them. And I'm a good girl, I am.

HIGGINS: Very well, then, what on earth is all this fuss about? The girl doesnt belong to anybody—is no use to anybody but me. [*He goes to Mrs Pearce and begins coaxing.*] You can adopt her, Mrs Pearce: I'm sure a daughter would be a great amusement to you. Now dont make any more fuss. Take her downstairs; and—

MRS PEARCE: But whats to become of her? Is she to be paid anything? Do be sensible, sir.

HIGGINS: Oh, pay her whatever is necessary: put it down in the housekeeping book. [*Impatiently.*] What on earth will she want with money? She'll have her food and her clothes. She'll only drink if you give her money.

LIZA [*turning on him*]: Oh you are a brute. It's a lie: nobody ever saw the sign of liquor on me. [*To Pickering.*] Oh, sir: youre a gentleman: dont let him speak to me like that.

PICKERING [*in good-humored remonstrance*]: Does it occur to you, Higgins, that the girl has some feelings?

HIGGINS [*looking critically at her*]: Oh no, I dont think so. Not any feelings that we need bother about. [*Cheerily.*] Have you, Eliza?

LIZA: I got my feelings same as anyone else.

HIGGINS [*to Pickering, reflectively*]: You see the difficulty?

PICKERING: Eh? What difficulty?

HIGGINS: To get her to talk grammar. The mere pronunciation is easy enough.

LIZA: I dont want to talk grammar. I want to talk like a lady in a flower-shop.

MRS PEARCE: Will you please keep to the point, Mr Higgins. I want to know on what terms the girl is to be here. Is she to have any wages? And what is to become of her when youve finished your teaching? You must look ahead a little.

HIGGINS [*impatiently*]: Whats to become of her if I leave her in the gutter? Tell me that, Mrs Pearce.

MRS PEARCE: Thats her own business, not yours. Mr Higgins.

HIGGINS: Well, when Ive done with her, we can throw her back into the gutter; and then it will be her own business again; so thats all right.

LIZA: Oh, youve no feeling heart in you: you dont care for nothing but yourself. [*She rises and takes the floor resolutely.*] Here! Ive had enough of this. I'm going [*making for the door*]. You ought to be ashamed of yourself, you ought.

HIGGINS [*snatching a chocolate cream from the piano, his eyes suddenly beginning to twinkle with mischief*]: Have some chocolates, Eliza.

LIZA [*halting, tempted*]: How do I know what might be in them? Ive heard of girls being drugged by the like of you.

[*Higgins whips out his penknife; cuts a chocolate in two; puts one half into his mouth and bolts it; and offers her the other half.*]

HIGGINS: Pledge of good faith. Eliza. I eat one half: you eat the other. [*Liza opens her mouth to retort: he pops the half chocolate into it.*] You shall have boxes of them, barrels of them, every day. You shall live on them. Eh?

LIZA [*who has disposed of the chocolate after being nearly choked by it*]: I wouldnt have ate it, only I'm too ladylike to take it out of my mouth.

HIGGINS: Listen, Eliza. I think you said you came in a taxi.

LIZA: Well, what if I did? Ive as good a right to take a taxi as anyone else.

HIGGINS: You have, Eliza; and in future you shall have as many taxis as you want. You shall go up and down and round the town in a taxi every day. Think of that, Eliza.

MRS PEARCE: Mr Higgins: youre tempting the girl. It's not right. She should think of the future.

HIGGINS: At her age! Nonsense! Time enough to think of the future when you havnt any future to think of. No, Eliza: do as this lady does: think of other people's futures; but never think of your own. Think of chocolates, and taxis, and gold, and diamonds.

LIZA: No: I dont want no gold and no diamonds. I'm a good girl, I am. [*She sits down again, with an attempt at dignity.*]

HIGGINS: You shall remain so, Eliza, under the care of Mrs Pearce. And you shall marry an officer in the Guards, with a beautiful moustache: the son of a marquis, who will disinherit him for marrying you, but will relent when he sees your beauty and goodness—

PICKERING: Excuse me, Higgins: but I really must interfere. Mrs Pearce is quite right. If this girl is to put herself in your hands for six months for an experiment in teaching, she must understand thoroughly what she's doing.

HIGGINS: How can she? She's incapable of understanding anything. Besides, do any of us understand what we are doing? If we did, would we ever do it?

PICKERING: Very clever, Higgins; but not to the present point. [*To Eliza.*] Miss Doolittle—

LIZA [*overwhelmed*]: Ah-ah-ow-oo!

HIGGINS: There! Thats all youll get out of Eliza. Ah-ah-ow-oo! No use explaining. As a military man you ought to know that. Give her her orders: thats enough for her. Eliza: you are to live here for the next six months, learning how to speak beautifully, like a lady in a florist's shop. If youre good and do whatever youre told, you shall sleep in a proper bedroom, and have lots to eat, and money to buy chocolates and take rides in taxis. If youre naughty and idle you will sleep in the back kitchen among the black beetles, and be walloped by Mrs Pearce with a broomstick. At the end of six months you shall go to Buckingham Palace in a car- riage, beautifully dressed. If the King finds out youre not a lady, you will be taken by the police to the Tower of London, where your head will be cut off as a warning to other presumptuous flower girls. If you are not found out, you shall have a present of seven-and-sixpence to start life with as a lady in a shop. If you refuse this offer you will be a most ungrateful wicked girl; and the angels will weep for you. [*To Pickering.*] Now are you satisfied, Pickering? [*To Mrs Pearce.*] Can I put it more plainly and fairly, Mrs Pearce?

MRS PEARCE [*patiently*]: I think youd better let me speak to the girl properly in private. I dont know that I can take charge of her or consent to the arrangement at all. Of course I know you dont mean her any harm; but when you get what you call interested in people's accents, you never think or care what may happen to them or you. Come with me, Eliza.

HIGGINS: Thats all right. Thank you, Mrs Pearce. Bundle her off to the bathroom.

LIZA [*rising reluctantly and suspiciously*]: Youre a great bully, you are. I wont stay here if I dont like. I wont let nobody wallop me. I never asked to go to Bucknam Palace, I didnt. I was never in trouble with the police, not me. I'm a good girl—

MRS PEARCE: Dont answer back, girl. You dont understand the gentleman. Come with me. [*She leads the way to the door, and holds it open for Eliza.*]

LIZA [*as she goes out*]: Well, what I say is right. I wont go near the King, not if I'm going to have my head cut off. If I'd known what I was letting myself in for, I wouldnt have come here. I always been a good girl; and I never offered to say a word to him; and I dont owe him nothing; and I dont care; and I wont be put upon; and I have my feelings the same as anyone else—

[*Mrs Pearce shuts the door; and Eliza's plaints are no longer audible.*]

*   *   *

Eliza is taken upstairs to the third floor greatly to her surprise; for she expected to be taken down to the scullery. There Mrs Pearce opens a door and takes her into a spare bedroom.

MRS PEARCE: I will have to put you here. This will be your bedroom.

LIZA: O-h, I couldnt sleep here, missus. It's too good for the likes of me. I should be afraid to touch anything. I aint a duchess yet, you know.

MRS PEARCE: You have got to make yourself as clean as the room: then you wont be afraid of it. And you must call me Mrs Pearce, not missus. [*She throws open the door of the dressing-room, now modernized as a bathroom.*]

LIZA: Gawd! whats this? Is this where you wash clothes? Funny sort of copper[5] I call it.

---

5. Kettle to boil laundry.

MRS PEARCE: It is not a copper. This is where we wash ourselves, Eliza, and where I am going to wash you.

LIZA: You expect me to get into that and wet myself all over! Not me. I should catch my death. I knew a woman did it every Saturday night; and she died of it.

MRS PEARCE: Mr Higgins has the gentlemen's bathroom down-stairs; and he has a bath every morning, in cold water.

LIZA: Ugh! He's made of iron, that man.

MRS PEARCE: If you are to sit with him and the Colonel and be taught you will have to do the same. They wont like the smell of you if you dont. But you can have the water as hot as you like. There are two taps: hot and cold.

LIZA [weeping]: I couldnt. I dursnt. Its not natural: It would kill me. Ive never had a bath in my life: not what youd call a proper one.

MRS PEARCE: Well, dont you want to be clean and sweet and decent, like a lady? You know you cant be a nice girl inside if youre a dirty slut outside.

LIZA: Boohoo!!!!

MRS PEARCE: Now stop crying and go back into your room and take off all your clothes. Then wrap yourself in this [taking down a gown from its peg and handing it to her] and come back to me. I will get the bath ready.

LIZA [all tears]: I cant. I wont. I'm not used to it. Ive never took off all my clothes before. It's not right: it's not decent.

MRS PEARCE: Nonsense, child. Dont you take off all your clothes every night when you go to bed?

LIZA [amazed]: No. Why should I? I should catch my death. Of course I take off my skirt.

MRS PEARCE: Do you mean that you sleep in the underclothes you wear in the daytime?

LIZA: What else have I to sleep in?

MRS PEARCE: You will never do that again as long as you live here. I will get you a proper nightdress.

LIZA: Do you mean change into cold things and lie awake shivering half the night? You want to kill me, you do.

MRS PEARCE: I want to change you from a frowzy[6] slut to a clean respectable girl fit to sit with the gentlemen in the study. Are you going to trust me and do what I tell you or be thrown out and sent back to your flower basket?

LIZA: But you dont know what the cold is to me. You dont know how I dread it.

MRS PEARCE: Your bed wont be cold here: I will put a hot water bottle in it. [Pushing her into the bedroom.] Off with you and undress.

LIZA: Oh, if only I'd a known what a dreadful thing it is to be clean I'd never have come. I didnt know when I was well off. I—[Mrs Pearce pushes her through the door, but leaves it partly open lest her prisoner should take to flight.]

[Mrs Pearce puts on a pair of white rubber sleeves, and fills the bath, mixing hot and cold, and testing the result with the bath thermometer. She perfumes it with a handful of bath salts and adds a palmful of mustard. She then takes a formidable looking long handled scrubbing brush and soaps it profusely with a ball of scented soap.

Eliza comes back with nothing on but the bath gown huddled tightly round her, a piteous spectacle of abject terror.]

MRS PEARCE: Now come along. Take that thing off.

LIZA: Oh I couldnt, Mrs Pearce: I reely couldnt. I never done such a thing.

6. Dirty, untidy.

MRS PEARCE: Nonsense. Here: step in and tell me whether it's hot enough for you.

LIZA: Ah-oo! Ah-oo! It's too hot.

MRS PEARCE [*deftly snatching the gown away and throwing Eliza down on her back*]: It wont hurt you. [*She sets to work with the scrubbing brush.*]

[*Eliza's screams are heartrending.*]

* * *

Meanwhile the Colonel has been having it out with Higgins about Eliza. Pickering has come from the hearth to the chair and seated himself astride of it with his arms on the back to cross-examine him.

PICKERING: Excuse the straight question, Higgins. Are you a man of good character where women are concerned?

HIGGINS [*moodily*]: Have you ever met a man of good character where women are concerned?

PICKERING: Yes: very frequently.

HIGGINS [*dogmatically, lifting himself on his hands to the level of the piano, and sitting on it with a bounce*]: Well, I havnt. I find that the moment I let a woman make friends with me, she becomes jealous, exacting, suspicious, and a damned nuisance. I find that the moment I let myself make friends with a woman, I become selfish and tyrannical. Women upset everything. When you let them into your life, you find that the woman is driving at one thing and youre driving at another.

PICKERING: At what, for example?

HIGGINS [*coming off the piano restlessly*]: Oh, Lord knows! I suppose the woman wants to live her own life; and the man wants to live his; and each tries to drag the other on to the wrong track. One wants to go north and the other south; and the result is that both have to go east, though they both hate the east wind. [*He sits down on the bench at the keyboard.*] So here I am, a confirmed old bachelor, and likely to remain so.

PICKERING [*rising and standing over him gravely*]: Come, Higgins! You know what I mean. If I'm to be in this business I shall feel responsible for that girl. I hope it's understood that no advantage is to be taken of her position.

HIGGINS: What! That thing! Sacred. I assure you. [*Rising to explain.*] You see, she'll be a pupil; and teaching would be impossible unless pupils were sacred. Ive taught scores of American millionairesses how to speak English: the best looking women in the world. I'm seasoned. They might as well be blocks of wood. I might as well be a block of wood. It's—

[*Mrs Pearce opens the door. She has Eliza's hat in her hand. Pickering retires to the easy-chair at the hearth and sits down.*]

HIGGINS [*eagerly*]: Well, Mrs Pearce: is it all right?

MRS PEARCE [*at the door*]: I just wish to trouble you with a word, if I may, Mr Higgins.

HIGGINS: Yes, certainly. Come in. [*She comes forward.*] Dont burn that, Mrs Pearce. I'll keep it as a curiosity. [*He takes the hat.*]

MRS PEARCE: Handle it carefully, sir, please. I had to promise her not to burn it; but I had better put it in the oven for a while.

HIGGINS [*putting it down hastily on the piano*]: Oh! thank you. Well, what have you to say to me?

PICKERING: Am I in the way?

MRS PEARCE: Not at all, sir. Mr Higgins: will you please be very particular what you say before the girl?

HIGGINS [*sternly*]: Of course. I'm always particular about what I say. Why do you say this to me?

MRS PEARCE [*unmoved*]: No sir: youre not at all particular when youve mislaid anything or when you get a little impatient. Now it doesnt matter before me: I'm used to it. But you really must not swear before the girl.

HIGGINS [*indignantly*]: I swear! [*Most emphatically.*] I never swear. I detest the habit. What the devil do you mean?

MRS PEARCE [*stolidly*]: Thats what I mean, sir. You swear a great deal too much. I dont mind your damning and blasting, and what the devil and where the devil and who the devil—

HIGGINS: Mrs Pearce: this language from your lips! Really!

MRS PEARCE [*not to be put off*]: —but there is a certain word I must ask you not to use. The girl used it herself when she began to enjoy the bath. It begins with the same letter as bath.[7] She knows no better: she learnt it at her mother's knee. But she must not hear it from your lips.

HIGGINS [*loftily*]: I cannot charge myself with having ever uttered it, Mrs Pearce. [*She looks at him steadfastly. He adds, hiding an uneasy conscience with a judicial air.*] Except perhaps in a moment of extreme and justifiable excitement.

MRS PEARCE: Only this morning, sir, you applied it to your boots, to the butter, and to the brown bread.

HIGGINS: Oh, that! Mere alliteration, Mrs Pearce, natural to a poet.

MRS PEARCE: Well, sir, whatever you choose to call it. I beg you not to let the girl hear you repeat it.

HIGGINS: Oh, very well, very well. Is that all?

MRS PEARCE: No, sir. We shall have to be very particular with this girl as to personal cleanliness.

HIGGINS: Certainly. Quite right. Most important.

MRS PEARCE: I mean not to be slovenly about her dress or untidy in leaving things about.

HIGGINS [*going to her solemnly*]: Just so. I intended to call your attention to that. [*He passes on to Pickering, who is enjoying the conversation immensely.*] It is these little things that matter, Pickering. Take care of the pence and the pounds will take care of themselves is as true of personal habits as of money. [*He comes to anchor on the hearthrug, with the air of a man in an unassailable position.*]

MRS PEARCE: Yes, sir. Then might I ask you not to come down to breakfast in your dressing-gown, or at any rate not to use it as a napkin to the extent you do, sir. And if you would be so good as not to eat everything off the same plate, and to remember not to put the porridge saucepan out of your hand on the clean table-cloth, it would be a better example to the girl. You know you nearly choked yourself with a fishbone in the jam only last week.

HIGGINS [*routed from the hearthrug and drifting back to the piano*]: I may do these things sometimes in absence of mind; but surely I dont do them habitually. [*Angrily.*] By the way: my dressing-gown smells most damnably of benzine.

MRS PEARCE: No doubt it does, Mr Higgins. But if you will wipe your fingers—

HIGGINS [*yelling*]: Oh very well, very well: I'll wipe them in my hair in future.

MRS PEARCE: I hope youre not offended, Mr Higgins.

---

7. The word in question is "bloody" which, at the time the play was written and produced, was a vulgar term not used in polite society.

HIGGINS [*shocked at finding himself thought capable of an unamiable sentiment*]: Not at all, not at all. Youre quite right, Mrs Pearce: I shall be particularly careful before the girl. Is that all?

MRS PEARCE: No, sir. Might she use some of those Japanese dresses you brought from abroad? I really cant put her back into her old things.

HIGGINS: Certainly. Anything you like. Is that all?

MRS PEARCE: Thank you, sir. Thats all. [*She goes out.*]

HIGGINS: You know, Pickering, that woman has the most extraordinary ideas about me. Here I am, a shy, diffident sort of man. Ive never been able to feel really grown-up and tremendous, like other chaps. And yet she's firmly persuaded that I'm an arbitrary overbearing bossing kind of person. I cant account for it.

[*Mrs Pearce returns.*]

MRS PEARCE: If you please, sir, the trouble's beginning already. Theres a dustman downstairs, Alfred Doolittle, wants to see you. He says you have his daughter here.

PICKERING [*rising*]: Phew! I say!

HIGGINS [*promptly*]: Send the blackguard[8] up.

MRS PEARCE: Oh, very well, sir. [*She goes out.*]

PICKERING: He may not be a blackguard, Higgins.

HIGGINS: Nonsense. Of course he's a blackguard.

PICKERING: Whether he is or not, I'm afraid we shall have some trouble with him.

HIGGINS [*confidently*]: Oh no: I think not. If theres any trouble he shall have it with me, not I with him. And we are sure to get something interesting out of him.

PICKERING: About the girl?

HIGGINS: No, I mean his dialect.

PICKERING: Oh!

MRS PEARCE [*at the door*]: Doolittle, sir. [*She admits Doolittle and retires.*]

[*Alfred Doolittle is an elderly but vigorous dustman, clad in the costume of his profession, including a hat with a back brim covering his neck and shoulders. He has well marked and rather interesting features, and seems equally free from fear and conscience. He has a remarkably expressive voice, the result of a habit of giving vent to his feelings without reserve. His present pose is that of wounded honor and stern resolution.*]

DOOLITTLE [*at the door, uncertain which of the two gentlemen is his man*]: Professor Iggins?

HIGGINS: Here, Good morning. Sit down.

DOOLITTLE: Morning, Governor. [*He sits down magisterially.*] I come about a very serious matter, Governor.

HIGGINS [*to Pickering*]: Brought up in Hounslow. Mother Welsh, I should think. [*Doolittle opens his mouth, amazed. Higgins continues.*] What do you want, Doolittle?

DOOLITTLE [*menacingly*]: I want my daughter: thats what I want. See?

HIGGINS: Of course you do. Youre her father, arnt you? You dont suppose anyone else wants her, do you? I'm glad to see you have some spark of family feeling left. She's upstairs. Take her away at once.

DOOLITTLE [*rising, fearfully taken aback*]: What!

HIGGINS: Take her away. Do you suppose I'm going to keep your daughter for you?

DOOLITTLE [*remonstrating*]: Now, now, look here, Governor. Is this reasonable? Is it fairity[9] to take advantage of a man like this? The girl belongs to me. You got her. Where do I come in? [*He sits down again.*]

___

8. Scoundrel.   9. Fair play.

HIGGINS: Your daughter had the audacity to come to my house and ask me to teach her how to speak properly so that she could get a place in a flower-shop. This gentleman and my housekeeper have been here all the time. [*Bullying him.*] How dare you come here and attempt to blackmail me? You sent her here on purpose.

DOOLITTLE [*protesting*]: No, Governor.

HIGGINS: You must have. How else could you possibly know that she is here?

DOOLITTLE: Dont take a man up like that, Governor.

HIGGINS: The police shall take you up. This is a plant—a plot to extort money by threats. I shall telephone for the police. [*He goes resolutely to the telephone and opens the directory.*]

DOOLITTLE: Have I asked you for a brass farthing? I leave it to the gentleman here: have I said a word about money?

HIGGINS [*throwing the book aside and marching down on Doolittle with a poser[1]*]: What else did you come for?

DOOLITTLE [*sweetly*]: Well, what would a man come for? Be human, Governor.

HIGGINS [*disarmed*]: Alfred: did you put her up to it?

DOOLITTLE: So help me, Governor, I never did. I take my Bible oath I aint seen the girl these two months past.

HIGGINS: Then how did you know she was here?

DOOLITTLE [*"most musical, most melancholy"*]: I'll tell you, Governor, if youll only let me get a word in. I'm willing to tell you. I'm wanting to tell you. I'm waiting to tell you.

HIGGINS: Pickering: this chap has a certain natural gift of rhetoric. Observe the rhythm of his native woodnotes wild. "I'm willing to tell you: I'm wanting to tell you: I'm waiting to tell you." Sentimental rhetoric! Thats the Welsh strain in him. It also accounts for his mendacity[2] and dishonesty.

PICKERING: Oh, please, Higgins: I'm west country[3] myself. [*To Doolittle.*] How did you know the girl was here if you didnt send her?

DOOLITTLE: It was like this, Governor. The girl took a boy in the taxi to give him a jaunt. Son of her landlady, he is. He hung about on the chance of her giving him another ride home. Well, she sent him back for her luggage when she heard you was willing for her to stop here. I met the boy at the corner of Long Acre and Endell Street.

HIGGINS: Public house. Yes?

DOOLITTLE: The poor man's club, Governor: why shouldnt I?

PICKERING: Do let him tell his story, Higgins.

DOOLITTLE: He told me what was up. And I ask you, what was my feelings and my duty as a father? I says to the boy, "You bring me the luggage," I says—

PICKERING: Why didnt you go for it yourself?

DOOLITTLE: Landlady wouldnt have trusted me with it, Governor. She's that kind of woman: you know. I had to give the boy a penny afore he trusted me with it, the little swine. I brought it to her just to oblige you like, and make myself agreeable. Thats all.

HIGGINS: How much luggage?

DOOLITTLE: Musical instrument, Governor. A few pictures, a trifle of jewlery, and a bird-cage. She said she didn't want no clothes. What was I to think from that, Governor? I ask you as a parent what was I to think?

---

1. Puzzle
2. Tendency to lie.

3. From the west of England—perhaps even Wales.

HIGGINS: So you came to rescue her from worse than death eh?

DOOLITTLE [*appreciatively: relieved at being so well understood*]: Just so, Governor. Thats right.

PICKERING: But why did you bring her luggage if you intended to take her away?

DOOLITTLE: Have I said a word about taking her away? Have I now?

HIGGINS [*determinedly*]: Youre going to take her away, double quick. [*He crosses to the hearth and rings the bell.*]

DOOLITTLE [*rising*]: No, Governor. Dont say that. I'm not the man to stand in my girl's light. Heres a career opening for her as you might say; and—
[*Mrs Pearce opens the door and awaits orders.*]

HIGGINS: Mrs Pearce: this is Eliza's father. He has come to take her away. Give her to him. [*He goes back to the piano, with an air of washing his hands of the whole affair.*]

DOOLITTLE: No. This is a misunderstanding. Listen here—

MRS PEARCE: He cant take her away, Mr Higgins: how can he? You told me to burn her clothes.

DOOLITTLE: Thats right. I cant carry the girl through the streets like a blooming monkey, can I? I put it to you.

HIGGINS: You have put it to me that you want your daughter. Take your daughter. If she has no clothes go out and buy her some.

DOOLITTLE [*desperate*]: Wheres the clothes she come in? Did I burn them or did your missus here?

MRS PEARCE: I am the housekeeper, if you please. I have sent for some clothes for the girl. When they come you can take her away. You can wait in the kitchen. This way, please.
[*Doolittle, much troubled, accompanies her to the door; then hesitates: finally turns confidentially to Higgins.*]

DOOLITTLE: Listen here, Governor. You and me is men of the world, aint we?

HIGGINS: Oh! Men of the world, are we? Youd better go, Mrs Pearce.

MRS PEARCE: I think so, indeed, sir. [*She goes, with dignity.*]

PICKERING: The floor is yours, Mr Doolittle.

DOOLITTLE [*to Pickering*]: I thank you, Governor. [*To Higgins, who takes refuge on the piano bench, a little overwhelmed by the proximity of his visitor; for Doolittle has a professional flavor of dust about him.*] Well, the truth is, Ive taken a sort of fancy to you, Governor; and if you want the girl, I'm not so set on having her back home again but what I might be open to an arrangement. Regarded in the light of a young woman, she's a fine handsome girl. As a daughter she's not worth her keep; and so I tell you straight. All I ask is my rights as a father; and youre the last man alive to expect me to let her go for nothing; for I can see youre one of the straight sort, Governor. Well, whats a five-pound note to you? and whats Eliza to me? [*He turns to his chair and sits down judicially.*]

PICKERING: I think you ought to know, Doolittle, that Mr Higgins's intentions are entirely honorable.

DOOLITTLE: Course they are, Governor. If I thought they wasn't, I'd ask fifty.

HIGGINS [*revolted*]: Do you mean to say that you would sell your daughter for £50?

DOOLITTLE: Not in a general way I wouldnt; but to oblige a gentleman like you I'd do a good deal, I do assure you.

PICKERING: Have you no morals, man?

DOOLITTLE [*unabashed*]: Cant afford them, Governor. Neither could you if you was as poor as me. Not that I mean any harm, you know. But if Liza is going to have a bit out of this, why not me too?

HIGGINS [*troubled*]: I dont know what to do, Pickering. There can be no question that as a matter of morals it's a positive crime to give this chap a farthing. And yet I feel a sort of rough justice in his claim.

DOOLITTLE: Thats it, Governor. Thats all I say. A father's heart, as it were.

PICKERING: Well, I know the feeling; but really it seems hardly right—

DOOLITTLE: Dont say that, Governor. Dont look at it that way. What am I, Governors both? I ask you, what am I? I'm one of the undeserving poor: thats what I am. Think of what that means to a man. It means that he's up agen middle class morality all the time. If theres anything going, and I put in for a bit of it, it's always the same story: "Youre undeserving: so you cant have it." But my needs is as great as the most deserving widow's that ever got money out of six different charities in one week for the death of the same husband. I dont need less than a deserving man: I need more. I dont eat less hearty than him; and I drink a lot more. I want a bit of amusement, cause I'm a thinking man. I want cheerfulness and a song and a band when I feel low. Well, they charge me just the same for everything as they charge the deserving. What is middle class morality? Just an excuse for never giving me anything. Therefore, I ask you, as two gentlemen, not to play that game on me. I'm playing straight with you. I aint pretending to be deserving. I'm undeserving; and I mean to go on being undeserving. I like it; and thats the truth. Will you take advantage of a man's nature to do him out of the price of his own daughter what he's brought up and fed and clothed by the sweat of his brow until she's growed big enough to be interesting to you two gentlemen? Is five pounds unreasonable? I put it to you: and I leave it to you.

HIGGINS [*rising, and going over to Pickering*]: Pickering: if we were to take this man in hand for three months, he could choose between a seat in the Cabinet and a popular pulpit in Wales.

PICKERING: What do you say to that, Doolittle?

DOOLITTLE: Not me, Governor, thank you kindly. Ive heard all the preachers and all the prime ministers—for I'm a thinking man and game for politics or religion or social reform same as all the other amusements—and I tell you it's a dog's life any way you look at it. Undeserving poverty is my line. Taking one station in society with another, it's—it's—well, it's the only one that has any ginger in it, to my taste.

HIGGINS: I suppose we must give him a fiver.

PICKERING: He'll make a bad use of it, I'm afraid.

DOOLITTLE: Not me, Governor, so help me I wont. Dont you be afraid that I'll save it and spare it and live idle on it. There wont be a penny of it left by Monday: I'll have to go to work same as if I'd never had it. It wont pauperize me, you bet. Just one good spree for myself and the missus, giving pleasure to ourselves and employment to others, and satisfaction to you to think it's not been throwed away. You couldnt spend it better.

HIGGINS [*taking out his pocket book and coming between Doolittle and the piano*]: This is irresistible. Lets give him ten. [*He offers two notes to the dustman.*]

DOOLITTLE: No. Governor. She wouldnt have the heart to spend ten; and perhaps I shouldnt neither. Ten pounds is a lot of money: it makes a man feel prudent like; and then good-bye to happiness. You give me what I ask you, Governor: not a penny more, and not a penny less.

PICKERING: Why dont you marry that missus of yours? I rather draw the line at encouraging that sort of immorality.

DOOLITTLE: Tell her so. Governor: tell her so. I'm willing. It's me that suffers by it. Ive no hold on her. I got to be agreeable to her. I got to give her presents. I got to buy her clothes something sinful. I'm a slave to that woman, Governor, just because I'm not her lawful husband. And she knows it too. Catch her marrying me! Take my advice, Governor—marry Eliza while she's young and dont know no better. If you dont youll be sorry for it after. If you do, she'll be sorry for it after; but better her than you, because youre a man, and she's only a woman and dont know how to be happy anyhow.

HIGGINS: Pickering: If we listen to this man another minute, we shall have no convictions left. [To Doolittle.] Five pounds I think you said.

DOOLITTLE: Thank you kindly, Governor.

HIGGINS: Youre sure you wont take ten?

DOOLITTLE: Not now. Another time, Governor.

HIGGINS [handing him a five-pound note]: Here you are.

DOOLITTLE: Thank you, Governor. Good morning. [He hurries to the door, anxious to get away with his booty. When he opens it he is confronted with a dainty and exquisitely clean young Japanese lady in a simple blue cotton kimono printed cunningly with small white jasmine blossoms. Mrs Pearce is with her. He gets out of her way deferentially and apologizes.] Beg pardon, miss.

THE JAPANESE LADY: Garn! Dont you know you own daughter?

DOOLITTLE: [exclaiming] Bly me! It's Eliza!
HIGGINS: {simul-} Whats that? This!
PICKERING: [taneously] By Jove!

LIZA: Dont I look silly?

HIGGINS: Silly?

MRS PEARCE [at the door]: Now, Mr Higgins, please dont say anything to make the girl conceited about herself.

HIGGINS [conscientiously]: Oh! Quite right, Mrs Pearce. [To Eliza.] Yes: damned silly.

MRS PEARCE: Please, sir.

HIGGINS [correcting himself]: I mean extremely silly.

LIZA: I should look all right with my hat on. [She takes up her hat; puts it on; and walks across the room to the fireplace with a fashionable air.]

HIGGINS: A new fashion, by George! And it ought to look horrible!

DOOLITTLE: [with fatherly pride]: Well, I never thought she'd clean up as good looking as that, Governor. She's a credit to me, aint she?

LIZA: I tell you, it's easy to clean up here. Hot and cold water on tap, just as much as you like, there is. Woolly towels, there is; and a towel horse[4] so hot, it burns your fingers. Soft brushes to scrub yourself, and a wooden bowl of soap smelling like primroses. Now I know why ladies is so clean. Washing's a treat for them. Wish they could see what it is for the like of me!

HIGGINS: I'm glad the bathroom met with your approval.

LIZA: It didnt: not all of it; and I dont care who hears me say it. Mrs Pearce knows.

HIGGINS: What was wrong, Mrs Pearce?

MRS PEARCE [blandly]: Oh, nothing, sir. It doesnt matter.

LIZA: I had a good mind to break it. I didn't know which way to look. But I hung a towel over it, I did.

HIGGINS: Over what?

4. Towel rack.

MRS PEARCE: Over the looking-glass sir.

HIGGINS: Doolittle: you have brought your daughter up too strictly.

DOOLITTLE: Me! I never brought her up at all, except to give her a lick of a strap now and again. Dont put it on me, Governor. She aint accustomed to it, you see: thats all. But she'll soon pick up your free-and-easy ways.

LIZA: I'm a good girl, I am; and I wont pick up no free-and-easy ways.

HIGGINS: Eliza: if you say again that youre a good girl, your father shall take you home.

LIZA: Not him. You dont know my father. All he come here for was to touch you for some money to get drunk on.

DOOLITTLE: Well, what else would I want money for? To put into the plate in church, I suppose. [*She puts out her tongue at him. He is so incensed by this that Pickering presently finds it necessary to step between them.*] Dont you give me none of your lip; and dont let me hear you giving this gentleman any of it neither, or youll hear from me about it. See?

HIGGINS: Have you any further advice to give her before you go, Doolittle? Your blessing, for instance.

DOOLITTLE: No, Governor: I aint such a mug as to put up my children to all I know myself. Hard enough to hold them in without that. If you want Eliza's mind improved, Governor, you do it yourself with a strap. So long, gentlemen. [*He turns to go.*]

HIGGINS [*impressively*]: Stop. Youll come regularly to see your daughter. It's your duty, you know. My brother is a clergyman; and he could help you in your talks with her.

DOOLITTLE [*evasively*]: Certainly. I'll come, Governor. Not just this week, because I have a job at a distance. But later on you may depend on me. Afternoon, gentlemen. Afternoon, maam. [*He touches his hat to Mrs Pearce, who disdains the salutation and goes out. He winks at Higgins, thinking him probably a fellow-sufferer from Mrs Pearce's difficult disposition, and follows her.*]

LIZA: Dont you believe the old liar. He'd as soon you set a bull-dog on him as a clergyman. You wont see him again in a hurry.

HIGGINS: I dont want to, Eliza. Do you?

LIZA: Not me. I dont want never to see him again. I dont. He's a disgrace to me, he is, collecting dust, instead of working at his trade.

PICKERING: What is his trade, Eliza?

LIZA: Talking money out of other people's pockets into his own. His proper trade's a navvy[5]; and he works at it sometimes too—for exercise—and earns good money at it. Aint you going to call me Miss Doolittle any more?

PICKERING: I beg your pardon, Miss Doolittle. It was a slip of the tongue.

LIZA: Oh, I dont mind; only it sounded so genteel. I should just like to take a taxi to the corner of Tottenham Court Road and get out there and tell it to wait for me, just to put the girls in their place a bit. I wouldnt speak to them, you know.

PICKERING: Better wait til we get you something really fashionable.

HIGGINS: Besides, you shouldnt cut your old friends now that you have risen in the world. Thats what we call snobbery.

LIZA: You dont call the like of them my friends now, I should hope. Theyve took it out of me often enough with their ridicule when they had the chance; and now I mean to get a bit of my own back. But if I'm to have fashionable clothes, I'll wait.

5. Manual laborer.

I should like to have some. Mrs Pearce says youre going to give me some to wear in bed at night different to what I wear in the daytime; but it do seem a waste of money when you could get something to shew. Besides, I never could fancy changing into cold things on a winter night.

MRS PEARCE [coming back]: Now, Eliza. The new things have come for you to try on.

LIZA: Ah-ow-oo-ooh! [She rushes out.]

MRS PEARCE [following her]: Oh, dont rush about like that, girl. [She shuts the door behind her.]

HIGGINS: Pickering: we have taken on a stiff job.

PICKERING [with conviction]: Higgins: we have.

*   *   *

There seems to be some curiosity as to what Higgins's lessons to Eliza were like. Well, here is a sample: the first one.

Picture Eliza, in her new clothes, and feeling her inside put out of step by a lunch, dinner, and breakfast of a kind to which it is unaccustomed, seated with Higgins and the Colonel in the study, feeling like a hospital out-patient at a first encounter with the doctors.

Higgins, constitutionally unable to sit still, discomposes her still more by striding restlessly about. But for the reassuring presence and quietude of her friend the Colonel she would run for her life, even back to Drury Lane.

HIGGINS: Say your alphabet.

LIZA: I know my alphabet. Do you think I know nothing? I dont need to be taught like a child.

HIGGINS [thundering]: Say your alphabet.

PICKERING: Say it, Miss Doolittle. You will understand presently. Do what he tells you; and let him teach you in his own way.

LIZA: Oh well, if you put it like that—Ahyee, bə yee, cə yee, də yee—

HIGGINS [with the roar of a wounded lion]: Stop. Listen to this, Pickering. This is what we pay for as elementary education. This unfortunate animal has been locked up for nine years in school at our expense to teach her to speak and read the language of Shakespear and Milton. And the result is Ahyee, Bə -yee, Cə - yee, Də -yee. [To Eliza.] Say A, B, C, D.

LIZA [almost in tears]: But I'm saying it. Ahyee, Bə yee, Cə -yee—

HIGGINS: Stop. Say a cup of tea.

LIZA: A cappə tə -ee.

HIGGINS: Put your tongue forward until it squeezes against the top of your lower teeth. Now say cup.

LIZA: C-c-c—I cant. C-Cup.

PICKERING: Good. Splendid, Miss Doolittle.

HIGGINS: By Jupiter, she's done it at the first shot. Pickering: we shall make a duchess of her. [To Eliza.] Now do you think you could possibly say tea? Not tə - yee, mind: if you ever say bə -yee cə -yee də -yee again you shall be dragged round the room three times by the hair of your head. [Fortissimo.] T, T, T, T.

LIZA [weeping]: I cant hear no difference cep that it sounds more genteel-like when you say it.

HIGGINS: Well, if you can hear that difference, what the devil are you crying for? Pickering: give her a chocolate.

PICKERING: No, no. Never mind crying a little, Miss Doolittle: you are doing very well; and the lessons wont hurt. I promise you I wont let him drag you round the room by your hair.

HIGGINS: Be off with you to Mrs Pearce and tell her about it. Think about it. Try to do it by yourself: and keep your tongue well forward in your mouth instead of trying to roll it up and swallow it. Another lesson at half-past four this afternoon. Away with you.

[*Eliza, still sobbing, rushes from the room.*]

And that is the sort of ordeal poor Eliza has to go through for months before we meet her again on her first appearance in London society of the professional class.

ACT 3

It is Mrs Higgins's at-home day.[1] Nobody has yet arrived. Her drawing room, in a flat on Chelsea Embankment, has three windows looking on the river; and the ceiling is not so lofty as it would be in an older house of the same pretension. The windows are open, giving access to a balcony with flowers in pots. If you stand with your face to the windows, you have the fireplace on your left and the door in the right-hand wall close to the corner nearest the windows.

Mrs Higgins was brought up on Morris[2] and Burne Jones[3]; and her room, which is very unlike her son's room in Wimpole Street, is not crowded with furniture and little tables and nicknacks. In the middle of the room there is a big ottoman; and this, with the carpet, the Morris wallpapers, and the Morris chintz window curtains and brocade covers of the ottoman and its cushions, supply all the ornament, and are much too handsome to be hidden by odds and ends of useless things. A few good oil-paintings from the exhibitions in the Grosvenor Gallery thirty years ago (the Burne Jones, not the Whistler[4] side of them) are on the walls. The only landscape is a Cecil Lawson[5] on the scale of a Rubens[6]. There is a portrait of Mrs Higgins as she was when she defied the fashion in her youth in one of the beautiful Rossettian[7] costumes which, when caricatured by people who did not understand, led to the absurdities of popular estheticism in the eighteen-seventies.

In the corner diagonally opposite the door Mrs Higgins, now over sixty and long past taking the trouble to dress out of the fashion, sits writing at an elegantly simple writing-table with a bell button within reach of her hand. There is a Chippendale chair further back in the room between her and the window nearest her side. At the other side of the room, further forward, is an Elizabethan chair roughly carved in the taste of Inigo Jones. On the same side a piano in a decorated case. The corner between the fireplace and the window is occupied by a divan cushioned in Morris chintz.

It is between four and five in the afternoon.

The door is opened violently; and Higgins enters with his hat on.

MRS HIGGINS [*dismayed*]: Henry! [*Scolding him.*] What are you doing here today? It is my at-home day: you promised not to come. [*As he bends to kiss her, she takes his hat off, and presents it to him.*]

HIGGINS: Oh bother! [*He throws the hat down on the table.*]

MRS HIGGINS: Go home at once.

HIGGINS [*kissing her*]: I know, mother. I came on purpose.

MRS HIGGINS: But you mustnt. I'm serious, Henry. You offend all my friends: they stop coming whenever they meet you.

HIGGINS: Nonsense! I know I have no small talk; but people dont mind. [*He sits on the settee.*]

---

1. Reception of visitors in one's home in genteel society.
2. William Morris (1834–1896), English graphic artist, poet, and social reformer.
3. Sir Edward Coley Burne-Jones (1833–1898), English painter and designer.
4. James Abbott McNeill Whistler (1834–1903), American avant-garde painter who did much of his work living in London.
5. Cecil Gordon Lawson (1851–1882), English landscape painter.
6. Peter Paul Rubens (1577–1640), Flemish painter.
7. Dante Gabriel Rossetti (1828–1882), painter and poet, founder of the Pre-Raphaelite Brotherhood.

MRS HIGGINS: Oh! dont they? Small talk indeed! What about your large talk? Really, dear, you mustnt stay.

HIGGINS: I must. Ive a job for you. A phonetic job.

MRS HIGGINS: No use, dear. I'm sorry; but I cant get round your vowels; and though I like to get pretty postcards in your patent shorthand, I always have to read the copies in ordinary writing you so thoughtfully send me.

HIGGINS: Well, this isnt a phonetic job.

MRS HIGGINS: You said it was.

HIGGINS: Not your part of it. Ive picked up a girl.

MRS HIGGINS: Does that mean that some girl has picked you up?

HIGGINS: Not at all. I dont mean a love affair.

MRS HIGGINS: What a pity!

HIGGINS: Why?

MRS HIGGINS: Well, you never fall in love with anyone under forty-five. When will you discover that there are some rather nice-looking young women about?

HIGGINS: Oh, I cant be bothered with young women. My idea of a lovable woman is somebody as like you as possible. I shall never get into the way of seriously liking young women: some habits lie too deep to be changed. [Rising abruptly and walking about, jingling his money and his keys in his trouser pockets.] Besides, theyre all idiots.

MRS HIGGINS: Do you know what you would do if you really loved me, Henry?

HIGGINS: Oh bother! What? Marry, I suppose.

MRS HIGGINS: No. Stop fidgeting and take your hands out of your pockets. [With a gesture of despair, he obeys and sits down again.] Thats a good boy. Now tell me about the girl.

HIGGINS: She's coming to see you.

MRS HIGGINS: I dont remember asking her.

HIGGINS: You didnt. I asked her. If youd known her you wouldnt have asked her.

MRS HIGGINS: Indeed! Why?

HIGGINS: Well, It's like this. She's a common flower-girl. I picked her off the kerbstone.

MRS HIGGINS: And invited her to my at-home!

HIGGINS [rising and coming to her to coax her]: Oh, thatll be all right. Ive taught her to speak properly; and she has strict orders as to her behavior. She's to keep to two subjects: the weather and everybody's health—Fine day and How do you do, you know—and not to let herself go on things in general. That will be safe.

MRS HIGGINS: Safe! To talk about our health! About our insides! Perhaps about our outsides! How could you be so silly, Henry?

HIGGINS [impatiently]: Well, she must talk about something. [He controls himself and sits down again.] Oh, she'll be all right; dont you fuss. Pickering is in it with me. Ive a sort of bet on that I'll pass her off as a duchess in six months. I started on her some months ago; and she's getting on like a house on fire. I shall win my bet. She has a quick ear; and she's been easier to teach than my middle-class pupils because she's had to learn a complete new language. She talks English almost as you talk French.

MRS HIGGINS: Thats satisfactory, at all events.

HIGGINS: Well, it is and it isnt.

MRS HIGGINS: What does that mean?

HIGGINS: You see, Ive got her pronunciation all right; but you have to consider not only how a girl pronounces, but what she pronounces; and thats where—

[*They are interrupted by the parlormaid, announcing guests.*]

THE PARLORMAID: Mrs and Miss Eynsford Hill. [*She withdraws.*]

HIGGINS: Oh Lord! [*He rises: snatches his hat from the table; and makes for the door; but before he reaches it his mother introduces him.*]

[*Mrs and Miss Eynsford Hill are the mother and daughter who sheltered from the rain in Covent Garden. The mother is well bred, quiet, and has the habitual anxiety of straitened means. The daughter has acquired a gay air of being very much at home in society; the bravado of genteel poverty.*]

MRS EYNSFORD HILL [*to Mrs Higgins*]: How do you do? [*They shake hands.*]

MISS EYNSFORD HILL: How d'you do? [*She shakes.*]

MRS HIGGINS [*introducing*]: My son Henry.

MRS EYNSFORD HILL: Your celebrated son! I have so longed to meet you, Professor Higgins.

HIGGINS [*glumly, making no movement in her direction*]: Delighted. [*He backs against the piano and bows brusquely.*]

MISS EYNSFORD HILL [*going to him with confident familiarity*]: How do you do?

HIGGINS [*staring at her*]: Ive seen you before somewhere. I havnt the ghost of a notion where; but Ive heard your voice. [*Drearily*] It doesnt matter. Youd better sit down.

MRS HIGGINS: I'm sorry to say that my celebrated son has no manners. You mustnt mind him.

MISS EYNSFORD HILL [*gaily*]: I dont. [*She sits in the Elizabethan chair.*]

MRS EYNSFORD HILL [*a little bewildered*]: Not at all. [*She sits on the ottoman between her daughter and Mrs Higgins, who has turned her chair away from the writing-table.*]

HIGGINS: Oh, have I been rude? I didnt mean to be.

[*He goes to the central window, through which, with his back to the company, he contemplates the river and the flowers in Battersea Park on the opposite bank as if they were a frozen desert.*

The parlormaid returns, ushering in Pickering.]

THE PARLORMAID: Colonel Pickering. [*She withdraws.*]

PICKERING: How do you do, Mrs Higgins?

MRS HIGGINS: So glad youve come. Do you know Mrs Eynsford Hill—Miss Eynsford Hill? [*Exchange of bows. The Colonel brings the Chippendale chair a little forward between Mrs Hill and Mrs Higgins, and sits down.*]

PICKERING: Has Henry told you what weve come for?

HIGGINS [*over his shoulder*]: We were interrupted: damn it!

MRS HIGGINS: Oh Henry, Henry, really!

MRS EYNSFORD HILL [*half rising*]: Are we in the way?

MRS HIGGINS [*rising and making her sit down again*]: No, no. You couldnt have come more fortunately; we want you to meet a friend of ours.

HIGGINS [*turning hopefully*]: Yes, by George! We want two or three people. Youll do as well as anybody else.

[*The parlormaid returns, ushering Freddy.*]

THE PARLORMAID: Mr Eynsford Hill.

HIGGINS [*almost audibly, past endurance*]: God of Heaven! Another of them.

FREDDY [*shaking hands with Mrs Higgins*]: Ahdedo?

MRS HIGGINS: Very good of you to come. [*Introducing.*] Colonel Pickering.

FREDDY [*bowing*]: Ahdedo?

MRS HIGGINS: I dont think you know my son, Professor Higgins.

FREDDY [*going to Higgins*]: Ahdedo?

HIGGINS [*looking at him much as if he were a pickpocket*]: I'll take my oath Ive met you before somewhere. Where was it?

FREDDY: I dont think so.

HIGGINS [*resignedly*]: It dont matter, anyhow. Sit down.

> [*He shakes Freddy's hand and almost slings him on to the ottoman with his face to the window; then comes round to the other side of it.*]

HIGGINS: Well, here we are, anyhow! [*He sits down on the ottoman next Mrs Eynsford Hill, on her left.*] And now, what the devil are we going to talk about until Eliza comes?

MRS HIGGINS: Henry: you are the life and soul of the Royal Society's soirées; but really youre rather trying on more commonplace occasions.

HIGGINS: Am I? Very sorry. [*Beaming suddenly.*] I suppose I am, you know. [*Uproariously.*] Ha, ha!

MISS EYNSFORD HILL [*who considers Higgins quite eligible matrimonially*]: I sympathize. I havnt any small talk. If people would only be frank and say what they really think!

HIGGINS [*relapsing into gloom*]: Lord forbid!

MRS EYNSFORD HILL [*taking up her daughter's cue*]: But why?

HIGGINS: What they think they ought to think is bad enough, Lord knows; but what they really think would break up the whole show. Do you suppose it would be really agreeable if I were to come out now with what I really think?

MISS EYNSFORD HILL [*gaily*]: Is it so very cynical?

HIGGINS: Cynical! Who the dickens said it was cynical? I mean it wouldnt be decent.

MRS EYNSFORD HILL [*seriously*]: Oh! I'm sure you dont mean that, Mr Higgins.

HIGGINS: You see, we're all savages, more or less. We're supposed to be civilized and cultured—to know all about poetry and philosophy and art and science, and so on; but how many of us know even the meanings of these names? [*To Miss Hill.*] What do you know of poetry? [*To Mrs Hill.*] What do you know of science? [*Indicating Freddy.*] What does he know of art or science or anything else? What the devil do you imagine I know of philosophy?

MRS HIGGINS [*warningly*]: Or of manners, Henry?

THE PARLORMAID [*opening the door*]: Miss Doolittle. [*She withdraws.*]

HIGGINS [*rising hastily and running to Mrs Higgins*]: Here she is, mother. [*He stands on tiptoe and makes signs over his mother's head to Eliza to indicate to her which lady is her hostess.*]

> [*Eliza, who is exquisitely dressed, produces an impression of such remarkable distinction and beauty as she enters that they all rise, quite fluttered. Guided by Higgins's signals, she comes to Mrs Higgins with studied grace.*]

LIZA [*speaking with pedantic correctness of pronunciation and great beauty of tone*]: How do you do, Mrs Higgins? [*She gasps slightly in making sure of the H in Higgins, but is quite successful.*] Mr Higgins told me I might come.

MRS HIGGINS [*cordially*]: Quite right: I'm very glad indeed to see you.

PICKERING: How do you do, Miss Doolittle?

LIZA [*shaking hands with him*]: Colonel Pickering, is it not?

MRS EYNSFORD HILL: I feel sure we have met before, Miss Doolittle. I remember
your eyes.

LIZA: How do you do? [*She sits down on the ottoman gracefully in the place just left
vacant by Higgins.*]

MRS EYNSFORD HILL [*introducing*]: My daughter Clara.

LIZA: How do you do?

CLARA [*impulsively*]: How do you do? [*She sits down on the ottoman beside Eliza,
devouring her with her eyes.*]

FREDDY [*coming to their side of the ottoman*]: Ive certainly had the pleasure.

MRS EYNSFORD HILL [*introducing*]: My son Freddy.

LIZA: How do you do?

[*Freddy bows and sits down in the Elizabethan chair, infatuated.*]

HIGGINS [*suddenly*]: By George, yes: It all comes back to me! [*They stare at him.*]
Covent Garden! [*Lamentably.*] What a damned thing!

MRS HIGGINS: Henry, please! [*He is about to sit on the edge of the table.*] Dont sit on
my writing-table: youll break it.

HIGGINS [*sulkily*]: Sorry.

[*He goes to the divan, stumbling into the fender and over the fire-irons on his way; ex-
tricating himself with muttered imprecations; and finishing his disastrous journey by
throwing himself so impatiently on the divan that he almost breaks it. Mrs Higgins looks
at him, but controls herself and says nothing.*

A long and painful pause ensues.]

MRS HIGGINS [*at last, conversationally*]: Will it rain, do you think?

LIZA: The shallow depression in the west of these islands is likely to move slowly in
an easterly direction. There are no indications of any great change in the baro-
metrical situation.

FREDDY: Ha! ha! how awfully funny!

LIZA: What is wrong with that, young man? I bet I got it right.

FREDDY: Killing!

MRS EYNSFORD HILL: I'm sure I hope it wont turn cold. Theres so much influenza about. It runs right through our whole family regularly every spring.

LIZA [*darkly*]: My aunt died of influenza: so they said.

MRS EYNSFORD HILL [*clicks her tongue sympathetically*]: !!!

LIZA [*in the same tragic tone*]: But it's my belief they done the old woman in.

MRS HIGGINS [*puzzled*]: Done her in?

LIZA: Y-e-e-e-es, Lord love you! Why should she die of influenza? She come through
diphtheria right enough the year before. I saw her with my own eyes. Fairly blue
with it, she was. They all thought she was dead; but my father he kept ladling gin
down her throat til she came to so sudden that she bit the bowl off the spoon.

MRS EYNSFORD HILL [*startled*]: Dear me!

LIZA [*piling up the indictment*]: What call would a woman with that strength in her
have to die of influenza? What become of her new straw hat that should have
come to me? Somebody pinched it; and what I say is, them as pinched it done her
in.

MRS EYNSFORD HILL: What does doing her in mean?

HIGGINS [*hastily*]: Oh, thats the new small talk. To do a person in means to kill
them.

MRS EYNSFORD HILL [*to Eliza, horrified*]: You surely dont believe that your aunt was killed?

LIZA: Do I not! Them she lived with would have killed her for a hat-pin, let alone a hat.

MRS EYNSFORD HILL: But it cant have been right for your father to pour spirits down her throat like that. It might have killed her.

LIZA: Not her. Gin was mother's milk to her. Besides, he'd poured so much down his own throat that he knew the good of it.

MRS EYNSFORD HILL: Do you mean that he drank?

LIZA: Drank! My word! Something chronic.

MRS EYNSFORD HILL: How dreadful for you!

LIZA: Not a bit. It never did him no harm what I could see. But then he did not keep it up regular. [*Cheerfully.*] On the burst, as you might say, from time to time. And always more agreeable when he had a drop in. When he was out of work, my mother used to give him fourpence and tell him to go out and not come back until he'd drunk himself cheerful and loving-like. Theres lots of women has to make their husbands drunk to make them fit to live with. [*Now quite at her ease.*] You see, it's like this. If a man has a bit of a conscience, it always takes him when he's sober; and then it makes him low-spirited. A drop of booze just takes that off and makes him happy. [*To Freddy, who is in convulsions of suppressed laughter.*] Here! What are you sniggering at?

FREDDY: The new small talk. You do it so awfully well.

LIZA: If I was doing it proper, what was you laughing at? [*To Higgins.*] Have I said anything I oughtnt?

MRS HIGGINS [*interposing*]: Not at all, Miss Doolittle.

LIZA: Well, thats a mercy, anyhow. [*Expansively.*] What I always say is—

HIGGINS [*rising and looking at his watch*]: Ahem!

LIZA [*looking round at him; taking the hint; and rising*]: Well: I must go. [*They all rise. Freddy goes to the door.*] So pleased to have met you. Goodbye. [*She shakes hands with Mrs Higgins.*]

MRS HIGGINS: Goodbye.

LIZA: Goodbye, Colonel Pickering.

PICKERING: Goodbye, Miss Doolittle. [*They shake hands*].

LIZA [*nodding to the others*]: Goodbye, all.

FREDDY [*opening the door for her*]: Are you walking across the Park, Miss Doolittle? If so—

LIZA [*perfectly elegant diction*]: Walk! Not bloody likely. [*Sensation.*] I am going in a taxi. [*She goes out.*]

[*Pickering gasps and sits down. Freddy goes out on the balcony to catch another glimpse of Eliza.*]

MRS EYNSFORD HILL [*suffering from shock*]: Well, I really cant get used to the new ways.

CLARA [*throwing herself discontentedly into the Elizabethan chair*]: Oh, it's all right, mamma, quite right. People will think we never go anywhere or see anybody if you are so old-fashioned.

MRS EYNSFORD HILL: I daresay I am very old-fashioned; but I do hope you wont begin using that expression, Clara. I have got accustomed to hear you talking about men as rotters, and calling everything filthy and beastly; though I do think it horrible and unladylike. But this last is really too much. Dont you think so, Colonel Pickering?

PICKERING: Dont ask me, Ive been away in India for several years; and manners have changed so much that I sometimes dont know whether I'm at a respectable dinner-table or in a ship's forecastle.

CLARA: It's all a matter of habit. Theres no right or wrong in it. Nobody means anything by it. And it's so quaint, and gives such a smart emphasis to things that are not in themselves very witty. I find the new small talk delightful and quite innocent.

MRS EYNSFORD HILL [rising]: Well, after that, I think it's time for us to go.
   [Pickering and Higgins rise.]

CLARA [rising]: Oh yes: we have three at-homes to go to still. Goodbye, Mrs Higgins. Goodbye, Colonel Pickering. Goodbye, Professor Higgins.

HIGGINS [coming grimly at her from the divan, and accompanying her to the door]: Goodbye. Be sure you try on that small talk at the three at-homes. Dont be nervous about it. Pitch it in strong.

CLARA [all smiles]: I will. Goodbye. Such nonsense, all this early Victorian prudery!

HIGGINS [tempting her]: Such damned nonsense!

CLARA: Such bloody nonsense!

MRS EYNSFORD HILL [convulsively]: Clara!

CLARA: Ha! ha! [She goes out radiant, conscious of being thoroughly up to date, and is heard descending the stairs in a stream of silvery laughter.]

FREDDY [to the heavens at large]: Well, I ask you—[He gives it up, and comes to Mrs Higgins.] Goodbye.

MRS HIGGINS [shaking hands]: Goodbye. Would you like to meet Miss Doolittle again?

FREDDY [eagerly]: Yes, I should, most awfully.

MRS HIGGINS: Well, you know my days.

FREDDY: Yes. Thanks awfully. Goodbye. [He goes out.]

MRS EYNSFORD HILL: Goodbye, Mr Higgins.

HIGGINS: Goodbye. Goodbye.

MRS EYNSFORD HILL [to Pickering]: It's no use. I shall never be able to bring myself to use that word.

PICKERING: Dont. It's not compulsory, you know. Youll get on quite well without it.

MRS EYNSFORD HILL: Only, Clara is so down on me if I am not positively reeking with the latest slang. Goodbye.

PICKERING: Goodbye. [They shake hands.]

MRS EYNSFORD HILL [to Mrs Higgins]: You mustnt mind Clara. [Pickering, catching from her lowered tone that this is not meant for him to hear, discreetly joins Higgins at the window.] We're so poor! and she gets so few parties, poor child! She doesnt quite know. [Mrs Higgins, seeing that her eyes are moist, takes her hand sympathetically and goes with her to the door.] But the boy is nice. Dont you think so?

MRS HIGGINS: Oh, quite nice. I shall always be delighted to see him.

MRS EYNSFORD HILL: Thank you, dear. Goodbye. [She goes out.]

HIGGINS [eagerly]: Well? Is Eliza presentable? [He swoops on his mother and drags her to the ottoman, where she sits down in Eliza's place with her son on her left.]
   [Pickering returns to his chair on her right.]

MRS HIGGINS: You silly boy, of course she's not presentable. She's a triumph of your art and of her dressmaker's; but if you suppose for a moment that she doesnt give herself away in every sentence she utters, you must be perfectly cracked about her.

PICKERING: But dont you think something might be done? I mean something to eliminate the sanguinary element from her conversation.

MRS HIGGINS: Not as long as she is in Henry's hands.

HIGGINS [*aggrieved*]: Do you mean that my language is improper?

MRS HIGGINS: No, dearest: it would be quite proper—say on a canal barge; but it would not be proper for her at a garden party.

HIGGINS [*deeply injured*]: Well I must say—

PICKERING [*interrupting him*]: Come, Higgins: you must learn to know yourself. I havnt heard such language as yours since we used to review the volunteers in Hyde Park twenty years ago.

HIGGINS [*sulkily*]: Oh, well, if you say so, I suppose I dont always talk like a bishop.

MRS HIGGINS [*quieting Henry with a touch*]: Colonel Pickering: will you tell me what is the exact state of things in Wimpole Street?

PICKERING [*cheerfully: as if this completely changed the subject*]: Well, I have come to live there with Henry. We work together at my Indian Dialects; and we think it more convenient—

MRS HIGGINS: Quite so. I know all about that: it's an excellent arrangement. But where does this girl live?

HIGGINS: With us, of course. Where should she live?

MRS HIGGINS: But on what terms? Is she a servant? If not, what is she?

PICKERING [*slowly*]: I think I know what you mean, Mrs Higgins.

HIGGINS: Well, dash me if *I* do! Ive had to work at the girl every day for months to get her to her present pitch. Besides, she's useful. She knows where my things are, and remembers my appointments and so forth.

MRS HIGGINS: How does your housekeeper get on with her?

HIGGINS: Mrs Pearce? Oh, she's jolly glad to get so much taken off her hands; for before Eliza came, she used to have to find things and remind me of my appointments. But she's got some silly bee in her bonnet about Eliza. She keeps saying "You dont think, sir": doesnt she, Pick?

PICKERING: Yes: thats the formula. "You dont think, sir." Thats the end of every conversation about Eliza.

HIGGINS: As if I ever stop thinking about the girl and her confounded vowels and consonants. I'm worn out, thinking about her, and watching her lips and her teeth and her tongue, not to mention her soul, which is the quaintest of the lot.

MRS HIGGINS: You certainly are a pretty pair of babies, playing with your live doll.

HIGGINS: Playing! The hardest job I ever tackled: make no mistake about that, mother. But you have no idea how frightfully interesting it is to take a human being and change her into a quite different human being by creating a new speech for her. It's filling up the deepest gulf that separates class from class and soul from soul.

PICKERING [*drawing his chair closer to Mrs Higgins and bending over to her eagerly*]: Yes: it's enormously interesting. I assure you. Mrs Higgins, we take Eliza very seriously. Every week—every day almost—there is some new change. [*Closer again.*] We keep records of every stage—dozens of gramophone disks and photographs—

HIGGINS [*assailing her at the other ear*]: Yes, by George: it's the most absorbing experiment I ever tackled. She regularly fills our lives up: doesnt she, Pick?

PICKERING: We're always talking Eliza.

HIGGINS: Teaching Eliza.

PICKERING: Dressing Eliza.

MRS HIGGINS: What!

HIGGINS: Inventing new Elizas.

HIGGINS: ⎫ ⎧You know, she has the most extraordinary quickness of ear;
PICKERING: ⎬ ⎨I assure you, my dear Mrs Higgins, that girl
HIGGINS: ⎫ ⎧just like a parrot. Ive tried her with every
PICKERING: ⎬ ⎨is a genius. She can play the piano quite beautifully.
HIGGINS: ⎫ ⎧possible sort of sound that a human being can make—
PICKERING: ⎬ ⎨We have taken her to classical concerts and to music
HIGGINS: ⎫ [*speaking* ⎧Continental dialects, African dialects, Hottentot
PICKERING: ⎬ *together*] ⎨halls; and it's all the same to her: she plays everything
HIGGINS: ⎫ ⎧clicks, things it took me years to get hold of; and
PICKERING: ⎬ ⎨she hears right off when she comes home, whether it's
HIGGINS: ⎫ ⎧she picks them up like a shot, right away, as if she had
PICKERING: ⎬ ⎨Beethoven and Brahms or Lehar and Lionel Monckton;
HIGGINS: ⎫ ⎧been at it all her life.
PICKERING: ⎭ ⎩though six months ago, she'd never as much as touched a piano—

MRS HIGGINS [*putting her fingers in her ears, as they are by this time shouting one another down with an intolerable noise*]: Sh-sh-sh—sh!
    [*They stop.*]

PICKERING: I beg your pardon. [*He draws his chair back apologetically.*]

HIGGINS: Sorry. When Pickering starts shouting nobody can get a word in edgeways.

MRS HIGGINS: Be quiet, Henry, Colonel Pickering: dont you realize that when Eliza walked into Wimpole Street, something walked in with her?

PICKERING: Her father did. But Henry soon got rid of him.

MRS HIGGINS: It would have been more to the point if her mother had. But as her mother didnt something else did.

PICKERING: But what?

MRS HIGGINS [*unconsciously dating herself by the word*]: A problem.

PICKERING: Oh I see. The problem of how to pass her off as a lady.

HIGGINS: I'll solve that problem. Ive half solved it already.

MRS HIGGINS: No, you two infinitely stupid male creatures: the problem of what is to be done with her afterwards.

HIGGINS: I dont see anything in that. She can go her own way, with all the advantages I have given her.

MRS HIGGINS: The advantages of that poor woman who was here just now! The manners and habits that disqualify a fine lady from earning her own living without giving her a fine lady's income! Is that what you mean?

PICKERING [*indulgently, being rather bored*]: Oh, that will be all right, Mrs Higgins. [*He rises to go.*]

HIGGINS [*rising also*]: We'll find her some light employment.

PICKERING: She's happy enough. Dont you worry about her. Goodbye. [*He shakes hands as if he were consoling a frightened child, and makes for the door.*]

HIGGINS: Anyhow, theres no good bothering now. The thing's done. Goodbye, mother. [*He kisses her, and follows Pickering.*]

PICKERING [*turning for a final consolation*]: There are plenty of openings. We'll do whats right. Goodbye.

HIGGINS [*to Pickering as they go out together*]: Lets take her to the Shakespear exhibition at Earls Court.

PICKERING: Yes: lets. Her remarks will be delicious.

HIGGINS: She'll mimic all the people for us when we get home.

PICKERING: Ripping. [Both are heard laughing as they go down-stairs.]

MRS HIGGINS [rises with an impatient bounce, and returns to her work at the writing-table. She sweeps a litter of disarranged papers out of the way; snatches a sheet of paper from her stationery case; and tries resolutely to write. At the third time she gives it up; flings down her pen; grips the table angrily and exclaims]: Oh, men! men!! men!!!

* * *

Clearly Eliza will not pass as a duchess yet; and Higgins's bet remains unwon. But the six months are not yet exhausted; and just in time Eliza does actually pass as a princess. For a glimpse of how she did it imagine an Embassy in London one summer evening after dark. The hall door has an awning and a carpet across the sidewalk to the kerb, because a grand reception is in progress. A small crowd is lined up to see the guests arrive.

A Rolls-Royce car drives up. Pickering in evening dress, with medals and orders, alights, and hands out Eliza, in opera cloak, evening dress, diamonds, fan, flowers and all accessories. Higgins follows. The car drives off; and the three go up the steps and into the house, the door opening for them as they approach.

Inside the house they find themselves in a spacious hall from which the grand staircase rises. On the left are the arrangements for the gentlemen's cloaks. The male guests are depositing their hats and wraps there.

On the right is a door leading to the ladies' cloakroom. Ladies are going in cloaked and coming out in splendor. Pickering whispers to Eliza and points out the ladies' room. She goes into it. Higgins and Pickering take off their overcoats and take tickets for them from the attendant.

One of the guests, occupied in the same way, has his back turned. Having taken his ticket, he turns round and reveals himself as an important looking young man with an astonishingly hairy face. He has an enormous moustache, flowing out into luxuriant whiskers. Waves of hair cluster on his brow. His hair is cropped closely at the back, and glows with oil. Otherwise he is very smart. He wears several worthless orders. He is evidently a foreigner, guessable as a whiskered Pandour[8] from Hungary: but in spite of the ferocity of his moustache he is amiable and genially voluble.

Recognizing Higgins, he flings his arms wide apart and approaches him enthusiastically.

WHISKERS: Maestro, maestro. [He embraces Higgins and kisses him on both cheeks.] You remember me?

HIGGINS: No I dont. Who the devil are you?

WHISKERS: I am your pupil: your first pupil, your best and greatest pupil. I am little Nepommuck, the marvellous boy. I have made your name famous throughout Europe. You teach me phonetic. You cannot forget ME.

HIGGINS: Why dont you shave?

NEPOMMUCK: I have not your imposing appearance, your chin, your brow. Nobody notices me when I shave. Now I am famous: they call me Hairy Faced Dick.

HIGGINS: And what are you doing here among all these swells?

NEPOMMUCK: I am interpreter. I speak 32 languages. I am indispensable at these international parties. You are great cockney specialist: you place a man anywhere in London the moment he open his mouth. I place any man in Europe.

[A footman hurries down the grand staircase and comes to Nepommuck.]

FOOTMAN: You are wanted upstairs. Her Excellency cannot understand the Greek gentleman.

NEPOMMUCK: Thank you, yes, immediately.

8. Member of the legendarily cruel Croatian militia.

[*The footman goes and is lost in the crowd.*]

NEPOMMUCK. [*to Higgins*]: This Greek diplomatist pretends he cannot speak nor understand English. He cannot deceive me. He is the son of a Clerkenwell watchmaker. He speaks English so villainously that he dare not utter a word of it without betraying his origin. I help him to pretend; but I make him pay through the nose. I make them all pay. Ha ha! [*He hurries upstairs.*]

PICKERING: Is this fellow really an expert? Can he find out Eliza and blackmail her?

HIGGINS: We shall see. If he finds her out I lose my bet.

[*Eliza comes from the cloakroom and joins them.*]

PICKERING: Well, Eliza, now for it. Are you ready?

LIZA: Are you nervous, Colonel?

PICKERING: Frightfully. I feel exactly as I felt before my first battle. It's the first time that frightens.

LIZA: It is not the first time for me, Colonel. I have done this fifty times—hundreds of times—in my little piggery in Angel Court in my day-dreams. I am in a dream now. Promise me not to let Professor Higgins wake me; for if he does I shall forget everything and talk as I used to in Drury Lane.

PICKERING: Not a word, Higgins. [*To Eliza.*] Now ready?

LIZA: Ready.

PICKERING: Go.

[*They mount the stairs, Higgins last. Pickering whispers to the footman on the first landing.*]

FIRST LANDING FOOTMAN: Miss Doolittle, Colonel Pickering, Professor Higgins.

SECOND LANDING FOOTMAN: Miss Doolittle, Colonel Pickering, Professor Higgins.

[*At the top of the staircase the Ambassador and his wife, with Nepommuck at her elbow, are receiving.*]

HOSTESS [*taking Eliza's hand*]: How d'ye do?

HOST [*same play*]: How d'ye do? How d'ye do, Pickering?

LIZA [*with a beautiful gravity that awes her hostess*]: How do you do? [*She passes on to the drawing room.*]

HOSTESS: Is that your adopted daughter, Colonel Pickering? She will make a sensation.

PICKERING: Most kind of you to invite her for me. [*He passes on.*]

HOSTESS [*to Nepommuck*]: Find out all about her.

NEPOMMUCK [*bowing*]: Excellency—[*He goes into the crowd.*]

HOST: How d'ye do, Higgins? You have a rival here tonight. He introduced himself as your pupil. Is he any good?

HIGGINS: He can learn a language in a fortnight—knows dozens of them. A sure mark of a fool. As a phonetician, no good whatever.

HOSTESS: How d'ye do, Professor?

HIGGINS: How do you do? Fearful bore for you this sort of thing. Forgive my part in it. [*He passes on.*]

[*In the drawing room and its suite of salons the reception is in full swing. Eliza passes through. She is so intent on her ordeal that she walks like a somnambulist in a desert instead of a débutante in a fashionable crowd. They stop talking to look at her, admiring her dress, her jewels, and her strangely attractive self. Some of the younger ones at the back stand on their chairs to see.*]

1044   Bernard Shaw

The Host and Hostess come in from the staircase and mingle with their guests. Higgins, gloomy and contemptuous of the whole business, comes into the group where they are chatting.]

HOSTESS: Ah, here is Professor Higgins: he will tell us. Tell us all about the wonderful young lady, Professor.

HIGGINS [*almost morosely*]: What wonderful young lady?

HOSTESS: You know very well. They tell me there has been nothing like her in London since people stood on their chairs to look at Mrs Langtry.[9]

[*Nepommuck joins the group, full of news.*]

HOSTESS: Ah, here you are at last, Nepommuck. Have you found out all about the Doolittle lady?

NEPOMMUCK: I have found out all about her. She is a fraud.

HOSTESS: A fraud! Oh no.

NEPOMMUCK: YES, yes. She cannot deceive me. Her name cannot be Doolittle.

HIGGINS: Why?

NEPOMMUCK: Because Doolittle is an English name. And she is not English.

HOSTESS: Oh, nonsense! She speaks English perfectly.

NEPOMMUCK: Too perfectly. Can you shew me any English woman who speaks English as it should be spoken? Only foreigners who have been taught to speak it speak it well.

HOSTESS: Certainly she terrified me by the way she said How d'ye do. I had a schoolmistress who talked like that; and I was mortally afraid of her. But if she is not English what is she?

NEPOMMUCK: Hungarian.

ALL THE REST: Hungarian!

NEPOMMUCK: Hungarian. And of royal blood. I am Hungarian. My blood is royal.

HIGGINS: Did you speak to her in Hungarian?

NEPOMMUCK: I did. She was very clever. She said "Please speak to me in English: I do not understand French." French! She pretends not to know the difference between Hungarian and French. Impossible: she knows both.

HIGGINS: And the blood royal? How did you find that out?

NEPOMMUCK: Instinct, maestro, instinct. Only the Magyar races can produce that air of the divine right, those resolute eyes. She is a princess.

HOST: What do you say, Professor?

HIGGINS: I say an ordinary London girl out of the gutter and taught to speak by an expert. I place her in Drury Lane.

NEPOMMUCK: Ha ha ha! Oh, maestro, maestro, you are mad on the subject of cockney dialects. The London gutter is the whole world for you.

HIGGINS [*to the Hostess*]: What does your Excellency say?

HOSTESS: Oh, of course I agree with Nepommuck. She must be a princess at least.

HOST: Not necessarily legitimate, of course. Morganatic[1] perhaps. But that is undoubtedly her class.

HIGGINS: I stick to my opinion.

HOSTESS: Oh, you are incorrigible.

9. Lillie Langtry (1852–1929), English actress and celebrity spokesperson for Pears' soap.
1. Form of marriage in which partners of unequal social station agree that neither the lower-ranking spouse nor any children will have a claim to the higher-ranking spouse's titles or property.

[*The group breaks up, leaving Higgins isolated. Pickering joins him.*]

PICKERING: Where is Eliza? We must keep an eye on her.

[*Eliza joins them.*]

LIZA: I dont think I can bear much more. The people all stare so at me. An old lady has just told me that I speak exactly like Queen Victoria. I am sorry if I have lost your bet. I have done my best: but nothing can make me the same as these people.

PICKERING: You have not lost it, my dear. You have won it ten times over.

HIGGINS: Let us get out of this. I have had enough of chattering to these fools.

PICKERING: Eliza is tired; and I am hungry. Let us clear out and have supper somewhere.

ACT 4

The Wimpole Street laboratory. Midnight. Nobody in the room. The clock on the mantelpiece strikes twelve. The fire is not alight: it is a summer night.

Presently Higgins and Pickering are heard on the stairs.

HIGGINS [*calling down to Pickering*]: I say, Pick: lock up, will you? I shant be going out again.

PICKERING: Right. Can Mrs Pearce go to bed? We dont want anything more, do we?

HIGGINS: Lord, no!

[*Eliza opens the door and is seen on the lighted landing in all the finery in which she has just won Higgins's bet for him. She comes to the hearth, and switches on the electric lights there. She is tired: her pallor contrasts strongly with her dark eyes and hair; and her expression is almost tragic. She takes off her cloak; puts her fan and gloves on the piano; and sits down on the bench, brooding and silent. Higgins, in evening dress, with overcoat and hat, comes in, carrying a smoking jacket which he has picked up downstairs. He takes off the hat and overcoat; throws them carelessly on the newspaper stand; disposes of his coat in the same way; puts on the smoking jacket; and throws himself wearily into the easy-chair at the hearth. Pickering, similarly attired, comes in. He also takes off his hat and overcoat, and is about to throw them on Higgins's when he hesitates.*]

PICKERING: I say: Mrs Pearce will row if we leave these things lying about in the drawing room.

HIGGINS: Oh, chuck them over the bannisters into the hall. She'll find them there in the morning and put them away all right. She'll think we were drunk.

PICKERING: We are, slightly. Are there any letters?

HIGGINS: I didnt look. [*Pickering takes the overcoats and hats and goes downstairs. Higgins begins half singing half yawning an air from La Fanciulla del Golden West. Suddenly he stops and exclaims.*] I wonder where the devil my slippers are!

[*Eliza looks at him darkly; then rises suddenly and leaves the room.*

Higgins yawns again, and resumes his song.

Pickering returns, with the contents of the letterbox in his hand.]

PICKERING: Only circulars, and this coroneted billet-doux[1] for you. [*He throws the circulars into the fender, and posts himself on the hearthrug, with his back to the grate.*]

HIGGINS [*glancing at the billet-doux*]: Money-lender. [*He throws the letter after the circulars.*]

1. Love letter.

[*Eliza returns with a pair of large down-at-heel slippers. She places them on the carpet before Higgins, and sits as before without a word.*]

HIGGINS [*yawning again*]: Oh Lord! What an evening! What a crew! What a silly tomfoolery! [*He raises his shoe to unlace it, and catches sight of the slippers. He stops unlacing and looks at them as if they had appeared there of their own accord.*] Oh! theyre there, are they?

PICKERING [*stretching himself*]: Well, I feel a bit tired. It's been a long day. The garden party, a dinner party, and the reception! Rather too much of a good thing. But youve won your bet, Higgins. Eliza did the trick, and something to spare, eh?

HIGGINS [*fervently*]: Thank God it's over!

[*Eliza flinches violently; but they take no notice of her; and she recovers herself and sits stonily as before.*]

PICKERING: Were you nervous at the garden party? *I* was. Eliza didnt seem a bit nervous.

HIGGINS: Oh, she wasnt nervous. I knew she'd be all right. No: it's the strain of putting the job through all these months that has told on me. It was interesting enough at first, while we were at the phonetics; but after that I got deadly sick of it. If I hadnt backed myself to do it I should have chucked the whole thing up two months ago. It was a silly notion: the whole thing has been a bore.

PICKERING: Oh come! the garden party was frightfully exciting. My heart began beating like anything.

HIGGINS: Yes, for the first three minutes. But when I saw we were going to win hands down, I felt like a bear in a cage, hanging about doing nothing. The dinner was worse: sitting gorging there for over an hour, with nobody but a damned fool of a fashionable woman to talk to! I tell you, Pickering, never again for me. No more artificial duchesses. The whole thing has been simple purgatory.

PICKERING: Youve never been broken in properly to the social routine. [*Strolling over to the piano.*] I rather enjoy dipping into it occasionally myself: it makes me feel young again. Anyhow, it was a great success: an immense success. I was quite frightened once or twice because Eliza was doing it so well. You see, lots of the real people cant do it at all: theyre such fools that they think style comes by nature to people in their position; and so they never learn. Theres always something professional about doing a thing superlatively well.

HIGGINS: Yes: thats what drives me mad: the silly people dont know their own silly business. [*Rising.*] However, it's over and done with; and now I can go to bed at last without dreading tomorrow.

[*Eliza's beauty becomes murderous.*]

PICKERING: I think I shall turn in too. Still, it's been a great occasion: a triumph for you. Goodnight. [*He goes.*]

HIGGINS [*following him*]: Goodnight. [*Over his shoulder, at the door.*] Put out the lights, Eliza; and tell Mrs Pearce not to make coffee for me in the morning: I'll take tea. [*He goes out.*]

[*Eliza tries to control herself and feel indifferent as she rises and walks across to the hearth to switch off the lights. By the time she gets there she is on the point of screaming. She sits down in Higgins's chair and holds on hard to the arms. Finally she gives way and flings herself furiously on the floor, raging.*]

HIGGINS [*in despairing wrath outside*]: What the devil have I done with my slippers? [*He appears at the door.*]

LIZA [*snatching up the slippers, and hurling them at him one after the other with all her force*]: There are your slippers. And there. Take your slippers; and may you never have a day's luck with them!

HIGGINS [*astounded*]: What on earth—! [*He comes to her.*] Whats the matter? Get up. [*He pulls her up.*] Anything wrong?

LIZA [*breathless*]: Nothing wrong—with you. Ive won your bet for you, havnt I? Thats enough for you. *I* dont matter, I suppose.

HIGGINS: You won my bet! You! Presumptuous insect! *I* won it. What did you throw those slippers at me for?

LIZA: Because I wanted to smash your face. I'd like to kill you, you selfish brute. Why didnt you leave me where you picked me out of—in the gutter? You thank God it's all over, and that now you can throw me back again there, do you? [*She crisps her fingers frantically.*]

HIGGINS [*looking at her in cool wonder*]: The creature is nervous, after all.

LIZA [*gives a suffocated scream of fury, and instinctively darts her nails at his face*]: !!

HIGGINS [*catching her wrists*]: Ah! would you? Claws in, you cat. How dare you shew your temper to me? Sit down and be quiet. [*He throws her roughly into the easy-chair.*]

LIZA [*crushed by superior strength and weight*]: Whats to become of me? Whats to become of me?

HIGGINS: How the devil do I know whats to become of you? What does it matter what becomes of you?

LIZA: You dont care. I know you dont care. You wouldnt care if I was dead. I'm nothing to you—not so much as them slippers.

HIGGINS [*thundering*]: Those slippers.

LIZA [*with bitter submission*]: Those slippers. I didnt think it made any difference now.

[*A pause. Eliza hopeless and crushed. Higgins a little uneasy.*]

HIGGINS [*in his loftiest manner*]: Why have you begun going on like this? May I ask whether you complain of your treatment here?

LIZA: No.

HIGGINS: Has anybody behaved badly to you? Colonel Pickering? Mrs Pearce? Any of the servants?

LIZA: No.

HIGGINS: I presume you dont pretend that *I* have treated you badly?

LIZA: No.

HIGGINS: I am glad to hear it. [*He moderates his tone.*] Perhaps youre tired after the strain of the day. Will you have a glass of champagne? [*He moves towards the door.*]

LIZA: No. [*Recollecting her manners.*] Thank you.

HIGGINS [*good-humored again*]: This has been coming on you for some days. I suppose it was natural for you to be anxious about the garden party. But thats all over now. [*He pats her kindly on the shoulder. She writhes.*] Theres nothing more to worry about.

LIZA: No. Nothing more for you to worry about. [*She suddenly rises and gets away from him by going to the piano bench, where she sits and hides her face.*] Oh God! I wish I was dead.

HIGGINS [*staring after her in sincere surprise*]: Why? In heaven's name, why? [*Reasonably, going to her.*] Listen to me, Eliza. All this irritation is purely subjective.

LIZA: I dont understand. I'm too ignorant.

HIGGINS: It's only imagination. Low spirits and nothing else. Nobody's hurting you. Nothing's wrong. You go to bed like a good girl and sleep it off. Have a little cry and say your prayers: that will make you comfortable.

LIZA: I heard your prayers. "Thank God it's all over!"

HIGGINS [impatiently]: Well, dont you thank God it's all over? Now you are free and can do what you like.

LIZA [pulling herself together in desperation]: What am I fit for? What have you left me fit for? Where am I to go? What am I to do? Whats to become of me?

HIGGINS [enlightened, but not at all impressed]: Oh, thats whats worrying you, is it? [He thrusts his hands into his pockets, and walks about in his usual manner, rattling the contents of his pockets, as if condescending to a trivial subject out of pure kindness.] I shouldnt bother about it if I were you. I should imagine you wont have much difficulty in settling yourself somewhere or other, though I hadnt quite realized that you were going away. [She looks quickly at him: he does not look at her, but examines the dessert stand on the piano and decides that he will eat an apple.] You might marry, you know. [He bites a large piece out of the apple and munches it noisily.] You see, Eliza, all men are not confirmed old bachelors like me and the Colonel. Most men are the marrying sort (poor devils!); and youre not bad-looking: it's quite a pleasure to look at you sometimes—not now, of course, because youre crying and looking as ugly as the very devil; but when youre all right and quite yourself, youre what I should call attractive. That is, to the people in the marrying line, you understand. You go to bed and have a good nice rest; and then get up and look at yourself in the glass; and you wont feel so cheap.

[Eliza again looks at him, speechless, and does not stir.

The look is quite lost on him: he eats his apple with a dreamy expression of happiness, as it is quite a good one.]

HIGGINS [a genial afterthought occurring to him]: I daresay my mother could find some chap or other who would do very well.

LIZA: We were above that at the corner of Tottenham Court Road.

HIGGINS [waking up]: What do you mean?

LIZA: I sold flowers. I didnt sell myself. Now youve made a lady of me I'm not fit to sell anything else. I wish youd left me where you found me.

HIGGINS [slinging the core of the apple decisively into the grate]: Tosh, Eliza. Dont you insult human relations by dragging all this cant about buying and selling into it. You neednt marry the fellow if you dont like him.

LIZA: What else am I to do?

HIGGINS: Oh, lots of things. What about your old idea of a florist's shop? Pickering could set you up in one: he has lots of money. [Chuckling.] He'll have to pay for all those togs you have been wearing today; and that, with the hire of the jewellery, will make a big hole in two hundred pounds. Why, six months ago you would have thought it the millennium to have a flower shop of your own. Come! youll be all right. I must clear off to bed: I'm devilish sleepy. By the way, I came down for something: I forget what it was.

LIZA: Your slippers.

HIGGINS: Oh yes, of course. You shied them at me. [He picks them up, and is going out when she rises and speaks to him.]

LIZA: Before you go, sir—

HIGGINS [dropping the slippers in his surprise at her calling him Sir]: Eh?

LIZA: Do my clothes belong to me or to Colonel Pickering?

HIGGINS [*coming back into the room as if her question were the very climax of unreason*]: What the devil use would they be to Pickering?

LIZA: He might want them for the next girl you pick up to experiment on.

HIGGINS [*shocked and hurt*]: Is that the way you feel towards us?

LIZA: I dont want to hear anything more about that. All I want to know is whether anything belongs to me. My own clothes were burnt.

HIGGINS: But what does it matter? Why need you start bothering about that in the middle of the night?

LIZA: I want to know what I may take away with me. I dont want to be accused of stealing.

HIGGINS [*now deeply wounded*]: Stealing! You shouldnt have said that. Eliza. That shews a want of feeling.

LIZA: I'm sorry. I'm only a common ignorant girl; and in my station I have to be careful. There cant be any feelings between the like of you and the like of me. Please will you tell me what belongs to me and what doesnt?

HIGGINS [*very sulky*]: You may take the whole damned houseful if you like. Except the jewels. Theyre hired. Will that satisfy you? [*He turns on his heel and is about to go in extreme dudgeon.²*]

LIZA [*drinking in his emotion like nectar, and nagging him to provoke a further supply*]: Stop, please. [*She takes off her jewels.*] Will you take these to your room and keep them safe? I dont want to run the risk of their being missing.

HIGGINS [*furious*]: Hand them over. [*She puts them into his hands.*] If these belonged to me instead of to the jeweller, I'd ram them down your ungrateful throat. [*He perfunctorily thrusts them into his pockets, unconsciously decorating himself with the protruding ends of the chains.*]

LIZA [*taking a ring off*]: This ring isnt the jeweller's: it's the one you bought me in Brighton. I dont want it now. [*Higgins dashes the ring violently into the fireplace, and turns on her so threateningly that she crouches over the piano with her hands over her face, and exclaims.*] Dont you hit me.

HIGGINS: Hit you! You infamous creature, how dare you accuse me of such a thing? It is you who have hit me. You have wounded me to the heart.

LIZA [*thrilling with hidden joy*]: I'm glad. Ive got a little of my own back, anyhow.

HIGGINS [*with dignity, in his finest professional style*]: You have caused me to lose my temper: a thing that has hardly ever happened to me before. I prefer to say nothing more tonight. I am going to bed.

LIZA [*pertly*]: Youd better leave a note for Mrs Pearce about the coffee; for she wont be told by me.

HIGGINS [*formally*]: Damn Mrs Pearce; and damn the coffee: and damn you; and [*wildly*] damn my own folly in having lavished my hard-earned knowledge and the treasure of my regard and intimacy on a heartless guttersnipe. [*He goes out with impressive decorum, and spoils it by slamming the door savagely*].

[*Eliza goes down on her knees on the hearthrug to look for the ring. When she finds it she considers for a moment what to do with it. Finally she flings it down on the dessert stand and goes upstairs in a tearing rage.*]

*   *   *

2. Anger, irritation.

The furniture of Eliza's room has been increased by a big wardrobe and a sumptuous dressing-table. She comes in and switches on the electric light. She goes to the wardrobe; opens it; and pulls out a walking dress, a hat, and a pair of shoes, which she throws on the bed. She takes off her evening dress and shoes: then takes a padded hanger from the wardrobe: adjusts it carefully in the evening dress; and hangs it, in the wardrobe, which she shuts with a slam. She puts on her walking shoes, her walking dress, and hat. She takes her wrist watch from the dressing-table and fastens it on. She pulls on her gloves: takes her vanity bag; and looks into it to see that her purse is there before hanging it on her wrist. She makes for the door. Every movement expresses her furious resolution.

She takes a last look at herself in the glass.

She suddenly puts out her tongue at herself; then leaves the room, switching off the electric light at the door.

Meanwhile, in the street outside, Freddy Eynsford Hill, lovelorn, is gazing up at the second floor, in which one of the windows is still lighted.

The light goes out.

FREDDY: Goodnight, darling, darling, darling.

[*Eliza comes out, giving the door a considerable bang behind her.*]

LIZA: Whatever are you doing here?

FREDDY: Nothing. I spend most of my nights here. It's the only place where I'm happy. Dont laugh at me, Miss Doolittle.

LIZA: Dont you call me Miss Doolittle, do you hear? Liza's good enough for me. [*She breaks down and grabs him by the shoulders.*] Freddy: you dont think I'm a heartless guttersnipe, do you?

FREDDY: Oh no, no, darling: how can you imagine such a thing? You are the loveliest, dearest—

[*He loses all self-control and smothers her with kisses. She, hungry for comfort, responds. They stand there in one another's arms.*

An elderly police constable arrives.]

CONSTABLE [*scandalized*]: Now then! Now then!! Now then!!!

[*They release one another hastily.*]

FREDDY: Sorry, constable. Weve only just become engaged.

[*They run away.*

The constable shakes his head, reflecting on his own courtship and on the vanity of human hopes. He moves off in the opposite direction with slow professional steps.

The flight of the lovers takes them to Cavendish Square. There they halt to consider their next move.]

LIZA [*out of breath*]: He didnt half give me a fright, that copper. But you answered him proper.

FREDDY: I hope I havnt taken you out of your way. Where were you going?

LIZA: To the river.

FREDDY: What for?

LIZA: To make a hole in it.

FREDDY [*horrified*]: Eliza, darling. What do you mean? What's the matter?

LIZA: Never mind. It doesnt matter now. Theres nobody in the world now but you and me, is there?

FREDDY: Not a soul.

[*They indulge in another embrace, and are again surprised by a much younger constable.*]

SECOND CONSTABLE: Now then, you two! What's this? Where do you think you are? Move along here, double quick.

FREDDY: As you say, sir, double quick.

[*They run away again, and are in Hanover Square before they stop for another conference.*]

FREDDY: I had no idea the police were so devilishly prudish.

LIZA: It's their business to hunt girls off the streets.

FREDDY: We must go somewhere. We cant wander about the streets all night.

LIZA: Cant we? I think it'd be lovely to wander about for ever.

FREDDY: Oh, darling.

[*They embrace again, oblivious of the arrival of a crawling taxi. It stops.*]

TAXIMAN: Can I drive you and the lady anywhere, sir?

[*They start asunder.*]

LIZA: Oh, Freddy, a taxi. The very thing.

FREDDY: But, damn it, Ive no money.

LIZA: I have plenty. The Colonel thinks you should never go out without ten pounds in your pocket. Listen. We'll drive about all night; and in the morning I'll call on old Mrs Higgins and ask her what I ought to do. I'll tell you all about it in the cab. And the police wont touch us there.

FREDDY: Righto! Ripping. [*To the Taximan.*] Wimbledon Common. [*They drive off.*]

ACT 5

Mrs Higgins's drawing room. She is at her writing-table as before. The parlormaid comes in.

THE PARLORMAID [*at the door*]: Mr Henry, maam, is downstairs with Colonel Pickering.

MRS HIGGINS: Well, shew them up.

THE PARLORMAID: Theyre using the telephone, maam. Telephoning to the police, I think.

MRS HIGGINS: What!

THE PARLORMAID [*coming further in and lowering her voice*]: Mr Henry is in a state, maam. I thought I'd better tell you.

MRS HIGGINS: If you had told me that Mr Henry was not in a state it would have been more surprising. Tell them to come up when theyve finished with the police. I suppose he's lost something.

THE PARLORMAID: Yes, maam [*Going.*]

MRS HIGGINS: Go upstairs and tell Miss Doolittle that Mr Henry and the Colonel are here. Ask her not to come down til I send for her.

THE PARLORMAID: Yes, maam.

[*Higgins bursts in. He is, as the parlormaid has said, in a state.*]

HIGGINS: Look here, mother: heres a confounded thing!

MRS HIGGINS: Yes, dear. Good morning. [*He checks his impatience and kisses her, whilst the parlormaid goes out.*] What is it?

HIGGINS: Eliza's bolted.

MRS HIGGINS [*calmly continuing her writing*]: You must have frightened her.

HIGGINS: Frightened her! nonsense! She was left last night, as usual, to turn out the lights and all that; and instead of going to bed she changed her clothes and went right off: her bed wasnt slept in. She came in a cab for her things before seven this morning; and that fool Mrs Pearce let her have them without telling me a word about it. What am I to do?

MRS HIGGINS: Do without, I'm afraid, Henry. The girl has a perfect right to leave if she chooses.

HIGGINS [*wandering distractedly across the room*]: But I cant find anything. I dont know what appointments Ive got. I'm—[*Pickering comes in. Mrs Higgins puts down her pen and turns away from the writing-table.*]

PICKERING [*shaking hands*]: Good morning. Mrs Higgins. Has Henry told you? [*He sits down on the ottoman.*]

HIGGINS: What does that ass of an inspector say? Have you offered a reward?

MRS HIGGINS [*rising in indignant amazement*]: You dont mean to say you have set the police after Eliza?

HIGGINS: Of course. What are the police for? What else could we do? [*He sits in the Elizabethan chair.*]

PICKERING: The inspector made a lot of difficulties. I really think he suspected us of some improper purpose.

MRS HIGGINS: Well, of course he did. What right have you to go to the police and give the girl's name as if she were a thief, or a lost umbrella, or something? Really! [*She sits down again, deeply vexed.*]

HIGGINS: But we want to find her.

PICKERING: We cant let her go like this, you know, Mrs Higgins. What were we to do?

MRS HIGGINS: You have no more sense, either of you, than two children. Why— [*The parlormaid comes in and breaks off the conversation.*]

THE PARLORMAID: Mr Henry: a gentleman wants to see you very particular. He's been sent on from Wimpole Street.

HIGGINS: Oh, bother! I cant see anyone now. Who is it?

THE PARLORMAID: A Mr Doolittle, sir.

PICKERING: Doolittle! Do you mean the dustman?

THE PARLORMAID: Dustman! Oh no, sir: a gentleman.

HIGGINS [*springing up excitedly*]: By George, Pick, it's some relative of hers that she's gone to. Somebody we know nothing about. [*To the parlormaid.*] Send him up, quick.

THE PARLORMAID: Yes, sir. [*She goes.*]

HIGGINS [*eagerly, going to his mother*]: Genteel relatives! now we shall hear something. [*He sits down in the Chippendale chair.*]

MRS HIGGINS: Do you know any of her people?

PICKERING: Only her father: the fellow we told you about.

THE PARLORMAID [*announcing*]: Mr Doolittle. [*She withdraws*].

[*Doolittle enters. He is resplendently dressed as for a fashionable wedding, and might, in fact, be the bridegroom. A flower in his buttonhole, a dazzling silk hat, and patent leather shoes complete the effect. He is too concerned with the business he has come on to notice Mrs Higgins. He walks straight to Higgins, and accosts him with vehement reproach.*]

DOOLITTLE [*indicating his own person*]: See here! Do you see this? You done this.

HIGGINS: Done what, man?

DOOLITTLE: This, I tell you. Look at it. Look at this hat. Look at this coat.

PICKERING: Has Eliza been buying you clothes?

DOOLITTLE: Eliza! not she. Why would she buy me clothes?

MRS HIGGINS: Good morning, Mr Doolittle. Wont you sit down?

DOOLITTLE [*taken aback as he becomes conscious that he has forgotten his hostess*]: Asking your pardon, maam. [*He approaches her and shakes her proffered hand.*] Thank you. [*He sits down on the ottoman, on Pickering's right.*] I am that full of what has happened to me that I cant think of anything else.

HIGGINS: What the dickens has happened to you?

DOOLITTLE: I shouldnt mind if it had only happened to me: anything might happen to anybody and nobody to blame but Providence, as you might say. But this is something that you done to me: yes, you, Enry Iggins.

HIGGINS: Have you found Eliza?

DOOLITTLE: Have you lost her?

HIGGINS: Yes.

DOOLITTLE: You have all the luck, you have. I aint found her: but she'll find me quick enough now after what you done to me.

MRS HIGGINS: But what has my son done to you. Mr Doolittle?

DOOLITTLE: Done to me! Ruined me. Destroyed my happiness. Tied me up and delivered me into the hands of middle class morality.

HIGGINS [rising intolerantly and standing over Doolittle]: Youre raving. Youre drunk. Youre mad. I gave you five pounds. After that I had two conversations with you, at half-a-crown an hour. Ive never seen you since.

DOOLITTLE: Oh! Drunk am I? Mad am I? Tell me this. Did you or did you not write a letter to an old blighter in America that was giving five millions to found Moral Reform Societies all over the world, and that wanted you to invent a universal language for him?

HIGGINS: What! Ezra D. Wannafeller! He's dead. [He sits down again carelessly.]

DOOLITTLE: Yes: he's dead; and I'm done for. Now did you or did you not write a letter to him to say that the most original moralist at present in England, to the best of your knowledge, was Alfred Doolittle, a common dustman?

HIGGINS: Oh, after your first visit I remember making some silly joke of the kind.

DOOLITTLE: Ah! You may well call it a silly joke. It put the lid on me right enough. Just give him the chance he wanted to shew that Americans is not like us: that they reckonize and respect merit in every class of life, however humble. Them words is in his blooming will, in which, Henry Higgins, thanks to your silly joking, he leaves me a share in his Pre-digested Cheese Trust worth three thousand a year on condition that I lecture for his Wannafeller Moral Reform World League as often as they ask me up to six times a year.

HIGGINS: The devil he does! Whew! [Brightening suddenly.] What a lark!

PICKERING: A safe thing for you, Doolittle. They wont ask you twice.

DOOLITTLE: It aint the lecturing I mind. I'll lecture them blue in the face, I will, and not turn a hair. It's making a gentleman of me that I object to. Who asked him to make a gentleman of me? I was happy. I was free. I touched pretty nigh everybody for money when I wanted it, same as I touched you, Enry Iggins. Now I am worrited[1]: tied neck and heels: and everybody touches me for money. It's a fine thing for you, says my solicitor. Is it? says I. You mean it's a good thing for you, I says. When I was a poor man and had a solicitor once when they found a pram in the dust cart, he got me off, and got shut of me and got me shut of him as quick as he could. Same with the doctors: used to shove me out of the hospital before I could hardly stand on my legs, and nothing to pay. Now they finds out that I'm not a healthy man and cant live unless they looks after me twice a day. In the house I'm not let do a hand's turn for myself: somebody else must do it and touch me for it. A year ago I hadnt a relative in the world except two or three that wouldnt speak to me. Now Ive fifty, and not a decent week's wages among the lot of them. I have to live for others and not for myself: thats middle class morality. You talk of losing Eliza. Dont you be anxious: I bet she's on my doorstep by this:

1. Worried.

she that could support herself easy by selling flowers if I wasnt respectable. And the next one to touch me will be you, Enry Iggins. I'll have to learn to speak middle class language from you, instead of speaking proper English. Thats where youll come in; and I daresay thats what you done it for.

MRS HIGGINS: But, my dear Mr Doolittle, you need not suffer all this if you are really in earnest. Nobody can force you to accept this bequest. You can repudiate it. Isnt that so, Colonel Pickering?

PICKERING: I believe so.

DOOLITTLE [softening his manner in deference to her sex]: Thats the tragedy of it, maam. It's easy to say chuck it; but I havnt the nerve. Which of us has? We're all intimidated. Intimidated, maam: thats what we are. What is there for me if I chuck it but the workhouse in my old age? I have to dye my hair already to keep my job as a dustman. If I was one of the deserving poor, and had put by a bit, I could chuck it; but then why should I, acause[2] the deserving poor might as well be millionaires for all the happiness they ever has. They dont know what happiness is. But I, as one of the undeserving poor, have nothing between me and the pauper's uniform but this here blasted three thousand a year that shoves me into the middle class. (Excuse the expression, maam; youd use it yourself if you had my provocation.) Theyve got you every way you turn: it's a choice between the Skilly of the workhouse and the Char Bydis[3] of the middle class; and I havnt the nerve for the workhouse. Intimidated: thats what I am. Broke. Bought up. Happier men than me will call for my dust, and touch me for their tip; and I'll look on helpless, and envy them. And thats what your son has brought me to. [He is overcome by emotion.]

MRS HIGGINS: Well, I'm very glad youre not going to do anything foolish, Mr Doolittle. For this solves the problem of Eliza's future. You can provide for her now.

DOOLITTLE [with melancholy resignation]: Yes, maam: I'm expected to provide for everyone now, out of three thousand a year.

HIGGINS [jumping up]: Nonsense! he cant provide for her. He shant provide for her. She doesnt belong to him. I paid him five pounds for her. Doolittle: either youre an honest man or a rogue.

DOOLITTLE [tolerantly]: A little of both, Henry, like the rest of us: a little of both.

HIGGINS: Well, you took that money for the girl; and you have no right to take her as well.

MRS HIGGINS: Henry: dont be absurd. If you want to know where Eliza is, she is upstairs.

HIGGINS [amazed]: Upstairs!!! Then I shall jolly soon fetch her downstairs. [He makes resolutely for the door.]

MRS HIGGINS [rising and following him]: Be quiet, Henry. Sit down.

HIGGINS: I—

MRS HIGGINS: Sit down, dear; and listen to me.

HIGGINS: Oh very well, very well, very well. [He throws himself ungraciously on the ottoman, with his face towards the windows.] But I think you might have told us this half an hour ago.

MRS HIGGINS: Eliza came to me this morning. She told me of the brutal way you two treated her.

2. Because.
3. In his odyssey to return home to Ithaca, the Greek hero Odysseus had to sail carefully between the paired hazards of Scylla, a monster who would pluck and eat mariners who passed too close, and Charybdis, an enormous whirlpool.

HIGGINS [*bouncing up again*]: What!

PICKERING [*rising also*]: My dear Mrs Higgins, she's been telling you stories. We didnt treat her brutally. We hardly said a word to her; and we parted on particularly good terms. [*Turning on Higgins.*] Higgins: did you bully her after I went to bed?

HIGGINS: Just the other way about. She threw my slippers in my face. She behaved in the most outrageous way. I never gave her the slightest provocation. The slippers came bang into my face the moment I entered the room—before I had uttered a word. And used perfectly awful language.

PICKERING [*astonished*]: But why? What did we do to her?

MRS HIGGINS: I think I know pretty well what you did. The girl is naturally rather affectionate, I think. Isnt she, Mr Doolittle?

DOOLITTLE: Very tender-hearted, maam. Takes after me.

MRS HIGGINS: Just so. She had become attached to you both. She worked very hard for you, Henry. I dont think you quite realize what anything in the nature of brain work means to a girl of her class. Well, it seems that when the great day of trial came, and she did this wonderful thing for you without making a single mistake, you two sat there and never said a word to her, but talked together of how glad you were that it was all over and how you had been bored with the whole thing. And then you were surprised because she threw your slippers at you! I should have thrown the fire-irons at you.

HIGGINS: We said nothing except that we were tired and wanted to go to bed. Did we, Pick?

PICKERING [*shrugging his shoulders*]: That was all.

MRS HIGGINS [*ironically*]: Quite sure?

PICKERING: Absolutely, Really, that was all.

MRS HIGGINS: You didnt thank her, or pet her, or admire her, or tell her how splendid she'd been.

HIGGINS [*impatiently*]: But she knew all about that. We didnt make speeches to her, if thats what you mean.

PICKERING [*conscience stricken*]: Perhaps we were a little inconsiderate. Is she very angry?

MRS HIGGINS [*returning to her place at the writing-table*]: Well, I'm afraid she wont go back to Wimpole Street, especially now that Mr Doolittle is able to keep up the position you have thrust on her; but she says she is quite willing to meet you on friendly terms and to let bygones be bygones.

HIGGINS [*furious*]: Is she, by George? Ho!

MRS HIGGINS: If you promise to behave yourself, Henry, I'll ask her to come down. If not, go home: for you have taken up quite enough of my time.

HIGGINS: Oh, all right. Very well. Pick: you behave yourself. Let us put on our best Sunday manners for this creature that we picked out of the mud. [*He flings himself sulkily into the Elizabethan chair.*]

DOOLITTLE [*remonstrating*]: Now, now, Enry Iggins! Have some consideration for my feelings as a middle class man.

MRS HIGGINS: Remember your promise, Henry. [*She presses the bell-button on the writing-table.*] Mr Doolittle: will you be so good as to step out on the balcony for a moment. I dont want Eliza to have the shock of your news until she has made it up with these two gentlemen. Would you mind?

DOOLITTLE: As you wish, lady. Anything to help Henry to keep her off my hands. [*He disappears through the window.*]

[*The parlormaid answers the bell. Pickering sits down in Doolittle's place.*]

MRS HIGGINS: Ask Miss Doolittle to come down, please.

THE PARLORMAID: Yes, maam. [*She goes out.*]

MRS HIGGINS: Now, Henry: be good.

HIGGINS: I am behaving myself perfectly.

PICKERING: He is doing his best, Mrs Higgins.

[*A pause. Higgins throws back his head; stretches out his legs; and begins to whistle.*]

MRS HIGGINS: Henry, dearest, you dont look at all nice in that attitude.

HIGGINS [*pulling himself together*]: I was not trying to look nice, mother.

MRS HIGGINS: It doesnt matter, dear. I only wanted to make you speak.

HIGGINS: Why?

MRS HIGGINS: Because you cant speak and whistle at the same time.

[*Higgins groans. Another very trying pause.*]

HIGGINS [*springing up, out of patience*]: Where the devil is that girl? Are we to wait here all day?

[*Eliza enters, sunny, self-possessed, and giving a staggeringly convincing exhibition of ease of manner. She carries a little work-basket, and is very much at home. Pickering is too much taken aback to rise.*]

LIZA: How do you do, Professor Higgins? Are you quite well?

HIGGINS [*choking*]: Am I— [*He can say no more.*]

LIZA: But of course you are: you are never ill. So glad to see you again, Colonel Pickering. [*He rises hastily; and they shake hands.*] Quite chilly this morning, isnt it? [*She sits down on his left. He sits beside her.*]

HIGGINS: Dont you dare try this game on me. I taught it to you; and it doesnt take me in. Get up and come home; and dont be a fool.

[*Eliza takes a piece of needlework from her basket, and begins to stitch at it, without taking the least notice of this outburst.*]

MRS HIGGINS: Very nicely put, indeed, Henry. No woman could resist such an invitation.

HIGGINS: You let her alone, mother. Let her speak for herself. You will jolly soon see whether she has an idea that I havnt put into her head or a word that I havnt put into her mouth. I tell you I have created this thing out of the squashed cabbage leaves of Covent Garden; and now she pretends to play the fine lady with me.

MRS HIGGINS [*placidly*]: Yes, dear; but youll sit down, wont you?

[*Higgins sits down again, savagely.*]

LIZA [*to Pickering, taking no apparent notice of Higgins, and working away deftly*]: Will you drop me altogether now that the experiment is over, Colonel Pickering?

PICKERING: Oh dont. You mustnt think of it as an experiment. It shocks me, somehow.

LIZA: Oh, I'm only a squashed cabbage leaf—

PICKERING [*impulsively*]: No.

LIZA [*continuing quietly*]: —but I owe so much to you that I should be very unhappy if you forgot me.

PICKERING: It's very kind of you to say so, Miss Doolittle.

LIZA: It's not because you paid for my dresses. I know you are generous to everybody with money. But it was from you that I learnt really nice manners; and that is what makes one a lady, isnt it? You see it was so very difficult for me with the example of Professor Higgins always before me. I was brought up to be just like him, unable to control myself, and using bad language on the slightest provocation. And I should never have known that ladies and gentlemen didnt behave like that if you hadnt been there.

HIGGINS: Well!!

PICKERING: Oh, thats only his way, you know. He doesnt mean it.

LIZA: Oh, I didnt mean it either, when I was a flower girl. It was only my way. But you see I did it; and thats what makes the difference after all.

PICKERING: No doubt. Still, he taught you to speak; and I couldnt have done that, you know.

LIZA [trivially]: Of course: that is his profession.

HIGGINS: Damnation!

LIZA [continuing]: It was just like learning to dance in the fashionable way: there was nothing more than that in it. But do you know what began my real education?

PICKERING: What?

LIZA [stopping her work for a moment]: Your calling me Miss Doolittle that day when I first came to Wimpole Street. That was the beginning of self-respect for me. [She resumes her stitching.] And there were a hundred little things you never noticed, because they came naturally to you. Things about standing up and taking off your hat and opening doors—

PICKERING: Oh, that was nothing.

LIZA: Yes: things that shewed you thought and felt about me as if I were something better than a scullery-maid; though of course I know you would have been just the same to a scullery-maid if she had been let into the drawing room. You never took off your boots in the dining room when I was there.

PICKERING: You mustnt mind that. Higgins takes off his boots all over the place.

LIZA: I know. I am not blaming him. It is his way, isnt it? But it made such a difference to me that you didnt do it. You see, really and truly, apart from the things anyone can pick up (the dressing and the proper way of speaking, and so on), the difference between a lady and a flower girl is not how she behaves, but how she's treated. I shall always be a flower girl to Professor Higgins, because he always treats me as a flower girl, and always will; but I know I can be a lady to you, because you always treat me as a lady, and always will.

MRS HIGGINS: Please dont grind your teeth. Henry.

PICKERING: Well, this is really very nice of you, Miss Doolittle.

LIZA: I should like you to call me Eliza, now, if you would.

PICKERING: Thank you. Eliza, of course.

LIZA: And I should like Professor Higgins to call me Miss Doolittle.

HIGGINS: I'll see you damned first.

MRS HIGGINS: Henry! Henry!

PICKERING [laughing]: Why dont you slang back at him? Dont stand it. It would do him a lot of good.

LIZA: I cant. I could have done it once but now I cant go back to it. You told me, you know, that when a child is brought to a foreign country, it picks up the language in a few weeks, and forgets its own. Well, I am a child in your country. I have forgotten my own language, and can speak nothing but yours. Thats the real break-off with the corner of Tottenham Court Road. Leaving Wimpole Street finishes it.

PICKERING [much alarmed]: Oh! but youre coming back to Wimpole Street, arnt you? Youll forgive Higgins?

HIGGINS [*rising*]: Forgive! Will she, by George! Let her go. Let her find out how she can get on without us. She will relapse into the gutter in three weeks without me at her elbow.

[*Doolittle appears at the centre window. With a look of dignified reproach at Higgins, he comes slowly and silently to his daughter, who, with her back to the window, is unconscious of his approach.*]

PICKERING: He's incorrigible, Eliza. You wont relapse, will you?

LIZA: No: not now. Never again. I have learnt my lesson. I dont believe I could utter one of the old sounds if I tried. [*Doolittle touches her on her left shoulder. She drops her work, losing her self-possession utterly at the spectacle of her father's splendor.*] A-a-a-a-a-ah-ow-ooh!

HIGGINS [*with a crow of triumph*]: Aha! Just so. A-a-a-a-ahowooh! A-a-a-ahowooh! A-a-a-a-ahowooh! Victory! Victory! [*He throws himself on the divan, folding his arms, and spraddling arrogantly.*]

DOOLITTLE: Can you blame the girl? Dont look at me like that, Eliza. It aint my fault. Ive come into some money.

LIZA: You must have touched a millionaire this time, dad.

DOOLITTLE: I have. But I'm dressed something special today. I'm going to St George's. Hanover Square. Your stepmother is going to marry me.

LIZA [*angrily*]: Youre going to let yourself down to marry that low common woman!

PICKERING [*quietly*]: He ought to, Eliza. [*To Doolittle.*] Why has she changed her mind?

DOOLITTLE [*sadly*]: Intimidated, Governor. Intimidated. Middle class morality claims its victim. Wont you put on your hat, Liza, and come and see me turned off?

LIZA: If the Colonel says I must. I—I'll [*almost sobbing*] I'll demean myself. And get insulted for my pains, like enough.

DOOLITTLE: Dont be afraid: she never comes to words with anyone now, poor woman! respectability has broke all the spirit out of her.

PICKERING [*squeezing Eliza's elbow gently*]: Be kind to them, Eliza. Make the best of it.

LIZA [*forcing a little smile for him through her vexation*]: Oh well, just to shew theres no ill feeling. I'll be back in a moment. [*She goes out.*]

DOOLITTLE [*sitting down beside Pickering*]: I feel uncommon nervous about the ceremony, Colonel. I wish youd come and see me through it.

PICKERING: But youve been through it before, man. You were married to Eliza's mother.

DOOLITTLE: Who told you that, Colonel?

PICKERING: Well, nobody told me. But I concluded—naturally—

DOOLITTLE: No: that aint the natural way, Colonel: It's only the middle class way. My way was always the undeserving way. But dont say nothing to Eliza. She dont know: I always had a delicacy about telling her.

PICKERING: Quite right. We'll leave it so, if you dont mind.

DOOLITTLE: And youll come to the church, Colonel, and put me through straight?

PICKERING: With pleasure. As far as a bachelor can.

MRS HIGGINS: May I come, Mr Doolittle? I should be very sorry to miss your wedding.

DOOLITTLE: I should indeed be honored by your condescension, maam; and my poor old woman would take it as a tremenjous compliment. She's been very low, thinking of the happy days that are no more.

MRS HIGGINS [*rising*]: I'll order the carriage and get ready. [*The men rise, except Higgins.*] I shant be more than fifteen minutes. [*As she goes to the door Eliza comes in, hatted and buttoning her gloves.*] I'm going to the church to see your father married, Eliza. You had better come in the brougham[4] with me. Colonel Pickering can go on with the bridegroom.

[*Mrs Higgins goes out. Eliza comes to the middle of the room between the centre window and the ottoman. Pickering joins her.*]

DOOLITTLE: Bridegroom! What a word! It makes a man realize his position, somehow. [*He takes up his hat and goes towards the door.*]

PICKERING: Before I go, Eliza, do forgive Higgins and come back to us.

LIZA: I dont think dad would allow me. Would you, dad?

DOOLITTLE [*sad but magnanimous*]: They played you off very cunning, Eliza, them two sportsmen. If it had been only one of them, you could have nailed him. But you see, there was two; and one of them chaperoned the other, as you might say. [*To Pickering.*] It was artful of you, Colonel: but I bear no malice: I should have done the same myself. I been the victim of one woman after another all my life, and I dont grudge you two getting the better of Liza. I shant interfere. It's time for us to go, Colonel. So long, Henry. See you in St George's, Eliza. [*He goes out.*]

PICKERING [*coaxing*]: Do stay with us, Eliza. [*He follows Doolittle.*]

[*Eliza goes out on the balcony to avoid being alone with Higgins. He rises and joins her there. She immediately comes back into the room and makes for the door; but he goes along the balcony quickly and gets his back to the door before she reaches it.*]

HIGGINS: Well, Eliza, youve had a bit of your own back, as you call it. Have you had enough? and are you going to be reasonable? Or do you want any more?

LIZA: You want me back only to pick up your slippers and put up with your tempers and fetch and carry for you.

HIGGINS: I havnt said I wanted you back at all.

LIZA: Oh, indeed. Then what are we talking about?

HIGGINS: About you, not about me. If you come back I shall treat you just as I have always treated you. I cant change my nature; and I dont intend to change my manners. My manners are exactly the same as Colonel Pickering's.

LIZA: Thats not true. He treats a flower girl as if she was a duchess.

HIGGINS: And I treat a duchess as if she was a flower girl.

LIZA: I see. [*She turns away composedly, and sits on the ottoman, facing the window.*] The same to everybody.

HIGGINS: Just so.

LIZA: Like father.

HIGGINS [*grinning, a little taken down*]: Without accepting the comparison at all points, Eliza, it's quite true that your father is not a snob, and that he will be quite at home in any station of life to which his eccentric destiny may call him. [*Seriously.*] The great secret, Eliza, is not having bad manners or good manners or any other particular sort of manners, but having the same manner for all human souls: in short, behaving as if you were in Heaven, where there are no third-class carriages, and one soul is as good as another.

LIZA: Amen. You are a born preacher.

HIGGINS [*irritated*]: The question is not whether I treat you rudely, but whether you ever heard me treat anyone else better.

4. Four-wheeled horse carriage.

LIZA [*with sudden sincerity*]: I dont care how you treat me. I dont mind your swearing at me. I shouldnt mind a black eye: Ive had one before this. But [*standing up and facing him*] I wont be passed over.

HIGGINS: Then get out of my way; for I wont stop for you. You talk about me as if I were a motor bus.

LIZA: So you are a motor bus: all bounce and go, and no consideration for anyone. But I can do without you: dont think I cant.

HIGGINS: I know you can. I told you you could.

LIZA [*wounded, getting away from him to the other side of the ottoman with her face to the hearth*]: I know you did, you brute. You wanted to get rid of me.

HIGGINS: Liar.

LIZA: Thank you. [*She sits down with dignity.*]

HIGGINS: You never asked yourself, I suppose, whether I could do without you.

LIZA [*earnestly*]: Dont you try to get round me. Youll have to do without me.

HIGGINS [*arrogant*]: I can do without anybody. I have my own soul: my own spark of divine fire. But [*with sudden humility*] I shall miss you, Eliza. [*He sits down near her on the ottoman.*] I have learnt something from your idiotic notions: I confess that humbly and gratefully. And I have grown accustomed to your voice and appearance. I like them, rather.

LIZA: Well, you have both of them on your gramophone and in your book of photographs. When you feel lonely without me, you can turn the machine on. It's got no feelings to hurt.

HIGGINS: I cant turn your soul on. Leave me those feelings; and you can take away the voice and the face. They are not you.

LIZA: Oh, you are a devil. You can twist the heart in a girl as easy as some could twist her arms to hurt her. Mrs Pearce warned me. Time and again she has wanted to leave you; and you always got round her at the last minute. And you dont care a bit for her. And you dont care a bit for me.

HIGGINS: I care for life, for humanity; and you are a part of it that has come my way and been built into my house. What more can you or anyone ask?

LIZA: I wont care for anybody that doesnt care for me.

HIGGINS: Commercial principles, Eliza. Like [*reproducing her Covent Garden pronunciation with professional exactness*] s'yollin voylets, isnt it?

LIZA: Dont sneer at me. It's mean to sneer at me.

HIGGINS: I have never sneered in my life. Sneering doesnt become either the human face or the human soul. I am expressing my righteous contempt for Commercialism. I dont and wont trade in affection. You call me a brute because you couldnt buy a claim on me by fetching my slippers and finding my spectacles. You were a fool: I think a woman fetching a man's slippers is a disgusting sight: did I ever fetch your slippers? I think a good deal more of you for throwing them in my face. No use slaving for me and then saying you want to be cared for: who cares for a slave? If you come back, come back for the sake of good fellowship; for youll get nothing else. Youve had a thousand times as much out of me as I have out of you; and if you dare to set up your little dog's tricks of fetching and carrying slippers against my creation of a Duchess Eliza. I'll slam the door in your silly face.

LIZA: What did you do it for if you didnt care for me?

HIGGINS [*heartily*]: Why, because it was my job.

LIZA: You never thought of the trouble it would make for me.

HIGGINS: Would the world ever have been made if its maker had been afraid of making trouble? Making life means making trouble. Theres only one way of escaping trouble; and thats killing things. Cowards, you notice, are always shrieking to have troublesome people killed.

LIZA: I'm no preacher: I dont notice things like that. I notice that you dont notice me.

HIGGINS [*jumping up and walking about intolerantly*]: Eliza: youre an idiot. I waste the treasures of my Miltonic mind by spreading them before you. Once for all, understand that I go my way and do my work without caring twopence what happens to either of us. I am not intimidated, like your father and your stepmother. So you can come back or go to the devil: which you please.

LIZA: What am I to come back for?

HIGGINS [*bouncing up on his knees on the ottoman and leaning over it to her*]: For the fun of it. Thats why I took you on.

LIZA [*with averted face*]: And you may throw me out tomorrow if I dont do everything you want me to?

HIGGINS: Yes; and you may walk out tomorrow if I dont do everything you want me to.

LIZA: And live with my stepmother?

HIGGINS: Yes, or sell flowers.

LIZA: Oh! If I only could go back to my flower basket! I should be independent of both you and father and all the world! Why did you take my independence from me? Why did I give it up? I'm a slave now, for all my fine clothes.

HIGGINS: Not a bit. I'll adopt you as my daughter and settle money on you if you like. Or would you rather marry Pickering?

LIZA [*looking fiercely round at him*]: I wouldnt marry you if you asked me; and youre nearer my age than what he is.

HIGGINS [*gently*]: Than he is: not "than what he is."

LIZA [*losing her temper and rising*]: I'll talk as I like. Youre not my teacher now.

HIGGINS [*reflectively*]: I dont suppose Pickering would, though. He's as confirmed an old bachelor as I am.

LIZA: Thats not what I want; and dont you think it. Ive always had chaps enough wanting me that way. Freddy Hill writes to me twice and three times a day, sheets and sheets.

HIGGINS [*disagreeably surprised*]: Damn his impudence! [*He recoils and finds himself sitting on his heels.*]

LIZA: He has a right to if he likes, poor lad. And he does love me.

HIGGINS [*getting off the ottoman*]: You have no right to encourage him.

LIZA: Every girl has a right to be loved.

HIGGINS: What! By fools like that?

LIZA: Freddy's not a fool. And if he's weak and poor and wants me, may be he'd make me happier than my betters that bully me and dont want me.

HIGGINS: Can he make anything of you? Thats the point.

LIZA: Perhaps I could make something of him. But I never thought of us making anything of one another; and you never think of anything else. I only want to be natural.

HIGGINS: In short, you want me to be as infatuated about you as Freddy? Is that it?

LIZA: No I dont. Thats not the sort of feeling I want from you. And dont you be too sure of yourself or of me. I could have been a bad girl if I'd liked. Ive seen more of some things than you, for all your learning. Girls like me can drag gentle-men down to make love to them easy enough. And they wish each other dead the next minute.

HIGGINS: Of course they do. Then what in thunder are we quarrelling about?

LIZA [*much troubled*]: I want a little kindness. I know I'm a common ignorant girl, and you a book-learned gentleman; but I'm not dirt under your feet. What I done [*correcting herself*] what I did was not for the dresses and the taxis: I did it because we were pleasant together and I come—came—to care for you; not to want you to make love to me, and not forgetting the difference between us, but more friendly like.

HIGGINS: Well, of course. Thats just how I feel. And how Pickering feels. Eliza: youre a fool.

LIZA: Thats not a proper answer to give me [*she sinks on the chair at the writing-table in tears*].

HIGGINS: It's all youll get until you stop being a common idiot. If youre going to be a lady, youll have to give up feeling neglected if the men you know dont spend half their time snivelling over you and the other half giving you black eyes. If you cant stand the coldness of my sort of life, and the strain of it, go back to the gutter. Work til youre more a brute than a human being: and then cuddle and squabble and drink til you fall asleep. Oh, it's a fine life, the life of the gutter. It's real: it's warm: it's violent: you can feel it through the thickest skin: you can taste it and smell it without any training or any work. Not like Science and Literature and Classical Music and Philosophy and Art. You find me cold, unfeeling, selfish, dont you? Very well: be off with you to the sort of people you like. Marry some senti-mental hog or other with lots of money, and a thick pair of lips to kiss you with and a thick pair of boots to kick you with. If you cant appreciate what youve got, youd better get what you can appreciate.

LIZA [*desperate*]: Oh, you are a cruel tyrant. I cant talk to you: you turn everything against me: I'm always in the wrong. But you know very well all the time that youre nothing but a bully. You know I cant go back to the gutter, as you call it, and that I have no real friends in the world but you and the Colonel. You know well I couldnt bear to live with a low common man after you two; and it's wicked and cruel of you to insult me by pretending I could. You think I must go back to Wimpole Street because I have nowhere else to go but father's. But dont you be too sure that you have me under your feet to be trampled on and talked down. I'll marry Freddy, I will, as soon as I'm able to support him.

HIGGINS [*thunderstruck*]: Freddy!!! that young fool! That poor devil who couldnt get a job as an errand boy even if he had the guts to try for it! Woman: do you not understand that I have made you a consort for a king?

LIZA: Freddy loves me: that makes him king enough for me. I dont want him to work: he wasnt brought up to it as I was. I'll go and be a teacher.

HIGGINS: Whatll you teach, in heaven's name?

LIZA: What you taught me. I'll teach phonetics.

HIGGINS: Ha! Ha! ha!

LIZA: I'll offer myself as an assistant to that hairyfaced Hungarian.

HIGGINS [*rising in a fury*]: What! That impostor! That humbug! That toadying ignoramus! Teach him my methods! my discoveries! You take one step in his direction and I'll wring your neck. [*He lays hands on her.*] Do you hear?

LIZA [*defiantly non-resistant*]: Wring away. What do I care? I knew youd strike me some day. [*He lets her go, stamping with rage at having forgotten himself, and recoils so hastily that he stumbles back into his seat on the ottoman.*] Aha! Now I know how to deal with you. What a fool I was not to think of it before! You cant take away the knowledge you gave me. You said I had a finer ear than you. And I can be civil and kind to people, which is more than you can. Aha! [*Purposely dropping her aitches to annoy him.*] Thats done you, Enry Iggins, it az. Now I dont care that [*snapping her fingers*] for your bullying and your big talk. I'll advertize it in the papers that your duchess is only a flower girl that you taught, and that she'll teach anybody to be a duchess just the same in six months for a thousand guineas. Oh, when I think of myself crawling under your feet and being trampled on and called names, when all the time I had only to lift up my finger to be as good as you, I could just kick myself.

HIGGINS [*wondering at her*]: You damned impudent slut, you! But it's better than snivelling; better than fetching slippers and finding spectacles, isnt it? [*Rising.*] By George, Eliza, I said I'd make a woman of you; and I have. I like you like this.

LIZA: Yes: you can turn round and make up to me now that I'm not afraid of you, and can do without you.

HIGGINS: Of course I do, you little fool. Five minutes ago you were like a millstone round my neck. Now youre a tower of strength: a consort battleship. You and I and Pickering will be three old bachelors instead of only two men and a silly girl.

[*Mrs Higgins returns, dressed for the wedding. Eliza instantly becomes cool and elegant.*]

MRS HIGGINS: The carriage is waiting, Eliza. Are you ready?

LIZA: Quite. Is the Professor coming?

MRS HIGGINS: Certainly not. He cant behave himself in church. He makes remarks out loud all the time on the clergyman's pronunciation.

LIZA: Then I shall not see you again, Professor. Goodbye. [*She goes to the door.*]

MRS HIGGINS [*coming to Higgins*]: Goodbye, dear.

HIGGINS: Goodbye, mother. [*He is about to kiss her, when he recollects something.*] Oh, by the way, Eliza, order a ham and a Stilton cheese, will you? And buy me a pair of reindeer gloves, number eights, and a tie to match that new suit of mine. You can choose the color. [*His cheerful, careless, vigorous voice shews that he is incorrigible.*]

LIZA [*disdainfully*]: Number eights are too small for you if you want them lined with lamb's wool. You have three new ties that you have forgotten in the drawer of your washstand. Colonel Pickering prefers double Gloucester to Stilton; and you dont notice the difference. I telephoned Mrs Pearce this morning not to forget the ham. What you are to do without me I cannot imagine. [*She sweeps out.*]

MRS HIGGINS: I'm afraid youve spoilt that girl, Henry. I should be uneasy about you and her if she were less fond of Colonel Pickering.

HIGGINS: Pickering! Nonsense: she's going to marry Freddy. Ha ha! Freddy! Freddy!! Ha ha ha ha ha!!!!! [*He roars with laughter as the play ends.*]

Sequel

The rest of the story need not be shewn in action, and indeed, would hardly need telling if our imaginations were not so enfeebled by their lazy dependence on the ready-mades and reach-me-downs of the ragshop in which Romance keeps its stock of "happy endings" to misfit all stories. Now, the history of Eliza Doolittle, though called a romance because the transfiguration it records seems exceedingly improbable, is common enough. Such transfigurations have been achieved by hundreds of resolutely ambitious young women since Nell Gwynne[1] set them the example by playing queens and fascinating kings in the theatre in which she began by selling oranges. Nevertheless, people in all directions have assumed, for no other reason than that she became the heroine of a romance, that she must have married the hero of it. This is unbearable, not only because her little drama, if acted on such a thoughtless assumption, must be spoiled, but because the true sequel is patent to anyone with a sense of human nature in general, and of feminine instinct in particular.

Eliza, in telling Higgins she would not marry him if he asked, was not coquetting: she was announcing a well-considered decision. When a bachelor interests, and dominates, and teaches, and becomes important to a spinster, as Higgins with Eliza, she always, if she has character enough to be capable of it, considers very seriously indeed whether she will play for becoming that bachelor's wife, especially if he is so little interested in marriage that a determined and devoted woman might capture him if she set herself resolutely to do it. Her decision will depend a good deal on whether she is really free to choose; and that, again, will depend on her age and income. If she is at the end of her youth, and has no security for her livelihood, she will marry him because she must marry anybody who will provide for her. But at Eliza's age a good-looking girl does not feel that pressure: she feels free to pick and choose. She is therefore guided by her instinct in the matter. Eliza's instinct tells her not to marry Higgins. It does not tell her to give him up. It is not in the slightest doubt as to his remaining one of the strongest personal interests in her life. It would be very sorely strained if there was another woman likely to supplant her with him. But as she feels sure of him on that last point, she has no doubt at all as to her course, and would not have any, even if the difference of twenty years in age, which seems so great to youth, did not exist between them.

As our own instincts are not appealed to by her conclusion, let us see whether we cannot discover some reason in it. When Higgins excused his indifference to young women on the ground that they had an irresistible rival in his mother, he gave the clue to his inveterate old-bachelordom. The case is uncommon only to the extent that remarkable mothers are uncommon. If an imaginative boy has a sufficiently rich mother who has intelligence, personal grace, dignity of character without harshness, and a cultivated sense of the best art of her time to enable her to make her house beautiful, she sets a standard for him against which very few women can struggle, besides effecting for him a disengagement of his affections, his sense of beauty, and his idealism from his specifically sexual impulses. This makes him a standing puzzle to the huge number of uncultivated people who have been brought up in tasteless homes by commonplace or disagreeable parents, and to whom, consequently, literature, painting, sculpture, music, and affectionate personal relations come as modes of sex if they come at all. The word passion means nothing else to them; and that Higgins could have a passion for phonetics and idealize his mother instead of Eliza, would seem to them absurd and unnatural. Nevertheless, when we look round and see that hardly anyone is too ugly or disagreeable to find a wife or a husband if he or she wants one, whilst many old maids and bachelors are above the average in quality and culture, we

1. Nell Gwynne (1650–1687), London theatre vendor, actor, and later mistress of Charles II.

cannot help suspecting that the disentanglement of sex from the associations with which it is commonly confused, a disentanglement which persons of genius achieve by sheer intellectual analysis, is sometimes produced or aided by parental fascination.

Now, though Eliza was incapable of thus explaining to herself Higgins's formidable powers of resistance to the charm that prostrated Freddy at the first glance, she was instinctively aware that she could never obtain a complete grip of him, or come between him and his mother (the first necessity of the married woman). To put it shortly, she knew that for some mysterious reason he had not the makings of a married man in him, according to her conception of a husband as one to whom she would be his nearest and fondest and warmest interest. Even had there been no mother-rival, she would still have refused to accept an interest in herself that was secondary to philosophic interests. Had Mrs Higgins died, there would still have been Milton and the Universal Alphabet. Landor's remark that to those who have the greatest power of loving, love is a secondary affair, would not have recommended Landor to Eliza. Put that along with her resentment of Higgins's domineering superiority, and her mistrust of his coaxing cleverness in getting round her and evading her wrath when he had gone too far with his impetuous bullying, and you will see that Eliza's instinct had good grounds for warning her not to marry her Pygmalion.

And now, whom did Eliza marry? For if Higgins was a predestinate old bachelor, she was most certainly not a predestinate old maid. Well, that can be told very shortly to those who have not guessed it from the indications she has herself given them.

Almost immediately after Eliza is stung into proclaiming her considered determination not to marry Higgins, she mentions the fact that young Mr Frederick Eynsford Hill is pouring out his love for her daily through the post. Now Freddy is young, practically twenty years younger than Higgins: he is a gentleman (or, as Eliza would qualify him, a toff[2]), and speaks like one. He is nicely dressed, is treated by the Colonel as an equal, loves her unaffectedly, and is not her master, nor ever likely to dominate her in spite of his advantage of social standing. Eliza has no use for the foolish romantic tradition that all women love to be mastered, if not actually bullied and beaten. "When you go to women" says Nietzsche[3] "take your whip with you." Sensible despots have never confined that precaution to women: they have taken their whips with them when they have dealt with men, and been slavishly idealized by the men over whom they have flourished the whip much more than by women. No doubt there are slavish women as well as slavish men; and women, like men, admire those that are stronger than themselves. But to admire a strong person and to live under that strong person's thumb are two different things. The weak may not be admired and hero-worshipped; but they are by no means disliked or shunned; and they never seem to have the least difficulty in marrying people who are too good for them. They may fail in emergencies: but life is not one long emergency: it is mostly a string of situations for which no exceptional strength is needed, and with which even rather weak people can cope if they have a stronger partner to help them out. Accordingly, it is a truth everywhere in evi-

2. Fashionable gentleman.
3. Friedrich Nietzsche (1844–1900), German philosopher whose rejection of traditional Judeo-Christian ethics and

belief in the natural moral superiority of certain individuals fascinated Shaw, finding its most direct expression in his play *Man and Superman* (1903).

dence that strong people, masculine or feminine, not only do not marry stronger people, but do not shew any preference for them in selecting their friends. When a lion meets another with a louder roar "the first lion thinks the last a bore." The man or woman who feels strong enough for two, seeks for every other quality in a partner than strength.

The converse is also true. Weak people want to marry strong people who do not frighten them too much: and this often leads them to make the mistake we describe metaphorically as "biting off more than they can chew." They want too much for too little; and when the bargain is unreasonable beyond all bearing, the union becomes impossible: it ends in the weaker party being either discarded or borne as a cross, which is worse. People who are not only weak, but silly or obtuse as well, are often in these difficulties.

This being the state of human affairs, what is Eliza fairly sure to do when she is placed between Freddy and Higgins? Will she look forward to a lifetime of fetching Higgins's slippers or to a lifetime of Freddy fetching hers? There can be no doubt about the answer. Unless Freddy is biologically repulsive to her, and Higgins biologically attractive to a degree that overwhelms all her other instincts, she will, if she marries either of them, marry Freddy.

And that is just what Eliza did.

Complications ensued; but they were economic, not romantic. Freddy had no money and no occupation. His mother's jointure,[4] a last relic of the opulence of Largelady Park, had enabled her to struggle along in Earlscourt with an air of gentility, but not to procure any serious secondary education for her children, much less give the boy a profession. A clerkship at thirty shillings a week was beneath Freddy's dignity, and extremely distasteful to him besides. His prospects consisted of a hope that if he kept up appearances somebody would do something for him. The something appeared vaguely to his imagination as a private secretaryship or a sinecure of some sort. To his mother it perhaps appeared as a marriage to some lady of means who could not resist her boy's niceness. Fancy her feelings when he married a flower girl who had become disclassed under extraordinary circumstances which were now notorious!

It is true that Eliza's situation did not seem wholly ineligible. Her father, though formerly a dustman, and now fantastically disclassed, had become extremely popular in the smartest society by a social talent which triumphed over every prejudice and every disadvantage. Rejected by the middle class, which he loathed, he had shot up at once into the highest circles by his wit, his dustmanship (which he carried like a banner), and his Nietzschean transcendence of good and evil. At intimate ducal dinners he sat on the righthand of the Duchess; and in country houses he smoked in the pantry and was made much of by the butler when he was not feeding in the dining room and being consulted by cabinet ministers. But he found it almost as hard to do all this on four thousand a year as Mrs Eynsford Hill to live in Earlscourt on an income so pitiably smaller that I have not the heart to disclose its exact figure. He absolutely refused to add the last straw to his burden by contributing to Eliza's support.

Thus Freddy and Eliza, now Mr and Mrs Eynsford Hill, would have spent a penniless honeymoon but for a wedding present of £500 from the Colonel to Eliza. It

4. Estate settled upon a widow by her late husband.

lasted a long time because Freddy did not know how to spend money, never having had any to spend, and Eliza, socially trained by a pair of old bachelors, wore her clothes as long as they held together and looked pretty, without the least regard to their being many months out of fashion. Still, £500 will not last two young people for ever; and they both knew, and Eliza felt as well, that they must shift themselves in the end. She could quarter herself on Wimpole Street because it had come to be her home; but she was quite aware that she ought not to quarter Freddy there, and that it would not be good for his character if she did.

Not that the Wimpole Street bachelors objected. When she consulted them, Higgins declined to be bothered about her housing problem when that solution was so simple. Eliza's desire to have Freddy in the house with her seemed of no more importance than if she had wanted an extra piece of bedroom furniture. Pleas as to Freddy's character, and the moral obligation on him to earn his own living, were lost on Higgins. He denied that Freddy had any character, and declared that if he tried to do any useful work some competent person would have the trouble of undoing it: a procedure involving a net loss to the community, and great unhappiness to Freddy himself, who was obviously intended by Nature for such light work as amusing Eliza, which, Higgins declared, was a much more useful and honorable occupation than working in the city. When Eliza referred again to her project of teaching phonetics, Higgins abated not a jot of his violent opposition to it. He said she was not within ten years of being qualified to meddle with his pet subject: and as it was evident that the Colonel agreed with him, she felt she could not go against them in this grave matter, and that she had no right, without Higgins's consent, to exploit the knowledge he had given her: for his knowledge seemed to her as much his private property as his watch: Eliza was no communist. Besides, she was superstitiously devoted to them both, more entirely and frankly after her marriage than before it.

It was the Colonel who finally solved the problem, which had cost him much perplexed cogitation. He one day asked Eliza, rather shyly, whether she had quite given up her notion of keeping a flower shop. She replied that she had thought of it, but had put it out of her head, because the Colonel had said, that day at Mrs Higgins's, that it would never do. The Colonel confessed that when he said that, he had not quite recovered from the dazzling impression of the day before. They broke the matter to Higgins that evening. The sole comment vouchsafed by him very nearly led to a serious quarrel with Eliza. It was to the effect that she would have in Freddy an ideal errand boy.

Freddy himself was next sounded on the subject. He said he had been thinking of a shop himself; though it had presented itself to his pennilessness as a small place in which Eliza should sell tobacco at one counter whilst he sold newspapers at the opposite one. But he agreed that it would be extraordinarily jolly to go early every morning with Eliza to Covent Garden and buy flowers on the scene of their first meeting: a sentiment which earned him many kisses from his wife. He added that he had always been afraid to propose anything of the sort, because Clara would make an awful row about a step that must damage her matrimonial chances, and his mother could not be expected to like it after clinging for so many years to that step of the social ladder on which retail trade is impossible.

This difficulty was removed by an event highly unexpected by Freddy's mother. Clara, in the course of her incursions into those artistic circles which were the highest within her reach, discovered that her conversational qualifications were expected to include a grounding in the novels of Mr H. G. Wells.[5] She borrowed them in various directions so energetically that she swallowed them all within two months. The result was a conversion of a kind quite common today. A modern Acts of the Apostles would fill fifty whole Bibles if anyone were capable of writing it.

Poor Clara, who appeared to Higgins and his mother as a disagreeable and ridiculous person, and to her own mother as in some inexplicable way a social failure, had never seen herself in either light; for, though to some extent ridiculed and mimicked in West Kensington like everybody else there, she was accepted as a rational and normal—or shall we say inevitable?—sort of human being. At worst they called her The Pusher; but to them no more than to herself had it ever occurred that she was pushing the air, and pushing it in a wrong direction. Still, she was not happy. She was growing desperate. Her one asset, the fact that her mother was what the Epsom greengrocer called a carriage lady, had no exchange value, apparently. It had prevented her from getting educated, because the only education she could have afforded was education with the Earlscourt greengrocer's daughter. It had led her to seek the society of her mother's class; and that class simply would not have her, because she was much poorer than the greengrocer, and, far from being able to afford a maid, could not afford even a house-maid, and had to scrape along at home with an illiberally treated general servant. Under such circumstances nothing could give her an air of being a genuine product of Largelady Park. And yet its tradition made her regard a marriage with anyone within her reach as an unbearable humiliation. Commercial people and professional people in a small way were odious to her. She ran after painters and novelists; but she did not charm them; and her bold attempts to pick up and practise artistic and literary talk irritated them. She was, in short, an utter failure, an ignorant, incompetent, pretentious, unwelcome, penniless, useless little snob; and though she did not admit these disqualifications (for nobody ever faces unpleasant truths of this kind until the possibility of a way out dawns on them) she felt their effects too keenly to be satisfied with her position.

Clara had a startling eyeopener when, on being suddenly wakened to enthusiasm by a girl of her own age who dazzled her and produced in her a gushing desire to take her for a model, and gain her friendship, she discovered that this exquisite apparition had graduated from the gutter in a few months time. It shook her so violently, that when Mr H. G. Wells lifted her on the point of his puissant pen, and placed her at the angle of view from which the life she was leading and the society to which she clung appeared in its true relation to real human needs and worthy social structure, he effected a conversion and a conviction of sin comparable to the most sensational feats of General Booth[6] or Gypsy Smith.[7] Clara's snobbery went bang. Life suddenly began to move with her. Without knowing how or why, she began to make friends and enemies. Some of the acquaintances to whom she had been a tedious or indifferent or ridiculous affliction, dropped her: others became cordial. To her amazement she found that some "quite nice" people were saturated with Wells, and that this accessibility to ideas was the secret of their niceness. People she had thought deeply religious and had tried to conciliate on that tack with disastrous results, suddenly took an interest in her, and

---

5. H(erbert) G(eorge) Wells (1866–1946), English novelist and writer of science fiction, who shared Shaw's zeal for social reform, while their passion meant they were often at odds.

6. ("General") William Booth (1829–1912), English religious reformer and founder of the Salvation Army.
7. Rodney ("Gypsy") Smith (1860–1947), popular British preacher and evangelist.

revealed a hostility to conventional religion which she had never conceived possible except among the most desperate characters. They made her read Galsworthy; and Galsworthy exposed the vanity of Largelady Park and finished her. It exasperated her to think that the dungeon in which she had languished for so many unhappy years had been unlocked all the time, and that the impulses she had so carefully struggled with and stifled for the sake of keeping well with society, were precisely those by which alone she could have come into any sort of sincere human contact. In the radiance of these discoveries, and the tumult of their reaction, she made a fool of herself as freely and conspicuously as when she so rashly adopted Eliza's expletive in Mrs Higgins's drawing room; for the new-born Wellsian had to find her bearings almost as ridiculously as a baby; but nobody hates a baby for its ineptitudes, or thinks the worse of it for trying to eat the matches; and Clara lost no friends by her follies. They laughed at her to her face this time; and she had to defend herself and fight it out as best she could.

When Freddy paid a visit to Earlscourt (which he never did when he could possibly help it) to make the desolating announcement that he and his Eliza were thinking of blackening the Largelady scutcheon by opening a shop, he found the little household already convulsed by a prior announcement from Clara that she also was going to work in an old furniture shop in Dover Street, which had been started by a fellow Wellsian. This appointment Clara owed, after all, to her old social accomplishment of Push. She had made up her mind that, cost what it might, she would see Mr Wells in the flesh; and she had achieved her end at a garden party. She had better luck than so rash an enterprise deserved, Mr Wells came up to her expectations. Age had not withered him, nor could custom stale his infinite variety in half an hour. His pleasant neatness and compactness, his small hands and feet, his teeming ready brain, his unaffected accessibility, and a certain fine apprehensiveness which stamped him as susceptible from his topmost hair to his tipmost toe, proved irresistible. Clara talked of nothing else for weeks and weeks afterwards. And as she happened to talk to the lady of the furniture shop, and that lady also desired above all things to know Mr Wells and sell pretty things to him, she offered Clara a job on the chance of achieving that end through her.

And so it came about that Eliza's luck held, and the expected opposition to the flower shop melted away. The shop is in the arcade of a railway station not very far from the Victoria and Albert Museum; and if you live in that neighborhood you may go there any day and buy a buttonhole from Eliza.

Now here is a last opportunity for romance. Would you not like to be assured that the shop was an immense success, thanks to Eliza's charms and her early business experience in Covent Garden? Alas! the truth is the truth: the shop did not pay for a long time, simply because Eliza and her Freddy did not know how to keep it. True, Eliza had not to begin at the very beginning: she knew the names and prices of the cheaper flowers; and her elation was unbounded when she found that Freddy, like all youths educated at cheap, pretentious, and thoroughly inefficient schools, knew a little Latin. It was very little, but enough to make him appear to her a Porson or Bentley,[8] and to put him at his ease with botanical nomenclature. Unfortunately he knew nothing else; and Eliza, though she could count money up to eighteen shillings or so, and had acquired a certain familiarity with the language

---

8. Richard Porson (1759–1808), English classical scholar; Richard Bentley (1662–1742), English classical scholar satirized by Jonathan Swift in *The Battle of the Books*.

of Milton from her struggles to qualify herself for winning Higgins's bet, could not write out a bill without utterly disgracing the establishment. Freddy's power of stating in Latin that Balbus built a wall[9] and that Gaul was divided into three parts did not carry with it the slightest knowledge of accounts or business: Colonel Pickering had to explain to him what a cheque book and a bank account meant. And the pair were by no means easily teachable. Freddy backed up Eliza in her obstinate refusal to believe that they could save money by engaging a bookkeeper with some knowledge of the business. How, they argued, could you possibly save money by going to extra expense when you already could not make both ends meet? But the Colonel, after making the ends meet over and over again, at last gently insisted; and Eliza, humbled to the dust by having to beg from him so often, and stung by the uproarious derision of Higgins, to whom the notion of Freddy succeeding at anything was a joke that never palled, grasped the fact that business, like phonetics, has to be learned.

On the piteous spectacle of the pair spending their evenings in shorthand schools and polytechnic classes, learning book-keeping and typewriting with incipient junior clerks, male and female, from the elementary schools, let me not dwell. There were even classes at the London School of Economics, and a humble personal appeal to the director of that institution to recommend a course bearing on the flower business. He, being a humorist, explained to them the method of the celebrated Dickensian essay on Chinese Metaphysics by the gentleman who read an article on China and an article on Metaphysics and combined the information. He suggested that they should combine the London School with Kew Gardens. Eliza, to whom the procedure of the Dickensian gentleman seemed perfectly correct (as in fact it was) and not in the least funny (which was only her ignorance), took the advice with entire gravity. But the effort that cost her the deepest humiliation was a request to Higgins, whose pet artistic fancy, next to Milton's verse, was calligraphy, and who himself wrote a most beautiful Italian hand, that he would teach her to write. He declared that she was congenitally incapable of forming a single letter worthy of the least of Milton's words; but she persisted; and again he suddenly threw himself into the task of teaching her with a combination of stormy intensity, concentrated patience, and occasional bursts of interesting disquisition on the beauty and nobility, the august mission and destiny, of human handwriting. Eliza ended by acquiring an extremely uncommercial script which was a positive extension of her personal beauty, and spending three times as much on stationery as anyone else because certain qualities and shapes of paper became indispensable to her. She could not even address an envelope in the usual way because it made the margins all wrong.

Their commercial schooldays were a period of disgrace and despair for the young couple. They seemed to be learning nothing about flower shops. At last they gave it up as hopeless, and shook the dust of the shorthand schools, and the polytechnics, and the London School of Economics from their feet for ever. Besides, the business was in some mysterious way beginning to take care of itself. They had somehow forgotten their objections to employing other people. They came to the conclusion that their own way was the best, and that they had really a remarkable talent for business. The Colonel, who had been compelled for some years to keep a sufficient sum on current account at his bankers to make up their deficits, found that the provision was unnecessary: the young people were prospering. It is true that there was not quite fair play between them

9. From Cicero's *Letters to Atticus* 12.2; a common schoolboy's Latin translation exercise.

and their competitors in trade. Their week-ends in the country cost them nothing, and saved them the price of their Sunday dinners; for the motor car was the Colonel's; and he and Higgins paid the hotel bills. Mr F. Hill, florist and greengrocer (they soon discovered that there was money in asparagus; and asparagus led to other vegetables), had an air which stamped the business as classy; and in private life he was still Frederick Eynsford Hill, Esquire. Not that there was any swank about him; nobody but Eliza knew that he had been christened Frederick Challoner. Eliza herself swanked like anything.

That is all. That is how it has turned out. It is astonishing how much Eliza still manages to meddle in the housekeeping at Wimpole Street in spite of the shop and her own family. And it is notable that though she never nags her husband, and frankly loves the Colonel as if she were his favorite daughter, she has never got out of the habit of nagging Higgins that was established on the fatal night when she won his bet for him. She snaps his head off on the faintest provocation, or on none. He no longer dares to tease her by assuming an abysmal inferiority of Freddy's mind to his own. He storms and bullies and derides; but she stands up to him so ruthlessly that the Colonel has to ask her from time to time to be kinder to Higgins; and it is the only request of his that brings a mulish expression into her face. Nothing but some emergency or calamity great enough to break down all likes and dislikes, and throw them both back on their common humanity—and may they be spared any such trial!—will ever alter this. She knows that Higgins does not need her, just as her father did not need her. The very scrupulousness with which he told her that day that he had become used to having her there, and dependent on her for all sorts of little services, and that he should miss her if she went away (it would never have occurred to Freddy or the Colonel to say anything of the sort) deepens her inner certainty that she is "no more to him than them slippers"; yet she has a sense, too, that his indifference is deeper than the infatuation of commoner souls. She is immensely interested in him. She has even secret mischievous moments in which she wishes she could get him alone, on a desert island, away from all ties and with nobody else in the world to consider, and just drag him off his pedestal and see him making love like any common man. We all have private imaginations of that sort. But when it comes to business, to the life that she really leads as distinguished from the life of dreams and fancies, she likes Freddy and she likes the Colonel; and she does not like Higgins and Mr Doolittle. Galatea never does quite like Pygmalion; his relation to her is too god-like to be altogether agreeable.

<hr />

Thomas Hardy
1840–1928

Thomas Hardy led a double life: one of the great Victorian novelists, he abandoned fiction in 1896 and reinvented himself as a poet. In a series of volumes published from 1898 through the early decades of the twentieth century, Hardy emerged as one of the most compelling voices in modern poetry. How should this strangely bifurcated literary career be read? There are continuities as well as divergences between Hardy's fiction and his poetry, and the shifts in his work provide a telling instance of the interwoven links and discontinuities between the Victorian era and the new modernism of the twentieth century.

Hardy was born and reared in the village of Higher Bockhampton, Stinsford, in the rural county of Dorset in southern England. He left home in his early twenties and worked as a church architect in London for five years, then returned to the family home in 1867; he continued to accept architectural commissions while trying his hand at fiction and poetry. In early poems such as *Hap* and *Neutral Tones* Hardy revealed his abiding sense of a universe ruled by a blind or hostile fate, a world whose landscapes are etched with traces of the fleeting stories of their inhabitants. He was not able to find a publisher for such works, and he largely stopped writing poetry, but his first novel, *Desperate Remedies,* was published in 1871. By 1874 he was earning a steady income from his writing and was able to marry Emma Lavinia Gifford, the sister-in-law of a rector whose church he had been restoring. He produced twenty novels within a twenty-five year period, achieving fame, popularity, and no little controversy for the provocative and dark worlds he created. In *Far from the Madding Crowd, The Return of the Native, Tess of the d'Urbervilles,* and *Jude the Obscure,* Hardy transformed the realist novel of manners into tragic accounts of the industrialization of rural Britain, the bankruptcy of religious faith, and irreconcilable tensions between social classes and between men and women. Though he had become a master of characterization and plot, in his later novels Hardy grew increasingly preoccupied with fundamentally lyrical questions of interiority, subjective perception, and personal voice. After the sexual frankness of *Jude the Obscure* provoked shocked reviews—the Bishop of Wakefield went so far as to burn the book—Hardy decided to abandon his prose writing altogether and to mine his chosen territory with the tools of a poet.

He began by recreating in poetry the landscape of his fiction. Hardy's first poetry collection, published when he was fifty-eight, was *Wessex Poems* (1898), its title referring to the imaginary countryside that he had created in his novels, loosely based on regions in the south of England but named for a long-vanished medieval kingdom. Hardy's "Wessex" was a place whose towns and roads and forests and fields were breathed into life by the novelist. The Wessex novels were published with maps of the territory, and the landmarks were to remain constant throughout the disparate books. The region took such a hold on readers' imaginations that a Wessex tourist industry emerged, one which is still in place today. Hardy was as painstaking in giving the precise (although imaginary) coordinates of a village pathway as he was in tracing the path of a character's destiny.

Many of Hardy's poems take root in this same creative landscape, now viewed by an intensely self-aware speaker who retraces his personal history, himself "tracked by phantoms having weird detective ways," as he says in *Wessex Heights.* Burning logs, a photograph, a diminishing figure on a train platform, a deer at a window all provide "moments of vision" (the title of one of his collections) that foreshadow the modernist "epiphanies" of Joyce and Woolf. Like the major modernists, Hardy explored the workings of memory, of perception, and of individual vision. In other poems, he focused on contemporary events, most notably in a series of poems written during World War I, unsparing in their presentation both of the necessity of waging the conflict and of its horrifying waste.

In his poetry as in his prose, Hardy's modern themes are typically set in a rural landscape with ancient roots. A constant feature of the Wessex novels involves characters setting off on one of the myriad footpaths connecting obscure villages and solitary cottages with one another. Hardy invented his own geography for Wessex, but the footpaths really existed and were the most important trails carved into the landscape by travelers over many years. Called "ley lines" in folk culture, such footpaths are thought to gather their energy over time, as hundreds of people gradually wear down a shared path and leave traces of themselves in the form of memory and tradition. Hardy's poems move between personal, historical, and natural levels of experience, but it is the landscape above all that conveys the power of these events.

Hardy embodied his moments of vision in poems that recall old oral and religious forms of verse, especially those of ballads and hymns. Like Wordsworth, Burns, and Kipling, Hardy was fascinated by the power of popular verse forms to convey deep truths in seemingly simple meters and diction; like his predecessors, Hardy brought his traditional forms to life by subtle modulations of their elements. The lines of Hardy's poetry are measured with extreme care and precision—not in any way approaching "free verse." As W. H. Auden wrote of Hardy's poetry: "No English poet, not even Donne or Browning, employed so many and so complicated stanza forms. Anyone who imitates his style will learn at least one thing, how to make words fit into a complicated structure." With architectural care, Hardy built up his words into complicated structures, lines, and stanzas following well-used poetic paths. With its compelling mixture of tradition and modernity, stoic calm and deep emotional intensity, Hardy's poetry has become a touchstone for modern poets writing in English, from Ezra Pound, who said he "needed no other poet," to Philip Larkin, Seamus Heaney, and Derek Walcott. "Auden worshiped his honesty, Eliot disliked his heresy," the critic Irving Howe has commented; "but Hardy prepared the ground for both."

Hardy mined his native landscape, and his own memory, until his death, composing many of his best poems in his seventies and eighties. He had built a house on the outskirts of Dorchester in 1885, and he lived there for the rest of his life, with his wife Emma until her death in 1912, and subsequently with his secretary, Florence Dugdale, whom he married in 1914. When he died, his body was buried in Westminster Abbey; but his heart, as he had directed, was buried in the grave of his wife Emma, next to his father's grave, in the Stinsford churchyard.

Hap°

chance

If but some vengeful god would call to me
From up the sky, and laugh: "Thou suffering thing,
Know that thy sorrow is my ecstasy,
That thy love's loss is my hate's profiting!"

5   Then would I bear it, clench myself, and die,
Steeled by the sense of ire unmerited;
Half-eased in that a Powerfuller than I
Had willed and meted° me the tears I shed.   *given*

But not so. How arrives it joy lies slain,
10 And why unblooms the best hope ever sown?
—Crass Casualty obstructs the sun and rain,
And dicing° Time for gladness casts a moan. . . .   *gambling*
These purblind° Doomsters had as readily strown   *half-blind*
Blisses about my pilgrimage as pain.

1866   1898

Wessex Heights

There are some heights in Wessex,[1] shaped as if by a kindly hand
For thinking, dreaming, dying on, and at crises when I stand,

---

1. An imaginary county in southwest England that forms the setting for Hardy's writings; the place names that follow are in "Wessex."

Say, on Ingpen Beacon eastward, or on Wylls-Neck westwardly,
I seem where I was before my birth, and after death may be.

5   In the lowlands I have no comrade, not even the lone man's friend—
Her who suffereth long and is kind;[2] accepts what he is too weak to mend:
Down there they are dubious and askance; there nobody thinks as I,
But mind-chains do not clank where one's next neighbour is the sky.

In the towns I am tracked by phantoms having weird detective ways—
10   Shadows of beings who fellowed with myself of earlier days:
They hang about at places, and they say harsh heavy things—
Men with a wintry sneer, and women with tart disparagings.

Down there I seem to be false to myself, my simple self that was,
And is not now, and I see him watching, wondering what crass cause
15   Can have merged him into such a strange continuator as this,
Who yet has something in common with himself, my chrysalis.

I cannot go to the great grey Plain; there's a figure against the moon,
Nobody sees it but I, and it makes my breast beat out of tune;
I cannot go to the tall-spired town, being barred by the forms now passed
20   For everybody but me, in whose long vision they stand there fast.
There's a ghost at Yell'ham Bottom chiding loud at the fall of the night,
There's a ghost in Froom-side Vale, thin-lipped and vague, in a shroud
       of white,
There is one in the railway train whenever I do not want it near,
I see its profile against the pane, saying what I would not hear.

25   As for one rare fair woman, I am now but a thought of hers,
I enter her mind and another thought succeeds me that she prefers,
Yet my love for her in its fulness she herself even did not know;
Well, time cures hearts of tenderness, and now I can let her go.

So I am found on Ingpen Beacon, or on Wylls-Neck to the west,
30   Or else on homely Bulbarrow, or little Pilsdon Crest,
Where men have never cared to haunt, nor women have walked with me,
And ghosts then keep their distance; and I know some liberty.

1898

The Darkling Thrush[1]

I leant upon a coppice° gate   *wood*
   When Frost was spectre-gray,
And Winter's dregs made desolate
   The weakening eye of day.
5   The tangled bine-stems° scored the sky   *stems of bushes*
   Like strings of broken lyres,
And all mankind that haunted nigh
   Had sought their household fires.

---

2. Cf. Corinthians 13.4: "Charity suffereth long, and is   1. The poem was published on 31 December 1900.
kind."

   The land's sharp features seemed to be
10   The Century's corpse outleant,[2]
   His crypt the cloudy canopy,
    The wind his death-lament.
   The ancient pulse of germ° and birth   *seed*
    Was shrunken hard and dry,
15 And every spirit upon earth
    Seemed fervourless as I.

   At once a voice arose among
    The bleak twigs overhead
   In a full-hearted evensong
20   Of joy illimited;
   An aged thrush, frail, gaunt, and small,
    In blast-beruffled plume,
   Had chosen thus to fling his soul
    Upon the growing gloom.

25 So little cause for carolings
    Of such ecstatic sound
   Was written on terrestrial things
    Afar or nigh around,
   That I could think there trembled through
30   His happy good-night air
   Some blessed Hope, whereof he knew
    And I was unaware.

On the Departure Platform

   We kissed at the barrier; and passing through
   She left me, and moment by moment got
   Smaller and smaller, until to my view
    She was but a spot;

5   A wee white spot of muslin fluff
   That down the diminishing platform bore
   Through hustling crowds of gentle and rough
    To the carriage door.

   Under the lamplight's fitful glowers,
10 Behind dark groups from far and near,
   Whose interests were apart from ours,
    She would disappear,

   Then show again, till I ceased to see
   That flexible form, that nebulous white;
15 And she who was more than my life to me
    Had vanished quite. . . .

---

2. As if leaning out from a coffin.

We have penned new plans since that fair fond day,
And in season she will appear again—
Perhaps in the same soft white array—
20 But never as then!

—"And why, young man, must eternally fly
A joy you'll repeat, if you love her well?"
—O friend, nought happens twice thus; why,
  I cannot tell!

                1909

The Convergence of the Twain
(Lines on the loss of the "Titanic")[1]

1

In a solitude of the sea
Deep from human vanity,
And the Pride of Life that planned her, stilly couches she.

2

Steel chambers, late the pyres
5 Of her salamandrine° fires,   *white-hot*
Cold currents thrid°, and turn to rhythmic tidal lyres. *thread*

3

Over the mirrors meant
To glass the opulent
The sea-worm crawls—grotesque, slimed, dumb, indifferent.

4

10 Jewels in joy designed
To ravish the sensuous mind
Lie lightless, all their sparkles bleared and black and blind.

5

Dim moon-eyed fishes near
Gaze at the gilded gear
15 And query: "What does this vaingloriousness down here?" . . .

6

Well: while was fashioning
This creature of cleaving wing,
The Immanent Will that stirs and urges everything

7

Prepared a sinister mate
20 For her—so gaily great—
A Shape of Ice, for the time far and dissociate.[2]

8

And as the smart ship grew
In stature, grace, and hue,
In shadowy silent distance grew the Iceberg too.

---

1. The largest ocean-liner of its day, the supposedly unsinkable *Titanic* sank on 15 April 1912 on its maiden voyage after colliding with an iceberg; two thirds of its 2,200 passengers died.
2. According to Hardy, the Immanent Will is that which secretly guides events.

9

25   Alien they seemed to be:
    No mortal eye could see
  The intimate welding of their later history,

10

    Or sign that they were bent
    By paths coincident
30 On being anon twin halves of one august event,

11

    Till the Spinner of the Years
    Said "Now!" And each one hears,
  And consummation comes, and jars two hemispheres.

1912   1912

Channel Firing[1]

That night your great guns, unawares,
Shook all our coffins as we lay,
And broke the chancel window-squares,
We thought it was the Judgment-day

5 And sat upright. While drearisome
Arose the howl of wakened hounds:
The mouse let fall the altar-crumb,
The worms drew back into the mounds,
The glebe° cow drooled. Till God called, "No;   *field*
10 It's gunnery practice out at sea
Just as before you went below;
The world is as it used to be:

"All nations striving strong to make
Red war yet redder. Mad as hatters
15 They do no more for Christés sake
Than you who are helpless in such matters.

"That this is not the judgment-hour
For some of them's a blessed thing,
For if it were they'd have to scour
20 Hell's floor for so much threatening. . . .

"Ha, ha. It will be warmer when
I blow the trumpet (if indeed
I ever do; for you are men,
And rest eternal sorely need)."

25 So down we lay again. "I wonder,
Will the world ever saner be,"
Said one, "than when He sent us under
In our indifferent century!"

---

1. The poem refers to military exercises in the English Channel prior to World War I.

And many a skeleton shook his head.
30   "Instead of preaching forty year,"
My neighbour Parson Thirdly said,
"I wish I had stuck to pipes and beer."

Again the guns disturbed the hour,
Roaring their readiness to avenge,
35   As far inland as Stourton Tower,
And Camelot, and starlit Stonehenge.[2]

April 1914   1914

In Time of "The Breaking of Nations"[1]

1

Only a man harrowing clods
         In a slow silent walk
With an old horse that stumbles and nods
         Half asleep as they stalk.

2

5   Only thin smoke without flame
         From the heaps of couch-grass;
Yet this will go onward the same
         Though Dynasties pass.

3

Yonder a maid and her wight°   man
10   Come whispering by:
War's annals will cloud into night
         Ere their story die.

1915   1916

Logs on the Hearth
A Memory of a Sister[1]

The fire advances along the log
         Of the tree we felled,
Which bloomed and bore striped apples by the peck°   basketful
Till its last hour of bearing knelled.

5   The fork that first my hand would reach
         And then my foot
In climbings upward inch by inch, lies now
         Sawn, sapless, darkening with soot.

2. The town of Stour Head, which Hardy calls Stourton, is in the county of Dorset. According to legend, Camelot was the site of King Arthur's court; Stonehenge is a prehistoric site in southwest England.

1. Cf. Jeremiah 51.20: "Thou art my battle axe and weapons of war: for with thee will I break in pieces the nations, and with thee will I destroy kingdoms."
1. Hardy's sister Mary died in November 1915.

Where the bark chars is where, one year,
10   It was pruned, and bled—
Then overgrew the wound. But now, at last,
Its growings all have stagnated.

My fellow-climber rises dim
From her chilly grave—
15   Just as she was, her foot near mine on the bending limb,
Laughing, her young brown hand awave.

1915   1917

Afterwards

When the Present has latched its postern° behind my tremulous stay,   *gate*
And the May month flaps its glad green leaves like wings,
Delicate-filmed as new-spun silk, will the neighbours say,
"He was a man who used to notice such things"?

5   If it be in the dusk when, like an eyelid's soundless blink,
The dewfall-hawk comes crossing the shades to alight
Upon the wind-warped upland thorn, a gazer may think,
"To him this must have been a familiar sight."

If I pass during some nocturnal blackness, mothy and warm,
10   When the hedgehog travels furtively over the lawn,
One may say, "He strove that such innocent creatures should come to no harm,
But he could do little for them; and now he is gone."

If, when hearing that I have been stilled at last, they stand at the door,
Watching the full-starred heavens that winter sees,
15   Will this thought rise on those who will meet my face no more,
"He was one who had an eye for such mysteries"?

And will any say when my bell of quittance is heard in the gloom,
And a crossing breeze cuts a pause in its outrollings,
Till they rise again, as they were a new bell's boom,
20   "He hears it not now, but used to notice such things"?

1917

Epitaph

I never cared for Life: Life cared for me,
And hence I owed it some fidelity.
It now says, "Cease; at length thou hast learnt to grind
Sufficient toll for an unwilling mind,
And I dismiss thee—not without regard
That thou didst ask no ill-advised reward,
Nor sought in me much more than thou couldst find."

1922

━═← PERSPECTIVES ←═━
The Great War: Confronting the Modern

The multiplying technological, artistic, and social changes at the turn of the twentieth century impressed that generation's artists as a rupture with the past. And no event so graphically suggested that human history had "changed, changed utterly," as World War I—"the Great War."

Great Britain, like its enemy Germany, entered the war with idealistic aims. Prime Minister H. H. Asquith put the justice of the British case this way in a speech to the House of Commons on 7 August 1914: "I do not think any nation ever entered into a great conflict—and this is one of the greatest that history will ever know—with a clearer conscience or stronger conviction that it is fighting not for aggression, not for the maintenance of its own selfish ends, but in defence of principles the maintenance of which is vital to the civilization of the world." But cynicism set in quickly—first among ground troops on the Western Front, dug into trenches and watching "progress" that could be measured in yards per day. Soon the British public became disillusioned with the war effort, partly as a result of technological advances in the news media. Daily papers in England carried photographs from the front, and while editorial policy generally supported the British government and printed heroic images of the fighting, this sanitized version of the war was largely offset by the long published lists of casualties; during the four years and three months that Britain was involved in the war, more than a million British troops—an average of fifteen hundred per day—were killed in action.

The war's lasting legacy was a sense of bitterly rebuffed idealism, bringing with it a suspicion of progress, technology, government, bureaucracy, nationalism, and conventional morality—themes probed in new ways by the period's writers. Just as the war had involved radically new strategies and new technologies, writers intensified their search for new forms and modes of expression as they and their compatriots found themselves in the midst of a conflict unlike anything previously known in the annals of history.

━━◆⊠━━

Blast

Wyndham Lewis (1884–1957), founder of the provocative arts magazine *Blast,* was often at odds with his sometime co-conspirator Ezra Pound: indeed both men were usually at odds with most of their friends. But they did agree on one thing: that the writers of Edwardian and Georgian England had failed to throw off the deadening literary mannerisms of the previous century. "As for the nineteenth century," Pound wrote, "with all respects to its achievements, I think we shall look back upon it as a rather blurry, messy sort of a period, a rather sentimentalistic, mannerish sort of a period."

Some violent corrective was needed. The name of Lewis's magazine was intended to suggest an explosive charge that would blow away tired literary and social conventions. It was a calculated assault on good taste, both in its contents and, more immediately, in its form: an oversized, bright pink cover with the single word *BLAST* splashed diagonally across it. Lewis carefully oversaw the details of typography; visually and rhetorically, *Blast* is indebted to the polemical style of the Italian artist F. T. Marinetti (1876–1944), the founder of Italian futurism. Marinetti's vivid manifestos for futurism celebrated a modern aesthetic of speed, technology, and power. Lewis in turn founded a movement he called Vorticism, and *Blast* bore the subtitle *The Review of the Great English Vortex.*

The definition of *vorticism* was left intentionally hazy; as canny an observer as the Vorticist painter William Roberts, one of the signatories of the manifesto, claimed that Vorticism was first and foremost "a slogan." In 1915 Lewis defined it this way: "By Vorticism we mean (a) ACTIVITY as opposed to the tasteful PASSIVITY of Picasso; (b) SIGNIFICANCE as opposed to the

Wyndham Lewis, *The Creditors* (design for *Timon of Athens*), 1912–1913.

dull or anecdotal character to which the Naturalist is condemned; (c) ESSENTIAL MOVEMENT and ACTIVITY (such as the energy of a mind) as opposed to the imitative cinematography, the fuss and hysterics of the Futurists."

In its disorienting layout of typography, the *Vorticist Manifesto* is as much a visual as a literary statement, reflecting the multiple and always skewed interest of its primary author, Lewis. Born on a yacht off the coast of Nova Scotia, he had moved to London with his mother when his parents separated in 1893. A precocious painter, he won a scholarship to the progressive Slade School of Art at age sixteen, but moved to Paris before completing his studies. He returned to London in 1909 and began a career as a painter and writer. During the War, he served both as an artillery officer and as a commissioned war artist. He also wrote an experimental novel, *Tarr* (1918), and went on to produce a range of works in the dozen years thereafter, including pro-fascist political theory in *The Art of Being Ruled* (1926) and more general cultural criticism in *Time and Western Man* (1927), in which he attacked the modern cult of subjectivity. During the thirties, he became increasingly unpopular in London, first as a result of a satirical novel, *The Apes of God,* which lampooned figures in the literary and art world and their patrons; following two libel actions against him, publishers became wary of taking on his works. Lewis and his wife spent the years of World War II living in poverty in America and Canada; after the war, he returned to England, where he became an art critic for the British Broadcasting Corporation. He continued to draw, paint, and write memoirs, satirical stories, and an allegorical fantasy in several volumes.

Along with the *Vorticist Manifesto,* the first issue of *Blast* included poetry by Pound, fiction by Ford Madox Ford and Rebecca West, a play by Lewis, and illustrations by Lewis and others. The timing of the first issue couldn't have been worse: after delays caused by typesetting difficulties, *Blast* went on sale in London on 20 June 1914; World War I began just a few weeks later. While Lewis and his confederates had declared war on conventional artistic and literary taste with their "puce monster"—an advertisement for the first issue announced the "END OF THE CHRISTIAN ERA"—they were usurped by a much more pressing conflict. As Lewis later wrote, "In 1914 I produced a huge review called *Blast*, which for the most part I wrote myself. That was my first public appearance. Immediately the War broke out and put an end to all that." Lewis brought out a second issue in July 1915, attempting to fend off charges of irrelevancy with a special "War Number" that included T. S. Eliot's "Preludes" and "Rhapsody on a Windy Night" and a manifesto from the sculptor Henri Gaudier-Brzeska, "written from the trenches," which concludes poignantly with an obituary for Gaudier, "Mort pour la Patrie" (died for the fatherland). But by this time, *Blast* itself was for all intents and purposes dead; its second issue was its last. Short-lived though it was, however, *Blast* was remarkably important in clearing the way for the new art of modernism.

VORTICIST MANIFESTO
LONG LIVE THE VORTEX!

Long live the great art vortex sprung up in the centre of this town!

We stand for the Reality of the Present—not for the sentimental Future, or the sacripant[1] Past.

We want to leave Nature and Men alone.

We do not want to make people wear Futurist Patches, or fuss men to take to pink and sky-blue trousers.

We are not their wives or tailors.

The only way Humanity can help artists is to remain independent and work unconsciously.

WE NEED THE UNCONSCIOUSNESS OF HUMANITY—their stupidity, animalism and dreams.

We believe in no perfectibility except our own.

Intrinsic beauty is in the Interpreter and Seer, not in the object or content.[2]

We do not want to change the appearance of the world, because we are not Naturalists, Impressionists or Futurists (the latest form of Impressionism), and do not depend on the appearance of the world for our art.

WE ONLY WANT THE WORLD TO LIVE, and to feel its crude energy flowing through us.

It may be said that great artists in England are always revolutionary, just as in France any really fine artist had a strong traditional vein.

Blast sets out to be an avenue for all those vivid and violent ideas that could reach the Public in no other way.

Blast will be popular, essentially. It will not appeal to any particular class, but to the fundamental and popular instincts in every class and description of people, **TO THE INDIVIDUAL.** The moment a man feels or realizes himself as an artist, he ceases to belong to any milieu or time. Blast is created for this timeless, fundamental Artist that exists in everybody.

---

1. Boasting of valor.
2. Although the Vorticists go on to differentiate themselves from the Impressionists, this statement is very close

to the impressionism articulated by Walter Pater in *The Renaissance* (1873).

The Man in the Street and the Gentleman are equally ignored.

Popular art does not mean the art of the poor people, as it is usually supposed to. It means the art of the individuals.

Education (art education and general education) tends to destroy the creative instinct. Therefore it is in times when education has been non-existent that art chiefly flourished.

But it is nothing to do with "the People."

It is a mere accident that that is the most favourable time for the individual to appear.

To make the rich of the community shed their education skin, to destroy politeness, standardization and academic, that is civilized, vision, is the task we have set ourselves.

We want to make in England not a popular art, not a revival of lost folk art, or a romantic fostering of such unactual conditions, but to make individuals, wherever found.

We will convert the King if possible.

A VORTICIST KING! WHY NOT?

DO YOU THINK LLOYD GEORGE[3] HAS THE VORTEX IN HIM?

MAY WE HOPE FOR ART FROM LADY MOND?[4]

We are against the glorification of "the People," as we are against snobbery. It is not necessary to be an outcast bohemian, to be unkempt or poor, any more than it is necessary to be rich or handsome, to be an artist. Art is nothing to do with the coat you wear. A top-hat can well hold the Sixtine.[5] A cheap cap could hide the image of Kephren.

AUTOMOBILISM (Marinetteism) bores us. We don't want to go about making a hullo-bulloo about motor cars, anymore than about knives and forks, elephants or gas-pipes.

Elephants are **VERY BIG.** Motor cars go quickly.

Wilde gushed twenty years ago about the beauty of machinery. Gissing,[6] in his romantic delight with modern lodging houses was futurist in this sense.

The futurist is a sensational and sentimental mixture of the aesthete of 1890 and the realist of 1870.

The "Poor" are detestable animals! They are only picturesque and amusing for the sentimentalist or the romantic! The "Rich" are bores without a single exception, *en tant que riches* [so far as they are rich]!

We want those simple and great people found everywhere.

Blast presents an art of Individuals.

MANIFESTO.

1

BLAST First (from politeness) ENGLAND

CURSE ITS CLIMATE FOR ITS SINS AND INFECTIONS

DISMAL SYMBOL, SET round our bodies,

of effeminate lout within.

---

3. David Lloyd George, British statesman, and Prime Minister 1916–1922.
4. A leader of fashionable London society.

5. The Sistine Chapel in the Vatican.
6. George Gissing (1857–1903), naturalist novelist.

VICTORIAN VAMPIRE, the LONDON cloud sucks
the TOWN'S heart.

A 1000 MILE LONG, 2 KILOMETER Deep

BODY OF WATER even, is pushed against us
from the Floridas, TO MAKE US MILD.
OFFICIOUS MOUNTAINS keep back DRASTIC WINDS

SO MUCH VAST MACHINERY TO PRODUCE

THE CURATE of "Eltham"
BRITANNIC AESTHETE
WILD NATURE CRANK
DOMESTICATED POLICEMAN
LONDON COLISEUM
SOCIALIST-PLAYWRIGHT
DALY'S MUSICAL COMEDY
GAIETY CHORUS GIRL
TONKS[7]

CURSE

the flabby sky that can manufacture no snow, but can only drop the sea on us in a drizzle like a poem by Mr. Robert Bridges.[8]

CURSE

the lazy air that cannot stiffen the back of the **SERPENTINE,** or put Aquatic steel half way down the **MANCHESTER CANAL.**

———

But ten years ago we saw distinctly both snow and ice here.
May some vulgarly inventive, but useful person, arise, and restore to us the necessary **BLIZZARDS.**

LET US ONCE MORE WEAR THE ERMINE
OF THE NORTH.

WE BELIEVE IN THE EXISTENCE OF THIS USEFUL
LITTLE CHEMIST IN OUR MIDST!

---

7. Henry Tonks, a teacher at the Slade School of Art (where Lewis and other Vorticists studied) who resisted as "contamination" such modern innovations as Post-Impressionism and Cubism.
8. Poet Laureate from 1913 until his death in 1930, noted for his technical skill and high moral tone.

2
OH BLAST FRANCE

pig plagiarism
BELLY
SLIPPERS
POODLE TEMPER
BAD MUSIC

SENTIMENTAL GALLIC GUSH
SENSATIONALISM
FUSSINESS.

PARISIAN PAROCHIALISM.

Complacent young man, so much respect for Papa and his son!—Oh!—Papa is wonderful: but all papas are!

BLAST

APERITIFS (Pernots, Amers picon)
Bad change
Naively seductive Houri salon-
  picture Cocottes
Slouching blue porters (can carry
  a pantechnicon)
Stupidly rapacious people at
  every step
Economy maniacs
Bouillon Kub (for being a bad pun)

PARIS.

Clap-trap Heaven of amative
  German professor.
Ubiquitous lines of silly little trees.
Arcs de Triomphe.
Imperturbable, endless prettiness.
Large empty cliques, higher up.
Bad air for the individual.

BLAST
MECCA OF THE AMERICAN

because it is not other side of Suez Canal, instead of an afternoon's ride from London.

3
CURSE
WITH EXPLETIVE OF WHIRLWIND
THE BRITANNIC AESTHETE

CREAM OF THE SNOBBISH EARTH
ROSE OF SHARON OF GOD-PRIG
OF SIMIAN VANITY
SNEAK AND SWOT OF THE SCHOOL-ROOM
IMBERB (or Berbed when in Belsize)-PEDANT

PRACTICAL JOKER
DANDY
CURATE

BLAST all products of phlegmatic cold
Life of **LOOKER-ON.**
CURSE

SNOBBERY
(disease of feminity)
FEAR OF RIDICULE
(arch vice of inactive, sleepy)
PLAY
STYLISM
SINS AND PLAGUES
of this LYMPHATIC finished
(we admit in every sense
finished)
VEGETABLE HUMANITY.

4
BLAST

THE SPECIALIST
"PROFESSIONAL"
"GOOD WORKMAN"
"GROVE-MAN"
ONE ORGAN MAN

BLAST THE

AMATEUR
SCIOLAST
ART-PIMP
JOURNALIST
SELF MAN
NO-ORGAN MAN

5
BLAST HUMOUR

Quack ENGLISH drug for stupidity and sleepiness.
Arch enemy of REAL, conventionalizing like

gunshot, freezing supple
REAL in ferocious chemistry
of laughter.

BLAST SPORT
HUMOUR'S FIRST COUSIN AND ACCOMPLICE.

Impossibility for Englishman to be grave and
keep his end up, psychologically.
Impossible for him to use Humour as well
and be persistently grave.
Alas! necessity for big doll's show in front
of mouth.
Visitation of Heaven on
English Miss
gums, canines of **FIXED GRIN**
Death's head symbol of Anti-Life.

CURSE those who will hang over this
Manifesto with SILLY CANINES exposed.

6
BLAST

years 1837 to 1900

Curse abysmal inexcusable middle-class (also Aristocracy and
Proletariat).

BLAST

pasty shadow cast by gigantic BOEHM[9]
(Imagined at introduction of BOURGEOIS VICTORIAN
VISTAS).
WRING THE NECK OF all sick inventions born in that pro-
gressive white wake.

9. Joseph Edgar Boehm (1834–1890), sculptor for Queen Victoria.

BLAST   their weeping whiskers—hirsute
RHETORIC of EUNUCH and STYLIST—
SENTIMENTAL HYGIENICS
ROUSSEAUISMS (wild Nature cranks)
FRATERNIZING WITH MONKEYS
DIABOLICS—raptures and roses
of the erotic bookshelves
culminating in
PURGATORY OF PUTNEY.[1]

CHAOS OF ENOCH ARDENS[2]

laughing Jennys[3]
Ladies with Pains
good-for-nothing Guineveres.

SNOBBISH BORROVIAN running after
GIPSY KINGS and ESPADAS[4]

bowing the knee to
wild Mother Nature,
her feminine contours,
Unimaginative insult to
MAN.

DAMN

all those to-day who have taken on that Rotten Menagerie, and still crack
their whips and tumble in Piccadilly Circus, as though London were a
provincial town.

WE WHISPER IN YOUR EAR A GREAT SECRET.

LONDON IS NOT A PROVINCIAL TOWN.

We will allow Wonder Zoos. But we do not want the
GLOOMY VICTORIAN CIRCUS in
Piccadilly Circus.

IT IS PICCADILLY'S CIRCUS!

NOT MEANT FOR MENAGERIES trundling
out of Sixties DICKENSIAN CLOWNS,
CORELLI[5] LADY RIDERS, TROUPS
OF PERFORMING GIPSIES (who
complain besides that 1/6 a night
does not pay fare back to Clapham).

1. A middle-class suburb of London.
2. *Enoch Arden* (1864), a sentimental narrative poem by Tennyson.
3. From Dante Gabriel Rossetti's popular poem *Jenny* (1870), again disliked for its sentimentality.

4. Refers to the contemporary popularity of the gypsy romances of George Borrow, such as *The Zincali* (1841).
5. Marie Corelli, pseud. of Mary Mackay (1855–1924), author of best-selling religious novels and romances.

BLAST[6]

The Post Office   Frank Brangwyn   Robertson Nicol
Rev. Pennyfeather   Galloway Kyle
(Bells)   (Cluster of Grapes)
Bishop of London and all his posterity
Galsworthy   Dean Inge   Croce   Matthews
Rev Meyer   Seymour Hicks
Lionel Cust   C. B. Fry   Bergson Abdul Bahai
Hawtrey   Edward Elgar   Sardlea
Filson Young   Marie Corelli   Geddes
Codliver Oil   St. Loe Strachey   Lyceum Club
Rhabindraneth Tagore   Lord Glenconner of Glen
Weiniger   Norman Angel   Ad. Mahon
Mr. and Mrs. Dearmer   Beecham   Ella
A. C. Benson   (Pills, Opera, Thomas)   Sydney Webb
British Academy   Messrs. Chapell
Countess of Warwick   George Edwards
Willie Ferraro   Captain Cook   R. J. Campbell
Clan Thesiger   Martin Harvey   William Archer
George Grossmith   R. H. Benson
Annie Besant   Chenil   Clan Meynell
Father Vaughan   Joseph Holbrooke   Clan Strachey

1

BLESS ENGLAND!

BLESS ENGLAND

FOR ITS SHIPS

which switchback on Blue, Green and
Red **SEAS** all around the **PINK
EARTH-BALL,**

BIG BETS ON EACH.

BLESS ALL SEAFARERS.

THEY exchange not one LAND for another, but one ELEMENT for
ANOTHER. The MORE against the LESS ABSTRACT.

---

6. The list of those blasted by the Vorticists falls, according to the critic William Wees, into seven categories: (1) members of the (literary and cultural) Establishment (e.g., William Archer, drama critic of the *Nation*); (2) people who represented popular or snobbish fads (e.g., Sir Abdul Baha Bahai, leader of the Bahai faith); (3) high-minded popular writers, (e.g., Marie Corelli); (4) mediocre but popular figures (e.g., the poet Ella Wheeler Wilcox); (5) fuzzy-minded reformers and idealists (e.g., Sidney Webb, a leader of the Fabian Socialist organization); (6) "popular figures whom the Vorticists just didn't like" (e.g., C. B. Fry, a cricket player); and (7) "blasting just for the fun of it . . . or blasting that grew from special circumstances and private reasons known only to insiders" (e.g., the Post Office and Cod Liver Oil). See William C. Wees, *Vorticism and the English Avant-Garde* (1972), pp. 217–27.

BLESS the vast planetary abstraction of the **OCEAN.**

————————

BLESS THE ARABS OF THE **ATLANTIC.**
THIS ISLAND MUST BE CONTRASTED WITH THE BLEAK WAVES.

————————

BLESS ALL PORTS.

PORTS, RESTLESS MACHINES of

> scooped out basins
> heavy insect dredgers
> monotonous cranes
> stations
> lighthouses, blazing
>   through the frosty
>   starlight, cutting the
>   storm like a cake
> beaks of infant boats,
>   side by side,
> heavy chaos of
>   wharves,
> steep walls of
>   factories
> womanly town

BLESS these **MACHINES** that work the little boats across
clean liquid space, in beelines.

BLESS the great **PORTS**

> HULL
> LIVERPOOL
> LONDON
> NEWCASTLE-ON-TYNE
> BRISTOL
> GLASGOW

BLESS ENGLAND,

Industrial Island machine, pyramidal workshop,
its apex at Shetland, discharging itself on the sea.

BLESS

> cold ————————
> magnanimous
> delicate
> gauche
> fanciful
> stupid

ENGLISHMEN.

2
BLESS the HAIRDRESSER.

He attacks Mother Nature for a small fee.
Hourly he ploughs heads for sixpence,
Scours chins and lips for threepence.
He makes systematic mercenary war on this
   WILDNESS.
He trims aimless and retrograde growths
   into CLEAN ARCHED SHAPES and
   ANGULAR PLOTS.

   BLESS this HESSIAN (or SILESIAN) **EXPERT**[7]
correcting the grotesque anachronisms
   of our physique.

3
BLESS ENGLISH HUMOUR

It is the great barbarous weapon of
the genius among races.
The wild MOUNTAIN RAILWAY from IDEA
to IDEA, in the ancient Fair of LIFE.

BLESS **SWIFT**   for his solemn bleak
                       wisdom of laughter.

SHAKESPEARE   for his bitter Northern
                   Rhetoric of humour.

BLESS ALL ENGLISH EYES
   that grow crows-feet with their
   FANCY and ENERGY.

BLESS this hysterical WALL built round
   the EGO.

BLESS the solitude of LAUGHTER.

BLESS the separating, ungregarious
   BRITISH GRIN.

4
BLESS FRANCE

for its BUSHELS of VITALITY
to the square inch.

---

7. From German industrial regions.

HOME OF MANNERS (the Best, the WORST and interesting mixtures).

MASTERLY PORNOGRAPHY (great enemy of progress).
COMBATIVENESS
GREAT HUMAN SCEPTICS
DEPTHS OF ELEGANCE
FEMALE QUALITIES
FEMALES
BALLADS of its PREHISTORIC APACHE
Superb hardness and hardiesse of its
Voyou° type, rebellious adolescent.   *disreputable*
Modesty and humanity of many there.
GREAT FLOOD OF LIFE pouring out
of wound of 1797.[8]
Also bitterer stream from 1870.[9]
STAYING POWER, like a cat.

BLESS[1]

Bridget   Berrwolf   Bearline   Cranmer Byng
Frieder Graham   The Pope   Maria de Tomaso
Captain Kemp   Munroe   Gaby   Jenkins
R. B. Cuningham Grahame   Barker
(not his brother)   (John and Granville)
Mrs. Wil Finnimore   Madame Strindberg   Carson
Salvation Army   Lord Howard de Walden
Capt. Craig   Charlotte Corday   Cromwell
Mrs. Duval   Mary Robertson   Lillie Lenton
Frank Rutter   Castor Oil   James Joyce
Leveridge   Lydia Yavorska   Preb. Carlyle   Jenny
Mon. le compte de Gabulis   Smithers   Dick Burge
33 Church Street   Sievier   Gertie Millar
Norman Wallis   Miss Fowler   Sir Joseph Lyons
Martin Wolff   Watt   Mrs. Hepburn
Alfree   Tommy   Captain Kendell   Young Ahearn
Wilfred Walter   Kate Lechmere   Henry Newbolt
Lady Aberconway   Frank Harris   Hamel
Gilbert Canaan   Sir James Mathew Barry
Mrs. Belloc Lowndes   W. L. George   Rayner
George Robey   George Mozart   Harry Weldon

8. The rise of Napoleon Bonaparte.
9. Beginning of Franco-Prussian War and end of the Second Empire, led by Napoleon Bonaparte's nephew Napoleon III.
1. This list of the blessed falls, according to William Wees, into four categories: (1) "some of the blessings, like most of the blasts, seemed designed to affront respectable public opinion" (e.g., the Pope and the Salvation Army); (2) "working class entertainments such as boxing and music halls"; (3) "a few selected representatives of the fine arts" (e.g., James Joyce); and (4) "friends of the Vorticists or of the avant-garde in general" (e.g., Frank Rutter and P. J. Konody, two sympathetic art critics).

Chaliapine   George Hirst   Graham White
Hucks   Salmet   Shirley Kellogg   Bandsman Rice
Petty Officer Curran   Applegarth   Konody
Colin Bell   Lewis Hind   LEFRANC
Hubert   Commercial Process Co.

MANIFESTO.

I.

1 Beyond Action and Reaction we would establish ourselves.
2 We start from opposite statements of a chosen world. Set up violent structure of adolescent clearness between two extremes.
3 We discharge ourselves on both sides.
4 We fight first on one side, then on the other, but always for the SAME cause, which is neither side or both sides and ours.
5 Mercenaries were always the best troops.
6 We are Primitive Mercenaries in the Modern World.
7 Our <u>Cause</u> is NO-MAN'S.
8 We set Humour at Humour's throat.
   Stir up Civil War among peaceful apes.
9 We only want Humour if it has fought like Tragedy.
10 We only want Tragedy if it can clench its side-muscles like hands on its belly, and bring to the surface a laugh like a bomb.

II.

1 We hear from America and the Continent all sorts of disagreeable things about England: "the unmusical, anti-artistic, unphilosophic country."
2 We quite agree.
3 Luxury, sport, the famous English "Humour," the thrilling ascendancy and idée fixe of Class, producing the most intense snobbery in the World; heavy stagnant pools of Saxon blood, incapable of anything but the song of a frog, in home-counties:—these phenomena give England a peculiar distinction in the wrong sense, among the nations.
4 This is why England produces such good artists from time to time.
5 This is also the reason why a movement towards art and imagination could burst up here, from this lump of compressed life, with more force than anywhere else.
6 To believe that it is necessary for or conducive to art, to "improve" life, for instance—make architecture, dress, ornament, in "better taste," is absurd.
7 The Art-instinct is permanently primitive.
8 In a chaos of imperfection, discord, etc., it finds the same stimulus as in Nature.
9 The artist of the modern movement is a savage (in no sense an "advanced," perfected, democratic, Futurist individual of Mr. Marinetti's limited imagination): this enormous, jangling, journalistic, fairy desert of modern life serves him as Nature did more technically primitive man.

[10] As the steppes and the rigours of the Russian winter, when the peasant has to lie for weeks in his hut, produces that extraordinary acuity of feeling and intelligence we associate with the Slav; so England is just now the most favourable country for the appearance of a great art.

III.

[1] We have made it quite clear that there is nothing Chauvinistic or picturesquely patriotic about our contentions.

[2] But there is violent boredom with that feeble Europeanism, abasement of the miserable "intellectual" before anything coming from Paris, Cosmopolitan sentimentality, which prevails in so many quarters.

[3] Just as we believe that an Art must be organic with its Time,
So we insist that what is actual and vital for the South, is ineffectual and unactual in the North.

[4] Fairies have disappeared from Ireland (despite foolish attempts to revive them)[2] and the bull-ring languishes in Spain.

[5] But mysticism on the one hand, gladiatorial instincts, blood and asceticism on the other, will be always actual, and springs of Creation for these two peoples.

[6] The English Character is based on the Sea.

[7] The particular qualities and characteristics that the sea always engenders in men are those that are, among the many diagnostics of our race, the most fundamentally English.

[8] That unexpected universality as well, found in the completest English artists, is due to this.

IV.

[1] We assert that the art for these climates, then, must be a northern flower.

[2] And we have implied what we believe should be the specific nature of the art destined to grow up in this country, and models of whose flue decorate the pages of this magazine.

[3] It is not a question of the characterless material climate around us.
Were that so the complication of the Jungle, dramatic Tropic growth, the vastness of American trees, would not be for us.

[4] But our industries, and the Will that determined, face to face with its needs, the direction of the modern world, has reared up steel trees where the green ones were lacking; has exploded in useful growths, and found wilder intricacies than those of Nature.

V.

[1] We bring clearly forward the following points, before further defining the character of this necessary native art.

2. The Celtic Revival was a nostalgic movement in Irish arts and letters.

2 At the freest and most vigorous period of ENGLAND'S history, her literature, then chief Art, was in many ways identical with that of France.

3 Chaucer was very much cousin of Villon[3] as an artist.

4 Shakespeare and Montaigne[4] formed one literature.

5 But Shakespeare reflected in his imagination a mysticism, madness and delicacy
peculiar to the North, and brought equal quantities of Comic and Tragic
together.

6 Humour is a phenomenon caused by sudden pouring of culture into Barbary.[5]

7 It is intelligence electrified by flood of Naivety.

8 It is Chaos invading Concept and bursting it like nitrogen.

9 It is the Individual masquerading as Humanity like a child in clothes too big for him.

10 Tragic Humour is the birthright of the North.

11 Any great Northern Art will partake of this insidious and volcanic chaos.

12 No great ENGLISH Art need be ashamed to share some glory with France,
tomorrow it may be with Germany, where the Elizabethans did before it.

13 But it will never be French, any more than Shakespeare was, the most catholic
and subtle Englishman.

VI.

1 The Modern World is due almost entirely to Anglo-Saxon genius,—its appearance and its spirit.

2 Machinery, trains, steam-ships, all that distinguishes externally our time, came
far more from here than anywhere else.

3 In dress, manners, mechanical inventions, LIFE, that is, ENGLAND, has influenced Europe in the same way that France has in Art.

4 But busy with this LIFE-EFFORT, she has been the last to become conscious
of the Art that is an organism of this new Order and Will of Man.

5 Machinery is the greatest Earth-medium: incidentally it sweeps away the doctrines of a narrow and pedantic Realism at one stroke.

6 By mechanical inventiveness, too, just as Englishmen have spread themselves all
over the Earth, they have brought all the hemispheres about them in their
original island.

7 It cannot be said that the complication of the Jungle, dramatic tropic growths,
the vastness of American trees, is not for us.

8 For, in the forms of machinery, Factories, new and vaster buildings, bridges and
works, we have all that, naturally, around us.

VII.

1 Once this consciousness towards the new possibilities of expression in present life has come, however, it will be more the legitimate property of Englishmen than of any other people in Europe.

2 It should also, as it is by origin theirs, inspire them more forcibly and directly.

---

3. François Villon (1431–1463?), French poet.
4. Michel de Montaigne (1533–1592), French essayist.

5. An old name for the western part of North Africa; possibly used here to mean "barbarity."

3   They are the inventors of this bareness and hardness, and should be the great enemies of Romance.

4   The Romance peoples will always be, at bottom, its defenders.

5   The Latins are at present, for instance, in their "discovery" of sport, their Futuristic gush over machines, aeroplanes, etc., the most romantic and sentimental "moderns" to be found.

6   It is only the second-rate people in France or Italy who are thorough revolutionaries.

7   In England, on the other hand, there Is no vulgarity in revolt.

8   Or, rather, there is no revolt, it is the normal state.

9   So often rebels of the North and the South are diametrically opposed species.

10   The nearest thing in England to a great traditional French artist, is a great revolutionary English one.

Signatures for Manifesto[6]

R. Aldington

Arbuthnot

L. Atkinson

Gaudier Brzeska

J. Dismorr

C. Hamilton

E. Pound

W. Roberts

H. Sanders

E. Wadsworth

Wyndham Lewis

Rupert Brooke
1887–1915

Rupert Brooke was the first of Britain's "war poets," and the last poem he completed during his short lifetime—*The Soldier*—is alone enough to guarantee his lasting place in modern poetry.

Brooke rose with extraordinary speed to the center of the British literary establishment. While an undergraduate, he worked with the *Cambridge Review* and came into contact with such influential writers as Henry James, W. B. Yeats, Virginia Woolf, and Lytton Strachey, and the editor and publisher Edward Marsh. In 1912, after the publication of his first volume of poetry, Brooke suffered a nervous breakdown; after a short recovery period, he spent most of the next three years traveling. World War I began shortly after he returned to England in the spring of 1914; Brooke enlisted immediately and was commissioned on a ship that sailed to Antwerp, Belgium, where Brooke saw no action through early 1915. During this lull, Brooke

6. The signatories to the manifesto are Richard Aldington, English writer and man of letters; Malcolm Arbuthnot, professional photographer; Lawrence Atkinson, Vorticist artist; Henri Gaudier-Brzeska, Vorticist sculptor and contributor to *Blast* who was killed in the trenches in World War I and whose obituary was included in *Blast II*; Jessica Dismoor, artist whose illustrations were included in *Blast*; Cuthbert Hamilton, avant-garde artist; Ezra Pound; William Roberts, painter; Helen Saunders, Vorticist designer; Edward Wadsworth, Vorticist painter; and Wyndham Lewis.

wrote the war sonnets for which he is best remembered today. While his ship was sailing to Gallipoli, Brooke died of blood poisoning, before seeing combat duty.

It is nearly impossible, even at this late date, to separate Brooke the myth from Brooke the poet; he was something of a national hero even before his death, thanks to the popular reception of his volume of war sonnets, *Nineteen Fourteen*. In Brooke's writings about the war, the irony of early poems like *Heaven* ("And in that Heaven of all their wish, / There shall be no more land, say fish") falls away. These patriotic poems—and most especially *The Soldier*, in which Brooke seemed to have foreseen his own death—meshed perfectly with the temperament of the British people as the nation entered into war. When *The Soldier* was read aloud at Saint Paul's Cathedral in London on Easter Sunday, 1915, Brooke the man—whom Yeats called "the handsomest man in England"—was permanently immortalized as the symbol of English pride.

The Great Lover

I have been so great a lover: filled my days
So proudly with the splendour of Love's praise,
The pain, the calm, and the astonishment,
Desire illimitable, and still content,
5   And all dear names men use, to cheat despair,
For the perplexed and viewless streams that bear
Our hearts at random down the dark of life.
Now, ere the unthinking silence on that strife
Steals down, I would cheat drowsy Death so far,
10   My night shall be remembered for a star
That outshone all the suns of all men's days.
Shall I not crown them with immortal praise
Whom I have loved, who have given me, dared with me
High secrets, and in darkness knelt to see
15   The inenarrable° godhead of delight?   *indescribable*
Love is a flame;—we have beaconed the world's night.
A city:—and we have built it, these and I.
An emperor:—we have taught the world to die.
So, for their sakes I loved, ere I go hence,
20   And the high cause of Love's magnificence,
And to keep loyalties young, I'll write those names
Golden for ever, eagles, crying flames,
And set them as a banner, that men may know,
To dare the generations, burn, and blow
25   Out on the wind of Time, shining and streaming . . . .

These I have loved:
                    White plates and cups, clean-gleaming,
Ringed with blue lines; and feathery, faëry dust;
Wet roofs, beneath the lamp-light; the strong crust
Of friendly bread; and many-tasting food;
30   Rainbows; and the blue bitter smoke of wood;
And radiant raindrops couching in cool flowers;
And flowers themselves, that sway through sunny hours,
Dreaming of moths that drink them under the moon;
Then, the cool kindliness of sheets, that soon
35   Smooth away trouble; and the rough male kiss

Of blankets; grainy wood; live hair that is
Shining and free; blue-massing clouds; the keen
Unpassioned beauty of a great machine;
The benison° of hot water; furs to touch;   *benediction*
40   The good smell of old clothes; and other such—
The comfortable smell of friendly fingers,
Hair's fragrance, and the musty reek that lingers
About dead leaves and last year's ferns. . . .
                                      Dear names,
And thousand other throng to me! Royal flames;
45   Sweet water's dimpling laugh from tap or spring;
Holes in the ground; and voices that do sing;
Voices in laughter, too; and body's pain,
Soon turned to peace; and the deep-panting train;
Firm sands; the little dulling edge of foam
50   That browns and dwindles as the wave goes home;
And washen stones, gay for an hour; the cold
Graveness of iron; moist black earthen mould;
Sleep; and high places; footprints in the dew;
And oaks; and brown horse-chestnuts, glossy-new;
55   And new-peeled sticks; and shining pools on grass;—
All these have been my loves. And these shall pass,
Whatever passes not, in the great hour,
Nor all my passion, all my prayers, have power
To hold them with me through the gate of Death.
60   They'll play deserter, turn with the traitor breath,
Break the high bond we made, and sell Love's trust
And sacramented covenant to the dust.
—Oh, never a doubt but, somewhere, I shall wake,
And give what's left of love again, and make
New friends, now strangers. . . .
65   But the best I've known,
Stays here, and changes, breaks, grows old, is blown
About the winds of the world, and fades from brains
Of living men, and dies.
Nothing remains.

                O dear my loves, O faithless, once again
70   This one last gift I give: that after men
Shall know, and later lovers, far-removed,
Praise you, "All these were lovely"; say, "He loved."

MATAIEA, 1914

The Soldier

If I should die, think only this of me:
    That there's some corner of a foreign field
That is forever England. There shall be
    In that rich earth a richer dust concealed;
5   A dust whom England bore, shaped, made aware,

Gave, once, her flowers to love, her ways to roam,
A body of England's, breathing English air,
　Washed by the rivers, blest by suns of home.

And think, this heart, all evil shed away,
10　　A pulse in the Eternal mind, no less
　　　Gives somewhere back the thoughts by England given,
Her sights and sounds; dreams happy as her day;
　And laughter, learnt of friends; and gentleness,
　　In hearts at peace, under an English heaven.

Siegfried Sassoon
1886–1967

It is tempting to describe a poet like Siegfried Sassoon by emphasizing his differences from the hugely popular Rupert Brooke. Sassoon was born to a wealthy Jewish family, who made their fortune in India; he lived a life of ease before the war, writing slight Georgian poetry and hunting foxes. World War I suddenly and unequivocally changed all that. Sassoon served with the Royal Welch Fusiliers, and before the end of 1915 saw action in France; he helped a wounded soldier to safety during heavy fire, for which he was awarded a Military Cross. After being wounded himself, Sassoon refused to return to battle; from his hospital bed, he wrote an open letter to the war department suggesting that the war was being unnecessarily prolonged, and as a result, he narrowly avoided a court-martial. Owing to the intervention of his fellow soldier the poet Robert Graves, he was instead committed to a hospital and treated for "shell-shock." He returned to the front in 1919, and was wounded a second time.

　　Where the war poetry of Brooke is patriotic to the point of sentimentality, Sassoon's verse is characterized by an unrelentingly realistic portrayal of the horrors of modern warfare. And where Brooke's poetry was eagerly welcomed by an anxious public, Sassoon's was largely rejected as either unpatriotic or unnecessarily grotesque. After the war, he lived in seclusion in the country, writing memoirs and poetry—though rarely with the shock value of his early war poems.

Glory of Women

You love us when we're heroes, home on leave,
Or wounded in a mentionable place.
You worship decorations; you believe
That chivalry redeems the war's disgrace.
5　You make us shells. You listen with delight,
By tales of dirt and danger fondly thrilled.
You crown our distant ardours while we fight,
And mourn our laurelled memories when we're killed.
You can't believe that British troops "retire"
10　When hell's last horror breaks them, and they run,
Trampling the terrible corpses—blind with blood.
　O German mother dreaming by the fire,
While you are knitting socks to send your son
His face is trodden deeper in the mud.

Craiglockhart,[1] 1917

---

1. A hospital near Edinburgh, Scotland, where Sassoon (along with Wilfred Owen) was treated for shell shock.

Everyone Sang

Everyone suddenly burst out singing;
And I was filled with such delight
As prisoned birds must find in freedom,
Winging wildly across the white
5   Orchards and dark-green fields; on—on—and out of sight.
Everyone's voice was suddenly lifted;
And beauty came like the setting sun:
My heart was shaken with tears; and horror
Drifted away . . . O, but Everyone
10   Was a bird; and the song was wordless; the singing will never be done.
April 1919

Wilfred Owen
1893–1918

The poet C. Day Lewis wrote that Wilfred Owen's poems were "certainly the finest written by
any English poet of the First War." In his small body of poems Owen manages to combine his
friend Siegfried Sassoon's outrage at the horror of the war with a formal and technical skill
reminiscent of his idols Keats and Shelley. Sassoon himself characterized their differences as
poets this way: "My trench-sketches were like rockets, sent up to illuminate the darkness. . . .
It was Owen who revealed how, out of realistic horror and scorn, poetry might be made."

Owen grew up on the Welsh border in Shropshire, the landscape A. E. Housman was to
celebrate in his poetry. After finishing technical school, Owen spent two years in training with
an evangelical Church of England vicar, trying to decide whether to pursue formal training as
a clergyman. As a result of his experiences, Owen became dissatisfied with the institutional
church's response to the poverty and suffering of England's least privileged citizens. In October
1915 he enlisted with the Artists' Rifles, and on 29 December 1916, he left for France as a lieutenant with the Lancashire Fusiliers.

Owen quickly became disillusioned with the war; as a result of almost unimaginable privations, which included being blown into the air while he slept in a foxhole, Owen suffered a
breakdown, and was sent to the Craiglockhart War Hospital in Edinburgh. Owen composed
nearly all of his poetry in the fourteen months of his rehabilitation, between August 1917 and
September 1918; though hard to imagine, it is quite possible that if he had not been sent back
to Great Britain to recover from his "shell shock," we might now know nothing of his poetry.
While at Craiglockhart he met Sassoon and found his true voice and mode; he published his
first poems on war themes anonymously in the hospital's magazine, which he edited. In September 1918 Owen returned to the battlefields of France; he was killed in action at Sambre
Canal on 4 November 1918, one week before the Armistice. Dylan Thomas called Owen "one
of the four most profound influences upon the poets who came after him"—the others being
Hopkins, Yeats, and Eliot.

Anthem for Doomed Youth

What passing-bells for these who die as cattle?
   Only the monstrous anger of the guns.
   Only the stuttering rifles' rapid rattle
Can patter out their hasty orisons.°   *prayers*
5   No mockeries now for them; no prayers nor bells,

Nor any voice of mourning save the choirs,—
The shrill, demented choirs of wailing shells;
    And bugles calling for them from sad shires.

What candles may be held to speed them all?
10   Not in the hands of boys, but in their eyes
Shall shine the holy glimmers of good-byes.
    The pallor of girls' brows shall be their pall;[1]
Their flowers the tenderness of patient minds,
And each slow dusk a drawing-down of blinds.

Strange Meeting

It seemed that out of battle I escaped
Down some profound dull tunnel, long since scooped
Through granites which titanic wars had groined.°   *joined together*
Yet also there encumbered sleepers groaned,
5   Too fast in thought or death to be bestirred.
Then, as I probed them, one sprang up, and stared
With piteous recognition in fixed eyes,
Lifting distressful hands as if to bless.
And by his smile, I knew that sullen hall,
10 By his dead smile I knew we stood in Hell.
With a thousand pains that vision's face was grained;
Yet no blood reached there from the upper ground,
And no guns thumped, or down the flues made moan.
"Strange friend," I said, "here is no cause to mourn."
15 "None," said that other, "save the undone years,
The hopelessness. Whatever hope is yours,
Was my life also; I went hunting wild
After the wildest beauty in the world,
Which lies not calm in eyes, or braided hair,
20 But mocks the steady running of the hour,
And if it grieves, grieves richlier than here.
For of my glee might many men have laughed,
And of my weeping something had been left,
Which must die now. I mean the truth untold,
25 The pity of war, the pity war distilled.
Now men will go content with what we spoiled,
Or, discontent, boil bloody, and be spilled.
They will be swift with swiftness of the tigress.
None will break ranks, though nations trek from progress.
30 Courage was mine, and I had mystery,
Wisdom was mine, and I had mastery:
To miss the march of this retreating world
Into vain citadels that are not walled.
Then, when much blood had clogged their chariot-wheels,
35 I would go up and wash them from sweet wells,
Even with truths that lie too deep for taint.
I would have poured my spirit without stint

1. The cloth draped over a coffin.

But not through wounds; not on the cess of war.
Foreheads of men have bled where no wounds were.
40   I am the enemy you killed, my friend.
I knew you in this dark: for so you frowned
Yesterday through me as you jabbed and killed.
I parried; but my hands were loath and cold.
Let us sleep now . . . ."

Dulce Et Decorum Est[1]

Bent double, like old beggars under sacks,
Knock-kneed, coughing like hags, we cursed through sludge,
Till on the haunting flares we turned our backs
And towards our distant rest began to trudge.
5   Men marched asleep. Many had lost their boots
But limped on, blood-shod. All went lame; all blind;
Drunk with fatigue; deaf even to the hoots
Of tired, outstripped Five-Nines[2] that dropped behind.

Gas! Gas! Quick, boys!—An ecstasy of fumbling,
10   Fitting the clumsy helmets just in time;
But someone still was yelling out and stumbling
And flound'ring like a man in fire or lime[3] . . .
Dim, through the misty panes and thick green light,
As under a green sea, I saw him drowning.

15   In all my dreams, before my helpless sight,
He plunges at me, guttering, choking, drowning.

If in some smothering dreams you too could pace
Behind the wagon that we flung him in,
And watch the white eyes writhing in his face,
20   His hanging face, like a devil's sick of sin;
If you could hear, at every jolt, the blood
Come gargling from the froth-corrupted lungs,
Obscene as cancer, bitter as the cud
Of vile, incurable sores on innocent tongues,—
25   My friend, you would not tell with such high zest
To children ardent for some desperate glory,
The old Lie: Dulce et decorum est
Pro patria mori.

---

1. From the *Odes* of the Roman satirist Horace (65–8 B.C.): Dulce et decorum est pro patria mori [sweet and fitting it is to die for your fatherland].
2. Artillery shells used by the Germans.

3. Calcium oxide, a powerfully caustic alkali used, among other purposes, for cleaning the flesh off the bones of corpses.

Isaac Rosenberg
1890–1918

World War I was the spur that goaded some poets, like Wilfred Owen, into the writing of poetry; for Isaac Rosenberg the war was simply the catalyst for a more vivid and powerful verse. Rosenberg began writing poetry on Jewish themes when he was just fifteen; he had published two volumes of poems and a verse play, *Moses*, by the time he joined the army in 1916. Rosenberg's experience of the war was, in important ways, different from the other poets represented here. To begin with, he was the son of Lithuanian Jewish immigrants who had settled in the East End, London's Jewish ghetto. As a child, Rosenberg lived with severe poverty; he was forced to leave school at fourteen to help support his family. He went to war not as an officer, but as a private; as the critic Irving Howe writes, "No glamorous fatality hangs over Rosenberg's head: he was just a clumsy, stuttering Jewish doughboy." He was killed while on patrol outside the trenches—a private's dangerous assignment.

His experiences on the Western Front seem to have provided him with the perfect canvas for his essentially religious art. Siegfried Sassoon, alluding to Rosenberg's training as an artist at the Slade School, later described his poems as "scriptural and sculptural": "His experiments were a strenuous effort for impassioned expression; his imagination had a sinewy and muscular aliveness; often he saw things in terms of sculpture, but he did not carve or chisel; he *modeled* words with fierce energy and aspiration." His less-than-genteel background also made Rosenberg impatient with the patriotic sentiments of a poet like Rupert Brooke, for whose "begloried sonnets" he had nothing but contempt. In the poetry of Rosenberg, by contrast—according to Sassoon—"words and images obey him, instead of leading him into over-elaboration." Interest in Rosenberg's poetry has recently been revived by critics interested in his use of Jewish themes; the critic Harold Bloom, for instance, calls Rosenberg "an English poet with a Jewish difference," and suggests that he is "the best Jewish poet writing in English that our century has given us."

Break of Day in the Trenches

The darkness crumbles away—
It is the same old druid[1] Time as ever.
Only a live thing leaps my hand—
A queer sardonic rat—
As I pull the parapet's poppy
To stick behind my ear.
Droll rat, they would shoot you if they knew
Your cosmopolitan sympathies.
Now you have touched this English hand
You will do the same to a German—
Soon, no doubt, if it be your pleasure
To cross the sleeping green between.
It seems you inwardly grin as you pass
Strong eyes, fine limbs, haughty athletes
Less chanced than you for life,
Bonds to the whims of murder,
Sprawled in the bowels of the earth,
The torn fields of France.

1. Member of an ancient Celtic religion.

What do you see in our eyes
20   At the shrieking iron and flame
        Hurled through still heavens?
        What quaver—what heart aghast?
        Poppies whose roots are in man's veins
        Drop, and are ever dropping;
25   But mine in my ear is safe,
        Just a little white with the dust.

1916   1922

Dead Man's Dump

        The plunging limbers over the shattered track
        Racketed with their rusty freight,
        Stuck out like many crowns of thorns,
        And the rusty stakes like sceptres old
5   To stay the flood of brutish men
        Upon our brothers dear.

        The wheels lurched over sprawled dead
        But pained them not, though their bones crunched,
        Their shut mouths made no moan.
10   They lie there huddled, friend and foeman,
        Man born of man, and born of woman,
        And shells go crying over them
        From night till night and now.

        Earth has waited for them,
15   All the time of their growth
        Fretting for their decay:
        Now she has them at last!
        In the strength of their strength
        Suspended—stopped and held.

20   What fierce imaginings their dark souls lit?
        Earth! have they gone into you!
        Somewhere they must have gone,
        And flung on your hard back
        Is their soul's sack
25   Emptied of God-ancestralled essences.
        Who hurled them out? Who hurled?

        None saw their spirits' shadow shake the grass,
        Or stood aside for the half used life to pass
        Out of those doomed nostrils and the doomed mouth,
30   When the swift iron burning bee
        Drained the wild honey of their youth.

        What of us who, flung on the shrieking pyre,°   funeral bonfire
        Walk, our usual thoughts untouched,
        Our lucky limbs as on ichor[1] fed,

---

1. The vital fluid flowing in the veins of the Gods in classical mythology.

35   Immortal seeming ever?
Perhaps when the flames beat loud on us,
A fear may choke in our veins
And the startled blood may stop.

The air is loud with death,
40   The dark air spurts with fire,
The explosions ceaseless are.
Timelessly now, some minutes past,
These dead strode time with vigorous life,
Till the shrapnel called 'An end!'
45   But not to all. In bleeding pangs
Some borne on stretchers dreamed of home,
Dear things, war-blotted from their hearts.

Maniac Earth! howling and flying, your bowel
Seared by the jagged fire, the iron love,
50   The impetuous storm of savage love.
Dark Earth! dark Heavens! swinging in chemic smoke,
What dead are born when you kiss each soundless soul
With lightning and thunder from your mined heart,
Which man's self dug, and his blind fingers loosed?

55   A man's brains splattered on
A stretcher-bearer's face;
His shook shoulders slipped their load,
But when they bent to look again
The drowning soul was sunk too deep
60   For human tenderness.

They left this dead with the older dead,
Stretched at the cross roads.

Burnt black by strange decay
Their sinister faces lie,
65   The lid over each eye,
The grass and coloured clay
More motion have than they,
Joined to the great sunk silences.

Here is one not long dead;
70   His dark hearing caught our far wheels,
And the choked soul stretched weak hands
To reach the living word the far wheels said,
The blood-dazed intelligence beating for light,
Crying through the suspense of the far torturing wheels
75   Swift for the end to break
Or the wheels to break,
Cried as the tide of the world broke over his sight.

Will they come? Will they ever come?
Even as the mixed hoofs of the mules,

80   The quivering-bellied mules,
      And the rushing wheels all mixed
      With his tortured upturned sight.
      So we crashed round the bend,
      We heard his weak scream,
85   We heard his very last sound,
      And our wheels grazed his dead face.

David Jones
1895–1974

David Jones's long narrative poem *In Parenthesis* is arguably the great literary text of World War I. While other poets have more vividly recreated the horrors of the war, and prose chroniclers like Robert Graves have analyzed more precisely the futility and banality of trench warfare, Jones's "writing"—the only generic label he was willing to assign *In Parenthesis*—combines the resources of both poetry and prose, and brings to bear a historical, religious, and mythical framework through which to understand the war. In Jones's text the Great War is revealed to be just the most recent battle in the great war that is human history.

Jones was born near London to an English mother and Welsh father; his father impressed upon him the richness of his Welsh heritage. After leaving grammar school, Jones enrolled in art school; when war broke out, however, he was quick to enlist, and joined the Royal Welch Fusiliers as an infantryman in January 1915. He served on the Western Front until March 1918, having been wounded at the battle of the Somme in June 1916; he remarked later that the war "had a permanent effect upon me and has affected my work in all sorts of ways." After the war, Jones went to Ditchling Common, a Catholic artists' guild run by the writer and sculptor Eric Gill. Jones was attracted to Gill's regimen of work and prayer; he converted to Roman Catholicism in 1921 and soon joined the guild, where he lived and worked until 1933.

Jones did not begin to write *In Parenthesis* until 1928. The poem tells the story of Private John Ball, from his embarkation from England in December 1915 to the battle of the Somme. The text modulates from straightforward narrative to a kind of prose poetry to stretches of pure poetry, incorporating echoes and allusions of texts, from the Welsh epic *The Mabinogion* to the medieval battle epic *Y Gododdin* to Malory's *Morte d'Arthur* to Shakespeare's history plays to Eliot's *The Waste Land*—as well as drawing from "subliterary" sources such as soldier's slang. *In Parenthesis* is difficult and allusive, as are many other monumental works of modernist literature, like Joyce's *Ulysses* and *Finnegans Wake*, Pound's *Cantos*, and Eliot's *The Waste Land*. While this difficulty has sometimes kept away the readers Jones deserves, the critic Thomas Dilworth calls *In Parenthesis* "the only authentic and successful epic poem in the language since *Paradise Lost*."

In Parenthesis differs from other war poetry in argument as well as form; the poem is not simply a protest against the war but rather an attempt to place the war into a world-historical context. As the critic Samuel Rees writes, it "is not a poem either to provoke or to end a war . . . except as it adds to the accumulation of testimony to the stupidities and brutality of history that each age must learn from or, more likely, ignore." In the writing he produced after *In Parenthesis* Jones continued to be concerned with contemporary society's loss of interest in the past, and with the depersonalizing effects of technology; his other great poem, *The Anathemata*, was judged by W. H. Auden to be "probably the finest long poem in English in this century."

from **In Parenthesis**[1]
Part 1. The Many Men So Beautiful[2]

'49 Wyatt, 01549 Wyatt.
Coming sergeant.
Pick 'em up, pick 'em up—I'll stalk within yer chamber.
Private Leg . . . sick.
Private Ball . . . absent.
'01 Ball, '01 Ball, Ball of No. 1.
Where's Ball, 2501 Ball—you corporal,
Ball of your section.
Movement round and about the Commanding Officer.
Bugler, will you sound "Orderly Sergeants."
    A hurrying of feet from three companies converging on the little group apart where on horses sit the central command. But from "B" Company there is no such darting out. The Orderly Sergeant of "B" is licking the stub end of his lead pencil; it divides a little his fairish moist moustache.
    Heavily jolting and sideway jostling, the noise of liquid shaken in a small vessel by a regular jogging movement, a certain clinking ending in a shuffling of the feet sidelong—all clear and distinct in that silence peculiar to parade grounds and to refectories. The silence of a high order, full of peril in the breaking of it, like the coming on parade of John Ball.
    He settles between numbers 4 and 5 of the rear rank. It is as ineffectual as the ostrich in her sand. Captain Gwynn does not turn or move or give any sign.
    Have that man's name taken if you please, Mr. Jenkins.
    Take that man's name, Sergeant Snell.
    Take his name, corporal.
    Take his name take his number—charge him—late on parade—the Battalion being paraded for overseas—warn him for Company Office.
    Have you got his name Corporal Quilter.
    Temporary unpaid Lance-Corporal Aneirin Merddyn Lewis had somewhere in his Welsh depths a remembrance of the nature of man, of how a lance-corporal's stripe is but held vicariously and from on high, is of one texture with an eternal economy. He brings in a manner, baptism, and metaphysical order to the bankruptcy of the occasion.
    '01 Ball is it—there was a man in Bethesda late for the last bloody judgment.
    Corporal Quilter on the other hand knew nothing of these things.
    Private Ball's pack, ill adjusted and without form, hangs more heavily on his shoulder blades, a sense of ill-usage pervades him. He withdraws within himself to soothe himself—the inequity of those in high places is forgotten. From where he stood heavily, irksomely at ease, he could see, half-left between 7 and 8 of the front rank, the profile of Mr. Jenkins and the elegant cut of his war-time rig and his flax

---

1. In his preface, Jones writes: "This writing is called 'In Parenthesis' because I have written it in a kind of space between—I don't know between quite what—but as you turn aside to do something; and because for us amateur soldiers (and especially for the writer, who was not only an amateur, but grotesquely incompetent, a knocker-over of piles, a parade's despair) the war itself was a parenthe- sis—how glad we thought we were to step outside its brackets at the end of '18—and also because our curious type of existence here is altogether in parenthesis."
2. Coleridge, *Ancient Mariner*, part iv, verse 4 [Jones's note]. "The many men, so beautiful! / And they all dead did lie: / And a thousand thousand slimy things / Lived on; and so did I."

David Jones, frontispiece to *In Parenthesis*, 1937.

head held front; like San Romano's[3] foreground squire, unhelmeted; but we don't have lances now nor banners nor trumpets. It pains the lips to think of bugles—and did they blow Defaulters[4] on the Uccello horns.

He put his right hand behind him to ease his pack, his cold knuckles find something metallic and colder.

No mess-tin cover.

Shining sanded mess-tin giving back the cold early light. *Improperly dressed, the Battalion being paraded for overseas.* His imaginings as to the precise relationship of this general indictment from the book to his own naked mess-tin were with suddenness and most imperatively impinged upon, as when an animal hunted, stopping in some ill-chosen covert to consider the wickedness of man, is started into fresh effort by the cry and breath of dogs dangerously and newly near. For the chief huntsman is winding his horn, the officer commanding is calling his Battalion by name—whose own the sheep are.

3. Cf. painting, "Rout of San Romano." Paolo Uccello (Nat. Gal.) [Jones's note].   4. Soldiers convicted by a court-martial.

55th Battalion!
Fifty-fifth Bat-tal-i-on
'talion!!

From "D" to "A" his eyes knew that parade. He detected no movement. They were properly at ease.

Reverberation of that sudden command broke hollowly upon the emptied huts behind "D" Company's rear platoons. They had only in them the rolled mattresses, the neatly piled bed-boards and the empty tea-buckets of the orderly-men, emptied of their last gun-fire.[5]

Stirrups taut and pressing upward in the midst of his saddle he continues the ritual words by virtue of which a regiment is moved in column of route:
. . . the Battalion will move in column of fours to the right—"A" Company—"A" Company leading.

Words lost, yet given continuity by that thinner command from in front of No. 1. Itself to be wholly swallowed up by the concerted movement of arms in which the spoken word effected what it signified.

"A" Company came to the slope, their files of four turn right. The complex of command and heel-iron turned confuse the morning air. The rigid structure of their lines knows a swift mobility, patterns differently for those sharp successive cries.

Mr. P. D. I. Jenkins who is twenty years old has now to do his business:
No. 7 Platoon—number seven.
number seven—right—by the right.
How they sway in the swing round for all this multiplicity of gear.
Keept'y'r dressing.
Sergeant Snell did his bit.
Corporal Quilter intones:
Dress to the right—no—other right.
Keep those slopes.
Keep those sections of four.
Pick those knees up.
Throw those chests out.
Hold those heads up.
Stop that talking.
Keep those chins in.
Left left lef'—lef' righ' lef'—you Private Ball it's you I'v got me glad-eye on.

So they came outside the camp. The liturgy of a regiment departing has been sung. Empty wet parade ground. A campwarden, some unfit men and other details loiter, dribble away, shuffle off like men whose ship has sailed.

The long hutment lines stand. Not a soul. It rains harder: torn felt lifts to the wind above Hut 10, Headquarter Company; urinal concrete echoes for a solitary whistler. Corrugated iron empty—no one. Chill gust slams the vacant canteen door.

Miss Veronica Best who runs the hut for the bun-wallahs[6] stretches on her palliasse,[7] she's sleepy, she can hear the band: We've got too many buns—and all those wads[8]—

5. Tea served to troops before first parade. Rouse parade [Jones's note].
6. Person pertaining to: e.g. staff-wallah; person addicted to: e.g. bun-wallah [Jones's note].
7. Straw mattress.
8. Canteen sandwiches [Jones's note].

you knew they were going—why did you order them—they won't be in after rouse-parade even—they've gone.

Know they've gone—shut up—Jocks from Bardown move in Monday. Violet turns to sleep again.

Horses' tails are rather good—and the way this one springs from her groomed flanks.

He turns slightly in his saddle.

You may march at ease.

No one said march easy Private Ball, you're bleedin' quick at some things ain't yer.

The Squire from the Rout of San Romano smokes Melachrino No. 9.

The men may march easy and smoke, Sergeant Snell.

Some like tight belts and some like loose belts—trussed-up pockets—cigarettes in ammunition pouches—rifle-bolts, webbing, buckles and rain—gotta light mate—give us a match chum. How cold the morning is and blue, and how mysterious in cupped hands glow the match-lights of a concourse of men, moving so early in the morning.

The body of the high figure in front of the head of the column seemed to change his position however so slightly. It rains on the transparent talc of his map-case.

The Major's horse rubs noses with the horse of the superior officer. Their docked manes brush each, as two friends would meet. The dark horse snorts a little for the pulling at her bridle rein.

In "D" Company round the bend of the road in the half-light is movement, like a train shunting, when the forward coaches buffer the rear coaches back. The halt was unexpected. How heavy and how top-heavy is all this martial panoply and how the ground seems to press upward to afflict the feet.

The bastard's lost his way already.

Various messages are passed.

Some lean on their rifles as aged men do on sticks in stage-plays. Some lean back with the muzzle of the rifle supporting the pack in the position of gentlewomen at field sports, but not with so great assurance.

It's cold when you stop marching with all this weight and icy down the back.

Battalion cyclists pass the length of the column. There is fresh stir in "A" Company.

Keep your column distance.

The regular rhythm of the march has re-established itself.

The rain increases with the light and the weight increases with the rain. In all that long column in brand-new overseas boots weeping blisters stick to the hard wool of grey government socks.

I'm bleedin' cripple already Corporal, confides a limping child.

Kipt' that step there.

Keep that proper distance.

Keep't' y'r siction o' four—can't fall out me little darlin'.

Corporal Quilter subsides, he too retreats within himself, he has his private thoughts also.

It's a proper massacre of the innocents in a manner of speaking, no so-called seven ages o' man only this bastard military age.

Keep that step there.

Keep that section distance.

Hand us thet gas-pipe young Saunders—let's see you shape—you too, little Benjamin—hang him about like a goddam Chris'us tree—use his ample shoulders for an armoury-rack—it is his part to succour the lambs of the flock.

With some slackening of the rain the band had wiped their instruments. Broken catches on the wind-gust came shrilly back:

Of Hector and Lysander and such great names as these—the march proper to them.[9]

So they went most of that day and it rained with increasing vigour until night-fall. In the middle afternoon the outer parts of the town of embarkation were reached. They halted for a brief while; adjusted puttees,[1] straightened caps, fastened undone buttons, tightened rifle-slings and attended each one to his own bedraggled and irregular condition. The band recommenced playing; and at the attention and in excellent step they passed through the suburbs, the town's centre, and so towards the docks. The people of that town did not acclaim them, nor stop about their business—for it was late in the second year.[2]

By some effort of a corporate will the soldierly bearing of the text books maintained itself through the town, but with a realisation of the considerable distance yet to be covered through miles of dock, their frailty reasserted itself—which slackening called for fresh effort from the Quilters and the Snells, but at this stage with a more persuasive intonation, with almost motherly concern.

Out of step and with a depressing raggedness of movement and rankling of tempers they covered another mile between dismal sheds, high and tarred. Here funnels and mastheads could be seen. Here the influence of the sea and of the tackle and ways of its people fell upon them. They revived somewhat, and for a while. Yet still these interminable ways between—these incessant halts at junctions. Once they about-turned. Embarkation officers, staff people of all kinds and people who looked as though they were in the Navy but who were not, consulted with the Battalion Commander. A few more halts, more passing of messages,—a further intensifying of their fatigue. The platoons of the leading company unexpectedly wheel. The spacious shed is open at either end, windy and comfortless. Multifarious accoutrements, metal and cloth and leather sink with the perspiring bodies to the concrete floor.

Certain less fortunate men were detailed for guard, John Ball amongst them. The others lay, where they first sank down, wet with rain and sweat. They smoked; they got very cold. They were given tins of bully beef and ration biscuits for the first time, and felt like real expeditionary soldiers. Sometime between midnight and 2 a.m. they were paraded. Slowly, and with every sort of hitch, platoon upon platoon formed single file and moved toward an invisible gangway. Each separate man found his own feet stepping in the darkness on an inclined plane, the smell and taste of salt and machinery, the texture of rope, and the glimmer of shielded light about him.

So without sound of farewell or acclamation, shrouded in a dense windy darkness, they set toward France. They stood close on deck and beneath deck, each man upholstered in his life-belt. From time to time a seaman would push between them about some duty belonging to his trade.

---

9. *The British Grenadiers* is the ceremonial march of all Grenadier and Fusilier Regiments [Jones's note].

1. Leggings.

2. That is to say in December 1915 [Jones's note].

Under a high-slung arc-light whose cold clarity well displayed all their sea weariness, their long cramped-upness and fatigue, they stumblingly and one by one trickled from the ship on to French land. German prisoners in green tunics, made greener by the light, heavily unloading timber at a line of trucks—it still rained, and a bitter wind in from the sea.

A young man, comfortable in a short fleece jacket, stood smoking, immediately beneath the centre of the arc—he gave orders in a pleasant voice, that measured the leisure of his circumstances and of his class. Men move to left and right within the orbit of the light, and away into the half darkness, undefined, beyond it.

"B" Company were conducted by a guide, through back ways between high shuttered buildings, to horse-stalls, where they slept. In the morning, they were given Field Service postcards—and sitting in the straw they crossed out what did not apply, and sent them to their mothers, to their sweethearts.

Toward evening on the same day they entrained in cattle trucks; and on the third day, which was a Sunday, sunny and cold, and French women in deep black were hurrying across flat land—they descended from their grimy, littered, limb restricting, slatted vehicles, and stretched and shivered at a siding. You feel exposed and apprehensive in this new world.

from *Part 7. The Five Unmistakable Marks*[3]

At the gate of the wood you try a last adjustment, but slung so, it's an impediment, it's of detriment to your hopes, you had best be rid of it—the sagging webbing and all and what's left of your two fifty—but it were wise to hold on to your mask.

You're clumsy in your feebleness, you implicate your tin-hat rim with the slack sling of it.

Let it lie for the dews to rust it, or ought you to decently cover the working parts.

Its dark barrel, where you leave it under the oak, reflects the solemn star that rises urgently from Cliff Trench.

It's a beautiful doll for us
it's the Last Reputable Arm.

But leave it—under the oak.

leave it for a Cook's tourist to the Devastated Areas[4] and crawl as far as you can and wait for the bearers.

Mrs. Willy Hartington has learned to draw sheets and so has Miss Melpomené;[5] and on the south lawns,
men walk in red white and blue
under the cedars
and by every green tree

---

3. Printed here is the conclusion to the chapter, which closes In Parenthesis. The chapter's title comes from Lewis Carroll's narrative poem The Hunting of the Snark, which concerns a voyage in search of the Snark; "warranted, genuine Snarks" can be identified by "five unmistakable marks." The poem ends with the death of the explorer who discovers the Snark.

4. This may appear to be an anachronism, but I remember in 1917 discussing with a friend the possibilities of tourist activity if peace ever came. I remember we went into details and wondered if the inexploded projectile lying near us would go up under a holiday-maker, and how people would stand to be photographed on our parapets. I recall feeling very angry about this, as you do if you think of strangers ever occupying a house you live in, and which has, for you, particular associations [Jones's note].

5. Greek muse of tragedy.

and beside comfortable waters.
But why dont the bastards come—
Bearers!—stret-cher bear-errs!
or do they divide the spoils at the Aid-Post.[6]

But how many men do you suppose could bear away a third of us: drag just a little further—he yet may counter-attack.

Lie still under the oak
next to the Jerry
and Sergeant Jerry Coke.

The feet of the reserves going up tread level with your forehead; and no word for
you; they whisper one with another; pass on, inward;
these latest succours:
green Kimmerii[7] to bear up the war.

Oeth and Annoeth's hosts they were
who in that night grew
younger men
younger striplings.[8]

The geste says this and the man who was on the field . . . and who wrote the book . . .
the man who does not know this has not understood anything.[9]

⇒→ END OF PERSPECTIVES: THE GREAT WAR ←⇐

•—⇥✦⇤—•

William Butler Yeats
1865–1939

Beginning his career as a poet during the languid 1880s and 1890s, William Butler Yeats
fought, as Ezra Pound said of T. S. Eliot, to modernize himself on his own. At a time when
Irish poetry seemed to be in danger of ossifying into a sentimental, self-indulgent luxury, Yeats
instead forged a verse that would serve as an exacting instrument of introspection and national inquiry. As a consequence, all modern Irish writing—most clearly poetry, but prose, drama,
and literary nonfiction as well—is directly in his debt.

---

6. The R.A.M.C. was suspected by disgruntled men of the
fighting units of purloining articles from the kit of the
wounded and the dead. Their regimental initials were
commonly interpreted: "Rob All My Comrades" [Jones's
note].
7. In Homer, the kimmerioi were a race who lived in eternal darkness, "on whom the sun never looks."
8. Cf. Englyn 30 of the *Englynion y Beddeu*, "The Stanzas
of the Graves." See Rhys, *Origin of the Englyn, Y Cymm-
rodor*, vol. xviii. Oeth and Annoeth's hosts occur in
Welsh tradition as a mysterious body of troops that seem

to have some affinity with the Legions. They were said to
"fight as well in the covert as in the open." Cf. *The Iolo
MSS* [Jones's note].
9. Cf. Chanson de Roland, lines 2095–8:

Co dit la geste e cil qui el camp fur,
[Li ber Gilie por qui Deus fait vertuz]
E fist la chartre [el muster de Loum].
Ki tant ne set, ne l'ad prod entendut.

I have used Mr. Rene Hague's translation [Jones's note].

Yeats was born in the Dublin suburb of Sandymount, but his spiritual home, the land of his mother Susan Pollexfen and her people, was the countryside of County Sligo. His father, John Butler Yeats, was an amateur philosopher, an insolvent painter, and a refugee from the legal profession; his grandfather and great-grandfather were both clergymen of the Church of Ireland. Through his mother's family, Yeats traced a close connection with the countryside of Ireland, and the myths and legends of the Irish people. Both parents belonged to the Anglo-Irish Protestant ascendancy, a heritage Yeats remained fiercely proud of all his life; but the success of his poetry, in part, lay in his ability to reconcile the British literary tradition with the native materials of the Irish Catholic tradition.

As he tells it in his autobiography, Yeats's childhood was not a happy one; in 1915 he wrote: "I remember little of childhood but its pain." His father, though a talented painter, lacked the ability to turn his gifts to profit; he would linger over a single portrait for months and sometimes years, revising ceaselessly. When Yeats was three, his father moved his family to London in order to put himself to school as a painter; their existence, though intellectually and artistically rich and stimulating, was quite straitened financially. The young Yeats found London sterile and joyless; fortunately for his imagination, and his future poetry, portions of each year were spent in the Sligo countryside, where Yeats spent time gathering the local folklore and taking long, wide-ranging walks and pony rides. The family remained in London until 1875, and had four more children (though one brother died in childhood). All his surviving siblings were to remain important to Yeats in his artistic life: his brother Jack B. Yeats became an important Irish painter, and his sisters Lily and Lolly together founded the Dun Emer Press, later called the Cuala Press, which published limited-edition volumes of some of Yeats's poetry.

In 1880 the family returned permanently to Ireland, settling first in Howth, in Dublin Bay; the city of Dublin, with its largely unsung history and tradition, fueled Yeats's imagination in a way that London never had. When the time for college came, Yeats was judged unlikely to pass Trinity College's entrance exams, and he was sent instead to the Metropolitan School of Art, apparently in preparation to follow in his father's footsteps. His true gift, it soon appeared, was not for drawing and painting but for poetry. He steeped himself in the Romantic poets, especially Shelley and Keats, as well as the English poet of Irish residence Edmund Spenser. His first poems were published in the *Dublin University Review* in March 1885.

Yeats's early work is self-evidently apprentice work; it draws heavily on the late-Romantic, Pre-Raphaelite ambience so important in the painting of his father and his father's colleagues. He also began to take an active interest in the various mystical movements that were then finding a foothold in Dublin and London, and with friends formed a Hermetic Society in Dublin as an antidote to the humanist rationalism to which his father was so passionately attached. At the same time—almost as a self-administered antidote to the teachings of mystics like the Brahmin teacher Mohini Chatterji—Yeats began to attend the meetings of several Dublin political and debating societies, and became increasingly interested in the nationalist artistic revival that would become known as the Irish Renaissance or Celtic Revival. Unlike most of his debating society comrades, Yeats imagined this political and cultural renaissance as resulting from a marriage of Blakean opposites: "I had noticed that Irish Catholics among whom had been born so many political martyrs had not the good taste, the household courtesy and decency of the Protestant Ireland I had known, yet Protestant Ireland seemed to think of nothing but getting on in the world. I thought we might bring the halves together if we had a national literature that made Ireland beautiful in the memory, and yet had been freed from provincialism by an exacting criticism, a European pose."

The Yeats family moved back to London in 1887; finances were difficult as ever, and Yeats contributed to the family's upkeep by editing two anthologies, *Poems and Ballads of Young Ireland* (1888) and *Fairy and Folk Tales of the Irish Peasantry* (1888). His own first collection of poems, *The Wanderings of Oisin and Other Poems*, was published in the following year; the poems are resolutely romantic, Yeats himself describing his manner at the time as "in all things Pre-Raphaelite." The poems were well received, but the praise of one reader in particular caught Yeats's attention. The statuesque beauty Maud Gonne appeared at Yeats's door with an introduction from the Irish revolutionary John O'Leary, and declared that the title poem had brought her to tears. It was a fateful meeting; throughout five decades Yeats continued to write to Gonne, for Gonne—the critic M. L. Rosenthal has suggested that "virtually every poem celebrating a woman's beauty or addressing a beloved woman has to do with her." Rosenthal might have added, every poem decrying the sacrifice of life to politics, including *No Second Troy*, *Easter 1916*, *A Prayer for My Daughter*, and others, all of which lament Gonne's increasing political fanaticism. This fanaticism, which Gonne considered simply patriotism, made impossible the spiritual and emotional consummation that Yeats so fervently desired. He proposed marriage, but she declined, marrying instead an Irish soldier who would later be executed for his role in the Easter Rising of 1916. Yeats is, among his other distinctions, a great poet of unrequited love.

The 1890s in London were heady times for a young poet. Yeats became even more active in his studies of the occult, studying with the charismatic Theosophist Madame Blavatsky and attending meetings of the Order of the Golden Dawn, a Christian cabalist society. The practical upshot of these activities for his later poetry was a confirmed belief in a storehouse of all human experience and knowledge, which he called variously the *Spiritus Mundi* and *Anima Mundi*, invoked in later poems like *The Second Coming* (1920). In 1891 Yeats, together with Ernest Rhys, founded the Rhymers' Club, which brought him into almost nightly contact with such important literary figures as Lionel Johnson, Ernest Dowson, Arthur Symons, and Oscar Wilde; during this same period, he established the Irish Literary Society in London, and the National Literary Society in Dublin. Clearly, something of a program for modern Irish poetry was beginning to emerge, even if Yeats himself wasn't yet quite ready to write it. Yeats also spent the years from 1887 to 1891 studying the writings of that most mystic of English poets, William Blake; working with his father's friend Edwin Ellis, he produced an edition of and extended commentary on Blake's prophetic writings. Summing up the lesson of Blake's writings, Yeats wrote: "I had learned from Blake to hate all abstractions."

Romantic abstraction was easier to abjure in principle than in practice; Yeats's poetry of the 1890s still hankers after what one of his dramatis personae would later call "the loveliness that has long faded from the world." As one critic has written, "Early Yeats was the best poetry in English in late Victorian times; but they were bad times." Yeats began the process of throwing off the false manners of his Pre-Raphaelite upbringing with his play *The Countess Cathleen*, first performed by the Abbey Theatre, funded by subscriptions collected by his good friend Lady Augusta Gregory. Yeats's play, like Synge's *Playboy of the Western World* years later on that same stage, offended Irish sensibilities; in it, Cathleen sells her soul in order to protect Irish peasants from starvation. Yeats's volume *The Wind Among the Reeds* (1899) closes out the 1890s quite conveniently; it is ethereal, beautiful, and mannered. With this volume, Yeats's early phase comes to a close.

The early years of the twentieth century found Yeats concentrating his energies on the writing of poetic dramas, including, *The Pot of Broth* (1902) and *On Baile's Strand* (1904), for his fledgling Irish National Theatre. In 1903, the small Dun Emer Press published his volume of poems *In the Seven Woods*. These poems, including *Adam's Curse*, show Yeats working in a more spare idiom, the cadences and rhythms closer to those of actual speech—a consequence, some have argued, of his years writing for the stage. New poems published in *The Green Helmet and Other Poems* (1910) display Yeats as an increasingly mature and confident poet; his treatment of Maud Gonne in *No Second Troy*, for instance, shows a tragic acceptance of the fact that he will never have her, nor master her indomitable spirit. In *A Coat*, the poem that closes the 1914 collection *Responsibilities*, Yeats writes of the embroidered cloak he had fashioned for himself in his early poems, whose vanity is now brought home to him by the gaudiness of his imitators. He resolves, in the volume's closing lines, to set his cloak aside, "For there's more enterprise / In walking naked." This sense was strengthened by his close work, during the winter of 1912–1913, with Ezra Pound, in a cottage in rural Sussex. Both studied the stripped-down Japanese Noh drama and the Orientalist Ernest Fennollosa's work on the Chinese ideogram, and both men no doubt reinforced one another's increasing desire for a poetry that would be, in Pound's phrase, "closer to the bone."

The Easter Rising of 1916 took Yeats by surprise; he was in England at the time and complained of not having been informed in advance. A number of the rebel leaders were personal friends; he writes their names into Irish literature in *Easter 1916*, an excruciatingly honest, and ambivalent, exploration of the nature of heroism and nationalism. Yeats's mixed feelings about the revolution derived in part from a concern that some of his early writings, like the nationalist *Cathleen ní Houlihan*, might have contributed to the slaughter that followed in the wake of Easter 1916; as he wrote many years later, he couldn't help but wonder, "Did that play of mine send out / Certain men the English shot?"

The intricacies of Yeats's emotional and romantic life would require an essay of their own. His first marriage proposal to Maud Gonne in 1891, politely refused, set a pattern that was to remain in place for many years; though a number of poems try to reason through the affair, Yeats remained tragically attracted to this woman who did not return his affection, and multiple proposals were turned down as routinely as the first. He would have done as well, he was to write years later, to profess his love "to a statue in a museum." In the summer of 1917 things reached such a pass that Yeats proposed to Maud Gonne's adopted daughter Iseult; here, again, he was refused. Then, hastily, in October 1917 he married a longtime friend Georgiana ("George") Hyde-Lees. For all the tragicomedy leading up to the marriage, Yeats could not have chosen better; George was intelligent and sympathetic, and she brought the additional gift of an interest in mysticism and a facility in automatic writing that Yeats was soon to take full advantage of. Since early childhood, Yeats had heard voices speaking to him, and when he was twenty-one a voice commanded him "Hammer your thoughts into unity"; this charge had weighed on his mind for years, and his various experiments in mysticism and esoteric religions were intended to discover the system wherein his thoughts might be made to cohere.

With George, Yeats finally created that system on his own; its fullest exposition is found in *A Vision* (1928), though elements of it turn up in his poems beginning as early as *No Second Troy*. The system is complicated enough to fill out over 300 pages in the revised (1937) edition; at the heart of the system, though, is a simple diagram of two interpenetrating cones, oriented horizontally, such that the tip of each cone establishes the center of the base of the opposite cone. These two cones describe the paths of two turning gyres, or spirals, representing two alternating antithetical ages which make up human history. Yeats saw history as composed of cycles of approximately 2,000 years; his apocalyptic poem *The Second Coming*, for instance, describes the anxiety caused by the recognition that the 2,000 years of Christian (in Yeats's terms, "primary") values were about to be succeeded by an antithetical age—the "rough beast" of a time characterized by values and beliefs in every way hostile to those of the Christian era. For Yeats, however, as for William Blake, this vacillation and tension between contraries was not to be regretted; Blake taught that "without Contraries is no progression," and Yeats, that "all the gains of man come from conflict with the opposite of his true being."

Yeats's greatest phase begins with the poems of *Michael Robartes and the Dancer* (1921). His mytho-historical system informs a number of the poems written in the 1920s and after; it explains, for instance, why Yeats saw the brutal rape of Leda by Zeus in the form of a swan as a precursor of the traditional Christian iconography of the Virgin Mary "visited" by God the Father in the form of a dove. A logical corollary of Yeats's belief in historical recurrence was the philosophy, articulated best in his late poem *Lapis Lazuli*, of tragic joy: "All things fall and are built again, / And those that build them again are gay." In a letter inspired by the gift of lapis lazuli that the poem celebrates, Yeats wrote to a friend: "To me the supreme aim is an act of faith or reason to make one rejoice in the midst of tragedy." The influence of the writing of Nietzsche, whom Yeats had been reading, is apparent in these formulations.

While continuing to push at the boundaries of modern literature and modern poetry, Yeats also enjoyed the role of statesman. In the fall of 1922, Yeats was made a senator of the new Irish Free State; in 1923 he was awarded the Nobel Prize for literature, the first Irish writer ever to receive the award. The 1930s also saw Yeats flirt briefly with fascism, as did other writers like Pound and Wyndham Lewis. Yeats's belief in the importance of an aristocracy, and his disappointment over the excesses of revolutionary zeal demonstrated in the Irish civil war, for a time during the 1930s made the fascist program of the Irish Blueshirt movement look attractive. He composed *Three Songs to the Same Tune* as rallying songs for the Blueshirts, but the poems were too recherché for any such use. He soon became disillusioned with the party.

Yeats continued to write major poetry almost until his death; his growing ill health seems only to have made his poetry stronger and more defiant, as evidenced in such sinuous and clearsighted poems as *Lapis Lazuli* and the bawdy Crazy Jane poems. In the work published as *Last Poems* (1939), Yeats most satisfactorily put into practice what he had much earlier discovered in theory: that he must, as he wrote in *The Circus Animals' Desertion*, return for his poetry to "the foul rag-and-bone shop of the heart." After a long period of heart trouble, Yeats died on 28 January 1939; he was buried in Roquebrune, France, where he and George had been spending the winter. In 1948 he was reinterred, as he had wished, in Drumcliff churchyard near Sligo, where his grandfather and great-grandfather had served as rectors. Again according to his wishes, his epitaph is that which he wrote for himself in *Under Ben Bulben*:

> Cast a cold eye
> On life, on death.
> Horseman, pass by!

The Lake Isle of Innisfree[1]

I will arise and go now, and go to Innisfree,
And a small cabin build there, of clay and wattles° made: *woven twigs*
Nine bean-rows will I have there, a hive for the honey-bee,
And live alone in the bee-loud glade.

5   And I shall have some peace there, for peace comes dropping slow,
Dropping from the veils of the morning to where the cricket sings;
There midnight's all a glimmer, and noon a purple glow,
And evening full of the linnet's° wings.   *song bird*

I will arise and go now, for always night and day
10   I hear lake water lapping with low sounds by the shore;
While I stand on the roadway, or on the pavements grey,
I hear it in the deep heart's core.

1890   1890

---

1. A small island in Lough Gill outside the town of Sligo, near the border with Northern Ireland.

Who Goes with Fergus?[1]

Who will go drive with Fergus now,
And pierce the deep wood's woven shade,
And dance upon the level shore?
Young man, lift up your russet brow,
5 And lift your tender eyelids, maid,
And brood on hopes and fear no more.

And no more turn aside and brood
Upon love's bitter mystery;
For Fergus rules the brazen° cars,   *brass*
10 And rules the shadows of the wood,
And the white breast of the dim sea
And all dishevelled wandering stars.

                                                                      1893

No Second Troy[1]

Why should I blame her that she filled my days
With misery, or that she would of late
Have taught to ignorant men most violent ways,
Or hurled the little streets upon the great,
5 Had they but courage equal to desire?
What could have made her peaceful with a mind
That nobleness made simple as a fire,
With beauty like a tightened bow, a kind
That is not natural in an age like this,
10 Being high and solitary and most stern?
Why, what could she have done, being what she is?
Was there another Troy for her to burn?

1908   1910

The Wild Swans at Coole[1]

The trees are in their autumn beauty,
The woodland paths are dry,
Under the October twilight the water
Mirrors a still sky;
5 Upon the brimming water among the stones
Are nine-and-fifty swans.

The nineteenth autumn has come upon me
Since I first made my count;
I saw, before I had well finished,
10 All suddenly mount
And scatter wheeling in great broken rings
Upon their clamorous wings.

---

1. The poem is a lyric from the second scene of Yeats's play *The Countess Cathleen*. Fergus was an ancient Irish king who gave up his throne to feast, fight, and hunt.
1. Yeats here compares Maud Gonne to Helen of Troy;
the Trojan War began from two kings' rivalry over Helen.
1. Coole Park was the name of the estate of Yeats's patron Lady Gregory in Galway.

I have looked upon those brilliant creatures,
And now my heart is sore.
15   All's changed since I, hearing at twilight,
The first time on this shore,
The bell-beat of their wings above my head,
Trod with a lighter tread.

Unwearied still, lover by lover,
20   They paddle in the cold
Companionable streams or climb the air;
Their hearts have not grown old;
Passion or conquest, wander where they will,
Attend upon them still.

25   But now they drift on the still water,
Mysterious, beautiful;
Among what rushes will they build,
By what lake's edge or pool
Delight men's eyes when I awake some day
30   To find they have flown away?

1916   1917

Easter 1916[1]

I have met them at close of day
Coming with vivid faces
From counter or desk among grey
Eighteenth-century houses.
5   I have passed with a nod of the head
Or polite meaningless words,
Or have lingered awhile and said
Polite meaningless words,
And thought before I had done
10   Of a mocking tale or a gibe°   *taunt*
To please a companion
Around the fire at the club,
Being certain that they and I
But lived where motley° is worn: *jester's outfit*
15   All changed, changed utterly:
A terrible beauty is born.

That woman's days were spent
In ignorant good-will,
Her nights in argument
20   Until her voice grew shrill.[2]
What voice more sweet than hers
When, young and beautiful,
She rode to harriers?°   *hunting dogs*

---

1. The Irish Republic was declared on Easter Monday, 24 April 1916.
2. Countess Markiewicz, née Constance Gore-Booth, played a prominent part in the Easter Rising and was sentenced to be executed; her sentence was later reduced to imprisonment.

This man[3] had kept a school
25 And rode our wingèd horse;
This other[4] his helper and friend
Was coming into his force;
He might have won fame in the end,
So sensitive his nature seemed,
30 So daring and sweet his thought.
This other man[5] I had dreamed
A drunken, vainglorious lout.
He had done most bitter wrong
To some who are near my heart,
35 Yet I number him in the song;
He, too, has resigned his part
In the casual comedy;
He, too, has been changed in his turn,
Transformed utterly:
40 A terrible beauty is born.

Hearts with one purpose alone
Through summer and winter seem
Enchanted to a stone
To trouble the living stream.
45 The horse that comes from the road,
The rider, the birds that range
From cloud to tumbling cloud,
Minute by minute they change;
A shadow of cloud on the stream
50 Changes minute by minute;
A horse-hoof slides on the brim,
And a horse plashes within it;
The long-legged moor-hens dive,
And hens to moor-cocks call;
55 Minute by minute they live:
The stone's in the midst of all.

Too long a sacrifice
Can make a stone of the heart.
O when may it suffice?
60 That is Heaven's part, our part
To murmur name upon name,
As a mother names her child
When sleep at last has come
On limbs that had run wild.
65 What is it but nightfall?
No, no, not night but death;
Was it needless death after all?
For England may keep faith
For all that is done and said.

3. Padraic Pearse.
4. Thomas MacDonagh, poet executed for his role in the rebellion.
5. Major John MacBride, briefly married to Maud Gonne, was also executed.

70   We know their dream; enough
      To know they dreamed and are dead;
      And what if excess of love
      Bewildered them till they died?
      I write it out in a verse—
75   MacDonagh and MacBride
      And Connolly[6] and Pearse
      Now and in time to be,
      Wherever green is worn,
      Are changed, changed utterly:
80   A terrible beauty is born.
1916   1916

COMPANION READING

Proclamation of the Irish Republic: Poblacht na h Eireann[1]

THE PROVISIONAL GOVERNMENT OF THE IRISH REPUBLIC

TO THE

PEOPLE OF IRELAND

Irishmen and Irishwomen:

In the name of God and of the dead generations from which she receives her old tradition of nationhood, Ireland, through us, summons her children to her flag and strikes for her freedom.

Having organised and trained her manhood through her secret revolutionary organisation, the Irish Republican Brotherhood, and through her open miltary organisations, the Irish Volunteers and the Irish Citizen Army, having patiently perfected her discipline, having resolutely waited for the right moment to reveal itself, she now seizes that moment, and, supported by her exiled children in America and by gallant allies in Europe, but relying in the first on her own strength, she strikes in full confidence of victory.

We declare the right of the people of Ireland to the ownership of Ireland, and to the unfettered control of Irish destinies, to be sovereign and indefeasible. The long usurpation of that right by a foreign people and government has not extinguished the right, nor can it ever be extinguished except by the destruction of the Irish people. In every generation the Irish have asserted their right to National freedom and sovereignty; six times during the past three hundred years they have asserted it in arms. Standing on that fundamental right and again asserting it in arms in the face of the world, we hereby proclaim the Irish Republic as a Sovereign Independent State, and we pledge our lives and the lives of our comrades-in-arms to the cause of its freedom, of its welfare, and of its exaltation among the nations.

The Irish Republic is entitled to, and hereby claims, the allegiance of every Irishman and Irishwoman. The Republic guarantees religious and civil liberty, equal rights and equal opportunities to all its citizens, and declares its resolve to pursue the happiness and prosperity of the whole nation and of all its parts, cherishing all the

---

6. James Connolly, Marxist commander-in-chief of the Easter rebels; also executed.

1. *Irish Republic*, in the Irish language.

children of the nation equally, and oblivious of the differences carefully fostered by an alien government, which have divided a minority from the majority in the past.

Until our arms have brought the opportune moment for the establishment of a permanent National Government, representative of the whole people of Ireland and elected by the suffrages of all her men and women,[2] the Provisional Government, hereby constituted, will administer the civil and military affairs of the Republic in trust for the people.

We place the cause of the Irish Republic under the protection of the Most High God, Whose blessing we invoke upon our arms, and we pray that no one who serves that cause will dishonor it by cowardice, inhumanity, or rapine. In this supreme hour the Irish nation must, by its valour and discipline and by the readiness of its children to sacrifice themselves for the common good, prove itself worthy of the august destiny to which it is called.

Signed on Behalf of the Provisional Government,

THOMAS J. CLARKE,
SEAN MACDIARMADA,
THOMAS MACDONAGH,
P. H. PEARSE,
EAMONN CEANNT,
JAMES CONNOLLY,
JOSEPH PLUNKETT.

Easter 1916

⁓

The Second Coming[1]

Turning and turning in the widening gyre°   *circle or spiral*
The falcon cannot hear the falconer;
Things fall apart; the centre cannot hold;
Mere anarchy is loosed upon the world,
5   The blood-dimmed tide is loosed, and everywhere
The ceremony of innocence is drowned;
The best lack all conviction, while the worst
Are full of passionate intensity.

Surely some revelation is at hand;
10   Surely the Second Coming is at hand.
The Second Coming! Hardly are those words out
When a vast image out of *Spiritus Mundi*[2]
Troubles my sight: somewhere in sands of the desert
A shape with lion body and the head of a man,
15   A gaze blank and pitiless as the sun,
Is moving its slow thighs, while all about it
Reel shadows of the indignant desert birds.
The darkness drops again; but now I know
That twenty centuries° of stony sleep   *the Christian era*

---

2. This call for women's suffrage in the Irish Republic predates full British women's suffrage by 12 years, and American women's suffrage by four years.
1. Traditionally, the return of Christ to earth on Judgment Day.
2. A storehouse of images and symbols common to all humankind; similar to Carl Jung's notion of the collective unconscious.

20   Were vexed to nightmare by a rocking cradle,
And what rough beast, its hour come round at last,
Slouches towards Bethlehem to be born?

1919   1921

A Prayer for My Daughter[1]

Once more the storm is howling, and half hid
Under this cradle-hood and coverlid
My child sleeps on. There is no obstacle
But Gregory's wood and one bare hill
5   Whereby the haystack- and roof-levelling wind,
Bred on the Atlantic, can be stayed;
And for an hour I have walked and prayed
Because of the great gloom that is in my mind.

I have walked and prayed for this young child an hour
10 And heard the sea-wind scream upon the tower,
And under the arches of the bridge, and scream
In the elms above the flooded stream;
Imagining in excited reverie
That the future years had come,
15 Dancing to a frenzied drum,
Out of the murderous innocence of the sea.

May she be granted beauty and yet not
Beauty to make a stranger's eye distraught,
Or hers before a looking-glass, for such,
20 Being made beautiful overmuch,
Consider beauty a sufficient end,
Lose natural kindness and maybe
The heart-revealing intimacy
That chooses right, and never find a friend.

25 Helen[2] being chosen found life flat and dull
And later had much trouble from a fool,
While that great Queen,[3] that rose out of the spray,
Being fatherless could have her way
Yet chose a bandy-leggèd smith[4] for man.
30 It's certain that fine women eat
A crazy salad with their meat
Whereby the Horn of Plenty is undone.
In courtesy I'd have her chiefly learned;
Hearts are not had as a gift but hearts are earned
35 By those that are not entirely beautiful;
Yet many, that have played the fool
For beauty's very self, has charm made wise,
And many a poor man that has roved,
Loved and thought himself beloved,

---

1. Anne Butler Yeats was born 26 February 1919.
2. Helen of Troy, who left her husband Menelaus for Paris.
3. Aphrodite, Greek goddess of love, born from the sea.
4. Aphrodite's husband Hephaestus, the god of fire, was lame.

40   From a glad kindness cannot take his eyes.

May she become a flourishing hidden tree
That all her thoughts may like the linnet° be,   *song bird*
And have no business but dispensing round
Their magnanimities of sound,
45   Nor but in merriment begin a chase,
Nor but in merriment a quarrel.
O may she live like some green laurel
Rooted in one dear perpetual place.

My mind, because the minds that I have loved,
50   The sort of beauty that I have approved,
Prosper but little, has dried up of late,
Yet knows that to be choked with hate
May well be of all evil chances chief.
If there's no hatred in a mind
55   Assault and battery of the wind
Can never tear the linnet from the leaf.

An intellectual hatred is the worst,
So let her think opinions are accursed.
Have I not seen the loveliest woman born
60   Out of the mouth of Plenty's horn,
Because of her opinionated mind
Barter that horn and every good
By quiet natures understood
For an old bellows full of angry wind?

65   Considering that, all hatred driven hence,
The soul recovers radical innocence
And learns at last that it is self-delighting,
Self-appeasing, self-affrighting,
And that its own sweet will is Heaven's will;
70   She can, though every face should scowl
And every windy quarter howl
Or every bellows burst, be happy still.

And may her bridegroom bring her to a house
Where all's accustomed, ceremonious;
75   For arrogance and hatred are the wares
Peddled in the thoroughfares.
How but in custom and in ceremony
Are innocence and beauty born?
Ceremony's a name for the rich horn,
80   And custom for the spreading laurel tree.

June 1919   1919

Sailing to Byzantium[1]

1

That is no country for old men. The young
In one another's arms, birds in the trees,

---

1. Constantinople, now called Istanbul, capital of the Byzantine Empire and the holy city of Eastern Christianity.

—Those dying generations—at their song,
The salmon-falls, the mackerel-crowded seas,
5   Fish, flesh, or fowl, commend all summer long
Whatever is begotten, born, and dies.
Caught in that sensual music all neglect
Monuments of unageing intellect.

2

An aged man is but a paltry thing,
10   A tattered coat upon a stick, unless
Soul clap its hands and sing, and louder sing
For every tatter in its mortal dress,
Nor is there singing school but studying
Monuments of its own magnificence;
15   And therefore I have sailed the seas and come
To the holy city of Byzantium.

3

O sages standing in God's holy fire
As in the gold mosaic of a wall,
Come from the holy fire, perne° in a gyre,   *spin*
20   And be the singing-masters of my soul.
Consume my heart away; sick with desire
And fastened to a dying animal
It knows not what it is; and gather me
Into the artifice of eternity.

4

25   Once out of nature I shall never take
My bodily form from any natural thing,
But such a form as Grecian goldsmiths make
Of hammered gold and gold enamelling
To keep a drowsy Emperor awake;—
30   Or set upon a golden bough to sing
To lords and ladies of Byzantium
Of what is past, or passing, or to come.

1926   1927

Leda and the Swan[1]

A sudden blow: the great wings beating still
Above the staggering girl, her thighs caressed
By the dark webs, her nape caught in his bill,
He holds her helpless breast upon his breast.

5   How can those terrified vague fingers push
The feathered glory from her loosening thighs?
And how can body, laid in that white rush,
But feel the strange heart beating where it lies?

A shudder in the loins engenders there
10   The broken wall, the burning roof and tower

---

1. In Greek mythology, Zeus came to Leda in the form of a swan and raped her; Helen of Troy and Clytemnestra were their offspring.

And Agamemnon[2] dead.
                              Being so caught up,
So mastered by the brute blood of the air,
Did she put on his knowledge with his power
Before the indifferent beak could let her drop?

1923   1924

Among School Children

1

I walk through the long schoolroom questioning;[1]
A kind old nun in a white hood replies;
The children learn to cipher and to sing,
To study reading-books and history,
5   To cut and sew, be neat in everything
In the best modern way—the children's eyes
In momentary wonder stare upon
A sixty-year-old smiling public man.

2

I dream of a Ledaean[2] body, bent
10   Above a sinking fire, a tale that she
Told of a harsh reproof, or trivial event
That changed some childish day to tragedy—
Told, and it seemed that our two natures blent
Into a sphere from youthful sympathy,
15   Or else, to alter Plato's parable,
Into the yolk and white of the one shell.[3]

3

And thinking of that fit of grief or rage
I look upon one child or t'other there
And wonder if she stood so at that age—
20   For even daughters of the swan can share
Something of every paddler's heritage—
And had that colour upon cheek or hair,
And thereupon my heart is driven wild:
She stands before me as a living child.

4

25   Her present image floats into the mind—
Did Quattrocento[4] finger fashion it
Hollow of cheek as though it drank the wind
And took a mess of shadows for its meat?
And I though never of Ledaean kind
30   Had pretty plumage once—enough of that,
Better to smile on all that smile, and show
There is a comfortable kind of old scarecrow.

2. Brother of Menelaus, husband of Helen. When she was abducted by Paris, Agamemnon fought to rescue her. He was murdered by his wife Clytemnestra on his return home.
1. While an Irish senator, Yeats visited St. Otteran's School in Waterford.

2. Of Leda, the mother of Helen of Troy (or Helen herself).
3. According to Plato's parable in the *Symposium*, male and female were once the two halves of a single body; it was subsequently cut in half like a hard-boiled egg.
4. Fifteenth-century artists of Italy's Renaissance.

5

What youthful mother, a shape upon her lap
Honey of generation had betrayed,
35   And that must sleep, shriek, struggle to escape
As recollection or the drug decide,
Would think her son, did she but see that shape
With sixty or more winters on its head,
A compensation for the pang of his birth,
40   Or the uncertainty of his setting forth?

6

Plato thought nature but a spume° that plays   *froth*
Upon a ghostly paradigm of things;
Solider Aristotle played the taws[5]
Upon the bottom of a king of kings;
45   World-famous golden-thighed Pythagoras[6]
Fingered upon a fiddle-stick or strings
What a star sang and careless Muses heard:
Old clothes upon old sticks to scare a bird.

7

Both nuns and mothers worship images,
50   But those the candles light are not as those
That animate a mother's reveries,
But keep a marble or a bronze repose.
And yet they too break hearts—O Presences
That passion, piety or affection knows,
55   And that all heavenly glory symbolise—
O self-born mockers of man's enterprise;

8

Labour is blossoming or dancing where
The body is not bruised to pleasure soul,
Nor beauty born out of its own despair,
60   Nor blear-eyed wisdom out of midnight oil.
O chestnut tree, great rooted blossomer,
Are you the leaf, the blossom or the bole?
O body swayed to music, O brightening glance,
How can we know the dancer from the dance?

1926   1927

Byzantium

The unpurged images of day recede;
The Emperor's drunken soldiery are abed;
Night resonance recedes, night-walkers' song
After great cathedral gong;
5   A starlit or a moonlit dome disdains
All that man is,
All mere complexities,
The fury and the mire of human veins.

---

5. A leather strap, used to spin a top.
6. A 6th-century B.C. Greek philosopher who developed   a mathematical basis for the universe and music.

Before me floats an image, man or shade,
10   Shade more than man, more image than a shade;
For Hades' bobbin° bound in mummy-cloth   spool
May unwind the winding path;
A mouth that has no moisture and no breath
Breathless mouths may summon;
15   I hail the superhuman;
I call it death-in-life and life-in-death.

Miracle, bird or golden handiwork,
More miracle than bird or handiwork,
Planted on the starlit golden bough,
20   Can like the cocks of Hades crow,
Or, by the moon embittered, scorn aloud
In glory of changeless metal
Common bird or petal
And all complexities of mire or blood.

25   At midnight on the Emperor's pavement flit
Flames that no faggot° feeds, nor steel has lit,   bundle of sticks
Nor storm disturbs, flames begotten of flame,
Where blood-begotten spirits come
And all complexities of fury leave,
30   Dying into a dance,
An agony of trance,
An agony of flame that cannot singe a sleeve.

Astraddle on the dolphin's mire and blood,
Spirit after spirit! The smithies break the flood,
35   The golden smithies of the Emperor!
Marbles of the dancing floor
Break bitter furies of complexity,
Those images that yet
Fresh images beget,
40   That dolphin-torn, that gong-tormented sea.
1930   1932

Crazy Jane Talks with the Bishop

I met the Bishop on the road
And much said he and I.
"Those breasts are flat and fallen now
Those veins must soon be dry;
5   Live in a heavenly mansion,
Not in some foul sty."

"Fair and foul are near of kin,
And fair needs foul," I cried.
"My friends are gone, but that's a truth
10   Nor grave nor bed denied,
Learned in bodily lowliness
And in the heart's pride.

"A woman can be proud and stiff
When on love intent;
15   But Love has pitched his mansion in
The place of excrement;
For nothing can be sole or whole
That has not been rent."

1931   1932

Lapis Lazuli[1]
(For Harry Clifton[2])

I have heard that hysterical women say
They are sick of the palette and fiddle-bow,
Of poets that are always gay,
For everybody knows or else should know
5   That if nothing drastic is done
Aeroplane and Zeppelin will come out,
Pitch like King Billy bomb-balls[3] in
Until the town lie beaten flat.

All perform their tragic play,
10   There struts Hamlet, there is Lear,
That's Ophelia, that Cordelia;[4]
Yet they, should the last scene be there,
The great stage curtain about to drop,
If worthy their prominent part in the play,
15   Do not break up their lines to weep.
They know that Hamlet and Lear are gay;
Gaiety transfiguring all that dread.
All men have aimed at, found and lost;
Black out; Heaven blazing into the head:
20   Tragedy wrought to its uttermost.
Though Hamlet rambles and Lear rages,
And all the drop scenes drop at once
Upon a hundred thousand stages,
It cannot grow by an inch or an ounce.

25   On their own feet they came, or on shipboard,
Camel-back, horse-back, ass-back, mule-back,
Old civilisations put to the sword.
Then they and their wisdom went to rack:
No handiwork of Callimachus[5]
30   Who handled marble as if it were bronze,
Made draperies that seemed to rise
When sea-wind swept the corner, stands;

1. A rich blue mineral producing the pigment ultramarine; used by the ancients for decoration.
2. A friend who gave Yeats a carving in lapis lazuli on his birthday.
3. German bombs; "King Billy" is a nickname for Kaiser Wilhelm II. Yeats may also mean to invoke King William

I of England, "William of Orange," whose defeat of King James II at the Battle of the Boyne in 1690 resulted in the Protestant ascendancy in Ireland.
4. Characters from *Hamlet* and *King Lear*.
5. Greek poet, grammarian, critic, and sculptor (c. 310–c. 240 B.C.).

His long lamp chimney shaped like the stem
Of a slender palm, stood but a day;
35   All things fall and are built again
And those that build them again are gay.

Two Chinamen, behind them a third,
Are carved in Lapis Lazuli,
Over them flies a long-legged bird
40   A symbol of longevity;
The third, doubtless a serving-man,
Carries a musical instrument.

Every discolouration of the stone,
Every accidental crack or dent
45   Seems a water-course or an avalanche,
Or lofty slope where it still snows
Though doubtless plum or cherry-branch
Sweetens the little half-way house
Those Chinamen climb towards, and I
50   Delight to imagine them seated there;
There, on the mountain and the sky,
On all the tragic scene they stare.
One asks for mournful melodies;
Accomplished fingers begin to play.
55   Their eyes mid many wrinkles, their eyes,
Their ancient, glittering eyes, are gay.

1936   1938

✦❖✦

James Joyce
1882–1941

James Joyce was one of the great innovators who brought the novel into the modern era. As T. S. Eliot put it, Joyce made "the modern world possible for art." The poet Edith Sitwell wrote that by the turn of the century, "language had become, not so much an abused medium, as a dead and outworn thing, in which there was no living muscular system. Then came the rebirth of the medium, and this was effected, as far as actual vocabularies were concerned, very largely by such prose writers as Mr. James Joyce and Miss Gertrude Stein." Joyce objected to this flaccidity, citing examples in the work of George Moore, the most important Irish novelist of the first decade of the twentieth century; Moore's novel *The Untilled Field*, Joyce complained to his brother Stanislaus, was "damned stupid," "dull and flat," and "ill written." In a comment that would have pleased Joyce, one critic writing in 1929 declared that Joyce had by that date "conclusively reduced all the pretensions of the realistic novel to absurdity."

James Augustus Aloysius Joyce was born in Rathgar, a middle-class suburb of Dublin; though he was to leave Ireland more or less permanently at age twenty-two, Ireland generally, and "Dear Dirty Dublin" specifically, were never far from his mind and writing. He was the eldest surviving son in a large family consisting, according to his father, of "sixteen or seventeen children." His father, John Stanislaus Joyce, born and raised in Cork, was a tax collector and sometime Parnellite political employee; his mother was Mary Jane Joyce, née Murray.

There is no better imaginative guide to the twists and turns of Joyce's family fortunes, and their effect on the young writer, than his first novel, *A Portrait of the Artist as a Young Man;* the life of Joyce's autobiographical hero Stephen Dedalus closely follows Joyce's own. The novel brings young Stephen from his earliest memories, through his Catholic schooling at Clongowes Wood College and Belvedere College, up to his graduation from University College, Dublin, and departure for Paris. Like Stephen, Joyce in these years first considered entering the priesthood, then began regarding Catholicism with increasing skepticism and irony, coming to view religion, family, and nation as three kinds of net or trap. One of the most important events of the early part of Joyce's life was the betrayal and subsequent death of "the uncrowned king of Ireland," Charles Stewart Parnell, the political leader who was working hard to make Home Rule for Ireland a reality; his demise, after his adulterous affair with Kitty O'Shea was discovered, was remembered by Joyce in his first poem, *Et Tu, Healy*—which he wrote at the age of eight— and in a haunting story, *Ivy Day in the Committee Room.* Joyce moved to Paris after graduation in 1902 and began medical studies, but he soon had to return to Dublin, as his mother was dying. Joyce gave up the idea of a medical career, which his father could not afford to finance in any event; he briefly tried teaching school and sought to define himself as a writer.

Like Dedalus, the young Joyce first concentrated on writing poetry. The majority of his early poems were collected in the volume *Chamber Music* (1907); both the strength and weakness of the poems is suggested by the praise of Arthur Symons, who in his review in the *Nation* described the lyrics as "tiny, evanescent things." Poetry was ultimately to prove a dead end for Joyce; though he brought out one more volume of thirteen poems during his lifetime (*Pomes Penyeach,* 1927), and wrote one forgettable play (*Exiles,* 1918), prose fiction is the primary area in which Joyce's influence continues to be felt.

The year 1904 proved to be an absolute watershed in Joyce's development as a writer. In January 1904—indeed, perhaps in the single day 7 January 1904—Joyce wrote an impressionistic prose sketch which would ultimately serve as the manifesto for his first novel. From this beginning, Joyce shaped his novel, which was to have been called *Stephen Hero;* and though he worked on it steadily for more than three years, and the manuscript grew to almost a thousand pages, the novel was not coming together in quite the way Joyce had hoped. Hence in the fall of 1907, he began cutting and radically reshaping the material into what would become *A Portrait of the Artist as a Young Man,* one of the finest examples of the *Künstlerroman* (novel of artistic growth) in English; H. G. Wells called it "by far the most living and convincing picture that exists of an Irish Catholic upbringing."

June 16, 1904, in particular is a crucial day in the Joycean calendar, for it is "Bloomsday"— the day on which the events narrated in *Ulysses* take place—and according to legend, it is the day that Nora Barnacle first agreed to go out walking with Joyce. Joyce's father thought Nora's maiden name a good omen, suggesting that she would "stick to him," and indeed she did; without the benefit of marriage, she agreed to accompany him four months later on his artistic exile to the Continent, and though they were not legally married until 1931, she proved a faithful and devoted partner, a small spot of stability amidst the chaos of Joyce's life. They settled for several years in Trieste, Italy, where Joyce taught English at a Berlitz school and where their two children, Giorgio and Lucia, were born. Joyce returned briefly to Ireland in 1909, seeking unsuccessfully to get work published and to start a movie theater; after another brief visit in 1912, he never returned. He spent most of World War I in Zurich, then moved to Paris, where he eked out an existence with the help of several benefactors as his reputation began to grow.

He had begun his first book in June or July 1904, invited by the Irish man of letters "A. E." (George Russell) to submit a short story to his paper *The Irish Homestead.* Joyce began writing the series of fifteen stories that would be published in 1914 as *Dubliners.* In letters to London publisher Grant Richards about his conception for the short stories, Joyce wrote that he planned the volume to be a chapter of Ireland's "moral history" and that in writing it he had "taken the first step towards the spiritual liberation of my country." Richards, however, objected to the stark realism—or sordidness—of several scenes, and pressed Joyce to eliminate vulgarisms;

Joyce refused. Finally, desperate to have the book published, Joyce wrote to Richards: "I seriously believe that you will retard the course of civilisation in Ireland by preventing the Irish people from having one good look at themselves in my nicely polished looking-glass."

During this period, Joyce also experimented with a form of short prose sketch that he called the "epiphany." An epiphany, as it is defined in *Stephen Hero*, is "a sudden spiritual manifestation, whether in the vulgarity of speech or of gesture or in a memorable phase of the mind itself." It consequently falls to the artist to "record these epiphanies with extreme care, seeing that they themselves are the most delicate and evanescent of moments." One benefit of Joyce's experimentation with prose epiphanies is that the searching realism and psychological richness of the stories in *Dubliners* are conveyed with a lucid economy of phrasing—what Joyce called "a style of scrupulous meanness"—and by a similar penchant for understatement on the level of plot. The stories often seem to "stop," rather than end; time and again, Joyce withholds the tidy conclusion that conventional fiction had trained readers to expect. In story after story, characters betray what Joyce termed their "paralysis"—a paralysis of the will that prevents them from breaking out of deadening habit. The final story of the collection, *The Dead*—written after the volume had ostensibly been completed, and comprising a broader scope and larger cast of characters than the other stories—is Joyce's finest work of short fiction, and justly praised as one of the great stories of our time; it was filmed, quite sensitively and beautifully, by director John Huston, the last film project before his death.

A second decisive year for Joyce was 1914. Having completed *Dubliners*, Joyce seems never to have thought seriously about writing short fiction again; and throughout the period he was writing his stories, he continued to work on *A Portrait*. As was the case with *Dubliners*, negotiations for the publication of *A Portrait* were extremely difficult; despite its dazzling language, few editors could get beyond the opening pages, with their references to bedwetting and their use of crude slang. Even though the novel had been published serially in *The Egoist* beginning in 1914, and was praised by influential writers like W. B. Yeats, H. G. Wells, and Ezra Pound, the book was rejected by every publisher in London to whom Joyce offered it, before finally being accepted by B. W. Huebsch in New York, and published in December 1916.

With both his stories and his first novel between hard covers, Joyce was finally able to concentrate his energies on the one novel for which, more than any other, he will be remembered—*Ulysses*; that work, too, had begun in 1914. The novel is structured, loosely, on eighteen episodes from Homer's *Odyssey*; Leopold Bloom, advertising salesman, is a modern-day Ulysses, the streets of Dublin his Aegean Sea, and Molly Bloom his (unfaithful) Penelope. Stephen Dedalus, stuck teaching school and estranged from his real father, is an unwitting Telemachus (Ulysses' son) in search of a father. Critics have disagreed over the years as to how seriously readers should take these Homeric parallels; Eliot understood them to be of the utmost importance—"a way of controlling, of ordering, of giving a shape and a significance to the immense panorama of futility and anarchy which is contemporary history"—while the equally supportive Pound suggested that the parallel structure was merely "the remains of a medieval allegorical culture; it matters little, it is a question of cooking, which does not restrict the action, nor inconvenience it, nor harm the realism, nor the contemporaneity of the action."

Concomitant with the Homeric structure, Joyce sought to give each of his eighteen chapters its own style. Chapter 12, focusing on Bloom's encounter with Dublin's Cyclops, called "the Citizen," is written in a style of "gigantism"—full of mock-epic epithets and catalogues, playfully suggestive of the style of ancient Celtic myth and legend. Chapter 13, which parallels Odysseus's encounter with Nausicaa, is written in the exaggerated style of Victorian women's magazines and sentimental fiction, a style which Joyce characterized as "a namby-pamby jammy marmalady drawersy (alto-là!) style with effects of incense, mariolatry, masturbation, stewed cockles, painter's palette, chitchat, circumlocutions, etc etc." While realist writers sought constantly to flush artifice from their writing, to arrive finally at a style which would be value-neutral, Joyce takes the English language on a voyage in the opposite direction; each

Photo of Sackville Street (now O'Connell Street), Dublin, with view of Nelson's Pillar.

chapter, as he wrote to his patron Harriet Shaw Weaver, left behind it "a burnt-up field." It would be difficult to overestimate the influence that *Ulysses* has had on modern writing; Eliot's candid response to the novel, reported in a letter to Joyce, was "I have nothing but admiration; in fact, I wish, for my own sake, that I had not read it."

Other people wanted to make sure that no one else would read it. *Ulysses* was promptly banned as obscene, in Ireland, England, and many other countries. Copies were smuggled into the United States, where a pirated edition was published, paying Joyce no royalties. Finally in 1933, in a landmark decision, a federal judge found that the book's frank language and sexual discussions were fully justified artistically—though he allowed that "*Ulysses* is a rather strong draught to ask some sensitive, though normal, persons to take."

In 1923, with *Ulysses* completed, Joyce suddenly reinvented himself and his writing once again, and turned his attention to the writing of the novel that would occupy him almost until his death—*Finnegans Wake*. If *Ulysses* attacks the novel form at the level of style, *Finnegans Wake* targets the very structures of the English language, using a neologismic amalgam of more than a dozen modern and ancient languages—a hybrid that devotees call "Wakese"; when questioned as to the wisdom of such a strategy, Joyce replied that *Ulysses* had proved English to be inadequate. "I'd like a language," he told his friend Stefan Zweig, "which is above all languages, a language to which all will do service. I cannot express myself in English without enclosing myself in a tradition."

On 13 January 1941, Joyce died of a perforated ulcer; his illness and death almost certainly owed something to an adult life of rather heavy drinking and surely to the pain of his self-exile. Though his oeuvre consists largely of one volume of short stories and three novels, his importance for students of modern literature is extraordinary. As Richard Ellmann writes at the opening of his magisterial biography, "We are still learning to be James Joyce's contemporaries, to understand our interpreter."

from DUBLINERS
Clay

The matron had given her leave to go out as soon as the women's tea was over and Maria looked forward to her evening out. The kitchen was spick and span: the cook said you could see yourself in the big copper boilers. The fire was nice and bright and on one of the side-tables were four very big barmbracks.[1] These barmbracks seemed uncut; but if you went closer you would see that they had been cut into long thick even slices and were ready to be handed round at tea. Maria had cut them herself.

Maria was a very, very small person indeed but she had a very long nose and a very long chin. She talked a little through her nose, always soothingly: *Yes, my dear,* and *No, my dear.* She was always sent for when the women quarrelled over their tubs and always succeeded in making peace. One day the matron had said to her:

—Maria, you are a veritable peace-maker!

And the sub-matron and two of the Board ladies[2] had heard the compliment. And Ginger Mooney was always saying what she wouldn't do to the dummy[3] who had charge of the irons if it wasn't for Maria. Everyone was so fond of Maria.

The women would have their tea at six o'clock and she would be able to get away before seven. From Ballsbridge to the Pillar, twenty minutes; from the Pillar to Drumcondra, twenty minutes; and twenty minutes to buy the things. She would be there before eight. She took out her purse with the silver clasps and read again the words *A Present from Belfast.* She was very fond of that purse because Joe had brought it to her five years before when he and Alphy had gone to Belfast on a Whit-Monday[4] trip. In the purse were two half-crowns and some coppers. She would have five shillings clear after paying tram fare. What a nice evening they would have, all the children singing! Only she hoped that Joe wouldn't come in drunk. He was so different when he took any drink.

Often he had wanted her to go and live with them; but she would have felt herself in the way (though Joe's wife was ever so nice with her) and she had become accustomed to the life of the laundry. Joe was a good fellow. She had nursed him and Alphy too; and Joe used often say:

—Mamma is mamma but Maria is my proper mother.

After the break-up at home the boys had got her that position in the *Dublin by Lamplight* laundry,[5] and she liked it. She used to have such a bad opinion of Protestants but now she thought they were very nice people, a little quiet and serious, but still very nice people to live with. Then she had her plants in the conservatory and she liked looking after them. She had lovely ferns and wax-plants and, whenever anyone came to visit her, she always gave the visitor one or two slips from her conservatory. There was one thing she didn't like and that was the tracts[6] on the walls; but the matron was such a nice person to deal with, so genteel.

When the cook told her everything was ready she went into the women's room and began to pull the big bell. In a few minutes the women began to come in by twos and threes, wiping their steaming hands in their petticoats and pulling down the

---

1. Speckled cakes or currant buns.
2. Members of the governing board of the Dublin by Lamplight Laundry.
3. Slang for a mute person.
4. Holiday following Whitsunday, the seventh Sunday after Easter.

5. Joyce's invented benevolent society, run by Protestant women, "saves" Dublin's prostitutes from a life on the streets by giving them honest work in a laundry. Maria works for the laundry but appears not to be a reformed prostitute herself.
6. Evangelical religious texts.

sleeves of their blouses over their red steaming arms. They settled down before their huge mugs which the cook and the dummy filled up with hot tea, already mixed with milk and sugar in huge tin cans. Maria superintended the distribution of the barm-brack and saw that every woman got her four slices. There was a great deal of laugh-ing and joking during the meal. Lizzie Fleming said Maria was sure to get the ring and, though Fleming had said that for so many Hallow Eves, Maria had to laugh and say she didn't want any ring or man either; and when she laughed her grey-green eyes sparkled with disappointed shyness and the tip of her nose nearly met the tip of her chin. Then Ginger Mooney lifted up her mug of tea and proposed Maria's health while all the other women clattered with their mugs on the table, and said she was sorry she hadn't a sup of porter[7] to drink it in. And Maria laughed again till the tip of her nose nearly met the tip of her chin and till her minute body nearly shook itself asunder because she knew that Mooney meant well though, of course, she had the notions of a common woman.

But wasn't Maria glad when the women had finished their tea and the cook and the dummy had begun to clear away the tea-things! She went into her little bedroom and, remembering that the next morning was a mass morning, changed the hand of the alarm from seven to six. Then she took off her working skirt and her house-boots and laid her best skirt out on the bed and her tiny dress-boots beside the foot of the bed. She changed her blouse too and, as she stood before the mirror, she thought of how she used to dress for mass on Sunday morning when she was a young girl; and she looked with quaint affection at the diminutive body which she had so often adorned. In spite of its years she found it a nice tidy little body.

When she got outside the streets were shining with rain and she was glad of her old brown raincloak. The tram was full and she had to sit on the little stool at the end of the car, facing all the people, with her toes barely touching the floor. She arranged in her mind all she was going to do and thought how much better it was to be independent and to have your own money in your pocket. She hoped they would have a nice evening. She was sure they would but she could not help thinking what a pity it was Alphy and Joe were not speaking. They were always falling out now but when they were boys together they used to be the best of friends: but such was life.

She got out of her tram at the Pillar and ferreted her way quickly among the crowds. She went into Downes's cakeshop but the shop was so full of people that it was a long time before she could get herself attended to. She bought a dozen of mixed penny cakes, and at last came out of the shop laden with a big bag. Then she thought what else would she buy: she wanted to buy something really nice. They would be sure to have plenty of apples and nuts. It was hard to know what to buy and all she could think of was cake. She decided to buy some plumcake but Downes's plumcake had not enough almond icing on top of it so she went over to a shop in Henry Street. Here she was a long time in suiting herself and the stylish young lady behind the counter, who was evidently a little annoyed by her, asked her was it wedding-cake she wanted to buy. That made Maria blush and smile at the young lady; but the young lady took it all very seriously and finally cut a thick slice of plumcake, parcelled it up and said:

—Two-and-four, please.

She thought she would have to stand in the Drumcondra tram because none of the young men seemed to notice her but an elderly gentleman made room for her. He

7. A heavy, dark brown ale.

was a stout gentleman and he wore a brown hard hat; he had a square red face and a greyish moustache. Maria thought he was a colonel-looking gentleman and she reflected how much more polite he was than the young men who simply stared straight before them. The gentleman began to chat with her about Hallow Eve and the rainy weather. He supposed the bag was full of good things for the little ones and said it was only right that the youngsters should enjoy themselves while they were young. Maria agreed with him and favoured him with demure nods and hems. He was very nice with her, and when she was getting out at the Canal Bridge she thanked him and bowed, and he bowed to her and raised his hat and smiled agreeably; and while she was going up along the terrace, bending her tiny head under the rain, she thought how easy it was to know a gentleman even when he has a drop taken.

Everybody said: O, *here's Maria!* when she came to Joe's house. Joe was there, having come home from business, and all the children had their Sunday dresses on. There were two big girls in from next door and games were going on. Maria gave the bag of cakes to the eldest boy, Alphy, to divide and Mrs Donnelly said it was too good of her to bring such a big bag of cakes and made all the children say:

—Thanks, Maria.

But Maria said she had brought something special for papa and mamma, something they would be sure to like, and she began to look for her plumcake. She tried in Downes's bag and then in the pockets of her raincloak and then on the hallstand but nowhere could she find it. Then she asked all the children had any of them eaten it—by mistake, of course—but the children all said no and looked as if they did not like to eat cakes if they were to be accused of stealing. Everybody had a solution for the mystery and Mrs Donnelly said it was plain that Maria had left it behind her in the tram. Maria, remembering how confused the gentleman with the greyish moustache had made her, coloured with shame and vexation and disappointment. At the thought of the failure of her little surprise and of the two and fourpence she had thrown away for nothing she nearly cried outright.

But Joe said it didn't matter and made her sit down by the fire. He was very nice with her. He told her all that went on in his office, repeating for her a smart answer which he had made to the manager. Maria did not understand why Joe laughed so much over the answer he had made but she said that the manager must have been a very overbearing person to deal with. Joe said he wasn't so bad when you knew how to take him, that he was a decent sort so long as you didn't rub him the wrong way. Mrs Donnelly played the piano for the children and they danced and sang. Then the two next-door girls handed round the nuts. Nobody could find the nutcrackers and Joe was nearly getting cross over it and asked how did they expect Maria to crack nuts without a nutcracker. But Maria said she didn't like nuts and that they weren't to bother about her. Then Joe asked would she take a bottle of stout[8] and Mrs Donnelly said there was port wine too in the house if she would prefer that. Maria said she would rather they didn't ask her to take anything: but Joe insisted.

So Maria let him have his way and they sat by the fire talking over old times and Maria thought she would put in a good word for Alphy. But Joe cried that God might strike him stone dead if ever he spoke a word to his brother again and Maria said she was sorry she had mentioned the matter. Mrs Donnelly told her husband it was a great shame for him to speak that way of his own flesh and blood but Joe said that Alphy was no brother of his and there was nearly being a row[9] on the head of it. But

8. An extra-strength ale.   9. Argument.

Joe said he would not lose his temper on account of the night it was and asked his wife to open some more stout. The two next-door girls had arranged some Hallow Eve games[1] and soon everything was merry again. Maria was delighted to see the children so merry and Joe and his wife in such good spirits. The next-door girls put some saucers on the table and then led the children up to the table, blindfold. One got the prayer-book and the other three got the water; and when one of the next-door girls got the ring Mrs Donnelly shook her finger at the blushing girl as much as to say: *O, I know all about it!* They insisted then on blindfolding Maria and leading her up to the table to see what she would get; and, while they were putting on the bandage, Maria laughed and laughed again till the tip of her nose nearly met the tip of her chin.

They led her up to the table amid laughing and joking and she put her hand out in the air as she was told to do. She moved her hand about here and there in the air and descended on one of the saucers. She felt a soft wet substance with her fingers and was surprised that nobody spoke or took off her bandage. There was a pause for a few seconds; and then a great deal of scuffling and whispering. Somebody said something about the garden, and at last Mrs Donnelly said something very cross to one of the next-door girls and told her to throw it out at once: that was no play. Maria understood that it was wrong that time and so she had to do it over again: and this time she got the prayer-book.

After that Mrs Donnelly played Miss McCloud's Reel for the children and Joe made Maria take a glass of wine. Soon they were all quite merry again and Mrs Donnelly said Maria would enter a convent before the year was out because she had got the prayer-book. Maria had never seen Joe so nice to her as he was that night, so full of pleasant talk and reminiscences. She said they were all very good to her.

At last the children grew tired and sleepy and Joe asked Maria would she not sing some little song before she went, one of the old songs. Mrs Donnelly said *Do, please, Maria!* and so Maria had to get up and stand beside the piano. Mrs Donnelly bade the children be quiet and listen to Maria's song. Then she played the prelude and said *Now, Maria!* and Maria, blushing very much, began to sing in a tiny quavering voice. She sang *I Dreamt that I Dwelt,*[2] and when she came to the second verse she sang again:

> I dreamt that I dwelt in marble halls
> > With vassals and serfs at my side
> And of all who assembled within those walls
> > That I was the hope and the pride.
> I had riches too great to count, could boast
> > Of a high ancestral name,
> But I also dreamt, which pleased me most,
> > That you loved me still the same.

But no one tried to show her her mistake;[3] and when she had ended her song Joe was very much moved. He said that there was no time like the long ago and no music

---

1. The primary game that Maria and the girls play is a traditional Irish Halloween game. In its original version, a blindfolded girl would be led to three plates, and would choose one. Choosing the plate with a ring meant that she would soon marry; water meant she would emigrate (probably to America); and soil, or clay, meant she would

soon die. In modern times, a prayer book was substituted for this unsavory third option, suggesting that the girl would enter a convent.
2. Aria from Act 2 of *The Bohemian Girl*.
3. Maria repeats the first verse rather than singing the second.

for him like poor old Balfe, whatever other people might say; and his eyes filled up so much with tears that he could not find what he was looking for and in the end he had to ask his wife to tell him where the corkscrew was.

The Dead

Lily, the caretaker's daughter, was literally run off her feet. Hardly had she brought one gentleman into the little pantry behind the office on the ground floor and helped him off with his overcoat than the wheezy hall-door bell clanged again and she had to scamper along the bare hallway to let in another guest. It was well for her she had not to attend to the ladies also. But Miss Kate and Miss Julia had thought of that and had converted the bathroom upstairs into a ladies' dressing-room. Miss Kate and Miss Julia were there, gossiping and laughing and fussing, walking after each other to the head of the stairs, peering down over the banisters and calling down to Lily to ask her who had come.

It was always a great affair, the Misses Morkan's annual dance. Everybody who knew them came to it, members of the family, old friends of the family, the members of Julia's choir, any of Kate's pupils that were grown up enough and even some of Mary Jane's pupils too. Never once had it fallen flat. For years and years it had gone off in splendid style as long as anyone could remember; ever since Kate and Julia, after the death of their brother Pat, left the house in Stoney Batter[1] and taken Mary Jane, their only niece, to live with them in the dark gaunt house on Usher's Island,[2] the upper part of which they had rented from Mr Fulham, the cornfactor on the ground floor. That was a good thirty years ago if it was a day. Mary Jane, who was then a little girl in short clothes, was now the main prop of the household for she had the organ in Haddington Road.[3] She had been through the Academy[4] and gave a pupils' concert every year in the upper room of the Antient Concert Rooms. Many of her pupils belonged to better-class families on the Kingstown and Dalkey line.[5] Old as they were, her aunts also did their share. Julia, though she was quite grey, was still the leading soprano in Adam and Eve's,[6] and Kate, being too feeble to go about much, gave music lessons to beginners on the old square piano in the back room. Lily, the caretaker's daughter, did housemaid's work for them. Though their life was modest they believed in eating well; the best of everything: diamond-bone sirloins, three-shilling tea and the best bottled stout.[7] But Lily seldom made a mistake in the orders so that she got on well with her three mistresses. They were fussy, that was all. But the only thing they would not stand was back answers.

Of course they had good reason to be fussy on such a night. And then it was long after ten o'clock and yet there was no sign of Gabriel and his wife. Besides they were dreadfully afraid that Freddy Malins might turn up screwed.[8] They would not wish for worlds that any of Mary Jane's pupils should see him under the influence; and when he was like that it was sometimes very hard to manage him. Freddy Malins always came late but they wondered what could be keeping Gabriel: and that was what brought them every two minutes to the banisters to ask Lily had Gabriel or Freddy come.

---

1. A district in northwest Dublin.
2. Two adjoining quays on the south side of the River Liffey.
3. Played the organ in a church on the Haddington Road.
4. Royal Academy of Music.

5. The train line connecting Dublin to the affluent suburbs south of the city.
6. A Dublin church.
7. An extra-strength ale.
8. Drunk.

—O, Mr Conroy, said Lily to Gabriel when she opened the door for him, Miss Kate and Miss Julia thought you were never coming. Good-night, Mrs Conroy.

—I'll engage[9] they did, said Gabriel, but they forget that my wife here takes three mortal hours to dress herself.

He stood on the mat, scraping the snow from his goloshes, while Lily led his wife to the foot of the stairs and called out:

—Miss Kate, here's Mrs Conroy.

Kate and Julia came toddling down the dark stairs at once. Both of them kissed Gabriel's wife, said she must be perished alive and asked was Gabriel with her.

—Here I am as right as the mail, Aunt Kate! Go on up. I'll follow, called out Gabriel from the dark.

He continued scraping his feet vigorously while the three women went upstairs, laughing, to the ladies' dressing-room. A light fringe of snow lay like a cape on the shoulders of his overcoat and like toecaps on the toes of his goloshes; and, as the buttons of his overcoat slipped with a squeaking noise through the snow-stiffened frieze, a cold fragrant air from out-of-doors escaped from crevices and folds.

—Is it snowing again, Mr Conroy? asked Lily.

She had preceded him into the pantry to help him off with his overcoat. Gabriel smiled at the three syllables she had given his surname and glanced at her. She was a slim, growing girl, pale in complexion and with hay-coloured hair. The gas in the pantry made her look still paler. Gabriel had known her when she was a child and used to sit on the lowest step nursing a rag doll.

—Yes, Lily, he answered, and I think we're in for a night of it.

He looked up at the pantry ceiling, which was shaking with the stamping and shuffling of feet on the floor above, listened for a moment to the piano and then glanced at the girl, who was folding his overcoat carefully at the end of a shelf.

—Tell me, Lily, he said in a friendly tone, do you still go to school?

—O no, sir, she answered. I'm done schooling this year and more.

—O, then, said Gabriel gaily, I suppose we'll be going to your wedding one of these fine days with your young man, eh?

The girl glanced back at him over her shoulder and said with great bitterness:

—The men that is now is only all palaver[1] and what they can get out of you.

Gabriel coloured as if he felt he had made a mistake and, without looking at her, kicked off his goloshes and flicked actively with his muffler at his patent-leather shoes.

He was a stout tallish young man. The high colour of his cheeks pushed upwards even to his forehead where it scattered itself in a few formless patches of pale red; and on his hairless face there scintillated restlessly the polished lenses and the bright gilt rims of the glasses which screened his delicate and restless eyes. His glossy black hair was parted in the middle and brushed in a long curve behind his ears where it curled slightly beneath the groove left by his hat.

When he had flicked lustre into his shoes he stood up and pulled his waistcoat down more tightly on his plump body. Then he took a coin rapidly from his pocket.

—O Lily, he said, thrusting it into her hands, it's Christmas-time, isn't it? Just . . . here's a little. . . .

He walked rapidly towards the door.

—O no, sir! cried the girl, following him. Really, sir, I wouldn't take it.

9. Wager.   1. Empty talk.

—Christmas-time! Christmas-time! said Gabriel, almost trotting to the stairs and waving his hand to her in deprecation.

The girl, seeing that he had gained the stairs, called out after him:

—Well, thank you, sir.

[He waited outside the drawing-room door until the waltz should finish, listening to the skirts that swept against it and to the shuffling of feet.] He was still discomposed by the girl's bitter and sudden retort. It had cast a gloom over him which he tried to dispel by arranging his cuffs and the bows of his tie. Then he took from his waistcoat pocket a little paper and glanced at the headings he had made for his speech. He was undecided about the lines from Robert Browning for he feared they would be above the heads of his hearers. Some quotation that they could recognise from Shakespeare or from the Melodies[2] would be better. The indelicate clacking of the men's heels and the shuffling of their soles reminded him that their grade of culture differed from his. He would only make himself ridiculous by quoting poetry to them which they could not understand. They would think that he was airing his superior education. He would fail with them just as he had failed with the girl in the pantry. He had taken up a wrong tone. His whole speech was a mistake from first to last, an utter failure.

Just then his aunts and his wife came out of the ladies' dressing-room. His aunts were two small plainly dressed old women. Aunt Julia was an inch or so taller. Her hair, drawn low over the tops of her ears, was grey; and grey also, with darker shadows, was her large flaccid face. Though she was stout in build and stood erect her slow eyes and parted lips gave her the appearance of a woman who did not know where she was or where she was going. Aunt Kate was more vivacious. Her face, healthier than her sister's, was all puckers and creases, like a shrivelled red apple, and her hair, braided in the same old-fashioned way, had not lost its ripe nut colour.

They both kissed Gabriel frankly. He was their favourite nephew, the son of their dead elder sister, Ellen, who had married T.J. Conroy of the Port and Docks.

—Gretta tells me you're not going to take a cab back to Monkstown[3] to-night, Gabriel, said Aunt Kate.

—No, said Gabriel, turning to his wife, we had quite enough of that last year, hadn't we. Don't you remember, Aunt Kate, what a cold Gretta got out of it? Cab windows rattling all the way, and the east wind blowing in after we passed Merrion. Very jolly it was. Gretta caught a dreadful cold.

Aunt Kate frowned severely and nodded her head at every word.

—Quite right, Gabriel, quite right, she said. You can't be too careful.

[—But as for Gretta there, said Gabriel, she'd walk home in the snow if she were let.] Mrs Conroy laughed.

—Don't mind him, Aunt Kate, she said. He's really an awful bother, what with green shades for Tom's eyes at night and making him do the dumb-bells, and forcing Eva to eat the stirabout.[4] The poor child! And she simply hates the sight of it! . . . O, but you'll never guess what he makes me wear now!

She broke out into a peal of laughter and glanced at her husband, whose admiring and happy eyes had been wandering from her dress to her face and hair. The two aunts laughed heartily too, for Gabriel's solicitude was a standing joke with them.

---

2. Thomas Moore's *Irish Melodies*, a perennial favorite volume of poetry.
3. An elegant suburb south of Dublin.
4. Porridge.

—Goloshes! said Mrs Conroy. That's the latest. Whenever it's wet underfoot I must put on my goloshes. Tonight even he wanted me to put them on, but I wouldn't. The next thing he'll buy me will be a diving suit.

Gabriel laughed nervously and patted his tie reassuringly while Aunt Kate nearly doubled herself, so heartily did she enjoy the joke. The smile soon faded from Aunt Julia's face and her mirthless eyes were directed towards her nephew's face. After a pause she asked:

—And what are goloshes, Gabriel?

—Goloshes, Julia! exclaimed her sister. Goodness me, don't you know what goloshes are? You wear them over your . . . over your boots, Gretta, isn't it?

—Yes, said Mrs Conroy. Guttapercha[5] things. We both have a pair now. Gabriel says everyone wears them on the continent.

—O, on the continent, murmured Aunt Julia, nodding her head slowly.

Gabriel knitted his brows and said, as if he were slightly angered:

—It's nothing very wonderful but Gretta thinks it very funny because she says the word reminds her of Christy Minstrels.[6]

—But tell me, Gabriel, said Aunt Kate, with brisk tact. Of course, you've seen about the room. Gretta was saying . . .

—O, the room is all right, replied Gabriel. I've taken one in the Gresham.[7]

—To be sure, said Aunt Kate, by far the best thing to do. And the children, Gretta, you're not anxious about them?

—O, for one night, said Mrs Conroy. Besides, Bessie will look after them.

—To be sure, said Aunt Kate again. What a comfort it is to have a girl like that, one you can depend on! There's that Lily, I'm sure I don't know what has come over her lately. She's not the girl she was at all.

Gabriel was about to ask his aunt some questions on this point but she broke off suddenly to gaze after her sister who had wandered down the stairs and was craning her neck over the banisters.

—Now, I ask you, she said, almost testily, where is Julia going? Julia! Julia! Where are you going?

Julia, who had gone halfway down one flight, came back and announced blandly:

—Here's Freddy.

At the same moment a clapping of hands and a final flourish of the pianist told that the waltz had ended. The drawing-room door was opened from within and some couples came out. Aunt Kate drew Gabriel aside hurriedly and whispered into his ear:

—Slip down, Gabriel, like a good fellow and see if he's all right, and don't let him up if he's screwed. I'm sure he's screwed. I'm sure he is.

Gabriel went to the stairs and listened over the banisters. He could hear two persons talking in the pantry. Then he recognised Freddy Malins' laugh. He went down the stairs noisily.

—It's such a relief, said Aunt Kate to Mrs Conroy, that Gabriel is here. I always feel easier in my mind when he's here. . . . Julia, there's Miss Daly and Miss Power will take some refreshment. Thanks for your beautiful waltz, Miss Daly. It made lovely time.

5. Rubberized fabric.   7. The most elegant hotel in Dublin.
6. A 19th-century minstrel show.

A tall wizen-faced man, with a stiff grizzled moustache and swarthy skin, who was passing out with his partner said:

—And may we have some refreshment, too, Miss Morkan?

—Julia, said Aunt Kate summarily, and here's Mr Browne and Miss Furlong. Take them in, Julia, with Miss Daly and Miss Power.

—I'm the man for the ladies, said Mr Browne, pursing his lips until his moustache bristled and smiling in all his wrinkles. You know, Miss Morkan, the reason they are so fond of me is—

He did not finish his sentence, but, seeing that Aunt Kate was out of earshot, at once led the three young ladies into the back room. The middle of the room was occupied by two square tables placed end to end, and on these Aunt Julia and the caretaker were straightening and smoothing a large cloth. On the sideboard were arrayed dishes and plates, and glasses and bundles of knives and forks and spoons. The top of the closed square piano served also as a sideboard for viands[8] and sweets. At a smaller sideboard in one corner two young men were standing, drinking hop-bitters.[9]

Mr Browne led his charges thither and invited them all, in jest, to some ladies' punch, hot, strong and sweet. As they said they never took anything strong he opened three bottles of lemonade for them. Then he asked one of the young men to move aside, and, taking hold of the decanter, filled out for himself a goodly measure of whisky. The young men eyed him respectfully while he took a trial sip.

—God help me, he said, smiling, it's the doctor's orders.

His wizened face broke into a broader smile, and the three young ladies laughed in musical echo to his pleasantry, swaying their bodies to and fro, with nervous jerks of their shoulders. The boldest said:

—O, now, Mr Browne, I'm sure the doctor never ordered anything of the kind.

Mr Browne took another sip of his whisky and said, with sidling mimicry:

—Well, you see, I'm like the famous Mrs Cassidy, who is reported to have said: *Now, Mary Grimes, if I don't take it, make me take it, for I feel I want it.*

His hot face had leaned forward a little too confidentially and he had assumed a very low Dublin accent, so that the young ladies, with one instinct, received his speech in silence. Miss Furlong, who was one of Mary Jane's pupils, asked Miss Daly what was the name of the pretty waltz she had played; and Mr Browne, seeing that he was ignored, turned promptly to the two young men who were more appreciative.

A red-faced young woman, dressed in pansy, came into the room, excitedly clapping her hands and crying:

—Quadrilles![1] Quadrilles!

Close on her heels came Aunt Kate, crying:

—Two gentlemen and three ladies, Mary Jane!

—O, here's Mr Bergin and Mr Kerrigan, said Mary Jane. Mr Kerrigan, will you take Miss Power? Miss Furlong, may I get you a partner, Mr Bergin. O, that'll just do now.

—Three ladies, Mary Jane, said Aunt Kate.

The two young gentlemen asked the ladies if they might have the pleasure, and Mary Jane turned to Miss Daly.

—O, Miss Daly, you're really awfully good, after playing for the last two dances, but really we're so short of ladies to-night.

—I don't mind in the least, Miss Morkan.

---

8. Meats.
9. Dry ale.

1. A French square dance.

—But I've a nice partner for you, Mr Bartell D'Arcy, the tenor. I'll get him to sing later on. All Dublin is raving about him.

—Lovely voice, lovely voice! said Aunt Kate.

As the piano had twice begun the prelude to the first figure Mary Jane led her recruits quickly from the room. They had hardly gone when Aunt Julia wandered slowly into the room, looking behind her at something.

—What is the matter, Julia? asked Aunt Kate anxiously. Who is it?

Julia, who was carrying in a column of table-napkins, turned to her sister and said, simply, as if the question had surprised her:

—It's only Freddy, Kate, and Gabriel with him.

In fact right behind her Gabriel could be seen piloting Freddy Malins across the landing. The latter, a young man of about forty, was of Gabriel's size and build, with very round shoulders. His face was fleshy and pallid, touched with colour only at the thick hanging lobes of his ears and at the wide wings of his nose. He had coarse features, a blunt nose, a convex and receding brow, tumid and protruded lips. His heavy-lidded eyes and the disorder of his scanty hair made him look sleepy. He was laughing heartily in a high key at a story which he had been telling Gabriel on the stairs and at the same time rubbing the knuckles of his left fist backwards and forwards into his left eye.

—Good-evening, Freddy, said Aunt Julia.

Freddy Malins bade the Misses Morkan good-evening in what seemed an off-hand fashion by reason of the habitual catch in his voice and then, seeing that Mr Browne was grinning at him from the sideboard, crossed the room on rather shaky legs and began to repeat in an undertone the story he had just told to Gabriel.

—He's not so bad, is he? said Aunt Kate to Gabriel.

Gabriel's brows were dark but he raised them quickly and answered:

—O no, hardly noticeable.

—Now, isn't he a terrible fellow! she said. And his poor mother made him take the pledge on New Year's Eve. But come on, Gabriel, into the drawing-room.

Before leaving the room with Gabriel she signalled to Mr Browne by frowning and shaking her forefinger in warning to and fro. Mr Browne nodded in answer and, when she had gone, said to Freddy Malins:

—Now, then, Teddy, I'm going to fill you out a good glass of lemonade just to buck you up.

Freddy Malins, who was nearing the climax of his story, waved the offer aside impatiently but Mr Browne, having first called Freddy Malins' attention to a disarray in his dress, filled out and handed him a full glass of lemonade. Freddy Malins' left hand accepted the glass mechanically, his right hand being engaged in the mechanical readjustment of his dress. Mr Browne, whose face was once more wrinkling with mirth, poured out for himself a glass of whisky while Freddy Malins exploded, before he had well reached the climax of his story, in a kink of high-pitched bronchitic laughter and, setting down his untasted and overflowing glass, began to rub the knuckles of his left fist backwards and forwards into his left eye, repeating words of his last phrase as well as his fit of laughter would allow him.

Gabriel could not listen while Mary Jane was playing her Academy piece, full of runs and difficult passages, to the hushed drawing-room. He liked music but the piece she was playing had no melody for him and he doubted whether it had any melody for the other listeners, though they had begged Mary Jane to play something. Four young men, who had come from the refreshment-room to stand in the door-way at the sound of the piano, had gone away quietly in couples after a few minutes. The only persons who seemed to follow the music were Mary Jane herself, her hands racing along the key-board or lifted from it at the pauses like those of a priestess in momentary imprecation, and Aunt Kate standing at her elbow to turn the page.

Gabriel's eyes, irritated by the floor, which glittered with beeswax under the heavy chandelier, wandered to the wall above the piano. A picture of the balcony scene in *Romeo and Juliet* hung there and beside it was a picture of the two murdered princes[2] in the Tower which Aunt Julia had worked in red, blue and brown wools when she was a girl. Probably in the school they had gone to as girls that kind of work had been taught, for one year his mother had worked for him as a birthday present a waistcoat of purple tabinet,[3] with little foxes' heads upon it, lined with brown satin and having round mulberry buttons. It was strange that his mother had had no musical talent though Aunt Kate used to call her the brains carrier of the Morkan family. Both she and Julia had always seemed a little proud of their serious and matronly sister. Her photograph stood before the pierglass.[4] She held an open book on her knees and was pointing out something in it to Constantine who, dressed in a man-o'-war suit, lay at her feet. It was she who had chosen the names for her sons for she was very sensible of the dignity of family life. Thanks to her, Constantine was now senior curate in Balbriggan[5] and, thanks to her, Gabriel himself had taken his degree in the Royal University.[6] A shadow passed over his face as he remembered her sullen opposition to his marriage. Some slighting phrases she had used still rankled in his memory; she had once spoken of Gretta as being country cute and that was not true of Gretta at all. It was Gretta who had nursed her during all her last long illness in their house at Monkstown.

He knew that Mary Jane must be near the end of her piece for she was playing again the opening melody with runs of scales after every bar and while he waited for the end the resentment died down in his heart. The piece ended with a trill of octaves in the treble and a final deep octave in the bass. Great applause greeted Mary Jane as, blushing and rolling up her music nervously, she escaped from the room. The most vigorous clapping came from the four young men in the doorway who had gone away to the refreshment-room at the beginning of the piece but had come back when the piano had stopped.

Lancers[7] were arranged. Gabriel found himself partnered with Miss Ivors. She was a frank-mannered talkative young lady, with a freckled face and prominent brown eyes. She did not wear a low-cut bodice and the large brooch which was fixed in the front of her collar bore on it an Irish device.

When they had taken their places she said abruptly:

—I have a crow to pluck with you.

—With me? said Gabriel.

She nodded her head gravely.

—What is it? asked Gabriel, smiling at her solemn manner.

—Who is G. C.? answered Miss Ivors, turning her eyes upon him.

Gabriel coloured and was about to knit his brows, as if he did not understand, when she said bluntly:

2. The young sons of Edward IV, murdered in the Tower of London by order of their uncle, Edward III.
3. Silk and wool fabric.
4. A large high mirror.

5. Seaport 19 miles southeast of Dublin.
6. The Royal University of Ireland, established in 1882.
7. A type of quadrille for 8 or 16 people.

—O, innocent Amy! I have found out that you write for *The Daily Express*.[8] Now, aren't you ashamed of yourself?

—Why should I be ashamed of myself? asked Gabriel, blinking his eyes and trying to smile.

—Well, I'm ashamed of you, said Miss Ivors frankly. To say you'd write for a rag like that. I didn't think you were a West Briton.[9]

A look of perplexity appeared on Gabriel's face. It was true that he wrote a literary column every Wednesday in *The Daily Express*, for which he was paid fifteen shillings. But that did not make him a West Briton surely. The books he received for review were almost more welcome than the paltry cheque. He loved to feel the covers and turn over the pages of newly printed books. Nearly every day when his teaching in the college was ended he used to wander down the quays to the second-hand booksellers, to Hickey's on Bachelor's Walk, to Webb's or Massey's on Aston's Quay, or to O'Clohissey's in the by-street. He did not know how to meet her charge. He wanted to say that literature was above politics. But they were friends of many years' standing and their careers had been parallel, first at the University and then as teachers: he could not risk a grandiose phrase with her. He continued blinking his eyes and trying to smile and murmured lamely that he saw nothing political in writing reviews of books.

When their turn to cross had come he was still perplexed and inattentive. Miss Ivors promptly took his hand in a warm grasp and said in a soft friendly tone:

—Of course, I was only joking. Come, we cross now.

When they were together again she spoke of the University question[1] and Gabriel felt more at ease. A friend of hers had shown her his review of Browning's poems. That was how she had found out the secret: but she liked the review immensely. Then she said suddenly:

—O, Mr Conroy, will you come for an excursion to the Aran Isles[2] this summer? We're going to stay there a whole month. It will be splendid out in the Atlantic. You ought to come. Mr Clancy is coming, and Mr Kilkelly and Kathleen Kearney. It would be splendid for Gretta too if she'd come. She's from Connacht,[3] isn't she?

—Her people are, said Gabriel shortly.

—But you will come, won't you? said Miss Ivors, laying her warm hand eagerly on his arm.

—The fact is, said Gabriel, I have already arranged to go—

—Go where? asked Miss Ivors.

—Well, you know, every year I go for a cycling tour with some fellows and so—

—But where? asked Miss Ivors.

—Well, we usually go to France or Belgium or perhaps Germany, said Gabriel awkwardly.

—And why do you go to France and Belgium, said Miss Ivors, instead of visiting your own land?

—Well, said Gabriel, it's partly to keep in touch with the languages and partly for a change.

—And haven't you your own language to keep in touch with—Irish? asked Miss Ivors.

8. A conservative paper opposed to the struggle for Irish independence.
9. Disparaging term for people wishing to identify Ireland as British.
1. Ireland's oldest and most prestigious university, Trinity College, was open only to Protestants; the "University question" involved, in part, the provision of quality university education to Catholics.
2. Islands off the west coast of Ireland where the people still retained their traditional culture and spoke Irish.
3. A province on the west coast of Ireland.

—Well, said Gabriel, if it comes to that, you know, Irish is not my language.

Their neighbours had turned to listen to the cross-examination. Gabriel glanced right and left nervously and tried to keep his good humour under the ordeal which was making a blush invade his forehead.

—And haven't you your own land to visit, continued Miss Ivors, that you know nothing of, your own people, and your own country?

—O, to tell you the truth, retorted Gabriel suddenly, I'm sick of my own country, sick of it!

—Why? asked Miss Ivors.

Gabriel did not answer for his retort had heated him.

—Why? repeated Miss Ivors.

They had to go visiting together and, as he had not answered her, Miss Ivors said warmly:

—Of course, you've no answer.

Gabriel tried to cover his agitation by taking part in the dance with great energy. He avoided her eyes for he had seen a sour expression on her face. But when they met in the long chain he was surprised to feel his hand firmly pressed. She looked at him from under her brows for a moment quizzically until he smiled. Then, just as the chain was about to start again, she stood on tiptoe and whispered into his ear:

—West Briton!

When the lancers were over Gabriel went away to a remote corner of the room where Freddy Malins' mother was sitting. She was a stout feeble old woman with white hair. Her voice had a catch in it like her son's and she stuttered slightly. She had been told that Freddy had come and that he was nearly all right. Gabriel asked her whether she had had a good crossing. She lived with her married daughter in Glasgow and came to Dublin on a visit once a year. She answered placidly that she had had a beautiful crossing and that the captain had been most attentive to her. She spoke also of the beautiful house her daughter kept in Glasgow, and of all the nice friends they had there. While her tongue rambled on Gabriel tried to banish from his mind all memory of the unpleasant incident with Miss Ivors. Of course the girl or woman, or whatever she was, was an enthusiast but there was a time for all things. Perhaps he ought not to have answered her like that. But she had no right to call him a West Briton before people, even in joke. She had tried to make him ridiculous before people, heckling him and staring at him with her rabbit's eyes.

He saw his wife making her way towards him through the waltzing couples. When she reached him she said into his ear:

—Gabriel, Aunt Kate wants to know won't you carve the goose as usual. Miss Daly will carve the ham and I'll do the pudding.

—All right, said Gabriel.

—She's sending in the younger ones first as soon as this waltz is over so that we'll have the table to ourselves.

—Were you dancing? asked Gabriel.

—Of course I was. Didn't you see me? What words had you with Molly Ivors?

—No words. Why? Did she say so?

—Something like that. I'm trying to get that Mr D'Arcy to sing. He's full of conceit, I think.

—There were no words, said Gabriel moodily, only she wanted me to go for a trip to the west of Ireland and I said I wouldn't.

His wife clasped her hands excitedly and gave a little jump.

—O, do go, Gabriel, she cried. I'd love to see Galway again.

—You can go if you like, said Gabriel coldly.

She looked at him for a moment, then turned to Mrs Malins and said:

—There's a nice husband for you, Mrs Malins.

While she was threading her way back across the room Mrs Malins, without adverting to the interruption, went on to tell Gabriel what beautiful places there were in Scotland and beautiful scenery. Her son-in-law brought them every year to the lakes and they used to go fishing. Her son-in-law was a splendid fisher. One day he caught a fish, a beautiful big big fish, and the man in the hotel boiled it for their dinner.

Gabriel hardly heard what she said. Now that supper was coming near he began to think again about his speech and about the quotation. When he saw Freddy Malins coming across the room to visit his mother Gabriel left the chair free for him and retired into the embrasure of the window. The room had already cleared and from the back room came the clatter of plates and knives. Those who still remained in the drawing-room seemed tired of dancing and were conversing quietly in little groups. Gabriel's warm trembling fingers tapped the cold pane of the window. How cool it must be outside! How pleasant it would be to walk out alone, first along by the river and then through the park! The snow would be lying on the branches of the trees and forming a bright cap on the top of the Wellington Monument.[4] How much more pleasant it would be there than at the supper-table!

He ran over the headings of his speech: Irish hospitality, sad memories, the Three Graces, Paris, the quotation from Browning. He repeated to himself a phrase he had written in his review: *One feels that one is listening to a thought-tormented music.* Miss Ivors had praised the review. Was she sincere? Had she really any life of her own behind all her propagandism? There had never been any ill-feeling between them until that night. It unnerved him to think that she would be at the supper-table, looking up at him while he spoke with her critical quizzing eyes. Perhaps she would not be sorry to see him fail in his speech. An idea came into his mind and gave him courage. He would say, alluding to Aunt Kate and Aunt Julia: *Ladies and Gentlemen, the generation which is now on the wane among us may have had its faults but for my part I think it had certain qualities of hospitality, of humour, of humanity, which the new and very serious and hypereducated generation that is growing up around us seems to me to lack.* Very good: that was one for Miss Ivors. What did he care that his aunts were only two ignorant old women?

A murmur in the room attracted his attention. Mr Browne was advancing from the door, gallantly escorting Aunt Julia, who leaned upon his arm, smiling and hanging her head. An irregular musketry of applause escorted her also as far as the piano and then, as Mary Jane seated herself on the stool, and Aunt Julia, no longer smiling, half turned so as to pitch her voice fairly into the room, gradually ceased. Gabriel recognised the prelude. It was that of an old song of Aunt Julia's—*Arrayed for the Bridal.*[5] Her voice, strong and clear in tone, attacked with great spirit the runs which embellish the air and though she sang very rapidly she did not miss even the smallest of the grace notes. To follow the voice, without looking at the singer's face, was to feel and share the excitement of swift and secure flight. Gabriel applauded

4. A monument to the Duke of Wellington, an Irish-born English military hero, located in Phoenix Park, Dublin's major public park.

5. A popular but challenging song set to music from Bellini's opera *I Puritani* (1835).

loudly with all the others at the close of the song and loud applause was borne in from the invisible supper-table. It sounded so genuine that a little colour struggled into Aunt Julia's face as she bent to replace in the music-stand the old leather-bound song-book that had her initials on the cover. Freddy Malins, who had listened with his head perched sideways to hear her better, was still applauding when everyone else had ceased and talking animatedly to his mother who nodded her head gravely and slowly in acquiescence. At last, when he could clap no more, he stood up suddenly and hurried across the room to Aunt Julia whose hand he seized and held in both his hands, shaking it when words failed him or the catch in his voice proved too much for him.

—I was just telling my mother, he said, I never heard you sing so well, never. No, I never heard your voice so good as it is to-night. Now! Would you believe that now? That's the truth. Upon my word and honour that's the truth. I never heard your voice sound so fresh and so . . . so clear and fresh, never.

Aunt Julia smiled broadly and murmured something about compliments as she released her hand from his grasp. Mr Browne extended his open hand towards her and said to those who were near him in the manner of a showman introducing a prodigy to an audience:

—Miss Julia Morkan, my latest discovery!

He was laughing very heartily at this himself when Freddy Malins turned to him and said:

—Well, Browne, if you're serious you might make a worse discovery. All I can say is I never heard her sing half so well as long as I am coming here. And that's the honest truth.

—Neither did I, said Mr. Browne. I think her voice has greatly improved.

Aunt Julia shrugged her shoulders and said with meek pride:

—Thirty years ago I hadn't a bad voice as voices go.

—I often told Julia, said Aunt Kate emphatically, that she was simply thrown away in that choir. But she never would be said by me.

She turned as if to appeal to the good sense of the others against a refractory child while Aunt Julia gazed in front of her, a vague smile of reminiscence playing on her face.

—No, continued Aunt Kate, she wouldn't be said or led by anyone, slaving there in that choir night and day, night and day. Six o'clock on Christmas morning! And all for what?

—Well, isn't it for the honour of God, Aunt Kate? asked Mary Jane, twisting round on the piano-stool and smiling.

Aunt Kate turned fiercely on her niece and said:

—I know all about the honour of God, Mary Jane, but I think it's not at all honourable for the pope to turn out the women out of the choirs that have slaved there all their lives and put little whipper-snappers of boys over their heads. I suppose it is for the good of the Church if the pope does it. But it's not just, Mary Jane, and it's not right.

She had worked herself into a passion and would have continued in defence of her sister for it was a sore subject with her but Mary Jane, seeing that all the dancers had come back, intervened pacifically:

—Now, Aunt Kate, you're giving scandal to Mr Browne who is of the other persuasion.

Aunt Kate turned to Mr Browne, who was grinning at this allusion to his religion, and said hastily:

—O, I don't question the pope's being right. I'm only a stupid old woman and I wouldn't presume to do such a thing. But there's such a thing as common everyday politeness and gratitude. And if I were in Julia's place I'd tell that Father Healy straight up to his face . . .

—And besides, Aunt Kate, said Mary Jane, we really are all hungry and when we are hungry we are all very quarrelsome.

—And when we are thirsty we are also quarrelsome, added Mr Browne.

—So that we had better go to supper, said Mary Jane, and finish the discussion afterwards.

On the landing outside the drawing-room Gabriel found his wife and Mary Jane trying to persuade Miss Ivors to stay for supper. But Miss Ivors, who had put on her hat and was buttoning her cloak, would not stay. She did not feel in the least hungry and she had already overstayed her time.

—But only for ten minutes, Molly, said Mrs Conroy. That won't delay you.

—To take a pick itself, said Mary Jane, after all your dancing.

—I really couldn't, said Miss Ivors.

—I am afraid you didn't enjoy yourself at all, said Mary Jane hopelessly.

—Ever so much, I assure you, said Miss Ivors, but you really must let me run off now.

—But how can you get home? asked Mrs Conroy.

—O, it's only two steps up the quay.

Gabriel hesitated a moment and said:

—If you will allow me, Miss Ivors, I'll see you home if you really are obliged to go.

But Miss Ivors broke away from them.

—I won't hear of it, she cried. For goodness sake go in to your suppers and don't mind me. I'm quite well able to take care of myself.

—Well, you're the comical girl, Molly, said Mrs Conroy frankly.

—*Beannacht libh*,[6] cried Miss Ivors, with a laugh, as she ran down the staircase.

Mary Jane gazed after her, a moody puzzled expression on her face, while Mrs Conroy leaned over the banisters to listen for the hall-door. Gabriel asked himself was he the cause of her abrupt departure. But she did not seem to be in ill humour: she had gone away laughing. He stared blankly down the staircase.

At that moment Aunt Kate came toddling out of the supper-room, almost wringing her hands in despair.

—Where is Gabriel? she cried. Where on earth is Gabriel? There's everyone waiting in there, stage to let, and nobody to carve the goose!

—Here I am, Aunt Kate! cried Gabriel, with sudden animation, ready to carve a flock of geese, if necessary.

A fat brown goose lay at one end of the table and at the other end, on a bed of creased paper strewn with sprigs of parsley, lay a great ham, stripped of its outer skin and peppered over with crust crumbs, a neat paper frill round its shin and beside this was a round of spiced beef. Between these rival ends ran parallel lines of side-dishes: two little minsters of jelly, red and yellow; a shallow dish full of blocks of blancmange and red jam, a large green leaf-shaped dish with a stalk-shaped handle, on which lay bunches of purple raisins and peeled almonds, a companion dish on which lay a solid rectangle of Smyrna figs, a dish of custard topped with grated nutmeg, a small bowl full of chocolates and sweets wrapped in gold and silver papers and a glass vase in

6. Farewell (Irish).

which stood some tall celery stalks. In the centre of the table there stood, as sentries to a fruit-stand which upheld a pyramid of oranges and American apples, two squat old-fashioned decanters of cut glass, one containing port and the other dark sherry. On the closed square piano a pudding in a huge yellow dish lay in waiting and behind it were three squads of bottles of stout and ale and minerals, drawn up according to the colours of their uniforms, the first two black, with brown and red labels, the third and smallest squad white, with transverse green sashes.

Gabriel took his seat boldly at the head of the table and, having looked to the edge of the carver, plunged his fork firmly into the goose. He felt quite at ease now for he was an expert carver and liked nothing better than to find himself at the head of a well-laden table.

—Miss Furlong, what shall I send you? he asked. A wing or a slice of the breast?

—Just a small slice of the breast.

—Miss Higgins, what for you?

—O, anything at all, Mr Conroy.

While Gabriel and Miss Daly exchanged plates of goose and plates of ham and spiced beef Lily went from guest to guest with a dish of hot floury potatoes wrapped in a white napkin. This was Mary Jane's idea and she had also suggested apple sauce for the goose but Aunt Kate had said that plain roast goose without apple sauce had always been good enough for her and she hoped she might never eat worse. Mary Jane waited on her pupils and saw that they got the best slices and Aunt Kate and Aunt Julia opened and carried across from the piano bottles of stout and ale for the gentlemen and bottles of minerals for the ladies. There was a great deal of confusion and laughter and noise, the noise of orders and counter-orders, of knives and forks, of corks and glass-stoppers. Gabriel began to carve second helpings as soon as he had finished the first round without serving himself. Everyone protested loudly so that he compromised by taking a long draught of stout for he had found the carving hot work. Mary Jane settled down quietly to her supper but Aunt Kate and Aunt Julia were still toddling round the table, walking on each other's heels, getting in each other's way and giving each other unheeded orders. Mr Browne begged of them to sit down and eat their suppers and so did Gabriel but they said there was time enough so that, at last, Freddy Malins stood up and, capturing Aunt Kate, plumped her down on her chair amid general laughter.

When everyone had been well served Gabriel said, smiling:

—Now, if anyone wants a little more of what vulgar people call stuffing let him or her speak.

A chorus of voices invited him to begin his own supper and Lily came forward with three potatoes which she had reserved for him.

—Very well, said Gabriel amiably, as he took another preparatory draught, kindly forget my existence, ladies and gentlemen, for a few minutes.

He set to his supper and took no part in the conversation with which the table covered Lily's removal of the plates. The subject of talk was the opera company which was then at the Theatre Royal. Mr Bartell D'Arcy, the tenor, a dark-complexioned young man with a smart moustache, praised very highly the leading contralto of the company but Miss Furlong thought she had a rather vulgar style of production. Freddy Malins said there was a negro chieftain singing in the second part of the Gaiety pantomime who had one of the finest tenor voices he had ever heard.

—Have you heard him? he asked Mr Bartell D'Arcy across the table.

—No, answered Mr Bartell D'Arcy carelessly.

—Because, Freddy Malins explained, now I'd be curious to hear your opinion of him. I think he has a grand voice.

—It takes Teddy to find out the really good things, said Mr Browne familiarly to the table.

—And why couldn't he have a voice too? asked Freddy Malins sharply. Is it because he's only a black?

Nobody answered this question and Mary Jane led the table back to the legitimate opera. One of her pupils had given her a pass for *Mignon.* Of course it was very fine, she said, but it made her think of poor Georgina Burns. Mr Browne could go back farther still, to the old Italian companies that used to come to Dublin—Tietjens, Ilma de Murzka, Campanini, the great Trebelli, Giuglini, Ravelli, Aramburo.[7] Those were the days, he said, when there was something like singing to be heard in Dublin. He told too of how the top gallery of the old Royal used to be packed night after night, of how one night an Italian tenor had sung five encores to *Let Me Like a Soldier Fall,* introducing a high C every time, and of how the gallery boys would sometimes in their enthusiasm unyoke the horses from the carriage of some great *prima donna* and pull her themselves through the streets to her hotel. Why did they never play the grand old operas now, he asked, *Dinorah, Lucrezia Borgia*? Because they could not get the voices to sing them: that was why.

—O, well, said Mr Bartell D'Arcy, I presume there are as good singers to-day as there were then.

—Where are they? asked Mr Browne defiantly.

—In London, Paris, Milan, said Mr Bartell D'Arcy warmly. I suppose Caruso,[8] for example, is quite as good, if not better than any of the men you have mentioned.

—Maybe so, said Mr Browne. But I may tell you I doubt it strongly.

—O, I'd give anything to hear Caruso sing, said Mary Jane.

—For me, said Aunt Kate, who had been picking a bone, there was only one tenor. To please me, I mean. But I suppose none of you ever heard of him.

—Who was he, Miss Morkan? asked Mr Bartell D'Arcy politely.

—His name, said Aunt Kate, was Parkinson. I heard him when he was in his prime and I think he had then the purest tenor voice that was ever put into a man's throat.

—Strange, said Mr Bartell D'Arcy. I never even heard of him.

—Yes, yes, Miss Morkan is right, said Mr Browne. I remember hearing of old Parkinson but he's too far back for me.

—A beautiful pure sweet mellow English tenor, said Aunt Kate with enthusiasm.

Gabriel having finished, the huge pudding was transferred to the table. The clatter of forks and spoons began again. Gabriel's wife served out spoonfuls of the pudding and passed the plates down the table. Midway down they were held up by Mary Jane, who replenished them with raspberry or orange jelly or with blancmange and jam. The pudding was of Aunt Julia's making and she received praises for it from all quarters. She herself said that it was not quite brown enough.

—Well, I hope, Miss Morkan, said Mr Browne, that I'm brown enough for you because, you know, I'm all brown.

All the gentlemen, except Gabriel, ate some of the pudding out of compliment to Aunt Julia. As Gabriel never ate sweets the celery had been left for him. Freddy

7. Famous 19th-century operatic singers. 8. Enrico Caruso (1874–1921), a famous tenor.

Malins also took a stalk of celery and ate it with his pudding. He had been told that celery was a capital thing for the blood and he was just then under doctor's care. Mrs Malins, who had been silent all through the supper, said that her son was going down to Mount Melleray[9] in a week or so. The table then spoke to Mount Melleray, how bracing the air was down there, how hospitable the monks were and how they never asked for a penny-piece from their guests.

—And do you mean to say, asked Mr Browne incredulously, that a chap can go down there and put up there as if it were a hotel and live on the fat of the land and then come away without paying a farthing?

—O, most people give some donation to the monastery when they leave, said Mary Jane.

—I wish we had an institution like that in our Church, said Mr Browne candidly.

He was astonished to hear that the monks never spoke, got up at two in the morning and slept in their coffins. He asked what they did it for.

—That's the rule of the order, said Aunt Kate firmly.

—Yes, but why? asked Mr Browne.

Aunt Kate repeated that it was the rule, that was all. Mr Browne still seemed not to understand. Freddy Malins explained to him, as best he could, that the monks were trying to make up for the sins committed by all the sinners in the outside world. The explanation was not very clear for Mr Browne grinned and said:

—I like that idea very much but wouldn't a comfortable spring bed do them as well as a coffin?

—The coffin, said Mary Jane, is to remind them of their last end.

As the subject had grown lugubrious it was buried in a silence of the table during which Mrs Malins could be heard saying to her neighbour in an indistinct undertone:

—They are very good men, the monks, very pious men.

The raisins and almonds and figs and apples and oranges and chocolates and sweets were now passed about the table and Aunt Julia invited all the guests to have either port or sherry. At first Mr Bartell D'Arcy refused to take either but one of his neighbours nudged him and whispered something to him upon which he allowed his glass to be filled. Gradually as the last glasses were being filled the conversation ceased. A pause followed, broken only by the noise of the wine and by unsettlings of chairs. The Misses Morkan, all three, looked down at the tablecloth. Someone coughed once or twice and then a few gentlemen patted the table gently as a signal for silence. The silence came and Gabriel pushed back his chair and stood up.

The patting at once grew louder in encouragement and then ceased altogether. Gabriel leaned his ten trembling fingers on the tablecloth and smiled nervously at the company. Meeting a row of upturned faces he raised his eyes to the chandelier. The piano was playing a waltz tune and he could hear the skirts sweeping against the drawing-room door. People, perhaps, were standing in the snow on the quay outside, gazing up at the lighted windows and listening to the waltz music. The air was pure there. In the distance lay the park where the trees were weighted with snow. The Wellington Monument wore a gleaming cap of snow that flashed westward over the white field of Fifteen Acres.[1]

He began:

—Ladies and Gentlemen.

---

9. Site of a Trappist monastery in the south of Ireland.   1. A section of Phoenix Park.

—It has fallen to my lot this evening, as in years past, to perform a very pleasing task but a task for which I am afraid my poor powers as a speaker are all too inadequate.

—No, no! said Mr Browne.

—But, however that may be, I can only ask you tonight to take the will for the deed and to lend me your attention for a few moments while I endeavour to express to you in words what my feelings are on this occasion.

—Ladies and Gentlemen. It is not the first time that we have gathered together under this hospitable roof, around this hospitable board. It is not the first time that we have been the recipients—or perhaps, I had better say, the victims—of the hospitality of certain good ladies.

He made a circle in the air with his arm and paused. Everyone laughed or smiled at Aunt Kate and Aunt Julia and Mary Jane who all turned crimson with pleasure. Gabriel went on more boldly:

—I feel more strongly with every recurring year that our country has no tradition which does it so much honour and which it should guard so jealously as that of its hospitality. It is a tradition that is unique as far as my experience goes (and I have visited not a few places abroad) among the modern nations. Some would say, perhaps, that with us it is rather a failing than anything to be boasted of. But granted even that, it is, to my mind, a princely failing, and one that I trust will long be cultivated among us. Of one thing, at least, I am sure. As long as this one roof shelters the good ladies aforesaid—and I wish from my heart it may do so for many and many a long year to come—the tradition of genuine warm-hearted courteous Irish hospitality, which our forefathers have handed down to us and which we in turn must hand down to our descendants, is still alive among us.

A hearty murmur of assent ran round the table. It shot through Gabriel's mind that Miss Ivors was not there and that she had gone away discourteously: and he said with confidence in himself:

—Ladies and Gentlemen.

—A new generation is growing up in our midst, a generation actuated by new ideas and new principles. It is serious and enthusiastic for these new ideas and its enthusiasm, even when it is misdirected, is, I believe, in the main sincere. But we are living in a sceptical and, if I may use the phrase, a thought-tormented age: and sometimes I fear that this new generation, educated or hypereducated as it is, will lack those qualities of humanity, of hospitality, of kindly humour which belonged to an older day. Listening to-night to the names of all those great singers of the past it seemed to me, I must confess, that we were living in a less spacious age. Those days might, without exaggeration, be called spacious days: and if they are gone beyond recall let us hope, at least, that in gatherings such as this we shall still speak of them with pride and affection, still cherish in our hearts the memory of those dead and gone great ones whose fame the world will not willingly let die.

—Hear, hear! said Mr Browne loudly.

—But yet, continued Gabriel, his voice falling into a softer inflection, there are always in gatherings such as this sadder thoughts that will recur to our minds: thoughts of the past, of youth, of changes, of absent faces that we miss here to-night. Our path through life is strewn with many such sad memories: and were we to brood upon them always we could not find the heart to go on bravely with our work among the living. We have all of us living duties and living affections which claim, and rightly claim, our strenuous endeavours.

—Therefore, I will not linger on the past. I will not let any gloomy moralising intrude upon us here to-night. Here we are gathered together for a brief moment from the bustle and rush of our everyday routine. We are met here as friends, in the spirit of good-fellowship, as colleagues, also to a certain extent, in the true spirit of *camaraderie*, and as the guests of—what shall I call them?—the Three Graces[2] of the Dublin musical world.

The table burst into applause and laughter at this sally. Aunt Julia vainly asked each of her neighbors in turn to tell her what Gabriel had said.

—He says we are the Three Graces, Aunt Julia, said Mary Jane.

Aunt Julia did not understand but she looked up, smiling, at Gabriel, who continued in the same vein:

—Ladies and Gentlemen.

—I will not attempt to play to-night the part that Paris[3] played on another occasion. I will not attempt to choose between them. The task would be an invidious one and one beyond my poor powers. For when I view them in turn, whether it be our chief hostess herself, whose good heart, whose too good heart, has become a byword with all who know her, or her sister, who seems to be gifted with perennial youth and whose singing must have been a surprise and a revelation to us all to-night, or, last but not least, when I consider our youngest hostess, talented, cheerful, hard-working and the best of nieces, I confess, Ladies and Gentlemen, that I do not know to which of them I should award the prize.

Gabriel glanced down at his aunts and, seeing the large smile on Aunt Julia's face and the tears which had risen to Aunt Kate's eyes, hastened to his close. He raised his glass of port gallantly, while every member of the company fingered a glass expectantly, and said loudly:

—Let us toast them all three together. Let us drink to their health, wealth, long life, happiness and prosperity and may they long continue to hold the proud and self-won position which they hold in their profession and the position of honour and affection which they hold in our hearts.

All the guests stood up, glass in hand, and, turning towards the three seated ladies, sang in unison, with Mr Browne as leader:

> *For they are jolly gay fellows,*
> *For they are jolly gay fellows,*
> *For they are jolly gay fellows,*
> *Which nobody can deny.*

Aunt Kate was making frank use of her handkerchief and even Aunt Julia seemed moved. Freddy Malins beat time with his pudding-fork and the singers turned towards one another, as if in melodious conference, while they sang, with emphasis:

> *Unless he tells a lie,*
> *Unless he tells a lie.*

Then, turning once more towards their hostesses, they sang:

> *For they are jolly gay fellows,*
> *For they are jolly gay fellows,*
> *For they are jolly gay fellows,*
> *Which nobody can deny.*

---

2. Companions to the Muses in Greek mythology.
3. Paris was the judge of a divine beauty contest in which

Hera, Athena, and Aphrodite competed; his selection of Aphrodite was, indirectly, the cause of the Trojan War.

The acclamation which followed was taken up beyond the door of the supper-room by many of the other guests and renewed time after time, Freddy Malins acting as officer with his fork on high.

The piercing morning air came into the hall where they were standing so that Aunt Kate said:

—Close the door, somebody. Mrs Malins will get her death of cold.

—Browne is out there, Aunt Kate, said Mary Jane.

—Browne is everywhere, said Aunt Kate, lowering her voice.

Mary Jane laughed at her tone.

—Really, she said archly, he is very attentive.

—He has been laid on here like the gas, said Aunt Kate in the same tone, all during the Christmas.

She laughed herself this time good-humouredly and then added quickly:

—But tell him to come in, Mary Jane, and close the door. I hope to goodness he didn't hear me.

At that moment the hall-door was opened and Mr Browne came in from the doorstep, laughing as if his heart would break. He was dressed in a long green over-coat with mock astrakhan cuffs and collar and wore on his head an oval fur cap. He pointed down the snow-covered quay from where the sound of shrill prolonged whistling was borne in.

—Teddy will have all the cabs in Dublin out, he said.

Gabriel advanced from the little pantry behind the office, struggling into his overcoat and looking round the hall, said:

—Gretta not down yet?

—She's getting on her things, Gabriel, said Aunt Kate.

—Who's playing up there? asked Gabriel.

—Nobody. They're all gone.

—O no, Aunt Kate, said Mary Jane. Bartell D'Arcy and Miss O'Callaghan aren't gone yet.

—Someone is strumming at the piano, anyhow, said Gabriel.

Mary Jane glanced at Gabriel and Mr Browne and said with a shiver:

—It makes me feel cold to look at you two gentlemen muffled up like that. I wouldn't like to face your journey home at this hour.

—I'd like nothing better this minute, said Mr Browne stoutly, than a rattling fine walk in the country or a fast drive with a good spanking goer between the shafts.

—We used to have a very good horse and trap at home, said Aunt Julia sadly.

—The never-to-be-forgotten Johnny, said Mary Jane, laughing.

Aunt Kate and Gabriel laughed too.

—Why, what was wonderful about Johnny? asked Mr Browne.

—The late lamented Patrick Morkan, our grandfather, that is, explained Gabriel, commonly known in his later years as the old gentleman, was a glue-boiler.

—O, now, Gabriel, said Aunt Kate, laughing, he had a starch mill.

—Well, glue or starch, said Gabriel, the old gentleman had a horse by the name of Johnny. And Johnny used to work in the old gentleman's mill, walking round and round in order to drive the mill. That was all very well; but now comes the tragic part about Johnny. One fine day the old gentleman thought he'd like to drive out with the quality to a military review in the park.

—The Lord have mercy on his soul, said Aunt Kate compassionately.

—Amen, said Gabriel. So the old gentleman, as I said, harnessed Johnny and put on his very best tall hat and his very best stock collar and drove out in grand style from his ancestral mansion somewhere near Back Lane, I think.

Everyone laughed, even Mrs Malins, at Gabriel's manner and Aunt Kate said:

—O now, Gabriel, he didn't live in Back Lane, really. Only the mill was there.

—Out from the mansion of his forefathers, continued Gabriel, he drove with Johnny. And everything went on beautifully until Johnny came in sight of King Billy's statue:[4] and whether he fell in love with the horse King Billy sits on or whether he thought he was back again in the mill, anyhow he began to walk round the statue.

Gabriel paced in a circle round the hall in his goloshes amid the laughter of the others.

—Round and round he went, said Gabriel, and the old gentleman, who was a very pompous old gentleman, was highly indignant. Go on, sir! What do you mean, sir? Johnny! Johnny! Most extraordinary conduct! Can't understand the horse!

The peals of laughter which followed Gabriel's imitation of the incident were interrupted by a resounding knock at the hall-door. Mary Jane ran to open it and let in Freddy Malins. Freddy Malins, with his hat well back on his head and his shoulders humped with cold, was puffing and steaming after his exertions.

—I could only get one cab, he said.

—O, we'll find another along the quay, said Gabriel.

—Yes, said Aunt Kate. Better not keep Mrs Malins standing in the draught.

Mrs Malins was helped down the front steps by her son and Mr Browne and, after many manoeuvres, hoisted into the cab. Freddy Malins clambered in after her and spent a long time settling her on the seat, Mr Browne helping him with advice. At last she was settled comfortably and Freddy Malins invited Mr Browne into the cab. There was a good deal of confused talk, and then Mr Browne got into the cab. The cabman settled his rug over his knees, and bent down for the address. The confusion grew greater and the cabman was directed differently by Freddy Malins and Mr Browne, each of whom had his head out through a window of the cab. The difficulty was to know where to drop Mr Browne along the route and Aunt Kate, Aunt Julia and Mary Jane helped the discussion from the doorstep with cross-directions and contradictions and abundance of laughter. As for Freddy Malins he was speechless with laughter. He popped his head in and out of the window every moment, to the great danger of his hat, and told his mother how the discussion was progressing till at last Mr Browne shouted to the bewildered cabman above the din of everybody's laughter:

—Do you know Trinity College?

—Yes, sir, said the cabman.

—Well, drive bang up against Trinity College gates, said Mr Browne, and then we'll tell you where to go. You understand now?

—Yes, sir, said the cabman.

—Make like a bird for Trinity College.

—Right, sir, cried the cabman.

The horse was whipped up and the cab rattled off along the quay amid a chorus of laughter and adieus.

---

4. Statue of William of Orange, who defeated the Irish Catholic forces in the Battle of the Boyne in 1690, which stood in College Green in front of Trinity College in the heart of Dublin. It was seen as a symbol of British imperial oppression.

Gabriel had not gone to the door with the others. He was in a dark part of the hall gazing up the staircase, a woman was standing near the top of the first flight, in the shadow also. He could not see her face but he could see the terracotta and salmonpink panels of her skirt which the shadow made appear black and white. It was his wife. She was leaning on the banisters, listening to something. Gabriel was surprised at her stillness and strained his ear to listen also. But he could hear little save the noise of laughter and dispute on the front steps, a few chords struck on the piano and a few notes of a man's voice singing.

He stood still in the gloom of the hall, trying to catch the air that the voice was singing and gazing up at his wife. There was grace and mystery in her attitude as if she were a symbol of something. He asked himself what is a woman standing on the stairs in the shadow, listening to distant music, a symbol of. If he were a painter he would paint her in that attitude. Her blue felt hat would show off the bronze of her hair against the darkness and the dark panels of her skirt would show off the light ones. *Distant Music* he would call the picture if he were a painter.

The hall-door was closed; and Aunt Kate, Aunt Julia and Mary Jane came down the hall, still laughing.

—Well, isn't Freddy terrible? said Mary Jane. He's really terrible.

Gabriel said nothing but pointed up the stairs towards where his wife was standing. Now that the hall-door was closed the voice and the piano could be heard more clearly. Gabriel held up his hand for them to be silent. The song seemed to be in the old Irish tonality and the singer seemed uncertain both of his words and of his voice. The voice, made plaintive by distance and by the singer's hoarseness, faintly illuminated the cadence of the air with words expressing grief:

> O, the rain falls on my heavy locks
> And the dew wets my skin,
> My babe lies cold . . .

—O, exclaimed Mary Jane. It's Bartell D'Arcy singing and he wouldn't sing all the night. O, I'll get him to sing a song before he goes.

—O do, Mary Jane, said Aunt Kate.

Mary Jane brushed past the others and ran to the staircase but before she reached it the singing stopped and the piano was closed abruptly.

—O, what a pity! she cried. Is he coming down, Gretta?

Gabriel heard his wife answer yes and saw her come down towards them. A few steps behind her were Mr Bartell D'Arcy and Miss O'Callaghan.

—O, Mr D'Arcy, cried Mary Jane, it's downright mean of you to break off like that when we were all in raptures listening to you.

—I have been at him all the evening, said Miss O'Callaghan, and Mrs Conroy too and he told us he had a dreadful cold and couldn't sing.

—O, Mr D'Arcy, said Aunt Kate, now that was a great fib to tell.

—Can't you see that I'm as hoarse as a crow? said Mr D'Arcy roughly.

He went into the pantry hastily and put on his overcoat. The others, taken aback by his rude speech, could find nothing to say. Aunt Kate wrinkled her brows and made signs to the others to drop the subject. Mr D'Arcy stood swathing his neck carefully and frowning.

—It's the weather, said Aunt Julia, after a pause.

—Yes, everybody has colds, said Aunt Kate readily, everybody.

—They say, said Mary Jane, we haven't had snow like it for thirty years; and I read this morning in the newspapers that the snow is general all over Ireland.

—I love the look of snow, said Aunt Julia sadly.

—So do I, said Miss O'Callaghan. I think Christmas is never really Christmas unless we have the snow on the ground.

—But poor Mr D'Arcy doesn't like the snow, said Aunt Kate, smiling.

Mr D'Arcy came from the pantry, full swathed and buttoned, and in a repentant tone told them the history of his cold. Everyone gave him advice and said it was a great pity and urged him to be very careful of his throat in the night air. Gabriel watched his wife who did not join in the conversation. She was standing right under the dusty fanlight and the flame of the gas lit up the rich bronze of her hair which he had seen her drying at the fire a few days before. She was in the same attitude and seemed unaware of the talk about her. At last she turned towards them and Gabriel saw that there was colour on her cheeks and that her eyes were shining. A sudden tide of joy went leaping out of his heart.

—Mr D'Arcy, she said, what is the name of that song you were singing?

—It's called *The Lass of Aughrim*, said Mr D'Arcy, but I couldn't remember it properly. Why? Do you know it?

—*The Lass of Aughrim*, she repeated. I couldn't think of the name.

—It's a very nice air, said Mary Jane. I'm sorry you were not in voice to-night.

—Now, Mary Jane, said Aunt Kate, don't annoy Mr D'Arcy. I won't have him annoyed.

Seeing that all were ready to start she shepherded them to the door where good-night was said:

—Well, good-night, Aunt Kate, and thanks for the pleasant evening.

—Good-night, Gabriel. Good-night, Gretta!

—Good-night, Aunt Kate, and thanks ever so much. Good-night, Aunt Julia.

—O, good-night, Gretta, I didn't see you.

—Good-night, Mr D'Arcy. Good-night, Miss O'Callaghan.

—Good-night, Miss Morkan.

—Good-night, again.

—Good-night, all. Safe home.

—Good-night. Good-night.

The morning was still dark. A dull yellow light brooded over the houses and the river; and the sky seemed to be descending. It was slushy underfoot; and only streaks and patches of snow lay on the roofs, on the parapets of the quay and on the area railings. The lamps were still burning redly in the murky air and, across the river, the palace of the Four Courts[5] stood out menacingly against the heavy sky.

She was walking on before him with Mr Bartell D'Arcy, her shoes in a brown parcel tucked under one arm and her hands holding her skirt up from the slush. She had no longer any grace of attitude but Gabriel's eyes were still bright with happiness. The blood went bounding along his veins; and the thoughts went rioting through his brain, proud, joyful, tender, valorous.

She was walking on before him so lightly and so erect that he longed to run after her noiselessly, catch her by the shoulders and say something foolish and affectionate into her ear. She seemed to him so frail that he longed to defend her against something and then to be alone with her. Moments of their secret life together burst like stars upon his memory. A heliotrope envelope was lying beside his breakfast-cup and he was caressing it with his hand. Birds were twittering in the ivy and the sunny web of the

5. The Irish law courts.

curtain was shimmering along the floor: he could not eat for happiness. They were standing on the crowded platform and he was placing a ticket inside the warm palm of her glove. He was standing with her in the cold, looking in through a grated window at a man making bottles in a roaring furnace. It was very cold. Her face, fragrant in the cold air, was quite close to his; and suddenly she called out to the man at the furnace:

—Is the fire hot, sir?

But the man could not hear her with the noise of the furnace. It was just as well. He might have answered rudely.

(A wave of yet more tender joy escaped from his heart and went coursing in warm flood along his arteries. Like the tender fires of stars moments of their life together, that no one knew of or would ever know of, broke upon and illumined his memory. He longed to recall to her those moments, to make her forget the years of their dull existence together and remember only their moments of ecstasy. For the years, he felt, had not quenched his soul or hers. Their children, his writing, her household cares had not quenched all their souls' tender fire. In one letter that he had written to her then he had said: *Why is it that words like these seem to me so dull and cold? Is it because there is no word tender enough to be your name?*

Like distant music these words that he had written years before were borne towards him from the past. He longed to be alone with her.) When the others had gone away, when he and she were in their room in the hotel, then they would be alone together. He would call her softly:

—Gretta!

Perhaps she would not hear at once: she would be undressing. Then something in his voice would strike her. She would turn and look at him. . . .

At the corner of Winetavern Street they met a cab. He was glad of its rattling noise as it saved him from conversation. She was looking out of the window and seemed tired. The others spoke only a few words, pointing out some building or street. The horse galloped along wearily under the murky morning sky, dragging his old rattling box after his heels, and Gabriel was again in a cab with her, galloping to catch the boat, galloping to their honeymoon.

As the cab drove across O'Connell Bridge Miss O'Callaghan said:

—They say you never cross O'Connell Bridge without seeing a white horse.

—I see a white man this time, said Gabriel.

—Where? asked Mr Bartell D'Arcy.

Gabriel pointed to the statue, on which lay patches of snow. Then he nodded familiarly to it and waved his hand.

—Good-night, Dan,[6] he said gaily.

When the cab drew up before the hotel Gabriel jumped out and, in spite of Mr Bartell D'Arcy's protest, paid the driver. He gave the man a shilling over his fare. The man saluted and said:

—A prosperous New Year to you, sir.

—The same to you, said Gabriel cordially.

She leaned for a moment on his arm in getting out of the cab and while standing at the curbstone, bidding the others good-night. She leaned lightly on his arm, as lightly as when she had danced with him a few hours before. He had felt proud

---

6. A statue of Daniel O'Connell, 19th-century nationalist leader, stands at the south end of Sackville Street (now called O'Connell Street).

and happy then, happy that she was his, proud of her grace and wifely carriage[But now, after the kindling again of so many memories, the first touch of her body, musical and strange and perfumed, sent through him a keen pang of lust.]Under cover of her silence he pressed her arm closely to his side; and, as they stood at the hotel door, he felt that they had escaped from their lives and duties, escaped from home and friends and run away together with wild and radiant hearts to a new adventure.

An old man was dozing in a great hooded chair in the hall. He lit a candle in the office and went before them to the stairs. They followed him in silence, their feet falling in soft thuds on the thickly carpeted stairs. She mounted the stairs behind the porter, her head bowed in the ascent, her frail shoulders curved as with a burden, her skirt girt tightly about her. He could have flung his arms about her hips and held her still for his arms were trembling with desire to seize her and only the stress of his nails against the palms of his hands held the wild impulse of his body in check. The porter halted on the stairs to settle his guttering candle. They halted too on the steps below him. In the silence Gabriel could hear the falling of the molten wax into the tray and the thumping of his own heart against his ribs.

The porter led them along a corridor and opened a door. Then he set his unstable candle down on a toilet-table and asked at what hour they were to be called in the morning.

—Eight, said Gabriel.

The porter pointed to the tap of the electric-light and began a muttered apology but Gabriel cut him short.

—We don't want any light. We have light enough from the street. And I say, he added, pointing to the candle, you might remove that handsome article, like a good man.

The porter took up his candle again, but slowly for he was surprised by such a novel idea. Then he mumbled good-night and went out. Gabriel shot the lock to.

A ghostly light from the street lamp lay in a long shaft from one window to the door. Gabriel threw his overcoat and hat on a couch and crossed the room towards the window. He looked down into the street in order that his emotion might calm a little. Then he turned and leaned against a chest of drawers with his back to the light. She had taken off her hat and cloak and was standing before a large swinging mirror, unhooking her waist. Gabriel paused for a few moments, watching her, and then said:

—Gretta!

She turned away from the mirror slowly and walked along the shaft of light towards him. Her face looked so serious and weary that the words would not pass Gabriel's lips. No, it was not the moment yet.

—You looked tired, he said.

—I am a little, she answered.

—You don't feel ill or weak?

—No, tired: that's all.

She went on to the window and stood there, looking out. Gabriel waited again and then, fearing that diffidence was about to conquer him, he said abruptly:

—By the way, Gretta!

—What is it?

—You know that poor fellow Malins? he said quickly.

—Yes. What about him?

—Well, poor fellow, he's a decent sort of chap after all, continued Gabriel in a false voice. He gave me back that sovereign I lent him and I didn't expect it really. It's a pity he wouldn't keep away from that Browne, because he's not a bad fellow at heart.

He was trembling now with annoyance. Why did she seem so abstracted? He did not know how he could begin. Was she annoyed, too, about something? If she would only turn to him or come to him of her own accord! To take her as she was would be brutal. No, he must see some ardour in her eyes first. He longed to be master of her strange mood.

—When did you lend him the pound? she asked, after a pause.

Gabriel strove to restrain himself from breaking out into brutal language about the sottish Malins and his pound. He longed to cry to her from his soul, to crush her body against his, to overmaster her. But he said:

—O, at Christmas, when he opened that little Christmas-card shop in Henry Street.

He was in such a fever of rage and desire that he did not hear her come from the window. She stood before him for an instant, looking at him strangely. Then, suddenly raising herself on tiptoe and resting her hands lightly on his shoulders, she kissed him.

—You are a very generous person, Gabriel, she said.

Gabriel, trembling with delight at her sudden kiss and at the quaintness of her phrase, put his hands on her hair and began smoothing it back, scarcely touching it with his fingers. The washing had made it fine and brilliant. His heart was brimming over with happiness. Just when he was wishing for it she had come to him of her own accord. Perhaps her thoughts had been running with his. Perhaps she had felt the impetuous desire that was in him and then the yielding mood had come upon her. Now that she had fallen to him so easily he wondered why he had been so diffident.

He stood, holding her head between his hands. Then, slipping one arm swiftly about her body and drawing her towards him, he said softly:

—Gretta dear, what are you thinking about?

She did not answer nor yield wholly to his arm. He said again, softly:

—Tell me what it is, Gretta. I think I know what is the matter. Do I know?

She did not answer at once. Then she said in an outburst of tears:

—O, I am thinking about that song, *The Lass of Aughrim.*

She broke loose from him and ran to the bed and, throwing her arms across the bed-rail, hid her face. Gabriel stood stock-still for a moment in astonishment and then followed her. As he passed in the way of the cheval-glass he caught sight of himself in full length, his broad, well-filled shirt-front, the face whose expression always puzzled him when he saw it in a mirror and his glimmering gilt-rimmed eye-glasses. He halted a few paces from her and said:

—What about the song? Why does that make you cry?

She raised her head from her arms and dried her eyes with the back of her hand like a child. A kinder note than he had intended went into his voice.

—Why, Gretta? he asked.

—I am thinking about a person long ago who used to sing that song.

—And who was the person long ago? asked Gabriel, smiling.

—It was a person I used to know in Galway when I was living with my grand-mother, she said.

The smile passed away from Gabriel's face. A dull anger began to gather again at the back of his mind and the dull fires of his lust began to glow angrily in his veins.

—Someone you were in love with? he asked ironically.

—It was a young boy I used to know, she answered, named Michael Furey. He used to sing that song, *The Lass of Aughrim*. He was very delicate.

Gabriel was silent. He did not wish her to think that he was interested in this delicate boy.

—I can see him so plainly, she said after a moment. Such eyes as he had: big dark eyes! And such an expression in them—an expression!

—O then, you were in love with him? said Gabriel.

—I used to go out walking with him, she said, when I was in Galway.

A thought flew across Gabriel's mind.

—Perhaps that was why you wanted to go to Galway with that Ivors girl? he said coldly.

She looked at him and asked in surprise:

—What for?

Her eyes made Gabriel feel awkward. He shrugged his shoulders and said:

—How do I know? To see him perhaps.

She looked away from him along the shaft of light towards the window in silence.

—He is dead, she said at length. He died when he was only seventeen. Isn't it a terrible thing to die so young as that?

—What was he? asked Gabriel, still ironically.

—He was in the gasworks, she said.

Gabriel felt humiliated by the failure of his irony and by the evocation of this figure from the dead, a boy in the gasworks. While he had been full of memories of their secret life together, full of tenderness and joy and desire, she had been comparing him in her mind with another. A shameful consciousness of his own person assailed him. He saw himself as a ludicrous figure, acting as a pennyboy[7] for his aunts, a nervous well-meaning sentimentalist, orating to vulgarians and idealising his own clownish lusts, the pitiable fatuous fellow he had caught a glimpse of in the mirror. Instinctively he turned his back more to the light lest she might see the shame that burned upon his forehead.

He tried to keep up his tone of cold interrogation but his voice when he spoke was humble and indifferent.

—I suppose you were in love with this Michael Furey, Gretta, he said.

—I was great with him at that time, she said.

Her voice was veiled and sad. Gabriel, feeling now how vain it would be to try to lead her whither he had purposed, caressed one of her hands and said, also sadly:

—And what did he die of so young, Gretta? Consumption, was it?

—I think he died for me, she answered.[8]

A vague terror seized Gabriel at this answer as if, at that hour when he had hoped to triumph, some impalpable and vindictive being was coming against him, gathering forces against him in its vague world. But he shook himself free of it with an effort of reason and continued to caress her hand. He did not question her again for he felt that she would tell him of herself. Her hand was warm and moist: it did not respond to his touch but he continued to caress it just as he had caressed her first letter to him that spring morning.

—It was in the winter, she said, about the beginning of the winter when I was going to leave my grandmother's and come up here to the convent. And he was ill at the time

---

7. Errand boy.

8. Gretta here echoes the words of Yeats's Cathleen ní Houlihan: "Singing I am about a man I knew one time, yellow-haired Donough that was hanged in Galway. . . .

He died for love of me: many a man has died for love of me." The play was first performed in Dublin on 2 April 1902.

in his lodgings in Galway and wouldn't be let out and his people in Oughterard[9] were written to. He was in decline, they said, or something like that. I never knew rightly.

She paused for a moment and sighed.

—Poor fellow, she said. He was very fond of me and he was such a gentle boy. We used to go out together, walking, you know, Gabriel, like the way they do in the country. He was going to study singing only for his health. He had a very good voice, poor Michael Furey.

—Well; and then? asked Gabriel.

—And then when it came to the time for me to leave Galway and come up to the convent he was much worse and I wouldn't be let see him so I wrote a letter saying I was going up to Dublin and would be back in the summer and hoping he would be better then.

She paused for a moment to get her voice under control and then went on:

—Then the night before I left I was in my grandmother's house in Nuns' Island, packing up, and I heard gravel thrown up against the window. The window was so wet I couldn't see so I ran downstairs as I was and slipped out the back into the garden and there was the poor fellow at the end of the garden, shivering.

—And did you not tell him to go back? asked Gabriel.

—I implored him to go home at once and told him he would get his death in the rain. But he said he did not want to live. I can see his eyes as well as well! He was standing at the end of the wall where there was a tree.

—And did he go home? asked Gabriel.

—Yes, he went home. And when I was only a week in the convent he died and he was buried in Oughterard where his people came from. O, the day I heard that, that he was dead!

She stopped, choking with sobs, and, overcome by emotion, flung herself face downward on the bed, sobbing in the quilt. Gabriel held her hand for a moment longer, irresolutely, and then, shy of intruding on her grief, let it fall gently and walked quietly to the window.

She was fast asleep.

Gabriel, leaning on his elbow, looked for a few moments unresentfully on her tangled hair and half-open mouth, listening to her deep-drawn breath. So she had had that romance in her life: a man had died for her sake. It hardly pained him now to think how poor a part he, her husband, had played in her life. He watched her while she slept as though he and she had never lived together as man and wife. His curious eyes rested long upon her face and on her hair: and, as he thought of what she must have been then, in that time of her first girlish beauty, a strange friendly pity for her entered his soul. He did not like to say even to himself that her face was no longer beautiful but he knew that it was no longer the face for which Michael Furey had braved death.

Perhaps she had not told him all the story. His eyes moved to the chair over which she had thrown some of her clothes. A petticoat string dangled to the floor. One boot stood upright, its limp upper fallen down: the fellow of it lay upon its side. He wondered at his riot of emotions of an hour before. From what had it proceeded? From his aunt's supper, from his own foolish speech, from the wine and dancing, the merry-making when saying good-night in the hall, the pleasure of the walk along the

9. A small village in Western Ireland.

river in the snow. Poor Aunt Julia! She, too, would soon be a shade with the shade of Patrick Morkan and his horse. He had caught that haggard look upon her face for a moment when she was singing *Arrayed for the Bridal*. Soon, perhaps, he would be sitting in that same drawing-room, dressed in black, his silk hat on his knees. The blinds would be drawn down and Aunt Kate would be sitting beside him, crying and blowing her nose and telling him how Julia had died. He would cast about in his mind for some words that might console her, and would find only lame and useless ones. Yes, yes: that would happen very soon.

The air of the room chilled his shoulders. He stretched himself cautiously along under the sheets and lay down beside his wife. One by one they were all becoming shades. Better pass boldly into that other world, in the full glory of some passion, than fade and wither dismally with age. He thought of how she who lay beside him had locked in her heart for so many years that image of her lover's eyes when he had told her that he did not wish to live.

Generous tears filled Gabriel's eyes. He had never felt like that himself towards any woman but he knew that such a feeling must be love. The tears gathered more thickly in his eyes and in the partial darkness he imagined he saw the form of a young man standing under a dripping tree. Other forms were near. His soul had approached that region where dwell the vast hosts of the dead. He was conscious of, but could not apprehend, their wayward and flickering existence. His own identity was fading out into a grey impalpable world: the solid world itself which these dead had one time reared and lived in was dissolving and dwindling.

A few light taps upon the pane made him turn to the window. It had begun to snow again. He watched sleepily the flakes, silver and dark, falling obliquely against the lamplight. The time had come for him to set out on his journey westward. Yes, the newspapers were right: snow was general all over Ireland. It was falling on every part of the dark central plain, on the treeless hills, falling softly upon the Bog of Allen and, farther westward, softly falling into the dark mutinous Shannon waves.[1] It was falling, too, upon every part of the lonely churchyard on the hill where Michael Furey lay buried. It lay thickly drifted on the crooked crosses and headstones, on the spears of the little gate, on the barren thorns. His soul swooned slowly as he heard the snow falling faintly through the universe and faintly falling, like the descent of their last end, upon all the living and the dead.

ULYSSES   *Ulysses* boldly announced that modern literature had set itself new tasks and devised new means to "make it new." In his review of the novel, T. S. Eliot wrote that Joyce had discovered "a way of controlling, of ordering, of giving a shape and a significance to the panorama of futility and anarchy which is contemporary history. . . . It is, I seriously believe, a step toward making the modern world possible for art . . . ." The technique with which Joyce shaped his materials Eliot called (at Joyce's suggestion) the mythical method—using ancient myth to suggest "a continuous parallel between contemporaneity and antiquity." Joyce's purposes in using myth—in the case of *Ulysses*, a series of parallels to Homer's *Odyssey*—are open to debate; but he was quite frank about the fact that each of the novel's eighteen chapters was modeled, however loosely, on one of Odysseus's adventures. Thus Leopold Bloom, the novel's advertising-salesman protagonist, is in some sense a modern-day Odysseus; rather than finding his way back from Troy and the Trojan Wars, he simply navigates his way through a very full day in Dublin on 16 June 1904. This day, however, has its perils. Bloom, a Jew, is set upon by

1. Where Ireland's longest river, the Shannon, empties into the sea.

anti-Semites, threatened with violence, and driven from the pub where he drinks; much later, in Dublin's red-light district, he rescues a very drunk young poet, Stephen Dedalus, from arrest, and takes him back to his home for a cup of cocoa and conversation. Foremost among Bloom's tests on this particular day, however, is his knowledge that his wife Molly will consummate an affair with the brash, egotistical tenor Blazes Boylan—an affair which, owing to his own shortcomings as a husband, Bloom is unwilling to stop.

The chapter given here is the thirteenth chapter, the "Nausicaa" episode. We find Bloom killing time on the beach at Sandymount, trying to stay away from his home long enough that his wife's new lover, Blazes Boylan, will be gone before his return. He has just narrowly escaped bodily injury at the hands of the unnamed ultra-Nationalist Citizen in Chapter 12, "Cyclops"; finding his way to the seaside for a bit of fresh air and relaxation, Bloom is happy to come across the self-consciously displayed feminine commodity Gerty MacDowell, who, having been stood up by young Reggie Wylie, is willing to suffer Bloom's sensual and sexual gaze. Her poignant fate as a young woman in a country missing half its young men is also clear. In the episode from the *Odyssey* on which this chapter is loosely based, Odysseus finds himself in the land of the seafaring Phaeacians, and in the company of Princess Nausicaa and her ladies, who have come to the water to do the laundry. In the *Odyssey*, Odysseus sheds his disguise, reveals himself to Nausicaa, and begs for her help in returning to home (Ithaca) and wife (Penelope); in Joyce's version, it is Nausicaa who does the revealing, to an admiring Odysseus who is carefully avoiding his return journey home. Joyce uses the scene to comment on the nature of attraction, beauty, and desire, and the ways in which sentimental fiction, commodity culture, and Bloom's own profession of advertising have affected the way we understand and seek to satisfy our deepest desires.

from **Ulysses**
[CHAPTER 13. "NAUSICAA"]

The summer evening had begun to fold the world in its mysterious embrace.[1] Far away in the west the sun was setting and the last glow of all too fleeting day lingered lovingly on sea and strand, on the proud promontory of dear old Howth[2] guarding as ever the waters of the bay, on the weedgrown rocks along Sandymount shore and, last but not least, on the quiet church[3] whence there streamed forth at times upon the stillness the voice of prayer to her who is in her pure radiance a beacon ever to the stormtossed heart of man, Mary, star of the sea.

The three girl friends were seated on the rocks, enjoying the evening scene and the air which was fresh but not too chilly. Many a time and oft were they wont to come there to that favourite nook to have a cosy chat beside the sparkling waves and discuss matters feminine, Cissy Caffrey and Edy Boardman with the baby in the pushcar and Tommy and Jacky Caffrey, two little curlyheaded boys, dressed in sailor suits with caps to match and the name H. M. S.[4] Belleisle printed on both. For Tommy and Jacky Caffrey were twins, scarce four years old and very noisy and spoiled twins sometimes but for all that darling little fellows with bright merry faces and endearing ways about them. They were dabbling in the sand with their spades and buckets, building castles as children do, or playing with their big coloured ball, happy as the

---

1. The prose style of the first half of this chapter is to some extent modeled on the overripe prose of sentimental 19th-century "women's" fiction, like Maria Cummins's novel *The Lamplighter* (1854), which Gerty MacDowell has read and which pops up in her thoughts later in the chapter.

2. The northeast headland of Dublin Bay, visible from the shore at Sandymount, where this chapter takes place.
3. The church would be the Roman Catholic Church of Mary, Star of the Sea, near Sandymount Strand.
4. His Majesty's Ship.

day was long. And Edy Boardman was rocking the chubby baby to and fro in the pushcar while that young gentleman fairly chuckled with delight. He was but eleven months and nine days old and, though still a tiny toddler, was just beginning to lisp his first babyish words. Cissy Caffrey bent over him to tease his fat little plucks and the dainty dimple in his chin.

—Now, baby, Cissy Caffrey said. Say out big, big. I want a drink of water.

And baby prattled after her:

—A jink a jink a jawbo.

Cissy Caffrey cuddled the wee chap for she was awfully fond of children, so patient with little sufferers and Tommy Caffrey could never be got to take his castor oil unless it was Cissy Caffrey that held his nose and promised him the scatty heel of the loaf or brown bread with golden syrup on. What a persuasive power that girl had! But to be sure baby was as good as gold, a perfect little dote in his new fancy bib. None of your spoilt beauties, Flora Mac Flimsy sort, was Cissy Caffrey. A truerhearted lass never drew the breath of life, always with a laugh in her gipsylike eyes and a frolicsome word on her cherryripe red lips, a girl lovable in the extreme. And Edy Boardman laughed too at the quaint language of little brother.

But just then there was a slight altercation between Master Tommy and Master Jacky. Boys will be boys and our two twins were no exception to this golden rule. The apple of discord was a certain castle of sand which Master Jacky had built and Master Tommy would have it right go wrong that it was to be architecturally improved by a frontdoor like the Martello tower[5] had. But if Master Tommy was headstrong Master Jacky was selfwilled too and, true to the maxim that every little Irishman's house is his castle, he fell upon his hated rival and to such purpose that the wouldbe assailant came to grief and (alas to relate!) the coveted castle too. Needless to say the cries of discomfited Master Tommy drew the attention of the girl friends.

—Come here, Tommy, his sister called imperatively, at once! And you, Jacky, for shame to throw poor Tommy in the dirty sand. Wait till I catch you for that.

His eyes misty with unshed tears Master Tommy came at her call for their big sister's word was law with the twins. And in a sad plight he was after his misadventure. His little man-o'-war top and unmentionables were full of sand but Cissy was a past mistress in the art of smoothing over life's tiny troubles and and very quickly not one speck of sand was to be seen on his smart little suit. Still the blue eyes were glistening with hot tears that would well up so she kissed away the hurtness and shook her hand at Master Jacky the culprit and said if she was near him she wouldn't be far from him, her eyes dancing in admonition.

—Nasty bold Jacky! she cried.

She put an arm round the little mariner and coaxed winningly:

—What's your name? Butter and cream?

—Tell us who is your sweetheart, spoke Edy Boardman. Is Cissy your sweetheart?

—Nao, tearful Tommy said.

—Is Edy Boardman your sweetheart? Cissy queried.

—Nao, Tommy said.

—I know, Edy Boardman said none too amiably with an arch glance from her shortsighted eyes. I know who is Tommy's sweetheart, Gerty is Tommy's sweetheart.

5. One of a series of towers on the Irish coast built by the British at the start of the 19th century to protect against a sea invasion by the French during the Napoleonic Wars.

—Nao, Tommy said on the verge of tears.

Cissy's quick motherwit guessed what was amiss and she whispered to Edy Boardman to take him there behind the pushcar where the gentlemen couldn't see and to
mind he didn't wet his new tan shoes.

But who was Gerty?

Gerty MacDowell who was seated near her companions, lost in thought, gazing far
away into the distance was in very truth as fair a specimen of winsome Irish girlhood as
one could wish to see. She was pronounced beautiful by all who knew her though, as
folks often said, she was more a Giltrap than a MacDowell. Her figure was slight and
graceful, inclining even to fragility but those iron jelloids she had been taking of late
had done her a world of good much better than the Widow Welch's female pills and
she was much better of those discharges she used to get and that tired feeling. The wax-
en pallor of her face was almost spiritual in its ivorylike purity though her rosebud
mouth was a genuine Cupid's bow, Greekly perfect. Her hands were of finely veined
alabaster with tapering fingers and as white as lemon juice and queen of ointments
could make them though it was not true that she used to wear kid gloves in bed or take
a milk footbath either. Bertha Supple told that once to Edy Boardman, a deliberate lie,
when she was black out at daggers drawn with Gerty (the girl chums had of course their
little tiffs from time to time like the rest of mortals) and she told her not let on whatever she did that it was her that told her or she'd never speak to her again. No. Honour
where honour is due. There was an innate refinement, a languid queenly *hauteur*[6] about
Gerty which was unmistakably evidenced in her delicate hands and higharched instep.
Had kind fate but willed her to be born a gentlewoman of high degree in her own right
and had she only received the benefit of a good education Gerty MacDowell might easily have held her own beside any lady in the land and have seen herself exquisitely
gowned with jewels on her brow and patrician[7] suitors at her feet vying with one
another to pay their devoirs[8] to her. Mayhap it was this, the love that might have been,
that lent to her softlyfeatured face at whiles a look, tense with suppressed meaning, that
imparted a strange yearning tendency to the beautiful eyes, a charm few could resist.
Why have women such eyes of witchery? Gerty's were of the bluest Irish blue, set off by
lustrous lashes and dark expressive brows. Time was when those brows were not so silk-
ily seductive. It was Madame Vera Verity, directress of the Woman Beautiful page of
the Princess novelette, who had first advised her to try eyebrowleine which gave that
haunting expression to the eyes, so becoming in leaders of fashion, and she had never
regretted it. Then there was blushing scientifically cured and how to be tall increase
your height and you have a beautiful face but your nose?[9] That would suit Mrs Dignam
because she had a button one. But Gerty's crowning glory was her wealth of wonderful
hair. It was dark brown with a natural wave in it. She had cut it that very morning on
account of the new moon and it nestled about her pretty head in a profusion of luxuriant clusters and pared her nails too, Thursday for wealth.[1] And just now at Edy's words
as a telltale flush, delicate as the faintest rosebloom, crept into her cheeks she looked so
lovely in her sweet girlish shyness that of a surety God's fair land of Ireland did not hold
her equal.

6. Arrogance.
7. Aristocratic.
8. Respects.
9. The phrases that comprise this sentence are modeled
on claims from advertisements for various cosmetics and
beauty treatments, such as would be advertised in
women's magazines of the period (1904).
1. Gerty's actions here are suggested by a number of common superstitions and folk beliefs.

For an instant she was silent with rather sad downcast eyes. She was about to retort but something checked the words on her tongue. Inclination prompted her to speak out: dignity told her to be silent. The pretty lips pouted a while but then she glanced up and broke out into a joyous little laugh which had in it all the freshness of a young May morning. She knew right well, no-one better, what made squinty Edy say that because of him cooling in his attentions when it was simply a lover's quarrel. As per usual somebody's nose was out of joint about the boy that had the bicycle always riding up and down in front of her window. Only now his father kept him in the evenings studying hard to get an exhibition in the intermediate[2] that was on and he was going to Trinity college to study for a doctor when he left the high school like his brother W. E. Wylie who was racing in the bicycle races in Trinity college university. Little recked[3] he perhaps for what she felt, that dull aching void in her heart sometimes, piercing to the core. Yet he was young and perchance he might learn to love her in time. They were protestants in his family and of course Gerty knew Who came first and after Him the blessed Virgin and then Saint Joseph. But he was undeniably handsome with an exquisite nose and he was what he looked, every inch a gentleman, the shape of his head too at the back without his cap on that she would know anywhere something off the common and the way he turned the bicycle at the lamp with his hands off the bars and also the nice perfume of those good cigarettes and besides they were both of a size and that was why Edy Boardman thought she was so frightfully clever because he didn't go and ride up and down in front of her bit of a garden.

Gerty was dressed simply but with the instinctive taste of a votary[4] of Dame Fashion for she felt that there was just a might that he might be out. A neat blouse of electric blue, selftinted by dolly dyes (because it was expected in the *Lady's Pictorial* that electric blue would be worn), with a smart vee opening down to the division and kerchief pocket (in which she always kept a piece of cottonwool scented with her favourite perfume because the handkerchief spoiled the sit) and a navy threequarter skirt cut to the stride showed off her slim graceful figure to perfection. She wore a coquettish little love of a hat of wideleaved nigger straw contrast trimmed with an underbrim of eggblue chenille and at the side a butterfly bow to tone. All Tuesday week afternoon she was hunting to match that chenille but at last she found what she wanted at Clery's[5] summer sales, the very it, slightly shopsoiled but you would never notice, seven fingers two and a penny. She did it up all by herself and what joy was hers when she tried it on then, smiling at the lovely reflection which the mirror gave back to her! And when she put it on the waterjug to keep the shape she knew that that would take the shine out of some people she knew. Her shoes were the newest thing in footwear (Edy Boardman prided herself that she was very *petite* but she never had a foot like Gerty MacDowell, a five, and never would ash, oak or elm[6]) with patent toecaps and just one smart buckle at her higharched instep. Her wellturned ankle displayed its perfect proportions beneath her skirt and just the proper amount and no more of her shapely limbs encased in finespun hose with highspliced heels and wide garter tops. As for undies they were Gerty's chief care and who that knows the fluttering hopes and fears of sweet seventeen (though Gerty would never see seventeen again) can find it in his

2. I.e., to be ranked highly in his class upon graduation, so as to secure a spot at Dublin's protestant university, Trinity College.
3. Cared.
4. Religious devotee.
5. The biggest department store in downtown Dublin.
6. Till the end of time.

heart to blame her? She had four dinky sets, with awfully pretty stitchery, three garments and nighties extra, and each set slotted with different coloured ribbons,
rosepink, pale blue, mauve and peagreen and she aired them herself and blued them
when they came home from the wash and ironed them and she had a brickbat to keep
the iron on because she wouldn't trust those washerwomen as far as she'd see them
scorching the things. She was wearing the blue for luck, hoping against hope, her own
colour and the lucky colour too for a bride to have a bit of blue somewhere on her
because the green she wore that day week brought grief because his father brought him
in to study for the intermediate exhibition and because she thought perhaps he might
be out because when she was dressing that morning she nearly slipped up the old pair
on her inside out and that was for luck and lovers' meetings if you put those things on
inside out so long as it wasn't of a Friday.

   And yet and yet! That strained look on her face! A gnawing sorrow is there all
the time. Her very soul is in her eyes and she would give worlds to be in the privacy
of her own familiar chamber where, giving way to tears, she could have a good cry
and relieve her pentup feelings. Though not too much because she knew how to cry
nicely before the mirror. You are lovely, Gerty, it said. The paly light of evening falls
upon a face infinitely sad and wistful. Gerty MacDowell yearns in vain. Yes, she had
known from the first that her daydream of a marriage has been arranged and the wed-
dingbells ringing for Mrs Reggy Wylie T. C. D.[7] (because the one who married the
elder brother would be Mrs Wylie) and in the fashionable intelligence Mrs Gertrude
Wylie was wearing a sumptuous confection of grey trimmed with expensive blue fox
was not to be. He was too young to understand. He would not believe in love, a
woman's birthright. The night of the party long ago in Stoers' (he was still in short
trousers) when they were alone and he stole an arm round her waist she went white
to the very lips. He called her little one in a strangely husky voice and snatched a
half kiss (the first!) but it was only the end of her nose and then he hastened from
the room with a remark about refreshments. Impetuous fellow! Strength of character
had never been Reggy Wylie's strong point and he who would woo and win Gerty
MacDowell must be a man among men. But waiting, always waiting to be asked and
it was leap year[8] too and would soon be over. No prince charming is her beau ideal to
lay a rare and wondrous love at her feet but rather a manly man with a strong quiet
face who had not found his ideal, perhaps his hair slightly flecked with grey, and who
would understand, take her in his sheltering arms, strain her to him in all the
strength of his deep passionate nature and comfort her with a long long kiss. It would
be like heaven. For such a one she yearns this balmy summer eve. With all the heart
of her she longs to be his only, his affianced bride for riches for poor, in sickness in
health, till death us two part, from this to this day forward.

   And while Edy Boardman was with little Tommy behind the pushcar she was just
thinking would the day ever come when she could call herself his little wife to be. Then
they could talk about her till they went blue in the face, Bertha Supple too, and Edy, the
spitfire, because she would be twentytwo in November. She would care for him with
creature comforts too for Gerty was womanly wise and knew that a mere man liked that
feeling of hominess. Her griddlecakes done to a goldenbrown hue and queen Ann's pudding of delightful creaminess had won golden opinions from all because she had a lucky

---

7. Trinity College, Dublin; a Trinity graduate would be
allowed to use these initials after his name.

8. Traditionally, a woman may propose marriage to a man
only during a leap year.

hand also for lighting a fire, dredge in the fine selfraising flour and always stir in the same direction then cream the milk and sugar and whisk well the white of eggs though she didn't like the eating part when there were any people that made her shy and often she wondered why you couldn't eat something poetical like violets or roses and they would have a beautifully appointed drawingroom with pictures and engravings and the photograph of grandpapa Giltrap's lovely dog Garryowen that almost talked, it was so human, and chintz covers for the chairs and that silver toastrack in Clery's summer jumble sales like they have in rich houses. He would be tall with broad shoulders (she had always admired tall men for a husband) with glistening white teeth under his carefully trimmed sweeping moustache and they would go on the continent for their honeymoon (three wonderful weeks!) and then, when they settled down in a nice snug and cosy little homely house, every morning they would both have brekky,[9] simple but perfectly served, for their own two selves and before he went out to business he would give his dear little wifey a good hearty hug and gaze for a moment deep down into her eyes.

Edy Boardman asked Tommy Caffrey was he done and he said yes, so then she buttoned up his little knickerbockers for him and told him to run off and play with Jacky and to be good now and not to fight. But Tommy said he wanted the ball and Edy told him no that baby was playing with the ball and if he took it there'd be wigs on the green[1] but Tommy said it was his ball and he wanted his ball and he pranced on the ground, if you please. The temper of him! O, he was a man already was little Tommy Caffrey since he was out of pinnies.[2] Edy told him no, no and to be off now with him and she told Cissy Caffrey not to give in to him.

—You're not my sister, naughty Tommy said. It's my ball.

But Cissy Caffrey told baby Boardman to look up, look up high at her finger and she snatched the ball quickly and threw it along the sand and Tommy after it in full career, having won the day.

—Anything for a quiet life, laughed Ciss.

And she tickled tiny tot's two cheeks to make him forget and played here's the lord mayor, here's his two horses, here's his gingerbread carriage and here he walks in, chinchopper, chinchopper, chinchopper chin. But Edy got as cross as two sticks about him getting his own way like that from everyone always petting him.

—I'd like to give him something, she said, so I would, where I won't say.

—On the beeoteetom, laughed Cissy merrily.

Gerty MacDowell bent down her head and crimsoned at the idea of Cissy saying an unladylike thing like that out loud she'd be ashamed of her life to say, flushing a deep rosy red, and Edy Boardman said she was sure the gentleman opposite heard what she said. But not a pin cared Ciss.

—Let him! she said with a pert toss of her head and a piquant tilt of her nose. Give it to him too on the same place as quick as I'd look at him.

Madcap Ciss with her golliwog curls. You had to laugh at her sometimes. For instance when she asked you would you have some more Chinese tea and jaspberry ram and when she drew the jugs too and the men's faces on her nails with red ink make you split your sides or when she wanted to go where you know she said she wanted to run and pay a visit to the Miss White. That was just like Cissycums. O, and will you ever forget the evening she dressed up in her father's suit and hat and the burned cork moustache and walked down Tritonville road, smoking a cigarette.

9. Breakfast.
1. A fistfight or altercation.

2. Pinafores. "Out of pinnies" would mean something like "out of diapers."

There was none to come up to her for fun. But she was sincerity itself, one of the bravest and truest hearts heaven ever made, not one of your twofaced things, too sweet to be wholesome.

And then there came out upon the air the sound of voices and the pealing anthem of the organ. It was the men's temperance retreat conducted by the missioner, the reverend John Hughes S. J.[3] rosary, sermon and benediction of the Most Blessed Sacrament. They were there gathered together without distinction of social class (and a most edifying spectacle it was to see) in that simple fane[4] beside the waves, after the storms of this weary world, kneeling before the feet of the immaculate, reciting the litany of Our Lady of Loreto, beseeching her to intercede for them, the old familiar words, holy Mary, holy virgin of virgins. How sad to poor Gerty's ears! Had her father only avoided the clutches of the demon drink, by taking the pledge or those powders the drink habit cured in Pearson's Weekly, she might now be rolling in her carriage, second to none. Over and over had she told herself that as she mused by the dying embers in a brown study without the lamp because she hated two lights or oftentimes gazing out of the window dreamily by the hour at the rain falling on the rusty bucket, thinking. But that vile decoction which has ruined so many hearths and homes had cast its shadow over her childhood days. Nay, she had even witnessed in the home circle deeds of violence caused by intemperance and had seen her own father, a prey to the fumes of intoxication, forget himself completely for if there was one thing of all things that Gerty knew it was the man who lifts his hand to a woman save in the way of kindness deserves to be branded as the lowest of the low.

And still the voices sang in supplication to the Virgin most powerful, Virgin most merciful. And Gerty, rapt in thought, scarce saw or heard her companions or the twins at their boyish gambols[5] or the gentleman off Sandymount green that Cissy Caffrey called the man that was so like himself passing along the strand taking a short walk. You never saw him anyway screwed but still and for all that she would not like him for a father because he was too old or something or on account of his face (it was a palpable case of doctor Fell) or his carbuncly nose with the pimples on it and his sandy moustache a bit white under his nose. Poor father! With all his faults she loved him still when he sang *Tell me, Mary, how to woo thee* or *My love and cottage near Rochelle* and they had stewed cockles and lettuce with Lazenby's salad dressing for supper and when he sang *The moon hath raised* with Mr Dignam that died suddenly and was buried, God have mercy on him, from a stroke.[6] Her mother's birthday that was and Charley was home on his holidays and Tom and Mr Dignam and Mrs and Patsy and Freddy Dignam and they were to have had a group[7] taken. No-one would have thought the end was so near. Now he was laid to rest. And her mother said to him to let that be a warning to him for the rest of his days and he couldn't even go to the funeral on account of the gout and she had to go into town to bring him the letters and samples from his office about Catesby's cork lino, artistic standard designs, fit for a palace, gives tiptop wear and always bright and cheery in the home.

A sterling good daughter was Gerty just like a second mother in the house, a ministering angel too with a little heart worth its weight in gold. And when her mother had those raging splitting headaches who was it rubbed on the menthol cone on her

3. Society of Jesus; the Jesuits.
4. Temple or church.
5. Frolics.
6. The funeral of Patrick ("Paddy") Dignam has taken place this morning, at Glasnevin Cemetery; that he died of a "stroke" is a polite euphemism, since it appears he has died of cirrhosis or another alcohol-related disease.
7. A group photograph.

forehead but Gerty though she didn't like her mother taking pinches of snuff and that was the only single thing they ever had words about, taking snuff. Everyone thought the world of her for her gentle ways. It was Gerty who turned off the gas at the main every night and it was Gerty who tacked up on the wall of that place[8] where she never forgot every fortnight the chlorate of lime Mr Tunney the grocer's christmas almanac the picture of halcyon days where a young gentleman in the costume they used to wear then with a threecornered hat was offering a bunch of flowers to his ladylove with oldtime chivalry through her lattice window. You could see there was a story behind it. The colours were done something lovely. She was in a soft clinging white in a studied attitude and the gentleman was in chocolate and he looked a thorough aristocrat. She often looked at them dreamily when she went there for a certain purpose and felt her own arms that were white and soft just like hers with the sleeves back and thought about those times because she had found out in Walker's pronouncing dictionary that belonged to grandpapa Giltrap about the halcyon days what they meant.

The twins were now playing in the most approved brotherly fashion, till at last Master Jacky who was really as bold as brass there was no getting behind that deliberately kicked the ball as hard as ever he could down towards the seaweedy rocks. Needless to say poor Tommy was not slow to voice his dismay but luckily the gentleman in black who was sitting there by himself came gallantly to the rescue and intercepted the ball. Our two champions claimed their plaything with lusty cries and to avoid trouble Cissy Caffrey called to the gentleman to throw it to her please. The gentleman aimed the ball once or twice and then threw it up the strand[9] towards Cissy Caffrey but it rolled down the slope and stopped right under Gerty's skirt near the little pool by the rock. The twins clamoured again for it and Cissy told her to kick it away and let them fight for it so Gerty drew back her foot but she wished their stupid ball hadn't come rolling down to her and she gave a kick but she missed and Edy and Cissy laughed.

—If you fail try again, Edy Boardman said.

Gerty smiled assent and bit her lip. A delicate pink crept into her pretty cheek but she was determined to let them see so she just lifted her skirt a little but just enough and took good aim and gave the ball a jolly good kick and it went ever so far and the two twins after it down towards the shingle. Pure jealousy of course it was nothing else to draw attention on account of the gentleman opposite looking. She felt the warm flush, a danger signal always with Gerty MacDowell, surging and flaming into her cheeks. Till then they had only exchanged glances of the most casual but now under the brim of her new hat she ventured a look at him and the face that met her gaze there in the twilight, wan[1] and strangely drawn, seemed to her the saddest she had ever seen.

Through the open window of the church the fragrant incense was wafted and with it the fragrant names of her who was conceived without stain of original sin, spiritual vessel, pray for us, honourable vessel, pray for us, vessel of singular devotion, pray for us, mystical rose. And careworn hearts were there and toilers for their daily bread and many who had erred and wandered, their eyes wet with contrition but for all that bright with hope for the reverend father Hughes had told them what the great saint Bernard said in his famous prayer of Mary, the most pious Virgin's inter-

8. Gerty's euphemism for the outhouse, or outdoor toilet. It is her job to change the chlorate of lime, used as a disinfectant and deodorant.

9. Seashore.
1. Pale.

cessory power that it was not recorded in any age that those who implored her power-ful protection were ever abandoned by her.

The twins were now playing again right merrily for the troubles of childhood are but as fleeting summer showers. Cissy played with baby Boardman till he crowed with glee, clapping baby hands in air. Peep she cried behind the hood of the pushcar and Edy asked where was Cissy gone and then Cissy popped up her head and cried ah! and, my word, didn't the little chap enjoy that! And then she told him to say papa.

—Say papa, baby. Say pa pa pa pa pa pa pa.

And baby did his level best to say it for he was very intelligent for eleven months everyone said and big for his age and the picture of health, a perfect little bunch of love, and he would certainly turn out to be something great, they said.

—Haja ja ja haja.

Cissy wiped his little mouth with the dribbling bib and wanted him to sit up properly and say pa pa pa but when she undid the strap she cried out, holy saint Denis, that he was possing wet and to double the half blanket the other way under him. Of course his infant majesty was most obstreperous at such toilet formalities and he let everyone know it:

—Habaa baaaahabaaa baaaa.

And two great big lovely big tears coursing down his cheeks. It was all no use soothering him with no, nono, baby, no and telling him about the geegee and where was the puffpuff but Ciss, always, readywitted, gave him in his mouth the teat of the suckingbottle and the young heathen was quickly appeased.

Gerty wished to goodness they would take their squalling baby home out of that and not get on her nerves no hour to be out and the little brats of twins. She gazed out towards the distant sea. It was like the paintings that man used to do on the pave-ment with all the coloured chalks and such a pity too leaving them there to be all blotted out, the evening and the clouds coming out and the Bailey light[2] on Howth and to hear the music like that and the perfume of those incense they burned in the church like a kind of waft. And while she gazed her heart went pitapat. Yes, it was her he was looking at and there was meaning in his look. His eyes burned into her as though they would search her through and through, read her very soul. Wonderful eyes they were, superbly expressive, but could you trust them? People were so queer. She could see at once by his dark eyes and his pale intellectual face that he was a for-eigner the image of the photo she had of Martin Harvey, the matinée idol, only for the moustache which she preferred because she wasn't stagestruck like Winny Rip-pingham that wanted they two to always dress the same on account of a play but she could not see whether he had an aquiline nose or a slightly retroussé[3] from where he was sitting. He was in deep mourning,[4] she could see that, and the story of a haunting sorrow was written on his face. She would have given worlds to know what it was. He was looking up so intently, so still and he saw her kick the ball and perhaps he could see the bright steel buckles of her shoes if she swung them like that thoughtfully with the toes down. She was glad that something told her to put on the transparent stock-ings thinking Reggy Wylie might be out but that was far away. Here was that of which she had so often dreamed. It was he who mattered and there was joy on her face because she wanted him because she felt instinctively that he was like no-one

2. The lighthouse perched at the tip of Howth Head.
3. An aquiline nose is hooked; a retroussé nose is turned-up.

4. The as-yet unnamed gentleman on the strand has attended the funeral of Paddy Dignam and is wearing black.

else. The very heart of the girlwoman went out to him, her dreamhusband, because she knew on the instant it was him. If he had suffered, more sinned against than sinning, or even, even, if he had been himself a sinner, a wicked man, she cared not. Even if he was a protestant or methodist she could convert him easily if he truly loved her. There were wounds that wanted healing with heartbalm. She was a womanly woman not like other flighty girls, unfeminine, he had known, those cyclists showing off what they hadn't got and she just yearned to know all, to forgive all if she could make him fall in love with her, make him forget the memory of the past. Then mayhap he would embrace her gently, like a real man, crushing her soft body to him, and love her, his ownest girlie, for herself alone.

Refuge of sinners. Comfortress of the afflicted. *Ora pro nobis*.[5] Well has it been said that whosoever prays to her with faith and constancy can never be lost or cast away: and fitly is she too a haven of refuge for the afflicted because of the seven dolours[6] which transpierced her own heart. Gerty could picture the whole scene in the church, the stained glass windows lighted up, the candles, the flowers and the blue banners of the blessed Virgin's sodality[7] and Father Conroy was helping Canon O'Hanlon at the altar, carrying things in and out with his eyes cast down. He looked almost a saint and his confessionbox was so quiet and clean and dark and his hands were just like white wax and if ever she became a Dominican nun in their white habit perhaps he might come to the convent for the novena of Saint Dominic. He told her that time when she told him about that in confession crimsoning up to the roots of her hair for fear he could see, not to be troubled because that was only the voice of nature and we were all subject to nature's laws, he said, in this life and that that was no sin because that came from the nature of woman instituted by God, he said, and that Our Blessed Lady herself said to the archangel Gabriel be it done unto me according to Thy Word. He was so kind and holy and often and often she thought and thought could she work a ruched teacosy[8] with embroidered floral design for him as a present or a clock but they had a clock she noticed on the mantelpiece white and gold with a canary bird that came out of a little house to tell the time the day she went there about the flowers for the forty hours' adoration[9] because it was hard to know what sort of a present to give or perhaps an album of illuminated views of Dublin or some place.

The exasperating little brats of twins began to quarrel again and Jacky threw the ball out towards the sea and they both ran after it. Little monkeys common as ditchwater. Someone ought to take them and give them a good hiding for themselves to keep them in their places, the both of them. And Cissy and Edy shouted after them to come back because they were afraid the tide might come in on them and be drowned.

—Jacky! Tommy!

Not they! What a great notion they had! So Cissy said it was the very last time she'd ever bring them out. She jumped up and called them and she ran down the slope past him, tossing her hair behind her which had a good enough colour if there had been more of it but with all the thingamerry she was always rubbing into it she couldn't get it to grow long because it wasn't natural so she could just go and throw her hat at it. She ran with long gandery strides it was a wonder she didn't rip up her skirt at the side that

---

5. From the Litany of Our Lady: "Pray for us."
6. Sorrows.
7. A lay group within a religious order.
8. A padded, lace-edged cover for a teapot, to help keep the tea warm.
9. A period of prayer and devotion instituted by Pope Clement VIII, in memory of the 40 hours Jesus spent in the tomb before the Resurrection.

was too tight on her because there was a lot of the tomboy about Cissy Caffrey and she was a forward[1] piece whenever she thought she had a good opportunity to show off and just because she was a good runner she ran like that so that he could see all the end of her petticoat running and her skinny shanks up as far as possible. It would have served her just right if she had tripped up over something accidentally on purpose with her high crooked French heels on her to make her look tall and got a fine tumble. *Tableau!*[2] That would have been a very charming exposé for a gentleman like that to witness.

Queen of angels, queen of patriarchs, queen of prophets, of all saints, they prayed, queen of the most holy rosary and then Father Conroy handed the thurible[3] to Canon[4] O' Hanlon and he put in the incense and censed the Blessed Sacrament and Cissy Caffrey caught the two twins and she was itching to give them a ringing good clip on the ear but she didn't because she thought he might be watching but she never made a bigger mistake in all her life because Gerty could see without looking that he never took his eyes off of her and then Canon O'Hanlon handed the thurible back to Father Conroy and knelt down looking up at the Blessed Sacrament and the choir began to sing *Tantum ergo*[5] and she just swung her foot in and out in time as the music rose and fell to the *Tantumer gosa cramen tum*. Three and eleven she paid for those stockings in Sparrow's of George's street on the Tuesday, no the Monday before Easter and there wasn't a brack on them and that was what he was looking at, transparent, and not at her insignificant ones that had neither shape nor form (the cheek of her!) because he had eyes in his head to see the difference for himself.

Cissy came up along the strand with the two twins and their ball with her hat anyhow on her to one side after her run and she did look a streel[6] tugging the two kids along with the flimsy blouse she bought only a fortnight before like a rag on her back and a bit of her petticoat hanging like a caricature. Gerty just took off her hat for a moment to settle her hair and a prettier, a daintier head of nutbrown tresses was never seen on a girl's shoulders, a radiant little vision, in sooth,[7] almost maddening in its sweetness. You would have to travel many a long mile before you found a head of hair the like of that. She could almost see the swift answering flush of admiration in his eyes that set her tingling in every nerve. She put on her hat so that she could see from underneath the brim and swung her buckled shoe faster for her breath caught as she caught the expression in his eyes. He was eying her as a snake eyes its prey. Her woman's instinct told her that she had raised the devil in him and at the thought a burning scarlet swept from throat to brow till the lovely colour of her face became a glorious rose.

Edy Boardman was noticing it too because she was squinting at Gerty, half smiling, with her specs, like an old maid, pretending to nurse the baby. Irritable little gnat she was and always would be and that was why no-one could get on with her, poking her nose into what was no concern of hers. And she said to Gerty:

—A penny for your thoughts.

—What? replied Gerty with a smile reinforced by the whitest of teeth. I was only wondering was it late.

1. Bold, impertinent.
2. In a popular parlor game, participants would strike poses to convey scenes or *tableaux*. In this context, Gerty means something like, "Wouldn't that be a picture!"
3. A censer; an implement for burning and wafting the smoke of incense in a church service.

4. Title of respect for the member of a religious order.
5. Gerty's rhythmical rendition of the hymn which begins, in Latin, *Tantum ergo Sacramentum*, "So great a sacrament."
6. A loose or disreputable woman.
7. In truth.

Because she wished to goodness they'd take the snottynosed twins and their baby home to the mischief out of that so that was why she just gave a gentle hint about its being late. And when Cissy came up Edy asked her the time and Miss Cissy, as glib as you like, said it was half past kissing time, time to kiss again. But Edy wanted to know because they were told to be in early.

—Wait, said Cissy, I'll ask my uncle Peter over there what's the time by his conundrum.[8]

So over she went and when he saw her coming she could see him take his hand out of his pocket, getting nervous, and beginning to play with his watchchain, looking at the church. Passionate nature though he was Gerty could see that he had enormous control over himself. One moment he had been there, fascinated by a loveliness that made him gaze and the next moment it was the quiet gravefaced gentleman, selfcontrol expressed in every line of his distinguishedlooking figure.

Cissy said to excuse her would he mind telling her what was the right time and Gerty could see him taking out his watch, listening to it and looking up and clearing his throat and he said he was very sorry his watch was stopped but he thought it must be after eight because the sun was set. His voice had a cultured ring in it and though he spoke in measured accents there was a suspicion of a quiver in the mellow tones. Cissy said thanks and came back with her tongue out and said uncle said his waterworks were out of order.

Then they sang the second verse of the *Tantum ergo* and Canon O'Hanlon got up again and censed the Blessed Sacrament and knelt down and he told Father Conroy that one of the candles was just going to set fire to the flowers and Father Conroy got up and settled it all right and she could see the gentleman winding his watch and listening to the works and she swung her leg more in and out in time. It was getting darker but he could see and he was looking all the time that he was winding the watch or whatever he was doing to it and then he put it back and put his hands back into his pockets. She felt a kind of a sensation rushing all over her and she knew by the feel of her scalp and that irritation against her stays that that thing must be coming on because the last time too was when she clipped her hair on account of the moon. His dark eyes fixed themselves on her again drinking in her every contour, literally worshipping at her shrine. If ever there was undisguised admiration in a man's passionate gaze it was there plain to be seen on that man's face. It is for you, Gertrude MacDowell, and you know it.

Edy began to get ready to go and it was high time for her and Gerty noticed that that little hint she gave had the desired effect because it was a long way along the strand to where there was the place to push up the pushcar and Cissy took off the twins' caps and tidied their hair to make herself attractive of course and Canon O'Hanlon stood up with his cope[9] poking up at his neck and Father Conroy handed him the card to read off and he read out *Panem de coelo praestitisti eis*[1] and Edy and Cissy were talking about the time all the time and asking her but Gerty could pay them back in their own coin and she just answered with scathing politeness when Edy asked her was she heartbroken about her best boy throwing her over. Gerty winced sharply. A brief cold blaze shone from her eyes that spoke volumes of scorn immeasurable. It hurt. O yes, it cut deep because Edy had her own quiet way of saying things like that she knew would wound like the confounded little cat she was. Gerty's lips parted swiftly to frame the word but she fought back the sob that rose to her throat, so slim, so flawless, so beauti-

8. Puzzle (Cissy is using the word nonsensically).
9. A long ecclesiastical mantle.

1. You have given them bread from Heaven (Latin).

fully moulded it seemed one an artist might have dreamed of. She had loved him better than he knew. Lighthearted deceiver and fickle like all his sex he would never understand what he had meant to her and for an instant there was in the blue eyes a quick stinging of tears. Their eyes were probing her mercilessly but with a brave effort she sparkled back in sympathy as she glanced at her new conquest for them to see.

—O, responded Gerty, quick as lightning, laughing, and the proud head flashed up. I can throw my cap at who I like because it's leap year.

Her words rang out crystalclear, more musical than the cooing of the ringdove but they cut the silence icily. There was that in her young voice that told that she was not a one to be lightly trifled with. As for Mr Reggy with his swank and his bit of money she could just chuck him aside as if he was so much filth and never again would she cast as much as a second thought on him and tear his silly postcard into a dozen pieces. And if ever after he dared to presume she could give him one look of measured scorn that would make him shrivel up on the spot. Miss puny little Edy's countenance fell to no slight extent and Gerty could see by her looking as black as thunder that she was simply in a towering rage though she hid it, the little kinnatt,[2] because that shaft had struck home for her petty jealousy and they both knew that she was something aloof, apart in another sphere, that she was not of them and there was somebody else too that knew it and saw it so they could put that in their pipe and smoke it.

Edy straightened up baby Boardman to get ready to go and Cissy tucked in the ball and the spades and buckets and it was high time too because the sandman was on his way for Master Boardman junior and Cissy told him too that Billy Winks was coming and that baby was to go deedaw and baby looked just too ducky, laughing up out of his gleeful eyes, and Cissy poked him like that out of fun in his wee fat tummy and baby, without as much as by your leave, sent up his compliments on to his brandnew dribbling bib.

—O my! Puddeny pie! protested Ciss. He has his bib destroyed.

The slight *contretemps*[3] claimed her attention but in two twos she set that little matter to rights.

Gerty stifled a smothered exclamation and gave a nervous cough and Edy asked what and she was just going to tell her to catch it while it was flying but she was ever ladylike in her deportment so she simply passed it off with consummate tact by saying that that was the benediction because just then the bell rang out from the steeple over the quiet seashore because Canon O'Hanlon was up on the altar with the veil that Father Conroy put round him round his shoulders giving the benediction with the Blessed Sacrament in his hands.

How moving the scene there in the gathering twilight, the last glimpse of Erin, the touching chime of those evening bells and at the same time a bat flew forth from the ivied belfry through the dusk, hither, thither, with a tiny lost cry. And she could see far away the lights of the lighthouses so picturesque she would have loved to do with a box of paints because it was easier than to make a man and soon the lamplighter would be going his rounds past the presbyterian church grounds and along by shady Tritonville avenue where the couples walked and lighting the lamp near her window where Reggy Wylie used to turn his freewheel like she read in that book *The*

2. Brat.   3. Set to; argument; fight.

Lamplighter by Miss Cummins,[4] author of *Mabel Vaughan* and other tales. For Gerty had her dreams that no-one knew of. She loved to read poetry and when she got a keepsake from Bertha Supple of that lovely confession album with the coralpink cover to write her thoughts in she laid it in the drawer of her toilettable which, though it did not err on the side of luxury, was scrupulously neat and clean. It was there she kept her girlish treasures trove, the tortoiseshell combs, her child of Mary badge, the whiterose scent, the eyebrowleine, her alabaster pouncetbox and the ribbons to change when her things came home from the wash and there were some beautiful thoughts written in it in violet ink that she bought in Hely's of Dame Street for she felt that she too could write poetry if she could only express herself like that poem that appealed to her so deeply that she had copied out of the newspaper she found one evening round the potherbs.[5] *Art thou real, my ideal?* it was called by Louis J. Walsh, Magherafelt,[6] and after there was something about *twilight, wilt thou ever?* and ofttimes the beauty of poetry, so sad in its transient loveliness, had misted her eyes with silent tears that the years were slipping by for her, one by one, and but for that one shortcoming she knew she need fear no competition and that was an accident coming down Dalkey hill and she always tried to conceal it. But it must end, she felt. If she saw that magic lure in his eyes there would be no holding back for her. Love laughs at locksmiths. She would make the great sacrifice. Her every effort would be to share his thoughts. Dearer than the whole world would she be to him and gild his days with happiness. There was the allimportant question and she was dying to know was he a married man or a widower who had lost his wife or some tragedy like the nobleman with the foreign name from the land of song had to have her put into a madhouse, cruel only to be kind. But even if—what then? Would it make a very great difference? From everything in the least indelicate her finebred nature instinctively recoiled. She loathed that sort of person, the fallen women off the accommodation walk beside the Dodder[7] that went with the soldiers and coarse men, with no respect for a girl's honour, degrading the sex and being taken up to the police station. No, no: not that. They would be just good friends like a big brother and sister without all that other in spite of the conventions of Society with a big ess. Perhaps it was an old flame he was in mourning for from the days beyond recall. She thought she understood. She would try to understand him because men were so different. The old love was waiting, waiting with little white hands stretched out, with blue appealing eyes. Heart of mine! She would follow her dream of love, the dictates of her heart that told her he was her all in all, the only man in all the world for her for love was the master guide. Nothing else mattered. Come what might she would be wild, untrammelled, free.

Canon O'Hanlon put the Blessed Sacrament back into the tabernacle[8] and the choir sang *Laudate Dominum omnes gentes*[9] and then he locked the tabernacle door because the benediction was over and Father Conroy handed him his hat to put on and crosscat Edy asked wasn't she coming but Jacky Caffrey called out:

—O, look, Cissy!

And they all looked was it sheet lightning but Tommy saw it too over the trees beside the church, blue and then green and purple.

—It's fireworks, Cissy Caffrey said.

---

4. Maria Cummins's 1854 novel *The Lamplighter* supplies the stylistic template for the first half of this chapter.
5. Herbs or greens cooked in a pot.
6. A small village in northeastern Ireland.

7. One of the four rivers that runs through Dublin.
8. Ceremonial receptacle for the Eucharist.
9. Give praise to the Lord, O ye nations (Latin).

And they all ran down the strand to see over the houses and the church, hel-terskelter, Edy with the pushcar with baby Boardman in it and Cissy holding Tommy and Jacky by the hand so they wouldn't fall running.

—Come on, Gerty, Cissy called. It's the bazaar fireworks.

But Gerty was adamant. She had no intention of being at their beck and call. If they could run like rossies[1] she could sit so she said she could see from where she was. The eyes that were fastened upon her set her pulses tingling. She looked at him a moment, meeting his glance, and a light broke in upon her. Whitehot passion was in that face, passion silent as the grave and it had made her his. At last they were left alone without the others to pry and pass remarks and she knew he could be trusted to the death, steadfast, a sterling man, a man of inflexible honour to his fingertips. His hands and face were working and a tremour went over her. She leaned back far to look up where the fireworks were and she caught her knee in her hands so as not to fall back looking up and there was no-one to see only him and her when she revealed all her graceful beautifully shaped legs like that, supply soft and delicately rounded, and she seemed to hear the panting of his heart, his hoarse breathing, because she knew about the passion of men like that, hotblooded, because Bertha Supple told her once in dead secret and made her swear she'd never about the gentleman lodger that was staying with them out of the Congested Districts Board[2] that had pictures cut out of papers of those skirtdancers and highkickers and she said he used to do something not very nice that you could imagine sometimes in the bed. But this was altogether differ-ent from a thing like that because there was all the difference because she could almost feel him draw her face to his and the first quick hot touch of his handsome lips. Besides there was absolution[3] so long as you didn't do the other thing before being married and there ought to be women priests that would understand without your telling out and Cissy Caffrey too sometimes had that dreamy kind of dreamy look in her eyes so that she too, my dear, and Winny Rippingham so mad about actors' pho-tographs and besides it was on account of that other thing coming on the way it did.

And Jacky Caffrey shouted to look, there was another and she leaned back and the garters were blue to match on account of the transparent and they all saw it and shouted to look, look there it was and she leaned back ever so far to see the fireworks and some-thing queer was flying about through the air, a soft thing to and fro, dark. And she saw a long Roman candle going up over the trees up, up, and, in the tense hush, they were all breathless with excitement as it went higher and higher and she had to lean back more and more to look up after it, high, high, almost out of sight, and her face was suffused with a divine, an entrancing blush from straining back and he could see her other things too, nainsook knickers, the fabric that caresses the skin, better than those other petti-width, the green, four and eleven, on account of being white and she let him and she saw that he saw and then it went so high it went out of sight a moment and she was trembling in every limb from being bent so far back that he had a full view high up above her knee where no-one ever not even on the swing or wading and she wasn't ashamed and he wasn't either to look in that immodest way like that because he couldn't resist the sight of the wondrous revealment half offered like those skirtdancers behaving so immodest before gentlemen looking and he kept on looking, looking. She would fain have cried to him chokingly, held out her snowy slender arms to him to come, to feel his lips laid on

1. A loose or disreputable woman (cf. "streel").
2. A board established to address problems of urban over-
crowding and poverty.
3. A remission of sin.

her white brow, the cry of a young girl's love, a little strangled cry, wrung from her, that cry that has rung through the ages. And then a rocket sprang and bang shot blind blank and O! then the Roman candle burst and it was like a sigh of O! and everyone cried O! O! in raptures and it gushed out of it a stream of rain gold hair threads and they shed and ah! they were all greeny dewy stars falling with golden, O so lovely! O so soft, sweet, soft!

Then all melted away dewily in the grey air: all was silent. Ah! She glanced at him as she bent forward quickly, a pathetic little glance of piteous protest, of shy reproach under which he coloured like a girl. He was leaning back against the rock behind. Leopold Bloom (for it is he) stands silent, with bowed head before those young guileless eyes. What a brute he had been! At it again? A fair unsullied soul had called to him and, wretch that he was, how had he answered? An utter cad he had been. He of all men! But there was an infinite store of mercy in those eyes, for him too a word of pardon even though he had erred and sinned and wandered. Should a girl tell? No, a thousand times no. That was their secret, only theirs, alone in the hiding twilight and there was none to know or tell save the little bat that flew so softly through the evening to and fro and little bats don't tell.

Cissy Caffrey whistled, imitating the boys in the football field to show what a great person she was: and then she cried:

—Gerty! Gerty! We're going. Come on. We can see from farther up.

Gerty had an idea, one of love's little ruses. She slipped a hand into her kerchief pocket and took out the wadding and waved in reply of course without letting him and then slipped it back. Wonder if he's too far to. She rose. Was it goodbye? No. She had to go but they would meet again, there, and she would dream of that till then, tomorrow, of her dream of yester eve. She drew herself up to her full height. Their souls met in a last lingering glance and the eyes that reached her heart, full of a strange shining, hung enraptured on her sweet flowerlike face. She half smiled at him wanly, a sweet forgiving smile, a smile that verged on tears, and then they parted.

Slowly without looking back she went down the uneven strand to Cissy, to Edy, to Jacky and Tommy Caffrey, to little baby Boardman. It was darker now and there were stones and bits of wood on the strand and slippy seaweed. She walked with a certain quiet dignity characteristic of her but with care and very slowly because, because Gerty MacDowell was. . . .

Tight boots? No. She's lame! O![4]

Mr Bloom watched her as she limped away. Poor girl! That's why she's left on the shelf and the others did a sprint. Thought something was wrong by the cut of her jib. Jilted beauty. A defect is ten times worse in a woman. But makes them polite. Glad I didn't know it when she was on show. Hot little devil all the same. Wouldn't mind. Curiosity like a nun or a negress or a girl with glasses. That squinty one is delicate. Near her monthlies, I expect, makes them feel ticklish. I have such a bad headache today.[5] Where did I put the letter? Yes, all right. All kinds of crazy longings. Licking pennies. Girl in Tranquilla convent that nun told me liked to smell rock oil. Virgins go mad in the end I suppose. Sister? How many women in Dublin have it today? Martha, she. Something in the air. That's the moon. But then why don't all women menstruate at the same time with same moon, I mean? Depends on the time they were

---

4. At this point in the chapter, the narrative point of view shifts from primarily Gerty's to Leopold Bloom's.
5. This sentence is remembered by Bloom from the letter he has received earlier in the day from his secret correspondent, Martha Clifford, with whom he is carrying on a postal "affair."

born, I suppose. Or all start scratch then get out of step. Sometimes Molly and Milly[6] together. Anyhow I got the best of that. Damned glad I didn't do it in the bath this morning over her silly I will punish you letter. Made up for that tramdriver this morning. That gouger M'Coy stopping me to say nothing. And his wife engagement in the country valise, voice like a pickaxe. Thankful for small mercies. Cheap too. Yours for the asking. Because they want it themselves. Their natural craving. Shoals of them every evening poured out of offices. Reserve better. Don't want it they throw it at you. Catch em alive, O. Pity they can't see themselves. A dream of wellfilled hose. Where was that? Ah, yes. Mutoscope[7] pictures in Capel street: for men only. Peeping Tom. Willy's hat and what the girls did with it. Do they snapshot those girls or is it all a fake. *Lingerie* does it. Felt for the curves inside her *deshabillé*.[8] Excites them also when they're. I'm all clean come and dirty me. And they like dressing one another for the sacrifice. Milly delighted with Molly's new blouse. At first. Put them all on to take them all off. Molly. Why I bought her the violet garters. Us too: the tie he[9] wore, his lovely socks and turnedup trousers. He wore a pair of gaiters the night that first we met. His lovely shirt was shining beneath his what? of jet. Say a woman loses a charm with every pin she takes out. Pinned together. O Mairy lost the pin of her. Dressed up to the nines for somebody. Fashion part of their charm. Just changes when you're on the track of the secret. Except the east: Mary, Martha: now as then. No reasonable offer refused. She wasn't in a hurry either. Always off to a fellow when they are. They never forget an appointment. Out on spec probably. They believe in chance because like themselves. And the others inclined to give her an odd dig. Girl friends at school, arms round each other's necks or with ten fingers locked, kissing and whispering secrets about nothing in the convent garden. Nuns with whitewashed faces, cool coif and their rosaries going up and down, vindictive too for what they can't get. Barbed wire.[1] Be sure now and write to me. And I'll write to you. Now won't you? Molly and Josie Powell. Till Mr Right comes along, then meet once in a blue moon. *Tableau!* O, look who it is for the love of God! How are you at all? What have you been doing with yourself? Kiss and delighted to, kiss, to see you. Picking holes in each other's appearance. You're looking splendid. Sister souls showing their teeth at one another. How many have you left? Wouldn't lend each other a pinch of salt.

   Ah!

   Devils they are when that's coming on them. Dark devilish appearance. Molly often told me feel things a ton weight. Scratch the sole of my foot. O that way! O, that's exquisite! Feel it myself too. Good to rest once in a way. Wonder if it's bad to go with them then. Safe in one way. Turns milk, makes fiddlestrings snap. Something about withering plants I read in a garden. Besides they say if the flower withers she wears she's a flirt. All are. Daresay she felt I. When you feel like that you often meet what you feel. Liked me or what? Dress they look at. Always know a fellow courting:

---

6. Molly is Marion ("Molly") Bloom, Leopold's 33-year-old wife, to whom he has been married for 15 years; Milly is Millicent ("Milly") Bloom, their daughter, who turned 15 the day before that on which the action of the novel is set.

7. A device for viewing sequential stop-action photographs, comprising a primitive motion picture. The mutoscope show Bloom recalls was pornographic.

8. Revealing or inadequately concealing, garment. The word *deshabillé*, along with other phrases like "opulent curves," is remembered in Bloom's interior monologue

from the pornographic book *Sweets of Sin* that he has examined and purchased at a second-hand bookseller earlier in the day.

9. The masculine pronouns here, and elsewhere in the pages that follow, frequently refer to Hugh "Blazes" Boylan, the Dublin singer and impresario who will be leaving on a musical tour to Belfast with Molly Bloom later in the summer; the two have inaugurated a love affair earlier this same afternoon.

1. Bloom here thinks of the (apocryphal) story that barbed wire was invented by a nun.

collars and cuffs. Well cocks and lions do the same and stags. Same time might prefer a tie undone or something. Trousers? Suppose I when I was? No. Gently does it. Dislike rough and tumble. Kiss in the dark and never tell. Saw something in me. Wonder what. Sooner have me as I am than some poet chap with bearsgrease plastery hair, lovelock over his dexter optic.[2] To aid gentleman in literary. Ought to attend to my appearance my age. Didn't let her see me in profile. Still, you never know. Pretty girls and ugly men marrying. Beauty and the beast. Besides I can't be so if Molly. Took off her hat to show her hair. Wide brim bought to hide her face, meeting someone might know her, bend down or carry a bunch of flowers to smell. Hair strong in rut. Ten bob I got for Molly's combings when we were on the rocks in Holles street. Why not? Suppose he gave her money. Why not? All a prejudice. She's worth ten, fifteen, more a pound. What? I think so. All that for nothing. Bold hand. Mrs Marion.[3] Did I forget to write address on that letter like the postcard I sent to Flynn. And the day I went to Drimmie's without a necktie. Wrangle with Molly it was put me off. No, I remember. Richie Goulding. He's another. Weighs on his mind. Funny my watch stopped at half past four. Dust. Shark liver oil they use to clean could do it myself. Save. Was that just when he, she?[4]

O, he did. Into her. She did. Done.

Ah!

Mr Bloom with careful hand recomposed his wet shirt. O Lord, that little limping devil. Begins to feel cold and clammy. After effect not pleasant. Still you have to get rid of it someway. They don't care. Complimented perhaps. Go home to nicey bread and milky and say night prayers with the kiddies. Well, aren't they. See her as she is spoil all. Must have the stage setting, the rouge, costume, position, music. The name too. *Amours* of actresses. Nell Gwynn, Mrs Bracegirdle, Maud Branscombe. Curtain up. Moonlight silver effulgence. Maiden discovered with pensive bosom. Little sweetheart come and kiss me. Still I feel. The strength it gives a man. That's the secret of it. Good job I let off there behind coming out of Dignam's. Cider that was. Otherwise I couldn't have. Makes you want to sing after. *Lacaus esant taratara.*[5] Suppose I spoke to her. What about? Bad plan however of you don't know how to end the conversation. Ask them a question they ask you another. Good idea if you're in a cart. Wonderful of course if you say: good evening, and you see she's on for it: good evening. O but the dark evening in the Appian way I nearly spoke to Mrs Clinch O thinking she was. Whew! Girl in Meath street that night. All the dirty things I made her say all wrong of course. My arks she called it. It's so hard to find one who. Aho! If you don't answer when they solicit must be horrible for them till they harden. And kissed my hand when I gave her the extra two shillings. Parrots. Press the button and the bird will squeak. Wish she hadn't called me sir. O, her mouth in the dark! And you a married man with a single girl! That's what they enjoy. Taking a man from another woman. Or even hear of it. Different with me. Glad to get away from other

2. A monocle worn in the right eye (in Bloom's imagination, associated with the stereotypical image of a poet).
3. The phrases are associated in Bloom's mind with the letter he brought upstairs to Molly that morning, addressed in a "bold hand" by Blazes Boylan to "Mrs. Marion [rather than, as decorum would dictate, Mrs. Leopold] Bloom." The letter probably confirmed the details of their afternoon rendezvous, as Bloom knows all too well.

4. Bloom here wonders if his watch stopped just at the moment that Molly and Boylan were committing their adultery against him (4:30 P.M.). Evidence from elsewhere in the book does suggest that the two events were nearly coincident.
5. Bloom's rhythmical rendition of *La causa è santa*, "The cause is sacred," from the Italian version of Giacomo Meyerbeer's opera, *Les Hugenots* (1836).

chap's wife. Eating off his cold plate. Chap in the Burton today spitting back gum-chewed gristle. French letter still in my pocketbook. Cause of half the trouble. But might happen sometime, I don't think. Come in. All is prepared. I dreamt. What? Worst is beginning. How they change the venue when it's not what they like. Ask you do you like mushrooms because she once knew a gentleman who. Or ask you what someone was going to say when he changed his mind and stopped. Yet if I went the whole hog, say: I want to, something like that. Because I did. She too. Offend her. Then make it up. Pretend to want something awfully, then cry off for her sake. Flatters them. She must have been thinking of someone else all the time. What harm? Must since she came to the use of reason, he, he and he. First kiss does the trick. The propitious moment. Something inside them goes pop. Mushy like, tell by their eye, on the sly. First thoughts are best. Remember that till their dying day. Molly, lieutenant Mulvey that kissed her under the Moorish wall beside the gardens. Fifteen she told me. But her breasts were developed. Fell asleep then. After Glencree dinner that was when we drove home the featherbed mountain. Gnashing her teeth in sleep. Lord mayor had his eye on her too. Val Dillon. Apoplectic.

There she is with them down there for the fireworks. My fireworks. Up like a rocket, down like a stick. And the children, twins they must be, waiting for something to happen. Want to be grownups. Dressing in mother's clothes. Time enough, understand all the ways of the world. And the dark one with the mop head and the nigger mouth. I knew she could whistle. Mouth made for that. Like Molly. Why that high class whore in Jammet's wore her veil only to her nose. Would you mind, please, telling me the right time? I'll tell you the right time up a dark lane. Say prunes and prisms forty times every morning, cure for fat lips. Caressing the little boy too. Onlookers see most of the game. Of course they understand birds, animals, babies. In their line.

Didn't look back when she was going down the strand. Wouldn't give that satisfaction. Those girls, those girls, those lovely seaside girls.[6] Fine eyes she had, clear. It's the white of the eye brings that out not so much the pupil. Did she know what I? Course. Like a cat sitting beyond a dog's jump. Women never meet one like that Wilkins in the high school drawing a picture of Venus with all his belongings on show. Call that innocence? Poor idiot! His wife has her work cut out for her. Never see them sit on a bench marked *Wet Paint*. Eyes all over them. Look under the bed for what's not there. Longing to get the fright of their lives. Sharp as needles they are. When I said to Molly the man at the corner of Cuffe street was goodlooking, thought she might like, twigged at once he had a false arm. Had too. Where do they get that? Typist going up Roger Greene's stairs two at a time to show her understandings. Handed down from father to mother to daughter, I mean. Bred in the bone. Milly for example drying her handkerchief on the mirror to save the ironing. Best place for an ad to catch a woman's eye on a mirror.[7] And when I sent her for Molly's Paisley shawl to Presscott's, by the way that ad I must, carrying home the change in her stocking. Clever little minx! I never told her. Neat way she carries parcels too. Attract men, small thing like that. Holding up her hand, shaking it, to let the blood flow back when it was red. Who did you learn that from? Nobody. Something the nurse taught me. O, don't they know? Three years old she was

6. From the song of which Milly Bloom's letter to her father makes mention, and which Blazes Boylan is known for singing, "Seaside Girls." The later phrase "Your head it simply swirls" is also from this song.

7. Bloom's profession is advertising canvasser, selling advertising space in newspapers to various retail concerns.

in front of Molly's dressingtable just before we left Lombard street west. Me have a nice pace. Mullingar. Who knows? Ways of the world. Young student. Straight on her pins anyway not like the other. Still she was game. Lord, I am wet. Devil you are. Swell of her calf. Transparent stockings, stretched to breaking point. Not like that frump today. A. E. Rumpled stockings. Or the one in Grafton street. White. Wow! Beef to the heel.

A monkey puzzle rocket burst, spluttering in darting crackles. Zrads and zrads, zrads, zrads. And Cissy and Tommy ran out to see and Edy after with the pushcar and then Gerty beyond the curve of the rocks. Will she? Watch! Watch! See! Looked round. She smelt an onion. Darling, I saw your. I saw all.

Lord!

Did me good all the same. Off colour after Kiernan's, Dignam's.[8] For this relief much thanks. In *Hamlet*, that is.[9] Lord! It was all things combined. Excitement. When she leaned back felt an ache at the butt of my tongue. Your head it simply swirls. He's right. Might have made a worse fool of myself however. Instead of talking about nothing. Then I will tell you all. Still it was a kind of language between us. It couldn't be? No, Gerty they called her. Might be false name however like my and the address Dolphin's barn a blind.[1]

> Her maiden name was Jemima Brown
> And she lived with her mother in Irishtown.

Place made me think of that I suppose. All tarred with the same brush. Wiping pens in their stockings. But the ball rolled down to her as if it understood. Every bullet has its billet. Course I never could throw anything straight at school. Crooked as a ram's horn. Sad however because it lasts only a few years till they settle down to potwalloping and papa's pants will soon fit Willy and fullers' earth[2] for the baby when they hold him out to do ah ah. No soft job. Saves them. Keeps them out of harm's way. Nature. Washing child, washing corpse. Dignam. Children's hands always round them. Cocoanut skulls, monkeys, not even closed at first, sour milk in their swaddles and tainted curds. Oughtn't to have given that child an empty teat to suck. Fill it up with wind. Mrs Beaufoy, Purefoy. Must call to the hospital.[3] Wonder is nurse Callan there still. She used to look over some nights when Molly was in the Coffee Palace. That young doctor O'Hare I noticed her brushing his coat. And Mrs Breen and Mrs Dignam once like that too, marriageable. Worst of all at night Mrs Duggan told me in the City Arms. Husband rolling in drunk, stink of pub off him like a polecat. Have that in your nose in the dark, whiff of stale boose. Then ask in the morning: was I drunk last night? Bad policy however to fault the husband. Chickens come home to roost. They stick by one another like glue. Maybe the women's fault also. That's where Molly can knock spots off them. It is the blood of the south. Moorish. Also the form, the figure. Hands felt for the opulent. Just compare for instance those others. Wife locked up at home, skeleton in the cupboard. Allow me to introduce my. Then they trot you out some kind of a nondescript, wouldn't know what to call her. Always see a fellow's weak point in his wife. Still there's destiny in it, falling

8. Kiernan's is the pub Barney Kiernan's, where Bloom got into a heated argument with a jingoistic Irish nationalist, The Citizen, in the previous chapter; Dignam's is the funeral of Paddy Dignam, recounted in Chapter 6.
9. *Hamlet*, 1.1.8.
1. Bloom here considers for the moment the possibility that this mysterious girl on the beach might be the same

mysterious woman, "Martha Clifford," with whom he is carrying on his intrigue by post.
2. Material used for cleaning the grease from clothing.
3. The next chapter of *Ulysses*, known as "Oxen of the Sun," takes place at the Holles Street National Maternity Hospital, where family friend Mina Purefoy is undergoing a long and difficult labor.

in love. Have their own secrets between them. Chaps that would go to the dogs if some woman didn't take them in hand. Then little chits of girls, height of a shilling in coppers, with little hubbies. As God made them He matched them. Sometimes children turn out well enough. Twice nought makes one. Or old rich chap of seventy and blushing bride. Marry in May and repent in December. This wet is very unpleasant. Stuck. Well the foreskin is not back. Better detach.

Ow!

Other hand a sixfooter with a wifey up to his watchpocket. Long and the short of it. Big he and little she. Very strange about my watch. Wristwatches are always going wrong. Wonder is there any magnetic influence between the person because that was about the time he. Yes, I suppose at once. Cat's away the mice will play. I remember looking in Pill lane. Also that now is magnetism. Back of everything magnetism. Earth for instance pulling this and being pulled. That causes movement. And time? Well that's the time the movement takes. Then if one thing stopped the whole ghesabo would stop bit by bit. Because it's all arranged. Magnetic needle tells you what's going on in the sun, the stars. Little piece of steel iron. When you hold out the fork. Come. Come. Tip. Woman and man that is. Fork and steel. Molly, he. Dress up and look and suggest and let you see and see more and defy you if you're a man to see that and, like a sneeze coming, legs, look, look and if you have any guts in you. Tip. Have to let fly.

Wonder how is she feeling in that region. Shame all put on before third person. More put out about a hole in her stocking. Molly, her underjaw stuck out, head back, about the farmer in the ridingboots and spurs at the horse show. And when the painters were in Lombard street west. Fine voice that fellow had. How Giuglini[4] began. Smell that I did, like flowers. It was too. Violets. Came from the turpentine probably in the paint. Make their own use of everything. Same time doing it scraped her slipper on the floor so they wouldn't hear. But lots of them can't kick the beam, I think. Keep that thing up for hours. Kind of a general all round over me and half down my back.

Wait. Hm. Hm. Yes. That's her perfume. Why she waved her hand. I leave you this to think of me when I'm far away on the pillow. What is it? Heliotrope? No, Hyacinth? Hm. Roses, I think. She'd like scent of that kind. Sweet and cheap: soon sour. Why Molly likes opoponax. Suits her with a little jessamine mixed. Her high notes and her low notes. At the dance night she met him, dance of the hours. Heat brought it out. She was wearing her black and it had the perfume of the time before. Good conductor, is it? Or bad? Light too. Suppose there's some connection. For instance if you go into a cellar where it's dark. Mysterious thing too. Why did I smell it only now? Took its time in coming like herself, slow but sure. Suppose it's ever so many millions of tiny grains blown across. Yes, it is. Because those spice islands, Cinghalese this morning, smell them leagues off. Tell you what it is. It's like a fine fine veil or web they have all over the skin, fine like what do you call it gossamer and they're always spinning it out of them, fine as anything, rainbow colours without knowing it. Clings to everything she takes off. Vamp of her stockings. Warm shoe. Stays. Drawers: little kick, taking them off. Byby till next time. Also the cat likes to sniff in her shift on the bed. Know her smell in a thousand. Bathwater too. Reminds me of strawberries and cream. Wonder where it is really. There or the armpits or under the neck. Because you get it out of all holes and corners. Hyacinth perfume

4. Italian tenor Antonio Giuglini (1827–1865) enjoyed great success in Dublin.

made of oil or ether or something. Muskrat. Bag under their tails one grain pour off odour for years. Dogs at each other behind. Good evening. Evening, How do you sniff? Hm. Hm. Very well, thank you. Animals go by that. Yes now, look at it that way. We're the same. Some women for instance warn you off when they have their period. Come near. Then get a hogo[5] you could hang your hat on. Like what? Potted herrings gone stale or. Boof! Please keep off the grass.

Perhaps they get a man smell off us. What though? Cigary gloves Long John had on his desk the other. Breath? What you eat and drink gives that. No. Mansmell, I mean. Must be connected with that because priests that are supposed to be are different. Women buzz round it like flies round treacle. Railed off the altar get on to it at any cost. The tree of forbidden priest. O father, will you? Let me be the first to. That diffuses itself all through the body, permeates. Source of life and it's extremely curious the smell. Celery sauce. Let me.

Mr Bloom inserted his nose. Hm. Into the. Hm. Opening of his waistcoat. Almonds or. No. Lemons it is. Ah no, that's the soap.[6]

O by the by that lotion. I knew there was something on my mind. Never went back and the soap not paid. Dislike carrying bottles like that hag this morning. Hynes might have paid me that three shillings. I could mention Meagher's just to remind him. Still if he works that paragraph. Two and nine. Bad opinion of me he'll have. Call tomorrow. How much do I owe you? Three and nine? Two and nine, sir. Ah. Might stop him giving credit another time. Lose your customers that way. Pubs do. Fellows run up a bill on the slate and then slinking around the back streets into somewhere else.

Here's this nobleman passed before. Blown in from the bay. Just went as far as turn back. Always at home at dinnertime. Looks mangled out: had a good tuck in. Enjoying nature now. Grace after meals. After supper walk a mile. Sure he has a small bank balance somewhere, government sit.[7] Walk after him now make him awkward like those newsboys me today. Still you learn something. See ourselves as others see us. So long as women don't mock what matter? That's the way to find out. Ask yourself who is he now. *The Mystery Man on the Beach*, prize titbit story by Mr Leopold Bloom. Payment at the rate of one guinea per column. And that fellow today at the graveside in the brown macintosh. Corns on his kismet however. Healthy perhaps absorb all the. Whistle brings rain they say. Must be some somewhere. Salt in the Ormond damp. The body feels the atmosphere. Old Betty's joints are on the rack. Mother Shipton's prophecy that is about ships around they fly in the twinkling. No. Signs of rain it is. The royal reader. And distant hills seem coming nigh.

Howth. Bailey light. Two, four, six, eight, nine. See. Has to change or they might think it a house. Wreckers. Grace darling. People afraid of the dark. Also glowworms, cyclists: lightingup time. Jewels diamonds flash better. Light is a kind of reassuring. Not going to hurt you. Better now of course than long ago. Country roads. Run you through the small guts for nothing. Still two types there are you bob against. Scowl or smile. Pardon! Not at all. Best time to spray plants too in the shade after the sun. Some light still. Red rays are longest. Roygbiv Vance taught us: red, orange, yellow, green, blue, indigo, violet. A star I see. Venus? Can't tell yet. Two, when three it's night. Were those nightclouds there all the time? Looks like a phantom ship. No. Wait. Trees are they? An optical illusion. Mirage. Land of the setting sun this. Homerule sun setting in the southeast. My native land, goodnight.

---

5. Flavor or, in this case, odor.
6. In Chapter 5 ("Lotus Eaters"), Bloom has purchased a bar of lemon soap, which he carries in his pants pocket, and put in an order for hand lotion.
7. Situation, or position.

Dew falling. Bad for you, dear, to sit on that stone. Brings on white fluxions. Never have little baby then less he was big strong fight his way up through. Might get piles myself. Sticks too like a summer cold, sore on the mouth. Cut with grass or paper worst. Friction of the position. Like to be that rock she sat on. O sweet little, you don't know how nice you looked. I begin to like them at that age. Green apples. Grab at all that offer. Suppose it's the only time we cross legs, seated. Also the library today: those girl graduates. Happy chairs under them. But it's the evening influence. They feel all that. Open like flowers, know their hours, sunflowers, Jerusalem artichokes, in ballrooms, chandeliers, avenues under the lamps. Nightstock in Mat Dillon's garden where I kissed her shoulder. Wish I had a full length oilpainting of her then. June that was too I wooed. The year returns. History repeats itself. Ye crags and peaks I'm with you once again. Life, love, voyage round your own little world. And now? Sad about her lame of course but must be on your guard not to feel too much pity. They take advantage.

All quiet on Howth now. The distant hills seem. Where we. The rhododendrons.[8] I am a fool perhaps. He gets the plums and I the plumstones. Where I come in. All that old hill has seen. Names change: that's all. Lovers: yum yum.

Tired I feel now. Will I get up? O wait. Drained all the manhood out of me, little wretch. She kissed me. My youth. Never again. Only once it comes. Or hers. Take the train there tomorrow. No. Returning not the same. Like kids your second visit to a house. The new I want. Nothing new under the sun. Care of P. O. Dolphin's barn. Are you not happy in your? Naughty darling. At Dolphin's barn charades in Luke Doyle's house. Mat Dillon and his bevy of daughters: Tiny, Atty, Floey, Maimy, Louy, Hetty. Molly too. Eightyseven that was. Year before we. And the old major partial to his drop of spirits. Curious she an only child, I an only child. So it returns. Think you're escaping and run into yourself. Longest way round is the shortest way home. And just when he and she. Circus horse walking in a ring. Rip van Winkle we played. Rip: tear in Henny Doyle's overcoat. Van: breadvan delivering. Winkle: cockles and periwinkles. Then I did Rip van Winkle coming back. She leaned on the sideboard watching. Moorish eyes. Twenty years asleep in Sleepy Hollow. All changed. Forgotten. The young are old. His gun rusty from the dew.

Ba. What is that flying about? Swallow? Bat probably. Thinks I'm a tree, so blind. Have birds no smell? Metempsychosis.[9] They believed you could be changed into a tree from grief. Weeping willow. Ba. There he goes. Funny little beggar. Wonder where he lives. Belfry up there. Very likely. Hanging by his heels in the odour of sanctity. Bell scared him out, I suppose. Mass seems to be over. Could hear them all at it. Pray for us. And pray for us. And pray for us. Good idea the repetition. Same thing with ads. Buy from us. And buy from us. Yes, there's the light in the priest's house. Their frugal meal. Remember about the mistake in the valuation when I was in Thom's. Twentyeight it is. Two houses they have. Gabriel Conroy's[1] brother is curate. Ba. Again. Wonder why they come out at night like mice. They're a mixed breed. Birds are like hopping mice. What frightens them, light or noise? Better sit still. All instinct like the bird in drouth got water out of the end of a jar by throwing in pebbles. Like a little man in a cloak he is with tiny hands. Weeny bones. Almost

8. In the closing chapter of *Ulysses*, "Penelope," Molly Bloom recounts in poetic language the early days of her courtship with and marriage to Leopold, including a romantic episode on the rhododendron-covered hillsides of Howth Head.

9. The belief that, after death, the soul is reborn in another body. Molly has earlier asked Leopold to define this term for her in Chapter 4, "Calypso."

1. Gabriel Conroy is the proud protagonist of the great short story that closes *Dubliners*, "The Dead."

see them shimmering, kind of a bluey white. Colours depend on the light you see. Stare the sun for example like the eagle then look at a shoe see a blotch blob yellowish. Wants to stamp his trademark on everything. Instance, that cat this morning on the staircase. Colour of brown turf. Say you never see them with three colours. Not true. That half tabbywhite tortoiseshell in the *City Arms* with the letter em on her forehead. Body fifty different colours. Howth a while ago amethyst. Glass flashing. That's how that wise man what's his name with the burning glass. Then the heather goes on fire. It can't be tourists' matches. What? Perhaps the sticks dry rub together in the wind and light. Or broken bottles in the furze act as a burning glass in the sun. Archimedes. I have it! My memory's not so bad.

Ba. Who knows what they're always flying for. Insects? That bee last week got into the room playing with his shadow on the ceiling. Might be the one bit me, come back to see. Birds too never find out what they say. Like our small talk. And says she and says he. Nerve they have to fly over the ocean and back. Lots must be killed in storms, telegraph wires. Dreadful life sailors have too. Big brutes of oceangoing steamers floundering along in the dark, lowing out like seacows. *Faugh a ballagh.*[2] Out of that, bloody curse to you. Others in vessels, bit of a handkerchief sail, pitched about like snuff at a wake when the stormy winds do blow. Married too. Sometimes away for years at the ends of the earth somewhere. No ends really because it's round. Wife in every port they say. She has a good job if she minds it till Johnny comes marching home again. If ever he does. Smelling the tail end of ports. How can they like the sea? Yet they do. The anchor's weighed. Off he sails with a scapular or a medal on him for luck. Well? And the tephilim[3] no what's this they call it poor papa's father had on his door to touch. That brought us out of the land of Egypt and into the house of bondage. Something in all those superstitions because when you go out never know what dangers. Hanging on to a plank or astride of a beam for grim life, lifebelt round round him, gulping salt water, and that's the last of his nibs till the sharks catch hold of him. Do fish ever get seasick?

Then you have a beautiful calm without a cloud, smooth sea, placid, crew and cargo in smithereens, Davy Jones' locker. Moon looking down. Not my fault, old cockalorum.

A lost long candle wandered up the sky from Mirus bazaar in search of funds for Mercer's hospital and broke, drooping, and shed a cluster of violet but one white stars. They floated, fell: they faded. The shepherd's hour: the hour of folding: hour of tryst. From house to house, giving his everwelcome double knock, went the nine o'clock postman, the glowworm's lamp at his belt gleaming here and there through the laurel hedges. And among the five young trees a hoisted lintstock[4] lit the lamp at Leahy's terrace. By screens of lighted windows, by equal gardens a shrill voice went crying, wailing: *Evening Telegraph, stop press edition! Result of the Gold Cup races!* and from the door of Dignam's house a boy ran out and called. Twittering the bat flew here, flew there. Far out over the sands the coming surf crept, grey. Howth settled for slumber tired of long days, of yumyum rhododendrons (he was old) and felt gladly the night breeze lift, ruffle his fell of ferns. He lay but opened a red eye unsleeping, deep and slowly breathing, slumberous but awake. And far on Kish bank the anchored lightship twinkled, winked at Mr Bloom.

Life those chaps out there must have, stuck in the same spot. Irish Lights board. Penance for their sins. Coastguards too. Rocket and breeches buoy and lifeboat. Day we went out for the pleasure cruise in the Erin's King, throwing them the sack of old

2. Irish, "Clear the way" (a battle cry).
3. The *tephilim* is a leather pouch containing passages from the first five books of the Hebrew bible; Bloom is instead thinking of a *mezuzah*, a piece of parchment inscribed with passages from the books of Deuteronomy, affixed to the doorpost of Jewish households.
4. A stake notched at one end to hold a lighted match.

papers. Bears in the zoo. Filthy trip. Drunkards out to shake up their livers. Puking overboard to feed the herrings. Nausea. And the women, fear of God in their faces. Milly, no sign of funk. Her blue scarf loose, laughing. Don't know what death is at that age. And then their stomachs clean. But being lost they fear. When we hid behind the tree at Crumlin. I didn't want to. Mamma! Mamma! Babes in the wood. Frightening them with masks too. Throwing them up in the air to catch them. I'll murder you. Is it only half fun? Or children playing battle. Whole earnest. How can people aim guns at each other. Sometimes they go off. Poor kids. Only troubles wildfire and nettlerash. Calomel purge I got her for that. After getting better asleep with Molly. Very same teeth she has. What do they love? Another themselves? But the morning she chased her with the umbrella. Perhaps so as not to hurt. I felt her pulse. Ticking. Little hand it was: now big. Dearest Papli.[5] All that the hand says when you touch. Loved to count my waistcoat buttons. Her first stays I remember. Made me laugh to see. Little paps to begin with. Left one is more sensitive, I think. Mine too. Nearer the heart. Padding themselves out if fat is in fashion. Her growing pains at night, calling, wakening me. Frightened she was when her nature came on her first. Poor child! Strange moment for the mother too. Brings back her girlhood. Gibraltar. Looking from Buena Vista. O'Hara's tower. The seabirds screaming. Old Barbary ape that gobbled all his family. Sundown, gunfire for the men to cross the lines. Looking out over the sea she told me. Evening like this, but clear, no clouds. I always thought I'd marry a lord or a gentleman with a private yacht. *Buenas noches, señorita. El hombre ama la muchaha hermosa.*[6] Why me? Because you were so foreign from the others.

   Better not stick here all night like a limpet. This weather makes you dull. Must be getting on for nine by the light. Go home. Too late for *Leah, Lily of Killarney*. No. Might be still up. Call to the hospital to see. Hope she's over. Long day I've had. Martha, the bath, funeral, house of keys, museum with those goddesses, Dedalus' song. Then that bawler in Barney Kiernan's. Got my own back there. Drunken ranters. What I said about his God made him wince.[7] Mistake to hit back. Or? No. Ought to go home and laugh at themselves. Always want to be swilling in company. Afraid to be alone like a child of two. Suppose he hit me. Look at it other way round. Not so bad then. Perhaps not to hurt he meant. Three cheers for Israel. Three cheers for the sister-in-law he hawked about, three fangs in her mouth. Same style of beauty. Particularly nice old party for a cup of tea. The sister of the wife of the wild man of Borneo has just come to town. Imagine that in the early morning at close range. Everyone to his taste as Morris said when he kissed the cow. But Dignam's put the boots on it. Houses of mourning so depressing because you never know. Anyhow she wants the money. Must call to those Scottish widows as I promised. Strange name. Takes it for granted we're going to pop off first. That widow on Monday was is outside Cramer's that looked at me. Buried the poor husband but progressing favourably on the premium. Her widow's mite. Well? What do you expect her to do? Must wheedle her way along. Widower I hate to see. Looks so forlorn. Poor man O'Connor wife and five children poisoned by mussels here. The sewage. Hopeless. Some good matronly woman in a porkpie hat to mother him.

---

5. Papli is Milly's affectionate name for her father, with which she opens the letter he has received that morning.
6. Good evening, Miss. The man loves the beautiful young girl (Spanish).
7. Bloom here gives a very brief summary of his day to this point: "Martha," Martha Clifford, his amorous correspondent from whom he has received a letter; "the bath," in which Bloom indulges himself in the "Lotus Eaters" chapter; the "funeral" of Paddy Dignam is recounted in Chapter 6, "Hades"; "house of keys" refers to the motif of an ad he is attempting to sell to Alexander Keyes, Wine & Tea Merchant, in Chapter 7, "Aeolus"; in Chapter 8, "Lestrygonians," Bloom wanders over to the museum to ascertain whether or not Greek statues indeed have anal sphincters; and in Chapter 11, "Sirens," Bloom has heard Simon Dedalus sing "Come, Thou Lost One," from the opera *Martha*. For "that bawler in Barney Kiernan's," see n. 8, page 1184.

Take him in tow, platter face and a large apron. Ladies' grey flanelette bloomers, three shillings a pair, astonishing bargain. Plain and loved, loved for ever, they say. Ugly: no woman thinks she is. Love, lie and be handsome for tomorrow we die. See him sometimes walking about trying to find out who played the trick. U. p: up.[8] Fate that is. He, not me. Also a shop often noticed. Curse seems to dog it. Dreamt last night? Wait. Something confused. She had red slippers on. Turkish. Wore the breeches. Suppose she does. Would I like her in pyjamas? Damned hard to answer. Nannetti's gone. Mailboat. Near Holyhead by now. Must nail that ad of Keyes's. Work Hynes and Crawford. Petticoats for Molly. She has something to put in them. What's that? Might be money.

Mr Bloom stooped and turned over a piece of paper on the strand. He brought it near his eyes and peered. Letter? No. Can't read. Better go. Better. I'm tired to move. Page of an old copybook. All those holes and pebbles. Who could count them? Never know what you find. Bottle with story of a treasure in it thrown from a wreck. Parcels post. Children always want to throw things in the sea. Trust? Bread cast on the waters. What's this? Bit of stick.

O! Exhausted that female has me. Not so young now. Will she come here tomorrow? Wait for her somewhere for ever. Must come back. Murderers do. Will I?

Mr Bloom with his stick gently vexed the thick sand at his foot. Write a message for her. Might remain. What?

I.

Some flatfoot tramp on it in the morning. Useless. Washed away. Tide comes here a pool near her foot. Bend, see my face there, dark mirror, breathe on it, stirs. All these rocks with lines and scars and letters. O, those transparent! Besides they don't know. What is the meaning of that other world. I called you naughty boy because I do not like.[9]

AM. A.

No room. Let it go.

Mr Bloom effaced the letters with his slow boot. Hopeless thing sand. Nothing grows in it. All fades. No fear of big vessels coming up here. Except Guinness's barges. Round the Kish in eighty days. Done half by design.

He flung his wooden pen away. The stick fell in silted sand, stuck. Now if you were trying to do that for a week on end you couldn't. Chance. We'll never meet again. But it was lovely. Goodbye, dear. Thanks. Made me feel so young.

Short snooze now if I had. Must be near nine. Liverpool boat long gone. Not even the smoke. And she can do the other. Did too. And Belfast. I won't go.[1] Race there, race back to Ennis.[2] Let him. Just close my eyes a moment. Won't sleep though. Half dream. It never comes the same. Bat again. No harm in him. Just a few.

O sweety all your little girlwhite up I saw dirty bracegirdle made me do love sticky we two naughty Grace darling she him half past the bed met him pike hoses frillies for Raoul to perfume your wife black hair heave under embon *señorita* young eyes Mulvey plump years dreams return tail end Agendath swoony lovey showed me her next year in drawers return next in her next her next.[3]

---

8. "U.p: up" is the text of a mysterious postcard received by Dennis Breen; he has gone to investigate filing suit against its (anonymous) sender. The message seems to be mocking Breen sexually, suggesting that he is so constantly aroused that he can only urinate upward.
9. The preceding two sentences are from Martha Clifford's letter.

1. Bloom is thinking here of Molly's upcoming singing tour, on which she will be accompanied by Blazes Boylan.
2. Bloom himself is planning a memorial trip to Ennis, where his father committed suicide on 27 June 1886.
3. This paragraph represents the unstructured thought fragments of Bloom as he drifts off to sleep.

A bat flew. Here. There. Here. Far in the grey a bell chimed. Mr Bloom with open mouth, his left boot sanded sideways, leaned, breathed. Just for a few

    Cuckoo
    Cuckoo
    Cuckoo.

The clock on the mantelpiece in the priest's house cooed where Canon O'Hanlon and Father Conroy and the reverend John Hughes S. J. were taking tea and sodabread and butter and fried mutton chops with catsup and talking about

    Cuckoo
    Cuckoo
    Cuckoo.

Because it was a little canarybird bird that came out of its little house to tell the time that Gerty MacDowell noticed the time she was there because she was as quick as anything about a thing like that, was Gerty MacDowell, and she noticed at once that that foreign gentleman that was sitting on the rocks looking was

    Cuckoo
    Cuckoo
    Cuckoo.

T. S. Eliot
1888–1965

T. S. Eliot was one of the dominant forces in English-language poetry of the twentieth century. When the entire body of Eliot's writing and influence is taken into account—not only his relatively modest poetic and dramatic production, but his literary criticism, his religious and cultural criticism, his editorial work at the British publishing house Faber and Faber, his influence on younger poets coming up in his wake, and quite simply his *presence* as a literary and cultural icon—no one looms larger. As one of those younger poets, Karl Shapiro, has written: "Eliot is untouchable; he is Modern Literature incarnate and an institution unto himself." Eliot's obituary in *Life* magazine declared that "Our age beyond any doubt has been, and will continue to be, the Age of Eliot."

Thomas Stearns Eliot was born in Saint Louis, Missouri. The roots of Eliot's family tree go deep into American, and specifically New England, soil. His ancestor Andrew Eliot was one of the original settlers of the Massachusetts Bay Colony, emigrating from East Coker, in Somerset, England, in the mid-seventeenth century; he later became one of the jurors who tried the Salem "witches." The Eliots became a distinguished New England family; the Eliot family tree includes a president of Harvard University and three U.S. Presidents (John Adams, John Quincy Adams, and Rutherford B. Hayes). In 1834 the Reverend William Greenleaf Eliot, the poet's grandfather, graduated from Harvard and moved to Saint Louis, where he established the city's first Unitarian church; he went on to found Washington University, and became its chancellor in 1872. It was into this family environment—redolent of New England, New England religion (Unitarianism), and New England educational tradition (Harvard)—that Eliot was born in 1888. And yet in a 1960 essay, Eliot wrote, "My urban imagery was that of Saint Louis, upon which that of Paris and London had been superimposed." The sights and sounds of Saint Louis impressed themselves deeply on Eliot's young imagination, especially the looming figure of the Mississippi River (which he was to call "a strong brown god" in *The Dry Salvages*).

From age ten Eliot attended Smith Academy in Saint Louis—also founded by his grandfather—and spent his last year of secondary school at the Milton Academy in Milton, Massachusetts, in preparation for his entrance into Harvard in 1906. Eliot went on to take his A.B. (1909) and M.A. (1910) degrees from Harvard and largely completed a Ph.D. in philosophy from Harvard, first spending a relatively unstructured year in Paris, attending lectures at the Sorbonne and hearing Henri Bergson lecture at the Collège de France. He wrote a doctoral dissertation on the neo-idealist philosopher F. H. Bradley in 1916, which was accepted by the philosophy department at Harvard, but he never returned to Cambridge to defend the dissertation and take the degree. Eliot's year in Paris was crucial in many ways; in addition to breathing in the vital Parisian intellectual and artistic scene, he soaked up the writing of late-nineteenth-century French poets like Jules Laforgue, Tristan Corbière, and Charles Baudelaire.

Eliot's poems are deeply indebted both to French and to British poets. The poem with which Eliot broke onto the modern poetry scene was *The Love Song of J. Alfred Prufrock*, composed between 1910 and 1911. In a strikingly new and jarring idiom, the poem builds on the dramatic monologues of Robert Browning, breaking up the unified voice at the center of Browning's experiments with startling juxtapositions and transitions, and adding the violent and disturbing imagery of the French symbolist poets. The resulting poem is a heavily ironic "love song" in which neither lover nor beloved exists with any solidity outside the straitjacket of "a formulated phrase"; Prufrock, like modern European humanity whom he represents, is unable to penetrate the thick husk of habit, custom, and cliché to arrive at something substantial.

Eliot, and the poem, came to the notice of modern literature impresario Ezra Pound; in 1915 Pound saw to it that *Prufrock* was published in Harriet Monroe's influential *Poetry* magazine, as well as in his own *Catholic Anthology*, which brought Eliot to the notice of the (largely hostile) British literary establishment in the person of reviewers like the *Quarterly Review*'s Arthur Waugh. Eliot wrote three other great poems in this early period, *Portrait of a Lady*, *Preludes*, and *Rhapsody on a Windy Night*. Like *Prufrock*, the poems deal unflinchingly with loneliness, alienation, isolation; while isolation is hardly a new theme for poetry, Eliot suggests in a particularly modernist form in these poems that our isolation from others derives from, and tragically mirrors, our isolation from ourselves. This internalized alienation was also one of the themes of Eliot's early and influential review essay *The Metaphysical Poets* (1921); in that piece, he suggested that English poetry had suffered through a long drought, dating from about the time of Milton, caused by what Eliot termed a "dissociation of sensibility." At the time of the metaphysical poets (in the seventeenth century), a poet, or any sensitive thinker, was a unified whole; "A thought to Donne," Eliot writes, "was an experience; it modified his sensibility. . . . the ordinary man's experience is chaotic, irregular, fragmentary." That chaotic consciousness seemed to Eliot especially pronounced in the early decades of the twentieth century; though not sanguine of easy solutions, he did believe that modern poets, writing a poetry that would synthesize the seemingly unrelated sensations and experiences of modern men and women, might show a way out of "the immense panorama of futility and anarchy which is contemporary history," as he wrote in 1923 in a review of Joyce's *Ulysses*.

A collection of Eliot's early poems was published in 1917 as *Prufrock and Other Observations* by the Egoist Press, through the offices of Pound. For the remainder of the decade, however, Eliot's poetic output was small; feeling himself at a creative cul de sac, he wrote a few poems in French in 1917, including *Dans le Restaurant* which later appeared, trimmed and translated, as a part of *The Waste Land*. On Pound's suggestion, Eliot set himself, as a formal exercise, to write several poems modeled on the quatrains of Théophile Gautier. Arguably the most significant and influential of Eliot's early writings, however, were his many critical essays and book reviews; between 1916 and 1921 he wrote nearly a hundred essays and reviews, many of which were published in 1920 as *The Sacred Wood*. Critics still disagree as to whether Eliot's poetry or critical prose has been the more influential; the most important of Eliot's critical precepts, such as the "impersonality" of poetry and the inherent difficulty of modern writing, have entered wholesale into the way that modern literature is studied and taught. Eliot's critical principles, complemented and extended by academics such as I. A. Richards, make up the foundation of what came to be known as the New Criticism, a major mode of reading that emphasizes close attention to verbal textures and to poetic ironies, paradoxes, and tensions between disparate elements—all prominent features of Eliot's own poetry.

Eliot lived in modest circumstances for several years, working as a schoolteacher and then a bank clerk between 1916 and 1922. He then edited an increasingly influential quarterly, *The Criterion* (1922–1939), and became an editor at Faber and Faber, a post he retained until his death. His reputation as a poet was confirmed in 1922 with *The Waste Land*, the epochal work that remains Eliot's best-known and most influential poem; Pound called it "about enough . . . to make the rest of us shut up shop." More than any other text of the century, *The Waste Land* forcibly changed the idiom that contemporary poetry must adopt if it were to remain contemporary. Perhaps the poem's most impressive formal achievement, created in no small part through Ezra Pound's judicious editorial work, is its careful balance between structure and chaos, unity and fragmentation; this poise is created in the poem in equal parts by the mythical structures Eliot used to undergird the contemporary action and the pedantic footnotes he added to the poem, after its periodical publication in the *Dial*, to call the reader's attention to those structures. *The Waste Land*—like *Ulysses*, *Finnegans Wake*, Pound's *Cantos*, and a number of other important texts—looks unified largely because we readers look for it to be unified. Such a style of reading is one of the great triumphs of modernism, and one Eliot was instrumental in teaching to readers and teachers alike.

The Waste Land is justly celebrated for giving voice to the nearly universal pessimism and alienation of the early decades of the twentieth century Europe—though Eliot maintained to the end that he was not a spokesperson for his generation or for anything else, and that the poem was "only the relief of a personal and wholly insignificant grouse against life; it is just a piece of rhythmical grumbling." Owing to the development of recording technology, to "give voice" in this case is not merely a metaphor, for Eliot's recording of *The Waste Land*, in what Virginia Woolf called Eliot's "sepulchral voice," has been tremendously influential on two generations of poets and students. Eliot's critical principle of "impersonality," however, has sometimes served to obscure how very personal, on one level, the poem is. The poem was completed during Eliot's convalescence at a sanatorium in Margate, England ("On Margate Sands. / I can connect / Nothing with nothing," the speaker despairs in section 3, "The Fire Sermon") and in Lausanne, Switzerland; the speaker, like the poet, is reduced to shoring the fragments of a disappearing civilization against his ruin. The poem also bears painful testimony to the increasingly desperate state of Eliot's wife Vivien Haigh-Wood, whom he had married in 1915; she suffered terribly from what was at the time called "nervousness," and had finally to be institutionalized in 1938. Whole stretches of one-sided "dialogue" from the "A Game of Chess" section would seem to have been taken verbatim from the couple's private conversations: "My nerves are very bad to-night. Yes, bad. Stay with me. / Speak to me. Why do you never speak? Speak." On the draft of the poem, Pound wrote "photography" alongside this passage. *The Waste Land* remains one of the century's most incisive and insightful texts regarding the breakdown of social, communal, cultural, and personal relationships.

In 1930 Eliot's next important poem, the introspective and confessional *Ash Wednesday*, was published; in the time since the publication of *The Waste Land*, however, Eliot's personal belief system had undergone a sea change. In June 1927 he was baptized into the Anglican church; five months later, he was naturalized as a British citizen. In his 1928 monograph *For Lancelot Andrewes*, Eliot declared himself to be "classicist in literature, royalist in politics, and Anglo-Catholic in religion." His poem *Journey of the Magi*, published as a pamphlet a month after his baptism, addresses the journey Eliot himself had made through death to a rebirth—precisely the rebirth which, in the opening lines of *The Waste Land*, seems an impossibility.

The 1930s also saw Eliot's entry into the theater, with three poetic dramas: *The Rock* (1934), *Murder in the Cathedral* (1935), and *The Family Reunion* (1939). In his later years, these highbrow dramas were complemented with a handful of more popular social dramas, *The Cocktail Party* (1950), *The Confidential Clerk* (1954), and *The Elder Statesman* (1959). Though celebrated by critics at the time for their innovative use of verse and their willingness to wrestle with both modern problems and universal themes, the plays have slipped in popularity in recent years. Nevertheless, as fate would have it, Eliot is the posthumous librettist of one of the most successful musicals in the history of British and American theater: his playful children's book *Old Possum's Book of Practical Cats* (1939), light verse written for the enjoyment of his godchildren, was transformed by Andrew Lloyd Webber in 1980 into the smash-hit musical *Cats*.

Eliot's final poetic achievement—and, for many, his greatest—is the set of four poems published together in 1943 as *Four Quartets*. Eliot believed them to be the best of his writing; "The *Four Quartets*: I rest on those," he told an interviewer in 1959. Structurally—though the analogy is a loose one—Eliot modeled the *Quartets* on the late string quartets of Beethoven, especially the last, the A Minor Quartet; as early as 1931 he had written the poet Stephen Spender, "I have the A Minor Quartet on the gramophone, and I find it quite inexhaustible to study. There is a sort of heavenly or at least more than human gaiety about some of his later things which one imagines might come to oneself as the fruit of reconcilliation and relief after immense suffering; I should like to get something of that into verse before I die."

Eliot's last years were brightened by increasing public accolades, including the Nobel Prize for literature in 1948; he became a very popular speaker on the public lecture circuit, attracting an audience of 15,000, for instance, at a lecture at the University of Minnesota in 1956, later published as *The Frontiers of Criticism*. These public appearances largely took the place of creative writing after 1960. In January 1947 Vivien Eliot died in an institution; a decade later, he married Esme Valery Fletcher, and enjoyed a fulfilling companionate marriage until his death in January 1965. Like Hardy and Yeats, Eliot expressed his wish to be buried in his ancestors' parish church, in his case at East Coker, the home of his ancestor Andrew Eliot; thus, in his death and burial, the opening of his poem *East Coker* is literalized: "In my beginning is my end."

The Love Song of J. Alfred Prufrock

> *S'io credessi che mia risposta fosse*
> *a persona che mai tornasse al mondo,*
> *questa fiamma staria senza più scosse.*
> *Ma per ciò che giammai di questo fondo*
> *non tornò vivo alcun, s'i'odo il vero,*
> *senza tema d'infamia ti rispondo.*[1]

Let us go then, you and I,
When the evening is spread out against the sky
Like a patient etherised upon a table;
Let us go, through certain half-deserted streets,
5   The muttering retreats

---

1. From Dante's *Inferno* (27.61–66). Dante asks one of the damned souls for its name, and it replies: "If I thought my answer were for one who could return to the world, I would not reply, but as none ever did return alive from this depth, without fear of infamy I answer thee."

Of restless nights in one-night cheap hotels
And sawdust restaurants with oyster-shells:
Streets that follow like a tedious argument
Of insidious intent

10　To lead you to an overwhelming question . . .
Oh, do not ask, "What is it?"
Let us go and make our visit.

In the room the women come and go
Talking of Michelangelo.

15　The yellow fog that rubs its back upon the window-panes,
The yellow smoke that rubs its muzzle on the window-panes,
Licked its tongue into the corners of the evening,
Lingered upon the pools that stand in drains,
Let fall upon its back the soot that falls from chimneys,

20　Slipped by the terrace, made a sudden leap,
And seeing that it was a soft October night,
Curled once about the house, and fell asleep.

And indeed there will be time
For the yellow smoke that slides along the street

25　Rubbing its back upon the window-panes;
There will be time, there will be time
To prepare a face to meet the faces that you meet;
There will be time to murder and create,
And time for all the works and days of hands

30　That lift and drop a question on your plate;
Time for you and time for me,
And time yet for a hundred indecisions,
And for a hundred visions and revisions,
Before the taking of a toast and tea.

35　In the room the women come and go
Talking of Michelangelo.

And indeed there will be time
To wonder, "Do I dare?" and, "Do I dare?"
Time to turn back and descend the stair,

40　With a bald spot in the middle of my hair—
(They will say: "How his hair is growing thin!")
My morning coat, my collar mounting firmly to the chin,
My necktie rich and modest, but asserted by a simple pin—
(They will say: "But how his arms and legs are thin!")

45　Do I dare
Disturb the universe?
In a minute there is time
For decisions and revisions which a minute will reverse.

For I have known them all already, known them all—

50　Have known the evenings, mornings, afternoons,
I have measured out my life with coffee spoons;
I know the voices dying with a dying fall
Beneath the music from a farther room.

So how should I presume?

55   And I have known the eyes already, known them all—
The eyes that fix you in a formulated phrase,
And when I am formulated, sprawling on a pin,
When I am pinned and wriggling on the wall,
Then how should I begin
60   To spit out all the butt-ends of my days and ways?
        And how should I presume?

And I have known the arms already, known them all—
Arms that are braceleted and white and bare
(But in the lamplight, downed with light brown hair!)
65   Is it perfume from a dress
That makes me so digress?
Arms that lie along a table, or wrap about a shawl.
        And should I then presume?
        And how should I begin?
                    . . .

70   Shall I say, I have gone at dusk through narrow streets
And watched the smoke that rises from the pipes
Of lonely men in shirt-sleeves, leaning out of windows? . . .

I should have been a pair of ragged claws
Scuttling across the floors of silent seas.
                    . . .

75   And the afternoon, the evening, sleeps so peacefully!
Smoothed by long fingers,
Asleep . . . tired . . . or it malingers,
Stretched on the floor, here beside you and me.
Should I, after tea and cakes and ices,
80   Have the strength to force the moment to its crisis?
But though I have wept and fasted, wept and prayed,
Though I have seen my head (grown slightly bald) brought
        in upon a platter,[2]
I am no prophet—and here's no great matter;
I have seen the moment of my greatness flicker,
85   And I have seen the eternal Footman hold my coat, and snicker,
And in short, I was afraid.

And would it have been worth it, after all,
After the cups, the marmalade, the tea,
Among the porcelain, among some talk of you and me,
90   Would it have been worth while,
To have bitten off the matter with a smile,
To have squeezed the universe into a ball
To roll it towards some overwhelming question,
To say: "I am Lazarus, come from the dead,
95   Come back to tell you all, I shall tell you all"[3]—

2. Cf. Matthew 14. John the Baptist was beheaded by
Herod and his head was brought to his wife, Herodias, on
a platter.

3. Cf. John 11. Jesus raised Lazarus from the grave after
he had been dead four days.

If one, settling a pillow by her head,
    Should say: "That is not what I meant at all.
    That is not it, at all."

And would it have been worth it, after all,
100   Would it have been worth while,
After the sunsets and the dooryards and the sprinkled streets,
After the novels, after the teacups, after the skirts that trail
    along the floor—
And this, and so much more?—
It is impossible to say just what I mean!
105   But as if a magic lantern[4] threw the nerves in patterns on a
    screen:
Would it have been worth while
If one, settling a pillow or throwing off a shawl,
And turning toward the window, should say:
    "That is not it at all,
110   That is not what I meant, at all."
          · · ·
No! I am not Prince Hamlet, nor was meant to be;
Am an attendant lord, one that will do
To swell a progress, start a scene or two,
Advise the prince; no doubt, an easy tool,
115   Deferential, glad to be of use,
Politic, cautious, and meticulous;
Full of high sentence, but a bit obtuse;
At times, indeed, almost ridiculous—
Almost, at times, the Fool.

120   I grow old . . . I grow old . . .
I shall wear the bottoms of my trousers rolled.

Shall I part my hair behind? Do I dare to eat a peach?
I shall wear white flannel trousers, and walk upon the beach.
I have heard the mermaids singing, each to each.

125   I do not think that they will sing to me.

I have seen them riding seaward on the waves
Combing the white hair of the waves blown back
When the wind blows the water white and black.

We have lingered in the chambers of the sea
130   By sea-girls wreathed with seaweed red and brown
Till human voices wake us, and we drown.

---

4. A device that employs a candle to project images, rather like a slide projector.

✃

COMPANION READINGS

Arthur Waugh:[1] [*Cleverness and the New Poetry*]

Cleverness is, indeed, the pitfall of the New Poetry. There is no question about the ingenuity with which its varying moods are exploited, its elaborate symbolism evolved, and its sudden, disconcerting effect exploded upon the imagination. Swift, brilliant images break into the field of vision, scatter like rockets, and leave a trail of flying fire behind. But the general impression is momentary; there are moods and emotions, but no steady current of ideas behind them. Further, in their determination to surprise and even to puzzle at all costs these young poets are continually forgetting that the first essence of poetry is beauty; and that, however much you may have observed the world around you, it is impossible to translate your observation into poetry, without the intervention of the spirit of beauty, controlling the vision, and reanimating the idea.

The temptations of cleverness may be insistent, but its risks are equally great: how great indeed will, perhaps, be best indicated by the example of the "Catholic Anthology," which apparently represents the very newest of all the new poetic movements of the day. This strange little volume bears upon its cover a geometrical device, suggesting that the material within holds the same relation to the art of poetry as the work of the Cubist school hold to the art of painting and design. The product of the volume is mainly American in origin, only one or two of the contributors being of indisputably English birth. But it appears here under the auspices of a house associated with some of the best poetry of the younger generation, and is prefaced by a short lyric by Mr W. B. Yeats, in which that honoured representative of a very different school of inspiration makes bitter fun of scholars and critics, who

> Edit and annotate the lines
> That young men, tossing on their beds,
> Rhymed out in love's despair
> To flatter beauty's ignorant ear.

The reader will not have penetrated far beyond this warning notice before he finds himself in the very stronghold of literary rebellion, if not of anarchy. Mr Orrick Johns may be allowed to speak for his colleagues, as well as for himself:

> This is the song of youth,
> This is the cause of myself;
> I knew my father well and he was a fool,
> Therefore will I have my own foot in the path before I take a step;
> I will go only into new lands,
> And I will walk on no plank-walks.
> The horses of my family are wind-broken,
> And the dogs are old,
> And the guns rust;
> I will make me a new bow from an ash-tree,
> And cut up the homestead into arrows.

---

1. Influential publisher, editor, and critic (1866–1943); father of novelist Evelyn Waugh. The *Catholic Anthology* (1914), which Waugh attacks in this review from the *Quarterly Review* (London), was edited by Ezra Pound and included Eliot's *The Love Song of J. Alfred Prufrock* and printed W. B. Yeats's *The Scholars* as a preface.

And Mr Ezra Pound takes up the parable in turn, in the same wooden prose, cut into battens:

> Come, my songs, let us express our baser passions.
> Let us express our envy for the man with a steady job and no worry about the future.
> You are very idle, my songs,
> I fear you will come to a bad end.
> You stand about the streets. You loiter at the corners and bus-stops,
> You do next to nothing at all.
> You do not even express our inner nobility,
> You will come to a very bad end.
> And I? I have gone half cracked.[2]

It is not for his audience to contradict the poet, who for once may be allowed to pronounce his own literary epitaph. But this, it is to be noted, is the "poetry" that was to say nothing that might not be said "actually in life—under emotion,"[3] the sort of emotion that settles down into the banality of a premature decrepitude:

> I grow old. . . . I grow old . . .
> I shall wear the bottoms of my trousers rolled.
> Shall I part my hair behind? Do I dare to eat a peach?
> I shall wear white flannel trousers, and walk upon the beach.
> I have heard the mermaids singing, each to each.
> I do not think that they will sing to me.

Here, surely, is the reduction to absurdity of that school of literary license which, beginning with the declaration "I knew my father well and he was a fool" naturally proceeds to the convenient assumption that everything which seemed wise and true to the father must inevitably be false and foolish to the son. Yet if the fruits of emancipation are to be recognised in the unmetrical, incoherent banalities of these literary "Cubists," the state of Poetry is indeed threatened with anarchy which will end in something worse even than "red ruin and the breaking up of laws." From such a catastrophe the humour, commonsense, and artistic judgment of the best of the new "Georgians" will assuredly save their generation; nevertheless, a hint of warning may not be altogether out of place. It was a classic custom in the family hall, when the feast was at its height, to display a drunken slave among the sons of the household, to the end that they, being ashamed at the ignominious folly of his gesticulations, might determine never to be tempted into such a pitiable condition themselves. The custom had its advantages; for the wisdom of the younger generation was found to be fostered more surely by a single example than by a world of homily and precept.

Ezra Pound: Drunken Helots and Mr. Eliot[1]

Genius has I know not what peculiar property, its manifestations are various, but however diverse and dissimilar they may be, they have at least one property in common. It makes no difference in what art, in what mode, whether the most conservative, or the most ribald-revolutionary, or the most diffident; if in any land, or upon

---

2. From Pound's *Further Instructions*.
3. Waugh here paraphrases Wordsworth's prescription in the Preface to *Lyrical Ballads*.

1. Pound replied to Waugh's review in the *Egoist*, June 1917. A "helot" is a serf or slave.

any floating deck over the ocean, or upon some newly contrapted craft in the aether, genius manifests itself, at once some elderly gentleman has a flux of bile from his liver; at once from the throne or the easy Cowperian[2] sofa, or from the gutter, or from the oeconomical press room there bursts a torrent of elderly words, splenetic, irrelevant, they form themselves instinctively into large phrases denouncing the inordinate product.

This peculiar kind of *rabbia* [madness] might almost be taken as the test of a work of art, mere talent seems incapable of exciting it. "You can't fool me, sir, you're a scoundrel," bawls the testy old gentleman.

Fortunately the days when "that very fiery particle" could be crushed out by the "Quarterly" are over, but it interests me, as an archaeologist, to note that the firm which no longer produces Byron, but rather memoirs, letters of the late Queen, etc., is still running a review, and that this review is still where it was in 1812, or whatever the year was; and that, not having an uneducated Keats to condemn, a certain Mr. Waugh is scolding about Mr. Eliot.[3]

All I can find out, by asking questions concerning Mr. Waugh, is that he is "a very old chap," "a reviewer." From internal evidence we deduce that he is, like the rest of his generation of English *gens-de-lettres* [men of letters], ignorant of Laforgue; of De Régnier's "Odelettes," of his French contemporaries generally, of De Gourmont's "Litanies," of Tristan Corbière, Laurent Tailhade.[4] This is by no means surprising. We are used to it from his "b'ilin'."[5]

However, he outdoes himself, he calls Mr. Eliot a "drunken helot." So called they Anacreon[6] in the days of his predecessors, but from the context in the "Quarterly" article I judge that Mr. Waugh does not intend the phrase as a compliment, he is trying to be abusive, and moreover, he in his limited way has succeeded.

Let us sample the works of the last "Drunken Helot." I shall call my next anthology "Drunken Helots" if I can find a dozen poems written half so well as the following:

[Quotes *Conversation Galante*]

Our helot has a marvellous neatness. There is a comparable finesse in Laforgue's "Votre âme est affaire d'oculiste," but hardly in English verse.

Let us reconsider this drunkenness:

[Quotes *La Figlia Che Piange*]

And since when have helots taken to reading Dante and Marlowe? Since when have helots made a new music, a new refinement, a new method of turning old phrases into new by their aptness? However the "Quarterly," the century old, the venerable, the praeclarus,[7] the voice of Gehova[8] and Co., Sinai and 51A Albemarle Street, London, W. 1, has pronounced this author a helot. They are all for an aristocracy made up of, possibly, Tennyson, Southey and Wordsworth, the flunkey, the dull and

---

2. After 18th-century poet William Cowper.
3. Pound is invoking the savage review of Keats that appeared in the *Quarterly Review* and was believed by his friends to have hastened Keats's death.
4. A series of French writers and texts that Pound admired. Jules Laforgue (1860–1887) was a French poet who helped develop free verse; he was an important influence on Eliot's early poetry. Henri de Régnier (1864–1936) was a French symbolist poet; Remy de Gourmont (1858–1915) was an influential French poet,

novelist, essayist, publisher, and literary critic; Tristan Corbière, pseudonym for Édouard Joachim Corbière (1854–1919), was a French poet who worked with common speech and slang; and Laurent Tailhade (1854–1919) was a satiric French poet.
5. Byline, identifying the author of a newspaper article.
6. Greek writer of love poems and drinking songs.
7. Preeminent.
8. Jehovah.

the duller. Let us sup with the helots. Or perhaps the good Waugh is a wag,[9] perhaps he hears with the haspirate[1] and wishes to pun on Mr. Heliot's name: a bright bit of syzygy.[2]

I confess his type of mind puzzles me, there is no telling what he is up to.

I do not wish to misjudge him, this theory may be the correct one. You never can tell when old gentlemen grow facetious. He does not mention Mr. Eliot's name; he merely takes his lines and abuses them. The artful dodger,[3] he didn't (sotto voce[4]) "he didn't want 'people' to know that Mr. Eliot was a poet".

The poem he chooses for malediction is the title poem, "Prufrock." It is too long to quote entire.

[Quotes portion of *Prufrock*]

Let us leave the silly old Waugh. Mr. Eliot has made an advance on Browning. He has also made his dramatis personae contemporary and convincing. He has been an individual in his poems. I have read the contents of this book over and over, and with continued joy in the freshness, the humanity, the deep quiet culture. "I have tried to write of a few things that really have moved me" is so far as I know, the sum of Mr. Eliot's "poetic theory." His practice has been a distinctive cadence, a personal modus of arrangement, remote origins in Elizabethan English and in the modern French masters, neither origin being sufficiently apparent to affect the personal quality. It is writing without pretence. Mr. Eliot at once takes rank with the five or six living poets whose English one can read with enjoyment.

The "Egoist" has published the best prose writer of my generation. It follows its publication of Joyce by the publication of a "new" poet who is at least unsurpassed by any of his contemporaries, either of his own age or his elders.

It is perhaps "unenglish" to praise a poet whom one can read with enjoyment. Carlyle's generation wanted "improving" literature, Smile's "Self-Help"[5] and the rest of it. Mr. Waugh dates back to that generation, the virus is in his blood, he can't help it. The exactitude of the younger generation gets on his nerves, and so on and so on. He will "fall into line in time" like the rest of the bread-and-butter reviewers. Intelligent people will read "J. Alfred Prufrock"; they will wait with some eagerness for Mr. Eliot's further inspirations. It is 7.30 p.m. I have had nothing alcoholic to-day, nor yet yesterday. I said the same sort of thing about James Joyce's prose over two years ago. I am now basking in the echoes. Only a half-caste rag for the propagation of garden suburbs, and a local gazette in Rochester, N.Y., U.S.A., are left whining in opposition. * * *

However, let us leave these bickerings, this stench of the printing-press, weekly and quarterly, let us return to the gardens of the Muses,

Till human voices wake us and we drown,

as Eliot has written in conclusion to the poem which the "Quarterly" calls the *reductio ad absurdum*:[6]

---

9. Joker.
1. To aspirate is to add the "h" sound to the beginning of a word: thus Eliot becomes "Hel[i]ot."
2. Any two related things (either similar or opposite).
3. The Artful Dodger is the name of Fagan's favorite pickpocket in Dickens's *Oliver Twist*.

4. In a low voice.
5. Samuel Smiles's *Self-Help* (1859) preached the Victorian gospel of self-improvement.
6. Reduction to absurdity (Latin), the rhetorical technique of pushing the consequences of an idea to the point where it looks ridiculous.

I have seen them riding seaward on the waves
Combing the white hair of the waves blown back
When the wind blows the water white and black.

We have lingered in the chambers of the sea
By sea-girls wreathed with seaweed red and brown
Till human voices wake us, and we drown.

The poetic mind leaps the gulf from the exterior world, the trivialities of Mr. Prufrock, diffident, ridiculous, in the drawing-room, Mr. Apollinax's laughter "submarine and profound" transports him from the desiccated new-statesmanly atmosphere of Professor Canning-Cheetah's. Mr. Eliot's melody rushes out like the thought of Fragilion "among the birch-trees."[7] Mr. Waugh is my bitten macaroon at this festival.

⟨∞⟩

THE WASTE LAND   Like Conrad's *Heart of Darkness*—from which Eliot had originally planned to take his epigraph, "The horror! the horror!"—*The Waste Land* has become part of the symbolic landscape of twentieth-century Western culture; the text, like Conrad's, has been appropriated by commentators high and low, left and right, as an especially apt description of the psychosocial and interpersonal malaise of modern Europeans. Late in 1921 Eliot, who was suffering under a number of pressures both personal and artistic, took three months' leave from his job at Lloyd's Bank and went for a "rest cure" at a clinic in Lausanne, Switzerland. On his way he passed through Paris and showed the manuscript of the poem—really manuscripts of a number of fragments, whose interrelationship Eliot was trying to work out—to Ezra Pound; Pound and Eliot went through the poem again as Eliot returned to London in January 1922. Pound's editorial work was considerable, as the facsimile edition of the draft reveals; Pound said that he performed the poem's "caesarian operation," and Eliot dedicated *The Waste Land* to Pound—*il miglior fabbro* ("the better craftsman," a phrase from Dante).

The most obvious feature of *The Waste Land* is its difficulty. Eliot was perhaps the first poet and literary critic to argue that such "difficulty" was not just a necessary evil but in fact a constitutive element of poetry that would come to terms with the modern world. In his review of a volume of metaphysical poetry, Eliot implicitly links the complex poetry of Donne and Marvell with the task of the modern poet: "We can only say that it appears likely that poets in our civilization, as it exists at present, must be *difficult*. Our civilization comprehends great variety and complexity, and this variety and complexity, playing upon a refined sensibility, must produce various and complex results." In the case of *The Waste Land*, the difficulty lies primarily in the poem's dense tissue of quotations from and allusions to other texts; as Eliot's own footnotes to the poem demonstrate, the poem draws its strength, and achieves a kind of universality, by making implicit and explicit reference to texts as widely different as Ovid's *Metamorphoses* and a World War I Australian marching song.

Beyond the density of the poem's quotations and allusions, Eliot hoped to suggest the possibilty of an order beneath the chaos. In his review of Joyce's *Ulysses* (published in November 1923) Eliot was to describe the "mythical method," deploying allusions to classical mythology to suggest an implicit (and recurring) order beneath contemporary history; and while his use of

---

7. The names and images in this sentence not taken from *Prufrock* are from another of Eliot's early poems, Mr. *Apollinax*. The poem ends with the lines, "Of dowager Mrs. Phlaccus, and Professor and Mrs. Cheetah / I remember a slice of lemon, and a bitten macaroon."

myth was not so methodical as Joyce's, his use of vegetation myth and romance structures points outside the world of the poem to "another world," where the brokenness of the waste land might be healed. At the time of writing the poem, however, Eliot could not see clearly where that healing might come from.

The Waste Land[1]

"Nam Sibyllam quidem Cumis ego ipse oculis meis vidi in ampulla pendere, et cum illi pueri dicerent: Σίβυλλα τί θέλεις; respondebat illa: ἀποθανεῖν θέλω."[2]

FOR EZRA POUND
il miglior fabbro.

I. THE BURIAL OF THE DEAD

April is the cruellest month, breeding
Lilacs out of the dead land, mixing
Memory and desire, stirring
Dull roots with spring rain.
5 Winter kept us warm, covering
Earth in forgetful snow, feeding
A little life with dried tubers.
Summer surprised us, coming over the Starnbergersee[3]
With a shower of rain; we stopped in the colonnade,
10 And went on in sunlight, into the Hofgarten,[4]
And drank coffee, and talked for an hour.
Bin gar keine Russin, stamm' aus Litauen, echt deutsch.[5]
And when we were children, staying at the arch-duke's,
My cousin's, he took me out on a sled,
15 And I was frightened. He said, Marie,
Marie, hold on tight. And down we went.
In the mountains, there you feel free.
I read, much of the night, and go south in the winter.

---

1. Not only the title, but the plan and a good deal of the incidental symbolism of the poem were suggested by Miss Jessie L. Weston's book on the Grail legend: *From Ritual to Romance* (Cambridge). Indeed, so deeply am I indebted, Miss Weston's book will elucidate the difficulties of the poem much better than my notes can do; and I recommend it (apart from the great interest of the book itself) to any who think such elucidation of the poem worth the trouble. To another work of anthropology I am indebted in general, one which has influenced our generation profoundly; I mean *The Golden Bough*; I have used especially the two volumes *Adonis, Attis, Osiris.* Anyone who is acquainted with these works will immediately recognize in the poem certain references to vegetation ceremonies [Eliot's note]. Sir James Frazer (1854–1941)

brought out the 12 volumes of *The Golden Bough*, a vast work of anthropology and comparative mythology and religion, between 1890 and 1915, with a supplement published in 1936.
2. From the *Satyricon* of Petronius (first century A.D.). "For once I myself saw with my own eyes the Sybil at Cumae hanging in a cage, and when the boys said to her, 'Sybil, what do you want?' she replied, 'I want to die.'" The Sybil was granted anything she wished by Apollo, if only she would be his; she made the mistake of asking for everlasting life, without asking for eternal youth.
3. A lake near Munich.
4. A public park in Munich, with a zoo and cafés.
5. I'm not a Russian at all; I come from Lithuania, a true German. (German)

What are the roots that clutch, what branches grow
20   Out of this stony rubbish? Son of man,[6]
You cannot say, or guess, for you know only
A heap of broken images, where the sun beats,
And the dead tree gives no shelter, the cricket no relief,[7]
And the dry stone no sound of water. Only
25   There is shadow under this red rock,
(Come in under the shadow of this red rock),
And I will show you something different from either
Your shadow at morning striding behind you
Or your shadow at evening rising to meet you;
30   I will show you fear in a handful of dust.
                    Frisch weht der Wind
                    Der Heimat zu
                    Mein Irisch Kind,
                    Wo weilest du?[8]
35   "You gave me hyacinths first a year ago;
They called me the hyacinth girl."
—Yet when we came back, late, from the hyacinth garden,
Your arms full, and your hair wet, I could not
Speak, and my eyes failed, I was neither
40   Living nor dead, and I knew nothing,
Looking into the heart of light, the silence.
Oed' und leer das Meer.[9]

Madame Sosostris, famous clairvoyante,
Had a bad cold, nevertheless
45   Is known to be the wisest woman in Europe,
With a wicked pack of cards.[1] Here, said she,
Is your card, the drowned Phoenician Sailor,
(Those are pearls that were his eyes.[2] Look!)
Here is Belladonna, the Lady of the Rocks,
50   The lady of situations.
Here is the man with three staves, and here the Wheel,
And here is the one-eyed merchant, and this card,
Which is blank, is something he carries on his back,
Which I am forbidden to see. I do not find

6. Cf. Ezekiel II, i [Eliot's note]. Ezekiel 2.1 reads: "But thou, son of man, hear what I say unto thee; Be not thou rebellious like that rebellious house: open thy mouth, and eat that I give thee."

7. Cf. Ecclesiastes 12.5 [Eliot's note]. "They shall be afraid of that which is high, and fears shall be in the way, and the almond tree shall flourish, and the grasshopper shall be a burden, and desire shall fail."

8. V. *Tristan and Isolde*, i, verses 5–8 [Eliot's note]. In Wagner's opera, Tristan sings this about Isolde, the woman he is leaving behind as he sails for home: "Fresh blows the wind to the homeland; my Irish child, where are you waiting?"

9. Id. iii, verse 24 [Eliot's note]. Tristan is dying and waiting for Isolde to come to him, but a shepherd, whom Tristan has hired to keep watch for her ship, reports only "Desolate and empty the sea."

1. I am not familiar with the exact constitution of the Tarot pack of cards, from which I have obviously departed to suit my own convenience. The Hanged Man, a member of the traditional pack, fits my purpose in two ways: because he is associated in my mind with the Hanged God of Frazer, and because I associated him with the hooded figure in the passage of the disciples to Emmaus in Part V. The Phoenician Sailor and the Merchant appear later; also the "crowds of people," and Death by Water is executed in Part IV. The Man with Three Staves (an authentic member of the Tarot pack) I associate, quite arbitrarily, with the Fisher King Himself [Eliot's note].

2. From Ariel's song, in Shakespeare's *The Tempest*: "Full fathom five thy father lies; / Of his bones are coral made; / Those are pearls that were his eyes: / Nothing of him that doth fade, / But doth suffer a sea-change" (1.2.399–403).

55 The Hanged Man.³ Fear death by water.
I see crowds of people, walking round in a ring.
Thank you. If you see dear Mrs. Equitone,
Tell her I bring the horoscope myself:
One must be so careful these days.

60 Unreal City,⁴
Under the brown fog of a winter dawn,
A crowd flowed over London Bridge, so many,
I had not thought death had undone so many.⁵
Sighs, short and infrequent, were exhaled,⁶
65 And each man fixed his eyes before his feet.
Flowed up the hill and down King William Street,
To where Saint Mary Woolnoth kept the hours
With a dead sound on the final stroke of nine.⁷
There I saw one I knew, and stopped him, crying: "Stetson!
70 You who were with me in the ships at Mylae!⁸
That corpse you planted last year in your garden,
Has it begun to sprout? Will it bloom this year?
Or has the sudden frost disturbed its bed?
O keep the Dog far hence, that's friend to men,⁹
75 Or with his nails he'll dig it up again!
You! hypocrite lecteur!—mon semblable,—mon frère!"¹

II. A GAME OF CHESS²

The Chair she sat in, like a burnished throne,³
Glowed on the marble, where the glass
Held up by standards wrought with fruited vines
80 From which a golden Cupidon peeped out
(Another hid his eyes behind his wing)
Doubled the flames of sevenbranched candelabra
Reflecting light upon the table as
The glitter of her jewels rose to meet it,
85 From satin cases poured in rich profusion.
In vials of ivory and coloured glass
Unstoppered, lurked her strange synthetic perfumes,
Unguent, powdered, or liquid—troubled, confused
And drowned the sense in odours; stirred by the air
90 That freshened from the window, these ascended
In fattening the prolonged candle-flames,

3. The tarot card that depicts a man hanging by one foot from a cross.
4. Cf. Baudelaire: "Fourmillante cité, cité pleine de rêves, / Où le spectre en plein jour raccroche le passant" [Eliot's note].
5. Cf. Inferno, iii.55–7: "si lunga tratta / di gente, ch'io non avrei mai creduto / che morte tanta n'avesse disfatta" [Eliot's note]. "Such an endless train, / Of people, it never would have entered in my head / There were so many men whom death had slain."
6. Cf. Inferno, iv. 25–7: "Quivi, secondo che per ascoltare, / non avea pianto, ma' che di sospiri, / che l'aura eterna face-

van tremare" [Eliot's note]. "We heard no loud complaint, no crying there, / No sound of grief except the sound of sighing / Quivering forever through the eternal air."
7. A phenomenon which I have often noticed [Eliot's note].
8. The Battle of Mylae (260 B.C.) in the First Punic War.
9. Cf. the Dirge in Webster's White Devil [Eliot's note].
1. V. Baudelaire, Preface to Fleurs du Mal [Eliot's note]. "Hypocrite reader—my double—my brother!"
2. Cf. Thomas Middleton's drama A Game at Chess (1625), a political satire.
3. Cf. Antony and Cleopatra, II. ii. 190 [Eliot's note].

Flung their smoke into the laquearia,[4]
Stirring the pattern on the coffered ceiling.
Huge sea-wood fed with copper
95   Burned green and orange, framed by the coloured stone,
In which sad light a carvèd dolphin swam.
Above the antique mantel was displayed
As though a window gave upon the sylvan scene[5]
The change of Philomel, by the barbarous king[6]
100   So rudely forced; yet there the nightingale[7]
Filled all the desert with inviolable voice
And still she cried, and still the world pursues,
"Jug Jug" to dirty ears.
And other withered stumps of time
105   Were told upon the walls; staring forms
Leaned out, leaning, hushing the room enclosed.
Footsteps shuffled on the stair.
Under the firelight, under the brush, her hair
Spread out in fiery points
110   Glowed into words, then would be savagely still.

"My nerves are bad to-night. Yes, bad. Stay with me.
Speak to me. Why do you never speak. Speak.
⠀⠀⠀What are you thinking of? What thinking? What?
I never know what you are thinking. Think."

115   I think we are in rats' alley[8]
Where the dead men lost their bones.

"What is that noise?"
⠀⠀⠀⠀⠀⠀⠀⠀⠀⠀The wind under the door.[9]
"What is that noise now? What is the wind doing?"
120   ⠀⠀⠀⠀⠀⠀⠀⠀⠀⠀Nothing again nothing.

⠀⠀⠀⠀⠀⠀⠀⠀⠀⠀⠀⠀⠀⠀⠀⠀⠀"Do
"You know nothing? Do you see nothing? Do you remember
Nothing?"
⠀⠀⠀I remember
125   Those are pearls that were his eyes.
"Are you alive, or not? Is there nothing in your head?"[1]
⠀⠀⠀⠀⠀⠀⠀⠀⠀⠀⠀⠀⠀⠀⠀⠀⠀⠀⠀But

---

4. Laquearia. V. *Aeneid*, I.726: "dependent lychni laque-aribus aureis / incensi, et noctem flammis funalia vin-cunt." [Eliot's note]. "Burning lamps hang from the gold-panelled ceiling / And torches dispel the night with their flames"; a *laquearia* is a panelled ceiling. The passage from Virgil's *Aeneid* describes the banquet given by Dido for her lover Aeneas.
5. Sylvan scene. V. Milton, *Paradise Lost*, iv. 140 [Eliot's note]. "And over head up grew / Insuperable height of loftiest shade, / Cedar, and Pine, and Fir, and branching Palm, / A Silvan Scene, and as the ranks ascend / Shade above shade, a woody Theatre / Of stateliest view" The

passage describes the Garden of Eden, as seen through Satan's eyes.
6. V. Ovid, *Metamorphoses*, vi, Philomela [Eliot's note]. Philomela was raped by King Tereus, her sister's husband, and was then changed into a nightingale.
7. Cf. Part III, l. 204 [Eliot's note].
8. Cf. Part III, l. 195 [Eliot's note].
9. Cf. Webster: "Is the wind in that door still?" [Eliot's note]. From John Webster's *The Devil's Law Case*, 3.2.162. The doctor asks this question when he discovers that a "murder victim" is still breathing.
1. Cf. Part I, l. 37, 48 [Eliot's note].

O O O O that Shakespeherian Rag—[2]
It's so elegant
130 So intelligent
"What shall I do now? What shall I do?"
"I shall rush out as I am, and walk the street
With my hair down, so. What shall we do tomorrow?
What shall we ever do?"
135   The hot water at ten.
And if it rains, a closed car at four.
And we shall play a game of chess,
Pressing lidless eyes and waiting for a knock upon the door.[3]

When Lil's husband got demobbed,° I said—   *demobilized*
140 I didn't mince my words, I said to her myself,
HURRY UP PLEASE ITS TIME[4]
Now Albert's coming back, make yourself a bit smart.
He'll want to know what you done with that money he gave you
To get yourself some teeth. He did, I was there.
145 You have them all out, Lil, and get a nice set,
He said, I swear, I can't bear to look at you.
And no more can't I, I said, and think of poor Albert,
He's been in the army four years, he wants a good time,
And if you don't give it him, there's others will, I said.
150 Oh is there, she said. Something o' that, I said.
Then I'll know who to thank, she said, and give me a straight look.
HURRY UP PLEASE ITS TIME
If you don't like it you can get on with it, I said.
Others can pick and choose if you can't.
155 But if Albert makes off, it won't be for lack of telling.
You ought to be ashamed, I said, to look so antique.
(And her only thirty-one.)
I can't help it, she said, pulling a long face,
It's them pills I took, to bring it off, she said.
160 (She's had five already, and nearly died of young George.)
The chemist[5] said it would be all right, but I've never been the same.
You *are* a proper fool, I said.
Well, if Albert won't leave you alone, there it is, I said,
What you get married for if you don't want children?
165 HURRY UP PLEASE ITS TIME
Well, that Sunday Albert was home, they had a hot gammon,°   *ham*
And they asked me in to dinner, to get the beauty of it hot—
HURRY UP PLEASE ITS TIME
HURRY UP PLEASE ITS TIME
170 Goonight Bill. Goonight Lou. Goonight May. Goonight.
Ta ta. Goonight. Goonight.
Good night, ladies, good night, sweet ladies, good night, good night.[6]

2. Quoting an American ragtime song featured in Zieg-
field's Follies of 1912.
3. Cf. the game of chess in Middleton's *Women beware
Women* [Eliot's note].
4. A British pub-keeper's call for a last round before
closing.

5. Pharmacist.
6. Ophelia speaks these words in Shakespeare's *Hamlet*,
and they are understood by the King as certain evidence
of her insanity: "Good night ladies, good night. Sweet
ladies, good night, good night" (4.5.72–73).

III. The Fire Sermon

The river's tent is broken; the last fingers of leaf
Clutch and sink into the wet bank. The wind
175 Crosses the brown land, unheard. The nymphs are departed.
Sweet Thames, run softly, till I end my song.[7]
The river bears no empty bottles, sandwich papers,
Silk handkerchiefs, cardboard boxes, cigarette ends
Or other testimony of summer nights. The nymphs are departed.
180 And their friends, the loitering heirs of City directors;
Departed, have left no addresses.
By the waters of Leman[8] I sat down and wept . . .
Sweet Thames, run softly till I end my song,
Sweet Thames, run softly, for I speak not loud or long.
185 But at my back in a cold blast I hear
The rattle of the bones, and chuckle spread from ear to ear.

A rat crept softly through the vegetation
Dragging its slimy belly on the bank
While I was fishing in the dull canal
190 On a winter evening round behind the gashouse
Musing upon the king my brother's wreck
And on the king my father's death before him.[9]
White bodies naked on the low damp ground
And bones cast in a little low dry garret,
195 Rattled by the rat's foot only, year to year.
But at my back from time to time I hear[1]
The sound of horns and motors, which shall bring[2]
Sweeney to Mrs. Porter in the spring.
O the moon shone bright on Mrs. Porter[3]
200 And on her daughter
They wash their feet in soda water
Et O ces voix d'enfants, chantant dans la coupole![4]

Twit twit twit
Jug jug jug jug jug jug
205 So rudely forc'd.
Tereu

Unreal City
Under the brown fog of a winter noon
Mr. Eugenides, the Smyrna[5] merchant

---

7. V. Spenser, *Prothalamion* [Eliot's note]; Spenser's poem (1596) celebrates the double marriage of Lady Elizabeth and Lady Katherine Somerset.
8. Lake Geneva. The line echoes Psalm 137, in which, exiled in Babylon, the Hebrew poets are too full of grief to sing.
9. Cf. *The Tempest*, I. ii [Eliot's note].
1. Cf. Marvell, *To His Coy Mistress* [Eliot's note]. "But at my back I always hear / Time's wingèd chariot hurrying near."
2. Cf. Day, *Parliament of Bees:* "When of the sudden, listening, you shall hear, / A noise of horns and hunting, which shall bring / Actaeon to Diana in the spring, /

Where all shall see her naked skin . . ." [Eliot's note].
3. I do not know the origin of the ballad from which these are taken: it was reported to me from Sydney, Australia [Eliot's note]. Sung by Australian soldiers in World War I: "O the moon shone bright on Mrs. Porter / And on the daughter / Of Mrs. Porter / They wash their feet in soda water / And so they oughter / To keep them clean."
4. V. Verlaine, *Parsifal* [Eliot's note]. "And O those children's voices singing in the dome." Paul Verlaine's sonnet describes Parsifal, who keeps himself pure in hopes of seeing the holy grail, and has his feet washed before entering the castle.
5. Seaport in western Turkey.

210   Unshaven, with a pocket full of currants
         C.i.f.⁶ London: documents at sight,
         Asked me in demotic° French   *vulgar*
         To luncheon at the Cannon Street Hotel⁷
         Followed by a weekend at the Metropole.⁸

215   At the violet hour, when the eyes and back
         Turn upward from the desk, when the human engine waits
         Like a taxi throbbing waiting,
         I Tiresias,⁹ though blind, throbbing between two lives,
         Old man with wrinkled female breasts, can see
220   At the violet hour, the evening hour that strives
         Homeward, and brings the sailor home from sea,¹
         The typist home at teatime, clears her breakfast, lights
         Her stove, and lays out food in tins.
         Out of the window perilously spread
225   Her drying combinations touched by the sun's last rays,
         On the divan are piled (at night her bed)
         Stockings, slippers, camisoles, and stays.
         I Tiresias, old man with wrinkled dugs
         Perceived the scene, and foretold the rest—
230   I too awaited the expected guest.
         He, the young man carbuncular,° arrives,   *pimply*
         A small house agent's clerk, with one bold stare,
         One of the low on whom assurance sits
         As a silk hat on a Bradford² millionaire.
235   The time is now propitious, as he guesses,

6. The currants were quoted at a price "carriage and insurance free to London"; and the Bill of Lading, etc., were to be handed to the buyer upon payment of the sight draft [Eliot's note].
7. A hotel in London near the train station used for travel to and from continental Europe.
8. An upscale seaside resort hotel in Brighton.
9. Tiresias, although a mere spectator and not indeed a "character," is yet the most important personage in the poem, uniting all the rest. Just as the one-eyed merchant, seller of currants, melts into the Phoenician Sailor, and the latter is not wholly distinct from Ferdinand Prince of Naples, so all the women are one woman, and the two sexes meet in Tiresias. What Tiresias *sees*, in fact, is the substance of the poem. The whole passage from Ovid is of great anthropological interest: ". . . Cum Iunone iocos et 'maior vestra profecto est / Quam, quae contingit maribus,' dixisse, 'voluptas.' / Illa negat; placuit quae sit sententia docti / Quaerere Tiresiae: venus huic erat utraque nota. / Nam duo magnorum viridi coeuntia silva / Corpora serpentum baculi violaverat ictu / Deque viro factus, mirabile, femina septem / Egerat autumnos; octavo rursus eosdem / Vidit et 'est vestrae si tanta potentia plagae,' / Dixit 'ut auctoris sortem in contraria mutet, / Nunc quoque vos feriam!' percussis anguibus isdem / Forma prior rediit genetivaque venit imago. / Arbiter hic igitur sumptus de lite iocosa / Dicta Iovis firmat; gravius Saturnia iusto / Nec pro materia fertur doluisse suique / Iudicis aeterna damnavit lumina nocte, / At pater omnipotens (neque enim licet inrita cuiquam / Facta dei fecisse deo) pro lumine adempto / Scire futura dedit poenamque lev-
avit honore" [Eliot's note]. This passage from Ovid's *Metamorphoses* describes Tiresias's sex change: "[The story goes that once Jove, having drunk a great deal,] jested with Juno. He said, 'Your pleasure in love is really greater than that enjoyed by men.' She denied it; so they decided to seek the opinion of the wise Tiresias, for he knew both aspects of love. For once, with a blow of his staff, he had committed violence on two huge snakes as they copulated in the green forest; and—wonderful to tell—was turned from a man into a woman and thus spent seven years. In the eighth year he saw the same snakes again and said: 'If a blow struck at you is so powerful that it changes the sex of the giver, I will now strike at you again.' With these words he struck the snakes, and his former shape was restored to him and he became as he had been born. So he was appointed arbitrator in the playful quarrel, and supported Jove's statement. It is said that Saturnia [i.e., Juno] was quite disproportionately upset, and condemned the arbitrator to perpetual blindness. But the almighty father (for no god may undo what has been done by another god), in return for the sight that was taken away, gave him the power to know the future and so lightened the penalty paid by the honor."
1. This may not appear as exact as Sappho's lines but I had in mind the "longshore" or "dory" fisherman, who returns at nightfall [Eliot's note]. "Hesperus, thou bringst home all things bright morning scattered: thou bringest the sheep, the goat, the child to the mother."
2. An industrial town in Yorkshire; many of its residents became wealthy during World War I.

The meal is ended, she is bored and tired,
Endeavours to engage her in caresses
Which still are unreproved, if undesired.
Flushed and decided, he assaults at once;
240   Exploring hands encounter no defence;
His vanity requires no response,
And makes a welcome of indifference.
(And I Tiresias have foresuffered all
Enacted on this same divan or bed;
245   I who have sat by Thebes below the wall
And walked among the lowest of the dead.)
Bestows one final patronising kiss,
And gropes his way, finding the stairs unlit . . .

She turns and looks a moment in the glass,
250   Hardly aware of her departed lover;
Her brain allows one half-formed thought to pass:
"Well now that's done: and I'm glad it's over."
When lovely woman stoops to folly and[3]
Paces about her room again, alone,
255   She smoothes her hair with automatic hand,
And puts a record on the gramophone.

"This music crept by me upon the waters"[4]
And along the Strand, up Queen Victoria Street.
O City city, I can sometimes hear
260   Beside a public bar in Lower Thames Street,
The pleasant whining of a mandoline
And a clatter and a chatter from within
Where fishmen lounge at noon: where the walls
Of Magnus Martyr[5] hold
265   Inexplicable splendour of Ionian white and gold.

The river sweats[6]
Oil and tar
The barges drift
With the turning tide
270   Red sails
Wide
To leeward, swing on the heavy spar.
The barges wash
Drifting logs
275   Down Greenwich reach

---

3. V. Goldsmith, the song in *The Vicar of Wakefield*
[Eliot's note]. Oliver Goldsmith's character Olivia, on
returning to the place where she was seduced, sings,
"When lovely woman stoops to folly / And finds too late
that men betray / What charm can soothe her melancholy, / What art can wash her guilt away? / The only art
her guilt to cover, / To hide her shame from every eye, /
To give repentance to her lover / And wring his bosom—
is to die."
4. V. *The Tempest*, as above [Eliot's note].

5. The interior of St. Magnus Martyr is to my mind one of
the finest among Wren's interiors. See *The Proposed
Demolition of Nineteen City Churches* (P.S. King & Son,
Ltd.) [Eliot's note].
6. The Song of the (three) Thames-daughters begins
here. From line 292 to 306 inclusive they speak in turn.
V. *Götterdämmerung*, III.I: the Rhine-daughters [Eliot's
note]. In Richard Wagner's opera, *Twilight of the Gods*,
the Rhine maidens, when their gold is stolen, lament that
the beauty of the river is gone.

Past the Isle of Dogs.[7]
    Weialala leia
    Wallala leialala

Elizabeth and Leicester[8]

280 Beating oars
The stern was formed
A gilded shell
Red and gold
The brisk swell

285 Rippled both shores
Southwest wind
Carried down stream
The peal of bells
White towers

290   Weialala leia
    Wallala leialala

"Trams and dusty trees.
Highbury bore me. Richmond and Kew[9]
Undid me. By Richmond I raised my knees

295 Supine on the floor of a narrow canoe."

"My feet are at Moorgate,[1] and my heart
Under my feet. After the event
He wept. He promised 'a new start.'
I made no comment. What should I resent?"

300 "On Margate Sands.[2]
I can connect
Nothing with nothing.
The broken fingernails of dirty hands.
My people humble people who expect

305 Nothing."
        la la
To Carthage then I came[3]

Burning burning burning burning[4]
O Lord Thou pluckest me out[5]

---

7. Greenwich is a borough on the south bank of the River Thames; the Isle of Dogs is a peninsula in East London formed by a sharp bend in the Thames called Greenwich Reach.

8. V. Froude, *Elizabeth*, vol. I, Ch. iv, letter of De Quadra to Philip of Spain: "In the afternoon we were in a barge, watching the games on the river. (The Queen) was alone with Lord Robert and myself on the poop, when they began to talk nonsense, and went so far that Lord Robert at last said, as I was on the spot there was no reason why they should not be married if the queen pleased" [Eliot's note].

9. Cf. *Purgatorio*, V. 133: "Ricorditi di me, che son la Pia; / Siena mi fe', disfecemi Maremma." [Eliot's note]. "Remember me, that I am called Piety; / Sienna made me and Maremma undid me." Highbury, Richmond, and Kew are suburbs of London near the Thames.

1. A slum in East London.

2. A seaside resort in the Thames estuary.

3. V. St. Augustine's *Confessions*: "to Carthage then I came, where a cauldron of unholy loves sang all about mine ears" [Eliot's note].

4. The complete text of the Buddha's Fire Sermon (which corresponds in importance to the Sermon on the Mount) from which these words are taken, will be found translated in the late Henry Clarke Warren's *Buddhism in Translation* (Harvard Oriental Series). Mr. Warren was one of the great pioneers of Buddhist studies in the Occident [Eliot's note].

5. From St. Augustine's *Confessions* again. The collocation of these two representatives of eastern and western asceticism, as the culmination of this part of the poem, is not an accident [Eliot's note]. Augustine writes: "I entangle my steps with these outward beauties, but thou pluckest me out, O Lord, Thou pluckest me out."

310   O Lord Thou pluckest

     burning

IV. DEATH BY WATER

Phlebas the Phoenician, a fortnight dead,
Forgot the cry of gulls, and the deep sea swell
And the profit and loss.
315   A current under sea
Picked his bones in whispers. As he rose and fell
He passed the stages of his age and youth
Entering the whirlpool.
                     Gentile or Jew
320 O you who turn the wheel and look to windward,
Consider Phlebas, who was once handsome and tall as you.

V. WHAT THE THUNDER SAID[6]

After the torchlight red on sweaty faces
After the frosty silence in the gardens
After the agony in stony places
325 The shouting and the crying
Prison and palace and reverberation
Of thunder of spring over distant mountains
He who was living is now dead
We who were living are now dying
330 With a little patience

Here is no water but only rock
Rock and no water and the sandy road
The road winding above among the mountains
Which are mountains of rock without water
335 If there were water we should stop and drink
Amongst the rock one cannot stop or think
Sweat is dry and feet are in the sand
If there were only water amongst the rock
Dead mountain mouth of carious° teeth that cannot spit   *rotting*
340 Here one can neither stand nor lie nor sit
There is not even silence in the mountains
But dry sterile thunder without rain
There is not even solitude in the mountains
But red sullen faces sneer and snarl
345 From doors of mudcracked houses
                      If there were water
And no rock
If there were rock
And also water
350 And water
A spring

---

6. In the first part of Part V three themes are employed: the journey to Emmaus, the approach to the Chapel Perilous (see Miss Weston's book), and the present decay of eastern Europe [Eliot's note].

A pool among the rock
If there were the sound of water only
Not the cicada
355   And dry grass singing
But sound of water over a rock
Where the hermit-thrush sings in the pine trees
Drip drop drip drop drop drop drop[7]
But there is no water

360   Who is the third who walks always beside you?
When I count, there are only you and I together[8]
But when I look ahead up the white road
There is always another one walking beside you
Gliding wrapt in a brown mantle, hooded
365   I do not know whether a man or a woman
—But who is that on the other side of you?

What is that sound high in the air[9]
Murmur of maternal lamentation
Who are those hooded hordes swarming
370   Over endless plains, stumbling in cracked earth
Ringed by the flat horizon only
What is the city over the mountains
Cracks and reforms and bursts in the violet air
Falling towers
375   Jerusalem Athens Alexandria
Vienna London
Unreal

A woman drew her long black hair out tight
And fiddled whisper music on those strings
380   And bats with baby faces in the violet light
Whistled, and beat their wings
And crawled head downward down a blackened wall
And upside down in air were towers
Tolling reminiscent bells, that kept the hours
385   And voices singing out of empty cisterns and exhausted wells

In this decayed hole among the mountains
In the faint moonlight, the grass is singing

---

7. This is *Turdus aonalaschkae pallasii*, the hermit-thrush which I have heard in Quebec County. Chapman says (*Handbook of Birds of Eastern North America*) "it is most at home in secluded woodland and thickety retreats. . . . Its notes are not remarkable for variety or volume, but in purity and sweetness of tone and exquisite modulation they are unequalled." Its "water-dripping song" is justly celebrated [Eliot's note].
8. The following lines were stimulated by the account of one of the Antarctic expeditions (I forget which, but I think one of Shackleton's): it was related that the party of explorers, at the extremity of their strength, had the constant delusion that there was one more member than could actually be counted [Eliot's note]. There seems also to be an echo of the account of Jesus meeting his disciples on the road to Emmaus: "Jesus himself drew near, and

went with them. But their eyes were holden that they should not know him" (Luke 24.13–16).
9. Cf. Hermann Hesse, *Blick ins Chaos*: "Schon ist halb Europa, schon ist zumindest der halbe Osten Europas auf dem Wege zum Chaos, fährt betrunken im heiligen Wahn am Abgrund entlang und singt dazu, singt betrunken und hymnisch wie Dmitri Karamasoff sang. Ueber diese Lieder lacht der Bürger beleidigt, der Heilige und Seher hört sie mit Tränen" [Eliot's note]. "Already half of Europe, already at least half of Eastern Europe, on the way to chaos, drives drunk in sacred infatuation along the edge of the precipice, singing drunkenly, as though singing hymns, as Dmitri Karamazov sang. The offended bourgeois laughs at the songs; the saint and the seer hear them with tears."

Over the tumbled graves, about the chapel
There is the empty chapel, only the wind's home.
390   It has no windows, and the door swings,
Dry bones can harm no one.
Only a cock stood on the rooftree
Co co rico co co rico
In a flash of lightning. Then a damp gust
395   Bringing rain

Ganga[1] was sunken, and the limp leaves
Waited for rain, while the black clouds
Gathered far distant, over Himavant.[2]
The jungle crouched, humped in silence.
400   Then spoke the thunder
DA
Datta: what have we given?[3]
My friend, blood shaking my heart
The awful daring of a moment's surrender
405   Which an age of prudence can never retract
By this, and this only, we have existed
Which is not to be found in our obituaries
Or in memories draped by the beneficent spider[4]
Or under seals broken by the lean solicitor
410   In our empty rooms
DA
Dayadhvam: I have heard the key[5]
Turn in the door once and turn once only
We think of the key, each in his prison
415   Thinking of the key, each confirms a prison
Only at nightfall, aethereal rumours
Revive for a moment a broken Coriolanus[6]
DA
Damyata: The boat responded
420   Gaily, to the hand expert with sail and oar
The sea was calm, your heart would have responded
Gaily, when invited, beating obedient
To controlling hands

1. The river Ganges.
2. The Himalayas.
3. "Datta, dayadhvam, damyata" (Give, sympathize, control). The fable of the meaning of the Thunder is found in the *Brihadaranyaka—Upanishad*, 5, 1. A translation is found in Deussen's *Sechzig Upanishads des Vada*, p. 489 [Eliot's note]. "That very thing is repented even today by the heavenly voice, in the form of thunder, in the form of thunder as 'Da,' 'Da,' 'Da,' . . . . Therefore one should practice these three things: self-control, alms-giving, and compassion."
4. Cf. Webster, *The White Devil*, v. vi: ". . . they'll remarry / Ere the worm pierce your winding-sheet, ere the spider / make a thin curtain for your epitaphs" [Eliot's note].
5. Cf. *Inferno*, xxxiii. 46: "ed io sentii chiavar l'uscio di sotto / all'orrible torre." Also F. H. *Bradley, Appearance*

and Reality, p. 346: "My external sensations are no less private to myself than are my thoughts or my feelings. In either case my experience falls within my own circle, a circle closed on the outside; and, with all its elements alike, every sphere is opaque to the others which surround it. . . . In brief, regarded as an existence which appears in a soul, the whole world for each is peculiar and private to that soul." [Eliot's note]. In the passage from the *Inferno*, Ugolino tells Dante of his imprisonment and starvation until he became so desperate that he ate his children: "And I heard below me the door of the horrible tower being locked."
6. In Shakespeare's play of the same name, Coriolanus is a Roman general who is exiled and later leads the enemy in an attack against the Romans.

425 I sat upon the shore
Fishing, with the arid plain behind me[7]
Shall I at least set my lands in order?
London Bridge is falling down falling down falling down
Poi s'ascose nel foco che gli affina[8]
Quando fiam uti chelidon—O swallow swallow[9]
430 *Le Prince d'Aquitaine à la tour abolie*[1]
These fragments I have shored against my ruins
Why then Ile fit you. Hieronymo's mad againe.[2]
Datta. Dayadhvam. Damyata.
Shantih   shantih   shantih[3]

Journey of the Magi[1]

"A cold coming we had of it,
Just the worst time of the year
For a journey, and such a long journey:
The ways deep and the weather sharp,
5   The very dead of winter."
And the camels galled, sore-footed, refractory,
Lying down in the melting snow.
There were times we regretted
The summer palaces on slopes, the terraces,
10 And the silken girls bringing sherbet.
Then the camel men cursing and grumbling
And running away, and wanting their liquor and women,
And the night-fires going out, and the lack of shelters,
And the cities hostile and the towns unfriendly
15 And the villages dirty and charging high prices:
A hard time we had of it.
At the end we preferred to travel all night,
Sleeping in snatches,
With the voices singing in our ears, saying
20 That this was all folly.

Then at dawn we came down to a temperate valley,
Wet, below the snow line, smelling of vegetation,
With a running stream and a water-mill beating the darkness
And three trees on the low sky.
25 And an old white horse galloped away in the meadow.

---

7. V. Weston, *From Ritual to Romance*; chapter on the Fisher King [Eliot's note].
8. V. *Purgatorio*, xxvi.148: "Ara vos prec per aquella valor / que vos condus al som de l'escalina, / sovegna vos a temps de ma dolor." / Poi s'ascose nel foco che gli affina" [Eliot's note]. In this passage, the poet Arnaut Daniel speaks to Dante: "Now I pray you, by the goodness that guides you to the top of this staircase, be mindful in time of my suffering."
9. V. *Pervigilium Veneris*. Cf. Philomela in Parts II and III [Eliot's note]. Philomel asks, "When shall I be a swallow?"
1. V. Gerard de Nerval, Sonnet *El Desdichado* [Eliot's note]. "The Prince of Aquitane in the ruined tower."

2. V. Kyd's *Spanish Tragedy* [Eliot's note]. The subtitle of Kyd's play is, "Hieronymo's Mad Againe." His son having been murdered, Hieronymo is asked to compose a court play, to which he responds "Why then Ile fit you"; his son's murder is revenged in the course of the play.
3. Shantih. Repeated as here, a formal ending to an Upanishad. "The Peace which passeth understanding" is a feeble translation of the content of this word [Eliot's note]. The Upanishads are poetic commentaries on the Hindu Scriptures.
1. The narrative of the poem is based upon the tradition of the three wise men who journeyed to Bethlehem to worship the infant Christ; cf. Matthew 2.1–12.

Then we came to a tavern with vine-leaves over the lintel,
Six hands at an open door dicing for pieces of silver,
And feet kicking the empty wine-skins.
But there was no information, and so we continued
30   And arrived at evening, not a moment too soon
Finding the place; it was (you may say) satisfactory.

All this was a long time ago, I remember,
And I would do it again, but set down
This set down
35   This: were we led all that way for
Birth or Death? There was a Birth, certainly,
We had evidence and no doubt. I had seen birth and death,
But had thought they were different; this Birth was
Hard and bitter agony for us, like Death, our death.
40   We returned to our places, these Kingdoms,
But no longer at ease here, in the old dispensation,
With an alien people clutching their gods.
I should be glad of another death.

                                                            1927

Tradition and the Individual Talent

1

In English writing we seldom speak of tradition, though we occasionally apply its name in deploring its absence. We cannot refer to "the tradition" or to "a tradition"; at most, we employ the adjective in saying that the poetry of So-and-so is "tradition-al" or even "too traditional." Seldom, perhaps, does the word appear except in a phrase of censure. If otherwise, it is vaguely approbative,[1] with the implication, as to the work approved, of some pleasing archaeological reconstruction. You can hardly make the word agreeable to English ears without this comfortable reference to the reassuring science of archaeology.

Certainly the word is not likely to appear in our appreciations of living or dead writers. Every nation, every race, has not only its own creative, but its own critical turn of mind; and is even more oblivious of the shortcomings and limitations of its critical habits than of those of its creative genius. We know, or think we know, from the enormous mass of critical writing that has appeared in the French language the critical method or habit of the French; we only conclude (we are such unconscious people) that the French are "more critical" than we, and sometimes even plume our-selves a little with the fact, as if the French were the less spontaneous. Perhaps they are; but we might remind ourselves that criticism is as inevitable as breathing, and that we should be none the worse for articulating what passes in our minds when we read a book and feel an emotion about it, for criticizing our own minds in their work of criticism. One of the facts that might come to light in this process is our tendency to insist, when we praise a poet, upon those aspects of his work in which he least resembles any one else. In these aspects or parts of his work we pretend to find what is individual, what is the peculiar essence of the man. We dwell with satisfaction upon the poet's difference from his predecessors, especially his immediate predeces-

1. Approving.

sors; we endeavour to find something that can be isolated in order to be enjoyed. Whereas if we approach a poet without this prejudice we shall often find that not only the best, but the most individual parts of his work may be those in which the dead poets, his ancestors, assert their immortality most vigorously. And I do not mean the impressionable period of adolescence, but the period of full maturity.

Yet if the only form of tradition, of handing down, consisted in following the ways of the immediate generation before us in a blind or timid adherence to its successes, "tradition" should positively be discouraged. We have seen many such simple currents soon lost in the sand; and novelty is better than repetition. Tradition is a matter of much wider significance. It cannot be inherited, and if you want it you must obtain it by great labour. It involves, in the first place, the historical sense, which we may call nearly indispensable to any one who would continue to be a poet beyond his twenty-fifth year; and the historical sense involves a perception, not only of the pastness of the past, but of its presence; the historical sense compels a man to write not merely with his own generation in his bones, but with a feeling that the whole of the literature of Europe from Homer and within it the whole of the literature of his own country has a simultaneous existence and composes a simultaneous order. This historical sense, which is a sense of the timeless as well as of the temporal and of the timeless and of the temporal together, is what makes a writer traditional. And it is at the same time what makes a writer most acutely conscious of his place in time, of his own contemporaneity.

No poet, no artist of any art, has his complete meaning alone. His significance, his appreciation is the appreciation of his relation to the dead poets and artists. You cannot value him alone; you must set him, for contrast and comparison, among the dead. I mean this as a principle of aesthetic, not merely historical, criticism. The necessity that he shall conform, that he shall cohere, is not onesided; what happens when a new work of art is created is something that happens simultaneously to all the works of art which preceded it. The existing monuments form an ideal order among themselves, which is modified by the introduction of the new (the really new) work of art among them. The existing order is complete before the new work arrives; for order to persist after the supervention[2] of novelty, the whole existing order must be, if ever so slightly, altered; and so the relations, proportions, values of each work of art toward the whole are readjusted; and this is conformity between the old and the new. Whoever has approved this idea of order, of the form of European, of English literature will not find it preposterous that the past should be altered by the present as much as the present is directed by the past. And the poet who is aware of this will be aware of great difficulties and responsibilities.

In a peculiar sense he will be aware also that he must inevitably be judged by the standards of the past. I say judged, not amputated, by them; not judged to be as good as, or worse or better than, the dead; and certainly not judged by the canons of dead critics. It is a judgment, a comparison, in which two things are measured by each other. To conform merely would be for the new work not really to conform at all; it would not be new, and would therefore not be a work of art. And we do not quite say that the new is more valuable because it fits in; but its fitting in is a test of its value—a test, it is true, which can only be slowly and cautiously applied, for we are none of us infallible judges of conformity. We say: it appears to conform, and is

---

2. The appearance of something additional.

perhaps individual, or it appears individual, and may conform; but we are hardly likely to find that it is one and not the other.

To proceed to a more intelligible exposition of the relation of the poet to the past: he can neither take the past as a lump, an indiscriminate bolus,[3] nor can he form himself wholly on one or two private admirations, nor can he form himself wholly upon one preferred period. The first course is inadmissible, the second is an important experience of youth, and the third is a pleasant and highly desirable supplement. The poet must be very conscious of the main current, which does not at all flow invariably through the most distinguished reputations. He must be quite aware of the obvious fact that art never improves, but that the material of art is never quite the same. He must be aware that the mind of Europe—the mind of his own country—a mind which he learns in time to be much more important than his own private mind—is a mind which changes, and that this change is a development which abandons nothing *en route*, which does not superannuate either Shakespeare, or Homer, or the rock drawing of the Magdalenian draughtsmen.[4] That this development, refinement perhaps, complication certainly, is not, from the point of view of the artist, any improvement. Perhaps not even an improvement from the point of view of the psychologist or not to the extent which we imagine; perhaps only in the end based upon a complication in economics and machinery. But the difference between the present and the past is that the conscious present is an awareness of the past in a way and to an extent which the past's awareness of itself cannot show.

Some one said: "The dead writers are remote from us because we *know* so much more than they did." Precisely, and they are that which we know.

I am alive to a usual objection to what is clearly part of my programme for the *métier* of poetry. The objection is that the doctrine requires a ridiculous amount of erudition (pedantry), a claim which can be rejected by appeal to the lives of poets in any pantheon. It will even be affirmed that much learning deadens or perverts poetic sensibility. While, however, we persist in believing that a poet ought to know as much as will not encroach upon his necessary receptivity and necessary laziness, it is not desirable to confine knowledge to whatever can be put into a useful shape for examinations, drawing-rooms, or the still more pretentious modes of publicity. Some can absorb knowledge, the more tardy must sweat for it. Shakespeare acquired more essential history from Plutarch than most men could from the whole British Museum. What is to be insisted upon is that the poet must develop or procure the consciousness of the past and that he should continue to develop this consciousness throughout his career.

What happens is a continual surrender of himself as he is at the moment to something which is more valuable. The progress of an artist is a continual self-sacrifice, a continual extinction of personality.

There remains to define this process of depersonalization and its relation to the sense of tradition. It is in this depersonalization that art may be said to approach the condition of science. I, therefore, invite you to consider, as a suggestive analogy, the action which takes place when a bit of finely filiated[5] platinum is introduced into a chamber containing oxygen and sulphur dioxide.

---

3. A lump; a mass of chewed food.
4. Drawings of hunting scenes, rendered in caves in

France and Spain, c. 13,000–10,000 B.C.
5. Eliot apparently means "made into filaments."

2

Honest criticism and sensitive appreciation are directed not upon the poet but upon the poetry. If we attend to the confused cries of the newspaper critics and the *susurrus* [buzzing] of popular repetition that follows, we shall hear the names of poets in great numbers; if we seek not Blue-book[6] knowledge but the enjoyment of poetry, and ask for a poem, we shall seldom find it. I have tried to point out the importance of the relation of the poem to other poems by other authors, and suggested the conception of poetry as a living whole of all the poetry that has ever been written. The other aspect of this Impersonal theory of poetry is the relation of the poem to its author. And I hinted, by an analogy, that the mind of the mature poet differs from that of the immature one not precisely in any valuation of "personality," not being necessarily more interesting, or having "more to say," but rather by being a more finely perfected medium in which special, or very varied, feelings are at liberty to enter into new combinations.

The analogy was that of the catalyst. When the two gases previously mentioned are mixed in the presence of a filament of platinum, they form sulphurous acid. This combination takes place only if the platinum is present; nevertheless the newly formed acid contains no trace of platinum, and the platinum itself is apparently unaffected; has remained inert, neutral, and unchanged. The mind of the poet is the shred of platinum. It may partly or exclusively operate upon the experience of the man himself; but, the more perfect the artist, the more completely separate in him will be the man who suffers and the mind which creates; the more perfectly will the mind digest and transmute the passions which are its material.

The experience, you will notice, the elements which enter the presence of the transforming catalyst, are of two kinds: emotions and feelings. The effect of a work of art upon the person who enjoys it is an experience different in kind from any experience not of art. It may be formed out of one emotion, or may be a combination of several; and various feelings, inhering for the writer in particular words or phrases or images, may be added to compose the final result. Or great poetry may be made without the direct use of any emotion whatever: composed out of feelings solely. Canto XV of the *Inferno* (Brunetto Latini) is a working up of the emotion evident in the situation; but the effect, though single as that of any work of art, is obtained by considerable complexity of detail. The last quatrain gives an image, a feeling attaching to an image, which "came," which did not develop simply out of what precedes, but which was probably in suspension in the poet's mind until the proper combination arrived for it to add itself to.[7] The poet's mind is in fact a receptacle for seizing and storing up numberless feelings, phrases, images, which remain there until all the particles which can unite to form a new compound are present together.

If you compare several representative passages of the greatest poetry you see how great is the variety of types of combination, and also how completely any semi-ethical criterion of "sublimity" misses the mark. For it is not the "greatness," the intensity, of the emotions, the components, but the intensity of the artistic process, the pressure, so to speak, under which the fusion takes place, that counts. The

6. Official government publication.
7. He [Brunetto Latini] turned then, and he seemed, / across that plain, like one of those who run / for the green cloth at Verona; and of those, / more like the one who wins, than those who lose (*Inferno*, 15.119–22).

episode of Paolo and Francesca employs a definite emotion, but the intensity of the poetry is something quite different from whatever intensity in the supposed experience it may give the impression of. It is no more intense, furthermore, than Canto XXVI, the voyage of Ulysses, which has not the direct dependence upon an emotion.[8] Great variety is possible in the process of transmutation of emotion: the murder of Agamemnon,[9] or the agony of Othello, gives an artistic effect apparently closer to a possible original than the scenes from Dante. In the *Agamemnon*, the artistic emotion approximates to the emotion of an actual spectator; in *Othello* to the emotion of the protagonist himself. But the difference between art and the event is always absolute; the combination which is the murder of Agamemnon is probably as complex as that which is the voyage of Ulysses. In either case there has been a fusion of elements. The ode of Keats contains a number of feelings which have nothing particular to do with the nightingale, but which the nightingale, partly, perhaps, because of its attractive name, and partly because of its reputation, served to bring together.

The point of view which I am struggling to attack is perhaps related to the metaphysical theory of the substantial unity of the soul: for my meaning is, that the poet has, not a "personality" to express, but a particular medium, which is only a medium and not a personality, in which impressions and experiences combine in peculiar and unexpected ways. Impressions and experiences which are important for the man may take no place in the poetry, and those which become important in the poetry may play quite a negligible part in the man, the personality.

I will quote a passage which is unfamiliar enough to be regarded with fresh attention in the light—or darkness—of these observations:

> And now methinks I could e'en chide myself
> For doating on her beauty, though her death
> Shall be revenged after no common action.
> Does the silkworm expend her yellow labours
> For thee? For thee does she undo herself?
> Are lordships sold to maintain ladyships
> For the poor benefit of a bewildering minute?
> Why does yon fellow falsify highways,
> And put his life between the judge's lips,
> To refine such a thing—keeps horse and men
> To beat their valours for her? . . . [1]

In this passage (as is evident if it is taken in its context) there is a combination of positive and negative emotions: an intensely strong attraction toward beauty and an equally intense fascination by the ugliness which is contrasted with it and which destroys it. This balance of contrasted emotion is in the dramatic situation to which the speech is pertinent, but that situation alone is inadequate to it. This is, so to

8. Dante's *Inferno*, Canto 5, tells the story of the lovers Paolo and Francesca; Canto 26 tells of the suffering of Ulysses in hell.
9. In Aeschylus's drama *Agamemnon*, Clytemnestra kills her husband Agamemnon for having sacrificed her daughter, Iphigenia, to the goddess Artemis.
1. From Cyril Tourneur's *The Revenger's Tragedy* (1607), 3.4; the speaker is addressing the skull of his former beloved, murdered after she refused to respond to an evil duke's advances. The revenger will make up the skull to look alive, putting poison on its lips; the evil Duke then dies when he kisses this supposed maiden in a dusky garden.

speak, the structural emotion, provided by the drama. But the whole effect, the dominant tone, is due to the fact that a number of floating feelings, having an affinity to this emotion by no means superficially evident, have combined with it to give us a new art emotion.

It is not in his personal emotions, the emotions provoked by particular events in his life, that the poet is in any way remarkable or interesting. His particular emotions may be simple, or crude, or flat. The emotion in his poetry will be a very complex thing, but not with the complexity of the emotions of people who have very complex or unusual emotions in life. One error, in fact, of eccentricity in poetry is to seek for new human emotions to express; and in this search for novelty in the wrong place it discovers the perverse. The business of the poet is not to find new emotions, but to use the ordinary ones and, in working them up into poetry, to express feelings which are not in actual emotions at all. And emotions which he has never experienced will serve his turn as well as those familiar to him. Consequently, we must believe that "emotion recollected in tranquillity"[2] is an inexact formula. For it is neither emotion, nor recollection, nor, without distortion of meaning, tranquillity. It is a concentration, and a new thing resulting from the concentration, of a very great number of experiences which to the practical and active person would not seem to be experiences at all; it is a concentration which does not happen consciously or of deliberation. These experiences are not "recollected," and they finally unite in an atmosphere which is "tranquil" only in that it is a passive attending upon the event. Of course this is not quite the whole story. There is a great deal, in the writing of poetry, which must be conscious and deliberate. In fact, the bad poet is usually unconscious where he ought to be conscious, and conscious where he ought to be unconscious. Both errors tend to make him "personal." Poetry is not a turning loose of emotion, but an escape from emotion; it is not the expression of personality, but an escape from personality. But, of course, only those who have personality and emotions know what it means to want to escape from these things.

3

ὁ δὲ νοῦς ἴσως θειότερον τι καὶ ἀπαθές ἐστιν.[3]

This essay proposes to halt at the frontier of metaphysics or mysticism, and confine itself to such practical conclusions as can be applied by the responsible person interested in poetry. To divert interest from the poet to the poetry is a laudable aim: for it would conduce to a juster estimation of actual poetry, good and bad. There are many people who appreciate the expression of sincere emotion in verse, and there is a smaller number of people who can appreciate technical excellence. But very few know when there is an expression of *significant* emotion, emotion which has its life in the poem and not in the history of the poet. The emotion of art is impersonal. And the poet cannot reach this impersonality without surrendering himself wholly to the work to be done. And he is not likely to know what is to be done unless he lives in what is not merely the present, but the present moment of the past, unless he is conscious, not of what is dead, but of what is already living.

2. This is Wordsworth's famous description of poetry in the Preface to *Lyrical Ballads*; see page 212.
3. The mind is doubtless something more divine and unimpressionable (from Aristotle's *De Anima* [*On the Soul*]).

Virginia Woolf

1882–1941

Virginia Woolf is the foremost woman writer of the twentieth century, writing in any language; within British literature, Woolf is in the company of James Joyce, T. S. Eliot, William Butler Yeats, and few others as a major author, of whatever gender. To take account of the transformations in modern English literature—in language, in style, and in substance—requires reckoning with Virginia Woolf, one of the chief architects of literary modernism. By 1962 Edward Albee could sardonically title a play *Who's Afraid of Virginia Woolf?*, knowing that her name would signify the greatness of modern literature. Woolf wrote luminous and intricate novels, two pivotal books on sexual politics, society, and war, several volumes of short stories and collected essays, reviews and pamphlets, and thirty volumes of a remarkable diary. Woolf was a woman of letters in an almost old-fashioned sense, one of the century's subtlest observers of social and psychic life, and a hauntingly beautiful prose writer.

Woolf's writing career began in childhood but was officially launched in 1915 with the publication of her first novel, *The Voyage Out*, when she was thirty-three. *The Voyage Out* was an emblematic beginning for her public career as a novelist, with its title suggesting the need to venture forth, to make a voyage into the world and out of the imprisonments of life and language. This novel paid special homage to *Heart of Darkness*, Joseph Conrad's story of a voyage through Africa that uncovers the heart of Europe's imperial encounter with the African continent and its exploited people. The theme resonated for Woolf throughout her books, because she too concentrated on the costs—both social and personal—of attempting to gain freedom. With the exception of *Orlando* (1928), a playful and flamboyant novel with a few scenes set in Turkey and Russia, Woolf was never again to set a novel outside the geographical confines of England. Voyaging out had become a matter of voyaging within. Woolf does not turn away from the larger world; she sets that larger world and its history squarely in England.

Woolf's own roots went deep in Victorian literary culture. She was born in 1882 into a privileged and illustrious British professional family with connections to the world of letters on both sides. She was the third child of the marriage of Leslie Stephen and Julia Duckworth, both of whom had been widowed; Leslie Stephen had married a daughter of the novelist William Thackeray, and Julia had been the wife of a publisher, and was connected to a long line of judges, teachers, and magistrates. Woolf's father, eventually to become Sir Leslie, was a prominent editor and a striving philosopher, who was appointed president of the London Library. His fame was to come not from his philosophical work but from his massive *Dictionary of National Biography*, a book that placed, and ranked, the leading figures of British national life for many centuries. Woolf's *Orlando*, with its subtitle: *A Biography*, spoofed the entire enterprise of the biography of great men by having *her* great man, Orlando, unexpectedly turn into a woman halfway through the novel.

Woolf grew up as an intensely literary child, surrounded by her father's project of arbitrating the greatness of the (mostly) men of letters she nonetheless sought to emulate. Her mother Julia was a famed beauty, whose magical grace was captured in the photographs of her equally famous relative, the photographer Julia Margaret Cameron. Woolf was to provide a haunting portrait of both her mother and father in her novel *To the Lighthouse* (1927), where the beautiful and consummately maternal Mrs. Ramsay ministers to her irascible and intellectually tormented philosopher husband, Mr. Ramsay, until her sudden death deprives the family and its circle of friends of their ballast in life. Julia Stephen's premature death in 1895 had cast just such a pall over her own family, especially over thirteen-year-old Virginia, who had a mental breakdown. Breakdowns would recur at intervals throughout her life.

Virginia Woolf and T. S. Eliot.

The death-haunted life characteristic of the Victorian family was Virginia Woolf's own experience. Two years after Julia died, Woolf's beloved half-sister and mother substitute, Stella Duckworth, died in childbirth at the age of twenty-seven. Woolf was also to lose her difficult but immensely loved father in 1904 (not so coincidentally, the same year Virginia was to publish her first essay and review), and her brother Thoby died of typhoid contracted on a trip to Greece with her in 1906. The novel *Jacob's Room* (1922) deals with a young man named Jacob and his college room, as perceived by his sister after his death in World War I. The items in Jacob's room are cloaked in memory and live in the consciousness of the sister as far more than precious objects—memory infuses them with shared life. The dead return again and again in Woolf's imagination and in her imaginative work; her development of the "moment of consciousness" in her writing, her novels' concentration on the binding powers of memory, and her invocation of the spreading, intertwining branches of human relations persisting even after death, may be the effect of her painful tutelage in loss.

As upper-class women, Woolf and her sisters were not given a formal education, while Thoby and Adrian both went to fine schools and ultimately to university. The sense of having been deliberately shut out of education by virtue of her sex was to inflect all of Woolf's writing and thinking. Education is a pervasive issue in her novels, and an enormous issue in her essays on social and political life, *A Room of One's Own* (1929) and *Three Guineas* (1938). Woolf became an autodidact, steeping herself in English literature, history, political theory, and art history, but she never lost the keen anguish nor the self-doubt occasioned by the closed doors of the academy to women. Education became for Woolf perhaps the key to transforming the role and the perception of women in society, and writing became her own mode of entry into the public world.

In 1912, Virginia Stephen married Leonard Woolf, like herself a member of the Blooms-bury group, but unlike her in being a Jew and coming from a commercial and far less illustrious family. Leonard Woolf was an "outsider" in anti-Semitic Britain no less than Virginia, who as a great woman writer was equally outside the norm. An accomplished writer in his own right, a political theorist and an activist in socialist issues and in anti-imperialist causes, Leonard Woolf devoted himself to Virginia and to her writing career. They established and ran the Hogarth Press together, an imprint that was to publish all of Virginia's books, as well as many important works of poetry, prose, and criticism from others. Virginia Woolf's erotic and emo-tional ties to women, and, in particular, her romance with Vita Sackville-West, while not nec-essarily explicitly sexual—no one seems to know for a certainty—were indubitably of the great-est importance to her life. Despite this, she placed Leonard Woolf and their marriage at the center of her being, and their rich and complex partnership weathered Virginia's numerous mental breakdowns. When she felt another episode of depression overtaking her in 1941, it was partly her reluctance to subject Leonard to what she saw as the burden of her madness that tragically led her to drown herself in the river near their home and their beloved press.

Woolf's themes and techniques as a writer are all distilled in her gem of a story *The Lady in the Looking-Glass: A Reflection* (1929), which is a parable about the dangers and the tran-scendence of writing. The lady of the title is absent for most of the brief story; an invisible nar-rator builds a world around her absence by recounting only what can be seen or sensed in the mirror to be glimpsed above the mantel. One of the oldest metaphors for literary art is the mir-ror, and with it, the notion that literature "holds up the mirror to nature," or reality. Literary art was long considered to be an imitation of reality, its mirrored reflection, its "re-presenta-tion." Woolf's story takes the garden shears of her missing character and tears representation to pieces, so to speak. Language cannot simply mirror something, her prose tells us, because it is too mysterious and subtle and wayward to do so. No imitation can ever capture subjective reality, and even inanimate objects are, for Woolf, filled with subjectivity. Finally, the story takes a "lady," a woman, as its subject because Woolf indicates that representation which tries to be realistic or real is instead a cruel violation, almost a form of rape. Truth in art is neither a representation nor a reflection: truth can only be gotten at sideways, in fragments, and with the fluidity of consciousness, in a subjective moment. "Examine for a moment an ordinary mind on an ordinary day," Woolf wrote in an essay on *Modern Fiction* in 1925:

> The mind receives a myriad impressions—trivial, fantastic, evanescent, or engraved with the sharpness of steel. From all sides they come, an incessant shower of innumerable atoms; and, as they fall, as they shape themselves into the life of Monday or Tuesday, the accent falls differently from of old; the moment of importance came not here but there; so that, if a writer were a free man and not a slave, if he could write what he chose, not what he must, if he could base his work upon his own feeling and not upon convention, there would be no plot, no comedy, no tragedy, no love interest or catastrophe in the accepted style, and perhaps not a single button sewn on as the Bond Street tailors would have it.

Woolf's stories are written out of her own painfully won freedom of observation; the passage that follows from *A Room of One's Own* meditates on the ways in which society and even human character would have to change in order for such freedom to spread.

The Lady in the Looking-Glass: A Reflection[1]

People should not leave looking-glasses hanging in their rooms any more than they should leave open cheque books or letters confessing some hideous crime. One could

---

1. Published in *Harper's Magazine*, December 1929.

not help looking, that summer afternoon, in the long glass that hung outside in the hall. Chance had so arranged it. From the depths of the sofa in the drawing-room one could see reflected in the Italian glass not only the marble-topped table opposite, but a stretch of the garden beyond. One could see a long grass path leading between banks of tall flowers until, slicing off an angle, the gold rim cut it off.

The house was empty, and one felt, since one was the only person in the drawing-room, like one of those naturalists who, covered with grass and leaves, lie watching the shyest animals—badgers, otters, kingfishers—moving about freely, themselves unseen. The room that afternoon was full of such shy creatures, lights and shadows, curtains blowing, petals falling—things that never happen, so it seems, if someone is looking. The quiet old country room with its rugs and stone chimney pieces, its sunken book-cases and red and gold lacquer cabinets, was full of such nocturnal creatures. They came pirouetting across the floor, stepping delicately with high-lifted feet and spread tails and pecking allusive beaks as if they had been cranes or flocks of elegant flamingoes whose pink was faded, or peacocks whose trains were veined with silver. And there were obscure flushes and darkenings too, as if a cuttlefish had suddenly suffused the air with purple; and the room had its passions and rages and envies and sorrows coming over it and clouding it, like a human being. Nothing stayed the same for two seconds together.

But, outside, the looking-glass reflected the hall table, the sunflowers, the garden path so accurately and so fixedly that they seemed held there in their reality unescapably. It was a strange contrast—all changing here, all stillness there. One could not help looking from one to the other. Meanwhile, since all the doors and windows were open in the heat, there was a perpetual sighing and ceasing sound, the voice of the transient and the perishing, it seemed, coming and going like human breath, while in the looking-glass things had ceased to breathe and lay still in the trance of immortality.

Half an hour ago the mistress of the house, Isabella Tyson, had gone down the grass path in her thin summer dress, carrying a basket, and had vanished, sliced off by the gilt rim of the looking-glass. She had gone presumably into the lower garden to pick flowers; or as it seemed more natural to suppose, to pick something light and fantastic and leafy and trailing, traveller's joy, or one of those elegant sprays of convolvulus that twine round ugly walls and burst here and there into white and violet blossoms. She suggested the fantastic and the tremulous convolvulus rather than the upright aster, the starched zinnia, or her own burning roses alight like lamps on the straight posts of their rose trees. The comparison showed how very little, after all these years, one knew about her; for it is impossible that any woman of flesh and blood of fifty-five or sixty should be really a wreath or a tendril. Such comparisons are worse than idle and superficial—they are cruel even, for they come like the convolvulus itself trembling between one's eyes and the truth. There must be truth; there must be a wall. Yet it was strange that after knowing her all these years one could not say what the truth about Isabella was; one still made up phrases like this about convolvulus and traveller's joy. As for facts, it was a fact that she was a spinster; that she was rich; that she had bought this house and collected with her own hands—often in the most obscure corners of the world and at great risk from poisonous stings and Oriental diseases—the rugs, the chairs, the cabinets which now lived their nocturnal life before one's eyes. Sometimes it seemed as if they knew more about her than we, who sat on them, wrote at them, and trod on them so carefully, were allowed to know. In each of these cabinets were many little drawers, and each almost certainly held letters, tied with bows of ribbon, sprinkled with sticks of lavender or rose leaves. For it was another fact—if facts were what one wanted—that Isabella had known many people, had had many friends; and thus if one had the audacity to open a drawer and read her letters, one would find the traces of many agitations, of appointments to meet, of upbraidings for not having met, long letters of intimacy and affection, violent letters of jealousy and reproach, terrible final words of parting—for all those interviews and assignations had led to nothing—that is, she had never married, and yet, judging from the mask-like indifference of her face, she had gone through twenty times more of passion and experience than those whose loves are trumpeted forth for all the world to hear. Under the stress of thinking about Isabella, her room became more shadowy and symbolic; the corners seemed darker, the legs of chairs and tables more spindly and hieroglyphic.

Suddenly these reflections were ended violently and yet without a sound. A large black form loomed into the looking-glass; blotted out everything, strewed the table with a packet of marble tablets veined with pink and grey, and was gone. But the picture was entirely altered. For the moment it was unrecognisable and irrational and entirely out of focus. One could not relate these tablets to any human purpose. And then by degrees some logical process set to work on them and began ordering and arranging them and bringing them into the fold of common experience. One realised at last that they were merely letters. The man had brought the post.

There they lay on the marble-topped table, all dripping with light and colour at first and crude and unabsorbed. And then it was strange to see how they were drawn in and arranged and composed and made part of the picture and granted that stillness and immortality which the looking-glass conferred. They lay there invested with a new reality and significance and with a greater heaviness, too, as if it would have needed a chisel to dislodge them from the table. And, whether it was fancy or not, they seemed to have become not merely a handful of casual letters but to be tablets graven with eternal truth—if one could read them, one would know everything there was to be known about Isabella, yes, and about life, too. The pages inside those marble-looking envelopes must be cut deep and scored thick with meaning. Isabella would come in, and take them, one by one, very slowly, and open them, and read them carefully word by word, and then with a profound sigh of comprehension, as if she had seen to the bottom of everything, she would tear the envelopes to little bits and tie the letters together and lock the cabinet drawer in her determination to conceal what she did not wish to be known.

The thought served as a challenge. Isabella did not wish to be known—but she should no longer escape. It was absurd, it was monstrous. If she concealed so much and knew so much one must prize her open with the first tool that came to hand— the imagination. One must fix one's mind upon her at that very moment. One must fasten her down there. One must refuse to be put off any longer with sayings and doings such as the moment brought forth—with dinners and visits and polite conversations. One must put oneself in her shoes. If one took the phrase literally, it was easy to see the shoes in which she stood, down in the lower garden, at this moment. They were very narrow and long and fashionable—they were made of the softest and most flexible leather. Like everything she wore, they were exquisite. And she would be standing under the high hedge in the lower part of the garden, raising the scissors that were tied to her waist to cut some dead flower, some overgrown branch. The sun would beat down on her face, into her eyes; but no, at the critical moment a veil of cloud covered the sun, making the expression of her eyes doubtful—was it mocking or tender, brilliant or dull? One could only see the indeterminate outline of her rather faded, fine face looking at the sky. She was thinking, perhaps, that she must order a new net for the strawberries; that she must send flowers to Johnson's widow; that it was time she drove over to see the Hippesleys in their new house. Those were the things she talked about at dinner certainly. But one was tired of the things that she talked about at dinner. It was her profounder state of being that one wanted to catch and turn to words, the state that is to the mind what breathing is to the body, what one calls happiness or unhappiness. At the mention of those words it became obvious, surely, that she must be happy. She was rich; she was distinguished; she had many friends; she travelled—she bought rugs in Turkey and blue pots in Persia. Avenues of pleasure radiated this way and that from where she stood with her scissors raised to cut the trembling branches while the lacy clouds veiled her face.

Here with a quick movement of her scissors she snipped the spray of traveller's joy and it fell to the ground. As it fell, surely some light came in too, surely one could penetrate a little farther into her being. Her mind then was filled with tenderness and regret. . . . To cut an overgrown branch saddened her because it had once lived, and life was dear to her. Yes, and at the same time the fall of the branch would suggest to her how she must die herself and all the futility and evanescence of things. And then again quickly catching this thought up, with her instant good sense, she thought life had treated her well; even if fall she must, it was to lie on the earth and moulder sweetly into the roots of violets. So she stood thinking. Without making any thought precise—for she was one of those reticent people whose minds hold their thoughts enmeshed in clouds of silence—she was filled with thoughts. Her mind was like her room, in which lights advanced and retreated, came pirouetting and stepping delicately, spread their tails, pecked their way; and then her whole being was suffused, like the room again, with a cloud of some profound knowledge, some unspoken regret, and then she was full of locked drawers, stuffed with letters, like her cabinets. To talk of "prizing her open" as if she were an oyster, to use any but the finest and subtlest and most pliable tools upon her was impious and absurd. One must imagine—here was she in the looking-glass. It made one start.

She was so far off at first that one could not see her clearly. She came lingering and pausing, here straightening a rose, there lifting a pink to smell it, but she never stopped; and all the time she became larger and larger in the looking-glass, more and more completely the person into whose mind one had been trying to penetrate. One verified her by degrees—fitted the qualities one had discovered into this visible body. There were her grey-green dress, and her long shoes, her basket, and something sparkling at her throat. She came so gradually that she did not seem to derange the pattern in the glass, but only to bring in some new element which gently moved and altered the other objects as if asking them, courteously, to make room for her. And the letters and the table and the grass walk and the sunflowers which had been waiting in the looking-glass separated and opened out so that she might be received among them. At last there she was, in the hall. She stopped dead. She stood by the table. She stood perfectly still. At once the looking-glass began to pour over her a light that seemed to fix her; that seemed like some acid to bite off the unessential and superficial and to leave only the truth. It was an enthralling spectacle. Everything dropped from her—clouds, dress, basket, diamond—all that one had called the creeper and convolvulus. Here was the hard wall beneath. Here was the woman herself. She stood naked in that pitiless light. And, there was nothing. Isabella was perfectly empty. She had no thoughts. She had no friends. She cared for nobody. As for her letters, they were all bills. Look, as she stood there, old and angular, veined and lined, with her high nose and her wrinkled neck, she did not even trouble to open them.

People should not leave looking-glasses hanging in their rooms.

A ROOM OF ONE'S OWN   *A Room of One's Own* is difficult to categorize—it is a long essay, a nonfiction novella, a political pamphlet, and a philosophical discourse all in one. Its effects have not been so difficult to categorize—Virginia Woolf's idiosyncratic text has been recognized as a classic from the time of its publication in 1929. The book was a departure from Woolf's output until then; she was a major literary figure, having already published such key novels as *Jacob's Room, Mrs Dalloway, To the Lighthouse,* and *Orlando,* and she was an established essayist with a formidable reputation as an arbiter of the literary tradition. One way of characterizing this book is to see that it represents Woolf's scrutiny of her own position as a woman writer, a self-examination of her public position that inevitably became a political document. The focus is not on Woolf's life or her work per se, but rather on the social and psychological conditions that would make such a life generally possible. The book creates a microcosm of such possibility in the "room" of its title; the book itself is a room within which its author contemplates and analyzes the dimensions of social space for women. Woolf recognizes that seemingly neutral social space, the room of cultural agency just as the room of writing, is in truth a gendered space. She directs her political inquiry toward the making and remaking of such rooms.

A *Room of One's Own* comes from established traditions of writing as well. It draws on the conversational tone and novelistic insight of the literary essay as perfected in the nineteenth century by such writers as Charles Lamb—whose *Oxford in the Vacation* was certainly in Woolf's mind when she wrote the opening chapter of her essay. At the same time, Woolf's book joins a lineage of feminist political philosophy, whose most eloquent exponent prior to Woolf herself was Mary Wollstonecraft, who joined the rhetorical ranks of Rousseau and John Stuart Mill with the publication of *A Vindication of the Rights of Woman,* her passionately reasoned exhortation for the equal and universal human rights of women. (Selections from Wollstonecraft's *Vindication* can be found on page 152.) The century and a half since Wollstonecraft had produced a rich history of feminist agitation and feminist thought. Virginia Woolf draws on this less-known tradition, invoking nineteenth-century figures from the women's movement like Emily Davies, Josephine Butler, and Octavia Hill. She also places her deliberations in the context of the suffragist movement and its fraught history in Britain. Virginia Woolf was strongly engaged in the debates of the suffrage movement, and its divisions over radical action or more conciliatory political approaches. Much of Woolf's long essay is devoted to demonstrating the subversive quality of occupying the blank page and wielding the printed word.

As politically motivated as *A Room of One's Own* is, it is equally a literary text. Woolf draws on all the intricacies of literary tropes and figures to mount her argument for women's education, women's equality, and women's social presence. Not the least of her strategies is her manipulation of the rhetoric of address—in other words, the audience implied by the language of a text. Woolf creates an ironic space, or room, in which she is a playfully ambiguous speaker addressing an uncertain audience: women at the colleges where she has been invited to speak, but also men and women alike who will read her printed text. By doing so, she keeps an ironic tension in play, holding at bay her anger at being censored or silenced by male readers by creating a sense of privacy and secrecy among women. This underscores Woolf's primary argument, the need for autonomy and self-determination. Her modest proposal, although faintly ironic, is also eminently pragmatic—the room of one's own that is her metaphor for the college classroom or the blank canvas or the book's page is at the same time the actual room, paid for and unintruded upon by domestic worries or social codes, whose possession permits a woman to find out who she may be.

from A Room of One's Own
Chapter 1

But, you may say, we asked you to speak about women and fiction—what has that got to do with a room of one's own?[1] I will try to explain. When you asked me to speak about women and fiction I sat down on the banks of a river and began to wonder what the words meant. They might mean simply a few remarks about Fanny Burney; a few more about Jane Austen; a tribute to the Brontës and a sketch of Haworth Parsonage under snow; some witticisms if possible about Miss Mitford; a respectful allusion to George Eliot; a reference to Mrs Gaskell and one would have done.[2] But at second sight the words seemed not so simple. The title women and fiction might mean, and you may have meant it to mean, women and what they are like; or it might mean women and the fiction that they write; or it might mean women and the fiction that is written about them; or it might mean that somehow all three are inextricably mixed together and you want me to consider them in that light. But when I began to consider the subject in this last way, which seemed the most interesting, I soon saw that it had one fatal drawback. I should never be able to come to a conclusion. I should never be able to fulfil what is, I understand, the first duty of a lecturer—to hand you after an hour's discourse a nugget of pure truth to wrap up between the pages of your notebooks and keep on the mantelpiece for ever. All I could do was to offer you an opinion upon one minor point—a woman must have money and a room of her own if she is to write fiction; and that, as you will see, leaves the great problem of the true nature of woman and the true nature of fiction unsolved. I have shirked the duty of coming to a conclusion upon these two questions—women and fiction remain, so far as I am concerned, unsolved problems. But in order to make some amends I am going to do what I can to show you how I arrived at this opinion about the room and the money. I am going to develop in your presence as fully and freely as I can the train of thought which led me to think this. Perhaps if I lay bare the ideas, the prejudices, that lie behind this statement you will find that they have some bearing upon women and some upon fiction. At any rate, when a subject is highly controversial—and any question about sex is that—one cannot hope to tell the truth. One can only show how one came to hold whatever opinion one does hold. One can only give one's audience the chance of drawing their own conclusions as they observe the limitations, the prejudices, the idiosyncrasies of the speaker. Fiction here is likely to contain more

---

1. Woolf delivered her essay in a shorter version to meetings first at two women's colleges, Newnham and Girton,   Cambridge University, in October 1928.
2. Important 19th-century novelists.

truth than fact. Therefore I propose, making use of all the liberties and licences of a novelist, to tell you the story of the two days that preceded my coming here—how, bowed down by the weight of the subject which you have laid upon my shoulders, I pondered it, and made it work in and out of my daily life. I need not say that what I am about to describe has no existence; Oxbridge is an invention; so is Fernham;[3] "I" is only a convenient term for somebody who has no real being. Lies will flow from my lips, but there may perhaps be some truth mixed up with them; it is for you to seek out this truth and to decide whether any part of it is worth keeping. If not, you will of course throw the whole of it into the wastepaper basket and forget all about it.

Here then was I (call me Mary Beton, Mary Seton, Mary Carmichael[4] or by any name you please—it is not a matter of any importance) sitting on the banks of a river a week or two ago in fine October weather, lost in thought. That collar I have spoken of, women and fiction, the need of coming to some conclusion on a subject that raises all sorts of prejudices and passions, bowed my head to the ground. To the right and left bushes of some sort, golden and crimson, glowed with the colour, even it seemed burnt with the heat, of fire. On the further bank the willows wept in perpetual lamentation, their hair about their shoulders. The river reflected whatever it chose of sky and bridge and burning tree, and when the undergraduate had oared his boat through the reflections they closed again, completely, as if he had never been. There one might have sat the clock round lost in thought. Thought—to call it by a prouder name than it deserved—had let its line down into the stream. It swayed, minute after minute, hither and thither among the reflections and the weeds, letting the water lift it and sink it, until—you know the little tug—the sudden conglomeration of an idea at the end of one's line: and then the cautious hauling of it in, and the careful laying of it out? Alas, laid on the grass how small, how insignificant this thought of mine looked; the sort of fish that a good fisherman puts back into the water so that it may grow fatter and be one day worth cooking and eating. I will not trouble you with that thought now, though if you look carefully you may find it for yourselves in the course of what I am going to say.

But however small it was, it had, nevertheless, the mysterious property of its kind—put back into the mind, it became at once very exciting, and important; and as it darted and sank, and flashed hither and thither, set up such a wash and tumult of ideas that it was impossible to sit still. It was thus that I found myself walking with extreme rapidity across a grass plot. Instantly a man's figure rose to intercept me. Nor did I at first understand that the gesticulations of a curious-looking object, in a cut-away coat and evening shirt, were aimed at me. His face expressed horror and indignation. Instinct rather than reason came to my help; he was a Beadle; I was a woman. This was the turf; there was the path. Only the Fellows and Scholars are allowed here; the gravel is the place for me.[5] Such thoughts were the work of a moment. As I regained the path the arms of the Beadle sank, his face assumed its usual repose, and though turf is better walking than gravel, no very great harm was done. The only

3. "Oxbridge" was in fact the common slang term for Oxford and Cambridge universities. "Fernham" suggests Newnham College.
4. Three of the four Marys who by tradition were attendants to Mary Queen of Scots (executed in 1567), and who figure in many Scottish ballads; the fourth was Mary Hamilton.
5. A beadle is a disciplinary officer. The fellows of Oxbridge colleges typically tutor the undergraduates, who are divided into scholars and commoners. The commoners form the majority of the student body.

charge I could bring against the Fellows and Scholars of whatever the college might happen to be was that in protection of their turf, which has been rolled for 300 years in succession, they had sent my little fish into hiding.

What idea it had been that had sent me so audaciously trespassing I could not now remember. The spirit of peace descended like a cloud from heaven, for if the spirit of peace dwells anywhere, it is in the courts and quadrangles of Oxbridge on a fine October morning. Strolling through those colleges past those ancient halls the roughness of the present seemed smoothed away; the body seemed contained in a miraculous glass cabinet through which no sound could penetrate, and the mind, freed from any contact with facts (unless one trespassed on the turf again), was at liberty to settle down upon whatever meditation was in harmony with the moment. As chance would have it, some stray memory of some old essay about revisiting Oxbridge in the long vacation brought Charles Lamb to mind—Saint Charles, said Thackeray,[6] putting a letter of Lamb's to his forehead. Indeed, among all the dead (I give you my thoughts as they came to me), Lamb is one of the most congenial; one to whom one would have liked to say, Tell me then how you wrote your essays? For his essays are superior even to Max Beerbohm's, I thought, with all their perfection, because of that wild flash of imagination, that lightning crack of genius in the middle of them which leaves them flawed and imperfect, but starred with poetry. Lamb then came to Oxbridge perhaps a hundred years ago. Certainly he wrote an essay—the name escapes me—about the manuscript of one of Milton's poems which he saw here.[7] It was *Lycidas* perhaps, and Lamb wrote how it shocked him to think it possible that any word in *Lycidas* could have been different from what it is. To think of Milton changing the words in that poem seemed to him a sort of sacrilege. This led me to remember what I could of *Lycidas* and to amuse myself with guessing which word it could have been that Milton had altered, and why. It then occurred to me that the very manuscript itself which Lamb had looked at was only a few hundred yards away, so that one could follow Lamb's footsteps across the quadrangle to that famous library where the treasure is kept. Moreover, I recollected, as I put this plan into execution, it is in this famous library that the manuscript of Thackeray's *Esmond* is also preserved. The critics often say that *Esmond* is Thackeray's most perfect novel. But the affectation of the style, with its imitation of the eighteenth century, hampers one, so far as I remember; unless indeed the eighteenth-century style was natural to Thackeray —a fact that one might prove by looking at the manuscript and seeing whether the alterations were for the benefit of the style or of the sense. But then one would have to decide what is style and what is meaning, a question which—but here I was actually at the door which leads into the library itself. I must have opened it, for instantly there issued, like a guardian angel barring the way with a flutter of black gown instead of white wings, a deprecating, silvery, kindly gentleman, who regretted in a low voice as he waved me back that ladies are only admitted to the library if accompanied by a Fellow of the College or furnished with a letter of introduction.

That a famous library has been cursed by a woman is a matter of complete indifference to a famous library. Venerable and calm, with all its treasures safe locked within its breast, it sleeps complacently and will, so far as I am concerned, so sleep for ever. Never will I wake those echoes, never will I ask for that hospitality again, I

---

6. William Makepeace Thackeray (1811–1863), novelist and journalist, Woolf's father's first father-in-law.
7. Lamb's *Oxford in the Vacation*—describing the locales Lamb himself was too poor to attend in term time. The manuscript of Milton's elegy *Lycidas* (1638) is in the Wren Library of Trinity College, Cambridge, together with that of Thackeray's novel *The History of Henry Esmond* (1852).

vowed as I descended the steps in anger. Still an hour remained before luncheon, and what was one to do? Stroll on the meadows? sit by the river? Certainly it was a lovely autumn morning; the leaves were fluttering red to the ground; there was no great hardship in doing either. But the sound of music reached my ear. Some service or celebration was going forward. The organ complained magnificently as I passed the chapel door. Even the sorrow of Christianity sounded in that serene air more like the recollection of sorrow than sorrow itself; even the groanings of the ancient organ seemed lapped in peace. I had no wish to enter had I the right, and this time the verger might have stopped me, demanding perhaps my baptismal certificate, or a letter of introduction from the Dean. But the outside of these magnificent buildings is often as beautiful as the inside. Moreover, it was amusing enough to watch the congregation assembling, coming in and going out again, busying themselves at the door of the chapel like bees at the mouth of a hive. Many were in cap and gown; some had tufts of fur on their shoulders; others were wheeled in bath-chairs; others, though not past middle age, seemed creased and crushed into shapes so singular that one was reminded of those giant crabs and crayfish who heave with difficulty across the sand of an aquarium. As I leant against the wall the University indeed seemed a sanctuary in which are preserved rare types which would soon be obsolete if left to fight for existence on the pavement of the Strand.[8] Old stories of old deans and old dons came back to mind, but before I had summoned up courage to whistle—it used to be said that at the sound of a whistle old Professor —— instantly broke into a gallop—the venerable congregation had gone inside. The outside of the chapel remained. As you know, its high domes and pinnacles can be seen, like a sailing-ship always voyaging never arriving, lit up at night and visible for miles, far away across the hills. Once, presumably, this quadrangle with its smooth lawns, its massive buildings, and the chapel itself was marsh too, where the grasses waved and the swine rooted. Teams of horses and oxen, I thought, must have hauled the stone in wagons from far countries, and then with infinite labour the grey blocks in whose shade I was now standing were poised in order one on top of another, and then the painters brought their glass for the windows, and the masons were busy for centuries up on that roof with putty and cement, spade and trowel. Every Saturday somebody must have poured gold and silver out of a leathern purse into their ancient fists, for they had their beer and skittles presumably of an evening. An unending stream of gold and silver, I thought, must have flowed into this court perpetually to keep the stones coming and the masons working; to level, to ditch, to dig and to drain. But it was then the age of faith, and money was poured liberally to set these stones on a deep foundation, and when the stones were raised, still more money was poured in from the coffers of kings and queens and great nobles to ensure that hymns should be sung here and scholars taught. Lands were granted; tithes were paid. And when the age of faith was over and the age of reason had come, still the same flow of gold and silver went on; fellowships were founded; lectureships endowed; only the gold and silver flowed now, not from the coffers of the king, but from the chests of merchants and manufacturers, from the purses of men who had made, say, a fortune from industry, and returned, in their wills, a bounteous share of it to endow more chairs, more lectureships, more fellowships in the university where they had learnt their craft. Hence the libraries and laboratories; the observatories; the splendid equipment of costly and delicate instruments which now stands on glass shelves, where centuries ago the grasses waved and

---

8. A thoroughfare in central London.

the swine rootled. Certainly, as I strolled round the court, the foundation of gold and silver seemed deep enough; the pavement laid solidly over the wild grasses. Men with trays on their heads went busily from staircase to staircase. Gaudy blossoms flowered in window-boxes. The strains of the gramophone blared out from the rooms within. It was impossible not to reflect—the reflection whatever it may have been was cut short. The clock struck. It was time to find one's way to luncheon.

It is a curious fact that novelists have a way of making us believe that luncheon parties are invariably memorable for something very witty that was said, or for something very wise that was done. But they seldom spare a word for what was eaten. It is part of the novelist's convention not to mention soup and salmon and ducklings, as if soup and salmon and ducklings were of no importance whatsoever, as if nobody ever smoked a cigar or drank a glass of wine. Here, however, I shall take the liberty to defy that convention and to tell you that the lunch on this occasion began with soles, sunk in a deep dish, over which the college cook had spread a counterpane of the whitest cream, save that it was branded here and there with brown spots like the spots on the flanks of a doe. After that came the partridges, but if this suggests a couple of bald, brown birds on a plate you are mistaken. The partridges, many and various, came with all their retinue of sauces and salads, the sharp and the sweet, each in its order; their potatoes, thin as coins but not so hard; their sprouts, foliated as rosebuds but more succulent. And no sooner had the roast and its retinue been done with than the silent serving-man, the Beadle himself perhaps in a milder manifestation, set before us, wreathed in napkins, a confection which rose all sugar from the waves. To call it pudding and so relate it to rice and tapioca would be an insult. Meanwhile the wineglasses had flushed yellow and flushed crimson; had been emptied; had been filled. And thus by degrees was lit, halfway down the spine, which is the seat of the soul, not that hard little electric light which we call brilliance, as it pops in and out upon our lips, but the more profound, subtle and subterranean glow, which is the rich yellow flame of rational intercourse. No need to hurry. No need to sparkle. No need to be anybody but oneself. We are all going to heaven and Vandyck[9] is of the company—in other words, how good life seemed, how sweet its rewards, how trivial this grudge or that grievance, how admirable friendship and the society of one's kind, as, lighting a good cigarette, one sunk among the cushions in the window-seat.

If by good luck there had been an ash-tray handy, if one had not knocked the ash out of the window in default, if things had been a little different from what they were, one would not have seen, presumably, a cat without a tail. The sight of that abrupt and truncated animal padding softly across the quadrangle changed by some fluke of the subconscious intelligence the emotional light for me. It was as if some one had let fall a shade. Perhaps the excellent hock was relinquishing its hold. Certainly, as I watched the Manx cat pause in the middle of the lawn as if it too questioned the universe, something seemed lacking, something seemed different. But what was lacking, what was different, I asked myself, listening to the talk. And to answer that question I had to think myself out of the room, back into the past, before the war indeed,[1] and to set before my eyes the model of another luncheon party held in rooms not very far distant from these; but different. Everything was different. Meanwhile the talk went on among the guests, who were many and young, some of this sex, some of that; it went on swimmingly, it went on agreeably, freely, amusingly. And as it went on I set it against the background

9. Sir Anthony Van Dyck, prominent 17th-century soci-   1. World War I.
ety painter.

of that other talk, and as I matched the two together I had no doubt that one was the descendant, the legitimate heir of the other. Nothing was changed; nothing was different save only—here I listened with all my ears not entirely to what was being said, but to the murmur or current behind it. Yes, that was it—the change was there. Before the war at a luncheon party like this people would have said precisely the same things but they would have sounded different, because in those days they were accompanied by a sort of humming noise, not articulate, but musical, exciting, which changed the value of the words themselves. Could one set that humming noise to words? Perhaps with the help of the poets one could. A book lay beside me and, opening it, I turned casually enough to Tennyson. And here I found Tennyson was singing:

> There has fallen a splendid tear
>   From the passion-flower at the gate.
> She is coming, my dove, my dear;
>   She is coming, my life, my fate;
> The red rose cries, "She is near, she is near";
>   And the white rose weeps, "She is late";
> The larkspur listens, "I hear, I hear";
>   And the lily whispers, "I wait."[2]

Was that what men hummed at luncheon parties before the war? And the women?

> My heart is like a singing bird
>   Whose nest is in a water'd shoot;
> My heart is like an apple tree
>   Whose boughs are bent with thick-set fruit;
> My heart is like a rainbow shell
>   That paddles in a halcyon sea;
> My heart is gladder than all these
>   Because my love is come to me.[3]

Was that what women hummed at luncheon parties before the war?

There was something so ludicrous in thinking of people humming such things even under their breath at luncheon parties before the war that I burst out laughing, and had to explain my laughter by pointing at the Manx cat, who did look a little absurd, poor beast, without a tail, in the middle of the lawn. Was he really born so, or had he lost his tail in an accident? The tailless cat, though some are said to exist in the Isle of Man, is rarer than one thinks. It is a queer animal, quaint rather than beautiful. It is strange what a difference a tail makes—you know the sort of things one says as a lunch party breaks up and people are finding their coats and hats.

This one, thanks to the hospitality of the host, had lasted far into the afternoon. The beautiful October day was fading and the leaves were falling from the trees in the avenue as I walked through it. Gate after gate seemed to close with gentle finality behind me. Innumerable beadles were fitting innumerable keys into well-oiled locks; the treasure-house was being made secure for another night. After the avenue one comes out upon a road—I forget its name—which leads you, if you take the right

---

2. From Tennyson's *Maud* (1855), lines 908–915.　　3. The first stanza of Christina Rossetti's poem *A Birthday* (1857).

turning, along to Fernham.[4] But there was plenty of time. Dinner was not till half-past seven. One could almost do without dinner after such a luncheon. It is strange how a scrap of poetry works in the mind and makes the legs move in time to it along the road. Those words—

> There has fallen a splendid tear
> From the passion-flower at the gate.
> She is coming, my dove, my dear—

sang in my blood as I stepped quickly along towards Headingley. And then, switching off into the other measure, I sang, where the waters are churned up by the weir:

> My heart is like a singing bird
> Whose nest is in a water'd shoot;
> My heart is like an apple tree—

What poets, I cried aloud, as one does in the dusk, what poets they were!

In a sort of jealousy, I suppose, for our own age, silly and absurd though these comparisons are, I went on to wonder if honestly one could name two living poets now as great as Tennyson and Christina Rossetti were then. Obviously it is impossible, I thought, looking into those foaming waters, to compare them. The very reason why the poetry excites one to such abandonment, such rapture, is that it celebrates some feeling that one used to have (at luncheon parties before the war perhaps), so that one responds easily, familiarly, without troubling to check the feeling, or to compare it with any that one has now. But the living poets express a feeling that is actually being made and torn out of us at the moment. One does not recognize it in the first place; often for some reason one fears it; one watches it with keenness and compares it jealously and suspiciously with the old feeling that one knew. Hence the difficulty of modern poetry; and it is because of this difficulty that one cannot remember more than two consecutive lines of any good modern poet. For this reason—that my memory failed me—the argument flagged for want of material. But why, I continued, moving on towards Headingley, have we stopped humming under our breath at luncheon parties? Why has Alfred ceased to sing

> She is coming, my dove, my dear?

Why has Christina ceased to respond

> My heart is gladder than all these
> Because my love is come to me?

Shall we lay the blame on the war? When the guns fired in August 1914, did the faces of men and women show so plain in each other's eyes that romance was killed? Certainly it was a shock (to women in particular with their illusions about education, and so on) to see the faces of our rulers in the light of the shell-fire. So ugly they looked—German, English, French—so stupid. But lay the blame where one will, on whom one will, the illusion which inspired Tennyson and Christina Rossetti to sing so passionately about the coming of their loves is far rarer now than then. One has

---

4. Both Girton and Newnham colleges, established only in the late 19th century, are outside the old university area of Cambridge.

only to read, to look, to listen, to remember. But why say "blame"? Why, if it was an illusion, not praise the catastrophe, whatever it was, that destroyed illusion and put truth in its place? For truth . . . those dots mark the spot where, in search of truth, I missed the turning up to Fernham. Yes indeed, which was truth and which was illusion, I asked myself. What was the truth about these houses, for example, dim and festive now with their red windows in the dusk, but raw and red and squalid, with their sweets and their boot-laces, at nine o'clock in the morning? And the willows and the river and the gardens that run down to the river, vague now with the mist stealing over them, but gold and red in the sunlight—which was the truth, which was the illusion about them? I spare you the twists and turns of my cogitations, for no conclusion was found on the road to Headingley, and I ask you to suppose that I soon found out my mistake about the turning and retraced my steps to Fernham.

As I have said already that it was an October day, I dare not forfeit your respect and imperil the fair name of fiction by changing the season and describing lilacs hanging over garden walls, crocuses, tulips and other flowers of spring. Fiction must stick to facts, and the truer the facts the better the fiction—so we are told. Therefore it was still autumn and the leaves were still yellow and falling, if anything, a little faster than before, because it was now evening (seven twenty-three to be precise) and a breeze (from the south-west to be exact) had risen. But for all that there was something odd at work:

> My heart is like a singing bird
>   Whose nest is in a water'd shoot;
> My heart is like an apple tree
>   Whose boughs are bent with thick-set fruit—

perhaps the words of Christina Rossetti were partly responsible for the folly of the fancy—it was nothing of course but a fancy—that the lilac was shaking its flowers over the garden walls, and the brimstone butterflies were scudding hither and thither, and the dust of the pollen was in the air. A wind blew, from what quarter I know not, but it lifted the half-grown leaves so that there was a flash of silver grey in the air. It was the time between the lights when colours undergo their intensification and purples and golds burn in window-panes like the beat of an excitable heart; when for some reason the beauty of the world revealed and yet soon to perish (here I pushed into the garden, for, unwisely, the door was left open and no beadles seemed about), the beauty of the world which is so soon to perish, has two edges, one of laughter, one of anguish, cutting the heart asunder. The gardens of Fernham lay before me in the spring twilight, wild and open, and in the long grass, sprinkled and carelessly flung, were daffodils and bluebells, not orderly perhaps at the best of times, and now wind-blown and waving as they tugged at their roots. The windows of the building, curved like ships' windows among generous waves of red brick, changed from lemon to silver under the flight of the quick spring clouds. Somebody was in a hammock, somebody, but in this light they were phantoms only, half guessed, half seen, raced across the grass—would no one stop her?—and then on the terrace, as if popping out to breathe the air, to glance at the garden, came a bent figure, formidable yet humble, with her great forehead and her shabby dress—could it be the famous scholar, could it be J——H—— herself?[5] All was dim, yet intense too, as if the scarf which the dusk had flung over the garden were torn asunder by star or sword—the flash of some terrible reality leaping, as its way is, out of the heart of the spring. For youth——

---

5. Jane Harrison, a famous classical scholar.

Here was my soup. Dinner was being served in the great dining-hall. Far from being spring it was in fact an evening in October. Everybody was assembled in the big dining-room. Dinner was ready. Here was the soup. It was a plain gravy soup. There was nothing to stir the fancy in that. One could have seen through the transparent liquid any pattern that there might have been on the plate itself. But there was no pattern. The plate was plain. Next came beef with its attendant greens and potatoes—a homely trinity, suggesting the rumps of cattle in a muddy market, and sprouts curled and yellowed at the edge, and bargaining and cheapening, and women with string bags on Monday morning. There was no reason to complain of human nature's daily food, seeing that the supply was sufficient and coal-miners doubtless were sitting down to less. Prunes and custard followed. And if any one complains that prunes, even when mitigated by custard, are an uncharitable vegetable (fruit they are not), stringy as a miser's heart and exuding a fluid such as might run in misers' veins who have denied themselves wine and warmth for eighty years and yet not given to the poor, he should reflect that there are people whose charity embraces even the prune. Biscuits and cheese came next, and here the water-jug was liberally passed round, for it is the nature of biscuits to be dry, and these were biscuits to the core. That was all. The meal was over. Everybody scraped their chairs back; the swing-doors swung violently to and fro; soon the hall was emptied of every sign of food and made ready no doubt for breakfast next morning. Down corridors and up staircases the youth of England went banging and singing. And was it for a guest, a stranger (for I had no more right here in Fernham than in Trinity or Somerville or Girton or Newnham or Christchurch),[6] to say, "The dinner was not good," or to say (we were now, Mary Seton and I, in her sitting-room), "Could we not have dined up here alone?" for if I had said anything of the kind I should have been prying and searching into the secret economies of a house which to the stranger wears so fine a front of gaiety and courage. No, one could say nothing of the sort. Indeed, conversation for a moment flagged. The human frame being what it is, heart, body and brain all mixed together, and not contained in separate compartments as they will be no doubt in another million years, a good dinner is of great importance to good talk. One cannot think well, love well, sleep well, if one has not dined well. The lamp in the spine does not light on beef and prunes. We are all *probably* going to heaven, and Vandyck is, we *hope*, to meet us round the next corner—that is the dubious and qualifying state of mind that beef and prunes at the end of the day's work breed between them. Happily my friend, who taught science, had a cupboard where there was a squat bottle and little glasses—(but there should have been sole and partridge to begin with)—so that we were able to draw up to the fire and repair some of the damages of the day's living. In a minute or so we were slipping freely in and out among all those objects of curiosity and interest which form in the mind in the absence of a particular person, and are naturally to be discussed on coming together again—how somebody has married, another has not; one thinks this, another that; one has improved out of all knowledge, the other most amazingly gone to the bad—with all those speculations upon human nature and the character of the amazing world we live in which spring naturally from such beginnings. While these things were being said, however, I became shamefacedly aware of a current setting in of its own accord and carrying everything forward to an end of its own. One might be talking of Spain or Portugal,

---

6. Trinity, Girton, and Newnham are colleges of Cambridge University; Somerville and Christchurch are at Oxford.

of book or racehorse, but the real interest of whatever was said was none of those things, but a scene of masons on a high roof some five centuries ago. Kings and nobles brought treasure in huge sacks and poured it under the earth. This scene was for ever coming alive in my mind and placing itself by another of lean cows and a muddy market and withered greens and the stringy hearts of old men—these two pictures, disjointed and disconnected and nonsensical as they were, were for ever coming together and combating each other and had me entirely at their mercy. The best course, unless the whole talk was to be distorted, was to expose what was in my mind to the air, when with good luck it would fade and crumble like the head of the dead king when they opened the coffin at Windsor. Briefly, then, I told Miss Seton about the masons who had been all those years on the roof of the chapel, and about the kings and queens and nobles bearing sacks of gold and silver on their shoulders, which they shovelled into the earth; and then how the great financial magnates of our own time came and laid cheques and bonds, I suppose, where the others had laid ingots and rough lumps of gold. All that lies beneath the colleges down there, I said; but this college, where we are now sitting, what lies beneath its gallant red brick and the wild unkempt grasses of the garden? What force is behind the plain china off which we dined, and (here it popped out of my mouth before I could stop it) the beef, the custard and the prunes?

Well, said Mary Seton, about the year 1860—Oh, but you know the story, she said, bored, I suppose, by the recital. And she told me—rooms were hired. Committees met. Envelopes were addressed. Circulars were drawn up. Meetings were held; letters were read out; so-and-so has promised so much; on the contrary, Mr——won't give a penny. The *Saturday Review* has been very rude. How can we raise a fund to pay for offices? Shall we hold a bazaar? Can't we find a pretty girl to sit in the front row? Let us look up what John Stuart Mill said on the subject.[7] Can any one persuade the editor of the——to print a letter? Can we get Lady——to sign it? Lady——is out of town. That was the way it was done, presumably, sixty years ago, and it was a prodigious effort, and a great deal of time was spent on it. And it was only after a long struggle and with the utmost difficulty that they got thirty thousand pounds together.[8] So obviously we cannot have wine and partridges and servants carrying tin dishes on their heads, she said. We cannot have sofas and separate rooms. "The amenities," she said, quoting from some book or other, "will have to wait."[9]

At the thought of all those women working year after year and finding it hard to get two thousand pounds together, and as much as they could do to get thirty thousand pounds, we burst out in scorn at the reprehensible poverty of our sex. What had our mothers been doing then that they had no wealth to leave us? Powdering their noses? Looking in at shop windows? Flaunting in the sun at Monte Carlo? There were some photographs on the mantel-piece. Mary's mother—if that was her picture—may have been a wastrel in her spare time (she had thirteen children by a minister of the church), but if so her gay and dissipated life had left too few traces of its pleasures on her face. She was a homely body; an old lady in a plaid shawl which was fastened

7. In 1869 Mill published his essay *The Subjection of Women*, which argued forcefully for women's suffrage and their right to equality with men.
8. "We are told that we ought to ask for £30,000 at least. ... It is not a large sum, considering that there is to be but one college of this sort for Great Britain, Ireland and the Colonies, and considering how easy it is to raise immense sums for boys' schools. But considering how few people really wish women to be educated, it is a good deal."–Lady Stephen, *Life of Miss Emily Davies* [Woolf's note].
9. Every penny which could be scraped together was set aside for building, and the amenities had to be postponed.–R. Strachey, *The Cause* [Woolf's note].

by a large cameo; and she sat in a basket-chair, encouraging a spaniel to look at the camera, with the amused, yet strained expression of one who is sure that the dog will move directly the bulb is pressed. Now if she had gone into business; had become a manufacturer of artificial silk or a magnate on the Stock Exchange; if she had left two or three hundred thousand pounds to Fernham, we could have been sitting at our ease tonight and the subject of our talk might have been archaeology, botany, anthropology, physics, the nature of the atom, mathematics, astronomy, relativity, geography. If only Mrs Seton and her mother and her mother before her had learnt the great art of making money and had left their money, like their fathers and their grandfathers before them, to found fellowships and lectureships and prizes and scholarships appropriated to the use of their own sex, we might have dined very tolerably up here alone off a bird and a bottle of wine; we might have looked forward without undue confidence to a pleasant and honourable lifetime spent in the shelter of one of the liberally endowed professions. We might have been exploring or writing; mooning about the venerable places of the earth; sitting contemplative on the steps of the Parthenon, or going at ten to an office and coming home comfortably at half-past four to write a little poetry. Only, if Mrs Seton and her like had gone into business at the age of fifteen, there would have been—that was the snag in the argument—no Mary. What, I asked, did Mary think of that? There between the curtains was the October night, calm and lovely, with a star or two caught in the yellowing trees. Was she ready to resign her share of it and her memories (for they had been a happy family, though a large one) of games and quarrels up in Scotland, which she is never tired of praising for the fineness of its air and the quality of its cakes, in order that Fernham might have been endowed with fifty thousand pounds or so by a stroke of the pen? For, to endow a college would necessitate the suppression of families altogether. Making a fortune and bearing thirteen children—no human being could stand it. Consider the facts, we said. First there are nine months before the baby is born. Then the baby is born. Then there are three or four months spent in feeding the baby. After the baby is fed there are certainly five years spent in playing with the baby. You cannot, it seems, let children run about the streets. People who have seen them running wild in Russia say that the sight is not a pleasant one. People say, too, that human nature takes its shape in the years between one and five. If Mrs Seton, I said, had been making money, what sort of memories would you have had of games and quarrels? What would you have known of Scotland, and its fine air and cakes and all the rest of it? But it is useless to ask these questions, because you would never have come into existence at all. Moreover, it is equally useless to ask what might have happened if Mrs Seton and her mother and her mother before her had amassed great wealth and laid it under the foundations of college and library, because, in the first place, to earn money was impossible for them, and in the second, had it been possible, the law denied them the right to possess what money they earned. It is only for the last forty-eight years that Mrs Seton has had a penny of her own. For all the centuries before that it would have been her husband's property—a thought which, perhaps, may have had its share in keeping Mrs Seton and her mothers off the Stock Exchange.[1] Every penny I earn, they may have said, will be taken from me and disposed of

---

1. The late 19th century saw the passage of legislation designed to improve the legal status of women. In 1870 the Married Women's Property Act allowed women to retain £200 of their own earnings (which previously had automatically become the property of her husband); in 1884 a further act gave married women the same rights over property as unmarried women, and allowed them to carry on trades or businesses using their property.

according to my husband's wisdom—perhaps to found a scholarship or to endow a fellowship in Balliol or Kings,[2] so that to earn money, even if I could earn money, is not a matter that interests me very greatly. I had better leave it to my husband.

At any rate, whether or not the blame rested on the old lady who was looking at the spaniel, there could be no doubt that for some reason or other our mothers had mismanaged their affairs very gravely. Not a penny could be spared for "amenities"; for partridges and wine, beadles and turf, books and cigars, libraries and leisure. To raise bare walls out of the bare earth was the utmost they could do.

So we talked standing at the window and looking, as so many thousands look every night, down on the domes and towers of the famous city beneath us. It was very beautiful, very mysterious in the autumn moonlight. The old stone looked very white and venerable. One thought of all the books that were assembled down there; of the pictures of old prelates and worthies hanging in the panelled rooms; of the painted windows that would be throwing strange globes and crescents on the pavement; of the tablets and memorials and inscriptions; of the fountains and the grass; of the quiet rooms looking across the quiet quadrangles. And (pardon me the thought) I thought, too, of the admirable smoke and drink and the deep armchairs and the pleasant carpets: of the urbanity, the geniality, the dignity which are the offspring of luxury and privacy and space. Certainly our mothers had not provided us with anything comparable to all this—our mothers who found it difficult to scrape together thirty thousand pounds, our mothers who bore thirteen children to ministers of religion at St Andrews.

So I went back to my inn, and as I walked through the dark streets I pondered this and that, as one does at the end of the day's work. I pondered why it was that Mrs Seton had no money to leave us; and what effect poverty has on the mind; and what effect wealth has on the mind; and I thought of the queer old gentlemen I had seen that morning with tufts of fur upon their shoulders; and I remembered how if one whistled one of them ran; and I thought of the organ booming in the chapel and of the shut doors of the library; and I thought how unpleasant it is to be locked out; and I thought how it is worse perhaps to be locked in; and, thinking of the safety and prosperity of the one sex and of the poverty and insecurity of the other and of the effect of tradition and of the lack of tradition upon the mind of a writer, I thought at last that it was time to roll up the crumpled skin of the day, with its arguments and its impressions and its anger and its laughter, and cast it into the hedge. A thousand stars were flashing across the blue wastes of the sky. One seemed alone with an inscrutable society. All human beings were laid asleep—prone, horizontal, dumb. Nobody seemed stirring in the streets of Oxbridge. Even the door of the hotel sprang open at the touch of an invisible hand—not a boots was sitting up to light me to bed, it was so late.

from *Chapter 3*

It would have been impossible, completely and entirely, for any woman to have written the plays of Shakespeare in the age of Shakespeare. Let me imagine, since facts are so hard to come by, what would have happened had Shakespeare had a wonderfully gifted sister, called Judith, let us say. Shakespeare himself went, very probably—his mother was an heiress—to the grammar school, where he may have learnt Latin—Ovid, Virgil, and Horace—and the elements of grammar and logic. He was, it

2. Balliol is a college of Oxford University; King's is at Cambridge.

is well known, a wild boy who poached rabbits, perhaps shot a deer, and had, rather sooner than he should have done, to marry a woman in the neighbourhood, who bore him a child rather quicker than was right. That escapade sent him to seek his fortune in London. He had, it seemed, a taste for the theatre; he began by holding horses at the stage door. Very soon he got work in the theatre, became a successful actor, and lived at the hub of the universe, meeting everybody, knowing everybody, practising his art on the boards, exercising his wits in the streets, and even getting access to the palace of the queen. Meanwhile his extraordinarily gifted sister, let us suppose, remained at home. She was as adventurous, as imaginative, as agog to see the world as he was. But she was not sent to school. She had no chance of learning grammar and logic, let alone of reading Horace and Virgil. She picked up a book now and then, one of her brother's perhaps, and read a few pages. But then her parents came in and told her to mend the stockings or mind the stew and not moon about with books and papers. They would have spoken sharply but kindly, for they were substantial people who knew the conditions of life for a woman and loved their daughter—indeed, more likely than not she was the apple of her father's eye. Perhaps she scribbled some pages up in an apple loft on the sly, but was careful to hide them or set fire to them. Soon, however, before she was out of her teens, she was to be betrothed to the son of a neighbouring wool-stapler. She cried out that marriage was hateful to her, and for that she was severely beaten by her father. Then he ceased to scold her. He begged her instead not to hurt him, not to shame him in this matter of her marriage. He would give her a chain of beads or a fine petticoat, he said; and there were tears in his eyes. How could she disobey him? How could she break his heart? The force of her own gift alone drove her to it. She made up a small parcel of her belongings, let herself down by a rope one summer's night and took the road to London. She was not seventeen. The birds that sang in the hedge were not more musical than she was. She had the quickest fancy, a gift like her brother's, for the tune of words. Like him, she had a taste for the theatre. She stood at the stage door; she wanted to act, she said. Men laughed in her face. The manager—a fat, loose-lipped man—guffawed. He bellowed something about poodles dancing and women acting—no woman, he said, could possibly be an actress. He hinted—you can imagine what. She could get no training in her craft. Could she even seek her dinner in a tavern or roam the streets at midnight? Yet her genius was for fiction and lusted to feed abundantly upon the lives of men and women and the study of their ways. At last—for she was very young, oddly like Shakespeare the poet in her face, with the same grey eyes and rounded brows—at last Nick Greene the actor-manager took pity on her; she found herself with child by that gentleman and so—who shall measure the heat and violence of the poet's heart when caught and tangled in a woman's body?—killed herself one winter's night and lies buried at some cross-roads where the omnibuses now stop outside the Elephant and Castle.[3]

That, more or less, is how the story would run, I think, if a woman in Shakespeare's day had had Shakespeare's genius. But for my part, I agree with the deceased bishop, if such he was—it is unthinkable that any woman in Shakespeare's day should have had Shakespeare's genius. For genius like Shakespeare's is not born among labouring, uneducated, servile people. It was not born in England among the Saxons and the Britons. It is not born today among the working classes. How, then, could it have been born among women whose work began, according to Professor

---

3. A tavern on the outskirts of South London.

Trevelyan,[4] almost before they were out of the nursery, who were forced to it by their parents and held to it by all the power of law and custom? Yet genius of a sort must have existed among women as it must have existed among the working classes. Now and again an Emily Brontë or a Robert Burns blazes out and proves its presence. But certainly it never got itself on to paper. When, however, one reads of a witch being ducked, of a woman possessed by devils, of a wise woman selling herbs, or even of a very remarkable man who had a mother, then I think we are on the track of a lost novelist, a suppressed poet, of some mute and inglorious Jane Austen, some Emily Brontë who dashed her brains out on the moor or mopped and mowed about the highways crazed with the torture that her gift had put her to. Indeed, I would venture to guess that Anon, who wrote so many poems without signing them, was often a woman. It was a woman Edward Fitzgerald,[5] I think, suggested who made the ballads and the folk-songs, crooning them to her children, beguiling her spinning with them, or the length of the winter's night.

This may be true or it may be false—who can say?—but what is true in it, so it seemed to me, reviewing the story of Shakespeare's sister as I had made it, is that any woman born with a great gift in the sixteenth century would certainly have gone crazed, shot herself, or ended her days in some lonely cottage outside the village, half witch, half wizard, feared and mocked at. For it needs little skill in psychology to be sure that a highly gifted girl who had tried to use her gift for poetry would have been so thwarted and hindered by other people, so tortured and pulled asunder by her own contrary instincts, that she must have lost her health and sanity to a certainty. No girl could have walked to London and stood at a stage door and forced her way into the presence of actor-managers without doing herself a violence and suffering an anguish which may have been irrational—for chastity may be a fetish invented by certain societies for unknown reasons—but were none the less inevitable. Chastity had then, it has even now, a religious importance in a woman's life, and has so wrapped itself round with nerves and instincts that to cut it free and bring it to the light of day demands courage of the rarest. To have lived a free life in London in the sixteenth century would have meant for a woman who was poet and playwright a nervous stress and dilemma which might well have killed her. Had she survived, whatever she had written would have been twisted and deformed, issuing from a strained and morbid imagination. And undoubtedly, I thought, looking at the shelf where there are no plays by women, her work would have gone unsigned. That refuge she would have sought certainly. It was the relic of the sense of chastity that dictated anonymity to women even so late as the nineteenth century. Currer Bell, George Eliot, George Sand,[6] all the victims of inner strife as their writings prove, sought ineffectively to veil themselves by using the name of a man. Thus they did homage to the convention, which if not implanted by the other sex was liberally encouraged by them (the chief glory of a woman is not to be talked of, said Pericles, himself a much-talked-of man), that publicity in women is detestable.[7] Anonymity runs in their blood. The desire to be veiled still possesses them. They are not even now as concerned about the health of their fame as men are, and, speaking generally, will pass a tombstone or a signpost without feeling an irresistible desire to cut their names on it,

---

4. George Trevelyan (1876–1962), historian.
5. Poet and translator (1809–1883).
6. Currer Bell, pen name of Charlotte Brontë; George Eliot, pen name of Mary Ann Evans; George Sand, pen name of Amandine Aurore Lucille Dupin (1804–1876).

7. The Athenian statesman Pericles was reported by the historian Thucydides to have said, "That woman is most praiseworthy whose name is least bandied about on men's lips, whether for praise or dispraise."

as Alf, Bert or Chas. must do in obedience to their instinct, which murmurs if it sees a fine woman go by, or even a dog, Ce chien est à moi [that dog is mine]. And, of course, it may not be a dog, I thought, remembering Parliament Square, the Sieges Allee[8] and other avenues; it may be a piece of land or a man with curly black hair. It is one of the great advantages of being a woman that one can pass even a very fine negress without wishing to make an Englishwoman of her.

That woman, then, who was born with a gift of poetry in the sixteenth century, was an unhappy woman, a woman at strife against herself. All the conditions of her life, all her own instincts, were hostile to the state of mind which is needed to set free whatever is in the brain. * * * There would always have been that assertion—you cannot do this, you are incapable of doing that—to protest against, to overcome. Probably for a novelist this germ is no longer of much effect; for there have been women novelists of merit. But for painters it must still have some sting in it; and for musicians, I imagine, is even now active and poisonous in the extreme. The woman composer stands where the actress stood in the time of Shakespeare. Nick Greene, I thought, remembering the story I had made about Shakespeare's sister, said that a woman acting put him in mind of a dog dancing. Johnson repeated the phrase two hundred years later of women preaching.[9] And here, I said, opening a book about music, we have the very words used again in this year of grace, 1928, of women who try to write music. "Of Mlle. Germaine Tailleferre one can only repeat Dr. Johnson's dictum concerning a woman preacher, transposed into terms of music. 'Sir, a woman's composing is like a dog's walking on his hind legs. It is not done well, but you are surprised to find it done at all.'"[1] So accurately does history repeat itself.

Thus, I concluded, shutting Mr Oscar Browning's life and pushing away the rest, it is fairly evident that even in the nineteenth century a woman was not encouraged to be an artist. On the contrary, she was snubbed, slapped, lectured and exhorted. Her mind must have been strained and her vitality lowered by the need of opposing this, of disproving that. For here again we come within range of that very interesting and obscure masculine complex which has had so much influence upon the woman's movement; that deep-seated desire, not so much that she shall be inferior as that he shall be superior, which plants him wherever one looks, not only in front of the arts, but barring the way to politics too, even when the risk to himself seems infinitesimal and the suppliant humble and devoted. Even Lady Bessborough, I remembered, with all her passion for politics, must humbly bow herself and write to Lord Granville Leveson-Gower:[2] ". . . notwithstanding all my violence in politics and talking so much on that subject, I perfectly agree with you that no woman has any business to meddle with that or any other serious business, farther than giving her opinion (if she is ask'd)." And so she goes on to spend her enthusiasm where it meets with no obstacle whatsoever upon that immensely important subject, Lord Granville's maiden speech in the House of Commons. The spectacle is certainly a strange one, I thought. The history of men's opposition to women's emancipation is more interesting perhaps than the story of that emancipation itself. An amusing book might be made of it if some young student at Girton or Newnham would collect examples and deduce a theory— but she would need thick gloves on her hands, and bars to protect her of solid gold.

---

8. Victory Road, a thoroughfare in Berlin.
9. Samuel Johnson (1709–1784), poet and man of letters.
1. A Survey of Contemporary Music, Cecil Gray, page 246

[Woolf's note].
2. Lady Bessborough (1761–1821), correspondent of the British statesman Lord Granville.

But what is amusing now, I recollected, shutting Lady Bessborough, had to be taken in desperate earnest once. Opinions that one now pastes in a book labelled cock-a-doodle-dum and keeps for reading to select audiences on summer nights once drew tears, I can assure you. Among your grandmothers and great-grandmothers there were many that wept their eyes out. Florence Nightingale shrieked aloud in her agony.[3] Moreover, it is all very well for you, who have got yourselves to college and enjoy sitting-rooms—or is it only bed-sitting-rooms?—of your own to say that genius should disregard such opinions; that genius should be above caring what is said of it. Unfortunately, it is precisely the men or women of genius who mind most what is said of them. Remember Keats. Remember the words he had cut on his tombstone. Think of Tennyson; think—but I need hardly multiply instances of the undeniable, if very unfortunate, fact that it is the nature of the artist to mind excessively what is said about him. Literature is strewn with the wreckage of men who have minded beyond reason the opinions of others.

And this susceptibility of theirs is doubly unfortunate, I thought, returning again to my original enquiry into what state of mind is most propitious for creative work, because the mind of an artist, in order to achieve the prodigious effort of freeing whole and entire the work that is in him, must be incandescent, like Shakespeare's mind, I conjectured, looking at the book which lay open at *Antony and Cleopatra*. There must be no obstacle in it, no foreign matter unconsumed.

For though we say that we know nothing about Shakespeare's state of mind, even as we say that, we are saying something about Shakespeare's state of mind. The reason perhaps why we know so little of Shakespeare—compared with Donne or Ben Jonson or Milton—is that his grudges and spites and antipathies are hidden from us. We are not held up by some "revelation" which reminds us of the writer. All desire to protest, to preach, to proclaim an injury, to pay off a score, to make the world the witness of some hardship or grievance was fired out of him and consumed. Therefore his poetry flows from him free and unimpeded. If ever a human being got his work expressed completely, it was Shakespeare. If ever a mind was incandescent, unimpeded, I thought, turning again to the bookcase, it was Shakespeare's mind.

from *Chapter 4*

The extreme activity of mind which showed itself in the later eighteenth century among women—the talking, and the meeting, the writing of essays on Shakespeare, the translating of the classics—was founded on the solid fact that women could make money by writing. Money dignifies what is frivolous if unpaid for. It might still be well to sneer at "blue stockings with an itch for scribbling," but it could not be denied that they could put money in their purses. Thus, towards the end of the eighteenth century a change came about which, if I were rewriting history, I should describe more fully and think of greater importance than the Crusades or the Wars of the Roses. The middle-class woman began to write. For if *Pride and Prejudice* matters, and *Middlemarch* and *Villette* and *Wuthering Heights* matter,[4] then it matters far more than I can prove in an hour's discourse that women generally, and not merely the lonely aristocrat shut up in her country house among her folios and her flatterers,

3. See *Cassandra*, by Florence Nightingale, printed in *The Cause*, by R. Strachey [Woolf's note].
4. *Pride and Prejudice* (1813), a novel by Jane Austen; *Middlemarch* (1871–1872) by George Eliot; *Villette* (1853) by Charlotte Brontë; *Wuthering Heights* (1847) by Emily Brontë.

took to writing. Without those forerunners, Jane Austen and the Brontës and George Eliot could no more have written than Shakespeare could have written without Marlowe, or Marlowe without Chaucer, or Chaucer without those forgotten poets who paved the ways and tamed the natural savagery of the tongue. For masterpieces are not single and solitary births; they are the outcome of many years of thinking in common, of thinking by the body of the people, so that the experience of the mass is behind the single voice. Jane Austen should have laid a wreath upon the grave of Fanny Burney, and George Eliot done homage to the robust shade of Eliza Carter—the valiant old woman who tied a bell to her bedstead in order that she might wake early and learn Greek. All women together ought to let flowers fall upon the tomb of Aphra Behn[5] which is, most scandalously but rather appropriately, in Westminster Abbey, for it was she who earned them the right to speak their minds. It is she—shady and amorous as she was—who makes it not quite fantastic for me to say to you tonight: Earn five hundred a year by your wits.

Here, then, one had reached the early nineteenth century. And here, for the first time, I found several shelves given up entirely to the works of women. But why, I could not help asking, as I ran my eyes over them, were they, with very few exceptions, all novels? The original impulse was to poetry. The "supreme head of song" was a poetess. Both in France and in England the women poets precede the women novelists. Moreover, I thought, looking at the four famous names, what had George Eliot in common with Emily Brontë? Did not Charlotte Brontë fail entirely to understand Jane Austen? Save for the possibly relevant fact that not one of them had a child, four more incongruous characters could not have met together in a room—so much so that it is tempting to invent a meeting and a dialogue between them. Yet by some strange force they were all compelled, when they wrote, to write novels. Had it something to do with being born of the middle class, I asked; and with the fact, which Miss Emily Davies a little later was so strikingly to demonstrate,[6] that the middle-class family in the early nineteenth century was possessed only of a single sitting-room between them? If a woman wrote, she would have to write in the common sitting-room. And, as Miss Nightingale was so vehemently to complain,—"women never have an half hour . . . that they can call their own"—she was always interrupted. Still it would be easier to write prose and fiction there than to write poetry or a play. Less concentration is required. Jane Austen wrote like that to the end of her days. "How she was able to effect all this," her nephew writes in his Memoir, "is surprising, for she had no separate study to repair to, and most of the work must have been done in the general sitting-room, subject to all kinds of casual interruptions. She was careful that her occupation should not be suspected by servants or visitors or any persons beyond her own family party."[7] Jane Austen hid her manuscripts or covered them with a piece of blotting-paper. Then, again, all the literary training that a woman had in the early nineteenth century was training in the observation of character, in the analysis of emotion. Her sensibility had been educated for centuries by the influences of the common sitting-room. People's feelings were impressed on her; personal relations were always before her eyes. Therefore, when the middle-class

---

5. A dramatist and the first English woman to earn a living by writing (1640–1689). Westminster Abbey, in central London, is the burial place of many of the English kings and queens, as well as of famous poets and statesmen.

6. (Sarah) Emily Davies was prominent in the movement to secure university education for women in the 19th century and was chief founder of Girton College, Cambridge (1873).

7. *Memoir of Jane Austen*, by her nephew, James Edward Austen-Leigh [Woolf's note].

woman took to writing, she naturally wrote novels, even though, as seems evident enough, two of the four famous women here named were not by nature novelists. Emily Brontë should have written poetic plays; the overflow of George Eliot's capacious mind should have spread itself when the creative impulse was spent upon history or biography. They wrote novels, however; one may even go further, I said, taking *Pride and Prejudice* from the shelf, and say that they wrote good novels. Without boasting or giving pain to the opposite sex, one may say that *Pride and Prejudice* is a good book. At any rate, one would not have been ashamed to have been caught in the act of writing *Pride and Prejudice*. Yet Jane Austen was glad that a hinge creaked, so that she might hide her manuscript before any one came in. To Jane Austen there was something discreditable in writing *Pride and Prejudice*. And, I wondered, would *Pride and Prejudice* have been a better novel if Jane Austen had not thought it necessary to hide her manuscript from visitors? I read a page or two to see; but I could not find any signs that her circumstances had harmed her work in the slightest. That, perhaps, was the chief miracle about it. Here was a woman about the year 1800 writing without hate, without bitterness, without fear, without protest, without preaching. That was how Shakespeare wrote, I thought, looking at *Antony and Cleopatra*; and when people compare Shakespeare and Jane Austen, they may mean that the minds of both had consumed all impediments; and for that reason we do not know Jane Austen and we do not know Shakespeare, and for that reason Jane Austen pervades every word that she wrote, and so does Shakespeare. If Jane Austen suffered in any way from her circumstances it was in the narrowness of life that was imposed upon her. It was impossible for a woman to go about alone. She never travelled; she never drove through London in an omnibus or had luncheon in a shop by herself. But perhaps it was the nature of Jane Austen not to want what she had not. Her gift and her circumstances matched each other completely. But I doubt whether that was true of Charlotte Brontë, I said, opening *Jane Eyre* and laying it beside *Pride and Prejudice*.[8]

I opened it at chapter twelve and my eye was caught by the phrase, "Anybody may blame me who likes." What were they blaming Charlotte Brontë for, I wondered? And I read how Jane Eyre used to go up on to the roof when Mrs Fairfax was making jellies and looked over the fields at the distant view. And then she longed—and it was for this that they blamed her—that "then I longed for a power of vision which might overpass that limit; which might reach the busy world, towns, regions full of life I had heard of but never seen: that then I desired more of practical experience than I possessed; more of intercourse with my kind, of acquaintance with variety of character than was here within my reach. I valued what was good in Mrs Fairfax, and what was good in Adèle; but I believed in the existence of other and more vivid kinds of goodness, and what I believed in I wished to behold.

"Who blames me? Many, no doubt, and I shall be called discontented. I could not help it: the restlessness was in my nature; it agitated me to pain sometimes. . . .

"It is vain to say human beings ought to be satisfied with tranquillity: they must have action; and they will make it if they cannot find it. Millions are condemned to a

---

8. Woolf goes on to describe parts of the plot of *Jane Eyre*; Jane Eyre, a penniless orphan, having suffered greatly during her schooling, takes up the post of governess to Adele, the daughter of Mr. Rochester, a man of strange moods. Rochester falls in love with Jane, who agrees to marry him; however this is prevented by Rochester's mad wife—whom Rochester has locked in the attic, concealing her existence from Jane—who tears Jane's wedding veil on the eve of the marriage. Rochester at first tells Jane that Grace Poole, a servant, had been responsible for this and other strange events, including the uncanny laughter occasionally heard in the house.

stiller doom than mine, and millions are in silent revolt against their lot. Nobody knows how many rebellions ferment in the masses of life which people earth. Women are supposed to be very calm generally: but women feel just as men feel; they need exercise for their faculties and a field for their efforts as much as their brothers do; they suffer from too rigid a restraint, too absolute a stagnation, precisely as men would suffer; and it is narrow-minded in their more privileged fellow-creatures to say that they ought to confine themselves to making puddings and knitting stockings, to playing on the piano and embroidering bags. It is thoughtless to condemn them, or laugh at them, if they seek to do more or learn more than custom has pronounced necessary for their sex.

"When thus alone I not unfrequently heard Grace Poole's laugh . . . ."

That is an awkward break, I thought. It is upsetting to come upon Grace Poole all of a sudden. The continuity is disturbed. One might say, I continued, laying the book down beside *Pride and Prejudice*, that the woman who wrote those pages had more genius in her than Jane Austen; but if one reads them over and marks that jerk in them, that indignation, one sees that she will never get her genius expressed whole and entire. Her books will be deformed and twisted. She will write in a rage where she should write calmly. She will write foolishly where she should write wisely. She will write of herself where she should write of her characters. She is at war with her lot. How could she help but die young, cramped and thwarted?

One could not but play for a moment with the thought of what might have happened if Charlotte Brontë had possessed say three hundred a year—but the foolish woman sold the copyright of her novels outright for fifteen hundred pounds; had somehow possessed more knowledge of the busy world, and towns and regions full of life; more practical experience, and intercourse with her kind and acquaintance with a variety of character. In those words she puts her finger exactly not only upon her own defects as a novelist but upon those of her sex at that time. She knew, no one better, how enormously her genius would have profited if it had not spent itself in solitary visions over distant fields; if experience and intercourse and travel had been granted her. But they were not granted; they were withheld; and we must accept the fact that all those good novels, *Villette, Emma, Wuthering Heights, Middlemarch,* were written by women without more experience of life than could enter the house of a respectable clergyman; written too in the common sitting-room of that respectable house and by women so poor that they could not afford to buy more than a few quires of paper at a time upon which to write *Wuthering Heights* or *Jane Eyre*. One of them, it is true, George Eliot, escaped after much tribulation, but only to a secluded villa in St John's Wood. And there she settled down in the shadow of the world's disapproval.[9] "I wish it to be understood," she wrote, "that I should never invite any one to come and see me who did not ask for the invitation"; for was she not living in sin with a married man and might not the sight of her damage the chastity of Mrs Smith or whoever it might be that chanced to call? One must submit to the social convention, and be "cut off from what is called the world." At the same time, on the other side of Europe, there was a young man living freely with this gipsy or with that great lady; going to the wars; picking

9. Following a strictly religious childhood, the novelist George Eliot lost her faith and eloped with G. H. Lewes, a married man, with whom she lived for the rest of his life; her family never forgave her.

up unhindered and uncensored all that varied experience of human life which served him so splendidly later when he came to write his books. Had Tolstoi lived at the Priory in seclusion with a married lady "cut off from what is called the world," however edifying the moral lesson, he could scarcely, I thought, have written *War and Peace*. * * *

* * * I do not want, and I am sure that you do not want me, to broach that very dismal subject, the future of fiction, so that I will only pause here one moment to draw your attention to the great part which must be played in that future so far as women are concerned by physical conditions. The book has somehow to be adapted to the body, and at a venture one would say that women's books should be shorter, more concentrated, than those of men, and framed so that they do not need long hours of steady and uninterrupted work. For interruptions there will always be. Again, the nerves that feed the brain would seem to differ in men and women, and if you are going to make them work their best and hardest, you must find out what treatment suits them—whether these hours of lectures, for instance, which the monks devised, presumably, hundreds of years ago, suit them—what alternations of work and rest they need, interpreting rest not as doing nothing but as doing something but something that is different; and what should that difference be? All this should be discussed and discovered; all this is part of the question of women and fiction. And yet, I continued, approaching the bookcase again, where shall I find that elaborate study of the psychology of women by a woman? If through their incapacity to play football women are not going to be allowed to practise medicine——

Happily my thoughts were now given another turn.

from Chapter 6

Next day the light of the October morning was falling in dusty shafts through the uncurtained windows, and the hum of traffic rose from the street. London then was winding itself up again; the factory was astir; the machines were beginning. It was tempting, after all this reading, to look out of the window and see what London was doing on the morning of the twenty-sixth of October 1928. And what was London doing? Nobody, it seemed, was reading *Antony and Cleopatra*. London was wholly indifferent, it appeared, to Shakespeare's plays. Nobody cared a straw—and I do not blame them—for the future of fiction, the death of poetry or the development by the average woman of a prose style completely expressive of her mind. If opinions upon any of these matters had been chalked on the pavement, nobody would have stooped to read them. The nonchalance of the hurrying feet would have rubbed them out in half an hour. Here came an errand-boy; here a woman with a dog on a lead. The fascination of the London street is that no two people are ever alike; each seems bound on some private affair of his own. There were the business-like, with their little bags; there were the drifters rattling sticks upon area railings; there were affable characters to whom the streets serve for clubroom, hailing men in carts and giving information without being asked for it. Also there were funerals to which men, thus suddenly reminded of the passing of their own bodies, lifted their hats. And then a very distinguished gentleman came slowly down a doorstep and paused to avoid collision with a bustling lady who had, by some means or other, acquired a splendid fur coat and a bunch of Parma violets. They all seemed separate, self-absorbed, on business of their own.

At this moment, as so often happens in London, there was a complete lull and suspension of traffic. Nothing came down the street; nobody passed. A single leaf detached itself from the plane tree at the end of the street, and in that pause and suspension fell. Somehow it was like a signal falling, a signal pointing to a force in things which one had overlooked. It seemed to point to a river, which flowed past, invisibly, round the corner, down the street, and took people and eddied them along, as the stream at Oxbridge had taken the undergraduate in his boat and the dead leaves. Now it was bringing from one side of the street to the other diagonally a girl in patent leather boots, and then a young man in a maroon overcoat; it was also bringing a taxi-cab; and it brought all three together at a point directly beneath my window; where the taxi stopped; and the girl and the young man stopped; and they got into the taxi; and then the cab glided off as if it were swept on by the current elsewhere.

   The sight was ordinary enough; what was strange was the rhythmical order with which my imagination had invested it; and the fact that the ordinary sight of two people getting into a cab had the power to communicate something of their own seeming satisfaction. The sight of two people coming down the street and meeting at the corner seems to ease the mind of some strain, I thought, watching the taxi turn and make off. Perhaps to think, as I had been thinking these two days, of one sex as distinct from the other is an effort. It interferes with the unity of the mind. Now that effort had ceased and that unity had been restored by seeing two people come together and get into a taxi-cab. The mind is certainly a very mysterious organ, I reflected, drawing my head in from the window, about which nothing whatever is known, though we depend upon it so completely. Why do I feel that there are severances and oppositions in the mind, as there are strains from obvious causes on the body? What does one mean by "the unity of the mind," I pondered, for clearly the mind has so great a power of concentrating at any point at any moment that it seems to have no single state of being. It can separate itself from the people in the street, for example, and think of itself as apart from them, at an upper window looking down on them. Or it can think with other people spontaneously, as, for instance, in a crowd waiting to hear some piece of news read out. It can think back through its fathers or through its mothers, as I have said that a woman writing thinks back through her mothers. Again if one is a woman one is often surprised by a sudden splitting off of consciousness, say in walking down Whitehall,[1] when from being the natural inheritor of that civilisation, she becomes, on the contrary, outside of it, alien and critical. Clearly the mind is always altering its focus, and bringing the world into different perspectives. But some of these states of mind seem, even if adopted spontaneously, to be less comfortable than others. In order to keep oneself continuing in them one is unconsciously holding something back, and gradually the repression becomes an effort. But there may be some state of mind in which one could continue without effort because nothing is required to be held back. And this perhaps, I thought, coming in from the window, is one of them. For certainly when I saw the couple get into the taxi-cab the mind felt as if, after being divided, it had come together again in a natural fusion. The obvious reason would be that it is natural for the sexes to co-operate. One has a profound, if irrational, instinct in favour of the theory that the union of man and woman makes for the greatest satisfaction, the most complete happiness. But the sight of the two people getting into the taxi and the satisfaction it gave me made me also ask whether there are two sexes in the mind corresponding to the two sexes in the body, and whether they also require to be united in order to get complete satisfaction and happiness. And I went on amateurishly to sketch a plan of the soul so that in each of us two powers preside, one male,

---

1. A main thoroughfare in central London and site of government offices.

one female; and in the man's brain, the man predominates over the woman, and in the woman's brain, the woman predominates over the man. The normal and comfortable state of being is that when the two live in harmony together, spiritually co-operating. If one is a man, still the woman part of the brain must have effect; and a woman also must have intercourse with the man in her. Coleridge perhaps meant this when he said that a great mind is androgynous.[2] It is when this fusion takes place that the mind is fully fertilised and uses all its faculties. Perhaps a mind that is purely masculine cannot create, any more than a mind that is purely feminine, I thought. * * *

* * * One must turn back to Shakespeare then, for Shakespeare was androgynous; and so was Keats and Sterne and Cowper and Lamb and Coleridge. Shelley perhaps was sexless. Milton and Ben Jonson had a dash too much of the male in them. So had Wordsworth and Tolstoi. In our time Proust was wholly androgynous, if not perhaps a little too much of a woman. But that failing is too rare for one to complain of it, since without some mixture of the kind the intellect seems to predominate and the other faculties of the mind harden and become barren. However, I consoled myself with the reflection that this is perhaps a passing phase; much of what I have said in obedience to my promise to give you the course of my thoughts will seem out of date; much of what flames in my eyes will seem dubious to you who have not yet come of age.

Even so, the very first sentence that I would write here, I said, crossing over to the writing-table and taking up the page headed Women and Fiction, is that it is fatal for any one who writes to think of their sex. It is fatal to be a man or woman pure and simple; one must be woman-manly or man-womanly. It is fatal for a woman to lay the least stress on any grievance; to plead even with justice any cause; in any way to speak consciously as a woman. And fatal is no figure of speech; for anything written with that conscious bias is doomed to death. It ceases to be fertilised. Brilliant and effective, powerful and masterly, as it may appear for a day or two, it must wither at nightfall; it cannot grow in the minds of others. Some collaboration has to take place in the mind between the woman and the man before the act of creation can be accomplished. Some marriage of opposites has to be consummated. The whole of the mind must lie wide open if we are to get the sense that the writer is communicating his experience with perfect fullness. There must be freedom and there must be peace. Not a wheel must grate, not a light glimmer. The curtains must be close drawn. The writer, I thought, once his experience is over, must lie back and let his mind celebrate its nuptials in darkness. He must not look or question what is being done. Rather, he must pluck the petals from a rose or watch the swans float calmly down the river. And I saw again the current which took the boat and the undergraduate and the dead leaves; and the taxi took the man and the woman, I thought, seeing them come together across the street, and the current swept them away, I thought, hearing far off the roar of London's traffic, into that tremendous stream.

Here, then, Mary Beton ceases to speak. She has told you how she reached the conclusion—the prosaic conclusion—that it is necessary to have five hundred a year and a room with a lock on the door if you are to write fiction or poetry. She has tried to lay bare the thoughts and impressions that led her to think this. She has asked you to follow her flying into the arms of a Beadle, lunching here, dining there, drawing pictures in the British Museum, taking books from the shelf, looking out of the window. While she has been doing all these things, you no doubt have been observing

2. The poet Samuel Taylor Coleridge made the remark in September 1832—"a great mind must be androgynous"—and it was duly recorded in his Table Talk.

her failings and foibles and deciding what effect they have had on her opinions. You have been contradicting her and making whatever additions and deductions seem good to you. That is all as it should be, for in a question like this truth is only to be had by laying together many varieties of error. And I will end now in my own person by anticipating two criticisms, so obvious that you can hardly fail to make them.

No opinion has been expressed, you may say, upon the comparative merits of the sexes even as writers. That was done purposely, because, even if the time had come for such a valuation—and it is far more important at the moment to know how much money women had and how many rooms than to theorise about their capacities— even if the time had come I do not believe that gifts, whether of mind or character, can be weighed like sugar and butter, not even in Cambridge, where they are so adept at putting people into classes and fixing caps on their heads and letters after their names. I do not believe that even the Table of Precedency which you will find in Whitaker's *Almanac*[3] represents a final order of values, or that there is any sound reason to suppose that a Commander of the Bath will ultimately walk in to dinner behind a Master in Lunacy. All this pitting of sex against sex, of quality against quality; all this claiming of superiority and imputing of inferiority, belong to the private-school stage of human existence where there are "sides," and it is necessary for one side to beat another side, and of the utmost importance to walk up to a platform and receive from the hands of the Headmaster himself a highly ornamental pot. As people mature they cease to believe in sides or in Headmasters or in highly ornamental pots. At any rate, where books are concerned, it is notoriously difficult to fix labels of merit in such a way that they do not come off. Are not reviews of current literature a perpetual illustration of the difficulty of judgment? "This great book," "this worthless book," the same book is called by both names. Praise and blame alike mean nothing. No, delightful as the pastime of measuring may be, it is the most futile of all occupations, and to submit to the decrees of the measurers the most servile of attitudes. So long as you write what you wish to write, that is all that matters; and whether it matters for ages or only for hours, nobody can say. But to sacrifice a hair of the head of your vision, a shade of its colour, in deference to some Headmaster with a silver pot in his hand or to some professor with a measuring-rod up his sleeve, is the most abject treachery, and the sacrifice of wealth and chastity which used to be said to be the greatest of human disasters, a mere flea-bite in comparison.

Next I think that you may object that in all this I have made too much of the importance of material things. * * * Intellectual freedom depends upon material things. Poetry depends upon intellectual freedom. And women have always been poor, not for two hundred years merely, but from the beginning of time. Women have had less intellectual freedom than the sons of Athenian slaves. Women, then, have not had a dog's chance of writing poetry. That is why I have laid so much stress on money and a room of one's own. However, thanks to the toils of those obscure women in the past, of whom I wish we knew more, thanks, curiously enough, to two wars, the Crimean which let Florence Nightingale out of her drawing-room, and the European War which opened the doors to the average woman some sixty years later, these evils are in the way to be bettered. Otherwise you would not be here tonight, and your chance of earning five hundred pounds a year, precarious as I am afraid that it still is, would be minute in the extreme. * * *

---

3. A compendium of general information first published in 1868.

Here I would stop, but the pressure of convention decrees that every speech must end with a peroration. And a peroration addressed to women should have something, you will agree, particularly exalting and ennobling about it. I should implore you to remember your responsibilities, to be higher, more spiritual; I should remind you how much depends upon you, and what an influence you can exert upon the future. But those exhortations can safely, I think, be left to the other sex, who will put them, and indeed have put them, with far greater eloquence than I can compass. When I rummage in my own mind I find no noble sentiments about being companions and equals and influencing the world to higher ends. I find myself saying briefly and prosaically that it is much more important to be oneself than anything else. Do not dream of influencing other people, I would say, if I knew how to make it sound exalted. Think of things in themselves.

And again I am reminded by dipping into newspapers and novels and biographies that when a woman speaks to women she should have something very unpleasant up her sleeve. Women are hard on women. Women dislike women. Women . . . but are you not sick to death of the word? I can assure you that I am. Let us agree, then, that a paper read by a woman to women should end with something particularly disagreeable.

But how does it go? What can I think of? The truth is, I often like women. I like their unconventionality. I like their subtlety. I like their anonymity. I like—but I must not run on in this way. That cupboard there,—you say it holds clean table-napkins only; but what if Sir Archibald Bodkin were concealed among them?[4] Let me then adopt a sterner tone. Have I, in the preceding words, conveyed to you sufficiently the warnings and reprobation of mankind? I have told you the very low opinion in which you were held by Mr Oscar Browning. I have indicated what Napoleon once thought of you and what Mussolini thinks now. Then, in case any of you aspire to fiction, I have copied out for your benefit the advice of the critic about courageously acknowledging the limitations of your sex. I have referred to Professor X and given prominence to his statement that women are intellectually, morally and physically inferior to men. I have handed on all that has come my way without going in search of it, and here is a final warning—from Mr John Langdon Davies.[5] Mr John Langdon Davies warns women "that when children cease to be altogether desirable, women cease to be altogether necessary." I hope you will make a note of it.

How can I further encourage you to go about the business of life? Young women, I would say, and please attend, for the peroration is beginning, you are, in my opinion, disgracefully ignorant. You have never made a discovery of any sort of importance. You have never shaken an empire or led an army into battle. The plays of Shakespeare are not by you, and you have never introduced a barbarous race to the blessings of civilisation. What is your excuse? It is all very well for you to say, pointing to the streets and squares and forests of the globe swarming with black and white and coffee-coloured inhabitants, all busily engaged in traffic and enterprise and love-making, we have had other work on our hands. Without our doing, those seas would be unsailed and those fertile lands a desert. We have

4. Sir Archibald Bodkin was then Director of Public Prosecutions; his office had been responsible for the 1928 prosecution of Radclyffe Hall's novel *The Well of Loneliness* on a charge of obscenity. It was subsequently banned. Woolf had wanted to give evidence in the book's defense at the trial, but expert witnesses were not allowed by the presiding magistrate.
5. *A Short History of Women*, by John Langford Davies [Woolf's note].

borne and bred and washed and taught, perhaps to the age of six or seven years, the one thousand six hundred and twenty-three million human beings who are, according to statistics, at present in existence, and that, allowing that some had help, takes time.

There is truth in what you say—I will not deny it. But at the same time may I remind you that there have been at least two colleges for women in existence in England since the year 1866; that after the year 1880 a married woman was allowed by law to possess her own property; and that in 1919—which is a whole nine years ago—she was given a vote? May I also remind you that the most of the professions have been open to you for close on ten years now? When you reflect upon these immense privileges and the length of time time during which they have been enjoyed, and the fact that there must be at this moment some two thousand women capable of earning over five hundred a year in one way or another, you will agree that the excuse of lack of opportunity, training, encouragement, leisure and money no longer holds good. Moreover, the economists are telling us that Mrs Seton has had too many children. You must, of course, go on bearing children, but, so they say, in twos and threes, not in tens and twelves.

Thus, with some time on your hands and with some book learning in your brains—you have had enough of the other kind, and are sent to college partly, I suspect, to be uneducated—surely you should embark upon another stage of your very long, very laborious and highly obscure career. A thousand pens are ready to suggest what you should do and what effect you will have. My own suggestion is a little fantastic, I admit; I prefer, therefore, to put it in the form of fiction.

I told you in the course of this paper that Shakespeare had a sister; but do not look for her in Sir Sidney Lee's life of the poet. She died young–alas, she never wrote a word. She lies buried where the omnibuses now stop, opposite the Elephant and Castle. Now my belief is that this poet who never wrote a word and was buried at the crossroads still lives. She lives in you and in me, and in many other women who are not here tonight, for they are washing up the dishes and putting the children to bed. But she lives; for great poets do not die; they are continuing presences; they need only the opportunity to walk among us in the flesh. This opportunity, as I think, it is now coming within your power to give her. For my belief is that if we live another century or so—I am talking of the common life which is the real life and not of the little separate lives which we live as individuals—and have five hundred a year each of us and rooms of our own; if we have the habit of freedom and the courage to write exactly what we think; if we escape a little from the common sitting-room and see human beings not always in their relation to each other but in relation to reality; and the sky, too, and the trees or whatever it may be in themselves; if we look past Milton's bogey, for no human being should shut out the view; if we face the fact, for it is a fact, that there is no arm to cling to, but that we go alone and that our relation is to the world of reality and not only to the world of men and women, then the opportunity will come and the dead poet who was Shakespeare's sister will put on the body which she has so often laid down. Drawing her life from the lives of the unknown who were her forerunners, as her brother did before her, she will be born. As for her coming without that preparation, without that effort on our part, without that determination that when she is born again she shall find it possible to live and write her poetry, that we cannot expect, for that would be impossible. But I maintain that she would come if we worked for her, and that so to work, even in poverty and obscurity, is worth while.

➤ PERSPECTIVES ➤
Regendering Modernism

Changes in the understanding of gender and sexuality are at the heart of modernity, and the modernist writing of the twentieth century is characterized by entirely new conceptions of what it means to be a woman, to be a man, to be a desiring, sexual being. Modernist literature did not simply "reflect" the enormous transformations in gender roles, divisions of labor, social institutions such as marriage and the family, and investigations of the self and psyche that emerged during this period: instead, this literature was partly responsible for shaping such transformations and giving people a shared vocabulary with which to name these changes.

This process can be described as "regendering." While "sex" refers to the biological differences between the female sex and the male sex, "gender" is a cultural term, a name for the ways that a culture constructs genders as identities, and how those identities are then organized. In the twentieth century much of what had been taken as a "natural" difference between the sexes— with women as weaker, more irrational, less intellectual, more virtuous, lacking in sexual desire, designed by nature for maternity, incapable of leadership and most public professions—came to be understood as the construction of gender, a state of affairs that was not innate, but rather had been created and reinforced by culture. Having "made" gender, culture could also remake it.

Gender cut to the quick of all the reconsiderations modernity made possible: the relation between self and other, in encounters of all kinds from the domestic to the imperial; the nature of selfhood and subjectivity itself, when complete self-awareness had been shown by Freud and others to be an impossibility. Gender governs the distinctions between public and private that underwrite every aspect of society, from the family to the school to the hospital to the factory to the courts, establishing the binaries that shape a culture—good/evil, rational/irrational, nature/culture, savage/civilized.

The first few decades of the twentieth century saw social and political upheavals in gender politics, as the movement for women's suffrage spread widely and occasioned actions from the symbolic to the fatal, as in the hunger strikes of imprisoned suffragists and the suicide of a leading feminist as she leapt into the path of a royal racehorse. Quite often the literary activities of women writers such as Woolf were in tandem with the movement, if not directly allied with it, as in the many lectures Woolf gave for working-class women and men in extension schools, and her clarion calls for women's educational and political rights. Ironically, several of the writers included here disdained the feminist label, Rebecca West chief among them, in part for the understandable reason that being lumped in with feminist agitation put their writing in a female ghetto. Much antifeminist sentiment among women writers was an attempt to have their work taken seriously as art, rather than viewed as a type of gender propaganda.

The widespread emphasis on gender issues in modernism, even where the changing of gender roles is feared or resisted, should not be taken to imply that modernism had an easy time breaking barriers or forging new vocabularies for gender and sexuality: many modernist works and their authors suffered powerful censorship, public attacks and even silencing altogether. Joyce's *Ulysses* was banned in Britain and Ireland, and was put on trial in the United States, chiefly for its frank acknowledgment of female and male desires alike. Lawrence's works with their overt focus on sexuality experienced much censorship, the trial over *Lady Chatterley's Lover* being only the most sensational. The great modernist writer E. M. Forster was unable to publish any of his explicitly homosexual work until shortly before his death in 1970; while the homoerotic aspects of his writing could be glimpsed between the lines, during the lifetime of modernism, homosexuality was still a crime in Britain. The gender hierarchies that had prevented many women from getting higher education and precluded them from full citizenship, also meant that the publishing world was dominated by men, in turn permitting many journals, presses, and magazines to remain male clubs of a sort; all this made it especially hard for women writers to break into print or to remain noticed once they had. Virginia Woolf lamented this imbalance

Leaders of the Actresses' Franchise League. One of the remarkable features of the suffragist movement in Britain was the spectacular manner it often adopted, from the carefully costumed and
staged protest rallies of groups like the Actresses' Franchise League to the hunger strikes, and consequent forced feedings, later instigated by more militant feminists impatient with the pace of
change. Women's Social and Political Union member Kitty Marion, for instance, recalled the dismay expressed by a Bishop who had enjoyed the "beautiful processions" of the early days of the
movement. "Yes," Marion replied, "but our beautiful processions didn't get us the vote . . . and we
want the vote!"

and tried to rectify it in part by establishing the Hogarth Press with her husband Leonard Woolf,
an imprint that published her work along with a host of modern writing by men and women.

Even writers who have been labeled as misogynists were far more invested in new attitudes
about gender and sex than this label allows. T. S. Eliot involved himself in encouraging the
careers of many women writers, and his poetry, while conservative in its gender politics, makes
clear that sexuality is fluid and mysterious, belonging to women as much as to men, and serving
not simply as a procreative duty but as a way of knowing oneself. D. H. Lawrence was excoriated by American feminist critic Kate Millett in the 1970s for what she saw as his virulent hatred
of women, yet even a swift review of his novels and stories reveals some of the strongest, most
explicitly sexual female characters in the canon and a good deal of homoerotic byplay on both
sides of the sexual divide. The varied selections presented here show a range of writers exploring the endlessly suggestive ambiguities and dislocations of modern gender identities.

━━ ⊰◈⊱ ━━

Virginia Woolf
1882–1941

People have often read Virginia Woolf's *Orlando* as a literary spoof, concentrating on its playfulness, its dedication to her intimate friend Vita Sackville-West, its glossy surface and constantly ironic tone. If we consider, though, that Woolf is taking on a form brought to its
national, imperial, Victorian height by her own father, then the gender politics of *Orlando*
becomes something else again. His work on the *Dictionary of National Biography* gave enormous
cultural power to her father, in the sense that he could be an arbiter of someone's importance
to the national life; the connection to the British empire is direct too, because it only became

necessary to have such a reference work at the point that Britain was spreading itself out over the globe. *Orlando* is subtitled "A Biography" and even includes illustrations it pretends are portraits of "Orlando," as well as a photograph of Vita Sackville-West captioned "Orlando today." A biography of a person who won't neatly die within one historical "age," who won't produce documented accomplishments and who won't even conform to the sanctity of sexual identity means that all bets are off: the regendering work of modernism has begun.

This "biography," moreover, is wrapped around the literary tradition of England, since Orlando is a writer whose writings we never really get to read. Interlaced with Britain's imperial identity (Orlando is an ambassador), this mock biography shows the linkage of sexism in England and racism abroad. *Orlando* is not a novel in which we identify with the hero/heroine, or are moved by the characters' losses and courage, as happens in *Mrs Dalloway*; we are kept at arm's length from Orlando because through ironic distance Woolf wants to invalidate the assumptions of her father's time: that gender identity is fixed, that only great men create history, that literature is the work of male genius, and that sexual desire, failure, and silence are to be feared. *Orlando* is filled with gender-bending and the oscillations of sexual desire; Orlando masquerades as a man and as a woman, has sexual partners of both sexes, and at one point marries a gypsy—a gesture to Sackville-West's Spanish and Roma heritage. In *Orlando*, no judgment of the biographical subject can be made, and this stymies the whole notion of fixing an identity. Orlando defies categories, boundaries, traditions, and expectations. S/he is beyond the Victorian pale.

from Orlando

At length, with a gesture of extraordinary majesty and grace, first bowing profoundly, then raising himself proudly erect, Orlando took the golden circlet of strawberry leaves and placed it, with a gesture which none that saw it ever forgot, upon his brows.[1] It was at this point that the first disturbance began. Either the people had expected a miracle—some say a shower of gold was prophesied to fall from the skies—which did not happen, or this was the signal chosen for the attack to begin; nobody seems to know; but as the coronet settled on Orlando's brows a great uproar rose. Bells began ringing; the harsh cries of the prophets were heard above the shouts of the people; many Turks fell flat to the ground and touched the earth with their foreheads. A door burst open. The natives pressed into the banqueting rooms. Women shrieked. A certain lady, who was said to be dying for love of Orlando, seized a candelabra and dashed it to the ground. What might not have happened, had it not been for the presence of Sir Adrian Scrope and a squad of British bluejackets,[2] nobody can say. But the Admiral ordered the bugles to be sounded; a hundred bluejackets stood instantly at attention; the disorder was quelled, and quiet, at least for the time being, fell upon the scene.

So far, we are on the firm, if rather narrow, ground of ascertained truth. But nobody has ever known exactly what took place later that night. The testimony of the sentries and others seems, however, to prove that the Embassy was empty of company, and shut up for the night in the usual way by two A.M. The Ambassador was seen to go to his room, still wearing the insignia of his rank, and shut the door. Some say he locked it, which was against his custom. Others maintain that they heard music of a rustic kind, such as shepherds play, later that night in the courtyard under the Ambassador's window. A washer-woman, who was kept awake by a toothache said that she saw a man's figure, wrapped in a cloak or dressing gown, come out upon

---

1. This part of the novel takes place in Istanbul, Turkey, as Orlando is being made a British duke in a ceremony at   the British Embassy.
2. Sailors.

the balcony. Then, she said, a woman, much muffled, but apparently of the peasant class was drawn up by means of a rope which the man let down to her on to the balcony. There, the washer-woman said, they embraced passionately 'like lovers,' and went into the room together, drawing the curtains so that no more could be seen.

Next morning, the Duke, as we must now call him, was found by his secretaries sunk in profound slumber amid bed clothes that were much tumbled. The room was in some disorder, his coronet having rolled on the floor, and his cloak and garter being flung all of a heap on a chair. The table was littered with papers. No suspicion was felt at first, as the fatigues of the night had been great. But when afternoon came and he still slept, a doctor was summoned. He applied the remedies which had been used on the previous occasion, plasters, nettles, emetics, etc., but without success. Orlando slept on. His secretaries then thought it their duty to examine the papers on the table. Many were scribbled over with poetry, in which frequent mention was made of an oak tree.[3] There were also various state papers and others of a private nature concerning the management of his estates in England. But at length they came upon a document of far greater significance. It was nothing less, indeed, than a deed of marriage, drawn up, signed, and witnessed between his Lordship, Orlando, Knight of the Garter, etc. etc. etc., and Rosina Pepita, a dancer, father unknown, but reputed a gipsy, mother also unknown but reputed a seller of old iron in the marketplace over against the Galata Bridge. The secretaries looked at each other in dismay. And still Orlando slept. Morning and evening they watched him, but, save that his breathing was regular and his cheeks still flushed their habitual deep rose, he gave no sign of life. Whatever science or ingenuity could do to waken him they did. But still he slept.

On the seventh day of his trance (Thursday, May the 10th) the first shot was fired of that terrible and bloody insurrection of which Lieutenant Brigge had detected the first symptoms. The Turks rose against the Sultan, set fire to the town, and put every foreigner they could find, either to the sword or to the bastinado. A few English managed to escape; but, as might have been expected, the gentlemen of the British Embassy preferred to die in defence of their red boxes, or, in extreme cases, to swallow bunches of keys rather than let them fall into the hands of the Infidel.[4] The rioters broke into Orlando's room, but seeing him stretched to all appearance dead they left him untouched, and only robbed him of his coronet and the robes of the Garter.[5]

And now again obscurity descends, and would indeed that it were deeper! Would, we almost have it in our hearts to exclaim, that it were so deep that we could see nothing whatever through its opacity! Would that we might here take the pen and write Finis[6] to our work! Would that we might spare the reader what is to come and say to him in so many words, Orlando died and was buried. But here, alas, Truth, Candour, and Honesty, the austere Gods who keep watch and ward by the inkpot of the biographer, cry No! Putting their silver trumpets to their lips they demand in one blast, Truth! And again they cry Truth! and sounding yet a third time in concert they peal forth, The Truth and nothing but the Truth!

At which—Heaven be praised! for it affords us a breathing space—the doors gently open, as if a breath of the gentlest and holiest zephyr[7] had wafted them apart, and three

---

3. Throughout the novel, Orlando writes a poem about an oak tree that changes over the centuries as literary styles develop.
4. Non-Muslims.
5. While the book is fiction, this description of an insur-rection against the Ottoman Empire, in which the British played a role, is historical.
6. The end.
7. Breeze.

figures enter.[8] First, comes our Lady of Purity; whose brows are bound with fillets of the whitest lamb's wool; whose hair is an avalanche of the driven snow; and in whose hand reposes the white quill of a virgin goose. Following her, but with a statelier step, comes our Lady of Chastity; on whose brow is set like a turret of burning but unwasting fire a diadem of icicles; her eyes are pure stars, and her fingers, if they touch you, freeze you to the bone. Close behind her, sheltering indeed in the shadow of her more stately sisters, comes our Lady of Modesty, frailest and fairest of the three; whose face is only shown as the young moon shows when it is thin and sickle shaped and half hidden among clouds. Each advances towards the centre of the room where Orlando still lies sleeping; and with gestures at once appealing and commanding, *Our Lady of Purity* speaks first:

"I am the guardian of the sleeping fawn; the snow is dear to me; and the moon rising; and the silver sea. With my robes I cover the speckled hen's eggs and the brindled[9] sea shell; I cover vice and poverty. On all things frail or dark or doubtful, my veil descends. Wherefore, speak not, reveal not. Spare, O spare!"

Here the trumpets peal forth.

"Purity Avaunt! Begone Purity!"

Then *Our Lady Chastity* speaks:

"I am she whose touch freezes and whose glance turns to stone. I have stayed the star in its dancing, and the wave as it falls. The highest Alps are my dwelling place; and when I walk, the lightnings flash in my hair; where my eyes fall, they kill. Rather than let Orlando wake, I will freeze him to the bone. Spare, O spare!"

Here the trumpets peal forth.

"Chastity Avaunt! Begone Chastity!"

Then *Our Lady of Modesty* speaks, so low that one can hardly hear:

"I am she that men call Modesty. Virgin I am and ever shall be. Not for me the fruitful fields and the fertile vineyard. Increase[1] is odious to me; and when the apples burgeon[2] or the flocks breed, I run, I run; I let my mantle fall. My hair covers my eyes. I do not see. Spare, O Spare!"

Again the trumpets peal forth:

"Modesty Avaunt! Begone Modesty!"

With gestures of grief and lamentation the three sisters now join hands and dance slowly, tossing their veils and singing as they go:

"Truth, come not out from your horrid den. Hide deeper, fearful Truth. For you flaunt in the brutal gaze of the sun things that were better unknown and undone; you unveil the shameful; the dark you make clear. Hide! Hide! Hide!"

Here they make as if to cover Orlando with their draperies. The trumpets, meanwhile, still blare forth:

"The Truth and nothing but the Truth."

At this the Sisters try to cast their veils over the mouths of the trumpets so as to muffle them, but in vain, for now all trumpets blare forth together.

"Horrid Sisters, go!"

The Sisters become distracted and wail in unison, still circling and flinging their veils up and down.

"It has not always been so! But men want us no longer; the women detest us. We go; we go. I (*Purity says this*) to the hen roost. I (*Chastity says this*) to the still unrav-

---

8. What follows is an ironic version of an allegorical masque, a form of court drama.
9. Mottled.

1. Reproduction.
2. Grow.

ished heights of Surrey. I (*Modesty says this*) to any cosy nook where there are curtains in plenty.

"For there, not here (all speak together joining hands and making gestures of farewell and despair towards the bed where Orlando lies sleeping) dwell still in nest and boudoir, office and lawcourt those who love us; those who honour us, virgins and city men; lawyers and doctors; those who prohibit; those who deny; those who reverence without knowing why; those who praise without understanding; the still very numerous (Heaven be praised) tribe of the respectable; who prefer to see not; desire to know not; love the darkness; those still worship us, and with reason; for we have given them Wealth, Prosperity, Comfort, Ease. To them we go, you we leave. Come, Sisters come! This is no place for us here."

They retire in haste, waving their draperies over their heads, as if to shut out something that they dare not look upon and close the door behind them.

We are, therefore, now left entirely alone in the room with the sleeping Orlando and the trumpeters. The trumpeters, ranging themselves side by side in order, blow one terrific blast:—

"THE TRUTH!"

at which Orlando woke.

He stretched himself. He rose. He stood upright in complete nakedness before us, and while the trumpets pealed Truth! Truth! Truth! we have no choice left but confess—he was a woman.

The sound of the trumpets died away and Orlando stood stark naked. No human being, since the world began, has ever looked more ravishing. His form combined in one the strength of a man and a woman's grace. As he stood there, the silver trumpets prolonged their note, as if reluctant to leave the lovely sight which their blast had called forth; and Chastity, Purity, and Modesty, inspired, no doubt, by Curiosity, peeped in at the door and threw a garment like a towel at the naked form which, unfortunately, fell short by several inches. Orlando looked himself up and down in a long looking-glass, without showing any signs of discomposure, and went, presumably, to his bath.

We may take advantage of this pause in the narrative to make certain statements. Orlando had become a woman—there is no denying it. But in every other respect, Orlando remained precisely as he had been. The change of sex, though it altered their future, did nothing whatever to alter their identity. Their faces remained, as their portraits prove, practically the same. His memory—but in future we must, for convention's sake, say "her" for "his," and "she" for "he"—her memory then, went back through all the events of her past life without encountering any obstacle. Some slight haziness there may have been, as if a few dark drops had fallen into the clear pool of memory; certain things had become a little dimmed; but that was all. The change seemed to have been accomplished painlessly and completely and in such a way that Orlando herself showed no surprise at it. Many people, taking this into account, and holding that such a change of sex is against nature, have been at great pains to prove (1) that Orlando had always been a woman, (2) that Orlando is at this moment a man. Let biologists and psychologists determine. It is enough for us to state the simple fact; Orlando was a man till the age of thirty; when he became a woman and has remained so ever since.

But let other pens treat of sex and sexuality; we quit such odious subjects as soon as we can. Orlando had now washed, and dressed herself in those Turkish coats and trousers which can be worn indifferently by either sex; and was forced to consider her position. That it was precarious and embarrassing in the extreme must be the first thought of every reader who has followed her story with sympathy. Young, noble, beautiful, she had woken to find herself in a position than which we can conceive

none more delicate for a young lady of rank. We should not have blamed her had she
rung the bell, screamed, or fainted. But Orlando showed no such signs of perturbation.
All her actions were deliberate in the extreme, and might indeed have been thought
to show tokens of premeditation. First, she carefully examined the papers on the table;
took such as seemed to be written in poetry, and secreted them in her bosom; next she
called her Seleuchi hound, which had never left her bed all these days, though half
famished with hunger, fed and combed him; then stuck a pair of pistols in her belt;
finally wound about her person several strings of emeralds and pearls of the finest orient which had formed part of her Ambassadorial wardrobe. This done, she leant out of
the window, gave one low whistle, and descended the shattered and bloodstained
staircase, now strewn with the litter of waste paper baskets, treaties, despatches, seals,
sealing wax, etc., and so entered the courtyard. There, in the shadow of a giant fig tree
waited an old Gipsy on a donkey. He led another by the bridle. Orlando swung her leg
over it; and thus, attended by a lean dog, riding a donkey, in company of a gipsy, the
Ambassador of Great Britain at the Court of the Sultan left Constantinople. * * *

And as she drove, we may seize the opportunity, since the landscape was of a simple English kind which needs no description, to draw the reader's attention more particularly than we could at the moment to one or two remarks which have slipped in
here and there in the course of the narrative. For example, it may have been observed
that Orlando hid her manuscripts when interrupted. Next, that she looked long and
intently in the glass[3]; and now, as she drove to London, one might notice her starting
and suppressing a cry when the horses galloped faster than she liked. Her modesty as
to her writing, her vanity as to her person, her fears for her safety all seem to hint that
what was said a short time ago about there being no change in Orlando the man and
Orlando the woman, was ceasing to be altogether true. She was becoming a little more
modest, as women are, of her brains, and a little more vain, as women are, of her person. Certain susceptibilities were asserting themselves, and others were diminishing.
The change of clothes had, some philosophers will say, much to do with it. Vain trifles
as they seem, clothes have, they say, more important offices than merely to keep us
warm. They change our view of the world and the world's view of us. For example,
when Captain Bartolus saw Orlando's skirt, he had an awning stretched for her immediately, pressed her to take another slice of beef, and invited her to go ashore with him
in the long boat. These compliments would certainly not have been paid her had her
skirts, instead of flowing, been cut tight to her legs in the fashion of breeches. And
when we are paid compliments, it behoves us[4] to make some return. Orlando curt-
seyed; she complied; she flattered the good man's humours as she would not have done
had his neat breeches been a woman's skirts, and his braided coat a woman's satin
bodice. Thus, there is much to support the view that it is clothes that wear us and not
we them; we may make them take the mould of arm or breast, but they mould our
hearts, our brains, our tongues to their liking. So, having now worn skirts for a considerable time, a certain change was visible in Orlando, which is to be found even in her
face. If we compare the picture of Orlando as a man with that of Orlando as a woman
we shall see that though both are undoubtedly one and the same person, there are certain changes. The man has his hand free to seize his sword; the woman must use hers
to keep the satins from slipping from her shoulders. The man looks the world full in
the face, as if it were made for his uses and fashioned to his liking. The woman takes a

3. Mirror.   4. We should.

sidelong glance at it, full of subtlety, even of suspicion. Had they both worn the same clothes, it is possible that their outlook might have been the same too.

That is the view of some philosophers and wise ones, but on the whole, we incline to another. The difference between the sexes is, happily, one of great profundity. Clothes are but a symbol of something hid deep beneath. It was a change in Orlando herself that dictated her choice of a woman's dress and of a woman's sex. And perhaps in this she was only expressing rather more openly than usual—openness indeed was the soul of her nature—something that happens to most people without being thus plainly expressed. For here again, we come to a dilemma. Different though the sexes are, they intermix. In every human being a vacillation[5] from one sex to the other takes place, and often it is only the clothes that keep the male or female likeness, while underneath the sex is the very opposite of what it is above. Of the complications and confusions which thus result every one has had experience; but here we leave the general question and note only the odd effect it had in the particular case of Orlando herself.

For it was this mixture in her of man and woman, one being uppermost and then the other, that often gave her conduct an unexpected turn. The curious of her own sex would argue how, for example, if Orlando was a woman, did she never take more than ten minutes to dress? And were not her clothes chosen rather at random, and sometimes worn rather shabby? And then they would say, still, she has none of the formality of a man, or a man's love of power. She is excessively tender-hearted. She could not endure to see a donkey beaten or a kitten drowned. Yet again, they noted, she detested household matters, was up at dawn and out among the fields in summer before the sun had risen. No farmer knew more about the crops than she did. She could drink with the best and liked games of hazard. She rode well and drove six horses at a gallop over London Bridge. Yet again, though bold and active as a man, it was remarked that the sight of another in danger brought on the most womanly palpitations. She would burst into tears on slight provocation. She was unversed in geography, found mathematics intolerable, and held some caprices[6] which are more common among women than men, as for instance, that to travel south is to travel down hill. Whether, then, Orlando was most man or woman, it is difficult to say and cannot now be decided. For her coach was now rattling over the cobbles. She had reached her home in the city. The steps were being let down; the iron gates were being opened. She was entering her father's house at Blackfriar's which, though fashion was fast deserting that end of the town, was still a pleasant, roomy mansion, with gardens running down to the river, and a pleasant grove of nut trees to walk in.

⊷ ⊰◊⊱ ⊶

E. M. Forster
1879–1970

Edward Morgan Forster, fondly referred to by friends as Morgan or "Bunny," had an enormous effect on modern British literature and letters over the course of his long life. Born in 1879, Forster died at 91 in 1970, having traversed the course of British culture from its Victorian and imperial peak to the postimperial world of the Beatles and the waning of the British novel. His prolific output of novels, short stories, literary criticism, travel writing, and political essays had also waned by the time of his death, partly because the subject he most wished to write

5. Movement.   6. Whimsical beliefs.

about—male homosexual love—was the final taboo of British literature he did not live to see broken. His autobiographical novel *Maurice*, describing an upper-class Englishman's finding of true love with a working-class man employed on a friend's estate, was published only in 1971, after Forster's death. The novels of Forster's youth and middle age remain classics of modern British literature—and the basis for several films in recent years. *Howards End* (1910) explores the fault lines between classes in British society, while *A Passage to India* (1924) defines the processes that would lead inexorably to the loss of Britain's empire.

Forster had a privileged upbringing, and a private education that led him to King's College, Cambridge, and degrees in classics and history. His family wealth allowed him to live in Greece, Italy, and Egypt after graduation in 1901; he spent part of World War I as a Red Cross volunteer in Alexandria, Egypt. He first traveled to India in 1912–1913, and later served as private secretary to the Maharajah of Dewas in 1921. Observing the tensions of empire firsthand, he became a journalist for the Labor Party's *Daily Herald*, later a radio broadcaster in the cause of Indian independence and a reviewer for the *New Statesman* and *Nation*. After Indian independence was achieved in 1947, he was brought to India in public tribute for his actions on behalf of the political solution to independence.

Forster was close to Virginia Woolf as friend and as literary influence: Woolf's *Mrs Dalloway* (1925) is modeled in part on *A Passage to India*, in that it takes one of its central characters from London to India and back. Like Woolf's novel, *A Passage to India* is notable for its use of multiple perspectives; Forster employed the shifting viewpoints of an elderly British woman, a Muslim Indian physician, and a male British educator and civil servant of empire, writing his story across the lines of difference of race, religion, gender, and culture. *The Life to Come*, coming from a body of work published posthumously, fuses Forster's concern for the expression of homosexual love with his equally distinctive and lifelong focus on the wrongs of Britain's empire and the harsh inequities of imperialism. Set in a nameless colony, the story is an allegory of the costs of suppressing others and the supreme price paid by suppressing oneself. Sexual desire, friendship and love between colonizer and colonized, master and servant, "superior" and "inferior" were the very things that, for Forster, could break down the barriers of empire abroad, and the inequalities of society at home. Reverend Pinmay, a prim, repressed colonial master in a clerical collar, can't accept Chief Vithobai as an equal, but he reaps the destruction he has sown. One of Forster's most famous lines is from an essay on literary form: "Only connect," he wrote, and that call to make connection, whether in narrative form, or between classes, races, sexes, and countries, is the hallmark of his fiction.

The Life to Come

1. Night

Love had been born somewhere in the forest, of what quality only the future could decide. Trivial or immortal, it had been born to two human bodies as a midnight cry. Impossible to tell whence the cry had come, so dark was the forest. Or into what worlds it would echo, so vast was the forest. Love had been born for good or evil, for a long life or a short.

There was hidden among the undergrowth of that wild region a small native hut. Here, after the cry had died away, a light was kindled. It shone upon the pagan limbs and the golden ruffled hair of a young man. He, calm and dignified, raised the wick of a lamp which had been beaten down flat, he smiled, lit it, and his surroundings trembled back into his sight. The hut lay against the roots of an aged tree, which undulated[1] over its floor and surged at one place into a natural couch, a sort of throne, where the young

---

1. Flowed.

man's quilt had been spread. A stream sang outside, a firefly relit its lamp also. A remote, a romantic spot . . . lovely, lovable . . . and then he caught sight of a book on the floor, and he dropped beside it with a dramatic moan as if it was a corpse and he the murderer. For the book in question was his Holy Bible. "Though I speak with the tongues of men and of angels, and have not—" a scarlet flower hid the next word, flowers were everywhere, even round his own neck. Losing his dignity, he sobbed "Oh, what have I done?" and not daring to answer the question he hurled the flowers through the door of the hut and the Bible after them, then rushed to retrieve the latter in an agony of grotesque remorse. All had fallen into the stream, all were carried away by the song. Darkness and beauty, darkness and beauty. "Only one end to this," he thought. And he scuttled back for his pistol. But the pistol was not with him, for he was negligent in his arrangements and had left it over with the servants at the further side of the great tree; and the servants, awoken from slumber, took alarm at his talk of firearms. In spite of all he could say, they concluded that an attack was impending from the neighbouring village, which had already proved unfriendly, and they implored their young master not to resist, but to hide in the brushwood until dawn and slip away as soon as the forest paths were visible. Contrary to his orders, they began packing, and next morning he was riding away from the enchanted hut, and descending the watershed into the next valley. Looking back at the huge and enigmatic masses of the trees, he prayed them to keep his unspeakable secret, to conceal it even from God, and he felt in his unhinged state that they had the power to do this, and that they were not ordinary trees.

When he reached the coast, the other missionaries there saw at once from his face that he had failed. Nor had they expected otherwise. The Roman Catholics, far more expert than themselves, had failed to convert Vithobai, the wildest, strongest, most stubborn of all the inland chiefs. And Paul Pinmay (for this was the young man's name) was at that time a very young man indeed, and had partly been sent in order that he might discover his own limitations. He was inclined to be impatient and headstrong, he knew little of the language and still less of native psychology, and indeed he disdained to study this last, declaring in his naïve way that human nature is the same all over the world. They heard his story with sympathy but without surprise. He related how on his arrival he had asked for an audience, which Vithobai had granted inside his ancestral stockade. There, dictionary in hand, he had put the case for Christ, and at the end Vithobai, not deigning to reply in person, had waved to a retainer and made him answer. The retainer had been duly refuted, but Vithobai remained impassive and unfriendly behind his amulets and robes. So he put the case a second time, and another retainer was put up against him, and the audience continued on these lines until he was so exhausted that he was fain to withdraw. Forbidden to sleep in the village, he was obliged to spend the night all alone in a miserable hut, while the servants kept careful watch before the entrance and reported that an attack might be expected at any moment. He had therefore judged it fitter to come away at sunrise. Such was his story— told in a mixture of missionary jargon and of slang—and towards the close he was looking at his colleagues through his long eyelashes to see whether they suspected anything.

"Do you advise a renewed attempt next week?" asked one of them, who was addicted to irony.

And another: "Your intention, I think, when you left us, was to get into touch with this unapproachable Vithobai personally, indeed you declared that you would not return until you had done so."

And a third: "But you must rest now, you look tired."

He was tired, but as soon as he lay down his secret stole out of its hiding-place beyond the mountains, and lay down by his side. And he recalled Vithobai, Vithobai the unapproachable, coming into his hut out of the darkness and smiling at him. Oh how delighted he had been! Oh how surprised! He had scarcely recognized the sardonic chief in this gracious and bare-limbed boy, whose only ornaments were scarlet flowers. Vithobai had laid all formality aside. "I have come secretly," were his first words. "I wish to hear more about this god whose name is Love." How his heart had leapt after the despondency of the day! "Come to Christ!" he had cried, and Vithobai had said, "Is that your name?" He explained No, his name was not Christ, although he had the fortune to be called Paul after a great apostle, and of course he was no god but a sinful man, chosen to call other sinners to the Mercy Seat. "What is Mercy? I wish to hear more," said Vithobai, and they sat down together upon the couch that was almost a throne. And he had opened the Bible at 1. Cor. 13, and had read and expounded the marvellous chapter, and spoke of the love of Christ and of our love for each other in Christ, very simply but more eloquently than ever before, while Vithobai said, "This is the first time I have heard such words, I like them," and drew closer, his body aglow and smelling sweetly of flowers. And he saw how intelligent the boy was and how handsome, and determining to win him there and then imprinted a kiss on his forehead and drew him to Abraham's bosom.[2] And Vithobai had lain in it gladly—too gladly and too long—and had extinguished the lamp. And God alone saw them after that.

Yes, God saw and God sees. Go down into the depths of the woods and He beholds you, throw His Holy Book into the stream, and you destroy only print and paper, not the Word. Sooner or later, God calls every deed to the light. And so it was with Mr Pinmay. He began, though tardily, to meditate upon his sin. Each time he looked at it its aspect altered. At first he assumed that all the blame was his, because he should have set an example. But this was not the root of the matter, for Vithobai had shown no reluctance to be tempted. On the contrary . . . and it was his hand that beat down the light. And why had he stolen up from the village if not to tempt? . . . Yes, to tempt, to attack the new religion by corrupting its preacher, yes, yes, that was it, and his retainers celebrated his victory now in some cynical orgy. Young Mr Pinmay saw it all. He remembered all that he had heard of the antique[3] power of evil in the country, the tales he had so smilingly dismissed as beneath a Christian's notice, the extraordinary uprushes of energy which certain natives were said to possess and occasionally to employ for unholy purposes. And having reached this point he found that he was able to pray; he confessed his defilement (the very name of which cannot be mentioned among Christians), he lamented that he had postponed, perhaps for a generation, the victory of the Church, and he condemned, with increasing severity, the arts of his seducer. On the last topic he became truly eloquent, he always found something more to say, and having begun by recommending the boy to mercy he ended by asking that he might be damned.

"But perhaps this is going too far," he thought, and perhaps it was, for just as he finished his prayers there was a noise as of horsemen below, and then all his colleagues came dashing into his room. They were in extreme excitement. Cried one: "News from the interior, news from the forest. Vithobai and the entire of his people have embraced Christianity." And the second: "Here we have the triumph of youth, oh it puts us to shame." While the third exclaimed alternately "Praise be to God!" and "I beg your pardon." They rejoiced one with another and rebuked their own hardness of heart and want of faith in the Gospel method, and they thought the more

2. Forster is using Paul Pinmay's religious rhetoric for double meanings: "drew him to Abraham's bosom" means both that Pinmay tried to convert Vithobai to Christian-

ity, but also that he embraced him.
3. Ancient.

highly of young Pinmay because he was not elated by his success, on the contrary, he appeared to be disturbed, and fell upon his knees in prayer.

2. Evening

Mr Pinmay's trials, doubts and final triumphs are recorded in a special pamphlet, published by his Society and illustrated by woodcuts. There is a picture called "What it seemed to be", which shows a hostile and savage potentate threatening him; in another picture, called "What it really was!," a dusky youth in western clothes sits among a group of clergymen and ladies, looking like a waiter, and supported by under-waiters, who line the steps of a building labelled "School." Barnabas (for such was the name that the dusky youth received at his baptism)—Barnabas proved an exemplary convert. He made mistakes, and his theology was crude and erratic, but he never backslid, and he had authority with his own people, so that the missionaries had only to explain carefully what they wanted, and it was carried out. He evinced abundant zeal, and behind it a steadiness of purpose all too rare. No one, not even the Roman Catholics, could point to so solid a success.[4]

Since Mr Pinmay was the sole cause of the victory, the new district naturally fell to his charge. Modest, like all sincere workers, he was reluctant to accept, refusing to go although the chief sent deputation after deputation to escort him, and only going in the end because he was commanded to do so by the Bishop. He was appointed for a term of ten years. As soon as he was installed, he set to work energetically—indeed, his methods provoked criticism, although they were fully justified by their fruits. He who had been wont to lay such stress on the Gospel teaching, on love, kindness, and personal influence, he who had preached that the Kingdom of Heaven is intimacy and emotion, now reacted with violence and treated the new converts and even Barnabas himself with the gloomy severity of the Old Law. He who had ignored the subject of native psychology now became an expert therein, and often spoke more like a disillusioned official[5] than a missionary. He would say: "These people are so unlike ourselves that I much doubt whether they have really accepted Christ. They are pleasant enough when they meet us, yet probably spread all manner of ill-natured gossip when our backs are turned. I cannot wholly trust them." He paid no respect to local customs, suspecting them all to be evil, he undermined the tribal organization, and—most risky of all—he appointed a number of native catechists of low type from the tribe in the adjoining valley. Trouble was expected, for this was an ancient and proud people, but their spirit seemed broken, or Barnabas broke it where necessary. At the end of the ten years the Church was to know no more docile sons.

Yet Mr Pinmay had his anxious moments.

His first meeting with Barnabas was the worst of them.

He had managed to postpone it until the day of his installation by the Bishop, and of the general baptism. The ceremonies were over, and the whole tribe, headed by their chief, had filed past the portable font and been signed on the forehead with the cross of Christ. Mistaking the nature of the rite, they were disposed to gaiety. Barnabas laid his outer garment aside, and running up to the group of missionaries like any young man of his people said, "My brother in Christ, oh come quickly," and stroked Mr Pinmay's flushed face, and tried to kiss his forehead and golden hair.

Mr Pinmay disengaged himself and said in a trembling voice: "In the first place send your people each to his home."

4. A number of Christian sects are competing to convert the "heathen."   5. A colonial civil servant.

The order was given and obeyed.

"In the second place, let no one come before me again until he is decently clad," he continued, more firmly.

"My brother, like you?"

The missionary was now wearing a suit of ducks[6] with shirt, vest, pants and cholera belt, also sun-helmet, starched collar, blue tie spotted with white, socks, and brown boots. "Yes, like me," he said. "And in the third place are you decently clad yourself, Barnabas?"

The chief was wearing but little. A cincture[7] of bright silks supported his dagger and floated in the fresh wind when he ran. He had silver armlets, and a silver necklet, closed by a falcon's head which nestled against his throat. His eyes flashed like a demon, for he was unaccustomed to rebuke, but he submitted and vanished into his stockade.

The suspense of the last few weeks had quite altered Mr Pinmay's character. He was no longer an open-hearted Christian knight[8] but a hypocrite whom a false step would destroy. The retreat of Barnabas relieved him. He saw that he had gained an ascendancy over the chief which it was politic to develop. Barnabas respected him, and would not willingly do harm—had even an affection for him, loathsome as the idea might seem. All this was to the good. But he must strike a second blow. That evening he went in person to the stockade, taking with him two colleagues who had recently arrived and knew nothing of the language.

The chief received them in soiled European clothes—in the interval he had summoned one of the traders who accompanied the baptismal party. He had mastered his anger, and speaking courteously he said: "Christ awaits us in my inner chamber."

Mr Pinmay had thought out his line of action. He dared not explain the hideous error, nor call upon his fellow sinner to repent; the chief must remain in a state of damnation for a time, for a new church depended on it. His reply to the unholy suggestion was "Not yet."

"Why not yet?" said the other, his beautiful eyes filling with tears. "God orders me to love you now."

"He orders me to refrain."

"How can that be, when God *is* Love?"

"I have served him the longer and I know."

"But this is my palace and I am a great chief."

"God is greater than all chiefs."

"As it was in your hut let it here be. Dismiss your companions and the gate will be barred behind them, and we close out the light. My body and the breath in it are yours. Draw me again to your bosom. I give myself, I, Vithobai the King."

"Not yet," repeated Mr Pinmay, covering his eyes with his hand.

"My beloved, I give myself . . . take me . . . I give you my kingdom." And he fell prone.

"Arise, Barnabas. . . . We do not want your kingdom. We have only come to teach you to rule it rightly. And do not speak of what happened in the hut. Never mention the hut, the word hut, the thought, either to me or to anyone. It is my wish and my command."

"Never?"

"Never."

6. Cotton canvas.
7. Loose belt.

8. A reference to the Crusades, where the Knights Templar killed rather than converted their Muslim enemy.

"Come, my gods, come back to me," he cried, leaping up and wrenching at his clothes. "What do I gain by leaving you?"

"No, no, no!" prevaricated Mr Pinmay. "I said Never speak, not that I would never come."

The boy was reassured. He said: "Yes. I misunderstood. You do come to Christ, but not yet. I must wait. For how long?"

"Until I call you. Meanwhile obey all my orders, whether given directly or through others."

"Very well, my brother. Until you call me."

"And do not call me your brother."

"Very well."

"Or seek my company." Turning to the other missionaries, he said, "Now let us go." He was glad he had brought companions with him, for his repentance was still insecure. The sun was setting, the inner chamber garlanded, the stockade deserted, the boy wild with passion, weeping as if his heart had broken. They might have been so happy together in their sin and no one but God need have known.

3. Day

The next crisis that Mr Pinmay had to face was far less serious, yet it shocked him more, because he was unprepared for it. The occasion was five years later, just before his own marriage. The cause of Christ had progressed greatly in the interval. Dancing had been put down, industry encouraged, inaccurate notions as to the nature of religion had disappeared, nor in spite of espionage had he discovered much secret immorality. He was marrying one of the medical missionaries, a lady who shared his ideals, and whose brother had a mining concession above the village.

As he leant over the veranda, meditating with pleasure on the approaching change in his life, a smart European dogcart[9] drove up, and Barnabas scrambled out of it to pay his congratulations. The chief had developed into an affable and rather weedy[1] Christian with a good knowledge of English. He likewise was about to be married—his bride a native catechist from the adjoining valley, a girl inferior to him by birth, but the missionaries had selected her.

Congratulations were exchanged.

Mr Pinmay's repentance was now permanent, and his conscience so robust that he could meet the chief with ease and transact business with him in private, when occasion required it. The brown hand, lying dead for an instant in his own, awoke no reminiscences of sin.

Wriggling rather awkwardly inside his clothes, Barnabas said with a smile: "Will you take me a short drive in your dog-cart, Mr Pinmay?"

Mr Pinmay replied that he had no dog-cart.

"Excuse me, sir, you have. It stands below. It, and the horse, are my wedding gift to you."

The missionary had long desired a horse and cart, and he accepted them without waiting to ask God's blessing. "You should not have given me such an expensive present," he remarked. For the chief was no longer wealthy; in the sudden advent of civilization he had chanced to lose much of his land.

---

9. Carriage.   1. Shaggy.

"My reward is enough if we go one drive, sir."

As a rule he did not choose to be seen pleasuring with a native—it undermined his authority—but this was a special occasion. They moved briskly through the village, Barnabas driving to show the paces of the horse, and presently turned to the woods or to what remained of them; there was a tolerable road, made by the timber-fellers, which wound uphill towards a grove. The scene was uninteresting, and pervaded by a whitish light that seemed to penetrate every recess. They spoke of local affairs.

"How much of the timber is earmarked for the mines?" inquired Mr Pinmay, in the course of the conversation.

"An increasing amount as the galleries extend deeper into the mountain. I am told that the heat down there is now so great that the miners work unclad. Are they to be fined for this?"

"No. It is impossible to be strict about mines. They constitute a special case."

"I understand. I am also told that disease among them increases."

"It does, but then so do our hospitals."

"I do not understand."

"Can't you grasp, Barnabas, that under God's permission certain evils attend civilization, but that if men do God's will the remedies for the evils keep pace? Five years ago you had not a single hospital in this valley."

"Nor any disease. I understand. Then all my people were strong."

"There was abundant disease," corrected the missionary. "Vice and superstition, to mention no others. And intertribal war. Could you have married a lady from another valley five years ago?"

"No. Even as a concubine[2] she would have disgraced me."

"All concubines are a disgrace."

"I understand. In regard to this marriage, sir, there is, however, a promise that you made me once."

"About the mining concession, of course? Exactly. Yes, I never thought you were treated fairly there. I will certainly approach my future brother-in-law to get you some compensation. But you ought to have been more careful at the time. You signed your rights away without consulting me. I am always willing to be consulted."

"It is not the mining concession," said Barnabas patiently; although a good steward for the Church, he had grown careless where his own affairs were concerned. "It is quite another promise." He seemed to be choosing his words. Speaking slowly and without any appearance of emotion, he said at last: "Come to Christ."

"Come to Him indeed," said Mr Pinmay in slightly reproving tones, for he was not accustomed to receive such an invitation from a spiritual inferior.

Barnabas paused again, then said: "In the hut."

"What hut?" He had forgotten.

"The hut with the Mercy Seat."

Shocked and angry, he exclaimed: "Barnabas, Barnabas, this is disgraceful. I forbad you ever to mention this subject."

At that moment the horse drew up at the entrance of the grove. Civilization tapped and clinked behind them, under a garish sun. The road ended, and a path where two could walk abreast continued into the delicate gray and purple recesses of the trees. Tepid, impersonal, as if he still discussed public affairs, the young man said:

2. A formal mistress.

"Let us both be entirely reasonable, sir. God continues to order me to love you. It is my life, whatever else I seem to do. My body and the breath in it are still yours, though you wither them up with this waiting. Come into the last forest, before it is cut down, and I will be kind, and all may end well. But it is now five years since you first said Not yet."

"It is, and now I say Never."

"This time you say Never?"

"I do."

Without replying, Barnabas handed him the reins, and then jerked himself out of the cart. It was a most uncanny movement, which seemed to proceed direct from the will. He scarcely used his hands or rose to his feet before jumping. But his soul uncoiled like a spring, and thrust the cart violently away from it against the ground. Mr Pinmay had heard of such contortions, but never witnessed them; they were startling, they were disgusting. And the descent was equally sinister. Barnabas lay helpless as if the evil uprush had suddenly failed. "Are you ill?" asked the clergyman.

"No."

"Then what ails you?"

"No."

"Do you repent of your words?"

"No."

"Then you must be punished. As the head of the community you are bound to set an example. You are fined one hundred pounds for backsliding."

"No." Then as if to himself he said: "First the grapes of my body are pressed. Then I am silenced. Now I am punished. Night, evening and a day. What remains?"[3]

What should remain? The remark was meaningless. Mr Pinmay drove back alone, rather thoughtful. He would certainly have to return the horse and cart—they had been intended as a bribe—and the hundred pounds must be collected by one of his subordinates. He wished that the whole unsavoury business had not been raked up into the light just before his wedding. Its senselessness alarmed him.

4. Morning

The concluding five years of Mr Pinmay's ministry were less satisfactory than their predecessors. His marriage was happy, his difficulties few, nothing tangible opposed him, but he was haunted by the scene outside the grove. Could it signify that he himself had not been pardoned? Did God, in His mystery, demand from him that he should cleanse his brother's soul before his own could be accepted? The dark erotic perversion that the chief mistook for Christianity—who had implanted it? He had put this question from him in the press of his earlier dangers, but it intruded itself now that he was safe. Day after day he heard the cold voice of the somewhat scraggy and unattractive native inviting him to sin, or saw the leap from the cart that suggested a dislocated soul. He turned to the Christianity of the valley, but he found no consolation there. He had implanted that too: not in sin, but in reaction against sin, and so its fruits were as bitter. If Barnabas distorted Christ, the valley ignored Him. It was hard, it lacked personality and beauty and emotion and all that Paul Pinmay had admired in his youth. It could produce catechists and organizers, but never a saint.

---

3. Barnabas has a seizure in the road, akin to Saul being stricken on the road to Damascus, and becoming Paul, a Christian. Barnabas instead "falls out" of Christianity when Pinmay rejects his love.

What was the cause of the failure? The hut, the hut. In the concluding years of his stay, he ordered it to be pulled down.

He seldom met Barnabas now. There was no necessity for it, since the chief's usefulness decreased as the community developed and new men pushed their way to the top. Though still helpful when applied to, he lost all capacity for initiative. He moved from his old stockaded enclosure with its memories of independence, and occupied a lofty but small modern house at the top of the village, suitable to his straitened[4] circumstances. Here he and his wife and their children (one more every eleven months) lived in the semi-European style. Sometimes he worked in the garden, although menial labour was regarding as degrading, and he was assiduous at prayer meetings, where he frequented the back row. The missionaries called him a true Christian when they called him anything, and congratulated themselves that witchcraft had no rallying-point; he had served their purpose, he began to pass from their talk. Only Mr Pinmay watched him furtively and wondered where his old energies had gone. He would have preferred an outburst to this corrupt acquiescence; he knew now that he could deal with outbursts. He even felt weaker himself, as if the same curse infected them both, and this though he had again and again confessed his own share of the sin to God, and had acquired a natural loathing for it in consequence of his marriage.

He could not really feel much sorrow when he learned that the unfortunate fellow was dying.

Consumption[5] was the cause. One of the imported workers had started an epidemic, and Mr and Mrs Pinmay were busied up to the moment of their own departure, negotiating an extension to the cemetery. They expected to leave the valley before Barnabas did, but during the last week he made, so to speak, a spurt, as if he would outstrip them. His was a very rapid case. He put up no fight. His heart seemed broken. They had little time to devote to individuals, so wide was the scope of their work, still they hurried over to see him one morning, hearing that he had had a fresh haemorrhage, and was not likely to survive the day. "Poor fellow, poor lad, he was an important factor ten years back—times change," murmured Mr Pinmay as he pushed the Holy Communion under the seat of the dog-cart—Barnabas's own cart, as it happened, for Mrs Pinmay, knowing nothing of the incident, had acquired it cheaply at a sale a couple of years back. As he drove it briskly up through the village Mr Pinmay's heart grew lighter, and he thanked God for permitting Barnabas, since die we must, to pass away at this particular moment; he would not have liked to leave him behind, festering, equivocal, and perhaps acquiring some sinister power.

When they arrived, Mrs Barnabas told them that her husband was still alive, and, she thought, conscious, but in such darkness of spirit that he would not open his eyes or speak. He had been carried up onto the roof, on account of the heat in his room, and his gestures had indicated that he would be left alone. "But he must not be left alone," said Mr Pinmay. "We must watch with him through this dark hour. I will prepare him in the first place." He climbed the staircase that led through a trapdoor onto the roof. In the shadow of the parapet lay the dying man, coughing gently, and stark naked.

"Vithobai!" he cried in amazement.

He opened his eyes and said: "Who calls me?"

"You must have some covering, Barnabas," said Mr Pinmay fussily. He looked round, but there was nothing on the roof except a curious skein[6] of blue flowers

4. Reduced.
5. Tuberculosis.

6. Woven or braided.

threaded round a knife. He took them up. But the other said, "Do not lay those upon me yet," and he refrained, remembering that blue is the colour of despair in that valley, just as red is the colour of love. "I'll get you a shawl," he continued. "Why, you are not lying upon a mattress, even."

"It is my own roof. Or I thought it was until now. My wife and household respected my wishes. They laid me here because it is not the custom of my ancestors to die in a bed."

"Mrs Barnabas should have known better. You cannot possibly lie on hard asphalt."

"I have found that I can."

"Vithobai, Vithobai," he cried, more upset than he expected.

"Who calls me?"

"You are not going back to your old false gods?"

"Oh no. So near to the end of my life, why should I make any change? These flowers are only a custom, and they comfort me."

"There is only one comforter . . . ." He glanced around the roof, then fell upon his knees. He could save a soul without danger to himself at last. "Come to Christ," he said, "but not in the way that you suppose. The time has come for me to explain. You and I once sinned together, yes, you and your missionary whom you so reverence. You and I must now repent together, yes, such is God's law." And confusedly, and with many changes of emotion and shiftings of his point of view and reservations, he explained the nature of what had happened ten years ago and its present consequences.

The other made a painful effort to follow, but his eyes kept closing. "What is all this talk?" he said at last. "And why do you wait until I am ill and you old?"

"I waited until I could forgive you and ask your forgiveness. It is the hour of your atonement and mine. Put away all despair, forget those wicked flowers. Let us repent and leave the rest to God."

"I repent, I do not repent . . ." he wailed.

"Hush! Think what you say."

"I forgive you, I do not forgive, both are the same. I am good I am evil I am pure I am foul, I am this or that, I am Barnabas, I am Vithobai. What difference does it make now? It is my deeds that await me, and I have no strength left to add to them. No strength, no time. I lie here empty, but you fill me up with thoughts, and then press me to speak them that you may have words to remember afterwards. . . . But it is deeds, deeds that count, O my lost brother. Mine are this little house instead of my old great one, this valley which other men own, this cough that kills me, those bastards that continue my race; and that deed in the hut, which you say caused all, and which now you call joy, now sin. How can I remember which it was after all these years, and what difference if I could? It was a deed, it has gone before me with the others to be judged."

"Vithobai," he pleaded, distressed because he himself had been called old.

"Who calls me the third time?"

"Kiss me."

"My mouth is down here."

"Kiss my forehead—no more—as a sign that I am forgiven. Do not misunderstand me this time . . . in perfect purity . . . the holy salutation of Christ. And then say with me: Our Father which art in Heaven, hallowed be Thy name . . . ."

"My mouth is down here," he repeated wearily.

Mr Pinmay feared to venture the kiss lest Satan took an advantage. He longed to do something human before he had the sinking man carried down to receive the

Holy Communion, but he had forgotten how. "You have forgiven me, my poor fellow," he worried on. "If you do not, how can I continue my vocation, or hope for the forgiveness of God?"

The lips moved.

"If you forgive me, move your lips once more, as a sign."

He became rigid, he was dying.

"You do still love me?"

"My breast is down here."

"In Christ, I mean." And uncertain of what he ought to do he laid his head hesitatingly upon the poor skeleton. Vithobai shivered, then looked at him with surprise, pity, affection, disdain, with all, but with little of any, for his spirit had mainly departed, and only the ghosts of its activities remained. He was a little pleased. He raised a hand painfully, and stroked the scanty hair, golden no longer. He whispered, "Too late," but he smiled a little.

"It is never too late," said Mr Pinmay, permitting a slow encircling movement of the body, the last it would ever accomplish. "God's mercy is infinite, and endureth for ever and ever. He will give us other opportunities. We have erred in this life but it will not be so in the life to come."

The dying man seemed to find comfort at last. "The life to come," he whispered, but more distinctly. "I had forgotten it. You are sure it is coming?"

"Even your old false religion was sure of that."

"And we shall meet in it, you and I?" he asked, with a tender yet reverent caress.

"Assuredly, if we keep God's commandments."

"Shall we know one another again?"

"Yes, with all spiritual knowledge."

"And will there be love?"

"In the real and true sense, there will."

"Real and true love! Ah, that would be joyful." His voice gained strength, his eyes had an austere beauty as he embraced his friend, parted from him so long by the accidents of earth. Soon God would wipe away all tears. "The life to come," he shouted. "Life, life, eternal life. Wait for me in it." And he stabbed the missionary through the heart.

The jerk the knife gave brought his own fate hurrying upon him. He had scarcely the strength to push the body onto the asphalt or to spread the skein of blue flowers. But he survived for a moment longer, and it was the most exquisite he had ever known. For love was conquered at last and he was again a king, he had sent a messenger before him to announce his arrival in the life to come, as a great chief should. "I served you for ten years," he thought, "and your yoke was hard, but mine will be harder and you shall serve me now for ever and ever." He dragged himself up, he looked over the parapet. Below him were a horse and cart, beyond, the valley which he had once ruled, the site of the hut, the ruins of his old stockade, the schools, the hospital, the cemetery, the stacks of timber, the polluted stream, all that he had been used to regard as signs of his disgrace. But they signified nothing this morning, they were flying like mist, and beneath them, solid and eternal, stretched the kingdom of the dead. He rejoiced as in boyhood, he was expected there now. Mounting on the corpse, he climbed higher, raised his arms over his head, sunlit, naked, victorious, leaving all disease and humilitation behind him, and he swooped like a falcon from the parapet in pursuit of the terrified shade.[7]

7. Ghost.

Rebecca West
1892–1983

Rebecca West is increasingly appreciated as a writer of fiction, literary criticism, political commentary, and biography, as well as one of the most important journalists of the century. Born Cicely Fairfield in Ireland, she was educated in Edinburgh after her father died when she was ten years old. She became an actress in London, taking the stage name "Rebecca West" from a heroine she had played in Ibsen's drama *Rosmersholm*. By the time she was twenty, she was becoming active in left-wing journalism and in agitation for women's rights. In 1914, when she wrote *Indissoluble Matrimony*, she was involved in a love affair with the free-thinking but married novelist H. G. Wells, with whom she had a son; at the same time, she was working on a critical biography of Henry James. She went on to write searching and sometimes critical essays on male modernists like Joyce, Eliot, and Lawrence, and perceptive essays on Virginia Woolf and Katherine Mansfield. Throughout her life, she wrote both novels and political journalism, notably a major study of Balkan politics and culture, *Black Lamb and Grey Falcon* (1942), and a series of brilliant reports on the Nuremberg trials of Nazi war criminals at the end of World War II, collected as *A Train of Powder* (1955). She was made Dame Commander of the British Empire in 1959. Like her political writing, her fiction is notable for its irreverent probing of modernity's fault lines. Though never an orthodox feminist, West demonstrated a keen insight into the psychology of women and men, and portrayed the straitened thinking that made feminism's ultimate victory anything but a foregone conclusion.

Indissoluble Matrimony

When George Silverton opened the front door he found that the house was not empty for all its darkness. The spitting noise of the striking of damp matches and mild, growling exclamations of annoyance told him that his wife was trying to light the dining-room gas. He went in and with some short, hostile sound of greeting lit a match and brought brightness into the little room. Then, irritated by his own folly in bringing private papers into his wife's presence, he stuffed the letters he had brought from the office deep into the pockets of his overcoat. He looked at her suspiciously, but she had not seen them, being busy in unwinding her orange motor-veil. His eyes remained on her face to brood a little sourly on her moving loveliness, which he had not been sure of finding: for she was one of those women who create an illusion alternately of extreme beauty and extreme ugliness. Under her curious dress, designed in some pitifully cheap and worthless stuff by a successful mood of her indiscreet taste— she had black blood in her—her long body seemed pulsing with some exaltation. The blood was coursing violently under her luminous yellow skin, and her lids, dusky with fatigue, drooped contentedly over her great humid black eyes. Perpetually she raised her hand to the mass of black hair that was coiled on her thick golden neck, and stroked it with secretive enjoyment, as a cat licks its fur. And her large mouth smiled frankly, but abstractedly, at some digested pleasure.

There was a time when George would have looked on this riot of excited loveliness with suspicion. But now he knew it was almost certainly caused by some trifle— a long walk through stinging weather, the report of a Socialist victory at a by-election, or the intoxication of a waltz refrain floating from the municipal band-stand across the flats of the local recreation ground. And even if it had been caused by some amorous interlude he would not have greatly cared. In the ten years since their marriage he had lost the quality which would have made him resentful. He now believed that quality to be purely physical. Unless one was in good condition and responsive to the messages sent out by the flesh Evadne could hardly concern one. He turned the bitter thought over in his heart and stung himself by deliberately gazing unmoved upon her beautiful joyful body.

"Let's have supper now!" she said rather greedily.

He looked at the table and saw she had set it before she went out. As usual she had been in an improvident hurry: it was carelessly done. Besides, what an absurd supper to set before a hungry solicitor's clerk! In the centre, obviously intended as the principal dish, was a bowl of plums, softly red, soaked with the sun, glowing like jewels in the downward stream of the incandescent light. Besides them was a great yellow melon, its sleek sides fluted with rich growth, and a honey-comb glistening on a willow-pattern dish. The only sensible food to be seen was a plate of tongue laid at his place.

"I can't sit down to supper without washing my hands!"

While he splashed in the bathroom upstairs he heard her pull in a chair to the table and sit down to her supper. It annoyed him. There was no ritual about it. While he was eating the tongue she would be crushing honey on new bread, or stripping a plum of its purple skin and holding the golden globe up to the gas to see the light filter through. The meal would pass in silence. She would innocently take his dumbness for a sign of abstraction and forbear to babble. He would find the words choked on his lips by the weight of dullness that always oppressed him in her presence. Then, just about the time when he was beginning to feel able to formulate his obscure grievances against her, she would rise from the table without a word and run upstairs to her work, humming in that uncanny, negro way of hers.

And so it was. She ate with an appalling catholicity of taste, with a nice child's love of sweet foods, and occasionally she broke into that hoarse beautiful croon. Every now and then she looked at him with too obvious speculations as to whether his silence was due to weariness or uncertain temper. Timidly she cut him an enormous slice of the melon, which he did not want. Then she rose abruptly and flung herself into the rocking chair on the hearth. She clasped her hands behind her head and strained backwards so that the muslin stretched over her strong breasts. She sang softly to the ceiling.

There was something about the fantastic figure that made him feel as though they were not properly married.

"Evadne?"

"S?"

"What have you been up to this evening?"

"I was at Milly Stafordale's."

He was silent again. That name brought up the memory of his courting days. It was under the benign eyes of blonde, plebeian Milly that he had wooed the distracting creature in the rocking chair.

Ten years before, when he was twenty-five, his firm had been reduced to hysteria over the estates of an extraordinarily stupid old woman, named Mrs. Mary Ellerker. Her stupidity, grappling with the complexity of the sources of the vast income which rushed in spate from the properties of four deceased husbands, demanded oceans of explanations even over her weekly rents. Silverton alone in the office, by reason of a certain natural incapacity for excitement, could deal calmly with this marvel of imbecility. He alone could endure to sit with patience in the black-panelled drawing-room amidst the jungle of shiny mahogany furniture and talk to a mass of darkness, who rested heavily in the window-seat and now and then made an idiotic remark in a bright, hearty voice. But it shook even him. Mrs. Mary Ellerker was obscene. Yet she was perfectly sane and, although of that remarkable plainness noticeable in most oft-married women, in good enough physical condition. She merely presented the loathsome spectacle of an ignorant mind, contorted by the artificial idiocy of coquetry, lack of responsibility, and hatred of discipline, stripped naked by old age. That was the real horror of her. One feared to think how many women were really like Mrs. Ellerker under their armour of physical perfection or social grace. For this reason he turned eyes of hate on Mrs. Ellerker's pretty little companion, Milly Stafordale, who smiled at him over her embroidery with wintry northern brightness. When she was old she too would be obscene.

This horror obsessed him. Never before had he feared anything. He had never lived more than half-an-hour from a police station, and, as he had by some chance missed the melancholy clairvoyance of adolescence, he had never conceived of any horror with which the police could not deal. This disgust of women revealed to him that the world is a place of subtle perils. He began to fear marriage as he feared death. The thought of intimacy with some lovely, desirable and necessary wife turned him sick as he sat at his lunch. The secret obscenity of women! He talked darkly of it to his friends. He wondered why the Church did not provide a service for the absolution of men after marriage. Wife desertion seemed to him a beautiful return of the tainted body to cleanliness.

On his fifth visit to Mrs. Ellerker he could not begin his business at once. One of Milly Stafordale's friends had come in to sing to the old lady. She stood by the piano against the light, so that he saw her washed with darkness. Amazed, of tropical fruit. And before he had time to apprehend the sleepy wonder of her beauty, she had begun to sing. Now he knew that her voice was a purely physical attribute, built in her as she lay in her mother's womb, and no index of her spiritual values. But then, as it welled up from the thick golden throat and clung to her lips, it seemed a sublime achievement of the soul. It was smouldering contralto such as only those of black blood can possess. As she sang her great black eyes lay on him with the innocent shamelessness of a young animal, and he remembered hopefully that he was good looking. Suddenly she stood in silence, playing with her heavy black plait. Mrs. Ellerker broke into silly thanks. The girl's mother, who had been playing the accompaniment, rose and stood rolling up her music. Silverton, sick with excitement, was introduced to them. He noticed that the mother was a little darker than the conventions permit. Their name was Hannan—Mrs. Arthur Hannan and Evadne. They moved lithely and quietly out of the room, the girl's eyes still lingering on his face.

The thought of her splendour and the rolling echoes of her voice disturbed him all night. Next day, going to his office, he travelled with her on the horse-car that bound his suburb to Petrick. One of the horses fell lame, and she had time to tell him that she was studying at a commercial college. He quivered with distress. All the time he had a dizzy illusion that she was nestling up against him. They parted shyly. During the next few days they met constantly. He began to go and see them in the evening at their home—a mean flat crowded with cheap glories of bead curtains and Oriental hangings that set off the women's alien beauty. Mrs. Hannan was a widow and they lived alone, in a wonderful silence. He talked more than he had ever done in his whole life before. He took a dislike to the widow, she was consumed with fiery subterranean passions, no fit guardian for the tender girl.

Now he could imagine with what silent rapture Evadne had watched his agitation. Almost from the first she had meant to marry him. He was physically attractive, though not strong. His intellect was gently stimulating like a mild white wine. And it was time she married. She was ripe for adult things. This was the real wound in his soul. He had tasted of a divine thing created in his time for dreams out of her rich beauty, her loneliness, her romantic poverty, her immaculate youth. He had known love. And Evadne had never known anything more than a magnificent physical adventure which she had secured at the right time as she would have engaged a cab to take her to the station in time for the cheapest excursion train. It was a quick way to light-hearted living. With loathing he remembered how in the days of their engagement she used to gaze purely into his blinking eyes and with her unashamed kisses incite him to extravagant embraces. Now he cursed her for having obtained his spiritual revolution on false pretences. Only for a little time had he had his illusion, for their marriage was hastened by Mrs. Hannan's sudden death. After three months of savage mourning Evadne flung herself into marriage, and her excited candour had enlightened him very soon.

That marriage had lasted ten years. And to Evadne their relationship was just the same as ever. Her vitality needed him as it needed the fruit on the table before him. He shook with wrath and a sense of outraged decency.

"O George!" She was yawning widely.

"What's the matter?" he said without interest.

"It's so beastly dull."

"I can't help that, can I?"

"No." She smiled placidly at him. "We're a couple of dull dogs, aren't we? I wish we had children."

After a minute she suggested, apparently as an alternative amusement, "Perhaps the post hasn't passed."

As she spoke there was a rat-tat and the slither of a letter under the door. Evadne picked herself up and ran out into the lobby. After a second or two, during which she made irritating inarticulate exclamations, she came in reading the letter and stroking her bust with a gesture of satisfaction.

"They want me to speak at Longton's meeting on the nineteenth," she purred.

"Longton? What's he up to?"

Stephen Longton was the owner of the biggest iron works in Petrick, a man whose refusal to adopt the livery of busy oafishness thought proper to commercial men aroused the gravest suspicions.

"He's standing as Socialist candidate for the town council."

". . . Socialist!" he muttered.

He set his jaw. That was a side of Evadne he considered as little as possible. He had never been able to assimilate the fact that Evadne had, two years after their marriage, passed through his own orthodox Radicalism[1] to a passionate Socialism, and that after reading enormously of economics she had begun to write for the Socialist press and to speak successfully at meetings. In the jaundiced recesses of his mind he took it for granted that her work would have the lax fibre of her character: that it would be infected with her Oriental crudities. Although once or twice he had been congratulated on her brilliance, he mistrusted this phase of her activity as a caper of the sensualist. His eyes blazed on her and found the depraved, over-sexed creature, looking milder than a gazelle, holding out a hand-bill to him.

"They've taken it for granted!"

He saw her name—his name—

---

1. An extreme form of Liberalism, still comfortably within the continuum of British democratic politics; Socialism, which Evadne has embraced, advocates the abolition of the current system and is thus too extreme for George's bourgeois attitudes.

Mrs. Evadne Silverton.[2]

It was at first the blaze of stout scarlet letters on the dazzling white ground that made him blink. Then he was convulsed with rage.

"Georgie dear!"

She stepped forward and caught his weak body to her bosom. He wrenched himself away. Spiritual nausea made him determined to be a better man than her.

"A pair of you! You and Longton—!" he snarled scornfully. Then, seeing her startled face, he controlled himself.

"I thought it would please you," said Evadne, a little waspishly.

"You mustn't have anything to do with Longton," he stormed.

A change passed over her. She became ugly. Her face was heavy with intellect, her lips coarse with power. He was at arms with a Socialist lead. Much he would have preferred the bland sensualist again.

"Why?"

"Because—his lips stuck together like blotting-paper—he's not the sort of man my wife should—should—"

With movements which terrified him by their rough energy, she folded up the bills and put them back in the envelope.

"George. I suppose you mean that he's a bad man." He nodded.

"I know quite well that the girl who used to be his typist is his mistress." She spoke it sweetly, as if reasoning with an old fool. "But she's got consumption. She'll be dead in six months. In fact, I think it's rather nice of him. To look after her and all that."

"My God!" He leapt to his feet, extending a shaking forefinger. As she turned to him, the smile dying on her lips, his excited weakness wrapped him in a paramnesic illusion:[3] it seemed to him that he had been through all this before—a long, long time ago. "My God, you talk like a woman off the streets!"

Evadne's lips lifted over her strong teeth. With clever cruelty she fixed his eyes with hers, well knowing that he longed to fall forward and bury his head on the table in a transport of hysterical sobs. After a moment of this torture she turned away, herself distressed by a desire to cry.

"How can you say such dreadful, dreadful things!" she protested, chokingly.

He sat down again. His eyes looked little and red, but they blazed on her. "I wonder if you are," he said softly.

"Are what?" she asked petulantly, a tear rolling down her nose.

"You know," he answered, nodding.

"George, George, George!" she cried.

"You've always been keen on kissing and making love, haven't you, my precious? At first you startled me, you did! I didn't know women were like that." From that morass he suddenly stepped on to a high peak of terror. Amazed to find himself sincere, he cried—"I don't believe good women are!"

"Georgie, how can you be so silly!" exclaimed Evadne shrilly. "You know quite well I've been as true to you as any woman could be." She sought his eyes with a liquid glance of reproach. He averted his gaze, sickened at having put himself in the

---

2. Evadne would have been addressed in polite society as "Mrs. George Silverton"; George reads this breach of decorum as one more sign that his wife is out of control. Leopold Bloom, the protagonist of James Joyce's *Ulysses*, makes a similar observation when his wife Molly receives a letter from her lover addressed to "Mrs. Marion Bloom."
3. A condition in which fact and fiction become confused.

wrong. For even while he degraded his tongue his pure soul fainted with loathing of her fleshliness.

"I—I'm sorry."

Too wily to forgive him at once, she showed him a lowering profile with downcast lids. Of course, he knew it was a fraud: an imputation against her chastity was no more poignant than a reflection on the cleanliness of her nails—rude and spiteful, but that was all. But for a time they kept up the deception, while she cleared the table in a steely silence.

"Evadne, I'm sorry. I'm tired." His throat was dry. He could not bear the discord of a row added to the horror of their companionship. "Evadne, do forgive me—I don't know what I meant by—"

"That's all right, silly!" she said suddenly and bent over the table to kiss him. Her brow was smooth. It was evident from her splendid expression that she was preoccupied. Then she finished clearing up the dishes and took them into the kitchen. While she was out of the room he rose from his seat and sat down in the armchair by the fire, setting his bull-dog pipe alight. For a very short time he was free of her voluptuous presence. But she ran back soon, having put the kettle on and changed her blouse for a loose dressing-jacket, and sat down on the arm of his chair. Once or twice she bent and kissed his brow, but for the most part she lay back with his head drawn to her bosom, rocking herself rhythmically. Silverton, a little disgusted by their contact, sat quite motionless and passed into a doze. He revolved in his mind the incidents of his day's routine and remembered a snub from a superior. So he opened his eyes and tried to think of something else. It was then that he became conscious that the rhythm of Evadne's movement was not regular. It was broken as though she rocked in time to music. Music? His sense of hearing crept up to hear if there was any sound of music in the breaths she was emitting rather heavily every now and then. At first he could hear nothing. Then it struck him that each breath was a muttered phrase. He stiffened, and hatred flamed through his veins. The words came clearly through her lips. . . . "The present system of wage-slavery . . . ."

"Evadne!" He sprang to his feet. "You're preparing your speech!"

She did not move. "I am," she said.

"Damn it, you shan't speak!"

"Damn it, I will!"

"Evadne, you shan't speak! If you do I swear to God above I'll turn you out into the streets—." She rose and came towards him. She looked black and dangerous. She trod softly like a cat with her head down. In spite of himself, his tongue licked his lips in fear and he cowered a moment before he picked up a knife from the table. For a space she looked down on him and the sharp blade.

"You idiot, can't you hear the kettle's boiling over?"

He shrank back, letting the knife fall on the floor. For three minutes he stood there controlling his breath and trying to still his heart. Then he followed her into the kitchen. She was making a noise with a basinful of dishes.

"Stop that row."

She turned round with a dripping dish-cloth in her hand and pondered whether to throw it at him. But she was tired and wanted peace: so that she could finish the rough draft of her speech. So she stood waiting.

"Did you understand what I said then? If you don't promise me here and now—"

She flung her arms upwards with a cry and dashed past him. He made to run after her upstairs, but stumbled on the threshold of the lobby and sat with his ankle twisted under him, shaking with rage. In a second she ran downstairs again, clothed in a big cloak with black bundle clutched to her breast. For the first time in their married life she was seized with a convulsion of sobs. She dashed out of the front door and banged it with such passion that a glass pane shivered to fragments behind her.

"What's this? What's this?" he cried stupidly, standing up. He perceived with an insane certainty that she was going out to meet some unknown lover. "I'll come and tell him what a slut you are!" he shouted after her and stumbled to the door. It was jammed now and he had to drag at it.

The night was flooded with the yellow moonshine of midsummer: it seemed to drip from the lacquered leaves of the shrubs in the front garden. In its soft clarity he could see her plainly, although she was now two hundred yards away. She was hastening to the north end of Sumatra Crescent, an end that curled up the hill like a silly kitten's tail and stopped abruptly in green fields. So he knew that she was going to the young man who had just bought the Georgian Manor, whose elm-trees crowned the hill. Oh, how he hated her! Yet he must follow her, or else she would cover up her adulteries so that he could not take his legal revenge. So he began to run—silently, for he wore his carpet slippers. He was only a hundred yards behind her when she slipped through a gap in the hedge to tread a field-path. She still walked with pride, for though she was town-bred, night in the open seemed not at all fearful to her. As he shuffled in pursuit his carpet slippers were engulfed in a shining pool of mud: he raised one with a squelch, the other was left. This seemed the last humiliation. He kicked the other one off his feet and padded on in his socks, snuffling in anticipation of a cold. Then physical pain sent him back to the puddle to pluck out the slippers; it was a dirty job. His heart battered his breast as he saw that Evadne had gained the furthest hedge and was crossing the stile into the lane that ran up to the Manor gates.

"Go on, you beast!" he muttered, "Go on, go on!" After a scamper he climbed the stile and thrust his lean neck beyond a mass of wilted hawthorn bloom that crumbled into vagrant petals at his touch.

The lane mounted yellow as cheese to where the moon lay on his iron tracery of the Manor gates. Evadne was not there. Hardly believing his eyes he hobbled over into the lane and looked in the other direction. There he saw her disappearing round the bend of the road. Gathering himself up to a run, he tried to think out his bearings. He had seldom passed this way, and like most people without strong primitive instincts he had no sense of orientation. With difficulty he remembered that after a mile's mazy wanderings between high hedges this lane sloped suddenly to the bowl of heather overhung by the moorlands, in which lay the Petrick reservoirs, two untamed lakes.

"Eh! she's going to meet him by the water!" he cursed to himself. He remembered the withered ash tree, seared by lightning to its root, that stood by the road at the bare frontier of the moor. "May God strike her like that," he prayed," "as she fouls the other man's lips with her kisses. O God! let me strangle her. Or bury a knife deep in her breast." Suddenly he broke into a lolloping run. "O my Lord, I'll be able to divorce her. I'll be free. Free to live alone. To do my day's work and sleep my night's sleep without her. I'll get a job somewhere else and forget her. I'll bring her to the dogs. No clean man or woman in Petrick will look at her now. They won't have her to speak at that meeting now!" His throat swelled with joy, he leapt high in the air.

"I'll lie about her. If I can prove that she's wrong with this man they'll believe me if I say she's a bad woman and drinks. I'll make her name a joke. And then—"

He flung wide his arms in ecstasy: the left struck against stone. More pain than he had thought his body could hold convulsed him, so that he sank on the ground hugging his aching arm. He looked backwards as he writhed and saw that the hedge had stopped; above him was the great stone wall of the county asylum. The question broke on him—was there any lunatic in its confines so slavered with madness as he himself? Nothing but madness could have accounted for the torrent of ugly words, the sea of uglier thoughts that was now a part of him. "O God, me to turn like this!" he cried, rolling over full-length on the grassy bank by the roadside. That the infidelity of his wife, a thing that should have brought out the stern manliness of his true nature, should have discovered him as lecherous-lipped as any pot-house[4] lounger, was the most infamous accident of his married life. The sense of sin descended on him so that his tears flowed hot and bitterly. "Have I gone to the Unitarian chapel every Sunday morning and to the Ethical Society every evening for nothing?" his spirit asked itself in its travail. "All those Browning lectures for nothing . . . ."[5] He said the Lord's Prayer several times and lay for a minute quietly crying. The relaxation of his muscles brought him a sense of rest which seemed forgiveness falling from God. The tears dried on his cheeks. His calmer consciousness heard the sound of rushing waters mingled with the beating of blood in his ears. He got up and scrambled round the turn of the road that brought him to the withered ash-tree.

He walked forward on the parched heatherland to the mound whose scarred sides, heaped with boulders, tufted with mountain grasses, shone before him in the moonlight. He scrambled up to it hurriedly and hoisted himself from ledge to ledge till he fell on his knees with a squeal of pain. His ankle was caught in a crevice of the rock. Gulping down his agony at this final physical humiliation he heaved himself upright and raced on to the summit, and found himself before the Devil's Cauldron, filled to the brim with yellow moonshine and the fiery play of summer lightning. The rugged crags opposite him were a low barricade against the stars to which the mound where he stood shot forward like a bridge. To the left of this the long Lisbech pond lay like a trailing serpent; its silver scales glittered as the wind swept down from the vaster moorlands to the east. To the right under a steep drop of twenty feet was the Whimsey pond, more sinister, shaped in an unnatural oval, sheltered from the wind by the high ridge so that the undisturbed moonlight lay across it like a sharp-edged sword.

He looked about for some sign of Evadne. She could not be on the land by the margin of the lakes, for the light blazed so strongly that each reed could be clearly seen like a black dagger stabbing the silver. He looked down Lisbech and saw far east a knot of red and green and orange lights. Perhaps for some devilish purpose Evadne had sought Lisbech railway station. But his volcanic mind had preserved one grain of sense that assured him that, subtle as Evadne's villainy might be, it would not lead her to walk five miles out of her way to a terminus which she could have reached in fifteen minutes by taking a train from the station down the road. She must be under cover somewhere here. He went down the gentle slope that fell from the top of the ridge to Lisbech pond in a disorder of rough heather, unhappy patches of cultivated grass, and coppices of silver birch, fringed with flaming broom that seemed faintly tarnished in the moonlight. At the bottom was a roughly hewn path which he followed in hot aimless hurry. In a little he approached a riot of falling waters. There was a slice ten feet broad carved out of the ridge, and to this narrow channel of black

---

4. Tavern.
5. George's activities—Unitarian church, Ethical Society, Browning Society—suggest that he participated in public exercises of a high moral nature without giving himself over to traditional religious faith, which he would have seen as "irrational" and "unmanly."

shining rock the floods of Lisbech leapt some feet and raced through to Whimsey. The noise beat him back. The gap was spanned by a gaunt thing of paint-blistered iron, on which he stood dizzily and noticed how the wide step that ran on each side of the channel through to the other pond was smeared with sinister green slime. Now his physical distress reminded him of Evadne, whom he had almost forgotten in contemplation of these lonely waters. The idea of her had been present but obscured, as sometimes toothache may cease active torture. His blood lust set him on and he staggered forward with covered ears. Even as he went something caught his eye in a thicket high up on the slope near the crags. Against the slender pride of some silver birches stood a gnarled hawthorn tree, its branches flattened under the stern moorland winds so that it grew squat like an opened umbrella. In its dark shadows, faintly illumined by a few boughs of withered blossom, there moved a strange bluish light. Even while he did not know what it was it made his flesh stir.

The light emerged. It was the moonlight reflected from Evadne's body. She was clad in a black bathing dress, and her arms and legs and the broad streak of flesh laid bare by a rent down the back shone brilliantly white, so that she seemed like a grotesquely patterned wild animal as she ran down to the lake. Whirling her arms above her head she trampled down into the water and struck out strongly. Her movements were full of brisk delight and she swam quickly. The moonlight made her the centre of a little feathery blur of black and silver, with a comet's tail trailing in her wake.

Nothing in all his married life had ever staggered Silverton so much as this. He had imagined his wife's adultery so strongly that it had come to be. It was now as real as their marriage; more real than their courtship. So this seemed to be the last crime of the adulteress. She had dragged him over those squelching fields and these rough moors and changed him from a man of irritations, but no passions, into a cold designer of murderous treacheries, so that he might witness a swimming exhibition! For a minute he was stunned. Then he sprang down to the rushy edge and ran along in the direction of her course, crying—"Evadne! Evadne!" She did not hear him. At last he achieved a chest note and shouted—"Evadne! come here!" The black and silver feather shivered in mid-water. She turned immediately and swam back to shore. He suspected sullenness in her slowness, but was glad of it, for after the shock of this extraordinary incident he wanted to go to sleep. Drowsiness lay on him like lead. He shook himself like a dog and wrenched off his linen collar, winking at the bright moon to keep himself awake. As she came quite near he was exasperated by the happy, snorting breaths she drew, and strolled a pace or two up the bank. To his enragement the face she lifted as she waded to dry land was placid, and she scrambled gaily up the bank to his side.

"O George, why did you come!" she exclaimed quite affectionately, laying a damp hand on his shoulder.

"O damn it, what does this mean!" he cried, committing a horrid tenor squeak. "What are you doing?"

"Why. George," she said," "I came here for a bathe."

He stared into her face and could make nothing of it. It was only sweet surfaces of flesh, soft radiances of eye and lip, a lovely lie of comeliness. He forgot this present grievance in a cold search for the source of her peculiar hatefulness. Under this sick gaze she pouted and turned away with a peevish gesture. He made no sign and stood silent, watching her saunter to that gaunt iron bridge. The roar of the little waterfall did not disturb her splendid nerves and she drooped sensuously over the hand-rail, sniffing up the sweet night smell; too evidently trying to abase him to another apology.

A mosquito whirred into his face. He killed it viciously and strode off towards his wife, who showed by a common little toss of the head that she was conscious of his coming.

"Look here, Evadne!" he panted. "What did you come here for? Tell me the truth and I promise I'll not—I'll not—"

"Not WHAT, George?"

"O please, please tell me the truth, do Evadne!" he cried pitifully.

"But, dear, what is there to carry on about so? You went on so queerly about my meeting that my head felt fit to split, and I thought the long walk and the dip would do me good." She broke off, amazed at the wave of horror that passed over his face.

His heart sank. From the loose-lipped hurry in the telling of her story, from the bigness of her eyes and the lack of subtlety in her voice, he knew that this was the truth. Here was no adulteress whom he could accuse in the law courts and condemn into the street, no resourceful sinner whose merry crimes he could discover. Here was merely his good wife, the faithful attendant of his hearth, relentless wrecker of his soul.

She came towards him as a cat approaches a displeased master, and hovered about him on the stone coping of the noisy sluice.

"Indeed!" he found himself saying sarcastically. "Indeed!"

"Yes, George Silverton, indeed!" she burst out, a little frightened. "And why shouldn't I? I used to come here often enough on summer nights with poor Mamma—"

"Yes!" he shouted. It was exactly the sort of thing that would appeal to that weird half-black woman from the back of beyond. "Mamma!" he cried tauntingly, "Mamma!"

There was a flash of silence between them before Evadne, clutching her breast and balancing herself dangerously on her heels on the stone coping, broke into gentle shrieks. "You dare talk of my Mamma, my poor Mamma, and she cold in her grave! I haven't been happy since she died and I married you, you silly little misery, you!" Then the rage was suddenly wiped off her brain by the perception of a crisis.

The trickle of silence overflowed into a lake, over which their spirits flew, looking at each other's reflection in the calm waters: in the hurry of their flight they had never before seen each other. They stood facing one another with dropped heads, quietly thinking.

The strong passion which filled them threatened to disintegrate their souls as a magnetic current decomposes the electrolyte, so they fought to organise their sensations. They tried to arrange themselves and their lives for comprehension, but beyond sudden lyric visions of old incidents of hatefulness—such as a smarting quarrel of six years ago as to whether Evadne had or had not cheated the railway company out of one and eightpence on an excursion ticket—the past was intangible. It trailed behind this intense event as the pale hair trails behind the burning comet. They were pre-occupied with the moment. Quite often George had found a mean pleasure in the thought that by never giving Evadne a child he had cheated her out of one form of experience, and now he paid the price for this unnatural pride of sterility. For now the spiritual offspring of their intercourse came to birth. A sublime loathing was between them. For a little time it was a huge perilous horror, but afterwards, like men aboard a ship whose masts seek the sky through steep waves, they found a drunken pride in the adventure. This was the very absolute of hatred. It cheapened the memory of the fantasias of irritation and ill-will they had performed in the less boring moments of their marriage, and they felt dazed, as amateurs who had found themselves creating a masterpiece. For the first time they were possessed by a supreme emotion and they felt a glad desire to strip away restraint and express it nakedly. It was ecstasy; they felt tall and full of blood.

Like people who, bewitched by Christ, see the whole earth as the breathing body of God, so they saw the universe as the substance and the symbol of their hatred. The stars trembled overhead with wrath. A wind from behind the angry crags set the moonlight on Lisbech quivering with rage, and the squat hawthorn-tree creaked slowly like the irritation of a dull little man. The dry moors, parched with harsh anger, waited thirstily and, sending out the murmur of rustling mountain grass and the cry of wakening fowl, seemed to huddle closer to the lake. But this sense of the earth's sympathy slipped away from them and they loathed all matter as the dull wrapping of their flame-like passion. At their wishing matter fell away and they saw sarcastic visions. He saw her as a toad squatting on the clean earth, obscuring the stars and pressing down its hot moist body on the cheerful fields. She felt his long boneless body coiled round the roots of the lovely tree of life. They shivered fastidiously. With an uplifting sense of responsibility they realised that they must kill each other.

A bird rose over their heads with a leaping flight that made it seem as though its black body was bouncing against the bright sky. The foolish noise and motion precipitated their thoughts. They were broken into a new conception of life. They perceived that God is war and his creatures are meant to fight. When dogs walk through the world cats must climb trees. The virgin must snare the wanton, the fine lover must put the prude to the sword. The gross man of action walks, spurred on the bloodless bodies of the men of thought, who lie quiet and cunningly do not tell him where his grossness leads him. The flesh must smother the spirit, the spirit must set the flesh on fire and watch it burn. And those who were gentle by nature and shrank from the ordained brutality were betrayers of their kind, surrendering the earth to the seed of their enemies. In this war there is no discharge. If they succumbed to peace now, the rest of their lives would be dishonourable, like the exile of a rebel who has begged his life as the reward of cowardice. It was their first experience of religious passion, and they abandoned themselves to it so that their immediate personal qualities fell away from them. Neither his weakness nor her prudence stood in the way of the event.

They measured each other with the eye. To her he was a spidery thing against the velvet blackness and hard silver surfaces of the pond. The light soaked her bathing dress so that she seemed, against the jagged shadows of the rock cutting, as though she were clad in a garment of dark polished mail. Her knees were bent so clearly, her toes gripped the coping so strongly. He understood very clearly that if he did not kill her instantly she would drop him easily into the deep riot of waters. Yet for a space he could not move, but stood expecting a degrading death. Indeed, he gave her time to kill him. But she was without power too, and struggled weakly with a hallucination. The quarrel in Sumatra Crescent with its suggestion of vast and unmentionable antagonisms; her swift race through the moon-drenched countryside, all crepitant with night noises: the swimming in the wine-like lake: their isolation on the moor, which was expressedly hostile to them, as nature always is to lonely man: and this stark contest face to face, with their resentments heaped between them like a pile of naked swords—these things were so strange that her civilised self shrank back appalled. There entered into her the primitive woman who is the curse of all women: a creature of the most utter femaleness, useless, save for childbirth, with no strong brain to make her physical weakness a light accident, abjectly and corruptingly afraid of man. A squaw, she dared not strike her lord.

The illusion passed like a moment of faintness and left her enraged at having forgotten her superiority even for an instant. In the material world she had a thousand times been defeated into making prudent reservations and practising unnatural docilities. But in the world of thought she had maintained unfalteringly her masterfulness in spite of the strong yearning of her temperament towards voluptuous surrenders. That was her virtue. Its violation whipped her to action and she would have killed him at once, had not his moment come a second before hers. Sweating horribly, he had dropped his head forward on his chest: his eyes fell on her feet and marked the plebeian moulding of her ankle, which rose thickly over a crease of flesh from the heel to the calf. The woman was coarse in grain and pattern.

He had no instinct for honourable attack, so he found himself striking her in the stomach. She reeled from pain, not because his strength overcame hers. For the first time her eyes looked into his candidly open, unveiled by languor or lust: their hard brightness told him how she despised him for that unwarlike blow. He cried out as he realised that this was another of her despicable victories and that the whole burden of the crime now lay on him, for he had begun it. But the rage was stopped on his lips as her arms, flung wildly out as she fell backwards, caught him about the waist with abominable justness of eye and evil intention. So they fell body to body into the quarrelling waters.

The feathery confusion had looked so soft, yet it seemed the solid rock they struck. The breath shot out of him and suffocation warmly stuffed his ears and nose. Then the rock cleft and he was swallowed by a brawling blackness in which whirled a vortex that flung him again and again on a sharp thing that burned his shoulder. All about him fought the waters, and they cut his flesh like knives. His pain was past belief. Though God might be war, he desired peace in his time, and he yearned for another God—a child's God, an immense arm coming down from the hills and lifting him to a kindly bosom. Soon his body would burst for breath, his agony would smash in his breast bone. So great was his pain that his consciousness was strained to apprehend it, as a too tightly stretched canvas splits and rips.

Suddenly the air was sweet on his mouth. The starlight seemed as hearty as a cheer. The world was still there, the world in which he had lived, so he must be safe. His own weakness and loveableness induced enjoyable tears, and there was a delicious moment of abandonment to comfortable whining before he realised that the water would not kindly buoy him up for long, and that even now a hostile current clasped his waist. He braced his flaccid body against the sucking blackness and flung his head back so that the water should not bubble so hungrily against the cords of his throat. Above him the slime of the rock was sticky with moonbeams, and the leprous light brought to his mind a newspaper paragraph, read years ago, which told him that the dawn had discovered floating in some oily Mersey dock, under walls as infected with wet growth as this, a corpse whose blood-encrusted finger-tips were deeply cleft. On the instant his own finger-tips seemed hot with blood and deeply cleft from clawing at the impregnable rock. He screamed gaspingly and beat his hands through the strangling flood. Action, which he had always loathed and dreaded, had broken the hard mould of his self-possession, and the dry dust of his character was blown hither and thither by fear. But one sharp fragment of intelligence which survived this detrition of his personality perceived that a certain gleam on the rock about a foot above the water was not the cold putrescence of the slime, but certainly the hard and merry light of a moon-ray striking on solid metal. His left hand clutched upwards at it, and he swung from a rounded projection. It was, his touch told him, a leaden ring hanging obliquely from the rock, to which his memory could visualise precisely in some past drier time when Lisbech sent no flood to Whimsey, a waterman mooring a boat strewn with pale-bellied perch. And behind the stooping waterman he remembered a flight of narrow steps that led up a buttress to a stone shelf that ran through the cutting. Unquestionably he was safe. He swung in a happy rhythm from the ring, his limp body trailing like a caterpillar through the stream to the foot of the steps, while he gasped in strength. A part of him was in agony, for his arm was nearly dragged out of its socket and a part of him was embarrassed because his hysteria shook him with a deep rumbling chuckle that sounded as though he meditated on some unseemly joke; the whole was pervaded by a twilight atmosphere of unenthusiastic gratitude for his rescue, like the quietly cheerful tone of a Sunday evening sacred concert. After a minute's deep breathing he hauled himself up by the other hand and prepared to swing himself on to the steps.

But first, to shake off the wet worsted rags, once his socks, that now stuck uncomfortably between his toes, he splashed his feet outwards to midstream. A certain porpoise-like surface met his left foot. Fear dappled his face with goose flesh. Without turning his head he knew what it was. It was Evadne's fat flesh rising on each side of her deep-furrowed spine through the rent in her bathing dress.

Once more hatred marched through his soul like a king: compelling service by his godhead and, like all gods, a little hated for his harsh lieu[6] on his worshipper. He saw his wife as the curtain of flesh between him and celibacy, and solitude and all those delicate abstentions from life which his soul desired. He saw her as the invisible worm destroying the rose of the world with her dark secret love.[7] Now he knelt on the lowest stone step watching her wet seal-smooth head bobbing nearer on the waters. As her strong arms, covered with little dark points where her thick hairs were clotted with moisture, stretched out towards safety he bent forward and laid his hands on her head. He held her face under water. Scornfully he noticed the bubbles that rose to the surface from her protesting mouth and nostrils, and the foam raised by her arms and her thick ankles. To the end the creature persisted in turmoil, in movement, in action. . . .

She dropped like a stone. His hands, with nothing to resist them, slapped the water foolishly and he nearly overbalanced forward into the stream. He rose to his feet very stiffly. "I must be a very strong man," he said, as he slowly climbed the steps. "I must be a very strong man," he repeated, a little louder, as with a hot and painful rigidity of the joints he stretched himself out at full length along the stone shelf. Weakness closed him in like a lead coffin. For a little time the wetness of his clothes persisted in being felt: then the sensation oozed out of him and his body fell out of knowledge. There was neither pain nor joy nor any other reckless ploughing of the brain by nerves. He knew unconsciousness, or rather the fullest consciousness he had ever known. For the world became nothingness, and nothingness which is free from the yeasty nuisance of matter and the ugliness of generation was the law of his being. He was absorbed into vacuity, the untamed substance of the universe, round which he conceived passion and thought to circle as straws caught up by the wind. He saw God and lived.

In Heaven a thousand years are a day. And this little corner of time in which he found happiness shrank to a nut-shell as he opened his eyes again. This peace was hardly printed on his heart, yet the brightness of the night was blurred by the dawn. With the grunting carefulness of a man drunk with fatigue, he crawled along the stone shelf to the iron bridge, where he stood with his back to the roaring sluice and rested. All things seemed different now and happier. Like most timid people he disliked the night, and the commonplace hand which the dawn laid on the scene

---

6. Discipline.
7. A reference to William Blake's poem *The Sick Rose*, in which a worm has entered a rose's "bed / of crimson joy; / And his dark secret love / Does thy life destroy."

seemed to him a sanctification. The dimmed moon sank to her setting behind the crags. The jewel lights of Lisbech railway station were weak, cheerful twinklings. A steaming bluish milk of morning mist had been spilt on the hard silver surface of the lake, and the reeds no longer stabbed it like little daggers, but seemed a feathery fringe, like the pampas grass in the front garden in Sumatra Crescent. The black crags became brownish, and the mist disguised the sternness of the moor. This weakening of effects was exactly what he had always thought the extinction of Evadne would bring the world. He smiled happily at the moon.

Yet he was moved to sudden angry speech. "If I had my time over again," he said, "I wouldn't touch her with the tongs." For the cold he had known all along he would catch had settled in his head, and his handkerchief was wet through.

He leaned over the bridge and looked along Lisbech and thought of Evadne. For the first time for many years he saw her image without spirits, and wondered without indignation why she had so often looked like the cat about to steal the cream. What was the cream? And did she ever steal it? Now he would never know. He thought of her very generously and sighed over the perversity of fate in letting so much comeliness.

"If she had married a butcher or a veterinary surgeon she might have been happy," he said, and shook his head at the glassy black water that slid under the bridge to that boiling sluice.

A gust of ague[8] reminded him that wet clothes clung to his fevered body and that he ought to change as quickly as possible, or expect to be laid up for weeks. He turned along the path that led back across the moor to the withered ash tree, and was learning the torture of bare feet on gravel when he cried out to himself: "I shall be hanged for killing my wife." It did not come as a trumpet-call, for he was one of those people who never quite hear what is said to them, and this deafishness extended in him to emotional things. It stole on him clamly, like a fog closing on a city. When he first felt hemmed in by this certainty he looked over his shoulder to the crags, remembering tales of how Jacobite fugitives had hidden on the moors for many weeks. There lay at least another day of freedom. But he was the kind of man who always goes home. He stumbled on, not very unhappy, except for his feet. Like many people of weak temperament he did not fear death. Indeed, it had a peculiar appeal to him; for while it was important, exciting, it did not, like most important and exciting things try to create action. He allowed his imagination the vanity of painting pictures. He saw himself standing in their bedroom, plotting this last event, with the white sheet and the high lights of the mahogany wardrobe shining ghostly at him through the darkness. He saw himself raising a thin hand to the gas bracket and turning on the tap. He saw himself staggering to their bed while death crept in at his nostrils. He saw his corpse lying in full daylight, and for the first time knew himself certainly, unquestionably dignified.

He threw back his chest in pride: but at that moment the path stopped and he found himself staggering down the mound of heatherland and boulders with bleeding feet. Always he had suffered from sore feet, which had not exactly disgusted but, worse still, disappointed Evadne. A certain wistfulness she had always evinced when she found herself the superior animal had enraged and humiliated him many times. He felt that sting him now, and flung himself down the mound cursing. When he stumbled up to the withered ash tree he hated her so much that it seemed as though she were alive again, and a sharp wind blowing down from the moor terrified him like her touch.

8. Fever.

He rested there. Leaning against the stripped grey trunk, he smiled up at the sky, which was now so touched to ineffectiveness by the dawn that it looked like a tent of faded silk. There was the peace of weakness in him, which he took to be spiritual, because it had no apparent physical justification: but he lost it as his dripping clothes chilled his tired flesh. His discomfort reminded him that the phantasmic night was passing from him. Daylight threatened him: the daylight in which for so many years he had worked in the solicitor's office and been snubbed and ignored. "'The garish day,'" he murmured disgustedly, quoting the blasphemy of some hymn writer. He wanted his death to happen in this phantasmic night.

So he limped his way along the road. The birds had not yet begun to sing, but the rustling noises of the night had ceased. The silent highway was consecrated to his proud progress. He staggered happily like a tired child returning from a lovely birthday walk: his death in the little bedroom, which for the first time he would have to himself, was a culminating treat to be gloated over like the promise of a favourite pudding for supper. As he walked he brooded dozingly on large and swelling thoughts. Like all people of weak passions and enterprise he loved to think of Napoleon, and in the shadow of the great asylum wall he strutted a few steps of his advance from murder to suicide, with arms crossed on his breast and thin legs trying to strut massively. He was so happy. He wished that a military band went before him, and pretended that the high hedges were solemn lines of men, stricken in awe to silence as their king rode out to some nobly self-chosen doom. Vast he seemed to himself, and magnificent like music, and solemn like the Sphinx. He had saved the earth from corruption by killing Evadne, for whom he now felt the unremorseful pity a conqueror might bestow on a devastated empire. He might have grieved that his victory brought him death, but with immense pride he found that the occasion was exactly described by a text. "He saved others, Himself He could not save."[9] He had missed the stile in the field above Sumatra Crescent and had to go back and hunt for it in the hedge. So quickly had his satisfaction borne him home.

The field had the fantastic air that jerry-builders[1] give to land poised on the knife-edge of town and country, so that he walked in romance to his very door. The unmarred grass sloped to a stone-hedge of towers of loose brick, trenches and mounds of shining clay, and the fine intentful spires of the scaffolding round the last unfin-ished house. And he looked down on Petrick. Though to the actual eye it was but a confusion of dark distances through the twilight, a breaking of velvety perspectives, he saw more intensely than ever before its squalid walls and squalid homes where mean men and mean women enlaced their unwholesome lives. Yet he did not shrink from entering for his great experience: as Christ did not shrink from being born in a stable. He swaggered with humility over the trodden mud of the field and the new white flags of Sumatra Crescent. Down the road before him there passed a dim figure, who paused at each lamp post and raised a long wand to behead the yellow gas-flow-ers that were now wilting before the dawn: a ghostly herald preparing the world to be his deathbed. The Crescent curved in quiet darkness, save for one house, where blazed a gas-lit room with undrawn blinds. The brightness had the startling quality of a scream. He looked in almost anxiously as he passed, and met the blank eyes of a man in evening clothes who stood by the window shaking a medicine. His face was like a wax mask softened by heat: the features were blurred with the suffering which comes from the spectacle of suffering. His eyes lay unshiftingly on George's face as he went by and he went on shaking the bottle. It seemed as though he would never stop.

9. These are the words of the priests and elders mocking   1. Low-wage, slipshod workers.
Jesus at his crucifixion; Matthew 27.42.

In the hour of his grandeur George was not forgetful of the griefs of the little human people, but interceded with God for the sake of this stranger. Everything was beautiful, beautiful, beautiful.

His own little house looked solemn as a temple. He leaned against the lamppost at the gate and stared at its empty windows and neat bricks. The disorder of the shattered pane of glass could be overlooked by considering a sign that this house was a holy place: like the Passover blood on the lintel. The propriety of the evenly drawn blind pleased him enormously. He had always known that this was how the great tragic things of the world had accomplished themselves: quietly. Evadne's raging activity belonged to trivial or annoying things like spring-cleaning or thunderstorms. Well, the house belonged to him now. He opened the gate and went up the asphalt path, sourly noticing that Evadne had as usual left out the lawn-mower, though it might very easily have rained, with the wind coming up as it was. A stray cat that had been sleeping in the tuft of pampas grass in the middle of the lawn was roused by his coming, and fled insolently close to his legs. He hated all wild homeless things, and bent for a stone to throw at it. But instead his fingers touched a slug, which reminded him of the feeling of Evadne's flesh through the slit in her bathing dress. And suddenly the garden was possessed by her presence: she seemed to amble there as she had so often done, sowing seeds unwisely and tormenting the last days of an ailing geranium by insane transplantation, exclaiming absurdly over such mere weeds as morning glory. He caught the very clucking of her voice. . . . The front door opened at his touch.

The little lobby with its closed doors seemed stuffed with expectant silence. He realised that he had come to the theatre of his great adventure. Then panic seized him. Because this was the home where he and she had lived together so horribly he doubted whether he could do this splendid momentous thing, for here he had always been a poor thing with the habit of failure. His heart beat in him more quickly than his raw feet could pad up the oil-clothed stairs. Behind the deal door at the end of the passage was death. Nothingness! It would escape him, even the idea of it would escape him if he did not go to it at once. When he burst at last into its presence he felt so victorious that he sank back against the door waiting for death to come to him without turning on the gas. He was so happy. His death was coming true.

But Evadne lay on his deathbed. She slept there soundly, with her head flung back on the pillows so that her eyes and brow seemed small in shadow, and her mouth and jaw huge above her thick throat in the light. Her wet hair straggled across the pillow on to a broken cane chair covered with her tumbled clothes. Her breast, silvered with sweat, shone in the ray of the street lamp that had always disturbed their nights. The counterpane rose enormously over her hips in rolls of glazed linen. Out of mere innocent sleep her sensuality was distilling a most drunken pleasure.

Not for one moment did he think this a phantasmic appearance. Evadne was not the sort of woman to have a ghost.

Still leaning against the door, he tried to think it all out: but his thoughts came brokenly, because the dawnlight flowing in at the window confused him by its pale glare and that lax figure on the bed held his attention. It must have been that when he laid his murderous hands on her head she had simply dropped below the surface and swum a few strokes under water as any expert swimmer can. Probably he had never even put her into danger, for she was a great lusty creature and the weir was a little place. He had imagined the wonder and peril of the battle as he had imagined his victory. He sneezed exhaustingly, and from his physical distress realised how absurd it was ever to have thought that he had killed her. Bodies like his do not kill bodies like hers.

Now his soul was naked and lonely as though the walls of his body had fallen in at death, and the grossness of Evadne's sleep made him suffer more unlovely a destitution than any old beggarwoman squatting by the roadside in the rain. He had thought he had had what every man most desires: one night of power over a woman for the business of murder or love. But it had been a lie. Nothing beautiful had ever happened to him. He would have wept, but the hatred he had learnt on the moors obstructed all tears in his throat. At least this night had given him passion enough to put an end to it all.

Quietly he went to the window and drew down the sash. There was no fireplace, so that sealed the room. Then he crept over to the gas bracket and raised his thin hand, as he had imagined in his hour of vain glory by the lake.

He had forgotten Evadne's thrifty habit of turning off the gas at the main to prevent leakage when she went to bed.

He was beaten. He undressed and got into bed: as he had done every night for ten years, and as he would do every night until he died. Still sleeping, Evadne caressed him with warm arms.

+—➤⊞◈➤—+

Katherine Mansfield
1888–1923

Katherine Mansfield was one of the twentieth century's most gifted writers of short fiction. As Elizabeth Bowen has written, Mansfield realized that "the short story . . . is not intended to be the medium either for exploration or long-term development of character. Character cannot be more than *shown*. . . ." Mansfield thus turned the short story away from contrived plot conventions, and toward the illumination of small events as they reveal the fabric of a life, making of short fiction an almost dramatic form.

Mansfield was born in Wellington, New Zealand. She moved to England more or less permanently before her twentieth birthday, but many of her most successful stories return to her childhood and her homeland for their subject. The path to this mature fiction was complicated, however; when she arrived in London in 1908, Mansfield was pregnant. She quickly married and the same day left her husband, who was not the child's father; she went to a German spa, where she miscarried. This tumultuous background is reflected in the bitter stories of her first volume, *In a German Pension*. In 1911 Mansfield met John Middleton Murray, editor and man of letters, with whom she remained until the end of her life.

Paradoxically, the horrors of World War I (in which her brother Leslie was killed) had an uplifting effect on Mansfield's writing. The result of the war, she wrote, is that "Now we know ourselves for what we are. In a way its a tragic knowledge. Its as though, even while we live again we face death. But *through Life*: thats the point. We see death in life as we see death in a flower that is fresh unfolded. Our hymn is to the flower's beauty—we would make that beauty immortal because we *know*."

One important element of Mansfield's "tragic knowledge" was the awareness that she was dying; she suffered her first tubercular hemorrhage in 1918, and never regained her health. She remained dedicated to her art until the very end, however, producing nineteen major stories during the last nineteen months of her life; Virginia Woolf, who admired and even envied Mansfield's talent, wrote that "No one felt more seriously the importance of writing than she did." The story included here, *The Daughters of the Late Colonel*, diagnoses with both tenderness and horror the spiritual death that Mansfield saw around her. It invokes a theme that has been important in twentieth-century literature from Henry James's *The Beast in the Jungle* to Samuel Beckett's *Waiting for Godot*, and beyond: that, as John Lennon put it, "Life is what happens to you / While you're busy making other plans."

The Daughters of the Late Colonel

1

The week after was one of the busiest weeks of their lives. Even when they went to bed it was only their bodies that lay down and rested; their minds went on, thinking things out, talking things over, wondering, deciding, trying to remember where . . .

Constantia lay like a statue, her hands by her sides, her feet just overlapping each other, the sheet up to her chin. She stared at the ceiling.

"Do you think father would mind if we gave his top-hat to the porter?"

"The porter?" snapped Josephine. "Why ever the porter? What a very extraordinary idea!"

"Because," said Constantia slowly, "he must often have to go to funerals. And I noticed at—at the cemetery that he only had a bowler." She paused. "I thought then how very much he'd appreciate a top-hat. We ought to give him a present, too. He was always very nice to father."

"But," cried Josephine, flouncing on her pillow and staring across the dark at Constantia, "father's head!" And suddenly, for one awful moment, she nearly giggled. Not, of course, that she felt in the least like giggling. It must have been habit. Years ago, when they had stayed awake at night talking, their beds had simply heaved. And now the porter's head, disappearing, popped out, like a candle, under father's hat. . . . The giggle mounted, mounted; she clenched her hands; she fought it down; she frowned fiercely at the dark and said "Remember" terribly sternly.

"We can decide to-morrow," she sighed.

Constantia had noticed nothing; she sighed.

"Do you think we ought to have our dressing-gowns dyed as well?"

"Black?" almost shrieked Josephine.

"Well, what else?" said Constantia. "I was thinking—it doesn't seem quite sincere, in a way, to wear black out of doors and when we're fully dressed, and then when we're at home—"

"But nobody sees us," said Josephine. She gave the bedclothes such a twitch that both her feet became uncovered, and she had to creep up the pillows to get them well under again.

"Kate does," said Constantia. "And the postman very well might."

Josephine thought of her dark-red slippers, which matched her dressing-gown, and of Constantia's favourite indefinite green ones which went with hers. Black! Two black dressing-gowns and two pairs of black woolly slippers, creeping off to the bathroom like black cats.

"I don't think it's absolutely necessary," said she.

Silence. Then Constantia said, "We shall have to post the papers with the notice in them to-morrow to catch the Ceylon mail. . . . How many letters have we had up till now?"

"Twenty-three."

Josephine had replied to them all, and twenty-three times when she came to "We miss our dear father so much" she had broken down and had to use her handkerchief, and on some of them even to soak up a very light-blue tear with an edge of blotting-paper. Strange! She couldn't have put it on—but twenty-three times. Even now, though, when she said over to herself sadly. "We miss our dear father so much" she could have cried if she'd wanted to.

"Have you got enough stamps?" came from Constantia.

"Oh, how can I tell?" said Josephine crossly. "What's the good of asking me that now?"

"I was just wondering," said Constantia mildly.

Silence again. There came a little rustle, a scurry, a hop.

"A mouse," said Constantia.

"It can't be a mouse because there aren't any crumbs," said Josephine.

"But it doesn't know there aren't," said Constantia.

A spasm of pity squeezed her heart. Poor little thing! She wished she'd left a tiny piece of biscuit on the dressing-table. It was awful to think of it not finding anything. What would it do?

"I can't think how they manage to live at all," she said slowly.

"Who?" demanded Josephine.

And Constantia said more loudly than she meant to, "Mice."

Josephine was furious. "Oh, what nonsense, Con!" she said. "What have mice got to do with it? You're asleep."

"I don't think I am," said Constantia. She shut her eyes to make sure. She was.

Josephine arched her spine, pulled up her knees, folded her arms so that her fists came under her ears, and pressed her cheek hard against the pillow.

2

Another thing which complicated matters was they had Nurse Andrews staying on with them that week. It was their own fault; they had asked her. It was Josephine's idea. On the morning—well, on the last morning, when the doctor had gone, Josephine had said to Constantia, "Don't you think it would be rather nice if we asked Nurse Andrews to stay on for a week as our guest?"

"Very nice," said Constantia.

"I thought," went on Josephine quickly, "I should just say this afternoon, after I've paid her, 'My sister and I would be very pleased, after all you've done for us, Nurse Andrews, if you would stay on for a week as our guest.' I'd have to put that in about being our guest in case—"

"Oh, but she could hardly expect to be paid!" cried Constantia.

"One never knows," said Josephine sagely.

Nurse Andrews had, of course, jumped at the idea. But it was a bother. It meant they had to have regular sit-down meals at the proper times, whereas if they'd been alone they could just have asked Kate if she wouldn't have minded bringing them a tray wherever they were. And meal-times now that the strain was over were rather a trial.

Nurse Andrews was simply fearful about butter. Really they couldn't help feeling that about butter, at least, she took advantage of their kindness. And she had that maddening habit of asking for just an inch more bread to finish what she had on her plate, and then, at the last mouthful, absent-mindedly—of course it wasn't absent-mindedly—taking another helping. Josephine got very red when this happened, and she fastened her small, beadlike eyes on the tablecloth as if she saw a minute strange insect creeping through the web of it. But Constantia's long, pale face lengthened and set, and she gazed away—away—far over the desert, to where that line of camels unwound like a thread of wool. . . .

"When I was with Lady Tukes," said Nurse Andrews, "she had such a dainty little contrayvance for the buttah. It was a silvah Cupid balanced on the—on the bordah of a glass dish, holding a tayny fork. And when you wanted some buttah you simply pressed his foot and he bent down and speared you a piece. It was quite a gayme."

Josephine could hardly bear that. But "I think those things are very extravagant" was all she said.

"But whey?" asked Nurse Andrews, beaming through her eye-glasses. "No one, surely, would take more buttah than one wanted—would one?"

"Ring, Con," cried Josephine. She couldn't trust herself to reply.

And proud young Kate, the enchanted princess, came in to see what the old tabbies wanted now. She snatched away their plates of mock something or other and slapped down a white, terrified blancmange.

"Jam, please, Kate," said Josephine kindly.

Kate knelt and burst open the sideboard, lifted the lid of the jam-pot, saw it was empty, put it on the table, and stalked off.

"I'm afraid," said Nurse Andrews a moment later, "there isn't any."

"Oh, what a bother!" said Josephine. She bit her lip. "What had we better do?"

Constantia looked dubious. "We can't disturb Kate again," she said softly.

Nurse Andrews waited, smiling at them both. Her eyes wandered, spying at everything behind her eye-glasses. Constantia in despair went back to her camels. Josephine frowned heavily—concentrated. If it hadn't been for this idiotic woman she and Con would, of course, have eaten their blancmange without. Suddenly the idea came.

"I know," she said. "Marmalade. There's some marmalade in the sideboard. Get it, Con."

"I hope," laughed Nurse Andrews, and her laugh was like a spoon tinkling against a medicine-glass—"I hope it's not very bittah marmalayde."

3

But, after all, it was not long now, and then she'd be gone for good. And there was no getting over the fact that she had been very kind to father. She had nursed him day and night at the end. Indeed, both Constantia and Josephine felt privately she had rather overdone the not leaving him at the very last. For when they had gone in to say good-bye Nurse Andrews had sat beside his bed the whole time, holding his wrist and pretending to look at her watch. It couldn't have been necessary. It was so tactless, too. Supposing father had wanted to say something—something private to them. Not that he had. Oh, far from it! He lay there, purple, a dark, angry purple in the face, and never even looked at them when they came in. Then, as they were standing there, wondering what to do, he had suddenly opened one eye. Oh, what a difference it would have made, what a difference to their memory of him, how much easier to tell people about it, if he had only opened both! But no—one eye only. It glared at them a moment and then . . . went out.

4

It had made it very awkward for them when Mr Farolles, of St John's, called the same afternoon.

"The end was quite peaceful, I trust?" were the first words he said as he glided towards them through the dark drawing-room.

"Quite," said Josephine faintly. They both hung their heads. Both of them felt certain that eye wasn't at all a peaceful eye.

"Won't you sit down?" said Josephine.

"Thank you, Miss Pinner," said Mr Farolles gratefully. He folded his coat-tails and began to lower himself into father's armchair, but just as he touched it he almost sprang up and slid into the next chair instead.

He coughed. Josephine clasped her hands; Constantia looked vague.

"I want you to feel, Miss Pinner," said Mr Farolles, "and you, Miss Constantia, that I'm trying to be helpful. I want to be helpful to you both, if you will let me. These are the times," said Mr Farolles, very simply and earnestly, "when God means us to be helpful to one another."

"Thank you very much, Mr Farolles," said Josephine and Constantia.

"Not at all," said Mr Farolles gently. He drew his kid gloves through his fingers and leaned forward. "And if either of you would like a little Communion, either or both of you, here and now, you have only to tell me. A little Communion is often very help—a great comfort," he added tenderly.

But the idea of a little Communion terrified them. What! In the drawing-room by themselves—with no—no altar or anything! The piano would be much too high, thought Constantia, and Mr Farolles could not possibly lean over it with the chalice. And Kate would be sure to come bursting in and interrupt them, thought Josephine. And supposing the bell rang in the middle? It might be somebody important—about their mourning. Would they get up reverently and go out, or would they have to wait . . . in torture?

"Perhaps you will send round a note by your good Kate if you would care for it later," said Mr Farolles.

"Oh yes, thank you very much!" they both said.

Mr Farolles got up and took his black straw hat from the round table.

"And about the funeral," he said softly. "I may arrange that—as your dear father's old friend and yours, Miss Pinner—and Miss Constantia?"

Josephine and Constantia got up too.

"I should like it to be quite simple," said Josephine firmly, "and not too expensive. At the same time, I should like—"

"A good one that will last," thought dreamy Constantia, as if Josephine were buying a nightgown. But of course Josephine didn't say that. "One suitable to our father's position." She was very nervous.

"I'll run round to our good friend Mr Knight," said Mr Farolles soothingly. "I will ask him to come and see you. I am sure you will find him very helpful indeed."

5

Well, at any rate, all that part of it was over, though neither of them could possibly believe that father was never coming back. Josephine had had a moment of absolute terror at the cemetery, while the coffin was lowered, to think that she and Constantia had done this thing without asking his permission. What would father say when he found out? For he was bound to find out sooner or later. He always did. "Buried. You two girls had me *buried*!" She heard his stick thumping. Oh, what would they say? What possible excuse could they make? It sounded such an appalling heartless thing to do. Such a wicked advantage to take of a person because he happened to be helpless at the moment. The other people seemed to treat it all as a matter of course. They were strangers; they couldn't be expected to understand that father was the very last person for such a thing to happen to. No, the entire blame for it all would fall on her and Constantia. And the expense, she thought, stepping into the tight-buttoned cab. When she had to show him the bills. What would he say then?

She heard him absolutely roaring, "And do you expect me to pay for this gim-crack excursion of yours?"

"Oh," groaned poor Josephine aloud, "we shouldn't have done it, Con!"

And Constantia, pale as a lemon in all that blackness, said in a frightened whisper, "Done what, Jug?"

"Let them bu-bury father like that," said Josephine, breaking down and crying into her new, queer-smelling mourning handkerchief.

"But what else could we have done?" asked Constantia wonderingly. "We couldn't have kept him, Jug—we couldn't have kept him unburied. At any rate, not in a flat that size."

Josephine blew her nose; the cab was dreadfully stuffy.

"I don't know," she said forlornly. "It is all so dreadful. I feel we ought to have tried to, just for a time at least. To make perfectly sure. One thing's certain"—and her tears sprang out again—"father will never forgive us for this—never!"

6

Father would never forgive them. That was what they felt more than ever when, two mornings later, they went into his room to go through his things. They had discussed it quite calmly. It was even down on Josephine's list of things to be done. *Go through father's things and settle about them*. But that was a very different matter from saying after breakfast:

"Well, are you ready, Con?"

"Yes, Jug—when you are."

"Then I think we'd better get it over."

It was dark in the hall. It had been a rule for years never to disturb father in the morning, whatever happened. And now they were going to open the door without knocking even. . . . Constantia's eyes were enormous at the idea; Josephine felt weak in the knees.

"You—you go first," she gasped, pushing Constantia.

But Constantia said, as she always had said on those occasions, "No, Jug, that's not fair. You're eldest."

Josephine was just going to say—what at other times she wouldn't have owned to for the world—what she kept for her very last weapon, "But you're tallest," when they noticed that the kitchen door was open, and there stood Kate. . . .

"Very stiff," said Josephine, grasping the door-handle and doing her best to turn it. As if anything ever deceived Kate!

It couldn't be helped. That girl was . . . Then the door was shut behind them, but—but they weren't in father's room at all. They might have suddenly walked through the wall by mistake into a different flat altogether. Was the door just behind them? They were too frightened to look. Josephine knew that if it was it was holding itself tight shut; Constantia felt that, like the doors in dreams, it hadn't any handle at all. It was the coldness which made it so awful. Or the whiteness—which? Everything was covered. The blinds were down, a cloth hung over the mirror, a sheet hid the bed; a huge fan of white paper filled the fireplace. Constantia timidly put out her hand; she almost expected a snowflake to fall. Josephine felt a queer tingling in her nose, as if her nose was freezing. Then a cab klop-klopped over the cobbles below, and the quiet seemed to shake into little pieces.

"I had better pull up a blind," said Josephine bravely.

"Yes, it might be a good idea," whispered Constantia.

They only gave the blind a touch, but it flew up and the cord flew after, rolling round the blindstick, and the little tassel tapped as if trying to get free. That was too much for Constantia.

"Don't you think—don't you think we might put it off for another day?" she whispered.

"Why?" snapped Josephine, feeling, as usual, much better now that she knew for certain that Constantia was terrified. "It's got to be done. But I do wish you wouldn't whisper, Con."

"I didn't know I was whispering," whispered Constantia.

"And why do you keep on staring at the bed?" said Josephine, raising her voice almost defiantly. "There's nothing on the bed."

"Oh, Jug, don't say so!" said poor Connie. "At any rate, not so loudly."

Josephine felt herself that she had gone too far. She took a wide swerve over to the chest of drawers, put out her hand, but quickly drew it back again.

"Connie!" she gasped, and she wheeled round and leaned with her back against the chest of drawers.

"Oh, Jug—what?"

Josephine could only glare. She had the most extraordinary feeling that she had just escaped something simply awful. But how could she explain to Constantia that father was in the chest of drawers? He was in the top drawer with his handkerchiefs and neckties, or in the next with his shirts and pyjamas, or in the lowest of all with his suits. He was watching there, hidden away—just behind the door-handle—ready to spring.

She pulled a funny old-fashioned face at Constantia, just as she used to in the old days when she was going to cry.

"I can't open," she nearly wailed.

"No, don't, Jug," whispered Constantia earnestly. "It's much better not to. Don't let's open anything. At any rate, not for a long time."

"But—but it seems so weak," said Josephine, breaking down.

"But why not be weak for once, Jug?" argued Constantia, whispering quite fiercely. "If it is weak." And her pale stare flew from the locked writing-table—so safe—to the huge glittering wardrobe, and she began to breathe in a queer, panting way. "Why shouldn't we be weak for once in our lives, Jug? It's quite excusable. Let's be weak—be weak, Jug. It's much nicer to be weak than to be strong."

And then she did one of those amazingly bold things that she'd done about twice before in their lives; she marched over to the wardrobe, turned the key, and took it out of the lock. Took it out of the lock and held it up to Josephine, showing Josephine by her extraordinary smile that she knew what she'd done, she'd risked deliberately father being in there among his overcoats.

If the huge wardrobe had lurched forward, had crashed down on Constantia, Josephine wouldn't have been surprised. On the contrary, she would have thought it the only suitable thing to happen. But nothing happened. Only the room seemed quieter than ever, and bigger flakes of cold air fell on Josephine's shoulders and knees. She began to shiver.

"Come, Jug," said Constantia, still with that awful callous smile, and Josephine followed just as she had that last time, when Constantia had pushed Benny into the round pond.

7

But the strain told on them when they were back in the dining-room. They sat down, very shaky, and looked at each other.

"I don't feel I can settle to anything," said Josephine, "until I've had something. Do you think we could ask Kate for two cups of hot water?"

"I really don't see why we shouldn't," said Constantia carefully. She was quite normal again. "I won't ring. I'll go to the kitchen door and ask her."

"Yes, do," said Josephine, sinking down into a chair. "Tell her, just two cups, Con, nothing else—on a tray."

"She needn't even put the jug on, need she?" said Constantia, as though Kate might very well complain if the jug had been there.

"Oh no, certainly not! The jug's not at all necessary. She can pour it direct out of the kettle," cried Josephine, feeling that would be a labour-saving indeed.

Their cold lips quivered at the greenish brims. Josephine curved her small red hands round the cup; Constantia sat up and blew on the wavy stream, making it flutter from one side to the other.

"Speaking of Benny," said Josephine.

And though Benny hadn't been mentioned Constantia immediately looked as though he had.

"He'll expect us to send him something of father's, of course. But it's so difficult to know what to send to Ceylon."

"You mean things get unstuck so on the voyage," murmured Constantia.

"No, lost," said Josephine sharply. "You know there's no post. Only runners."

Both paused to watch a black man in white linen drawers running through the pale fields for dear life, with a large brown-paper parcel in his hands. Josephine's black man was tiny; he scurried along glistening like an ant. But there was something blind and tireless about Constantia's tall, thin fellow, which made him, she decided, a very unpleasant person indeed. . . . On the veranda, dressed all in white and wearing a cork helmet, stood Benny. His right hand shook up and down, as father's did when he was impatient. And behind him, not in the least interested, sat Hilda, the unknown sister-in-law. She swung in a cane rocker and flicked over the leaves of the *Tatler*.

"I think his watch would be the most suitable present," said Josephine.

Constantia looked up; she seemed surprised.

"Oh, would you trust a gold watch to a native?"

"But of course I'd disguise it," said Josephine. "No one would know it was a watch." She liked the idea of having to make a parcel such a curious shape that no one could possibly guess what it was. She even thought for a moment of hiding the watch in a narrow cardboard corset-box that she'd kept by her for a long time, waiting for it to come in for something. It was such beautiful firm cardboard. But, no, it wouldn't be appropriate for this occasion. It had lettering on it: *Medium Women's 28. Extra Firm Busks*. It would be almost too much of a surprise for Benny to open that and find father's watch inside.

"And of course it isn't as though it would be going—ticking, I mean," said Constantia, who was still thinking of the native love of jewellery. "At least," she added, "it would be very strange if after all that time it was."

8

Josephine made no reply. She had flown off on one of her tangents. She had suddenly thought of Cyril. Wasn't it more usual for the only grandson to have the watch?

And then dear Cyril was so appreciative, and a gold watch meant so much to a young man. Benny, in all probability, had quite got out of the habit of watches; men so seldom wore waistcoats in those hot climates. Whereas Cyril in London wore them from year's end to year's end. And it would be so nice for her and Constantia, when he came to tea, to know it was there. "I see you've got on grandfather's watch, Cyril." It would be somehow so satisfactory.

Dear boy! What a blow his sweet, sympathetic little note had been! Of course they quite understood; but it was most unfortunate.

"It would have been such a point, having him," said Josephine.

"And he would have enjoyed it so," said Constantia, not thinking what she was saying.

However, as soon as he got back he was coming to tea with his aunties. Cyril to tea was one of their rare treats.

"Now, Cyril, you mustn't be frightened of our cakes. Your Auntie Con and I bought them at Buszard's this morning. We know what a man's appetite is. So don't be ashamed of making a good tea."

Josephine cut recklessly into the rich dark cake that stood for her winter gloves or the soling and heeling of Constantia's only respectable shoes. But Cyril was most unmanlike in appetite.

"I say, Aunt Josephine, I simply can't. I've only just had lunch, you know."

"Oh, Cyril, that can't be true! It's after four," cried Josephine. Constantia sat with her knife poised over the chocolate-roll.

"It is, all the same," said Cyril. "I had to meet a man at Victoria, and he kept me hanging about till . . . there was only time to get lunch and to come on here. And he gave me—phew"—Cyril put his hand to his forehead—"a terrific blow-out," he said.

It was disappointing—to-day of all days. But still he couldn't be expected to know.

"But you'll have a meringue, won't you, Cyril?" said Aunt Josephine. "These meringues were bought specially for you. Your dear father was so fond of them. We were sure you are, too."

"I *am*, Aunt Josephine," cried Cyril ardently. "Do you mind if I take half to begin with?"

"Not at all, dear boy; but we mustn't let you off with that."

"Is your dear father still so fond of meringues?" asked Auntie Con gently. She winced faintly as she broke through the shell of hers.

"Well, I don't quite know, Auntie Con," said Cyril breezily. At that they both looked up.

"Don't know?" almost snapped Josephine. "Don't know a thing like that about your own father, Cyril?"

"Surely," said Auntie Con softly.

Cyril tried to laugh it off. "Oh, well," he said, "it's such a long time since—" He faltered. He stopped. Their faces were too much for him.

"Even *so*," said Josephine.

And Auntie Con looked.

Cyril put down his teacup. "Wait a bit," he cried. "Wait a bit, Aunt Josephine. What am I thinking of?"

He looked up. They were beginning to brighten. Cyril slapped his knee.

"Of course," he said, "it was meringues. How could I have forgotten? Yes, Aunt Josephine, you're perfectly right. Father's most frightfully keen on meringues."

They didn't only beam. Aunt Josephine went scarlet with pleasure; Auntie Con gave a deep, deep sigh.

"And now, Cyril, you must come and see father," said Josephine. "He knows you were coming to-day."

"Right," said Cyril, very firmly and heartily. He got up from his chair; suddenly he glanced at the clock.

"I say, Auntie Con, isn't your clock a bit slow? I've got to meet a man at—at Paddington just after five. I'm afraid I shan't be able to stay very long with grandfather."

"Oh, he won't expect you to stay *very* long!" said Aunt Josephine.

Constantia was still gazing at the clock. She couldn't make up her mind if it was fast or slow. It was one or the other, she felt almost certain of that. At any rate, it had been.

Cyril still lingered. "Aren't you coming along, Auntie Con?"

"Of course," said Josephine, "we shall all go. Come on, Con."

9

They knocked at the door, and Cyril followed his aunts into grandfather's hot, sweetish room.

"Come on," said Grandfather Pinner. "Don't hang about. What is it? What've you been up to?"

He was sitting in front of a roaring fire, clasping his stick. He had a thick rug over his knees. On his lap there lay a beautiful pale yellow silk handkerchief.

"It's Cyril, father," said Josephine shyly. And she took Cyril's hand and led him forward.

"Good afternoon, grandfather," said Cyril, trying to take his hand out of Aunt Josephine's. Grandfather Pinner shot his eyes at Cyril in the way he was famous for. Where was Auntie Con? She stood on the other side of Aunt Josephine; her long arms hung down in front of her; her hands were clasped. She never took her eyes off grandfather.

"Well," said Grandfather Pinner, beginning to thump, "what have you got to tell me?"

What had he, what had he got to tell him? Cyril felt himself smiling like a perfect imbecile. The room was stifling, too.

But Aunt Josephine came to his rescue. She cried brightly, "Cyril says his father is still very fond of meringues, father dear."

"Eh?" said Grandfather Pinner, curving his hand like a purple meringue-shell over one ear.

Josephine repeated, "Cyril says his father is still very fond of meringues."

"Can't hear," said old Colonel Pinner. And he waved Josephine away with his stick, then pointed with his stick to Cyril. "Tell me what she's trying to say," he said.

(My God!) "Must I?" said Cyril, blushing and staring at Aunt Josephine.

"Do, dear," she smiled. "It will please him so much."

"Come on, out with it!" cried Colonel Pinner testily, beginning to thump again.

And Cyril leaned forward and yelled, "Father's still very fond of meringues."

At that Grandfather Pinner jumped as though he had been shot.

"Don't shout!" he cried. "What's the matter with the boy? *Meringues!* What about 'em?"

"Oh, Aunt Josephine, must we go on?" groaned Cyril desperately.

"It's quite all right, dear boy," said Aunt Josephine, as though he and she were at the dentist's together. "He'll understand in a minute." And she whispered to Cyril, "He's getting a bit deaf, you know." Then she leaned forward and really bawled at

Grandfather Pinner, "Cyril only wanted to tell you, father dear, that *his* father is still very fond of meringues."

Colonel Pinner heard that time, heard and brooded, looking Cyril up and down.

"What an esstrordinary thing!" said old Grandfather Pinner. "What an esstrordinary thing to come all this way here to tell me!"

And Cyril felt it *was*.

"Yes, I shall send Cyril the watch," said Josephine.

"That would be very nice," said Constantia. "I seem to remember last time he came there was some little trouble about the time."

10

They were interrupted by Kate bursting through the door in her usual fashion, as though she had discovered some secret panel in the wall.

"Fried or boiled?" asked the bold voice.

Fried or boiled? Josephine and Constantia were quite bewildered for the moment. They could hardly take it in.

"Fried or boiled what, Kate?" asked Josephine, trying to begin to concentrate. Kate gave a loud sniff. "Fish."

"Well, why didn't you say so immediately?" Josephine reproached her gently. "How could you expect us to understand, Kate? There are a great many things in this world, you know, which are fried or boiled." And after such a display of courage she said quite brightly to Constantia, "Which do you prefer, Con?"

"I think it might be nice to have it fried," said Constantia. "On the other hand, of course boiled fish is very nice. I think I prefer both equally well . . . Unless you . . . In that case—"

"I shall fry it," said Kate, and she bounced back, leaving their door open and slamming the door of her kitchen.

Josephine gazed at Constantia; she raised her pale eyebrows until they rippled away into her pale hair. She got up. She said in a very lofty, imposing way, "Do you mind following me into the drawing-room, Constantia? I've something of great importance to discuss with you."

For it was always to the drawing-room they retired when they wanted to talk over Kate.

Josephine closed the door meaningly. "Sit down, Constantia," she said, still very grand. She might have been receiving Constantia for the first time. And Con looked round vaguely for a chair, as though she felt indeed quite a stranger.

"Now the question is," said Josephine, bending forward, "whether we shall keep her or not."

"That is the question," agreed Constantia.

"And this time," said Josephine firmly, "we must come to a definite decision."

Constantia looked for a moment as though she might begin going over all the other times, but she pulled herself together and said, "Yes, Jug."

"You see, Con," explained Josephine, "everything is so changed now." Constantia looked up quickly. "I mean," went on Josephine, "we're not dependent on Kate as we were." And she blushed faintly. "There's not father to cook for."

"That is perfectly true," agreed Constantia. "Father certainly doesn't want any cooking now, whatever else—

" Josephine broke in sharply. "You're not sleepy, are you, Con?"

"Sleepy, Jug?" Constantia was wide-eyed.

"Well, concentrate more," said Josephine sharply, and she returned to the subject. "What it comes to is, if we did"—and this she barely breathed, glancing at the door—"give Kate notice"—she raised her voice again—"we could manage our own food."

"Why not?" cried Constantia. She couldn't help smiling. The idea was so exciting. She clasped her hands. What should we live on, Jug?"

"Oh, eggs in various forms!" said Jug, lofty again. "And, besides, there are all the cooked foods."

"But I've always heard," said Constantia, "they are considered so very expensive."

"Not if one buys them in moderation," said Josephine. But she tore herself away from this fascinating bypath and dragged Constantia after her.

"What we've got to decide now, however, is whether we really do trust Kate or not."

Constantia leaned back. Her flat little laugh flew from her lips.

"Isn't it curious, Jug," said she, "that just on this one subject I've never been able to quite make up my mind?"

11

She never had. The whole difficulty was to prove anything. How did one prove things, how could one? Suppose Kate had stood in front of her and deliberately made a face. Mightn't she very well have been in pain? Wasn't it impossible, at any rate, to ask Kate if she was making a face at her? If Kate answered "No"—and of course she would say "No"—what a position! How undignified! Then again Constantia suspected, she was almost certain that Kate went to her chest of drawers when she and Josephine were out, not to take things but to spy. Many times she had come back to find her amethyst cross in the most unlikely places, under her lace ties or on top of her evening Bertha. More than once she had laid a trap for Kate. She had arranged things in a special order and then called Josephine to witness.

"You see, Jug?"

"Quite, Con."

"Now we shall be able to tell."

But, oh dear, when she did go to look, she was as far off from a proof as ever! If anything was displaced, it might so very well have happened as she closed the drawer; a jolt might have done it so easily.

"You come, Jug, and decide. I really can't. It's too difficult."

But after a pause and a long glare Josephine would sigh, "Now you've put the doubt into my mind, Con, I'm sure I can't tell myself."

"Well, we can't postpone it again," said Josephine. "If we postpone it this time—"

12

But at that moment in the street below a barrel-organ struck up. Josephine and Constantia sprang to their feet together.

"Run, Con," said Josephine. "Run quickly. There's sixpence on the—"

Then they remembered. It didn't matter. They would never have to stop the organ-grinder again. Never again would she and Constantia be told to make that monkey take his noise somewhere else. Never would sound that loud, strange bellow when father thought they were not hurrying enough. The organ-grinder might play there all day and the stick would not thump.

It never will thump again,
It never will thump again,

played the barrel-organ.

What was Constantia thinking? She had such a strange smile; she looked different. She couldn't be going to cry.

"Jug, Jug," said Constantia softly, pressing her hands together. "Do you know what day it is? It's Saturday. It's a week to-day, a whole week."

> A week since father died,
> A week since father died,

cried the barrel-organ. And Josephine, too, forgot to be practical and sensible; she smiled faintly, strangely. On the Indian carpet there fell a square of sunlight, pale red; it came and went and came—and stayed, deepened—until it shone almost golden.

"The sun's out," said Josephine, as though it really mattered.

A perfect fountain of bubbling notes shook from the barrel-organ, round, bright notes, carelessly scattered.

Constantia lifted her big, cold hands as if to catch them, and then her hands fell again. She walked over to the mantelpiece to her favourite Buddha. And the stone and gilt image, whose smile always gave her such a queer feeling, almost a pain and yet a pleasant pain, seemed to-day to be more than smiling. He knew something; he had a secret. "I know something that you don't know," said her Buddha. Oh, what was it, what could it be? And yet she had always felt there was . . . something.

The sunlight pressed through the windows, thieved its way in, flashed its light over the furniture and the photographs. Josephine watched it. When it came to mother's photograph, the enlargement over the piano, it lingered as though puzzled to find so little remained of mother, except the earrings shaped like tiny pagodas and a black feather boa. Why did the photographs of dead people always fade so? wondered Josephine. As soon as a person was dead their photograph died too. But, of course, this one of mother was very old. It was thirty-five years old. Josephine remembered standing on a chair and pointing out that feather boa to Constantia and telling her that it was a snake that had killed their mother in Ceylon. . . . Would everything have been different if mother hadn't died? She didn't see why. Aunt Florence had lived with them until they had left school, and they had moved three times and had their yearly holiday and . . . and there'd been changes of servants, of course.

Some little sparrows, young sparrows they sounded, chirped on the window-ledge. Yeep-eyeep-yeep. But Josephine felt they were not sparrows, not on the window-ledge. It was inside her, that queer little crying noise. Yeep-eyeep-yeep. Ah, what was it crying, so weak and forlorn?

If mother had lived, might they have married? But there had been nobody for them to marry. There had been father's Anglo-Indian friends before he quarreled with them. But after that she and Constantia never met a single man except clergymen. How did one meet men? Or even if they'd met them, how could they have got to know men well enough to be more than strangers? One read of people having adventures, being followed, and so on. But nobody had ever followed Constantia and her. Oh yes, there had been one year at Eastbourne a mysterious man at their boarding-house who had put a note on the jug of hot water outside their bedroom door! But by the time Connie had found it the steam had made the writing too faint to read; they couldn't even make out to which of them it was addressed. And he had left next day. And that was all. The rest had been looking after father, and at the same time keeping out of father's way. But now? But now? The thieving sun touched Josephine gently. She lifted her face. She was drawn over to the window by gentle beams. . . .

Until the barrel-organ stopped playing Constantia stayed before the Buddha, wondering, but not as usual, not vaguely. This time her wonder was like longing. She remembered the times she had come in here, crept out of bed in her nightgown when the moon was full, and lain on the floor with her arms outstretched, as though she was crucified. Why? The big, pale moon had made her do it. The horrible dancing figures on the carved screen had leered at her and she hadn't minded. She remembered too how, whenever they were at the seaside, she had gone off by herself and got as close to the sea as she could, and sung something, something she had made up, while she gazed all over that restless water. There had been this other life, running out, bringing things home in bags, getting things on approval, discussing them with Jug, and taking them back to get more things on approval, and arranging father's trays and trying not to annoy father. But it all seemed to have happened in a kind of tunnel. It wasn't real. It was only when she came out of the tunnel into the moonlight or by the sea or into a thunderstorm that she really felt herself. What did it mean? What was it she was always wanting? What did it all lead to? Now? Now?

She turned away from the Buddha with one of her vague gestures. She went over to where Josephine was standing. She wanted to say something to Josephine, something frightfully important, about—about the future and what . . .

"Don't you think perhaps—" she began.

But Josephine interrupted her. "I was wondering if now—" she murmured. They stopped; they waited for each other.

"Go on, Con," said Josephine.

"No, no, Jug; after you," said Constantia.

"No, say what you were going to say. You began," said Josephine.

"I . . . I'd rather hear what you were going to say first," said Constantia.

"Don't be absurd, Con."

"Really, Jug."

"Connie!"

"Oh, Jug!"

A pause. Then Constantia said faintly, "I can't say what I was going to say, Jug, because I've forgotten what it was . . . that I was going to say."

Josephine was silent for a moment. She stared at a big cloud where the sun had been. Then she replied shortly, "I've forgotten too."

—•—══◊══—•—

Jean Rhys
1890–1979

Jean Rhys is the pen name of Ella Gwendolyn Rees Williams, born a Creole of Scottish, Irish, and Welsh descent on the British-held island of Dominica in the British West Indies. Her family history, her place of birth, and her social, economic, and cultural positions were all to play important roles in her writings, as she incorporated fictionalized versions of the family history and her own childhood in the Caribbean into her major novels *Voyage in the Dark* (1934) and *Wide Sargasso Sea* (1966), and wove this unusual background into her short fiction as well. Jean Rhys's writing is an example of postcolonial fiction before the fact, in that she moved to London and wrote for decades before most of the British colonies in the Caribbean became independent. Yet Rhys's fiction shows the features of postcolonial contemporary writing in English found in the work of Salman Rushdie, Derek Walcott, Seamus Heaney, Ngugi wa-Thiongo, and others in this anthology: like them, she addresses the complex and painful identity of nations and individuals once belonging to the British empire in a tongue and a literary tradition shared by colonizer and colonized alike. Rhys's work is marked by the prevalence in it of outsiders and outcasts, through whose alien perspectives she observes and critiques the norms and conventions of British society. Narrative voice is a key element of her writing, and its shifting points of view with no one authoritative voice echo the problem of authority and even authorship in a postcolonial world. To this dizzying sense of homelessness and alienation from place Rhys adds also a trenchant consideration of the effect of displacement on women, whose voices are silenced and to whom cultural authority was seldom granted. Her story *Mannequin* voices precisely the vertigo experienced by a young girl, Anna, who is thrown out into the world to make her way as a fashion model or mannequin, experiencing the coldness of Europe after the rich friendships of her Caribbean home, feeling the disdain of the British for her outsider status, and suffering exploitation by the men and women who treat her like a commodity—a piece of beautiful property to be bought and sold.

Rhys left Dominica in 1907 to enter the proper Perse School for girls, where she took first prize in Roman history on the college exams for Oxford and Cambridge. She was never to go to a university, however, because when her father died in the West Indies in 1910 she was left penniless and alone in England, and refused to return to Dominica. Taking the stage name Vivian Gray, she broke with middle-class conventions and with all the rules of propriety for women and joined a traveling musical variety troupe as a chorus girl. Rhys had a checkered history for many years, employed fleetingly as a model, an actress, a secretary and a prostitute, undertaking three rocky marriages and a literary life that vacillated between Paris and London. The destitution she had suffered from her father's death was repeated many times, in crises ranging from her own alcoholism to the financial frauds committed by at least one husband. As a writer, though, Rhys blossomed under the unlikely sponsorship of the great modernist Ford Madox Ford, who published her piece *Triple Sec,* ironically named after a liqueur, in his prestigious *Transatlantic Review,* and who involved her in the vibrant literary scene in Paris at the time. Her first collection of short fiction, *The Left Bank, and Other Stories* (1927) had an introduction by Ford; the next decade saw the publication of *Postures* (1928), and three strong and stunning autobiographical novels, among her best works: *After Leaving Mr. MacKenzie* (1930), *Voyage in the Dark* (1934), and *Good Morning, Midnight* (1939).

The war years of the 1940s and England's difficult aftermath in the economically and culturally devastated 1950s saw Rhys sink into obscurity and hard times. A second patron, however, the actress Selma Vas Dias, tracked her down only by advertising for her in a newspaper after adapting *Good Morning, Midnight* as a BBC radio play; with her encouragement Rhys began to write again at what might have been the end of her career. In 1957 she got a book contract for an idea she had of retelling *Jane Eyre* from the perspective of Bertha Mason, the Caribbean first wife of Rochester, who has gone mad and is sequestered in his castle's attic. Her hidden presence is discovered by the intrepid Jane on the verge of the latter's wedding night, which she calls off. Jane returns to marry Rochester only after Bertha has set the great house afire, killing herself and blinding her husband. In Charlotte Brontë's classic novel, Bertha Mason is a terrifying "other," a frightening reminder of Britain's involvement in colonialism and the slave trade, and there is more than a hint that her Creole lineage includes African blood.

In *Wide Sargasso Sea* (1966), Rhys's acknowledged masterpiece and now itself a classic of postcolonial fiction, the tables are turned. The book begins in the West Indies, and follows its main character as she is essentially sold to a British nobleman who can never be reconciled to her "strangeness," her cultural difference, and her ties to the Caribbean land and its people—black, white, and Creole. Her insanity is hardly the madness of a wild savage, as Brontë's book had described it; instead, the woman is driven mad by her treatment as the ultimate outsider.

Jean Rhys was seventy-six years old when she achieved literary fame by her rewriting of the British literary tradition. She lived on, famously cranky and bitter, and hugely productive, publishing two collections of short fiction written from a range of female perspectives, old and young, white and of color. Rhys's truth-telling about gender oppression, her understanding that it was linked to racism and colonial exploitation, and her frankness about sex and power masquerading as love were ahead of her time. *Tigers Are Better-Looking* came out in 1968, *Sleep it Off, Lady* in 1976, until Jean Rhys the British Creole writer slept it off for good in 1979.

Mannequin[1]

Twelve o'clock. Déjeuner chez Jeanne Veron,[2] Place Vendôme.

Anna, dressed in the black cotton, chemise-like garment of the mannequin off duty was trying to find her way along dark passages and down complicated flights of stairs to the underground from where lunch was served.

She was shivering, for she had forgotten her coat, and the garment that she wore was very short, sleeveless, displaying her rose-coloured stockings to the knee. Her hair was flamingly and honestly red; her eyes, which were very gentle in expression, brown and heavily shadowed with kohl; her face small and pale under its professional rouge. She was fragile, like a delicate child, her arms pathetically thin. It was to her legs that she owed this dazzling, this incredible opportunity.

Madame Veron, white-haired with black eyes, incredibly distinguished, who had given them one sweeping glance, the glance of the connoisseur, smiled imperiously and engaged her at an exceedingly small salary. As a beginner, Madame explained, Anna could not expect more. She was to wear the jeune fille[3] dresses. Another smile, another sharp glance.

Anne was conducted from the Presence by an underling who helped her to take off the frock she had worn temporarily for the interview. Aspirants for an engagement are always dressed in a model of the house.

She had spent yesterday afternoon in a delirium tempered by a feeling of exaggerated reality, and in buying the necessary make up. It had been such a forlorn hope, answering the advertisement.

The morning had been dreamlike. At the back of the wonderful decorated salons she had found an unexpected sombreness; the place, empty, would have been dingy and melancholy, countless puzzling corridors and staircases, a rabbit warren and a labyrinth. She despaired of ever finding her way.

In the mannequins' dressing-room she spent a shy hour making up her face—in an extraordinary and distinctive atmosphere of slimness and beauty; white arms and faces vivid with rouge; raucous voices and the smell of cosmetics; silken lingerie. Coldly critical glances were bestowed upon Anna's reflection in the glass. None of them looked at her directly . . . A depressing room, taken by itself, bare and cold, a very inadequate conservatory for these human flowers. Saleswomen in black rushed in and out, talking in sharp voices; a very old woman hovered, helpful and shapeless, showing Anna where to hang her clothes, presenting to her the black garment that Anna was wearing, going to lunch. She smiled with professional motherliness, her little, sharp, black eyes travelling rapidly from la nouvelle's hair to her ankles and back again.

She was Madame Pecard, the dresser.

Before Anna had spoken a word she was called away by a small boy in buttons to her destination in one of the salons: there, under the eye of a vendeuse,[4] she had to learn the way to wear the innocent and springlike air and garb of the jeune fille. Behind a yellow, silken screen she was hustled into a leather coat and paraded under the cold eyes of an American buyer. This was the week when the spring models are

---

1. French term for fashion model.
2. Lunch at Jeanne Veron's.

3. Young girl.
4. Saleswoman.

shown to important people from big shops all over Europe and America: the most critical week of the season . . . The American buyer said that he would have that, but with an inch on to the collar and larger cuffs. In vain the saleswoman, in her best English with its odd Chicago accent, protested that that would completely ruin the chic of the model. The American buyer knew what he wanted and saw that he got it.

The vendeuse sighed, but there was a note of admiration in her voice. She respected Americans: they were not like the English, who, under a surface of annoying moroseness of manner, were notoriously timid and easy to turn round your finger.

"Was that all right?" Behind the screen one of the saleswomen smiled encouragingly and nodded. The other shrugged her shoulders. She had small, close-set eyes, a long thin nose and tight lips of the regulation puce colour. Behind her silken screen Anna sat on a high white stool. She felt that she appeared charming and troubled. The white and gold of the salon suited her red hair.

A short morning. For the mannequin's day begins at ten and the process of making up lasts an hour. The friendly saleswoman volunteered the information that her name was Jeannine, that she was in the lingerie, that she considered Anna *rudement jolie*,[5] that noon was Anna's lunch hour. She must go down the corridor and up those stairs, through the big salon then . . . Anyone would tell her. But Anna, lost in the labyrinth, was too shy to ask her way. Besides, she was not sorry to have time to brace herself for the ordeal. She had reached the regions of utility and oilcloth: the decorative salons were far overhead. Then the smell of food—almost visible, it was so cloudlike and heavy—came to her nostrils, and high-noted, and sibilant, a buzz of conversation made her draw a deep breath. She pushed a door open.

She was in a big, very low-ceilinged room, all the floor space occupied by long wooden tables with no cloths . . . She was sitting at the mannequins' table, gazing at a thick and hideous white china plate, a twisted tin fork, a wooden-handled stained knife, a tumbler so thick it seemed unbreakable.

There were twelve mannequins at Jeanne Veron's: six of them were lunching, the others still paraded, goddess-like, till their turn came for rest and refreshment. Each of the twelve was a distinct and separate type: each of the twelve knew her type and kept to it, practising rigidly in clothing, manner, voice and conversation.

Round the austere table were now seated Babette, the gamine, the traditional blonde enfant: Mona, tall and darkly beautiful, the femme fatale, the wearer of sumptuous evening gowns. Georgette was the garçonne;[6] Simone with green eyes Anna knew instantly for a cat whom men would and did adore, a sleek, white, purring, long-lashed creature . . . Eliane was the star of the collection.

Eliane was frankly ugly and it did not matter: no doubt Lilith,[7] from whom she was obviously descended, had been ugly too. Her hair was henna-tinted, her eyes small and black, her complexion bad under her thick make-up. Her hips were extraordinarily slim, her hands and feet exquisite, every movement she made was as graceful as a flower's in the wind. Her walk . . . But it was her walk which made her the star there and earned her a salary quite fabulous for Madame Veron's, where large salaries were not the rule . . . Her walk and her "chic of the devil" which lit an expression of admiration in even the cold eyes of American buyers.

Eliane was a quiet girl, pleasant-mannered. She wore a ring with a beautiful emerald on one long, slim finger, and in her small eyes were both intelligence and mystery.

---

5. Awfully cute.
6. Boyish girl.

7. Mythical rejected first wife of Adam.

Madame Pecard, the dresser, was seated at the head of the mannequin's table, talking loudly, unlistened to, and gazing benevolently at her flock.

At other tables sat the sewing girls, pale-faced, blackfrocked—the workers heroically gay, but with the stamp of labour on them: and the saleswomen. The mannequins, with their sensual, blatant charms and their painted faces were watched covertly, envied and apart.

Babette the blonde enfant was next to Anna, and having started the conversation with a few good, round oaths at the quality of the sardines, announced proudly that she could speak English and knew London very well. She began to tell Anna the history of her adventures in the city of coldness, dark and fogs . . . She had gone to a job as a mannequin in Bond Street and the villainous proprietor of the shop having tried to make love to her and she being rigidly virtuous, she had left. And another job, Anna must figure to herself, had been impossible to get, for she, Babette, was too small and slim for the Anglo-Saxon idea of a mannequin.

She stopped to shout in a loud voice to the woman who was serving: "Hé, my old one, don't forget your little Babette . . ."

Opposite, Simone the cat and the sportive Georgette were having a low-voiced conversation about the tristeness of a monsieur of their acquaintance. "I said to him," Georgette finished decisively, "Nothing to be done, my rabbit. You have not looked at me well, little one. In my place would you not have done the same?"

She broke off when she realized that the others were listening, and smiled in a friendly way at Anna.

She too, it appeared, had ambitions to go to London because the salaries were so much better there. Was it difficult? Did they really like French girls? Parisiennes?

The conversation became general,

"The English boys are nice," said Babette, winking one divinely candid eye. "I had a chic type who used to take me to dinner at the Empire Palace. Oh, a pretty boy . . ."

"It is the most chic restaurant in London," she added importantly.

The meal reached the stage of dessert. The other tables were gradually emptying; the mannequins all ordered very strong coffee, several liqueur. Only Mona and Eliane remained silent; Eliane, because she was thinking of something else; Mona, because it was her type, her genre to be haughty.

Her hair swept away from her white, narrow forehead and her small ears: her long earrings nearly touching her shoulders, she sipped her coffee with a disdainful air. Only once, when the blonde enfant, having engaged in a passage of arms with the waitress and got the worst of it was momentarily discomfited and silent, Mona narrowed her eyes and smiled an astonishingly cruel smile.

As soon as her coffee was drunk she got up and went out.

Anna produced a cigarette, and Georgette, perceiving instantly that here was the sportive touch, her genre, asked for one and lit it with a devil-may-care air. Anna eagerly passed her cigarettes round, but the Mère Pecard interfered weightily. It was against the rules of the house for the mannequins to smoke, she wheezed. The girls all lit their cigarettes and smoked. The Mère Pecard rumbled on: "A caprice, my children. All the world knows that mannequins are capricious. Is it not so?" She appealed to the rest of the room.

As they went out Babette put her arm round Anna's waist and whispered: "Don't answer Madame Pecard. We don't like her. We never talk to her. She spies on us. She is a camel."[8]

That afternoon Anna stood for an hour to have a dress draped on her. She showed this dress to a stout Dutch lady buying for the Hague, to a beautiful South American with pearls, to a silver-haired American gentleman who wanted an evening cape for his daughter of seventeen, and to a hook-nosed, odd English lady of title who had a loud voice and dressed, under her furs, in a grey jersey and stout boots.

The American gentleman approved of Anna, and said so, and Anna gave him a passionately grateful glance. For, if the vendeuse Jeannine had been uniformly kind and encouraging, the other, Madame Tienne, had been as uniformly disapproving and had once even pinched her arm hard.

About five o'clock Anna became exhausted. The four white and gold walls seemed to close in on her. She sat on her high white stool staring at a marvellous nightgown and fighting an intense desire to rush away. Anywhere! Just to dress and rush away anywhere, from the raking eyes of the customers and the pinching fingers of Irene.

"I will one day. I can't stick it," she said to herself. "I won't be able to stick it." She had an absurd wish to gasp for air.

Jeannine came and found her like that.

"It is hard at first, hein? . . . One ask oneself: Why? For what good? It is all idiot. We are all so. But we go on. Do not worry about Irene." She whispered: "Madame Vernon likes you very much. I heard her say so."

At six o'clock Anna was out in the rue de la Paix; her fatigue forgotten, the feeling that now she really belonged to the great, maddening city possessed her and she was happy in her beautifully cut tailor-made and beret.

Georgette passed her and smiled; Babette was in a fur coat.

All up the street the mannequins were coming out of the shops, pausing on the pavements a moment, making them as gay and as beautiful as beds of flowers before they walked swiftly away and the Paris night swallowed them up.

━━◆━━

Angela Carter
1940–1992

When Angela Carter broke onto the British literary scene in 1966 with her first novel, *Shadow Dance*, realist narrative strategies were the order of the day. The British experience of the second world war, and the fragmentation of the Empire it accelerated, seemed to demand a gritty, topical, engaged variety of writing which would detail Britannia's newly straitened circumstances; the Angry Young Men and the "kitchen sink" school of drama, along with the unsentimental poetry of writers like Philip Larkin, set a no-nonsense tone for literary production.

8. In French slang, "camel" is equivalent to "bitch."

Carter was having none of it: near the end of her career, she summed up her outlook by saying, "I am the pure product of an advanced, industrialised, post-imperialist country in decline." Her writing, from the start, was characterized by strategies that parallel the main activity of her characters in *Shadow Dance*: rummaging through the junk shop of the past. Words, phrases, images, characters, plots in Carter's novels and short stories most often have invisible quotation marks surrounding them: she is supremely aware, and works to make her readers aware, that part of the burden of postmodernism is the awareness that it has all already been said. As she said to an interviewer, "In a period like this of transition and conflicting ideologies, when there isn't a prevalent ideology, really all artists can do is go round mopping up."

As a result, self-conscious echoing of other literary texts—what critics call *intertextuality*—runs throughout Carter's writing. That first novel closes with an ironic reworking of a scene from Russian writer Fyodor Dostoevsky's novel *The Idiot*; the opening of her 1969 novel *Heroes and Villains* parodies the opening of Jane Austen's canonical 1816 novel, *Emma*. At the same time, Carter brought to contemporary British fiction a sensibility which, almost instinctively, sought to bring down the arbitrary barriers erected between "literary" and "genre" fiction. Her stories and novels deploy the resources, variously, of fairy tales, pornography, fantasy, science fiction, myth, and romance to address, finally, universals of the human condition.

Before her death from cancer at age fifty-one, Carter had published, together with ten novels, plays, film scripts, an opera, a feminist study of (paradoxically) the profoundly misogynist Marquis de Sade, and a great trove of short stories. One collection, *The Bloody Chamber* (1979), rewrites a number of timeless fairy tales through the lenses of contemporary feminism and Freudian theory (she had translated and introduced *The Fairy Tales of Charles Perrault* in 1977). The story reprinted here first appeared in the 1974 collection *Fireworks: Nine Profane Pieces*.

Penetrating to the Heart of the Forest

The whole region was like an abandoned flower bowl, filled to overflowing with green, living things; and, protected on all sides by the ferocious barricades of the mountains, those lovely reaches of forest lay so far inland the inhabitants believed the name, Ocean, that of a man in another country, and would have taken an oar, had they ever seen one, to be a winnowing fan. They built neither roads nor towns; in every respect like Candide,[1] especially that of past ill-fortune, all they did now was to cultivate their gardens.

They were the descendants of slaves who, many years before, ran away from plantations in distant plains, in pain and hardship crossed the arid neck of the continent, and endured an infinity of desert and tundra, before they clambered the rugged foothills to scale at last the heights themselves and so arrive in a region that offered them in plentiful fulfilment all their dreams of a promised land. Now, the groves that skirted those forests of pine in the central valley formed for them all of the world they wished to know and nothing in their self-contained quietude concerned them but the satisfaction of simple pleasures. Not a single exploring spirit had ever been curious enough to search to its source the great river that watered their plots, or to penetrate to the heart of the forest itself. They had grown far too contented in their lost fastness to care for anything but the joys of idleness.

They had brought with them as a relic of their former life only the French their former owners had branded on their tongues, though certain residual, birdlike flutings of forgotten African dialects put unexpected cadences in their speech and, with the years, they had fashioned an arboreal argot[2] of their own to which a French grammar

---

1. After a series of tragedies, Candide—the protagonist of Voltaire's philosophical novel—settles on a small farm, and resolves, in the face of life's sorrow and pain, "we must cultivate our garden."
2. Specialized vocabulary.

would have proved a very fallible guide. And they had also packed up in their ragged bandanas a little, dark, voodoo folklore. But such bloodstained ghosts could not survive in sunshine and fresh air and emigrated from the village in a body, to live only the ambiguous life of horned rumours in the woods, becoming at last no more than shapes with indefinable outlines who lurked, perhaps, in the green deeps, until, at last, one of the shadows modulated imperceptibly into the actual shape of a tree.

Almost as if to justify to themselves their lack of a desire to explore, they finally seeded by word of mouth a mythic and malign tree within the forest, a tree the image of the Upas Tree of Java whose very shadow was murderous, a tree that exuded a virulent sweat of poison from its moist bark and whose fruits could have nourished with death an entire tribe. And the presence of this tree categorically forbade exploration—even though all knew, in their hearts, that such a tree did not exist. But, even so, they guessed it was safest to be a stay-at-home.

Since the woodlanders could not live without music, they made fiddles and guitars for themselves with great skill and ingenuity. They loved to eat well so they stirred themselves enough to plant vegetables, tend goats and chickens and blend these elements together in a rustic but voluptuous cookery. They dried, candied and preserved in honey some of the wonderful fruits they grew and exchanged this produce with the occasional traveller who came over the single, hazardous mountain pass, carrying bales of cotton fabrics and bundles of ribbons. With these, the women made long skirts and blouses for themselves and trousers for their menfolk, so all were dressed in red and yellow flowered cloth, purple and green checkered cloth, or cloth striped like a rainbow, and they plaited themselves hats from straw. They needed nothing more than a few flowers before they felt their graceful toilets were complete and a profusion of flowers grew all around them, so many flowers that the straw-thatched villages looked like inhabited gardens, for the soil was of amazing richness and the flora proliferated in such luxuriance that when Dubois, the botanist, came over the pass on his donkey, he looked down on that paradisial landscape and exclaimed: "Dear God! It is as if Adam had opened Eden to the public!"

Dubois was seeking a destination whose whereabouts he did not know, though he was quite sure it existed. He had visited most of the out-of-the-way parts of the world to peer through the thick lenses of his round spectacles at every kind of plant. He gave his name to an orchid in Dahomey, to a lily in Indo-China and to a dark-eyed Portuguese girl in a Brazilian town of such awesome respectability that even its taxis wore antimacassar. But, because he loved the frail wife whose grave eyes already warned him she would live briefly, he rooted there, a plant himself in alien soil, and, out of gratitude, she gave him two children at one birth before she died.

He found his only consolation in a return to the flowering wilderness he had deserted for her sake. He was approaching middle age, a rawboned, bespectacled man who habitually stooped out of a bashful awareness of his immense height, hirsute and gentle as a herbivorous lion. The vicissitudes of a life in which his reticence had cheated him of the fruits of his scholarship, together with the forlorn conclusion of his marriage, had left him with a yearning for solitude and a desire to rear his children in a place where ambition, self-seeking and guile were strangers, so that they would grow up with the strength and innocence of young trees.

But such a place was hard to find.

His wanderings took him to regions ever more remote from civilisation but he was never seized with a conviction of home-coming until that morning, as the sun irradiated the mists and his donkey picked its way down a rough path so overgrown with dew-drenched grass and mosses it had become no more than the subtlest intimation of a direction.

It took him circuitously down to a village sunk in a thicket of honeysuckle that filled with languorous sweetness the rarefied air of the uplands. On the dawning light hung, trembling, the notes of a pastoral aubade[3] somebody was picking out on a guitar. As Dubois passed the house, a plump, dark-skinned woman with a crimson handkerchief round her head threw open a pair of shutters and leaned out to pick a spray of morning glory. As she tucked it behind her ear, she saw the stranger and smiled like another sunrise, greeting him with a few melodious phrases of his native language she had somehow mixed with burned cream and sunshine. She offered him a little breakfast which she was certain he must need since he had travelled so far and, while she spoke, the yellow-painted door burst open and a chattering tide of children swept out to surround the donkey, turning up to Dubois faces like sunflowers.

Six weeks after his arrival among the Creoles,[4] Dubois left again for the house of his parents-in-law. There, he packed his library, notebooks and records of researches; his most precious collections of specimens and his equipment; as much clothing as he felt would last him the rest of his life; and a crate containing objects of sentimental value. This case and his children were the only concessions he made to the past. And, once he had installed all those safely in a wooden farmhouse the villagers had interrupted their inactivity long enough to make ready for him, he closed the doors of his heart to everything but the margins of the forest, which were to him a remarkable book it would take all the years that remained to him to learn to read.

The birds and beasts showed no fear of him. Painted magpies perched reflectively on his shoulders as he pored over the drawings he made among the trees, while fox cubs rolled in play around his feet and even learned to nose in his capacious pockets for cookies. As his children grew older, he seemed to them more an emanation of their surroundings than an actual father, and from him they unknowingly imbibed a certain radiant inhumanity which sprang from a benign indifference towards by far the greater part of mankind—towards all those who were not beautiful, gentle and, by nature, kind.

"Here, we have all become *homo silvester*, men of the woods," he would say. "And that is by far superior to the precocious and destructive species, *homo sapiens*—knowing man. Knowing man, indeed; what more than nature does man need to know?"

Other carefree children were their playfellows and their toys were birds, butterflies and flowers. Their father spared them enough of his time to teach them to read, to write and to draw. Then he gave them the run of his library and left them alone, to grow as they pleased. So they thrived on a diet of simple food, warm weather, perpetual holidays and haphazard learning. They were fearless since there was nothing to be afraid of, and they always spoke the truth because there was no need to lie. No hand or voice was ever raised in anger against them and so they did not know what anger was; when they came across the word in books, they thought it must mean the mild fretfulness they felt when it rained two days together, which did not happen often. They quite forgot the dull town where they had been born. The green world took them for its own and they were fitting children of their foster mother, for they were strong, lithe and supple, browned by the sun to the very colour of the villagers whose liquid *patois*[5] they spoke. They resembled one another so closely each could have

---

3. A song evoking daybreak, or lovers departing at daybreak.
4. People of mixed African descent.
5. Regional dialect.

used the other as a mirror and almost seemed to be different aspects of the same person for all their gestures, turns of phrase and manner of speech were exactly similar. Had they known how, they would have been proud, because their intimacy was so perfect it could have bred that sense of loneliness which is the source of pride and, as they read more and more of their father's books, their companionship deepened since they had nobody but one another with whom to discuss the discoveries they made in common. From morning to evening, they were never apart, and at night they slept together in a plain, narrow bed on a floor of beaten earth while the window held the friendly nightlight of a soft, southern moon above them in a narrow frame. But often they slept under the moon itself, for they came and went as they pleased and spent most of their time out of doors, exploring the forests until they had gone further and seen more than ever their father had.

At last, these explorations took them into the untrodden, virginal reaches of the deep interior. Here, they walked hand in hand beneath the vaulted architraves of pines in a hushed interior like that of a sentient cathedral. The topmost branches twined so thickly that only a subdued viridian[6] dazzle of light could filter through and the children felt against their ears a palpable fur of intense silence. Those who felt less kinship with the place might have been uneasy, as if abandoned among serene, voiceless, giant forms that cared nothing for man. But, if the children sometimes lost their way, they never lost themselves for they took the sun by day and the stars by the otherwise trackless night for their compass and could discern clues in the labyrinth that those who trusted the forest less would not have recognised, for they knew the forest too well to know of any harm it might do them.

Long ago, in their room at home, they began work on a map of the forest. This was by no means the map an authentic cartographer would have made. They marked hills with webs of feathers of the birds they found there, clearings with an integument of pressed flowers and especially magnificent trees with delicate, brightly coloured drawings on whose watercolour boughs they stuck garlands of real leaves so that the map became a tapestry made out of the substance of the forest itself. At first, in the centre of the map, they put their own thatched cottage and Madeline drew in the garden the shaggy figure of their father, whose leonine mane was as white, now, as the puff ball of a dandelion, bending with a green watering can over his pots of plants, tranquil, beloved and oblivious. But as they grew older, they grew discontented with their work for they found out their home did not lie at the heart of the forest but only somewhere in its green suburbs. They were seized with the desire to pierce more and yet more deeply into the unfrequented places and now their expeditions lasted for a week or longer. Though he was always glad to see them return, their father had often forgotten they had been away. At last, nothing but the discovery of the central node of the unvisited valley, the navel of the forest, would satisfy them. It grew to be almost an obsession with them. They spoke of the adventure only to one another and did not share it with the other companions who, as they grew older, grew less and less necessary to their absolute intimacy, since, lately, for reasons beyond their comprehension, this intimacy had been subtly invaded by tensions which exacerbated their nerves yet exerted on them both an intoxicating glamour.

Besides, when they spoke of the heart of the forest to their other friends, a veil of darkness came over the woodlanders' eyes and, half-laughing, half-whispering,

---

6. Blue-green.

they could hint at the wicked tree that grew there as though, even if they did not believe in it, it was a metaphor for something unfamiliar they preferred to ignore, as one might say: "Let sleeping dogs lie. Aren't we happy as we are?" When they saw this laughing apathy, this incuriosity blended with a tinge of fear, Emile and Madeline could not help but feel a faint contempt, for their world, though beautiful, seemed to them, in a sense, incomplete—as though it lacked the knowledge of some mystery they might find, might they not? in the forest, on their own.

In their father's books they found references to the Antiar or Antshar of the Indo-Malay archipelago, the *antiaris toxicaria* whose milky juice contains a most potent poison, like the quintessence of belladonna.[7] But their reason told them that not even the most intrepid migratory bird could have brought the sticky seeds on its feet to cast them down here in these land-locked valleys far from Java. They did not believe the wicked tree could exist in this hemisphere; and yet they were curious. But they were not afraid.

One August morning, when both were thirteen years old, they put bread and cheese in their knapsacks and started out on a journey so early the homesteads were sleeping and even the morning glories were still in bud. The settlements were just as their father had seen them first, prelapsarian[8] villages where any Fall was inconceivable; his children, bred in those quiet places, saw them with eyes pure of nostalgia for lost innocence and thought of them only with that faint, warm claustrophobia which the word, "home," signifies. At noon, they ate lunch with a family whose cottage lay at the edges of the uninhabited places and when they bade their hosts goodbye, they knew, with a certain anticipatory relish, they would not see anyone else but one another for a long time.

At first, they followed the wide river which led them directly into the ramparts of the great pines and, though days and nights soon merged together in a sonorous quiet where trees grew so close together that birds had no room to sing or fly, they kept a careful tally of the passing time for they knew that, five days away from home, along the leisurely course of the water, the pines thinned out.

The bramble-covered riverbanks, studded, at this season, with flat, pink discs of blossom, grew so narrow that the water tumbled fast enough to ring out various carillons while grey squirrels swung from branch to low branch of trees which, released from the strait confines of the forest, now grew in shapes of a feminine slightness and grace. Rabbits twitched moist, velvet noses and laid their ears along their backs but did not run away when they saw the barefoot children go by and Emile pointed out to Madeline how a wise toad, squatting meditatively among the kingcups, must have a jewel in his head because bright beams darted out through his eyes, as though a cold fire burned inside his head. They had read of this phenomenon in old books but never seen it before.

They had never seen anything in this place before. It was so beautiful they were a little awe-struck.

Then Madeline stretched out her hand to pick a water-lily unbudding on the surface of the river but she jumped back with a cry and gazed down at her finger with a mixture of pain, affront and astonishment. Her bright blood dripped down on to the grass.

"Emile!" she said. "It bit me!"

---

7. A poisonous herb of Eurasia.
8. "Before the Fall," the state of innocence before humankind's fall from grace narrated in the first two chapters of Genesis.

They had never encountered the slightest hostility in the forest before. Their eyes met in wonder and surmise while the birds chanted recitatives to the accompaniment of the river. "This is a strange place," said Emile hesitantly. "Perhaps we should not pick any flowers in this part of the forest. Perhaps we have found some kind of carnivorous water-lily."

He washed the tiny wound, bound it with his handkerchief and kissed her cheek, to comfort her, but she would not be comforted and irritably flung a pebble in the direction of the flower. When the pebble struck the lily, the flower unfurled its close circle of petals with an audible snap and, bewildered, they glimpsed inside them a set of white, perfect fangs. Then the waxen petals closed swiftly over the teeth again, concealing them entirely, and the water-lily again looked perfectly white and innocent.

"See! It *is* a carnivorous water-lily!" said Emile. "Father *will* be excited when we tell him."

But Madeline, her eyes still fixed on the predator as if it fascinated her, slowly shook her head. She had grown very serious.

"No," she said. "We must not talk of the things we find in the heart of the forest. They are all secrets. If they were not secrets, we would have heard of them before."

Her words fell with a strange weight, as heavy as her own gravity, as if she might have received some mysterious communication from the perfidious[9] mouth that wounded her. At once, listening to her, Emile thought of the legendary tree; and then he realised that, for the first time in his life, he did not understand her, for, of course, they had heard of the tree. Looking at her in a new puzzlement, he sensed the ultimate difference of a femininity he had never before known any need or desire to acknowledge and this difference might give her the key to some order of knowledge to which he might not yet aspire, himself, for all at once she seemed far older than he. She raised her eyes and fixed on him a long, solemn regard which chained him in a conspiracy of secrecy, so that, henceforth, they would share only with one another the treacherous marvels round them. At last, he nodded.

"Very well, then," he said. "We won't tell father."

Though they knew he never listened when they spoke to him, never before had they consciously concealed anything from him.

Night was approaching. They walked a little further, until they found pillows of moss laid ready for their heads beneath the branches of a flowering tree. They drank clear water, ate the last of the food they had brought with them and then slept in one another's arms as if they were the perfect children of the place, although they slept less peacefully than usual for both were visited by unaccustomed nightmares of knives and snakes and suppurating[1] roses. But though each stirred and murmured, the dreams were so strangely inconsequential, nothing but fleeting sequences of detached, malign images, that the children forgot them as they slept and woke only with an irritable residue of nightmare, the dregs of unremembered dreaming, knowing only they had slept badly.

In the morning, they stripped and bathed in the river. Emile[2] saw that time was subtly altering the contours of both their bodies and he found he could no longer ignore his sister's nakedness, as he had done since babyhood, while, from the way she

---

9. Treacherous.
1. Discharging fluid.
2. The name "Emile" is borrowed from Jean-Jacques Rousseau's novel on male education of the same name.

Rousseau's Emile needed to know only nature, supposedly; the references to Adam and Eve and to Madeline / Magdalen suggest human nature is more complex.

suddenly averted her own eyes after, in her usual playful fashion, she splashed him with water, she, too, experienced the same extraordinary confusion. So they fell silent and hastily dressed themselves. And yet the confusion was pleasurable and made their blood sting. He examined her finger and found the marks of the lily's teeth were gone; the wound had healed over completely. Yet he still shuddered with an unfamiliar thrill of dread when he remembered the fanged flower.

"We have no food left," he said. "We should turn back at noon."

"Oh, no!" said Madeline with a mysterious purposefulness that might have been rooted, had he known it, only in a newborn wish to make him do as she wanted, against his own wishes. "No! I'm sure we shall find something to eat. After all, this is the season for wild strawberries."

He, too, knew the lore of the forest. At no time of the year could they not find food—berries, roots, salads, mushrooms, and so on. So he saw she knew he had only used a pale excuse to cover his increasing agitation at finding himself alone with her so far from home. And now he had used up his excuse, there was nothing for it but to go on. She walked with a certain irresolute triumph, as though she were aware she had won an initial victory which, though insignificant in itself, might herald more major battles in the future, although they did not even know the formula for a quarrel, yet.

And already this new awareness of one another's shapes and outlines had made them less twinned, less indistinguishable from one another. So they fell once more to their erudite botanising, in order to pretend that all was as it had always been, before the forest showed its teeth; and now the meandering path of the river led them into such magical places that they found more than enough to talk about for, by the time the shadows vanished at noon, they had come into a landscape that seemed to have undergone an alchemical change, a vegetable transmutation, for it contained nothing that was not marvellous.

Ferns uncurled as they watched, revealing fronded fringes containing innumerable, tiny, shining eyes glittering like brilliants where the ranks of seeds should have been. A vine was covered with slumbrous, purple flowers that, as they passed, sang out in a rich contralto with all the voluptuous wildness of flamenco—and then fell silent. There were trees that bore, instead of foliage, brown, speckled plumage of birds. And when they had grown very hungry, they found a better food than even Madeline had guessed they might, for they came to a clump of low trees with trunks scaled like trout, growing at the water's edge. These trees put out shell-shaped fruit and, when they broke these open and ate them, they tasted oysters. After they consumed their fishy luncheon, they walked on a little and discovered a tree knobbed with white, red-tipped whorls that looked so much like breasts they put their mouths to the nipples and sucked a sweet, refreshing milk.

"See?" said Madeline, and this time her triumph was unconcealed. "I told you we should find something to nourish us!"

When the shadows of the evening fell like a thick dust of powdered gold on the enchanted forest and they were beginning to feel weary, they came to a small valley which contained a pool that seemed to have no outlet or inlet and so must be fed by an invisible spring. The valley was filled with the most delightful, citronesque fragrance as sharply refreshing as a celestial eau-de-cologne and they saw the source of the perfume at once.

"Well!" exclaimed Emile. "This certainly isn't the fabled Upas Tree! It must be some kind of incense tree, such as the incense trees of Upper India where, after all, one finds a similar climate, or so I've read."

The tree was a little larger than a common apple tree but far more graceful in shape. The springing boughs hung out a festival of brilliant streamers, long, aromatic sprays of green, starlike flowers tipped with the red anthers of the stamens, cascading over clusters of leaves so deep a green and of such a glossy texture the dusk turned to discs of black glass those that the sunset did not turn to fire. These leaves hid secret bunches of fruit, mysterious spheres of visible gold streaked with green, as if all the unripe suns in the world were sleeping on the tree until a multiple, universal dawning should wake them all in splendour. As they stood hand in hand gazing at the beautiful tree, a small wind parted the leaves so they would see the fruit more clearly and, in the rind, set squarely in the middle of each faintly flushed cheek, was a curious formation—a round set of serrated indentations exactly resembling the marks of a bite made by the teeth of a hungry man. As if the sight stimulated her own appetite, Madeline laughed and said: "Goodness, Emile, the forest has even given us dessert."

She sprang towards the exquisite, odoriferous tree which, at that moment, suffused in a failing yet hallucinatory light the tone and intensity of liquefied amber, seemed to her brother a perfect equivalent of his sister's amazing beauty, a beauty he had never seen before that filled him, now, with ecstasy. The dark pool reflected her darkly, like an antique mirror. She raised her hand to part the leaves in search of a ripe fruit but the greenish skin seemed to warm and glow under her fingers so the first one she touched came as easily off the stem as if it had been brought to perfection by her touch. It seemed to be some kind of apple or pear. It was so juicy the juice ran down her chin and she extended a long, crimson, newly sensual tongue to lick her lips, laughing.

"It tastes so good!" she said. "Here! Eat!"

She came back to him, splashing through the margins of the pool, holding the fruit out towards him on her palm. She was like a beautiful statue which has just come to life. Her enormous eyes were lit like nocturnal flowers that had been waiting only for this especial night to open and, in their vertiginous[3] depths, reveal to her brother in expressible entirety the hitherto unguessed at, unknowable, inexpressible vistas of love.

He took the apple; ate; and, after that, they kissed.

➤ END OF PERSPECTIVES: REGENDERING MODERNISM ➤

⇥◆⇤

D. H. Lawrence
1885–1930

D. H. Lawrence's meteoric literary life ended in Venice, Italy, in 1930, where he died at the age of forty-five, far from his birthplace in Nottinghamshire, the coal-mining heart of England. If Lawrence was something of a comet in British literature, arcing across its skies with vibrant energy and controversy while he lived, he was equally visible after his death in the excitement and danger that persisted like a halo around his texts. A formidable poet, an exceptional essayist and literary critic, and a major novelist, Lawrence created works that were pioneering in

---

3. Revolving, dizzying.

their defiant eroticism, their outspoken treatment of class politics, and their insistence on see-ing British literature as part of world literature in a time of global crisis. Many of his writings were censored and unavailable in England until long after his death, or published in expurgated versions or in private printings. Their frank concentration on sexuality, and on female as well as male desire, continues to make Lawrence's novels provocative and even controversial today.

David Herbert Lawrence was the son of a coal miner. As a primarily self-educated writer who studied and taught at Nottingham University College, instead of Oxford or Cam-bridge, he was unlike many of his literary peers in being lower-class and outside the privi-leged literary and social circles they moved in. He essentially invented himself, drawing on the support and encouragement of his mother, and nurturing a clear-eyed and furious analy-sis of British class structure that pervades many of his novels. The sexual frankness of his work is accompanied by its economic frankness, its willingness to point out all the ways that culture and taste are fashioned by income as much as by ideas. The sense of being an out-sider to the gentlemanly world of letters fed Lawrence's need to live and work outside Britain, and he traveled restlessly to Europe and America, to Australia and Mexico. Lawrence is deeply associated with many of the countries and places he lived in; with Italy, above all, in the power of his writing about Italian culture and landscape; with the United States, in classic analysis of American literature, and in works set in New Mexico and San Francisco; with France, Germany, and Switzerland as backdrops for his literary works and their cultural theorizing; with Australia for his commentary on this distant British colony and its indigenous peoples, in novels like *Kangaroo*; with Mexico and the primitivism and exoticism he explored in *The Plumed Serpent* and *Aaron's Rod*.

As peripatetic and as open to experience as Lawrence was, his great writing begins with novels and stories set in England. Some of his early and most exceptional works are, in fact, modernist versions of a central nineteenth-century literary genre, the *bildungsroman*, or the story of a personal education. Lawrence's *Sons and Lovers* (1912) has the autobiographical overtones that often accompany a coming-of-age narrative. Written after the death of his devoted mother Lydia Lawrence in 1910, the book delineates the experience of a young man who was as socially and economically disadvantaged as Lawrence himself, and the almost incestuous love between mother and son that allows him to break free from the crushing life in the mines that might have been his only option, and to follow his deep need for love, imagination, and poetry into the writing of literature. His later novel *The Rainbow* (pub-lished in an expurgated version in 1915) is also a *bildungsroman*, but featuring as its protago-nist a female character and specifically feminine issues of education and freedom. In a pref-ace to the novel, Lawrence wrote that he insisted on portraying characters that were not the old-fashioned character portraits of the past, relying on "the old stable ego." For Lawrence, people were internally fragmented, not completely self-aware, and above all governed by sexual currents that exceeded their conscious knowledge and control. In this Lawrence was profoundly influenced by Freud's discovery of the prominence and power of the uncon-scious. All of Lawrence's writing engages with the invisible and largely silent realm of the uncon-scious, whose wishes and impulses are a kind of dynamic dance running under the surface of the conscious sense of self.

To this dance of the unconscious rhythms of life Lawrence added an abiding fascination with myth. He joined most modernist writers in his interest in showing the persistence of myth in modern culture: Joyce, Woolf, Eliot, and Faulkner all structured work around myth-ic parallels or mythic figures. For Lawrence, myth loomed importantly because it allowed for the discussion of hidden patterns and cycles in human action and human relationships, pat-terns that are much larger than the individual human being. Our personalities are illusions, Lawrence's fiction claims, because they mask deeper mythic forms. In *The Rainbow*, Lawrence draws his mythic structure from the Bible, and the cycles of birth, death, and rebirth in the story of Noah and the flood, with the rainbow of God's promise starting the cycle of rebirth over and over again.

One of Lawrence's greatest novels is *Women in Love*, a story of two sisters confronting modern life as they move out of their country's orbit and take on independence, sexual freedom, and careers in the world. He began writing it in 1916, during World War I. The war was as shattering to Lawrence as it was to every other British writer; for Lawrence, it was the apotheosis and the logical conclusion of the machine culture he hated for having spoiled England even before the war wreaked its devastation. Lawrence sharply criticized industrial capitalism, but not from the vantage point of an aristocratic worldview that regretted the loss of the landed estates. He thought and wrote as the son of a worker whose life was maimed by industrial toil in the mines, and as a school teacher of the impoverished children of miners and laborers who had lost their self-sufficient way of life on the land. Lawrence did not dream of a return to a golden feudal age, but he did dissect the ravages of industry and the connections between world war, capital, and modernization. *Women in Love* embraces these themes and more, as it turns to Europe and its classical culture to try to find a way out of the cultural impasse and sterility Lawrence saw around him. However, in this novel and others Lawrence writes of a death instinct visible for him in European culture, including its philosophy and art. At times, Lawrence's intense hatred of modernity led him to flirt with fascism, which occasionally seemed to him to promise a way out of the dead end of modern society and its hideous conflagrations in war. In order to rescue the life-affirming capacities of human society Lawrence sought out exotic and foreign cultures, and what he termed "primitive" cultures around the world—ostensibly unspoiled agricultural societies still predicated on myth rather than machine. These exotic alternatives, as Lawrence saw, were hardly utopian either, and most such societies were contaminated by colonization and Western influences. Lawrence did seek a less rationalized and less materialistic perspective in the "primitive" or archaic worlds he explored, and found that these cultures were more open to the life-giving force of sexuality. At once intense and engaging, his travel writing gives a sense of immediacy mingled with deep reflection.

Sexuality is the force in human life that most clearly derives from unconscious fantasies and desires, and on that basis it is at the heart of Lawrence's writing. Lawrence's work was thought shocking because it takes for granted the erotic elements hidden in the family— what Freud had called the "family romance." The alliances and the divisions between family members have an erotic component for Lawrence; in addition, relations to friends and to all others one encounters are sexualized in mysterious ways, often involving a powerful homoerotic current. Much of Lawrence's fiction seems to idealize a sexual state beyond words and beyond conscious understanding, and to depict this Lawrence draws on a beautiful incantatory style, filled with a highly musical repetition and rhythm.

Lawrence's own erotic career is as famous as his writing. The passion and frustrations of his marriage to the formidable Frieda Weekely (born Frieda von Richthofen) remained a hidden presence in all his writing after their marriage in 1914. When they met, Frieda was a married woman with an impressive erotic career behind her; she became a close partner in his political and cultural essay writing, and in his restless travels. They lived in Germany, Italy, and in Taos, New Mexico, among other locales. After his death in Italy, she and her then lover transported Lawrence's ashes back to Taos, and the two built a kind of shrine to Lawrence on the grounds of what had been his home with Frieda. It was in this region that they had explored Hispanic and Indian cultures under the sponsorship of a patron of the avant-garde, Mabel Dodge Luhan. Up until the mid-1980s it was possible to pay a dollar to the manager of the Taos Hotel and be admitted into his office, where numerous paintings by D. H. Lawrence were on display. Lawrence was a fascinating, if not a major, painter; the exhibits of his paintings in England were subject to the same censorship and public outrage as his novels. A viewer of the paintings could read them as an allegory for many of the disquieting themes of his literary work: the majority of them depict a couple, usually male and female, locked in an embrace that is as urgent as it is suffocating; around the edges of these couplings Lawrence painted menacing wolves and dogs, often with teeth bared or fangs dripping with blood, emblematic of the intensity and even the destructiveness of erotic relationships.

In his 1923 essay *Surgery for the Novel—or a Bomb*, Lawrence expresses his impatience with the endlessly refined analyses of modernists like Proust and Joyce. "What is the underlying impulse in us," he asks, "that will provide the motive power for a new state of things, when this democratic-industrial-lovey-dovey-darling-take-me-to-mama state of things is bust? *What next?*" His own efforts to forge a new mythic realism can be seen in his novella *The Fox*, also from 1923, which explores the interpenetration of human and animal, nature and social constraint, masculinity and feminity, sexual desire and deep aggression. The story's rural setting becomes a place at once of poverty and of beauty, in which Lawrence can counterpoint pursuits and entrapments on several levels, giving symbolic resonance to sharply observed naturalistic detail.

Lawrence's poetry explores related concerns. Like Thomas Hardy before him, Lawrence was equally gifted in both literary endeavors. Lawrence's poetry emanates from the same image-suffused, musically rhythmic, and tautly modern space as his prose works. Like Lawrence himself, his art desires to move *beyond*—beyond the old stable fictions of the ego in his prose, and beyond the old stable fiction of the lyric voice. In his poetry he accomplishes this by a preternatural immediacy, an intensity of "thereness" that includes what might in the past have seemed to be incoherent elements or fragmentary perspectives. What has been silent, veiled, or unconscious, in personal and in public life, rears up and announces itself in Lawrence's writing, appears on the page and defies silencing.

Odour of Chrysanthemums

1

The small locomotive engine Number 4, came clanking, stumbling down from Selston[1] with seven full wagons. It appeared round the corner with loud threats of speed, but the colt that it startled from among the gorse,[2] which still flickered indistinctly in the raw afternoon, out-distanced it at a canter A woman, walking up the railway line to Underwood,[3] drew back into the hedge, held her basket aside, and watched the footplate of the engine advancing. The trucks thumped heavily past, one by one, with slow inevitable movement, as she stood insignificantly trapped between the jolting black wagons and the hedge; then they curved away towards the coppice where the withered oak leaves dropped noiselessly, while the birds, pulling at the scarlet hips beside the track, made off into the dusk that had already crept into the spinney.[4] In the open, the smoke from the engine sank and cleaved to the rough grass. The fields were dreary and forsaken, and in the marshy strip that led to the whimsey, a reedy pit-pond, the fowls had already abandoned their run among the alders, to roost in the tarred fowl-house. The pit-bank loomed up beyond the pond, flames like red sores licking its ashy sides, in the afternoon's stagnant light. Just beyond rose the tapering chimneys and the clumsy

---

1. Mining village in Nottinghamshire, central England.
2. Wild, yellow-flowered shrub.
3. Small village in central England.
4. A small thicket.

black headstocks of Brinsley Colliery. The two wheels were spinning fast up against the sky, and the winding engine rapped out its little spasms. The miners were being turned up.

The engine whistled as it came into the wide bay of railway lines beside the colliery, where rows of trucks stood in harbour.

Miners, single, trailing and in groups, passed like shadows diverging home. At the edge of the ribbed level of sidings squat a low cottage, three steps down from the cinder track. A large bony vine clutched at the house, as if to claw down the tiled roof. Round the bricked yard grew a few wintry primroses. Beyond, the long garden sloped down to a bushcovered brook course. There were some twiggy apple trees, winter-crack trees, and ragged cabbages. Beside the path hung dishevelled pink chrysanthemums, like pink cloths hung on bushes. A woman came stooping out of the felt-covered fowl-house, half-way down the garden. She closed and padlocked the door, then drew herself erect, having brushed some bits from her white apron.

She was a tall woman of imperious mien, handsome, with definite black eyebrows. Her smooth black hair was parted exactly. For a few moments she stood steadily watching the miners as they passed along the railway: then she turned towards the brook course. Her face was calm and set, her mouth was closed with disillusionment. After a moment she called:

"John!" There was no answer. She waited, and then said distinctly:

"Where are you?"

"Here!" replied a child's sulky voice from among the bushes. The woman looked piercingly through the dusk.

"Are you at that brook?" she asked sternly.

For answer the child showed himself before the raspberrycanes that rose like whips. He was a small, sturdy boy of five. He stood quite still, defiantly.

"Oh!" said the mother, conciliated. "I thought you were down at that wet brook—and you remember what I told you——"

The boy did not move or answer.

"Come, come on in," she said more gently, "it's getting dark. There's your grandfather's engine coming down the line!"

The lad advanced slowly, with resentful, taciturn movement. He was dressed in trousers and waistcoat of cloth that was too thick and hard for the size of the garments. They were evidently cut down from a man's clothes.

As they went slowly towards the house he tore at the ragged wisps of chrysanthemums and dropped the petals in handfuls among the path.

"Don't do that—it does look nasty," said his mother. He refrained, and she, suddenly pitiful, broke off a twig with three or four wan flowers and held them against her face. When mother and son reached the yard her hand hesitated, and instead of laying the flower aside, she pushed it in her apron-band. The mother and son stood at the foot of the three steps looking across the bay of lines at the passing home of the miners. The trundle of the small train was imminent. Suddenly the engine loomed past the house and came to a stop opposite the gate.

The engine-driver, a short man with round grey beard, leaned out of the cab high above the woman.

"Have you got a cup of tea?" he said in a cheery, hearty fashion.

It was her father. She went in, saying she would mash.[5] Directly, she returned.

5. Separate tea from the leaves.

"I didn't come to see you on Sunday," began the little greybearded man.

"I didn't expect you," said his daughter.

The engine-driver winced; then, reassuming his cheery, airy manner, he said:

"Oh, have you heard then? Well, and what do you think——?"

"I think it is soon enough," she replied.

At her brief censure the little man made an impatient gesture, and said coaxingly, yet with dangerous coldness:

"Well, what's a man to do? It's no sort of life for a man of my years, to sit at my own hearth like a stranger. And if I'm going to marry again it may as well be soon as late—what does it matter to anybody?"

The woman did not reply, but turned and went into the house. The man in the engine-cab stood assertive, till she returned with a cup of tea and a piece of bread and butter on a plate. She went up the steps and stood near the footplate of the hissing engine.

"You needn't 'a' brought me bread an' butter," said her father. "But a cup of tea"—he sipped appreciatively—"it's very nice." He sipped for a moment or two, then: "I hear as Walter's got another bout on," he said.

"When hasn't he?" said the woman bitterly.

"I heerd tell of him in the 'Lord Nelson' braggin' as he was going to spend that b—— afore he went: half a sovereign that was."

"When?" asked the woman.

"A' Sat'day night—I know that's true."

"Very likely," she laughed bitterly. "He gives me twenty-three shillings."

"Aye, it's a nice thing, when a man can do nothing with his money but make a beast of himself!" said the grey-whiskered man. The woman turned her head away. Her father swallowed the last of his tea and handed her the cup.

"Aye," he sighed, wiping his mouth. "It's a settler, it is——"

He put his hand on the lever. The little engine strained and groaned, and the train rumbled towards the crossing. The woman again looked across the metals. Darkness was settling over the spaces of the railway and trucks: the miners, in grey sombre groups, were still passing home. The winding engine pulsed hurriedly, with brief pauses. Elizabeth Bates looked at the dreary flow of men, then she went indoors. Her husband did not come.

The kitchen was small and full of firelight; red coals piled glowing up the chimney mouth. All the life of the room seemed in the white, warm hearth and the steel fender reflecting the red fire. The cloth was laid for tea; cups glinted in the shadows. At the back, where the lowest stairs protruded into the room, the boy sat struggling with a knife and a piece of white wood. He was almost hidden in the shadow. It was half-past four. They had but to await the father's coming to begin tea. As the mother watched her son's sullen little struggle with the wood, she saw herself in his silence and pertinacity; she saw the father in her child's indifference to all but himself. She (seemed to be) occupied by her husband. He had probably gone past his home, slunk past his own door, to drink before he came in, while his dinner spoiled and wasted in waiting. She glanced at the clock, then took the potatoes to strain them in the yard. The garden and fields beyond the brook were closed in uncertain darkness. When she rose with the saucepan, leaving the drain steaming into the night behind her, she saw the yellow lamps were lit along the high road that went up the hill away beyond the space of the railway lines and the field.

Then again she watched the men trooping home, fewer now and fewer.

Indoors the fire was sinking and the room was dark red. The woman put her saucepan on the hob, and set a batter-pudding near the mouth of the oven. Then she stood unmoving. Directly, gratefully, came quick young steps to the door. Someone hung on the latch a moment, then a little girl entered and began pulling off her out-door things, dragging a mass of curls, just ripening from gold to brown, over her eyes with her hat.

Her mother chid her for coming late from school, and said she would have to keep her at home the dark winter days.

"Why, mother, it's hardly a bit dark yet. The lamp's not lighted, and my father's not home."

"No, he isn't. But it's a quarter to five! Did you see anything of him?"

The child became serious. She looked at her mother with large, wistful blue eyes.

"No, mother, I've never seen him. Why? Has he come up an' gone past, to Old Brinsley? He hasn't, mother, 'cos I never saw him."

"He'd watch that," said the mother bitterly, "he'd take care as you didn't see him. But you may depend upon it, he's seated in the 'Prince o' Wales.' He wouldn't be this late."

The girl looked at her mother piteously.

"Let's have our teas, mother, should we?" said she.

The mother called John to table. She opened the door once more and looked out across the darkness of the lines. All was deserted: she could not hear the winding-engines.

"Perhaps," she said to herself, "he's stopped to get some ripping[6] done."

They sat down to tea. John, at the end of the table near the door, was almost lost in the darkness. Their faces were hidden from each other. The girl crouched against the fender slowly moving a thick piece of bread before the fire. The lad, his face a dusky mark on the shadow, sat watching her who was transfigured in the red glow.

"I do think it's beautiful to look in the fire," said the child.

"Do you?" said her mother. "Why?"

"It's so red, and full of little caves—and it feels so nice, and you can fair smell it."

"It'll want mending directly," replied her mother, "and then if your father comes he'll carry on and say there never is a fire when a man comes home sweating from the pit. A public-house[7] is always warm enough."

There was silence till the boy said complainingly: "Make haste, our Annie."

"Well, I am doing! I can't make the fire do it no faster, can I?"

"She keeps wafflin' it about so's to make 'er slow," grumbled the boy.

"Don't have such an evil imagination, child," replied the mother.

Soon the room was busy in the darkness with the crisp sound of crunching. The mother ate very little. She drank her tea determinedly, and sat thinking. When she rose her anger was evident in the stern unbending of her head. She looked at the pudding in the fender, and broke out:

"It is a scandalous thing as a man can't even come home to his dinner! If it's crozzled up to a cinder I don't see why I should care. Past his very door he goes to get to a public-house, and here I sit with his dinner waiting for him——"

She went out. As she dropped piece after piece of coal on the red fire, the shadows fell on the walls, till the room was almost in total darkness.

"I canna see," grumbled the invisible John. In spite of herself, the mother laughed.

6. Tearing a vein of coal from the earth.   7. Pub; tavern.

"You know the way to your mouth," she said. She set the dust-pan outside the door. When she came again like a shadow on the hearth, the lad repeated, complaining sulkily:

"I canna see."

"Good gracious!" cried the mother irritably, "you're as bad as your father if it's a bit dusk!"

Nevertheless, she took a paper spill from a sheaf on the mantelpiece and proceeded to light the lamp that hung from the ceiling in the middle of the room. As she reached up, her figure displayed itself just rounding with maternity.

"Oh, mother——!" exclaimed the girl.

"What?" said the woman, suspended in the act of putting the lamp-glass over the flame. The copper reflector shone handsomely on her, as she stood with uplifted arm, turning to face her daughter.

"You've got a flower in your apron!" said the child, in a little rapture at this unusual event.

"Goodness me!" exclaimed the woman, relieved. "One would think the house was afire." She replaced the glass and waited a moment before turning up the wick. A pale shadow was seen floating vaguely on the floor.

"Let me smell!" said the child, still rapturously, coming forward and putting her face to her mother's waist.

"Go along, silly!" said the mother, turning up the lamp. The light revealed their suspense so that the woman felt it almost unbearable. Annie was still bending at her waist. Irritably, the mother took the flowers out from her apron-band.

"Oh, mother—don't take them out!" Annie cried, catching her hand and trying to replace the sprig.

"Such nonsense!" said the mother, turning away. The child put the pale chrysanthemums to her lips, murmuring:

"Don't they smell beautiful!"

Her mother gave a short laugh.

"No," she said, "not to me. It was chrysanthemums when I married him, and chrysanthemums when you were born, and the first time they ever brought him home drunk, he'd got brown chrysanthemums in his button-hole."

She looked at the children. Their eyes and their parted lips were wondering. The mother sat rocking in silence for some time. Then she looked at the clock.

"Twenty minutes to six!" In a tone of fine bitter carelessness she continued: "Eh, he'll not come now till they bring him. There he'll stick! But he needn't come rolling in here in his pit-dirt, for I won't wash him. He can lie on the floor——Eh, what a fool I've been, what a fool! And this is what I came here for, to this dirty hole, rats and all, for him to slink past his very door. Twice last week—he's begun now——"

She silenced herself, and rose to clear the table.

While for an hour or more the children played, subduedly intent, fertile of imagination, united in fear of the mother's wrath, and in dread of their father's home-coming, Mrs. Bates sat in her rocking-chair making a 'singlet' of thick cream-coloured flannel, which gave a dull wounded sound as she tore off the grey edge. She worked at her sewing with energy, listening to the children, and her anger wearied itself, lay down to rest, opening its eyes from time to time and steadily watching, its ears raised to listen. Sometimes even her anger quailed and shrank, and the mother suspended her sewing, tracing the footsteps that thudded along the sleepers outside; she would lift her head sharply to bid the children 'hush', but she recovered herself in time, and the footsteps went past the gate, and the children were not flung out of their play-world.

But at last Annie sighed, and gave in. She glanced at her wagon of slippers, and loathed the game. She turned plaintively to her mother.

"Mother!"—but she was inarticulate.

John crept out like a frog from under the sofa. His mother glanced up.

"Yes," she said, "just look at those shirt-sleeves!"

The boy held them out to survey them, saying nothing. Then somebody called in a hoarse voice away down the line, and suspense bristled in the room, till two people had gone by outside, talking.

"It is time for bed," said the mother.

"My father hasn't come," wailed Annie plaintively. But her mother was primed with courage.

"Never mind. They'll bring him when he does come—like a log." She meant there would be no scene. "And he may sleep on the floor till he wakes himself. I know he'll not go to work to-morrow after this!"

The children had their hands and faces wiped with a flannel. They were very quiet. When they had put on their night-dresses, they said their prayers, the boy mumbling. The mother looked down at them, at the brown silken bush of intertwining curls in the nape of the girl's neck, at the little black head of the lad, and her heart burst with anger at their father, who caused all three such distress. The children hid their faces in her skirts for comfort.

When Mrs. Bates came down, the room was strangely empty, with a tension of expectancy. She took up her sewing and stitched for some time without raising her head. Meantime her anger was tinged with fear.

2

The clock struck eight and she rose suddenly, dropping her sewing on her chair. She went to the stair-foot door, opened it, listening. Then she went out, locking the door behind her.

Something scuffled in the yard, and she started, though she knew it was only the rats with which the place was over-run. The night was very dark. In the great bay of railway lines, bulked with trucks, there was no trace of light, only away back she could see a few yellow lamps at the pit-top, and the red smear of the burning pit-bank on the night. She hurried along the edge of the track, then, crossing the converging lines, came to the stile by the white gates, whence she emerged on the road. Then the fear which had led her shrank. People were walking up to New Brinsley; she saw the lights in the houses; twenty yards farther on were the broad windows of the 'Prince of Wales', very warm and bright, and the loud voices of men could be heard distinctly. What a fool she had been to imagine that anything had happened to him! He was merely drinking over there at the 'Prince of Wales'. She faltered. She had never yet been to fetch him, and she never would go. So she continued her walk towards the long straggling line of houses, standing back on the highway. She entered a passage between the dwellings.

"Mr. Rigley?—Yes! Did you want him? No, he's not in at this minute."

The raw-boned woman leaned forward from her dark scullery and peered at the other, upon whom fell a dim light through the blind of the kitchen window.

"Is it Mrs. Bates?" she asked in a tone tinged with respect.

"Yes. I wondered if your Master was at home. Mine hasn't come yet."

"'Asn't 'e! Oh, Jack's been 'ome an' 'ad 'is dinner an' gone out. 'E's just gone for 'alf an hour afore bed-time. Did you call at the 'Prince of Wales'?"

"No——"

"No, you didn't like——! It's not very nice." The other woman was indulgent. There was an awkward pause. "Jack never said nothink about—about your Master," she said.

"No!—I expect he's stuck in there!"

Elizabeth Bates said this bitterly, and with recklessness. She knew that the woman across the yard was standing at her door listening, but she did not care. As she turned:

"Stop a minute! I'll just go an' ask Jack if 'e knows anythink," said Mrs. Rigley.

"Oh no—I wouldn't like to put——!"

"Yes, I will, if you'll just step inside an' see as th' childer doesn't come downstairs and set theirselves afire."

Elizabeth Bates, murmuring a remonstrance,[8] stepped inside. The other woman apologised for the state of the room.

The kitchen needed apology. There were little frocks and trousers and childish undergarments on the squab and on the floor, and a litter of playthings everywhere. On the black American cloth of the table were pieces of bread and cake, crusts, slops, and a teapot with cold tea.

"Eh, ours is just as bad," said Elizabeth Bates, looking at the woman, not at the house. Mrs. Rigley put a shawl over her head and hurried out, saying:

"I shanna be a minute."

The other sat, noting with faint disapproval the general untidiness of the room. Then she fell to counting the shoes of various sizes scattered over the floor. There were twelve. She sighed and said to herself: "No wonder!"—glancing at the litter. There came the scratching of two pairs of feet on the yard, and the Rigleys entered. Elizabeth Bates rose. Rigley was a big man, with very large bones. His head looked particularly bony. Across his temple was a blue scar, caused by a wound got in the pit, a wound in which the coal-dust remained blue like tattooing.

"'Asna 'e come whoam yit?" asked the man, without any form of greeting, but with deference and sympathy. "I couldna say wheer he is—'e's non ower theer!"—he jerked his head to signify the 'Prince of Wales'.

"'E's 'appen[9] gone up to th' 'Yew'," said Mrs. Rigley.

There was another pause. Rigley had evidently something to get off his mind:

"Ah left 'im finishin' a stint,"[1] he began. "Loose-all 'ad bin gone about ten minutes when we com'n away, an' I shouted: 'Are ter comin', Walt?' an' 'e said: 'Go on, Ah shanna be but a'ef a minnit,' so we com'n ter th' bottom, me an' Bowers, thinkin' as 'e wor just behint, an' 'ud come up i' th' next bantle[2]——"

He stood perplexed, as if answering a charge of deserting his mate. Elizabeth Bates, now again certain of disaster, hastened to reassure him:

"I expect 'e's gone up to th' 'Yew Tree', as you say. It's not the first time. I've fretted myself into a fever before now. He'll come home when they carry him."

"Ay, isn't it too bad!" deplored the other woman.

"I'll just step up to Dick's an' see if 'e is theer," offered the man, afraid of appearing alarmed, afraid of taking liberties.

"Oh, I wouldn't think of bothering you that far," said Elizabeth Bates, with emphasis, but he knew she was glad of his offer.

8. Protestation or objection.
9. Perhaps, maybe.

1. Amount of work to be done.
2. Carload.

As they stumbled up the entry, Elizabeth Bates heard Rigley's wife run across the yard and open her neighbour's door. At this, suddenly all the blood in her body seemed to switch away from her heart.

"Mind!" warned Rigley. "Ah've said many a time as Ah'd fill up them ruts in this entry, sumb'dy 'll be breakin' their legs yit."

She recovered herself and walked quickly along with the miner.

"I don't like leaving the children in bed, and nobody in the house," she said.

"No, you dunna!" he replied courteously. They were soon at the gate of the cottage.

"Well, I shanna be many minnits, Dunna you be frettin' now, 'e'll be all right," said the butty.[3]

"Thank you very much, Mr. Rigley," she replied.

"You're welcome!" he stammered, moving away. "I shanna be many minnits."

The house was quiet. Elizabeth Bates took off her hat and shawl, and rolled back the rug. When she had finished, she sat down. It was a few minutes past nine. She was startled by the rapid chuff of the winding-engine at the pit, and the sharp whirr of the brakes on the rope as it descended. Again she felt the painful sweep of her blood, and she put her hand to her side, saying aloud: "Good gracious!—it's only the nine o'clock deputy going down," rebuking herself.

She sat still, listening. Half an hour of this, and she was wearied out.

"What am I working myself up like this for?" she said pitiably to herself, "I s'll only be doing myself some damage."

She took out her sewing again.

At a quarter to ten there were footsteps. One person! She watched for the door to open. It was an elderly woman, in a black bonnet and a black woollen shawl—his mother. She was about sixty years old, pale, with blue eyes, and her face all wrinkled and lamentable. She shut the door and turned to her daughter-in-law peevishly.

"Eh, Lizzie, whatever shall we do, whatever shall we do!" she cried.

Elizabeth drew back a little, sharply.

"What is it, mother?" she said.

The elder woman seated herself on the sofa.

"I don't know, child, I can't tell you!"—she shook her head slowly. Elizabeth sat watching her, anxious and vexed.

"I don't know," replied the grandmother, sighing very deeply. "There's no end to my troubles, there isn't. The things I've gone through, I'm sure it's enough——!" She wept without wiping her eyes, the tears running.

"But, mother," interrupted Elizabeth, "what do you mean? What is it?"

The grandmother slowly wiped her eyes. The fountains of her tears were stopped by Elizabeth's directness. She wiped her eyes slowly.

"Poor child! Eh, you poor thing!" she moaned. "I don't know what we're going to do, I don't—and you as you are—it's a thing, it is indeed!"

Elizabeth waited.

"Is he dead?" she asked, and at the words her heart swung violently, though she felt a slight flush of shame at the ultimate extravagance of the question. Her words sufficiently frightened the old lady, almost brought her to herself.

"Don't say so, Elizabeth! We'll hope it's not as bad as that; no, may the Lord spare us that, Elizabeth. Jack Rigley came just as I was sittin' down to a glass afore

3. Fellow coal miner.

going to bed, an' 'e said: '''Appen you'll go down th' line, Mrs. Bates. Walt's had an accident. 'Appen you'll go an' sit wi' 'er till we can get him home.' I hadn't time to ask him a word afore he was gone. An' I put my bonnet on an' come straight down, Lizzie. I thought to myself: 'Eh, that poor blessed child, if anybody should come an' tell her of a sudden, there's no knowin' what'll 'appen to 'er.' You mustn't let it upset you, Lizzie—or you know what to expect. How long is it, six months—or is it five, Lizzie? Ay!"—the old woman shook her head—"time slips on, it slips on! Ay!"

Elizabeth's thoughts were busy elsewhere. If he was killed—would she be able to manage on the little pension and what she could earn?—she counted up rapidly. If he was hurt—they wouldn't take him to the hospital—how tiresome he would be to nurse!—but perhaps she'd be able to get him away from the drink and his hateful ways. She would—while he was ill. The tears offered to come to her eyes at the picture. But what sentimental luxury was this she was beginning? She turned to consider the children. At any rate she was absolutely necessary for them. They were her business.

"Ay!" repeated the old woman, "it seems but a week or two since he brought me his first wages. Ay—he was a good lad, Elizabeth, he was, in his way. I don't know why he got to be such a trouble, I don't. He was a happy lad at home, only full of spirits. But there's no mistake he's been a handful of trouble, he has! I hope the Lord'll spare him to mend his ways. I hope so, I hope so. You've had a sight o' trouble with him, Elizabeth, you have indeed. But he was a jolly enough lad wi' me, he was, I can assure you. I don't know how it is . . . ."

The old woman continued to muse aloud, a monotonous irritating sound, while Elizabeth thought concentratedly, startled once, when she heard the winding-engine chuff quickly, and the brakes skirr with a shriek. Then she heard the engine more slowly, and the brakes made no sound. The old woman did not notice. Elizabeth waited in suspense. The mother-in-law talked, with lapses into silence.

"But he wasn't your son, Lizzie, an' it makes a difference. Whatever he was, I remember him when he was little, an' I learned to understand him and to make allowances. You've got to make allowances for them——"

It was half-past ten, and the old woman was saying: "But it's trouble from beginning to end; you're never too old for trouble, never too old for that——" when the gate banged back, and there were heavy feet on the steps.

"I'll go, Lizzie, let me go," cried the old woman, rising. But Elizabeth was at the door. It was a man in pit-clothes.

"They're bringin' 'im, Missis," he said. Elizabeth's heart halted a moment. Then it surged on again, almost suffocating her.

"Is he—is it bad?" she asked.

The man turned away, looking at the darkness:

"The doctor says 'e'd been dead hours. 'E saw 'im i' th' lamp-cabin."

The old woman, who stood just behind Elizabeth, dropped into a chair, and folded her hands, crying: "Oh, my boy, my boy!"

"Hush!" said Elizabeth, with a sharp twitch of a frown. "Be still, mother, don't waken th' children: I wouldn't have them down for anything!"

The old woman moaned softly, rocking herself. The man was drawing away. Elizabeth took a step forward.

"How was it?" she asked.

"Well, I couldn't say for sure," the man replied, very ill at ease. " 'E wor finishin' a stint an' th' butties 'ad gone, an' a lot o' stuff come down atop 'n 'im."

"And crushed him?" cried the widow, with a shudder.

"No," said the man, "it fell at th' back of 'im. 'E wor under th' face, an' it niver touched 'im. It shut 'im in. It seems 'e wor smothered."

Elizabeth shrank back. She heard the old woman behind her cry:

"What?—what did 'e say it was?"

The man replied, more loudly: "'E wor smothered!"

Then the old woman wailed aloud, and this relieved Elizabeth.

"Oh, mother," she said, putting her hand on the old woman, "don't waken th' children, don't waken th' children."

She wept a little, unknowing, while the old mother rocked herself and moaned. Elizabeth remembered that they were bringing him home, and she must be ready. "They'll lay him in the parlour," she said to herself, standing a moment pale and perplexed.

Then she lighted a candle and went into the tiny room. The air was cold and damp, but she could not make a fire, there was no fireplace. She set down the candle and looked round. The candlelight glittered on the lustre-glasses, on the two vases that held some of the pink chrysanthemums, and on the dark mahogany. There was a cold, deathly smell of chrysanthemums in the room. Elizabeth stood looking at the flowers. She turned away, and calculated whether there would be room to lay him on the floor, between the couch and the chiffonier.[4] She pushed the chairs aside. There would be room to lay him down and to step round him. Then she fetched the old red tablecloth, and another old cloth, spreading them down to save her bit of carpet. She shivered on leaving the parlour; so, from the dresser drawer she took a clean shirt and put it at the fire to air. All the time her mother-in-law was rocking herself in the chair and moaning.

"You'll have to move from there, mother," said Elizabeth. "They'll be bringing him in. Come in the rocker."

The old mother rose mechanically, and seated herself by the fire, continuing to lament. Elizabeth went into the pantry for another candle, and there, in the little pent-house under the naked tiles, she heard them coming. She stood still in the pantry doorway, listening. She heard them pass the end of the house, and come awkwardly down the three steps, a jumble of shuffling footsteps and muttering voices. The old woman was silent. The men were in the yard.

Then Elizabeth heard Matthews, the manager of the pit, say: "You go in first, Jim. Mind!"

The door came open, and the two women saw a collier backing into the room, holding one end of a stretcher, on which they could see the nailed pit-boots of the dead man. The two carriers halted, the man at the head stooping to the lintel of the door.

"Wheer will you have him?" asked the manager, a short, white-bearded man.

Elizabeth roused herself and came from the pantry carrying the unlighted candle.

"In the parlour," she said.

"In there, Jim!" pointed the manager, and the carriers backed round into the tiny room. The coat with which they had covered the body fell off as they awkwardly turned through the two doorways, and the women saw their man, naked to the waist, lying stripped for work. The old woman began to moan in a low voice of horror.

4. Chest of drawers.

"Lay th' stretcher at th' side," snapped the manager, "an' put 'im on th' cloths. Mind now, mind! Look you now——!"

One of the men had knocked off a vase of chrysanthemums. He stared awkwardly, then they set down the stretcher. Elizabeth did not look at her husband. As soon as she could get in the room, she went and picked up the broken vase and the flowers.

"Wait a minute!" she said.

The three men waited in silence while she mopped up the water with a duster.

"Eh, what a job, what a job, to be sure!" the manager was saying, rubbing his brow with trouble and perplexity. "Never knew such a thing in my life, never! He'd no busines to ha' been left. I never knew such a thing in my life! Fell over him clean as a whistle, an' shut him in. Not four foot of space, there wasn't—yet it scarce bruised him."

He looked down at the dead man, lying prone, half naked, all grimed with coal-dust.

"''Sphyxiated', the doctor said. It *is* the most terrible job I've ever known. Seems as if it was done o' purpose. Clean over him, an' shut 'im in, like a mouse-trap"—he made a sharp, descending gesture with his hand.

The colliers standing by jerked aside their heads in hopeless comment.

The horror of the thing bristled upon them all.

Then they heard the girl's voice upstairs calling shrilly: "Mother, mother—who is it? Mother, who is it?"

Elizabeth hurried to the foot of the stairs and opened the door:

"Go to sleep!" she commanded sharply. "What are you shouting about? Go to sleep at once—there's nothing—"

Then she began to mount the stairs. They could hear her on the boards, and on the plaster floor of the little bedroom. They could hear her distinctly:

"What's the matter now?—what's the matter with you, silly thing?"—her voice was much agitated, with an unreal gentleness.

"I thought it was some men come," said the plaintive voice of the child. "Has he come?"

"Yes, they've brought him. There's nothing to make a fuss about. Go to sleep now, like a good child."

They could hear her voice in the bedroom, they waited whilst she covered the children under the bedclothes.

"Is he drunk?" asked the girl, timidly, faintly.

"No! No—he's not! He—he's asleep."

"Is he asleep downstairs?"

"Yes—and don't make a noise."

There was silence for a moment, then the men heard the frightened child again:

"What's that noise?"

"It's nothing, I tell you, what are you bothering for?"

The noise was the grandmother moaning. She was oblivious of everything, sitting on her chair rocking and moaning The manager put his hand on her arm and bade her "Sh—sh!!"

The old woman opened her eyes and looked at him. She was shocked by this interruption, and seemed to wonder.

"What time is it?" the plaintive thin voice of the child, sinking back unhappily into sleep, asked this last question.

"Ten o'clock," answered the mother more softly. Then she must have bent down and kissed the children.

Matthews beckoned to the men to come away. They put on their caps and took up the stretcher. Stepping over the body, they tiptoed out of the house. None of them spoke till they were far from the wakeful children.

When Elizabeth came down she found her mother alone on the parlour floor, leaning over the dead man, the tears dropping on him.

"We must lay him out," the wife said. She put on the kettle, then returning knelt at the feet, and began to unfasten the knotted leather laces. The room was clammy and dim with only one candle, so that she had to bend her face almost to the floor. At last she got off the heavy boots and put them away.

"You must help me now," she whispered to the old woman. Together they stripped the man.

When they arose, saw him lying in the naïve dignity of death, the women stood arrested in fear and respect. For a few moments they remained still, looking down, the old mother whimpering. Elizabeth felt countermanded.[5] She saw him, how utterly inviolable he lay in himself. She had nothing to do with him. She could not accept it. Stooping, she laid her hand on him, in claim. He was still warm, for the mine was hot where he had died. His mother had his face between her hands, and was murmuring incoherently. The old tears fell in succession as drops from wet leaves; the mother was not weeping, merely her tears flowed. Elizabeth embraced the body of her husband, with cheek and lips. She seemed to be listening, inquiring, trying to get some connection. But she could not. She was driven away. He was impregnable.

She rose, went into the kitchen, where she poured warm water into a bowl, brought soap and flannel and a soft towel.

"I must wash him," she said.

Then the old mother rose stiffly, and watched Elizabeth as she carefully washed his face, carefully brushing the big blond moustache from his mouth with the flannel. She was afraid with a bottomless fear, so she ministered to him. The old woman, jealous, said:

"Let me wipe him!"—and she kneeled on the other side drying slowly as Elizabeth washed, her big black bonnet sometimes brushing the dark head of her daughter-in-law. They worked thus in silence for a long time. They never forgot it was death, and the touch of the man's dead body gave them strange emotions, different in each of the women; a great dread possessed them both, the mother felt the lie was given to her womb, she was denied; the wife felt the utter isolation of the human soul, the child within her was a weight apart from her.

At last it was finished. He was a man of handsome body, and his face showed no traces of drink. He was blond, full-fleshed, with fine limbs. But he was dead.

"Bless him," whispered his mother, looking always at his face, and speaking out of sheer terror. "Dear lad—bless him!" She spoke in a faint, sibilant ecstasy of fear and mother love.

Elizabeth sank down again to the floor, and put her face against his neck, and trembled and shuddered. But she had to draw away again. He was dead, and her living flesh had no place against his. A great dread and weariness held her: she was so unavailing. Her life was gone like this.

5. Overruled, contradicted.

"White as milk he is, clear as a twelve-month baby, bless him, the darling!" the old mother murmured to herself. "Not a mark on him, clear and clean and white, beautiful as ever a child was made," she murmured with pride. Elizabeth kept her face hidden.

"He went peaceful, Lizzie—peaceful as sleep. Isn't he beautiful, the lamb? Ay—he must ha' made his peace, Lizzie. 'Appen he made it all right, Lizzie, shut in there. He'd have time. He wouldn't look like this if he hadn't made his peace. The lamb, the dear lamb. Eh, but he had a hearty laugh. I loved to hear it. He had the heartiest laugh, Lizzie, as a lad——"

Elizabeth looked up. The man's mouth was fallen back, slightly open under the cover of the moustache. The eyes, half shut, did not show glazed in the obscurity. Life with its smoky burning gone from him, had left him apart and utterly alien to her. And she knew what a stranger he was to her. In her womb was ice of fear, because of this separate stranger with whom she had been living as one flesh. Was this what it all meant—utter, intact separateness, obscured by heat of living? In dread she turned her face away. The fact was too deadly. There had been nothing between them, and yet they had come together, exchanging their nakedness repeatedly. Each time he had taken her, they had been two isolated beings, far apart as now. He was no more responsible than she. The child was like ice in her womb. For as she looked at the dead man, her mind, cold and detached, said clearly: "Who am I? What have I been doing? I have been fighting a husband who did not exist. He existed all the time. What wrong have I done? What was that I have been living with? There lies the reality, this man." And her soul died in her for fear: she knew she had never seen him, he had never seen her, they had met in the dark and had fought in the dark, not knowing whom they met nor whom they fought. And now she saw, and turned silent in seeing. For she had been wrong. She had said he was something he was not; she had felt familiar with him. Whereas he was apart all the while, living as she never lived, feeling as she never felt.

In fear and shame she looked at his naked body, that she had known falsely. And he was the father of her children. Her soul was torn from her body and stood apart. She looked at his naked body and was ashamed, as if she had denied it. After all, it was itself. It seemed awful to her. She looked at his face, and she turned her own face to the wall. For his look was other than hers, his way was not her way. She had denied him what he was—she saw it now. She had refused him as himself. And this had been her life, and his life. She was grateful to death, which restored the truth. And she knew she was not dead.

And all the while her heart was bursting with grief and pity for him. What had he suffered? What stretch of horror for this helpless man! She was rigid with agony. She had not been able to help him. He had been cruelly injured, this naked man, this other being, and she could make no reparation. There were the children—but the children belonged to life. This dead man had nothing to do with them. He and she were only channels through which life had flowed to issue in the children. She was a mother—but how awful she knew it now to have been a wife. And he, dead now, how awful he must have felt it to be a husband. She felt that in the next world he would be a stranger to her. If they met there, in the beyond, they would only be ashamed of what had been before. The children had come, for some mysterious reason, out of both of them. But the children did not unite them. Now he was dead, she knew how eternally he was apart from her, how eternally he had nothing more to do with her. She saw this episode of her life closed. They had denied each other in life. Now he had withdrawn. An anguish came over her. It was finished then: it had become hopeless between them long before he died. Yet he had been her husband. But how little!

"Have you got his shirt, 'Lizabeth?"

Elizabeth turned without answering, though she strove to weep and behave as her mother-in-law expected. But she could not, she was silenced. She went into the kitchen and returned with the garment.

"It is aired," she said, grasping the cotton shirt here and there to try. She was almost ashamed to handle him; what right had she or anyone to lay hands on him; but her touch was humble on his body. It was hard work to clothe him. He was so heavy and inert. A terrible dread gripped her all the while: that he could be so heavy and utterly inert, unresponsive, apart. The horror of the distance between them was almost too much for her—it was so infinite a gap she must look across.

At last it was finished. They covered him with a sheet and left him lying, with his face bound. And she fastened the door of the little parlour, lest the children should see what was lying there. Then, with peace sunk heavy on her heart, she went about making tidy the kitchen. She knew she submitted to life, which was her immediate master. But from death, her ultimate master, she winced with fear and shame.

⊶ ⫘⬥⫘ ⊷

W. H. Auden
1907–1973

Wystan Hugh Auden's fantastically wrinkled face is a familiar icon from photographs taken in his later years. Often depicting Auden posing with his ever-present cigarette against a cityscape or airport, the photographs reveal part of Auden's continuing allure, which is that he was a witness, in his writing and in his person, to the changing scene of life and letters in the middle decades of the twentieth century. Auden came to embody a British literary Golden Age that lived on after the conditions that had brought it into being had changed utterly. His imperturbable face, looking much older than it was, had a sagelike quality of wisdom and the measurement of time passing: a map of modern experience.

Born in York, England, Auden had a pampered childhood, and was too young to see service in World War I. He was of the postwar generation, a group of gifted poets and writers who sought to replace the terrible losses of the war, its literary as well as its human casualties. Auden attended Christ Church College, Oxford, where his precocious literary career began in 1928 with the private publication of his *Poems*, thirty copies of which were put together by his friend and fellow writer Stephen Spender at Oxford. Auden joined a number of his friends and peers in heading to Berlin; his friend Christopher Isherwood's *I Am a Camera* (later the basis for the musical *Cabaret*) documented the phenomenon of these expatriate British writers spending their youthful careers in a decadent and exciting Berlin. Like many of the rest—though some died fighting fascism in Spain—Auden returned to England; he became a teacher in Scotland and England while writing feverishly. The cultural ferment of the thirties led Auden in many directions: chiefly, he wrote poetry, but he also became a noted literary critic, and he collaborated with Isherwood and others on plays and screenplays.

Auden's literary and political wanderlust took him to Iceland in 1936, where he wrote *Letters from Iceland* with Louis MacNeice; to Spain, which resulted in much poetry and occasional writing; to China, Japan, and the United States, culminating in the book *On the Frontier*. In 1939 he took an epochal step: he settled in the United States, where he became a citizen in 1946. In this he was a reverse T. S. Eliot—Eliot was an American who became a British citizen and is usually included as a premier writer of British, not American, literature. Auden was an American citizen who is always included in British anthologies, and rarely, if ever, in American collections. Part of Auden's desire to live in America had to do with his need to escape a stifling set of expectations for him that obtained in England—social, literary, and even personal expectations. In 1935, he had married Thomas Mann's daughter Erika, largely to protect her from political persecution in Germany, since Auden was a homosexual and lived for most of his adult life with the poet Chester Kallman, whom he met in 1939.

It was during Auden's teaching and fellowship years in the United States that he began to produce the large oeuvre of his poetry and his criticism. He taught and lectured at many colleges and universities, and read widely, taking a particular interest in the existentialist theology of Søren Kierkegaard. Increasingly impatient with Marxist materialism, Auden found a renewed commitment to Christianity in his later decades. During these years he published such notable milestones as his *Collected Shorter Poems*, *The Age of Anxiety*, and the critical work *The Enchafèd Flood*. In 1958 his definitive *Selected Poetry* was published, followed in 1962 by his magisterial work of criticism, *The Dyer's Hand*. His peripatetic and sometimes difficult teaching life led him to accept an offer from Oxford in 1956, to spend summers in Italy and in Austria, and to make a final move to Oxford and Christ Church College in 1972. However, he died shortly thereafter in 1973, in Austria, where he shared a summer house with Kallman.

The title of one of Auden's major long poems, *The Age of Anxiety*, summons up a reigning motif of Auden's poetic writing. Auden's poetry is edgy, tense, worried, psychoanalytic and yet despondent of the powers of psychoanalysis to allay anxiety. Anxiety is in some ways Auden's muse. This arises from the seriousness with which Auden had gauged the world political situation. Having witnessed the depression, the rise of Nazism, totalitarianism, World War II, the Holocaust, the atomic bomb, and the Cold War, Auden's political realism is tinged inevitably with disillusionment. Modern history is one primary source for Auden's poetry; in poems like *September 1, 1939*, he makes no retreat to purely aesthetic subject matter, or to the past, or to pure experimentation. Auden's is a poetry of waiting rooms, radio broadcasts, armed battalions, and of snatched pleasures treasured all the more for their fleeting magic.

Paradoxically, Auden's moral and political engagements coexist with an anarchic streak, a wry wit, and a love of leisure and play. Auden developed one of the most seductively varied voices in modern poetry, creating an endlessly inventive style that draws at will on Latin elegy, Anglo-Saxon alliterative verse forms, Norse runes and "kennings," technical scientific discourse, and the meters and language of British music hall songs and of American blues singers. All these elements can be present in a single stanza, to sometimes dizzying effect; in other poems, these radically different materials are blended and modulated into a deceptively plain style of great power.

A topic of special concern for Auden was the survival of literary language. How would poetry make claims for its relevance, given that it was now surrounded by so many other voices, from those of mass culture to the exigent rhetoric of war? Auden often compared himself poetically to William Butler Yeats, as another political poet in a time when poetry was seen as largely irrelevant or even antithetical to politics.

Auden's poetry remains a profoundly lyric poetry: that is, it celebrates the singular human voice that sings its lines. It is not surprising that he wrote opera librettos, notably *The Rake's Progress*, which he wrote with Chester Kallman for Igor Stravinsky. Auden was an intellectual inheritor of Freud and Marx—he knew the ways that the self could remain unknown to itself, and the ways that history could relentlessly rush on oblivious of the human lives swept up in its current. Still, the human voice of poetry goes on, even in the age of anxiety, framing its lyric songs. In the late phase of his poetry, Auden had despaired of systems, and returned even more to the meticulous versification he was so well versed in. His poems become almost defiant vehicles of traditional rhyme and meter, lodged in the modern, everyday world, where "in the deserts of the heart," Auden would "let the healing fountain start."

Musée des Beaux Arts[1]

About suffering they were never wrong,
The Old Masters: how well they understood
Its human position; how it takes place
While someone else is eating or opening a window or just walking dully along;
5   How, when the aged are reverently, passionately waiting
For the miraculous birth, there always must be
Children who did not specially want it to happen, skating
On a pond at the edge of the wood:
They never forgot
10   That even the dreadful martyrdom must run its course
Anyhow in a corner, some untidy spot
Where the dogs go on with their doggy life and the torturer's horse
Scratches its innocent behind on a tree.

In Brueghel's *Icarus*, for instance: how everything turns away
15   Quite leisurely from the disaster; the ploughman may
Have heard the splash, the forsaken cry,
But for him it was not an important failure; the sun shone
As it had to on the white legs disappearing into the green
Water; and the expensive delicate ship that must have seen
20   Something amazing, a boy falling out of the sky,
Had somewhere to get to and sailed calmly on.

1938   1940

In Memory of W. B. Yeats

(d. January 1939)

1

He disappeared in the dead of winter:
The brooks were frozen, the air-ports almost deserted,
And snow disfigured the public statues;
The mercury sank in the mouth of the dying day.
5   O all the instruments agree
The day of his death was a dark cold day.

Far from his illness
The wolves ran on through the evergreen forests,
The peasant river was untempted by the fashionable quays;
10   By mourning tongues

1. The Musées Royaux des Beaux-Arts in Brussels contain a collection of paintings by the Flemish painter Pieter Brueghel (1525–1569) that includes *The Fall of Icarus*; Brueghel is famous for his acute observation of ordinary life. A figure from Greek mythology, Icarus had wings of wax and feathers but flew too close to the sun, which melted the wax and caused him to fall into the sea.

The death of the poet was kept from his poems.

But for him it was his last afternoon as himself,
An afternoon of nurses and rumours;
The provinces of his body revolted,
15   The squares of his mind were empty,
Silence invaded the suburbs,
The current of his feeling failed: he became his admirers.

Now he is scattered among a hundred cities
And wholly given over to unfamiliar affections;
20   To find his happiness in another kind of wood
And be punished under a foreign code of conscience.
The words of a dead man
Are modified in the guts of the living.

But in the importance and noise of to-morrow
25   When the brokers are roaring like beasts on the floor of the Bourse,[1]
And the poor have the sufferings to which they are fairly accustomed,
And each in the cell of himself is almost convinced of his freedom;
A few thousand will think of this day
As one thinks of a day when one did something slightly unusual.
30   O all the instruments agree
The day of his death was a dark cold day.

2

You were silly like us: your gift survived it all;
The parish of rich women, physical decay,
Yourself; mad Ireland hurt you into poetry.
35   Now Ireland has her madness and her weather still,
For poetry makes nothing happen: it survives
In the valley of its saying where executives
Would never want to tamper; it flows south
From ranches of isolation and the busy griefs,
40   Raw towns that we believe and die in; it survives,
A way of happening, a mouth.

3

Earth, receive an honoured guest;
William Yeats is laid to rest:
Let the Irish vessel lie
Emptied of its poetry.

45   Time that is intolerant
Of the brave and innocent,
And indifferent in a week
To a beautiful physique,

Worships language and forgives
50   Everyone by whom it lives;
Pardons cowardice, conceit,
Lays its honours at their feet.

1. Stock exchange.

Time that with this strange excuse
Pardoned Kipling and his views,
55   And will pardon Paul Claudel,[2]
Pardons him for writing well.

In the nightmare of the dark
All the dogs of Europe bark,
And the living nations wait,
60   Each sequestered in its hate;

Intellectual disgrace
Stares from every human face,
And the seas of pity lie
Locked and frozen in each eye.

65   Follow, poet, follow right
To the bottom of the night,
With your unconstraining voice
Still persuade us to rejoice;

With the farming of a verse
70   Make a vineyard of the curse,
Sing of human unsuccess
In a rapture of distress;

In the deserts of the heart
Let the healing fountain start,
75   In the prison of his days
Teach the free man how to praise.

February 1939   1940

September 1, 1939[1]

I sit in one of the dives
On Fifty-Second Street
Uncertain and afraid
As the clever hopes expire
5   Of a low dishonest decade:
Waves of anger and fear
Circulate over the bright
And darkened lands of the earth,
Obsessing our private lives;
10   The unmentionable odour of death
Offends the September night.

Accurate scholarship can
Unearth the whole offence

2. Rudyard Kipling (1865–1936), short-story writer, poet, and novelist remembered for his celebration of British imperialism; Paul Claudel (1868–1955), French poet and diplomat noted for his conservative views.

1. Auden arrived in New York City, where he was to spend World War II and much of the rest of his life, in January 1939. German forces marched into Poland on 1 September 1939; Britain and France declared war on 3 September.

From Luther[2] until now
15   That has driven a culture mad,
Find what occurred at Linz,[3]
What huge imago made
A psychopathic god:[4]
I and the public know
20   What all schoolchildren learn,
Those to whom evil is done
Do evil in return.

Exiled Thucydides[5] knew
All that a speech can say
25   About Democracy,
And what dictators do,
The elderly rubbish they talk
To an apathetic grave;
Analysed all in his book,
30   The enlightenment driven away,
The habit-forming pain,
Mismanagement and grief:
We must suffer them all again.

Into this neutral air
35   Where blind skyscrapers use
Their full height to proclaim
The strength of Collective Man,
Each language pours its vain
Competitive excuse:
40   But who can live for long
In an euphoric dream;
Out of the mirror they stare,
Imperialism's face
And the international wrong.

45   Faces along the bar
Cling to their average day:
The lights must never go out,
The music must always play,
All the conventions conspire
50   To make this fort assume
The furniture of home;
Lest we should see where we are,
Lost in a haunted wood,
Children afraid of the night
55   Who have never been happy or good.

2. Martin Luther, German religious reformer (1483–1546), whose criticisms of Roman Catholic doctrine sparked the Protestant Reformation in Europe.
3. Linz, Austria, was Adolf Hitler's birthplace.
4. In the psychological terminology developed by C. G. Jung (1875–1961), an *imago* is an idealized mental image of self or others, especially parental figures.
5. Fifth-century Athenian historian and general in the Peloponnesian War between Athens and Sparta (431–404 B.C.). In his famous *History of the Peloponnesian War*, which follows events until 411 B.C., Thucydides records the Athenian statesman Pericles' *Funeral Oration*, given at the end of the first year of the war. In it, Pericles describes the benefits and possible dangers of democratic government as it was then practiced at Athens. Thucydides himself was exiled from Athens in 424 B.C., following a military defeat incurred under his leadership.

The windiest militant trash
Important Persons shout
Is not so crude as our wish:
What mad Nijinsky wrote
60   About Diaghilev
Is true of the normal heart;[6]
For the error bred in the bone
Of each woman and each man
Craves what it cannot have,
65   Not universal love
But to be loved alone.

From the conservative dark
Into the ethical life
The dense commuters come,
70   Repeating their morning vow,
"I *will* be true to the wife,
I'll concentrate more on my work,"
And helpless governors wake
To resume their compulsory game:
75   Who can release them now,
Who can reach the deaf,
Who can speak for the dumb?

All I have is a voice
To undo the folded lie,
80   The romantic lie in the brain
Of the sensual man-in-the-street
And the lie of Authority
Whose buildings grope the sky:
There is no such thing as the State
85   And no one exists alone;
Hunger allows no choice
To the citizen or the police;
We must love one another or die.

Defenceless under the night
90   Our world in stupor lies;
Yet, dotted everywhere,
Ironic points of light
Flash out wherever the Just
Exchange their messages:
95   May I, composed like them
Of Eros and of dust,
Beleaguered by the same
Negation and despair,
Show an affirming flame.

1939   1940

6. Vaslav Nijinsky (1890–1950), principal male dancer in the Ballets Russes company under the direction of Sergei Pavlovich Diaghilev (1872–1929). The company revolutionized the world of dance, causing a sensation on its visit to Paris in 1909. Auden borrowed the following lines from Nijinsky's (1937) *Diary:* "Diaghilev does not want universal love, but to be loved alone."

⟫+ PERSPECTIVES +⟪

World War II and the End of Empire

World War I had been a catastrophe of unprecedented proportions. Never before in world history had a preponderance of national powers joined together into two warring alliances; never before had the theater of war included such a wide expanse of the globe. But for Great Britain, at least, the war was foreign rather than domestic; as demoralizing and bleak as the fighting was, it was "over there," and never touched the British Isles. World War II would be a very different story.

World War II started, technically, with Hitler's invasion of Poland on 1 September 1939; as is the case with all world-historical conflicts, however, the war's genesis can be traced further back—in this case, back two decades to the peace treaties with which World War I was uneasily concluded. The victors of World War I never quite got what they hoped for, and the defeated nations had their defeat transformed into ritual diplomatic humiliation. Meanwhile, a worldwide economic depression had begun in the United States in 1929 and spread to Europe by the early 1930s, weakening democratic governments and lending a seductive edge to the rhetoric of political extremists. As a result, when Hitler began to rise to power in a beleaguered Germany during the 1930s, his message of empowerment was one that many Germans wanted to hear. Beginning with Poland, Hitler overran Denmark, Luxembourg, the Netherlands, Belgium, and Norway in quick succession, and by June 1940 had conquered even France. Britain was next on Hitler's list, as the major remaining obstacle to the domination of Europe.

Hitler hoped to paralyze and demoralize the British by a devastating series of attacks by air. This drew out to become the ten-month-long Battle of Britain, in which the German Luftwaffe (air force) engaged Britain's Royal Air Force in the previously inviolable air space over England's green and pleasant land. The battle brought enormous costs—especially during the eight months of nightly air raids over British metropolitan centers known as the Blitz. The bombing caused great destruction to London, which was bombed every night between 7 September and 2 November 1940; more than 15,000 civilians were killed in London (30,000 nationwide), over half a million left homeless, and important cultural and architectural treasures, such as the House of Commons and Buckingham Palace, were damaged or destroyed. This violation of England's homeland was costly in psychological and emotional terms as well; one poignant register of the broad impact of the air raids can be seen in Virginia Woolf's final novel *Between the Acts*, where the sound of bombs falling on distant London unnerves the residents and guests of Pointz Hall. As Woolf's diaries and letters make clear, the sound of those bombs were also a crucial factor in her decision to take her own life in March 1941.

In May 1941, Germany finally gave up its attempt to conquer Britain from the air. With the bombing of Pearl Harbor by the Japanese in December 1941, the United States entered the war on the side of the Allies; with their help, Britain was able to mount an offensive against Germany on the European mainland and retake land that had been invaded by Germany. In 1942, Britain and the United States began to plan an invasion across the English Channel. The first attempt, a raid staged at the French port of Dieppe in the summer of 1942, was a disappointing failure. The Allies regrouped, however, and planned the offensive known as D-Day. On 6 June 1944, Allied troops, under the command of General Dwight D. Eisenhower, crossed the channel with 2,700 ships and 176,000 soldiers and overcame German defenses; by the end of the month, about a million Allied troops were on the ground in France, and the tide of the war had turned. In April 1945 Hitler committed suicide; one week later, Germany signed a statement of unconditional surrender, with Japan following suit on 2 September.

World War II was over; in some important arenas, however, its influence had just begun to be felt. With such a great proportion of its able-bodied young men going off to war, millions of women in both Britain and the United States took employment outside the home for the first time; that trend, once started, has only gained momentum in the years since. The economic and personal freedom ceded to women during the wartime emergency laid the groundwork for the contemporary women's movement in Great Britain; Margaret Thatcher, Britain's first woman Prime Minister (1979–1990), was a postwar inheritor of Winston Churchill's legacy.

At the same time, the United States and the Soviet Union emerged from the war as the preeminent world powers; Britain, while on the winning side, saw its global prestige in eclipse, and found itself in the midst of an economic crisis. At the height of the war, Britain was devoting 54 percent of its gross national product to the war effort; by the war's end it had expended practically all of its foreign financial resources and was several billion pounds in debt to its wartime allies. In short, Britain was bankrupt. As its colonial possessions increased their protests against British rule, Britain had neither the military nor the economic power to control them; India, which had begun its independence movement during World War I, finally won full independence on 15 August 1947, and Burma and Ceylon (now Sri Lanka) quickly followed suit in early 1948. At about the same time, Britain was forced to withdraw from Palestine, and from all of Egypt except for the Suez Canal; the Canal itself was nationalized by Egypt in the summer of 1956. The 1960s saw increased Irish Republican activity in Northern Ireland, degenerating into armed sectarian violence in 1968; recent years have seen periodic waves of IRA violence in support of independence for Ulster, alternating with largely unsuccessful diplomatic attempts to forge a lasting peace in Northern Ireland. In the spring of 1982 Prime Minister Thatcher sent British troops to liberate the Falkland Islands, a small self-governing British colony off the coast of Argentina, from an Argentinian occupying force; Thatcher won a resounding reelection the following year on the strength of the British success, suggesting that pride in the British Empire, while diminishing in importance, was by no means yet extinct.

Sir Winston Churchill
1874–1965

British historian A. J. P. Taylor has written of a unique paradox of World War II: though it was a time of unprecedented stress and anxiety for the British people, "Great Britain was never so free from political controversy." The reason? Winston Churchill's ability to forge a partnership between himself and the British people. "There have been many great British leaders," Taylor continues; "There has only been one whom everyone recognized as the embodiment of the national will." The pictures of Churchill—watch-chain draped across his waistcoat, cigar drooping from his jowly face (above his bow tie and beneath his homburg), index and middle fingers raised in the V of Victory—is perhaps the most familiar and bouyant icon of Allied victory in the war.

Winston Churchill was born at Blenheim Palace, the ancestral home of his grandfather, the seventh duke of Marlborough; his father, Lord Randolph Churchill, had a distinguished career as a Conservative member of Parliament. Young Winston proved not to be an outstanding scholar, however, and instead of university, was sent to the Royal Military Academy. This military training, and his subsequent combat experience on the Western Front and in the Sudan, was to prove invaluable as he led his country as prime minister through the darkest days of World War II. Equally important to Churchill the statesman was his early work as a journalist and essayist; the economist John Kenneth Galbraith suggested that Churchill's power as an orator derived from his "fearsome certainty that he was completely right," a certainty made manifest in "his use of language as a weapon." In Churchill's well-known phrases, like "blood, toil, tears and sweat," a nation at war found its rallying cries.

Winston Churchill, June 1943. Returning to 10 Downing Street after meeting with American president Franklin Roosevelt in Washington, D.C., and visiting Allied armies in North Africa, the Prime Minister flashes his famous "V for Victory" sign to reporters.

Two Speeches Before the House of Commons

["Blood, Toil, Tears and Sweat"][1]

I beg to move,

> That this House welcomes the formation of a Government representing the united and inflexible resolve of the nation to prosecute the war with Germany to a victorious conclusion.

On Friday evening last I received His Majesty's Commission to form a new Administration. It was the evident wish and will of Parliament and the nation that this should be conceived on the broadest possible basis and that it should include all parties, both those who supported the late Government and also the parties of the Opposition. I have completed the most important part of this task. A War Cabinet has been formed of five Members, representing, with the Opposition Liberals, the unity of the nation. The three party Leaders have agreed to serve, either in the War Cabinet or in high executive office. The three Fighting Services have been filled. It was necessary that this should be done in one single day, on account of the extreme

1. Delivered in the House of Commons, 13 May 1940.

urgency and rigour of events. A number of other positions, key positions, were filled yesterday, and I am submitting a further list to His Majesty to-night. I hope to complete the appointment of the principal Ministers during to-morrow. The appointment of the other Ministers usually takes a little longer, but I trust that, when Parliament meets again, this part of my task will be completed, and that the administration will be complete in all respects.

I considered it in the public interest to suggest that the House should be summoned to meet to-day. Mr Speaker agreed, and took the necessary steps, in accordance with the powers conferred upon him by the Resolution of the House. At the end of the proceedings to-day, the Adjournment of the House will be proposed until Tuesday, 21st May, with, of course, provision for earlier meeting, if need be. The business to be considered during that week will be notified to Members at the earliest opportunity. I now invite the House, by the Motion which stands in my name, to record its approval of the steps taken and to declare its confidence in the new Government.

To form an Administration of this scale and complexity is a serious undertaking in itself, but it must be remembered that we are in the preliminary stage of one of the greatest battles in history, that we are in action at many other points in Norway and in Holland, that we have to be prepared in the Mediterranean, that the air battle is continuous and that many preparations, such as have been indicated by my hon. Friend below the Gangway, have to be made here at home. In this crisis I hope I may be pardoned if I do not address the House at any length to-day. I hope that any of my friends and colleagues, or former colleagues, who are affected by the political reconstruction, will make allowance, all allowance, for any lack of ceremony with which it has been necessary to act. I would say to the House, as I said to those who have joined this Government: "I have nothing to offer but blood, toil, tears and sweat."

We have before us an ordeal of the most grievous kind. We have before us many, many long months of struggle and of suffering. You ask, what is our policy? I can say: It is to wage war, by sea, land and air, with all our might and with all the strength that God can give us; to wage war against a monstrous tyranny, never surpassed in the dark, lamentable catalogue of human crime. That is our policy. You ask, what is our aim? I can answer in one word: It is victory, victory at all costs, victory in spite of all terror, victory, however long and hard the road may be; for without victory, there is no survival. Let that be realised; no survival for the British Empire, no survival for all that the British Empire has stood for, no survival for the urge and impulse of the ages, that mankind will move forward towards its goal. But I take up my task with buoyancy and hope. I feel sure that our cause will not be suffered to fail among men. At this time I feel entitled to claim the aid of all, and I say, "Come then, let us go forward together with our united strength."

["WARS ARE NOT WON BY EVACUATIONS"][1]

From the moment that the French defenses at Sedan and on the Meuse[2] were broken at the end of the second week of May, only a rapid retreat to Amiens[3] and the south could have saved the British and French Armies who had entered Belgium at the

---

1. Delivered in the House of Commons 4 June 1940. This speech exemplifies Churchill's ability to rally his people amid the greatest difficulties—here, the disastrous defeat of the British and French armies in April–May 1940. What might have been seen as the humiliation of the British army becomes, in Churchill's stirring account, the

heroic achievement of a successful evacuation against all odds.
2. A river flowing through France, Belgium, and the Netherlands.
3. A city located on the Somme River in northern France.

appeal of the Belgian King; but this strategic fact was not immediately realized. The French High Command hoped they would be able to close the gap, and the Armies of the north were under their orders. Moreover, a retirement of this kind would have involved almost certainly the destruction of the fine Belgian Army of over 20 divisions and the abandonment of the whole of Belgium. Therefore, when the force and scope of the German penetration were realized and when a new French Generalissimo,[4] General Weygand, assumed command in place of General Gamelin, an effort was made by the French and British Armies in Belgium to keep on holding the right hand of the Belgians and to give their own right hand to the newly created French Army which was to have advanced across the Somme[5] in great strength to grasp it.

However, the German eruption swept like a sharp scythe around the right and rear of the Armies of the north. Eight or nine armored divisions, each of about four hundred armored vehicles of different kinds, but carefully assorted to be complementary and divisible into small self-contained units, cut off all communications between us and the main French Armies. It severed our own communications for food and ammunition, which ran first to Amiens and afterwards through Abbeville, and it shore its way up the coast to Boulogne and Calais, and almost to Dunkirk.[6] Behind this armored and mechanized onslaught came a number of German divisions in lorries, and behind them again there plodded comparatively slowly the dull brute mass of the ordinary German Army and German people, always so ready to be led to the trampling down in other lands of liberties and comforts which they have never known in their own.

I have said this armored scythe-stroke almost reached Dunkirk—almost but not quite. Boulogne and Calais were the scenes of desperate fighting. The Guards defended Boulogne for a while and were then withdrawn by orders from this country. The Rifle Brigade, the 60th Rifles, and the Queen Victoria's Rifles, with a battalion of British tanks and 1,000 Frenchmen, in all about four thousand strong, defended Calais to the last. The British Brigadier was given an hour to surrender. He spurned the offer, and four days of intense street fighting passed before silence reigned over Calais, which marked the end of a memorable resistance. Only 30 unwounded survivors were brought off by the Navy, and we do not know the fate of their comrades. Their sacrifice, however, was not in vain. At least two armored divisions, which otherwise would have been turned against the British Expeditionary Force, had to be sent to overcome them. They have added another page to the glories of the light divisions, and the time gained enabled the Graveline water lines to be flooded and to be held by the French troops.

Thus it was that the port of Dunkirk was kept open. When it was found impossible for the Armies of the north to reopen their communications to Amiens with the main French Armies, only one choice remained. It seemed, indeed, forlorn. The Belgian, British and French Armies were almost surrounded. Their sole line of retreat was to a single port and to its neighboring beaches. They were pressed on every side by heavy attacks and far outnumbered in the air.

When, a week ago today, I asked the House to fix this afternoon as the occasion for a statement, I feared it would be my hard lot to announce the greatest military disaster in our long history. I thought—and some good judges agreed with me—that perhaps 20,000 or 30,000 men might be re-embarked. But it certainly seemed that the whole of the French First Army and the whole of the British Expeditionary Force

---

4. Supreme commander of the French forces.
5. A river in northern France.

6. Seaports in northern France.

north of the Amiens-Abbeville gap would be broken up in the open field or else would have to capitulate for lack of food and ammunition. These were the hard and heavy tidings for which I called upon the House and the nation to prepare themselves a week ago. The whole root and core and brain of the British Army, on which and around which we were to build, and are to build, the great British Armies in the later years of the war, seemed about to perish upon the field or to be led into an ignominious and starving capacity.

That was the prospect a week ago. But another blow which might well have proved final was yet to fall upon us. The King of the Belgians[7] had called upon us to come to his aid. Had not this Ruler and his Government severed themselves from the Allies, who rescued their country from extinction in the late war, and had they not sought refuge in what was proved to be a fatal neutrality, the French and British Armies might well at the outset have saved not only Belgium but perhaps even Poland. Yet at the last moment, when Belgium was already invaded, King Leopold called upon us to come to his aid, and even at the last moment we came. He and his brave, efficient Army, nearly half a million strong, guarded our left flank and thus kept open our only line of retreat to the sea. Suddenly, without prior consultation, with the least possible notice, without the advice of his Ministers and upon his own personal act, he sent a plenipotentiary[8] to the German Command, surrendered his Army, and exposed our whole flank and means of retreat.

I asked the House a week ago to suspend its judgment because the facts were not clear, but I do not feel that any reason now exists why we should not form our own opinions upon this pitiful episode. The surrender of the Belgian Army compelled the British at the shortest notice to cover a flank to the sea more than 30 miles in length. Otherwise all would have been cut off, and all would have shared the fate to which King Leopold had condemned the finest Army his country had ever formed. So in doing this and in exposing this flank, as anyone who followed the operations on the map will see, contact was lost between the British and two out of the three corps forming the First French Army, who were still farther from the coast than we were, and it seemed impossible that any large number of Allied troops could reach the coast.

The enemy attacked on all sides with great strength and fierceness, and their main power, the power of their far more numerous Air Force, was thrown into the battle or else concentrated upon Dunkirk and the beaches. Pressing in upon the narrow exit, both from the east and from the west, the enemy began to fire with cannon upon the beaches by which alone the shipping could approach or depart. They sowed magnetic mines in the channels and seas; they sent repeated waves of hostile aircraft, sometimes more than a hundred strong in one formation, to cast their bombs upon the single pier that remained, and upon the sand dunes upon which the troops had their eyes for shelter. Their U-boats, one of which was sunk, and their motor launches took their toll of the vast traffic which now began. For four or five days an intense struggle reigned. All their armored divisions—or what was left of them—together with great masses of infantry and artillery, hurled themselves in vain upon the ever-narrowing, ever-contracting appendix within which the British and French Armies fought.

Meanwhile, the Royal Navy, with the willing help of countless merchant seamen, strained every nerve to embark the British and Allied troops; 220 light warships and 650 other vessels were engaged. They had to operate upon the difficult coast, often in adverse weather, under an almost ceaseless hail of bombs and an increasing concentration of artillery fire. Nor were the seas, as I have said, themselves free from mines and torpedoes. It was in conditions such as these that our men carried on, with little or no rest, for days and nights on end, making trip after trip across the dangerous waters, bringing with them always men whom they had rescued. The numbers they have brought back are the measure of their devotion and their courage. The hospital ships, which brought off many thousands of British and French wounded, being so plainly marked were a special target for Nazi bombs; but the men and women on board them never faltered in their duty.

Meanwhile, the Royal Air Force, which had already been intervening in the battle, so far as its range would allow, from home bases, now used part of its main metropolitan fighter strength, and struck at the German bombers and at the fighters which in large numbers protected them. This struggle was protracted and fierce. Suddenly the scene has cleared, the crash and thunder has for the moment—but only for the moment—died away. A miracle of deliverance, achieved by valor, by perseverance, by perfect discipline, by faultless service, by resource, by skill, by unconquerable fidelity, is manifest to us all. The enemy was hurled back by the retreating British and French troops. He was so roughly handled that he did not hurry their departure seriously. The Royal Air Force engaged the main strength of the German Air Force, and inflicted upon them losses of at least four to one; and the Navy, using nearly 1,000 ships of all kinds, carried over 335,000 men, French and British, out of the jaws of death and shame, to their native land and to the tasks which lie immediately ahead. We must be very careful not to assign to this deliverance the attributes of a victory. Wars are not won by evacuations. But there was a victory inside this deliverance, which should be noted. It was gained by the Air Force. Many of our soldiers coming back have not seen the Air Force at work; they saw only the bombers which escaped its protective attack. They underrate its achievements. I have heard much talk of this; that is why I go out of my way to say this. I will tell you about it.

This was a great trial of strength between the British and German Air Forces. Can you conceive a greater objective for the Germans in the air than to make evacuation from these beaches impossible, and to sink all these ships which were displayed, almost to the extent of thousands? Could there have been an objective of greater military importance and significance for the whole purpose of the war than this? They tried hard, and they were beaten back; they were frustrated in their task. We got the Army away; and they have paid fourfold for any losses which they have inflicted. Very large formations of German aeroplanes—and we know that they are a very brave race—have turned on several occasions from the attack of one-quarter of their number of the Royal Air Force, and have dispersed in different directions. Twelve aeroplanes have been hunted by two. One aeroplane was driven into the water and cast away by the mere charge of a British aeroplane, which had no more ammunition. All of our types—the Hurricane, the Spitfire and the new Defiant—and all our pilots have been vindicated as superior to what they have at present to face.

When we consider how much greater would be our advantage in defending the air above this Island against an overseas attack, I must say that I find in these facts a sure basis upon which practical and reassuring thoughts may rest. I will pay my tribute to these young airmen. The great French Army was very largely, for the time being, cast back and disturbed by the onrush of a few thousands of armored vehicles. May it not also be that the cause of civilization itself will be defended by the skill and devotion of a few thousand airmen? There never has been, I suppose, in all the world, in all the history of war, such an opportunity for youth. The Knights of the Round Table, the Crusaders, all fall back into the past—not only distant but prosaic; these young men, going forth every morn to guard their native land and all that we stand for, holding in their hands these instruments of colossal and shattering power, of whom it may be said that

> Every morn brought forth a noble chance
> And every chance brought forth a noble knight,[9]

deserve our gratitude, as do all the brave men who, in so many ways and on so many occasions, are ready, and continue ready to give life and all for their native land.

I return to the Army. In the long series of very fierce battles, now on this front, now on that, fighting on three fronts at once, battles fought by two or three divisions against an equal or somewhat larger number of the enemy, and fought fiercely on some of the old grounds that so many of us knew so well—in these battles our losses in men have exceeded 30,000 killed, wounded and missing. I take occasion to express the sympathy of the House to all who have suffered bereavement or who are still anxious. The President of the Board of Trade [Sir Andrew Duncan] is not here today. His son has been killed, and many in the House have felt the pangs of affliction in the sharpest form. But I will say this about the missing: We have had a large number of wounded come home safely to this country, but I would say about the missing that there may be very many reported missing who will come back home, some day, in one way or another. In the confusion of this fight it is inevitable that many have been left in positions where honor required no further resistance from them.

Against this loss of over 30,000 men, we can set a far heavier loss certainly inflicted upon the enemy. But our losses in materiel are enormous. We have perhaps lost one-third of the men we lost in the opening days of the battle of 21st March, 1918, but we have lost nearly as many guns—nearly one thousand—and all our transport, all the armored vehicles that were with the Army in the north. This loss will impose a further delay on the expansion of our military strength. That expansion had not been proceeding as far as we had hoped. The best of all we had to give had gone to the British Expeditionary Force, and although they had not the numbers of tanks and some articles of equipment which were desirable, they were a very well and finely equipped Army. They had the first-fruits of all that our industry had to give, and that is gone. And now here is this further delay. How long it will be, how long it will last, depends upon the exertions which we make in this Island. An effort the like of which has never been seen in our records is now being made. Work is proceeding everywhere, night and day, Sundays and week days. Capital and Labor have cast aside their interests, rights, and customs and put them into the common stock. Already the flow of munitions has leaped forward. There is no reason why we should not in a few months overtake the sudden and serious loss that has come upon us, without retarding the development of our general program.

Nevertheless, our thankfulness at the escape of our Army and so many men, whose loved ones have passed through an agonizing week, must not blind us to the fact that what has happened in France and Belgium is a colossal military disaster. The French Army has been weakened, the Belgian Army has been lost, a large part of those fortified lines upon which so much faith had been reposed is gone, many valuable mining

---

9. Churchill misquotes slightly Tennyson's poem *Morte d'Arthur*, lines 280–81.

districts and factories have passed into the enemy's possession, the whole of the Channel ports are in his hands, with all the tragic consequences that follow from that, and we must expect another blow to be struck almost immediately at us or at France. We are told that Herr Hitler has a plan for invading the British Isles. This has often been thought of before. When Napoleon lay at Boulogne for a year with his flat-bottomed boats and his Grand Army, he was told by someone. "There are bitter weeds in England." There are certainly a great many more of them since the British Expeditionary Force returned.

The whole question of home defense against invasion is, of course, powerfully affected by the fact that we have for the time being in this Island incomparably more powerful military forces than we have ever had at any moment in this war or the last. But this will not continue. We shall not be content with a defensive war. We have our duty to our Ally. We have to reconstitute and build up the British Expeditionary Force once again, under its gallant Commander-in-Chief, Lord Gort. All this is in train; but in the interval we must put our defenses in this Island into such a high state of organization that the fewest possible numbers will be required to give effective security and that the largest possible potential of offensive effort may be realized. On this we are now engaged. It will be very convenient, if it be the desire of the House, to enter upon this subject in a secret Session. Not that the government would necessarily be able to reveal in very great detail military secrets, but we like to have our discussions free, without the restraint imposed by the fact that they will be read the next day by the enemy; and the Government would benefit by views freely expressed in all parts of the House by Members with their knowledge of so many different parts of the country. I understand that some request is to be made upon this subject, which will be readily acceded to by His Majesty's Government.

We have found it necessary to take measures of increasing stringency, not only against enemy aliens and suspicious characters of other nationalities, but also against British subjects who may become a danger or a nuisance should the war be transported to the United Kingdom. I know there are a great many people affected by the orders which we have made who are the passionate enemies of Nazi Germany. I am very sorry for them, but we cannot, at the present time and under the present stress, draw all the distinctions which we should like to do. If parachute landings were attempted and fierce fighting attendant upon them followed, these unfortunate people would be far better out of the way, for their own sakes as well as for ours. There is, however, another class, for which I feel not the slightest sympathy. Parliament has given us the powers to put down Fifth Column[1] activities with a strong hand, and we shall use those powers subject to the supervision and correction of the House, without the slightest hesitation until we are satisfied, and more than satisfied, that this malignancy in our midst has been effectively stamped out.

Turning once again, and this time more generally, to the question of invasion, I would observe that there has never been a period in all these long centuries of which we boast when an absolute guarantee against invasion, still less against serious raids, could have been given to our people. In the days of Napoleon the same wind which would have carried his transports across the Channel might have driven away the blockading fleet. There was always the chance, and it is that chance which has excited and befooled the imaginations of many Continental tyrants. Many are the tales

1. Traitorous: a term coined by a Spanish fascist general in 1936, who attacked Madrid with four columns of troops, and later boasted that he had been aided by a "fifth column" of secret fascist supporters inside the city.

that are told. We are assured that novel methods will be adopted, and when we see the originality of malice, the ingenuity of aggression, which our enemy displays, we may certainly prepare ourselves for every kind of novel stratagem and every kind of brutal and treacherous maneuver. I think that no idea is so outlandish that it should not be considered and viewed with a searching, but at the same time, I hope, with a steady eye. We must never forget the solid assurances of sea power and those which belong to air power if it can be locally exercised.

I have, myself, full confidence that if all do their duty, if nothing is neglected, and if the best arrangements are made, as they are being made, we shall prove ourselves once again able to defend our Island home, to ride out the storm of war, and to outlive the menace of tyranny, if necessary for years, if necessary alone. At any rate, that is what we are going to try to do. That is the resolve of His Majesty's Government— every man of them. That is the will of Parliament and the nation. The British Empire and the French Republic, linked together in their cause and in their need, will defend to the death their native soil, aiding each other like good comrades to the utmost of their strength. Even though large tracts of Europe and many old and famous States have fallen or may fall into the grip of the Gestapo and all the odious apparatus of Nazi rule, we shall not flag or fail. We shall go on to the end, we shall fight in France, we shall fight on the seas and oceans, we shall fight with growing confidence and growing strength in the air, we shall defend our Island, whatever the cost may be, we shall fight on the beaches, we shall fight on the landing grounds, we shall fight in the fields and in the streets, we shall fight in the hills; we shall never surrender, and even if, which I do not for a moment believe, this Island or a large part of it were subjugated and starving, then our Empire beyond the seas, armed and guarded by the British Fleet, would carry on the struggle, until, in God's good time, the New World, with all its power and might, steps forth to the rescue and the liberation of the old.

— ⌗◆⌗ —

Stephen Spender
1909–1995

Stephen Spender was an important member of the group of poets writing in the wake of World War I and in the rising shadow of fascism and the approach of World War II. World War I, Spender said, "knocked the ballroom-floor from under middle-class English life"; his first important volume, *Poems*, was published in 1933—the year that Hitler rose to the chancellor-ship of the Third Reich. Thus the turn toward politics that characterizes the poetry of Spender and the other young Oxford poets who allied themselves with W. H. Auden—the so-called "Auden Generation"—seems in retrospect not so much a decision as an inevitability. Spender speaks this way, too, about his brief affiliation with communism, suggesting that the embrace of communism by British intellectuals in the 1930s was not a matter of economic theory but of conscience. For Spender, Auden, Cecil Day-Lewis and others, fascism was such an obvious, and obviously powerful, evil that only communism appeared strong enough to keep it at bay.

The complex energies and tensions of the 1930s drew forth from Spender his most ideal-istic and passionate poetry; he will be remembered primarily for the poetry he wrote in his twenties. Some of the energy of his writing derives from his sense of exclusion from English society; his mixed German-Jewish-English ancestry and his bisexuality led him to find, as he wrote, that "my feeling for the English was at times almost like being in love with an alien race." After World War II, Spender wrote little poetry, but continued to work in literary and cultural criticism. His *Collected Poems* was published in 1985.

Icarus[1]

He will watch the hawk with an indifferent eye
    Or pitifully;
Nor on those eagles that so feared him, now
    Will strain his brow;
5   Weapons men use, stone, sling and strong-thewed° bow   *strong-muscled*
    He will not know.

This aristocrat, superb of all instinct,
    With death close linked
Had paced the enormous cloud, almost had won
10   War on the sun;
Till now, like Icarus mid-ocean-drowned,
    Hands, wings, are found.

                                                       1929

What I Expected

What I expected, was
Thunder, fighting,
Long struggles with men
And climbing.
5   After continual straining
I should grow strong;
Then the rocks would shake
And I rest long.

What I had not foreseen
10   Was the gradual day
Weakening the will
Leaking the brightness away,
The lack of good to touch,
The fading of body and soul
15   Smoke before wind,
Corrupt, unsubstantial.

The wearing of Time,
And the watching of cripples pass
With limbs shaped like questions
20   In their odd twist,
The pulverous° grief   *dusty*
Melting the bones with pity,
The sick falling from earth—
These, I could not foresee.

25   Expecting always
Some brightness to hold in trust
Some final innocence

---

1. In Greek mythology, Icarus was the son of Daedalus, the inventor. To escape from Crete, Daedalus fashioned wings for his son and himself out of wax. Daedalus warned Icarus not to fly too high, for the heat of the sun would melt the wax wings; but Icarus, intoxicated by the power of flight, ignored his father's warning and plunged to his death in the sea.

Exempt from dust,
That, hanging solid,
30   Would dangle through all
Like the created poem,
Or the faceted crystal.

1933

The Express

After the first powerful plain manifesto
The black statement of pistons, without more fuss
But gliding like a queen, she leaves the station.
Without bowing and with restrained unconcern
5   She passes the houses which humbly crowd outside,
The gasworks, and at last the heavy page
Of death, printed by gravestones in the cemetery.
Beyond the town, there lies the open country
Where, gathering speed, she acquires mystery,
10   The luminous self-possession of ships on ocean.
It is now she begins to sing—at first quite low
Then loud, and at last with a jazzy madness—
The song of her whistle screaming at curves,
Of deafening tunnels, brakes, innumerable bolts.
15   And always light, aerial underneath
Retreats the elate metre of her wheels.
Steaming through metal landscape on her lines,
She plunges new eras of white happiness
Where speed throws up strange shapes, broad curves
20   And parallels clean like trajectories from guns.
At last, further than Edinburgh or Rome,
Beyond the crest of the world, she reaches night
Where only a low stream-line brightness
Of phosphorus, on the tossing hills is white.
25   Ah, like a comet through flame, she moves entranced
Wrapt in her music no bird-song, no, nor bough,
Breaking with honey buds, shall ever equal.

1933

The Pylons

The secret of these hills was stone, and cottages
Of that stone made,
And crumbling roads
That turned on sudden hidden villages.

5   Now over these small hills, they have built the concrete
That trails black wire;
Pylons, those pillars
Bare like nude, giant girls that have no secret.

The valley with its gilt and evening look
10   And the green chestnut

Of customary root,
Are mocked dry like the parched bed of a brook.

But far above and far as sight endures
Like whips of anger
15   With lightning's danger
There runs the quick perspective of the future.

This dwarfs our emerald country by its trek
So tall with prophecy:
Dreaming of cities
20   Where often clouds shall lean their swan-white neck.

1933

━ ᚷ ━

Elizabeth Bowen
1899–1973

Elizabeth Bowen was born into a world that was, at the turn of the century, on the verge of disappearing forever: the world of the Anglo-Irish ascendancy, the privileged world of the Protestant "big house" tradition. Bowen's Court, an estate in County Cork, had been in her family since an ancestor in the service of Oliver Cromwell had come to Ireland in 1749; the estate passed out of the family in 1960, when Elizabeth could no longer afford to maintain the property, and it was torn down by its new owner in 1963.

In stark contrast to her proud Anglo-Irish heritage, Bowen's childhood was rootless in the extreme. As a young child, the family's time was split between Bowen's Court, in the country, and Dublin, where her father was a barrister; in 1906, he suffered a nervous breakdown, and Elizabeth moved to London with her mother. Bowen's mother died of cancer in 1912, and Elizabeth was shuttled between various relatives. During World War I, she returned to neutral Ireland, where she worked in a hospital with veterans suffering from "shell shock"; she returned to London in 1918 to attend art school and lived primarily in London for the rest of her life.

Bowen was in London during the Blitz. She again volunteered her services to the victims of war, working for the Ministry of Information as an air-raid warden. She wrote a number of vivid, powerful stories about the ravages of war in London during the Blitz—among them *Mysterious Kôr* (1946), which the American novelist and short-story writer Eudora Welty has called the "most extraordinary story of those she wrote out of her life in wartime London."

Bowen's writing was not confined to short fiction; in addition to her more than eighty short stories, she was the author of ten novels—the most popular of which are *The Death of the Heart* (1938) and *The Heat of the Day* (1949)—as well as a great deal of newspaper and magazine writing and a history of her ancestral home, *Bowen's Court* (1964), published the year after it was demolished.

Mysterious Kôr

Full moonlight drenched the city and searched it; there was not a niche left to stand in. The effect was remorseless: London looked like the moon's capital—shallow, cratered, extinct. It was late, but not yet midnight; now the buses had stopped the polished roads and streets in this region sent for minutes together a ghostly unbroken reflection up. The soaring new flats and the crouching old shops and houses looked equally brittle under the moon, which blazed in windows that looked its way. The futility of the black-out[1] became laughable: from the sky, presumably, you could see every slate in the roofs, every whited kerb, every contour of the naked winter flowerbeds in the park; and the lake, with its shining twists and tree-darkened islands would be a landmark for miles, yes, miles, overhead.

However, the sky, in whose glassiness floated no clouds but only opaque balloons, remained glassy-silent. The Germans no longer came by the full moon. Something more immaterial seemed to threaten, and to be keeping people at home. This day between days, this extra tax, was perhaps more than senses and nerves could bear. People stayed indoors with a fervour that could be felt: the buildings strained with battened-down human life, but not a beam, not a voice, not a note from a radio escaped. Now and then under streets and buildings the earth rumbled: the Underground[2] sounded loudest at this time.

Outside the now gateless gates of the park, the road coming downhill from the north-west turned south and became a street, down whose perspective the traffic lights went through their unmeaning performance of changing colour. From the promontory of pavement outside the gates you saw at once up the road and down the street: from behind where you stood, between the gateposts, appeared the lesser strangeness of grass and water and trees. At this point, at this moment, three French soldiers, directed to a hostel[3] they could not find, stopped singing to listen derisively to the waterbirds wakened up by the moon. Next, two wardens coming off duty emerged from their post and crossed the road diagonally, each with an elbow cupped inside a slung-on tin hat. The wardens turned their faces, mauve in the moonlight, towards the Frenchmen with no expression at all. The two sets of steps died in opposite directions, and, the birds subsiding, nothing was heard or seen until, a little way down the street, a trickle of people came out of the Underground, around the anti-panic brick wall. These all disappeared quickly, in an abashed way, or as though dissolved in the street by some white acid, but for a girl and a soldier who, by their way of walking, seemed to have no destination but each other and to be not quite certain even of that. Blotted into one shadow he tall, she little, these two proceeded towards the park. They looked in, but did not go in; they stood there debating without speaking. Then, as though a command from the street behind them had been received by their synchronized bodies, they faced round to look back the way they had come.

His look up the height of a building made his head drop back, and she saw his eyeballs glitter. She slid her hand from his sleeve, stepped to the edge of the pavement and said: "Mysterious Kôr."

"What is?" he said, not quite collecting himself.

"This is—

> Mysterious Kôr thy walls forsaken stand,
> Thy lonely towers beneath a lonely moon—

—this is Kôr."[4]

"Why," he said, "it's years since I've thought of that."

1. During the Blitz, all lights were ordered concealed or extinguished at night so that enemy planes would have difficulty locating their targets.
2. The London subway system.
3. An inn.
4. Kôr is the lost city of H. Rider Haggard's 1887 adventure novel *She*. These lines are from a poem by Andrew Lang (1844–1912). The central character Ayesha, whose name means *She-who-must-be-obeyed*, is incessantly described as "mysterious." One of Ayesha's statements—"My empire is of the imagination"—may have had an ironic resonance for Bowen, writing about the condition of England during World War II.

She said: "I think of it all the time—"

> Not in the waste beyond the swamps and sand,
> The fever-haunted forest and lagoon,
> Mysterious Kôr thy walls———

—a completely forsaken city, as high as cliffs and as white as bones, with no history———"

"But something must once have happened: why had it been forsaken?"

"How could anyone tell you when there's nobody there?"

"Nobody there since how long?"

"Thousands of years."

"In that case, it would have fallen down."

"No, not Kôr," she said with immediate authority. "Kôr's altogether different; it's very strong; there is not a crack in it anywhere for a weed to grow in; the corners of stones and the monuments might have been cut yesterday, and the stairs and arches are built to support themselves."

"You know all about it," he said, looking at her.

"I know, I know all about it."

"What, since you read that book?"

"Oh, I didn't get much from that; I just got the name. I knew that must be the right name; it's like a cry."

"Most like the cry of a crow to me." He reflected, then said: "But the poem begins with 'Not'—'Not in the waste beyond the swamps and sand—' And it goes on, as I remember, to prove Kôr's not really anywhere. When even a poem says there's no such place—"

"What it tries to say doesn't matter: I see what it makes me see. Anyhow, that was written some time ago, at that time when they thought they had got everything taped, because the whole world had been explored, even the middle of Africa. Everything and place had been found and marked on some map; so what wasn't marked on any map couldn't be there at all. So they thought: that was why he wrote the poem. 'The world is disenchanted,' it goes on. That was what set me off hating civilization."

"Well, cheer up," he said; "there isn't much of it left."

"Oh, yes, I cheered up some time ago. This war shows we've by no means come to the end. If you can blow whole places out of existence, you can blow whole places into it. I don't see why not. They say we can't say what's come out since the bombing started. By the time we've come to the end, Kôr may be the one city left: the abiding city. I should laugh."

"No, you wouldn't," he said sharply. "You wouldn't—at least, I hope not. I hope you don't know what you're saying—does the moon make you funny?"

"Don't be cross about Kôr; please don't, Arthur," she said.

"I thought girls thought about people."

"What, these days?" she said. "Think about people? How can anyone think about people if they've got any heart? I don't know how other girls manage: I always think about Kôr."

"Not about me?" he said. When she did not at once answer, he turned her hand over, in anguish, inside his grasp. "Because I'm not there when you want me—is that my fault?"

"But to think about Kôr is to think about you and me."

"In that dead place?"

"No, ours—we'd be alone here."

Tightening his thumb on her palm while he thought this over, he looked behind them, around them, above them—even up at the sky. He said finally: "But we're alone here."

"That was why I said 'Mysterious Kôr.'"

"What, you mean we're there now, that here's there, that now's then? . . . I don't mind," he added, letting out as a laugh the sigh he had been holding in for some time. "You ought to know the place, and for all I could tell you we might be any-where: I often do have it, this funny feeling, the first minute or two when I've come up out of the Underground. Well, well: join the Army and see the world." He nodded towards the perspective of traffic lights and said, a shade craftily: "What are those, then?"

Having caught the quickest possible breath, she replied: "Inexhaustible gases; they bored through to them and lit them as they came up; by changing colour they show the changing of minutes; in Kôr there is no sort of other time."

"You've got the moon, though: that can't help making months."

"Oh, and the sun, of course; but those two could do what they liked; we should not have to calculate when they'd come or go.'

"We might not have to," he said, 'but I bet I should."

"I should not mind what you did, so long as you never said, 'What next?'"

"I don't know about 'next,' but I do know what we'd do first."

"What, Arthur?"

"Populate Kôr."

She said: "I suppose it would be all right if our children were to marry each other?"

But her voice faded out; she had been reminded that they were homeless on this his first night of leave. They were, that was to say, in London without any hope of any place of their own. Pepita shared a two-roomed flatlet with a girl friend, in a by-street off the Regent's Park Road, and towards this they must make their halfhearted way. Arthur was to have the sitting-room divan, usually occupied by Pepita, while she herself had half of her girl friend's bed. There was really no room for a third, and least of all for a man, in those small rooms packed with furniture and the two girls' belongings: Pepita tried to be grateful for her friend Callie's forbearance—but how could she be, when it had not occurred to Callie that she would do better to be away tonight? She was more slow-witted than narrow-minded—but Pepita felt she owed a kind of ruin to her. Callie, not yet known to be home later than ten, would be now waiting up, in her house-coat, to welcome Arthur. That would mean three-sided chat, drinking cocoa, then turning in: that would be that, and that would be all. That was London, this war—they were lucky to have a roof—London, full enough before the Americans came. Not a place: they would even grudge you sharing a grave—that was what even married couples complained. Whereas in Kôr . . .

In Kôr . . . Like glass, the illusion shattered: a car hummed like a hornet towards them, veered, showed its scarlet tail-light, streaked away up the road. A woman edged round a front door and along the area railings timidly called her cat; mean-while a clock near, then another set further back in the dazzling distance, set about striking midnight. Pepita, feeling Arthur release her arm with an abruptness that was the inverse of passion, shivered; whereat he asked brusquely: "Cold? Well, which way?—we'd better be getting on."

Callie was no longer waiting up. Hours ago she had set out the three cups and saucers, the tins of cocoa and household milk and, on the gas-ring, brought the kettle to just short of the boil. She had turned open Arthur's bed, the living-room divan, in the neat inviting way she had learnt at home—then, with a modest impulse, replaced the cover. She had, as Pepita foresaw, been wearing her cretonne[5] housecoat, the nearest thing to a hostess gown that she had; she had already brushed her hair for the night, rebraided it, bound the braids in a coronet round her head. Both lights and the wireless[6] had been on, to make the room both look and sound gay: all alone, she had come to that peak moment at which company should arrive—but so seldom does. From then on she felt welcome beginning to wither in her, a flower of the heart that had bloomed too early. There she had sat like an image, facing the three cold cups, on the edge of the bed to be occupied by an unknown man.

Callie's innocence and her still unsought-out state had brought her to take a proprietary pride in Arthur; this was all the stronger, perhaps, because they had not yet met. Sharing the flat with Pepita, this last year, she had been content with reflecting the heat of love. It was not, surprisingly, that Pepita seemed very happy— there were times when she was palpably on the rack, and this was not what Callie could understand. "Surely you owe it to Arthur," she would then say, "to keep cheer- ful? So long as you love each other————" Callie's calm brow glowed—one might say that it glowed in place of her friend's; she became the guardian of that ideality which for Pepita was constantly lost to view. It was true, with the sudden prospect of Arthur's leave, things had come nearer to earth: he became a proposition, and she would have been as glad if he could have slept somewhere else. Physically shy, a brotherless virgin, Callie shrank from sharing this flat with a young man. In this flat you could hear everything: what was once a three-windowed Victorian drawing- room had been partitioned, by very thin walls, into kitchenette, living-room, Callie's bedroom. The living-room was in the centre; the two others open off it. What was once the conservatory, half a flight down, was now converted into a draughty bath- room, shared with somebody else on the girl's floor. The flat, for these days, was cheap—even so, it was Callie, earning more than Pepita, who paid the greater part of the rent: it thus became up to her, more or less, to express good will as to Arthur's making a third. "Why, it will be lovely to have him here," Callie said. Pepita accept- ed the good will without much grace—but then, had she ever much grace to spare?— she was as restlessly secretive, as self-centred, as a little half-grown black cat. Next came a puzzling moment: Pepita seemed to be hinting that Callie should fix herself up somewhere else. "But where would I go?" Callie marvelled when this was at last borne in on her. "You know what London's like now. And, anyway"—here she laughed, but hers was a forehead that coloured as easily as it glowed—"it wouldn't be proper, would it, me going off and leaving just you and Arthur; I don't know what your mother would say to me. No, we may be a little squashed, but we'll make things ever so homey. I shall not mind playing gooseberry, really, dear."

But the hominess by now was evaporating, as Pepita and Arthur still and still did not come. At half-past ten, in obedience to the rule of the house, Callie was obliged to turn off the wireless, whereupon silence out of the stepless street began seeping into the slighted room. Callie recollected the fuel target and turned off her dear little table lamp, gaily painted with spots to make it look like a toadstool, thereby leaving only the hanging light. She laid her hand on the kettle, to find it gone cold again and sigh for the wasted gas if not for her wasted thought. Where are they? Cold crept up her out of the kettle; she went to bed.

5. Cotton fabric with a printed pattern.   6. Radio.

Callie's bed lay along the wall under the window: she did not like sleeping so close up under glass, but the clearance that must be left for the opening of door and cupboards made this the only possible place. Now she got in and lay rigidly on the bed's inner side, under the hanging hems of the window curtains, training her limbs not to stray to what would be Pepita's half. This sharing of her bed with another body would not be the least of her sacrifice to the lovers' love; tonight would be the first night—or at least, since she was an infant—that Callie had slept with anyone. Child of a sheltered middle-class household, she had kept physical distances all her life. Already repugnance and shyness ran through her limbs; she was preyed upon by some more obscure trouble than the expectation that she might not sleep. As to *that*, Pepita was restless; her tossings on the divan, her broken-off exclamations and blurred pleas had been to be heard, most nights, through the dividing wall.

Callie knew, as though from a vision, that Arthur would sleep soundly, with assurance and majesty. Did they not all say, too, that a soldier sleeps like a log? With awe she pictured, asleep, the face that she had not yet, awake, seen—Arthur's man's eyelids, cheekbones and set mouth turned up to the darkened ceiling. Wanting to savour darkness herself, Callie reached out and put off her bedside lamp.

At once she knew that something was happening—outdoors, in the street, the whole of London, the world. An advance, an extraordinary movement was silently taking place; blue-white beams overflowed from it, silting, dropping round the edges of the muffling black-out curtains. When, starting up, she knocked a fold of the curtain, a beam like a mouse ran across her bed. A searchlight, the most powerful of all time, might have been turned full and steady upon her defended window; finding flaws in the blackout stuff, it made veins and stars. Once gained by this idea of pressure she could not lie down again; she sat tautly, drawn-up knees touching her breasts, and asked herself if there were anything she should do. She parted the curtains, opened them slowly wider, looked out—and was face to face with the moon.

Below the moon, the houses opposite her window blazed back in transparent shadow; and something—was it a coin or a ring?—glittered half-way across the chalk-white street. Light marched in past her face, and she turned to see where it went: out stood the curves and garlands of the great white marble Victorian mantel-piece of that lost drawing-room; out stood, in the photographs turned her way, the thoughts with which her parents had faced the camera, and the humble puzzlement of her two dogs at home. Of silver brocade, just faintly purpled with roses, became her housecoat hanging over the chair. And the moon did more: it exonerated and beautified the lateness of the lovers' return. No wonder, she said herself, no wonder—if this was the world they walked in, if this was whom they were with. Having drunk in the white explanation, Callie lay down again. Her half of the bed was in shadow, but she allowed one hand to lie, blanched, in what would be Pepita's place. She lay and looked at the hand until it was no longer her own.

Callie woke to the sound of Pepita's key in the latch. But no voices? What had happened? Then she heard Arthur's step. She heard his unslung equipment dropped with a weary, dull sound, and the plonk of his tin hat on a wooden chair. "Sssh-sssh!" Pepita exclaimed, "she *might* be asleep!"

Then at last Arthur's voice: "But I thought you said—"

"I'm not asleep; I'm just coming!" Callie called out with rapture, leaping out from her form in shadow into the moonlight, zipping on her enchanted house-coat over her nightdress, kicking her shoes on, and pinning in place, with a trembling firmness, her plaits in their coronet round her head. Between these movements of hers she heard not another sound. Had she only dreamed they were there? Her heart beat: she stepped through the living-room, shutting her door behind her.

Pepita and Arthur stood on the other side of the table; they gave the impression of being lined up. Their faces, at different levels—for Pepita's rough, dark head came only an inch above Arthur's khaki shoulder—were alike in abstention from any kind of expression; as though, spiritually, they both still refused to be here. Their features looked faint, weathered—was this the work of the moon? Pepita said at once: "I suppose we are very late?"

"I don't wonder," Callie said, "on this lovely night."

Arthur had not raised his eyes; he was looking at the three cups. Pepita now suddenly jogged his elbow, saying, "Arthur, wake up; say something; this is Callie—well, Callie, this is Arthur, of course."

"Why, yes of course this is Arthur," returned Callie, whose candid eyes since she entered had not left Arthur's face. Perceiving that Arthur did not know what to do, she advanced round the table to shake hands with him. He looked up, she looked down, for the first time: she rather beheld than felt his red-brown grip on what still seemed her glove of moonlight. "Welcome, Arthur," she said. "I'm so glad to meet you at last. I hope you will be comfortable in the flat."

"It's been kind of you," he said after consideration.

"Please do not feel that," said Callie. "This is Pepita's home, too, and we both hope—don't we, Pepita?—that you'll regard it as yours. Please feel free to do just as you like. I am sorry it is so small."

"Oh, I don't know," Arthur said, as though hypnotized; "it seems a nice little place."

Pepita, meanwhile, glowered and turned away.

Arthur continued to wonder, though he had once been told, how these two unalike girls had come to set up together—Pepita so small, except for her too-big head, compact of childish brusqueness and of unchildish passion, and Callie, so sedate, waxy and tall—an unlit candle. Yes, she was like one of those candles on sale outside a church; there could be something votive even in her demeanour. She was unconscious that her good manners, those of an old fashioned country doctor's daughter, were putting the other two at a disadvantage. He found himself touched by the grave good faith with which Callie was wearing that tartish house-coat, above which her face kept the glaze of sleep; and, as she knelt to relight the gas-ring under the kettle, he marked the strong, delicate arch of one bare foot, disappearing into the arty green shoe. Pepita was now too near him ever again to be seen as he now saw Callie—in a sense, he never *had* seen Pepita for the first time: she had not been, and still sometimes was not, his type. No, he had not thought of her twice; he had not remembered her until he began to remember her with passion. You might say he had not seen Pepita coming: their love had been a collision in the dark.

Callie, determined to get this over, knelt back and said: "Would Arthur like to wash his hands?" When they had heard him stumble down the half-flight of stairs, she said to Pepita: "Yes, I was so glad you had the moon."

"Why?" said Pepita. She added: "There was too much of it."

"You're tired. Arthur looks tired, too."

"How would you know? He's used to marching about. But it's all this having no place to go."

"But, Pepita, you——"

But at this point Arthur came back: from the door he noticed the wireless, and went direct to it. "Nothing much on now, I suppose?" he doubtfully said.

"No; you see it's past midnight; we're off the air. And, anyway, in this house they don't like the wireless late. By the same token," went on Callie, friendly smiling, "I'm afraid I must ask you, Arthur, to take your boots off, unless, of course, you mean to stay sitting down. The people below us——"

Pepita flung off, saying something under her breath, but Arthur, remarking, "No, I don't mind," both sat down and began to take off his boots. Pausing, glancing to left and right at the divan's fresh cotton spread, he said: "It's all right is it, for me to sit on this?"

"That's my bed," said Pepita. "You are to sleep in it."

Callie then made the cocoa, after which they turned in. Preliminary trips to the bathroom having been worked out, Callie was first to retire, shutting the door behind her so that Pepita and Arthur might kiss each other good night. When Pepita joined her, it was without knocking: Pepita stood still in the moon and began to tug off her clothes. Glancing with hate at the bed, she asked: "Which side?"

"I expected you'd like the outside."

"What are you standing about for?"

"I don't really know: as I'm inside I'd better get in first."

"Then why not get in?"

When they had settled rigidly, side by side, Callie asked: "Do you think Arthur's got all he wants?"

Pepita jerked her head up. "We can't sleep in all this moon."

"Why, you don't believe the moon does things, actually?"

"Well, it couldn't hope to make some of us *much* more screwy."

Callie closed the curtains, then said: "What do you mean? And—didn't you hear?—I asked if Arthur's got all he wants."

"That's what I meant—have you got a screw loose, really?"

"Pepita, I won't stay here if you're going to be like this."

"In that case, you had better go in with Arthur."

"What about me?" Arthur loudly said through the wall. "I can hear practically all you girls are saying."

They were both startled—rather that than abashed. Arthur, alone in there, had thrown off the ligatures[7] of his social manner: his voice held the whole authority of his sex—he was impatient, sleepy, and he belonged to no one.

"Sorry," the girls said in unison. Then Pepita laughed soundlessly, making their bed shake, till to stop herself she bit the back of her hand, and this movement made her elbow strike Callie's cheek. "Sorry," she had to whisper. No answer: Pepita fingered her elbow and found, yes, it was quite true, it was wet. "Look, shut up crying, Callie: what have I done?"

Callie rolled right round, in order to press her forehead closely under the window, into the curtains, against the wall. Her weeping continued to be soundless: now and then, unable to reach her handkerchief, she staunched her eyes with a curtain, disturbing slivers of moon. Pepita gave up marvelling, and soon slept: at least there is something in being dog-tired.

A clock struck four as Callie woke up again—but something else had made her open her swollen eyelids. Arthur, stumbling about on his padded feet, could be heard next door attempting to make no noise. Inevitably, he bumped the edge of the table. Callie sat up: by her side Pepita lay like a mummy rolled half over, in

7. Restrictions.

forbidding, tenacious sleep. Arthur groaned. Callie caught a breath, climbed lightly over Pepita, felt for her torch[8] on the mantelpiece, stopped to listen again. Arthur groaned again: Callie, with movements soundless as they were certain, opened the door and slipped through to the living-room. "What's the matter?" she whispered. "Are you ill?"

"No; I just got a cigarette. Did I wake you up?"

"But you groaned."

"I'm sorry; I'd no idea."

"But do you often?"

"I've no idea, really, I tell you," Arthur repeated. The air of the room was dense with his presence, overhung by tobacco. He must be sitting on the edge of his bed, wrapped up in his overcoat—she could smell the coat, and each time he pulled on the cigarette his features appeared down there, in the fleeting, dull reddish glow. "Where are you?" he said. "Show a light."

Her nervous touch on her torch, like a reflex to what he said, made it flicker up for a second. "I am just by the door; Pepita's asleep; I'd better go back to bed."

"Listen. Do you two get on each other's nerves?"

"Not till tonight," said Callie, watching the uncertain swoops of the cigarette as he reached across to the ashtray on the edge of the table. Shifting her bare feet patiently, she added: "You don't see us as we usually are."

"She's a girl who shows things in funny ways—I expect she feels bad at our putting you out like this—I know I do. But then we'd got no choice, had we?"

"It is really I who am putting you out," said Callie.

"Well, that can't be helped either, can it? You had the right to stay in your own place. If there'd been more time, we might have gone to the country, though I still don't see where we'd have gone there. It's one harder when you're not married, unless you've got the money. Smoke?"

"No, thank you. Well, if you're all right, I'll go back to bed."

"I'm glad she's asleep—funny the way she sleeps, isn't it? You can't help wondering where she is. You haven't got a boy, have you, just at present?"

"No. I've never had one."

"I'm not sure in one way that you're not better off. I can see there's not so much in it for a girl these days. It makes me feel cruel the way I unsettle her: I don't know how much it's me myself or how much it's something the matter that I can't help. How are any of us to know how things could have been? They forget war's not just only war; it's years out of people's lives that they've never had before and won't have again. Do you think she's fanciful?"

"Who, Pepita?"

"It's enough to make her—tonight was the pay-off. We couldn't get near any movie or any place for sitting; you had to fight into the bars, and she hates the staring in bars, and with all that milling about, every street we went, they kept on knocking her even off my arm. So then we took the tube to that park down there, but the place was as bad as daylight, let alone it was cold. We hadn't the nerve—well, that's nothing to do with you."

"I don't mind."

"Or else you don't understand. So we began to play—we were off in Kôr."

8. Flashlight.

"Core of what?"

"Mysterious Kôr—ghost city."

"Where?"

"You may ask. But I could have sworn she saw it, and from the way she saw it I saw it, too. A game's a game, but what's a hallucination? You begin by laughing, then it gets in you and you can't laugh it off. I tell you, I woke up just now not knowing where I'd been; and I had to get up and feel round this table before I even knew where I was. It wasn't till then that I thought of a cigarette. Now I see why she sleeps like that, if that's where she goes."

"But she is just as often restless; I often hear her."

"Then she doesn't always make it. Perhaps it takes me, in some way—Well, I can't see any harm: when two people have got no place, why not want Kôr, as a start? There are no restrictions on wanting, at any rate."

"But, oh, Arthur, can't wanting want what's human?"

He yawned. "To be human's to be at a dead loss." Stopping yawning, he ground out his cigarette: the china tray skidded at the edge of the table. "Bring that light here a moment—that is, will you? I think I've messed ash all over these sheets of hers."

Callie advanced with the torch alight, but at arm's length: now and then her thumb made the beam wobble. She watched the lit-up inside of Arthur's hand as he brushed the sheet; and once he looked up to see her white-nightgowned figure curving above and away from him, behind the arc of light. "What's that swinging?"

"One of my plaits of hair. Shall I open the window wider?"

"What, to let the smoke out? Go on. And how's your moon?"

"Mine?" Marvelling over this, as the first sign that Arthur remembered that she was Callie, she uncovered the window, pushed up the sash, then after a minute said: "Not so strong."

Indeed, the moon's power over London and the imagination had now declined. The siege of light had relaxed; the search was over; the street had a look of survival and no more. Whatever had glittered there, coin or ring, was now invisible or had gone. To Callie it seemed likely that there would never be such a moon again; and on the whole she felt this was for the best. Feeling air reach in like a tired arm round her body, she dropped the curtains against it and returned to her own room.

Back by her bed, she listened; Pepita's breathing still had the regular sound of sleep. At the other side of the wall the divan creaked as Arthur stretched himself out again. Having felt ahead of her lightly, to make sure her half was empty, Callie climbed over Pepita and got in. A certain amount of warmth had travelled between the sheets from Pepita's flank, and in this Callie extended her sword-cold body: she tried to compose her limbs; even they quivered after Arthur's words in the dark, words to the dark. The loss of her own mysterious expectation, of her love for love, was a small thing beside the war's total of unlived lives. Suddenly Pepita flung out one hand: its back knocked Callie lightly across the face.

Pepita had now turned over and lay with her face up. The hand that had struck Callie must have lain over the other, which grasped the pyjama collar. Her eyes, in the dark, might have been either shut or open, but nothing made her frown more or less steadily: it became certain, after another moment, that Pepita's act of justice had been unconscious. She still lay, as she had lain, in an avid dream, of which Arthur had been the source, of which Arthur was not the end. With him she looked this way, that way, down the wide, void, pure streets, between statues, pillars and shadows, through archways and colonnades. With him she went up the stairs down which nothing but moon came; with him trod the ermine[9] dust of the endless halls, stood on terraces, mounted the extreme tower, looked down on the statued squares, the wide, void, pure streets. He was the password, but not the answer: it was to Kôr's finality that she turned.

━◂ ═◆═ ▸━

George Orwell
1903–1950

The critic Irving Howe called George Orwell (pseudonym of Eric Arthur Blair) "the greatest moral force in English letters during the past several decades," as well as "the best English essayist since Hazlitt." He was one of the most consistently provocative British writers of the 1930s and 1940s; his characteristic mode was the polemic, whether that polemic was cloaked in the form of an essay or literary criticism, a novel or even travel writing.

Orwell was born in India into a lower-middle-class family, his father a British civil servant working as an administrator in the Opium Department of the Government of India. His mother managed to gain his entrance into Eton, an elite preparatory school, on a scholarship. The snobbism of his more affluent classmates was to leave a permanent mark. Unable to afford college, Orwell followed in his father's footsteps and enlisted in the Indian Imperial Police. Unlike his father, however, he was disgusted by the inhumanity of colonial rule that he witnessed while stationed in Burma; his revulsion is vividly depicted in essays like *Shooting an Elephant* and *A Hanging*, as well as in his early novel *Burmese Days* (1934). His distaste for police work caused Orwell to leave after five years, determined to establish himself as a writer; he became convinced of the importance of establishing an art of political writing. His 1945 political allegory *Animal Farm* is most specifically an indictment of the Soviet Union during the Cold War, but it conveys timeless larger lessons—that totalitarianism lurks just below the surface of every civil government, that absolute power in the hands of any government leads to the abolition of personal freedoms. Schoolchildren in both the United Kingdom and the United States are familiar with the novel's famous slogan: "All animals are equal . . . but some are more equal than others." These same themes are explored in Orwell's dystopian novel *Nineteen Eighty-Four* (1949), which has entered the contemporary imagination through its images of tyranny and oppression, through phrases like "newspeak" and "double-think," and through the foreboding, forbidding image of Big Brother, who is always "watching you."

Before his untimely death from tuberculosis, Orwell did important work in literary and cultural criticism. His criticism, Evelyn Waugh complained, insisted that the critic ask of every text: "What kind of man wrote or painted this? What were his motives, conscious or unconscious? What sort of people like his work? Why?" They were questions under which, as his disparaging mention of Waugh in *Inside the Whale* suggests, most of the fiction written during the 1930s did not fare well. He also became a defender of British popular culture in the 1940s; his essays on such "subliterary" forms as boys' magazines, seaside resort postcards, and personal ads, for instance, anticipate the recent interest in material culture at the center of British and American cultural studies. Almost half a century after his death, Orwell's enduring importance would seem to be his thoroughgoing distrust of "smelly little orthodoxies," be they literary, aesthetic, political, or linguistic.

9. White.

Shooting an Elephant

In Moulmein, in Lower Burma,[1] I was hated by large numbers of people—the only time in my life that I have been important enough for this to happen to me. I was sub-divisional police officer of the town, and in an aimless, petty kind of way anti-European feeling was very bitter. No one had the guts to raise a riot, but if a European woman went through the bazaars alone somebody would probably spit betel[2] juice over her dress. As a police officer I was an obvious target and was baited whenever it seemed safe to do so. When a nimble Burman tripped me up on the football field and the referee (another Burman) looked the other way, the crowd yelled with hideous laughter. This happened more than once. In the end the sneering yellow faces of young men that met me everywhere, the insults hooted after me when I was at a safe distance, got badly on my nerves. The young Buddhist priests were the worst of all. There were several thousands of them in the town and none of them seemed to have anything to do except stand on street corners and jeer at Europeans.

All this was perplexing and upsetting. For at that time I had already made up my mind that imperialism was an evil thing and the sooner I chucked up my job and got out of it the better. Theoretically—and secretly, of course—I was all for the Burmese and all against their oppressors, the British. As for the job I was doing, I hated it more bitterly than I can perhaps make clear. In a job like that you see the dirty work of Empire at close quarters. The wretched prisoners huddling in the stinking cages of the lock-ups, the grey, cowed faces of the long-term convicts, the scarred buttocks of the men who had been flogged with bamboos—all these oppressed me with an intolerable sense of guilt. But I could get nothing into perspective. I was young and ill-educated and I had had to think out my problems in the utter silence that is imposed on every Englishman in the East. I did not even know that the British Empire is dying, still less did I know that it is a great deal better than the younger empires that are going to supplant it. All I knew was that I was stuck between my hatred of the empire I served and my rage against the evil-spirited little beasts who tried to make my job impossible. With one part of my mind I thought of the British Raj[3] as an unbreakable tyranny, as something clamped down, *in saecula saeculorum*,[4] upon the will of prostrate peoples; with another part I thought that the greatest joy in the world would be to drive a bayonet into a Buddhist priest's guts. Feelings like these are the normal by-products of imperialism; ask any Anglo-Indian official, if you can catch him off duty.

One day something happened which in a roundabout way was enlightening. It was a tiny incident in itself, but it gave me a better glimpse than I had had before of the real nature of imperialism—the real motives for which despotic governments act. Early one morning the sub-inspector at a police station the other end of the town rang me up on the phone and said that an elephant was ravaging the bazaar. Would I please come and do something about it? I did not know what I could do, but I wanted to see what was happening and I got on to a pony and started out. I took my rifle, an old 44 Winchester and much too small to kill an elephant, but I thought the noise

1. Republic in southeast Asia, bordered by Bangladesh, India, China, Laos, and Thailand.
2. An East Indian pepper plant, the leaves of which are chewed.
3. "Rule" (Hindi).
4. Forever and ever (Latin).

might be useful *in terrorem*.[5] Various Burmans stopped me on the way and told me about the elephant's doings. It was not, of course, a wild elephant, but a tame one which had gone "must".[6] It had been chained up as tame elephants always are when their attack of "must" is due, but on the previous night it had broken its chain and escaped. Its mahout,[7] the only person who could manage it when it was in that state, had set out in pursuit, but he had taken the wrong direction and was now twelve hours' journey away, and in the morning the elephant had suddenly reappeared in the town. The Burmese population had no weapons and were quite helpless against it. It had already destroyed somebody's bamboo hut, killed a cow and raided some fruit-stalls and devoured the stock; also it had met the municipal rubbish van, and, when the driver jumped out and took to his heels, had turned the van over and inflicted violence upon it.

The Burmese sub-inspector and some Indian constables were waiting for me in the quarter where the elephant had been seen. It was a very poor quarter, a labyrinth of squalid bamboo huts, thatched with palm-leaf, winding all over a steep hillside. I remember that it was a cloudy stuffy morning at the beginning of the rains. We began questioning the people as to where the elephant had gone, and, as usual, failed to get any definite information. That is invariably the case in the East; a story always sounds clear enough at a distance, but the nearer you get to the scene of events the vaguer it becomes. Some of the people said that the elephant had gone in one direction, some said that he had gone in another, some professed not even to have heard of any elephant. I had almost made up my mind that the whole story was a pack of lies, when we heard yells a little distance away. There was a loud, scandalised cry of "Go away, child! Go away this instant!" and an old woman with a switch in her hand came round the corner of a hut, violently shooing away a crowd of naked children. Some more women followed, clicking their tongues and exclaiming; evidently there was something there that the children ought not to have seen. I rounded the hut and saw a man's dead body sprawling in the mud. He was an Indian, a black Dravidian[8] coolie,[9] almost naked, and he could not have been dead many minutes. The people said that the elephant had come suddenly upon him round the corner of the hut, caught him with its trunk, put its foot on his back and ground him into the earth. This was the rainy season and the ground was soft, and his face had scored a trench a foot deep and a couple of yards long. He was lying on his belly with arms crucified and head sharply twisted to one side. His face was coated with mud, the eyes wide open, the teeth bared and grinning with an expression of unendurable agony. (Never tell me, by the way, that the dead look peaceful. Most of the corpses I have looked devilish.) The friction of the great beast's foot had stripped the skin from his back as neatly as one skins a rabbit. As soon as I saw the dead man I sent an orderly to a friend's house nearby to borrow an elephant rifle. I had already sent back the pony, not wanting it to go mad with fright and throw me if it smelled the elephant.

The orderly came back in a few minutes with a rifle and five cartridges, and meanwhile some Burmans had arrived and told us that the elephant was in the paddy fields below, only a few hundred yards away. As I started forward practically the whole population of the quarter flocked out of their houses and followed me. They had seen the rifle and were all shouting excitedly that I was going to shoot

5. To frighten it (Latin).
6. A period of heightened aggressiveness and sexual activity in male elephants, during which violent frenzies occur.
7. Elephant driver (Hindi).
8. Native of southeast India or Sri Lanka.
9. A derogatory term for an unskilled Asian laborer.

the elephant. They had not shown much interest in the elephant when he was merely ravaging their homes, but it was different now that he was going to be shot. It was a bit of fun to them, as it would be to an English crowd; besides, they wanted the meat. It made me vaguely uneasy. I had no intention of shooting the elephant—I had merely sent for the rifle to defend myself if necessary—and it is always unnerving to have a crowd following you. I marched down the hill, looking and feeling a fool, with the rifle over my shoulder and an ever-growing army of people jostling at my heels. At the bottom, when you got away from the huts, there was a metalled road and beyond that a miry waste of paddy fields a thousand yards across, not yet ploughed but soggy from the first rains and dotted with coarse grass. The elephant was standing eighty yards from the road, his left side towards us. He took not the slightest notice of the crowd's approach. He was tearing up bunches of grass, beating them against his knees to clean them and stuffing them into his mouth.

I had halted on the road. As soon as I saw the elephant I knew with perfect certainty that I ought not to shoot him. It is a serious matter to shoot a working elephant—it is comparable to destroying a huge and costly piece of machinery—and obviously one ought not to do it if it can possibly be avoided. And at that distance, peacefully eating, the elephant looked no more dangerous than a cow. I thought then and I think now that his attack of "must" was already passing off; in which case he would merely wander harmlessly about until the mahout came back and caught him. Moreover, I did not in the least want to shoot him. I decided that I would watch him for a little while to make sure that he did not turn savage again, and then go home.

But at that moment I glanced round at the crowd that had followed me. It was an immense crowd, two thousand at the least and growing every minute. It blocked the road for a long distance on either side. I looked at the sea of yellow faces above the garish clothes—faces all happy and excited over this bit of fun, all certain that the elephant was going to be shot. They were watching me as they would watch a conjuror about to perform a trick. They did not like me, but with the magical rifle in my hands I was momentarily worth watching. And suddenly I realised that I should have to shoot the elephant after all. The people expected it of me and I had got to do it; I could feel their two thousand wills pressing me forward, irresistibly. And it was at this moment, as I stood there with the rifle in my hands, that I first grasped the hollowness, the futility of the white man's dominion in the East. Here was I, the white man with his gun, standing in front of the unarmed native crowd—seemingly the leading actor of the piece; but in reality I was only an absurd puppet pushed to and fro by the will of those yellow faces behind. I perceived in this moment that when the white man turns tyrant it is his own freedom that he destroys. He becomes a sort of hollow, posing dummy, the conventionalised figure of a sahib.[1] For it is the condition of his rule that he shall spend his life in trying to impress the "natives" and so in every crisis he has got to do what the "natives" expect of him. He wears a mask, and his face grows to fit it. I had got to shoot the elephant. I had committed myself to doing it when I sent for the rifle. A sahib has got to act like a sahib; he has got to appear resolute, to know his own mind and do definite things. To come all that way, rifle in hand, with two thousand people marching at my heels, and then to trail feebly away, having done nothing—no, that was impossible. The crowd would laugh at me. And my whole life, every white man's life in the East, was one long struggle not to be laughed at.

1. White gentleman (Urdu).

But I did not want to shoot the elephant. I watched him beating his bunch of grass against his knees, with that preoccupied grandmotherly air that elephants have. It seemed to me that it would be murder to shoot him. At that age I was not squeamish about killing animals, but I had never shot an elephant and never wanted to. (Somehow it always seems worse to kill a *large* animal.) Besides, there was the beast's owner to be considered. Alive, the elephant was worth at least a hundred pounds; dead, he would only be worth the value of his tusks—five pounds, possibly. But I had got to act quickly. I turned to some experienced-looking Burmans who had been there when we arrived, and asked them how the elephant had been behaving. They all said the same thing: he took no notice of you if you left him alone, but he might charge if you went too close to him.

It was perfectly clear to me what I ought to do. I ought to walk up to within, say, twenty-five yards of the elephant and test his behaviour. If he charged I could shoot, if he took no notice of me it would be safe to leave him until the mahout came back. But also I knew that I was going to do no such thing. I was a poor shot with a rifle and the ground was soft mud into which one would sink at every step. If the elephant charged and I missed him, I should have about as much chance as a toad under a steam-roller. But even then I was not thinking particularly of my own skin, only the watchful yellow faces behind. For at that moment, with the crowd watching me, I was not afraid in the ordinary sense, as I would have been if I had been alone. A white man mustn't be frightened in front of "natives"; and so, in general, he isn't frightened. The sole thought in my mind was that if anything went wrong those two thousand Burmans would see me pursued, caught, trampled on and reduced to a grinning corpse like that Indian up the hill. And if that happened it was quite probable that some of them would laugh. That would never do. There was only one alternative. I shoved the cartridges into the magazine and lay down on the road to get a better aim.

The crowd grew very still, and a deep, low, happy sigh, as of people who see the theatre curtain go up at last, breathed from innumerable throats. They were going to have their bit of fun after all. The rifle was a beautiful German thing with cross-hair sights. I did not then know that in shooting an elephant one should shoot to cut an imaginary bar running from ear-hole to ear-hole. I ought therefore, as the elephant was sideways on, to have aimed straight at his ear-hole; actually I aimed several inches in front of this, thinking the brain would be further forward.

When I pulled the trigger I did not hear the bang or feel the kick—one never does when a shot goes home—but I heard the devilish roar of glee that went up from the crowd. In that instant, in too short a time, one would have thought, even for the bullet to get there, a mysterious, terrible change had come over the elephant. He neither stirred nor fell, but every line of his body had altered. He looked suddenly stricken, shrunken, immensely old, as though the frightful impact of the bullet had paralysed him without knocking him down. At last, after what seemed a long time—it might have been five seconds, I dare say—he sagged flabbily to his knees. His mouth slobbered. An enormous senility seemed to have settled upon him. One could have imagined him thousands of years old. I fired again into the same spot. At the second shot he did not collapse but climbed with desperate slowness to his feet and stood weakly upright, with legs sagging and head drooping. I fired a third time. That was the shot that did for him. You could see the agony of it jolt his whole body and knock the last remnant of strength from his legs. But in falling he seemed for a moment to rise, for as his hind legs collapsed beneath him he seemed to tower upwards like a huge rock toppling, his trunk reaching skyward like a tree. He trumpeted, for the first and only time. And then down he came, his belly towards me, with a crash that seemed to shake the ground even where I lay.

I got up. The Burmans were already racing past me across the mud. It was obvious that the elephant would never rise again, but he was not dead. He was breathing very rhythmically with long rattling gasps, his great mound of a side painfully rising and falling. His mouth was wide open—I could see far down into caverns of pale pink throat. I waited a long time for him to die, but his breathing did not weaken. Finally I fired my two remaining shots into the spot where I thought his heart must be. The thick blood welled out of him like red velvet, but still he did not die. His body did not even jerk when the shots hit him, the tortured breathing continued without a pause. He was dying, very slowly and in great agony, but in some world remote from me where not even a bullet could damage him further. I felt that I had got to put an end to that dreadful noise. It seemed dreadful to see the great beast lying there, powerless to move and yet powerless to die, and not even to be able to finish him. I sent back for my small rifle and poured shot after shot into his heart and down his throat. They seemed to make no impression. The tortured gasps continued as steadily as the ticking of a clock.

In the end I could not stand it any longer and went away. I heard later that it took him half an hour to die. Burmans were arriving with dahs[2] and baskets even before I left, and I was told they had stripped his body almost to the bones by the afternoon.

Afterwards, of course, there were endless discussions about the shooting of the elephant. The owner was furious, but he was only an Indian and could do nothing. Besides, legally I had done the right thing, for a mad elephant has to be killed, like a mad dog, if its owner fails to control it. Among the Europeans opinion was divided. The older men said I was right, the younger men said it was a damn shame to shoot an elephant for killing a coolie, because an elephant was worth more than any damn Coringhee[3] coolie. And afterwards I was very glad that the coolie had been killed; it put me legally in the right and it gave me a sufficient pretext for shooting the elephant. I often wondered whether any of the others grasped that I had done it solely to avoid looking a fool.

Salman Rushdie
b. 1947

Born in Bombay on the day India achieved independence from Britain, Salman Rushdie was raised in Pakistan after the partition of the subcontinent. He then settled in England, where he soon became one of the most noted writers about the aftermath of empires. His magisterial novel *Midnight's Children* was awarded not only the prestigious Booker McConnell Prize for the best British novel of 1981 but later the "Booker of Bookers," as the best novel in the first twenty-five years of the prize's history. Like Saleem Sinai, the protagonist and narrator of *Midnight's Children*, Rushdie delights in telling its story, in a mixture of history, fantasy, fable, and sheer stylistic exuberance that has come to be known (through the works of Latin American writers like Gabriel Garcia Marquez) as magic realism. At once an Indian and a British writer, Rushdie enjoys a double status as both insider and outsider that allows him to comment both on the history of his native land and on the contemporary politics of Britain with savage and comic incisiveness.

---

2. Large knives.   3. Burmese place-name.

Unfortunately, most who do not know Rushdie's writing well know his name from the publicity surrounding his 1988 novel *The Satanic Verses*; the novel was judged to be an affront to Islam, and on Valentine's Day in 1989 the late Iranian leader Ayatollah Ruhollah Khomeini issued a *fatwa*, or death threat, against both Rushdie and his publisher, carrying a multimillion dollar bounty. As a result, Rushdie was forced to go underground; for nearly ten years he moved from place to place protected by full-time bodyguards, making but unable to receive phone calls, and generally staying out of the public eye and out of harm's way. Under Islamic law, a *fatwa* can be lifted only by the man who imposed it; since Khomeini died with the *fatwa* still in effect, it technically will remain in effect until Rushdie's death, although subsequent Iranian leaders have suggested that the edict would not be enforced. Rushdie has, in recent years, begun a boldly public life in England and the United States.

It is both appalling and intriguing that the written word still has this much power. The book that followed *The Satanic Verses* was *Haroun and the Sea of Stories*, a tale often (mistakenly) labeled "juvenile." It is in fact an allegory of the power of language—its power to liberate, and the desperate attempts of what political philosopher Louis Althusser calls the "ideological state apparatus" to silence this free, anarchic speech. The story did indeed begin as a bath-time entertainment for Rushdie's son Zafar; but as the affair over the *Satanic Verses* grew and festered, the story matured into a parable of the responsibility of the artist to speak from the heart and conscience, regardless of the political consequences. Rushdie's story *Christopher Columbus and Queen Isabella of Spain Consummate Their Relationship* mixes history and fantasy, popular culture and high literary art to comment on the sometimes callow ways of power.

Christopher Columbus and Queen Isabella of Spain Consummate Their Relationship

Columbus, a foreigner, follows Queen Isabella for an eternity without entirely giving up hope.

— *In what characteristic postures?*

Proud yet supplicant, the head held high but the knee bent. Fawning yet fearless; possessed of a certain saucy vulgarity, he gets away with it by virtue of his confidence-man's charm. However, as time passes, the ingratiating aspects of his stance are emphasised; the sea-dog raffishness[1] wears a little thin. As do his shoes.

= *His hope. It is of what?*

Obvious answers first. He hopes for preferment. He wants to tie the Queen's favour to his helmet, like a knight in a romance. (He owns no helmet.) He has hopes of cash, and of three tall ships, *Niña Pinta Santa Maria*; of, in fourteen hundred and ninety-two, sailing across the ocean blue. But, on his first arrival at court, when the Queen herself asked him what he desired, he bowed over her olive hand and, with his lips a breath away from the great ring of her power, murmured a single, dangerous word.

"Consummation."

— *These unspeakable foreigners! The nerve! "Consummation," indeed! And then following in her footsteps, month after month, as if he stood a chance. His coarse epistles, his tuneless serenades beneath her casement windows, obliging her to have them closed, shutting out the cooling breeze. She had better things to do, a world to conquer & so forth, who did he think he was?*

---

1. Vulgarity.

= Foreigners can be dogged. And can also, on account of language difficulties, fail to take a hint. Then again, let us not forget, it is considered de rigueur[2] to keep a few foreigners around. They lend the place a certain cosmopolitan tone. They are often poor and consequently willing to perform divers[3] necessary but dirty jobs. They are, moreover, a warning against complacency, their existence in our midst reminding us that there are quarters in which (hard as it is to accept) we ourselves would be considered foreign, too.

— But to speak so to the Queen!

= Foreigners forget their place (having left it behind). Given time, they begin to think of themselves as our equals. It is an unavoidable hazard. They introduce into our austerities their Italianate blandishments. Nothing for it: turn a deaf ear, look the other way. They rarely mean real harm, and go too far only infrequently. The Queen, be assured, can look after herself.

Columbus at Isabella's court is quickly burdened with the reputation of being a crazy man. His clothes are excessively colourful and he drinks, also, to excess. When Isabella wins a military victory she celebrates it with eleven days of psalms and the sonorous severities of priests. Columbus crashes about outside the cathedral, waving a wineskin. He is a one-man debauch.

— See him, the drunkard, his huge, shaggy head filled with nonsenses! A fool with a glittering eye dreaming of a golden paradise beyond the Western Edge of Things.

"Consummation."

The Queen plays with Columbus.

At luncheon she promises him everything he wants; then cuts him dead later the same afternoon, looking through him as if he were a veil.

On his saint's day she summons him to her inmost boudoir, dismisses her girls, permits him to braid her hair and, for a moment, to fondle her breasts. Then she summons her guards. She banishes him to the stables and piggeries for forty days. He sits forlorn on horse-munched hay while his thoughts run on distant, fabled gold. He dreams of the Queen's perfumes but awakes, gagging, in a pigsty.

Toying with Columbus pleases the Queen.

And pleasing the Queen, he reminds himself, may help him to achieve his purpose. Pigs rootle by his feet. He grits his teeth.

"Pleasing the Queen is good."

Columbus ponders:

Does she torment him merely for sport?

Or: because he is foreign, and she is unused to his ways and meanings.

Or: because her ring finger, still hot with the memory of his lips his breath, has been — how-you-say? — touched. Yes: tentacles of warmth spread backward from her fingers towards her heart. A turbulence has been aroused.

Or: because she is torn between the possibility of embracing his scheme with a lover's abandon, and the more conventional, and differently (maliciously) pleasurable option of destroying him by laughing, finally, after much foreplay, in his foolish, supplicant face.

2. Compulsory.   3. Various.

Columbus consoles himself with possibilities. Not all possibilities are consoling, however.

She is an absolute monarch. (Her husband is an absolute zero: a blank, couldn't be colder. We will not speak further of him.) She is a woman whose ring is often kissed. It means nothing to her. She is no stranger to flatteries. She resists them effortlessly.

She is a tyrant, who numbers among her possessions a private menagerie of four hundred and nineteen fools, some grotesquely malformed, others as beauteous as the dawn. He, Columbus, is merely her four hundred and twentieth idiot. This, too, is a plausible scenario.

Either: she understands his dream of a world beyond the world's end, and is moved by it, so profoundly that it spooks her, and she turns first towards it, then away;

Or: she doesn't understand him at all, nor cares to understand.

"Take your pick."

What's certain is that *he* doesn't understand *her*. Only the facts are plain. She is Isabella, all-conquering Queen. He is her invisible (though raucous, multicoloured, wine-bibbing) man.

"Consummation."

The sexual appetites of the male decline; those of the female continue, with the advancing years, to grow. Isabella is Columbus's last hope. He is running out of possible patrons, sales talk, flirtatiousness, hair, steam.

Time drags by.

Isabella gallops around, winning battles, expelling Moors from their strongholds, her appetites expanding by the week. The more of the land she swallows, the more warriors she engulfs, the hungrier she gets. Columbus, aware of a slow shrivelling inside him, scolds himself. He should see things as they are. He should come to his senses. What chance does he have here? Some days she makes him clean latrines. On other days he is on body-washing duty, and after a battle the bodies are not clean. Soldiers going to war wear man-sized diapers under their armour because the fear of death will open the bowels, will do it every time. Columbus was not cut out for this sort of work. He tells himself to leave Isabella, once and for all.

But there are problems: his advancing years, the patron shortage. Once he decamps, he will have to forget the western voyage.

The body of philosophical opinion which holds that life is absurd has never appealed to him. He is a man of action, revealing himself in deeds. But without the western voyage he will be obliged to accept the meaninglessness of life. This, too, would be a defeat. Invisible in hot tropical colours, unrequited, he remains, dogging her footsteps, hoping for the ecstasy of her glance.

"The search for money and patronage," Columbus says, "is not so different from the quest for love."

———

—   *She is omnipotent. Castles fall at her feet. The Jews have been expelled. The Moors prepare their last surrender. The Queen is at Granada, riding at her armies' head.*

=   *She overwhelms. Nothing she has wanted has ever been refused.*

—   *All her dreams are prophecies.*

= Acting upon information received while sleeping, she draws up her invincible battle plans, foils the conspiracies of assassins, learns of the infidelities and corruptions for which she blackmails both her loyalists (to ensure their support) and her opponents (to ensure theirs). The dreams help her forecast the weather, negotiate treaties, and invest shrewdly in trade.

— She eats like a horse and never gains an ounce.

= The earth adores her footfall. Its shadows flee before the brilliance of her eyes.

— Her face is a lush peninsula set in a sea of hair.

= Her treasure chests are inexhaustible.

— Her ears are soft question-marks, suggesting some uncertainty.

= Her legs.

— Her legs are not so great.

= She is full of discontents.

— No conquest satisfies her, no peak of ecstasy is high enough.

= See: there at the gates of the Alhambra is Boabdil the Unlucky, the last Sultan of the last redoubt[4] of all the centuries of Arab Spain. Behold: now, at this very instant, he surrenders the keys to the citadel into her grasp . . . there! And as the weight of the keys falls from his hand into hers, she . . . she . . . yawns.

Columbus gives up hope.

While Isabella is entering the Alhambra in listless triumph, he is saddling his mule. While she dawdles in the Court of the Lions, he departs in a flurry of whips elbows hooves, all rapidly obscured by a dust cloud.

Invisibility claims him. He surrenders to its will. Knowing he is abandoning his destiny, he abandons it. He rides away from Queen Isabella in hopeless anger, rides day and night, and when his mule dies under him he shoulders his ridiculous gypsy-patchwork bags, their rowdy colours muted now by dirt; and walks.

Around him stretches the rich plain her armies have subdued. Columbus sees none of it, neither the land's fertility nor the sudden barrenness of the vanquished castles looking down from their pinnacles. The ghosts of defeated civilisations flow unnoticed down the rivers whose names — Guadalthis and Guadalthat — retain an echo of the annihilated past.

Overhead, the arabesque wheelings of the patient buzzards.

Jews pass Columbus in long columns, but the tragedy of their expulsion makes no mark on him. Somebody tries to sell him a Toledo sword; he waves the man away. Having lost his own dream of ships, Columbus leaves the Jews to the ships of their exile, waiting in the harbour of Cadiz. Exhaustion strips him of his senses. This old world is too old and the new world is an unfound land.

"The loss of money and patronage," Columbus says, "is as bitter as unrequited love."

He walks beyond fatigue, beyond the limits of endurance and the frontiers of self, and somewhere along this path he loses his balance, he falls off the edge of his sanity, and out here beyond his mind's rim he sees, for the first and only time in his life, a vision.

4. A small fortification.

It is a dream of a dream.

He dreams of Isabella, languidly exploring the Alhambra, the great jewel she has seized from Boabdil, last of the Nasrids.

She is staring into a large stone bowl held aloft by stone lions. The bowl is filled with blood, and in it she sees—*that is, Columbus dreams her seeing*—a vision of her own.

The bowl shows her that everything, all the known world, is now hers. Everyone in it is in her hands, to do with as she pleases. And when she understands this— *Columbus dreams*—the blood at once congeals, becoming a thick and verminous sludge. Whereupon the Isabella of Columbus's weary, but also vengeful, imaginings is shaken to her very marrow by the realisation that she will never, *never*, NEVER! be satisfied by the possession of the Known. Only the Unknown, perhaps even the Unknowable, can satisfy her.

All at once she remembers Columbus (*he envisions her remembering him*). Columbus, the invisible man who dreams of entering the invisible world, the unknown and perhaps even unknowable world beyond the Edge of Things, beyond the stone bowl of the everyday, beyond the thick blood of the sea. Columbus in this bitter dream makes Isabella see the truth at last, makes her accept that her need for him is as great as his for her. Yes! She knows it now! She must must must give him the money, the ships, any-thing, and he must must must carry her flag and her favour beyond the end of the end of the earth, into exaltation and immortality, linking her to him for ever with bonds far harder to dissolve than those of any mortal love, the harsh and deifying ties of history.

"Consummation."

In Columbus's savage dream, Isabella tears her hair, runs from the Court of the Lions, screams for her heralds.

"Find him," she commands.

But Columbus in his dream refuses to be found. He wraps around himself the dusty patchwork cloak of his invisibility, and the heralds gallop hither and yon in vain.

Isabella screeches, beseeches, implores.

Bitch! Bitch! How do you like it now, Columbus sneers. By absenting himself from her court, by this final and suicidal invisibility, he has denied her her heart's desire. Serves her right.

Bitch!

She murdered his hopes, didn't she? Well, then. In doing so she has laid herself low as well. Poetic justice. Fair's fair.

At the dream's end he permits her messengers to find him. Their hoofbeats, their waving frantic arms. They plead, cajole, offer bribes. But it's too late. Only the sweet self-lacerating joy of murdering Possibility remains.

He answers the heralds: a shake of the head.

"No."

He comes to his senses.

He is on his knees in the fertility of the plains, waiting for death. He hears the hoofbeats approaching and raises his eyes, half expecting to see the Exterminating Angel, riding towards him like a conqueror. Its black wings, the boredom on its face.

Isabella's heralds surround him. They offer him food, drink, a horse. They are shouting.
— *Good news! The Queen has summoned you.*
= *Your voyage: wonderful news.*
— *She saw a vision, and it scared her.*
= *All her dreams are prophecies.*

The heralds dismount. They offer bribes, plead, cajole.
— *She ran from the Court of the Lions, shouting out your name.*
= *She will send you beyond the stone bowl of the known world, beyond the thick blood of the sea.*
— *She's waiting for you in Santa Fé.*
= *You must come at once.*
He stands up, like a requited lover, like a groom on his wedding day. He opens his mouth, and what almost spills out is the bitter refusal: no.
"Yes," he tells the heralds. *Yes. I'll come.*

—◢ END OF PERSPECTIVES: WORLD WAR II AND THE END OF EMPIRE ◣—

——•◇•——

Dylan Thomas
1914–1953

One of the most important facts of Dylan Thomas's biography is his birthplace: Swansea, South Wales. Thomas was Welsh first, English second. Although Wales is entirely contained within the borders of England, it has its own language, unrelated to English. The Welsh language is a living and thriving one, and it is visible in Wales in place names, street signs, church music, and a host of other daily manifestations. Thomas uses the words of the English language in making his poems, plays, and stories, but these words are defamiliarized, are made strange, by virtue of their having been laid on top, as it were, of absent Welsh words and phrasings that echo nonetheless through the English lines. A common criticism made about Dylan Thomas's poetry by English critics who were his contemporaries was that the poetry was overly emotional and excessively musical, and that it lacked "rigor." These charges against the poems sound all too familiarly like the complaints against the Welsh and the Irish peoples—too emotional, too lyrical, too irrational. The innovative and densely lyrical patterns of Thomas's poetry and his prose style come partially out of his "Welshification" of English, a process that has effects on both the style and the subject matter of his work. In another register, he can be seen as the last of the Romantic poets, writing precocious lyrics infused with an intense sense of self.

Dylan Thomas's earliest volume, *18 Poems*, appeared in 1934 when Thomas was twenty years old, a suite of poems based on the cycle of life, birth, childhood, and death in Swansea. It caused a sensation for the magic of its wordplay and the intensely personal focus of the poems. The book was received ecstatically in Britain, but not so in Wales, whose provincial proprieties Thomas always viewed with a half-affectionate sarcasm. Like James Joyce, Thomas felt the necessity of escape; at the age of twenty-one he moved to the metropolitan center, to London, to pursue his hopes of a literary career. There he worked for the BBC as a writer and a performer on radio broadcasts. The short stories of his collection *Portrait of the Artist as a Young Dog* (1940) wittily recount, in obvious homage and parody of Joyce's *Portrait of the Artist as a*

Young Man, the travails of the would-be writer who hopes to break through the barriers of class and nation. He spent the years of World War II in London as well, but as a conscientious objector, not a combatant, and, as a Welshman, to a certain degree as an outsider within. The war was traumatizing for him as for so many others, and Thomas's pacifism and despair led to the superb poetry of his volume *Deaths and Entrances*.

Poetry alone could not pay the bills and allow Thomas and his young family to live in London. After the war he turned to screenplays and to short stories. In the late 1940s, Thomas returned to his poetry, this time less as a poet than as a performer or public reader of his own work. His vibrant and sonorous Welsh-accented voice (akin to that of the Welsh actor Richard Burton), melded with the incantatory lyricism of his poetic language, proved to be irresistible to the public, both in England and in the United States. His brilliant poetry readings instigated a new popularity for poetry itself on both sides of the Atlantic, and his captivating talents as a reader and indeed an actor created for him the persona of Dylan Thomas, Bohemian poet, which he wore until his early death in New York City, after an overdose of whiskey following a poetry reading. He was on his way to California to stay with Igor Stravinsky, with whom he planned to write an epic opera.

The great American poet John Berryman described certain recurrent words as the "unmistakable signature" of Dylan Thomas's poetry. Berryman chose a list of forty "key words" in Thomas's work, including among them: blood, sea, ghost, grave, death, light, time, sun, night, wind, love, and rain. Berryman noted the symbolic value Thomas made these seemingly simple words carry across the span of many poems. Thomas's themes were agreed by most critics to be simple and elemental ones—related to the cycles of life, to nature and childhood, to life's meaning. Berryman argued fiercely that while these were simple themes on the surface, what a poem means *is* its imagery, the way its words are put into relation to one another: "A poem that works well demonstrates an insight, and the insight may consist, not in the theme, but in the image-relations or the structure-relations." Thomas himself aimed at using wordplay and fractured syntax to create sound as a "verbal music." The musicality of his poems and his prose is stunningly evident, and rarely more so than in his play *Under Milk Wood*, a kind of oratorio for disembodied voices. In the play, published posthumously in 1954, Thomas gives voice to the inhabitants of the Welsh village of Llaregyub, whose voices weave together the actions of nature and humans on one single rural day. There is no "plot," and the actors simply stand on stage and read, taking on many voices as these ebb and flow musically through them.

Oral speech and song are more important than written language in rural countries and cultures, especially when one's written language is officially discouraged or even forbidden. Social memory is passed on in story and song; tales and jokes and sermons and performances loom larger in the society of a country town than do written artifacts. Dylan Thomas was very much a writer, yet his poetry and prose are written to be heard, to exist in the ear of the listener as much as the eye of the reader. The lush richness of Thomas's poetic voice is a verbal music that passes on a tradition of oral culture and its precious gifts. The spoken or sung word is a word accompanied by breath; breath is related in most cultures, but certainly in those of Wales and Ireland, to the spirit. One collection of Dylan Thomas's poetry and sketches he titled *The World I Breathe*. This title could as easily be *The Word I Breathe*.

The Force That Through the Green Fuse Drives the Flower

The force that through the green fuse drives the flower
Drives my green age; that blasts the roots of trees

Is my destroyer.
And I am dumb to tell the crooked rose
My youth is bent by the same wintry fever.

The force that drives the water through the rocks
Drives my red blood; that dries the mouthing streams
Turns mine to wax.
And I am dumb to mouth unto my veins
How at the mountain spring the same mouth sucks.

The hand that whirls the water in the pool
Stirs the quicksand; that ropes the blowing wind
Hauls my shroud sail.
And I am dumb to tell the hanging man
How of my clay is made the hangman's lime.

The lips of time leech to the fountain head;
Love drips and gathers, but the fallen blood
Shall calm her sores.
And I am dumb to tell a weather's wind
How time has ticked a heaven round the stars.

And I am dumb to tell the lover's tomb
How at my sheet goes the same crooked worm.

1933

Do Not Go Gentle into That Good Night

Do not go gentle into that good night,
Old age should burn and rave at close of day;
Rage, rage against the dying of the light.

Though wise men at their end know dark is right,
Because their words had forked no lightning they
Do not go gentle into that good night.

Good men, the last wave by, crying how bright
Their frail deeds might have danced in a green bay,
Rage, rage against the dying of the light.

Wild men who caught and sang the sun in flight,
And learn, too late, they grieved it on its way,
Do not go gentle into that good night.

Grave men, near death, who see with blinding sight
Blind eyes could blaze like meteors and be gay,
Rage, rage against the dying of the light.

And you, my father, there on the sad height,
Curse, bless, me now with your fierce tears, I pray.
Do not go gentle into that good night.
Rage, rage against the dying of the light.

1951

⊷ ⛭ ⊶

Samuel Beckett
1906–1989

On January 5, 1953, *En Attendant Godot* (*Waiting for Godot*) premiered at the Théâtre de Baby-lone, Paris—and the shape of twentieth-century drama was permanently changed. *Godot* helped to strip the modern stage of everything but its essentials: two characters, seemingly without past or future or worldly possessions, and a spare stage: "A country road. A tree. Evening." Critics would subsequently find in Beckett's bleak stage suggestions of a postnuclear holocaust landscape, as they would in the later *Fin de partie* (*Endgame*, 1957); and for the remainder of his long and productive career, Beckett would continue to explore, with unparal-leled honesty and courage, that realm of being that he called in one story *Sans*—"lessness."

April 13, 1906—Good Friday—is the date usually given for Samuel Barclay Beckett's birth, though the birth certificate shows May 13. He was born in the family home of Cooldrinagh in Foxrock, an upper-class Protestant suburb south of Dublin, to William Beckett, surveyor, and Mary (May) Roe, the daughter of a wealthy Kildare family. "You might say I had a happy childhood," Beckett later recalled; "my father did not beat me, nor did my mother run away from home." Beck-ett attended private academies in Dublin, then in 1920 was enrolled in Portora Royal School in Enniskillen, Northern Ireland, where he excelled more in sports than studies as star bowler on the cricket team, captain of rugby and swimming, and light-heavyweight champion in boxing. In 1923 Beckett entered Trinity College, Dublin, studying modern languages; he also enjoyed the freedom of the city, frequenting the Gate Theatre (for the drama of Pirandello and O'Casey), the music hall, and the movies (especially Charlie Chaplin, Laurel and Hardy, Buster Keaton, and the Marx Brothers). All would prove formative influences on his later drama and fiction.

In 1927 Beckett received his B.A. degree, first in his class in modern languages, and went off on fellowship to France to teach for two years at the École Normale Supérieure in Paris. While in Paris he became a friend of James Joyce, who influenced him profoundly. Besides aid-ing Joyce in various ways with his work, Beckett wrote an important essay, *Dante . . . Bruno . . . Vico . . . Joyce,* on *Finnegans Wake*—for a volume of critical writing published before the novel itself was completed. With characteristic understatement, Beckett has said that "Paris in the twenties was a good place for a young man to be"; at the same time, learning the craft of writing in Paris under the shadow of fellow Irish expatriate James Joyce would be enough to provoke the anxiety of influence in even the best of writers. However, Beckett's respect and admiration for Joyce were boundless and never wavered. In 1969 Beckett admitted that Joyce had become "an ethical ideal" for him: "Joyce had a moral effect on me. He made me realize artistic integrity."

The term of his fellowship in Paris having run out, Beckett returned to Dublin to assume teaching at Trinity College. That he was ill-suited to this role was immediately apparent to stu-dents, colleagues, and Beckett himself. "I saw that in teaching," Beckett later said, "I was talk-ing of something I knew little about, to people who cared nothing about it. So I behaved very badly." The bad behavior to which Beckett refers was his resignation by mail while on spring holidays in Germany during his second year. Beckett returned briefly to Paris, where it became clear that the unwelcome attentions of Joyce's daughter Lucia were straining Beckett's relation-ship with the elder writer. He returned to the family home for a time in 1933, where he worked on his first published fiction, the Joycean collection of short stories *More Pricks than Kicks*.

The 1930s found Beckett shuttling back and forth between poverty in London and the frustrating comforts of home in Dublin; Paris seemed to him forbidden, owing to the break with Joyce. In spite of his difficult living circumstances, however, and occasional crippling attacks of clinical depression, Beckett managed to complete his first novel, *Murphy*. The man-uscript was rejected by forty-one publishers before being accepted by Routledge in 1937. At the end of 1937, Beckett overcame his reluctance and moved back to Paris. From then on, he wrote largely in French. During the early years of World War II, he attempted to write but found it increasingly difficult to maintain the neutrality required of him by his Irish citizenship in light of the German invasion of France. He abandoned that neutrality in October 1940, when he joined one of the earliest French Resistance groups; he helped in Paris with Resistance activities until his group had been penetrated and betrayed, and just in the nick of time he and his lover Suzanne Deschevaux-Dumesnil (the two had met in 1938, and would eventually marry in 1961) were smuggled into Unoccupied France. At the end of the war Beckett returned to Paris, where he was awarded the *Croix de Guerre* and the *Médaille de la Résistance* by the French government.

While hiding from the Germans from 1942 to 1945 in the village of Roussillon in southeast France, Beckett wrote *Watt*, a complex and aridly witty novel that was never to enjoy the attention devoted to Beckett's other fiction. Meanwhile, Beckett continued his experiments with drama. Though it is drama for which Beckett is best known, he always put more stock in his fiction; "I turned to writing plays," he once said dismissively, "to relieve myself of the awful depression the prose led me into."

At an impasse in the writing of what would prove to be his greatest novels, the trilogy *Molloy, Malone Dies,* and *The Unnameable* (1951–1953), Beckett took off three months to write *Waiting for Godot;* it took four years to get the play produced. It is easy enough, in retrospect, to understand the producers' reservations: *Godot* breaks with the conventions of the well-made play at just about every turn, even down to its symmetrical, mirror-image two-act structure. The Irish critic Vivian Mercier wittily described *Godot* as a play in which "nothing happens, twice." Beckett's play *Krapp's Last Tape* (1960) uses a tape recorder (which, at the time of writing, Beckett had never seen) as a stage metaphor for the struggle over memory. In this play Beckett went farther than ever in stripping down his action, now involving just a single character. The play is less a monologue, though, than Krapp's dialogue with his past and future selves—and with the machine on which the selves of different years have recorded their fragmentary observations and memories.

After the success of his plays of the fifties and early sixties, Beckett turned to shorter and shorter forms, both in drama and fiction; he produced a number of very powerful, very short plays (*Not I,* 1973; *Footfalls,* 1976; *Rockabye,* 1981) and short, poetic texts that he called by a variety of self-deprecating names ("fizzles," "residua," "texts for nothing"). He sought an intensified power in the increasing economy of his works. In 1969 Beckett was awarded the Nobel Prize for literature, for "a body of work," as the citation declares, "that, in new forms of fiction and the theatre, has transmuted the destitution of modern man into exaltation."

Krapp's Last Tape

A late evening in the future.

Krapp's den.

Front centre a small table, the two drawers of which open towards the audience.

Sitting at the table, facing front, i.e. across from the drawers, a wearish old man: Krapp.

Rusty black narrow trousers too short for him. Rusty black sleeveless waistcoat, four capacious pockets. Heavy silver watch and chain. Grimy white shirt open at neck, no collar. Surprising pair of dirty white boots, size ten at least, very narrow and pointed.

White face. Purple nose. Disordered grey hair. Unshaven.

Very near-sighted (but unspectacled). Hard of hearing.

Cracked voice. Distinctive intonation.

Laborious walk.

On the table a tape-recorder with microphone and a number of cardboard boxes containing reels of recorded tapes.

Table and immediately adjacent area in strong white light. Rest of stage in darkness.

Krapp remains a moment motionless, heaves a great sigh, looks at his watch, fumbles in his pockets, takes out an envelope, puts it back, fumbles, takes out a small bunch of keys, raises it to his eyes, chooses a key, gets up and moves to front of table. He stoops, unlocks first drawer, peers into it, feels about inside it, takes out a reel of tape, peers at it, puts it back, locks drawer, unlocks second drawer, peers into it, feels about inside it, takes out a large banana, peers at it, locks drawer, puts keys back in his pocket. He turns, advances to edge of stage, halts, strokes banana, peels it, drops skin at his feet, puts end of banana in his mouth and remains motionless, staring vacuously before him. Finally he bites off the end, turns aside and begins pacing to and fro at edge of stage, in the light, i.e. not more than four or five paces either way, meditatively eating banana. He treads on skin, slips, nearly falls, recovers himself, stoops and peers at skin and finally pushes it, still stooping, with his foot over edge of stage into pit. He resumes his pacing, finishes banana, returns to table, sits down, remains a moment motionless, heaves a great sigh, takes keys from his pockets, raises them to his eyes, chooses key, gets up and moves to front of table, unlocks second drawer, takes out a second large banana, peers at it, locks drawer, puts back keys in his pocket, turns, advances to edge of stage, halts, strokes banana, peels it, tosses skin into pit, puts end of banana in his mouth and remains motionless, staring vacuously before him. Finally he has an idea, puts banana in his waistcoat pocket, the end emerging, and goes with all the speed he can muster backstage into darkness. Ten seconds. Loud pop of cork. Fifteen seconds. He comes back into light carrying an old ledger and sits down at table. He lays ledger on table, wipes his mouth, wipes his hands on the front of his waistcoat, brings them smartly together and rubs them.

KRAPP [*briskly*]: Ah! [*He bends over ledger, turns the pages, finds the entry he wants, reads.*] Box . . . thrree . . . spool . . . five. [*He raises his head and stares front. With relish.*] Spool . . . [*Pause.*] Spooool! [*Happy smile. Pause. He bends over table, starts peering and poking at the boxes.*] Box . . . thrree . . . thrree . . . four . . . two . . . [*with surprise*] nine! good God! . . . seven . . . ah! the little rascal! [*He takes up box, peers at it.*] Box thrree. [*He lays it on table, opens it and peers at spools inside.*] Spool . . . [*he peers at ledger*] . . . five . . . [*he peers at spools*] . . . five . . . five . . . ah! the little scoundrel! [*He takes out a spool, peers at it.*] Spool five. [*He lays it on table, closes box three, puts it back with the others, takes up the spool.*] Box thrree, spool five. [*He bends over the machine, looks up. With relish.*] Spooool! [*Happy smile. He bends, loads spool on machine, rubs his hands.*] Ah! [*He peers at ledger, reads entry at foot of page.*] Mother at rest at last. . . . Hm. . . . The black ball. . . . [*He raises his head, stares blankly front. Puzzled.*] Black ball? . . . [*He peers again at ledger, reads.*] The dark nurse. . . . [*He raises his head, broods, peers again at ledger, reads.*] Slight improvement in bowel condition. . . . Hm. . . . Memorable . . . what? [*He peers closer.*] Equinox, memorable equinox. [*He raises his head, stares blankly front. Puzzled.*] Memorable equinox? . . . [*Pause. He shrugs his shoulders, peers again at ledger, reads.*] Farewell to—[*he turns page*]—love. [*He raises his head, broods, bends over machine, switches on and assumes listening posture, i.e. leaning forward, elbows on table, hand cupping ear towards machine, face front.*]

TAPE [*strong voice, rather pompous, clearly Krapp's at a much earlier time*]: Thirty-nine today, sound as a—[*Settling himself more comfortably he knocks one of the boxes off the table, curses, switches off, sweeps boxes and ledger violently to the ground, winds tape back to beginning, switches on, resumes posture.*] Thirty-nine today, sound as a bell, apart from my old weakness, and intellectually I have now every reason to suspect at the . . . [*hesitates*] . . . crest of the wave—or thereabouts. Celebrated the awful occasion, as in recent years, quietly at the Winehouse. Not a soul. Sat before the fire with closed eyes, separating the grain from the husks. Jotted down a few notes, on the back of an envelope. Good to be back in my den, in my old rags. Have just eaten I regret to say three bananas and only with difficulty refrained from a fourth. Fatal things for a man with my condition. [*Vehemently.*] Cut'em out! [*Pause.*] The new light above my table is a great improvement. With all this darkness round me I feel less alone. [*Pause.*] In a way. [*Pause.*] I love to get up and move about in it, then back here to . . . [*hesitates*] . . . me. [*Pause.*] Krapp.

[*Pause.*]

The grain, now what I wonder do I mean by that, I mean . . . [*hesitates*] . . . I suppose I mean those things worth having when all the dust has—when all *my* dust has settled. I close my eyes and try and imagine them.

[*Pause. Krapp closes his eyes briefly.*]

Extraordinary silence this evening, I strain my ears and do not hear a sound. Old Miss McGlome always sings at this hour. But not tonight. Songs of her girlhood, she says. Hard to think of her as a girl. Wonderful woman though. Connaught,[1] I fancy. [*Pause.*] Shall I sing when I am her age, if I ever am? No. [*Pause.*] Did I sing as a boy? No. [*Pause.*] Did I ever sing? No.

[*Pause.*]

Just been listening to an old year, passages at random. I did not check in the book, but it must be at least ten or twelve years ago. At that time I think I was still living on and off with Bianca in Kedar Street. Well out of that, Jesus yes! Hopeless business. [*Pause.*] Not much about her, apart from a tribute to her eyes. Very warm. I suddenly saw them again. [*Pause.*] Incomparable! [*Pause.*] Ah well? [*Pause.*] These old P.M.s are gruesome, but I often find them—[*Krapp switches off, broods, switches on.*]—a help before embarking on a new . . . [*hesitates*] . . . retrospect. Hard to believe I was ever that young whelp. The voice! Jesus! And the aspirations! [*Brief laugh in which Krapp joins.*] And the resolutions! [*Brief laugh in which Krapp joins.*] To drink less, in particular. [*Brief laugh of Krapp alone.*] Statistics. Seventeen hundred hours, out of the preceding eight thousand odd, consumed on licensed premises[2] alone. More than 20 per cent, say 40 per cent of his waking life. [*Pause.*] Plans for a less . . . [*hesitates*] . . . engrossing sexual life. Last illness of his father. Flagging pursuit of happiness. Unattainable laxation.[3] Sneers at what he calls his youth and thanks to God that it's over. [*Pause.*] False ring there. [*Pause.*] Shadows of the opus . . . magnum.[4] Closing with a—[*brief laugh*]—yelp to Providence. [*Prolonged laugh in which Krapp joins.*] What remains of all that misery? A girl in a shabby green coat, on a railway-station platform? No?

[*Pause.*]

When I look—

[*Krapp switches off, broods, looks at his watch, gets up, goes backstage into darkness. Ten seconds. Pop of cork. Ten seconds. Second cork. Ten seconds. Third cork. Ten seconds. Brief burst of quavering song.*]

KRAPP [*sings*]:   Now the day is over,
                        Night is drawing nigh-igh,
                        Shadows—

[*Fit of coughing. He comes back into light, sits down, wipes his mouth, switches on, resumes his listening posture.*]

1. A province in northwestern Ireland.
2. Pubs licensed to sell alcohol.
3. Movement of the bowels.

4. A "magnum opus" is a great work; a magnum is a large wine bottle.

TAPE: —back on the year that is gone, with what I hope is perhaps a glint of the old eye to come, there is of course the house on the canal where mother lay a-dying, in the late autumn, after her long viduity [*Krapp gives a start*] and the—[*Krapp switches off, winds back tape a little, bends his ear closer to machine, switches on*]—a-dying, after her long viduity, and the—

[*Krapp switches off, raises his head, stares blankly before him. His lips move in the syllables of "viduity." No sound. He gets up, goes backstage into darkness, comes back with an enormous dictionary, lays it on table, sits down and looks up the word.*]

KRAPP [*reading from dictionary*]: State—or condition—of being—or remaining—a widow—or widower. [*Looks up. Puzzled.*] Being—or remaining? . . . [*Pause. He peers again at dictionary. Reading.*] "Deep weeds of viduity." . . . Also of an animal, especially a bird . . . the vidua or weaver-bird. . . . Black plumage of male. . . . [*He looks up. With relish.*] The vidua-bird!

[*Pause. He closes dictionary, switches on, resumes listening posture.*]

TAPE: —bench by the weir from where I could see her window. There I sat, in the biting wind, wishing she were gone. [*Pause.*] Hardly a soul, just a few regulars, nursemaids, infants, old men, dogs. I got to know them quite well—oh by appearance of course I mean! One dark young beauty I recollect particularly, all white and starch, incomparable bosom, with a big black hooded perambulator, most funeral thing. Whenever I looked in her direction she had her eyes on me. And yet when I was bold enough to speak to her—not having been introduced—she threatened to call a policeman. As if I had designs on her virtue! [*Laugh. Pause.*] The face she had! The eyes! Like . . . [*hesitates*] . . . chrysolite![5] [*Pause.*] Ah well. . . . [*Pause.*] I was there when—[*Krapp switches off, broods, switches on again.*]—the blind went down, one of those dirty brown roller affairs, throwing a ball for a little white dog as chance would have it. I happened to look up and there it was. All over and done with, at last. I sat on for a few moments with the ball in my hand and the dog yelping and pawing at me. [*Pause.*] Moments. Her moments, my moments. [*Pause.*] The dog's moments. [*Pause.*] In the end I held it out to him and he took it in his mouth, gently, gently. A small, old, black, hard, solid rubber ball. [*Pause.*] I shall feel it, in my hand, until my dying day. [*Pause.*] I might have kept it. [*Pause.*] But I gave it to the dog.

[*Pause.*]

Ah well. . . .

[*Pause.*]

Spiritually a year of profound gloom and indigence until that memorable night in March, at the end of the jetty, in the howling wind, never to be forgotten, when suddenly I saw the whole thing. The vision at last. This I fancy is what I have chiefly to record this evening, against the day when my work will be done and perhaps no place left in my memory, warm or cold, for the miracle that . . . [*hesitates*] . . . for the fire that set it alight. What I suddenly saw then was this, that the belief I had been going on all my life, namely—[*Krapp switches off impatiently, winds tape forward, switches on again*]—great granite rocks the foam flying up in the light of the lighthouse and the wind-gauge spinning like a propeller, clear to me at last that the dark I have always struggled to keep under is in reality my most—[*Krapp curses, switches off, winds tape forward, switches on again*]—unshatterable association until my dissolution of storm and night with the light of the under-

---

5. Green gemstone.

standing and the fire—[*Krapp curses louder, switches off, winds tape forward, switches on again*]—my face in her breasts and my hand on her. We lay there without moving. But under us all moved, and moved us, gently, up and down, and from side to side.

[*Pause.*]

Past midnight. Never knew such silence. The earth might be uninhabited.

[*Pause.*]

Here I end—

[*Krapp switches off, winds tape back, switches on again.*]

—upper lake, with the punt,[6] bathed off the bank, then pushed out into the stream and drifted. She lay stretched out on the floorboards with her hands under her head and her eyes closed. Sun blazing down, bit of a breeze, water nice and lively. I noticed a scratch on her thigh and asked her how she came by it. Picking gooseberries, she said. I said again I thought it was hopeless and no good going on and she agreed, without opening her eyes. [*Pause.*] I asked her to look at me and after a few moments—[*Pause.*]—after a few moments she did, but the eyes just slits, because of the glare. I bent over her to get them in the shadow and they opened. [*Pause. Low.*] Let me in. [*Pause.*] We drifted in among the flags[7] and stuck. The way they went down, sighing, before the stem! [*Pause.*] I lay down across her with my face in her breasts and my hand on her. We lay there without moving. But under us all moved, and moved us, gently, up and down, and from side to side.

[*Pause.*]

Past midnight. Never knew—

[*Krapp switches off, broods. Finally he fumbles in his pockets, encounters the banana, takes it out, peers at it, puts it back, fumbles, brings out envelope, fumbles, puts back envelope, looks at his watch, gets up and goes backstage into darkness. Ten seconds. Sound of bottle against glass, then brief siphon. Ten seconds. Bottle against glass alone. Ten seconds. He comes back a little unsteadily into light, goes to front of table, takes out keys, raises them to his eyes, chooses key, unlocks first drawer, peers into it, feels about inside, takes out reel, peers at it, locks drawer, puts keys back in his pocket, goes and sits down, takes reel off machine, lays it on dictionary, loads virgin reel on machine, takes envelope from his pocket, consults back of it, lays it on table, switches on, clears his throat and begins to record.*]

KRAPP: Just been listening to that stupid bastard I took myself for thirty years ago, hard to believe I was ever as bad as that. Thank God that's all done with anyway. [*Pause.*] The eyes she had! [*Broods, realizes he is recording silence, switches off, broods. Finally.*] Everything there, everything, all the—[*Realizes this is not being recorded, switches on.*] Everything there, everything on this old muckball, all the light and dark and famine and feasting of . . . [*hesitates*] . . . the ages! [*In a shout.*] Yes! [*Pause.*] Let that go! Jesus! Take his mind off his homework! Jesus! [*Pause. Weary.*] Ah well, maybe he was right. [*Pause.*] Maybe he was right. [*Broods. Realizes. Switches off. Consults envelope.*] Pah! [*Crumples it and throws it away. Broods. Switches on.*] Nothing to say, not a squeak. What's a year now? The sour cud and the iron stool.[8] [*Pause.*] Revelled in the word spool. [*With relish.*] Spoool! Happiest moment of the past half million. [*Pause.*] Seventeen copies sold, of which eleven at trade price to free circulating libraries beyond the seas. Getting known. [*Pause.*] One pound six and something, eight I have little doubt. [*Pause.*] Crawled

---

6. A small, flat-bottomed boat.
7. Reeds.

8. Indigestion and constipation.

out once or twice, before the summer was cold. Sat shivering in the park, drowned in dreams and burning to be gone. Not a soul. [*Pause.*] Last fancies. [*Vehemently.*] Keep 'em under! [*Pause.*] Scalded the eyes out of me reading *Effie*[9] again, a page a day, with tears again. Effie. . . . [*Pause.*] Could have been happy with her, up there on the Baltic, and the pines, and the dunes. [*Pause.*] Could I? [*Pause.*] And she? [*Pause.*] Pah! [*Pause.*] Fanny came in a couple of times. Bony old ghost of a whore. Couldn't do much, but I suppose better than a kick in the crutch. The last time wasn't so bad. How do you manage it, she said, at your age? I told her I'd been saving up for her all my life. [*Pause.*] Went to Vespers[1] once, like when I was in short trousers. [*Pause. Sings.*]

> Now the day is over,
> Night is drawing nigh-igh,
> Shadows—[*coughing, then almost inaudible*]—of the evening
> Steal across the sky.

[*Gasping.*] Went to sleep and fell off the pew. [*Pause.*] Sometimes wondered in the night if a last effort mightn't—[*Pause.*] Ah finish your booze now and get to your bed. Go on with this drivel in the morning. Or leave it at that. [*Pause.*] Leave it at that. [*Pause.*] Lie propped up in the dark—and wander. Be again in the dingle[2] on a Christmas Eve, gathering holly, the red-berried. [*Pause.*] Be again on Croghan[3] on a Sunday morning, in the haze, with the bitch, stop and listen to the bells. [*Pause.*] And so on. [*Pause.*] Be again, be again. [*Pause.*] All that old misery. [*Pause.*] Once wasn't enough for you. [*Pause.*] Lie down across her.

   [*Long pause. He suddenly bends over machine, switches off, wrenches off tape, throws it away, puts on the other, winds it forward to the passage he wants, switches on, listens staring front.*]

TAPE: —gooseberries, she said. I said again I thought it was hopeless and no good going on and she agreed, without opening her eyes. [*Pause.*] I asked her to look at me and after a few moments—[*Pause.*]—after a few moments she did, but the eyes just slits, because of the glare. I bent over to get them in the shadow and they opened. [*Pause. Low.*] Let me in. [*Pause.*] We drifted in among the flags and stuck. The way they went down, sighing, before the stem! [*Pause.*] I lay down across her with my face in her breasts and my hand on her. We lay there without moving. But under us all moved, and moved us, gently, up and down, and from side to side.

   [*Pause. Krapp's lips move. No sound.*]

Past midnight. Never knew such silence. The earth might be uninhabited.

   [*Pause.*]

Here I end this reel. Box—[*Pause.*]—three, spool—[*Pause.*]—five. [*Pause.*] Perhaps my best years are gone. When there was a chance of happiness. But I wouldn't want them back. Not with the fire in me now. No, I wouldn't want them back.

   [*Krapp motionless staring before him. The tape runs on in silence.*]

CURTAIN

---

9. Theodor Fontane's sentimental novel *Effi Briest* (1895).   2. Valley.
1. Evening church service.   3. Mountain in County Wicklow in Southeastern Ireland.

from Texts for Nothing[1]

8

Only the words break the silence, all other sounds have ceased. If I were silent I'd hear nothing. But if I were silent the other sounds would start again, those to which the words have made me deaf, or which have really ceased. But I am silent, it sometimes happens, no, never, not one second. I weep too without interruption. It's an unbroken flow of words and tears. With no pause for reflection. But I speak softer, every year a little softer. Perhaps. Slower too, every year a little slower. Perhaps. It is hard for me to judge. If so the pauses would be longer, between the words, the sentences, the syllables, the tears, I confuse them, words and tears, my words are my tears, my eyes my mouth. And I should hear, at every little pause, if it's the silence I say when I say that only the words break it. But nothing of the kind, that's not how it is, it's for ever the same murmur, flowing unbroken, like a single endless word and therefore meaningless, for it's the end gives the meaning to words. What right have you then, no, this time I see what I'm up to and put a stop to it, saying, None, none. But get on with the stupid old threne[2] and ask, ask until you answer, a new question, the most ancient of all, the question were things always so. Well I'm going to tell myself something (if I'm able), pregnant I hope with promise for the future, namely that I begin to have no very clear recollection of how things were before (I was!), and by before I mean elsewhere, time has turned into space and there will be no more time, till I get out of here. Yes, my past has thrown me out, its gates have slammed behind me, or I burrowed my way out alone, to linger a moment free in a dream of days and nights, dreaming of me moving, season after season, towards the last, like the living, till suddenly I was here, all memory gone. Ever since nothing but fantasies and hope of a story for me somehow, of having come from somewhere and of being able to go back, or on, somehow, some day, or without hope. Without what hope, haven't I just said, of seeing me alive, not merely inside an imaginary head, but a pebble sand to be, under a restless sky, restless on its shore, faint stirs day and night, as if to grow less could help, ever less and less and never quite be gone. No truly, no matter what, I say no matter what, hoping to wear out a voice, to wear out a head, or without hope, without reason, no matter what, without reason. But it will end, a desinence[3] will come, or the breath fail better still, I'll be silence, I'll know I'm silence, no, in the silence you can't know, I'll never know anything. But at least get out of here, at least that, no? I don't know. And time begin again, the steps on the earth, the night the fool implores at morning and the morning he begs at evening not to dawn. I don't know, I don't know what all that means, day and night, earth and sky, begging and imploring. And I can desire them? Who says I desire them, the voice, and that I can't desire anything, that looks like a contradiction, it may be for all I know. Me, here, if they could open, those little words, open and swallow me up, perhaps that is what has happened. If so let them open again and let me out, in the tumult of light that sealed my eyes, and of men, to try and be one again. Or if I'm guilty let me be forgiven and graciously authorized to expiate, coming and going in passing time, every day a little purer, a little deader. The mistake I make is to try and think, even the way I do, such as I am I shouldn't be able, even the way I do. But whom can I have offended so grievously, to be punished in this inexplicable way, all is inexplicable, space and time, false and inexplicable, suffering and tears, and even the old convulsive cry, It's not me, it can't be me.

---

1. Having completed his *Molloy* trilogy in 1950, Beckett wrote this series of short texts between 1950 and 1952 as "an attempt to get out of the attitude of disintegration" established in his trilogy—an attempt, Beckett later said, that failed.
2. Song of lamentation.
3. Termination.

But am I in pain, whether it's me or not, frankly now, is there pain? Now is here and here there is no frankness, all I say will be false and to begin with not said by me, here I'm a mere ventriloquist's dummy, I feel nothing, say nothing, he holds me in his arms and moves my lips with a string, with a fish-hook, no, no need of lips, all is dark, there is no one, what's the matter with my head, I must have left it in Ireland, in a saloon, it must be there still, lying on the bar, it's all it deserved. But that other who is me, blind and deaf and mute, because of whom I'm here, in this black silence, helpless to move or accept this voice as mine, it's as him I must disguise myself till I die, for him in the meantime do my best not to live, in this pseudo-sepulture[4] claiming to be his. Whereas to my certain knowledge I'm dead and kicking above, somewhere in Europe probably, with every plunge and suck of the sky a little more overripe, as yesterday in the pump of the womb. No, to have said so convinces me of the contrary, I never saw the light of day, any more than he, ah if no were content to cut yes's throat and never cut its own. Watch out for the right moment, then not another word, is that the only way to have being and habitat? But I'm here, that much at least is certain, it's in vain I keep on saying it, it remains true. Does it? It's hard for me to judge. Less true and less certain in any case than when I say I'm on earth, come into the world and assured of getting out, that's why I say it, patiently, variously, trying to vary, for you never know, it's perhaps all a question of hitting on the right aggregate. So as to be here no more at last, to have never been here, but all this time above, with a name like a dog to be called up with and distinctive marks to be had up with, the chest expanding and contracting unaided, panting towards the grand apnoea.[5] The right aggregate, but there are four million possible, nay probable, according to Aristotle, who knew everything. But what is this I see, and how, a white stick and an ear-trumpet, where, Place de la République, at pernod[6] time, let me look closer at this, it's perhaps me at last. The trumpet, sailing at ear level, suddenly resembles a steam-whistle, of the kind thanks to which my steamers forge fearfully through the fog. That should fix the period, to the nearest half-century or so. The stick gains ground, tapping with its ferrule[7] the noble bassamento of the United Stores, it must be winter, at least not summer. I can also just discern, with a final effort of will, a bowler hat which seems to my sorrow a sardonic synthesis of all those that never fitted me and, at the other extremity, similarly suspicious, a complete pair of brown boots lacerated and gaping. These insignia, if I may so describe them, advance in concert, as though connected by the traditional human excipient,[8] halt, move on again, confirmed by the vast show windows. The level of the hat, and consequently of the trumpet, hold out some hope for me as a dying dwarf or at least hunchback. The vacancy is tempting, shall I enthrone my infirmities, give them this chance again, my dream infirmities, that they may take flesh and move, deteriorating, round and round this grandiose square which I hope I don't confuse with the Bastille,[9] until they are deemed worthy of the adjacent Père Lachaise[1] or, better still, prematurely relieved trying to cross over, at the hour of night's young thoughts. No, the answer is no. For even as I moved, or when the moment came, affecting beyond all others, to hold out my hand, or hat, without previous song, or any other form of concession to self-respect, at the terrace of a café, or in the mouth of the underground, I would know it was not me, I would know I was here, begging in another dark, another silence, for another alm, that of being or of ceasing, better still, before having been. And the hand old in vain would drop the mite and the old feet shuffle on, towards an even vainer death than no matter whose.

---

4. Tomb.
5. Cessation of breathing.
6. A licorice-flavored liqueur.
7. Metal-capped tip.

8. Glue.
9. Parisian prison destroyed during the French Revolution in 1789.
1. Parisian cemetery.

⟞ PERSPECTIVES ⟝
Whose Language?

Though Britain's last major overseas colony, Hong Kong, rejoined China in 1997, at least one important reminder of British rule remains in countries as far-flung as India, South Africa, and New Zealand: the English language itself. Twentieth-century linguists, following on the pioneering work of Benjamin Lee Whorf and Edward Sapir, are nearly unanimous in their belief that languages do not merely serve to describe the world but in fact help to create that world, establishing both a set of possibilities and a set of limits.

The politics of language thus becomes important for writers, especially writers in colonial and postcolonial cultures. In an episode from Joyce's *A Portrait of the Artist as a Young Man*, the Irish protagonist Stephen Dedalus converses with the English-born Dean of Studies at University College, Dublin, where Stephen is a student. In the course of the conversation it becomes clear that Stephen is already a more supple and cunning user of the English language than his teacher, and yet he feels himself at a disadvantage in having to use the language of the invader; he muses: "The language in which we are speaking is his before it is mine. How different are the words *home, Christ, ale, master*, on his lips and on mine! I cannot speak or write these words without unrest of spirit. His language, so familiar and so foreign, will always be for me an acquired speech. I have not made or accepted its words. My voice holds them at bay. My soul frets in the shadow of his language." The Penal Acts of 1695 and 1696 had made the Irish language illegal in Ireland; after 500 years of trying to subdue the "wild Irish," British lawmakers realized that the Irish natives would never be brought under English rule until their tongues were bound. In his poem *Traditions*, Seamus Heaney meditates on the enduring cost of what he has called elsewhere "the government of the tongue":

> Our guttural muse
> was bulled long ago
> by the alliterative tradition,
> her uvula grows
> vestigial, forgotten.

In much colonial and postcolonial writing, however, the confusion of tongues inflicted by British rule has been seen by the writers of Empire as a positive linguistic resource. Nadine Gordimer in South Africa both mixes local dialect with standard English to take the measure of reality a far cry from London. Salman Rushdie, explaining his decision to use English rather than his native Hindi, writes: "Those of us who do use English do so in spite of our ambiguity towards it, or perhaps because of that, perhaps because we can find in that linguistic struggle a reflection of other struggles taking place in the real world, struggles between the cultures within ourselves and the influences working upon our societies. To conquer English may be to complete the process of making ourselves free." Thus a great deal of contemporary English-language writing—especially in countries where English was once the language of the conqueror (such as Ireland, Scotland, Wales, South Africa, India, and Kenya)—meditates on the blindnesses and insights inherent in using English. Some writers, like the Irish poet Nuala Ní Dhomhnaill, write in defiance of English; if one's native tongue is a minority language like Irish, this decision necessarily narrows a writer's potential audience. More common is the decision made by Rushdie, and by James Joyce before him: to write English as an "outsider," attesting to an alien's perspective on the majority language.

Philip Larkin
1922–1985

Philip Larkin's lifetime production of poems was quite small, but highly influential; he is best known for his three last volumes, *The Less Deceived* (1955), *The Whitsun Weddings* (1964), and *High Windows* (1974), which together collect fewer than one hundred poems. During his lifetime, however, he fulfilled the role—a role that every society seems to require—of the crotchety traditionalist poet, becoming famous for what the poet and critic Donald Hall has called a "genuine, uncultivated, sincere philistinism."

Born in Coventry, Larkin completed a B.A. and M.A. at Oxford (where he was a friend of the novelist Kingsley Amis), and became a professional librarian, working at the University of Hull from 1955 until his death. After two modestly successful novels (*Jill* and *A Girl in Winter*) and two undistinguished volumes of poetry (*The North Ship* and *XX Poems*), Larkin established himself as a new and important voice in British poetry with his collection *The Less Deceived*. According to most critics, the influence of Thomas Hardy's poetry was decisive; Seamus Heaney writes that the "slips and excesses" of his first two volumes—consisting, primarily, of embarrassing echoes of W. B. Yeats—led Larkin "to seek the antidote of Thomas Hardy."

Larkin was attracted to Hardy's bleak outlook on life, as well as his skilled versification and spare language. Larkin's dark vision remained unremitting as late as *Aubade*, the last poem to be published during his lifetime:

> I work all day, and get half drunk at night.
> Waking at four to soundless dark, I stare.
> In time the curtain-edges will grow light.
> Till then I see what's really always there:
> Unresting death, a whole day nearer now,
> Making all thought impossible but how
> And where and when I shall myself die.

Like the most famous postwar British playwright, Samuel Beckett, the most important postwar British poet was not above having a laugh at his own despair; in an oft-repeated remark, Larkin told an interviewer that "deprivation is for me what daffodils were for Wordsworth."

Larkin is one of the most English of modern British poets; he refused to read "foreign" literature—including most American poetry—or to travel abroad; Hull became the center and circumference of his poetic world. He kept to himself to an extraordinary degree; he never married, nor did he maintain any longstanding intimate relationship. In his obituary for Larkin, Kingsley Amis described him as "a man much driven in upon himself, with increasing deafness from early middle age cruelly emphasizing his seclusion."

Even in his solitude, though, Larkin kept up a running dialogue with the outside world, not only as a poet but as a jazz reviewer for many years. His encyclopedic knowledge of jazz provides the basis for his probing, dyspeptic account of modernity in the opening essay of his collection *All What Jazz*. In this essay as in his verse, Larkin's writing is pointed, skeptical, acerbic—and always self-consciously English.

Talking in Bed

> Talking in bed ought to be easiest,
> Lying together there goes back so far,
> An emblem of two people being honest.
>
> Yet more and more time passes silently.
> Outside, the wind's incomplete unrest

5

Builds and disperses clouds about the sky,

And dark towns heap up on the horizon.
None of this cares for us. Nothing shows why
At this unique distance from isolation

10   It becomes still more difficult to find
Words at once true and kind,
Or not untrue and not unkind.

1960   1964

MCMXIV[1]

Those long uneven lines
Standing as patiently
As if they were stretched outside
The Oval or Villa Park,
5   The crowns of hats, the sun
On moustached archaic faces
Grinning as if it were all
An August Bank Holiday lark;

And the shut shops, the bleached
10   Established names on the sunblinds,
The farthings and sovereigns,
And dark-clothed children at play
Called after kings and queens,
The tin advertisements
15   For cocoa and twist, and the pubs
Wide open all day;

And the countryside not caring:
The place-names all hazed over
With flowering grasses, and fields
20   Shadowing Domesday[2] lines
Under wheat's restless silence;
The differently-dressed servants
With tiny rooms in huge houses,
The dust behind limousines;

25   Never such innocence,
Never before or since,
As changed itself to past
Without a word—the men
Leaving the gardens tidy,
30   The thousands of marriages
Lasting a little while longer:
Never such innocence again.

1960   1964

---

1. 1914, in the style of a monument to the war dead.   value, and ownership of lands in England.
2. The Domesday Book is the medieval record of the extent,

High Windows

When I see a couple of kids
And guess he's fucking her and she's
Taking pills or wearing a diaphragm,
I know this is paradise

5   Everyone old has dreamed of all their lives—
Bonds and gestures pushed to one side
Like an outdated combine harvester,
And everyone young going down the long slide

To happiness, endlessly. I wonder if
10 Anyone looked at me, forty years back,
And thought, *That'll be the life;*
No God any more, or sweating in the dark

About hell and that, or having to hide
What you think of the priest. He
15 *And his lot will all go down the long slide*
Like free bloody birds. And immediately

Rather than words comes the thought of high windows:
The sun-comprehending glass,
And beyond it, the deep blue air, that shows
20 Nothing, and is nowhere, and is endless.

1967   1974

◄—— ✦◊✦ ——►

Seamus Heaney
b. 1939

More prominently than any poet since Yeats, Seamus Heaney has put Irish poetry back at the center of British literary studies. His first full-length collection, *Death of a Naturalist* (1966), ushered in a period of renewed interest in Irish poetry generally, and Ulster poetry in particular; the subsequent attention to poets like Derek Mahon, Michael Longley, Medbh McGuckian and Paul Muldoon owes a great deal to the scope of Heaney's popularity.

As a great number of Heaney's early poems bear poignant witness, he spent his childhood in rural County Derry, Northern Ireland; his family was part of the Catholic minority in Ulster, and his experiences growing up were for that reason somewhat atypical. The critic Irvin Ehrenpreis maps the matrix of Heaney's contradictory position as an Irish poet: "Speech is never simple, in Heaney's conception. He grew up as an Irish Catholic boy in a land governed by Protestants whose tradition is British. He grew up on a farm in his country's northern, industrial region. As a person, therefore, he springs from the old divisions of his nation." His experience was split not only along religious lines, then, but also national and linguistic ones; in some of his early poetry Heaney suggests the split through the paired names—"Mossbawn" (the very English name of his family's fifty-acre farm) and "Anahorish" (Irish *anach fhior uisce*, "place of clear water," where he attended primary school). As a result, Heaney's is a liminal poetry—a "door into the dark"—and Heaney stands in the doorway, with one foot in each world. Heaney makes brilliant use of the linguistic resources of both the traditions he inherited, drawing on the heritage of English Romanticism while also relying heavily on Irish-language assonance in lines like "There were dragon-flies, spotted butterflies, / But best of all was the warm thick slobber / of frogspawn that grew like clotted water / In the shade of the banks" (*Death of a Naturalist*).

When he was twelve, Heaney won a scholarship to a Catholic boarding school in London-derry (now Derry) then went on to Queen's University, Belfast, which was the center of a vital new poetic movement in the 1960s. He was influenced by poets who were able to transform the local into the universal, especially Ted Hughes and Robert Frost. As an "Ulster poet," it has fallen to Heaney to use his voice and his position to comment on Northern Ireland's sectarian violence; ironically enough, however, his most explicitly "political" poems were published before the flare-up of the Troubles that began in 1969, and his most self-conscious response to Ulster's strife, the volume *North* (1975), uses historical and mythological frameworks to address the current political situation obliquely. The Irish critic Seamus Deane has written, "Heaney is very much in the Irish tradition in that he has learned, more successfully than most, to conceive of his personal experience in terms of his country's history"; for Heaney, as the popular saying has it, the personal is the political, and the political the personal. His most successful poems dealing with Ulster's political and religious situation are probably those treating neolithic bodies found preserved in peat bogs. Heaney was living in Belfast, lecturing at Queen's University, at the inception of the Troubles; as a Catholic, he felt a need to convey the urgency of the situation without falling into the easy Republican—or Unionist, for that matter—rhetoric. It was at this point that Heaney discovered the anthropologist P. V. Glob's *The Bog People* (1969), which documents (with riveting photographs) the discovery of sacrificial victims preserved in bogs for 2,000 years. Heaney intuitively knew that he had found his "objective correlative"— what he has called his "emblems of adversity"—with which to explore the Troubles.

Like Yeats, Heaney has, from the very start, enjoyed both popular and critical acclaim. His poems have a surface simplicity; his early poetry especially relishes the carefully observed detail of rural Irish life.

The Toome Road

One morning early I met armoured cars
In convoy, warbling along on powerful tyres,
All camouflaged with broken alder branches,
And headphoned soldiers standing up in turrets.
5   How long were they approaching down my roads
As if they owned them? The whole country was sleeping.
I had rights-of-way, fields, cattle in my keeping,
Tractors hitched to buckrakes in open sheds,
Silos, chill gates, wet slates, the greens and reds
10   Of outhouse roofs. Whom should I run to tell
Among all of those with their back doors on the latch
For the bringer of bad news, that small-hours visitant
Who, by being expected, might be kept distant?
Sowers of seed, erectors of headstones . . .
15   O charioteers, above your dormant guns,
It stands here still, stands vibrant as you pass,
The invisible, untoppled omphalos.[1]

A Postcard from North Antrim

In Memory of Sean Armstrong

A lone figure is waving
From the thin line of a bridge

---

1. The navel, or central point (Greek).

Of ropes and slats, slung
Dangerously out between
5   The cliff-top and the pillar rock.
A nineteenth-century wind.
Dulse[1]-pickers. Sea campions.[2]

A postcard for you, Sean,
And that's you, swinging alone,
10   Antic, half-afraid,
In your gallowglass's[3] beard
And swallow-tail of serge[4]:
The Carrick-a-Rede Rope Bridge
Ghost-written on sepia.[5]

15   Or should it be your houseboat
Ethnically furnished,
Redolent of grass?
Should we discover you
Beside those warm-planked, democratic wharves
20   Among the twilights and guitars
Of Sausalito?[6]

Drop-out on a come-back,
Prince of no-man's land
With your head in clouds or sand,
25   You were the clown
Social worker of the town
Until your candid forehead stopped
A pointblank teatime bullet.

Get up from your blood on the floor.
30   Here's another boat
In grass by the lough[7] shore,
Turf smoke, a wired hen-run—
Your local, hoped for, unfound commune.
Now recite me *William Bloat*,
35   Sing of *the Calabar*

Or of Henry Joy McCracken
Who kissed his Mary Ann
On the gallows at Cornmarket.
Or Ballycastle Fair.
40   "Give us the raw bar!"
"Sing it by brute force
If you forget the air."

Yet something in your voice
Stayed nearly shut.

1. An edible red seaweed.
2. A flowering plant with red, pink, and white blossoms.
3. Foreign soldier.
4. A fabric used for suits.

5. A brown pigment used in old photographs.
6. A resort city on San Francisco Bay.
7. Lake.

45   Your voice was a harassed pulpit
       Leading the melody
       It kept at bay,
       It was independent, rattling, non-transcendent
       Ulster—old decency

50   And Old Bushmills,[8]
       Soda farls,[9] strong tea,
       New rope, rock salt, kale plants,
       Potato-bread and Woodbine[1].
       Wind through the concrete vents
55   Of a border check-point.
       Cold zinc nailed for a peace line.

       Fifteen years ago, come this October,
       Crowded on your floor,
       I got my arm round Marie's shoulder
60   For the first time.
       "Oh, Sir Jasper,[2] do not touch me!"
       You roared across at me,
       Chorus-leading, splashing out the wine.

The Singer's House

    When they said *Carrickfergus*[1] I could hear
    the frosty echo of saltminers' picks.
    I imagined it, chambered and glinting,
    a township built of light.

5   What do we say any more
    to conjure the salt of our earth?
    So much comes and is gone
    that should be crystal and kept,

    and amicable weathers
10   that bring up the grain of things,
    their tang of season and store,
    are all the packing we'll get.

    So I say to myself *Gweebarra*[2]
    and its music hits off the place
15   like water hitting off granite.
    I see the glittering sound

    framed in your window,
    knives and forks set on oilcloth[3],

---

8. Manufacturer of Irish whiskey.
9. Cakes.
1. Brand of cigarette.
2. Title of a traditional (and bawdy) rugby song.

1. Seaport just north of Belfast on the northeast coast of Ireland.
2. Bay in County Donegal, in the northwest of Ireland.
3. Stiff, waterproof cloth often used as tablecloth.

and the seals' heads, suddenly outlined,
20 scanning everything.

People here used to believe
that drowned souls lived in the seals.
At spring tides they might change shape.
They loved music and swam in for a singer

25 who might stand at the end of summer
in the mouth of a whitewashed turf-shed,
his shoulder to the jamb, his song
a rowboat far out in evening.

When I came here first you were always singing,
30 a hint of the clip of the pick
in your winnowing climb and attack.
Raise it again, man. We still believe what we hear.

The Skunk

Up, black, striped and damasked like the chasuble[1]
At a funeral Mass, the skunk's tail
Paraded the skunk. Night after night
I expected her like a visitor.

5 The refrigerator whinnied into silence.
My desk light softened beyond the verandah.
Small oranges loomed in the orange tree.
I began to be tense as a voyeur.

After eleven years I was composing
10 Love-letters again, broaching the word "wife"
Like a stored cask, as if its slender vowel
Had mutated into the night earth and air

Of California. The beautiful, useless
Tang of eucalyptus spelt your absence.
15 The aftermath of a mouthful of wine
Was like inhaling you off a cold pillow.

And there she was, the intent and glamorous,
Ordinary, mysterious skunk,
Mythologized, demythologized.
20 Snuffing the boards five feet beyond me.

It all came back to me last night, stirred
By the sootfall of your things at bedtime,
Your head-down, tail-up hunt in a bottom drawer
For the black plunge-line nightdress.

1. A sleeveless vest worn by priests.

25   Hear it calling out to every creature.
      And they drink these waters, although it is dark here
              because it is the night.

      I am repining for this living fountain.
      Within this bread of life I see it plain
30   although it is the night.

Punishment[1]

      I can feel the tug
      of the halter at the nape
      of her neck, the wind
      on her naked front.

5   It blows her nipples
      to amber beads,
      it shakes the frail rigging
      of her ribs.

      I can see her drowned
10   body in the bog,
      the weighing stone,
      the floating rods and boughs.

      Under which at first
      she was a barked sapling
15   that is dug up
      oak-bone, brain-firkin[2]:

      her shaved head
      like a stubble of black corn,
      her blindfold a soiled bandage,
20   her noose a ring

      to store
      the memories of love.
      Little adulteress,
      before they punished you

25   you were flaxen-haired,
      undernourished, and your
      tar-black face was beautiful.
      My poor scapegoat,

      I almost love you
30   but would have cast, I know,
      the stones of silence.
      I am the artful voyeur

      of your brain's exposed
      and darkened combs,

---

1. A young girl's body, dating from the first century A.D., was recovered from a German bog in 1951. The body exhibited various punishments bestowed upon adulterous women by ancient Germanic peoples.
2. A wooden container.

35   your muscles' webbing
      and all your numbered bones:

      I who have stood dumb
      when your betraying sisters,
      cauled³ in tar,
40   wept by the railings,⁴

      who would connive
      in civilized outrage
      yet understand the exact
      and tribal, intimate revenge.

from Station Island¹
12

      Like a convalescent, I took the hand
      stretched down from the jetty, sensed again
      an alien comfort as I stepped on ground

      to find the helping hand still gripping mine,
5   fish-cold and bony, but whether to guide
      or to be guided I could not be certain

      for the tall man in step at my side
      seemed blind, though he walked straight as a rush
      upon his ash plant, his eyes fixed straight ahead.²

10   Then I knew him in the flesh
      out there on the tarmac³ among the cars,
      wintered hard and sharp as a blackthorn bush.

      His voice eddying with the vowels of all rivers⁴
      came back to me, though he did not speak yet,
15   a voice like a prosecutor's or a singer's,

      cunning, narcotic, mimic, definite
      as a steel nib's⁵ downstroke, quick and clean,
      and suddenly he hit a litter basket

      with his stick, saying, 'Your obligation
20   is not discharged by any common rite.
      What you do you must do on your own.

      The main thing is to write
      for the joy of it. Cultivate a work-lust
      that imagines its haven like your hands at night

---

3. Capped.
4. In Belfast, women may still be shaven, stripped, tarred and handcuffed to railings by the Irish Republican Army for keeping company with British soldiers [Heaney's note].
1. *Station Island* is a sequence of dream encounters with familiar ghosts, set on Station Island on Lough Derg in County Donegal. The island is also known as St. Patrick's Purgatory because of a tradition that Patrick was the first to establish the penitential vigil of fasting and praying that still constitutes the basis of the three-day pilgrimage. Each unit of the contemporary pilgrim's exercises is called a "station" and a large part of each station involves walking barefoot and praying round the "beds," stone circles which are said to be the remains of early medieval monastic cells [Heaney's note].
2. The speaker alludes to James Joyce, who was nearly blinded by glaucoma and who affected an ashplant walking-stick.
3. Blacktop; pavement.
4. The "Anna Livia Plurabelle" section of Joyce's last novel *Finnegans Wake* is thick with the names of rivers.
5. Penpoint.

25   dreaming the sun in the sunspot of a breast.
      You are fasted now, light-headed, dangerous.
      Take off from here. And don't be so earnest,

      so ready for the sackcloth and the ashes.[6]
      Let go, let fly, forget.
30   You've listened long enough. Now strike your note.'

      It was as if I had stepped free into space
      alone with nothing that I had not known
      already. Raindrops blew in my face

      as I came to and heard the harangue and jeers
35   going on and on: 'The English language
      belongs to us. You are raking at dead fires,

      rehearsing the old whinges[7] at your age.
      That subject people stuff is a cod's[8] game,
      infantile, like this peasant pilgrimage.

40   You lose more of yourself than you redeem
      doing the decent thing. Keep at a tangent.
      When they make the circle wide, it's time to swim

      out on your own and fill the element
      with signatures on your own frequency,
45   echo-soundings, searches, probes, allurements,

      elver-gleams[9] in the dark of the whole sea.'
      The shower broke in a cloudburst, the tarmac
      fumed and sizzled. As he moved off quickly

      the downpour loosed its screens round his straight walk.

Postscript

      And some time make the time to drive out west
      Into County Clare,[1] along the Flaggy Shore,
      In September or October, when the wind
      And the light are working off each other
5   So that the ocean on one side is wild
      With foam and glitter, and inland among stones
      The surface of a slate-grey lake is lit
      By the earthed lightning of a flock of swans,
      Their feathers roughed and ruffling, white on white,
10   Their fully grown headstrong-looking heads
      Tucked or cresting or busy underwater.
      Useless to think you'll park and capture it
      More thoroughly. You are neither here nor there,
      A hurry through which known and strange things pass
15   As big soft buffetings come at the car sideways
      And catch the heart off guard and blow it open.

6. The dress of repentance and grief.
7. Complaints.
8. Fool's.

9. Young eels, especially those migrating up a stream from the ocean.
1. County in west Ireland.

➵➵➵➵➵

Nuala Ní Dhomhnaill
b. 1952

Ní Dhomhnaill was born in a coal mining region in England, to Irish parents; she was sent at the age of five, however, to live with relatives in the Gaeltacht (Irish-speaking area) on the Dingle Peninsula in West Kerry—"dropped into it cold-turkey," she says. She thus grew up bilingual, speaking English in the home, Irish out of it. Ní Dhomhnaill quickly learned that translation always picks up and leaves behind meaning; she tells this story: "I recall as a child someone asking my name in Irish. The question roughly translates as 'Who do you belong to?' Still most fluent in English, I replied, 'I don't belong to anybody. I belong to myself.' That became quite a joke in the village." In some ways, Ní Dhomhnaill's poetic career has been the process of discovering who, and whose, she is—and making those discoveries through the medium of the Irish language; her name itself, pronounced *nu-AH-la ne GOE-ne,* sounds different than it looks to English eyes.

"The individual psyche is a rather puny thing," she has said; "One's interior life dries up without the exchange with tradition." Ní Dhomhnaill's fruitful exchange with the Irish literary tradition has resulted in a poetry rich in the imagery of Irish folklore and mythology, and pregnant with the sense of contradiction and irony that undergirds Irish writing ("We [Celts] are truly comfortable only with ambiguity," she says). Ní Dhomhnaill's poetry in Irish includes the prize-winning volumes *An Dealg Droighin* (1981) and *Féar Suaithinseach* (1984), as well as a selection of poems from her volume *Feis* translated into English by the poet Paul Muldoon. The *Irish Literary Supplement* has called her "the most widely known and acclaimed Gaelic poet of the century"; by continuing to write in Irish, she has helped make it a viable language for modern poetry. Ní Dhomhnaill lives in Dublin and teaches at University College, Cork.

Parthenogenesis[1]

Once, a lady of the Ó Moores
(married seven years without a child)
swam in the sea in summertime.
She swam well, and the day
5   was fine as Ireland ever saw
not even a puff of wind in the air
all the bay calm, all the sea smooth—
a sheet of glass—supple, she struck out
with strength for the breaking waves
10   and frisked, elated by the world.
She ducked beneath the surface and there saw
what seemed a shadow, like a man's.
And every twist and turn she made
the shadow did the same
15   and came close enough to touch.
Heart jumped and sound stopped in her mouth
her pulses ran and raced, sides near burst.
The lower currents with their ice

---

1. Translated by Michael Hartnett. "Parthenogenesis" is the scientific term for virgin birth.

pierced her to the bone
20   and the noise of the abyss numbed all her limbs
then scales grew on her skin . . .
the lure of the quiet dreamy undersea . . .
desire to escape to sea and shells . . .
the seaweed tresses where at last
25   her bones changed into coral
and time made atolls of her arms,
pearls of her eyes in deep long sleep,
at rest in a nest of weed,
secure as feather beds . . .
30   But stop!
Her heroic heritage was there,
she rose with speedy, threshing feet
and made in desperation for the beach:
with nimble supple strokes she made the sand.
35   Near death until the day,
some nine months later
she gave birth to a boy.
She and her husband so satisfied,
so full of love for this new son
40   forgot the shadow in the sea
and did not see what only the midwife saw—
stalks of sea-tangle in the boy's hair
small shellfish and sea-ribbons
and his two big eyes
45   as blue and limpid as lagoons.
A poor scholar passing by
who found lodging for the night
saw the boy's eyes never closed
in dark or light and when all the world slept
50   he asked the boy beside the fire
"Who are your people?" Came the prompt reply
"Sea People."

This same tale is told in the West
but the woman's an Ó Flaherty
55   and tis the same in the South
where the lady's called Ó Shea:
this tale is told on every coast.
But whoever she was I want to say
that the fear she felt
60   when the sea-shadow followed her
is the same fear that vexed
the young heart of the Virgin
when she heard the angels' sweet bell
and in her womb was made flesh
65   by all accounts
the Son of the Living God.

1986

Labasheedy (The Silken Bed)[1]

I'd make a bed for you
in Labasheedy
in the tall grass
under the wrestling trees
5   where your skin
would be silk upon silk
in the darkness
when the moths are coming down.

Skin which glistens
10   shining over your limbs
like milk being poured
from jugs at dinnertime;
your hair is a herd of goats
moving over rolling hills,
15   hills that have high cliffs
and two ravines.

And your damp lips
would be as sweet as sugar
at evening and we walking
20   by the riverside
with honeyed breezes
blowing over the Shannon
and the fuchsias bowing down to you
one by one.

25   The fuchsias bending low
their solemn heads
in obeisance to the beauty
in front of them
I would pick a pair of flowers
30   as pendant earrings
to adorn you
like a bride in shining clothes.

O I'd make a bed for you
in Labasheedy,
35   in the twilight hour
with evening falling slow
and what a pleasure it would be
to have our limbs entwine
wrestling
40   while the moths are coming down.

1986

---

1. Translated by the author.

Why I Choose to Write in Irish,
The Corpse That Sits Up and Talks Back[1]

Not so long ago I telephoned my mother about some family matter. "So what are you writing these days?" she asked, more for the sake of conversation than anything else. "Oh, an essay for *The New York Times*," I said, as casually as possible. "What is it about?" she asked. "About what it is like to write in Irish," I replied. There was a good few seconds' pause on the other end of the line; then, "Well, I hope you'll tell them that it is mad." End of conversation. I had got my comeuppance. And from my mother, who was the native speaker of Irish in our family, never having encountered a single word of English until she went to school at the age of 6, and well up in her teens before she realized that the name they had at home for a most useful item was actually two words—"safety pin"—and that they were English. Typical.

But really not so strange. Some time later I was at a reception at the American Embassy in Dublin for two of their writers, Toni Morrison and Richard Wilbur. We stood in line and took our buffet suppers along to the nearest available table. An Irishwoman across from me asked what I did. Before I had time to open my mouth her partner butted in: "Oh, Nuala writes poetry in Irish." And what did I write about? she asked. Again before I had time to reply he did so for me: "She writes poems of love and loss, and I could quote you most of them by heart." This was beginning to get up my nose, and so I attempted simultaneously to deflate him and to go him one better. "Actually," I announced, "I think the only things worth writing about are the biggies: birth, death and the most important thing in between, which is sex." "Oh," his friend said to me archly, "and is there a word for sex in Irish?"

I looked over at the next table, where Toni Morrison was sitting, and I wondered if a black writer in America had to put up with the likes of that, or its equivalent. Here I was in my own country, having to defend the official language of the state from a compatriot who obviously thought it was an accomplishment to be ignorant of it. Typical, and yet maybe not so strange.

Let me explain. Irish (as it is called in the Irish Constitution; to call it Gaelic is not P.C. at the moment, but seen as marginalizing) is the Celtic language spoken by a small minority of native speakers principally found in rural pockets on the western seaboard. These Irish-speaking communities are known as the "Gaeltacht," and are the last remnants of an earlier historical time when the whole island was Irish-speaking, or one huge "Gaeltacht." The number of Irish speakers left in these areas who use the language in most of their daily affairs is a hotly debated point, and varies from 100,000 at the most optimistic estimate to 20,000 at the most conservative. For the sake of a round number let us take it to be 60,000, or about 2 percent of the population of the Republic of Ireland.

Because of the effort of the Irish Revival movement, and of the teaching of Irish in the school system, however, the language is also spoken with varying degrees of frequency and fluency by a considerably larger number of people who have learned it as a second language. So much so that census figures over the last few decades have consistently indicated that up to one million people, or 30 percent of the population of the Republic, claim to be speakers of Irish. To this can be added the 146,000 people in the Six Counties of Northern Ireland who also are competent in

---

1. Published in the *New York Times Book Review*, January 1995.

Irish. This figure of one million speakers is, of course, grossly misleading and in no way reflects a widespread use of the language in everyday life. Rather it can be seen as a reflection of general good will toward the language, as a kind of wishful thinking. Nevertheless that good will is important.

The fact that the Irish language, and by extension its literature, has a precarious status in Ireland at the moment is a development in marked contrast to its long and august history. I believe writing in Irish is the oldest continuous literary activity in Western Europe, starting in the fifth century and flourishing in a rich and varied manuscript tradition right down through the Middle Ages. During this time the speakers of any invading language, such as Norse, Anglo-Norman and English, were assimilated, becoming "more Irish than the Irish themselves." But the Battle of Kinsale in 1601, in which the British routed the last independent Irish princes, and the ensuing catastrophes of the turbulent 17th century, including forced population transfers, destroyed the social underpinning of the language. Its decline was much accelerated by the great famine of the mid-19th century; most of the one million who died of starvation and the millions who left on coffin ships for America were Irish speakers. The fact that the fate of emigration stared most of the survivors in the eye further speeded up the language change to English—after all, "What use was your Irish to you over in Boston?"

The indigenous high culture became the stuff of the speech of fishermen and small farmers, and this is the language that I learned in West Kerry in the 1950's at the age of 5 in a situation of total immersion, when I was literally and figuratively farmed out to my aunt in the parish of Ventry. Irish is a language of enormous elasticity and emotional sensitivity; of quick and hilarious banter and a welter of references both historical and mythological; it is an instrument of imaginative depth and scope, which has been tempered by the community for generations until it can pick up and sing out every hint of emotional modulation that can occur between people. Many international scholars rhapsodize that this speech of ragged peasants seems always on the point of bursting into poetry. The pedagogical accident that had me learn this language at an early age can only be called a creative one.

The Irish of the Revival, or "book Irish," was something entirely different, and I learned it at school. Although my first literary love affair was with the Munster poets, Aodhagán Ó Rathaille and Eoghan Rua Ó Suilleabháin, and I had learned reams and reams of poetry that wasn't taught at school, when I myself came to write it didn't dawn on me that I could possibly write in Irish. The overriding ethos had got even to me. Writing poetry in Irish somehow didn't seem to be intellectually credible. So my first attempts, elegies on the deaths of Bobby Kennedy and Martin Luther King published in the school magazine, were all in English. They were all right, but even I could see that there was something wrong with them.

Writing Irish poetry in English suddenly seemed a very stupid thing to be doing. So I switched language in mid-poem and wrote the very same poem in Irish, and I could see immediately that it was much better. I sent it in to a competition in *The Irish Times*, where it won a prize, and that was that. I never looked back.

I had chosen my language, or more rightly, perhaps, at some very deep level, the language had chosen me. If there is a level to our being that for want of any other word for it I might call "soul" (and I believe there is), then for some reason that I can never understand, the language that my soul speaks, and the place it comes from, is Irish. At 16 I had made my choice. And that was that. It still is. I have no other.

But if the actual choice to write poetry in Irish was easy, then nothing else about it actually is, especially the hypocritical attitude of the state. On the one hand, Irish is enshrined as a nationalistic token (the ceremonial *cúpla focal*—"few words"—at the beginning and end of speeches by politicians, broadcasters and even airline crews is an example). On the other hand, it would not be an exaggeration to speak of the state's indifference, even downright hostility, to Irish speakers in its failure to provide even the most basic services in Irish for those who wish to go about their everyday business in that language.

"The computer cannot understand Irish" leads the excuses given by the state to refuse to conduct its business in Irish, even in the Gaeltacht areas. Every single service gained by Irish speakers has been fought for bitterly. Thus the "Gaelscoileanna," or Irish schools, have been mostly started by groups of parents, often in the very teeth of fierce opposition from the Department of Education. And the only reason we have a single Irish radio station is that a civil rights group started a pirate station 20 years ago in the West and shamed the Government into establishing this vital service. An Irish television channel is being mooted[2] at present, but I'll believe it when I see it.

You might expect at least the cultural nationalists and our peers writing in English to be on our side. Not so. A recent television documentary film about Thomas Kinsella begins with the writer intoning the fact that history has been recorded in Irish from the fifth century to the 19th. Then there is a pregnant pause. We wait for a mention of the fact that life, experience, sentient consciousness, even history is being recorded in literature in Irish in the present day. We wait in vain. By an antiquarian sleight of hand it is implied that Irish writers in English are now the natural heirs to a millennium and a half of writing in Irish. The subtext of the film is that Irish is dead.

So what does that make me, and the many other writers of the large body of modern literature in Irish? A walking ghost? A linguistic specter?

Mind you, it is invidious of me to single out Thomas Kinsella; this kind of insidious "bad faith" about modern literature in Irish is alive and rampant among many of our fellow writers in English. As my fellow poet in Irish, Biddy Jenkinson, has said, "We have been pushed into an ironic awareness that by our passage we would convenience those who will be uneasy in their Irishness as long as there is a living Gaelic tradition to which they do not belong." Now let them make their peace with the tradition if they wish to, I don't begrudge them a line of it. But I'll be damned if their cultural identity is procured at the expense of my existence, or of that of my language.

I can well see how it suits some people to see Irish-language literature as the last rictus[3] of a dying beast. As far as they are concerned, the sooner the language lies down and dies, the better, so they can cannibalize it with greater equanimity, peddling their "ethnic chic" with nice little translations "from the Irish." Far be it from them to make the real effort it takes to learn the living language. I dare say they must be taken somewhat aback when the corpse that they have long since consigned to choirs of angels, like a certain Tim Finnegan,[4] sits up and talks back to them.

---

2. Debated.
3. Gasp.
4. In the vaudeville song *Tim Finnegan's Wake*, the hero takes a drunken fall and dies. At his wake, however, whiskey is spilled over his body and he comes back to life. James Joyce uses this story as the central structure for *Finnegans Wake*.

The fault is not always one-sided. The Gaels (Irish-language writers) often fell prey to what Terence Browne, a literary historian, has called an "atmosphere of national self-righteousness and cultural exclusiveness," and their talent did not always equal the role imposed on them. Nevertheless, long after the emergence of a high standard of literature in Irish with Seán Ó Riordáin, Máirtín Ó Direáin and Máire Mhac an tSaoi in poetry, and Máirtín Ó Cadhain in prose, writing in Irish was conspicuously absent from anthologies in the 1950's and 60's. Even as late as the 70's one of our "greats," Seán Ó Riordáin, could hear on the radio two of his co-writers in English saying how "poetry in Ireland had been quiescent in the 50's," thus consigning to nothingness the great work that he and his fellow poets in Irish had produced during that very decade. After a lifetime devoted to poetry, is it any wonder that he died in considerable grief and bitterness?

As for the cultural nationalists, Irish was never the language of nationalist mobilization. Unlike other small countries where nationalism rose throughout the 19th century, in Ireland it was religion rather than language that mostly colored nationalism. Daniel O'Connell, the Liberator, a native-Irish-speaking Kerryman, used to address his monster mass meetings from the 1820's to the 40's in English, even though this language was not understood by 70 percent of the people he was addressing. Why? Because it was at the reporters over from *The Times* of London and their readers that his words were being primarily directed. It is particularly painful to recall that while nationalism was a major motivator in developing modern literary languages out of such varied tongues as Norwegian, Hungarian, Finnish and Estonian, during that very same period the high literary culture of Irish was being reduced to the language of peasants. By the time the revival began, the damage had already been done, and the language was already in irreversible decline (spoken by only 14.5 percent in 1880). The blatant myopia of the cultural nationalists is still alive and glaringly obvious in the disgraceful underrepresentation of Irish in the recently published three-volume *Field Day Anthology of Irish Writing*.

It should not be surprising, then, that we poets and fiction writers in Irish who are included in the anthology feel as if we are being reduced to being exotic background, like Irish Muzak. Thus the cultural nationalists, without granting Irish the intellectual credibility of rational discourse or the popular base of the oral tradition, enshrine it instead as the repository of their own utopian fantasies; pristine, changeless, "creative," but otherwise practically useless.

How does all this affect me, as a poet writing in Irish? Well, inasmuch as I am human and frail and prone to vanity and clamoring for attention, of course it disturbs me to be misunderstood, misrepresented and finally all but invisible in my own country. I get depressed, I grumble and complain, I stand around in rooms muttering darkly. Still and all, at some very deep and fundamental level it matters not one whit. All I ever wanted was to be left alone so that I could go on writing poetry in Irish. I still remember a time when I had an audience I could count on the fingers of one hand. I was perfectly prepared for that. I still am.

But it has been gratifying to reach a broader audience through the medium of translations, especially among the one million who profess some knowledge of Irish. Many of them probably had good Irish when they left school but have had no chance of using it since for want of any functional context where it would make sense to use the language. I particularly like it when my poetry in English translation sends them back to the originals in Irish, and when they then go on to pick up the long-lost threads of the language that is so rightly theirs. I also find it pleasant and vivifying to make an occasional trip abroad and to reach a wider audience by means of dual-language readings and publications.

But my primary audience is those who read my work in Irish only. A print run for a book of poems in Irish is between 1,000 and 1,500 copies. That doesn't sound like much until you realize that that number is considered a decent run by many poets in English in Ireland, or for that matter even in Britain or America, where there's a much larger population.

The very ancientness of the Irish literary tradition is also a great source of strength to me as a writer. This works at two levels, one that is mainly linguistic and prosodic and another that is mainly thematic and inspirational. At the linguistic level, Old Irish, though undoubtedly very difficult, is much closer to Modern Irish than, say, Anglo-Saxon is to Modern English. Anyone like me with a basic primary degree in the language and a bit of practice can make a fair job of reading most of the medieval texts in the original.

Thematically too, the older literature is a godsend, though I am only now slowly beginning to assess its unique possibilities to a modern writer. There are known to be well over 4,000 manuscripts in Ireland and elsewhere of material from Old to Modern Irish. Apart from the great medieval codices, only about 50 other manuscripts date from before 1650. Nevertheless, the vast majority of the manuscripts painstakingly copied down after this time are exemplars of much earlier manuscripts that have since been lost. A lot of this is catalogued in ways that are unsatisfactory for our time.

Many items of enormous psychological and sexual interest, for example, are described with the bias of the last century as "indecent and obscene tales, unsuitable for publication." On many such manuscripts human eye has not set sight since they were so described. In addition, most scholarly attention has been paid to pre-Norman-Conquest material as the repository of the unsullied wellsprings of the native soul (those cultural nationalists again!), with the result that the vast area of post-Conquest material has been unfairly neglected. The main advantage of all this material to me is that it is proof of the survival until even a very late historical date of a distinct *Weltanschauung* [worldview] radically different from the Anglo mentality that has since eclipsed it.

Because of a particular set of circumstances, Irish fell out of history just when the modern mentality was about to take off. So major intellectual changes like the Reformation, the Renaissance, the Enlightenment, Romanticism and Victorian prudery have never occurred in it, as they did in the major European languages.

One consequence is that the attitude to the body enshrined in Irish remains extremely open and uncoy. It is almost impossible to be "rude" or "vulgar" in Irish. The body, with its orifices and excretions, is not treated in a prudish manner but is accepted as *an nádúir*, or "nature," and becomes a source of repartee and laughter rather than anything to be ashamed of. Thus little old ladies of quite impeccable and unimpeachable moral character tell risqué stories with gusto and panache. Is there a word for sex in Irish, indeed! Is there an Eskimo word for snow?

By now I must have spent whole years of my life burrowing in the department of folklore at University College, Dublin, and yet there are still days when my hands shake with emotion holding manuscripts. Again, this material works on me on two levels. First is when I revel in the well-turned phrase or nuance or retrieve a word that may have fallen into disuse. To turn the pages of these manuscripts is to hear the voices of my neighbors and my relatives—all the fathers and grandfathers and uncles come to life again. The second interest is more thematic. This material is genuinely ineffable, like nothing else on earth.

Indeed, there is a drawer in the index entitled "Neacha neamhbeo agus nithe nach bhfuil ann" ("Unalive beings and things that don't exist"). Now I am not the greatest empiricist in the world but this one has even me stumped. Either they exist or they don't exist. But if they don't exist why does the card index about them stretch the length of my arm? Yet that is the whole point of this material and its most enduring charm. Do these beings exist? Well, they do and they don't. You see, they are beings from *an saol eile*, the "otherworld," which in Irish is a concept of such impeccable intellectual rigor and credibility that it is virtually impossible to translate into English, where it all too quickly becomes fey and twee and "fairies-at-the-bottom-of-the-garden."

The way so-called depth psychologists go on about the subconscious nowadays you'd swear they had invented it, or at the very least stumbled on a ghostly and ghastly continent where mankind had never previously set foot. Even the dogs in the street in West Kerry know that the "otherworld" exists, and that to be in and out of it constantly is the most natural thing in the world.

This constant tension between reality and fantasy, according to Jeffrey Gantz, the translator of *Early Irish Myths and Sagas*, is characteristic of all Celtic art, but manifests itself particularly in the literature of Ireland. Mr Gantz believes that it is not accidental to the circumstances of the literary transmission but is rather an innate characteristic, a gift of the Celts. It means that the "otherworld" is not simply an anticipated joyful afterlife; it is also—even primarily—an alternative to reality.

This easy interaction with the imaginary means that you don't have to have a raving psychotic breakdown to enter the "otherworld." The deep sense in the language that something exists beyond the ego-envelope is pleasant and reassuring, but it is also a great source of linguistic and imaginative playfulness, even on the most ordinary and banal of occasions.

Let's say I decide some evening to walk up to my aunt's house in West Kerry. She hears me coming. She knows it is me because she recognizes my step on the cement pavement. Still, as I knock lightly on the door she calls out, "An de bheoaibh nó de mhairbh thu?" ("Are you of the living or of the dead?") Because the possibility exists that you could be either, and depending on which category you belong to, an entirely different protocol would be brought into play. This is all a joke, of course, but a joke that is made possible by the imaginative richness of the language itself.

I am not constructing an essentialist argument here, though I do think that because of different circumstances, mostly historical, the strengths and weaknesses of Irish are different from those of English, and the imaginative possibilities of Irish are, from a poet's perspective, one of its greatest strengths. But this is surely as true of, say, Bengali as it is of Irish. It is what struck me most in the Nobel Prize acceptance speech made by the Yiddish writer Isaac Bashevis Singer. When often asked why he wrote in a dead language, Singer said he was wont to reply that he wrote mostly about ghosts, and that is what ghosts speak, a dead language.

Singer's reply touched a deep chord with his Irish audience. It reminded us that the precariousness of Irish is not an Irish problem alone. According to the linguist Michael Krause in *Language* magazine, minority languages in the English language sphere face a 90 percent extinction rate between now and some time in the next century. Therefore, in these days when a major problem is the growth of an originally Anglo-American, but now genuinely global, pop monoculture that reduces everything to the level of the most stupendous boredom, I would think that the preservation of minority languages like Irish, with their unique and unrepeatable way of looking at the world, would be as important for human beings as the preservation of the remaining tropical rain forests is for biological diversity.

Recently, on a short trip to Kerry with my three daughters, I stayed with my brother and his wife in the old house he is renovating on the eastern end of the Dingle peninsula, under the beetling brow of Cathair Chonroi promontory fort. My brother said he had something special to show us, so one day we trooped up the mountain to Derrymore Glen. Although the area is now totally denuded of any form of growth other than lichens and sphagnum moss, the name itself is a dead giveaway: Derrymore from *Doire Mór* in Irish, meaning "Large Oak Grove."

A more desolate spot you cannot imagine, yet halfway up the glen, in the crook of a hanging valley, intricate and gnarled, looking for all the world like a giant bonsai, was a single survivor, one solitary oak tree. Only the top branches were producing leaves, it was definitely on its last legs and must have been at least 200 to 300 years old. How it had survived the massive human and animal depredation of the countryside that occurred during that time I do not know, but somehow it had.

It was very much a *bile*, a sacred tree, dear to the Celts. A fairy tree. A magic tree. We were all very moved by it. Not a single word escaped us, as we stood in the drizzle. At last Ayse, my 10-year-old, broke the silence. "It would just give you an idea," she said, "of what this place was like when it really was a '*Doire Mór*' and covered with oak trees." I found myself humming the air of *Cill Cais*, that lament for both the great woods of Ireland and the largess of the Gaelic order that they had come to symbolize:

> Cad a dhéanfaimid feasta gan adhmad?
> Tá deireadh na gcoillte ar lár.
> Níl trácht ar Chill Cais ná a theaghlach
> is ní chlingfear a chling go brách.

> What will we do now without wood
> Now that the woods are laid low?
> Cill Cais or its household are not mentioned
> and the sound of its bell is no more.

A week later, back in Dublin, that question is still ringing in the air. I am waiting for the children to get out of school and writing my journal in Irish in a modern shopping mall in a Dublin suburb. Not a single word of Irish in sight on sign or advertisement, nor a single sound of it in earshot. All around me are well-dressed and articulate women. I am intrigued by snatches of animated conversation, yet I am conscious of a sense of overwhelming loss. I think back to the lonely hillside, and to Ayse. This is the answer to the question in the song. This is what we will do without wood.

At some level, it doesn't seem too bad. People are warm and not hungry. They are expressing themselves without difficulty in English. They seem happy. I close my notebook with a snap and set off in the grip of that sudden pang of despair that is always lurking in the ever-widening rents of the linguistic fabric of minority languages. Perhaps my mother is right. Writing in Irish is mad. English is a wonderful language, and it also has the added advantage of being very useful for putting bread on the table. Change is inevitable, and maybe it is part of the natural order of things that some languages should die while others prevail.

And yet, and yet . . . I know this will sound ridiculously romantic and sentimental. Yet not by bread alone. . . . We raise our eyes to the hills. . . . We throw our bread upon the waters.[5] There are mythical precedents. Take for instance Moses' mother, consider her predicament. She had the choice of giving up her son to the Egyptian soldiery, to have him cleft in two before her very eyes, or to send him down the Nile in a basket, a tasty dinner for crocodiles. She took what under the circumstances must have seemed very much like *rogha an dá dhiogha* ("the lesser of two evils") and Exodus and the annals of Jewish history tell the rest of the story, and are the direct results of an action that even as I write is still working out its inexorable destiny. I know it is wrong to compare small things with great, yet my final answer to why I write in Irish is this:

Ceist 'na Teangan

> Curirim mo dhóchas ar snámh
> i mbáidn´ teangan
> faoi mar a leagfá naíonán
> i gcliabhán
> a bheadh fite fuaite
> de dhuilleoga feileastraim
> is bitiúman agus pic
> bheith cuimilte lena thóin
>
> ansan é a leagadh síos
> i measc na ngiolcach
> is coigeal na mban sí
> le taobh na habhann,
> féachaint n'fheadaráis
> cá dtabharfaidh an sruth é,
> féachaint, dála Mhaoise,
> an bhfóirfidh iníon Fharoinn?

The Language Issue

> I place my hope on the water
> in this little boat
> of the language, the way a body might put
> an infant
>
> in a basket of intertwined
> iris leaves,
> its underside proofed
> with bitumen and pitch,
>
> then set the whole thing down amidst
> the sedge
> and bulrushes by the edge
> of a river

5. Echoing three biblical affirmations of the need to look beyond immediate material wants (Matthew 4.4, Psalm 121.1, Ecclesiastes 11.1). In the first passage cited, Jesus is fasting in the wilderness and rejects Satan's tempting suggestion that he turn stones into bread: "he answered, 'It is written, "Man shall not live by bread alone, but by every word that proceeds from the mouth of God." '"

only to have it borne hither and thither,
not knowing where it might end up;
in the lap, perhaps,
of some Pharaoh's daughter.[6]

— ✠ —

Ngugi wa Thiong'o
b. 1938–

The great novelist and postcolonial theorist Ngugi wa Thiong'o is a crucial figure to bring into the debate about the ownership of English. Like Nuala Ní Dhomhnaill, the Irish poet who has decided to write in Irish and have her work translated by others into English, even though English is her first language, Ngugi has political reasons for questioning the use of English by African writers who, as he once did, write the literature of modern Africa in European languages. Ngugi achieved prominence in Africa and in Britain and America for his English-language novels of the African struggle for self-determination, especially the revolution in Kenya that led to its independence from Great Britain. After two years of imprisonment by the Kenyan government in 1977 for what it considered a subversive play, Ngugi made the decision to stop writing in English and has since done his creative work in Gĩkũyũ, offering English translations, while continuing to write critical works and political essays in English for worldwide audiences. Despite his love of English and the global impact of his novels, Ngugi wa Thiong'o believes English can never be one of Africa's true languages of liberation and cultural creation.

A Kenyan of the Gĩkũyũ tribe, Ngugi was born James Ngugi, one of twenty-eight children of a peasant farmer who squatted on the land of an African landlord. Kenya was under British colonial rule then, and James's early education was at missionary-run primary schools. Political agitation for independence reached a peak in the 1950s, and when a "State of Emergency" was declared in Kenya in 1952 by the British, English became the official language of instruction. Ngugi won a place at the prestigious Alliance High School and received a thorough training in English literature. The struggle for independence powerfully affected him and his community; upon arriving home on a school vacation, for example, Ngugi found his home destroyed by the colonial soldiers, whose policy of "protecting" villages from insurgency was actually designed to cut off the supply of food the villagers gave to the freedom fighters. This trauma is registered at the heart of Ngugi's writing; his novels almost all contain the motif of a thwarted attempt to return home.

Ngugi graduated from Makerere University College in Kampala with an honors degree in English; in the heady postcolonial atmosphere he read not only English classics but was also exposed to the new literature of Africa and the Caribbean by writers like Chinua Achebe and George Lamming. By 1966 James Ngugi had gone to England to study for an M.A. in English at Leeds University, although his main subject was to be Caribbean literature. Ngugi never finished his thesis, which was ironically a boon to world literature, because he was immersed in completing his important novel *A Grain of Wheat* (1966). Two novels had preceded it, the autobiographical *Weep Not, Child* (1964) and *The River Between* (1965). Throughout this time Ngugi continued to write plays; the last work he published as James Ngugi was a collection of short plays *This Time Tomorrow* (1970). While teaching as a visiting professor at several universities, Ngugi wa Thiong'o wrote one of his most impressive novels, *Petals of Blood* (1977).

---

6. As happened with Moses when the Israelites were enslaved in Egypt (Exodus 2). Fearing their growing numbers, Pharaoh had ordered all male Hebrew infants to be drowned in the Nile; Moses's mother instead set him adrift in a reed basket, which was found by the Pharaoh's daughter, who adopted him and raised him as an Egyptian. As an adult, Moses led the Israelites out of Egypt to the Promised Land.

As its title suggests, the novel also treats the bloody trauma of breaking away as a new nation, a nation inevitably haunted by its former colonial existence.

The two years Ngugi spent in prison crystallized his thoughts about decolonization, which he had come to see was not merely a political event but demanded an entire change in the minds of those who had been dominated. The price of becoming free and establishing a viable culture entailed giving up the language of the colonizer. The president of Kenya, Daniel Arap Moi, has permanently banned Ngugi from Kenya as a political threat. From the time of his sentence on, although living in exile and far from his Gĩkũyũ roots in Kenya, Ngugi's fiction, plays, and poetry have been written in Gĩkũyũ language. His first post-English novel, *Caitaani Muthara-ini* (*Devil on the Cross*, 1980), was written in jail on sheets of the coarse toilet paper provided him in his prison cell and smuggled out by a sympathetic guard. With the strokes of his worn pencil on that rough and precious paper, Ngugi proved his dedication to creating an African literature in its indigenous tongues and ceased to be what he now calls an Afro-European writer. Ngugi has not been back to Kenya since 1982, and his books are banned in his homeland. He has written several novels in the past decade, as well as screenplays for African cinema and many more plays; he founded and edited the first Gĩkũyũ language literary journal *Mutiri*. Ngugi taught all over the world as a visiting professor at such institutions as Beyreuth University, Auckland University, and Yale University, among others, until finding an academic home at New York University in 1992, where he is the Erich Maria Remarque Professor of Languages and Literatures.

Paradoxically, perhaps, Ngugi wrote his great theoretical analysis of the political and spiritual process of decolonization, *Decolonizing the Mind* (1980), in English, and it has circulated globally as a worldwide touchstone of liberation. An excerpt chosen from this lasting book represents Ngugi's uncompromising answer to the question "whose language?" English can never belong to Africans until the languages of Africa create a literary home where English is not the master, but only an invited guest.

from DECOLONIZING THE MIND
Native African Languages
3

I was born into a large peasant family: father, four wives and about twenty-eight children. I also belonged, as we all did in those days, to a wider extended family and to the community as a whole.

We spoke Gĩkũyũ as we worked in the fields. We spoke Gĩkũyũ in and outside the home. I can vividly recall those evenings of story-telling around the fireside. It was mostly the grown-ups telling the children but everybody was interested and involved. We children would re-tell the stories the following day to other children who worked in the fields picking the pyrethrum flowers, tea-leaves or coffee beans of our European and African landlords.

The stories, with mostly animals as the main characters, were all told in Gĩkũyũ. Hare, being small, weak but full of innovative wit and cunning, was our hero. We identified with him as he struggled against the brutes of prey like Lion, Leopard, Hyena. His victories were our victories and we learnt that the apparently weak can outwit the strong. We followed the animals in their struggle against hostile nature— drought, rain, sun, wind—a confrontation often forcing them to search for forms of co-operation. But we were also interested in their struggles amongst themselves, and particularly between the beasts and the victims of prey. These twin struggles, against nature and other animals, reflected real-life struggles in the human world.

Not that we neglected stories with human beings as the main characters. There were two types of characters in such human-centred narratives: the species of truly human beings with qualities of courage, kindness, mercy, hatred of evil, concern for others; and a man-eat-man two-mouthed species with qualities of greed, selfishness, individualism and hatred of what was good for the larger co-operative community. Co-operation as the ultimate good in a community was a constant theme. It could unite human beings with animals against ogres and beasts of prey, as in the story of how Dove, after being fed with castoroil seeds, was sent to fetch a smith working far away from home and whose pregnant wife was being threatened by these man-eating two-mouthed ogres.

There were good and bad story-tellers. A good one could tell the same story over and over again, and it would always be fresh to us, the listeners. He or she could tell a story told by someone else and make it more alive and dramatic. The differences really were in the use of words and images and the inflexion of voices to effect different tones.

We therefore learnt to value words for their meaning and nuances. Language was not a mere string of words. It had a suggestive power well beyond the immediate and lexical meaning. Our appreciation of the suggestive magical power of language was reinforced by the games we played with words through riddles, proverbs, transpositions of syllables, or through nonsensical but musically arranged words. So we learnt the music of our language on top of the content. The language, through images and symbols, gave us a view of the world, but it had a beauty of its own. The home and the field were then our pre-primary school but what is important, for this discussion, is that the language of our evening teach-ins, and the language of our immediate and wider community, and the language of our work in the fields were one.

And then I went to school, a colonial school, and this harmony was broken. The language of my education was no longer the language of my culture. I first went to Kamaandura, missionary run, and then to another called Maanguuũ run by nationalists grouped around the Gĩkũyũ Independent and Karinga Schools Association. Our language of education was still Gĩkũyũ. The very first time I was ever given an ovation for my writing was over a composition in Gĩkũyũ. So for my first four years there was still harmony between the language of my formal education and that of the Limuru peasant community.

It was after the declaration of a state of emergency over Kenya in 1952 that all the schools run by patriotic nationalists were taken over by the colonial regime and were placed under District Education Boards chaired by Englishmen. English became the language of my formal education. In Kenya, English became more than a language: it was *the* language, and all the others had to bow before it in deference.

Thus one of the most humiliating experiences was to be caught speaking Gĩkũyũ in the vicinity of the school. The culprit was given corporal punishment—three to five strokes of the cane on bare buttocks—or was made to carry a metal plate around the neck with inscriptions such as I AM STUPID or I AM A DONKEY. Sometimes the culprits were fined money they could hardly afford. And how did the teachers catch the culprits? A button was initially given to one pupil who was supposed to hand it over to whoever was caught speaking his mother tongue. Whoever had the button at the end of the day would sing who had given it to him and the ensuing process would bring out all the culprits of the day. Thus children were turned into witch-hunters and in the process were being taught the lucrative value of being a traitor to one's immediate community.

The attitude to English was the exact opposite: any achievement in spoken or written English was highly rewarded; prizes, prestige, applause; the ticket to higher realms. English became the measure of intelligence and ability in the arts, the sciences, and all the other branches of learning. English became *the* main determinant of a child's progress up the ladder of formal education.

As you may know, the colonial system of education in addition to its apartheid racial demarcation had the structure of a pyramid: a broad primary base, a narrowing secondary middle, and an even narrower university apex. Selections from primary into secondary were through an examination, in my time called Kenya African Preliminary Examination, in which one had to pass six subjects ranging from Maths to Nature Study and Kiswahili. All the papers were written in English. Nobody could pass the exam who failed the English language paper no matter how brilliantly he had done in the other subjects. I remember one boy in my class of 1954 who had distinctions in all subjects except English, which he had failed. He was made to fail the entire exam. He went on to become a turn boy in a bus company. I who had only passes but a credit in English got a place at the Alliance High School, one of the most elitist institutions for Africans in colonial Kenya. The requirements for a place at the University, Makerere University College, were broadly the same: nobody could go on to wear the undergraduate red gown, no matter how brilliantly they had performed in all the other subjects unless they had a credit—not even a simple pass!—in English. Thus the most coveted place in the pyramid and in the system was only available to the holder of an English language credit card. English was the official vehicle and the magic formula to colonial elitedom.

Literary education was now determined by the dominant language while also reinforcing that dominance. Orature (oral literature) in Kenyan languages stopped. In primary school I now read simplified Dickens and Stevenson alongside Rider Haggard. Jim Hawkins, Oliver Twist, Tom Brown—not Hare, Leopard and Lion—were now my daily companions in the world of imagination. In secondary school, Scott and G. B. Shaw vied with more Rider Haggard, John Buchan, Alan Paton, Captain W. E. Johns. At Makerere I read English: from Chaucer to T. S. Eliot with a touch of Graham Greene.

Thus language and literature were taking us further and further from ourselves to other selves, from our world to other worlds.

What was the colonial system doing to us Kenyan children? What were the consequences of, on the one hand, this systematic suppression of our languages and the literature they carried, and on the other the elevation of English and the literature it carried?

9

I started writing in Gĩkũyũ language in 1977 after seventeen years of involvement in Afro-European literature, in my case Afro-English literature. It was then that I collaborated with Ngũgĩ wa Mĩriĩ in the drafting of the playscript, *Ngaahika Ndeenda* (the English translation was *I Will Marry When I Want*). I have since published a novel in Gĩkũyũ, *Caitaani Mũtharabainĩ* (English translation: *Devil on the Cross*) and completed a musical drama, *Maitũ Njugĩra*, (English translation: *Mother Sing for Me*); three books for children, *Njamba Nene na Mbaathi i Mathagu*, *Bathitoora ya Njamba Nene*, *Njamba Nene na Cibũ Kĩng'ang'i*, as well as another novel manuscript: *Matigari Ma Njirũũngi*. Wherever I have gone, particularly in Europe, I have been confronted with the question: why are you now writing in Gĩkũyũ? Why do you now write in an African language? In some academic quarters I have been confronted with the rebuke, 'Why have you abandoned us?' It was almost as if, in choosing to write in Gĩkũyũ, I was doing something abnormal. But Gĩkũyũ is my mother tongue! The very fact that what common sense dictates in the literary practice of other cultures is being questioned in an African writer is a measure of how far imperialism has distorted the view of African realities. It has turned reality upside down: the abnormal is viewed as normal and the normal is viewed as abnormal. Africa actually enriches Europe: but Africa is made to believe that it needs Europe to rescue it from poverty. Africa's natural and human resources continue to develop Europe and America: but Africa is made to feel grateful for aid from the same quarters that still sit on the back of the continent. Africa even produces intellectuals who now rationalise this upside-down way of looking at Africa.

I believe that my writing in Gĩkũyũ language, a Kenyan language, an African language, is part and parcel of the anti-imperialist struggles of Kenyan and African peoples. In schools and universities our Kenyan languages—that is the languages of the many nationalities which make up Kenya—were associated with negative qualities of backwardness, underdevelopment, humiliation and punishment. We who went through that school system were meant to graduate with a hatred of the people and the culture and the values of the language of our daily humiliation and punishment. I do not want to see Kenyan children growing up in that imperialist-imposed tradition of contempt for the tools of communication developed by their communities and their history. I want them to transcend colonial alienation.

* * *

Chinua Achebe once decried the tendency of African intellectuals to escape into abstract universalism in the words that apply even more to the issue of the language of African literature:

> Africa has had such a fate in the world that the very adjective *African* can call up hideous fears of rejection. Better then to cut all the links with this homeland, this liability, and become in one giant leap the universal man. Indeed I understand this anxiety. *But running away from oneself seems to me a very inadequate way of dealing with an anxiety* [italics mine]. And if writers should opt for such escapism, who is to meet the challenge?

Who indeed?

We African writers are bound by our calling to do for our languages what Spenser, Milton and Shakespeare did for English; what Pushkin and Tolstoy did for Russian; indeed what all writers in world history have done for their languages by meeting the challenge of creating a literature in them, which process later opens the languages for philosophy, science, technology and all the other areas of human creative endeavours.

Nadine Gordimer
b. 1923

Nadine Gordimer was born in South Africa to Jewish emigrant parents from London. Thus her childhood, like those of the children of countless middle-class colonial families, was somewhat complex and contradictory. In an interview, Gordimer offers this explanation: "I think when you're born white in South Africa, you're peeling like an orange. You're sloughing off all the conditioning that you've had since you were a child." In Gordimer's case, that "sloughing off" of white, British prejudices and habits of mind has been thorough; the novelist Paul Theroux, for instance, suggests that "Gordimer's vision of Africa is the most complete one we have, and in time to come, when we want to know everything there is to know about a newly independent black African country, it is to this white South African woman . . . that we will turn."

Since Gordimer published her first collection of short stories in 1949 her writing has been praised for its evenhanded and scrupulously honest treatment of the political terrain of South Africa; over the years she has become, in the words of one critic, "the literary voice and conscience of her society." Among her gifts are an ear sensitive to the cadences and idiosyncrasies of spoken English, and a gift for social satire in service of a finally moral purpose. The longstanding subject of Gordimer's writing—her great theme—is, as critic Michiko Kakutani describes it, "the consequences of apartheid on the daily lives of men and women, the distortions it produces in relationships among both blacks and whites." In Gordimer's writing, these distortions are always shown rather than explained; her presentation is essentially dramatic, a trait she shares with modern masters of short fiction like Chekhov and Joyce.

Gordimer has been faulted for the emphasis in politics in her writing. Her response to this charge is eloquent: "The real influence of politics on my writing is the influence of politics on people. Their lives, and I believe their very personalities, are changed by the extreme political circumstances one lives under in South Africa. I am dealing with people; here are people who are shaped and changed by politics. In that way my material is profoundly influenced by politics." To date, Gordimer has published more than ten novels, including the celebrated *A Guest of Honour* (1970) and *The Conservationist* (1974; cowinner of the Booker McConnell Prize), and more than a dozen collections of short stories. *Jump and Other Stories*, which includes *What Were You Dreaming?*, was published in 1991, the same year Gordimer was awarded the Nobel Prize for Literature. In this story, the disjunction between black and white South African English is the starting-point for an exploration of blocked communication between races and genders alike.

What Were You Dreaming?

I'm standing here by the road long time, yesterday, day before, today. Not the same road but it's the same—hot, hot like today. When they turn off where they're going, I must get out again, wait again. Some of them they just pretend there's nobody there, they don't want to see nobody. Even go a bit faster, *ja*. Then they past, and I'm waiting. I combed my hair; I don't want to look like a *skollie* [ruffian]. Don't smile because they think you being too friendly, you think you good as them. They go and they go. Some's got the baby's napkin hanging over the back window to keep out this sun. Some's not going on holiday with their kids but is alone; all alone in a big car. But they'll never stop, the whites, if they alone. Never. Because these *skollies* and that kind've spoilt it all for us, sticking a gun in the driver's neck, stealing his money, beating him up and taking the car. Even killing him. So it's buggered up for us. No white wants some guy sitting behind his head. And the blacks—when they stop for you, they ask for money. They want you must pay, like for a taxi! The blacks!

But then these whites: they stopping; I'm surprised, because it's only two—empty in the back—and the car it's a beautiful one. The windows are that special glass, you can't see in if you outside, but the woman has hers down and she's calling me over with her finger. She ask me where I'm going and I say the next place because they don't like to have you for too far, so she say get in and lean into the back to move along her stuff that's on the back seat to make room. Then she say, lock the door, just push that button down, we don't want you to fall out, and it's like she's joking with someone she know. The man driving smiles over his shoulder and say something—I can't hear it very well, it's the way he talk English. So anyway I say what's all right to say, yes master, thank you master, I'm going to Warmbad. He ask again, but man, I don't get it—*Ekskuus?* Please? And she chips in—she's a lady with grey hair and he's a young chap—My friend's from England, he's asking if you've been waiting a long time for a lift. So I tell them—A long time? Madam! And because they white, I tell them about the blacks, how when they stop they ask you to pay. This time I understand what the young man's saying, he say, And most whites don't stop? And I'm careful what I say, I tell them about the blacks, how too many people spoil it for us, they robbing and killing, you can't blame white people. Then he ask where I'm from. And she laugh and look round where I'm behind her. I see she know I'm from the Cape, although she ask me. I tell her I'm from the Cape Flats[1] and she say she suppose I'm not born there, though, and she's right, I'm born in Wynberg, right there in Cape Town. So she say, And they moved you out?

Then I catch on what kind of white she is; so I tell her, yes, the government kicked us out from our place, and she say to the young man, You see?

He want to know why I'm not in the place in the Cape Flats, why I'm so far away here. I tell them I'm working in Pietersburg.[2] And he keep on, why? Why? What's my job, everything, and if I don't understand the way he speak, she chips in again all the time and ask me for him. So I tell him, panel beater.[3] And I tell him, the pay is very low in the Cape. And then I begin to tell them lots of things, some things is real and some things I just think of, things that are going to make them like me, maybe they'll take me all the way there to Pietersburg.

I tell them I'm six days on the road. I not going to say I'm sick as well, I been home because I was sick—because *she's* not from overseas, I suss that, she know that old story. I tell them I had to take leave because my mother's got trouble with my brothers and sisters, we seven in the family and no father. And s'true's God, it seem like what I'm saying. When do you ever see him except he's drunk. And my brother is trouble, trouble, he hangs around with bad people and my other brother doesn't help my mother. And that's no lie, neither, how can he help when he's doing time; but they don't need to know that, they only get scared I'm the same kind like him, if I tell about him, assault and intent to do bodily harm. The sisters are in school and my mother's only got the pension. *Ja.* I'm working there in Pietersburg and every week, madam, I swear to you, I send my pay for my mother and sisters. So then he say, Why get off here? Don't you want us to take you to Pietersburg? And she say, of course, they going that way.

And I tell them some more. They listening to me so nice, and I'm talking, talking. I talk about the government, because I hear she keep saying to him, telling about this law and that law. I say how it's not fair we had to leave Wynberg and go to the Flats. I tell her we got sicknesses—she say what kind, is it unhealthy there? And I don't have to think what, I just say it's *bad, bad,* and she say to the man, *As I told you.* I tell about the house we had in Wynberg, but it's not my grannie's old house where we was all living together so long, the house I'm telling them about is more the kind of house they'll know, they wouldn't like to go away from, with a tiled bathroom, electric stove, everything. I tell them we spend three thousand rands fixing up that house—my uncle give us the money, that's how we got it. He give us his savings, three thousand rands. (I don't know why I say three; old Uncle Jimmy never have three or two or one in his life. I just say it.) And then we just kicked out. And panel beaters getting low pay there; it's better in Pietersburg.

---

1. A small town near Cape Town.
2. A city in northeastern South Africa.
3. A person who does body work on automobiles.

He say, but I'm far from my home? And I tell her again, because she's white but she's a woman too, with that grey hair she's got grown-up kids—Madam. I send my pay home every week, s'true's God, so's they can eat, there in the Flats. I'm saying, *six days on the road*. While I'm saying it, I'm thinking; then I say, look at me, I got only these clothes, I sold my things on the way, to have something to eat. *Six days on the road*. He's from overseas and she isn't one of those who say you're a liar, doesn't trust you—right away when I got in the car, I notice she doesn't take her stuff over to the front like they usually do in case you pinch something of theirs. Six days on the road, and am I tired, tired! When I get to Pietersburg I must try borrow me a rand to get a taxi there to where I live. He say, Where do you live? Not in town? And she laugh, because he don't know nothing about this place, where whites live and where we must go—but I know they both thinking and I know what they thinking; I know I'm going to get something when I get out, don't need to worry about that. They feeling bad about me, now. Bad. Anyhow it's God's truth that I'm tired, tired, that's true.

They've put up her window and he's pushed a few buttons, now it's like in a super-market, cool air blowing, and the windows like sunglasses: that sun can't get me here.

The Englishman glances over his shoulder as he drives.

"Taking a nap."

"I'm sure it's needed."

All through the trip he stops for everyone he sees at the roadside. Some are not hitching at all, never expecting to be given a lift anywhere, just walking in the heat outside with an empty plastic can to be filled with water or paraffin or whatever it is they buy in some country store, or standing at some point between departure and destination, small children and bundles linked on either side, baby on back. She hasn't said anything to him. He would only misunderstand if she explained why one doesn't give lifts in this country; and if she pointed out that in spite of this, she doesn't mind him breaking the sensible if unfortunate rule, he might misunderstand that, as well—think she was boasting of her disregard for personal safety weighed in the balance against decent concern for fellow beings.

He persists in making polite conversation with these passengers because he doesn't want to be patronizing; picking them up like so many objects and dropping them off again, silent, smelling of smoke from open cooking fires, sun and sweat, there behind his head. They don't understand his Englishman's English and if he gets an answer at all it's a deaf man's guess at what's called for. Some grin with pleasure and embarrass him by showing it the way they've been taught is acceptable, invoking him as *baas* and *master* when they get out and give thanks. But although he doesn't know it, being too much concerned with those names thrust into his hands like whips whose purpose is repugnant to him, has nothing to do with him, she knows each time that there is a moment of annealment[4] in the air-conditioned hired car belonging to nobody—a moment like that on a no-man's-land bridge in which an accord between warring countries is signed—when there is no calling of names, and all belong in each other's presence. He doesn't feel it because he has no wounds, neither has inflicted, nor will inflict any.

This one standing at the roadside with his transistor radio in a plastic bag was actually thumbing a lift like a townee; his expectation marked him out. And when her companion to whom she was showing the country inevitably pulled up, she read

4. Tempering by heating.

the face at the roadside immediately: the lively, cajoling, performer's eyes, the salmon-pinkish cheeks and nostrils, and as he jogged over smiling, the unselfconscious gap of gum between the canines.

A sleeper is always absent; although present, there on the back seat.

"The way he spoke about black people, wasn't it surprising? I mean—he's black himself."

"Oh no he's not. Couldn't you see the difference? He's a Cape Coloured. From the way he speaks English—couldn't you hear he's not like the Africans you've talked to?"

But of course he hasn't seen, hasn't heard: the fellow is dark enough, to those who don't know the signs by which you're classified, and the melodramatic, long-vowelled English is as difficult to follow if more fluent than the terse, halting responses of blacker people.

"Would he have a white grandmother or even a white father, then?"

She gives him another of the little history lessons she has been supplying along the way. The Malay slaves brought by the Dutch East India Company[5] to their supply station, on the route to India, at the Cape in the seventeenth century; the Khoikhoi who were the indigenous inhabitants of that part of Africa; add Dutch, French, English, German settlers whose back-yard progeniture with these and other blacks began a people who are all the people in the country mingled in one bloodstream. But encounters along the road teach him more than her history lessons, or the political analyses in which they share the same ideological approach although he does not share responsibility for the experience to which the ideology is being applied. She has explained Acts, Proclamations, Amendments. The Group Areas Act, Resettlement Act, Orderly Movement and Settlement of Black Persons Act. She has translated these statute-book euphemisms: people as movable goods. People packed onto trucks along with their stoves and beds while front-end loaders scoop away their homes into rubble. People dumped somewhere else. Always somewhere else. People as the figures, decimal points and multiplying zero-zero-zeros into which individual lives—Black Persons Orderly-Moved, -Effluxed, -Grouped—coagulate and compute. Now he has here in the car the intimate weary odour of a young man to whom these things happen.

"Half his family sick . . . it must be pretty unhealthy, where they've been made to go."

She smiles. "Well, I'm not too sure about that. I had the feeling, some of what he said . . . they're theatrical by nature. You must take it with a pinch of salt."

"You mean about the mother and sisters and so on?"

She's still smiling, she doesn't answer.

"But he couldn't have made up about taking a job so far from home—and the business of sending his wages to his mother? That too?"

He glances at her.

Beside him, she's withdrawn as the other one, sleeping behind him. While he turns his attention back to the road, she is looking at him secretly, as if somewhere in his blue eyes registering the approaching road but fixed on the black faces he is trying to read, somewhere in the lie of his inflamed hand and arm that on their travels have been plunged in the sun as if in boiling water, there is the place through which the worm he needs to be infected with can find a way into him, so that he may host it

5. Occupied South Africa from 1652–1795 while it was a Dutch Cape Colony.

and become its survivor, himself surviving through being fed on. Become like her. Complicity is the only understanding.

"Oh it's true, it's all true . . . not in the way he's told about it. Truer than the way he told it. All these things happen to them. And other things. Worse. But why burden us? Why try to explain to us? Things so far from what we know, how will they ever explain? How will we react? Stop our ears? Or cover our faces? Open the door and throw him out? They don't know. But sick mothers and brothers gone to the bad—these are the staples of misery, mmh? Think of the function of charity in the class struggles in your own country in the nineteenth century; it's all there in your literature. The lord-of-the-manor's compassionate daughter carrying hot soup to the dying cottager on her father's estate. The "advanced" upper-class woman comforting her cook when the honest drudge's daughter takes to whoring for a living. *Shame*, we say here. Shame. You must've heard it? We think it means, what a pity; we think we are expressing sympathy—for them. *Shame*. I don't know what we're saying about ourselves." She laughs.

"So you think it would at least be true that his family were kicked out of their home, sent away?"

"Why would anyone of them need to make that up? It's an everyday affair."

"What kind of place would they get, where they were moved?"

"Depends. A tent, to begin with. And maybe basic materials to build themselves a shack. Perhaps a one-room prefab. Always a tin toilet set down in the veld,[6] if nothing else. Some industrialist must be making a fortune out of government contracts for those toilets. You build your new life round that toilet. His people are Coloured, so it could be they were sent where there were houses of some sort already built for them; Coloureds usually get something a bit better than blacks are given."

"And the house would be more or less as good as the one they had? People as poor as that—and they'd spent what must seem a fortune to them, fixing it up."

"I don't know what kind of house they had. We're not talking about slum clearance, my dear; we're talking about destroying communities because they're black, and white people want to build houses or factories for whites where blacks live. I told you. We're talking about loading up trucks and carting black people out of sight of whites."

"And even where he's come to work—Pietersburg, whatever-it's-called—he doesn't live in the town."

"Out of sight." She has lost the thought for a moment, watching to make sure the car takes the correct turning. "Out of sight. Like those mothers and grannies and brothers and sisters far away on the Cape Flats."

"I don't think it's possible he actually sends all his pay. I mean how would one eat?"

"Maybe what's left doesn't buy anything he really wants."

Not a sound, not a sigh in sleep behind them. They can go on talking about him as he always has been discussed, there and yet not there.

Her companion is alert to the risk of gullibility. He verifies the facts, smiling, just as he converts, mentally, into pounds and pence any sum spent in foreign coinage. "He didn't sell the radio. When he said he'd sold all his things on the road, he forgot about that."

"When did he say he'd last eaten?"

"Yesterday. He said."

6. Plains.

She repeats what she has just been told: "Yesterday." She is looking through the glass that takes the shine of heat off the landscape passing as yesterday passed, time measured by the ticking second hand of moving trees, rows of crops, country-store stoeps,[7] filling stations, spiny crook'd fingers of giant euphorbia.[8] Only the figures by the roadside waiting, standing still.

Personal remarks can't offend someone dead-beat in the back. "How d'you think such a young man comes to be without front teeth?"

She giggles whisperingly and keeps her voice low, anyway. "Well, you may not believe me if I tell you . . ."

"Seems odd . . . I suppose he can't afford to have them replaced."

"It's—how shall I say—a sexual preference. Most usually you see it in their young girls, though. They have their front teeth pulled when they're about seventeen."

She feels his uncertainty, his not wanting to let comprehension lead him to a conclusion embarrassing to an older woman. For her part, she is wondering whether he won't find it distasteful if—at her de-sexed age—she should come out with it: for cock-sucking. "No one thinks the gap spoils a girl's looks, apparently. It's simply a sign she knows how to please. Same significance between men, I suppose ? A form of beauty. So everyone says. We've always been given to understand that's the reason."

"Maybe it's just another sexual myth. There are so many."

She's in agreement. "Black girls. Chinese girls. Jewish girls."

"And black men?"

"Oh my goodness, you bet. But we white ladies don't talk about that, we only dream, you know! Or have nightmares."

They're laughing. When they are quiet, she flexes her shoulders against the seat-back and settles again. The streets of a town are flickering their text across her eyes. "He might have had a car accident. They might have been knocked out in a fight."

They have to wake him because they don't know where he wants to be set down. He is staring at her lined white face (turned to him, calling him gently), stunned for a moment at this evidence that he cannot be anywhere he ought to be; and now he blinks and smiles his empty smile caught on either side by a canine tooth, and gulps and gives himself a shake like someone coming out of water. "Sorry! Sorry! Sorry madam!"

What about, she says, and the young man glances quickly, his blue eyes coming round over his shoulder: "Had a good snooze?"

"Ooh I was finished, master, finished, God bless you for the rest you give me. And with an empty stummick, you know, you dreaming so real. I was dreaming, dreaming, I didn't know nothing about I'm in the car!"

It comes from the driver's seat with the voice (a real Englishman's from overseas) of one who is hoping to hear something that will explain everything. "What were you dreaming?"

But there is only hissing, spluttery laughter between the two white pointed teeth. The words gambol. "Ag, nothing, master, nothing, all non-sunce—"

The sense is that if pressed, he will produce for them a dream he didn't dream, a dream put together from bloated images on billboards, discarded calendars picked up, scraps of newspapers blown about—but they interrupt, they're asking where he'd like to get off.

---

7. Verandas.   8. An African shrub.

"No, anywhere. Here it's all right. Fine. Just there by the corner. I must go look for someone who'll praps give me a rand for the taxi, because I can't walk so far, I haven't eaten nothing since yesterday . . . just here, the master can please stop just here—"

The traffic light is red, anyway, and the car is in the lane nearest the kerb. Her thin, speckled white arm with a skilled flexible hand, but no muscle with which to carry a load of washing or lift a hoe, feels back to release the lock he is fumbling at. "Up, up, pull it up." She has done it for him. "Can't you take a bus?"

"There's no buses Sunday, madam, this place is ve-ery bad for us for transport, I must tell you, we can't get nowhere Sundays, only work-days." He is out, the plastic bag with the radio under his arm, his feet in their stained, multi-striped jogging sneakers drawn neatly together like those of a child awaiting dismissal. "Thank you madam, thank you master, God bless you for what you done."

The confident dextrous hand is moving quickly down in the straw bag bought from a local market somewhere along the route. She brings up a pale blue note (the Englishman recognizes the two-rand denomination of this currency that he has memorized by colour) and turns to pass it, a surreptitious message, through the open door behind her. *Goodbye master madam.* The note disappears delicately as a tit-bit finger-fed. He closes the door, he's keeping up the patter, *goodbye master, goodbye madam,* and she instructs—"No, bang it. Harder. That's it." *Goodbye master, goodbye madam*—but they don't look back at him now, they don't have to see him thinking he must keep waving, keep smiling, in case they should look back.

She is the guide and mentor; she's the one who knows the country. She's the one—she knows that too—who is accountable. She must be the first to speak again. "At least if he's hungry he'll be able to buy a bun or something. And the bars are closed on Sunday."

+—— ◄◆► ——+

Eavan Boland
b. 1944

The question posed by this final section of the anthology—"whose language?"—asks to whom the English language belongs. The poet Eavan Boland puts a special spin on this question throughout her work. As an Irish writer, she has a complex relationship to the language and the literary tradition shared with England, of course. But the thrust of Boland's questioning is directed more toward Irish literature in English and above all to modern Irish poetry. In that rich poetic tradition, Boland sees an absence, hears a silence: the woman poet in Ireland has been, she argues, shut out of poetry in a distinctive way.

The *Field Day Anthology of Irish Literature* was a monumental undertaking; published to wide acclaim in the early 1990s, and edited by Seamus Heaney and Brian Friel among others, the anthology had an ambitious scope, intending to collect all the major writing in the Irish tradition up to the present day. Eavan Boland made a bold stand in print and in person after its publication, declaring that the absence of more female editors and more works by women was evidence of a long-standing gender problem in Irish literature, even today. Ireland was traditionally represented in poetry and fiction by the figure of a suffering woman, whether she was an old country crone, "the old sow that eats its farrow" in Joyce's *Ulysses*, the beautiful Countess Cathleen Ní Houlihan in Yeats's play, the grieving mother of the famine literature, or the magical ancient Queen Mab. Poetry was written about these metaphorical women, standing in for Ireland and symbolizing the country, but almost never, Boland asserts, in a woman's voice. Women had been sidelined in Irish history altogether, despite having played many active roles, turned by poetic language into beautiful icons or sorrowing mothers in the literature that articulated Irish independence. All of Eavan Boland's complex and distinguished poetry before and since her quarrel with the *Field Day* anthology has been devoted to supplying those absent women's voices. Boland's eloquent poetry is regarded as among the finest women's writing of our time.

Eavan Boland was born in Dublin in 1944; since her father was a diplomat, she spent considerable time outside Ireland growing up, in London when her father was Ambassador to the Court of St. James's from 1950 to 1956, and in New York City from 1956 to 1964 when he served as the Irish ambassador to the United Nations. She returned to Ireland and Dublin for college, receiving a first-class honors degree in English from Trinity College. She spent a year at Trinity as a junior lecturer, but then left the academic life to write full time, raise a family of two children with her novelist husband, and teach sporadically at the School of Irish Studies in Dublin. Her first full-length book of poems, *New Territory*, came out in 1967, followed eight years later by *The War Horse*.

Boland's third collection was a watershed for her: *In Her Own Image* (1980) inaugurated her concentration on bringing the inner lives of women to poetic voice. A fountain of volumes has emerged since then, as well as awards to match them. Among the books are *The Journey and Other Poems* (1983), *Selected Poems 1980–1990* (1990), *In a Time of Violence* (1994), *An Origin Like Water: Collected Poems* (1996), and *The Lost Land* (1998); the awards include a Lannan Foundation Award in Poetry and the American Ireland Fund Literary Award. Eavan Boland is currently almost as well known for her essays and reviews, and for her cultural journalism in the *Irish Times*, as for her prominence as a reader of her own poetry. And she has come full circle since leaving academe; Boland is currently a professor of English at Stanford University.

The poems by Eavan Boland collected for this anthology are diverse and complicated, yet each works to restore missing voices, missing narratives, most of them female. *Anorexic* voices the paradoxical self-destruction of starving for love and power; *The Pomegranate* is a beautiful rewriting of the myth of Persephone, the Greek maiden whose mother, Ceres, the goddess of fertility, was forced to let her daughter spend the winter each year underground with Hades, the god of death, in order to let spring come again. Narrated in the voice of a contemporary mother gazing at her own teenage daughter, separated from her by the girl's need to acquire independence, the poem modernizes the cycle of human seasons and probes the nature of maternal regret. Boland brings the intimacy of such feelings to her meditations on history, violence, and Ireland itself. *Mise Eire* is a dazzling play on words from its title onward; a defiant female voice repudiates Ireland, rejects it for naming her "the woman" in its poetry, not seeing beyond that designation to the real woman who once stood on the deck of the *Mary Belle*, headed to America, a half-dead infant in her arms. "A new language is a scar," the poem tells us. Eavan Boland's poetic task has been to heal those scars by uncovering them, to give voice to the absent throng of women in the Irish past.

The Pomegranate

The only legend I have ever loved is
The story of a daughter lost in hell.
And found and rescued there.
Love and blackmail are the gist of it.
5   Ceres and Persephone the names.
And the best thing about the legend is
I can enter it anywhere. And have.
As a child in exile in

A city of fogs and strange consonants,

10   I read it first and at first I was

An exiled child in the crackling dusk of

The underworld, the stars blighted. Later

I walked out in a summer twilight

Searching for my daughter at bedtime.

15   When she came running I was ready

To make any bargain to keep her.

I carried her back past whitebeams.

And wasps and honey-scented buddleias.

But I was Ceres then and I knew

20   Winter was in store for every leaf

On every tree on that road.

Was inescapable for each one we passed.

And for me.

It is winter

25   And the stars are hidden.

I climb the stairs and stand where I can see

My child asleep beside her teen magazines,

Her can of Coke, her plate of uncut fruit.

The pomegranate! How did I forget it?

30   She could have come home and been safe

And ended the story and all

Our heartbroken searching but she reached

Out a hand and plucked a pomegranate.[1]

She put out her hand and pulled down

35   The French sound for apple and

The noise of stone and the proof

That even in the place of death,

At the heart of legend, in the midst

Of rocks full of unshed tears

40   Ready to be diamonds by the time

The story was told, a child can be

Hungry. I could warn her. There is still a chance.

The rain is cold. The road is flint-coloured.

The suburb has cars and cable television.

45   The veiled stars are above ground.

It is another world. But what else

Can a mother give her daughter but such

Beautiful rifts in time?

If I defer the grief I will diminish the gift.

50   The legend must be hers as well as mine.

She will enter it. As I have.

She will wake up. She will hold

The papery, flushed skin in her hand.

And to her lips. I will say nothing.

---

1. In the classical myth, Persephone would have emerged from the underworld unharmed except for the fact that she broke a command to bring nothing back: by plucking a pomegranate, she became liable to death. The next lines recall the derivation of the term "pomegranate" from Old French *pomme granade*, "seeded apple."

A Woman Painted on a Leaf

I found it among curios and silver.
in the pureness of wintry light.

A woman painted on a leaf.

Fine lines drawn on a veined surface
5 in a handmade frame.

This is not my face. Neither did I draw it.

A leaf falls in a garden.
The moon cools its aftermath of sap.
The pith of summer dries out in starlight.

10 A woman is inscribed there.

This is not death. It is the terrible
suspension of life.

I want a poem
I can grow old in. I want a poem I can die in.

15 I want to take
this dried-out face,
as you take a starling from behind iron,
and return it to its element of air, of ending—
so that autumn
20 which was once
the hard look of stars,
the frown on a gardener's face,
a gradual bronzing of the distance,

will be,
25 from now on,
a crisp tinder underfoot. Cheekbones. Eyes. Will be
a mouth crying out. Let me.

Let me die.

Mise Eire[1]

I won't go back to it—

my nation displaced
into old dactyls,[2]
oaths made
5 by the animal tallows
of the candle—

land of the Gulf Stream,
the small farm,
the scalded memory,

---

1. I am Ireland (Gaelic). Mise Eire also reads as "misery," a pun.

2. The English adapted "Eire" to "Ireland," drawing the word out into dactylic meter.

10   the songs
        that bandage up the history,
        the words
        that make a rhythm of the crime

        where time is time past.
15   A palsy of regrets.
        No. I won't go back.
        My roots are brutal:

        I am the woman—
        a sloven's mix
20   of silk at the wrists,
        a sort of dove-strut
        in the precincts of the garrison—

        who practices
        the quick frictions,
25   the rictus[3] of delight
        and gets cambric for it,
        rice-colored silks.

        I am the woman
        in the gansy-coat[4]
30   on board the *Mary Belle*,
        in the huddling cold,

        holding her half-dead baby to her
        as the wind shifts East
        and North over the dirty
35   water of the wharf

        mingling the immigrant
        guttural with the vowels
        of homesickness who neither
        knows nor cares that

40   a new language
        is a kind of scar
        and heals after a while
        into a passable imitation
        of what went before.

÷—◆—÷

Derek Walcott
b. 1930

Over the last five decades, Derek Walcott has articulated the tensions of living between two worlds—the competing claims and traditions of the West Indies, his home, and Europe. A concern with issues of national identity runs throughout Walcott's large body of poetry and drama; his poetry exploits the resources of a European literary tradition in the service of Caribbean themes and concerns. No poet, as T. S. Eliot insisted, can write important poetry

---

3. Frozen smile.   4. A cheap cloth coat.

without tapping into some cultural or literary tradition; in the poem *Forest of Europe*, Walcott puts the question this way:

> What's poetry, if it is worth its salt,
> but a phrase men can pass from hand to mouth?
> From hand to mouth, across the centuries,
> the bread that lasts when systems have decayed.

Walcott was born in Castries, Saint Lucia, an isolated, volcanic island in the West Indies. Saint Lucia is a former British colony, and Walcott's education there was thoroughly British. In the introduction to *Dream on Monkey Mountain and Other Plays* (1970), Walcott writes, "The writers of my generation were natural assimilators. We knew the literature of Empires, Greek, Roman, British, through their essential classics; and both the patois of the street and the language of the classroom hid the elation of discovery." Empire and slavery left their impress on the Walcott family; both of his grandmothers were said to be descended from slaves. Walcott attended University College of the West Indies in Jamaica on a British government scholarship; he completed a degree in English in 1953, and from 1954 until 1957 taught in West Indian schools. In 1958 a Rockefeller Fellowship allowed him to spend a year in New York studying theater; the following year he moved to Trinidad and founded the Little Carib Theatre Workshop. It was in his playwriting that Walcott first accomplished the fusion of native and European elements he sought; his 1958 play *Drums and Colours*, for instance, employs calypso music, mime, and carnival masks to "carnivalize" the smooth surface of European drama, creating a literary form which, while written in English, is uniquely Caribbean in character. *O Babylon!* (1976), his most popular play, focuses on the Rastafarians of Jamaica. He is also a talented painter, and his poems are notable for the vivid clarity of their images.

Walcott has written more than fifteen volumes of poetry as well as a dozen plays. His first important poetry collection was *In a Green Night* (1962), which includes his best-known poem, *A Far Cry from Africa*. Walcott himself has never settled in one place for long, and for many years he has split his time between his home in Trinidad and a teaching post at Boston University. Walcott's poems create a landscape of historical and personal memory, overlaying empires, centuries, continents, and stages of his own life. He developed his themes most expansively in his verse novel *Omeros* (1991), which rewrites Homer's *Iliad* as a Caribbean story, interspersed with scenes of the poet's own life and travels in Boston, London, and Dublin. Walcott was awarded the Nobel Prize for literature in 1992, "for a poetic oeuvre of great luminosity, sustained by a historical vision, the outcome of a multicultural commitment."

A Far Cry from Africa

> A wind is ruffling the tawny pelt
> Of Africa. Kikuyu,[1] quick as flies,
> Batten° upon the bloodstreams of the veldt.°   *fasten / open country*
> Corpses are scattered through a paradise.
> 5 Only the worm, colonel of carrion, cries:
>   "Waste no compassion on these separate dead!"
> Statistics justify and scholars seize
> The salients of colonial policy.
> What is that to the white child hacked in bed?
> 10 To savages, expendable as Jews?
>
> Threshed out by beaters, the long rushes break
> In a white dust of ibises[2] whose cries

---

1. Indigenous people of Kenya.   2. Wading birds resembling storks.

Have wheeled since civilization's dawn
From the parched river or beast-teeming plain.
15   The violence of beast on beast is read
As natural law, but upright man
Seeks his divinity by inflicting pain.
Delirious as these worried beasts, his wars
Dance to the tightened carcass of a drum,
20   While he calls courage still that native dread
Of the white peace contracted by the dead.

Again brutish necessity wipes its hands
Upon the napkin of a dirty cause, again
A waste of our compassion, as with Spain,
25   The gorilla wrestles with the superman.
I who am poisoned with the blood of both,
Where shall I turn, divided to the vein?
I who have cursed
The drunken officer of British rule, how choose
30   Between this Africa and the English tongue I love?
Betray them both, or give back what they give?
How can I face such slaughter and be cool?
How can I turn from Africa and live?

1962

from **Midsummer**
50

I once gave my daughters, separately, two conch shells
that were dived from the reef, or sold on the beach, I forget.
They use them as doorstops or bookends, but their wet
pink palates are the soundless singing of angels.
5   I once wrote a poem called "The Yellow Cemetery,"
when I was nineteen. Lizzie's age. I'm fifty-three.
These poems I heaved aren't linked to any tradition
like a mossed cairn;[1] each goes down like a stone
to the seabed, settling, but let them, with luck, lie
10   where stones are deep, in the sea's memory.
Let them be, in water, as my father, who did watercolours,
entered his work. He became one of his shadows,
wavering and faint in the midsummer sunlight.
His name is Warwick Walcott. I sometimes believe
15   that his father, in love or bitter benediction,
named him for Warwickshire.[2] Ironies
are moving. Now, when I rewrite a line,
or sketch on the fast-drying paper the coconut fronds
that he did so faintly, my daughters' hands move in mine.
20   Conches move over the sea-floor. I used to move
my father's grave from the blackened Anglican headstones
in Castries[3] to where I could love both at once—

1. A heap of stones marking a trail.
2. Birthplace of Shakespeare. Warwick Walcott, journalist, occasional poet, and printer, died when his son was a
young child.
3. Port and capital of Saint Lucia.

the sea and his absence. Youth is stronger than fiction.

52

I heard them marching the leaf-wet roads of my head,
the sucked vowels of a syntax trampled to mud,
a division of dictions, one troop black, barefooted,
the other in redcoats bright as their sovereign's blood;
5   their feet scuffled like rain, the bare soles with the shod.
One fought for a queen, the other was chained in her service,
but both, in bitterness, travelled the same road.
Our occupation and the Army of Occupation
are born enemies, but what mortar can size
10   the broken stones of the barracks of Brimstone Hill
to the gaping brick of Belfast? Have we changed sides
to the moustached sergeants and the horsy gentry
because we serve English, like a two-headed sentry
guarding its borders? No language is neutral;
15   the green oak of English is a murmurous cathedral
where some took umbrage,[4] some peace, but every shade, all,
helped widen its shadow. I used to haunt the arches
of the British barracks of Vigie.[5] There were leaves there,
bright, rotting like revers of epaulettes,[6] and the stenches
20   of history and piss. Leaves piled like the dropped aitches
of soldiers from rival shires, from the brimstone trenches
of Agincourt to the gas of the Somme.[7] On Poppy Day[8]
our schools bought red paper flowers. They were for Flanders.[9]
I saw Hotspur cursing the smoke through which a popinjay
25   minced from the battle. Those raging commanders
from Thersites to Percy,[1] their rant is our model.
I pinned the poppy to my blazer. It bled like a vowel.

54

The midsummer sea, the hot pitch road, this grass, these shacks that made me,
jungle and razor grass shimmering by the roadside, the edge of art;
wood lice are humming in the sacred wood,
nothing can burn them out, they are in the blood;
5   their rose mouths, like cherubs, sing of the slow science
of dying—all heads, with, at each ear, a gauzy wing.
Up at Forest Reserve, before branches break into sea,
I looked through the moving, grassed window and thought "pines,"
or conifers of some sort. I thought, they must suffer
10   in this tropical heat with their child's idea of Russia.

---

4. In two senses: offence, shade.
5. Vigie Beach near Castries, Saint Lucia.
6. Turned-up edges of ornamental shoulder pieces worn on uniforms.
7. French sites of important battles in 1415 and in World War I.
8. Veterans Day.

9. Scene of a disastrous World War I offensive—"the battle of the mud"—in which the British lost 324,000 soldiers.
1. The headstrong Sir Henry Percy (1364–1403) became known as "Hotspur"; he serves as rival to Prince Hal in Shakespeare's *Henry IV*. Thersites accuses Achilles of cowardice in Homer's *Iliad*.

Then suddenly, from their rotting logs, distracting signs
of the faith I betrayed, or the faith that betrayed me—
yellow butterflies rising on the road to Valencia[2]
stuttering "yes" to the resurrection; "yes, yes is our answer,"
15   the gold-robed Nunc Dimittis[3] of their certain choir.
Where's my child's hymnbook, the poems edged in gold leaf,
the heaven I worship with no faith in heaven,
as the Word turned toward poetry in its grief?
Ah, bread of life, that only love can leaven!
20   Ah, Joseph, though no man ever dies in his own country,[4]
the grateful grass will grow thick from his heart.

1984

═╬ END OF PERSPECTIVES: WHOSE LANGUAGE? ╬═

---

2. A seaport in Eastern Spain.
3. "Lord, now let thy servant depart in peace," sung at the end of Mass.
4. The line echoes Jesus's comment that no prophet is honored in his own country (Mark 6.4). On one level, Joseph may be Jesus's father, mourning his son's early death. *Midsummer* as a whole is addressed to Walcott's friend Joseph Brodsky, the exiled Russian poet.

BIBLIOGRAPHIES
The Romantics and Their Contemporaries

Bibliographies, General Collections, General Reference • Annual bibliographies are published by the Modern Language Association of America, the Modern Humanities Research Association, the *Keats-Shelley Journal*, *The Romantic Movement*, and *The Year's Work in English Studies* • *Encyclopedia of the Romantic Era, 1760–1860* (Fitzroy, Dearborn), 2002. • Stuart Curran, ed., *The Cambridge Companion to British Romanticism*, 1993. • Frank Jordan, ed., *The English Romantic Poets: A Review of Research and Criticism*, 4th ed. 1985 [covers Blake, W. Wordsworth, Coleridge, Byron, P. B. Shelley, Keats]. • Karl Kroeber and Gene Ruoff, eds., *Romantic Poetry: Recent Revisionary Criticism*, 1993. • Iain McCalman, *An Oxford Companion to The Romantic Age: British Culture 1176–1832*, 1999. • Jerome McGann, ed., *The New Oxford Book of Romantic Period Verse*, 1993. • Anne K. Mellor and Richard Matlak, eds., *British Literature 1780–1830*, 1996. • Michael O'Neill, ed., *Literature of the Romantic Period: A Bibliographical Guide*, 1998. • David Perkins, ed., *English Romantic Writers*, 2d ed., 1995. • Duncan Wu, ed., *A Companion to Romanticism*, 1997. • Duncan Wu, ed., *Romanticism, An Anthology*, 1994. • Duncan Wu, ed., *Romanticism, A Critical Reader*, 1995 [essays on Blake, W. Wordsworth, Coleridge, P. B. Shelley, Byron, Keats, Clare, M. Shelley, Austen]. • Several volumes in the series *Approaches to Teaching World Literature* published by the Modern Language Association are devoted to writers in our period: among others, Blake (ed. Robert Gleckner and Mark Greenberg); Byron (ed. F. W. Shilstone); Coleridge (ed. Richard Matlak); Keats (ed. Walter Evert and Jack Rhodes); Mary Shelley (ed. Stephen Behrendt); Percy Shelley (ed. Spencer Hall); and Wordsworth (ed. Spencer Hall and Jonathan Ramsey). • *Studies in English Literature* publishes an annual omnibus review in each fall issue: "Recent Studies in the Nineteenth Century." • Website hub for a wealth of resources on authors, issues, as well as visual images is the award-winning *Romantic Circles*, ed. Stephen Jones and Neil Fraistat. http://www.rc.umd.edu

History and Literary History • M. H. Abrams "English Romanticism: The Spirit of the Age," 1963; repr. in *Romanticism and Consciousness: Essays in Criticism*, ed. Harold Bloom, 1970. • Derek Beales, *From Castlereagh to Gladstone 1815–85*, 1969. • Marilyn Butler, *Romantics, Rebels, and Reactionaries: English Literature and Its Background, 1760–1830*, 1981. • Marilyn Butler, "Romanticism in England," *Romanticism in National Context*, eds. Roy Park and Mikulá Teich, 1988. • James Chandler, *England in 1819*, 1998. • James Chandler, ed., *The Cambridge History of Romanticism*, 2002. • Ian R. Christie, *Wars and Revolutions*, in *New History of England*, vol. 7, 1982. • J. C. D. Clark, *English Society 1688–1832*, 1985. • Linda Colley, *Britons: Forging the Nation 1707–1837*, 1992. • Jeffrey N. Cox, *Poetry and Politics in the Cockney School: Keats, Shelley, Hunt and their Circle*, 1998. • M. J. Daunton, *Progress and Poverty: An Economic and Social History of Britain 1700–1850*, 1995. • Lee Erickson, *The Economy of Literary Form: English Literature and the Industrialization of Publishing 1800–1850*, 1996. • Norman Gash, *Aristocracy and People: Britain 1815–1865*, 1979. • Marilyn Gaull, *English Romanticism: The Human Context*, 1988. • Élie Halévy, *A History of the English People in 1815*, trans. 1924, repr. 1987. • Ian Jack, *English Literature, 1815–1832*, 1963. • Jon Klancher, *The Making of English Reading Audiences, 1790–1832*, 1987. • John B. Owen, *The Eighteenth Century 1714–1815*, 1974. • Harold Perkin, *Origins of Modern English Society*, 1969. • Roy Porter, *English Society in the Eighteenth Century*, 1982. • W. L. Renwick, *English Literature, 1789–1815*, 1963. • Alan Richardson, *Literature, Education, and Romanticism*, 1994. • E. P. Thompson, *The Making of the English Working Class*, 1963. • E. P. Thompson, *Customs in Common*, 1991. • R. J. White, *Waterloo to Peterloo*, 1957. • Raymond Williams, *Culture and Society 1780–1950*, 1960. • Raymond Williams, *The Country and The City*, 1973. • Susan J. Wolfson and William H. Galperin, eds., "The Romantic Century," *European Romantic Review* 11, 2000. • Susan J. Wolfson, "Our Puny Boundaries:

Why the Craving to Carve Up the Nine-teenth Century?" *PMLA* 116, 2001. • Carl Woodring, *Politics in English Romantic Poetry*, 1970.

Contemporary Reception • John O. Hayden, *The Romantic Reviewers 1802–24*, 1969. • Theodore Redpath, ed., *The Young Romantics and Critical Opinion, 1807–1824: Poetry of Byron, Shelley, and Keats as Seen by Their Contemporary Critics*, 1973. • Donald H. Reiman, *The Romantics Reviewed: Contemporary Reviews of British Romantic Writers*, 1972.

Poetic Form and Genres • M. H. Abrams, "Structure and Style in the Greater Romantic Lyric," 1965, repr. in *Romanticism and Consciousness*, ed. Harold Bloom 1970. • M. H. Abrams, *Natural Supernaturalism: Tradition and Revolution in Romantic Literature*, 1971. • Harold Bloom, "The Internalization of Quest-romance," 1969, repr. in *Romanticism and Consciousness*, ed. Harold Bloom, 1970. • Harold Bloom, *The Anxiety of Influence: A Theory of Poetry*, 1973. • Douglas Bush, *Mythology and the Romantic Tradition in English Poetry*, 1937. • Stuart Curran, *Poetic Form and British Romanticism*, 1986. • Geoffrey Hartman, *Beyond Formalism*, 1970. • John Hollander, "Romantic Verse Form and the Metrical Contract," 1965, repr. in *Romanticism and Consciousness*, ed. Harold Bloom, 1970. • David Perkins, "The Construction of 'The Romantic Movement' as a Literary Classification," *Nineteenth-Century Literature*, 1990. • Thomas Vogler, *Preludes to Vision: On the Epic Venture in Blake, Wordsworth, Keats, and Hart Crane*, 1971. • Brian Wilkie, *Romantic Poets and Epic Tradition*, 1965. • W. K. Wimsatt, "The Structure of Romantic Nature Imagery," in *The Verbal Icon*, 1954; repr. in *Romanticism and Consciousness*, ed. Harold Bloom, 1970.

Theory and Criticism • M. H. Abrams, *The Mirror and the Lamp: Romantic Theory and Critical Tradition*, 1953. • M. H. Abrams, *Natural Supernaturalism*, 1971. • M. H. Abrams, *The Correspondent Breeze: Essays on English Romanticism*, 1984. • John Beer, ed., *Questioning Romanticism*, 1995. • Edward E. Bostetter, *The Romantic Ventriloquists: Wordsworth, Coleridge, Shelley, Keats, Byron*, 1963. • Paul de Man, *The Rhetoric of Romanticism*, 1984. • Paul de Man, "The Rhetoric of Temporality," in his *Blindness and Insight*, 2d ed., 1983. • William

H. Galperin, *The Return of the Visible in British Romanticism*, 1993. • Karl Kroeber, *British Romantic Art*, 1986. • Jerome McGann, *The Romantic Ideology: A Critical Investigation*, 1983. • Jerome McGann, *The Poetics of Sensibility: A Revolution in Literary Style*, 1996. • Anne K. Mellor, *English Romantic Irony*, 1980. • David Perkins, *The Quest for Permanence: The Symbolism of Wordsworth, Shelley, and Keats*, 1959. • Tilottama Rajan, *Dark Interpreter: The Discourse of Romanticism*, 1980. • Charles R. Rzepka, *The Self as Mind: Vision and Identity in Wordsworth, Coleridge, and Keats*, 1986. • David Simpson, *Irony and Authority in Romantic Poetry*, 1979. • Susan J. Wolfson, *Formal Charges: The Shaping of Poetry in British Romanticism*, 1997. • Marshall Brown, ed., *The Cambridge History of Literary Criticism*, vol. 5, *Romanticism*, 2000. • Susan J. Wolfson, ed., "Ideology and Romantic Aesthetics: a Forum," *Studies in Romanticism* 37, 1998: essays on P. B. Shelley, Keats, Barbauld, Coleridge, the Elgin Marbles, Wollstonecraft • Jerome Christensen, *Romanticism at the End of History*, 2000. • Alan Richardson, *British Romanticism and the Science of the Mind*, 2001. • Willard Spiegelman, *Majestic Indolence: English Romantic Poetry and the Work of Art*, 1995. • Stuart M. Sperry, "Towards a Definition of Romantic Irony," in *Romantic and Modern: Revaluations of Literary Tradition*, ed. George Bornstein, 1977. • Earl R. Wasserman, "The English Romantics: The Grounds of Knowledge," *Studies in Romanticism*, 1964.

Perspectives: The Rights of Man and the Revolution Controversy • Headnote: Coleridge is quoted from *Table Talk*, 4 January 1823; Wordsworth is quoted from a letter of 30 March 1835.

Criticism. • Simon Bainbridge, *Napoleon and English Romanticism*, 1996. • Stephen Blakemore, *Crisis in Representation: Thomas Paine, Mary Wollstonecraft, Helen Maria Williams, and the Rewriting of the French Revolution*, 1997; and *Intertextual War: Edmund Burke and the French Revolution in the Writings of Mary Wollstonecraft, Thomas Paine, and James Mackintosh*, 1997. • Marilyn Butler, ed., *Burke, Paine, Godwin, and the Revolution Controversy*, 1984. • Ceri Crossley and Ian Small, eds., *The French Revolution and British Culture*, 1989. • Seamus Deane, *The French Revolution and Enlightenment England 1789–1832*, 1988. • H. T. Dickinson, *British Radicalism and the French Revolution*, 1985. • Clive Emsley, *British Society and* the French Wars 1793–1815, 1979. • Burton R. Friedman, *Fabricating History: English Writers and the French Revolution*, 1988. • Kevin Gilmartin, *Print Politics: The Press and Radical Opposition in Early Nineteenth-Century England*, 1996. • Albert Goodwin, *The Friends of Liberty*, 1979. • E. J. Hobsbawm, *The Age of Revolution 1789–1848*, 1962. • Howard Mumford Jones, *Revolution and Romanticism*, 1974. • Anne K. Mellor, "English Women Writers and the French Revolution," in *Rebel Daughters: Women and the French Revolution*, eds. Sara Melzer and Leslie Rabine, 1992. • Ronald Paulson, *Representations of Revolution, 1789–1820*, 1983. • Mark Philp, ed., *The French Revolution and British Popular Politics*, 1991. • Mark Philp, "Vulgar Conservatism, 1792–1793," *English Historical Review*, 1995. • Esther Schor, *Bearing the Dead: The British Culture of Mourning from the Enlightenment to Victoria*, 1994. • David Simpson, *Romanticism, Nationalism, and the Revolt Against Theory*, 1993. • Olivia Smith, *The Politics of Language 1791–1819*, 1984. • Bruce Woodcock and John Coates. *Combative Styles: Romantic Writing and Ideology*, 1995.

The Anti-Jacobin • *Context.* • M. Dorothy George, *English Political Caricature: A Study of Opinion and Propaganda, 1793–1832*, 1959.

Text. • Charles Edmonds, ed., *Poetry of the Anti-Jacobin* 1890.

Perspectives: The Abolition of Slavery and the Slave Trade • *General Studies.* • Roger Anstey, *The Atlantic Slave Trade and British Abolition, 1760–1810*, 1975. • Joan Baum, *Mind-forg'd Manacles: Slavery and the English Romantic Poets*, 1994. • Robin Blackburn, *The Overthrow of Colonial Slavery, 1776–1848*, 1988. • Reginald Coupland, *The British Anti-Slavery Movement*, 1933. • Michael Craton, *Sinews of Empire: A Short History of British Slavery*, 1974. • Michael Craton, James Walvin, and David Wright, eds., *Slavery, Abolition and Emancipation: Black Slaves and the British Empire*, 1976 [an anthology of important documents, including the "Mansfield decision" (Somerset v. Stewart, June 1772), and a succinct history]. • David Brion Davis, *The Problem of Slavery in the Age of Revolution*, 1975. • Eva Dyke, *The Negro in English Romantic Thought*, 1942. • Moira Ferguson, *Subject to Others: British Women Writers and Colonial Slavery, 1670–1834*, 1992 [including a massive bibliography]. • Tim Fulford and Peter J. Kitson, eds., *Romanticism and Colonialism*, 1998. • Sonia Hofkosh and Alan Richardson, eds., *Romanticism, Race and Imperial Culture*, 1996. • Edith F. Hurwitz, *Politics and Public Conscience: Slave Emancipation and the Abolitionist Movement in Britain*, 1973. • Margaret Kirkham, *Jane Austen, Feminism and Fiction*, 1983 [on the Mansfield Decision and *Mansfield Park*]. • Frank Joseph Klingberg, *The Anti-Slavery Movement in England: A Study in English Humanitarianism*, 1926. • Gordon K. Lewis, *Slavery, Imperialism, and Freedom Studies in English Radical Thought*, 1978. • Dale H. Porter, *The Abolition of the Slave Trade in England, 1784–1807*, 1970. • Helen Thomas, *Romanticism and Slave Narratives*, 2000. • James Walvin, *Black and White: The Negro and English Society, 1555–1945*, 1973. • James Walvin, *Slavery and British Society, 1776–1846*, 1982. • James Walvin, *England, Slaves, and Freedom 1776–1838*, 1986. • Eric Williams, *Capitalism and Slavery*, 1944.

Specific Figures. • Reginald Coupland, *Wilberforce: A Narrative*, 1923. • E. L. Griggs, *Thomas Clarkson: The Friend of the Slaves*, 1938. • Edmund Heward, *Lord Mansfield*, 1979. • Robert Isaac and Samuel Wilberforce, *The Life of William Wilberforce*, 1835. • C. L. R. James, *The Black Jacobins: Toussaint L'Ouverture and the San Domingo Rebellion*, 1938; repr. 1963. • Oliver M. Warner, *William Wilberforce and His Times*, 1962. See also the entries on *Olaudah Equiano* and *Mary Prince*.

Gender, Women Writers, The Rights of Woman • *Editions.* • Paula Feldman, ed., *British Women Poets of the Romantic Era, An Anthology*, 1997. • Duncan Wu, ed., *Romantic Women Poets, An Anthology*, 1997.

Criticism. • Stephen C. Behrendt and Harriet Kramer Linkin, eds., *Approaches to Teaching British Women Poets of the Romantic Period*, 1997. • Stuart Curran, "Romantic Poetry: The 'I' Altered," in *Romanticism & Feminism*, ed., Anne Mellor • Paula Feldman, and Theresa M. Kelley, eds., *Romantic Women Writers: Voices and Countervoices*, 1995. • Harriet Kramer Linkin and Stephen C. Behrendt and eds., *Romanticism and Women Poets: Opening the Doors of Reception*, 1999. • Diane Long Hoeveler, *Romantic Androgyny: The Women Within*, 1990. • Sonia Hofkosh, *Sexual Politics and the Romantic Author*, 1998. • Jerome McGann, *The Poetics of Sensibility*, 1996. • Anne K. Mellor, *Mothers of the Nation:*

Women's Political Writing in England, 1780–1830, 2000. • Anne K. Mellor, ed., *Romanticism and Feminism*, 1988. • Anne K. Mellor, *Romanticism and Gender*, 1993. • Judith Pascoe, *Romantic Theatricality: Gender, Poetry, and Spectatorship*. 1997. • Marlon Ross, *The Contours of Masculine Desire: Romanticism and the Rise of Women's Poetry*, 1989. • Irene Tayler and Gina Luria, "Women in British Romantic Literature," in *What Manner of Woman*, ed. Marlene Springer, 1977. • Carol Shiner Wilson and Joel Haefner, eds., *Revisioning Romanticism: British Women Writers, 1776–1837*, 1994. • Jonathan Wordsworth, *The Bright Work Grows: Women Writers of the Romantic Age*, 1997.

A Vindication in Context: The Wollstonecraft Controversy and the Rights of Women • *Textual Reference*. • Anna Laetitia Le Breton, *Memoir of Mrs. Barbauld*, 1874 [Barbauld's letter to Edgeworth, 4 September 1804].

General Studies. • Leonore Davidoff and Catherine Hall, *Family Fortunes: Men and Women of the English Middle Class, 1780–1850*, 1987. • Bridget Hill, *Women, Work, and Sexual Politics in Eighteenth-Century England*, 1989. • Gary Kelly, *Women, Writing, and Revolution, 1790–1827*, 1993. • Anne K. Mellor, *Romanticism and Gender*, 1993. • Mitzi Myers, "Reform or Ruin: 'A Revolution in Female Manners,'" in *Studies in Eighteenth-Century Culture*, 1982. • Mary Poovey, *The Proper Lady and the Woman Writer*, 1984. • Katharine Rogers, *Feminism in Eighteenth-Century England*, 1982. • For Barbauld, Southey, Blake, and More, see the main entries under their names.

Perspectives: The Sublime, the Beautiful, and the Picturesque • *General Criticism*. • Malcolm Andrews, *The Search for the Picturesque*, 1989. • Andrew Ashfield and Peter de Bolla, eds., *The Sublime: A Reader in British Eighteenth-Century Aesthetic Theory*, 1996. • John Barrell, *The Idea of Landscape and a Sense of Place*, 1972; and *The Dark Side of the Landscape: The Rural Poor in English Painting 1730–1840*, 1980. • Ann Bermingham, *Landscape and Ideology*, 1986. • Stephen Copley and Peter Garside, eds., *The Politics of the Picturesque*, 1994. • Peter de Bolla, *The Discourse of the Sublime*, 1989. • Frances Ferguson, *Solitude and the Sublime*, 1992. • Neil Hertz, *The End of the Line*, 1985. • Walter John Hipple, Jr., *The Beautiful, the Sublime, and the Picturesque in Eighteenth-*

Century British Aesthetic Theory, 1957. • Christopher Hussey, *The Picturesque*, 1927. • Elizabeth W. Manwaring, *Italian Landscape in Eighteenth-Century England*, 1925. • Samuel H. Monk, *The Sublime*, 1935. • Thomas Weiskel, *The Romantic Sublime*, 1976.

The writers surveyed. • Donald Greene, "The Original of Pemberley," *Eighteenth-Century Fiction*, 1998 (on Austen's *Pride and Prejudice*). • Burke's *Sublime and Beautiful*, ed. J. T. Boulton, 1968. • W. D. Templeman, *The Life and Work of William Gilpin*, 1937. • C. P. Barbier, *William Gilpin*, 1963. • René Wellek, *Immanuel Kant in England 1793–1838*, 1938. • Giuseppe Micheli, *The Early Reception of Kant's Thought in England 1785–1805*, 1990. • For more on Austen and Wollstonecraft, see the main author entries, and Ruskin in the Victorian era.

Our texts. • Jane Austen, *Pride and Prejudice*, 1813. • Edmund Burke, *A Philosophical Enquiry into the Origin of Our Ideas of the Sublime and Beautiful*, 1757; 1812 edn. • William Gilpin, *Three Essays*, 2d edn., 1794. • Immanuel Kant, *The Critique of Judgement*, tr. James Creed Meredith, 1952. • John Ruskin, *Modern Painters*, 1968. • Mary Wollstonecraft, *A Vindication of the Rights of Men*, 1790.

Jane Austen • *Letters*. • Deirdre Le Faye, ed., *Jane Austen's Letters*, 1997.

Life and Background. • Park Honan, *Jane Austen: Her Life*, 1987. • David Nokes, *Jane Austen*, 1997. • Clare Tomalin, *Jane Austen: A Life*, 1997.

Edition. • Claudia L. Johnson and Susan J. Wolfson, eds., *Pride and Prejudice*, a Longman Cultural Edition, 2002.

Criticism. • Wayne Booth, *The Rhetoric of Fiction*, 1961. • Marilyn Butler, *Jane Austen and the War of Ideas*, 1975.

Criticism and Reference. • Edward Copeland and Juliet McMaster, eds., *The Cambridge Companion to Jane Austen*, 1997. • Alistair Duckworth, *The Improvement of the Estate, A Study of Jane Austen's Novels*, 1971 • William H. Galperin, *The Historical Austen*, 2002. • Sandra Gilbert and Susan Gubar, *The Madwoman in the Attic: The Woman Writer and the Nineteenth-Century Literary Imagination*, 1979. • Claudia Johnson, *Jane Austen: Women, Politics, and the Novel*, 1988. • Claudia Johnson, *Equivocal Beings: Politics, Gender, and Sentimentality in the 1790s*, 1995. • Arnold Kettle, *An Introduction to the*

English Novel, 1951. • Margaret Kirkham, *Jane Austen, Feminism, and Fiction*, 1983. • U. C. Knoepflmacher, "The Importance of Being Frank: Character and Letter-Writing in *Emma*," *SEL* 1967. • A. Walton Litz, *Jane Austen: A Study of Her Artistic Development*, 1965. • Susan Morgan, *In the Meantime: Character and Perception in Jane Austen's Fiction*, 1980. • Judith Lowder Newton, *Women, Power and Subversion: Social Strategies in British Fiction, 1778–1860*, 1981. • Warren Roberts, *Jane Austen and the French Revolution*, 1979. • Tony Tanner, *Jane Austen*, 1986. • Sir Walter Scott, review of *Emma*, *Quarterly Review*, 1815.

Our Texts. • *The Novels of Jane Austen* (Edinburgh 1911); *Jane Austen's Letters*, ed. R. W. Chapman, 1932.

Anna Letitia Barbauld • *Biography and Editions*. • Lucy Aikin, "Memoir" in *The Works of Anna Letitia Barbauld*, 1825. • William McCarthy and Elizabeth Kraft, eds., *The Poems of Anna Letitia Barbauld*, 1994.

Edition. • William McCarthy and Elizabeth Kraft, eds., *Anna Letitia Barbauld, Selected Poetry and Prose*, 2002. • Betsy Rodgers, *Georgian Chronicle: Mrs. Barbauld and her Family*, 1958.

Criticism. • Isobel Armstrong, "The Gush of the Feminine: How Can We Read Women's Poetry of the Romantic Period?" in *Romantic Women Writers*, eds. Theresa Kelley and Paula Feldman, 1995. • William Keach, "A Regency Prophecy and the End of Anna Barbauld's Career," *Studies in Romanticism*, 1994. • William McCarthy, " 'We Hoped the *Woman* Was Going to Appear': Repression, Desire, and Gender in Anna Letitia Barbauld's Early Poems," in *Romantic Women Writers*, eds. Kelley and Feldman, 1995. • William McCarthy, "The Posthumous Reception of Anna Letitia Barbauld," in Linkin and Behrendt, *Romanticism and Women Poets*, 1999. • Marlon B. Ross, "Configurations of Feminine Reform: The Woman Writer and the Tradition of Dissent," in *Revisioning Romanticism*, eds. Carol Shiner Wilson and Joel Haefner, 1994. • Jonathan Wordsworth, *The Bright Work Grows: Women Writers of the Romantic Age*, 1997.

Our Texts. • "The Mouse's Petition," "On a Lady's Writing," "Washing Day," and "Eighteen Hundred and Eleven" from *A Selection From the Poems . . . of Anna Letitia Barbauld*, ed. Grace Ellis, 1874; "Inscription for an Ice-House," "The First Fire," from *The Works of*

Anna Laetitia Barbauld, ed. Lucy Aikin, 1825; "To the Poor and "To A Little Invisible Being" from *The Poems of Anna Laetitia Barbauld*, eds. McCarthy and Kraft, 1994.

William Blake • *Biography*. • Peter Ackroyd, *Blake*, 1996. • Alexander Gilchrist, *The Life of William Blake, Pictor Ignotus*, 1863. • Mona Wilson, *The Life of William Blake*, 1927.

Illuminations. • Oxford University Press: paperback color-plate editions, with commentary by Geoffrey Keynes, of *The Songs of Innocence and of Experience*, 1967; *The Marriage of Heaven and Hell*, 1975; *Visions of the Daughters of Albion*, 1980. • Princeton University Press, of the *Songs*, 1991. All plates are reproduced in black and white photographs, with commentary, in David V. Erdman, *The Illuminated Blake*, 1974. • http://www.blakearchive.org • see also "Romantic Circles" for guidance: http://www.rc.umd.edu

Criticism. • Harold Bloom, *The Visionary Company*, 1961, rev. 1971. • Harold Bloom, *Blake's Apocalypse*, 1963, rev. 1970. • Leopold Damrosch, *Symbol and Truth in Blake's Myth*, 1980. • Jackie DiSalvo, *War of the Titans: Blake's Critique of Milton and the Politics of Religion*, 1984. • Vincent Arthur de Luca, *Words of Eternity: Blake and the Poetics of the Sublime*, 1991. • Morris Eaves, *William Blake's Theory of Art*, 1982. • Morris Eaves, *The Counter-Arts Conspiracy: Art and Industry in the Age of Blake*, 1992. • Morris Eaves, ed., *The Cambridge Companion to William Blake*, 2002. • David V. Erdman, *Blake: Prophet Against Empire*, 1969. • Robert Essick, *William Blake, Printmaker*, 1980. • Robert Essick, *William Blake and the Language of Adam*, 1989. • Michael Ferber, " 'London' and Its Politics," *ELH*, 1981. • Michael Ferber, *The Poetry of William Blake*, 1981. • Northrop Frye, *Fearful Symmetry*, 1947. • Robert Gleckner, *The Piper and the Bard*, 1959. • Heather Glen, *Vision and Disenchantment: Blake's "Songs" and Wordsworth's "Lyrical Ballads,"* 1983. • Nancy Moore Goslee, "Slavery and Sexual Character: Questioning the Master Trope in *Visions of the Daughters of Albion*," *ELH*, 1990. • Jean H. Hagstrum, *William Blake: Poet and Painter*, 1964. • Zachary Leader, *Reading Blake's Songs*, 1981. • John Mee, *Dangerous Enthusiasm: William Blake and the Culture of Radicalism in the 1790s*, 1992. • W. J. T. Mitchell, *Blake's Composite Art*, 1978. • Martin K. Nurmi, "Fact and Symbol in 'The Chimney Sweeper' of Blake's *Songs of Innocence*," *Bulletin* of the New York Public Library, 1964. • Morton Paley, Energy and the Imagination: A Study of the Development of Blake's Thought, 1970. • Mark Schorer, William Blake: the Politics of Vision, 1946. • Irene Tayler, "The Woman Scaly" [on Visions of the Daughters of Albion], 1973; repr. Norton Critical Edition of Blake's Poetry and Designs. • E. P. Thompson, Witness Against the Beast: William Blake and Moral Law, 1993. • Joseph Viscomi, Blake and the Idea of the Book, 1993. • Thomas Vogler, "'In Vain the Eloquent Tongue': An Un-Reading of Visions of the Daughters of Albion," in Blake and the Argument of Method, eds. Dan Miller, Mark Bracher, and Donald Ault, 1987.

Our Texts. • Edited for this volume with reference to the design of Blake's illuminated plates.

Edmund Burke • Biographical Studies. • Carl B. Cone, Burke and the Nature of Politics, 2 vols., 1957, 1964. • C. B. Macpherson, Burke, 1980. • Conor Cruise O'Brien, The Great Melody: A Thematic Biography and Commented Anthology of Edmund Burke, 1992.

Criticism and Context. • James T. Boulton, The Language of Politics in the Age of Wilkes and Burke, 1963. • Alfred Cobban, Edmund Burke and the Revolt Against the Eighteenth Century, 1929, repr. 1962. • Tom Furniss, Edmund Burke's Aesthetic Ideology: Language, Gender, and Political Economy in Revolution, 1993. • J. G. A. Pocock, "Burke and the Ancient Constitution: A Problem in the History of Ideas," in Politics, Language, and Time, 1971. • J. G. A. Pocock "The Political Economy of Burke's Analysis of the French Revolution," in Virtue, Commerce, and History, 1985.

Our Text. • The Works of Edmund Burke, 1894.

Robert Burns • Biographical Studies. • Raymond Bentman, Robert Burns, 1987. • David Daiches, Robert Burns and His World, 1971. • John Delancey Ferguson, Pride and Passion: Robert Burns, 1939. • James Mackay, A Biography of Robert Burns, 1992.

Editions. • John Delancey Ferguson, ed., The Letters of Robert Burns, 2 vols., rev. ed. by G. Ross Roy, 1985. • James Kinsley, ed., The Poems and Songs of Robert Burns, 3 vols., 1968.

Criticism. • Thomas Crawford, Burns: A Study of the Poems and Songs, 1960. • Thomas Crawford, ed., Robert Burns and Cultural Authority, 1997. • Leopold Damrosch, "Burns, Blake, and the Recovery of Lyric," Studies in Romanticism, 1982. • R. D. S. Jack and Andrew Noble, eds., The Art of Robert Burns, 1982. • Donald A. Low, ed., Critical Essays on Robert Burns, 1975. • Carol McGuirk, Robert Burns and the Sentimental Era, 1985.

Our Texts. • The Centenary Burns, eds. Ernest Henley and Thomas F. Henderson, 1896–1897; the second version of "Comin' Thro' the Rye" and "The Fornicator" from The Merry Muses of Caledonia, 1799–1800.

George Gordon, Lord Byron • Biography. • Benita Eisler, Byron: Child of Passion, Fool of Fame, 1999. • Leslie A. Marchand, Byron: A Biography, 3 vols., 1957; abridged and revised in one volume as Byron: A Portrait, 1970.

Editions. • E. H. Coleridge and R. E. Prothero, eds., The Works of Lord Byron, 13 vols., 1898–1904. • Leslie A. Marchand, ed., Byron's Letters and Journals, 12 vols., 1973–82. • Jerome J. McGann, ed., Lord Byron: The Complete Poetical Works, 7 vols., 1980–93. • Susan J. Wolfson and Peter J. Manning, eds., Lord Byron: Selected Poems, 1998.

Criticism. • Bernard Beatty, Byron's Don Juan, 1985. • Drummond Bone, ed., The Cambridge Companion to Byron, 2002. • Jerome Christensen, Lord Byron's Strength: Romantic Writing and Commercial Society, 1993. • Michael G. Cooke, The Blind Man Traces the Circle: On the Patterns and Philosophy of Byron's Poetry, 1969. • Louis Crompton, Byron and Greek Love, 1985. • Charles Donelan, Romanticism and Male Fantasy in Byron's "Don Juan," 2000. • Gary Dyer, "Being Flash to Don Juan," PMLA 116, 2001. • Andrew Elfenbein, Byron and the Victorians, 1995. • W. Paul Elledge, Byron and the Dynamics of Metaphor, 1968. • W. Paul Elledge, "Parting Shots: Byron Ending Don Juan I," Studies in Romanticism, 1988. • Caroline Franklin, Byron's Heroines, 1992. • Robert F. Gleckner, Byron and the Ruins of Paradise, 1967. • Robert F. Gleckner, ed., Critical Essays on Lord Byron, 1991. • Peter W. Graham, Don Juan and Regency England, 1990. • Peter Graham, Lord Byron, 1998. • Sonia Hofkosh, "Women and the Romantic Author: The Example of Byron," in Romanticism and Feminism, ed. Anne Mellor, 1988. • M. K. Joseph, Byron the Poet, 1964. • Malcolm Kelsall, Byron's Politics, 1987. • Alice Levine and Robert N. Keane, eds., Rereading Byron, 1993. • Peter J. Manning, Byron and His Fictions, 1978. • Peter J. Manning, "Don Juan and Byron's Imperceptiveness to the English

Word," *Studies in Romanticism*, 1979; repr. in his *Reading Romantics*, 1990. • Peter J. Manning, "*Don Juan* and the Revisionary Self," in *Romantic Revisions*, eds. Robert Brinkley and Keith Hanley, 1992. • Jerome J. McGann, *Byron and Wordsworth*, 1999; *Fiery Dust: Byron's Poetic Development*, 1968. • Jerome J. McGann, *Don Juan in Context*, 1976. • Jerome J. McGann, "The Book of Byron and the Book of a World," in his *The Beauty of Inflections*, 1988. • Jerome McGann, *Byron and Wordsworth*, 1999. • Donald H. Reiman, "*Don Juan* in Epic Context," in *Studies in Romanticism*, 1977, repr. in his *Romantic Texts and Contexts*, 1987 • Alan Richardson, on *Manfred*, in *A Mental Theater: Poetic Drama and Consciousness in the Romantic Age*, 1988. • George M. Ridenour, *The Style of Don Juan*, 1960. • Andrew Rutherford, *Byron: A Critical Study*, 1961. • Frederick W. Shilstone, *Byron and the Myth of Tradition*, 1988. • Stuart M. Sperry, "Byron and the Meaning of *Manfred*," *Criticism* 16, 1974. • Jane Stabler, ed., *Byron, A Longman Critical Reader*, 1998 • Peter L. Thorslev, *The Byronic Hero: Types and Prototypes*, 1962. • Francis Wilson, ed., *Byromania*, 1999. • Susan J. Wolfson, "Hemans and the Romance of Byron," in Sweet and Melnyck, eds., *Felicia Hemans: Reimagining Poetry in the Nineteenth Century*.

Our Texts. • *The Works of Lord Byron, with his Letters and Journals, and His Life*, by Thomas Moore, 1832–34; *Byron's Letters and Journals*, ed. Leslie A. Marchand, 1973–1982.

John Clare • *Biography.* • William J. Howard, *John Clare*, 1981. • Edward Storey, *A Right to Song: The Life of John Clare*, 1982. • J. W. Tibble and Anne Tibble, *John Clare: A Life*, rev. 1972.

Criticism. • John Barrell, *The Idea of Landscape and the Sense of Place, 1730–1840: An Approach to the Poetry of John Clare*, 1972. • John Goodridge and Simon Kövesi, eds., *John Clare: New Approaches*, 2000 (with complete bibliography, several essays; and a bibliography of the copyright dispute). • Hugh Haughton, Adam Phillips, and Geoffrey Summerfield, eds., *John Clare in Context*, 1994. • Elizabeth Helsinger, "Clare and the Place of the Peasant Poet," *Critical Inquiry*, 1987. • James C. McKusick, " 'A Language that is Ever Green': The Ecological Vision of John Clare," *University of Toronto Quarterly*, 1991–92. • James McCusick, *Green Writing: Romanticism and Ecology*, 2000 • James C. McKusick, "John Clare and The Tyranny of Grammar," *Studies in Romanticism*,

1994. • Mark Storey, *The Poetry of John Clare: A Critical Introduction*, 1974. • L. J. Swingle, "Stalking the Essential John Clare: Clare in Relation to His Romantic Contemporaries," *Studies in Romanticism*, 1975. • Anne Wallace, "Farming on Foot: Tracking Georgic in Clare and Wordsworth," *Texas Studies in Language and Literature*, 1992. • Sarah Zimmerman, *Romanticism, Lyricism, and History*, 1999.

Our Texts. • Eric Robinson and David Powell, eds., *John Clare*, 1984; "Written in November" also from *The Village Minstrel*, 1821.

Samuel Taylor Coleridge • *Biography.* • Rosemary Ashton, *The Life of Samuel Taylor Coleridge*, 1996. • Walter Jackson Bate, *Coleridge*, 1968. • Richard Holmes, *Coleridge: Early Visions*, 1990.

Editions. • Kathryn Coburn, ed., *The Collected Works of Samuel Taylor Coleridge*, Bollingen Series 75, 1969—. Includes (among others): *Essays on His Times*, ed. David V. Erdman, 3 vols., 1978; *Lectures 1808–19 On Literature*, ed. R. A. Foakes, 2 vols., 1987; *Lay Sermons*, ed. R. J. White, 1972; *Biographia Literaria*, ed. James Engell and Walter Jackson Bate, 2 vols., 1983; *Poetical Works*, ed. J. C. C. Mays, 3 vols. (forthcoming). • E. H. Coleridge, ed., *Complete Poetical Works*, 2 vols., 1912. • R. A. Foakes, ed., *Coleridge on Shakespeare: The Text of the Lectures of 1811–12*, 1971. • Paul H. Fry, ed., *The Rime of the Ancient Mariner*, ed. 1999 (texts and critical contexts). • E. L. Griggs, ed., *Collected Letters of Samuel Taylor Coleridge*, 6 vols., 1956–71. • William Keach, ed., *Samuel Taylor Coleridge: The Complete Poems*, 1997. • Thomas M. Raysor, ed., *Coleridge's Shakespearian Criticism*, 2 vols., 1960. • Martin Wallen, ed., *Coleridge's Ancient Mariner: An Experimental Edition of Texts and Revisions 1798–1828*, 1993.

Criticism. • M. H. Abrams, *The Mirror and the Lamp*, 1953. • J. A. Appleyard, *Coleridge's Philosophy of Literature*, 1965. • John Beer, *Coleridge the Visionary*, 1959. • John Beer, *Coleridge's Poetic Intelligence*, 1977. • Frederick Burwick, ed., *Coleridge's Biographia Literaria: Text and Meaning*, 1989. • Jerome Christensen, *Coleridge's Blessed Machine of Language*, 1981. • George Dekker, *Coleridge and the Literature of Sensibility*, 1978. • Susan Eilenberg, *Strange Power of Speech: Wordsworth, Coleridge, and Literary Possession*, 1992. • Kelvin Everest, *Coleridge's Secret Ministry: The Context of the Conversation Poems*, 1979. • Frances Ferguson, "Coleridge and the Deluded Reader: 'The Rime of the Ancient Mariner,' " *Georgia Review*, 1977. •

Norman Fruman, *Coleridge: The Damaged Archangel*, 1971. • Christine Gallant, ed., *Coleridge's Theory of Imagination Today*, 1989. • William H. Galperin, "'Desynonymizing' the Self in Wordsworth and Coleridge," *Studies in Romanticism*, 1987. • Paul Hamilton, *Coleridge's Poetics*, 1984. • Anthony John Harding, *Coleridge and the Inspired Word*, 1985. • Alethea Hayter, *Opium and the Romantic Imagination*, 1968. • William Heath, *Wordsworth and Coleridge: A Study of Their Literary Relations in 1801–02*, 1972. • Patrick Keane, *Coleridge's Submerged Politics: The Ancient Mariner and Robinson Crusoe*, 1994. • John Livingston Lowes, *The Road to Xanadu*, 1927. • Paul Magnuson, *Coleridge's Nightmare Poetry*, 1974. • Paul Magnuson, *Coleridge and Wordsworth: A Lyrical Dialogue*, 1989. • Thomas McFarland, *Coleridge and the Pantheist Tradition*, 1969. • Thomas McFarland, *Romanticism and The Forms of Ruin*, 1981. • Jerome J. McGann, "*The Ancient Mariner*: The Meaning of Meanings," in *The Beauty of Inflections*, 1985. • James C. McKusick, *Coleridge's Philosophy of Language*, 1986. • Raimonda Modiano, *Coleridge and the Concept of Nature*, 1985. • Raimonda Modiano, "Word and 'Languageless' Meaning: Limits of Expression in *The Rime of the Ancient Mariner*," *Modern Language Quarterly*, 1977. • John Morrow, *Coleridge's Political Thought: Property, Morality, and the Limits of Traditional Discourse*, 1990. • Roy Park, "Coleridge's Two Voices as a Critic of Wordsworth," *ELH*, 1969. • Reeve Parker, *Coleridge's Meditative Art*, 1975. • Arden Reed, *Romantic Weather*, 1983. • Nicholas Roe, *Wordsworth and Coleridge: The Radical Years*, 1988. • Gene W. Ruoff, *Wordsworth and Coleridge: The Making of the Major Lyrics, 1802–1804*, 1989. • Elizabeth Schneider, *Coleridge, Opium, and Kubla Khan*, 1953. • Max F. Schuli, *The Poetic Voices of Coleridge*, 1963. • Elinor Shaffer, *Coleridge, Kubla Khan, and the Fall of Jerusalem*, 1985. • Karen Swann, "Christabel: The Wandering Mother and the Enigma of Form," *Studies in Romanticism*, 1984. • Karen Swann, "Literary Gentlemen and Lovely Ladies: The Debate on the Character of *Christabel*," *ELH*, 1985. • Kathleen M. Wheeler, *Sources, Processes, and Methods in Coleridge's Biographia Literaria*, 1980.

Our Texts. • *The Complete Works of Samuel Taylor Coleridge*, ed. W. G. T. Shedd, 7 vols., 1853; "The Rime of the Ancyent Marinere" from *Lyrical Ballads*, 1798.

William Cowper • *Biography.* • David Cecil, *The Stricken Deer*, 1929. • M. J. Quinlan, *Cowper:*

A Critical Life, 1953. • Charles Ryskamp, *William Cowper of the Inner Temple*, 1959.

Editions. • John D. Baird and Charles Ryskamp, eds., *Poems of William Cowper*, 3 vols., 1980. • James King and Charles Ryskamp, eds., *Letters and Prose Writings of William Cowper*, 5 vols., 1979–86.

Criticism. • Morris Golden, *In Search of Stability: The Poetry of William Cowper*, 1960. • Vincent Newey, *Cowper's Poetry*, 1982.

Our Texts. • *Poems*, 1851.

Olaudah Equiano • *Editions.* • Angelo Costanzo, ed., *The Interesting Narrative of the Life of Olaudah Equiano* (with contextual materials), 2001. • Werner Sollors, ed., *Narrative of the Life of Olaudah Equiano* (with contextual materials and critical essays), 2001.

Criticism. • William L. Andrews, *To Tell a Free Story: The First Century of Afro-American Autobiography*, 1986. • Angelo Costanzo, *Surprizing Narrative: Olaudah Equiano and the Beginnings of Black Autobiography*, 1987. • Srinivas Aravamudan, *Tropicopolitans*, 1999. • Henry L. Gates, Jr., *The Signifying Monkey: A Theory of Afro-American Literary Criticism*, 1988. • Sonia Hofkosh, "Capitalism, Abolition, and the Romantic Individual," in *Romanticism, Race, and Imperial Culture*, ed. Hofkosh and Richardson. • Susan M. Marren, "Between Slavery and Freedom: The Transgressive Self in Olaudah Equiano's Autobiography," *PMLA*, 1993. • Dwight McBride, *Impossible Witnesses: Truth, Abolitionism, and Slave Testimony*, 2001. • Geraldine Murphy, "Olaudah Equiano, Accidental Tourist," *Eighteenth-Century Studies*, 1994. • Adam Potkay, "Olaudah Equiano and the Art of Spiritual Autobiography," *Eighteenth-Century Studies*, 1994.

Our Text. • *The Life of Olaudah Equiano*, 1814.

Felicia Hemans • *Editions.* • Paula R. Feldman, *Records of Woman With Other Poems*, 1999. • Susan J. Wolfson, ed., *Felicia Hemans: Selected Poems, Letters, & Reception Materials*, 2000.

Biography. • Henry F. Chorley, *Memorials of Mrs. Hemans, with Illustrations of Her Literary Character from Her Private Correspondence*, 1836. • [Harriett Mary Hughes {Browne}; later Owen], *Memoir of the Life and Writings of Felicia Hemans: By Her Sister*, 1845. • Peter W. Trinder, *Mrs. Hemans*, 1984.

Criticism. • Isobel Armstrong, *Victorian Poetry: Poetry, Poetics and Politics*, 1993. • Norma

Clarke, *Ambitious Heights: Writing, Friendship, Love*, 1990. • George Gilfillan, "Female Authors. No. I–Mrs. Hemans," *Tait's Edinburgh Magazine*, 1847. • Anthony John Harding, "Felicia Hemans and the Effacement of Woman," in *Romantic Women Writers*, eds. Theresa Kelley and Paula Feldman, 1995. • Angela Leighton, *Victorian Woman Poets: Writing Against the Heart*, 1993. • Tricia Lootens, "Hemans and Home: Victorianism, Feminine 'Internal Enemies,' and the Domestication of National Identity," *PMLA*, 1994. • Jerome J. McGann, "Literary History, Romanticism, and Felicia Hemans," in *Revisioning Romanticism*, eds. Carol Shiner Wilson and Joel Haefner, 1994. • Anne Mellor, *Romanticism and Gender*, 1993. • Nanora Sweet and Julie Melnyck, eds., *Felicia Hemans: Reimagining Poetry in the Nineteenth Century*, 2001. • Herbert F. Tucker, "House Arrest: The Domestication of English Poetry in the 1820s," *ELH*, 1994. • Susan J. Wolfson, "'Domestic Affections' and 'the Spear of Minerva': Felicia Hemans and the Dilemma of Gender," in *Revisioning Romanticism*, eds. Wilson and Haefner, 1994. • Susan J. Wolfson, "Gendering the Soul," in *Romantic Women Writers*, eds. Kelley and Feldman, 1995. • Jonathan Wordsworth, *The Bright Work Grows: Women Writers of the Romantic Age*, 1997.

Our Texts. • All lifetime editions, for which see *Felicia Hemans*, ed. Wolfson.

Francis Jeffrey • *Biography.* • Henry Cockburn, *Life of Lord Jeffrey*, 2 vols., 1852.

Editions. • Francis Jeffrey, *Contributions to the Edinburgh Review*, 4 vols., 1844.

Criticism. • David Bromwich, "Romantic Poetry and the *Edinburgh* Ordinances," *Yearbook of English Studies*, 1986. • Jerome Christensen, "The Detection of the Romantic Conspiracy in Britain," *South Atlantic Quarterly*, 1996. • John Clive, *Scotch Reviewers: The Edinburgh Review 1802–1815*, 1957. • Philip Flynn, *Francis Jeffrey*, 1978. • Peter F. Morgan, *Literary Critics and Reviewers in Early 19th Century Britain*, 1983. • Mark Schoenfield, "Regulating Standards: The *Edinburgh Review* and the Circulations of Judgement," *The Wordsworth Circle*, 1993. • Kim Wheatley, "Paranoid Politics: The *Quarterly* and *Edinburgh* Reviews," *Prose Studies*, 1992.

Our Texts. • *Edinburgh Review*, 1 (October 1802), and 24 (November 1814).

John Keats • *Biography and Reception.* • Walter Jackson Bate, *John Keats*, 1963. • George H. Ford, *Keats and the Victorians: A Study of His Influence and Rise to Fame 1821–1895*, 1944. • G. M. Matthews, ed., *Keats: The Critical Heritage*, 1971. • Andrew Motion, *Keats*, 1998. • Aileen Ward, *John Keats: The Making of a Poet*, 1963. • Susan J. Wolfson, "Feminizing Keats," in *Critical Essays on John Keats*, ed. Hermione de Almeida, 1990.

Criticism. • John Barnard, *John Keats*, 1987. • Walter Jackson Bate, *The Stylistic Development of Keats*, 1945. • John Bayley, "Keats and Reality," *Proceedings of the British Academy*, 1962. • Cleanth Brooks, "Keats's Sylvan Historian: History without Footnotes," in *The Well Wrought Urn: Studies in the Structure of Poetry*, 1947. • Douglas Bush, *John Keats: His Life and Writings*, 1966. • Morris Dickstein, *Keats and His Poetry*, 1971. • Stuart Ende, *Keats and the Sublime*, 1976. • Geoffrey Hartman, "Spectral Symbolism and Authorial Self," in *The Fate of Reading*, 1975. • Wolf Z. Hirst, *John Keats*, 1981. • Margaret Homans, "Keats Reading Women, Women Reading Keats," *Studies in Romanticism*, 1990. • John Jones, *John Keats's Dream of Truth*, 1969. • William Keach, "Cockney Couplets: Keats and the Politics of Style," *Studies in Romanticism*, 1986. • Robert Kern, "Keats and the Problem of Romance," *Philological Quarterly*, 1979. • Marjorie Levinson, *Keats's Life of Allegory*, 1988. • Jerome J. McGann, "Keats and the Historical Method in Literary Criticism," 1979, repr. in *The Beauty of Inflections*, 1985. • Christopher Ricks, *Keats and Embarrassment*, 1976. • Jeffrey Robinson, *Reception and Poetics in Keats*, 1998. • Nicholas Roe, *John Keats and the Culture of Dissent*, 1997. • Stuart M. Sperry, *Keats the Poet*, 1973. • Jack Stillinger, "Imagination and Reality in the Odes" and "The Hoodwinking of Madeline," in *"The Hoodwinking of Madeline" and Other Essays on Keats's Poems*, 1971. • Karen Swann, "Harrassing the Muse," in *Romanticism and Feminism*, Anne Mellor, ed. 1988. • Helen Vendler, *The Odes of John Keats*, 1983. • Leon Waldoff, *Keats and the Silent Work of Imagination*, 1985. • Daniel P. Watkins, *Keats's Poetry and the Politics of the Imagination*, 1989. • Susan J. Wolfson, "Keats and the Manhood of the Poet," *European Romantic Review*, 1995. • Susan J. Wolfson, *The Questioning Presence: Wordsworth, Keats, and the Interrogative Mode in Romantic Poetry*, 1986. • Susan J. Wolfson, ed., *The Cambridge Companion to John Keats*, 2001.

Our Texts. • Poems published in Keats's lifetime are from first editions; posthumous publications are from Houghton's *Poetical Works*, 1891, checked against *The Poems of John Keats*, ed. Jack Stillinger, 1978, the best modern edition. • *The Letters of John Keats*, *1814–1821*, ed. Hyder E. Rollins, 1958.

Charles Lamb • *Biography.* • David Cecil, *A Portrait of Charles Lamb*, 1983. • Winifred F. Courtney, *Young Charles Lamb 1775–1802*, 1982. • E. V. Lucas, *Life of Charles Lamb*, rev. ed., 2 vols., 1921.

Editions. • E. V. Lucas, ed., *The Works of Charles and Mary Lamb*, 1903–1905. • E. W. Marrs, ed., *The Letters of Charles and Mary Anne Lamb*, 3 vols., 1975—.

Critical Studies. • Jane Aaron, *A Double Singleness: Gender and the Writing of Charles and Mary Lamb*, 1991. • George L. Barnett, *Charles Lamb*, 1976. • Robert Frank, *Don't Call Me Gentle Charles!*, 1976. • Richard Haven, "The Romantic Art of Charles Lamb," *ELH*, 1963. • Alison Hickey, "Double Bonds: Charles Lamb's Romantic Collaborations," *ELH*, 1996. • Gerald Monsman, *Confessions of a Prosaic Dreamer: Charles Lamb's Art of Autobiography*, 1984. • John Nabholtz, "My Reader My Fellow-Labourer": A Study of English Romantic Prose, 1986. • Roy Park, "Lamb, Shakespeare, and the Stage," *Shakespeare Quarterly*, 1982. • Mark Parker, " 'A Piece of Autobiography'; Reference in Charles Lamb's Essays," *Auto/Biography Studies*, 1986–1987. • Mark Parker, "Ideology and Editing: The Political Context of the Elia Essays," *Studies in Romanticism*, 1991. • F. V. Randel, *The World of Elia*, 1975. • See also the entry for Mary Lamb.

Our Texts. • *The Works of Charles and Mary Lamb*, ed. E. V. Lucas, 1903–1905.

Catherine Macaulay • *Criticism.* • Bridget Hill, *Republican Virago: The Life and Times of Catherine Macaulay*, 1992. • Jonathan Wordsworth, *The Bright Work Grows: Women Writers of the Romantic Age*, 1997.

Our Text. • *Letters on Education, With Observations on Religious and Metaphysical Subjects* (1790). Reprinted in *Feminist Controversy in England, 1788–1810*, ed. Gina Luria, 1974; excerpts from letters 4 and 21, and all of letters 22 and 23 are included in *A Vindication of the Rights of Woman*, ed. Carol Poston, 2nd ed. 1988.

Hannah More • *Biography.* • M. G. Jones, *Hannah More*, 1952. • W. Roberts, *Memoirs of the Life and Correspondence of Mrs. Hannah More*, 1834. • Mary Alden Hopkins, *Hannah More and Her Circle*, 1947.

Criticism. • Elizabeth Kowaleski-Wallace, *Their Fathers' Daughters: Hannah More, Maria Edgeworth and Patriarchal Complicity*, 1991. • Anne K. Mellor, *Mothers of the Nahm*, 2001. • Mitzi Myers, "Hannah More's Tracts for the Times: Social Fiction and Female Ideology," *Fetter'd or Free: British Women Novelists, 1670–1815*, eds. Mary Anne Schofield and Cecelia Macheski, 1986. • Alan Richardson, *Literature, Education, and Romanticism*, 1994. • G. H. Spinney, "Cheap Repository Tracts," in *The Library*, 1939. • Jonathan Wordsworth, *The Bright Work Grows: Women Writers of the Romantic Age*, 1997.

Our Texts. • *Village Politics*, 1792; *The Works of Hannah More*, 1830.

Thomas Paine • A. J. Ayer, *Thomas Paine*, 1988. • Eric Foner, *Thomas Paine and Revolutionary America*, 1976. • David F. Hawke, *Thomas Paine*, 1974. • John Keane, *Thomas Paine: A Political Life*, 1995. • Mark Philp, *Paine*, 1989.

Our Text. • *The Rights of Man*, 1790.

Thomas Percy • *Biographical Studies.* • Bertram H. Davis, *Thomas Percy*, 1981. • Bertram H. Davis, *Thomas Percy: A Scholar-Cleric in the Age of Johnson*, 1989.

Criticism. • William H. Matchett, "The Integrity of 'Sir Patrick Spence,' " *Modern Philology*, 1970. • Kathryn Sutherland, "The Native Poet: The Influence of Percy's Minstrel from Beattie to Wordsworth," *Review of English Studies*, 1982.

Our Text. • *Reliques of Ancient English Poetry*, 2 vols., 1906.

Mary Prince • Moira Ferguson, ed., *The History of Mary Prince*, 1987. • Moira Ferguson, *Subject to Others: British Women Writers and Colonial Slavery, 1670–1834*, 1992. • Jenny Sharpe, " 'Something Akin to Freedom': The Case of Mary Prince," in *Differences*, 1996.

Our Text. • *History of Mary Prince*, 1831.

Mary Robinson • *Edition.* • Judith Pascoe, ed., *Mary Robinson, Selected Poems*, 2000; with reception materials.

Biography. • Robert D. Bass, *The Green Dragoon: The Lives of Banastre Tarleton and Mary Robinson*, 1957. • Mary Robinson, *Memoirs of the Late Mrs. Robinson, Written by Herself: With Some Posthumous Pieces*, 1801. • Marguerite Steen, *The Lost One: A Biography of Mary (Perdita) Robinson*, 1937.

Criticism. • Stuart Curran, "Mary Robinson's *Lyrical Tales* in Context," in *Revisioning Romanticism*, ed. Carol Shiner Wilson and Joel Haefner, 1994. • Jerome McGann, *The Poetics of Sensibility* (ch. 10), 1996. • Judith Pascoe, *Romantic Theatricality* (ch. 5 and 6), 1995. • Daniel Robinson, "From 'Mingled Measure' to 'Ecstatic Measures': Mary Robinson's Poetic Reading of 'Kubla Khan,'" *The Wordsworth Circle*, 1995. • Jonathan Wordsworth, *The Bright Work Grows: Women Writers of the Romantic Age*, 1997.

Our Texts. • "The Haunted Beach," *Lyrical Tales* (1800); repr. Woodstock Press. Other poems: *Sappho and Phaon*, 1796; "The Camp" repr. in Jerome McGann, ed., *The New Oxford Book of Romantic Period Verse*, 1993; *Poetical Works of the Late Mrs. Mary Robinson*, 1806 (repr. 1824); "To the Poet Coleridge" (1801).

Criticism. • Sonia Hofkosh, "Mary Shelley's Gift-Book Stories," in *Sexual Politics and the Romantic Author*, 1998. • Peter J. Manning, "Wordsworth in the *Keepsake*, 1829," in *Literature in the Marketplace*, eds. John O. Jordan and Robert L. Patten, 1995. • Judith Pascoe, "Mary Shelley in the Annuals," *Mary Shelley in Her Times*, ed. Betty T. Bennett and Stuart Curran, 1999.

Percy Bysshe Shelley • *Biography.* • Kenneth Neill Cameron, *The Young Shelley*, 1950. • Richard Holmes, *Shelley: The Pursuit*, 1974. • Newman Ivey White, *Shelley*, 1940.

Editions. • Kelvin Everest and Geoffrey Matthews, *The Poems of Shelley*, 1989, 1999. • Donald Reiman and Neil Fraistat, eds., *The Complete Poetry of Percy Bysshe Shelley*, v. 1, 2000; more volumes to follow. • Donald Reiman and Neil Fraistat, eds., *Shelley's Poetry and Prose*. 2d edn, 2002; texts and critical essays.

Reception. • Mark Kipperman, "Absorbing a Revolution: Shelley Becomes a Romantic, 1889–1903," in *Nineteenth-Century Literature*, 1992. • Sylva Norman, *The Flight of the Skylark*, 1954. • N. I. White, *The Unextinguish'd Hearth*, 1938.

General Criticism. • Stephen C. Behrendt, *Shelley and His Audiences*, 1989. • Harold Bloom, *Shelley's Mythmaking*, 1959. • Judith Chernaik, *The Lyrics of Shelley*, 1972. • Frances Ferguson, "Shelley's *Mont Blanc*: What the Mountain Said," in *Romanticism and Language*, ed. Arden Reed, 1984. • Paul Foot, *Red Shelley*, 1980. • Jerrold Hogle, *Shelley's Process*, 1988. • William C. Keach, *Shelley's Style*, 1984. • Angela Leighton, *Shelley and the Sublime*, 1984. • Donald H. Reiman, *Percy Bysshe Shelley*, 1990. • Hugh Roberts, *Shelley and the Chaos of History*, 1997. • Michael Henry Scrivener, *Radical Shelley*, 1982. • Stuart Sperry, *Shelley's Major Verse*, 1988. • Earl R. Wasserman, *Shelley: A Critical Reading*, 1981. • Milton Wilson, *Shelley's Later Poetry*, 1959. • Ross G. Woodman, *The Apocalyptic Vision in the Poetry of Shelley*, 1964.

On The Mask of Anarchy. • *The Masque of Anarchy, A Poem*, with Preface by Leigh Hunt (1832), facsimile repr. ed. Jonathan Wordsworth, 1990. • Stuart Curran, *Shelley's Annus Mirabilis: The Maturing of an Epic Vision*, 1975. • Thomas R. Edwards, *Imagination and Power: A Study of Poetry on Public Themes*, 1971. • Stephen Goldsmith, *Unbinding Jerusalem: Apocalypse and Romantic Imagination*, 1993. • Donald H. Reiman, *"The Mask of Anarchy": A Facsimile Edition*, with Scholarly Introductions, Bibliographical Descriptions, and Annotations, 1985. • E. P. Thompson, *The Making of the English Working Class*, 1964. • Susan J. Wolfson, *Formal Charges*, 1997.

On Adonais. • James A. W. Heffernan, "*Adonais*: Shelley's Consumption of Keats," *Studies in Romanticism*, 1984. • Susan J. Wolfson, "Keats Enters History: Autopsy, Adonais, and the Fame of Keats," in *Keats and History*, ed. Nicholas Roe, 1994.

Our Texts. • *The Complete Poetical Works of Percy Bysshe Shelley*, ed. William Michael Rossetti, 1881, checked against modern editions; *The Mask of Anarchy* is checked against Reiman's 1985 facsimile edition of the 1819 *The Mask of Anarchy*.

Charlotte Smith • *Biography.* • Lorraine Fletcher, *Charlotte Smith: A Critical Biography*, 1998.

Editions. • *The Poems of Charlotte Smith*, ed. Stuart Curran, 1993.

Criticism. • Stuart Curran, "Charlotte Smith and British Romanticism," *South Central Review* 11.2, 1994. • Paula Feldman, headnote in *British Women Poets of the Romantic Era*,

1997. • Bishop C. Hunt, "Wordsworth and Charlotte Smith," *The Wordsworth Circle*, 1970. • Judith Pascoe, "Female Botanists and the Poetry of Charlotte Smith," in *Revisioning Romanticism*, eds. Carol Shiner Wilson and Joel Haefner, 1994. • Adela Pinch, *Strange Fits of Passion*, 1996. • Sarah Zimmerman, *Romanticism, Lyricism, and History*, 1999; and "Charlotte Smith and the Lyric's Audience," in Linkin and Behrendt, *Romanticism and Women Poets*, 1999.

Our Text. • *Elegiac Sonnets*, 5th ed., 1789.

William Thompson and Anna Wheeler • *Text, Biography.* • Richard Pankhurst's edition of *Appeal*, 1983; Pankhurst has also written a biography of Thompson, 1954.

Criticism (Wheeler). • Stephen Burke, "Letter from a Pioneer Feminist," *Studies in Labour History*, 1976. • Richard Pankhurst, "Anna Wheeler; A Pioneer Socialist and Feminist," *Philological Quarterly*, 1954.

Helen Maria Williams • *Edition.* • Neil Fraistat and Susan S. Lanser, eds., *Helen Maria Williams, Letters Written in France*, 2001 (with reviews and other contextual materials)

Criticism. • M. Ray Adams, "Helen Maria Williams and the French Revolution," *Wordsworth and Coleridge*, ed. Earl Leslie Griggs, 1939. • Mary Favret, *Romantic Correspondence: Women, Politics, and the Fiction of Letters*, 1993. • Chris Jones, "Helen Maria Williams and Radical Sensibility," *Prose Studies*, 1989. • Nicola Watson, *Revolution and the Form of the British Novel, 1790–1825*, 1994.

Our Texts. • *Letters from France*, 1790, 1796.

Mary Wollstonecraft • *Biography.* • Pamela Clemit and Gina Luria Walker, *Memoirs of the Author of A Vindication of the Rights of Woman, by William Godwin*, 2001. • William Godwin, *Memoirs of the Author of a Vindication of the Rights of Woman*, 1798 • Gary Kelly, *Revolutionary Feminism: The Mind and Career of Mary Wollstonecraft*, 1992. • Jennifer Lorch, *Mary Wollstonecraft: The Making of a Radical Feminist*, 1990. • Emily Sunstein, *A Different Face—The Life of Mary Wollstonecraft*, 1975. • Janet Todd, *Mary Wollstonecraft: A Revolutionary Life*, 2000. • Claire Tomalin, *The Life and Death of Mary Wollstonecraft*, 1974.

Criticism. • Claudia L. Johnson, ed., *The Cambridge Companion to Mary Wollstonecraft*, 2002. •

Claudia Johnson, *Equivocal Beings: Politics, Gender, and Sentimentality in the 1790s*, 1995. • Anne K. Mellor, *Romanticism and Gender*, 1993. • Ellen Moers, *Literary Women: The Great Writers*, 1963. • Mary Poovey, *The Proper Lady and the Woman Writer*, 1984. • In Carol Poston's edition are included appreciations by George Eliot, 1855; Emma Goldman, c. 1910; and Virginia Woolf, 1932; as well as Ferdinand Lundberg and Marynia Farnham's notorious "Mary Wollstonecraft and the Psychopathology of Feminism," 1947; and helpful essays by (among others) Carolyn W. Korsmeyer, "Reason and Morals in the Early Feminist Movement," 1976; Elissa Guralnick on radical politics in *Rights of Woman*, 1977; R. M. Janes, on the reception of *Rights of Woman*, 1978; and Mitzi Myers, "Reform or Ruin," 1982. • Timothy J. Reiss, "Revolution in Bounds: Wollstonecraft, Women, and Reason," in *Gender and Theory: Dialogues on Feminist Criticism*, ed. Linda Kauffman, 1989. • Virginia Sapiro, *A Vindication of Political Virtue: The Political Theory of Mary Wollstonecraft*, 1992. • Nicola Trott, "Sexing the Critic: Mary Wollstonecraft at the Turn of the Century," in Richard Cronin, ed., *1798: The Year of the "Lyrical Ballads,"* 1998. • Orrin Wang, "The Other Reasons," *Yale Journal of Criticism*, 1991.

On Vindication of the Rights of Men • Gary Kelly, "Mary Wollstonecraft as Vir Bonus," *English Studies in Canada*, 1979. • Mitzi Myers, "Politics from the Outside," *Studies in Eighteenth-Century Culture*, 1977.

On Maria, or the Wrongs of Woman. • Moira Ferguson, Introduction to the Norton edition, 1975. • Gary Kelly, Introduction to the Oxford edition, 1976; related remarks in *The English Jacobin Novel 1780–1805*, 1976, and *English Fiction of the Romantic Period 1789–1830*, 1989. • Anne K. Mellor, "Righting the Wrongs of Woman: Mary Wollstonecraft's *Maria*," *Nineteenth-Century Contexts* 19, 1996. • Tilottama Rajan, "Wollstonecraft and Godwin: Reading the Secrets of the Political Novel," *Studies in Romanticism*, 1988.

Our Texts. • *A Vindication of the Rights of Men, in a Letter to the Right Honourable Edmund Burke; Occasioned by His "Reflections on the Revolution in France,"* 2nd ed., 1790; *Vindication of the Rights of Woman*, ed. Carol Poston, 2nd ed., 1988; *Maria or the Wrongs of Woman* from William Godwin's edition in *The Posthumous Works*, 1798; repr. Norton, 1975.

Dorothy Wordsworth • *Biographies.* • Catherine Macdonald Maclean, *Dorothy and William Wordsworth*, 1927. • Robert Gittings and Jo Manton, *Dorothy Wordsworth*, 1985.

Editions. • Susan Levin, *The Collected Poems of Dorothy Wordsworth*, in *Dorothy Wordsworth & Romanticism*, 1987. • Ernest de Selincourt, ed., *Journals of Dorothy Wordsworth*, 1941. • Mary Moorman, ed., *Journals of Dorothy Wordsworth* (Alfoxden and Grasmere), 1971. • Pamela Woof, ed., *The Grasmere Journals*, 1991. • Alan G. Hill, ed., *Letters of Dorothy Wordsworth*, 1981.

Criticism. • Rachael Brownstein, "The Private Life," *Modern Language Quarterly* 34, 1971. • Robert Con Davis, "The Structure of the Picturesque: Dorothy Wordsworth's Journals," *The Wordsworth Circle* 9, 1978. • Thomas De Quincey, "Recollections of Grasmere," *Tait's Edinburgh Magazine*, 1839, reprinted in various collected works. • Kurt Heinzelman, "The Cult of Domesticity: Dorothy and William Wordsworth at Grasmere," in *Romanticism & Feminism*, ed. Mellor (above). • Margaret Homans, *Women Writers and Poetic Identity*, 1980; and *Bearing the Word: Language and Female Experience in Nineteenth-Century Women's Writing*, 1986. • Susan M. Levin, *Dorothy Wordsworth & Romanticism*, 1987. • Alan Liu, "On the Autobiographical Present: Dorothy Wordsworth's Grasmere Journals," *Criticism* 26, 1984. • Susan J. Wolfson, "Individual in Community," in *Romanticism & Feminism*, ed. Mellor (above). • Virginia Woolf, "Dorothy Wordsworth," *The Second Common Reader*, 1932.

Our texts. • Levin's *Poems.* • Moorman's *Journals*, with reference to Woof's. • Hill's *Letters.*

William Wordsworth • *Biography and Reference.* • Stephen Gill, *Wordsworth: A Life*, 1989. • John L. Mahoney, *William Wordsworth: A Poetic Life*, 1997. • Mary Moorman, *William Wordsworth: A Biography*, 2 vols., 1957–1965. • Mark L. Reed, *Wordsworth: The Chronology of the Early Years, 1770–1799*, 1967. • Mark L. Reed, *Wordsworth: The Chronology of the Middle Years, 1800–1815*, 1975. • Duncan Wu, *Wordsworth's Reading 1779–1799*, 1993. • Duncan Wu, *Wordsworth's Reading 1800–1815*, 1995.

Biography and Criticism. • Kenneth R. Johnston, *The Hidden Wordsworth*, 1998. • Duncan Wu, *Wordsworth: An Inner Life*, 2002.

Editions. • R. L. Brett, and A. R. Jones, eds., *Wordsworth and Coleridge: Lyrical Ballads*, 1968. • Beth Darlington, ed., *The Love Letters of William and Mary Wordsworth*, 1981. • Ernest de Selincourt, ed., *The Letters of William and Dorothy Wordsworth*, 2nd ed. rev.: *Early Years, 1787–1805*, ed. Chester L. Shaver, 1967; *Middle Years, Part 1, 1806–1811*, ed. Mary Moorman, 1969, *Part 2, 1812–1820*, ed. Alan G. Hill, 1970; *Later Years, Part 1, 1821–1828*, 1978, *Part 2, 1829–1834*, 1979, *Part 3, 1835–1839*, 1982, and *Part 4, 1840–1853*, 1988, all ed. Alan G. Hill. • Michael Mason, ed., *Lyrical Ballads*, 1992. • W. J. B. Owen and Jane Worthington Smyser, eds., *The Prose Works of William Wordsworth*, 3 vols., 1974. • Stephen Parrish, gen. ed., *The Cornell Wordsworth*, 1975–. This series, based on Wordsworth's earliest texts, thus far includes (among others): *The Prelude, 1798–1799*, ed. Stephen Parrish, 1977; *Poems, in Two Volumes and Other Poems 1800–1807*, ed. Jared Curtis, 1983; *The Fourteen-Book Prelude*, ed. W. J. B. Owen, 1985; *The Thirteen-Book Prelude*, ed. Mark L. Reed, 2 vols., 1991; *Shorter Poems, 1807–1820*, ed. Carl H. Ketcham, 1989; *Lyrical Ballads, and Other Poems, 1797–1800*, ed. James Butler and Karen Green, 1992. • Jonathan Wordsworth, M. H. Abrams, and Stephen Gill, eds., *The Prelude 1799, 1805, 1850*, 1979. • Ernest de Selincourt and Helen Darbishire, eds., *The Poetical Works of William Wordsworth*, 5 vols., 1940–1949. [Based on Wordsworth's final texts.]

Criticism. • Jonathan Arac, "Bounding Lines: *The Prelude* and Critical Revision," *boundary 2*, 1979. • James Averill, *Wordsworth and the Poetry of Human Suffering*, 1980. • Alan Bewell, *Wordsworth and the Enlightenment*, 1989. • Don Bialostosky, *Making Tales: The Poetics of Wordsworth's Narrative Experiments*, 1988. • James K. Chandler, *Wordsworth's Second Nature: A Study of the Poetry and Politics*, 1984. • David Collings, *Wordsworthian Errancies*, 1994. • Jared Curtis, *Wordsworth's Experiments with Tradition: The Lyric Poems of 1802*, 1971. • Paul de Man, "Time and History in Wordsworth," *Diacritics*, 1987. • David Ellis, *Wordsworth, Freud, and the Spots of Time*, 1985. • Elizabeth Fay, *Becoming Wordsworthian*, 1995. • Frances Ferguson, *Wordsworth: Language as Counter-Spirit*, 1977. • William H. Galperin, *Revision and Authority in Wordsworth*, 1989. • Frederick Garber, *Wordsworth and the Poetry of Encounter*, 1971. • George Gilpin, ed., *Critical Essays on William Wordsworth*, 1990. • Heather Glen, *Vision and*

Disenchantment: Blake's Songs and Wordsworth's Lyrical Ballads, 1983. • Alan Grob, The Philosophic Mind: A Study of Wordsworth's Poetry and Thought 1797–1805, 1973. • Geoffrey Hartman, Wordsworth's Poetry 1787–1814, 1964; repr. rev. 1971. • Geoffrey Hartman, The Unremarkable Wordsworth, 1987. • James A. W. Heffernan, Wordsworth's Theory of Poetry, 1969. • James Heffernan, "Wordsworth's 'Levelling' Muse in 1798," in 1798: The Year of the "Lyrical Ballads," ed. Richard Cronin, 1998. • Mary Jacobus, Romanticism, Writing, and Sexual Difference: Essays on The Prelude, 1989. • Mary Jacobus, Tradition and Experiment in Wordsworth's Lyrical Ballads, 1976. • Kenneth R. Johnston, Wordsworth and The Recluse, 1984. • Kenneth R. Johnston, "The Politics of 'Tintern Abbey,'" The Wordsworth Circle, 1983. • Kenneth R. Johnston and Gene W. Ruoff, eds., The Age of William Wordsworth, 1987. • John E. Jordan, Why the Lyrical Ballads?, 1976. • Theresa M. Kelley, Wordsworth's Revisionary Aesthetics, 1988. • J. Douglas Kneale, Monumental Writing: Aspects of Rhetoric in Wordsworth's Poetry, 1988. • Marjorie Levinson, Wordsworth's Great Period Poems, 1986. • Herbert Lindenberger, On Wordsworth's Prelude, 1963. • Alan Liu, Wordsworth: The Sense of History, 1989. • Peter J. Manning, Reading Romantics, 1990. • Richard J. Onorato, The Character of the Poet: Wordsworth in The Prelude, 1971. • Judith W. Page, Wordsworth and the Cultivation of Women, 1994. • Stephen M. Parrish, The Art of the Lyrical Ballads, 1973. • David Perkins, The Quest for Permanence: The Symbolism of Wordsworth, Shelley, and Keats, 1959. • Adela Pinch, "Female Chatter: Gender and Feeling in Wordsworth's Early Poetry," in Strange Fits of Passion, 1996. • Jeffrey C. Robinson, Radical Literary Education: A Classroom Experiment with Wordsworth's 'Ode', 1987. • Paul D. Sheats, The Making of Wordsworth's Poetry 1785–1798, 1973. • David Simpson, Wordsworth and the Figurings of the Real, 1982. • David Simpson, Wordsworth's Historical Imagination: The Poetry of Displacement, 1987. • Gayatri C. Spivak, "Sex and History in The Prelude (1805): Books Nine to Thirteen," Texas Studies in Language and Literature, 1981. • Keith G. Thomas, Wordsworth and Philosophy, 1989. • Douglas B. Wilson, The Romantic Dream: Wordsworth and the Poetics of the Unconscious, 1993. • Susan J. Wolfson, The Questioning Presence, 1986. • Jonathan Wordsworth, William Wordsworth: The Borders of Vision, 1982. • For the relations of Wordsworth and Coleridge, see also the entry under Samuel Taylor Coleridge.

Our Texts. • Lyrical Ballads, 1798; Complete Poetical Works, 1892, 1898, and 1911; The Thirteen-Book Prelude, ed. Mark L. Reed; The Excursion (1814); letter to Mary Ann Rawson from The Letters of William and Dorothy Wordsworth, 2nd ed., Later Years, Part 2, ed. Alan G. Hill, 1979.

The Victorian Period

Bibliographies • Brahma Chaudhuri, ed., Annual Bibliography of Victorian Studies, 1976–. • Brahma Chaudhuri, ed., A Comprehensive Bibliography of Victorian Studies, 1970–1984, 3 vols. • Modern Language Association International Bibliography, online. • David Nicholls, Nineteenth-Century Britain, 1815–1914. 1978. • Victorian Poetry. Annual "Guide to the Year's Work on Victorian Poetry." 1963–. • Studies in English Literature. Annual review of "Recent Studies in the Nineteenth Century" (autumn issue), 1961–. • Victorian Studies. Annual "Victorian Bibliography" (summer issue), 1957–.

Guides to Research • David J. DeLaura, Victorian Prose: A Guide to Research, 1973. • Frederic E. Faverty, The Victorian Poets: A Guide, to Research, 2nd ed., 1968. • Lionel Madden, How to Find Out About the Victorian Period, 1970. • Lionel Stevenson, ed. Victorian Fiction: A Guide to Research, 1964; supplemented by Victorian Fiction: A Second Guide to Research, ed. George H. Ford, 1978.

Cultural and Intellectual Background • Richard D. Altick, Victorian People and Ideas, 1973. • Asa Briggs, Victorian People: A Reassessment of Persons and Themes 1851–67, 1965. • Asa Briggs, Victorian Things, 1988. • Jerome H. Buckley, The Victorian Temper: A Study in Literary Culture, 1951. • Jerome H. Buckley, The Triumph of Time: A Study of the Victorian Concepts of Time, History, Progress, and Decadence, 1966. • David Cannadine, The Decline and Fall of the British Aristocracy, 1990. • A. Dwight Culler, The Victorian Mirror of History, 1985. • David J. Delaura, Hebrew and Hellene in Victorian England: Newman, Arnold, and Pater, 1969. • Peter Gay, The Bourgeois Experience: From Victoria to Freud, 2 vols., 1984–1986. • Robin Gilmour, The Victorian Period: The Intellectual and Cultural Context of English Literature, 1830–1890, 1993. • Christopher Herbert, Culture and Anomie: Ethnographic Imagination in the Nineteenth Century, 1991. • Thomas William Heyck, The Transformation of Intellectual Life in Victorian England, 1982. • Walter E. Houghton, The Victorian Frame of Mind, 1830–1870, 1957. • Richard Jenkyns, The Victorians and Ancient Greece, 1980. • Steven Marcus, The Other Victorians: A Study of Sexuality and Pornography in Mid-Nineteenth-Century England, 1964. • Sally Mitchell, ed., Victorian Britain: An Encyclopedia, 1988. • E. Royston Pike, ed., "Hard Times": Human Documents of the Industrial Revolution, 1966; "Golden Times": Human Documents of the Victorian Age, 1967; "Busy Times": Human Documents of the Age of the Forsytes, 1969. • Mary Poovey, Making a Social Body: British Cultural Formation, 1830–1864, 1995. • Thomas Richards, The Commodity Culture of Victorian England: Advertising and Spectacle, 1851–1914, 1990. • Edward Said, Orientalism, 1978. • Richard L. Stein, Victoria's Year: English Literature and Culture, 1837–1838, 1987. • George W. Stocking, Victorian Anthropology, 1987. • Herbert Sussman, Victorians and the Machine, 1968. • Herbert F. Tucker, ed., A Companion to Victorian Literature and Culture, 1999. • Frank M. Turner, Contesting Cultural Authority: Essays in Victorian Intellectual Life, 1993. • Basil Willey, Nineteenth Century Studies, 1949. • Basil Willey, More Nineteenth Century Studies, 1956. • Raymond Williams, Culture and Society 1780–1950, 1958. • Janet Wolff and John Seed, eds., The Culture of Capital: Art, Power and the Nineteenth-Century Middle Class, 1988. • G. M. Young, Victorian England: Portrait of an Age, 1936.

Fiction • Richard D. Altick, The Presence of the Present: Topics of the Day in the Victorian Novel, 1991. • Nancy Armstrong, Desire and Domestic Fiction: A Political History of the Novel, 1987. • Joseph W. Childers, Novel Possibilities: Fiction and the Formation of Early Victorian Culture, 1995. • Deirdre David, ed., The Cambridge Companion to the Victorian Novel, 2001. • Peter Garrett, The Victorian Multiplot Novel,

1980. • Barbara Hardy, Forms of Feeling in Victorian Fiction, 1985. • E. A. Horsman, The Victorian Novel, 1991. • George Levine, The Realistic Imagination: English Fiction from Frankenstein to Lady Chatterley, 1981. • D. A. Miller, The Novel and the Police, 1988. • J. Hillis Miller, The Form of Victorian Fiction, 1968. • Ira B. Nadel and William E. Fredeman, eds., Victorian Novelists Before 1885, in Dictionary of Literary Biography, vol. 21, 1983. • Robert Polhemus, Erotic Faith: Being in Love from Jane Austen to D. H. Lawrence, 1990. • Barry Qualls, The Secular Pilgrims of Victorian Fiction, 1982. • Elaine Showalter, A Literature of Their Own: British Women Novelists from Brontë to Lessing, 1977. • Lionel Stevenson, The English Novel: A Panorama, 1960. • Ronald R. Thomas, Dreams of Authority: Freud and the Fictions of the Unconscious, 1990.

Gender and Culture • Amanda Anderson, Tainted Souls and Painted Faces: The Rhetoric of Fallenness in Victorian Culture, 1993. • Nina Auerbach, Romantic Imprisonment: Women and Other Glorified Outcasts, 1985. • Nina Auerbach, Woman and the Demon: The Life of a Victorian Myth, 1982. • Francoise Basch, Relative Creatures: Victorian Women in Society and the Novel, 1974. • Susan Casteras and Linda H. Peterson, A Struggle for Fame: Victorian Women Artists and Authors, 1994. • Lloyd Davis, ed., Virgin Sexuality and Textuality in Victorian Literature, 1993. • Richard Dellamora, Masculine Desire: The Sexual Politics of Victorian Aestheticism, 1990. • Kristine Ottesen Garrigan, ed., Victorian Scandals: Representations of Gender and Class, 1992. • Sandra Gilbert and Susan Gubar, The Madwoman in the Attic: The Woman Writer and the Nineteenth-Century Literary Imagination, 1979. • A. James Hammerton, Cruelty and Companionship: Conflict in Nineteenth-Century Married Life, 1992. • Kathleen Hickok, Representations of Women: Nineteenth-Century British Women's Poetry, 1984. • Margaret Homans, Bearing the Word: Language and Female Experience in Nineteenth-Century Women's Writing, 1986. • Dorothy Mermin, Godiva's Ride: Women of Letters in England, 1830–1880, 1993. • Ellen Moers, Literary Women, 1976. • Deborah Epstein Nord, Walking the Victorian Streets: Women Representation, and the City, 1995. • Christopher Parker, ed., Gender Roles and Sexuality in Victorian Literature, 1995. • Eve Kosofsky Sedgwick, Between Men: English Literature and Male Homosocial Desire, 1985. • Alan Sinfield, Cultural Politics—Queer Reading, 1994.

History and Politics • Derek Beales, *From Castlereagh to Gladstone: 1815–1885*, 1970. • Patrick Brantlinger, *The Spirit of Reform: British Literature and Politics, 1832–1867*, 1977. • Asa Briggs, *A Social History of England*, 1983. • Barbara Dennis and David Skilton, eds., *Reform and Intellectual Debate in Victorian England*, 1987. • C. C. Eldridge, *Victorian Imperialism*, 1978. • E. J. Feuchtwanger, *Democracy and Empire: Britain, 1865–1914*, 1985. • Jose Harris, *Private Lives, Public Spirit: A Social History of Great Britain, 1870–1914*, 1993. • Patricia Jalland, *Women, Marriage, and Politics, 1860–1914*, 1987. • Patrick Joyce, *Visions of the People: Industrial England and the Question of Class, 1848–1914*, 1991. • J. P. Parry, *The Rise and Fall of Liberal Government in Victorian Britain*, 1994. • David Thomson, *England in the Nineteenth Century*, 1950. • E. P. Thompson, *The Making of the English Working Class*, 1963. • F. M. L. Thompson, *The Rise of Respectable Society: A Social History of Victorian Britain, 1830–1900*, 1988. • *Victorian Studies. Special Issue: Victorian Ethnographies*, vol. 41, no. 3, 1999.

Literature • William E. Buckler, *The Victorian Imagination: Essays in Aesthetic Exploration*, 1980. • Raymond Chapman, *The Sense of the Past in Victorian Literature*, 1986. • J. Hillis Miller, *The Disappearance of God: Five Nineteenth Century Writers*, 1963. • J. Hillis Miller, *Victorian Subjects*, 1990. • David Morse, *High Victorian Culture*, 1993. • John R. Reed, *Victorian Conventions*, 1975 • Ruth Robbins and Julian Wolfreys, eds., *Victorian Identities: Social and Cultural Formations in Nineteenth-Century Literature*, 1996.

Nonfiction Prose • Andrea Broomfield and Sally Mitchell, eds., *Prose by Victorian Women: An Anthology*, 1996. • Jerome H. Buckley, *The Turning Key: Autobiography and the Subjective Impulse since 1800*, 1984. • A. O. J. Cockshut, *The Art of Autobiography in 19th and 20th Century England*, 1984. • Mary Jean Corbett, *Representing Femininity: Middle-Class Subjectivity in Victorian and Edwardian Women's Autobiographies*, 1992. • Avrom Fleishman, *Figures of Autobiography: The Language of Self-Writing in Victorian and Modern England*, 1983. • Regenia Gagnier, *Subjectivities: A History of Self-Representation in Britain, 1832–1920*, 1991. • Heather Henderson, *The Victorian Self: Autobiography and Biblical Narrative*, 1989. • John Holloway, *The Victorian Sage*, 1953. •

George P. Landow, ed., *Approaches to Victorian Autobiography*, 1979. • A. L. Le Quesne, *Victorian Thinkers: Carlyle, Ruskin, Arnold, Morris*, 1993. • George Levine and William Madden, eds., *The Art of Victorian Prose*, 1968. • Laura Marcus, *Auto/biographical Discourses: Theory, Criticism, Practice*, 1995. • Thaïs E. Morgan, ed., *Victorian Sages and Cultural Discourse: Renegotiating Gender and Power*, 1991. • Linda Peterson, *Victorian Autobiography: The Tradition of Self-Interpretation*, 1986.

Poetry • Isobel Armstrong, *Victorian Poetry: Poetry, Poetics, and Politics*, 1993. • Douglas Bush, *Mythology and the Romantic Tradition in English Poetry*, 1937. • Carol T. Christ, *The Finer Optic: The Aesthetic of Particularity in Victorian Poetry*, 1975. • Carol T. Christ, *Victorian and Modern Poetics*, 1984. • Thomas J. Collins, ed., *The Broadview Anthology of Victorian Poetry and Poetic Theory*, 1999. • William E. Fredeman and Ira B. Nadel, eds., *Victorian Poets After 1850*, in *Dictionary of Literary Biography*, vol. 35, 1985. • William E. Fredeman, and Ira B. Nadel, eds., *Victorian Poets Before 1850*, in *Dictionary of Literary Biography*, vol. 32, 1984. • Eric Griffiths, *The Printed Voice of Victorian Poetry*, 1989. • Antony H. Harrison, *Victorian Poets and Romantic Poems: Intertextuality and Ideology*, 1990. • E. D. H. Johnson, *The Alien Vision of Victorian Poetry*, 1952. • Robert Langbaum, *The Poetry of Experience: The Dramatic Monologue in Modern Literary Tradition*, 1957. • Angela Leighton, *Victorian Women Poets: Writing Against the Heart*, 1992. • Angela Leighton, ed., *Victorian Women Poets: A Critical Reader*, 1996. • Angela Leighton and Margaret Reynolds, eds., *Victorian Women Poets: An Anthology*, 1995. • Laurence W. Mazzeno, *Victorian Poetry: An Annotated Bibliography*, 1995. • W. David Shaw, *The Lucid Veil: Poetic Truth in the Victorian Age*, 1987.

Reading and Readership • Richard D. Altick, *The English Common Reader: A Social History of the Mass Reading Public 1800–1900*, 1957. • Richard D. Altick, *Writers, Readers, and Occasions*, 1989. • N. N. Feltes, *Modes of Production of Victorian Novels*, 1986. • Kate Flint, *The Woman Reader, 1837–1914*, 1993. • John O. Jordan and Robert L. Patten, eds., *Literature in the Marketplace: Nineteenth-Century British Publishing and Reading Practices*, 1995. • Judith Kennedy, ed., *Victorian Authors and Their Works: Revision, Motivations, and Modes*, 1991. • Q. D. Leavis, *Fiction and the Reading Public*,

1932. • Joanne Shattock and Michael Wolff, eds., *The Victorian Periodical Press*, 1982. • John Sutherland, *Victorian Fiction: Writers, Publishers, Readers*, 1995. • David Vincent, *Literacy and Popular Culture: England 1750–1914*, 1990.

Theater • Michael R. Booth, ed., *English Plays of the Nineteenth Century*, 5 vols., 1969–1976. • Michael R. Booth, *Theater in The Victorian Age*, 1991. • Michael R. Booth, ed., *The Lights o'London and other Victorian Plays*, 1995. • Tracy C. Davis, *Actresses as Working Women: Their Social Identity in Victorian Culture*, 1991. • Anthony Jenkins, *The Making of Victorian Drama*, 1991. • Joel H. Kaplan and Sheila Stowell, *Theatre and Fashion: Oscar Wilde to the Suffragettes*, 1994.

Visual Arts • Richard Altick, *Paintings from Books: Art and Literature in Britain, 1760–1900*, 1985. • Kenneth Bendiner, *An Introduction to Victorian Painting*, 1985. Deborah Cherry, *Painting Women: Victorian Women Artists*, 1993. • Carol T. Christ and John O. Jordan, eds., *Victorian Literature and the Victorian Visual Imagination*, 1995. • Gerard Curtis, *Visual Words: Art and the Material Book in Victorian England*, 2000. • Linda Dowling, *The Vulgarization of Art: The Victorians and Aesthetic Democracy*, 1996. • William Gaunt, *The Pre-Raphaelite Dream*, 1966. • Helmut Gernsheim, *Julia Margaret Cameron: Her Life and Photographic Work*, 1975. • Heinz K. Henisch, *The Photographic Experience, 1839–1914*, 1994. • U. C. Knoepflmacher and G. B. Tennyson, eds., *Nature and the Victorian Imagination*, 1977. • Jeremy Maas, *Victorian Painters*, 1969. • Jan Marsh, *Pre-Raphaelite Sisterhood*, 1985. • Ira Bruce Nadel and F. S. Schwartzbach, eds., *Victorian Artists and the City*, 1980. • Pamela Gerrish Nunn, *Problem Pictures: Women and Men in Victorian Painting*, 1996. • Leslie Parris, ed., *The Pre-Raphaelites*, 1984. • Graham Reynolds, *Victorian Painting*, 1966; rev. 1987. • Lindsay Smith, *Victorian Photography, Painting, and Poetry: The Enigma of Visibility in Ruskin, Morris and the Pre-Raphaelites*, 1995. • Roy Strong, *And When Did You Last See Your Father?: The Victorian Painter and British History*, 1978. • Julian Treuherz, *Victorian Painting*, 1993. • Mike Weaver, *British Photography in the Nineteenth Century: The Fine Art Tradition*, 1989. • Christopher Wood, *The Pre-Raphaelites*, 1981.

World Wide Web Addresses. • *British Poetry 1780–1910: A Hypertext Archive of Scholarly Editions:* etext.lib.virginia.edu/britpo.html • *Northeast Victorian Studies Association:* fmc.utm.edu.nvsa/index.html [Maintains list of other Victorian web sites.] • *Victoria Research Web:* www.indiana.edu/~victoria/vwcont.html [Lists other Victorian web sites, and online Victorian journals and discussion groups.]. • George Landow's *Victorian Web:* www.stg.brown.edu/projects/hypertext/landow/victorian/victov.html • *Victorian Women Writers Project:* www.indiana.edu/~letrs/vwwp/.

Oscar Wilde in Context: Aestheticism, Decadence and the *Fin de Siècle* • *Anthologies.* Karl Beckson, ed., *Aesthetes and Decadents of the 1890s: An Anthology of British Poetry and Prose*, 1966; 1981. • Graham Hough and Eric Warner, eds., *Strangeness and Beauty: An Anthology of Aesthetic Criticism, 1840–1910*, 2 vols., 1983. • Sally Ledger and Roger Luckhurst, eds., *The Fin de Siècle: A Reader in Cultural History, c. 1880–1900*, 2000. • Ian Small, ed., *The Aesthetes: A Sourcebook*, 1979. • Derek Stanford, ed., *Poets of the 'Nineties: A Biographical Anthology*, 1965. • R. K. R. Thornton, ed., *Poetry of the Nineties*, 1970. • Stanley Weintraub, ed., *The Yellow Book: Quintessence of the Nineties*, 1964.

Criticism. • Karl Beckson, *London in the 1890s: A Cultural History*, 1992. • Gene H. Bell-Villada, *Art for Art's Sake and Literary Life: How Politics and Markets Helped Shape the Ideology and Culture of Aestheticism, 1790–1990*, 1996. • G. A. Cevasco, ed., *The 1890s: An Encyclopedia of British Literature, Art, and Culture*, 1993. • Richard Dellamora, *Masculine Desire: The Sexual Politics of Victorian Aestheticism*, 1990. • Linda C. Dowling, *Aestheticism and Decadence: A Selective Annotated Bibliography*, 1977. • Linda C. Dowling, *Hellenism and Homosexuality in Victorian Oxford*, 1994. • Linda C. Dowling, *Language and Decadence in the Victorian Fin de Siècle*, 1986. • Bram Dijkstra, *Idols of Perversity: Fantasies of Feminine Evil in Fin-de-Siècle Culture*, 1986. • Ian Fletcher, ed., *Decadence and the 1890s*, 1979. • Hilary Fraser, *Beauty and Belief: Aesthetics and Religion in Victorian Literature*, 1986. • William Gaunt, *The Aesthetic Adventure*, 1945. • Richard Gilman, *Decadence: The Strange Life of an Epithet*, 1979. • Walter Hamilton, *The Aesthetic Movement in England*, 1882. • Simon Houfe, *Fin de Siècle: The Illustrators of the 'Nineties*,

1992. • Graham Hough, *The Last Romantics*, 1947. • Holbrook Jackson, *The Eighteen Nineties*, 1913. • Sally Ledger and Scott McCracken, eds., *Cultural Politics at the Fin de Siècle*, 1995. • Patricia Marks, *Bicycles, Bangs, and Bloomers: The New Woman in the Popular Press*, 1990. • Linda Merrill, *A Pot of Paint: Aesthetics on Trial in "Whistler v. Ruskin,"* 1992. • John R. Reed, *Decadent Style*, 1985. • Elaine Showalter, *Sexual Anarchy: Gender and Culture at the Fin de Siècle*, 1990. • Chris Snodgrass, *Aubrey Beardsley: Dandy of the Grotesque*, 1995. • Robin Spencer, *The Aesthetic Movement: Theory and Practice*, 1972. • John Stokes, *In the Nineties*, 1989. • John Stokes, ed., *Fin de Siècle/Fin de Globe: Fears and Fantasies of the Late Nineteenth Century*, 1992. • Mikulas Teich and Roy Porter, eds., *Fin de Siècle and its Legacy*, 1990. • R. K. R. Thornton, *The Decadent Dilemma*, 1983.

Our Texts. • GILBERT: "If You're Anxious for to Shine" from *The Complete Plays of Gilbert and Sullivan*, 1941; WHISTLER: "Mr. Whistler's 'Ten O'Clock'" from *The Gentle Art of Making Enemies*, 2nd ed., 1892; "MICHAEL FIELD": "La Gioconda" and "A Pen-Drawing of Leda" from *Sight and Song*, 1892; "A Girl" from *Underneath the Bough*, 1893; LEVERSON: "Suggestion" from *The Yellow Book*, April 1895; SYMONS: "Pastel" and Preface from *Silhouettes*, 1896; "White Heliotrope" from *London Nights*, 2nd ed., 1897; "The Decadent Movement in Literature" from *Harper's New Monthly Magazine*, vol. 87 (Nov. 1893); LE GALLIENNE: "A Ballad of London" from *Robert Louis Stevenson: An Elegy and Other Poems*, 1895; JOHNSON: from *Complete Poems*, ed. Iain Fletcher, 1953; DOUGLAS: "Two Loves" from *Two Loves and Other Poems*, 1990; "Impression de nuit" from *The Collected Poems of Lord Alfred Douglas*, 1919; CUSTANCE: from *The Selected Poems of Olive Custance*, 1995; BEERBOHM: "Enoch Soames" from *Seven Men and Two Others*, 1950.

Perspectives: Imagining Childhood • *Anthologies.* • Patricia Demers, ed., *A Garland from the Golden Age: An Anthology of Children's Literature from 1850 to 1900*, 1983. • E. Royston Pike, ed., *Human Documents of the Victorian Golden Age, 1850–1875*, 1967.

Criticism. • Philippe Ariès, *Centuries of Childhood*, trans. R. Baldick, 1986. • Jacqueline Banerjee, *Through the Northern Gate:*

Childhood and Growing Up in British Fiction, 1719–1901, 1996. • Penny Brown, *The Captured World: The Child and Childhood in Nineteenth-Century Women's Writing in England*, 1993. • Humphrey Carpenter, *Secret Gardens: A Study of the Golden Age of Children's Literature*, 1985. • Peter Coveney, *The Image of Childhood*, 1967. • Charles Frey and John Griffith, *The Literary Heritage of Childhood: An Appraisal of Children's Classics in the Western Tradition*, 1987. • Mary Hilton, Morag Styles, and Victor Watson, eds., *Opening the Nursery Door: Reading, Writing and Childhood 1600–1900*, 1997. • Peter Hunt, ed., *Children's Literature: An Illustrated History*, 1995. • Thomas E. Jordan, *Victorian Childhood: Themes and Variations*, 1987. • U. C. Knoepflmacher, *Ventures into Childhood: Victorians, Fairy Tales, and Femininity*, 1998. • Antony and Peter Miall, *The Victorian Nursery Book*, 1980. • Lance Salway, ed., *A Peculiar Gift: Nineteenth Century Writings on Books for Children*, 1976. • Sharon Smulders, "Sound, Sense, and Structure in Christina Rossetti's *Sing-Song*," *Children's Literature* 22, 1994. • Carole G. Silver, *Strange and Secret Peoples: Fairies and Victorian Consciousness*, 1999. • James Walvin, *A Child's World: A Social History of English Childhood, 1800–1914*, 1982. • Jackie Wullschläger, *Inventing Wonderland: The Lives and Fantasies of Lewis Carroll, Edward Lear, J. M. Barrie, Kenneth Grahame and A. A. Milne*, 1995.

Our Texts. • DARWIN, "A Biographical Sketch of an Infant," 1877 • COOK, *Eliza Cook's Journal*, 1849 • HOFFMANN, *The English Strewwelpeter*, 1848 • T. MILLER, *Original Poems for My Children*, 1850 • W. MILLER, *Whistle-Binkie*, 1841 • LEAR, Limericks: *A Book of Nonsense* 1861; "The Owl and the Pussy-Cat" and "The Jumblies" from *Nonsense Songs*, 1871; "How Pleasant to know Mr. Lear!" from *The Complete Nonsense Book*, edited by Lady Strachey, 1912. • ROSSETTI, *Poetical Works*, 1906 • STEVENSON, *A Child's Garden of Verses*, 1885 • BELLOC, *The Bad Child's Book of Beasts*, 1897; *Cautionary Tales for Children*, 1907 • POTTER, *The Tale of Peter Rabbit*, 1902 • ASHFORD, *The Young Visiters; or, Mr. Salteena's Plan*, 1919 • JAMES, *What Maisie Knew*, 1897

Perspectives: The Industrial Landscape • *Anthologies.* • David J. Bradshaw and Suzanne Ozment, eds., *The Voice of Toil: Nineteenth-*

Century British Writings About Work, 2000. • F. P. Donovon, *The Railroad in Literature: A Brief Survey of Railroad Fiction, Poetry, Songs, Biography, Essays, Travel, and Drama in the English Language*, 1940. • E. Royston Pike, *"Hard Times": Human Documents of the Industrial Revolution*, 1966. • Jeremy Warburg, ed., *The Industrial Muse: The Industrial Revolution in English Poetry*, 1958.

Criticism. • John Belchem, *Industrialization and the Working Class: The English Experience; 1750–1900*, 1990. • Asa Briggs, *Victorian Cities*, 1963. • D. S. L. Cardwell, *The Norton History of Technology*, 1994. • Alice Chandler, *A Dream of Order: The Medieval Ideal in Nineteenth-Century English Literature*, 1970. • S. G. Checkland, *The Rise of Industrial Society in England, 1815–1885*, 1964. • Kenneth Clark, *The Gothic Revival: An Essay in the History of Taste*, 1928. • Bruce I. Coleman, ed., *The Idea of the City in Nineteenth-Century Britain*, 1973. • H. J. Dyos and Michael Wolff, eds., *The Victorian City: Images and Realities*, 2 vols., 1973. • Frank Ferneyhough, *The History of Railways in Britain*, 1975. • E. J. Hobsbawm, *Industry and Empire*, 1968. • Peter Keating, *The Working Classes in Victorian Fiction*, 1971. • David Levine, *The Making of an Industrial Society*, 1991. • Steven Marcus, *Engels, Manchester, and the Working Class*, 1974. • Ivan Melada, *The Captain of Industry in English Fiction, 1821–1871*, 1970. • Joel Mokyr, ed., *The British Industrial Revolution: An Economic Perspective*, 1993. • Joel Mokyr, ed., *The Economics of the Industrial Revolution*, 1986. • Deborah Epstein Nord, *Walking the Victorian Streets: Women, Representation, and the City*, 1995. • Ivy Pinchbeck, *Women Workers and the Industrial Revolution, 1750–1850*, 1930. • Sonya O. Rose, *Limited Livelihoods: Gender and Class in Nineteenth-Century England*, 1992. • Jack Simmons, *The Victorian Railway*, 1991. • Herbert Sussman, *Victorians and the Machine: The Literary Response to Technology*, 1968. • E. P. Thompson, *The Making of the English Working Class*, 1963. • Barrie Stewart Trinder, *The Making of the Industrial Landscape*, 1982. • Martha Vicinus, *The Industrial Muse: A Study of Nineteenth Century Working-Class Literature*, 1974. • James Walvin, *English Urban Life, 1776–1851*, 1984. • Raymond Williams, *The Country and the City*, 1973. • Edward A. Wrigley, *Continuity, Chance and Change: The Character of the Industrial Revolution in England*, 1989.

Our Texts. • "The Steam Loom Weaver" from Martha Vicinus, *The Industrial Muse*, 1974; KEMBLE: *Record of a Girlhood*, vol. 2, 1879; MACAULAY: "A Review of Southey's Colloquies" from *Edinburgh Review*, Jan. 1830; PARLIAMENTARY PAPERS: from *Victorian Women: A Documentary Account of Women's Lives*, eds. Hellerstein, Hume, and Offen, 1981; DICKENS: *Dombey and Son*, Charles Dickens Edition, 1867; *Hard Times*, 1854; DISRAELI: *Sybil* from *The Works of Benjamin Disraeli*, 1904; ENGELS: *The Condition of the Working Class in England, 1845*, trans. W. O. Henderson and W. H. Chaloner, 1958; MAYHEW: *London Labour and the London Poor*, vols. 1 and 2, 1861–1862; SMITH: "Glasgow" from *City Poems*, 1857.

Popular Short Fiction • Anthologies. • Nina Auerbach and U. C. Knoepflmacher, eds., *Forbidden Journeys: Fairy Tales and Fantasies by Victorian Women Writers*, 1992. • Everett F. Bleiler, ed., *A Treasury of Victorian Stories*, 1979. • Jonathan Cott, ed., *Beyond the Looking Glass: Extraordinary Works of Fairy Tale and Fantasy*, 1973. • Michael Cox, ed., *Victorian Detective Stories*, 1993. • Michael Cox and R. A. Gilbert, eds., *Victorian Ghost Stories*, 1991. • Richard Dalby, ed., *The Virago Book of Victorian Ghost Stories*, 1987. • Harold Orel, ed., *Victorian Short Stories: An Anthology*, 1987. • Harold Orel, ed., *Victorian Short Stories 2: The Trials of Love*, 1990. • Jack Zipes, ed., *Victorian Fairy Tales*, 1987.

Criticism. • Walter Allen, *The Short Story in English*, 1981. • Dean Baldwin, "The Tardy Evolution of the British Short Story," in *Studies in Short Fiction* 30 (1993). • Julia Briggs, *Night Visitors: The Rise and Fall of the English Ghost Story*, 1977. • Margaret Dalziel, *Popular Fiction 100 Years Ago*, 1958. • Alvar Ellegard, *The Readership of the Periodical Press in Mid-Victorian Britain*, 1957. • John R. Greenfield, ed., *British Short-Fiction Writers, 1800–1880*, in *Dictionary of Literary Biography*, vol. 159, 1996. • Clare Hanson, *Short Stories and Short Fictions, 1880–1980*, 1985. • Wendell V. Harris, *British Short Fiction in the Nineteenth Century: A Literary and Bibliographic Guide*, 1979. • Rosemary Jackson, *Fantasy: The Literature of Subversion*, 1981. • Peter Keating, *Working Class Stories of the 1890s*, 1972. • Lionel Madden and Diana Dixon, eds., *The Nineteenth-Century Periodical Press in Britain: A Bibliography of Modern Studies, 1901–1971*, 1976. • Harold Orel, *The Victorian*

Short Story: Development and Triumph of a Literary Genre, 1986. • Peter Penzoldt, The Supernatural in Fiction, 1952. • Stephen Prickett, Victorian Fantasy, 1979. • David Punter, The Literature of Terror: A History of Gothic Fictions from 1765 to the Present Day, 1980. • Joanne Shattock and Michael Wolff, eds., The Victorian Periodical Press: Samplings and Soundings, 1982. • Valerie Shaw, The Short Story: A Critical Introduction, 1983. • Alvin Sullivan, ed., British Literary Magazines, Vol. 3: The Victorian and Edwardian Age, 1837–1913, 1984. • Jack Sullivan, Elegant Nightmares: The English Ghost Story from Le Fanu to Blackwood, 1978. • William B. Thesing, ed., British Short-Fiction Writers, 1880–1914: The Realist Tradition, in Dictionary of Literary Biography, vol. 135, 1995. • Marshall B. Tymn et al., eds., Fantasy Literature: A Core Collection and Reference Guide, 1979.

Perspectives: Religion and Science • Anthologies. • Tess Cosslett, ed., Science and Religion in the Nineteenth Century, 1984. • Richard J. Helmstadter and Paul T. Phillips, eds., Religion in Victorian Society: A Sourcebook of Documents, 1985. • Gerald Parsons, ed., Religion in Victorian Britain, Vol. 3: Sources. 1988.

Criticism. • Peter Addinall, Philosophy and Biblical Interpretation: A Study in Nineteenth-Century Conflict, 1991. • D. W. Bebbington, Evangelicalism in Modern Britain: A History from the 1730s to the 1980s, 1989. • Gillian Beer, Open Fields: Science in Cultural Encounter, 1995. • P. J. Bowler, Evolution: The History of an Idea, 1984. • P. J. Bowler, The Invention of Progress: The Victorians and the Past, 1989. • Ian Bradley, The Call to Seriousness, 1976. • Douglas Bush, Science and English Poetry, 1590–1950, 1949. • Owen Chadwick, The Victorian Church, 2 vols., 1966, 1970. • Owen Chadwick, The Secularisation of the European Mind in the Nineteenth Century, 1975. • Tess Cosslett, The 'Scientific Movement' and Victorian Literature, 1982. • Sydney Eisen and Bernard V. Lightman, Victorian Science and Religion: A Bibliography, 1984. • Alan D. Gilbert, Religion and Society in Industrial England: Church, Chapel and Social Change, 1740–1914, 1976. • Stephen Jay Gould, Time's Arrow, Time's Cycle, 1987. • Richard J. Helmstadter and Bernard Lightman, eds., Victorian Faith in Crisis: Essays on Continuity and Change in Nineteenth-Century Religious Belief, 1990. • Elisabeth Jay, ed., The Evangelical and Oxford Movements, 1983. • Thomas W.

Laqueur, Religion and Respectability: Sunday Schools and Working Class Culture, 1780–1850, 1975. • George Levine, One Culture: Essays in Science and Literature, 1987. • Peter Morton, The Vital Science: Biology and the Literary Imagination, 1860–1900, 1984. • James Paradis and George C. Williams, eds., Evolution and Ethics: With New Essays on Its Victorian and Sociobiological Context, 1989. • James Paradis and Thomas Postlewait, eds., Victorian Science and Victorian Values: Literary Perspectives, 1985. • G. Parsons, ed., Religion in Victorian Britain, 4 vols., 1988. • Bernard M. G. Reardon, Religious Thought in the Victorian Age: A Survey from Coleridge to Gore, 1995. • Martin J. S. Rudwick, Scenes from Deep Time: Early Pictorial Representations of the Prehistoric World, 1992. • James A. Secord, Victorian Sensation: The Extraordinary Publication, Reception, and Secret Authorship of Vestiges of the Natural History of Creation, 2000. • A. Symondson, ed., The Victorian Crisis of Faith, 1970. • W. R. Ward, Religion and Society in England, 1790–1850, 1972. • W. R. Ward, The Protestant Evangelical Awakening, 1992. • Michael Wheeler, Death and the Future Life in Victorian Literature and Theology, 1990.

Our Texts. • MACAULAY: "Lord Bacon" from Critical and Historical Essays, vol. 2, 1865; DICKENS: Sunday Under Three Heads, 1836; STRAUSS: The Life of Jesus Critically Examined, 1846; BRONTE: Jane Eyre, 1848; CLOUGH: The Poems of Arthur Hugh Clough, ed. A. L. P. Norrington, 1968; COLENSO: The Pentateuch and Book of Joshua Critically Examined, 1863; NEWMAN: Apologia Pro Vita Sua, 1866; HUXLEY: Evolution and Ethics, 1894; GOSSE: Father and Son, 1907.

Perspectives: Victorian Ladies and Gentlemen • Anthologies. • Susan Groag Bell and Karen M. Offen, Woman, the Family, and Freedom: The Debate in Documents, 2 vols., 1983. • Erna Olafson Hellerstein, Leslie Parker Hume, and Karen M. Offen, eds., Victorian Women: A Documentary Account of Women's Lives, 1981. • Elizabeth K. Helsinger, Robin Lauterbach Sheets, and William Veeder, eds., The Woman Question: Society and Literature in Britain and America, 1837–1883, 3 vols., 1983. • Janet Murray, Strong-Minded Women and Other Lost Voices from Nineteenth-Century England, 1982.

Criticism. • James Eli Adams, Dandies and Desert Saints: Styles of Victorian Masculinity, 1995. • Patricia Branca, Silent Sisterhood: Middle-

Class Women in the Victorian Home, 1975. • Michael Brander, The Victorian Gentleman, 1975. • Joan N. Burstyn, Victorian Education and the Ideal of Womanhood, 1980. • David Castronovo, The English Gentleman: Images and Ideals in Literature and Society, 1987. • John Chandos, Boys Together: English Public Schools, 1800–1864, 1984. • Leonore Davidoff and Catherine Hall, Family Fortunes: Men and Women of the English Middle Class, 1780–1850, 1987. • Jonathan Gathorne-Hardy, The Public School Phenomenon, 1977. • Robin Gilmour, The Idea of the Gentleman in the Victorian Novel, 1981. • Mark Girouard, The Return to Camelot: Chivalry and the English Gentleman, 1981. • Deborah Gorham, The Victorian Girl and the Feminine Ideal, 1982. • Donald E. Hall, ed., Muscular Christianity: Embodying the Victorian Age, 1994. • Lee Holcombe, Victorian Ladies at Work: Middle-Class Women in England and Wales, 1850–1914, 1973. • Richard Holt, Sport and the British: A Modern History, 1989. • Margaret Homans, Royal Representations: Queen Victoria and British Culture, 1837–1876, 1998. • Margaret Homans and Adrienne Munich, eds., Remaking Queen Victoria, 1997. • J. R. de S. Honey, Tom Brown's Universe: The Development of the English Public School in the Nineteenth Century, 1977. • Kathryn Hughes, The Victorian Governess, 1993. • Elizabeth Langland, Nobody's Angels: Middle-Class Women and Domestic Ideology in Victorian Culture, 1995. • Anita Levy, Other Women: The Writing of Class, Race, and Gender, 1832–1898, 1991. • Elizabeth Longford, Eminent Victorian Women, 1981. • J. A. Mangan and James Walvin, eds., Manliness and Masculinity: Middle-Class Masculinity in Britain and America, 1800–1940, 1987. • Philip Mason, The English Gentleman: The Rise and Fall of an Ideal, 1982. • Claudia Nelson and Lynne Vallone, eds., The Girl's Own: Cultural Histories of the Anglo-American Girl, 1830–1915, 1994. • Mary Poovey, Uneven Developments: The Ideological Work of Gender in Mid-Victorian England, 1988. • Sonya O. Rose, Limited Livelihoods: Gender and Class in Nineteenth-Century England, 1992. • Brian Simon and Ian Bradley, eds., The Victorian Public School: Studies in the Development of an Educational Institution, 1975. • Herbert Sussman, Victorian Masculinities: Manhood and Masculine Poetics in Early Victorian Literature and Art, 1995. • Dorothy Thompson, Queen Victoria: The Woman, the Monarchy, and the People, 1990. • Norman Vance, The Sinews of

the Spirit: The Ideal of Christian Manliness in Victorian Literature and Religious Thought, 1985. • Martha Vicinus, ed., Suffer and Be Still: Women in the Victorian Age, 1972. • Martha Vicinus, ed., A Widening Sphere: Changing Roles of Victorian Women, 1977.

Our Texts. • COBBE: Life of Frances Power Cobbe, 1904; ELLIS: The Women of England, 1839; C. BRONTE: The Brontës: Their Lives, Friendships, and Correspondence, eds. Wise and Symington, Vol. 1, 1933; A. BRONTE: Agnes Grey, 1860; NEWMAN: The Idea of a University, 1873; NORTON: "A Letter to the Queen," 1855; HUGHES: Tom Brown's School Days, 1869; BEETON: The Book of Household Management, 1861; VICTORIA: see footnotes; KINGSLEY: The Works of Charles Kingsley, vol. 7, 1899; NEWBOLT: "Vitaï Lampada," The Island Race, 1898.

Matthew Arnold • Editions. • Kenneth Allott, ed., Arnold: The Complete Poems, 1965; 2nd ed., Miriam Allott, 1979. • Miriam Allott and R. H. Super, eds., Matthew Arnold, 1986 [annotated selection]. • Cecil Y. Lang, ed., The Letters of Matthew Arnold, 1996–. • Howard Foster Lowry, ed., The Letters of Matthew Arnold to Arthur Hugh Clough, 1968. • R. H. Super, ed., The Complete Prose Works of Matthew Arnold, 11 vols., 1960–1977.

Biography. • Ian Hamilton, A Gift Imprisoned: The Poetic Life of Matthew Arnold, 1999. • Park Honan, Matthew Arnold: A Life, 1981. • Nicholas Murray, A Life of Matthew Arnold, 1997.

Criticism. • Kenneth Allott, ed., Matthew Arnold, 1975. • Ruth Roberts, Arnold and God, 1983. • Harold Bloom, ed., Matthew Arnold, 1987. • William E. Buckler, On the Poetry of Matthew Arnold, 1982. • Douglas Bush, Matthew Arnold: A Survey of His Poetry and Prose, 1971. • Joseph Carroll, The Cultural Theory of Matthew Arnold, 1982. • Stefan Collini, Arnold, 1988. • Dwight Culler, Imaginative Reason, 1966. • Carl Dawson and John Pfordresher, eds., Matthew Arnold, the Poetry: The Critical Heritage, 1973; and Matthew Arnold, Prose Writings: The Critical Heritage, 1979. • T. S. Eliot, "Matthew Arnold," in his The Use of Poetry and the Use of Criticism, 1933. • T. S. Eliot, "Arnold and Pater," in his Selected Essays, 1932. • R. Giddings, ed., Matthew Arnold: Between Two Worlds, 1986. • Leon Gottfried, Matthew Arnold and the Romantics, 1983. • D. G. James, Matthew Arnold and the

Decline of English Romanticism, 1961. • Edward D. H. Johnson, The Alien Vision of Victorian Poetry, 1952. • James C. Livingston, Matthew Arnold and Christianity: His Religious Prose Writings, 1986. • David G. Riede, Matthew Arnold and the Betrayal of Language, 1988. • Alan Roper, Arnold's Poetic Landscapes, 1969. • G. Robert Stange, The Poet as Humanist, 1967. • Lionel Trilling, Matthew Arnold, 1949.

Our Texts. • The poems in this anthology are from Allott, Complete Poems; our prose selections are from Super, Complete Prose.

Elizabeth Barrett Browning • Editions. • Cora Kaplan, ed., Aurora Leigh and Other Poems, 1978. • Philip Kelley and Ronald Hudson, eds., The Brownings' Correspondence, 1984–. • Elvan Kintner, ed., The Letters of Robert Browning and Elizabeth Barrett Browning, 1845–1846, 2 vols., 1969. • Charlotte Porter and Helen Clarke, eds., Complete Works, 6 vols., 1900. • Harriet Waters Preston, ed., The Complete Poetical Works of Elizabeth Barrett Browning, 1900; 1974. • Margaret Reynolds, ed., Aurora Leigh, 1992; 1996.

Biography. • Angela Leighton, Elizabeth Barrett Browning, 1986. • Gardner B. Taplin, The Life of Elizabeth Barrett Browning, 1957.

Criticism. • Warner Barnes, A Bibliography of Elizabeth Barrett Browning, 1968. • Kathleen Blake, "Elizabeth Barrett Browning and Wordsworth: The Romantic Poet as a Woman," Victorian Poetry 24 (1986). • Helen Cooper, Elizabeth Barrett Browning, Woman and Artist, 1988. • Deirdre David, Intellectual Women and Victorian Patriarchy: Harriet Martineau, Elizabeth Barrett Browning, George Eliot, 1987. • Sandra M. Gilbert, "From Patria to Matria: Elizabeth Barrett Browning's Risorgimento." PMLA 99 (1984); repr. Victorian Women Poets, ed. Angela Leighton, 1996. • Alethea Hayter, Mrs. Browning: A Poet's Work and Its Setting, 1962. • Dorothy Mermin, Elizabeth Barrett Browning: The Origins of a New Poetry, 1989. • Virginia L. Radley, Elizabeth Barrett Browning, 1972. • Dolores Rosenblum, "Face to Face: Elizabeth Barrett Browning's Aurora Leigh and Nineteenth-Century Poetry," Victorian Studies 26 (1983). • Glennis Stephenson, Elizabeth Barrett Browning and the Poetry of Love, 1989. • Marjorie Stone, Elizabeth Barrett Browning, 1995. • Virginia Woolf, "Aurora Leigh," in The Second Common Reader, 1932. • Joyce Zonana, "The Embodied

Muse: Elizabeth Barrett Browning's Aurora Leigh and Feminist Poetics," Tulsa Studies in Women's Literature 8 (1989); repr. in Victorian Women Poets, ed. Angela Leighton, 1996.

Our Texts. • Charlotte Porter and Helen Clarke, eds., Complete Works, 6 vols., 1900.

Robert Browning • Editions. • Poetical Works of Robert Browning, 16 vols., 1888–1889. • Ian Jack, Margaret Smith, and Robert Inglesfield, eds., The Poetical Works of Robert Browning, 1983–. • Philip Kelley and Ronald Hudson, eds., The Brownings' Correspondence, 1984–. • John Pettigrew and Thomas J. Collins, eds., The Poems, 2 vols., 1981.

Biography. • William Irvine and Park Honan, The Book, the Ring, and the Poet, 1974. • John Maynard, Browning's Youth, 1977. • Mrs. Sutherland Orr, Life and Letters of Robert Browning, 1891; 1908. • Clyde de L. Ryals, The Life of Robert Browning: A Critical Biography, 1993.

Criticism. • Isobel Armstrong, ed., Robert Browning, 1974. • Walter Bagehot, "Wordsworth, Tennyson, and Browning," in Literary Studies, ed. R. H. Hutton, 1895. • Harold Bloom and Adrienne Munich, eds., Robert Browning: A Collection of Critical Essays, 1979. • Joseph Bristow, Robert Browning, 1991. • G. K. Chesterton, Robert Browning, 1903. • Norman B. Crowell, A Reader's Guide to Robert Browning, 1972. • William C. DeVane, A Browning Handbook, 1955. • Philip Drew, ed., Robert Browning: A Collection of Critical Essays, 1966. • Donald Hair, Browning's Experiments with Genre, 1972. • Ian Jack, Browning's Major Poetry, 1973. • Roma A. King Jr., The Bow and the Lyre, 1957. • Robert Langbaum, The Poetry of Experience: The Dramatic Monologue in Modern Literary Tradition, 1957. • Boyd Litzinger and K. L. Knickerbocker, eds., The Browning Critics, 1965. • Boyd Litzinger and Donald Smalley, eds., Browning: The Critical Heritage, 1970. • Loy Martin, Browning's Dramatic Monologues and the Post-Romantic Subject, 1985. • William S. Peterson, Robert and Elizabeth Barrett Browning: An Annotated Bibliography, 1951–1970, 1974. • W. O. Raymond, The Infinite Moment, 1965. • Herbert F. Tucker, Browning's Beginnings: The Art of Disclosure, 1980.

Our Texts. • From Poetical Works of Robert Browning, 16 vols., 1888–1889.

Thomas Carlyle • *Editions.* • C. R. Sanders, K. J. Fielding, Clyde de L. Ryals, et al., eds., *The Collected Letters of Thomas and Jane Welsh Carlyle,* 1970–. • H. D. Traill, ed., *The Works of Thomas Carlyle,* 30 vols., 1896–1899.

Biography. • J. A. Froude, *Thomas Carlyle: A History of the First Forty Years of his Life, 1795–1835,* 2 vols., 1882; *Thomas Carlyle: A History of his Life in London, 1834–1881,* 2 vols., 1884. • Fred Kaplan, *Thomas Carlyle: A Biography,* 1983.

Criticism. • Ruth Roberts, *The Ancient Dialect: Thomas Carlyle and Comparative Religion,* 1988. • K. J. Fielding and Rodger L. Tarr, eds., *Carlyle Past and Present,* 1976. • Michael Goldberg, *Carlyle and Dickens,* 1972. • John Holloway, *The Victorian Sage,* 1953. • Albert J. LaValley, *Carlyle and the Idea of the Modern,* 1968. • George Levine, *The Boundaries of Fiction: Carlyle, Macaulay, Newman,* 1968. • Emery Neff, *Carlyle and Mill,* 1926. • Barry Qualls, *The Secular Pilgrims of Victorian Fiction,* 1983. • John D. Rosenberg, *Carlyle and the Burden of History,* 1985. • Philip Rosenberg, *The Seventh Hero: Thomas Carlyle and the Theory of Radical Activism,* 1974. • Jules Paul Seigel, ed., *Thomas Carlyle: The Critical Heritage,* 1971. • Rodger Tart, *Thomas Carlyle: A Descriptive Bibliography,* 1990. • G. B. Tennyson, *"Sartor" Called "Resartus,"* 1965. • G. B. Tennyson, "Thomas Carlyle," in *Victorian Prose: A Guide to Research,* ed. David J. DeLaura, 1973. • Chris Vanden Bossche, *Carlyle and the Search for Authority,* 1991. • Basil Willey, *Nineteenth Century Studies,* 1949.

Our Texts. • Texts cited from H. D. Traill.

Lewis Carroll • *Editions.* • Morton N. Cohen, ed., *The Letters of Lewis Carroll,* 1979. • Martin Gardner, ed., *The Annotated Alice,* 1960. • Donald J. Gray, ed., *Alice in Wonderland,* 2nd ed., 1992. • Roger Lancelyn Green, ed., *The Diaries of Lewis Carroll,* 1953–54.

Biography. • Morton N. Cohen, *Lewis Carroll: A Biography,* 1995. • Morton N. Cohen, ed., *Lewis Carroll: Interviews and Recollections,* 1989. • Derek Hudson, *Lewis Carroll: An Illustrated Biography,* 1976.

Criticism. • Harold Bloom, ed., *Lewis Carroll,* 1987. • Edward Guiliano, ed., *Lewis Carroll: A Celebration,* 1982. • Michael Hancher, *The Tenniel Illustrations to the 'Alice' Books,* 1985. • Jo Elwyn Jones, *The Alice Companion: A Guide to Lewis Carroll's Alice Books,* 1998. • Robert Phillips, ed., *Aspects of Alice,* 1974. • Catherine Robson, *Men in Wonderland: The Lost Girlhood of the Victorian Gentlemen,* 2001.

Our Texts. • *The Complete Writings of Lewis Carroll,* 1939.

Charles Darwin • *Editions.* • Philip Appleman, ed., *Darwin,* 1970; 2nd ed., 1979. • Nora Barlow, ed., *The Autobiography of Charles Darwin, 1809–1882: With Original Omissions Restored,* 1958. • Paul H. Barrett and R. B. Freeman, eds., *The Works of Charles Darwin,* 29 vols., 1986. • Richard E. Leakey, abridged and introduced, *The Illustrated Origin of Species,* 1979; 1986.

Biography. • John Bowlby, *Charles Darwin: A New Life,* 1990. • Francis Darwin, ed., *The Life and Letters of Darwin,* 1887–1888. • Adrian Desmond and James Moore, *Darwin,* 1991.

Criticism. • Mea Allan, *Darwin and His Flowers: The Key to Natural Selection,* 1977. • Gillian Beer, *Darwin's Plots: Evolutionary Narrative in Darwin, George Eliot, and Nineteenth-Century Fiction,* 1983. • Peter Brent, *Charles Darwin: "A Man of Enlarged Curiosity,"* 1981. • Sir Gavin De Beer, *Charles Darwin: Evolution by Natural Selection,* 1964. • Loren Eiseley, *Darwin's Century: Evolution and the Men Who Discovered It,* 1958. • Michael T. Ghiselin, *The Triumph of the Darwinian Method,* 1984. • Stephen Jay Gould, *Ever Since Darwin,* 1977. • Stephen Jay Gould, *The Flamingo's Smile,* 1985. • David Kohn, ed., *The Darwinian Heritage,* 1985. • George Levine, *Darwin and the Novelists: Patterns of Science in Victorian Fiction,* 1988. • Jonathan Miller and Borin Van Loon, *Darwin for Beginners,* 1982. • John D. Rosenberg, "Mr. Darwin Collects Himself," in *Nineteenth-Century Lives,* ed. Laurence S. Lockridge et al., 1989. • Robert M. Young, *Darwin's Metaphor: Nature's Place in Victorian Culture,* 1985.

Our Texts. • *The Voyage of the Beagle,* 1860, repr. 1962, ed. Leonard Engel; *On the Origin of Species,* 1859, repr. 1968, ed. J. W. Burrow; *The Descent of Man,* 2 vols., 1871; *The Autobiography of Charles Darwin, 1809–1882: With Original Omissions Restored,* ed. Nora Barlow, 1958.

Charles Dickens • *Editions.* • Charles Dickens, *Works.* The Clarendon Edition. 1966–. •

Michael Patrick Hearn, *The Annotated Christmas Carol*, 1976. • Madeline House, Graham Storey, Katherine Tillotson et al., eds., *The Letters of Charles Dickens*, 1965–. • Michael Slater, ed., *The Christmas Books*, 2 vols., 1971.

Biography. • Peter Ackroyd, *Dickens*, 1990. • John Forster, *The Life of Charles Dickens*, 1872–1874. • Edgar Johnson, *Charles Dickens: His Tragedy and Triumph*, 1952. • Fred Kaplan, *Dickens: A Biography*, 1988.

Criticism. • Peter Ackroyd, *Introduction to Dickens*, 1991. • Nicolas Bentley, Michael Slater, and Nina Buris, *The Dickens Index*, 1989. • G. K. Chesterton, *Charles Dickens*, 1906. • Philip Collins, *Dickens and Crime*, 1962. • Philip Collins, ed., *Dickens: The Critical Heritage*, 1971. • Philip Collins, ed., *Dickens: Interviews and Recollections*, 2 vols., 1981. • Paul Davis, *The Lives and Times of Ebenezer Scrooge*, 1990. • *The Dickensian.* 89.3. 1993. Special issue on *A Christmas Carol.* • George H. Ford, *Dickens and His Readers*, 1955. • Robert Garis, *The Dickens Theatre*, 1965. • George Gissing, *Charles Dickens: A Critical Study*, 1903. • Ruth F. Glancy, *Dickens's Christmas Books, Christmas Stories, and Other Short Fiction: An Annotated Bibliography*, 1985. • Michael Goldberg, *Carlyle and Dickens*, 1972. • Patricia Ingham, *Dickens, Women, and Language*, 1992. • Steven Marcus, *Dickens: From Pickwick to Dombey*, 1965. • J. Hillis Miller, *Charles Dickens: The World of His Novels*, 1958. • George Orwell, "Charles Dickens," in his *A Collection of Essays*, 1954. • Robert Partlow, ed., *Dickens the Craftsman*, 1970. • Daniel Pool, *What Jane Austen Ate and Charles Dickens Knew: From Fox-Hunting to Whist: The Facts of Daily Life in Nineteenth-Century England*, 1993. • F. S. Schwarzbach, *Dickens and the City*, 1979. • Michael Slater, *Dickens and Women*, 1983. • Harry Stone, *Dickens and the Invisible World: Fairy Tales, Fantasy and Novel-Making*, 1979. • Angus Wilson, *The World of Charles Dickens*, 1970. • Edmund Wilson, "Dickens: The Two Scrooges," in his *The Wound and the Bow*, 1952.

Our Texts. • *The Christmas Books*, 2 vols., ed. Michael Slater, 1971; *Charles Dickens: A December Vision: His Social Journalism*, eds. Neil Philip and Victor Neuburg, 1986.

Arthur Conan Doyle • T. J. Binyon, *"Murder Will Out": The Detective in Fiction*, 1989. • John Dickson Carr, *The Life of Sir Arthur Conan Doyle*, 1949. • Dorothy Glover, *Victorian Detective Fiction*, 1966. • Richard Lancelyn Green, Introduction to *The Adventures of Sherlock Holmes*, 1993. • John A. Hodgson, ed., *Sherlock Holmes: The Major Stories with Contemporary Critical Essays*, 1994. • Rosemary Jann, *The Adventures of Sherlock Holmes: Detecting Social Order*, 1995. • Glenn W. Most, and William W. Stowe, eds., *The Poetics of Murder: Detective Fiction and Literary Theory*, 1983. • Pierre Nordon, *Conan Doyle*, trans. Frances Partridge, 1966. • Harold Orel, ed., *Critical Essays on Sir Arthur Conan Doyle*, 1992. • Ian Ousby, *Bloodhounds of Heaven: The Detective in English Fiction from Godwin to Doyle*, 1976. • Dennis Porter, *The Pursuit of Crime: Art and Ideology in Detective Fiction*, 1981. • Daniel Stashower, *Teller of Tales: The Life of Arthur Conan Doyle*, 1999. • Julian Symons, *Conan Doyle*, 1979. • Julian Symons, *Mortal Consequences: A History—from the Detective Story to the Crime Novel* [*Bloody Murder*], 1972; rev. 1985.

Our Text. • *Strand Magazine*, July 1891

Elizabeth Gaskell • W. A. Craik, *Elizabeth Gaskell and the English Provincial Novel*, 1975. • Angus Easson, *Elizabeth Gaskell*, 1979. • Angus Easson, ed., *Elizabeth Gaskell: The Critical Heritage*, 1991. • Rowena Fowler, "Cranford: Cow in Grey Flannel or Lion Couchant?" *SEL* 24 (1984). • Winifred Gérin, *Elizabeth Gaskell*, 1980. • Rae Rosenthal, "Gaskell's Feminist Utopia: The Cranfordians and the Reign of Goodwill," in *Utopian and Science Fiction by Women: Worlds of Difference*, eds. Jane L. Donawerth and Carol A. Kolmerten, 1994. • Hilary M. Schor, *Scheherezade in the Market Place: Elizabeth Gaskell and the Victorian Novel*, 1992. • Patsy Stoneman, *Elizabeth Gaskell*, 1987. • Jenny Uglow, *Elizabeth Gaskell: A Habit of Stories*, 1993. • Patricia A. Wolfe, "Structure and Movement in Cranford," in *Nineteenth-Century Fiction*, vol. 23, 1968. • Terence Wright, *Elizabeth Gaskell: "We are not angels": Realism, Gender, Values*, 1995.

Our Text. • *The Works of Mrs. Gaskell*, Knutsford Edition, 8 vols., 1906–1920. Ed. A. W. Ward. 1906–1911.

Gerard Manley Hopkins • *Editions.* • Claude C. Abbott, ed., *The Correspondence of Gerard Manley Hopkins and Richard Watson Dixon*, 2 vols., 1935; rev. 1955. • Claude C. Abbott, *Further Letters of Gerard Manley Hopkins*, 1938; 1956. • Claude C. Abbott, *The Letters of Gerard Manley Hopkins to Robert Bridges*,

1935; 1955. • Christopher Devlin, ed., *The Sermons and Devotional Writings of Gerard Manley Hopkins*, 1959. • Humphrey House and Graham Storey, eds., *Journals and Papers*, 1959. • Norman H. MacKenzie, ed., *The Poetical Works of Gerard Manley Hopkins*, 1990. • Catherine Phillips, ed., *Gerard Manley Hopkins*, 1986.

Biography. • Robert Bernard Martin, *Gerard Manley Hopkins: A Very Private Life*, 1991. • Norman White, *Hopkins: A Literary Biography*, 1992.

Criticism. • Tom Dunne, *Gerard Manley Hopkins: A Comprehensive Bibliography*, 1976 [annual updates in *Hopkins Quarterly*]. • William H. Gardner, G. M. *Hopkins: A Study of Poetic Idiosyncrasy in Relation to Poetic Tradition*, 2 vols., 1944; 1949. • Richard F. Giles, ed., *Hopkins Among the Poets: Studies in Modern Responses to Gerard Manley Hopkins*, 1985. • Daniel Harris, *Inspirations Unbidden: The "Terrible Sonnets" of Gerard Manley Hopkins*, 1982. • Norman H. MacKenzie, *A Reader's Guide to Gerard Manley Hopkins*, 1981. • Paul L. Mariani, *A Commentary on the Complete Poems of Gerard Manley Hopkins*, 1970. • Walter J. Ong, *Hopkins, the Self, and God*, 1986. • Alison Sulloway, *Gerard Manley Hopkins and the Victorian Temper*, 1972.

Our Texts. • W. H. Gardner, ed., *Poems of Gerard Manley Hopkins*, 1948; Humphrey House, and Graham Storey, eds., *Journals and Papers*, 1959; Claude C. Abbott, ed., *The Correspondence of Gerard Manley Hopkins and Richard Watson Dixon*, 2 vols., 1935; rev. 1955.

Rudyard Kipling • Editions. • *Works.* Sussex Edition, 35 vols., 1937–1939. • Thomas Pinney, ed., *The Letters of Rudyard Kipling*, 1872–1910, 1990–. • Thomas Pinney, ed., *Something of Myself*, 1937; 1990 [Kipling's autobiography]. • *Rudyard Kipling's Complete Verse: Definitive Edition*, 1940.

Biography. • Charles Carrington, *Rudyard Kipling: His Life and Work*, 1955; rev. 1978. • Philip Mason, *Kipling: The Glass, the Shadow, and the Fire*, 1975. • Angus Wilson, *The Strange Ride of Rudyard Kipling: His Life and Works*, 1977.

Criticism. • Helen Pike Bauer, *Rudyard Kipling: A Study of the Short Fiction*, 1994. • Francelia Butler, Barbara Rosen, and Judith A. Plotz, eds., *Children's Literature*, 20. Special

Kipling issue, 1992. • Louis Cornell, *Kipling in India*, 1966. • Elliot L. Gilbert, *The Good Kipling: Studies in the Short Story*, 1971. • Elliot L. Gilbert, ed., *Kipling and the Critics*, 1965. • Roger Lancelyn Green, *Kipling: The Critical Heritage*, 1971. • Peter Keating, *Kipling the Poet*, 1994. • Sandra Kemp, *Kipling's Hidden Narratives*, 1987. • Harold Orel, ed., *Critical Essays on Rudyard Kipling*, 1989. • Harold Orel, *Rudyard Kipling: Interviews and Recollections*, 2 vols., 1983. • Mark Paffard, *Kipling's Indian Fiction*, 1989. • Norman Page, *A Kipling Companion*, 1984. • Andrew Rutherford, ed., *Kipling's Mind and Art*, 1964. • Zohreh T. Sullivan, *Narratives of Empire: The Fictions of Rudyard Kipling*, 1993. • J. M. S. Tompkins, *The Art of Rudyard Kipling*, 1959.

Our Texts. • "Without Benefit of Clergy" *from Macmillan's Magazine*, 62 (June 1890); *Rudyard Kipling's Complete Verse: Definitive Edition*, 1940; *Just So Stories for Little Children*, 1912.

Thomas Babington Macaulay • John Clive, *Macaulay: The Shaping of the Historian*, 1973. • George Levine, *The Boundaries of Fiction*, 1968. • William Madden, "Macaulay's Style," in *The Art of Victorian Prose*, 1968. • Jane Millgate, *Macaulay*, 1973. • Thomas Pinney, *The Letters of Thomas Babington Macaulay*, 5 vols., 1974–81. • Sir G. O. Trevelyan, *Life and Letters of Lord Macaulay*, 1876. • Lady Trevelyan, ed. *The Works of Lord Macaulay*, 12 vols., 1898.

Our Text. • Macaulay, *Speeches: with his Minute on Indian Education*, 1935

John Stuart Mill • *Editions.* • John Robson et al., eds., *Collected Works*, 33 vols., 1963–1991. • Ann P. Robson and John M. Robson, eds., *Sexual Equality: Writings by John Stuart Mill, Harriet Taylor Mill, and Helen Taylor*, 1994. • David Spitz, ed., *On Liberty*, Norton critical edition, 1975.

Biography. • Alexander Bain, *John Stuart Mill*, 1882; 1969. • Michael St. J. Packe, *The Life of John Stuart Mill*, 1954.

Criticism. • Fred Berger, *Happiness, Justice, and Freedom*, 1984. • Janice Carlisle, *John Stuart Mill and the Writing of Character*, 1991. • Maurice Cowling, *Mill and Liberalism*, 1963. • F. W. Garforth, *Educative Democracy: John Stuart Mill on Education in Society*, 1980. • Peter Glassman, *The Evolution of a Genius*, 1985. • John Gray and G. W. Smith, eds., *J. S. Mill: On Liberty in Focus*, 1991. • Joseph

Hamburger, *Intellectuals in Politics,* 1985. • Michael Laine, *Bibliography of Writings on John Stuart Mill,* 1982. • Michael Laine, ed., *A Cultivated Mind: Essays on J.S. Mill Presented to John M. Robson,* 1991. • John M. Robson, *The Improvement of Mankind: The Social and Political Thought of J. S. Mill,* 1968. • Alan Ryan, *John Stuart Mill,* 1970. • J. B. Schneewind, ed., *Mill: A Collection of Critical Essays,* 1968. • F. Parvin Sharpless, *The Literary Criticism of John Stuart Mill,* 1967. • Lynn Zastoupil, *John Stuart Mill and India,* 1994.

Our Texts. • John Robson et al., eds., *Collected Works,* 33 vols., 1963–1991.

Christina Rossetti • *Editions.* • Rebecca W. Crump, ed., *The Complete Poems of Christina Rossetti: A Variorum Edition,* 3 vols., 1979–1990. • William M. Rossetti, ed., *The Poetical Works of Christina Rossetti,* 1904. • Rebecca W. Crump, ed., *The Family Letters of Christina Georgina Rossetti.* 1908; 1968.

Biography. • Kathleen Jones, *Learning Not to Be First: The Life of Christina Rossetti,* 1991. • Jan Marsh, *Christina Rosseetti: A Writer's Life,* 1995.

Criticism. • Mary Arseneau, Antony H. Harrison, and Lorraine Janzen Kooistra, eds., *The Culture of Christina Rossetti: Female Poetics and Victorian Contexts,* 1999. • Georgina Battiscombe, *Christina Rossetti: A Divided Life,* 1981. • Kathleen Blake, *Love and the Woman Question in Victorian Literature,* 1983. • Edna Kotin Chatles, *Christina Rossetti: Critical Perspectives, 1862–1982,* 1985. • Rebecca W. Crump, *Christina Rossetti: A Reference Guide,* 1976. • Antony H. Harrison, *Christina Rossetti in Context,* 1988. • Antony H. Harrison, ed., *Victorian Poetry:* special issue on Christina Rossetti, vol. 32, no. 3–4, 1994. • Elizabeth K. Helsinger, "Consumer Power and the Utopia of Desire: Christina Rossetti's Goblin Market." *ELH* 58 (1991). • David A. Kent, ed., *The Achievement of Christina Rossetti,* 1987. • Katherine J. Mayberry, *Christina Rossetti and the Poetry of Discovery,* 1989. • Jerome McGann, "Christina Rossetti's Poems: A New Edition and a Revaluation," *Victorian Studies* 23 (1980). • Jerome McGann, "The Religious Poetry of Christina Rossetti," *Critical Inquiry* 10 (1983). • Dorothy Mermin, "Heroic Sisterhood in Goblin Market," *Victorian Poetry* 21 (1983). • Dolores Rosenblum, *Christina Rossetti: The Poetry of Endurance,* 1986. • Sharon Smulders, *Christina Rossetti, Revisited,* 1996. •

Virginia Woolf, "I Am Christina Rossetti," in *The Second Common Reader,* 1932.

Our Texts. • Rebecca W. Crump, ed., *The Complete Poems of Christina Rossetti: A Variorum Edition,* 3 vols., 1979–1990.

John Ruskin • *Editions.* • Harold Bloom, ed., *The Literary Criticism of John Ruskin,* 1965. • Van Akin Burd, ed., *The Ruskin Family Letters, 1801–1843,* 2 vols., 1973. • E. T. Cook and Alexander Wedderburn, eds., *The Works of John Ruskin,* 39 vols., 1903–1912. • John D. Rosenberg, ed., *The Genius of John Ruskin: Selections from His Writings,* 1963.

Biography. • Joan Abse, *John Ruskin: The Passionate Moralist,* 1980. • Timothy Hilton, *John Ruskin: The Early Years, 1819–1859,* 1985. • John Dixon Hunt, *The Wider Sea: A Life of John Ruskin,* 1982.

Criticism. • Linda M. Austin, *The Practical Ruskin: Economics and Audience in the Late Work,* 1991. • Michael W. Brooks, *John Ruskin and Victorian Architecture,* 1987. • Susan Casteras et al., *John Ruskin and the Victorian Eye,* 1993. • Raymond Fitch, *The Poison Sky: Myth and Apocalypse in Ruskin,* 1982. • Elizabeth Helsinger, *Ruskin and the Art of the Beholder,* 1982. • Robert Hewison, *John Ruskin: The Argument of the Eye,* 1976. • Robert Hewison, ed., *New Approaches to Ruskin: Thirteen Essays,* 1981. • George P. Landow, *The Aesthetic and Critical Theories of John Ruskin,* 1971. • George P. Landow, *Ruskin,* 1985. • Linda Merrill, *A Pot of Paint: Aesthetics on Trial in Whistler v. Ruskin,* 1992. • John D. Rosenberg, *The Darkening Glass: A Portrait of Ruskin's Genius,* 1961. • J. C. Sherburne, *John Ruskin, or the Ambiguities of Abundance: A Study in Social and Economic Criticism,* 1972.

Our Texts. • E. T. Cook and Alexander Wedderburn, eds., *The Works of John Ruskin,* 39 vols., 1903–1912.

Robert Louis Stevenson • *Editions.* • Bradford A. Booth and Ernest Mehew, *The Letters of Robert Louis Stevenson,* 1994. • Janet Adam Smith, ed., *Robert Louis Stevenson: Collected Poems,* 2nd ed., 1971.

Biography. • Graham Balfour, *The Life of Robert Louis Stevenson,* 1901. • Jenni Calder, *R L S: A Life Study,* 1980. • Philip Callow, *Louis: A Life of Robert Louis Stevenson,* 2001. • Frank J. McLynn, *Robert Louis Stevenson: A*

Biography, 1993. • R. C. Terry, ed., *Robert Louis Stevenson: Interviews and Recollections*, 1996.

Criticism. • Jenni Calder, ed., *Stevenson and Victorian Scotland*, 1981. • Ed Cohen, "The Double Lives of Men: Narration and Identification in the Late Nineteenth-Century Representation of Ex-Centric Masculinities," *Victorian Studies* 36.3, 1993. • David Daiches, *Robert Louis Stevenson and His World*, 1973. • Edwin Eigner, *Robert Louis Stevenson and Romantic Tradition*, 1966. • Henry Geduld, ed., *The Definitive Dr. Jekyll and Mr. Hyde Companion*, 1983. • John R. Hammond, *A Robert Louis Stevenson Companion: A Guide to the Novels, Essays, and Short Stories*, 1984. • Robert Kiely, *Robert Louis Stevenson and the Fiction of Adventure*, 1964. • Paul Maixner, ed., *Robert Louis Stevenson: The Critical Heritage*, 1981. • Elaine Showalter, "Dr. Jekyll's Closet," in *The Haunted Mind: The Supernatural in Victorian Literature*, eds. Smith and Haas, 1999. • Judith Walkowitz, *City of Dreadful Night: Narratives of Sexual Danger in Victorian London*, 1992. • William Veeder and Gordon Hirsch, eds., *Dr. Jekyll and Mr. Hyde after One Hundred Years*, 1988.

Our Text. • *The Strange Case of Dr. Jekyll and Mr. Hyde*, 1886.

Alfred Tennyson • Editions. • Cecil Y. Lang and Edgar F. Shannon Jr., eds., *The Letters of Alfred, Lord Tennyson*, 3 vols., 1981–1990. • Christopher Ricks, ed., *Poems*, 3 vols., 1987. • Hallam Tennyson, ed., *Works*, 9 vols., 1907–1908.

Biography. • Robert B. Martin, *Tennyson: The Unquiet Heart*, 1980. • Hallam Tennyson, *Alfred, Lord Tennyson: A Memoir, by His Son*, 2 vols., 1897.

Criticism. • Daniel Albright, *Tennyson: The Muses' Tug-of-War*, 1986. • Kirk K. Beetz, *Tennyson: A Bibliography, 1827–1982*, 1984. • Jerome H. Buckley, *Tennyson: The Growth of a Poet*, 1960. • Philip Collins, ed., *Tennyson: Seven Essays*, 1993. • A. Dwight Culler, *The Poetry of Tennyson*, 1977. • Donald S. Hair, *Tennyson's Language*, 1991. • Arthur H. Hallam, "On Some Characteristics of Modern Poetry, and On the Lyrical Poems of Alfred Tennyson," *Englishman's Magazine* (August 1831). • Gerhard Joseph, *Tennyson and the Text: The Weaver's Shuttle*, 1992. • John D. Jump, ed., *Tennyson: The Critical Heritage*, 1967. • John Killham, ed., *Critical Essays on the Poetry of Tennyson*, 1960. • James R. Kincaid, *Tennyson's Major Poems: The Comic and Ironic*

Patterns, 1975. • Sir Harold Nicolson, *Tennyson: Aspects of His Life, Character, and Poetry*, 1923. • Norman Page, ed., *Tennyson: Interviews and Recollections*, 1983. • Timothy Peltason, *Reading In Memoriam*, 1985. • F. E. L. Priestley, *Language and Structure in Tennyson's Poetry*, 1973. • Christopher Ricks, *Tennyson*, 1972. • John D. Rosenberg, *The Fall of Camelot: A Study of Tennyson's "Idylls of the King,"* 1973. • Matthew Rowlinson, *Tennyson's Fixations: Psychoanalysis and the Topics of the Early Poetry*, 1994. • Marion Shaw, *An Annotated Critical Bibliography of Alfred, Lord Tennyson*, 1989. • W. David Shaw, *Tennyson's Style*, 1976. • Alan Sinfield, *Alfred Tennyson*, 1986. • Herbert F. Tucker, *Tennyson and the Doom of Romanticism*, 1988. • Herbert F. Tucker, ed., *Critical Essays on Alfred Lord Tennyson*, 1993. • Paul Turner, *Tennyson*, 1976.

Our Texts. • Hallam Tennyson, ed., *Works*, 9 vols., 1907–1908.

Oscar Wilde • Editions. • Richard Ellmann, ed., *The Artist as Critic: Critical Writings of Oscar Wilde*, 1969. • Rupert Hart-Davis, ed., *Letters*, 1962. • Rupert Hart-Davis, *More Letters*, 1985. • Isobel Murray, ed., *The Complete Shorter Fiction of Oscar Wilde*, 1979. • Isobel Murray, ed., *The Writings of Oscar Wilde*, 1989. • Robert Ross, ed., *First Collected Edition*, 14 vols., 1908.

Biography. • Richard Ellmann, *Oscar Wilde*, 1987. • Vyvyan Holland, *Oscar Wilde, a Pictorial Biography*, 1960. • Melissa Knox, *Oscar Wilde: A Long and Lovely Suicide*, 1994.

Criticism. • Karl Beckson, ed., *Oscar Wilde: The Critical Heritage*, 1970. • Patricia Flanagan Behrendt, *Oscar Wilde: Eros and Aesthetics*, 1991. • Harold Bloom, ed., *Oscar Wilde: Modern Critical Views*, 1985. • Harold Bloom, ed., *Oscar Wilde's "The Importance of Being Earnest": Modern Critical Interpretations*, 1988. • Ed Cohen, *Talk on the Wilde Side: Toward a Geneology of a Discourse on Male Sexualities*, 1993. • Richard Ellmann, ed., *Oscar Wilde: A Collection of Critical Essays*, 1969. • Regenia Gagnier, ed., *Critical Essays on Oscar Wilde*, 1991. • Regenia Gagnier, *Idylls of the Marketplace: Oscar Wilde and the Victorian Public*, 1986. • Christopher S. Nassaar, *Into the Demon Universe: A Literary Exploration of Oscar Wilde*, 1974. • Kerry Powell, *Oscar Wilde and the Theatre of the 1890s*, 1991. • Peter Raby, *The Importance of Being Earnest: A Reader's Companion*, 1995. • Peter Raby, ed., *The*

Cambridge Companion to Oscar Wilde, 1997. •
Epifanio San Juan Jr., The Art of Oscar Wilde,
1967. • Rodney Shewan, Oscar Wilde: Art and
Egotism, 1977. • John Stokes, Oscar Wilde:
Myths, Miracles, and Imitations, 1996.

Our Texts. • Poems from First Collected Edition, ed. Robert Ross, 1908; "The Soul of

Man under Socialism" from Fortnightly Re-
view (February 1891); "The Decay of Lying,"
from the Preface to The Picture of Dorian
Gray, and "The Importance of Being
Earnest" from The Writings of Oscar Wilde,
ed. Isobel Murray, 1989; "De Profundis" from
The Letters of Oscar Wilde, ed. Rupert Hart-
Davis, 1962.

The Twentieth Century

General Background • Joseph Bristow, Effemi-
nate England: Homoerotic Writing after 1885,
1995. • Carol T. Christ, Victorian and Modern
Poetics, 1984. • Valentine Cunningham,
British Writers of the Thirties, 1988. • Alistair
Davies, ed., An Annotated Critical Bibliography
of Modernism, 1982. • Marianne DeKoven,
Rich and Strange: Gender, History, Modernism,
1991. • Kevin J. H. Dettmar, ed., Rereading the
New: A Backward Glance at Modernism, 1992.
• Terry Eagleton, Fredric Jameson, Edward W.
Said, Nationalism, Colonialism, and Literature,
1990. • Maud Ellmann, The Poetics of Imper-
sonality: T. S. Eliot and Ezra Pound, 1987. •
David Gervais, Literary Englands: Versions of
"Englishness" in Modern Writing, 1993. • John
Halperin, Eminent Georgians: The Lives of King
George V, Elizabeth Bowen, St. John Philby, and
Nancy Astor, 1995. • Robert Hogan et al.,
Dictionary of Irish Literature, 1996. • Robert
Hughes, The Shock of the New, 1981. • Hugh
Kenner, The Pound Era, 1971. • Michael H.
Levenson, A Genealogy of Modernism: A Study
of English Literary Doctrine, 1908–1922, 1984.
• James Longenbach, Stone Cottage: Pound,
Yeats, and Modernism, 1988. • Perry Meisel,
The Myth of the Modern: A Study in British Lit-
erature and Criticism after 1850, 1987. • Peter
Nicholls, Modernisms: A Literary Guide, 1995.
• Michael North, The Political Aesthetic of
Yeats, Eliot, and Pound, 1991. • Michael
North, Reading 1922: A Return to the Scene of
the Modern, 1999. • Edward W. Said, Begin-
nings, 1981. • Herbert N. Schneidau, Waking
Giants: The Presence of the Past in Modernism,
1991. • Sanford Schwartz, The Matrix of Modernism: Pound, Eliot, and Early Twentieth-Century Thought, 1985. • C. K. Stead, Pound,
Yeats, Eliot, and the Modernist Movement,
1986. • George Watson, British Literature since
1945, 1991. • Stephen Watt and Kevin Dettmar, eds., Marketing Modernisms, 1996. •
David Weir, Anarchy and Culture, 1997.

Perspectives: Regendering Modernism • Shari
Benstock, Women of the Left Bank: Paris,
1900–1940, 1986. • Rita Felski, The Gender of
Modernity, 1995. • Susan Stanford Friedman,
Mappings: Feminism and the Cultural Geogra-
phies of Encounter, 1998. • Sandra Gilbert and
Susan Gubar, No Man's Land: The Place of the
Woman Writer in the Twentieth Century, 3 vols.,
1988–1994. • Gabriele Griffin, Difference in
View: Women and Modernism, 1994. • Gillian
Hanscombe & Virginia L. Smyers, Writing for
Their Lives: The Modernist Women 1910–1940,
1988. • Elizabeth Jane Harrison and Shirley
Peterson, eds., Unmanning Modernism: Gendered
Re-Readings, 1997. • Phyllis Lassner, British
Women Writers of World War II: Battlegrounds
of Their Own, 1998. • Anne McClintock, Im-
perial Leather, 1995. • Bonnie Kime Scott, ed.,
The Gender of Modernism: A Critical Anthology,
1990. • Karen Schneider, Loving Arms: British
Women Writing the Second World War, 1997. •
Anthea Trodd, Women's Writing in English:
Britain, 1900–1945, 1998.

**Perspectives: The Great War: Confronting the
Modern** • Adrian Barlow, The Great War in
British Literature, 2000. • Allyson Booth, Postcards from the Trenches: Negotiating the Space
between Modernism and the First World War,
1996. • Evelyn Cobley, Representing War:
Form and Ideology in First World War Narratives, 1993.• Paul Fussell, The Great War and
Modern Memory, 1975. • Dorothy Goldman,
ed., Women and World War I: The Written Response, 1993. • Klein-Holger, The First World
War in Fiction: A Collection of Critical Essays,
1976. • Pericles Lewis, Modernism, Nationalism,
and the Novel, 2000. • Mark Morrisson, The
Public Face of Modernism, 2001. • John Onions,
English Fiction and Drama of the Great War,
1918–1939, 1990. • Vincent Pecora, Self and
Form in Modern Narrative, 1989. • Lawrence
Rainey, Institutions of Modernism, 1998. • Michal

Tratner, *Modernism and Mass Politics*, 1995. • William C. Wees, *Vorticism and the English Avant-Garde*, 1972.

Perspectives: Whose Language? • Ian Baucom, *Out of Place: Englishness, Empire, and the Locations of Identity*, 1999. • Eugene Benson and L. W. Conolly, eds., *Encyclopedia of Post-Colonial Literatures in English*, 1994. • Elleke Boehmer, *Colonial and Postcolonial Literature: Migrant Metaphors*, 1995. • Robert Crawford, *Devolving English Literature*, 1992. • Michael Edward Gorra, *After Empire: Scott, Naipaul, Rushdie*, 1997. • Bruce King, ed., *New National and Post-Colonial Literatures: An Introduction*, 1996. • Patrick McGee, *Telling the Other*, 1992. • Judie Newman, *The Ballistic Bard: Postcolonial Fictions*, 1995. • Jahan Ramazani, *The Hybrid Muse: Postcolonial Poetry in English*, 2001. • Edward W. Said, *Culture and Imperialism*, 1993. • Jonathan White, ed., *Recasting the World: Writing after Colonialism*, 1993.

Perspectives: World War II and the End of Empire • Bill Ashcroft, Gareth Griffiths, and Helen Tiffin, *The Empire Writes Back: Theory and Practice in Post-Colonial Literatures*, 1989. • Bernard Bergonzi, *Wartime and Aftermath: English Literature and its Background, 1939–1960*, 1993. • Patrick Brantlinger, *Rule of Darkness: British Literature and Imperialism, 1830–1914*, 1988. • Alistair Davies and Alan Sinfield, eds., *British Culture of the Postwar: An Introduction to Literature and Society, 1945–1999*, 2000. • George Richard Esenwein, *Spain at War: The Spanish Civil War in Context, 1931–1939*, 1995. • Robert Hewison, *Under Siege: Literary Life in London, 1939–1945*, 1977. • Karen R. Lawrence, ed., *Decolonizing Tradition: New Views of Twentieth-Century "British" Literary Canons*, 1992. • David Leavitt, *While England Sleeps* [novel], 1993. • David Lloyd, *Anomalous States: Irish Writing and the Post-Colonial Moment*, 1993. • Robert H. MacDonald, *The Language of Empire: Myths and Metaphors of Popular Imperialism, 1880–1918*, 1994. • David Morgan, *The Battle for Britain: Citizenship and Ideology in the Second World War*, 1993. • John M. Muste, *Say That We Saw Spain Die: Literary Consequences of the Spanish Civil War*, 1966. • Mark Rawlinson, *British Writing of the Second World War*, 2000. • Andrew Sinclair, *War Like a Wasp: The Lost Decade of the 'Forties*, 1989. • Hugh Thomas, *The Spanish Civil War*, 1986. • Keith Williams, *British Writers and the Media, 1930–1945*, 1996.

W. H. Auden • *Biographies*. • Richard Davenport Hines, *Auden*, 1993. • Charles Osborne, *W. H. Auden: The Life of a Poet*, 1979.

Criticism. • George W. Bahlke, ed., *Critical Essays on W. H. Auden*, 1991. • John G. Blair, *The Poetic Art of W. H. Auden*, 1965. • Harold Bloom, ed., *W. H. Auden*, 1986. • John R. Boly, *Reading Auden: The Returns of Caliban*, 1991. • Frederick Buell, *W. H. Auden as a Social Poet*, 1973. • John Fuller, *A Reader's Guide to W. H. Auden*, 1970. • John Haffenden, ed., *W. H. Auden: The Critical Heritage*, 1983. • Anthony Hecht, *The Hidden Law: The Poetry of W. H. Auden*, 1993. • Lucy McDiarmid, *Saving Civilization: Yeats, Eliot, and Auden between the Wars*, 1984. • Lucy McDiarmid, *Auden's Apologies for Poetry*, 1990. • Edward Mendelson, ed., *W. H. Auden: A Tribute*, 1974. • Edward Mendelson, *Early Auden*, 1981. • Edward Mendelson, *Later Auden*, 1999. • Monroe K. Spears, *The Poetry of W. H. Auden: The Disenchanted Island*, 1963. • George T. Wright, *W. H. Auden*, 1969.

Samuel Beckett • *Biographies*. • Lois Gordon, *The World of Samuel Beckett, 1906–1946*, 1996. • James Knowlson, *Damned to Fame: The Life of Samuel Beckett*, 1996.

Criticism. • H. Porter Abbott, *Beckett Writing Beckett: the Author in the Autograph*, 1996. • James Acheson, *Samuel Beckett's Artistic Theory and Practice: Criticism, Drama, and Early Fiction*, 1997. • Richard Begam, *Samuel Beckett and The End of Modernity*, 1996. • Linda Ben-Zvi, *Samuel Beckett*, 1986. • Bob Cochran, *Samuel Beckett: A Study of the Short Fiction*, 1992. • Ruby Cohn, *Back to Beckett*, 1974. • Ruby Cohn, *Just Play: Beckett's Theater*, 1980. • J. E. Dearlove, *Accommodating the Chaos: Samuel Beckett's Nonrelational Art*, 1982. • S. E. Gontarski, ed., *The Beckett Studies Reader*, 1993. • S. E. Gontarski, ed., *On Beckett: Essays and Criticism*, 1986. • Lawrence Graver and Raymond Federman, eds., *Samuel Beckett: The Critical Heritage*, 1979. • Mel Gussow, ed., *Conversations With and About Beckett*, 1996. • Hugh Kenner, *Flaubert, Joyce, and Beckett: The Stoic Comedians*, 1962. • Hugh Kenner, *A Reader's Guide to Samuel Beckett*, 1973. • Hugh Kenner, *Samuel Beckett: A Critical Study*, 1968. • Charles R. Lyons, *Samuel Beckett*, 1990. • Patrick A. McCarthy, ed., *Critical Essays on Samuel Beckett*, 1986. • Vivian Mercier, *Beckett/Beckett*, 1977. • Kristin Morrison, *Canters* and Chronicles: The Use of Narrative in the Plays of Samuel Beckett and Harold Pinter, 1983. • Eoin O'Brien, The Beckett Country: Samuel Beckett's Ireland, 1993. • John Piling, ed., The Cambridge Companion to Beckett, 1994. • Christopher B. Ricks, Beckett's Dying Words: The Clarendon Lectures, 1990, 1993.

Eavan Boland • Eavan Boland, A Kind of Scar: The Woman Poet in a National Tradition, 1989. • Eavan Boland, Object Lessons: The Life of the Woman and the Poet in Our Time, 1995. • Patricia Boyle Haberstroh, Women Creating Women: Contemporary Irish Women Poets, 1996. • Debrah Raschke, "Eavan Boland's Outside History and In a Time of Violence: Rescuing Women, the Concrete, and Other Things Physical from the Dung Heap," Colby Quarterly 32.2 (1996), 135–42. • Marilyn Reizbaum, "An Interview with Eavan Boland," Contemporary Literature 30.4 (1989), 471–79.

Elizabeth Bowen • Biographies. • Elizabeth Bowen, Bowen's Court and Seven Winters: Memories of a Dublin Childhood, 1984. • Patricia Craig, Elizabeth Bowen, 1986.

Criticism. • Allan E. Austin, Elizabeth Bowen, 1989. • Andrew Bennett and Nicholas Royle, Elizabeth Bowen and the Dissolution of the Novel: Still Lives, 1995. • Harold Bloom, ed., Elizabeth Bowen, 1987. • Renée Hoogland, Elizabeth Bowen: A Reputation in Writing, 1994. • Heather B. Jordan, How Will the Heart Endure: Elizabeth Bowen and the Landscape of War, 1992. • Phyllis Lassner, Elizabeth Bowen: A Study of Short Fiction, 1991.

Rupert Brooke • Biographies. • Nigel H. Jones, Rupert Brooke: Life, Death & Myth, 1999. • John Lehmann, Rupert Brooke: His Life and His Legend, 1980.

Criticism. • Rupert Brooke, The Letters of Rupert Brooke, ed. Geoffrey Keynes, 1968. • Adrian Caesar, Taking It Like a Man: Suffering, Sexuality, and the War Poets: Brooke, Sassoon, Owen, Graves, 1993. • Paul Delany, The Neo-Pagans: Rupert Brooke and the Ordeal of Youth, 1987. • Pippa Harris, Song of Love: The Letters of Rupert Brooke and Noel Oliver, 1991. • William E. Laskowski, Rupert Brooke, 1994. • Jonathan Rutherford, Forever England: Reflections on Race, Masculinity and Empire, 1997.

Angela Carter • Aidan Day, Angela Carter: The Rational Glass, 1998 • Sarah Gamble, Angela Carter: Writing from the Front Line, 1997. • Alison Lee, Angela Carter, 1997. • Linden Peach, Angela Carter, 1998. • Lorna Sage, ed., Flesh and the Mirror: Essays on the Art of Angela Carter, 1994. • Lindsey Tucker, ed., Critical Essays on Angela Carter, 1998.

Sir Winston Churchill • Biographies. • Roy Jenkins, Churchill: A Biography, 2001. • William Manchester, The Last Lion: Winston Spencer Churchill Visions of Glory, 1874–1932, 1983. • William Manchester, The Last Lion: Winston Spencer Churchill: Alone, 1932–1940, 1989.

Criticism. • Winston S. Churchill, Memoirs of The Second World War, 1990. • Mark Donnelly, Britain in the Second World War, 1999 • Victor Feske, From Belloc to Churchill: Private Scholars, Public Culture, and the Crisis of British Liberalism, 1900–1939, 1996. • James Humes, Wit and Wisdom of Winston Churchill, 1995. • Warren F. Kimball, Churchill and Roosevelt, the Complete Correspondence, 3 vols., 1984. • Warren F. Kimball, Forged in War: Roosevelt, Churchill, and the Second World War, 1997. • Sheila Lawlor, ed., Churchill and the Politics of War, 1940–1941, 1994. • Keith Robbins, Churchill, 1993. • Manfred Weidhorn, Churchill's Rhetoric and Political Discourse, 1988.

Joseph Conrad • Biographies. • John Batchelor, The Life of Joseph Conrad: A Critical Biography, 1993. • Ford Madox Ford, Joseph Conrad: A Personal Remembrance, 1989. • Frederick Karl, Joseph Conrad: The Three Lives: A Biography, 1979. • Jeffrey Meyers, Joseph Conrad: A Biography, 1991. • Ian Watt, Joseph Conrad: A Critical Biography, 1979.

Criticism. • Chinua Achebe, "An Image of Africa." • Ted Billy, ed., Critical Essays on Joseph Conrad, 1987. • Harold Bloom, ed., Joseph Conrad's "Heart of Darkness," 1987. • Harold Bloom, ed., Joseph Conrad, 1986. • Harold Bloom, Marlow, 1992. • Keith Carabine, ed., Joseph Conrad: Critical Assessments, 4 vols., 1992. • Avrom Fleishman, Conrad's Politics: Community and Anarchy in the Fiction of Joseph Conrad, 1967. • Christopher L. GoGwilt, The Invention of the West: Joseph Conrad and the Double-Mapping of Europe and Empire, 1995. • Albert J. Guerard, Conrad the Novelist, 1958. • Geoffrey Harpham, One of Us: The Mastery of Joseph Conrad, 1996. • Nico Israel, Outlandish: Writing Between Exile and Diaspora, 2000. • Fredric Jameson, The

Political Unconscious: Narrative as a Socially Symbolic Act, 1981. • Frederick R. Karl and Laurence Davies, eds., *The Collected Letters of Joseph Conrad*, 1983–. • Owen Knowles and Gene Moore, eds., *The Oxford Reader's Companion to Conrad*, 2000. • Vincent P. Pecora, *Self and Form in Modern Narrative*, 1989. • Martin Ray, ed., *Joseph Conrad: Interviews & Recollections*, 1990. • Edward W. Said, *Joseph Conrad and the Fiction of Autobiography*, 1966. • Edward W. Said, *The World, the Text, and the Critic*, 1983. • Norman Sherry, ed., *Conrad: The Critical Heritage*, 1973. • J. H. Stape, ed., *The Cambridge Companion to Joseph Conrad*, 1996. • Bruce Teets, *Joseph Conrad: An Annotated Bibliography*, 1990. • Cedric P. Watts, *A Preface to Conrad*, 1993. • Mark A. Wollaeger, *Joseph Conrad and the Fictions of Skepticism*, 1990.

Nuala Ní Dhomhnaill • M. Louise Cannon, "The Extraordinary Within the Ordinary: The Poetry of Eavan Boland and Nuala Ni Dhomhnaill," *South Atlantic Review* 60 (1995). • Deborah McWilliams Consalvo, "The Lingual Ideal in the Poetry of Nuala Ni Dhomhnaill," *Eire-Ireland: A Journal of Irish Studies*, 30 (1995). • Patricia Boyle Haberstroh, *Women Creating Women: Contemporary Irish Women Poets*, 1996. • Frank Sewell, *Modern Irish Poetry: A New Alhambra*, 2000.

T. S. Eliot • *Biographies.* • Peter Ackroyd, *T. S. Eliot: A Life*, 1984. • Denis Donoghue, *Words Alone: The Poet T. S. Eliot*, 2000. • Lyndall Gordon, *Eliot's Early Years*, 1977. • Lyndall Gordon, *Eliot's New Life*, 1988. • Lyndall Gordon, *T. S. Eliot: An Imperfect Life*, 1998.

Criticism. • Harold Bloom, ed., *T. S. Eliot*, 1985. • Harold Bloom, ed., *T. S. Eliot's "The Waste Land,"* 1986. • Jewel Spears Brooker and Joseph Bentley, *Reading "The Waste Land": Modernism and the Limits of Interpretation*, 1990. • Ronald Bush, *T. S. Eliot: The Modernist in History*, 1991. • T. S. Eliot, *The Letters of T. S. Eliot*, ed. Valerie Eliot, 1988–. • T. S. Eliot, *"The Waste Land": A Facsimile and Transcript of the Original Drafts Including the Annotations of Ezra Pound*, ed. Valerie Eliot, 1971. • Maud Ellmann, *The Poetics of Impersonality: T. S. Eliot and Ezra Pound*, 1987. • Nancy K. Gish, *"The Waste Land": A Poem of Memory and Desire*, 1988. • Michael Grant, ed., *T. S. Eliot: The Critical Heritage*, 1982. • Frank Lentricchia, *Modernist Quartet*, 1994. •

James Longenbach, *Modernist Poetics of History: Pound, Eliot, and the Sense of the Past*, 1987. • Lucy McDiarmid, *Saving Civilization: Yeats, Eliot, and Auden Between the Wars*, 1984. • Gail McDonald, *Learning to Be Modern: Pound, Eliot, and the American University*, 1993. • Louis Menand, *Discovering Modernism: T. S. Eliot and His Context*, 1986. • Anthony David Moody, ed., *The Cambridge Companion to T. S. Eliot*, 1994. • Anthony David Moody, *Thomas Stearns Eliot, Poet*, 1979. • Jeffrey M. Perl, *Skepticism and Modern Enmity: Before and After Eliot*, 1989. • Christopher B. Ricks, *T. S. Eliot and Prejudice*, 1988. • John Paul Riquelme, *Harmony of Dissonances: T. S. Eliot, Romanticism and Imagination*, 1990. • Sanford Schwartz, *The Matrix of Modernism: Pound, Eliot, and Early Twentieth-Century Thought*, 1985. • Grover Cleveland Smith, *The Waste Land*, 1983. • Stanley Sultan, *Eliot, Joyce, and Company*, 1987. • Stanley Sultan, *"Ulysses," "The Waste Land," and Modernism: A Jubilee Study*, 1977.

E. M. Forster • *Biographies.* • Nicola Beauman, *Morgan: A Biography of the Novelist E. M. Forster*, 1994. • P. N. Furbank, *E. M. Forster: A Life*, 1994. • Mary Lago, *E. M. Forster: A Literary Life*, 1995.

Criticism. • Calvin Bedient, *Architects of the Self: George Eliot, D. H. Lawrence, and E. M. Forster*, 1972. • Harold Bloom, ed., *E. M. Forster*, 1987. • G. K. Das, *E. M. Forster's India*, 1977. • Philip Gardner, *E. M. Forster: The Critical Heritage*, 1973. • Christopher Gillie, *A Preface to Forster*, 1983. • B. J. Kirkpatrick, *A Bibliography of E. M. Forster*, 1986. • Mary Lago and P. N. Furbank, eds., *Selected Letters of E. M. Forster*, 1983–85. • Robert K. Martin and George Piggford, eds., *Queer Forster*, 1997. • Sara Suleri, *The Rhetoric of English India*, 1992. • J. H. Stape, ed., *E. M. Forster: Interviews and Recollections*, 1993. • Lionel Trilling, *E. M. Forster*, 1965. • Alan Wilde, *Critical Essays on E. M. Forster*, 1985.

Nadine Gordimer • *Biographies.* • Nadine Gordimer, *Writing and Being*, 1995. • Andries Walter Oliphant, ed., *A Writing Life: Celebrating Nadine Gordimer*, 1998.

Criticism. • Nancy T. Bazin and Marilyn D. Seymour, *Conversations with Nadine Gordimer*, 1990. • Stephen Clingman, *The Novels of Nadine Gordimer: History from the Inside*, 1986. •

Andrew V. Ettin, *Betrayals of the Body Politic: The Literary Commitments of Nadine Gordimer*, 1993. • Dominic Head, *Nadine Gordimer*, 1995. • Christopher Heywood, *Nadine Gordimer*, 1983. • Bruce King, ed., *The Later Fiction of Nadine Gordimer*, 1993. • Judie Newman, *Nadine Gordimer*, 1988. • Rowland Smith, ed., *Critical Essays on Nadine Gordimer*, 1990. • Kathrin Wagner, *Rereading Nadine Gordimer*, 1994.

Thomas Hardy • *Biographies*. • Simon Gatrell, *Hardy, the Creator: A Textual Biography*, 1988. • James Gibson, *Thomas Hardy: A Literary Life*, 1996. • Michael Millgate, *Thomas Hardy: A Biography*, 1982.

Criticism. • Harold Bloom, ed., *Thomas Hardy*, 1987. • Graham Clarke, ed., *Thomas Hardy: Critical Assessments*, 4 vols., 1993. • Reginald Gordon Cox, *Thomas Hardy: The Critical Heritage*, 1970. • Ronald P. Draper, *An Annotated Critical Bibliography of Thomas Hardy*, 1989. • Dale Kramer, *Critical Essays on Thomas Hardy: The Novels*, 1990. • Dale Kramer, ed., *The Cambridge Companion to Thomas Hardy*, 1999. • Robert Langbaum, *Thomas Hardy in Our Time*, 1995. • C. Day Lewis, *The Lyrical Poetry of Thomas Hardy*, 1970. • Perry Meisel, *Thomas Hardy: The Return of the Repressed: A Study of the Major Fiction*, 1972. • J. Hillis Miller, *Thomas Hardy: Distance and Desire*, 1970. • Michael Millgate, ed., *Selected Letters*, 1990. • Charles P. C. Pettit, ed., *New Perspectives on Thomas Hardy*, 1994. • Richard L. Purdy and Michael Millgate, eds., *The Collected Letters of Thomas Hardy*, 1978–88. • Rosemary Sumner, *A Route to Modernism: Hardy, Lawrence, Woolf*, 2000. • Merryn Williams, *A Preface to Hardy*, 1993. • Paul Zietlow, *Moments of Vision: The Poetry of Thomas Hardy*, 1974.

Seamus Heaney • *Biographies*. • Helen Hennessy Vendler, *Seamus Heaney*, 1998. • Michael Parker, *Seamus Heaney: The Making of the Poet*, 1993.

Criticism. • Elmer Andrews, *The Poetry of Seamus Heaney*, 1988. • Elmer Andrews, *The Poetry of Seamus Heaney*, 2000. • Harold Bloom, ed., *Seamus Heaney*, 1986. • Sidney Burris, ed., *The Poetry of Resistance: Seamus Heaney and the Pastoral Tradition*, 1990. • Neil Corcoran, *Seamus Heaney: A Faber Student Guide*, 1986. • Neil Corcoran, *The Poetry of Seamus Heaney: A Critical Study*, 1998. • Tony Curtis, ed., *The Art of Seamus Heaney*,

2001. • Tony Curtis, ed., *The Art of Seamus Heaney*, 1994. • Michael J. Durkan and Rand Brandes, *Seamus Heaney: A Reference Guide*, 1996. • Thomas C. Foster, *Seamus Heaney*, 1989. • Robert F. Garratt, *Critical Essays on Seamus Heaney*, 1995. • Henry Hart, *Seamus Heaney, Poet of Contrary Progressions*, 1992. • Catherin Malloy and Phyllis Carey, eds., *Seamus Heaney: The Shaping Spirit*, 1996. • Michael R. Molino, *Questioning Tradition, Language, and Myth: The Poetry of Seamus Heaney*, 1994. • Bernard O'Donoghue, *Seamus Heaney and the Language of Poetry*, 1994. • Daniel Tobin, *Passage to the Center: Imagination and the Sacred in the Poetry of Seamus Heaney*, 1999.

David Jones • *Biographies*. • René Hague, ed., *Dai Great-Coat: A Self-Portrait of David Jones in His Letters*, 1980.

Criticism. • Thomas Dilworth, *The Shape of Meaning in the Poetry of David Jones*, 1988. • Thomas Dilworth, ed., *Inner Necessities: The Letters of David Jones to Desmond Chute*, 1984. • René Hague, *David Jones*, 1975. • Jeremy Hooker, *David Jones: An Exploratory Study of the Writings*, 1975. • David Jones, *David Jones: Letters to Vernon Watkins*, ed. Ruth Pryor, 1976. • Jonathan Miles and Derek Shiel, *David Jones: The Maker Unmade*, 1996. • Kathleen Raine, *David Jones, Solitary Perfectionist*, 1974. • Kathleen Staudt, ed., *At the Turn of a Civilization: David Jones and Modern Poetics*, 1993.

James Joyce • *Edition*. • *Ulysses*, ed. Hans Walter Gabler, 1984.

Biographies. • Richard Ellmann, *James Joyce*, 1982. • Herbert S. Gorman, *James Joyce*, 1948. • Michael Seidel, *James Joyce: A Short Introduction*, 2002.

Criticism. • Derek Attridge, ed., *The Cambridge Companion to James Joyce*, 1990. • Richard Brown, *James Joyce and Sexuality*, 1989. • Frank Budgen, *James Joyce and the Making of "Ulysses,"* 1960. • Vincent Cheng, *Joyce, Race and Empire*, 1995. • Kevin J. H. Dettmar, *The Illicit Joyce of Postmodernism: Reading Against the Grain*, 1996. • Enda Duffy, *The Subaltern "Ulysses,"* 1994. • Christine Froula, *Modernisms's Body*, 1996. • Don Gifford, *Ulysses Annotated: Notes for Joyce's "Ulysses,"* 1988. • Stuart Gilbert, *James Joyce's "Ulysses": A Study*, 1930. • Clive Hart and David Hayman, eds., *James Joyce's "Ulysses": Critical Essays*,

1974. • Hugh Kenner, *Joyce's Voices*, 1978. • Hugh Kenner, *Ulysses*, 1987. • R. B. Kershner, *Joyce, Bakhtin, and Popular Literature: Chronicles of Disorder*, 1989. • Karen Lawrence, *The Odyssey of Style in "Ulysses,"* 1981. • Garry Leonard, *Advertising and Joyce*, 1999. • A. Walton Litz, *The Art of James Joyce: Method and Design in "Ulysses" and "Finnegans Wake,"* 1961. • Patrick McGee, *Joyce Beyond Marx*, 2001. • Vicki Mahaffey, *Reauthorizing Joyce*, 1988. • Dominic Manganiello, *Joyce's Politics*, 1980. • E. H. Mikhail, *James Joyce: Interviews and Recollections*, 1990. • Margot Norris, *Joyce's Web: The Social Unraveling of Modernism*, 1992. • Richard Pearce, *The Politics of Narration: James Joyce, William Faulkner, and Virginia Woolf*, 1991. • David Pierce, *James Joyce's Ireland*, 1992. • Arthur Power, *Conversations with James Joyce*, 1974. • Mary T. Reynolds, ed., *James Joyce: A Collection of Critical Essays*, 1993. • Bonnie K. Scott, *Joyce and Feminism*, 1984. • Fritz Senn, *Joyce's Dislocutions*, 1984. • Robert E. Spoo, *James Joyce and the Language of History: Dedalus's Nightmare*, 1994. • Joseph Valente, ed., *Quare Joyce*, 1998. • Jennifer Wicke, *Advertising Fictions: Literature, Advertising, and Social Reading*, 1988.

Philip Larkin • *Biographies*. • Andrew Motion, *Philip Larkin: A Writer's Life*, 1993.

Criticism. • James Booth, *Philip Larkin: Writer*, 1992. • James Booth, ed., *New Larkins for Old: Critical Essays*, 2000. • Richard Hoffpauir, *The Art of Restraint: English Poetry from Hardy to Larkin*, 1991. • Philip Larkin, *Selected Letters: 1940–1985*, ed. Anthony Thwaite, 1993. • Bruce K. Martin, *Philip Larkin*, 1978. • Janice Rossen, *Philip Larkin: His Life's Work*, 1990. • Dale Salwak, ed., *Philip Larkin: The Man and His Work*, 1988. • Andrew Swarbrick, *Out of Reach: The Poetry of Philip Larkin*, 1995. • Anthony Thwaite, *Larkin at Sixty*, 1982. • David Timms, *Philip Larkin*, 1973.

D. H. Lawrence • *Biographies*. • Mark Kinkead-Weekes, *D. H. Lawrence: Triumph to Exile, 1912–1922*, 1996. • Harry T. Moore, *The Priest of Love: A Life of D. H. Lawrence*, 1974. • John Worthen, *D. H. Lawrence: A Literary Life*, 1989.

Criticism. • James T. Boulton, ed., *The Letters of D. H. Lawrence*, 6 vols., 1979–. • Henry Coombes, *D. H. Lawrence: A Critical Anthology*, 1973. • James C. Cowan, *D. H. Lawrence: An Annotated Bibliography of Writings about Him*,

1982. • Paul Delany, *D. H. Lawrence's Nightmare: The Writer and His Circle in the Years of the Great War*, 1978. • R. P. Draper, *D. H. Lawrence: The Critical Heritage*, 1970. • Geoff Dyer, *Out of Sheer Rage*, 1977. • Elaine Feinstein, *Lawrence and the Women*, 1993. • Anne Fernihough, ed., *The Cambridge Companion to D. H. Lawrence*, 2001. • Sandra Gilbert, *Acts of Attention: The Poems of D. H. Lawrence*, 1972. • Leo Hamalian, *D. H. Lawrence: A Collection of Criticism*, 1973. • Philip Hobsbaum, *A Reader's Guide to D. H. Lawrence*, 1981. • Dennis Jackson and Fleda Brown Jackson, eds., *Critical Essays on D. H. Lawrence*, 1988. • Thomas Rice Jackson, *D. H. Lawrence: A Guide to Research*, 1983. • F. R. Leavis, *D. H. Lawrence, Novelist*, 1970. • Henry Miller, *The World of Lawrence: A Passionate Appreciation*, 1980. • Kate Millet, *Sexual Politics*, 1970. • Ross C. Murfin, *The Poetry of D. H. Lawrence: Texts and Contexts*, 1983. • Joyce Carol Oates, *The Hostile Sun: The Poetry of D. H. Lawrence*, 1973. • F. B. Pinion, *A. D. H. Lawrence Companion: Life, Thought, and Works*, 1979. • Tony Pinkney, *D. H. Lawrence and Modernism*, 1990. • Paul Poplawski, *D. H. Lawrence: A Reference Companion*, 1996. • Peter Preston and Peter Hoare, eds., *D. H. Lawrence in the Modern World*, 1989. • Warren Roberts, *A Bibliography of D. H. Lawrence*, 1982. • Keith Sagar, ed., *A D. H. Lawrence Handbook*, 1982. • Keith M. Sagar, *The Art of D. H. Lawrence*, 1975. • Carol Siegel, *Lawrence among the Women: Wavering Boundaries in Women's Literary Traditions*, 1991. • Stephen Spender, *D. H. Lawrence: Novelist, Poet, Prophet*, 1973. • Rosemary Sumner, *A Route to Modernism: Hardy, Lawrence, Woolfe*, 2000.

Katherine Mansfield • *Biographies*. • Gillian Boddy, *Katherine Mansfield: The Woman and the Writer*, 1988. • Claire Tomalin, *Katherine Mansfield: A Secret Life*, 1987.

Criticism. • Mary Burgan, *Illness, Gender, and Writing: The Case of Katherine Mansfield*, 1994. • Saralyn R. Daly, *Katherine Mansfield*, 1994. • Pamela Dunbar, *Radical Mansfield: Double Discourse in Katherine Mansfield Short Stories*, 1997. • Ian A. Gordon, *Undiscovered Country: The New Zealand Stories of Katherine Mansfield*, 1974. • Sydney J. Kaplan, *Katherine Mansfield and the Origins of Modernist Fiction*, 1990. • Jasper F. Kobler, *Katherine Mansfield: A Study of the Short Fiction*, 1990. • Patricia Moran, *Word of Mouth: Body Language in Katherine*

Mansfield and Virginia Woolf, 1996. • Patrick D. Morrow, *Katherine Mansfield's Fiction*, 1993. • Rhoda B. Nathan, ed., *Critical Essays on Katherine Mansfield*, 1993. • Vincent O'Sullivan and Margaret Scott, *The Collected Letters of Katherine Mansfield*, 1984–1996. • Jan Pilditch, ed., *The Critical Response to Katherine Mansfield*, 1996. • Roger Robinson, ed., *Katherine Mansfield: In from the Margin*, 1994.

Ngugi Wa Thiong'o • Simon Gikandi, *Ngugi wa Thiong'o*, 2000. • Oliver Lovesey, *Ngugi wa Thiong'o*, 2000. • Christopher Miller, *Theories of Africans*, 1998. • Peter Nazareth, ed., *Critical Essays on Ngugi wa Thiongo*, 2000. • Michael Parker and Roger Starkey, eds., *Postcolonial Literatures: Achebe, Ngugi, Desai, Walcott*, 1995. • Patrick Williams, *Ngugi wa Thiong'o*, 1999.

George Orwell • *Biographies*. • Peter Hobley Davison, *George Orwell: A Literary Life*, 1996. • Michael Shelden, *Orwell: The Authorized Biography*, 1991.

Criticism. • Harold Bloom, ed., *George Orwell*, 1987. • Peter Buitenhuis and Ira B. Nadel, *George Orwell, A Reassessment*, 1988. • Roger Fowler, *The Language of George Orwell*, 1995. • Jeffrey Meyers, ed., *George Orwell: The Critical Heritage*, 1997. • Valerie Meyers, *George Orwell*, 1991. • Bernard Oldsey and Joseph Browne, eds., *Critical Essays on George Orwell*, 1986. • Alok Rai, *Orwell and the Politics of Despair: A Critical Study of the Writings of George Orwell*, 1990. • John Rodden, *The Politics of Literary Reputation: The Making and Claiming of "St. George" Orwell*, 1991. • Bernard Schweizer, *Radicals on the Road: The Politics of English Travel Writing in the 1930s*, 2001. • Raymond Williams, *George Orwell*, 1971. • David Wykes, *A Preface to Orwell*, 1987.

Wilfred Owen • *Biographies*. • Harold Owen, *Journey from Obscurity; Wilfred Owen, 1893–1918*, 1963–1965. • Jon Stallworthy, *Wilfred Owen*, 1974.

Criticism. • Sven Bäckman, *Tradition Transformed: Studies in the Poetry of Wilfred Owen*, 1979. • Adrian Caesar, *Taking It Like a Man: Suffering, Sexuality, and the War Poets: Brooke, Sassoon, Owen, Graves*, 1993. • Desmond Graham, *The Truth of War: Owen, Rosenberg and Blunden*, 1984. • Dominic Hibberd, *Owen the Poet*, 1988. • Douglas Kerr, *Wilfred Owen's Voices: Language and Community*, 1993. •

Arthur E. Lane, *An Adequate Response: The War Poetry of Wilfred Owen and Siegfried Sassoon*, 1972. • Stephen MacDonald, *Not About Heroes: The Friendship of Siegfried Sassoon and Wilfred Owen*, 1983. • Wilfred Owen, *Wilfred Owen: Collected Letters*, eds. William H. Owen and John Bell, 1967. • Stuart Sillars, *Structure and Dissolution in English Writing, 1910–1920*, 1999.

Jean Rhys • *Biographies*. • Carole Angier, *Jean Rhys*, 1985.

Criticism. • Mary Lou Emery, *Jean Rhys at "World's End": Novels of Colonial and Sexual Exile*, 1990. • Veronica Marie Gregg, *Jean Rhys's Historical Imagination: Reading and Writing the Creole*, 1995. • Paula Le Gallez, *The Rhys Woman*, 1990. • Cheryl Alexander Malcolm, *Jean Rhys: A Study of the Short Fiction*, 1996. • Sylvie Maurel, *Jean Rhys*, 1998. • Sanford V. Sternlicht, *Jean Rhys*, 1997.

Issac Rosenberg • *Biographies*. • Joseph Cohen, *Journey to the Trenches: The Life of Isaac Rosenberg: 1890–1918*, 1975. • Jean Moorcroft Wilson, *Isaac Rosenberg, Poet and Painter: A Biography*, 1975.

Criticism. • Desmond Graham, *The Truth of War: Owen, Rosenberg and Blunden*, 1984.

Salman Rushdie • Anouar Abdallah, ed., *For Rushdie: A Collection of Essays by 100 Arabic and Muslim Writers*, 1994. • Fawzia Afzal-Khan, *Cultural Imperialism and the Indo-English Novel: Genre and Ideology in R. K. Narayan, Anita Desai, Kamala Markandaya, and Salman Rushdie*, 1993. • Lisa Appignanesi and Sara Maitland, eds., *The Rushdie File*, 1990. • M. Keith Booker, ed., *Critical Essays on Salman Rushdie*, 1999. • Timothy Brennan, *Salman Rushdie and the Third World: Myths of the Nation*, 1989. • Catherine Cundy, *Salman Rushdie*, 1997. • Michael Edward Gorra, *After Empire: Scott, Naipaul, Rushdie*, 1997. • James Harrison, *Salman Rushdie*, 1991. • Nico Israel, *Outlandish: Writing between Exile and Diaspora*, 2000. • Steve MacDonogh, ed., *The Rushdie Letters: Freedom to Speak, Freedom to Write*, 1993. • Daniel Pipes, *The Rushdie Affair: The Novel, the Ayatollah, and the West*, 1990. • Malise Ruthven, *A Satanic Affair: Salman Rushdie and the Rage of Islam*, 1990.

Siegfried Sassoon • *Biographies*. • Sanford V. Sternlicht, *Siegfried Sassoon*, 1993. • Jean

Moorcroft Wilson, *Siegfried Sassoon—The Making of a War Poet: A Biography 1886–1918*, 1999.

Criticism. • Adrian Caesar, *Taking It Like a Man: Suffering, Sexuality, and the War Poets: Brooke, Sassoon, Owen, Graves*, 1993. • Felicitas Corrigan, ed., *Siegfried Sassoon: Poet's Pilgrimage*, 1973. • John Hildebidle, "Neither Worthy Nor Capable: The War Memoirs of Graves, Blunden, and Sassoon," in *Modernism Reconsidered*, eds. Robert Kiely and John Hildebidle, 1983. • Arthur E. Lane, *An Adequate Response: The War Poetry of Wilfred Owen and Siegfried Sassoon*, 1972. • Stephen MacDonald, *Not About Heroes: The Friendship of Siegfried Sassoon and Wilfred Owen*, 1983. • Paul Moeyes, *Siegfried Sassoon, Scorched Glory: A Critical Study*, 1997. • Sigfried Sassoon, *Diaries*, 3 vols., ed. Rupert Hart-Davis, 1981–1985. • Stuart Sillars, *Structure and Dissolution in English Writing, 1910–1920*, 1999. • Michael Thorpe, *Siegfried Sassoon: A Critical Study*, 1966.

Bernard Shaw • *Biographies.* • Michael Holroyd, *Bernard Shaw*, 4 vols., 1988–93. • Stanley Weintraub, ed., *Shaw: An Autobiography, Selected from His Writings*, 2 Vols., 1969–70.

Criticism. • *The Bodley Head Bernard Shaw: Collected Plays and Their Prefaces*, Vol. 7. London: Reinhardt, Bodley Head, 1972. • Harold Bloom, ed., *George Bernard Shaw's Pygmalion*, 1988. • Ian Britain, *Fabianism and Culture: A Study in British Socialism and the Arts c. 1884–1918*, 1982. • R. F. Dietrich, *Bernard Shaw's Novels*, 1996. • T. F. Evans, ed., *Shaw and Politics*, 1991. • J. Ellen Gainor, *Shaw's Daughters: Dramatic and Narrative Constructions of Gender*, 1991. • A. M. Gibbs, ed., *Shaw: Interviews and Recollections*, 1990. • Gareth Griffith, *Socialism and Superior Brains: The Political Thought of Bernard Shaw*, 1992. • Michael Holroyd, *The Genius of Shaw: A Symposium*, 1979. • Christopher Innes, ed. *The Cambridge Companion to George Bernard Shaw*, 1998. • Dan H. Laurence and James Rambeau, eds., *Agitations: Letters to the Press, 1875–1950*, 1985. • Dan H. Laurence, ed., *Collected Letters, 1965–*. • Dan H. Laurence, *Bernard Shaw: A Bibliography*, 1983. • Sally Peters, *Bernard Shaw: The Ascent of the Superman*, 1996. • Jean Reynolds, *Pygmalion's Wordplay*, 1999. • J. P. Wearing, Elsie B. Adams, and Stanley Weintraub, eds., *G. B. Shaw: An Annotated Bibliography of Writings about Him*, 3 vols., 1986–87. • Stanley Weintraub, *Bernard*

Shaw: A Guide to Research, 1992. • Robert F. Whitman, *Shaw and the Play of Ideas*, 1977.

Stephen Spender • *Biographies.* • Hugh David, *Stephen Spender: A Portrait with Background*, 1992.

Criticism. • Hemant Balvantrao Kulkarni, *Stephen Spender: Poet in Crisis*, 1970. • David Adams Leeming, *Stephen Spender: A Life in Modernism*, 1999. • Michael O'Neill, *Auden, MacNeice, Spender: The Thirties Poetry*, 1992. • Surya Nath Pandey, *Stephen Spender: A Study in Poetic Growth*, 1982. • Stephen Spender, *Journals, 1939–1983*, 1986. • Stephen Spender, *Letters to Christopher: Stephen Spender's Letters to Christopher Isherwood, 1929–1939, with "The Line of the Branch"—Two Thirties Journals*, ed. Lee Bartlett, 1980. • Sanford Sternlicht, *Stephen Spender*, 1992. • A. K. Weatherhead, *Stephen Spender and the Thirties*, 1975.

Dylan Thomas • John Ackerman, *Thomas: His Life and Work*, 1996 • Walford Davies, *Dylan Thomas: New Critical Essays*, 1972. • Paul Ferris, ed., *The Collected Letters*, 1985. • Paul Ferris, *Dylan Thomas*, 1977. • Constantine Fitzgibbon, *Selected Letters of Dylan Thomas*, 1966. • Georg Gaston, ed., *Critical Essays on Dylan Thomas*, 1989. • John Goodby and Chris Wigginton, eds. *Dylan Thomas*, 2001. • R. B. Kershner, *Dylan Thomas*, 1976. • Ruskworth M. Kidder, *Dylan Thomas: The Country of the Spirit*, 1973. • Jacob Korg, *Dylan Thomas*, 1992. • William T. Moynihan, *The Craft and Art of Dylan Thomas*, 1966. • Andrew Sinclair, *Dylan Thomas: No Man More Magical*, 1975. • Caitlin Thomas, *Leftover Life to Kill*, 1957. • William York Tindall, *A Reader's Guide to Dylan Thomas*, 1962. • George Tremlett, *Dylan Thomas: In the Mercy of His Means*, 1992.

Derek Walcott • *Biographies.* • Bruce King, *Derek Walcott: A Caribbean Life*, 2000.

Criticism. • William Baer, ed., *Conversations with Derek Walcott*, 1996. • Edward Baugh, *Derek Walcott: Memory as Vision: Another Life*, 1978. • Paul Breslin, *Nobody's Nation: Reading Derek Walcott*, 2001. • Stewart Brown, ed., *Art of Derek Walcott*, 1991. • Paula Burnett, *Derek Walcott: Politics and Poetics*, 2000.• Robert D. Hamner, *Derek Walcott*, 1993. • Robert D. Hamner, ed., *Critical Perspectives on Derek Walcott*, 1993. • Bruce King, *Derek Walcott and West Indian Drama: Not Only a*

Playwright But a Company: The Trinidad Theatre Workshop 1959–1993, 1995. • Tejumola Olaniyan, *Scars of Conquest—Masks of Resistance: The Invention of Cultural Identities in African, African-American, and Caribbean Drama*, 1995. • Michael Parker and Roger Starkey, eds., *Postcolonial Literatures: Achebe, Ngugi, Desai, Walcott*, 1995. • Jahan Ramazani, *The Hybrid Muse: Postcolonial Poetry in English*, 2001. • Rei Terada, *Derek Walcott's Poetry: American Mimicry*, 1992. • John Thieme, *Derek Walcott*, 1999.

Rebecca West • *Biographies.* • Victoria Glendinning, *Rebecca West: A Life*, 1987. • J. R. Hammond, *H. G. Wells and Rebecca West*, 1991. • Carl E. Rollyson, *Rebecca West: A Life*, 1996.

Criticism. • Motley F. Deakin, *Rebecca West*, 1980. • Gordon N. Ray, *H. G. Wells and Rebecca West*, 1974. • Bernard Schweizer, *Radicals on the Road: The Politics of English Travel Writing in the 1930s*, 2001. • Bonnie Kime Scott, *Refiguring Modernism. Vol. I: The Women of 1928. Vol. II: Postmodern Feminist Readings of Woolf, West, and Barnes*, 1995. • Peter Wolfe, *Rebecca West: Artist and Thinker*, 1971.

Virginia Woolf • *Biographies.* • Gillian Beer, *Virginia Woolf: The Common Ground*, 1996. • Quentin Bell, *Virginia Woolf: A Biography*, 1972. • Lyndall Gordon, *Virginia Woolf: A Writer's Life*, 1993. • Mitchell Alexander Leaska, *Granite and Rainbow: The Life of Virginia Woolf*, 1998. • Hermione Lee, *Virginia Woolf*, 1998. • John Mepham, *Virginia Woolf: A Literary Life*, 1991.

Criticism. • Anne O. Bell, ed., *A Moment's Liberty: The Shorter Diary*, 1992. • Rachel Bowlby, *Feminist Destinations and Further Essays on Virginia Woolf*, 1997. • Alison Booth, *Greatness Engendered: George Eliot and Virginia Woolf*, 1992. • Rachel Bowlby, ed., *Virginia Woolf*, 1993. • Thomas C. Caramagno, *The Flight of the Mind: Virginia Woolf's Art and Manic-Depressive Illness*, 1992. • Pamela L. Caughie, *Virginia Woolf and Postmodernism: Literature in Quest and Question of Itself*, 1991. • Mary A. Caws, *Women of Bloomsbury: Virginia, Vanessa and Carrington*, 1991. • Emily Dalgarno, *Virginia Woolf and the Visible World*, 2001. • Margaret Homans, ed., *Virginia Woolf: A Collection of Critical Essays (20th Century Views)*, 1992. • Mark Hussey, *Virginia Woolf*

A to Z: A Comprehensive Reference for Students, Teachers, and Common Readers to Her Life, Work, & Critical Reception, 1996. • James King, *Virginia Woolf*, 1995. • Mitchell A. Leaska, ed., *A Passionate Apprentice: The Early Journals, 1897–1909*, 1992. • Eleanor McNees, ed., *Virginia Woolf: Critical Assessments*, 4 vols., 1994. • Andrew McNeillie, ed., *Essays of Virginia Woolf*, 4 vols. • Douglas Mao, *Solid Objects*, 1998. • Kathy J. Phillips, *Virginia Woolf Against Empire*, 1994. • Panthea Reid, *Art and Affection: A Life of Virginia Woolf*, 1996. • Sue Roe and Susan Sellers, eds., *The Cambridge Companion to Viriginia Woolf*, 2000. • S. P. Rosenbaum, ed., *Women and Fiction: The Manuscript Versions of "A Room of One's Own,"* 1992. • Bonnie Kime Scott, *Refiguring Modernism*, 2 vols., 1995. • Peter Stansky, *On Or about December 1910: Early Bloomsbury and Its Intimate World*, 1996. • J. H. Stape, *Virginia Woolf: Interviews and Recollections*, 1995. • J. H. Stape, *Congenial Spirits: The Selected Letters of Virginia Woolf*, 1991. • Jeanette Winterson, *Art Objects: Essays on Ecstasy and Effrontery*, 1996. • Alex Zwerdling, *Virginia Woolf and Real Life*, 1987.

William Butler Yeats • *Edition.* • *The Poems of W. B. Yeats: A New Edition*, ed. Richard J. Finneran, 1983.

Biographies. • Terence Brown, *The Life of W. B. Yeats: A Critical Biography*, 1999. • Richard Ellmann, *Yeats, the Man and the Masks*, 1948. • R. F. Foster, *W. B. Yeats: A Life*, 1997–.

Criticism. • Harold Bloom, *Yeats*, 1970. • Elizabeth B. Cullingford, *Gender and History in Yeats's Love Poetry*, 1993. • Elizabeth Butler Cullingford, *Gender and History in Yeats's Love Poetry*, 1996. • Una Mary Ellis-Fermor, *The Irish Dramatic Movement*, 1954. • Richard Ellmann, *Eminent Domain: Yeats among Wilde, Joyce, Pound, Eliot, and Auden*, 1967. • Richard J. Finneran, *Critical Essays on W. B. Yeats*, 1986. • Adrian Frazier, *Behind the Scenes: Yeats, Horniman, and the Struggle for the Abbey Theatre*, 1990. • Maud Gonne, *The Gonne-Yeats Letters 1893–1938*, eds. Anna MacBride White and A. Norman Jeffares, 1993. • A. Norman Jeffares, *A New Commentary on the Poems of W. B. Yeats*, 1984. • A. Norman Jeffares, *W. B. Yeats: The Critical Heritage*, 1977. • A. Norman Jeffares, *W. B. Yeats, Man and Poet*, 1996. • Frank Kermode,

Romantic Image, 1961. • Louis MacNeice, The Poetry of W. B. Yeats, 1941. • Vicki Mahaffey, States of Desire: Wilde, Yeats, Joyce, and the Irish Experiment, 1998. • Edward Greenway Malins, A Preface to Yeats, 1974. • Lucy McDiarmid, Saving Civilization: Yeats, Eliot, and Auden Between the Wars, 1984. • E. H. Mikhail, ed., W. B. Yeats: Interviews and Recollections, 2 vols., 1977. • David Pierce, Yeats's Worlds: Ireland, England and the Poetic Imagination, with photographs by Dan Harper, 1995. • John Quinn, The Letters of John Quinn to William Butler Yeats, ed. Alan Himber, with George Mills Harper, 1983. • Jahan Ramazani, The Hybrid Muse: Postcolonial Poetry in English, 2001. • Jahan Ramazani, Yeats and the Poetry of Death: Elegy, Self-Elegy, and the Sublime, 1990. • M. L. Rosenthal, Running to Paradise: Yeats's Poetic Art, 1994. • Michael J. Sidnell, Yeats's Poetry and Poetics, 1996. • Jon Stallworthy, Between the Lines: Yeats's Poetry in the Making, 1963. • William York Tindall, W. B. Yeats, 1966. • John Eugene Unterecker, A Reader's Guide to William Butler Yeats, 1959. • William Butler Yeats, Collected Letters of W. B. Yeats, eds. Warwick Gould, John Kelly, and Dierdre Toomey, 1986–.

CREDITS

INDEX